John Arlott, who introduces and edits this massive and comprehensive work of reference, is a distinguished broadcaster and journalist. He is cricket and wine correspondent of *The Guardian*. John Arlott is backed up here with a strong team of expert contributors. He lives near Winchester, Hampshire.

Edited by John Arlott

The Oxford Companion to Sports and Games

Line drawings by Carl James

Paladin

Granada Publishing Limited
Published in 1977 by Paladin
Frogmore, St Albans, Herts AL2 2NF

First published in Great Britain by
Oxford University Press 1976
Copyright © Oxford University Press 1976
Introduction Copyright © John Arlott 1976
Made and printed in Great Britain by
Richard Clay (The Chaucer Press) Ltd
Bungay, Suffolk

Preface

The Oxford Companion to Sports and Games was originally planned as an introduction to all sports and games which are the subject of national or international competition. While it was being compiled it was decided that, if it were fully to serve its purpose, it should be extended beyond those limits. It is intended to help the reader to understand a sport when he watches it for the first time. The descriptive section explains how it is played – as distinct from how to play it. If it is watched on television, the commentary may refer – often without opportunity for explanation – to technical devices, equipment, outstanding performers, events, clubs, and stadia, of which the most important are mentioned here.

The idea of a *Companion* to deal with all sports and games had to be abandoned at the earliest stage: such scope would have resulted in either an unwieldy volume or inadequate treatment. The first, and most important, editorial decision excluded blood sports. The choice lay between, for example, limiting the entry 'trout' to the dictionary definition, 'Kinds of freshwater fish esteemed as food and game', or, alternatively, describing the varieties of trout and the different fashions of catching them, rods, flies, and famous rivers. To give similar treatment to all the aspects of game and coarse angling and to all the animals shot and hunted would have resulted – alone, and without mention of athletic sports – in a book as large as this. Such a work may one day be compiled: but it would be complementary to this *Companion*, not part of it.

Board and table games are excluded, as essentially a different subject, on which an authoritative study already exists in R. C. Bell's *Board and Table Games from Many Civilizations*. Most street, folk, and children's games clearly required different treatment since they often lack not only the definition of uniform rules, but even a single precise name. Conclusively, too, they have been not only treated but related – as could not be done in a work of this kind – in two outstanding studies, *The Traditional Games of England, Scotland and Ireland* by Alice Bertha Gomme, and *Children's Games in Street and Playground* by Iona and Peter Opie. Thus only a few – and those relevant to modern adult games – are entered here.

There are some departures from the planned shape. Decisively, additions were made of subjects likely to be watched, particularly on television, by viewers who wished to know more about them. In most of these instances there were extra reasons. Coursing was included since the Waterloo Cup is a national competition. Other entries are of historically important ancestors of major modern sports; others again, of some antiquity – like knur and spell and stool ball – because they have endured to become part of a regional fabric and tradition.

As in the case of coursing, a separate conclusion had to be reached about bullfighting. A sport of such social and historic importance in several countries, which has produced such a canon of literature and art, clearly ought to be included in a reference book on sport. The point to be decided was whether it belonged in this volume or in one on blood sports. It is not strictly a blood sport because it is a contest as distinct from a hunt. It is, though, related to athletic pursuits in the techniques and disciplines of the bullfighter. Conclusively, it was included because it is likely to be watched – as a public spectacle or on television or film – by people who wish to be informed about it.

The primary aim, here, is that of every reference book – accuracy. Contributors (listed at p. viii) were drawn for the most part from the corps of sports correspondents of the national and international press. However, in the case of games with little literature or press coverage, and on which no established and fully informed writer was available, it was accepted that a senior administrator with playing experience, even though with no known writing ability, was the safest contributor. In editing contributions, the attempt was made to achieve uniform presentation without suppressing individual styles. In the reporting of many sports a jargon has become established; the editorial effort has been to hold a balance between cliché and technical usage.

The possibility of printing the rules or laws of each game was considered and rejected, partly on grounds of space; decisively they were not included because of the unwieldy nature of many codes, and the consequent difficulties of a person unfamiliar with the subject attempting to find a specific item within an arbitrary, but not necessarily logical, arrangement. It seemed preferable to incorporate a digested form of the laws within a 'course of play' description and to accompany it in most cases with a plan of the field, pitch, or court to clarify the description. Brief bibliographies and addresses of governing bodies are provided for most sports, for those who wish to study any of the sports in greater depth. Words printed in small capitals indicate a cross-reference, i.e. the first occurrence in an entry of a name or term for which there is a full entry elsewhere in the *Companion*.

The numerous line drawings included are to help demonstrate the play. The action photographs reflect the quality of outstanding performers and record pictorially some historic moments of sport.

The constant problem in compiling this *Companion*, and its chief shortcoming, is inherent in any book about sporting events – the simple fact that it is out of date before it is printed. In the other *Oxford Companions* – on themes more profound than sport – a preponderance of the content deals with the enduring truths of the subject: change is relatively slight. The great names remain undimmed, others join them, but only slowly. Some aspects of sport, too, are unchanging; technical criteria, basic laws, traditions, developments, the biographies of great performers of the past. The attempt has been made, too, to set the history of each sport in perspective rather than tie it tightly to the present. Nevertheless, sport changes rapidly; wherever measurement is possible, performance can be seen to improve. Every Olympic Games, every World Cup, every cycle of Test cricket, every generation of boxers, reveals and establishes new record-breakers and eminent performers. Only an annual publication can remain within hailing distance of the figures of such progress. This, however, is not a record book. With only changes of detail these games will be played in the manner described here for many years to come. The historical sections record, in most cases, the formative and establishing phases. The biographies of great sportsmen – in which high and international standards were set for inclusion – will endure.

Those wanting up-to-date statistics should not consult this book; for most sports that demand is met by annuals devised specifically to that end. The purpose here is to help the reader towards a basic understanding of a sport, its nature, structure, techniques, development, traditions and personalities as they were known at the beginning of 1974.

No reference book is free from errors; although considerable efforts have been made to avoid them here, they cannot have been completely successful and apologies are offered for those that have occurred.

Anyone who edits a book of this size for the first time must eventually be awed by the scale of the undertaking. Thanks are due to all those who prevented awe developing into despair by keeping time with their contributions; those who did not meet their obligations were few, but so distressing as to be ineradicably imprinted on memory. A deep gratitude is owed to several who contributed much more than simply their commissioned writing: among them Geoffrey Nicholson, Gordon Jeffery, David Frith, and David Hunn. Jon Stallworthy's counsel was invaluable in the early days; Jonathan Crowther and Carol Buckroyd helped through some heavy going. R. H. Havercroft did the initial sub-editing of a mass of material. Susan Stenderup was the resourceful picture researcher. Frank Keating especially, and Clifford Makins rendered expert assistance with the photographs. Carl James, the artist, and Roger Davies, the designer, helped to give the work its visual impact. Catharine Carver, with remarkable vision and practical skill, turned the vast files of the revised and re-revised entries into this book. In the mind of the editor the *Companion* will always be associated with her, and with David Edwards who, often in difficult circumstances, worked meticulously and illuminatingly on some complex – even obscure – contributions, and sustained both enthusiasm and momentum.

JOHN ARLOTT

Alresford, Hants
September, 1974

Contributors

Neil Allen, John Arlott, John Armitage, W. E. Armstrong, Radford Barrett, Howard Bass, Pat Besford, John Blake, William Boddy, Margaret Boyd, F. L. Briscoe, Malcolm Brodie, Raymond Brooks-Ward, Nigel Brown, Michael Clark, H. Edwards Clarke, Richard Cohen, C. D. Coppock, Hon. Dennis Craig, Allison Danzig, C.-L. de Beaumont, Peter Dobereiner, Alfred Drewry, David Edwards, Brian A. Fagg, Henri Fluchère, John Forbes, Major Peter Freeman, David Frith, David Frost, Brian Glanville, John Glasspool, John Goodbody, David Gray, Colonel A. F. Harper, E. G. Heath, Peter Hildreth, Eric Hill, James B. Hogg, J. H. Horry, David Hunn, Horace A. Jackson, Gordon Jeffery, Joanna Jeffery, Walter Johnston, C. M. Jones, M. M. Jones, T. F. Kelly, Asif Khan, J. F. Leaf, Major L. Lewis, Sydney Lipski, Jennifer A. Mander, Sheldon Meyer, Hon. Ivor Montagu, Ken Moses, Genevieve Murphy, Carl Myatt, Geoffrey Nicholson, M. A. Nicholson, Douglas Nye, Geoffrey Page, A. J. Palmer, Roy Pankhurst, Professor Lauri Pihkala, D. E. Porter, Jeremy Potter, Patrick Purcell, G. W. Rackham, John Radosta, John Rafferty, Major E. G. B. Reynolds, Harold Rosenthal, Irving Rosenwater, Charles Rous, Patrick Rowley, John Samuel, H. A. E. Scheele, Dr. L. M. Seewald, L. J. K. Setright, Dr. Harold Seymour, Peter Sherman, J. W. Solomon, Oscar State, A. P. Stoner, Rena B. Stratford, G. D. Stringer, F. J. Underhill, R. L. Vallintine, D. A. Wade, Ann Welch, M. D. Welch, Robin Welsh, Bryn Williams, P. O. Winkle, A. Wishart, Venlo Wolfsohn, Colin Young

A

AALTONEN, RAVNO (1938-   ), Finnish motor rally driver (see MOTOR RACING). He represented BMC, then BMW, Datsun, Lancia, and MERCEDES. He joined Ford for the World Cup Rally in 1970 and finished third.

AARON, HENRY LOUIS (1934-   ), American BASEBALL outfielder and batting star for the ATLANTA (formerly Milwaukee) BRAVES from 1954. He set numerous batting records, including the NATIONAL LEAGUE lifetime record for runs batted in—more than 2,000. He made more than 3,000 hits, and he was National League batting champion in 1956 and 1959. In 1957 he was chosen Most Valuable Player in the National League. But his outstanding achievement was hitting more than 700 home runs, which was to lead in 1974 to his breaking BABE RUTH's all-time record of 714.

A.B.A. (1) see AMATEUR BOXING ASSOCIATION; (2) see AMERICAN BASKETBALL ASSOCIATION.

ABDUL-JABBAR, KAREEM, see ALCINDOR, F. L.

ABEBE BIKILA (1932-73), MARATHON-runner for Ethiopia. The first man to win the Olympic marathon twice, Abebe Bikila was unknown and barefoot when he won the 1960 Olympic marathon at Rome. He retained his title, this time shod, at Tokyo in 1964. In each race he appeared unextended and improved the world's best performance, his time in 1964 being 2 hrs. 12 min. 11·2 sec. His emergence hinted at the existence of untapped reserves of African distance running talent, a supposition later endorsed by the performances of KEINO. A member of the Emperor Haile Selassie's bodyguard, Abebe Bikila was partially paralysed in a motoring accident in 1969 and subsequently took part as an archer in the PARAPLEGIC GAMES at Stoke Mandeville Hospital, England.

ABEL, ROBERT (1857-1936), cricketer for England and Surrey. An opening batsman, short of stature, and known as 'the Guv'nor', he scored heavily for his county, especially at the OVAL, until 1903, when failing eyesight forced him to retire. He carried his bat for 132 not out in a Test match at SYDNEY, and among his records were a score of 357 not out for Surrey, and a fourth-wicket stand of 448 with HAYWARD.

ABERDARE, 3rd Lord (formerly Hon. Clarence Napier Bruce) (1885-1957), British amateur cricketer and RACKETS and TENNIS player for Winchester College, Oxford University, and Middlesex. He was a master tactician at rackets and won the British amateur singles championship in 1922 and 1931 but also won the doubles title ten times, between 1921 and 1934, with four different partners.

ABERDEEN F.C., Scottish Association FOOTBALL club. It was founded in 1903, entered the Scottish League in 1905 and has played continuously in the top division. Aberdeen's most successful seasons date from the resumption of competitive football after the Second World War: it won the Scottish League Cup in 1946 (the first year of the competition) and in the 1955-6 season; the Scottish League championship in 1954-5; and the Scottish Cup in 1947 and 1970. Outstanding players include Hutton, Glen, JACKSON, Leggat, and B. Yorston.
COLOURS: Red shirts and white shorts.
GROUND: Pittodrie Park, Aberdeen.

ABRAHAMS, HAROLD MAURICE (1899-   ), sprinter for Great Britain, ATHLETICS administrator, and journalist. After a distinguished athletics career at Cambridge University, Abrahams won the Olympic 100 metres at Paris in 1924, equalling the Olympic record of 10·6 sec. three times. In the final he defeated, among others, the then 'world's fastest human', PADDOCK. After his retirement from active athletics, Abrahams devoted himself to administration and became a member of the General Committee of the Amateur Athletic Association in 1926. He also served on the British Amateur Athletics Board, being elected honorary treasurer in 1948 and chairman in 1968. He was athletics correspondent of the *Sunday Times* from 1925 to 1965 and a B.B.C. radio commentator for more than 45 years.

A.C. MILAN, Association FOOTBALL club. Founded in 1889, renamed Milano during the Fascist era, it became Milan again in 1945. It first won the Italian championship in 1901, and gained further titles in 1906 and 1907 but then did not win the championship again until 1951. Since then Milan has been one of the dominant Italian clubs and has made several appearances as the national champion in the European Champion Clubs Cup competition. The club reached the final of that competition on three occasions, losing to REAL MADRID in 1958 but beating BENFICA in 1963 and AJAX in 1969. Leading players have included De Vecchi, GREN, NORDAHL, LIEDHOLM, SCHIAFFINO, Altafini, and Rivera.
COLOURS: Red and black striped shirts, white shorts.

ADAM, KARL (1911-1976), West German ROWING coach whose methods revolutionized rowing in the 1950s and '60s. A world student BOXING champion before the Second World War, he had no previous rowing experience when he began coaching at RATZEBURG, near Lübeck, after the war. He ignored traditional ideas of rowing and coaching and relied on what he called the 'cybernetic system' of learning — an instinctive use of the sensory organs for balance, and co-ordination. He adapted interval training methods from athletics and introduced intensive land training in the winter months, based on the use of weights.
Employing a high rate of striking and virtually no body-swing, Adam's crews were almost immediately successful and from 1958 they won European, world, and Olympic titles. His eights were particularly successful and from 1959 to 1968 they were beaten only once in international championships. In 1965, Adam was appointed director of the Ratzeburg Rowing Academy.

ADAMOWICZ, TONY (1941-   ), American MOTOR RACING driver, 1969 FORMULA 5000 CHAMPIONSHIP winner, taking two victories in the series. In 1968 he won six TRANS-AM under-2-litre sedan (saloon) car races, leading PORSCHE to the manufacturer's title.

ADAMS TROPHY, see BOWLS, LAWN.

ADLINGTON, PAUL (1948-   ), British water skier. In August 1969 Adlington set a British national record of 3,765 points in the tricks event in the northern European championships at Princes Club near London.

ADMIRAL'S CUP, a YACHTING trophy competed for biennially by representative three-boat teams of offshore racing yachts. The competition comprises four races two off-shore and two inshore, sailed every odd-number year concurrent with Cowes Week. The final race of the series is the FASTNET.

ADMIRATION (1892) was the foundation mare of the Eyrefield Lodge Stud in Ireland, owned by Col. Loder. She was dam of PRETTY POLLY and ancestress of DONATELLO II and ST. PADDY.

AEROBATICS, see FLYING, SPORTING.

AERTS, JEAN (1907-   ), Belgian cyclist. He was the first man to win world road-race titles both as an amateur (1927) and as a professional (1935). A curiosity of his 1927 title is that amateurs and professionals rode together in the championship race at the NUR-BURGRING, Germany; Aerts came fifth, but was the highest-placed amateur.

A.F.L., see AMERICAN FOOTBALL LEAGUE.

AFRICAN GAMES, see PAN-AFRICAN GAMES.

AGA KHAN, H.H. the (1875-1957), the most successful race-horse owner-breeder and a lavish patron of the Turf. He headed the list of leading owners in England for a record 13 seasons, and won 784 races including 17 classics, and £1,026,510 in stakes. His five Derby winners were Blenheim, triple-crowned BAH-RAM, Mahmoud (who won in the record time of 2 min., 33·8 sec.), My Love, and TULYAR.

AGA KHAN TOURNAMENT, see HOCKEY, FIELD.

AGAPOV, GENNADI (1933-   ), race walker for U.S.S.R. who set a world record for 20 km. in 1969 and gained a silver medal in the European Games 50 km. in 1966. An erratic competitor, he was a leader in both the 1964 and 1968 OLYMPIC GAMES 50 km. but faded badly on both occasions, and was fifth in the LUGANO CUP final 20 km. in 1970.

AGOSTINI, GIACOMO (1944-   ), Italian racing motor-cyclist. After some domestic success in the 250 cc. class, he was invited to ride for MV AGUSTA in 1965 and became an immediate contender for the 350 and 500 cc. world championships, winning the larger class first in 1966 and in the following six years. In

1973 he had to content himself with the 350 cc. title; at the end of that season he transferred his services to the Yamaha team.

AHM, Mrs. TONNI (*née* Olsen) (1915-), Danish BADMINTON player. In the course of a career extending internationally for 23 years, she was one of her country's finest players and among the first to achieve world class. Between 1939 and 1952 she won 11 ALL-ENGLAND titles, including a hat-trick in both 1950 and 1952, and during her whole career more than 50 national championship titles.

AILLÈRES, GEORGES (1936-), RUGBY LEAGUE forward for France and Toulouse Olympique, first in the second row and later as prop forward, and captain of the national team. He made the first of his 36 international appearances in 1961-2, and captained the French international side in 1969-70.

AINTREE, race-course near Liverpool, where the GRAND NATIONAL STEEPLECHASE is run.

AIR PISTOL SHOOTING, see SHOOTING, AIR WEAPONS.

AIR RACING, see FLYING, SPORTING.

AIR RIFLE SHOOTING, see SHOOTING, AIR WEAPONS.

AIR TOURING, see FLYING, SPORTING.

AIRD TROPHY, see BOWLS, INDOOR.

AIROLO–CHIASSO RELAY, a Swiss event in road RACE WALKING for a five-man relay, held in mid-October over a total distance of 115 km. (72 miles). First held in 1962, it is unique in that it is the only relay event internationally accepted in race walking and now attracts national teams from the U.S.A., Czechoslovakia, and Romania as well as all the leading west European countries. Winners have included Sweden (1962-3, 1965), Italy (1966-9, 1970, 1972), and London (1967-8). The course record is held by East Germany, established in 1973.

The race starts at 6.30 a.m. and the first stage (27 km.) finishes at Giornico, the record-holder being Nigro (Italy) in 1969. This stage is downhill with numerous hairpin bends. The next section to Bellinzona (30 km.) is very flat. After a flat section of 8 km. the third stage finishes at the summit of Monte Ceneri following a difficult 6 km. climb. The next leg finishes in Lugano (19 km.) over an undulating route. The final stage to Chiasso

(25 km.) is often very difficult, due to the volume of motor traffic encountered. This section is flat for the first 16 km. and then undulating to the finish.

AJAX, Dutch Association FOOTBALL club, Amsterdam, was founded in 1900 and first won the Netherlands championship in 1917-18, subsequently winning it five more times in the 1930s. Outstanding among its players have been Muller, wing half, and CRUYFF, centre forward, in their powerful team of the late 1960s, which won the European Champions Cup in 1971, 1972, and 1973.
COLOURS: White shirts with broad red vertical band, white shorts.

AKERS-DOUGLAS, I. (*fl.* 1932-5), British amateur RACKETS player. He won the British amateur singles championship 1932-4 and the doubles championship with Wagg in 1932-3 and 1935.

ALABAMA, University of, American college FOOTBALL team, nicknamed the 'Crimson Tide', dominated the Southeastern Conference in the early 1930s, under coach Thomas, led by passer Howell and receiver HUTSON. Under coach Bryant, who had played in Alabama's 1935 Rose Bowl, Alabama compiled a 57-6-3 won-and-lost record between 1960 and 1965, with quarterback NAMATH outstanding. The 1973 team was unbeaten until the climactic Sugar Bowl game, when NOTRE DAME defeated them for the national championship.
COLOURS: Crimson and white.

ALAN BARBER CUP, see ETON FIVES.

ALBERT LUSTY TROPHY, see BICYCLE POLO.

ALBERT PARK, Melbourne. When in 1960 the Victorian government allocated part of Albert Park, on the outskirts of Melbourne, for various sports, the Victoria Squash Rackets Association obtained a site on which was built a six-court club including a championship court to accommodate about 450 spectators. It was here that the individual event of the 1967 international championships was played.

ALCIDE (1955), English race-horse by Alycidon (winner of the Ascot, Goodwood, and Doncaster Cups), who was bred and owned by Sir Humphrey de Trafford, trained by BOYD-ROCHFORT, and ridden by Carr. He won the KING GEORGE VI AND QUEEN ELIZABETH STAKES, the ST. LEGER, and six other races, together with £56,051 in stakes.

ALCINDOR, FERDINAND LEWIS (Kareem Abdul-Jabbar) (1947-   ), American BASKETBALL player, standing 7 ft. 1⅜ in. (2·17 m.) in height. In his three seasons at the University of California at Los Angeles, the U.C.L.A. BRUINS won 88 games, and lost only 2. They won the NATIONAL COLLEGIATE ATHLETIC ASSOCIATION title on each occasion, and Alcindor was voted the most valuable player of the play-offs at all three finals.

Alcindor declined the invitation to play in the 1968 OLYMPIC GAMES. He turned professional in 1969 with the MILWAUKEE BUCKS, of the NATIONAL BASKETBALL ASSOCIATION, with a contract reputedly for $1,400,000. In his first two seasons at Milwaukee the Bucks rose from last place to win the N.B.A. championship in 1971.

ALDWYCH SPEED SKATING CLUB, Britain's first roller speed skating (see ROLLER SKATING) club, formed in London in 1908, produced most of the best British racers until 1928, when the club's main activities were transferred to ice speed skating (see ICE SKATING). The collective skating ability of its members has been reflected by five team victories in the British 3 miles (4·828 km.) inter-club relay championship, 1923, 1924, 1925, 1927, and 1928, and by a tenth team victory in 1969 in the equivalent championship on ice, previous successes on ice including six wins in a row, 1939 to 1950—an unbeaten period including the inactive war years. Six outright wins were achieved in Britain's Southern and Midland Ice Speed Skating League club competition from 1939 to 1955.

ALES, Church, see FOLK SPORTS.

ALEXANDER, GROVER CLEVELAND (1887-1950), American BASEBALL pitcher who won 373 games, a NATIONAL LEAGUE record equalled only by MATHEWSON. The most dramatic incident in his 20-year major-league career occurred in the seventh and deciding game of the 1926 WORLD SERIES. In the seventh inning with two out and three NEW YORK YANKEE runners on base, he was called into the game and preserved the ST. LOUIS CARDINALS' 3-2 lead by striking out the dangerous hitter Lazzeri. He went on to hold New York scoreless in the remaining two innings and thus enabled the Cardinals to win their first world championship.

ALEXEEV, VASILI (1942-   ), Russian super heavyweight lifter and 1970, 1971, 1972, and 1973 world and European champion. He was the first lifter to total 600 kg.

(1,322·8 lb.) and to jerk 500 lb. (226·8 kg.), and eventually to press 500 lb. Alexeev has so far made 58 world records, more than any other lifter. He was the first lifter to total 400 kg. (881½ lb.) on the two lifts.

ALI, MUHAMMAD, see CLAY, C.

ALLAIS, ÉMILE (1914-   ), French ski racer who won all three gold medals at the world championships at Chamonix in 1937 and, in collaboration with a technician-theorist, Gignaux, devised the first exclusively French Alpine SKIING technique based on rotation of the body and heel-lift.

ALLAN CUP, the senior amateur league competition in ICE HOCKEY in Canada, first won in 1908 by Ottawa Cliffsides.

ALLARDICE, ROBERT BARCLAY (1779-1854), commonly known as 'Captain Barclay', performed a feat of extraordinary athletic endurance at Newmarket Heath in 1809. He walked 1,000 miles (1,609 km.) in 1,000 hours. His performance, for a wager, led to many similar attempts, to a great increase in professional ATHLETICS generally, as well as a public interest in them, and to an awareness among athletes of the need for sustained and rigorous training.

ALL-BLACKS, popular term for representative RUGBY UNION players of New Zealand, first used in 1905. It is derived from the black jerseys, black shorts, and black stockings which became the regular uniform for New Zealand representative players in 1901.

ALLEN, Dr. FOREST C. (Phog) (b. 1886), American BASKETBALL coach, who became one of the principal ambassadors of the game. Allen himself played the game in the 1890s, soon after its invention by NAISMITH. Allen was instrumental in achieving recognition for basketball as an Olympic sport in 1936, and was elected to the Hall of Fame (see NAISMITH) at its foundation in 1959. He held radical views regarding proposals for revisions of the rules, with the special intention of limiting the effect of the very tall player.

ALLEN, FREDERICK (1920-   ), RUGBY UNION five-eighth for New Zealand who captained his country on their 1949 tour of South Africa. He became one of the most celebrated coaches the game has known, leading the Auckland provincial side to a record number of 25 consecutive defences of the RANFURLY SHIELD between 1960 and 1963. Between

1966 and 1968, he coached New Zealand to an unbroken sequence of victories against the LIONS, France, Australia, England, Scotland, and Wales, and was assistant manager and coach of the 1967 ALL-BLACKS in Britain and France.

ALLEN, GEORGE OSWALD BROWNING (Gubby), C.B.E. (1902-   ), cricketer for England, Cambridge University, and Middlesex. A fast bowler and fine middle-order batsman, he captained England in 1936, and led the team to Australia in the following winter, winning the first two Tests but losing the remaining three. He was later an England selector, and president (1963-4) and, subsequently, treasurer of M.C.C.

ALLEN, RICHARD JAMES (1902-   ), HOCKEY goalkeeper for India and Port Commissioners (Calcutta). With CHAND and GENTLE, he holds a record of having won an Olympic gold medal for hockey three times (1928, 1932, 1936). He was an outstanding goalkeeper in the years between the two wars and did not concede a goal throughout the 1928 OLYMPIC GAMES tournament.

ALL-ENGLAND BADMINTON CHAMPIONSHIPS, the most important BADMINTON tournament; since the Second World War it has generally been regarded as the unofficial championship of the world. It has been held annually since 1899 (except during war years) and is organized by the Badminton Association of England in March.

ALL-ENGLAND CLUB, the most influential of all LAWN TENNIS clubs. The WIMBLEDON championships, the game's first and most important tournament, have always been played 'on the lawns of the All-England Club', whether at Worple Road, as they were from 1877 to 1921, or, as they have been since, at the 'new' ground at Church Road. The club was founded originally as the All-England Croquet Club in 1869. In 1877, as lawn tennis began to increase in importance, the name was changed to the All-England Croquet and Lawn Tennis Club and in 1882 lawn tennis finally took precedence when the present title of All-England Lawn Tennis and Croquet Club was adopted.

The All-England is a private club with 375 members and 90 temporary members who are elected from year to year. In addition, there are a number of honorary members, who usually include the singles champions. The championships are organized by the 12 members of the committee of the club and 7 representatives of the LAWN TENNIS ASSOCIATION.

ALL-ENGLAND XI. The spread of interest in CRICKET to the rural centres of England during the mid-nineteenth century owed much to the All-England XI, which was founded in 1846 by WILLIAM CLARKE, who captained and managed it. He was an accomplished slow bowler himself — he took 2,385 wickets between 1846 and 1853 (including 476 in 1853) — and the top-class players who toured with him usually overwhelmed the local opposition, who were invariably unskilled. Among his team were PARR, PILCH, MYNN, Guy, Dean, Felix (né Wanostrocht), J. Lillywhite, WISDEN, Hillyer, Martingell, Box, and the fearsome fast bowler, Jackson. The provincial sides had little chance against such a weight of talent, though they usually played as XVIIIs or XXIIs, or with 'given men'. Any success that local players managed to achieve against such illustrious opposition was greatly relished.

The missionary work of Clarke's XI continued after his death in 1856, though by this time a rival group known as the United England XI had been set up by Wisden and Dean after several of the All-England players from the south had taken exception to Clarke's autocratic manner and to his method of sharing profits. Parr had succeeded Clarke as captain, and after Clarke's death the All-England XI played the United England XI annually in what became recognized as the major match of the season, in aid of the Cricketers' Fund. The United England XI in turn suffered a split in its ranks in 1865, and before long organized county cricket became the main interest. The All-England XI, however, had harnessed the professional cricketing might of England and generated an enthusiasm that eventually raised the game to the level of a national pastime.

ALLHUSEN, Maj. DEREK (1917-   ), British three-day event (see EQUESTRIAN EVENTS) horseman. At the age of 54, he rode in the British team that won a gold medal in the 1968 OLYMPIC GAMES while individually he also won the silver medal. In the WINTER OLYMPIC GAMES of 1948, he represented Great Britain in the pentathlon and his interest in three-day events was fired by watching Olympic teams training for this competition during the same year. He first rode for Britain in 1957 on a home-bred mare called Laurien, but it was with Lochinvar that he achieved his success at the Mexico Olympics.

ALLSOP, TERENCE (1941-   ), LACROSSE player for England, South of England, Kent, and Cambridge University. He was considered by the Americans after the combined universities tour of 1961 to be the best goal-keeper in the world. His ability to assess the game, clear the ball accurately, and break down opposing attack moves proved to be a deciding factor in several games when he played for England on the 1967 tour of the States.

ALPE D'HUEZ, BOBSLEIGH course near Grenoble, France, constructed for the 1968 WINTER OLYMPIC GAMES but opened in time to stage the 1967 world championships. It is the only course in the world with a base constructed entirely of concrete, 2,450 cu. m. of concrete being used in 700 prefabricated sections. The course includes six corners, one hairpin bend, and four curves. The starting altitude is 2,000 m. (6,562 ft.). The course is 1,500 m. long, dropping 390 m. (1,280 ft.). Some of the corners are artificially frozen: 165 lighting installations enable competitions to be held at night, when ice conditions are often at their best. The two-man sleds can here average more than 113 km./h. (70 m.p.h.) on the banked and plummetting serpentine track.

ALPINE SKIING, see SKIING.

ALTCAR CLUB, COURSING club founded in 1825 by Lord Molyneux. The club originally staged two meetings each year on the SEFTON family estates at Altcar, Lancashire, one in early November for the Altcar Cup, the other in early February. This programme has been adhered to, save for bringing forward the February meeting by a month to make way for the WATERLOO CUP which, since 1836, has traditionally been run over the same ground.

Compared with the ups and downs of other coursing clubs, the Altcar has flourished until it is indisputably the principal coursing institution in the United Kingdom, if not the world. As membership is accorded only to those who have served a proper apprenticeship in the sport, to be a member of Altcar is regarded both as an honour and as the hallmark of the Leash. The club's two major trophies, the Altcar Cup and the Members' Plate, are the most coveted of coursing honours next to the Blue Riband itself.

ALTHAM, HARRY SURTEES, C.B.E., D.S.O., M.C. (1888-1965), cricketer for Oxford University, Surrey, and Hampshire, and CRICKET historian. His scholarly *History of Cricket* appeared in 1926 (with subsequent editions in collaboration with E. W. Swanton), and he continued to serve the game as administrator and as coach and mentor to young cricketers.

ALTIG, RUDI (1937-   ), German profes-

sional cyclist. An all-rounder, he won world pursuit titles as an amateur (1959) and as a professional (1960 and 1961) as well as the professional road-race championship of 1966. Although his road-race victories included the 1962 VUELTA A ESPAGNA, his limitations as a climber eventually made him turn much of his attention to six-day and other track racing.

ALTWEGG, JEANNETTE, C.B.E. (1930-   ), ice figure-skater for Great Britain. This methodical, imperturbable performer won the world and European titles in 1951. The following year, she retained the European title and won the Olympic gold medal in Oslo, a feat later to be recognized by the award of a C.B.E., the highest honour ever bestowed on a British skater. Four times national champion, 1947-50, Miss Altwegg had an ideal temperament for the big occasion and excelled particularly in the compulsory figures, attaining an exemplary standard which widened international respect for British achievement in this branch of the sport. She was also a finalist in the 1947 Wimbledon junior LAWN TENNIS championships.

ALVERA, RENZO (1933-   ), BOBSLEIGH rider for Italy, gained four consecutive world two-man titles as brakeman to MONTI, 1957-60. Alvera was also in two winning four-man world championship crews in 1960 and 1961, each time riding behind Monti; so he achieved a record number of six world titles as a brakeman.

AMATEUR BOXING ASSOCIATION (A.B.A.), founded in 1880 to 'encourage, develop, and control amateur BOXING in England'. There are separate bodies for the sport in Scotland and Wales. The A.B.A. was brought into being as a replacement for the Queensberry amateur championships which had begun in 1867 and which continued until 1885. The A.B.A. had only 12 clubs in affiliation at first but by 1924 that number had increased to 105. The high point of the A.B.A. season is its championships, in which all British amateurs may box, at the EMPIRE POOL, WEMBLEY, in April.

AMERICAN BASKETBALL ASSOCIATION (A.B.A.), professional BASKETBALL league in the U.S.A., formed in 1967 following the failure of the SAPERSTEIN-inspired American Basketball League (A.B.L.) to rival the NATIONAL BASKETBALL LEAGUE. The A.B.A. appointed MIKAN as league commissioner, and in 1969 Borgia became director of officials.

AMERICAN BOWLING CONGRESS
(A.B.C.), see BOWLING, TENPIN.

AMERICAN FOOTBALL LEAGUE
(A.F.L.), American professional FOOTBALL
organization, founded in 1960 under the
leadership of Lamar Hunt, owner of the Dallas
Texans, with war flying hero Foss as first
Commissioner. Presenting a challenge to the
well-established NATIONAL FOOTBALL LEAGUE
(N.F.L.), the A.F.L. had teams in New York,
Boston, Buffalo, Houston, Dallas (later Kansas City), Denver, Oakland, and Los Angeles
(later San Diego). After several years of
meagre attendance, the League began to succeed in the bidding war for college football
talent with the N.F.L. Werblin bought the
New York Titans, renamed them the NEW
YORK JETS, and moved the A.F.L. into major
position by signing ALABAMA quarterback
NAMATH and by negotiating a five-year television contract with the National Broadcasting
Company. The bidding war escalated. When
the NEW YORK GIANTS signed the Buffalo
kicker, Gogolak, the new A.F.L. Commissioner Davis, former Oakland coach, began
raiding N.F.L. quarterbacks. Soon (June
1966) the two Leagues agreed to merge. The
ten A.F.L. teams (the original eight, plus
Miami and Cincinnati) formed the American
Conference of the combined N.F.L. The New
York Jets were the first A.F.L. team to win the
Super Bowl, between the two League champions, in 1969.

AMERICAN LEAGUE, American professional BASEBALL league officially founded in
1901, with B. B. JOHNSON as guiding force. In
1903 the NATIONAL LEAGUE agreed to establish two major leagues, and the WORLD SERIES
between the two leagues' champions was first
held that year. The DETROIT TIGERS and BOS-
TON RED SOX were the strong teams of the first
20 years, while MACK'S PHILADELPHIA ATH-
LETICS won four titles between 1910 and 1914.
Mack then sold his stars to maintain solvency
in the face of declining attendance, as he
would later do in the early 1930s, after successive titles again, 1929-31. Following the 1919
World Series, several leading CHICAGO WHITE
SOX players were accused of 'throwing' the
series in return for payment from gamblers, a
scandal that removed Chicago as a league
power. In 1920 Boston sold BABE RUTH and
several other stars to the NEW YORK YANKEES
and thus helped start the greatest 'dynasty' in
baseball history. From 1921 to 1964, under
three great managers, among others
—Huggins in the 1920s, McCarthy in the
1930s, STENGEL in the 1950s—the Yankees
won 29 league titles and 20 World Series,

including an unprecedented five in a row from
1949 to 1953. In 1954 the ST. LOUIS BROWNS
shifted to Baltimore; the next year Philadelphia shifted to Kansas City. In 1962 the LOS
ANGELES (later California) ANGELS and the
MINNESOTA TWINS (shifted from Washington,
which in turn gained a new team) expanded
the league to ten teams. In 1968 Kansas City
shifted to Oakland, to be followed the next
year by league expansion to 12 teams, partly
to calm Kansas City's upset. The KANSAS CITY
ROYALS and SEATTLE PILOTS were formed, but
the inept Seattle organization was transferred
to Milwaukee the next year. In 1972 the
WASHINGTON SENATORS were transferred to
the Dallas–Fort Worth area and renamed the
TEXAS RANGERS, playing in Arlington. Thus
the nation's capital was left without a major-
league baseball team.

AMERICA'S CUP, named after the yacht
America which won it in 1851, is a ewer-
shaped trophy originally presented by the
Royal Yacht Squadron in 1851 for a race
round the Isle of Wight. In 1857 the Stevens
syndicate, owners of the *America*, gave the
cup to the New York Yacht Club as a perpetual international challenge trophy.

The *America*, a schooner-rigged yacht of
170 tons, was designed and built by Steers of
New York, based on the lines of the pilot
schooners for which he was famous. She was
financed at a cost of $30,000 by a syndicate
headed by Stevens.

AMES, LESLIE ETHELBERT GEORGE,
C.B.E. (1905-   ), cricketer for England and
Kent. His 102 centuries in first-class CRICKET
place him far above any other wicket-keeper
as a run-scorer, and he was first choice for
England throughout the 1930s, during which
he scored eight Test centuries, averaging
40·56, and made 98 dismissals.

AMIN, I. (1934-   ), the best Egyptian
amateur SQUASH RACKETS player since the
Second World War. He became Egyptian
amateur champion in 1958 and again in 1963
and 1964. He first came to Britain for the
1955-6 amateur championship which,
although unseeded, he won. Amin figured in
five subsequent finals of the amateur championship, winning only once again when, in
1960, he beat his compatriot Shafik.

AMR BEY, F. D. (Amr Pasha) (1910-   ),
Egyptian SQUASH RACKETS player who came to
prominence when serving in the Egyptian
Embassy in London. He first won the amateur
championship in 1931 and won the event six
times in all. He successfully challenged

BUTCHER for the Open championship in 1932 and defended his title against the same player once and against DEAR three times, retiring unbeaten in 1938.

AMSTELVEEN HOCKEY GROUND, near Amsterdam, the national ground of the Royal Netherlands Hockey Board. The ground was laid out in 1938 and redesigned in 1970 as a World Hockey Cup venue. At that time, 19 grass grounds were laid and a hard court with artificial lighting.

AMSTUTZ, WALTER (1902-   ), Swiss SKIING pioneer principally involved in the formation of the Swiss University Ski Club in 1924, who collaborated closely with ARNOLD LUNN and the KANDAHAR CLUB at Mürren, Switzerland, in introducing downhill and modern slalom racing.

ANDERLECHT R.S.C., Association FOOT-BALL club, Brussels. Founded in 1908, it dominated Belgian football after the Second World War, winning its initial championship in 1946-7, and going on to win the next two. The club competed regularly in the European Cup and its best players include MERMANS, JURION, and VAN HIMST.
COLOURS: Blue and mauve shirts, white shorts.

ANDERSEN, HJALMAR (1923-   ), ice speed-skater for Norway, who won three gold medals at the 1952 WINTER OLYMPIC GAMES in Oslo, over distances of 1,500, 5,000, and 10,000 metres. He was world over-all champion on three consecutive occasions, 1950-2.

ANDERSON, GARY (1940-   ), American who won seven world championships in either small-bore or high-power rifle SHOOT-ING during the period 1962 to 1968 while a theological student. He also won the Olympic Gold medals for free rifle, 300 metres (328 yds.) three positions, in 1964 at Tokyo and 1968 at Mexico. He set six world records in various rifle shooting categories.

ANDERSON, JESSIE, see VALENTINE, MRS. GEORGE.

ANDERSON, PAUL (1933-   ),- American heavyweight lifter, 1955 world champion, 1956 Olympic champion. He was the first lifter to total over 1,100 lb. (500 kg.) and to press 400 lb. (181·4 kg.). He was known as the 'Dixie Derrick' because of his amazing feats of strength, including a back lift of 6,270 lb. (2,844 kg.), the greatest weight ever lifted by one man.

ANDRADA, MANUEL (c. 1900-   ), Argentinian POLO player, one of the best of his day at 'back'. He played in the winning team in the Cup of the Americas v. U.S.A. in 1936 and in the losing team in 1932. Handicap 10.

ANDRADE, JOSÉ (fl. 1924-38), Association footballer for Uruguay, who played in the Olympic winning teams of 1924 and 1938, and the World Cup-winning team of 1930, in the half-back line known as 'la costilla metal-lica' (iron curtain).

ANDRADE, RODRIGUEZ (fl. 1950-4), Association footballer for Uruguay, a nephew of JOSÉ ANDRADE who played in Uruguay's 1930 World Cup-winning team, he was an outstanding member of the 1950 World Cup-winning side in Brazil, and of the 1954 World Cup side which came fourth in Switzerland.

ANDRETTI, MARIO (1940-   ), Italian MOTOR RACING driver, three-times United States Auto Club national champion — 1965, 1966, and 1968 — and winner of 32 U.S.A.C. national championship races including the 1969 INDIANAPOLIS 500. In road racing, he won the 1969 Pike's Peak Hill Climb in a speedway car; the 1970 and 1972 Sebring 12-hours with co-drivers; the 1971 Questor Grand Prix at Ontario; the 1971 South African Grand Prix, and in 1973, the 24 Hours of Daytona, the B.O.A.C. 1,000 Kilometres at BRANDS HATCH, and the Watkins Glen 6 Hours with co-driver Ickx.

ANDREYEV, VLADIMIR (1947-   ), BASKETBALL player for the U.S.S.R. A member of the TS.S.K.A. MOSCOW club, Andreyev stands 7 ft. 1 in. (2·15 m.) tall, and rapidly established himself as one of the finest centres in the history of the game in Europe.

ANGELO, DOMENICO (1717-1802), Italian fencer who came to London in 1754, founded an aristocratic Academy of Arms which lasted for more than a century and a half. He was riding and FENCING master to the royal family and author of École des Armes. The tradition was carried on by his son Harry Angelo II (1756-1835), his grandsons Henry Angelo III (1780-1852) and William Henry Angelo (1789-1853), and his great-grandson Henry Angelo IV who died about 1866.

ANILIN (1961), the best race-horse bred in the Soviet Union. Trained and ridden by Nasi-boff, he won the Bolshoi Derby, the Grand Prix of the socialist countries, and the Prix im U.S.S.R. twice, as well as scoring three consecutive wins in the PREIS VON EUROPA.

ANIMAL-BAITING, a pastime popular all
the year in the sixteenth century, included the
'blood' sports of cock-fighting, dog-fighting,
and even horse-fighting. Of the sports setting
animals against others of the same species,
cock-fighting was by far the most popular.
Cocks were carefully bred and trained to fight.
At first they fought with their natural weapons
of spur and beak, but by the seventeenth century the refinement of metal spurs had been
added. The best breeds of fighting cocks
included Piles, Blackreds, Pollcats, Pirchin
Ducks, Gingers, and Shropshire Reds. In 1697
the cock-pit in Whitehall was converted to the
Privy Council Room, but although royal
interest in cock-fighting may have declined,
the aristocracy, gentry, and commons retained
their liking for it, partly because of the
pleasure of watching the spectacle and partly
from the betting that accompanied each fight.

Fitzstephen, the chronicler of Henry II's
reign, records cock-fights and the baits that
were popular from at least that time until the
nineteenth century. He mentions the baiting
— that is the setting of dogs on to a tied-up and
sometimes blinded animal — of bulls, bears,
and boars. The baiting of the first two was to
continue for another 800 years. Sometimes
asses or horses were used, but the sport
offered was poor since the animals were not
aggressive enough.

The baits were attended by rich and poor
alike, and while the outcome of the fight was
usually inevitable, in that the bull or bear had
little chance of defeating or escaping from all
its attackers, there was still betting on the performance of individual dogs. The duration of
the fight would depend on the owner of the
bull or bear, or the owners of the dogs. Bears
were generally kept to fight again, since they
were expensive, but bulls were more expendable, although a bull that had acquired a reputation for providing good sport was a valuable
asset and was kept to fight repeatedly. The
Master of Bears was a crown office, with a
stipend of 16d. per day, and on 11 October
1561 Sir Saunders Duncombe was granted a
patent for 'the sole profit of the fighting and
combating of wild and domestic beasts in
England for the space of fourteen years',
which must have provided him with a good
income.

There were bear gardens in London,
notably one behind Shakespeare's Globe
theatre, on Bankside in Southwark, built in
1526. The royal palace contained a bear
garden, for the Tudors were especially fond of
the sport. When Mary Tudor had been
crowned and met her sister Elizabeth, later
Elizabeth I, they first attended mass and then
proceeded to watch a bear-bait. Laneham writ-

ing in 1575 describes a bait with the relish that
people of all classes felt when watching such a
fight: '...it is a sport very pleasent to see the
bear, with his pink eyes leering after his enemies approach....if he were taken once, then
by what shift with clawing, with roaring, with
tossing and tumbling he would work himself
from them... with the blood and slaver hanging about his physiognomy.' Four or five dogs
were generally loosed at the beginning of the
bait and it was by no means unusual for two to
be killed almost at once. Fresh dogs were
unleashed and the fight continued either until
the supply of dogs ran out, or until the bear
was too badly injured to fight on. The bears
were tended by bear-wards who saw to the
healing of their charges' wounds and kept
them in good health for the next combat. The
bear-wards often travelled from town to town
and led the bear through the streets as an
advertisement for the bait to come. Then local
people could bring their dogs to the bait.

Stubbes took the Puritan attitude to such
sports when he wrote in 1583: 'What Christian
heart can take pleasure to see one poor beast
rend, tear and kill another and all for his fool-
ish pleasure.' The Protectorate suppressed
baits but they were restored with the monarchy
in 1660. By this time not only Puritans were
revolted by the practice. Pepys wrote in 1666
of bull-baiting: 'It is a very rude and nasty
pleasure', and Evelyn in 1670 said of a visit to
Bankside, 'there was cock-fights, dog-fights
and bull and bear-baiting. It being a famous
day for all these butcherly sports or rather barbarous cruelties... all ended and I most
heartily weary of the rude and dirty pastime.'
But such sentiments were a minority view, and
it was not until 1802 that an attempt was made
in Parliament to introduce legislation to abolish the pastime. The attempt, despite its support by Sheridan and Wilberforce, was
defeated, largely by the efforts of Windham
who saw behind it a conspiracy of Methodists
and Jacobins to overthrow the established
order and undermine the traditional British
way of life. In 1835, however, another attempt
at abolition was made and this time it was successful. Even so, illegal baits were held at
Wirksworth in 1840, at Eccles in 1842, and at
West Derby in 1853.

Another variety of bull-baiting was the
annual Stamford bull-running. This event had
origins dating back to King John's reign. For
centuries a bull was turned loose in the streets
on 13 November and then chased through the
town by the inhabitants armed with sticks and
clubs. The hunt lasted all day and the exhausted animal was finally surrounded, killed,
and eaten. In 1788 the Lord Mayor and Lord
Exeter tried to stop it but without success.

The Society for the Prevention of Cruelty to Animals sent down representatives in 1836 and a riot ensued. The Home Secretary urged the town authorities to act, and in 1838 a large number of special constables, augmented by soldiers and police, tried again to end the hunt but without success. By 1840 the townspeople had presumably decided that the run caused more trouble than it was worth and the custom was abandoned, in Stamford and elsewhere. (See FOLK SPORTS.)

ANNE, H.R.H. Princess (1950-   ), British three-day event (see EQUESTRIAN EVENTS) horsewoman. The first member of the British royal family ever to compete in a European championship, she rode Doublet to win the individual title in 1971.

ANQUETIL, JACQUES (1934-   ), French professional road-race cyclist. The dominant figure in continental stage racing from 1957 to 1965, he achieved a record five TOUR DE FRANCE victories, four of them in succession (1961-4). His greatest attribute was his skill as a time trialist; he won the GRAND PRIX DES NATIONS nine times, and owed many of his Tour successes to the minutes and seconds he could count on regaining in the time-trial stages. However, he could make a show of strength, as in the 1963 Tour de France when he attacked and beat POULIDOR and BAHAMONTES on two mountain stages, and in the 1966 LIÈGE–BASTOGNE–LIÈGE when he broke alone 25 miles from the finish and won by nearly 5 minutes. He was the first man to win both the VUELTA A ESPAGNA and Tour de France in the same year (1963), and in the following season won the GIRO D'ITALIA and Tour de France double, which only COPPI had achieved. He retired as a professional rider at the end of 1969.

ANSELL, Col. Sir MICHAEL (1905-   ), British show jumping (see EQUESTRIAN EVENTS) administrator and former international rider. Though he lost his sight as the result of a war wound, he played a leading role in the British Show Jumping Association, of which he became chairman in December 1944.

ANSON, ADRIAN C. (1851-1922), American BASEBALL player for 27 years in the major leagues, and player-manager of the Chicago White Stockings for 19 seasons (1879-97), during which the team won five pennants. Anson batted 300 or higher 20 times, won the NATIONAL LEAGUE batting championship four times, and made more than 3,000 hits.

ANTHOINE, ÉMILE (1882-1968), French race walker, official, and administrator. While holding professional middle-distance running records he competed and finished second in the Bordeaux–Paris 611 km. (379 miles) walk in 1903. Creating many national records at varying distances, Anthoine was still competing with success well into his mid-sixties. Founder of the Union Française de Marche and the STRASBOURG–PARIS race (1926), he organized numerous long-distance competitions throughout France and was instrumental in making endurance walk events so popular among the French public.

ANTILLA, KALLE (*fl.* 1920-4), Finnish wrestler who won Olympic gold medals in 1920 and 1924. His style and speed brought him the freestyle lightweight title in 1920. He confirmed his position as Europe's finest competitor when he finished first in the world Graeco-Roman championships for the next two years in the featherweight category. He rounded off his successful career with a gold medal at Paris in 1924.

APARICIO, JULIO (1932-   ), *matador de toros*, who took his *alternativa* in 1950. Courageous and artistic in his early career, his *pases de castigo* are regarded as a hallmark of their kind.

APOLOGY (1871) was one of the champion fillies of the English Turf. She won the ST. LEGER, OAKS, ONE THOUSAND GUINEAS, CORONATION STAKES, and ASCOT GOLD CUP.

APPLE TREE GANG. Five pioneer American golfers who formed the St. Andrews Golf Club of Yonkers in 1888 became known as the Apple Tree Gang when they laid out a six-hole golf course in an orchard. The club later moved to its permanent home at Mount Hope, N.Y.

AQUABOBBING, a water sport, is a way to ski on water requiring no special athletic abilities. It is performed on a vehicle like a tricycle, with three water skis in place of wheels, which is towed over the water by a motor launch on the same principle as WATER-SKIING. As with a tricycle, no skill in maintaining equilibrium is needed. The aquabobber sits comfortably in an upright position in the saddle, holding the handlebars firmly, with his feet resting on the side skis, and skims over the water at 25 m.p.h. (40 km./h.) or more without any danger of falling.

The aquabob is built on a rustless steel frame. The three skis are of wood, the two side ones fixed rigidly to the frame, while the front ski, positioned slightly lower, is movable to allow steering. At the rear extremity of each ski is a small fin. The rubber-cushioned saddle is also of wood to ensure that the aquabob floats. The over-all length is 6 ft. (1·83 m.), width 2 ft. (0·61 m.), and the height of the saddle above water 1 ft. 6 in. (0·45 m.).

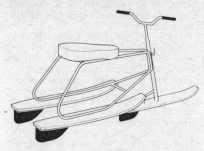

AQUABOB

No special dress is necessary, but for courses at high speed and stunting a Mae West rubber suit like that used by water-skiers is worn.

Aquabobbing requires a minimum of effort. Since motion is imparted solely by the vehicle being pulled there is practically no strain on the arms or legs. Only a twist of the handlebars, or a lean to right or left, is necessary to keep on course.

Runs are generally from 2 to 3 miles (3 to 5 km.). The start is made either touching the bottom or in deep water, the aquabobber lying on his stomach at full length on the saddle with his legs stretched out behind in an open scissors position to keep both machine and rider in balance. When the pulling rope is in tension, the go-ahead is given and the aquabobber waits until he is well out of the water and travelling at a good speed before sliding into the upright sitting position.

The ideal cruising speed of around 25 m.p.h. (40 km./h.) may be increased or diminished without danger. Slaloming across the waves at a speed approaching 40 m.p.h. (64 km./h.) is easily mastered and acrobatic feats are possible.

If the rider falls off the aquabob automatically slides free of the pulling rope. To bring the aquabob to a stop the rider waits until the boat slows almost to a halt and then jumps clear in the manner of a cyclist on a bicycle.

Aquabobbing first appeared in Switzerland in the spring of 1967 on the lake of Neuchâtel. In the previous winter GUGGI, a 22-year-old medical student at the University of Lausanne, was given the job of repairing his father's skibob.

He took it to a friend, GAILLE, who worked in the family factory making metal furniture fittings. The discussion over the skibob soon turned to water-skiing, which they both practised in the summer with considerable skill. The medical student wondered why the skibob could not go on the water. Guggi made a small model, Gaille manufactured a prototype, and the idea was born. Before the snow had left the lake shores the inventor in a powerful motor boat and the builder equipped with a frogman's suit made the first trials with the water tricycle. Within six weeks the aquabob was developed.

That summer a fleet of five aquabobs was in use on the lake of Neuchâtel and before the end of the season aquabobbing appeared on the neighbouring lake of Morat. Financial difficulties and a lack of efficient publicity for the launching of the new sport confined it during the next two years to the region in which it had been invented. Then, in March 1970, after being presented at the Salon des Inventions in Brussels where it was awarded the Médaille de Vermeil in the sports category, aquabobbing made its appearance on the sea in Belgium and Holland.

The sport is still in its infancy, but aquabobs are in use in Switzerland, Holland, and Yugoslavia.

ARCARO, EDWARD (*fl.* 1945-50), one of the leading jockeys in the U.S.A. The best horse he ever rode was probably CITATION.

ARCHER, FREDERICK (1857-86), champion jockey in England for 13 consecutive years, 1874-86. He rode five DERBY winners, four OAKS winners, and six ST. LEGER winners, including the triple crown (SEE HORSE RACING) on ORMONDE in 1886. Altogether Archer won 21 classic races and rode 2,748 winners, his highest number in any one season being 246 winners in 1885, a record unsurpassed until broken by RICHARDS in 1933.

ARCHER, JAY, SEE BIDDY BASKETBALL.

ARCHERY in its modern form is the art of shooting arrows from a bow at a target. Although it is essentially an individual pursuit, it may be desirable, but it is not necessary, to participate as a member of a team; the individual is encouraged to record his own performance with a view to improving his personal standard of shooting.

Though unchanged in principle, the instruments of archery today differ profoundly in detail from their early prototypes. The traditional English longbow, made of yew or other exotic woods, was commonly used for target archery up to the 1940s but was then rapidly replaced, firstly by tubular steel weapons and then by the modern composite bow made of wood, plastic, and fibreglass, whose construction derives from the ancient Asiatic bow used by the Saracens and the conquering hordes of Genghiz Khan. The modern bow has limbs which are rectangular in section, of adequate thickness to withstand twisting as the bow is drawn. The design aims at employing the whole limb, including the backward-curved ends, for storing energy, so that the stressed limb 'works' throughout with approximately the same stored energy in each unit of volume. The limb is built up on a thin strip of wood, usually hard maple, to both sides of which the plastic with embedded glass-fibre is bonded. The sculptured hand-grip, first developed to accommodate an archer with a weakened wrist, is shaped to ensure that force is applied by the bow hand at a constant point. Made to exacting specifications, in the hands of a skilled archer the modern composite bow gives a standard of accuracy never before known. Simple practice bows for beginners with reasonably good performance and of moderate cost may be made of solid fibreglass or wood.

Bows are graded by the number of pounds of effort required to draw back an arrow to its fullest extent, known as the bow weight. Men

PARTS OF A BOW

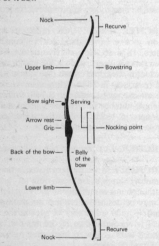

use bows of 32 to 42 lb. (14·51–19·05 kg.); those for women weigh 26 to 34 lb. (11·79–15·42 kg.). The special quality sought after in a bow is that of cast: its capacity to project an arrow swiftly and cleanly, provided

the archer is using it proficiently. The majority of modern target bows are equipped with an adjustable sighting device which varies in complexity according to the individual requirements of the archer. Some bow sights are simple sliding marks, other bows are furnished with precise threaded gauges and scales; under present-day rules, however, none may be equipped with optical lenses of any description.

The arrow, one of the simplest and most ingenious of man's inventions, was until recent years normally made of wood, provided with a steel 'pile', or point, and a reinforced 'nock', or string notch. Sometimes a hardwood foreshaft was added for extra strength and this was known as the footing. Today most arrows are made of aluminium alloy or fibreglass tubing furnished with a steel point (or pile) and a string notch (or nock) moulded from solid nylon. The vanes (or fletchings), which serve to steady the arrow in flight, are cut from the wing feathers of turkeys and usually dyed in various distinctive colours; alternatively, they may be cut from thin plastic. The usual number of fletchings is three, set at equidistant positions round the shaft, but occasionally four are used. Each arrow must carry the name or initials of its owner so that it can be identified in the target, and it is customary to add a distinctive coloured pattern, known as the cresting, for easy identification. The length of the arrow used is determined by the stature of the archer, and it is important that the flexibility of the arrow should be in correct proportion to the power of the bow. The thickness of the arrow, known as its 'spine', which determines its weight and flexibility, is graded by internationally recognized standards. It is essential to use a carefully matched set of arrows — a fact well known in Elizabethan times, when Michael Drayton wrote in his *Polyolbion*:

> Their arrows finely paired, for timber, and for
> feather,
> With birch and brazil pieced, to fly in any
> weather.

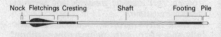

PARTS OF AN ARROW

In addition to his bow and a set of arrows (usually eight), the archer's equipment includes certain accessories: A finger tab or glove is used to protect the fingers of the hand which draws the string back. (Right-handed archers invariably hold the bow in the left hand and draw the string with the fingers of the right hand.) A bracer is fastened to the inside of the forearm of the bow arm to prevent the released bowstring from striking the arm. A quiver, used to store arrows ready for use, is slung at the waist for target archers and over the shoulder for other activities, such as field archery or hunting. A tassel, usually made in the colours of the archer's club, is used to clean arrows which may become muddy or dirty.

The most popular form of archery in Europe is TARGET ARCHERY, which consists of shooting arrows from various distances at a target of standard size. The target consists of a boss about 4 in. (10·16 cm.) thick and approximately 4 ft. (1·219 m.) in diameter, made of tightly coiled straw rope. On this is stretched a target face of canvas or similar material painted with coloured scoring rings. For the standard British five-zone target face, the arrangement is as follows: a circle in the centre measuring 9⅗ in. (24·4 cm.) ringed by four concentric bands each 4⅘ in. (12·2 cm.) wide. From the centre outwards the colours are yellow (called 'the gold'), red, blue, black, and white, their scoring values being 9, 7, 5, 3, and 1 respectively. The target is erected on a

central gold down to 1 for the outermost ring of the white.

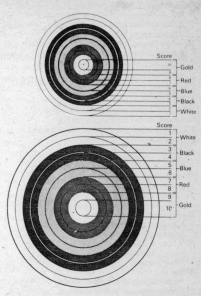

(*Above*) 80 cm. diameter: central gold, 8 cm., each band 4 cm.; (*below*) 122 cm. diameter: central gold, 12·2 cm., each band 6·1 cm.; scored as indicated.

The ideal archery range consists of a level area of closely cropped grass in a reasonably sheltered position. In the most favoured arrangement, the ground is laid out on a north-and-south axis, and the targets set up at the northern end. There should be a safety zone of at least 25 yds. (22·860 m.) behind the targets. Archers stand astride a clearly defined shooting line or mark to shoot, with a waiting line at least 5 yds. (4·572 m.) behind them. The various distances being shot are clearly defined on the ground by means of white lines, tapes, or spots, and the targets, which are set up at least 12 ft. (3·658 m.) apart for communal shooting, are usually numbered from left to right for identification purposes.

In target archery a *round*, consisting of a specified number of arrows shot at predetermined distances, must be completed before scores can be recorded. Rounds vary according to the standard of proficiency, the age and sex of the archer, and the particular form of archery chosen. The following are those officially recognized by the GRAND NATIONAL ARCHERY SOCIETY and the Fédération Internationale de Tir à l'Arc and are used in

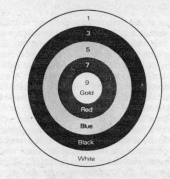

BRITISH STANDARD FIVE-ZONE TARGET FACE
Central zone (gold), 9⅗ in. (24·4 cm.); each band 4⅘ in. (12·2 cm.); scored as indicated.

wooden stand of a height such that its exact centre, the pin-hole, is 51¼ in. (130 cm.) vertically above the ground. Two sizes of target face are used for shooting under international rules, each at a different shooting distance. A 122-cm. (48 3/32 in.) target face is used for distances of 90, 70, and 60 m. (295 ft. 3 in., 229 ft. 8 in., and 196 ft. 10 in.), and an 80-cm. (31 31/64 in.) face for distances of 50 and 30 m. (164 ft. 1 in. and 98 ft. 5 in.). Both these faces are divided into 10 zones, each colour of the standard five-zone target face being halved, the scoring values then ranging from 10 for the

competitive shooting by clubs and societies affiliated to those authorities:

York Round (Gentlemen's championship round)
6 dozen arrows to be shot at 100 yds.
4 dozen arrows to be shot at 80 yds.
2 dozen arrows to be shot at 60 yds.

Hereford Round (Ladies' championship round)
6 dozen arrows to be shot at 80 yds.
4 dozen arrows to be shot at 60 yds.
2 dozen arrows to be shot at 50 yds.

F.I.T.A. (Gentlemen — under international rules)
3 dozen arrows to be shot at 90 m.
3 dozen arrows to be shot at 70 m.
3 dozen arrows to be shot at 50 m.
3 dozen arrows to be shot at 30 m.

F.I.T.A. (Ladies — under international rules)
3 dozen arrows to be shot at 70 m.
3 dozen arrows to be shot at 60 m.
3 dozen arrows to be shot at 50 m.
3 dozen arrows to be shot at 30 m.

St. George Round
3 dozen arrows to be shot at 100 yds.
3 dozen arrows to be shot at 80 yds.
3 dozen arrows to be shot at 60 yds.

New Western Round
4 dozen arrows to be shot at 100 yds.
4 dozen arrows to be shot at 80 yds.

New National Round
4 dozen arrows to be shot at 100 yds.
2 dozen arrows to be shot at 80 yds.

Albion Round
3 dozen arrows to be shot at 80 yds.
3 dozen arrows to be shot at 60 yds.
3 dozen arrows to be shot at 50 yds.

Long Western Round
4 dozen arrows to be shot at 80 yds.
4 dozen arrows to be shot at 60 yds.

Long National Round
4 dozen arrows to be shot at 80 yds.
2 dozen arrows to be shot at 60 yds.

Western Round
4 dozen arrows to be shot at 60 yds.
4 dozen arrows to be shot at 50 yds.

National Round
4 dozen arrows to be shot at 60 yds.
2 dozen arrows to be shot at 50 yds.

Windsor Round
3 dozen arrows to be shot at 60 yds.
3 dozen arrows to be shot at 50 yds.
3 dozen arrows to be shot at 40 yds.

American Round
30 arrows to be shot at 60 yds.
30 arrows to be shot at 50 yds.
30 arrows to be shot at 40 yds.

Short Metric Round
3 dozen arrows to be shot at 50 m.
3 dozen arrows to be shot at 30 m.

The following rounds are recognized for use by junior archers (under 18 years of age):

Bristol I Round
6 dozen arrows to be shot at 80 yds.
4 dozen arrows to be shot at 60 yds.
2 dozen arrows to be shot at 50 yds.

Bristol II Round
6 dozen arrows to be shot at 60 yds.
4 dozen arrows to be shot at 50 yds.
2 dozen arrows to be shot at 40 yds.

Bristol III Round
6 dozen arrows to be shot at 50 yds.
4 dozen arrows to be shot at 40 yds.
2 dozen arrows to be shot at 30 yds.

Bristol IV Round
6 dozen arrows to be shot at 40 yds.
4 dozen arrows to be shot at 30 yds.
2 dozen arrows to be shot at 20 yds.

St. Nicholas Round
3 dozen arrows to be shot at 50 yds.
3 dozen arrows to be shot at 40 yds.
3 dozen arrows to be shot at 30 yds.

Metric I Round
3 dozen arrows to be shot at 70 m.
3 dozen arrows to be shot at 60 m.
3 dozen arrows to be shot at 50 m.
3 dozen arrows to be shot at 30 m.

Metric II Round
3 dozen arrows to be shot at 60 m.
3 dozen arrows to be shot at 50 m.
3 dozen arrows to be shot at 50 m.
3 dozen arrows to be shot at 30 m.

Metric III Round
3 dozen arrows to be shot at 50 m.
3 dozen arrows to be shot at 40 m.
3 dozen arrows to be shot at 30 m.
3 dozen arrows to be shot at 20 m.

Metric IV Round
3 dozen arrows to be shot at 40 m.
3 dozen arrows to be shot at 30 m.
3 dozen arrows to be shot at 20 m.
3 dozen arrows to be shot at 10 m.

In the metric rounds the two longer distances are shot on a 122-cm. ten-zone target face and the two shorter distances on an 80-cm. ten-zone target face under F.I.T.A. target archery rules. In all other rounds the standard British 122-cm. five-zone target face is used. A metric round may be shot in one day or over two consecutive days, but all other rounds are to be shot in one day.

When a round is shot, each archer, after shooting six arrows as non-scoring sighters, shoots three arrows and then retires until all the other archers shooting at the same target have also shot three. A repetition of this process marks the completion of an 'end' of six arrows. Scores are then taken, the arrows withdrawn from the target, and the next end shot. Further ends are shot in this fashion until the total number of arrows in the round have been discharged. Lunch and tea breaks are arranged at convenient intervals during the shooting of a round. Although the score from a round cannot be officially recorded unless it is completed during one day's shooting, the only time limit imposed on the archers is a maximum of two and a half minutes allowed for each to shoot his three arrows.

Shooting has to be carefully controlled, for a thoughtless shot may be a fatal one. For this reason most suppliers of archery equipment emphasize the fact that there is no such thing as a 'toy' archery set. In addition to the stringent safety precautions included in the rules for archery there are several unwritten rules, based on good manners and etiquette. These involve consideration for others on the shooting line, and are accepted whenever archers shoot together. Four archers shooting together constitute the ideal arrangement; the third member of this group automatically becomes target captain. It is his responsibility to record the scores of all archers shooting on his target, with the help of the fourth man,

ARCHERY RANGE
The shooting line moves according to the round being shot.

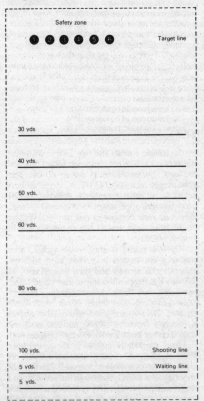

preme arbiter of the meeting. This unique and traditional office dates from the days when a lady of title or wealth gave her patronage to an archery tournament. Her duties are usually ornamental rather than functional, although it is customary for her to preside at the prize-giving after the meeting.

While shooting is taking place a number of special circumstances can arise which may call for the application of the *Rules of Shooting* published by the official body for archery in the United Kingdom, the Grand National Archery Society. Occasionally an arrow enters the target and cuts two colours, in which case the higher score is recorded. If an arrow hits another arrow and remains embedded in it, it is scored the same as the arrow struck. If an arrow bounces from a target, provided it has been carefully observed, another shot is allowed. If an arrow falls so far short that it can be touched by the archer's bow held at full length, it can be retrieved and shot again. These and several other eventualities are allowed for in the *Rules*, which are based on practical experience and long-established custom. The maximum score for one end is 54 — or 60 under international rules — when all six arrows are shot into the gold. This is termed a perfect end, the archer responsible being traditionally rewarded by a shilling (now 5p) from each archer shooting the same round. At a national meeting of several hundred archers such a reward can be worth collecting. However this custom is forbidden if the question of amateur status is involved, as it is for competitors in the OLYMPIC GAMES. Generally, archery is an amateur sport, although a small number of coaches act as professionals.

The Grand National Archery Society's Handicap and Classification Schemes operate for members of clubs affiliated to that body. Under the Handicap Scheme each archer is assessed on an average performance and is awarded a handicap figure which alters according to his changing proficiency. According to this figure, and depending on the type of round being shot, a handicap allowance is made enabling the archer to compete on equal terms with others of varying standards. The Classification Scheme operates independently of the handicapping system and lays down simple regulations by which archers may qualify as either Class 1, 2, or 3, Master Bowman, or — the highest grading of all — a Grand Master Bowman, by shooting a series of rounds up to predetermined standards. An active coaching organization operates under the auspices of the Society, the services of which are available to members of affiliated clubs throughout the United Kingdom. Other countries have different systems for training

designated lieutenant, who checks each entry on the score sheet. Any dispute which cannot be resolved by the target captain is referred to the judge or field captain. In the unusual circumstances of his not being able to give a decision, the matter is reserved for the attention of the 'lady paramount', who is the su-

archers; in some cases active assistance is granted from official and government sources.

Competitive target archery is regularly organized on the basis of friendly matches between clubs, in postal tournaments, and on a more serious level at county, regional, national, and international championship meetings. Every two years world archery championships are sponsored by the Fédération Internationale de Tir à l'Arc (F.I.T.A.), the international body for archery, and the venue of this meeting changes according to the country which acts as host. For international competition the *Rules of Shooting* published by F.I.T.A. apply. The official distances are based on the metric scale and the ten-zone target face, which has already been described, is used.

ARCHERY SCORE SHEET		

ARCHERY SCORE SHEET

Record scores at world championship tournaments are maintained by F.I.T.A. and national records are kept by each of the national archery associations; these include not only scores for target archery, but distance records, field archery records, and archery hunting trophy records. The introduction in 1931 of international rules for target shooting made possible the comparison of scores throughout the world. Under the system laid down by the Grand National Archery Society, each archery club affiliated to that body main-

tains a complete record of each member's scores, with a centralizing arrangement for team selection for county, regional, national, and international tournaments. Other national organizations operate similar systems.

FIELD ARCHERY consists of shooting at bold animal figures, which may be coloured to add realism, upon which are superimposed the scoring rings. They are fastened to straw bales or other suitable backstops and set up in positions as varied and as ingenious as the organizers can devise. The technique of shooting employed by field archers is termed instinctive, where no aids to sighting are used, and the archer becomes proficient by adopting a stance quite unsuited to other forms of archery. These techniques are similar in many respects to those used in hunting wild game with the bow and arrow. No special equipment is needed although most field archers employ a bow of a heavier weight than they would normally use in target practice. As the ground selected for field shooting is invariably rough, there is a danger of losing or breaking arrows. To prevent this, special arrows, having stouter shafts, heavier piles, and longer fletchings, are used for this form of shooting. American archers have excelled in field archery, although it has become increasingly popular in Europe where special tournaments are now regularly organized. The *Rules of Shooting for Field Archery*, prepared by F.I.T.A., are now generally recognized for this form of sport.

Other variants of archery include rovers, clout-shooting, flight-shooting, popinjay-shooting, and novelties such as archery golf and archery darts. ROVERS, in common with field archery, is practised in rough country; the distances are unspecified, and the same type of equipment can be used. The original form of rovers consisted simply of roving through the woods and fields picking out as a target any suitable mark such as a log or mound. The archer who scored a hit or made the best shot chose the next object to be aimed at. Rovers is still occasionally played in its original form and no standard rules are used.

The principal object of CLOUT-SHOOTING is to shoot arrows high in the air to fall on a target marked out on the ground at much greater distances than those used in normal target archery. The distances shot are measured by the score of yards and are from 8 to 10 score (146·304–182·880 m.) for men and from 6 to 8 score (109·728–146·304 m.) for women. The traditional 'clout' was a small target with a black aiming-spot set up in the centre of the marked-out target. This has now been replaced by a flag. The target measures 24 ft. (7·315 m.) in diameter and has five scoring areas defined by rings at radii of 18 in.

(0·457 m.), 3 ft. (0·914 m.), 6 ft. (1·829 m.), 9 ft. (2·743 m.), and 12 ft. (3·658 m.), respectively: by ancient custom these are designated 'a foot', 'half a bow', 'a bow', 'a bow and a half', and 'two bows'. Scoring, from the central ring outwards, is 5, 4, 3, 2, and 1.

FLIGHT-SHOOTING is a highly specialized pursuit with the sole object of reaching great distances — an exacting but extremely satisfying form of archery. Modern flight equipment is the result of advanced technological development and involves a short and powerful bow shooting slender lightweight arrows of special design. There are three classes in which competition may take place; the target-bow class, in which standard target equipment is used; the flight-bow class, which is reserved for competitors using specially made equipment; and a free-style class in which any form of shooting is allowed.

POPINJAY-SHOOTING is rarely seen outside the continent of Europe. The target consists of wooden cylinders with feathers attached, variously called cocks, hens, and chicks, set on a frame, called a roost, on top of a mast 85 ft. (25·908 m.) high. The object is to dislodge these 'birds', each of which has a score value, by shooting blunt-headed arrows vertically from the base of the mast.

For light relief from the more regular routines of target archery, modern archers occasionally choose some form of novelty shooting such as ARCHERY GOLF or ARCHERY DARTS. These forms of shooting are also valuable in providing additional training in aiming and accuracy. In matches between archers and golfers the tee shot of the golfer is duplicated with a flight shot from a bow, the approach shot is matched by shooting a standard target arrow, and the archer holes out by shooting at a white disc of card. Archery darts can be played against regular darts players. The archers use an enlarged target face patterned like a dart board and shoot at about 10 yds. (9·144 m.) while the darts players use their normal dart board. Scoring is as for a regular darts match.

Hunting live game by means of the bow and arrow has enjoyed a revival in recent years. To a large extent this is an individual pursuit, though records of special trophies of the hunt are maintained and clubs and societies have been formed which cater exclusively for this specialized form of archery. In America, where suitable terrain is more readily available and wild life more abundant, bow-hunters number several hundred thousand.

Fédération Internationale de Tir à l'Arc, *Rules of Shooting for the F.I.T.A. Round* (1968); Grand National Archery Society, *Rules of Shooting* (1968).

Archery can claim the oldest ancestry of any sport actively pursued today. There are clear indications that the bow and arrow were used by primitive hunters up to approximately 50,000 years ago. It is not certain when the bow was first invented but there is evidence of its use in different parts of the world at widely separated periods in the history of man.

The first type of bow to be used was undoubtedly of 'self' construction, that is comprised of one piece of wood, shaped to provide the necessary pliability. This primitive form has persisted throughout the ages and can still be found in use among the natives of parts of Africa, South America, and New Guinea. A refinement in the design of the self bow — the lengthening of the bow-stave so that a longer arrow could be shot from it with much greater force — produced the traditional English longbow of the Middle Ages whose basic design has not altered to this day.

The longbow made of yew (*Taxus baccata*) was cleverly fashioned to utilize the natural properties of that wood. A stave was cut which included sapwood and heartwood, which have opposed properties. The heartwood used to form the belly of the bow — the side nearest the archer when the bow is drawn — resists and springs back from compression. The sapwood, being elastic, becomes the back of the bow — the side furthest away from the archer — and, when the bow is drawn, it resists the tension set up. A bow of this type had to be long to minimize stresses and prevent breakage — hence 'longbow'.

Whereas the longbow was made entirely of wood, the oriental composite bow in use in Asia and the Near East from about 2500 B.C. was constructed of material in layers cunningly shaped and glued together to provide a weapon far more powerful than any previously known. The layers were so arranged that the compression, tension, and shear in the bent limbs occurred in each case in the material best adapted to withstand that force. Horn, which is compressible, was used as the belly of the bow; sinew, which has elastic properties, was used for the back; and the whole was built up on a wooden core and covered with moisture-proof lacquers. From a careful study of both the English longbow and the Asiatic composite present-day bowyers have produced the modern composite bow of wood and plastic.

Modern bow design owes much to experiments in mechanical performance and investigations into the science of ballistics by two American pioneers in this unusual field, Hickman, a research engineer, and Klopsteg, a university professor. Research and development during and after the Second World War produced plastics with excellent capacities for storing and releasing energy through stress loading and unloading. These new materials were soon applied to bowyery, and horn and sinew replaced by strong plastic with fibreglass reinforcements to match the bow now in use.

Some of the earliest references to the use of the bow for recreation date from ancient Egypt where the skill of nobles and princes in shooting at targets was carefully recorded. In Egypt, too, we discover records of the training of bowmen for war, and accounts of the effectiveness of the bow as a royal hunting weapon. Archery in war features in the earliest accounts of the Greeks, who used the composite bow with great success in battle. Homer makes reference to Odysseus' skill as a bowman in the famous incident in which the suitors for the hand of Penelope were invited to shoot through the apertures in twelve axes set up in line. Only Odysseus could successfully accomplish this feat, which indicates his familiarity with the special techniques necessary to attain such accuracy. Plato in his treatise on the *Laws* recommended that boys over six years of age should learn horsemanship and archery and mentioned the fact that the Scythians taught their youths to shoot both right-and left-handed. In other early civilizations — in China and India, for instance — archery is frequently mentioned in similar contexts: in war, in the chase, and as a purely sporting pastime.

When in the Middle Ages the wooden self bow developed into the longbow, shooting arrows with greater penetrative power, the simple hunting implement of primitive man was elevated to a sophisticated weapon of war. The disciplined deployment of a large number of bowmen could cause havoc among a closely packed concentration of the enemy. This was successfully put to the test in a number of notable engagements during the Hundred Years War; such battles as Crécy, Poitiers, and Agincourt were won primarily by bowmen. In English villages and towns, from the reign of Henry I to that of Elizabeth I, archery practice was compulsory; from their youth to advanced middle age men were directed to attend at the butts at regular times. The location of the butts can often be learned from the survival in a community of such names as Butt Field, The Butts, and Archery or Artillery Row. Practice at the butts became a regular social diversion and usually took place after church on Sundays or holy days. The village folk needed little persuasion to occupy themselves in such fashion and friendly competition soon became a popular pastime. There are many records of wagers and challenges at the butts. No doubt some unofficial poaching was indulged in, using the same bows and arrows as were used for training in peace and for the defence of the country in times of emergency.

But very soon the longbow ceased to be the officially prescribed weapon of the English army. By an ordinance of 1595, the Privy Council declared that archers should no longer be enrolled in the trained bands, but only arquebusiers, caliver-men, and musketeers. All bows had to be exchanged for hand guns and great stocks of archery equipment were made obsolete. A long argument then began concerning the relative merits of bow versus gun; among those who supported the retention of the bow were ROGER ASCHAM, the famous scholar, whose book *Toxophilus* (1545) was the first major work on archery written in English, and Bishop Latimer, who included a plea for the bow in one of his sermons before Edward VI. Inevitably, the bow was discarded. In 1801 Thomas Roberts, in his book *The English Bowman*, summed up the Englishman's affection for the weapon that he had known for so long:

…it had long been the safety of the realm, and had led the English to the greatest and most extraordinary victories that history had to record; securing their peace at home, and planting in the minds of their enemies a rooting terror, that did not terminate with them even in the grave; but survived, and was handed down to successive generations. It was the weapon, of all others most suited to their genius, prowess, and strength; with which they had been accustomed to form an acquaintance, very early in life; and it may, with truth, be said to have been the toy of their infancy, the pride of their manhood, and the boast of their old age.

In order to keep the memory of the bow alive a few keen and devoted followers banded themselves into societies with the object of regularly practising archery as a pastime. During the seventeenth century one of the most prominent of these societies was the Finsbury Archers, who used the open fields to the north of London as their shooting ground. In Edinburgh, the (ROYAL) COMPANY OF ARCHERS was founded in 1676 and subsequently became the Queen's Bodyguard for Scotland. The ancient SCORTON ARROW has been competed for since 1673, and this is undoubtedly the oldest sporting trophy for which an annual open competition takes place. The eighteenth century saw the formation of many important archery associations, the most important being the (ROYAL) TOXOPHILITE SOCIETY, founded in 1781 (the title 'Royal' being conferred in 1847), and the WOODMEN OF ARDEN, instituted in 1785. Both these societies, together with the Royal Company of Archers, are still thriving and shoot regularly in competition.

The revival of archery in the eighteenth century was due to a large extent to the encouragement given the sport by the Prince of Wales, later George IV. He was a patron of several of the societies of élite bowmen and regularly gave prizes for competition, and he laid down the scoring values of the standard target which are still in use today. He also determined the set distances which make up the York Round, still the basis for many championship meetings.

In the Victorian period archery found even greater popularity, although it was still reserved for the leisured classes. Many of the clubs of today had their beginnings on the country-house lawns of Victorian England, and much of the formal procedure of an archery meeting was formulated by the enthusiasts of this era. By this time, through the influence of a few zealous young gentlemen, archery had begun to attract a following in America and in a short while it became an established part of the sporting calendar.

Possibly the most important date in the history of competitive archery is 1844. During the August of that year the first Grand National Archery Meeting was held in York, the forerunner of a long series of championship meetings which have been held annually, apart from war years, ever since. In 1861 the Grand National Archery Society was founded, and assumed responsibility for this meeting, in due course becoming the official governing authority for archery in the United Kingdom. In 1879 the National Archery Association of America was founded, to be responsible for the organization of the sport in the U.S.A. A notable increase in the popularity of archery was observed after each of the two world wars, possibly as a reaction to the unsettled and tense way of living during times of emergency and a yearning for a more peaceful pastime.

The beginning of international archery can be confidently assigned to the year 1931, when Poland took the initiative and held an international tournament, and when the Fédération Internationale de Tir à l'Arc was instituted. By 1933 F.I.T.A. was firmly established and the annual meeting was considered a world championship event from that year. The original F.I.T.A. members were Belgium, France, Poland, and Sweden. During the following year (1932) Great Britain joined, to be followed in 1933 by the U.S.A. and Czechoslovakia. Gradually, as archery found new popularity, other countries applied for membership. F.I.T.A. now has affiliated to it no less than 45 member associations from all over the world. Many of these nations, such as Japan, Holland, Switzerland, and Turkey, boasted of centuries of archery traditions. Others, equally enthusiastic, although having less experience on which to draw, included New Zealand, Australia, Ireland, and Finland. In recent years the U.S.S.R., the United Arab Republic, China, and Rhodesia have joined. Individual membership in the national associations ranges from a few hundreds to many thousands; among the strongest are the U.S.A., Great Britain, and Japan.

The objects of F.I.T.A. include the promotion and encouragement of archery throughout the world, framing rules of shooting, and maintaining records or scores at world championships. In addition to the world championship meetings arranged by F.I.T.A., now held every two years, international tournaments are held annually in various parts of the world. Every year Great Britain organizes an international trial to which top archers from abroad are invited, and many other countries organize tournaments which are open to archers from member nations. Regular large-scale competitive meetings are held in America, in Russia, and in Europe. The problems of long-distance travel have been overcome by the regular postal shoots held throughout the world. In 1969 the first world championships for field archery were held, and this is to be a regular feature each year, as well as European championship meetings. The inclusion of archery among the events at the 1972 Olympic Games at Munich indicates a revival of international competition in archery not seen since the Games of 1908.

E. Burke, *The History of Archery* (1958); G. Grimley, *The Book of the Bow* (1958); G. A. Hansard, *The Book of Archery* (1840); E. G. Heath, *Archery, the Modern Approach* (1966), *The Grey Goose Wing* (1971), and *A History of Target Archery* (1973); *Archery: The Technical Side*, ed. C. N. Hickman, F. Nagler, and P. E. Klopsteg (1947); P. E. Klopsteg, *Bows and Arrows: A Chapter in the Evolution of Archery in America* (from the Smithsonian Report for 1962); Longman and Walrond, *Archery* (The Badminton Library, 1894); E. K. Milliken, *Archery in the Middle Ages* (1967); M. E. Richardson, *Teach Yourself Archery* (1970). GOVERNING BODY (WORLD): Fédération Internationale de Tir à l'Arc, 46 The Balk, Walton, Wakefield, West Yorkshire; (U.K.): Grand National Archery Society, 20 Broomfield Road, Chelmsford, Essex.

ARCHIDAMIA (1933) was the best racing filly in the history of the Italian turf. She won the Milan Grand Prix, Italian Grand Prix, Italian Derby, Oaks, Two Thousand Guineas, and One Thousand Guineas. She was raced by the Razza del Soldo and trained by Regoli.

ARENA, EDUARDO (*c.* 1926–   ), Peruvian surfer who was chairman of the International Surfing Federation from its inception in 1962.

ARKLE (1957) was the most popular steeplechase horse in England, whose thrilling battles with MILL HOUSE aroused much excitement in the 1960s. Arkle was bred in Ireland by Mrs. Baker, trained by Dreaper on behalf of Anne, Duchess of Westminster, and ridden by P. Taaffe. Arkle never fell and won the CHELTENHAM GOLD CUP three years running, as well as the Hennessy Gold Cup twice, Whitbread Gold Cup, King George VI Steeplechase, Irish Grand National, and 19 other races out of 35 starts, together with a jumping record £75,249 in prize money.

ARLBERG-KANDAHAR, the 'Derby' of ski racing, begun by ARNOLD LUNN and SCHNEIDER at ST. ANTON in 1928. The outstanding success of the Arlberg-Kandahar in 1928 and 1929 did much to bring about the recognition of downhill and slalom racing at the Fédération Internationale de Ski congress in Oslo in 1930. The Arlberg-Kandahar Cup was unusual in that it was awarded on the combined results of downhill and slalom, and the finishing number achieved in downhill governed the start number in slalom. It was intended as an event to encourage the allrounder rather than the specialist, but owing to World Cup requirements its inter-dependent starting system was discontinued. The race is held at Mürren, headquarters of the KANDAHAR CLUB, St. Anton, headquarters of the Arlberg S.C., Chamonix, Sestrière, and GARMISCH-Partenkirchen, on an annual rota basis.

ARLINGTON PARK, Chicago, the racetrack where the American Derby and Grand Prix Stakes are run.

ARMFIELD, JAMES (1935-   ), Association footballer for Blackpool, and England for whom he played in 43 full international matches. He made his first appearance with Blackpool in the League First Division in a match against PORTSMOUTH on Boxing Day 1954. In 1957 he was selected for England's Under-23 team, and made his first appearance in a full international against Brazil in May 1959. Chilean journalists voted him the best right back in the world following the 1962 World Cup championship. When HAYNES was badly injured in a car crash, Armfield took over as England's captain. He continued to play for Blackpool until 1971, when he was appointed manager of Bolton Wanderers.

ARMILLITA CHICO (Fermín Espinosa) (1911-   ), matador de toros (alternativa 1928), was one of the most complete Mexican toreros in all suertes including the banderillas. He was the first matador to cut a hoof in Mexico City, and won the Golden Ear trophy for four seasons there.

ARMOUR, THOMAS (1896-1968), Scottish (Edinburgh) golfer who represented Great Britain as an amateur in the team match against America in 1921. He subsequently became an American citizen and represented the U.S.A. in the professional team against Britain. He won the U.S. Open championship in 1927, the Open championship in 1931, and many other tournaments. On retirement from tournament plays he gained a considerable reputation as a teacher of GOLF.

ARMSTRONG, HENRY (1912-   ), American boxer and the only man to hold three world professional BOXING championships at once. In 1937 he won the featherweight (126 lb; 57·152 kg.), and the next year added the welterweight (147 lb; 66·678 kg.) and the lightweight (135 lb; 61·237 kg.) titles before relinquishing the featherweight championship at the end of 1938. After losing the lightweight he held the welterweight title for 20 successive defences until beaten in late 1940. Armstrong boxed a draw for the middleweight championship the same year and retired in 1945 after 175 bouts and 144 victories. He was renowned for all-out attack at great speed, and extraordinary stamina.

ARMSTRONG, WARWICK WINDRIDGE (1879-1947), cricketer for Australia and Victoria. First touring England in 1902, huge and uncompromising as batsman, slow bowler, and captain, he and his team defeated England eight times inside seven months in 1920-1. In 50 Test matches he made 2,863 runs and took 87 wickets.

ARMY, see UNITED STATES MILITARY ACADEMY.

ARRUZA, CARLOS (1920-66), matador de toros from 1940. He appeared frequently with MANOLETE whose sober toreo contrasted with the Mexican Arruza's athletic flamboyance. He revived the desplante known as the teléfono, placed his own banderillas, and performed all suertes with mastery.

ARSENAL F.C., Association FOOTBALL club, London, founded in 1886 by a group of workmen in a section of the Royal Arsenal establishment at Woolwich, and called Dial Square. Subsequently the name was changed to Royal Arsenal. The club became professional in 1891 and was elected to the Second Division of the Football League in 1893. It became Woolwich Arsenal in 1896, and adopted its present name in 1913 when it moved from Plumstead in south London to

Highbury, north of the river Thames. The club played in the Second Division of the League from 1893 to 1904, and again, after being relegated, in the two seasons 1913-14 and 1914-15; otherwise it competed in the First Division with an unbroken membership from 1919. The F.A. Cup was won in 1930 and 1936, and the Football League championship in the seasons 1930-1, 1932-3, 1933-4, 1934-5, and 1937-8 in the decade of the club's greatest successes. The club enjoyed its first success in European club competitions by winning the Fairs Cup in 1970. In 1971 Arsenal became the fourth club to win the F.A. Cup and League championship double by beating Liverpool 2-1 at Wembley after extra time. Outstanding players of the 1930s included BASTIN, Drake, HAPGOOD, JACK, JAMES, and B. JONES; after the war, Scott, Forbes, Macaulay, MERCER, Kelsey, and McLintock.
COLOURS: Red shirts with white sleeves and collars, white shorts.
GROUND: Highbury Stadium, London.

ART ROSS TROPHY, ICE HOCKEY trophy, awarded annually in the NATIONAL HOCKEY LEAGUE of North America to 'the player who leads the league in scoring points at the end of the regular season'. It was given in 1948 in honour of the former manager and coach of BOSTON BRUINS. Each winner receives $1,000. In 1962, G. HOWE of DETROIT RED WINGS won it for a record sixth time in a period spanning 13 seasons.

ARTURO A (1958), the richest money-winning race-horse produced in South America, known as the 'King of International Racing'. Arturo A won the GRAN PREMIO CARLOS PELLEGRINI, Gran Premio de Honor, and Gran Premio 25 de Mayo twice in the Argentine; the Grande Premio do Brasil, Grande Premio do São Paulo, and Derby Sudamericano in Brazil; and the Gran Premio Internacional Jose P. Ramirez in Uruguay.

ASCARI, ALBERTO (1918-55), Italian MOTOR RACING driver. His first performance of any note was in the 1940 Brescia Grand Prix where he drove a Tipo 815 FERRARI but retired with engine trouble. In postwar days he and his friend, Villoresi, drove for the Scuderia Ambrosiana, and he was at the wheel of the winning 4CLT/48 MASERATI on its début in the 1948 San Remo Grand Prix. For 1949 Ascari and Villoresi joined Ferrari for his struggles with the Alfa Romeo 158s, and Ascari finished second in the 1951 world championship and won both the German and Italian Grands Prix that year, coming second at SPA and REIMS.

When Alfa Romeo withdrew from racing and Grand Prix racing was held to Formula Two rules, Ascari and his 2-litre Ferrari almost completely dominated the scene, and he won the world championship in 1952 and 1953. In 1952 he won the Dutch, Belgian, French, British, German, and Italian races (every championship race except the Swiss) and also scored victories at Syracuse, Pau, Comminges, Marseilles, and La Baule. At LE MANS in 1953 he and Villoresi chased the leading Jaguars for much of the race, and, although their 4·5 Ferrari retired with clutch failure, Ascari set a new lap record of 112·63 m.p.h. (181 km./h.).

For 1954 Ascari and Villoresi joined the Lancia team to drive the new V-8 Grand Prix car. Ascari disliked sports car racing and the Mille Miglia in particular but agreed to drive one of Lancia's D.24 cars after Villoresi was injured in a practice crash. His was the sole D.24 to survive the race, and he won at 86·77 m.p.h. (139 km./h.). At MONACO in 1955 he was leading the race when a brake locked and the Lancia plunged into the harbour. Ascari was rescued, unhurt. Shortly afterwards he was killed practising at MONZA with a borrowed Ferrari sports car.

ASCHAM, ROGER (1515-68) was born during the reign of Henry VIII, in a village in Yorkshire, and became a noted English scholar and writer. In the summer of 1544 he wrote: 'I have written and dedicated to his King's majesty a book, which is now in the press, "On the Art of Shooting", and in which I have shown well it is fitted for Englishmen both at home and abroad, and how certain rules of the art may be laid down to ensure its being learnt thoroughly by all our fellow countrymen.' The title of the work was *Toxophilus, the Schole of Shootinge Conteyned in Two Bookes.* He formally presented it to the King at Greenwich and was promptly rewarded by a pension of £10, which was renewed and increased by Edward VI, Queen Mary, and Elizabeth I.

Ascham was tutor to Edward VI and to Elizabeth when she was a princess, and Latin secretary to Queen Mary. *Toxophilus* sets down the pleasant talk of the two college fellows, 'Lover of Learning' and 'Lover of Archery', as they discourse beside the wheatfields in the neighbourhood of Cambridge upon 'the Booke and the Bowe'. Although this work is not rigidly confined to the subject expressed by its title, it does contain, among other matters appertaining to shooting, the famous 'five pointes' of shooting—'Standyng, nocking, drawing, holdyng and lowsyng', which 'done as they shoulde be done, make fayre shootynge'. Much of what Ascham wrote on the art of ARCHERY is as true today as when it was written, and the principles he laid down, although then applicable to the longbow, are, with very little modification, of practical value to the modern archer.

ASCOT, race-course near Windsor, founded by Queen Anne in 1711. It is the venue of the ASCOT GOLD CUP, held annually in June, and a month later, the KING GEORGE VI AND QUEEN ELIZABETH STAKES.

ASCOT GOLD CUP is the most important long-distance event in the English HORSE RACING calendar. It was first run at Ascot in 1807 and it is still run at the Royal Meeting in June over 2½ miles (4,000 m.). Only three out of the eleven winners of the triple crown (see HORSE RACING) have also succeeded in winning the Gold Cup: WEST AUSTRALIAN, who won it in what was then the record time for the race; GLADIATEUR, who won it by 40 lengths; and ISINGLASS, one of the greatest of all race-horses.

ASHBOURNE CUP (1) see CAMOGIE; (2) see TOBOGGANING: CRESTA and CURZON CUP.

ASHE, ARTHUR ROBERT (1943-   ), American LAWN TENNIS player, the first Negro man to head the United States ranking list and the winner of the U.S. Open and national titles in 1968. A disciplined competitor with a remarkable ability to serve with great pace and accuracy for long periods, Ashe's victory at FOREST HILLS was the first gained there by an American since that of TRABERT in 1955. Ashe was a semi-finalist in the men's singles at WIMBLEDON in 1968 and 1969 and, as a member of the U.S. Davis Cup (see LAWN TENNIS) team from 1963 onwards, played a major part in the recapture of the trophy from a weakened Australian team at Melbourne in 1968. He turned professional in the autumn of 1970.

In 1970 Ashe also won the Australian title after being runner-up to EMERSON in 1966 and 1967. He became a centre of controversy when the South African government, in pursuance of its policy of apartheid, refused him permission to compete in the South African championships. This decision played an important part in hardening opinion against South Africa's participation in the Davis Cup. It was not until 1973 that he was allowed to compete at Johannesburg. He lost in the final to Connors.

ASHES, The, CRICKET term for the mythical trophy played for between England and Aus-

tralia. It originated in the *Sporting Times* which, on 29 August 1882, after Australia had for the first time beaten England in England, printed a mock obituary of English cricket, ending with, 'The body will be cremated and the Ashes taken to Australia.' An Ashes Urn, given by two ladies to the Hon. Ivo Bligh when his English team beat Australia in 1882-3, remains always in the pavilion at LORD'S, but it postdates the term. When either country 'wins the Ashes' it retains them until beaten, and this has led to the often criticized tendency of the holder to base strategy on avoidance of defeat, as distinct from playing every Test series as an objective in itself.

ASHTON, ERIC (1935-   ), RUGBY LEAGUE three-quarter for Great Britain and WIGAN. Captaining Wigan in six Challenge Cup finals between 1958 and 1965, he was a gifted leader. He began as a winger, but soon moved to centre, playing for Great Britain in the WORLD CUP in Australia in 1957, and leading the 1962 team in Australia. He played 26 times for Great Britain. In 1965 he was appointed player-coach of Wigan, for whom he scored 300 tries.

ASIAN GAMES, an area championship of the International Amateur Athletic Federation (see ATHLETICS, TRACK AND FIELD) contested by men and women from all Asian countries affiliated to the I.A.A.F. The Games were inaugurated in New Delhi, India, in 1951 and immediately ran into political trouble. Pakistan refused to take part because of the location and China because of the participation of Formosa. At the 1962 meeting in Indonesia, Formosa and Israel were excluded out of deference to China (who nevertheless did not take part) and the Arab states. There was an Arab boycott of the 1966 Games in Bangkok because Israel competed. So did Formosa, but by then the principal Communist countries of Asia, including China, had created GANEFO — the Games of the New Emerging Forces.

The Games became quadrennial from 1954. A full Olympic programme of track and field events is held, but the standard of performance has generally been poor by western international standards. From the start, Japanese athletes have dominated the Games, winning half the gold medals in the first six meetings.

A.S.K. RIGA, BASKETBALL team of the Red Army club, of Riga, Latvia. A.S.K. were the first winners of the EUROPEAN CUP FOR CHAMPION CLUBS, gaining the title in 1958, and retaining it in each of the two following seasons. The team was coached to these successes by GOMELSKI.

ASPAROUKHOV, GUNDI (1943-   ), Association footballer for Levski F.C. and Bulgaria. A consistent centre forward, he played once for the national Bulgarian team at Rancagua, Chile, in the 1962 world championship, and three times in both the 1966 and 1970 world championships.

ASSOCIATION CROQUET, see CROQUET.

ASSOCIATION FOOTBALL, see FOOTBALL, ASSOCIATION.

ASTOLFINA (1945), a notable Italian filly who won the Milan Grand Prix, Italian Oaks, Two Thousand Guineas, One Thousand Guineas, and Jockey Club Grand Prix for her owner Tesio. Ridden by CAMICI, she won 9 out of 11 races and more than 11 million lire in prize money.

ASTON VILLA F.C., Association FOOTBALL club, Birmingham, founded in 1874 and one of the original members of the Football League in 1888. McGregor, an official of the club, was the main instigator of the establishment of the League. The club first won the League championship in 1893-4 and won it four more times before competitive football ceased during the First World War. It gained a considerable reputation in F.A. Cup football with five final victories in the same pre-1915 period, during which, in 1897, the club won both the Cup and the championship — previously achieved only by PRESTON NORTH END in 1889. In the period between the two wars the club's success was limited to one F.A. Cup win in 1920; and since the Second World War to one F.A. Cup win in 1957 and one League Cup win in 1961. Outstanding players of the pre-1915 period included Hampton, HARDY, and SPENCER; of the 1919-39 period, Houghton, and WALKER; and in post-1945 football Hitchens, BLANCHFLOWER, and McParland.
COLOURS: Claret and light blue shirts, white shorts.
GROUND: Villa Park, Birmingham.

ASTOR, 2nd Viscount (1879-1952), a leading race-horse owner-breeder in England. He won the OAKS five times, and the ST. LEGER once with Book Law, but never succeeded in winning the DERBY, although no less than five horses wearing his colours finished second in this classic. Lord Astor founded his world-famous Cliveden Stud with the mare Conjure, bought for only £100 in 1900.

ASTRODOME (Harris County Sports Stadium) at Houston, Texas, was completed in 1965 at a cost of $20·5 million, the largest indoor stadium in the world, roofed by the world's largest dome. It has an inside diameter of 642 ft. (195 m.) and is 208 ft. (63 m.) high — tall enough to accommodate an 18-storey building. The whole stadium covers 9½ acres, has a performance area of 200,000 sq. ft. (18,390 sq. m.) and can hold 45,000 spectators for BASEBALL or 66,000 for BOXING. It is kept at a constant temperature of 72° F.

The HOUSTON ASTROS baseball team play there, and it has also been used for American and Association FOOTBALL, POLO, rodeos, circuses, and bullfights. CLAY twice defended his world heavyweight title there, against Williams and Terrell.

ASTRONOMIE (1932) was a most distinguished matron of the French race-horse stud owned by BOUSSAC. She was dam of Marsyas II (PRIX DU CADRAN four times), CARACALLA II (PRIX DE L'ARC DE TRIOMPHE and ASCOT GOLD CUP), Arbar (Prix du Cadran and Ascot Gold Cup), and Asmena (English OAKS).

ATANO III (Mariano Juaristi Mendizábal) (1904-   ), Spanish Basque PELOTA player. He was for twenty years supreme in his speciality, the *main nue*, or bare hand, form of the game. Before he appeared, in 1922 *main nue* was a rather slow and stately game; Atano, a small, wiry man charged with nervous energy, changed all that. He not only went for the 'early ball', but hit it low and hard, and if possible on the volley. Totally ambidextrous, he went straight for the ball, using either hand to attack or defend. Many times champion of Spain, he lost his title in 1948, but continued to play for many years. The citizens of Azcoitia erected a bust of him in the main square of his native town.

ATTELL, ABE (1884–1970), American boxer; world featherweight champion 1905-12. He won a disputed version of the world title at 17 and again at 19 and so may be regarded as the most precocious of all world BOXING champions. Skilful, hard, and cunning, he had 32 consecutive wins at the start of his career. In 1909 he met his master in Britain's DRISCOLL but he must still be considered one of the greatest at his weight.

ATHLETIC PARK, Wellington, New Zealand, venue for RUGBY UNION Test matches and home ground of the Wellington provincial side.

ATHLETICS, Indoor. The summer sport of track and field ATHLETICS finds an extension in the winter months, predominantly from January to April, in an indoor season. Meetings are staged on banked tracks with Tartan or other synthetic surfaces or, less often, on board, dirt, clay, or cinder tracks. Circuits are generally of 200 metres/220 yards per lap but 12 laps to the mile and other specifications are not uncommon. Competitors wear needle-spiked shoes on board tracks, the events staged being those normally contested on outdoor tracks with these exceptions: straight sprint and hurdle races are generally restricted to 50 or 60 metres, and the field-event programme is curtailed by the necessary omission of the HAMMER, DISCUS, and JAVELIN.

The first indoor meeting was held in New York in 1868 and American Amateur Athletic Union indoor championships have been held annually since 1906. In England the Amateur Athletic Association organized indoor championships at WEMBLEY, London, from 1935 to 1939, and they were revived there in 1962 before being moved to the R.A.F. arena at Cosford, Shropshire. Indoor meetings are also held in many countries throughout Europe. The European Indoor Games were inaugurated in 1966, an annual fixture of less importance than the EUROPEAN CHAMPIONSHIPS.

GOVERNING BODY (WORLD): International Amateur Athletic Federation, 162 Upper Richmond Road, London S.W.15.

ATHLETICS, Professional. Professional athletics no longer hold the interest of the general sporting public, though in America the signing of former international track stars for an athletics 'circus' became more frequent in the 1970s, when some British runners were included. There are nevertheless 1,200 regular professional competitors in Australia, and about 1,000 in Britain — confined almost entirely to performing in Scotland and the extreme north of England.

Probably born of expediency many centuries ago (see HIGHLAND GAMES), running for money became a private sport in Britain in the late eighteenth century. Rich sporting men who found a likely winner among the local workers, or on their own staff (probably one of the footmen who ran beside the gentleman's carriage), would challenge a neighbouring landowner to beat him. The nominees, heavily backed by their patron's wagers, would then race from one local landmark to another. By 1820, such races were being staged for public entertainment, and well-organized meetings were common in big industrial towns by the middle of the century, long before amateur athletics were established. Scotland proved particularly receptive to pedestrianism, as professional running was known, and the acquisition by promoters of POWDERHALL

Park, Edinburgh, in 1869, laid the foundations of what was to remain for nearly 100 years the mecca of the sport. It was not unusual for crowds of 10,000 to attend the regular meetings at Powderhall (weekly, for many years), and on 1 January 1909 there was a record attendance of 17,000.

Throughout the nineteenth century, and even up to the First World War, the standard of the professional athletes was far higher in most cases than that of the amateurs, much as it is today in boxing. Top amateurs, anxious to prove themselves against the best opposition, sometimes entered races against the 'peds' under assumed names, but this was far from being the most objectionable form of deceit that came to be practised in professional running.

Even after the formation of national or area bodies to organize and co-ordinate professional athletics, meetings were largely autonomous, each in the hands of an individual promoter. It had been found at an early stage that a system of handicaps led to a race that was more sporting than a scratch race, the handicap being based on known form. In London this led to a riot at the Lillie Bridge Stadium, Fulham, in 1887, where a crucial meeting between two of the fastest sprinters, HUTCHENS and Gent, was abandoned because, it was said, the competitors and their managers were unable to agree which of them should win. The stand was wrecked and the stadium virtually destroyed by spectators who had already laid a great deal of money in bets.

There was, and still is, more to professional athletics than pedestrian races. As nineteenth-century showmanship found its flair, there were sprints against cyclists and horses, and medley races in which the competitors had to run a mile, walk a mile, and ride a horse for a mile. Some were held as part of a circus, among them a 60-hour race in Dundee, in which the winner covered 352 miles (563 km.). Even after amateur athletics were standardized by the International Amateur Athletic Federation (see ATHLETICS, TRACK AND FIELD), the professionals tended to go their own way, maintaining races over 90 rather than 100 yards or metres, over 130, 300, 600, 1600, and so on.

Field events pursued basically the same path as in the amateur sport, with a few interesting additions and variations such as the HITCH AND KICK high jump, tossing the WEIGHT (a form of chained hammer-throwing in which either distance or height may be the object) and, in Scotland, tossing the CABER (a tree trunk). As the industrial towns of England lost interest, professional athletics were concentrated in a few rural areas, notably the Lake

District of Cumberland and Westmorland (the LAKELAND GAMES), the most southerly area of Scotland, around Hawick, Jedburgh, and Kelso (the BORDER GAMES), and among the mountain villages of Clackmannan, Fife, and Perthshire (the Highland Games).

By the end of the nineteenth century, professional running had taken a firm hold in some of the country areas of Australia, where some of the world's fastest sprinters run in the STAWELL GIFT HANDICAP.

Professionalism in Scotland was so deep-rooted that in some areas it was the only form of athletics. From 1950, in Britain and in America, two quite different and separate roads to professionalism opened. In Britain, several outstanding athletes turned professional after it became clear that they had given their best to the amateur sport. They included some of the finest middle-distance runners in the world, such as PIRIE, Ibbotson, Simpson, and Whetton, and the champion shot-putter ROWE, who became a Highland Games expert. For the runners, there has been little track competition, but their declared professional status has put them in the market to earn money from advertising, writing, broadcasting, lecturing, and coaching, none of which would be allowed under amateur rules.

Several American athletes have been induced to become professionals at the very peak of their careers, immediately after winning Olympic medals. They include the sprinters Evans and Hines, and long jumpers Boston and BEAMON. Several athletics 'circuses' have toured in the United States, with money prizes as large as contract tennis professionals can win, but public support has seldom justified the outlay. Former leading amateur athletes also frequently turn to professional gridiron FOOTBALL or BASKETBALL in America, as in Britain they occasionally do to RUGBY LEAGUE football.

The reverse may also be the case. Rugby League footballers, not allowed to compete in amateur athletics, often take part in professional meetings. The Powderhall sprint champion, MCNEILL, took up professional running because, as a former professional soccer player, he was barred from the amateur track. Tarrant, a remarkable long-distance runner, could not compete as an amateur in Britain because, as a teenager, he earned a few shillings in the boxing ring. Athletes under the age of 16 may compete at professional meetings without prejudicing their amateur status, provided they do not accept money prizes.

ATHLETICS, Track and Field. Known in Great Britain and the Commonwealth as athletics, or more fully in the U.S.A. as track and field athletics, this composite sport for amateurs embraces the group of outdoor activities concerned with running, jumping, and throwing contests: CROSS-COUNTRY RUNNING, DECATHLON, DISCUS, HAMMER, HIGH JUMP, HURDLING, JAVELIN, LONG-DISTANCE RUNNING, LONG JUMP, MARATHON, MIDDLE-DISTANCE RUNNING, PENTATHLON, POLE VAULT, RACE WALKING, RELAY RUNNING, ROAD RUNNING, SHOT PUT, SPRINTING, STEEPLECHASE, TRIPLE JUMP. All these events are contested by both men and women except the decathlon, hammer, marathon, pole vault, and steeplechase, contested only by men. (See also ATHLETICS, INDOOR; ATHLETICS, PROFESSIONAL.)

Athletics had its origins in remote antiquity; its history has been traced back as far as the ancient Greek OLYMPIC GAMES in the thirteenth century B.C. Evidence exists of athletic contests in England in about 1154, but the first organized competitions were held at the Royal Military Academy, Woolwich, London, in 1849. The first competition held regularly was probably that first staged at Exeter College, Oxford, in 1850.

The sport is governed at international level by the International Amateur Athletic Federation (I.A.A.F.), which defines an amateur as 'one who competes for the love of sport and as a means of recreation, without any motive of securing any material gain from such competition'. The most important international competition in athletics is the Olympic Games which embraces many other sports and is organized by the INTERNATIONAL OLYMPIC COMMITTEE.

A modern athletics stadium (from *stade*, the standard foot race in the Greek Olympic Games) comprises a running track, with all the necessary approach runways and circles for the standard track and field events, together with the impedimenta relevant to these events. Specifications for an athletics arena are laid down in the handbook of the International Amateur Athletic Federation. The largest stadia, including those used for the Olympic Games, can accommodate upwards of 100,000 spectators. Major stadia are situated at the venues of all major athletics championships, and countries affiliated to the I.A.A.F. have at least one, sometimes several, stadia, which may accommodate other sports.

Although reports of organized athletics meetings in the nineteenth century refer to 'cinder paths', competitions were then usually held on open fields, the running track being simply the available meadow or dirt surface. Cinder tracks, or tracks made of clay, or mixtures of these or similar materials, have been in common use throughout the history of modern athletics including the Olympic Games and other major championships up to 1964. Before this date, however, experiments had been made with asphalt or rubberized surfaces. Of these, the Tartan track, a synthetic resin surface patented in the U.S.A. and originally designed for HORSE RACING, has been widely accepted as the best all-round track both as regards performance in all weathers and ease of maintenance. It was used in the Olympic Games of 1968. The Tartan surface is employed not only for the running track itself but also for the approaches to the high jump, long jump, triple jump, pole vault, and javelin, which were formerly served by cinder approaches. The length of running tracks is standardized at 400 metres per lap with six or eight lanes marked out according to the specifications of the I.A.A.F.

Starting blocks, a metal or wooden device consisting of a central shaft with two angled surfaces connected to it against which a runner braces his feet at the start of a race, first came into general use after the Second World War. They are used especially in sprinting and hurdling but also to a lesser extent in the 800 metres and 880 yards. Nailed to the track before a race and easily removed afterwards, being light and portable, starting blocks obviate the delays formerly incurred when runners dug holes in the track from which to make their starts. They are usually supplied at major athletics arenas, but most athletes possess a set.

The starter, an official approved by the national association of the country in which an athletics meeting is held, has control of competitors at the start of all running and hurdling events, giving the signal to start by the report of a pistol. Under I.A.A.F. regulations, which must be adhered to if performances are to be regarded as valid or submitted for ratification as records, three official timekeepers are required to time the winner of a running or hurdling race. The manual stopwatches are set in motion on sight of the flash from the starter's pistol and stopped as soon as the runner's torso reaches the perpendicular plane of the nearer edge of the finish line.

Modern athletics stadia are usually equipped with photo-finish electrical timekeeping, which is increasingly used as a means of deciding both the result and the timing of the competitors in major athletics championships. A camera takes a continuous film of the finish line; the film, which revolves on a spool set immediately adjacent to the finish line, is set in motion by the starter's pistol. Timings, graduated to a hundredth of a second, are printed on the film so that the finishing order and the timing of each runner can be read off at a glance or transmitted by computer to the results indicator board. Since 1964 the official timing of competitors at the Olympic Games has been provided by photo-finish devices.

In running and hurdling events which involve running on a curve, allowance has to be made for runners in the outer lanes having to cover an additional distance. The runner in the inside lane starts from the scratch mark while those in each successive outer lane have an advanced starting mark ensuring that each competitor, keeping to his own lane throughout the race, will cover the same distance. 'Echelon', or staggered, starts, are normally employed for the 200 metres, 220 yards, 400 metres, 440 yards, for these distances on the flat and with hurdles, and also for the 4 × 100 metres, 4 × 110 yards, 4 × 400 metres, and 4 × 440 yards relays. In major championships echelon starts are also employed, for the first turn only, in the 800 metres and 880 yards.

In races where the number of competitors exceeds that which can be safely or conveniently accommodated in one race, heats (or preliminary races) are staged in order to reduce the number, by a process of elimination, to a manageable quota of 6 or 8 finalists in races run in lanes, or up to 12 finalists in longer track events. In the Olympic Games, two preliminary rounds of heats, followed by a semi-final, are sometimes found to be necessary. The composition of the heats is decided by a process known as 'seeding' (see LAWN TENNIS).

The basic items of clothing required by all competitors in athletics are a track suit, singlet, short pants, and shoes. The track suit is a two-piece overall garment, usually of fleece-back cotton or nylon, close fitting at the wrist and ankles. It should have zips at the ankles and preferably a zip-through jacket. The track suit is worn over the shorts and singlet during preliminary warming-up exercises before training or competition. It often carries the athlete's national or club colours and emblem. The singlet is sleeveless and is usually of cotton, and carries the competitor's number, front and back; it is often part of a team uniform, as are the running shorts. These are made of cotton, nylon, or satin, and are cut as brief as possible. The shorts are usually worn over a pair of briefs or an athletic support. Shoes are the most important item of an athlete's clothing. A pair of flat-soled rubber shoes for warming up and a pair of spiked shoes are the minimum requirement for competitors in all track and field events except the shot and discus which, being thrown from a concrete circle, do not call for spiked shoes. Race walkers use specially designed leather shoes. The I.A.A.F. lays down specifications for shoes in its Rule 142 and these have particular application in the high jump.

The I.A.A.F., founded in 1912, convened its first meeting, attended by 17 countries, in 1913. Only one member for each affiliated country — of which, in 1969, there were over 130 — may serve on the I.A.A.F. Great Britain and Northern Ireland are represented by the British Amateur Athletic Board.

The I.A.A.F.'s objects include the compilation of 'rules and regulations governing international competition for men and women in amateur athletics'; co-operating with the Organizing Committees of the Olympic Games; and the ratifying of world and Olympic records. World, area, or group championships for athletics are organized by the I.A.A.F., the Olympic Games being regarded as the world championships. The area and group championships, that is, any international championship involving five or more nations, include the ASIAN GAMES, the COMMONWEALTH GAMES, the EUROPA CUP, the EUROPEAN CHAMPIONSHIPS, the PAN-AFRICAN GAMES, and the PAN-AMERICAN GAMES.

Since 1913 the I.A.A.F. has listed as official records the best amateur athletic performances recorded anywhere in the world. Application for record acceptance must be submitted on an official form to the I.A.A.F. by the national association of the country in which the performance took place. The record must previously have been approved by the national association in question, must have been made out of doors, with official timekeepers or field judges present, and must have been achieved in bona fide scratch competition. Following ratification, a world record plaque is presented to the record-breaker by the I.A.A.F. Apart from world records, there are European records, Commonwealth records, and records for each of the major championships, including the Olympic Games. Championship records are not subject to ratification.

With effect from 1974, in events up to 400 metres/440 yards the I.A.A.F. recognized two sets of world records, those recorded by manual and those by full electrical timekeeping. This was done because electrical timekeeping is not available in many countries.

According to Rule 148 of the I.A.A.F. Regulations, information as to wind conditions must be made available when applying for world records in all sprinting and hurdling distances up to and including 220 yards (flat or on a turn), together with the long jump and triple jump. A device known as a wind-gauge, or anemometer, is used to measure the wind speed. If the wind component assisting the competitor exceeds 2 m. (6 ft. 6 in.) per second, the performance cannot be accepted as a record. A surveyor's certificate must also be filed, verifying that the arena was level.

Although Rule 141(3) of the I.A.A.F. Regulations lays down that 'All women's entries must be accompanied by a certificate as to sex, issued by a qualified medical doctor, recognized by the National Association', the I.A.A.F. have recently found it necessary to require women competitors at major international competitions to undergo a sex-determination test. This regulation was first implemented at the 1966 European championships from which there were several notable absentees. According to Rule 144 of the I.A.A.F. Regulations, 'Doping is the employment of drugs with the intention of increasing athletic efficiency by their stimulating action upon muscles or nerves, or by paralysing the sense of fatigue. Their use is strongly deprecated not only on moral grounds but also because of their danger to health.' The rule further states that athletes must submit to an anti-doping test if required to do so by the organizers of a meeting. Offenders are suspended during the pleasure of the I.A.A.F. Council.

I.A.A.F. Handbook (latest edition). R. L. Quercetani, *World History of Track and Field Athletics, 1864-1964* (1964).

GOVERNING BODY (WORLD): International Amateur Athletic Federation, 162 Upper Richmond Road, London S.W.15.

ATIF, Col. MANZOOR HUSSAIN (1929-), HOCKEY player, captain, selector, coach, and manager of Pakistan, one of the few players to win an Olympic gold medal and manage an Olympic gold medal-winning side. A tall, well-built player, he became one of the best full-backs in the world and represented Pakistan in four OLYMPIC GAMES (1952, 1956, 1960, and 1964), winning a gold medal in 1960 and two silver medals. He captained Pakistan at the 1964 Olympic Games and the 1962 ASIAN GAMES. He first managed the national team in 1965 and was manager of Pakistan's successful Olympic side of 1968.

ATKINS, G. W. T. (*fl.* 1952-71), British amateur RACKETS player. He won the world rackets championship in 1954, defeating DEAR at Queen's Club, and by 1971 had held the title for 17 years undefeated, the longest tenure of this title. He lost the amateur singles title to LEONARD in 1962 and to SWALLOW in 1964, but successfully defended the world title from challenges by Leonard in 1963 and 1968 and by Swallow in 1964 and 1970. He won the British amateur singles championship in

1952-3, 1956, 1960, and 1963 and also won the doubles championship with Kershaw in 1953 and 1961-2.

ATKINS, J. (1942-   ), leading British CYCLO-CROSS rider. A slightly-built, agile competitor, he won ten national titles during the period 1961-73), the last eight in successive years and the last five as a professional.

ATLANTA BRAVES, American professional BASEBALL team, began play in the NATIONAL LEAGUE in 1966, following the transfer of the franchise from Milwaukee. In 1969 Atlanta won the Western Division title, only to be eliminated by the WORLD SERIES winners, the NEW YORK METS. The outfielder AARON (who began playing with Milwaukee in 1954) has been their outstanding player; in 1974 he was to better BABE RUTH'S record in career home runs. (See BOSTON BRAVES; MILWAUKEE BRAVES.)

AUCKLAND CUP is the most important race for older horses in New Zealand and is run over 2 miles (3,200 m.) on the Ellerslie track on New Year's Day.

AUERBACH, ARNOLD J. (Red) (1917-   ), American BASKETBALL coach. Auerbach became coach to the BOSTON CELTICS in 1950, and took them to nine NATIONAL BASKETBALL ASSOCIATION titles. He became general manager to the Celtics on his retirement from coaching in 1966. He was elected to the Hall of Fame (see NAISMITH) in 1969.

AUFFRAY, GUY (1946-   ), French JUDO fighter who won the European middleweight title in 1971 and was runner-up in the two following years. He also won the bronze medal in the 1971 world championships.

AUGUSTA NATIONAL, U.S. GOLF course in Georgia. The inspiration of JONES and Roberts, Augusta is the home of the Masters tournament and embodies two courses in one. As a members' course it presents no insuperable difficulties. The fairways are vast and cut through groves of flowering trees and shrubs of a former nursery, and the greens are large. However, played from the moderately lengthened championship tees and with the holes cut in difficult places, Augusta becomes a stiff test. While par is comfortably within the compass of the professional, the birdies which he must score require immaculate placing of the drive and accurate approach work. In its planning and layout this is probably the most sophisticated golf course in the world.

AUREOLE (1950), a champion chestnut race-horse by HYPERION out of Angelola (by DONATELLO II) was bred at the Sandringham Stud, owned by H.M. Queen ELIZABETH II, trained by BOYD-ROCHFORT, and ridden by E. Smith and Carr. Aureole won the KING GEORGE VI AND QUEEN ELIZABETH STAKES, CORONATION CUP, Hardwicke Stakes, and £36,225 in prize money. At stud he was a successful stallion, sire of ST. PADDY and other good race-horses.

AURNESS, RALPH (c. 1952-   ), American surfer who came first in the world SURFING championships in Australia in 1970.

AUST BALL is a German bat-and-ball team game of the FIVES-tennis type and a forerunner of VOLLEYBALL. It is played between two teams of five players each. The ball, 65–71 cm. (25–28 in.) in diameter, and 300–350 g. (about 12½ oz.) in weight, is hit with one fist. The object of the game is to hit and return the ball over a rope 2 m. (78 in.) high.

No player may go nearer the rope than the line drawn 3 m. back from it on either side. A game consists of two 15-minute halves. It is decided on points, one of which is ceded to the other side when the ball bounces more than three times without being returned; is hit out of court; is struck with two fists or the open hand; or if it is played more than three times on one side without crossing the net.

AUSTIN, HENRY WILFRED (Bunny) (1906-   ), British LAWN TENNIS player, twice runner-up in the men's singles at WIMBLEDON and an important member of the successful British Davis Cup (see LAWN TENNIS) team of the 1930s. Comparatively frail in physique, he possessed a formidable armoury of ground strokes and a particularly effective forehand. He was at his best at Wimbledon, failing only once before the quarter-finals in the years between 1929 and 1939. VINES beat him in the 1932 final and he met BUDGE at the peak of his form in 1938.

AUSTRALIAN FOOTBALL COUNCIL (A.F.C.), see FOOTBALL, AUSTRALIAN RULES.

AUSTRALIAN NATIONAL ATHLETIC COUNCIL, the governing body in that country of professional ATHLETICS, which are more popular there than anywhere else in the world. Some 1,200 athletes are registered with the Council, under the aegis of which up to 200 meetings are held through the summer. The state of Victoria is the centre of the sport, which is also widely followed in Tasmania and New South Wales.

AUSTRALIAN RULES FOOTBALL, see FOOTBALL, AUSTRALIAN RULES.

AUTO RACING, see MOTOR RACING.

AUTO-UNION. The Auto-Union Grand Prix car was designed by Dr. Porsche, later to be responsible for the Volkswagen and for cars made under his own name. Encouraged by Hitler for reasons of prestige, the new concern developed the first practical rear-engined racing car. It was very fast, but required sensitive driving. Full advantage was taken of weight-saving materials to keep the car, the Type A, within the Formula weight limits. With MERCEDES, the Auto-Unions dominated the Grand Prix racing of the middle 1930s and provided some exciting racing. Rosemeyer was one of the most successful drivers to master the difficulties of handling these powerful vehicles, but he was killed in a speed record attempt. The last model to be produced before the war was the Type D with a V-12 engine of 2,990 cc. capacity developing 400 b.h.p. The company was later absorbed into the Volkswagen complex.

AUTOCROSS, a form of MOTOR RACING or speed event run on a grass or unsealed surface, against the clock. Dependent on the design of the circuit, two or more cars are run simultaneously to add competition and spectator interest. The circuits themselves are of a temporary nature, usually marked out with flags and straw bales in a field hired for the purpose by the organizing club.

Strict regulations governing the precise character of the event and the nature of the courses have been laid down by the British Royal Automobile Club (R.A.C.), and these in general apply to other countries where the sport has found a footing.

The course may not include a straight exceeding 200 yds. (182·8 m.) in length, and the radius of corners following immediately upon this straight is limited as a safety factor. The start line may not be situated within 50 yds. (45·7 m.) of the first corner, and great attention is given to spectator protection. If no barriers can be provided neither the paddock nor spectator areas may be within 100 ft. (30·5 m.) of the circuit's edge. Minimum permissible barriers are a double row of straw bales or their equivalent, placed approximately half-way between the course and the area to be protected. Where such barriers are provided, paddock and spectator areas may be allowed to approach to within 60 ft. (18·3 m.) of the course along the straights and 75 ft. (22·9 m.) on corners. Final course requirements stipulate that natural hazards such as trees and ditches must be avoided by at least 60 ft., and that strand or barbed wire fences should not be closer than 100 ft. from the edge of the circuit. Thus the designer of these temporary courses has parameters within which to work, and the plan of his proposed course must be submitted to the governing body for approval before an event licence will be granted.

Once the governing body has approved the date and venue, the meeting may proceed. Pure racing cars are prohibited from autocross, and specials with a capacity of more than 3 litres are also banned. Eligible cars comply with a number of regulations mainly designed to make the sport as safe as possible. Cars must have not less than four road wheels, must be of sound construction and mechanical condition, must have a sealed fireproof bulkhead, complete floor, flame-proof bonnet, and sprung suspensions.

Other technical specifications demand the inclusion of return springs acting directly on the throttle spindles (to prevent a jammed throttle taking a car into the crowd), clearly marked 'on/off' positions on the ignition switch, minimum thickness plastic windows, and laminated shatterproof screens.

The running of an autocross event depends largely upon the length and configuration of the course. If it is less than 30 ft. (9·1 m.) wide, cars may be started consecutively but not abreast. The second car will be flagged off when the first has gained a lead of 200 yds. (182·8 m.) or one-third of a lap, whichever is the lesser. If the course is under 30 ft. wide but more than 600 yds. (548·6 m.) long, three cars may be run consecutively but again 200-yard starting intervals must be observed. When the course exceeds 30 ft. in width and 600 yds. in length, two cars may be started simultaneously, and another pair may also be released simultaneously when the first have taken a lead of 300 yds. (274·3 m.).

Thus the regulations governing the organization and running of any autocross meeting are comprehensive and extensive. Nonetheless, the organization of events is an extremely popular promotion among the smaller and less wealthy motor clubs. Spectator appeal is at its greatest where longer courses with simultaneous running of the cars is concerned, and these are by far the most common of all competitions.

The length of the run may vary from meeting to meeting and course to course, but is usually less than five laps of the course, commonly three laps, and seldom less. Regulations demand that the course should be travelled in a clockwise direction (generally proved to be safer in a right-hand drive car), and striking a marker flag lining the course results in a five-second time penalty per flag.

Competitors will usually make practice runs and two true timed runs, the better of which decides the place of each in the competition. Awards are presented for both placings in class and over-all. Class demarcations are fairly simple; they cater for four distinct types of vehicle: front-wheel drive saloons, front-engined rear-wheel drive saloons, rear-engined cars, and sports cars and specials. Each of these sections may then be further split into capacity divisions, such as up to 850 cc., over 850 cc. and under 1300 cc., and over 1300 cc.

Extensive engine modifications to increase the peak power and torque which it produces are permitted. Care has to be taken to make sure that peak power occurs somewhere near the middle of the unit's rev. range, since it is low-speed power which makes all the difference on loose, dusty, or muddy surfaces. Too much gear-changing is usually to be avoided so that a car with ample torque and power low in the rev. range is well suited to autocrossing. Automatic transmission is a help in very bad conditions but its use is limited as yet. Four-wheel drive gives great tractional advantages and a 2·5 or 5 per cent time handicap has been placed on these vehicles.

Suspension modifications must be made, partly in order to make the car responsive and easy to drive, but mainly to avoid the possibility of suspension breakage over bumpy and rough circuits. Lowering and widening the suspension is usually the first move in this process, adding stability, while bigger wheels carrying larger tyres give better traction on dry surfaces. If the surface breaks up badly or becomes really muddy, narrower wheels and tyres have an advantage in cutting through the surface to firmer ground rather than 'floating' over the top.

Radial-ply cross-country tyres are usually preferred, although in very dry conditions ordinary smooth-tread radials prove faster, giving much less drag. To cut rolling resistance, tyre pressures are increased in drier going, while in snowy, wet, or muddy conditions very low tyre pressures will be used to ensure maximum grip. Only normal production tyres are permitted, and tubeless tyres are prohibited because they do not seal well, and grass, stones, and other debris may be wedged between the tyre and wheel rim.

Driving technique depends very much on the configuration of the car, but success in autocross demands a driver capable of adapting his style easily to changing conditions and with sufficient sensitivity to keep his car at the limit of adhesion. Cars with the weight of the engine over the driven wheels, such as the rear-engined Volkswagen or Imp and the front-engined front-wheel drive British Leyland Minis, have a tractive advantage over the front-engined rear-wheel drive cars. These therefore usually prove faster than their 'opposite end' opponents, and home-built autocross specials almost invariably feature engine-over-driven-wheels layouts. Fastest time of the day awards usually go to vehicles in the specials classes, but tuned and modified saloons give a very good account of themselves.

RALLYCROSS, a variation of autocross, uses sections of surfaced permanent motor racing circuits allied to unsurfaced sections over those circuits' infields, and differs from autocross in several respects apart from its mixed-surface venue.

Cars may be started simultaneously and four abreast in rallycross, these four competitors completing a series of against-the-clock three-lap runs during the meeting. Class and over-all awards are again offered. Tyre restrictions are not as severe as in pure autocross, and one-off racing and special tyres may be used to combat the mixture of hard and soft surfaces. Since the venues are all permanent racing circuits, very extensive protective barriers exist between car and spectator, so that the public are generally closer to the competition and get a better view of it.

Autocross originated in England soon after the Second World War, but its roots extend more deeply into the history of sporting motoring. Between the world wars, timed hill-climbs and speed trials had flourished until 1925, when an accident involving spectators caused a ban on open-road events. Such events retreated to private land and coastal beaches at Southport and Saltburn, and the so-called 'freak' hill-climb made its début in 1926. The idea was to produce a 'safe' hill-climb, a climb on land so steep and rough that forward speeds were very low and vertical progress was the exception rather than the rule. These events were popular briefly among the northern clubs, then reappeared in less savage form in the south of England in the early 1930s. These brought motor competitions off the road on to rough countryside and the step from there to dirt-track and grass-track circuit racing was but a short one.

Sporting activities ceased during wartime, but in 1946 rough-country 'trials' reappeared, the idea being to climb as high as possible on seemingly impassable mud slopes. Timed sections began to appear as competition became fiercer, vehicles more specialized, and ties occurred which had to be decided. The mating of grass or rough-track racing and timing of the trials kind soon followed in events which would now be called autocross; the date the name was coined is uncertain, but it was not this early. Credit for the organization of the first event of this kind has been given to the Hagley and District Light Car Club, at Easter 1947. Their venue was Rushmore Arena, just off the Stourbridge–Bridgnorth road in Shropshire, and the club experimented with a number of different circuits and modes of competition. On 26 July 1947, it ran an event consisting of two-at-a-time circuit races, a timed hill-climb, and a knock-out hill-climb. Cash prizes were offered and a crowd numbering several thousand attended. Competing cars included Allards, supercharged MG Midgets, and a variety of Ford-powered specials; Wharton was a prominent winner.

At this early stage, organizers were very self-reliant so far as the type of competition and its regulations were concerned. In 1951 a major autocross meeting was held on Dunstable Downs by the Sporting Owner-Drivers' Club and the London Motor Club, and this was followed by another true autocross meeting in 1953; held at Roke Down near Bere Regis, Dorset, and organized by the West Hants and Dorset Car Club. In 1954 the East Anglian Motor Club ran an 'autoscramble' at Earls Colne which was contested by cars and motor cycles alike and appears to have used a very rough and hilly course through a wood.

But it was on August Bank Holiday 1954 that autocross really came of age and appeared in its modern form, credit for this maturity going to the Taunton Motoring Club and its late president, W. Cawsey. They promoted regular autocross circuit events at West Country venues, and many other clubs followed their lead. In 1959 the Taunton M.C. became the first to be granted a national British meeting permit for an autocross, for by this time the sport had received official R.A.C. approval and a stringent set of standard regulations.

Many clubs in agricultural areas virtually specialized in autocross meetings, for the variety of venues available to them was almost limitless. Classes catered for open and closed cars, and specials were admitted if they had two seats and mudguards. Side-valve Ford-engined specials, built originally for trials use, proved very successful in autocross apart from their alarming proclivity towards overturning, caused by their great ground clearance and consequent high centre of gravity.

Various Allard models, the Dellow trials-type car, Morgan, and LOTUS Mark 6 sports cars all featured regularly in autocross results during the late 1950s and early 1960s, while Triumph Herald, Austin A30-35, Riley One-Point-Five, and Ford Anglia saloon cars obtained places in the closed-car divisions. The sport grew quickly from 1960, and while it flourished in the United Kingdom it also gained ground slowly on the Continent, although on a very much more restricted scale.

During this period competitors began to approach the particular problems posed by autocross in a more specialized and scientific manner. Tyres originally designed for rough-country work on tractors and dumper trucks found their way on to saloon, sports, and special cars; wheels had wider sections in order to carry bigger tyres; suspension modification and tuning became more important and four-wheel drive was introduced. Parkin's Cannon-ball Special, based on a Lotus 6 chassis, combined a home-built four-wheel drive system with a special 1650 cc. Ford engine, and dominated autocross meetings from early in 1962 and throughout the middle of the decade. In view of this car's success, and that of its imitators, a standard time penalty was imposed on all four-wheel drive machines.

Similar domination by two production-car designs also led to a reclassification of autocross entries. The introduction of the BMC Mini in 1959 and the successes of Manifold's Volkswagen 'Beetle' made competitors quickly realize the advantage of having the engine's mass over the driven wheels. With the introduction of the modified Mini-Coopers from 1962, such cars were quickly placed in a class of their own. In this way autocross fields became divided into the current front-wheel drive saloons, rear-engined saloons, front-engined rear-drive saloons, and sports and specials classes.

Because autocross had assumed such a large national following, the British Trials and Rally Drivers' Association founded a national championship. This came to prominence in the early 1960s, competitors scoring points from class placings in numerous events throughout the season. The scheme gave everyone an equal chance of success since it did not rely purely on over-all 'fastest time of the day' (FTD) results.

The Association of Central Southern Motor Clubs, the London Counties Association of Motor Clubs, and the Association of Welsh Motor Clubs followed with a string of regional championships, but none of them offered the enthusiastic competitor much in the way of financial reward for what was necessarily a fairly expensive sport. Commercial sponsorship came in 1966 when a tobacco company financed a championship organized by the East Midlands Clubs. This series was sufficiently successful to persuade the company to sponsor a national championship the following season, under the 'No. 6' brand name. The competition consisted of 32 qualifying rounds, four area semi-finals, and a national final. The national 'No. 6' autocross championship continued as the sport's main U.K. competition until 1970, when the company announced the withdrawal of their support.

Autocross was essentially a summer sport, but as early as 1963 a winter event had occurred which presaged the development of a spectacular new version. Shortly after the R.A.C. Rally of that year, a field of the leading cars in that event was assembled before television cameras to take part in an autocross-type event behind the BRANDS HATCH motor racing circuit's main grandstand. In the winter of 1967-8 the idea was revived, with television coverage, at Lydden Hill circuit, near Canterbury, Kent. The course used part of the surfaced racing circuit and much of the infield, and owed more to pure racing than autocross itself. Four cars were started simultaneously, timed over three laps, the fastest over all gaining the major award. This variation of autocross, known as rallycross, became a popular and well-supported winter sport.

Championships were sponsored by another tobacco company, by a lubricants manufacturer, and by Independent and BBC television. Regular events are held at Lydden Hill, Croft, and Cadwell Park, and while summer autocross continues to attract the enthusiastic amateur, the lure of television publicity attracted manufacturer's teams to rallycross. The British Ford, British Leyland, and Rootes/Chrysler concerns all ran specially prepared rallycross cars, but, none the less, private entrants such as Weldon, Williamson, Boulden, Chatfield, and Carotte proved extremely competitive with factory drivers Chapman, Rhodes, the Clark brothers, and Harper.

Sponsorship changed the character of autocross from that of a friendly amateur sport into one where acrimonious protests and counter-protests caused some drop in support.

With championship points and money at stake, the sport undoubtedly suffered, but it is now very firmly established in the United Kingdom, and has spread to Italy, to the Netherlands, and, in a limited form, to other countries of western Europe. Ford Motor Company demonstrations at Rome's Vallelunga racing circuit brought rallycross to Italy, and similar events take place — although on nothing like the British scale — in the Antipodes and in some parts of the U.S.A.

AUTUMN DOUBLE, see CAMBRIDGESHIRE HANDICAP and CESAREWITCH HANDICAP.

AVIATION, see FLYING, SPORTING.

AVUS RACE TRACK, German MOTOR RACING track opened in September 1921. The name is an abbreviation of *Automobil Verkehrs und Ubungs Strasse* (motor traffic and practice road). The track consisted of parallel straights divided dangerously by a narrow centre strip running from Charlottenburg to Nikolasse, with banked loops at either end. In 1936-7 the north loop was replaced by steeper banking, which reduced the length from 12·2 to 12 miles (19 km.). After the Second World War, the original south loop was in the Soviet sector so that an unbanked loop was substituted. The circuit length was thus reduced to 5·2 miles (8·3 km.). The track was the venue of the German Grand Prix in 1926 and 1959 but it was not used after 1967.

AYRSHIRE (1885), race-horse bred and owned by the Duke of PORTLAND, trained by DAWSON, and ridden by Barrett. He won 11 races, including the DERBY, TWO THOUSAND GUINEAS, ECLIPSE STAKES, and £35,915 in stakes. Ayrshire was inbred to four sets of full brothers and sisters.

AYUB ZONAL TROPHY, see CRICKET.

B

BAB AT THE BOWSTER (1866), COURS-
ING greyhound. Although denied the cachet of
a classic victory by MASTER MCGRATH in the
1869 WATERLOO CUP, this bitch was commonly regarded as the greatest of her sex ever
to course. The dual winner of the great Scarisbrick Champion Cup for 128 dogs, the Douglas Cup for 64, as well as the Altcar and Elston
Cups, she won no fewer than 62 of her 67
courses and stake money of some £1,500.

BACON, S. V., E. H., E. A., and E. (*fl.*
1911-24), brothers, British wrestlers in the
catch-as-catch-can and Cumberland and Westmorland styles. Between 1911 and 1924 they
held 22 British championships in these styles.

BADMINTON is an indoor game played by
one or two players opposing an equivalent
number across a net which is 5 ft. 1 in. (1·55
m.) high at the posts and 5 ft. (1·524 m.) high
in the centre, on a court whose over-all dimensions are 44 ft. (13·41 m.) by 20 ft. (6·10 m.).
The court must be laid out on a level and
smooth surface, wood or composition flooring
being most common, and the floor must not be
slippery. Other than the specifications laid
down for international and tournament play

there is no stipulation in the laws as to the
height of a court, but for international play a
minimum of 26 ft. (7·93 m.) from the floor
over the full court is prescribed. This is,
however, the absolute minimum, and many
national organizations have stipulated 30 ft.
(9·14 m.) as the minimum. A minimum of 4 ft.
(1·22 m.) is essential as clear space surrounding all four sides of the court, but this can be
slightly decreased where two or more courts
are marked out side by side. The markings on
the court are usually in white paint, though
white tape may also be used. The lines must be
1½ in. (4 cm.) wide.

For doubles play the entire court is used,
but the singles court is 3 ft. (91 cm.) narrower,
the two tramlines being ignored. The service
court in doubles is a rectangle bounded by the
short service line, the centre line, the long service line for doubles, and the side line, but in
singles the service court extends to the back
boundary line, and to the appropriate side line.

The net is supported by posts which are
fixed to the floor on the side lines of the
doubles court (irrespective of whether singles
or doubles is played). It should be made of
cord of a mesh of ⅝ to ¾ in. (1·5–2 cm.); it is 2
ft. 6 in. (76·2 cm.) deep with a 3-in. (7·5 cm.)

BADMINTON COURT
Diagonal measurements: full court (from corner to corner), 48 ft. 4 in. (14·723 m.); half court (from post to
back boundary line), 29 ft. 8¾ in. (9·061 m.).

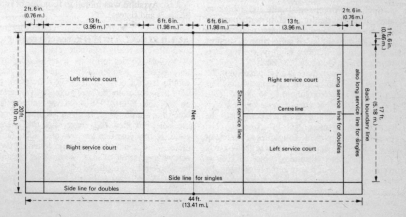

white tape doubled over the top and supported by a cord or cable through the top and strained over the top of the posts.

The game is played by both men and women and in doubles by mixed pairs as well as those of the same sex. In its athletic sense it is a racket-and-ball game, but the missile is a shuttle which is hit by the player with a racket. There are two types of shuttle, one of feathers, and the other of nylon. The base of the former is of cork, completely rounded except at the top, 1 to 1¼ in. (2·5–2·9 cm.) in diameter, and it is usually covered with white kid leather. A feather shuttle has 16 white goose feathers fixed into the top of the cork, firmly fastened with thread so as to strengthen them. The feathers are from 2½ to 2¾ in. (6·4–7·0 cm.) long from the tip to the top of the cork base, and they have a spread of up to 2¼ in. (6·4 cm.) at the top. A nylon shuttle is usually of one piece, that part which displaces the feathers often being called the skirt.

Shuttles are manufactured in many different speeds to conform to the atmosphere of the hall in which they are used; they weigh from 73 to 85 gr. (4·73–5·51 g.), but for really high altitudes, such as Johannesburg and Mexico City, even lighter ones are required. Because of its extreme lightness, the shuttle's speed is affected by the atmosphere, and the correct speed shuttle is that which when struck with a full underhand stroke from a spot above the back boundary line at an upward angle falls not less than 1 ft. (0·30 m.), and not more than 2 ft. 6 in. (0·76 m.) short of the other back boundary line. The life of a shuttle varies, for it can be damaged by mishits which will cause it not to fly truly, so that in championship play several shuttles may be used in one match.

Rackets have gone through many stages of development since the game was evolved, and the modern version is made of either hickory or steel, or with a steel shaft and a hickory head. It is strung very tightly with thin gut with about 16 strands horizontally and vertically. The handle is usually covered with a leather grip. Extremely whippy, the racket is 26 in. (66 cm.) long and the head is 8¼ in. (21 cm.) wide, though there is no stipulation in the laws as to its dimensions or composition. The weight will vary from about 3¼ to 5½ oz. (92 to 156 g.), so that it is a very fragile weapon.

In competitive play a match consists of the best of three games, each of 15 points. The laws, however, provide for games to consist of up to 21 points, but this method is used only in 'American' or 'Round Robin' handicap events. The toss of a coin at the beginning of a match decides which side is to serve first, and that side will continue serving from alternate courts until it loses a rally, when the advantage of serving passes to the other side. Only the server can add to his score (a point) by winning a rally. Should the receiving side win a rally, the score remains static but the service changes hands. A game of 15-up can therefore consist of many times that number of rallies before it is completed. In doubles play the first service takes place from the right-hand service court to the diagonally opposite service court. When a rally is won by the server's side, its members change courts and the same player serves from the left-hand service court to the court diagonally opposite. The two partners serve consecutively, and after both have been downed, the right to service passes to the opposing side, who will similarly commence from the right-hand service court. Thus, in doubles the receiving side requires to win two rallies before gaining the service.

A side loses a rally when it commits a fault: (a) if the service is not underhand or if the receiver allows it to drop and it falls outside the correct service court, (b) if either in service or play the shuttle hits the surface of the court, falls outside the boundaries, or does not pass the net: (c) if the shuttle is caught on the racket or slung, or if it is hit twice by the same player with two successive strokes; or if the shuttle is hit by a player and his partner successively; (d) if a player touches the net or intentionally baulks or obstructs an opponent.

'Double hit' is a term commonly used when a shuttle is struck by two distinct touches of the racket. Until 1968 any double hit was a fault, but in that year the law was altered to invalidate a hit only when the player made two strokes at the shuttle. 'Wood shot' is the term used for mishits when the shuttle is totally or partially struck by the frame of the racket. From 1949 until 1963 any stroke not made cleanly off the gut of the racket was a fault, but before and after these dates clean hits off the frame of the racket have been valid. The wood shot question has caused controversy ever since badminton was competitively organized, and it is difficult to envisage the evolution of a really satisfactory ruling.

A 'let' occurs only as a result of any unforeseen or accidental hindrance such as a shuttle from a neighbouring court interfering with play, or a shuttle being caught in or held on the net. Until 1958 a let was automatic when the shuttle in service touched the top of the net, provided the serve was otherwise good. In that year that law was abolished, and there is no penalty for a shuttle touching the net when passing over it. When a let occurs the whole rally is replayed.

If the score reaches 13-all, the player or pair which first reached 13 points has the option of 'setting' the game for a further 5 points, or of continuing the game only up to 15. When the game has been set, the score is called 'love-all' and the first side to score 5 points wins the game. Similarly at 14-all the game may be set a further 3 points. If a side has declined to set the game at 13-all this does not prevent its being set later if the score should reach 14-all. In games of 21-up the score may be similarly set at 19 or 20.

The women's singles game is a shorter one, of 11 points. If a game reaches 9-all it may be set for 3 points, and at 10-all for 2 points, in each case the score being called 'love-all'.

At the commencement of the second or third game, the winner of the preceding game serves, though in doubles only one service hand is permitted. At the end of each game the opponents change ends and remain at the same end of the court throughout that game except that in a third game the opponents change ends half-way through it, that is when one side's score has reached 8 in a game of 15, 6 in a game of 11, and 11 in a game of 21.

The service in badminton must be delivered underhand; the two main types are the short service where the shuttle just skims the net and is intended to fall just inside the short service line, and the high service where the shuttle is hit anything up to the full height of the hall with the intention of causing it to fall vertically, as near as possible to the long service line. There is also the drive service and the flick service. The former will cross the net only just above it, and be made to land near the long service line. The flick service is a deceptive high one delivered in exactly the same way as a short service, and it is intended to catch the receiver off his guard. The spot from which the service is hit can, and often is, varied.

Shuttles do not, of course, bounce so that all shots are volleys. The main strokes during the course of a rally are the clear, the smash, the drop, and the drive, all either forehand or backhand. The clear is sometimes called a 'lob' or 'toss', and is hit high in the air so as to land as near as possible to the back boundary line. Its object is to gain time or to drive the opponent to the back of the court. Maximum depth is of great importance in order to give the hitter of the clear the maximum time to deal with the smash which it invites. The smash is the natural reply to a clear, and though it is much more forceful on the forehand, it is also used on the backhand. It must be hit from a position as high as possible in order to obtain a steep angle. The smash wins more rallies than any other stroke. The drop is made from any part of the court and causes the shuttle to fall within a few feet of the other side of the net. It is achieved by a checking of

the wrist, and is most effective when the striking action is identical to that of the smash. Its object can be both attacking and defensive, and a surprise drop shot will end many a rally. The drive, both on the forehand and backhand, is a fast stroke with the shuttle only just crossing the net. It is made only from the side of the court but can be directed straight down or across court, and is frequently used in mixed doubles where the woman covers the net. There are many variations of these basic strokes.

The server must stand with both feet entirely within his service court, and neither foot must touch the line. Usually he stands a few feet behind, but sometimes only just behind, the short service line, and as near as possible to the centre service line so that the shuttle has the shortest distance to travel, thus giving the receiver the least possible time to deal with it.

The receiver will stand as near to the short service line as he dare in order that he may kill the imperfect short service, and yet be able to retreat to deal with a service over his head. Thus a good man will stand with his front foot as near as permitted to the short service line and leaning forward over it, but a woman will need to stand at least 3 or 4 ft. (say, 1 m.) behind the short service line in order to avoid being caught by an unexpected high service. Neither the server nor the receiver may alter the position of his feet until the shuttle is actually hit, but after the service has been delivered there is no restriction on the players' movements.

Badminton should be played entirely in white clothing, though there has been a tendency for players to practise in track suits. Men usually wear shorts and vests or shirts in light absorbent material, and woollen socks rolled down to the ankle. White sweaters may be worn for additional warmth. Many types of shoe are available but all must have crêpe or rubber soles, and no heels. Women are divided in their choice between shorts and frocks. In any case, clothing should be loose to allow freedom of movement.

Handicap events are very popular in the British Isles, though rarely played elsewhere. In these events a player or pair will be awarded a number of points' start or may be asked to owe points, with no limit to the number allowed. An additional method of handicapping in doubles is to cause a pair to owe a hand or to cause a pair to receive a hand. In these cases the pair which owes a hand will have only one hand when it gains the service instead of the customary two. (This obviously cannot apply to singles because its effect would be to deprive one player of serving at all.)

Setting is not permitted in handicap events, because the extension of a game would work unfairly against the inferior player. Thus all handicap games must end at 15, 21, or 11, as the case may be. The changing of ends in the third game of handicap matches is made at the half-way stage, and this can vary when one side is receiving odds or owing odds. For instance, a pair handicapped at plus 4 will change ends when its score has reached 10, that is, when it has scored half the required number of points (6 of 11).

Players or pairs will start at the odds allotted to them, except when both receive odds, or both owe odds. Then the player or pair due to receive or owe the smaller amount will start at 0, and the other player or pair will start at a figure in geometrical proportion to the original odds. Tables to show these have been officially adopted.

Tournaments provide the principal form of competitive play among individuals and, throughout the world, they are restricted to amateurs. There are open championships for challenge trophies, meetings restricted to county, state, or other residential qualifications, invitation tournaments, local tournaments, national and international championships, and so on. In most countries there are also promoted junior meetings for which the age limit is 18, as well as events for various younger age groups. Many countries also stage events for veterans.

Usually a tournament includes all five branches of the game (men's and women's singles and doubles and mixed doubles), and entries are required to be filed by a given date. Generally, competition is on the knock-out basis, but occasionally such tournaments are run on the 'American' principle with section winners playing off, both with and without handicaps. Handicap events are frequently included in British tournaments and are sometimes held as separate events.

The promotion of a tournament is always undertaken by a club or association affiliated to its national organization, and the draw for level events is seeded so that the best players are prevented from being drawn against each other in the early rounds. All national organizations have adopted regulations to govern the seeding and the draw. In cases where very large entries are expected, provision is often made for preceding qualifying rounds so that the main event is not unwieldy and does not impose too much play upon the more successful competitors.

Mostly, tournaments will require a minimum of four courts and two, three, and more days of play to enable them to be completed. A tournament is always under the management of a referee who is responsible for the order of play and for adherence to the laws of badminton and the regulations governing the competition. The individual matches are, when possible, played under the authority of an umpire, though often, owing to difficulties of finding suitable officials, the competitors umpire their own matches.

Team play is also a feature of competitive badminton, and most countries promote championships or other competitions between representative county, state, or provincial teams, sometimes for teams of men and women separately, but more often for mixed teams where the contest will embrace all branches of the game. Inter-club competitions are also common. Sometimes they are staged on the knock-out basis, but more often in leagues.

The International Badminton Federation Handbook, annually, which includes the laws of badminton. *The Badminton Association of England. — Annual Handbook.*

Badminton derives its name from the seat of the Duke of Beaufort at Badminton in Gloucestershire where the game is supposed to have evolved about 1870 from the ancient children's game of battledore and shuttlecock. From the outset it gained popularity with army officers who took it to India and played it out of doors.

The first laws were drawn up in Poona in the mid-1870s, and these were used by the several groups who adopted the game at English seaside resorts, shortly to be followed by some of the London suburbs. Variations soon occurred and when it was discovered that even sizes of courts differed to an alarming extent a meeting was convened at Southsea, Hampshire, in 1893 at which the representatives of 14 clubs founded the Badminton Association which there and then adopted a uniform set of laws. Slow progress was made in the formative years, but in 1899 the Association instituted its own tournament which was soon to become known as the ALL-ENGLAND CHAMPIONSHIPS.

The court dimensions adopted in 1893 were identical with the present except that the court was not rectangular. It was waisted at the centre to an hour-glass shape, being 4 ft. (1·219 m.) narrower at the net than at the back. This was a legacy of the Victorian salons where the door was in the centre of the large rooms; the shape enabled the door to be opened without taking down the net. Not until 1901 was the court made rectangular.

In the early days, shuttlecocks, or shuttles as they have come to be known, were entirely handmade, and could vary to a remarkable extent in their behaviour and weight.

The singles game was regarded as

extremely selfish, and, although rather primitive doubles were played, three-, four-, and five-a-side games were more usual. Inter-club matches made up the principal form of competitive play, and it was not until a few years before the First World War that tournaments became more popular.

The Badminton Association grew steadily. Geographically it had no limits and many Irish and Scottish clubs were also in membership. However, the Badminton Union of Ireland was formed in 1899, and the Scottish Badminton Union in 1911. The Irish open championships were first contested in 1902 and the Scottish in 1907, and both have continued regularly ever since. From the 1920s onwards the game developed apace throughout Great Britain and Ireland, and the Welsh Badminton Union came into being in 1928.

All the home unions were originally affiliated to the Badminton Association, which, when the game began to gain popularity abroad, was the prime mover in 1934 in founding the International Badminton Federation (I.B.F.), in which England, Ireland, Scotland, and Wales have always been regarded as separate national organizations. The I.B.F. had nine founder-members, and now has affiliated to it organizations in more than 70 countries, of which over 50 are national associations, the remainder being associate members in countries not yet granted full membership.

The I.B.F. is responsible for the international government of the game; among its main duties are the organization and management of the contests for the THOMAS CUP and the UBER CUP. It alone has power to alter the laws and regulations affecting international play and tournaments of international championship or higher status. The founder-president, Sir GEORGE THOMAS, retired after 21 years since when it has been customary to change presidents at least every two years.

On the formation of the Federation, the Badminton Association relinquished its hitherto unopposed international jurisdiction of the game and restricted its activities to England and the Channel Islands. At the same time it wisely added the words 'of England' to its title. By 1939 there were over 1,300 clubs affiliated, and the Badminton Association of England (B.A.E.) had decentralized many of its functions by the recognition of the numerous county associations which had come into being. It also instituted the inter-county championship, firstly as a simple group competition with winners playing off, but later as a competition in five divisions of play, according to standard, county associations each being permitted to enter up to three teams. Arrange-

ments were made for promotion and relegation by means of challenge ties at the end of the season, and in recent years as many as 100 teams have been entered annually. Teams now consist of up to six men and six women, and a tie includes all branches of the game. By the 1970s the 40 county associations of England had a joint membership of well over 3,000 clubs, for all of which many tournaments and inter-club competitions are arranged by the local body. Many of the bigger county associations also have district associations which have been formed for identical purposes.

The Badminton Association of England is governed by a council elected by the county associations, each of which is entitled to representation, and the work of the council is decentralized among numerous committees. The council works closely with the Sports Council, the Central Council of Physical Education, the British Commonwealth Games Organization (badminton has been included in the COMMONWEALTH GAMES since 1966) and the English Schools Badminton Association which it helped to found.

England has regular international fixtures with all the stronger European nations and from time to time with many non-European countries. She has always competed in the contests for the Thomas Cup and the Uber Cup, and has enjoyed considerable success in the latter, though without capturing the trophy. The All-England Championships are organized by the B.A.E. and are regarded as the world's leading tournament and the unofficial world championships. In their early years they were held at various halls in London: from 1910 to 1939 at the Royal Horticultural Hall; from 1947 to 1949 at Harringay Arena; and from 1950 until 1956 at the Empress Hall. Since 1957 they have been held at the EMPIRE POOL, WEMBLEY.

In the early days of the championships the title properly described the entry, and it was not until 1938 that more than the occasional player from outside the British Isles took part. Since the Second World War the tournament has always commanded a representative entry from all parts of the world. For many years it has been a four-day meeting, though since 1952 there have, additionally, been preceding qualifying rounds for all five events to cater for players not accepted directly into the main tournament. Not until 1939 did players from outside the British Isles win any of the titles, but since the war winners have come from Denmark, England, Indonesia, Japan, Malaysia, Sweden, and the U.S.A. Several additional countries amongst the 20 or so usually represented have provided runners-up. Since the entry has become thoroughly international, most singles victories have been achieved by the following: KOPS (Denmark) and HARTONO (Indonesia), 7; WONG PENG SOON and CHOONG EWE BENG (Malaysia), 4 each; and Mrs. HASHMAN (U.S.A.) 10. Prior to 1939 DEVLIN (Ireland) and Miss Lucas (England) each won 6 times; NICHOLS, Miss Thomson, and Mrs. Barrett (all of England) 5 times, and Sir George Thomas (England) 4 times; all these won the trophies outright, the requirement for which is 3 successive victories or 4 in all.

All-England junior championships have been promoted since 1949-50. But the one big shortcoming to the continued development of the game has been the general shortage of playing facilities, which leave much to be desired compared with what is available in other countries. Despite this difficulty, England can claim to have produced many of the world's most prominent players, though not since 1938 has she provided an All-England men's singles champion. However, Miss Ward (now Mrs. Nielsen), Miss Smith (now Mrs. Oakley), and Miss Beck have won the singles title for women. Doubles successes have been more frequent, and among the winners hailing from England in postwar years have been Mrs. UBER and Miss Allen (now Mrs. Webber), Mrs. ROGERS and Mrs. TIMPERLEY (three times), and Miss Boxall and Mrs. Whetnall (twice), all in ladies' doubles, and in mixed doubles Best and Miss Cooley (later Mrs. Rogers), JORDAN four times with three different partners — Mrs. Timperley, Miss Pritchard, and Miss Pound (Mrs. Whetnall), Mills and Miss Perrin (Mrs. Gilks), and Talbot and Mrs. Gilks.

In the Commonwealth Games, English players have gained more gold medals than all other countries put together, and in the European championships as many titles as all other countries together.

Though mostly in events which include women, England's representatives have been very successful in the international or open championships of many of the leading countries to which representative players are regularly sent. Official international teams have been dispatched at different times to Japan, Australasia, South Africa, the U.S.A., and other countries. Ireland and Scotland too have taken their part in international play, though never outside Europe except for the Commonwealth Games, and both have competed regularly in the two international team championships promoted by the I.B.F.

The Badminton Union of Ireland includes both the Republic of Ireland and Northern Ireland, and both the Irish Open and Close championships take place in some degree of rotation in both parts of the island. For many years the principal team championship in Ireland has been on a club basis, for the four provincial associations have always been too unevenly matched, though Leinster and Ulster have met annually with varying results ever since 1911. Ireland has produced a number of famous players, among them Devlin, MACK, Maconachie, Boyle, and Rankin, all of whom gained All-England Championship honours between the wars.

In Scotland the main inter-team event is known as the Inter-Group Competition in which the eight groups, into which the administration of the Scottish Badminton Union is divided, have competed regularly since 1927. In contrast to its counterpart in England this is staged on a knock-out basis over one week-end. Scottish groups as well as Welsh counties or regions are permitted to enter the English inter-county championship, but this is the only case where complete autonomy does not prevail. The west of Scotland has contested the final of this championship on several occasions without ever winning it.

Due to its smaller population, Wales has taken a lesser part in international play, though she has in recent years competed frequently in the Helvetia Cup, and in 1970 Port Talbot was the venue for the European championships. Pre-war Wales played international matches regularly against the other home countries, but latterly she has more often opposed continental nations with a fair degree of success. There are now nine county associations in Wales, though these do not compete against each other for any championship. North Wales and South Wales, however, have an annual encounter at which the South have proved much the more successful.

International matches. The first international took place in Dublin in the 1902-3 season, England beating Ireland by 5 matches to 2. Since then 43 countries have taken part in fixtures recognized by the I.B.F., and more than 800 have been fulfilled on the five continents of the world. Of these England has contested over 200, and Denmark, Ireland, and Scotland each more than 100. Most of these are friendly fixtures, though many have come within the competitions for the Thomas Cup and the Uber Cup, which are respectively recognized officially as the international badminton championship and the ladies' international badminton championship.

The Thomas Cup competition takes place only every third year, and to date has been won five times by Indonesia and four times by Malaysia. From 10 entrants in the inaugural year, the number has steadily risen and the largest number in any one contest was 26. Due to the different playing seasons throughout the world, one competition lasts about 12 months. In the nine events held up to 1973, 154 ties had been played off in all of the four continents (American, Asian, Australasian, and European) after which the zones are named.

The Uber Cup is also competed for every three years. The U.S.A. won the first three contests, but in 1966 the Cup was won by Japan and retained ever since. The number of nations competing has risen from the original 11 to 19 on the fifth occasion.

Other international team competitions are the Helvetia Cup (instituted in 1961-2 for annual competition between the weaker countries of Europe) and the team competitions which form part of the Asian championships and the ASIAN GAMES. Another trophy competed for is the Whyte Trophy between Australia and New Zealand who meet every two years; it was inaugurated in 1938.

The composition of teams and matches in international fixtures varies and is according to agreement between the interested parties. In most friendly fixtures teams are restricted to five men and three women, and seven matches form the basis of competition.

The European Badminton Union was founded in 1967 for the main purpose of organizing European championships for individuals. It is affiliated as an international member of the I.B.F. and claims the membership of most of the national organizations in Europe.

Senior European championships are held in April in alternate years, and always in a different country. So far they have been staged in West Germany, Wales, and Sweden, and the 1974 tournament was scheduled for Austria. In the intervening years the Union promotes European junior championships for players under 18 on the preceding 1 September. They are also held in April and have so far been held at The Hague, in Czechoslovakia, and at Edinburgh. International team events were added to the senior programme from 1972. Entry for European championships is restricted to five players of each sex per country who have to be selected by their national associations.

The Asian Badminton Confederation was founded in 1959 and its object is the promotion of Asian championships, both for individuals and for international teams. These tournaments are held every two or three years and have so far taken place at Kuala Lumpur, Lucknow, Manila, and Djakarta. Entries are restricted to players selected by the national associations of Asia, though sometimes non-Asian players have been invited. All national organizations in Asia which are affiliated to the International Badminton Federation are eligible for membership.

Australia. Badminton has not advanced as might have been expected in such a sport-conscious country, though it was introduced into Western Australia in 1900. Not until 1912 was it taken up in Victoria and 1923 in Tasmania. Other states commenced playing in the following few years, but until the mid-1930s competitive play was mostly restricted to Tasmania and Victoria, although the B.A. of Western Australia dates from 1924. The year 1929 saw the first inter-state meeting between Victoria and Tasmania, and these two states have been keen rivals ever since. Together with South Australia they founded the Australian Badminton Association in 1935, and slowly the other states affiliated.

The national body, as its first duty, instituted the annual Badminton Carnival at which are held the Australian championships and the inter-state team championship for the Clendinnen Shield, which was originally donated for competition between Tasmania and Victoria but was now thrown open to other states. The carnival, usually held in August, is promoted in each of the six states in turn, and has always attracted the best representatives of the Commonwealth. From 1937 to 1960 Victoria was a regular winner of the inter-state series of matches, but since then New South Wales, Tasmania, and Western Australia have had their years of success.

Since 1951 Australia has competed regularly for the Thomas Cup and the Uber Cup, but she has not been very successful. In 1938 she commenced regular fixtures with New Zealand, and has a slight advantage in the results. The country has been a regular participant in the Commonwealth Games, but few overseas teams, other than New Zealand, have visited Australia.

Canada. Military personnel were responsible for introducing badminton into Vancouver in the late 1890s, but the game was slow to spread to other parts. The first Open tournament was the British Columbia championships in the 1913-14 season, and, as soon as the First World War was over, the game was taken up in the east, so that in 1921-2 the Canadian Badminton Association was founded and the first Canadian championships held in Montreal. They have been held annually since, and ten different cities have staged the meeting which was restricted to Canadian players until 1957, in which year it was thrown open to the world.

The greatest advance of the game was made in the autumn of 1925 when a fairly representative team from the British Isles toured the length and breadth of Canada; its success caused the erection of specially built halls in many cities. Another British team toured five years later. Both were under the captaincy of Sir George Thomas. Even before the Second World War, Canadian champions occasionally competed in the All-England Championships — Mrs. Walton of Toronto won the women's singles in 1939.

Throughout the history of Canadian badminton, British Columbia and Ontario have generally provided the strongest players, though the 1970 men's singles winner at the Commonwealth Games (Paulson) came from Calgary.

Team play has not been a big feature of the game in Canada and inter-provincial honours, for which the Manitoba Trophy is the prize, have always been awarded as a result of individual successes in the Canadian championships.

Canada was a founder member of the International Badminton Federation and has taken part in all the competitions for the Thomas Cup and the Uber Cup, though without the success which might have been expected. Canada found the United States a stumbling block to progress in both events, though latterly she has won the American Zone of both contests.

Denmark. Badminton first became known as a result of exhibitions given by teams of British players in the late 1920s, and enthusiasm so quickly took root that, early in 1930, the Danish Badminton Association was formed with headquarters in Copenhagen. Soon after, national championship tournaments were inaugurated and the game spread to all parts of the kingdom. From 1933 Danish teams were sent to Great Britain, firstly to play matches against Wales and by 1938 to participate in the All-England Championships. The first of many successes in this tournament occurred in 1939 when Madsen captured the men's singles and a Danish pair won the ladies' doubles.

Denmark was a founder member of the International Badminton Federation and she has taken a prominent part in the triennial contests for the Thomas Cup. She won the European Zone in all of the first nine contests but has not yet won the cup, though her team was very close in 1964 when it lost to Indonesia in the challenge round by 5 matches to 4. In the Uber Cup she has not been so successful though she reached the last stage on two occasions.

There are now over 500 clubs in the Danish Association, and all of them use specially built halls, usually with several courts in each. The Danes were responsible for the spread of the game to other Nordic countries.

Many Danish players have gained All-England Championship honours. Four players have each won the men's or ladies' singles, Kops leading with seven victories. Danes with most successes in all events in those championships are KOBBERÖ, 15; Mrs. AHM, 12; Kops and Mrs. THORNDAHL, 11 each.

Danish Open championships were inaugurated in 1935-6, and they attract entries from many of the strongest countries of the world. In 1949 a successful nation-wide inter-club team championship was instituted, but inter-provincial meetings are rare, though several of the provinces have regular matches with similar organizations from abroad.

India. There is a long history of badminton, for the game was taken there in the 1870s by British army officers. But it was not until the 1920s that it became competitively organized, the Punjab leading the way with the inauguration of the first state championships in 1929. Curiously, these tournaments included three-a-side events until as late as 1936.

The Badminton Association of India, formerly the All-India Badminton Association, was founded only in 1935, and from then on the game took a big step forward with the institution of All-India Championships which have ever since been peripatetic and are preceded by the inter-state championship. Eighteen state associations are now part of the Badminton Association of India as well as a small number of occupational sports boards.

India has always taken part in the contests for the Thomas Cup and the Uber Cup, and one of her representatives was runner-up in the singles of the All-England Championships of 1947.

Indonesia. Badminton was played in various parts of Indonesia many years before the country's national governing body affiliated to the International Badminton Federation in 1953. Indonesia was first recognized as a major playing nation when one of her leading players, SONNEVILLE, won the Malayan open singles title in 1955 in the face of very strong international opposition. Two years later Indonesia entered the Thomas Cup for the first time, and took the trophy with convincing wins over Denmark, Thailand, and the holders, Malaya, in Singapore. There followed a long period of international successes, and on only one occasion, 1967, was the Thomas Cup not retained, when Indonesia withdrew after play in the challenge round had been stopped owing to spectator interference in Djakarta. But she regained the cup three years later.

Badminton is the most important sport in the country, and considerable national prestige attaches to its players, among the best being Hartono, who has been All-England singles champion annually since 1968. Two Indonesians won the All-England women's doubles title in the same year, and one of them, Miss MINARNI, was ranked among the finest players of the time. Indonesia has also competed in the Uber Cup since 1959, and in 1969 she reached the challenge round.

Japan. Though British residents played badminton in Japan from the early 1920s it was not until 1938 that the Japanese themselves took it up. The Nippon Badminton Association was formed in 1947 and a year later the first national championships were promoted. In 1952 Japan was elected to the International Badminton Federation and two years later made her début in the Thomas Cup. Not till 1963 was any player dispatched to Europe, but since then the Japanese have been prominent in all the major international tournaments of the world. In 1965 Japan made her initial entry in the Uber Cup and her team exceeded all expectations by winning the women's international championship at the first attempt, beating the holders, the U.S.A., in New Zealand. Since then she has retained the trophy, and in 1969 did so on her own courts in Tokyo when 10,000 spectators attended the challenge round.

Japanese players have made their mark in the All-England Championships, notably on the women's side with three singles wins and three doubles successes. In men's play for the Thomas Cup, Japan ran the holders and eventual champions, Indonesia, to 5-4 in 1970.

Malaysia. Badminton was played outdoors throughout Malaysia for many years before 1934, when the Badminton Association of Malaya was founded. Shortly afterwards Devlin, six times All-England singles champion who had recently turned professional, toured the country and was amazed at the extremely high standard of play. The first Malayan champion came to England in 1938-9 and Malaya took part in and won the first competition for the Thomas Cup in 1949. On her own courts she retained the Thomas Cup until defeated by Indonesia in 1958, but she regained the trophy in 1967, only to lose it again three years later.

Among Malaysia's most famous players have been Wong Peng Soon, Ooi Teik Hock, the Choong brothers, Ng Boon Bee, and Tan Aik Huang, all of whom have won titles in various parts of the world, including the All-England Championships. Women's play in Malaysia has never been of as high a standard as the men's.

Singapore was formerly part of the Badminton Association of Malaya, and the island provided Malaya with several of its leading players, including Wong Peng Soon, four times All-England singles champion, but since 1966 Singapore has been separately affiliated to the International Badminton Federation.

New Zealand. Although the game was originally introduced in Auckland around the turn of the century it was not until about 1920 that it gained ground and spread to other towns in the North Island. The first tournaments were held in Wanganui and Napier about 1925, and in 1927 the New Zealand Badminton Federation was founded. It immediately promoted the first New Zealand Championships which were held in a one-court hall in Wanganui. These have been held annually since then in as many as 14 different towns with regular representation from all over the country and with the occasional participation of visiting players. The New Zealand Badminton Federation was one of the nine founders of the I.B.F.

In 1934 an inter-provincial team championship was started, which is now held in three standards of play. The championship runs throughout the season and Auckland has been the most successful province, but other provinces which have won the Wisden Cup have been Waikato, Wellington, Otago, and Southland. New Zealand has been a regular competitor in the contests for the Thomas Cup and the Uber Cup; the final rounds of the latter were staged in New Zealand in 1966. Since 1938 New Zealand has played Australia in a regular series of international fixtures for the Whyte Trophy.

New Zealand has not yet produced any players of world domination, but if Robson (b. 1926) had been a European resident he might well have reached such eminence. Other leading players have included Purser and Miss Cox, both of whom, like Robson, have proved themselves on the courts of the world.

South Africa. Badminton was introduced into South Africa during the inter-war period and became very popular in the Transvaal and Cape Town areas, but because of marked atmospheric variations, which affected the flight of shuttles in the two centres, interprovincial rivalry was hindered until specially made shuttles were adopted. The South African Badminton Union was founded in 1939, and from five founding associations the number has increased to 19.

The first South African championships, intended for 1940 but postponed owing to the war, were staged in 1948. This large tournament, which is peripatetic and always preceded by the inter-provincial team championship for the Melvill Cup, usually takes place in July or August during the middle of the South African season. It is an open tournament and members of visiting teams have occasionally competed and won titles.

Since 1948 numerous official international

teams from countries including Canada, Denmark, England, West Germany, Sweden, and the U.S.A. have toured South Africa to play series of test matches, and South Africa has frequently competed in the contests for the Thomas Cup and the Uber Cup; she has also sent an official team to Australasia.

The strongest playing centres are southern Transvaal and the Western Province which between them have won the Melvill Cup on all but two occasions. They have also provided the largest representation in Springbok teams.

U.S.A. Although the game has not yet got beyond being a minor sport in the U.S.A., the country has produced some of the best players. Although badminton was known many years before, it was not until 1936 that the American Badminton Association was formed; the number of players participating in the game has always remained relatively small. One of the principal promoters in America was the late K. R. Davidson, a Scottish international and coach, and many Canadians also helped to raise the standard of the leading players, so that immediately after the war FREEMAN of California became recognized as the greatest singles player the game had known. Soon afterwards two women, the Misses Varner and Devlin (now Mrs. Hashman) attained equal eminence, and all achieved numerous international successes for their country, though Freeman scarcely played after 1949. Alston and Rogers, both of California, are other players with world reputations, and Miss Marshall of Buffalo, N.Y., who won the American singles title seven years running from 1947, could well have attained great international fame had she competed outside her own country in her best years.

The U.S.A. has been prominent in the competitions for the Thomas Cup and the Uber Cup. In the former she was undoubtedly the second strongest nation from 1948 to 1952, and she held the Uber Cup from 1956 until Japan wrested it from her ten years later.

The principal playing centre has always been California, though the whole of the country is represented in the American Badminton Association, and international players have come from almost all parts. On the Pacific coast the game is played competitively throughout the year, but in the east the season is identical with the winter months. Annual United States championships were commenced in 1937. Until 1954 they were restricted to American players, but since then numerous overseas visitors have gained championship honours at the peripatetic meeting which has rarely been held at the same place more than once.

The Badminton Gazette, 1907 to date; S. M. Massey, *Badminton* (1911); N. B. Radford, *Badminton* (1954); E. G. Richman, *Badminton in Australia and New Zealand* (1939); *Handbook of the All-India Badminton Association* (1944).
GOVERNING BODY (WORLD): International Badminton Federation, 4 Madeira Avenue, Bromley, Kent.

BADMINTON HORSE TRIALS, see EQUESTRIAN EVENTS.

BAERLEIN, E. M. (1880-1971), British amateur RACKETS and TENNIS player for Eton College, Cambridge University, and Manchester. A fine exponent of both games, he won the British amateur singles title at rackets nine times over a span of twenty years, 1903-23. He also won the rackets doubles championship with Miles in 1902 and 1904-5, with Ashworth in 1909, and with Kershaw in 1914 and 1920.

BAGSHOT SCRAMBLE, see CYCLO-CROSS.

BAHAMONTES, FEDERICO (1928-   ), Spanish professional road-race cyclist known, for his prowess on mountain ascents, as the 'Eagle of Toledo'. Between 1954 and 1964 he was six times King of the Mountains in the TOUR DE FRANCE, which he won in 1959.

BAHRAM (1932), English race-horse bred and owned by the AGA KHAN, trained by BUTTERS, and ridden by Fox and Smirke. Bahram won all his nine races and £43,086 in stakes. War years excepted, he was, until 1970, the only horse to win the English triple crown (1935) (see HORSE RACING), since ROCK SAND in 1903.

BAILEY, TREVOR EDWARD (1923-   ), cricketer for England, Cambridge University, and Essex. A stubborn batsman and fast-medium bowler who regularly overcame crises for England during the 1950s, he was at his dourest at Brisbane in 1958, scoring 68 in 458 minutes against Australia. In the course of 61 Tests he exceeded 2,000 runs and 100 wickets.

BAILEY, WILLIAM JOHN (1888-1971), British track cyclist. A tall, well-built rider who had played Association FOOTBALL for Middlesex, Bill Bailey won three consecutive world amateur sprint titles in 1909-11. Unable to compete in 1912, when the championships were held in the U.S.A., he won again in Berlin in 1913. He also won the outdoor track classic, the Grand Prix de Paris, four years running, 1910-13. Turning professional shortly before the First World War, he rode on the continental tracks into the 1920s.

BAKER, EDWIN PERCY (1895-   ), English lawn BOWLS player, until 1972 the only man to have won the English Bowling Association singles championship four times, in 1932, 1946, 1952, and 1955. He also won the pairs twice (1950, 1962) and the triples once (1960), and his tally of 7 English championship titles stood as a record until 1973 when BRYANT won the singles to bring his total up to 12. Baker is a slim, tall, and upright figure and his delivery had a quality of grace. The 1952 final in which he beat Allen is still referred to as the finest display of bowling ever seen in the E.B.A. championships. He represented England in the 1958 COMMONWEALTH GAMES at Cardiff, when he won a silver medal in singles, and played for England in 14 international team championship series from 1933 to 1959.

BALAS, IOLANDA (1936-   ), high jumper for Romania. Miss Balas was the first woman to jump 6 ft. (1·83 m.), a height which she cleared more than 50 times. Using the outmoded 'scissors' style, she won two Olympic (1960 and 1964) and two European (1958 and 1962) titles. She improved the world record 14 times between 1956 and 1961 when she jumped 6 ft. 3¼ in. (1·91 m.). Miss Balas married her coach, Ion Söter.

BALL, ALAN JAMES (1945-   ), Association footballer for Blackpool, EVERTON, ARSENAL, and England for whom he made his first appearance in a full international match on 9 May 1965, at the age of 19, against Yugoslavia in Belgrade. Just over a year later his brilliant midfield play was a major factor in England's success in the final of the 1966 world championship at WEMBLEY. He was then a Blackpool player, but his registration was soon transferred to Everton for a fee of £112,000. He became captain of Everton in 1970 and was in the team that were beaten in the 1968 F.A. Cup final but won the Football League championship in the 1969-70 season. He was transferred to Arsenal in 1971 and was in the team beaten in the F.A. Cup final in May 1972.

BALL, JOHN (1861-1940), golfer of Royal Liverpool golf club, probably the finest amateur England has produced. At the age of 15 he finished sixth in the Open championship. The amateur championship was not inaugurated until nine years later but even so he won the title a record eight times, the last occasion at the age of 51. He was the first amateur to win the Open (in 1890) and captained the English team from 1902 to 1911.

Like that other great amateur, the American JONES, Ball's enthusiasm for GOLF was a matter of intermittent mood and on occasions he took to playing the Hoylake links backwards, or left-handed, to give an added interest to his game.

BALLOONING, a form of unpowered flight dependent on the inflation of a spherical fabric container with a gas that is lighter than air. The container (balloon) rises, carrying the pilot and passengers in a basket beneath it. Descent is effected by the controlled release of the gas through a valve in the top of the container, operated by a cord from the basket.

There are two popular forms of inflation: by hydrogen, the lightest known gas, one cubic foot of which weighs only ·0055 lb. (·0023 kg.) and exerts a lift in standard conditions of ·0752 lb. (·0341 kg.); and by hot air, which expands within the container (its surplus mass escaping through a hole in the bottom) and causes the balloon to rise as the air inside becomes lighter than the cold air outside. Hydrogen-inflated ballooning, being absolutely silent, is regarded as the purest form of the sport and leads to longer flights, but has been largely superseded by the much cheaper hot-air method.

Inflation by hydrogen may cost £250 a flight, as well as about £1,500 for the balloon. It is still common in Europe, and particularly in Germany, where advertising banners are permitted on the balloons and flights are sponsored. In Britain and the U.S.A. few hydrogen-filled balloons are now found. Heating the air within the container by burning propane gas below it may be slightly dangerous — the flame is sometimes 6 ft. (1·8 m.) high — but it costs only a fraction of the hydrogen method.

Either method of ascent requires the co-operation of a ground crew of five or six people to hold down the basket with ropes until the inflation or heating is complete. To maintain altitude in a hot-air balloon, occasional re-heating is required during flight. The cross-country passage is at the mercy of the wind, but skilled pilots can navigate with remarkable accuracy. A favourite form of competitive ballooning is the so-called pilot-declared goal: the pilot, having taken account of the weather and atmospheric conditions, is required to pin-point his target — usually more than 5 miles (8 km.) from take-off — and is awarded marks for the accuracy of his landing in relation to the distance of his flight.

A wind of 10 knots is usually enough to prevent take-off, and can lead to hazardous landings. The rate of descent can be decreased by the emptying of ballast (usually sand) from the basket and by a rope drag-line that acts as an anchor. At the moment of impact, which may be quite severe, the rip cord is pulled. This opens a panel in the balloon to allow it to collapse immediately, but the basket is almost invariably overturned and balloonists are encouraged to wear boots and crash helmets.

The sport is organized by clubs and national associations, many of which hold frequent international meets. Balloons are classified for competition by the cubic capacity of their containers, in ten sections from less than 250 cu. m. to 4,000 cu. m. and over (327–5,232 cu. yds.).

Man's efforts to fly succeeded on 21 November 1783, when two Frenchmen, de Rozier and the Marquis d'Arlandes, were airborne under a balloon for 25 minutes and covered more than 5 miles (8·05 km.). The ascent was achieved by burning a mixture of straw and wool under the envelope. The men believed, apparently, that the gas thus produced had special properties: the fact that they had heated the air in the envelope was not, at the time, thought to be relevant. Nearly two years later de Rozier and another companion died when their balloon caught fire.

Only ten days after that first manned flight, two other Frenchmen, Charles and Robert, reached 2,000 ft. (610 m.) in a hydrogen balloon, with no fire and apparently little danger. The type became known as a Charlière. Hot-air balloons were called Montgolfières after their inventors, Jacques and Joseph Montgolfier, but they soon went out of use.

Ballooning in the nineteenth century was a story of steady and astonishing achievement in hydrogen balloons, with flights across the English Channel and the Alps, and one from St. Louis, Missouri, of 800 miles (1,287 km.). By the end of the century the sport was so fashionable in London as to be rated a social grace, and it continued so until the end of the Edwardian era, when it was deeply wounded by the coming of heavier-than-air flight.

Two lasting records were established by Germans shortly before the First World War; a flight lasting 87 hours by Kaulen in 1913, and a distance of 2,192 miles (3,527 km.) by Berliner in 1914. The eccentric American millionaire Bennett offered an annual international trophy for long-distance flight that was won outright by Belgium with three successive victories (1922-4). A new prize was put up by a Belgian, and was won six times by his fellow-countryman Demuyter. In the 1930s there was a surge of ballooning interest and achievement in Russia, but the sport took a long time to recover from the Second World War.

In Britain it remained dormant until a cross-Channel flight in a hot-air balloon reawakened interest in 1963. It led to a remarkable boom in the sport in Britain, where only two flights were recorded in 1965, and 565 flights in 1970. Britain was then the third most active nation in the ballooning world, after the U.S.A. and Germany.

GOVERNING BODY (WORLD): Fédération Aéronautique Internationale, 6 Rue Galilée, Paris 16, France.

BALLYMOSS (1954), a race-horse by Mossborough, bred by Ball,. owned by McShain, and trained in Ireland by O'BRIEN. Ballymoss won eight races and £107,165 in stakes (a British record), including the KING GEORGE VI AND QUEEN ELIZABETH STAKES, ST. LEGER, ECLIPSE STAKES, CORONATION CUP, IRISH SWEEPS DERBY, and PRIX DE L'ARC DE TRIOMPHE. At stud he sired ROYAL PALACE.

BALLYNENNAN MOON (1939), racing greyhound, a brindled dog, by Mr. Moon out of Banriogan Dan, winner of 65 of his 91 races, including 23 out of 24. Only a short-head defeat in his fifteenth race stopped him beating the consecutive wins record of MICK THE MILLER. He was trained by ORTON, and owned by Mrs. J. J. Cearns.

BALTIMORE BULLETS, American professional BASKETBALL team, playing in the NATIONAL BASKETBALL ASSOCIATION. Baltimore were original members of the league, and gained their only championship success in the opening year of competition, winning the 1948 play-offs. Their personnel has included MONROE and Unseld.
COLOURS: Black uniforms, with red and white trim.

BALTIMORE COLTS, American professional FOOTBALL team, started in the All America Football Conference in 1946 as the Miami Seahawks and shifted to Baltimore the next year. They were one of the three Conference teams absorbed into the NATIONAL FOOTBALL LEAGUE after the 1949 season. Baltimore came into prominence in 1958 when they won the League championship in a 'sudden death' play-off with the NEW YORK GIANTS, and repeated the next year. Unitas, who led them at quarterback, holds the N.F.L. passing yardage record. Other stars of that team were the end Berry, the fullback Ameche, and the defensive end Marchetti. The 1968 team won the N.F.L. title, only to lose in the Super Bowl to the NEW YORK JETS. In 1970 Baltimore switched to the American Football Conference, made up largely of old AMERICAN FOOTBALL LEAGUE teams, and in 1971 won the Super Bowl.
COLOURS: Blue, white, and silver.

BALTIMORE ORIOLES, American professional BASEBALL team, had a strong tradition in the NATIONAL LEAGUE in the 1890s, featuring the outfielder Keeler and the third baseman MCGRAW. The Orioles left the major leagues after the 1902 season and remained in the minor-league International League until 1954. In that year the ST. LOUIS BROWNS' franchise in the AMERICAN LEAGUE was shifted to Baltimore and the old Orioles name applied to the new team. Baltimore was very successful in the late 1960s, winning the American League titles in 1966, 1969, 1970, and 1971 and the WORLD SERIES in 1966 and 1970. Their inspirational leader was the outfielder FRANK ROBINSON, who joined them from the CINCINNATI REDS in 1966 and remained through 1971.

BAMBRICK, JOSEPH (1905-   ), Association footballer for Northern Ireland, GLENTORAN, LINFIELD, CHELSEA, and Walsall. A centre forward, he established a British international record when he scored six goals for Northern Ireland against Wales at CELTIC PARK, Belfast on 1 February 1930. He scored altogether 94 goals in the season of 1929-30, including 50 for Linfield in the Irish League.

BAMBRIDGE, E. CHARLES (b. 1862), Association footballer for Swifts, Corinthians, and England for whom he made the first of his 18 appearances, between 1879 and 1887, when he was only 17. He scored six of England's ten goals in his first three matches against Scotland. A brilliant outside left before the 'passing game' developed, 'Charlie Bam', a founder member of the Corinthians, served on the committee of the Football Association, first as the representative of the Swifts club and later of Wiltshire County F.A., while still an active player.

BANCROFT, WILLIAM JOHN (1870-1959), RUGBY UNION full-back for SWANSEA and Wales. An unorthodox and often incautious player, Bancroft nevertheless played 33 consecutive matches for Wales, 11 of them as captain, scoring 60 points. He is said to have invented the screw kick. In 1893 he scored the decisive penalty goal which gave Wales their first home victory over England, against the instructions of his captain, GOULD, taking a drop kick instead of placing the ball. His brother, Jack, became Welsh full-back in 1909, and scored 88 points, which remained a national record for 58 years.

BAND OF BROTHERS, see CRICKET.

BANDY approximates to HOCKEY played on an ice-covered football pitch. Originally an outdoor sport, a condensed version known as rink-bandy is played indoors in Holland, but the game proper lives on only in Finland, Mongolia, Norway, the Soviet Union (including Estonia and Latvia), and Sweden. In the Baltic countries its popularity is immense: Sweden, for example, has 1,265 bandy clubs and more than 100,000 players regularly engaged in the game. The world championship is held every second year.

The rules of bandy require that it shall be played by at the most 11 players a side, and not fewer than 8. The rink is roughly the size of an Association FOOTBALL pitch, and with similar tolerances, i.e. between 90 and 110 m. (approx. 98 and 120 yds.) long and between 45 and 65 m. (approx. 49 and 71 yds.) wide.

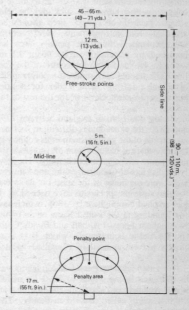

BANDY RINK

All players must wear ice skates and all except the goalkeeper carry curved wooden sticks similar to field hockey sticks: the length measured along the outside of the curve must not be more than 1·20 m. (3 ft. 11¼ in.). The ball is hard, usually red, and 6 cm. (2⅜ in.) in diameter — about half-way between a GOLF ball and a hockey ball. The goal cages are almost exactly the same size as in hockey: 2·1 m. (approx. 7 ft.) high and 3·5 m. (11 ft. 5¾ in.) wide.

The object of the game, which is started

from the centre circle, is to hit the ball into the opponents' goal. Skilled players display the speed and agility of skating seen in ICE HOCKEY, but, since bandy is played with a ball and not a puck, even greater skill with the stick is necessary. The great size of the rink, the duration of the match — two halves of 45 minutes each — and the speed at which it is played make top-class bandy a severe test of physical fitness.

The ball may not be touched with the hands, except by the goalkeeper, and the stick may not be raised higher than the level of the shoulders. The ball may be stopped by the skate, but kicking (except by the goalkeeper) is allowed only to position the ball so that the player himself may strike it. Restrictions as to impeding an opponent are similar to those in hockey: neither he nor his stick may be held, struck, pushed, or kicked. Free strokes are awarded for infringements, and serious infringements within the penalty area are punished by a penalty stroke taken 12 m. (approx. 13 yds.) from the centre of the goal line. The referee may send off a player guilty of a gross infringement, either for a brief period (as in ice hockey) or for the rest of the match.

Bandy was born in England between 1790 and 1820; the exact date is difficult to fix since no records of the game remain in its country of origin, where it has not been played since the early years of the twentieth century. The low-lying districts of Cambridgeshire and Lincolnshire were the home of the sport but its spread to other districts appears to have been slow. It had reached Nottingham by 1865, which saw the founding at the Forest Racecourse of the Nottingham Forest Football and Bandy Club. (In the Baltic countries in which it is now chiefly played, it used to be called 'winter football'.)

The first match between London teams was in 1875 and in the winter of 1890-1 a match was played between Haarlem, Holland, and an English club called Buzu-Fen-Bandy. The National Bandy Association was founded, and the first rules published, in 1891; but as a national sport in Britain it was short-lived, probably because there was seldom enough ice on which to play. From bandy developed the game of ice hockey.

Among other countries that have ceased to play bandy since 1910 are Austria, Denmark, Germany, and Switzerland.

BANKS, GORDON (1937-   ), Association footballer for Chesterfield, Leicester City, STOKE CITY, and England for whom he first kept goal in a full international match in April 1963 against Scotland at WEMBLEY. He made

his Football League début for Chesterfield in 1958-9, transferring at the end of the season to Leicester City for whom he was playing in 1966 when his performances for England in their world championship matches earned him the ranking of the world's best goalkeeper. Leicester City transferred him to Stoke in April 1967 for a fee of £25,000. In the season 1970-1 he was made captain of Stoke — a rare honour for a goalkeeper but a tribute to his ability and integrity. He played in goal for Stoke when the team defeated CHELSEA in the League Cup final in March 1972, but sustained eye injuries in a car accident the following October and subsequently retired as a player in first-class football.

BANNERMAN, JOHN MACDONALD (1901-69), RUGBY UNION lock forward for Glasgow H.S.F.P., Oxford University, and Scotland. His 37 international caps, won consecutively in the 9 seasons 1921-9, remained a Scottish record for over 30 years.

BANNISTER, Dr. ROGER GILBERT (1929-   ), middle-distance runner for Great Britain. Bannister was the first man to run the mile in under 4 minutes which, in its day, was the most coveted achievement in athletics. He did this on 6 May 1954 at the Iffley Road track, Oxford, clocking a time of 3 min. 59·4 sec. to break HÄGG's world record. In the same year Bannister defeated Landy of Australia, who had superseded him as world record-holder, to win the COMMONWEALTH GAMES mile title in his fastest time of 3 min. 58·8 sec. In his last race he won a gold medal in the 1954 European 1,500 metres championship. Bannister was also a member of the British team which broke the world 4×1 mile relay record in 1953 with a time of 16 min. 41·0 sec.

BARBARIAN F.C., RUGBY UNION touring club formed in 1890 at Bradford, Yorkshire by the BLACKHEATH forward, Carpmael, who at that time was leading a scratch side on a series of fixtures in the Midlands and Yorkshire. Membership, by invitation only, is extended to outstanding players — usually, though not invariably, internationals — from all countries. The club has six basic annual fixtures, against Penarth, CARDIFF, SWANSEA, and NEWPORT at Easter; against Leicester on Boxing Day; and against East Midlands (the Arthur Mobbs memorial match) at Northampton on the first Thursday in March. Since 1948 it has been the custom of major touring sides to conclude their British programme with a match against the Barbarians, who beat the third and fourth WALLABIES in 1948 and 1958,

and the fifth SPRINGBOKS in 1961. The Barbarians themselves toured Canada in 1957 and South Africa in 1958 and 1969.
COLOURS: Black and white hooped jerseys, black shorts.

BARBICAN CUP, see COURSING.

BARCELONA C.F., Spanish Association FOOTBALL club, was founded in 1899 by Gamper, a naturalized Swiss. Winners of the first Spanish League championship in 1928-9 and several times Spanish League and Spanish Cup winners since, the club were frequent contenders in European competitions reaching the final of the European Cup in 1961 and winning the Fairs Cup in 1958, 1960, and 1966. Outstanding players include KOCSIS (ex Hungary), SUAREZ, Kubala (ex Hungary), CRUYFF (ex Netherlands), and Ramallets.
COLOURS: Red and blue striped shirts, blue shorts.

BARCLAY, Capt., see ALLARDICE, R. B.

BARDSLEY, WARREN (1883-1954), cricketer for Australia and New South Wales. A left-handed opening batsman, sound yet equipped with a range of strokes, he became the first to score a century in each innings of a Test match when he made 136 and 130 against England in 1909. In 1926, on his fourth and final tour of England, he carried his bat through an innings at LORD'S. He also made three centuries against South Africa — two of them in England during the Triangular Tournament of 1912. At the time of his retirement he had more centuries (53) to his credit than any other Australian.

BARILLON, LOUIS (1926-   ), Swiss SKIBOBBING pioneer. He was one of the first demonstrators of the sport in the Alps and through his initiative skibobbing was established as a recreation for the general public in many of the leading winter sports centres in Switzerland and France. In 1969 he founded skibobbing championships for the world's best racing motorists, Championnats du Monde de Pilotes de Grand Prix Automobile, in Villars-sur-Ollon, Switzerland.

BARLEY-BREAK, a game otherwise known as 'Last couple in Hell', was supposed to have acquired its name because it was played among the barley stacks in the farmyard. A piece of ground was divided into three parts, the middle portion being called 'Hell'. In this a man and woman stood hand in hand, and tried to catch the other couples as they advanced from the outer sections. Those who

were caught had to take their stand in the middle, and the object of the game was to be the last couple caught. A somewhat similar game was PRISONERS' BASE, first mentioned in the reign of Edward III; Shakespeare in *Cymbeline* writes:

> He with two striplings, lads more like to run
> The country base than to count such slaughter
> Made good the passage.

(See FOLK SPORTS.)

BARNA, VICTOR (Györö Braun) (1911-72), by record the greatest of all TABLE TENNIS players, graceful in movement and with style so effective in attack close to the table, especially with backhand wrist-flick, that few noticed his equal mastery of the floating ball returned from distance in defence. Barna was five times men's singles world champion (four times in succession) and once runner-up, eight times men's doubles champion (seven times in succession, with three different partners), twice mixed doubles champion, all between 1930 and 1939. He was also five times winner of the English open men's singles, twice after breaking his right (playing) arm in a car accident, and seven times member of a winning SWAYTHLING CUP team. Born in Budapest, he emigrated to France, then to England, where he adopted British nationality and several times captained England teams. After retirement as a competitor he contributed much to the game as an exhibition player and adviser to the firm of Dunlop, and founded the Swaythling Club, a social club for former table tennis internationals of all countries.

BARNES, SYDNEY FRANCIS (1873-1967), cricketer for England, Warwickshire, Lancashire, and Staffordshire. Able to impart biting spin at a brisk pace, he was among the greatest of all bowlers. A masterful man, tall, determined, and strong-willed, because of disagreements with county committees over financial terms he played mainly league CRICKET; but in the highest — Test — class in only 27 matches he took 189 wickets: 34 in Australia in 1911-12 and 49 in only four Tests in South Africa two years later, his final series. He still took wickets cheaply in league cricket at the age of 61.

BARRE, EDMOND (1802-73), REAL TENNIS world champion, 1829-62.

BARRETT, Mrs. J. E., see MORTIMER, ANGELA.

BARRIÈRE, PAUL (1919-   ), president of the French RUGBY LEAGUE from 1946 to 1955. It was largely on his initiative that the

French Rugby League was re-formed after being suppressed by the Vichy government in 1940. His arrangement of financial guarantees made possible the first WORLD CUP tournament, played in France in 1954.

BARRINGTON, J. P. (1940-   ), British SQUASH RACKETS player. Barrington showed no special aptitude for squash in his early years and arrived in London in 1964 as a second-rate player; but with tremendous determination and dedication he raised his game to international standards within a year. He won the Open championship in December 1966 and the amateur championship in the following month. He retained the Open title in 1967 and the amateur title for the two following years. He also won the amateur championships of Australia, South Africa, and the U.A.R. He regained the Open championship at Birmingham in December 1969, beating HUNT in the longest final on record, and retained the title for the following three years. Barrington first played for Ireland in 1966, being qualified by reason of his father's birth. He turned professional in February 1969 after his second failure to win the international championships, and became the first professional to play exhibition matches all over the world.

BARRINGTON, KENNETH FRANK (1930-   ), cricketer for England and Surrey. A patient, dedicated batsman; after early disappointments he re-established himself in the England side in 1959 in the West Indies, and proceeded to score 20 centuries in Test CRICKET before illness forced his retirement in 1969, when his Test aggregate (6,806) was below only four others. Though capable of forcing innings, his most typical was a stubborn 256 against Australia, against whom his average was 63.96.

BARRY, ERNEST (1882-1968), world professional sculling (see ROWING) champion from 1912 to 1919 and again in 1920. Considered as, technically, the finest sculler of all time, he won the Doggett's Coat and Badge in 1903 and the British championship in 1908, setting a record time for the Putney to Mortlake course which stood for 25 years. He retired after regaining the world championship at the age of 38 and later became a professional coach in Germany and Denmark. He was one of four members of the Barry family to win the Doggett's Coat and Badge and his great nephew, W. L. Barry, was amateur champion of the Thames from 1963 to 1966.

BARRY, Mrs. JOYCE (*née* Cran) (d. 1964), LACROSSE player for Scotland before going to the U.S.A. in the early 1920s to teach physical education. She was one of the pioneer teachers of the game and a founder of the United States Women's Lacrosse Association of which she was the first president from 1931 to 1935.

BARTALI, GINO (1914-   ), Italian roadrace cyclist. He had an unusually long professional career of 26 years, and his two victories in the TOUR DE FRANCE (1938, 1948) were eleven seasons apart. A strong climber, he won the MILAN–SAN REMO four times and both the GIRO D'ITALIA and TOUR OF LOMBARDY three times.

BARTON, PAMELA (1917-43), amateur golfer, winner of two British ladies' championships, the French, and the American ladies' championships. An English and British international, she was killed in a plane crash while serving in the W.A.A.F.

BASEBALL is a nine-a-side game played with bat, ball, and glove, mainly in the U.S.A. Teams consist of a pitcher and catcher, called the battery; first, second, and third basemen, and shortstop, called the infield; and right, centre, and left fielders, called the outfield. Substitute players may enter the game at any time, but once a player is removed he cannot return.

The standard ball has a cork-and-rubber centre wound with woollen yarn and covered with horsehide. It weighs from 5 to 5¼ oz. (148 g.) and is from 9 to 9¼ in. (approx. 23 cm.) in circumference. For SOFTBALL, a modified form of baseball, a larger ball is used. The bat is a smooth, round, tapered piece of hardwood not more than 2¾ in. (approx. 7 cm.) in diameter at its thickest part and no more than 42 in. (1.07 m.) long.

BASEBALL AND BATS

Originally, fielders played barehanded, but gloves have been developed over the years. First basemen wear a special large mitt, and catchers use a large, heavily-padded mitt as well as a chest protector, shin guards, and a metal mask. Catchers were at first unprotected. Consequently, they stood back at a distance from home plate and caught pitched balls on the bounce, but the introduction of the large, round, well-padded mitt or 'pillow glove' and the face mask enabled them to move up close behind the plate and catch pitched balls on the fly. Players wear shoes with steel cleats and, while batting and running the bases, they use protective plastic helmets.

The game is played on a field containing four bases placed at the angles of a 90-ft. (27·4 m.) square (often called a diamond): home plate and, in counter-clockwise order, first, second, and third base. Two foul lines form the boundaries of fair territory. Starting at home, these lines extend past first and third base the entire length of the field, which is often enclosed by a fence at its farthest limits.

The object of each team is to score more runs than the other. A run is scored whenever a player circles all the bases and reaches home without being put out. The game is divided into innings, in each of which the teams alternate at bat and in the field. A team is allowed three outs in each half-inning at bat, and must then take up defensive positions in the field while the other team has its turn to try to score. Ordinarily, a game consists of nine innings; in the event of a tie, extra innings are played until one team outscores the other in the same number of innings.

The players take turns batting from home plate in regular rotation. The opposing pitcher throws the ball to his catcher from a slab (called the 'rubber') on the pitcher's mound, a slightly raised area of the field directly between home and second base. The rubber is 60 ft. 6 in. (18·4 m.) from home plate, which is 17 in. (43 cm.) wide and set flush in the ground. Bases are canvas bags fastened to metal pegs set in the ground.

The batter tries to reach base safely after hitting the pitched ball into fair territory. A hit that enables him to reach first base is called a 'single', a two-base hit is a 'double', a three-base hit a 'triple', and a four-base hit a 'home run'. A fair ball hit over an outfield fence is automatically a home run. A batter is also awarded his base if the pitcher delivers four pitches which, in the umpire's judgement, do not pass through the 'strike zone' — that is, over home plate between the batter's armpits and knees; or if he is hit by a pitched ball; or if the opposing catcher interferes when he swings the bat. To prevent the batter from hitting safely, baseball pitchers deliver the ball with great speed and accuracy and vary its speed and trajectory. Success in batting, therefore, requires courage and a high degree of skill.

After a player reaches base safely, his progress towards home depends largely on his team mates' hitting the ball in such a way that

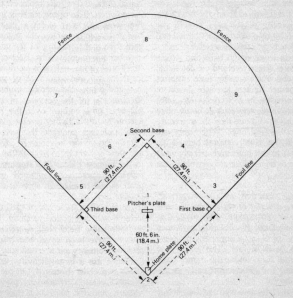

BASEBALL FIELD
(1) Pitcher; (2) catcher; (3) first baseman; (4) second baseman; (5) third baseman; (6) shortstop; (7) left fielder; (8) centre fielder; (9) right fielder.

he can advance. A base runner may also advance on his own, by 'stealing' — running for the next base as the pitcher delivers the ball to the batter, and reaching it before he is tagged out by an opposing fielder. A runner may try to move ahead if the pitcher makes a 'wild pitch' to the batter, or if the catcher allows a 'passed ball' by failing to catch a pitch. A runner may also advance if the pitcher commits a 'balk' by making an illegal move or delivery.

Players may be put out in various ways. A batter is out when the pitcher gets three 'strikes' on him. A strike is a pitch that crosses the plate in the strike zone, or any pitch that is struck at and missed or is hit into foul territory. After two strikes, however, foul balls do not count except when a batter 'bunts' — lets the ball meet the bat instead of swinging at it — and the ball rolls foul. A batter is also out if he hits the ball in the air anywhere in fair or foul territory and it is caught by an opponent before it touches the ground. He is out if he hits the ball on the ground and a fielder catches and throws it to a player at first base, or catches it and touches that base, before the batter (now become a base runner) gets there.

A base runner may be put out if, while off base, he is tagged by an opposing player with the hand or glove holding the ball, or if he is forced to leave his base to make room for another runner and fails to reach the next base before an opposing player tags him or the base; or if he is hit by a team mate's batted ball before it has touched or passed a fielder.

An umpire-in-chief 'calls' balls and strikes from his position directly behind the catcher at home plate, and one or more base umpires determine whether runners are safe or out at the other three bases. In WORLD SERIES games six umpires are used, one each at home plate and the three bases and one near the extremity of each of the two foul lines. When only one umpire is used, he usually stands behind the pitcher in order to call balls and strikes and at the same time to be as close as possible to the bases.

Baseball, long regarded as the American national game, evolved directly from the old English game of ROUNDERS. The myth that baseball was spontaneously invented by Abner Doubleday in 1839 at Cooperstown, New York, has no basis in fact. The game was played in simple form under the name 'base ball' in England and America as early as the eighteenth century.

The basic modern rules were written about 1845 by CARTWRIGHT of the New York Knickerbockers, generally considered the first organized team. The first match game played according to Cartwright's rules took place on 19 June 1846, at the Elysian Fields in Hoboken, New Jersey, between the Knickerbockers and the New York Base Ball Club. It lasted only four innings (the nine-inning rule not yet having been adopted), since by that time the New York nine had scored the requisite 21 'aces' (runs) for victory and had made two more for good measure, as against but one ace by the Knickerbockers.

Other organized clubs appeared before long as the sport gained popularity especially in New York, Brooklyn, and other parts of the northeast. Gradually the game developed from a polite amateur sport into a commercialized amusement played by professionals and controlled by promoters, who capitalized on its growing popularity and the need of urban dwellers for amusement by enclosing playing fields and charging admission. The Cincinnati Red Stockings of 1869, led by HARRY WRIGHT and his brother George, was the first openly professional team, and the first professional league, the National Association of Professional Base Ball Players, was formed in 1871. The Athletics of Philadelphia won the league's first championship pennant. The Boston Red Stockings captured all the others during the league's remaining four years.

In 1876 the NATIONAL LEAGUE of Professional Base Ball Clubs replaced the National Association. The prime movers in its formation were HULBERT and SPALDING. The new 'major league' separated the managing of the game from the playing of it and limited its membership to eight clubs. Each club received 'territorial rights' — that is, a monopoly of its local market and assurance of protection in it — and shortly the member clubs agreed not to compete for the services of each other's players. This control over the players was established through the 'reserve clause', a proviso in players' contracts that gave each club a continuing option to rehire its men each year and thus prevent them from selling their skills to the highest bidder in a free market. These restrictive practices remained in effect in professional baseball in spite of the anti-trust laws of the U.S.A.

After a bitter trade war in 1882 the National League was compelled to share the business with the rival eight-club American Association, which made lower admission charges, provided Sunday games, and sold beer on its grounds. The two outstanding teams of the 1880s were the National League's Chicago White Stockings, headed by player-manager ANSON, and the ST. LOUIS BROWNS of the American Association, who won four successive league championships.

Following renewed trade war between the

two major leagues in 1891, the American Association collapsed and left the National League, which absorbed four of the Association's clubs, supreme as a 12-club league. The most successful teams of the 1890s were the Boston Beaneaters, winners of five championships, and the BALTIMORE ORIOLES, who won the league pennant three times.

In 1903, after another fierce trade war, the National League, weakened by internal strife and the jettisoning of four of its clubs, had to recognize B. B. JOHNSON'S AMERICAN LEAGUE as a major league. The two leagues entered into an agreement with each other and in turn with the National Association, which comprised the various lesser (minor) leagues throughout the U.S.A. and, later on, in Canada and Latin America. This cartel-like structure, known as 'Organized Baseball', regulates and controls professional baseball by means of 'baseball law', an elaborate set of trade agreements among clubs and leagues. Whenever independent organizations have tried to enter the business, Organized Baseball has branded them 'outlaws' and either destroyed them by boycotts, raids on their players, and court injunctions, or absorbed them.

The peace settlement of 1903 provided for a three-man National Commission, composed of the two major-league presidents and a third baseball man selected by them, to govern Organized Baseball — an arrangement that lasted until 1920. The era of the National Commission saw an over-all rise in attendance and profits; the replacement of the old wooden grandstands with more spacious concrete-and-steel stadia; and the emergence of a new American institution, the so-called World Series, a post-season series of games played annually between the champion teams of each major league for the 'world championship'. Such outstanding players as COBB, WALTER JOHNSON, MATHEWSON, WAGNER, and YOUNG, such teams as the NEW YORK GIANTS, the CHICAGO CUBS, the PHILADELPHIA ATHLETICS, and the BOSTON RED SOX, and such team managers as MCGRAW and MACK commanded widespread interest and even devotion among baseball fans throughout the U.S.A.

Nevertheless, further trade wars, dissension among club owners, and a scandal involving an alleged rigging of the 1919 World Series marred Organized Baseball and contributed to the replacement of the National Commission in 1920 by a single commissioner, Judge LANDIS, who was elected by the major-league club owners and armed by them with broad executive and punitive powers over professional players and clubs. Landis, who remained in office until his death in 1945, was followed by several other commissioners none of whom,

however, received as much authority as he held.

The symbol of integrity that Landis provided and the magnetism of BABE RUTH with his prodigious home-run hitting and colourful personality quickly revived public confidence and interest in professional baseball. Attendance increased during the 1920s and reached a new high of 10 million for major-league games in 1930. During this decade RICKEY, vice-president of the St. Louis National League club, instituted the 'farm system', whereby the St. Louis club established ownership or control of a chain of minor-league teams ranging from the lowest level, Class D, to the highest, Class AAA, for the purpose of developing a steady supply of players for the parent club. Before long other major-league clubs emulated the Rickey system of vertical integration by creating farm systems of their own. The 1920s also marked the introduction of radio broadcasting, which all major-league clubs gradually permitted, and the beginning of the 'Yankee dynasty', so named because of the NEW YORK YANKEES' unmatched record of winning 29 league pennants and 20 world championships in the 44 years from 1921 to 1965.

Both the major and minor leagues suffered hardship during the depression. Not a year passed from 1931 to 1940 without at least five major-league clubs losing money, and several had to borrow funds from their leagues in order to continue operations. When the U.S.A. entered the Second World War, President Roosevelt granted Organized Baseball permission to carry on, and, in spite of the drain on its manpower, it continued to function by employing players over or under draft age or otherwise ineligible for conscription.

Interest in professional baseball heightened in the years immediately following the war. Major-league attendance rose to 20 million per year — double that of the best pre-war season — and profits averaged $4 million in the years 1946-9, while the number of minor leagues climbed to a new high of 60. Major-league players also gained substantial employment benefits, notably a pension plan and a salary minimum. Several times in the past the players had organized to seek redress of grievances. Their first organization, the Brotherhood of Professional Base Ball Players, formed in 1885, culminated in the sensational player revolt of 1890 when the players, led by WARD and supported by outside capitalists, formed their own league in competition with Organized Baseball, which destroyed the Players League after a year-long trade war. Later efforts at unionization likewise had little success until after the Second World War when the major-league club owners, faced with the twin threat of a players' union and raids on their players by the 'outlaw' Mexican League, granted concessions.

Another signal event occurred in 1947 when the BROOKLYN DODGERS signed JACKIE ROBINSON and thus erased a long-standing, unwritten rule that had barred Negroes from Organized Baseball. However, Robinson was not, as widely believed, the first Negro to play in major-league baseball. That distinction belongs to Moses Fleetwood Walker, who played with the Toledo club of the American Association, then a major league, in 1884, before the colour line was drawn. Since Robinson's début, numerous North American and Latin-American Negroes have achieved distinction, among them the outfielders AARON, MAYS, FRANK ROBINSON, and CLEMENTE, the infielder WILLS, the catcher CAMPANELLA, and the pitcher ROBERT GIBSON.

Under the peace agreement of 1903 the National and American Leagues established their 16 teams in ten cities — Boston, New York, Philadelphia, and Washington, along the eastern seaboard, and Pittsburgh, Cleveland, Chicago, Detroit, Cincinnati, and St. Louis in the midwest. This alignment of markets remained fixed for more than half a century despite population changes that made it increasingly unrealistic. Not until 1953 did the Boston National League club break the pattern by getting permission from the other major-league owners to transfer its franchise to Milwaukee. Since then a number of members of both major leagues have moved to other cities, and in addition each league has gradually expanded to 12 clubs in an effort to exploit new markets in cities of the west coast, southwest, and southeast.

The expansion of the major leagues, made feasible by air travel, was accompanied by the construction in practically all major-league cities of new, modern stadia financed wholly or partly out of public funds. An outstanding example is the ASTRODOME at Houston, Texas, a domed stadium where games are played on artificial turf in a fixed temperature, regardless of weather. Professional baseball has also come to rely heavily upon income from sale of television rights, particularly the World Series and the annual All-Star Game between the best players of each major league. Night baseball games were introduced to the major leagues by the Cincinnati club in 1935.

Baseball long remained undisputed as the premier game of Americans, played by boys and young men on city lots, in open fields, in schools and colleges, and in semi-professional and industrial-league teams throughout the country. Since the Second World War the growth and variety of leisure activities available to the public have brought professional baseball increasing competition, while FOOTBALL, BASKETBALL, and ICE HOCKEY challenged it as the favourite American game. Nevertheless, countless youths still play the game, mostly in highly-organized amateur leagues such as the Little League and the Babe Ruth League, classified according to the age of the participants. The most prominent of these are American Legion Junior Baseball, American Amateur Baseball Congress, Little League, National Amateur Baseball Federation, and National Baseball Congress. The impact of the game is still reflected in American speech and literature.

Baseball's influence has also reached beyond the U.S.A. Ever since Wright led two American teams on a tour of England in 1874, where they played baseball against each other and CRICKET against English teams, baseball enthusiasts have exhibited a missionary impulse, and the game has gained popularity abroad, particularly in Latin America, Japan, and, to a lesser degree, some European countries.

The Little Red Book of Baseball, annually; H. Seymour, *Baseball: The Early Years* (1960) and *Baseball: The Golden Age* (1971); *The Official Encyclopedia of Baseball*, ed. H. Turkin and S. C. Thomson (6th ed. rev., 1972); L. Watts, *The Fine Art of Baseball: A Complete Guide to Strategy, Skill and System* (1964).

BASEBALL, Welsh, an 11-a-side team game played with a wooden bat and hard ball, mainly in South Wales and part of north-west England. It differs in several respects, and notably in the matter of equipment, from the more widely-known form of BASEBALL played in the U.S.A. The clothing worn by the players is much simpler: ordinary football-style shirts and shorts, and either spiked running shoes or lightweight football boots. Catching gloves and other protective gear are not used.

The Welsh baseball bat more nearly resembles a CRICKET bat than it does a baseball bat. Made of willow, it has a flat striking surface and a deeply chamfered back. It may be altogether 3 ft. (91 cm.) long, and 3½ in. (8·9 cm.) broad at the base. Unlike that of a cricket bat, the face tapers evenly into the handle, a maximum breadth of 2½ in. (6·4 cm.) being allowed at a point 19 in. (48·3 cm.) above the base.

The ball is of approximately the same size and weight as a cricket ball, but covered in white chrome leather. It is delivered underarm by a bowler (not a pitcher) from a rectangle 10 ft. (3 m.) long and 2 ft. 6 in. (76 cm.) wide, the front edge of which is 50 ft. (15 m.) from the batting point. Behind the rectangle stands a referee. A fair ball must reach the batsman above his knee and below his chin, and in striking it his rear foot may not move beyond the centre line of the small batting diamond in which he stands. Behind the batsman stands a backstop, equivalent of the American baseball catcher.

The inner field of play is also shaped, as in American baseball, like a diamond, the four points of which are the four bases to which the batsman runs. The batting area (known as the centre peg) is 15 ft. (4·6 m.) in front of the fourth, or home, base, which is 100 ft. (30·5 m.) from the second base, at the opposite point of the diamond. The first and third bases are 86 ft. (26·2 m.) apart. Each base is represented not by a plate but by a pole stuck in the ground, which must be touched by the batsman reaching or passing it. All 11 members of a team bat before the innings is completed.

Supporters of this form of the sport claim that the American game grew from Welsh baseball. The ancient game of ROUNDERS flourished in the west of England, and almost certainly led to this refinement's building up in South Wales. It spread to isolated pockets in England, notably around Liverpool, and internationals have been played between the two countries since 1908. The first such match after the Second World War drew 16,000 spectators to the grounds of Cardiff Castle, and though its appeal has since waned, the B.B.C. televised a match from Cardiff in the summer of 1971.

The game is scarcely played in Wales beyond the areas of Cardiff and Newport, but enthusiasm for it is as intense there during the summer as it is for Association FOOTBALL during the winter. The Welsh National Baseball League has eight divisions, more than 60 clubs and about 1,400 adult players. Many thousands of children play it in schools in those areas and in Liverpool, with the great advantage that the Welsh baseball diamond can be easily pitched on comparatively rough ground. Even the adult game is played almost exclusively on common parkland and not in specially-prepared sports fields.

GOVERNING BODY (WALES): Welsh Baseball Union, 39 Pentyrch Street, Cathays, Cardiff; (ENGLAND): English Baseball Association, 7 Waltham Road, Anfield, Liverpool.

BASKETBALL, a five-a-side ball game which originated in the U.S.A. in 1891 but is now played worldwide. The object of the game as its inventor, NAISMITH, conceived it, is for one team to secure possession of the ball and to throw it into the opponents' basket, while attempting to prevent the other team

from securing the ball or scoring. A goal is scored when the ball enters the basket from above and remains in, or passes through, the net.

The goal consists of a basket made of a bottomless net of white cord, suspended from an orange-painted iron ring of 45 cm. (18 in.) inside diameter, and constructed of metal 20 mm. (approx. ¾ in.) in cross-sectional diameter. The net is constructed so as to check the ball momentarily as it passes through the basket. The ring lies in a horizontal plane, 3·05 m. (10 ft.) above the floor, and is rigidly attached to the backboard at a point equidistant from the two vertical edges and 30 cm. (1 ft.) above the bottom edge of this board.

Backboards are made of hard wood, painted white, or of a suitable transparent material of

BACKBOARD AND RING, WITH MARKINGS

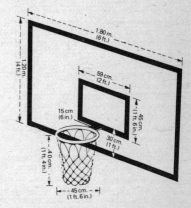

an equivalent rigidity. Each backboard measures 1·80 m. (6 ft.) horizontally, 1·20 m. (4 ft.) vertically, and has a plane front surface. It is rigidly mounted in a position at the end of the court in a perpendicular plane, parallel to the end lines, with its lower edge 2·75 m. (9 ft.) above the floor. The centre of the backboard lies in the perpendicular plane erected 1·20 m. (4 ft.) inside the court, opposite the mid-point of the end line. The supporting structures must be carefully constructed so as not to interfere with the playing area or the immediate out-of-bounds area.

The court is a rectangular hard surface, free from obstruction, 26 m. (85 ft.) between end lines and 14 m. (46 ft.) between the side lines. Its surface may be of any one of a number of suitable materials, but grass-covered courts are not permitted. The court is marked by clearly defined lines, 5 cm. (2 in.) in width.

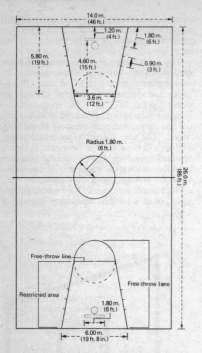

BASKETBALL COURT (F.I.B.A. RULES)

The ball used in basketball is spherical and is made of leather, rubber, or moulded nylon casing, or similar synthetic material, around a rubber inner bladder. The ball is between 75 and 78 cm. (about 30 in.) in circumference and weighs between 600 and 650 g. (21·16–22·92 oz.). It is inflated to a pressure such that when dropped on a hard surface from a height of 1·80 m. (6 ft.) measured to the bottom of the ball, it rebounds to a height of between 1·20 m. and 1·40 m. (4 ft.–4 ft. 8 in.), measured to the top of the ball. The ball is normally bright orange in colour, with black panel markings.

Each team consists of five players, up to five substitutes being allowed to each side. Each team wears a set of matching vests, or singlets, contrasting in colour with those of their opponents, brief-cut shorts, socks, and specially constructed shoes or boots with rubber soles and canvas uppers. Each player is numbered on the front and back of his vest. In international competition, only the numbers 4 to 15 inclusive may be used. No team mates may wear duplicate numbers.

The game begins with a 'jump-ball' at the centre circle. Two players, one from each team, stand in the centre circle, with their feet inside that half of the circle which is nearer to their own basket. The referee tosses the ball up between them, to a height greater than either player can reach by jumping. The players jump upwards and strive to tap the ball, after it has reached its highest point, in such a way that a member of their team gains possession. The jumpers are each allowed two taps of the ball, but they may not catch the ball until it has touched, or been touched by, one of the non-jumping players, the floor, a basket, or a backboard. During a jump-ball, the eight non-jumping players must remain outside the centre circle until the ball has been tapped.

Once a team has gained possession of the ball, its players may advance the ball either by passing it among themselves, or by dribbling it. The ball may be played only with the hands and players are not allowed to carry it more than a single pace. The swiftest and most efficient way of moving the ball about the court is by interpassing. There is no limit to the number of passes a team may make before attempting a shot at goal. It is usual for a team to make several passes before shooting, but there is never any obligation to pass the ball when one is in possession within the playing court.

The alternative method of advancing the ball is by dribbling. This allows an individual player to move the ball about the court unassisted. The dribble begins when a player bounces the ball on the floor and then touches it again, without the intrusion of another player. The dribbler may continue to bounce the ball for as long as he wishes, or is able, but once he catches it, or allows it to come to rest in his hand, he is not permitted to start another dribble. He must either pass or attempt a shot at goal. A proficient dribbler will be able to dribble using either hand and will not need to look at the ball, thereby enabling him to watch the positions of the players on the court.

The aim of passing and dribbling the ball is to attempt to reach a suitable shooting position. There is no restriction on which players are entitled to shoot or from where a shot may be taken. Any player in possession of the ball within the playing court is entitled to shoot, but naturally the nearer the basket the shot is taken, the greater the likelihood of success. A shot may be aimed directly into the ring or it may be bounced off the backboard into the basket.

If a shot misses, the ball will normally rebound back into play from the ring or the backboard and both teams may then attempt to secure control of it. The attacking team may attempt to tip the ball directly into the basket, or, having obtained possession, may attempt another shot. A team must try to shoot at goal within 30 seconds of gaining possession on the playing court. An infraction of this rule is a violation and possession is given to the opposing team.

The play in basketball is fast and free and on the comparatively small court it is essential that the rules governing personal contact be strictly framed to preserve Naismith's original concept of a game of skill. Every player must try to avoid personal contact at all times. If such contact occurs, a 'personal foul' is charged against the player responsible. A player is, however, entitled to take up any floor position that is not already occupied by an opponent, providing that this causes no personal contact. With this definition of a personal foul the game becomes one in which skill and power are of paramount importance.

If the player who had been fouled was in the act of shooting for goal, and if the shot proved unsuccessful, that player is awarded two free throws, i.e. two unhindered shots at the basket from immediately behind the 'free-throw line'. This is a line drawn parallel to the end line, 3·60 m. (12 ft.) in length and laid down 4·60 m. (15 ft.) from the face of the backboard. A free throw, if successful, is worth one point. The shooter must remain behind the free-throw line until the ball hits the ring or the backboard and no other player is allowed to enter the free-throw lane until that time. If the second throw is unsuccessful, and the ball rebounds from the ring, players of both sides may compete for the rebound in the normal way.

The non-offending team may waive its right to free throws, if it so desires, and accept possession of the ball opposite the half-way line. If the official considers that a foul is 'intentional' it is treated as having been committed against a player in the act of shooting and thus carries the free-throw penalty.

There is an alternative form of foul, known as a 'technical foul', which is charged for an offence not involving personal contact. This is normally an offence against the spirit of the game, and may be committed by a player, by the coach, or by a substitute. The penalty for a technical foul by a player is two free throws, to be taken by any member of the opposition, after which the ball remains in play in the normal way. For a technical foul by a coach, or substitute, the penalty is one free throw, followed by possession of the ball opposite the half-way line.

If a player commits five fouls during a match, he is automatically barred from taking any further part in the game. In the case of any flagrant infraction of the rules, a player may be disqualified immediately. In either case, a substitute may be introduced in place of the player who has been required to leave the game.

All breaches of the rules not considered to be fouls are known as 'violations'. Violations include running with the ball ('travelling'), kicking or punching the ball, making an illegal dribble, or causing the ball to go out of bounds.

In the case of a violation, or following a foul that does not carry the award of free throws, play is restarted by the ball's being placed at the disposal of a member of the non-offending team, out of bounds at the side line opposite the point at which the infringement occurred. That player must then pass the ball into the playing court within five seconds.

Following a goal scored during normal play, or a successful second free throw, the opposing team put the ball back into play from any point behind the end line.

The game is controlled by two officials, aided by several assistants. The officials (referee and umpire) operate on opposite sides of the playing court. The referee has the ultimate authority on all matters, but the two officials have equal jurisdiction during the normal course of the game. The assistants ('table officials') are the timekeeper, scorer, and '30-seconds operator', with the possible addition of a commissioner, chairman, and scoreboard operator. The officials conduct the game, blowing a whistle whenever it is necessary to make known a decision. They communicate with the table officials and the players by a system of signals.

The scorer keeps a chronological summary on the official score-sheet. He records the points scored, noting the number of the scorer, and indicates free throws and whether they scored or missed. He notes all fouls and charged time-outs. He indicates the number of fouls committed by a player by raising an appropriately numbered marker. In addition, the scorer is responsible for controlling substitutions, and for indicating charged time-outs by sounding his signal at the appropriate time.

The timekeeper controls the game clock and indicates the expiration of each period by sounding his signal. A match consists of two periods of 20 minutes each, although if a match is tied at the end of this time there is an extra period of 5 minutes — or as many such periods as are needed to break the tie. The game clock records actual playing time only. When an official sounds his whistle, the timekeeper stops the clock, which is not restarted until the ball is once again in play and is touched by a player on the playing court. The clock is stopped during the execution of free throws.

The '30-seconds operator' ensures that the team in possession attempts a shot within 30 seconds of having gained control of the ball. If they fail to do so, the '30-seconds operator' sounds his signal to indicate a violation.

The interval between halves is ten minutes and the game is re-started in the second half with a jump-ball at the centre circle. The game is also re-started by a jump-ball, at the nearest available circle, whenever both teams have equal claim to possession of the ball.

The team in possession of the ball must advance the ball into its front court (i.e. that half of the playing court nearer to the opponents' basket) within ten seconds of having gained possession on the playing court. This team cannot subsequently cause the ball to return to its back court. Infringement of this rule is a violation.

One of the players of each team must be designated captain. If he leaves the court for any valid reason, he must notify the officials which player will replace him as captain during his absence. The actual tactics of a team are, however, usually under the control of the team coach, who is responsible for deciding which of his players will start the game, whom to substitute, and when. There is no limit to the number of substitutions that may be made during a game and a team is always entitled to have five players on the court, if that many are still eligible to play. Substitutions can be effected only when the ball is dead and the clock stopped, and, if this is following a violation, only if the team that is substituting has possession of the ball. Since the whistle is not blown and the clock not stopped following a goal scored during normal play, no substitution may be effected at this time.

In addition to substitutions, a team coach may request a 'time-out'. He is allowed to have up to a maximum of two charged time-outs in each half, and one in each extra period. A charged time-out may be granted only when the ball is dead and the clock stopped. A time-out is for one minute, during which time the coach may address his team.

The game is won by the team scoring the greater number of points in the playing time; or if a team refuses to continue to play or has fewer than two players on court at any time, or if the referee so decides, that team forfeits the game.

Tactics. Because the goal is 3·05 m. (10 ft.) above the floor and the ball must enter it from above, the tall player has a natural advantage in basketball, and it is usual for the leading teams to include several players considerably over 6 ft. (1·8 m.). There is still opportunity, however, for the skilful smaller man to excel at the sport.

Basketball is a game in which every player on the court is involved in constant action, irrespective of which team is in possession, or of the part of the court in which the ball is located. It is usual for all five players of a team to attack when their team is in possession and to defend when the opposition has control of the ball.

There are no formal positions and teams will attack and defend in whatever formation the coach chooses. The attack employed by a team will naturally depend upon the ability and talents of its players and upon their comparison with the opposition. Such additional factors as the number of fouls already committed by individuals and the local conditions and rules of the competition will also influence the offensive style chosen by the coach.

EXAMPLES OF OFFENSIVE FORMATIONS

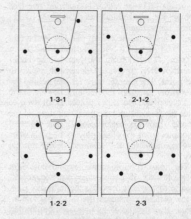

1·3·1   2·1·2

1·2·2   2·3

The method of attack by means of the 'fast break' gives a team the opportunity to exploit its speed and skill and to nullify its opponents' defensive tactics. Using the fast break, the team that had been defending, having gained possession, will immediately attempt to advance the ball up court and try to establish a numerical advantage near its opponents' goal. In this way, it is possible to make a worthwhile shot before the defence has time to form.

If it is not possible to use the fast break, or if this is incompatible with the tactics of the team, then that team will normally attempt to establish some form of controlled offence. The scope of offence is limitless but the guiding principles are few. The object is to gain the opportunity for making a shot with some probability of success, but at the same time a team will try to safeguard possession throughout its offensive manoeuvres.

The deployment of players is governed principally by their respective heights and the tactics employed by the defending team. The smaller, more agile, players work mainly in the mid-court area, some 6 m. (20 ft.) or more from the basket, and are known as guards or quarterbacks. These players are usually the most skilful dribblers and passers of the ball. The taller players, who normally play at the side or corner of the court, are known as forwards, while the tallest players of all, playing near the basket, are called pivots, centres, or posts. The actual formation employed is at the discretion of the coach. The terminology used to describe the offence is conventionally counted from the mid-court, towards the basket.

The defence employed by a team will depend on the personnel involved, the tactics chosen, and the state of the game. It may involve man-to-man principles, zone principles, or a combination of the two. In addition, the defence may be passive or may involve a degree of pressure.

In 'passive' defence, the team will defend the area close to the basket, seeking to deny the opposition the opportunity of shooting from this range, thus encouraging the longer shot in the hope that it will be unsuccessful and the defence obtain the rebound. In 'pressure' defence, the defending team make positive attempts to gain possession of the ball and prevent the shot being taken.

An extension to the principle of pressure defence leads to the 'press'. This is a form of defence in which pressure is applied over an

ZONE DEFENCES

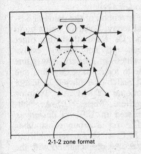 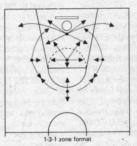 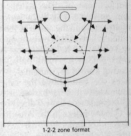

2-1-2 zone format   1-3-1 zone format   1-2-2 zone format

The one essential tactical restriction governing offensive formations is the need to have at least one guard to bring the ball up court so as to initiate the offence and maintain a suitable position to offer some defence against a possible fast break by the opposition.

The variety of defensive tactics is equally great. The basic defence involves strict man-to-man marking, where each defensive player is assigned responsibility for a member of the opposition. The position on the court at which the defender first assumes this responsibility, and the closeness with which he marks his opponent, will depend upon the over-all defensive strategy which his team is adopting.

The alternative principle is the system of 'zone' defence, in which each player is responsible for defending a loosely-defined area of the court and assumes responsibility for any attacking player within this area. He will also be ready to assist players in adjacent areas, when necessary. The shape of the zone is defined by a numerical system, counting from the mid-court, e.g. 2-1-2, 1-3-1, 1-2-2.

area far beyond that from which a shot would normally be taken. In the case of a 'full-court press', pressure is applied over the whole court whenever that team is defending. The 'press' may employ the principles of a zone, man-to-man defence, or a combination of the two.

In addition to the general scope of offence and defence, there are several facets of the game which require attention. These include jump-balls, free throws, out-of-bounds throws, and other special situations. The coach, who controls tactics, may be said to be the most important member of the team. He not only orders substitutions and time-outs, but may direct and change the team's tactics during these time-outs.

Rules. The rules for international competition are laid down by the Fédération Internationale de Basketball Amateur (F.I.B.A.) and are reviewed by its Technical Commission after each OLYMPIC GAMES. The rules quoted here were approved at Munich in 1972, but the rules of national federations sometimes contain minor variations when applied to domestic competition. This is especially so in the U.S.A. where there are further variations between the NATIONAL BASKETBALL ASSOCIATION (N.B.A.), the AMERICAN BASKETBALL ASSOCIATION (A.B.A.), the NATIONAL COLLEGIATE ATHLETIC ASSOCIATION (N.C.A.A.), and other ruling organizations.

The N.B.A., the A.B.A., the N.C.A.A., and the Amateur Athletic Union of the U.S.A. (A.A.U.) all have the following variations from the F.I.B.A. rules in common. Personal fouls committed against a player who is not in the act of shooting carry a penalty of one free throw, unless the ball is in the control of the team committing the foul. Beginning with the seventh personal foul committed by a team in each half, a bonus free throw is awarded if a player, having been awarded one free throw, is successful with this attempt. If a player is shooting for goal when he is fouled but the shot is successful, he is still awarded one, and only one, free throw.

The court marking in the U.S.A. differs from that of F.I.B.A. in various ways, most significantly in the shape of the restricted area, which is a rectangle measuring 5·80 m. (19 ft.) by 3·60 m. (12 ft.) under most American rules.

In N.C.A.A. rules only, the method of scoring known as 'dunking', whereby a player takes the ball above the ring and forces it downwards into the basket, is prohibited. The 30-seconds rule has no direct equivalent under N.C.A.A. rules. In the American professional leagues (N.B.A. and A.B.A.) the 30-seconds rule is replaced by a 24-seconds limit. A player is allowed to commit six fouls before he is automatically disqualified, and five time-outs are allowed during the course of the game. Under A.B.A. rules only, 3 points are awarded for successful shots taken from further than a stipulated distance.

Several other minor variations from the F.I.B.A. rules exist, but these require detailed reference to the relevant rules. (cf. National Collegiate Athletic Association, *Official Basketball Rules*.)

Official Basketball Rules, published by the Amateur Basket Ball Association.

The earliest evidence of a game that resembles basketball may be found in ancient Central and South American civilizations. In South America, on the Yucatan peninsula, playing 'courts' bounded by stone walls and set among groves of trees, have been found dating from the seventh century B.C. Overlooking the courts were sculptures of gods and other religious symbols, suggesting that the game normally took place as part of a religious festival. The game, known as *pok-tapok*, was played with a rubber ball filled with sacred plants. The object was to play the ball into the 'goal', using only the hips, thighs, and knees. A goal was situated at each end of the court and consisted of a flat stone slab with a hole cut through the centre. In Mexico, in the sixteenth century, the Aztec game of *ollamalitzli* required that the players propel a solid rubber ball through a fixed stone ring. The successful player was reputedly entitled to claim the clothing of all the spectators.

Omar Khayyám, the eleventh-century philosopher, seems to have made the first literary allusion to basketball in one of his epigrams, which may be translated as: 'You are a ball, played with by fate; a ball which God throws since the dawn of time into the catch-basket.'

An engraving made by de Bruys in 1603 shows a precursor of basketball, and Vieth in his *Encyclopaedia of Athletics* (1818) details a game played in Florida in which the players attempted to throw the ball into a basket attached to the top of a pole.

Credit for the invention of the game of basketball as played today, however, must go to the Canadian-born Dr. Naismith. Unlike other sports, basketball did not merely evolve —Naismith invented an entirely new game and it is possible to locate the exact time and place of the first match ever played. A leader at the International Y.M.C.A. Training School at Springfield, Mass., U.S.A., Naismith was instructed in 1891 to design an indoor team game for a group of students working for Y.M.C.A. secretarial qualifications who had become disenchanted with the compulsory formal gymnastics.

A game of skill which gave equal opportunity to every player, as Naismith intended, required the elimination of physical contact, which in turn meant that running with the ball must be prohibited. In an enclosed area it was necessary that the ball be played with the hands only. Naismith chose an Association football for the new game, since this was easy to handle, difficult to conceal, and had an even and predictable bounce. True to his intention that skill, and not strength, should prevail, Naismith decided to eliminate the concept of a goal line, or similar large target; his target, which was to permit little margin of error to the shooter, was placed not at ground level, nor in a vertical plane, but in a horizontal plane, suspended out of reach of the players.

Naismith formulated his first rules in December 1891 and, on 20 January 1892, organized the first game of basketball at the Y.M.C.A. gymnasium in Springfield. For goals he had two peach baskets nailed to the balcony, 10 ft. (3 m.) above the ground, one at each end of the gymnasium. The class comprised 18 students, so the game was played between two teams of 9. The game proved to be so popular that Naismith was soon inundated with requests for copies of the rules, and later in 1892 he published the first rule-book containing the 13 rules of the original game. Most of these are embodied in the modern game, the only significant difference being the absence of the dribble from Naismith's version of the game.

Naismith did not specify the number of players that should comprise a team, but suggested that the game could be played by any number, from three up to forty or more. Generally, though, it was agreed that the nine players on each side, for whom the game had been designed, was the ideal. Skill and mobility soon developed, however, and by 1895 it was agreed to limit the number of players on each side to five, seven, or nine, depending on the size of the gymnasium. Soon after this the number was finally standardized at the present five.

In 1895, the Y.W.C.A. organization requested a copy of the rules, which were adopted with certain restrictions to make the game less energetic, and more suitable for young women. From these rules the game of NETBALL subsequently developed independently.

In selecting the goal for his new game, Naismith had overlooked one factor, that of retrieving the ball. At first a ladder was used to collect the ball each time a goal was scored but, as the players' skill increased and scores became more frequent, this caused a tedious delay. By 1900, therefore, the peach basket had been replaced by an iron ring and a bottomless net.

Basketball competitions were held in the U.S.A. as early as 1895; the first intercollegiate conference was organized in 1901, and in the same year the game was featured in the Pan-American Exposition at Buffalo, N.Y.

A campaign to have basketball included in the Olympic Games was soon launched. In 1904, at the St. Louis Games, a tournament for American teams was organized as part of the Louisiana Purchase Exposition, but all the competing teams were from the U.S.A. and this event is now officially listed in the records as a demonstration. In 1924, at the VIIIth Olympiad, in Paris, the first international exhibition tournament took place; it included teams from France, Italy, Great Britain, and the U.S.A., and was won by London Central Y.M.C.A. Prior to the Amsterdam Olympics, in 1928, F. C. ALLEN began negotiations with the INTERNATIONAL OLYMPIC COMMITTEE and attempted without success to persuade the Los Angeles Olympic Organizing Committee to

include basketball as a demonstration sport at the 1932 Olympiad.

The Fédération Internationale de Basketball Amateur, the International Amateur Basketball Federation, which is the ruling body for all international competition in the sport, was formed in 1932, at a meeting in Geneva attended by representatives from Argentina, Czechoslovakia, Greece, Italy, Latvia, Portugal, Romania, and Switzerland. Bouffard, of Switzerland, was elected the first president, and R. WILLIAM JONES was appointed secretary-general. The membership of the F.I.B.A. reached 133 national federations in 1973. The original offices were in Rome, but permanent headquarters were later established in Munich.

The joint efforts and influence of Allen and Jones succeeded in getting basketball accepted for the programme of the XIth Olympiad, in Berlin in 1936, where, with 22 nations competing, the U.S.A. became the first Olympic champions. By 1952 the number of competing teams had reached 27 and it was agreed that in future the competition proper be limited to 16 countries, to be decided by a series of qualifying tournaments throughout the world. Meanwhile the sport had spread throughout the world, principally through the Y.M.C.A. leaders from Springfield and by the U.S. servicemen established in many parts of the world.

Several minor adjustments to the rules were made. The dribble was legalized, and the ball acquired its own identity. A backboard was added behind the basket, at first to prevent intervention by enthusiastic spectators in the balcony at the end of the court. The rebound shot, however, soon became an integral part of the game and the backboard an essential requirement. In the 1920s, legislation was introduced requiring a player who had been fouled to execute the free throws himself — prior to that time a team could have all its free throws taken by a 'specialist' freeshooter. In 1936, when the centre jump-ball which used to follow every score was eliminated, the tempo of the game was considerably increased; this led to some questioning as to whether the game was not 'now entirely too strenuous for the participants'.

Specific timing regulations which made the game longer and more accurately controlled were introduced, and the use of substitutions and time-outs was by now recognized. At the same time the 'three-seconds violation' was introduced. This penalized a player who remained in the restricted area for a period in excess of three seconds while his team was in control of the ball. The restricted area was later widened to combat further the effect of

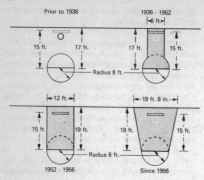

Prior to 1936

1936 - 1952

15 ft. 17 ft. 17 ft. 15 ft.

Radius 6 ft.

←12 ft.→ ←19 ft. 8 in.→

15 ft. 19 ft. 19 ft. 15 ft.

Radius 6 ft.

1952 - 1956   Since 1956

Increase in size of the restricted area under F.I.B.A. rules. (Shading denotes restricted area.)

the very tall player, and in 1956 F.I.B.A. again enlarged this area.

Basketball is generally accepted as one of the most popular spectator sports in the world today. As the game has developed, various competitions and championships have been set up. The F.I.B.A. is responsible for the organization of the world championships, the Inter-Continental Cup, and the championships within continents, including the European championships and European cup competitions. The first European championships were held in 1935, when Latvia were the winners. The championships, held in alternate years, are nowadays contested in two divisions. The eight leading nations in the previous championship automatically qualify for Division One. All other countries contest the Division Two championship, with the top four teams then qualifying to play in the Division One championship later in the year. World championships, introduced by the F.I.B.A. to fill the interim period between Olympic Games tournaments, were first held in Argentina in 1950 when the host country became the first champions. The EUROPEAN CUP FOR CHAMPION CLUBS began in 1958.

In America, the professional N.B.A. achieved major league status in 1949, and the N.C.A.A. championship was inaugurated in 1938.

B. E. Coleman, *Coaching Basketball*; *Basketball Officiating— Technique and Interpretations*; Amateur Basket Ball Association, *Official Year-Book* annually.

GOVERNING BODY (WORLD): Fédération Internationalale de Basketball Amateur, 19 Rugendas Strasse, Munich, West Germany; (U.K.): British and Irish Basketball Federation, P.O. Box I.W.3, Leeds 16.

BASS, CHARLES BURDETT (1886-1964), clay pigeon shooter for Great Britain and key British organizer of the sport for 40 years from 1914. A founder-member of the WALTHAM ABBEY GUN CLUB and its secretary from 1914 to 1939, Bass introduced skeet (see SHOOTING, CLAY PIGEON) to Britain in 1935. He represented England in international team matches from 1932 to 1937 and was winner of the first White City Cup in the floodlit tournament at White City, London in 1933. Bass supervised layouts of shooting grounds throughout the British Isles and the development of ammunition and target manufacture.

BASTIN, CLIFFORD (b. 1912), Association footballer for Exeter City, ARSENAL, and England for whom he made 21 appearances between 1932 and 1938 and scored 12 goals. By the time he was 21 he had won F.A. Cup-winners and League championship medals and had played for England. Originally an inside forward, he was converted by Arsenal to an outside left where, in partnership with JAMES, he contributed greatly to his club's successes throughout the 1930s. Subsequently he reverted to inside forward, where he played most often for England, and finally to wing half.

BATH, HARRY (1924-   ), Australian RUGBY LEAGUE forward and goal-kicker. He went to England in 1947 to join Barrow, was then transferred to WARRINGTON, and over the next nine years was an outstanding success. In 12 appearances for OTHER NATIONALITIES he and CLUES formed perhaps the best second-row pair in the game's history. Bath returned to Australia early in 1957 to coach ST. GEORGE and also the Australian Test team.

BATH CLUB, London. The old Bath Club in Dover Street was the scene of 16 successive amateur SQUASH RACKETS championships from 1923 to 1938. In these early days of the game a large gallery was not necessary and only 30 to 40 people could view the game on the main court. The club has always been a great supporter of squash and organizes the Bath Club Cup, a league competition for London West End social clubs which for many years was regarded as the game's most important tournament of its kind. It also founded in 1968 the Bath Club inter-schools tournament.

BATH ROAD 100, annual English 100-mile (160·934 km.) CYCLING time trial promoted by the Bath Road Club. Massed-start races over 100 miles from Bath to Hounslow date from 1874, but were banned, with all others, in 1894-5. Under the time-trial formula, the Bath

Road 100 was revived in 1903 and became the classic event of its kind.

BATINTON is a game for two or four players based on BADMINTON with a TABLE TENNIS scoring system. The game is played indoors or outdoors on any non-slippery surface. The standard size of an individual court is 36 ft. (10·97 m.) by 12 ft. (3·66 m.) but the width may vary between 10 ft. (3·05 m.) and 13 ft. (3·96 m.). If only 30 ft. (9·14 m.) is available, the back boundary lines may be extended 6 ft. (1·83 m.) vertically up the wall or background. Boundary lines should be approximately ¼ in. (1·27 cm.) in width. They are laid out with tape, linen, chalk, or any other material to suit the surface. A net is stretched across the centre of the court so that the middle of the net is 5 ft. (1·52 m.) above the playing surface. It is usual for several courts to be laid out side by side in a hall or gymnasium.

The game is played with a bat similar in construction to a table tennis bat, but longer: the hitting head is of wood covered with cork or plastic. The over-all length is 16 in. (41 cm.), the head 8½ in. (22 cm.) long and 6½ in. (16·5 cm.) wide. The shuttle is exactly the same as the rubber-nosed plastic shuttle used in badminton.

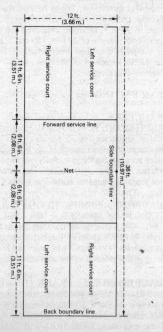

BATINTON COURT

Doubles, two players on each side of the net, is the usual form, although singles are often played.

The game commences with a service from the right-hand service court into the opponent's right-hand service court. The object is to hit the shuttle into the opponent's court or to force the opponent to hit the shuttle out of court or into the net. The player who achieves either wins the point. Each game is played until one player, or side, has reached 21 points, unless the score reaches 20-all when the game will continue until one side is 2 points ahead.

Each player serves in turn for five consecutive points. Service is taken alternately from the right and left service courts, always commencing in the right-hand court. Once play has commenced any type of stroke may be played to keep the shuttle moving from one end to the other. In doubles either partner may play the shot. The boundary lines constitute part of the court; if any part of the shuttle falls on the line it is in court.

In service the shuttle must be hit with an under-arm action in order to start play: the bat must be below the level of the elbow and both feet must be in contact with the surface of the service court. The three main strokes are, as in badminton: the drop shot, played either slowly or quickly so that the shuttle just clears the net and drops in the front of the opponent's court; the high back-court drive, played high into the air so that it is beyond the reach of an opponent close to the net (i.e. dropping close to the back boundary line); and the smash, played with the bat coming down on to the shuttle in order to hit it as steeply as possible into the opponent's court.

Batinton was 'invented', on the instructions of a New Zealand general in Cologne in 1918, by Bombing Officer Pat Hanna, O.C. Entertainment and Recreation, N.Z. Division on the Rhine. His instructions were: 'Organize entertainment, lay on laughter unlimited and rollicking recreation: games galore, games that every man can play.' The entertainment was easy to provide, but games for more than 30,000 men in restricted areas, games which everyone knew or could learn quickly and which needed little space, did not exist.

Hanna devised a new game and called it batinton. It was based on the ancient battledore and shuttlecock. Forty-eight people could play in the area of one tennis court. The game was simple yet skilful. It could be as fast and furious as the players wished and it could be played on any fairly even, non-slippery surface both indoors and outdoors. So popular was it that the supplies of shuttles ran out and the game drifted into obscurity.

At the onset of the Second World War the game was reintroduced and in 1940 it became available for general play in Australia. The shortage of shuttles again presented problems but developments within the plastics industry considerably helped the game. The first plastic bat, with plywood reinforcement, was introduced in 1952, and the plastic-skirted, rubber-nosed shuttle was produced in 1956.

The game was brought into England in 1961 and in 1963 a series of demonstrations were held in the C.C.P.R. Sports Arena at the Colex Exhibition at Olympia in London.

In 1965 the first plastic bat with cork face was produced and has largely replaced the wooden bat. By 1973 the game had spread from Australia and Great Britain to many countries in the world but had not had time to become extensively played.

BATTEN, WILLIAM (1890-1959), English RUGBY LEAGUE centre. His transfer fee from HUNSLET to Hull in 1913 (£600), his pay from Hull (£14 a match, plus bonuses), and his benefit match receipts in 1920 (£1,079) were all records at the time. He played eight times against Australia. A colourful player and fearless runner, Batten was generally regarded as the hardest tackler of his day.

BATTHYÁNY, Countess MARGIT (1911-   ), is the owner of the Gestüt Erlenhof, one of the leading German thoroughbred horse-breeding and racing establishments. An earlier member of this racing family, Prince Batthyány, bred ST. SIMON.

BAUGH, SAMUEL ADRIAN (1914-   ), American college and professional FOOTBALL player, the first prominent passing quarter-back. At Texas Christian University (1934-6), he passed three or four times as often as most passers and led punters (kickers) in college football. He played 16 years of professional football for the WASHINGTON REDSKINS and led them to League titles in 1937 and 1942. At retirement, he held League records for passes attempted, passes completed, most touchdown passes, most yardage (approximately 13 miles), and highest ratio of pass completions in a single season (70·3 per cent in 1945).

BAUMGARTEN, ELMER H. (1881-1961), former president of the American Bowling Congress and later executive secretary, who helped make tenpin BOWLING in the U.S.A. one of the world's largest participant sports.

BAYARDO (1906), English race-horse by Bay Ronald out of GALICIA (dam also of LEMBERG) tracing to QUEEN MARY, who won 22 out of his 25 races including the ST. LEGER, ECLIPSE STAKES, CHAMPION STAKES, and ASCOT GOLD CUP. At stud he sired two winners of wartime triple crowns (see HORSE RACING) in GAY CRUSADER and GAINSBOROUGH. Bayardo was bred and raced by Cox, trained by ALEC TAYLOR, and ridden by Maher and Dillon. He was one of the best horses never to win the DERBY.

BAYLOR, ELGIN (1934-   ), American BASKETBALL player. He graduated from Seattle College and turned professional with the MINNEAPOLIS (now Los Angeles) LAKERS in 1958. Baylor is considered to have been one of the greatest of all-round players.

BEACH COMBER (1945), racing greyhound, a brindled dog, by Soapy Hands out of More Taxes. A famous name in American greyhound history, he was a colourful 'character' who entertained race crowds with a 'victory roll' after each of his 200 races, lying down and rolling over on the track. He was the winner of 99 races between 1947 and 1950. U.S. tracks still hold 'Beach Comber nights' and run races in his memory.

BEAMON, ROBERT (1946-   ), long jumper for the U.S.A. When he won the 1968 Olympic LONG JUMP title with a leap of 29 ft. 2½ in. (8·90 m.), Beamon improved the world record by a margin of 21½ in. (55 cm.), a bigger advance than had been effected by the cumulative increases of the previous 40 years of record-breaking.

BEAR-BAITING, see ANIMAL-BAITING.

BEAUCLERK, Rt. Hon. and Revd. Lord FREDERICK, D.D. (1773-1850), a prominent amateur cricketer for 35 seasons from 1791; autocratic and often irascible, he bowled slow under-arm and batted gracefully, often playing matches for large side-stakes. He became in later years a prominent *habitué* at LORD'S.

BEAUFORT, HENRY HUGH ARTHUR FITZROY SOMERSET, 10th Duke of (1900-   ), founder of the Badminton Horse Trials, Britain's premier three-day event (see EQUESTRIAN EVENTS), which is held every spring in the grounds of his ancestral home.

BEAUREPAIRE, Sir FRANK (1891-1956), Australian freestyle swimmer who competed in all four OLYMPIC GAMES between 1908 and 1924. He was third in the 1,500 metres at three of these Games (1908, 1920, and 1924) and also won three silver medals.

BECKENBAUER, FRANZ (1945-   ), Association footballer for Bayern Munich and West Germany. He was an outstanding player in both the 1966 and 1970 world championships, and was to captain the West German side that won the World Cup in 1974. He also played for the Rest of the World XI against Brazil in 1968 in Rio de Janeiro.

BECKER, FRIEDRICH (d. 1938), German author of *The Breed of the Racehorse* and a leading exponent of the theory that a sire line does not thrive on the properties inherited from ancestors in straight male lineage, but that its continuation is mainly determined by the qualities of the maternal lines with which it is crossed. (See HORSE RACING.)

BEDI, BISHAN SINGH (1946-   ), cricketer for India, Northern Punjab, Delhi, and Northamptonshire. A slow, left-arm bowler of classical method, he first played for India in 1966-7, against West Indies, and by 1973 his 121 Test wickets placed him fourth among Indian bowlers. He joined Northamptonshire in 1972 and in 1973 was the leading wicket-taker in England with 105 wickets.

BEDSER, ALEC VICTOR, O.B.E. (1918-   ), cricketer for England and Surrey. With 236 wickets in 51 Tests, he was England's key bowler for a decade following the Second World War, swinging and cutting the ball off the pitch at a brisk pace and bowling inexhaustibly, often with little support. He and his twin brother, Eric, played a large part in Surrey's seven consecutive championships from 1952. In retirement he has served as assistant manager for M.C.C. in Australia and as chairman of selectors.

BEETON, E. AUDREY, see LEVICK, Mrs. MURRAY.

BEIGHTON CUP, see HOCKEY, FIELD.

BELCHER, JEM (1781-1811), British boxer who won the English bare-fist BOXING championship in 1800. He lost an eye playing RACKETS in 1803 but after retirement returned to the ring for three more championship defeats. Belcher was possibly the first to introduce to the prize ring refined footwork and boxing in retreat.

BELDHAM, WILLIAM (Silver Billy) (1766-1862), cricketer, chiefly for HAMBLEDON, playing at the highest level for 35 seasons. An all-rounder, at his peak he was unrivalled as a powerful, high-scoring batsman.

BELFAST CELTIC F.C., Association FOOTBALL club founded in 1881, they dropped out of the Irish League in the 1948-9 season after a U.S.A. tour in which they defeated Scotland 2-0 in New York. They won the Irish League championship in six successive seasons—1936, 1937, 1938, 1939, 1940, 1941. Outstanding players were SCOTT, Coulter, McCullough, VERNON, and Tully.
COLOURS: Green, and white stripes; white shorts.

BELGRAVE HARRIERS, English athletic club at Wimbledon, near London. Founded in 1887, the walking section has been at the forefront of the British scene for the past 45 years. Winners of numerous national, international, and team honours, its outstanding internationals have been GREEN, Bentley, Churcher, Hall, VICKERS, and Middleton. Members of the club have also played a major part in the organization and administration of British RACE WALKING since 1920.

BELIVEAU, JEAN (1931-   ), ICE HOCKEY player for MONTREAL CANADIENS from 1953. A centreman of great natural ability with a keen sense of anticipation and accurate marksmanship, calm-tempered, graceful, 6 ft. 3 in. (1·9 m.) tall and heavily built. By the time he was 20 he was already an outstanding amateur with Quebec Aces. He won the HART TROPHY twice, 1956 and 1964, the ART ROSS TROPHY in 1956, and the CONN SMYTHE TROPHY in 1965.

BELL, DeBENNVILLE (Bert) (1894-1959), American college and professional FOOTBALL player, coach, owner (the PHILADELPHIA EAGLES), and later Commissioner of the NATIONAL FOOTBALL LEAGUE (1946-59). His hard work, enthusiasm, good judgement, and faith in the game kept professional football on a steady course during its first great expansion. He fought successfully to keep gambling out of the game.

BELMONT, AUGUST (1852-1924), was the leading figure on the American Turf for many years and became president of the New York Jockey Club. He bought ROCK SAND for £25,000, and bred that stallion's son, TRACERY, as well as the mighty race-horse MAN O' WAR.

BELMONT PARK, New York, is the leading race-track in the U.S.A., where the BELMONT STAKES, COACHING CLUB AMERICAN OAKS, WITHERS STAKES, and JOCKEY CLUB GOLD CUP are run.

BELMONT STAKES, a horse-race founded

in 1867, is the third leg of the American triple crown and the only classic race run over $1\frac{1}{2}$ miles (2,400 m.) in the U.S.A., for which reason many racing people would place it above the KENTUCKY DERBY in importance. It is run at BELMONT PARK in early June.

BELMONTE, JUAN (1892-1962), *matador de toros* who, together with JOSELITO, revolutionized *toreo* following his *alternativa* in 1913. His practice of consistently deviating the bull round him (most earlier *toreros* had side-stepped, or caped the bull straight past them) added a new dimension to cape and *muleta* work, and earned him the title of 'the man who derailed the bull'. The style of his first period (1913-22) was *de frente* but his practice of citing recalcitrant bulls for *naturales* by advancing the right leg may well have originated the *toreo de tres cuartes* of the second stage of his career (1925-34). Although his repertoire was deliberately limited in the main to the fundamental *lances* and passes, his work was of such a distinctive nature as to make him one of the two greatest matadors of all time, the other being Joselito. In 1919 he appeared in 109 *corridas*, a record for that time.

BELOUSOVA, LUDMILA (1935-   ), ice figure-skater for the U.S.S.R. who, with PROTOPOPOV as partner, won two Olympic, four world, and four European pair-skating titles. She was born at Ulyanovsk, U.S.S.R.

BELOV, ALEKSANDR (1949-   ), BASKETBALL player from the U.S.S.R. Belov scored the winning basket for his country against the U.S.A. in the Olympic final in Munich in 1972, with less than three seconds left for play. He is a member of the A.S.K. RIGA club.

BELOV, SERGEI (1944-   ), BASKETBALL player born in Tomsk, Siberia, who later moved to Moscow, and joined the TS.S.K.A. MOSCOW club. Belov was a regular member of the U.S.S.R. national team for many years, and was voted the most valuable player of the championship at the 1972 OLYMPIC GAMES in Munich.

BEMROSE TROPHY, see MOTOR-CYCLE TRIALS.

BENAUD, RICHIE, O.B.E. (1930-   ), cricketer for Australia and New South Wales. Late in developing, he emerged as a match-winning all-rounder, batting powerfully, bowling leg-spin and its variations with life and accuracy (his 248 Test wickets are an Aus-

tralian record), and leading his country (1958-63) with perception and frequent audacity. His finest performance was at OLD TRAFFORD in 1961 when his 6 wickets for 70 won the match (and the ASHES) from a seemingly hopeless situation.

BENAUSSE, GILBERT (1930-   ), RUGBY LEAGUE player for France and Club-Carcassonne. He played in 46 international matches, mostly at stand-off half, but also at centre and on the wing. He was renowned for his ability to drop goals, and for his creative gifts in general play.

BEND OR (1877), race-horse bred and owned by the Duke of WESTMINSTER for whom he won the English DERBY, when ARCHER, with his left leg on the favourite's neck rounding Tattenham Corner, rode the race of his life to beat Robert the Devil by a head in 1880. At stud Bend Or was to achieve lasting fame, as sire of the unbeaten ORMONDE.

BENDIGO (William Thompson) (1811-80), British boxer who won the prize ring championship of England in 1839 though little more than a middleweight. He had sometimes to go down without being hit in order to avoid punishment from much heavier opponents. His ring name came from the fact that he was one of triplets called Shadrach, Meschach, and Abednego. A town in Australia was named after him.

BENDIX TROPHY, see FLYING, SPORTING.

BENFICA, Association FOOTBALL club, Lisbon, was founded in 1904 by Damiao, its first centre forward, and first won the League championship in 1936, two years after it had been initiated. The club retained the championship in 1937 and 1938, and then dominated club football competitions in Portugal from the early 1960s to 1968 during which time they won the European Cup in 1961 and 1962 and were the beaten finalists in 1965 and 1968. Among the outstanding players of recent years have been Aguas, COLUNA, Costa Pereira, EUSEBIO, Torres, Simeos, GERMANO, and Augusto.
COLOURS: Red shirts, white shorts.

BENGTSSON, STELLAN (1952-   ), Swedish TABLE TENNIS player, born in Falkenberg. A left-handed player of exceptional dedication, fitness, and speed of movement, he is the outstanding contestant, certainly in Europe, at the present day. His offensive is unwavering, he adapts his tactics skilfully to his opponents, and his backhand attack is extraordinarily strong. He started playing at 8, entered league play at 12, broke an arm at school a few years later. In 1970 he won the European junior title without dropping a game, in 1971 the world men's singles, in 1972 the English, French, Yugoslav, and European men's singles, in 1972 and 1973 the Swedish. At the world championships of 1973, besides helping his team (Sweden) to break the Far East monopoly of the SWAYTH-LING CUP (winning all his matches against both China and Japan), he took the men's doubles (with K. Johansson).

BENHAM, STANLEY (1913-   ), BOB-SLEIGH rider for the U.S.A., who drove the world title-winning four-man crews in 1949 at LAKE PLACID, N.Y., and the following year at CORTINA, Italy. He won two silver medals at the WINTER OLYMPIC GAMES, at Oslo in 1952.

BENJAMIN, Dr. NEIL (1901-   ), lawn BOWLS administrator from Sydney, Australia, who was primarily responsible for three major events in the history of international bowls. In 1961 he rewrote the constitution of the International Bowling Board, lobbied administrators around the world, and in November 1962 piloted the new constitution through the I.B.B. annual general meeting at Perth, Western Australia. Thus the previously British-dominated Board became more truly international in its control, paving the way for the first bowls championships of the world. This, the third and greatest of Benjamin's achievements, took place at KYEEMAGH, N.S.W. in October 1966 when he was president of the I.B.B.

BENNER, HUELETT L. (1925-   ), U.S.A. pistol SHOOTING champion in many events who won three world and two Pan-American titles.

At the Oslo world championships in 1952 he set a new world record in the rapid fire event with 582 points out of a possible 600. Two years later he won the same event at the world championships in Caracas, Venezuela and failed to win the centre-fire title by only one point. He won both free pistol and centre-fire pistol events in the 1955 PAN-AMERICAN GAMES.

BENNETT, ALEC (*fl.* 1924-32), Irish-Canadian racing motor-cyclist. The first man to win a TOURIST TROPHY at over 60 m.p.h. (1924) he won five TT races and rode four record laps. He was equally successful on the Continent, with a notable record in the Belgian and French Grands Prix. He retired from rac-ing in 1929, though he rode again as an amateur in 1932.

BENNETT, TERENCE (1936-   ), water skier for Australia. He set the first non-stop distance record in Australia by skiing 538 miles (865 km.) in 12 hrs. 15 min.

BENSON, VICTOR (1892-1967), British wrestler in catch-as-catch-can and Cumberland and Westmorland styles. Between 1919 and 1930, he held 13 British championships.

BENSON AND HEDGES CUP, a one-day competition in English CRICKET, conducted annually since 1972, which carries a gold trophy worth £2,000 and a cash award to the winners. The competing sides are the 17 first-class English counties, two representative teams of the Minor Counties (north and south), and, in alternate years, Oxford and Cambridge Universities. The country is split into four geographical zones, each containing five sides, which play on a league basis. The top two teams from each zone go forward to a knock-out stage, the final being staged at LORD'S in July. No matches are first-class in status, and each innings is restricted to 55 overs. A Gold Award (medallion) is presented to the outstanding individual performer in each match, and during the zonal matches a 'Team of the Week' award is made.

BENTINCK, Lord GEORGE (1802-48), was one of the ablest administrators in the history of HORSE RACING. Known as 'the Napoleon of the Turf', he introduced the practice of parading runners in the paddock before each event, numbering the horses to help in their identification, and starting races by lowering a flag.

BENTLEY, the racing car designed by Walter Bentley, occupies a special place in the history of the sport. The first 3-litre car appeared in 1921 and in 1924 won the LE MANS 24-hour race. This was privately entered, but the works teams were successful in the 1927-30 Le Mans races. Barnato, with various co-drivers, won the last three races and in 1929 the first three places were occupied by Bentleys; in 1930, the first two. The 3-litre type had been joined by the larger 4·5-litre model, capable of nearly 138 m.p.h. (222 km./h.) in special track form, and the 6·5-litre which was developed into the 'Speed Six'.

The drivers and backers of the Bentley were wealthy sportsmen who did much to give the car its glamorous image. When Bentley was taken over by Rolls-Royce there was no more official racing, but E. R. Hall's privately entered cars continued to make a good showing in the Tourist Trophy race.

BERESFORD, JACK, C.B.E. (1899-   ). The son of a famous oarsman, J. Beresford, sr., who won a silver medal in the 1912 OLYMPIC GAMES, he competed for Great Britain in five Olympics from 1920 to 1936 as sculler (see ROWING) and oarsman, winning a gold or silver medal on each occasion.

Primarily a sculler, he was second to the American, J. B. KELLY, SR., in the single sculls in 1920 but won the title in 1924. In 1928 he rowed in the THAMES ROWING CLUB eight which finished second and in 1932, again for Thames, in the coxless fours which won the gold medal. In 1936, at the age of 37, he won the double sculls with Southwood.

Beresford won the Diamond Sculls at HENLEY four times and had six other Henley wins, his last being in 1939 in the double sculls, again with Southwood, when they dead-heated with the Italians in the final. He won the WINGFIELD SCULLS for the amateur championship of the Thames on seven successive occasions and the PHILADELPHIA GOLD CUP for the world amateur championship in 1924 and 1925. In 1949, he received the Olympic Diploma of Merit and in 1971 he was elected president of Thames Rowing Club.

BERG, JACK (Kid) (1909-   ), British boxer. He won the world junior welterweight title in 1930 with his all-action style and had great success in the U.S.A. including a points victory over CANZONERI. Berg boxed professionally for 21 years.

BERGMANN, RICHARD (1920-70), outstanding match player at TABLE TENNIS, born in Vienna of a Polish father and Italian mother. He won four men's singles world championships, the first in his second season (1937), the last in 1950, and but for the Second World War would surely have bettered BARNA's singles total. Six times winner of the English open men's title, Bergmann was a relentless defender, wearing his opponent down by confidence and persistence and then breaking his spirit by a rare, flashing, forehand hit.

He played first for Austria, emigrated to escape the Anschluss, served in the British army during the war, took British nationality, and played for England, but finished up under the jurisdiction of the U.S. Table Tennis Association. First with Barna, then with LEACH (then promoting 'circuses'), and finally with the HARLEM GLOBETROTTERS, he was a tireless missionary exhibition player in all parts of the world and was dubbed 'Mr. Table Tennis' by the sporting press.

BERMUDA RACE, see YACHTING.

BESKOV, KONSTANTIN (1922-   ), Association footballer for DYNAMO MOSCOW and the Soviet Union at centre or inside forward. He was a member of the Dynamo Moscow team that toured Britain in 1945, and of the Soviet national team (which he later managed) in the 1952 OLYMPIC GAMES.

BEST, GEORGE (1946-   ), Association footballer for Northern Ireland and MANCHESTER UNITED. An accomplished forward with superb ball control, he was European and English 'Footballer of the Year' in 1968-9.

BEVAN, BRIAN (1924-   ), Australian RUGBY LEAGUE winger who joined WARRINGTON at the end of the Second World War and became the most prolific try-scorer in the history of the game. His career total of 834 tries when he retired in 1964 exceeded that of any other player by nearly 300, and he was among the leading try-scorers for 15 consecutive seasons despite intensive marking. He played 16 times for OTHER NATIONALITIES in the international championship.

BEVAN, JOHN (1943-   ), underwater swimmer. A scientific officer at the Royal Naval Physiological Laboratory, he completed a world record simulated dive to a depth of 1500 ft. (457 m.) in 1970, and won the Diver of the Year award in that year. He was the organizer of the sport of octopush (see UNDERWATER HOCKEY), 1969-73.

BIATHLON is a combined running and SWIMMING event introduced by the Modern Pentathlon Association of Great Britain in 1968. Senior men compete over the same distances as those for the modern PENTATHLON — 4,000 metres running, 300 metres swimming. At its introduction the standards set for the gold badge award of the Association were 15 minutes for the running, 4 min. 40 sec. for the swimming.

The sport is designed to produce modern pentathlon performers on the theory that it is desirable to teach swimming at an early age; that a certain proportion of capable swimmers are natural runners and that, if these two abilities are developed early, the other three skills of pentathlon — horse-riding, pistol-SHOOTING, and FENCING — can be acquired later.

(For another form of biathlon, see under SKIING.)

BIBBIA, NINO (1922-   ), tobogganist specializing on the Cresta run (see TOBOGGANING: CRESTA). Italian born, but subsequently living in St. Moritz, Bibbia remained the supreme Cresta rider from the end of the Second World War to 1970. He won the Olympic gold medal in 1948, one of two occasions when the Cresta formed part of the OLYMPIC GAMES. Bibbia won the GRAND NATIONAL every year from 1960 to 1964, and the CURZON CUP eight times in the 20 years from 1949 to 1969. His time of 54·67 seconds from Top on 22 January 1965 set a record for the full course. He also achieved the course record from Junction, on 17 January 1965, with 43·59 seconds. Bibbia's outstanding qualities included his fast starts, superior steering technique, and ability to weigh up the course and his rivals.

BICYCLE POLO is a form of POLO adapted to the use of bicycles instead of ponies; it is thus a team game in which the players' object is to score goals (the units of scoring) by driving a ball upfield with the long-handled mallet that each of them carries, and finally to strike the ball between the goal posts which the opposing team is defending.

The European version of the game —played mainly in Britain, Ireland, Belgium, and France—freely modifies the basic rules of polo; a smaller pitch is used, and the teams (of both men and women) number six, one of whom is a reserve, rather than four. As played in the United Arab Republic, India, Pakistan, Ceylon, Malaysia, and Singapore, it is a literal translation of polo, taking little account of the special characteristics of bicycle-riding.

The following description of bicycle polo is based upon the practice common to Britain and Ireland. The game is played on a rectangular grass pitch measuring between 110 yds. (100·6 m.) and 90 yds. (82·3 m.) along the touch lines, and between 80 yds. (73·2 m.) and 60 yds. (54·9 m.) along the goal lines; Association FOOTBALL fields, being of approximately these dimensions, are often used.

The goal, placed centrally on the goal line, consists of two upright posts 4 yds. (3·66 m.) apart, with a crossbar 9 ft. (2·74 m.) from the ground. A semi-circular penalty area in front of each goal is marked by a line along a radius of 15 yds. (13·7 m.) from the centre of the goal line. Parallel with each goal line, and 25 yds. (22·9 m.) from it, quarter-lines are marked to the full width of the field; and lengthways the playing area is divided by a centre, or sprinters', line which runs from the centre of one goal line to the other.

Although conventional roadster bicycles can be modified for use in the sport, a special-

ized machine is built for serious players. The main function of its design is to shorten the wheelbase to as little as 37 in. (939·8 mm.), and so increase the bicycle's manoeuvrability. This is effected by raising the angle of the head tube to approximately 70°, using straight forks, and curving the seat tube to fit the contour of the rear wheel. To compensate for this shortening, and to allow the rider more legroom, the saddle pillar is extended over the

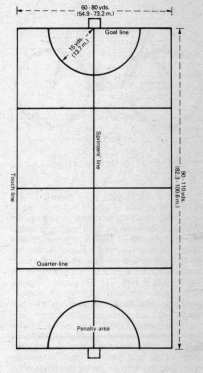

BICYCLE POLO PITCH

rear wheel, and short, almost upright handlebars are fitted.

Wheels of 26 in. (660 mm.) diameter, with heavy-gauge spokes, are used, and there is a fixed-wheel gearing of 39 in. (990·6 mm.) per revolution. The height to the bottom bracket is extended to 11¾ in. (298·5 mm.), which enables the rider to lean over without his pedal touching the ground. This facility is improved by bending outwards the already short cranks. It is obligatory, for safety's sake, to use pedals with rubber rather than metal treads, and without toe-clips or straps, and to fit rubber grips on the handlebars. There are no brakes since, with such a low gear, the rider can stop by simply treading back on the pedals.

The mallet used for striking the ball has a wooden head and a cane handle; it is about 32 in. (813 mm.) in length. The ball, made of bamboo root or plastic, is approximately 3½ in. (88·9 mm.) in diameter, and 4 oz. (113 g.) in weight. Players wear shorts, football jerseys, and protective knee-pads.

SPECIALIZED MACHINE FOR BICYCLE POLO
(1) saddle pillar, (2) head tube, (3) seat tube, (4) fork.

A game of bicycle polo consists of six 15-minute periods of play (chukkers), separated by intervals of one minute; teams change ends once, between the third and fourth chukkers. Substitution of players is permitted only during the intervals, but a player coming off the field at one interval may return at the next; thus it is customary for the six players in the team to rest in turn. The five players engaged in the game normally take up positions as goalkeeper, full-back, half-back, and two forwards.

At the start of a game or a chukker, or after a goal has been scored, the referee (who is on foot) places the ball on the sprinters' line at the centre of the field. On his signal, one man on either side (referred to, during this phase only, as the 'sprinter') races to gain possession of the ball from a standing start on the left-hand side of his goal. It is an offence for him to cross the sprinters' line before either he or the opposing sprinter has touched the ball (a ruling that reduces the likelihood of a head-on crash), or for any other player to approach within 10 yds. (9·14 m.) of the ball before this has been done.

The team which gains possession then attempts to work the ball up field either by individually driving it through or by inter-passing. The ball is normally trapped by blocking with the wheels of the bicycle, but a player is allowed to stop it with his body,

including his hand (although he may not catch it), and to kick it, provided that it is in the air. The most common foul is to lay the ball while dismounted, for playing the ball includes merely allowing it to touch one's body or bicycle, and to be dismounted it is sufficient simply to put a foot to the ground. It is not an offence to be dismounted at other times.

The defending player may tackle with his bicycle, shoulder-charge a player in possession, or hook his mallet, and he may ride-off an opponent challenging for the ball. However, he may not slash at the other's mallet, or play round him at a ball on the further side of the machine. While in his own penalty area, the goalkeeper may not be charged or obstructed, the onus of avoiding him being always on the attacker. Offside is limited to the area between the opponents' quarter-line and goal line, where an attacking player may legitimately receive the ball only if there is at least one defending player nearer the goal line.

For an offence committed by the defending side within its own penalty area, a penalty hit is awarded to the attacking side. This is taken from the centre of the penalty line, and only the goalkeeper may attempt to stop the ball. After any other infringement, a free hit is taken at the spot where it occurred by a member of the non-offending side.

If the ball crosses the touch line, a member of the side not responsible for putting it out of play takes a 'hit on'. This he does with a 'back hit' or 'cross hit' while facing away from the field; he may hit the ball in any direction. If the attacking side puts the ball over the opposing goal line, a defender takes a 'goal hit', during which the other side must retire behind the quarter-line. If a defending side puts the ball over its own goal line, the attacking side is awarded a 'corner hit'. This is taken from the junction of the quarter-line and the touch line on the appropriate side of the field. In the case of a deadlock in a scrimmage, the referee takes a 'roll in'; with all players standing at least 10 yds. away, he rolls the ball towards the centre of the field.

Bicycle polo was probably invented in Ireland in 1891 by R. J. Mecredy, a former racing cyclist who had remained an active member of the Ohnehast C.C., of Dublin, and was then editor of *Irish Cyclist*. It was the custom of the club at that period to make a Saturday excursion to the Scalp in Co. Wicklow, 20 miles from Dublin. On 10 October 1891 a report appeared in *Cycling*, under the heading 'Polo on Wheels', of the previous Saturday's club run when, on arriving at the Scalp, 'the game of cycling polo was inaugurated, and promises to be immensely popular with members'. The report continued: 'After a few games there were hardly any collisions, and these only occurred when the riders were travelling at very slow pace. One would think that polo is a sport which would peculiarly gladden the heart of the cycle-repairer, but there was not even a bent pedal. R. J. Mecredy is enthusiastic about it, and hopes to get a few matches when it is generally known.'

Forty cyclists were present at that first match, and Mecredy's optimism appears justified, for in 1901 an international match was played between England and Ireland at the Crystal Palace, London, Ireland winning 10-5. A further international was staged in London, at Shepherds Bush stadium, in 1908 — 'in connection with the OLYMPIC GAMES', although not part of the official programme — at which Ireland beat Germany 3-1. It is not known whether the Germans took the game from Ireland, or developed it spontaneously themselves.

The first Bicycle Polo Association was formed in London in 1895, and continued to promote the sport until the First World War. It then declined until 1930 when the present governing body within the U.K., the Bicycle Polo Association of Great Britain, was founded by Scott and five other members of the Corrance C.C. By 1937 the game was being played in many district leagues, and a year later the first of the modern series of home internationals between England, Ireland, and Scotland was staged. These were run off in 1938 and 1939, and in consecutive seasons between 1946 and 1951. There was then a lapse of 15 years, but the series was revived in 1966. The internationals are played on a knock-out basis at a tournament traditionally held in September, the winning country holding the Albert Lusty Trophy.

The sport in Britain is organized on the basis of local leagues reinforced by a number of national competitions. The most important of these are the inter-county challenge contest for the Apex Trophy, in which Warwickshire, Northamptonshire, Surrey, Kent, Sussex, the City of London, and Hampshire participate; the Champion of Champions competition between the league winners and the non-handicapped cup-winners; and the English Cup championship in which every club may take part. Some leading English clubs are the Catherine de Barnes, of Solihull, Birmingham, founded in 1963; the Norwood Paragon C.C., which has taken an interest in bicycle polo since 1930; and Crystal Palace, founded 1950.

In 1968 a world body, the International Cycle Polo Federation, was formed in Mexico City by representatives of India, the United Arab Republic, the U.S.A., Ceylon, Singapore, Belgium, and France. Britain applied for membership in 1970. The sport has developed strongly, although along different lines (see above), in the Far East; All-India internationals have been held, and the game has been included in the programme of the ASIAN GAMES.

BIDDY BASKETBALL, the original version of MINI-BASKETBALL. Invented in 1950 by the American youth leader, Jay Archer, the game is still played, as biddy basketball, in the U.S.A. It differs in some details of the rules from the international version.

BIENVENIDA (Antonio Mejías) (1922-), *matador de toros* who took the *alternativa* in 1942 and was still appearing in major *corridas* in 1973 at 51 years of age. A master of the *lidia* throughout his career, competent to the extreme with the cape and *muleta*, he had a profound knowledge of the possibilities and limitations of the bulls he faced, which he exploited to the full. As much an *aficionado* as a *torero*, in 1952 he exposed the horn-shaving being practised at that time.

BIG TEN, athletic conference of American colleges in the Midwest, originally consisting of the Universities of MINNESOTA, Iowa, Wisconsin, Illinois, MICHIGAN, Indiana, CHICAGO, and OHIO STATE, Purdue, and Northwestern Universities. Chicago dropped out of the conference in 1940, when FOOTBALL was abandoned at the University, and Michigan State University joined in 1950. Michigan, under YOST, dominated the conference in football in the 1900s; Chicago, under STAGG, was powerful through the 1920s; Minnesota, under Bierman, dominated most of the 1930s and 1940s; while Ohio State became a major force in the 1930s and remained so throughout the 1960s.

BIGNAL, MARY D., see RAND, Mrs.

BINDA, ALFREDO (1902-), Italian road-race cyclist. Although most of his successes were achieved within his own country, including five victories in the GIRO D'ITALIA, he had a notable record in world professional road-race championships at home and abroad. He won his three titles in Germany (1927), Liège (1930), and Rome (1932); he also took third place in Zurich (1929).

BINGHAM, WILLIAM (1932-), Association footballer for Northern Ireland, GLENTORAN, SUNDERLAND, Luton Town, EVERTON, and Port Vale. An outside right, he played for his country on 57 occasions, was Irish F.A. international team manager in 1967-71, Greek national coach 1971-3, and manager of Everton 1973-7.

BINGLEY, BLANCHE (later Mrs. G. W. Hillyard) (1863-1938), British LAWN TENNIS player, one of the indomitable early pioneers of the women's game. She competed in the first women's championship at WIMBLEDON in 1884, 'after learning the game at Ealing and Harrow with good men players', lost to Watson, the holder, in the challenge round the following year, and then defeated her to win the title in 1886.

BIRKENBEINERLAUF, a ski race instituted in 1932 by the Norwegian Ski Association to celebrate the rescue in 1205 of the two-year-old Haakon by the *Birkenbeiner*, a group who remained loyal to the king and his child. Two men rescued the child from the rebel Baglern and brought him across the deep snow of the Dovre mountains. Haakon grew up to become one of Norway's great leaders. The race starts at Lillehammer and ends at Rena, or vice versa, and is 57 km. (35 miles) long. It is run annually in February or March, depending on conditions.

BIRLING, see LOGROLLING.

BISLEY CAMP, Surrey, see SHOOTING, RIFLE.

BLACKBURN ROVERS F.C., Association FOOTBALL club formed in 1874 by old boys of Blackburn Grammar School. The club adopted professionalism in 1880 and won the F.A. Cup in 1884, 1885, and 1886. They were one of the 12 original members of the Football League in 1888 and were never relegated from the First Division until 1936. After the Second World War, Blackburn's time was divided between the First and Second Divisions until 1971 when they were relegated for the first time to the Third Division. Only Aston Villa, with seven F.A. Cup wins, have been more successful in the Cup competition than Blackburn Rovers who, in addition to the three wins in the 1880s, also won the Cup in 1890, 1891, and 1928.

The club's outstanding players from 1874 to 1914 included Forrest and J. M. Lofthouse (both of whom won five F.A. Cup-winners medals), CROMPTON, Houlker and Arthur; from 1919 to 1939, Cunliffe, Puddefoot, Rollo, and Healless; and from 1946, Clayton, Douglas, Eckersley, VERNON, and England.
COLOURS: Blue and white halved shirts, and white shorts.
GROUND: Ewood Park, Blackburn.

BLACKFRIARS RING was a most popular BOXING arena in south-east London until it was destroyed during an air raid in the Second World War. The Ring was originally an octagonal Nonconformist chapel which had fallen into disuse until it was opened in 1910 for weekly boxing promotions by Burge, a former British lightweight champion, and run, after his death, by his wife. Many outstanding boxers built their early reputations here including such world champions as LEWIS and WILDE.

BLACKHAM, JOHN McCARTHY (1853-1932), cricketer for Australia and Victoria. Known as 'the Prince of Wicket-keepers', he was a member of the first eight Australian teams to tour England and captain of the eighth. He stood at the stumps even to fast bowling, setting new standards and obviating the need for a longstop.

BLACKHEATH F.C., RUGBY UNION football club, formed in 1858, recognized as the oldest in existence with an open membership; only GUY'S HOSPITAL and EDINBURGH ACADEMICALS have a longer history. 'The Club', as it is sometimes known, played a leading role in abolishing the practice of hacking, in founding the Rugby Football Union in 1871, and in organizing the first international match against Scotland. Over 220 Blackheath players have won international caps.
HOME GROUND: Rectory Field, Blackheath.
COLOURS: Red and black hooped jerseys and black shorts.

BLACKHEATH HOCKEY CLUB, see HOCKEY, FIELD.

BLAIK, EARL HENRY (Red) (1897-   ), American college FOOTBALL coach, who played at both Miami (Ohio) University (1914-17) and at the UNITED STATES MILITARY ACADEMY (1918-19). Famed for 'methodical brilliance', he stressed hard work and perfect execution of fundamental plays, characteristics which his famous pupil, LOMBARDI, later applied to professional football. While he was coaching Dartmouth College (1934-40), Blaik's teams won 22 consecutive games. At Army (the U.S. Military Academy) from 1941 to 1958, his teams won 121 games, lost 33, tied 11. From 1944 to 1950, the teams won 57, lost 3, tied 4; won 2 consecutive national championships; were undefeated in 1944, 1945, and 1946; and had an undefeated run of 32 games (1944-7). He ended his career in 1958 with an unbeaten team.

BLAINE, ANTOINE (1910-   ), RUGBY LEAGUE player in the first French team to win the international championship (in 1939) and secretary of the French League from 1951 to 1964. He was manager of the highly successful touring team in Australia in 1951.

BLAKE, TERENCE MICHAEL (1921-), London-born gymnast and diver, who introduced TRAMPOLINING to England and became the first coach at the sport in England. Organizer of the first four world championships, and former vice-president of the International Trampoline Association.

BLANCHFLOWER, ROBERT DENNIS (1926-), Association footballer for Northern Ireland, GLENTORAN, Barnsley, ASTON VILLA, and TOTTENHAM HOTSPUR. Elected English 'Footballer of the Year' in 1958 and 1961, he captained the United Kingdom team which met the Rest of Europe in Irish F.A.'s seventy-fifth anniversary match on 13 August 1955. A thoughtful and constructive wing half-back, he captained the Tottenham Hotspur side which performed the remarkable 'double', winning the English Football League and the F.A. Cup in 1960-1; he played 57 times for his country.

BLANKERS-KOEN, Mrs. FRANCINA E. (1918-), sprinter, hurdler, jumper, and competitor in the PENTATHLON for the Netherlands. Probably the greatest all-round woman athlete of the century, Fanny Blankers-Koen accumulated nine gold medals in major championship events: the 1946 European 80 metres hurdles and 4 × 100 metres relay; the 1948 Olympic 100 metres, 200 metres, 80 metres hurdles, and 4 × 100 metres relay — a unique achievement; and the European 100 metres, 200 metres, and 80 metres hurdles in 1950. In addition she had bronze medals in the 1938 European 100 and 200 metres and a silver medal in the 1950 sprint relay. She set many world records between 1942 and 1951, the best of which were 10·8 sec. for 100 yards, 11·3 sec. for 100 metres, 24·2 sec. for 220 yards, 11·0 sec. for 80 metres hurdles, 5 ft. 7⅜ in. (1·71 m.) for the HIGH JUMP, 20 ft. 6 in. (6·25 m.) for the LONG JUMP, and 4,692 points for the pentathlon.

BLED is a magnificent lake among the mountains of northern Yugoslavia and one of the finest ROWING courses in the world, only fractionally longer than the prescribed international championship distance of 2,000 metres (1·2 miles). The European championships were held there in 1956, the world championships in 1966, and the junior championships in 1971.

BLEDISLOE CUP, the trophy presented in 1931 by Lord Bledisloe, Governor-General of New Zealand, for competition between the national RUGBY UNION teams of New Zealand and Australia. New Zealand was the first holder of the trophy, beating Australia 20-13 at Auckland on 12 September 1931. Australia won it for the first time in 1934 when they beat New Zealand 25-11 at Sydney in the first Test of the two-match series and drew the second 3-3, also at Sydney.

BLIND MAN'S BUFF, a boisterous STREET GAME, played by adults in the Middle Ages with greater emphasis on the buffs received by the blind man than in its later indoor children's party version, is an example of a sport with universal appeal. It was played in classical times when Pollux, tutor to the Emperor Commodus, described it under the name of *chalke muia*, the brazen fly or, possibly, the brass fly. As with the later blind man's buff, one player was hooded or had his eyes bandaged. He shouted that he would catch the brazen fly, the other players replying that he might chase the brazen fly but would not catch him. They proceeded to whip the 'blind man' with whips made from papyrus husks until one of them was caught.

There is a brave story behind the game in France and Belgium where it is called *Colin-maillard*, in memory of a warrior from Liège who was knighted by Robert the Pious, king of France, in 999. Although blinded in a battle against the Count of Louvain he continued to fight with such success that after his death the king introduced tournaments in one event of which blindfolded knights fought a group of other knights with blunted weapons.

The game is known in Italy as blind fly; in Germany and Austria, blind cow; in Denmark and Sweden, blind buck; while in one of its two main forms it is played in, among other countries, Finland, Russia, China, Japan, and India. In England, apart from such fairly generally used alternate names as Hoodman blind, blind hob, and hud-man blind, there are, or perhaps were, a number of regional names such as 'biggly' in Cumberland, 'blind Sim' in East Anglia, 'Willy blindy' in Durham, and 'belly blind' and 'Jockie blind man' in Scotland.

BLOOMER, STEPHEN (1874-1938), Association footballer for Derby County, Middlesbrough, and England for whom he made 23 appearances at inside right and scored 28 goals. He bridged the gap between the early individualistic style of play with its emphasis on dribbling and the developing appreciation of combined play with its emphasis on passing the ball. Above all he had a simple understanding that 'the purpose of play was the scoring of goals'. Helped by the ability, then almost unknown, to shoot instantaneously with either foot, he scored 352 goals in League matches for Derby County and Middlesbrough.

BLOSS, Mrs. W. G., see VARNER, M.

BLUE LARKSPUR (1926), race-horse bred in the U.S.A. by Col. BRADLEY, who won the BELMONT, Classic, and WITHERS STAKES, later becoming an outstanding sire of brood mares and possibly the prepotent influence in modern American race-horse pedigrees.

BLYTHE, COLIN (Charlie) (1879-1917), cricketer for England and Kent. With admirable control of flight, length, and spin, this sensitive slow left-arm bowler, who died in action in France, took 2,506 wickets in 16 seasons, 100 of them in Test matches (including 15 against South Africa at HEADINGLEY in 1907).

BMW, German firm of manufacturers of racing motor cycles, etc. Enjoying more success in record-breaking than in racing prior to 1939, BMW motor cycles were most successfully applied to sidecar racing after the Second World War, and in the hands of German and Swiss riders completely monopolized the international Grands Prix and the world championships for sidecars from 1954 to 1971.

BOAT RACE, The, the annual ROWING competition on the Thames in London between the eights of OXFORD and CAMBRIDGE Universities. Known simply as 'The Boat Race' throughout the world, it was first rowed at Henley in 1829 (when Oxford won). The second Race was not held until 1836, when it was rowed from Westminster to Putney, the then championship course for professional scullers. On this occasion, Cambridge were successful. The race became an annual affair in 1839 and in 1845 the course was moved to its present one from Putney to Mortlake, a distance of 4¼ miles (6·8 km.) on the outskirts of London. The record for the race was set in 1948 by Cambridge, with a time of 17 min. 50 sec.

Fortunes have fluctuated over the years, Cambridge recording the longest unbroken sequence of 13 wins between 1924 and 1936. Oxford have had two sequences of nine successive wins, the last from 1890 to 1898. There was one dead-heat in 1877 when a member of the Oxford crew broke his oar near the finish, the judge, 'Honest' John Phelps, recording the verdict as 'Dead-heat to Oxford by six feet'.

BOBET, LOUISON (1925-   ), French professional road-race cyclist. A rider of great tenacity rather than natural endowment, he was the first man to win three successive TOURS DE FRANCE (1953-5). He became world champion in 1954, and also scored single victories in six classic races. The manner of his retirement from his last Tour in 1959 was characteristic; having been unwell for several days, he forced himself to climb the 9,091 ft. (2,770 m.) Iseran pass, the highest in the Alps, before abandoning the race.

BOBSLEIGH, or bobsledding, a winter sport in which sleds, normally manned by four-man or two-man crews, are guided down a specially prepared, descending track of solid ice with banked bends.

The bobsled, originally of wooden construction, is now a precision-built machine of steel and aluminium. It has two axles, with two rounded runners mounted on each. The rear axle is fixed and the front one turns for steering. The sled may be steered either by ropes or a wheel. Americans tend to favour the steering-wheel, whereas most Europeans prefer the sensitivity of ropes.

The brake, a bar made of hardened steel located between the two rear runners, has a serrated edge which cuts into the ice. But because the ruts it makes can render the course dangerous, braking is not permitted during a competition except in emergency, when disqualification would be automatic.

The length of a two-man sled, often called a boblet, must not exceed 8 ft. 10 in. (2·7 m.). For four-man crews the length limit is 12 ft. 5 in. (3·8 m.). The width of either must not be greater than 2 ft. 2¼ in. (67 cm.). The crew seats are no more than 8 in. (20 cm.) above the ice. The front of the sled is fitted with a streamlined cowling which reduces wind resistance.

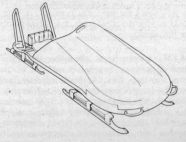

TWO-MAN BOBSLED, OR BOBLET

The maximum weight used to be 363 lb. for a two-man sled and 507 lb. for a four, but revised championship rules now stipulate a maximum weight of bobs with their teams, namely 375 kg. (827 lb.) for a two and 630 kg. (1,389 lb.) for a four. Within these limits additional weights may be bolted to the sled to assist light crews. All bobs with their team members are weighed before starting. Since 1952, this rule has eliminated the advantage heavy riders previously had when only the weight of the bob and not its crew was taken into account.

A championship event normally comprises four heats or runs for each sled, two on each of two consecutive days if conditions permit; the lowest aggregate of times for the four runs determines the winner.

Runs are timed electrically, nowadays a vital factor, when hundredths of a second frequently decide the issue. All important points on the course are linked by telephone, to ensure that the course is clear and safe and to keep spectators at all points informed by loudspeakers of progress elsewhere.

Championship bobsleigh courses are designed with permanent concrete or stone foundations on which wet snow and water freeze under suitable natural conditions. Consistently ideal ice at vital points of some courses is maintained by electrical refrigeration.

To comply with international championship regulations, a course must be at least 1,500 m. (1,640 yds.) long and contain a minimum of 15 banked turns. The walled banking at some turns rises to 20 ft. (6·1 m.), with an overturning lip of ice to help keep the sleds on the track.

The world's major championship courses have been established at ALPE D'HUEZ, France; CORTINA D'AMPEZZO, Italy; GARMISCH-Partenkirchen, West Germany; IGLS, Austria; LAKE PLACID, N.Y. (U.S.A.); and ST. MORITZ, Switzerland. All these have been WINTER OLYMPIC GAMES venues and all except that at St. Moritz were originally constructed for a specific Olympic occasion.

Bobsledding calls for considerable skill and nerve, but it is possible to reach world championship class after relatively little preparation — compared, that is, with the years of arduous training necessary to become a topflight figure skater or tennis player.

An intimate knowledge and experience of the course are of prior importance before participating in competitions. If one's bobsled touches the steep, packed ice banking, one is likely at least to lose a vital split second. At the start, initial impetus is given by members of the crew when they push, while holding

rear and side handles, before jumping into their seats.

Arts which help to reduce decimal time fractions include the driver's trick of turning his head before moving into a bend, the pace being too quick to enable him otherwise to realign his sights for the new direction on exit. The skill of weight transference to the necessary degree to correct a skidding sled has also to be acquired by trial and error.

The brakeman has to check skids and stop the sled at the end of the run. The official practice runs which usually take place on four of the five days preceding a championship are essential for learning the characteristics of a course.

The value of the two middle men in a crew of four is often underrated. They are much more than human ballast. Their synchronized timing of weight transference in cornering is a prime factor and the efficiency of their team work in pushing at the start can save more than half a second over other crews. Bobsledding bears certain similarities to ROWING, teaching a corresponding kind of team cohesion, and to MOTOR RACING, particularly in the aspect of waiting. The suspense between runs can tax a man's nerves far more than the actual racing. Near the course, in the building which houses the sleds, there is a feverish atmosphere reminiscent of motor-racing pits. Mechanics work on chassis, metal runners, and cowlings, conscious that a tiny adjustment may be decisive.

Although peak speeds on the hard and slithery surface sometimes exceed 90 m.p.h., there are fewer serious accidents than one might expect. Four-man bobs are slightly faster than twos. Goggles, crash helmets, knee pads, and elbow pads are essential items of equipment.

Although various forms of sleigh-riding on ice have been popular for centuries, bobsleigh — as a recognized sport distinct from TOBOGANING — originated in Switzerland in 1888, when an Englishman, Wilson Smith, connected two sleighs with a board to travel from St. Moritz to Celerina.

This relatively unsophisticated structure was quickly improved and the first organized competition was staged at St. Moritz in 1898 on the Cresta run, which had been built for one-man tobogganing and was not really suitable for the faster-moving bobsleds. A special, separate bob run, the world's first, was built at St. Moritz in 1902.

The world administration, now called the International Bobsleigh Federation, was formed in 1923 and was known as the International Federation of Bobsleigh and Tobogganing until 1957, when tobogganing became separately controlled. The Federation organized the first world and Olympic four-man championships, decided concurrently, at Chamonix, France, in 1924.

The first world title for two-man crews was contested in 1931 at Oberhof, Germany, and this category became an Olympic event the following year at Lake Placid, N.Y. Crews of five raced occasionally up to 1928; since then only events for crews of two and four have been recognized and all riders have been required to sit.

The first regular bobsled-maker was a Swiss blacksmith, Mathis, of St. Moritz, who worked during the early 1920s. The majority of championship sleds during the 1940s were Swiss Feierabends, made at Engelberg. From the early 1950s Italian Podars built at Cortina acquired a near monopoly until the mid-1960s, when mechanical improvements by the former Italian racer, SIORPAES, were frequently adopted; and nations and crews tended more to make their own developments.

The outstanding bobsledder in world championships has been the Italian driver, MONTI, who took 11 titles, 8 of them in two-man sleds, and retired in 1968 when he gained both Olympic gold medals. The most notable British racer has been NASH, who, with DIXON as his brakeman, won the Olympic and world two-man titles in 1964. They retained their world title in the following year.

FISKE, of the U.S.A., became the first man to win two Olympic gold medals in the event for larger crews. Another American, FORTUNE, who took part in the 1948 Winter Olympics and was still piloting one of the United States sleds in 1969, had an international career spanning 22 years. Among the sport's other most successful drivers have been FEIERABEND, KAPUS, and ENDRICH (Switzerland), KILIAN and OSTLER (Germany), BENHAM (U.S.A.), and EMERY (Canada).

The most consistently successful nation since the Second World War has been Italy, largely due to the Cortina track being more available than most for practice, to the technical influence of Monti, and also to the country's considerable mechanical success in sled-building.

During training for the 1969 world championship meeting at Lake Placid, an American four led by Fenner crashed, throwing and badly bruising all the riders. Only an hour later, they recovered enough to make the run in 1 min. 4 sec., easily the best time recorded on the course, representing an average speed of about 60 m.p.h. along the snaking mile-long track.

GOVERNING BODY (WORLD): International Bobsleigh Federation, Via Cerva 30, Milan, Italy.

BOCA JUNIORS, Association FOOTBALL club, Buenos Aires. Founded in 1908 and turned professional in 1931, the club won the Argentinian championship four times in the 1920s; four times in the 1930s, including twice the 'outlaw' league that operated during the period when the acceptance of professionalism was being disputed; and three times in the 1940s. The club reached the final of the South American Cup in 1963 and its outstanding players have included MONTI, Rattin, Angelillo, and Marzolini.

COLOURS: Blue shirts with yellow hoop.

BOGDANOV, ANATOLI (1926-   ), Russian who won six titles at the 1954 world rifle SHOOTING championships in Caracas, Venezuela, where he set a world record for the free rifle 300 metres (328 yds.) three positions category, and increased that record the following year and again four years later. He won the Olympic gold medal at Helsinki in 1952 for the 300 metres (328 yds.) event and four years later in Melbourne was winner of the 50 metres (54·7 yds.) free rifle three positions Olympic gold medal.

BOIARD (1870) was one of the best French race-horses of the nineteenth century, winning the GRAND PRIX DE PARIS, French Derby and St. Leger, PRIX DU CADRAN, and ASCOT GOLD CUP.

BOLD RULER (1954), a race-horse by Nasrullah (a son of NEARCO out of a granddaughter of LADY JOSEPHINE), the leading thoroughbred stallion in the U.S.A. for seven consecutive seasons.

BOLOGNA, Association FOOTBALL club. Founded in 1909 and three times Italian champions in the 1930s with an outstanding team, the club won its seventh championship title in 1964 after beating INTERNAZIONALE (Milan) in a play-off. Among the outstanding players have been Schiavio, Ceresoli, Andreolo (prior to 1939), Cappello, Pilmark, Jensen, Bulgarelli, and H. Nielsen.

COLOURS: Red and blue striped shirts.

BOMBITA (Ricardo Torres) (1879-1936), *matador de toros* who retired at the beginning of the 'Golden Era' (1913-20); he took the *alternativa* in 1899. He founded the Montepio de Toreros (the *toreros*' benefit association) and in 1923 was awarded the Cruz de la Beneficencia, Spain's highest civilian award. More than competent with çape and *muleta*, his forte, as was natural to the period, was the *suerte de matar*.

BONALLACK, MICHAEL FRANCIS (1934-   ), English amateur golfer. He was many times amateur champion, English champion, and WALKER CUP player and captain. One of the foremost English amateurs of all GOLF history, Bonallack won every notable amateur event in Britain, some of them several times. In the final of the English championship in 1968 he went round Ganton in 61 strokes but it could not be recognized as a record score because it was done in a match-play event.

BONNE BELLE CUP, see WIGHTMAN CUP.

BONNET, HONORÉ (1919-   ). As director of the French national ski team during the 1960s he introduced technical, physical, and psychological training methods which gave France the leading place in international ski racing. In 1966 at Portillo, Chile, France won six of the eight available gold medals at the world championships, and in 1968, the year of Bonnet's retirement, won each of the men's Olympic gold medals at Grenoble through KILLY. Bonnet introduced summer training, graded groups, and technological aids, such as walkie-talkies, on a scale that was hitherto unknown.

BONVIN, PIERRE-JOSEPH (1949-   ), Swiss skibobber who was world champion in 1969 and Swiss champion in 1968-70. In 1969 he became the first competitor to break the long series of successes of the Austrians who had until then dominated international SKIBOBBING competition.

BORDEAUX–PARIS CYCLE RACE, French professional classic claimed to be the longest continuous cycle race in annual competition. Its distance, depending on the route taken, is 345 to 382 miles (555–615 km.), and from the start at 1 a.m. it takes over 16 hours to complete. The first 150 miles or so, during the hours of darkness, are ridden as a conventional road race; then from Chatellerault or Poitiers to the finish, each competitor is paced by a Derny motor cycle. The event was first staged in 1891; up to 1970 the highest average speed recorded was 24·8 m.p.h. (39·9 km./h.) by Van Coningsloo (Belgium) in 1967.

BORDER GAMES. British professional ATHLETICS meetings held in the south of Scotland. They reached a peak of popularity in the late nineteenth century, when they were known particularly for the variety of their jumps (which included the HITCH AND KICK) and the expertise of their jumpers, one of whom performed a TRIPLE JUMP of 49 ft. 9 in. (15·16 m.) in 1893 — an achievement that remained beyond the powers of amateur athletes in Britain for more than 50 years.

BORG, ARNE (1901-   ), Swedish swimmer who won the Olympic 1,500 metres in 1928, four other Olympic medals, and five European titles, including a clean sweep of the freestyle 100, 400, and 1,500 metres in 1927. A happy-go-lucky giant of his time, he broke 32 world records between 1921 and 1929 for all distances from 300 yards (274·3 m.) to one mile (1,609·3 m.).

BORJA, ENRICO (1945-   ), Association footballer for Universidad F.A. and Mexico, for whom he played at centre forward in the 1966 world championship matches in London. Excellent technically, Borja was the best all-round Mexican player of the 1960s.

BOROS, JULIUS (1920-   ), American professional golfer was U.S. Open champion in 1952 and 1963, a RYDER CUP player, and winner of many sponsored tournaments. Boros is one of the most successful and durable players on the U.S. circuit.

BOROTRA, JEAN (1898-   ), French LAWN TENNIS player, the first of the 'Four Musketeers' (the others were LACOSTE, COCHET, and BRUGNON) to win the men's singles title at WIMBLEDON. He was an unorthodox, audacious volleyer whose fitness and enthusiasm made it possible for him to compete in first-class lawn tennis 40 years after he won the title in 1924. TILDEN called him a 'goat-getter — a player who by his style and method set out to upset his opponents' mental poise'. Borotra's Basque beret made him a gift for cartoonists and the public loved his showmanship. Even in his late sixties, when appearing for sentiment's sake at Wimbledon or for the International Club of France, he retained his sense of theatre and his ability to command attention.

Fast surfaces suited him best, but his first major success was in 1924 when he beat Lacoste in the French final, a victory that he repeated a month later in the Wimbledon final. Borotra won the Australian title in 1928 and was French champion again in 1931, but apart from victories over VINES and Allison (U.S.A.) in the 1932 Davis Cup (see LAWN TENNIS) challenge round (before which he had pleaded that he was too old to play singles), the best results of his later years were either on wood — he won the British covered court title 11 times and the French indoor title 12 times — or in doubles with Brugnon, with whom he won two of his three Wimbledon titles.

BORRETT, NORMAN F. (1919-   ), British SQUASH RACKETS and HOCKEY player. Although he represented Cambridge for three years before 1939, it was not until after the war that he burst upon the squash scene and, virtually unknown, won the amateur championship in December 1946. He won the title for the next four years and then retired from the game. He returned, however, to captain the British team in South Africa in 1955. As an international hockey player he captained the British Olympic team, as a forward, in 1948 and was capped 37 times at hockey by England or Great Britain. He also played CRICKET for Essex and Devon.

BORZOV, VALERI (1949-   ), sprinter for the U.S.S.R. Arguably the greatest European sprinter of all time, Borzov first came to notice in 1969 when he won the European championship 100 metres at Athens while still practically unknown. During the next three years he was unbeaten in any important ATHLETICS competition including several visits to the United States, traditionally the home of the world's best sprinters. He defended his 100 metres title successfully in 1971 at Helsinki and added the 200 metres gold medal. At Munich in 1972 he became the first man since 1956 to win an Olympic sprint double, taking the 100 metres gold medal in 10·14 sec. and the 200 metres in 20·0 sec., a European record. His best 100 metres time of 10·0 sec. was also a European record.

BOSANQUET, BERNARD JAMES TIN-DAL (1877-1936), cricketer for England, Oxford University, and Middlesex. An all-rounder, his importance in CRICKET history lies in his discovery and exploitation of the 'googly' (known in Australia as the 'bosie' or 'wrong 'un') by means of which he substantially decided the Test series of 1903-4 and 1905 between England and Australia.

BOSBAAN, an artificial ROWING course in Holland on the outskirts of Amsterdam, it was originally intended for the 1928 Olympic rowing events but was not completed in time. Finished in the early 1930s, it was the first of its type in the world and set the standard for later artificial courses. One of the features of the Bosbaan is a road running the entire length of the 2,000 metre (1·2 mile) course, along which two moving grandstands follow the races. The European championships were held there on four occasions and a number of major regattas also take place each year. The Amsterdam Regatta in June is one of the premier European events.

BOSISTO, GLYN DE VILLIER (1899-   ), the most renowned lawn BOWLS player produced by Australia. Winner of the national singles title in 1949, 1951 and 1953, he also skipped the championship winning fours on two occasions, 1951 and 1957. Only two other players—Waxman (1914) and Stanley (1930)—have won both the singles and fours in one year. Author of *Bowling Along*, Bosisto advocated and practised complete dedication and found world fame through thoroughness. His methods appear better suited to fast Australian greens than to the slow ones found overseas, for he finished only sixth in the 1954 COMMONWEALTH GAMES singles at Vancouver and fifth at Cardiff in 1958.

BOSTON, WILLIAM JOHN (1934-   ), Welsh RUGBY LEAGUE winger who scored 475 tries for WIGAN between 1953 and 1968. He also scored 90 tries in representative matches, 58 of them for Great Britain on tour in Australia in 1954 and 1962 and during the WORLD CUP tournament there in 1957. Altogether he played in 33 international matches, and twice for OTHER NATIONALITIES. Immensely strong and possessed of a deceptive sidestep, he set a record for a United Kingdom player by scoring 60 tries in the season 1956-7.

BOSTON BRAVES, American professional BASEBALL team, a major force in NATIONAL LEAGUE play before 1900 under different nicknames. In a remarkable turnabout, the 1914 'Miracle Braves', under their manager Stallings, in last place on the 4th of July, rallied to capture the National League pennant and the WORLD SERIES. The Braves' other National League pennant occurred in 1948, led by the extraordinary pitching duo of Sain and Spahn. Sain had four 20-game-winning seasons, while the left-hander Spahn ranks as one of the pre-eminent pitchers in baseball history. When attendance dwindled in the early 1950s, the Braves' owner Perini convinced the National League to allow him to relocate in Milwaukee. (See ATLANTA BRAVES; MILWAUKEE BRAVES.)

BOSTON BRUINS, ICE HOCKEY club of Boston, in 1924 became the first United States professional team in the NATIONAL HOCKEY LEAGUE of North America. It first won the N.H.L. championship in 1929 and retained the title in 1930, but the club's best years were 1939-41, when the championship was won three times consecutively. The club also won the STANLEY CUP in 1929, 1939, 1941, 1970, and 1972.

Home matches are played at Boston Garden, with a 13,909 capacity. Team members train in Canada at London, Ontario, and best

players have included Brimsek, Clapper, Cowley, J. Crawford, Dumart, Hollett, ORR, Schmidt, SHORE, and Stewart.
COLOURS: Gold, black, and white.

BOSTON CELTICS, American professional BASKETBALL club with the best record in the history of the NATIONAL BASKETBALL ASSOCIATION. The club was founded in 1946 and entered the newly-formed National Basketball Association of America in that year. After four seasons, however, their efforts had been so unsuccessful that the owners, Boston Garden Corporation, decided to relinquish their ownership. The club then came under the private ownership of Brown and Pieri, whose enterprise enabled the club to survive.

In 1950 AUERBACH was appointed coach and COUSY joined the team the next year. In 1956 RUSSELL joined the Celtics and this combination achieved unprecedented success. From 1957, Boston Celtics gained the championship of the N.B.A., and recognition as the premier team in the world, in 11 of the next 13 seasons.
COLOURS: Green uniforms with white trim.

BOSTON RED SOX, American professional BASEBALL team, a member of the AMERICAN LEAGUE when it was founded in 1901 and winners of the first official WORLD SERIES in 1903, led by the pitcher CY YOUNG. The Red Sox also won the World Series in 1912, 1915, 1916, and 1918, led by the outfielder Speaker and, in the latter two years, by the star pitcher and sometime outfielder BABE RUTH. In 1920 Ruth and several other Red Sox stars were sold to the NEW YORK YANKEES, and the Red Sox ceased to be a major factor in American League competition for many years. In the 1930s they bought the first baseman Foxx from the PHILADELPHIA ATHLETICS and the shortstop Cronin from the WASHINGTON SENATORS but could not win a pennant. Cronin was later the team's manager, and still later became American League president. The Red Sox's greatest modern player was the outfielder TED WILLIAMS, who joined the team in 1939 and in 1946 led the Red Sox to the American League pennant.

BOTAFOGO, Association FOOTBALL club, Rio de Janeiro. Founded in 1904, they first won the Rio championship in 1910 but then had to wait until 1930 to win again. The outstanding players have included LEONIDAS, DIDÌ, GARRINCHA, Zagalo, and Amarildo.
COLOURS: Black and white striped shirts.

BOTTICELLI (1951), a race-horse by Blue

Peter out of Buonamica by NICCOLO DELL' ARCA, was bred in Italy by Tesio, and is the only race-horse ever to win as many as six of the most important races in that country, viz: the Milan and Italian Grand Prix, the Italian triple crown, and the Milan Gold Cup, as well as the ASCOT GOLD CUP. He wore the colours of the Marchese M. Incisa della Rocchetta, was trained by Penco, and ridden by CAMICI.

BOULE, see JEU PROVENÇAL and PÉTANQUE.

BOURDA OVAL, Georgetown, CRICKET ground in Guyana. Belonging to the Georgetown Cricket Club, which did much towards establishing inter-colonial cricket in the 1860s, it has one of the finest batting wickets in the world. West Indies achieved their first win over England there in 1929-30. Its capacity is 13,000.

BOUSSAC, MARCEL (1889-   ), was for many years the leading owner-breeder of race-horses in France. Champions to carry his colours included five winners of the PRIX DE L'ARC DE TRIOMPHE: Corrida (twice), DJEBEL, Ardan, CARACALLA II, and Coronation V. His horses were mostly trained by SEMBLAT and ridden by Johnstone and POINCELET.

BOWL-PLAYING or road bowling, as it is also called, is almost entirely confined to parts of the south and north of Ireland, although a similar game, called *Klootschien,* is played in Holland and some adjacent districts in West Germany. The game is quite simple; two players bowl or throw an iron ball along an ordinary public road, the less busy the better, and the winner is the player who covers a set distance with fewer throws.

The ball, made of solid iron and usually weighing 28 oz. (790 g.) (though lighter ones may be used) is called a bowl, but is often popularly termed the 'bullet'. If a player wins by one throw, he is said to have won by a 'bowl of odds'. Singles games, known as 'single-handed scores', are the more popular, although double scores, between pairs, are also common, with each man playing from the spot where his partner's throw rested.

One of the skills of the game is the negotiation of a bend in the road. In the south of Ireland, the players, using a wheel-like swing of the arm, develop great skill in lofting the ball round and over even the sharpest of bends, so that it lands on and continues safely along the roadway. This is essential, since a player is penalized if his bowl lands in or over the roadside fence. In the north, where the under-arm delivery is favoured, the players are extremely skilled at spinning the bowl along the ground round even the sharpest bends.

Bowl-playing devotees claim for their game a very ancient origin, but it manifestly could not have gained any wide popularity until a permanent road system existed. The heyday of the game was through much of the nineteenth century when traffic was slow and sparse on relatively good clay-and-stone roads. Later, the obstruction caused by bowl-players and their hundreds of followers led to confrontations with the law after the advent of the bicycle and the motor car. The game itself, however, was never made illegal. Nowadays bowl-playing on tarmacadam or concrete highways is not feasible, so the game has been relegated to the side roads.

Despite its wide popularity for so long in so many parts of Ireland, bowl-playing was conducted almost entirely on a local basis and no central body was formed until 1954 when *An Bol Cumann* (the Bowl-Playing Association) was set up. *An Bol Cumann* has about 100 affiliated branches, mainly in Co. Cork and in West Waterford, with a few in counties Limerick and Armagh.

International contests have been arranged, home and away, with Dutch and West German teams. At home, national competitions are held for the All-Ireland championship.

GOVERNING BODY: *An Bol Cumann*, Bandon, Co. Cork, Eire.

BOWLING, Tenpin, an indoor game for individual players or for teams, largely concentrated in the U.S.A., in which a player aims to knock down with a ball ten 'pins' placed in a triangle, the apex of which is 60 ft. (18·29 m.) away at the end of a 'lane' of smooth polished wood.

The modern pin is 15 in. (381 mm.) tall and 14·9729 in. in circumference. If made of wood, it may weigh between 3 lb. 2 oz. and 3 lb. 10 oz. (1·42–1·64 kg.), or between 3 lb. 4 oz. and 3 lb. 6 oz. (1·47–1·53 kg.) if of synthetic material. The ball must not have a circumference of more than 27 in. (685 mm.) and it may not weigh more than 16 lb. (7·26 kg.). Its diameter must be constant. It has one thumb-hole and two finger-holes.

The lane is 62 ft. 10$\frac{3}{16}$ in. (19·16 m.) long and 42 in. (1·06 m.) wide. Maple is used at the ends, where there is more wear-and-tear and likelihood of damage, and pitch-pine in the middle. There is usually about 16 ft. (4·87 m.) in front of the delivery point, or 'foul line'.

The ball is rolled and if the bowler knocks down all ten pins with his first delivery or after his second delivery, the pins are put up again by an automatic machine, known as a pin-spotter, and the balls are automatically returned to the bowling end of the lane. All modern tenpin bowling is played at specially constructed or adapted bowling centres.

The scoring is progressive. Ten frames of ten pins make up a game and points are awarded for the number of pins knocked down. If all the pins are knocked down by the first ball, called a 'strike', the player is rewarded by a bonus — 10 points plus the score of the next two balls bowled.

Thus in a game of ten frames, a player must bowl 12 strikes in succession in order to bowl a perfect game of 300 points. If two deliveries are needed to knock down the pins (called a 'spare'), 10 points are awarded plus the bonus of the next ball. When a 'spare' is scored in the tenth frame, a third ball is bowled. A score of 120 would be extremely good for a newcomer to the game and a player who regularly achieves 170 should be good enough for scratch league play.

Tenpin bowling is a modern, highly competitive, and commercialized version of the simple game which involved throwing a ball at a target. As this became more sophisticated, the number of targets increased and by hitting one or more in a certain way a player might also knock down others. Related games were played in ancient Egypt — a stone ball and nine stone pins were found in the tomb of a child buried in 5200 B.C. — and in the ancient Polynesian game of *ula naika* a player bowled at a target from 60 ft. (18·29 m.), the distance between delivery and pin in modern tenpin bowling.

According to Pehle, a German writer on bowls, members of the congregation in Germany would bowl in church cloisters in the third and fourth centuries. The *kegel*, which men carried for sport and protection, would be set up as a target, representing *Heide* (the Heathen One), and if the bowler hit it, he would be judged clean of sin. The term *kegling* or *kegeling* is still used for bowling in Germany and among German-Americans. Luther approved of the pastime and a successful *kegeler* was said to have 'knocked the Devil out of his ground'.

Early bowlers met with mixed receptions from their rulers. Edward III banned bowling in England; Henry VIII built alleys at Whitehall, and the Elizabethans, although mainly following the English preference for lawn BOWLS, used cannon-balls when they played. SKITTLE alleys and ninepin alleys (tenpin bowling nowadays prefers 'lane' to 'alley') were usually associated with taverns and fairs, and in time the ball was rolled on wood rather than on grass. The number of pins, usually between nine and fifteen, depended on local preference, and the popularity of pin-bowling attracted gamblers. In 1511 Henry VIII condemned the game because, it was said, 'the alleys are in operation in conjunction with saloons, or dissolute places, and bowling has ceased to be a sport, and rather a form of vicious gambling'.

Ninepins, a European game, was taken to America by settlers. The introduction of the tenth pin is shrouded in mystery, but there is a picture of tenpin bowling in Suffolk in 1803 and it was played in New York City in the 1820s. In *Rip Van Winkle* (1818) Washington Irving described thunder as like the sound of a ball rolling at pins. Gambling again began to spoil the reputation of the sport and in 1841 it was banned in Connecticut. According to one of the game's legends, the prohibition referred only to the ninepin diamond formation, and the tenth pin and the now familiar tenpin triangle brought legality. In the middle of the nineteenth century there was a boom in the building of indoor alleys in many American cities and in 1875 the first attempt to form a national bowling association was made in New York.

The sport did not, however, become organized until the formation of the American Bowling Congress (A.B.C.) in 1895. This body gave the game rules and standardized equipment. Under the leadership of the A.B.C., tenpin bowling has reached a stage where it can claim to be the largest participant sport in the world. More than 4,000,000 men are members of the A.B.C. and the Women's International Bowling Congress, founded at St. Louis in 1916, reached a membership of about 3,000,000. Modern bowling centres, with automatic pin-spotters and score-indicators, have replaced the rough, tough alleys, lit by kerosene lamps, which catered for saloon crowds in the early days of the twentieth century.

There were many early debates about the size and weight of the ball and one of the first and hardest tasks of the A.B.C. was to enforce the use of its standard ball. The battle against the loaded ball — or 'dodo' — caused particular controversy in 1913. The first tenpin balls were wooden (lignum vitae) and of such a density that they would not float. There were no finger-holes and the early ball had a tendency to crack, chip, and warp. The first balls with finger-holes appeared in the early 1900s and in 1905 the arrival of hard rubber balls ended the use of wood. The original rubber balls were red, but black became the popular choice until approval was given to the plastic ball in the 1960s when bright mottling became fashionable.

There has been little variation in the size of the pins since the A.B.C. adopted its first rules in 1895. The first pins were of maple, hard and highly polished, but, as the popularity of bowling increased and maple became more expensive, substitutes had to be found. Laminated pins were used and in 1950 the A.B.C. ordered the use of plastic bases, which maintained height and lasted longer. Nearly a million games were played before the plastic-coated pin was approved because the A.B.C. wanted to be sure that the game remained the same test of skill as it had been in 1895. In 1962 the entirely synthetic pin was developed and its adoption followed three years of tests by the governing body.

The A.B.C.'s great achievement is to have turned tenpin bowling into a respectable family sport, highly competitive and highly organized; modern technology has been called in to help to make bowling centres suitable for the exercise of the skills of the game. Enthusiasm for the game has increased in the years since the Second World War when the automatic pin-spotter increased the pace of playing. In the earlier years of the game pin-boys were employed to re-set the pins after each frame, a slow and costly process, and pin-boys tended to be unreliable. The pin-spotter, sweeping up the fallen pins and setting them up again mechanically, solved this problem. The equipment was approved by the A.B.C. in 1952. In Britain, the first automatic pin-spotters were installed at two U.S. Air Force bases in Suffolk.

The British Tenpin Bowling Association was formed in 1961 and soon afterwards Australia formed its national association. By 1974 tenpin bowling was played in 49 countries, each of which had its own national governing body. The Professional Bowlers' Association was formed in America in 1958, intending, as the U.S. Professional Golfers' Association (see GOLF) had, to promote lucrative tours for the top players.

In 1961 the A.B.C. accepted an invitation to become affiliated to the Fédération Internationale des Quilleurs (F.I.Q.), an international organization based at Helsinki which covers a number of bowling games.

GOVERNING BODY (WORLD): Fédération Internationale des Quilleurs (Tenpin Division), 19 Canterbury Road, Ilford, Essex; (U.S.A.): American Bowling Congress, 5301 South 76th Street, Greendale, Wisconsin, U.S.A.

BOWLS, Indoor, in the form of SKITTLES has been played at least since the sixteenth century but not until the start of the twentieth century was any serious attempt made to reproduce the standard International Bowling Board (I.B.B.) outdoor game (see BOWLS, LAWN) under cover. At that time, cricketers were practising throughout the year on indoor matting wickets and it was W. G. GRACE who exerted the greatest influence in persuading bowls-players that indoor play was also feasible for them.

In Scotland the Edinburgh Winter Bowling Association was founded in 1905 and competitive play took place in the Synod Hall on the Castle Terrace for many years. In the south Dr. Grace's association with the Crystal Palace, London, both as a cricketer and a bowls-player, and his position as president of the English Bowling Association (E.B.A.) led to the start of indoor play at the Crystal Palace on carpet-covered rinks laid along one of the long galleries. In north London, Alexandra Palace offered similar facilities and two years later a club was founded which played in one of the large halls attached to the Palace itself. In the 1930s the Crystal Palace club acquired a purpose-built hall which enabled the club to become one of the best in the south of England and quickly overcame the fire of 1936 which destroyed the Palace itself. The Alexandra Palace club has used the same floor since its formation although space permits only two rinks, each 99 ft. by 16 ft. (30·2 × 4·9 m.).

The early popularity of these two indoor clubs resulted in a search for other ready-made venues and the King's Hall, Wimbledon and the swimming bath at Kingston-on-Thames, Surrey, were soon in use. Stimulated by these developments, Welsh bowlers began winter play although the lack of suitable halls restricted them to sub-length church and chapel halls until long after the Second World War. This was also the case in Ireland, but in Scotland the Kelvin Hall, Glasgow, provided ample space, and in 1935 a four-rink purpose-built hall was opened in Ayr by E. Ecrepont, himself an international indoor player.

In that year the thriving PADDINGTON BOWLS CLUB in Maida Vale, London, opened what remains one of the largest indoor 'greens' in Britain with eight rinks 39 yds. long and 13 ft. wide (35·7 × 4 m.). This consists of an accurately laid wooden floor and an underlay, on top of which a new type of carpet was installed in 1970.

In 1933 the need for a controlling organization was acknowledged. A recommendation formally set down on 8 April 1933 at the Berners Hotel, London, read 'the indoor game of bowls should be organized in future as a section of the E.B.A.' Autonomy was granted in December 1970 when the English Indoor Bowling Association was born at the annual general meeting of the E.B.A.

The Alexandra Palace, Bognor Regis, Bournemouth, Crouch Hill, Crystal Palace, Lyons, Margate, Newport (I.o.W.), South-East London, Southend, Temple, and West London clubs were represented at the 1933 meeting. By April 1934, 25 clubs were affiliated, a number increased to 28 by the end of the second year. The Second World War halted temporarily what had become a strong upward trend, and, though a revival did not begin until the early 1950s, by 1973 there were 125 affiliated clubs. There were many clubs in Scotland, including the 12-rink 'monster' at Shawbridge, and full championship-size halls had long been operative at Cardiff and Belfast.

The primary object in 1906 was year-round recreation but there is little doubt that the competitive side of the game sparked the considerable development of the past decade. Practically every specialist hall stages either (or both) a winter league or an open tournament, usually for fours, while the inter-club championship team matches are a major feature of the English and Scottish winter programmes. The DENNY CUP was founded in 1935, the English indoor singles championship in the winter of 1960-1, the pairs in 1963-4, the fours in 1966-7, and the triples in 1971.

Internationally, the annual team matches for the Hilton Cup began in the winter of 1935-6 when England, Scotland, and Wales competed, and Ireland joined during the winter of 1962-3. Like Wales until 1961, Ireland was seriously handicapped before the opening of her first full-size green at Belfast in 1966-7. By the 1970 series, however, Ireland beat Wales and lost only to England, champions 12 times from 1955 to 1970.

The meeting of the I.B.B. in 1962 at Perth, Western Australia, revealed the necessity for the diversification of international control, and led to the formation of the British Isles Bowling Council (B.I.B.C.). Inevitably the growth of the indoor game necessitated a parallel body and the National Indoor Bowls Council came into being in 1965. Apart from general administrative duties, this council was intended to widen the scope of international indoor bowls and, to that end, the first British Isles indoor championships were staged in 1967, BRYANT (England) winning the singles; Knowling and Spooner (England) the pairs; and Wales, skipped by Humphreys, the fours.

At the start of the 1970s indoor bowls, I.B.B. style, had spread to Australia and Switzerland, and there was the probability of further expansion in America and Canada. Thus the likelihood of world indoor championships could be foreseen.

One important change had become apparent during the 1960s. Before then the majority of associations were essentially 'clubs': non-profit-making, with the surpluses — if any — going to club funds for general improvements. The larger, more ambitious centres which then began to proliferate possessed commercial possibilities. Some were run by individuals who, even though they were bowls-players, received profits. Several, especially in Scotland, became partial investments because membership entailed a loan on which interest — usually 5 per cent p.a. — was paid. The failure of tenpin BOWLING to prove as financially attractive as some entrepreneurs had hoped led to the closure of many centres and investigations of traditional bowls as an alternative. The future may well see further developments along these lines.

Indoor championship bowls need only 7 sq. yds. (6 sq. m.) per participant, while indoor LAWN TENNIS requires 200 sq. yds. (approx. 170 sq. m.) per player in doubles. Thus the financial return per square yard per session is very high, and with old-age pensioners and women's clubs sharing a green, there are many indoor centres arranging five sessions per day. This high-occupancy factor has not been lost on municipal authorities and some have assisted private clubs in various forms of partnership, while others operate indoor halls themselves, notably at swimming baths which are covered with floors during the winter months.

Women's indoor bowls. Indoor play flourishes in Britain. The English Women's Indoor Bowling Association (E.W.I.B.A.), founded in 1951, administers the game for more than 60 affiliated clubs; as in the outdoor game, there is an official separation of the sexes on the green. There are similar associations in Ireland, Scotland, and Wales.

The Aird Trophy competition was launched by the E.W.I.B.A. in the winter of 1968-9 in memory of Hilda Aird, president in 1956-7. It is based on a two-wood triples formula, open to all members of affiliated clubs with no restriction on the number of entries per club.

The Yetton Trophy, founded in 1953-4 (when Richmond beat Birmingham in the final), is the premier English indoor bowls championship for women. Each club affiliated to the E.W.I.B.A. is entitled to enter one or two teams of eight players. These are divided into fours, one playing the opposing team's 'away' four on the home green, the other four travelling to the opponents' green to meet their 'home' four. The two individual results are added to give an over-all result. The championship begins in November each winter, the semi-finals and final taking place on a given day in March of the following year.

English Bowling Association Indoor Year Book, annually; *English Indoor Bowling Association Official Year Book,* annually; *English Women's Indoor Bowls Association Year Book,* annually; D. J.

Bryant, *Bryant on Bowls, Outdoor and Indoor* (1970); C. M. Jones, *Bowls: How to Become a Champion* (1972); Arthur Sweeney, *Indoor Bowls* (1966).

GOVERNING BODIES: English Indoor Bowling Association, 46 Triumph House, Alderman Avenue, Barking, Essex; National Indoor Bowls Council, 130 Longhill Road, Catford, London S.E.6; English Women's Indoor Bowling Association, 22 Frobisher Close, Worthing, West Sussex.

BOWLS, Lawn. The game approved by the International Bowling Board (I.B.B.) for world competition is played on a flat lawn or green which in championship play is usually at least 40 by 40 yds. (36·6 m.) in size. The green is surrounded by a ditch approximately 2 in. (51 mm.) deep and 12 in. (305 mm.) wide and enclosed by a bank sloping at an angle of 35° from the perpendicular. The green is divided by boundaries of fine string into six 'rinks' the length of the green, and 19 to 21 ft. (5·8–6·4 m.) wide. A match may be man against man (singles), two against two (pairs), three against three (triples), or four against four (now fours but once rinks, a term still used quite frequently).

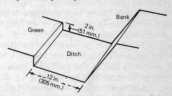

PERIMETER DITCH
The top of the sloping bank must be at least 9 in. (228 mm.) higher than the green.

In contests between clubs, counties, countries, or other groups it is customary for several individual matches to take place, usually simultaneously. Six rinks of fours is the most popular inter-group formula, but in Scotland there is one annual contest of 80 'four against four', while the Denny Cup (national indoor club championship) in England is for four fours, two matches played on each club's indoor green (actually a carpet).

In singles and pairs each man has four bowls (circumference not exceeding 16¼ in. — 419 mm.), known as 'woods', whether they be made of composition, hardened rubber, or lignum vitae. In triples each man has three woods and in fours, two. The woods are delivered alternately by the opposing players towards a smaller white ball (the 'jack', 'kitty', or 'cot') 2⅝ in. (63·5 mm.) in diameter. The object of each man or group is to position as many woods as possible nearer to the jack than the nearest opposing wood. Each wood fulfilling that object scores a point, so that in singles it is possible to score a maximum of 4 shots per full set of deliveries (an end), in triples 9, and in pairs or fours 8.

A player must make each delivery with at least one foot on or over a mat, towards the jack which has been bowled and then centred on the green at a distance not less than 25 yds. (22·9 m.) from the edge of the mat facing the jack. The mat is usually made of rubber and is 24 in. long by 14 in. wide (610 × 356 mm.); delivery is said to be complete at the moment the bowl leaves the player's hand.

The right to bowl first on the opening end is decided by the toss of a coin and the winner usually goes first, though he may decide to hand over the right to his opponent or to the opposing side. The player bowling first places the mat on the centre line of the rink with its back edge 4 ft. (1·2 m.) from the ditch. It must remain in that position until completion of the end. If it is displaced accidentally it must be replaced as nearly as possible in the same position. In all subsequent ends the back edge of the mat must be not less than 4 ft. from the rear ditch or the front edge not less than 27 yds. (24·7 m.) from the front ditch, its actual position between these two extremes being decided by the player in singles, or the lead of the group who won the preceding end. A bowler is said to be in possession of the green from the moment he steps on the mat until his bowl comes to rest at the far end. While in possession he must not be impeded or disturbed. Apart from varying the actual placing of the mat between the permissible extremes, skilled players make additional tactical use of it by changing the position on the mat itself from which they actually deliver their bowls.

If the jack is thrown less than 25 yds. (22·9 m.) from the front of the mat it is returned to the mat and the opposing player (or the lead in group matches) throws it. Before doing so he may, if he wishes, change the position of the mat, but after delivering the jack he must make way for the man or lead of the team who won the preceding end to deliver the first bowl. Any bowl travelling less than 15 yds. (13·7 m.) from the front of the mat is deemed dead and moved from the green to the bank. Bowls which come to rest outside the strings bounding the rink on which play is taking place are also deemed dead, as are those which go into the ditch without touching the jack when first delivered.

Bowls that hit the jack on their initial run — whether or not they cannon on to it via another bowl or bowls — remain live and potential scorers until completion of the end. They are called 'touchers', are marked with chalk, and remain where they are whenever they run or are cannoned into the ditch. Any toucher in the ditch and nearer to the jack than the best opposing bowl counts in the score. A jack cannoned into the ditch and within the strings marking the width of the rink on which play is taking place remains in play. Its position is indicated to bowlers at the delivery end by a 'suitable object' — usually a strip of metal painted white — stuck into the bank behind the jack. Touchers cannot be established after the jack has gone into the ditch.

When all bowls have been delivered from one end of the rink to the jack and the score agreed by the two players in singles or the opposing skips in pairs, triples, or fours, the end is said to be complete. The jack and all bowls are then delivered from the mat down the green in the reverse direction, the score is agreed upon — and so the game continues.

In pairs and fours the opposing groups play 21 ends and in triples 18 ends. In tournament play, if the score be tied, an extra end is bowled to determine the winner. In multi-rink club, county, or international matches or in tournaments staged on an all-against-all league basis, however, it is customary to record the tie. In singles there is no predetermined number of ends. Victory goes instead to the player first scoring 21.

Bowls are black or brown, and made of wood, rubber, or composition. Each bowl of a set must bear the player's distinguishing mark on each side. Bowls made of wood (lignum vitae) must not exceed 16¼ in. (419 mm.) in circumference, nor 3½ lb. (1·59 kg.) in weight. Metal loading of bowls made of wood is strictly prohibited. For international and COMMONWEALTH GAMES matches, bowls with a major diameter of 4¾ to 5⅛ in. (121–130 mm.) may be of a maximum weight of 3½ lb. (1·59 kg.). For all other matches, the weight of bowls made of rubber or composition must be in accordance with the rules adopted by each national association for its domestic competitions. Before the I.B.B. meeting at Perth in November 1962, the weight of a bowl was governed by its size in all international play. The British Isles Bowls Council (B.I.B.C.) elected at that meeting to retain this rule for internal tournaments.

All bowls are flattened slightly on one side, this imbalance being termed the 'bias', which causes a bowl to travel in a curved path instead of a straight one. The amount a bowl may be biased by shaping — it is forbidden to attach or insert leaden or other weights — is governed by standard bowls, against which all bowls have to be tested and approved every ten years.

Each official tester is authorized to stamp the I.B.B. or B.I.B.C. approval sign on bowls which have a bias equal to or greater than that of the standard bowl. Full details of the stamping of bowls are printed each year in the English Bowling Association (E.B.A.) Year Book. The stamping is based on a test currently accepting that there are no absolute criteria of bias because the amount of swing is affected by the running surface of the green.

A system of grading was developed by Taylor who produced five standard bowls, numbered 'No. 1 bias' to 'No. 5 bias', against which all other bowls could be compared on a test table. Number 1 bias ran comparatively straight, the amount of swing increasing with each number up to the maximum. These standards were universally adopted, and replicas produced, and all I.B.B. recognized testers possess a set. In games governed by the I.B.B., no bowl 'straighter' in run than a No. 3 bias is permissible, but there is no limit to amounts of bias greater than No. 3. In the crown green game straighter-running bowls are permitted, No. 2 being the commonest in general use.

There are occasions when the player would prefer the bowls to run in a straight line and a few attempt sometimes to achieve this by delivering a bowl so that the bias rotates over and over instead of remaining at the side. They claim that this 'tilting' counters the sideways drag and so allows the bowl to travel in a straight line. By varying the angle of tilt they can control the amount of the curve.

Tilting was more prevalent when the majority of bowlers used lignum vitae bowls because these were more nearly spherical than most present-day composition bowls. A spherical bowl is less affected in run by the axis on which it is propelled. Many composition bowls are circular along their running circumference but seriously elliptical when delivered at $90°$ from the running angle. Thus they bump along rather than glide and this destroys all control. Few present-day bowlers exploit tilt because nearly all use composition bowls.

The amount of 'land'—the term used to describe the width of the curve taken by a bowl on its way to the jack—is related to the pace of the green. The longer the green permits the bowl to trickle before stopping, the more land will be needed for it to finish on a straight line between mat and jack.

The apparently innocuous law known as 'weight for size' threatened to sever the home countries from the International Bowling Board when that body abolished it in 1962. The law came into being before the advent of composition bowls and related the permissible weight of a bowl to the diameter of its running surface. This relationship, in fact, was virtu-ally ordained by nature since the density of lignum vitae, from which most bowls were made, is a constant. Only by varying the shape of the bowl along the axis of its running circumference could this weight-size ratio be varied.

The density of composition can be controlled so that it is possible to make a minimum-size bowl of maximum weight. This, the I.B.B. believes, removes the disadvantage suffered by men with hands only large enough to use minimum-size bowls. The British countries consider such bowls as 'marbles' and thus contrary to the true skills of bowls. The controversy still existed in 1972 although the B.I.B.C. accepted the democratic vote in 1962 so far as non-domestic play is concerned.

In 1918 a dedicated Australian bowls craftsman, W. D. Hensell, in conjunction with the Dunlop Rubber Company, produced 12 moulded rubber bowls which complied with official test requirements. Before the end of 1918, Dunlop-Hensell vulcanite or ebonite bowls were in use on Victorian greens and by 1924 Australia had ceased to import lignum vitae bowls. Hensell persisted with his experiments and at the end of 1930 produced standard-size, standard-weight bowls made of plastic. Henselite bowls are now the most widely used in the world. Vitalite, made in England, are also much used.

To afford satisfactory playing conditions, a bowling *green* must be flat, true, and resistant to wear. It should drain sufficiently fast to permit play soon after rain yet also be unaffected by drought. In southern England it should have a running time around 14 seconds, in the north perhaps 2 seconds less.

Generally, sea-washed turf is superior to inland turf. Experiments have been carried out in England with rubberized greens as well as artificial grass carpets. Though the latter are splendid indoors, they had yet to prove themselves outdoors at the start of the 1970s.

The path of a bowl delivered down a green is governed by the speed of the green. This, in turn, is controlled by a number of factors including the length and density of the grass, its nap (sunlight attracts grass towards it and so makes the bowl travel slightly further in one direction than the other), the state of the surface (which is often dependent on the amount of rain), and, to some degree, the sub-surface.

In Britain it is customary to use unspecific terms like 'slow', 'heavy', 'free', 'fast', etc. to describe a green. This was superseded long ago in countries like Australia, South Africa, and the U.S.A. where they determine the pace of a green by means of a stop watch, noting the time a bowl takes from leaving the hand until it comes to rest, normally at a point 30 yds. (27·4 m.) from its delivery position. Players are frequently baffled because a '9 seconds green' sounds faster than '12 seconds' whereas, in fact, it is the other way round. The comparison is with a billiard table, on which the longer a ball keeps running, the faster the table is said to be.

The last feet of run demonstrate a bowl's unique character because its bias slowly becomes a stronger force than its forward propulsion, causing it to follow a curving path. The extent of this curve can reach 180° on a 16-seconds green. The speed of the average green in southern England in mid-summer is approximately 12 seconds for a start-to-stop running distance of 30 yds. (27·4 m.). This drops to about 10 seconds in the north, while at Balgreen, Edinburgh, during the 1970 Commonwealth Games, the pace seldom exceeded 9 seconds. Each extra yard (0·91 m.) of full travel takes approximately half a second, raising the time to 14 seconds for a start-to-stop distance of 34 yds. (31·1 m.).

The speed of a green affects to some extent the ratio of the various basic *shots* used in any particular match. Nevertheless, whether the green be sun-baked and fast or rain-soaked and slow, the most frequently used shot is known as 'drawing to the jack' or 'draw'.

As the term implies, the player seeks to impart to his bowl sufficient pace and the correct direction for it to come to rest adjacent or touching the jack. A right-handed player delivering his bowl on a line to his right as he looks down the green is said to be using the forehand; bowls delivered on a line to his left are on the backhand. The relationship is to the bowler, not the rink on which he is playing, so that a left-handed bowler's forehand is to his left as he looks down the green and the backhand to his right. The terms forehand and backhand apply to all shots.

Occasionally a bowler delivers a bowl which runs on to the jack and stays with it while pushing it a foot or so farther up the green. Basically this is a draw shot delivered with a marginal increase of strength with the object of trailing the jack to a more advantageous position. It is one of the most useful and most difficult shots in the game, demanding great precision of touch. Thus on fast greens — timed at 16 seconds or more — it is scarcely possible to judge strength with sufficient accuracy to trail the jack, say 12 in. (305 mm.), and this shot is virtually unknown in Australia and New Zealand.

Its near relative is the firm or yard-on shot. It is usually played when a bowler wishes to remove — 'rest-out' — an opposition bowl which is preventing a big score, or to open up the bowls at the head without driving the jack beyond the boundaries of the rink, thus rendering the end dead and necessitating its replay.

When the position is so poor that nothing seems likely to stop the opposition scoring, most competitive bowlers resort to the firing shot, or drive as it is called in Australia. Delivered with full force, the intention normally is to crash the jack beyond the confines of the rink, so causing a dead end. Because of the force of forward propulsion, the bias has little or no chance to take effect and the bowl travels in a straight line. This often enables it to find gaps not open to a bowl following a curved path and makes the firing shot suitable for crashing the jack away from opposition bowls and into the ditch in order to score with bowls lying nearer to the ditch than any of the opponents'. It is the most spectacular shot in the game.

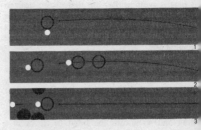

THREE BASIC SHOTS
(1) The draw shot; (2) trailing the jack; (3) the firing shot, or drive.

Sometimes intentionally (but more often not) a bowler delivers a bowl which starts off course, only to cannon — 'wick' — from a stray bowl well off centre on to the target jack or bowl.

Order of play. The first man of any group — be it pair, triple, or four — to deliver is known as the lead or, in Australia, leader. Before actually delivering he must first, if he or his group won the preceding end, place the mat and deliver the jack to the length he or his skip, who bowls last in the group, considers to be of greatest advantage to the group as a whole. He then seeks to draw his bowls closer to the jack than those of the opposition.

In triples and fours the lead is followed by the number two. Many experts deem this the most important position of all. It demands great precision, especially in delivering bowls to blank, yet key, positions on the rink, always a more difficult task than delivering to the jack or another bowl.

In fours the number two is followed by the third man, a position demanding ability at every shot in the game as well as a temperament which remains undisturbed. The last man to bowl in a pair, triple, or four is called the skip or, in Australia, rink director. Once positions have been established for a match they cannot be changed, at least in the I.B.B. game. Positional changes are allowed at any time in the English Bowling Federation (E.B.F.) game. Occasionally, a skip will surrender tactical control to one of his colleagues, although he must still bowl last.

In fours and triples play the duty of filling in the score-card after each end is delegated to the number two and in pairs to the lead. In singles it is undertaken by a marker who also centres the jack, removes the mat at the conclusion of each end, and generally acts as an assistant to the two competitors. He should not announce the position of bowls or give other information unless asked to do so by either player.

In the event of two bowls being so positioned that their relative distances from the jack cannot be agreed by the players, the marker must be called upon to measure, though his measure is not necessarily decisive. In the event of further disagreement, a player must call for the umpire in charge of the green. The umpire is the final arbiter of disputes of fact and law on the green, though even his decision can later be questioned by written objection to the tournament committee. His decision stands for the match being played though the objection can lead to an official I.B.B. interpretation of a law.

Until 1957 and the advent of coloured discs, the ability to memorize the side to which each bowl belonged was considered essential to a good bowler. The I.B.B. decided that coloured discs would be used in the July 1957 international matches at Bournemouth; England were to have yellow discs, Scotland blue, Wales red, and Ireland green. This move considerably simplified both playing and watching and the custom developed until it is now automatic in all international championships.

Points. Apart from orthodox games, there are a number of novelties which are sometimes introduced, the most popular of which is probably 'points', a game devised for bowlers who wish to practise the four vital shots in bowls, the draw, the guard, the trail, and the firing shot. The game consists of 32 shots, 8 in each of the four categories. For draw shots three concentric circles with their centre 100 ft. (30·5 m.) from the front of the mat are marked by chalk or string, their radii being 1, 2, and 3 ft. (305, 610, 914 mm.) respectively. A jack is placed on the centre mark and two bowls, 5 ft. (1·5 m.) apart, are placed 15 ft. (4·6 m.) in front of the jack. Points are awarded (3, 2, 1) according to the circle in which each bowl comes to rest. Similar situations are created for the other shots so that a maximum of 96 points can be scored.

The spider, one of many systems used by bowlers to raise money for charity, is particularly popular in Australia. This usually takes place when every member is at the club and a small entrance fee is charged. All bowlers take up positions equidistant from each other round the four sides of the green while the official in charge places a jack in the middle of the green before retiring to the bank. At his signal, all members deliver their bowls simultaneously towards the jack. The owner of the bowl nearest to the jack, when it (even if cannoned) and all other bowls have come to rest, is declared the winner of the spider. He is awarded either a special prize or a percentage of the pool, the rest of the money being given to the nominated charity.

Bowls probably evolved from the earliest days of history when primitive man, in moments of relaxation, threw rocks or large stones at smaller stones or other targets. Its existence as a disciplined game may be safely traced back some 7,000 years, for Sir Flinders Petrie, the great Egyptologist, discovered implements for a game similar to modern tenpin BOWLING in the grave of an Egyptian child buried about 5200 B.C. The ancient Polynesians, including some who emigrated to New Zealand in the fourteenth century, played a version of bowls with pieces of whetstone 3 to 4 in. (76–102 mm.) in diameter, about 1 in. (25 mm.) across at their running edges, and shaped very precisely into an ellipse. The game spread from Egypt to Greece and Rome, and thence to other regions of Europe during the time of Roman colonization. Sculptured and painted antiquities of ancient Greece and Rome indicate that games based on rolling bowls or hoops at targets existed several thousands of years ago. There are even suggestions that a version of bowls was played in England during the first century A.D., though it was of such a vigorous nature that it might be regarded as a forerunner of throwing the JAVELIN rather than of the gentler game of bowls.

The transition to a game where proximity to the target counted, as distinct from contact, was slow. A manuscript in the Royal Archives at Windsor depicts thirteenth-century bowls showing two men bowling towards a small cone in a manner suggesting that proximity is important. Strutt, an early nineteenth-century authority on medieval games, dates this type of bowls to the Middle Ages. Certainly the inherently beautiful and true turf found in England encouraged the rolling of bowls along the ground, and the SOUTHAMPTON BOWLS

CLUB annually promotes a traditional tournament on a green dating back to 1299. In 1361 Edward III passed an edict (which continued in varying forms until 1845) prohibiting 'the hurling of stones'; he feared that bowls might lessen the time spent on ARCHERY practice and so endanger his armies in battle.

Despite such restrictions, the game continued to flourish, and in the middle of the sixteenth century bowls with an intentional imbalance (bias) were introduced, possibly by Charles Brandon (also known as the Duke of Suffolk) although the mathematician Reide mentions bias in *The Castle of Knowledge*, published in 1556. Bias changed the entire concept of the game by allowing bowls to run in curved paths which took them round obstructions on the way to their desired positions. The previously limited game gave way to one in which movement of the target — the jack — and nearby bowls by the delivered bowl offered great tactical scope.

Every British child has been taught that on 19 July 1588 Sir Francis Drake was playing bowls on Plymouth Hoe when news was brought that the Spanish Armada had been sighted. Drake's reply, 'There is plenty of time to win this game and to thrash the Spaniards too', has become legendary. It is fashionable to discount this legend, but three pieces of evidence strongly support it. The first is a number of biased bowls of the period dug up on the Hoe; the second is Drake's known liking for the game; and the third is the published report of the incident in *Vox Populi*, a political pamphlet of 1624. The story is made more credible by the fact that the news reached Drake when the tide was low and conditions unsuitable for putting so cumbersome a fleet to sea.

The game of bowls developed slowly but steadily, especially among the Scots. The earliest recorded green in Scotland was at Holyrood Palace where James IV competed with his friends for small stakes. Bowls was very popular in Edinburgh during the sixteenth century and its popularity spread round the country.

In 1848-9 a committee was formed to draw up a code of laws. The task was delegated to W. W. Mitchell, a Glasgow solicitor, who prepared a code that was immediately accepted as standard and which has remained in force for virtually unchanged ever since. The Scots were also responsible for the development of level greens and the spread of the game overseas. The Scottish Bowling Association (S.B.A.) was formed in 1892. At the start of the 1970s the Association was responsible for approximately 800 clubs and district associations. Apart from general policy-framing and administrative duties, the S.B.A. promotes and organizes the Scottish championships each year.

In England, prior to the drawing up of standardized rules by Mitchell, bowls developed in piecemeal fashion. From 1850 the pattern changed and there was a gradual movement of clubs towards the Mitchell code. Local and regional associations evolved, beginning with the Northumberland and Durham B.A. in 1882 and followed by others such as the London and Southern Counties (1895), the Midland Counties (1895), and London Parks (1901).

The Australian touring CRICKET team of 1899 included several bowls administrators and a co-ordinating body, the Imperial Bowling Association, was formed; though it was overtaken in importance by the English Bowling Association which was inaugurated on 8 June 1903 with the cricketer W. G. GRACE as its first president. The E.B.A., largest and most important bowls association in the British Isles, was a founder member of the International Bowling Board and connects its 34 affiliated counties and approximately 2,700 clubs with the world game played in Australia, South Africa, and the U.S.A.

The International Bowling Board, the world governing body of lawn bowls, was formed at the Park Hotel, Cardiff, Wales, on 11 July 1905. It succeeded the Imperial Bowling Association, which had been formed primarily to arrange matches between countries within the Commonwealth. The 1905 meeting was attended by representatives from England, Ireland, Scotland, and Wales, although by the 1970 meeting, held during the Commonwealth Games in Edinburgh, the total number of countries had risen to 18.

The Board comprises delegates appointed by member nations, executive powers over routine matters normally resting in the hands of the president and honorary secretary. The presidency changes every two years and there is no permanent headquarters. The main function of the I.B.B. is to draw up laws governing all aspects of the international game and these rules are operative in all open international events sanctioned by the I.B.B., though many countries modify the laws for their domestic championships.

Bowls in England developed according to three main codes: the I.B.B. code, the English Bowling Federation code, and the crown green code. Two of these have many common laws, but the third (see below) contains distinct differences.

The I.B.B. game, the largest, is governed by the English Bowling Association. The English Bowling Federation, founded in 1945, has a common ancestry with the E.B.A., and was formed because groups of players in counties which now comprise the E.B.F. preferred their own variant game to the one governed by I.B.B. laws. The Federation is divided into two sections, the northern, comprising Durham, Northumberland, Derbyshire, and Nottinghamshire; and the southern, Lincolnshire, Norfolk, Northamptonshire, North Cambridgeshire, and Suffolk. Within the E.B.F. itself there are several local variations which apply for specific competitions.

The differences between the E.B.F. and E.B.A. codes fall into two categories, one basic, the other one of form. Both are flat-green games but an E.B.A. green must be surrounded by a ditch whereas this is unnecessary for the E.B.F. game. In the E.B.A. game the jack and any bowls which touch it during their original delivery remain live and are not moved. In the E.B.F. game all bowls running off the green (and the jack if driven off the green) become dead and the end is rendered dead. Under E.B.A. rules any bowl nearer to the jack than the opponent's best scores, but in the E.B.F. game it does not count if it is beyond a radius of 6 ft. (1·8 m.) from the jack.

The E.B.F. game began at the Mansfield, Nottinghamshire, club, probably in 1712. Historically, E.B.F. bowlers never used more than two bowls, whether in singles, pairs, or triples, although recently a four-woods singles championship was introduced. In the E.B.A. game four bowls are delivered in singles and pairs, three in triples, and two in fours, a form of bowls not in the E.B.F. code. Thus the time taken for each end is significantly reduced and major E.B.F. team matches are of 31 ends against the E.B.A.'s 21.

The E.B.F. permits rinks 16 ft. (4·9 m.) wide (against the 19–21 ft. (5·8–6·4 m.) of the E.B.A.) and is therefore known as the 'small-green clubs' association. Many eastern counties have flourishing leagues which could not be recognized by the county E.B.A. As in the E.B.A., county champions compete for the Federation championships and segregation of the sexes is not complete; during the annual championship week at Skegness the Howard Touring Trophy is competed for by teams of four ladies.

The British Isles Bowls Council was formed after the I.B.B. meeting at Perth in November 1962 when world control, which had always lain with the home countries, passed more into the hands of Australia and the southern hemisphere group. Hitherto sanction of all tours, tournaments, etc. had had to be obtained from the I.B.B., but it was realized that it was no longer feasible for the world authority to govern every detail. The B.I.B.C. came into being to control bowls within the British Isles, including the sanction of tournaments and domestic matches. This included the right to vary the laws of the game for these tournaments, though such variations could not be applied in events governed by the I.B.B. like the Commonwealth Games.

England, Ireland, Scotland, and Wales may each send four representatives of their outdoor associations plus one each from their indoor associations to the Council.

Lawn bowls took an important forward step at the start of the 1900s while Grace was president of the E.B.A. Always eager for competitive sport, he experimented with indoor play on a carpet laid along one of the galleries at the Crystal Palace. The experiments succeeded and the first indoor club, Crystal Palace, was formed in 1906. In 1933 the E.B.A. Indoor Section, now the E.I.B.A., took over what was by then a thriving game (see BOWLS, INDOOR). Thus the game now takes place twelve months of the year all over Britain where once this only happened in temperate Cornwall. Floodlit bowls is very popular in Australia and South Africa and there are a few isolated outdoor greens in England under lights.

Australia. Bowls was first played in Australia at the Beach Tavern, Hobart, in 1844 but organized bowls did not come about until 4 July 1867 at a meeting at the Bull and Mouth hotel in Melbourne, where a number of clubs attempted to standardize the rules. (There were then almost as many different sets as there were clubs.) The first bowling association in the world came into being on 2 May 1880 with the birth of the New South Wales Bowling Association, to be followed two months and one day later by the Victorian B.A. Because of intense rivalry between these and subsequent state associations, Moody of the South Australia B.A. organized a one-week carnival in 1906. This proved so successful that it was decided to hold one every four years and this agreement led to the foundation of the Australian Bowling Council, which was ratified by all state associations on 22 September 1911.

New Zealand. The game was introduced into New Zealand in 1860, the first club was founded, at Auckland, in 1861, and the original New Zealand B.A. formed in 1886. In fact, this represented clubs only in South Island. The game, however, spread to North Island and in 1913 the New Zealand B.A. and Northern B.A. merged to form the present N.Z.B.A.

U.S.A. There is evidence of lawn bowls being played in the U.S.A. soon after the start of the seventeenth century. For geographical reasons, the game developed in pockets but a truly national association slowly evolved and the American Lawn B.A., formed in 1937, was finally accepted by the International Bowling Board in July 1938.

South Africa. The Port Elizabeth Club opened on 5 February 1884 and the South African B.A. was formed on 5 April 1904.

Bowls for beginners. There are no professionals under the E.B.A. code in Britain, but professional coaches abound in Australia and it is customary in many clubs in the 18 member countries of the I.B.B. to have members whose duty it is to teach beginners. Regular courses of instruction are held in England in May each year, organized by the Central Council for Physical Education in conjunction with a number of county bowling associations, mostly in the south of England.

Bowls for the blind. By blowing a whistle when standing over the jack, a skip or marker can indicate length and position and so enable a blind man to play bowls. Such has become the skill of some sightless men that they have been able to secure and hold positions in Australian 'pennant' fours, the highest standard of play in that country. The system was introduced to Britain in 1955 and well over 50 blind bowlers entered the 1970 tournament at Hastings.

English Bowling Association Official Year Book, annually; *English Bowling Federation Official Year Book,* annually. D. J. Bryant, *Bryant on Bowls* (1970); Humphrey J. Dingley, *Touchers and Rubs* (1893); Dr. John W. Fisher, *World Bowls* (1956); C. M. Jones, *The Watney Book of Bowls* (1967) and *Bowls: How to Become a Champion* (1972); *World Bowls* magazine, monthly.

GOVERNING BODIES (WORLD): International Bowling Board, c/o English Bowling Association, 4 Lansdowne Crescent, Bournemouth, Hampshire; (ENGLAND): English Bowling Association, 4 Lansdowne Crescent, Bournemouth, Hampshire; English Bowling Federation, 5 Milton Street, Ipswich, Suffolk; (SCOTLAND): Scottish Bowling Association, 50 Wellington Street, Glasgow, Scotland.

Crown green bowls.

In southern England and round the world in countries affiliated to the I.B.B., bowls is played on a level green. In the northern areas of England and Wales and in the Isle of Man, there persists a variation in which the centre of the green is higher than its boundaries, so giving the game its name. This game shares a common ancestry with all other forms of bowls, dating back to the old target-hitting days of 5200 B.C. It is believed to have evolved through the difficulties once experienced in producing level greens in some of the poorer areas of industrial northern England where small greens abounded behind public houses.

The game is played on a square area of short grass varying in size from 30 to 60 yds. (27.4–54.9 m.) but usually about 40 yds. (36.6 m.) square. The surface of the green slopes gently upwards from the sides to a central crown 8 to 18 in. (203–457 mm.) higher than the sides. Unlike the greens used for flat-green play (see above), the surface tends to be irregular, adding a further variable to that caused by the crown.

Three points are clearly marked on all greens: (1) the centre; (2) the official entrance, which must be near the middle of one of the sides; and (3) a 4-yd. (3.7 m.) distance from the edges of the green, which is indicated by pegs at the four corners.

Pairs — two players per side — are sometimes played but the usual game is singles. Each player delivers, alternately, two bowls per end, whether the game be singles or pairs. Each delivery is made with one foot on a circular mat about 12 in. (305 mm.) in diameter — called the 'footer' — and is termed a cast.

The object is to cast each bowl nearer to a smaller bowl — the 'jack' — than any or all of the opposition's bowls. Each bowl finishing nearer to the jack than the best opposition bowl scores a point. The standard game is won by the first player or pair scoring 21 but some tournaments are run at anything between 11 and 41 up, the latter figure applying to matches organized by the Lancashire Professional Bowling Association for their panel of bowlers.

Strangely, there is no rule covering the bowls which may be used. Thus the permissible variations are infinite and the governing body was forced in 1968 to give a ruling prohibiting the use of jacks as bowls, a manoeuvre tried by two players in tournaments earlier that year. However, the dynamics of play dictate standards and so most bowls in use weigh between 2 lb. 6 oz. and 3 lb. (1.1–1.4 kg.). They tend to be smaller in diameter than those used in flat-green bowls. Each bowl has a bias which causes it to follow a curved path when delivered along a flat green. The bias is imparted by flattening one side of the bowl. The amount of bias is measured in flat-green bowls against standard bowls approved by the International Bowling Board (I.B.B.) and is graded from No. 1 to No. 5. There are no upper or lower limits in the crown green game but experience shows that a 2½ bias is the average. However, professionals and keen competitive bowlers usually own several sets, the choice depending on each green and its condition on match days.

A definition of the standard jack specifies that jacks of No. 2 full bias as approved by the British Crown Green Amateur Bowling Asso-

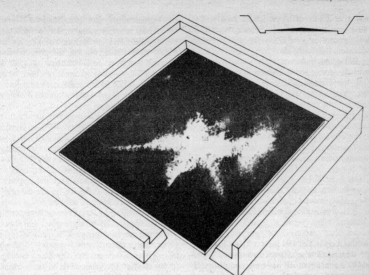

CROWN GREEN
Shaded area indicates sloping surface. (Section shows elevation of crown green in relation to flat green.)

ciation and the British Parks and Recreation Amateur Bowling Association respectively shall weigh 21 oz. (595 g.), with a minimum of 20 oz. (567 g.) and maximum of 23 oz. (652 g.). The diameter should be 3¾ in. (95·3 mm.) minimum with maximum 3⅞ in. (98·4 mm.). However, as there is no rule dictating their use in all tournaments, the standard seems of academic rather than practical value though many efforts have been made to bring such jacks into general use.

The rule governing the use of the footer is much more specific than in the flat-green game. Every player must place his toe on the footer when bowling either the jack or the bowl. A player bowling the jack with his right hand must play his bowls with his right hand and must have his right toe on the footer, and vice versa for a left-handed player. A player must bowl with the same hand throughout the game and any bowl not so played may be stopped by the referee and must then be played again. If a player again breaks this rule during the course of the game, the bowl wrongly played is deemed dead.

The referee has far wider powers than the marker in a flat-green singles. His functions are to settle any dispute not provided for in the laws of the game; to ensure strict adherence to the laws without waiting for either player to register an objection; to give decisions when players disagree; and, if necessary, to remove a bowl so measuring may be carried out. The decision of the referee on any point is final.

In amateur matches play must begin within 3 yds. (2·7 m.) of the clearly marked official entrance to the green. Professional matches begin from the centre, the bowlers using a footer which is only 4 in. (102 mm.) in diameter. One foot must remain in contact with this throughout the cast.

The jack may be thrown in any direction — forward, sideways, diagonally — by the bowler winning the toss and, later, each end. To be 'live' (make a mark) it must be at least 21 yds. (19·2 m.) from the footer, but on heavy greens a player may claim a limit on length to prevent a strong bowler constantly using the full 56 yds. (51·2 m.) diagonal of a green 40 yds. (36·6 m.) square. It is not a 'mark' if the jack comes to rest inside a radius of 3 yds. (2·7 m.) from the centre of the green which is clearly marked; nor is it a mark if both jack and footer are less than 4 yds. (3·7 m.) from the same edge of the green.

If the jack is delivered so that its bias supplements the slope of the green it will swing round in a wide arc; so, too, will a bowl. Such casts are known as 'round pegs'. When the bowl is cast with bias towards the centre of the green, so countering the effects of the slope, it is known as a 'square peg'. The difficulty of keeping round peg casts on the green means that bowls are usually less strongly biased than in the flat-green game.

On fast greens the tendency is to use light-weight, unpolished bowls which come to rest sooner than heavy bowls. On damp, heavy greens a 3 lb. (1·36 kg.) bowl is probably preferable providing the player is strong enough to cast accurately over the full diagonal. So far lignum vitae bowls heavily outnumber compositions, partly because it is not possible to obtain so wide a range with composition bowls. However, lignum vitae bowls can lose over 8 oz. (227 g.) of weight in a year, so there is a swing to compositions.

On highly-crowned greens it is sometimes good tactics to use strongly-biased bowls and cast them straight peg to jacks delivered along the edges of the green. If the opponent is using weak-bias bowls he will have to find his own 'land' all the time and may experience great difficulty in preventing his bowls sliding off into the ditch.

As in flat-green play, the main scoring shot is the draw to the jack. With only two bowls per player in place of four, positional and promotional play is virtually non-existent. Nevertheless, the firing shot has a useful and effective role to play when the opponent has cast two potential scoring shots in positions which appear unbeatable. Then it is wise to fire confidently and so strongly that the bias has little or no chance to cause a change of direction.

If the jack is cannoned off the green, the end becomes void. The bowler who set the mark delivers the jack to a new mark and the end is resumed from (a) the original position of the footer if more than half the bowls remain to be played, or (b) a point 1 yd. (0·91 m.) from the edge of the green nearest to where the jack left the green if half the bowls have been played.

Because it is customary for several games to take place on a green simultaneously, there are provisions covering interference, generally without penalty. The jack must be returned and delivered again if it is either impeded in any way while running or if it comes to rest in the direct path of the bowls of another game. If jacks from two different games are bowled to positions near to one another, the first one bowled makes the mark and the other is returned for re-delivery. When a mark has been established the end becomes void if the jack is moved by the jack or bowl from another game or if it is displaced by an exterior cause and the players fail to agree about the spot on which it should be replaced. The end also becomes void if a player hits the jack with his bowl and the jack cannons into a bowl or jack from another game or any person on the green. If the jack is cannoned into by any bowl of the game being played, the jack remains in its new position until disturbed again or until the end is completed. If a running bowl is impeded, other than by the caster, it must be played again. If the caster impedes it, the bowl is taken out of play.

Unlike the flat-green game, in which running up the green behind bowls is commonplace, there are strict limitations on what a bowler may do after casting. He must not approach nearer to his bowl than 3 yds. (2·7 m.) before it stops rolling. If he follows it across the green he must give his opponent a clear view of the bowl in its course. On no account may he attempt to slow down or speed up the bowl during its travel. Severe penalties may be applied to transgressors. On the first occasion, he is cautioned. A second offence gives the opponent two points. The third infringement is final; the offender's bowls are removed from the green and the game awarded to his opponent.

Measurement to determine which of two or more bowls is nearer to the jack differs in one respect from the flat-green game. Occasionally a bowl rests on the jack or another bowl and the measurement cannot be made without removing the obstructing bowl. Such removals should be made by the referee and if the remaining bowl falls to a new position after removal of the support, the new position is the one which counts. In flat-green play the remaining bowl would, before removal of the support, be wedged in position.

Once a match has begun it should be played to completion. If bad light or exceptionally heavy rain cause an interruption or postponement, the score stands and the position of the jack is marked so that play may be resumed from its point of interruption.

Betting is widespread in the crown green game, both among participants and between members of the public and bookmakers. This privilege is claimed under a clause from the Betting Commission Report of 1924 which states that betting between a bookmaker and a member of the public on a racecourse or on any enclosed place to which the public have a restricted right of access is legal unless (in the case of an enclosed place) at or near every public entrance there is displayed a notice prohibiting betting.

Crown green bowls is governed by the British Crown Green Bowling Association (B.C.G.B.A.) which was founded in 1932 following the demise of the National Crown Green Amateur Bowling Association and the British Crown Green Amateur Association.

The new organization's officials came from among those running its two predecessors. The professional game is, however, governed separately by the two professional associations of Lancashire and Yorkshire. The total number of professionals is not high, being of the order of 60. Amateurs are not allowed to compete with them and there have been cases of suspension for breach of that ruling. There are, however, difficulties in defining amateurism as applied to all bowls, a situation which has arisen in many other games.

The B.C.G.B.A.'s council follows the normal pattern and is made up of delegates from the various county associations. These are, in chronological order of formation, Lancashire (organized with Cheshire in 1888), Yorkshire (1892), Warwickshire and Worcestershire (1897), Staffordshire (1902), Cheshire (which separated from Lancashire in 1910), Derbyshire (1911 — although it was playing county matches before that year), Shropshire (1913 — including the Bishop Castle Club which was founded in the middle of the seventeenth century), North Wales (1925), and North Midlands (1951).

Many clubs — Tally Ho, Birmingham for example — possess both a flat and a crown green and members play both games though usually one of them is treated as a relaxation from the other, according to the bowler's predilection.

League play flourishes and in the Midlands it was once an almost inviolate rule that when a public house was built and room existed, a crown green was laid by the brewers. The Hand of Providence, Cradley Heath, was a splendid example and Saturday night league matches were events of great importance, with the manager's son collecting the sixpenny green fees and taking orders for drinks.

Changing patterns of social life began to have their effect during the 1960s. Wives went out more with their husbands and public houses took on a new look, lounges where both sexes mix replacing the exclusively male retreats. Such developments necessitated space and many crown greens suffered 'development'. However, municipal authorities, aware of the game's great social virtues, have played an important part in fostering it, and in the Manchester area alone there are over 70 municipal greens. Unlike the flat-green game, there is virtually no indoor play and there are very few covered halls.

Tournaments abound and many of them attract huge entries. Most clubs run a competition on President's Day and each county has an individual 'merit' event. The quarter finalists in each of these go forward to the national championship which is played off each August. Newspapers, too, promote competitions, some of which attract as many as 5,000 entries. The game has two 'classic' tournaments, the Talbot and the Waterloo, both of which are staged in Blackpool, Lancashire.

The Talbot Handicap, first staged in 1873 by Robert Nickson, owner of the Talbot Hotel, has become the most famous competition in crown green bowls. Originally conceived as a grand finale and extension to a season which in those days finished in September, it was first won by Joseph Fielding. The tournament caught the imagination of the crown green world and by 1881 the entry reached 88. This figure rose to 1,000 in 1910, and hit a record of 1,580 for the 'victory' meeting of 1919. Since then the entry has been restricted to 1,024, necessitating ten rounds to determine the winner. It is open to all bowlers, but professionals are normally severely handicapped, perhaps owing seven to good amateurs.

The tournament has been held every year except 1939 since its inception. From 1873 until 1966, before the hotel was demolished in 1967, all but 11 of the 92 tournaments took place on the Talbot green. In 1941, the Ministry of Aircraft Production having commandeered the Talbot, the tournament was staged at the old Number 3 Hotel — a noted centre of bowls — and for the next ten years at the Raikes Hotel, to which it has now returned.

Like the Talbot Handicap, the Waterloo Handicap is a classic of crown green bowls. Founded in 1907, it is held at the Waterloo Hotel, Blackpool, and entry is restricted to 1,024 bowlers. Play normally begins at 1 p.m. each day, two games of 41 up being played. Licensed betting is permitted and wagers are made between punters from beginning to end of each match. The panel is often supplemented by non-panel professionals. Although a considerable amount of money may change hands in the course of an afternoon there is no question of large fortunes being won or lost. Most punters are happy to show a couple of pounds profit on the afternoon. The Association maintains strict control over betting and is justifiably proud that over the course of the years such ventures have raised in excess of £100,000 for charity.

Undoubtedly the crown green game is thriving but it still lacks the co-ordinated, efficient, national control exercised by the E.B.A. over the flat-green game and this is a handicap to its expansion, especially into the southern areas of England.

British Crown Green Amateur Bowling Association Official Year Book, annually; E. A. Lundy, *Crown Bowls* (1961).

GOVERNING BODY: British Crown Green Amateur

Bowling Association, Highbridge, Scisset, Huddersfield, West Yorkshire.

Women's bowls. Homer tells us that the ball was invented by the Lydians and that Anagalla, a native of Corcyra, was the first to make a ball for play. Princess Nausicaa was taught to use it, though the game she and her handmaidens played seems to have been the forerunner of HANDBALL and its many derivatives. Nevertheless, female participation in ball games dates from then and fourteenth-century illustrations show mixed bowls in progress.

In 1902 women in the midlands and north-west of England were playing both the flat and crown green games and in 1906 the London County Council decreed that one rink on each park should be reserved for women's play. At that time play was 'friendly' except for occasional competitions promoted by men's clubs. The Kingston Canonbury Ladies' Bowling Club was formed in 1910, soon to be followed by others. County associations were the next logical step and the Somerset Women's Bowling Association, formed on 16 April 1928, was followed by Leicestershire in 1930 and Sussex in 1931. The latter county's first president was Clara Johns (1880-1967), known as the 'Mother of English Women's Bowling', who was the driving force behind the formation of the English Women's Bowling Association (E.W.B.A.) in October 1931, the year of the first tournament for women.

The inter-county championship began in 1953 and is played for the Johns Trophy, of which Surrey were the first winners. Important though this is, it gains less attention than the individual championships which are staged at Wimbledon Park, London, each August. These comprise the singles (inaugurated 1932), pairs (1932), triples (1933), fours (1932), and two-wood singles (1939). (Incidentally, women have not adopted the official name 'fours' for four-a-side play but have retained the old-fashioned 'rink'.)

Today more than 53,000 women play bowls at clubs affiliated to the E.W.B.A. In national competitions there is complete separation of the sexes; the women's game is governed by the E.W.B.A. and by the English Women's Bowling Federation (E.W.B.F.) for the Federation code. Both bodies organize a comprehensive network of championships and, in the case of the Association code, there are annual international series of team matches, both outdoor and indoor, between the home countries.

In some of the smaller district competitions under the Federation code it is usual for fours to be made up in any combination of men and women. Although there is a women's fours event in the E.B.F. championships at Skegness, and although mixed pairs events are held at many seaside resorts under licence from the B.I.B.C., there has not yet been an English mixed pairs championship. Indeed, it is difficult to see how a national event could be introduced without a change of I.B.B. laws which suggest that bowls is a game for men only.

The Adams Trophy is the women's county team championship of the E.B.F. Each match is of 31 ends between teams of six triples. The championship is divided into two geographical areas, the winning county from each meeting on the last Saturday in August each year. In 1969 the long-accepted method of awarding victory to the team scoring the greater number of shots was abandoned. In its place the E.B.F. introduced a points system making it possible for a county to lose on five of the six rinks yet still win on aggregate score.

Women's bowls is established in Australia and South Africa and Test matches between ladies' teams of the two countries began in 1969. The Victorian Ladies B.A., formed in 1907, is the oldest women's bowls association in the world.

The formation of a women's International Board of Control came a step nearer in December 1969 when the Australian Women's Bowling Council promoted the first women's international championships at the Elizabethan W.B.C., Rockdale, N.S.W. Six countries entered representatives. The first women's world championships were staged in Australia at the end of 1973.

English Women's Bowling Association Year Book, annually.
GOVERNING BODIES: English Women's Bowling Association, 22 Bloomfield Park, Bath, Somerset; English Women's Bowling Federation, 4 Neatherd Road, Dereham, Norfolk; Australian Women's Bowling Council, c/o The Elizabethan Women's Bowling Council, West Botany Street, Rockdale, N.S.W., Australia.

BOX LACROSSE, see LACROSSE.

BOXE FRANÇAIS, French boxing, is a localized French form of combat in which both gloved fists and feet are employed. Derived from SAVATE and *chausson,* it is performed in a roped ring similar to that for BOXING. Although it was an interesting and highly athletic pursuit in which established and outstanding orthodox boxers took part, it was essentially a single (French) national interest and, as such, could not compete in significance with the international sport of boxing. It is now little more than an exhibition sport.

BOXING, fist-fighting with gloves worn by two men in a roped square, is both an amateur and professional sport with wide international following and participation. Though the majority of world professional champions have come from the U.S.A., many outstanding boxers have been produced in Europe, Central and South America and, in recent years, in Asia. Amateur boxing, which is on the Olympic programme of sports, is also widely practised in the Communist countries where there is no professional sport.

Boxing is basically a simple sport though it is sometimes made seemingly complex by the lack of one authoritative governing professional body. This causes disagreements over rules and occasionally as to who should be called world champion. But the aim for all boxers is to win either on points, by scoring more blows on the target (defined as 'any part of the front or sides of the head or body above the belt') or to outclass an opponent so that he is unable to defend himself, or is counted out within ten seconds for a 'knock-out'.

Boxing is practised in a three-roped 'ring' of between 14 and 20 ft. (4·27–6·1 m.) square, and, since the ring is usually set on a stage, the floor should project not less than 18 in. (457 mm.) outside the ropes. Gloves, according to the rules of the various governing bodies, should weigh 6 or 8 oz. (170 or 227 g.), and the boxer's hands are further protected by wrappings of soft and adhesive bandage. The amateur wears a singlet, shorts, and high-ankled soft leather boots and uses 8-oz. gloves; the professional is stripped to the waist and in Britain his gloves weigh 6 oz. Boxers are protected by a rubber gum-shield in their mouths and a protector-cup guarding the groin.

All rounds boxed by both senior amateurs and professionals are of three minutes' duration followed by a minute's rest, when the boxers may be seated in their corners. Amateur bouts are all of three rounds but the professionals box from six rounds for beginners up to the championship distance of 15 rounds. If a boxer of either code is knocked down at the end of any round, except the last, the count must be continued past the bell until the boxer rises.

Points-scoring systems in professional boxing have differed for many years. The British Boxing Board of Control scores 10 points for the winner of a round and then fractions down to a theoretical maximum division of 5-4¼ for any one round. The remaining governing bodies in professional boxing are all inclining towards the 'five must' rule in which rounds can be scored 5-5, 5-4, 5-3, or even 5-2.

In Britain professional bouts are controlled and scored only by a referee. In the U.S.A. a points decision — if the bout goes the scheduled distance without a stoppage or a knock-out — is made by the referee and two judges seated at the ring-side. During 1970-3, the European Boxing Union (E.B.U.) which organizes European professional championships experimented with the use of a referee and two judges — all amateur.

After much difference of opinion the various governing bodies of professional boxing agreed from 1 September 1970 on a uniform scale of weights for the recognized divisions — though this was no guarantee of perpetuity. The weight limits agreed were:

Flyweight, 8 st. (112 lb.; 50·802 kg.)
Bantamweight, 8 st. 6 lb. (118 lb.; 53·525 kg.)
Featherweight, 9 st. (126 lb.; 57·152 kg.)
Junior lightweight, 9 st. 4 lb. (130 lb.; 58·967 kg.)
Lightweight, 9 st. 9 lb. (135 lb.; 61·237 kg.)
Junior welterweight, 10 st. (140 lb.; 63·503 kg.)
Welterweight, 10 st. 7 lb. (147 lb.; 66·678 kg.)
Junior middleweight, 11 st. (154 lb.; 69·853 kg.)
Middleweight, 11 st. 6 lb. (160 lb.; 72·574 kg.)
Light-heavyweight, 12 st. 7 lb. (175 lb.; 79·378 kg.)
Heavyweight, any weight

The Association Internationale de Boxe Amateur (A.I.B.A.) which controls amateur boxing, including the tournament in the OLYMPIC GAMES, recognizes 11 weight divisions with the following limits:

Light-flyweight, not exceeding 48 kg. (105 lb. 13 oz. 2 dr.)
Flyweight, over 48 kg. (105 lb. 13 oz. 2 dr.) not exceeding 51 kg. (112 lb. 6 oz. 15 dr.)
Bantamweight, over 51 kg. and not exceeding 54 kg. (119 lb. 0 oz. 12 dr.)
Featherweight, over 54 kg. and not exceeding 57 kg. (125 lb. 10 oz. 9 dr.)
Lightweight, over 57 kg. and not exceeding 60 kg. (132 lb. 4 oz. 7 dr.)
Light-welterweight, over 60 kg. and not exceeding 63·5 kg. (139 lb. 15 oz. 14 dr.)
Welterweight, over 63·5 kg. and not exceeding 67 kg. (147 lb. 11 oz. 5 dr.)
Light-middleweight, over 67 kg. and not exceeding 71 kg. (156 lb. 8 oz. 7 dr.)
Middleweight, over 71 kg. and not exceeding 75 kg. (165 lb. 5 oz. 8 dr.)
Light-heavyweight, over 75 kg. and not exceeding 81 kg. (178 lb. 9 oz. 3 dr.)
Heavyweight, over 81 kg. (178 lb. 9 oz. 3 dr.)

In international amateur boxing, contestants at all weights are required to be ready to weigh in on the first morning of the competition and may have only one attempt at making the limit. In Britain professional boxers have to weigh in at 1 p.m. for evening promotions and are allowed one hour of grace from that time to make the weight. If a boxer involved in a British championship cannot make the weight, the contest automatically becomes a non-title bout.

In major international amateur tournaments, like the Olympic Games and the European championships, the contest is controlled by the referee but he does not score the bout. Instead, scoring papers are marked by five judges seated at the ring-side. At the end of each of the three rounds the 'better' (more skilful) boxer receives 20 points and his opponent proportionally less. After an equal round each boxer may receive 20 points: but, unlike the position in professional boxing, there can be no draw. If a judge finds boxers are equal on points he awards the decision to the man who has done 'most of the leading off or who has shown the better style or defence'. The A.I.B.A. rules state that no extra points shall be awarded for a knock-down.

Boxers may be disqualified for a wide range of infringements. The rules of the European Boxing Union states that a boxer must not: hit below the belt; pretend to have been struck below the belt; lean on his opponent or push him backward; push the head of his opponent backward with the open glove and hit with the other; hold a rope with his glove; hide behind his gloves to avoid boxing; strike his opponent when he is on the floor or, after having been down, is trying to get up; hold his opponent or deliberately prolong a clinch; hold his opponent with one hand and strike him with the other; hit with the shoulder or the head or make use of the knees; hit with the inside or lower part of the hand, the wrist, or the elbow; hit or slap with the open glove; strike with back-hand blows; hustle his opponent onto the ropes; deliberately strike his opponent low; use the pivot blow (throwing out the arm and fist while pivoting); insult his opponent, swear, or use vile or improper language; duck below the belt of his opponent.

The A.I.B.A. rules state that the competitor who commits fouls can, at the discretion of the referee, be cautioned, warned, or disqualified without warning. Only three formal warnings may be given to the same boxer in one contest before he is disqualified. The A.I.B.A. lists the following fouls: hitting or holding below the belt; tripping, kicking and butting with foot or knee; hits or blows with head, shoulder, forearm, elbow; throttling of the opponent; pressing with arm or elbow in the opponent's face; pressing the head of the opponent back over the ropes; hitting with open glove, the inside of the glove, wrist, or side of the hand; hits landing on the back of the opponent and especially any blow on the back of the neck or head and kidney punch; pivot blows; attack while holding the ropes or making any unfair use of the ropes; lying on, wrestling, and throwing in the clinch; an attack on an opponent who is down or who is in the act of rising; holding; holding or locking the opponent's arm or head, or pushing an arm underneath the arm of the opponent; holding and hitting or pulling and hitting; ducking below the belt of the opponent in a manner dangerous to his opponent; completely passive defence by means of double cover and intentionally falling to avoid a blow; useless, aggressive, or offensive utterances during the round; not stepping back when ordered to break; attempting to strike the opponent immediately after the referee has ordered 'Break' and before taking a step back. The A.I.B.A. adds that if a referee has any reason to believe that a foul has been committed which he himself has not seen he may consult the judges.

Both the professional E.B.U. and the amateur A.I.B.A. insist that any boxer knocked down should have a minimum respite of eight seconds whether or not he is ready to continue. The British Boxing Board of Control does not have the compulsory count, but it is included in New York, as is a rule whereby three knock-downs of a boxer in one round brings the bout to a close. However, the New York State Athletic Commission does not apply these regulations to any world professional championship staged in its territory.

All responsible boxing bodies endeavour to exercise strict medical control over boxers through examinations before contests, responsible and humane refereeing, and immediate medical attention for any boxer who has been knocked out or seriously hurt during a contest. The only haemostatic authorized to be used by seconds under the rules of the E.B.U. is adrenalin 1/1000. The British Boxing Board of Control forbids the use by seconds of iron chloride solution, monsol, and ammoniated liniments for massage, and alcohol.

The successful boxer aims at hitting his opponent without being hit in return. He needs speed, judgement, endurance, and fitness and, above all, courage; but he also needs a cool head.

There are four basic punches. These are the straight blow; the hook (with the arm bent at right angles); the swing; and the uppercut. These punches may be delivered with either hand and at the opponent's head or body. The chief methods of defence are to slip (avoid) a punch, block with forearm or open glove, deflect, duck, or side-step.

The normal stance for a boxer is left foot forward and left arm extended. 'Southpaws', those who stand with right foot and right glove first, are in the minority though they have included winners of world and European championships. The orthodox boxer is bound to do most work with his left hand whether he is scoring points or making openings for a two-handed attack. The left can be used for attack and as a defensive counter-attack when it stops a rushing opponent in his tracks. The right represents the heavy artillery in attack but is also a vital part of the defence as it can so often be used to block or deflect the opponent's left leads to face or body.

This, however, is a somewhat simplistic view of boxing technique. The speed at which modern contests are often fought over 10 or 15 rounds means that nimble footwork and the use of the whole ring are nearly as important as power and accuracy of punch. Boxers generally circle round the ring and quite often the man who can dominate the centre of the ring and move in the smaller circle is conserving energy.

Close-quarter boxing, or 'in-fighting', can play a big part in professional boxing because the length of the contests means that either man may wish to seek the refuge of a 'clinch'. In order to maintain pressure the proficient in-fighter must be able to drive away to the body and then switch his attack to the head. Such ability calls for excellence at 'combination punching' which begins with the classic one-two, or left and following right to the head, and can be developed to a rhythmic sequence of six or seven swift successive blows.

Amateur boxing, with bouts over only three rounds, is bound to be swifter, and sometimes more flurried, than professional contests. Nevertheless, the basic boxing principles of attack, defence, counter-attack, footwork, and ring strategy — backed by fitness, clear thinking, and courage — are common to both codes.

British Boxing Board of Control, *Referees' Guide* (1969).

Boxing may be said to date from the first time a fist was clenched and used as a weapon. The first record of its being practised as a major sport, however, dates from the ancient Greeks who introduced pugilism into the Olympic Games about 686 B.C. The boxers had much in common with their modern counterparts. They wore soft leather coverings for their hands and in training used primitive punching-bags and head-guards. Their technique was not very different save that body-punching and clinching were virtually unknown.

Gradually, boxing, which for the Greeks laid considerable emphasis on skill, became brutalized as spectators showed an increasing taste for blood. The Romans, perhaps influenced by Etruscan interest in gladiatorial contests, developed the cestus, an iron-studded gauntlet which could, if it landed flush upon

Left jab

Left hook

Straight right

Right uppercut

Basic stance

BOXING STANCE AND PUNCHES

an opponent's temple, cause his death. As the Roman populace demanded ever bloodier circuses, pugilism as such declined in interest and eventually disappeared during the fourth century A.D.

In subsequent centuries there must have been many unrecorded examples of fighting for fun, or a wager, or both. But the true revival of pugilism came in seventeenth- and eighteenth-century England. The first organized bare-knuckle fight in this country of which there is any record was in January 1681 when a bout was held for the entertainment of the Duke of Albemarle between his footman and a butcher.

Boxing historians generally regard the year 1719 as a vital one. It was then that FIGG set himself up in the area by Oxford Street, London, as a champion at self-defence with sword, quarterstaff (a long wooden pole), and fists. On his business card, designed for him by the artist Hogarth, Figg was described as 'Master of the Noble Science of Defence in Oxford Road near Adam and Eve court — teaches gentlemen the use of the small backsword and quarterstaff'. There was no mention of fist-fighting in Figg's publicity sheet but he is recognized as the first prize-fighting champion of England. He became known through his rugged exhibitions at Southwark Fair in south-east London: but after he had established himself at the Adam and Eve Inn, north of Oxford Street, he gained a rich patron in the Earl of Peterborough and built a school of arms with a raised circular stage and space for several hundred spectators.

When Figg defended the unofficial championship he had claimed, his opponent in 1727 was Sutton, a pipe-maker from Greenwich, and the audience is said to have included Sir Robert Walpole and the writers Swift and Pope. Figg and Sutton had three contests that morning, with broadsword, fists, and quarterstaff. Figg won the first by cutting Sutton on the shoulder, the second by flooring his opponent with a punch above the heart, and the third, with quarterstaff, by breaking Sutton's knee.

It was a primitive beginning to the history of modern boxing. Figg and Sutton faced each other almost square on with their feet firmly rooted to the stage. It was considered cowardly to break ground and in any case it was best to be near your man since wrestling was allowed and there was always a chance of throwing a rival heavily to the boards. A round ended when a man went down, a rule which applied all through the heyday of the English prize ring.

Figg was not only champion and an outstanding teacher; he can also claim to be the first promoter of an international match. When he was challenged to a boxing match by an Italian, Carini, Figg matched Carini with one of his pupils, Bob Whittaker, and, to his joy, saw him win. A contemporary report says that Whittaker was first knocked off the stage but 'Bob was not to be tolled out so soon and he jumped up on the stage like a gamecock to renew the attack.... He made a little stoop, ran boldly in beyond the heavy mallet, and with one English peg in the stomach brought the Italian on his breech.'

The spectators at Whittaker's victory included George I and the Prince of Wales, an indication of the patronage Figg had gained since his first days in London. At the end of the programme Figg sparred with a new fighter from Bristol named BROUGHTON. Six years after Figg had beaten Sutton it was Broughton who claimed the championship and subsequently became known as 'the Father of Boxing' for his part in framing the first set of rules for the sport.

Broughton, unlike the money-conscious Figg, was keen to defend his honours in fights rather than sparring. In April 1741 he took on Stevenson, a Yorkshire coachman, of whom it was written by Captain Godfrey, the author of the first textbook on boxing, 'he put in his blows faster than Broughton but then one of the latter's told for three of the former's.' Broughton eventually beat Stevenson with a right under the heart but when his opponent died from his injuries within a month Broughton said at first that he would never fight again.

Broughton decided to lessen the chance of any more such tragedies by drawing up his rules, which remained in force in England for nearly a hundred years. These rules, 'to be observed in all battles on the stage' and 'agreed by several gentlemen at Broughton's Amphitheatre 16 August 1743', were a vital contribution. They barred such practices as hitting a man below the belt or when he was down. Only wrestling holds above the waist were permitted. A round ended when a man was down so that, unlike the current three-minute round, it could last only a few seconds or nearly half an hour. Once a man was down he was allowed 30 seconds to recover before coming from his second's knee to a mark in the centre of the ring. If he could not toe the mark, or 'come up to scratch', he had lost.

Broughton's rules were so sensible that they formed the basis of the London Prize-ring Rules drawn up in 1838 (which introduced more regulations against fouls) and even of the QUEENSBERRY RULES introduced towards the end of the nineteenth century in London as a guide to the rest of the world.

Broughton, who was also responsible for the introduction of gloves (at first called 'mufflers') in sparring exhibitions, did much to add respectability to these early days of pugilism. But in April 1750 he met his downfall at the hands of Slack of Bristol, a city which later produced many outstanding prizefighters. After 14 minutes Broughton was blinded by his opponent's blows and his backer, the Duke of Cumberland, the 'Butcher' of Culloden, lost £10,000 in a wager and declared that he had been betrayed by his fighter. The agonized Broughton, groping for his opponent, pleaded unavailingly, 'I can't see my man, your Highness, I am blind but not beat. Only place me before him and he shall not gain the day yet.'

In spite of this sad ending to his career as champion, Broughton remained popular; when he died at 84 he left £7,000 and was buried in Westminster Abbey. In the years following his defeat, however, the prize ring fell into disrepute and it was not until Tom Johnson became champion in 1783 that a measure of skill returned to the sport.

But a much greater contribution was that of the Jewish boxer MENDOZA whose three battles with Humphries attracted crowds of almost 10,000 in inn-yards or the open countryside. Mendoza was only 5 ft. 7½ in. (1·7 m.) tall and, by modern standards, a middleweight. He made up for his lack of height with swift footwork and was so difficult to hit that he often beat much heavier men. At this time there were occasionally bouts for lighter boxers but the open championship was the only lucrative prize and drew all the public attention. When Mendoza lost the title in 1795 it was to JOHN JACKSON who was 5 ft. 11 in. (1·8 m.) tall and about 40 lb. (18 kg.) heavier.

'Gentleman' Jackson won the championship by holding Mendoza's curly black hair with one hand and belabouring him with the other. This was not considered particularly unsporting and any controversy was soon forgotten as Jackson's capacity for diplomacy and quiet dignity gave him a reputation in London society far above the dreams of his predecessors. He opened a gymnasium in Bond Street and abandoned fighting to teach such famous pupils as the poet Lord Byron, who described the champion as 'my friend and corporeal master and pastor'.

Jackson had only three recorded fights but his fame as a teacher of boxing, and his ability as an all-round athlete, made him a vital power behind the Pugilistic Club which was formed by aristocratic followers of the sport in 1814 as boxing's first unofficial governing body. He was an influential figure at the ringside and his successor, BELCHER, set new standards in speed and skill, especially in counterpunching. Belcher might have earned an even greater reputation but for the loss of an eye while playing rackets when he was only 22.

The next four champions were Pearce (1805), GULLY (1808), CRIBB (1809), and Spring (1823) and their reigns mark the final stage of the golden period of prize-fighting, though there were still notable figures to come. All four men retired from the ring without losing the title of champion. Pearce, like Belcher, died young; but Cribb and Spring both became publicans; and Gully prospered so mightily that he was eventually elected a member of Parliament and made a fortune in the coal industry and horse-racing.

Cribb's two victories over the black American MOLINEAUX in 1810 and 1811 marked the beginning of boxing as an international sport, although prize-fighting was still far removed from the modern ring. The fighters had no gloves to protect their hands and hitting had therefore to be done carefully. Considerable time was consumed by positioning, and the fact that contests, when not held on raised stages, were usually fought on the turf meant that spiked shoes were often worn. Since an opponent could be lifted in a wrestling hold and then slammed to the ground, the smaller man had to be so evasive that fights in the nineteenth century must often have been so slow-moving that they would have infuriated a modern audience.

Scientific training was unknown to most prize-fighters who, coming from poor homes, frequently lacked a proper diet in childhood. A notable exception in preparation was Cribb for his second fight with Molineaux, but the English champion had Captain Barclay (see R. B. ALLARDICE), a noted long-distance runner and walker, as trainer.

Few thought of pugilism as a full-time career unless they became champion and could cash in on their fame by becoming a landlord or giving lessons in the art of boxing. Payment for prize-fights usually came from rich sponsors or from bets laid by the boxers themselves. In 1805 Gully is said to have earned about £500 from a fight with Pearce. When Tom Johnson fought Perrins in 1789 his backer made £20,000 of which he gave £1,000 to Johnson. Cribb probably collected slightly less than that from his first fight with Molineaux in 1810.

The private lives of most of the prizefighters make tragic reading. The majority of them drank excessively between fights and lost all their hard-won earnings to spongers. After his second fight with Cribb the beaten Molineaux drank heavily and died, penniless, in an army barracks aged only 34.

In spite of the efforts of the aristocratic Pugilistic Club to see fair play, backed by such lively sporting writers as PIERCE EGAN, the prize ring was often overshadowed by deceit and double-cross. In 1812 Egan, who wrote plays, doggerel, and guides to the raffish life of London, brought out his first instalment of *Boxiana*, a chronicle of the prize ring which eventually amounted to five bound volumes.

It was said of Egan that 'he was flattered and petted by pugilists and peers: his patronage and countenance were sought for by all who considered the road to a prize-fight the road to reputation and honour. In his particular line he was the greatest man in England'. But even Egan's righteous championing of the ring could not stop a decline in standards towards the middle of the nineteenth century. Jem Ward and BENDIGO (William Thompson) were considered good champions of England but both were involved in controversial fights. The nobility, the 'Corinthians', disgustedly began to withdraw their presence and support from prize-fighting.

There was to be one more fine flourish. In April 1860 SAYERS, who had been champion of England for three years, met the American HEENAN, for £200 a side at Farnborough, Hampshire, and the whole country buzzed with excitement. Heenan was not unanimously regarded as champion of his country where a national title had first been contested in 1849. But with the retirement to politics of his conqueror, Morrissey, Heenan was recognized as the best American heavyweight.

In the end, however, there was no winner, for after 2 hrs. 20 min., with the ring ropes cut, the crowd out of control, and both men badly battered, the official result was a draw. Many members of Parliament and the writers Dickens and Thackeray were said to be among the crowd, though the fight had to be held in some secrecy because of the opposition of the police. Sayers suffered a torn tendon in his right arm and Heenan was virtually blinded by facial swellings at the chaotic finish. No one can be certain who was the better man but Sayers, no more than a middleweight, earned great fame and some £3,000 from a testimonial fund for his courage against a bigger, taller opponent.

The Sayers-Heenan fight marked the beginning of the end of the prize ring. The next great champion, MACE, fought both with bare knuckles and with the skin-tight gloves which were becoming common. Mace, like Sayers little more than a middleweight, had his last major contest in 1871 and died in 1910. By then the brutal, unorganized days of the prize ring were long over. Mace himself sowed the seeds of the sport both in the U.S.A., where he fought several times, and in Australia where he taught Foley, later the coach of many fine boxers. In New Zealand Mace is said to have been among the first to note the talent of English-born FITZSIMMONS, who subsequently won world titles at three different weights.

The rules for boxing with gloves, to which the Marquess of Queensberry lent his name and patronage, are believed to have been drafted around 1867 by Chambers. But it was not until 1892 that CORBETT became the first champion to win the title under the new rules using gloves, three-minute rounds, a minute's rest, a maximum of ten seconds following a knock-down, and no wrestling allowed. The Queensberry Rules did not lay down the length of a professional bout nor did they make any mention of a points decision. For a while the winner was still the man who lasted longest on his feet. The term 'ring' for a roped square, said to have been the original eighteenth-century name for an area of ground in London's Hyde Park fenced off specifically for impromptu fights, was kept in the Queensberry Rules. But there was now a carefully worded instruction that boxers should wear 'fair-sized boxing gloves of the best quality and new'.

SULLIVAN, who won the American title with bare fists in 1882, beat Kilrain after 2 hours in 1889 for the last bare-knuckle championship, and lost to Corbett in 1892 wearing 5-oz. (142 g.) gloves. Of the prize-ring rules Sullivan said: 'They allow too much leeway for the rowdy element to indulge in their practices. Such mean tricks as spiking, biting, gouging, strangling, butting with the head, falling down without being struck, scratching with the nails, kicking, falling on an antagonist with the knees are impossible under the Queensberry Rules. Fighting under the new rules before gentlemen is a pleasure.'

But it was Corbett, not Sullivan, who symbolized the new development of the sport. He was good-looking, well built, and a scientific fighter, in complete contrast to Sullivan who had depended chiefly upon strength and a knock-out punch in the right hand. It was typical of Corbett's inventive mind that when he broke two knuckles in his left hand he developed a short left hook which won him many fights. He was the first of the great stylists of the modern ring. But in 1897 he was beaten in 14 rounds by Fitzsimmons who landed a paralysing left hook to the stomach and became heavyweight champion at a weight of only 156 lb. (71 kg.).

In 1891 Fitzsimmons had become the second official middleweight champion of the world though for many years the weight limit, in this and other lighter divisions now gradually being established, fluctuated according to the needs of the reigning champion. The terms 'middleweight', 'lightweight', and 'welterweight' had occasionally been used during the years of the prize ring. But under Queensberry Rules it was not until 1909 that the NATIONAL SPORTING CLUB, London, drew up a complete list of the eight most important divisions and themselves created the lightest class of flyweight.

The generally-accepted first glove championships of the various professional weights are: light-heavyweight (1903), middleweight (1884), welterweight (1892), lightweight (1868), featherweight (1889), bantamweight (1888), flyweight (1909). The light-heavyweight class was invented by the manager of an American boxer named Root who could neither make the middleweight limit nor concede weight successfully to the leading heavyweights. From time to time during the 1920s and 1930s there were attempts to introduce other weights, including paperweight for the lightest of all, and dreadnoughts, or super-heavyweights; but it was only in the 1960s that the professional governing bodies accepted world titles at junior middleweight, junior welterweight, and junior lightweight.

As glove-fighting increased in popularity in Britain and the U.S.A. at the beginning of the twentieth century, the sport of boxing gained a toe-hold in Europe when Lerda, using the ring name of 'Kid' Adler, founded a 'school of English boxing' in Paris. The French boxing federation was established in 1903 and in 1920 CARPENTIER won the world light-heavyweight title for France. Boxing was not introduced in Germany on a large scale until about 1920 but ten years later SCHMELING won the heavyweight championship of the world.

Long before then the Americans, strengthened by their multi-racial society, had begun to establish their superiority in most of the major professional titles. Following the Irish-Americans Sullivan and Corbett, the Negroes (the featherweight DIXON, the lightweight GANS, and the heavyweight JACK JOHNSON) found a measure of social status for the descendants of slaves as they rose to the top. After them came the sons of poor immigrant Jewish, Polish, and Italian families literally fighting to find a place in the sun.

But the big prize for all of them, if they had the right physique, continued to be the world heavyweight championship. In 1899 Fitzsimmons, a mighty hitter for such a small man, was himself knocked out by the massive Jeffries. When Jeffries retired the Canadian-born Burns defended the title in Britain, Ireland, France, and Australia while he desperately

avoided the inevitable meeting with Jack Johnson, the new black challenger. Johnson beat Burns in 1908, caused race riots in the U.S.A. by defeating the previously all-conquering Jeffries, and remained a controversial but brilliant champion until he was beaten by Willard in 1915.

Willard's conqueror four years later was DEMPSEY, from Colorado, with whose appearance came the first million-dollar gates. Dempsey, who fought his way out of the copper mines and epitomized the 'hungry' fighter, unleashed a whirlwind attack against Willard to score seven knock-downs in the first round; amateur psychologists on the sports pages began to write about 'killer instinct'. Dempsey fought from a crouch which reminded some veterans of the compact style of Jeffries and was the antithesis of the erect, clean-cut stance of 'Gentleman Jim' Corbett.

When Dempsey's shrewd manager, Kearns, combined forces with the imaginative promoter RICKARD the result was a gate of $1,789,238 for the meeting of Dempsey and Carpentier in Jersey City on 2 July 1921. The crowd was estimated at 80,000 and for the first time a championship was broadcast by wireless. Professional boxing had now shown it was big business as well as a major sport. The point was rubbed in when in 1923 Dempsey successfully defended the title against Firpo from Argentina and a crowd of 85,000 paid more than a million dollars. All their expectations were fulfilled when Dempsey was knocked down, put Firpo down seven times, and then himself was knocked through the ropes, all in the first round. Dempsey won by a knock-out in the second. He was at his best against big, slow-moving men, and lost the title in 1927 to the intelligent TUNNEY who had spent many years noting the limitations of Dempsey's style. Tunney's skilful victory on points over ten rounds was very different from the bloody fights to the finish at the beginning of the century. But Tunney himself was not typical of the ring. He offended purists of the primitive school by reading books, and retired undefeated champion in 1928 with a rich wife and a fortune all his own.

Before he did so Tunney beat Dempsey in a return bout which produced the controversy of the long count. In the seventh round Dempsey put Tunney down and then stood over the fallen champion as he had done against Firpo. The referee insisted, in keeping with the rules of the Illinois Boxing Commission, that Dempsey should retire to a neutral corner. By the time the brief argument was over and Tunney had risen at the count of nine he had been down for an estimated 14 seconds. What is often forgotten is that Dempsey himself was down for a short count in the ninth round before Tunney won clearly on points. This bout drew a gate of $2,658,660; Tunney's share was $990,000 for 30 minutes of boxing.

After the retirement of Tunney the heavyweight championship declined in interest and standard until LOUIS became the second black world champion, in 1937. But the lighter divisions produced many remarkable champions in the first quarter of the twentieth century as the balance of power moved inexorably away from Britain to the U.S.A.

Before that the private sporting clubs in London provided some good examples of boxing administration. The Pelican Club, opened in Denman Street in 1887, had a remarkable manager in Fleming and when he moved to found the National Sporting Club at Covent Garden with Bettinson the N.S.C. became an internationally famous centre for the sport. The N.S.C. gave its 1,300 members, who traditionally wore dinner jackets and did not applaud during boxing, some remarkable programmes featuring many present and future world and British champions. The Club's greatest days were over by 1928 when its doors were opened to the public for the first time but it was most recently rejuvenated in 1955 at the Café Royal in Regent Street. In 1901 a trial for manslaughter of members of the N.S.C. after the death of a boxer ended with a verdict of not guilty. This case virtually legalized boxing in Britain.

It was in 1909 that the fifth Earl of Lonsdale presented the first of many championship belts to the N.S.C. Altogether the Club presented 22 of these LONSDALE BELTS which, in the years before the formation of the British Boxing Board of Control, greatly strengthened the unofficial control of the N.S.C. over boxing in Britain. A Board of Control with considerable N.S.C. representation was formed in 1919 but it was not until 1929 that a new board gained the independence which it now keeps through financially disinterested stewards. The Board continues to award Lonsdale Belts to boxers who win British titles; if a champion wins three title contests in the same division the belt becomes his.

In the U.S.A. there was no single governing body because of the almost autonomous governments of the various states. But the standard of boxing rose higher as the immigrants arriving from overseas produced hundreds of young men ready to try their luck in the professional ring. The Polish-American middleweight KETCHEL, the West Indian welterweight WALCOTT, and the Jewish-American lightweight LEONARD were all among the greatest of champions in their divisions. Ketchel and Walcott hit so hard they were not afraid to challenge heavyweights early in the twentieth century, and Leonard, at his peak around 1920, boxed with the precision of a chess-player and hit with shattering force. Now that boxing had forsaken such rudimentary stages as inn-yards, barges, and country fields, the fights were invariably held in New York, Boston, New Orleans, and the burgeoning California cities of San Francisco and Los Angeles. In the main the fighters were from the cities too but the black fighters often came from the depressed rural areas of the South.

All the evidence available on film, including the Corbett-Fitzsimmons heavyweight championship of 1897, shows that the early Queensberry world champions lacked versatility in footwork and punching. There was still a link with the old days of prize-fighting on turf in that boxers tended to move straight back and forward as though on railway lines. Fights to a finish, which came to mean over 45 rounds, tended to be conducted at a slow pace which would be intolerable to the crowds following boxing by the late 1920s. When a man like Jeffries could win the world heavyweight title in his 13th official contest it was obvious that the number of truly active professionals was at first comparatively small.

The black American boxers were often busier than the whites because they would take fights anywhere, at any time. The featherweight Dixon, who boxed between 1886 and 1906, and the light-heavyweight LANGFORD whose career lasted from 1902 to 1923, had more than 100 unofficial fights which do not appear on their record. The same is true of the British flyweight WILDE who learned his trade, not in the amateur ring, but in the Welsh boxing booths around 1910.

Despite the undeniable genius of some of the early champions, the highest all-round standard in the professional ring was reached between the late 1920s and mid-1930s. By then no world championship was staged over more than 15 rounds but great speed and fitness were demanded since a top boxer might well have 15 contests over 10 or 15 rounds in a year. GREB, a great American middleweight, had 43 bouts in 1919 but more than half were 'no decision' contests at a time when New York State's Frawley Law, repealed in 1920, stated that all bouts were merely exhibitions with no points decisions given unless a man won by a knockout. Just as impressive were the 27 bouts fought in 1937 by the triple world champion ARMSTRONG who won all but one inside the distance.

When Rickard died in 1929 he was succeeded as the leading organizer of professional boxing in the U.S.A. by Jacobs who had been chief assistant to Rickard. Jacobs promoted at

New York's MADISON SQUARE GARDEN arena from 1937 to 1949 and depended upon the heavyweight champion Louis and, to a lesser extent, Armstrong as his chief draws. Jacobs had official gross receipts of nearly $2 million for the second world championship between Louis and Conn in 1946 — part of the postwar boom in professional boxing.

The exciting appeal of the smoothly moving, hard-hitting Louis, who defended his title a record 25 times between 1937 and 1948, was a great stimulus to boxing. So, towards the end of Louis's career, were the middleweights Zale, Graziano, and 'Sugar Ray' ROBINSON whose return bout in 1951 with the British champion Turpin grossed $767,626 at the New York Polo Grounds. But it was the income from television in the 1960s, and closed-circuit theatre television in the following decade, which kept the sport alive as the number of boxers and spectators declined.

MARCIANO, a hard-punching Italian-American who was world heavyweight champion from 1952 to 1955, gave boxing another much-needed boost as the sport came under increasing criticism because of the danger of brain damage and even death to boxers. Ironically, one of the successors to Marciano was Johansson from Sweden, where professional boxing is now banned. In 1969 the Royal College of Physicians in London reported that studies of 224 retired professional boxers—in the main men who had finished boxing 20 years previously — showed some brain damage in 37 cases. The British Boxing Board of Control pointed out in answer to the report that in recent years there had been a considerable strengthening of medical precautions in British professional boxing.

None the less, the number of active professional boxers in Britain had declined from over 1,000 in the immediate postwar years to about 400 by 1970 with the increase of other, less hazardous occupations. This decline in participation was reflected in the U.S.A. and a larger percentage of leading challengers for world titles came from Latin America and Asia during the 1960s. Bassey from Nigeria was world featherweight champion from 1957 to 1959 and later his countryman, Dick Tiger, won first the middleweight and then the light-heavyweight title. Monzon of Argentina became world professional middleweight champion in 1970. While American domination was threatened at the top it became obvious that the base of the pyramid was also widening in Mexico, Puerto Rico, Japan, and elsewhere. The truly international appeal of the sport was emphasized when, during 1970, a Mexican defended a world title in Rome against a French-Australian with a British referee.

Before the American CLAY, who boxed professionally as Muhammad Ali after he became a Black Muslim, won the world heavyweight title in 1964 from Liston, the world had heard a great deal of him, for he used the press, radio, and television to launch his own publicity campaign. His slogan 'I am the greatest', and his ability to predict the round in which he would win were backed by considerable speed of hand and foot and a superb, though sometimes unorthodox, defence. Clay became world champion when he was just 22, after only 20 professional bouts.

Clay's boxing ability and his personal charisma gave professional boxing the lift it needed. At his best he epitomized the old cliché that boxing is 'the noble art of self-defence'; Clay made boxing look more akin to fencing than to primitive fist-fighting. He continued to be controversial as a symbol of black emancipation in the U.S.A. and refused to serve in the American forces at the time of the Vietnam war. For this he was deprived of his championship in 1967 though three years later, after FRAZIER had won the vacant title, Clay was again granted a licence to box.

Clay's mercurial rise to the top came at a time when the use of communications satellites and, later, closed-circuit theatre television allowed his bouts to be watched live by huge audiences. Closed-circuit television had first made its impact in 1955 when receipts from the Marciano-Moore bout were $1,125,000. Thereafter the most money from closed-circuit came through the following contests:

1962: Patterson v. Liston, $4,500,000
1964: Clay v. Liston, $3,640,000
1961: Patterson v. Johansson, $2,544,000
1960: Patterson v. Johansson, $2,251,161
1958: Robinson v. Basilio, $1,400,000

Thus the golden age of Dempsey was at last surpassed financially as the electronic era of sport made huge rewards possible. When Clay met Frazier, his successor as world champion, in a title fight at Madison Square Garden in March 1971, the 'live' audience was 20,455 with receipts of $1,352,500. But the really big money came from closed-circuit television across the States and television in 35 other countries. This championship, for which Clay and Frazier, the winner on points over 15 rounds, each received $2,500,000, must have grossed more than $20 million.

The athletic, graceful style of Clay did much to remove the shadows of disapproval which had gathered over boxing since the deaths in world championships of the welterweight Paret in 1962 and the featherweight Moore in 1963. But the obvious dangers in professional boxing, which had been underlined as far back as 1741 with the death of Broughton's opponent, Stevenson, continued to arouse strong criticism among doctors and educationalists, if not among the general public. It was obvious that the brutal pastime of nineteenth-century England would have to adopt a more civilized approach if it was to survive through the twentieth century.

Professional boxing has continued to be handicapped by the lack of a single, authoritative governing body. The nearest to an international authority is the World Boxing Council (W.B.C.), started in Mexico City in 1963 and reconstituted in 1969. It includes the Latin American, North American, and Oriental federations, as well as the European Boxing Union and the British Board of Control, and has 27 member countries. The New York State Athletic Commission, though technically separate, has a working agreement with the Council. Its chief rival, the World Boxing Association, stems from the National Boxing Association, founded in 1920, and is basically a grouping of some of the American states. Like the W.B.C. it issues monthly ratings of boxers in all divisions and names its own world champions. Just as in the 1930s and 1940s there were disputes between the National Boxing Association and the New York State Athletic Commission over the world championship, so dissension continues today between the two 'world' bodies: at the end of 1970, to take one example, there were *two* recognized world champions at 4 of the 11 weights, and disagreement over two other championships.

AMATEUR BOXING. Though members of the London gentry sparred with 'Gentleman' Jackson in his Oxford Street rooms in the early nineteenth century, there was no official amateur boxing until a few of the loosely organized amateur clubs already in existence met together in 1866 and decided to hold championships, for trophies presented by the Marquess of Queensberry, in 1867, at lightweight, middleweight, and heavyweight. The last Queensberry amateur championships were held in 1885, five years after the formation of the AMATEUR BOXING ASSOCIATION (A.B.A.). This new body, which followed a meeting of representatives of several London clubs, went much further in its rules than the Queensberry regulations in defining the 'target', 'attack', and 'defence'. But the greatest difference was that the A.B.A. did not frown upon infighting, or close-quarter attacks, whereas in the Queensberry championships it was not uncommon for the referee to caution a boxer with the words: 'Box. Don't fight.' Ironically the first president of the A.B.A. was Anderson

who had been disqualified 'for fighting' when competing in the Queensberry middleweight championship. But Douglas, whose son became Olympic champion in 1908, was three times a Queensberry champion and for 18 years also the president of the A.B.A. The first A.B.A. championships were held under the new rules on 18 April 1881 at St. James's Hall, Piccadilly. They consisted of four weights, feather (9 st.), light (10 st.), middle (11 st. 4 lb.), and heavy (any weight).

The A.B.A. were the forefathers of international amateur boxing. In 1902 their championships were entered by Americans, and by 1906 the A.B.A. had made firm contact with France, Australia, and South Africa. Boxing was first introduced into the Olympic programme in 1904, and in the Games of 1908, held in London, all five Olympic titles were won by members of the A.B.A. team. Among the gold medallists was J. W. H. T. Douglas, later to distinguish himself for England on the CRICKET field. Apart from its exclusion from the Games at Stockholm in 1912, and a subsequent break because of war, boxing has played an important part in the Olympic programme ever since. In 1920 in Antwerp MALLIN won the Olympic middleweight title for Britain and retained it four years later in Paris, after which he retired. But his 1924 triumph was attended by one of the more famous controversies in the sport, when his opponent in the semi-final was disqualified for biting. Harry Mallin never lost an amateur bout, and it is remarkable that his brother Fred later won five successive A.B.A. middleweight championships.

Prior to 1939 the world body controlling amateur boxing was the Fédération Française de Boxe, but this organization ceased to exist during the Second World War. The present Amateur International Boxing Association was formed at a conference held in London in 1946, called by the Amateur Boxing Association of England and the Fédération Française de Boxe, which was attended by 24 national governing bodies from all five continents. The Association is now the world body controlling amateur boxing for the Olympic Games, continental, regional, and inter-nation championships and tournaments in every part of the world. The boxing competition of the 1948 Olympic Games in London was the first to be conducted under A.I.B.A. rules, as have been all subsequent Olympic Games and international tournaments. The growth and development of world amateur boxing can be gauged from the entry figures in the Olympic boxing competitions. In 1948, 206 boxers took part from 39 countries. In Mexico in 1968, when the light-flyweight division was added to the programme of ten weights, 337 boxers took part from 69 countries. That record was beaten in Munich in 1972 with 357 entries. The A.I.B.A. has continued over the years to press for a higher standard of judging as well as medical control.

Olympic champions who have gone on to win world professional titles include the American flyweights Genaro (1920) and La Barba (1924), the Argentine flyweight Perez (1948), and the American heavyweight Frazier (1964). PATTERSON was Olympic middleweight champion for the U.S.A. in 1952 and professional world heavyweight champion by 1956, and Clay won the Olympic light-heavyweight title in 1960 before he became professional heavyweight champion. PAPP of Hungary was Olympic middleweight gold-medallist in 1948 and light-middleweight champion in 1952 and 1956 before turning professional and winning the European middleweight championship in 1962.

The European amateur championships were started in Paris in 1924. From about 1953 they became dominated by the outstandingly fit boxers from Poland and the Soviet Union who, though they might not have succeeded as professionals, were able to box the amateur three three-minute rounds at great speed. In 1961 the Russians won five European amateur titles; in 1963 seven; and in 1965 they took eight out of the ten weights. They tended to produce aggressive two-handed fighters but one of the most skilful on the Continent was their light-middleweight Lagutin. The Poles won 18 European and 5 Olympic titles between 1953 and 1969 but Italy won 3 Olympic gold medals in Rome in 1960, including the welterweight title through Benvenuti who was twice champion of Europe and later professional middleweight champion of the world. But the majority of boxers taking part in the Olympics and the European amateur championships never turn professional, particularly since no countries in the Communist bloc practise professional sport.

The Communist countries maintain a very high standard of technical skills, and for the next few years will probably stave off the challenge of Africa, now emerging as a major force in amateur boxing. In Nigeria, Kenya, Ghana, and Zambia, boxing is now a thriving sport. In changing social patterns, the black Africans, with their innate strength and ability, will challenge strongly in future Olympic boxing competitions. (But in the 1972 Munich Olympics it was Cuba which won three gold medals, one more than the Soviet Union.) African amateur boxers first made their impact in the British COMMONWEALTH GAMES, which they gradually began to dominate. At Edinburgh in 1970 they won 8 out of 11 titles.

D. Batchelor, *The Big Fight* (1956); H. Carpenter, *Masters of Boxing* (1964); N. Fleischer, *Ring Record Book* (1971); D. James, *Better Boxing* (1970); P. Wilson, *More Ringside Seats* (1959).

GOVERNING BODY (PROFESSIONAL): World Boxing Council, 106 Quezon Boulevard, Quezon City, Philippines; (AMATEUR): International Amateur Boxing Association, 8 New Square, Lincoln's Inn, London W.C.2.

BOXING, Chinese, correctly called Chinese martial art, has been described by people who do not understand it as 'shadow-boxing'. It is far from that. Chinese boxing, with its various forms and styles minutely copied from the movements of animals, was first created and used for self-defence and, in the days of the divided kingdoms, taught to and used by soldiers. However, as dynasties changed, Chinese philosophers and boxing masters began a search for a means of using this martial exercise to make man live longer. Thus was born the modern form of the soft school of martial art — *Tai Chi, Paat Kwa*, and *Luk Hop Paat Faat*. Today, the Chinese and a small number of westerners are taking this art as a sport, and as a health exercise.

Although Chinese boxing is used now solely for self-defence and body-building, in the past warriors and warrior-emperors made their mark in Chinese history because of their prowess in a particular fighting style. Ngok Fei, who lived a century before the start of the Sung Dynasty (A.D. 1127-1280), was credited with a fighting style, *ying yi*, and the use of the lance. Another style, *hau kuen* ('monkey fist'), is linked with a legend dating back to the Tang Dynasty (A.D. 618-907) in which the goddess of mercy ordered the monkey god to escort a Buddhist monk, Tong Sam Chong, to Tibet to collect Buddha's scriptures. The warrior-emperor, Kuen Lung Wong, was the third in the Ching Dynasty (1644-1912). A wanderer righting wrongs, he was said to have been trained by the masters at Siu Lam Chi. He burned down a temple while seeking the rebels who were plotting to overthrow the Ching empire in an attempt to re-establish the Ming Dynasty (A.D. 1368-1644).

Chinese boxing is divided into two schools: the soft and the hard. *Siu Lam Pai* embraces all the present hard forms, one of which, *Hung Kuen* ('Red Fist'), was adapted by the Japanese and became the popular KARATE. The soft school of Chinese boxing was formulated by a scholar called Chan Tuan who lived just before Chiu Hon Yang became the first emperor in the Sung Dynasty (960-1127). The first soft style was *Luk Hop Paat Faat*, from which other soft styles possibly derived. These include *Tai Chi*, created by a Taoist monk, Cheung Sam Fung, in the Yuan Dynasty.

Today, Chinese boxing is still practised widely in Asia and in all Chinese communities in western countries. The centres are in Hong Kong, Taiwan, China, and south-east Asia. Chinese boxing tournaments are held once every two years. The 1967 event was held in Taiwan, and the venue was Singapore in 1969 and 1971.

BOXING, Thai, is a sporting form of self-defence indigenous to Thailand. Blows with the feet, knees, and elbows are permitted as well as those with the gloved fist used in BOX-ING under QUEENSBERRY RULES. It is at once a science and an art, and is also of deeply traditional significance to the Thai people, all the males of whom are expected to master at least its fundamentals.

Combatants are dressed as normal boxers are, except that the feet are bare and bandaged from the ankle to the instep. Blows may be aimed at any part of the opponent's body above the abdomen, a high kick to the head, carried out with remarkable speed and dexterity, being one of the most common.

An essential skill of the sport is the ability to land a combination of blows in different places: while in-fighting, for instance, a boxer may be upper-cutting with his fists and at the same time deliver a damaging blow to the ribs with his knee. Clinches are frequent, but the throwing of an opponent, while not an offence, is discouraged and may lead to a loss of points. Butting, eye-gouging, and smothering are not permitted. The fight is controlled by a referee in the ring and two judges outside it, who award a maximum of five points per round. Matches are made within weight classes similar to those of the Queensberry Rules of boxing.

The incidental trappings to a Thai boxing bout are as vital as the fight itself. Each boxer enters the ring beforehand for a ritual which has its roots deep in the history of his country. It opens with a form of prayer to the sacred objects held in veneration by all the Thai, and a ceremonial salute to the boxer's instructor and trainers, followed by homage to the king. Then comes a demonstration of shadow-boxing, the form of which denotes the area from which the boxer comes. It is intended both to loosen the muscles and to strike fear into the heart of the opponent.

Meanwhile the accompanying music has started; this plays throughout the fight as well as the preliminaries. It is provided by a ring-side orchestra of pipe, two long drums, and cymbals. The musicians, under the leadership of the piper, change their tune spontaneously to suit the mood of the fight and sometimes raise the tempo to bring life to a dull bout.

The enthusiasm of the crowd is a major part of the entertainment, which is by far the most popular sport in Thailand. There are two main stadia in Bangkok, each staging a programme twice a week. Queensberry and Thai boxing are often seen in the same evening, and many experts in the native sport become excellent international boxers in the lighter weights.

BOYCOTT, GEOFFREY (1940-   ), cricketer for England and Yorkshire. One of the most dedicated batsmen in CRICKET history, he was dropped from the England side in 1967 after making a tedious 246 not out against India — his highest Test score. His 146 in the 1965 GILLETTE CUP final was exhilarating, and in the 1970s bowlers began to find greater difficulty in containing him. An opening batsman who wears contact lenses, he provided England with a great solidity. He was appointed captain of Yorkshire in 1971, when he became the first Englishman to average 100 in a first-class season at bat.

BOYD, MARGARET, O.B.E. (1913-   ), LACROSSE player for Bedford College of Physical Education, Boxmoor Ladies, and England from 1934 to 1951. A strong defence wing, she captained the English team from 1937 to 1951 and the first official English team to the U.S.A. in 1949. She was responsible for keeping the game alive in England during the Second World War and for establishing the national schools' tournaments which are held annually at the end of the season. She is the author of *Lacrosse — Playing and Coaching* and was the organizer and manager of the combined United States and British team which made the first tour to Australia, New Zealand, and Tokyo in 1969. In 1973 she was elected the first president of the International Federation of Women's Lacrosse Associations.

BOYD-ROCHFORT, Capt. Sir CECIL (b. 1887), a leading English race-horse trainer at Freemason Lodge, Newmarket, until he retired in 1968. He headed the list of winning trainers five times, and trained AUREOLE for Queen ELIZABETH II, MELD for Lady WERNHER, and ALCIDE and Parthia for Sir Humphrey de Trafford.

BOZSIK, JOSEF (1925-   ), Association footballer for Honved F.C. and Hungary, who played at right half in the Hungarian team of the early 1950s that inflicted the first home defeat on England at WEMBLEY in 1953 by 6-3, and were unluckily beaten in the final of the 1954 world championship. A member of parliament in Hungary, he stayed with the national team after the 1956 revolution and played in the 1958 world championship.

BRABHAM, JACK (1926-   ), the first of a long line of successful MOTOR RACING drivers from the antipodes to break into European racing. Brabham drove a COOPER-Bristol in Australian events during 1953-4. In his first European season in 1955 he drove a Cooper rear-engined sports car with a Bristol engine; he then took this back home and won the 1955 Australian Grand Prix. Brabham returned to Europe in 1956 to drive works Cooper sports cars and, when they became available, Formula Two cars. For his Continental Grand Prix début at Monaco in 1957, he drove a 1,960 cc. Cooper to take sixth place. At the wheel of a 2·5-litre Cooper-Climax, he won the drivers' world championship in 1959 and 1960. Brabham remained with the Cooper team in 1961 but in the early part of the season was forced to drive the uncompetitive 4-cylinder cars. During 1961 he drove a special 2·7-litre Cooper-Climax into ninth place at INDIANAPOLIS, U.S.A.

At the end of that year he left the Cooper team, and, until his own Grand Prix car was ready, he drove a LOTUS 24-Climax. At the 1962 German Grand Prix his car made its début, and his successes since then were at the wheel of his own cars. He was world champion again in 1966 but retired in 1970.

BRABOURNE STADIUM, Bombay, CRICKET ground in India. Opened in 1937-8, it is administered by the private Cricket Club of India. It is essentially a modern ground, with a residential club in the large pavilion which provides facilities for swimming, tennis, squash, billiards, and dancing. The ground holds 50,000 spectators, most of them seated and under cover. The cricket pitch lacks bounce, and a large proportion of matches there —particularly Test matches—have been drawn.

BRADFORD 50 KM., an English event in road RACE WALKING. It has been held every year since 1903 and has the distinction of being the oldest continuous annual event in race walking. The course has varied over the years; originally being from Bradford to York, 39¼ miles (63 km.), since 1946 it has been over the international distance of 50 km. (31¼ miles). The walk is organized by the Bradford and District Walking Association.

Winners include Olympic 50 km. champions, GREEN (1930, 1932, and 1933), and WHITLOCK (1933, 1936-8, 1940, 1952) while A. Johnson had eight consecutive victories (1954-61). The course is a gruelling one over the Yorkshire moors including many difficult climbs and descents. The race starts at 9.30 a.m. every Whit Monday.

BRADLEY, Col. EDWARD RILEY (1859-1946), an American who in 1906 founded the renowned Idle Hour Stock Farm and Racing Stable near Lexington, Kentucky. In 1930 he bought, for 1,250 guineas, LA TROIENNE, destined to become the most successful brood mare in the history of bloodstock-breeding in the U.S.A. Bradley also bred BLUE LARKSPUR and four winners of the KENTUCKY DERBY.

BRADLEY, WILLIAM WARREN (1943-   ), American BASKETBALL player. Bradley was recognized as one of the finest players in collegiate history during his time at Princeton University. After appearing as a member of the gold medal-winning team at the 1964 OLYMPIC GAMES in Tokyo, he was offered a lucrative professional scholarship, but he refused it, preferring to accept a Rhodes scholarship to Oxford University. During his two years at Oxford, Bradley played for Simmenthal (Milan) and helped them to win the EUROPEAN CUP FOR CHAMPION CLUBS in 1966. On his return to the U.S.A., Bradley signed a four-year contract with the NEW YORK KNICK-ERBOCKERS for a reputed $500,000, and helped New York win the NATIONAL BASKETBALL ASSOCIATION championship in 1970.

BRADMAN, Sir DONALD GEORGE (1908-   ), cricketer for Australia, New South Wales, and South Australia. His 117 centuries in 338 first-class innings make him statistically the most successful batsman in CRICKET history. His career, extending from 1927 to 1949, was studded with batting records achieved by tireless, relentless effort, keen eyesight, extraordinary co-ordination, and superlative footwork. His 452 not out stood as the highest first-class innings for 29 years, and his aggregate of 974 runs in the 1930 Test series (his first in England) remains a record, as do his 29 Test centuries (two over 300) and over-all average of 99·94 (6,996 runs). His influence upon attendances was as immense as his impact upon opposing bowlers: the 'body-line' attack was contrived primarily against him. As captain of Australia he never lost a rubber, and after his retirement he became an active administrator. He was the first Australian cricketer to receive a knighthood (in 1949).

BRAEMAR GATHERING, British professional ATHLETICS meeting held in the highlands of Aberdeenshire, Scotland, not far from the royal residence of Balmoral Castle. The frequent presence of royalty at these games, from Queen Victoria onwards, ensured that their prestige and popularity remained high when other Scottish highland meetings lost some of their appeal.

BRAGINA, LYUDMILA (1943-   ), middle-distance runner for the U.S.S.R. Few athletes have been able to win an Olympic gold medal coupled with a world record. Bragina accomplished the threefold feat of breaking the world record in heat, semi-final, and final of the Olympic 1,500 metres, a distance newly introduced to the programme at Munich in 1972. Her time in the final was 4 min. 1·4 sec. The Russian prodigy came to prominence only two months before the Games when she improved the world 1,500 metres record for the first time with 4 min. 6·9 sec. Then just three weeks later she sliced over 16 sec. from the world 3,000 metres record with a time of 8 min. 52·0 sec.

BRAID, JAMES (1870-1950), Scottish professional golfer. The first man to win the Open championship five times, he completed, with VARDON and TAYLOR, the so-called 'Great Triumvirate' of GOLF who dominated the professional game in Britain from 1894 until the outbreak of the Great War in 1914. A founder member of the Professional Golfers Association, whose match-play championship he won four times, his name will always be associated with Walton Heath, the Surrey Club he served for 45 years, helping to make it one of Britain's finest inland courses.

BRAITHWAITE, ROBERT (1925-   ), clay pigeon shooter for Great Britain. He won Britain's first Olympic gold medal when, at Mexico City in 1968, he scored 198 — only two short of maximum — equalling the Olympic record set at the previous Games by MATTARELLI. Braithwaite's 198 included an unprecedented run of 189 successive hits.

BRANDS HATCH, motor circuit near Farningham in Kent, opened for Formula Three racing in 1949, and now one of the best-known and most frequently used British circuits, both for MOTOR RACING and test driving. It has permanent amenities similar to the pre-war BROOKLANDS. The course is short and spectacular. Corners follow one another in rapid succession and the course is undulating, with very little passing room except along the Bottom straight, with Paddock Hill bend a hazardous corner. The original distance was 1 mile (1·6 km.), but this was extended to 1·24 miles — 1·9 km. (the present club circuit) — in 1954. The full Grand Prix circuit with a length of 2·65 miles (4·2 km.) was opened in 1960. Brands Hatch was the venue of the British Grand Prix in 1964, 1966, 1968, 1970, 1972, and 1974.

BRÄNNBOLL, see PESÄPALLO.

BRANTÔME (1931), champion French racehorse who won the PRIX DE L'ARC DE TRIOMPHE, French St. Leger, French Two Thousand Guineas, Prix Lupin, and PRIX DU CADRAN. He was bred and owned by Baron E. DE ROTHSCHILD, trained by Robert, and ridden by Bouillon. Brantôme won 12 out of 14 races and prize money totalling 2,048,302 francs.

BRASHER, CHRISTOPHER (1928-   ), mountaineer and English Olympic athlete associated with BANNISTER in the first 4-minute mile at Oxford in 1954. He won the gold medal in the 3000 metres STEEPLECHASE at the Melbourne OLYMPIC GAMES (1956) and immediately retired from track ATHLETICS. He was subsequently attracted to ORIENTEERING and with DISLEY, a fellow Olympic steeplechaser and mountaineer, pioneered the sport in Britain; he was the first chairman of the British Orienteering Federation (1967).

BREMNER, WILLIAM (1942-   ), Association footballer for LEEDS UNITED and Scotland, both of which he captained. He made his Football League début for Leeds in January 1960 against CHELSEA. He made his first appearance for Scotland in a full international in May 1965 against Spain, captained Scotland for the first time in Copenhagen against Denmark in October 1968 and was to lead them in the finals of the 1974 World Cup. He won the F.A. Cup-Winners and runners-up medals, and Football League championship and Second Division championship medals, in addition to Fairs Cup-winners medals — all with Leeds United.

BRENTER, ENGELBERT (1897-   ), ERICH (1940-   ), and WILLI (1942-   ). Engelbert Brenter, Austrian skier and skibob pioneer, made the first ski with metal sides, and was the inventor of *patinettes*, the short foot-skis for skibobbers. His elder son, Erich, was the winner of the first skibob competition held in Obertauern, Austria, in 1950, and from 1958, when international SKIBOBBING contests began, he shared alternately with his brother Willi, for nearly a decade, the first places in these events. He was European champion in 1964. Willi Brenter was world champion in 1967, European champion in

1963, 1965, and 1966, and Austrian champion in 1964-5. In 1966 he was the fastest skibobber in the world, creating a record of 102 m.p.h. (164 km./h.) at Cervinia, Italy. He built the first modern skibob in the family factory in 1960.

BRIDGE, Mrs. KATHLEEN (*née* Lidderdale) (1898-1973), HOCKEY player who represented England as a forward and full-back. She was first selected at the age of 15, to become the youngest player ever to represent England at women's hockey. A member of the England team 1913-14 and 1920-5 and captain of England in 1923, she toured the U.S.A. with the England touring team in 1921.

BRIGADIER GERARD (1968), race-horse trained by Hern, ridden by Mercer, and owned and trained by HISLOP. One of the outstanding middle-distance performers of all time, he was beaten only once in 18 races. His only defeat was inflicted by Roberto, a DERBY winner, in record time at York, and his victories included the TWO THOUSAND GUINEAS in 1971. He retired to stud at the end of his four-year-old career.

BRIGGS, BARRY (1935-   ), motorcycle speedway rider from New Zealand. He first rode in the world championship in 1954, since when he has had a consistent and successful record on the Czechoslovakian Jawa machines.

BRIGGS, JOHN (1862-1902), cricketer for England and Lancashire. Originally an all-rounder, he served England best as a slow left-arm bowler from 1884 to 1899, toured Australia six times and South Africa once. His best Test performance was 15 wickets for 28 against South Africa, and he did the hat-trick at SYDNEY in 1892.

BRISTOL R.F.C., leading RUGBY UNION football club in the West Country, founded 1888. Noted for its attacking Rugby in the years after the Second World War, it scored 834 points in the 1959-60 season. Bristol internationals include Tucker, Corbett, Hosen, and Pullin.

HOME GROUND: Memorial Ground, Bristol.
COLOURS: Blue and white hooped jerseys and white shorts.

BRITANNIA CUP, see HENLEY ROYAL REGATTA.

BRITISH COLUMBIA LIONS, Canadian professional FOOTBALL team, joined the Canadian Football League in 1954, won the Western Conference League title in 1963 and 1964, when they won only the Grey Cup (see FOOTBALL, CANADIAN). The quarterback Kapp led them to the titles and later returned to the U.S. to lead the MINNESOTA VIKINGS to a National Football Conference title in 1969.
COLOURS: Orange and black.

BRITISH EMPIRE AND COMMON-WEALTH GAMES, see COMMONWEALTH GAMES.

BRITISH LIONS, see LIONS.

BRITTON, JACK (1885-1962), American boxer who won the world welterweight title in 1915, 1916, and again in 1919, holding it until 1922. He engaged in a series of 20 bouts, covering 222 rounds, with Britain's LEWIS. Britton started his professional career in 1904 and ended with two victories in 1930. A boxer rather than a puncher, he lost only 25 out of 320 contests and was beaten only once (in 1905) inside the distance.

BRM, racing car built by Mays, of pre-war ERA fame, who obtained support from British industry and individuals to manufacture a competitor for Grands Prix. The enterprise, called British Racing Motors, made its first appearance at SILVERSTONE in 1950. Unfortunately, by the time the supercharged V-16 engine had overcome its many teething troubles, the Formula had changed and the whole enterprise, in financial difficulties, was sold to Sir Alfred Owen. The new 2·5-litre cars proved excellent in the opening stages of events, but then all too frequently failed mechanically. In 1962, however, BRM won the world championship, due largely to GRAHAM HILL's driving as well as to the improved speed and reliability of the cars themselves. BRM was second in the 1963, 1964, and 1965 world championships, and showed considerably improved form, after many setbacks, at the opening of the 1974 season. BRM engines have been used to power other cars, notably the COOPER.

BROAD-HALFPENNY DOWN, Hambledon, a CRICKET ground in Hampshire, retains a place of permanent fame as the ground on which the celebrated HAMBLEDON cricketers perfected their skills in the eighteenth century. The ground itself is about two miles to the north of the village of Hambledon, and cricket was certainly played on it as early as 1756, if not before. Many of the great matches by Hambledon against England, Kent, and Surrey were played there, the ground being 'administered' by Richard Nyren, father of JOHN NYREN. Close to the ground there stood — and still stands — the Bat and Ball inn, of which Richard Nyren was landlord. In about 1782 the Duke of Dorset and others complained of the bleakness of Broad-Halfpenny Down, and a move was thereupon made to WINDMILL DOWN. The turf from Broad-Halfpenny was taken to the new venue.

BROAD JUMP, see LONG JUMP.

BROEKHUYSEN, NICO, see KORFBALL.

BROMFIELD, PERCIVAL (1886-1947), English TABLE TENNIS champion in 1904 (the last season before the 18-year period during which the game lapsed) and again in 1924. One of the first specialists in exploiting the pimple rubber-covered racket and first perfecter of the backhand flick, a fast attacking stroke executed with the wrist and taking the opponent far to left or right, he contributed much to reviving the game on the right lines. Bromfield captained the first English SWAYTHLING CUP team in 1926. His daughter, Valerie (1912-   ) won the English Open women's singles title in 1931.

BROOK, ERIC F. (1908-65), Association footballer for Barnsley, MANCHESTER CITY, and England for whom he made 18 appearances in full international matches between 1929 and 1937. Nominally an outside left, 'Wandering Eric' had a liking for taking up positions towards the centre of the forward line from where more goals were possible with his exceptionally powerful shooting. He scored ten goals for England, including two in the 3-2 victory against Italy at Highbury in November 1934. He was a member of the Manchester City team that lost to EVERTON in the 1933 F.A. Cup final but won a year later against PORTSMOUTH.

BROOKES, Sir NORMAN EVERARD (1877-1968), Australia's first notable LAWN TENNIS player and the first overseas competitor to win the men's singles title at WIMBLEDON. Brookes was an astute tactician and a clever left-handed volleyer, and with WILDING, a New Zealander, he disturbed the early supremacy of the British and the Americans by capturing the Davis Cup (see LAWN TENNIS) for Australasia in 1907 and holding it until 1912. The Australasian pair regained the Cup in 1914, and in 1919 Brookes, aided by PATTERSON, led the team which retained it when the competition was resumed. His last Davis Cup appearance was in the 1920 challenge round. Altogether, he played in 39 rubbers, 22 of which were in challenge rounds.

He came to England in 1905 and surprised the lawn tennis world by reaching the challenge round at Wimbledon where H. L. DOHERTY beat him 8-6, 6-2, 6-4. In 1907 Brookes won the title, beating A. W. GORE 6-4, 6-2, 6-2. In 1911 he won the Australian title but did not return to Wimbledon until 1914 when he defeated Froitzheim (Germany) in the all-comers' final and Wilding in the challenge round. When the war ended, Brookes was 42 and Patterson, another player from Melbourne, who was 18 years his junior, took his title. In 1924, in his forty-seventh year, he reached the last 16 at Wimbledon by beating Hunter 3-6, 6-3, 6-4, 5-7, 6-3.

BROOKLANDS RACE TRACK or motor course, was built near Weybridge, Surrey, in 1906-7 and opened in the summer of the latter year. The track was oval-shaped, its long turns steeply banked, one of these bankings being taken over the River Wey on a ferro-concrete bridge of ingenious construction. The track cost £150,000 in terms of 1907 currency. It was laid out on horse-race lines because being the world's first special motor course, there was no previous experience to rely on. It proved invaluable to British motor manufacturers and inventors who were hampered when testing their products and ideas by the prevailing 20 m.p.h. speed limit on British roads. MOTOR RACING at Brooklands was conducted on very sound, gentlemanly lines, with no competitions on Sundays.

The track was closed during the First World War but otherwise racing took place there from 1907 to 1939, the course being converted for aeroplane manufacture during the Second World War and never subsequently repaired.

Various circuits were contrived within the 2¾ miles (4·4 km.) of the main track, which enabled imitation road races to be run. The first Royal Automobile Club British Grand Prix was held at Brooklands in 1926. The outer circuit, rendered very fast by the banked turns designed to allow 'hands-off' steering at up to 120 m.p.h. (193 km./h.), encouraged the construction of special track cars and one of these, Cobb's 24-litre aero-engined Napier Railton, set the eventual lap record of 143·44 m.p.h. (230·8 km./h.) and was officially timed over the kilometre at 151·97 m.p.h. (244·5 km./h.).

Racing at Brooklands was administered officially by the Brooklands Automobile Racing Club but many other clubs organized events, ranging from driving tests and high-speed trials to important long-distance races for sports cars or pure racing cars. The latter

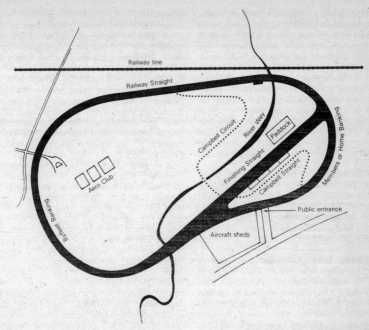

BROOKLANDS RACE TRACK
The long turns of the oval-shaped track in use from 1907 to 1939 were steeply banked.

included the Junior Car Club's 'Double Twelve' over a course with corners made from sandbank markers, a race of 24 hours' duration with the competing cars locked away during the night, and the British Racing Drivers Club's 500-mile outer-circuit race for cars of all types, which up to 1936 was the fastest long-distance race in the world.

By an individual system of handicapping it was possible for cars of all types and ages to race effectively in the shorter Brooklands races. This system was instituted by Ebblewhite, the celebrated Brooklands handicapper and starter of races for most of the track's life.

Because local residents complained about the noise of cars and motor cycles on the track, special silencers became compulsory from 1924 onwards and night running was prohibited, hence the 'Double Twelve' race. Apart from races, all manner of records, from half-mile sprints to 'Double Twelve' runs were established and broken at the famous Weybridge track in the 1920s and 1930s.

BROOKLYN DODGERS, American professional BASEBALL team, received its name from fans who 'dodged' tram traffic on the way to the ball park. A member of the NATIONAL LEAGUE in 1890, the Dodgers won 12 league titles up until 1957 but only triumphed in the WORLD SERIES in 1955. In the 1920s, under the benevolent control of its manager Robinson, the team's eccentric behaviour became famous. Its best players were the outfielders Wheat and Herman, perpetrator of some of the most bizarre happenings; Grimes and Vance led its pitchers. McPhail came from Cincinnati as general manager in the late 1930s and revived Dodger fortunes. In 1941 Brooklyn won the National League pennant, and, with the arrival of RICKEY as general manager in 1943, the Dodgers soon became a baseball power. In 1945 Rickey changed baseball history by signing the Negro JACKIE ROBINSON, who joined the Dodgers in 1947, and the success of the team in the decade that followed — including six league titles — resulted partly from Negro stars like Robinson, the catcher CAMPANELLA, the pitcher Newcombe, as well as other players like the first baseman Hodges, the outfielder Snider, and the shortstop Reese. The controversial Durocher served as manager from 1939 to 1948, followed by Shotton and Dressen, and since 1954 Alston.

Brooklyn had an intense community identity, revealed in baseball's most fervid, rabid fans and its most bitter sports rivalry, with its intra-city foes, the NEW YORK GIANTS. The changing nature of the community surrounding the Brooklyn ball park led the Brooklyn owner O'Malley to demand new facilities from the New York City government. When they were not forthcoming, and despite the fact that the Dodgers were the only league team to show a profit over the previous five years, O'Malley moved the team to Los Angeles in 1958, where they retained the Dodger name. (See LOS ANGELES DODGERS.)

BROOMBALL, a rather exclusive game played in the U.S.S.R. which is literally HOCKEY on ice. Russian-type brooms, about 18 in. (45·7 cm.) are used instead of sticks. Skates are not permitted. A similar game 'hockey with a ball' is also played on ice in the U.S.S.R., but with hockey sticks.

BROOME, DAVID (1940-   ), British show jumping (see EQUESTRIAN EVENTS) rider. He achieved most of his successes with horses that were going badly before he teamed up with them. This is especially true of the ex-troop-horse Wildfire, with whom he first jumped on a British international team (at Rotterdam in 1959) and Sunsalve, his mount for the 1960 OLYMPIC GAMES in Rome, where he won the individual bronze medal. The following year, again on Sunsalve, he won the men's European championship. In 1966, he established his highly successful partnership with Mister Softee, on whom he won two more European championships (1967 and 1969), as well as his second individual bronze medal, at the 1968 Olympic Games in Mexico. In 1970, riding Beethoven at La Baule, he became the first British rider to win the men's world championship title. Riding Manhattan, he was a member of the British team which finished fourth in the 1972 Olympic Games in Munich.

BROOMFIELD, N. H. R. A. (1937-   ), British SQUASH RACKETS player, the youngest player to win the amateur championship (at the age of 20). He repeated his win in the following year against the same player, the Egyptian AMIN. His fine physique helped him to many successes in junior squash, culminating in winning the Drysdale Cup at the age of 15, a record at that time. He won the Drysdale Cup on two other occasions, being the only player to win this, the junior championship, three times. He became South African champion in 1958 and represented Great Britain in Australia in 1959 and England against South Africa in 1967.

BROUGH, A. LOUISE (1923-   ), American LAWN TENNIS player, one of the most effective exponents of the service and volley game. She won the U.S. singles title in 1947, defeating her doubles partner, OSBORNE, in the final, only to lose it to her in the following year. In 1948 and 1950 Brough won all three titles at WIMBLEDON and in 1949 she failed to repeat her success only when she and Bromwich were beaten in the mixed doubles final by Sturgess and Summers. After her singles reign had been interrupted by Hart and CONNOLLY, she regained the title by beating Fleitz in 1955.

Altogether Brough won the women's doubles at Wimbledon five times and reached the final on three other occasions. In the U.S. doubles she and Osborne were undefeated from 1942 to 1950 and again from 1955 to 1957. Brough won the mixed doubles four times in both championships, the Australian singles and doubles in 1950, and the French doubles in 1946, 1947, and 1949. She won all 22 of her WIGHTMAN CUP rubbers.

BROUGH, JAMES (1904-   ), a RUGBY UNION full-back who played for England in 1924 while with Silloth, Cumberland, and turned professional for LEEDS RUGBY LEAGUE CLUB in 1925. He was a member of the 1928 and 1936 British RUGBY LEAGUE teams in Australia, as captain on the second occasion.

BROUGHTON, JACK (1704-89), British boxer who held the English prize ring championship from 1734 to 1750. He is an important figure in the development of BOXING because he drew up the first set of rules governing contests on a stage surrounded by ropes in 1743 and introduced the use of gloves, then known as 'mufflers', for sparring. A hard hitter, Broughton prepared his rules after an opponent had died from the effects of his blows. He is known as 'the Father of Boxing'.

BROWN, JAMES (1936-   ), American college and professional FOOTBALL player. As a fullback, he was perhaps the greatest ball-carrier in the history of professional football. He was prominent as a football and LACROSSE player at Syracuse University (1954-6) and then played professional football with the CLEVELAND BROWNS, starting in 1957. He led the NATIONAL FOOTBALL LEAGUE 8 times in rushing (running yardage), and in his playing lifetime carried the ball 2,359 times, for 12,312 yards. He held the single-season record of 1,863 yards rushing and left football after the 1965 season for a career in films and politics.

BROWN, PAUL E. (1908-   ), American college and professional FOOTBALL coach who played college football at Miami (Ohio) University. After a successful high school coaching career, he led OHIO STATE university to a national championship in 1942. During the Second World War he coached the Great Lakes Naval Training Station team. His CLEVELAND BROWNS were champions of the All-America Conference in all four years of its existence (1946-9). In the NATIONAL FOOTBALL LEAGUE, Cleveland won championships in 1950, 1954, and 1955. Brown stressed simple, fundamental football, and criticism about his 'unimaginative' style resulted in his retirement at the end of the 1962 season. In 1968 he joined a group which purchased an AMERICAN FOOTBALL LEAGUE franchise for the Cincinnati Bengals, and in 1970, after the consolidation of the N.F.L. and A.F.L. teams, Cincinnati won the Central Division title in the American Football Conference.

BROWN JACK (1924), a remarkable gelding, one of the most popular race-horses of this century, and the favourite mount of DONOGHUE. He won the longest race in the English calendar, the Queen Alexandra Stakes at ASCOT (2 miles, 6 fur., 34 yds. — 4,430 m.) six years in succession from 1929 to 1934, in addition to the EBOR HANDICAP, Ascot Stakes, Chester, Goodwood, and Doncaster Cups, and other races including the CHAMPION HURDLE CHALLENGE CUP at Cheltenham, and over £20,000 in stakes.

BROWNE, WILLIAM FRASER (1903-31), RUGBY UNION back-row forward for HARLE-QUINS, Army, United Services and Ireland. Although he won only 12 caps, during the 1920s, he is remembered as the first man to discipline the Irish pack so that its efforts lasted the full 80 minutes of the game.

BROWNLOW, CHARLES (1882-1924), an early secretary of the Australian Rules Football Club of Geelong, Victoria. He was also a vice-president of the VICTORIAN FOOTBALL LEAGUE, and the CHARLES BROWNLOW MEDAL was named in his honour.

BRUCE, Hon. C. N., see ABERDARE, 3rd Lord.

BRUGNON, JACQUES (Toto) (1895-   ), French LAWN TENNIS player, the doubles specialist of the 'Four Musketeers' (the other three were BOROTRA, COCHET, and LACOSTE), who won the Davis Cup (see LAWN TENNIS) for France in 1927 and held it until 1932. He lost only 9 of the 32 doubles rubbers which he played for France between 1921 and 1934, partnering either Lacoste, Borotra, or Cochet, and in nine years he reached the WIMBLEDON final seven times, winning twice with Cochet and twice with Borotra. He gained the French title twice with Cochet and three times with Borotra, and in 1928 he and Borotra won the Australian championship. Their last important tournament appearance was in the French championships of 1939, when Brugnon was 44 and Borotra 40. They had a match point in the final against the Americans, Harris and McNeill, before losing 10-8 in the final set.

BRULEUR (1910) was perhaps the best stallion ever to stand in France, where he handed down the most important French sire line descending from The FLYING DUTCHMAN. The most notable son of Bruleur was KSAR.

BRUMEL, VALERI NIKOLAYEVICH (1942-   ), high jumper for the U.S.S.R. One of the greatest exponents of the 'straddle' style, Brumel won an Olympic silver medal in 1960 when only 18 and in the same year set a European record of 7 ft. 2¾ in. (2·20 m.). He raised the world record in six instalments from 1961 to 1963, reaching 7 ft. 5¾ in. (2·28 m.), was European champion in 1962, and Olympic champion in 1964.

BRUNDAGE, AVERY (1887-1975), international ATHLETICS administrator for the U.S.A. Although he was a first-class athlete and represented the U.S.A. in the 1912 Olympic DECATHLON, Brundage's primary importance is as an indefatigable champion of the Olympic amateur code. He was president of the United States Olympic Association from 1929 to 1953 and president of the INTERNATIONAL OLYMPIC COMMITTEE from 1952 to 1972.

BRUSTAD, ARNE (fl. 1936-8), Association footballer for Lyn F.C. and Norway. He scored in both the 1936 OLYMPIC GAMES in Berlin and the 1938 world championship in France. He also appeared in the Rest of Europe team against England at Highbury in October 1938 in a match arranged as part of the seventy-fifth birthday celebrations of the Football Association.

BRYANT, DAVID JOHN, M.B.E. (1931-   ), English lawn BOWLS player and winner of gold medals in the 1966 world singles championship, the 1962 COMMONWEALTH GAMES singles and fours, and the 1970 Commonwealth Games singles, Bryant has a record which sets him far ahead of any other player in the history of the game. Apart from these four titles, he has won all the three British Isles championships and twelve English Bowling Association championships; this last put him ahead of BAKER's seven while still in his thirties. He is the only man to have his name on all four championship trophies, and to have won the singles five times, including a hat-trick in 1971/72/73.

In 1957, aged 25, he won his first English title by skipping his father and the Harrises (father and son) to the fours championship. Bryant's technical skill derives from an experimental approach based on the belief that accepted styles are not beyond improvement. A measure of his skill is his record in the world championship singles at Sydney in 1966, the Commonwealth Games singles at Perth in 1962, and Balgreen, Edinburgh, in 1970. Unbeaten at Perth, he lost only to Evans (Wales) in Sydney and Motroni (Scotland) at Balgreen, making his record 39 wins in 41 matches against the best players in the world on three separate occasions. He is the author of *Bryant on Bowls* (1970).

BUCHAN, CHARLES MURRAY (1891-1960), Association footballer whose appearances for England were limited to six full international matches and one 'Victory' match between 1913 and 1924, partly because of the war, but mainly because his individual, quick-thinking football brain made it difficult for players not accustomed to his style to combine effectively with him. He was 18 when SUNDERLAND paid £1,000 for his registration in 1911. In the next three full seasons before the wartime suspension of the League programme he scored 65 goals for Sunderland. After the war he returned to Sunderland until 1925 when CHAPMAN, newly installed as manager of ARSENAL, obtained his registration for the unusual fee of £2,000 plus £100 for each goal he scored in his first season with the London club—he scored 19. He continued to play for Arsenal until 1928 when he became a football writer with the *Daily Chronicle* (later *News Chronicle*) and subsequently founder-editor of the football magazine that bore his name.

BUCKLE, FRANK (1766-1832), was the outstanding English jockey of his day. Known as 'the Pocket Hercules', he rode five winners of the DERBY, nine of the OAKS, two of the ST. LEGER, five of the TWO THOUSAND GUINEAS, and six of the ONE THOUSAND GUINEAS, a record total of 27 classic winners, as well as 'all the good things at Newmarket'.

BUCKLEY, WILLIAM GEORGE (1907-73), chief spokesman for RUGBY LEAGUE in Australia after succeeding FLEGG in 1960 as president of the New South Wales League and chairman of the Australian Board of Control (later renamed the Australian Rugby League). An energetic and forthright administrator, he was, in 1948-9, joint manager of the Australian touring team in England and France.

BUCKMASTER, W. S. (b. 1872), English POLO player in the winning team for the Westchester Cup in 1902. He played between 1892 and 1914. Handicap 10.

BUCKPASSER (1963), a race-horse by Tom Fool out of Busanda by WAR ADMIRAL out of Businesslike by BLUE LARKSPUR out of LA TROIENNE, champion in the U.S.A., winning the American Derby, Arlington Classic, TRAVERS STAKES, JOCKEY CLUB GOLD CUP, Brooklyn, Metropolitan, and Suburban Handicaps, together with $1,462,014 in stakes for 25 victories out of 31 starts. In 1967, Buckpasser was syndicated for stud at a record price of $4,800,000. He was bred and raced by Phipps, president of the American Jockey Club.

BUDGE, JAMES DONALD (1916-   ), American LAWN TENNIS player, the first man to capture all four major singles titles in one year and one of the most completely successful competitors in the history of the game. Budge used the whole court and had no weakness for an opponent to exploit. His most powerful weapon was his heavy, rolled backhand and he maintained relentless pressure on his opponents.

He played at WIMBLEDON for the first time in 1935 and beat AUSTIN. His best years were 1937 and 1938 when he won all three titles at Wimbledon and FOREST HILLS. In 1938, the year of his 'grand slam', he lost only one set in the whole of the Wimbledon tournament. He was the first player to win the men's singles there without losing a set since the abolition of the challenge round in 1922; he was equally successful in the mixed doubles with MARBLE; and he and Mako yielded only one set in the men's doubles. In the same year he won the French and Australian titles and turned professional. Budge played a major part in the recapture of the Davis Cup (see LAWN TENNIS) by the U.S.A. in 1937, winning three rubbers against Great Britain.

BUDOKWAI, JUDO club, London. Founded in 1918, it was the first judo club to be established in Europe and has remained the most distinguished ever since. It was opened by KOIZUMI and was the centre of European judo until the Second World War. The first international match was held between a Budokwai team and a German national side in 1926 which the London club won.

The Budokwai helped form the British Judo Association and the European Judo Union in 1949 and moved from its original premises in Lower Grosvenor Place to its present location in Gilston Road, South Kensington, in 1954. The club celebrated its silver jubilee with its fiftieth annual display at the Royal Albert Hall, London, in 1968.

BUENO, MARIA ESTHER (1939-   ), Brazilian LAWN TENNIS player, one of the most graceful and artistic of all WIMBLEDON champions. She won the title in 1959 on her second appearance at the tournament, defeating Hard (U.S.A.), who was later to win many doubles events with her, and retained it with a victory over Reynolds (South Africa) the following year. Then began a series of matches against the powerful and athletic MARGARET SMITH between 1960 when Miss Smith, then an unknown junior, defeated her in the semi-finals of the Australian championships, and 1968 when ill-health forced the Brazilian player to retire. Smith won most of these matches, but Bueno beat her in a dramatic Wimbledon final in 1964 by 6-4, 7-9, 6-3, only to fail against her the following year and to fall to Mrs. KING (U.S.A.) in the 1966 final. She won the U.S. singles title four times between 1959 and 1966, the Wimbledon doubles five times, and the U.S. doubles four times.

BUGATTI, racing car which appeared in 1908 and was prominent in races of all types until 1939. The Type 35 first appeared in 1924 and scored literally thousands of wins in Grand Prix and sports car racing in the 1920s. The Type 59 won its first Grand Prix (the Belgian) in 1934, and went on to successes in other Grand Prix and sports car races. Their manufacturer, Ettore Bugatti, died in 1947 and his factory was absorbed into the Hispano-Suiza concern.

BUGATTI CIRCUIT, MOTOR RACING circuit near LE MANS, designed by Deutsch, chief engineer of the French Department of Bridges and Roads and a partner in the former D.B. competition car concern and the builder of C.D. competition sports cars, was completed in 1965. It has a length of 2·71 miles (4·3 km.) and incorporates the pit straight of the main 24-hour circuit. It was used for the 1967 French Grand Prix. In 1967 GRAHAM HILL'S Lotus - Cosworth 49 set the lap record to 102·824 m.p.h. (165·48 km./h.).

BULA (1965), National Hunt race-horse trained by WINTER and ridden by Kelleway and Pitman. Successor to PERSIAN WAR as champion hurdler (see CHAMPION HURDLE CHALLENGE CUP), he failed to win the title for a third time in 1973, and became a top-class steeplechaser.

BULL, one of the earliest of DECK GAMES, still popular with passengers. The playing pieces are either rubber discs or canvas bags filled with sand, as they probably were centuries ago. Each player has six discs or bags and he throws them on the numbered squares of the board, from a distance agreed upon by the players, and in a sequence that may vary slightly according to the custom followed by the ships of different companies. There are twelve squares on the board, made up of four rows of three squares each with the furthest row showing the right-hand bull, the number 10, and the left-hand bull. The remaining numbers (1 to 9) are allocated to the three lower rows such that the aggregate number in each line is 15 with the usual sequence of numbers 8-1-6; 3-5-7; and 4-9-2. The winner is the person who first completes the full sequence of the board and this usually means covering numbers 1 to 10 onsecutively, followed by the right-hand and finally the left-hand bull, and then returning in the reverse order to number 1.

When a player has thrown his six discs, the last division or square he covered in his correct sequence is noted, and the next player takes his six throws. Discs must rest in a square without touching the lines but a disc may be driven completely into a square by another one and, if in the correct sequence, count. The rules differ as to what penalty should follow a disc being thrown or moved into the wrong bull square but generally this means going back to the start and re-commencing the entire sequence, while a player whose disc or bag falls off the board is penalized by dropping back one number.

BULL-BAITING, see ANIMAL-BAITING.

BULLEN, JANE (1948-   ), British three-day event (see EQUESTRIAN EVENTS) horsewoman. The first woman to represent Britain in the Olympic three-day event, she won a team gold medal at Mexico (1968), riding Our Nobby, little more than a pony. She was the first woman to win an Olympic medal in the three-day event.

BULLER, JOHN SIDNEY, M.B.E. (1909-70), cricketer for Yorkshire and Worcestershire, and first-class umpire. After keeping wicket regularly for Worcestershire from 1935 to 1946 he earned universal respect as an umpire, appearing in 33 Test matches, including that at LORD's in 1960 when he 'called' the South African, Griffin, for throwing. He died during a county match in which he was officiating.

BULLFIGHTING, which is mainly to be found in Spain, where it is the national spectacle, is also widely practised in the same form in some parts of Latin America and southern France. Other variations take place elsewhere, principally in Portugal and the Provençal region of France.

The English word 'bullfighting' is a misnomer, since a contest is implied where none exists. In this the *corrida de toros* (running of the bulls) differs from other sports, the intended outcome of the encounter being the death of the bull and the survival of the man, although the latter frequently sustains serious injury and is sometimes killed. (Official records indicate an average of two deaths a year in Spain over the past two centuries, but this figure is well below the actual death rate. Leading matadors may expect to be seriously injured several times each season.) In Spain the *corrida* is viewed by adherents as an art, by detractors as a relic of barbaric times.

The formal Spanish *corrida de toros* generally consists of the putting to death of six *toros de lidia* (fighting bulls) by three *matadores de toros* (killers of bulls) in a public *plaza de toros* (bull ring) in accordance with a prescribed pattern of events.

The *corrida* is publicized in advance by *carteles* (posters) announcing the place, time, and date of event, the cost of the tickets, the name of the three participating matadors and their assistants, the breed of the bulls, and the location of the offices where tickets may be bought. Prices vary in descending order from *barreras* (front row seats) to *andanadas* (upper gallery), those in *sombra* (shade) being more expensive than *sol y sombra* (sun and shade) and *sol* (sunny sector) respectively, the most expensive seats being *barrera sombra* and the cheapest *andanada sol*.

Five in the afternoon is the traditional hour of the *corrida* (which may be varied to suit local weather conditions and working hours). Just before the *corrida* begins, the president and his entourage take their places in a box, identifiable by richly decorated drapes, located in the centre of the *sombra* sector immediately above the uncovered section of the tiers of public seats. From this vantage point the president (usually a local dignitary) controls the sequence and duration of each phase of the proceedings, and ensures (by the

imposition of fines and if necessary the arrest of offending participants) compliance with the regulations which, by law, govern the conduct of the *corrida*. In addition to his guests, the president has with him the paid *asesor* (technical adviser), usually a retired matador, whose counsel he enlists, particularly when deciding the duration of the various *suertes* (stages) which are determined by the changing condition of each bull. The signal for the change of *suerte* is made by draping a

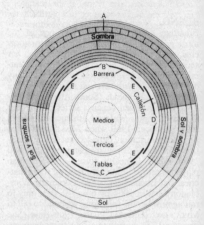

PLAZA DE TOROS
(A) President's box; (B) main gate — 'gate of honour'; (C) *toril*, from which bulls enter; (D) *puerta de cuadrillas*, entrance for parade of *toreros*; (E) *burladeros*. Seats in the front row of the *sombra* (shade) sector are the most expensive.

handkerchief, the colour of which signifies a specific instruction, over the sill of the presidential box. Instructions for fines or other action to be taken for infractions of the regulations are telephoned to the *callejón* (alleyway round the bull ring) below.

At the appointed hour, the president drapes a white handkerchief over the sill of his box, the band above the *toril* (the pen from which the bull enters the plaza) opposite sounds a fanfare of trumpets, the gates are opened and the *paseillo* (parade) of the *toreros* (general term for all active participants in the *corrida*) begins.

The *paseillo* is led, on horseback, by two *alguaciles* (constables who transmit the orders of the president to the *toreros* during the *corrida* and deliver any awards to the matadors) dressed in the plumed hats and black velvet costume of Felipe II.

Immediately following are the three matadors dressed in the *traje de luces* ('suit of lights'), consisting of the *casaquilla* (jacket) which, although heavy, affords no protection against the horns of the bull, and the *taleguilla* (tight-fitting three-quarter-length breeches), both of which are made of coloured silk richly ornamented with gold braid. The remainder of the costume consists of the *camisa de torear* (a ruffled white lace shirt) and tie, the *medias* (pink thigh-length silk hose), the *zapatillas* (black leather slippers), and the *montera* (a winged black hat of unique design). The *montera* is carried, not worn, if the matador is making his first appearance in a particular ring or is taking his *alternativa* (the doctorate *corrida* in which *novilleros*—apprentice matadors—graduate from confronting three-year-old to four-year-old bulls). As they approach, the matadors are placed to the right, left, and centre, in order of descending seniority, based on the date of their *alternativa*.

Each matador is followed in file, invariably out of step by token of some unwritten tradition, by his *cuadrilla*. This is a team of three *banderilleros* (assistants on foot) and two *picadores* (mounted assistants) who are generally retained throughout the season by the matador for all his appearances. The *banderilleros* also wear *traje de luces* of coloured silk except that these are less ornate and embellished in silver, black, or white braid instead of gold. On entering the ring, matadors and *banderilleros* wear the *capote de paseillo* (parade cape, richly embroidered and embellished) wrapped tightly over one shoulder. The picadors wear a similar *casaquilla* to the *banderilleros*, but the *montera* is replaced by the *castoreño* (round-topped wide-brimmed beaver hat), and the *taleguilla* and *zapatillas* are replaced by *calzonas* (chamois leather trousers buttoned up on the sides), *botas* (heavy leather boots), and *monas* (heavy steel leggings).

The *cuadrillas* of the matadors are succeeded by personnel provided by the impresario of the plaza, consisting of two reserve picadors, the *puntillero* (the dagger-man who administers the *coup de grâce* in the event that a fallen bull is not killed by the sword), the *monosabios* (red-shirted attendants whose function is to help remount a picador after a fall), the *areneros* (attendants who level the sand of the ring during intervals), the *carpinteros* (carpenters who repair any section of the barriers which may become broken during the *corrida*), and the *mulilleros* (the mule-handlers) accompanied by the mules which are used to drag the dead bulls out of the arena.

The entire procession advances to immediately below the president's box and the matadors and their *cuadrillas* bow in salutation and are acknowledged by the president. Then all members of the parade clear the ring by taking up their positions in the *callejón*, while the two mounted *alguaciles* make a half-circuit in opposite directions to arrive back beneath the presidential box to receive the key to the *toril*. In smaller rings the key will be thrown down and caught in the *alguacil*'s hat; in larger rings it will be passed down. Having delivered the key to the guardian of the *toril* on the opposite side of the plaza, the *alguaciles* leave the ring, and on the showing of the president's white handkerchief the *toril* door is flung open and the senior matador and his public await the first bull of the afternoon.

At mid-morning on the day of the *corrida*, the *peones de confianza* (the trusted representatives of the matadors taking part, usually their senior *banderilleros*) have assembled at the corrals to assess the bulls on the basis of presence, conformation, and temperament, and agree their order of acceptability. The numbers and names of the bulls are written on three slips of cigarette paper in pairs, the best three being paired off with the remainder to ensure an equitable distribution of good and bad characteristics between the three matadors. The three slips of paper are screwed up, placed in a hat, and the *sorteo* (draw) takes place. The first pair drawn are for the senior matador and are the first and fourth bulls of the *corrida* respectively; the second pair for the second matador appear in the second and fifth place; the third pair for the junior matador are the third and last bulls of the *corrida*.

A few minutes before the start of the *corrida*, the door of the pen of the first bull is opened to allow it to enter the *toril*. Through an aperture above the *toril* the *mayoral* (breeder's foreman) thrusts a small barb carrying the *divisa* (ribbons indicating the breeder's colours) into the thick upper loin of the bull's back.

Suerte de varas. When, at the signal of the president, the *toril* door is flung open, the bull charges into the arena and gallops round it, encouraged by the *banderilleros* who emerge from behind the *burladeros* (short barriers which shield the four gaps in the *barrera* —main barrier around the arena—through which the *toreros* gain access to the ring) briefly to flap their *capotes de brega* (working capes, having the appearance of a 270° circular sector of about 2·3 m. (7 ft. 6 in.) diameter when spread on the ground, made of bright magenta raw silk on the outside and golden yellow cotton percale inside) for which they exchanged their *capotes de paseillo* at the end of the parade.

(More rarely, should the matador make an instantaneous decision on the entry of the bull that it is charging well, he receives it with a *larga cambiada de rodillas*—a one-handed kneeling pass — spreading the cape before him on the sand and deflecting the charge of the bull from his body by flaring the cape with one hand over his opposite shoulder.)

When the characteristics of the bull's first few wild charges have been evaluated, either the matador steps on to the sand, or if he requires further confirmation of the animal's tendencies, his senior *banderillero* goes in with the bull and executes some *lances* (passes with the cape) which generally take the form of *largas* (one-handed passes) in which the edge of the cape is trailed on the sand beneath the muzzle of the animal so that the matador can observe such idiosyncrasies as a preference for one horn, or a tendency to turn quickly after charging or to stop suddenly during an assault.

When the matador, alone in the ring, accepts the initial onslaughts of the bull the

charge). Additionally, since the early part of this century, the canon of *cargar la suerte* (deliberately to accept the onus of deviating the bull round the man's body instead of permitting it to travel in a straight line past him — generally achieved by stepping into the bull's path with the leg opposite the oncoming animal) has come to have great significance. The style of *lances* with the *capote* (and passes with the *muleta*) can loosely be divided into the *Sevillano* (feet together) school and the school of Ronda (feet apart). Additionally all *toreo* can be classified into three forms, *de frente* (frontal), *tres cuartos* (three-quarter), and *perfil* (profile), which relate to the stance of the matador when accepting the bull's charge.

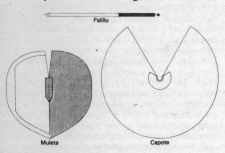

TORERO'S CAPE AND MULETA

The *muleta*, of scarlet cloth half lined with yellow percale, is draped over the *palillo*; its pointed end, like a nail, goes through the cloth, and the screw-eye at the other end fixes the *muleta* to it.

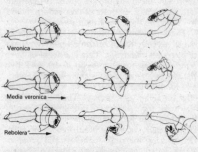

BASIC LANCES WITH THE CAPOTE

lances, now performed with both hands, are low (to slow down its speed), and if the animal shows a reluctance to return to the encounter the matador will follow through with the cape to retain its attention as it emerges from the cloth. Having captured the attention of the *toro* and slowed it down, the matador then begins to execute *lances* in series, upon which his ability with the *capote* is judged.

The form of these *lances* is very much dependent on the style and personality of the individual matador, but if worthy of merit they conform with the age-old traditional canons of good *toreo* (work with the *capote* and *muleta* — a scarlet cloth on a stick) which consist of *parar* (to receive the charge of the bull with feet firmly planted), *mandar* (to control the trajectory of the bull from the inciting of its charge to the exit from the pass), and *templar* (to adjust the movement of the *muleta* in harmony with the changing velocity of the bull's

Each series of *lances* executed by the matador is terminated by a *remate* (finishing pass) which cuts short the bull's charge by turning it sharply, giving the matador a brief respite to take up a new position for the next series of *lances*. The fundamental *lance* with the *capote* is the *veronica* in which the matador cites the bull with the *capote* raised and extended towards the animal with the near hand; when the bull comes close, the matador extends the cloth away from himself with the other hand, at the same time dropping the near hand to thigh level to give the bull the impression that the moving target is going away from its original position. The *remate* for a series of these *lances* is either the *media veronica*, which begins as a *veronica* except that midway through the *lance* the *capote* is swirled sharply into the small of the back; or the *rebolera* in which the *capote* is fanned out horizontally with one hand. The latter manoeuvre gives the matador the opportunity to terminate the series with the *capote* behind his back should he wish to begin a series of *gaoneras*, in which the bull is passed in a truncated form of a *veronica* with the man in front of the cape. Other typical *lances* are *chicuelinas* which begin somewhat like a *veronica* except that in mid-pass the matador swivels in the reverse direction to the passage of the bull, winding the cape round his body so that it disappears from view. Dozens of variations of these basic *lances* and *remates* make for variety in the matador's work with the *capote*. His performance is judged, not only by his adherence to the canons mentioned, but for the versatility displayed, the grace and style with which he executes the manoeuvres, the degree to which he works close to the bull, and the extent to which he eliminates unwanted characteristics in the bull's behaviour by corrective capework.

The *toro de lidia*, in common with other animals with limited vision, is extremely susceptible to movement, which is in itself sufficient stimulus to put escape reactions (which in the case of the *toro de lidia* take the form of attack) into operation. As with other ungulates, the bull's eyes are set on either side of the head, causing the reception of two separate images, while frontal vision can be achieved only to a limited extent and with some difficulty. By remaining stationary while moving the lure, the *torero* induces the bull to reject the stationary image and concentrate on the moving target. Excessive exploitation of this shortcoming, working with the *ojo contrario* (opposite eye), is deprecated by the serious *aficionado* (bullfight enthusiast) and is greeted with protests by the public. Almost no *torero* is aware of the scientific basis of his ability to manipulate the bull's charge, relying instead on his experience and intuition.

When he considers that the matador has performed sufficient capework, having regard to the condition of the bull, the president signals with a white handkerchief for the entry of the picadors. (Should the bull have shown signs of a physical defect, such as lameness, the president rejects the bull by a signal with a green handkerchief and the *cabestros*—steers —are brought in to return the animal to the corrals; the substitute takes its place.) The three *banderilleros* enter the ring to distract the attention of the bull while the two mounted picadors make their entry through a gate in the *barrera* and take up their positions on opposite sides of the ring. Only the senior picador is intended to participate; the reserve picador is present in case his companion is unhorsed. The two other matadors are also in the arena, to take part in the *quites* (taking the bull away from the horse) in which all three matadors alternate. This provides the opportunity for a display of competitive capework.

The picadors are mounted on horses, more robust than elegant, whose sole qualifications are that they must be a minimum of 1·47 m.

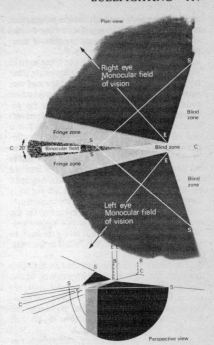

VISUAL SYSTEM OF THE BULL
In the plan view of the bull's vision arrowheads denote: to infinity. Lines protruding from the tonal areas represent total extent of vision. The depth of the blind zone, EY, is 5 ft. (1·524 m.). In the 'fringe' zones the bull's vision is confused with objects, to infinity. Divisions between the fields and zones of vision are in reality muted, not sharp as shown here. The monocular field of vision is actually a cone, as shown in the perspective view below of the left eye, section SS (shown in white lines) of the larger diagram, from the centre of the visual area. (E) eye; (BB) relative length of bull; (CC) imaginary centre line.

(15 hands) high and in good health. Each is examined by the veterinaries before the *corrida* and a red cord with a lead seal placed round its neck to indicate its fitness. The horses are caparisoned by the *peto*, a 25 kg. (55 lb.) mattress-like protective covering introduced by royal order in 1928 largely due to government concern about the effect on tourists of eviscerated horses in the bull rings. The efficacy of the measure is debatable since the *peto* does little to discourage the picadors from preventing the bull from making contact with the horse. Few horses survive more than a few dozen *corridas* and minor injuries are frequent. The right eye of each horse is covered with a red blindfold to prevent panic if

the bull were seen to attack, and in most plazas the horses' ears are plugged with cotton-wool and they are given a minute quantity of morphine before the *corrida*.

The picadors carry the *vara* (a lance used to weaken the bull sufficiently to lower its head for the moment of the kill so that the matador may make his entry with the sword by going in over the horns). The *vara* comprises the *garrocha* (a beech pole about 2·6 m. (8 ft. 6 in.) long and 30 mm. (1⅛ in.) in diameter) to the end of which is attached the *puya*, a cylindrical steel goad with a crosspiece. (The cylindrical part is covered with coiled cord and is 36 mm. (1⅜ in.) in diameter and 75 mm. (3 in.) long, fitted at the end with a pyramid-shaped tip 29 mm. (1⅛ in.) long.) The *garrocha* is slightly curved so that the picador can ensure, by aligning it in the cradle of his arm, that the cutting edge of the *puya* is not uppermost, which would cause it to skid along the back of the bull instead of embedding itself in the muscle.

The senior matador capes the first bull into position, the cape discreetly vanishing at the last moment to reveal the picador and his mount. As the bull charges the horse, the picador leans over and thrusts the *puya* into the bull, leaning on the *garrocha* with his full weight to ward off the attack.

Contrary to popular belief, the *puya* is not placed in the *morillo* (the hump of tossing-muscle), which would cripple the bull entirely, but in the *lomo alto* (the upper loin) at a point midway between the end of the *morillo* and the middle of the bull's back. The muscle here is sufficiently thick to prevent the point of the *puya* from striking bone, which would also incapacitate the bull. The object of wounding the bull in the *lomo alto* is ultimately to lower the animal's head. The veins which pass through the *lomo alto* supply the *morillo*, from which muscle the bull derives the enormous strength in its head. When the *morillo* is weakened due to an inadequate blood supply, the head becomes lowered and the matador is thus able to enter to kill in a straight line over

the horns, bringing relatively swift death by severing one of the main arteries to the rear of the heart.

When it is considered that the first *puyazo* (pike-thrust) has been sufficiently effective, the senior matador makes the *quite*, taking the bull away from the horse with his *capote* out into the centre of the arena where he performs further capework before returning it for a second *puyazo*. (Should the matadors experience difficulty in bringing the bull to the horse, the *banderilleros* intervene to expedite matters.) The process is repeated by the second and third matadors in turn unless, as frequently happens, the president decides that the bull has already been sufficiently weakened, in which case he will signal with a white handkerchief a change of *suerte*. Three *puyazos* are provided for by the regulations. Should the matador to whom the bull is allocated consider that his animal has lost sufficient strength, and wish to conserve the animal for the later stages, he petitions for a change of act by raising his *montera* towards the president. This request is often granted.

The weakening of the bull by the picadors is subject to regulations intended to prevent excessive debilitation of the animal's faculties. The *puya* may not be placed anywhere other than in the *lomo alto*; the picador may not practise the manoeuvre known as the *carioca*, in which, by urging his mount in a clockwise direction, he prevents the bull from disengaging itself and partially extracts the *puya* and re-inserts it in the same wound; nor may he cross the outside circle marked on the sand 7 m. (22 ft. 9 in.) from the edge of the arena, and the bull must be kept within the inside circle (9 m. — 29 ft. 6 in. — from the edge) when being positioned for the *suerte*. Infraction of such regulations, or ignoring the president's signal (a trumpet call) to discontinue the *suerte*, results in a fine.

Suerte de banderillas. When the *suerte de varas* (the first phase of each bull, involving the capework and the participation of the picadors) has concluded, the horsemen and their

WEAPONS
Puntilla and barbs are not to scale.

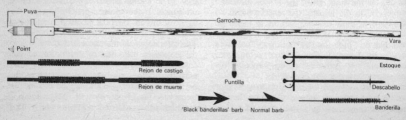

Puya

Garrocha

Vara

Point

Rejon de castigo

Estoque

Rejon de muerte

Puntilla

Descabello

'Black banderillas' barb   Normal barb

Banderilla

mounts leave the arena and the *suerte de ban-derillas* begins. The *banderillas*, 20 mm. (¾ in.) in diameter by 70 cm. (2 ft. 3 in.) long, are round beechwood sticks decorated with coloured paper, fitted with steel barbs 40 mm. (1½ in.) long at the end. They are placed in the hide of the bull to the rear of the *lomo alto* in pairs, the number being decided by the president according to the animal's condition. The function of the *suerte de banderillas* is to enliven the bull after the chastening effect of the *suerte de varas* by confronting it with a man without protection to be attacked with relative impunity. The barbs of the *banderillas* serve to aggravate rather than pain the bull.

For placing of the *banderillas*, the bull is manoeuvred into a position, by a *banderillero* with the *capote*, from which it sights the senior *banderillero* who walks towards it with a swaying motion, and makes a dash off to the side, or runs swiftly in the form of a figure eight until the bull starts to charge. In the *al cuarteo* (quarter-circle) method, as the bull charges the man runs in a wide arc obliquely towards the line of the charge, shortening the distance between himself and the animal, timing the collision so that at the moment of their encounter he is in the lee of the bull whose limited turning circle places the man beyond reach of the horns. The *banderillas* are rammed home, the standard of performance being judged by the correct positioning and proximity of the two darts. The *banderillero* escapes by running in a zigzag towards the *barrera*, which he is frequently obliged to vault, while his companions distract the bull's attention by flapping their capes. The procedure is repeated until the president's white handkerchief and a further clarion call bring the *suerte* to an end.

Some matadors, especially those of Latin American origin, choose to demonstrate their versatility by placing the *banderillas* themselves. In most cases they elect to do so alone in the arena. While they may place one or two pairs *al cuarteo*, they generally try to introduce such variations as running directly at the bull in the *poder a poder* (head on) method, the direct run-in being made with a slightly weaving motion; as the bull lowers its head to hook, the darts are thrust home and used as a crutch to enable the *torero* to spiral away from the horns. Another variation is the *al sesgo* (on the bias), usually performed with a recalcitrant animal, in which the run-in is very fast at an acute angle, the matador relying on the speed of his entry to surprise the bull. Probably the most spectacular is the *al quiebro* (body feint) manoeuvre in which the matador provokes the attack by a series of jumps, calling on the bull until it charges head on; when only a few feet

separate them, the man makes a swift movement with one foot to the side at the same time inclining his body. As the bull swerves in response to the feint, the matador resumes his former position and places the *banderillas* from his original stance.

Should a bull have been dealt with inadequately in the *suerte de varas*, on rare occasions the president, by a signal with a red handkerchief, orders black *banderillas* to be inserted. These are covered in black paper and the steel tip is double-barbed followed by a spear-shaped section 20 mm. (¾ in.) wide. They are placed in the same way as ordinary *banderillas* but their effect is more debilitating. At one time *banderillas de fuego* (fire *banderillas*), tipped with a cartridge which ignited a charge of powder and firecrackers, were used, but these were abandoned in 1950.

On completion of the *suerte de banderillas*, the *banderilleros* distract the attention of the bull while the matador makes his way to beneath the presidential box. He carries the *estoque*—a tempered steel sword with a channelled blade 20 mm. (¾ in.) wide and 85 cm. (2 ft. 9 in.) long, the blade being slightly curved towards the tip, with a small open handle, fitted with a metal crosspiece, terminating in a round leather-covered cork pommel. The sword (which at this stage may be a dummy sword of aluminium or light wood if the matador has suffered a recent wrist injury) is carried, together with the *muleta*, in the left hand, the right hand extending the *montera* aloft towards the president to whom the matador is obliged, by the regulations, to dedicate the death of his first bull. (Afterwards, if he so chooses, he may make a dedication to a friend or some celebrity in the audience.) He turns on his heel towards the bull, throws his *montera* over his left shoulder, and the *suerte de matar* (the act of the kill) begins. This begins with the *faena* (work with the *muleta*) and ends with the death of the bull.

Suerte de matar. The *faena* almost invariably begins with the lure in the right hand. The *torero* grasps the *palillo* (the stick inside the *muleta*) at the centre, together with the handle of the sword, the point of which extends the draped cloth to present a larger target. The *muleta* is of heavy red serge cloth and lined on the inside, generally with the same yellow cotton percale used for the *capote*, to give it more weight and shape, and to improve the flow of the material.

The passes used for the initiation of the *faena* depend on the condition of the bull. If he is lively, charges straight, follows the cloth, and appears to have good, balanced vision, the matador opens his *faena* with *ayudados por alto* (high passes assisted with the sword). The most spectacular of these is the *pase de la muerte* (death pass) in which the extended cloth is advanced towards the bull on a level with its head as it attacks. The matador, standing quite still, moves the cloth rhythmically just ahead of the horns as they pass and repass his body, raising the cloth to give the bull an exit at the end of each charge. The manoeuvre is so named because the horns are level with the man's heart. If the matador is confident of the bull, he sometimes performs the *ayudados por alto* sitting on the *estribo* (the step at the bottom of the *barrera* used by *toreros* to vault out of the ring).

If the bull is too impetuous or sluggish, charges erratically, has a tendency to hook, or appears to have defective vision, the matador opens his *faena* with *pases de castigo* (punishing passes), offering the animal both sides of the cloth alternately in a chopping motion in swift succession until he has caught the bull's attention. The matador then begins to compose his *faena*, customarily with *derechazos* (right-handed passes, in all of which the *muleta* is extended by the sword) progressing to *naturales* (left-handed passes in which the *muleta* is not supported by the sword and therefore offers a smaller target). Each series of passes is terminated by a *remate* (finishing pass) in which the bull loses sight of the cloth, giving the matador a brief respite in which to take up a new position for the succeeding series.

In each series of *derechazos*, in which the bull passes from left to right of the *torero*, the cloth is kept low, turning the bull in a slow quarter-circle so that it continues to follow the lure for the succeeding pass; at the end of each series of *derechazos* the matador presents the animal with the reverse side of the cloth, passing it from right to left, raising the *muleta* high at the end of the pass so that the bull loses the target and temporarily abandons interest. This *remate* is called the *pase cambiado por alto con la derecha* (reverse high right-handed pass). The next series of *derechazos* is again initiated by the *torero* inciting the bull, extending the *muleta* in invitation, using the *toque* (a light flick of the cloth to provoke the charge), shuffling across the line of attack while moving the *muleta* behind his back if the bull does not respond.

The procedure for each series of *naturales* is identical to that above, but in the reverse direction. The *remate* for a series of *naturales* is called the *pase de pecho* (breast pass).

The criterion of the quality of the matador's execution of the *derechazos*, *naturales*, and their respective *remates*, which are the basis of the *faena*, is that they should be performed with grace and individual style while observing the canons of *parar*, *mandar*, *templar*, and

Pase natural →

Pase de la muerte →

Pase de pecho →

Manoletina →

PASSES WITH THE MULETA

cargar la suerte previously mentioned, always providing that the condition of the bull permits. Conversely, adherents of *tremendisme* (sensational *toreo*) deprecate the regimentation implied by observance of these canons, preferring *toreo* of a more flamboyant and individualistic character in which the matador manifests more originality and bravado than style.

Either category of *torero* spices his *faena* with *pases de adorno* (decorative passes) interspersed with the basic *derechazos* and *naturales*. Passes such as the *manoletina* (in which the lure is held in the right hand at waist level, slightly behind the *torero*, with the left hand grasping the inside edge of the *muleta* in the small of the back, the cloth being swirled over the horns of the bull as they pass under the man's armpit); the *molinete* (a right-handed or left-handed pass in which the arm is extended across the chest and the reverse side of the *muleta* is proffered to the bull at the height of the horns, the man spinning into the cloth in a reverse direction to the charge, so that the lure furls around his body, disappearing from view as the *toro* reaches him); the *afarolado* (a pass made with either hand, citing as though for a *pase cambiado por alto con la derecha* or a *pase de pecho* spiralling the *muleta* over the head midway through the pass while spinning the body in the reverse direction to the charge); and the *arrucina* (a right-handed pass with the *muleta* completely behind the *torero*, the knuckles of the right hand situated in the small of the back, the bull attacking the small fragment of cloth visible to the left of the man's body. These, and many other varieties of *pases de adorno*, some of which are named after their inventors, are used to lend variety to the *faena*, and to enliven the bull when the *pases por bajo* (low passes) such as the classic *derechazo* and *natural* have begun to take their toll on the animal's strength.

Towards the end of the *faena*, the matador may decide that he has the bull sufficiently under control to enable him to execute some *desplantes* (seemingly injudicious feats which usually take the form of a theatrical gesture close to the animal). The *desplantes* have no functional value and serve only to demonstrate the extent to which the matador has dominated the *toro*. They take the form of touching the horn of the bull, kneeling before the animal while discarding the sword and *muleta* on the sand sometimes with the back to the bull; or, in the case of the *teléfono*, the *torero*, chin in hand, places his elbow on the animal's forehead.

When the matador decides that he has expended the animal's possibilities in terms of the number and variety of passes he can perform, and that the fatigue induced by the *faena* has lowered its head sufficiently, be begins to prepare the bull for the kill. Generally he endeavours to execute a number of *naturales* towards the end of the *faena*, in order to persuade the bull that its quarry is to the left of the cloth. This is done so that when the matador enters for the kill, the bull instinctively tends to hook to the left, while the man's natural exit in this manoeuvre is along the animal's right flank.

To line up the bull for the kill, having exchanged the dummy sword — if one has been used — for the *estoque*, the matador employs *trastear* (manipulating the bull into the required position by fanning the reverse side of the *muleta* from side to side under the muzzle). His ultimate object is to *cuadrar* (square up) the bull so that it is standing with its front feet 15 to 25 cm. (6 in. to 10 in.) apart. If the feet are too close together the bull is unstable and may move during the kill; if one foot is in front of the other or the feet are too far apart, the shoulder blades move together and restrict the entry of the sword; should any of these conditions obtain, the bull is repositioned.

When the animal is correctly aligned, the matador stands in front of it about 1·5 m. (5 ft.) away, with the left foot pointing towards the bull and the right foot at right angles behind it. He furls the *muleta* towards the muzzle of the animal with a clockwise gesture with the folds just touching the ground, raises the sword to eye level, and sights along it towards the bull's withers. Immediately before executing the sword-thrust, he swivels his

right foot into alignment with the left and arches his body forward on the balls of his feet.

The sword-thrust is performed by three basic techniques with minor variations. The most commonly practised is the *volapié* (fleet-of-foot) method in which the matador takes a straight run at the bull, reaching it before it attacks, extending his sword arm as he goes in to make the thrust, at the same time crossing the *muleta* in his left hand upwards towards his right, guiding the bull's horns with the cloth

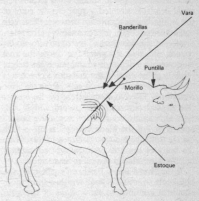

ANATOMY OF THE BULL AT THE KILL
Arrows indicate the placing of the various weapons; the matador's sword, entering at the *cruz de rubios*, is placed correctly at a 45° angle to sever the aorta and kill cleanly. The *puntilla* entering at the base of the skull administers the *coup de grâce*.

away from his body under his right armpit. If, while he is in the citing position, the bull involuntarily charges, or the matador causes it to do so by a sharp flick of the cloth, the feat is called *recibiendo* (receiving), the *torero* having received the attack without moving forward. If both man and bull start to move at the same time and meet midway, the *suerte* is called *a un tiempo* (at the same time). If, in a *volapié*, the bull launches an attack just prior to the man reaching it, the *suerte* is said to have been executed *arrancando* (with a sudden start); in *aguantado* (standing one's ground) the *suerte* starts *recibiendo* but the matador begins to move forward just before the bull reaches him. The *al cuarteo* method where the matador runs in a short circle away to the side of the bull, as if placing *banderillas*, is considered reprehensible except if the bull's head is still too high to permit a direct entry over the horns, or if, by virtue of the animal's having impaired vision or an excessively mettlesome disposition, a straight entry presents too great a degree of danger. In the event of the entry to kill being made *al cuarteo*, instead of the sword entering the bull perpendicularly at an angle of about 45°, bringing almost instantaneous death by severing the rear aorta, *vena cava*, or one of the major arteries to the rear of the heart, the sword enters the animal obliquely, usually penetrating the lungs and resulting in a protracted death by pulmonary haemorrhage.

The *cruz de rubios* (the area in the bull's back where the sword should enter to ensure a rapid death) is situated slightly to the right of the animal's spinal column between the fourth and sixth vertebrae, approximately at the intersection of the *morillo* and the *lomo alto*, and is roughly the size of a small fist. Since the area is located in a near horizontal plane at a height roughly at the level of the matador's chest, it is difficult to strike it with any accuracy; the matador is aided to some extent by the *muerte* (the bowed portion of the sword which consists of a shallow curve for about the last 15 cm. (6 in.) of the blade before the tip) which also permits the blade to continue to travel into the body of the bull at about 45° although it has been introduced at a more acute angle.

If the sword-thrust has been successful, the bull keels over and is dead within a short time; should it continue to show signs of life after falling, the *puntillero* delivers the *coup de grâce* by severing the spinal cord at the base of the skull with the *puntilla* (a dagger with a spear-shaped point, the blade of which is 40 mm. (1½ in.) wide, 15 cm. (6 in.) long, and 6 mm. (¼ in.) thick; the wooden handle is 12 cm. (4¾ in.) long).

If, as is sometimes the case, the sword-thrust has been unsuccessful, one of a number of courses of action may be taken. If the sword has failed to enter at all, or inflicted only a shallow wound, the matador is obliged to make a further attempt. Once he has succeeded in lodging a sword partway into the bull, he may at his own discretion, if he considers that its effect is likely to be lethal, await the outcome. If he does not consider his attempt to have been effective, he may place further swords until the bull succumbs. At any time after he has achieved a partial entry he may elect to use the *descabello* (a sword of much heavier and more rigid design than the *estoque*, equipped with a rigid tip, 25 mm. (1 in.) by 10 cm. (4 in.) long, terminating in a crosspiece). This implement is generally used when the bull has all but expired, retaining its feet with difficulty, with lowered head; in making use of it, the matador may seek the help of his *banderilleros* who attract the bull's attention and further lower its head by spreading a *capote* on the sand under its muzzle to enable the matador to sever the spinal cord, holding the sword almost vertically, in the same manner as the *puntillero*.

From the beginning of the *faena* to the death of the bull the matador is allowed 15 minutes. After ten minutes, at the signal of the president's white handkerchief, the first *aviso* (warning) is given by the sounding of a trumpet. Three minutes later the second *aviso* is given. After a further two minutes the third *aviso* announces the failure of the matador and the bull is returned to the corrals and ultimately slaughtered. Failure is unusual; generally the bull succumbs to the matador's sword. If the performance has been successful, the public immediately petition the president for recognition of the matador's skill by waving white handkerchiefs. The recognition of the quality of a performance is by the award of one or two of the ears of the bull killed. The custom originated in the compensating of *toreros* in the early days of the village *corrida*, when they were not paid for their participation, by conceding them the meat of the animal they had killed for subsequent sale; the ear of the dead animal was severed and retained by the *torero* as evidence of ownership.

The evaluation of the work of a matador is based not only on the merit of his *toreo* but on his command of the *lidia* (the progressive preparation of the bull for its death, taking into consideration the changing condition of the animal throughout the three phases, getting the best out of it in each of them). The over-all surveillance of the *lidia* is the responsibility of the senior matador, but each individual matador is judged on his capacity for recognizing the nature of behavioural changes and applying progressive remedial measures to develop the potential of the bull to the full. These measures take the form of keeping the bull under control at all times so that it does not arrive at the *muleta* in a distracted condition; making certain that the animal is not excessively enfeebled during the *suerte de varas* due to tardy *quites*, having its strength sapped to the extent that it is unable to respond adequately in the *faena*; ensuring that the same condition does not obtain due to excessive caping or unduly brusque *remates* which wrench the animal's neck; applying corrective measures if the bull shows a preference for one horn by using severe passes on that side and moderate passes on the other until the caprice is eliminated; inducing a recalcitrant bull to charge by moving in close to the horns; curtailing the length of charge of the bull which loses the cloth by following through with the lure so that the bull wheels to the attack once more, and reducing excessive force in an over-impetuous animal by sharp *remates* and *pases de castigo*. Each bull has a *lidia* appropriate to it, a *lidia* which is subject to continuous adjustment requiring considerable experience and skill to assess and apply. The final criterion of the matador's work is his capacity with the sword, the principal elements of which are honesty of entry, accuracy of location, and the efficacy of the sword-thrust.

The combined elements of *toreo, lidia*, and proficiency in the *suerte de matar* are all taken into consideration in determining any awards to be made.

The award of ears is signalled by the display of the president's white handkerchief, the first ear being awarded in recognition of the volume of public acclaim, and the second in accordance with his own evaluation. In response to the president's signals, the *alguacil* collects the appropriate trophies from the *puntillero* who has severed them, and presents them to the matador on behalf of his superior. In minor rings, the trophies may include a tail or even a hoof, although such awards are proscribed by the regulations.

The team of mules is brought into the ring and tethered to the horns of the dead bull by a special harness equipped with a tow bar, and the *arrastre* (dragging of the bull out of the arena) takes place. If the bull has displayed exceptional qualities, a signal from the president with a blue handkerchief awards it a *vuelta al ruedo* (lap of the ring), and the body of the bull is dragged around the arena in a wide circle in recognition of the breeder's achievement. It is then removed to the butcher's yard.

As soon as the *arrastre* has taken place, if the matador has gained any awards he makes a triumphal lap of the arena holding his trophies aloft, and is often showered with garlands and bouquets of flowers, cigars, chocolates, and similar gifts.

All personnel retire from the plaza except the *areneros* who sprinkle fresh sand on any areas stained with blood and rake the arena level in preparation for the entry of the second bull. The remaining five bulls are dispatched in a similar fashion.

In the event of a matador being so badly injured that he is unable to continue, the animals allotted to him are allocated to the next senior remaining matador. If two matadors become incapacitated, all remaining animals are dealt with by the survivor, and should he suffer the same fate, the dispatch of the remainder becomes the responsibility of the *sobresaliente* (substitute matador). If he is injured the *corrida* is abandoned, although this is rare.

Three other forms of bullfighting which take place on a significant scale are *rejoneo* (bullfighting on horseback) in Spain, the *tourada a la portuguesa* (Portuguese bullfight), and the *course à la cocarde* (the 'rosette' bullfight) of southern France.

REJONEO, in which the bull is killed, is presented in Spain as an adjunct to the normal *corrida*, the *rejoneador* (mounted bullfighter) either appearing at the beginning of the performance, or after the third bull. (Sometimes a *corrida* exclusively featuring *rejoneadores* takes place.) The bull is a three-year-old *novillo* which has almost invariably had the tips of its horns removed, and the mounts (generally three or four are used, being changed between *suertes*) are highly-trained elegant Peninsular thoroughbreds often of Arab, English, or Irish extraction. The *rejoneador* is dressed in a *de luxe* version of the *traje de campo* (suit used for the *tienta*), with a *chaquetilla* (short waistcoat-length jacket) of ornately embroidered black velvet, meticulously tooled *zahones* (leather chaps), and the wide-brimmed flat-topped Andalusian *sombrero cordobés*. His horse, its mane braided with coloured ribbons and its hooves varnished, is equipped with a standard high Andalusian saddle and wears no protection. It weighs usually less than 400 kg. (880 lb.), and stands about 1·5 m. (15 hands) high. It has a square head, full chest, slightly depressed flanks, a short back, a not unduly large croup, and although not as fast as the English racehorse it handles more smoothly because of its compact length. It is accomplished in Spanish dressage, and is trained to obey commands by leg movements when the *rejoneador*'s hands are otherwise occupied. In the *paseillo*, the *rejoneador* rides slightly behind the *alguaciles*. He is supported in his performance by two *toreros*, and a *sobresaliente* on foot, who may kill the bull if his superior fails to do so from horseback. The sequence of events in *rejoneo* is that the horseman firstly places, in the *lomo alto*, three *rejones de castigo* (castigating lances) 1·4 m. (4 ft. 7 in.) long, with a steel blade 15 cm. (6 in.) long, 40 mm. (1½ in.) wide, and 5 mm. (¼ in.) thick, which has a leaf-shaped single-sided hooked barb for about a third of its length, thereafter reducing to a 5 mm. (¼ in.) square section. The blade is separated from the wooden shaft by a flange 6 cm. (2⅜ in.) in diameter. The wooden shaft of the *rejón de castigo* is broken off by the horseman after the blade has entered, releasing a small flag, which, fluttering from the end of the broken shaft, is used to provoke the charge of the bull as it circles the arena in pursuit of the wheeling horseman.

The second stage consists of placing three pairs of *banderillas*, 80 cm. (2 ft. 7½ in.) long and terminating in a barb 7 cm. (2¾ in.) long and is 18 mm. (¾ in.) wide, to the rear of the *lomo alto*. The third *suerte* comprises putting the animal to death by placing the *rejón de muerte* (the killing lance, which is identical to the *rejón de castigo* except that the blade is 50 cm. (1 ft. 7⅝ in.) long, parallel for most of its length, reducing thereafter to a point) in the same locality as the sword used by the matador on foot. Throughout the performance the *rejoneador* uses the movement of the horse to manipulate and position the bull in the same way as the *torero* on foot uses the *capote*. As with pedestrian *toreo*, the manoeuvres that appear to be most difficult generally involve less risk, and vice versa. (Placing the *banderillas* while urging the horse through a flank-width gap between the bull and the *barrera*, although demanding perfect timing, is less hazardous than the same feat with the bull with its back to the *barrera*. In the former, the bull has its agility impeded by the fence as it emerges from the encounter, and the rider and his mount have the whole ring to work in, whereas in the latter, the opposite is the case. If the first *rejón de muerte* fails to bring about the death of the bull, further attempts may be made, but if the bull has not been despatched within five minutes of the president's signal for the final *suerte*, the *rejoneador* or his *sobresaliente* are obliged to try to kill the animal using a sword and *muleta* on foot, from which time they are subject to the regulations relating to the regular foot *toreros* from the sounding of the first *aviso*. Awards to the *rejoneador* are based on the skill and grace demonstrated during the three *suertes,* supplemented by additional consideration for his merit if he has placed the *banderillas* with two hands instead of holding them in one hand while controlling the horse with the other, or if he has practised the *suerte de la rosa* (a manoeuvre in which a single *banderilla*, which may be as little as 15 cm. (6 in.) long, ornamented with a large rosette) is placed by the horseman who has to stand in the stirrup and lean over the horns to do so.

In the *TOURADA PORTUGUESA*, which takes place only in the plazas of Portugal, where the public killing of bulls was made illegal in 1933, the animal is not put to death in the ring, but is removed to the slaughterhouse where it is generally despatched on the following day. Since 1941 no *picadeiros* are used and although *espadas* (swordsmen) sometimes participate, their performance is restricted to work with the cape and *muleta*, finishing with a simulated kill by placing a *bandarilha* where the sword should pierce the bull. The *passeio* (parade) of the *tourada* generally consists of one or two teams of eight *forcados* (catchers)

and two or more *cavaleiros* (mounted bullfighters), each of whom is accompanied by two *peãos* (capemen on foot). The *forcados* are dressed in flower-patterned coats, khaki breeches, and red and green stocking caps. The *cavaleiros* are dressed in a seventeenth-century costume of gold-embroidered thigh-length coats, three-cornered hats, tight-fitting breeches, and silver-spurred top-boots. *Espadas* and *peãos* wear the costume of their Spanish counterparts. The *passeio* also includes the *campinos* (bull-herders) with bright scarlet waistcoats and white stockings, carrying long poles.

The *tourada* begins with the mounted *cavaleiro* awaiting the entry of the bull (whose horns have had the tips removed or covered with leather padding) opposite the gate of the *touril* (bull pen). He is armed with a *farpa* (a *bandarilha* similar to its Spanish equivalent but about 1·4 m. — 4 ft. 7 in. — long). The horseman is flanked by two *peãos*, who play the bull when it enters to familiarize the *cavaleiro* with its movements. The *farpa* is then placed, using techniques analogous to Spanish *toreo*, the shaft of the *farpa* breaking off to unfurl a small flag which is used to play the bull. Thereafter a number of *bandarilhas* of various lengths, becoming progressively shorter, are placed, using a wide variety of citing techniques and equestrian manoeuvres. When the *cavaleiro* leaves the arena the *peãos* cape the bull further to reduce its impetuosity.

The last phase of the *tourada*, the *pega*, is the catching of the bull by the *forcados*. The eight men enter the ring while the *peãos* divert the bull's attention on the far side. The *forcados* approach the animal from behind, strung out in single file. When at close quarters, the leading *forcado* claps his hands, calling and challenging the bull. The bull turns round quickly and generally charges straight and fast at the strutting *forcado* who waits it with his hands behind his back. At the last moment, the man takes a step or two backward to soften the blow, and flings himself between the horns, locking his hands underneath the bull's neck. The impetus carries the bull into the rest of the team, who move to right and left in turn, so that eventually there are two at the head, two at the neck, one holding the tail, and the remaining two clinging to the forepart of the animal. When the bull is brought to a standstill, the seven men make their escape. Their companion hangs on to the tail of the bull while the animal circles trying to catch him. Ultimately the man releases his hold and walks away, and oxen are brought in to remove the bull.

The *COURSE À LA COCARDE*, which originated in Provence more than four centuries ago, still flourishes in many parts of southern France, notably, in Arles, Nîmes, Avignon, Marseilles, and Montpellier.

The Camargue bull, which is a feature of this event, is not injured during the encounter, and may take part in about half a dozen *courses* each season, frequently enjoying a fame which eclipses that of the human participants.

The object of the latter is to remove, without recourse to any lure other than the human body, a small *cocarde* (cloth rosette) attached to the horns by a string harness, followed by the retrieval of two small woollen pompons attached to the base of the horns by elastic bands. Money prizes are awarded, generally supplemented by donations from the spectators, the *cocarde* earning the highest reward, followed by the string harness and the pompons.

The performers in the *course à la cocarde* are dressed in white trousers and short-sleeved shirts, and they wear running shoes.

The bull begins its career at about three years old, and although usually castrated, it is nevertheless nearly as aggressive as its Spanish counterpart, from which it differs considerably in conformation, the weight being more evenly distributed and the horns pointing upward.

The removal of the trophies is done in three ways, in all of which the only implement employed is the *crochet* (a four-pronged metal comb held in the palm of the hand) which was introduced in 1900.

The most difficult technique is the *razet* (the ploy involving a lone man) which consists of attracting the bull's attention, running towards it head on, swerving at the last moment to slow down and deflect the charge while passing the arm between the horns to snatch the prize. The escape, made at high speed, ends with the man leaping over the barrier with the horns a fraction behind him.

The *à la reprise* (retake) method involves the intervention of a *tourneur* (an aide who turns the bull round by running in a tight circle) to position the bull to enable the *razeteur* to perform his task. The feat is also performed *à la bourre* (taking the animal by surprise when it is in pursuit of another object) by the involvement of a number of *razeteurs* who run at the bull in quick succession until one of them gets within reach of the prize.

The *course à la cocarde* is also known as the *course libre*.

The Spanish bull used for *corridas* is completely different in breeding, physique, and temperament from the domestic bovine animal. For about four years it lives only with other bulls occasionally tended by a mounted ranch hand. The terrain on which it is reared is selected to provide adequate distance between its food and water supplies to ensure ample exercise to build muscular strength. It has little experience of man on foot at close quarters and until it is sent to the plaza it knows nothing of confinement. The bull is reared from a sire chosen for its physical conformation, and a dam selected for a ready disposition to attack at the slightest provocation. This derives from a popular (but scientifically unsubstantiated) belief on the part of the breeders that a bull inherits its *trapio* (physical presence) from the male parent and its aggressive characteristics from the female.

The selection of the parent cow is established on the ranch at a *tienta* (the testing of two-year-old *vacas bravas*—fighting cows —to determine their suitability for reproducing *toros de lidia*. Young bulls are never tested in the *tienta* bull ring unless they are going to be used for stud purposes. The cows selected for consideration are herded into the corrals of a miniature bull ring on the ranch. There they are separated by a system of multiple doors and open-topped passageways which permit their being manipulated from the walls above with *garrochas* which are also carried by the *vaqueros* (mounted herdsmen) in the open countryside to ward off an unexpected attack. The cows are let into the small arena one at a time at a signal from the *ganadero* (the bull-breeder who owns the ranch) who sits in a box overlooking the small plaza accompanied by his *mayoral* (foreman) and a few guests. When the cow is let into the arena it meets a mounted *vaquero* (armed with a *garrocha* with a small spiked end) on the opposite side of the plaza and a *torero* on foot (armed with a cape). If it is a spirited animal, the cow will attack the mounted *vaquero* who wards it off by thrusting the pointed end of the *garrocha* into the summit of the animal's withers. The extent to which the *vaca* continues to attack and the number of times when, having disengaged itself, it returns to the encounter spontaneously are a measure of its suitability for the breeding of *toros de lidia*. While the *ganadero* and the *mayoral* make notes on its comportment, the *vaca* is then played, first with the cape and then with the *muleta* by the *torero* on foot.

The *torero* is generally a matador, a *novillero*, an *aspirante* (before becoming a *novillero* every *torero* must have made at least ten public appearances in this category, in which he is required to face two-year-old bulls in *corridas* without picadors), or a *maletilla*. The *maletilla* is an itinerant unqualified *torero* who roams the countryside in the hope of being allowed to appear in *capeas*, village bullfights in improvised rings of piled ox-carts, often featuring older bulls which have been previously caped. Though illegal, due to the high death and accident rate, *capeas* are nevertheless frequently held. For *tientas*, too, the *maletillas* turn up in droves in the mostly forlorn hope of being allowed to gain some practice and perhaps be noticed by someone sufficiently influential in the taurine world to further their careers. In addition to the professional and aspiring *toreros* who take part in *tientas*, it is not unusual for the *ganadero* and members of his family and friends to take part in the event. Traditional dress for participants in the *tienta* is the *traje de campo*, consisting of the *chaquetilla* (short waistcoat-length jacket), *calzonas* (three-quarter-length trousers), *botas camperas* (high leather country boots), and *zahones* (leather chaps).

After each cow has been tested it is taken from the ring, usually by a *vaquero* on foot without implements who incites the charge of the animal by running across its line of vision, deftly side-stepping at the last moment to reveal a door through which the *vaca* charges back into the corral. The classification of each animal is entered in the breeder's register: '*toro*' (indicating its suitability for breeding for the bull ring) or '*buey*' (indicating that it is suitable only for beef production). In the event of the latter classification, the scrupulous breeder has the animal re-branded or otherwise prominently marked to ensure that it is not used to breed bulls destined for the *plaza de toros*. Sometimes the cows selected for breeding for the ring are tested again in the following year to ensure that their quality has been maintained.

Cows are also sometimes tested by *acoso y derribo* (pursuit and tumble) in which they are chased by mounted *vaqueros* and overturned by the thrusting of blunt *garrochas* into their flanks. A *vaquero* on horseback with a spiked *garrocha* and a *torero* stand by to check the animal's reaction to the experience.

The cows used for breeding *toros de lidia* are from three to ten years old, are on heat at three-weekly intervals two or three times each spring, and shed their young in the winter after slightly more than nine months' gestation. The *semental* (stud bull) ideally is from three to six years old, but may be older, and is placed with a herd of from twenty to fifty cows for four or five months during the spring. The *semental*, although principally selected for its appearance, also has its aggressive characteristics taken into account, and its blood lines carefully traced to maintain continuity of the qualities required, in line with the established principles of selective breeding. After their birth, the calves are milk-fed until the autumn when they are separated from their mothers. Their diet thereafter consists of pasturage, complemented in inclement weather by beans, oats, rye, fodder, and feed containing a balance of protein, vitamin, and mineral elements calculated to develop the physique compatible with their ultimate role in the *corrida*.

When the bull calf is separated from its mother it is branded with the *hierro* (hot-iron brand mark) of the breeder on its right rear flank, and with a registration number on its side. Additionally a separate single digit indicates the year of birth to prevent the fraudulent presentation of under-age bulls in the *plaza*. The ears are also notched further to denote the identity of the breeder, and then sterilized, as are the brand marks. The calf is then released into the main male herd and spends the next three years living in the open country. On the ranch, *cabestros* (steers) which are domesticated and have been trained for the purpose are used in a similar fashion to sheep-dogs to crowd the *toros de lidia* into herd formation and manoeuvre them from one place to another.

In the *plazas de toros*, the insecurity engendered by the isolation of the bull from the herd, coupled with the sense of confinement of the bull ring upon an animal unaccustomed to restraint, impels the bull to attack as a defensive measure. The *toro bravo* is not 'brave' ('*bravo*' is intended in the sense of 'wild' or savage), and its attack is the reflex action of an animal 'fleeing forwards' because of the fear engendered by unfamiliar circumstances.

By the time the *toro de lidia* is four years old it weighs more than the 460 kg. (1014 lb.) demanded by the regulations for *corridas de toros*. In physical appearance it differs considerably from the domestic bull, being comparatively light, enabling it to turn very rapidly after charging. Immediately behind the nape of the neck, the *morillo* is considerably distended and becomes more so when the animal attacks. The horns are long, tapering from about 76 mm. (3 in.) thick at the base forward and upwards to fine inturned points.

The age of the bull, which is verified by the veterinaries after the *corrida* to ensure that the animal was of regulation age, can be determined to some extent by the *anillos* (rings) at the base of the horns, one ring denoting a three-year-old, two a four-year-old, an additional ring forming each year; additionally, the bull's age can be verified from its dental formation, a three-year-old bull having four permanent and four milk teeth, a four-year-old having six permanent and two milk teeth, the eight teeth being fully formed when the bull is six years old. The dental method can be inaccurate if the animal has been given artificial feed which accelerates dental growth.

The four-year-old bull can outpace a race-horse over a short distance, and its strength is such that it can lift a rider and his mount and topple them over the barrier (1·6 m. — 5 ft. 3 in. — high) around the public bull ring.

The bulls are sent to the public *plaza de toros* by truck in *cajones* (individual crates, 2 m. (6 ft. 6 in.) high, 2·5 m. (8 ft. 3 in.) long, the width of 80 cm. (2 ft. 7½ in.) being just adequate to permit entry of the bull's body) a few days before the *corrida*. The bulls are rounded up and separated at the ranch plaza by the same method as used for the *tienta*. From the pen they are driven up a narrow ramp, the end of which is level with the base of the *cajón* which is already in place on the truck. As each bull is boxed, the open end of the *cajón* is closed by the dropping of a vertical sliding gate into place. The truck is then manoeuvred into position and the next bull is loaded in the same way. The *mayoral* generally travels with the bulls to the plaza to supervise the unloading at their destination and to ensure that the animals are not tampered with *en route*. Generally, seven bulls are provided by the *ganadero*, one being the *sobrero* (reserve substitute) which will be used in the event that one of the six bulls destined for the *corrida* is accidentally injured or rejected by the plaza veterinaries for some defect. At the plaza the bulls are unloaded and placed together in a corral where they are fed and watered daily by the *mayoral* or a *vaquero* from the ranch until the day of the *corrida*.

On the evening previous to, or the early morning of, the *corrida* the bulls are inspected in the corrals by the veterinaries, whose principal function is to ensure that they appear to be in sound health, free of physical defects, and of sufficient size and presence for the type of *corrida* being held in the particular category of plaza.

On the morning of the *corrida*, immediately after the *sorteo*, the *apartado* (the separating and penning of the bulls) takes place, by the use of *cabestros* and a system of doors and passageways similar to that used at the ranch. The pens are dimly lit to relax the bull; they are not in darkness since emergence into the bright sunlight would impair the animal's vision, a faculty which requires to be preserved intact if the bull is to be successfully deceived by the *torero*'s lures.

Despite the regulations governing the *corrida*, malpractices occur, particularly with respect to manipulation of the natural faculties of the bull. In a profession where injury entails the loss of a substantial number of contracts, the participants are encouraged to practise chi-canery, not from lack of courage, which they are called upon to display daily, but because of the substantial loss of revenue which results from their being incapacitated. The most common method of reducing the lethal attributes of the bull is *afeitar* (horn-shaving). If a bull which has become accustomed to the disposition of the tips of its horns has a portion of them removed, it is in a similar position to a boxer were it possible for him to have the length of his arms reduced. Any blow falls short of the mark. The method of shortening a bull's horns is to saw about 75 mm. (3 in.) off the tips, resharpen them with a file, and then cover up the evidence by working a viscous staining fluid (generally sump oil) into the horns to restore the natural texture. This is carried out at times at the ranch, if the breeder is unscrupulous, where the animal is constrained in a *mueco* (a cradle in which it can be firmly tethered for medical treatment), or in the transport *en route* for the plaza if the aid of the *mayoral* can be enlisted. Periodically, in response to public outcry, the authorities tighten up the regulations in an attempt to stamp out the practice, but that it persists is evidenced by the number of fines imposed every season.

Another method used to reduce the bull's faculties is the administration of a salt diet. Again, providing that the co-operation of the *mayoral* or the *vaquero* can be enlisted, before the *corrida* the bull is given large quantities of salt, to which it is partial, then allowed to drink large quantities of water to assuage its thirst. The result is almost instantaneous diarrhoea which considerably weakens the animal and renders it much more manageable in the bull ring. Again, although not widespread, there is continuing evidence of this practice.

Other malpractices, such as placing the bull head downwards in an inclined crate to disorientate it, sandbagging the kidney region to induce debility, and the administration of drugs, have been abandoned because of the difficulty of assessing the dosage and timing, and the high risk of catalepsy involved.

While bull-breeding traditionally has been the indulgent privilege of rich landowners (the high costs of breeding and rearing the *toro de lidia*, together with the vast tracts of land needed, and the fact that frequently less than 20 per cent of the stock reared can be disposed of to the bull rings, combine to make the venture unprofitable), in recent years a new type of commercial breeder has emerged who produces on a large scale the bulls with the qualities required by the *toreros*.

The first quality that the expert *apoderado* (matador's manager) looks for in a bull for his protégé is *nobleza* (the quality of an animal which charges straight without vacillation, follows the cloth, and continues to attack regardless of its condition; these characteristics are determined by breeding and are present in some breeds more than others).

The second requirement is that the horns should be such that they will provide ample evidence to the public of the lethal potential of the animal while offering as little risk to the *torero* as possible. The preferred configuration of horns is that they point forward while slightly inturned at the tips, since a bull so armed will tend to attack in a direct line, throwing his horns squarely into the lure. Widespread horns are not favoured because the *torero* has to allow them a respectful distance, since the slightest deviation of the head may result in a *cornada* (wound). Horns which turn inward are not favoured because bulls so equipped will tend to hook as a natural consequence. Horns which turn too far inward are also not in favour because the absence of distance between the tips makes a *cornada* unlikely and the *torero*'s performance will be diminished by the obvious absence of danger. Horns with thick tips are obviously preferable to those with fine points.

The last requirement of the *apoderado* is that the bull should have good presence and bulk, without undue muscularity, so that its appearance is acceptable to the public without presenting its *torero* with an animal comprised of solid muscle which could arrive at the *muleta* with such excessive vigour that the *faena* suffers for it. Ideally the bull should arrive at the *muleta parado* (stopped) to the extent that it will not charge involuntarily, while retaining sufficient vigour to attack when incited.

Most matadors have preferences for certain breeds of bull, and the commercial breeders try to accommodate their requirements. However, some of the traditional breeders whose bulls have been prominent for generations continue to breed animals which by virtue of their presence and temperament are infrequently seen in *corridas*, and then are almost invariably faced by matadors of the second category.

The most notable of these is the Miura breed of Seville, referred to as the 'Bulls of Death', a strain which has accounted for the deaths of nine *toreros* in the past century including the unfortunate MANOLETE. In 1908 the leading *toreros* formed a pact banning these bulls entirely. The Miura bull is reputed to possess *sentido* (the ability to distinguish between the man and the lure) and has now all but disappeared from the major scene. Pressure of public opinion ensures that the scrupulous breeder still has a substantial outlet for his products, although the market is dominated to some extent by ranches which conform to the requirements of the top matadors.

For either category of breeder the market is relatively substantial. About 600 *corridas de toros* and 400 *novilladas* are held in Spain each season, and almost 100 events of both varieties take place in France, bringing the total of bulls killed to well over 6,000 each year. The value of a four-year-old *toro de lidia* is about £400. The principal bull-breeding areas of Spain are Andalusia, the Central Zone, and Salamanca. There are almost 300 registered breeders.

Bullfighting, in one form or another, has existed for more than 40,000 years, since Palaeolithic man, in his quest for food, engaged the Stone Age bull in mortal combat.

The implements used by the prehistoric *torero* were clubs, knives, axes, and spears, the efficacy of which was considerably improved by the discovery of the cutting properties of flint. One of the animals then greatly in evidence was the auroch, now extinct, which stood 6 ft. high (1·8 m.) at the shoulder and had vast horns. It was a remote ancestor of the Spanish *toro de lidia*. Stone Age man left a very revealing record of his bullfighting activities in Europe. For some 25,000 years, the walls of caves have borne evidence in drawings depicting bulls not very dissimilar to the *toro* of today; often the animals are shown bloody or disembowelled, and menaced by the implements used to kill it.

As a breeder, Neolithic man some 12,000 years ago recognized the bull's powerful procreative capacity without at first associating it with his own activity; as a grower of crops, he observed the increased yield of ground broken by the bull. Even the invention of the plough did not dispel his delusion, since the implement was attached to the animal's horns. The bull and its horns became a powerful symbol of fertility which led to its worship and the eventual attempt to gain possession of its mystical force by ritual killing, the forerunner of the *corrida*.

Five thousand years ago, in Mesopotamia and India, the bull was worshipped and ritually sacrificed. The Babylonian legend of the slaying of the Bull of Heaven by Gilgamesh is the oldest written account of a bullfight. The sacred Hindu manuscript, the *Rig-Veda*, describes ritual sacrifices, some of them involving entire herds of bulls. The cult spread to Egypt, Africa, and the Levant.

In Crete, nearly 4,000 years ago, during the spring fertility rites wild bulls were taken to the arena at Knossos. Various exploits were performed with them, all involving the touching of the bull's horns to procure the benefit of the fertility they were believed to possess. The Cretan *corrida* was initiated with a ritual which involved young men and women confronting a bull, awaiting its onslaught, and at the last moment, grasping the horns and somersaulting, to land feet first on the animal's back or on the ground. There are many representations of the feat in the form of metal-worked urns and sculptures from the period. The Cretan *corrida* also featured the ritual killing of bulls by grasping one horn and the muzzle and breaking the animal's neck, or by stabbing or bleeding it to death. The last two methods appear to have been practised only by priests and kings.

Three thousand years ago, in Greece, devotees of the bull-god Dionysus, after drinking large quantities of sacramental wine, dismembered live bulls and ate the raw flesh. Worshippers of Zeus conducted more complex ceremonies such as the *Bouphonia* (ox- or bull-murder), a ritual contrived to provide evidence for a subsequent trial which condemned the sacrificial knife to be flung into the sea, absolving the participants of blame.

Between 1200 and 600 B.C., many Greek and Etruscan tribes migrated to Italy, taking their bull-cults with them. Their rituals included the sacrifice of bulls, which was preceded by hunts in which youths ran alongside the herd, overturning the animals by grasping them by their horns and forelegs. Likewise, the inhabitants of Italia (land of cattle) venerated the bull-god.

When Rome finally conquered the peninsula, the bull-hunting and ritual killing activities of rural Italy became transformed into the spectacles of the Roman arena. Julius Caesar introduced the auroch. One bullfighter who achieved considerable success with the aurochs was Martial as Karpophorus. Most of these early bullfights consisted of the slaying of a bull by a single man armed with a sword and a small shield; Ovid says that a red cloth was used to induce the animal to charge. At times Christians were thrown into the arena to abate the initial ferocity of the bull.

By 206 B.C. Spain was under the dominance of Rome, which within the century declared the bull-cult of Mithras an official religion. Its rites included a baptismal ceremony in which a bull was slaughtered on a wooden grille over a pit occupied by converts who became drenched in blood. The Roman *corrida* and the Mithraic rituals were popularly received by the Iberian people, who had come into contact with most of the bull-cults of the old world, including that of the Celts who had invaded Iberia in 400 B.C. and occupied most of the peninsula. The Iberians practised bull-worship long before the Romans came and undoubtedly held improvised bull-fights, but it was the invaders who built the arenas and amphitheatres in the principal cities in which organized spectacles took place.

When Christianity ousted Mithraism, towards the end of the fourth century, Theodosius the Great in Christian Rome issued an edict banning animal sacrifices under penalty of death. Early in the fifth century, the invasion of Spain by the Visigoths resulted in a regeneration of the *corrida*, although by this time it had lost most of its religious significance and largely took the form of displays of prowess in jousting.

After the arrival of the Moors at the beginning of the eighth century, the *corrida* took on a more formalized pattern. It is highly probable that the Moors, accustomed to boar-hunts on foot and horseback, saw in the bull ring a new outlet for their aptitude with the javelin. Moorish ballads of the period describe the *paseillo* of horsemen accompanied by music, and the custom of dedicating the death of the bull to royal patrons and friends.

The first public announcement of a *corrida* was that celebrating the marriage in Avila of the Infante Sancho de Estrada in 1080. A *corrida* was held in 1107 for the marriage of Blasco Muñoz; another was held at Varea, Logroño, in 1133 to celebrate the coronation of Alfonso VII; and yet another in Léon in 1140 honoured the marriage of his daughter.

At the time of the eviction of the Moors at the end of the fifteenth century, the *corrida* consisted largely of the participation of nobles on horseback armed with lances and javelins, accompanied by *peones* on foot armed with a variety of weapons such as spears, lances, knives, and cloth lures which may have been capes.

Royal patronage, and at times participation, favoured the *corrida* in the sixteenth and seventeenth centuries, although this period was subject to a number of Papal interdictions. Charles V fought a bull in Valladolid in 1527 to honour the birth of his son. Philip IV also took part in *corridas*.

The modern *corrida de toros* came into being at the beginning of the eighteenth century. Philip V was strongly opposed to the bullfight, and concerned at the number of nobles and potential knightly warriors it disabled. In deference to his wishes, the nobles began to abandon the arena.

For some time the exploits of the *peones* in manoeuvring the animals for the horsemen, and dispatching bulls which had not succumbed to the lance, had attracted the interest of the public, and *corridas* involving commoners began to take place. Initially, pride of place was given to the picador who had replaced the knight on horseback, and to the awesome appearance and ferocity of his adversary. The matador for a time was relegated to a subordinate role, ultimately to be reversed.

Practically nothing is known of these early *corridas*, but about 1726 a matador named FRANCISCO ROMERO became a celebrity and from thereon the history of the *corrida* is better documented. He is said by some to have invented the *muleta*, but it is known to have existed previously.

From 1726 onwards, the status of the matador gradually increased until, by the end of the nineteenth century, the importance of his role and the sequence of the events of the *corrida* were much the same as they are today.

By the turn of the century, although the public still attached great importance to the size and ferocity of the bulls and the skill of the picador, the matador had become the focal point. Although the measure of his ability was largely confined to his skill with the sword, and his capework and *muletazos* were mainly viewed as functional manoeuvres to enable the *suerte de varas* and the kill to be efficiently executed, the significance of *toreo*, in the modern sense of the term, was beginning to take shape.

By 1913, when BELMONTE took the *alternativa*, work with the *capote* and *muleta* were as important as ability with the sword. Between 1913 and 1920, the 'Golden Age' of *toreo*, Belmonte and JOSELITO frequently appeared together, competing for supremacy. The style adopted during this period was *toreo de frente*. The bulls of the 'Golden Era' were said to be five years old and to weigh 570 kg. (1254 lb.). The present regulations provide for bulls of 460 kg. (1012 lb.) minimum and four years old.

By 1930, when ORTEGA appeared, *toreo de tres cuartos* was being practised. It had begun to emerge some time previously, and may well have been originated by Belmonte's custom with recalcitrant bulls of advancing the right leg to incite the attack when initiating a *naturale*; when he swivelled on the balls of his feet during the pass, it took him into the *toreo de tres cuartos* position.

By the end of the Spanish Civil War in 1939, *toreo de perfil* was already in fashion; detractors attribute its perpetuation to Manolete, while extolling him as one of the greatest matadors of all time.

Tremendismo, which was encountered periodically before the advent of EL CORDOBES in 1963, has since become a major vogue for a new genre of *aficionado*, hitherto rarely seen in the *plaza de toros*.

Matadors become public figures in a variety of ways. Taurine schools exist, but no leading modern matador has ever graduated from one. Frequently he is a continuation of a dynasty of *toreros* in a family which has contributed to taurine history for several generations; at times matadors have originated as penniless urchins. At first almost all matadors pay impresarios for the privilege of appearing in a public *plaza de toros*. Thereafter for a season or two they are fortunate to receive their bare expenses for the *corridas* in which they take part. It is usually not until a matador has begun to command a following that he is able to charge fees for his participation. While initially such fees will be relatively low (in view of the expenses which a matador has to meet for payment to his *cuadrilla*, hotel and travelling expenses, and the purchase and upkeep of equipment), should he be sufficiently fortunate and talented to become a national figure his earnings can amount to a million pounds sterling in two or three seasons at the top of his profession. In most cases a substantial proportion of this income reverts to his backers who financed his early days.

The life of a matador at the summit is arduous, not only in terms of physical risk and intense strain. Additionally he is subjected to the fatigue imposed by travelling thousands of miles each season, mostly by road at night, trying to sleep while his car travels the uneven, undulating roads of Spain to keep his engagements. *Toreros* have been known to appear in a different plaza in a different town every day for a month at a time, and most of the élite will undertake fifty to a hundred engagements during the six months of the season. The matador frequently arrives in a town during the early morning, rests until noon, eats a small lunch (his food intake before a *corrida* has to be minimal to avoid complications should he find himself on the operating-table later in the day), dresses for his rendezvous with the bulls, fulfils his function in the *corrida*, and leaves immediately afterwards for an assignment the following day in another part of the country.

The training of a matador initially takes the form of *toreo de salón* (practising with the cape and *muleta*, with a colleague armed with a pair of horns playing the part of the bull; the horns are also mounted on a *carretón*—a wooden carriage constructed to simulate the vital regions of the bull, mounted on a bicycle wheel and equipped with handles — for practice with the *banderillas* and sword). Thereafter he takes part in as many *tientas* as possible, and may slip into the fields at night to cape bulls in the open country. This is illegal and punishable by heavy penalties, because the animals gain from the experience and are dangerous when brought to the bull ring. The matador's first public performances take place in villages in improvised rings, frequently with no medical facilities, where he faces *morucho* (half-breed) cattle of both sexes (the female being the more dangerous because absence of testicles permits a much shorter turning circle) some of which have been caped before and are therefore more dangerous. If he survives the ordeal and surmounts the financial obstacles to become a prominent *torero*, he is afforded the privilege of selecting, or having selected for him by experts, the breeds and types of bulls he faces.

The principal bull rings of Spain are in Madrid, Barcelona, Seville, Valencia, San Sebastian, Bilbao, and Zaragoza. The *plaza Monumental* in Madrid holds 23,000 spectators. There are some 400 permanent *plazas de toros* in Spain, the oldest being that of Bejar (Salamanca) which was inaugurated in 1707. The average size of plaza has a diameter of 50 m. (164 ft.).

The recognized Spanish season commences with the Feria of Valencia in March and concludes with the Feria of Zaragoza in October, but *corridas* are more and more frequently held outside these dates.

The Spanish form of *corrida* is also to be found on a major scale in Latin America in Mexico (where the principal plaza holds 46,000), Peru, Venezuela, Colombia, and Ecuador, and many Spanish *toreros* spend their winter season in these countries. Likewise, Latin American *toreros* are a feature of the Spanish scene, but on a lesser scale. The Spanish version is also encountered in France, notably in Provence and regions north of the Pyrenees, where the law permits performances in places where it is traditional to the locality, failure to hold a *corrida* for a period of one year involving permanent forfeiture of franchise under penalty of prosecution.

There are 41 bull rings in Portugal in which the *tourada* is held. The event also takes place outside Portugal — in Lourenço Marques, Beira, Luanda, Lobito, and Benguela. In addition to providing animals for their own events, Portuguese breeders send bulls to the Spanish rings with some success.

Bullfighting has taken place in England on an almost negligible scale; the last *corrida*, which involved the participation of Spanish matadors, was held at the Royal Agricultural Hall, London, on 18 March 1870. While it was in progress, the event was suspended on the intervention of the R.S.P.C.A. and the *toreros* were fined £1 each. Bloodless *corridas*, which were held in the U.S.A. in the late 1960s, in which *banderillas* were placed in a foam pad attached to the animals and the *suerte de matar* omitted, were poorly attended. A direct television transmission via satellite to America of a *corrida* held in Spain in 1970 brought public protest.

Antonio Abad Ojuel and Emilio L. Oliva, *Los Toros* (1966); José Silva Aramburu, *Enciclopedia Taurina* (1961); Huldine Beamish, *Cavaliers of Portugal* (1966); Eduardo Bonet, Luis Fernández Salcedo, *et al*, *Bulls and Bullfighting* (1970); Barnaby Conrad, *Encyclopedia of Bullfighting* (1962) and *How to Fight a Bull* (1968); Gregorio Corrochano, *Teoria de las Corridas de Toros* (1962) and *Qué es torear?* (1966); José Maria de Cossío, *Los Toros* (vols. I-IV) (1943); Ernest Hemingway, *Death in the Afternoon* (1932); Jose Delgado Hillo, *La Tauromaquia* (1894); Auguste Lafront, *Encyclopédie de la Corrida* (1950); Néstor Lujan, *Historia del Toreo* (1954); Angus Macnab, *Fighting Bulls* (1959); Benito Madariaga, *El Toro de Lidia* (1966); John Marks, *To the Bullfight Again* (1966); John McCormick and Mario Sevilla Mascarenas, *The Complete Aficionado* (1967); J. Sánchez de Neira, *El Toreo* (1879); Domingo Ortega, *El Arte de Toreo* (1950); Claude Popelin, *Le Taureau et son combat* (1952) and *La Tauromachie* (1970); Manuel Lozano Sevilla, *La Fiesta de los Toros* (1965); R. H. Smythe, *Animal Vision* (1961).

BULTEEL, Sir JOHN CROCKER (1891-1956), was the most outstanding clerk of the course in the history of HORSE RACING, holding this appointment at ASCOT for some ten years.

BUMPING RACES, see ROWING.

BUNBURY, Sir CHARLES (1740-1821), was the first uncrowned 'King of the Turf' and almost 'perpetual president' of the English JOCKEY CLUB for more than forty years. He owned Diomed, winner of the first race for the DERBY STAKES in 1780; Eleanor, the first filly to win the Derby and OAKS; and Smolensko, the first colt to win the Derby and TWO THOUSAND GUINEAS.

BUNTON, HAYDN (1911-56), Australian Rules footballer who won the CHARLES BROWNLOW MEDAL three times; he played for Fitzroy as a rover. He had abundant energy and stamina. In his first two seasons in the VICTORIAN FOOTBALL LEAGUE (1931 and 1932) he won Brownlow medals, and he won another in 1935. He later transferred to Western Australia where he won the Sandover Medal (the equivalent of the Charles Brownlow Medal) three times. He finished his FOOTBALL career in South Australia.

BURGE, FRANK (1896-1958), Australian RUGBY LEAGUE player. He was perhaps the greatest try-scoring forward in the game's history. His achievement in scoring 33 tries during the Australian tour of England in 1921-2 was outstanding. Long-striding, fast, and powerful, he had a keen sense of anticipation and was also a strong tackler. He played in nine tests against Great Britain.

BURGHLEY, Lord, see EXETER, Marquess of.

BURGIS, GORDON (c. 1945-   ), British surfer and snow skier from Jersey. He came first in the European SURFING championships held in Jersey in 1969 and represented Great Britain in the world championship held in Australia in 1970.

BURNY, JEAN PIERRE (fl. 1968-70), Belgian canoeist of the Ghent Canoe Club whose ability covers both flat-water and rough-water canoe racing. In 1968 he was a finalist in the K2 event at the Mexico Olympic Games, while in the following year he won the world championship event in K1 of the down-river race at Bourg St. Maurice, France. This was followed in 1970 by his winning a bronze medal at the world sprint championships in Copenhagen in the men's K1 500 metres.

BURTON, Mrs. BERYL (1937-   ), British amateur cyclist on road and world CYCLING championships during the 1960s and early 1970s, Mrs. Burton is chiefly remarkable for her achievements in the domestic field of time-trialling. The only woman consistently to beat top-class male riders in open events, in 1967 she covered 277¼ miles (446·19 km.) in a 12-hour time trial — 5¾ miles (9·25 km.) more than the existing British men's record; and in 1968 she rode 100 miles (160·934 km.) in 3 hrs. 55 min. 5 sec., although it was not until 1956 that the men's record had been brought under 4 hrs. She set one world record of 28 min. 58·4 sec. for 20 km. (12·427 miles) at Milan in 1960, and also held national women's records at 10 miles (16·093 km.), 25 miles (40·234 km.), and 50 miles (80·467 km.) on the road, and at 1 mile (1·609 km.) and 5 miles (8·047 km.) on the track. She held the British women's Best All-Rounder title every year between 1959 and 1973. Although she found the atmosphere of the world championships less congenial, up to 1970 Mrs. Burton had won five gold, three silver, and three bronze medals in the pursuit event, and two gold and one silver in the road race; only ERMOLAEVA (Russia) showed a comparable success in world championships.

BUSBY, Sir MATTHEW, C.B.E. (1909-   ), Association footballer for MANCHESTER CITY, LIVERPOOL, and Scotland for whom he made one appearance in a full international match. Originally an inside forward, he settled to a successful playing career at wing half with Manchester City, with whom he played in the F.A. Cup finals of 1933 and 1934, and Liverpool to whom he was transferred in 1936. After the war he became manager of MANCHESTER UNITED and achieved his greatest ambition in 1968 at WEMBLEY when they beat BENFICA in the final of the European Champion Clubs Cup. Eight months later he announced his retirement as team manager but retained his interest in the club as general manager. Manchester United with Busby as manager won the League championship five times and were six times runners-up, and reached the F.A. Cup final four times and were twice the winners. Busby was given the freedom of Manchester in 1967, and knighted in 1968.

BUTCHER, D. G. (1905-   ), British professional SQUASH RACKETS player. He won the British Open championship in 1930 by beating Read (who had been designated champion) in the first challenge of that event. He beat off a challenge by Arnold in the following year but in 1932 and 1934 he was beaten by AMR BEY. Butcher was professional champion, 1930-5 and professional doubles champion, 1937-8. He was professional at the Conservative and LANSDOWNE CLUBS in London and at the Hampstead Squash Club before emigrating to Australia in 1955.

BUTTERS, (JOSEPH ARTHUR) FRANK (1878-1957) was eight times the leading racehorse trainer in England and won 15 classic races for his patrons. Among many famous horses who passed through his Fitzroy House stable at Newmarket were FAIRWAY, for Lord DERBY, and the triple-crown winner (see HORSE RACING) BAHRAM for the AGA KHAN.

BUTTON, DICK (1929-   ), ice figure-skater for the U.S.A. who once held five titles simultaneously, a unique distinction. He was world champion five consecutive times, 1948-52; twice Olympic champion, 1948 and 1952; thrice North American champion, 1947, 1949, and 1951; seven times United States champion, 1946-52; and once European champion, 1948, the last occasion when the latter was open to Americans.

He began skating at the age of 12, won the U.S. junior championship when 15, and, at 16, became the youngest man to hold the U.S. senior title. The first skater to perform a triple jump (three mid-air revolutions before landing), Button achieved the first real triple loop jump in time for the 1952 WINTER OLYMPIC

GAMES in Oslo and began a new era of athleticism in jumping on skates. Button has favoured dropping compulsory figures from championships and deciding titles solely on free skating. In 1949 he was awarded the Sullivan Trophy by the U.S. Amateur Athletic Union, presented to the nation's outstanding athlete of the year. After 1952, he turned professional to appear in ice shows, and afterwards became a television commentator on skating.

BUXTON, Mrs. MARJORIE (*née* Lockley) (1906-   ), a versatile LACROSSE player for Wales and captain of the first touring team to Ireland and to Jersey. She was usually a home. She and her sisters were active in establishing clubs and in forming the Welsh association. She went to the U.S.A. with the coaching team in 1934, which led to many years of coaching lacrosse teams in that country.

BYERLEY TURK (*c.* 1682) was one of the three foundation fathers of the thoroughbred race-horse, together with the DARLEY ARABIAN and the GODOLPHIN BARB. The Byerley Turk became the paternal great-great-grandsire of HEROD.

C

C.A. MONTREUIL is a French walking club on the outskirts of Paris. The leading club in the Union Française de Marche, prior to 1960, it then contained the two principals of the STRASBOURG–PARIS race in the 1950s, ROGER and Godart (jnr.), and the then outstanding junior, Delerue, in its ranks. The club included most of the leading modern national long-distance competitors, C. Bédee, Bracq, and Facquet being outstanding.

CABER, Tossing the, best-known of all events featured in meetings of Scottish professional athletes, and also practised in other parts of the Commonwealth. The caber is a tree trunk of unspecified size, but according to the rules of the SCOTTISH GAMES ASSOCIATION, it should be 'of a length and weight beyond the powers of the best athlete to turn'.

The caber is presented vertically to the competitor, who makes a platform of his hands to take its weight, his arms stretched down in front of him. In the perfect toss, the caber will revolve longitudinally, landing with its base pointing away from the competitor. It should point in the exact direction he was facing at the moment of throw (known as a 'twelve o'clock toss'), and not be angled to left or right.

In competition, the thrower has three trials and is judged on the best of his hands to his satisfaction, even if he subsequently drops it. There are no restrictions on the length of his run nor the mark from which he makes the throw.

Caber-tossers who compete regularly in the same area become familiar with the individual characteristics of each caber, which, once it has been tossed, must never be cut. One of the greatest challenges in Scotland is presented by the Braemar caber, which weighs more than 120 lb. (54·5 kg.) and is 19 ft. (5·79 m.) long. It was first tossed in 1951 by George Clark, who was then 51 years old.

A new caber, never tossed, may be shortened if none of the competing athletes is able to toss it successfully.

CAGANCHO (Joaquín Rodríguez) (1903-), Mexican *matador de toros*, one of the purest and most classical of *toreros*, renowned for his revolutionary configurations with the cape.

CALCUTTA CUP, RUGBY UNION perpetual challenge trophy at issue since 1878 in the annual match between England and Scotland. On the disbandment of the Calcutta Football Club in 1877, the heavily ornamented cup, 18 in. (45·72 cm.) high, was made by Indian craftsmen from the silver rupees remaining in the club funds. It was presented to the Rugby Football Union, who retain possession whether or not England wins the match.

CALDER MEMORIAL TROPHY, ICE HOCKEY trophy, awarded annually in the NATIONAL HOCKEY LEAGUE (N.H.L.) of North America to 'the player selected as the most proficient in his first year of the competition'. It was donated in 1937 by Frank Calder, first N.H.L. president, and renamed after his death in 1943. Each winner receives $1,000 and is selected by a poll of sports writers and broadcasters.

CALE GREEN, Stockport, England, the traditional home of LACROSSE in the north of England; major games have been staged there over the past 80 years. Australian, American, Canadian, and All-England sides have used the ground, and crowds of up to 10,000 have watched the matches. It is the home ground of the Stockport Lacrosse Club.

CALGARY STAMPEDERS, Canadian professional FOOTBALL team, joined the Western Interprovincial Rugby Union as the 'Bronks' in 1936, but changed their name after the Second World War. Since 1937 they have won the Western Conference title eight times; in 1948 their unbeaten team also captured the Grey Cup (see FOOTBALL, CANADIAN); in 1971 they won both the Western title and the Grey Cup. Bright led all Canadian Football League runners in yards gained rushing, with 10,909 in 13 seasons; Kwong was third, with 9,022 in 11 seasons; both men ended their careers with the EDMONTON ESKIMOS.
COLOURS: Red and white.

CALHOUN, LEE QUENCY (1933-), high hurdler for the U.S.A. The first man to win the Olympic 110 metres hurdles twice (1956 and 1960), Calhoun was technically one of the most accomplished high hurdlers of all time. He equalled the world record of 13·2 sec. in 1960.

CALIFORNIA ANGELS, American professional BASEBALL team, joined the AMERICAN LEAGUE in 1961 as the Los Angeles Angels when it expanded to ten teams. Retaining the nickname of the Los Angeles minor-league Pacific coast team, the Angels shared a ball park with the NATIONAL LEAGUE team the LOS ANGELES DODGERS and made a creditable third-place finish in 1962. In 1965 the team changed its name to California Angels and in 1966 moved into a new stadium in Anaheim close to Disneyland. In their first decade the Angels were never a contender in the American League. The pitcher Nolan Ryan set a major-league season's record of 383 strikeouts in 1973.

CALUMET FARM, Lexington, Kentucky, is one of the best-known thoroughbred horsebreeding and racing establishments in the U.S.A. It headed the winners list for many years and, in 1947, was the first to account for 100 wins and record earnings of $1,402,436 in a single season.

CAMANACHD, see SHINTY.

CAMBRIDGE UNIVERSITY BOAT CLUB. Although college ROWING at Cambridge had become established some years earlier, the University Boat Club was not founded until 1827, when regular inter-collegiate bumping races began. This pre-dates the OXFORD UNIVERSITY BOAT CLUB by 11 years.

Apart from the annual BOAT RACE against Oxford, representative Cambridge crews have competed at HENLEY and in international championships. In 1950, rowing under the colours of their reserve club, the GOLDIE BOAT CLUB, the Cambridge eight finished third in the European championship, and in 1951 Cambridge produced the first British eight to win the European championship. In 1906 Cambridge defeated Harvard in a private race over the Putney to Mortlake course, and in 1951, on a visit to the U.S.A., they were unbeaten in a series of races against American universities, including Harvard and Yale.
COLOURS: Light blue.

CAMBRIDGESHIRE HANDICAP, inaugurated in 1839, is a horse race run over 1 mile 1 furlong (1,800 m.) at NEWMARKET in early October, and is the first leg of the 'Autumn Double', the second being the CESAREWITCH HANDICAP.

CAMEL GT CHALLENGE, a series of eight to ten professional motor races on road courses conducted in the U.S.A. by the International Motor Sports Association (I.M.S.A.). The competition is open to international Touring and Grand Touring cars designated Groups 1,2,3, and 4 by the Fédération Internationale de l'Automobile (F.I.A.), the world governing body of MOTOR RACING. The F.I.A. rules of the Camel GT Challenge are much the same as the F.I.A. regulations that govern the 24 Hours of Le Mans and other classic endurance races.

Varying with the preferences of the organizers and spectators, Camel GT Challenge events range from 200 miles (322 km.) to endurance events of 12 hours. They attract audiences of more than 30,000, and entry lists of approximately 100 cars. The basic drama of this type of race is provided by the contrasting performance of the huge 7-litre Chevrolet Corvettes and Camaros, which are strong on the long straights, against the smaller-engine 3-litre PORSCHE 911 RS Carreras and similar sports cars, which are more nimble in the corners and which require fewer pit stops to replenish fuel supply. Other cars in the competition include Ford Mustang, A.M.C. Javelin, Alfa Romeo, BMW, RS Capri, and Pantera.

To fill what was then a gap in the American road-racing spectrum, the series was started without commercial sponsorship in 1971 by the young and aggressive International Motor Sports Association. That year Gregg and Haywood, co-driving a Porsche 914-6, tied for the championship. In 1972 the series acquired sponsorship by a cigarette manufacturer and became known as the Camel GT Challenge. With larger budgets for purses, promotion, and point funds, the series expanded to ten events, most of them in the eastern U.S.A. Haywood won the 1972 championship by repulsing the challenge of the big cars in a Porsche 911S powered by a 2.5-litre engine. In 1973 the series consisted of nine races with money prizes exceeding $225,000. Gregg won the championship, this time in a Porsche Carrera.

One of the races in 1973 was a 12-hour event at Sebring, Florida, formerly the site of a 12-hour race in the world manufacturers' championship. Other courses used in the series included Mid-Ohio Sports Car Course in Ohio, Lime Rock Park in Connecticut, Road Atlanta in Georgia, and Daytona International Speedway in Florida. With still greater budgets and more prestigious drivers, I.M.S.A. plans to expand its domain to several California venues.

The Camel GT Challenge is the model on which the TRANS-AM CHAMPIONSHIP of the

Sports Car Club of America is based. But because of its economic advantages and its skilful promotion, the GT series is more successful than the Trans-Am.

In 1973 I.M.S.A. was admitted to membership in the Automobile Competition Committee for the United States – F.I.A. This membership opened the way for I.M.S.A. to obtain listings on the international sporting calendar of the F.I.A. for future events in the growing GT series. Another prospect was co-operation with the United States Auto Club in presenting race events as joint ventures, featuring different kinds of cars and races in one week-end.

CAMICI, ENRICO, was for many years the leading jockey in Italy, being retained by the DORMELLO-OLGIATA stables, for whom he rode the champions Tenerani, BOTTICELLI, and RIBOT.

CAMINO, PACO (1941-   ), *matador de toros* who took the *alternativa* on 17 April 1960, is a master of all *suertes*, and although at times predisposed to *toro de perfil* he is quite capable of all forms of *toreo,* including *de frente.*

CAMIRA FLASH (1966), racing greyhound, a white and fawn dog, by Prairie Flash out of Duet Fire. The first greyhound owned by a member of the royal family, he won the 1968 GREYHOUND DERBY for H.R.H. Prince Philip, earning £8,231 for the Duke of Edinburgh Award Scheme. Trained by R. Singleton, he was attached to White City, London.

CAMOGIE, Ireland's native field sport for women, is a 12-a-side stick-and-ball game. Since it is a modified form of HURLING, the rules are very similar, but body-charging, or any other unnecessary physical contact with an opponent, is expressly forbidden. The pitch is also shorter (100 to 120 yds. long — 91–110 m.) and narrower (60 to 75 yds. wide — 55–68 m.) than the standard hurling ground. The crooked, broad-bladed stick, called the *camog*—a diminutive of the hurler's *caman* — is lighter and shorter than the hurley, being usually about 3 ft. (91 cm.) long in the handle. The ball is similar to a hurling ball, 9 to 10 in. (23–25 cm.) in circumference, but somewhat lighter.

A distinctive feature of camogie is a second crossbar across the top of the goal posts, which are 20 ft. (6·1 m.) high. A point is scored when the ball passes between the crossbars in this upper scoring space. A ball driven under the lower crossbar, which is 7 ft. (2·1 m.) high, counts as a goal and equals 3 points. The goal posts are 15 ft. (4·6 m.) apart.

As in hurling, the ball may be struck with the stick when in the air and may be lifted from ground to hand by means of the stick, but may not be picked up off the ground with the

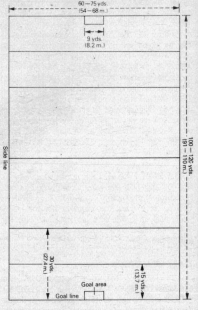

CAMOGIE PITCH

hand. If a defender fouls within her own goal area, the attacking side is awarded a free stroke from the 15-yard line opposite the spot where the infringement occurred. If a player deflects a ball over her own end line, a free stroke is given to the attacking side from a line 30 yds. (27 m.) out, at a point opposite the spot where the ball crossed the line.

The team comprises a goalkeeper, fullback, right back, centre back, left back, right wing, mid-field, left wing, right forward, centre forward, left forward, and full forward. Championship games are of 50 minutes' duration, in two halves of 25 minutes each way; a maximum of three substitutes may be introduced, and games are controlled by a referee, assisted by two goal umpires at each end and a touch judge on each side line.

The official dress is a sleeveless tunic, blouse, and black tights, together with light studded boots. Most players also like to wear short ankle-socks. The outlawing of physical contact means that success in camogie can be ensured only by complete control of stick and ball alike and the game, as played between top-class teams, can be both thrilling and artistic.

Feminism was relatively late in arriving on the Irish sports fields, and it was not until the opening years of the twentieth century that girl members of some of the Dublin branches of the national language movement, the Gaelic League, evolved, from hurling, a game all their own, which they named camogie.

The game was first played competitively in public at Navan in the autumn of 1904 and a controlling body, the Camogie Association of Ireland, was founded later that year. Little progress was made outside Dublin city and some parts of Co. Louth, and the game did not receive its first real boost until an annual inter-university competition, the Ashbourne Cup, was organized in 1915. The university cities of Dublin, Belfast, Cork, and Galway are still the great urban strongholds of the sport. But for many years the Ashbourne Cup remained the only nation-wide competition; organization, because of political troubles, was difficult until the mid-1920s.

CAMOGIE TEAM LINE-OUT
(G) Goalkeeper; (FB) full-back; (B) back; (CB) centre back; (W) wing; (MF) mid-field; (F) forward; (CF) centre forward; (FF) full forward.

		G		
		FB		
B		CB		B
W		MF		W
F		CF		F
		FF		

The Camogie Association, which for more than a decade had been almost entirely confined to Dublin, Cork, and Galway, was reorganized on a national basis in 1932. The inauguration in that year of an All-Ireland championship for county teams caused the game to spread quickly, but it was dominated by those counties which draw their strength from the big cities, Dublin, Cork, and Antrim — Dublin won more titles between 1932 and 1970 than all other counties combined. Since 1950, however, organization in the provinces has been improving steadily. Coaching courses for players and officials have raised the standard of play in the rural areas and such counties as Wexford, Kilkenny, and Tipperary have moved into the top grade.

By the beginning of 1974 there were 27 county committees affiliated to the Camogie Association, with a total of over 400 clubs and some 10,000 playing members. The Association organizes All-Ireland and provincial championships on a county basis in senior and junior and minor grades and there is an All-Ireland championship for individual schools and colleges. County championships are organized by the county committees.

The Camogie Association, although a completely independent organization, has many close links with the GAELIC ATHLETIC ASSOCIATION (G.A.A.), since both have the same objective — the advancement of native Irish games. As a result, the Camogie Association has never attempted to acquire any large enclosed grounds, since, by agreement, its championship matches are played on G.A.A. pitches.

Dublin, the leading county, has understandably produced the most outstanding personalities of the game, notably Mills, who won 15 All-Ireland medals, playing on the left wing, and O'Connor, a full forward, who won 13.

Camogie Association of Ireland, *Playing Rules and Constitution.*
GOVERNING BODY: Camogie Association of Ireland, 11 Glenbeigh Road, Dublin 7, Eire.

CAMP, WALTER CHAUNCEY (1859-1925), American college FOOTBALL player and coach, called the 'father of American football', played football at Yale from 1876 to 1881. A member of college football's rules and legislative committees from 1878 until his death, he conceived most of the basic rules that transformed American football from a variation of RUGBY into a distinctive game of its own.

In 1880 he substituted the scrimmage for the Rugby scrummage and thus established the principle of orderly possession of the ball when it was put into play. He also reduced the number of players in each team from 15 to 11 and established the alignment that became standard — seven linemen, a quarterback, two halfbacks, and a fullback. In 1882 he introduced a system of 'downs' and 'yards to gain' (then five yards in three downs), and also employed signals to call plays. In 1883 he instituted a numerical scoring system assigning point values to touchdowns, field goals, points after touchdowns, and safeties. In 1888 he persuaded the rules committee to permit tackling the ball-carrier below the waist. He was YALE's first football coach (1888-92), and then coached Stanford (1891 and 1894-5).

He was also famous for selecting an 'All-America Team' of the 11 outstanding college football players of the year by position, the first in 1889. From 1899 until his death his selections appeared annually in *Collier's*

Weekly, and were recognized as final authority on the merits of college players.

CAMP PERRY, Ohio (U.S.A.), see SHOOTING, RIFLE.

CAMPANELLA, ROY (1921-   ), American BASEBALL catcher for the BROOKLYN DODGERS, 1948 through 1957. He set a career record for home runs by a NATIONAL LEAGUE catcher, 242. He was selected as the National League's Most Valuable Player in 1951, 1953, and 1955, and was also elected to baseball's Hall of Fame.

CAMPBELL, Brig. COLIN A. (1901-   ), Canadian curler. A past president of the Canadian Curling Association, chairman of the Canadian Committee dealing with overseas tours, captain of the Canadian team in Scotland 1960, and elected president of the International Curling Federation in 1969, he was made an honorary member of the ROYAL CALEDONIAN CURLING CLUB in 1965.

CAMPBELL-LAMERTON, MICHAEL JOHN (1933-   ), RUGBY UNION lock forward for Halifax, LONDON SCOTTISH, Army, Scotland, and British LIONS. Aged 27 before he won his first Scottish cap, he went on to make 27 international appearances and captain the Lions touring party to Australasia in 1966.

CAMSELL, GEORGE H. (*fl.* 1926-36), Association footballer for Middlesbrough and England for whom he made nine appearances in full international matches between 1929 and 1936. A strongly built centre forward, he set a League scoring record in the season 1926-7 with 59 goals for Middlesbrough in the Second Division. One season later DEAN scored 60 goals for EVERTON in First Division matches to establish a new record. It was the arrival of Dean, and later Waring and Drake, that limited Camsell's appearances for England, but his 18 goals for England, including at least one in every match in which he played, is clear evidence of his exceptional ability.

CANADA CUP, see WORLD CUP (2).

CANADA MATCH, see SHOOTING, RIFLE: SERVICE CALIBRE.

CANADIAN FOOTBALL LEAGUE, see FOOTBALL, CANADIAN.

CAN-AM, the Canadian-American Challenge Cup, is an annual series of motor races, six held in the U.S.A. and two in Canada, offering the world's fastest road racing. The series, administered by the Sports Car Club of America (S.C.C.A.), has grown in attendance and prestige since its inception in 1966, with annual purses and prizes totalling close to $1 million. For the first five seasons the 'Canadian-American' champions were foreigners on holiday from Grand Prix racing. The British driver Surtees won the first championship in 1966. For the next four years the Can-Am was monopolized by two New Zealanders of Team McLaren, based at Colnbrook, near London: MCLAREN won the title in 1967 and 1969; his colleague, HULME, won in 1968 and again in 1970, after McLaren's death. It was not until 1971 that an American, REVSON, won the championship, after he had joined Team McLaren.

Revson's win was a dramatic demonstration of the invincibility of the orange Team McLaren cars. Their machines were disappointing in the opening year of 1966, but from 1967 to 1971 they won 37 of the 43 races scheduled. Two of the six events the McLaren team failed to win were taken by other teams using McLaren cars.

Team McLaren's superiority was ended in 1972 with the advent of the Turbo-charged PORSCHES, derivations of the 910s that had previously dominated the world manufacturers' championship. The 910s were modified for the shorter Can-Am races. The most important changes were a reduction in weight and replacement of the normally aspirated 5-litre engine by a turbo-charged 5-litre engine; by 1973 the turbo-charged engine was generating up to 1,100 h.p. on the dynamometer.

The turbo-Porsches — the 917-10 in 1972 and the 917-30 in 1973 — simply overwhelmed the opposition. Team McLaren won only two of the eight Can-Ams in 1972; in 1973 McClaren did not even enter the Can-Am because its normally aspirated Chevrolet V-8 engines of up to 8 litres, producing more than 700 h.p., were no match for the turbo-Porsches.

The Canadian-American Challenge Cups of 1972 and 1973 were won in works turbo-Porsches prepared by the American racing entrepreneur Penske. In 1972 the winning driver was Follmer, hurriedly substituted after Penske's premier driver, DONOHUE, was injured in a testing accident. In 1973 Donohue won the championship with six consecutive victories in the Porsche 917-30. The other two races that year were won by independently entered turbo-Porsche 917-10s, carryovers from the 1972 season.

Until 1973 Can-Am races were run as close as practicable to 200 miles (322 km.), in one sprint. In 1973 the format was changed to a qualifying heat of 75 miles (121 km.) and a feature race of 125 miles (201 km.). Eligible cars are two-seat sports/racing cars conforming to the Appendix J, Group 7 category under the Fédération Internationale de l'Automobile (F.I.A.) rules (see MOTOR RACING, INTERNATIONAL). Can-Am cars have no limit on engine size, body contours, over-all dimensions, total weight, or size of wheels and tyres. A competitive Group 7 car exceeds 200 m.p.h. (322 km./h.) on the straights; from a standing start it easily accelerates to 100 m.p.h. (161 km./h.) and returns to a complete stop within 10 seconds.

The typical Can-Am car is aerodynamic, with ground clearance of 3 to 4 in. (76-102 cm.) and stability enhanced by aerofoils and tyres 20 in. (508 cm.) wide. It is built of the lightest materials, such as aluminium, magnesium, titanium, or fibreglass. The engine most frequently used is the Chevrolet V-8 with a piston displacement of up to 8 litres. With fuel injection and other modifications, this generates more than 700 h.p. at 7,000 r.p.m. Virtually all Can-Am cars — McLaren, Lola, and modified Porsches and FERRARIS — are manufactured in Europe.

Because of Group 7's freedom from restrictions, designers work beyond established formulas, and many represent an individual way of thinking. This latitude has attracted the best engineering talents — men like Herd, McLaren, Hall, Broadley, Terry, Bailey, Bryant, Harris, and the anonymous designers of Porsche and Ferrari. There have been unusual, even exotic designs, among them Hall's bizarre 'vacuum cleaner' Chaparral 2J, built on a principle of physics known as ground-effect; Harris's tiny AVS Shadow; Bryant's titanium Ti-22; but none has ever won a Can-Am. The Team McLaren cars are noted not for innovation but for superb construction from an integrated, total concept, built with painstaking attention to fundamentals and details.

Similarly, the Porsches are noted for superb craftsmanship, durability, and reliability. Porsche 917s had competed before 1972, but with conventional engines and negligible success. The turbo-charged engines made them winners once the Porsche engineers (and Donohue, himself an engineer) conquered such problems as throttle lag.

For 1974 the Sports Car Club of America placed a limit of 73 gals. (332 l.) on the amount of petrol permitted each car — 25 gals. on board for the 75-mile race, and 7 gals. available in the pits for replenishment. Ostensibly the principal consideration was the world fuel shortage, but it also was apparent that the S.C.C.A. was trying to elevate non-Porsches

into a competitive position. Because the turbo-Porsches consumed considerable petrol (their tanks had a 110-gal. — 500 l. — capacity), the 73-gal. limitation severely hampered the car if it did not completely force it out of the series. At the start of 1974 Porsche was protesting the rules change and threatening to withdraw from the Can-Am.

CÁNDIDO, JOSÉ (1734-71), *matador de toros* who took the *alternativa* in 1758, was the first full matador to be killed by a bull. He was gored by the Bornos bull Coriano in Puerta de Santa Maria on 23 June 1771, and died the following day.

CANNE is a French individual combat sport which developed over centuries from a form of QUARTERSTAFF to something nearer FENCING. It is played with a cane, which is held in one hand. Whirling, as well as the parrying and lungeing of fencing, is part of the method adopted. The *canne*, a walking stick, shorter than the baton used two-handed in the parent game, is a weapon which can be rapidly employed. The sport derives from the same sources as SAVATE. A *canne à épée*, or *canne armée*, is a swordstick.

CANNON, JOHN (1937-), London-born MOTOR RACING driver who won the 1970 FORMULA 5000 CHAMPIONSHIP and three races in the series. In 1969, he won three continental races being placed fourth in the final standings. He won the 1968 Laguna Seca CAN-AM Challenge Cup race.

CANOE POLO, a form of WATER POLO in which the participants are in short, low canoes known as bats, and use double paddles. Teams are five a side, passing to each other a ball about the size of a football, with the object of scoring a goal by throwing it against a vertical board 1 m. (3 ft. 3 in.) square on the opposing goal line.

Deliberate ramming and unseemly use of the paddle are offences, punishable by a free throw, but bumping and brushing of canoes is almost incessant. The game may be played in any convenient area, either in swimming baths or on a roped-off course on open water. In baths, ropes are also used to keep play at least 1 metre away from the perimeter to avoid damage. A game usually lasts for two periods of seven minutes each.

Canoe polo is popular among canoeists in several European countries, notably Germany, and Britain held national team championships at Crystal Palace in London from 1969.

CANOEING is a sport and pastime performed

on water in a small craft, pointed at both ends (a canoe or kayak), propelled by one or more persons kneeling or sitting in a forward-facing position roughly in the centre of the boat, using a single-bladed or double-bladed paddle. As a sport, canoeing divides into three groups: slalom, wild water (sometimes referred to as down-river racing), and long-distance racing and sprint racing. A further variation, canoe sailing, has a limited popularity.

The term 'canoe' is used in Britain to describe almost any craft pointed at both ends in which the paddler faces forward, though the craft may well be a kayak. In the North Americas and on the Continent the terms 'canoe' and 'kayak' are used more precisely to refer to two distinct types of craft: the *canoe*, pointed at both ends, with the paddler kneeling in a forward-facing position and propelling it with the use of a single-bladed paddle; and the *kayak*, pointed at both ends, with the paddler sitting in a forward-facing position and using a double-bladed paddle.

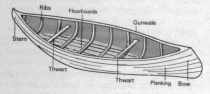

CANADIAN CANOE (TRADITIONAL)

As the canoe originated in North America it is now generally referred to as the Canadian canoe, and craft of traditional lines — although of modern materials — can still be obtained today. Development of the Canadian canoe for competition was twofold — slalom and wild-water racing, and sprint racing.

The Canadian canoe for slalom and wild water — known as the C1 or C2 (the figure following the 'C' being the number of persons paddling the craft) — was first used in rough-water events almost to traditional lines.

The Canadian canoe for sprint racing — classifications C1, C2, C6, or C7 — was introduced during the 1950s. The craft still retains the open deck, the paddler or paddlers kneeling on one knee only, but the gunwale line is very low and sleek, with all the traditional lines of the original Canadian version lost. It is now a very highly specialized craft purely for sprint racing.

Although there are still some enthusiasts who paddle designs of the original Eskimo kayak, today's craft is as different from the original as is the canoe. For sprint racing the

kayak is a long sleek wood-veneer craft with a small rudder fitted under the stern to enable the paddler to steer without breaking his stroke. From the single-seat Eskimo kayak, the racers now have designs for double- and four-seat variants. The rough-water kayak is completely of fibreglass, the slalom version being quite short and highly manoeuvrable, while for down-river racing the craft has a deep bow for cutting through the water. For touring, the range is almost unlimited, the design in many ways little changed from that of the 1930s, but the materials range from canvas, wood panels, and veneer, to fibreglass.

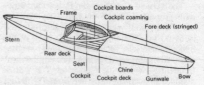

KAYAK (RIGID, FRAME/CANVAS)

The Struer craft, racing kayaks and canoes designed by Samson and manufactured in Denmark of wood veneer, have probably had more influence on sprint racing than any other, and every major country uses them for national and international events.

Following are regulation dimensions and weights for kayaks and canoes in the various forms of canoe sport:

Slalom:
K1   Min. length 4·00 m. (13 ft. 1 in.), min. width 0·60 m. (1 ft. 11¾ in.); no weight restriction.
C1   Min. length 4·00 m. (13 ft. 1 in.), min. width 0·70 m. (2 ft. 3⅝ in.); no weight restriction.
C2   Min. length 4·58 m. (15 ft.), min. width 0·80 m. (2 ft. 7½ in.); no weight restriction.
Wild water or down-river racing:
K1   Max. length 4·50 m. (14 ft. 9 in.), min. width 0·60 m. (1 ft. 11¾ in.); no weight restriction.
C1   Max. length 4·30 m. (14 ft. 1 in.), min. width 0·80 m. (2 ft. 7½ in.); no weight restriction.
C2   Max. length 5·00 m. (16 ft. 5 in.), min. width 0·80 m. (2 ft. 7½ in.); no weight restriction.
Flat-water sprint or long-distance racing:
K1   Max. length 5·20 m. (17 ft. 1 in.), min. width 0·51 m. (1 ft. 8¼ in.), min. weight 12 kg. (26 lb.).
K2   Max. length 6·50 m. (21 ft. 4 in.), min. width 0·55 m. (1 ft. 9⅝ in.), min. weight 18 kg. (40 lb.).
K4   Max. length 11·00 m. (36 ft.), min. width 0·60 m. (1 ft. 11¾ in.), min. weight 30 kg. (66 lb.).
C1   Max. length 5·20 m. (17 ft. 1 in.), min. width 0·75 m. (2 ft. 5½ in.), min. weight 16 kg. (35 lb.).
C2   Max. length 6·50 m. (21 ft. 4 in.), min. width 0·75 m. (2 ft. 5½ in.), min. weight 20 kg. (44 lb.).
C7   Max. length 11·00 m. (36 ft.), min. width 0·85 m. (2 ft. 9¼ in.), min. weight 50 kg. (110 lb.).

Single-ended paddles are used with canoes. At the top of the shaft (or 'loom') is a rounded grip; the blade is longer and narrower than those of the double paddle used with a kayak. These blades are offset at 90° to each other ('feathered') and vary in profile to suit touring, slalom, down-river or sprint racing.

A small waterproof skirt ('spraydeck') may be worn by paddlers competing on rough water, but is not generally used in sprint racing. This fits round the waist and over the cockpit coaming of the canoe or kayak to prevent water entering the craft in rough conditions or during the 'Eskimo roll' — a righting manoeuvre (variously called a *steyr* or *pawlata*) in which a canoeist remains in his capsized craft.

SLALOM is the most exciting and spectacular of canoe sports, not only for the paddler but also for the spectator. It is performed on the roughest of rivers where falls are steep, rapids thunder and boil, and rocks jut from the water. The canoeists, wearing lifejackets and crash hats, start singly at set intervals and race down the half-mile (0·8 km.) course, the fastest paddler or crew being the winner.

The main principles of canoe slalom are borrowed from SKIING; snow-covered slopes and skis are exchanged for racing water and fibreglass kayaks. Thus the paddler does not simply race down stream from start to finish, but must negotiate a number of 'gates' which are hung just above the water. The gate consists of two poles, at least 1·8 m. (5 ft. 11 in.) long with a diameter of 35 to 50 mm. (1·4–2·0 in.). The right-hand pole has green and white rings, the left-hand pole red and white.

The gates are adjustable in height and position, and the width of each gate must be from 3·5 to 1·2 m. (11 ft. 6 in.–4 ft.). Above each gate is a board indicating its number and perhaps the letter 'R' for a reverse gate, or 'T' for a team gate. A free gate — which may be taken in reverse or forwards from any direction — is marked with black and white rings. The canoeist must pass cleanly through the gates in their numbered order, either forwards or in reverse, time penalties being added for incorrect taking or hitting of the gates. Two separate runs are allowed, the better score only to count.

Scoring and technical terms may best be illustrated by tracing a canoeist over part of a slalom course such as that at Bourg St. Maurice, France, where the world championship was held in 1969. As the paddler passes through the start gate, an automatic timer is started in the control centre. The canoeist traverses the rough water and goes down through gate 1 which is a forward gate in the main stream, followed by gate 2 which is just off the main stream and must be taken in an up-stream direction. This requires a 'break-out' (a stroke forcing the craft out of the main stream) whereby the paddler gains the slack water and goes through the gate. Perhaps the stern of his kayak clips the right-hand pole and a penalty of 10 seconds is marked down by the gate judge. (At international and world championship events, each gate on the slalom course is supervised by two gate judges, one from the organizing nation, the other if possible from one of the competing nations. In addition, there are also section umpires responsible for a number of gates, a finishing judge, and a chief umpire. Protests are settled by the competition committee.)

The canoeist will now ride high into the rough water to allow time to align for gate 3, over the standing wave, through the 'stopper' — a term given to a rough-water condition. With fast-flowing water falling over rocks or a weir, it creates a situation where the water will roll back on itself and is thus flowing both down stream and up stream. Anything passing through this point will be checked or temporarily held — hence stopper. The heavier the water and the bigger the drop, the more severe the stopper. (In the U.S.A., Australia, and New Zealand, this water condition is termed 'pressure wave'.)

On gate 4 the canoeist catches the left-hand pole with his paddle, while the kayak gunwale touches the right-hand pole. This incurs a 20 seconds penalty, 10 for each touch, although additional touches of each pole from the inside cannot incur further penalties. Our paddler now inadvertently passes through gate 5 sideways and for this he incurs 50 seconds for incorrect presentation to the gate. Caught off balance, he capsizes only to 'Eskimo roll' immediately, but not in time to miss hitting the outside of gate 6. For this he receives another 50 seconds penalty.

Forward gate 7 he takes cleanly and now passes down the main fall with an attempted break-out for gate 8. However, let us suppose the paddler fails at this and is sped on to gate 9 and, although in a reverse position, hits the outside of the left-hand pole. Under the rules, two gates following the one just completed are counted as 'live' and a touch on the second gate — in this case gate 9 — incurs 50 seconds for the miss of gate 8 (which may not now be attempted) and another 50 seconds for the outside touch of gate 9. However, gate 9 may be re-attempted and, providing the paddler goes through the gate line in the correct direction, even if hitting one or both poles, the 50 seconds penalty is reduced to only 20 seconds. If the canoeist now passes correctly through all other gates and eventually over the finish, the timer in control stops and all penalties from the gate judges are accounted. To a course time of, say, 443·54 seconds, penalties of 460

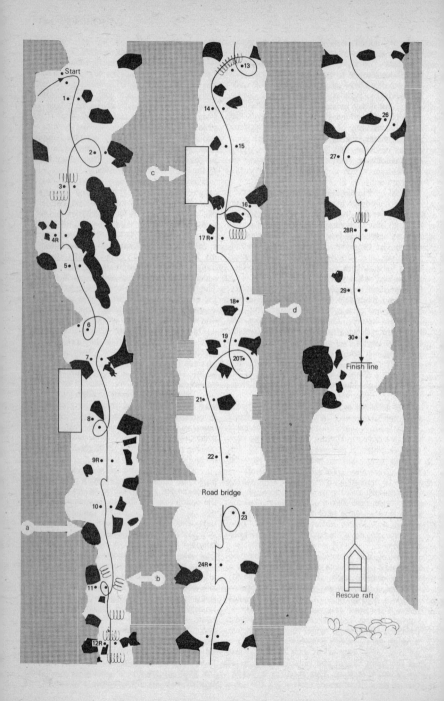

seconds are added, making a total score of 903·54 points. A second run will give him another score. In the event of a tie between paddlers the winner is then decided by the lowest of each paddler's second score.

The slalom course for international and world championship events must have a maximum length of 800 m. (½ mile), with a water flow of not less than 2 m./sec. (6 ft. 7 in./ sec.). The course should include natural or artificial hazards such as rapids, rocks, weirs, and bridges. The course must include a minimum of 15 gates.

Giant slalom is an event not often now performed. It is a combination of slalom and down-river racing (see below). The course is as for down-river racing, but with the addition of 20 to 25 gates, all of which are of the forward type and placed in the main current. Points consist of the course time combined with gate penalties (10 seconds for a complete miss and 5 seconds for incorrect negotiation of a gate missed but touched).

Throughout Europe and in the U.S.A. there are recognized slalom sites where competitions of international or world championship standard are held annually. These include (with Bourg St. Maurice, France): Spittal, Austria; Lipno, Czechoslovakia; Zwickau, East Germany; Monschau and Augsburg, West Germany; Llangollen, North Wales, Great Britain; Merano, Italy; Tacen, Yugoslavia; Szczawnicze, Poland; Arkansas, U.S.A.

DOWN-RIVER or WILD-WATER RACING is the straightforward racing version of rough-water canoeing. Here there are no gates to be negotiated as in slalom, the only hazards being natural ones in the shape of rocks, fallen trees, bridges, or other obstacles in the river. It is a straight race from start to finish, the fastest man over the course being the winner. Contestants are started singly at intervals, the course being a minimum of 3 km. (1·9 miles) on water not less than grade III (see below). Classes are for:

Men: K1, C1, and C2.
Women: K1.
Mixed: C2.

Team events for three boats in each of the above classes are also held.

All the popular touring and rough-water rivers are graded to an international standard of difficulty, as follows:

(*Opposite*) SLALOM COURSE, BOURG ST. MAURICE
Shaded area denotes river bank; black dots with numbers show position of gate poles over the top of the water. Arrows indicate (a) rock jutting into river current; (b) stopper or standing wave; (c) temporary stand alongside or in the water; (d) exposed rock in the river course.

Grade I. Flat water.
Grade II. Flat water with minor rapids.
Grade III. Fast flowing water with rapids, many quite heavy.
Grade IV. Very fast water, heavy rapids.
Grade VI. Very fast flowing water, very heavy rapids with standing waves.
Grade VII. Water conditions present grave risk to life and should not be attempted.

LONG-DISTANCE RACING in canoe sport is as cross-country racing is to athletics or car-rallying to motor racing. In Britain the season starts early in the year (first events taking place in February) and goes on well into November, with some 25 national ranking races and a number of other events. Unlike slalom and sprint racing, long-distance racing is not officially recognized by the International Canoe Federation (I.C.F.). However, the sport is popular in several countries including South Africa, Spain, Denmark, and Ireland, and, to a lesser extent, Holland, Belgium, Sweden, and Austria. Some events are described as 'international'; these include the SELLA DESCENT, the LIFFEY DESCENT, the international and national long-distance championships of Great Britain, and the international Gudenea marathon. Courses vary a great deal and this seems to be one of the main attractions of the competitions. Weather conditions, too, are variable and the average course of about 12 miles (20 km.) can provide a testing experience.

Long-distance racing may take place on any type of river, lake, or open water. The distance is usually 10 to 15 miles (16–24 km.), but some races are as long as 70 to 140 miles (112–225 km.). In the early years of the sport there were a great number of classes covering both single and double kayaks of varying lengths. Later the classes were whittled down to single and double kayaks (K1, K2, touring single, and touring double). Massed starts are used, usually by class or at times by all singles classes or all double classes of senior, junior, or women's events. On many rivers where there is no great width and the entry large, a good start can almost win the race for a paddler; thus at such events there is much jockeying for position as the starting time gets near. In most races at least two or three locks have to be portaged (i.e. the craft carried round) and five or six crews arriving at a portage simultaneously create great excitement and sense of competition.

SPRINT RACING for canoe or kayak is competed on flat water (a regatta course) over a straight distance of 500 metres, 1000 metres, or a circuit of 10,000 metres (547 yds., 1094 yds., 6·2 miles). Each race has a mass start (at international events a maximum of nine lanes is permitted), the winner being the paddler whose bow first crosses the finish line. At international regattas, for all but the 10,000 metre event, each competitor or crew must stay in their buoyed lane and be at least 5 m. (16 ft. 5 in.) away from all other paddlers at any time. This is to prevent 'wash-hanging', where a following paddler may contrive to get his kayak to plane on the bow wave of a leading paddler, thereby conserving strength. In the 10,000 metre event crews must adhere to the 5 metre rule for the first and last 1000 metres. It is not usually possible to provide a straight 10,000 metre course and the event is then run over a circuit with up to four turns. Water should be 3 m. (9 ft. 10 in.) deep over the entire course.

Annual world championships are held but although times are recorded for each event, there are no world records since conditions vary greatly and the depth of water has a great influence on speed. Classes for sprint racing championships are:

Men: 1000 m. and 10,000 m. in K1, K2, K4, C1, and C2; 500 m. in K1 and K2; 4 × 500 m. relay in K1.

Women: 500 m. in K1, K2, and K4.

World championship events are held separately for seniors and juniors in these classes. International events are combined regattas for seniors and juniors based on age qualifications. At such events there may also be classes for aspirants over 500 m. and 300 m.

In OLYMPIC GAMES classes for sprint racing are:

Men: 1000 m. in K1, K2, K4, C1, and C2; 500 m. in K1, K2, C1, C2.

Women: 500 m. in K1 and K2.

CANOE SAILING. The sailing canoe bears very little resemblance, apart from its pointed ends, to a canoe or kayak. However, the craft is a direct descendant of the Rob Roy kayak and is called the International 10 sq. metre sailing canoe (I.C.). It comes under racing rules drawn up by the Canoe Sailing Committee of the I.C.F. but is highly specialized and has only limited appeal. International events are held and a number of federations, including Germany, Great Britain, Sweden, and the U.S.A. organize races.

The origins of the canoe can be traced directly to the North American Indians when early craft were built with birch bark stitched over a light framework. Although the Indians used their canoes for hunting and hostile activities, the early trappers and fur traders used them for carrying goods, the canoe being the major means of transport in the pioneer days of the New Territories. The canoe also features in the adventures of missionaries and explorers of North America. The craft was built to varying lengths, commonly around 20 ft. (6·1 m.), but much greater lengths were seen in the *voyageurs'* canoes, which were upwards of 35 ft. (10·67 m.) and carried great loads and many people.

Although early man may have used a craft similar in dimensions by hollowing out a log, the kayak as we know it today is descended from those used by the Eskimos of Greenland and Alaska at a much later date. The Eskimo kayak was a very light craft, being made of a framework, either of driftwood or bone, over which was stitched a covering of sealskin, greased with animal fat to make it waterproof. The hull was usually around 18 ft. (5·49 m.) long — although greater lengths were known — and very narrow, about 2 ft. (0·61 m.) at the widest point. The deck was completely closed save for a small round hole in which the paddler sat. The occupant wore a small skirt round the waist, fitted over the cockpit coaming; thus, in the event of a capsize, the kayak was completely watertight and by use of a manoeuvre (the Eskimo roll), it was possible to right the craft without leaving it.

The history of canoeing as a sport starts with the founding of the ROYAL CANOE CLUB in England in 1866 (then known as the Canoe Club). MacGREGOR, who founded the club and designed the first kayak for leisure and sport, toured in his craft throughout the rivers of Europe. MacGregor's 'Rob Roy' kayak was a clinker-built craft of cedar wood to which was later added a mast and sail, leaving the paddles only for occasional use.

After an energetic start in England, paddling waned by the 1900s, although the sport of canoe sailing was at a peak and the Royal Canoe Club was very strong, with many other clubs across the country. However, on the Continent a young German named Klepper designed and manufactured a light folding kayak that was to revolutionize the sport. Klepper founded in 1907 a firm that was to produce the finest kayaks in the world and lead in canoe and kayak design by the middle of the century. The 'Klepper' had a light ash frame, over which fitted a tailored skin of canvas, the whole craft packing down into two bags. By the 1930s the folding kayak was in use across Europe; but canoeists in eastern Europe were using a rigid kayak built on traditional Eskimo lines. This kayak was brought to a Scout Jamboree in Britain and became known as the 'Scout' kayak. To it can be traced the popularity of canoeing today in Britain.

Canoe sport on the Continent gained in popularity and in 1936 Germany requested its introduction to the Olympic Games. This was flat-water racing and, with Olympic status, the sport progressed across the Atlantic. Canoe slalom was only in its early stages but the excitement of racing the wild water soon caught the imagination of many European countries. Slalom was introduced in Britain in 1939 but did not take real hold until 1948. Later years saw its introduction to America, Canada, New Zealand, and Australia. At the 1969 world championships, the Japanese and Dutch competed for the first time, while in the following year the Russians competed for the first time at the Zwickau international in East Germany. Slalom gained Olympic status with its introduction in the 1972 Games in Munich, but seems likely not to be included in the 1976 Games in Montreal.

The International Canoe Federation's member nations include Argentina, Australia, Austria, Belgium, Bolivia, Bulgaria, Canada, Cuba, Czechoslovakia, Denmark, Finland, France, Germany (East and West), Great Britain, Hungary, Iran, Ireland, Italy, Ivory Coast, Japan, People's Republic of Korea, Luxemburg, Mexico, Netherlands, New Zealand, Norway, Poland, Romania, South Africa (temporarily suspended), Spain, Sweden, Switzerland, U.S.A., U.S.S.R., and Yugoslavia.

Long-distance racing was started in Britain about 1947-8 although the first recorded event was in December 1867, when a 12 mile (19 km.) race was organized by the Royal Canoe Club at Teddington on the Thames.

As the sport progressed, the design of kayaks became more specialized. The racing paddlers demanded more speed, the slalomists more manoeuvrability, and the tourists wanted lighter and faster craft, although still retaining a good carrying capacity. In 1948 the first cold-moulded wood veneer racing kayaks appeared in Britain — soon to be replaced by hot-moulded craft from Denmark — while in the following decade an entirely new material — glass fibre — was introduced.

Canoes for slalom and rough water remained open-decked, although the deck was covered by a canvas spraydeck with openings for the paddlers, and the craft were built to touring specifications of wood veneer or planking. With the introduction of fibreglass in the 1950s craft became more specialized, international specifications were agreed, and four models of boat were built — C1 and C2 for slalom, C1 and C2 for wild water. The decks were completely covered in, save for rounded holes for the paddlers, hard gunwale lines became rounded, and small half-seats were incorporated on the rear of the cockpit coaming, but still the basic kneeling position was retained. The canoe became a specialized form of slalom transport with its capability for touring or load-carrying lost.

P. W. Blandford, *Canoeing Waters* (1966); British Canoe Union, *Guide to the Waterways of the British Isles* (1964) and *The Eskimo Roll, No. 4*; A. Byde, *Living Canoeing* (1969) and *Beginners' Guide to Canoeing* (1973); F. S. Chapman, *Watkins' Last Expedition* (1960); J. de Liège, *Canoe-Kayak en France* (Touring Club of France, 1961); J. MacGregor, *A Thousand Miles in the Rob Roy* (reissue, 1963); N. McNaught, *The Canoeing Manual* (1956); A. Skilling and D. Sutcliffe, *Canoeing Complete* (1966); C. Sutherland, *Modern Canoeing* (1964); P.D. Whitney, *White Water Sport* (1960); *Canoeing Magazine*, monthly; *Canoe-Kayak Magazine*, quarterly (in French).

GOVERNING BODY (WORLD): International Canoe Federation, Via G. Massaia 59, Florence, Italy.

CANZONERI, TONY (1908-59), American boxer who won the world featherweight and junior welterweight titles and was twice lightweight champion, as well as boxing a draw for the bantamweight title when only 18. Between 1927 and 1937 he engaged in 21 bouts for world titles. Though renowned for his speed, he demonstrated his punching power when winning the lightweight title with a knock-out in 66 seconds of the first round.

CAPANNELLE, LA, race-course in Rome where the Italian Derby, Two Thousand Guineas, One Thousand Guineas, and the important PREMIO ROMA are run.

CAPE OF GOOD HOPE DERBY, horse-race run over the Kenilworth course in Cape Town, in February over 12 furlongs (2,400 m.), is the most important race for three-year-olds in South Africa.

CARACALLA II (1942), French race-horse by Tourbillon out of ASTRONOMIE, the winner of all his eight races, including the PRIX DE L'ARC DE TRIOMPHE, GRAND PRIX DE PARIS, French St. Leger, and ASCOT GOLD CUP. He was bred and owned by BOUSSAC, trained by SEMBLAT, and ridden by Elliott.

CARBAJAL, ANTONIO (1929–   ), Association footballer for Leon and Mexico for whom he kept goal in the five successive World Cup competitions of 1950, 1954, 1958, 1962, and 1966.

CARDIFF ARMS PARK, headquarters of the Welsh RUGBY UNION and, since 1954, the venue for all Welsh home internationals. It is also the home ground of CARDIFF R.F.C. who now, however, play not on the national pitch but on an adjoining field. In the late 1960s, a rebuilding programme was started to increase the spectator capacity by 1982 from just over

58,000 to 74,000, 31,000 of whom were to be seated.

CARDIFF R.F.C., Welsh RUGBY UNION football club, founded in 1876. It became a first-class club in the mid-1880s, under the captaincy of Hancock, who developed the four-three-quarter system there. The club lost only the last game in seasons 1885-6 and 1905-6, and in 1947-8, won 39 of its 41 games, scoring over 800 points. In 1907 Cardiff beat the South African touring side (who, otherwise, lost only to Scotland); in 1947-8, the Australians; and in 1953-4, New Zealand. Famous Cardiff players include NICHOLLS, Gabe, C. W. Jones, TANNER, B. L. WILLIAMS, C. I. MORGAN, EDWARDS, and JOHN.
HOME GROUND: Cardiff Arms Park.
COLOURS: Black and Cambridge blue hooped jerseys and navy shorts.

CARDUS, Sir NEVILLE (1889-   ), CRICKET writer. Knighted in 1967, he wrote between the two world wars essays and reports for the *Manchester Guardian* that were of an unprecedented — and subsequently unapproached — vivacity and evocative quality. He wrote in addition a number of books on the game, notably *A Cricketer's Book* (1922), *Days in the Sun* (1924), *The Summer Game* (1929), *Cricket* (1930), *Good Days* (1934), *Australian Summer* (1937), *Autobiography* (1947), and *Cricket All the Year* (1952).

CAREY, JOHN JOSEPH (1919-   ), Association footballer for MANCHESTER UNITED and Ireland, who played first in international football for the southern Irish team at inside left against Norway in November 1937, in a qualifying competition match for the 1938 world championship. He was a member of the Manchester United team that won promotion to the First Division of the Football League in 1938 and, after the war, playing mainly at fullback (but his exceptionally fine all-round ability enabled him to play in any position with calm distinction), captained the club when it won the F.A. Cup in 1948 and the League championship in 1952. From 1946 to 1950 he was one of the small number of Irish footballers to play for, and in his case also to captain, both the Irish F.A. (Northern Ireland) and the F.A. of Ireland (Eire) in international matches. After retiring as a player he managed several F.L. clubs, including Nottingham Forest and EVERTON, but was mainly associated, as team and later general manager, with BLACKBURN ROVERS.

CARISBROOK, Dunedin, New Zealand, venue for RUGBY UNION Test matches and home ground of the Otago provincial side.

CARLAW PARK, Auckland, New Zealand, a football ground owned by the New Zealand RUGBY LEAGUE. It has been the main venue for New Zealand's Test matches since it was opened in 1921. The capacity is 30,000.

CARLING, ELIZABETH (1928-   ), LACROSSE player for England from 1952 to 1962 and captain 1956-62. She played throughout her international career as a wing defence. She was a member of the British touring team to the U.S.A. in 1954 and was vice-captain of a similar team to tour the States in 1960.

CARNICERITO DE MÉJICO (José González) (1907-47), *matador de toros*, killed in Vilaviciosa (Portugal) on 14 September 1947, when a bull of Estaban Oliveira severed his femoral artery, although its horns had been shaved.

CARNOUSTIE, Scottish GOLF course. In the opinion of many golfers, Carnoustie, on the Angus coast, is the toughest of the championship courses. It is flat, relieved only by dunes of modest proportion, and rather drab in appearance, but, like many other Scottish links, the character of Carnoustie cannot be considered simply in terms of its physical properties. These, by themselves, are undistinguished. What makes Carnoustie is the weather; there is nearly always a changeable coastal wind of some force and this makes the playing of the course a matter of limitless variety and keen judgement. Winding burns add to the interest of the closing holes.

CARPENTIER, GEORGES (1894-1975), French boxer who won the world light-heavyweight title, was European champion at four divisions, and boxed in every one of the eight professional weights. Carpentier, a man of good looks and great charm, attracted women spectators to the sport in large numbers for the first time. Evidence of his appeal came in his unsuccessful challenge in 1921 for the world heavyweight title, held by DEMPSEY, when, for the first time, receipts totalled more than $1 million.

CARR, JOSEPH B. (1922-   ), Irish amateur golfer. His achievements include: amateur champion 1953, 1958, 1960; Irish Open champion 1946, 1950, 1954, 1956; Irish close champion 1954, 1957, 1963, 1964, 1965, 1967; R. T. Jones award for outstanding sportsmanship in GOLF, 1961; Walter Hagen award for contributions to international golf, 1967: WALKER CUP player and captain. Carr won every Irish area championship and most leading amateur events in Britain.

CARRARO, FRANCO (1936-   ), Italian water ski administrator and ex-Italian national ski champion, who was chairman of the European technical committee in 1968 and president of the World Water Ski Union in 1971. As an all-round sportsman he is also noted for his work as president of the INTER-NAZIONALE Milano Football Club.

CARSON, WILLIAM (1942-   ), jockey, who took over from PIGGOTT as champion jockey in 1972 and retained the title in 1973.

CARTER, FRANK (1880-1937), a leading race-horse trainer in France, who turned out 23 classic winners, the best of which was PEARL CAP.

CARTER, HORATIO S. (1913-   ), Association footballer with SUNDERLAND his home town, Derby County, Hull City, and, briefly, Cork Athletic. He was an excellent inside right who made 13 appearances for England in full international matches and 3 in 'Victory' international games. In the course of a long playing career (1931-53) he won League championship and F.A. Cup-winners' medals with Sunderland; a F.A. Cup-winners' medal with Derby County; a F.L. Third Division (North) championship medal with Hull City; and a F.A. of Ireland Cup-winners' medal with Cork Athletic. He was manager as well as player with Hull City and he had subsequent spells as manager of LEEDS UNITED, Mansfield Town, and Middlesbrough.

CARTWRIGHT, ALEXANDER JOY, Jr. (1820-92), member of the Knickerbocker Base Ball Club of New York who, in 1845, formulated the basic rules of BASEBALL.

CARTWRIGHT, WILLIAM EDWARD (1916-   ), introduced SKIBOBBING in America. It was through his initiative that skibobbing was recognized by the Amateur Athletic Union in 1966 as a national sport in the U.S.A. He is a member of the Fédération Internationale de Skibob committee.

CASEMENT PARK, sports ground in Andersonstown, Belfast, and the chief GAELIC ATHLETIC ASSOCIATION venue in Ulster. It has a capacity of 40,000 of which 5,000 are covered seats.

CASLAVSKA, VERA (1942-   ), brilliant Czech female gymnast who won the combined exercises gold medals at the 1964 and 1968 OLYMPIC GAMES. In all she won 22 titles in Olympics and world and European championships. An attractive blonde standing 5 ft. 3 in.

(1·60 m.), from Prague, she initially showed great promise as an ice-skater. But, when 15 years old, she was invited to take part in nationwide trials to find gymnastic talent, and, trained by Bosakova, the 1956 Olympic silver medallist, she made her international début at the 1958 world championships, winning a silver medal in the team event. Her first European title was gained the following year on the beam. By 1962 only LATYNINA stood between her and the world title and she narrowly missed winning the gold medal in the combined exercises.

At the Tokyo Olympics in 1964, Caslavska was at her peak and finished a clear winner over-all and in addition took gold medals in the beam and vault. In the 1965 European championships at Sofia she equalled Latynina's achievement of gaining a gold medal in every event, a performance she was to repeat two years later in Amsterdam. She competed closely with Latynina's successor, KUCHIN-SKAYA, at the 1966 world championships but won the combined exercises gold medal. In addition she helped her country break Russia's monopoly of the team championship. But it was at the 1968 Olympics in Mexico that she reached her peak as a competitor by beating the Russians Voronina and Kuchinskaya. The highlight was her floor routine, the 'Mexican Hat Dance', which brought rapturous applause. She rounded off her career with four gold medals and two silver, and celebrated by marrying Odlozil, the 1964 1,500 metres silver medallist.

CASPER, BILL (1931-   ), American professional golfer, one of the most consistent and highest-earning players of his era. He won the U.S. Open championship in 1959 and 1966, the U.S. Masters in 1970, and in his first 16 years as a tournament professional won some 40 sponsored events. Casper was a RYDER CUP player. He is an elder of the Mormon Church.

CASSIDY, MARSHALL (1892-1968), was the most powerful 'back-room boy' in American HORSE RACING. As executive secretary of the New York Jockey Club, he introduced *inter alia* the starting gate, elevated vantage points for racing officials, the photo-finish camera, the film patrol, the saliva test for doping, lip-tattooing for horse identification, and blood tests for determining disputed parentage. More than any other individual, Cassidy shaped racing into its modern form.

CATCHPOLE, KENNETH (1939-   ), RUGBY UNION scrum half for Australia and one of the great scrum halves in the game's history, excelling in the quickness of his passing. His first game for Australia was in 1961, and he and HAWTHORNE formed an outstanding half-back partnership for Australia in the 1960s.

CAULFIELD, VIVIAN (1874-1958), English artist and writer whose book, *How to Ski,* published in 1910, analysed SKIING dynamics for the first time. He discussed and illustrated unweighting, counter-rotation, and parallel swings, and the technique he propounded was widely taken up in Central Europe. His criticism of the method of turning and braking with a single stick marked progress to the modern style of skiing with a stick in each hand.

CAULFIELD CUP, an Australian handicap horse race run over 1¼ miles (2,000 m.) at Caulfield, near Melbourne, in October.

CAVANAGH, ROBERT (1916-   ), Argentinian POLO player who was one of the best heavyweights and strongest hitters that ever played. He was in the winning Argentine team *v.* U.S.A. in the Cup of the Americas in 1936 and 1950.

C.C.C., see CLUB CRICKET CONFERENCE.

CELTIC F.C., Association FOOTBALL club, Glasgow, formed in 1887 by Irish Catholics in the east end of Glasgow with the aim of raising money to provide meals for needy children. Three years later the club became a founder member of the Scottish League from which it has never been relegated. The Catholic, and Irish, support has remained with the club but by no means exclusively. Celtic's first major success was in 1892 when they won the Scottish Cup for the first time. A year later they won the Scottish League in the last season before a Second Division was added. In 1972, when for the fourth time in six seasons Celtic won both Cup and championship, it was the twenty-sixth time the championship had been won and the twenty-second time the Cup, while the championship victory of 1973 was the eighth in a row. Celtic and their Glasgow rivals, RANGERS, have dominated, almost monopolized, Scottish football for over 70 years but in the 1960s Celtic, under the managership of Stein, emerged as a major force in European club competitions and became the first British club to win the European Champion Clubs Cup when, in Lisbon in 1967, Celtic beat INTERNAZIONALE (Milan) 2-1. Among many outstanding players were Hay, McMenemy, Quinn, and Orr before 1914; Kennaway, Hogg, Delaney, and

McGrory between the wars; and Evans, Fernie, Tully, McNeill, Johnstone, and Crerand in recent years.

COLOURS: Green and white hooped shirts, white shorts.

GROUND: Celtic Park, commonly called Parkhead, Glasgow.

CELTIC PARK, Belfast, Association FOOTBALL ground formerly of BELFAST CELTIC F.C. which decided to withdraw from football in the 1948-9 season. It has a capacity of 40,000 and is now used for GREYHOUND RACING.

CENTENARIO STADIUM, Association FOOTBALL ground in Montevideo, Uruguay, constructed in 1930 both as part of the independence centenary celebrations and as the venue for the first F.I.F.A. world football championship. The stadium is owned by the Uruguayan F.A. and used for international matches and the more important games played by Uruguay's leading clubs, PENAROL and NACIONAL. The capacity of the ground, which is uncovered but largely seated, is about 75,000.

CENTRAL PARK, Wigan, Lancashire, ground of WIGAN RUGBY LEAGUE CLUB, it is used regularly for international matches and other important games. The capacity is 47,747, a figure reached for the League match against ST. HELENS on 27 March 1959.

CENTURIONS, a RACE WALKING organization, has been described as the 'most exclusive athletic body in the world'. Originally an all-British membership, over the past 20 years it has opened its doors to walkers from all over the world. Centurions are exclusively amateur walkers who have walked 100 miles (161 km.) within 24 hours in a bona fide competition.

The club was formed in 1911 with Fowler-Dixon, who achieved his 100 miles in 1877, some 25 years before anyone else did so, as its first president. There are now over 500 members and at least one race per year is promoted in England over the 100 miles distance.

CERAR, MIROSLAV (1939-   ), a magnificent Yugoslav gymnast who was particularly proficient on the pommel-horse. Standing 5 ft. 8 in. (1·73 m.) and weighing 11 st. 2 lb. (71 kg.), he used his height and strength to dominate his speciality during the 1960s and in addition was twice over-all European champion. His circles and scissor-swings were extremely smooth and he was a dedicated trainer. He won world titles in 1962, 1966, and 1970 and Olympic gold medals in 1964 and 1968. He also finished first on the parallel bars in the 1962 world championships.

CESAREWITCH HANDICAP, a horse race inaugurated in 1839, run over 2 miles 2 furlongs (3,600 m.) at NEWMARKET in late October. It is the second leg of the 'Autumn Double', the first being the CAMBRIDGESHIRE HANDICAP.

(See also GREYHOUND RACING.)

CESTA PUNTA, see PELOTA.

CHALLENGE CUP, see RUGBY LEAGUE.

CHALLENGE PENNANT OF AMERICA, ICE YACHTING award, instituted by the NEW HAMBURGH ICE YACHT CLUB in 1881, for competition open to craft from any country. It was contested regularly until 1902, all winners being local Hudson River yachts. The event was not held again for 20 years. On resumption in 1922, it was won by Millard's *Scout,* skippered by Captain Drake, of the New Hamburgh club. In 1951, Drake presented the trophy to the Eastern Ice Yachting Association. The original silk pennant was placed beside the hull of the *Icicle,* several times its winner, in the Roosevelt Memorial Library at Hyde Park, New York. A replica of the old pennant was unfurled when the competition was again revived at Greenwood Lake, New Jersey, in 1951, when the winner was Rollberg's *Black Magic,* a class E skeeter from Fox Lake Ice Yacht Club, Illinois. In 1953, Perrigo's *Thunderjet,* a skeeter of the same class, won for the Pewaukee Ice Yacht Club, of Pewaukee, Wisconsin. This was the occasion when *Thunderjet* broke the 1907 *Wolverine* record, covering 30 miles (48 km.) in 29 min. 4 sec.

CHALLENGE TROPHY, see SHINTY.

CHAMBERLAIN, WILTON NORMAN (1936-), American professional BASKETBALL player, standing 7 ft. 1¼ in. (2·16 m.), Chamberlain graduated from Kansas University, first played as a professional for the Philadelphia (now San Francisco) Warriors, then for the PHILADELPHIA 76ERS and subsequently, after a brief spell with the HARLEM GLOBETROTTERS, for the LOS ANGELES LAKERS. Universally known as 'Wilt the Stilt', Chamberlain graduated as the leading scorer in collegiate history and as a professional became the all-time leading scorer, reaching a total of 30,000 points in 1972. He also set the record of most points in a season, with 4,029 in 1961-2, and became the first man to score 100 points in a single game in the NATIONAL BAS-

KETBALL ASSOCIATION, against the NEW YORK KNICKERBOCKERS on 2 March 1962.

CHAMBERS, Mrs. LAMBERT, see DOUGLASS, DOROTHEA K.

CHAMPION HURDLE CHALLENGE CUP, a horse race run over 2 miles 200 yds. (3,400 m.) at Cheltenham in mid-March, it is the 'Derby' for hurdlers in England. It was won three years in succession by Hatton's Grace, Sir Ken, and PERSIAN WAR, who must consequently be considered as the champion hurdlers of all time.

CHAMPION STAKES, one of the most important English races for three-year-olds and older horses on weight-for-age terms; it is run over 1 mile 2 furlongs (2,000 m.) at NEWMARKET in mid-October.

CHAND, Maj. DHYAN (1905-), HOCKEY player for India, United Provinces, Indian Army, and Jhansi Heroes. Chand was one of the greatest hockey players the world has seen. He was a centre forward whose goalscoring ability was almost incredible: he scored 133 goals during India's 1932 world tour and 201 goals, in 43 games, during a tour of Australia and New Zealand in 1935. During his career, he played for India in every continent of the world and his skill played an important part in India's reputation as the outstanding hockey nation of the world. He won Olympic gold medals at three successive OLYMPIC GAMES (1928, 1932, 1936). In the 1936 Olympic final, Chand scored six goals to help India beat Germany 8-1. In 1952, he published his memoirs under the title *Goal.*

CHANNEL SWIMMING, see SWIMMING.

CHAPADMALAL in Argentina is the most celebrated thoroughbred stud-horse farm in South America. The *haras Comalal* section is now owned by Don Miguel Martinez de Hoz, and the *haras Malal Hué* section by his brother Don José Alfredo Martinez de Hoz and sons.

CHAPMAN, HERBERT (1875-1934), Association FOOTBALL club manager who was primarily responsible for a major tactical evolution in the history of football when, after the change in the offside rule in 1925, he countered the greater freedom offered to centre forwards by withdrawing his centre half to a centre back position, and filled the space left in midfield by using his inside forwards, the whole team conforming roughly to a WM pattern. Chapman, an average player for TOTTEN-

HAM HOTSPUR before the 1914-18 war, was prepared to resume an engineering career when he had the unexpected chance to play and manage Northampton Town. When the club won the Southern League in 1909 he was confirmed as a football club manager, and, after some pre-war seasons with LEEDS, he became manager of HUDDERSFIELD TOWN and developed the teams that won the F.A. Cup in 1922 and the League championship in the successive seasons 1923-4 and 1924-5. At that time Chapman was persuaded to move to Highbury to manage ARSENAL. In the eight years before his death in 1934, Arsenal twice won the championship (and were heading the table at the time of his death), were twice runners-up in the championship, won the F.A. Cup, and were twice the beaten finalists. Moreover the club had attained a high reputation that has remained.

CHAPMAN, VERA (1930-   ), outstanding HOCKEY forward for England, South of England, Surrey, and Southern Railway. She first played for England at the age of 18. She was a member of the England team 1948-50 and 1952-61 and a member of the England touring teams in 1954 (South Africa), 1956 (Australia), 1958 (Germany), and 1959 (Netherlands).

CHAPOT, FRANK (1934-   ), American show jumping (see EQUESTRIAN EVENTS) rider. A regular member of the U.S.A. team from 1955, he made his début at the OLYMPIC GAMES in 1956 and four years later won a team silver medal in Rome with Trail Guide. He won another team silver medal in 1972 when he rode White Lightning at the Olympic Games in Munich. He also won two team gold medals at the PAN-AMERICAN GAMES (in 1959 on Diamant and 1963 on San Lucas).

CHAPOT, Mrs. MARY (née Mairs) (1944-   ), American show jumping (see EQUESTRIAN EVENTS) rider. She was the first American to win an individual Games gold medal when she rode Tomboy at the PAN-AMERICAN GAMES in 1963. She won a second gold medal at the same event when the U.S.A. team beat Argentina and Chile. She also competed in the 1964 and 1968 OLYMPIC GAMES.

CHAPPELL, GREGORY STEPHEN (1948-   ), cricketer for Australia, South Australia, Somerset, and Queensland. After two seasons in English county CRICKET his career in Australia progressed to a point where in 1970-1 he scored 108 at Perth in his first Test innings against England and, in the following series, 131 at LORD'S and 113 at the

OVAL. With subsequent successes against Pakistan and West Indies he became, as a forcing, upright batsman, medium-pace bowler, and fine fieldsman, an important figure in a rebuilt Australian team. He is a grandson of former Australian captain V. Y. Richardson and brother of I. M. CHAPPELL.

CHAPPELL, IAN MICHAEL (1943-   ), cricketer for Australia, South Australia, and Lancashire. He succeeded LAWRY as Australia's captain in 1971 and led a young team through a shared series in England and to victory over Pakistan and West Indies, showing enterprise in the field and in his batting. He scored 10 centuries in his first 50 Test matches.

CHARLES, ROBERT (1936-   ), New Zealand professional golfer who in 1963 became the first left-handed winner of the Open championship. A consistent player and outstanding putter, Charles won many tournaments on each of the major world GOLF circuits.

CHARLES, W. JOHN (1932-   ), Association footballer for LEEDS UNITED, JUVENTUS, Roma, Cardiff City, and Wales for whom he made his first appearance at the age of 18 years and 71 days. Swansea-born and signed as an amateur by Leeds United when he was only 15, the tall, magnificently-built Charles was developed as a centre half but became better known as a goal-scoring centre forward with an aggregate of 154 League goals for Leeds (including 42 in 1953-4) from 1948 until he was transferred to the Italian club, Juventus, in 1957. He enjoyed five prosperous years in Italian football without impairing his reputation for good sportsmanship. After a short return to Leeds, he played again briefly for Roma in Italian football, before settling in the U.K. as a player for Cardiff City and later as player-manager of the Southern League clubs, Hereford United and Merthyr Tydfil.

CHARLES BROWNLOW MEDAL, regarded as the most coveted award in Australian Rules FOOTBALL. Named after a former vice-president of the VICTORIAN FOOTBALL LEAGUE, it was instituted in 1924, and is presented to the player selected as the best and fairest in the League. The votes are recorded throughout the season by the field umpires and remain in sealed envelopes until they are counted just prior to the first semi-final.

CHARLOTTOWN (1963), English racehorse by Charlottesville (Grand Prix and French Derby) out of MELD, was bred and owned by Lady WERNHER, trained by Gosden and Smyth, and ridden by Lindley and Breasley. Charlottown won seven races and £101,210, including the DERBY and CORONATION CUP.

CHARLTON, ANDREW (Boy) (1908-1975), the first great Australian swimmer of the 1920s, who won five Olympic middle- and long-distance medals and set five world records between 1923 and 1928. He won the Olympic 1,500 metres in 1924 in a world record time of 20 min. 06·6 sec. which was more than 1 minute faster than any man had done before.

CHARLTON, JOHN, O.B.E. (1935-   ), Association footballer for LEEDS UNITED, and England for whom he made his first appearance in a full international at centre half against Scotland at WEMBLEY in April 1965 — only one month before his thirtieth birthday, and 12 years after making his Football League début for Leeds United. When, at an age when most 'uncapped' players assume that international recognition has eluded them, he was selected for the same team as his younger brother, R. CHARLTON, for the match against Scotland in April 1965, it was the first time in the twentieth century that brothers had played together in an England team in a full international match. He played twice in the 1970 world championships in Mexico — the last time at the age of 35 against Czechoslovakia at Guadalajara. He retired as a player at the end of the 1972-3 season and became manager of Middlesbrough.

CHARLTON, ROBERT, C.B.E. (1937-   ), Association footballer for MANCHESTER UNITED, and England for whom he made his first appearance in a full international against Scotland at Hampden Park in April 1958, and his last against West Germany in the quarter-final of the 1970 world championship at Guadalajara in June 1970. The latter was his 106th appearance for England and broke the record for English international appearances previously held by WRIGHT. He was the younger of two famous brothers (see J. CHARLTON) and an English schoolboy international footballer before he signed for Manchester United. In May 1968 he was a member of the Manchester United team that won the European Champion Clubs Cup at WEMBLEY. Two years before he had been in the England team that won the world championship. He retired as a player at the end of the 1972-3 season and became manager of PRESTON NORTH END.

CHAUSSON, see SAVATE and BOXE FRANÇAIS.

CHEAPE, LESLIE St. C. (1882-1916), English POLO player in the 1914 winning team for the Westchester Cup v. U.S.A. He was possibly the best-ever English player. Handicap 10.

CHEF CONFRÉRIE ROYALE ET CHEVALIÈRE DE SAINT MICHEL, Belgian FENCING guild and club founded at Ghent in 1613. It still occupies its original *salle d'armes* in the Halle aux Draps, constructed in 1425, in Ghent.

CHELSEA F.C., Association FOOTBALL club, London. Founded in 1904 and accepted into membership of the Second Division of the Football League, Chelsea had a remarkably successful first season for a new club, finishing in third place and scoring 90 goals in 38 League matches — still the club's scoring record. One season later Chelsea were second in the table and promoted to the First Division. Chelsea won the League championship in the season ending 1955 and reached the quarter-final of the second competition for the Fairs Cup in 1959.

Relegated in 1962, Chelsea returned to the First Division in 1963-4 to enjoy their most consistently successful period, finishing third in the Football League in 1965 and 1970, and reaching the F.A. Cup final in 1967, and in 1970 when they beat LEEDS UNITED. In European club competitions, Chelsea reached the semi-final of the Fairs Cup in 1966 and won the Cup-Winners Cup in 1971. WOODWARD was the club's outstanding player in the period 1905 to 1914. Between the wars leading players included B. Howard Baker, Woodley, GALLACHER, and JACKSON, while since 1946 a long list of fine players includes LAWTON, GREAVES, Evans, Bonetti, Tambling, Cooke, and Osgood.
COLOURS: Royal blue shirts and shorts.
GROUND: Stamford Bridge, London.

CHELTENHAM GOLD CUP is the most important steeplechase (see HORSE RACING) run in England at level weights, all competitors carrying 12 stone (76 kg.), unlike the GRAND NATIONAL which is a handicap. The National Hunt meeting at Cheltenham is held in mid-March, and the Gold Cup, run over 3 miles 2 furlongs 76 yds. (5,250 m.) is the main event. GOLDEN MILLER won the race five years in succession, 1932-6, as well as winning the Grand National in 1934; Cottage Rake won the Cup three years running from

1948 to 1950; MILL HOUSE in 1963; and ARKLE in 1964-6.

CHESTER, FRANK (1896-1957), cricketer for Worcestershire, and first-class umpire. After his promise as a player had been terminated by the loss of a hand in the First World War, he turned at an unusually early age to umpiring, and soon established a high reputation. He officiated in 48 Test matches.

CHEUCA, see HOCKEY, FIELD.

CHICAGO, University of, American college FOOTBALL team, nicknamed the 'Maroons', entered football in 1892, the year the University was founded, under coach STAGG, who remained until 1932, when football was 'de-emphasized'. Chicago was a major factor in the BIG TEN from the turn of the century through to the 1920s. Particularly outstanding were the teams from 1904 to 1909. The 1905 team gave MICHIGAN its first defeat in five years, was national champion, and was led by the excellent quarterback and drop-kicker Eckersall. From 1905 to 1909 Chicago lost only twice and had unbeaten records in 1907 and 1908. Even the anaemic teams of the 1930s boasted a master strategist as coach in Shaughnessy, who created the T-formation for the CHICAGO BEARS professional team. In 1940 Chicago abandoned college football and only resumed the game on a modest scale in 1969.
COLOURS: Maroon.

CHICAGO BEARS, American professional FOOTBALL team, have one of the most illustrious traditions in American sports. They began in 1920 as the Decatur (Illinois) Staleys, formed from the nucleus of a naval training team by the end HALAS, who coached them for nearly 40 years and owned them from the 1920s on. In 1925 the most famous college football player of the era, GRANGE of Illinois, joined them. From 1930 to the mid-1940s the Bears were a dominant force in professional football, famous for their rough, brutal play — featuring linemen such as Hewitt, Stydahar, Fortmann, Musso, and Turner. They were supported by the powerful fullback NAGURSKI: this rugged tradition was upheld by the tackle Connor around 1950 and the linebacker Butkus in the 1960s. The Bears contrasted this violent style with nimble running backs like Grange, Feathers in the 1930s, McAfee in the 1940s, and Sayers in the 1960s. When Halas introduced the T-formation, the team, led by the quarterback Luckman, routed the WASHINGTON REDSKINS in the 1940 title game, 73-0, and started what soon became a universal acceptance of the T as the basic foot-ball offensive formation. During NATIONAL FOOTBALL LEAGUE history the Bears, nicknamed the 'Monsters of the Midway', have won seven League titles and more victories (over 400) than any other team.
COLOURS: Orange, navy blue, and white.

CHICAGO BLACK HAWKS, ICE HOCKEY club of Chicago, joined the professional NATIONAL HOCKEY LEAGUE of North America in 1926. STANLEY CUP winners in 1934, 1938, and 1961, the club did not become N.H.L. champions until 1967. The players train and play home matches at the Chicago Stadium, which seats 16,666 spectators. Among the club's most successful players have been Bentley, Gardiner, HULL, Mikita, Mosienko, and Siebert.
COLOURS: Red, black, and white.

CHICAGO CARDINALS, American professional FOOTBALL team, entered the NATIONAL FOOTBALL LEAGUE in 1920 as the Racine (Wisconsin) Cardinals and lived during much of their career under the shadow of their rival CHICAGO BEARS, although their halfback Nevers was one of the authentic stars of the 1920s. Their one League title came in 1947, led by the 'dream backfield' — quarterback Christman, halfbacks Trippi and Angsman, and fullback Harder (league scoring leader 1947-9). In 1960 they became the St. Louis Cardinals.
COLOURS: Red, white, and black.

CHICAGO CUBS, American professional BASEBALL team, began as the Chicago White Stockings even before the founding of the NATIONAL LEAGUE in 1876. Under the first-baseman-manager ANSON, the White Stockings dominated baseball before 1890, winning six National League titles. The first-baseman-manager Chance led them to National League titles as the Cubs four times between 1906 and 1910. In these years Chance was part of the famous, overrated 'double-play' combination, Tinkers to Evers to Chance; the pitcher Mordecai 'Three-Finger' Brown won more than 20 games in six straight seasons: 1906-11. In the years 1929 to 1938 the Cubs won five more league titles (without being able to win the WORLD SERIES) with the outfielders Stevenson and Wilson (who still holds the major-league season record for runs batted in with 190 in 1930) as leading hitters. The Cubs have not won a league title since 1945, but the pitcher Jenkins equalled Brown's earlier record by winning 20 games in six successive seasons, 1967-72.

CHICAGO WHITE SOX, American professional BASEBALL team, entered the major leagues with the founding of the AMERICAN LEAGUE in 1901, and won the league's first title. Comiskey was general manager and soon owner of the franchise. The 1906 team, called the 'hitless wonders', with a team batting average of ·228, upset the highly favoured CHICAGO CUBS to win the WORLD SERIES. In the early period the pitcher Walsh was their outstanding star, winning 40 games in 1908. Led by the pitchers Faber and Cicotte and the outfielder Jackson, the White Sox won the 1917 World Series but lost in 1919. Soon after the so-called 'Black Sox' scandal broke. A number of White Sox players, including Cicotte and Jackson, were accused of 'throwing' the series to benefit gamblers; the accused were subsequently banned from baseball by Commissioner LANDIS. The White Sox did not win another American League title for 40 years. The pitcher Lyons (winner of 206 games) and the shortstop Appling (a lifetime ·310 batting average) led them in their meagre years. The Venezuelan-born Aparicio, who played for Chicago in 1956-62 and 1968-70, took part in more major-league games than any other shortstop in history.

CHICHESTER, Sir FRANCIS (1901-72), English yachtsman and airman who sailed alone in the ketch *Gipsy Moth IV* round the world 1966-7. He was the winner of the first single-handed transatlantic yacht race in 1960 and finished second in the second race in 1964. In 1931 he made the first east-west solo flight from New Zealand to Australia across the Tasman Sea.

CHICLANERO, El (José Redondo) (1818-53), *matador de toros* (*alternativa* 1842), who died of exhaustion at the height of his career, which was noteworthy for his capacity in all *suertes*, particularly the kill.

CHIQUITO DE CAMBO (Joseph Apesteguy) (1881-1956), French Basque PELOTA player, the greatest exponent of *grand chistera* who has yet appeared. Due to his influence, big courts that could contain the game — *places libres* and *frontons*— were built in Paris and Nice, Toulouse and Bordeaux, and — naturally — almost everywhere in the Basque provinces and south-western France. Although *grand chistera* was his speciality, he was brilliant at most forms of pelota. He won with many different partners, for he had the true champion's faculty of raising, by energy and example, the game of even inferior players. He once defeated two experienced *pilotaris* wielding, instead of a *chistera*, an empty champagne bottle. He made a great deal of money in a long professional career, but died

poor. His home town raised a memorial and named its new *fronton* after him, now one of the most famous pelota courts in the world.

CHIQUITO D'EIBAR (Indalecio Sarasqueta) (1860-1928). This Basque was Spain's first international PELOTA champion, and perhaps the first player to make the game his life as a full-time professional. Called Chiquito (Spanish, 'little one') because of his small physique and apparent delicacy, he was a prodigy who, at 16, beat Spain's reigning champion in a renowned match at Eibar — hence his sobriquet. He is important as an innovator and pioneer. It was he who introduced the basket-glove — *chistera*— from its birthplace, France, into Spain, and was the first to use it in the Argentine, where he went in 1884. The modern era of pelota in South America began with Chiquito's visit there, and his dramatic and successive triumphs over Payrandú of the Argentine, and Uruguay's Vergara.

CHOCHOSHVILI, SHOTA (1950-   ), Russian JUDO fighter who caused the upset of the light-heavyweight class at the 1972 Olympics by throwing Japan's SASAHARA and then taking the gold medal.

CHOONG EWE BENG (Eddy Choong) (1930-   ), Malayan BADMINTON player. Only 5 ft. 2 in. (1·58 m.) tall, he was a dynamic player who during a European playing career between 1950 and 1957 won practically all the honours open to him. He won the ALL-ENGLAND CHAMPIONSHIP singles four times and the men's doubles three times with his elder brother Choong Ewe Leong (David). He was a member of the winning Malayan THOMAS CUP team in 1955 and also played in the two following contests.

CHRISTOPHERSON, STANLEY (1861-1949), a former president of the M.C.C. (1939-46), and the only Englishman to have played CRICKET and HOCKEY for England. He scored a hat-trick on his début in international hockey.

CHUANG TSE-TUNG (1942-   ), Chinese TABLE TENNIS player and long outstanding world champion at men's singles, winning three times running, in 1961, 1963, and 1965. Chuang first started training at the age of 14 in the Children's Palace, Chingshan Park, Peking. Then, still a schoolboy, he distinguished himself against a Hungarian touring team in 1958 and a year later on a Chinese tour of Sweden. A fast and courageous hitter of great determination, he was daring with half-volley hits from the left and especially severe with the return of service and the 'third ball' attack (the scoring of winners off the opponent's return of service). In each of his successful world finals he defeated in hard struggle Li Fu-jung of Shanghai, who was one year younger and himself otherwise unbeaten in singles in the three world championships. A student at a physical culture college, Chuang, was appointed a member of the National People's Congress in 1964. After the Cultural Revolution he resumed international competition briefly after 1970.

CHUKHARIN, VIKTOR (*fl.* 1952-6), the first of the famous Russian male gymnasts, he won the combined exercises gold medals at the 1952 and 1956 OLYMPIC GAMES and the 1954 world championships. This magnificent competitor, who excelled on the parallel bars, collected a total of ten gold medals in these three events. At the Helsinki Olympics he was first in the pommel-horse and vault with a display that revolutionized the sport. Two years later in Rome he won the parallel bars but had to share first place with his compatriot, Muratov. He was back at his best for the Melbourne Olympics to win the over-all gold medal from the Japanese, Ono, and help his country to another team title.

CHURCHILL, CLIVE (1927-   ), Australia's foremost RUGBY LEAGUE full-back. After joining SOUTH SYDNEY from Newcastle, N.S.W. in 1947, he was chosen for the Australian tour of England and France in 1948-9. He was an outstanding success, played in more than 40 consecutive international matches, and toured again in 1952-3 (as captain) and 1956-7. He was fast and elusive, and kicked accurately. He later coached South Sydney successfully.

CHURCHILL DOWNS, Louisville, Kentucky, the race-track in the U.S.A. where the KENTUCKY DERBY and KENTUCKY OAKS are competed for annually in May.

CHURRUCA, FRANCISCO (1936-   ), Spanish Basque PELOTA player who is an outstanding *cesta punta* specialist, and the best *arrière* the game has so far produced. This popularity came from an engaging presence, a generous attitude to the game, and a wide-swinging classical style. In 1970, partnered by Egurbide, he won the world professional championship — the first to be organized in St. Jean-de-Luz, France.

CINCINNATI REDS, American professional BASEBALL team, a founding member of the NATIONAL LEAGUE as the Red Stockings up to 1880, who re-entered in 1890 as the Reds. Its first WORLD SERIES title came in the tainted 1919 'Black Sox' series against the CHICAGO WHITE SOX. The Reds won league titles in 1939 and 1940, led by the pitchers Derringer and Walters and the catcher Lombardi. In 1935 the Reds' general manager McPhail staged the first major-league night game. (A generation later, virtually all week-day major-league baseball games were played at night.) In 1938 Vander Meer hurled no-hit games on two successive pitching turns for the Reds, the only time the feat has been accomplished in baseball history. Cincinnati won league titles in 1961 and 1970, and 1972, with the catcher Bench the outstanding player in latter years.

CINCINNATI ROYALS, American professional BASKETBALL team. The club was formed originally as the Rochester Royals and gained the NATIONAL BASKETBALL ASSOCIATION title in 1951. After moving to Cincinnati, the team has included ROBERTSON and LUCAS.

CITATION (1945), a race-horse by Bull Lea out of Hydroplane by HYPERION out of Toboggan (English OAKS) was bred at CALUMET FARM, owned by Mr. and Mrs. Wright, trained by Jones, and ridden by ARCARO. Citation won 32 out of 45 races, including the American triple crown, the American Derby, Jockey Club Gold Cup, and Hollywood Gold Cup, together with $1,085,760 in stake money, thus becoming the first equine 'dollar millionaire' with a new world record in prize money for a race-horse.

CLAIBORNE FARM STUD, Paris, Kentucky, has for many years been one of the most important thoroughbred horse-breeding centres in America, where champions like KELSO, ROUND TABLE, NASHUA, and WHIRLAWAY were bred. For 16 successive seasons the leading stallion in the U.S.A., stood at Claiborne; Nasrullah, being followed in turn by Princequillo, Ambiorix, and BOLD RULER. Now NIJINSKY and SECRETARIAT are in residence.

CLARK, EARL HARRY (Dutch) (1906-   ), American college and professional FOOTBALL player and coach, who played football and BASEBALL at Colorado College (1927-9). An extremely versatile quarterback, he was an exceptional runner, passer, dropkicker, and punter (kicker). A member of both the college and the professional football Hall of Fame, he played in the NATIONAL FOOTBALL LEAGUE for the Portsmouth Spartans (1931-2) and the DETROIT LIONS (1934-8) and led the League in scoring in 1932, 1935, and 1936. In his last two playing years he also coached Detroit, and later coached the Cleveland Rams (1939-42) and then, in college, the University of Detroit for five years.

CLARK, JIM (1937-68), Scottish MOTOR RACING driver considered to be one of the greatest of all time. He drove many different cars between 1955 and 1959, including SUNBEAM-Talbot, PORSCHE, and the Jaguar D-type. He also drove an Aston Martin DBR1 in 1960 and a works DB4GT in 1961. His main occupation in 1960, however, was to drive Formula Junior cars for Team LOTUS. After the death of Stacey in the Belgian Grand Prix, he appeared for the Formula One team and took third place in the Portuguese Grand Prix. During 1961 he was number two to Ireland for Team Lotus and was third in the Dutch and French Grands Prix and fourth in the German Grand Prix. In 1962 he became team leader for Lotus and his fortunes and those of the make became inseparable.

He won the drivers' championship in 1963 and 1965, won at INDIANAPOLIS in 1965, and his total of major Grand Prix wins exceeded that of FANGIO by one. Clark was killed in a crash at HOCKENHEIM that has never been satisfactorily explained.

CLARKE, E. R., captain of the English women's LACROSSE team from 1913 until 1922. She was closely associated with the growth and development of the women's game during the early decades of the century through her work in schools and training colleges and she helped found and played for the first women's club, the Southern Ladies. She was involved in the foundation of the Ladies' Lacrosse Association in 1912 and was a member of the first executive committee.

CLARKE, RONALD WILLIAM (1937-), middle-distance and long-distance runner for Australia. The most prolific record-breaker since ZATOPEK, Clarke set 17 world records, at distances ranging from 2 miles to the one-hour run, between 1963 and 1968. He was the first man to better 13 min. for 3 miles, clocking 12 min. 52·4 sec. in the course of a world 5,000 metres record of 13 min. 16·6 sec. in 1965. Again, as the first man to better 28 min. for 10,000 metres, he did so by a huge margin, with 27 min. 39·4 sec., and reduced the 6 miles record to 26 min. 47·0 sec. His other world records included: 8 min. 19·6 sec. for 2 miles, 47 min. 12·8 sec. for 10 miles, 59 min. 22·8 sec. for 20,000 metres, and 12 miles 1,006 yds. for the one-hour run. However, Clarke failed to do himself justice by winning a major title. His consolations were silver medals in the COMMONWEALTH GAMES 3 miles (1962 and 1966) and the 6 miles in 1966, and an Olympic bronze medal in the 10,000 metres in 1964.

CLARKE, WILLIAM (1798-1856), cricketer for Nottinghamshire and ALL-ENGLAND XI. Known as 'Old Clarke', he was a calculating and eminently successful under-arm bowler when quite advanced in years. Besides founding TRENT BRIDGE cricket ground, he took CRICKET, in the form of his All-England XI, to many outlying parts of the country.

CLAY, CASSIUS (later Muhammad Ali) (1942-), American boxer who won the world heavyweight title in 1964, four years after winning the Olympic light-heavyweight championship. He had his licence to box withdrawn because his adherence to the Black Muslim faith made him refuse to serve in the U.S. Armed Forces. Clay is a vital figure in the history of the sport both for his physical skill and his colourful, controversial character. Probably the best athlete, in the generic sense, to hold the heavyweight championship, his great speed allied to a formidable physique carried him unbeaten through 19 professional contests before he beat Liston for the title. He defended the championship nine times before being inactive for three years until his licence was restored in 1970. The next year he was outpointed by FRAZIER when trying to regain the title, but the income from this and subsequent bouts brought his total ring earnings to more than $20 million.

CLAY PIGEON SHOOTING, see SHOOTING, CLAY PIGEON.

CLELAND, COOK (1916-), colourful American naval pilot, who flew in the Second World War and Korea. He became famous for his Thompson Trophy racing with 3,500 h.p. modified Corsair fighters. The only man other than the even more colourful Col. Roscoe Turner to win this race twice, he did so in 1949 at 397 m.p.h. (638 km./h.), the fastest closed-circuit speed ever set in piston-engined aircraft.

CLEMENTE, ROBERTO WALKER (1934-72), American BASEBALL outfielder for the PITTSBURGH PIRATES of the NATIONAL LEAGUE, 1955 through 1972. He was one of the few to make 3,000 hits, and four times he led the National League in batting: 1961, 1964, 1965, and 1967. He was named the Most Valuable Player of the National League in 1966. When his career was cut short by a fatal airplane accident following the 1972 season, the Hall of Fame election committee waived the requirement that a five-year period must elapse before a player is eligible, and he was immediately elected.

CLENDINNEN SHIELD, see BADMINTON.

CLEVELAND BROWNS, American professional FOOTBALL team, dominated the All-America Football Conference (A.A.C.) from its founding in 1946 until 1950, when the Browns were merged into the NATIONAL FOOTBALL LEAGUE (N.F.L.). Coach PAUL BROWN stressed precise execution of a limited number of plays; his teams won 47 of 54 games in A.A.C. play and all four League titles. After joining the N.F.L., the Browns won six straight Eastern Conference titles and four League titles — 1950, 1954, 1955, 1964. The team was led by the astute quarterback Graham, the ends Speedie and Lavelli, the bruising fullback Motley, and the exceptional kicker Groza. From 1957 to 1965 the Browns boasted professional football's greatest running back JIM BROWN, seven times league rushing leader and all-time leader in yards gained running.
COLOURS: Brown, orange, and white.

CLEVELAND INDIANS, American professional BASEBALL team, an initial member of the AMERICAN LEAGUE in 1901. Among its outstanding stars have been the second baseman Lajoie, who had a lifetime ·339 batting average; the outfielder Speaker, star of Cleveland's 1920 WORLD SERIES win, with a lifetime ·344 average; and the pitcher Feller, six times a 20-game winner, with 266 wins between 1936 and 1956. The 'boy-manager' Boudreau led the 1948 Indians to a league play-off win over the BOSTON RED SOX and a Series win over the BOSTON BRAVES.

CLIFTONVILLE F.C., Association FOOTBALL club, Belfast. Founded in 1879, Cliftonville is Ireland's oldest club and the only remaining all-amateur one in the Irish League. They won the Irish Cup in 1882-3; 1886-7; 1887-8; 1896-7; 1899-1900; 1900-1; 1906-7.
COLOURS: Red shirts, white shorts.

CLUB BALL was an ancient pastime played with a stick and a ball and of 'rude and unadulterated simplicity'. Its history as a game is obscure but it is important because by at least Tudor times the use of a relatively straight bat (as distinct from the curved sticks with knobs on the end that were used in early forms of HURLING, GOLF, and HOCKEY) and, it seems, the placing of fielders to catch the ball, were

features of club ball that combined with the use of the stool as a wicket in STOOLBALL to evolve a form of CRICKET in the true line of the modern game.

At a time when stoolball was a popular rural game in south and west England, the Worcestershire regional name for a low wooden stool, such as would have been used as the wicket in stoolball, was 'cricket' and it has been suggested that cricket got its name from this direct association with stoolball. There seems however to be a wider claim that the name cricket derived from the Anglo-Saxon word *criec* meaning a staff, stick, or club. Nyren in *The Cricketers of My Time* (1833) accepted that derivation and at the same time cast doubt on Strutt's earlier contention that the ancient game of club ball got its name from the compound of the Welsh and Danish words *clwppa* and *bol*. Nyren preferred to date club ball from the earlier Saxon period.

A game played by hitting a ball with a club is known to have been played at least as early as the middle of the twelfth century, and a sport called *creag* is mentioned in Edward I's Wardrobe Account for 1300 as one of the games played by the 16-year-old Prince Edward. Later, in the reign of Edward IV (1461-83), club ball was among the games outlawed because they diverted persons 'strong and able of bodie' from using their bows. The enactment failed to have the desired effect and most of the games and pastimes, too deeply rooted to be killed off, were still flourishing some fifty years later when the bowyers, fletchers, stringers, and arrowhead-makers of the reign of Henry VIII, getting short of employment, persuaded the king to authorize another similar enactment that made some concession at least to the noblemen in allowing them to play BOWLS and tennis within the precincts of their houses.

The common people, despite the new enactment, continued to play club ball, a game that required only a stick and a ball by way of equipment, and an area of open space in which to play. Nyren thought that it had 'similar laws and customs prescribed in the playing at it' as TRAPBALL that followed it and which carried with it an air of refinement in the 'march of mechanism'.

CLUB CRICKET CONFERENCE (C.C.C.). Founded in 1915, the C.C.C. was originally formed by, and in the interests of, London CRICKET clubs. Its chief aim was to preserve club cricket against the disruptions caused by the First World War, but as interest spread throughout England the membership was widened. Well over 2,000 clubs are now affiliated. The main functions of the Conference are to foster cricket at club level, to assist clubs by offering fixtures in emergencies, to maintain a register of approved umpires, to advise on the preservation of private grounds, to arrange representative matches — with players drawn from member clubs — and generally to co-ordinate amateur club cricket.

CLUES, ARTHUR (1924-   ), the first Australian RUGBY LEAGUE Test player to be signed by an English club after the Second World War. He played three times against Great Britain in 1946 and joined LEEDS in January 1947. A penetrative and constructive second-row forward, he played 14 times for OTHER NATIONALITIES in the international championship. He transferred to HUNSLET in 1954 and retired in 1957.

COACHING, the sport of driving and of racing a coach and horses, was at its peak in popularity in the nineteenth century. Before that time, the condition of the roads and of conveyances had restricted speeds, but the eighteenth century had seen large-scale improvements in the roads, as well as advances in the technique of coach-building. Gentlemen, who once would have considered travelling by coach as a particularly uncomfortable and arduous means of transport, now eagerly wagered on the outcome of races and participated in them.

In general the coaches used were of the mail-coach variety, heavy vehicles with two or four horses, and, after the introduction in 1818 of the macadam system of road-surfacing, the speeds increased dramatically, as indeed did the risks involved. The coaches were controlled by a driver, who sat out front, sometimes accompanied by another driver, a guard, or an unfortunate passenger for whom there was no other place. The standard of driving often tended to be enthusiastic rather than safe, not surprising when the amounts at stake in the races are considered. In 1820 a law was passed against 'wanton or furious driving', and offenders could be punished. But road-users continued to be disturbed by coach races. Sometimes smaller vehicles, faster and lighter than mail-coaches, were used, especially if two gentlemen or, more likely, their representatives were racing.

Closely related to coaching was tandem driving, popular in the first half of the nineteenth century. Tandems differed from coaches in that horses driven in tandem were harnessed behind each other, generally one behind one, whereas in a mail-coach, a drag, or a landau there were generally four horses, harnessed in two pairs. Tandems were lighter and more manoeuvrable. They were not gener-

ally driven at flat-out speeds, but at a constant trot, a pace very difficult to maintain, so that a successful tandem-driver had to be extremely skilful.

In 1784 Sir John Palmer drove a coach from Bath in Somerset to London at an average speed of 7 m.p.h. (11.3 km./h.), and this feat heralded the golden age of coaching. Hitherto there had usually been three horses in a team, but after this record-breaking run the generally accepted number became four, so that the pace was more even, and more easily controlled. The *Sporting Magazine* of June 1807 reported that on the North Road a coach went between London and Stamford, a distance of 90 miles (145 km.) in only 9 hrs. 4 min. The following year the driver of the coach that ran between Portsmouth and London was drunk at the reins, and overturned the coach at Putney. One passenger died as a result, and such accidents were by no means uncommon in the history of coaching. But not all coachmen were incapable and unreliable. One, Poynter, drove the Lewes Stage for 30 years, and retired with the proud record of not a single accident.

As early as the very beginning of the eighteenth century the dangers incipient in coaching had been recognized, and a bill of 1709 imposed a fine of £5 if a driver, through his carelessness, upset a coach. The *St. James Chronicle* for 15 July 1815 reported on a race between Hinckley and Leicester, in which five of the passengers were killed and another four received fractured limbs. The *Chronicle* comments disapprovingly: 'It is time the magistrates put a stop to these outrageous proceedings.' *The Times* frequently listed such mishaps. Cases also occurred of teams of horses starting off of their own accord, unaccompanied by a driver. And so, in 1806, it was made a punishable offence for a driver to leave a team of horses without someone responsible in charge.

There were frequent races between public stage-coaches, for example on 7 August 1808. On this day a coach called *Patriot* from Leicester and another coach called *Defiance* raced from Leicester to Nottingham. The distance covered in this race was 26 miles (42 km.) and the horses were to be exchanged for a new team at Loughborough. Thousands turned out to watch the event, which started at eight o'clock. It was eventually won by *Patriot* which arrived two minutes before its opponent, completing the race in 2 hrs. 10 min., carrying 12 passengers all the while.

After macadam road-surfacing became universal, coaches could cover greater distances in shorter times than ever before, and from about 1825 to 1838 coaching was at its peak, in popularity and in technique. By 1838 the mail was transferred to the railways, and interest in and facilities for coaching declined. The equipment used was sometimes suspect. The horses were often scarcely broken in, and were rarely in good condition. Horses known as 'bo-kickers' (those that would only gallop) were especially unreliable when they were on a flat surface. Such an unregulated speed could be disastrous. Race-horses, having passed their prime, often ended up 'on the road'. Mendoza, which won eight races at Newmarket in 1791-3, became one of a team in the Catterick and Gretna Bridge mail-coach, and in 1807 was still at work.

But all these races were between public coaches. It was inevitable that the nobility and gentry, when they became interested in the sport, should wish to make their own particular brand as exclusive as possible. Accordingly driving clubs grew up. These imposed stringent conditions of entrance, and their members were as carefully selected as for the other clubs to which a nineteenth-century gentleman might seek to belong. In 1835, 'Nimrod' records that in 1825 'thirty or forty four-in-hand equipages were constantly to be seen about town'. But the fashion was short-lived; 'One is stared at now.'

'Meets' of barouche landaus (light, open carriages) were held; the carriages drove in slow procession for their occupants to dine at Bedfont or Windsor. The costume worn was designed to demonstrate the exclusiveness of the members, and was therefore sometimes somewhat bizarre. In 1808 the Whip Club was founded as a rival to the Benson, earliest of the driving clubs, and on 6 June the Whip's members met in Park Lane, London, to drive to Harrow. They wore pale brown, single-breasted coats with mother-of-pearl buttons. Their waistcoats were striped blue and yellow, and their breeches of silk plush. The carriage was no less colourful; its body was painted yellow, and the 'cattle', or horses, were bright bay. Such excesses invited parody, and in 1809 a young Etonian made an appearance at the procession in a low phaeton (a light, four-wheeled, open carriage) with a four-in-hand of donkeys, and brought up the rear around Grosvenor Square.

The premier driving club was the Benson, founded in 1807. In 1851, Thackeray described Sir Henry Peyton, one of its early members, as still driving the 'solitary four-in-hand' in the London parks. By 1853 the Benson had faded, the Whip had ended in 1838. The Defiance club had been founded in 1809 but this was short-lived. In 1838 the Richmond Drag Club was founded (a 'drag' was a vehicle similar in build to a mail-coach, and drawn by four horses); its membership was restricted to the friends of Lord Chesterfield.

In 1802 the *Sporting Magazine* recorded a race between two mail-coaches racing concurrently with each other instead of trying to beat a record previously set. These two coaches were the London Mail, with four greys, and the Plymouth mail pulled by four blacks. In 1811 Seward undertook to drive a four-in-hand for 15 miles (24 km.) in a time of 50 minutes. He drove from Hyde Park Corner to Staines, and failed to fulfil his boast by only 3 min. 20 sec. In May 1805 Buxton, the inventor of a bit and also the founder of the Whip, raced against Hall, a horse dealer, driving non-broken horses.

In 1820 racing was made a criminal offence, because of the casualties and disturbance that it involved. But May Day racing continued. On 1 May 1830 the independent *Tally-Ho* raced from London to Birmingham, a distance of 108 miles (174 km.), and covered the distance in 7 hrs. 39 min. In the late 1860s, the Duke of Beaufort and others raced the Brighton coach against others from London to Brighton.

In 1888, Selby raced from the White Horse Cellar in London to Brighton and back again in 7 hrs. 50 min. Such speeds depended to a great extent on the alacrity with which grooms could unhitch the tired team and harness up the new horses at each change. In 1908, Miss Brocklebank's grooms won the Hon. Adam Beck's prize for the 'Best Coach and appointments and quickest change of teams'. These grooms managed their change in 48 seconds.

Coaching still continued as a pastime with pleasant traditional overtones, but the furious competitive races had ceased by the turn of the century. Tandem racing died out even earlier. In 1807 an edict of 10 March from the Vice-Chancellor of Cambridge forbade undergraduates to drive tandems, because of the accidents and disturbances that had occurred as a result of reckless and dangerous driving. On 14 April 1819 Buxton announced his intention to trot from Hounslow to Hare Hatch, a distance of 24 miles (39 km.), in 2 hours. But he 'broke' his trot and allowed the horses to accelerate into a canter. The *Sporting Magazine* for 19 May 1824 reported that Capt. Swann had engaged to drive 12 miles (19 km.) at a trot. He broke only once in the distance, in the seventh mile. In 1824 too, Capt. Ramsden drove from Theale to London, a distance of 43 miles (69 km.), at a trot, in 3 hrs. 29 min.

Tandem driving went out of fashion in about 1840, although the Tandem Club was re-established after the Crimean War (1856), and some interest in the sport lingered on.

COACHING CLUB AMERICAN OAKS is the fillies' equivalent of the BELMONT STAKES and the most important event in the U.S.A. for female race-horses. It is run over 1¼ miles (2,000 m.) at BELMONT PARK, N.Y., in June.

COAKES, MARION, see MOULD, Mrs.

COBB, TYRUS RAYMOND (1886-1961), American BASEBALL outfielder, star batter, and base-runner for the Detroit and Philadelphia AMERICAN LEAGUE teams from 1905 to 1928. He led his league in batting 12 times —9 times in succession—and stole 892 bases. Three times he batted over ·400, and he held the highest lifetime batting average, ·367. Only a handful of players have made 3,000 or more hits; Cobb stood alone with more than 4,000.

COBHAM, Sir ALAN, K.B.E., A.F.C. (1894-1973), British pioneer of flight refuelling techniques, was principally known for his Air Circus which introduced popular flying to Britain through National Air Days in 1932-3 and displays in 1934-5. He competed in the first King's Cup in 1922 and undertook numerous survey and record flights in 1921-31. More than any other man, he symbolized the sport of flying in Britain in this period.

COCHET, HENRI (1901-   ), French LAWN TENNIS player, one of the 'Four Musketeers' (BOROTRA, BRUGNON, and LACOSTE were the others) who captured the Davis Cup (see LAWN TENNIS) for France, and one of the game's instinctive geniuses. Lean and slight, a master of the spectacular volley and half-volley, sharp-reflexed and splendidly versatile, Cochet played for France for 11 years until he joined TILDEN on a professional tour in 1933. He won the French singles title five times between 1922 and 1932, WIMBLEDON twice (1927 and 1929, beating Borotra in the final on both occasions) and FOREST HILLS in 1928.

Cochet was reinstated as an amateur in 1945 and won a number of tournaments. As late as 1950, he won the British covered court doubles title with DROBNY. He played in six challenge rounds and won 44 Davis Cup rubbers out of 58 in 26 ties between 1922 and 1933.

COCK-FIGHTING, see ANIMAL-BAITING.

COLEMAN, JOHN (1928-73), Australian Rules footballer, was regarded as one of the best full-forwards since the Second World War. Playing for Essendon in the VICTORIAN FOOTBALL LEAGUE, he kicked 100 goals in his first season in 1949 and a further 120 in the following season. He exceeded 100 in 1952, but a knee injury forced his premature retirement in 1954, when he had kicked 537 goals in 98 matches.

COLLEDGE, CECILIA (1920-   ), ice figure-skater for Great Britain. Tracing some of the technically best skating figures seen before the war, she won early recognition in 1933 when coming second to Miss HENIE in the European championship. She became world champion in 1937, took the European title three times in succession, 1937-9, and was Olympic runner-up, again to Miss Henie, in 1936.

She was the only girl to win six British titles, 1935-46. These were consecutive but, because of the intervening war, spanned 12 years which suggests how many more victories she might have achieved in peacetime conditions. In 1946 she turned professional and has since coached at Boston Skating Club for more than 20 years.

COLOMBES, the stadium in the suburbs of Paris where France played most of their RUGBY UNION international matches until 1972, and the home ground of the Racing Club de France.

COLORADO KING (1960), a champion race-horse in South Africa, bred by Birch Bros., leased to Louw, and trained by Laird. He won the Cape Mellow-wood Guineas and the CAPE OF GOOD HOPE DERBY, both in record time, and crowned his brilliant career with a spectacular victory in the ROTHMAN'S JULY HANDICAP, as the shortest-priced favourite ever to win the most important event on the South African turf. Colorado King was then sold to America, where he won the Hollywood Gold Cup.

COLUNA, MARIO (1935-   ), Association footballer for BENFICA (Lisbon) and Portugal in both wing half and inside forward positions. Born in Angola, he was a prominent member of the Benfica teams that won the European Champion Clubs Cup in both 1961, when he scored the winning goal, and 1962, and were the beaten finalists in 1963, 1965, and 1968. For many years Benfica's captain, he was also captain of the Portuguese team that finished in third place in the 1966 World Cup championship held in England.

COMMONWEALTH GAMES. Originally called the British Empire Games, these are now officially named the British Commonwealth Games. ATHLETICS is the main sport at these Games which are a major championship of the International Amateur Athletic Federation (see ATHLETICS, TRACK AND FIELD). The Games were held in Hamilton, Canada, in 1930; London in 1934; Sydney, Australia, in 1938; Auckland, New Zealand, in 1950; and subsequently at four-year intervals. Women's events were first introduced in 1934.

COMMONWEALTH MATCH, see SHOOTING, RIFLE: SERVICE CALIBRE.

COMPTON, DENIS CHARLES SCOTT, C.B.E. (1918-   ), cricketer for England and Middlesex; Association footballer for England and Arsenal. His career figures, though imposing, fail to convey his true worth as an entertaining and improvising batsman. The Second World War interrupted a promising beginning, but 1947, his peak year, found him transposing his ability into record-breaking figures: 3,816 runs and 18 centuries. In 1948 he played two memorable innings against Australia, one in poor light, the other after sustaining a cut eyebrow. In the following winter in South Africa he hit the fastest triple century in first-class cricket. At times a penetrative left-arm spin bowler, and during his younger days a fine soccer wing forward, he had to curtail both careers because of a knee injury.

CONIBEAR, HIRAM (d. 1917), American ROWING coach. Originally a BASEBALL trainer, he was appointed rowing coach at Washington University in 1907. After studying the methods of other American coaches, he developed his own system which eventually spread throughout United States collegiate rowing. Many famous American university coaches learnt to row in Conibear's Washington crews and his methods were widely used until the early 1960s.

The characteristics of the Conibear stroke were a powerful leg-drive, a short swing, fast finish, and steady sliding. Conibear crews generally adopted a low rate of striking and were renowned for their staying power.

CONN SMYTHE TROPHY, ICE HOCKEY trophy, awarded annually in the STANLEY CUP competition contested by the leading teams in the NATIONAL HOCKEY LEAGUE of North America. Donated in 1965 by Maple Leaf Gardens, Toronto, and named after the former TORONTO MAPLE LEAFS coach, manager, president, and owner. It goes to 'the most valuable player for his team in the entire play-offs'. Each winner, who receives $1,000, is selected by the League governors.

CONNOLLY,   HAROLD   VINCENT

(1931-   ), hammer-thrower for the U.S.A. One of the most remarkable sportsmen ever to triumph over a physical disability, Connolly was handicapped by a birth injury which made his left arm three inches shorter than his right. He was Olympic champion in 1956 and broke the world record seven times between 1956 and 1965, becoming the first man to surpass 70 metres with 230 ft. 9 in. (70·34 m.) in 1960. His best performance was 233 ft. 9½ in. (71·26 m.). He married Olga Fikotova, the 1956 Olympic DISCUS champion from Czechoslovakia.

CONNOLLY,   MAUREEN   (1934-69), American LAWN TENNIS player, the first woman to win all four of the major singles titles in a year and one of the game's supreme ground stroke players. She won the U.S. singles title in 1951 at the age of 16 and then lost only four more matches in the rest of her career, failing twice against Hart, once against Fry, and once against Fleitz. The WIMBLEDON finals in which she beat BROUGH — by 7-5, 6-3 in 1952 and by 6-2, 7-5 in 1954 — and Hart by 8-6, 7-5 in 1953, were regarded as classic matches. In both 1953 and 1954 she lost only 19 games in winning the title. Besides her three Wimbledon victories, she won twice in Paris, three times at FOREST HILLS, and took the Australian title in 1953, the year of her 'grand slam'. She broke a leg in a riding accident in July 1954, and retired from competition. She married Brinker, a U.S. Olympic horseman, and, as a coach, she helped many promising players, but her last years were a constant battle against illness. She died on the eve of Wimbledon.

CONROY, JOHN VALENTINE (1928-   ), HOCKEY player for Europe, Great Britain, England, Combined Services, South of England, Middlesex, Army, Mid-Surrey, and Hornets. An inside forward of outstanding skill and speed, he developed into a fine tactician. Born in India, he was the first Anglo-Indian to be picked for Great Britain at hockey. His influence led to a higher premium being put on pure skill in British hockey. He played in 55 internationals (23 for Great Britain, 32 for England), filling four different forward positions, and was a vital member of Britain's 1952 and 1956 Olympic teams. He won a bronze medal in 1952. Generally regarded as Britain's greatest-ever forward, he was still playing senior hockey in his 40s.

CONSOLINI, ADOLFO (1917-69), discus-thrower for Italy. Perhaps the greatest and certainly the most durable of European discus-throwers, Consolini won the A.A.A. championship in London in 1938, the European championship in 1946, 1950, and 1954, the Olympic title in 1948, and the Olympic silver medal in 1952. He broke the world record three times between 1941 and 1948 when he threw 55·33 m.

CONSTANTINE, Lord LEARIE NICHOLAS (1901-71), cricketer for West Indies and Trinidad. A prodigious, unorthodox hitter of the ball, dynamic fast bowler, and, as a catcher, uninhibited and unexcelled, he drew crowds wherever he played, and attracted much early recognition for West Indian CRICKET. For several seasons he played Lancashire League cricket with conspicuous success. Later activity in political spheres resulted in his being created a life peer in 1969.

COOK, Sir THEODORE ANDREA (1867-1928), for many years editor-in-chief of *The Field*, was also the author of *A History of the English Turf*, first published in 1904 and immediately accepted as the classic work on the subject.

COOLEY, IRIS L., see ROGERS, MRS. W. C. E.

COOPER, British racing car. The first version was built in 1946 by John Cooper and his father, Charles. It was a 500 cc. single-cylinder model made from available components and the two men turned out a large number of these JAP-engined Formula Three cars in the following years. They went on to other, and larger, racing cars and in 1955 produced the rear-engined version which, with a Bristol engine, won the Australian Grand Prix of that year with BRABHAM driving. With a Coventry-Climax engine it dominated Grand Prix racing in 1959 and the 1960s, winning the world championship. The 1·5-litre was not as successful, but nevertheless won many races in 1961 and 1962. For 1966 and the new 3-litre Formula, Cooper turned to MASERATI for their power unit and for 1968 to BRM. Coopers were pioneers of the lightweight Grand Prix car with the engine in the tail.

COOPER, ALBERT ARTHUR (1910-), a race walker for Great Britain and Woodford Green A.C., who set world records for 3 km. and 5 km. in 1935 and won the Amateur Athletic Association (A.A.A.) 2-mile championship seven times in succession (1932-8). A very stylish walker, he won the Fowler-Dixon style medal (awarded only in A.A.A. championships) on no fewer than ten occasions.

COOPER, LIONEL (1923-), Australian RUGBY LEAGUE winger who played in three Tests against Great Britain in 1946 and joined HUDDERSFIELD early in 1947. Immensely strong as well as fast and elusive, Cooper set a Huddersfield club record by scoring 432 tries before returning to Australia in 1955. On 17 November 1951, against Keighley, he became the first to score 10 tries in a match between senior clubs. He played ten times for OTHER NATIONALITIES in the international championship and headed the League try-scoring list three times.

COOPER, MARGARET JOYCE (1909-), English swimmer who won four out of a possible five gold medals at the first British Empire Games in 1930. Her SWIMMING talent embraced all styles and distances except the breaststroke. A medallist at two OLYMPIC GAMES and two European championships, she married the British Olympic ROWING gold medallist, John Badcock.

COPPI, FAUSTO (1919-60), Italian road-race cyclist, known as the 'Campionissimo', the champion of champions. Although already 26 when international cycling resumed after the Second World War, Coppi took more major prizes than any rider before him. He won the GIRO D'ITALIA five times, the TOUR DE FRANCE twice, and was the first to win both in the same year. His classic victories included the TOUR OF LOMBARDY (five times), the MILAN–SAN REMO thrice, the GRAND PRIX DES NATIONS twice and the world road-race championship of 1953. On the track he set a world hour record in 1942, and took world pursuit titles in 1947 and 1949. Coppi was noted for the manner as well as the number of his victories. His one weakness was in the sprint, so he used his phenomenal strength to draw away from the field, often on a climb, some distance from the finish. Thus he won the FLÈCHE WALLONNE by 6 minutes, the 1946 Milan–San Remo by 14 minutes, and an Alpine stage in the Tour de France by 7 minutes.

CORBALLY, CYRIL (1881-1946), one of three outstanding CROQUET players from Ireland. He first appeared on the English croquet scene in 1902 and won the open championship at his first attempt. He entered it on only seven occasions and won it on five. One who saw him play a good deal wrote, '...He was a splendid tactician. He was both brilliant and accurate. There was no stroke that he was not master of.' Corbally won the men's championship once, and the mixed doubles twice, during a very short croquet career.

CORBETT, JAMES J. (1866-1933), American boxer who won the world heavyweight title in 1892 from SULLIVAN in the first championship under the QUEENSBERRY RULES. Corbett, who was first a bank clerk, brought an image of respectability to professional BOXING and earned high regard during the latter part of the nineteenth century for his skill in the ring. After losing the title to FITZSIMMONS in 1897 he twice made brave attempts to regain it from JEFFRIES.

CORBILLON CUP, see MARCEL CORBILLON CUP.

CORDOBÉS, El (Manuel Benítez (1937-), *matador de toros* who took the *alternativa* in 1963, and became a millionaire in two years as a result of his professional achievements in the bull ring. The high priest of *tremendismo*, the range of *toreo* practised by him includes passes executed while hopping on his knees in front of the bull, and leaping on the animal's back. His great experience (in 1965 he appeared in 111 *corridas*) gave him an understanding of bulls: His *capotazos* are inelegant, his work with the *muleta* a parody of *toreo*, but his immense courage endeared him even to detractors of his work as a serious *torero*.

CORK CONSTITUTION R.F.C., Irish RUGBY UNION football club. It was formed in 1894 by the staff of the (now defunct) newspaper after which it was named. Its most notable internationals are KIERNAN, N. F. Murphy, and his son N. A. MURPHY .
GROUND: Temple Hill.
COLOURS: Blue, black, and white.

CORNISH, PETER (1938-), underwater swimmer and expedition leader who successfully organized the lifting and recovery from the seabed of a Beaufighter aircraft (1971), H.M.S. 'X-E 8', a mini-sub (1972), and a Halifax bomber (1973). He won the Diver of the Year award in 1972.

CORONACH (1923), English race-horse by Hurry On, bred and owned by Lord Woolavington, trained by DARLING, and ridden by Childs, won the DERBY in a canter by five lengths, the ST. LEGER in record time, the ECLIPSE STAKES, and the CORONATION CUP, together with £48,224 in stakes.

CORONATION CUP is an important weight-for-age horse race run in England over the Derby course of 1½ miles (2,400 m.) at EPSOM on the day after the DERBY.

CORTINA, BOBSLEIGH course at Cortina d'Ampezzo in the Dolomites, Italy. It was completed in time for the 1939 world championships. The bobsleigh events of the 1956 WINTER OLYMPIC GAMES were held here and other world championship meetings in 1950, 1954 and 1960. It is usually open for a larger proportion of the winter than other courses, a factor which has given an advantage in training to the Italian crews, who have also benefited from the fact that the Podar sleds are made near the course, which facilitates mechanical experiments and tests.

COSIC, KRESIMIR (1948-), BASKETBALL player from Zadar, Yugoslavia, who stands at 6 ft. 11 in. (2·11 m.). He was selected for the All-Europe team and helped his country to win the silver medal at the 1968 OLYMPIC GAMES. He then received a scholarship to attend Brigham Young University, in Utah (U.S.A.), and in 1972 became the first non-American to be included in the All-American selection.

COSTILLARES (Joaquín Rodríguez) (1729-1800), *matador de toros* who invented the *volapié*, and perhaps the *veronica*. He was one of the first *toreros* to use the *muleta* decoratively instead of functionally.

COTSWOLD GAMES, an obsolete English rural sports meeting, probably dating back to the sixteenth century. The games were revived in 1604, with royal approval, by Robert Dover, who called them Cotswold's Olympick Games. They soon became known as Dover's Games, as which they lasted until 1850.

COTTER, EDMOND PATRICK CHARLES (1904-) English CROQUET player, was the first to bring a new look to the game in the postwar era and quickly rose to fame. Having played as a boy he took up the game again in 1948 and the following year won the President's Cup at the first attempt. He adopted an attacking approach which defeated the defensive attitude that had developed since the war. A fast and attractive player, Cotter brought the triple peel back as an objective of each game. He captained England in the MAC-ROBERTSON trophy competitions in 1956 and 1963, and between 1948 and 1969 won two open championships, four men's, ten open doubles (with SOLOMON), and the President's Cup six times. He played bridge for England on many occasions, won the world bridge championship in 1938, and played GOLF to a scratch handicap.

COTTON, THOMAS HENRY, M.B.E.

(1907-   ), English professional golfer and Open champion 1934, 1937, and 1948. The most distinguished English golfer of his generation, Cotton did much to raise the status of the professional. Winner of many national titles and sponsored tournaments, he was, with HAGEN and LOCKE, one of the first three professionals to be made honorary members of the Royal and Ancient. At the end of his playing career he turned to golf-course architecture.

COUBERTIN, Baron PIERRE DE, see OLYMPIC GAMES.

COUNTRY CLUB, Brookline, Massachusetts, U.S. GOLF course distinguished more by its history than by intrinsic merit. Built in 1882, it was the scene in 1913 of the U.S. Open championship victory of the amateur, OUIMET in a play-off against VARDON and RAY. Fifty years later it was again the scene of the U.S. Open championship. Venerable, honourable, and a good course of the park variety, it is hardly a great one.

COURSING has been defined as the pursuit of game by hounds hunting by sight and not by scent. The game coursed varies with the geographical habitat and the species of the greyhound breed indigenous to that locality. Speaking of the greyhound in England, Dr. John Caius wrote that it was used in 'taking the bucke, the harte, the dowe, the foxe and other beastes of semblable kindes ordained for the game of hunting. Some are of a greater sorte and some of a lesser sorte, some are smooth-skynned and some are curled. The bigger therefore are appointed to hunt the bigger beastes, the smaller serve to hunt the smaller accordingly.'

Whereas the wolf, the hart, and the gazelle have been the quarry of the borzoi, the deerhound, and the Saluki throughout the ages, in the twentieth century the hare is the game pursued in all those countries where coursing is conducted as an established and organized sport. Certainly in England, Ireland, America, Australia, Portugal, and Spain, the hare is the sole quarry coursed by the various breed clubs catering for the field sport: the National Coursing Club, the Whippet Coursing Club, the Saluki Coursing Club, the Deerhound Coursing Club.

Although the hare is pursued by beagles and harriers also, the distinction is that, in coursing, a brace — two greyhounds which pursue solely by sight — are used, whereas beagles and harriers hunt in packs of a score or more and pursue by scent alone.

While there is evidence that coursing was practised as a sport in Greece more than 2,000 years ago, the sole object then was the amusement of watching the contest between two dogs and the hare. Out of the enjoyment of watching dogs behind their natural quarry there developed a competitive interest, a desire to match greyhounds to test their respective merits.

At first sight the rules for judging the merits of two hounds competing for possession of their game appear complex and difficult. The key lies in the various qualities and characteristics of the greyhound breed which are to be tested. Primarily the two basic qualities are speed and agility. Speed, with which the greyhound is naturally endowed above all other dogs, is commonly regarded as the most important. The rules are designed to award points to the dog showing greater pace and agility in comparison with its rival.

The traditional organization and form of club coursing is by way of stakes, invariably for 8, 16, 32 dogs or, in the case of national events like the WATERLOO, Barbican, and Irish Cups, 64 dogs. Entries are made and fees paid by a stipulated date to the club secretary. Names are drawn from a hat in pairs and dogs compete in that order. The running of the stake then proceeds on a knock-out basis, the winner of the first brace meeting the winner of the second brace and so on, until the ultimate winners in the top and bottom halves of the card meet in the final. The stake money, comprising the entry fees less a proportion towards the cost of the meeting, is divided between the winner, the runner-up, and the semi-finalists on a pre-arranged basis, with the winner invariably being awarded a trophy.

The two dogs to be matched are handed over by their owners or trainers to the slipper — the official responsible for releasing them simultaneously behind a suitable hare. He buckles each dog into a collar attached to a hollow leather leash, the other end of which is attached to his wrist. A wire cable running through the centre of this leash, or slip, is attached to a pin in each of the collars. By releasing his grip on the leash, the slipper automatically draws the pins from the collars which open and release both dogs. At meetings where hares are beaten towards him, as distinct from those meetings where he walks up the field with his dogs, the slipper usually takes up his stance and conceals himself in a small moveable hide — commonly called the slipper's 'shy' or 'hurdle'.

Before releasing the dogs, the slipper must ensure that the hare has had a fair start — not less than 80 yds. (73 m.) is stipulated by the rules. From this moment of fair release the determination of the relative merits of the two dogs is the sole responsibility of the judge (invariably clad in hunting pink) who takes up his position some 100 yds. (91 m.) ahead of the slipper, mounted to enable him to keep sufficiently in touch with the work of both dogs to count their scores.

The first dog to reach the hare is awarded 1, 2, or 3 points for his superior pace in the run-up — the race from the slipper to the hare. The points are based on the distance one dog leads the other to the hare, 1 point for a lead of one length, 2 points for a lead of two lengths, to a maximum of 3 points (a length being deemed the length of the animal, as in horse racing).

The other meter of pace is the go-by — the degree of pace revealed when a dog in the course races from one length behind to one length in front of its rival — for which again 1, 2, or 3 points are awarded. The 3 points awarded for being virtually three lengths faster than its opponent during the course is on a par with the 3 points awarded for similar speed in the run-up.

The dog first reaching the hare and forcing her to make her characteristic right-angled jink is awarded 1 point for his agility. For each subsequent turn that a dog forces his quarry to make in its escape manoeuvres, he scores a further point. If a dog merely wrenches a hare when he is pursuing it — does little more than force it to deviate slightly from its straight line of escape — then for this lesser exhibition of agility he scores but a half-point.

The other facets of the course for which points are awarded, the trip (when a hare is thrown off her legs), the wrench (a turn of less than a right angle), and the kill, are of minor importance. The latter is not even point-worthy, unless it is achieved by marked cleverness on the part of the greyhound. The judge's decision is based solely on the number of points each dog scores during the course. As the hare escapes in approximately six out of seven courses, the kill clearly cannot be a decisive issue in determining the winner.

The geographical setting against which the slipper and judge perform their duties depends upon the size and importance of the meeting. At the majority of meetings staged by members' clubs — one-day affairs — the normal pattern is for the slipper with his brace of dogs buckled in his slips to walk up a large stubble or pasture field with the judge some 100 yds. (91·4 m.) ahead on the flank. The spectators and owners either bring up the rear or range along the hedge or dike-side. For identification, the dogs wear either a red or white woollen collar. The judge signifies the winner by raising a red or white handkerchief.

At the larger two-day meetings, and such three-day events as the Waterloo or Barbican Cups which attract widespread interest and support, the hares are brought to the slipper and judge, within view of the spectators, by large-scale drives of the surrounding countryside. These drives, by a converging semicircle of beaters through adjacent root and stubble fields, are arranged to force hares one at a time across a flat pasture some 600 yds. (550 m.) long and 300 yds. (275 m.) wide, past the slipper in his shy whence he releases his charges once the hare is running true and straight up the field.

At all meetings under National Coursing Club rules the passage of hares must be completely unhampered. All fields in which coursing is staged in England must be open, with no form of fence, hedge, or paling to prevent or impede the escape of the game.

Consequent on the passing of the Ground Game Act 1880, which gave the tenant equal rights with his landlord to the ground game on his holding, thus threatening to decimate the hare population in many parts of England, a form of enclosed coursing was conceived, primarily to provide facilities and preserve hares for the continuation of coursing.

At Plumpton, a typical enclosed meeting, a park was laid out comprising a breeding preserve and an area of artificial cover into which hares could be driven when wanted for coursing. At the other end of the field, some 600 yds. (550 m.) long, there was an ingenious escape fence which enabled the hare to elude her pursuers and end the course. As the hares were carefully fed and trained so that they knew their way up field to the escape, the proportion of hares that escaped was even larger than under the old open system.

Park coursing, however, was considered to put an undue emphasis on the importance of speed and as an all-round test of merit it did not compare with the sport in such open grounds as Altcar and Newmarket. Its popularity proved to be short-lived, and the last enclosed park meeting in England was held in 1890. Coursing on park lines is still actively organized in Eire.

Coursing is probably the oldest of all sports. It is as old as the various species of the greyhound breed itself. The drawings of domesticated hunting dogs, clearly of greyhound type, depicted on the murals of the tombs of Amten in the valley of the Nile and on the sepulchral walls of Rechmara, dating back to 1500 B.C., are proof both of the pride and pleasure that man has taken in his sporting hounds and of the antiquity of coursing which extends far beyond the origins of Christianity itself. There is even scriptural authority (Prov. 30: 29-31) for the antiquity of the breed:

'There be three things which go well, yea, four are comely in going:

A lion which is strongest among beasts, and turneth not away for any;

A greyhound; an he goat also; and a king, against whom there is no rising up.

Coursing may have been introduced into Britain from the east by the Phoenicians about 500 B.C. Certainly Flavius Arrianus in his *Cynegeticus* (A.D. 150) — the earliest and most exhaustive treatise on coursing — refers consistently to the greyhound as the 'Celtic hound'. His description of the manner and spirit in which coursing should be conducted, written some 1,800 years ago, is still a model for the sport today:

Whoever courses with greyhounds should neither slip them near the hare nor more than a brace at a time for though the hare is remarkably swift footed and has often beaten many dogs yet being started from her form she cannot but be flustered at heart and terrified at the halluing and the hounds pressing close upon her, and in this way many a noble hare has often ignobly perished without an effort showing no diversion worth mentioning. Let the hare therefore keep away from her form as if unperceived and recover her presence of mind, and then if she be a racer she will prick up her ears and bound away from her seat with long strides, and the greyhounds having capered about as if they were dancing will stretch out at full speed after her, and at this time is the spectacle worthy indeed of the pains that must be bestowed upon these dogs.

The rigour with which Norman and Angevin kings enforced the cruel Forest Laws in the eleventh to fourteenth centuries is proof enough of the extent to which greyhounds were kept and employed as a vital and necessary means of obtaining food for the commoners' very survival. The emergence of a competitive element, the arrangement of matches between two dogs, dates back to the sixteenth century, when Elizabeth I appointed her Earl Marshal, Thomas, Duke of Norfolk, to codify the many varying conventions and local practices that had grown up around the sport and to draw up a uniform code of rules to define the points of a course and to judge the relative merit of each dog's efforts. With Norfolk's Laws of the Leash subscribed to and accepted by the principal nobility, coursing could be said to have graduated from the category of an enjoyable sporting pot-hunting pastime into an organized competitive sport.

The earliest coursing under the new rules was almost certainly conducted in private on such royal estates or baronial manors as Cowdray Park in Sussex and Kenilworth in Warwickshire. Although there are records of matches being decided in public in the reign of Charles I, it was not until the close of the eighteenth century that the first clubs were established for the purpose of promoting sport and good fellowship among their members.

The first, the SWAFFHAM CLUB, was formed in 1776 at the instigation of the celebrated but eccentric Lord Orford who is regarded as the father of modern coursing. He is believed to have been the first breeder to introduce the bulldog cross from which the brindle colour is supposed to stem. Lord Orford died in 1797 while watching his famous bitch Czarina — unbeaten in 47 courses — defeat her opponent Maria. With the success of the Swaffham Club, and the growing popularity of organized coursing, others quickly followed: 1780, the Ashdown Park Club; 1781, the Malton Club; 1805, the Newmarket Society; 1822, the Amesbury Club; and 1825, the ALTCAR CLUB.

Some of these clubs have long since ceased to exist. Others have had a fitful existence, lapsing and being revived only to relapse and be revived again. Others, although still in existence, have lost their original identity and suffered a change of name consequent on amalgamation or association with neighbouring clubs. In such cases the thread connecting the original club or society with the present-day club is the territory over which they pursue their sport, e.g. the Louth Coursing Society which was formed in 1806 coursed over much the same land as the present North Lincolnshire Coursing Club.

One of the memorable meetings in coursing history was staged by the Amesbury Club in 1864 on the downs at Stonehenge — the Altcar Club *v.* the World, the Altcar having challenged the World to produce 16 bitch puppies, 16 dog puppies, and 16 all-age greyhounds to match against theirs. The Altcar Club ultimately won the match by two events to one, the club winning the Challenge Bracelet for bitch puppies and the all-age Challenge Cup, and the World the Challenge Bracelet for dog puppies. In addition to these stakes, there was also the Great Western Cup for 74 bitch puppies and the Druid Cup for 46 dog puppies. Altogether the meeting extended for seven days, and on the second day alone the judge, Warwick, used four horses.

Not all the old original clubs formed in the first quarter of the nineteenth century have been lost. Noteworthy exceptions being the Swaffham, SOUTH OF ENGLAND, and Altcar Clubs, which still stage some first-class coursing meetings.

Consequent on the upsurge in the popularity of coursing, four impelling needs soon manifested themselves: (*a*) an up-to-date and uniform code of rules; (*b*) a complete and official record of results at coursing meetings; (*c*) a register of pedigree, a stud-book, as a guarantee of breed purity; (*d*) an authoritative body to control, organize, and administer the sport on central lines.

Although Norfolk's Laws of the Leash had remained authoritative for close on 200 years, it was now apparent that these in turn were in need of being brought up to date. In 1834 Thacker published his *Courser's Companion*, the main feature of which was the codification and consolidation of the various sets of rules and regulations that had grown up around Norfolk's original laws. Thacker's Rules, as they became known, ultimately formed the basis of the official rules drawn up and authorized later by the National Coursing Club. In addition Thacker also produced in 1842 the *Courser's Annual Remembrancer* or stud-book, the first of an annual set of 17 volumes which represented the first systematic attempt to record the results and publish the returns of all coursing meetings in the United Kingdom. As such it was the forerunner of the official *Coursing Calendar* which superseded Thacker's annual efforts when the National Coursing Club took over in 1858.

The first seeds of a reliable and authoritative stud-book were sown by Goodlake who, having edited the notes of the Revd. E. W. Barnard, published them in 1828 as the *Courser's Companion and Stud-Book*. The inclusion in this work of the parentage of greyhounds constitutes the first serious and systematic attempt to compile a breed register. Goodlake's proposal in 1801 to hold a dinner in London in Derby week for the representatives of all coursing clubs to meet and arrange a large stake for the championship of England, anticipated by some 35 years the first truly national event, the Waterloo Cup, and by some 51 years the formation of the National Coursing Club.

Although the formation of a controlling body to organize and administer the sport was an obvious and logical step, the National Coursing Club was not formed to act as a supreme authority on coursing matters until 1858. In addition to framing a new code of rules based largely on Thacker's, it also set out a code of conduct and administered the laws of the club and arbitrated on all disputes. The National Coursing Club acted for coursing exactly as the Jockey Club acted for racing. The club, constructed on a liberal elective basis, consists of members elected by the constituent coursing clubs in the United Kingdom, each of which can nominate two members. The club thus formed can elect up to 30 additional members from well-known supporters

of the sport. The club is administered by a standing committee appointed by the members and consisting of the president and not less than nine members, three of whom retire annually in rotation. Up to 1972, when the last Earl died, the Earls of SEFTON have traditionally been presidents of the club.

In addition to codifying and bringing the rules up to date, the National Coursing Club also introduced in 1881 the first volume of its stud-book and stipulated that every dog that ran at a public meeting must be registered therein by name, description, pedigree, and owner — a momentous decision which effectively and henceforth ensured the purity of blood and authentic lineage of the breed.

As supporters of a sport of the countryside, of the vast stubbles of Hampshire, the downs of Wiltshire, the flats of Lancashire, and the fens of Lincolnshire, coursing devotees were largely people with rural interests.

In the Middle Ages the effect of the repressive Forest Laws from 1014 to 1377 was that ownership of a greyhound was restricted to royalty and nobility. Serfs and villeins were expressly prohibited from keeping greyhounds on pain of death; even a freeman could not keep a greyhound within ten miles of a royal forest unless the dog was lamed to ensure that it did not trespass and hunt the royal game. 'No manner of artificers, labourers or any other laymen which hath not lands or tenements to the value of £10 by year, nor any Priest nor other Clerk if he be not advanced to the value of £10 by year, shall keep from henceforth any greyhound.'

Against such a background it was understandable that the majority of coursing devotees up to the formation of the National Coursing Club in 1858 were among the landed aristocracy, the hereditary landlords, the squires, and large yeoman farmers. The Industrial Revolution in the second half of the nineteenth century, however, saw the sport fortified and stimulated by the new blood of such enthusiastic industrialists as Messrs. Rank, Pilkington, and Dennis, just as in the 1930s, the social and economic base of the sport was broadened by the interest and enthusiasm of many dog-owners from GREYHOUND RACING.

The effect of these social, economic, and political changes in the fabric of coursing can best be viewed in the decline of the great kennels. Prior to the First World War most greyhounds were kept in big private kennels, some with as many as 60 dogs in training. From 1930 the greyhound population was predominantly in the kennels of smaller owners with from five to ten dogs.

That a sport with such deep roots should

have its traditional trophies, its classics, on a par with the Turf, is understandable. Of these the Waterloo Cup, the Blue Riband of the Leash, is the most keenly coveted and takes precedence over all other events in the coursing calendar. Among the sport's other major events the Barbican Cup, the only other 64-dog stake, which has been staged by the South of England and East of England Clubs at venues as far removed as Kent, Wiltshire, and Lincolnshire, ranks as one of the sport's classics, as do the Altcar Cup, the South of England Cup, and the Huntingdon Silver. In Ireland the Irish Cup, which dates from 1906, the National Derby, and the Oaks are the premier trophies.

Foremost among the kennels noteworthy for their record of success in the Waterloo Cup was that of G. F. and C. T. Fawcett. Dogs from their kennel at Saughall, Cheshire, dominated coursing for the period 1890 to 1905; those trained by Tom Wright won five Waterloo Cups with Fabulous Fortune (1896), Fearless Footsteps (1900 and 1901), Farndon Ferry (1902), and Father Flint (1903). In addition the Fawcetts' dogs were runners-up for the Waterloo Cup on three occasions, Faster & Faster (1891), Fitz Fife (1892), and Fortuna Favente (1895).

The confederacy of J. E. and S. M. Dennis won the Waterloo classic on no fewer than four occasions with Dendraspis (1909), Dilwyn (1914), Dee Rock (1935), and Dee Flint (1940).

In addition to winning the Blue Riband on four occasions, the Sefton family's kennel has provided the beaten finalist on six occasions, Sold Again (1933), Shy Bess (1942), String (1943), Scorpion (1950), Sucker (1953), and Streakaway (1970).

The most successful owner of the postwar era, LUCAS, won the Waterloo Cup in 1949 and 1964 with Lifeline and Latin Lover, and was runner-up for the honour in 1948 and 1951 with Lady of the Lamp and Lily of Laguna. He won three Barbican Cups with dogs trained by Lewis Reynolds: Latin Lexicon (1948), Landlocked (1950), and Lentenloaf (1951).

The Wright family holds a unique place in the annals of training coursing greyhounds. Joseph Wright trained Burnaby and Thoughtless Beauty, the Cup winners of 1888 and 1895. His brother Tom turned out the five winners for the Fawcetts between 1896 and 1903. The 1895 final was noteworthy for the fact that not only did the brothers Joseph and Thomas train the two finalists, Thoughtless Beauty and Fortuna Favente, but a third brother, Robert, also officiated as slipper.

The three cousins, Hardy, John, and Harold Wright, in the period 1912 to 1960 trained the winners of 16 Blue Ribands between them to bring the Wright family total to 25 Cup-winners over a period of 65 years. Harold's record of nine winners with Tide Time (1912), Guards Brigade (1922), Bryn Truthful (1934), Dee Rock (1935), Dee Flint (1940), Swinging Light (1941 and 1942), Bryn Tritoma (1945), and Maesydd Michael (1946), represents a training record for the Waterloo Cup. The only trainer with a record comparable to that of Thomas and Harold Wright is Denny Smith with six winners to his credit: Heavy Weapon (1910), Hung Well (1913), Winning Number (1915), Jovial Judge (1926), Genial Nobleman (1933), and Hand Grenade (1936).

Against the background of 135 years of coursing history some greyhounds naturally stand out as celebrated star performers, of which the black and white MASTER MCGRATH, the brindle dog FULLERTON, and the bitch BAB AT THE BOWSTER, are supreme. Famous and talented, but overshadowed by this brilliant trio, the names of the bitches Cerito and Bed of Stone are noteworthy — Cerito for her three victories in the Waterloo Cups of 1850, 1852, and 1853, when it was still admittedly a 32-dog event. Bed of Stone has the unique record of winning all three Altcar trophies, the Purse in 1870, the Plate in 1871, and the Cup in 1872.

The only comparable successes in this century were those of the bitch, Fearless Footsteps, and Swinging Light, who achieved their memorable dual successes in 1900 and 1901 and 1941 and 1942 respectively. By general accord, however, the circumstances underlying the achievement of Rotten Row in winning the Blue Riband in 1937 and reaching the finals in 1936 and 1938, stamped him as one of the outstanding coursing greyhounds of this century.

Edward C. Ash, *The Book of the Greyhound* (1933); H. Edwards Clarke, *The Modern Greyhound* (1949), *A Complete Study of the Modern Greyhound* (1963), *The Greyhound* (1969); Harding Cox and Gerald Lascelles, *Coursing and Falconry* (1892); Hugh Dalziel, *The Greyhound* (1888); Adair Dighton, *The Greyhound and Coursing* (1921); James Matheson, *The Greyhound* (1930); 'Stonehenge' (Dr. Walsh), *The Greyhound* (1875).
GOVERNING BODY: National Coursing Club, 82 Borough High Street, London S.E.1.

COURT, Mrs. B. M., see SMITH, MARGARET.

COURT TENNIS, see REAL TENNIS.

COURTINE, HENRI (1930-   ), French JUDO fighter whose timing with ankle sweeps secured him a position as one of Europe's finest competitors. He was a member of the

French team which won the European championships team title in 1952, 1954, 1955, and 1962. Although only a middleweight he was extremely impressive in the open category events since most of his career was before weight classes were introduced. He was 4th *Dan* champion of Europe in 1959, world championships semi-finalist in 1958, and middleweight gold medallist in 1962.

COUSTEAU, JACQUES-YVES (1910-), French underwater explorer who developed the modern aqualung (see UNDERWATER SWIMMING) together with engineer Gagnan. He undertook much underwater research including a one-mile descent in the bathyscaphe, and developed underwater vehicles and habitats. He was president of the Confédération Mondiale des Activités Subaquatiques (C.M.A.S.) and producer of underwater films, the best-known being *The Silent World.* His books include: *The Silent World, The Living Sea, World Without Sun.*

COUSY, ROBERT (1928-), American professional BASKETBALL player. Although comparatively small for a leading player, Cousy is considered by many to have been the greatest player in basketball history. He graduated from Holy Cross College and turned professional with the Tri-Cities (Illinois) Hawks in 1950. When this club was dissolved, Cousy was passed over by Boston and joined the Chicago Stags. In 1951 he finally joined the BOSTON CELTICS, with whom he spent the rest of his career until his retirement in 1963. During his time with Boston, Cousy became famed as a play-maker and set a record with 715 assists in 1959-60. He helped the Celtics to win six NATIONAL BASKETBALL ASSOCIATION championships. After his retirement as a player, Cousy returned to his college as coach and in 1969 was appointed coach to the CINCINNATI ROYALS.

COVENTRY, CORDON (1901-68), Australian Rules footballer. A full-forward for Collingwood, he holds the VICTORIAN FOOTBALL LEAGUE record with 1,299 goals. He played a record 306 games (between 1920 and 1936) for his club and was a member of the side for five League premierships. He won the League goal-kicking awards from 1926 to 1930 and in 1937. In four of these seasons he kicked over 100 goals.

COVENTRY R.F.C., leading RUGBY UNION football club in the Midlands, formed in 1874. Its most successful period was in the late 1950s and early 1960s when it regularly sup-

plied a dozen players to the Warwickshire side which won the county championship seven times in eight seasons. Its most prominent players include Rotherham, JACKSON, Judd, and Duckham.

HOME GROUND: Coundon Road.
COLOURS: Blue and white banded jerseys, navy shorts.

COWAN, ANDREW (1936-), British motor rally driver (see MOTOR RACING). He won the 10,000-mile Sydney Marathon in 1970, and twice won the Scottish International Rally, the first time in 1961 only three years after taking up the sport. He won the 1964 Tour de France with Proctor but crashed in the Andes in the 1970 World Cup Rally.

COWDREY, MICHAEL COLIN, C.B.E. (1932-), cricketer for England, Oxford University, and Kent. A boy prodigy, an England batsman at 22, Test captain intermittently from 1960, holder of a record number of catches (117) in Tests, and the first to receive 100 Test caps, he has often appeared to be unconvinced of his own exceptional talent. His easy style and his ability to time the ball and place it through the field have given way on occasion to cramped, circumspect batsmanship.

Withal, his achievements have been formidable and his overseas tours numerous, including five to Australia. In 1970 he exceeded HAMMOND's record aggregate in Tests (7,249). A fourth-wicket stand of 411 with MAY against West Indies in 1957, an opening stand of 290 with Pullar against South Africa in 1960, and an innings of 307 against South Australia are among his successes, but a heel injury in 1969 inflicted the most serious of his setbacks. In 1973 he became the sixteenth player to score 100 hundreds.

COX, Dr. L. D. (1883-), American LACROSSE player, coach, manager, and administrator, and professor of landscape architecture at Syracuse University. As coach at Harvard University, he initiated the practice of selecting the All-America intercollegiate lacrosse squads. At Syracuse his teams were four times national champions. In 1933 he was responsible for a major modification of the game when he introduced the ten-a-side game incorporating substitution, the offside rule, and time-out penalties for rule infringements. This effected a rapid increase in the popularity of lacrosse as a field game in America. The international rules are based on his concept of modern lacrosse.

COX PLATE is a valuable weight-for-age

horse race in Australia. It is competed for over 1¼ miles (2,000 m.) at Moonee Valley race-track near Melbourne.

CRABOS, RENÉ (1899-1964), RUGBY UNION centre three-quarter and administrator for France. He played 17 times for his country between 1920 and 1924, captaining the side but having his career cut short by breaking a leg against Ireland in Dublin in 1924. As an administrator, he was first a national selector and subsequently president of the Fédération Française de Rugby. As president he was responsible for the recall from semi-retirement of MIAS who was destined to lead France to win the home international championship unshared for the first time in 1959.

CRAPOM (1930) was the second Italian race-horse to win the French PRIX DE L'ARC DE TRIOMPHE, ORTELLO having already won this race in 1929. Crapom also won the Milan Grand Prix, St. Leger, and Two Thousand Guineas in his own country. He was owned by Crespi, trained by Regoli, and ridden by Ca-prioli.

CRAPP, LORRAINE (1938-   ), Austral-ian swimmer who was the first woman to break 5 minutes for the 400 metres freestyle, a feat that stands alongside the first 4-minute athletics mile by BANNISTER. She did this in 1956, breaking a world record that had stood for 16 years. In the same swim, she set world records for 200 metres and 220 and 440 yards. She repeated these four records in one swim in 1956 and won two British Empire and COM-MONWEALTH GAMES titles in 1954 and the Olympic 400 metres in 1956, when she was also second in the 100 metres and a member of Australia's winning relay team.

CRAVEN, Dr. DANIEL HARTMAN (1911-   ), RUGBY UNION player and ad-ministrator for South Africa. He played in four positions, scrum half, stand-off half, centre three-quarter, and No. 8 forward, in 16 Tests for his country between 1931 and 1938. He captained South Africa in the series against the 1938 LIONS, became coach to the University of Stellenbosch, and then president of the South African Rugby Board in 1956.

CRAWFORD, JOHN HERBERT (1908-   ), Australian LAWN TENNIS player, the last of the great champions to rely almost entirely on ground strokes. Even in 1933, when he won one of WIMBLEDON's finest finals against the fierce-serving VINES, his style seemed reminiscent of a past golden age. He seldom had to volley. Using an old-

fashioned square-headed racket, he took the ball astonishingly early, rallied rhythmically, and hit accurate and effective passing shots.

He won the first of his four Australian titles in 1931 and his victory in Paris in 1933, when he beat COCHET in the final, was the first there by a player outside the circle of the 'Four Mus-keteers' (BOROTRA, BRUGNON, Cochet, and LACOSTE) since the French championships were opened to all comers in 1925. Between 1928 and 1937 he won 36 out of 58 Davis Cup (see LAWN TENNIS) rubbers.

CRESTA RUN, see TOBOGGANING: CRESTA.

CRIBB, TOM (1781-1848), British boxer who won the prize ring championship of England in 1809 by beating BELCHER. The fol-lowing year Cribb gained the first of two vic-tories over the American MOLINEAUX in the first of the great international battles of the ring. Noted for his counter-punching, he was probably not one of the outstanding champions and his first victory over Molineaux was par-tially secured by the trickery of Cribb's seconds. But Cribb was so respected by his contemporaries that pugilism gained great publicity.

CRICKET, an 11-a-side bat-and-ball game played mainly in English-speaking countries. The chief centres of first-class cricket are England, Australia, South Africa, the West Indies, New Zealand, India, and Pakistan: the game is also established, on a lower level of performance, in Scotland, Wales, Ireland, Sri Lanka, East and West Africa, Fiji, Bermuda, Argentina, the U.S.A., Canada, Hong Kong, Singapore, Holland, and Denmark.

Cricket, which has evolved over several centuries, is a complicated game, and those who are not familiar with it as part of their environment often find it difficult to follow. It has been described as 'casting a ball at three straight sticks and defending the same with a fourth', but in addition to defending the 'sticks' (stumps which form the wicket), the batsman attempts to score a run (the unit of scoring) or runs. The winning team is that with the greater aggregate of runs in a completed match, which may last from a few hours to as much as six days in some Test (international) matches.

Cricket is traditionally and usually played on turf, but in some areas where durable grass does not grow matches take place on matting stretched over earth or concrete, or on other artificial surfaces. The ground may be of any shape, and it is sometimes quite large, but the full playing area is contained within a defined boundary line, ideally at least 75 yds. (68·58 m.) from the playing pitch. The pitch, which is set as nearly as possible centrally on the ground, is 22 yds. (20·12 m.) long, and is marked out in whiting.

The cylindrical wooden stumps (each 28 in. — 71·12 cm. — high) are set up at the centre of the bowling crease at both ends of the pitch in two groups of three, called the wickets, and surmounted by two bails (each 4⅜ in. — 11·11 cm. — long) which rest in grooves cut in the tops of the stumps and project no more than ½ in. (1·27 cm.) above the stumps. (*Note:* In Australia 'stumps' is a term meaning the end of play for the day. The term 'wicket' is also often used as a synonym for pitch or, in the plural, for the number of batsmen dismissed or still to bat: the context indicates the meaning intended.)

The size of the wicket has varied since it was first set, in 1744, at 22 in. (55·88 cm.)

8 ft. 8 in. (2.64 m.)

minimum 4 ft. (1.22 m.) 4 ft. (1.22 m.)

minimum 12 ft. (3.66 m.)

22 yds. (20.12 m.)

Popping crease

Return crease   Bowling crease   Return crease

CRICKET PITCH

high and 6 in. (15·24 cm.) wide — with only two stumps supporting one bail. The middle stump was added around 1776. Since 1931 the dimensions of the wicket have been 28½ in. (72·39 cm.) high and 9 in. (22·86 cm.) wide.

Before a match begins, it is agreed whether each team shall have one or two opportunities of scoring runs; if one, it is called a one-innings match, if two, a two-innings match. Generally, a match of one day or less is of one innings; of two days or more, invariably of two innings. The teams, each consisting of eleven players, bat alternately except where one follows on (see below).

Each team has a captain, whose powers are wider and more significant than in any other game, and whose decisions frequently decide a match. The captains of the two teams toss a coin and the winner may choose whether his team or his opponent's shall bat first ('take first innings'). The side which does not bat first is known as the fielding side, and it takes the field first. Usual clothing is white or cream

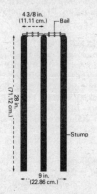

4 3/8 in. (11.11 cm.)   Bail

28 in. (71.12 cm.)

Stump

9 in. (22.86 cm.)

WICKET
Bails project ½ in. (1·27 cm.) above the stump.

shirts and flannel trousers, white leather or canvas boots generally with spiked soles, sweaters (if needed), and caps with peaks designed to shield the eyes from the sun. One member of the fielding side, known as the wicket-keeper, wears leg guards (pads), large leather gauntlets (wicket-keeping gloves), and, usually, padding for the lower part of the body. He is a key member of the fielding side, occupying a position at a suitable distance behind the stumps at the batting end. His duties are to receive balls untouched by the batsman, to catch edged strokes, to stump a batsman who has left his ground, and to gather returns from the fieldsmen.

A cricket match is controlled by two

umpires, one for each end, who are 'the sole judges of fair and unfair play', and to whom all decisions are referred. They communicate their awards and decisions to players and official scorers by a code of signals.

Although the primitive cricket ball was made of anything that would roll or tie into spherical shape, by the middle of the eighteenth century it was bound in red-dyed leather and was required to weigh between 5 and 6 oz. (142 and 170 g.). There was then already a flourishing industry in the manufacture of cricket balls in west Kent. Now the ball is formed of a cork and twine core and a red leather outer casing. It must weigh between 5½ and 5¾ oz. (156–163 g.), and be between 8¹³⁄₁₆ and 9 in. (22·38–22·86 cm.) in circumference. Its seam can be employed by the bowler to make the ball 'break' or swing.

The implement used by the batsman to stop or strike the ball was, in early years, similar in shape to a modern HOCKEY stick. It has always been made of wood, but the tendency has been towards decreasing weight. Modern bats weigh between 2 lb. 4 oz. and 2 lb. 6 oz. (1020 and 1077 g.), but there is no legal restriction. The present shape — straight-sided, with a bulge (known as 'meat') at the back of the bat towards the bottom ('toe') — evolved around 1775. The blade is carved from willow; the handle is made from cane reinforced with layers of rubber and bound in twine. A rubber grip usually covers the handle, which extends into the blade of the bat in a V shape (the splice). The permitted maximum dimensions are 38 in. (96·52 cm.) long over-all by 4¼ in. (10·80 cm.) wide.

The captain of the side which takes the first innings (the batting side) decides the order in which his batsmen will take their individual innings, and the first two start the batting. They each have a bat and will almost certainly wear padded batting gloves, pads for the legs, and a protector for the lower abdomen.

One batsman (the 'striker') goes to the crease from which he will face the bowler; the other (the 'non-striker') goes to the opposite crease. The batsman may bat right- or left-handed. The two sides of the ground are known as the 'on' (or 'leg') side (to a right-handed batsman's left as he faces the bowler), and the 'off' side (to his right).

The captain of the fielding side selects his first bowler, the wicket-keeper takes up position, and the other nine members of the fielding side are disposed by the captain in appropriate positions, depending on whether the batsman is right-handed or left-handed.

Bowling. The bowler, a member of the fielding side, bowls, propels, or delivers the ball by hand. Essentially, 'the ball must be bowled, not thrown or jerked' — otherwise it is an unfair delivery (or 'no ball'). There have been attempts further to define fair bowling and they may be summarized by saying that there should be no bending or straightening of the arm at the elbow during the final armswing at the end of which the ball is released.

The bowler may bowl with his right arm or left, under-arm, round-arm, or over-arm, although he may not change from one to the other without informing the umpire, who will warn the batsman of the coming change. Virtually all bowling nowadays is over-arm. The bowler may also bowl over the wicket, or from the other side of the stumps, called 'round the wicket'.

A delivery is called by the umpire as a 'no-ball' unless, at the moment of delivery, the bowler has at least some part of his front foot behind the popping crease, and both feet within — and not touching — the return crease.

Basically the bowler is trying to dismiss the batsman — i.e. to end his individual innings — by one of four means. The batsman may be:

(1) 'Bowled' — when, regardless of whether the ball has touched the batsman or his bat, it breaks the wicket, i.e. completely removes either bail from the top of the stumps.

(2) 'Caught' — when the ball, after touching any part of the bat or the batsman's hand or glove, is held by a fieldsman before it touches the ground. (*Note:* The catcher must have no part of himself grounded outside the playing area when making the catch or immediately afterwards.)

(3) 'Leg before wicket' (usually abbreviated to 'l.b.w.') — when a ball which has pitched on the line of the stumps, or outside the line of the off stump (i.e. the stump furthest from the batsman — the others are 'middle' and 'leg'), and, without contact with the bat, would, in the opinion of the umpire, have hit the wicket had it not been stopped — voluntarily or involuntarily, the point of contact being between wicket and wicket — by any part of the batsman's body or clothing except his hand (holding the bat). If he deliberately pads away a ball outside the off stump, even though the contact is made outside the line of the stumps, he is out (provided, as always, that the ball would have hit the wicket).

(4) 'Stumped' — when the batsman, although not attempting a run, has no part of his body or bat grounded behind the popping crease and the wicket-keeper breaks the wicket with a hand holding the delivered ball.

A fifth method of dismissal — 'hit wicket' — may only rarely be attributable to the bowler's deliberate intent, but it is credited to him in the score-book. It happens when, while playing at the ball, the batsman breaks his wicket with his bat or any part of his body or clothing.

The batsman is out also (though his dismissal is *not* credited to the bowler) if he: (*a*) is 'run out' — when the wicket he has left (if the batsmen have not crossed) or the one to which he is running (if they have crossed) is broken by the ball while he is 'out of his ground'

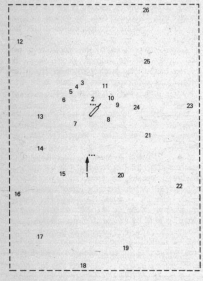

CRICKET FIELD PLACINGS

(1) Bowler; (2) wicket-keeper; (3) first slip; (4) second slip; (5) third slip; (6) gully; (7) silly mid-off; (8) silly mid-on; (9) and (10) short leg; (11) leg-slip; (12) third man; (13) cover point; (14) extra cover; (15) mid-off; (16) deep extra cover; (17) long-off; (18) straight hit; (19) long-on; (20) mid-on; (21) mid-wicket; (22) deep mid-wicket; (23) deep square leg; (24) square leg; (25) fine leg; (26) long leg.

(when no part of his body or the bat he is holding is grounded behind the line of the popping crease); (*b*) handles the ball except at the request of one of the fielding side; (*c*) having stopped the ball, deliberately hits it a second time in an attempt to score runs; (*d*) wilfully obstructs a fieldsman.

An appeal (in the words 'How's that?'), which may be made by any member of the fielding side, covers all forms of dismissal, and must be answered by an umpire in the terms 'Out' or 'Not out'.

As each batsman is out, he is replaced by the next in the batting order, which the captain may vary at any time.

Scoring of runs. Batting is a complex and precarious skill but its aims are simple — to prevent the bowler and fieldsmen from dismissing the batsman and to score runs.

Runs are scored by a batsman when he strikes the ball and he and his partner both run and make good their ground behind the popping creases at the ends opposite those at which they started, before the fielding side can return the ball and break the wicket: thus one run is scored. If they turn, run, cross, and make good their ground a second, third, or any number of times, they score two, three, or other appropriate number of runs. If either batsman fails to make good his ground while running two or more runs the umpire will cancel that run by calling and signalling 'Short run'.

In the case of boundary hits, the batsman need not run to score. If he hits the ball and it crosses the boundary line after having touched the ground, he automatically scores a 'boundary' — four runs. If the ball passes over the boundary line without touching the ground, six runs are added to the striker's score.

'Extras' (called 'sundries' in Australia) are added to the team's total, but not to the batsman's individual score, for:

(1) A 'no ball': one extra is scored for a no ball unless the batsman hits the delivery for runs, as he may do and count them to his score. It is in effect a free hit for him: he cannot be out in any of the ways credited to a bowler, but only for handling the ball, hitting the ball twice, obstructing the field, or by being run out.

(2) A 'bye' — when the batsman misses the ball or allows it to pass, and the wicket-keeper fails to stop it, the batsmen may run, or count a boundary, as the case may be.

(3) A 'wide' — if the ball is bowled so high or wide that the umpire considers it to have been out of the batsman's reach, one run is scored; but, if the wicket-keeper does not stop a wide ball, the batsmen may take as many runs as they can, as in the case of byes.

The ball becomes 'dead' after its return by a fielder to the wicket-keeper or bowler, and the cycle of play begins again as the bowler commences his run-up for the next delivery.

The course of play. The first bowler bowls an 'over' of six balls (eight in Australia), not inclusive of wides or no balls, from the end at which he started. The second bowler then bowls an over from the opposite end and, provided overs are bowled from alternate ends, bowlers may be changed as often as the captain of the fielding side desires, except that a bowler may not bowl two successive overs.

An innings may continue until ten batsmen have been dismissed (except in limited-overs matches, e.g. GILLETTE CUP): the remaining batsman of the 11 is described as 'not out' and he does not continue to bat when he no longer has a batting partner.

The result. A cricket match is won by the team which scores most runs in a completed match. At its simplest: if, in a single-innings match, team A scores 200 runs and team B, 100, team A wins by 100 runs. Similarly, in a two-innings match, if team A scores 150 in its first innings and 200 in its second, team B 100 in its first innings and 150 in its second, team A wins by 100 runs.

On the other hand, if the team batting second scores enough runs to win without all its batsmen being out (i.e. without losing all its wickets) it does not need to go on batting. Thus, if team A scores 200 runs and team B reaches 201 when only, say, four of its batsmen are out, the scores are said to be team A 200, team B 201 'for four wickets', and team B is said to have won by six wickets.

To expedite a result a captain may 'declare' his team's innings closed, or in other circumstances he may invite the other team to bat again immediately after its first innings ('follow-on'). Again, examples will make this clear:

The captain of a team may declare its innings closed at any time. If team A has scored 400 runs with only, say, two batsmen out, and the captain considers this a probable winning total, he may declare the innings closed (or ended). If team B is then dismissed for 300, the final score would read: team A 400 'for two wickets declared', team B 300. Team A wins by 100 runs.

In a two-innings match, a captain may often declare his team's second innings closed to achieve a positive result within the time remaining. Then the scores might read: team A 350 and 200 for six wickets declared, team B 200 and 150. Team A wins by 200 runs. Alternatively: team A 300 for eight wickets declared and 200 for six wickets declared, team B 200 and 301 for eight wickets. Team B wins by two wickets (i.e. having two of its ten second-innings wickets remaining).

The 'follow-on' is a device introduced into English cricket in 1835 and universally adopted ever since, though its numerical conditions have been readjusted from time to time. The follow-on is only possible in a two-innings match, when the side which bats first and eventually achieves a first-innings lead of 200 runs (in a match of more than three days), 150 (in a match of three days), 100 (in a two-day match), or 75 (in a one-day match), shall have the option of making the other side bat again to follow its own innings. Thus, if team A bats first and scores 400, and then puts out team B for 240 (in a three-day match), the captain of team A may ask team B to bat again immediately. Then a score might read: team A 400, team B 240 and 150: result, team A wins by an innings and 10 runs.

By enforcing the follow-on, team A does not necessarily forfeit its second innings, and the sequence of innings could be: team A 400, team B 240 and 200, team A 41 for two wickets. Team A wins by eight wickets. A team batting first, even though not entitled to enforce the follow-on, may *forfeit* its second innings.

It is possible also for a team batting second to win by taking only one innings to its opponents' two, thus: team A 220, team B 440, team A (second innings) 200. Team B wins by an innings and 20 runs.

A match in which the final scores are level is a 'tie' (but only if the last innings has been completed). An uncompleted match is termed a 'draw'. An 'abandoned' match is one in which no play takes place, invariably because of unfavourable weather or pitch conditions.

In a Test match played between two countries from among those having Test status, the teams are chosen by the duly appointed selectors of the respective countries' governing bodies for international cricket. Usually a Test match is one of a series of matches — most frequently five in number — played between the two countries, one of them a touring side, in the same season.

Bowling technique. Bowling is a profound skill with many facets. A good bowler relies on two basic qualities to restrict the batsman's run-scoring, while he employs any of some seven technical resources to achieve his dismissal. The two primary requisites are direction and length. In the case of direction — sometimes called 'line' — the ball must be directed so accurately on the line of the wicket or slightly to a selected side of it that the batsman cannot hit it freely or to areas free of fieldsmen. A ball of 'good length' is one which pitches at such a point that the batsman cannot use either of the two kinds of batting stroke — forward or back — with command.

Length depends upon the batsman and the pace of the bowling. A tall batsman can hit on the half-volley a ball which a shorter man would have to play as of good length. Again, a good-length ball from a slow bowler will pitch substantially nearer the batsman than one from a fast bowler. In effect, a good-length ball is not sufficiently full-pitched to be driven nor short enough to be cut or hooked.

The bowler generally hopes to dismiss a batsman by one of several of the following means: speed, swing, swerve, finger-spin, wrist-spin, flight, or change of pace.

Speed is self-evident: the batsman is defeated by the pace of the ball. 'Swing' is the term used to describe a ball's curve through the air. The later this occurs in flight the more difficult it is to combat. It is most easily practised when the ball is new, its seam sharp, and its surface shiny. It may be out-swing, which moves away from the outside edge of the bat, or in-swing, which moves from the off side towards, or outside, the batsman's legs. Persistent in-swing bowling concentrated on the batsman's leg stump and pads (known as 'leg theory') usually presents a dull cricket spectacle, especially when accompanied by restrictive leg-side field-placing which ensures that most attempts at scoring are fruitless. 'Swerve' is the term used to describe a similar, generally slower, more uniform curve through the air, produced by spinning the ball.

The following references to spin bowling refer to right-arm bowlers and right-handed batsmen. The 'leg break' is bowled by imparting anti-clockwise spin (as viewed from behind the bowler) to the seam of the ball by finger — and, ideally, wrist — action. On a responsive pitch so delivered will turn (or 'break') upon pitching, from leg to off, often having swerved in flight slightly from off to leg. The 'off break' is bowled by 'cutting' the index finger across the seam of the ball and causing it to spin from off to leg. In addition to turning in this direction off the pitch, it will sometimes have swerved in flight towards the slips. The 'googly' (developed by BOSANQUET) is an off break bowled with a leg-break action but with the axis of spin reversed by turning the wrist so that the ball is delivered from *behind* the hand. Another bowling variation is the 'top-spinner', where 'over-spin' applied to the ball causes it to dip in flight and hurry through low off the pitch.

'Flight' is variation of the ball's arc through the air which causes the batsman to mistime his stroke through misjudging the point at which the ball will pitch. The batsman may here contribute to his own defeat, as with a 'yorker', which is a full toss which he is misled into playing as if it were a half-volley, or any ball which surprises and defeats him by its swiftness and fullness of length.

'Change of pace' is the attempt, by disguising action, to deliver a faster or slower ball than the batsman anticipates and thus make him play too late or too soon. 'Body-line' is used of fast, intimidatory leg-theory bowling.

Batting technique. The bases of batting are founded upon either forward or back play, whether in attack or defence.

The preparatory stance should be comfortable and balanced. From this position the batsman needs to judge the pace, length, and line of the ball as it is delivered by the bowler, and to apply the appropriate stroke to it by means of correct footwork, wrist control, and general co-ordination of trunk and limbs.

One of the prime aims is to maintain (perhaps anatomically unnaturally) a perpendicular bat (a 'straight bat') immediately prior to and during impact, except in the case of certain attacking strokes squarish to either side of the wicket. These consist chiefly of, to the leg side, the 'pull' and the 'hook' to rising balls, and the 'sweep' to the half-volley; to the off side, the 'cut' anywhere in an arc from just forward of cover-point to fine third man. In each of these the right hand supplies most of the power (conversely in the case of a left-handed batsman).

Of the straight-batted strokes, the drive — with or without the intent to score runs — is the most prominent. The forward defensive stroke is merely a defensive parry. Increased power and improved timing develop this into an attacking drive 'off the front foot', the direction of the drive being influenced in the first place by the line of the bowled ball and in the second place by the positioning of the batsman and the direction of the face of his bat. The drive is played with the full face and may be directed to mid-wicket or mid-on ('on drive'), past the bowler's umpire ('straight drive'), through mid-off ('off drive'), through cover-point ('cover drive'), or to square third man ('square drive'). In the last four the left hand usually controls direction.

It is generally considered advisable (because it eliminates the chance of being caught) to hit the ball along the ground, although the lofted stroke may be profitable when played into vacant areas of the field or hit strongly enough to clear the boundary.

The backward strokes played with a straight bat ('off the back foot') emanate from the back defensive (played to short deliveries) and develop into deflection strokes such as the 'leg glance' (or 'glide'), which sends the leg-side delivery in the arc from square-leg to fine-leg (this may also be played off the front foot) or any of the drives mentioned earlier, with the difference that the batsman's weight is on his back leg (i.e. right leg for a right-handed batsman) in response to the greater rise of the ball (it having pitched shorter). Back play enables a batsman to utilize the ground between the creases.

The batsman may often need to advance to the pitch of the ball to ensure the success of his stroke, particularly to well-flighted slow bowling of testing length. Against hostile fast bowling he may even prefer to take evasive action by ducking under short, fast balls; and to certain deliveries which pitch on a good length and deviate, it may be advisable to withdraw the bat and play no stroke if none may be played profitably and without serious risk of dismissal.

Many batsmen are remembered for their distinctive styles of play, but almost every successful batsman has been orthodox in *basic* technique.

M.C.C., *The Laws of Cricket*, annually; R. S. Rait Kerr, *Cricket Umpiring and Scoring* (1950) and various editions.

Cricket grew most strongly in England but its precise origins are not known. An apparent reference to its being played in Kent is contained in the wardrobe accounts of Edward I for 1300. An Elizabethan coroner testified that, in about 1550, he and other scholars of the free school of Guildford went to a piece of land in the parish of Holy Trinity and 'did runne and play there at creckett'. There are regular references to it during the seventeenth century and William Goldwin's Latin poem '*In Certamen Pilae; Anglice*, A Cricket-Match (1706) describes unmistakably the game which, modified and altered, is today known as cricket.

The basic pattern of one person casting a ball at a target — hurdle, gate, stool, or stone — defended by another who tries to hit the ball away with a stick is so simple that it may well have separate origins in different communities; Celtic, Scandinavian, and French origins have been suggested for it. It is generally accepted that the English form of the game originated in the sheep country of south-eastern England, where, on the short, downland grass, a ball of rag or wool, literally bowled — all along the ground — would run truly. The bowler's target was the wicket-gate of the sheepfold as the term 'wicket' indicates; and the shepherd's crook which the batsman used to hit the ball away would account for the fact that the earliest known cricket bats were long with a curving blade. In the early seventeenth century Cotgrave referred to a 'crosse' as 'the crooked staff wherewith boys play at cricket'.

In its early stages it was a naïve peasant game and, later, one of the apprentices' rowdy diversions in urban areas. By the end of the seventeenth century, however, its players were more mature and sophisticated: probably the highest standards of play were in Sussex — where Slindon was a noted 'nursery', Kent and, significantly, London.

In 1730 a match took place on the Artillery Ground at Finsbury, London (which is still in use). Cricket had now spread from the agricul-

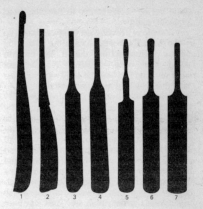

EVOLUTION OF THE CRICKET BAT
(1) The oldest bat in existence (1750); (2) eighteenth-century curved bat; (3) bat inscribed 'Ring little Joey 1793'; (4) bat stamped 'E. Bagot'; (5) bat of Robert Robinson; (6) bat used by W. G. Grace (1900); (7) bat used by Denis Compton (1947).

tural south to the industrial north and midlands: it was played throughout England at levels from those of children on village greens and young artisans in towns, to the public schools, the Services, the universities, on the estates of wealthy landowners, and, soon, on the grounds such as White Conduit and LORD'S, created for the wealthy members of London clubs.

In or about the 1760s a club was founded in the Hampshire downland village of HAMBLE-DON. It was controlled by wealthy patrons, but its outstanding cricketers were the village craftsmen and small farmers, like SMALL, BELDHAM, HARRIS, and John and Richard NYREN, who established techniques of batting and bowling which still apply. By the 1790s the centre of the game was moving away from Kent, Sussex, and Hampshire to London, especially to Lord's ground, where the MARYLEBONE CRICKET CLUB (M.C.C.) had its headquarters.

In the first quarter of the nineteenth century, round-arm bowling — whereby the bowler raised his bowling arm in delivery towards and as high as shoulder level — was employed although it was forbidden by the laws. It represented progress in that it extended the scope of bowlers and, after many earlier attempts at its legal introduction (Walker of Hambledon and Willes of Kent had evoked scorn by their exploitation of it), it was officially sanctioned from 1835. A series of matches between Sussex and England in 1827 had demonstrated that round-arm bowling would not be as dangerous to batsmen as its opponents claimed.

A completely revised set of laws, drawn up by the M.C.C. in 1835, gave the advancing game a formal setting that it had hitherto lacked. This code — although it underwent major revision in 1884 and 1947 — is still basically that which governs cricket today.

The role of the public schools in the early championing of cricket had far-reaching effects that have nourished the game in England for a century and a half. Eton, Winchester, Westminster, and Harrow were all playing cricket in the eighteenth century, and with the game thriving at both the schools and the universities, a corpus of amateur players of high merit grew up strong enough to challenge — though not always to beat — the professionals at their own art. Thus was born the Gentlemen v. Players fixture, which was first staged at Lord's in 1806, and thereafter played as a major event in the cricketing calendar until the formal demise of the amateur in first-class cricket before the start of the 1963 season. The annual fixture at Lord's — even after the introduction of Test cricket to England in 1880 — remained a natural highlight which attracted large crowds and much enthusiasm. It was always a considerable honour to be chosen for this game.

From the beginning, the amateur element had a strong influence both on play and administration. The evils that had crept into the game — notably overt betting and the 'selling' of matches by well-known players — quickly subsided and eventually disappeared. The popularity of cricket, which had once depended on the presence of high stakes, increased as individual skills in both batting and bowling became more scientific, each department of the game facing the challenge of the other with careful and accurate adjustments, the result of shrewd observation of strengths and weaknesses. The most significant major change in technique came in 1864 when, after persistent pressure from certain cricketers — Willsher prominent among them — the bowler was finally freed of restriction on the height of his arm at the point of delivering the ball. Over-arm — as distinct from the lower bowling actions (under-arm and round-arm) — had a profound effect upon the character of the game, and it has been employed almost exclusively ever since.

The surfaces on which cricket was played had, with but rare exceptions, little attention paid them until well into the second half of the nineteenth century. Added to the absence of boundary lines on most grounds until the 1860s, this tended to make scoring low, though it indicated no lack of ability, and

because of wholly different conditions no comparisons of batting and bowling performances with those after 1890 are strictly valid. The perfection of pitches in the last decade of the nineteenth century brought a standard of batsmanship that had only been hinted at hitherto — though the hint had been a powerful one.

That hint — an expression of cricket's unending potential — was provided by the game's first great popular hero, W. G. GRACE, who made his début in first-class cricket in 1865. By the end of the 1870s he had transformed batsmanship, and with it the whole art of cricket. There had been heroes before him, though not quite possessing the same ability or nation-wide prestige. Three of these heroes were contemporaries in the powerful Kent XI of the 1840s — Felix, MYNN, and PILCH, all of them commanding and stylish batsmen. Mynn in addition was a fine, fast, and accurate round-arm bowler whose strength in every department of the game earned him the sobriquet 'The Lion of Kent'. Mynn and Felix (né Wanostrocht) played each other at single-wicket before great crowds, which found that form of cricket a splendid spectacle principally in the 1830s and 1840s. Pilch, born in Norfolk, was a professional and must be accounted the first of the truly great batsmen since Small 'found out cricket' in the days of Hambledon.

Two great bowlers of cricket's emergent period — and certainly the wiliest — were LILLYWHITE, of Sussex, and CLARKE, of Nottinghamshire, both born in the 1790s. Both were endowed with great force of character and confidence. Lillywhite bowled medium-pace round the wicket and Clarke bowled slow under-arm lobs, and they 'thought out' their victims with uncanny ability, sometimes, it seemed, to the point of mesmerism.

It was Clarke's enterprise that was responsible for the most far-reaching event of the middle of the nineteenth century — the founding in 1846 of his ALL-ENGLAND XI, which, comprised of the foremost amateurs and professionals of the time, toured all parts of the country, spreading the gospel of cricket against local sides, who were quick to imitate the methods of the great players, to the obvious benefit of the game. Great interest was aroused by this and subsequent similar touring teams, and although most of the matches were really of an exhibition nature and played on extremely poor grounds, the popularity of the game increased rapidly. The venture, too, was a financial success for Clarke.

The rival United England XI, principally engineered by WISDEN, proved, if unconsciously, that the number of fine cricketers in the land was increasing, and the missionary activities of these teams, which extended to the late 1870s, began to see serious cricket flourish in many counties. Spectators learned to appreciate more keenly the skills of good cricket, and an appetite for competitive matches was born, fostered by such players as PARR (Clarke's successor on his death) and Jackson of Nottinghamshire, Caffyn and Stephenson of Surrey, and HAYWARD and Carpenter of Cambridgeshire (which, up to 1871, was a formidable cricketing county).

But the greatest influence — *the* giant among cricketers — was Grace, whose exploits with bat and ball (but chiefly as a technically unparalleled batsman of his day) made him a national figure and 'the Champion'. He arrived on the scene when famous amateur clubs like Free Foresters (founded 1856) and I Zingari (founded 1845) were raising standards, and his complete mastery of all bowling that he encountered, professional and amateur alike, made his native Gloucestershire, hitherto a county of modest achievement, a power in the land. W.G.'s brothers — E.M., older than 'the Champion', and G.F., younger — with much moral and practical support from their mother, gave rise to the legend of 'the county of the Graces': the scene was set for inter-county competition in England on an organized basis.

COUNTY CRICKET. Although inter-county rivalry dated back well into the eighteenth century and an unofficial form of county championship existed in the 1860s, it was not until the introduction of qualification rules for players in 1873 that the championship assumed a realistic shape; because of its vague nature before then it is usually reckoned to have begun in that year. Even then it was not official, the newspapers compiling tables of merit and declaring the winners. At all events, first-class cricket in England after 1873 became increasingly centred on the county championship, and its advance and popularity as a domestic competition in due course set the pattern *mutatis mutandis* for all the other first-class countries.

Nine counties competed in the championship of 1873, and the position remained unchanged until the end of 1887. These original nine counties were:

Derbyshire. Founded in 1870, its colours are chocolate, amber, and pale blue, and its badge the rose and crown. The chief grounds are Derby, Chesterfield, Buxton, and Ilkeston. The county dropped out of the championship after 1887, was readmitted in 1895, and has competed regularly since then. Never a powerful force in English cricket, it has nevertheless produced several very fine fast bowlers of Test match class.

Gloucestershire. Formally instituted in 1871 (though playing as a county before that), its colours are blue, gold, brown, sky-blue, green, and red, and its crest the coat of arms of the City and County of Bristol. The chief grounds are Ashley Down (Bristol), Gloucester, and Cheltenham. The county owed its early fame principally to the family of Graces, but it later produced outstanding players such as JESSOP, C. W. L. Parker, HAMMOND, Goddard, and GRAVENEY. Among them, however, only the Graces ever shared in a championship-winning year.

Kent. Formed in 1859 and reorganized by amalgamation in 1870, its colours are red and white and its crest a white horse. The chief ground is the ST. LAWRENCE GROUND (Canterbury), with matches freely spread through many towns in the county. Kent has a noble tradition, and its batting has been stimulated by a strong strain of amateur enterprise, though its most prolific performers have been the professionals WOOLLEY (who was the leading run-scorer) and FREEMAN (who took the most wickets). AMES, both as wicket-keeper and batsman, and after his playing days as secretary-manager, served the county handsomely. COWDREY was captain for 15 years (1957-71) before stepping down, and his influence was felt throughout the whole of English cricket.

Lancashire. Founded in 1864, its colours are red, green, and blue and the crest a red rose. The chief ground is at OLD TRAFFORD (Manchester), with occasional matches at Liverpool, Southport, and Blackpool. Up to 1939 one of the great powers in English cricket — with five championships in nine years between 1926 and 1934 — the club languished somewhat until the coming of the JOHN PLAYER LEAGUE in 1969 revived its prowess. Great players include MACLAREN, Spooner, J. T. and E. TYLDESLEY, McDonald, Duckworth, Paynter, WASHBROOK, and STATHAM.

Middlesex. Founded in 1863, its colours are dark blue, and the crest consists of three seaxes. The county plays solely at Lord's, as a tenant of the M.C.C. Apart from occasional spells, it has been one of the leading sides in the country through most of its history, though, strangely, championship-winner only on rare occasions. Its most significant player was WARNER, a magnificent captain; others who rank high are HENDREN, Hearne, ALLEN, Robins, W. J. EDRICH, COMPTON, and Titmus.

Nottinghamshire. Formed in 1841 and reorganized in 1866, its colours are green and gold, and its badge the county badge of Nottinghamshire. The chief ground is at TRENT BRIDGE (Nottingham), though matches are occasionally played at Newark and Worksop. A fine breeding-ground for cricketers, the county, in the early days of the championship, was mainly professional, and it has a proud record marred only by less satisfactory performances in the years since the Second World War. The Gunn family (George, William, and John) were notable players, as were SHREWSBURY, SHAW, A. O. Jones, A. W. Carr, Hardstaff (father and son), LARWOOD, Voce, and R. T. Simpson. The county's two twentieth-century championships (in 1907 and 1929) are not a true reflection of prowess.

Surrey. Founded in 1845, its colours are chocolate, and its badge the Prince of Wales's feathers. The chief ground is at the OVAL (London), and occasional matches are played at Guildford. After Yorkshire, it is the most successful side in championship history. In the nine years 1887-95 it failed to come top only once, and it won outright seven years in succession from 1952. Among its truly outstanding players have been RICHARDSON, LOCKWOOD, LOHMANN, HOBBS, STRUDWICK, A. V. BEDSER, MAY, LOCK, and LAKER.

Sussex. Founded in 1839 and reorganized in 1857, its colours are dark blue, light blue, and gold, and its badge the county arms of six martlets. The chief grounds are HOVE, Eastbourne, and Hastings. It is the only one of the original sides in the championship never to have won the title. At the turn of the century, great batting feats were performed by FRY and RANJITSINHJI, while in the 1920s TATE was one of the country's leading bowlers, and DULEEPSINHJI briefly one of the most talented batsmen. In the 1960s DEXTER batted with a panache uncommon in postwar cricket.

Yorkshire. Founded in 1863 and reorganized in 1891, its colours are dark blue, light blue, and gold, and the crest a white rose. The chief grounds are HEADINGLEY (Leeds), Scarborough, Bradford, and Huddersfield. It is the only county club which insists that its players be born within the county. Yorkshire has won the championship more often than any other county and has produced consistently skilful teams. Among a large number of highly talented players have been HIRST, RHODES, H. SUTCLIFFE, LEYLAND, VERITY, HUTTON, TRUEMAN, and BOYCOTT.

These nine counties played 31 games between them in the championship season of 1873. Thereafter the expansion of the championship reflected the increase both in county pride and public interest in competitive and regular cricket of high standard. Derbyshire dropped out after 1887 — they had won only one match in four years — but in 1891 Somerset came in, and by 1895 Essex, Hampshire, Leicestershire, Warwickshire, and Derbyshire (readmitted) were all competing.

With 14 counties in the county championship of 1895, English cricket entered what historians generally agree to be its Golden Age. The five new counties playing in 1895 were:

Essex. Founded in 1876, its colours are blue, gold, and red, and its badge three scimitars with the word 'Essex' beneath. The chief grounds are Chelmsford, Colchester, Leyton, Brentwood, Ilford, Romford, Southend, and Westcliff. The county has never finished higher than third in the championship (in 1897), and has suffered because many of its best amateurs have been able to turn out only irregularly. Some, however, notably Douglas, Pearce, Insole, and BAILEY, rendered distinguished service as players and captains, and other fine players have included Kortright, Fane, McGahey, Perrin, Russell, O'Connor, Nichols, T. P. B. Smith, Farnes, and B. R. Knight.

Hampshire. Founded in 1863, its colours are blue, gold, and white, and its badge the Tudor rose and crown. Before the mid-1950s, it was rarely a force in the County Championship, and usually finished in the lower half of the table. Under the captaincies of Eagar (1946-57) and Ingleby-Mackenzie (1958-65), the county experienced its finest moments: it finished third in 1955, second in 1958, and first in

1961. Inspired by the brilliance of the South African batsman, B. A. Richards, Hampshire won the title again in 1973. Its greatest cricketers have been MEAD, who scored most runs and hundreds, and Shackleton, who took most wickets. From 1919 to 1933 the Hon. L. H. (Lord) Tennyson was one of the most flamboyant captains in county cricket, and Kennedy and Newman were a fine pair of all-rounders who served their county long and well. In the 1950s and 1960s, Marshall, the West Indian Test cricketer, was the freest opening batsman in county cricket.

Leicestershire. Founded in 1879, its colours are scarlet and dark green, and its badge a gold running fox on a green background. The chief ground is at Leicester (Grace Road). One of the weaker counties in the history of the championship, it finished joint-third in 1953, under the inspiring captaincy of Palmer; and then, after Lock assumed the captaincy in 1966, it was joint-second in 1967. Among the side's prominent players have been J. H. King, C. J. B. Wood, A. E. Knight, Astill, Geary, Dempster, Berry, Walsh, and the two former Yorkshiremen, Watson and ILLINGWORTH.

Somerset. Formed in 1875, and reorganized in 1885, its colours are black, white, and maroon, and its badge the Wessex wivern. The chief ground is at Taunton, and matches are also played at Bath, Glastonbury, and Weston-super-Mare. The county was promoted to first-class status in 1891, but has never finished higher than third, and was bottom four years in succession from 1952 to 1955. Up to the Second World War, it rarely had a settled side, and much use was made of amateurs, among whom two captains, S. M. J. Woods (1894-1906) and Daniell (1919-26), are remembered as exceptional men. Other notable players include Braund, Palairet, J. C. White, Wellard, F. S. Lee, Gimblett, McCool, Alley, and K. E. Palmer.

Warwickshire. Founded in 1884, its colours are dark blue, gold, and silver, and its badge a bear and ragged staff. The chief ground is at EDGBASTON (Birmingham), and matches are occasionally played at Coventry and Nuneaton. The county has had an inconsistent career in the championship: after being fourteenth in 1910, they finished top the year after; they won the title for the second time in 1951, only to drop to tenth place in the next year. In 1972, under the captaincy of A. C. Smith, Warwickshire again won the championship. The most prominent players have been Lilley, E. J. Smith, Quaife, Foster, Wyatt, Dollery, Hollies, Cartwright, and M. J. K. SMITH.

When the season of 1895 began W. G. Grace was in his 47th year, but he was still the foremost batsman in the country, scoring 1,000 runs in May and passing his century of centuries in first-class cricket. The 20 years up to 1914 were a period characterized by style and gracefulness, with the amateur playing a larger part in English cricket than at any time thereafter. The standard at the schools and the universities was notably high, and the talented amateur was as much in demand on country-house occasions as on more public ones. The heyday of English country-house cricket was

In late Victorian and Edwardian times, when wealthy owners of great houses vied with each other to stage congenial cricket encounters, at which the social proprieties were as important as the play. Little expense was spared to ensure lavish enjoyment — all carefully screened from press publicity.

This was the era, too, of the famous amateur clubs — Free Foresters, I Zingari, Band of Brothers, Eton Ramblers, Harrow Wanderers, and many others. These had all been founded many years before, and indeed still have full fixture lists, but the Golden Age saw them at their strongest, gayest, and most influential. It was not unusual to find many first-class cricketers in their ranks, and much of the spirit of their play was carried to the sterner fields of county and Test match cricket.

The backbone of county cricket was nevertheless supplied by the professional. His pay was never high, and his life certainly drab compared with the amateur's: but he rarely complained, and he looked forward to a benefit — in reality, usually a meagre one — towards the end of his career. Coaching posts at public schools were normally filled from the ranks of retired county professionals. Lord Hawke, who captained Yorkshire from 1883 to 1910, paid special attention to the personal welfare of the professionals in his team, and Yorkshire produced such a high standard of efficiency that it was clear his policy was right. From 1895 to 1914 Yorkshire played 445 county matches and lost only 68 of them: except in 1910 and 1911, they never finished below fourth. Two of the finest all-rounders of all time, Hirst and Rhodes, helped Yorkshire to her eminence.

Another great county side emerged before the First World War in Kent. The Tonbridge nursery had been established in 1897, run on sound lines. The players it produced — among them BLYTHE and Woolley — joined some wonderfully adventurous amateurs, including Hutchings, Mason, Dillon, and Blaker, to put Kent where it had not been since the 1840s. Kent were county champions in 1906, 1909, 1910, and 1913, and in two other years in this period they were second.

Two new sides entered the English county championship in the Golden Age after the expansion of 1895. These were:

Worcestershire. Founded in 1865, its colours are dark green and black and its badge a shield argent bearing fesse between three pears sable. The chief ground is at Worcester, and matches are also played at Dudley and Kidderminster. It was promoted to first-class status in 1899, but experienced much playing and financial difficulty up to 1939: between 1920 and 1938 the side's best position was tenth. The best players in the early years were the brothers

Foster, Bowley, Arnold, Simpson-Hayward, followed by Root, the elder Nawab of PATAUDI, Walters, Gibbons, Perks, Jenkins, Kenyon, D'Oliveira, and — after his days with Gloucestershire — Graveney. The county won the championship in 1964 and 1965. It did not take part in the competition in 1919.

Northamptonshire. Founded in 1820 and reorganized in 1878, its colours are maroon and its badge the Tudor rose. The county was admitted to the championship in 1905, but up to the Second World War it had the poorest record of all the counties: it finished bottom five years in succession (1934-8) and was last or one from last in 12 of the 13 playing seasons between 1930 and 1948. A revival followed under the captaincy of F. R. Brown in 1949, and the county has not since slipped back to its former ingloriousness. It has, however, never won the championship. Its leading players have been G. J. Thompson, Jupp, E. W. Clark, Bakewell, D. Brookes, Tribe, K. V. Andrew, Subba Row, and Tyson.

The First World War brought a hiatus in first-class cricket in England, though a limited amount of club and league cricket continued. Afterwards, in 1919, the experiment of two-day county championship matches was tried, with extended hours of play on each day, but this was pronounced at once to be a failure. The reversion to the traditional three-day games was made in 1920, and there has been no change since.

The highlights of the immediate postwar years were the successive championship wins, in 1920 and 1921, of Middlesex. The year 1920 marked the final season in county cricket of the celebrated Warner, and in an amazing finale to a memorable career, he captained Middlesex to nine successive victories in their last nine games to win the title when a single slip would have lost it.

The ruthless Yorkshire side, however, was not long in establishing its ascendancy. They won four years in succession from 1922, and had two further hat-tricks of wins before the Second World War. At one stage between 1924 and 1927, they went through 70 consecutive county games without being beaten, their brilliant attack consisting of Rhodes, G. G. Macaulay, Kilner, Waddington, and E. Robinson. The opening batsmen, Holmes and H. Sutcliffe, were rivalled as an opening pair in England only by Hobbs and SANDHAM of Surrey. In 1930, with a record number of wickets behind him, Rhodes retired, and in his stead arrived another left-arm bowler, Verity, who, in less than a decade, took 1,956 first-class wickets. He and the fast bowler, Bowes, under the shrewd captaincy of Sellers, did much to keep Yorkshire on top.

The championship reached its final number of 17 participants after the First World War with the admission in 1921 of Glamorgan.

Glamorgan. Founded in 1888, its colours are blue and gold, and its badge a gold daffodil. The chief grounds are at Cardiff and Swansea, and matches are also played at Neath and Colwyn Bay. Glamorgan played as a second-class county until elevated in 1921, and then found competition at the highest level a severe strain until 1939. The early stalwarts included Riches, Clay, Turnbull — all fine captains, E. Davies, Dyson, and Wooller; and after the Second World War, Watkins, W. E. Jones, Parkhouse, Walker, Shepherd, and A. R. Lewis. Wooller led the side to its first championship in 1948, and Lewis to its second in 1969.

Between the wars Hammond scored prolifically for Gloucestershire, but though his county twice finished second (in 1930 and 1931) it never won. Neither did Surrey — with Hobbs in the side for much of the time — nor Kent, who possessed the biggest wicket-taker in England in Freeman, the best wicketkeeper-batsman in Ames, and the ever-prolific Woolley. Standards in the county championship were probably never higher than in the inter-war years.

In 1927 the legal size of the ball was reduced slightly to its present maximum circumference of 9 in. (22·86 cm.) and in 1931 the height of the wicket was increased by 1 in. to 28 in. (71·12 cm.). An experimental use of eight-ball overs in first-class cricket in England was tried in 1939 and never repeated; but the most signficant alteration in the laws came in 1937 when, after a two seasons' trial, the 'l.b.w.' law was extended to include the ball pitched on the off side of the wicket. This met with a mixed reception from cricketers, some of whom unambiguously blamed it for many of the batting evils that afflicted the game in future years.

England's Test match programme between the wars widened significantly with the entry into the Test fold of the West Indies (in 1928), New Zealand (in 1929-30), and India (in 1932). These countries were met both home and away, as well as, of course, Australia and South Africa. The great Hobbs-Sutcliffe opening partnership flourished between 1924 and 1930, during which time they shared 15 century opening stands for England; and in the period from 1928-9 to 1939, Hammond — who turned amateur to captain England in 1938 — himself scored 22 Test hundreds. In Test matches in England between the wars, apart from defeats by strong Australian sides (especially those of 1921 and 1930), England lost only a solitary Test, to South Africa in 1935.

In 1930 four-day Tests were introduced to England for the first time, and that year marked the first visit to England of BRADMAN. He quite overwhelmed England's bowlers with his devastating efficiency, scoring the record number of 974 runs in the Test series a the phenomenal average of 139·14. His shat tering success caused England's captain, o the next meeting with Australia, in 1932-3, t put into action a questionable method of bowl ing, quickly named 'body-line', whereby fas rising balls were directed at ot just outside th leg stump to a packed leg-side field, to mak ordinary scoring strokes either impossible o especially hazardous. JARDINE, England' captain in Australia who directed this policy had as principal bowlers to execute it Larwoo and Voce. A controversy at once flared up and irate cables were exchanged by the Aus tralian Board and the M.C.C. When passion finally subsided it was generally agreed tha such bowling was not only dangerous bu against the best interests of the game. In 193 the M.C.C. issued formal instructions t umpires to prevent its recurrence.

The Second World War caused the longes gap in first-class cricket that England has eve known, but when an improvised programm was arranged for 1945 (including a series o 'Victory' Tests against a side chosen from Australian servicemen in England), publi response was swift and keen.

A completely revised code of laws— though firmly based on the existing one — wa in active preparation by the M.C.C. from 1944. It became the 1947 code and operate from the start of the 1948 season. With subse quent amendments, it has governed the con duct of the game at all levels and in all parts o the world to the present time.

Immediate postwar interest in first-clas cricket in England was intense. Between 194 and 1950 championship and Test matc crowds gave no cause for administrative con cern, and though Test matches continue thereafter to attract healthy gates — especiall the matches against Australia and the We Indies — the 1950s saw the beginning of steady decline in the attractions of three-da inter-county cricket. The glorious summer o 1947 gave no hint of future difficulties. In tha year both Compton and W. J. Edrich exceede the previous record aggregate in a season o Hayward in 1906, and Compton also made th record number of 18 centuries in a season Middlesex, with a batting strength and spee of scoring unapproached by any other side and led with rare flair by Robins, won thei first championship since 1921. An equall splendid summer followed in 1948, when suc was the enthusiasm for the visiting Australian that they returned home with a profit of abou £75,000 to accompany their unbeaten record Glamorgan, to the surprise of many, won th championship that year, for the first time sinc their elevation to first-class status in 1921: t was a fitting end to the career of Clay, who had played for the county from the start.

The 1948 season saw the introduction of five-day Tests to England, and apart from the 1949 series against New Zealand, this remained the pattern thereafter. A new force burst on the English scene in 1950, when some powerful, compelling cricket by the touring West Indians caused English cricketers and spectators thenceforth to place them in the highest bracket as performers, and this estimate was fully justified in the course of time. The 1950 tour emphasized to league clubs in the north of England the real potential of the new West Indian cricketer, and many Caribbean players were attracted into the leagues as professionals, to add lustre to the legends created by CONSTANTINE, who had begun with Nelson in the Lancashire League in 1929. Test players from all over the world, as well as from England, attracted the attention of league officials, and large sums were paid for their services. At the same time, the experience of English pitches and the peculiar demands of the half-day game proved of much benefit even to the most capable of overseas players, most of whom freely acknowledge that they became better cricketers for the experience.

After Warwickshire won the championship in 1951 — their only previous success had been in 1911 — English cricket in the 1950s was dominated by the famous Surrey side, which performed the unprecedented feat of winning the title seven years in succession from 1952 to 1958. Surridge, their captain in the first five years, was followed by May, who scored nearly 8,000 runs in county matches in this golden period for Surrey. The bowling strength included A. V. Bedser, Loader, Lock, and Laker — an attack few counties could combat. Altogether, in their seven years of success, Surrey won 122 of their 195 county matches.

In the midst of these triumphs, Laker had an even greater personal triumph when he routed Australia in the Test series in England in 1956, taking 46 wickets at only 9·60 runs each, including the record number of 19 in one match at Old Trafford. The Australians that year won only 9 first-class matches out of 31, and for the first time in history Australia began the first Test without a single victory against a county side.

The 1950s also saw an important advancement in the field of umpiring in England, following the formation of the Association of Cricket Umpires in 1953. This body is quite independent of the panel of first-class and Test umpires and exercises its surveillance over club cricket; principally by lectures and examinations it has raised the standard and status of club umpires.

From the 1950s a series of small amendments to the conditions which governed first-class play were introduced in an effort to defeat defensive tactics and to combat the effects of 'dead' wickets. No truly satisfactory formula was evolved, and administrators recognized that the means to attract spectators in numbers to county cricket lay principally with the players themselves. Meanwhile, most counties began to show regular losses, which were offset only by the share they received from annual Test match profits.

During the M.C.C.'s tour of Australia in 1958-9, certain Australian bowlers were accused of having suspect bowling actions. The issue — dubbed 'the throwing controversy' — had sufficient substance for legislators to make a determined effort to end it. England's own house was by no means in order, but it was made so, as was Australia's. Subsequently, a great furore, accompanied by photographic evidence, broke over the alleged dubiety of the action of Griffith, the West Indian fast bowler, who had a wonderfully successful first tour of England in 1963. He was never actually no-balled for throwing in any of his 28 Tests, and so the allegations — which were in respect of the occasional faster ball anyway — remain 'not proven'. Allied to debates on throwing, the problem of 'drag' by a bowler's back foot in delivery also received close attention from ruling bodies throughout the world.

At the beginning of 1963, the ancient distinction between the amateur and professional in English first-class cricket was abolished, and with it went the traditional Gentlemen v. Players fixture. All participants in county and Test cricket thereafter were known as 'cricketers', though naturally they were free, if they so wished, to negotiate contracts with the counties for whom they played. Professionalism still continued in league cricket. The most profound innovation affecting the playing strength of sides was the dispensation in 1968 which enabled counties to engage one overseas cricketer on immediate registration, without residential qualification. Most counties — Yorkshire remaining staunchly aloof — took quick advantage. There was strong competition for the gifted SOBERS, who accepted the offer of Nottinghamshire.

In 1968, a new 'government' for English cricket was created, the CRICKET COUNCIL, which formally assumed most of the functions of the M.C.C., other than the responsibility for the laws. In the same year the Test and County Cricket Board replaced the Board of Control for Test Matches at Home (established in 1898) and the Advisory County Cricket Committee (which had been formed in 1904 at the request of the counties, an important administrative step). By the end of the 1960s, two new competitions were a regular feature of the English scene — the Gillette Cup (which was inaugurated in 1963) and the John Player League, for Sunday competition only, which was first played in 1969. In 1970 the 'l.b.w.' law was altered for the first time since 1937.

On the field, Yorkshire reasserted its dominance and won the championship seven times in the ten years up to 1968. But cricket found itself increasingly involved in politics around this time as a result of the internal policies of South Africa which, *inter alia*, prevented contact on the field between white and non-white cricketers and effectively debarred any non-white cricketer from being a member of the national team. D'Oliveira, a Cape Coloured cricketer of high merit, had been obliged through lack of opportunity to leave South Africa for England, and when he was included in the proposed English party to tour the republic in 1968-9, the South African government promptly objected; the tour was cancelled. Mounting pressure against South Africa also caused the cancellation of the South African tour of England scheduled for 1970, and these events caused many harrowing hours for cricket's administrators.

In 1970-1 England, under Illingworth, regained the ASHES in Australia, after Australia had held them since 1958-9. The struggle was hard, despite the fact that Australia was experiencing a period of temporary decline, but the batting of Boycott and the bowling of SNOW were potent factors. England had previously regained the Ashes in 1953 — in England.

Australia made a valiant effort to win the series in England in 1972, the fast bowlers Lillee and Massie creating an especially fine impression and taking 54 wickets between them in the five Tests. But the rubber was shared, with two victories to each side, although Australia gave clear evidence of its intention to return to the very top as a cricketing nation.

The introduction in England in 1972 of a new one-day competition — the BENSON AND HEDGES CUP — placed even more emphasis on the growing interest in limited-over cricket at major level. A reduced county championship programme, however, continued to provide the basic first-class fare for spectators in England.

INTERNATIONAL CRICKET. The Imperial Cricket Conference, with M.C.C., Australia, and South Africa as the original members, first met in 1909, at Lord's, and one of its early decisions was to hold a Triangular Tournament in England in 1912 between the three member countries, a venture which duly took place but was never repeated. The Conference became a common meeting place for the ruling bodies of the Test-playing countries, and membership was confined to countries within the British Commonwealth. India, New Zealand, and the West Indies were elected in 1926, and Pakistan in 1952. South Africa forfeited membership on leaving the Commonwealth in 1961. The Conference was renamed the International Cricket Conference in 1965 and new rules allowed membership to countries outside the Commonwealth, and created the status of associate membership, open to non-Test-playing countries whose cricket is genuinely organized and governed. The U.S.A., Ceylon (now Sri Lanka), and Fiji were elected associate members in 1965, Bermuda, Holland, Denmark, and East Africa in 1966, Malaysia in 1967, Canada in 1968, Gibraltar and Hong Kong in 1969, and Papua and New Guinea in 1973.

Australia was the first country to show a significant challenge to the authority of England, and from the beginning has produced cricketers of great merit — untutored, but basically as adept as professionals. Coaching has certainly played its part in Australia since Caffyn, of Surrey, coached in Melbourne and Sydney in the 1860s, having remained behind after touring with an English side. But many of Australia's greatest players, especially batsmen, have been allowed to develop along their own lines with the minimum of organized instruction. Professionalism has at no time been a feature of Australian first-class cricket, with the minor exceptions of imported players from England and the West Indies who began to play there in the 1960s.

An English side first went to Australia in 1861-2, under H. H. Stephenson, and PARR led a side two years later. These were primitive days, both in terms of playing strength and conditions, but interest was mounting quickly, especially within the colonies of Victoria and New South Wales, whose annual competitions (started in March 1856) were already the sporting highlights of the summer. The team captained by W. G. Grace in 1873-4 brought a further surge of interest, so historically it was no surprise to find a combined Australian side taking the field against — and beating — the English side under J. Lillywhite jr. at Melbourne in March 1877. This was the first Test match.

In 1878 the first official Australian team came to England (though an aboriginal side had toured ten years before). This team beat a powerful M.C.C. side at Lord's in a single day — and Australian cricket had reached full maturity. SPOFFORTH was the first of a long line of great Australian fast bowlers, and the standards he set in those early days served to keep his country's cricket on the highest plateau thereafter.

Australia played its first Test in England in 1880, and except during the two world wars the regular interchange of visits between the two countries has continued ever since. The 200th Test match between the countries was played at Lord's in 1968, and by common consent it is in these games that the highest standard of cricket in the world is seen. Australia has played Tests against all the other first-class countries — South Africa (first in 1902-3), West Indies (1930-1), New Zealand (1945-6), India (1947-8), and Pakistan (1956-7). Australia is second only to England in the number of Tests played.

The entire composition of Australian Test sides is drawn from the country's only domestic first-class competition — the SHEFFIELD SHIELD, which was instituted in 1892-3, and in which the quality of cricket played has always been high.

Australian cricket administration until the 1900s centred largely on the Melbourne Cricket Club, which made itself responsible both for sending national sides abroad and for inviting teams to visit Australia. The players themselves had much to say in the organization of tours and the destination of profits. In 1905 the Australian Board of Control for International Cricket was established to undertake these and other roles, and apart from one major fracas with the leading Australian players in 1911-12, it has grown in strength and influence, with a widening of functions, so that its voice is a powerful one in the world government of the game. The Board's appointed selectors choose both home Test sides and Australian teams to tour overseas. The two most formidable sides since the Board's creation have been those which visited England in 1921 and 1948. The 1921 side, under ARMSTRONG, remained undefeated until the end of August, and possessed a pair of superlative opening bowlers in GREGORY and E. A. McDonald, who took 254 first-class wickets between them in England that summer. MAILEY and Armstrong himself also took 100 wickets each, and MACARTNEY and BARDSLEY were in outstanding form with the bat: they each scored 8 centuries and passed 2,000 runs, Macartney getting 345 in one day against Nottinghamshire at Trent Bridge. The 1948 team, captained by Bradman (on his fourth and final tour of England as a player), not only won four of the five Tests but were unbeaten in their entire programme of 34 matches (31 of

them first-class). No other team has gone through a tour of England without defeat. As many as seven batsmen reached 1,000 runs, and Bradman himself, HASSETT, and MORRIS all averaged over 70. In a single day against Essex at Southend-on-Sea, the side scored 721 runs. LINDWALL and K. R. MILLER, as opening bowlers, made as great an impression as Gregory and McDonald had done before them. In all departments of the game the side was immensely strong, though, as in 1921, English cricket had not yet recovered from the setbacks of war.

Australian sides in England have never been weak, and outside the Tests they have been especially difficult to beat. After Hampshire had beaten the 1912 side, it was not until 1956 that another county (Surrey) beat them, and their success in England between the wars reflects creditably on their four able captains — Armstrong (1921), H. L. Collins (1926), WOODFULL (1930 and 1934), and Bradman (1938). The 1961 captain BENAUD, also ranks high among the significant leaders.

The general excellence of Australian pitches has encouraged the emergence of many prolific batsmen, the most celebrated being TRUMPER, HILL, Macartney, PONSFORD, MCCABE, and Bradman. Bradman averaged 110·19 in Sheffield Shield matches alone (for New South Wales and South Australia between 1927 and 1949). Among Australia's great bowlers have been Spofforth, C. T. B. TURNER, TRUMBLE, Gregory, Mailey, GRIMMETT, O'REILLY, and Lindwall. All-rounders have also played an important part in Australian domestic and Test cricket from its earliest times, and Australia has produced more than any other country, players like GIFFEN, NOBLE, Armstrong, Miller, Benaud, and DAVIDSON.

South Africa was first visited by an English side in 1888-9, with C. Aubrey (later Sir Aubrey) Smith as captain. Test matches with South Africa date from that season, though the game was already firmly established in South Africa by the 1840s. The CURRIE CUP tournament, the national domestic competition, began in 1889-90. The two most successful sides have been Transvaal and Natal, and the other principal sides that have taken part are Western Province, Eastern Province, Rhodesia, Orange Free State, Border, and Griqualand West.

South African cricket took a comparatively long time to emerge as a redoubtable force. When the first team visited England, in 1894, none of the matches was first-class, though by that time the South African Cricket Association — the governing body for first-class and international cricket in South Africa — had been formed (in 1890). This body's jurisdiction has extended over the sphere of white cricket in South Africa, and the considerable element of non-white cricketers has its own administration, first set up in 1897 as the South African Coloured Cricket Board.

The Edwardian era saw South African cricket make important strides. Teams visited England in 1901, 1904, and 1907, the last tour marking South Africa's début in Test cricket in England. It was not, however, until 1935 that South Africa won a Test match on English soil. A fine trio of googly bowlers in 1907 (Schwarz, Vogler, and G. C. White) engendered a new respect for South Africa. England had already lost the series of 1905-6, and it lost again in 1909-10. When H. W. TAYLOR, a batsman of special gifts, appeared, it seemed that South Africa's cricketing future was assured.

The decline in effectiveness of its googly bowlers marked the end of South Africa's challenge. A very ordinary side visited England for the Triangular Tournament (with Australia also competing) of 1912. With BARNES in brilliant bowling form for England in 1913-14, South Africa was crushed. Meanwhile Australia had paid its first visit to South Africa in 1902-3 and the first return visit to Australia was made in 1910-11, when FAULKNER showed remarkable all-round skill.

Between the wars South African cricket languished. Matting pitches persisted in some centres even up to 1939, but their gradual replacement by good turf pitches was an important step, bringing forth such fine batsmen as MITCHELL, Melville, and the younger A. D. NOURSE. One of the most famous of all matches was played at Durban in March 1939, when the Test match against England was left drawn after ten days in order to allow the English players to catch their ship home.

A young side of largely inexperienced players did service for South Africa from the early 1950s, their unusually splendid fielding being an asset that surprised many observers. Adcock and Heine formed a formidable pair of fast bowlers, and TAYFIELD, especially on hard pitches, was an off-spin bowler to rank with the world's best. The all-rounder GODDARD was a constant tower of strength. It was not until the 1960s, with the blossoming of R. G. POLLOCK and his brother P. M. (a fast bowler), that South Africa was a real force again. Barlow, a pugnacious opening batsman, was an integral part of the new team, moulded by van der Merwe's captaincy and inspired in the field by Bland's rare agility and accuracy. Events off the field, however, had a sad effect on South African cricket in this period. After South Africa left the (then) Imperial Cricket Conference on becoming a republic in 1961, proposed tours by England to South Africa in 1968-9 and by South Africa to England in 1970 were cancelled.

West Indies. During the period of South Africa's postwar revival, a younger cricketing nation, the West Indies, was also performing great deeds. They were called 'Champions of the World', though it had not always been so. The organization of cricket in the many West Indian islands was still largely disjointed when R. Slade Lucas took the first English team there in 1895, but a special enthusiasm existed which was to ensure the eventual ripening of talent, in particular in the four territories of Barbados, Trinidad, British Guiana (now Guyana), and Jamaica. A combined West Indian team made its initial tour of England in 1900, but it was not strong enough to be reckoned first-class. Since 1891 an inter-colonial tournament had existed, though hampered by difficulties of distance and providing only spasmodic competition at high level.

Various English sides, including two sent by the M.C.C., visited West Indies before the First World War, and in 1906 the Barbadian, Austin, captained the first West Indian side to play first-class matches in England. It was not, however, until 1923 that another side came, again under Austin, though the standard of the visitors had not advanced significantly in the interim. Constantine was introduced to English grounds in 1923 and he remained a compelling personality as fast bowler, fearless hitter, and outstanding fielder until 1939. He appeared in league cricket in Lancashire when not needed for his country.

The West Indies Cricket Board of Control was formed in 1926, and when the next team visited England, in 1928, it was accorded Test status. In 1930-1 the first West Indian side went to Australia and encountered Bradman at his best; but in HEADLEY, of Jamaica, they had a batsman of world stature. West Indies recorded their first win in a Test series, beating England by two games to one, with one draw, in 1934-5 — a warning of things to come. The warning was more distinct when wartime matches in the West Indies threw up the genius of the 'three Ws' — WORRELL, WEEKES, and WALCOTT, all batsmen of immense power and skill. Under J. D. C. Goddard's captaincy, and with the spin bowlers VALENTINE and RAMADHIN at their most destructive, the West Indies surprised England in 1950 and won a Test match (and a series) in England for the first time. After that tour West Indies played five-match Test series.

In 1953-4 England was obliged for the first time to send the most powerful side it could muster to tour the West Indies, and the Test series was drawn. It saw the introduction to Test cricket of the remarkable Sobers, whose presence was to dominate not only West Indian, but world, cricket. With colleagues in KANHAI, GIBBS, and the two fast bowlers, w. w. HALL and Griffith, Sobers helped to make West Indies supreme, and few more popular sides ever visited England than that of 1963, under Worrell, whom Sobers succeeded as captain.

Despite the enormous advance of the West Indies as a Test power — due in large measure to natural talent within the islands — inter-territorial cricket was not placed on a firmly constituted basis until the introduction in 1965-6 of the SHELL SHIELD, a sponsored tournament designed to ensure that each first-class territory played the other at least once. A combined Windward and Leeward Islands team also plays in this tournament, though both these groups of islands had played competitive cricket amongst themselves since before the First World War.

New Zealand. Although cricket in New Zealand has been played continuously since the early 1840s, and though it has always been — and remains — the premier summer sport, it has never developed sufficiently to make New Zealand challengers for world supremacy. Rather, the game has progressed in a minor key; fine players have been produced, but never in sufficient abundance to make any real impact on strong opponents.

Inter-provincial cricket was born at Wellington in March 1860, when Wellington met Auckland. Such matches, between the principal provinces, have continued since then to be the basic portion of New Zealand's cricketing programme. The contests were placed on a competitive basis from the season of 1906-7, when the PLUNKET SHIELD was introduced, and the four major provinces — Auckland, Canterbury, Otago, and Wellington — have been regular participants. In 1950-1 an area designated Central Districts joined the competition, followed in 1956-7 by Northern Districts.

Despite her proximity to Australia, New Zealand's cricket relations with her powerful neighbour have never been especially strong, and for the regular appearance of renowned players on its fields, New Zealand has looked much more to England. The visits by M.C.C. teams at the end of tours of Australia have been great occasions for New Zealand, and although the Englishmen have generally had things very much their own way, the enthusiasm engendered has been vastly to the good of New Zealand cricket.

The first English side to go to New Zealand was Parr's, which went primarily to visit Australia, in 1863-4; this team visited Dunedin and Christchurch, where it provided a strong local impetus for the furtherance of the game. Before the end of the century several professional coaches from English counties had been engaged with success by provincial associations, and in December 1894, the New Zealand Cricket Council was formed in Christchurch. New Zealand has been well served administratively since that time, though money has never been plentiful.

The first representative Australian team — other than a side from one colony — to play first-class matches in New Zealand was that led by Noble in 1904-5; the first South African team played in 1931-2; the first from the West Indies in 1951-2 (after one two-day game in 1930-1); the first Pakistani side in 1964-5; and the first from India in 1967-8. New Zealand, in its turn, has played at first-class level in all the Test countries of the world.

Although New Zealand became a Test nation in 1929-30 — having first toured England in 1927 without playing Tests — its first victory in a Test did not come until 1955-6, when the West Indies were beaten at Auckland. At that time, B. SUTCLIFFE and REID virtually carried New Zealand on their shoulders, and their deeds surpassed those of earlier fine cricketers — Blunt, Dempster, James, Merritt, Lowry, Hadlee, DONNELLY, Wallace, and Burtt.

India. Cricket in India is of considerable antiquity, dating at least from 1721. Englishmen imported the game and not until the 1840s did Indians themselves begin to take part in organized matches. Its popularity, however, was so strong that in due course all communities in every corner of the sub-continent were enjoying the game, often with a fervour that excluded all other forms of sporting activity. Successive viceroys lent their distinguished patronage, and, at a time when Indian princes ruled with colossal wealth and power, it was their unstinted support for cricket at every level that raised the game to permanent popularity.

Parsee teams toured England in 1886 and 1888, and Vernon took out the first English team to India in 1888-9. Then in 1892-3 there began the long series of Presidency Matches — played at Bombay and Poona — between Europeans and Parsees, which became the Bombay Triangular Tournament in 1907-8 with the entry of the Hindus. The Muslims entered from 1912-13, when the tournament became Quadrangular, and subsequently — with a Rest side entering — Pentangular from 1937-8 until 1945-6.

Meanwhile, representative Indian sides had

toured England in 1911, 1932, and 1936, and on the 1932 tour India played its first Test match. The first M.C.C. side to India toured in 1926-7, and on the second visit — under Jardine in 1933-4 — the first Test matches were played on Indian soil. The Indian Board of Control was formed in 1927, though India had already been represented at the Imperial Cricket Conference held in London in 1926.

Following the great interest created by the English visit of 1933-4, and with a desire to perpetuate the memory of Ranjitsinhji, the Indian Board instituted the RANJI TROPHY competition in November, 1934. It was on the perfect Ranji Trophy wickets that MERCHANT and Hazare made many of their great wartime scores which attracted huge crowds.

India first toured Australia in 1947-8, the West Indies in 1952-3, Pakistan in 1954-5, and New Zealand in 1967-8. There has been no contact at first-class level between India and South Africa.

Pakistan, created a nation in 1947, is the youngest of the first-class and Test-playing countries. It received its first touring side — the West Indians — in 1948-9, and the first M.C.C. visit was in 1951-2. Meanwhile, in 1949, the Board of Control had been formed, and since 1952 Pakistan has been a member of the International Cricket Conference.

Pakistan played its first Tests in India in 1952-3, under Kardar, and made her first Test tour of England in 1954, drawing the four-match series. HANIF MOHAMMAD, a batsman of monumental patience and future captain of Pakistan, was the sheet-anchor in Pakistan's early years in Test cricket, and the medium-fast bowling of FAZAL MAHMOOD, both on turf and on matting, carried much of the attack.

In domestic cricket Hanif Mohammad established the world record individual score in first-class cricket with an innings of 499 for Karachi *v.* Bahawalpur at Karachi in January 1959, and he later became the first Pakistani to reach 10,000 runs in first-class matches. The two competitions played at first-class level in Pakistan are the QUAID-I-AZAM TROPHY (instituted in 1953-4) and the Ayub Zonal Trophy (instituted in 1960-1), with Karachi the most successful side in both.

Cricket is played in many countries outside the orbit of Test cricket. Among them are:

Scotland. A large amount of club and league cricket has long flourished in Scotland, where the earliest known game was played in 1785. The Grange C.C. of Edinburgh exerted much influence until the Scottish Cricket Union, after an early failure, was reformed in 1908. Scottish national sides have appeared since 1865 and have opposed many first-class touring teams from overseas. The major event, however, is the clash with Ireland, and regular matches take place in both countries.

Ireland. The major towns and cities boast many clubs, some of them of respectable age. The first recorded match was played at Phoenix Park, Dublin, in 1792. Irish cricketers have toured the United States — the first visit was in 1879 — and they have made many ventures to England. Occasional first-class touring sides to England have played in Ireland, and in 1969 Ireland dismissed the West Indians at Londonderry for 25. Much of the country's domestic cricket is on a league basis.

Wales. Many Welsh county clubs have in former days appeared in the Minor Counties championship, and today still play each other. The North Wales Cricket Association is especially active, and in South Wales there is a good standard of league cricket. A side styled 'Wales' formerly took the field, but national aspirations — as well as the best players — have for many years now been concentrated on Glamorgan County Cricket Club.

U.S.A. As early as 1709 a form of cricket was played in Virginia, and the United States first met Canada in 1844, to start the oldest international cricket match in the world. The first English team toured North America in 1859, and the Australians paid a brief visit in 1878. The first Philadelphian team played in England in 1884, and until 1914 the game in Philadelphia reached a notable height of popularity and ability: J. B. King, a fast bowler, performed well both in England and America. The game has also flourished among enthusiasts in Chicago, New York, and Southern California, and in 1961 the United States Cricket Association was founded. The U.S.A. was elected to associate membership of the International Cricket Conference in 1965.

Canada. The first organized clubs date from the 1830s, and there was early contact with the U.S.A. Several English sides visited Canada before the first Canadian team came to England in 1880. Though matches with the United States continued, much of the interest in Canada was centred on Montreal and Toronto, and the game never made notable progress. In 1954 a Canadian side played some first-class matches in England, and many Canadian Colts sides — under the aegis of the Canadian Cricket Association, the ruling body — have made tours to England since the 1950s. Canada joined the International Cricket Conference as an associate member in 1968.

Netherlands. Nowhere on the European mainland is cricket played more extensively than in Holland. The game began there in the late 1850s, and the Nederlandsche Cricket Bond — later accorded the prefix 'Royal' — was founded in 1883 as the national ruling body. English coaches were engaged from 1889, and in 1892 a Dutch team first toured England. A great number of English clubs — notably the M.C.C. and the Free Foresters — have visited Holland, and among Dutch clubs the most influential have been the Hague C.C. and the Flamingos. About 250 teams participate in Saturday and Sunday league cricket on matting wickets.

Denmark. After Holland, Denmark is the principal cricket-playing country on the continent of Europe. The game was certainly played as early as 1866, and within twenty years many clubs had sprung up.

English sides have frequently toured there, and the first M.C.C. visit was in 1922. In 1926 the first Danish team — the Gentlemen of Denmark — visited England. A Danish XI and a Dutch XI first met in 1947, and regular international matches between these countries resulted. The Danish Cricket Union was formed in 1953, and, like Holland, Denmark was admitted to associate membership of the International Cricket Conference in 1966.

Fiji Islands. Many keen, uninhibited cricketers — often in bare feet — have played in Fiji since the 1870s. In 1895 a Fijian team toured New Zealand, but it was not until 1946 that the Fiji Cricket Association was formed. There have been subsequent visits to New Zealand and Australia, and occasional first-class sides passing Fiji have played there.

Argentina is the principal South American cricket country, where standards were particularly high between the two world wars. The first M.C.C. side toured there in 1911-12, and the Argentine Cricket Association was formed in 1913, though it had operated under a different name since 1899. Regular matches have been played against Brazil and Chile, and several Argentinian players were in the combined South American side that visited England in 1932.

Bermuda. The game has been played in Bermuda since the 1840s, and in the decade up to 1914 there was much competition with Philadelphia. English, Australian, and West Indian sides have visited Bermuda, and, since 1960, occasional Bermudian sides have toured England. Bermuda became an associate member of the International Cricket Conference in 1966.

Hong Kong. The premier club, the Hong Kong C.C., was founded in 1851 and has had a continuous existence since then. Between 1866 and 1948 a series of inter-port fixtures with Shanghai was played, and occasional teams from England, Australia, and New Zealand have played in Hong Kong. The cricket ground there is reputed to be the most valuable, in monetary terms, in the world. Hong Kong became an associate member of the International Cricket Conference in 1969.

Singapore. Cricket in Singapore can be traced back to the 1830s, and later regular matches were played against Hong Kong and Shanghai. First-class sides from England and Australia have toured there, and in 1948 the Singapore Cricket Association was formed. The game, however, has never been a significant force there.

Ceylon. The Colombo C.C. was formed in 1832, since when enormous enthusiasm in schools and clubs has been a feature of the island's cricket. Since the Hon. Ivo Bligh's side played there in 1882, most of the famous names in English cricket have played in Ceylon *en route* to Australia. Sinhalese sides have frequently visited India, but never England. Since 1922 the Ceylon Cricket Association and the Ceylon Board of Control have governed the game. In 1965 Ceylon (now Sri Lanka) became an associate member of the International Cricket Conference.

East Africa. After the First World War, matches between Kenya, Tanganyika, and Uganda at club level grew steadily in number in all territories. The Kenya Kongonis was an influential club in Nairobi, and the fixtures between Officials and Settlers and Europeans and Asians were highlights of the season. The first match between the representative strengths of Kenya and Tanganyika took place in 1951, when the East African Cricket Conference was formed. In 1966 East Africa joined the International Cricket Conference as an associate member.

West Africa. The game has never been particularly strong in West Africa, though cricket is played in Nigeria, Ghana, Liberia, Gambia, and Sierra Leone. Southern Nigeria played the Gold Coast as early as 1904, but the standard in West Africa has rarely attracted overseas sides.

Women's Cricket. The first women's cricket match was played in 1745, and, though the women's game has undergone fluctuations in popularity, it has been pursued with enthusiasm — often before large gatherings — ever since. Rowlandson's 'Cricket Match Extraordinary' depicts a rural women's match which was played for high stakes in 1811, and in Hambledon days several noblemen gave the women's game encouragement and support.

Although the first club, the White Heather, was formed in 1887, women's cricket was less in evidence in late Victorian and Edwardian days. Country-house cricket flourished, and references were made to 'lady' cricketers. It could be said that the game at large had been influenced by women, for Willes, an early propounder and exponent of round-arm bowling, allegedly had noted the potential value of such a delivery in the bowling action of his sister, Christina, whose crinolines had debarred under-arm deliveries. Further, W. G. Grace owed much to the early encouragement of his mother.

In 1890 the 'Original English Lady Cricketers', under assumed names, toured the country and played exhibition matches before huge concourses, but they disbanded at the end of the season.

After the First World War, cricket regained popularity, particularly in girls' public schools, and this, together with the increasing emancipation of women, made the Women's Cricket Association, founded in 1926, a necessity. The W.C.A. adopted the M.C.C.'s Laws of Cricket, except that the ball was to be smaller (5 oz. — 142 g.) than in men's cricket.

Soon the numbers of women cricketers and followers of the game were increasing rapidly. A regular magazine was started by Marjorie Pollard; an annual week of festival cricket was begun at Colwall; and a match between London and District and the Rest of England was the successful forerunner of other representative fixtures. Some of the men's county grounds were made available for women's matches, and by 1939 17 county associations had been formed. In 1934-5 an England team visited Australia and New Zealand, and played the first women's Test matches. Tours have since been exchanged at regular intervals, the players finding their own fares and purchasing their own equipment.

One of the most outstanding English woman cricketers was Hide, who captained England from 1937 to 1954. She and Maclagan, who scored the first Test century, have been compared in method with eminent male counterparts. Others who have drawn attention by their performances have been Duggan, Heyhoe (now Mrs. Flint), and Bakewell (who did the 'double' of 1,000 runs and 100 wickets on the 1968-9 tour of Australia and New Zealand). For Australia, Betty Wilson was the finest player throughout the 1950s.

In 1973 a World Cup was staged for the first time; England was the host country, and emerged as winners.

The formation of the International Women's Cricket Council in 1958 ensured that there would be a continuous exchange of ideas between England, Australasia, South Africa, the West Indies, and Holland, together with other countries where women's cricket is likely to respond to encouragement.

H. S. Altham and E. W. Swanton, *A History of Cricket*, 2 vols. (5th ed., 1962); Rowland Bowen, *Cricket: A History of its Growth and Development throughout the World* (1970); Bill Frindall, *The Kaye Book of Cricket Records* (1968); E. V. Lucas, ed., *The Hambledon Men* (1907); R. S. Rait Kerr, *The Laws of Cricket: their History and Growth* (1950); E. W. Swanton, ed., *The World of Cricket* (1966); Roy Webber, *The County Cricket Championship* (1957); Arthur Wrigley, *The Book of Test Cricket 1876-1964* (1965); *Wisden Cricketers' Almanack*, annually, 1864-date.

GOVERNING BODY (WORLD): International Cricket Conference, Lord's Cricket Ground, St. John's Wood Road, London N.W.8; (ENGLAND): Cricket Council, Lord's Cricket Ground, St. John's Wood Road, London N.W.8.

CRICKET, Deck, see DECK CRICKET.

CRICKET COUNCIL, the governing body of the game of CRICKET in England, is responsible for major policy other than the framing and alteration of the laws. It was established in 1968, following a Governmental request to the MARYLEBONE CRICKET CLUB to create a body that would be eligible for grant aid along the lines of other sports. Its chairman and vice-chairman are respectively the president and treasurer of the M.C.C., and its other members consist of nine M.C.C. representatives nominated by the M.C.C. committee, seven Test and County Cricket Board representatives (including its chairman and the chairman of the Minor Counties Cricket Association), and ten representatives nominated by the National

Cricket Association, of whom one is its chairman and three represent coaching and youth cricket. The National Cricket Association itself is composed of representatives of all branches of cricket in England below county level, embracing clubs, schools, the Services, universities, women's cricket, umpiring, and coaching.

CRITCHLEY, Brig.-Gen. ALFRED CECIL (1890-1964), greyhound promoter, who launched GREYHOUND RACING in Britain when he built and operated the first track, at Belle Vue, Manchester, in 1926, in conjunction with a fellow Canadian, Munn, and Maj. Lyne-Dixon. He was known as 'the father of greyhound racing' in Britain.

CROCKETT, ROBERT W. (1863-1935), first-class CRICKET umpire. The most outstanding of early Australian umpires, he officiated in 33 Test matches from 1901-2 to 1924-5, winning esteem for his sound judgement and good humour.

CROKE PARK, sports arena in Dublin, Ireland, and the headquarters of the GAELIC ATHLETIC ASSOCIATION. It has a capacity of 75,000 of which 30,000 are covered seats.

CROMPTON, ROBERT (b. 1879), Association footballer for BLACKBURN ROVERS and England for whom he made 41 appearances at right back at a time of few international matches. He was unchallenged in his position in the national team from 1902 to 1914. He was captain both of his club and of England and after retiring from active football became a director of the Blackburn club.

CROQUET, Association, is a lawn game played with balls and a mallet on a court measuring approximately 35 yds. by 28 yds. (31·95 × 25·56 m.), on which are set out six hoops and one central peg. The hoops are made of round iron ⅝ in. (1·59 cm.) thick and have a square crown, the crown of the first hoop being coloured blue and that of the last, or rover hoop, red. They stand 1 ft. (30·5 cm.) out of the ground and the inside measurement between the uprights is 3¾ in. (9·53 cm.). Four coloured clips corresponding to the colour of the balls are used to show which hoop each ball next has to make. They are placed on the crown of the hoop for hoops 1 to 6 and on one of the uprights on the return journey. The peg is made of wood 1½ in. (3·8 cm.) in diameter and stands 18 in. (45·72 cm.) out of the ground, exclusive of a detachable portion at the top to hold the clips.

The balls are made of compressed cork covered with a layer of composition or plastic and coloured respectively blue, red, black, and yellow. They weigh 1 lb. (453·6 g.) and have a diameter of 3⅝ in. (9·21 cm.) and are therefore ⅛ in. (0·32 cm.) smaller than the hoops.

The mallet (which the player has to provide for himself) is made of wood and weighs between 2¾ and 3¾ lb. (1·247–1·701 kg.). The commonest weight is between 3 and 3¼ lb. (1·360–1·474 kg.). The head for heavier mallets is usually made of lignum vitae, although this is increasingly difficult to find in seasoned condition. Lighter mallets are made of boxwood. The size of the head is ideally 9 in. (22·86 cm.) long and between 2¼ and 2½ in. square (5·71–6·35 cm.). Round-headed mallets are as popular as square ones and both are usually bound with brass, set back ¼ in. (0·64 cm.) from each face, to prevent splitting. The

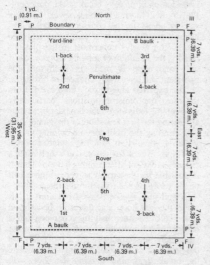

STANDARD CROQUET COURT AND SETTING
(P) corner pegs; (F) corner flags. The Willis setting now in use was introduced in 1922.

best shafts are hickory, with ash, which is rather brittle, or malacca, which is too resilient, as alternatives. Metal and nylon shafts have been extensively experimented with but they are far too springy.

The object of the game is to score all 12 hoops (each hoop in both directions) and the peg point in the correct order with each ball. The side which does so first is the winner and the number of strokes taken to achieve this is immaterial. There are 26 points in a full game

and the score is described as the difference between the maximum and that achieved by the loser. Thus if the loser has not scored a single hoop (which is by no means unusual, particularly in first-class play), the winner has won +26. If the loser has scored, say, 17 points, he has lost −9, and the winner has won +9. (In Australia and New Zealand the scores are given perhaps more logically as 26-0, 26-17, etc.).

Four balls are always used; in singles each player has two balls. Blue and black are always partners against red and yellow. The striker strikes with his mallet only one of his balls during any turn. The winner of the toss may choose either whether to play first or second, or which colour balls to play with.

The boundary of the court is defined by a white line, the inside edge of which is the actual boundary. The balls are played into the court from either of the baulks, which are part of the yard-line, an imaginary line which runs right round the court 1 yd. (0·91 m.) in from the boundary. The A baulk runs from the Ist corner spot to the middle of the south boundary and the B baulk from the IIIrd corner spot to the middle of the north boundary.

When all four balls are in play, the sides play alternately but the balls need not be played in sequence. Thus the player of blue and black could play blue for as many turns as he wishes. In doubles, each player plays the same ball throughout, but one player of a partnership can play several consecutive turns of his side.

A turn consists initially of one stroke, but this can be extended if that stroke is a roquet — made when the striker's ball hits one of the other three balls — or scores a hoop. A roquet entitles the striker to two further strokes — a croquet stroke, played with the striker's ball touching the roqueted ball, and then one further ordinary stroke, called the continuation stroke. On this continuation stroke the striker may roquet one of the other balls and then take croquet in the same way, but he may roquet each ball only once in each turn unless a hoop is scored. Running a hoop entitles the striker to another ordinary stroke and also the right to roquet the other three balls again. Thus, every time a hoop is run the sequence of roquet and croquet can begin again and, by a combination of these strokes and running hoops (called making a break), the turn can be extended even until the peg has been reached. The turn does not end if a ball is sent off the court unless it is either the croqueted ball or the striker's ball in a croquet stroke.

The making of a break follows a basic pattern. In a four-ball break the striker will have one ball (called the 'pioneer') waiting at his next hoop, say the second. Another ball (called the 'pivot') will be about half-way between that and his present hoop, the first. His own ball will be in front of the first hoop with the remaining ball (called the 'pilot') off which he will make his hoop.

He approaches the first hoop on the croquet stroke, sending his own ball in front of the hoop and the pilot behind it. He now runs the hoop and can roquet the pilot again. He croquets this to the third hoop as his pioneer for that, at the same time going to the pivot in the middle. He roquets that and in the croquet stroke following goes to the ball at the second hoop which has now become the pilot for that hoop, leaving the pivot ball in the middle. He roquets the new pilot, makes the second hoop in the same way as he made the first and afterwards sends the pilot ball to the fourth hoop as his pioneer, going back to the pivot and from there to the new pilot waiting at the third hoop.

However perfect a break, its advantage can be entirely wiped out if the leave at the end is not a good one. Normally it should be such that the opponents are separated and the striker's balls are together, but they should lie in such a way that they are strategically placed for his next turn, to play either with that ball or his partner's. At the same time they should not offer the opponent the chance of a break if he should hit. A good player can frequently leave the balls so that he will have a break in his next turn *if* he plays one or two very good shots. His opponent therefore may think that, if he shoots at any of the other balls, he will eliminate the necessity for these good shots and decide to go off to a distant corner in the hope that an error will be made and the break will not materialize.

Playing a break, although presenting enough problems in the controlling of all the balls accurately enough to maintain it, is perhaps the easiest part of a turn. More often than not, the break will have to be gathered in, a very formidable undertaking if all the balls are on the boundaries. Frequently the break will have to be only a three-ball one, played without the pivot ball; sometimes a two-ball break is all that can be managed, and in this case it is unlikely that more than two or three hoops will be made.

Croquet is a complicated game to follow until the main essentials have been grasped, and the beginning is most confusing of all to the novice. One would expect to see the first shots played towards the first hoop, which after all is the immediate object. But the chances of running the hoop from 6 yds. (5.49 m.) with a margin for error of only $\frac{1}{8}$ in. (0.32 cm.) are very slight indeed; the probability is that the ball will rebound from the hoop and be a sitting target for the second player, who has a good chance of roqueting it, making the hoop, and, if he has sufficient ability, making several more hoops from such an opening. The opening normally employed therefore is to avoid all proximity to the first hoop, the first player usually playing his ball off the east boundary just outside the IVth corner. The second player will then lay a 'tice' about 10 yds. (9.14 m.) down the west boundary from the Ist corner, near enough to entice the opponent to shoot at it but far enough for there to be no certainty that he will hit it. The third ball may then join up with its partner in the IVth corner, or may shoot at the opponent's tice from the Ist corner so that if he misses it he will end up in the IInd corner well out of harm's way.

The game now develops into a tactical battle with the object of securing the innings if possible or alternatively of avoiding the presentation of an easy break to the opponent. Players will normally think seven or eight strokes ahead in the course of a break and experts can think up to seventeen or eighteen ahead. But always uppermost in the player's mind is the intention of making a break, for if only one hoop is made in each turn the opponent will have many chances of hitting in.

The expert is able to pick up a break from the most unpromising positions, particularly when all the balls are on the boundaries as they are during the first few shots of the game. Any ball crossing the boundary or coming to rest within 1 yd. (.91 m.) of it is replaced on the yard-line, except for the striker's ball after a croquet stroke, or after running a hoop. Thus it is possible for the striker to get behind a ball on the yard-line and roquet it into the court.

A ball may not be pegged out until it has made the last hoop and therefore becomes a rover ball. Another ball may not peg out a rover unless it is itself a rover. The end of the game may be straightforward if one ball is on the peg. The partner ball has only to complete the break, and after making the rover will croquet its partner on to the peg and peg out itself in the following stroke. On the other hand, a good many complications can arise, such as pegging out an opponent if one of his balls is a rover, producing an interesting three-ball situation.

Although in theory the sequence of roquet and croquet and running hoops can go on to the finish, the player will not go so far as to peg his first ball out because of the disadvantage of being left with only one ball, and because in first-class play there are penalties to be conceded at certain points in the form of lifts and contacts. Under the lift rule, introduced in 1928, a player is prevented from leaving his opponent 'cross-wired' at the first hoop, for at the end of his first break, if he has made 1-back, the opponent may lift either of his balls and play from the baulk. The contact rule provides that, if a player has made both 1-back and 4-back in the same turn with his first ball before his other ball has made 1-back, his opponent has the option of placing either of his balls in contact with any other ball at the beginning of his turn. Both rules were devised to prevent a player from making an all-round break to the peg while his opponent might have only one shot, of as much as 30 yds. (27·43 m.), in which to save the game.

Strokes. The croquet stroke, played after a roquet has been made, is probably the most important stroke in the game. The striker's ball is placed in contact with the roqueted ball, wherever that has come to rest. The player then strikes his own ball in such a way that both balls move. If either ball goes off the court the turn ends. The croquet stroke has a number of different names according to the type of stroke played. A stop-shot is a croquet stroke in which the croqueted ball goes as far as possible in relation to the striker's ball, probably at least seven or eight times as far. In a half-roll, the croqueted ball travels two or three times as far, and in a full-roll about the same distance as the striker's ball. A pass-roll is a roll in which the striker's ball travels further than the croqueted ball. Although croquet strokes are divided for convenience into these four groups, each merges imperceptibly into the next as all the possible permutations between the distances each ball travels are covered.

In describing croquet strokes one assumes that the balls are travelling in much the same direction. They can however be played at any angle from the straight up to a maximum of about 85° from each other. When the balls travel in different directions the stroke is also known as a split shot, but falls into the categories described above, e.g. split stop-shot, split pass-roll, etc. A player may *not* put his foot on his ball when playing this, or any other, shot. A split shot played at an angle of about 85°, in which the croqueted ball stays practically where it is (though it must at least shake), is called a take-off. In a roll stroke, follow-through must be imparted to the backward ball but it is a foul if there is any push or if the mallet remains in contact with the backward ball after the balls have parted.

The 'rush' is a form of roquet in which the roqueted ball is sent to a particular spot. Expert players might consider a rush of 3 yds. (2·74 m.) as possible. Lesser players would be doubtful that they could rush a ball more than 2 yds. (1·83 m.) away and many no more than 1 yd. (0·91 m.).

The importance of a rush is that it overcomes the necessity for long rolls and split shots. The rush-line is also an important aspect of break-making.

The 'peel' is a stroke putting a ball other than the striker's through its hoop. To achieve an extra hoop for one's partner in the course of a break is, of itself, completely immaterial. A valid reason for a peel would be if one's partner ball wanted the rover hoop, in which case to peel that ball through the rover in the course of the break would enable the game to be won in that same turn. Alternatively the partner ball might be for the third hoop; if it will be impossible to lie up in the IIIrd corner near that hoop because a lift has to be conceded at the end of the turn, it would be advantageous to peel through the third hoop and lie up in the IVth corner. Or, since a ball peeled through 1-back or 4-back does not concede a lift, players beginning a turn with a ball on either of these two hoops will sometimes peel their ball through, particularly if the opponent has put one or both of his balls in baulk.

An attacking form of peeling would be to peel one's opponent ball through the last hoop in order to peg it out of the game. Expert players are often prepared to take the risk of peeling the *opponent* in this way and players therefore frequently stop their first break at the penultimate hoop which would then necessitate a double peel. To achieve this the first peel is normally done when making the sixth hoop and the rover peel when making the rover.

The introduction of the contact rule virtually prevented the first ball of each side from making more than the first nine hoops. This offered the opportunity and challenge of finishing the game by peeling this ball through its last three hoops on the second break. The standard triple is achieved by peeling through 4-back when making the third hoop, thus leaving a double peel to be completed. If, as frequently happens, a peel fails, then the whole operation becomes a delayed one and opportunities must be found, or contrived, to peel through the required hoops.

The triple peel was once regarded as the peak of a player's skill, and although more advanced peels were possible they were regarded more as showmanship than anything else. Quadruple and quintuple peels should not arise except on rare occasions because the first ball round should not have stopped at 3-back or 2-back unless forced to by an error. There is, however, a valid reason for attempting the sextuple peel, namely the possibility of completing the game without offering the

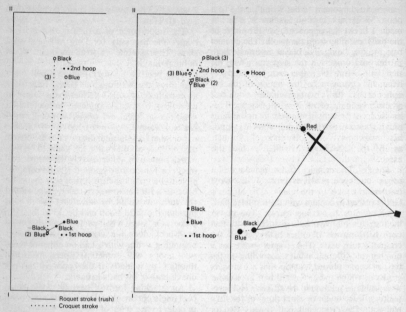

——— Roquet stroke (rush)
· · · · · · · Croquet stroke

USING THE RUSH

(*Below left*) Blue has run the first hoop but has run past black. Assuming red and yellow are in opposite corners, blue can only (2) roquet black and (3) roll up to the second hoop, about 20 yds. (18·29 m.) away. (*Centre*) Blue has run the first hoop but has obtained a rush on black to the second hoop. He can now (2) roquet black, rushing it to a spot a yard or two in front of the second hoop, and (3) approach the hoop from there. (*Right*) Blue wants to get a rush on red to a distant hoop. He can roquet black and take-off to red, but an error of a yard either side of the rush-line may prove fatal. His better course is to rush black to the spot marked in the diagram with a black square and take-off from there, *along the rush-line;* with a similar error he will still have a rush, even though a long one.

opponent a lift. The sextuple is most commonly attempted by adopting a set position at the end of the first break. The opponent balls are cross-wired at the first hoop, leaving the striker's ball in the jaws of 1-back with its partner ball between that hoop and the north boundary. As 1-back has not been made the opponent has no lift and can only shoot at the one ball left open to him, or retire to a corner. The sextupler must now rush his ball through 1-back, peel through 2-back when making the first hoop, 3-back when making the fourth hoop, and thereafter take any opportunity he can contrive to achieve the remaining three peels. A sextuple has only once been completed in a championship event, by Wylie in the final of the open championships in 1971. No peel is regarded as completed unless both the peeled ball and the striker's ball are pegged out in that turn.

Handicap games have their own form of tactics, particularly in doubles play, according to whether bisques are being given or

received. A bisque, or extra turn which may be taken at any time in the course of the game, offers a player a turn consecutive to his ordinary turn without the adversary's play intervening to upset the arrangement of the balls. Bisques may be used defensively, to get out of trouble when, for instance, the player has missed a hoop with an opponent ball very close. Offensive use of a bisque occurs when the player has enough bisques to use one or even two to establish a break by bringing the balls in from the boundary, and then take· another to start the break he has established.

A half-bisque is an extra turn in which no hoop can be scored and its main use is therefore to set the balls up in a break position preparatory to taking a full bisque. Each player is handicapped according to his known form and record. The lowest handicap in the U.K. in 1973 was −5 and the highest 16. Half-bisques are not given in a player's handicap above the level of 7½.

An unusual feature of handicapping is that a player does not have the same number of bisques in every game, since he receives only the difference between the two handicaps, the better player being regarded as though he were in the position of a scratch player. Thus, the number of bisques a player receives (or gives) depends entirely on the handicap of his opponent. It will also be a matter of chance whether he is in receipt of a half-bisque. If his handicap is $5\frac{1}{2}$ he will not receive one if he is playing someone with a handicap of $3\frac{1}{2}$, but if his handicap is 6 he will receive $2\frac{1}{2}$ bisques against the same player. In doubles the odds are half the difference between the combined handicaps of each pair, fractions under a half being counted as a half and over a half being counted as a whole bisque.

Golf croquet is a simple game played with the same equipment as Association croquet but having little relation to it. It differs from it in one fundamental way, namely, that the croquet stroke is not used. Thus it is a version of Victorian croquet, and is played normally in the gardens of private houses.

Golf croquet should properly be played with four balls coloured blue, red, black, and yellow. Blue and black are partners against red and yellow, and in singles each player plays two balls. The game begins from the B baulk and after the first stroke the balls are always played in sequence: blue, red, black, yellow. Each turn consists of one stroke only, the object being to score the hoops in order. But all the balls are always for the same hoop so that as soon as a hoop is scored all the balls progress to the next hoop. The order of the hoops is the same as in croquet except that the peg is not played. If there is an equality of points after the rover hoop, the third hoop is contested to decide the game; otherwise the game ends as soon as one side has scored a majority of the points to be played. The player is not allowed to make his ball jump over another.

The Laws of Association Croquet, latest edition.

It is popularly supposed that croquet was played in Pall Mall (Pell-Mell, or Pale-maille) in the early sixteenth century. An account of about this time describes a game 'where-in a round box ball is struck with a mallet through a high arch which he that can do at the fewest blows or at the number agreed upon wins'. The precise form of the game is uncertain, but it is reasonable to assume that it had originated in France, because so many of the terms then used were French. The connection of *maille* and 'mallet' is certainly indicative, and it is thought that a form of the game was played on the sands of northern France with bent willow

boughs in which a ball was hit by something like a shepherd's crook and apparently called *croquet*. It is said that Louis XIV was fond of playing an open-air game which is the ancestor of modern croquet. It was called *le jeu de mail*, the ball being played with a mallet through successive hoops on the ground.

The development of croquet from these early beginnings is obscure until John Jaques, a manufacturer of sports goods, made the first sets and wrote a book on the game in about 1857. The game must have flourished considerably, for in 1867 Walter Jones-Whitmore organized the first championships at Evesham, Worcestershire. The setting consisted of nine hoops and two pegs and the court was approximately 66 ft. by 48 ft. (20·11 × 14·63 m.). The hoops were 8 in. wide (20·32 cm.) and the balls certainly not more than $3\frac{1}{4}$ in. (8·89 cm.) in diameter.

In 1870 the championships were transferred to the All-England Croquet and Lawn Tennis Club (as it then was) at Wimbledon, and in the same year a conference of croquet-players met to formulate and agree upon rules. The size of the court was increased to 50 yds. by 35 yds. (45·72 × 31·95 m.) and the width of the hoops reduced to 6 in. (15·24 cm.). In the following year this was further reduced to 4 in. (10·16 cm.) and the Hale setting of six hoops and two pegs was introduced and was to remain the standard setting for the next fifty years.

The Hale setting had made the best use of the space, which had been greatly reduced to the size in use today, by increasing the 'size' of the shots. The reduction in the number of hoops inaugurated the double circuit, and the strange 'cage', a crossed hoop with a bell hanging from it which had to be rung as the ball passed through, had been done away with.

From about 1882 croquet went into a decline, though it was still played at house-parties and provincial clubs, no doubt by those who regarded themselves as too old for the new sport of lawn tennis. In 1896 the Croquet Association was formed but its influence on the development of the game was not immediate. What did undoubtedly influence the game was the appearance of the great players from Ireland where croquet had unaccountably flourished. CORBALLY, O'CALLAGHAN, and MATHEWS brought such skill and enterprise to the game that they all but transformed it, and among other things introduced the 'Irish Grip'.

From its earliest days the essence of croquet lay in the fact that the balls were played in sequence; blue, red, black, yellow. The inevitable consequence was that each player, at the end of his turn, put out of the game the next ball to play. By 1914, however, the

194   CROQUET

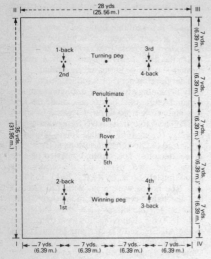

THE HALE SETTING (1871-1922)

ball game came the adoption of the 3⅜-inch (9·53 cm.) hoop — ⅛ in. (0·32 cm.) wider than the ball — still in use today. The greatest skill was now essential for it is vital to run a hoop through to a particular spot if control of the break is to be maintained. As a consequence, very few surprise results are to be seen in the prize-lists today.

Two more major innovations in the format of the game were still to come. In 1922 came the Willis setting, as used today. The turning peg was done away with and the winning peg moved to the centre of the court. This meant that the two centre hoops were placed further apart, thereby eliminating the easy 'ladies' mile' down the centre of the court. The accurate placing of the pioneer balls at the next hoop now became of paramount importance and is still, of course, the most obvious hallmark of the expert player.

In 1928 came the lift shot, introduced because the rise in the standard of play which had taken place after the turn of the century, despite, or perhaps because of, the extreme difficulty occasioned by the narrow hoops, had resulted in far too many one-sided games. At championship level the game was frequently won or lost on the initial toss, for the advantage which the lead at that time offered could result in an all-round break to the peg. If the player at the first hoop missed with his single long shot, as was often the case, his opponent had only to complete a simple break without the effort of even picking it up. The introduction of the rule by which a player, at the end of his opponent's first break, was able to lift either of his balls and play from the baulk line, reduced the length of shot from over 30 yds. (27·43 m.) to a maximum of 19 (17·37 m.), with an alternative, though slightly more risky, shot of only 13 yds. (11·89 m.). Moreover, the shot that he could now take was comparatively safe as it offered him the refuge of a friendly corner if he should miss.

The lift shot did much to redress the balance of the game and had the added attraction that it encouraged the art of the triple peel, since the first ball of either side to get going did not usually make the 4-back hoop for fear of being peeled out of the game. An extension to the lift principle was soon made with the addition of the contact law (see above). But since to give contact is in effect to give up the innings, it is a manoeuvre rarely employed nowadays.

Croquet has never been a spectator sport. It was, and to some extent still is, a sport of the privileged few, at any rate so far as the United Kingdom is concerned. As in Victorian times, it is played only at private clubs to which the public are not admitted, although the member-

establishment of the either-ball game, the most far-reaching innovation to be introduced, was virtually complete. The whole concept of the game was changed, for although the play of the break during a turn had remained the same, it had been the leave at the end of the turn which dictated the course of the game. In the sequence game a break could still be left for one's partner ball at the end of a turn, by leaving the 'dead' ball at one's partner's next hoop. The fact that the next ball to play was some 30 yds. (27·43 m.) away at the other end of the court made the continuation of one's innings a matter of some certainty. That the opponent could now play either of his balls meant that no easy break could be left for the next turn, for the opponent would remove the most useful ball to a safe position.

It was not long, however, before ingenious ways round this difficulty were devised. The most expert of these was for the first player to get in to go round to the peg, leaving the opponent 'cross-wired' at the first hoop and his own two balls in the IIIrd corner. With one of these tucked up close behind the third hoop, the opponent had a shot at only one ball at a range of about 30 yds. If this shot was not hit the game was virtually over, for a ball was still waiting at the first hoop to start the next break going. About the turn of the century, the principle of the 'open' shot had been introduced; before that it had been permissible to leave the opponent no ball to shoot at at all.

Together with the introduction of the either-

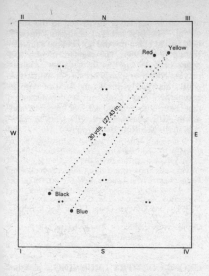 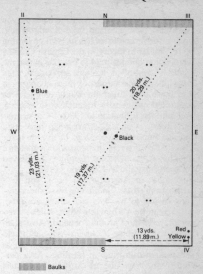

THE LIFT
(*Left*) The leave before the introduction of the lift; (*right*) the leave after the lift was introduced.

ship is now much more heterogeneous. But in recent years it has shown a marked increase in popularity in the sports facilities offered by commercial firms to their employees.

Another encouraging sign has been the sudden influx of young players into a game normally thought of as being exclusively for older people. In this the universities, notably Cambridge, have played a major part. Although there were in the past occasional instances of young people taking up the game (G. F. Stone was severely frowned on when he appeared at a tournament with a bucket and spade at the age of twelve, before the First World War), they did not play a permanent role until 1948, when SOLOMON was first in a train of teenagers which has grown till they now all but dominate the championship class.

Miss STEEL, undoubtedly the greatest woman player of all time, with fifteen wins in the women's championship (eight of them in succession) and four in the open championship, proved that equality of play between the sexes is possible.

Solomon by 1970 had won the open championship ten times and represented England in every international match held over a period of twenty years. But the domination of croquet since the last war by the triumvirate of HICKS, COTTER, and Solomon was partially shattered when, in 1965, Bolton won the President's Cup at the age of 18. There is the likelihood

that a new generation of young people, particularly Aspinall and Wylie, will at least equal and probably take over, the position of the older generation.

The Croquet Association, whose president since 1967 has been RECKITT, great chronicler of the sport, is the body which administers croquet in the United Kingdom. From its headquarters at the Hurlingham Club, it organizes the principal championship events, the more important of which are the open championships, both singles and doubles, the men's, women's, and mixed doubles championships, and four invitation events the chief of which is the President's Cup. These are staged not only at the Hurlingham Club but also at provincial clubs throughout the country. In 1967 came the introduction of the Stoker Bowl for the championship of champions, in which the winner of the President's Cup challenged the winner of the open championship for the right to play the holder. This was withdrawn after Solomon had won it four times in succession.

In addition to these official events the main clubs have annual tournaments which attract the principal players and provide a constant opportunity for competitive play. Croquet is essentially an individual sport and team and inter-club competitions are almost nonexistent in the United Kingdom.

Outside the United Kingdom, Association

croquet is played on an organized basis only in Australia, New Zealand, and South Africa. Each of these countries has its own governing body, similar in theory to the English Croquet Association but different in practice in that the game is controlled through individual state associations. The largest of these countries in membership is Australia where croquet was controlled exclusively by each state association until the formation in 1950 of the Australian Croquet Council, since when inter-state and dominion championships have been held. The first of a series of international matches for the MACROBERTSON trophy was played between Australia and England in 1925.

Croquet in Australia has been, and to a large extent still is, dominated by women, perhaps owing to the fact that clubs are often adjuncts to men's bowling clubs. Miss Morrison played a most prominent part in Australian croquet, first in the Victorian Association and later in the Australian Croquet Council, which she was instrumental in forming. As a performer she was one of Australia's greatest players, winning her first championship in 1916-17 and her seventh title in that event in 1957-8. She played in the MacRobertson trophy in 1935 and 1937. Many of the top Australian honours, both in state and dominion championships, have gone to men. Howat, who won his first open title in 1955 and his ninth in 1967, is a natural player, though not a stylish one, and has done much tuition during his travels in Australia.

In New Zealand croquet became a fully organized sport as early as 1920 when the New Zealand Croquet Council was formed, although the first dominion championships were held in Christchurch in 1913. The Council controls the sport through twenty district associations and competition is based much more on inter-club contests than on individual events. As in Australia there is a strict division of players into A, B, and C grades according to handicap, which offers little or no opportunity for weaker players to gain experience against more expert ones.

New Zealand's greatest player is ROSS who has had an enormous influence on the game over a period of fifty years. As in the United Kingdom the younger generation is beginning to make its presence felt, a process which began in 1945 with Heenan who, with only limited time available, won five opens and four men's titles. Prince entered the scene at the age of 16 when he was called into the New Zealand team against England in 1963. In 1969 he captained New Zealand and has won four open and eight men's titles.

Croquet was probably established in South Africa before either Australia or New Zealand and yet it has never flourished to the same extent. The first national championship was held in 1911, but this did not become a regular feature until 1935. The standard of play has never been as high as in the other croquet-playing countries, partly because of indifferent courts and partly due to the lack of regular competitive play. Clubs are at such distances that inter-club events are not possible and South Africa has not entered a team to compete in the MacRobertson trophy.

D. Miller and J. Thorpe, *Croquet and How to Play It* (1966); M. B. Reckitt, *Croquet Today* (1956); J. W. Solomon, *Croquet* (1966).

GOVERNING BODY (U.K.): The Croquet Association, Hurlingham Club, London S.W.6.; (AUSTRALIA): The Australian Croquet Council, 16 Maldon Street, Footscray, Victoria, N.S.W.; (NEW ZEALAND): The New Zealand Croquet Council, 43a Argyle Street, Hawera, N.Z.; (SOUTH AFRICA): The South African Croquet Association, 4 The Olivers, 148 Pietermaritz Street, Pietermaritzburg, Natal.

CROSS-COUNTRY RUNNING, as the name implies, is foot racing over country terrain including natural obstacles, though on the Continent races are often held on formal racecourses with man-made hurdles.

Cross-country running was first organized in 1867 by members of the THAMES ROWING CLUB at Putney, London, as a means of keeping fit before the ROWING season began. The sport's origins can also be traced to the early-nineteenth-century sports of HARE AND HOUNDS and PAPER-CHASING. The English championship was first decided in 1877 and is now organized by the English Cross-Country Union (founded 1883). It is contested annually by as many as 1,000 runners competing for club and individual honours. The first international race was held between France and England in 1898. The international championship, which is recognized by the International Amateur Athletic Federation (see ATHLETICS, TRACK AND FIELD), was first run in 1903, the year in which the International Cross-Country Union was founded. Again team and individual titles are at issue, and teams from Europe, the Americas, and the Commonwealth are entered. Championship races are usually decided over seven-mile or nine-mile courses, the continental distances being somewhat shorter.

Cross-country is a popular sport not only with runners who specialize in it but also among middle-distance and long-distance track runners who find it a useful form of winter conditioning. Cross-country for women is a well-established, though less popular, sport, with both national and international races held annually at distances of two or three miles. Cross-country events were omitted from the athletics programme in the OLYMPIC GAMES after 1924, but a cross-country race is included in the Olympic modern PENTATHLON schedule.

CROWN GREEN BOWLS, see BOWLS, LAWN: CROWN GREEN.

CRUYFF, JOHAN (1974-   ), Association footballer for AJAX of Amsterdam, BARCELONA, and the Netherlands. One of the most talented and exciting of European centre forwards, he first played for Ajax in the Netherlands league in 1965 at the age of 19 and had established himself among the leading goalscorers in Dutch football, when he moved to Barcelona in 1973. He was to captain the Dutch side which reached the final of the 1974 World Cup.

CRYSTAL PALACE CIRCUIT, difficult MOTOR RACING road circuit in the centre of the London suburb at Sydenham. Opened in 1937, when the lap distance was 2 miles (3·2 km.), it was re-opened in 1953, and in postwar form the length was 1·39 miles (2·2 km.). The circuit has since been closed for motor racing.

CÚCHARES (Francisco Arjona) (1818-68), *matador de toros*, held in such high esteem that *toreo* to this day is referred to as 'the art of Cúchares'. He took his *alternativa* in 1840, and died of yellow fever in Cuba. He was a pupil of ROMERO and CANDIDO in Seville.

CUDGEL-PLAYING, see QUARTER-STAFF.

CULCHETH, BRIAN (1938-   ), British motor rally driver (see MOTOR RACING) for British Leyland. He finished second, with Syer, in the 1970 World Cup Rally.

CULLIS, STANLEY (1917-   ), Association footballer for WOLVERHAMPTON WANDERERS, and England for whom he made 12 appearances in full international matches, including one in March 1938 against the Rest of Europe, and 20 appearances in wartime international matches. He first captained Wolverhampton Wanderers in 1936-7, playing at centre half, when only 19 years old. He made his début for England against Ireland in October 1937 and played what, because of the outbreak of war, proved to be his last full international, against Romania in Bucharest in May 1939. He was manager of Wolverhampton Wanderers from 1949 to 1963, and of Birmingham City from 1965 to 1970.

CUMBERLAND CUP, see SQUASH RACKETS.

CUMBERLAND AND WESTMORLAND, see WRESTLING.

CUMMING, ERIC (1922-64), Australian professional athlete, one of the finest Commonwealth sprinters in history, amateur or professional. He won the POWDERHALL Sprint of 1952, from a 2-yard handicap, covering the snow-bound 130-yard (118·9 m.) course, against the wind, in 12·2 sec. The previous year he was judged to have run a Powderhall heat fractionally faster than that, but lost the final. The Eric Cumming Memorial Sprint, over 90 metres (98·5 yds.), is now held every year at the Edinburgh New Year Footracing Gala (the 'Powderhall' meeting).

CUNNINGHAM, WILLIAM (1943-   ), American BASKETBALL player. He graduated in 1965 from the University of North Carolina, turned professional, and joined the PHILADELPHIA 76ERS, in the NATIONAL BASKETBALL ASSOCIATION.

CURLING is a game akin to BOWLS played on ice, usually by two teams of four players (a match played by any large gathering is a 'bonspiel'), each player using two curling stones and playing them, at the direction of his 'skip' (captain), alternately with his opposite number. A curler throws the stones over 40 yds. (36·58 m.) to circles (the 'house') cut on the ice and often coloured.

The ice on which curlers play is called the rink (also the name for a team of four players). At either end are cut circles having a radius of 6 ft. (1·83 m.), whose centres (or tees) are 38 yds. (34·75 m.) apart. Inner circles may also be drawn at 2 ft. (60·96 cm.) intervals. In alignment with each tee, a centre line may be drawn to a point 4 yds. (3·66 m.) behind the tee. Four scores are drawn across the rink at right angles to the centre line: (*a*) the tee; (*d*) the hog score, one-sixth of the distance between the foot score and the farther tee.

The object of the game is to place more stones nearer the tee (called the 'button' in Canada and the U.S.A.) than the opponents. (A stone which does not pass the hog score, or 'hog', is removed from the ice; similarly, a stone which passes the back score is removed.) All games are decided by a majority of shots. A team (or rink) scores one shot for every stone which is nearer the tee than any stone of the opposing rink. All measurements are taken from the tee to the nearest part of the

CURLING RINK
Inner circles and centre lines, shown in fine line, are optional.

stone. Every stone which is not clearly outside the outer circle is eligible to count.

The first player in a team is called the 'lead' and the rotation of play and the system of scoring is the same as for lawn bowls. ('Points' is a version played by individual curlers with a series of different shots.) An end (or 'head') is completed when the eight players have played their sixteen stones and the players then play the next end on the same sheet of ice in the opposite direction. A game is played by time or a fixed number of ends.

The average weight of a curling stone is 40 lb. (18·1 kg.). The handle, fitted by a bolt through a hole in the centre of the stone, adds a further 1½ lb. (0·7 kg.) so that the total weight thrown by a curler is 41½ lb. (18·8 kg.).

Under the ROYAL CALEDONIAN CURLING CLUB rules, all curling stones are of a circular shape. No stone, including bolt and handle, may be of greater weight than 44 lb. (19·9 kg.), or of greater circumference than 36 in. (91·4 cm.), or of less height than one-eighth part of its greatest circumference.

Curling stones, which traditionally come from Scotland, are known as 'granites'. The stones are fine-grained to provide a strong interlocking quality and have a low water absorbency and a consistent hardness to give even wear. With normal use, good stones will last the lifetime of a curler; when in constant use in matched sets of stones on indoor ice rinks, they will last for perhaps ten years —five years' running on each side.

Stone-making is a highly specialized art. Round blocks, weighing roughly 100 lb. (45·36 kg.), are rough-hewn and matched in colour and texture. Each stone is reduced to a size 12 lb. (5·4 kg.) heavier than the final weight, a hole is bored in the centre, and the stone is reduced again to within 2 lb. (0·9 kg.) of the final weight. The stone is ground and a concave cup and circular rim are formed, a precise process since the stone runs on the rim. The stone is then polished, the running rim is finished, and the striking band (which will receive a pounding from other stones) added. Finally, the hole in the centre is countersunk square to take the iron bolt which holds the handle.

A curler chooses his curling boots (or shoes) with special care. The choice is a personal one and is dependent on the method adopted by the player to deliver his curling stones. Certain types of rubber sole will grip on sticky ice and the curler will stumble awkwardly instead of sliding smoothly forward on the left foot as he delivers his stone. Most players experiment with various types of sole until they find the one best suited to their needs. Many curlers prefer a sliding sole on the left foot and a sole with more grip on the right foot. Some prefer soles which provide for a short slide as they throw their stones. Others, including younger curlers who use the long-sliding delivery, wear soles which give the maximum slide. Some carry a slip-on sole and fit it on the left foot when about to play.

Each curler carries a brush, or broom. The broom (or besom) has a long and varied history. The earliest was a cutting from the osier tree, the slender, pliant branches of which were ideal for sweeping snow and other impediments from the path of a curling stone. Twigs of broom bound together were later used. These old-time implements were called 'kowes' or 'cowes'. Today, two main types of broom are used, the brush in Europe and the corn broom in Canada and the U.S.A. The best brush is made of horsehair but many other materials are used. The skip holds his broom in a vertical position in the circles to direct his player, who throws his stone towards the broom.

An iron sheet on which a player stands to throw a curling stone is called the 'crampit'. It is 3 or 4 ft. (91·4 or 121·9 cm.) long by about 12 in. (30·5 cm.) wide and has spikes on the underside to grip the ice. (The earliest known footwear for curling, also called a crampit, or 'cramp', or 'tramp', was a pronged iron sole attached by straps to the boot.) In use for more than a century, the crampit is now almost a thing of the past, although still seen on outdoor ice. The 'hack' is now in universal use as a foothold for curlers. As the name implies, a hack was originally a hole cut in outdoor ice as a foothold from which the curler could throw his stone. The most efficient modern hack is the type used in Canada and the U.S.A. — a hole cut in the ice and lined with serrated rubber to prevent slipping. This type is not used on Scottish ice rinks because the ice is also used for skating and it is not practical to fill in the holes prior to skating and cut new holes before the next curling session. In Scotland and elsewhere, a raised hack, with prongs which fit small holes bored in the ice, is used.

To throw his stone, a curler places his right foot on the hack (positioned on the foot score) for purchase and adopts a sitting position, with his left foot comfortably on the ice and slightly ahead of him. He grips the handle of the stone in his right hand and holds his broom in the left. With his eye firmly fixed on the skip's broom at the other end of the ice, the curler lines up his shot and, with an under-arm pendulum action, draws the stone back, lifts it off the ice, and brings it forward to release it with a follow-through directed at the skip's broom. During the backward swing, the curler raises his body to place all his weight on the right foot, possibly swinging the left leg to the left to counter the weight of the stone on the right side.

The curler twists the handle of his stone when delivering it. This imparts 'draw' to the stone which makes it run with a controlled swing to the left or right. A stone delivered smoothly and squarely on to the ice is said to be 'well soled': the rocking movement of a stone not properly soled is a 'kiggle-caggle'.

The other two players in the team run alongside the moving stone and wait for the skip's call to sweep. The player's side may sweep the ice from the nearest hog score to the sweeping score, except when snow is falling or drifting, when the limits are sweeping score to sweeping score. Efficient sweeping in front of a running stone can make the stone travel 12 ft. (3·66 m.) further than an unswept stone. In addition, sweeping reduces the amount of draw so that sweepers can bring a stone past a guard (a stone placed in front of another). Sweeping removes dust and impurities from the path of a stone, reduces the atmospheric pressure (thus drawing the stone on), and causes a temporary melting of the ice, lowering the friction at the leading side of the stone.

A stone aimed at the broom but thrown inside it is termed 'narrow' (or 'thin' or 'tight'), outside it is 'wide'. A fast shot aimed to hit another stone is a 'strike'; the movement of one stone hitting another and rebounding at an angle is a 'wick' and a stone struck forward is said to be 'raised' or 'promoted'. A stone is 'burned' when touched by mistake, and one

which finishes within the circles without touching another stone is called a 'draw'. To come as close as possible to another stone is to 'freeze' (the old Scottish expression being to 'crack an egg'), the space between the two is the 'port'. A stone lying on the tee is called a 'pot-lid'.

The sliding delivery, a modern method of throwing a curling stone, was introduced by Canadians in the last thirty years and has now been widely adopted, particularly by young curlers. This delivery starts in the same way as the conventional delivery but, as the stone is swung forward, the player thrusts strongly from the hack and slides far out on the ice with a slippery sole on his left shoe.

A curler must complete his delivery and stop before he has reached the nearest hog score. This is one of the basic curling rules which, by tradition, are short and simple. There are only 18 playing rules and umpires are seldom asked to act except when measuring the distance of stones from the tee at the conclusion of an end. Curlers themselves are expected to interpret the rules sportingly and to observe the courtesies of the game.

The origins of curling, 'Scotland's ain game', are unknown and there is still doubt whether the game started in Scotland or the Low Countries. The case for Holland rests on paintings by Breughel, two of whose landscapes show a game similar to curling being played on frozen ponds. Scotland's claim is supported by references in early literature and by many examples of old curling stones which, over hundreds of years, have been unearthed in digging and salvaged from lochs throughout the country. The fact that no such finds have been made in Holland would seem to indicate that Breughel's game on ice was played with frozen clods of earth which disintegrated when the thaw came. Scottish curlers claim that curling is played with curling stones and that a game without stones cannot reasonably be called curling. It is certain that Scotland takes credit for nurturing curling through lean periods in its early history and for providing the impetus which has made modern curling a highly-organized game in fifteen countries.

'The Muses Threnodie' by Henry Adamson (1638) contains what is believed to be the first written reference to curling. When his friend, James Gall, died of consumption in Perth, Adamson wrote an 'In Memoriam' in verse which included the line, 'his allay bowles and curling-stones'. Ministers of the Scottish kirk have contributed the major portion of curling literature. The earliest curling book, *An Account of the Game of Curling*, was written by the Revd. John Ramsay, a member of the famous Duddingston Curling Society, in 1811. The Revd. James Taylor's *Curling, The Ancient Scottish Game* was published in 1884, and the classic book on the history and growth of the game is the Revd. John Kerr's *History of Curling* (1890).

Sir Walter Scott wrote of curling in *Guy Mannering* and three of Scotland's best-known poets, Robert Burns, Allan Ramsay, and James Hogg (the Ettrick Shepherd) are represented in curling libraries. 'Tam Samson's Elegy' (1786) by Burns contains the most famous curling verses:

When winter muffles up his cloak,
And binds the mire like a rock;
When to the loughs the curlers flock
　Wi' gleesome speed,
Wha will they station at the cock?
　Tam Samson's dead!

He was the king o' a' the core,
To guard, or draw, or wick a bore,
Or up the rink like Jehu roar
　In time o' need;
But now he lags on Death's 'hog-score',
　Tam Samson's dead!

In the middle of the nineteenth century, Sir George Harvey, president of the Royal Scottish Academy, painted an animated curling scene, 'The Curlers', etchings and variations of which decorate the walls of ice rinks and the homes of curlers throughout the world. 'Grand Match at Linlithgow Loch' (1848) by Charles Lees, R.S.A., is another famous curling painting. Owned by the Royal Caledonian Curling Club, it hangs in the Central Scotland Ice Rink in Perth.

The earliest relic of the game is the 'Stirling Stone'. This, with the date 1511 etched on it, lies in the Smith Institute in Stirling. It is a 26-pound (11·79 kg.) kuting (or quoiting) stone, the first type used for curling, and has rough finger-holds so that the stone could be thrown along the ice with a quoiting action. These early stones are also called 'channel stanes' (because they were taken from the channels of rivers and were thus worn smooth) and 'loofies' — a reference to the shape of the stone which resembled a *loof* (the old Scots word for the palm of a hand).

The Minute Books of old Scottish curling clubs contain many references to the social and political history of Scotland and a wealth of country humour and earthy anecdotes about the parish bonspiels (challenge matches between neighbouring villages and districts) which were the forerunners of modern competitions and international matches.

The earliest stones, with notches for fingers and thumb, were superseded in the early part of the seventeenth century by stones with handles, and curling stones were then delivered as they are now, by swinging the arm straight back and forward in an under-arm motion before throwing (not pushing) the stone along the ice. The rough handles, made of iron, wood, or thorn, were often inserted by the local blacksmith. This revolutionary step introduced the strong-arm era in curling, when bigger and ever bigger stones of all shapes and sizes were hurled down the ice to scatter opposition stones. Another advantage of a big stone was that, once in position, it was not easily dislodged. Examples of these massive blocks still exist, many of them weighing more than 100 lb. (45·36 kg.) and it is clear that only men of remarkable strength could have wielded them. The biggest curling stone known, the 'Jubilee Stone' weighing 117 lb. (53·07 kg.), is on display in Perth, with other Royal Caledonian Curling Club relics, in the Central Scotland Ice Rink.

Towards the end of the eighteenth century, curling progressed from these trials of strength to become a game of skill and finesse. Curlers noticed that stones more spherical than others gave a more consistent performance. This led to the rounding of the stone, a simple development which transformed every aspect of play. Rounded stones not only ran consistently but rebounded from other stones at angles which could be predetermined, like cannons in billiards. At the same time, curlers discovered that by turning the handle of a rounded stone to apply 'in-hand' or 'out-hand' motions they could control the run of the stone, like using the bias in bowls. The game became a test of skill and accuracy, requiring brain not brawn. The chaos of old-time curling was replaced by order and uniformity, and, with a premium on accuracy, new tactical moves were evolved to exploit the finer points of the game.

As the new order gained momentum, challenge games between Scottish provinces became widespread and variations of rules in different districts caused violent controversies on such basic issues as the size of stones and the composition of rinks. The need for co-ordinated planning and national regulations became urgent and this led to the formation of the Royal Caledonian Curling Club in 1838. The Club based its rules on the first set of curling rules, framed by the most influential of the old curling clubs, the Duddingston Curling Society (founded in Edinburgh in 1795), and quickly became established as the 'mother club' of the game in the world.

John Cairnie of Curling Hall, Largs, the driving force behind the formation of the Royal Club, and its first president, was famous for many curling innovations. Cairnie built the first artificial pond at Curling Hall, invented the foot-iron (crampit), and was the author of *Essay on Curling and Artificial Pond-Making* (1833).

The Royal Club's *Annual* is now circulated to all British clubs and all curling countries. The international function of the Royal Club has been enhanced by the introduction and encouragement of international exchange tours, the first tour, by Scots to Canada in 1902, being followed by visits to and from many countries. The growth of overseas curling tours is one of the principal features of the modern game.

The Royal Club also initiated meetings which led to the founding of the International Curling Federation in 1966. The Club called a meeting of 'Administrators and Personalities' from overseas associations in Perth, Scotland, in 1965. The chairman was Maj. Cameron of Allangrange, then president of the Royal Club, who became the Federation's first president. Representatives from Scotland, Canada, the U.S.A., Switzerland, Sweden, Norway, France, Germany, Italy, Denmark, and England now attend Federation meetings annually to discuss international affairs and world rules.

When indoor ice rinks were built, in the early years of this century, well-prepared sheets of ice raised the quality of play to a level undreamed of in the era of outdoor curling, when players had to contend with rough and heavily biased ice and a surface which constantly changed with variations of weather. Today, outdoor curling is still played in Scotland, and elsewhere, when hard frost provides suitable ice. Six inches of black ice are required for the Royal Club's 'Grand Match' between the north and south of Scotland, when 2,500 curlers congregate on a big Scottish loch for this, one of Scotland's most spectacular sporting occasions. But all major competitions are now played indoors. National championships are held in almost every curling country, in addition to a wide variety of other events.

The old Scottish adage, 'what we have we hold', has not been observed in curling, for Scots have exported their national game to many parts of the world. Canada, where the game was introduced by Scottish fur traders and soldiers after the siege of Quebec, is now easily the strongest curling country, with well over half-a-million curlers. The Royal Montreal Curling Club, the first curling club in Canada and the first sporting club of any kind in the North American continent, was founded by Scots in 1807. The Canadian championship for the Macdonald Brier Tankard was launched in 1927 and is the world's biggest and most competitive curling event.

Eight Scottish curlers formed the first curling club in the U.S.A., the Orchard Lake Club in Michigan, in 1832. The Grand National Curling Club of America was established in 1867. The first United States national championship was held in the Chicago Stadium in 1957 and the United States Men's Curling Association was founded in 1958.

Scots introduced curling in St. Moritz 90 years ago and thousands of curling visitors throng the Swiss mountain resorts each year. The installation of artificial ice in the Alpine areas and the building of large indoor ice rinks in the lowland cities have contributed further to the growth of the game in Switzerland.

A Scot, William Andrew Macfie, launched curling in Sweden in 1846 — at Uddevalla on the west coast — but the game did not become widespread until the early years of this century. The Swedish Curling Association was founded in 1916. The top competition in Sweden is the Swedish Cup, an international event which is staged every second year.

The first record of curling in Norway is contained in minutes of the Scottish club, Evenie Water, which had a happy association with the Elverhae Club, the members of each being honorary members of the other, in 1880. Tours by Scots in the last twenty years inspired the growth of modern curling in Norway and the first indoor ice rink, at Asker near Oslo, has further stimulated expansion.

About 100 years ago, Scots took curling to New Zealand, where the game is played exclusively by men on frozen dams in the mountainous country of central Otago, from Ranfurly west to Alexandra. There are 27 New Zealand clubs, the two main curling centres being Naseby and Oturehua.

The WINTER OLYMPIC GAMES at Chamonix in 1924, the only time curling has been included as an Olympic gold medal sport, focused the interest of curlers in France. The French championship, started soon after, has been held ever since. Most of the growing number of French clubs are in the Haute Savoie area but curling has been introduced in a number of the main cities, including Paris.

The Olympic Ice Stadium at Cortina d'Ampezzo in the Dolomites is the focal point of Italian curling. An annual international summer bonspiel at Cortina is the country's principal curling attraction. Kitzbühel in the Tyrol is the principal centre of curling in Austria. The success of the Kitzbühel Curling Club, founded in 1955, prompted the Tourist Board to build an artificial rink in the town. Other Tyrolean resorts have introduced curling in their winter sports programmes. A curling competition at Garmisch-Partenkirchen in 1961 launched modern curling in Germany. Garmisch, with its Olympic Stadium, is one of several main curling venues in Germany. The

German Curling Association was instituted in 1966.

An enthusiastic curler, Mme Francis, returned from a curling trip to Switzerland in 1964 to inspire the formation of the Curling Club Liège, the first curling club in Belgium.

Curling was launched in Holland with the formation of the Amsterdam Curling Club in 1961. The cost of building an indoor rink has limited the growth of the game but the Dutch members maintain curling interest by making annual visits to Switzerland, Scotland, Denmark, and elsewhere.

A gift of curling stones from Scotland led to the foundation of the Copenhagen Curling Club in 1966. This first curling club in Denmark quickly gained in stature and, in 1968, held an international bonspiel (for the Mermaid Cup) which attracted entries from Sweden, Norway, Switzerland, and Scotland.

England has only two curling centres—the Richmond Ice Rink at East Twickenham, London, and the Blackpool Ice Drome, which serves the small but enthusiastic group of curlers in the First English Province of the Royal Caledonian Curling Club.

An international gathering of curlers meets annually during the week of the World Curling Championship, a tournament which began in 1959 when the Scotch Whisky Association launched the Scotch Whisky Cup, an international competition between the champion rinks of Scotland and Canada. In 1968, the Scotch Whisky Association withdrew, and, in cooperation with the Royal Caledonian Curling Club, Air Canada assumed sponsorship of the world championship and presented the Silver Broom trophy which is now played for annually in different parts of the world. The champion rinks of ten countries now compete in the world championship. Canada has dominated world championship play. In the first fifteen years of the event, the Canadian stranglehold has been broken on only three occasions, by the U.S.A. in 1965, by Scotland in 1967, and by Sweden in 1973.

A principal feature of world curling since the Second World War has been the spectacular growth of ladies' and junior clubs. Ladies' competitions and tours are now firmly established on the curling calendar and the accent on youth grows stronger each year.

Standard curling stones, equal in weight and performance, and the high quality of ice-making and equipment in up-to-date ice rinks make modern curling a game of delicate skill and precision. But, despite the advances in technique and performance, curling is still called 'a slippery game', because of the swings of fortune caused by lucky 'rubs' and rolls; and curlers everywhere enjoy the fellowship of the game and are united in the 'brotherhood of the rink'.

The Revd. John Kerr, *History of Curling* (1890); Robin Welsh, *Beginner's Guide to Curling* (1969).
GOVERNING BODIES: International Curling Federation, c/o Royal Caledonian Curling Club, Edinburgh, Scotland; Royal Caledonian Curling Club, Edinburgh, Scotland.

CURRAGH, The, a race-course near Dublin where most of the important horse races in Ireland are run, including the IRISH SWEEPS DERBY and IRISH GUINNESS OAKS, Irish St. Leger, Two Thousand Guineas, and One Thousand Guineas. Races run there for older horses are the Gladness, Ballymoss, Desmond, and Blandford Stakes, while the principal two-year-old races are the Railway, Anglesey, National, and Beresford Stakes.

CURRIE CUP (1), CRICKET trophy of South Africa. Presented by Sir Donald Currie, a ship-owner and philanthropist, for competition between the South African provinces, it was first won by Transvaal, in 1889-90, the season of the tournament's introduction. The competition, which is divided into 'A' and 'B' sections—with the lowest team in 'A' relegated to 'B' and the winner of 'B' promoted to 'A' each season—has been intermittent, and until the late 1960s it was never held when an overseas Test team was visiting South Africa. Transvaal were the most frequent winners of the Cup before the Second World War, since when Natal have been dominant. Since 1972 the tournament has been sponsored by a brewing company.

(2) Trophy awarded to the province winning the inter-provincial RUGBY UNION competition in South Africa. This gold cup was originally presented by Sir Donald Currie, of the Castle Shipping Line, to Maclaglan, captain of the 1891 British team, the first touring side to visit South Africa. The presentation was made in Southampton before the tourists set sail, and the idea was that the cup should be given to the South African team who put up the best opposition to the British side. The cup was duly given to the Griqualand West Rugby Union, but they in turn handed it over to the South African Rugby Football Board in 1892 as a trophy for inter-provincial competition.

CURTIS CUP, GOLF tournament played in alternate years between teams of women amateur golfers representing Great Britain and Ireland and the U.S.A.

CURZON CUP, one of the two classics of the Cresta run skeleton-TOBOGGANING season at

St. Moritz, Switzerland. The cup was given by the Hon. F. N. Curzon in 1910, replacing the Ashbourne Cup which was won outright by Thoma-Badrutt in 1909. The cup goes to the rider with the best aggregate of six runs from Junction, the shortened course with which the Cresta season begins.

CUTHBERT, BETTY (1938-   ), sprinter for Australia. Winner in 1956, at 18, of three Olympic gold medals, for the 100 metres, 200 metres, and 4 × 100 metres relay. Betty Cuthbert had a long period of limited success before she emerged again as an Olympic gold medallist in 1964, this time over 400 metres in 52·0 sec. She held 16 world records between 1956 and 1963 at distances from 60 metres to 440 yards. Her best times for 100 and 220 yards were 10·4 and 23·2 sec. respectively.

CYCLE BALL, an amateur CYCLING ball-game derived from Association FOOTBALL in which the ball is trapped, driven forward, and shot at goal by the rider manipulating the front wheel of his bicycle. It is played indoors between teams of two riders, and as a field game between teams of six. World championships are held annually, those in 1970 being contested by representatives of Czechoslovakia, East and West Germany, Austria, Switzerland, Belgium, and France.

GOVERNING BODY: Commission Internationale de Cyclisme en Salle (a subsidiary of the Fédération Internationale Amateur de Cyclisme), Viale Tiziano, 70 Rome, Italy.

CYCLING is both a sport and a non-competitive pastime. As the sport of riding a cycle in various tests of speed, skill, and endurance, it is practised in all European countries, Australia, New Zealand, Japan, and the West Indies, and to a lesser extent in North Africa, South Africa, and the Americas. As a recreation, pursued for exercise and exploration, it is almost universal.

The cycle used for sport (in most cases a single bicycle, though occasionally a tandem or tricycle) is defined more by common usage than by a set of official regulations. Organizers may impose restrictions on gearing, the use of fixed rear wheels, etc., but riders are generally free to assemble their machines from such components as are commercially available or which they choose to have built. This process of natural selection has led, in fact, to a broad uniformity of cycle design within any one section of the sport, though there are variations in mechanical detail, styling, and materials.

The racing bicycle used on the road weighs 22 to 24 lb. (10–10·9 kg.), which is as light as is presently consistent with the need for strength, variable gearing, and other mechanical features. Lightness is achieved by the use of alloys; by paring down and drilling components; by drawing the spokes to narrow their gauge in the centre, and reducing their number to 24 to 28, against the usual average of 36; and by using a narrow plastic saddle, tape binding on the handlebars in place of solid grips, and tubular tyres weighing only 6 to 9 oz. (170–255 g.) each. No inessential features such as mudguards, bells, or lamps are carried.

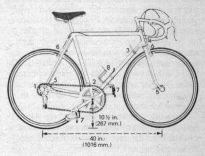

ROAD RACE BICYCLE
(1) Sprocket block; (2) double chain-wheel; (3) and (4) gear levers; (5) quick-release lever; (6) caliper brakes; (7) toe-clip; (8) carrier.

Most models are fitted with *derailleur* gears, a mechanism by which the chain can be transferred between up to six different sprockets assembled in a 'block' on the back hub. Twice this number of gear ratios can be achieved by combining the *derailleur* with a double chain-wheel, one wheel having fewer teeth than the other. The *derailleur* and the chain-wheel changes are operated by levers attached either to the down tube or the end of the handlebars.

The tubular tyres are cylindrical in cross-section, with the inner tube encased in a covering which is sewn together at the base. Since there is no wire stiffening to hold the tyre in place, it is stuck to the rim with adhesive. The thin tread reduces weight and friction, but, as tubulars are sometimes more liable to puncture, hubs are fitted with quick-release levers to facilitate wheel changes.

Cable-operated caliper brakes are always used. The pedal has a metal rather than a rubber tread, the rider's foot being held by a toe-clip and strap, and by a metal plate in the sole of the shoe which slots into the tread. On the down tube is a wire carrier; this takes the water bottle (usually known by its French name, *bidon*).

Although accessories tend to be standard

manufacturers' products, nearly every serious rider has his cycle frame specially built to suit the length of his legs and arms and his riding posture. The wheelbase is frequently shorter than in cycles for everyday use, perhaps 40 in. (1016 mm.) compared with the normal 42 in. (1067 mm.). The standard height to the bottom bracket is 10½ in. (267 mm.).

The track bicycle used for sprinting weighs only 18 to 20 lb. (8·17–9·07 kg.) over-all, despite the fact that the frame is more sturdily built, and the rear stays and the fork crown are more heavily constructed to prevent 'whip' and to give the rider more control. For similar reasons, the heavier road rim is used with 28 to 36 spokes, and the wheel is built with a larger flange, since there is no need for the small road flange which 'floats' in the middle of the wheel and cushions the effect of bumpy surfaces. For rigidity, too, the wheelbase tends to be fractionally shortened to 39 to 40 in. (990–1016 mm.).

The saving in weight and wind resistance is achieved by dispensing with any variable gear mechanism (the rear wheel is fixed), quick-release hubs, and even brakes. Lighter silk-covered or, on wooden tracks, cotton-covered tubular tyres are normally fitted, weighing as little as 4 oz. (113 g.).

A downward-sloping Sacchi stem is often used to give the rider a lower crouching position. And the bottom bracket height is raised to 11 in. (279 mm.) for greater clearance, enabling the rider to stand still on the banking with less risk of his right pedal touching the track.

The tandem used in sprinting is, in effect, a version of the track bicycle, elongated, strengthened, and equipped for two riders. Frame design varies widely, but it is basically a 'double diamond' with an extra bar running diagonally through it to prevent whip. It has stronger seat stays, heavier, plain-gauge

TRACK BICYCLE
(1) Rear stays; (2) fork crown; (3) flange; (4) Sacchi stem.

spokes, and a second handlebar fixed rigidly to the front seat-pillar. Components are of steel.

There are alternative types of transmission. In one, the drive is from a front chain-wheel on the left to a rear chain-wheel on the left, and through the bottom bracket-spindle to a rear chain-wheel on the right which transmits the hub. In the other, the chain-wheels are in line on the right.

Cycling is a highly fragmented sport. For the most part it can be divided into road and track events, but these exist in great variety, and outside either category are the games of BICYCLE POLO and CYCLE BALL, the cross-country sport of CYCLO-CROSS, and the simulated racing of cycle-roller contests (see below).

ROAD EVENTS. Here 'road' means any surface, other than that of a specially constructed cycle track, which is suitable for vehicles. It may be streets and highways, a motor-racing circuit, or a course marked out on an aerodrome or seaside promenade. It may be open or closed to other traffic.

Road racing. There are no standard distances in this sport. A road race may cover anything from 20 miles (32 km.) to more than 3,000 miles (4,828 km.), and last under an hour or, broken into daily stages, several weeks. At whatever length, the basis of competition remains the same; the riders move off together at the start of the race or any subsequent stage, and the winner is the person covering the total course in the shortest time. Hence the title, massed-start racing, to distinguish this from time-trialling.

It is rarely the case that the strongest rider wins by simply outstripping the others, as the strongest runner might in an athletics MARATHON. Certain physical principles, peculiar to cycling, have led to the development of team tactics which can either nullify or reinforce individual prowess. The basic principle is that it requires less effort to ride in the shelter of another cyclist (either directly behind him, or slightly to the side if there is a cross-wind) than it does to ride alone or in the lead. It therefore follows (a) that the second rider is conserving energy which may enable him to beat a stronger man in the end, and (b) that if each of two good riders takes it in turn to pace and shelter the other, together they can maintain a faster pace than a single rider of equal, or greater, strength and determination, who is pursuing or trying to elude them. Three good riders working together will be a more potent force than two, and so on, although in practice the maximum advantage is probably gained when the group numbers eight to ten.

As a result, a road race is only exceptionally decided by an all-out individual effort from start to finish. It is rather made up of quiet spells interspersed with attacks, chases, counter-attacks, and regroupings dictated by the tactics of the moment. The riders compete in teams, generally of six to twelve men. One is the leader, although there may be one or two other protected riders; the remainder are supporting members of the team, or in the widely-used French term, *domestiques*.

The job of the *domestique* is to help close the gap if a rival breaks away: to pace his leader up to the break; to pace him back to the main bunch (or *peloton*) if he punctures and drops behind; to exchange bicycles with him if he has mechanical trouble; to hinder pursuit if he escapes, by blocking at the front of the *peloton* and slowing its progress; and in a mass finish, to lead him out in the final sprint.

The moves in a road race are often difficult to interpret because of their constantly changing pattern. Two or three members of rival teams, for instance, may form a temporary coalition in order to establish a break, and not become opponents again until the last few miles. During the course of a race the team may switch its support to a different rider; if the nominal leader is not well placed to win, it will work instead to get its best sprinter into a breakaway. And frequently a *domestique*, having attached himself to a strong breakaway on behalf of his leader, will find himself with no helpful alternative but to contest the finish.

There are exceptional circumstances in which tactics play little part. One is where the race is decided by 'selection from behind', usually in an arduous event like the PARIS–ROUBAIX, where the winner does not make a clean break from the field, but sets such a hard pace at the front that the other riders drop behind. Another is on mountainous stretches where, since pace-making is of little value, the rider must strike out for himself.

Team or neutral service cars follow the race; if a rider has mechanical trouble they will usually provide him with a new bicycle until his old one is repaired, and if he punctures will replace the wheel (rather than the tyre). The team or race organization is also responsible for handing up rations at feeding-stations along the route. The food is contained in a light cotton satchel, called a *musette*, which the rider snatches up as he rides through, and then jettisons after transferring the food to his racing jersey pockets.

The clothing worn in road races consists of lightweight, perforated shoes with metal insets laminated between the layers of the sole; white ankle socks; tight-fitting woollen shorts which reach half-way down the thigh; racing jersey with large pouches across the chest and at the

hip; cotton racing cap; and mitts to protect the knuckles from grazing.

Of the many forms of road racing, the following are most common:

Stage races are, in effect, series of massed-start races, sometimes punctuated by time trials (see below), in which the riders move on to a new destination each day. They may, as in the TOUR DE FRANCE, complete the entire circuit of a country. Each stage is an event in itself, with its own prize list; but, more important, it counts towards the over-all placings in the race. These are shown on the General Classification table which is published at the end of each stage after the first, and gives a running total of the time each rider has taken so far in the race. The rider who finishes at the top of the General Classification table is the winner. The system is often complicated by the award of time bonuses — of from one minute to five seconds — to the first six to cross the line at the end of a stage. These are deducted only from the riders' over-all times.

Next in importance to over-all victory are the points and mountain prizes. A daily Points Classification is drawn up, based upon stage finishing positions. Two methods are used to award the points. Either 1 point is given for a stage win, 2 points for second place, and so on, the rider with the fewest points leading the table, or 15 points are given for first place, 14 for second, etc., in which case the aim is to accumulate the highest total. The purpose of the points prize is to reward the specialist road-race sprinter who may finish consistently well on the flatter stages but loses too much time in the mountains ever to win the race.

Similarly the mountain prize is an encouragement to the exceptional climber who may not have the sprinting ability to win many stages. On mountainous stretches certain summits are designated as *primes*, and are placed in one of perhaps four categories according to the severity of the ascent. The first riders to the top receive a diminishing number of points down to an agreed number of places; the higher the category of the *prime*, the more points there are at issue. The prize, and usually the title 'King of the Mountains', goes to the rider who gains most points. Although the mountain prize is more characteristic of stage races, it may be included in a suitable one-day race.

One-day races may take the form of a race from one town or landmark to another, an uninterrupted tour beginning and ending in the same place, or a circuit race covering so many laps of a road course. Classic races usually take one or other of the first two forms since these offer a greater variety of terrain and physical challenge. National and world championships, however, are nearly always held on circuits which can more conveniently be closed to other traffic.

Distinctive types of circuit racing are the *criterium* and the *kermesse*, both designed as public spectacles. A *criterium* is a race, or series of races, through the closed streets of a town or the roads linking a group of villages; it has laps of roughly 2 to 4 miles (3·2–6·4 km.). The *kermesse* uses an even smaller urban circuit of perhaps no more than half a mile. In both the competitors ride as individuals rather than as members of a team.

Although popular on the track (see below), *motor-paced races* are becoming comparatively rare on the road. The greater part of the BORDEAUX–PARIS, however, is ridden behind motor cycles.

Time-trialling is a system of competition which removes the element of pacing and therefore the tactics based upon it. Riders are started singly at one-minute intervals, and are individually timed on completing the course. They must not allow themselves to be paced even when overtaking or being overtaken, and have to depend upon their own self-knowledge and discipline to set a speed which will yield the best return over the distance. Unless they gain on the 'minute man' in front of them, they meet no visible opposition; hence the French term for time trial, *course contre la montre*, 'race against the watch'.

In Britain, time-trialling is practised by cycle clubs as a separate amateur sport, particularly on Sunday morning in spring and summer. For men there are national championships over 25, 50, and 100 miles (40, 80·5, and 161 km.), and 12 and 24 hours, with a hill climb conducted on the same principle; for women the championships are over 25, 50, and 100 miles, and 12 hours. These are open to competitors on single bicycles or tricycles. Club events are over these and intermediate distances, and in some cases tandem riders are eligible to compete.

This special interest has led to the development of a British time-trial bicycle which has no counterpart elsewhere. It has a light frame with elaborately cut and fretted lugs (the metal sleeves by which the frame is joined at its angles) or so constructed that it dispenses with lugs altogether. The bracket is drilled or slotted; the lightest practicable wheels are fitted; and a single chain-wheel is used with a five-gear block and a handlebar *derailleur* control.

On the Continent, time trials are rarely promoted as self-contained events, a major exception being the GRAND PRIX DES NATIONS, which has become an amateur and professional classic. Individual and team time trials,

however, play an important part in most stage races.

Team time trials are run on similar lines. The members of a team start and keep together, but while they take it in turn to pace each other, they may accept no pacing assistance from outside. In events run for their own sake, teams are composed of two, three, or four riders, although in stage races the whole road team of up to a dozen riders is necessarily engaged. Two-man teams start at intervals of two minutes, and the time is taken on the second man to cross the line; three-man and four-man teams start at three-minute intervals, and the time is taken on the third finisher; stage races adapt the rules to their own circumstances.

Road records are also pursued with more enthusiasm in Britain than elsewhere. Official recognition is given to records over 50, 100, and 1,000 miles (80·5, 161, and 1,609 km.), 12 and 24 hours, and 12 specified place-to-place courses (e.g. Land's End to John o' Groats, London to Brighton and back). These may be set on single or tandem bicycles, or single or tandem tricycles. The rider must previously declare his intention to tackle a record, and the attempt must be officially observed and recorded. Nowadays only unpaced records are accepted.

TRACK EVENTS. A track specially constructed for cycling is symmetrical and approximately oval in shape, but with two straight sections — a back straight and a finishing straight — parallel with its greater axis. It is generally banked all round, though far more steeply on the curves than on the straights. The surface of an open-air track is made of concrete, asphalt, shale, cinders, or, occasionally, wood. Technically its circumference must be less than 1 km., but distances of 250, 333⅓, 400, and 500 m. (or the British equivalent in yards or fractions of a mile) are popular. Indoor tracks are nearly always made of wooden slats or plywood panels; the circuit is often under 200 m. and rarely over 300 m. (219–328 yds.), having shorter straights and steeper end banking, which may be angled up to 50 to 55 degrees. Racing is always anticlockwise.

The circumference of a track is measured along the gauge line, a 20-mm. (¾ in.) blue band painted 20 cm. (8 in.) from the inner edge of the track. A black or white sprinters' line, 40 mm. (1½ in.) wide, is marked concentrically 90 cm. (35 in.) from the inner edge, and a blue stayers' line, of the same width, at one-third the breadth of the track from the inner edge. In, respectively, sprint and motor-paced races, competitors may not cross these lines if such action would baulk an opponent.

There are many types of track events, of which six form the basis of competition at world championship level:

Except in special challenge matches, *sprint races* are organized within a knock-out competition, with three riders on the track in the earlier rounds, and two or three in the finals. Each race is held over 1 km. (or 500 m. for women), but only the last 200 m. or 220 yds. is timed. This is because the first part of the race is traditionally given up to manoeuvres in which the riders switch across the width of the track, slow down, and sometimes stand still in an effort to force each other to take the lead. All else being equal, it is easier to use the other man as pace-maker and to accelerate from behind him in the final straight than it is to win from the front.

Tandem sprints, although faster over the last 200 m., cover the same distance and take the same general form as singles sprints. The front man in the team controls the racing; the man behind, who provides the extra power and is often called the 'stoker', also acts as lookout if an opposing team is to the rear.

Motor-paced races are the longest track events; the championship distance for professionals is 100 km. (62·1 miles), while for amateurs the final lasts an hour. Each competitor is paced by a specially built motor-cycle of between 125 c.c. and 650 c.c., and, riding in the shelter of its driver, he is able to maintain average speeds of 80 km./h. (50 m.p.h.) and more.

The rules governing the design of the motor-cycle and cycle, and even the amount of clothing worn by the pacer, strike a balance between speed and safety. The motor-cycle has a roller fitted horizontally behind the back wheel, and at right angles to it, 13½ to 15½ in. (343–394 mm.) from the ground; this prevents the rider getting too close to his pace, and travelling dangerously fast. However, to gain the maximum advantage, he rides a cycle with a small front wheel (the permitted minimum is a diameter of 60 cm. or 23⅝ in.) set between forks which are offset to the rear instead of to the front. The other characteristics of his machine are that the tyres are heavier and taped, as well as shellacked to the rims, and the chain-wheel is extremely large. The rider wears a solid crash helmet.

Each competitor is highly dependent upon his pacemaker's appreciation of the strength of his own rider and of the opposition. A rider can only go as fast as the pacer lets him, and if the pacer increases speed the rider must try to keep in contact with him. Yet in spite of the noise of the motors, it is possible for the two to communicate; the pacer's helmet has an ear-phone opening through which he can hear shouted messages.

Motor-paced racing is termed in French *demi-fond* (i.e. middle distance, because at one time there were track races held over even longer distances), and the specialist riders are universally known by their English title, stayers.

A distinctive feature of sprint and motor-paced races is the *repêchage*. This is an extra heat in which riders eliminated during the qualifying rounds are given a second chance to win a place in the next stage of the competition.

In the *1,000 metres time trial* the rider has the track to himself, and from a standing start tries to cover 1 km. in the shortest possible time.

Individual pursuit is an event contested by professionals over 5 km., by amateurs over 4 km., and by women over 3 km. Two riders take part in each race, starting from stations on opposite sides of the track and attempting to gain on each other. Victory goes to the first rider to reach his home station on completing the distance or, less often, to the rider who overtakes his opponent.

In the track time trial and individual pursuit, as well as in record attempts, less rigidity is needed in the bicycle since the rider is not competing close to others. The machine is therefore often reduced in weight to 15 to 16 lb. (6·8–7·3 kg.). The frame is lightened; wheels have smaller flanges, fewer spokes (24–28), and less sturdy rims; and the lightest tyres are fitted.

Although following the same principle as the individual pursuit, *team pursuit,* over 4 km., is between amateur teams of four riders. Each rider leads the team for one lap or half a lap, then swings up on the end banking and drops back to the end of the file. Thus, after another three laps or another lap and a half he finds himself leading the team once more. The weakest man can afford to drop out near the finish as the time is taken on the third man to reach the team's home station.

While these six events form the basis of the programme at most indoor or outdoor track meetings, other types of event are often included:

Madison racing is a contest between teams of two or three riders, only one of whom is in the race at any given moment. While he is riding in earnest on the inside of the track, his partner (or one of his partners) circles slowly above the stayers' line. After two, three, or any agreed number of laps, the resting partner will move down and the active partner will relay him into the race by some form of physical contact, a push or a hand-sling, and then slip away up the banking. The manoeuvre is reversed after a similar interval. If the team is composed of three men, each takes it in turn to leave the track to rest. In this way, although no rider is continually racing, the event itself can be prolonged for many hours. The object of the race is to gain laps. This is done by a team breaking away from the front of the racing group, and circling the track to catch up with its tail. This is rarely achieved by one partner alone, and may require several relay changes to complete.

Devil-take-the-hindmost is an elimination race in which, every so many laps (the number will vary according to the size of the track), the last man across the finishing line drops out. The process continues until only two men are left to contest the final sprint.

Though not an elimination contest, *point-to-point* resembles a devil-take-the-hindmost in reverse. At regular lap intervals the first man across the line is awarded a certain number of points, and the winner is not necessarily the rider who takes the final sprint (though this may carry an extra points bonus) but the one with the highest points total.

Australian pursuit is a form of individual pursuit in which a number of riders start from equidistant stations around the track. Any riders who are overtaken are eliminated, and the winner is the first man home of those who remain when the distance is completed.

Italian pursuit is a variation on the team pursuit in which each team sheds one rider at the completion of every lap until it is represented by only one man for the final circuit of the track.

Omnium is a contest to find the best all-rounder at a track meeting. Points are given for placings in four or five key events, the prize going to the rider with the highest total. Frequently the *omnium*, and its particular events, is restricted to certain star riders, and the remainder simply provide a supporting programme.

The *six-day race* is a highly specialized event staged on indoor tracks during the winter months and confined to an exclusive circle of professional riders. For the six days the racing traditionally runs from the middle of one morning until the early hours of the next, during which time there is always one rider from each of the two-man or three-man teams on the track. There has been a tendency, however, to shorten the hours and increase the variety of the racing.

Madison racing remains at the heart of the six-day race, and over-all victory goes to the team that gains most laps. Interspersed in the programme, however, are sprints, elimination races, motor-paced races, and kilometre time trials. Prizes are awarded for these, and in some cases points which are used to separate teams which have gained the same number of laps. Another feature of the six is the *prime* prizes offered to the next team to gain a lap; these are often donated by members of the crowd to enliven the racing.

Grass-track racing, largely associated with country fêtes and fairs, is a diminishing sport, but national championships exist at 800 m. (874·9 yds.) and 5 km. (3·1 miles) for amateurs, and at 800 m. for women. Often the cycling is held on athletics tracks, and although ordinary track bicycles are ridden, they require a greater clearance beneath the bottom bracket since there is no banking at the corners; without this the riders would touch ground with their pedals in leaning over. Tyres with heavily-studded treads are fitted.

Cycle speedway, a form of racing modelled on motor-cycle speedway (SEE MOTOR-CYCLE RACING), is generally conducted on shale tracks 85 to 125 yds. (77·7–114·3 m.) in circumference. Riders compete in fours, and cover four laps in each race.

There are nine basic distances and times at which world records can be set on the track: 1 km. (0·62 miles), 5 km. (3·1 miles), 10 km. (6·2 miles), 20 km. (12·4 miles), 100 km. (62·1 miles), and one hour standing start, and 200 m. (219 yds.), 500 m. (546·8 yds.), and 1 km. flying start. Separate records are kept for indoor and outdoor tracks, and for amateurs and professionals, making 36 categories in all. Nearly 200 national British records may be contested, including those for women, but not all have been established.

The clothing worn in track events is similar to that of road racing except that the shorts are of lighter material, the jersey has no pockets, and a crash helmet is obligatory. The hat is an open framework of leather-covered sorbo strips, fitting close to the head and fastened by a chin strap.

An unofficial form of contest existing outside the general classes of cycle sport is *cycle-roller racing*. The cycle-roller is a home training device on which it is possible to ride a normal, but stationary, bicycle. By attaching instruments to count the number of revolutions of the rollers, it is possible to calculate the theoretical speed of the rider and the distance he would have covered, and therefore to compare his performance with another's. The measure is not sufficiently precise for serious competition.

British Cycling Federation Racing Handbook, latest edition; *Road Time Trials Council Handbook,* latest edition.

The first cycle race took place at the Parc de St. Cloud, in the suburbs of Paris, on 31 May 1868; it was over 1,200 m. (1,312 yds.), and was won by an English resident, James Moore. The first inter-town road race, between Paris and Rouen, followed 18 months later; from 325 starters, Moore was again the winner, covering the 83 miles (133·57 km.) in 10 hrs. 25 min. Yet while these are recognized landmarks in the history of organized cycle racing, informal challenge matches and speed trials date back to the earliest development of the bicycle, the object of each designer being to show that his machine was faster and more reliable than its predecessors.

The forerunner of the bicycle was the *célerifère*, or *velocifère*, built for the Comte de Sivrac and demonstrated in the gardens of the Palais Royale, Paris, in 1791. It consisted of a wooden horse mounted on two small wheels which ran in line, and was propelled by the rider sitting astride the horse and pushing at the ground with alternate feet; it had no steering mechanism. Slimmer, lighter versions were manufactured, and it became a regular pastime to race these along the Champs Elysées.

In 1817 a more significant advance was made by the German engineer, Baron von Drais de Sauerbrun, who introduced a pivoting front wheel which enabled him to steer the machine by a handlebar, and an arm-rest against which he could press forward as he thrust back with his feet. Thus he was able to maintain an average speed of 8 m.p.h. (12·9 km./h.) over reasonably level ground; and another rider on a *draisienne* travelled the 37 km. (23 miles) between Beaune and Dijon at an average of 15 km./h. (9·3 m.p.h.). From 1818 British manufacturers made the *draisienne* by the hundred, usually under the name of 'hobby-horse' or 'dandy-horse', but its vogue was brief.

Experiment with two-wheeled machines then declined until 1839 when Macmillan, a blacksmith at Courthill, Dumfriesshire, Scotland, developed a method of treadle propulsion, the treadles being connected by levers and cranks directly to the rear wheel. Macmillan's discovery showed that a rider could drive himself forward, and still keep his balance, without touching his feet to the ground. But the general significance of the machine —although the object of local curiosity —went unrecognized until the end of the century, and the next development was reached independently in Paris around 1863.

A coachbuilder, Michaux, was asked to build *draisienne* hobby-horses for private customers, and experimented by fitting to the front wheel a cranked axle which the rider could turn with his feet. By 1865 his workshop was producing annually 400 velocipedes —later popularly known as 'bone-shakers'

—and in 1868 one of them was brought to England by Rowley Turner, Paris agent of the Coventry Sewing Machine Company. Later changing its name to the Coventry Machinists Company, this firm began building Michaux velocipedes for the French and British market, as a consequence of which the city of Coventry was to become the world's centre of bicycle manufacture.

For the next 20 years, the velocipede went through a period of intensive technical development. Solid rubber tyres replaced iron rims in 1868, and a year later wire spokes held in tension, rather than rigid iron struts, were introduced. Early on, Michaux had increased the size of the front wheel so that a faster speed was achieved with the same number of pedal revolutions, but it was another Parisian, Magée, who designed the Ordinary or high-wheel bicycle (the term 'penny farthing' was not commonly used until the 1890s, when the machine was already becoming obsolete) in 1869, carrying the trend to its mechanical conclusion. The saddle was moved forward above the front wheel so that the only factor limiting the wheel's size was the length of the rider's legs. By the mid-1870s the front wheel was typically 54 in. (1·37 m.) in diameter compared with a rear or trailing wheel of only 17 in. (432 mm.). On racing models, however, the front wheel might be of 58 to 60 in. (1·47–1·52 m.), while the over-all weight was reduced to 20 lb. (9 kg.) against the 50 lb. (22·68 kg.) of a touring Ordinary. The high-wheel bicycle might seem cumbersome, but it was a fast and efficient engineering structure which could be exploited for serious racing, especially on prepared tracks. It was on an Ordinary in 1882 that Cortis became the first cyclist to cover 20 miles (32·187 km.) within an hour.

The ascendancy of the high-wheel bicycle lasted for some 20 years, and the main development towards a more stable form of transport took place in the field of tricycles. The first positive move in designing the low-wheeled safety bicycle was made in 1879 when Lawson's Bicyclette (a generic term adopted by the French) was produced with a chain-wheel drive to the rear wheel; its front wheel, however, was still 40 in. (1·016 m.) in diameter compared with the 24 in. (609 mm.) of the back wheel, and it was not a commercial success.

The machine that finally changed the shape of the bicycle was the Rover safety model —in its 1885 version rather than the experimental form of the previous year —which was produced by Starley, a one-time employee of the Coventry Machinists Company. The later Rover had a rear-wheel chain drive, a front wheel of 32 in. (813 mm.) and a rear wheel of 30 in. (762 mm.), and, although its lines were curved, a basic diamond frame. It was not until 1962 that Moulton, of Bradford-on-Avon, successfully challenged the diamond-frame contour when he designed a bicycle with 16 in. (406 mm.) wheels and an open frame; even then the great majority of racing cyclists remained loyal to the traditional structure derived from Starley.

Within five years of its introduction, the Rover, and models based upon its general design, had supplanted the high-wheeler both as a touring and racing machine. There have been continuous technical refinements since then: in 1881 the free-wheel was invented; pneumatic tyres were first commercially produced by Dunlop in 1888; from the 1890s there were experiments with hub and *derailleur* gears; in 1897 Reynolds and Hewitt brought in the butt-ended tube, which served to lighten frame design; and in 1901 Raleigh introduced the first all-steel bicycle. By the turn of the century, however, the basic technical development had been completed, and the shift in sporting interest from the machines themselves to the men who rode them became even more marked.

Early cycle racing. The bicycle had been primarily devised as a means of sport and recreation (as well as an exercise in mechanical invention) rather than a mode of transport. The cost of a new high-wheeler was approximately £12 (the rough equivalent of £75 a century later), which placed it beyond the means of those who might have ridden it to work. The early cyclists, therefore, were generally young men of the middle class (in 1879, the first British two-mile track champion was the younger brother of the Earl of Kintore). And what attracted them to the sport was its speed; motor cars were not allowed on the British highways until 1896, and were restricted to 12 m.p.h. (19 km./h.) until 1903; meanwhile bicycles were generally faster than carriages on the road, if not as fast as horses on the turf.

From 1868 there was continuous cycle sport of one kind or another. Some racing over short distances took place on the public roads, but since the coming of the railways and the abandonment of the toll-gate system, these were in a worse state of repair than at the start of the century, and unsuitable for racing at length or in numbers. However, they were adequate for recreation, and for setting individual distance and place-to-place records, activities which greatly increased. Genuine racing men required better surfaces, and the professional events which began in England in 1871 — attracting entries from 'J. Moore, of Paris' among others — were held in enclosed areas like the Star Grounds, Fulham, London, and the Aston Cross Grounds, Birmingham. From this it was the logical step to build special cycle tracks, which rapidly increased in number and improved in quality through the 1880s and 1890s. Of the early tracks, Paddington (London) was built of ash, Herne Hill (London) partly of ash and wooden battens, Manchester of shale, and Coventry of gravel, while Bristol and many others were covered with grass. In 1891, however, the first cement track was laid at Putney velodrome (London), and the best of the others followed suit.

A significant development in track racing was the introduction of pacing. Promoters first put single riders into the race to go to the front and stir it up. Then they introduced tandems to pace whichever riders could keep up with them. And from that point they built up multiple-pacing machines, from triplets, quads, quints to a 10-man bicycle (in the U.S.A. a 15-man 'quindicuplet' was manufactured). By this time each rider had his own pacer or series of pacers, which were often provided, at a fee, by the Dunlop tyre company to any rider whose cycle was fitted with Dunlop tyres; it is estimated that in the early 1890s Dunlop employed a regular force of 60 pacemakers, and took on extra men for important meetings. The pacers were used both in races and record attempts, pushing up the speeds and adding to the spectacle, which frequently attracted crowds of 10,000–15,000. Cycle manufacturers like Humber, Rudge, and Swift, as well as Dunlop, sponsored teams of professional riders to advertise their products, and there was widespread betting, through bookmakers, at the tracks.

These developments to some extent alienated the original enthusiasts for cycling who came from the middle classes, and the split widened between track racing and the wholly amateur road cycling. In spite of the unsatisfactory conditions, road racing continued, and there were continual record attempts (in which, as on the track, pacemaking was permitted). When the Road Records Association was formed in 1888, among the first records it ratified was 3 hrs. 15 min. 29 sec. for 50 miles and 6 hrs. 39 min. 5 sec. for 100 miles, both set in 1885; 295 miles in 24 hrs., set in 1886; and a Land's End to John o' Groats run on a tricycle in 6 days 15 hrs. 22 min. However, the police had set a speed limit of 12 m.p.h. for cyclists, and many hundreds were successfully prosecuted for 'furious riding'. After the death of a woman whose horse had reared when frightened by cyclists, road racing was discontinued, and some established races were reluctantly transferred to the track.

There was a similar craze for cycle racing in

the 1890s in the U.S.A., Australia, France, and Germany; the six-day race was developed in New York from 1891; and long-distance road racing became established on an annual basis on the continent of Europe within the next few years. England, however, was acknowledged as the centre of activity. In 1886 there were estimated to be 68 bicycle factories in England; ten years later there were 700, with an annual production of 750,000 machines. Many foreign riders competed for British titles, including the American, Zimmermann, who was the first world 1-mile and 10-miles champion. Having formed the National Cyclists' Union (N.C.U. — now the British Cycling Federation) as early as 1878, England took the lead in founding a world body, the International Cyclist Association (I.C.A.), in 1892. Its original members were England, Belgium, Denmark, Germany, France, Holland, U.S.A., and Canada.

The great wave of interest in cycling had begun to recede in Britain by the end of the century. Many tracks closed down, and with recession in the cycle industry, which had been over-producing, fewer professionals found sponsors. In 1900 discontent with British influence in I.C.A. led to the formation of a new world body, the Union Cycliste Internationale, with headquarters in Geneva, and England had to apply for membership a few years later. British riders continued to succeed in the world track championships well into the 1920s; but the growing section of the sport was road racing, from which English cyclists were debarred. So, from that period, British (which essentially meant English) and continental cycling went separate ways and developed their own styles.

British cycle racing. Track racing continued to attract fair support up to the First World War, and produced two notable amateur world champions in the sprinter, BAILEY, and the stayer, Meredith, who won seven gold medals in the period 1904-13. It also enjoyed a revival after the Second World War, influenced by the international successes of HARRIS and PORTER and by the reintroduction of six-day racing (see below).

For 50 years, however, cycling on the highways was confined to three main activities which had no true counterpart in other areas of the world. One of these, touring, was purely recreational although highly organized. The Cyclists' Touring Club, formed in 1878, had about 60,000 members in the early years of the century, and played an important part in encouraging an interest in cycling as such. The second was record-making, which, conducted with circumspection, was able to continue without attracting much hostility from the authorities. The last was time-trialling which England alone built into a separate and self-contained sport.

Its originator was Bidlake, a member of the NORTH ROAD club whose 24-hour road race had been affected by the N.C.U. ban and had been transferred to the track. Although this had brought faster times, it was not a satisfactory solution to run so long a race in the monotonous setting of a stadium, and the event had attracted fewer spectators. Bidlake therefore devised a form of road competition which would avoid the notice of, or inconvenience to, the public. Riders would dress inconspicuously, and would start at intervals, being individually timed over the same course. The first time trial, over 50 miles, took place on 5 October 1895 and is thus described in the club's history: 'The scratchmen went off first, each starting separately, and pacing was strictly barred. There were 22 entrants, and of these six finished....The day was not a good one, and the race was not a brilliant success, but it was at least felt that the experiment had justified itself, and that another trial on a better day would be warranted.' Characteristically, the history does not record the place where the trial took place, and 75 years later it was still the practice to refer to courses by a system of codes.

Even though the N.C.U. in 1897 had specifically banned time-trialling, along with other forms of road racing, to its licence-holders, the sport grew spontaneously in various parts of the country and kept to certain common practices. The riders' clothing was unobtrusive, the customary dark jacket and black tights; a bell was carried on the bicycle to comply with normal use; no prior publicity was given to events; courses were kept secret and generally chosen for their remoteness; and the trials were held in the early hours of the morning. These self-imposed rules persisted until the Second World War, even though black tights had become highly conspicuous. The clothing regulations were relaxed in stages, and since 1950 riders have competed in club jerseys.

Various factors have accounted for the growth of trialling. More efficient machines and better road surfaces, as well as improvements in technique, have resulted in progressively faster times. In 1922 the Road Racing Council — renamed the Road Time Trials Council (R.T.T.C.) in 1937 — took charge of organizing and promoting the sport. A national championship was introduced in 1930, the rider showing the best aggregate times over 50 and 100 miles, and 12 hours, being awarded the title of British Best All-Rounder. And in 1967 the first of a series of international invitation time trials was held near Newbury in Berkshire.

Up to the Second World War both the N.C.U. and the R.T.T.C. were opposed to massed-start road racing on the grounds that it might attract legislation which would hamper other forms of cycle sport; road races were staged, however, on the BROOKLANDS racing track. There were sufficient enthusiasts to form a British League of Racing Cyclists (which later surrendered its authority to the British Cycling Federation), and from 1942, when the first modern massed-start race was held on public roads between Llangollen and Wolverhampton, the sport has gradually become more attractive to cyclists and more acceptable to the authorities. There have been two significant developments. In 1951 the first TOUR OF BRITAIN was staged, seven years later becoming an annual event as the Milk Race. And in 1965 a full professional class was formed, where previously there had been only an 'independent' or semi-professional class, and riders like ROBINSON and SIMPSON, who wished to make a career of cycling, had to look for opportunities on the Continent.

European cycle racing. Similar obstacles have never been put in the way of road racing on the Continent, and in France, Belgium, Holland, and Italy it has become the national summer sport. Many of the classic races like the Bordeaux–Paris, Paris–Roubaix, and LIÈGE–BASTOGNE–LIÈGE, which are still run annually, were founded in the 1890s, and the Tour de France dates from 1903. This has enabled a strong professional class to grow up, and in general continental cycling is more frankly commercial than in Britain. The interests that employ professional teams also sponsor amateur clubs, treating them as nurseries and relieving promising young riders of the necessity to earn a living outside the sport during the summer season.

Until the Second World War it was the manufacturers of cycles and components who sponsored the trade teams, but the industry suffered through the postwar increase in car-ownership, and many firms cut their commitment in racing. Magni, an Italian professional, is credited with having found a solution to this problem during the 1950s. He suggested that it was to the commercial advantage of companies unconnected with cycling to have their trade names displayed on the riders' clothing and mentioned in the race results. Magni himself rode in the name of a hand cream, and in subsequent seasons the cycle firm sponsors were replaced by petrol, vermouth, tobacco, and beer producers.

The professional racing season follows a set pattern. In February the teams establish their training camps around the Mediterranean coast, and compete in the short *criteriums* of the south of France, and the less strenuous stage races, like the Tour of Sardinia and the Paris-Nice, until early March. Then comes a series of hard, one-day classics — the MILAN –SAN REMO, TOUR OF FLANDERS, and Paris –Roubaix — working up to the first of the national tours, the VUELTA A ESPAGNA. This is followed by the Belgian classics, the Liège –Bastogne–Liège and FLÈCHE WALLONNE, and the GIRO D'ITALIA.

Either or both of the Spanish and Italian tours may be missed, but it is unusual for an ambitious professional rider not to enter the Tour de France, which comes at the end of June and lasts three weeks. This is the pinnacle of the season, a rider's reputation depending more upon his success in the Tour than in any other race; so much so that the winner traditionally receives none of the prize money, but divides it among the members of his team, knowing that he will be recompensed by contracts to appear in the small one-day races and track meetings that fill the remainder of the season. After the Tour, the rider is not required by his team (although he may appear individually in the world championships, Bordeaux–Paris, or Grand Prix des Nations) until October when the two autumn classics, the PARIS-TOURS and TOUR OF LOMBARDY, complete the season.

The amateur season follows much the same pattern: one-day races followed by stage races, and then the *criteriums* of late summer. The difference for riders in eastern Europe is that there is no professional class; and while cyclists of a certain standard will compete internationally within their own areas, those of the east and west will only meet at world championships and at a limited number of races, like the TOUR DE L'AVENIR and the PEACE RACE, which enjoy considerable prestige.

World cycling championships. Many races unofficially entitled world championships, particularly over a distance of 1 mile, were held before the formation of the International Cyclist Association in 1892. Official championships began in the following year at Chicago. They consisted of three amateur events — over 1 mile (1·609 km.), 10 miles (16·094 km.) and 100 km. (62·136 miles) paced — Zimmerman winning the first two, and Meintjes of South Africa the last; Meintjes's medal was the only one of nine that Americans did not win. In 1894 a similar programme was put on at Antwerp, where medals were shared by riders from six countries; but at Cologne in 1895 the 1 mile and 10 mile events were replaced by a sprint; the 100 km. paced race for amateurs was retained; and in addition there was a sprint and 100 km. paced for professionals.

This remained the basic pattern up to the First World War, and although entries became more broadly international, only France and Germany were successful in challenging the lead of Great Britain and the U.S.A. In amateur events during that period, Britain won 30 medals, France 21, Germany 17, and America 16 (a more remarkable record considering that 19 of the 22 championships were held in Europe). Taking amateur and professional results together, France won 53 medals, Britain 41, America 32, and Germany 31.

It was in the postwar years, as cycle racing in Britain and America contracted, that the championships came to be dominated by the continental nations of western Europe. In the half-century after the championships restarted in 1920, Britain won only 38 medals and 12 titles in the growing number of men's events, while the U.S.A. took one silver medal and one bronze. The shift in the sport's centre of interest is also reflected in the choice of championship venues. Exceptionally, the 1922 programme was begun in Britain (at New Brighton and in Shropshire), but due to bad weather and disputes over the organization it was completed in Paris; Leipzig was selected for all events in 1934, and the amateur in 1960; similarly the amateur races were held separately at Montevideo (Uruguay) in 1968, and at Brno (Czechoslovakia) in 1969; in 1970 the complete championships were staged in Leicester; and the 1974 championships were scheduled to take place in Montreal. In every other case, however, the host countries have been chosen from among those in western Europe where cycling has the benefit of heavy commercial sponsorship.

There have been a number of changes in the championship programme. The amateur paced race was not revived after 1918, but in 1921 an amateur road race was included; for the first two years, and again in 1931, it was run as a time trial, but on other occasions has been a massed-start race. The professional road race began in 1927.

In the last championships before the Second World War, at Milan in 1939, amateur and professional individual pursuits were introduced, although only the heats were run off before the meeting was abandoned. They were revived at Zurich in 1946; so was the amateur paced race in 1958, but with the final run over one hour instead of 100 km. In that year, too, after lobbying by Great Britain, and support from Holland, Belgium, and certain eastern European countries, women's events were introduced: sprint, individual pursuit, and

road race. The amateur team time trial and team pursuit were added in 1962, and the amateur tandem sprint and 1,000 m. (1,094 yds.) time trial four years later, thus making up the modern programme of 15 events which are spread over approximately 11 days.

The prizes awarded in the championships, either for amateurs or professionals, are medals to the first three riders placed, and a 'rainbow jersey' to the winner; this is a white jersey with a broad horizontal band composed of blue, red, black, yellow, and green stripes, the national colours of member countries of the Union Cycliste Internationale. For western amateurs, however, a world title is often regarded as the means of gaining a professional contract, and for professionals the opportunity to gain more and better-paid engagements in the end-of-season races.

Six-day cycle racing developed separately from the rest of professional cycling, although from time to time it has recruited prominent riders from the road and track. It was designed to create the longest possible test of endurance for the competitors, while still not offending against the laws which prohibited Sunday entertainment. Thus in its early years, races began at a minute after midnight on Sunday and continued until midnight on Saturday; and the successful six-day formula was retained even after such laws were relaxed and events were allowed to run through the weekend.

The first six-day race was held at the Islington, London, track in 1878, when the winner, Carns of Yorkshire, covered 1,060 miles (1,706 km.) riding an Ordinary. The race was introduced to America in 1891, however, and its main development took place there around the turn of the century. From MADISON SQUARE GARDEN, New York — where there were annual promotions from 1899, and often three events a year during the 1920s and 1930s — the sport spread to Philadelphia in 1902, Buffalo in 1910, and Chicago in 1915.

New York's most important contribution to the growth of the sport was the introduction of two-man teams; this began the slow change in emphasis from a trial by physical exhaustion to a sporting contest in which stamina was simply one of many attributes required. Although it was still the rule that at least one rider from every team had to be on the track at all times, each partner could take it in turn to rest (for a maximum of three hours) in the early morning when few spectators remained. Another natural development from two-man teams was the Madison relay (see above), which became the basic activity of the event.

The same system was adopted when six-day racing was reimported into Europe — by Berlin 1909, Frankfurt 1911, Brussels 1912, and

Paris 1913 — and taken to Toronto in Canada, and Melbourne and Sydney in Australia, all in the year 1912. Since the Second World War, western Europe has become the centre of the sport, with some 15 meetings promoted at indoor stadia between September and March. The greatest interest lies in Holland, Belgium, and Germany, where there is a strong tradition of winter track racing. In London the first six-day race in the modern style was held in 1923; five meetings followed in the 1930s, and two more in 1950-1; in 1967 the London six was revived at Earls Court, and from the following year continued on an annual basis at the EMPIRE POOL, WEMBLEY.

During the 1950s and 1960s there were further changes in the typical six-day programme. Madison racing was cut back to allow the inclusion of sprints, elimination races, and kilometre time trials; and since these made greater demands on the vitality of the competitors, the track was cleared from approximately 2 a.m. until the early afternoon to allow the riders to sleep.

Racing for many hours on end on small, steeply banked tracks requires specialized talents; and while current world champions are often included in the programme for the sake of publicity and public interest, the teams are mainly composed of perhaps a score of regular riders, who form what is known as 'the blue train', and move on from one event to the next. Its most notable members have been POST and VAN STEENBERGEN. This system, in which contracts to appear loom larger than the prizes for winning, has stressed the element of exhibition riding above that of open and determined competition.

Peter Clifford, *The Tour de France* (1965); Mike Daniell, *5..4..3..2..1..GO!* (1971); N. G. Henderson, *Continental Cycle Racing* (1970); Philip Sumner, *Early Bicycles* (1966); Dick Swann, *The Life and Times of Charley Barden* (1965); John Woodforde, *The Story of the Bicycle* (1970).

GOVERNING BODY (WORLD): Union Cycliste Internationale, 8 Rue Charles-Humbert, 1205 Geneva, Switzerland; (ENGLAND): British Cycling Federation, 26 Park Crescent, London W.1.

CYCLO-CROSS is a form of bicycle racing practised in winter on cross-country courses. Interest in the sport is mainly confined to Europe, where its strongest following is in Luxemburg, the Low Countries, and Russia, but it is also found in the U.S.A., especially around Chicago.

The recommended length for a cyclo-cross race is 10 to 15 miles (16–24 km.), which, depending upon the severity of the course, will give a duration of 60–75 minutes; most races are made up of successive laps of a circuit of half a mile to 2 miles (0·8–3·2 km.). Since courses, where possible, are left in their natural state, their characteristics vary considerably. No more than one-third of the distance may be composed of metalled road, and usually the proportion is much less. For the rest, organizers are officially encouraged to choose 'terrain calling for skilled machine-handling and balance'.

Such a terrain will usually include most of the following features: pasture or ploughed field and woodland; steep banks and flights of steps to climb or descend; walls, stiles, gates, fallen trees, streams, and ditches; narrow paths, bridges and gaps where it is difficult for one competitor to pass another. If the landscape does not provide sufficient obstacles, artificial hurdles may be added. Because the cyclo-cross season runs from September to mid-March, rain, snow, and ice often create additional hazards.

Point-to-point events are less common, but such as exist are often longer and more spectacular. An example is the annual Three Peaks Race in Yorkshire, during which competitors must pass over the summits of Pen-Y-Ghent, Whernside, and Ingleborough, each of which is more than 2,270 ft. (692 m.) above sea level. It takes the winner approximately 3 hrs. to complete the course.

All cyclo-cross races have a massed start, which must take place in an area wide enough for the whole field to assemble in not more than two lines abreast. Thereafter the cyclists tackle the course in their own way, riding where they are able, and when the going becomes too rough or steep, or where there are obstacles to cross, carrying their bicycles on their shoulders. Ability in cross-country running and nimbleness in vaulting are therefore required, but generally the advantage lies with those who can keep riding where others are forced to take to their feet.

Apart from basic strength and stamina, the qualities shown by the most successful competitors are dexterity in controlling the bicycle, nerve in taking steep, slippery, and uneven surfaces at speed, and judgement in selecting the best line where the course is broad enough to offer a choice. It is characteristic of cyclo-cross that the class of a rider is well defined, and that results are more predictable than in most sports.

The rider's initial objective is to make a fast start and be ahead at the first obstacle or narrow section; the leader has a clearer path than those who follow and get in each other's way. Races are often lost, if not won, in the first 200 yds. (183 m.). Beyond that the tactics of the sport are rudimentary. There are rarely stretches sufficiently fast and level for pacemaking between members of a team, and, while situations may occur during a breakaway in which they can work together against an opponent (e.g. by attacking and relaxing in turn to break the rhythm of his riding), a rider's effort needs to be self-sufficient.

The bicycle used in cyclo-cross is basically a steel-frame road machine (see CYCLING) with its weight reduced by the use of aluminium alloy for handlebars, brakes, and pedals, and of a plastic saddle and nylon gears. Five or six gears, with handlebar controls, are more common than ten or twelve; the chain-wheel is equipped with a flange or guide on either side to stop the chain jogging off on broken ground.

The bottom bracket height is often 11 in. (279 mm.) against the conventional 10½ in. (267 mm.), and additional clearance is provided beneath the fork crown as a precaution against mud from the tyres collecting there.

Normal road wheels are used, but with tyres of 10 oz. (284 g.) and upward, manufactured with deep treads. Double toe-clips are fitted for greater strength, and also double-sided pedals to enable the competitor to ride a short distance without having to put his feet into the toe-clips. Cables are taped, rather than clipped, to the frame, and all unnecessary projections are filed down to make the bicycle less uncomfortable to carry; carrying handles, however, although formerly standard equipment, have now gone out of fashion.

Serious contestants station helpers with spare machines round the course. This is not only a precaution in case of a puncture or mechanical trouble; after heavy rain a bicycle may pick up 5 lb. (2·27 kg.) of mud over the course, so that there is some gain in changing to a cleaner machine.

The clothing worn is similar to that in road

TYPICAL CYCLO-CROSS COURSE
(1) Leaf-mould—slimy descent through trees; (2) concrete bridge 10 ft. wide; (3) 20 steps; (4) narrow mud footpath; (5) less severe descent with narrow stream to step across; (6) metal fence to be vaulted—2 ft. of water with loose, soggy banks, then a 20° run-up through the trees; (7) narrow gap; (8) short, steep descent, very thick mud.

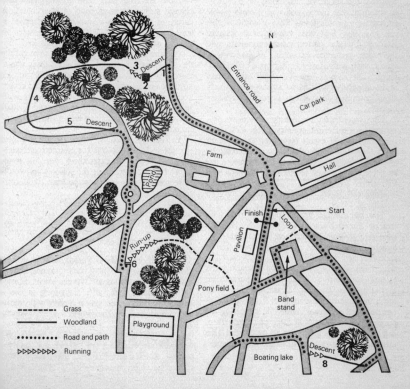

races, except that the jersey is without pockets and has long sleeves as a protection against the cold and scratches from thorns and branches. Depending on the condition of the ground, a rider may wear football studs or running spikes on his shoes.

The origins of cyclo-cross are obscure, although it is thought to have taken shape in France shortly after the turn of the century, and to have been influenced by the use of bicycles in military manoeuvres. Many so-called road races at that time, however, included sections of rough, unmade ground, and there can have been only a difference of degree between these and cyclo-cross events.

By 1925 the sport had become sufficiently well established on the Continent to justify an annual world championship which, from 1950, was officially recognized by the Union Cycliste Internationale. It was held as a single race, open to both amateurs and professionals, until 1967 when, for the first time, the classes were separated. One reason for this change was that the sport was attracting large crowds to international races, and was therefore able to sustain a professional class of some 50 riders. Another was that countries in eastern Europe did not permit professionalism and therefore, with the exception of Czechoslovakia, were unwilling to enter open championships. The move, however, had little effect and competitors still came almost exclusively from countries in western Europe and Scandinavia.

The world championships are now promoted in a different country each year, with the professional event following the amateur on the same day and over the same course; the amateurs simply ride fewer laps. Entries are restricted to national teams of up to four men in either event. In addition, national championships are held in approximately 15 countries.

The beginnings of cyclo-cross in Britain can be traced back to a Cyclists v. Harriers race held at Walsall, Staffordshire, from 1921, and its early progress ran parallel with that of motor-cycle scrambling, or MOTO-CROSS, which it resembles. A number of cyclo-cross events are still referred to as scrambles, including the Bagshot Scramble, the most important event in the south of England. Competition was informal, with riders treating the contests as an agreeable form of winter training rather than as a sport in its own right. This attitude, too, is evident from the facetiousness of race titles like 'Circuit of the Duckpond' and 'Tour of the Sinterland Woods'.

In 1954, when the British Cyclo-Cross Association was formed to control and promote the sport in England and Wales, only six annual races were established. After 19 years the winter programme included more than 140 senior events and over half that number for junior and schoolboy riders; approximately 255 cycle clubs were affiliated to the Association. In 1955 the first national championship was staged, and after 1967 both amateur and professional titles were awarded; on occasions when there has been a small professional entry, however, the two classes have competed together in a single championship race.

Specialist cyclo-cross riders also emerged during the 1950s, men who reversed the old order by using road races as a method of keeping fit for the winter. Bicycle design was adapted to the needs of the sport; by 1970 the weight of the machine had been reduced by 6 to 7 lb. (2·7–3·2 kg.), to 20 lb. (9·1 kg.); and, where previously the simplest transmission had been thought best for muddy conditions, variable gearing was introduced. The last change was a consequence of the changing nature of the courses themselves. There was a tendency in the early 1950s to make them as rugged as possible, so that competitors spent more time carrying their bicycles than riding them. On the Continent, however, there was a move towards faster circuits with longer stretches of roadway and more rideable cross-country sections. This gave a truer race with just rewards for skill and speed, and British events gradually began to adopt the continental pattern.

British cyclo-cross, while tending to be insular and unambitious for international competition, is still an expanding sport. Its main area of growth is among the schools and youth movements who see it as the least dangerous form of cycle racing.

GOVERNING BODY (WORLD): Union Cycliste Internationale, 8 Rue Charles-Humbert, 1205 Geneva, Switzerland; (ENGLAND): British Cyclo-Cross Association (affiliated to the British Cycling Federation), 26 Park Crescent, London W.1.

CYPRESS POINT, U.S. GOLF course in California. Perhaps the most photographed hole in golf is the sixteenth at Cypress Point. Something over 200 yds. (183 m.) long across a rocky bay to a green set on a narrow promontory, it is one of the world's great disaster holes.

CYRIAX CUP, see RUGBY FIVES.

D

DA SILVA, ADHEMAR FERREIRA (1927-   ), triple jumper for Brazil. Da Silva won five gold medals in major championships: at the OLYMPIC GAMES in 1952 and 1956 and the PAN-AMERICAN GAMES in 1951, 1955, and 1959. He improved the world record five times between 1950 and 1955 with a best distance of 54 ft. 4 in. (16·56 m.) in 1955.

DA SILVA, LEONIDAS, see LEONIDAS.

DAHLIA (1970), a race-horse trained by Zilber and ridden by Pyers. One of the best ever French fillies, she won the IRISH GUINNESS OAKS and KING GEORGE VI AND QUEEN ELIZABETH STAKES in 1973 when she also became the first filly to win the Washington International.

DAIGO, TOSHIRO (1926-   ), Japanese JUDO fighter who in 1950 was promoted to 6th Dan, the youngest person to be awarded this grade at the time. His powerful build (5 ft. 10 in. — 1·78 m., 16 st. — 102 kg.) and fine technique, particularly a neat *ko-uchi-gari* (minor inner reaping throw) brought him tremendous success in the early 1950s. He won the all-Japan championships in 1951 and 1954 and the Tokyo championships in 1950 and 1951. Later he was head of the KODOKAN *kenshusei* (special students).

DAKYU is an equestrian, ball-and-goal, team game which has been played in Japan for more than a thousand years. It might be described as a form of mounted LACROSSE. The players carry a pole with a metal net at the end: their purpose is to catch the ball in the net and throw it into the opposing goal, which is a circle 61 cm. (24 in.) in diameter. The winning team is that which first scores 12 points.

DALINSH, JANIS (*c.* 1910-   ), a race walker who represented Latvia (now part of the U.S.S.R.), the first of this country's long line of world-beaters. He set a world best for 50 km. in 1933, was European 50 km. champion in 1934, and a bronze medallist in the Olympic event at the same distance in 1932. Near the end of his career he set a world's record for 30 km. in 1939.

DALLAS COWBOYS, American professional FOOTBALL team, entered the NATIONAL FOOTBALL LEAGUE (N.F.L.) in 1960 and built themselves into a contender by mid-decade. They had the reputation of losing the 'big' games, in 1947 losing the N.F.L. title to the GREEN BAY PACKERS in the final seconds in −13° weather; in 1971 they were beaten in the Super Bowl by the BALTIMORE COLTS, but they did triumph in 1972. In the 1960s the Cowboys were known for coach Landry's imaginative offence (attack). As a title contender in 1970-1 Landry changed to a fundamental, well-executed style, virtually without individual stars, except for the tackle Lilly. The team has benefited from an astute management, which has drafted well from college football and has made clever trades.
COLOURS: Silver blue, royal blue, and white.

DAMASCUS (1964), a race-horse bred in the U.S.A. and owned by Mrs. Bancroft, trained by Whitely, and ridden in most of his races by SHOEMAKER, won the BELMONT STAKES, PREAKNESS STAKES, American Derby, TRAVERS STAKES, JOCKEY CLUB GOLD CUP, and $1,176,781 in stakes.

DANIELS, CHARLES (1885-1973), America's first eminent swimmer, who won five medals, including three golds, at the 1904 OLYMPIC GAMES and a gold medal and a bronze at the 1908 London Olympics. An early exponent of the American crawl, he had great influence on the development of the stroke in Britain through his visits in 1906 and 1907 when he won the Amateur Swimming Association 100 yards (91·4 m.) titles.

DARA, Col. ALI IQTIDAR SHAH (1915-   ), the only player to represent both India and Pakistan at HOCKEY in the OLYMPIC GAMES. He was unlucky not to be chosen for the Indian Olympic teams of 1932 and 1936 but was sent to Berlin after the 1936 Olympic tournament had started and played in both the semi-final and winning final team. He scored two of India's goals in their 8-1 victory over Germany. He continued playing after the war and at the age of 33 captained the Pakistan team at the 1948 Olympics. He served as a member of the International Hockey Federation and International Hockey Rules Board for many years.

DARK MIRAGE (1965), a race-horse known as 'the mighty mite', was one of the most outstanding fillies in the history of racing in the U.S.A. She won the KENTUCKY OAKS, COACHING CLUB AMERICAN OAKS, Delaware Oaks, Monmouth Oaks, Acorn Stakes, Mother Goose Stakes, and La Troienne Stakes.

DARLEY ARABIAN (*c.* 1702), was bought in Aleppo (Halab), Syria, for James Darley in 1704 and became the paternal great-great-grandsire of ECLIPSE. He is one of the three foundation fathers of the thoroughbred race-horse, along with the BYERLEY TURK and the GODOLPHIN BARB.

DARLING, FRED (d. 1953), the Master of Beckhampton, was an outstanding English race-horse trainer with 19 classic winners to his credit, of which seven were DERBY winners, including CORONACH for Lord Woolavington. Darling headed the list of winning trainers six times.

DARLING, Hon. JOSEPH, C.B.E. (1870-1946), cricketer for Australia and South Australia. A forceful batsman and purposeful captain, he led the 1899, 1902, and 1905 Australian teams to England, and the 1902-3 team in South Africa, winning each rubber but the last. On home pitches he scored heavily, particularly during 1897-8, when he and another left-hander, HILL, dominated the series.

DARWIN, BERNARD, C.B.E. (1876-1961), English international amateur golfer, author, and journalist. A grandson of the evolutionist, Darwin played GOLF for England for 20 years, but his greatest contribution to the game was as a writer. He and his CRICKET-writer contemporary, CARDUS, brought wit, style, and high literary merit to the sports pages and set the standards for a new school of writing about games. Darwin was golf correspondent for *The Times* for most of his adult life and in 1937 was awarded the C.B.E. for services to literature. He was captain of the Royal and Ancient in 1934. His books include: *Golf Courses of Great Britain, Tee Shots and Others, Present Day Golf* (with GEORGE DUNCAN), *Golf: Some Hints and Suggestions, A Friendly Round, Green Memories, Out of the Rough, Playing the Like, Rubs of the Green*, and *British Golf.*

DAUGAWA (T.T.T.) RIGA, women's BASKETBALL team which represents the Tram and Trolleybus Trust of Riga, Latvia (U.S.S.R.). In the first 15 seasons of competition for the EUROPEAN CUP FOR CHAMPION CLUBS for women, 1959-73, Daugawa achieved the remarkable record of 13 wins, failing only in 1959 and 1963. The team was captained for much of this time by SMILDZINYA.

DAVIDSON, ALAN KEITH, M.B.E. (1929-), cricketer for Australia and New South Wales. A left-handed all-rounder, he took 186 wickets in Test CRICKET with his fast swing bowling, and his often vigorous batting turned the course of several matches. He was also a fine close fielder. After his retirement he became a cricket administrator.

DAVIES, LYNN (1942-), long jumper for Great Britain. The first Welsh athlete to win an Olympic gold medal, Davies upset the favourites to claim the 1964 title with 26 ft. 5½ in. (8·06 m.). He then went on to complete the first triple win of gold medals in ATHLETICS history by winning the 1966 Commonwealth and European titles. In 1968 he improved the United Kingdom record to 27 ft. (8·23 m.). He was silver medallist in the 1969 European championship and retained his Commonwealth championship at Edinburgh in 1970.

DAVIES, ROBERT (1924-), American BASKETBALL player. He graduated from Columbia University and played in the NATIONAL BASKETBALL ASSOCIATION for ten seasons with the ROCHESTER ROYALS, helping them to gain one N.B.A. title. He was elected to the 'all-League' team on seven occasions and is generally considered to have been among the finest players of all time.

DAVIES, RONALD (1942-), Association footballer for Chester, Luton, Norwich City, Southampton, PORTSMOUTH, and Wales, for whom he made his first appearance in a full international at Swansea on 15 April 1964 when, incidentally, BEST was making his début for the Irish opponents. A worthy successor to a notable line of Welsh centre forwards in postwar football that includes players as dissimilar as Ford and CHARLES, he made a major contribution to Southampton's early survival in the First Division and subsequent advance to higher placings that earned the club entry in the Fairs Cup competition in the 1969-70 season. He was transferred to Portsmouth in 1973.

DAVIES, WILLIAM JOHN ABBOTT (1890-1967), RUGBY UNION outside half for United Services, Portsmouth, Royal Navy and England. Noted for his running and left footed drop kick, Davies played most of his important games — at club, services, and international level — in partnership with KERSHAW, his junior by ten years. In their four seasons together, England once shared the international championship, and twice won it outright. Davies won 22 England caps, and was on the losing side only in his first international against South Africa in 1913.

DAVIS, DWIGHT F. (1879-1945), American LAWN TENNIS player, and donor of the Davis Cup, the trophy of the game's international team championship for men. A tall, powerful player, he was the runner-up in the U.S. singles championship in 1898 and 1899 and won the all-comers' doubles at WIMBLEDON in 1901 with Ward, falling to the DOHERTY brothers in the challenge round. He played singles and doubles without defeat in the first Davis Cup match against the British Isles at Boston in 1900, but in the second contest at New York in 1902 he and Ward lost to the Dohertys.

DAVIS, GLENN ASHBY (1934-   ), hurdler for the U.S.A. The first man to win the Olympic 400 metres hurdles twice (1956 and 1960) and, in 1956, the first man to break 50 seconds for that event, Davis also won a gold medal in the Olympic 4 × 400 metres relay in 1960 in world record time. He was holder of world records for the 400 metres hurdles, 440 yards hurdles, and 200 metres hurdles on a turn, with times of 49·2, 49·9, and 22·5 sec. respectively. Not a fluent hurdler, Davis used his immense power to win his races and held the world record for 440 yards flat in 45·7 sec. from 1958 to 1963.

DAVIS, JOHN (1921-   ), American Negro heavyweight lifter who was the youngest lifter to win a world title, aged 17 in 1938. He added seven Olympic and world titles, thus achieving eight in succession. 1951 Pan-American champion and 12 times U.S.A. champion, he was the first lifter to jerk 400 lb. 181·4 kg.).

DAVIS, JOHN (1939-   ), LACROSSE player for Canada and Ontario. A former member of the Green Gaels club, Oshawa, he is an attack player of outstanding ability and an expert stick-handler and tactician. For the Green Gaels he scored a total of 184 points, made up of 91 goals and 93 assists in 24 games played. More recently he joined the Peterborough club, Ontario, and in 1966 was awarded the Mike Kelly medal as the sports writers' choice of the most valuable club player in the Mann Cup (see LACROSSE) series.

DAVIS CUP, see LAWN TENNIS.

DAVOS S.C., ICE SKATING club formed in Switzerland in 1877, following the enthusiasm of British guests at the Hotel Belvedere; headquarters of the International Skating Union.

DAWES, JOHN, see LONDON WELSH F.C.

DAWSON, ALFRED RONALD (1932-   ), RUGBY UNION hooker for Wanderers, Ireland, and British LIONS. An outstanding leader and tactician, he was appointed captain of the Lions touring party to Australasia and Canada in 1959, after winning only 9 of his 27 international caps.

DAWSON, GEORGE (d. 1913), in his day the leading race-horse trainer in England. In 1889 his stable established a record of £77,914 won in stake money during a single flat-racing season, a record which was not surpassed until LAWSON broke it in 1931. Dawson trained AYRSHIRE, Donovan, and Memoir for the Duke of PORTLAND.

DAWSON, JERRY (1888-1970), footballer for England and Burnley. A native of Cliviger, a hamlet four miles from Burnley, he retired there after 23 years as the Burnley club's regular goalkeeper. He won two England caps and an F.A. Cup medal (1914), when he played in every tie except the final, which he missed because of injury. He is best remembered for his part in Burnley's championship win of 1920-1 (see FOOTBALL, ASSOCIATION). He missed only three appearances and played throughout the side's record-breaking run between September and March of 30 matches without defeat, during which he conceded only 17 goals while Burnley scored 68.

Dawson, a lean 5 ft. 10 in. (1·77 m.), had an extraordinary reach, a tigerish spring, and was famous for his elegant flicks over the crossbar. He was an excellent club cricketer, and a noted KNUR AND SPELL player.

DAY, JAMES (1946-   ), Canadian show jumping (see EQUESTRIAN EVENTS) rider and member of the team which won the gold medal at the 1968 OLYMPIC GAMES. Riding Canadian Club, he won the individual gold medal at the PAN-AMERICAN GAMES in 1967, and the partnership thus became an automatic choice for Mexico the following year, when Canada sent a show jumping team to compete in the Olympics for the first time.

DE ALVAREZ, LILLI (1905-   ), Spanish LAWN TENNIS player, celebrated for her aggressively artistic style. She lost in three successive WIMBLEDON finals — to Mrs. GOD-FREE in 1926 (her first appearance) and to WILLS in 1927 and 1928. She won the French doubles title in 1929 and all three Italian and Argentinian titles in 1930.

DE BEAUMONT, CHARLES-LOUIS (1902-72), British fencer. Hon. secretary of the Amateur Fencing Association, 1936-56 and president from 1956, founder of the British Commonwealth Fencing Federation and president from 1950, he won the British épée championship in 1936, 1937, 1938, and 1953, and won the first British Commonwealth épée championship in 1950. He captained the British FENCING team at the OLYMPIC GAMES in 1936, 1948, 1952, 1956, 1960, 1964, and 1968, and was made *Membre d'Honneur* of the Fédération Internationale d'Escrime in 1949. He was the author of eight books on fencing.

DE BEAUMONT CENTRE, headquarters of the British Amateur Fencing Association and of the LONDON FENCING CLUB — the 'centre court' of British FENCING. Built in 1963, it confirmed the remarkable growth of British fencing as a national sport and was the first building in the world built solely for fencing.

DE HAVILLAND, Capt. GEOFFREY, see FLYING, SPORTING.

DE LA HUNTY, Mrs. SHIRLEY (1925-   ), hurdler and sprinter for Australia. The only woman to win the Olympic 80 metres hurdles twice (1952 and 1956), Mrs. de la Hunty was also a considerable sprinter, who won a silver medal with the Australian 4 × 100 metres relay team in the 1948 OLYMPIC GAMES and a gold medal in 1956. She also won gold medals in the 1950 COMMONWEALTH GAMES 80 metres hurdles and medley relay, and held world records for 80 metres hurdles in 10·9 sec. and 100 metres in 11·3 sec.

DE LUMNICZER, S. (*fl.* 1929-39), clay pigeon shooter for Hungary. He was three times world champion in 1929, 1933, and 1939, and twice European champion, in 1933 and 1937.

DE VICENZO, ROBERTO (1923-   ), Argentinian professional golfer. He was Open champion in 1967, winner of 30 national championships in Europe and the Americas and of more than 100 sponsored tournaments — many of them on the American Professional Golfers Association circuit — and a WORLD CUP player.

DE VLAEMINCK, ERIC (1945-   ), Belgian CYCLO-CROSS rider, winner of the world championship in 1966 and in the six successive seasons 1968-73. When he took the professional title in 1968, his brother Roger won the amateur title on the same day.

DEAN, WILLIAM RALPH (1906-   ), Association footballer for Tranmere, EVERTON, and England for whom he made 16 appearances from 1927 to 1932 and scored 17 goals — 12 of them in his first five international appearances in 1927. The last of these five matches was against France in Paris on 26 May at the end of England's close-season tour. When the new Football League season started, his zest for goal-scoring continued and at the end of the season (1927-8) he had set a record for the Football League with 60 goals for Everton in 39 First Division matches. This tally, that beat by one goal the record set up only one season before by CAMSELL, included five goals in one match, four goals in another, five hat-tricks, and fourteen matches in which he scored twice. In the same season he scored three goals in F.A. Cup-ties, four goals for England in international matches against France and Belgium, and six goals for the Football League in matches against the Scottish and Irish Leagues. A tall, strongly-built centre forward, he had exceptional ability, not least in the power and the direction of his heading.

DEANS, ROBERT GEORGE (1883-1908), RUGBY UNION centre three-quarter for New Zealand. He was the centre of a controversy on 16 December 1905 as the man many people thought scored a try that afternoon for New Zealand against Wales at Cardiff. The referee disagreed. Wales won the match 3-0, the only defeat suffered by these New Zealanders on their tour of 33 matches.

DEAR, J. P. (1909-   ), highly versatile British professional player of court games. He was world RACKETS champion from 1947-54 and previously Open SQUASH RACKETS champion. He was world TENNIS champion 1955-7.

DEAUVILLE, France, is the setting for the principal French thoroughbred race-horse sales of yearlings in August, and of all types of bloodstock in November.

DECATHLON, a standard event on the programme of all major ATHLETICS championships which has featured in the OLYMPIC GAMES since 1912, the decathlon is an all round test of SPRINTING, HURDLING, MIDDLE DISTANCE RUNNING, and a range of field events. The ten-event programme is distributed over two days as follows: first day — 100 metres, LONG JUMP, SHOT PUT, HIGH JUMP, and 400 metres; second day — 110 metres hurdles, DISCUS, POLE VAULT, JAVELIN, and 1,500 metres. Performance is rated according to a points-scoring system. Each competitor must start in every event and the winner is the athlete with the largest points total. The official points table has undergone periodic revision, the current scale being that first introduced by the International Amateur Athletic Federation (see ATHLETICS, TRACK AND FIELD) in 1962 and in use since 1964.

The I.A.A.F. Scoring Table for Men's Track and Field Events (latest edition).

DECK CRICKET, a form of CRICKET first played on shipboard with a tethered ball. Few players found that satisfactory and the bigger ships sought to allocate a considerable area of deck space for the game. Possibly to avoid losing too many cricket balls, or more likely as a necessary means of preventing injury to other passengers, nets rigged from awning spars to the deck enclosed the playing area that was about 30 ft. wide and 60 ft. long (9·1 × 18·3 m.). A strip of coconut matting was laid the full length of the pitch, and the stumps set in a block of wood. The pattern of play was the same as for the game on land except that scoring was related to the area the ball reached before being fielded. An area, stretching the width of the playing space and reaching 8 ft. (2·4 m.) from a line drawn about 15 ft. (4·6 m.) from the stumps, was worth one run; the next area extending for a further 8 ft. was worth 2 runs; a slightly bigger area, extending for a further 9 ft. 6 in. (2·9 m.) was worth 3 runs; and beyond that was the boundary and 4 runs.

Like most DECK GAMES, deck cricket was appreciated by spectators as well as by the players themselves, but the game did take up a relatively large amount of the available deck space and it needed its special protective netting. It was losing favour, perhaps with the shipping companies more than the passengers, even before the post-1945 increase in air passenger traffic persuaded shipping companies to build smaller vessels with consequent reduction in deck space for the smaller number of passengers. Some passengers may try their own improvised games of cricket but as part of the organized programme of deck games it is out of fashion.

DECK GAMES, as organized diversions and means of recreation for passengers on board ships, particularly those on holiday cruises, date only from the 1920s, but games were played aboard ship several centuries earlier and some few of them, like BULL, SWINGING THE MONKEY, and SHUFFLEBOARD are still played today even though the former two linger on the programme of many shipping lines more by reason of sentiment than because of popular demand.

Small sailing ships offered little clear deck space in which games could be played, nor did the conditions under which they lived and worked leave seamen much time or energy for sport. Before about the fifteenth century, sailors showed little aptitude or enthusiasm for playing games when on board their ships.

The situation changed when the fighting ships needed more men. The unwilling landsmen caught by the press gang and forced to serve in the fighting ships from the fifteenth until well into the nineteenth century had been accustomed to playing games in their rural environment and sought to adopt some of them to preserve a link with their previous existence. It is probably not a coincidence that one of the earliest known deck games was called Bull and involved the use of a bag known as a 'bull's head'. Regular seamen would have given the game a name and symbols with more nautical associations.

On the whole, however, it seems likely that the wretched crews of ships, particularly fighting vessels, were too fatigued with work, suffering, and sickness to play many games — even if space and opportunity permitted. It was probably only the increase in the emigrant trade in the last days of sail that kept alive the deck games that did survive until the post-1918 fashion for cruising ships revived them and established a host of new ones.

The emigrant trade meant the presence of a large number of passengers on board ships which had not been designed for this. The accommodation was wretched, sometimes intolerably so; the journeys were long, and the passage slow. It was then, not from any particular interest in games themselves but to overcome boredom and possibly as a means of keeping a measure of good health, that the emigrants played such games as they could.

The post-1918 extension of passenger traffic on ships coincided with an increase in interest in sports generally that showed itself in the added enthusiasm of most nations for the OLYMPIC GAMES, and in the introduction of a world FOOTBALL championship. It was reflected in the demand for more opportunities for playing games on the decks of ships, and it was not long before shipping companies acknowledged the situation by allocating additional space for games and by introducing a new term in the plans for passenger vessels — a 'sports deck'.

Most of the games introduced had a direct connection with the most popular of games played ashore, notably DECK TENNIS, deck bowls, DECK QUOITS, deck golf, DECK CRICKET, and deck croquet. Sea voyages, even cruises, no longer occupied months, and apart from the immediate response expected from passengers towards a game they played, or had played, ashore, it was an obvious advantage that deck games had familiar playing terms even if the rules and equipment had usually to be modified.

Consideration of space, even on the largest passenger vessels, has probably been the main reason for the decline in popularity, indeed the virtual demise, of many of the deck games introduced in the first boom period. (In addition to those deck games mentioned above, see also HORSE-RACING and STEEPLECHASING.)

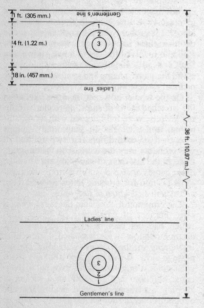

DECK QUOITS LAYOUT

DECK QUOITS can be played wherever convenient on the deck but, in practice, most ships have brass marks sunk into the deck that minimize the necessity of measuring and chalking before each game. The object of the game is simple enough — to place quoits (rope rings) as near as possible to the centre mark (the jack) since the circles closest to the jack attract the highest points. Each player has either three or four quoits and the game is won by the player (or pair of players in a doubles match) first scoring 21 points. A match is won by the player or pair winning the most of three games. Opponents stand together at the ends of the pitch in the singles game, and play from each end alternately. In doubles, partners stand at opposite ends, that is to say, each against an opponent.

Only those quoits nearer the jack than the best quoit of the opposite player or pair are counted as scoring. The rules vary slightly but generally they are: (1) quoits must be thrown backhand and over the centre line; (2) women must stand with their feet behind the chalk line, and not outside the ends; (3) men must stand with the foremost foot inside the small circle; (4) quoits falling short of the dead line (or ladies' line) do not count and must be removed promptly; (5) a quoit touching a circle will score the number of the outer ring; (6) bumping one's own or opponents' quoits to further one's own interests is permitted; (7) riding quoits do not count.

DECK TENNIS is a combination of TENNIS and quoits, and it has been, since the 1920s, one of the most popular of all DECK GAMES. Like many other such games, deck tennis sought to adapt to shipboard conditions a game already known to passengers as a land sport. It is a measure of the success of this particular adaptation that deck tennis is now established as a land game known as RING TENNIS or beach tennis.

Deck tennis is played by either two or four people who throw a quoit or rubber ring to one another across a net suspended over the centre of the court, which is divided like a LAWN TENNIS court. The size of the courts, whether for singles or for doubles, varies. There are exceptions but generally singles courts are between 30 and 40 ft. (9·1–12·2 m.) long, and from 10 to 15 ft. (3–4·6 m.) wide. In the faster doubles game, the length may be less, say between 28 and 34 ft. (8·5–10·4 m.), but the width should be not less than 14 ft. (4·3 m.) and not more than 15 ft. (4·6 m.). Whatever the over-all dimensions of the court, there must be a neutral space extending for 3 ft. (0·9 m.) on either side of the net across the width of the court. Parallel to the neutral line, and between 6 and 8 ft. (1·8–2·4 m.) from each end of the court, there are other lines known as back lines. The centre line, making four divisions, extends from the middle of the back line to the middle of the neutral line on each side of the net.

There are no definitive rules for deck tennis, for the simple reason that a court has to be marked out in whatever deck space is available and often surrounding influences, deck fit-

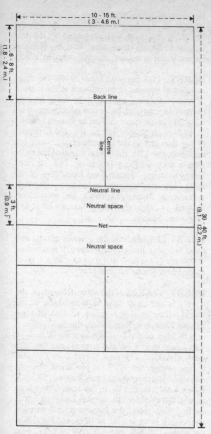

DECK TENNIS COURT

quoit touches the net in service it must be played again, if it drops within bounds. Players standing over the neutral line are faulted.

After a serve all four players may run or stand anywhere in the playing area on their own side. Players may stretch their hands over the neutral line but not over the net.

If the quoit touches an outside object it counts against the player delivering it. The quoit must be returned by the player receiving it from the position in the court in which he catches it. If the quoit falls within the neutral space the point is lost. If a player's hand touches, but drops the quoit, it will count against him. Should the quoit strike a boundary line and pass out of bounds, it is considered to have fallen within bounds. Even if the quoit is already out of bounds, anyone attempting to catch it, and failing to do so, will lose the point.

Should both players touch the quoit, it is counted a fault. Players must not hold on to a quoit unnecessarily, or use both hands, and a quoit touching any part of the body is faulted. Players are not allowed to serve or return the quoit with both feet off the deck.

If the quoit falls on the deck in the proper court when serving, or within bounds in subsequent play, it counts against the player who fails to catch it. A quoit falling untouched out of the proper court when served, or out of bounds in subsequent play, will lose the point for those serving or delivering the quoit.

Scoring advances 15, 30, 40, advantage, game; there are six games to a set.

DEEV, PAVEL (1941-   ), Russian three-day event (see EQUESTRIAN EVENTS) horseman. A member of the Russian team which won the European championship in 1962, when it was staged in England, he has ridden in two OLYMPIC GAMES and came close to winning the individual gold medal at Mexico in 1968.

DELAGE. The first racing car bearing this name, built by Louis Delage, appeared in 1911 and won the Coupe de l'Auto race. Delage Grand Prix cars were successful in the Grand Prix de France in 1912. After wins with the 2-litre V-12 GP car in 1925, Delage produced a complicated straight-eight 1·5-litre type for the 1926 and 1927 seasons. In the latter they were first in a number of Grands Prix including the European at MONZA and the Royal Automobile Club at BROOKLANDS.

DELFORCE, Mrs. ELIZABETH (*née* Poulton) (1920-   ), HOCKEY player for England, East of England, Kent, and Atlanta.

tings, the convenience of other passengers, and the welfare of the players and spectators, have enforced amendments and revision of the more generally accepted rules.

The server stands on the back line of the right-hand court and delivers the quoit over the net to his opponent in the diagonally opposite court. The quoit must be delivered in an upward direction for at least 6 in. (152 mm.) after it leaves the hand. The server's hand may pass over the back line before the ring leaves it, but the quoit must not be delivered flat and, although 'wobblers' are allowed, they are not considered good form. Forehand and backhand deliveries must be given but not overhand ones or deliveries from a height above the shoulder. Feints at delivery or baulking in any form are forbidden. If the

A really fine full-back, she represented England from 1949 to 1957 and was recalled in 1960; she was a member of the England touring team to Holland in 1948; and captained England for six years (1952-7).

DEMPSEY, JACK (1895-　), American boxer who held the world heavyweight title between 1919 and 1926. He featured in four championship bouts and one non-title contest which drew more than $1 million, including his second meeting with TUNNEY in 1927 which grossed $2,658,660. These figures, extraordinary before the advent of television, reflected the great appeal of Dempsey, whose persistent attack and savage punching invariably made him one of the most exciting boxers to watch. Dempsey learned his craft the hard way, fighting in the back rooms of saloons and dance-halls. After he was managed by the shrewd Kearns, the young fighter from Colorado rose steadily to the top. In 1919 he gave away 58 lb. (26 kg.) to Willard and won the title in three rounds. In 1921 Dempsey defended the title against CARPENTIER and the appeal of the bout, thanks to the genius of the promoter, RICKARD, produced the first gate of more than $1 million. Unpopular during his early reign as champion because he had done no military service during the First World War, Dempsey later became a respected figure as well as a rich man.

DEN OUDEN, WILEMIJNTJE (1918-　), Dutch woman who had the distinction of holding a world SWIMMING record for the longest time. This was her 64·6 seconds for 100 metres in 1936 which stood, unchallenged, for six days short of 20 years. She won four gold and five silver medals in OLYMPIC GAMES and European championships between 1931 and 1938.

DENNY CUP, colloquial term for what is virtually the English indoor club championship of BOWLS. It is played between the months of October and March and clubs affiliated to the English Indoor Bowling Association are allowed to nominate one team of 16 players. The draw is made on the knock-out system. Each match is normally played on a home-and-away basis, eight men versus eight men on the greens of each of the two clubs; the scores of these two meetings are added together to give the result, extra ends being played to obtain a winner and loser whenever there is an over-all tie after 21 ends at each venue. Clubs may agree to play both legs on one green. The quarter-finals are staged at a neutral club unless both participants in a match agree to use the home-and-away system of ear-lier rounds. The semi-finals and finals are staged at an indoor club chosen by the E.I.B.A. The cup was presented by the late Leonard Denny and was won by Crystal Palace in the inaugural championship in 1935.

DERBY, 17th Earl of (1865-1948), the most influential breeder of bloodstock in the history of HORSE RACING, and top of the list of leading owners in England on seven occasions, winning 20 classic races. When he won the DERBY in 1924 with Sansovino, he was the first peer of his line to win the premier classic since his ancestor, the 12th Earl, who founded the race, won it with Sir Peter Teazle in 1787. At Lord Derby's Stanley House Stud stood four of the most important stallions in modern pedigrees: SWYNFORD, Pharos, FAIRWAY, and HYPERION; as well as celebrated brood mares like SCAPA FLOW and Selene.

DERBY ITALIANO, the premier classic and most valuable horse race in Italy. It is run over 2,400 m. (1½ miles) at La CAPANNELLE racecourse near Rome early in May.

DERBY STAKES, 'the Blue Riband of the Turf', is the most famous horse race in the world. Run over 1½ miles (2,400 m.) on Epsom Downs in England on the last Wednesday in May or the first Wednesday in June, it was founded in 1780 and named after the 12th Earl of DERBY. The race, worth over £66,000 to the winner in 1973, is for three-year-old colts and fillies, colts to carry 9 stone (57 kg.), fillies 8 st. 9 lb. (55 kg.). The hottest favourite to win the premier classic was Ladas at 9 to 2 on in 1894, while the longest-priced winners of the race were Jeddah in 1898, the filly, Signorinetta, in 1908, and Aboyeur in 1913, who all started at 100 to 1 against. Six fillies have won the Derby: Eleanor in 1801, Blink Bonny in 1857, Shotover in 1882, Signorinetta in 1908, Tagalie in 1912, and Fifinella (a wartime Derby) in 1916.

Lord Egremont and the AGA KHAN both won the Derby five times; Robson, PORTER, and DARLING each trained seven winners; and ROBINSON and DONOGHUE both rode six winners.

The most exciting finishes were probably when Cadland and The Colonel ran a dead-heat in 1828 (Cadland later winning the run-off); when BEND OR, ridden by ARCHER, beat Robert the Devil by a head in 1880; when St. Gatien and Harvester ran a dead-heat in 1884 (stakes divided); when PERSIMMON, in the royal colours, defeated St. Frusquin by a neck in record time in 1896; and when Roberto beat RHEINGOLD by a short head in 1972.

(See also GREYHOUND RACING.)

DESJARDINS, PETE (1908-), diver for the U.S.A. and Stanford University. Winner of both springboard and high DIVING in the OLYMPIC GAMES at Amsterdam, 1928, he averaged 9·2 judges' points for all his dives, and for two dives he received 10 points (the maximum) from each judge. In 1931 he toured Great Britain, lecturing and demonstrating the latest diving techniques. He presented the Pete Desjardins trophy for the English national 1-metre springboard championship to encourage divers to learn their dives on the 1-metre board before progressing to the higher boards. His visits were so successful in rousing enthusiasm for diving that he was invited again in 1934 and each year until 1937.

DESPERDICIOS (Manuel Domínguez) (1816-86), *matador de toros* whose pseudonym means 'garbage' or 'offal'. He acquired this gruesome nickname in a *corrida* in Puerta de Santa Maria on 1 June 1857, when a bull gored him in the eye, which he promptly tore out and cast disdainfully away before continuing his performance. After his *alternativa* in 1836, he went to South America.

DETROIT LIONS, American professional FOOTBALL team, entered the NATIONAL FOOTBALL LEAGUE in 1930 as the Portsmouth (Michigan) Spartans. In 1934 they became the Detroit Lions and had a good record during the 1930s, with an exceptional backfield, featuring the versatile quarterback CLARK, the running backs Caddel and Cardwell, and the fullback Gutowsky. They won the 1935 League title, and won successive titles in 1952 and 1953, led by the flamboyant quarterback Layne and the halfback Walker.
COLOURS: Blue and silver.

DETROIT RED WINGS, ICE HOCKEY club of Detroit, member of the professional NATIONAL HOCKEY LEAGUE of North America. The club first won the STANLEY CUP in 1936, retaining it the following year and winning it again in 1943, 1950, 1952, 1954, and 1955; they were N.H.L. champions 13 times and the first club to win it seven times in a row, 1949-55. Their home rink, Olympia Stadium, Detroit, has a capacity of 15,692 and an ice surface measuring 83 by 200 ft. (25 × 60 m.). Outstanding players have included G. HOWE, S. Howe, Kelly, Quackenbush, SAWCHUK, and J. Stewart.
COLOURS: Red and white.

DETROIT TIGERS, American professional BASEBALL team, an initial member of the AMERICAN LEAGUE in 1901. Under its manager Jennings Detroit won three straight league titles (1907-09). Later the Tigers captured the WORLD SERIES in 1935, 1945, and 1968. Detroit's greatest player in the early period (1905-26) was TY COBB, manager from 1921 to 1926, who has the highest major-league lifetime batting average of ·367. From 1914 to 1929 the outfielder Heilman batted ·342. In the 1930s the outfielder Greenberg (lifetime average ·313), the second baseman Gehringer (lifetime average ·320), and the catcher-manager (1934-7) Cochrane led the Tigers.

DEUTSCHES DERBY is the premier classic horse race in Germany, run over 2,400 m. (1½ miles) at Hamburg-Horn at the end of June.

DEVERNOIS, CLAUDE (1904-), president of the French RUGBY LEAGUE from 1955 to 1964.

DEVIL AMONG THE TAILORS, see SKITTLES.

DEVIZES TO WESTMINSTER MARATHON, 125 mile (201 km.) race, begun in 1949, for double crews only of canoe or kayak. It starts at Devizes in Wiltshire, England, and is raced for 54 miles along the Kennet and Avon Canal to join the Thames at Reading, then 71 miles down to Westminster in London. This event is held annually at Easter and has proved of great interest to Service crews who for many years have held the record. First canoeists over the course were content to aim for a time under 100 hours but by 1970 the winners were down to under 20 hours.

DEVLIN, J. FRANK (1899-), Irish BADMINTON player who, at the height of his career, was probably the finest the game had known. Included in his numerous successes were six ALL-ENGLAND CHAMPIONSHIP singles wins, six men's doubles titles, and five mixed doubles wins. In 1931 he became a teaching professional and took up a post in Canada. He is the father of Mrs. HASHMAN and Mrs. Peard, both outstanding players who represented the U.S.A.

DEVLIN, JUDITH M., see HASHMAN, MRS. G. C. K.

DEVON AND CORNWALL, see WRESTLING.

DEWAR MATCH, see SHOOTING, RIFLE: SMALL-BORE.

DEXTER, EDWARD RALPH (1935-   ), cricketer for England, Cambridge University, and Sussex. An exciting batsman, one of the few to rate comparison with those of CRICKET's Golden Age before the First World War, he seemed to fear no bowler, and often paid for this indifference. His courage was epitomized in an innings of 70 at LORD's against a fiery West Indies attack, and an eight-hour innings of 174 against Australia in 1964 revealed a self-discipline not often displayed. Captain of England in 25 Tests, he is also a top-class golfer.

DI MAGGIO, JOSEPH PAUL (1914-   ), American BASEBALL player for the NEW YORK YANKEES (1936-51), known for his batting ability and his graceful outfield play. He led his team twice in batting and twice in home runs. In 1941 he set a new record by batting safely at least once in 56 consecutive games.

DI STEFANO, ALFREDO (1926-   ), Association footballer for RIVER PLATE (Buenos Aires), Milionarios (Bogota), REAL MADRID, Argentina, and Spain. One of the greatest footballers of all time, he played for River Plate in his home country before joining the procession of South American players who signed for Colombian clubs which could afford to pay high wages to their imported star players. Subsequently he took Spanish nationality and played regularly for the Spanish national team. He will be remembered for his performances at centre forward for Real Madrid when they won the European Champion Clubs Cup in each of the first five seasons of the competition. At the end of his playing career he became a coach and in 1971 managed Valencia to success in the Spanish League championship.

DIAMOND JUBILEE (1897), English racehorse, full brother to PERSIMMON by ST. SIMON out of PERDITA II, was bred at the Sandringham Stud, owned by the Prince of WALES (later Edward VII), trained by MARSH, and ridden by his stable attendant, Herbert Jones, who was perhaps the only person able to control this evil-tempered animal. Diamond Jubilee won 13 races, including the DERBY and ST. LEGER, both in record time, the TWO THOUSAND GUINEAS and ECLIPSE STAKES, with a total of £29,185 in stake money.

DIAMOND SCULLS, see HENLEY ROYAL REGATTA.

DICKINSON, JAMES W., M.B.E. (1925-   ), Association footballer for PORTSMOUTH, and England for whom he made the first of his 48 appearances in full international matches against Norway in Oslo on 18 May 1949 and his last in a World Cup qualifying match against Denmark in Wolverhampton on 5 December 1956. He was a member of the Portsmouth team until 1965 after playing a record 764 Football League matches for the club in the First, Second, and Third Divisions. Between 1948 and 1950 when Portsmouth won the League championship in two successive seasons, a major factor in the team's fine all-round play was the excellent understanding between the wing halves, Dickinson and Scoular. He remained with his only professional club after retiring as a player, firstly as public relations officer and later as secretary.

DIDI (Waldir Pereira) (1928-   ), Association footballer for BOTAFOGO (Rio) and Brazil for whom he played in midfield in the successful World Cup finals of 1958 and 1962. A tall, elegant player, he became renowned for his 'falling leaf' free kick and was an established world-class player of vast experience when he left his Brazilian club, Botafogo, to play for REAL MADRID. There was too much similarity of style and thinking in his play and that of DI STEFANO for the two ever to blend in the Real Madrid side. After returning to South America, he became a coach in Peru and was later appointed to prepare the Peruvian national team for their qualifying matches of the 1970 World Cup championship.

DIDRIKSON, MILDRED (Babe) (later Mrs. Zaharias) (1914-56), all-round athlete for the U.S.A. When she was only 16, Miss Didrikson broke the world JAVELIN record with 133 ft. 3¼ in. (40·62 m.), and when still only 18, won Olympic gold medals in 1932 for the 80 metres hurdles and javelin, together with a silver medal in the HIGH JUMP. Her time of 11·7 sec. in the hurdles final broke the world record which she had equalled in the preliminaries. In the high jump she also equalled the world record with 5 ft. 5¼ in. (1·66 m.), but had to concede first place because the judges did not approve her unorthodox head-first style.

Having thus no more than hinted at her immense ATHLETICS potential, Miss Didrikson went on to earn even greater fame and rewards as a professional golfer, winning the U.S. national women's amateur championship and the British ladies' championship, and, as a professional, the U.S. Open three times.

DIETRICH, WERNER (1933-   ), West German wrestler who won titles at both freestyle and Graeco-Roman. He was outstandingly consistent in the Olympics, winning a heavyweight gold medal in 1960 at freestyle and silver and bronze medals at other celebrations. He might have pressed the great freestyle competitor, MEDVED, even harder at the 1968 Olympics but he damaged a knee in the final pool and finished third. He retired after the 1972 Olympics.

DILLARD, HARRISON (1923-), hurdler and sprinter for the U.S.A. Favourite for the Olympic 110 metres hurdles title in 1948, Dillard failed in the final U.S. Olympic trials at his chosen event but succeeded instead in winning a place in the 100 metres, which he went on to win in 10·3 sec. to equal the Olympic record. In 1952 he made amends for his hurdles disappointment by winning the 110 metres event at Helsinki in 13·7 sec. for another Olympic record. In both his Olympic appearances he contributed his considerable speed to American victories in the 4 × 100 metres relay. Dillard held world records for 120 yards hurdles in 13·6 sec. and 220 yards hurdles on a straight track in 22·3 sec. and was virtually unbeatable in indoor competition, winning the American A.A.U. 60 yards hurdles in seven successive years.

DINNIE, DONALD (1837-1916), Scottish professional athlete of immense power and versatility, who was still drawing crowds all over the world when he was more than 50 years old. His achievements, notably in field events, were so spectacular that by the end of the nineteenth century their accuracy was often questioned. He put the SHOT nearly 50 ft. (15·24 m.) and threw the 16-lb. (7·2 kg.) HAMMER 138 ft. (42·06 m.). He was almost invincible in many HIGHLAND GAMES events, and was also a high jumper, wrestler, and weightlifter of extraordinary ability.

D'INZEO, PIERO (1923-), Italian show jumping (see EQUESTRIAN EVENTS) rider. Acknowledged as two of the most stylish and talented riders in the world, Piero and his brother RAIMONDO D'INZEO have, between them, won every major individual show jumping title. As a young lieutenant in the Italian cavalry, Piero made his Olympic début in 1949, when he represented Italy in both the show jumping and the three-day event. His successes include four Olympic team medals (silver, 1956; bronze, 1960, 1964, and 1972) and two individual medals (bronze, 1956, on Uruquay; silver, 1960, on The Rock). He has also won the European championship once (1959, on Uruquay) and finished second twice (1958, on The Rock; 1961, on Pioneer).

D'INZEO, RAIMONDO (1925-), Italian show jumping (see EQUESTRIAN EVENTS) rider. He spent two years at Rome University before opting to make riding his career by joining the Italian cavalry. In 1950, he was transferred to the *carabinieri* and, two years later, he had his first ride in the OLYMPIC GAMES. His successes include an individual Olympic gold medal (1960, on Posillipo) and an individual silver (1956, on Merano), as well as the same team medals as his brother, PIERO D'INZEO (silver, 1956; bronze 1960, 1964, and 1972). He has also won the men's world championship twice (1956, on Merano; 1960, on Gowran Girl).

DISCUS, a standard field event for men and women on the programme of all major ATHLETICS championships; performances are eligible for acceptance as records by the International Amateur Athletic Federation (see ATHLETICS, TRACK AND FIELD). The discus is also one of the events in the DECATHLON.

Throwing the discus is mentioned in the writings of Homer, and was first contested in the ancient Greek OLYMPIC GAMES in about 708 B.C. The discus is circular, tapering from its thickest point at the centre to the rim. Constructed of wood with metal plates set flush into the sides, it weighs 4 lb. 6·547 oz. (2 kg.) for men, and 2 lb. 3·274 oz. (1 kg.) for women. The discus is thrown with one hand from within the limits of a circle 8 ft. 2⅜ in. (2·50 m.) in diameter. A competitor is allowed six throws, which are measured from the landing point to the circumference of the circle. The thrower commences his throw from the back of the circle, holding the discus flat against his hand with his fingers curled round the rim. After a few preliminary swings of the throwing arm, the athlete drives across the circle, turning as he goes, and landing in the front half of the circle in a position to release the discus.

DISLEY, JOHN (1928-), mountaineering instructor and English Olympic athlete who won a bronze medal in the 3000 metres STEEPLECHASE at the Helsinki OLYMPIC GAMES (1952). He then turned his interest to ORIENTEERING and with BRASHER, a fellow international athlete, was responsible for the development of the sport in Britain. He succeeded Brasher as chairman of the British Orienteering Federation (1970).

DIVING is an individual competitive sport, with separate events for men and women, in which the diver projects himself into the air from an elevated board and executes either a simple header or more complicated somersaults, before entering the water.

Diving, meaning basically 'to plunge into water', is used generally to describe any method of descending beneath the surface of the water. We speak of a submarine diving, of a diving bell, and of pearl-divers. In survival swimming and life-saving we speak of the surface dive which is used to descend quickly to the bottom when swimming. In the sport of sub-aqua (see UNDERWATER SWIMMING) we have 'skin-diving' using the snorkel, and of aqualung diving using the compressed-air container. Swimmers use the racing dive to enter the water from the side of the pool (see SWIMMING). In these instances the dive is used as a means to an end, descending deep or, in the case of the racing dive, projecting the body as far forward as possible beneath the surface. In competitive diving, however, the water is just the landing medium as the mat is for the gymnast. It is the flight through the air that is the dive and provides the challenge; competitive diving is actually aerial gymnastics.

Diving as practised today means taking off from a height and aiming to remain in the air for as long as possible before entering the water. To do so the diver requires height, which is obtained either by diving from a high fixed board or projecting oneself high into the air from a springboard.

The high board is a rigid platform with a resilient hardwood surface, covered with coconut or other non-slip matting. It is installed at heights of 5 m., 7·5 m., and 10 m. (16 ft. 5 in., 24 ft. 7 in., and approx. 33 ft.) above the water level. Because of the higher tariff value, all divers in international competition use the 10-metre platform. The regulations require that the 10-metre platform be 2 m. (6 ft. 7 in.) wide and 6 m. (19 ft. 8 in.) long. It is usually mounted on reinforced concrete or steel. The front of the platform must project at least 1·5 m. (4 ft. 11 in.) beyond the edge of the bath, and the back and sides must be surrounded by hand rails. Each platform must be accessible by suitable stairs (not ladders). Mechanical surface agitation must be installed under the diving facilities to aid divers in their visual perception of the surface of the water.

The modern springboard is a flexible, tapered, precision instrument from which the diver springs upward to obtain extra height in his dive, giving him more time in the air. An expert can rise 4 to 5 ft. (1·2 to 1·5 m.) above the board. Springboards are installed at heights of 1 m. and 3 m. (3 ft. 3½ in. and 9 ft. 10 in.) above the water level. The regulations require that the springboards be at least 4·8 m. (15 ft. 9 in.) long and 0·5 m. (1 ft. 8 in.) wide,

and covered along the whole length with rough coconut matting, unless provided with a satisfactory non-slip surface. The springboards for the OLYMPIC GAMES, regional games, continental championships, and international contests must be provided with movable fulcrums easily adjustable by the diver. The boards must be new and must project at least 1·5 m. (4 ft. 11 in.) beyond the edge of the bath. The modern springboard, consisting of timber strips glued together and totally encased in fibreglass, has been superseded in international competition by the light and more springy aluminium-alloy board.

The only personal equipment the male diver needs is a well-fitting pair of trunks with an internal tying cord (external belts cannot withstand the impact with the water). Women need a one-piece costume with strong shoulder straps.

When describing a dive it is convenient to divide it into four parts: (1) the starting position on the board; (2) the take-off from the board; (3) the flight through the air; (4) the entry into the water. In practice the dive is one continuous movement, and in competition it is judged as a whole and not in parts.

The *starting position* for standing dives is at the front end of the board with the body erect, hands by the sides or above the head. For running dives the erect position with hands by the sides is taken up at least four paces back from the front end of the board.

The *take-off* comprises every movement the diver makes from the time he assumes the starting position until the moment his feet leave the board. For running dives from the fixed platform, the run is on the balls of the feet followed by a low hop, to land on the end of the board. From the springboard the 'run' is in reality a three-step walk, followed by a high leap into the air from one foot, called the hurdle step, and a landing on the end of the board with both feet together. Before the diver loses contact with the board at the completion of the take-off, three objects must be achieved: (*a*) the body must be projected upwards with maximum velocity to obtain height, with its resultant gain in time; (*b*) the body must be set in motion away from the board, for safety; (*c*) the body movements necessary to produce the forward or backward rotation must be completed. After the diver has lost contact with the board there is little he can do to alter his dive.

The *flight* is that part of the dive when the body is free in the air, and is finished the moment any part of the body touches the water. During the flight the body may be carried in one of three recognized body positions: (*a*) straight — the body is not bent either at the hips or knees; (*b*) pike — the body is bent at the hips (90° or more) but the legs are straight at the knees; (*c*) tuck — the whole body is bunched up with the knees together, hands on the lower legs. In each position the feet are together with toes pointed. The positions are assumed soon after take-off and held for varying lengths of time during the flight, depending on the requirements of the dive being performed. Just prior to the entry the body is straightened. During his time in the air the diver is able to control his rate of rotation (angular velocity) within certain limits. The tighter he tucks, the faster he spins, and when

Straight

Pike

Tuck

BODY POSITIONS

he stretches out for the entry he is rotating at his slowest.

The *entry* begins the moment any part of the body touches the water and is completed (as is the dive) the moment the body is totally submerged. From the high platform the diver plummets into the water at about 32½ m.p.h. (52 km./h.). To avoid the shock to his system, he aims to enter the water as nearly vertical as possible, with his body perfectly straight. When entering feet first, the arms are held close to the body, but for head-first entries the arms are stretched above the head, hands close together.

All dives are some form of somersault. The simple header is a half-somersault. This is followed by the single somersault, 1½ somersault, double somersault, 2½ somersault, triple somersault, and finally the 3½ somersault. The direction of the rotation (somersault) can be either forward or backward. The half, 1½, 2½, and 3½ somersault dives are head-first entries, but the single, double, and triple somersault dives enter feet first. As feet-first entries are

more difficult to control, the majority of divers select head-first entry dives in competition. The diver takes off from the board either facing, or with his back to, the water, and there are four basic groups of dives: (1) forward dive — forward start with forward rotation; (2) back dive — back start with backward rotation; (3) reverse dive — forward start with backward rotation; (4) inward dive — back start with forward rotation.

There is a fifth group—'twist'—comprising any dive in which the body rotates laterally about its long axis in addition to any somersaulting rotation. There is also a sixth group, 'arm-stand', used from fixed boards only, in which the diver commences his dive from a position balanced on his hands.

Diving installations may be indoor or outdoor. The diving area in the modern pool complex is usually separated from the swimming area. This enables the required water temperature of 83° to 86° F. (28° to 30° C.) (to be obtained against that of 76° F. (24° C.) required for the swimming area. Minimum and preferred depths of water over a specified area for each height of board are laid down by the Fédération Internationale de Natation Amateur (F.I.N.A.) for reasons of safety, using the plummet line — a vertical line extending through the centre point of the front edge of the diving springboard or platform — as a basic measuring point of reference. These depths are reviewed by F.I.N.A. every four years, immediately after the Olympic Games, and revised if necessary. The regulations also include minimum distances to the nearest wall in all directions.

(*a*) Depth of water at plummet
    1-metre springboard: 3·40 m. minimum (3·80 m. preferred)
    3-metre springboard: 3·80 m. minimum (4·00 m. preferred)
    5-metre platform: 3·80 m. minimum (4·00 m. preferred)
    10-metre platform: 4·50 m. minimum (5·00 m. preferred)
(*b*) Depth at 6·00 m. ahead of plummet
    1-metre springboard: 3·30 m. minimum (3·70 m. preferred)
    3-metre springboard: 3·70 m. minimum (3·90 m. preferred)
    5-metre platform: 3·70 m.
Depth at 12·00 m. ahead of plummet
    10-metre platform: 4·25 m.
(*c*) Distance from plummet to pool wall ahead
    1-metre springboard: 9·00 m.
    3-metre springboard: 10·50 m.
    5-metre platform: 11·00 m.
    10-metre platform: 13·50 m.
(*d*) Distance from plummet back to pool wall
    1-metre and *3-metre springboard:* 1·50 m. minimum (1·80 m. preferred)
    5-metre and *10-metre platform:* 1·50 m.

(*e*) Distance from plummet to side pool wall
  1-metre springboard: 2·50 m.
  3-metre springboard: 3·50 m.
  5-metre platform: 4·50 m.
  10-metre platform: 5·25 m.
(*f*) Distance between boards
  1-metre and *3-metre springboards:* 1·90 m. minimum (2·40 m. preferred)

In pools used for the Olympic Games the depths must be the preferred dimensions. The depth of water anywhere in the diving pool must be not less than 1·8 m. (5 ft. 11 in.) and the angle of slope of the pool bottom must not exceed 30° (approx. 1:2) at any point.

All diving competitions organized at international games are subject to the regulations of F.I.N.A. The men's springboard competitions comprise five required dives (forward, back, reverse, and inward dives, and forward dive ½ twist) and six voluntary dives, including one from each of the five groups. The ladies' springboard competitions comprise five required dives, as in the men's springboard competitions, but only five voluntary dives selected from the five groups.

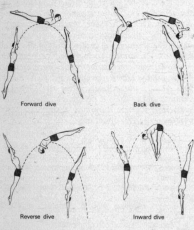

Forward dive

Back dive

Reverse dive

Inward dive

FOUR BASIC DIVES

The men's high-board competitions comprise six basic dives and four voluntary dives. In each section each dive is selected from a different group. The dives may be performed from either the 5-metre or 10-metre platform. The ladies' high-board competitions comprise four required dives (forward, back, reverse, and inward dives) and four voluntary dives from four different groups performed from either the 10-metre or 5-metre platform. Where there are more than 12 competitors, there are preliminary and final contests.

Dives are judged on execution only. The degree of difficulty of the dive is reflected in the tariff value allocated to it. The diver has to decide whether to risk a more difficult high-tariff position with a possible low award from the judges if he 'flops'. The judges' awards are multiplied by the degree of difficulty value to arrive at the final score.

The judging panel is composed of the referee and the judges. In Olympic and continental championships seven judges are required; for an official inter-nation competition five judges are sufficient. The referee is in charge of the competition. Two recorders (secretaries) record the judges' awards on the score sheet, cancel out the highest and lowest award, add the remainder, and multiply by the degree of difficulty. In contests where there are seven judges, the score is divided by 5 and multiplied by 3 in order to establish a score comparable to that obtained in contests where there are five judges. Points are awarded as follows:

> Completely failed, 0 points
> Unsatisfactory, ½–2 points
> Deficient, 2½–4½ points
> Satisfactory, 5–6 points
> Good, 6½–8 points
> Very good, 8½–10 points

A diver is allowed only one attempt at each dive. If he balks and has to restart, the referee will subtract 2 points from each award. If he balks a second time, the referee will declare it a failed dive. The winner is the competitor who obtains the largest number of points.

The International Diving Committee of F.I.N.A. meet immediately after the Olympic Games and whenever otherwise necessary, to consider and if necessary revise the rules for diving from proposals received from any country. They also investigate, study, and are prepared to recommend equipment for international or Olympic competitions.

Amateur Swimming Association, *International Rules for Diving,* latest edition.

Until the beginning of the nineteenth century, all references to diving in the books on swimming refer to a simple plunge from the side of a pool as a means of entering the water for the purpose of swimming. This eventually developed into the 'racing dive' used as the start of some competitive swimming events.

It is difficult to say at what period in history man first dived head first into water. The first swimming obviously took place in the rivers and the neighbouring sea in countries near the tropics. The original object of the dive (to enter the water to swim) gave way to jumping, and then to diving for its own sake. The challenge and the satisfaction came from the flight

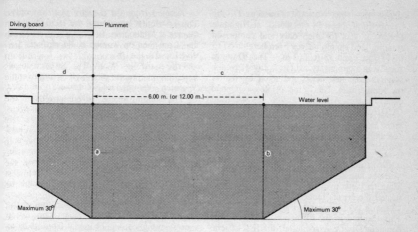

DIAGRAMMATIC CROSS-SECTION OF DIVING POOL
(a) Depth of water at plummet; (b) depth at 6·00 m. (12·00 m. for 10-metre platform) ahead of plummet; (c) distance from plummet to pool wall ahead; (d) distance from plummet back to pool wall. (Not shown in diagram: distance from plummet to side pool wall; distance between boards.)

through the air, and men jumped and dived from greater and greater heights.

In more recent history, professional divers have dived from temporary towers, often over 60 ft. (18·29 m.) high, into tanks of water for the amusement of the crowds at fairgrounds and carnivals. People began jumping from bridges in Europe and the U.S.A., later diving head first from them. Indians in Mexico were adept at jumping and diving from high cliffs into the sea. During a visit to Hawaii in the late nineteenth century, Lady Brassey observed how the natives leaped, dived, and somersaulted from considerable heights, often into pools at the bottom of waterfalls, for the sheer excitement of it.

At the beginning of the nineteenth century a new form of diving was developing in Europe, mainly in Germany and Sweden where formal gymnastics was popular. During the summer months, gymnastic apparatus was transferred to the beach. The flying rings, the trapeze, and the springboard were erected and used from high platforms to enable gymnastics to be performed over the water. This was the beginning of 'fancy diving', the name later given to aerial acrobatics over the water. (Until this time, most diving was 'plain' — the simple forward header with the body held straight and arms extended sideways — known in the early days in Europe as the 'Swedish swallow' and later in the U.S.A. as the 'swan dive'.) The trapeze and rings were gradually discarded and diving from platform and springboard incorporating gymnastic somersaults developed as a separate sport, becoming known as springboard diving and fancy high diving.

Diving as a competitive event began in Great Britain. In 1893 the Amateur Swimming Association (A.S.A.) (England) inaugurated the plunging championship, which consisted of a standing head-first dive. The entry was near horizontal, the body descending to about 2 ft. (0·61 m.). It was open to men only, the winner being the person who travelled the farthest distance, the plunge terminating at the expiration of 60 seconds. The English amateur record — 86 ft. 8 in. (26·4 m.) — was made by Parrington at Bootle in 1933. (Parrington won this event eight times.) Big heavy men had the advantage over smaller men in plunging, and the plunging championship ceased from 1937. Diving for its own sake had already developed from the plunge, and the take-off was being attempted from greater heights. Thomas, the noted swimming historian, urged the adoption of the term 'springing' to apply to entering the water from an elevation. By this time, however, the word 'dive' had become so firmly established that it was too late to change it. In 1889 the first diving championship took place in Scotland. It included a dive from the side and a dive from a height of about 6 ft. (1·8 m.). In 1893 the first diving stage in England was erected at the Highgate Ponds, London. It was a firm board fixed at a height of about 15 ft. (4·6 m.) above the surface.

In 1895, the Royal Life Saving Society

staged the first National Graceful Diving Competition, open to the world, at Highgate Ponds. It was for men only and comprised standing and running dives from heights of 15 ft. (4·6 m.) and 33 ft. (10 m.). The 10-metre stage was a temporary structure, fitted up each summer for a few weeks and taken down after the competition. This competition was handed over to the Amateur Diving Association (A.D.A.) in 1920 and taken over by the A.S.A., who renamed it the Plain Diving Championship of the A.S.A. in 1935. It was held outdoors until 1953, when it was transferred to the indoor Derby Bath at Blackpool; in 1961 the competition was discontinued.

In the late 1800s, Johansson, Hagberg, and Mauritzi came over from Sweden and demonstrated the art of 'fancy high diving' from the 10-metre platform erected at Highgate Ponds. This resulted in the formation in 1901 of the Amateur Diving Association, the first official organization in the world devoted to the sport of diving. There were more facilities for platform diving in Europe than in the U.S.A., and the European divers from England or northern Europe dominated the plain diving events. In England and most of Europe divers graduated from plain diving, taking off from platforms, to fancy diving from platforms and then to springboards. Plain diving events were included in the Olympic Games until 1924, but in 1928 the men's plain and fancy high diving events were amalgamated into one competition and renamed 'high-board diving'. The word 'fancy' disappeared from the diver's vocabulary. Fancy dives had been included for the first time in competition in 1903; springboard diving was included in the Olympic Games at St. Louis in 1904 and platform diving in the supplementary Olympic Games at Athens in 1906. Diving at this time was very little known in southern Europe despite the advantages of a warmer climate.

Tariff tables giving a degree of difficulty value to each dive were drawn up and used for the first time at the Olympic Games at White City, London, in 1908. Women were allowed in the Olympic diving events for the first time at the Olympic Games in Stockholm in 1912 in a plain diving contest. Diving was considered unsuitable for women at that time and it was not until 1920, at the Olympic Games in Antwerp, that women were allowed to compete in springboard events. Women were allowed to compete in a high-board (fancy) diving event for the first time at the Amsterdam Olympics in 1928 (the men's and women's plain diving events having been discontinued after the 1924 Games). It was decided, however, that certain dives were not to be performed by women at all, and some other dives were to be performed

by women from the 5-metre platform only. This restriction lasted until the 1956 Olympic Games at Melbourne. In 1957 it was removed and from then on women could perform any dive listed in the tables.

Prior to the First World War, Sweden dominated the plain and fancy high diving events. The men's springboard events were dominated by the German divers, who won all bronze, silver, and gold medals. The one exception was the event won by Sheldon (U.S.A.) at the St. Louis Games in 1904. The First World War brought diving to a halt in Europe, and the U.S.A. divers forged ahead to such an extent that, when the Olympic Games restarted in 1920 at Antwerp, they swept the board, gaining all six springboard medals in the men's and women's events.

This started the U.S.A. domination of the Olympic diving events. They won every men's springboard gold medal from 1920 to 1968 and all the silvers until Dibiasi (Italy) won the silver in 1968. Of the 11 platform gold medals, the U.S.A. men won 9, and the U.S.A. women won every springboard medal in the period from 1920 to 1948. Mrs. MCCORMICK (U.S.A.) won the Olympic springboard and high diving events in both 1952 and 1956, a remarkable feat. The U.S.A. women's run of gold medals was broken by Miss KRAMER (Germany) who won both the springboard and high diving at Rome in 1960 and the springboard at Tokyo in 1964.

European championships were introduced in 1926 under the jurisdiction of the European Swimming League .(L.E.N.) to take place between the Olympic years. As the U.S.A. divers were not eligible, Germany dominated these events, winning more medals than any other nation. Britain's only gold medallists were Miss Slade (springboard) in 1938 at the EMPIRE POOL, Wembley, and PHELPS, who, at the age of 14, won the high-board event with ease at Budapest in 1958; he repeated his success in 1962 at Leipzig.

The British Empire and Commonwealth Games (now the COMMONWEALTH GAMES) were first held at Hamilton, Ontario, in 1930 with 11 competing countries, and provided encouragement to England, who could not break the power of the U.S.A. and Germany in world diving events. Until 1966, England had won half the available Commonwealth gold medals. Phelps emerged as the most successful diver, becoming springboard and high-board champion in 1962 at Perth, Australia, and repeating his success in 1966 at Kingston, Jamaica.` In 1966, England won all four events — men's and women's springboard and high-board.

The PAN-AMERICAN GAMES between countries on the American continent are usually a repeat of the Olympic Games, with the U.S.A. dominating the diving events. The world supremacy of the U.S.A. men divers is due largely to their national collegiate programme. An analysis of the men and women champions in the U.S.A. since 1948 shows that they are all from the state of California with its suitable climate, excellent diving facilities, and good diving coaches; but as more indoor diving facilities are provided elsewhere, the gap between the U.S.A. and the rest of the world is gradually being reduced. Over the years, diving contest conditions have undergone constant revision and have been altered in the light of experience. In the period before 1924 the diving tables were very complex. There were six methods of executing each forward or reverse dive. The take-off could be either standing, a running take-off from one foot, or a running take-off from both feet, and in each case a head-first entry could be made 'with or without hands' (in the latter case the arms were held by the sides). The competition itself consisted of ten compulsory dives and two 'post' dives. The post dives were drawn by number out of a hat, and as they consisted of some of the most difficult dives on the list, it was an unnerving experience for a diver waiting for his post dive to be drawn. The 1928 Olympic diving competitions consisted of compulsory dives and voluntary dives. The compulsory dives were selected after each Olympic Games and were in force for the following four years. This form of competition continued until the 1948 Games in London. From 1949 to 1956 all dives were voluntary dives on both springboard and high board, and very rarely were the basic dives seen in competition. After 1956, the regulations were revised again to include five required basic dives from the springboard. This brought a new look to diving and did a great deal to ensure that divers mastered their basic dives before being encouraged to attempt the more difficult ones.

In the early 1920s most dives were performed in the straight position from both spring and firm boards. The English Amateur Diving Association stated in 1921 that: 'Certain somersaults may be made with a bend at the hips and knees if the board is not sufficiently high to allow the limbs to be kept straight. "Back Front" dives should be performed with no bend at the hips or knees, but from a low board it will be found necessary to bend at the hips.' As multiple-somersault dives came into being it became necessary to ball (tuck) the body up to complete the necessary rotation and so the tuck and pike positions eventually became recognized in addition to the straight position. In the 1920 Olympics at Antwerp the diving list included the header forward (straight), the hunch dive (tuck position), and the pike dive as three separate dives. It was later decided to make them one dive, i.e. 'forward dive' to be performed in any one of the three positions at the choice of the diver. This applies now to all dives in each group.

The Paris Olympic Games in 1924 were notable for the introduction of the first standard international springboard with a movable fulcrum, brought over from the U.S.A. The American men and women divers, who made a clean sweep of all six springboard medals, produced on these boards a standard of execution that put them in a class well above any other country. In 1928 an American diver, DESJARDINS, won both the high-board and springboard diving events at the Amsterdam Games. He demonstrated dives from the springboard never seen before, such as the forward $1\frac{1}{2}$ somersault with a full twist. Early wooden springboards were crude by comparison with the boards now used. Modern standardization of springboards, with the general adoption of the metal alloy board first produced in the U.S.A., has had a tremendous influence on the progress of international diving. Divers are now able to perform the forward $1\frac{1}{2}$ somersault with three twists.

After the Second World War, diving was in the doldrums in Europe. In the 1948 Olympic Games in England, the diving events were held at the Empire Pool, Wembley, and again the U.S.A. divers were outstanding. Mrs. Draves won both springboard and high diving events, demonstrating a grace and excellence not seen before. But it was LEE, from California, who captured the imagination of the spectators when he won the men's high diving. He went on to repeat his success in 1952 in Helsinki. Platform diving had come a long way in a few years. Each country that stages the Olympic Games must provide full diving facilities and, while most countries build them outdoors if possible (such as at Los Angeles in 1932, Berlin in 1936, Helsinki in 1952, and Rome in 1960), some countries build covered pools. This was done at Melbourne in 1956 and at Tokyo, when the YOYOGI NATIONAL GYMNASIUM was built in 1964.

A covered 10-metre diving stage is a costly project, but as new building techniques and materials began to be available it became a practical possibility. Indoor 10-metre diving facilities are now found in most countries, allowing high-board training to take place all the year round instead of for just a few weeks in the summer season. The Crystal Palace National Sports Centre in England, which opened in 1964, heralded the introduction of a new type of sports complex which included a separate covered diving pool with a 10-metre stage and hostel accommodation for the competitors. Many unique designs for diving stages have been produced, with Germany leading the way. Some have elevators to transport the diver to the higher boards.

The early high diving stages were erected over whatever water happened to be available. It was usually outdoors, often cold and murky. When indoor pools became available (the first was built in 1828 at Liverpool) they were built for swimming. The maximum depth at the deep end was never more than 6 ft. (1·8 m.). As diving became more popular, springboards and tiered diving stages were erected at some pools. The shallow water, however, made vertical entries impossible. To avoid hitting the bottom, divers would aim to enter at about 45°. The modern filtration plant was unknown, and it was often not possible to see the bottom. Divers would instinctively arch up on entry to avoid going too deep. Today the water is kept clear and hygienic, and is heated to between 76° F. (24° C.) and 86° F. (30° C.). It is possible to see the bottom through 16 ft. (4·88 m.) of water.

The English Amateur Diving Association specified in 1921 that the minimum depth of water for a 3-metre springboard should be 8 ft. 6 in. (2·6 m.), for a 5-metre board 10 ft. (3 m.), and for a 10-metre board 12 ft. (3·7 m.). With the evolution of diving these depths became inadequate and were increased in response to divers' requests in 1936, in 1952, and again in 1968.

Although the modern male diving attire consists only of brief trunks, the regulations in 1920 required that 'cloth drawers' at least 6 cm. wide at the sides must be worn under the costume. The costume itself covered the whole of the trunk, with arm holes no lower than 7½ cm. from the armpit. The costume also had legs reaching half-way down the thigh. Ladies' costumes were 'cut straight round the neck and provided with shaped arms of at least 7½ cm. length'. The regulations also stated that 'as identification marks, competitors shall wear caps of different colours which will be supplied by the swimming committee'. As many dives in those days required an entry into the water with 'arms close to sides' the hat afforded protection for the head. Later, these 'handless' dives were deleted and hats were not needed for protective purposes and so went out of favour.

Diving is an individual sport, but in order to compete it is necessary to belong to an association affiliated to the governing body of the sport. (F.I.N.A., the International Swimming Federation, founded in London in 1908, is the world governing body for diving as well as for swimming.) In the U.S.A. many divers are affiliated through their universities. Most other divers are members of swimming clubs; diving clubs as such are relatively unknown outside Great Britain. As diving has increased in popularity, groups of enthusiasts have banded together to form clubs devoted solely to diving, the most famous being the HIGH-GATE DIVING CLUB, London, formed in 1928.

In the early days of diving it was often a case of the survival of the fittest. Only those with courage combined with a high degree of gymnastic ability attempted it. For many years there were no textbooks to explain the complexities of the sport, and training was based on trial and error. In later years a more scientific approach to diving has been achieved, and the laws of mechanics applied to diving movements. This has resulted in a remarkable advance in the standard of performance of established dives and an increase in the complexity of new dives. Dives are being performed today by schoolchildren which, fifty years ago, would have been considered impossible for experienced adults.

Amateur Swimming Association, *Competitive Swimming* (1962); G. W. Rackham, *Diving* (1969).
GOVERNING BODY (WORLD): Fédération Internationale de Natation Amateur, 555 North Washington Street, Naperville, Ill. 60540, U.S.A.; (U.K.): Amateur Swimming Association of Great Britain, Harold Fern House, Derby Square, Loughborough, Leicestershire.

DIXON, GEORGE (1870-1909), American boxer, who won both the bantamweight and the featherweight world titles and was the first Negro to become a champion. 'Little Chocolate', as he was known, boxed from 1886 to 1906 with a bodyweight ranging from 87 lb. (39 kg.) to 122 lb. (55 kg.). He took part in so many unofficial contests that he may have had more than 700 bouts and it is a measure of his genius in the ring that he did so well when Negro boxers had to fight against racial intolerance. Dixon won the bantamweight title in London in 1890 and the featherweight championship the following year. Pound for pound he may be considered one of the greatest boxers at any weight.

DIXON, Hon. ROBIN (1935-   ), BOB-SLEIGH rider for Great Britain, was brakeman for NASH when they won the Olympic and world two-man titles at IGLS, Austria, in 1964 and retained the world championship the following year at ST. MORITZ, Switzerland. The two achieved so close an understanding that their names are seldom mentioned separately. Dixon is heir to Lord Glentoran.

DJEBEL (1937) was a notable French race-horse, bred and owned by BOUSSAC, who won the PRIX DE L'ARC DE TRIOMPHE, GRAND PRIX DE SAINT-CLOUD, and Prix des Sablons (now PRIX GANAY), together with the French St. Leger and English TWO THOUSAND GUINEAS.

DKW, German firm of manufacturers of motor cycles. Established in 1919, it was notable for highly developed and specialized racing machines, always with two-stroke engines. They dominated the lightweight category in international racing during the late 1930s, and were again a force to reckon with between 1950 and 1956.

DO NASCIMENTO, EDSON ARANTES, see PELÉ.

DOBBIE, JOHN MOORE (1914-   ), lawn BOWLS player who skipped Australia in the fours and triples at the inaugural world bowls championships at KYEEMAGH in October 1966, winning a gold medal in the triples and a silver medal in the fours. Secretary of the Royal Victorian Bowling Association, Dobbie represented Australia in the 1970 COMMONWEALTH GAMES at Balgreen, Edinburgh, and the 1972 world championships at Worthing.

DR. GERO CUP, an important Central European international Association FOOTBALL competition, known variously as the Nations Cup, the International Cup, and the Europe Cup. It took its present, and probably final, name in 1955 in tribute to Dr. Josef Gero, the president of the Austrian Football Association who had died in the previous year. First contested between 1927 and 1929, much as a result of the drive and organizing ability of MEISL, the leading figure in Austrian football between the wars, this competition contributed as significantly to the development of international football in Central Europe as did the MITROPA CUP for the leading clubs of the region. Austria, Czechoslovakia, Hungary, Italy, and Switzerland took part in each of the three completed competitions (and the one unfinished competition) held before the war. The competitions were spread over two years, each country playing the other four at home and away for a total of eight matches. Italy won twice, Austria once, and Hungary were leading the competition that began in 1936 but ceased when Austria and Czechoslovakia lost their national sovereignty. The competition was resumed in 1948 with the same five countries competing, but was not completed until 1953 with Hungary the winners. Two years later a further competition, with Yugoslavia an additional entrant, began. This, won by Czechoslovakia, was concluded in 1960, by which time the first European Nations Cup competition had been contested. The European Nations Cup has grown into the EUROPEAN FOOTBALL CHAMPIONSHIP and it is unlikely that national associations will find room in their crowded fixture lists for further competitions for the Dr. Gero Cup.

DOD, CHARLOTTE (1871-1962), British LAWN TENNIS player, the game's first prodigy. In 1887, at the age of 15 years and 10 months, Lottie Dod won the women's singles title at WIMBLEDON, retained it the following year, beating BINGLEY in the final, did not compete for two years, and then returned to win three more times. Only in 1893, at their last meeting, did Bingley (Mrs. Hillyard) manage to take a set from her. After so many easy victories, Dod lost interest in competitive lawn tennis. She became a champion golfer, a HOCKEY international, a fine skater, and the best woman archer in England.

On court, she was known as 'the little wonder' at the age of 12. Two years later she could beat many men. Her anticipation was so remarkable that she never seemed to have to make a hurried shot; her forehand had 'the power and direction of a man's'; and she volleyed and smashed effectively, which was rare in a Victorian woman player.

DOGGETT'S COAT AND BADGE, see ROWING.

DOGU, YASAR (*fl.* 1946-52), Turkish wrestler, was the outstanding winner in the 1948 Olympics. He took the freestyle welterweight title at the first postwar European championships in Stockholm and then pinned four competitors at the 1948 Olympics before beating Merrill (U.S.A.) and GARRARD (Australia) for the gold medal. The following year, he won the European middleweight title and in 1951 moved up yet another class to finish first in the world light-heavyweight championship.

DOHERTY, HUGH LAWRENCE, see DOHERTY, REGINALD FRANK.

DOHERTY, PETER DERMONT (1913-   ), Association footballer for Northern Ireland, Coleraine, GLENTORAN, Blackpool, MANCHESTER CITY, Derby County, and HUDDERSFIELD TOWN; manager of Doncaster Rovers (1949-58) and Bristol City (1958-60). A commanding and inventive inside forward, he made 16 international appearances for his country, won an English F.A. Cup medal with Derby County in the 1945-6 season, and was

Northern Ireland's international team manager 1951-62.

DOHERTY, REGINALD FRANK (1874-1910) and HUGH LAWRENCE (1876-1919), British LAWN TENNIS players, who played a major part in popularizing the game at the time when, after the retirement of the RENSHAWS, WIMBLEDON badly needed new heroes. The Dohertys were graceful and spectacular competitors, superb volleyers who moved swiftly. They competed at Wimbledon for the first time in 1896. Both were beaten in the first round of the singles, but R.F. ('Reggie' or 'Big Do') played superbly in the doubles with Nisbet, and H.L. ('Laurie' or 'Little Do') failed against A. W. GORE in the final of the first competition for the All-England Plate, Wimbledon's consolation event. Thereafter R.F. won the singles title from 1897 to 1900 and then, after Gore had beaten him in 1901, H.L. ruled from 1902 to 1906. The brothers won the doubles from 1897 to 1901 and from 1903 to 1905. In 1902 S. H. Smith and Riseley upset them and then defeated them again in the final in 1906 in what proved to be the brothers' last appearance at Wimbledon. Between them, the Dohertys had won 17 championships in ten years. Burrow commented: 'With them departed the home country's unquestioned supremacy at lawn tennis'.

Abroad, H.L. won the U.S. singles title in 1903 and, with his brother, won the doubles in 1902 and 1903. R.F. won the South African title in 1909. Their supremacy in the British covered court championship was comparable to their command at Wimbledon. In the Davis Cup (see LAWN TENNIS) H.L. was never beaten; he won 12 rubbers in 5 challenge rounds between 1902 and 1906.

DOLEZAL, JOSEF (1920-   ), race walker for Czechoslovakia and U.D.A. Prague. He was a versatile performer who set world records for several distances between 5 and 20 miles (8–32 km.) during 1952-5. In his long career Dolezal competed in three Olympic and two European Games gaining one Olympic silver, one European gold and silver medals. His performance in the 1954 European Games at Berne, when he won the 10 km. track race and, a day later, was second in the 50 km. road event, has never been approached. He is the only European walker ever to have competed in China. In his own country's classic, PRAGUE–PODEBRADY, he recorded eight wins (1946, 1949-55).

DOMECQ, ALVARO (1918-   ), one of the foremost *rejoneadores* (see BULLFIGHTING) of the twentieth century, he was rivalled only by PERALTA, and is also famous as a bull-breeder and sherry vintner. His son, Alvarito Domecq, is also an exponent of *rejoneo*.

DOMINGUÍN (Domingo del Campo) (1873-1905), *matador de toros* who took the *alternativa* in 1898, was one of the last of the old-time rugged swordsmen from the nineteenth century. On 7 October 1905 he was fatally gored by the Miura bull Desertor in the Barcelona plaza.

DOMINGUÍN, LUIS MIGUEL (1926-   ), *matador de toros*, who took the *alternativa* on 2 August 1944. Dominguín knew more about the bulls than any other *torero* of his generation, and he coupled this knowledge with a style which was serene and unhurried. Although capable of great art, his sang-froid in the presence of the bull, and the arrogance with which he executed his *toreo*, alienated him from the public, although his capability was commensurate with that of MANOLETE and ORDÓÑEZ.

DONALDSON, JACK (1886-1933), Australian professional sprinter who held almost all professional records from 65 yards (59·4 m.) to 400 yards (365·76 m.). Among his most remarkable achievements were 130 yards (118·9 m.) in 12 sec. in 1907, and 100 yards (91·4 m.) in 9·38 sec. in 1909, a time that would have been a world (amateur) record nearly forty years later. In 1908 he ran 130 yards against the Olympic 100-metre gold medallist, R. Walker, and beat him by 5 yards.

DONATELLO II (1934), race-horse, by Blenheim (English DERBY) out of Delleana (Italian Grand Prix, Two Thousand Guineas, and One Thousand Guineas) tracing to PRETTY POLLY, was bred, owned, and ridden by Gubellini and trained by Tesio. He won the Milan Grand Prix, the Italian Grand Prix, and the Italian Derby before being bought by Esmond for £45,500, and sent to stand at stud in England in 1938. He was the first 'foreign' stallion to exercise an important influence on the breed of the new 'international' race-horse, becoming sire of Alycidon, winner of the Ascot, Goodwood, and Doncaster Cups, and of Crepello, winner of the Derby and TWO THOUSAND GUINEAS.

DONCASTER, race-course on the Town Moor in Yorkshire, is run by a race committee of the Corporation. The last classic race of the season, the ST. LEGER STAKES, is run here, and other important races are the Doncaster Cup for stayers, the Park Hill Stakes for three-year-old fillies, the OBSERVER GOLD CUP for two-year-olds, and the Portland Handicap for sprinters.

DONINGTON PARK CIRCUIT, MOTOR RACING circuit, near Derby, opened in March 1933. Its original length was 2·19 miles (3·5 km.), but it was extended in 1934 to 2·55 miles (4·1 km.) and in 1937 to 3·125 miles (5 km.). It was a true road circuit, with short straights, a wide variety of bends, and steep uphill and downhill sections, situated in typical English parkland. The circuit has been used for club meetings, long-distance sports-car classics (the Tourist Trophy, the Junior Car Club 200-Mile Race, etc.) but its major events were the British or Donington Grand Prix races of 1937 and 1938, when the German G.P. teams made their début in England, AUTO-UNION winning on both occasions. It is hoped that the circuit will be re-opened, in modified form, by its new owner, Wheatcroft, before the end of the 1974 season.

DONNELLY, MARTIN PATERSON (1917-   ), cricketer for New Zealand, Wellington, Canterbury, Oxford University, Middlesex, and Warwickshire. He played some stirring innings in a brief career: for the Dominions, for the University, for the Gentlemen, and for New Zealand (with 206 at LORD'S in 1949 the highest for his country against England). Short in stature, left-handed, and exquisite of style, he also played once for England at RUGBY football.

DONOGHUE, STEPHEN (1884-1945), was champion jockey in England from 1914 to 1923. He won the DERBY six times; wartime substitute races at NEWMARKET on POMMERN (1915) and GAY CRUSADER (1917), the hat-trick at EPSOM on Humorist (1921), Captain Cuttle (1922), and Papyrus (1923), and yet again on Manna (1925). His favourite mount, however, was BROWN JACK, whom he rode to victory in the Queen Alexandra Stakes at Royal Ascot for six consecutive years.

DONOHUE, MARK (1937-1975), American MOTOR RACING driver. Although primarily a road racer, he won the 1972 INDIANAPOLIS 500, having finished second in 1970, and won the 1971 Pocono 500 and Michigan 200 on speedways. On road circuits, he was the 1967 and 1968 U.S. road racing championship winner with 11 victories in 16 races. He was second in the 1966 CAN-AM Challenge Cup standings, third in 1967, and 1973 champion with six straight victories. He won 26 TRANS-AM sedan (saloon) car races between 1968 and 1971. With Parsons, he won the 24 Hours of

Daytona in 1969. In 1973, he won the Riverside, California, road race for Grand National stock cars. He retired from racing in early 1974 after winning the final heat of the International Race of Champions, and is now associated in the racing enterprises of Roger Penske, formerly his car owner and team manager.

DORDONI, GIUSEPPE (1928-   ), race walker for Italy and G.S. Diana, Padua. Regarded by many authorities as the finest stylist yet seen, Dordoni was a world-class performer at all distances up to 50 km. during the period 1948-61. Olympic 50 km. champion in 1952 and European champion at the same distance two years earlier, his career included four Olympiads and two European Games. Winner of countless Italian classic races, his duals with PAMICH during the years 1955 to 1961 helped to popularize the sport in his home country. Several clashes with VICKERS both in England and on the Continent resulted in some of the finest exhibitions of speed walking ever seen. Dordoni became an international judge and coach to the Italian team and has produced several outstanding protégés in recent years.

D'ORIOLA, CHRISTIAN (1928-   ), French fencer. An outstanding technician with a natural sense of time and distance, d'Oriola dominated world foil FENCING in the decade following the Second World War; he learned to fence in the village of Perpignan, where he was taught by the local publican. He won the world foil championship at Lisbon in 1947 at the age of 17 at his first appearance in international fencing. He was Olympic foil champion in 1952 and 1956 and world foil champion in 1947, 1949, 1953, and 1954, a record which has not yet been equalled. He retired from fencing after his 1956 win.

D'ORIOLA, PIERRE JONQUÈRES (1920-   ), French show jumping (see EQUESTRIAN EVENTS) rider. The winner of two individual gold medals (in 1952 and 1964), he remained at the top of international show jumping for more than two decades. Before the 1952 OLYMPIC GAMES, he had ridden the ex-polo pony, Ali Baba, only three times, but he nevertheless won the individual gold medal. His successes also include a team silver medal (with Nagir) in the 1968 Olympics, and the men's world championship (with Pomone) at Buenos Aires in 1966.

DORMELLO-OLGIATA is the Italian racehorse stud farm, breeding establishment, and racing stable made world-famous by Tesio. Here were bred such notable performers as Cavaliere d'Arhino, Apelle, DONATELLO II, NEARCO, Bellini, NICCOLO DELL' ARCA, Torbido, Tenerani, Daumier, BOTTICELLI, Braque, and 'the best horse in the world', RIBOT.

DOS SANTOS, MANOEL FRANCISCO, see GARRINCHA.

DOUGLASS, DOROTHEA K. (Mrs. Lambert Chambers) (1878-1960), British LAWN TENNIS player, the most successful woman competitor in the years preceding the First World War. Miss Douglass won the women's singles at WIMBLEDON seven times, a record surpassed only by WILLS.

She was the champion in 1903-4, 1906, 1910-11, and 1913-14. In her challenge rounds she lost only to overseas players. Sutton from California beat her in 1905; she gained her revenge in 1906, but lost to the American girl again in 1907. In 1919, she was beaten by the young LENGLEN, after holding two match points in the long, dramatic, classic final. She played doubles in the WIGHTMAN CUP in 1925 and 1926, and became a professional in 1928.

DOWNING, KEOUNE (c. 1952-   ), Hawaiian surfer, son of George Downing, manager of the 1970 Hawaiian team. He came fifth in the world championships in Australia in 1970.

DRAG BOAT RACING, see POWERBOAT RACING.

DRAG RACING, see MOTOR RACING, AMERICAN.

DRESSAGE, see EQUESTRIAN EVENTS.

DRISCOLL, JIM (1881-1925), British boxer, who claimed the world featherweight title in 1909 after having much the better of a ten-rounds no-decision contest with the American world champion ATELL. Generally regarded as the best BOXING technician Britain has ever produced, Driscoll earned an equally high reputation in the U.S.A. when he boxed there during 1908 and 1909. He was undoubtedly the best exponent of the upright British style, founded on the use of the straight left.

DROBNY, JAROSLAV (1921-   ), Czech LAWN TENNIS player who became a British citizen, one of the finest postwar clay court competitors and the winner of the WIMBLEDON title in 1954 after failing in two previous finals. He played ICE HOCKEY for Czechoslovakia at the age of 15 and was a member of their team in the 1948 OLYMPIC GAMES.

A left-hander with a fierce service, formidable strength on the forehand and a considerable armoury of delicate shots, he played at Wimbledon for the first time in 1938 and won the French title in 1951 and 1952, the Italian in 1950, 1951, and 1953, and the German championship in 1950. His most dramatic performances were reserved for Wimbledon. In 1946 he beat KRAMER, the favourite, and his losing finals were against Schroeder (U.S.A.) in 1949 and SEDGMAN in 1951, but in 1954, when it seemed that he was past his best, he beat the 19-year-old Australian, ROSEWALL, 13-11, 4-6, 6-2, 9-7 in one of the longest postwar finals. In an earlier round the previous year he had beaten his old rival, Patty, 6-8, 18-16, 6-3, 6-8, 12-10 in a contest which lasted for 4 hrs. 20 min., setting a record for length of match at Wimbledon which stood until 1969 when GONZALES met Pasarell.

DROUYA, PETER (c. 1949-   ), Australian surfer who came third in the world championships in Australia in 1970.

DRYSDALE CUP, see SQUASH RACKETS.

DU PONT, Mrs. W., see OSBORNE, MARGARET.

DUBLIN UNIVERSITY F.C., the oldest RUGBY UNION football club in Ireland formed in 1856 by students at the university (also known as Trinity College, Dublin). Among its notable internationals are Lloyd, Sugden, Parke, and Clinch.

DUDDLESTON CUP, see FENLAND SKATING.

DUKE, GEOFFREY, O.B.E. (1923-   ), English racing motor-cyclist. Appointed leader of the NORTON team in 1950 after a brief period of riding as an amateur, he won the 350 and 500 cc. world championships in 1951 and the 350 cc. championship again in the following year. In 1953 he became leader of the GILERA team, again winning the 500 cc. world championship in that and the two following years. The most impeccable rider ever seen in international racing, he found it difficult to recover his form after a lengthy absence from racing and he retired in 1959.

DUKLA PRAGUE, Association FOOTBALL club, Prague. The club was formed as the club of the army in 1947 and named A.T.K. Subsequently it was renamed U.D.A. (Central Army

Club) in 1953, and finally Dukla in 1956 in honour of the Carpathian village of that name where Czechs withstood the Germans during the Second World War. For several years in the 1950s and 1960s the club had the pick of Czechoslovakian footballers and were eight times the winners of the Czechoslovakian League between 1953 and 1966, and, as the national club champions, fairly regular contenders for the European Cup, reaching the quarter-final stage in 1963. Outstanding players included Novak, Pluskal, MASOPUST, Kucera, and Geleta.

COLOURS: Red shirts and yellow shorts.

DULEEP TROPHY, Indian CRICKET trophy named after the late DULEEPSINHJI, who was chairman of the All-India Council of Sports. It is awarded to the winner of an inter-zone knock-out competition first played in 1961-2.

DULEEPSINHJI, KUMAR SHRI (1905-59), cricketer for England, Cambridge University, and Sussex. A nephew of RANJITSINHJI, he played first-class CRICKET from 1924 to 1932, establishing a unique reputation for his ease and grace as a batsman. His most famous innings was his first — and highest — in Tests: 173 against Australia at LORD's in 1930.

DUNCAN, GEORGE (1884-1964), Scottish professional golfer. He won the 1920 Open championship, having tied with MITCHELL in the Victory championship the previous year when the Open was in abeyance because of the war. He represented Great Britain in the RYDER CUP and in his later years gained a reputation as a fine coach.

DUNSTABLE GLIDING CLUB, lat. 51° 44′ N, long. 0° 33′ W, near Luton, Bedfordshire, was the first British club to become internationally famous, and the largest single club on its own site. Situated at the foot of the chalk downs of the Chiltern Hills, with grass landing ground, it has been the starting place for many national records.

DUPRÉ, FRANÇOIS (1888-1966), a prominent French breeder and owner of thoroughbred race-horses. TANTIÈME and Bella Paola (OAKS, ONE THOUSAND GUINEAS, CHAMPION STAKES, and PRIX VERMEILLE) were two of the best horses to carry his colours, and he also bred from his remarkable mare RELANCE three other champion race-horses in MATCH III, RELKO, and RELIANCE.

DURACK, FANNY (1894-1960), Australian swimmer who was the first woman Olympic champion. She won the 100 metres freestyle at the 1912 Games in Stockholm in a world record time. The cancellation of the 1916 Games, because of the First World War, robbed her of further Olympic honours but she broke nine world records between 1912 and 1918, from 100 yards (91·4 m.) to one mile (1,609·3 m.), setting standards for women that took many years to emulate.

DURNAN, BILL (1922-   ), ICE HOCKEY player for MONTREAL CANADIENS from 1943 to 1950, and one of the greatest goalminders. Ambidextrous, he had a rare ability to catch and block shots with either hand, which he used with spectacular effect almost as much as he used his stick and pads. He used his height of 6 ft. (1·8 m.) to full advantage, and the fact that he won the VEZINA TROPHY in six of his seven NATIONAL HOCKEY LEAGUE (N.H.L.) seasons is testimony to his technique. In the 1948-9 season he achieved ten shut-outs, including a record run of four games without conceding a goal — a record shut-out playing time of 5 hrs., 9 min., 21 sec. He totalled 34 shut-out games during his seven N.H.L. seasons. In that time, he played 901 games, letting through an average of only 2·35 goals per game.

A deep head gash from another player's skate caused his premature retirement in 1950.

DYNAMO MOSCOW, Association FOOTBALL club, Moscow, traditionally associated with and sponsored by the N.K.V.D., now the K.G.B. Founded in 1887 by the English Charnock brothers who were manufacturers at Orekhovo-Zuyevo, near Moscow, the club was known as Orekhovo Klub Sport, Morosovsti, and then Dynamo Moscow when it was sponsored by the Electrical Trades Union. It was the first Soviet club to attract attention outside the U.S.S.R. when it made a successful British tour in 1945. In 1972 the club reached the final of the European Cup-Winners Cup before losing 2-3 to Glasgow RANGERS in Barcelona. Outstanding players have included BESKOV, Bobrov, YASHIN, Khomich, Semichastny, and Chislenko.

COLOURS: Blue shirts, white shorts.

DYSON, GEOFFREY HARRY GEORGE (1914-   ), ATHLETICS coach and physical educationalist for Great Britain. Dyson was adviser to many outstanding British track and field athletes including Maureen Gardner, 1948 Olympic 80 metres hurdles silver medallist, whom he subsequently married. He was chief coach to the English Amateur Athletic Association from 1947 to 1961 and in 1963 took up an appointment as national director of the Royal Canadian Legion's Sports Training

Plan. In 1968 he returned to England as director of Physical Education at Winchester College. His publication, *The Mechanics of Athletics,* is a standard work in its field.

DZAJIC, DRAGAN (1946-   ), Association footballer for RED STAR BELGRADE and Yugoslavia, both of whom he captained. An excellent outside left, he came to the forefront in European football by his performances in the Yugoslavian national side in the semi-final and final of the European Football Championship in Italy in 1968. He scored the only goal of the match against England in the semi-final. Subsequently he was chosen to play for the Rest of the World XI against Brazil in Rio.

E

EBOR HANDICAP is the most valuable horse race of its kind in England. Founded in 1843, it is run over 1¾ miles (2,800 m.) at York during August.

ECLIPSE (1764-89), was bred by the Duke of Cumberland, third son of George II, and owned by Col. O' Kelly. He was the most famous race-horse of the eighteenth century, and, together with HEROD and MATCHEM, ancestor in direct male line of all thoroughbred race-horses throughout the world. Eclipse did not run on the race-course until he was five years old and then won easily all the races and matches in which he took part.

ECLIPSE STAKES, horse race founded in 1886, one of the most important weight-for-age races in England, run over 1¼ miles (2,000 m.) at SANDOWN PARK in July.

EDEN PARK, Auckland, New Zealand, venue for RUGBY UNION test matches and home ground of the Auckland provincial side.

EDGBASTON, CRICKET ground in a suburb of Birmingham, is the headquarters of the Warwickshire County Cricket Club, which plays the majority of its home matches there. It is one of the best-appointed grounds in England. Commodious stands surround the field, prominent among them being the west wing, named the William Ansell Stand, after the man who did much to help secure the ground. It was first used by Warwickshire in 1886, and staged its first Test match in 1902. After 1929, however, Test cricket did not return to Edgbaston until 1957, since when it has been a regular Test venue. The ground holds over 30,000, and some 83,000 attended the entire Test against Australia in 1961.

EDINBURGH ACADEMICALS R.F.C., the oldest RUGBY UNION club in Scotland, founded in 1857-8 by former pupils of Edinburgh Academy. Among its leading past players are Maclaglan, captain of the first British team in South Africa, Macpherson, and Elliot.
GROUND: Raeburn Place.
COLOURS: Blue and white.

EDINBURGH S.C., ICE SKATING club formed in 1742, the first in the world.

EDINBURGH WANDERERS R.F.C., RUGBY UNION football club founded in 1869 for players living in the city but ineligible to join the dominant former pupils' clubs. Until the late 1960s its players had included 49 Scottish, 11 English, 11 Irish, 3 Welsh internationals, and 1 Australian. In 1937 it provided the captains for the two opposing international sides at Swansea: Rees for Wales, and Logan for Scotland.
GROUND: Murrayfield.
COLOURS: Red and black jerseys, black shorts.

EDMONTON ESKIMOS, Canadian professional FOOTBALL team, entered the Western Conference League in 1949 and dominated the entire Canadian Football League in the 1950s. Under coach Ivy, they captured both Conference titles and the Grey Cup (see FOOTBALL, CANADIAN) in the years 1954 to 1956, with the quarterback Parker chosen as the League's outstanding player each year. They were Western Conference champions in 1973.
COLOURS: Green and gold.

EDRICH, JOHN HUGH (1937-   ), cricketer for England and Surrey. In a chequered career, begun with seven centuries during 1959, he eventually became a regular and dependable opening batsman for England in 1968, having scored 120 four years earlier in his first Test against Australia (off whom he scored heavily in subsequent series). A left-hander, he made a hard-hit 310 not out against New Zealand in 1965.

EDRICH, WILLIAM JOHN, D.F.C. (1916-   ), cricketer for England and Middlesex. A courageous batsman and whole-hearted fast bowler, he eventually fulfilled early promise with an innings of 219 against South Africa in 1938-9, but the Second World War interrupted his progress. Resuming in 1946, he continued to give staunch service to England and to his county. In 1947 he made 3,539 runs in first-class CRICKET, an aggregate exceeded only by his colleague, COMPTON, in the same championship-winning season.

EDWARD VII, H.M. King, see WALES, PRINCE OF.

EDWARDS, DUNCAN (1936-58), Association footballer for MANCHESTER UNITED, and England for whom he made 18 appearances in full international matches, having made his début for England's A team at left half-back against Scotland in April 1955 when he was only 18½ years of age. He was a member of the Manchester United team that won the Football League championship in the seasons ending 1956 and 1957, and in the team that drew with RED STAR BELGRADE in February 1958 to gain United an aggregated two-leg victory that took the club to the semi-final of the European Champion Clubs Cup. On the journey home the aircraft carrying the team crashed on take-off at Munich; he survived the crash but died three weeks later from his injuries.

EDWARDS, GARETH OWEN (1947-   ), RUGBY UNION scrum half for CARDIFF, Wales, and British LIONS. Wiry and versatile, Edwards played at full-back, outside half, and centre as well as scrum half during the 1967 Cardiff tour of South Africa. He was first capped before his twentieth birthday, and was the youngest player ever to captain Wales when he led the side against Scotland at the age of 20 years and 7 months.

EGAN, JOSEPH (1919-   ), RUGBY LEAGUE player. Unrivalled as England's first choice hooker from 1945 to 1950, he was generally considered to have been the best in his position in the game's history. After 13 years with WIGAN, he left in 1950 to be player-coach at Leigh. Clever in the loose and an inspiring leader, he toured Australia in 1946 and 1950. He played in 14 Tests, and 16 times for England in the international championship.

EGAN, PIERCE (c. 1772-1849), a leading British sporting journalist, whose knowledge of fields as different as bull-baiting and the theatre was unsurpassed among his contemporaries. He was an Irishman but lived most of his life in London, and made a considerable impact with his magazines, books, and plays focused upon the sports and entertainments of the bustling city. His vivid style was allied to considerable technical knowledge of sport. After several years of writing for the *Weekly Dispatch* he published the five-volume *Boxiana* (or *Sketches of Ancient and Modern Pugilism; from the days of Broughton and Slack to the Heroes of the Present Milling Era*). The first volume appeared in London in 1813, followed by others in 1818, 1821, 1824, and 1828. They contained full round-by-round descriptions of all the significant bare-fist prize-fights and profiles of all the leading pugilists, and *Boxiana* is the basic source for the early history of BOXING. It has been claimed that Egan's writing was an important influence on the dialogue and personality of Cockney characters in the novels of Dickens.

EISENHOWER TROPHY, International amateur GOLF event for men's teams, played in alternate years.

ELCHO SHIELD, see SHOOTING, RIFLE: SERVICE CALIBRE.

ELDER, JAMES (1934-   ), Canadian show jumping (see EQUESTRIAN EVENTS) rider. A member of the gold medal team at the Mexico OLYMPIC GAMES in 1968, he was one of the few riders to succeed in both three-day event and show jumping. He twice rode in Canada's Olympic three-day event team (1956 and 1960), winning a team bronze medal at his first attempt. He also won a team gold medal in the three-day event at the PAN-AMERICAN GAMES of 1959.

ELEK, ILONA (1907-   ), Hungarian women's Olympic FENCING champion, 1936 and 1948; Olympic silver medallist, 1952; women's world fencing champion, 1934, 1935, and 1951. She has won more Olympic and world championship titles than any other woman fencer.

ELIZABETH II, H.M. Queen (1926-   ), royal patron of the turf. The Queen has a profound knowledge of HORSE RACING, and her horses met with considerable success shortly after she ascended the throne. AUREOLE won the KING GEORGE VI AND QUEEN ELIZABETH STAKES, CORONATION CUP, and Hardwicke Stakes; Carozza the OAKS; and Pall Mall the TWO THOUSAND GUINEAS in the royal racing colours. The Queen headed the list of winning owners in England in 1954 and again in 1957, the first reigning monarch ever to achieve this feat twice.

ELLABY, ALFRED (1902-   ), England's most prolific RUGBY LEAGUE try-scorer; his total of 487 was later exceeded by an Australian, BEVAN, and a Welshman, BOSTON. He toured Australia in 1928 and 1932 during his career with ST. HELENS, and played in a total of nine Tests against Australia. An exceptionally fast, graceful runner, with a keen anticipation, he joined WIGAN in 1934, but returned to St. Helens in 1937.

ELLIOTT, HERBERT JAMES (1938-   ), middle-distance runner for Australia. Never beaten in open competition in a mile or 1,500 metres race, Elliott won gold medals in the 1958 COMMONWEALTH GAMES 880 yards and mile and in the 1960 Olympic 1,500 metres. His world record of 3 min. 36·0 sec. in 1958, improved by him to 3 min. 35·6 sec. in the 1960 Olympic final, was unbeaten until 1967. He also held the world mile record at 3 min. 54·5 sec. from 1958 to 1962 and bettered 4 minutes for the mile 17 times.

ELLIOTT, SEAMUS (1934-71), most successful of Irish road-race cyclists, 'Shay' Elliott, a Dubliner, rode on the Continent from 1955, holding the race lead in the VUELTA A ESPAGNA of 1962 and the TOUR DE FRANCE of 1963.

ELLIS PARK, Johannesburg,. South Africa, venue for RUGBY UNION Test matches and the home ground of the Transvaal provincial team. A record crowd of 95,000 attended the first Test there between South Africa and the LIONS in 1955.

ELMER, ROBERT POTTER (1878-1951) was once known as the man who 'almost invented archery'. A graduate of Princeton University in 1899, he qualified as a physician in 1903. His untiring efforts in research on all aspects of ARCHERY and its history did much to aid the great modern revival of the sport. He was champion archer of the U.S.A. eight times, president of the American National Archery Association, president of the United Bowmen of Philadelphia, vice-president of the GRAND NATIONAL ARCHERY SOCIETY and a life member of the ROYAL TOXOPHILITE SOCIETY.

Dr. Elmer published several books on archery which are still considered standard works on the subject, including *Archery* (1926), *Target Archery* (1946), and, in collaboration with other authors, *The Book of the Long Bow* (1929) and *Arab Archery* (1945).

ELMIRA (Harris Hill), N.Y., GLIDING centre, lat. 42° 05' N, long. 76° 55' W, 170 miles north of New York City. Developed in 1930 as the glider capital of America, home of regionals and class contests, such as the Schweizer 1:26 competitions, it is a grass airfield with one strip on a hilltop: the Schweizer Sailplane factory on Elmira-Corning airfield is three miles distant, in the valley.

EMERSON, ROY S. (1936-   ), a swift and athletic LAWN TENNIS player who re-asserted Australia's supremacy after LAVER had turned professional in 1962. Emerson was the most successful competitor in the last lean years of the amateur game before the introduction of open tournaments, winning all four of the major singles titles — WIMBLEDON (1964

and 1965), FOREST HILLS (1961 and 1964), Paris (1963 and 1965), and Australia (1961 and 1963-7), without ever completing a 'grand slam'. In 1966 he was expected to equal PERRY's record, which was unique at the modern Wimbledon, of winning the men's singles for three years in succession, but he fell and damaged a shoulder in his match against Davidson and lost by 1-6, 6-3, 6-3, 6-4.

Emerson won a large number of major doubles titles with a variety of partners, notably FRASER, Laver, STOLLE, and SANTANA, and he was one of Australia's finest Davis Cup (see LAWN TENNIS) players, playing in 18 ties, including 9 successive challenge rounds, and winning 36 rubbers out of 40 between 1959 and 1967. He turned professional in 1968.

EMERY, VICTOR (1933-   ), BOBSLEIGH rider for Canada, and the first driver to win a world championship for that country. Emery won the world and Olympic four-man titles at IGLS, Austria, in 1964 and retained the world title the following year at ST MORITZ, Switzerland.

EMPIRE MATCH, see SHOOTING, RIFLE: SERVICE CALIBRE.

EMPIRE POOL, Wembley (London), opened in 1934 for the Empire Games (see COMMONWEALTH GAMES) SWIMMING and DIVING events. The building, 200 ft. (60·96 m.) wide, 417 ft. (127 m.) long, and 80 ft. (24·38 m.) high, cost £150,000, and has seating accommodation for between 8,000 and 11,000. It housed the first indoor 10-metre diving stage in Great Britain and was used for the 1936 Olympic swimming and diving trials and for the 1938 European Games. The swimming and diving events for the 1948 OLYMPIC GAMES were also held there. Diving suffered a great blow when it was decided to close the pool after the Games. It was converted into a sports arena and used for various events including ice pantomimes.

ENDERLEIN, ORTRUN (1943-   ), luge TOBOGGANING rider for East Germany, winner of three consecutive women's world titles, 1964-5-7, and Olympic winner in 1964.

ENDO, YUKIO (1937-   ), the only gymnast to be a member of all the Japanese teams which won three Olympic titles and two world championships during the 1960s. In addition Endo, 5 ft. 3 in. (1·60 m.) and 9 st. 4 lb. (59 kg.), won the most important competition for a Japanese gymnast — the over-all gold medal at the Tokyo OLYMPIC GAMES when he also finished first on the parallel bars. A member of the Japanese squad which upset the Russians for the team title at the 1960 Olympics, he showed he was one of the finest competitors of the era when he finished second over-all to the Russian TITOV at the 1962 world championships. After Tokyo he lost his leadership in the sport but was still good enough to win a silver medal in the 1968 Olympics in the vault and help Japan to her third successive team title at the Games.

ENDRICH, FELIX (1921-   ), BOBSLEIGH rider for Switzerland; winner of one Olympic and four world titles. As two-man boblet driver, he gained an Olympic gold medal in 1948 at ST. MORITZ, Switzerland, and with it the world championship. He also won the world two-man event as driver in 1949 at LAKE PLACID, U.S.A., and in 1953 at GARMISCH, Germany. He was previously in the winning four-man bob, with FEIERABEND as driver, in the 1947 world championships at St. Moritz.

ENGELHARD, CHARLES W. (1916-71), one of the world's leading race-horse owners. He bought as yearlings Ribocco for $35,000, Ribero for $50,000, and Ribofilio 'the last of the cheap RIBOTS' for $100,000. Ribocco won the OBSERVER GOLD CUP, IRISH SWEEPS DERBY, and English ST. LEGER, together with £121,764 in stakes; Ribero also won the Irish Sweeps Derby and English St. Leger; but Ribofilio only managed to finish second in the same two races. Then, in 1968, Engelhard bought as a yearling, for $84,000, NIJINSKY with whom he won the English triple crown (see HORSE RACING) in 1970.

ENGLISH MATCH, see SHOOTING, RIFLE: SMALL-BORE.

EPSOM, race-course in Surrey, is the venue for the DERBY, OAKS, and CORONATION CUP races. Horse racing has taken place on Epsom Downs since 1730.

EQUESTRIAN EVENTS are competitive events for horse and rider designed to test the horse's development and training, his jumping ability, endurance, speed, and agility, and the all-round ability of horse and rider.

DRESSAGE. The French term for the training of horses, *dressage*, has been adopted by the equestrian world generally for a series of movements which test a horse's development and state of training. The Fédération Équestre Internationale (F.E.I.) gives the following definition: 'The object of dressage is the harmonious development of the physique and ability of the horse. As a result, it makes the horse calm, supple, and keen, thus achieving perfect understanding with its rider. These qualities are revealed by: the freedom and regularity of the paces; the harmony, lightness, and ease of movements; the lightening of the forehand and the engagement of the hindquarters; the horse remaining absolutely straight in any movement along a straight line and bending accordingly when moving on curved lines. The horse thus gives the impression of doing of his own accord what is required of him.'

Dressage competitions are designed to assess how far these objects have been achieved. The tests for international competitions cover varying standards compiled by the F.E.I. They consist of a series of movements, graded in difficulty according to the standard of competitors. Each movement is marked individually by the judges and the total marks are then averaged to give each horse's final score.

The dressage test was first included in the OLYMPIC GAMES in 1912. The Olympic Grand Prix de Dressage is described by the F.E.I. as 'expert competition'; there is also the Intermediate Competition ('of advanced difficulty'), and the Prix St.-Georges ('of medium difficulty'). All tests are judged in an area measuring 60 m. by 20 m. (66 × 22 yds.).

SHOW JUMPING, in which horse and rider jump a set course of fences specially designed and built for each contest, has three main categories of competition: those which primarily test jumping ability but use time as the deciding factor in order to reach a final result; those which test jumping ability alone; and those which put a premium on speed and agility.

Most competitions come into the first category, with time counting in the first round or, more frequently, in the first or second jump-off. Jumping ability is of prime importance, since time counts only when there is equality of faults and a horse with a slow clear round will therefore beat a fast one with four faults. These competitions are judged under Table (or *Barème*) A, and faults are incurred as follows:

Fence knocked down — 4 faults
One or more feet in the water, or on the landing tape — 4 faults
Refusals (including running-out or circling)
   First — 3 faults
   Second — 6 faults
   Third — Elimination
Fall of horse and/or rider — 8 faults
For each second over the time allowed — ½ fault
Exceeding the time limit (which is double the time allowed) — Elimination

Competitors may be eliminated for other reasons, which rarely apply. These include failure to start within 60 seconds of the starting signal, taking the wrong course, and receiving unauthorized assistance.

. The competition which tests jumping ability alone is known as a *Puissance* and this, too, is judged under Table A rules. In this case there is no recourse to the clock, since the object is to test the horse over 'a limited number of large obstacles'. During successive jump-offs, the fences are reduced to a minimum of two (one spread and one upright) and these are made progressively more difficult. The F.E.I. imposes a limit of four jump-offs in *Puissance* competitions and, if there is still equality after the fourth jump-off, the first prize is divided.

Some riders dislike the idea of testing a horse to the limit of its ability because, they maintain, it is liable to undermine a show jumper's confidence. These views, which are particularly strong in Britain, have resulted in an increase of *Puissance* contests for which there is a limit of three jump-offs.

Tables B and C cover the international rules for speed competitions, in which faults are converted into seconds. Under Table B a knock-down, or a foot in the water jump, incurs a 10-second penalty; in Table C the penalty may vary between 3 and 17 seconds, depending on the length of the course and the number of fences.

Classes run under Tables B and C rules are judged purely on a time basis, which means that speed and agility are all-important. Even with the penalty for a knock-down added to its time, the horse that is fast and agile will invariably beat one that jumps a slow clear round. The F.E.I. lays down the rules and regulations for all international shows, the most important of which are known as the *Concours de Saut Internationale Officiel* (C.S.I.O.). It is at these 'official' internationals that Nations Cup competitions are held.

The Nations Cup, open to international teams of four riders, is decided over two rounds in each of which the team's worst score is discarded. A nation may be represented by only three riders (when a fourth is not available), though in practice such a necessity rarely arises. The Olympic team competition was originally contested by only three riders from each country, with every score counting. In December 1970, the F.E.I. ruled that the Olympic contest should be brought into line with the Nations Cup, and that a full team would therefore consist of four riders instead of three.

The President's Cup, instituted in 1965 and awarded annually, is based on the results of Nations Cups and is virtually a world team championship. The number of points awarded for a Nations Cup victory is dependent on the number of teams taking part; if there are three,

four, or five, the winner earns 5 points towards the President's Cup; for six teams the top score is 6 points; for seven or more teams it is 7 points. The result is determined by adding together each nation's six best scores.

Next to the Olympic Games, the principal individual contest is the men's world championship, which is open to two riders from each nation. The title is decided during three preliminary competitions and a unique final, in which the four qualifiers ride their own and each other's horses. Clearly this involves a searching test of the riders' skill; it also gives a head start to the finalist with a particularly difficult mount, since such a horse is likely to incur many more faults with a strange rider than with the regular partner who knows all its quirks.

There is a separate world championship for women riders, which does not involve the changing of horses, and, since there are fewer top women internationals, it carries less weight than the men's title.

The men's and women's European championships are decided by three or four different types of competition, which are designed to find the best all-round horse and rider. Unlike the men's world championship, points are carried forward to the final contest, so that the rider who scores in the last leg of the championship is not necessarily the one who wins the title.

Juniors, who are defined by the F.E.I. as riders under the age of 18, are debarred from the Olympic Games and the other major

SHOW JUMPING OBSTACLES

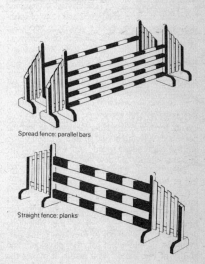

Spread fence: parallel bars

Straight fence: planks

international classes. Those under the minimum age of 14 are also ineligible for the junior European championships, which include a team as well as an individual title.

Show jumping has been described as a test in which the course designer is the examiner and the competitors the examinees. Since courses are specially designed for each individual competition, the rider's ability to 'read' the problems correctly is vital. These problems relate to the positioning of the fences just as much as to their height and width. Combination fences, which comprise two or more jumps within 12 m. (39 ft. 4 in.) of each other, become considerably more difficult when a distance problem is involved. The F.E.I. lays down rules to which course designers must adhere, but there is still considerable scope for individuality. All international courses have their own characteristics, which is particularly noticeable in the case of Aachen, the home of the German international, where the fences are reputed to be bigger and tougher than anywhere else in the world.

The THREE-DAY EVENT is an equestrian competition designed to test the all-round ability of horse and rider. It is also known as horse trials and, because it originated as a test for officers' chargers, it is still referred to on the Continent as the *militaire*. The name given to the sport by the F.E.I. describes it more precisely as the *Concours Complet d'Équitation*. The event consists of three distinct parts, or phases, which test the horse in dressage, then speed, endurance, and cross-country, and finally in show jumping. The phases take place on three separate days, hence the name.

The dressage phase (see above) is designed to test the horse's obedience and state of training, as well as the rider's ability to apply the aids correctly. The test consists of a series of movements at the walk, trot, and canter, which the rider must memorize in advance. Each movement is marked separately by the judges and points are also awarded for 'general impression'. Points are deducted if a rider forgets the test and carries out the movements in the wrong order.

For scoring purposes, the judges' marks are averaged and then deducted from the maximum possible total, to give a penalty score. This penalty is then multiplied by the 'multiplying factor' (which can vary between 1 and $2\frac{1}{3}$) to give the actual penalty points that the competitor will carry through to the next phase. It is through the multiplying factor that the dressage phase can be made to exert 'the correct influence on the whole competition'. The figure used will vary according to the severity of the second phase and, to a lesser extent, of the final show jumping test.

The second phase, which is designed to test the speed, endurance, and jumping ability of the true cross-country horse, is the most important, as well as the toughest, part of the competition. The length of the course varies according to the importance of the competition, which means that riders in the Olympic Games and the world or continental championships cover the longest distance, up to a maximum of 32·3 km. (about 20 miles).

The course for such an event would be divided as follows: (1) and (3) roads and tracks — totalling 16 to 20 km. (about 10 to $12\frac{1}{2}$ miles); (2) steeplechase — 3·6 to 4·2 km. ($2\frac{1}{4}$ to $2\frac{1}{2}$ miles); (4) cross-country — 7·2 to 8·1 km. ($4\frac{1}{2}$ to 5 miles).

Though the two roads and tracks sections contribute to the endurance aspect of the test, penalties are rarely incurred on them. There is no jumping involved and competitors can therefore be penalized only by failing to complete each of these sections within the allotted time of 240 m. (262 yds.) per minute. Since all riders carry a stop-watch, such mistakes in timing rarely occur.

The first acid test comes on the steeplechase course, for it is here that time bonus marks can be earned and jumping penalties incurred. The time factor calls for a fine judgement of pace, since the horse's energies have to be conserved for the long journey ahead. The maximum bonus (which may vary between 37·6 and 44 points in major international competitions) is obtained when a horse completes the course in a specified time, and it is therefore a waste of effort to go any faster. An alternative method of scoring, which is used fairly extensively, involves translating bonuses into penalties. This means that the horse which would have achieved maximum bonus under the original system is credited with a zero penalty score instead.

After the second section of roads and tracks, there is a compulsory ten-minute halt, during which the horse is inspected by a veterinary surgeon to ensure that it is fit enough to continue. Competitors then set out on the cross-country course, containing between 30 and 35 fixed obstacles, by far the most difficult part of the test.

The height for cross-country obstacles (excluding brush fences where horses can jump through the top six inches) is limited to 1·2 m. (3 ft. 11 in.). This means that the main problems are posed by the shape and siting of the obstacles rather than their size. A typical cross-country course would include one or more jumps into water, obstacles built on a steep downhill gradient, and several 'drop-fences' where the landing is considerably lower than the take-off.

Penalties on the cross-country and steeple-chase courses are incurred as follows:

Refusals (including running-out or circling)
First — 20 penalties
Second (at the same obstacle) — 40 penalties
Third (at the same obstacle) — Elimination
Fall of horse and/or rider within the 'penalty.zone' which surrounds each fence — 60 penalties
Second fall of horse and/or rider within the 'penalty zone' on the steeplechase course — Elimination
Third fall of horse and/or rider within the 'penalty zone' on the cross-country course — Elimination
Taking the wrong course — Elimination

It is on the cross-country section that competitors can earn the biggest time bonus (between 80·8 and 90·8 in major international classes). Penalties are incurred for exceeding the 'time allowed', at the rate of 0·4 of a penalty for each second over.

On the final morning of a three-day event, each horse still in the competition must undergo a thorough veterinary examination. Those which fail to pass this examination are automatically withdrawn. The test on the third day is not an ordinary show jumping competition, nor a test of style or endurance. Its object is to prove that, on the day after a severe test of endurance, horses are still able to continue in service. The course is designed with this object in mind and it is not a difficult test of the horse's jumping ability.

Show jumping penalties in the three-day event are incurred as follows:

Fence knocked down — 10 penalties
One or more feet in the water, or on the landing tape — 10 penalties
Refusals (including running-out or circling)
First — 10 penalties
Second — 20 penalties
Third — Elimination
Fall of horse and/or rider — 30 penalties
For each second over the time allowed — ¼ penalty
Exceeding the time limit — Elimination

The principal international three-day events (apart from those included in the Olympic and PAN-AMERICAN GAMES) are the world and European championships. Both are open to men and women riders over the age of 18, and they carry a team as well as an individual title. As in the Olympic Games, each team consists of four riders and the final result is assessed by adding together the best three over-all scores.

Riders between the ages of 14 and 18 have the chance to gain international experience in the junior European championships, which also carry a team and individual title.

In most countries, horses and riders compete in one-day events before tackling the full-scale three-day test. As the name implies, these are events on a smaller scale which are completed in a single day, by omitting the steeplechase and the roads and tracks sections from the second phase. One-day events are particularly popular in Britain, where national championships are held at the end of each season.

F.E.I. Rules for Dressage Events, Jumping Events, and Three-Day Events, annually.

The training of horses by means of gymnastic exercises has probably existed ever since man began training horses more than 3,000 years ago. Originally dressage was connected solely with the basic training of war horses and, unlike the advanced form of equitation known as high school (*haute école*), it was regarded only as a means to an end. The first Olympic Grand Prix de Dressage had repercussions throughout the equestrian world and, at competition level, dressage has become an end in itself. Since the end of the Second World War, the Olympic test has included advanced movements, which come into the category of high school 'airs'.

Though the precise venue and date of the first show jumping competition are unknown, the sport gained popularity in a number of countries towards the end of the nineteenth century. The Royal Dublin Society, founded in 1731, was responsible for some of the earliest contests since they ran classes for 'wide' and 'high' leaps at their show in 1865. This was only four years after the Society organized their first show classes, which were then for agricultural horses. Russia organized show jumping competitions at much the same time, and the French followed shortly afterwards.

About 1875 agricultural shows in Britain began to include 'leaping' or 'lepping' contests in their programme. Rules were non-existent and judges were therefore at liberty to decide whether style or jumping ability would be the deciding factor. This led to dissatisfaction among the competitors, who believed — with justification in many cases — that the results had been decided long before the competition began.

At the second modern Olympic Games, at Paris in 1900, three jumping classes were included in the programme, but it was not for another 12 years that equestrian sports became accepted as a regular part of the Olympics. Meanwhile Britain had staged her first International Horse Show, at Olympia, London, in 1907, which included 11 show jumping competitions. Seven overseas countries were represented and the Dutch and the Belgians took the lion's share of the prize money.

Two years later, international classes were staged at Lucerne and at MADISON SQUARE GARDEN, New York, where the National Horse Show had been thriving since 1883. The sport was also growing in other parts of the world. Russian riders were preparing for an onslaught on the team competition at London's International, which they won from 1911 to 1913; Sweden was laying the foundations for her team gold medal at the 1912 Olympic Games (which proved to be the first of a hat-trick that was completed in 1920 and 1924).

The Swedish Count von Rosen played a major role in the history of show jumping; it was through his initiative that the sport was accepted for the Olympic Games of 1912. He had made an abortive attempt to get equestrian sports included in the IVth Olympiad four years earlier in London, and renewed his efforts when it was decided that the 1912 Olympics would be held at Stockholm.

The rules for the Olympic show jumping competitions in 1912 were much more complicated than today's. The use of 'slats' (thin strips of wood on the top of each fence) meant that horses were penalized for 'touching' a jump (and thus dislodging the slat) and, since the penalty was greater if the touch were made with the horse's forelegs, the scoring system was largely dependent on the judge's eyesight. Though still used in Britain (and some other countries) up to the late 1940s, slats had been abolished for Olympic competitions before the Antwerp Games of 1920. The distinction between faults made with the horse's fore- or hindlegs continued until a simplified system of judging was introduced for the Los Angeles Games of 1932.

The most far-reaching event for show jumping between the two World Wars was the birth of the Fédération Équestre Internationale, the ruling body for international equestrian sport. The need for a complete set of international rules and regulations had become increasingly pressing and it was on the instigation of Baron de Coubertin, who had been responsible for reviving the Olympic Games, that a meeting of the leading equestrians was arranged. The ensuing conferences, in which France and Sweden played a prominent part, resulted in the founding of the F.E.I. in May 1921. The other founder members were Belgium, Denmark, Italy, Japan, Norway, and the U.S.A. The British Show Jumping Association was formed in 1923.

International jumping between the wars was almost entirely confined to army officers but, as the number of cavalry regiments declined, civilian riders moved into the international sphere. The 1948 Olympic Games in London, in which the 44 show jumping competitors were all military men, marked the final phase of the army's monopoly.

During the next two decades much was done to popularize jumping as a spectator sport. Courses, hitherto very dull, became far more imaginative; national federations followed the F.E.I.'s example and adopted the simplified scoring system (with a knock-down by fore- or hindlegs counting as four faults); time was introduced as the arbiter in the first round or deciding jump-off of many contests. Generous sponsorship in the 1960s brought greatly increased prize money, and television coverage a vast new audience. In Germany, show jumping became second only to football as a popular spectator sport.

The three-day event developed from cavalry endurance tests which took the form of long-distance rides of varying lengths, the severity being measured by the speed required as much as by the actual distance. Since the practice of jumping fences came into vogue only in the latter part of the eighteenth century, these early rides were all on the flat, mainly on roads and tracks. Among the endurance tests were 'long-distance rides from Vienna to Wiener Neustadt (in 1687), from Vienna to Berlin (in 1892), and a disastrous event from Brussels to Ostend (in 1902), which resulted in the death of 16 of the 29 horses who completed the journey.

Meanwhile France was developing the *raid militaire*, a long-distance cross-country ride, run as a military exercise and not as a competition. The course for one *raid* went from Biarritz to Paris.

The French staged what was probably the first all-round test with the inauguration of their *Championnat du Cheval d'Armes* in 1902. The test comprised four sections — dressage, steeplechase, a long-distance ride on roads and tracks covering 50·4 km. (31 miles), and show jumping. It was immediately acclaimed a resounding success. The idea was developed in cavalry regiments in other parts of the world and the sport took a decisive step forward when it was included in the Olympic Games of 1912.

The Olympic 'military' or 'pentathlon on horseback', which later developed into the present three-day event, was divided into five phases when it first appeared on the Olympic programme: (1) long-distance ride of 55 km. (34 miles), incorporating a cross-country course of 5 km. (3 miles); (2) steeplechase of 3·5 km. (2 miles); (3) prize jumping (show jumping); (4) prize riding (dressage). The competition was confined to army officers riding military horses and, though the rules allowed civilians to compete from 1924 onwards, the Olympic three-day event was to remain a military stronghold until after the Games in London in 1948.

Though British officers serving in India took part in similar tests during the 1920s, the cavalry regiments at home in England showed little interest in this developing equestrian sport. Four British riders did take part in the Olympic 'military' of 1912 but, since none of them succeeded in completing the full test, their performances did little to stimulate interest in the sport at home.

The dressage phase was dropped at the next Olympic Games, at Antwerp in 1920, and a second endurance phase took its place. The complete test thus became: (1) endurance and cross-country and (2) endurance and speed (steeplechase) — total distance 74 km. (46 miles); (3) show jumping. Dressage was reinstated in 1924 when, for the first time, the present pattern of three-day events took shape. The total distance of the endurance phase was reduced to 36 km. (22 miles).

Though Britain had made a dismal Olympic début in three-day events, she was to play a dominant part in the sport after the Second World War. Between 1953 and 1972 British teams won three Olympic gold medals, seven out of eleven European championships, and one out of two world championships.

The seed of these successes was sown in 1949, a year after the Olympic Games in London, when the Duke of BEAUFORT launched the Badminton Horse Trials, then called the Badminton Olympic Three-Days Event. The sport, with its long military associations, was scarcely known to the civilian riders of Britain and, perhaps on account of its novelty, interest in the inaugural Badminton was immense. This event marked the beginning of a civilian takeover at both national and international levels.

The Daily Telegraph Book of Show Jumping (1970); Lt.-Col. C. E. G. Hope, *The Horse Trials Story* (1969); E. Schmit-Jensen, *Equestrian Olympic Games* (1948).

GOVERNING BODY (WORLD): Fédération Équestre Internationale, Avenue Hamoir 38, 1180 Brussels, Belgium.

EQUINE RESEARCH STATION of the Animal Health Trust was established in 1947 at Balaton Lodge, Newmarket, under the direction of Prof. Miller. Research has been conducted into sterility, uterine and other bacterial infections in mares, redworm and diseases in foals, equine rhinopneumonitis, and many other ailments liable to afflict the horse.

ERMOLAEVA, GALINA (1937-   ), Russian sprint cyclist, and winner of 14 world championship medals — 6 gold, 5 silver, and 3 bronze — during the period 1958-70.

ESPARTERO, El (Manuel García) (1866-94), *matador de toros* who took the *alternativa* in 1885, was one of the end-of-the-century

toreros who had little command of the cape and *muleta*, but were highly competent with the sword. On 27 May 1894, in the *plaza de toros* of Madrid, with his body already bearing 13 cicatrices as evidence of encounters with the same herd, he was gored in the stomach by the Miura bull Perdigon and died within 20 minutes.

ESTADIO BERNABEU, Association FOOTBALL ground of REAL MADRID. The stadium, which has a capacity of 135,000, was built and developed between 1943 and 1953, and named after the president of the Real Madrid club. Its completion coincided with the rise of the club to first place in European club football in the late 1950s.

ESTUDIANTES DE LA PLATA, Association FOOTBALL club, founded by students of La Plata University in 1905, which entered the First Division of the Argentinian League in 1912. The club played without conspicuous success until the middle 1960s when with an outstanding team of young players it finished high enough in the Argentinian League to qualify for entry in the South American Cup for clubs. Against strong opposition, Estudiantes won and went on to beat the European club champions, MANCHESTER UNITED, in the unofficial world club championship in 1968. Although retaining the South American title in the following two competitions they were beaten for the world championship by A.C. MILAN in 1969 and FEIJENOORD in 1970. Leading players have included Malbernat, Veron, and Poletti.

COLOURS: Red and white striped shirts, black shorts.

ETCHEBASTER, PIERRE (1893-   ), REAL TENNIS world champion 1928-55. Etchebaster was a trinquet and PELOTA champion, who learned tennis at Bordeaux before moving to Paris as *paumier*, and in 1928 won the world championship from Covey, the first Frenchman to hold the title since BARRE's defeat in 1862. In 1930 Etchebaster went to New York to become head professional at the Racquet and Tennis Club. There he has remained, retaining his world title undefeated for 26 years and continuing afterwards to raise the standard of play in America.

ETON COLLEGE, see ETON FIELD GAME; ETON FIVES; ETON WALL GAME.

ETON COLLEGE BOAT CLUB, the most famous school ROWING club in the world, whose origins date back to 1793. Eton oarsmen played a major part in the development of rowing at Oxford and Cambridge during the nineteenth century and Eton crews could hold their own with the best in the country. Eton crews won the Ladies' Plate at HENLEY on seven successive occasions in the 1890s. Despite the challenge of other schools in the twentieth century, Eton remained the most powerful force. An Eton eight won the first International Youth Regatta at RATZEBURG in 1967 and another was second in 1968.

ETON FIELD GAME is a form of football confined to Eton College, and one of several versions of the game current when Association FOOTBALL was evolved in the 1860s. The field game, an 11-a-side game, must be distinguished from the ETON WALL GAME. Whereas the wall game is played only by the 70 scholars and a few enthusiasts from the rest of the school, the field game is taught to every Eton boy in his first year. It is still the 'official' football game at Eton. There is a school field team, which plays regularly against scratch teams of visitors and masters, and house colours are awarded partially on performance in the field game House Ties, a fiercely contested knock-out competition, which is held every March between the 26 houses.

Several features distinguish the field game from other codes of football: (a) the relatively small size of the goal, with no handling of the ball by any player; (b) the enforcement of a strict offside rule, which prevents any passing of the ball; (c) the possibility of scoring 'rouges' on the goal line, in addition to kicking actual goals.

The object of the field game is to propel the ball towards the opponents' goal line and score there. It is played on a large number of rectangular pitches throughout Eton, of varying dimensions. The goals are of uniform size, being the same as that of HOCKEY goals, 12 ft. wide by 7 ft. high (3·66 × 2·13 m.). There is only one 'standard' pitch, known as The Field, on which all really important matches are played. Its dimensions are 130 yds. (from goal to goal) × 90 yds. (118·87 × 82·29 m.). It is bounded by touch lines at either side and goal lines at either end, marked in whiting. In the field of play 3 yds. (2·74 m.) from each goal line and parallel to it a dotted line called the 3-yard line is marked. Fifteen yards (13·72 m.) from each goal line and parallel to it there is a continuous line called the 15-yard line. A round ball is used, similar to a small soccer ball.

The chief centre of activity in the field game is the 'bully'. This is a group of 8 out of the 11 players on each side, who keep as close together as possible, once play has started. Their centripetal tendency is caused by the

rule against passing, which obliges the bully to play as far as possible 'as one man'. Any bully player who becomes detached from the main mass must take no part in the game until he rejoins the bully. But if a bully player overruns the ball, another immediately behind him may take it on. The three players on each side who are not in the bully are called 'behinds', and act as defensive 'backs' behind the bully. The bully players are designated as one post, two sideposts, one back-up post (b.u.p.), three corners, one fly (flying man). The behinds are called 'short', 'long', and 'goals'.

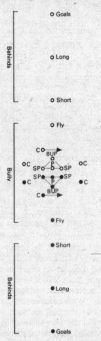

POSITIONS IN A 'SET BULLY', ETON FIELD GAME
(C) Corner; (P) post; (SP) sidepost; (BUP) back-up post.

When a 'set bully' is formed, the posts, sideposts, and b.u.p.s bind together in tight formation. Each side has 'heads' in alternate bullies, i.e. has the right to form down first. This means that the front row (post and sideposts) of the side with 'heads' put their heads down, while the front row of the side without 'heads' are obliged to stand upright, and so are at a disadvantage in applying pressure and observing the ball. The b.u.p.s on either side bind on behind their posts with their heads down, and, together with their front row, push forward as soon as the ball is put in from the side by one of the corners. The immediate aim of each side is to make ground forwards, or at any rate not lose it. The three corners on either side maintain a fairly loose contact with the more tightly formed part of the bully, ready to pounce on the ball as soon as it appears. The fly informs his bully as to the whereabouts of the ball and directs operations generally, being ready to receive the ball if it is kicked through the bully by the opposing side.

The set bully may in certain circumstances begin a period of play, but on other occasions play may be initiated by the ball being kicked off by one of the behinds. In this case the members of the bully spread themselves across the field, trying if possible to be 'unmarked' by an opponent. An individual bully player is then entitled to take on the ball after the behind has kicked it, but the other members of the bully must immediately group themselves together round him, in the manner previously described, if they are to take any part in the game. An individual bully player in normal circumstances will dribble the ball forward as fast as possible. He ought to be backed up by at least one other member of the bully to take over the ball if he loses control of it, or is tackled. Collectively the bully will normally proceed with heads down and the ball at their feet in what is known as a 'bully-rush'.

The basic task of the behinds is to stop opposing bully players from getting through towards the behind's goal or goal line. After tackling an opposing player (in which no use of the arm is permitted) or in any other way gaining access to the ball, the behind's normal task is to return it to his own bully, who ought to be grouping themselves together to receive it. The opposing bully will also join the group, since if they become detached from it they will all be 'offside'. With as little delay as possible the behind kicks the ball in such a way as, ideally, to fall at the feet of his own bully, so that they may take it on in the direction of the opposing goal. The offside rule does not apply to a behind when he kicks the ball forward towards, or preferably over, the heads of his bully players.

Scoring may be done by means of goals, which count 4 points each, or 'rouges', which count 3. To score a goal involves kicking the ball between the goal posts, which is comparatively difficult, since the goal is so small. An alternative method of scoring, somewhat more frequently employed, is to obtain a rouge on the goal line. There are various rather complicated conditions under which a rouge may be scored, but the principle is always the same, that the ball is touched when beyond the line by an attacker after a mistake of some sort by a

defender. Typically a rouge occurs when a defender inadvertently kicks the ball backward over his own line. If an attacker then succeeds in touching it before a defender can do so a rouge is scored. Similarly a rouge may be scored if the ball is kicked by an attacker, rebounds off a defender backwards over the line, and is touched by an attacker. While 'on the line' (i.e. within three yards of the goal line) the ball must be kept in motion by the attackers. If it stops, a kick-out is awarded to the defenders. If a 'rougeable ball' is touched by the defenders, the attacking side have the choice of scoring 1 point (followed by a kick-off by the defenders) or scoring no points, in which case a bully is formed three yards from the goal line with attackers' 'heads'. A heavy or powerful bully who made the latter choice might have a good chance of scoring a rouge.

Once a rouge has been scored, the attackers are allowed to attempt to convert it into a goal by means of a 'ram'. This is a set piece in which the defending bully group themselves in the goal mouth, while a picked body of attackers (normally three or four) form up one behind the other and make an organized rush into the middle of the defenders, in an effort to force the ball through the goal mouth. If successful, they gain 2 extra points.

The game is officially controlled by two umpires, and the main *penalties* are as follows: A set bully is awarded for cornering (passing sideways) and furking (heeling the ball backward in the tight or loose bully). A free kick is awarded for sneaking (passing forward), passing back, playing while on the ground, or any type of fouling. If the ball goes out but not behind, a set bully is formed one-quarter of the way across the field of play and (a) opposite the place where it was last touched by a player (if he was outside his own 15-yard area), or (b) on the 15-yard line (if he was not), or (c) (when this is to the disadvantage of his side) opposite the place where the ball went out. A kick-off takes place if the attackers kick the ball over the defenders' goal line without scoring a rouge. If a goal of any kind is scored the ball is kicked off from the centre of the field.

The most noticeable features of the field game from the spectator's point of view are:
(1) A requirement to 'keep the ball close', leading to loose 'bully-rushes' by the bully as a whole, or fast dribbling 'runs-down' by individual players.
(2) Spectacularly high kicking by the behinds, for whom there is a great advantage either in volleying the ball or playing it immediately while in motion, rather than wasting time by steadying it. The aim of the high kick is to clear the heads of other players and enable the

behind's own bully to 'charge up', thus gaining ground before taking the ball on when it comes down at their feet. In practice, before this can happen, the ball often reaches an opposing behind, who makes another high kick back, and thus much effort is wasted by the two bullies charging backward and forward between two rival behinds indulging in alternate high kicks.

(3) The processional progress along the goal line towards the goal, as the attackers try to induce the defenders to give away a rouge, while the defenders endeavour to 'clear' the ball.

(4) The great amount of exercise taken by all players except goals and possibly long.
Laws of the Game of Football as Played in the Field at Eton, revised 1971.

Football at Eton in some form or other dates back to the Middle Ages. In 1519 the headmaster, William Horman, produced a book of Latin sentences based on school life which included the words: 'We will play with a ball full of wynde'. But organized football came into existence only during the nineteenth century. About 1830 hockey was being played concurrently with football, hence perhaps the persistence of hockey-type goals. At this time football was being played at Eton in a more or less unorganized form by a number of voluntary 'clubs' whose varied rules were determined partly by their individual traditions and partly by the nature of the terrain on which they regularly played. During the same period we find the term 'rouge' applied to any episode of violent activity, as in the expressions: 'smart and prolonged rouges', 'in the thick of every rouge and rally for two hours', or as a verb, 'pushing and rouging'.

Out of this fluid situation three distinct types of football evolved, the wall game, the field game, and 'Lower College', whose scoring in shies and goals suggests that it combined some of the characteristics of both wall and field. Towards the middle of the century football throughout Britain was gradually becoming more highly organized, and 1850 is a useful rough dividing date between the crude unorganized varieties of the game in the first half of the century and the Victorian conception of organized compulsory games, which became a characteristic of public school life in the second half. At Eton 'Lower College' finally disappeared in 1863, the year of the foundation of the Football Association.

Amid the development of RUGBY and Association football as national games the field game held its own as the main game at Eton, and it is clear that Alfred Lubbock, writing of his own experience of the field game in the

1850s and 1860s, is describing a game very similar to that played today. Records of keepers of the field begin in 1855, and in 1862 the school field colours of light blue and red were instituted. Since 1850 the rules of the field game have been altered slightly from time to time, and the current rules, entitled *Laws of the Game of Football as Played in the Field at Eton*, are obtainable at the Eton School Stores Stationery Department.

In 1971 a radical change took place in the conditions under which football was played at Eton. Previously the field game was played in the Michaelmas term, and soccer and Rugby had to do as best they could in the Lent term. Fair competition against other schools was impossible, and the standard of the Eton teams in these two national games was comparatively low. In 1971 soccer and Rugby were transferred to the Michaelmas term and the field game to the Lent. At the same time the rules of the field game were altered with two main aims in view: (*a*) to reduce the number of drawn games, and (*b*) to discourage deliberate kicking to touch, which was beginning to spoil the game.

Those interested in the field game are recommended to watch either the school field matches, which now take place throughout February and the first part of March, or the last rounds of the House Ties in the middle of March.

A. C. Ainger, *Eton 60 Years Ago* (1917); Alfred Lubbock, *Memories of Eton* (1899); G. W. Lyttelton, articles in the *Eton College Magazine*, 1827; J. J. Pawson, *The Eton Field Game* (1935); *Fifty Years of Sport* (Eton, Harrow, Winchester) (1922).

ETON FIVES, a hand-ball game played by pairs in a three-walled court, the design of which is based on an area outside the chapel at Eton College where for centuries among the strange collection of ledges, steps, and drainholes, boys played with bare hands and balls of varying size and hardness.

Eton fives is played at over 50 centres throughout England, mainly in London, the Midlands, and the south-eastern counties of England, and in Australia, Malaysia, Nigeria, and Europe. It is one of three versions of the game, each named after the public school of its origin. (See also RUGBY FIVES; WINCHESTER FIVES.)

The fives ball is a composition of cork and rubber, painted white, and approximately the size of a GOLF ball. Gloves are of leather and the fingers and palm should be evenly but thinly padded, so that control can be given to placing and 'cut'. The gloves prevent bruised hands and also protect the fingers and knuckles from injury against the many projections in the court. Dress is usually white shirt and shorts as in court games, and it should allow complete freedom of movement of waist, arms, and legs.

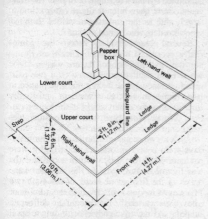

SECTION OF AN ETON FIVES COURT

Looking through the right-hand corner of the front wall towards the pepper box on the left-hand wall; the lower court, 15 ft. 3 in. (4·65 m.) deep, with buttresses at either end, is not shown.

Courts vary in dimensions, but all have a ledge running across the front wall making a horizontal line 4 ft. 6 in. (1·37 m.) from the ground. Running across the court is a shallow step 10 ft. (3·05 m.) from the front wall, dividing the court into an inner or upper court and an outer or lower court. The lower court is 15 ft. 3 in. (4·65 m.) in depth and 14 ft. (4·27 m.) wide. At the end of the step, projecting from the left-hand wall, is a buttress (known as 'the pepper box').

One player guards the upper court and his partner the lower court. To start the game, the ball must be served to the opponent's liking. Generally it should bounce to shoulder height and should be lobbed, thrown, or bowled with no spin imparted so that it falls true without breaking. The player receiving ('cutting' or 'slogging') has the right to refuse any number of serves if they are not to his liking. The receiver then strikes the ball as the 'first cut' to return it above the front ledge within certain limits aiming to make it impossible to retrieve. If the server or his partner returns the ball, the rally continues until a side fails to hit the ball 'up' and the striker and his partner lose that rally. Points are scored only by the pair serving.

Game ball is reached at 11 points when the server, apart from still having to provide an ideal service for his opponent, has to place one foot in the lower court and not move till the ball has been hit. A game consists of 12 points and matches are generally the best of five games. If 11-all is reached, the game may be 'set' to three; or at 10-all, to three or five.

The foremost stroke is the 'first cut'. The laws allow two forms, either (1) that which hits first the right-hand wall and then the front wall above the ledge; or (2) that which hits first the front wall above the ledge between the right-hand wall and the vertical ('blackguard') line marked on the front wall 3 ft. 8 in. (1·12 m.) from the right-hand corner.

The purpose of the player on the top step, who serves, is to dominate the game. This requires skill, speed, an accurate eye, and volleys with either hand. The volley on the top step is the essence of success and delay can cost the rally. Co-operation in partnership, however, is essential, and a volley which would be difficult for the top court player may be possible for his partner. The player in the lower court should back up every stroke by his partner on the top step who can often miss the ball entirely or change his mind at the last moment.

While footwork is instinctive to natural games players, frequently the game moves so fast that a shot has to be played off the wrong foot. To be able to hit a fives ball equally hard and accurately with both hands is the aim of all players, but particular emphasis is placed on the left hand in Eton fives by the shape of the court which is very much to the benefit of a left-hander. Frequently the ball should be hit no harder than is necessary; the modern composition ball is more likely to fall dead if hit firmly but gently into the pepper box. Another basic principle is the necessity for a loose wrist for the majority of shots.

Every effort should be made to avoid getting in the way of opponents as they attempt to make their shots, but such is the speed of the game that it is not always possible to move quickly enough to allow an opponent to play a stroke as he wishes, and in every case a 'let' should be offered before it is asked for. The spirit of the game is such that an umpire or marker is generally not necessary; nor would an umpire be practical, as the best view of any situation on the court would probably be masked by the players themselves. In the finals of the various championships, however, a marker is usually appointed merely as someone to appeal to if need arises.

The word 'fives' has been used to denote many different games and pastimes in which a ball was propelled either across a net or against a wall with the hand. It has also meant

BOXING, the fives court for a period being the 'ring' of today.

The derivation of the word is uncertain, but that it is from playing with the five fingers of the hand is generally accepted. Other theories are that scoring was a multiple of fives, there may have been five persons in a match (four players and an umpire), or the game may have involved five players a side.

The latter view is supported by Nicholas's chronicle, *Progresses of Queen Elizabeth*: 'The same day after dinner, about three of the clocke, ten of my Lord of Hartford's servants, all Somersetshire men, in a square green court, before Her Majesty's window, did lay up lines, squaring out the forme of a tennis court, and making a crosse line in the middle. In this square they (being stript of their doublets) played, five to five, with the hand ball at bord and cord (as they terme it), to so great liking of Her Highness.' This is not fives as known today, nor HANDBALL, but TENNIS or *jeu de paume*, and this particular game was probably played with the hand.

Dr. Johnson's dictionary describes 'fives' as 'a kind of play with a bowl' and 'bowl' as 'a round mass which may be rolled along the ground'.

The Eton variation of the game originated outside the chapel at the college where boys waited for roll-call. At the foot of the stairs leading up to the north door of the chapel there was a space between two buttresses, partially obstructed on the left by the end of a stone balustrade known today as the 'pepper box'. There four boys could play together, two of them between the buttresses, and the other two behind them on a level platform a little lower down. A convenient sloping ledge at a height of 4 ft. 6 in. (1·37 m.) formed the play-line and another ledge about 2 ft. (0·6 m.) from the ground formed an additional hazard. The bull's-eye of the court, known as the 'dead man's hole', which would make the ball irretrievable, was no more than a drain.

Such was the popularity of the game that in 1840 the headmaster, Dr. E. C. Hawtrey, instigated, on a more suitable site, the building of the first four Eton fives courts, incorporating the characteristics of the chapel court, but with modifications to make the game easier and faster. Eight more courts were built in 1847. Today Eton has about 40 courts, the largest number in the world, and is frequently the venue for national competitions.

It was not until much later that the game spread to other schools. Harrow was the second school to build courts, in 1870. Charterhouse, Highgate, and Westminster adopted the game next in 1886, and over a dozen courts were built at Cambridge between 1890

and 1900. Open courts were also constructed in country houses all over England. In those days, however, accurate dimensions were not considered necessary as they are today and this accounted for the low standard of play. In later years courts were built at many other schools largely due to the enthusiasm of old Etonian schoolmasters who joined the staff.

Several years elapsed before the game really prospered at schools other than Eton, and the first inter-school fixture was in 1885 when Eton challenged Harrow to a one-pair match. Eton won easily but the match stimulated interest and the standard gradually improved at the other schools, so that by the First World War there were a considerable number of inter-school matches.

As with most games, the laws in the early days were based on oral tradition and it was not until 1877 that they were first codified. It was then that A. C. Ainger, an old Etonian, drew up the first set of *Rules of the Game of Fives as Played at Eton*. Even then, individual rules were variously interpreted by different schools and the first authoritative set of laws was published by the Eton Fives Association (E.F.A.) in 1931.

Before the Second World War London was generally regarded as the main centre of the game, due largely to the popularity of the Queen's Club courts and also to the fact that it was mainly at the schools in and around London that the game was most popular. Since the war, however, it has become increasingly popular at schools all over England and there are over 30 public and grammar schools which play the game regularly. Fives has been credited with half-blue status at Oxford and Cambridge universities. Nearly all the schools which possess courts have active old boys' clubs.

That Eton fives has not developed to any large extent must be due to the complicated and costly design of the court, the lack of spectator appeal, and the absolute necessity for four players to one game.

In 1924 Lord Kinnaird gave a challenge cup to innovate a knock-out competition for old boys' pairs. It was not competed for until 1926, and, to give it a greater showing of importance, the competition was later renamed the amateur championship for the Kinnaird Cup. It is played over an extended period during the season (September to April) and the semi-finals and final are of a particularly high standard. The initial rounds, organized during a week-end at Eton, see a gathering of over 60 pairs from all parts of the country. Ludgrove, the preparatory school at Wokingham, Berkshire, site of two of the most accurate Eton fives courts in the world, has frequently been the venue for the final.

The Alan Barber Cup was introduced in 1966 as a three-pair knock-out competition among the old boys' clubs and stimulated considerable interest.

The Public Schools Competition has inevitably varied in standard throughout the years, but at times has produced fives of very high quality and has always been well supported.

The pre-war fives ball was produced by hand, using a mixture of tightly-wound felt cloth and a hand-sewn leather cover. This had a very characteristic bounce which was dependent on the skill of the maker. The balls did not last very long — after only one game the seam would begin to break. They could be repaired by sewing on a new leather cover.

The major supplier of balls before the war was the firm of Jefferies Malings Ltd. which started in 1852 as manufacturers of balls for RACKETS, ROUNDERS, STOOLBALL, yardball, and fives. During the Second World War a bomb destroyed the London factory and the premises did not re-open. An acute shortage of balls developed and there was concern whether the game could continue.

At this time the Eton Fives Association set up a committee to investigate alternative sources and an unsuccessful effort was made to produce plastic balls. In 1960, Baden Fuller became interested in the project and offered to investigate the problem. After two years' work he produced the formula for the composition fives ball which is now used. This is a complex chemical mixture mainly based on rubber and cork with a specially formulated white coating (applied three to five times) with high resistance to scuffing. Baden Fuller offered to produce the ball in conjunction with the Eton Fives Association so that its price could be kept low. It was produced in 1963 as the E.F.A. ball.

During 1964 many complaints were made that this ball was much faster than the leather-covered one. After further development, a slower version of the ball was produced and accepted as a suitable alternative for certain fast courts. However, during the following year players became used to the higher speed and appeared to enjoy the fast game, leaving the Association with large stocks of slow balls which thereafter were suitable only for preparatory schools.

Fives was first introduced on the Continent largely through the efforts of Spencer, a master at Zuoz College, Switzerland, in 1924 when three open-air courts were built. In the 1930s a team from the Eton Fives Association visited Zuoz and from time to time the college has sent teams to England. The game at Zuoz has remained popular, helped by an annual visit from the Old Citizens and visits by Highgate and Berkhamsted Schools. Three more courts were added in 1966. There are also courts at the Institut Montana at Zugerberg bei Zug, near Zurich, and four courts were built in the late 1920s at the Alpine College at Arvey bei Villars, near Bex. In 1962 the old Zuozers built a court in Zurich and such has been its popularity that it has since been covered and lit, and the old Zuozers now send teams to play matches in England. Other courts on the Continent include one at Düsseldorf and one built in the middle 1950s at Wellenburg Castle, near Augsburg, by Prince Fugger, an old boy of Zuoz. There is also a court at Salzburg on the premises of the Hotel Mönchstein.

Charlesworth, an old Salopian schoolmaster at Shrewsbury, introduced the game to Australia at Geelong Church of England Grammar School on an exchange visit in 1954, when one court was built.

In Malaya, two courts were built in 1905 when Malay College, Perak, was founded and the courts have been in frequent use.

The game was introduced to Nigeria by Hogben, who built two courts in November 1922 while teaching at the Birnin Kebbi Provincial School. They were built of mud and are now in decay, but new courts have been built in many of the main towns in the northern region. In 1963 a team from Eton College toured Nigeria. The Eton Fives Association sent a team there in 1965 and the Nigerian Fives Association accepted the invitation to tour England in 1966. In Nigeria the game is played with a tennis ball and bare hands. One of the objectives of the Eton Fives Association's visit was to introduce gloves and the hard ball in an effort at uniformity.

Rackets, Squash-Rackets, Tennis, Fives and Badminton (The Lonsdale Library, 1933); *How to Play Fives* (Spalding's Sports and Athletics Library); *Almanack of Sport* (1966).

GOVERNING BODY (WORLD): Eton Fives Association, 171 Carshalton Road, Sutton, Surrey.

ETON WALL GAME is one of the oldest forms of FOOTBALL in existence and certainly one of the oddest of sporting survivals. It is played only on a site at Eton college, where a red brick wall separates the playing fields from the Slough Road.

Originally it was a game for 11-a-side, but after the Second World War the number was reduced to 10. Play takes place in a narrow strip, roughly 4 to 5 yds. wide and 118 yds. long (3.66–4.57 m. × 107.89 m.), adjoining the wall, which is about 11 ft. (3.35 m.) high. The surface begins as grass, but in the course of a season becomes reduced to bare earth,

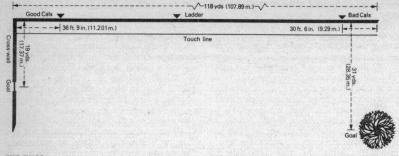

THE WALL
Not drawn to scale. A goal is outlined on the trunk of the tree at right.

dust, or varying consistencies of mud, according to weather conditions. The wall game is quite different from any other kind of football, in that from a spectator's point of view it is mainly static, with only rare moments of rapid movement. These characteristics are largely determined by the site.

At its left-hand end the wall terminates in a cross-wall going off at right angles. Nineteen yds. (17·37 m.) from the junction is a door in the cross-wall, which is one of the two goals. At the other end there is no cross-wall, and the goal line is marked in whiting. The goal at this end, 31 yds. (28·35 m.) away from the wall, is an old elm tree, with a section of its trunk, approximate in shape to the door, outlined in whitewash. At either end of the wall is a scoring area marked off by a white line on the wall and known as Calx (the Latin for 'chalk'). The presence of the cross-wall makes scoring easier there; hence the area at that end (36 ft. 9 in. — 11·201 m.) is known as Good Calx and that at the other end (30 ft. 6 in. — 9·29 m.) as Bad Calx. Somewhat nearer Good Calx than Bad, there is a metal ladder up the wall on the Slough Road side, the bolts of which are visible on the side where the game is played, and in each half of the game, or after a goal is scored, play starts at the ladder. The object of the game is to propel the ball into the opponent's Calx and score there.

The ball is round and about the size of a child's soccer ball. The functions of the players are highly specialized, depending on their position, which must be adapted to their build. They are designated as follows: three walls, two seconds, a third, a fourth, a lines, a fly, and a long. Walls are chosen for a combination of tall stature, long reach, and weight. They play in 'line astern', typically right up against the wall itself. Seconds must be short and stocky, as they play at or under the walls' feet, normally in a crouching position. Third,

fourth, and lines are designated 'outsides'. The third and fourth are sturdy, general-purpose footballers, and play in 'line abreast' outside the walls and seconds. Lines must be a quick, agile player with a reliable kick, as he must kick the ball at once if it appears near the touch line. Finally come the two 'behinds', fly

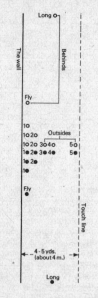

BASIC POSITIONS
Plan view shows players on both sides when formed up at the commencement of a new period of play. (1) Wall; (2) second; (3) third; (4) fourth.

('flying man') who stands behind the main mass (known as the 'bully'), and long, who stands some way back. The eleventh player, formerly employed, was a third behind, called 'goals', who had very little to do.

Rules. Without going into detail it is suitable here to mention some of the main rules. The ball may not be handled, and the only passing allowed is directly sideways — no forward passing or 'heeling' of the ball backward is allowed. If a player finds himself in front of the ball he must drop round to the back of his own bully, as he is in an 'offside' position. An active player may not touch the ground with any part of his body except his hands and feet. Walls and seconds may 'knuckle' their opponents with the outside only of their 'outside hand', but no striking or kicking of an opponent is allowed. Serious injuries are comparatively rare in the wall game, but if a player feels that he is being crushed into an intolerable position, he is entitled to shout 'air', at which, if he can be heard, the bully breaks up immediately. If the ball is kicked outside the touch line, it becomes 'dead' when it stops, or when it makes any contact with another player (or spectator). The next bully is formed opposite the point where the ball went dead, not where it crossed the touch line. To begin or resume play the ball is rolled into the bully by the thirds alternately.

The game consists of two periods of half an hour each, with a five-minute break and a change of ends at half-time. On official occasions the game is administered by two umpires and a referee. Normally one umpire is considered sufficient.

The pattern of play varies according to the position of the ball relative to the wall. Ground may be made: (*a*) along the wall, in tight formation; (*b*) by 'loose' bully rushes; (*c*) by kicking.

In tight bully-play along the wall, the player with the ball attempts to force his way forward through the opposition, keeping the ball up against the wall, which he uses as a support on one side. His opponents try to force him off the ball and gain control of it themselves. Other players assist those on or near the ball by applying pressure in suitable places so that constant heaving and shoving is characteristic of play at the wall. Progress is very slow, or non-existent, unless a player is skilful or lucky enough to 'break through' with the ball, in which case he may dribble it forward or kick it out, thus making a lot of ground.

In loose bully work, if the ball comes 'loose' away from the wall, players group themselves round it and try to rush forward with the ball at their feet. Occasionally a group of players may form in a 'phalanx', crouching down beside each other and passing the ball from side to side in an effort to confuse the opposition as to its whereabouts. Most frequently the outcome of loose bully play is that the ball will be returned to the wall, or will go out (and hence become dead) with a certain amount of ground made.

Any player who gets the opportunity may kick the ball in the direction of the opponents' Calx. This makes far more ground than any other method, but the attendant risk is greater, since, unless the ball is kicked out over the touch-line, it is likely to be returned, with interest, by the opposing behind. Thus the ideal kick is forward and outward and very high, so as to clear the heads of other players. A good kick may decide the whole fortune of a game, and it will be appreciated that the fatal crime in the wall game is to 'cool' (i.e. to lose control of the ball forward), since such an error is liable to be severely punished by a kick from the opposition.

Scoring. Once the ball is in Calx the character of the play changes. 'Furking' (heeling, or passing the ball backward) is now allowed, and the object of the attackers is to touch up a 'shy', which counts 1 point.

This is normally achieved by means of a Calx bully, an elaborate set-piece in which the ball is put in by one of the umpires. Each side then struggles to furk back the ball, so as to get full possession of it. If the attackers contrive to touch the ball while it is off the ground and up against the wall, they may claim a shy. If granted, this allows the attackers a free throw at the goal. In practice the goal is very rarely hit (on an average in about one game every two years) and the game is normally won or lost by the number of shies rather than goals scored. If neither side reaches Calx, it is bound to be a draw.

A goal may be kicked, rather than thrown, but this is rarer still. A thrown goal is the equivalent of ten shies, and a kicked goal of five. If the defenders gain control of the ball in Good Calx they try to kick it forward and out of Calx. In Bad Calx they may furk it over the back line, after which they are entitled to a kick-out. If they fail to do either of these things, a new Calx bully forms either where the shy was touched up, or (normally) where the ball went dead in Calx.

The mobility, or otherwise, of the game is greatly affected by the conditions. At the beginning of the season, when the ground is firm, movement can be quite free, and a decisive score is the rule rather than the exception. Towards the end of a rainy season the mud may be so thick that the ball can only be moved with difficulty. In these conditions Calx may never be reached, so that pointless draws are more common.

The flying man on each side, in addition to playing as a behind, has the duty of reporting on the position of the ball to his side and directing the efforts of his players. Also, a penalty is not normally awarded by the umpire unless a verbal appeal is made to him. In consequence of both these activities the game takes place amid much shouting by the players. The penalties themselves usually consist either of a newly formed bully on the same spot for minor infringement, or an award of ten yards' distance against the offending side for severer offences.

Rules of the Game of Football as Played at The Wall at Eton.

Eton College was founded in 1440. Part of the foundation consisted of a school for boys comprising 70 scholars, or 'Collegers', as they later became known, and a number of other boys who came to be educated there, and were later called 'Oppidans' (townsmen). These terms are important to the history and practice of the wall game, as the main match of the season is between teams chosen from Collegers and Oppidans respectively.

The wall game cannot have been played before 1717, which was when the wall was built. It does not seem to have been played regularly until the beginning of the nineteenth century. At first it appears to have been merely one variety of football at Eton (though the most formalized and the most popular), which included a wall as a prominent feature of the game, but was played on a comparatively wide area beside it. The technique may have been transferred from 'passage football', a familiar pastime in Eton boys' houses at that time, which is still occasionally played.

Early in the history of the game an annual match arose between Collegers and Oppidans, which is still regularly played on the nearest Saturday to St. Andrew's Day (30 November). This match is the only occasion on which the wall game reaches the public eye and it is regularly reported in the national press. It goes back at least to 1820, but full records do not begin until 1845. The rules were first codified in 1849 and have changed little since. Wall colours date from around 1852, College wall wearing narrow purple and white stripes and Oppidan wall broad purple and orange stripes. The survival of the school wall colour (mixed wall) of red and blue stripes is in continual jeopardy.

The wall game has always been a speciality of the Collegers, who start playing it as soon as they arrive at Eton. The skill and experience thus acquired enables a team chosen from the 70 scholars to compete on equal terms with one chosen from over 1,100 Oppidans, who make up in strength and footballing skill what they lack in experience of this particular game.

The season starts towards the end of September, and for the next two months the College and Oppidan teams compete regularly against scratch sides of old boys or masters, in preparation for the St. Andrew's Day match, the only occasion on which they meet face to face.

On St. Andrew's Day between 1845 and 1973 the Collegers and Oppidans won roughly the same number of matches each, with rather more draws than decisive games. Only three goals have been scored in the St. Andrew's Day match, though in 1842 College won by a goal and 19 shies, which amounts to 29 points. The most famous player of the wall game is J. K. Stephen (College Keeper 1876 and 1877) who is reputed to have carried the whole Oppidan bully on his back. His memory is kept alive by a toast: '*In piam memoriam* J.K.S.' drunk in College after every St. Andrew's Day match.

The wall game, which shares many features with the ETON FIELD GAME, shows every chance of survival and has a peculiar appeal of its own; why should it not be played elsewhere? The rules, entitled *Rules of the Game of Football as Played at The Wall at Eton* are available at the Eton School Stores Stationery Department. Formerly the game was not confined to one wall at Eton — until the 1850s it was also played along another wall beside the Field — which shows that the existing goals and the cross-wall are more a quaint local feature than a physical or spiritual necessity.

A. C. Ainger, *Eton 60 Years Ago* (1917); Alfred Lubbock, *Memories of Eton* (1899); B. J. W. Hill, *Eton Medley* (1948); W. Sterry, *Annals of Eton* (1898); *Fifty Years of Sport* (Eton, Harrow, Winchester) (1922).
AUTHORITY: The Keeper of Mixed Wall, Eton College, Windsor.

EUROPA CUP, a major team championship of international ATHLETICS open to European national associations affiliated to the International Amateur Athletic Federation (see ATHLETICS, TRACK AND FIELD). First staged in 1965 at Stuttgart (men) and Kassel (women), this competition consists of a qualifying round in three groups, followed by a semi-final round and a six-nation final. Each nation enters one competitor per event, the result being determined on a points-scoring basis. The Europa Cup final was staged at Kiev in 1967, at Stockholm in 1970, at Edinburgh in 1973, and is to be held thereafter in a four-year cycle.

EUROPEAN CHAMPIONSHIPS, a major championship of the International Amateur Athletic Federation (see ATHLETICS, TRACK AND FIELD), first staged in Turin in 1934 with men only competing. In 1938 the men's championships were decided in Paris and the women's in Vienna. Thenceforward men and women competed at the same venue, in Oslo, 1946; Brussels, 1950; Berne, 1954; Stockholm, 1958; Belgrade, 1962; Budapest, 1966; Athens, 1969; Helsinki, 1971. In 1974 the championships reverted to the four-year cycle and were staged in Rome.

EUROPEAN CUP, see HOCKEY, FIELD.

EUROPEAN CUP FOR CHAMPION CLUBS, an annual inter-club BASKETBALL competition organized by the Fédération Internationale de Basketball Amateur. The competition is open to the men's basketball clubs rated as national champions by each of the affiliated nations in Europe and the Mediterranean basin, and there is a parallel competition for women's clubs.

The men's cup was presented by the French sporting newspaper *L'Équipe*, of Paris, and was first contested in the season 1957-8. The first winners of the trophy were A.S.K. RIGA. The trophy was not won by a club outside the Soviet Union until 1964, when REAL MADRID were the victors. One of the most prized trophies in basketball, by 1973 it had been won by clubs from only three nations, U.S.S.R., Spain, and Italy.

The women's cup was presented by *Naroden Sport*, of Sofia, and was first contested in 1958-9. The first winners of the trophy were SLAVIA SOFIA, but the competition has since been dominated by DAUGAWA (T.T.T.) RIGA, with 13 victories in the first 15 years of the competition.

EUROPEAN CUP-WINNERS CUP, an annual inter-club BASKETBALL competition organized by the Fédération Internationale de Basketball Amateur. The competition is open to the clubs which have won the national cup in the preceding season in each of the affiliated nations in Europe and the Mediterranean basin. The cup was presented by *Przeglad Sportowy*, of Warsaw, Poland, and was first competed for in 1966-7. The first winners of the trophy were IGNIS VARESE, of Italy. A parallel competition for women's teams was introduced in 1971-2. The first winners were Spartak Leningrad.

EUROPEAN FOOTBALL CHAMPIONSHIP, originally the European Nations Cup, is an Association FOOTBALL competition open to the full national sides of the member-associations of the Union des Associations Européennes de Football (U.E.F.A.). The idea of the competition was discussed for

many years before the setting-up of the European Federation, but such a competition needed the central organization of an authoritative body. It eventually began in 1958 with a rather disappointing entry of 17 Associations, only slightly more than half those entitled to enter. The four British national Associations were among the non-competitors. The first competition, won by the Soviet Union, was organized on a cup system with each country playing twice against the same opponent on a home-and-away basis in each round up to and including the quarter-finals. The matches for the semi-finals, third and fourth places, and the final were played as single matches in the country of one of the semi-finalists. The same method of play was used for the second competition, won by Spain, in 1964, when the entry had encouragingly increased to 29.

The success of the first two competitions and the increased entry persuaded U.E.F.A. to change the method of play to correspond more closely to the Fédération Internationale de Football Associations (F.I.F.A.)'s world championship, and the first European Football Championship commenced in 1966 with only Iceland and Malta of the 33 member Associations not competing. The pattern now established is that this competition will be played during the two seasons which follow the final competition of the world championship and will be organized on a combined league (for the qualifying competition) and cup (for the final competition) system, with the league matches and the quarter-finals played on a home-and-away basis, and the final competition staged in the country of one of the semi-finalists. The first championship determined in this manner was won by Italy in 1968, with Yugoslavia runner-up, England third, and the U.S.S.R. fourth. The second championship, concluded in 1972, was won by West Germany, with the U.S.S.R. second, Belgium third, and Hungary fourth.

EUROPEAN INDOOR GAMES, see ATHLETICS, INDOOR.

EUSEBIO, FERREIRA DA SILVA (1943-), Association footballer for BENFICA (Lisbon) and Portugal. Playing for his country, he was the leading goal-scorer in the 1966 World Cup championship held in England. Although he had not established a regular place in the Benfica side that won the 1961 European Champion Clubs Cup, he fully warranted inclusion in the team from the commencement of the 1961-2 season. He retained his place while Benfica won the Champion Clubs Cup in 1962, were the beaten finalists in

1963, 1965, and 1968, and won the Portuguese championship in 1971.

EVANS, ERIC (1925-), RUGBY UNION hooker for Sale and England. Although not established in the England side until he was 26, Evans won 30 international caps, only one short of WAKEFIELD's record, and finished his career by leading England through two unbeaten seasons.

EVANS, MALDWYN (1937-), left-handed Welsh lawn BOWLS player, who scored the only win over BRYANT at KYEEMAGH, N.S.W., when Bryant won the world championship in 1966, and then took that title from him at Worthing in 1972.

EVANS, THOMAS GODFREY, C.B.E. (1920-), cricketer for England and Kent. A small and spectacular wicket-keeper and an animated batsman who made two Test centuries, he represented England without serious challenge from 1946 to 1959, claiming a record 219 dismissals in 91 Tests.

EVERTON F.C., Association FOOTBALL club, Liverpool. It was founded in 1878 by young men associated with a Sunday school and known as St. Domingo Church Sunday School Club. Within a year the name was changed to Everton; the club became professional in 1885 and one of the original members of the Football League three years later. Everton won the championship in 1891, 1915, and 1928, but were relegated for the first time in 1930. The club stayed only one year in the Second Division, finishing the 1930-1 season in top place and proceeding to win the First Division championship in 1931-2 and 1938-9.

In the 1960s they resumed a leading position in English football with the championship won in 1963 and 1970, and the F.A. Cup in 1966. Outstanding players with the club included Chadwick, Hardman, and Makepeace, in the pre-1914 period; Cresswell, DEAN, LAWTON, MERCER, and Sagar between the wars; and BINGHAM, Collins,

VERNON, Wilson, Labone, YOUNG, and BALL since 1946.

COLOURS: Royal blue shirts, white shorts.
GROUND: Goodison Park, Liverpool.

EWBANK, WILBUR (Weeb) (1907-), American FOOTBALL coach who started professionally under PAUL BROWN with the CLEVELAND BROWNS. He was the only coach to win professional championships in each major league—the NATIONAL FOOTBALL LEAGUE in 1958 with the BALTIMORE COLTS and the American Conference of the League with the NEW YORK JETS against his old Baltimore team in the 1969 Super Bowl.

EXBURY (1959), French race-horse who won a European record £166,696 in stakes, including the PRIX DE L'ARC DE TRIOMPHE, GRAND PRIX DE SAINT-CLOUD, PRIX GANAY, and CORONATION CUP. Exbury was bred and owned by Baron G. DE ROTHSCHILD, trained by Watson, and ridden by Deforge.

EXETER, David George Brownlow Cecil, 6th Marquess of (1905-), hurdler and international ATHLETICS administrator for Great Britain. As Lord Burghley he was perhaps the most renowned hurdler of his day, holding the British records for 120, 220, and 440 yards hurdles and for the 400 metres hurdles, at which distance he won the Olympic title in 1928. In 1932 he finished fourth in the Olympic 400 metres hurdles with his best time of 52.2 sec. This was unbeaten as a British record until 1954. In 1932 he also won a silver medal in the Olympic 4 × 400 metres relay. He briefly held the world record for the 440 yards hurdles and in the 1930 Empire Games won three gold medals: the 120 and 440 yards hurdles and the 4 × 440 yards relay. Lord Exeter became president of the Amateur Athletic Association in 1936 and of the International Amateur Athletic Federation (see ATHLETICS, TRACK AND FIELD) in 1946, in which capacities he resolutely championed the amateur code.

EXETER TRIAL, see MOTOR-CYCLE TRIALS.

F

F.A. CUP, see FOOTBALL, ASSOCIATION.

FAHRBACH SCHUSTER CUP, see TRAMPOLINING.

FAIR PLAY (1905) was the most outstanding stallion in the U.S.A. during the first quarter of this century. He was sire of MAN O' WAR.

FAIRBAIRN, STEPHEN (1862-1938), Australian ROWING coach whose influence on the sport was worldwide. He was one of the first to appreciate the importance of the subconscious, and he deplored coaching for 'style' and 'body-form', thus anticipating the West German coach, K. ADAM. An exceptional athlete, Fairbairn rowed four times for Cambridge University but did not make his mark as a coach until he was over 40, when he began to coach his old college, Jesus. His crews were highly successful, causing prolonged arguments between his followers and devotees of orthodox rowing in the 1920s and 1930s. In 1926, he founded the Head of the River race.

FAIRWAY (1925), English race-horse by Phalaris out of SCAPA FLOW, bred and owned by Lord DERBY, trained by BUTTERS, and ridden by Weston. Fairway won 12 races worth £42,722, including the ST. LEGER, ECLIPSE STAKES, and CHAMPION STAKES twice. At stud he was outstanding, heading the list of winning sires four times.

FALL, TONY (1940-   ), British motor rally driver (see MOTOR RACING), whose first notable success was a class-win in the 1964 Royal Automobile Club Rally. He took a Coupe des Alpes in the French Alpine of 1965 and won the Polish, Scottish, and Irish rallies of 1967.

FALLOWFIELD, WILLIAM (1914-   ), secretary of the RUGBY LEAGUE in England since 1946 and secretary of the Rugby League International Board since its inception in 1948. He played RUGBY UNION for Northampton and the Royal Air Force, and for England in Services internationals during the Second World War. It was at his instigation that the WORLD CUP tournament was organized, and he has often served as manager and coach of international teams.

FALLOWFIELD STADIUM, Manchester, built in 1892, is the oldest cycle track extant in the north of England; it is made of concrete, measures 509 yds. (465·94 m.) in circumference, and has 30° bankings. Its major annual event is the Manchester Wheelers' meeting on the second Saturday in July. It has ATHLETICS and other facilities; the F.A. Cup Final (see FOOTBALL, ASSOCIATION) was played there in 1893.

FALMOUTH, 6th Viscount (1819-89), race-horse owner who paid ARCHER a retaining fee of £100 per annum to ride his horses, which included Silvio, winner of the DERBY and ST. LEGER.

FANGIO, JUAN MANUEL (1911-   ), Argentinian MOTOR RACING driver. Five times world champion, he started his racing career in 1938 with a Ford Special and during 1939-42 and 1947 he was seen at the wheel of a Chevrolet; in 1948 he drove a European car (MASERATI) for the first time in the Buenos Aires Grand Prix. He continued to drive Chevrolets until the end of 1949, but the same year came to Europe to drive a Maserati. He won the San Remo, Pau, Perpignan, Marseilles (with a Simca), Autodrome, and Albi Grands Prix. As a result, he was invited to join the Alfa Romeo team and came second in the 1950 drivers' championship, having won the MONACO, Belgian, and French Grands Prix. He remained with the team for 1951 and won the championship after successes at Bremgarten, Rheims, and Barcelona and second places at SILVERSTONE and the NURBURGRING.

When Alfa Romeo withdrew from racing, Fangio joined Maserati with whom he remained until the appearance of the new MERCEDES-BENZ W.196 at the French Grand Prix in 1954. He won the Argentine and Belgian races for Maserati and the French, German, Swiss, and Italian for Mercedes, thereby gaining his second world championship. His third world championship came in 1955, when he won the Argentine, Belgian, Dutch, and Italian races and was second in the British.

Mercedes withdrew from racing at the end of 1955, and Fangio became a member of the FERRARI team. His wins at Silverstone and the Nurburgring, combined with the points gained when he took over Musso's car to win the

Argentine race and Collins's car to finish second at Monaco and MONZA, gave him his fourth world championship. Fangio's final full year of racing was 1957, and, as he had not been happy with Ferrari, he returned to Maserati. With the now ageing 250F Maserati he won the Argentine, Monaco, French, and German races and was second at Pescara and Monza, gaining his fifth and final world championship. Fangio went into semi-retirement at the end of 1957, and his last race was the 1958 French Grand Prix, in which he finished fourth with a Maserati.

FARLEY, GORDON JOSEPH (1944-   ), British MOTOR-CYCLE TRIALS champion in 1970 after being runner-up to MILLER three years running. A former Triumph and Greeves works rider, he ended Miller's 11-year domination when he won the title on a Montesa.

FARRELLY, BERNARD (c. 1943-   ), Australian surfer who won the first world SURFING title in 1963 at Sydney, and came second in the same event in Australia in 1970.

FASTNET RACE, an offshore yacht race, sailed biennially over a 605-mile (968 km.) course from Cowes, Isle of Wight, round the Isles of Scilly to the Fastnet Rock, off the south-west coast of Ireland, and back to Plymouth.

FAULKNER, Maj. GEORGE AUBREY, D.S.O. (1881-1930), cricketer for South Africa and Transvaal. Originally a leg-break/'googly' bowler, he became a consistent, high-scoring batsman, reaching his peak in 1910-11 in Australia when he scored 732 runs in five Tests. After the First World War he became well known as a coach and opened a coaching school in London.

FAULKNER, MAX (1916-   ), English professional golfer, winner of the 1951 Open championship and many sponsored tournaments and European national championships. He was a RYDER CUP player, and British Seniors champion, 1968.

FAZAL MAHMOOD (1927-   ), cricketer for Pakistan, Northern India, North Zone, Punjab, and Lahore. A fast-medium bowler, at times almost unplayable on matting wickets, he did much from 1952 in establishing Pakistan as a Test match power. In 1956-7 he took 13 wickets in a Test against Australia, and his career total of 139 wickets in Test CRICKET was a Pakistan record.

FEDERATION CUP, see LAWN TENNIS.

FEIERABEND, FRITZ (1908-   ), BOBSLEIGH rider for Switzerland, the first driver to win three world four-man titles, 1939, 1947, and 1954, in a war-interrupted career spanning 19 years. He was also the first man to pilot three world championship-winning two-man crews, in 1947, 1950, and 1955. Feierabend took part in three WINTER OLYMPIC GAMES, winning two silver medals (1936 and 1948) and a bronze (1952) in the two-man events, and a silver (1936) and a bronze (1952) in the four-man events. He afterwards manufactured the Feierabend bobsled at Engelberg, Switzerland, his models being used by most nations during the years immediately following the Second World War, until the Italian Podars gained popularity in the early 1950s.

FEIJENOORD S.C., Association FOOTBALL club, Rotterdam. Founded in 1908, the club first won the Netherlands championship in 1924 and it has emerged in recent years as one of the most successful of Dutch clubs both in national and European competitions. Feijenoord reached the semi-final of the European Cup in 1963 and the final, in which they beat CELTIC 2-1, in 1970. The club added the unofficial world title to their European one by beating the Argentinian club, ESTUDIANTES. Outstanding players include Van Heel, Kreyermaat, Pieters-Graafland, and Moulijn.
COLOURS: Red shirts with broad white vertical band, and black shorts.

FEIJENOORD STADIUM, Association FOOTBALL ground of the Rotterdam club, FEIJENOORD. It is owned by the local authority, has a capacity of 64,500 with two-thirds of the spectators seated, and is served by its own railway station with several platforms so that a capacity crowd can be transported from the stadium within half an hour of the end of a match.

FEILDEN, Maj.-Gen. Sir RANDLE (1904-   ), a leading figure in the administration and modernization of the English Turf, both as senior steward, until he retired in 1973, of the JOCKEY CLUB and as Chairman of the Turf Board and the Joint Racing Board.

FEISTMANTL, JOSEF (1940-   ), luge TOBOGGANING rider for Austria, world singles champion in 1969; world and Olympic pairs titles winner, with Stengl as partner, in 1964.

FELL RUNNING, an endurance test for both distance runners and mountaineers, deriving its name from the hills of northern England where it is mainly contested, though annual events take place also in the Midlands, Wales,

Scotland, and elsewhere in the British Isles. Courses, either 'out-and-back' or circuitous, may vary in distance from 2 to over 40 miles (3·22–64 km.), but may not have any formal route. For example, one Scottish challenge is won by the competitor who scales the largest number of peaks in 24 hours. In tests of such extreme severity the over-all speed may not exceed a layman's walking pace and, in the event of fog or mist on the upland sections, a map and compass are often used as in ORIENTEERING. Fell runners have not infrequently lapsed into unconsciousness and occasional fatalities have been reported. An outstanding performer in the longer events was the late Eric Beard of Yorkshire who broke records in many regular events including the Welsh 'Three-Thousander'. This originated before the Second World War, and involves starting on a peak 3,000 ft. (914 m.) high and racing a 'switchback' across the top of 13 other peaks of similar altitude. Beard's record for this was 5 hrs. 27 min. One of the more important longer events, dating from 1895, is the Ben Nevis race, a 12-mile (19 km.) return course from Fort William to the top of Ben Nevis (4,406 ft., 1342·9 m.) mountain. The record of 1 hr. 38 min. 56 sec. was set by Peter Hall of Barrow, the 1964 winner. The nearest equivalent to a national title in fell running is the Three Peaks race, an annual event in north-west Yorkshire since 1954. Mike Davies of Reading won it for the fourth time in 1968 when he set a record of 2 hrs. 40 min. 34 sec. for the 22-mile (35 m.) route.

FENCING, the dexterous use of a sword for attack or defence, has a long and fascinating history with its roots in the traditions of chivalry. Today, it is a sport practised increasingly throughout the world with three weapons: the foil, the épée, and the sabre.

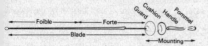

PARTS OF THE SWORD

In each case the weapon consists of a blade and mounting. The tang of the blade passes through the mounting to a pommel, or locking nut, which often serves also to balance the weapon. The mounting consists of a metal guard or *coquille* which protects the sword hand, and a handle or grip which is the part usually held by the sword hand. At foil and épée a small cushion inside the *coquille* protects the fingers. The half of the blade nearest to the guard is called the forte; the remainder of the blade is called the foible.

The foil, a light weapon evolved in the seventeenth century as a practice weapon for the short court sword, was never made for use in duels. Its maximum total length is 110 cm. (3 ft. 7 in.), and its maximum weight 500 g. (17⅝ oz.). It has a quadrangular tapering blade and a small, bell-shaped guard. It may have a curved French handle, an Italian handle with a cross-bar, or the so-called orthopaedic grip shaped to the hand.

The épée is the duelling sword, developed in the nineteenth century to practise in the schools for an actual duel. It is a heavier weapon than the foil — maximum weight 770 g. (27¼ oz.) — though its maximum length is the same. It has a larger bell-guard and a stiffer, triangular, fluted blade. It too may have a curved French handle or an Italian handle with a cross-bar, or an orthopaedic handle shaped to the hand.

The sabre is the cut-and-thrust weapon evolved from the backsword and the heavy cavalry sabre. Its maximum length is 105 cm. (41¾ in.) and its maximum weight 500 g. (17⅝ oz.). It has a flattened V-shaped blade with a blunted cutting edge and a point folded over to form a button. There is a half-circular guard to protect the sword hand from cuts.

Fencing equipment, in addition to the weapon, includes a mask, jacket, and glove. Breeches and stockings complete the outfit. Traditionally jacket and breeches were made of canvas, but nylon is increasingly used today. There is hardly any danger in fencing, provided protective clothing which is of adequate strength for the weapon used, and a mask and glove in good condition, are worn at all times.

Fencing demands quick thinking, poise, balance, and muscular control combined with mental discipline, rather than strength. Much practice is required before muscles and mind are trained to carry out complex fencing movements automatically, leaving the brain free to analyse the opponent's game and devise the strategy and tactics necessary to outwit him. Fencing has been likened to a game of chess played at lightning speed.

Basic movements. In a bout, or assault between two fencers in which hits are counted, the fencer takes up a stance, or prepared position — 'on guard' — with his arms, weapon, body, and feet so placed as to give him the best possible balance for attack or defence, movement forward or back, or the lunge. When the fencers cross swords they are said to be 'engaged'; otherwise they are fencing with 'absence of blade'. When they are in the 'on guard' position, the distance between the two constitutes the 'fencing measure'. The

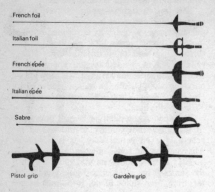

French foil

Italian foil

French épée

Italian épée

Sabre

Pistol grip

Gardère grip

FENCING WEAPONS
Two kinds of orthopaedic grips are shown below.

distance normally maintained is that where each fencer feels safe from a direct attack yet in a position to launch an attack of his own. Obviously, where fencers are of different heights, each will be jockeying for the fencing measure most suitable to himself.

The sequence of fencing movements exchanged during a bout is called a 'phrase'. An attack may be simple, such as a straight thrust; or indirect, when it has to pass the point of the weapon to the opposite side of the opponent's blade; or compound or composed, when it includes one or more false attacks — feints or preparatory movements — in order to create an opening for a final scoring movement. A lunge is the extension of the sword arm, body, and legs to carry the point or edge of the weapon forward from the 'on guard' position to score a hit on the opponent's target (see below). The lunge and the recovery from the lunge to the 'on guard' position are known as the 'development' and the 'return to guard'.

A hit is an offensive action which lands the point or edge of the weapon on the opponent. If a hit lands on the opponent's target it is a valid hit; otherwise it is a non-valid, or off-target, hit. A hit made with any part of the front edge or the first third of the back of a sabre is known as a cut. A stop-hit is a form of counter-attack delivered into the oncoming attack, which, ideally, does literally 'stop' the opponent.

A parry is a defensive action which deflects an attacker's blade clear of the target. An important principle of defence in fencing is to oppose the forte of the blade to the foible of the opponent's blade when making a parry. There are three types of parry: (a) the simple, or direct, parry, the instinctive reaction of moving the sword laterally across the target to protect the line along which the attack is approaching; (b) the indirect parry, made by moving the sword in a semi-circle from a high-line engagement to deflect an attack into a low-line or vice versa; (c) a circular or counter-parry, made by a circular movement of the defender's blade which gathers the attacker's blade and brings it back to the original line of engagement.

A riposte is the offensive action which follows a successful parry. A riposte may be simple, made with one blade movement (either direct or indirect); or it may be compound, that is, preceded by one or more feints or preparatory movements. If a riposte is parried, the next offensive action from the defender is known as a counter-riposte. A feint is an offensive movement made to draw a reaction from an opponent — usually to change his line of defence, leaving the originally defended line open to the attacker's thrust.

Fencing time — *temps d'escrime* — is the time required to perform one simple fencing movement, such as a single blade movement, an arm movement, or a movement of the foot, e.g. a step forward. Fencing time varies according to the speed of reaction of each individual fencer. Counter-time — also called a 'second-intention attack' — is effected by drawing the opponent's stop-hit by invitations or exposing the target during a simulated attack, parrying the stop-hit, and scoring with a riposte.

In quartata is an attacking movement made while moving the body out of line with a side-step. *Passata sotto* is the action of avoiding an attacker's blade by ducking below it. *Sentiment de fer* is the term used for feeling an opponent's reactions through contact of the blades, and thus anticipating his movements.

Doighte means finger-play, controlling and directing the weapon by using the fingers only. The first finger and thumb of the sword hand, known as the 'manipulators', direct the weapon. The point is raised or lowered by alternately pulling with the thumb and pushing with the forefinger, or vice versa. A circular movement is imparted to the blade by rolling the handle between the manipulators. The remaining fingers, called the 'aids', serve to steady the handle.

Rules and conventions. The valid target within which hits may be counted is different for each of the three weapons. At foil, valid hits are restricted to those made with the point on the trunk only. Hits which arrive on the head, arms, or legs are not counted as good. At épée, hits may be made with the point on any part of the opponent or his equipment. In sabre fencing, hits may be scored with the whole of the front edge or the third of the back edge nearest to the point (cuts), as well as with the point. Valid hits are restricted to those which arrive with point or edge on the head, arms, or trunk down to line of the hips when 'on guard'.

In foil fencing, the fencer who initiates an attack, that is the one who straightens his sword arm with the point of his weapon threatening his opponent's target, has the 'right of way' until the attack is deflected or parried, after which the right of way passes to his opponent for his riposte. If in turn the riposte is parried, the right of way reverts to the original attacker for his counter-riposte, and so on through the series of movements which build up a fencing phrase. However, an exception is made if an attack is fenced slowly or with a bent arm, or is preceded by a number of false attacks or feints; if the opponent lands a stop-hit before the attack is completed, it will be counted as valid if it arrives a period of fencing time before the attack.

The lightness of the foil gives ease of manipulation and this makes it the best weapon with which to acquire *doigte* and blade control. Further, the rules and conventions of foil fencing teach appreciation of fencing time, while the closer distance maintained at this weapon, in which the trunk alone is the valid target, develops reflex actions.

Épée is fenced competitively as near to the conditions of a duel as possible. The rules and conventions of foil play do not apply, and priority, if both competitors are hit, is a question of the timing of the arrival of hits. If a hit arrives not less than $\frac{1}{25}$ th of a second before the other it alone scores. If no such time-interval exists, a double hit — a hit against each fencer — is scored, on the principle that in an actual duel both would be wounded.

Although the sabre was a duelling weapon, it is fenced competitively according to the rules and conventions that apply to foil fencing, with the difference in valid target noted above.

Competitions, judging, and scoring. Fencing competitions take place on a *piste* which is 2 m. (6 ft. 7 in.) wide and 14 m. (46 ft.) long. An extension of 2 m. (6 ft. 7 in.) to the *piste* at either end serves as a 'run-back' at foil and épée; a 1973 ruling provides for a *piste* of 24 m. (78 ft. 9 in.) for sabre. The *piste* is marked with lines which indicate the initial positions 'on guard' and at which a competitor is warned when he is a certain distance from the rear limit of the *piste*. If after having been warned at the warning line (1 m. — 3 ft. 3 in. — at foil, and 2 m. — 6 ft. 7 in. — at épée and sabre, from the rear limit) a competitor retires with both feet over the rear limit, a hit

Foil (for women and men)

Épée

Sabre

THE VALID TARGET

is scored against him. At sabre, under the 1973 ruling, when a fencer retreats over the rear limit both fencers are brought back to the 'on guard' lines; the regulations then continue as for épée.

A bout between men at foil, épée, or sabre is fenced for five hits, i.e. the fencer against whom five hits are scored loses the bout. At women's foil a bout is fenced for four hits. The time limits for a bout are six minutes of actual fencing for men, and five minutes for women. The competitors are warned when one minute remains for fencing. If the time limit expires at foil or sabre, the fencer who is leading (say 3-2) wins the bout and the hits are brought up to the full number (in this case the

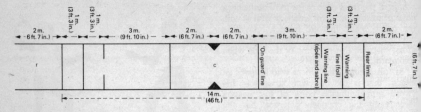

score will be 5-4). At épée, if the fencers reach 5-5 (say by a double hit) before time expires they continue to fence until one has scored a decisive hit. If no decisive hit is scored and time expires, a double defeat is scored.

Senior foil and épée competitions are judged by an electrical judging apparatus which registers hits exactly. Each weapon is fitted with a spring-loaded point connected by fine wires which run down a groove in the blade to a plug inside the guard. Before coming 'on guard' a fencer plugs his 'body wire' into this plug. The body wire runs up inside the sleeve of the jacket and emerges at the back where it in turn is plugged to a wire from a spring-loaded spool placed at the end of the *piste*. This takes up the slack as the fencers move up and down the *piste*. The spools have connecting wires to the central apparatus placed beside the centre of the *piste*. The central apparatus registers hits by light and sound signals. The *piste* is entirely covered with a metal mesh overlay, kept taut. Hits on the ground (metal *piste*) or on the guards of the weapons are not registered by the apparatus.

At foil the fencers wear a metallic over-jacket which exactly covers the valid target. A hit on the target is registered on the apparatus by a coloured light while a hit which arrives off the target (head, arms, or legs) causes a white light. Simultaneous white and coloured lights on the same side of the apparatus show that there has been a hit off the target before a valid hit. Otherwise the foil apparatus does not indicate any priority between the arrival of hits so that the president or referee is required to 'read the phrase' and award hits according to the rules and conventions applicable to foil fencing. Because of the expense of the electrical foil equipment, beginners or junior competitors use non-electric, or 'steam' foils, for which judging is the same as for sabre (see below).

All épée is fenced with electrical apparatus, which judges completely and automatically because it can time exactly the arrival of hits.

Thus if a hit arrives more than $\frac{1}{25}$ th of a second before the opponent's hit, only the first will be recorded. If both arrive within that interval, the apparatus registers a double hit.

No electrical apparatus is at present used for judging sabre. It is therefore necessary to have two pairs of judges to observe hits and to decide whether the hit is on or off the target, and a president to control the bout and award hits according to the rules and conventions applicable to sabre fencing.

Swords were used before the dawn of recorded history and there are many examples of these weapons dating from the Bronze Age. Fencing, the skilful use of a sword according to established rules and movements, was practised by all the ancient races — the Persians, Egyptians, Greeks, and Romans — not only in war but as a pastime.

The earliest representation of a fencing match occurs in a relief carving in the temple of Madinet-Habu, near Luxor, built by Rameses III about 1190 B.C. It records a practice bout or tournament and not a duel. Care is taken to avoid injury: the swords have well-covered points, and the fencers are wearing masks fitted with bibs, padded over the ears, and tied to their wigs; narrow shields strapped to the arm are used for defence. Judges and organizers carry feathered wands, and there are a large number of spectators.

In the Middle Ages the general use of armour meant that a battle axe, mace, or long, double-handed sword was required to bludgeon the well-protected opponent into submission. As a result, swords were heavy and clumsy, needing strength rather than skill for their use. But the introduction of gunpowder in the fourteenth century made the wearing of complete armour largely redundant. Swords were still used for close-quarter fighting, but there was a sudden transformation of weapons to lighter and more manageable forms. Skilful swordplay became of paramount importance.

Guilds of fencing masters, such as the famous Marxbrüder of Frankfurt, sprang up all over Europe to develop the art of swordsmanship, and these fencing schools became very powerful. Early methods were somewhat rough-and-ready and included many tricks borrowed from wrestling. Fencing masters 'discovered' strokes guaranteed to bring instant success in duels or battles and sold them to their pupils for large sums. These strokes, some of which are still in current use, were assiduously practised in strict secrecy and suddenly produced in combat, to great effect. Examples are the *coup de Jarnac*, a cut inside the knee, and the *botte de Nevers*, a stop-hit delivered between the eyes.

The Italians are credited with the discovery of the effective use of the point rather than relying exclusively on the edge of the sword. By the end of the sixteenth century, their lighter weapons and controlled swordplay had spread throughout Europe, and rapier fencing was established. From then on, the emphasis was on skill and speed rather than forcefulness. Wrestling tricks were mostly abandoned, the lunge was discovered, and fencing became established as an art.

The rapier was a long, well-balanced sword, excellent for keeping the opponent at a distance and for making attacks, but too heavy to carry out all the movements required in combat. Defence was therefore effected mostly with the left hand, which was armed with a dagger or protected by a glove or cloak. The opponent's thrusts were often avoided by ducking (*passata sotto*) or by side-stepping (*in quartata*). Rapier fencing was thus a two-handed game, during which the fencers circled each other, seeking advantage from the light or the terrain.

During the seventeenth century, the Spaniards evolved a very complex method of rapier fencing. Lines were drawn inside a large circle, and fencers moved inside these according to very strict and precise rules. This method does not seem to have been very successful, and was never adopted as widely as the Italian forms of fencing.

The evolution of swordsmanship altered dramatically in the seventeenth century with a change of fashion in dress. At the court of Louis XIV silks and satins, breeches, stockings, and brocade coats were worn, for which the long trailing rapiers which had accompanied the doublet and hose and the top-boots and cloaks of earlier times were not suitable. Yet every gentleman had to carry a sword; so fashion decreed the wearing of a light, short, court sword. Though at first regarded with derision as a 'toy', the short court sword was soon recognized by fencers as an ideal light weapon; all attacking and defensive movements could be made with a single weapon wielded with one hand, the left hand no longer being used. Swift and subtle swordplay became possible, hits were made almost exclusively with the point, and defence was effected mostly with the blade alone. The court of the *roi soleil* set the tone for all Europe; the light court sword displaced the rapier, and fencing as we understand it in Europe today became a reality.

The mask was unknown in Europe until the end of the eighteenth century, and practice with the light court sword, with swift blade movements made at close quarters, involved the risk of injury to the eyes. It was said that no good fencing master could hope to end his days with both eyes intact. To minimize risk, rules and conventions were imposed to regulate fencing with the court sword and its practice counterpart, the foil. Fencers came to adopt a special stance, when on guard, with the weight on the rear foot and the head well back, while valid hits were restricted to those arriving on the right breast. The fencer who initiated an attack had the 'right of way' — this took priority over any movement made against him by his opponent at the same time. If this movement was parried, however, the right of way passed to his opponent for his riposte.

About 1780 the French master La Boëssière 'invented' the mask, making it possible to engage in more complex swordplay without risk of injury. However, the traditional rules and conventions were kept, and indeed amplified, because otherwise swift and complex blade movements made at close quarters, instead of building up a fencing phrase, would have degenerated into a brawl of simultaneous actions, and these rules and conventions have remained the basis of the modern rules which govern fencing with foil and sabre.

Foil fencing in the schools became increasingly stylized, but duelling still continued, for the orthodox, controlled swordplay which encouraged subtle phrases of absorbing interest was of little account when meeting a determined opponent with a heavier weapon and a disregard for all conventions, one cold grey morning on the duelling ground.

In the mid-nineteenth century, the *épée de combat* was evolved so that those taking part in a duel could practise in the *salle d'armes* under realistic conditions. The épée, now an established competition weapon, is a regulation duelling sword and is used without limitations or other conventions, and under rules approximating as closely to the conditions of a duel as the use of protective equipment allows.

The heavy cutting weapons of the Middle Ages continued as the backsword or broadsword, known as the Englishman's traditional weapon in the days of the first Queen Elizabeth. In the late eighteenth century the Hungarians introduced the Eastern scimitar for use by their cavalry and it was soon adopted throughout Europe. The military sabre and the naval cutlass were used in the fencing schools throughout the nineteenth century.

In the last quarter of the nineteenth century, the Italians introduced a light sabre which was used with a special style developed by the famous Milanese master RADAELLI. His method was later considerably modified by the Hungarian school founded by Santelli. Although the light sabre was a recognized duelling weapon, sabre fencing in schools and competitions became an academic pursuit governed by conventional rules similar to those at foil.

Swordsmanship as a mode of defence was practised in Britain, as in most European countries, from the earliest times. For a long time, however, fencing schools were regarded by the authorities as places which encouraged brawling, duelling, and ruffianism of the baser sort. Edward I had enacted a statute in 1285 which forbade the teaching of fencing or the holding of tournaments within the precincts of the City of London. This view of the sport continued until Henry VIII, a great lover of swordplay, sometime before 1540 granted letters patent to a Corporation of Masters of Defence. The Corporation brought together the leading masters in the country, both English and foreign, and was granted many privileges, including the lucrative monopoly of teaching fencing. It thus became the first governing body for fencing—and, it is claimed, for any sport—in Great Britain. It was granted a coat of arms, a sword pendant argent. Its traditions are carried on today by the British Academy of Fencing, the governing body for professional fencing, which uses the same coat of arms. Because the first organization for fencing in Britain had been founded by a Tudor king, Edward VII in 1906 granted the Amateur Fencing Association permission to adopt the Tudor rose as the badge to be worn by British fencers of international rank.

From the sixteenth century prize fights, later associated with BOXING, were displays and trials of skill with swords. They were extremely popular and were often patronized by royalty. A stage was erected in a hall or public garden and the champions challenged each other to bouts with a variety of weapons. Often 'sharps' were called for and there then followed very sanguinary encounters. Bouts were by single combat or sometimes in a mêlée and the winner was the one who 'held the stage' to the end.

In England, towards the middle of the eighteenth century, FIGG, the first British boxing champion and also champion of the Corporation of Masters of Defence, introduced fisticuff bouts into the prize fights. These knuckle fights became so popular that they eventually ousted bouts with the sword and, with the virtual cessation of duelling, fencing was relegated to the status of a provincial amusement with backswords, single stick, and quarterstaff.

No doubt the stimulus of duelling kept fencing alive on the Continent, but it was neglected in Britain in the early Victorian period. A few schools, such as that of the famous ANGELOS and the LONDON FENCING CLUB, founded in 1848, kept the sport alive in a few London salles, some public schools, and the universities.

Interest in fencing in England revived with its inclusion in the curriculum of the Army School of Physical Training in 1861. The enthusiasm of Captain HUTTON, F.S.A., an authority on ancient weapons and author of many textbooks, spread this interest in civilian circles so that in 1902 the Amateur Fencing Association was formed (with Hutton as its first president) as the governing body for fencing in the United Kingdom.

Competitive fencing as a sport commenced on the continent of Europe in the last quarter of the nineteenth century. Fencing has been an Olympic sport since the first modern OLYMPIC GAMES were held at Athens in 1896.

There are records of women's fencing from the eighteenth century, but few women's competitions were held before the beginning of the twentieth century. A women's individual foil event was first included in the Olympic Games in 1924, but their team event was not added to the Olympic programme until 1960.

Fencing had long been a traditional sport in France, Italy, and adjacent western European countries, and in Hungary and to a lesser extent in Poland. As a result France and Italy dominated world competition at foil and épée and Hungary and Italy at sabre virtually until 1955, although notable champions emerged from time to time from other countries such as Cuba, Denmark, Sweden, Britain, and Germany. In the mid-1950s, partly due to the introduction of the electrical judging apparatus at foil, a new school of fencing based on simplified technique, with the emphasis on speed and athletic qualities, emerged in eastern Europe. Within a decade the U.S.S.R., Poland, Hungary, and Romania had largely displaced the western European countries as leaders in world competition at all weapons.

Fencing has spread very rapidly throughout the world in the last twenty years, and strong teams are now appearing from such widely different countries as Japan, Cuba, Mexico, and Sweden. Teams from North Africa and Latin America are also competing internationally.

The Fédération Internationale d'Escrime, the world governing body for fencing, was founded on the initiative of LACROIX (France) at a meeting held at the Automobile Club in Paris on 29 November 1913. European championships for different weapons were held from 1921. The first European championships to include all weapons with both team and individual events were held at Liège in 1930 and have continued to be held annually except in Olympic Games years. From 1936 they were called world championships.

World youth championships have been organized annually at Easter since 1950. Originally confined to fencers under 21 years of age, the championships now admit competitors under 20 and comprise individual events for all weapons. One noticeable development in recent years has been the number of under-20 fencers who have regularly reached the finals of senior events.

Bob Anderson, *All About Fencing* (1970); Z. Beke and J. Polgar, *The Methodology of Sabre Fencing* (1963); Egerton Castle, *Schools and Masters of Fence* (1870; reprinted 1970); Maître R. Clery, *Escrime* (1965); R. Crosnier, *Fencing with the Electric Foil* (1961), *Fencing with the Épée* (1958), *Fencing with the Foil* (1967), and *Fencing with the Sabre* (1966); C.-L. de Beaumont, *Fencing—Ancient Art and Modern Sport* (1970) and *Modern British Fencing*: vol. I, to 1948, vol. II, 1949-1956, vol. III, 1957-1964 (in preparation); E. Mangiarotti and A. Cerchiari, *La Vera Scherma* (1966).

GOVERNING BODY (WORLD): Fédération Internationale d'Escrime, 53 Rue Vivienne, Paris 2, France; (ENGLAND): Amateur Fencing Association, 83 Perham Road, West Kensington, London W.14.

FENLAND SKATING, a form of ice speed-skating (see ICE SKATING) developed on natural, seasonal ice along a stretch of some 80 miles (129 km.) of the low-lying Fenland district of England, mainly in Lincolnshire and Cambridgeshire. In this area the shallow water which flooded the flat meres made, when frozen, large expanses for safe skating. The facilities gradually diminished as the water was systematically drained by pumps during the nineteenth century. Until 1850 Whittlesea Mere could provide some 2,000 acres of ice.

Although rudimentary ice skating as a means of travel may have been practised in the Fen district as early as the twelfth century, it is unlikely that any sporting or recreative aspect was realized until at least 500 years later. Although not the first, the earliest recorded skating races took place in 1814, when Young of Mepal was the outstanding exponent.

A *Handbook of Fen Skating* by Neville Goodman was published in London in 1882. It included a line drawing of a 'skaiting match at Chatteris', with top-hatted spectators watching from Carter's Bridge and from a horse-drawn stage-coach. The date of the event illustrated was 23 January 1823.

Professionalism is recorded as early as 1820, when 4,000 spectators at Croyland watched four racers compete over a distance of two miles for a prize of five guineas, won by Gittam of Nordelph, Norfolk. Heats were usually decided between two racers over two miles; these turned round barrels at each end of a half-mile stretch.

In 1823, J. Young of Nordelph beat May of Upwell over this distance in a time of 5 min., 33 sec. In the same year Gittam covered a mile in 2 min., 29 sec. with a flying start and a favourable wind at Padnall, near Ely.

In 1854, W. Smart of Welney emerged to dominate Fenland skating for ten years. His low, crouching style and powerful stride fascinated crowds who travelled miles to see him race. He was reported to have covered a mile in 2 min., 2 sec., but times in those days were rough guidance, because the marked distances were paced out and allowed scope for errors of judgement.

Championships of the time were based on the knock-out principle so that, if sixteen competed in eight heats, the winners would compete against each other in a second round of four heats to produce semi-finals and a final. This 'sudden death' element excited the crowds and, when timekeeping became more accurate, the requirement that each competitor need complete the course only once to qualify by time alone for the final was not a popular change.

If the appearance of leading performers was sufficiently publicized, spectators came in thousands from such Fenland and neighbouring towns as Boston, Bourne, Cambridge, Chatteris, Ely, Lincoln, Littleport, Lynn, March, Peterborough, Sleaford, Spalding, and Wisbech. Collections were made to offset expenses.

In 1875, G. Smart took over the title from his uncle and held the British championship from 1879 until 1889, when his brother, J. Smart, succeeded him: the family name was kept well to the fore until the turn of the century. The most successful professionals since then have been F. Ward, 1900 and 1905; Greenhall, 1908 and 1912; Pearson, 1929, 1933, and 1936; and N. Young, 1952, 1954, 1956, and 1962.

The formation of the National Skating

Association (N.S.A.) of Great Britain in 1879 led to an organized distinction between professional and amateur; official outdoor amateur championships began in the following year and national titles decided over a distance of one and a half miles. All were contested on the Fens except, oddly enough, the first, held in 1800 at the Welsh Harp, Hendon, London. The most frequent venues since have been Lingay Fen and Bury Fen. F. Norman won the first two championships. Those winning the amateur title most times since have been (in chronological order) Tebbit, four (1895, 1900, 1902, and 1905); Dix, three (1908, 1909, and 1912); Horn, four (1927, 1929, and 1933, Jan. and Dec.); and Holwell, three (1952, 1954, and 1955).

Since 1894, a one-mile (1·609 m.) amateur race for the Duddleston Cup has been a well supported event, held mostly at Lingay Fen. The first to win this three times was Horn, 1927, 1929, and 1933. Several other events are also still held on the Fenlands when weather conditions permit, including the Prince of Orange Bowl (one and a half miles), open to overseas entrants and first won by an American, Donoghue, at Lingay Fen in 1890.

Excelling during the particularly severe winters of 1889-92 and 1895, the Fenmen dominated English ice speed-skating until the 1930s, when racing on mechanically-frozen ice at indoor rinks transformed the sport's scope. The N.S.A., however, still retains a special Fens Centre committee to administer the Fenland skating activities which, naturally, fluctuate as unpredictably as the weather.

Alan Bloom, *The Skaters of the Fens* (1957).

FEOLA, VICENTE (1909-   ), Brazilian Association FOOTBALL coach and manager. He made his name with the São Paulo club and had charge of the first Brazilian team to win the World Cup — in Sweden, 1958. For a period he managed BOCA JUNIORS in Buenos Aires. He missed the 1962 World Cup through illness, but returned to manage the 1966 Brazilian side in England.

FERENCVAROS, Association FOOTBALL club, Budapest. Founded in 1899 as F.T.C., it changed its name to Kinizsi in 1945 and was later amalgamated for a while with the army club, Honved. After the 1956 revolution, the club was re-formed as a separate entity under its present name. It has always been among the leading clubs in Hungarian football and won the national championship 20 times between 1903 and 1968. In European club competitions, Ferencvaros has been most successful in the Fairs Cup which it won in 1965 and was

the beaten finalist in 1968. Outstanding players have included Schlosser, Sarosi, Matrai, Bukovi, and Albert.

COLOURS: Green and white.

FERRARI, a racing car. Enzo Ferrari originally worked for Alfa Romeo and took over its competition activities with his organization Scuderia Ferrari. This arrangement ended in 1938, and in 1946 the first true Ferrari 375 was a 4·5-litre V-12 model which dominated Grand Prix racing in 1951. After the withdrawal from racing of Lancia, the Lancia D50 was handed to Ferrari who modified it and had many successes in 1956 and 1957 Grand Prix racing. The Dino Ferrari was developed for the 1957 season and HAWTHORN in particular performed well with it in 1958, 1959, and 1960, although not the superior of the COOPERS of the later years. The Tipo 156 1·5-litre had no serious challengers in 1961 and won the manufacturers' world championship while its successor, the 158, did the same in 1964. The 3-litre model, the 312, was second to BRABHAM in the 1966 world championship. Many different types of Ferrari have been produced for sports car, Formula Two, Prototype, and Tasman racing. Ferrari continues active in sports/racing and Formula One contests, and in 1974 was to field the flat-12 F1 12-cylinder 312B cars.

FERRIER, ROBERT (1900-71), Association footballer for Motherwell, he captained that team when they won the Scottish championship in 1931-2 — the only club, apart from CELTIC and RANGERS, to do so between 1904 and 1948. A brilliant outside left in a period of great wingers, he was born in Sheffield but taken back to his father's native Scotland at the age of three weeks and lived there for the rest of his life. He was thus the finest player of his time not to receive international recognition but left a remarkable scoring record for a winger of around 300 goals for Motherwell in 626 League appearances, including 32 in 37 matches in the 1929-30 season.

FETTESIAN-LORETTONIANS, Scottish RUGBY UNION football club formed in 1881 with the main object of raising an annual touring side for New Year matches. The founder members were former pupils of Fettes College and Loretto who were at Oxford and Cambridge Universities. The club was most influential, in its display of skills and tactics, during the 1880s and 1890s; only one of the 1883-4 side failed to win an international cap.

F.F.G.G. ROMA, an Italian sports club composed of members working as national guards (civil and military). The walking section is the leading Italian RACE WALKING club. Under the celebrated coach Corsaro, numerous national titles have been gained and internationals among its ranks include Busca, De Vito, Carpentier, and Zambaldo.

F.I.A. (Fédération Internationale de l'Automobile), see MOTOR RACING.

F.I.B.A. (Fédération Internationale de Basketball Amateur), see BASKETBALL.

FIELD HOCKEY, see HOCKEY, FIELD.

F.I.F.A. (Fédération Internationale de Football Associations), see FOOTBALL, ASSOCIATION.

FIGG, JAMES (1695-1734), British boxer, the first recognized champion of the English prize ring. After gaining a reputation as a teacher of FENCING and an expert with sword and cudgel, Figg declared himself champion from about 1719 after giving exhibitions of his skill at Southwark Fair, London, where his visiting card was designed for him by Hogarth, and at his own 'amphitheatre' in Tottenham Court Road. In 1727 Figg defeated his chief rival, Sutton, with fists, sword, and cudgel on the stage and established his position as champion. His pupils included BROUGHTON, subsequently champion himself, and Captain Godfrey whose *Treatise of the Useful Science of Defence* stemmed from the lessons he had received. Figg may be regarded as the first boxing coach, manager, and promoter though fighting with stick and sword were as vital as fists to his reputation.

FIGURE-SKATING, see ICE SKATING; ROLLER SKATING.

F.I.N.A. (Fédération Internationale de Natation Amateur), see DIVING, SWIMMING, WATER POLO.

FINGERLE, Dieter (*fl.* 1959-67), roller pair-skater (see ROLLER SKATING) for West Germany, the first person to win four world roller pair-skating titles, partnered by Miss Schneider in 1959 and by Miss Keller in 1965, 1966, and 1967.

FINNEY, THOMAS (1922-   ), Association footballer for PRESTON NORTH END and England for whom he made 76 appearances in full international matches between 1947 and 1959 and scored 30 goals. An outstanding outside right for Preston for whom he first played during the war, his appearances for England

seemed limited at first to games when MATTHEWS was not available. Arguably a more *complete* player than Matthews, he was successfully 'switched' to the left wing, and even to centre forward, in many of the matches he played for England. His long career with Preston North End ended in April 1960.

FINNISH SPORTS, see KUNINGASPALLO; PESÄPALLO; TOUCH BALL.

FISKE, WILLIAM (1911-41), BOBSLEIGH rider for the U.S.A., the first driver to win two Olympic gold medals in the event for larger crews, 1928 and 1932. The 1928 victory was the last occasion when five-man crews were permitted. Fiske died in a flying accident in 1941, while on active service.

F.I.T.A. (Fédération Internationale de Tir à l'Arc), see ARCHERY.

FITZSIMMONS, BOB (1862-1917), British-born boxer who won world titles at middleweight (1891), heavyweight (1897), and light-heavyweight (1903). As a boy he left England for New Zealand where he took up BOXING professionally with the encouragement of MACE. Fitzsimmons weighed no more than 167 lb. (76 kg.) when he knocked out CORBETT for the heavyweight title with a much publicized 'solar plexus' punch. Then 34, Fitzsimmons continued to be a terror to much bigger men even after he lost the title to JEFFRIES and once beat an opponent to whom he was conceding 140 lb. (64 kg.) in two rounds. He fought his last bout, over six rounds, when he was 52.

FIVES, see ETON FIVES; RUGBY FIVES; WINCHESTER FIVES.

F.K. AUSTRIA, Association FOOTBALL club, Vienna. Founded in 1894 as Vienna Cricket and Football Club, it became Wiener Amateur Sportverein in 1911, F.K. (Fussball Klub) Austria in 1925, and first won the Austrian championship 1923-4. Austria won a hat-trick of championships, 1961-3, and competed in the European Cup. Among the club's leading players have been NAUSCH, Seszta, and SINDELAR, before the Second World War, and OCWIRK and Melchior after it.

COLOURS: Violet shirts, white sleeves, white shorts.

FLAMINGOS, see CRICKET.

FLASHY SIR (1943), racing greyhound, a brindled dog, by Lucky Sir out of Flashy Harmony. The shining star of American greyhound tracks in 1944-7, he is regarded by U.S.

experts as the greatest track dog in racing history. Flashy Sir won an estimated $50,000, and, in 80 starts, won 60 races and finished second ten times. He set track records at Flagler, Taunton, Raynham, Biscayne, Wonderland, and St. Petersburg.

FLÈCHE WALLONNE CYCLE RACE, Belgian professional classic founded in 1936. The race has no fixed course, but traditionally starts at Liège, finishes at Charleroi, and covers 128 to 155 miles (206–249 km.) of laborious climbing along the Ardennes mountain roads. With the older LIÈGE–BASTOGNE–LIÈGE event, it makes up what is called *Le Week-End Ardennais*, although the combined classification was officially recognized only in the years 1950-64.

FLEGG, HARRY (Jersey) (1878-1960), one of the pioneers of Australian RUGBY LEAGUE, and a power in the game for 52 years. Born at Bradford, Yorkshire, he was taken to Australia as a child and became the first secretary and first captain of the Eastern Suburbs club in Sydney in 1908. Dedicated, robust, and tenacious, his worth to the game was widely recognized. He was president of the New South Wales League for the last 32 years of his life and chairman of the Australian Rugby League (then the Board of Control) for many years. He was a New South Wales and Australian selector for nearly 20 years.

FLEISCHER, NAT (1887-1972), an American BOXING reporter and historian, who founded *The Ring* (monthly magazine) in 1922 and the annual *Ring Record Book* in 1942. Fleischer, who saw his first world championship in 1899 at the age of 12, acted as referee or judge in many world championships and wrote more than 60 books on the sport. He published international rankings of current boxers in his magazine from 1925.

FLEMINGTON, a race-course at Melbourne, Australia, where the MELBOURNE CUP, Queen Elizabeth Stakes, Victoria Derby, V.R.C. Oaks, and Maribyrnong Plate for two-year-olds are run.

FLINTHAM, GEORGE HENRY (1892-1963), greyhound owner, the most prolific winner of every type of greyhound race in the history of the sport; but he never achieved his ambition of winning a GREYHOUND DERBY.

FLUMINENSE, Association FOOTBALL club, Rio de Janeiro. Founded in 1902 and co-founders of the Rio League in 1906, the club won the championship that year and retained it in 1907, 1908, and 1909. Between 1911 and 1959, the club won 13 more titles in the Rio region of Brazil and the Rio Cup in 1952. The leading players have included Tim, Ademir, Jair, and Castilho.

COLOURS: White shirts with green and red diagonal stripes, white shorts.

FLY BALL is a bat-and-ball game of the TENNIS type played with a shuttlecock. The racket, of the shape of a TABLE TENNIS bat, has a net hitting surface; the shuttlecock is like that used in BADMINTON.

The court is 7 m. (23 ft.) long and 3·20 m. (10 ft. 6 in.) (4·20 m. — 13 ft. 9¾ in. — for doubles) in width. The net is 1·30 m. (51 in.) high. Points are scored as in badminton; a game is of 30 points and a match goes to the player, or pair, which first wins two games.

FLYING, Sporting, embraces all those aspects of flying which have no specific military, commercial, or other working connotation. It has developed in a manner similar to any other sport relying upon a mechanical device for its fulfilment and most countries of the world now have their own aero clubs.

Air touring developed from the cross-country capabilities of the aeroplane; aerobatics from its method of control; air racing from its developing potential for increased speed. Record-breaking followed inevitably from the early competition from pilots and manufacturers for supreme performance. The greater part of sporting flying is undertaken by pilots who either learned to fly in an air force or who have been attracted to flying by the presence of a flying club. Most of them fly on a private pilot's licence, but some are professional civil or military pilots.

AIR TOURING is the most widely practised form of sporting flying. It is a continuation of the cross-country training given during instruction for the private pilot's licence and it requires no special skills or aptitudes. In its more deliberate form it takes shape as an organized air rally, but in private flying, where a very large part of the appeal is still simply in flying itself, there is a considerable sporting element in the approach to any but the most prosaic of local flights.

The advent of the true light aeroplane in the late 1920s was the real beginning of air touring. As the realization dawned that the aeroplane was capable of overcoming such natural barriers as the English Channel and could reduce, if not entirely destroy, the barriers of time and distance, so it gradually became a part of the leisure life of the world.

While the light aircraft developed in the late

1920s and early 1930s started as the toy of the wealthy or dedicated man, developments over the succeeding years into the 1950s and 1960s, speeded up by the war, have radically altered the picture. Light-aircraft touring was initially an adventure — and a rather bizarre adventure at that — confined to those daring enough to risk their lives with elementary maps, few instruments, and only partially reliable engines, flying to otherwise inaccessible parts of the globe. The development of the industry has totally altered the picture.

The sporting element of touring by air has been maintained in Europe by international air rallies, largely social gatherings, but relieved and enhanced by arrival and landing competitions, treasure hunts, and navigational exercises. Dozens of these week-end meetings take place in western Europe every year, the most important being the biennial Air Tour of Europe of the Fédération Aéronautique Internationale (F.A.I.), when some 80–100 light aircraft fly through six to eight countries.

In America, the sporting element has concentrated more on competitive events, such as races, and air touring has become a new manifestation of the basic American urge to travel, the light aircraft having become a swift, far-ranging successor to the automobile, extending the week-end trip — devoted to other sports such as sailing, fishing, and hunting — by some hundreds of miles.

To the pilot attracted by AIR RACING or AEROBATICS, the only problems are of aptitude and economics. Both demand skills in aircraft handling that are not beyond the average man or woman, but their development depends, as in other sports, on enthusiasm and an initial aptitude. In both it is possible to enjoy oneself at the basic levels of the sport without too much specialized equipment; in both, ultimate success depends on considerable financial outlay, constant training, and the selection of the right aircraft.

Air racing, along with record-breaking, was the earliest form of competitive sport connected with aeroplanes. The year 1909, the golden year of the aeroplane, saw the first true competitive international meeting at Reims (France was the cradle of competitive flying). From then until the First World War, air racing grew rapidly in popularity in France, Germany, Italy, the U.K. and the U.S.A., the most famous meetings being those held every week-end at Hendon, the London aerodrome run by Grahame-White.

In 1919, the pre-war Aerial Derby, a race round London, was revived, and in 1922 the King's Cup air race, for a trophy presented to the Royal Aero Club by King George V to encourage sporting aviation, was introduced.

The annual race is open to British-registered aircraft.

The pre-war international Gordon Bennett races, introduced at Reims by the American who gave them their name, disappeared after the 1920 meeting, but the Schneider Trophy, an international event for 'hydro-aeroplanes' (seaplanes) first run in 1913, continued for nearly two decades and led to the development of the Spitfire aircraft which played a major part in the Battle of Britain. The rules of the competition provided for seaworthiness trials in addition to a racing circuit of not less than 150 nautical miles (275 km.). What proved to be the final race in the series took place in 1931; it was won by a British aircraft and, since no challenger appeared within five years, the trophy became the property of the Royal Aero Club.

Among major American air races are the Pulitzer Trophy, which began in 1920 and finished in 1929; the Thompson Trophy, which started in 1930, and the Bendix Trophy, in the following year, both survived the Second World War and formed the basis of the National Air Races.

In Britain, handicap racing over circuits varying from 12 to 25 miles (19–40 km.), and longer events over straight or triangular courses, still continues. Over forty aircraft compete and provide finishes that can bring 30 aircraft across the line in a space of two minutes. In 1969-70 formula or class racing was introduced from America, with aircraft designed to a rigid specification based on the successful series of single-seater midget racer events sponsored by the Goodyear Company just after the Second World War.

Long before it was realized that an aeroplane will function, given certain basic requirements, regardless of its attitude in relation to the ground, the first aerobatic pilots were discovering the possibilities of flight in unusual attitudes. Lt. Nesterov of the Imperial Russian Air Service carried out the first aerobatic manoeuvre — a loop — but he recurs only once in flying history, and it was a Frenchman, Pégoud, who became the first aerobatic display pilot in 1913.

Between 1919 and 1939 aerobatics remained largely a method of amusing crowds at flying displays. Individual pilots such as Detroyat and Doret in France, Tyson and Turner-Hughes in England, and Udet and Fieseler in Germany, developed the art, greatly improved the disciplines of the sport and, in individual competition, introduced the one great new element in aerobatics — competitive flying.

While display flying, that is flying aerobatics of a kind calculated to excite a crowd, is still an important part of the sport, competition aerobatics has entirely taken hold of those who fly this kind of discipline as an art in itself. The basic manoeuvres remain the loop, the roll, the stall turn, and the spin. In competitive work, however, performed before critical judges, the ability of a performer is assessed by his skill in performing sequences of pre-set or free manoeuvres, to a rigid scoring system and within a box of air small enough to tax the highest skills. The standard international aerobatic contest consists of three or more sequences, each of from 15 to 30 individual manoeuvres, including a first sequence of pre-set figures, a second sequence of figures shown to the pilots only 24 hours before they fly it, and one or more 'free' sequences designed by the pilot himself to demonstrate his mastery over his machine.

Under the international scoring system devised by Col. Aresti of Spain, each manoeuvre has a 'difficulty coefficient' between 1 and about 35, which is multiplied by a mark —from 0 to 10—given by the judges in accordance with their assessment of the skill with which each manoeuvre is performed. Total scores in an international contest can be only tens apart, from a possible of perhaps 20,000, such is the equality of skill among top aerobatic pilots.

For international contests and for the world championships, held every two years, the arena for the contest is a box of air, the top 1,000 m. (3,280 ft.) and the base 100 m. (328 ft.) from the ground, and 1,000 m. by 800 m. (3,280 × 2,624 ft.) in plan. Linesmen or instruments guard the edges and barographs record the heights attained—infringements are subject to heavy penalties.

RECORD-BREAKING. The setting of records for the fastest, furthest, or highest flight has been part of sporting flying since the first aircraft. It is the most exacting side of competitive aviation, seeking the ultimate in aircraft performance. From the beginning, the F.A.I. has set precise and carefully controlled requirements for the timing and measurement of all official records, since the validity and accuracy of the results must be beyond doubt. Because of the publicity value of breaking records, especially the speed record, these regulations are complex and set to limits of, in the case of measurements and apparatus, ·01 per cent of error.

In order to beat a previous record, a fresh attempt must exceed the previous figure by a minimum of 1 per cent. As aircraft have grown more complex and diverse, more different classes of record have been introduced by the F.A.I. A record may be set up in any of these classes (from balloons to spaceships), in any of the different categories of record; in the more important categories, the best performance, regardless of class, is taken as a world record.

The preparation for a record attempt can be prodigious. Speed records are run over carefully surveyed courses and, with modern jet aircraft, which give their best performance at height, complex tracking equipment is required to follow the flight. An average of runs in either direction over the course is taken, to eliminate the effects of wind. In height records, measuring apparatus (either a barograph on the aircraft or ground equipment) has to be installed and checked, and the results analysed after the attempt. In records involving a weight categorization or the carriage of a given load, most careful and accurate weighing of aircraft or load must take place.

The most popular record has always been world speed. Today, when only research and fighter aircraft are capable of the speeds required, emphasis is on nationality rather than the man or even the machine. (Records are attributed to the country of origin of the pilot.) Because of the very high costs and the special aircraft involved, the struggle to be the 'fastest man alive' has been restricted during the 1960s and 1970s to the U.S.A. and U.S.S.R.

With the reliability of aircraft outpacing man's physical limits in the 1930s and 1940s, the endurance record became less important, and was replaced by distance in straight line or distance in closed circuit (over a surveyed closed course). With attempts on world speed records taking place only rarely, the most attractive of record categories is the speed over a recognized route, commonly referred to as point-to-point records. This category is one of speed between two capital cities or major towns in different countries. The nature of such an attempt and the fact that it is a record highly suitable for light aircraft, have made it the most popular—and most publicized—attempt in recent years. Because they are inevitably the only truly sporting attempts in any class, light-aircraft records are of considerable public interest.

An attempt on a record may be made for various reasons; many sporting pilots simply like the idea of tackling a more exacting and unusual flight than their normal routine. In the case of commercial or military aircraft, the sporting or competitive element is inevitably combined with the value in terms of publicity for a service, product, or airline, accruing from a successful attempt.

The method of setting up a record is much the same in all cases. The relevant national aero club supervises all attempts by its nationals, who will have applied to it for the services required. Officials for weighing, recording, analysing, and interpreting the necessary data to produce results are provided by the club. The file of results and documents is forwarded to the F.A.I. for checking, the record having been certified as a national performance, and if all is correct the F.A.I. confirms the attempt and publishes it in its bulletin of records.

During the years since 1905-6, when the earliest records were set up, the method of classifying records has undergone many changes, as the F.A.I. *Code Sportif* reflected differing developments in aviation. The rapid growth of light aircraft, for example, led to the introduction of a whole new section in the 1920s, entirely for light aeroplanes, subdivided into sub-classes (to cater for the widely differing types of aircraft) in accordance with engine size. After the Second World War, when engines became standardized in power and aircraft design had improved to the point where engine size was no longer a suitable means of categorization, the present system of sub-division of light aircraft for record purposes was introduced based on total weight. In similar fashion, the F.A.I. Sporting Commission has amended or added to its record classes and methods as need arose.

All national, international, and world events (certain very important international events in aerobatics, parachuting, gliding, and aero-modelling qualify for world status) must be run under F.A.I. rules, as must record attempts. 'Invitation', as against 'open' events, however, may be organized nationally on a private basis. The F.A.I. maintains an annual calendar of sporting flying events which is circulated to all member national clubs, with news of recent record attempts, and publishes an annual bulletin which contains reports on the activities of the F.A.I. during the past year and an up-to-date list of all current records.

From the start of flying as a practical proposition, around 1909, until the beginning of the First World War, practically all flying was undertaken as a sport. Specifically competitive flights were classed either as records or as displays, for the entertainment of the public. Aerobatics had begun to make an appearance in 1913, racing was developing in France and England, and, as the military and commercial possibilities of the aircraft emerged, the purely sporting aspect became specialized.

After 1918, following a period when exponents of sporting flying (then referred to under a general title of 'private aviation') consisted mostly of wealthy amateurs and ex-military pilots flying ex-military machines, strenuous efforts were made to popularize and above all to cheapen the sport. This resulted in the production of large numbers of aircraft, usually in prototype only, intended to sell on grounds of economy. In consequence almost all were too small and light to be practical and powered by engines far too feeble for normal flight.

The period of the 'motor glider' or *'avionette'* lasted until 1924 and was characterized by a large number of different designs in France, Britain, and the U.S.A. Motor-glider competitions were held in Britain in 1923 and two-seater competitions in 1924 but little of lasting value emerged. In 1925 de Havilland introduced the first 'Moth', powered by a 60 h.p. Cirrus engine. This aircraft became the foundation of sporting flying throughout the world and established a British ascendancy in the light-aircraft market which lasted until 1939. It was a simple biplane of wood and fabric construction, with an economical but sufficiently powerful engine, reliable, and easy to fly. Its top speed was 91 m.p.h. (146 km./h.).

With this aircraft, its successors, and its rivals, the popularity of light-aeroplane records, air touring, and rallies grew. Around it formed the network of flying clubs that put learning to fly on a regularized basis. De Havilland had, in fact, discovered the correct formula for the light aeroplane and although light-aircraft design has altered considerably, almost every successful sporting aircraft up to 1939 followed his inspiration. In 1925 also, flying clubs began to multiply, as suitable aircraft appeared. The major developments in sporting flying were taking place in France, Germany, Britain, and the U.S.A. In Germany, apart from the universal search for economy and simplicity, the terms of the Treaty of Versailles did not permit the expansion of aviation beyond light, sporting aeroplanes. Most other European countries, notably Italy, Belgium, and Holland, were developing sporting flying in the 1920s and 1930s and a major national effort to introduce aviation to its people was being made in Russia through government-sponsored flying organizations.

The period 1925-38 was characterized by increasingly frenzied record attempts, many of them in light aircraft, the peak period coming roughly between 1927 and 1932. Aerial touring increased steadily in Europe. By 1938, however, the picture began to change. Increasing costs in most countries, together with a failure to appreciate the changing circumstances as aviation became more commonplace, put many clubs in peril. In Britain, the government subsidy for certain clubs (5 in 1925, 64 in 1938) was withdrawn, and only the introduction of the Civil Air Guard scheme for building up a reserve of pilots in time of war alleviated the shock.

In the U.S.A., where sporting flying had developed on more individual lines, flying clubs in the European sense did not exist; training came from professional schools. The natural American accent on individuality and the spirit of the inter-war period threw greater emphasis on exhibitionism rather than on serious competitive or sporting events.

Following the Second World War, the resurgence of sporting flying largely awaited, as in 1919, the emergence of suitable aircraft. This time, the impetus came from the U.S.A. In Britain, where the aviation industry had been totally committed, by agreement with the Americans, to military aircraft design and production, there were, after 1945, only the de-requisitioned pre-war aircraft released by the R.A.F. from wartime communications duties. In America, however, where civil aircraft development had continued throughout the war, light-aircraft design established a world lead it never lost. In France, to keep the economy running and the aircraft industry in being, factories which had been building communications aircraft for the Germans during the war were given contracts by the postwar government to continue. The aircraft produced were handed over to flying clubs and a subsidy scheme introduced to encourage sporting flying.

In the years 1946-55, sporting flying became increasingly specialized and racing and aerobatics became almost professional sports. While in Europe the aeroplane was primarily a touring and recreational vehicle, the U.S.A., with its greater distances and more commercial approach, was developing the light aeroplane as a business and working tool.

Because of the greater opportunities for international competition, it was in Europe that competitive flying had its greatest development. True sporting flying in the U.S.A. was tending, in the 1940s and 1950s, towards individual effort, resulting in a growing absorption in amateur design and construction which ideally suited the national temperament. In Britain, with the surviving supply of pre-war light aeroplanes coming to an end and with no prospect of a practical modern revival of interest in light aircraft in the industry, progress was slowing down. Economic conditions did not favour the expansion of what was largely a private sector of flying; such designs as were in production were very largely pre-war in conception.

In 1958-9, those conditions had improved to the point where dollar restrictions on the import of American light aircraft could be lifted and the resultant supply of modern sporting and touring aircraft had profound effects on European sporting flying. While racing and aerobatic aircraft continued to be, until about 1962, pre-war or war-time aircraft, air touring and rally flying absorbed the new concept of light aircraft, born of the American technological developments in aviation and their competitive, booming economy. France alone, in Europe, continued to develop a strong native light-aircraft industry. Considerably more air-minded than Britain, she dominated the European and world scene in competitive flying in almost all its aspects until the early 1960s, when competition from other nations began to make itself felt. By 1970, American aircraft and engines had reached a position of dominance in sporting aviation. In the more specialized forms of flying sport, however, which now demanded specialized equipment, European designs still held the lead.

The Fédération Aéronautique Internationale, founded in 1905, was principally concerned in the early days of flying before the First World War, when all flying was 'sporting', in formulating the rules for record-breaking, racing, and international aviation meets. Modified from time to time over the years, these rules became the universal standards for all member countries and are embodied in the *Code Sportif* of the F.A.I., in which are set out the definitions of sporting flying, the duties of officials, the methods of timekeeping and observing competitive or record events, penalties, protests and appeals, and the other details of sporting aviation events.

The F.A.I. maintains a close watch on the progress of sporting flying in its national and international aspects and has an active interest in seeing that legislation at both levels is helpful, rather than inimical, to its kind of flying. It has an observer at the International Civil Aviation Organization in Montreal and one of its major functions is to make international travel by light aircraft as simple and regulation-free as possible. In this it has succeeded to a great degree, with the virtual abolition of customs *carnets*.

The national aero clubs are appointed by the F.A.I. to govern all sporting flying activities within their borders and to look after and protect the interests of their nationals when operating anywhere as private pilots. They have under their jurisdiction the control of all open meetings and record attempts and are responsible for the proper documentation of these, and the provision of stewards timekeepers, handicappers, and judges. They issue the sporting licences that entitle the holders to compete in open contests, and the various certificates of competence required in different branches of the sport. Examples of these certificates of competence are the pilot's certificate for private pilots (once synonymous with a pilot's licence, though the latter is now generally issued by state departments); gliding certificates A, B, and C in silver or gold; and parachuting and ballooning certificates. Most national aero clubs award annually gold, silver, and bronze medals and other aviation awards and are entitled to nominate candidates for the various F.A.I. awards each year.

In addition, national aero clubs host international and world competitions in the various branches of sporting flying. Certain clubs, notably those in the United Kingdom, France, and Germany and most of the East European countries (where sporting flying is on a highly organized, state-aided basis) also support, sponsor, or organize other national or international events.

In the U.K., one of the more active countries in this field, the Royal Aero Club annually organizes a series of air races, pilot-instruction clinics, aerobatic competitions, and social events, and awards cups and trophies in the course of these series. In many cases, the events are sponsored and organized, and the awards presented, by other bodies — usually a local flying club or aviation organization — who call upon the Club to supply a permit for the meeting, approve the course for races and the regulations for the meeting, and nominate the necessary officials under the *Code Sportif* of the F.A.I.

Although many national aero clubs, such as the one in West Germany, still control directly all the sporting activities within their boundaries, others have permitted or encouraged the formation of autonomous or semi-autonomous bodies around each specialized sport. Thus, in the U.K. there exist, in conjunction with the Royal Aero Club (since 1 April 1971, by merger, the United Service and Royal Aero Club), the British Gliding Association, the British Parachute Association, the Society of Model Aeronautical Engineers, and the Popular Flying Association (amateur construction and ultra-light aircraft). The United Service and Royal Aero Club fulfils the functions of a national aero club in regard to F.A.I. commitments, while control of the sporting or competitive side of light aviation is vested in the British Light Aviation Centre. B.L.A.C. grew out of a merger between the Association of British Aero Clubs and the Royal Aero Club Aviation Centre, and looks after the interests of private pilots and clubs and the control, under national and international legislative

bodies — the Department of Trade and Industry Aviation Branch and the International Civil Aviation Organization (I.C.A.O.) — of flying training. Both bodies are very closely integrated and share many officials and departments.

Terence Boughton, *The Story of the British Light Aeroplane* (1967); C. H. Gibbs-Smith, *Aviation: An Historical Survey* (1970); B. J. Hurren, *Fellowship of the Air* (1951). *Bulletins of the Fédération Aéronautique Internationale*, annually; *Flight International*, weekly since 1909.

GOVERNING BODY (WORLD): Fédération Aéronautique Internationale, 6 Rue Galilée, Paris 14, France; (U.K.): United Service and Royal Aero Club, 116 Pall Mall, London S.W.1.

FLYING DUTCHMAN, The (1846), famous English race-horse by the DERBY and TWO THOUSAND GUINEAS winner Bay Middleton out of Barbelle, bred and owned by Lord Eglinton. He won 15 out of the 16 races in which he ran, including the Derby, ST. LEGER, and ASCOT GOLD CUP, being the first horse ever to win all three great races. His only defeat was in the Doncaster Cup in 1850, when that season's Derby and St. Leger winner, VOLTIGEUR, beat him by a neck. The Dutchman, however, obtained his revenge at York the following spring by defeating his old rival by a short length in the most celebrated match in the history of the turf.

FLYING FOX (1896), English race-horse by Orme (son of ORMONDE), bred and owned by the Duke of WESTMINSTER, trained by PORTER, and ridden by Cannon. He won nine races and £40,096, including the triple crown (see HORSE RACING) and the ECLIPSE STAKES. On the death of the Duke in 1900, Flying Fox was sold to Blanc for 37,500 guineas, setting a new world record price for a thoroughbred.

FOLK SPORTS are the games and pastimes, including competitive, athletic, and recreational activities, which are traditional and have been, or were, played both by the nobility and the commons. They include simple diversions which are now no longer practised and also more sophisticated sports which have become refined and adapted into today's pastimes. The games are sometimes played universally, but with regional variations, or were of a purely local origin and nature.

Since they were the sports of the people, who, for the most part, had little time for recreational activities, the opportunities for folk sports were infrequent and limited generally to high days and holidays, Sundays, and festivals.

By the sixteenth century many sports already had a flourishing tradition behind them, and by the following century many sports of indigenous popular growth were formalized. The Puritan tradition tended to discourage such sports, partly because of their possible pagan origin, and partly because they were often played on a Sunday; and the Interregnum forbade many folk sports, particularly bull-baiting and bear-baiting (see ANIMAL-BAITING).

The Restoration saw the revival of folk sports, but often in a debased and dubious form. Events were 'revived' which had never existed before — in Bishop's Stortford a cross-country follow-my-leader was held on Michaelmas Day, in the course of which everyone was 'bumped' and women generally stayed at home 'except those not of a scrupulous character'. While games like kit-cat, BARLEY-BREAK, STOOLBALL, and ninepins had been little interrupted by the Protectorate, the Restoration gave formal approval to activities like FOOTBALL and CRICKET. This was a period of aristocratic interest in sport, mainly because of the wagering on the outcome of horse-races, cricket matches, and cock-fights.

In medieval and Tudor times, court ladies shared in some sports (Elizabeth I hunted and hawked), but generally the only physical aspect of a woman's education was dancing. Less well-born women had more scope for athletic activities. The women traditionally played stoolball and barley-break on Shrove Tuesday. Smock races were popular all over the country; at Maidenhead the smock was competed for by 'five damsels under twenty years of age, chaste in principle, bandy legs and humped backs not being permitted to start'. Elsewhere, races for women seem almost as frequent as those for men. Eighteenth-century cricketers engaged in a match on Wandsworth Common to subscribe for a 'Holland smock of one guinea value which will be run for by two jolly wenches, one known by the name of "the little bit o'blue" (the handsome Broom girl) at the fag end of Kent Street and Black Bess of the Mint . . .excellent sport is expected.' By the end of the century women were even taking part in BOXING matches, incurring the criticism of the Wesleyan, Richard Graves, that such women 'exhibit themselves before the whole assembly in a dress hardly reconcilable with the rules of decency'.

An important stage in the preservation of folk sports comes with the revival of the COTSWOLD GAMES by Robert Dover. The Games had declined in popularity because of Puritanism and had been wholly plebeian in character. Dover, a traditionalist and a Royalist, attempted to restore and improve them after the Restoration. He introduced diversions such as chess and gaming to attract men of other ranks. Considerable numbers participated in these games. A contemporary, Wallington, commented:

'Who durst assemble such a troop as he
    But might of insurrection charged be?
For though some of thy sports most manlike be
    Yet are they linl,ed with peace and modesty.
Here all in th'one and self same sphere do move
    Nor strive so much to win by force as love.
So well the rudest and most rustic swains
    Are managed by thy industrious pains.'

The games were originally of the type described by Shakespeare in *The Winter's Tale*, presided over by a shepherd king, whose flock had produced the first lamb. The revival Games included leaping, leapfrog, a contest of shinkicking, WRESTLING, throwing the HAMMER, and foot races. There was no ARCHERY, the 'military' exercises being single-stick fighting (see QUARTER-STAFF) and handling the pike. Dover's Games were welcomed as a return to an already idealized concept of 'merrie' pre-Protectorate England. Drayton typifies this attitude when he describes Dover as 'one who in these dull iron times dost revive the Golden Age's glories'. This conscious invocation of the past robbed the sports of much of their original spontaneity, and although various sports continued until the beginning of the twentieth century and later, it was generally only in comparatively remote and isolated areas that they retained their original character and composition.

Many folk sports had their origin in religious festivals or occasions. Wakes (from an Old English word *wacian*, meaning watch) were all-night vigils kept by both the religious and the lay to mark the anniversary of the dedication of a church. Merrymaking and a fair would follow, and gradually the wake became not a vigil but a secular fair, including all the usual attractions of competitive races: women for a smock, men for a silver spoon, chasing a pig, sack races, climbing a greasy pole, and trials of strength. There were also grinning matches in which the contestants vied with each other in contorting their faces into the most hideous spectacle, while their heads were framed by a horse collar. The contestants were often old women and the usual prize was tobacco. Dugdale, in *The Antiquites of Warwickshire* (1656), described wakes and their fairs: 'The people fell to lecherie and songs, daunces, harping, piping and also to glotony and sinne, and so turned holinesse to cursydnesse.' And Stubbes wrote: 'Many spend more at one of the wakesses than in all the whole yere besides.' The growth of such Puritan thinking curtailed wakes and Sunday festivals.

Church ales had been important social and money-raising functions in the Tudor and Stuart periods. The churchwardens at this time sold, or distributed free of charge, ale and food, sometimes in the church house or perhaps in a barn or in the church itself. The purpose was to attract the local residents to the church where the wardens might then induce them to pay their parish rates. There was usually also a feast, dances, and games. At the King ale in Whitsuntide a Lord and Lady of the Ale were chosen to preside over the celebrations. These larger ales sometimes went on for several days. Sometimes a private individual might hold an ale for the benefit of the parish, as at Shere in Surrey, where in 1536 John Redford 'made a drinking, at his own expense' and £7 4s. 3d. was raised. Poor families might hold 'bride ales' where the bride would sell her own ale to try to cover the cost of the wedding.

Wassails took place on New Year's Eve. The name probably derives from *Waes hael*, meaning 'Health to you', which was, traditionally at least, the greeting of Rowena, the daughter of Hengist, an early Norse invader of Britain. The wassailers, usually the younger men and women of the village, went round to all the houses, singing and mumming, and wherever they stopped the inhabitants refreshed them with food and drink before they continued on their way. The origin of the wassail and its accompanying songs and chants was a pagan ceremony of propitiation to the gods of the fields and the crops. To ensure heavy crops and a good harvest, a matter of life and death to the villagers, the wassailers went to all the cornfields, the orchards, and the farms. They sang invocations and poured out mead, ostensibly to encourage the growth of the crop, but originally as a libation to the responsible god. In the orchards they would strike the trees with their sticks during the songs. Gradually the time for such activities was changed to twelfth day. Records of wassailing processions continue until the seventeenth century, after which they become less widespread and change from being an integral part of the village's preparations for the sowing and planting of a new crop in spring to an excuse for the youth of the village to collect, at first food and ale, but later presents or money. In 1852 there is a record of what was obviously wassailing although it was called 'apple-howling' at the time. The 'howlers' went to the orchards in traditional style, and rapped on the trees with their sticks. As they rapped they sang:

'Stand fast root, bear well top.
  Pray the god send us a good howling crop.

Every twig, apples big.
  Every bough, apples enow.
Hats full, caps full.
  Full quarters, sacks full.'

Local occasions often meant festivities of a purely local character and origin. In Leicestershire on Easter Monday there was a football match between Hallaton and Medbourne for a dummy bottle of ale. In the West Country the May celebrations were mainly an opportunity for wrestling. Ascension Day was traditionally a time for beating the bounds of a parish and also for foot races. What began as a perambulation of the parish gradually became a race. Sometimes HURLING took place during this beating of the bounds, as at Helston and Bodmin, where even today the bounds are still occasionally beaten. At Truro the unmarried men played the married, and at Helston the inhabitants of two streets played everyone else. The bounds-beating at Bodmin covers 18 miles (29 km.) over the moorland, and the proceedings are interspersed with games of hurling.

In the twentieth century, folk games left their origins behind. Some are lost and forgotten; others remain purely as children's games; some have been forcibly suppressed; and others persist, either as 'games' or as highly specialized 'sports'. The religious element has faded, as has much of the cruelty. Originally these folk sports were for participants, not for spectators, and all took part regardless of individual skill. Now, activities which were once part of pagan ritual survive as family games. (See also HAXEY HOOD, NINE MEN'S MORRIS, WAKES, WASSAILS.)

T. Thistleton Dyer, *British Popular Customs, Past and Present* (1876); F. W. Hackwood, *Old English Sports* (1907); C. Hole, *English Sports and Pastimes* (1949); J. Strutt, *The Sports and Pastimes of the People of England* (1801); N. Wymer, *Sport in England* (1950).

FOLKESTONE FESTIVAL, the best-known HOCKEY festival in the world. Started in 1906, it is held annually at Easter at this south-east coastal resort in England.

FONTAINE, JUSTE (1933-   ), Association footballer for Nice, REIMS, and France who, playing at centre or inside forward, established a World Cup scoring record with 13 goals in Sweden in 1958. He was always at his best as part of a 'tandem' with KOPA; the most successful years of Reims, in the French League and in the European Champion Clubs Cup, and later of the French national side, which finished third in the 1958 World Cup championship, were coincident with the years of the Fontaine and Kopa partnership.

FOOTBALL, American (college) is an 11-a-side team game played with an oval leather ball, inflated to 12½–13½ p.s.i. and weighing 14–15 oz. (396–425 g.). It is played on a rectangular field, usually of grass, but often of synthetic turf, 300 ft. (91·4 m.) between the goal lines and 160 ft. (48·8·m.) wide, with end-zone extensions 30 ft. (9·1 m.) deep beyond each goal line. At the limit of each zone, goal posts are erected. The uprights are 23 ft. 4 in. (7·1 m.) apart, they extend at least 20 ft. (6·1 m.) above ground, and are connected by a crossbar 10 ft. (3·05 m.) above ground. The field is marked by horizontal lines the entire width of the playing area and 5 yds. (4·57 m.) apart from goal line to goal line, giving it the appearance of a gridiron. The 50-yard line marks the centre of the field.

The object of the game is to outscore the opposing team. Points are scored on touchdowns (6 points), field goals (3), and conversion tries (2 or 1). 'Safeties' result in the award of 2 points to the opposing team.

A team advances the ball by running and/or passing it by hand forward and/or laterally until it is brought across the opponent's goal line through a series of plays or in one fell swoop. A touchdown thereby results, and it entitles the scoring team to try for an extra point by a conversion placement kick through the goal posts, or for an extra 2 points by running the ball or completing a pass across the goal line. The conversion try, in each instance, starts from scrimmage with the ball placed 3 yds. (2·7 m.) from the goal line of the defending team. The field goal is usually attempted when the advance by running and/or passing has stopped short of a touchdown but is within the defensive team's territory so that the goal posts are within range for the kicking specialist, who boots the ball as it is held on the ground for him by a team mate (a placement kick). A safety is registered when a player in possession of the ball is 'downed' in his own end zone.

The team winning the toss usually elects to take the kick-off. It is made from the 40-yard line of the kicking team. The receiving team returns the kick-off, or, if the ball crosses its goal line, may elect to down it in the end zone, in which event a 'touchback' results and the ball is brought out to its 20-yard line. On rare occasions the ball is run back all the way (100 yards or more from the end zone) resulting in a touchdown.

At the point where the receiver of the kick-off is downed (short of a touchdown), the ball is put in play by his side. A scrimmage results. The two teams line up facing each other, separated by the neutral zone, approximately 11 in. (279 mm.) — the length of the ball. The seven men in the forward line of the team in possession of the ball are crouched low, prepared to block out the opponents in solid body contact and open the way for their ball-carrier to advance or to protect their passer, almost invariably the quarterback, who is stationed directly behind the centre in the T-formation that is virtually universal. The three other backs (the two halfbacks and fullback) are

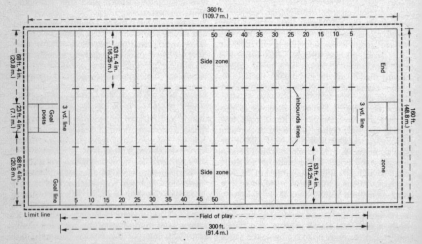

AMERICAN COLLEGE FOOTBALL FIELD
Broken line surrounding the rectangular field is the limit line, 5 ft. (1·5 m.) outside the playing area. Goal posts are at least 20 ft. (6·1 m.) high; the crossbar is 10 ft. (3·05 m.) above the ground.

Defensive alignment | Single-wing offence | T-formation offence

```
E  T  G  G  T  E    |  E  T  C  G  G  T  E  |  E  T  G  C  G  T  E
   L        L        |              Q   H   |          Q
 H              H    |        F            |       H        H
       S             |           H         |              F
```

OFFENSIVE AND DEFENSIVE ALIGNMENTS
(C) Centre; (G) guard; (T) tackle; (E) end; (Q) quarterback; (H) halfback; (F) fullback; (L) line-backer; (S) safety.

positioned two or more yards behind him; or one or more may move out, or one may move sideways before the play starts. In addition to the centre, the men in the forward line are the two ends, two tackles, and two guards. Those in the forward line of the defending team, who may vary from four to eight, or, occasionally, even more, are also in a crouching position or they may stand more erect, prepared to break through and try to get to the ball-carrier or passer and suppress him by force.

Traditionally the defence consisted of two ends, two tackles, and two guards on the line, with the centre and a back as 'line-backers' directly behind the defensive line, two backs stationed behind and outside the line-backers, and a 'safety' slightly deeper between these backs. The supporting backs and line-backers are prepared to tackle the carrier if he gets through the line and to knock or intercept the ball if it is thrown, pursuing the oncoming pass-receivers to intervene between them and the ball, but restrained from laying hands on them before the ball is touched. In a kicking situation, usually on the fourth 'down' (play), the defence concentrates on breaking through to block the punt, and some fall back down the field and block to open the way for their team mate who catches the kick and runs it back.

Before the team in possession of the ball takes its position for the scrimmage, it goes into a huddle some 10 yds. (9·14 m.) behind the spot where the ball is stationed. The quarterback will tell his team mates what offensive play will be tried and then will prepare the players for the start of the play at the line of scrimmage by calling out a series of numbers, whose sequence indicates when the centre will move the ball to begin the play. The defensive team usually huddles to prepare an alignment against the play the quarterback is calling. Play then starts when the centre on the offensive team, who is bent over the ball, with one or both hands on it, 'snaps' or hands it back and up to his quarterback.

To maintain possession of the ball, a team must advance it 10 yards by running and/or passing in four downs. If it fails to make the 10 yards in three plays, it will usually kick

(punt) the ball to the opponent on the fourth down. Each time the 10 yards (or more) are made, a 'first down' is gained, and the team continues to advance the ball until it scores by a touchdown or field goal, or until it gives up possession by kicking, or failure to make a first down, or through loss of the ball on a fumble or interception of a pass.

A game lasts one hour, divided into quarters of 15 minutes each, with a 15-minute interval between the halves and an interval of one minute between the first and second, and the third and fourth, periods. Each half starts with a kick-off, and the teams change ends after the first and third periods. In practice, with the interval, 'time-outs' taken for injuries, moving the ball by the referee, penalties, and allowing for television commercials, a game usually lasts two and a quarter hours or more. Each team is allowed three time-outs each half; these are commonly used to slow down offensive drives or to gain extra time for the offence in the closing minutes of a game.

A test of little more than brute strength and endurance in its early years, the game has become so specialized that, whereas for roughly the first 75 years the 11 men who started a game probably played almost throughout and few substitutes were used, now offensive and defensive units are used, each group having its own substitutes drilled only in the one phase. Special units are selected and trained also for kick-offs and punts, both offensively and defensively, and individually or in combinations for defence when the offence (attack) is threatening the goal line.

In a game of rugged body contact that may become violent because of the speed with which the players move and may strike one another in blocking and tackling, there are many penalties for the protection of the men as well as for the enforcement of fair play. Penalties are most frequently awarded for the following offences and result in the loss of 5 to 15 yards for the guilty team: 'offside' (a player, offensive or defensive, penetrating the neutral zone of the line of scrimmage before the ball is played); illegal procedure (usually a back in forward motion or an offensive lineman moving before the play begins) — both 5-yard penalties; 'holding', in which an offensive or defensive player detains an opposing player by using his hands, the penalty being 15 yards on offence and 5 yards and a loss of down on defence; 'clipping', in which a player blocks an opponent from behind — 15 yards from the point of the foul; and pass interference, wherein a defensive player (although it may also be an attacking player) actively prevents an opponent from catching a pass, the penalty being possession of the ball at the point of the foul. Play is supervised by a referee, an umpire, a lineman, a field judge, and usually a back judge.

A head guard with a face mask and knee pads are required protective equipment for each player. Thigh and shin guards, knee braces, and shoe cleats, all conforming to regulations, may be worn but are not mandatory. Jerseys of contrasting colours for the players are required; they carry numbers on the front and back.

Football in the U.S.A. dates as far back as 1609, when colonists from England were kicking an air-filled bladder, as they had done in Britain. It was a crude form of football, really Association football in its most elemental form, and two hundred years were to pass before the sport was taken up in the colleges.

In 1867, the Princeton Rules were drawn up. They were for soccer, with teams of 25-a-side. Rutgers formulated rules about the same time and in late 1867 a patent was taken on the first covering for a football — a canvas layer to go over the rubber bladder. On 6 November 1869, PRINCETON and Rutgers met at New Brunswick, New Jersey, under Rutgers rules, a modification of the code of the London Football Association (L.F.A.). They specified a maximum of 25 players a side, the team first scoring six goals to be the winner, the grounds to measure 360 ft. by 225 ft. (109·7 × 68·6 m.), the goals 24 ft. (7·3 m.) wide, a round inflated ball to be used which could be kicked or batted with the hand. Running with it and throwing it were barred. The Princeton rules, under which a player making a fair catch was allowed a free kick, were used in a second game a week later. Rutgers won the first, 6 goals to 4, and Princeton the second, 8-0. The following year, Columbia entered the intercollegiate lists and lost to Rutgers, 6-3. The Cornell Football Association was formed but did not seek outside games. The Yale Football Association was organized on 31 October 1872, with rules based on those of the L.F.A.

At HARVARD, football was revived in 1871 and what was known as the 'Boston Game' was played. It was largely soccer, but the round rubber ball could be picked up and the holder could run with it if pursued. On 3 December 1872, the Harvard Football Association was formed, but it did not seek outside competition. With Harvard abstaining, the leading college football powers set up on 19 October 1873 the first intercollegiate rules in the United States. The code was again based on that of the L.F.A. Harvard found a rival in McGill University Football Club of Montreal, which played under the code of the Rugby Football Union of England. They met in three games in 1874. Harvard was so taken with English RUGBY that it approached YALE and gained acceptance of 'concessionary rules' that established the most famous college football rivalry on 13 November 1875. Yale liked running with the ball and went over to English Rugby. So did Princeton representatives, who saw the game, and invited Yale, Harvard, and Columbia to meet in 1876 to form the Intercollegiate Football Association. The association adopted the English Rugby Union code except for a change in the scoring rule.

In 1880 the evolution of the American game began. One man far more than any other was responsible for the transformation, CAMP of Yale. He conceived most of the basic changes and advocated them forcefully, to create a game far more imaginative and diverse and putting a greater premium upon tactics and strategy.

The first of these changes, in 1880, was the substitution of the scrimmage for the Rugby scrummage, establishing the principle of orderly possession of the ball in putting it in play and introducing the quarterback, who was to become the most attractive figure in the game. After three years of effort, Camp succeeded in reducing the number of players from 15 to 11, and he devised the arrangement that became standard — seven linemen, a quarterback, two halfbacks, and a fullback. The block tactics used by Princeton and Yale in their 1880 and 1881 games to maintain uninterrupted possession of the ball for an entire half by each without trying to score resulted in great public dissatisfaction, and in 1882 brought about the system of downs and 'yards to gain' (five in three downs, ultimately ten in four downs), necessitating the marking off of the field with horizontal lines five yards apart, giving it the appearance of a gridiron. It was now necessary to put far greater emphasis upon strategy in planning an attack and on defence as well.

The distinctive American version of football was now taking shape. Meanwhile, the game had become so brutal, with many injuries, some fatal, that there were protests across the country and demands for the game's abolition from college campuses. This trend was accentuated by the momentum mass plays that originated in the 1890s. Men were pulled back from the line and massed with backs to form a wedge of blockers hurling ahead of the ball-carrier and smashing opponents out of the way. Ironically, the man who originated the first of these pulverizing plays was one of the most revered figures in football history, STAGG. In 1890 he brought the ends back and stationed them in the backfield as interferers.

His formation marked the first change from the seven-man offensive line, since the number of players on a team was reduced. In 1891, Stagg originated a second momentum mass play — the 'turtleback', a solid oval of players converging on the opposing tackle. In 1892 the most dreaded of all mass assaults was sprung by Harvard in the 'flying wedge', a kick-off manoeuvre that sent a phalanx of blockers downfield, each hanging on to the clothing of the man ahead, with the ball-carrier following along in the wake of the carnage the 'wedge' produced. This had become the standard kick-off procedure by 1893.

Football was becoming so rough and hazardous that it came under increasingly heavy criticism. In 1894, representatives of Yale, Harvard, Princeton, Pennsylvania, and the U.S. Naval Academy revised the rules to put a stop to the flying wedge and to limit the massing of men behind the line. Also, the duration of the game was cut from 90 to 70 minutes. But the brutal play continued. Indeed, new mass plays were introduced. The roughness continued throughout the 1890s, for, while some colleges outlawed the mass plays, others exploited them, particularly Pennsylvania, which won 65 of 66 games in 1894-8 with its 'Guards Back' attack.

In 1903 the rules required that seven men be on the offensive line of scrimmage between the 25-yard lines. In 1904, six, rather than five, were required on the line, regardless of the position. Still the roughness continued, with 1905 one of the worst seasons, resulting in 18 deaths and 159 other injuries. There was such a storm of protest that President Theodore Roosevelt summoned representatives of Yale, Harvard, and Princeton and told them that the brutality and foul play must be eliminated.

In December 1905, representatives of 62 colleges and universities organized the Intercollegiate Athletic Association of the United States, with Capt. Pierce of West Point as its head. (In 1910 it was to become the NATIONAL COLLEGIATE ATHLETIC ASSOCIATION — N.C.A.A.) It appointed a rules committee which met in session with the American Football Rules Committee, headed by Camp.

The most significant change, in 1906, was the legalization of the forward pass. The length of the game was reduced from 70 to 60 minutes. A neutral zone was established between the offensive and defensive lines at scrimmage. It was now necessary to gain 10 yards instead of 5 in three downs. Ball-carriers could no longer 'hurdle' tacklers, and linemen were restricted from dropping back on offence. But the game still remained hazardous. Interlocked interference continued, with only six men required on the line. Linemen playing the tackle positions were to take even heavier punishment with the forward pass in the game. The halfbacks, who formerly worked close behind them to stop the running attack, now fell back to defend against the pass. In 1909 six tackles died of injuries, and this caused the rules committee in 1910 to put an end to momentum mass assault. Seven men were now required on the line of scrimmage on offence. Interlocked interference was banned, along with pushing and pulling the ball-carrier. The changes not only made for a safer game but bolstered the defence so much that in 1912, to restore the balance, a fourth down was allowed in which to make 10 yards; the length of the field was reduced from 110 to 100 yds. (100·6 m. to 91·4 m.) with end zones 10 yards deep in which passes could be completed for touchdowns, and the many restrictions on the pass were gradually removed to encourage its use. The 20-yard limit on the distance the ball could be thrown beyond the line was removed in 1912, when the value of the touchdown was increased from 5 to 6 points.

So far as fundamentals were concerned, American football's evolution from Rugby was now complete. It was some years before the pass was adopted extensively, particularly in the East. NOTRE DAME emphasized its potential when they defeated the heavily favoured UNITED STATES MILITARY ACADEMY at West Point, N.Y., in 1913 by 35-13, in the inaugural game of what became football's most celebrated intersectional rivalry.

Among the major teams in the early period were the Yale team of 1888 which scored 698 points to 0 by its 13 opponents; the Yale teams of 1891 to 1894, which lost only one game out of 53; Woodruff's Pennsylvania teams, which won 65 of 66 games from 1894 to 1898; YOST's 'Point-a-Minute' teams at MICHIGAN, featuring runner Heston, who scored 72 touchdowns from 1901 to 1904; Stagg's virtually invincible University of CHICAGO teams of 1904 to 1906, with quarterback Eckersall, who twice drop-kicked five field goals in a single game, and the equally successful 1907 to 1909 teams; and Harvard's 'golden era' from 1908 to 1915 (coached by the disciplinarian and strategist, Haughton), which included a run of 33 wins.

The first Rose Bowl game was held on New Year's Day in Pasadena, California, in 1902, with Michigan defeating Stanford, 49-0. The series was not resumed until 1916, and since then has been held virtually every year. By the 1930s it had spawned a number of imitation games in the Sugar Bowl (New Orleans) in 1935, the Sun Bowl (El Paso, Texas) in 1936, the Orange Bowl (Miami) and the Cotton Bowl (Dallas), both in 1937. The period after the Second World War saw a proliferation of various other 'bowl' games and 'all-star' contests around New Year's Day. The Rose Bowl remains the most prestigious and matches the champions of the BIG TEN (Midwest) and Pacific Coast conferences.

After the First World War, college football underwent its period of greatest expansion. Important games attracted immense attention in the press. With crowds of 60,000 and more commonplace (the Army-Navy game of 1926 attracted 110,000 in Chicago), football had become big business. Commercialism was rampant, even at the most respectable colleges, which went heavily into debt to build large stadia. The successful coach commanded a high salary. High school and prep. school athletes were recruited for college teams in scandalous fashion; they were often given athletic scholarships in violation of amateur regulations and at the sacrifice of academic standards. The depression years in the 1930s altered conditions only to a limited degree.

The 1920s saw the ascendancy of ROCKNE's Notre Dame teams. The most glamorous was the Four Horsemen with their linemen, the Seven Mules, of 1924. Equally outstanding were Notre Dame's national champions of 1929 and 1930. The 1920s was a period of famous players: Illinois's GRANGE; MINNESOTA's NAGURSKI, and Stanford's Nevers.

The 1930s saw the rise of the South and South-west as football powers, a trend that continued into the 1970s. ALABAMA's 1935 team won the Rose Bowl and featured a great passing combination, Howell to HUTSON. Tennessee, Louisiana State, and Duke were other Southern football powers. The South-west developed a wide-open game that relied heavily on the forward pass. In 1935 Southern Methodist and Texas Christian, bitter rivals from the neighbouring Texas cities of Dallas and Fort Worth respectively, staged a passing duel that brought Southern Methodist the national championship. The outstanding player, however, was Texas Christian's quarterback, BAUGH, the most illustrious passer of the period, who in college and later in professional football (with the WASHINGTON REDSKINS) helped revolutionize football offence by putting emphasis on passing. Texas Christian's 1938 national champions had another brilliant passer, O'Brien (later a professional with the PHILADELPHIA EAGLES).

SOUTHERN CALIFORNIA dominated the West Coast for most of the decade. Its 1931 team broke a long Notre Dame winning run and instituted a bitter and continuous intersectional rivalry. Minnesota, coached by Bierman, won all but one game from 1934 to 1936 and ruled as national champion in 1934 and 1936, as well as in 1940 and 1941. Michigan had outstanding teams in the early 1930s, and in the late 1930s featured the greatest running back of the period, Harmon. OHIO STATE, an important Midwest team, had major contests with Notre Dame in the 1930s. In the East, Pittsburgh was famous for a tough defence and a crushing offence; Princeton was undefeated from 1933 to 1935, except for a loss to Yale in 1934. The most versatile athlete was Colorado's WHITE, who later played professionally.

After the attack on Pearl Harbour in December 1941, many colleges dropped football. The game kept going largely because of the Navy Pre-Flight training programme introduced by a former Navy player and coach, in which football players and other athletes were allowed to take part in varsity competition as part of their naval training at the colleges to which they were assigned. Some of them played for more than one college as they were transferred; on occasion they played against their Alma Mater.

The T-formation — the basic modern offence — was developed in the late 1930s by HALAS and his CHICAGO BEARS staff in conjunction with Shaughnessy, then at the University of Chicago. Some of the principles of the attack had been experimented with by Stagg as early as 1894 and 1905 from the old standard T. This modern version, with a back in motion wide before the ball was snapped and ends stationed wide of the line, created a sensation in 1940 for the speed and deception with which it struck through quick openings through the line. That year Stanford University, where Shaughnessy had gone as coach, beat every opponent with the T and defeated Nebraska in the Rose Bowl. Leahy and BLAIK went to Notre Dame and Army, respectively, in 1941 and began using the T. In 1943 Leahy developed what was regarded as the best Notre Dame team in history, and in 1944 to 1946 Army won every game except for a 0-0 tie with Notre Dame in 1946. That was enough to start a swing to the T-formation which, with variations, has been the standard ever since. Faurot at Missouri developed the split-T in 1941, with wider line-spacing and the quarterback carrying the ball much of the time. Faurot's 1943 Iowa Pre-Flight team used it with conspicuous success. WILKINSON and Tatum were on his staff, and they used the split-T most effectively in the 1950s, Wilkinson at OKLAHOMA and Tatum at Maryland. A later variation, the wishbone-T, was developed by a Wilkinson pupil, Royal, at TEXAS in the 1960s. In this formation, the fullback is stationed in front of the halfbacks. The quarterback is mostly a runner, moving laterally along the line and having the option to pass off to other running backs if about to be tackled.

The use of platoons started in 1945 at Michigan. Because of the shortage of manpower in wartime, coach Crisler used different units for offence and defence in the line only. Two years later, he was using backs as well as linemen — entire teams — in separate units for offence and defence. In time the use of platoons became so general that, in 1953, substitutions were again restricted to one player at a time. In the 1960s, the rules were liberalized gradually until by 1965 wholesale substitutions were again permitted.

The later 1940s were dominated by Notre Dame and Army. Notre Dame was unbeaten in 1941, and two years later was national champion, although beaten in the final game by Great Lakes Naval Training Station. When Leahy returned from the services in 1946, Notre Dame began an unbeaten run of 38 games that lasted until 1950 and brought national championships in 1946, 1947, and 1949. Meanwhile Army achieved a 3-year unbeaten run from 1944 to 1946, marred only by the tie with Notre Dame in the latter year. Halfback Davis and fullback Blanchard were the most effective pair of running backs in college football history, and each in turn was selected as best player of the year. Army started another unbeaten run in 1948 that stretched to 28 games before a defeat by Navy. Crisler's 1947 Michigan team was undefeated and beat Southern California in the Rose Bowl, while the 1948 Michigan team was national champion.

As the 1940s drew to a close, Wilkinson started a remarkable coaching record at Oklahoma. From 1948 until the Sugar Bowl game of 1951 (when Kentucky beat them), Oklahoma, using the split-T, won 31 games in a row. After losing opening games to Notre Dame in 1952 and 1953, and being tied by Pittsburgh in the latter year, Oklahoma remained unbeaten until 1957 (when Notre Dame beat them) — establishing a run of 47 consecutive wins.

National champions in 1950, 1955, and 1956, Oklahoma was also unbeaten in its Big Six (later Big Eight) conference from 1947 to 1958. In the most famous game of the decade, their 1955 team overwhelmed unbeaten Maryland in the 1956 Orange Bowl.

At Maryland, Tatum had unbeaten teams in 1951, 1953, and 1955 (until the Oklahoma loss). Tennessee, Georgia Tech, and Louisiana State, with coach Dietzel's famous 1958 defensive platoon, the 'Chinese bandits', were prominent football powers in the South. U.C.L.A. rose to challenge Southern California in the West, although Southern California's 1952 team (which defeated U.C.L.A., 14-13) was probably the area's strongest of the decade. Michigan State became a new Midwest power, being national champion in 1952, while Ohio State was national champion in 1954 and 1955. In 1958 Blaik closed his coaching career at Army by devising a 'lonely end' formation, where Carpenter was stationed far out wide and never took part in the huddle; the formation, together with running backs Dawkins and Anderson, brought Army an unbeaten season. Syracuse was unbeaten in 1959 and 1960.

The 1960s saw major competition in the South-west between Royal's Texas team and Broyles's Arkansas team. Texas was unbeaten in 1962-3, Arkansas in 1964-5, and Texas again in 1969-70 (but upset by Notre Dame in the Cotton Bowl after the last season). The South continued strong with Alabama, the major force. Bryant, who had had unbeaten teams at Kentucky and Texas A. & M. in the 1950s, returned to coach Alabama and produced national champions in 1961, 1964, and 1965, with the unbeaten 1964 team including NAMATH at quarterback.

Southern California was national champion in 1962 and 1967 and spoiled Notre Dame's unbeaten season in 1964. Notre Dame participated in one of the most publicized games in history in 1966, when, before an estimated 33 million television viewers, they played to a 10-10 tie with Michigan State, 'freezing' the ball in the final minutes. The two teams shared the national championship. Ohio State, with a remarkable sophomore team, was national champion in 1968, and lost only two games in succeeding years. Nebraska was unbeaten and national champion in 1970 and 1971, winning the latter championship in the 1972 Orange Bowl against previously unbeaten Alabama. Southern California was the unbeaten national champion in 1972. Notre Dame won the 1973 championship by defeating previously unbeaten Alabama in the Sugar Bowl.

In the 1960s college football faced a serious challenge to its popularity from professional football (see below), which underwent an enormous boom. The professionals agreed to avoid games on Saturday afternoon (except after the close of the college season) and Friday and Saturday nights, so as not to compete on television with college games. The N.C.A.A. allowed only one college game to be televised into any specific area on Saturday afternoon (although some exceptions were made for Saturday night games). College football has fully held its own against the professional challenge. Every year since 1954, attendance has increased. It also recognized black athletes more and more. Not only were black players prominent on many college teams in the North, but teams in the Deep South began actively to recruit them. And black colleges, which had operated in almost total obscurity, gained recognition for their football, especially Grambling College in Louisiana, which has sent more players into professional football than virtually any other college.

By the 1970s, college football in the major conferences was increasingly being played at virtually a professional level by teams that could afford the expense of recruiting high school players, paying them athletic scholarships, maintaining special training facilities and having extensive high-salaried coaching staffs to guide them.

Allison Danzig, *Oh, How They Played the Game: The Early Days of Football and the Heroes Who Made Them Great* (1971); John McCallum and Charles H. Pearson, *College Football U.S.A., 1869-1971* (1971).

American professional football closely resembles college football (see above). There are some differences, most of which have contributed to a more mobile and wide-open (attacking) game. The dimensions of the field are the same, as are the basic objectives and manoeuvres. The offensive team must make 10 yards (9·14 m.) in four downs or lose the ball. The scoring is the same, except that conversions (extra points) count only 1 point and are usually accomplished by place-kicks. The conversion try takes place from the 2-yard line, and the goal posts are closer together than in college football (18 ft. 6 in. — 5·6 m.).

In the 1930s the goal posts were put on the goal line rather than at the end of the end zone, 10 yards removed from the goal line. This created a stronger incentive for kicking field goals, since the ball had to travel a shorter distance to be a successful goal. At about the same time, a forward pass was permitted from anywhere behind the line of scrimmage, instead of the 5-yard distance behind that college football required, which gave the passer greater flexibility and increased the use of the forward pass as an offensive weapon. A ball

carrier was also allowed to get up and keep running if his knee hit the ground without a defensive player touching him, in contrast to college football, where the ball was 'dead' once the ball carrier's knee touched the ground.

Although college football pioneered in allowing unlimited substitutions of players, specialization of functions reached its highest development in professional football from the mid-1950s on. Different sets of players made up the offensive and defensive teams, while there were even special units for kick-offs and punts, called 'special teams' or, more colourfully, 'suicide squads', who hurtled down the field at full speed either, as offence, to block for the kick-receiver or, as defence, to knock the kick-receiver down. The increased specialization expanded team rosters. As low as 20 players in 1934, they eventually grew to the present 40 players 30 years later. Since its development by the Chicago Bears in 1940, the T-formation has remained the basic 'pro' offence formation.

The basic offensive and defensive alignments date from the 1950s. The traditional alignment had put seven men on the line of scrimmage, with a centre over the ball, a guard, then a tackle, and then an end lined up close by on both left and right side of the centre. In the new alignment one end was split very wide of the rest of the line and called a 'split end'. The other end, who was a more burly athlete, usually weighing about 225 lb. (102 kg.), remained close to the line and was used much of the time as a blocker; he was designated a 'tight end'. One of the halfbacks was stationed wide of and slightly behind the line, usually on the opposite side from the 'split end', and was called a 'flanker', while the remaining backs, who could line up alongside each other or one behind the other directly behind the quarterback, in what was called an 'I' formation, were called simply 'running backs'. The new alignment greatly opened up the offensive game and put a premium on passing and on swift receivers as flankers and split ends.

To counteract this offensive, the defence was realigned. The traditional defensive line of six or seven men, with one or two linebackers, two halfbacks, and safety, changed with the availability of defence specialists. In the mid-1950s Landry, the defensive coach of the NEW YORK GIANTS, reduced the defensive line to four (two ends, two tackles), and this 'front four', which was quickly adopted by all professional teams, depended on huge athletes — usually well over 6 ft. (1·8 m.) and weighing more than 250 lb. (113 kg.) — who could harass the passer and block running plays.

```
E    T  G  C  G  T   E
        Q            H

   RB      RB
```

Standard offence

```
      E    T    T    E
    L      L         L
CB                      CB
      S         S
```

Standard defence

OFFENSIVE AND DEFENSIVE ALIGNMENTS
(C) Centre; (G) guard; (T) tackle; (E) end; (Q) quarterback; (H) halfback; (RB) running back; (L) line-
backer; (CB) corner back; (S) safety.

Three line-backers were stationed behind this
line, with the middle line-backer calling
defensive signals to counteract offensive
alignments; these men had to be equally adept
at tackling the ball-carrier or guarding against
the forward pass. The 'defensive secondary'
now consisted of two 'corner backs' and two
'safeties'. The corner backs, swift runners
who had to be unerring tacklers and possessed
of an excellent sense of anticipation against
passes, were primarily responsible for
preventing ball-carriers from running wide
round the defensive end and for covering the
fastest and most adept pass-receivers, the
flankers and split ends. The safeties were the
last line against penetration by ball-carriers.
The 'free safety' helped the corner backs cover
the swift pass-receivers, while the 'tight
safety' had primary responsibility for the 'tight
end'.

Professional teams usually had an elaborate
system to evaluate college football players
(from whose ranks virtually all professionals
are drawn) based on a pool of scouting information which rates player-performance by
computer. A general manager will supervise
personnel and evaluate scouting information;
while the head coach will have assistant
coaches for the offensive and defensive lines,
offensive backfields and secondaries, with
often offensive and defensive 'co-ordinators'
over them reporting directly to the head coach.
Some teams have special coaches for quarterbacks, pass-receivers, 'special teams', and/or
kickers. Coaching is now a full-time job, with
most of the time away from games and practice fields spent viewing films to evaluate the
team's players and its future opponents.

The first American professional football
game was played in Latrobe, Pennsylvania, on
31 August 1895. In the following years in
western Pennsylvania, players like WARNER
and HEFFELFINGER emerged. Upper New York
state formed teams after 1900 at Buffalo,
Syracuse, and some smaller towns. Before
1920, though, the centre of professional football was Ohio, in towns such as Canton, Mas-
sillon, Akron, Columbus, and Dayton.
THORPE first played professionally for the
Canton Bulldogs and coached them in 1919-
20. At Canton in July 1919 a league, called the
American Professional Football Association,
was formed, the precursor of the National
Football League (N.F.L.) which began operations in 1922 and has been the dominant force
in professional football ever since.

By 1920 the sport had spread to Indiana and
Illinois, many of whose leading players had
been members of the Great Lakes Naval Training Station team of 1918 that won the 1919
Rose Bowl. The most important influence was
Halas, who joined the Decatur (Illinois)
Staleys in 1920 as end and coach. By 1922 the
Staleys had become the Chicago Bears, who
dominated the league for much of the period
up to the Second World War. Halas induced
the leading college football player of the time,
Grange, to join the Bears after his final game
with the University of Illinois in 1925 and to
go on a whirlwind tour that, at one point,
included seven games in nine days, and helped
to attract national attention to the sport. With
Grange, the Bears played to a crowd of 73,000
in New York, more than double the attendance
for any professional game until that time. In
1921 the GREEN BAY PACKERS entered the
professional league. Endowed with fanatical
fans and two exceptional coaches, Lambeau
before the Second World War and LOMBARDI
after 1960, the Packers have remained for over
50 years one of the most colourful and successful teams in the sport.

In 1933, along with the changes placing the
goal posts on the goal line and allowing forward passes from any point behind the line of
scrimmage, the league was split into two divisions, Eastern and Western, whose champions
met in a title game. The Chicago Bears and
New York Giants competed for the title in
both 1933 and 1934, with the Giants outwit-
ting the Bears in 1934 by having their players
switch from cleated shoes to basketball shoes
to gain traction on a playing field that was
covered in ice. In 1934 the *Chicago Tribune*
sponsored an 'All-Star Game' between the
N.F.L. champion (the Bears) and a specially
selected group of the best college players of
the previous year, an event that has continued
ever since, and is usually played early in
August.

Perhaps the most far-reaching proposal in
National Football League history was put for-

ward by the Philadelphia owner, BELL, in 1935 when he advocated and saw adopted a plan by which college football players in their final year of eligibility were drafted by professional football teams. Starting in 1936, the team in last place in the N.F.L. could choose first among all players graduating from college during that academic year. Each N.F.L. team then 'drafted' in turn in reverse order to their final placing in that autumn's N.F.L. standing. The same procedure was continued for each succeeding round (originally 30 rounds, but since the 1960s only 17). This ingenious system assures the weakest teams of acquiring the most talented college players or of surrendering their position for comparable value in seasoned professional players from another team. It is thus possible for a weak team, through astute drafting and trading, to improve their position immeasurably within two or three years. Professional basketball later adopted the same system.

In the 1930s, college football dominated American autumn sports. Professional football games, except for title contests, were not particularly well attended. The game was developing leading players and teams, though, with the Chicago Bears, New York, Green Bay, and the DETROIT LIONS, and the Washington (formerly Boston) Redskins dominating. Marshall bought a dormant Boston franchise in 1932 and brought in new ideas such as a League title play-off game. He also pushed the forward-pass rule that greatly encouraged passing as an offensive weapon. When Boston failed to support his Eastern Division champions in 1936, he moved the team to Washington, where it remained. Marshall was a colourful promoter who introduced marching bands and other crowd-pleasing devices to attract fans. His most effective manoeuvre, however, was signing Baugh, the quarterback from Texas Christian University, who became the leading passer during his 16 years at Washington and proved the efficacy of the passing change that Marshall had advocated years earlier. Baugh led Washington to the league title in his first year (1937) and again in 1942.

Before the Second World War, the Chicago Bears featured such stars as player-coach Halas and Hewitt at end, Grange and Feathers as runners, Manders as halfback and kicker, and the overpowering fullback Nagurski. New York had Leemans as a runner, Strong as kicker, and the redoubtable Hein as centre and line-backer. Detroit featured a remarkable backfield, with Caddel, Presnell, and fullback Gutowsky, but the team revolved around the versatile quarterback, CLARK, who excelled as runner, passer, play-caller, and drop-kicker. Green Bay featured strong runners in Hinkle

and the dedicated 'Johnny Blood' (real name, McNally), but its principal strength was a passing attack that featured, first, Herber and then Isbell as passers, but depended largely on the spectacular pass-receiving of Hutson, certainly the most influential pass-catcher in professional history. During Hutson's career (1935-45), Green Bay won League titles in 1936, 1939, and 1944. Hutson held League pass-receiving and scoring records at the time of his retirement. The most versatile athlete was White, who was paid the then staggering salary of $15,800 by the PITTSBURGH STEELERS in 1937. White was a 'triple-threat' player, passing, punting, and running, and led the League in rushing in 1938 at Pittsburgh and in 1940 at Detroit.

The most famous team of the early 1940s was the Chicago Bears, arguably the greatest professional football team of all time. In the 1940s the Bears routed an excellent Washington Redskin team by the incredible score of 73 to 0. The Bears employed the T-formation, with quarterback Luckman guiding the team and passing masterfully. The game established the T as the basic offensive alignment. In the early 1940s the Bears featured centre Turner, guard Fortmann, tackle Stydahar, end Kavanaugh, halfback McAfee, and fullbacks Osmanski and Standlee.

The growing popularity of the game immediately before the war, and the return of many former college football players after the war, encouraged the formation of a rival professional league, the All-America Football Conference (A.A.C.), in 1946, with teams in New York, Brooklyn, Chicago, Miami, Buffalo, Cleveland, Los Angeles, and San Francisco. A costly bidding competition for college players between the leagues followed, and this finally led the new League to sue for peace after the 1949 season. The A.A.C. was also handicapped in that the CLEVELAND BROWNS, under their coach PAUL BROWN, dominated the League, winning all four League titles and 47 out of 54 regular League games in the 1946-9 period. Three A.A.C. teams — Cleveland, San Francisco, and Baltimore (who had replaced Miami in 1947) — joined the National Football League after the 1950 merger.

Cleveland promptly won the N.F.L. title in its first year in the League. Brown had begun building the nucleus of a team while coaching the Great Lakes Naval Training Station during the Second World War. His teams stressed superb execution of a limited number of plays. They also featured an exceptional quarterback in Graham, an excellent strategist who passed accurately to two sure-handed receivers, Lavelli and Speedie, and a crushing fullback,

Motley. Motley and the San Francisco full-back Perry (the third leading runner in N.F.L. history) were two of many black players given a first chance to play professional football by the All-America Football Conference. Black athletes played professional football in the first days of the N.F.L.'s predecessor, the American Professional Football Association. Pollard, the first black All-American college player from Brown University, and the actor-singer, Paul Robeson, both played for the Akron Pros in 1919-20. Although there were black college players in the 1930s, none of them was welcomed into professional football. All of this changed after the Second World War. Indeed, by 1970 approximately one-third of all professional football players were black; and the outstanding running back of the postwar era was JIM BROWN, All-America star at Syracuse University, who in his professional years (1957-65) established all-time records for yards-rushing, yards rushed in a single season, and the number of times leading the League in rushing.

The Philadelphia Eagles and CHICAGO CARDINALS were the leading National Football League teams in the late 1940s, the Eagles being built around the back Van Buren, the pass-receiver and defensive end Pihos, and the centre Bednarik, who played in college at the University of Pennsylvania and then at Philadelphia from 1949 to 1962. The Cardinals relied principally upon their quarterback Christman, halfbacks Trippi and Angsman, and fullback Harder, a running back and place-kicker who led the League in scoring in 1947-9. The 1950s saw a full conversion to two-platoon football and a realignment of offence and defence formations. The Cleveland Browns continued to be prominent and other strong teams were the LOS ANGELES RAMS and the DETROIT LIONS. Los Angeles had two exceptional quarterbacks, the astute Waterfield and the classic passer Van Brocklin; Layne was the quarterback and inspirational leader of Detroit, and the running back Walker and the offensive end (and later fullback) Hart the supporting attacking players.

The title games of 1958 and 1959 were struggles between the BALTIMORE COLTS and New York Giants. Baltimore, relying on the passing of Unitas, his receiver Berry, and the running of Ameche, won both games. The 1958 play-off changed the face of professional football. The game was tied at the end of the regulation four quarters and then went into a 'sudden death' period, the first in professional football history, with Ameche scoring the winning touchdown on the thirteenth play of the extra time. The excitement generated by the game confirmed the acceptance of profes-

sional football as a leading television attraction. Television interest was enhanced by instant replay, by which the spectacular plays could be re-run, usually in slow motion, soon after they occurred. The N.F.L. Commissioner, Bell, instituted a vital restriction by banning television coverage of all games within a 75-mile (120 km.) radius of every professional game being played, thus guaranteeing that fans in the area had to attend a team's home games in order to see them. (This restriction was dropped in 1973 by Congressional act, with mixed results, although public interest in the game remained high.)

In 1960 the most vigorous challenge to the established National Football League was launched by a group led by the Texan Lamar Hunt. Well-financed in some cities, but operating precariously in others, the new AMERICAN FOOTBALL LEAGUE (A.F.L.) started with teams in New York, Boston, Buffalo, Houston, Dallas (soon to be Kansas City), Denver, Oakland, and Los Angeles (later San Diego). The League struggled through the first few seasons with heavy losses due to meagre attendance and the increased bidding competition with the N.F.L. for each year's college football players. Werblin, the retired head of the Music Corporation of America, bought the moribund New York Titan franchise in 1963, changed the team's name to the NEW YORK JETS, and within two years, through two moves, made the new League a serious threat to the established N.F.L. First, he was instrumental in negotiating a five-year contract for the weekly televising of A.F.L. games with the National Broadcasting Company — for a total fee of $36 million — with each club to share in the revenue, thus assuring a firm financial basis for the new league. Second, in 1965, Werblin followed his show-business instincts by discovering a player of special 'star' quality — quarterback Namath of the University of Alabama — whom he signed for a record three-year contract of $427,000. Namath proved to be an astute investment, because the terms of his contract generated massive publicity for himself, the Jets, and the League.

The bidding war between the two Leagues for college football players became increasingly ruinous for the individual owners and teams, with some individual players' contracts exceeding $600,000. Meanwhile the A.F.L. Buffalo place-kicker, Gogolak, was signed by the N.F.L. New York Giants. In retaliation, the former Oakland Raiders' coach Davis, who had been made commissioner of the A.F.L., immediately encouraged A.F.L. teams to offer extremely generous contracts to such prominent quarterbacks in the National

Football League as Gabriel of Los Angeles and Brodie of San Francisco. Soon after, negotiations were started between the Leagues, with the N.F.L. commissioner, ROZELLE, who had succeeded Bell in 1959, being instrumental in bringing together the owner's committees of each league and guiding the agreement to merge the leagues through the U.S. Congress. The merger agreement of 8 June 1966 provided for a full integration of all 26 professional football teams for the 1970 season and established an inter-league championship (to be played in the following January), which was quickly dubbed the 'Super Bowl'. The Green Bay Packers won the first two games in 1967 and 1968, beating Kansas City and Oakland respectively, while the Namath mystique received a strong boost from the New York Jets' upset of Baltimore in the 1969 game, a victory that Namath had predicted the week before. Kansas City defeated the MINNESOTA VIKINGS in 1970, Baltimore beat Dallas in 1971, and Dallas won in 1972 by defeating Miami. The Miami Dolphins, guided by coach Shula (who previously led Baltimore), were unbeaten in the 1972 season, the first such team in over 30 years. They beat Washington in the Super Bowl in 1973, and the next year became the first team since Green Bay to win two consecutive Super Bowls when they defeated Minnesota in 1974. The warm-weather cities like Los Angeles, Miami, Houston (in its enclosed ASTRODOME), and New Orleans have staged the mid-January event.

In the National Football League during the 1960s, the New York Giants, Cleveland Browns, and Baltimore Colts were strong teams, with the DALLAS COWBOYS, under the Giants' former defensive coach, Landry, a growing power in the later years. The dominant team of the decade, though, was the Green Bay Packers, drilled thoroughly by Lombardi, featuring powerful running, aggressive defensive play, and superior conditioning. A remarkably close-knit team, it did not depend upon individual players. Its most attractive player, halfback Hornung, was suspended for a year in 1963, for failure to report a bribe offer, and retired soon after. The team's quarterback, Starr, was an astute tactician who served on the field as an *alter ego* for Lombardi.

In 1970 the League was divided into two conferences, the National and the American. The National Conference encompassed former N.F.L. teams — the New York Giants, Philadelphia, Washington, Atlanta, Detroit, Chicago, Green Bay, St. Louis, Minnesota, New Orleans, Dallas, Los Angeles, and San Francisco. To produce an equivalent 13 teams in the American Conference, three N.F.L. teams — Cleveland, Baltimore, and Pittsburgh — joined the New York Jets, Boston (soon to become New England), Buffalo, Miami, Cincinnati, Houston, Kansas City, Denver, San Diego, and Oakland. Each conference has three divisions, with the winner of each division and the second place team with the best record conducting semi-final playoffs, and the winners then meeting for the divisional championship. The divisional champions then meet in the Super Bowl.

Television has been instrumental in bringing professional football to its peak of popularity as a spectator sport, and the income from this source keeps the 26 professional football teams solvent. In 1971 professional football games were watched weekly on television by approximately 75 million spectators. The 1972 Super Bowl was the most widely watched regularly scheduled television event in American history. Some 65 million people viewed the game in approximately 27·5 million homes — both television records.

In an opinion poll covering 1971, football (particularly professional football) was rated as the favourite spectator sport of 36 per cent of all Americans. Ten years before, football polled 21 per cent to baseball's 34 per cent.

Roger Treat, *Official Encyclopedia of Football* (9th ed. rev., 1971); *Official Record Book of the National Football League* (1970).

FOOTBALL, Association, is an 11-a-side ball-and-goal game played at first-class level throughout the world. Soccer, as it is often called, is played with a spherical, usually leather-covered, ball with a circumference of not more than 28 in. (0·71 m.) and not less than 27 in. (0·69 m.), weighing, at the start of a game, not more than 16 oz. nor less than 14 oz. (453–396 g.) on a pitch not more than 130 yds. by 100 yds. (120 × 90 m.) and not less than 100 yds. by 50 yds. (90 × 45 m.). The pitch must be rectangular in shape so that the length must in all cases exceed the breadth.

The positions of the players became generally established in the early years of this century, and are still accepted in most of Britain, as: goalkeeper, right back, left back, right half-back, centre half-back, left half-back, outside right, inside right, centre forward, inside left, outside left. In recent years most countries in practice and many in name have accepted that the former centre half-back has now become a centre back; and the development towards a more fluid form of play has led to a less rigid positioning. Nevertheless, most of the names of the positions continue to exist though less definitively than formerly.

The fundamental object of the game is for

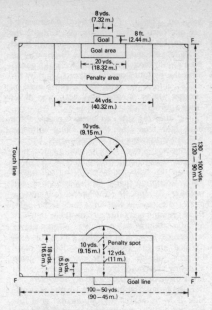

ASSOCIATION FOOTBALL PITCH
Metric dimensions are those agreed by the International Football Association Board. (F) corner flags; optional flagstaff at either end of centre line.

one set of players to force the ball into the goal (a pair of upright posts across which is mounted the crossbar) defended by their opponents. The object of the game is not defined in the laws as authorized by the International Football Association Board but, for all matches played with the approval of national Associations or their affiliated local Associations, the size of pitches, the size, weight, and material of the ball, width between goal posts and height of the crossbar from the ground, and duration of the periods of play are all regulated. However, providing the principles of the laws affecting those matters are maintained, they may be modified in their application to players of school age. The maximum number of players is now defined by Law III, which states: 'A match shall be played between two teams, each consisting of not more than 11 players, one of whom shall be the goalkeeper.' The International Board leave the minimum number of players in a team to the discretion of national Associations but recommend that: 'A match should not be considered valid if there are fewer than seven players in either of the teams.'

At the beginning of a match, the choice of ends or the opportunity to kick-off is decided by the toss of a coin, with the team winning the toss having the option of choosing which end of the pitch they wish to defend or to kick-off. The referee gives the signal for the game to start when he is satisfied that every player is in his own half of the field and every player of the team opposing that of the player kicking-off is not less than 10 yds. (9·15 m.) away from the kicker. Play begins when the ball has travelled the distance of its own circumference and it must not be played for a second time by the player kicking-off until it has been touched or played by another player.

Once play has started, no player, except the goalkeepers within their own penalty areas, may intentionally handle the ball. By kicking or heading it the players of one team seek to move the ball from one another until one of their side is in a position to shoot the ball into the goal of the opposing side with his foot or head. The law relating to the method of scoring reads: 'A goal is scored when the whole of the ball has passed over the goal line, between the goal posts and under the crossbar, provided it has not been thrown, carried, or propelled by hand or arm, by a player of the attacking side, except in the case of a goalkeeper, who is within his own penalty area.'

Opponents can obtain possession of the ball by intercepting passes between members of the attacking side, or by tackling opposing players when they are in possession of the ball. Tackles may be made by the feet, in which case the intention must be to play the ball and force it away from the control of the opponent's feet, or by charging the player fairly, i.e. charging shoulder against shoulder. Players are penalized if they charge in a violent or dangerous manner, kick or attempt to kick an opponent, trip him, jump at him, charge him from behind (unless he is obstructing), strike, hold, or push him, or handle the ball. The penalty for any of those infringements is the award of a direct free kick at the ball by the opposing side from the place where the offence occurred. If the place was within the offending player's penalty area, the offence is penalized by a penalty kick, in which case the ball is placed on the penalty spot and, when it is being taken, all players with the exception of the player taking the kick, and the opposing goalkeeper, must be within the field of play but outside the penalty area, and at least 10 yds. (9·15 m.) from the penalty spot. The opposing goalkeeper must stand (without moving his feet) on his own goal line, between the goal posts, until the ball is kicked. The player taking the kick must kick the ball forward; he must not play the ball a second time until it has been touched or played by another player. A goal can, of course, be scored from a penalty kick and, similarly, directly from any of the other free kicks awarded against a side for the offences already mentioned.

In the case of a number of other offences (such as charging fairly but when the ball is not within playing distance of the players concerned, intentionally obstructing a player when not playing the ball, or indulging in time-wasting tactics), an *indirect* free kick is awarded to the non-offending side. A goal cannot be scored directly from such a kick.

The ball is in play, except when it has wholly crossed the goal line or touch line (whether on the ground or in the air) or when the game has been stopped by the referee. The majority of cases when play has been stopped by the referee will involve the award of a free kick and the game is re-started by the taking of the kick. In the less frequent case of a temporary suspension of the game while the ball is still in play, e.g. because of suspected serious injury to a player, the game is re-started by the referee dropping the ball where it was when he suspended play. It is deemed in play when it touches the ground and no player may play the ball until it has touched the ground. When the ball is out of play because it has passed wholly over a touch line, it must be thrown in from the point where it crossed the line, in any direction, by a player of the team opposite to that of the player who last touched the ball. The thrower at the moment of delivering the ball must face the field of play and part of each foot must be either on the touch line or on the ground outside the touch line. The thrower must use both hands and deliver the ball from behind and over his head. The ball is in play immediately it enters the field of play, but the thrower cannot again play the ball until it has been touched by another player. Nor can a goal be scored direct from a throw-in.

When the ball goes out of play by wholly passing over the goal line (excluding that portion between the goal posts), if it was last played by one of the attacking team, the game is re-started by a member of the defending side kicking the ball from a point within that half of the goal area nearest to where it crossed the line, so that it passes beyond the penalty area, at which point the ball is again in play. Players of the team opposing that of the player taking the goal-kick must remain outside the penalty area while the kick is being taken. If the ball before wholly crossing the goal line had, on the other hand, been last played by one of the defending team, a member of the attacking side takes a corner kick, i.e. the whole of the ball must be placed within the quarter circle at the nearest corner flag, which must not be moved, and the ball must be kicked from that

position. Players of the defending team must not approach within 10 yds. (9·15 m.) of the ball until it is in play, that is to say until it has been kicked and travelled the distance of its own circumference. As with free kicks generally, the ball may not be touched again by the kicker until it has been touched or played by another player. A goal may be scored direct from a corner kick.

An attacking side can lose possession of the ball, and thus lose the attacking initiative which then passes to their opponents, by misplacing a pass that is intercepted by an opposing player, by being beaten in a tackle, or by playing the ball last before it passed out of play. Accepting that a shot or header at goal saved by the opposing goalkeeper falls into the same category as that of a misplaced pass, there remains one other circumstance in which an attack breaks down. This is when a player is deemed to be 'out of play', as it was first defined in the rules. Later 'out of play' became 'offside' and the rule of the game affecting this point has ever been among the most discussed of the relatively few laws. As defined today, the law reads: 'A player is offside if he is nearer his opponents' goal line than the ball *at the moment the ball is played unless*: (*a*) he is in his own half of the field of play; (*b*) there are two of his opponents nearer to their own goal line than he is; (*c*) the ball last touched an opponent or was last played by him; (*d*) he receives the ball direct from a goal kick, a corner kick, a throw-in, or when it was dropped by the referee.' The penalty for such an infringement is the award of an indirect free kick to the opposing team and there is an addition to the law noting that: 'A player in an offside position shall not be penalized unless, in the opinion of the referee, he is interfering with the play or with an opponent, or is seeking to gain an advantage by being in an offside position.'

When a goal is scored, the game is re-started by a player of the team conceding the goal kicking-off in the same way as when the match itself was started. Similarly, when the game is re-started after half-time, that is to say after 45 minutes of a match that, unless mutually agreed otherwise, has a duration of two periods of that time, the teams change ends and the kick-off is taken by a player of the opposite team to that which started the game. At the end of the match the team scoring the greater number of goals is the winner; if no goals, or an equal number of goals is scored by both sides, the game is termed a draw.

At basic level the only equipment needed for a game of football is a ball, that is to say, anything spherical or nearly so. The goals can be, and indeed have been and still are, anything from chalk marks on a wall, piles of coats, the width of a street, or the respective ends of a town or village square. The dress of the players in such games is optional. The equipment worn by a player under Football Association (F.A.) rules usually consists of a jersey or shirt; shorts; stockings; and boots. The laws of the game are concerned only that: 'A player shall not wear anything which is dangerous to another player'; and, although that general wording gives the referee authority to send a player off the field for adjustment to his equipment if he is wearing anything — for example, a ring or plaster bandage — that might be dangerous, in practice it mainly applies to footwear.

This remained little changed from the 1880s to the early 1950s, when the postwar increase in international and inter-club football matches, and a grudging acceptance that the greater mobility and agility shown by South American footballers in particular was partly made possible by the lighter boots they wore, started a general fashion for lighter, more flexible equipment. The change was accelerated by the introduction of new, synthetic materials with boots or perhaps more correctly, shoes, being made of plastic with plastic studs that can be screwed into the soles — and can easily be changed to suit ground conditions. The law relating to the standard to which bars and studs must conform has had to be often amended to take account of manufacturing changes, but the intention has been constant — that of outlawing the wearing of anything dangerous to other players. The law itself does not insist that football boots must be worn but the International Football Association Board's opinion is that 'in competition matches, referees should not allow one or a few players to play without wearing football boots, when all the other players do wear them'.

Originally there was no requirement that the goalkeeper should wear anything distinctive from the jerseys worn by the other players in his team. It was the Football League at its annual meeting in June 1909 which decided that, to assist the referee, goalkeepers must play in distinctive colours of scarlet, royal blue, or white (green was added three years later), and the sensible practice soon became generally adopted. It remains, however, a matter for various league committees, and the organizing committees of other football competitions, what regulations are agreed about the colours of shirts worn by competing teams. Generally, clubs are required to notify their normal colours and their second choice so that when a visiting club is due to play against a club whose colours are the same or very similar, the obligation is with it to wear its second choice of colours. The respective goalkeepers may wear the same coloured jersey but that colour must be distinct from the colours of the outfield players of both sides.

By the early 1970s the increased pace of most games of football had encouraged clubs to seek the 'strip' that gave their players the maximum freedom of movement with brief shorts, lightweight shirts (except in very cold weather), and thin stockings.

Football, as it is now played throughout the world in accordance with the laws of the game authorized by the International Football Association Board, began in England in the mid-nineteenth century, but there is evidence that a form of football was played centuries before the birth of Christ. In China, for example, a game called *Tsu chu* was played 2,500 years ago. *Tsu* may be translated as 'to kick the ball with feet' and *chu* as 'a ball made of leather, and stuffed'. In Sinj on the Dalmatian coast of Yugoslavia there is a Roman stele dating from the second century A.D. that depicts a young man holding a ball made of hexagonal sections, as are many footballs now used on the Continent. According to Yugoslavian archaeologists, the ball was probably made of leather and from this and other Roman monuments in Dalmatia it is certain that ball games, including a form of football, were popularly played during the Roman epoch.

The Greeks had a word for the game — *episkyros* — and, although it seems they used a very large ball, they and the Romans when they played *harpastum* and the Chinese, when they played *Tsu chu*, agreed that football was a competition between two teams.

England. There are records of football being played in England in the twelfth century in the fields that surrounded the City of London but it was when the players were forced to use the streets as their pitches that kingly disapproval was shown in 1314 by Edward II proclaiming: Forasmuch as there is a great noise in the city caused by hustling over large balls, from which many evils may arise, which God forbid, we command and forbid, on behalf of the King, on pain of imprisonment, such game to be used in the city in future.'

Neither that ban, nor similar edicts of Edward III (1349), Richard II (1389), Henry IV (1401), and the Scottish statutes of 1457 and 1491, stopped the playing of football; but Richard II's act was revealing in that it also decreed that archery should be encouraged as an alternative. He was less concerned with the noise and 'the many evils' than with the disinclination of his subjects to practise archery, a sport with potential military value.

Football in Tudor England (1485-1603) was

a brutal game played without rules except unwritten ones of local custom, and not only authority frowned on it. In the sixteenth century, Stubbes, in his *Anatomie of Abuses*, wrote that football caused 'fighting, brawling, contention, quarrel picking, murder, homicide, and great effusion of blood, as daily experience teacheth'. Royal displeasure was somewhat assuaged over the years, perhaps because of the obvious ineffectiveness of the edicts, perhaps because of the lessening importance of archery in warfare. In 1615 James I may have been the first monarch to attend a football match, played in Wiltshire. Charles II approved of the game and watched a match between a team of the Royal Household and a team of the Duke of Albemarle's servants in 1681.

The inclination to kick at a round object was as strong and natural in England during the eighteenth century as it had been in China 200 years B.C., in Roman-occupied Dalmatia in the second century, or in fourteenth-century England, but the opportunities to play football were becoming increasingly limited to 'mob' games on Shrove Tuesday when perhaps 500 a side started play in the market-place at midday and continued until sunset. A vast social and economic revolution enveloped England throughout the greater part of the late eighteenth and the nineteenth centuries. Agriculture ceased to be the most important item in the English economy as new uses were discovered for coal and iron and, in particular, the textile industries were developed. The change from an agricultural to an industrial nation and the growth of the railway system combined to bring about in a period of a hundred years a vast movement of the population. Before the Industrial Revolution the bulk of the country's population was in the southern half, principally around London and the Thames valley, and Bristol and the Severn valley. After it, although a handful of large towns — London, Bristol, Southampton, Portsmouth, and Plymouth — remained in the south the population was most dense in the textile areas of Lancashire and part of Yorkshire, in the Black Country of the Midlands, and in the coal and shipbuilding areas of the north-east coast and South Wales. This movement of population was to be a major factor in the subsequent development of football in England but, at the time, forms of football were being played regularly only in the public schools.

The majority of the football-playing public schools were in the south — Winchester, Charterhouse, and Eton being among the most prominent. They all played football but the game varied according to the tradition and custom of the school. House matches became a feature at most schools (wherein lay the idea that became the Football Association Challenge Cup) but matches between teams from different schools were infrequent since difficulties obviously arose from teams playing to varying rules. Thus, one school permitted limited handling of the ball while another did not. It was these differences in the rules and traditions that made difficult the continuation of football-playing by boys going up as young men to the Universities at Oxford and Cambridge. They found themselves limited to matches arranged between two sides from old boys of the same school. Not surprisingly, HOCKEY was then the most popular winter sport at the Universities.

Clearly, if organized football was to be played seriously, the solution was to find acceptable common rules. At Cambridge, as early as 1846, an attempt was made by two old Salopians, de Winton and Thring, who persuaded some old Etonians to join them in forming a football club. Two years later a more positive step was taken when representatives of most of the public schools met and agreed upon a common code called the Cambridge Rules. Matches under these rules were played for many years at Cambridge and those who played were later to popularize the rules further as they joined and formed clubs after leaving the University. The immediate effect, however, was slight and had little impact in the country as a whole.

In 1862, Thring drew up the following ten rules for what he aptly described as the 'Simplest Game':

(1) A goal is scored whenever the ball is forced through the goal and under the bar, except it be thrown by the hand.
(2) Hands may be used only to stop a ball and place it on the ground before the feet.
(3) Kicks must be aimed only at the ball.
(4) A player may not kick the ball whilst in the air.
(5) No tripping-up or heel-kicking allowed.
(6) Whenever a ball is kicked beyond the side flags, it must be returned by the player who kicked it, from the spot it passed the flag line in a straight line towards the middle of the ground.
(7) When a ball is kicked behind the line of goal, it shall be kicked off from that line by one of the side whose goal it is.
(8) No player may stand within six paces of the kicker when he is kicking-off.
(9) A player is out of play immediately he is in front of the ball, and must return behind the ball as soon as possible. If the ball is kicked by his own side past a player, he may not touch it, or advance, until one of the other side has first kicked it, or one of his own side, having followed it up, has been able, when in front of him, to kick it.
(10) No charging is allowed when a player is out of play — i.e. immediately the ball is behind him.

Only a year after Thring presented his ten rules, two meetings, independent of each other, were convened in October 1863. A set of rules came out of each of these meetings, both sets longer and more explicit than Thring's. In many essentials, however, Thring's rules have remained valid. Five of them (Nos. 1, 3, 5, 7, and 10) have remained applicable over more than a hundred years of organized football; No. 4, in itself an indication perhaps of the danger of trying to be too simple in framing a rule, never appeared in subsequent rules drawn up by either Cambridge University or the Football Association (whose first version allowed a player to *catch* the ball), but kicking at the ball in the air in circumstances that could cause injury to an opponent is forbidden as 'playing in a dangerous manner'; No. 8 remains applicable save only that the distance is defined as ten yards rather than Thring's six paces; No. 9 contains the elements of the off-side law; No. 6 shows two interesting changes of emphasis in that the F.A.'s first laws preferred that the ball should be thrown in from touch and not kicked, and that originally both Thring and the F.A. gave the kick or the throw to the player who had put the ball into touch; No. 2 is the only one of Thring's rules wholly inappropriate to the modern game of football. In its way, however, in 1862 it put greater emphasis upon footing the ball and not handling it than did the Football Association when it was formed and agreed a set of rules one year later.

Early in October 1863, players at Cambridge again took the lead in drafting better regulations and appointed a committee under the chairmanship of the Revd. H. Burn, an old boy of Shrewsbury School. Other schools represented on the committee were Eton, Harrow, Rugby, Marlborough, and Westminster. This committee produced a revised set of the Cambridge University Football Rules — 14 of them, beginning with their definition of the size of a pitch and ending with '*All* charging is fair; but holding, pushing with the hands, tripping-up, and shinning are forbidden.'

These Cambridge rules had gone some way towards reconciling many of the diverse codes of play, at least so far as the University, old boys', Army, and Civil Service clubs were concerned. Elsewhere, particularly in Sheffield, where the first football club had been founded in 1855, matches were being played to local rules with not even an awareness of the Cambridge and London moves towards uniformity.

The London meeting was held late in October 1863 in the Freemasons' Tavern, Great Queen Street, and was attended by delegates representing the following clubs:

Crystal Palace, Blackheath, Percival House and Blackheath School, Kensington Grammar School, Barnes, Charterhouse, Blackheath Proprietary School, Forest (Epping Forest), No Names (Kilburn), and Crusaders. Also present were others who played the game and were interested in the attempt to agree a uniform set of rules, but were not formally representing any club. At the meeting a resolution was carried that the clubs should form themselves into an Association to be called 'The Football Association'.

It is noticeable that the clubs represented were all from London and the home counties. This is not surprising — it was scarcely to be expected that clubs elsewhere would have known about the meeting or been prepared to come to London had they done so, but what was surprising, and disappointing, was that only one public school was represented, and that one, Charterhouse, abstained when the meeting came to the point of enrolling clubs at the annual subscription of one guinea. Correspondence from Morley, the appointed hon. sec., failed to gain a response in the schools but there were encouraging approaches from outside clubs, and by the fourth meeting on 24 November draft rules had been prepared. At the same time the secretary drew the members' attention to the Cambridge Rules and suggested they should also be considered. There is an element of confusion about what happened next but, although the voting on an amendment as announced by the president and recorded in the minutes was subsequently challenged, the effective course of business was that Alcock proposed 'that the Cambridge Rules appear to be the most desirable for the Association to adopt'; Morley, the secretary, moved an amendment 'that the rules of the Cambridge University embrace the true principles of the game with greatest simplicity, and therefore, that a committee be appointed to enter into communication with the Committee of the University, to endeavour to induce them to modify some of the rules which appear to the Association to be too lax and liable to give rise to disputes'; F. W. Campbell of Blackheath moved a further amendment that merely noted that the Cambridge Rules were 'worthy of consideration' — without suggesting any actual consideration of them.

There were two important points of difference between the Cambridge Rules and those proposed by the Association. Law IX as proposed by the Association allowed a player 'to run with the ball towards his adversaries' goal if he makes a fair catch, or catches the ball on the first bound'; Law X allowed an opponent 'to charge, hold, trip, or hack' any player running with the ball. The Cambridge Rules, on the other hand, made no mention of running with the ball, and though charging was allowed, holding, pushing with the hands, tripping-up, and shinning were forbidden. Thus Alcock's proposal was for rules that excluded running with the ball and hacking an opponent; Campbell's amendment was to include them; the secretary's amendment was designed to permit further consideration and his was the amendment that the meeting carried.

The fifth meeting was held a week later — on 1 December. There had been considerable discussion within clubs about the proposed rules during the previous week. Campbell challenged the minutes of the previous meeting by contending that the votes cast for both Morley's and his own amendment had failed to show a majority of the 19 members present, a circumstance which, in respect of Morley's amendment, the president suggested, was due to the fact that not everybody present voted, either for or against the amendment. Campbell persisted but his proposal that the resolutions of Alcock and Morley be expunged was defeated. The minutes were accordingly signed with a protest registered by Campbell on behalf of the Blackheath club.

The secretary went on to deal with matters of correspondence that included a long communication from the strong Sheffield Football Club in which their secretary, Chesterman, in addition to enclosing the club's subscription for enrolment, put forward their point of view that the Association's proposed rules permitting running with the ball and hacking were directly opposed to *football* and were more suggestive of wrestling.

It was sentiments such as Sheffield's that influenced Alcock and Morley to move that the rules allowing hacking and running should be expunged. The secretary made it plain that although he had little personal objection, 'if we carry those two rules it will be seriously detrimental to the great majority of the football clubs'. He suggested that Blackheath's fondness for hacking already made it difficult for them to arrange matches with other clubs and concluded: 'If we have "hacking", no one who has arrived at the years of discretion will play at football, and it will be entirely relinquished to schoolboys.' Predictably, Campbell immediately rose to oppose, fearing that the alteration proposed would do 'away with the skill shown in the game at Harrow and Eton, and the pluck so necessary in the game as played at Rugby'.

Despite Blackheath's opposition, the motion expunging the running and hacking laws was carried, and at the next meeting it was agreed that Lillywhite should print and publish the rules and laws of the game as now settled by the Association. The first committee, with Campbell of Blackheath as treasurer, was appointed, and arrangements made for a friendly game to be played by members using the new rules on some public ground on Saturday, 2 January, 1864. The meeting was about to end when Campbell announced that while his club entirely approved of the objects of the Association, it was their view that the adopted laws destroyed the game and took away all interest in it. Blackheath therefore wished to be withdrawn from membership. Efforts were made to persuade Blackheath to wait until the new rules had been tried for a year but these failed and subsequently Blackheath were prominent among the clubs who, in 1871, formed the Rugby Union. Ironically, when there was again contention over hacking, it was Blackheath who led the opposition to it and finally had it expunged from the Rugby laws.

Although from the beginning of 1864 the F.A.'s laws of the game became increasingly known and studied, it was scarcely to be expected that they would be immediately adopted by every club, either those in the London area or, particularly, those that were springing up in the provinces. The area of greatest growth outside London was Sheffield where the Sheffield club had been among the first of the provincials to seek membership of the Football Association. Several other clubs were formed in the area until, in 1867, there were sufficient for Sheffield to form its own Football Association. It was the forerunner of the county F.A.s that were later to become an integral part of the organization in England. Sheffield rules had variations from those of the F.A., but nevertheless two matches were played in 1866 between teams representing Sheffield and London.

The success of these first representative matches encouraged the Football Association to plan further games between county sides. In September 1867 they advised the press that: 'After four years' discussion and mature consideration the Rules of The Football Association have been reduced to a form which it is generally admitted will leave little to be amended or altered. A strong desire has been expressed by many of the principal players in and around London that the Rules should be tested in a county match Middlesex *v.* Kent and Surrey and the game will be played on Saturday, 2 November, 1867, at Beaufort House.'

That match took place, was judged a success, and others followed but still these, and most of the effective influence of the Football Association, were limited to the southern counties. Something more was needed to capture the imagination of clubs throughout England and, for that matter, Scotland, Wales, and Ireland. It is most unlikely that Alcock, the newly-elected hon. sec. of the F.A., anticipated quite what the effect would be on the popularity of football when he suggested that the clubs be invited·to subscribe towards purchasing (at a cost of some £20) a cup to be competed for by all clubs belonging to the Football Association.

A meeting in July 1871 gave the committee authority to make some preliminary enquiries and on 16 October it was decided: 'That a Challenge Cup be established open to all clubs belonging to the Football Association.' Represented at that meeting were the following clubs: Royal Engineers, Barnes, Wanderers (formerly the Forest club), Harrow Chequers, Clapham Rovers, Hampstead Heathens, Civil Service, Crystal Palace, Upton Park, Windsor House Park, and Lausanne. All except the last two entered for the competition as did Hitchin, Maidenhead, Marlow, Donington School, Reigate Priory, and QUEEN'S PARK, Glasgow — the last the same amateur club that still graces the senior Scottish football scene and which, although its income for the year amounted to only £6, sent a guinea towards the cost of purchasing the trophy for the competition.

All the entrants, with the exceptions of Donington School (from near Spalding in Lincolnshire) and Queen's Park, were based in or near London and special consideration was given to the Scottish club in view of the distance involved. After a bye in the first round, Queen's Park were drawn against Donington School in the second, but the school scratched. Meanwhile, Clapham Rovers, Maidenhead, and Barnes by virtue of wins over Upton Park, Marlow, and Civil Service respectively had reached the second round of the first competition for the F.A. Cup; Wanderers and Royal Engineers had done so because their due opponents, Harrow Chequers and Reigate Priory, had scratched; and Crystal Palace and Hitchin were permitted to play in the second round because they had drawn their first round match and a rule of the competition at the time allowed that 'in the case of a drawn match the Clubs shall be drawn in the next ties or shall compete again, at the discretion of the Committee'.

Wanderers, Crystal Palace, Royal Engineers, and Hampstead Heathens (who had a bye in the first round) won their second round matches to join Queen's Park in the third. Those five remaining clubs were neatly whittled down to four semi-finalists, Queen's Park being afforded another bye, Wanderers and Crystal Palace drawing their match, and

both being allowed to go forward, and Royal Engineers beating Hampstead Heathens. The R.E.s were thus the only semi-finalist to have won a third round tie. Wanderers and Queen's Park drew their match but then the Scottish club, faced with the journey to the OVAL for a replay, scratched. Royal Engineers beat Crystal Palace, and on 16 March 1872 a crowd of some 2,000 people at Kennington Oval saw Wanderers beat the Royal Engineers 1-0 to become the first winners of a Football Association Cup competition. Within six years the number of entries for the competition had grown to 43 and although London and southern clubs still predominated, new names were beginning to appear.

The success of the competition was an incentive to clubs to seek membership of the Football Association either directly or through county Associations. In Turton, situated between Blackburn and Bolton, the village schoolmaster and the son of the lord of the manor organized scratch matches under Harrow rules for many years before deciding in 1872 actually to form a football club in the village. In 1874 Turton decided to embrace the 'London rules' and under the influence of their village team, new clubs sprang up in Blackburn, Bolton, Darwen, and other places until the Lancashire F.A. was formed in 1878. The Berkshire and Buckinghamshire and the Cheshire County Football Associations were formed in the same year. Birmingham in 1875, Staffordshire, Sheffield New (later renamed Hallam and later again amalgamated with the Sheffield Association), and Surrey in 1877, had all followed the Sheffield Association of 1867. Northumberland and Durham came into being a year after Lancashire and almost every year saw further county and district Associations being formed. Not all of them immediately allied themselves with the Football Association but steadily the authority of the F.A. grew, probably the most significant recognition coming in 1877 when the oldest of the county or district Associations, Sheffield, agreed to bring their own laws of play in line. By the end of the 1870s only one Association, that of Scotland, was at variance with the Football Association over points of law.

The newer county and district Associations started their own Challenge Cup competitions — the Birmingham District and County Association in 1877, the Staffordshire Association in 1878 (when Stoke were the first winners), and the Lancashire Association in 1879. Their better clubs tested their strength in these regional competitions but the target was the F.A. Cup. Familiar midland and northern club names appeared among the entrants. In

1879-80 came ASTON VILLA, Nottingham Forest, and BLACKBURN ROVERS, with Forest for the second successive season reaching the semi-final. A year later a club from further north reached the semi-final — Darwen, the first from Lancashire to progress so far in the competition. In the fourth round Darwen had beaten Sheffield Wednesday whose turn it was to reach the semi-final the following season. More, they were drawn against Blackburn Rovers and so, in 1881-2, for the first time a northern club was certain to reach the F.A. Cup final. It was Blackburn Rovers who beat Sheffield Wednesday 5-1 in a replay after a goalless first match.

Blackburn Rovers failed against Old Etonians in the final of 1882 but a second Blackburn club, the Olympics, revenged them a year later. Two old boys' clubs and two from the north — Blackburn Olympics and NOTTS COUNTY — had reached the semi-finals. Olympics disposed of Old Carthusians 4-0 while Notts County were beaten by Old Etonians who thus, for the second final in succession, faced opposition from Blackburn. This time the Lancashire club won and a year later every semi-finalist came from outside London and the south — the two Blackburn clubs, Notts County again, and, sole survivor of the 'old guard', Queen's Park. Blackburn Rovers won the final, beating Queen's Park by 2-1.

Increasing attendances at the F.A. Cup finals indicated the rapid growth of popularity of the game. Until 1892, by which time the Surrey County Cricket Club (see CRICKET) became perturbed about the damage that large crowds might do to the pitch, the finals continued to be played at the Oval with the attendances growing from 16,000 to 25,000. In 1893 the final was played at Fallowfield (Manchester) where 45,000 spectators watched the game between WOLVERHAMPTON and EVERTON. The following year Bolton and Notts County took the field at Everton before 37,000. The London-based Football Association feeling that, for all the northern domination, the F.A. Cup was their national competition, decided that the finals should be staged in London and from 1895 until the First World War the venue was Crystal Palace with 42,500 spectators watching the first final staged there and 65,891 the final of 1897. In 1901 — in contrast to the crowd of nearly 2,000 that watched the first final at the Oval in 1872 — 110,820 spectators packed the Crystal Palace ground. The majority of that attendance had probably come hoping to see a London club, TOTTENHAM HOTSPUR, beat their Yorkshire opponents, Sheffield United, and to end the northern domination of the competition. Football had over the previous quarter of a century

become something more than a game played for 90 minutes by two teams of 11 players.

The most significant change in the entries for the F.A. Cup competition between, say, 1872 and 1882 was not that their number increased from the original 15 (of whom only 11 actually played a match) to 73, but that the *class* of the competing clubs was different. Originally the clubs were all of middle- or upper-class origin but as the game grew rapidly in popularity, and as greater opportunities for leisure time were gained for the working class in the industrial areas of the midlands and the north of England, more clubs with a working-class basis were formed and the best of them soon entered the F.A. Cup competition. When Blackburn Olympic visited Kennington Oval in 1883 and beat the Old Etonians in the Cup final, they included in their team several working lads: spinners and weavers from the cotton trade of Lancashire, a picture-framer, a moulder's mate, a dentist's assistant; their captain, Warburton, was a master-plumber, and at least two players appeared to follow no occupation except that of playing football.

The issue of professionalism was brought into the open the following year when first Accrington, after they had beaten Park Road, and then PRESTON NORTH END, after they had beaten Upton Park, were excluded from the competition on the grounds that they had professional players. Upton Park made their protest to the F.A. and Maj. Sudell, who was trying to make Preston a club to emulate their neighbours, Blackburn Rovers, admitted that his players were paid but went on to assert that paying players was common practice with northern and midland clubs. The issue could no longer be ignored. It could have resulted in a division within Association football, similar to that which later divided RUGBY UNION and RUGBY LEAGUE football, but fortunately there were a majority on the F.A. Council who remained constant to their original intention of regulating a universal game. The campaign to legalize professionalism had to be patiently and diplomatically managed through the machinery of the F.A. but when the 1885-6 season began the professional need no longer hide the fact that he was getting paid. There was, however, some division, with the London F.A. and other southern county F.A.s refusing for many years to admit professional clubs to their membership, while the competition between the professional clubs in the north and the midlands led to a steady improvement in the standards of play, shown by their domination in the F.A. Cup competition. Yet the same professionalism caused these clubs increasing concern about their financial situation. There was no tidy fixture list at the time when the F.A. officially accepted professionalism. Friendly matches, local and county cup-ties, county representative matches, and F.A. Cup-ties were arranged haphazardly. Sometimes fixtures clashed, sometimes opponents failed to materialize.

The time was ripe for McGregor, of the Aston Villa (Birmingham) club, to formulate the idea of regular competitive matches — a suggestion which had been made by others before him but not acted upon. The result was the formation in March 1888 of the Football League. It grew out of professionalism, and the League system and the growth of professional clubs have gone hand-in-hand ever since. As originally proposed and formed, the Football League was intended to be a *national* league, but it was many years before this intention was fulfilled. Twelve clubs competed in the first season, 1888-9. Six clubs were from Lancashire — Preston North End, who were the first champions; Blackburn Rovers; Bolton Wanderers; Everton; and Burnley; three from Staffordshire — Wolverhampton Wanderers, West Bromwich Albion, and STOKE CITY — and one each from Derbyshire (Derby County), Nottinghamshire (Notts County), and Warwickshire (Aston Villa). Stoke dropped out after two seasons and SUNDERLAND, who replaced them, were the first north-eastern club to play in the Football League. A year later Stoke returned and Darwen, yet another Lancashire club, were admitted to make the strength of the Football League up to 14 for its fourth season.

One of the original proposals was that there should be 'two classes of League club — First and Second', and the Second Division duly appeared in 1892-3. The full strength of the Football League was now 28, with 16 clubs playing in the First Division and 12 in the Second. Clubs in London and the south were still either unwilling or of insufficient standing to be admitted, and geographically, the 28 clubs were distributed as Lancashire 10; Staffordshire 6; Warwickshire, Yorkshire, Lincolnshire, Nottinghamshire, Cheshire 2 apiece; and Derby and Durham 1 each.

Even before the Football League started its Second Division, McGregor and his associates had plenty of evidence of the success of the system. Other Leagues were formed (the Irish in 1890 and the Scottish in 1891) or their formation actively discussed; while the results of Football League matches and the activities of clubs were discussed far beyond the towns of the north and the midlands.

London and the south were ready for League football. Unfortunately the leadership and control of the London F.A. was in the hands of those who had failed in efforts to persuade the F.A. to 'outlaw' professional players and clubs. Within the London area they remained determined to prevent their own clubs being outclassed by the professionals by keeping London 'clean', a citadel of out-and-out amateurism. Other county Associations in the south were less prejudiced. Hampshire, for example, never made any distinction between paid and unpaid players except when forced to by the regulations governing competitions over which they had no direct control. The London F.A.'s attitude did none the less considerably influence the feeling in the south that, however delightful it was to follow from afar the progress of the professional clubs, there was something undignified about professionalism.

In spite of the lack of leadership from the London F.A., eager enthusiasts did form clubs and leagues while the London F.A. reserved their own efforts for organizing their senior and junior cup competitions and, increasingly, their Charity Cup for which a separate committee was appointed and for which the London F.A. specifically invited clubs to compete each year. One of the first Leagues in the London area was Woolwich, formed in 1891 — the same year in which the Royal Arsenal club, frustrated by the lack of progress of the game in London, turned professional (see ARSENAL) and thus cast themselves off from the London F.A.

More local Leagues followed and slowly their representatives gained seats on the Council of the London F.A. whose meetings were said often to have been as vigorous and heated as those of any borough council on which rival political parties were evenly numbered. It was not until 1906 that the London F.A. at long last came into line with the F.A. itself, and with every other county and district F.A., and agreed to admit the paid player, although, even when professionalism had been accepted by a two-thirds majority vote, the die-hards refused to accept the change. The Middlesex and Surrey members, representing still predominantly old boys' clubs, withdrew and subsequently formed first the Amateur Football Defence Federation and later the Amateur Football Association (A.F.A.) as a rival body to the F.A. that, in 1885, had declared itself ready to cater for all clubs whether amateur, professional, or neither wholly one nor the other. From 1907 until 1914 the clubs who followed the A.F.A. lingered in a football wilderness.

Since the original clubs in membership of the Football League were from Lancashire and the midlands, and the immediate newcomers were from those areas, Yorkshire, Lincolnshire, and the north-east, it was logical that, with the spread of professionalism to the south of England, a League should be formed for that area. In the season 1894-5 the Southern League began with two divisions; and for nearly a quarter of a century it was the most important professional League apart from the Football League and the Scottish League. Its clubs increased in power; Tottenham Hotspur won the F.A. Cup in 1901 and Southampton reached the final in 1900 and 1902. At the end of the season 1919-20 all 22 clubs in the First Division of the Southern League were elected to the Football League. The Southern League itself declined in power between the two wars. Since 1946, however, it has steadily increased in size: member clubs range from East Anglia, Warwickshire, Herefordshire into east Wales and all areas south of that line.

What the twenty years of refusal to comply with the development of football had not done in London and the south was to prevent the introduction of professionalism. Clubs, beginning with Royal Arsenal in 1891, had turned professional and resigned from, or been expelled by, the London F.A. They had gone their own way and the 1906 decision meant little or nothing to them. The delay in allowing the game to develop meant, however, that for most of these clubs the door of the Football League was closed and it remained so until 1920.

Royal Arsenal became the first southern club to play in the Football League in the season 1893-4. Luton Town were elected to the Second Division of the Football League four seasons later but only stayed in the League for three seasons; Bristol City made their entry into the Second Division in 1901-2; and CHELSEA and Clapton Orient in 1905. Before they were admitted to the Football League, the Royal Arsenal had taken the initiative in calling a meeting of representatives of southern clubs in the opinion that some effort should be made to improve the game in the south of England so that clubs might approach the standard of efficiency attained by many of those in the northern and midland counties. The Royal Arsenal club felt that this could 'be done by the strongest clubs in the south forming themselves into a combination or league'. Several meetings were held to discuss the proposed new League but before it was formed the Royal Arsenal was admitted into the Football League. The idea remained live, however, and the Southern League started in the season 1894-5. It remained for a quarter of a century not only, as it is still today, the principal professional league outside of the Football League in England, but nearly an equal partner with the senior

League. McGregor, writing in 1905 about the origin and the future of the Football League, commented upon the fact that it was not yet a truly national body, and added a qualification in respect of the Southern League: 'While it [the Football League] does not include Southampton, PORTSMOUTH, and Tottenham Hotspur, it cannot be said to be truly representative. Whether the League will grow at the expense of the Southern League, I do not for a moment pretend to say. I would not willingly see the Southern League lessened in influence by reason of the growth of the League. But I should say the tendency is in the direction of a national League, but this is more likely to come by evolution than revolution.'

McGregor's foresight was as accurate as any hindsight could be. The Southern League enjoyed many great years in the first phase of its existence before the evolutionary changes took place; years that saw the formation, growth, and maturing of almost every one of today's leading professional clubs in London and the south. Royal Arsenal (Woolwich Arsenal as they became known in 1896 and simply Arsenal in 1913) are the notable exception.

The Football League, as McGregor had foreseen, became a truly national league by evolution when, on the resumption of regular competitive fixtures after the First World War, an approach was made on the suggestion of the then president of the Football League, Sutcliffe, to leading members of the Southern League for them to form a Third Division of the Football League. In the season 1920-1, after Cardiff City had been elected to the Second Division of the Football League, the remaining 21 clubs of the previous season's Southern League First Division joined Grimsby Town, relegated from the Second Division of the Football League, to make up the Football League's Third Division (South). In fact for that one season there was no Third Division (North), but even without that partner on the lowest rung of the ladder, it was obvious that the southerners were the junior members. Despite occasional periods of ascendancy by clubs like Arsenal, Portsmouth, Tottenham, and Chelsea, the northern and midland clubs have maintained their initial advantages in the Football League competition.

It was the clubs themselves who, both in the north and midlands in the 1880s and in the south a decade later, formed the Football and Southern Leagues — the first to meet the economic needs of already-formed professional clubs, the second to raise the standard of football that, in itself, led to an acceptance of professionalism. The Football League, already a powerful force in football in England before its growth in 1920, exists for the benefit of the professional clubs who are its members. Its role has thus always been different from that of the Football Association who had formed their Cup competition with the intention of increasing interest in the game itself.

The magic has remained with the F.A. Cup competition but the strength of football, and not only of the professional game, is the regular week-by-week programme of League matches. At the same time, because of the historic reasons for their formation, the Football Association and the Football League in England have remained separate bodies with separate spheres of interest and, inevitably, some occasional conflict of interest. Countries coming later to football have been able to streamline their organization with one national association controlling all aspects of the game.

The Football League has its headquarters at Lytham St. Annes, Lancashire, and employs a full-time staff of nearly 30 people. Each of the 44 First and Second Division clubs hold one share that entitles them to vote on all proposals. Clubs relegated from the Second to the Third Division at the end of the season pass their share at the annual general meeting to the clubs promoted from the Third Division in their places. All clubs in the Third and Fourth Divisions are associate members of the Football League and, by F.A. regulations, are allowed only 1 vote for every 11 clubs, i.e. a total of 4 votes for the present 48 associate members. The League is governed by a management committee of nine members, directors of clubs elected by the vote of the clubs. This committee deals with all matters affecting F.L. clubs during the year between the annual general meetings.

INTERNATIONAL FOOTBALL. Before the advent of professionalism, the formation of any county or district Football Association with the exception of that of Sheffield, or before the uniform set of rules was being used by all but a handful of clubs, the first international football match was played. On 1 November 1872, 22 young sportsmen strolled on to the field of the West of Scotland Cricket Club at Hamilton Crescent, Partick, to engage in a game of football.

Accounts of the attendance at that match vary. Arnott, who played for Scotland regularly between 1883 and 1894, once recalled how as a boy of ten he had walked nearly five miles to reach the ground, 'but after reaching our destination, found that there was no chance of getting inside the ground unless we paid at the gate. What few coppers we had among us were gone by this time; and how disappointed we felt, after such a weary walk, at the poor prospect of our getting a view of

the game. Just when we had given up all hope, we earnestly begged a cabman to accommodate us on the top of his cab, and it was from that perch that I witnessed the first encounter between the two nations. There would not be any more than 2,000 spectators present; but I well recollect the great excitement there was among them when the play was going on.' The result of the match was a goalless draw and almost a hundred years were to pass before, on 25 April 1970, another match between the two countries ended without a score.

When England and Scotland played their historic match at Partick, the Franco-Prussian War had just ended and France was still stunned from the catastrophes of the Battle of Sedan, the surrender of Paris to the Prussians, and the portents of the Commune. Europe generally was troubled with wars and rumours of war, revolutions, and rumblings of revolt while Britain began to enjoy the fruits of the Industrial Revolution. British engineers, businessmen, artisans, and seamen travelled to many parts of Europe and South America to sell, exploit, and deliver the products of British industry, and, incidentally, to teach their hosts how to play football. Thus it was the representatives of British firms who founded the first two football clubs in Vienna, and called them First Vienna F.C. (by which name the club is still known), and the Vienna Cricket and Football Club (from which, via the Wiener Amateur S.V., the present F.K. AUSTRIA descended).

Vienna was then the capital of the old Austrian Monarchy and the game soon gained adherents in Prague and Graz as well as in Vienna. In 1887, a year before Blackburn Rovers became founder-members of the Football League, a man named Charnock, working in his family's textile mill near Moscow, sent to England for footballs and 'shirts made up of blue-and-white hand-woven calico in the Blackburn Rovers colours, and white calico knickers'. The mill's team were prominent in popularizing football in the Moscow area despite fears by the Tsarist authorities that football clubs formed by those of 'low birth' would be used as revolutionary cells. A similar fear delayed the growth of the game in the Russian-controlled provinces of Poland, but elsewhere, in the areas under German and Austrian control, football became popular from the beginning of the twentieth century, Cracovia F.C. (1906) being one of the earliest Polish clubs. In the Russian-controlled provinces it was left to British engineers to form the first football club in Lodz. Political repressions retarded the development of the game in the turbulent area of the Balkans, but around 1895 the first football match played in Turkey took place at Izmir between teams of British residents and Greek students. British sailors had brought the game to Greece as they had to the ports of most mercantile nations.

In Sweden, British members of the Embassy staff and residents played both Rugby and Association football, and perhaps a mixture of both, in the Stockholm parks. The locals watched and tried to copy them but, possibly from some confusion between the two codes, the rules of play varied from one part of Sweden to another. In 1891 the Velocipede Ball Club of Malmö obtained a set of the English F.A.'s rules, and had it translated and circulated. As in England a quarter of a century earlier, the existence of a uniform set of rules hastened the increase in the popularity of the game and in 1896 the first Swedish championship was organized. Seven years earlier the first two national Football Associations outside Britain had been formed in Denmark, and in the Netherlands, where students, particularly those who had been to public schools in England, had played the game from as early as the 1870s. Belgium and Switzerland each formed Associations in 1895. Two years later the Swiss championship commenced and was won by a club still prominent in Swiss football, Grasshoppers. The club's name is an indication of the English influence found in club names throughout the world. In Austria and Italy, Vienna and Milan respectively retain the original anglicized version of the names of their cities; Switzerland have the Young Boys' club; Argentina have RIVER PLATE; Bolivia, Always Ready; Uruguay, Liverpool; and the Netherlands, Go Ahead and Be Quick.

The formation of national Football Associations was an essential preliminary to the control of national championships and the arranging of international matches. The England-Scotland matches continued annually from 1872; England first played Wales in 1879; and in 1882 Ireland entered the international arena with matches against England and Wales. In the same year Scotland and Wales met for the first time. When, in the following season, 1883-4, Scotland v. Ireland also became an annual fixture, the stage was set for the British international championship that, with the exceptions of the years covered by the two world wars, has been competed every season since then. Representative matches, mainly inter-city, steadily increased on the Continent from the late 1890s onwards, and on 12 October 1902 Austria beat Hungary 5-0 in Vienna in the first international match between non-British countries. In 1904 another pair of neighbouring countries met for their first international matches — Belgium and France drawing 3-3 in Brussels, and a year later France, in addition to again playing against Belgium, entertained Switzerland in Paris, while Belgium played home and away matches with the Netherlands. Three years later England sent their full international side to play matches against Austria, Hungary, and Bohemia in Vienna, Budapest, and Prague; but generally, in an age when to travel long distances was still an event, international matches were confined to neighbouring countries.

In Paris, on 21 May 1904, delegates from Belgium, Denmark, France, the Netherlands, Spain, Sweden, and Switzerland attended a meeting that decided to form the Fédération Internationale de Football Associations (F.I.F.A.), and a Frenchman, Guerin, became the first president. Guerin was in office for only two years before Woolfall took over until the end of the First World War. After the war, when F.I.F.A.'s activities grew in importance, another Frenchman, Rimet, became president and remained in that post until June 1954. The idea of organizing a world football championship had ever been in the minds of those who first campaigned for a world body such as F.I.F.A., when the first World Cup competition was organized to take place in 1930, it was called the Jules Rimet Cup.

There was, it seems in retrospect, an even greater element of unreality about the 1904 meeting than there had been about the meeting at the Freemasons' Tavern, in October 1863. Of the six countries represented at the Paris meeting, France had played their first full international match only twenty days before; Denmark were not to play their first until four years later in 1908 when the Olympics were held in London; Switzerland's first matches took place in that same year, while Spain did not commence her international matches until the OLYMPIC GAMES of 1920. Moreover, in the case of three of the countries, France, Spain, and Sweden, national Football Associations had still to be formed.

Conspicuous by their absence from the meeting at which F.I.F.A. was founded were representatives of the Football Association, and of the national Football Associations of Scotland, Ireland, and Wales. The F.A. had not been indifferent to the development of the game, for which they had drawn up the laws, outside England. In 1882 it was they who proposed that there should be a meeting between themselves and the national F.A.s of Ireland, Scotland, and Wales to agree over the laws of the game. The Scottish F.A. had been reluctant to participate in such a meeting because they preferred to retain their own version of the rules of play and because they feared any interference with their independence. The

F.A. thereupon threatened to discontinue the series of annual international matches between England and Scotland that had commenced ten years before. Eventually the Scottish F.A. agreed to attend the meeting which was held at Manchester on 6 December 1882. This resulted in agreement on a uniform set of laws and the establishment of the International Football Association Board as the only body with authority to make any alterations to the laws of the game. That authority remains, the only change being that the Board now consists of 20 members, 16 appointed by the 4 British Associations, each of whom nominates 4 members, and 4 members appointed by the Executive Committee of F.I.F.A. (Article 18 of the Regulations of F.I.F.A.).

For some years before the first F.I.F.A. meeting in 1904, continental associations had been in touch with the F.A. in London. Belgium, towards the end of the 1890s, suggested an agreement with the F.A. The Netherlands F.A. early in 1902 wrote proposing the founding of an international Association to promote football in Europe. The F.A. were evasive, passed the Dutch suggestion to the International Board, received it back for consideration by the national Associations of Scotland, Ireland, and Wales, but did advise the Netherlands F.A. that they would be convening a conference to be held shortly in England. When, however, one of the French Associations wrote in November 1903 also proposing the formation of a federation of the European Football Associations, the secretary of the F.A. replied directly that 'the Council of the Football Association cannot see the advantages of such a Federation'.

None the less, once the European Associations had formed F.I.F.A., the F.A. moved quickly and within ten days had appointed a special committee 'to consider the new continental aspect and the desirability of holding a Conference in London on the eve of the England v. Scotland international match the following year'. The conference, attended by the representatives of several continental Associations, was held in April 1905 and ended with the British Associations not joining F.I.F.A. but accepting its intentions and objects and offering co-operation. The F.A. were soon persuaded to adopt a more positive attitude as members became increasingly concerned at the way F.I.F.A. were interpreting some of the laws of the game and were defining amateurism. Accordingly, four F.A. representatives attended an international conference in Berne in June 1906 from which the effective growth of F.I.F.A. dates, and which opened the door for the entry of the British Associations.

The representatives' report back to the F.A. Council began by recalling that 'a Federation of various Nations was formed at Paris in 1904: the object being to develop and control international football', and went on to report how 'after a discussion lasting several hours, we find that as yet it is not a complete organization for governing Continental International football'. Credit was given to the Federation for the assistance it had already given in the development of the game throughout the Continent, 'but it has not had the opportunities of settling principles to control International play. International matches, inter-Association matches, and inter-club matches are all played on the Continent, but it appears to be the custom to call as many of the matches as possible "Internationals". Your representatives discussed with the other representatives the position they considered an International Federation should occupy, and all were of the opinion that the constitution of the Federation should be revised.'

At the conference, agreement was reached on a number of points that were to be used as the basis for framing articles for an amended constitution. These included: that 'The Laws of the Game as promulgated by the Football Association (England) should be strictly adhered to by all members of the Association'; that 'Each Association admitted to the Federation must be the actual National body controlling all Association football within that country'; and that 'International matches should only be those played between Representative Teams of National Associations selected by the National Associations concerned in the matches.'

The war of 1914-18 brought a halt to the progress of international football and to the work of F.I.F.A. but it had made considerable progress despite internal difficulties in some of the countries, such as France, that had been most active in its creation. The consideration of various Football Associations occupied a large part of F.I.F.A.'s conference time. In 1908 they refused an application for membership by the A.F.A. that had split from the F.A. The decision was entirely in line with the F.I.F.A. regulation that each Association must be the national body controlling all Association football within its country.

Football on an international scale was resumed after the First World War with an almost immediate disagreement between the British Associations and the organizational framework that was F.I.F.A. F.I.F.A. intended to pick up in 1919 their membership of 1914 — so far as the redrawn map of Europe allowed. England, in particular, had other ideas, and the F.A. were to the fore in arranging a conference in Brussels in December 1919, attended by delegates from the Associations of Belgium, England, France, Ireland, Scotland, Wales, and Luxemburg. The nations present reaffirmed that they were not prepared to entertain any relations with the former enemy countries of Austria, Germany, and Hungary. They went further in also resolving 'not to meet neutral Associations nor neutral clubs who had played against the Associations or the clubs of the Central Empires'. This firm attitude was in direct opposition to the decision of the Associations of Denmark, Finland, Norway, and Sweden who, in a conference held in Göteborg at the same time, affirmed their right to continue football relations with all other national Associations according to the rules of F.I.F.A. About the same time, the Italian F.A. stated that they were ready to resume relations with all countries, including those of the Central Powers. The Associations represented at the Brussels conference closed ranks by setting up a new organization called the Federation of National Football Associations, but it was not long before the F.A. had to accept that even Belgium and France had doubts about the wisdom of the boycott of the 'neutrals'. Belgium were particularly concerned since the 1920 Olympics were being held in Antwerp and there were hopes that the football tournament would be more keenly contested than had been the ones of 1908 and 1912.

The F.A. co-operated with the team, officially labelled Great Britain, that competed in the 1920 Olympic football tournament, but went ahead with their already declared intention of withdrawing from membership of F.I.F.A. The Scottish, Irish, and Welsh F.A.s did the same and later in the same year a proposal by the Irish F.A. to exclude the F.I.F.A. representation from the International Football Board was carried unanimously.

The British break from F.I.F.A. lasted only four years, of which the last two were concerned mainly with formalities. For some years to come England, Scotland, Ireland, and Wales maintained their boycott of the countries of the Central Powers but international matches against the neutral nations were resumed. F.I.F.A. itself had been no more than an organizational shell but soon it had to deal with the awkward situation that had arisen in Irish football as a consequence of the political partition of the north and south. Many clubs in southern Ireland had ceased their membership of the Irish F.A. and in June 1921 formed themselves into the Football Association of Ireland (F.A.I.). A number of republican-minded clubs in Ulster, particularly in Belfast, joined the F.A.I. Undismayed

at their non-recognition by the F.A., the Football Association of Ireland made application to F.I.F.A. and were admitted to membership in August 1923, when England, Scotland, Wales, and Ireland were not members. By this time, however, F.I.F.A. were anxious for British support in getting some momentum into the work of the Federation and invited the F.A. to take the initiative in seeking to resolve the Irish question. This was done for the time being (see below under *Republic of Ireland*), though it was not until 1954 that positive F.I.F.A. decisions finally clarified the position of the 'two' Irelands in respect of both nomenclature and the qualification of players for international matches.

The solution of the immediate problem of the two Irish Associations probably further impressed upon F.I.F.A. the need for British support and the international body sent an invitation to the United Kingdom Associations to rejoin the Federation. The invitation was discussed at a meeting of representatives of England, Scotland, Wales, and Ireland and a reply was sent by Wall, secretary of the F.A., indicating that British dissatisfaction with F.I.F.A. was not confined to the matter of membership of the countries of the Central Powers. The British Associations had not forgotten efforts made before the war to replace the International Football Board by F.I.F.A.; the attempt to treat the four separate national Associations as one for voting purposes; and what they felt to be a policy of making F.I.F.A. all-powerful in football affairs at the expense of the British Associations. The F.A. wrote on 19 October 1923:

We have long established Laws of the Game and Rules of the Associations which are suitable to our wishes and requirements. In some respects these do not appear to be suitable or acceptable to some other National Associations. We do not desire to interfere with the action of other Associations who may not agree with all our Rules, nor do we desire that they interfere with ours. We observe that the work of the Federation is to control and develop the sport as an International Game. Are we to assume that this control includes the control of the Laws of the Game and the individual Associations forming the Federations?

Two months later, on 21 December 1923, four representatives of F.I.F.A. attended a meeting in London with delegates of the four British Associations. The F.I.F.A. representatives were the president, Rimet; Seeldrayers, a Belgian, who was later to be briefly president of F.I.F.A. after Rimet's long term ended in June 1954; Delaunay; and the secretary, Hirschman. At times, during his long period in office as president of F.I.F.A., Rimet was to complain that he found it difficult to understand the attitude of one or the other, or all, of the British Football Associations, but there was little room for misunderstanding about the four conditions the United Kingdom bodies set out as prerequisites to their return to F.I.F.A. These were that, (1) the articles of the International Federation should not affect the inter-relations of the Football Associations of the United Kingdom; (2) the articles providing for a percentage of the receipts from international matches being paid to the International Feder-ation should not apply to matches played between the Football Associations of the United Kingdom; (3) the International Asso-ciation Football Board be asked to reinsert in its rules the rule giving representation to the International Federation, and providing that there shall not be any alteration in the laws of the game without the consent of at least four-fifths of the representatives present and voting at the International Board; (4) the Federation would not interfere with the rules of an Asso-ciation relating to its internal management.

The meeting reached agreement on the four conditions under which the British Associa-tions would rejoin the Federation, but not on a second major point on the agenda for the meeting — the definition of an amateur. It was not long before the issue, left unresolved at the London meeting, was to come to the fore in circumstances that caused a rift between the British Associations and F.I.F.A. that lasted for 20 important years in the history of the game. The F.A. had finally resolved its own searching arguments about legalizing profes-sionalism in football 40 years before the December 1923 meeting. Having themselves made honest men of professionals, the British Associations found little difficulty in present-ing F.I.F.A. with a positively worded defini-tion in the following terms:

Players are either amateur or professional. Any player registered with his National Association as a professional, or receiving remuneration or consider-ation of any sort above his necessary hotel and travelling expenses actually paid, shall be a profes-sional. Training expenses, other than the wages paid to a trainer or a coach, must be paid by the players themselves. A player competing for any money prize in a football contest shall be a professional.

The F.I.F.A. representatives, aware of the varying attitudes adopted by national associa-tions in their membership, were unable to accept the British definition. They were no more able to accept it at the Rome congress of F.I.F.A. in 1926 when they were faced by what amounted to an ultimatum from the INTERNATIONAL OLYMPIC COMMITTEE in respect of participation in the 1928 Amster-dam Olympic Games. A year before, at the Prague congress, there had been disagreement

with the Olympic Games Committee who had stated that it wished to control the football tournament at the Games. Thereupon the F.I.F.A. congress passed a resolution declar-ing that: 'it considers the F.I.F.A. as the highest authority on all football matters, and that it cannot accept the interference or gui-dance of anybody else in such matters.' The phrasing of the resolution proved unfortunate. Considered in isolation from the circum-stances, the resolution was a contradiction of the guarantees given by the F.I.F.A. represen-tatives at the December 1923 meeting in Lon-don, and it needed a conciliatory letter from Rimet to Clegg, president of the F.A., and further discussions at the 1926 Rome congress of F.I.F.A., before the British Associations, and in particular the F.A. who were the spokesmen for them in most matters affecting the International Board and F.I.F.A., were placated.

The resolution no doubt goaded the Interna-tional Olympic Committee to remind F.I.F.A. that a prerequisite for participation in the 1928 Amsterdam Olympic Games was that amateur-ism should be regarded in its narrowest terms. This brought F.I.F.A. back to the situation left unresolved in the December 1923 meeting with the British Associations. Nor at the Rome congress of 1926 was anything like agreement reached among the 22 national Associations represented. After considerable discussion and explanations of the practice in different coun-tries, the following resolution proposed by Switzerland was adopted by 12 votes to 8, with two national associations abstaining:

It is not allowed to pay compensation for 'broken time' except in some well-circumscribed cases, to be fixed by each National Association. However, full compensation for 'broken time' shall never be reimbursed, and it shall not be given in such a way that the player will be tempted to put sport before his work. The Regulations of National Associations concerning this matter shall be previously approved by the Executive Committee, who will take account in fixing the number of days for which compensa-tions may be given, with the idea mentioned here-above and the geographical conditions of each coun-try. The National Associations are at liberty to allow compensation for 'broken time' or not.

What happened next was surprising, and, eventually, harmful for the organizational development of football. The Olympic Games Committee who but a short time before had been clear in their intention of controlling football in the 1928 Olympic Games, when faced by the demand of F.I.F.A. that their members would only take part in the Games if payment for 'broken time' was officially recognized, gave way completely and reversed their earlier decision in favour of the more strict definition of amateurism. F.I.F.A. were satisfied but the British Associations were not. They withdrew from the Amsterdam Olympic Games and on 17 February 1928, at a conference of the United Kingdom Associations, resolved unanimously to withdraw from F.I.F.A. In the letter notifying F.I.F.A. of this decision, Wall, writing on behalf of the Associations of the United Kingdom, concluded by expressing the desire still 'to maintain friendly relations with the Federation and its affiliated Associations, and to co-operate with them on all suitable occasions'. Efforts were made at F.I.F.A.'s next executive committee meeting to reach a new agreement with the U.K. Associations but a majority, led by Hirschman, were opposed to this so that, ostensibly over the issue of 'broken time', the British Associations for the second time ceased membership of F.I.F.A. It was an exclusion that lasted until the Federation was revived in the season 1946-7.

During the period from 1928 until the outbreak of the Second World War the standard of play in British football failed to advance to the extent that it did in many countries in Europe and in South America, and the disassociation from F.I.F.A. was the main reason for what amounted to stagnation — the consequences of which were not appreciated until competitive international football was resumed after the war. At the same time, although there was a considerable growth in membership and the world championships were successfully inaugurated, F.I.F.A. suffered from contact with the British Associations that was limited to meetings of the International Association Board and to the exchange of opinions. F.I.F.A.'s main contribution to the development of football in the decade immediately before the outbreak of the Second World War was the establishment of the world championship, the greatest competition in the game.

From at least 1908 onwards there were countries entitled to claim the position of world football champions by reason of success in the football competitions arranged as part of or, originally, parallel to, the organization of the four-yearly Olympic Games. The obvious defect in accepting the Olympics as the means of deciding the world's leading football nation was that, in football perhaps more than in any other world sport, professionalism had been accepted in the land of its birth before the game was ever exported. It is true that a team of amateurs from Great Britain won the football Olympics in both 1908 (when six teams competed including a France A and a France B when that country had not formed a national football Association) and 1912 when 11

nations competed. But apart from the fact that Olympic rules required a Great Britain entry, the best players under the control of the four British Associations as, for example, England's goalkeeper and backs of the time, HARDY, CROMPTON, and PENNINGTON, were not eligible to play, thus from the beginning minimizing the Olympic football tournament as a world championship. None the less the Olympics did offer the opportunity for competitive international football of which F.I.F.A. were prepared to assume full control. Some time before the 1928 disputes, however, Rimet and Delaunay had realized that professionalism, open or screened, was increasing in most leading football-playing nations.

While the British Associations had been fighting their battles over the payment of 'broken time', Austria, Hungary, and Czechoslovakia, three of the countries that had, as Delaunay said, recognized professionalism, had accepted that they would not be entering for the 1928 Olympics. They were, of course, foremost among the supporters of the motion proposed by Delaunay at the 1928 F.I.F.A. congress that plans should be prepared for the staging of the first world championship. The Scandinavian nations, Denmark, Finland, Norway, and Sweden, and Estonia voted against the motion, but there were 25 approving votes, and Delaunay and MEISL, one of the first of the great international referees and the leading figure in Austrian football between the wars, began the organizational preparations. Meisl had recently seen the implementation of two of his ideas for an extension of competitive play among both the leading club sides and the national sides of the Central European countries. On 14 August 1927 the opening match had been played between Belgrado and Hungaria in Belgrade for the MITROPA CUP. Two clubs each from Austria, Czechoslovakia, Hungary, and Yugoslavia, took part in the first competition. Later, clubs from Italy, Romania, and Switzerland took part in a competition that is still extant but has been superseded in importance by the European Champions Cup, the European Cup-Winners Cup, and the European Fairs Cup, which embrace all European countries, but which owe their success to some extent to the pioneering years of the Mitropa Cup.

A month after the opening Mitropa Cup match in Belgrade, the national sides of Czechoslovakia and Austria met in Prague on 18 September 1927, for the opening match of the Cup competition that was to be known variously as the Nations Cup, the International Cup, the Europe Cup, and finally the DR. GERO CUP. Austria, Czechoslovakia, Hungary,

Italy, and Switzerland took part in the first competition.

These two competitions not only did much to popularize the game, they also showed the value of inter-club and international competitions in exchanging tactical ideas. They were, however, confined to, at the most, seven European nations. Delaunay and Meisl were concerned with the organization of a *world* football competition which, from 1924, demanded the inclusion of the South American countries.

The game had been steadily developing in South America from 1886, when an Englishman, Poole, professor at Montevideo University, formed the Albion F.C. in Uruguay. In 1888 the São Paulo Athletic Club in Brazil added football to the games its members played. At the turn of the century the arrival of Italian immigrants in Argentina gave impetus to the game previously introduced by the large British community in Buenos Aires. International football began in 1902 when Uruguay and Argentina played the first in their long series of matches for the Lipton Cup, presented by Sir Thomas Lipton. The SOUTH AMERICAN CHAMPIONSHIP began unofficially in 1916 in Buenos Aires, and officially the following year in Montevideo; Uruguay were the winners on each occasion. The championship and other inter-national competitions continued throughout the First World War, the standard of play improving with experience until in 1924 Uruguay entered for the Paris Olympics. Two years before a split developed in the Uruguayan F.A. over the issue of professionalism and PENAROL and other leading clubs, with the exception of NACIONAL, formed their own federation. Uruguay were thus without many of the country's better players when they came to Paris in 1924. Their football was, nevertheless, a revelation to European spectators and they won the Olympic football tournament. Four years later, with differences settled, Uruguay returned to Europe for the Amsterdam Olympics, together with Chile, Argentina, and Mexico.

The European nations were weakened by the absence of Austria, Hungary, and Czechoslovakia, who had openly acknowledged that their best players were professionals; the British four, who declined to send a Great Britain amateur XI because they doubted the amateur status of many of those playing for other countries; and Poland, Romania, and Sweden who had not entered. Italy was the only European entrant to challenge seriously the South American domination and they were beaten in the semi-final by Uruguay. In the final Uruguay met Argentina and, after drawing the first match 1-1, retained

their title by winning the replay 2-1. There was little difference between Uruguay and Argentina and both were clearly superior to the non-professional European entrants. Uruguay's wins in 1924 and 1928 were factors to be considered when the 1929 F.I.F.A. congress in Barcelona discussed the choice of country to organize the first world championship. In the end the four possible European candidates, Italy, the Netherlands, Spain, and Sweden, withdrew and left the field to Uruguay. Apart from winning the two previous Olympics, Uruguay had emphasized that in 1930 the country was to celebrate the hundredth anniversary of its independence. An international football tournament would fit into the pattern of festivities, and the CENTENARIO STADIUM in Montevideo, to be built for the world championship and named after the anniversary, would be ready in time for the matches to be played there.

It was a fitting gesture, but holding the first world championship in South America considerably reduced the number of entrants. Only 13 nations took part and 9 of them were from the American continent. Europe's four competing countries were France, Belgium, Romania, and Yugoslavia; not surprisingly the honours went to South America: Uruguay beat Argentina 4-2 in the final.

The selection of Italy as the venue for the 1934 world championship had the anticipated result of increasing the number of entries, and creating the need for the introduction of group qualifying competitions to reduce the 32 who entered to 16 for the final tournament. Uruguay were notable absentees, partly because the long-delayed official recognition of professionalism had led to fierce competition between clubs and a consequent opposition to releasing players for the national team, but also because of ill-feeling between the Uruguayan and Argentinian national Associations. Argentina did enter but, like Brazil, was beaten in the first round, and eight European teams made up the entire quarter-final field. As in 1930, the host country won the competition, Italy beating Czechoslovakia 2-1 in extra time. The British Associations had not entered but, with the appearance of Austria, Hungary, Czechoslovakia, Spain, Italy, Portugal, Germany, Poland, the Netherlands, the Irish Free State, and indeed of almost every European country, the competition had clearly established itself and F.I.F.A.'s authority had been vastly enhanced. Rimet and Delaunay were entitled to believe that their 1904 dream of a world championship had come true, and were delighted at the prospect of their own country, France, acting as host for the 1938 championship. It was not the fault of F.I.F.A. that 1938 was not the best of years to be sanguine about the spread of international fellowship. Austria, who had qualified for the finals, had been occupied by German troops and its national Football Association had ceased to exist before the final tournament was held. F.I.F.A., who regularly sent invitations to the British Associations to take part despite their non-membership, offered the F.A. the vacant place. England declined, while Uruguay, still having internal football troubles, Argentina, and Spain, plunged into civil war, did not enter. It was, though, indicative of the extension of F.I.F.A.'s influence that the number of entries had increased to 36, and included countries like Costa Rica, Dutch Guiana, and Japan. The French made strenuous efforts to ensure the success of the tournament despite the absence of some of the best teams. The COLOMBES STADIUM in Paris was considerably enlarged; new stadiums were constructed in Bordeaux and Marseilles; special postage stamps were issued; and publicity campaigns were launched to advertise the championship. Although war was soon to stop European competitive football, the 1938 world championship, in which Italy retained their title by beating Hungary 4-2, pointed the way to the success of the competition in postwar years.

The 'splendid isolation' of the British, as Dr. Schricker, then secretary of F.I.F.A. and an admirer of British football, sadly called it, was never so real as it appeared to be so far as the F.A. were concerned. Ireland and Wales did not play international matches against non-British countries until after the Second World War, and Scotland did not make regular visits to the Continent until the late 1930s, but England played against continental opposition in international matches both at home and away. In all, between 1929 and May 1939, England played 23 matches on the Continent against France three times, Belgium three times, Germany twice, Austria twice, Italy twice, Switzerland twice, Spain, Hungary, the Netherlands, Norway, Sweden, Finland, Czechoslovakia, Yugoslavia, and Romania. At home England entertained France, Spain, Germany, Austria, Italy, Hungary, Norway, and Czechoslovakia. In addition, as part of the celebrations of the seventy-fifth anniversary of the formation of the Football Association, F.I.F.A. selected and made the arrangements for a team representing the Continent to play England at Highbury on 26 October 1938.

Nor were British, and in particular English, contacts with European football confined to international matches. Despite the fact that their national Associations were no longer members of F.I.F.A., club tours of Europe remained popular, but with different results from those generally attained in the period up to 1930. Wall, the secretary of the F.A. from 1895 to 1934, was not the most internationally-minded of men, but his assessment of the position as he saw it in 1934 was unclouded. In his book, *Fifty Years of Football*, he observed that: 'the countries of the Continent have so greatly advanced in the playing of the game, having for many years been taught by professionals from Britain, that we have said "Good-bye" to all the nonsense about the stopping of counting after British teams have scored ten goals. The day is past when these trips can be taken as a holiday after a long and arduous season of League matches and Cup-ties.'

Wall saw that in comparison with other countries the standard of British football was, if not declining, being reached and perhaps surpassed. Not that England's international record over the period was a poor one against foreign opponents. Of 23 matches played on the Continent, England won 11, drew 4, and lost 8. The very first defeat by a foreign country was in Madrid against Spain on 15 May 1929 when England lost 4-3, and the other defeats were, surprisingly, against France in 1931 (2-5); Austria in 1936 (1-2); and Switzerland in 1938 (1-2). At home, England won every one of the eight matches played against foreign visitors, gaining revenge by beating Spain 7-1 in 1931.

F.I.F.A. turned to South America for the first world football championship after the end of the Second World War and Brazil were invited to act as host. The Argentinian F.A. was then in dispute with the Brazilian F.A. and declined to enter. High hopes that the Soviet Union would enter for the first time, raised by the successful tour of the DYNAMO MOSCOW club in Britain shortly after the end of the war, had been dashed by the deterioration in relations between the West and the Soviet countries between then and 1950 when the championship was held. None of the Soviet countries entered; the Austrians did not feel their team good enough; and West Germany were still excluded from international competition. The over-all entry made qualifying groups a necessity but there was some lack of enthusiasm for the competition and only 13, instead of 16, qualifiers arrived in Brazil for the final tournament. Two vacancies occurred because of a complete withdrawal of nations in a qualifying group. The third was in Group V where it was decided that the annual British home championship should be used as a qualifying group for two of the four British Associations making their first appearances in the world championship. England headed the group and Scotland were second but the Scots had made it plain that they would go to Brazil only if they were the British champions.

There were no volunteers to fill the vacancies and, although Uruguay beat Brazil 2-1 when they met in what was coincidentally the final match of the tournament that had been contested on a league basis, the imbalance of the first-round groups had meant that whereas Brazil played a total of six matches, Uruguay played only four. The organization was better in 1954 when the world championship was held in Switzerland, and every match was played within a 100-mile radius of the headquarters at Berne. Moreover, for the first time, television took the matches into the homes of millions of Europeans.

F.I.F.A.'s membership had been steadily growing since the end of the Second World War. It had been 51 in 1938; it was 73 in 1950; and 84 in 1954 when the world championship was staged in Switzerland. F.I.F.A. was thus firmly established as the only body responsible for the administration of football on a world scale. It commanded universal respect and its work was growing rapidly outside of the established football areas of Europe and South America. It was time that consideration was given to a second layer in the organization of international football. This already existed in South America where a confederation had been formed in 1916 that was responsible, among other things, for the organization of the South American championship. That disputes between various national Associations in South America frequently caused one or the other of them to retreat into isolation was no argument against the desirability of continental federations, and in June 1954 the Union des Associations Européennes de Football (U.E.F.A.) was founded. The Asian Football Confederation was founded in the same year, the African Football Confederation in 1956, the Confederación Norte-Centroamericana y del Caribe de Fútbol (CONCACAF) in 1961, and finally the Oceania Football Confederation (O.F.C.), covering Australia, Fiji, New Zealand, and Papua and New Guinea, in 1966. These new confederations and the stronger, reconstituted Confederación Sudamericana de Fútbol (CONMEBOL), have played important parts in the development of football in recent years. By far the biggest and most important of them has always been U.E.F.A., who found themselves involved soon after formation in a difficult situation involving matters not envisaged in their statutes. The confederations, like F.I.F.A. itself, are open for membership to national Football Associations with the implied concern with organizing international competitions. High in the list of aims behind the formation of U.E.F.A. was the setting up of a regular European championship or cup to be competed for by their member national associations.

Instead, U.E.F.A. found themselves faced with demands for a European *club* competition. Professionalism in football demands that the clubs who pay the players are commercially successful, and the financial rewards from taking part in competitions with clubs from other countries had long seemed attractive to continental clubs. In the early years of the twentieth century the cost and the time involved in long journeys was an obvious deterrent, but the Mitropa Cup for the leading clubs of many Central European countries had been popular and lucrative from 1927 to the outbreak of the Second World War, and in the early 1950s plans were afoot to revive it. More ambitious plans were beginning to concern Hanot, the football editor of the French sporting paper *L'Équipe*, at around the same time. He had always appreciated that for any European club competition to be successful there had to be participation by British, and particularly English, clubs. The televising of the 1954 world championship matches had made a considerable impact on football enthusiasts in England. When Wolverhampton Wanderers played at home against the Hungarian club, Honved, in December 1954, it was obvious that a large proportion of those who paid to watch matches in England were eager to see English clubs take on foreign challengers. That match was being played as Hanot and his friends finalized the plans for a European cup competition that appeared the next day in *L'Équipe*, but the impact the match made in Britain confirmed that the time was right for a competition open to one club from each Football Association, and in which progress would be made after the playing of home and away matches in midweek under floodlights, with the final being contested in Paris in a single match. Some national Associations had doubts about aspects of the proposed competition, but in general the reaction was favourable. The problem was finding the organization to run it; both F.I.F.A. and the newly-formed U.E.F.A. pointed out that they were concerned with competitions between the representative teams of national Associations, and not with individual clubs. *L'Équipe* decided to go ahead without either F.I.F.A. or U.E.F.A. and invited representatives of 18 leading European clubs to a meeting in Paris in April 1955. Fifteen of the clubs sent representatives while another, the Edinburgh club, HIBERNIAN, notified their support by telegram. A committee was elected from the meeting and matches arranged for the first round to be played in autumn 1955. Faced with this clear indication of support for such a competition, F.I.F.A.'s emergency committee again discussed the project and decided to authorize the competition providing that, in accordance with the long-established statutes of F.I.F.A., the participating clubs received the approval of their national Association to compete; that U.E.F.A. took over responsibility for organizing the competition, and that, as the name Europe Cup had long been mentioned in connection with an inter-nation competition, it should not be used for this club competition. In June 1955, U.E.F.A. did take over the organization and the competition was named the European Champion Clubs Cup.

About the same time, U.E.F.A. were discussing a European competition between representative teams of the national Associations but, in 1954, nothing came immediately of the suggestion which was opposed by the F.A. whose secretary, ROUS, explained in the 1955-6 F.A. Year-book that:

quite apart from the difficulty of fitting another major competition in with our own annual international Championship and our very full programme of league matches, it was felt that what was needed were more 'friendlies'. We hope that the new European Federation will lead to many more of these kind of international matches being played — without trophies, medals, or problems of national prestige! Let us hope that more 'friendlies' at every level may be played between the peoples of Europe — between clubs, cities, factories, youth organizations, schools, and others.

The reference to matches between cities is particularly interesting because Rous had been concerned with the organization of a competition between cities that was being discussed at almost exactly the same time as Hanot and L'Équipe were formulating their competition. The prime mover behind the competition was Thommen, the Swiss vice-president of F.I.F.A. He had been impressed by the circumstances that surrounded a match played in 1950 between Basle and Belgrade but it was not until 1954 that a small but influential committee was formed consisting of Thommen, Dr. Barassi, the president of the Italian F.A. and a prominent member of U.E.F.A., and Rous.

The competition was called, somewhat awkwardly, the 'Inter-City Industrial Fairs Cup' and, as that name implied, the participants were to represent cities that organized industrial or trade fairs. Moreover, it was hoped that the football fixtures would coincide with the holding of the fairs. In April 1955 the representatives of 12 cities in 10 countries met in Basle to discuss details of the competition at roughly the same time as the 15 representatives of clubs were meeting in Paris to discuss L'Équipe's project. More immediate progress was made at Basle where it was agreed that to avoid fixture congestion in the participating countries, the competition should be spread over two years; that only two cities could enter from any one nation; and that the competition should be placed under the authority of U.E.F.A. Twelve cities entered for the first competition and these were divided into four groups of three. The opening match was played, appropriately, in Basle, on 4 June 1955 when the Swiss city's opponents were London. The visitors won 5-0.

The opening match in the European Champion Clubs Cup did not take place until three months later when on 4 September the Sporting Club of Portugal drew 3-3 with Partizan Belgrade in Lisbon. The first competition for the Champions Cup was completed on 13 June 1956 when REAL MADRID beat REIMS 4-3 in Paris. The Fairs Cup first competition on the other hand extended far beyond the two years and the final match between BARCELONA, the first winners of the Cup, and London was not played until 1 May 1958. In less than a month from then Real Madrid were to win the European Champion Clubs Cup for the third successive time. Rous's sentiments about an extension of 'friendly' matches, although not wholly outmoded because at amateur and junior levels there had been a steady increase in contact between minor clubs, were not applicable to senior football. Nor, as the difference between the Champions Cup and the Fairs Cup in their early years showed, were spectators moved by the idea of a representative city XI rather than identifying with a club. It was significant that when the second competition for the Fairs Cup began in September 1958, London were represented by a team drawn wholly from Chelsea and played under the name of that club.

The European Champion Clubs Cup was an overwhelming success both in terms of the standard of football and in the financial rewards it brought to successful clubs. The arrangements made with Eurovision for the televising of matches helped financially and added to the interest shown in Europe. In 1968, for example, U.E.F.A. could report that 30 European television authorities had arranged to take the televised finals of the Champions Cup and the Cup-Winners Cup. The only countries not taking the match were Albania, Iceland, and Turkey. The European Cup-Winners Cup, first played for in the season 1960-1, was in itself evidence of the interest that had been created by the Champion Clubs Cup competition. Only one club per country could enter for the Champion Clubs

Cup—a circumstance that has added to the reward for winning the championship of every national league in Europe but which left many clubs disappointed. So, logically, the Cup-Winners Cup competition was started for the winners of the cup competition in each European country. In truth many of them either had no such competition or in the past had cared little about it. With entry into Europe as the bait, interest has revived in national cup competitions. Similarly pressure from national associations who have been themselves pushed by their clubs, changed the character of the Fairs Cup into an annual competition with usually double the number of participants of the other two European club competitions so that as many as three, occasionally four, clubs from the major footballing nations in Europe have been able to take part, until from the season 1971-2 it was taken over by U.E.F.A. and re-named the U.E.F.A. Cup.

The increased participation of a larger number of clubs in these European competitions has frequently brought into focus a clash of interest between clubs and national Associations in the selection of players for international matches. The number of these, too, has increased with the European Cup for Nations introduced between 1958 and 1960, and repeated between 1962 and 1964. These competitions, conducted on a home-and-away knock-out basis, followed immediately after the completion of the 1958 and 1962 world football championships, both of which were won by Brazil. No sooner were the final matches played in the Nations Cup than countries began the qualifying competition for the following world championship. From 1966, when England won the world championship, the form of the European Nations competition has been changed. It is now called the EUROPEAN FOOTBALL CHAMPIONSHIP and the qualifying matches to produce eight countries for the quarter-finals are decided on a group basis—with a consequential increase in the number of matches that have to be played. The quarter-finals are decided on a home-and-away basis, and the semi-finals and final played on a knock-out basis in the country of one of the semi-finalists.

Europe remains much the strongest of the continental confederations but the game is developing very quickly in Africa and Asia, both of which organize competitions for the national sides of their members' associations, and for their champion clubs, along the same lines as those well-established in Europe. The confederations have played a large part in the organization and development of football in various continents but Rous, in his summing-up of world football as it stood at the end of

1970, was concerned with ways in which the confederations and F.I.F.A. could work even more closely together in the future. His suggestion was that the president of each confederation should become a vice-president of F.I.F.A. thus making 'Confederations feel that their points of view were being put directly at the centre on matters of administration and organization within F.I.F.A. It would also mean that F.I.F.A. would be better informed about what constituent members are thinking.' The constituent members then numbered 138 national Associations compared with the few who gathered at the Freemasons' Tavern in London in October 1863.

Scotland. On the night of 9 July 1867, a number of men met in Glasgow to form a football club. This was Queen's Park, the first in Scotland, and for many years the history of football in Scotland was the history of Queen's Park.

Queen's Park played their first challenge match in 1868 against Thistle F.C. and the letter of acceptance, which they still preserve, shows the fluid state of the rules. Twenty players a side was suggested and two hours for the duration of the match. The visitors were asked to bring their own ball.

Football was accepted as worthy of newspaper comment when a report of the match between Queen's Park and Hamilton Grammarians appeared in the *Glasgow Herald* on 2 June 1869. It was the first report of a football match in Scotland.

Queen's Park found opposition difficult to come by and they joined the F.A. to widen their horizon. Their membership was confirmed on 9 November 1870, and in the first F.A. Cup competition they played a no-scoring semi-final tie against Wanderers at the Oval, London, but could not afford the travelling expenses for the replay and had to scratch.

In February 1873 eight clubs formed themselves into the Scottish Football Association and sponsored a Scottish Cup. The clubs were Queen's Park, Third Lanark, Vale of Leven, Clydesdale, Eastern, Dumbreck, Granville, and Kilmarnock. Only Queen's Park and Kilmarnock survive.

Sixteen clubs entered for the first Scottish Cup competition. RANGERS, who were later so successful, did not compete, for their entry was received too late. Queen's Park won the inaugural competition and won again in the following two years, and by 1893, the last time they won, they had taken the cup ten times. By the time the third tournament had been played the entries had risen to 49.

The F.A. legalized professionalism in England in 1885, but the struggle to preserve amateurism persisted longer in Scotland, with

Queen's Park leading the opposition. Professionalism was legalized in Scotland in May 1893 and by the end of the following season 83 clubs had registered around 800 players.

The pattern of Scottish football was formed in 1890 when after several meetings in Glasgow the Scottish League was formed. Those sponsoring the proposal argued that this was the only way to have certainty of fixtures but Queen's Park led the opposition on the grounds that a league favoured professionalism.

The first league comprised 11 clubs, Abercorn, CELTIC, Cowlairs, Cambuslang, Dumbarton, HEART OF MIDLOTHIAN, Rangers, St. Mirren, Renton, Third Lanark, and Vale of Leven. Queen's Park did not join until 1900 and only did so because they were finding it increasingly difficult to arrange fixtures. Division II of the League was formed in 1894 but the two divisions were run separately and not until the season of 1921-2 did they work together and automatic promotion and relegation were instituted. Rangers in the season of 1898-9 set a record when, led by Hamilton, they won all the 18 games played.

The first international with representative teams was played at Hamilton Crescent, the ground of West of Scotland Cricket Club, on St. Andrew's Day 1872. When that first match was played there were 100 clubs in England and ten in Scotland. The second international was at Kennington Oval when four Englishmen played in the Scotland team because the funds allowed only seven travelling players. The inaugural international in each country was thus played on a cricket ground.

There were no regular venues for internationals in the last decade of the century. Hampden was the favourite ground because of the popularity of Queen's Park but when Celtic built a new ground, the best-appointed in Great Britain, the game against England was played there.

A significant step in the moulding of Scottish football was the establishment in Glasgow in 1888 of Celtic in opposition to Rangers. Their rivalry was to become bitter and lucrative and to overshadow all else in Scottish football. Rangers had been formed in 1873 by a number of young men whose main interest was rowing on the river Clyde but who had been inspired by the Eastern Club which played on the Flesher's Haugh on the river bank. Celtic were formed late in 1887 and played their first match the following year.

The Celtic club quickly asserted itself under the direction of Maley who, as player and then manager, influenced the club for 52 years. He retired from the managership in 1940 at the age of 71. Until the First World War Celtic held the mastery in Scotland. Between the start of the century and the start of the war they won the Scottish Cup seven times and the league championship in six successive years from 1905 and then four times in succession from 1914.

At the end of the war the appointment of Struth as trainer was to foreshadow a new era for Rangers. He was appointed manager when Wilton died in 1920, and he established the modern Rangers. He was strong on discipline and dignity. He resigned as manager in April 1953 and under him the club had its most successful years. They dominated Scottish football and provided such captains for the international teams as Meiklejohn, Simpson, Brown, Shaw, and YOUNG. Struth's success began with the signing of MORTON from the amateur Queen's Park in 1920; he became one of the greatest left wingers of all time. He played until 1932-3 and then was elected to the board of directors of Rangers.

Under Struth, Rangers started an 11-year spell in which they won the Scottish Cup four times and the Scottish League championship nine times. The League run was broken by Celtic in 1926 and Motherwell in 1932 and the latter was the only intrusion into the monopoly of Rangers and Celtic between the wars. Motherwell lost only two league games during that season and were famed for their left wing Stevenson and Ferrier and for their centre forward McFadyen who scored 52 goals in 34 matches (a Scottish League record).

The third Hampden Park, the present one, was opened in 1903 and Scottish international football settled there, but the international cult was not fully developed until Scotland first played England in the new WEMBLEY STADIUM in 1924. Then the annual trek of 30,000 spectators across the border was established. The first match at Wembley was a dull affair before 60,000 spectators, but the following year, at Hampden, Scotland played the first team composed entirely of home players since 1895 and beat England 2-0, with Morton the tormentor of the English. This raised the excitement for the most famous Scotland team between the wars which beat England at Wembley in 1928 by 1-5.

In Scotland the biennial games against England established many records. In 1931 there were 129,810 spectators at Hampden Park to set a new world record for a sporting event. In 1933, the year of the depression, there were 134,710 spectators, and GILLESPIE of Queen's Park captained Scotland, the last amateur to do so. In 1937 there was the first all-ticket match: 150,000 tickets were sold and 149,407 turned up at the newly extended Hampden with its North Stand. The drawings were over £20,000 and the players were paid £6. Scotland won 3-1.

The Scottish Cup between the wars held as much interest as the internationals. There was a remarkable final in 1928 when Rangers won the cup for the first time in 25 years. Their failure in the competition had been a music-hall joke. Meiklejohn, the captain, scored the first goal from a penalty kick amidst tremendous tension and Rangers eventually won 4-0. In 1931 Motherwell led Celtic 2-0 in the final with but five minutes to be played. Celtic scored two goals to tie the scores and won the replay 4-2. In 1938 East Fife, a Second Division club, won the Cup by beating Kilmarnock 4-2 in a replay.

Football in Scotland was interrupted during the war and a system of regional leagues was formed. Kilmarnock, whose ground was taken over by the army, suffered the most serious disruption. After being closed down for four years they were relegated and it took them seven seasons to win promotion again to the first division.

At the re-start of football a new force appeared, Hibernian. A forward line of all the talents, Smith, Johnstone, Reilly, Turnbull, and Ormond, established the brightest era in the history of the club and was probably the best forward line ever to play in Scotland.

Hibernian won the Scottish League championship in 1948 and again in 1951 and in 1952. Smith, an elegant winger, was later to win championship medals with Heart of Midlothian and Dundee. Rangers were less dominant after the war although they built a magnificent defence with Young and Shaw at full-back behind McColl, Woodburn, and Cox, nicknamed the 'Iron Curtain'.

First Hibernian, then Celtic and ABERDEEN halted their championship runs and Heart of Midlothian were developing a new image with three inside forwards, Conn, Bauld, and Wardhaugh and a powerful half-back Mackay, who later went to Tottenham Hotspur, adding spirit. Heart of Midlothian finally broke through in 1957 to win the championship which they repeated in 1960. They might have won again in 1965 but lost to Kilmarnock, under the former Rangers player Waddell, 2-0. It was Kilmarnock's first championship win and it broke a frustrating run of near-success. They had four times been runners-up in the previous five seasons as well as being beaten finalists in the Scottish Cup.

Stein became manager of Celtic near the end of that season. He had been a player with the club, captain, and later coach. He left to become manager of Dunfermline, who under him won the Scottish Cup. He moved to Hibernian and they won the Summer Cup.

When he returned to Celtic they were immediately successful and established the most complete domination ever in the Scottish game. In 1966-7 they won every competition in which they played, including the European Champions Cup — the first British team to win that competition. They won the cup in a memorable final in Lisbon when, after conceding a goal, they beat INTERNAZIONALE (Milan) 2-1. Gemmell and Chalmers scored the goals.

The following season Celtic, trying for the world championship, played the South American champions, RACING, Buenos Aires, and lost the play-off in Montevideo. They reached the final of the European Champions Cup again in 1969-70 but surprisingly lost in extra time to FEIJENOORD in Milan.

In the 1950s economic problems complicated Scottish football. The main support was centralized on Celtic and Rangers and in the low-population areas gates diminished. When the maximum wage was abolished in England, dissatisfaction was rife among the top players outside Celtic and Rangers and they pressed their clubs for transfers to England. The clubs themselves, mostly poverty-stricken, favoured the idea and by the 1960s a steady export trade in footballers had been built up, with clubs outside Celtic and Rangers having to sell a player a year to survive.

English clubs saw a cheaper way of acquiring Scottish players by by-passing the clubs and signing youngsters from school — LAW and BREMNER went to England in this way. In the late 1960s almost every successful English club had a strong backbone of Scottish players and yet the Scottish international team made little impact outside the home championship. They had a particularly dismal record in the World Cup despite having great players available. Even with Baxter, Law, White, Crerand, and Mackay available they could not qualify for the final stages.

Scotland made a miserable start to the World Cup in 1950. They could have taken part in the final stages in Brazil as runners-up in the British championship but they had previously declared that they would go only as champions. In 1954 in Switzerland and in 1958 in Sweden they took part but failed to win a game. They failed to qualify for Chile in 1962; with good players in 1966 they lost a home match to Poland and with it the qualification and were further annoyed when they beat the England team that won at Wembley the following season. In 1970 the chance of competing in Mexico was lost to West Germany by a single goal, but in 1974 they managed to reach the finals.

In the various European club competitions,

Dundee in 1963 eliminated Cologne, Sporting (Lisbon), and ANDERLECHT, and were stopped only by the eventual winners A.C. Milan in the semi-final and still won the home game against Milan. In 1967, the year Celtic won the Champions Cup, Rangers went to the final of the Cup-Winners Cup and were beaten in extra time.

In the 1970s Scotland's problem was not so much producing good football players as holding them for the adornment of the home game. Celtic and Rangers were becoming ever richer with the help of giant pools and social clubs and money was being drawn away from the provincial clubs. The system and the economy were ludicrously out of balance with all but two clubs being little more than 'player farms', rearing footballers for the export market.

Northern Ireland. The Irish Football Association (I.F.A.) was formed at the Queen's Hotel, Belfast, by a group of businessmen, in 1880. Since then it has played a major role in developing the laws of the game and, frequently, acting as peacemaker in international disputes.

The first major Association football match was played in Northern Ireland on 24 October 1878, when the Ulster and Windsor Rugby Football Club organized an exhibition game between two Scottish teams, Queen's Park and Caledonians, at the Ulster Cricket Grounds, Belfast. Caledonians won 3-2, but the result was merely consequential; the entertainment and excitement gripped the public imagination.

As a result, McAlery, a leading city merchant, decided to form a club and on 11 October 1879 CLIFTONVILLE officially came into existence. Soon, others in Belfast followed until eventually the need for a governing body was apparent. Once again McAlery took the initiative by arranging the meeting of the seven clubs who founded the Irish Football Association.

Their first priority was organizing a competition, the Irish Cup, which was introduced in 1881. Cliftonville, who have remained amateur throughout, and Distillery, first professional club in Ireland, are the only survivors of seven teams which took part in the initial series. The others were Knock, Oldpark, Avoniel, Moyola Park, and Alexandra. Relationships were far from harmonious in those early days; in the opening round Oldpark lodged two unsuccessful protests against Cliftonville over the interpretation of rules, while an objection by Avoniel that a Moyola player 'had long nails in his boots' was officially rejected. Moyola were the first winners of the Irish Cup, a competition which still remains

the most important of Irish football. Sixteen clubs, the twelve of the Irish League and four from junior football who qualify through two preliminary rounds, compete in the first round proper.

Ireland's first international match, on 18 February 1882, at Knock, resulted in a 0-13 win for England. A newspaper report stated: 'The weather was shocking, but in spite of that, there was a large number of spectators—proof that the new game is rapidly attaining popularity in our midst.'

The writer had not far to seek for an excuse for so heavy a defeat. 'The Association game had only been three years in existence in this district, so that it can scarcely be expected that players could have arrived at such perfection to compete against a team so experienced as that representing England, the majority of whom have played the game from boyhood!'

The Irish team took the field, not in the now familiar green, but in 'a costume consisting of royal blue jersey and hose with white knickers, each player wearing his international badge on his left breast'. Kennedy, then assistant hon. sec. of the Irish F.A., was the referee and had the assistance of two 'umpires'. A week later, Ireland met Wales at Wrexham. Again the defeat was heavy—by 7-1. One explanation put forward was 'the rough passage across the Channel'.

By 1886 professionalism was introduced and on 14 March 1890 the Irish League, next in national legislative importance to the Irish F.A., was formed. It is responsible for the administration of the League championship, the Ulster, City, and Gold Cups as well as the inter-league series with England, Scotland, and the Republic of Ireland. It consists of 12 senior clubs with a B Division of 18 clubs, including some reserve XIs of senior sides. It is a league with a locally-confined history, and, apart from a match against Lega Nazionale (Italian semi-professional league) in May 1963, has not ventured competitively beyond the United Kingdom. The member clubs are Ards, Ballymena United, Bangor, Cliftonville, Coleraine, Crusaders, Distillery, Glenavon, GLENTORAN, Larne (replacing Derry City, who withdrew in November 1972 due to effects of the civil unrest), LINFIELD, and Portadown.

The game rapidly spread in 1890 from Ulster to the other Irish provinces of Munster, Connaught, and Leinster. All teams, including those in the then comparatively inaccessible parts of the west of Ireland, became affiliated to the Belfast-based body which established a council, representing all the areas, to govern the game throughout Ireland.

Much football history has been turbulent,

none more so than that of the Irish F.A. Two major crises occurred in 1911 and 1920; in 1911 the County Antrim Divisional Association was suspended for failing to obey an I.F.A. ruling and the Irish Cup was awarded to Linfield, the only club to remain loyal to the parent body.

Linfield arranged matches with Dublin and with cross-Channel teams during the next season, while the County Antrim F.A. sides staged their own competition. These included a new 'Irish Cup' which, when the dispute was ultimately settled in 1912, was handed over to the Irish League, and became the Gold Cup.

As a result of the 1920 flare-up, the Leinster, Munster, and Connaught clubs broke away from the Irish F.A. This dispute resulted from an Irish Cup semi-final between BELFAST CELTIC and Glentoran at Cliftonville, Belfast, during the height of the country's political troubles and civil unrest. Revolver shots were fired among the crowd and it culminated in a riot, with the referee, McClean (Belfast), ordering the teams to leave the field. Subsequently, Celtic were successful in their claim for the tie on the grounds that Glentoran had included an ineligible player, McIlveen. Then, however, the Senior Clubs Protest and Appeals Committee, responsible for arrangements, suspended Celtic, whose next move was to issue a writ, which was later withdrawn by agreement after the Irish F.A. had paid a sum of money in compensation, and the suspension was removed.

The Irish political unrest affected virtually every issue in the country. Football did not escape. When the Protest and Appeals Committee ordered Shelbourne back to Belfast for a drawn Irish Cup semi-final replay against Glenavon in 1921, all the southern clubs withdrew from the Irish F.A. The split had become complete.

Many attempts were made to heal the North-South breach; they all failed. So, in 1922, the Irish Free State F.A. was formed. Its clubs were immediately suspended by the Irish F.A. who, anxious to maintain the homogeneity of the Association, saw no reason why there should be two football Associations in an area which hitherto had been content with one. The vital point was that the clubs in the new Free State who left the Irish F.A. thus made themselves non-members. In 1922 and again in 1923 the new body's application to the British Associations for recognition and membership of the International Board was refused.

Following correspondence between F.I.F.A. and the English Football Association, a conference was held in Liverpool on 18 October 1923 with the object of clarifying the complex position. The four British Associations met representatives of the new Association and agreed that the two Irish bodies would exercise full jurisdiction within their own areas. The conference further decided that the Irish Free State F.A. would be recognized as an Association of Dominion status. On that basis the Irish F.A. removed the suspensions and enabled the new body and its affiliated clubs to have friendly relations with other Associations and clubs. Today, the Irish F.A. is entitled to use the name 'Ireland' in home countries championship games; for those under F.I.F.A. auspices, it must be 'Northern Ireland'.

The I.F.A.'s finest achievement was the performance of Northern Ireland in the 1958 World Cup series in Sweden — seven months after they had defeated England 2-3 at Wembley on 7 November 1957. The side, managed by the accomplished inside forward, DOHERTY (who resigned in 1962 for domestic reasons — to be succeeded by PEACOCK, BINGHAM, and then Neill), won its qualifying section against Italy (0-1, 2-1) and Portugal (1-1, 3-0). Bingham and BLANCHFLOWER were the most capped players with 57 appearances, but this record was surpassed by Neill in the 1971-2 season; he played on 59 occasions before retiring to concentrate on management. Northern Ireland lost in the quarter-final to France, mainly through lack of sufficient reserves and having to include players not fully fit. Such, however, was the prestige gained that Northern Ireland has since been regarded as a force in international football in marked contrast to its former 'poor relation' status.

In the 1962 World Cup series the I.F.A. found that some of its 1958 stars were on the wane and there were insufficient competent young players to replace them. In consequence, the team did not qualify against West Germany and Greece for the 1962 finals in Chile; and they failed again in 1966 and in 1970 when BEST (Manchester United) was unavailable for the decisive, qualifying-group match with the Soviet Union in Moscow. The 1974 qualifying series against Bulgaria, Cyprus, and Portugal was equally depressing, with the ultimate humiliation a 1-0 defeat by Cyprus in Nicosia on 14 February 1973. Because of the political troubles all home matches had to be staged at English venues.

The I.F.A. also take part in amateur internationals and won the British championship when it was inaugurated in 1948; it reached the final of the 1963 European youth international series, to be defeated 4-0 by England at Wembley. B, under-23, and schoolboy internationals are staged, too, but the Irish Schools

F.A. is a separate organization with no official affiliation to the Irish F.A., although they work in close harmony.

In the Irish Cup, the premier domestic tournament, Linfield were the leading team until 1896-9, when Belfast Celtic first entered, and for many years, these Belfast rivals dominated affairs. Belfast Celtic dropped out in 1921, remaining inactive until 1925, but when they returned they did not enter the Irish League. Instead, they competed in the Intermediate League. Even in this, they proved a force. They made a direct entry to the Irish Cup and beat Linfield 3-2 in the final. They left Northern Ireland competitions again in 1949 and the club's intentions remained a mystery. From the end of the 1948-9 season, after a tour of the U.S.A. during which they defeated Scotland 2-0 in New York, their playing pitch at CELTIC PARK on the Donegall Road was kept in perfect condition, although used only for occasional charity games and thrice-weekly greyhound race meetings. Then in March 1973 rioters and vandals wrecked the offices and stands. A year earlier Distillery were forced to vacate Grosvenor Park for similar reasons, and now share Seaview with Crusaders.

Linfield's record is unsurpassed in the 80-year history of the Irish Cup. They have won it 30 times, and are followed by Distillery with 11, Belfast Celtic and Glentoran with 8 each, and Cliftonville with 7. In two seasons, 1921-2 and 1961-2, Linfield won the seven trophies available to Irish League clubs.

The Irish Cup has twice been won by teams never in membership of the Irish League. They were Willowfield (1928) and Dundela (1955). These clubs qualified for entry as Intermediate Cup semi-finalists. Such entry is not automatic — the teams are invited — but the I.F.A. have never departed from the tradition of bringing junior teams into the competition in this way. Only two of the present 12 Irish League sides, Bangor and Portadown, have never won the Irish Cup.

Amateur football in Northern Ireland, apart from that of the mainly amateur Irish League club, Cliftonville, consists primarily of junior competitions, although Irish League clubs sometimes include a small number of amateurs. The League clubs provide almost all the members of the Northern Ireland teams in the home countries amateur international championship.

Republic of Ireland. When Ireland was partitioned after the First World War there was an immediate defection of many clubs in southern Ireland from the Irish F.A., and in June 1921 these clubs set up the Football Association of Ireland (F.A.I.). The Associations of England, Scotland, and Wales declined to recognize the new Association while the Irish F.A. suspended the breakaway clubs. This was not a negative move because in addition to southern Irish clubs, a number of republican-minded clubs in Ulster, particularly some in Belfast and Derry, had also been accepted into membership of the Dublin-centred F.A. of Ireland.

The reaction of the F.A.I. was to apply for membership of F.I.F.A. and in this they were successful in August 1923, at which time the British associations were out of F.I.F.A. membership (see above). However, at the request of F.I.F.A. and the F.A.I., the Football Association convened a meeting between representatives of the four British Associations and the F.A.I. As a result of this the new Association agreed to change its name to that of the F.A. of the Irish Free State (I.F.S.); to the Irish Football Association and themselves exercising full jurisdiction within their own areas; and to the mutual recognition of suspensions. At the same time the F.A. agreed to recognize the F.A. of the Irish Free State as an Association with Dominion status; the Irish, Welsh, and Scottish Associations equally recognized the new Association so that clubs from each association could freely play each other; while, finally, the Irish F.A. agreed to remove the suspensions they had imposed. Over the period between the two world wars when the British Associations were generally out of competitive contact with the wider world of football, a sprinkling of players from lesser English clubs, like Lincoln and Walsall, were playing in international matches for the Irish Free State. It was under that name that the southern Irishmen made their start in international football in the 1924 Paris Olympics. A bye in the first round took them to the last-16 stage and a victory over Bulgaria by 1-0 (centre forward Duncan was the scorer) carried them into the quarter-finals. Here progress was stopped by the Netherlands but only, after extra time, by 2-1. Before leaving Paris the Irish Free State played, and won, a third match — against Estonia who had been knocked out by the U.S.A. in the first round. A fortnight later the U.S.A., on their way home from Europe, went to Dublin and played against the Irish Free State. The result was a win for the Irish whose first four international matches had resulted in three wins and one defeat.

From 1921-2 the Association had encouraged the Football League of Ireland to organize a League championship that has been contested without a break since then, and a Shield competition that, among other advantages, serves to augment the fixture list for clubs competing in a national League of usually only

12 clubs. In 1934 the Irish entered for the world championship and were placed in a qualifying group with the Netherlands and Belgium. The Netherlands beat the Irish 5-2 in Amsterdam, and Belgium 4-2 in Antwerp. The first group match between the I.F.S. and Belgium had been drawn 4-4 in Dublin and with two from the group qualifying for the world championship finals in Italy, the Irish were unfortunate to be eliminated with a goal average of 0·66 compared with Belgium's 0·75. Friendly international matches against Hungary (three times), Switzerland (three times), Germany (twice), the Netherlands, Luxemburg, and France followed, before two matches against Norway in 1937 in a qualifying group for the 1938 world championship. The Irish, who by 1936 were describing themselves as Ireland and not the I.F.S., lost 3-2 in Oslo and could only draw 3-3 in Dublin.

In deliberately describing themselves as Ireland, the Dublin Association were seeking to bring into the open their frequent complaints to the Belfast Irish Football Association that the latter persisted in describing their representative teams as Ireland although they controlled football in only six of Ireland's 32 counties. There was at the time no possibility of any potential national opponent being faced with a choice of two Irish national sides since from 1919 to 1939 the Northern Irish F.A. played international matches against only England, Scotland, and Wales, none of whom arranged international matches against the Irish Free State, although there had been since 1924 regular matches between the Welsh League and the League of Ireland (southern Ireland).

The Football Association made occasional efforts to act as intermediary between the Belfast- and Dublin-based associations but generally the F.A. and the other British Associations took the attitude that this question of nomenclature and other problems could be resolved only within Ireland. The Dublin body did try to reach an agreement with the older association whereby the selection and control of international matches involving Ireland as a whole, rather than only either Ulster or the Irish Free State, would be governed by a joint committee. The I.F.A. refused to accept the suggestion but they did, with the English, Welsh, and Scottish F.A.s making no protest, continue to select and play southern Irishmen in their teams. It was not until the British Associations were, like the southern Irish, in membership of F.I.F.A. that the confused position was clarified by positive decisions from F.I.F.A. The I.F.A. may include players from the Republic of Ireland in their championship matches against England, Scotland,

and Wales, but for all other matches their players must have been born in Northern Ireland and, by a decision of June 1954, the I.F.A. teams should be officially described as Northern Ireland. The Football Association of Ireland, as the southern Association is now officially described, use the name Republic of Ireland to describe their national team.

It is a team that has not enjoyed spectacular success in international football but has competed in every world championship competition except the first in 1930, and in all the European Nations Cup and, later, European Football Championship competitions — the first of which was ignored by the English, Scottish, Welsh, and Northern Ireland Associations. England were the first of the U.K. countries to play against the Republic of Ireland in an international match — at Dublin in September 1946. The return was played at Goodison Park, Liverpool, three years later, and resulted in a win for the Irish by 0-2. Purists have argued that this, and not the Hungarian win at Wembley in 1953, should be recorded as England's first home defeat by a 'foreign' country, but with the Irish team including nine players employed by English Football League clubs there seems a distinction to be made. It is seldom in recent seasons that players with Irish clubs are selected for the Republic of Ireland national side, unless the best of the home players who have been attracted to the richer professional clubs of England and Scotland are refused permission by their clubs to appear in the international match because of club commitments. Football in Ireland has had to accept that the best players will go to English and Scottish clubs. In the south too, football has had to compete with the rival claims of Gaelic FOOTBALL.

Argentina. There has long been a vigorous English colony in Buenos Aires, so it is not surprising that the game should have been brought early to Argentina; the Argentinian Football Federation was set up in 1893. The names of clubs such as Newell's Old Boys and River Plate denote the English influence, but, despite a number of visits from such clubs as Southampton, Tottenham Hotspur, Everton, and the Corinthians, the game stubbornly refused to take root. Sir Thomas Lipton, in presenting a trophy for competition between Argentina and Uruguay, did what he could, but it was only with the mass immigration of Italians that enthusiasm grew among the native population. Indeed, the great names of Argentinian football bear witness to the fact: MONTI, ORSI (both of whom played for Italy's World Cup-winning team), DI STEFANO, Rossi, Sivori, Angelillo, LABRUNA.

The native Argentinian style was, until the

middle 1960s, distinguished by its extreme virtuosity. Though many tough players like Monti were produced, the crowds appreciated artistry above all. In 1928 Argentina sent their first touring team to Europe, where it distinguished itself in a remarkable Olympic tournament in Amsterdam. Monti was the captain, Orsi, at outside left, the star forward, scoring three goals in the exciting 6-3 defeat of Belgium. In the final, Argentina met the holders, Uruguay, who, like the Argentinians themselves and many other entrants, were really a team of 'disguised' professionals. The first match was drawn, the second narrowly won, 2-1, by the Uruguayans, who two years later beat Argentina 4-2 in Montevideo in the final of the first World Cup. The Argentinian attack that day was led by the gifted Stabile, who was later their international team manager for twenty years.

In 1934, annoyed by the depredations of Italian clubs, Argentina deliberately sent a weakened team to the World Cup. In 1938 and 1950 they refused to compete, and it was not until 1958 that they were seen again in the World Cup finals — disastrously, for the Czechs beat them 6-1 in Sweden, and their team was pelted with rubbish on its return to Buenos Aires airport.

In the late 1940s Argentinian football was decimated by an exodus of almost all the best professionals to Colombia, which was not then a member of F.I.F.A. Di Stefano, a brilliant centre forward, never went back, ending his career with Real Madrid. It was a very long time before the game recovered, though Argentina continued to dominate the South American Championship. In the 1960s a reaction against being beaten by the more 'systematic' of the world's teams, including Brazil, led to a new emphasis on negative play and toughness. The Argentinian teams which won the 1967 and 1968 world club titles — Racing Club and ESTUDIANTES — were destructive, physical, and cynically efficient. They bore scant resemblance to those teams which, in the past, had made Argentinian football respected throughout the world. But a warning had already been given during the 1966 World Cup, in a notorious match against England at Wembley when Rattin, Argentina's captain, was sent off the field.

COLOURS: Broad blue and white stripes on shirts, blue shorts.
SEASON: April–December.

Austria. The game was introduced by English expatriates working in Vienna in the 1890s. Gardeners employed by Baron Rothschild formed the First Vienna club, playing in the Rothschild colours of blue and yellow. Their main rivals were the Vienna Cricket and Football Club, who played only football, and later matured into F.K. Austria. The two clubs met in the first match ever played on Austrian soil, on 15 November 1894, the Cricketers winning 4-0. That same year, Nicholson, a sportsman in every sense of the word, arrived to work for the Thomas Cook agency in Vienna, played for First Vienna, and became the first president of the Austrian Football Union. In 1900 Southampton became the first British club to play in Austria.

The real father of Austrian football, however, was Hugo Meisl, the son of a wealthy Jewish businessman who was so disturbed by his son's enthusiasm for the sport that he banished him for a time to Trieste. Meisl was an early member of the Cricketers and it was he who, in 1912, brought to Vienna Jimmy Hogan, perhaps the most influential and talented of all coaches. Hogan made a poor beginning, but, after a long talk with Meisl, he grasped the way to put his ideas over to the Viennese, who came to idolize him.

After the First World War, Meisl — whose brother Willy was an international goalkeeper and an outstanding journalist — combined with Hogan to build the so-called *Wunder team*. Playing football of what came to be known as the Vienna School, based on exquisite control and the short pass, Austria became the outstanding team on the Continent, even though it never won a World Cup. In 1932 Austria came to Stamford Bridge and ran England to 4-3. Among its finest players were Smistik, the attacking centre half, and SINDELAR, the tall, blond centre forward.

A weary Austrian team took only fourth place in the 1934 World Cup, and by 1938, after the anschluss, had ceased to exist as a separate entity. Following the war, there was a brief efflorescence in the early 1950s, when an elegant team was motivated by another great attacking centre half, OCWIRK. But, by the 1954 World Cup, when Austria took a meaningless third place, the Vienna School was in ruins, the 'third back' game had replaced it and the ensuing years saw an increasing emphasis on power rather than technique, a tipping of the balance of power from Vienna and its great clubs — RAPID, F.K. Austria, Wacker — to the provinces. Nevertheless, in the 1965-6 season, Austria became one of the very few teams ever to defeat England at Wembley.

Among other leading postwar players have been Melchior, outside right, Stojaspal, inside left, and Zeman, a goalkeeper in the tradition of HIDEN, the Viennese baker who kept goal so spectacularly for the *Wunderteam* and then travelled the world. Hanappi not only played a record number of matches for his country, but successfully appeared in positions as varied as right back and centre forward.

COLOURS: White shirts with black shorts and stockings.
SEASON: August–June.

Belgium. Although Belgium began playing the England amateur team as early as 1908, when they lost 2-8 in Brussels, they did not compete in an Olympic tournament until they staged, and won, that of 1920. Their outstanding player before the First World War was Six, one of the finest centre forwards of all time.

The Belgian team of the 1920s contained a number of very gifted players, particularly Bastin, an Antwerp shipping clerk who played outside left, Gillis, at inside right, and Debie in goal, while Vlaminck also played in the Leicester City attack. The coach was the former Scottish international, Maxwell.

The 1920 Olympic side beat Spain 3-1 and Holland 3-0, and were leading Czechoslovakia 2-0 after 40 minutes of the final when the Czechs walked off. In the same year, Belgium recorded their first victory over the England amateur side, while in 1923 they became the first foreign team to meet a full professional England team in England, losing 6-1 at Highbury. The following season, however, England were held to a 2-2 draw in Antwerp, England equalizing eight minutes from the end. Thirteen years later Belgium, in Brussels, beat England for the first time.

In 1934 they entered the World Cup, losing 5-2 in the first round, in Florence, to Germany, Voorhoof scoring both goals. Langenus of Belgium was the leading referee of the competition.

In 1938 they again went out in the first round of the World Cup, this time to France, in Paris. Braine, their inside forward, later that year played for the Rest of Europe against England.

The leading Belgian player of the early postwar years was unquestionably MERMANS of Anderlecht, the centre forward, closely followed by the Beerschot centre forward, Coppens. Belgium reached the finals of the 1954 World Cup, holding England to a 4-4 draw, after extra time, in Basle, but losing 4-1 to Italy and failing to qualify. Belgium did not qualify for the 1958, 1962, or 1966 World Cup finals, but in the meanwhile produced an outstanding club team in Anderlecht, which regularly played an honourable part in the European Cup. Among its chief players were JURION, a bespectacled inside right, who captained the national side, and VAN HIMST, the centre forward. Standard Liège, who competed frequently in the European Cup-Winners Cup, provided the chief opposition during this period, but were rather more inclined than Anderlecht to import foreign players.

Gormlie, who played for a number of English clubs as goalkeeper, coached both Anderlecht and the Belgian national team, after the war, while mention should also be made of Lambrechts, who played at outside right for the Rest of Europe against Great Britain in Glasgow in May 1947.

COLOURS: Red shirts, black shorts.
SEASON: September–May.

Brazil. The chief pioneer of the game in Brazil was Charles Miller. Born of English parents in São Paulo, he went back to England and played for Southampton, in the 1890s. Later he returned to Brazil with his soccer kit and a couple of footballs to find the game virtually unknown. In São Paulo he formed clubs with the English Gas Company, São Paulo Railways, for whom he worked, and the London Bank, while he persuaded São Paulo Athletic Club to play football as well as cricket. In 1898, the local Mackenzie College became the first chiefly Brazilian football club. In 1902, a São Paulo championship was flourishing, while Englishmen in Rio founded the FLU-MINENSE club.

In 1910 the Corinthians, invited by Fluminense, made the first tour of Brazil by a British side, visiting São Paulo as well as Rio. The São Paulo Corinthians side was named after them. In 1913 the Corinthians returned, and actually lost to a Rio side, 2-1. In 1914 Torino came to tour and stayed many months, because of the outbreak of war. That September, Brazil beat Argentina 1-0 in the first international match between the two countries, and in 1916 the first South American Championship was played in Montevideo.

Brazilian football was revolutionized by the emergence of the black player, but for many years there was great discrimination — the slaves had been emancipated only in 1888. The mulatto Friedenreich, the first outstanding coloured player, was bitterly upset when picked for the Blacks against the Whites. Manteiga, of America F.C., Rio, was the first black player to win a regular place in a major team; many players and supporters at once left America for Fluminense, one of the last bastions of prejudice. But, by the 1930s, coloured players had forced their way through by sheer talent, and the outstanding member of Brazil's fine 1938 World Cup team was its black centre forward, LEONIDAS.

Brazil entered the first World Cup in 1930, in Uruguay, and were narrowly eliminated in their pool, losing 2-1 to Yugoslavia, but beating the Bolivians 4-0. In Italy four years later, Leonidas and De Britto were splendid forwards, but the more disciplined Spaniards knocked Brazil out 3-1. In 1938, Brazil came up with another gifted forward in Tim, and a superb full-back in Da Guia. They beat the Poles 6-5 in an astonishing game, and the Czechs 2-1 in a replay. They then surprisingly left out both Tim and Leonidas, and went down 2-1 to Italy in the semi-final.

In 1950 Brazil put on the World Cup themselves, deploying a superb inside forward trio of Zizinoo, Ademir, and Jair. But, though they won their group and beat Spain and Sweden in the final pool, their traditional rivals, Uruguay, surprised them 2-1 in the decisive match, played at the spectacular new MARACAÑA STADIUM before a 200,000 crowd.

After this reverse, Brazil abandoned the 'diagonal' system of marking for a rather unhappy eight-year flirtation with the 'third back' game. In 1954 they sent a talented side to the Swiss World Cup, but went down in the quarter-finals 4-2 to Hungary in a notoriously violent match in Berne. Julinho, their outside right, was a superb player, but in Sweden in 1958 even he was outstripped by the brilliance of GARRINCHA. There, playing the 4-2-4 system, Brazil took the World Cup at last, their astonishingly talented side thrashing France 5-2 in the semi-final and Sweden by the same margin in the final. They had splendid backs in Djalma and NILTON SANTOS, fine midfield players in DIDÌ and Zito, and a remarkable prodigy in the coloured 17-year-old PELÉ, scorer of two memorable goals in the final.

In Chile four years later, playing a more cautious 4-3-3 after the withdrawal through injury of Pelé, Brazil retained the World Cup; they beat the Czechs 3-1 in the final, using eight of their 1958 side. Garrincha was their outstanding match-winner. But in 1966, in England, a similar faith in the old guard proved misplaced, and they failed to qualify for the quarter-finals. When however in 1970 the final stages were contested in Mexico in conditions more favourable to the Brazilian style, they were successful for the third time and took the Jules Rimet trophy (the original World Cup) into their permanent keeping. Four years later in West Germany they were to disappoint.

The main rivalry in Brazil has always been between Rio and São Paulo, each with its own championship, and only lately has the huge state of Minas Gerais, for long a major source of talent, begun to play a role in club football. Pelé's club, SANTOS, was one of the world's best throughout the 1960s, twice winning the world club title.

COLOURS: Yellow shirts and green shorts; originally blue shirts and white shorts.
SEASON: February–December.

Bulgaria. The Bulgarian Federation was established in 1923, but not until after the Second World War did Bulgaria make any impact on the European game, and not until 1962 did they compete in the finals of the World Cup. It was only a year, however, before the newly-founded association sent a team to a major tournament: the Olympics of 1924. There, it acquitted itself most honourably, losing only 1-0 to Ireland in its solitary second round match. It was not seen in another Olympiad until 1952, when it gave Russia a surprisingly close game in the first round of the Finnish tournament, losing 1-2.

By the 1956 Olympic tournament, Bulgaria had an extremely talented team, with notable stars in Kolev, the little, dark-haired inside left Bojkov, the right half, who became team manager in the late 1960s; and Panayotov, a deep-lying centre forward. All three played for the C.D.N.A. Army club, which dominated football in Bulgaria in that era. Later it changed its name to C.S.K.A., and was strongly challenged by the Levski club and by Lokomotiv of Sofia.

The 1956 team beat Great Britain 6-1 in Sofia, then drew with them 3-3 at Wembley in their eliminating group, but had to play and beat them again (6-1) in Australia, since Britain were re-admitted to the tournament. Bulgaria then defeated India 3-0, but once again lost 2-1 to Russia, this time in the semi-final. Many thought them the more talented team.

Beating France in a play-off in Milan — the goal was scored by a new star, the inside left Yakimov — they qualified for the Rancagua group of the 1962 World Cup in Chile. There, they lost narrowly to Argentina in their first game, went down 6-1 to Hungary in their second (it was the World Cup début of ASPAROUKHOV), drew a dismal match 0-0 with England, and thus failed to qualify for the quarter-finals.

But in 1966 they again came through to the finals, this time playing in the Liverpool group, in England. Asparoukhov was suffering from an ankle injury, and the team lost all three of its games, 2-0 to Brazil, 3-0 to Portugal, and 3-1 to Hungary, the latter matches being at Old Trafford, Manchester.

In 1968 a Bulgarian team which was more or less the equivalent of a B international side — there are no fine distinctions about professionalism — got into the final of the Mexican Olympic tournament, after narrowly beating the Mexicans themselves in the semi-finals.

The final, played at the Aztec Stadium against Hungary, was disastrous for Bulgaria, three of whose players were sent off, somewhat contentiously, in the first half, at a time when they were already two goals down. They ultimately lost 3-1, their goal being scored by the first of their players to be sent off, Dimitrov. Jekov was an effective centre forward, and at that time leading scorer in the Bulgarian League championship.

COLOURS: All white.

SEASON: March–November.

Chile. A vigorous British community in Chile during the late nineteenth century ensured an early start to the game; the Chilean Federation was formed in 1895.

Chile entered for the first World Cup in 1930, in Uruguay, and gave a very good account of themselves, winning two of their three matches but losing the third, to Argentina, who won the group to qualify for the semi-finals. In their first match, Chile easily beat Mexico, 3-0, Subiabre, their inside right, scoring twice. He also scored the only goal against Argentina in the second match, and the goal which beat France in the third. The Argentinian game degenerated into a brawl when an Argentinian kicked at Torres, the Chilean left half, as he jumped to head a ball.

It was twenty years before Chile qualified again for the World Cup finals, and once more it was in South America, in Brazil. They brought back Robledo, the Newcastle United inside forward who had been born at Iquique of a Chilean father and a Yorkshire mother, to play. The team was captained by a spectacular goalkeeper, Eves. Again Chile gave a useful account of herself, losing even games 2-0 both to England and Spain, and easily defeating the U.S.A. team which had beaten England.

Twelve years later, the Chileans themselves put on the World Cup, building a number of fine new stadia, notably in Santiago, the capital, and, on a smaller, more compact scale, at Viña del Mar. Other qualifying groups played at Rancagua in a stadium owned by the Braden Copper Company, and north, near the Peruvian border, at Arica. The Chileans themselves did remarkably well, taking third place. They qualified by coming second in their Santiago group, beating the Swiss and the Italians — in a notoriously violent game — and then losing to the West Germans.

But, in the quarter-finals at Arica, they surprisingly beat Russia, the powerful shooting of their left half, Rojas, playing a decisive part. Other outstanding members of the team were Toro, the inside right — he linked with Rojas in a 4-2-4 formation — and the outside left, L. Sanchez, who was, however, lucky not to be sent off for striking an opponent in the Italian match. The team manager was RIERA, who the following year took charge of the Rest of the World selection, and subsequently had a period in charge of the BENFICA club of Lis-

bon. Brazil beat Chile 4-2 in Santiago in the semi-final, but in the third-place match against Yugoslavia a goal from long range by Rojas gave Chile the victory.

Among the leading clubs are Colo Colo — for whom Robledo later became a player and a coach — Universidad Cattolica, and Green Cross.

Chile qualified for the 1966 World Cup but showed disappointing form. Playing in the north-eastern English group, they lost 2-0 to Italy, drew 1-1 with North Korea, and lost 2-1 to Russia. Of the leading members of the 1962 side, only Sanchez survived.

COLOURS: Red, blue shorts.

SEASON: April–December

Czechoslovakia. Czech football began, largely in Prague, in the latter days of the Habsburg Empire. John Dick, a Scot who used to play for Woolwich Arsenal, was the chief pioneering coach, imparting to the native game the short-passing, elegant Scots style which became the familiar mark of 'Danubian' football. As early as 1906, Celtic played in Prague, while an F.A. touring team actually played and won there, 8-0, in 1899. Two famous clubs, Slavia and Sparta, sprang up in the city and dominated Czech football for many years, though after the Russian *coup* in 1948, each was forced to change its name for a period. In 1908 a strong England team played Bohemia in Prague, and won by only 4-0. There was something of a riot and a spectator who kicked the formidable referee, John Lewis of Bolton, was seized by him.

In 1920 Czechoslovakia sent a team to the Olympic Games in Antwerp, which played excellent football, but disgraced itself in the final. Curiously enough, Lewis was again the referee. He sent off a Czech player guilty of a serious foul against a Belgian, whereupon the whole team left the field. The Belgians, whose two goals were said by some critics to be dubiously allowed, were thus left 2-0 in the lead and were awarded the victory, the Czechs being disqualified. Previously, the Czechs had beaten Yugoslavia 9-0, and Norway 4-0.

In 1924 they entered the Paris Olympics, defeating Turkey 5-0 in the first round, but then going out 1-0 to Switzerland after a 1-1 draw. They did not appear again in an Olympic Games football tournament until after the Second World War.

In 1934 they entered the World Cup for the first time, and their extremely talented team reached the final. It was most unlucky to be beaten 2-1 in Rome by Italy after extra time, Orsi's equalizing goal being something of a freak. Puc, an excellent left winger, had scored the Czech goal. Perhaps the most celebrated member of the team was its splendid goalkeeper, PLANICKA, while Nejedly was an outstanding inside forward. The Czechs beat Romania, Switzerland, and Germany on the way to the final. A few weeks earlier, they had defeated England 2-1 in Prague.

In 1937, the Czechs played at Tottenham: Crayston, England's right half, was injured, but England just won, 5-4, thanks to a hat-trick by MATTHEWS, who moved to inside right and scored all the goals with his left foot.

Czech football was slow to recover after the war, in which it was dominated for many years by U.D.A. (later DUKLA), the Army team. Czechoslovakia competed without distinction in the 1954 World Cup, where they were heavily defeated 5-0 by Austria, but by 1958 they had a far better World Cup team, capable of defeating Argentina 6-1. POPLUHAR (Slovan Bratislava), the centre half, and MASOPUST, the fine left half who became 'European Footballer of 1962', played in the final, four years later. Northern Ireland knocked the team out in Malmö in a play-off.

By 1962, Dukla had made a name in European club competition, and a very gifted national team went to Chile, losing 3-1 to Brazil in a close final. Qualifying by taking second place in the Viña del Mar group, the Czechs then surprisingly beat Hungary in the quarter-final at Rancagua (Schroiff keeping goal superbly), and Yugoslavia in Viña del Mar. They played a 4-2-4 formation, Masopust being well abetted by the lanky Kvasniak in midfield. Perhaps if the country's outstanding opportunist, Kucera, had not missed the tournament through a knee injury, the result of the final might have been different.

COLOURS: Red shirts, white shorts, blue stockings.
SEASON: August–June.

Denmark. No country made a quicker beginning than Denmark, though they were overtaken after the First World War, when other, larger countries took more seriously to the game. The first football is said to have been sent to an English boy at the Soro Akademi. In 1879 two Englishmen named Smart and Gibson formed the English Football Club in Copenhagen, and in the same year the Copenhagen Boldklub began to play a game combining elements of both soccer and Rugby. In 1889 the Danske Boldspil Union (Danish Ball Union) was born, administering soccer among other sports. A league championship was immediately formed and for years was dominated by K.B. (Boldklub) and A.B. (Akademisk Boldklub).

In 1913 a national championship was instituted, the provincial clubs playing off to decide who would confront the champions of Copenhagen. K.B. were the first winners, beating B. 1901 by 6-2.

In 1908 Denmark sent an outstandingly good team to the Olympic tournament in London. Two years previously, they were good enough to defeat Glasgow Celtic 2-1 in Copenhagen. Now, with the famous Middelboe brothers in the half-back line (Nils captained Chelsea in the early 1920s) they beat both French entrants, and lost only 2-0 to the powerful United Kingdom team in the final. Many thought that theirs was the better passing, but their finishing was poor, even though Sophus Nielsen scored ten goals against France.

In 1912 when the Olympics were held in Stockholm, Denmark again reached the final, and were extremely unlucky. Their chief scorer, Nielsen, was unfit, while Buchwald, the right half, went off with a dislocated elbow after only 15 minutes. The United Kingdom beat them 4-2, but 'lost' the second half 1-0. Denmark had won the unofficial Olympic tournament of 1906, first beating a team from Smyrna which included five English brothers, then winning 9-0 against a Greek side which refused to come back for the second half.

Remaining steadfastly amateur, the Danes sent a distinguished side to London for the Olympiad of 1948, taking third place by beating Great Britain 5-3 at Wembley. Of this team, JOHN HANSEN and Carl Hansen later formed a famous left-wing partnership for JUVENTUS of Turin, with Karl Aage Hansen at inside right. In the ensuing years, Danish football was veritably pillaged by Italian clubs. Among those who went to Italy were a fine pair of wing half-backs, Pilmark and Jensen (Bologna), and Nielsen, centre forward of the Danish 1960 Olympic team. This team gallantly reached the final, in which it lost narrowly to Yugoslavia. Its outstanding feat was to beat a very strong side of young Hungarian League players, including Albert and Gorocs, in the semi-final, in Rome.

There are over 180,000 registered players in Denmark, more or less equally divided between those under and those over the age of 16. A pleasing feature of the late 1960s was the emergence as leading players of the sons of John and Karl Hansen.

COLOURS: Red shirts, white shorts.
SEASON: April–November.

Finland. Finland's national association was founded in 1907, and in 1912 they entered a team for the Olympic tournament in Stockholm. There they beat Italy 3-2 in the first round, Russia 2-1 in the second, and finally went out 4-0 to the powerful United Kingdom side, the eventual winners of the tournament.

They were not to be found in another Olympic tournament until 1936, in Germany, when they succumbed in the first round, 7-3 to Peru.

here was a further gap, until Finland themselves organized the Olympiad of 1952, when
the Finnish team drew a bye in the first round,
losing narrowly by 4-3 to Austria in the
second.

Finland have yet to qualify for the finals of
World Cup or a European Nations Cup
though they compete regularly in both. The
amateurism of their players has undoubtedly
been a handicap, though in the later 1960s
they began to recall for international matches
footballers who had gone abroad to play
professionally. Peltonen, a forward who
played successfully in West German football,
was the outstanding Finnish attacker of his
decade, as Lehovirta had been in the 1950s.

Finnish clubs have been competing in the
European Cup since the season 1958-9, when
Allosura entered.

COLOURS: Blue shirts, white shorts, blue stockings.
SEASON: April–November.

France. Though professionalism did not
become legal till the early 1930s, football
gained a strong hold in France before the
nineteenth century was over, and the French
played a leading part in forming the International Federation in 1904, just as French initiative, notably that of Rimet, led to the initiation
of the World Cup and, much later, through
Manot, of the European Cup.

In 1908 the French actually sent two teams
to the Olympic soccer tournament in London,
but each lost in the first round, and, after the
Danes had soundly beaten one team 17-1, all
the players were brusquely taken home, thus
putting an end to plans for a consolation tournament.

By 1930, however, the French were able to
send a respectable team to the World Cup in
Uruguay, including Pinel at centre half, THÉ
POT in goal, and Mattler at full-back. It was
most unfortunate to be beaten 1-0 by the eventual finalist, Argentina. In 1934 at Turin, the
French were again narrowly defeated, this
time 3-2 by Austria after extra time. Thépot
and Mattler were still in the team, which was
captained by Nicolas, who later became the
inspiration of the brilliant 1958 World Cup
team.

In 1938 France put on the World Cup most
successfully. Their own side knocked out Belgium 3-1 in Paris in the first round, Mattler
captaining the eleven, but lost 3-1 to the eventual victors, Italy, in the second round. France
withdraw from the 1950 World Cup, objecting
to the long distances they were asked to travel
in Brazil, and failed to qualify for the quarter-
finals in Switzerland in 1954.

The members of the 1958 team trained
together at Kopparberg in Sweden before the
start of the World Cup finals, in which they
played superbly. The deep-lying centre forward, KOPA, from Noeux-les-Mines, the son
of a Polish miner and a Frenchwoman, was
France's inspiration. He made infinite chances
for the centre forward, FONTAINE, whose 13
goals in the tournament constituted a record.
France took third place, after losing to Brazil
in the semi-final. The team failed to qualify
for Chile in 1962, played disappointingly in
England four years later, being eliminated in
its qualifying group, and again failed to qualify for both the 1970 and 1974 World Cup
final stages.

In the 1950s and 1960s French professional
football ran into troubled waters, and even so
famous a club as Racing Club de Paris, which
played a long series of matches with Arsenal
between the wars, temporarily ceased to exist
as an independent team.

Reims, the outstanding French club of the
1950s, twice reached the final of the European
Cup, inspired by Kopa, losing on each occasion to Real Madrid. Among other distinguished clubs are Bordeaux, Nice, St.
Étienne, and Monaco, which plays traditionally in French League football. Many fine
players have been 'imported' from North
Africa and the French African colonies,
notably Mekloufi, who played for St. Étienne,
Algeria, and France, and, in the late 1960s,
Keita, from Mali, who also played for St.
Étienne. In *France Football*, France has the
world's leading football magazine, which
organizes the European 'Footballer of the
Year' Award.

COLOURS: Blue shirts, white shorts, red stockings.
SEASON: September–June.

Germany. Football in Germany began in
the universities, and as early as 1899 the
English F.A. sent a mixed team of amateurs
and professionals to make a tour of the country. Two years later, the Germans sent an
international team to England, which was
heavily beaten, first at Tottenham, by an
England team of amateurs, then at Manchester, by a team of professionals.

A form of soccer is said to have been played
in Germany by English schoolboys as early as
1865. The first recorded soccer club,
however, was the English F.C. of Dresden, in
1890. The two Schricker brothers — who borrowed money from their mother to finance the
F.A. tour of 1899 — and Bensemann were the
most vigorous early promoters of the sport.
The Germans sent a team to the 1912 Olympic
tournament in Stockholm where, in the consolation tournament, a forward called Fuchs
set up a long-standing international record by
scoring ten goals against Russia.

After the First World War, the game grew

swiftly in Germany, helped by the presence as national coach of Hogan. Among his discoveries was HOFMANN of Dresden, who scored all three goals when Germany drew 3-3 with England in Berlin in 1930.

Disciplined and physical, rather than brilliant, the Germans took an honourable third place in the World Cup of 1934, beating the Austrians for the position at Naples. But four years later they not only lost 6-3 at home to England, though their team was reinforced by Austrians, but were put out in the first round of the World Cup by Switzerland in Paris.

After the Second World War, both East Germany and West Germany formed their own associations. German teams were not readmitted to the World Cup till 1954 — when West Germany surprisingly won it. Cleverly managed by HERBERGER, who had taken office in 1937, they put out a deliberately weak team to lose 8-3 to Hungary, but qualified nevertheless, and, a week later, beat the Hungarians 3-2 in the final in Berne. Two of the goals were scored by the powerful right winger, Rahn, but the orchestrator of the side was its captain and inside forward, the clever veteran, FRITZ WALTER.

In Sweden, four years later, Sweden beat West Germany 3-1 at Göteborg, in a contentious semi-final. In Chile they lost 1-0 in the quarter-final to Yugoslavia. In the 1966 final, they were beaten 4-2 by England after extra time, in a thrilling game, after they had equalized in the very last minute. SEELER played with power and distinction at centre forward in all these three World Cups. In 1970 in Mexico, they defeated England 3-2 after extra time to reach the semi-final, at which stage they lost 3-4 to Italy, but subsequently beat Uruguay 1-0 in the match between the beaten semi-finalists to earn third place in the championship. West Germany were the host country in 1974, when they were to win the Cup in a 2-1 victory over the Netherlands.

Only in the 1960s did West Germany forsake regional football for the national *Bundesliga*. East Germany, considerably smaller in resources, follows the Iron Curtain pattern of ostensible amateurism, though their players would certainly be considered professionals in western Europe. Until the 1974 competition they had never managed to qualify for the World Cup finals, but they have participated successfully in Olympiads and have strong club sides such as Vorwaerts (Army) and Motor Jena.

COLOURS: (West Germany) White shirts with black facings, black shorts; (East Germany) white shirts, blue shorts, white stockings.
SEASON: (West Germany) August–June; (East Germany) September–June.

Greece. Association football is playe throughout Greece, as it has been since Britis sailors and engineers introduced the game particularly in the Athens, Piraeus, and Salo nika areas, which remain the centres for th leading clubs such as Panathinaikos, Olym piakos, and Aris. The Greeks were quick t learn the game and several football clubs wer in being before the turn of the century. It wa not, however, until 14 November 1926 that Football Association was formed in Athen with sufficient support from clubs in othe Greek cities to be generally accepted as th national Association (Elliniki Podosfairil Omospondia).

Before this, Greek teams had taken part i international competitions. As early as 190 when an intermediate Olympics was held i Athens, Greece decided to introduce a compe titive football tournament. Only Denmark se along a representative football team and th Greeks increased the entry to four with team representing Athens, Salonika, and Smyrna The last-named was made up to full strengt with volunteers from various countries wh were taking part in the Olympic ATHLETIC but the Athens and Salonika XIs were strongl partisan and their match ended in one of th first of the stormy scenes that have fair regularly enlivened the Greek football scen That it happened emphasizes the regional fee ing that historically had hampered the d velopment of the national football team ar delayed the establishment of a national asse ciation for so many years.

A year after the foundation of the Gree F.A. a successful application was made affiliate to F.I.F.A., and during the 1930s, a brief period of calm in the Balkans, Gree took part regularly in competitions for the Ba kan Cup against the opposition of Bulgari Romania, and Yugoslavia, and also entere for the 1934 and 1938 world championship Defeats outnumbered victories, which we confined to matches played in Athens, wi the exception of the 3-1 win in the 1938 Wor Cup qualifying competition over Palestine Tel-Aviv.

After the Second World War and the end the civil war in Greece, the political hostili between Greece and her Balkan neighbou precluded an immediate resumption of intern tional football between them. Instead, som what ironically, Greece marked her return international football in 1948 and 1949 wi matches in Athens and Istanbul against Tu key, a country studiously avoided by th Greeks in pre-war football. Friendly match against Syria and Egypt resulted in rare wi away from home, but up to the end of t 1968-9 season, in a programme of intern tional matches largely in the competitive world and European championships, Greece had still to win an away match against European opponents.

A similar situation of more than average disparity between home and away performances, stemming possibly from the poor, grassless pitches on which the Greeks usually play their home matches, exists in the European Champions Cup in which Greek clubs have taken part since the season of 1959-60. Not until November 1969 was victory gained on an opponent's ground — by A.E.K. Athens against Akademisk B.K. in Copenhagen by 2-0. This win took A.E.K. Athens to the quarter-final stage of the competition — much the best performance to that date by a Greek club. Olympiakos and Panathinaikos have also played in the competition and the same three clubs have been the only Greek representatives in the Cup-Winners Cup competition.

COLOURS: White shirts, blue shorts, blue stockings with white trims.

Hungary made a precocious start to football, receiving a number of British touring sides before the First World War. She entered a team for the 1908 Olympic tournament but withdrew it, owing to political troubles, and entered the 1912 tournament in Stockholm, but was beaten 7-0 by the United Kingdom. The consolation tournament, however, was won by the Hungarians, who beat Austria 3-0 in the final, after beating Germany 3-1.

The first football is reputed to have been brought into Hungary by a student called Ray, who had been at Zurich University. The Budapesti Torna Club, previously given to the practice of gymnastics, took up the game, which had early preceptors in Stobbe and Iszer. On 9 May 1897 a hundred spectators watched two of the Budapest Torna teams play on the Millanaris field. The game was locally criticized as being dangerous, but such objections were brushed aside. In 1901 the Hungarian Football Association was formed and, in the same year, Southampton made an influentially important and impressive tour, winning 8-0 and 13-0. Seven years later the England team beat Hungary 7-0 in Budapest. In 1909 England came once more, winning 4-2 and 8-2. The Hungarian left winger was one of their first great stars, Schlosser, who won more than 80 caps.

The turning point in the history of the game came when Hogan arrived in Budapest during the First World War, bringing with him his traditionally Scottish methods of football. The Hungarians paid graceful tribute to the fact in November 1953, when they invited him to Wembley Stadium, where he saw them beat England 6-3 — the first foreign international team ever to win on English soil.

After the war Hogan returned for a while to Hungary, discovering two famous players, Braun and Orth, and, although Hungary were traumatically defeated 3-0 by Egypt in the Paris Olympic tournament of 1924, they improved remarkably. In the 1934 World Cup, they had their revenge over Egypt, 4-2 at Naples, but lost a rough game to Austria in the second round at Bologna. That same year they defeated England 2-1 at Budapest. In 1938, an artistic team reached the World Cup final in Paris, but lost 4-2 to the more powerful and efficient Italians. It was captained from centre forward by the gifted Dr. Sarosi.

During the late 1940s and early 1950s, Hungary remained in hibernation behind the Iron Curtain, emerging to win the 1952 Olympic tournament in Helsinki with a team which had at last added finishing power to technique. It included the marvellous inside forwards, KOCSIS, a superb header of a ball, and PUSKAS, with his formidable left foot. BOZSIK was the attacking right half. In 1953, with HIDEGKUTI playing brilliantly as a deep-lying centre forward and scoring three goals, they beat England at Wembley, following that up in May 1954 by overwhelming them 7-1 in Budapest.

Winning the World Cup seemed a formality, but an injury to Puskas disrupted them. He returned for the final, before he was truly fit, and West Germany won 3-2 after Hungary had taken an early 2-0 lead. The 1956 revolution found Honved, the Army club to which most star players had been inducted since the war, abroad. Players such as Puskas, Kocsis, and the winger, Czibor, did not go home, and a great team fell to pieces.

Since then, there has been a revival, thanks to such talented forwards as Bene, Albert, and Farkas, all of whom were outstanding in the 1966 World Cup, when Brazil, the holders, were spectacularly beaten at Everton; but Russia beat Hungary in the quarter-finals. Hungary won the Olympic tournaments of 1952, 1964 in Tokyo, and 1968 in Mexico City. In common with other Iron Curtain countries, there is no true distinction between amateurs and professionals.

COLOURS: Cherry red shirts, white shorts.
SEASON: August–December, February–June, Cup and League.

Italy. Football was brought to Italy in 1887 by a Torinese businessman, Bosio, though the first organized club was Genoa — *il vecchio Genoa*, as it is known. It was founded in 1892 by resident Englishmen, and not until five years later, after the arrival of the vigorous Dr. Spensley, were Italians admitted to the club.

Pozzo, who died at the end of 1968, was a Torinese and a founder member of the celebrated Torino club. It was he, as *commissario tecnico*, or manager, of the Italian national team who perhaps did more than any single person to develop the game in his country. He assumed this position as early as 1912, when he was asked at the last moment to take an Italian team to the Stockholm Olympics, after a split in the young Federation. After the war he resumed the position of national manager and held it for over 20 years until 1948, twice (in 1934 and 1938) winning the World Cup.

Pozzo modelled his victorious teams of the 1930s on the Manchester United tactics which he observed before the First World War, when a student in the midlands, and which he discussed with the great United centre half of that period, Roberts. Italian football had no truck with the 'third back' game until Genoa introduced it in the early 1940s. An attacking centre half was encouraged to distribute the ball with long passes to the wings.

Italy staged and won the 1934 World Cup, but the event was used too blatantly in the cause of Fascist propaganda; as the Belgian referee, Langenus, remarked, the Italians made it overplain that they had put on the World Cup in order to win it. This they did by the skin of their teeth, after extra time in Rome, beating the Czechs 2-1. There were three Argentinians, Monti, Orsi (who got the vital equalizing goal), and Guaita in the Italian team. Under Italian law each enjoyed double nationality.

In 1938 Italy had a better team with only one *oriundo* (Italian of foreign birth), Andreolo, a Uruguayan who succeeded Monti at centre half. This team was superior to the 1934 side, from which it included only two survivors — the inside forwards, MEAZZA and Ferrari. The centre forward was the powerful opportunist, PIOLA, with Meazza the finest leader ever produced by the Italian game. Italy defeated Hungary 4-2 in the final, played in Paris.

After the Second World War, Italian football was immersed in a wild maelstrom of professionalism. Foreign players were imported, paid huge salaries, and periodically banned; e.g. in 1953, and after the World Cup of 1966, when Italy lost 1-0 to North Korea. They included the 'Gre-no-li' trio of GREN, NORDAHL, and LIEDHOLM, who played for Milan, and the three Danish forwards, John and Karl Hansen and Carl Praxest for Juventus.

Juventus dominated the Italian championship between the wars, but in the 1940s their fellow Turin club, Torino, were dominant. Torino took five titles in a row until the

Superga air crash removed virtually the whole team and its reserves with one dreadful blow. It was equally a disaster for the Italian national side, which then included seven or eight Torino players. Not surprisingly, Italy fared poorly in the 1950 World Cup in Brazil, losing to Sweden (most of whose players were subsequently engaged by Italian clubs) and failing to reach the final pool.

In 1954 Italy qualified for Switzerland but were beaten by the home team. In 1958 Northern Ireland surprisingly eliminated them before the competition proper. In Chile the Italians were involved in a particularly violent match against the Chileans in Santiago, and again did not reach the quarter-finals, a fate which once more overtook them in 1966. In 1970, in Mexico, they reached the final before losing to Brazil 1-4, and in 1974 were to be eliminated after the early rounds of the finals in West Germany.

Italian footballers tend to be athletic, technically skilled, combative, and inventive. A long line of distinguished players passes from de Vecchi, through Meazza, Piola, and Boniperti, to such as Rivera and Riva. In 1968, Italy staged and won the European Nations Cup, beating Yugoslavia in a replayed final.

COLOURS: Blue shirts, white shorts.
SEASON: September–June.

Japan. According to one version, Association football was first demonstrated in Japan by an English teacher named Johns, at Kogakuryo School in 1874. Johns's demonstrations probably made only a slight and passing impression, but football had gained enough support by 1917 for Japan to stage the third Far East championship in Tokyo. The national Football Association (Nippon Shukyu Kyokai) was not founded until 1921, when the first national championship took place and the national side journeyed abroad for the first time — to Shanghai for the fifth Far East championship. Affiliation to F.I.F.A. followed in 1929, and participation in competitions beyond the Far East in 1936, when Japan was represented at the Berlin Olympics. A quarter-final defeat by 8-0 against Italy, the eventual winners, was less surprising than Japan's earlier victory over Sweden by 3-2.

The 1946 F.I.F.A. Congress in Luxemburg decided that 'no relations be permitted between Japan and its clubs and other F.I.F.A. Associations or their clubs', and Japanese football remained isolated until, following a review of the ban decided upon by the F.I.F.A. congress in Rio in June 1950, their national Association was readmitted to the world body in December 1950. Japan immediately entered for the football section of the first ASIAN GAMES, staged in New Delhi in 1951, and followed this with entry for the 1954 world championship and the 1956 and 1960 Olympics. Results fluctuated between an encouraging qualification, at the expense of South Korea, for the 1956 Olympic final tournament, and a mediocre display in Melbourne against a poor Australian side. Failure to qualify for the final stages of the 1960 Olympics finally persuaded the Japanese F.A. that their native endeavour and enthusiasm needed the guidance of an experienced European coach. With the help and the advice of the West German F.A. and F.I.F.A., Japan were able to persuade the German coach, Cramer, to work for them in Japan. In separate spells of six weeks in 1960, nearly a year between 1961 and 1962, and ten weeks in 1963, Cramer not only taught those already playing the game modern techniques but, more importantly, trained the Japanese to be coaches themselves.

The game that had been confined largely to high-school boys and university students is now flourishing throughout the country under the leadership of an Association whose members in 1964 had to meet after work in their homes, but who now have offices and a full-time secretary in Tokyo. Significantly, not only is the game now played in primary schools throughout Japan, but large industrial concerns sponsor many clubs who take part in the National League that was started in 1965. Tokyo, Osaka, Yokohama, and Hiroshima are the main centres, with the leading club, Toyo Kogyo, situated in Hiroshima. Hiroshima since the war has been in the fore of Japanese football because it was largely occupied by British troops who enjoyed themselves playing football, while elsewhere in Japan the occupying American troops, not welcomed in Hiroshima, were playing baseball. The first outstanding player of world class is Kamamoto.

COLOURS: Blue shirts, white shorts, blue stockings.

Luxemburg. The Luxemburg Football Federation was founded in 1908, but the progress of the country's football has been badly impeded by the depredations of its neighbours, Belgium and France, who are wont to sign its best players for their professional clubs.

In 1920 Luxemburg entered the Olympic football tournament for the first time, sending a team to Antwerp which went out 3-0 to Holland in the first round. In 1924 in the French Olympic tournament, Luxemburg drew a bye in the first round, then lost 2-0 to Italy, in the second. In 1928 Luxemburg competed again, in Amsterdam, and again lost in the initial round, this time to Belgium, 5-3. In 1936, in Berlin, Germany beat them 9-0, again in the first round.

After the Second World War, Luxemburg continued to compete in the Olympic tournament, and once more lost in the first round in London in 1948, this time to Yugoslavia, 6-1. But in 1952, they at long last succeeded in winning a match, beating the Great Britain amateur team 5-3, after extra time, in Finland. In their second game, they lost narrowly (2-1) to Brazil. One of the outstanding members of the team was the inside forward, Nuremberg, who had been playing regularly for Nice in the French championship.

Luxemburg enters regularly for the World Cup, though it has not succeeded in qualifying for the finals. Its finest achievement was in the eliminating competition for the 1962 tournament, when it most surprisingly overcame Portugal at home.

In the later 1960s, under the skilful team managership of a German, Heinz, Luxemburg took to recalling their expatriated professional players for international games, and put up stronger resistance. Their midfield player, Pilot, who joined Standard Liège in the Belgian championship, emerged as one of the most skilful European footballers of his day.

Luxemburg clubs began to compete in the European Cup in 1956-7, when their champions, Spora, entered. Subsequently, such clubs as Jeunesse Esch, Dudelange, and U.S. Luxemburg have also competed.

COLOURS: Red shirts, white shorts.
SEASON: August–June.

Mexico. The Mexican Federation was established in 1927, and three years later Mexico competed in the World Cup in Uruguay. There they lost all three of their matches, 4-1 to France, 3-0 to Chile, and 6-3 to Argentina, thus failing to qualify for the semi-finals. Their team was captained by the right back, Gutierrez.

In the years following the Second World War, Mexican football was considerably influenced by Argentinian players, who actually preponderated in some of the leading teams, although in the 1960s the tendency was generally to engage Brazilians.

Mexico did not compete again in the finals of a World Cup until 1950, while their first two appearances in Olympiads were unhappy: in 1928 they were beaten 7-1 in the first round by Spain, in Holland; in 1948, in London, they went down 5-3, again in the first round to Korea.

After the Second World War, they were able to qualify regularly for the World Cup finals, being consistently drawn in a weak Central and North American group, which they were easily able to dominate. In 1950, they opened the final stages of the tournament in Brazil, losing 4-0 to Brazil herself. They also lost their other two qualifying group matches, 4-1 to Yugoslavia and 2-1 to Switzerland. Their goalkeeper in all three matches, and in the 1954, 1958, 1962, and 1966 World Cups, was CARBAJAL, perhaps the finest player Mexico had produced. In 1954, in Switzerland, Mexico lost both matches in Pool I: 5-0 to Brazil, when Carbajal was unable to play, and, more closely, 3-2 to France. Cardenas, who played right half not only in that team but in the succeeding two World Cups, was appointed team manager of Mexico for their South American tour of 1968.

In 1958, in Sweden, Mexico acquired their first point in a World Cup tournament when they drew 1-1 with Wales, but Sweden beat them 3-0, Hungary 4-0. Nevertheless, they had a talented player in Reyes, their inside right, who went on to the next two World Cups.

In Chile, four years later, at long last Mexico won their first game in a World Cup final tournament, beating Czechoslovakia 3-1 in Viña del Mar, after honourable defeats (2-0, 1-0) by Brazil and Spain.

In 1966 the Mexicans played uncharacteristically defensive football in London, losing 2-0 to England at Wembley, but drawing with both France and Uruguay. BORJA, the centre forward, emerged as a player of unusual gifts.

In the 1968 Olympic tournament, Mexico, playing at home, fielded a team of young professionals which disappointingly failed to get beyond the semi-finals, losing to France, 4-1, Bulgaria (in the semi-finals) 3-2, and finally and humiliatingly 2-0 to Japan in the match for third place. The advantage of playing so high above sea-level — over 7,200 ft. (2,194 m.) — in Mexico City was diminished by the fact that the visiting teams had time to get acclimatized. Mexico staged the 1970 World Cup and reached the quarter-final stage before losing 1-4 to Italy. Then surprisingly they failed to qualify for the 1974 competition when Haiti, the host country, headed the final qualifying table for Central and North American entrants.

COLOURS: Green with white shorts.
SEASON: March–December.

Netherlands. Dutch football made an early beginning and matches with the England amateur side were initiated as early as 1907, when the Dutch were beaten 8-1 at The Hague and 12-2 at Darlington. But, by the following year, when a team was sent to the Olympic soccer tournament in London, great improvement had been worked by the coaching of Chadwick, the former Everton and England player. A powerfully-built team in which almost every player stood over six feet (1·8 m.) lost only 4-0 to the United Kingdom, and eventually took third place, beating Sweden 2-1.

In 1912, Netherlands reached the Olympic semi-finals in Stockholm, beating Sweden, the hosts, 4-3 and Austria 3-1, but losing to Denmark 4-1. The following year, at The Hague, Netherlands defeated the England amateur team 2-1, for the first time.

In the 1920 Antwerp tournament, Netherlands beat Luxemburg and Sweden, lost to Belgium, and then to Spain in the play-off for second and third places. Another fine effort was made in Paris four years later, when fourth place was gained, Sweden winning the third-place match 3-1. But in 1928, playing hosts in Amsterdam, Netherlands went out 2-0 in the first round to the eventual winners, Uruguay. Mutters, of Netherlands, refereed the two final matches and the third-place game.

Thereafter Netherlands concentrated on the World Cup and in 1934, they lost 3-2 in Milan to Switzerland in the first round. Andetiesen captained the Dutch team from centre half. The following season the only inter-war match between Netherlands and England took place, a scratch England team winning 1-0 in Amsterdam.

In 1938 a Dutch team, including five of the 1934 World Cup side, forced Czechoslovakia to extra time in the first round at Le Havre, but then went out 3-0. At outside left was the young De Harder, who was to play successfully for Bordeaux after the war.

In 1947, WILKES of the Xerxes club of Rotterdam played for the Rest of Europe at inside left against Britain in Glasgow, later joining Internazionale of Milan. Several other talented Dutch forwards of the era went to France, among them De Kubber, Appel, and Timmermans.

In 1948 the full Dutch international team was knocked out by Great Britain's amateurs in the first round of the Olympic tournament at Highbury, in an exciting match. Since then, Dutch first-class football has become fully and overtly professional.

AJAX of Amsterdam and Feijenoord of Rotterdam have competed with distinction in European competitions; these have been the outstanding postwar Dutch teams. Netherlands failed to reach the finals of a World Cup between 1938 and 1970, but a number of outstanding players emerged in the 1960s, particularly the Feijenoord outside left, Moulijn, and the Ajax (and later Barcelona) centre forward, CRUYFF, perhaps the most gifted Dutch attacker since Wilkes. The striking improvement in Dutch football resulted in Feijenoord winning the European Cup in 1970 and Ajax in 1971, 1972, and 1973, and in the qualification of the national team for the final stages of the 1974 World Cup competition, in which they were to lose 2-1 to West Germany.

COLOURS: Orange shirts, white shorts.

SEASON: August–June.

North Korea. During the long Japanese occupation, Korea had no football team of its own, but a number of gifted players emerged and played for Japan; in particular for the Japanese Olympic team which surprisingly beat Sweden in Germany in 1936. In 1948 a Korean side was sent to the Olympic tournament in London. It did remarkably well to beat Mexico 5-3 in the first round, but, in the second, it was severely beaten 12-0 by the eventual winners, Sweden.

After the split between the North and South Korean territories, little more was heard of North Korean football until the World Cup eliminating tournament of 1965, though progress was made under Russian coaches. For the World Cup, in which she was drawn in the Afro-Asian group, North Korea followed the policy previously embraced by Communist countries in Europe; that is to say, drafting its star players into a Central Army team in the capital, Pyongyang, regardless of their clubs of origin.

There the players, each of whom was given an officer's rank, were kept in monastically strict collective training under the national coach, Myung Rye Hyun. The withdrawal, almost *en masse*, of the Afro-Asian group from the World Cup qualifying competition left only North Korea and Australia to play off for a position in the finals. Both matches were played in Cambodia. Australia were favoured, but the North Koreans played splendid attacking football in the second half of the first game; 1-0 ahead at half-time, they eventually won 6-1. The Koreans were small and light but very fast and fit. Australia improved in the return match, but lost again, 3-1.

In the 1966 World Cup finals, North Korea played all their qualifying matches on the ground of Middlesbrough, where the local crowd warmly supported them. They began poorly, losing 3-0 to Russia, but in their second match they played with much more aggressive spirit, and deserved better than a draw against Chile. Their third match was one of the most astonishing in the history of the competition, as they beat the powerful Italian side 1-0, with a goal by their excellent inside forward, Pak Do Ik, one of several players who had been seconded to the Army team from their clubs of origin.

In the quarter-final, at Everton, they went into a brisk and still more unexpected 3-0 lead over Portugal, who, however, eventually outstripped them and won 5-3, thanks largely to the prowess of EUSEBIO. The North Koreans

learned with remarkable speed as the competition progressed. Their most inspirational player was Pak Seung Jin, born at Wonsan in 1941, striker or deep-lying centre forward, who was the scorer of three of the goals against Australia and of the first-minute goal against Portugal.

The most unusual feature of the team's success was that it appeared to be achieved virtually without previous foreign contacts. After the 1966 World Cup North Korean football again withdrew into isolation.

COLOURS: All white, with a North Korean flag on the chest.

Norway. The Norwegian Football Association was founded in 1902. Ten years later, the Norwegians entered for the Olympic tournament in Stockholm for the first time, but were knocked out in their first match 7-0 by the powerful and more experienced Danes. But in the consolation tournament the Norwegians put up a brave show against Austria, going down by the only goal of a close game.

By 1920 they had improved sufficiently to knock the Great Britain amateur side out of the Antwerp Olympiad 3-1 in the first round. Czechoslovakia, however, proved much too strong for the Norwegians, beating them 4-0 in the second round.

The Norwegians did not reappear in an Olympic tournament until 1936, when they played, with extraordinary success, in Germany. As genuine amateurs, they were quite properly able to field their complete national side, and, after trouncing Turkey 4-0, they actually beat the Germans 2-0 in the Olympic Stadium, under the gaze of Hitler. This left them to play Italy in the semi-finals. Italy had a team of alleged students which, in fact, consisted largely of experienced young professionals. Again the match took place in the Olympic Stadium. BRUSTAD, Norway's excellent outside left, one of the best forwards she has produced, equalized Italy's first goal, in the thirteenth minute. The match went into extra time, and not until then could Italy score the goal whereby she squeezed into the Olympic final.

In charge of the Norwegian team was the distinguished sportsman Halvorsen who, as a student, played centre half for the famous German club, S.V. Hamburg. It was therefore particularly ironic that, during the Second World War, he should be tortured by the S.S. for his refusal to allow the Norwegian international team to play under Nazi auspices. He died as a consequence of his ill-treatment. That day, the Italians and Norwegians returned to the Olympic Village together, the Italians deliberately refraining from singing, to avoid hurting the Norwegians' feelings.

Two years later, when Italy, by a curious coincidence, just defeated Norway 2-1, again in extra time, in Marseilles, there was another chivalrous gesture. The huge, blond Norwegian centre forward, Brunyldsen, who tormented Italy's defence throughout the match (Pozzo called him 'A cruel thorn in my crown of roses') unleashed, just before full-time, with the score 1-1, a tremendous high shot. Olivieri, Italy's goalkeeper, made a stupendous save — and Brunyldsen stepped forward to shake his hand. Brustad was again the Norwegian goal-scorer. Later that year, Pozzo chose him for the Rest of Europe against England, at Highbury.

Norway have yet to reach the finals of a World Cup, and since the war they have not produced a team as successful as that of the late 1930s. Among Norway's most talented players has been Bredesen, who played for Lazio of Rome as an attacker in the 1950s.

COLOURS: Red shirts, white shorts, blue stockings.
SEASON: Mid-April–mid-October.

Paraguay. The Paraguayan national football association was founded in 1906. Though never among the leading South American footballing countries, Paraguay has had her moments, and players, of great distinction. She has also produced, in Solitch, one of the finest coaches of the modern era, who, while working in Rio, was probably the pioneer of the 4-2-4 system.

Under Solitch Paraguay won the South American Championship for the first time, in 1953, in Lima, beating Brazil 3-2 in a decisive match. The team had a fine goalkeeper in Riquelme, an excellent 18-year-old centre forward in Romero, and a powerful centre half in Leguizamon. Six of the team soon afterwards emigrated to play for clubs in other South American countries, which has long been the pattern in Paraguayan football.

Erico, the best Paraguayan footballer of all time, a centre forward, went to Argentina in 1934, to play for INDEPENDIENTE. The previous year another fine Paraguayan forward, Carceres, had gone to Boca Juniors, of Buenos Aires, remaining in Argentina for 12 years.

Paraguay were runners-up in the South American Championship in 1922, 1927, 1937, 1947, 1949, and 1963. In 1930, they entered for the first World Cup, in Montevideo, and were drawn in Pool IV, losing 3-0 to the U.S.A., but defeating Belgium 1-0 with a goal by their captain and outside left, Pena.

They qualified again in 1950, when the team which went to Brazil was captained by its inside left, Fretes. Sweden were held to a draw, 2-2, in Curitiba, but Italy beat Paraguay 2-0, in São Paulo. Unzaim, the team's outside left, later played successfully for Lazio of Rome, and in France.

In 1958, Paraguay accomplished the considerable feat of knocking out Uruguay in the World Cup eliminators, thus qualifying for the finals in Sweden. The matches against Uruguay resulted in a 5-0 victory for Paraguay in Asunción, and a 2-0 defeat in Montevideo.

In Sweden, a team whose general was Parodi, a clever inside forward who had played for Genoa in the Italian championship, began badly, losing 7-3 to France at Norrköping. In its second match, however, it defeated Scotland 3-2, on the same ground, and finally drew 3-3 with Yugoslavia at Ekilstuna. The young centre half, Lezcano, helped Penarol to win the world cup championship for clubs in 1966. Achucarro and Villalba were excellent wing halves.

In 1960, the Olimpia club of Asunción lost on aggregate by a single goal to Penarol (0-1, 1-1) in the first final of the South American Liberators Cup.

COLOURS: Red and white jerseys, blue shorts.
SEASON: March–October.

Peru founded their Association in 1919 and entered the first World Cup 11 years later. They lost their first match (a rough one in which their captain was sent off the field) 3-1 to Romania, but their second saw them give a notable performance. Opposed to Uruguay, the powerful hosts, they lost by only a single goal, and their goalkeeper, Pardon, and the left back, Maquilon, were exceptional.

Six years later Peru competed in the Olympic tournament in Germany. Their gifted team beat Finland 7-3, and were then drawn against Austria. At full-time the score was 2-2, in extra time Peru got two more goals to make it 4-2, but since they had substituted a player, they were ordered to replay. This they refused to do, so Austria were given a bye to the final. From then until 1970, no Peruvian team appeared in the finals of a World Cup or an Olympiad, although they competed regularly in the World Cup qualifying stages and, with distinction, in the South American Championship.

They staged the championship themselves in 1927, 1939 (when they won it), 1953, and 1957. It was in the late 1950s that they had perhaps the best team they had ever possessed, pressing Brazil very hard in the qualifying phase of the 1958 World Cup (they lost by only 1-0 in the decisive match in Rio) and distinguishing themselves in the South American Championship of 1959 in Buenos Aires. There, they held Brazil, the World Cup holders, to a 2-2 draw, then defeated Uruguay 5-3. Four of their players, Azca, the goalkeeper, Benitez, then a left back, Gomez-

Sanchez, the outside right, and Joya, centre forward, were chosen by journalists for an All-South America selection, while Seminario, the outside left, was equally effective. Later in the year, they defeated England 4-1 in Lima.

The team then broke up, most of the leading players going abroad. Joya, now a left winger, won a world club championship medal with Penarol of Montevideo in 1966, Benitez was right half· in the Milan team which won the 1963 European Cup, while Seminario played in Spain and Portugal. The coach of the 1959 team was Orth, the celebrated former Hungarian centre half, who had become a naturalized Peruvian.

In the late 1960s the national side was managed for a time by the great Brazilian inside forward, Didì, who also had charge of the leading Cristal club of Lima. The national side qualified for the 1970 World Cup final stages and, after beating Bulgaria 3-2 and Morocco 3-0 in the first round, were only beaten 2-4 by the eventual winners, Brazil, in an exciting quarter-final.

COLOURS: Red and white stripes.
SEASON: All year.

Poland. Polish football, although the national Association was founded in 1919, made no true impact on the world game until the late 1930s and then, understandably, was a long time recovering from the Second World War. The season runs from March to November, but leading clubs, particularly the dominant postwar team, GORNIK ZABRZE, participate regularly outside that period in the various European championships.

The first appearance of a Polish team in international competition was in the Olympic tournament of 1924 in Paris, when it was defeated 5-0 by Hungary in the first round. In 1936, however, the Poles went as far as the semi-finals of the Olympic tournament in Berlin. Hungary were most impressively beaten 3-0 and Britain 5-4. In the semi-finals, however, Poland went down 3-1 to Austria, while in the third-place match they lost 3-2 to Norway.

They now had the basis of an excellent team, and qualified for the finals of the World Cup, in France, after a season in which they beat Denmark 3-1 and the Republic of Ireland 6-1. In their first match, at Strasbourg, Poland were drawn against Brazil, and lost 5-4 in extra time, after a very exciting game. The fair-haired Polish inside left, Willimowski, scored all the team's four goals. Gora, Nytz, and Dytko made up a fine half-back line.

Immediately after the war, a Polish Army team, the Carpathians, toured England, playing skilful football. In Poland itself, the clubs were reorganized, and often renamed on the Communist pattern. There was little contact with countries beyond the Iron Curtain, but Poland entered the 1958 World Cup and beat Russia in Warsaw in an eliminating group which the Russians eventually won.

In 1960 the Poles sent their full international team to compete in the Olympic tournament in Italy. They beat Tunisia 6-1 in Rome, but lost 2-1 to Denmark at Livorno and 2-0 to Argentina at Naples, and so did not qualify in their group. The leading Polish player of this epoch was the Gornik inside forward, Pohl, a superb striker of the ball with either foot and a diligent worker in midfield.

In the late 1960s there emerged a still more talented Gornik forward in LUBANSKI, who became a regular member — and scorer — of the international side while still in his teens. Yet, although fine stadia were built in Warsaw and Katowice and the popularity of the game grew, no Polish team had qualified for the World Cup finals between 1938 and 1970. Gwardia of Warsaw entered the first European Cup competition in the 1955-6 season, but was eliminated in the first round by Djurgarden of Sweden. Not until 1962-3 did a Polish team, Polonia Bytom, get beyond this stage, and not until 1968 did one advance beyond the second round. This was when Gornik got to the quarter-finals, playing two memorable games against the eventual winners, Manchester United, whom they actually beat 1-0 in the return match in Poland. Since then Polish football has continued to improve, with Gornik reaching the final of the European Cup-Winners Cup in 1970, and the national team winning the Olympic football tournament in Munich in 1972 and later qualifying for the final stages of the 1974 World Cup by eliminating England and Wales.

COLOURS: White shirts, red shorts.
SEASON: March–November.

Portugal. Though the Portuguese Federation was founded in 1912, there is surprisingly little history until the 1950s. Not, indeed, until 1966 did Portugal succeed in reaching the finals of the World Cup, although then it was to take an honourable third place, after narrowly losing to the winners, England, in the semi-finals.

It might almost be said that the effective history of Portuguese football runs concurrently with that of the Benfica club of Lisbon. Under the managership of the Hungarian, GUTTMANN, Benfica built up an outstanding team in the early 1960s, thanks partly to the importing of players from Portugal's African colonies.

In the 1940s, however, Portugal had already produced two outstanding inside forwards in Vasques and Travassos. The latter played with distinction in the Rest of Europe team which beat Great Britain 4-1 in Belfast in August 1955. Earlier that year, Portugal, who lost 10-0 in Lisbon to England in 1948, had enjoyed a measure of revenge when they beat England 3-1 in Oporto. Their star that day was a coloured inside forward called Matateu, the precursor of Eusebio and COLUNA.

It was Coluna, an inside left and later half-back from Angola, who scored the decisive goal for Benfica against Barcelona in the European Cup Final of 1961 in Berne, with a characteristically powerful left-footed shot. Benfica were now to take over from the Sporting Club of Lisbon as the dominant team in Portuguese football. They had other outstanding footballers in GERMANO, a powerful and splendidly mobile centre half, and Aguas, a versatile centre forward.

In 1962 they retained the European Cup, after knocking out Tottenham Hotspur on aggregate in the semi-final. By now, they had in their attack the finest Portuguese forward of all time, the inside forward Eusebio from Mozambique. He had been put into the team earlier that season, at the age of 19, in Uruguay, when the club played for and lost the world title against Penarol. In the final, played in Amsterdam against Regl Madrid, his tremendous right-footed shooting contrasted with the spectacular left-footed shooting of Puskas on the other side. Benfica won memorably, 5-3, and at the end of the match, Puskas presented Eusebio with his jersey.

Benfica reached the final a third time, in 1963, losing unluckily to Milan at Wembley, while in 1968 they were beaten after extra time (again at Wembley) by MANCHESTER UNITED. Wembley was also the scene of Portugal's 2-1 defeat by England and their triumph over Russia in the third place match of the 1966 World Cup, in which Eusebio was immensely successful. He scored four goals to rally the team in the quarter-finals, when they were 3-0 down to North Korea. His Benfica club-mate, the huge Torres, was also a great success at centre forward (where he had succeeded Aguas), while Simoes, yet another Benfica player, had emerged as a fine winger.

COLOURS: Red shirts, blue shorts.
SEASON: September–May.

Romania. The Romanian Soccer Federation was founded in 1910. Immediately after the First World War many of the leading players were Hungarian. A team was entered for the 1924 Olympics, but was beaten 6-0 by Holland in its first match.

In 1930 Romania entered for the first World Cup in Uruguay. King Carol, whose first act on ascending the throne was to grant an amnesty to all suspended footballers, chose the Romanian team, player by player, and then interceded with their various employers for permission for them to make the long journey to South America. In its first match, Romania beat Peru 3-1, Staucin, their centre forward, scoring twice. Vogl, the centre half and captain, and Robe, the right half, were the foremost members of a useful team which, however, lost 4-0 to Uruguay.

In 1934 Romania qualified for the World Cup finals in Italy, and a team which included only one member of the 1930 side, Covaci, narrowly lost, 2-1, to the Czechs at Trieste in the first round, after holding a 1-0 lead at half-time. Only two marvellous saves by the Czech goalkeeper, Planicka, prevented the quick, clever Romanian side from at least equalizing.

In 1938 Romania surprisingly lost to Cuba in the French World Cup at Toulouse, after a replay. Covaci played in his third World Cup, and the French linesman gave Cuba's winning goal offside.

Thereafter Romania failed for many years to qualify for the final stages of any major tournament. For a decade after the war they had little to do with European countries on the other side of the Iron Curtain, though they developed one or two useful club teams, particularly the Army side, C.C.A. of Bucharest, with its clever inside right, Constantin.

Romanian club sides have competed steadily in the three European cup competitions, and in the later 1960s a useful international side was built, with a particularly talented right winger in Pircalab, while no fewer than six of the Nunweiller brothers became successful footballers. The leading teams were now Dynamo and Steaua of Bucharest, and Petrolul of Ploesti.

England, who had defeated Romania 2-0 in Bucharest in 1939, were twice met and twice held to a draw, in the 1968-9 season. A year later England and Romania met again, in the 1970 World Cup in Mexico. Romania did not advance beyond the first round but they beat Czechoslovakia 2-1 and were only beaten by England 0-1, and by Brazil 2-3.

COLOURS: Yellow shirts, blue shorts, red stockings.
SEASON: March–July, September–December.

South Africa has been producing first-class talent for over 40 years and receiving F.A. touring teams since 1910 (until her withdrawal from the Commonwealth), but has yet to develop a viable professional organization and, in consequence, a strong international team. During the 1960s, moreover, the policies of apartheid made South Africa *persona non grata* with F.I.F.A.

The 1910 English touring side was extremely powerful, containing such players as Holley, Wedlock, and WOODWARD. It won all its 23 games, scoring 143 goals against 16; yet in the three international matches, South Africa did remarkably well, going down 3-0, 6-2, and 6-3. After the First World War, there were three further tours, in 1920, 1929, and 1939, England winning all nine international matches, but on three occasions having to be content with odd-goal victories. But the immense popularity of Rugby football was something against which soccer, largely centred in Cape Town and Johannesburg, could scarcely prevail.

In 1924, South Africa made an impressive tour of Britain. Liverpool began to make a practice of signing South African players, with enormous success. Hodgson, a centre forward, not only won several full caps for England, but set a League scoring record with the club during the 1920s and 1930s which stood until January 1969. Riley was a capable goalkeeper, Nieuwenhuys an outside right of considerable skill.

After the war, a South African winger, Priday, helped Liverpool to win the championship, but it was Charlton Athletic, above all, who encouraged South African talent. In 1946, they used O'Linn — later a Test cricketer — and Forbes in their League team, while in the 1950s the two forwards, Leary and Firmani, were a formidable pair of strikers. Leary went on to play cricket for Kent, Firmani to join Sampdoria of Genoa, to play for Italy, and also to figure in the attack of Internazionale, Milan. In 1967 Charlton appointed him their manager.

Blackpool's South African left-winger, Perry, scored the winning goal for them in the Cup final of 1953, and was capped for England; Kelly played in goal for Barnsley and Ireland; and Stuart gave WOLVERHAMPTON many years of service at right back. In 1959 a professional League was begun in Johannesburg, and, especially after South Africa left the Commonwealth, the tide began to move in the opposite direction. Veteran British professional players tended to go to play in South Africa.

In 1954 and 1958 South Africa sent touring teams to England again, playing largely amateur teams or the reserve teams of professional clubs.

COLOURS: Green shirts, white shorts, green and gold stockings.
SEASON: Mid-January–mid-September.

Spain. The Spanish Federation was founded in 1905. The first time the international team entered a tournament was in 1920, on the occasion of the 1920 Olympiad, and with remarkable success. Denmark were favoured to win the competition, but Spain

defeated them, 1-0. Unfortunately they were obliged on the very next day to meet Belgium, the hosts, who were quite fresh, and they lost, 3-1. In the consolation tournament, however, they beat Sweden, Italy (though reduced to nine sound men), and Holland, and were awarded second place in the competition, the Czechs having been disqualified.

In the 1924 Olympics Italy had their revenge in Paris, winning 1-0 before a crowd of 30,000. It was a match which revealed the vast talents of ZAMORA, the finest Spanish goalkeeper of all time. His only unhappy match for Spain coincided with his solitary appearance in London when, on a muddy day in 1931, his nervousness caused him to give away some easy goals to England, who won 7-1. This was England's revenge for defeat by Spain in Madrid in May 1929, when the Spaniards became the first foreign side ever to defeat the full English international team. On this occasion Zamora played superbly, and the Spanish forwards played with high skill in the intense heat, which much affected the English players.

The previous year, in the 1928 Olympiad, Spain entered a genuinely amateur team which, after drawing 1-1 with Italy's 'disguised' professionals, could not sustain such form in the replay, and lost 7-1.

Spain entered the World Cup for the first time in 1934, when they once again fell to Italy, this time at Florence in the second round in two violent games. Zamora, by now a veteran, was superb in the first, but was so roughly treated that he was unfit for the second. Quincoces was an excellent full-back.

In 1938, the civil war made entry for the World Cup impossible, but, in 1950, Spain competed in Brazil, beat England 1-0 in Rio, qualified for the final pool, but finished fourth, scoring only one point for a draw with Uruguay. Their outstanding players were Zarra, the centre forward, Basora, outside right, and Ramallets, who kept goal splendidly against England.

The 1950s saw the rise of the Real Madrid club, the development of their immense Bernabeu Stadium (named after their resourceful president), and their amazing domination of the European Cup, which they won five times consecutively. Foreign players, particularly their superb Argentinian centre forward, Di Stefano, and Puskas, who came into the team in 1959, played a major part. Barcelona, another excellent team, lost in the European Cup final of 1961 to Benfica.

The international team failed to qualify for the World Cup in 1954 or 1958, were eliminated in their qualifying group at Viña del Mar in Chile in 1962, and again, in England, four years later, and failed to qualify for the 1970 final stages.

They did, however, win the European Nations Cup in 1964, beating Russia in the final in Madrid. A great contribution was made by SUAREZ, the former Barcelona inside forward, by then playing for Internazionale of Milan.

Spain has also contributed to the game a famous referee and, later, administrator, in Escartin.

COLOURS: Red shirts, blue shorts.
SEASON: September–June.

Sweden. Though not as swift starters as their neighbours the Danes, Sweden overhauled them between the wars, and have produced an array of fine players, many of whom have played for clubs in other lands. The Swedes sent a team to the London Olympics of 1908, but it was crushed 12-1 by the United Kingdom in the first round. They played a 'consolation' match against Holland, however, and lost only 2-0.

Between then and the 1912 Olympics, which they themselves staged, they played five matches against the England amateur team, losing them all. But the extent of their progress was shown when, in the first round of the Olympic tournament, they lost only 4-3 to the Dutch. In the consolation tournament, Italy defeated them, 1-0. They were to lose to Holland yet a third time: 5-4 in the 1920 Olympics, held in Antwerp.

But, by 1923, they were good enough to play hosts, and give a reasonable account of themselves, against the full English professional team, going down only by 4-2 and 3-1. The following year they did remarkably well in the Paris Olympic tournament, losing only 2-1 to Switzerland in a close semi-final, and at last getting the better of Holland, 3-1, in the third-place match.

1934 saw them enter the World Cup for the first time. At Bologna, they showed talent and temperament in defeating Argentina 3-2; Jonasson proved an excellent centre forward. In the next round, however, Germany beat them 2-1 in Milan, the Swedes pulling back a goal after they had been reduced to ten men.

1936 saw their defeat at the Berlin Olympics by Japan; but they again contested the World Cup finals in France in 1938. Their captain was the 35-year-old Keller, inside right and general of the attack, who has been a member of their 1924 Olympic side. That team had beaten the holders, Belgium, 8-1, and this one, drawing a bye in the first round, proceeded to beat Cuba 8-0. The outstanding player was Westerstroem, a winger. But Hungary beat them 5-1 in the semi-final.

The war years allowed Sweden, uninvolved, to develop prodigiously and by 1946 NORRKÖPING had an outstanding club side, including the three brothers Nordahl — Gunnar, Knud, and Bertil — and the immensely versatile Liedholm. All of them, plus the brilliant inside right, Gren, later helped Sweden to win the 1948 Olympic tournament, defeating Yugoslavia 3-1 at Wembley in the final, and all eventually played for clubs in Italy, where Gren, Gunnar Nordahl, and Liedholm formed the famous 'Gre-no-li' trio for Milan.

The mass pillaging by Italian clubs meant that Raynor, Sweden's gifted little team manager from Yorkshire, had to build a new side for the 1950 World Cup in Brazil. Yet it was good enough to knock out Italy in the qualifying group and eventually to take third place. Among its stars were the inside forwards, Skoglund and Palmer, Knud Nordahl, and the centre forward, Jeppson. All, once again, turned professional with Italian clubs. The Swedes themselves did not adopt part-time professionalism for nearly a decade.

In 1958 Raynor returned, and took advantage of the new dispensation to bring star players such as Hamrin, Skoglund, and Liedholm back from abroad. With Gren also in the World Cup team, the Swedes, playing hosts, reached the finals of the competition. They defeated Russia in the quarter-finals, West Germany in the semi-finals, and ultimately lost 5-2 to Brazil in Stockholm in the final, after taking an early lead through Liedholm.

During the 1960s their best players, such as Kindvall (to Holland), Persson (to Glasgow Rangers), and Magnusson (to Italy, Germany, and France) continued to go abroad, and Sweden did not qualify for the World Cup finals of 1962 or 1966. They qualified in 1970 but failed to advance beyond the first round, and qualified again for the 1974 finals after a play-off with Austria.

COLOURS: Yellow shirts, blue shorts.
SEASON: April–November.

Switzerland. The Swiss Football Federation was founded as early as 1895. It was not until 1920, however, that the Swiss entered an Olympic tournament, and then they conceded a walk-over in the first round to France in Antwerp. From 1924, however, when they reached the final of the Olympic tournament in Paris, the Swiss have been sturdy competitors in the international field, frequently reaching the final stages of the World Cup.

In the 1924 Olympics they beat Lithuania 9-0 in the first round, knocked out the Czechs 1-0 after a 1-1 draw, defeated Italy 2-1 in the semi-finals, but lost 3-0 to Uruguay in the final. In 1928, however, in Holland, they lost their first round match 4-0 to Germany, and have not subsequently competed in an Olympic tournament.

The Swiss first entered the World Cup in 1934, reached the finals in Italy, and won their first round match in Milan, defeating Holland 3-2 in a close game. Kilholz, their centre forward, got two of the goals; the other went to Abegglen III, one of three brothers who all played for their country with distinction. In the second round, Switzerland lost in a very tight game to the Czechs, 3-2, Kielholz and Abegglen again being the scorers.

1938 was a fine year for Swiss football. Not only were the World Cup finals reached again, but a powerful England team was defeated 2-1 in Zurich. In the first round of the World Cup in Paris, the Swiss drew 1-1 with Germany after extra time, Abegglen III scoring their goal, and then splendidly won the replay 4-2, Abegglen III scoring two more goals. One of the others went to Bickel, who was still playing for his famous Zurich club, the Grasshoppers, in the 1950s.

After the war, Swiss football was dominated by the *verrou* pattern of football — with a sweeper-up — introduced by the Austrian coach, Rappan. Steffen, a huge, blond left back, played for the Rest of Europe against Britain in 1947, the year in which he also made a number of appearances for Chelsea.

In 1950 Switzerland travelled to the World Cup, where they nearly beat Brazil at São Paulo; the result was a 2-2 draw. Antenen and Fatton were particularly dangerous wingers, Neury an excellent full-back.

In 1954 Switzerland staged the World Cup, and their own team reached the quarter-final, twice defeating Italy, losing 2-0 to England, and going out 7-5 to Austria in an extraordinary quarter-final. Antenen and Fatton played again; Vonlanthen, the inside forward, eventually played for Internazionale of Milan.

Switzerland did not qualify for the 1958 World Cup, but competed in the Santiago group in Chile in 1962, where Antenen competed in his third World Cup, and in the Midland group in England in 1966. In neither case did the team qualify for the quarter-final round, nor did it for the final stages of the 1970 and 1974 competitions.

COLOURS: Red shirts with a white cross, white shorts, white stockings.
SEASON: September–May.

Turkey. The Turkish Football Association was founded in 1923. The leading clubs, Fenerbahce, Galatassaray, and Besiktas all come from Istanbul, and have competed regularly in the European Cup competitions. Goztepe Izmir have taken part with some success in the European Fairs Cup.

For many years the Istanbul League was much the strongest in the country, but, in 1959, national first and second division tournaments were initiated.

A Turkish side first entered the Olympic football tournament in 1936 in Germany, being defeated 4-0 in the first round by Norway. They again competed in London in 1948, defeating China 4-0 in the first round, but going down 3-1 to Yugoslavia in the second. In 1952, in Finland, they received a bye in the first round, knocked out the Dutch Antilles 2-1, and were then beaten 7-1 by Hungary, the ultimate winners, in the quarter-finals. They did not qualify for the finals of 1956, 1960, 1964, or 1968.

The Turks reached the finals of the World Cup in 1954, when they eliminated Spain, in a play-off match in Rome, on the toss of a coin. In Berne, they lost 4-1 to West Germany, and beat South Korea 7-0 in Geneva. This led to a play-off against West Germany in Zurich, which the Germans won 7-2. Turgay, the Turkish captain and goalkeeper, was not fit and missed the game. An outstanding member of the team was the inside left, Lefter, who two years later inspired the 3-1 defeat in Istanbul, of the powerful Hungarian side. Lefter played with success for the Nice and Fiorentina clubs.

Among other outstanding Turkish footballers have been Can, a fine outside left or inside forward, who in the early 1960s played for a number of Italian clubs, including Venice and Fiorentina; Metin, a centre forward who played for Palermo; and Ozcan, a goalkeeper who represented S.V. Hamburg in the European Cup-Winners Cup final of 1968.

Fenerbahce eliminated the English champions, MANCHESTER CITY, in the first round of the 1968-9 European Cup on full merit.

COLOURS: White shirts with white star and crescent in red hoop, white shorts, red and white stockings.
SEASON: September–May.

U.S.A. Although various attempts have been made, soccer has obstinately refused to take root in the United States. It has for many years been extensively played at a minor level, particularly in Philadelphia, where there has long been a proliferation of leagues, and in St. Louis, where it is very popular in the schools.

In the early 1920s a number of American clubs, notably that owned by the vast Bethlehem Steel Corporation, began to poach players from Britain — Scotland in particular — hoping to give the game an impetus. The outlawed American Soccer League, in contention with the United States Soccer Association, offered good players some £20 a week, at a time when the top wage in Britain was £8. Among those who accepted these terms were

Wattie JACKSON, the Kilmarnock centre forward, and his younger brother, Alec, from the Dumbarton club, later to return to Britain to become an outstanding right winger with ABERDEEN, HUDDERSFIELD, and Chelsea. Harper, the Scottish international goalkeeper, Chedgzoy, an Everton and England outside right, Howieson, from Hull City, and Blair, of Manchester City, were all still in the U.S.A. in 1929, Harper with the Boston club, the others with New Bedford. In 1932, after the tragic death of Thomson, Glasgow Celtic brought back Kennaway from the Fall River club, to keep goal for them.

The experiment failed, though the game was kept going by such as Jeffrey, who arrived during the 1920s to work on the railroad, play soccer for a works team, eventually become a highly successful coach at Penn State University, and at last manage the U.S.A. team which beat England in the World Cup of 1950.

In 1930, boosted by their British stars, the U.S.A. entered for the first World Cup, in Uruguay, where they acquitted themselves honourably. Captained by their inside right, Florie, the U.S.A. defeated Belgium 3-0 in their first match, and kept the same XI to beat Paraguay by the same score. This put them at the head of their group and into the semi-finals, in which Argentina were too strong for them, winning 6-1. Four years later the U.S.A. team got as far as a preliminary World Cup match in Rome against Italy, which they lost 7-1.

In 1950 Jeffrey took a scratch team to Brazil, which astonished the footballing world by beating the powerful England side 1-0 at Belo Horizonte. The only goal was headed by the centre forward, the Haitian-born Gaetjens. McIlvenney, a free-transfer Scottish player from Wrexham F.C., was the right half and captain. The Americans also put up a fine performance against Spain, but lost 5-2 to Chile and did not reach the final pool.

The game, however, still obstinately failed to capture the imagination of a public brought up on the more violent native product, and, even when a group of optimistic millionaires decided to impose it 'from above' in 1967, they met with indifferent success.

Unfortunately, two rival bodies, the official United States Soccer Association (which invited foreign teams to play in an invitational league) and the 'outlawed' National Professional Soccer League (N.P.S.L.), came into being. The N.P.S.L. imported players, in a great hurry, from all over the world, and established particularly impressive clubs in Atlanta, Baltimore, and St. Louis. In 1968, the two factions made peace and amalgamated to form the North American Soccer League,

but huge sums of money were lost by all concerned, and on 1 November, at a meeting at Chicago, the League ceased to exist in its comprehensive form.

Nevertheless, clubs had been established and, after a brief alarm that league competition would die entirely, a provisional competition was laboriously put together. Meanwhile, there was vastly increased activity in high schools and colleges.

COLOURS: White shirts, blue shorts, red stockings.
SEASON: March–December.

U.S.S.R. Football was brought to Russia by the English brothers Charnock in 1887 when they formed the earliest football team at their cotton mills in Orekhovo-Zuyevo, partly as an antidote to revolutionary activity among their workers. Strap-piercers in the mill were used to attach studs to the players' boots. Before the outbreak of the First World War, there was already a vigorous league of factory teams in the Moscow region, sometimes drawing crowds as large as 15,000.

Russia sent a team to the Olympic tournament of 1912, where it lost 2-1 in the first round to Finland, and then, humiliatingly, 16-0 to Germany in the consolation tournament.

After the Revolution, Russian football continued to develop, with the formation of such clubs as Dynamo Moscow, but there were no contacts at all with the world game until 1945, when the famous and talented Dynamo Moscow side was sent to Britain. They made an unbeaten tour of four matches, drawing with Chelsea and Rangers, beating Arsenal 4-3 in a contentious match refereed by Latychev (who took charge of the 1962 World Cup final), and Cardiff City by 10-1. On the way home, they narrowly beat the Swedish club, Norrköping. The team played smooth, attacking football, and had a remarkable inside-forward trio of Kartsev, BESKOV, and Bobrov.

After this, Russia again withdrew from international competition until 1952, when they sent a team to the Helsinki Olympics, with Bobrov at centre forward. They drew an extraordinary match 5-5 with Yugoslavia, but lost 3-1 in the replay. Since all Russian players are nominally amateurs, this was the full international team; as it was when it proceeded to win the Olympic tournament of 1956 in Melbourne, defeating Yugoslavia 1-0 in the final.

In 1958 Russia entered the World Cup for the first time, qualified for the quarter-final by beating England 1-0 in a play-off in Göteborg, but were then defeated by Sweden. By now, the pattern of Russian football had set into one of physical power and rather unimaginative efficiency. There were, however, outstanding players such as the attacking wing half,

NETTO, the centre forward, Simonian, and above all the tall goalkeeper, YASHIN, who was twice to play for world representative teams. He was a product of Dynamo Moscow.

The first Russian club to enter European competition was Dynamo Kiev which reached the semi-finals of the Cup-Winners Cup in 1965-6, while Torpedo of Moscow competed in the European Cup in the following season.

Russia won the first European Nations Cup in Paris in 1960, defeating Yugoslavia in the final, and lost 2-1 to Spain in the 1964 final in Madrid. In 1968 England beat them 2-0 in Rome in the third-place match and in 1972 in Brussels they were beaten 0-3 in the final by West Germany.

Russia were eliminated in the quarter-final in the 1962 World Cup in Chile, when Yashin had one of his rare poor spells, while in 1966, at Everton, West Germany knocked them out in the semi-final and Portugal beat them in the third-place match. In 1970 in Mexico they were again eliminated at the quarter-final stage, and were to refuse a qualifying match against Chile for the 1974 Cup.

The tendency during the 1960s was for power to shift from Moscow into the provinces, where Dynamo Kiev in particular emerged as a successful club, and later national championships were won by Zaria Voroshilovgrad (1972) and Ararat Erevan (1973).

COLOURS: Red shirts, white shorts.

SEASON: South: March–December; Central Russia: April–October; North: May–September.

Uruguay. Stimulated by the donation of the Lipton Cup for matches against Argentina, football in Uruguay was already a fairly sturdy growth in the early years of the twentieth century. The Federation was founded in 1900, but it was in the 1920s that football really flowered. Outstanding teams, highly trained and virtually professional, were sent to the Olympics of 1924 and 1928, in each case winning the football tournament. They included such outstandingly gifted footballers as the full-back, J. ANDRADE, and the forwards, Petrone and Scarone.

In 1930 Uruguay staged the first World Cup, to coincide with the centenary of their independence. The long journey by sea deterred most of the leading European teams from competing, a circumstance taken gravely amiss by Uruguay, who retaliated by refusing to enter the European World Cups of 1934 and 1938. A new stadium, the Centenario Stadium, was built in Montevideo, though it was completed only after the tournament began, and the Uruguayan international team went into 'concentration' for weeks beforehand in a house furnished from top to bottom by local firms. A vigilant curfew was imposed on the players, and when the celebrated goalkeeper, Mazzali, was caught entering the house after hours, he was expelled without more ado.

Uruguay duly won the competition, after an uncertain start. Beating Peru only 1-0, they more easily defeated Romania, 4-0, qualified for the semi-finals, in which they beat Yugoslavia 6-1, and finally beat Argentina 4-2 in the final, after being 2-1 behind.

Four years later the Uruguayans were still having trouble with the problem of overt professionalism, but despite their tiny population (2,000,000), the quality of their football remained as high as ever. In 1950, they again won the World Cup, thanks in no small measure to the play of two forwards, who participated in 1949 in a South American Championship, which proved disastrous for Uruguay, who sent only a skeleton team owing to a strike by the professionals. The outstanding forwards were SCHIAFFINO, inside left, and Ghiggia, outside right, who scored the two goals in a dramatic 2-1 win over Brazil in the Maracaña Stadium in the decisive match. The captain of the team was its roving centre half, the powerful VARELA, who was outstanding, while R. ANDRADE, nephew of the former international player, had a superb game in defence.

Uruguay, whose championship has long been dominated by the two Montevideo clubs, Penarol and Nacional, reached the semi-finals of the World Cup in Switzerland in 1954, when they were unlucky to lose a classically exciting match to Hungary 4-2 in extra time. Schiaffino and Varela were again members of a team which beat Scotland 7-0, and beat England 4-2 in the quarter-finals.

In 1958 Uruguay failed to qualify for Sweden, being eliminated by Paraguay. In 1962, now playing 4-2-4, the Uruguayans reached the final pool, but failed to qualify, in Arica, Chile, for the quarter-final matches, while in 1966, playing with a sweeper-up, they were beaten by West Germany at Sheffield in a violent quarter-final, during which they had two men sent off. Their team was much weakened by the depredations of Argentinian clubs. In 1970 however in Mexico they reached fourth place after losing 1-3 to Brazil in the semi-final and 0-1 to West Germany in the match between the defeated semi-finalists, and were again to qualify for the finals in 1974.

COLOURS: Light blue shirts, black shorts.

SEASON: April–December.

Yugoslavia. The Yugoslav Federation was founded in 1919, and the national team plunged almost immediately into international competition, losing 9-0 to the much more experienced Czechs in the 1920 Olympic tournament in Antwerp. Within a decade, however, they were good enough to defeat Brazil and to reach the semi-finals of the first World Cup.

Meanwhile they were again heavily beaten in the first round of the 1924 Olympic tournament in France: 7-0 by Uruguay who were to knock them out of the World Cup in 1930 by 6-1. In 1928, in Amsterdam, they drew a bye in the Olympic competition, before succumbing 2-1 to the Portuguese.

The 1930 World Cup team had an excellent right wing in Tirnanic, who managed the national team after the Second World War, and Marianovic. Stefanovic, centre half, and Beck, the centre forward, had played in Sete's French cup-winning team two months earlier, an honour won by the left winger Seculic the following season, with Montpellier. Seculic preceded Tirnanic as Yugoslavia's team manager up to 1954. Beck, then only 21, won 15 caps for his country, and then took French nationality and played for France. Having defeated the more technically skilled Brazilians, the Yugoslavs beat Bolivia 4-0, qualified for the semi-finals, and went to Uruguay. They did not qualify again for the World Cup finals until 1950, although in 1939 they beat a strong England team 2-1 in Belgrade.

After the Second World War their football recovered very quickly; they were Olympic runners-up in 1948. Several clubs were renamed and reorganized — Dynamo Zagreb, Partizan, and RED STAR of Belgrade — though the outstanding club of the early 1950s was Hajduk of Split. The 1950 Yugoslav World Cup team which went to Brazil was immensely talented, with superb inside forwards in MITIC (later team manager) and Bobek, a fine right half in Cjaicowski, a brilliant goalkeeper in Beara. A head injury to Mitic as he took the field in Rio contributed to a 2-0 defeat by Brazil, but they easily beat Switzerland and Mexico. Thus Yugoslavia unluckily failed to qualify for the final pool.

In Switzerland four years later, having been runners-up in the 1952 Olympic tournament, they again fielded a most gifted team, which reached the quarter-finals and lost 2-0 to West Germany. To Mitic, Bobek, Beara, and Cjaicowski were added the equally talented VUKAS and ZEBEC.

In 1956, Russia beat Yugoslavia 1-0 in the Olympic final in Melbourne. Yugoslavia finally won the Olympic crown in 1960 in Rome, beating the Danes, although their most consistent scorer, Galic, was sent off. In the 1958 World Cup, a team which now included the outstanding inside forward Sekularac, with Zebec at centre half, lost in the quarter-finals

1-0 to West Germany at Malmö; a result which was reversed in the quarter-finals of the Chilean World Cup at Santiago. In the semifinals, however, the Czechs beat them at Viña del Mar, and Yugoslavia lost the third-place match to Chile. Sekularac was their foremost player, Soskic a fine goalkeeper.

They did not qualify for the 1966 or 1970 World Cups, but were to contest the finals in 1974; despite enormous depredations of their players by foreign teams, they reached the finals of the 1968 Nations Cup (for the second time), losing on a replay to Italy in Rome. In DZAJIC, outside left, the Yugoslavs had the most admired player of the competition.

COLOURS: Blue with white shorts.

SEASON: August–June.

R. C. Churchill, *English League Football* (1961); Maurice Golesworthy, *The Encyclopaedia of Association Football*, latest edition; Maurice Golesworthy and Roger Macdonald, *The AB-Z of World Football* (1966); Geoffrey Green, *The History of the Football Association* (1953) and *The Official History of the F.A. Cup* (1949); Gordon Jeffery, *European International Football* (1963); Willy Meisl, *Soccer Revolution* (1955).

GOVERNING BODY (WORLD): Fédération Internationale de Football Associations (F.I.F.A.), F.I.F.A. House, Hitziweg 11, 8032 Zurich, Switzerland; (ENGLAND): The Football Association, 22 Lancaster Gate, London W.2.

FOOTBALL, Australian Rules

is a fast-moving game with few rules apart from those aimed at protecting the player. High marking and long kicking from man to man (to advance the ball up field) are the main features of the sport, which draws crowds that are claimed by the Australian National Football Council (A.F.C.) to be the largest in the world *per capita*. The field has no definite size, but minimum and maximum standards have been set. The oval must have a minimum width of 120 yds. (110 m.) and a maximum of 170 yds. (155 m.). The minimum length is 150 yds. (135 m.) and the maximum 200 yds. (185 m.).

A team consists of 18 players with two reserves. A game consists of four quarters of 25 minutes each plus 'time on' for delays in play. The teams change ends at each quarter, and there is a 15-minute break at half time and a five-minute break at three-quarter time, when the coaches are allowed to address their team on the field.

The scoring consists of 'goals' and 'behinds'. A goal is scored when the ball passes through the two centre goal posts, which are 7 yds. (6·40 m.) apart; 6 points are recorded. A behind is scored when the ball passes outside the centre posts but between a centre post and a behind post (which is situated 7 yds. to the side of each centre post); 1

point is recorded. The ball must be kicked clearly through the centre posts to register the 6 points. If it is touched by any player on its way through the posts, only 1 point is recorded. If the ball hits the goal post, again 1 point only is scored.

The ball is oval in shape, and measures 29½ in. (736 mm.) by 22¾ in. (572 mm.) when firmly inflated. It must weigh between 16 and 17 oz. (454 and 482 g.). Before a match the rival captains must approve the quality of the ball, which is shown to them by the field umpire.

A team is made up of three full-forwards, three half-forwards, three centres, three half-backs, three full-backs, and three players known as the 'ruck'. The ruck consists of two followers and a rover, who moves with the flow of the play to all parts of the ground. The reserves are used to replace injured players at any time, but once a player leaves the ground he is not permitted to return. Play is not held up when a player is injured, and the replacement cannot enter the playing area until the injured player has left it.

The officials consist of five umpires: one field umpire, two boundary umpires, and two goal umpires. The goal umpires (stationed one at each end of the ground between the goal posts), determine whether a goal or a behind has been scored, and signal the score by means of flags. Two flags are waved for a goal, one flag for a behind. The goal umpire at the opposite end of the ground acknowledges the score by waving his flags similarly, and both goal umpires keep a scoring-card. The field umpire is in sole control of the match. He interprets the laws of the game during play and awards free kicks for infringements. The two boundary umpires are stationed on either side of the playing area. They signal to the field umpire when the ball goes 'out of bounds' (out of the playing arena) and when the ball is kicked over the boundary line on the full (free kick to the nearest opponent).

The main feature of the game is the long kicking which takes place from player to player. Their chief aim is to kick to a team mate, who, though guarded by an opposing player, endeavours to give a 'lead out' by breaking away from the opposing player and taking a 'mark', which entitles him to a free kick. From the mark, he endeavours to dispose of the ball to another player of the same team (nearer the goal) who is in a position to pass it on to the forward line. Goals are often kicked from 60 to 70 yds. (55–64 m.). There is no offside rule in the game, nor is there the knock-on rule which applies in Rugby. This helps the game to flow freely.

At the start of a match the two captains toss a coin for the choice of ends. The field umpire bounces the ball in the centre circle, which is 10 ft. (3·048 m.) in diameter. It is here that the rucks, who are usually well over 6 ft. (1·83 m.) in height, go for the 'hit-out', which sends the ball into play with the rovers, who vie with each other to gain possession of the ball and move it up field towards the opposition's goal. The ball is bounced in the centre circle each time a goal is scored, the ball having been returned by the boundary umpires, who sprint to the centre to maintain the fast pace of the game.

When a ball goes out of bounds but is not

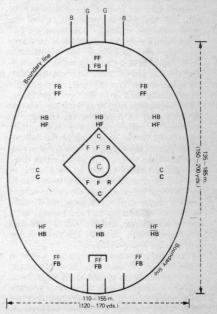

PLAYING FIELD WITH TEAM FORMATIONS, AUSTRALIAN RULES FOOTBALL
Bold-face letters indicate position of team attacking the top goal, light-face letters their opponents. (C) Centre; (F) follower and (R) rover (the ruck); (HF) half-forward; (HB) half-back; (FF) full-forward; (FB) full-back. Goal posts (G) and behind posts (B) are 6·4 m. (7 yds.) apart; goal square in 9 m. (approx. 10 yds.) deep; square at centre is 45·72 m. (approx. 50 yds.) along each side.

kicked out on the full, the boundary umpire stands on the boundary line facing away from the arena and throws the ball high into the air over his head 10 to 15 yds. (9·14–13·72 m.) into the arena. The rucks usually go for these throw-ins, but any player can go for a hit-out if the rucks are not up with the play.

A player may run with the ball providing that he bounces it at least every 10 yds. (9·14 m.). He may kick the ball off the ground or hand-pass to a member of his team. In hand-passing, the ball must be held in one hand and hit with the clenched fist of the other hand. Throwing is not permitted, and is punished by a penalty free kick to the nearest opposition player.

A 'mark' is allowed when a player catches a ball which has been kicked more than 10 yds. by another player. From the time it is kicked until it is marked, it must not touch the ground or be touched by another player.

Free kicks are given for: (*a*) throwing the ball; (*b*) grasping an opponent around the neck, shoulder, or legs; (*c*) retaining the ball when firmly held by an opponent (a player must hand-pass or kick the ball immediately he is firmly held by an opponent); (*d*) dropping the ball when firmly held by an opponent; (*e*) lying on or over the ball; (*f*) pushing a player in the back or in the face; (*g*) tripping (or attempting to trip) or striking (or attempting to strike) an opponent; (*h*) charging an opponent by rushing at him or pushing him when he is not in possession of the ball; (*i*) holding or tackling a player who is not in possession of the ball; (*j*) wilfully wasting time, or wilfully kicking or forcing the ball out of bounds; (*k*) running with the ball more than 10 yds. without bouncing it. In the case of (*c*) and (*d*), the player shall not be penalized if, when in the act of kicking or hand-balling, he is swung off balance, and his boot or hand does not connect with the ball. The field umpire will give the order to play on.

Play also continues when a player is bumped and the ball falls from his hands; when his hands are pinned to his sides, causing him to drop the ball; when he is knocked on the arm or elbow, causing him to drop the ball. When the ball is held to his body by another player the umpire takes possession of it and bounces it up; if the ground is too muddy he throws it into the air.

A player may not be sent off the field for foul play. However, any of the five umpires on the field may report a player, first having notified him that he is being reported, and taking his number. A report of the offence must be handed to the club officials immediately after the match, and the player is then summoned to a tribunal of independent administrators who deal with the matter accordingly. Evidence is given by the umpires and the players concerned, and the tribunal, which may be presided over by a stipendiary magistrate, dismisses the charge or suspends the player for a number of matches.

A player is allowed to 'check', or block, an opponent from tackling a team mate who is in possession of the ball, providing that the checking — which is also referred to as 'shepherding' — is done without any infringement of the rules, and that the ball is not more than 5 yds. (4·57 m.) away. Shepherding is not, however, permitted at the centre bounce, or at the boundary throw-in. A player can tackle an opponent by 'meeting' him with his hip or his shoulder when he is in possession of the ball, and pushing him on the side, or holding him around the waist to retard his progress.

When a behind is scored, the ball is not returned to the centre of the field, but is kicked out of the goal square, a 10 yd. (9 m.) rectangle immediately in front of the goal posts in the playing area, by the full-back, or a player from the opposing team. A ball is also out of bounds if a player kicking for goal fails to send the ball between either the goal or behind posts. If it is kicked out on the full a free kick is awarded to the nearest opponent at the spot where the ball crossed the boundary line.

When a player takes a mark and when taking his kick, his opposite number may attempt to baulk him by jumping up in front of him, calling out, or waving his arms. However, if he moves over the mark from which the free kick has been awarded, he can be penalized 15 yds. (13·72 m.) and the player taking the free kick can advance that distance nearer the goal. A player may also have a 15 yd. penalty awarded against him if, after being penalized, he refuses to return the ball to his opponent, thus delaying play and wasting time.

Place-kicking is allowed in Australian Rules football but it is seldom employed as it is regarded as time-wasting.

Australian Rules football is the national code throughout the Australian Commonwealth, although it is played mostly in the southern states, Western Australia, and Papua–New Guinea. New South Wales and Queensland tend to be dominated by the Rugby codes, but Australian football is spreading rapidly throughout these states. Although the game has been streamlined over the years, and new laws have been introduced, it is still basically the original game.

Australian football officially dates back to 1858, when H. C. A. HARRISON and his cousin, T. W. Wills, decided to devise a purely Australian game. About this time, Irish garrison troops — many of whom were on the gold diggings — played their Gaelic type of football (see FOOTBALL, GAELIC), and the presence of the English game of Rugby in the same area created some confusion when these early matches were played. Harrison and Wills were cricketers, as were their colleagues, and the CRICKET influence in the game probably accounts for the oval shape of the Australian Rules football field. In its early days, the game was played on cricket grounds controlled by cricket clubs.

The first club to be formed was the Melbourne Football Club, the oldest club in Australia. It celebrated its centenary in 1958. The club was sponsored by the Melbourne Cricket Club as a means of keeping its members fit during the winter months.

The game was of a rough-and-tumble nature as there were few rules and no defined area for the playing field. The first recorded match, on 7 August 1858, was between the Scotch College and Melbourne Church of England Grammar School. The teachers and boys did battle with forty a side, and the goal posts were nearly a mile apart. The site for this match was where the MELBOURNE CRICKET GROUND stands today, with its capacity for more than 120,000 spectators.

Other clubs were formed shortly after the Melbourne Club, and the first two (according to the Australian Football Council in its history of the game) were South Yarra and Richmond. The following year the Geelong Club was formed by Wills. All these clubs, with the exception of South Yarra, are still members of the VICTORIAN FOOTBALL LEAGUE (V.F.L.).

The early game was a mixture of soccer, Rugby, Gaelic football, and improvisation. A round ball was used and the match was started with the teams lined up on each side of the centre; the ball was kicked into play and the players rushed to their respective positions. Matches lasted until one team had scored two goals, and in some cases went on over two or three days before decisions were reached. This type of football did not last for long. Harrison and Wills, assisted by their colleagues, Hammersley and Thompson, held a meeting at the Freemason's Hotel in Swanston Street, Melbourne, on 8 May 1866 to revise the laws. They drew up what could be termed the first set of rules for the Australian game, the main points being: (1) The size of the ground was not to be more than 200 yds. (182·88 m.) long and 150 yds. (137·16 m.) wide, with the goal posts 7 yds. (6·40 m.) apart. (2) The side losing the toss would start the game by kicking off from the centre. (3) 'Little marks' were introduced when a player caught the ball directly from the foot or the leg. (4) Tripping was prohibited, although players could be pushed with the hands or the body if they were in motion, and players could be held if they were in possession of the ball. (5) Running with the ball, which up to this stage had been a feature of the game, was practically eliminated

by reducing the permitted distance to 7 yds. (6·40 m.). (6) Boundary lines were introduced, which brought in the throw-in from the boundary. (7) Throwing the ball was not permitted. (8) Captains awarded the penalties — the nearer captain having the final say.

New clubs were formed in many centres and the game spread rapidly into country areas. The movement of the troops and the miners from Victoria to South Australia and Western Australia aroused interest in the 'new game' in these states, and there was an immediate demand for its introduction in Adelaide and Perth. Groups of other football adherents switched to what was already being referred to as the 'Victorian game'. The Adelaide Club was formed in 1860.

The oval ball was being universally used by 1867, in place of the round one. Teams playing in competitive matches in Melbourne that year were: Melbourne, South Yarra, Richmond, Geelong, Emerald Hill, Prahran, and St. Kilda.

In 1869 the practice of awarding the match to the first team to score two goals was discontinued. The winner was now to be the highest scorer (goals only being counted) in a limited time. The actual playing time was never defined, but was agreed upon by the captains before the start of the game. The captains played a major role as they not only declared goals when scored, but they also awarded penalties for breaches of the rules. This responsibility was taken from them, however, in 1872, following a further revision of the rules, and umpires were introduced.

Other improvements were made, including the changing of ends at half-time instead of when a goal was scored, and penalties for breaches of the laws were introduced. The umpire also decided on whether a legitimate goal had been kicked. Although at this time there were behind posts, behinds were not counted; 'near misses' (or behinds) entitled a player of the defending side to take the ball into the playing area and kick it back towards the centre.

A year later, in 1873, uniforms were introduced, although the coloured caps which had distinguished the players up to that time were retained. Uniforms consisted of woollen jerseys or leather jackets in the colours of the clubs, and shorts stretching below the knee (many players wore knickerbockers tucked into their socks). As the game became faster the shorts became shorter and the uniform neater in appearance and more streamlined.

There were now regular conferences on the laws, and it became clear that the administrators aimed to develop the most spectacular of all codes of football. The game became increasingly popular, and by public demand the clubs in Melbourne formed themselves in 1877 into the VICTORIAN FOOTBALL ASSOCIATION (V.F.A.), which is now the oldest football body in Australia. The South Australian Football Association was created in 1878, and the first inter-state match (or inter-colonial match as it was called in those days) was played in Melbourne between Victoria and South Australia in 1879. The game was also flourishing in Perth, and the Western Australian League was formed to control matches in Perth, although there were many matches being played in the area of the Kalgoorlie and Coolgardie goldfields.

In 1896 a breakaway movement started in Victoria when the Victorian Football League was formed, and most of the major clubs transferred to it. The little mark was abolished, and the system of scoring by points was introduced, so that near-misses or behinds were included in the score. By 1897 the League had spread into New South Wales as the railway line was built between Albury and Sydney. The flow of the game was accelerated in 1903 when boundary umpires were appointed, thus relieving the field umpire of the job of throwing in the ball from the boundary.

The game was now being played in all states of Australia, although the main strength was in the southern and western states, where regular inter-state matches were becoming a feature and creating great rivalry. The movement of players between states was causing considerable concern between clubs and states, and the need for a national controlling body was discussed by the administrators.

The Australian Football Council (A.F.C.) was formed in 1906. The meeting was convened by Wilson, the secretary of the Victorian Football League, and delegates from all states and from New Zealand were in attendance. Hickey, a delegate of the Victorian League, was appointed chairman. The Council immediately set about tightening up inter-state clearances and permit rules and controlling the laws of the game throughout all the Australian states as well as Papua–New Guinea. The first Australian championship was played in Melbourne in 1908 and it was won by the Victorian Football League. Since then the all-Australian championship has been played in all the capital cities at regular intervals. Of the 17 championships held, the Victorian Football League team has won all but three. Inter-state matches are arranged between the states annually, but the championships are held only triennially.

The Victorian Football Association still flourishes, but it operates only in Melbourne.

The laws are the same as in the League, but it has only 16 a side, with 2 additional men as emergencies.

Until 1969, up to which date it played in the national championships, the Association was a member of the Australian Football Council, but in that year it withdrew over a dispute involving the switching of players from one body to the other. A League player may switch to an Association club without a permit, but if the same player wishes to return to a League club later he has to refrain from playing football for 12 months. If an Association player switches to a League club without receiving a clearance from the V.F.A. he is automatically disqualified from playing but only with a V.F.A. club. Outside Victoria the Victorian Football Association maintains harmonious relations with the other states playing the national football, and the interchange of players is considered by the Permits Committee who sanction the necessary arrangements. The Victorian Football Association is gradually building up its strength by playing most of its major games on Sundays. It allows, for a fee, direct television coverage, which has greatly boosted attendances.

By contrast the League does not allow direct telecasts of its matches, even if all seats have been sold for one of the final series. Television stations are allowed to show replays of the main League matches one hour after they have finished. All League matches are played on a Saturday in competition with other major sports, except in New South Wales and Queensland, where the matches are played on Sundays.

Australian Rules has become a vital part of the way of life in the southern and western states, where generation after generation of a family follows a particular team. Although the sport has not made the same progress in New South Wales and Queensland — the RUGBY LEAGUE stronghold of Australia—Queensland is showing an increased interest, and the sport has never been stronger in that state than at present, despite the fact that in the north of Queensland, even in the middle of winter, the temperature is in the middle 80s (F.). North Queensland had the distinction of having sent the first teams of Australian footballers outside the Commonwealth when they played Papua–New Guinea in 1957. The game is also played extensively in Darwin, in the Northern Territory, where the temperature is seldom under 90° F. Many aboriginals have been developed into top-class players by the leading clubs.

There are 12 teams in the Victorian Football League, which covers the metropolitan area of Melbourne as well as Geelong, which is 45 miles away. At the six matches played every week-end, the average attendance is 180,000, although the population of Melbourne is only a little over two million. During the final series, crowds of up to 120,000 pack the Melbourne Cricket Ground and the V.F.L.'s own stadium at Waverly to watch the teams that have reached the 'final five'.

Although attendance figures in Perth, Melbourne, Adelaide, and Hobart provide indisputable proof of the great interest in the capital cities, Australian football faces one major problem in the international sphere: the area necessary for the playing of Australian Rules at its best has to be unusually large. Interest from overseas countries has been short-lived when the grounds have proved to be inadequate in size. It is significant that the states where Australian Rules has thrived have had the best facilities for sport in the country. Attempts have been made to introduce the game overseas, and Australian teams have toured New Zealand, Hawaii, Japan, the U.S.A., Europe, England, and Ireland as a part of the end-of-season trips arranged by supporters' clubs, but they have not been able to show off the game as the spectacle it has proved to be on the large Australian grounds.

GOVERNING BODY: Australian Football Council, 6 Collins Street, Melbourne, Australia.

FOOTBALL, Canadian, developed from RUGBY in the same way as American football and closely resembles the U.S. game (see FOOTBALL, AMERICAN). The fundamental differences are: (1) the Canadian field is much larger — 110 yds. (100·58 m.) long against the American 100 (91·44 m.), 65 yds. (59·44 m.) wide against 53 (48·46 m.), with much deeper end zones — 25 yds. (22·86 m.) against 10 (9·14 m.); (2) the Canadian game has 12 players per side instead of the American 11, the additional player acting as a fifth back on offence (attack) and as a line-backer or defensive back on defence; (3) Canadian football allows the offensive (attacking) team only three downs in which to make 10 yards to retain control of the ball, in contrast to American football's four downs; (4) before the ball is put into play, all offensive backs may be running forward, sideways or backward, where in the American game only one back may be in motion before the ball is snapped, and then only sideways or backward, never forward; (5) a defensive line player may not be nearer than one yard to the ball being put in play, while the American football defensive linemen may be 'nose to nose' with the offensive line; (6) a punt or unsuccessful field-goal attempt is a 'live' ball and may be recovered by the kicking team, while the receiver of the

kick must be allowed 5 yards to field the ball, and the receiver's team mates are not allowed to block for him (in American football the receiver may run back a kick, signal for a 'fair catch', which means the receiver cannot be tackled, or in turn run back the kick, or he may allow the kicked ball to roll 'dead' and thereby gain possession); (7) points are the same (6 points for a touchdown, 3 for a field goal, and 1 for a conversion try) except for a 'rouge', a single point scored if the receiving team is unsuccessful in bringing the return of a kick out of its own end zone; (8) the conversion try occurs from the 10-yard line, either by a kick or by a scrimmage that runs or passes the ball over the goal line, while in American professional football the try occurs from the 2-yard line and the ball must be place-kicked. These differences make the Canadian game much more open, exciting, and attacking.

In 1874 McGill University of Montreal devised the rules for a hybrid game of Rugby that were first used that year in a HARVARD-McGill game. The rules were then adopted by Harvard and became the basis for the rules of both Canadian and American football. In 1891 the Canadian Rugby Union was established. In 1907 the Interprovincial Rugby Union was formed, consisting of teams from Hamilton, Toronto, Ottawa, and Montreal; it became known as the 'Big Four' — the same four teams from the Eastern Football Conference of the present Canadian Football League. In 1909 Lord Grey, the Governor-General of Canada, donated a trophy to be awarded annually for the Rugby Football Championship of Canada. The University of Toronto defeated the Parkdale Canoe Club, 26-6, in the first Grey Cup game.

In 1921 the number of players per side was reduced from 14 to 12, and the ball was put into play by the 'snap back', who passed the ball between his legs, instead of its being 'heeled in', as before. Although a forward pass was thrown in a game in 1929, the Canadian Rugby Union did not recognize this move until 1931.

In the 1930s the Grey Cup gradually became a professional contest, as intercollegiate teams (1936) dropped out of the competition. Most finals have been held at Toronto (including a famous game in 1962 that had to be suspended because of fog nine minutes before its end; the final nine minutes were concluded the next day). In the competition the third-place team plays a 'sudden death' game on the home field of the second-place team — the games being held on the first Sunday in November in both the Eastern and Western Conferences. In the Eastern Conference, the play-off winner plays the first-place conference winner in a two-game match over the following two week-ends, while in the Western Conference the play-off winner and the first-place winner play a best-of-three-game series over the same two-week period. The Grey Cup final matches the winners on the last Sunday in November.

By 1954 the current alignment of professional teams was established, with Hamilton, Toronto, Ottawa, and Montreal in the Eastern Football Conference, and with Winnipeg, Saskatchewan (Regina), Calgary, Edmonton, and British Columbia (Vancouver) in the Western. The Canadian Football Council was formed in 1956 and the value of a touchdown was increased from 5 to 6 points. The Canadian Football League replaced the Canadian Rugby Union in 1960, and Halter was appointed as Commissioner. In 1968 Gaudaur was named Commissioner at the same time as a new constitution was adopted.

The Canadian professional game is dominated by American players, although Ottawa's JACKSON was an outstanding Canadian-born quarterback in the 1960s. In order to limit American influence, each Canadian team may carry only 14 American citizens on a roster of 32 active players. In recruiting American players, Canadian teams have frequently offered off-season job security, and many American players in the Canadian professional league have chosen to stay in Canada after their football careers have ended.

Canadian Football League: Official Record and Information Manual, ed. Greg Fulton (1971).

FOOTBALL, Gaelic, a 15-a-side ball-and-goal game which, superficially, looks like a compromise between Association FOOTBALL and RUGBY. It is played almost exclusively in Ireland, although British and American teams compete in the All-Ireland championships.

A side consists of three full-forwards, three half-forwards, two mid-fields, three half-backs, three full-backs, and a goalkeeper. Some important competitions are played 13-a-side, one full-forward and one full-back being omitted. The players are positioned as for HURLING, the kindred Irish stick-and-ball game.

The pitch is usually 150 yds. (137 m.) long and 90 yds. (82 m.) wide with goal posts at each end 16 ft. (4·88 m.) high and 21 ft. (6·40 m.) apart, with a crossbar 8 ft. (2·44 m.) from the ground.

The ball may weigh between 13 and 15 oz. (368–425 g.) and measure 27 to 29 in. (685–736 mm.) in circumference. Its cover is of leather, usually horsehide which is now often plastic-coated, with an inflated bladder of rubber. To score a goal, equal to 3 points, the ball must be kicked or punched between the posts and under the crossbar. One point is scored when the ball is driven between the posts but over the crossbar.

If the defending side puts the ball over its own end line, the attackers are awarded a free kick, from a line 50 yds. (45·72 m.) out, at a point opposite where the ball crossed the end line. If the ball is driven over the side lines, a free kick is given against the side responsible at the place where the ball crossed the line.

A goal area, based on the end line, 15 yds. (13·72 m.) by 5 yds. (4·57 m.) extends in front of the goal posts. If a defender fouls inside this area (known as the 'parallelogram' or the

GAELIC FOOTBALL LINE-OUT
(G) Goalkeeper; (FB) full-back; (HB) half-back; (MF) mid-field; (HF) half-forward; (FF) full-forward.

'square') a penalty kick is awarded to the opposition from a spot 14 yds. (12·80 m.) out and directly in front of the goal posts. All other players, except the kicker and the goalkeeper, must remain outside the 21-yd. (19·20 m.) line until the kick is taken. The goalkeeper is allowed to move along his goal line to anticipate the kick, but may not advance until the ball is kicked. When the ball is driven wide of the goal posts and over the end line by the attacking side, it is kicked out from the corner of the parallelogram by a defender. After a score, the ball is kicked out from the 21-yd. line.

The rules of Gaelic, as distinct from all other European football codes, include no offside rule, and allow the players to play the ball both on and off the ground with foot or hand. A player is not, however, permitted to pick the ball directly from the ground with the hand, but he can lift it or chip it from the ground into his hand with his foot, and this constitutes one of the basic skills of the game. The ball may be caught when in flight or on the bounce, and may be passed or punched with the closed fist. Throwing is not permitted. A player in possession of the ball may carry it for four paces, but must then either 'hop' (bounce) it — only one hop is permitted if the ball has been caught — or kick or fist it away.

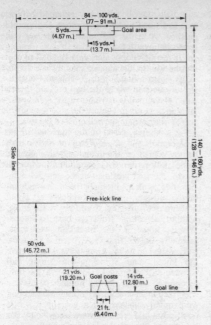

GAELIC FOOTBALL PITCH
Goal area is also known as the parallelogram.

However, the player may 'carry' the ball on a solo run in two different ways. He may, hopping the ball every three steps, run in possession as long as he wishes, provided the ball has not been caught. He may also run as far as he wishes providing he bounces the ball from toe to hand every four steps.

Pulling, pushing, tripping, or elbowing an opponent is a foul, and punished by a free kick to the opposing side. A Rugby-style tackle is similarly penalized, as is a frontal charge or a charge in the back. A fair and square shoulder charge is permitted, however, and is much appreciated by the spectators. Any player who kicks or strikes an opponent, or who abuses or strikes the referee or other officials, is sent from the field and automatically suspended for a period of from one month to two years, depending on the gravity of his offence.

Games are controlled by a referee, who has sole charge of the play, assisted by four goal umpires, two at each end, and a touch judge on each side line. The referee starts the game by throwing in the ball between the mid-field players at the beginning of each half. He is also the sole adjudicator on playing time.

All regular Gaelic football matches last 60 minutes — 30 minutes each half — except for the senior finals of the provincial championships and the semi-finals and finals of the All-Ireland senior championships. These are extended to 80 minutes, with halves of 40 minutes.

Teams are allowed three substitutes in the course of a game, irrespective of whether the player being replaced is injured.

In its earliest days, with 21 players a side, and a ball that was much larger, heavier, and less lively than today's, the sport did not call for any remarkable tactical skills. It was a game for tall, strong men who battled for possession of the ball, mainly at close quarters, and compensated by power for what they might lack in mobility.

Today, the high, overhead fielding of the livelier ball, and the ability to hold on to it once it has been caught, remain the most effective, and spectacular, skills of the game. The long, straight punt, whether off the ground or from the hand, is another fundamental accomplishment. The drop-kick is also useful, but the majority of players today tend to neglect the fly-kick, which was formerly very much in favour. While admittedly risky when the ball is in the air, the fly-kick can be a most useful tactic when the ball is on the ground.

Catch-and-kick was the predominant strategy on the Gaelic fields until comparatively recently. Since the game is strictly amateur, tactical development has been slow; training facilities were limited and full-time training was outlawed many years ago as not being in accordance with the game's amateur status. But by 1970 a most effective blend of the old and the new, assimilating the traditional skills of high catching and long kicking with slick inter-passing, clever combination, and intelligent running 'off the ball' had been successfully achieved.

Gaelic Athletic Association, *Official Guide*, latest edition.

Despite claims that Gaelic football is as old as hurling, there is no distinctive reference to the game in the Irish sagas. Indeed, not until 1527 does the first direct mention of football in Ireland occur, when a parliamentary measure, the Statutes of Galway, forbade hurling and all other ball games that might threaten the practice of ARCHERY 'except alone football with the grate ball'.

But football in Ireland failed to receive any literary recognition again for more than a century and a half. Then the Gaelic poet Mac-Curta described a game he had seen in his youth (c. 1660) on the banks of the river Boyne. MacCurta's poem makes clear that the snatching and carrying of the ball were features of the pastime, while wrestling between the players was permitted. Wrestling was still a noteworthy part of the game when the English traveller, Dunton, saw football played 'according to the Irish style' in north Co. Dublin towards the end of the seventeenth century. Co. Dublin is still a stronghold of the game; it was this countryside that produced what is possibly the first narrative poem in English to describe a football match.

The poet Concanen wrote his lay to celebrate the victory of his native village, Swords, some seven miles north of Dublin, over the neighbouring village of Lusk in a six-a-side game played at Swords in 1720. Concanen's composition reveals that the ball was of ox-hide, 'stuffed with finest hay'; the goals at each end of the field were formed of boughs of sally-wood bent into a bow; the ball could be caught and kicked overhead, kicked and rushed along the ground, or carried. Tripping and wrestling were not legal, but seem to have counted among the skills of the game.

Twenty years later, in the Omeath country beyond the Boyne, another poet, Redmond Murphy, described in Gaelic a 12-a-side football game. Wrestling, and snatching and running with the ball, were again featured. In Dangan, Co. Meath, 'a grate match at football' was played between married men and bachelors in 1731, while, ten years later, Dubliners watched a game on the frozen Liffey.

From the early nineteenth century there are records which show the popularity of Irish-style football in Kerry, Ireland's leading county in the code. There, before the great famine of 1847 depopulated the countryside, the pastime was known as *Caid*, the Gaelic name for the ovoid ball used. This ball was usually a pig's bladder, inflated, and covered with cured animal-skin. The game came in two varieties, field *Caid* and cross-country *Caid*. In the field game, boughs of trees were bent into an arch to form the goal. In the cross-country version, usually played between the entire male population, young and old, of two parishes, the objective was to bring the ball home from the bounds ditch where the match began.

Wrestling was permitted, in the form of tackling or holding. Carrying the ball was legal, and fleet runners, strategically stationed on the outskirts of the crush, often gained considerable ground if put in clear possession, and, if exceptionally lucky, might carry the *Caid* in triumph all the way home. *Caid* was usually played in winter, when the crops had been cleared from the land. The most popular period was through the 12 days of Christmas (25 December to 6 January) which remained very much a holiday season in Ireland until well into the nineteenth century.

By the 1860s, however, native Irish football had fallen away into a rough-and-tumble pastime. A leather ball stuffed with hay was used; there were few set rules, if any; tripping and wrestling were freely employed, and discipline was so lacking that these affairs sometimes ended in a free-for-all. This was in striking contrast to the tradition of *Caid*, which was 'played very fair and with great good humour'.

The foundation in 1884 of the GAELIC ATH-LETIC ASSOCIATION (G.A.A.), devoted to the preservation and popularizing of native Irish games, saved, rejuvenated, and, eventually, completely reformed Gaelic football. Maurice Davin, the first president of the new Association, had, with his brothers, been an exponent of the old-time game, and quickly set about drafting new rules that would revive the sport, without departing from its best traditions. Wisely, however, the transition was made gradually. In the first G.A.A. rules for football, issued in 1885, tripping, tackling above the knees, and wrestling—a single fall —were still permitted. Goals were the only recognized scores and the number of players was fixed at 21-a-side. Wrestling and tackling were quietly phased out a year later, while point-posts and crossbar were introduced, but no number of points could equal a goal.

When the first All-Ireland championships began in 1887, further rule changes quickly suggested themselves. In 1888 5 points were declared equal to a goal, the number of players in a team was reduced to 17 in 1892, while, in 1896, a goal was made equal to 3 points (a ratio that still stands) and the height of the crossbar was reduced from 10 ft. 6 in. (3·20 m.) to 8 ft. (2·44 m.).

Until the 1890s, however, the ball was too big and heavy to allow very lengthy kicking, with the result that the fly-kick was more common than nowadays, while a player who had caught the ball often preferred to strike it with the rigid forearm, a tactic greatly admired at the time and a method of moving the ball that, when expertly used, could drive it remarkable distances.

In those early championship days, however, ground football probably predominated. Groups of players in close formation, something like the 'flying wedge' of old-time American FOOTBALL, strove to sweep the ball upfield. Their opponents, in similar force, frequently met them head on, and thus led to hectic struggles for possession in mid-field or goal mouth, with weight, strength, and determination the most valuable assets.

But the perfecting of the vulcanized rubber bladder, which ensured a much livelier ball, plus the reduction of the number of players to

17-a-side, changed the game dramatically. A renowned Dublin club side, Young Irelands, quickly worked out a new technique in which a player went high to secure the ball and then punted it upfield to an unattended colleague. This catch-and-kick style soon superseded the old kick-and-rush.

Dublin dominated the late 1890s and the early years of the new century, but the pastime received an even greater fillip when Kerry and Kildare, who first introduced the tactic of hand-passing, met in three exciting games for the All-Ireland title of 1903 that set a new standard of excellence in the code. Kerry won, and thus began a great career in the All-Ireland championship. Even the reduction of teams to 15-a-side in 1913 did not affect the power of the Kerry teams.

By this time the All-Ireland football finals were drawing the largest attendances at any sporting event in the country. New records were again set in the 1915 final when 30,000 spectators saw Wexford beat the Kerry champions and start a four-in-a-row title sequence of their own. The Irish revolution, and the civil war that followed, hindered progress through the next decade, but, for the second time, the players of Kerry and Kildare set new standards in the 1926 final, the Kerry team winning a replay before a new record attendance of 40,000. Kerry came back again three years later to equal that Wexford record by winning four championships in succession from 1929 to 1932.

In the following year Cavan gave the championship a new dimension by bringing the title and trophy to Ulster for the first time, while, later in the 1930s, Galway and Mayo succeeded in taking the senior crown west of the Shannon for the first time. Since then the standard in all four provinces has been remarkably well balanced.

This levelling of standards has also been demonstrated in the inter-provincial competition, introduced, together with the national leagues, in 1926. In the early years, Munster and Leinster were supreme. Then, first Connacht, and afterwards Ulster, who took some time to become established, fared even better than the more traditional centres. Indeed Ulster teams were the dominant force in this inter-provincial competition through the 1960s. In the championship, too, Ulster sides steadily improved ever since Cavan won two successive All-Ireland titles in the late 1940s Other Ulster sides from Armagh and Derry were the first from across the political boundary to reach the All-Ireland finals and try to take the title home. Where they failed, Down succeeded and brought the championship to Nothern Ireland in 1960 and 1961.

The Down mentors built these champion teams on new techniques of all-the-year-round training, on team-work and tactics perfected as much in the class-room as on the playing field. They played precision football right out of defence, and adapted coaching and physical training techniques from other sports to set new standards in fitness, combination, and expertise.

After Down came an outstanding Galway team that made Gaelic football even more entertaining to watch, by introducing new concepts of forward play, in which clever running when 'off the ball' played an important part. Then, at the end of the 1960s, back came the old champions, Kerry, with an amalgam of traditional skills and up-to-the-minute techniques that illustrated exactly how Gaelic football has become a spectacular blend of the old and the new.

While training and coaching techniques altered the whole approach to the game, changes through 50 years have been few and far between. In changing circumstances, however, many keen students of the game believe that experiments should be made. A special committee recommended that the number of players be further reduced to 13-a-side (as is already the case in college competitions), that players be permitted to take the ball direct from the ground with the hand, that the solo run be restricted, and that the palmed hand-pass be restored instead of the fisted pass.

During its early years, Gaelic football was confined to Ireland. It was later carried overseas by Irish emigrants, but only in Australia where the Australian Rules game (see FOOTBALL, AUSTRALIAN RULES) is manifestly based on the old-time Kerry pastime of *Caid*, did football 'after the Irish style' really take root. Yet, though both Gaelic and Australian Rules have a common origin and still have so many similarities — scoring system, high fielding, limitations on carrying, field-placings — the codes never came together until 1967, when an Australian Rules side, the Galahs, came to Ireland and drew large crowds by the brilliance of their play and the ease with which they adapted to Gaelic rules.

A second team of Australian tourists received a similar welcome a year later, while All-Ireland champions Meath, in 1968, and Kerry, in 1970, travelled to Australia, but failed to arouse as much interest and enthusiasm as the Australians had in Ireland. Long-term negotiations took place in an effort to find an agreed set of laws that would provide both Gaelic football and Australian Rules with the one attribute both most sorely needed, international competition.

Gaelic football has long been popular among the Irish exiles in Britain and the U.S.A. British teams compete regularly in the lesser grades of the All-Ireland championships, while selected New York sides have performed creditably in various competitions with Irish champion teams. The 1947 All-Ireland football final was played in New York and led to such a revival of Gaelic games in the U.S.A. that tours to New York and beyond by Irish teams became annual events, while New York teams came regularly across the Atlantic to challenge Ireland's best.

Heretofore Gaelic football teams from Britain and New York have been almost exclusively composed of Irish-born players. More recently juvenile sides have been formed, both in Britain and America. Such teams have, in Britain, reached a high level of proficiency.

Since Gaelic football, like hurling, is so closely confined to Ireland, the stars of the game can only be measured by national standards. The renowned Kerry goalkeeper, O'Keeffe, set a new record in 1946 when he became the first player to win seven All-Ireland senior football medals. O'Keeffe's inter-county career extended from 1930 to 1949. Another distinguished player is O'Connell, a native of Valentia Island. One of the greatest mid-fielders the game has known, he was the stylist supreme, and a delight to watch.

P. Foley, *Kerry's Football Story* (1945); J. Lennon, *Coaching Gaelic Football* (1964) and *Fitness for Gaelic Football* (1969); J. Mahon, *Twelve Glorious Years* (1965); P. D. Mehigan, *Gaelic Football* (1944); Dr. E. O'Sullivan, *The Art and Science of Gaelic Football* (1958); R. Smith, *The Football Immortals* (1969).

GOVERNING BODY: Gaelic Athletic Association, Croke Park, Dublin 1, Eire.

FOOTBALL, Harrow, is an 11-a-side game evolved at Harrow School and played nowhere else. It is played with a large ball shaped like a flattened sphere, 10 in. (25·4 cm.) in diameter in one direction, 11 in. (27·94 cm.) in the other, on an ordinary RUGBY pitch, marked only with a half-way line, and with a pair of goal posts 6 yds. (5·5 m.) apart at each end. The object of the game is to propel the ball between the opponents' goal posts, i.e. to score a 'base'. The side that scores most bases wins. There is no crossbar between the posts, and it does not matter how high the ball is when it passes between them. If it is kicked higher than the top of the posts the umpires have to decide whether or not it has passed between their line continued straight up. If it has, a base is scored. A shot that goes straight over the goal post — a 'poler' — does not count as a base.

The two features of the game that particularly contribute to its unique character are the offside rule and 'yards'. If a player is in front of the ball when one of his own side touches it he is offside (except at a throw-in from touch, or when the ball has been put over the base line by an attacker and is being punted back into play by the defending side — a 'base-kick'). It is thus impossible to pass the ball forward; and to work the ball up the field a player must dribble it along, for preference with a few of his own side in close support, ready to continue the movement if he is tackled or overruns the ball.

Whenever the ball is kicked in the air, except at a base-kick, any player who is onside may catch it and shout 'Yards'. The game then stops and he is entitled to a free punt, which will be aimed at the opponents' base if it is within range. The usual method of scoring is to take 'yards', either from one of the player's own side or from a careless kick in the air by an opponent, and punt the ball through: for, though a base may be scored by kicking the ball straight off the ground, this is not easy.

The taking of 'yards' is not limited to potential scoring situations, and a competent player will take 'yards' whenever he can in any part of the field. Even if he is out of range of the base, he can make much ground by punting the ball as far as possible up the field, for preference placing his kick so that the opponents cannot catch it and punt it straight back again. In difficult situations a player near his own base may 'knock down "Yards"' — i.e. prevent an opponent taking 'yards': otherwise handling is not allowed.

During play little time is lost for stoppages, for the ball is never intentionally kicked into touch. If it does go out, the side that put it there may easily lose 20 or 30 yards from the resulting throw-in, for the ball may be hurled — usually one-handed — in any direction from the place where it went out, and the offside rule does not apply. From a base-kick, up to half the length of the field may be lost, for the ball is punted up the field from the base line, and again the offside rule does not apply. A corner can be conceded (by the defender kicking it out behind his own base line) with impunity, since the attackers have to throw the ball in in a direction parallel to the touch line and from the point at which it went out; but to concede a corner is at best a last-ditch defensive measure, and a more skilful player will attempt rather to bounce the ball out off an opponent, thus securing a base-kick or throw for his own side.

On a wet ground the ball becomes so heavy that it is difficult to kick it 20 yards, but in dry conditions a good kicker may well be able to score from the half-way line. The nature of the game thus changes radically with the weather — the heavy slog in the mud of a wet January becomes, on the hard ground of a dry March, a hectic chase after a ball that balloons wildly in the air, is carried by every gust of wind, and is desperately difficult to control.

Most players find that the ball is too massive to be headed, and use their shoulders to stop it in the air. This is called 'fouling' the ball, and so the cry 'Well fouled' is one of applause without sarcastic overtones.

The 11 players consist of four centres, four wings (inside and outside on the left, inside and outside on the right), and three backs (left, centre, and right). The descriptions 'top' and 'bottom' are sometimes used instead of 'left' and 'right', because the field is usually not quite level and it is customary for the players to stay on the same side of it throughout the game, e.g. the left back in the first half is the right back in the second.

The centres follow the ball wherever it goes and often form a loose scrum round it, and since no heeling is allowed, the ball has to be worked forward. The wings work in pairs and their aim is to dribble the ball rapidly up the field and give 'yards'. The inside wings will be close to any scrum and almost work in with the centres, while the outside wings are a few feet away in support. The backs' aim is to kick the ball farther up the field than their opponents can kick it back again, which can best be achieved by placing a kick where it cannot be caught, and then taking 'yards' off the opponents' return.

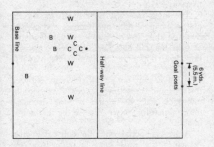

HARROW FOOTBALL PITCH
Positioning of one side is shown: (C) centre; (W) wing; (B) back, with the ball.

There is thus much scope for skilful positioning. The centre back is always close behind the play, ready to take 'yards' from his own side or stop a breakthrough by the opposition, and the wing back on whose side of the field play is will also be well up. The other wing back stays just far enough behind to ensure that the ball cannot be kicked over his head, since there is no goalkeeper and he is the last line of defence; but when the ball crosses to his side of the field he must be ready to move up rapidly.

There are virtually no penalties and so, in the words of the *Obiter Dicta*, 'rules have to be kept for the sake of conscience, and the benefit of the doubt is habitually given to the opposition. If you inadvertently break a rule, stand away at once.' If an infringement occurs from which the offending side gains no advantage, the game is allowed to continue. If there is an advantage to the offending side, the umpire stops the game and re-starts it with a 'bounce' — throwing the ball a foot or two in the air, with several players from each side standing as near as they like. They may not touch the ball until it bounces, but as soon as it does the game continues.

The only circumstances in which the umpire may take action which penalizes the offending side are when there is an infringement by the attackers near the base. Whether or not there is an advantage to the offending side, he stops the game and awards a base-kick to the defending side (the phrase 'near the base' works perfectly well without precise definition — there is no need for a marked penalty area). A player in a House match can be sent off if he wilfully breaks the rules, but though players have sometimes to be reminded of this provision, the threat has seldom if ever had to be carried out.

The players can normally run the game very well by themselves, but in matches it is necessary to have an impartial observer who can determine matters of fact about which there may be a difference of opinion. It is possible for one umpire to control a game with the aid of two touch judges — or even without, if the players are warned that they will have to settle for themselves whether the ball is out or not — but it is better to have two umpires and no touch judges, in which case the umpires take one side of the field each and act as their own touch judges. Their decision is final on matters of fact, but they are at liberty to refer any question of law to the committee of the Philathletic Club if they feel unable to decide it at the time. The umpires do not have a whistle, but it is convenient for them to carry a stick (for pointing).

The game evolved as a form of football that could be played in extremely muddy conditions with few or many players on each side. From the mid-nineteenth century it was played on the present football fields, the rules gradually becoming fixed, with the number of players on each side usually 11. Since 1927, with the introduction of Rugby football in the winter term, Harrow football has been played in the Easter term only.

Though the first XI plays several matches against old Harrovians and one against the masters, the main interest of the season lies in the House matches. There are a few Sixth Form games, for the selection and training of the school team, which are taken by the master-in-charge, but otherwise all arrangements are on a House basis and are entirely organized by boys.

P. H. M. Bryant, *Harrow* (1937); E. D. Laborde, *Harrow School, Yesterday and Today* (1948).

FOOTBALL, Rugby, see RUGBY LEAGUE; RUGBY UNION.

FOOTBALL, Winchester College, is a 15-a-side or 6-a-side code of football, with a unique terminology. It is played exclusively at Winchester College, with a round ball as in Association FOOTBALL, but in some other respects it resembles RUGBY. The ground is 80 yds. long by 27 yds. wide (73·15 × 24·69 m.), bounded on the two long sides by netting 8 ft. (2·44 m.) high (called 'canvas') with, a yard inside the netting and running parallel with it, a rope 3 ft. (91 cm.) high, supported by nine posts set at 10 yd. (9·14 m.) intervals. Between the posts at either end — a distance of 25 yds. (22·86 m.) — is a shallowly trenched goal line (though there is no goal in terms of posts) called 'worms'. The remaining yard of width between the last post and the netting on each side, which is not part of the goal line, is called 'under-ropes'.

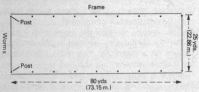

Frame

Post

Worms

25 yds.
(22·86 m.)

Post

80 yds
(73.15 m.)

WINCHESTER COLLEGE FOOTBALL PITCH
Diagram shows the iron frame carrying the netting, with nine posts on either side carrying the rope. The goal line extends only from last post to last post, leaving 1 yd. (914 mm.) at either end which is 'under ropes' and not part of 'worms'.

In the 15-a-side — XV — game, a team is composed of eight 'ups', four 'hotwatchers', and three 'behinds' or 'kicks'. In the six-a-side — VI — game, there are three ups, a hotwatcher, and two kicks. The ups correspond more or less to forwards in Rugby, and form the 'hot' (or scrum): they pack 3-2-3 or 3-4-1, including one 'over-the-ball' in the

front row whose duties are similar to those of the hooker in Rugby; or one up may be detached to act as an extra hotwatcher. The hotwatchers act at times like three-quarters and at others like half-backs in Rugby: the kicks discharge the duties of full-backs and three-quarters in Rugby.

A game lasts an hour, and each half opens with a set hot at the centre of the ground. The fundamental aim of each side is to kick the ball over their opponents' goal line. Progress is by kicking or scrummaging (known as 'hotting'). In the hot, dribbling is allowed but hard kicking is illegal: this is directly opposite to the case in open play.

When the ball has last been touched by an opponent it may be kicked to any height (a 'flyer'). If a player kicks a ball hard he may follow up and play it again; but such a kick must not rise above shoulder height (an 'own-side' kick). If a player receives the ball from a member of his own side who is nearer the opponents' goal line — a back pass — he may make an ownside kick. Whenever a ball is played, however, any member of the same side nearer to the opponents' goal line is offside and can take no immediate part in the play without incurring a penalty.

When the ball is kicked out of 'ropes' or a kick is deflected by the rope, then, if it is next caught, only an ownside kick is allowed. Any player may catch a ball kicked by, or bouncing off, an opponent but he must then 'bust' (punt) it within three strides unless opponents try to collar him, in which case he may run with it from them until they bring him down or cease to try to do so.

The kicks may use their hands to stop the ball; they must then put it down and take an ownside kick. If a player kicks the ball gently, he may 'back it up', i.e. stand over it so as to impede an opponent; but he must not play it (a dribble).

A player may not go into the space between the rope and the netting ('ropes'), although he may kick at the ball under the rope, or kick it into the netting, in which case the rebound is in play.

A goal is scored when the ball passes over 'worms' (the goal line) untouched by the defence, at any height from a flyer, but under shoulder height from an ownside kick. Either such goal counts 3 points. If the ball passes over the base line between the last post and 'canvas', or over 'worms', (1) after being last touched by a defender, or (2), from 'ropes', this constitutes a 'behind' and counts 1 point to the attack. Thereupon, the whole of both sides, except only the three attacking kicks, retire behind 'worms'; the ball is kicked out from the centre of 'worms' by one of the defence; and if the attacking side returns it, by the *first* kick, untouched by a defender, over 'worms', they score 2 more points.

The hot differs from a Rugby scrum in that the ball is placed between the two over-the-balls and may not be played until one side has driven the other back sufficiently for the front row to dribble the ball forward or, by allowing it to pass the front row, to bring the hot to an end, whereupon the over-the-ball passes it out sideways between the front and second row to the hotwatcher, waiting at the side of the hot.

A team is penalized for infringement of the rules or kicking the ball out of play ('over canvas') by a hot, midway between 'canvases', and one 'post' (i.e. 10 yds.) back towards the goal defended by the offending side. This means that hots are frequent, and the penalizing by loss of distance of the side which kicks the ball out of play means that a hot is preferable to kicking out and therefore there is little kicking for touch as in Rugby. The hot may be used defensively by dribbling the ball forward, or offensively by passing out to the hotwatcher. The side which controls the hot

DISPOSITION OF PLAYERS FOR A 'HOT'
(*Left*) A hot in the centre of the ground; two 'hotwatchers' (H) close in, two 'on ropes', with 'second behind', 'middle behind', and 'last behind' (B) disposed in depth. (*Right*) A less standardized form of hot in 'down ropes' play: four 'ups' (U) hanging over the rope and 'hotting' sideways; three 'ups' forming a second row and 'hotting' straight down 'canvas'; one 'up' acting as an extra hotwatcher; and the three 'kicks' (B) disposed in depth.

can open up the play or close it down according to the state of the game and the wind.

Tactically, the side in defence seeks to carry the ball forward by the slow process of driving it along 'ropes', whence no goal can be scored. The side in attack seeks to carry it out in a quick rush diagonally forward from under 'ropes'. In open play, tactics are principally directed to denying flyers to the opposing kicks by quick following up.

The art of XV is to train a number of players to manoeuvre in a confined space. The problem of VI is to dispose a few players so as best to cover a considerable area. The basic strategy of VI is as in XV — the same defensive and offensive use of the hot and 'down ropes' play; the same recourse to 'ropes' in defence and avoidance of 'ropes' when in attack. It is found, however, that the possibilities of defence are very much less than in XV and that it pays to exploit the open spaces and attack.

The main difference is tactical. In the early 1900s VI was played as a miniature XV. The three ups and the hotwatcher toiled up in a usually fruitless attempt to charge down the opponents' kick, had the ball kicked over their heads and toiled back to put themselves onside, and repeat the process. Eventually the principle was evolved of 'hunting in pairs' — one pair in attack, the other pair lying back, helping the kicks to cover the empty spaces and ready to go up in attack the moment their kick has played the ball. This saving of time greatly increases the chance of a successful attack upon the opponents' kick. Meanwhile the previously forward pair falls back in defence on either 'ropes'.

There are, of course, three possible ways of pairing — hotwatcher with over-the-ball (the most usual); or hotwatcher with either wing. Which pairing is employed is often decided by the various players' efficiency with the left foot.

For a first view of Winchester football, VI is preferable. The long kicks and the resounding 'plants' when the up charges down an opponent's kick; the shorter hots and less time spent 'down ropes' — all combine to make it more amusing to watch and easier to understand. It is true that a heavy ground kills the long kicking and a strong wind keeps the play all at one end; but, played on a light ground and without too much wind, it is a pretty game.

XV has a better balance of attack and defence, and it can be maintained that a perfect wheel of the set hot as it carries the ball to the safety of 'ropes', or a concentrated rush as the ups bring the ball out from 'ropes', require greater skill than anything in VI. Unskilfully played, however, it can become a meaningless mêlée.

Winchester College football is one of the many forms of the basic kicking-into-goal game shaped in isolation by local conditions, in this case by its somewhat curious cradle. Until 1790 the school's only playground was a mile away within the circle of the ancient British camp which crowns St. Catherine's Hill. A Latin poem (c. 1650) mentions football among the games played on 'Hills'. Furthermore, the Winchester Table of the Laws (c. 1560) refers to going to 'Hills' and by this date football was a national pastime. The game played there was, no doubt, the simplest possible — four corner posts, the whole end as goal, and two lines of juniors to keep the ball in play. The rough ground would tend to produce long kicking rather than dribbling.

In 1790 the Governing Body made over to College (i.e. the Scholars) an area, now known as 'Meads', within the boundary wall as their playground. Some years later a field a short distance from the school was secured for Commoners. The limited area of 'Meads' dictated the size of the ground (now 80 yds. by 27). The first step in its development in 'Meads' was the introduction of a line of posts carrying a rope down each side of the ground. It had been found that the juniors interfered with play; the rope curbed, but did not entirely prevent, their activities.

In 1840 it was suggested that the juniors' labours in keeping the ball in play should be reduced by a canvas, mounted on an iron frame 8 ft. high, running down the sides of the ground. Not surprisingly, the resistance to wind offered by the canvas resulted in the rending of the canvas or the uprooting of the frame. In this experiment the posts and rope were retained to save the players from colliding with the iron frame. Some years later netting was used: it has the advantage that it can be stretched tighter on the frame than canvas. As a legacy from the experiment with canvas, the term 'canvas' is still used for the netting and has been extended to the whole ground, e.g. 'middle game canvas'.

The next problem concerned 'ropes'. The rope was passed through a hole bored 4 in. (101 mm.) below the top of each post and was hitched round each post. Merely strained by hand, it was not taut enough to stand up to the impact of 16 struggling forwards. In the early 1880s a winch was adopted which strained the rope, now passed direct from hole to hole, sufficiently to support the players and keep them on their feet.

By 1820 College was playing an annual match against Commoners at 22-a-side and, later in the term, at 6-a-side. The disposition of the 22 was a 'last behind', a 'second behind', and 20 ups. Later one more was withdrawn from the 'ups'.

At first the disposition in XV was 3 behinds and 12 ups. Early in the 1870s we read 'so and so shirked the "hots"', and a year or two later 'so and so, who took no part in the "hots"',

did some good things'. Before long 'hotwatch' was an accepted position — three at first and ultimately four.

Until 1863 there was no serious disparity of numbers between College and Commoners. The addition of new houses, however, led in 1868 to the formation of a third side — Old Tutors' Houses (O.T.H. for short). In the same year it was decided to play 15-a-side instead of 22. From 1868 until quite recently the three sides played a complete series of matches at XV and VI. Now, in view of the increased disparity of numbers, College play Commoners and O.T.H. at 10-a-side instead of 15.

From the earliest times Winchester football was played in the Christmas term and Association FOOTBALL, when introduced, in the Easter term. In 1965, however, the games were changed over and Winchester College football is now played in the Easter term. For about eight years, between 1866 and 1875, Winchester College football was played in the Parks at Oxford during the Michaelmas term: in 1876 it gave way to Association football.

The Revd. G. Ogilvie, an old Wykehamist, when he was principal of the Diocesan College, Rondebosch, 1862-85, introduced Winchester College football into his school. It spread over Cape Colony and for a time was quite popular, until it gave way to Rugby. Now the game is confined to Winchester.

FOOTBALL LEAGUE, see FOOTBALL, ASSOCIATION.

FORD, BERNARD, M.B.E. (1947-   ), ice dance-skater for Great Britain who attained with his partner, Miss TOWLER, a technique ahead of that of any contemporaries or predecessors. Champions of the world for four consecutive years, 1966-9, throughout which time they also held the European and British titles, Ford and Towler acquired a rare ability to retain elegant postures while leaning at acute backward angles. Their smooth-flowing body sway, with movements of their free, non-skating legs exceptionally well-synchronized, with their versatile footwork and slick changing of tempo were prime characteristics.

In 1966, their career could have ended abruptly and tragically when Ford fell 40 feet from a London building. He narrowly missed spiked railings and, in the circumstances, was fortunate to suffer only three crushed vertebrae and a chipped ankle bone from which he made a full recovery in six months. In 1969, they were each awarded the M.B.E., relinquished amateur status to coach at the Streatham ice rink in London, and became world professional ice-dance champions at Wembley. Ford was born in London.

FORD, HORACE ALFRED (1822-80) was champion archer of Great Britain 11 times in consecutive years, 1849-59, and in 1867. He wrote *Archery, its Theory and Practice* (1856), in which he presented a completely fresh approach to ARCHERY resulting from a logical and intelligent application of a series of simple principles to the art of shooting. His performance with a longbow has never been equalled and his record score for the championship double York Round at Cheltenham in 1857 was 1,250 points.

FORDHAM, GEORGE (1837-87), known as 'The Demon', was head of the winning jockey's table in England 14 times between 1855 and 1871. During his career in the saddle, he rode 2,587 winners, including 15 classic successes.

FOREST HILLS, Long Island, N.Y., a suburb of New York City, is the home of the U.S. LAWN TENNIS championships, the second most important tournament of the lawn tennis year. The event is played on the grounds of the West Side Lawn Tennis Club, which was founded in 1892 on a site near Central Park and twice moved before settling at Forest Hills.

In 1915 the club acquired the right to hold the U.S. championships from the Newport Casino, where the event had been staged since 1881. After its main Stadium Court, which seats 14,000 spectators, had been built in 1923 Forest Hills became the permanent home of the tournament. The second most important court, the equivalent to No. 1 court at WIMBLEDON, is known as the Grandstand Court. Altogether, there are about 23 grass courts and a number of clay courts.

FORMOSA (1865), celebrated English racing filly who won the ST. LEGER, OAKS, and ONE THOUSAND GUINEAS, and, after running a dead-heat for first place in the TWO THOUSAND GUINEAS, was defeated in the run-off. Her success was not bettered until 1902, when SCEPTRE won the same four classic races outright.

FORMULA 5000 CHAMPIONSHIP, a series of motor races, usually eight to ten a year, conducted by the Sports Car Club of America for single-seat, open-wheel formula cars powered by engines with a maximum piston displacement of 5,000 cc. Most events are run on American road courses and one or two in Canada for total purses and prizes of more than $400,000. The first three champions were

Americans — Hutchison in 1967, Sell in 1968, and ADAMOWICZ in 1969. Later, foreign drivers dominated. The 1970 champion was CANNON, English by birth and Canadian by citizenship; in 1971 it was Hobbs, an Englishman with considerable Grand Prix experience. They were followed in 1972 by a New Zealander, McRae, and in 1973 by a South African, Scheckter.

The series began in 1967, with smaller machines and a different name, and quickly gained popularity. One reason was the competitiveness of Formula 5000 entries — the rules equalize the cars, thus placing a premium on driving skill. (Formula 5000 has also proliferated in Europe and elsewhere; indeed, it is the foundation of the Tasman Series in New Zealand and Australia.)

In appearance, the Formula 5000 car, which occasionally is called Formula A, is a hybrid of the classic Grand Prix Formula One and the 'Indy' cars of the INDIANAPOLIS 500. The engine most widely used is the Chevrolet V-8, tuned to produce approximately 500 h.p. To limit costs, certain restrictions are imposed. The engine must be produced in quantities of at least 1,000 a year. It must be 'stock block', which means its valves must be actuated by pushrods, not overhead cams. However, extensive substitution of race-quality parts — pistons, connecting-rods, valve gear, etc. — is permitted.

Races are 75 to 100 miles long (121–161 km.), with the order of the grid determined by a pair of shorter qualifying heats. In its most successful seasons, 1971 through 1973, the series was sponsored by a cigarette manufacturer and during that period it was designated the L. & M. 5000 Championship.

FORO ITALICO, Rome, home of the Italian LAWN TENNIS championships, the second most important clay court tournament, and, with the possible exception of the Monte Carlo Country Club, the most dramatic setting for a major lawn tennis event. The courts are part of the complex of sports arenas planned by Mussolini for the OLYMPIC GAMES which the war prevented. They are administered by the Italian Olympic Committee and hired for the tournament by the Italian Lawn Tennis Federation. The main court is magnificent, with its stands of white marble, decorated with huge white statues. There are six other courts and the ground is surrounded by pine trees. Many players regard the Italian championships as the pleasantest and most exciting of all tournaments.

FORT BOVISAND, near Plymouth, Devon, underwater centre organizing courses in nautical archaeology, diver training, commercial diver training, underwater photography, and marine biology for divers. Founded in 1969, it became the first British Sub Aqua Club (see UNDERWATER SWIMMING) regional centre in 1974.

FORTUNA (Diego Mazquiarán) (1895-1940), *matador de toros* who achieved only moderate success, because of ill-health, but is renowned for having caped a bull which had escaped from the corrals into the streets of Madrid, injuring eleven people and killing another, on 22 January 1928.

FORTUNE, FREDERICK (1921-   ), BOBSLEIGH rider for the U.S.A., who had a record length of international career spanning 22 seasons. He took part in the 1948 WINTER OLYMPIC GAMES at ST. MORITZ, Switzerland, gaining a bronze medal in the two-man event, and was still driving one of the United States sleds in the 1969 world championships at LAKE PLACID, N.Y.

FOSBURY, RICHARD (1947-   ), high jumper for the U.S.A. The originator of what came to be known as the 'Fosbury flop' style of jumping, Fosbury ranked no better than 48th in the world in 1967. In 1968 he won the Olympic gold medal with a height of 7 ft. 4¼ in. (2·24 m.) using his unprecedented head-first, face-upwards technique which caused him, literally, to land on his back.

FOSTER, H. K., British amateur RACKETS player who won the British amateur singles championship eight times in 1894-1900 and 1904. He also won the doubles championship eight times between 1893 and 1903. He also played CRICKET for Worcestershire.

FOX, NEIL (1940-   ), English RUGBY LEAGUE player, the most prolific scorer of his time. When he left to join Bradford Northern in 1969, he had scored 4,191 points, including 238 tries and 1,442 goals, for WAKEFIELD TRINITY since 1955. He returned to Wakefield as a player-coach in the following season and reached a total of 5,000 points in 1973-4. As a powerful centre (6 feet — 1·83 m. — tall, weighing 15 stone. — 95·25 kg.), he made the first of his 30 international appearances at the age of 19 and toured Australia in 1962.

FOX, UFFA (1898-1972), English yacht and dinghy designer, and helmsman, the author of a series of books on yacht design and performance. A pioneer in the design of light-displacement craft and planing dinghies, he served an apprenticeship in boat-building and studied naval architecture. He designed and built the International 14-ft. class dinghy *Avenger*, based on his experience with high-speed hulls. *Avenger* was a breakthrough in dinghy design because of her ability to lift out of the water, or plane, at suitable wind speeds.

FOXHALL (1878) was the only American race-horse to win both the ASCOT GOLD CUP and the French Grand Prix as well as the CAMBRIDGESHIRE and CESAREWITCH handicaps in the same season.

FOXHUNTER (1941), British show jumping (see EQUESTRIAN EVENTS) horse who won 78 international competitions between 1947 and 1953. Bought by LLEWELLYN in 1947, he made such rapid progress that he was chosen for the OLYMPIC GAMES in London the following year, where he contributed to the team's bronze medal. He was also in the British team which won the gold medal at Helsinki in 1952.

FOYT, A. J. (1935-   ), American MOTOR RACING driver who was three-times INDIANAPOLIS 500 winner, 1961, 1964, and 1967, and Pocono 500 winner in 1973. Winner of United States Auto Club national championship five times, 1960, 1961, 1963, 1964, and 1967 and winner of 45 U.S.A.C. national championship races. He was 1972 U.S.A.C. national dirt track champion. Driving stock cars, he won the U.S.A.C. title in 1968; the 1964 and 1965 Daytona 400s and 1972 Daytona 500; the 1970 Riverside 500-mile road race; and the 1971 and 1972 Ontario 500s and the 1971 Atlanta 500 in the N.A.S.C.A.R. Grand National championship. He won the 1967 LE MANS 24 Hours with GURNEY.

FRAMPTON, TREGONWELL (1641-1727) has been called the 'father of the English Turf'. He was supervisor of the royal race-horses at Heath House, Newmarket, under William III, Queen Anne, and the first two Georges.

FRANCE, WILLIAM H. G. sr. (1909-   ), principal organizer and president of the American National Association for Stock-Car Auto Racing (N.A.S.C.A.R.) from its founding in 1947 until his retirement in January 1972, after which he served as head of the firm operating the Daytona and Alabama (Talladega) speedways which he built. He created the Grand National championship in 1949.

FRANCIS DRAKE FELLOWSHIP, the most famous of the benevolent organizations in lawn BOWLS, founded in 1928 for all members of bowling clubs where the flat-green game is played. It is dedicated to providing funds for the relief of needy dependants of players who were members of the fellowship.

FRANK, RÉNÉ GEORGE (1898-   ), international HOCKEY official, who was largely responsible for the development and growth of the Fédération Internationale de Hockey (F.I.H.) in the years following the Second World War. During his playing days, he represented Ling University, Hornsey (London), La Rasante, and Daring. He was hon. treas. of the Belgian Hockey Association from 1934 and hon. sec. from 1946. Elected a member of the council of the F.I.H. in 1946, he became secretary-general of that organization in 1950, and president in 1966, a position to which he was re-elected in 1970. He played a very important part in the introduction of a hockey World Cup, in the development of continental championships, and in the amalgamation of the F.I.H. and the International Hockey Rules Board.

FRANK WORRELL TROPHY. Instituted in 1960-1 by the Australian Cricket Board of Control in commemoration of the tied Test match between Australia and West Indies at Brisbane during the series of that season, it is named after the late SIR FRANK WORRELL, who led West Indies in that match, and it is for competition between the two countries.

FRANKE, GUSTAV (1941-   ), German MOTOR-CYCLE TRIALS rider who was the first non-Briton to become famous in the sport. He rode a 250 cc. Zundapp to win the 'unofficial' European championship of 1965.

FRANKLIN, NEIL (1923-   ), Association footballer for STOKE CITY, Hull City, Stockport County, and England for whom he made his first appearance in a full international match when these were resumed after the Second World War on 28 September 1946 in Belfast against Northern Ireland. A tall, stylish centre half, he had played in 12 wartime and 'Victory' international matches. After playing against Northern Ireland in the first postwar international match, he took part in every one of England's next 26 matches to the end of the 1949-50 season. His final match was against Scotland on 15 April 1950 when England's win ensured qualification for the world championship.

FRANKLIN, SYDNEY (1903-   ), *matador de toros*, took the *alternativa* in Nuevo Laredo, Mexico, in 1932, and was the second American to claim the achievement.

FRASCUELO (Salvador Sánchez) (1844-98), *matador de toros* whose *alternativa* took place on 27 October 1867, was an extremely competent all-round *torero* of the period and his rivalry with Lagartijo provided 23 years of intense competition in the bull ring.

FRASER, DAWN (1937-   ), Australian swimmer who was the only competitor, man or woman, to win the same Olympic title at three successive Games. This was for 100 metres freestyle, which she won in 1956, 1960, and 1964. She was the first woman to break 1 minute for 100 metres and 110 yards (100·6 m.) and her 27 individual world records, in a remarkable nine-year career from 1956 to 1964, included nine successive records for 100 metres.

FRASER, NEALE ANDREW (1933-   ), a left-handed Australian LAWN TENNIS player with a powerful service, who won the WIMBLEDON title in 1960, the U.S. title in 1959 and 1960, and played a major part in his country's recapture of the Davis Cup (see LAWN TENNIS) in 1959. This was his first appearance as a singles player in a challenge round, but he beat both the leading Americans, Olmedo and MacKay, and, with EMERSON, defeated Buchholz and Olmedo in the doubles. He continued to play for Australia until 1963, notably in 1962 when he again won three rubbers in a difficult challenge round against Mexico.

Fraser's victory at Wimbledon was dramatic; it was his seventh attempt on the title and his career there had begun in the qualifying competition in 1954. In 1958 Cooper beat him in the final and in 1960 he was five times within a point of defeat in his quarter-final against Buchholz. Eventually the American retired with cramp in the thirty-first game of the fourth set. In Wimbledon's first all-left-handed final Fraser beat LAVER, then aged 21, 6-4, 3-6, 9-7, 7-5. He beat Olmedo and Laver in his U.S. finals and in 1962 he and his brother, J. G. Fraser, achieved the record, unique at the modern Wimbledon, of becoming the first pair of brothers to reach the semi-finals of the singles. Neither reached the final, but only the RENSHAWS (1882, 1883, and 1889) and the DOHERTYS (1898) improved upon that feat. In 1973 he captained the Australian team which regained the Davis Cup from the U.S.A. at Cleveland.

FRAZIER, JOE (1944-   ), American boxer who won the world heavyweight title in 1970 after CLAY had been deprived of his championship. Frazier became the first man to beat Clay professionally when the two met in March 1971 and Frazier won on points over 15 rounds. Their bout in MADISON SQUARE GARDEN drew a crowd of 20,455 who paid $1,352,500 to see the bout, but it grossed more than $20 million thanks to closed-circuit television income. Frazier who, like Clay, was paid $2,500,000 for this unique meeting of two undefeated world heavyweight champions, was Olympic gold medallist in 1964. He gained the recognition of the New York State Athletic Commission as world champion in 1968 but was more widely regarded as the title holder when he beat Ellis, the 'champion' of the World Boxing Association (see BOXING), in February 1970. Frazier's early career showed him to be an explosive left hooker and a tenacious in-fighter but probably his great fitness paid the highest dividends against Clay. In 1973 in Jamaica he lost the title to Foreman, another former Olympic champion, in the second round.

FREDRIKSSON, GERT (1919-   ), outstanding Swedish canoeist, whose record of Olympic, world championships, and national championship wins and placings is unlikely to be equalled. He was the winner of 56 individual K1 championship events spanning four OLYMPIC GAMES (1948-60) and four world championships (1948, 1950, 1954, 1958). He won a total of 44 gold medals for the individual K1 event, 35 gold medals in the relay event, and 3 gold medals in the K2 event between 1953 and 1960, and, at the age of 41, won the bronze K1 1000 metres and gold K2 medals at the Rome Olympics.

FREE DIVING, see UNDERWATER SWIMMING.

FREE FORESTERS, see CRICKET.

FREEMAN, ALFRED PERCY (Tich) (1888-1965), cricketer for England and Kent. He was very small, and, although playing only 12 times for England, he took 3,776 wickets in first-class CRICKET (well over half of them after turning 40), a career total second only to that of RHODES. With his leg-spin bowling he took 1,122 wickets in only four seasons to 1931, including a record 304 in 1928.

FREEMAN, Dr. DAVID GUTHRIE (1920-   ), American BADMINTON player. With only one season of serious international play, he acquired the reputation of being the greatest singles player the game has known. This great season was 1948-9 when, as a member of the first American THOMAS CUP team, he carried all before him, finishing by winning the ALL-ENGLAND singles title with 15-2, 15-4 and 15-1, 15-6 victories over the two top Malayan players. After the age of 18 he was never defeated, and was a clear winner of the American title six times running. In 1938 Freeman won both the singles and doubles in the United States junior LAWN TENNIS championships, but soon gave up the game.

FREEMAN, NOEL (1938-   ), race walker for Australia. He was Olympic silver medallist at 20 km. in 1960, and fourth in 1964, and winner of COMMONWEALTH GAMES 20 miles (32 km.) in 1970. The most successful Australian walker yet seen in international competition, Freeman was holder of several national records between 5 and 20 miles.

FREG, LUIS (1888-1934), Mexican *matador de toros* who, from the time of his *alternativa* in Alcalá de Henares, Spain, on 25 August 1911, was renowned for his swordsmanship. He popularized the *pase de la muerte*. Gored 57 times, he received the last rites five times, only to be drowned in his native land.

FRIGERIO, UGO (č. 1895-1969), race walker for Italy. Together with PAVESI, he was largely responsible for the Italian domination of the sport during the 1920s and was Olympic champion in 1920 at 3 km. and 10 km. and again in 1924 at 10 km. Eight years later in Los Angeles, Frigerio gained a bronze medal at 50 km. He was English Amateur Athletic Association champion at 2 miles in 1922 and at 7 miles in 1931. Frigerio had a most successful indoor season in the U.S.A. in 1925, being the first European walker to compete on the small board circuits that are used there. After his retirement from racing he contributed most valuable work on the international Walking Commission.

FRITH, FREDERICK, O.B.E. (*fl.* 1936-49), English racing motor-cyclist. The only man to be consistently successful in MOTOR-CYCLE RACING before and after the Second World War, he joined the NORTON team in 1936 and in the following year was the first rider to lap the TOURIST TROPHY course at over 90 m.p.h. (145 km./h.). In 1948 and 1949 he won many international events riding for Velocette, in the latter year winning the newly inaugurated world championship in the 350 cc. category. He retired at the end of that season and became the first motor-cyclist to be given recognition in the honours list.

FRY, Capt. CHARLES BURGESS (1872-1956), cricketer for England, Oxford University, Surrey, Sussex, and Hampshire; Association footballer for England, Corinthians, and

Southampton. A scholar and the most accomplished all-round sportsman of his time, he had a classic batting style. He headed the English national averages six times, scored 94 centuries, including six in succession in 1901, captained England, yet went on only one overseas tour (to South Africa in 1895-6). He was also a fast and agile RUGBY UNION three-quarter, and he equalled the world record for the long jump.

FUJII, SHOZO (1951-   ), Japanese JUDO fighter who won the world middleweight titles at the 1971 and 1973 world championships. His use of *seio-nage* (shoulder throw) brought him a number of quick wins even against the most stable of opponents. He was unlucky in being a contemporary of SEKINE and so missed selection for the 1972 Olympics when he would have been the probable gold medallist.

FULLERTON, (1887), COURSING grey-hound. Owned by Col. North, this brindle dog by Greentick out of Bit of Fashion, in addition to winning the Blue Riband outright in 1890, 1891, and 1892, also shared the final honours with a kennel-mate, Troughend, as a puppy in 1889. The winner of 31 out of 33 courses and of stakes amounting to £2,000, Fullerton is accepted as one of the greatest greyhounds in coursing history.

FULTON, A. G., M.B.E., D.C.M. (1887-1972), an outstanding British marksman with the rifle and the only man ever to win the King's Prize three times (1912, 1926, and 1931). His father, G. E. Fulton, won the Queen's Prize at Wimbledon in 1888, and in 1958, his son, Maj. R. A. Fulton, won the Queen's Prize at Bisley, thus completing an outstanding family record in British target shooting. A. G. Fulton started his shooting career in 1902. He joined the Queen's Westminster Rifles and in the First World War he was awarded the D.C.M. for his sniping exploits in France. In 1959 he was awarded the M.B.E. for services to rifle SHOOTING and two years later a presentation was made to him for the same reason by the Territorial Army Rifle Association. He had more King's/Queen's 'hundred' badges than any other marksman, having appeared in the final on 28 occasions. Besides representing Great Britain and England many times in all the principal British and Commonwealth team matches, and in the OLYMPIC GAMES, he won most of the major Bisley trophies on more than one occasion and gained many successes with touring teams in Australia and Canada.

FULTON, JOHN (1932-   ), American *matador de toros*, who by taking the *alternativa* in Seville on 18 July 1963, became the third U.S. citizen to do so.

FULTON, ROY (1914-   ), Irish lawn BOWLS player, bronze medallist in singles in the 1966 world championships at KYEEMAGH and also in the 1970 COMMONWEALTH GAMES singles at Edinburgh. Fulton was British Isles singles champion in 1967, pairs 1966 and 1967, and singles champion of Northern Ireland 1956, 1957, 1962, 1964, 1966, 1967. He has a controlled delivery and great sensitivity of touch.

G

G.A.A., see GAELIC ATHLETIC ASSOCIATION.

GABLE, DAN (1945-   ), American wrestler who won the 1972 Olympic freestyle lightweight title. His rugged training which sometimes included five daily sessions enabled him to enjoy an excellent career in which he lost only one bout.

GAELIC ATHLETIC ASSOCIATION (G.A.A.), organizes and controls the native Irish games of HURLING, Gaelic FOOTBALL, HANDBALL, and ROUNDERS. Despite its title, the Association does not now cater for track or field ATHLETICS, although it did so from its foundation in 1884 until 1921.

The Gaelic Athletic Association is the most powerful and popular sports organization in Ireland, equally strong north and south of the political boundary. Always unequivocally nationalistic in its ideals and its outlook, the G.A.A. was, in former years, entirely predominant in the sporting sphere throughout the provinces, particularly in the rural areas.

The basis of organization, now as in 1884 when it was founded, is the local club. In 1973, just over 3,000 clubs were affiliated to its central council. The vast majority of these were to be found throughout the 32 counties of Ireland, with the greatest number overseas in England, where there were 155; there were 5 in Scotland, and 29 from the American Board which controls parts of Canada and the U.S.A. outside New York. In addition, there are a number of clubs in and around New York which affiliate to the New York G.A.A., a body in close association with the G.A.A. in Ireland.

The G.A.A.'s chief activity is the organization of its hurling and football competitions. At inter-county level, these are the All-Ireland championships, which begin in April and finish in September, and the National Leagues, which commence in October, and reach their climax in May. The senior championships have been in continuous existence since 1887, but the National Leagues, which are senior competitions, were established in 1926 when they were set up to provide competitive fare at inter-county level through the autumn and spring.

The Gaelic Athletic Association is strictly amateur. Players are not allowed to accept payment of any kind, the value of prizes and trophies is strictly limited, and there is a fixed scale of travelling expenses, both for players and officials, and referees are not paid.

The origin of the G.A.A. derived from the confused situation in Irish athletics. Although the Irish Champion Athletic Club had existed through most of the 1870s, it was not a legislative body; its sole function was the organization of annual championships. By 1880 there were a number of athletic clubs, but most of these were in Dublin and catered almost exclusively for the leisured, professional, and business classes. On the foundation of the Amateur Athletic Association (A.A.A.) in England, moves were made to set up a corresponding body in Ireland. Much was talked and written, but nothing done. Eventually some clubs forced the issue by joining the English A.A.A., and thus brought the problem into the open. A group of athletes then founded the Gaelic Athletic Association at Thurles in County Tipperary on 1 November 1884. The new organization announced that it was independent of all outside control and that, while cultivating all accepted track and field sports, it would devote particular attention to preserving and promoting native Irish games and pastimes. The first president was the then father-figure of Irish athletics, Maurice Davin from Carrick-on-Suir, a former champion weight-thrower whose brother Pat set new world records in both the high and long jumps. The first secretary was Cusack, a Clare-born Dublin champion with the shot.

The new Association immediately gave a sensational fillip to Irish athletics by bringing into competition many who had been virtually barred hitherto because they worked for a living whereas most Irish meetings had catered only for gentleman-athletes. The immediate reaction from the Dublin clubs was the formation, in 1885, of an Irish Athletic Association. A brief 'war' of boycotting and counter-boycotting followed, but from 1886, and for 20 years afterwards, athletes from either association could compete freely at meetings organized by the other. This meant keener competition, and it was during the next two decades that Ireland produced such renowned athletes as Mitchell, Kiely, O'Connor

Horgan, and the Leahy brothers, who set many world records in the jumps, the weights, and the HAMMER and won several Olympic and many British titles.

But, from the very earliest years, the greater emphasis within the G.A.A. began to centre on the team games of hurling and Gaelic football, and by the end of the nineteenth century the All-Ireland hurling and football championships had become national events. By this time the control of the track and field sports had been delegated to an Athletic Council which, while still part of the G.A.A., had almost complete autonomy. This Council continued to run athletic championships until 1921 when, in an endeavour to promote athletic unity in Ireland, the Association withdrew completely from the organization of athletics.

A more militant nationalism was soon evident in the Association's general policy and 1904 saw the introduction of the rules banning from G.A.A. membership all those who played or supported any non-Irish game. These rules were slightly modified with the passing of time and, by the 1920s, the ban applied to four games only, RUGBY, soccer, CRICKET, and HOCKEY. Through the following 50 years the Ban Rules remained a constant cause of contention. After the end of the civil war in 1923, the G.A.A. membership was sharply divided between those who accepted the new Irish Free State and those who had fought the rearguard action for a republic. But the Association played an important role by bringing those who had so recently been enemies together again on the playing fields.

By the middle of 1924 the Association was back in full stride. The National Leagues were added to the championships to provide winter competition, inter-provincial games between selected teams were inaugurated, and the end of the decade saw the arrival of a dynamic new personality, Padraig O'Keeffe, who was appointed general secretary.

The Gaelic Athletic Association seemed to reach its peak of popularity through the late 1950s and early 1960s. The greatest crowds that had ever assembled for any Irish sporting events gathered to watch the All-Ireland hurling and football finals.

But by the late 1960s, the days when hurling and Gaelic football provided the pastimes of every leisure hour were gone for ever. The rural population, from which the Association had always drawn its greatest strength, was declining steadily. Moreover, the challenge from other games suddenly became a very real threat to the G.A.A.'s supremacy on the Irish sportsfields. The Ban Rules, which had been one of the Association's great bulwarks in

other days, were now considered, especially by many of the younger generation, to be more of a hindrance than a help to the continued progress of the G.A.A. Eventually, at the end of 1970, a referendum was taken of all clubs within the Association. They voted overwhelmingly for the abolition of all rules that banned non-Irish games. The subsequent county conventions followed the lead the clubs had given, only two counties out of 32 favouring retention. Finally, the annual congress, meeting at Queen's University in Belfast on 11 April 1971, swept out the Ban Rules without debate.

P. O'Neill, *Twenty Years of the G.A.A.* (1931); T. F. O'Sullivan, *Story of the G.A.A.* (1910); P. Purcell, *Sixty Glorious Years of the G.A.A.* (1947); *Our Games Annual*, annually since 1958.

GAELIC FOOTBALL, see FOOTBALL, GAELIC.

GAILLE, BLAISE (1942-   ), Swiss constructor of the first aquabob in 1967. He was the first demonstrator of AQUABOBBING, and in 1968 he made a record 10-mile (16 km.) nonstop run on the lake of Neuchâtel at an average speed of 45 m.p.h. (72 km./h.).

GAINSBOROUGH (1915), a race-horse by BAYARDO, was bred and owned by Lady James Douglas, trained by ALEC TAYLOR, and ridden by Childs. Gainsborough won an English wartime triple crown (see HORSE RACING) and substitute Gold Cup run at NEWMARKET, later becoming a leading stallion at stud, where he sired SOLARIO, winner of the ST. LEGER, ASCOT GOLD CUP, and CORONATION CUP, and HYPERION.

GALIA, JEAN (1905-48), French RUGBY LEAGUE player. He was chiefly responsible for introducing the game into France in 1933. A former RUGBY UNION international forward, he captained the first French Rugby League team to visit England and showed exceptional drive and ability in organizing the French League.

GALICIA (1898), a race-horse by Galopin out of Isoletta by ISONOMY, was a celebrated English brood mare and dam of BAYARDO and LEMBERG.

GALILEE (1963), the champion Australian race-horse, who won the Cup triple crown with victories in the MELBOURNE CUP and CAULFIELD CUP in 1966 and the Sydney Cup in 1967, as well as winning the Queen Elizabeth Stakes, Queen's Plate, and 11 other races, together with $163,430 in prize money. Galilee was bred by Otway at Trelawney Stud, Cambridge, New Zealand, and was owned by Mr. and Mrs. Bailey of Adelaide.

GALLACHER, HUGH (1902-57), Association footballer for Airdrieonians, NEWCASTLE UNITED, CHELSEA, Derby County, NOTTS COUNTY, Grimsby, Gateshead, and Scotland for whom he made his first appearance on 1 March 1924 against Ireland in Glasgow and the last of 19 appearances in home championship matches on 6 April 1935 against England in Glasgow. He had pluck and a quick football brain that enabled him, as centre forward, both to lead and to link attacks; but, above all, from close quarters and in crowded goal-mouths, he was able to shoot accurately the moment the chance was offered. He scored five goals in succession for the Scottish League against the Irish League in November 1925. Later, when with Newcastle, he again scored five goals, for Scotland against Ireland in February 1929, but he failed to score in what must have been the most memorable international match in which he played — on 31 March 1928 when Scotland beat England 5-1.

GALLAGHER, FRANK (1895-1966), English RUGBY LEAGUE loose forward. He played in seven Tests against Australia. A Dewsbury player when chosen for the 1920 tour, he moved to Batley before touring again in 1924. His last two seasons were spent with LEEDS, whom he joined in 1927. Inside backs who played alongside him claimed that there was no one to equal him in constructive ability.

GALLANT FOX (1927), an outstanding American race-horse, won the KENTUCKY DERBY, BELMONT, PREAKNESS, and LAWRENCE REALIZATION classic stakes, JOCKEY CLUB GOLD CUP, and Saratoga Cup, together with $328,165 in prize money, then a world record. Gallant Fox was bred and owned by WOODWARD, trained by Fitzsimmons, and ridden by SANDE.

Later he stood at the CLAIBORNE FARM STUD, producing two outstanding sons in Omaha, which won the Kentucky Derby, Belmont, Preakness, and Classic Stakes; and Granville, which won the Belmont, Classic, TRAVERS, and Lawrence Realization Stakes, as well as the Saratoga Cup.

GALLO, El (Rafael Gómez) (1882-1962), *matador de toros* of a most enigmatic disposition. He sometimes performed with brilliant courage, at other times with abject cowardice. His *alternativa* took place on 28 September 1902 and from thereon he retired and reappeared at frequent intervals until 1936. At one of his retirement *corridas*, he refused to face the bull because he believed that it had winked at him, and his brother, JOSELITO, was obliged to take his place. He killed 1,875 bulls during his career.

GANDAR DOWER, K. C. (1908-44), brilliant though unorthodox games player, who represented Cambridge in varsity matches in REAL TENNIS, LAWN TENNIS, RUGBY and ETON FIVES, SQUASH RACKETS, and billiards. He won the Eton fives amateur championship for the Kinnaird Cup with McConnell in 1929 and 1932, was Rugby fives amateur singles champion in 1932, and squash rackets amateur champion in 1938. He played lawn tennis for Great Britain and was an enigmatic explorer, author, and poet.

GANEFO (Games of the New Emerging Forces), an international ATHLETICS meeting in the Far East, held irregularly since 1963 when the competing nations were Cambodia, China, Indonesia, North Korea, and North Vietnam. Apparently a Communist-inspired answer to the ASIAN GAMES, GANEFO is not sanctioned by the International Amateur Athletic Federation (see ATHLETICS, TRACK AND FIELD) and performances are not eligible as world records.

In the first meeting, at Djakarta, Indonesia, the outstanding athlete was the North Korean SIN KIM DAN. Her times for the 400 metres (51·4 sec.) and the 800 metres (1 min. 59· sec.) were well inside the world records then existing. At Phnom Penh, Cambodia, in 1966 a Chinese high jumper, Ni Chihchin, came within $\frac{1}{8}$ in. (0·95 cm.) of BRUMEL's record of 7 ft. 5¾ in. (2·28 m.). At Shanghai in 1969, the same man passed the record with a jump of 2·29 m.

GANLEY, BERNARD (1930-   ), RUGBY LEAGUE full-back for Oldham. In 1957-8 he set up a record with 224 goals. He played three times for Great Britain, and in one of these matches, at Wigan on 23 November 1957, he kicked ten goals in ten attempts. His accuracy at kicking was an important factor in Oldham's League championship win in 1956-7.

GANS, JOE (1874-1910), American boxer who won the world lightweight title in 1902, holding it until 1908. He and LEONARD are generally considered the greatest of all lightweights. Gans was best known for his skill but his punch could be so powerful that he won the world title in less than a round. He was suffering from the early stages of tuberculosis when he was twice beaten by NELSON in championship contests and died only 15 months after his last bout.

GAONA, RUDOLFO (1888-   ), Mexican *matador de toros* (*alternativa* 1908) who invented the *gaonera* in which the cape is held behind the back. A pair of *banderillas* placed in Pamplona in 1915 is still regarded as the model for the *suerte*. Acthough he had to compete with BELMONTE and JOSELITO at their peak, he was one of the finest all-round *toreros* of history.

GARLITS, DONALD GLENN (1932-   ), American drag-racing (see MOTOR RACING) driver. A leading competitor in U.S. national events from late 1957 when he became the first driver to set a national record outside California, he broke the Kissimee, Florida, strip record in his 395 cu. in. Chrysler-powered slingshot *Swamp Rat*, and went on to exceed 180 m.p.h. (288 km./h.) terminal speeds in 1959, and 200 m.p.h. (322 km./h.) in 1964 — the first man to do so. He remained a leading competitor until 1970 when he suffered severe foot injuries due to his clutch exploding. He later staged a comeback, currently holding the highest terminal speed record of 243.90 m.p.h. (392.5 km./h.) — 6.175 seconds — set 19 March 1972, at Gainesville Dragway, Florida (U.S.A.).

GARMISCH, BOBSLEIGH course at Garmisch-Partenkirchen in the Bavarian Alps, West Germany. It was built for the 1936 WINTER OLYMPIC GAMES, but opened in time to stage the world championships in 1934. Other world championship meetings were held there in 1938, 1953, 1958, and 1962. A good course technically, it enjoys less reliable climatic conditions than ST. MORITZ or CORTINA.

GARRARD, ROBERT (*fl.* 1934-48), one of the British Commonwealth's finest wrestlers. This fast-moving Australian won the Commonwealth lightweight title in 1934, 1938, and 1950, and was a silver medallist in the welterweight class at the 1948 Olympics.

GARRINCHA (Manoel Francisco dos Santos) (1933-   ), Association footballer for the Rio clubs BOTAFOGO, Corinthians, and Flamengo, and for Brazil, a remarkable right winger. Although in 1971 he sought a job as a coach in France, he never took kindly as a player to a regimented, disciplined style of team play. His individual virtuosity contributed greatly to Brazil's win in the 1958 world championship when he was introduced into the team in the later stages of the tournament in Sweden. He remained a member of the national team that retained the championship title in Chile in 1962, and in the less happy team that competed in the 1966 championship in England.

GARRYOWEN R.F.C., RUGBY UNION football club in Doorodoyle, Co. Limerick, founded in 1884. Garryowen is also the term for a manoeuvre first employed by the club in Ulster Cup matches, in which the forwards charge up on a high kick ahead; if correctly executed, it should allow the forwards to reach the ball at their greatest momentum just as it drops to earth.

GASKOINA, El (The Gascon) (Jean Erratchun) (1817-1859), French Basque PELOTA player, chronologically the second seminal figure in the game's history after PERKAIN. As a player he was supreme in his time, but he is just as important as the link *pilotari* between Perkain's ancient pelota (leather glove, heavy ball, open courts) and the beginning of the modern game (wicker glove, faster ball, walled courts). He was contemporary with a generation of exceptional Spanish champions, with whom he had some memorable matches — the most celebrated being the meeting at Irun in 1846 which attracted a crowd of 12,000 and was the cause of frenetic gambling. A gritty personality, quite the opposite of the jaunty Perkain, Gaskoina grew hugely fat as he aged, but still held his own with the best by the finesse of his placing and his weight of shot.

GASNIER, REGINALD (1939-   ), Australian RUGBY LEAGUE player. He was perhaps the finest centre ever to play the game. He had exceptional speed and sharp reflexes, was skilled in fundamentals, and never lacked courage. Chosen for the 1959-60 tour of Britain and France after only half a season in first-grade football in Sydney, at the age of 20, his form was a revelation to English spectators. He scored three tries in his first Test. This was the first of three full tours to Britain, besides a WORLD CUP visit in 1960. He was captain of the 1967-8 Australian touring team, but a leg injury in the first Test and a further breakdown in France ended his playing career.

GAUDIN, LUCIEN (1886-1934), French fencer, Olympic foil and épée champion in 1924. He was technically the most perfect fencer of this century and declared *Hors Classe* by the French Fencing Federation, an honour never before bestowed on any fencer.

GAUL, CHARLY (1932-   ), Luxembourgeois road-race cyclist, celebrated for his ability as a climber. He was nicknamed 'the Angel of the Mountains' after winning, by nearly 14 minutes, a stage of the 1955 TOUR DE FRANCE which included the major climbs of Aravis, Telegraphe, and Galibier in the Alps. He was twice King of the Mountains in the Tour, which he won in 1958.

GAY CRUSADER (1914), a race-horse by BAYARDO, bred and owned by Cox, trained by ALEC TAYLOR, and ridden by DONOGHUE. Gay Crusader won an English wartime triple crown (see HORSE RACING), CHAMPION STAKES, and substitute Gold Cup run at NEWMARKET.

GAYFORD, THOMAS (1928-), Canadian show jumping (see EQUESTRIAN EVENTS) rider, one of the Canadian trio which sprang a major surprise by winning the Olympic team gold medal in Mexico (1968). He rode for Canada's three-day event team (winning a team gold medal at the 1959 PAN-AMERICAN GAMES) before specializing in show jumping. In 1967, he rode Big Dee to win a team bronze for show jumping at the Pan-American Games.

GEE, KENNETH (1916-), English RUGBY LEAGUE player. One of the finest prop forwards in the history of the game, he joined WIGAN in 1933 and was so consistent that he was playing in international football 20 years later. He played 33 times for England, and toured Australia in 1946 and 1950. Gee and his Wigan scrum partner, EGAN, played alongside each other in more than 20 internationals.

GEESINK, ANTON (1934-), Dutch JUDO fighter and the first man to beat the Japanese at their own sport. Geesink, 6 ft. 6 in. (1·98 m.) and 19 st. (121 kg.), dominated the sport from 1961 when he secured his first world title until his retirement six years later. He took 18 European individual titles between 1952 and 1967 and secured the gold medal at the 1964 OLYMPIC GAMES in the open category. His run of victories was due to his ability to combine speed and skill with his huge physique.

At the first world championships he finished third and in 1958 lost in the quarter-finals. Three years later in Paris, when the championships were held for the first time outside Japan, Geesink took the title. There was only one class—the open category—and in successive rounds he beat the three Japanese entrants, KAMINAGA, Koga, and SONE, the 1958 world champion, to take the title.

In 1964 the Japanese were determined to regain their position when the sport appeared for the first time in the Olympics in deference to the Japanese hosts. But before 15,000 spectators Geesink twice defeated Kaminaga, holding him down with *kesa-gatame* (scarf hold) in the final. In the 1965 world championships in Rio de Janeiro, Geesink defeated Matsunaga for the heavyweight title. He took his last major title when he beat KIKNADZE (U.S.S.R.) in the European championships open final at Rome in 1967, after which he took up professional instructing in Holland.

GEFÄLLER, GEORG (1895-), and GEORG jr. (1923-). The elder Gefäller was the German inventor of the modern ski-bob, the *Gefäller Ei* (Gefäller Egg), in 1947. His son Georg was the first president of the Fédération Internationale de Skibob, the international federation of SKIBOBBING, and the father of the sport. He organized the first official skibob race in the world in Kiefersfelden in Germany in 1951 and founded in the same year the first skibob federation and club in Bavaria.

GEISLER, ILSE (1941-), luge TOBOGGANING rider for East Germany; twice women's world champion, in 1962 and 1963.

GENTLE, RANDIR SINGH (1923-) an outstanding HOCKEY full-back for India Independent S.C. (Delhi), and Tata S.C (Bombay), he was also a remarkable scorer of penalty corner goals. With CHAND and ALLEN he holds the record of having won an Olympic hockey gold medal three times (1948, 1952 1956). In the 1956 Olympics, he scored six goals including the decisive goal in the final against Pakistan. Frequently chosen to tour with Indian national teams, he visited East Africa three times, New Zealand, Singapore Malaya, and the Far East. During his long career, he played in the Indian national championship 20 times. On retiring he proved an outstanding coach and was invited, at one time or another, to prepare the national teams of India, Malaya, and Spain. He also became an international umpire.

GENTLEMEN *v.* **PLAYERS,** see CRICKET.

GENTO, FRANCISCO (1933-), Association footballer for REAL MADRID and Spain both of whom he captained towards the end of a long and very successful career. A stockily-built man, he was noted for his quick acceleration and great speed down the left wing which he used to advantage as a member of the great Real Madrid side that won the first five competitions for the European Champion Clubs Cup between 1956 and 1960. He was also in the Real Madrid sides beaten in the finals of

962 and 1964 but successful for the sixth
me in 1966. In the latter year he played for
pain in the world championship tournament
England, as he had in the 1962 champion-
hip in Chile.

EREVICH, ALDAR (1910-   ), Hun-
arian fencer; Olympic sabre champion 1948
nd world sabre champion 1935, 1951, and
955; probably the greatest technician in the
istory of FENCING. Told in 1960, when
e was 50, that he was too old to compete for a
lace on the Hungarian Olympic team, he
hallenged the entire team and defeated them
l; he then went to the Rome OLYMPIC GAMES
d missed the sabre final by a single hit.

ERMANO, FIGUEIREDO (1932-   ),
ssociation footballer for BENFICA (Lisbon)
d Portugal, who was at the peak of his play-
g career in the period when, in the European
hampion Clubs Cup finals of 1961 and 1962,
enfica ended the REAL MADRID monopoly of
e competition by beating BARCELONA and
eal Madrid in the respective finals. An
xceptionally mobile defender, he missed the
uropean final of 1963 but was back in the
enfica side beaten in the 1965 final by INTER-
AZIONALE — a match in which he went into
al after Benfica's goalkeeper Pereira retired
jured.

EZIRA CLUB, Cairo. This, the main sport-
g club in Egypt, is situated close to the cen-
e of Cairo and was known to thousands of
ritish servicemen in both World Wars. With
ven SQUASH RACKETS courts and plans for a
rge galleried court designed by Shafik, one
the U.A.R.'s leading players, Gezira has
en the training ground for many of the coun-
y's leading squash players, both professional
d amateur.

IBBS, LANCELOT RICHARD (1934-
    ), cricketer for West Indies, Guyana,
uth Australia, and Warwickshire. An off-
in bowler possessing consummate control
er flight and length, he was the first West
dian to take 200 wickets in Test CRICKET,
d his skill contributed much towards West
dies' pre-eminence after 1960. Against Aus-
lia in 1960-1 he did the hat-trick at Ade-
de, and a year later he achieved his best
nings return — 8 wickets for 38 against
dia. He was the first player to bowl 20,000
lls in a Test career.

IBSON, ALTHEA (1927-   ), American
WN TENNIS player, the first Negro to
hieve major success in the game. She learnt
r lawn tennis by playing PADDLE TENNIS and

in her first notable match, at FOREST HILLS in
1950, she came close to beating BROUGH, the
reigning WIMBLEDON champion. Her game
was notable for strength and aggression and
she developed steadily as a match player. In
1956 she won the French and Italian singles
titles and the Wimbledon doubles with Buxton, a British player, and in 1957 and 1958 she
won the singles titles at both Wimbledon and
Forest Hills. In those two years she completely
dominated women's lawn tennis. Her only set-
back was a defeat by Truman, then 17, in the
WIGHTMAN CUP match at Wimbledon in 1958
which enabled the British to gain their first
postwar victory in the competition.

GIBSON, CAMERON MICHAEL HEN-
DERSON, M.B.E. (1942-   ), RUGBY
UNION centre and outside half for North of Ireland, Cambridge University, Ireland, and British LIONS. Capped 31 times for Ireland by the
end of the 1969-70 season, Gibson had
become one of the most reliable of all Irish
mid-field players.

Although increasingly selected at centre, it
was from outside half that he dropped two
goals and scored a try at Dublin against the
fifth WALLABIES in 1967. He played in all four
Lions' Tests in New Zealand, 1966, South
Africa, 1968, and New Zealand, 1971.

GIBSON, ROBERT (1935-   ), American
BASEBALL pitcher for the ST. LOUIS CARDI-
NALS, from 1959. He set a NATIONAL LEAGUE
lifetime record for strikeouts. In 1968 he set a
National League season record for lowest
earned-run average, 1·12, and received both
the award for best pitcher and the one for Most
Valuable Player in the league. In 1970 he was
again named best pitcher in the National
League.

GICHIN, FUNAKOSHI (1870-1957), Okinawan exponent of KARATE. He was invited to
Japan in 1923 to teach Tang Hand or *te*. He
combined *te* (the Okinawan hand-fighting)
with Japanese JU-JITSU, renaming it KARATE-
DO, and founded the Shotokan style of karate.

GIFFEN, GEORGE (1859-1927), cricketer
for Australia and South Australia. A strong-
willed man, always enduring and often powerful as a batsman, and tireless as a slow-
medium bowler, he was Australia's leading
player throughout his career, reaching his peak
in the 1894-5 Test series against England,
when he scored 475 runs and took 34 wickets.

GILERA, Italian motor-cycle firm prominent
in international racing from 1938, when it took
over the prototype four-cylinder 500 cc. Rondine and made it the fastest and most highly

developed racing machine in existence before the outbreak of the Second World War. After the war its design was completely revised, although remaining faithful to the basic concept, and the Gilera team dominated the larger capacity classes in international MOTOR-CYCLE RACING until the end of 1957. The 1957 machines still proved competitive when raced as a private venture under the management of DUKE (former Gilera rider) in 1963.

GILLESPIE, WILLIAM (1891-   ), Association footballer for Northern Ireland, Leeds City, Sheffield United, and Derry City. An ideal inside forward, and shrewd captain, he played 25 times for his country and won an F.A. Cup medal with Sheffield United in the 1924-5 season.

GILLETTE CUP, the trophy awarded annually to the winner of the Gillette Cup competition in English CRICKET. Conducted on a knock-out basis between the 17 first-class county sides and the 5 leading counties in the Minor Counties championship of the previous season, it was instituted in 1963 as an antidote to flagging interest in the county championship proper. It was an immediate success and has never lost its hold on the public, the final at LORD'S in September always producing a crowd of over 20,000. Though not first-class in status, this type of cricket consistently arouses great enthusiasm. The matches, which are of one innings a side, each limited to 60 overs, are intended to be completed in a single day, though weather interference may prolong a match. Subject to each bowler being limited to a maximum of 12 overs, the normal laws of cricket apply. In the early years of the competition Sussex proved especially adept at Gillette-style cricket, and did not suffer defeat until the third year of the competition. A 'Man of the Match' award is presented by an appointed adjudicator at the end of each game (in all rounds) for the most meritorious performance, irrespective of which side wins.

GILLI DANDA is an indigenous outdoor team or individual game akin to the English KNUR AND SPELL, played in India, Pakistan, and Ceylon with slight variations. It is also known as gulli danda or danda guli. It is played on an open field without any set boundary lines or prescribed shape. Two sticks are used — the gilli, about 5 in. (127 mm.) long and the danda, about 2 ft. (609 mm.) long. Both are smooth, round, about an inch (25 mm.) in diameter, and cut from the same piece of hard wood. The gilli is tapered to a point at each end, the danda at one. A small hole about

the size and shape of the gilli is dug in the ground and is called the guchhi.

Gilli danda is played between two teams, two individuals, or one against odds. There is no limit to the number of players on each side, but ideally it should not exceed seven. The side winning the toss chooses whether to field or to play first. The captain decides the order in which his players take their turn, depending on their ability and skill, and the rival captain arranges his field placements.

The player coming in first opens the innings by placing the gilli across the guchhi. He then inserts the tapered end of the danda under the gilli and lifts it into the air to propel it as far away as he can. The gilli may either fly or roll along the ground. The opponents, standing in front of the player at some distance, try to catch the gilli or stop it. If it is caught, the player is out. He is out also when a fielder, having failed to catch the gilli, hits the danda which has been placed across the guchhi by the player, with an accurate throw.

If the player overcomes these initial obstacles he is entitled to three attempts to hit the gilli. For the first, he may touch it and place it by hand near the guchhi; for the next two he may not.

The gilli pops up in the air as it is gently struck with the danda on either of its ends. While it is still above the ground, the player tries to hit it, again with the danda, clear of the fielders so that it can neither be caught nor intercepted by the fielders already stationed in the direction the gilli is likely to take. Also the farther he despatches the gilli, the more likely the player is to score more points. However, if the gilli drops to the ground before being hit, the player loses one try; he may fail again twice, in which case he is almost sure to get out since the fielders will have little difficulty in hitting the danda from close range. Alternatively, the gilli may have gone several hundred feet away from the guchhi if there has been perfect timing, proper impact, and considerable power behind the strokes.

When the player has had three attempts, he returns to the guchhi and lays his danda across it. One of the fielders then throws the gilli from the spot where it finally landed. If it hits the danda, or falls into the hole, the player is out. If it misses, the playing team demands a number of annas, or runs, depending on an estimate of the distance between the guchhi and the gilli's landing-spot (one anna being equal to the length of the danda). The opposition may grant the annas if they think the guess is right or they may challenge it. The distance is then measured with the danda in a straight line, irrespective of the course the gilli may have followed. If it is found to be adequate, the player gets the *annas*; otherwise he is out. If not out, he repeats the whole process again and again until such time as he is out. At the end of one team's innings, the other takes its turn, the number of innings being decided beforehand. The side with most *annas* at the end of the match wins.

Gilli danda is not a well-organized or standardized game — it is played with slight variations, but all of these have their own rules. In some versions, a player may continue hitting the *gilli* as long as he can connect with it while it is in the air. This is common in games where an individual plays against many, all of whom field at the same time. Each player takes his turn and joins the fielders again as soon as he is out. At the close of play *annas* scored by each individual are counted, and the one with the highest score wins.

In Ceylon, a similar game is known as *gudu*. Here the player does not place his long stick over the hole after lifting or propelling the *kuttiya*, as the *gilli* is known. He defends the hole when the *kuttiya* is thrown back by the fielders, after failing to catch it, and tries to hit it hard. If he misses and the *kuttiya* falls within a *danda*'s length of the hole, he is out. If he hits it, the distance between the point where it falls and the hole is measured by the *danda*. The player repeats the process until he gets out. The side scoring most *danda*-lengths wins.

As a further variation from the game in India or Pakistan, the winners in Ceylon penalize the losers. One of the players in the winning team stands by the hole, tosses the *kuttiya* in the air with his hand and hits it with the *danda*. He is followed by the rest of the players, each of whom hits the *kuttiya* from the spot where his previous colleague had sent it. After the last member has taken his turn, the losers must pick up the *kuttiya* and run back towards the hole in a relay. They are obliged to exhale as they run along, and must repeat the words '*gudu-gudu*' loudly as a proof that they do not inhale. If one of them fails to do so, the winners resume hitting the *kuttiya* from the spot and the losers must cover a longer distance.

Gilli danda is an ancient game. It was played, more or less in its present form, about 5,000 years ago. Despite its long history and popularity, no association or organization for its administration has been formed in India. Nor are there any tournaments for teams or individuals.

The game is particularly popular in northern India, where small boys play it in the streets.

GILPATRIC, GUY (d. 1939), American underwater swimmer, principal originator of the sport of UNDERWATER SWIMMING in the Mediterranean, 1920-30, and author of the first book on the sport, *The Compleat Goggler* (1938).

GILTINAN, JAMES JOHN (1866-1952), a leading figure in the introduction of RUGBY LEAGUE to Australia. An organizer of energy, enterprise, and powers of persuasion, he caused events to move rapidly once a decision had been taken to break away from the RUGBY UNION. Within a year he had organized eight city clubs and a team from Newcastle, N.S.W., to play in a league each Saturday in Sydney; provided the impetus for the foundation of the code in Queensland; and made arrangements for the visit of the All-Blacks and Maoris to Sydney and for an Australian team to tour England. He was appointed secretary of the newly formed New South Wales League in 1908, and in the same year he raised the money for, and managed, the first Australian team to tour England. He was secretary for only one year, but as a life member he continued to play a prominent part in the game's development for over 20 years.

GIMONDI, FELICE (1942-   ), Italian road-race cyclist ranking third to MERCKX and COPPI on the basis of truly international victories. After winning the TOUR DE L'AVENIR in 1964, he turned professional and won the TOUR DE FRANCE the following year, although included in the race only as a late replacement. An excellent climber and time triallist, and a proficient finishing sprinter, by the end of the 1970 season Gimondi had twice won the GIRO D'ITALIA and GRAND PRIX DES NATIONS, and once the VUELTA A ESPAGNA, PARIS–ROUBAIX, TOUR OF LOMBARDY, and PARIS–BRUSSELS. In both the Grand Prix des Nations (1968) and Paris–Brussels (1966) he had set up record times. His later career was overshadowed by Merckx, but in 1973 he beat him in the sprint to win the world road championship.

GIRARDENGO, CONSTANTE (1893-   ), professional cyclist, who was Italian road-race champion for the 13 years 1913-25. Allowing for a break during the First World War, he won nine successive national titles, a record for any country. Apart from two six-day races in central Europe, all his major victories occurred in Italy: six in the MILAN–SAN REMO (a record), three in the TOUR OF LOMBARDY, and two in the GIRO D'ITALIA.

GIRO D'ITALIA (Tour of Italy), an annual stage race for professional cyclists. First held in 1909, it was modelled on the TOUR DE

FRANCE but remained a largely domestic event until 1950 when, for the first time, it was won by a non-Italian, Koblet (Switzerland). Gaining recognition as a major international race, it was won by foreign riders seven times in the next 20 years. The Giro, run between the Spanish and French tours, lasts just under three weeks and takes a different route each year; up to 1970 the shortest was 1,496 miles (2,400 km.) in 1909, the longest 2,690 miles (4,325 km.) in 1954.

GLACIARIUM, the world's first mechanically-refrigerated ICE SKATING rink, near King's Road, Chelsea, London; built by John Gamgee in 1876 with an ice surface measuring 40 ft. by 24 ft. (12 × 7·3 m.). It was, as the *Illustrated London News* records, constructed in a permanent building with galleries for spectators, the walls being decorated with Swiss alpine and forest scenes painted by Durand of Paris.

GLADIATEUR (1862), a race-horse by MONARQUE, was one of the most notable horses of all time, winning the GRAND PRIX DE PARIS and the French St. Leger, the English triple crown (see HORSE RACING) and the ASCOT GOLD CUP by 40 lengths, together with £30,868 in prize money.

GLADIOLO (1943), a race-horse who won the Milan and Italian Grand Prix and the Italian triple crown. He was bred and raced by the Razza del Soldo, trained by Regoli, and ridden by Caprioli.

GLAHN, KLAUS (1942-   ), West German JUDO fighter whose skill made him one of Europe's finest heavyweights. He won a bronze medal in the open category at the 1964 OLYMPIC GAMES and was second to the Japanese entrants in the open category at the 1967 world championships and in the heavyweight class two years later at the Mexico City world championships. Only the presence of RUSKA prevented him from placing second in the 1971 world championships and Munich Olympics heavyweight categories. He retired after finishing third in the 1973 world championships.

GLENEAGLES, popular Scottish hotel GOLF course in the superb scenery of the Grampian foothills. Hilly and wooded, the Gleneagles courses are designed for tourists' enjoyment and cannot be considered great tests of golf. In their own context, for pleasure and beauty, they have few equals in the British Isles and, in keeping with the five-star way of life, are maintained in excellent order.

GLENTORAN F.C., Association FOOTBALL club, Belfast. Founded in 1882, Glentoran were the first Irish League club to compete in the Inter-Cities Fairs Cup, 1962-3. They also took part in the 1967 U.S. tournament. The club's outstanding players have included DOHERTY, BINGHAM, BLANCHFLOWER, MCILROY, and C. Martin.
COLOURS: Red, green, and black shirts, white shorts.

GLIDING is the sport of flying without the use of a motor, by utilizing currents of rising air. Skill is recognized in the award of individual proficiency badges, by the breaking of international or national records, and in championships.

The glider, a heavier-than-air machine without an engine, is launched into the air by aerotow, winch, or car-tow (see below), and flies by using gravity to maintain speed. Although the aircraft is all the time gliding downwards through the air, it is designed to do so at a flat angle — for a high-performance competition glider about 1:48. It will thus travel 48 miles for every 1 mile, or 5,280 ft. (1,609 m.), loss of height. When a glider is flown into rising air it is circled, or otherwise manoeuvred, to stay within the up-current, and is borne upwards. At the top of the lift, the glider is flown, usually fast, in the desired direction, gliding downwards again until another up-current is located. When no further lift can be found, the glider has to be landed.

Soaring is the art, or science, of finding and using up-currents, the three main sources of lift being thermals, slope lift, and wave lift. Most cross-country soaring is carried out by using *thermals*, flights of over 600 miles (1,000 km.) being made in this way. Thermals are separate rising bubbles of air found in the bottom few thousand feet of the atmosphere, and are caused by the irregular heating of the ground by the sun. Towns, sunny valleys, and dry dusty areas produce better thermals than damp ground or cool, windswept places. To be of use to a glider, thermals need to be not less than 200 yds. (180 m.), preferably up to 800 yds. (725 m.), across, and rising at not less than 150 ft. per min. (·75 m./sec.). In temperate regions, such as northern Europe, thermals rarely rise higher than 7,000 ft. (2,300 m.), but in hotter, continental areas such as Texas or Australia, they may go up to 15,000 ft. (4,600 m.), or higher. If the air is moist, condensation takes place in the rising, expanding, and cooling thermals and a cumulus cloud forms near the top. The small scattered cumulus clouds of a summer day indicate the locations of thermals. The lift continues up into the cloud. If the air is very unstable, the cloud may grow into a thunderhead in which the glider may climb to a height of 33,000 ft. (10,000 m.) or more, provided that the pilot is skilled and the glider is equipped with cloud-flying instruments and oxygen.

If a glider is properly used in strong thermal conditions, cross-country speeds averaging over 90 m.p.h. (145 km./h.) can be made. To achieve this, the glider has to be flown at speeds of over 120 m.p.h. (193 km./h.) between thermals and then slowed to about 50 m.p.h. (80 km./h.) on entering the next upcurrent. For practical purposes thermals develop only in daytime and are too weak to be of use in winter, other than in the tropics.

Slope soaring is possible above the wind-ward faces of hills more than 100 ft. (30 m.) high, and with a wind speed of more than 15 m.p.h. (25 km./h.). As long as the wind continues to blow up over the hill the glider will stay up if it is flown in the region of this lift. Lift does not normally extend more than 1,000 ft. (330 m.) above the crest, and is better over a long ridge than a round hill.

Wave soaring is also carried out in lift caused by hills and mountains, but to the lee, or downwind, of them. When air has been forced up over high ground it flows downward again on the lee side and then, under certain conditions, rebounds as a wave or series of waves. Some wave systems, such as those in the Southern Alps of New Zealand, or at Bishop in the Sierra Nevada of California, go up to 50,000 ft. (15,000 m.) or more. Lift can be very strong, as well as smooth, in the wave's upflow, but there are equally strong currents in the downflow. The existence of waves may be deduced by the appearance of lenticulars, hard-edged lens-shaped clouds which frequently develop at the crest of each wave and remain stationary in relation to the ground with the wind blowing through them. At a lower level, and nearer the lee face of the mountains, there may be turbulent reverse flow, sometimes made visible by a rotor cloud.

When flying across country in hilly or mountainous regions, the pilot may use slope and wave lift as well as thermals. Wave lift does not always develop when there are strong thermals, but often increases during the evening, when it is a useful means of prolonging a flight.

The glider is characterized by a large span wing of narrow width, or chord. The ratio of span to chord is termed aspect ratio; for training gliders this is about 15 to 20, and for competition gliders between 20 and 30. Thus a wing span of 20 m. would have a mean, or average, chord of 1 m. The weight of a single-seater glider is 400 to 500 lb. (180–225 kg.),

and a two-seater about 600 to 800 lb. (270–360 kg.), although some big competition single-seaters are above this weight. The wing-loading of a glider is the wing area divided by the combined weight of glider and pilot; for training gliders it is about 4 lb. (1·814 kg.) per sq. ft. and for competition gliders between 5 and 8 lb. (2·268–3·629 kg.) per sq. ft. The wing span of a training glider is usually about 50 to 55 ft. (15–17 m.)

Gliders are made of wood with a fabric covering, or metal — usually aluminium — or fibreglass, which is rapidly replacing wood as a constructional material. Fibreglass gliders are invariably white in colour to prevent their getting too hot in the sun.

The cockpit of a high-performance glider is slim and streamlined, and the pilot lies in a partially supine position. Such aircraft have a retractable landing wheel and great attention is given to surface finish in order to minimize drag. Because of the very flat gliding angle, landing in small fields would be difficult if some aid to shortening the glide path were not provided. This is usually in the form of air brakes — plates which can be made to protrude from the wing at will. By opening and closing these plates, the pilot can accurately control his glide path. Some gliders are fitted with a tail parachute which does much the same job either in addition to, or instead of, the air brakes. The parachute can also be jettisoned by the pilot in an emergency.

In addition to the aircraft itself a considerable quantity of instrumentation and equipment is needed by the soaring pilot:

Airspeed indicator (A.S.I.), which gives the speed at which the glider is flying through the air. It is correct at sea-level but under-reads progressively with increasing altitude. It does not give the speed over the ground for which a wind allowance must be made.

Altimeter, a barometer indicating changes in pressure in terms of height. If the altimeter is set at zero on an airfield, it will thereafter give the height of the aircraft above that airfield. If it is set for height above sea-level before take-off it will continue to show the height above sea-level during the flight. The altimeter is subject to discrepancy caused by changes in the prevailing air pressure: if the aircraft is flown towards lowering pressure the altimeter shows the aircraft to be higher than it actually is. Pressure corrections can be made in flight after obtaining the correct pressure from air-traffic control by radio.

Barograph, a recording barometer indicating pressure changes encountered by the aircraft in terms of height. The rotation of the drum also records the length of the flight. A barograph is required for record and proficiency-badge flight claims and must be sealed by an official observer before take-off.

Compass, normally a simple pivoted magnet calibrated in 360°. It is subject to variation error due to change of the earth's magnetic pattern and deviation error due to ferrous metal and other magnetic equipment (such as a camera exposure meter) in the cockpit.

Cloud-flying instruments. The artificial horizon is an electrically driven gyro instrument giving the attitude of the aircraft, permitting flight without visual reference to the ground. The turn-and-slip indicator is a less sophisticated instrument for the same purpose. One or other is essential for cloud flying.

Variometer, a very sensitive pressure instrument which indicates whether the glider is in rising air and going up, or in sinking air and going down. It will indicate sink or climb rates as slow as 20 ft. (6 m.) per min. It is the instrument most essential to soaring, and most pilots prefer to install two varios in their aircraft. Some variometers are total-energy compensated to eliminate misleading indications caused by changes in the aircraft's speed, some are electrically driven to minimize indication lag, and some give the signals audibly as a rising and falling note. Many variometers have an outer circular scale, called a Mac-Cready ring, which the pilot sets to show him the best speed to fly between thermals, depending on the strength of the available lift.

Radio equipment in a glider is normally VHF on allocated channels in the aircraft wave-band primarily for communication between pilots and retrieval crews. The pilot will also use air maps and a calculator. Aeronautical chart scales are 1:1,000,000, 1:500,000, and 1:250,000, corresponding to approximately 16, 8, and 4 miles (25·7, 12·9, 6·4 km.) to the inch respectively. The 'half-million' chart is the most widely used. Height above sea-level of hills, airfields, and obstructions are clearly given, but details insignificant from the air are left out. Maps are overprinted with controlled air-space information and radio navigation data. A calculator is a circular slide-rule to enable the pilot to work out the height needed to glide a particular distance, or alternatively the distance he could glide from a given height. Each calculator is calibrated to suit the performance of the type of glider in which it will be used.

Since sunshine is needed to provide good soaring weather and the pilot sits in a perspex bubble, suitable clothing for soaring includes light-coloured, long-sleeved shirt, trousers, sun hat, dark glasses, and boots if the glider may have to be landed in rough country. When training, particularly in winter, windproof clothing and waterproof shoes are essential.

Extra oxygen is necessary to supplement that available in the atmosphere above 15,000 ft. (4,600 m.). Oxygen is frequently used by glider pilots on long flights above 10,000 ft. (3,000 m.), to aid concentration. About 500 litres are normally carried with a demand-valve supply to a face mask.

Parachutes are usually worn. Originally intended to safeguard the pilot when flying primitive gliders in storm clouds, the practice has continued, mainly in case of collision, since gliders are flown close together in thermals. Parachutes are usually made of nylon, have a canopy diameter of about 28 ft. (8·5 m.), give a descent rate of 16 ft./sec. (5 m./ sec.) and weigh 15 to 20 lb. (7–9 kg.).

Various means of launching the glider are used. In *aerotowing*, the glider is towed by a light aeroplane on the end of a synthetic fibre (nylon, polypropylene) rope. The aeroplane climbs to approximately 2,000 ft. (630 m.) above the airfield. There the glider pilot releases the rope, the tug pilot having tried to find lift in order to give the glider the best start. Aerotowing can also be used to retrieve gliders from cross-country flights. The length of the tow rope is usually between 100 and 150 ft. (30–45 m.) and has a breaking strain of about 1,000 lb. (450 kg.).

In *winch-launching*, a powerful engine (about 100 h.p.) drives a drum on to which the launching cable is wound fast enough to launch the glider. The engine of the winch is usually mounted on a mobile chassis and placed on the windward edge of the airfield. The steel launching-cable is pulled, by a tractor, to the far side of the airfield and attached to the release hook of the glider which is facing into the wind. At a signal from the glider, the winch-driver winds in the cable at 40 to 50 m.p.h. (64–80 km./h.), enabling the glider to climb attached to the wire like a kite. At the top of the launch the glider pilot releases the cable. The height gained from a winch launch is approximately one-third of the length of the cable laid out on the ground, e.g. if the distance between the winch and the glider is 3,000 ft. (1,000 m.), the glider should be able to achieve a height of 1,000 ft. (300 m.). Launching cable may be of stranded steel of 2,000 lb. (900 kg.) breaking strain, with a 1,000 lb. (450 kg.) weak link, or it may be of mono-filament wire, such as piano wire.

Launching by *car-tow* is similar to winch-launching, except that the source of power is a car which is driven along a runway at some 50 m.p.h. (80 km./h.). An earlier method of launching by *bungey*, in which the glider was catapulted off a hilltop by a rubber rope, is now seldom used.

After an outlanding, the glider is usually

retrieved by car and trailer. Trailers are generally two-wheeled, about 26 ft. (8 m.) long, and may be open or covered with plywood, aluminium sheet, or fibreglass. On an open trailer the wings and fuselage of the glider may be protected by canvas covers. The glider is designed to be dismantled quickly for retrieval purposes, so it is not difficult to get the aircraft on to its trailer in 15 minutes. The trailer is also used for storage purposes.

Training of glider pilots is carried out in gliding clubs and schools on two-seater gliders with qualified instructors. The student learns either by taking his turn every week-end on a 'first come, first served' basis or by going on an instructional course of one to two weeks. Usually some 60 flights launched by winch, or about 20 flights using aerotows, are needed before the student is ready to go solo. He is taught how to handle the glider on the ground and in the air, to maintain the right speeds and to turn correctly, and how to land using air brakes to control his approach path. The student also learns emergency procedures, such as how to deal with a failure of the launch, recovery from a spin, collision avoidance, and how to carry out a daily inspection for safety in flight. The minimum age for solo flying in Britain is 16, in the U.S.A. and some other countries 14.

In some schools training is carried out on a two-seater motor glider — an aircraft with a small engine of about 40 h.p. possessing handling characteristics similar to a glider. Training is quicker since the motor glider can take off as soon as the instructor is ready, and each lesson can be better tailored both to the student and to the weather.

When a pilot goes solo he gains his B badge, after which he can try for the C, for which a simple soaring flight is required. This is followed, in Britain where there is no state licence, by the bronze C. The requirements include two soaring flights of at least half an hour each, a competence check with an instructor, and test papers on air law, etc.

The advanced soaring proficiency standards, starting with the silver badge, are international. For this the pilot has to soar across country for a distance of 50 km. (31·07 miles), climb 1,000 m. (3,280 ft.), and make a flight of at least five hours' duration. The silver badge is the minimum standard for entering championships. For the gold badge, the pilot must fly across country a distance of 300 km. (186·4 miles), and climb 3,000 m. (9,842 ft.). The highest achievements are the three diamonds, for which a distance flight of 500 km. (310·7 miles), a completed triangular course flight of 300 km. (186·4 miles), and a climb of 5,000 m. (16,400 ft.) are required, and the

1,000 km. (621 miles) diploma. After this the ambitious pilot pursues records.

International and national records can be claimed for the following types of flight, provided that the required minimum margin over the previous record has been exceeded:
Pure distance. A distance flight in any direction measured as a great circle course between the starting point and the landing place.
Distance to a declared goal. A distance flight ending at a point declared before departure.
Distance to a turn point and back to the starting place. Evidence of reaching the turn point may be given photographically; the turn point must be pre-declared.
Gain of height. The height climbed after release.
Absolute altitude. Height reached above sea level.
Speed over a triangular course. The glider is timed over start and finish lines by an official observer, and the pilot produces evidence that he reached the pre-declared turn points. A triangular course must not have any leg less than 28 per cent of the total distance.

An international or national record relates to the nationality of the pilot, regardless of where in the world the record was made. Some countries have local records where the nationality of the pilot is unimportant, but the flight must start in the country concerned.

Gliding championships consist of a period of 7 to 14 days in which a task is set on each day of suitable weather. Pilots attempt to complete the task and they gain daily points in relation to their performance. At the end of the period the daily points won by each glider are added, the champion being the pilot of the glider with the greatest total score.

The daily tasks may be for distance or for speed — for example, to attempt to fly as far as possible along a given route or set line, or to make the fastest time round a triangular or out-and-return course of, say, 300 km. (186·4 miles). Each pilot crosses the start line at the moment he thinks will give him the strongest lift over the course.

World championships are held approximately every two years, with the gliders divided into two classes, open and standard. In the latter there is a wing-span limit of 15 m. (49 ft. 3 in.), and other restrictions intended to keep down expense and complication. World championships usually attract about 80 gliders from 25 to 30 countries. Each glider is flown by a single pilot.

Although enough was known about bird flight and structures for a practical glider to have been made in the sixteenth century, no one succeeded in doing so before Otto Lilienthal

(1848-96). He fitted wings connected to a tail, made of osier wands and covered with shirt material, on to his shoulders and took off from a hilltop by running down into the wind, hanging from the framework and landing at the bottom, on his own feet. Lilienthal made over 2,000 flights in both monoplane and biplane hang gliders. In Britain, Percy Pilcher (1869-99) flew similar gliders from 1892 on. Both pilots were killed as a result of structural failure. The Wright brothers, Orville and Wilbur, built and flew several gliders, but also built and installed the first practical aeroengine, thus inventing the aeroplane. Gliding was forgotten until after the First World War when the Germans were forbidden by the Treaty of Versailles to make aeroplanes. Instead some pilots built and flew simple gliders in the Rhön mountains (see WASSERKUPPE) and so started the sport.

Hill, or slope, soaring was discovered in 1921, just in time to prevent the new sport from dying because of the tedium of bringing the aircraft back to the top of the mountain after every flight. The first international meeting was held at Iford, Sussex, in 1922, arranged by the *Daily Mail*. The prize for the longest flight was won by Maneyrol (France) in a world-record time of 3 hrs. 21 min.

Soaring by using lift under clouds was discovered in 1926 by Kegel and Nehring, and exploited by KRONFELD. Thermal soaring was developed largely by HIRTH, the first pure thermal flights being made in America. During the 1930s a great deal of soaring was done in Germany, some in Poland, France, the U.S.A., Britain, and some other European countries. By 1939 the distance record stood at 465 miles (749 km.) (Klepikova, Russia) and the altitude record at 22,560 ft. (6,838 m.) (Ziller, Germany). The first soaring flight across the English Channel was made by an Englishman, Stephenson. The international system of proficiency badges had been introduced and by 1939 the Germans had gained 813 silver badges and the British 40.

After the war the 'three diamonds' were introduced and records for duration flying banned after the death of a pilot attempting to beat the world record of 52 hours.

Gliding re-established itself as soon as equipment became available. Mount Cook (New Zealand) and Bishop (U.S.A.) were explored for wave, and many altitude and out-and-return records were broken. Thermal soaring increased all over the world, particularly in countries like Australia, the U.S.A. and South Africa where the weather is good and the sun hot. In Europe, Poland took the lead in gliding in the 1950s, but subsequently lost it to Germany.

The biggest development in recent years has been in glider design and construction permitting higher speeds. The performance of gliders, in terms of glide-angle, went up from 1:29 in 1950 to 1:45 in 1970, and progress was by no means at an end. Operating speeds increased from about 60 m.p.h. (96 km./h.) to over 100 m.p.h. (160 km./h.). The main reason for this jump in glider performance was the change during the 1960s to fibreglass construction. The first fibreglass glider, the Phoenix, designed by Nägle, flew in the 1960 world championships. By 1970, 70 out of 78 aircraft in the championships were constructed wholly of fibreglass, which enables an exact wing profile to be accurately maintained and permits an excellent surface finish.

In 1964 the first distance flight of over 1,000 km. (600 miles) was made in the U.S.A. by Parker. Twelve flights over 1,000 km. (621 miles) have now been made, including five out-and-return goal flights, four in the U.S.A. and one in New Zealand.

Altogether there are over 100,000 glider pilots and 12,000 gliders in the world. In Britain there are some 7,000 pilots and 700 gliders distributed between about 80 clubs.

Recently there has been a revival of hang gliding, particularly among young people. Simple cheap sailwings, such as the Rogallo, or rigid aerofoil hang gliders, such as the Icarus II or Volmer VJ-23, are built using new lightweight materials, a typical aircraft weight being 35 to 50 lb. (15-22 kg.). The longest flight by a hang glider so far is 8 hrs. 24 min. slope soaring in Hawaii.

N. Ellison, *British Sailplanes and Gliders, 1922-1970* (1971); D. Piggott, *Gliding: A Handbook on Soaring Flight* (1971); *The Gliding Book*, ed. R. Serjeant and A. Watson (1970); A. and L. Welch, *New Soaring Pilot* (1968) and *The Story of Gliding* (1965); P. Wills, *Free as a Bird* (1973).

GOVERNING BODY (WORLD): Commission Internationale Vol à Voile (C.I.V.V.) of the Fédération Aeronautique Internationale, 6 Rue Galilée, Paris 14, France; (UNITED KINGDOM): British Gliding Association, 75 Victoria Street, London S.W.1.

GLIMA, see WRESTLING.

GODDARD, TREVOR LESLIE (1931-), cricketer for South Africa and Natal. A left-handed opening batsman and medium-paced left-arm bowler who concentrated on the leg stump, he led South Africa creditably against Australia and England. In 38 Tests he scored 2,458 runs and took 114 wickets.

GODFREE, Mrs. L. A., see MCKANE, KATHLEEN.

GODOLPHIN BARB (*c.* 1724), a horse, probably an Arabian, believed to have been a present to the King of France from the Emperor of Morocco. He was bought in Paris in 1729 and later became the property of Lord Godolphin. Together with the DARLEY ARAB-IAN and the BYERLEY TURK, he was one of the three male progenitors of the thoroughbred race-horse, becoming the paternal grandsire of MATCHEM.

GOITSCHEL, MARIELLE (1944-), French Alpine ski racer who set new standards for women racers in the 1960s with her outstanding athleticism. She won six world or Olympic gold medals between 1962 and 1968.

GOLDEN GLOBE RACE, see YACHTING.

GOLDEN GLOVES, the most famous amateur BOXING match in the United States, began in 1928 as an inter-cities competition between Chicago and New York, sponsored by the *Chicago Tribune* and the New York *Daily News.* Winners received a gold medal and a pair of miniature golden gloves.

GOLDEN MILLER (1926) was the most famous steeplechase horse in the history of HORSE RACING in England. He was bred by Solomon, owned by the Hon. DOROTHY PAGET, trained by Briscoe, and ridden by Wilson and others. Golden Miller won the CHEL-TENHAM GOLD CUP five years in succession from 1932 to 1936, as well as the GRAND NATIONAL in record time in 1934, and 23 other races out of 55 starts. He is the only horse ever to win the double of the Grand National at Liverpool and the Gold Cup at Cheltenham.

GOLDEN SLIPPER STAKES is the most valuable and important horse race for two-year-olds in Australia. It is run over 6 furlongs (1,200 m.) at the Rosehill track, Sydney, in March.

GOLDIE BOAT CLUB. Named after a Cambridge oarsman, its colours are worn by the CAMBRIDGE UNIVERSITY reserve ROWING crew. Since 1965, the Goldie crew has raced its Oxford counterpart, ISIS, immediately before the BOAT RACE between the university senior crews.

GOLF is a club-and-ball game played throughout the world and to a high level of performance by at least a few players in almost every country.

It has been frequently observed that golf is two games in one. It is distinguished from other cross-country club-and-ball games of continental European origin.(see below) by the fact that, having propelled his ball considerable distances, using as much power as he can command, the golfer must then putt it into a small hole on a prepared surface — a matter of extreme delicacy and finesse. The object of the player is to play the ball from his starting point — the tee — to the hole in as few strokes as possible.

A golf course, usually between 5,000 and 7,000 yds. (4,572–6,400 m.) in length, is divided into 18 separate holes, each one of which may be anything from 100 to 600 yds. or more long. A hole will normally comprise the following features: a flat teeing ground from which the player makes his initial stroke, or drive in the case of long holes; a fairway of mown grass 30 to 100 yds. (27–90 m.) wide extending to the green; the green itself, the prepared putting surface into which the hole of 4¼ in. (108 mm.) diameter is sunk and marked by a flag. In addition, each hole will be embellished by hazards such as sand-filled bunkers, ponds, streams, drainage ditches, trees and shrubs, and other natural features sited to impede and penalize an inaccurate shot.

An 18-hole course can normally be accommodated easily within 150 acres (60 hectares). Where insufficient land is available for a full course, a nine-hole course is frequently built and, in this case, a round of golf consists of two circuits. It is sometimes the practice with nine-hole courses to provide two teeing grounds for each hole so that the golfer will encounter a different series of challenges the second time he goes round the course.

The golf ball, of 1·62 in. (41 mm.) minimum diameter (1·68 in. — 43 mm. — in the U.S.A. and Canada), and 1·62 oz. (46 g.) maximum weight, is made of elastic thread wound under tension around a central core and covered by a plastic casing. To propel it, the player may use a maximum of 14 golf clubs, woods and irons. Wooden clubs have longer shafts than iron clubs and are used when considerations of distance are paramount; in a normal set of clubs there are four woods. Irons are manufactured in sets numbered from 1 to 9 with the striking faces inclined at progressively increasing angles from 13° to about 47°. The higher-numbered clubs therefore produce a high trajectory, less distance, and greater accuracy. In addition, the golfer carries specialist clubs such as a putter, a sand-iron for bunker play, and a wedge for short approach shots and for recovering from heavy rough grass.

Between the wars, famous professional golfers were contracted to endorse different makes of golf club and were paid a fee for each individual club carried. This led to the practice of professionals, or their long-suffering caddies, carrying up to 30 clubs at a time and so, in 1938, the authorities fixed a legal limit at 14 clubs. This means that, from the set outlined above, the golfer must discard two. His choice will be influenced by the playing conditions, but it is usual to put aside the No. 1 iron and one of the woods, either the No. 2 or No. 3. Although common practice, it is not necessary for the golfer actually to remove the surplus clubs from his bag; he may simply declare before the round which of his clubs are out of play.

Golf is played in two main forms. In *stroke play* the golfer counts his total number of strokes for the round, or rounds, and the player with the lowest total wins. This is the form of golf used in all the major open championships and most professional tournaments: stroke play over 72 holes, or four rounds.

In *match play*, the game is contested hole by hole between sides of one or two players, the winner being the side which wins more

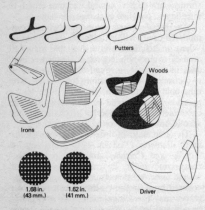

GOLF CLUBS AND BALL
The larger of the two balls, 1·68 in. in diameter, is standard in the U.S.A. and Canada, the smaller one elsewhere.

holes (i.e. takes fewer strokes at each) than there are holes left to play. The widest possible margin of victory in an 18-hole match is therefore '10 and 8', that is, winning the first 10 holes and having only 8 holes remaining.

In knock-out competition, in which an outright winner must emerge to go through to the next round, players tied, 'all square', after 18 holes, play extra holes, the first side to win a hole being the winners. Match play is virtually obsolete in the U.S.A. where the preference at all levels of the game is for stroke play. Else-where, match play predominates among club golfers and stroke play is reserved for organized competitions.

The basic conception of the game is simple — that the ball be played, as it lies, in successive strokes from the teeing ground into the hole, the ball furthest from the hole always to be played first. The complexities in the code arise from the need to provide for all occurrences (such as lost ball, ball out of bounds, ball lying in water, and interference from agencies over which the golfer has no control) which may frustrate straightforward play. On many courses there are also specific local rules, defined by notice in the club house and usually also on the score-cards.

The caddie, or golfer's attendant, carries his clubs and, by the rules, is the only person entitled to proffer advice to the player except in the case of foursomes where partners and their caddies may confer. Among the conventions and courtesies of golf is the cry of 'Fore!', the traditional word of warning. When a player, in making a stroke, displaces a turf (divot), golfing etiquette demands that he replace it and tread it down.

It is usual for the first shot at each hole to be played off a wooden or plastic tee-peg ('tee' or 'peg') which lifts the ball clear of the teeing ground. The tee-peg was invented in 1920 by Lowel of New Jersey. Previously, golfers teed their balls on a mound or pinch of sand from sand boxes provided on each teeing ground (they are still retained on many courses).

'Par' is the score in which a first-class player should play a hole in summer conditions. 'Bogey' is the score that should be taken at each hole by a scratch golfer, i.e. a player with a handicap (see below) of 0. In American golfing parlance it is a score of one stroke higher than the par for the hole. A 'birdie' is a score of one shot fewer than the par for the hole, an 'eagle' two strokes less, and an 'albatross' (in America a 'double eagle') three strokes less.

A player or team is said to be 'dormy' when leading in an 18-hole match by as many holes as are left to play. Three up and three to play would thus make the leader dormy.

If there is a tie in stroke play, or when players are all square after 18 holes in match play, the winner is determined by 'sudden death', that is to say the players start again at the first hole (unless regulations have been formulated specifying a different order of play) and the first one to win a hole is the winner.

Many terms are used to describe and define the many different vagaries of stroke. To 'press' is to try to hit the ball too hard, usually with a resultant mis-hit. To 'shank', or 'socket', is to hit the ball on that part of the club where the club-head is joined to the hosel, or neck: as a result the ball flies off at an angle. To 'sclaff' is the old-fashioned term for a mis-hit stroke in which the club-head scrapes the ground before coming into contact with the ball.

A 'push' is a shot which goes in a straight line to the right of the intended direction. A 'slice' is a stroke in which clockwise spin is imparted to the ball, usually inadvertently, causing it to veer to the right. Slice is synonymous with 'cut', both words being used as nouns and verbs. When clockwise spin is deliberately applied to curve the ball, the term used for the manoeuvre is 'fade'. A 'pull' is a stroke in which the ball goes in a straight line to the left of the intended direction. A 'hook' is a shot in which anti-clockwise spin is imparted to the ball, causing it to veer in flight from right to left. It is known as 'draw' when it is used deliberately to obtain greater length — the hooked or drawn ball tends to run further than those sliced, cut, or hit straight — when the sideways movement in the air is controlled. In its most acute and accidental form, when the ball swerves sharply to the left and barely rises from the ground it is known as the 'duck-hook'.

To 'top' obviously is to strike the top of the ball, which sends it scuttling along the ground. An 'air shot' or 'fresh air shot' is one that completely misses the ball: it counts as a stroke. 'Borrow' is the term used for aiming a ball in putting to one side of the hole to compensate for a slope of the green. A 'stymie', abolished in 1951, occurred when a ball lay in the path of another on the green. Before 1951 the deliberate laying of a stymie was an integral part of the game. The term 'rub of the green' is used to describe any untoward occurrence or stroke of fortune (good or bad) not specifically covered by the rules, such as when a moving ball is stopped or deflected by an outside agency.

Rules. The original 13 rules of golf have gradually proliferated to 41 main laws, most of which are further qualified by numerous sub-clauses, a written code of etiquette, 35 definitions, and a considerable body of case-law in the form of decisions which have been handed down by the rules committees in determining disputes.

The rules of etiquette follow the dictates of common sense and good manners, such as remaining still, quiet, and out of the line of vision of a player who is making a stroke; waiting until those ahead are clearly out of range before playing; playing without undue delay and, when held up to search for a ball, inviting the people behind to play through; leaving the course as you find it, by replacing divots and raking bunkers; and by observing the convention that two-ball matches take precedence on the course.

In general, the penalty for breaking a rule is 2 strokes in stroke play and the loss of the hole in match play. As noted above, the player must carry no more than 14 clubs which, like the ball, must conform to specifications. The honour of striking first from the tee is taken by the winner of the previous hole. In friendly games the convention is for the lowest handicap player to take the honour at the first hole. The ball must be teed within the teeing ground, which is defined by two markers and extends backward to a depth of two club-lengths. If the ball falls off the tee it may be replaced without penalty, but if the player makes a stroke at it, that stroke must be counted whether it makes contact or not. All such 'air' strokes anywhere on the course must be counted. Having driven off, the player furthest from the hole plays next until the hole is completed.

The player must play his ball as it lies and may touch it only to identify it, after which it must be replaced. He must not move, bend, or break anything fixed or growing to improve his lie, except as may happen in fairly taking his stance and making the stroke. The player is allowed to remove obstructions (anything artificial, or man-made, which is not a part of the construction of the course) in the vicinity of his ball, and he may remove 'loose impediments' (natural objects such as stones, leaves, twigs, and fir-cones), except in a hazard. If, in removing such debris, the player causes the ball to move he suffers a penalty of 1 stroke.

If a ball is lost, or out of bounds, or unplayable (and the player is the sole judge of whether his ball is unplayable), the standard procedure is the 'stroke and distance' rule. Under this procedure, another ball is played from where the original stroke was made, and 1 penalty stroke is added. Thus, if a tee shot is hit out of bounds, another ball is played from the tee and this stroke counts as the player's *third.* In the case of an unplayable ball, the player has two options in addition to the stroke and distance rule. He may drop the ball within two club-lengths, but not nearer the hole, under penalty of 1 stroke. Or he may drop the ball behind the point where it lay, keeping that point between himself and the hole, with no limit to how far behind that point the ball may be dropped.

If the ball is lost in a hazard, another ball may be dropped in the hazard without penalty or, under penalty, outside the hazard, keeping the point of entry between the golfer and the hole. The procedure for dropping is for the player to stand facing the hole and drop the ball over his shoulder. To save time, the rules allow for the playing of a provisional ball in cases where it is thought the original ball might be lost or out of bounds. If, on reaching the area, the player finds the original ball is indeed out of bounds or lost, he may continue to play with the provisional ball under the stroke and distance rule. Should the original ball be found and in play, the provisional ball must be abandoned.

A temporary accumulation of water, such as puddles, which is clearly visible after the player has taken his stance, is 'casual water' and a player is entitled to drop the ball without penalty at the nearest spot which avoids these conditions, but not nearer the hole; on the greens he may place the ball. Snow and ice may be treated as casual water or as loose impediments at the option of the player.

On the putting green, the player may have the flagstick attended or removed. If his ball hits an unattended flagstick from a stroke played on the green, the penalty in match play is loss of hole, or 2 strokes in stroke play.

The foregoing is merely an outline of the main rules. There are many further provisions, framed to cover unusual contingencies. For, although golf is basically a simple concept, golf courses, covering large areas of countryside and involving extremes of weather conditions, frequently present the player with problems of procedure. The complexities of the laws reflect the complexity of nature. The golfer who proceeds on the basis of 'play it as it lies' and accepts misfortune as the luck of the game will certainly be observing the spirit of golf and, in most cases, the laws. However, in golf as in life, justice and legality are not always synonymous. The obligation to accept relief where the rules allow is no less than the duty to endure penalties. It is perhaps unreasonable to expect the ordinary golfer to retain every clause and qualification in his memory. But the carrying of a book of rules as standard golfing equipment will help him in his objective observance of the rule of law.

The rules committees of the Royal and Ancient Golf Club of St. Andrews (the 'R. and A.') and the United States Golf Association (U.S.G.A.) are the supreme authorities and meet every four years to agree revisions; in only two details, the specification of the ball referred to above and the rules of amateur status, are the codes in operation on each side of the Atlantic at variance.

Handicapping. One of the attractions of golf is that, because of the method of handicapping, it is possible for a relative novice to meet a skilled player on level terms. In order to understand the handicap system, one must first learn something of how golf courses are rated and be familiar with the terms used in golf. There are slight differences in the system in various countries and what follows, except where specified, is the basis of the method used in the British Isles. It should therefore be seen as a typical method, not a universal one.

'Par', the word which golf has given to the English language as a synonym for 'the norm', in golf has a specific meaning, as explained above: the score in which a first-class player should play a hole in summer conditions. Holes up to 250 yds. (228·6 m.) long are rated 'par 3'; holes between 251 and 475 yds. (229–434·3 m.) are 'par 4'; holes of 476 yds. (435 m.) and over are 'par 5'.

The handicapping system is based not on par but on a rating known as the Standard Scratch Score (SSS). This is defined as the score in which a scratch player (i.e. with a handicap of 0) is expected to go round the course, playing from the medal tees, in summer conditions. Par is the rating of a hole, SSS is the rating of a course and is determined on the total length according to the following table of standard lengths of courses with the corresponding basic SSS:

7,100 yds. (6,492 m.) — 74
6,900 yds. (6,309 m.) — 73
6,700 yds. (6,126 m.) — 72
6,500 yds. (5,944 m.) — 71
6,300 yds. (5,761 m.) — 70
6,100 yds. (5,578 m.) — 69
5,900 yds. (5,395 m.) — 68
5,700 yds. (5,212 m.) — 67
5,500 yds. (5,029 m.) — 66
5,300 yds. (4,846 m.) — 65
5,100 yds. (4,663 m.) — 64
4,900 yds. (4,481 m.) — 63
4,700 yds. (4,298 m.) — 62
4,500 yds. (4,115 m.) — 61
4,300 yds. (3,932 m.) — 60
4,100 yds. (3,749 m.) — 59

Courses of exceptional difficulty may also receive an allowance, on the authority of the national union, to be added to the SSS. Golf-club committees are empowered to add one or two strokes to the SSS on the day of competition for exceptional weather conditions.

Handicaps are intended to enable a golfer to return, in summer conditions, a *net* score equal to the SSS of his home course. Thus a 10-handicap player whose course measures 4,900 yds. (4,481 m.) — SSS 63 — should go round in 73 strokes.

To obtain a handicap, a player should submit to his home club two attested cards for rounds played from the medal tees and preferably on the day of a competition. The club handicap committee will then allot him a handicap, the highest for men being 24, for women 36. From this it will be obvious that a player's handicap is valid only for his own course. When play takes place on a course with a different SSS, an adjustment must be made in accordance with a 'corresponding handicap' table, in which a player's handicap at his home club is augmented, or reduced, by a set number of strokes depending on the SSS of the course on which he is playing. For example, a player with a handicap of 16 strokes has 2 strokes added to his handicap when playing on a course whose SSS is from 7 to 10 higher than his home course; his handicap is reduced by 1 stroke when the course on which he is playing has an SSS of from 3 to 7 points lower than his home course. The complexities of this system brought it into disrepute and by 1973 it was virtually abandoned.

In the U.S.A., courses are assessed by experts and given a course rating using a common standard. American handicaps, which are scrupulously and frequently revised, often by computer, are therefore standardized and a 10-handicap man should be able to play to that handicap on any course.

Yet another system of course rating, not used in America, is by 'bogey'. This term, first used in 1891, derived from the song 'Hush, Hush, Hush, here comes the Bogey Man', because the player who could match the score was a regular bogey man (devil, goblin, or bugbear). The bogey of a hole, i.e. the score which a scratch man is expected to take, is very similar to par. Usually, the only difference is that the longer par-4 holes are rated as 'bogey-5s'. The term was recognized by the R. and A. in 1910 when the rules committee framed rules for bogey competitions. 'Bogey' is gradually passing from the vocabulary of golf, to be replaced by 'par'.

A knowledge 'of the outlines of the handicapping and course-rating systems is necessary for golfers to understand how the various forms of golf competition are played:

Stroke play: the player simply subtracts his full handicap from his total score.

Singles: the higher handicap man receives an allowance of three-quarters of the difference between the two players' handicaps. In computing stroke allowances, fractions of 0·5 and higher count as 1, smaller fractions count as 0. These handicap strokes must be taken at the holes specified on the card of the course.

Foursomes: a form of partner-golf in which players take alternate strokes at the same ball. The players drive alternately, no matter who may have played the last shot on the previous hole. The stroke allowance is three-eighths of the difference between the aggregate handicaps of the two sides.

Fourball: partner-golf in which each player plays his own ball. The better score of the partnership on each hole is counted. Handi-

capping is as for singles, i.e. three-quarters of the difference. However, for simplicity, it is best for the lowest-handicap player of the group to receive no strokes and for the rest of the players to compute their stroke allowance from him.

Bogey competition: the player competes against the bogey score of each hole, as if it were an opponent, receiving three-quarters of his handicap.

Greensome: a variation of foursome play, the difference being that both partners drive at each hole and then select the preferred ball before continuing the hole in alternate strokes. To handicap a partnership, multiply the lower handicap of the pair by 0·6 and multiply the higher handicap by 0·4. The aggregate of these two figures will be the medal handicap of the partnership. For matches and bogey competitions, take three-quarters of the difference.

Stableford: a system of scoring, invented in 1931, in which the objective is the acquisition of points. One point is gained for a score of 1 over bogey (or par, if there is no separate bogey-rating), 2 points for bogey, 3 points for 1 under bogey (birdie), and 4 points for 2 under (eagle). Handicap allowances in Stableford contests are determined as follows: singles — seven-eighths; bogey foursomes — seven-sixteenths of combined handicaps; mixed bogey foursomes — add 9 strokes to lady's handicap and then proceed as for bogey foursomes; greensome bogey competition — three-eighths of combined handicaps; fourball bogey — both partners receive seven-eighths of their handicaps.

Eclectic: played under stroke-play conditions over a number of rounds, the competitor selecting the lowest score he has made at each hole. Eclectic competitions can be played over a period of a month, or a year. In America this system is known as a 'ringer score'.

Bisque: an unofficial handicap stroke which may be agreed between two players. A bisque varies from a normal stroke allowance in that it may be taken at any time without prior announcement but before the player leaves the green. One bisque is, of course, much more valuable than a one-stroke allowance since it can be taken at the most telling moment and not at a predetermined hole.

There are many forms of wagering on golf — on a match, on stroke differential, on separate holes. There is also the Nassau, in which the players gamble on the outcome of the separate halves of a match and the match as a whole, i.e. three bets. Bingo-bango-bingo is a form of wagering in which players, who must meticulously observe the rule that whoever is furthest from the hole plays next, pay out on the first ball to reach the green, the ball nearest the hole when all balls are on the green, and the first ball into the hole.

Clubs and balls. The Roman game of *paganica* was played with a bent stick and a leather-covered ball stuffed with feathers. Some golf historians have accepted that since the technique and practice of making balls in this way had such a long and respectable ancestry, it followed that the first golf balls were made in this way; but that assumption is open to some doubt. A plausible case, for instance, can be made for the theory that golf was originally played with boxwood balls. Among the earliest written documents of golf are accounts for clubs and balls; at the beginning of the sixteenth century balls were sold for 4d. a dozen. It is known from later records that, in the course of a long and exhausting day, a craftsman could produce four feather balls. Making even the most generous allowances for the value of money in those days, it seems hardly probable that a man could live on a pittance of that order. A hundred years later, feather balls cost 5d. each, which again suggests, despite inflation, that the earlier balls were of a much simpler manufacture. Some circumstantial, though persuasive, support is given to the boxwood-ball theory by the earliest surviving clubs. These were discovered in a house in Hull, Yorkshire, in a cupboard which had been boarded up, together with a newspaper of 1741, the date of their incarceration. The clubs themselves, however, have been expertly dated as of Stuart origin (i.e. prior to 1714). These clubs, now at Troon golf club in Scotland, are immensely long and heavy by later standards and seem ill-suited to the task of striking a feather ball. As implements for playing a heavy and unyielding boxwood ball, they appear more appropriate.

The later evolution of golf equipment certainly follows a natural pattern of clubs being modified to suit the improvements in ball design. At all events, by the early seventeenth century, the feathery ball reigned unchallenged. James VI granted one James Melvill a monopoly to make and sell golf balls in Scotland for 21 years, a common and unscrupulous method of swelling the royal purse at the time. In the making of feathery balls, untanned bulls' hide was cut into four sectors (later modified to three and then two panels), stitched and turned inside out, leaving the smallest of openings for the insertion of feathers — traditionally, enough to fill a top hat — steamed for easier compression. The case of the ball was placed in a mould and the feathers packed in with a stuffing iron, a tapered iron rod with a wooden chest-brace on the end to give the ball-maker maximum pressure. The aperture was then stitched up, the

ball hammered into shape and painted. The result, from the hands of a master craftsman, was a remarkable missile. The stitched seams, which golfers sometimes felt were unsightly and impeded the flight through the air, in fact improved the ball's aerodynamics. On a frosty day, with a slight following wind, a French master at the Madras College, St. Andrews, drove a feathery ball 361 yds. (330 m.). It is not recorded what make of ball was used by Messieux on that winter's day in 1836 but it was almost certainly a Gourlay, from the workshop of the supreme ballmaker of the day, whose finest examples sold for as much as 5s. each. The great disadvantage of the feathery ball was that it became sodden in wet weather and liable to split. Similarly, a cut imparted by a badly aimed blow from the sharp edge of a club rendered the ball unfit for play.

Whether because of the coming of the feathery ball, or whether by a process of evolution, the art of club-making was refined to a point far removed from those unwieldy Stuart implements. The making of golf clubs was originally the job of the bow-makers. The accounts of the Lord High Treasurer of Scotland of 1502 record the purchase by James IV of clubs from the bowyer of St. Johnstoun (later Perth), but gradually the specialist clubmakers came on the scene and some, like Hugh Philp, became as esteemed by golfers as Chippendale and Hepplewhite were for their furniture. Originally all clubs were wooden, with shafts of hazel or seasoned ash spliced to heads of blackthorn. Thorn trees were planted horizontally in the side of a bank so that, in growing, they bent to form the neck, or scare, for splicing to the shaft. Golf courses, being built on common land, were often scarred by cart tracks and this not infrequently presented a problem to a golfer whose ball came to rest in a rut. The solution was an iron-headed club, the rut iron, and thus the forge and anvil were added to the saw, the plane, and the file in the clubmaker's workshop.

An even greater stimulus to the manufacture of iron clubs was the introduction of the gutta-percha ball in 1850. According to the legend, not accepted by all scholars entirely without reservation, a St. Andrews professor, the Revd. Dr. Paterson, receives the credit for the gutta-percha ball, which became known popularly as the 'gutta' or 'guttie'. The story tells how the professor received from India a marble statue of Vishnu which had been packed for protection with gutta-percha. Rolling a piece of this latex-like substance in his hands, the professor conceived the idea of using it for a golf ball.

The first experiments with gutta-percha

were woefully unsuccessful as the ball, being perfectly smooth, had poor aerodynamic qualities and dipped sharply back to earth after flying a short distance. However, the pioneers persisted and found that, as gutta-percha balls became scratched and nicked by the clubhead in play, they flew better. The Paterson Patent ball was launched, the first varieties being made to resemble the featheries, complete with moulded seams and stitches. Then the ball-makers discovered the trick of hammering indentations on the balls and, when eventually the process was mechanized, the moulds were made to impart dimples, or brambleberry markings, on the surface of the ball.

The guttie, much cheaper than the feathery, also had other superior qualities. It could, for example, be remade when it went out of shape, or was chipped, simply by soaking it in hot water and remoulding it. It held its flight better, particularly into the wind, and was a vast improvement for putting. Quite a mystique was built up around the guttie. It was eventually produced in a range of weights from 26, advancing in half-sizes, to 30. It is not entirely clear what these figures represented, whether the weight in drams avoirdupois at 16 to the ounce or, more likely, pennyweights Troy at 20 to the ounce (1 ounce = 28 g. approx.). In any case, the measurement does not seem from surviving examples to have been very exact but the golfers of the period discussed at length which size was most suitable for different conditions.

Gutties were at their best after they had matured for six months or so and this gave golfers another field for exercising acute judgement. Not only did they have to accumulate their sets of clubs one by one by a process of feel, trial, and intuition, they also had to judge when a ball was exactly 'ripe'. The guttie revolutionized golf. Gourlay, the master maker of featheries, watched a demonstration of the new guttie and was impressed to the point of shock. At that time he had a standing order from a client to send him featheries whenever he had any available. That evening Gourlay dispatched his entire stock of featheries, some six dozen, and turned his talents to the manufacture of the newcomer.

If the guttie transformed the ballmaking industry, it had scarcely less effect on the clubmakers. Being as hard as pipeclay, the guttie wrought havoc with wooden clubs. Some clubmakers began to face their wooden clubs with patches of leather to cushion the shock of impact. Others, such as Philp, sought softer woods such as apple and pear for clubheads. By this time hickory had become virtually the standard wood for shafts.

For fifty years the guttie was the standard ball for golf, its only challenger being the 'putty', or Eclipse ball. This was made of a secret composition thought to contain cork chippings and indiarubber among its ingredients. Judged from contemporary accounts, it was more lively and more durable than the guttie but these advantages were outweighed by the fact that it did not travel quite so far. And golfers of the nineteenth century were obsessed by the search for greater distance no less than their successors. Thus, like the solid composition balls of the 1960s, whose indestructability could not prevail against their reputation for a slight loss of length, the Eclipse was itself eclipsed.

The revolution produced by the discovery of the guttie was repeated, in reverse, with the invention in 1902 of the rubber-cored ball. Dr. Haskell, a dentist from Cleveland, Ohio, perfected a method of winding elastic thread under tension around a central core and, when finished with a gutta-percha casing, the resulting ball offered advantages immediately obvious to all but the most hidebound golfers. When the Scottish professional, HERD, won the 1902 Open championship with a Haskell, the days of the guttie were numbered.

The switch to rubber-core from gutta was not immediately universal. The old ball had its adherents and the merits of the two balls were keenly debated in much the same way, and using the same arguments, as the controversy some 65 years later over the variation in size between the British and American balls. By 1914, some 12 years after the appearance of the Haskell, the issue was still sufficiently open to create spirited public interest in a grand trial designed to prove once and for all whether the guttie could hold its own against the rubber-core. Four eminent professionals were gathered for the trial. VARDON and DUNCAN were paired together against BRAID and J. H. TAYLOR for the 36-hole four-ball contest at Sandy Lodge golf club. In the morning round, Vardon and Duncan, playing with rubber-cored balls, beat Braid and Taylor by 5 holes. Before the next round began they held a long-driving contest, the greatest distances recorded being: guttie, 240 yds. (219 m.); rubber-core, 278 yds. (254 m.). In the afternoon Vardon and Duncan played with gutties and lost by 4 holes to the rubber-cores of Braid and Taylor. With that convincing 9-hole victory for the rubber-core, the debate was finally over.

With the arrival of the rubber-core ball, the clubmakers once again had to revise their ideas, for now the ball was resilient and soft to impact. To gain maximum advantage from it, the faces of clubs had to be as hard as possible. Persimmon was imported for fashioning clubheads and faces were inset with ivory, bone, and metal. Irons really came into their own.

In 1921 the size of the ball was standardized at a minimum diameter of 1·62 in. (41 mm.) and the weight at a maximum of 1·62 oz. (46 g.). After experimenting with different patterns such as lattice and brambleberry, manufacturers discovered by trial that dimples ·013 in. (3·302 mm.) deep gave optimum flight characteristics and this arrangement was adopted universally.

This period in the 1920s was an important one for golf for it marked the beginning of the modern era in equipment. After a number of false starts, the steel shaft ousted hickory and was legalized in 1929. That same year the United States Golf Association decided that the rather coarser fairways of America called for a slightly larger ball and decided on a minimum diameter of 1·68 in. (43 mm.). The Americans also introduced a weight limit of 1·55 oz. (44 g.) at that time but rescinded this specification four years later, returning to the Royal and Ancient's standard of 1·62 oz. (46 g.). One other discrepancy between the ruling bodies is that the U.S.G.A. imposes a limit on the resilience of golf balls by means of an impact test. To be legal in America, a ball must not exceed 250 ft. (76·2 m.) per second initial velocity in this test. Moves to standardize the rules of golf throughout the world led to discussions about a uniform ball. In 1968 the British Professional Golfers Association (P.G.A.) embarked on a three-year trial period during which the 1·68 in. (43 mm.), or American, ball was used exclusively in events held under P.G.A. auspices. (The American ball was, of course, quite legal under the R. and A. definition specifying a *minimum* diameter of 1·62 in.)

With the introduction of mass-production methods in the manufacture of golf clubs it was felt that some method of standardization was required to measure the 'feel' of clubs. In other words, what was required was a scientific equivalent of the sensitive hands of the old clubmakers who matched clubs by hefting them and shaving down the shafts until they felt right. The system commonly used by manufacturers to produce matched sets is known as 'swingweight', based on a formula relating the weight of the components of a club to its length. This formula later came under criticism from scientists on the grounds that it is a static measurement whereas the only valid system of matching the feel of clubs must relate the properties of different clubs when being swung. Some manufacturers abandoned swingweight in favour of matching clubs by dynamic means. Variations in swingweight were achieved by using different weights of head and by fitting shafts of various degrees of flexibility (and therefore of differing weights). The introduction of aluminium alloy shafts during the 1960s achieved a saving of ½ oz. (14 g.) in shaft weight and thus enabled clubmakers to experiment with clubs of significantly different weight distribution. Further innovations in club-making, with shafts of fibreglass, lightweight steel, and carbon fibre followed aluminium.

With so many variables in golf clubs — a wide range of swingweights, five different degrees of shaft flex in either steel or aluminium, adjustments in length and angle of lie (the angle between the sole of the club and the shaft), and various types and thickness of grip — it is clear that the possible permutations are enormous. As with the ball, the general form and marking of golf clubs is strictly defined in the rules of golf. The golfer is wise to make sure that the clubs he buys are those best suited to his physique and golfing style.

IRONS, NOS. 2 TO 9

Specifications vary slightly among manufacturers but the following table of length, angle of loft, and performance — expressed as the average distance which a golfer hits (excluding run) in normal conditions — can be taken as typical.

Driver (No. 1 wood), 43 in. (1092 mm.), 11° — 230 yds. (210 m.)

Brassie (No. 2 wood), 42½ in. (1080 mm.), 13° — 220 yds. (201 m.)

Spoon (No. 3 wood), 42 in. (1063 mm.), 16° — 210 yds. (192 m.)

4-wood, 41½ in. (1050 mm.), 19° — 200 yds. (183 m.)

1-iron, 40 in. (1016 mm.), 17° — 215 yds. (197 m.)

2-iron, 39¾ in. (1010 mm.), 20° — 200 yds. (183 m.)

3-iron, 39½ in. (1003 mm.), 23° — 185 yds. (169 m.)

4-iron, 39 in. (991 mm.), 27° — 170 yds. (155 m.)

5-iron (formerly mashie), 38½ in. (978 mm.), 31° — 155 yds. (142 m.)

6-iron, 38 in. (965 mm.), 35° — 145 yds. (133 m.)

7-iron (formerly mashie-niblick), 37½ in. (952 mm.), 39° — 135 yds. (123 m.)

8-iron (formerly niblick), 37 in. (940 mm.), 43° — 125 yds. (114 m.)

9-iron, 36½ in. (927 mm.), 47° — 120 yds. (110 m.)

Wedge, 36 in. (912 mm.), 51° — 100 yds. (91 m.)

Sand-wedge (formerly 'blaster'), 36 in. (912 mm.), 56°

Putter, various lengths, 4°–10°

The course. Unlike most games which are played on standard pitches or courts as exactly uniform as it is possible to make them, golf is played on courses of the widest divergence of character and dimensions. The fact that golf courses can be built on every sort of natural country, from links to meadow, alp to swamp, and forest to desert, gives the game limitless variety and is one of its charms. The original golf was played on purely natural ground, unprepared by man in any way beyond the digging of the holes. Golfers, we may assume, made up holes from day to day, choosing whichever route took their fancy as they propelled their balls over the Scottish links.

In time, as the game caught the popular fancy, a regular route became established by custom, although the number of holes constituting a 'round' varied from place to place, according to the available space. The circumstances which gave St. Andrews pre-eminence in golf administration also established the OLD COURSE, with its 18 holes, as the pattern for others to follow. Features which occurred naturally at St. Andrews, such as sandy depressions, caused by wind erosion, were faithfully copied by those who laid out later courses during the days of the game's early expansion in Britain and abroad. Sand bunkers became sanctified as an essential feature of a golf course no matter how incongruous they might appear on the rolling landscape of a chalk down or inland park. In the same way, when the St. Andrews club of Yonkers, N.Y., which was laid out in an apple orchard, was the premier American club, there was a feeling among the pioneers, fortunately dispelled quite quickly, that apple trees were essential for true golf.

Other conventions crept into golf architecture. At some places rough ground or heather in front of the tee necessitates a slight elevation of the tee itself, and where the ground tends to be wet, greens, too, require to be built up to provide adequate drainage. Both these local expedients became established as standard features over the years and, together with artificial sand bunkers, vastly increased the expense of building golf courses.

With the arrival of the specialist (though not invariably expert, or even competent) golf architect, course design began to evolve into three distinct styles. The largest of these is the traditional school which simply continues in the conventional, and expensive, manner of superimposing elevated tees, greens, and bunkers on the land at appropriate places. Even more expensive is the method which can perhaps be described as 'landscape sculpture'. In this the architect who is fortunate enough to control a generous budget makes extensive use of earth-moving machinery. He can command mountains and lakes to appear and the success of his finished work depends on the quality of his original vision. The third method is naturalistic. Here the architect is concerned to preserve rather than to change. His skill is devoted to the siting of tees and greens in such a way as to make them blend into the scenery and to make the best use of the natural features, leaving the impression that the hand of man has not touched the course.

From the golfing point of view, the architect has to balance many factors, some seemingly contradictory. Ideally, he should provide three or four par-3 holes, the same number of par-5s, and the remainder as par-4s of varying length. The holes should run in various directions (to subject the player to differing wind conditions) and they should incorporate as much variety as possible and involve the use of the full range of clubs. From a playing point of view, they must offer a fair challenge, and fair rewards, to golfers of every level of skill.

Quite apart from aesthetic and golfing considerations, the architect has a wide range of technical responsibilities, such as providing suitable varieties of grass for the soil and climate, ensuring adequate drainage and irrigation, and providing a layout which can be easily maintained. It goes without saying that the architect is concerned to create a pleasant environment, for this is one of the game's greatest attractions, but here his scope is limited by the site itself. From a golfing aspect, his main preoccupation is to cause the player to think. The architect's aim is to introduce features which will lull the golfer into a feeling of over-confidence, or tempt him to over-reach himself, or to become inhibited because of obvious dangers. He will so plan the holes that the golfer who seeks to put his ball into the prime position must run the gauntlet of the direst potential trouble. The architect always provides a safe route for the conservative player to follow to par the hole, and a treacherous, narrow line which the golfer who is bold enough, and accurate enough, may take if he is to have the best chance of a birdie.

Holes which are straightforward or uniformly difficult, either through excessive length or narrowness, are bad golf holes. There should always be options for the player to ponder, and if the architect can sow a seed of doubt in the golfer's mind, then he has succeeded. To that extent the architect is an illusionist. Some of the greatest holes in golf are quite 'easy' in that they provide plenty of leeway for off-line shots and present no special difficulties in the matter of sloping lies or long carries. And yet they prove to be difficult because the architect has contrived an illusion of danger. To the uninitiated, the hitting of a golf ball is a purely physical act — and, indeed, that part of it is difficult enough for most players. But golf is played largely in the mind and it is there, exploiting the frailties of human psychology, that the best architects direct their attention.

Ranges. Unlike moving-ball games such as TENNIS, CRICKET, or FOOTBALL, golf requires no great degree of athleticism nor, apparently, any special gifts of co-ordination. The ball is stationary and the implements to strike it with

bunkers, par-3 courses, and indoor schools where the learner can be taught every shot he is likely to need on the course.

The seaside putting greens and pitch-and-putt courses are purely recreational, offering holidaymakers an opportunity to try a version, however far removed from the real thing, of the game of golf. The larger commercial enterprises, however, represent serious golf comparable to the nets of the cricketer. In some instances, notably in Japan; golf centres are a form of substitute golf. Because of the rapid expansion of the game, many would-be

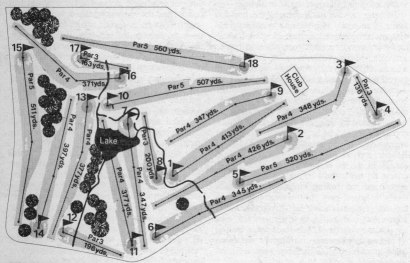

GOLF COURSE
Diagram, from an aerial view of the Portland, Oregon, Golf Club, shows a typical 18-hole course. Par strokes and yardage are shown for each hole. Total yardage for 9 holes: 3,082 yds. (par 35); for 18 holes: 6,541 yds. (par 72).

are easy to wield. The game, then, looks simple. Everyone who takes up the game quickly realizes that he has within him the potential to hit the ball well, and there is, after all, nothing to prevent such a consummation. This notion, which all too often proves fallacious in practice, frequently induces an obsessive element in golfers who believe that all they require is practice to make them expert.

In order to cater for this feeling, which is by no means always delusory, a number of peripheral activities have grown up around golf. Driving ranges, which originated in America, may be nothing more than a large field and a row of bays at which golfers stand and fire off shots. They may, however, embrace other facilities such as practice putting greens, practice

golfers are unable to become members of the overcrowded clubs and must restrict their golf to the substitute varieties until they reach a certain level of proficiency.

Not least of the virtues of driving ranges is that they can operate during darkness and so they offer a form of golf for the enthusiast, especially during winter evenings, when a real game is denied him. In Ireland, a country richly endowed with splendid golf courses, a substitute form of the game has developed as a separate game in its own right. There, pitch-and-putt is established, with clubs, championships, and rules entirely divorced from the parent game. Holes are limited to 75 yds. (68·58 m.) in length, greens are minuscule by normal golfing standards, and players use only two clubs, wedge and putter. Many pitch-and-putt players never indulge in the 'long game' as they call it.

The development of these fringe golf activities makes it difficult to form an accurate estimate of the number of people who play golf. A head count of golf-club members would be wildly short of the mark because of the thousands of people whose golf is restricted to ranges, golf centres, and fee-paying visits to private and municipal courses. It can be asserted with some confidence that with the exception of angling, which should perhaps be categorized as a hobby rather than a sport, golf is the major participant sport in Britain with something like 2 million adherents, representing a growth rate of perhaps a hundredfold in England over 50 years. In the North American continent the estimate of more than 10 million golfers represents an even more powerful explosion. Much the same story is true of the Commonwealth and the Far East. Where golfers were counted in hundreds at the turn of the century, they must now be numbered in their thousands and millions.

The Golfer's Handbook, annually.

No completely convincing evidence has been advanced to prove the origins of golf. Historians have sought to trace the ancestry of the game through other cross-country pursuits such as the Irish SHINTY, or hurly, the Belgian *chole*, Dutch *kolven*, and French *jeu de mail*. Medieval illustrations showing players wielding clubs in more or less golfing postures can be put forward as evidence and, superficially at least, the language of golf frequently appears to have a continental derivation. For example, there are the Dutch words *kolf* (club), *stuit mij* ('it stops me'), and *tuitje* (a pile of earth on which *chole* players placed the ball to drive off), which suggest 'golf', and 'stymie', and 'tee'.

Whether these linguistic signposts prove anything beyond the common root of their English counterparts is open to serious doubt. In attempting to trace the paternity of golf, one must first ask the question: what is golf? If the game is defined loosely as hitting a ball across country with a stick or club then it is seen to have some inherited characteristics of the games of continental Europe. If, on the other hand, the essence of golf is the manoeuvring of a ball as a preliminary to putting it into a small hole, then the claim that golf was a pure child of Scotland, untainted by foreign blood, is much strengthened. Assuming that golf sprang unprompted from Scottish ingenuity, conjecture gives way to fact when it comes to establishing its date of birth. In 1424 an Act of James I's parliament forbade the playing of football on the grounds that it interfered with ARCHERY practice. Thirty-three years later a similar Act, under James II, added golf to football as forbidden pastimes. Clearly then, between these two dates golf grew to such proportions as to become a serious diversion from the stern necessity of maintaining a trained citizen army.

Although these earliest written references to golf occur in disapproving royal decrees, it was royal patronage after the peace treaty of 1502, when the citizens were freed of irksome military duties, that stimulated the growth of the game. From that date all the Stuart monarchs played golf. One of the charges levelled against Mary Queen of Scots was that she had been observed playing golf within days of the murder of her husband, Darnley. When James VI of Scotland succeeded to the English throne (as James I) he brought golf south with him. In these early days the game was without established laws or form. It was played over the common links land bordering the sea which, as the only uncultivated open space available to them, the local population naturally used for such pursuits as drying washing on gorse bushes, walking, catching rabbits, or practising archery.

Club golf, from which developed rules and the established layout of a course, did not come into being until 1744 when the golfing community of Leith petitioned the Edinburgh city fathers to provide a trophy for open competition. From this beginning there evolved the Honourable Company of Edinburgh Golfers, followed in 1754 by a similar association of golfing enthusiasts in St. Andrews, which became the Royal and Ancient golf club.

The first club to be formed outside Scotland was Blackheath, near London, in 1766. The earliest surviving written rules are those drawn up by the St. Andrews golfers for their inaugural competition in 1754. These rules were admirably succinct, numbering 13 in all. It is possible that they were copied from laws, since lost, established by the golfers of Edinburgh, for they contain a reference to 'the Soldiers' Lines' which has puzzled historians. There was, however, a military camp at Leith and, if the St. Andrews code is applied to the Edinburgh trophy competition, the mystery vanishes.

The formation of other clubs which followed in rapid succession resulted in a proliferation of rules. Many were of a purely local nature and others were required as stroke play was introduced as a variation on match play.

The convention that 18 holes constitute a round of golf (a development which was to have the most profound significance on the later history of the game) came about by accident. Originally there was no prescribed number — Leith had only five holes, each over 400 yds. (366 m.) long. This course was later lengthened to seven holes and Blackheath followed suit, increasing their original five holes to seven. North Berwick also had seven holes and when the London Scottish Volunteers laid out their course on Wimbledon Common they took seven holes as the accepted number. Prestwick had 12 and St. Andrews 11. The St. Andrews golfers played out along the shoreline and then retraced their path, playing the same holes in reverse direction, a round thus constituting 22 holes. In 1764 the Royal and Ancient passed a resolution converting the first four holes into two and so a round became 18. St. Andrews came to be recognized as the supreme authority in golfing matters so that 18 holes were generally accepted. It was not until 1919 that a representative meeting of championship clubs officially vested the ultimate authority for golf in the R. and A., so that, legally speaking, the R. and A. is much junior to its American opposite number, the United States Golf Association (U.S.G.A.), which was formed in 1891.

Although some of the contests for the first golf trophies were technically open to any golfer, in practice they were no more than club events and the credit for introducing championship golf must go to the Prestwick club. In 1857 Prestwick inaugurated an annual competition, to be played at Prestwick and St. Andrews, for two-man teams from eight leading clubs. The following year the format was changed to individual match play. The Prestwick club was sufficiently encouraged by its success to subscribe for an ornamented belt for stroke-play competition among professionals in 1860. It was won by W. Park (Musselburgh) with a 36-hole score of 174 and, although the event was restricted to professionals, this contest is usually recognized as the first Open championship. The R. and A. celebrated the 1960 championship as the Centenary Open. The following year the Prestwick committee resolved that the championship on future occasions should be open to all. By winning the belt in successive years from 1868 to 1870, T. MORRIS, JR. made it his own property and a replacement trophy was required. The Open championship was held in abeyance in 1871 but the following year the R. and A. combined with Prestwick and the Honourable Company of Edinburgh Golfers in subscribing for a silver claret jug, the present Open championship trophy. The amateur championship, although not officially recognized as such until many years later, was inaugurated by the Royal Liverpool club in 1885 and played on their links at Hoylake.

With the establishment of the championships, the pattern was set for golf's further development. Since the middle of the nineteenth century, the history of golf has been one of expansion and adjustment to meet contemporary conditions although fundamentally the game remains unchanged.

Golf was spread beyond the borders of its native land by expatriate Scots, frequently by officers of Scottish regiments. Royal Calcutta (1829) and Royal Bombay (1842) are the oldest golf clubs outside the British Isles, but by the early 1880s the game was established in every corner of what was then the British Empire.

In view of the later position of the U.S.A. as the premier golfing nation it would be of particular interest if the origin of the American game could be established with certainty. Unfortunately, golf in America is of such respectable antiquity that the oldest surviving references to the game, in court records of complaints against players endangering the citizens of Fort Orange with their practices, are ambiguous. The translation of those records of 1657-9 may have mistaken golf for the Dutch game of *kolven*. Scottish officers were certainly playing golf in New York in 1779 and the South Carolina golf club was inaugurated at Charleston in 1786. Other clubs were formed in Southern states but the game did not catch on and the clubs declined.

The seed of golf was planted afresh with the establishment of the Oakhurst Club in West Virginia in 1884 and, even more important, the St. Andrews Club in Yonkers three years later. This time the game flourished. Five charter clubs set up the United States Golf Association and in 1900 the game received a strong public stimulus from an exhibition tour by Vardon, the leading English professional of the day. The professional game in America at this time was represented mainly by immigrant Scots, but in 1913 a native-born golfer, and an amateur at that, OUIMET, beat Vardon in a play-off to win the U.S. Open championship. The result inspired such interest in the game that within a few years America was the leading golfing nation of the world, both in numbers and subsequently in playing standards at the highest level.

The spread of golf across the world reflects in a small way the progress of Britain's imperial history in the nineteenth century. Just as trade followed the flag so golf, in due course, followed both. The Duke of Wellington's Peninsular campaign went so well that some of his officers actually managed to play a form of golf at Pau. They were so attracted by the place that they later returned on holiday to Pau with their clubs: in due course Pau golf club was formed and the town owed much of its subsequent prosperity as a resort to the existence of the club.

Elsewhere on the Continent, golf was slowly introduced, almost entirely as an added attraction for wealthy British visitors to the fashionable watering places, but native interest in the game was quickened by the successes of local players. As elsewhere, local boys who were recruited as caddies achieved proficiency at golf and became professionals. Men such as MASSY of France, who won the Open championship at Hoylake in 1907, and VAN DONCK of Belgium, did much to stimulate the growth of continental golf. Into the second half of the twentieth century, however, golf on the Continent was still for the most part a minority sport for the wealthy and privileged classes and its development was roughly on a par with the state of the game in England during the 'flapper' era of the 1920s.

The British community in India who worked so assiduously to transplant their middle-class culture to the tropics devoted much energy to the propagation of golf. The Royal Calcutta and the Royal Bombay golf clubs have the distinction of being the oldest clubs outside Great Britain and they were followed by a proliferation of clubs throughout the Far East. Rangoon, Bangkok, Singapore, Hongkong, and Shanghai all had flourishing clubs, mostly with the cachet of a 'Royal' prefix, before the end of the century. Golf in mainland China naturally suffered the fate of all bourgeois activities with the Communist revolution, but under American stimulus it flourished strongly in Formosa (Taiwan) and many Chinese professionals won international recognition. It is generally believed that golf in Japan, where the game is a national pastime of astonishing virility, began with the American army of occupation after the Second World War. In fact, Japan's first golf course, in Kobe, was built in 1903 and the Tokyo Club followed ten years later. The tragedy of Japanese golf is that the country is not large enough to accommodate the epidemic proportions of golf enthusiasm. Club membership therefore is vastly expensive and many 'players' are destined to spend their entire golfing lives without ever setting foot on a grass fairway. For them the game consists solely of hitting balls at driving ranges.

Golf came to Australia, New Zealand, Canada, and South Africa along with other imperial habits towards the end of the nineteenth century, although in the case of Canada there is a flimsy and earlier precedent in the form of a Glasgow sailor who in 1854 'carried his clubs to the heights of Abraham and there entertained himself in solitary con-

tentment'. Apart from Britain and the U.S.A. the game developed earlier in these countries and France than elsewhere, but since the Second World War there has been a general tendency towards levelling-up behind the United States.

In general, however, the spread of golf throughout the world was the result of individual enthusiasm. Small groups of British golfers laid out courses for their own amusement in every corner of the globe and in due time the game flourished and found its own native expression. Naturally, local conditions gave golf a local flavour. In some regions greens are still unknown and the ball is played to 'browns', areas of flattened sand bonded by oil: and even in South Africa and Japan putting surfaces are by no means uniformly good. In almost every case, however, golfers looked to St. Andrews as the temple of the game's traditions and the ultimate authority. The exception was Canada where golf came under American influence. Although Canadian golf retains some of the British traditions, it is Americanized to the extent of allegiance to the United States Golf Association rather than to the Royal and Ancient Club. In practical terms this meant a commitment during the modern years of the game's rapid expansion to the American big ball, while the rest of the world played with the smaller ball. In 1971 the two ruling bodies jointly considered a proposal for a uniform ball of 1·66 in. (42 mm.). After the inauguration of the two world-wide international competitions — the Canada (now WORLD) CUP for professionals and the EISENHOWER TROPHY for amateurs — such a ball, it was hoped, would complete the work of those early evangelists who took their clubs with them on their overseas adventures and unite the brotherhood of world golfers in the same game, played to the same rules with the same equipment.

Women's golf. Long after the allegation against Mary Queen of Scots, there is a reference to golf being played by women at Musselburgh in 1792, and a women's club was formed there in 1872, following those at St. Andrews (1867), and Westward Ho!, North Devon. Two years later, too, a women's club was formed at Pau.

At this time, however, women's courses were miniature versions of the men's, constructed on the assumption that a woman could not drive more than about 80 yds. (73·15 m.). Many of these women golfers were of a period, a class, and a type to be concerned with the emancipation of women; and observers of the period noted the women golfers, like the cyclists, as evidence of the emergent female. They were not long content to be banished to second-class accommodation, and by 1893 the (British) Ladies' Golf Union (L.G.U.) had been formed and held its first championship — at Lytham and St. Annes. There were 38 competitors and it was won by Lady Margaret Scott. A number of the ladies' clubs of the period had their own, independent courses and club houses, as the Wirral and Formby club still does. In general, however, women now play on the same courses as men, where they face the same problem except that of length.

The major achievement of the L.G.U. in the field of golf in general was the creation of a universally acceptable form of handicapping. It was devised by Purvis and supported by Miss Pearson (later Mrs. Miller), the first, and highly capable, hon. sec. of the L.G.U. Until then most handicaps meant nothing except in the club which set them; often the best player in a club was rated scratch and the remaining members were given relative figures; so that scratch players might well prove handicap 12 or 14 on a long or difficult course. There were some early errors but the L.G.U. had the essence of the matter and, by the early years of this century, their modified system was employed in men's golf also.

Many of the best early women golfers, such as Miss Mulligan, Miss Adair, and the Hezlet sisters, were Irish; but soon came the first Scot to win the 'Open' — Miss Campbell — and the Orr sisters: from England, Miss Dod, Miss LEITCH on each side of the First World War, and, after it, the remarkable Miss WETHERED. In America Mrs. ZAHARIAS, Miss Berg, and Miss SUGGS, after success as amateurs, proved highly accomplished and successful professional competition and exhibition players. The emancipation was complete.

Robert Browning, *A History of Golf* (1956); *The Royal and Ancient Game of Golf*, ed. Harold H. Hilton and Garden G. Smith (1912); *A History of Golf in Britain* (1952); Ben Hogan, *The Modern Fundamentals of Golf* (1957); *Golf*, ed. Horace G. Hutchinson (The Badminton Library, 1890); *Bobby Jones on Golf* (1968); Mark McCormack, *The World of Professional Golf*, annually; Charles Price, *The World of Golf* (1963); Harry Vardon, *The Complete Golfer* (1905); H. N. Wethered and T. Simpson, *The Architectural Side of Golf* (1929); Dr. David Williams, *The Science of the Golf Swing* (1969); Douglas Young, *St. Andrews Town and Gown Royal and Ancient* (1969).
GOVERNING BODIES (AMATEUR): Royal and Ancient Golf Club, St. Andrews, Fife, Scotland; United States Golf Association, Golf House, 40 East 38th Street, New York, N.Y. 10016, U.S.A.; (PROFESSIONAL): British Professional Golfers Association, The Oval, Kennington, London S.E. 11; Professional Golfers Association of America, 60 East 42nd Street, New York, N.Y. 10017, U.S.A.

GOLF CROQUET, see CROQUET.

GOLUBNICHI, VLADIMIR (1936-   ), race walker for U.S.S.R., regarded as the most consistent and durable 20 km. exponent yet seen. He set a 20 km. world record at 19 years of age and improved it three years later, the performance standing in the record books for nine years. His international record is outstanding: Olympic champion, 1960 and 1968, silver medallist 1972, bronze medallist 1964, second in the LUGANO CUP final 1966 and 1970, and third European 1966, all at 20 km. With tremendous competition from his own countrymen, Golubnichi's ability to be at his best for the big championships made him a most feared rival for over 15 years.

GOMELSKI, ALEXANDER, BASKETBALL coach for several years in charge of the U.S.S.R. national team. Gomelski, a mere 5 ft. 5 in. (1·65 m.) tall, never became a very successful player but was an extremely successful coach. He took his club, A.S.K. RIGA, from comparative obscurity to win three EUROPEAN CUP FOR CHAMPION CLUBS competitions. As coach to the U.S.S.R. national team, Gomelski led his team to the world championship title in 1967. They also won silver and bronze medals in the OLYMPIC GAMES and while under his control were undefeated in the European championships.

GONZALES, RICHARD A. (Pancho) (1928-   ), American LAWN TENNIS player, a fiercely aggressive player who dominated the professional game in the 1950s. Gonzales turned professional in 1949 after having won the U.S. singles title for the second successive year, and succeeded KRAMER, another Californian, as world champion. He was one of the most complete players of all time, possessing a devastating service, a powerful smash, great speed, a shrewd lawn tennis brain, remarkable concentration, and an armoury of delicate shots. Undoubtedly, he would have won many major championships if he had remained an amateur and when at last the traditional events were opened to the professionals in 1968, he was several years past his best. He still, however, managed to reach the semi-finals of the French Open in 1968 and occasionally to surprise the younger leaders of the game. At WIMBLEDON in 1969 he assured himself of a permanent place in the history of the game by beating Pasarell (U.S.A.) in a match which lasted 5 hrs. 20 min., an hour more than the tournament's previous longest match.

GOODWOOD, race-course originally laid

out by Lord BENTINCK in the Duke of Richmond's park on the Sussex Downs in England. The most important races run there are the SUSSEX STAKES, Goodwood Cup for stayers, King George Stakes for sprinters, Gordon Stakes and Nassau Stakes (fillies) for three-year-olds, Richmond Stakes and Molecomb Stakes (fillies) for two-year-olds, the Stewards' Cup, the Eytel Handicap for three-year-olds, and the P.T.S. Laurels Handicap.

GOODWOOD MOTOR CIRCUIT, MOTOR RACING track near Chichester on land belonging to the Duke of Richmond and Gordon, some way below the famous GOODWOOD racecourse. It was opened in September 1948 and had a length of 2·38 miles (3·8 km.). With the addition of a chicane in April 1952, the length was increased to 2·4 miles. It was a well-surfaced circuit, with excellent facilities, including a tunnel connecting the pits to the outside of the track.

The most important races were the Glover Trophy (also known as the Richmond Trophy) held on Easter Monday of each year, and the Goodwood Nine Hours race held in 1952, 1953, and 1955. The Richmond Trophy was a separate Formula One race in 1949 to 1952. The Tourist Trophy was held at Goodwood from 1958 to 1963. The track was closed in 1966 because it was considered unsafe for the very high speeds of the cars then racing, but was still used for testing.

GORDITO (Antonio Carmona) (1838-1920), *matador de toros* who invented the *al quiebro* method of placing the *banderillas*, and later did so with his feet tied together. He also placed *banderillas* while seated on a chair.

GORDON-WATSON, MARY (1948-   ), British three-day event (see EQUESTRIAN EVENTS) horsewoman. She won the individual European and world championships in 1969 and 1970 respectively. She was also a member of the British teams which won the world team title in 1970 and the Olympic gold medal in 1972. Her successes were achieved with her father's horse, Cornishman V, who proved to be one of the most talented and courageous three-day event horses of all time. Ridden by MEADE, Cornishman V was also in the Olympic gold medal team in 1968.

GORE, ARTHUR WENTWORTH (1868-1928), British LAWN TENNIS player, one of the most remarkable WIMBLEDON champions. A baseliner, spry and moustachioed, apt on big occasions to fortify himself in the middle of a hard match with a glass of champagne, he played at every Wimbledon from 1888 to 1927. He was almost a one-shot player, punching a flat forehand with the racket in a dead line with his outstretched arm. His backhand was said to be more of an efficient push than a stroke, and his service was soft, low-bounding, and shrewdly placed.

Gore won the title at his fourteenth attempt in 1901 when the luck of a ball off the net-cord helped him to frustrate Hillyard. His victory by 4-6, 7-5, 6-4, 6-4 over R. F. DOHERTY in the challenge round interrupted ten years of Doherty supremacy. In 1908, when BROOKES did not defend, Gore recaptured the title by beating Roper Barrett, and the following year, at the age of 41, became Wimbledon's oldest champion by beating Ritchie, who was a mere 39 years old, 6-8, 1-6, 6-2, 6-2, 6-2 in the challenge round. He won the doubles with Roper Barrett in that year and although WILDING took the singles title from him in 1910, Gore reached the challenge round again in 1912, only to lose to Wilding again.

He was a member of the first British Isles Davis Cup (see LAWN TENNIS) team which went to LONGWOOD in 1900 and lost to the U.S.A. — Whitman beat him, and his rubber against DAVIS was not finished — and in 1912 he was still needed for the first tie of the season against France. In 1926 he played another match which caught public attention. The Duke of York, later George VI, entered the doubles at Wimbledon with his equerry, Sir Louis Greig, and Gore and Roper Barrett, whose ages totalled 111, beat them.

GORE, SPENCER W. (1850-1906), English LAWN TENNIS player, the first WIMBLEDON champion and the first player to use the volley effectively. A RACKETS player and an old Harrovian, he beat Marshall 6-1, 6-2, 6-4 in the final of the first championship in 1877. Instead of waiting at the back of the court for his opponents to return his shots, as was customary at the time, Gore ran forward and whenever possible hit the ball before it bounced. This adventurous policy caused some controversy as to whether the volley and the overhead service, also used by some competitors, were legitimate strokes.

In 1878 Gore was beaten 7-5, 6-1, 9-7 in the challenge round by Hadow, another rackets player from Harrow, in the challenge round. Hadow countered Gore's volleys with another new weapon, the lob. Gore never competed at Wimbledon again and Hadow, who had won the title without losing a set, returned to Ceylon, and did not defend it.

GORMAN, TOM (1902-   ), Australian RUGBY LEAGUE player. A centre three-quarter from Queensland, Gorman played in ten successive Test matches against Great Britain from 1924, and was captain in the last seven. His positional sense made him an outstanding defender, and he had inspiring qualities as a leader, especially in tight situations.

GORNIK ZABRZE, Association FOOTBALL club, Zabrze. One of the clubs in the Silesia region of Poland that developed after the Second World War, Gornik won the Polish championship in 1961 and 1963-8. The club's many championship victories brought them regular appearances in the European Cup but they came nearest to success in European club competitions in the Cup-Winners Cup, in the final of which they were beaten by MANCHESTER CITY in 1970. Leading players have included Pohl and LUBANSKI.
·COLOURS: Blue.

GOROKHOVA, GALINA (1938-   ), Russian fencer, six times U.S.S.R. champion at foil and world champion in 1965 and 1970, as well as six times a member of the winning team for the world title. In 1971, in Vienna, she was disqualified during the final for having 'arranged' a fight with Pascu, who had 'thrown' her a fight in the semi-finals.

GOTCH, FRANK (*fl.* 1900-13), American wrestler who won the world catch-as-catch-can title from HACKENSCHMIDT in 1908 and held it until his retirement five years later. Gotch was beaten by JENKINS, the holder of the American title, in 1903 but turned the tables two years later. From then until his retirement he had 160 bouts, winning 154 of them. He did lose his title in 1906 (to Beall when he was thrown against an unpadded post and stunned) but regained it the following year. His quick-moving, attacking tactics upset Hackenschmidt at their first meeting in 1908 and the following year defeated Zybyszco in a controversial bout in Chicago. In 1911 he had a return bout with Hackenschmidt who was suffering from a damaged knee; he defeated the Russian again and retired two years later.

GOULD, ARTHUR JOSEPH (1864-1919), RUGBY UNION footballer for NEWPORT and Wales. Beginning his international career as a full-back, he made his name as a strong, decisive centre in the period of the three-three-quarters system; he initially resisted, but came to accept, the inclusion of a second centre in the three-quarter line. Gould won 27 international caps, and his 18 appearances as captain of Wales still remained a record after 74 years.

GOULD, JAY (1888-1935), REAL TENNIS player and winner of the Gold Medal at the 1908 Olympics; world champion 1914-16. When only 17 he won the Gold Racquet at Tuxedo and the amateur championship in New York. The next year, 1907, he became the first American to win the English amateur championship, and in 1908 he won the gold medal in the only OLYMPIC GAMES which have included real tennis. He remained American amateur champion from 1906 to 1925. He was the first amateur of any nation to become world champion.

GOULD, SHANE (1956-   ), Australian swimmer, winner of five medals at the 1972 Munich Olympics — three golds, a silver, and a bronze. During her short two and a half years of international competition, this talented all-round performer broke 11 notable world records, for all five freestyle distances, from 100 metres to 1,500 metres, and for the 200 metres medley. She turned professional at the tender age of 16 years.

GOULDING, GEORGE HENRY (*c.* 1890-   ), race walker for Canada. Olympic 10 km. champion in 1912, his 1-mile world record lasted for 29 years, while his American Amateur Athletic Union 7 miles championship winning time in 1915 remained an American record until 1966.

GRACE, Dr. WILLIAM GILBERT (1848-1915), cricketer for England, Gloucestershire, and London County. Large and bearded, the best-known of all cricketers in the history of the game, he stood supreme among his contemporaries. He began playing at the highest level while still a youth, when pitches generally were crudely prepared, and he played in his last Test match at the age of 50, by which time the game was well organized and playing conditions had vastly improved. In his long career he made 54,904 runs, with 126 centuries, took 2,876 wickets, and held 877 catches — peerless as a set of aggregates. In addition he made 95 centuries in minor matches. His records, many of which survive, were numerous, and he, more than any other, made CRICKET England's national summer game. In 1880 he made the first Test century against Australia, and he led his country 13 times, though taking part in only one Test tour (1891-2). For almost 30 years he scored heavily and consistently and took wickets in the blue riband matches between the Gentlemen and the Players. As late as 1895 he summoned prodigious form, scoring a thousand runs in May, hitting his hundredth century, and amassing 2,346 runs — the third highest total for one season in his prolific career. It created as much of a sensation as his unprecedented aggregate of 2,736 runs 24 years earlier.

One of a large sporting family, he had been an exceptional athlete when young. His cricket career with Gloucestershire ended after a disagreement with the committee in 1899. After 29 years of county captaincy he became captain-manager of the short-lived London County. He was keenly interested in BOWLS and in 1903 he was elected first president of the English Bowling Association.

GRAFSTRÖM, GILLES (1893-   ), ice figure-skater for Sweden; originator of the flying sit spin; winner of three Olympic gold medals, 1920, 1924, and 1928, and three world championships, 1922, 1924, and 1929.

GRAN CRITERIUM is the most important horse race for two-year-olds in Italy. It is run in mid-October over 1,500 m. (7½ furlongs) at Milan and forms the second leg of the big Italian two-year-old double, the first being the Criterium Nazionale, 1,200 m. (6 furlongs), also run at Milan in September.

GRAN PREMIO CARLOS PELLE-GRINO, a weight-for-age horse race in Argentina, open to three-year-olds and upwards, is the most important and valuable international race in South America. It is run early in November over 3,000 m. (15 furlongs) on the San Isidro track at Buenos Aires.

GRAN PREMIO D'ITALIA, a classic horse race for three-year-olds run in early June at Milan over 2,400 m. (1½ miles). It is virtually a repeat of the DERBY ITALIANO run over the same distance at Rome three weeks earlier.

GRAN PREMIO DEL JOCKEY CLUB, a horse race, is the middle leg of the triple crown for older horses in Italy. It is run over 2,400 m. (1½ miles) at SAN SIRO, Milan, in October, and is the most valuable horse race in Italy after the DERBY ITALIANO.

GRAN PREMIO DE MADRID is the most important horse race in Spain. It is for three-year-olds and upwards, and is run over 2,500 m. (12½ furlongs) on the Zarzuela course at Madrid. In 1968, the winner, Tebas, a five-year-old mare, was bred, owned, trained, and ridden to victory by a neck under top weight, by the Duque de Albuquerque.

GRAN PREMIO DI MILANO, horse race which is the first leg of the Italian triple crown of weight-for-age events, the other races being

the GRAN PREMIO DEL JOCKEY CLUB and the PREMIO ROMA. It is run on the SAN SIRO racecourse in Milan in mid-June over a distance of 3,000 m. (1 mile 7 furlongs).

GRAN PREMIO NACIONAL, a horse race, is the Argentine Derby, run over 2,500 m. (12½ furlongs) on the Palermo track, Buenos Aires, in October.

GRAND CHALLENGE CUP, see HENLEY ROYAL REGATTA.

GRAND CHISTERA, see PELOTA.

GRAND CRITERIUM is an important horse race for two-year-olds in France. Run over 1,600 m. (1 mile) at LONGCHAMP in October, this event forms the third leg of the French triple crown for two-year-olds, the first leg being the Prix Robert Papin over 1,100 m. (5½ furlongs) at Maisons Lafitte in late July, and the second, the Prix Morny over 1,200 m. (6 furlongs) at DEAUVILLE in mid-August.

GRAND NATIONAL, the outstanding event of the Cresta skeleton TOBOGGANING season at St. Moritz, Switzerland, from Top—i.e. the full length of the run. The competition was instituted in 1885 one year after a rudimentary version of the modern run was first built. A team from Davos met a team from St. Moritz, a Davos rider winning. The cup, presented by Liebert, is still competed for annually on the aggregate of three runs. (See also CURZON CUP.)

GRAND NATIONAL ARCHERY SOCIETY, the governing body for ARCHERY in the United Kingdom, was founded in 1861 with the sole object of organizing the Grand National Archery Meetings which began in 1844. Its present objects include the promotion and encouragement of archery and its functions include the holding of British national championships for target and other branches of archery, and the control of the selection and the management of British representative teams.

The Society is organized on a regional basis, and these regions, seven in number, are subject to the overriding control of the Society, and are self-governing within their own jurisdictional areas. Membership of the Society includes ordinary and junior members and approximately 600 associated clubs, plus a few overseas clubs. There are some 10,000 archers in the United Kingdom who, by reason of their club's affiliation to the governing body, automatically become associate members of the Grand National Archery Society.

The Society is a member association of the world authority for archery, the Fédération Internationale de Tir à l'Arc, and is affiliated to the British Olympic Association.

GRAND NATIONAL STEEPLECHASE is the most famous horse race in the world for jumpers 'over the sticks', and the most severe test for a horse ever devised. It was first run in England in 1839 and is now a handicap for horses, geldings, and mares, six years old and upwards, who have fulfilled certain qualifications in their previous appearances on the racecourse. The weights carried range from 12 stone (76 kg.) down to 10 stone (63 kg.). The Grand National is run near the end of March at AINTREE near Liverpool over a course of 4 miles 856 yds. (about 7,200 m.) with 30 jumps, including the notorious Becher's Brook, Canal Turn Rail and Fence, and Valentine's Brook. In 1973 it was worth more than £25,000 to the winner.

Abd-el-Kadir, Peter Simple, The Colonel, The Lamb, Manifesto, and Reynoldstown won the Grand National twice; Cloister, Jerry M, and Poethlyn carried top weight to victory, as did Manifesto when winning for the second time. When Cloister won in 1893, he finished 40 lengths ahead of his rivals in record time, since when Crackle, Kellsboro Jack, GOLDEN MILLER, and Red Rum have in turn set records, the latter completing the course in 9 min. 1·90 sec. in 1973.

There have been some very close finishes, notably when Shaun Goilin won by a neck in 1930, and when the American entire horse, Battleship (by MAN O' WAR) starting at odds of 40 to 1 against, won by a head in 1938, having previously won the American Grand National. Although beaten by three-quarters of a length by Red Rum, Crisp was responsible for the most memorable race in recent years when he attempted to make all the running under 12 stone (76 kg.) and was caught in the final strides. The only 'royal' winner of the Grand National was Ambush II in 1900, carrying the colours of the Prince of WALES to victory. Only Stevens has ever ridden five winners of the National: on Freetrader in 1856, on the full sisters, Emblem and Emblematic, in 1863 and 1864, and on The Colonel in 1869 and again, by a neck, in 1870.

With the LINCOLN HANDICAP, the Grand National makes up the 'Spring Double', first big betting event of the English racing year.

(See also GREYHOUND RACING.)

GRAND PRIX, see MOTOR RACING, INTERNATIONAL.

GRAND PRIX DE FRANKFURT, German road race for professional cyclists. Starting and finishing at Frankfurt's Henninger Tower, after which it is often named, it follows a fixed course of 140 miles (225 km.) through the Taunus mountains and includes three major climbs. Founded in 1962, it replaced the defunct PARIS–BRUSSELS race in 1967 in the list of classic events.

GRAND PRIX DES NATIONS, the only individual time trial included in the list of professional CYCLING classics. From its foundation in 1932 until 1955, the event was held over a course of 140 to 142 km. (87–88 miles) from Versailles to the PARC DES PRINCES, Paris. In 1970, after experiments with shorter distances, a new course of 100 km. (just over 62 miles) was used from Auffargis to the Stade Municipale de Vincennes; in 1973 the event was moved to an 80 km. (49·7 miles) course at St.-Jean-de-Monts (Vendée). The record number of victories was held by ANQUETIL with nine, and the highest average speed by GIMONDI with 47·5 km./h. (29·5 m.p.h.) over 73·5 km. (47 miles) in 1968.

GRAND PRIX DE PARIS, a horse race founded in 1863, is the French classic for three-year-olds run over 3,100 m. (1 mile 7½ furlongs) in late June at LONGCHAMP.

GRAND PRIX DE SAINT-CLOUD, a horse race (known, prior to 1940, as the Prix du Président de la République) which is the middle leg of the triple crown for older race-horses in France, the other two being the PRIX GANAY and the PRIX DE L'ARC DE TRIOMPHE. The race at Saint-Cloud early in July covers a distance of 2,500 m. (1 mile 4½ furlongs).

GRANERO, MANUEL (1902-22), *matador de toros* who took the *alternativa* in 1920. He was killed by the bull Pocapena, of Veragua, in the Madrid *plaza de toros* on 7 May 1922, as he was approaching the height of his career.

GRANGE, HAROLD (Red) (1903-   ), American college and professional FOOTBALL player. An All-America halfback at the University of Illinois (1923-5), he was the most elusive runner in college football history. Against the University of MICHIGAN in 1924 he ran for touchdowns the first four times he handled the ball (within 12 minutes), scored a fifth touchdown, and passed for a sixth later in the same game. Following the 1925 college season he signed to play professional football for the CHICAGO BEARS of the NATIONAL FOOTBALL LEAGUE and went on a tour that earned him $250,000 in two months and helped attract the first major popular attention to the professional game. He played for the New York Yankees in the AMERICAN FOOTBALL LEAGUE in 1926-7, and, after the collapse of the League, returned to the Chicago Bears in 1929 and played until 1934.

GRANT, R., III, American amateur RACKETS player who won the U.S. amateur singles championship ten times up to 1953. He was a very severe hitter who would have distinguished himself in the U.K. championships had he been able to compete.

GRASS SKIING is a sport of individual participation akin to SKIING, but practised on grassy slopes. The snow skis are replaced by freely-revolving caterpillar tracks or rollers that have more in common with roller skates than with skis. The main centres of the sport are in Germany, Austria, Switzerland, and France, though its rapid development has led to a considerable following in other countries with suitable hilly pasture-land, such as Italy, England, Andorra, Australia, Japan, and South Africa.

The only essential items of equipment are grass skis, which enable the wearer to glide down a grassy gradient much as the wearer of roller skates would move down a smoother and harder slope. The caterpillar tracks, one to each ski and about 1½ in. (3·81 cm.) wide, are usually formed of rigid plastic studs on a nylon belt, running freely in a steel frame about 4 in. (10·16 cm.) high and the same width as the sole of the shoe. The length varies from shoe length for the recreational skier to as much as 2 ft. 6 in. (76·2 cm.) for the top-class racing. A later English model replaces tracks with rollers, 3 in. (7·62 cm.) wide and 3½ in. (8·89 cm.) in diameter, five of which are used in each ski. These are not as fast as track skis, but are more stable, and unlike tracks permit a small amount of lateral movement. Strong boots, giving ankle support, are the most suitable footwear, and to these the ski frames are strapped or clipped.

Changes in direction are mainly accomplished, as in WATER SKIING or ROLLER SKATING, by changes in the inclination and emphasis of weight of the body. To attempt a skiing manoeuvre such as snowploughing usually brings disaster, though accidents are seldom serious as long as nursery slopes are being used.

Progress and stability are helped by the use of ski sticks. These need not be of the type used on snow, the points of which are too fine to be helpful in muddy conditions (grass skiing experts sometimes fit plastic bottle-tops to the tips to thicken them). Broom handles, roughly sharpened at one end, are quite suitable. Old

clothes are recommended, particularly for the novice.

Grass skiing is restricted to slopes, whatever their gradient, that are reasonably smooth, dry, and close-cropped. Long grass tends to clog the tracks and progress at any speed is impossible over wet mud. The ground must also be clear of rocks, ruts, and bumps, any of which are likely to cause a fall.

Grass skiing originated in Germany in 1967, where a Stuttgart sports goods manufacturer, Kaiser, developed the necessary equipment. It soon spread to neighbouring countries, reaching England in May 1970, when an international championship was held at Windermere, in the Lake District. The sport's popularity in all countries that adopted it grew quickly, and meets are held throughout the spring, summer, and autumn. Skis are usually available on hire at these meets, which often include simple competitions for novices as well as more involved events, such as a slalom. Many of the most expert grass skiers in Europe are found in areas already well known for skiing, among them Gstaad (Switzerland) and Lermoos (Austria). The sport is in most cases organized by grass ski committees of the national ski associations.

GRASS-TRACK RACING, Motor-cycle, see MOTOR-CYCLE RACING.

GRAVENEY, THOMAS WILLIAM, O.B.E. (1927-   ), cricketer for England, Gloucestershire, Worcestershire, and Queensland. Tall and elegant in style, he was the first batsman to score 40,000 runs and 100 centuries in postwar CRICKET. He left Gloucestershire in 1960 after 13 seasons, and scored heavily for Worcestershire during the next ten. In Test cricket he was not always a regular selection, but his 79 appearances (4,882 runs) included some notable innings, the highest being 258 against West Indies.

GRAY, WILLIAM (d. 1875), British RACKETS player who was world champion from 1866 to 1875. He was the professional at Eton College and the outstanding player of six brothers, two of whom were also world rackets champions; Henry Gray 1863-6, and Joseph Gray 1878-87.

GREAT NORTHERN DERBY, a horse race which is run over 1½ miles (2,400 m.) at Auckland, New Zealand, on 26 December.

GREAVES, JAMES (1940-   ), Association footballer for CHELSEA, A.C. MILAN, TOTTENHAM HOTSPUR, WEST HAM UNITED, and

England (for whom he scored 44 goals in 57 appearances in full international matches). One of the most prolific scoring inside forwards in all English football, Greaves scored his hundredth goal in League matches for Chelsea, his first club, at the early age of 20 years 9 months. In June 1961 he signed for the Italian club, A.C. Milan, but returned to England five months later when Tottenham paid Milan £98,000 for the transfer of his registration, and scored his two-hundredth League goal at exactly the same age as Dean had done over 30 years before — 23 years 290 days. In 1970, towards the end of his career, he was transferred to West Ham United.

GREB, HARRY (1894-1926), American boxer who held the world middleweight title between 1923 and 1926. Known as the 'Human Windmill' because of his seemingly tireless action, Greb had nearly 300 bouts and was knocked out only once, when he broke an arm as a 20-year-old. He boxed with great distinction against light-heavyweights and even heavyweights and is the only man to have beaten TUNNEY. Two months after losing the middleweight title to Flowers in 1926 Greb died following an eye operation. Later it was confirmed that he had boxed many of his later bouts when blind in one eye. Much has been made of Greb's love for fast living but his remarkable stamina was due to most conscientious roadwork.

GREEN, THOMAS WILLIAM (1893-), race walker for Great Britain and BELGRAVE HARRIERS. Olympic 50 km. champion in 1932, at 39 years of age, he was also winner of the LONDON–BRIGHTON race (1929-31, and 1933), MILAN 100 KM. (1930), BRADFORD 32 miles (1930-3), and MANCHESTER–BLACKPOOL 50 miles (1929-34). A prolific performer at the longer distances, his duels with WHITLOCK highlighted English walking in the 1930s.

GREEN BAY PACKERS, American professional FOOTBALL team, have had a long colourful tradition, joining the NATIONAL FOOTBALL LEAGUE (N.F.L.) in 1922, under coach Lambeau, who remained until 1949. Situated in a relatively small city in northern Wisconsin, the Packers have maintained a fierce independence and deep civic pride that have offset the small population base upon which their franchise was built. In the 1930s, the Packers had a leading passer in Herber and the League's pre-eminent pass-receiver in HUTSON, who won the pass-catching title no less than nine times; when Herber retired in the late 1930s, Isbell replaced him as Hutson's passer. In the early part of this era the Packers also featured the tackle Hubbard, the halfback 'Johnny Blood' (John McNally), and the fullback Hinkle. In the 1950s the team reached a low ebb; the franchise was only saved when the community purchased it. The collective ownership promptly hired the NEW YORK GIANTS offensive (attacking) coach LOMBARDI as general manager and coach. Between 1959 and 1968, when he retired from the Packers, Lombardi's teams won five League titles, plus the first two Super Bowls. A relentless perfectionist, Lombardi insisted on precise execution of a limited number of plays; his quarterback Starr acted as his *alter ego* on the field. The Packers' proud tradition lists more League titles—eight—than any other N.F.L. team.
COLOURS: Green and gold.

GREENE, NANCY (1944-), Canadian Alpine ski racer, and the first woman holder of the World Ski Cup (see SKIING), in 1967. She was Olympic gold medallist in the giant slalom at Grenoble in 1968, and helped to break the European domination of international Alpine skiing during the 1960s.

GREENFIELD, STUART, see KNUR AND SPELL.

GREGORY, JACK MORRISON (1895-1973), cricketer for Australia and New South Wales. Scorer of the fastest Test century — he reached 100 in 70 minutes against South Africa at Johannesburg in 1921-2 — he was a huge and hostile right-arm fast bowler who, bowling in partnership with E. A. McDonald, did much to make Australia invincible for several seasons after the First World War. His left-handed batting and magnificent fielding at slip made him a complete and dominant all-rounder.

GREGORY, SYDNEY EDWARD (1870-1929), cricketer for Australia and New South Wales. With a Test career stretching from 1890 to 1912, he played in a record number of Test matches — 52 — against England, making 201, the highest of his four centuries, in the 1894-5 series. He captained Australia against England and South Africa in the 1912 Triangular Tournament, and was the most distinguished member of a famous cricketing family.

GREN, GUNNAR (1920-), Association footballer for Göteborg, A.C. MILAN, Fiorentina, Genoa, and Sweden. He played in the Swedish side of amateurs that won the 1948 Olympics football tournament in London. An inside right, he was one of several fine players in that team who were then persuaded to sign as professionals in Italian football. By 1958 when the world championship was staged in Sweden, he had returned to his native Göteborg and, although a 'veteran', he played for Sweden.

GREY CUP, see FOOTBALL, CANADIAN.

GREYHOUND DERBY, the premier event in GREYHOUND RACING, held at White City, London. Prize money for this 525 yard (480 m.) race exceeds £25,000, the owner of the winning greyhound receiving approximately £12,500. The Derby has a fixed date in the greyhound calendar: the fourth Saturday in June; the eliminating races to produce the field of six from the 48 acceptances begin early in June.

GREYHOUND RACING, a sport in which greyhounds compete in pursuit of a mechanical imitation of a hare. The racing takes place on a track of an elliptical or oval shape with a circumference of approximately 400 to 550 yds. (366–493 m.), around which the artificial hare is made to move on an electrified rail. Racing is usually conducted over distances varying between 230 yds. (210 m.) for the sprint and 1,200 yds. (1,097 m.) for the marathon, and can be on the flat or over hurdles. Each race may comprise any number of greyhounds up to eight, although five or six is the general rule in Great Britain. Turf and sand are the most commonly used track surfaces.

The greyhound is an ancient canine breed which can be traced back over 70 centuries. The name bears no relationship to the colour grey. The history of the greyhound points to several possible derivations of the name: the early Greek gazehound, the Icelandic *greyhundr* (*grey* meaning 'dog'), or — the more popular theory — the *Greek-hound*, which is known to have arrived in England with the Gallic tribes. 'Greyhound' may be a corruption of the word 'Greek-hound', the 'k' being difficult to pronounce. Built entirely for speed, the racing greyhound remains one of the few canine pure breeds.

In 1486, Dame Juliana Berners wrote *The Boke of St. Albans,* which, for the first time in English literature, set out and described in full the whole subject of greyhounds and harehunting. The book contained what was, and still remains, the classical description of the greyhound's physical conformation:

A greyhound should be heeded lyke a snake,
And neckyd lyke a drake,
Backed lyke a bream,
Footed lyke a catte,
Taylled lyke a ratte.

The standard colourings of greyhounds, with their abbreviations as given on race-cards, are black (bk.), blue (be.), brindle (bd.), fawn (f.), red (r.), tickled — light or dark specks (tkd.), and white (w.). There can be combinations of colourings, e.g. fawn and white. The colouring is recorded in the dog's identity book, which, in Great Britain, each racing greyhound is required to have. This is its passport and record and must accompany it wherever it races on any course. The book, which gives all other particulars: birth date, sire and dam, measurements, marks, and racing record, is never in the hands of the dog's owner. If a greyhound is transferred from one course to another, the identity book goes with it for identification on arrival. Similar arrangements for identification exist in Ireland, Australia, and the U.S.A., where the information is recorded on a special Bertillon card.

Just before the start of a race, the greyhounds, wearing muzzles and distinguishing jackets of different colours with numbers affixed, are taken from the racing kennels and led into the paddock where the identity of each dog is corroborated with its identity book by a race-course official. The greyhound is then examined by a veterinary surgeon to ensure its fitness to race.

The colour of the jackets and numbers denotes the order across the track, starting from the inner rail, in which the greyhounds will commence to race. Different colours are used for the different positions in countries where greyhound racing is popular.

Great Britain and Spain: No. 1, red; No. 2, blue; No. 3, white; No. 4, black; No. 5, orange; No. 6, white and black stripes. *Great Britain only:* No. 7, light green with broad orange band; No. 8, red and white check.

Australia: No. 1, red; No. 2, black and white check; No. 3, white; No. 4, blue; No. 5, yellow; No. 6, brown; No. 7, black; No. 8, pink.

Ireland: No. 1, red; No. 2, blue; No. 3, white; No. 4, red and white stripes; No. 5, black; No. 6, orange.

U.S.A.: No. 1, red; No. 2, blue; No. 3, white; No. 4, green; No. 5, black; No. 6, yellow; No. 7, green and white; No. 8, yellow and black.

Immediately before the start of the race the artificial hare commences its 'run' from behind the traps. A mechanism fitted to the hare equipment automatically ensures that the traps are fully opened at the time the hare is approximately 12 yds. (11 m.) ahead of the starting traps.

From the start of the race, the greyhound's native intelligence and cunning teach it, with experience, to gain the position in the field which is most favourable to its particular style of racing. This might be the inside position nearest the rails, in which the greyhound will have less distance to cover, or an outside position, where the greyhound's run is less likely to be impeded.

The performance of the greyhounds at the bends, especially the first, when there may be very little distance between the first and the last greyhound so soon after leaving the traps, often influences the result of the race. It is at the bends on the track, with the hare having 'deviated' from its straight course, that the greyhounds are most likely to impede each other, and it is at these positions that the greyhound's track craft and experience count as much as speed in the winning of a race.

As the traps open for the start of the race, a special timing device is automatically set going and, as the nose of the leading greyhound touches an invisible ray projecting across the track at the winning post, the device is automatically stopped, thus showing the exact time of the race. The speed of the greyhounds may reach 40 m.p.h. (64 km./h.) from the traps and 35 m.p.h. (56 km./h.) over the finishing line.

The judge, who occupies a box opposite the winning post, is the sole arbiter in declaring the winner, i.e. the greyhound whose nose first reaches the winning line. He may call for a photo-finish to assist him in making his decision. Introduced to Britain at White City greyhound race-course, London, in October 1945, the photo-finish procedure is now universally accepted. (See also HORSE RACING.) The camera is placed on the winning line and the film moves in a steady, continuous movement across a slit aperture, normally $\frac{1}{32}$ in. (0·8 mm.). This takes a composite picture of the runners through the narrow aperture as, in turn, they reach the winning line. The photograph is used to confirm the judge's placing in the order of finishing, and prints are exhibited around the stadium for the public to see.

Racing at all the principal greyhound stadia in Great Britain is conducted under the Rules of Racing formulated by the National Greyhound Racing Club following the introduction of greyhound racing to Great Britain in 1926, and implemented on all the principal greyhound race-courses on 23 April 1928. They prescribe detailed rules for the conduct of the sport; the compulsory registration of all greyhounds racing on approved race-courses; the establishment of the identity of each and every greyhound; the licensing of track officials, trainers, and kennel staff; and the investigation of any reports of improper practices and breaches of the rules by owners, trainers, officials, or other persons.

A prominent feature of greyhound racing, as in horse racing, is the betting on race results. Each race-course must hold a track betting licence, issued by the licensing author-ity for a period of seven years, before betting can take place. Punters betting with a totalisator endeavour to select the dog or dogs they think will either win or obtain a place (first, second, or, where eight greyhounds are run, third place) or obtain the first and second place in correct order in the forecast pool. Some race-courses have multi-race pool betting which calls for the correct forecasting of the result of two, three, or more races. After the deduction of Government tax and operators' expenses, the whole of the pool is returned to the holders of the winning tickets. It is possible to ascertain the state of the betting at any time by reference to the large visual indicators which are displayed at greyhound race-courses.

The first computerized totalisator at a greyhound race-course was installed at the St. Petersburg, Florida, track in 1969. It is capable of making all the necessary calculations for the declaration of the dividends within a few seconds of the order of finish being declared. In most countries where greyhound racing is a major sport, the law provides for an accountant or state representative to be present at every meeting to ensure that the totalisator is operated properly and that the dividends and other calculations are correct.

National Greyhound Racing Club, Ltd. *Rules of Racing*, latest edition.

Greyhounds have been bred for speed, and the pursuit of the hare, for many centuries. Excavations in Mesopotamia date greyhounds back to 5,000 B.C. The tomb of the Egyptian King Amten in the Nile valley contains three carvings of greyhounds. Ptaheptep's sepulchre at Sakkara (2,500 B.C.) shows greyhounds starting a coursing race and the Metropolitan Museum of Art in New York has scenes of greyhounds taken from the tomb of Recem-koy (Fifth Dynasty), 2,500 B.C., and Achtoy (Eleventh Dynasty), 2,100 B.C.

Proof of the existence of greyhounds in England dates back 3,500 years; a skeleton of a greyhound was revealed when the Avebury stone circle was uncovered in 1959. Greyhounds have figured prominently among royalty and the nobility. King John accepted them in lieu of fines; Henry II, Henry VII, and Charles I had many greyhounds. When Robert Cecil, first Earl of Salisbury, built Hatfield House in 1611 he followed fashion by installing carved gates at the foot of the staircases to prevent the greyhounds from reaching the upper rooms. Frederick the Great is said to have carried a pet greyhound into his campaign, and Richard II had a greyhound with him when he was captured in the castle of Flint.

The first written code for greyhound COURS-ING was made by the Duke of Norfolk in 1776 following the organization of the Swaffham Coursing Society by the Earl of Orford, who spent many years experimenting in the breeding and training of greyhounds. The first coursing meetings in America were in 1878 and Gen. George Custer and his orderly, Maj. James (Hound Dog) Kelly, were enthusiasts.

In 1876 the first attempt to introduce 'simulated coursing' — the forerunner of greyhound racing — was made at the Welsh Harp, Hendon, near London. It was described in *The Times* dated 11 September 1876 under the headline 'Coursing by Proxy':

For a distance of 400 yards in a straight line a rail had been laid down on the grass. It has an apparatus like a skate on wheels. On this sort of shuttle is mounted an artificial hare. It is made to travel along the ground at any required pace and so naturally to resemble the living animal that it is eagerly pursued by the greyhounds. On Saturday afternoon at one-half past three, a trial was run of the new mechanical arrangement run by a windlass at West Harp. When the hour came, all that was seen was the artificial hare bounding away, quite naturally, from its bag, and followed at once by the greyhounds. The new sport is undoubtedly an exciting and interesting one.

Several meetings were held, but because the race-course was a straight run, the fastest, but not necessarily the cleverest, greyhound always won, and owners lost interest. In 1890, a patent was taken out for a circular greyhound track but no further action was taken.

An American, Owen Patrick Smith, was the pioneer who conceived the idea of greyhounds running a circular course behind the artificial hare and it happened almost accidentally. Smith was secretary of the Chamber of Commerce at Hot Springs, South Dakota, and in 1905 he decided to promote a coursing meeting as a tourist attraction. He asked a coursing man, George Sawyer of Dorchester, Nebraska, to tell him all he knew about greyhounds and, when his coursing venture was a success, dreamed of a nationwide series of meetings. The cautious Sawyer rejected Smith's ideas, but the imaginative Smith went ahead with an Intermountain Coursing Association meeting at Salt Lake City in 1907.

In face of a public outcry over the slaughter of live hares, Smith then conceived the idea of substituting an artificial lure and, despite opposition from greyhound trainers who doubted it would work, he raised money to build a small circular track near Salt Lake City, and stuffed a rabbit skin, attached it to a motor cycle, and sent it around the track. The greyhounds chased it — and the greyhound-racing industry was born.

It took a long time to get off the ground, however. Not until 1919 did Sawyer agree to join Smith in the venture and they built a track at Emeryville, California, under the banner of the Blue Star Amusement Company. It cost $40,000, no betting was allowed, and the partnership lost money; but Smith persisted. He improved the mechanical hare by mounting a motor engine on four wheels and putting a toy rabbit on top. George Heintz, who had shares in the company, designed a folding arm which made the rabbit disappear at the end of the race, but Smith would not accept this improvement and it became the subject of a long legal argument.

Smith and Sawyer formed the International Greyhound Racing Association at Tulsa in 1920 and Sawyer introduced betting — through bookmakers — regardless of Smith's protests. This time it was a success and the champion dog at the time — the first big name in greyhound racing — was Mission Boy, who won 28 out of 30 races.

In 1922 the sport moved to Florida, which is now the centre of American greyhound racing, when two property men, Curtiss and Bright, persuaded Smith to promote racing at the Hialeah track. More than 5,000 race-goers saw the first Miami Derby in March 1922.

Such was the success of the new sport in America that a businessman, Charles A. Munn, secured the rights of the mechanical lure and crossed the Atlantic to England, where he hawked the idea around. Eventually he met Maj. Lyne-Dixon, a coursing enthusiast, who introduced him to Brig.-Gen. CRITCHLEY and, within a few months, Critchley launched the Greyhound Racing Association.

With a capital of £25,000 a track was built at Belle Vue, Manchester, and opened on 24 July 1926. Although £50 was lost on the first meeting, which attracted a crowd of only 1,700, the directors were able to repay £10,000 to the bank after only 30 nights' racing. After the first year a 1 s. share was worth £37 10 s.

The first programme consisted of six races — three at 440 yds. (402 m.), two at 550 yds. (493 m.), and one hurdle race — and the first greyhound race was won by a dog called Mistley at a starting price of 6–1.

During 1926-7 greyhound racing rapidly became popular in Britain, attracting not only the attention of sporting men, but also company promoters. It came to London in the summer of 1927 with the opening of White City track, followed by tracks at Harringay and Wembley. By the end of 1927, over 40 greyhound race-courses were planned, or in completion, in Britain. The sport quickly established itself in the other principal greyhound-racing countries, Ireland and Australia.

Those at the head of the enterprise in Britain realized that, in a sport in which betting was an integral part, it was essential in the public interest that controlling bodies should be established. Accordingly, the National Greyhound Racing Club (N.G.R.C.) came into being in 1928. Composed of sportsmen of good position who had no financial interest in any greyhound racing promotion, it arose out of the general need for a national body which should be independent of the promoters, and which should draw up a set of rules of racing. Its main object was to protect the interest of the public.

The managements of the leading race-courses were among the first to see the necessity for such a body, and when the Club was established they agreed to accept its supervision and formed themselves, also in 1928, into the National Greyhound Racing Society of Great Britain Ltd. (N.G.R.S.). The race-courses which declined to accept the jurisdiction of the N.G.R.C. continued to operate independently. As the functions of the Club were to control the conduct of greyhound racing in Britain, so the business of the Society was to deal with administration, and it was recognized by departments of state and by local government authorities as the representative body dealing with administrative and legal matters affecting the sport, as with relations with Parliament, the press and the public.

In 1972 a single governing body, the National Greyhound Racing Club Ltd., replaced the N.G.R.C. and the N.G.R.S. and, under its secretary and chief officer F. J. Underhill, has assumed the functions of both these organizations.

In Australia, greyhound racing is supervised by the State Control Boards of New South Wales (controlling 42 race-courses, with headquarters at Lidcombe) and Victoria (controlling 10 race-courses, with headquarters in Melbourne), where greyhound racing is principally promoted. Similar Control Boards have been established in other states. In Ireland, a statutory body, Bord na gCon, is responsible for the general control of racing. The Bord, with its headquarters in Limerick, also operates race-courses at Shelbourne Park and Harolds Cross, in Dublin, and in Cork.

In the U.S.A., the racing is controlled by the state racing commissions in those states where it is permitted to operate. Greyhound racing has been legalized in the states of Alabama, Arizona, Arkansas, Colorado, South Dakota, Florida, Massachusetts, New Hampshire, and Oregon. The American Greyhound Track Operators Association is a national organization covering nearly all the managements of the 38 tracks in the U.S.A., whose headquarters are in Miami, Florida.

Greyhound racing is also established in Mexico, and, on a lesser scale, in Spain, where there are tracks at Barcelona, Madrid, and Valencia. The premier body there is the Federación Española Galguera, with headquarters in Madrid.

The world governing body, the World Greyhound Racing Federation, founded by Britain, Ireland, Spain, Australia, and the U.S.A., has as its principal purpose the promotion and development of international greyhound racing and the interchange of information as to the best procedures and administration for such racing. The Federation's headquarters are at the Bord na gCon, Limerick, Ireland, whose chief officer, S. P. Flanagan, is secretary general of the world body.

The sport is also promoted at a lower level than in the major greyhound-racing countries, in Indonesia, Italy, Macao, and New Zealand. There is track-racing, without betting, in Finland, Holland, and Sweden.

Until 1931, when the totalisator began to make its appearance on greyhound race-courses, betting was carried out solely by on-course bookmakers. The first totalisator betting system was invented in 1872 by a Frenchman called Oller, and was named the Pari-Mutuel (as it is still known in France and America). Oller's system was completely manual without any form of indication of the betting trends. The main disadvantage with this system was that it was very slow and always much behind the actual betting. It was not until 1912 that Julius (later Sir George Julius) invented a machine that answered this and many other problems.

The first mechanical totalisator equipment was installed at Ellerslie Race Track in New Zealand, and first came into operation in Great Britain, at a greyhound race-course, in 1930. The greyhound totalisator was declared illegal in 1933. The Betting and Lotteries Act of 1934 placed the greyhound totalisator on a proper statutory basis, although betting on the track with the totalisator was confined to not more than 104 days a year. Under a 1971 amendment to this law racing can now take place on 130 days in a licensing year.

The years immediately following the Second World War proved to be boom ones for greyhound racing, the sport providing a much-needed relief from the austerity and hazards of wartime life when other social and recreational amenities had not yet been fully restored. The popularity of the sport reached its peak in 1946 when attendances at greyhound stadia totalled 34 million.

Changes in the law governing all forms of betting and gaming (the Betting and Gaming Act, 1960) brought about a diminution of interest, although attendances were still averaging 9 million a year in the 1960s and 8 million in the early 1970s.

Over-all, there are approximately 100 greyhound race-courses in Great Britain, and most cities and large towns have at least one stadium. The more famous are White City, the 'Mecca' of greyhound racing, the internationally famous WEMBLEY STADIUM, Wimbledon, and Walthamstow, all in London; POWDERHALL, Edinburgh; Belle Vue, Manchester; Shawfield, Glasgow; and Hall Green, Birmingham.

Eleven classic greyhound races are held in Britain each year, the premier event being the GREYHOUND DERBY at White City, London. The remaining races are the Grand National (525 yds. — 480 m. — over hurdles), White City; the Gold Collar (575 yds. — 526 m. — flat), Catford; the Greyhound Oaks (525 yds. — 480 m. — flat), Harringay; the Scurry Gold Cup (460 yds. — 421 m. — flat), Slough; the St. Leger (700 yds. — 640 m. — flat), Wembley; the Cesarewitch (880 yds. — 805 m. — flat), Belle Vue, Manchester; the Grand Prix (700 yds. — 640 m.), Walthamstow; the Welsh Derby (525 yds. — 480 m.), Cardiff; the Scottish Derby (525 yds. — 480 m.), Shawfield, Glasgow. Greyhound classic races are also held in Australia, Ireland, Spain, and the U.S.A.

Edward C. Ash, *The Book of the Greyhound* (1933); William H. Bracht, *Greyhounds and Mechanical Lure Racing* (1973); H. Edwards Clarke, *The Greyhound* (1965); Roy Genders, *The Greyhound* (1960); H. Montagu-Harrison, *The Greyhound Trainer* (1962); C. G. E. Wimhurst, *The Book of the Greyhound* (1961).

GOVERNING BODY (WORLD): World Greyhound Racing Federation, Limerick, Ireland; (GREAT BRITAIN): National Greyhound Racing Club Ltd., St. Martin's House, 140 Tottenham Court Road, London W.1.

GRIFFIN, BRIAN (1941-   ), LACROSSE player for Australia and Victoria. A leading Australian attack player and a prolific goalscorer, he was a member of the Australian team which visited England in 1962, when he scored 51 of the touring team's 142 goals. In 1967 he was instrumental in his country's defeat of Canada and England in the international world field lacrosse tournament.

GRIFFO, YOUNG (1871-1927), Australian boxer who claimed the world featherweight title in 1890 and later three times held the renowned American DIXON to a draw. Griffo was a master of defence and even the best featherweights and lightweights of his time found it difficult to land a punch on him, although he often entered the ring drunk.

GRIMMETT, CLARENCE VICTOR (1891-   ), cricketer for Australia, Wellington, Victoria, and South Australia. Born in New Zealand, he finally settled in South Australia and made a late Test début in 1924-5. By the age of 43, at the time of his last Test match, he had become Australia's leading wicket-taker with 216 in only 37 Tests. He bowled leg breaks and variations with a low arm action and unusual accuracy.

GRIMSHAW, DAVID (1939-   ), president of the British Surfing Association and manager of the 1968 team in Puerto Rico.

GRINHAM, JUDITH BRENDA (1939-   ), the first British swimmer to win an Olympic title for 32 years and the first competitor to hold this crown and the British Empire and Commonwealth Games and European titles, and the world record at the same time. Her Olympic medal was for the 100 metres backstroke in Melbourne in 1956 and two years later she completed her gold medal hattrick in Cardiff and Budapest respectively.

GRONBERG, AXEL (*fl.* 1946-53), Swedish middleweight wrestler who excelled in the Graeco-Roman style. He won Olympic gold medals in 1948 and 1952, was second in the 1953 world championships, and won one European gold medal and one bronze. He also finished third in two European freestyle championships.

GROSSER PREIS VON BADEN, a horse race which is one of the most important international weight-for-age races in Germany. It takes place on the Iffezheim course at Baden-Baden early in September over 2,400 m. (1½ miles) and is the middle leg of the triple crown for older horses, the other two being the GROSSER PREIS VON NORDRHEIN-WESTFALEN at Düsseldorf in July, and the PREIS VON EUROPA at Cologne in October, both over a similar distance.

GROSSER PREIS VON NORDRHEIN-WESTFALEN, a horse race which is the first leg of the German triple crown for older horses on weight-for-age terms, run at Düsseldorf in July over 2,400 m. (1½ miles).

GROUT, ARTHUR THEODORE WALLACE (1927-68), cricketer for Australia and Queensland. Playing in his first Test at the age of 30, having been understudy to Tallon for many seasons, he went on to make 187 dismissals in 51 Test matches. Six times he took five or six wickets in an innings, and he provided an excellent foil to BENAUD and DAVIDSON, Australia's key bowlers from 1957 to 1963.

G.S. VARNAMO, Swedish walking club located midway between Göteborg and Stockholm. Led by J. LJUNGGREN, his brother V. Ljunggren, and Green, the club dominated Swedish RACE WALKING during the period 1948-60. The leading current performer, Ingvarsson, has been the most consistent Swedish walker during recent years.

GUDU, see GILLI DANDA.

GUERRITA (Rafael Guerra) (1862-1941), *matador de toros,* was regarded as a master *torero* from the time of his *alternativa* in 1887. He faced 2,547 bulls, none of which left the arena alive. He was the first matador to execute a pass sitting on the *estribo.* In 1895 he appeared in three *corridas* in one day.

GUGEN, OSCAR N. (1910-   ), underwater swimmer, founder chairman of the British Sub Aqua Club, 1953, and officer of the Confédération Mondiale des Activités Subaquatique (C.M.A.S.) (see UNDERWATER SWIMMING).

GUGGI, SERGE (1945-   ), Swiss inventor of the aquabob (1967).

GULLY, JOHN (1783-1863), British boxer; champion of the English prize ring in 1808. He was famous for his meteoric rise in society thanks largely to his BOXING ability and business sense. The son of a butcher, Gully was in a debtor's prison when he first made his name as a boxer. After retirement from the ring, he made a fortune in HORSE RACING, won the DERBY (three times), the OAKS, and the ST. LEGER, became a member of Parliament, and was presented at Court.

GURNEY, DAN (1931-   ), American sports car driver (see MOTOR RACING) who won three championship Grand Prix races before winning the 1967 Belgian Grand Prix in an Eagle, a car designed and built by his own firm. He won the 1958 and 1962 United States Auto Club road racing championships and was placed second in the 1968 and 1969 INDIANAPOLIS 500s and third in 1970. He won seven U.S.A.C. national championship races, all on road courses, and other successes include five Riverside 500-mile N.A.S.C.A.R. Grand National road races; the 1967 LE MANS 24 Hours with FOYT; and three CAN-AM Challenge Cup races. He retired as a racing driver in 1970 to concentrate on his own car design and construction firm.

GUTHRIE, JAMES (d. 1937), Scottish racing motor-cyclist. Very successful both in continental Grands Prix and in the Isle of Man TOURIST TROPHY, he spent much of his long riding career in the NORTON team (1928-9 and 1931-7). He died as a result of a crash at the last corner when leading the German Grand Prix of 1937.

GUTTMANN, BELA (1900-   ), Hungarian Association FOOTBALL coach and manager. An international centre half who played for M.Y.K. Budapest and Hakoah Vienna in the 1920s and 1930s, he afterwards became a successful manager in Italy (Milan), in Brazil (São Paulo), and, above all, in Portugal, where he directed the European Cupwinning teams of BENFICA in 1961 and 1962.

GUYON, JEAN-JACQUES (1932-   ) French three-day event (see EQUESTRIAN EVENTS) horseman and winner of the individual gold medal at the OLYMPIC GAMES in Mexico (1968). His first major success was in 1965 when he rode Mon Clos to win the French national three-day event championship.

GUY'S HOSPITAL R.F.C., the oldest RUGBY UNION football club in existence, dating from 1843. A founder member of the Rugby Football Union, 1871, it was the first club to win the HOSPITALS' CUP, introduced in 1875, and one of the earliest teams in England to formalize positions in the scrum.
HOME GROUND: Honor Oak Park, London.
COLOURS: Navy blue and gold jerseys, navy shorts.

GUZZI, or Moto Guzzi, Italian motor cycles prominent in racing since the foundation of the firm in 1921. Until 1957, their last year in international Grand Prix racing, Guzzi machines were generally among the fastest and invariably the most refined and yet unconventional in design.

GYARMATI, DEZSO (1927-   ), one of the world's greatest WATER POLO players, who won medals at five OLYMPIC GAMES — gold medals in 1952, 1956, and 1964, a silver in 1948, and a bronze, at the age of 33, in 1960. He was also a member of Hungary's European champion teams of 1954 and 1962. He could play as well with his right hand as with his left and at back as well as forward.

GYMNASTICS is one of the most graceful and artistic of sports and is popular all over the world, particularly in the Iron Curtain countries and Japan. The combination of strength, dexterity, and artistry makes it both an enthralling event in itself and an excellent training for other sports.

Competitions are graded to accommodate all levels of competitor from schools to internationals and the sport is practised by both sexes. Team events are staged in some international meetings like the world championships and OLYMPIC GAMES and also at a lower level. At local level, contests may consist of as few as one or two exercises — vaulting and agility being the most common — but at national and international level there are now six set exercises for men: floor exercises, vault, pommel-horse, parallel bars, horizontal bars, and rings; and four for women: floor exercises, vault, beam, and asymmetrical bars. In major events, medals are awarded for each individual exercise as well as for an over-all championship and team event. Competitors are awarded points by a team of four judges and there is also a referee.

Competitors must perform two sets of exercises on each apparatus — a compulsory (predetermined) set and a voluntary set (a routine of the competitor's own choice). The gymnast's score is obtained by averaging the two intermediate scores on the four cards, thus eliminating the highest and lowest marks. The contestant with the highest accumulated score is awarded the first place in the all-round individual category; the second highest is the second-placed competitor, and so on. The results of the team competition are obtained by aggregating the five highest scores of the six members of the group in each of the exercises. The first six competitors in an individual event participate in the finals for each apparatus and are registered with the average of the two initial scores (compulsory and voluntary). Each entrant then performs another voluntary exercise and scores afresh to determine the order for the individual apparatus. In the European championships however, in which, unlike the Olympic Games and world championships, there are no team championships and only voluntary competitions, three men and two women from each country compete in the six events. The judges select the six best men on each apparatus who then perform on the apparatus again and the total marks are aggregated to find the winner.

Judges display their marks simultaneously, awarding a maximum of ten. Penalties are incurred by faulty execution, lack of control, requiring assistance, falling from the apparatus, or exceeding time limits. The judges also take into consideration the difficulty of execution and the aesthetic appeal. Deductions

are made in tenths of a point. Judges work from the *Code de Pointage* — a book which is revised biennially and gives a mass of information for judges' guidance. All movements are given a rating of difficulty — A, B, or C — getting progressively harder. The 10·0-point voluntary exercise must have one exercise of C difficulty (two in the Olympics, world, and European championships) and four of B difficulty.

Many of the exercises consist of static positions requiring great strength linked by beautifully rhythmic movements. While certain of the exercises put a premium on power, others stress suppleness and subtle skill. Success in the six exercises for men and four for women requires that the gymnast develops a strong physique and all-round ability.

The FLOOR EXERCISES are usually the first of the events since they give competitors a chance to warm up with movements not requiring tremendous strength. They are probably the most picturesque of all the events but a comparatively new development in the sport. It was fashionable during the nineteenth century to stage massed floor exercises involving hundreds of thousands of performers in outdoor exhibitions. These were largely formal displays, but in the 1932 Olympics the individual event was first staged, women entering the event 20 years later. These competitions have given the sport some of its most memorable moments.

The mat on which the gymnasts compete is 12 m. (13 yds.) square and is placed inside an area 14 m. (15 yds.) square. The mat consists of a soft material 0·045 m. (1⅞ in.) thick. The large mat is comprised of 60 small mats, 2 m. (6 ft. 7 in.) by 1·20 m. (3 ft. 11¼ in.), which are linked together. During the 1960s a portable sprung floor, consisting of sections of thin ply-board with layers of sponge-rubber sandwiched between, was introduced.

Men perform for 70 seconds and women to a musical accompaniment for 90 seconds. Both aim to impress the judges with a sequence of blended leaps, spins, and balances, together with the elements of tumbling and acrobatics. Strength movements should be performed slowly and static positions must be held for at least two seconds. Somersaults should be done at shoulder height.

The VAULTING HORSE is also shared by both men and women. It is probably the simplest of all the events and outsiders have frequently won major international competitions. The horse consists of a leather-covered body similar to the pommel-horse, but without the pommels. For men its upper surface is 1·35 m. (4 ft. 5¼ in.) from the floor level. The horse is

Double handstand, horizontal bar

Rings

Single handstand, parallel bars

Vaulting horse

Floor exercise

GYMNASTICS EXERCISES FOR MEN

divided into three parts, one 0·40 m. (1 ft. 3¾ in.) long, the next 0·20 m. (8 in.), and the third 0·40 to 0·43 m. (1 ft. 3¾ in.–1 ft. 5 in.) long.

Men vault over the horse lengthways, passing first over the 'croup' and then the 'neck'. Women vault sideways, putting their hands on the middle of the horse which, at 1·10 m. (3 ft. 7¼ in.), is not as high as for men. Both men and women have a run-up of between 12·19 m. (40 ft.) and 18·29 m. (60 ft.). They take off with their feet together from a springboard,

1·20 m. (3 ft. 11¼ in.) by 0·60 m. (1 ft. 11¾ in.), which they may place at any distance from the horse. The competitor touches the horse and may twist or turn before landing in an upright position. Women are marked for how far they reach after touching the horse. Both sexes are also assessed on the difficulty of the movements they make during the leap and on the smoothness of the effort. Competitors must not stagger on landing.

The POMMEL-HORSE is an almost trapezoidal, leather-covered body on which only men compete since it requires great strength in the arms and shoulders. Its upper surface is 1·10 m. (3 ft. 7¼ in.) above the floor and measures 1·60 m. (5 ft. 3 in.) to 1·63 m. (5 ft. 4½ in.). It is 0·35 m. (1 ft. 1½ in.) thick. The pommels or handles are 0·12 m. (4¾ in.) high and 0·28 m. (11 in.) wide. They are centred along the upper surface of the horse 0·40 to 0·45 m. (1 ft. 3½ in.–1 ft. 5¾ in.) apart.

The event probably originated because of the need for soldiers to acquire the skills of horsemanship but JAHN developed it into what is now probably the most fascinating of all exercises for men. A competitor grasps the pommels, placing all his weight on them, and then begins a continuous swinging movement, passing one or both legs over the horse, executing forward and backward splits and preferably circular movements to the right and left with both legs. Competitors must swing their legs and not lift them. Even for single leg movements, legs should not be swung individually, one should be used to balance or assist the other. Hands may be placed on the horse as well as on the pommels. Outstanding competitors like CERAR are generally taller than most gymnasts and have long arms which help to keep their bodies further away from the horse while still maintaining balance.

The ALLOY RINGS is probably the exercise for which most strength is needed and it is practised only by men. The gymnast with short arms has a tremendous advantage since he can use his strength more easily, but in recent years the swinging skills introduced have given the event even more appeal. During his performance the competitor must hold static positions and execute two inverted positions—handstands—one based on strength and the other utilizing his momentum. The two rings hang from wire cables 0·50 m. (1 ft. 7¾ in.) apart. The cables and rings are joined by looped straps 0·70 m. (2 ft. 3½ in.) long and 0·035 m. (1¼ in.) wide. The inside diameter of the rings is 0·18 m. (7 in.). The overhead support which is rectangular is 5·50 m. (18 ft.) high and the rings hang at the most 2·50 m. (8 ft. 2½ in.) above floor level. The gymnast begins by leaping up to clutch the rings, one in each hand, and then performs his routine, concluding by landing on the floor with both legs together.

The PARALLEL BARS in their original form are used only by men. Jahn invented the apparatus when he discovered that German youth was lacking strength in the arms and for years athletes used them for 'pull-ups', 'dips', and 'press-ups'. But as the sport developed, skilled movements involving swinging were introduced. Skill is now more important than strength and usually the smaller gymnast with supple shoulders is ideal for the event. Probably the most important exercise is swinging from a hanging position through a somersault into the support position, as this is needed in any voluntary work. The gymnast is required to perform one movement in which both hands release the bars simultaneously and in C-difficulty routines he may perform movements such as going from a handstand between the bars and then resting again in another handstand. The bars are made of flexible wood and oval in cross section, 0·051 m. (2 in.) thick vertically and 0·041 m. (1½ in.) wide. They are 3·50 m. (11 ft. 5¾ in.) long, 0·42 m. (1 ft. 4½ in.) to 0·48 m. (1 ft. 7 in.) apart and 1·70 m. (5 ft. 7 in.) above the floor level. The supports of each bar are 2·30 m. (7 ft. 6½ in.) apart and are fastened to a heavy ground-plank.

Women use the ASYMMETRIC BARS as one of their four exercises and used to practise on parallel bars until just before the Second World War. Subsequently their programme was redesigned to cut out the more muscular exercises and a special piece of equipment — the asymmetric, sometimes known as the 'high and low bars' — was introduced. This has enabled women to bring an added aesthetic quality to the bars. The bars are still parallel and on the same plane but the upper bar is 2·30 m. (7 ft. 6½ in.) and the other is 1·50 m. (4 ft. 11 in.) above the ground. Emphasis is on the suspension and momentary bracing positions and the female gymnast must change bars by turning or executing elegant movements.

The HORIZONTAL or HIGH BAR produces probably the most exciting moments in gymnastics. Only men compete on it but women and children use it for training. The whirling actions and swinging movements have made it extremely popular. Here, any attempt to use strength will interfere with the rhythm of the movement. No held balances are required and any hesitation in the flow is penalized by the judges. The apparatus is mainly concerned with the full extension of the body and a firm hand-grip and gymnasts whose strength/weight ratio is lower than it should be can do well on the horizontal bars. A knowledge of mechanics is of help.

Jahn introduced the horizontal bar and originated a number of the exercises for it. At first a thick wooden bar was used but after a while steel became popular. Displays usually last between 15 and 30 seconds. The bar consists of a steel rod 2·40 m. (7 ft. 10½ in.) long and 0·028 m. (1⅛ in.) thick. It is mounted on posts 2·50 m. (8 ft. 2½ in.) above the ground.

The BALANCE BEAM is used only by women in competitions. It was originally envisaged as a method for women to demonstrate balance but in recent years many of the skills of the floor exercises have been introduced. Routines include spins, twists, held balances, sitting and prone exercises, steps, jumps, and turns, all grouped in rhythmic patterns. The exercises take place on a slightly rounded wooden beam 5 m. (16 ft. 4¾ in.) long and 0·10 m. (4 in.) wide. The beam is 0·16 m. (6¼ in.) thick. It is mounted on two adjustable supports and is set 1·20 m. (3 ft. 11¼ in.) above the floor level.

Training for the international events demands both tremendous mental concentration and also physical determination. Training largely involves repetition practice of the movements for competition, frequently under a coach. Some competitors use other sports like running and weight-training to increase their fitness but this is not widespread. But many female competitors use ballet, which is very close to many of the gymnastic movements.

Men wear wide long trousers with braces and white sleeveless vests; women are dressed in one-piece costumes. Both sexes wear very light slippers. For powerful, heavy movements men often use chalk to assist their grip and sometimes both sexes wear wrist-straps as the strain is considerable.

Although the different exercises require separate skills and various techniques, few leading competitors concentrate on one exercise. The aim is to bring performance on all the apparatus to the same level and in a two-hour session a competitor works on most of the pieces, although some gymnasts have a particular gift for certain movements. But the great gymnasts have always been amazingly uniform in their performances on the various apparatus and it is this amalgamation of all the physical skills that has made the sport so popular.

International Gymnastics Federation, *Code de Pointage* (reprinted bi-annually, two parts —one for men, the other for women).

The origin of gymnastics, one of the most graceful and picturesque of the Olympic sports, can be traced back to the ancient civilizations of China, Persia, India, and Greece. But as a modern competitive sport it has developed into its present form since the Second World War, with the introduction of the women's events and the staging of biennial world and European championships.

Although modern gymnastics was developed primarily in Germany, the most successful countries have been Russia, Japan, and Czechoslovakia. Towards the end of the 1960s, however, the wheel had turned full circle and the East Germans were becoming a major force in international events.

Most of the current competitive exercises may be attributed to the German, Jahn, but the ancient civilizations practised the sport. The Chinese had mass displays of free exercises, as they do at present, and both the Persians and the Indians followed a strict code of physical exercise. But it was the Greeks who really started to modernize the sport. Gymnastics derives from the word *gymnos* (naked) and the word 'gymnasium' originally meant a public place or building where the Greek youths exercised. The distinguished physician, Galen, provided some of the earliest literature on the sport and showed how knowledgeable the Greeks were about its fundamentals. Activities like rope-climbing were included in the ancient Olympic Games and, with the rise of the Roman Empire, the Greek method of physical culture spread.

Among the events the Romans introduced was the wooden horse on which they practised mounting and dismounting. Most of the exercises were used for military preparation, but when the ancient Olympic Games were abolished the sport fell into decline for nearly 1,500 years.

It was revived initially by men like Muth, Salzman, and Ling. Muth's book, *Gymnastics for Youth*, is the first major work on the subject, and Ling, a Swede, regulated a series of free exercises which a number of countries adopted. But the man who made the major contribution to the sport was Jahn. His invention of events like the parallel bars and the rings and his routines for the horizontal bars helped greatly with the modernization of gymnastics. There was a clash of views between Ling and Jahn, since the Swede felt that gymnastics was an educational system while Jahn viewed it as a club activity. Ling's movements were more rhythmic and fluent while Jahn gave more emphasis to strength movements.

Modern gymnastics is a mixture of both schools — the beauty of the floor exercises routines being balanced by the rugged power needed for the rings and parallel bars. But it is fair to say that Jahn was the more influential of the pair, for his Turnplatz, opened in Berlin in 1811, was an open-air gymnasium which started the spread of the sport throughout Europe. Clubs were founded in Britain and a number of schools included physical training in their curriculum. A major event in British gymnastics occurred in 1860 when the army selected 12 N.C.O.s and formed them into the Army Gymnastic Staff, later the Army Physical Training Corps. The Army, realizing after the Crimean War that soldiers needed to be fit, were in the forefront of the expansion of the sport in Britain. The leading clubs joined in 1890 to form the Amateur Gymnastic Association and the first championship was in 1896 — the year of the first modern Olympic Games.

Germany, predictably, dominated the first major international gymnastics competition, winning five gold medals. It took many years for the gymnastics events to settle down to their present programme. For example, eight years later there was a combined event of the horizontal bar, parallel bars, pommel-horse, 100 yards, LONG JUMP, and SHOT PUT — an interesting combination with ATHLETICS.

But the outstanding gymnast before the First World War was unquestionably the Italian, Braglia, who won the combined exercises gold medal at both the 1908 and 1912 Olympics. Tysall was the most successful British competitor, finishing second to Braglia at the 1908 Games. Unfortunately the reaction to war in Britain caused a decline in the sport, which was German-orientated. Despite the efforts of such fine coaches as Oberholzer of the Northern Polytechnic, gymnastics failed to make headway. There was also a curious lack of interest by physical education authorities, some of whom felt that gymnastics could overdevelop competitors' physiques. Some authorities even banned the teaching of apparatus gymnastics. The leading British competitor in this period was Whitford who won the national title every year from 1928 to 1939. At a time when Britain was so reactionary one bright spot was the start of the national women's championships.

Although women's international competitions were not staged in the big events, men's gymnastics continued to progress between the wars. Germany had regained leadership in the sport from Italy by the time the Olympics were staged in Berlin in 1936. Led by Schwarzmann, the over-all individual champion, they took the team title from Switzerland who were also a formidable force at the time. Among their star performers were Miesz, who was the combined exercises gold medallist in the 1928 Games, and Mack, runner-up to Schwarzmann eight years later.

Gymnastics became a true world-wide sport after the Second World War. The 1948 Olympics were still dominated by the western

European countries. The men's team championships went to Finland and Switzerland were highly placed in other events.

Basle was the venue for the first world championships in 1950 and Switzerland took seven of the eight men's titles. It was the last time that the western European countries were to dominate the sport. A hint of things to come was the result in the women's individual championships which were staged for the first time. Rakoczy (Poland), a slim, talented girl, took four gold medals including the over-all title.

The Russians arrived at the 1952 Olympics and transformed the sport. They brought with their immaculately prepared team one of the finest competitors in the history of the sport — CHUKHARIN — who was to be over-all champion in the 1952 Olympics, the 1954 world championships (shared with his compatriot, Muratov), and the 1956 Olympics. The Russian squad won five of the seven men's titles and four of the six women's events. The other two women's championships went to Hungarians — KELETI and Korondi. In the 1954 world championships in Rome the Japanese took two titles, including a win by the legendary IKEDA on the beam.

Two more brilliant Russian gymnasts made their Olympic début at Melbourne in 1956. Both of them — SHAKHLIN and LATYNINA — were to dominate the sport for the rest of the decade. Latynina just edged out Keleti for the gold medal in the women's combined exercises and also spear-headed Russia's victory in the team event. Shakhlin's artistry on the pommel-horse helped him to eighth place over-all and the event was won by Chukharin. But it was already clear that the Japanese would become a force to be reckoned with. Ono snatched the silver medal from Titov and finished only 0·05 points behind Chukharin.

Although the Japanese girls were placed surprisingly low, their style was appreciated by the audience and simply did not find favour with the judges. By now the need for artistry in the major international competitions was apparent and many of the Iron Curtain countries gave their outstanding competitors ballet lessons every week as part of their training. Latynina won all five events at the 1957 European championships and followed it up with five out of six gold medals at the 1958 world championships in Moscow. Shakhlin, competing in the same championships, swept to a record five out of eight possible titles for a male competitor.

Russia and Japan had a momentous meeting at the 1960 Olympics. Although Shakhlin took the over-all gold medal, the Japanese filled six of the first nine places — Ono again missing the individual gold medal by 0·05 of a point — and took the team event. The 42-year-old Takemoto was fifth over-all. But in the women's categories Latynina convincingly retained her title from the vivacious Muratova (the wife of the former world champion, Muratov) and the slender, graceful Astakhova. With another Russian girl, Nikolaeva, fourth, the team title went convincingly to the Soviet Union with Czechoslovakia just under 9 points behind.

There was a controversy on the asymmetrical bars when Ikeda introduced a back straddle to earn applause from the crowd but only fifth place from the judges. CASLAVSKA was a member of the Czechoslovak team that took the bronze medal in the team event. She was to gain the vault gold medal at the 1962 world championships in Prague and then take over the leadership of the sport from Latynina.

The Czechs, inspired by Bosakova, a 1956 Olympic silver medallist, were to mount a powerful challenge to the Russian domination. Bosakova herself won the beam at the 1962 world championships but Latynina clung to her combined-exercises title. In the men's events TITOV (Russia) captured the over-all championships but the Yugoslav, Cerar, was in magnificent form on both the parallel bars and pommel-horse, taking both gold medals.

The 1964 Olympics were held in Tokyo before a very knowledgeable crowd in the Metropolitan Stadium and the Japanese were in superb form. ENDO took the individual over-all gold medal and led the Japanese team to the team title 2·50 points ahead of the Russians who were weakened by a crucial injury to their champion, Kerdemilidi. Shakhlin, battling to retain his title, tied in second place with his compatriot Lisitsky and Tsurumi (Japan). Japan and Russia both profited from mistakes on the floor by Cerar, who had won the European title the year before, and by MENICHELLI (Italy) in the compulsory exercises. On the voluntary movements the latter outclassed everyone else and his innovative tumbling routine on the floor at last found favour with the judges to give him the title ahead of Lisitsky.

In the women's events, Latynina was supplanted as champion by the equally great Caslavska. But Russia just held on to the team title ahead of the Czechs. Caslavska collected three gold medals and missed a fourth, when she fell off the asymmetrical bars attempting a pirouette, and finished fifth. The Czech girl was even more successful a year later in the European championships in Sofia when she equalled Latynina's 1957 success by collecting five gold medals, a performance she repeated two years later in Amsterdam.

At the 1966 world championships Caslavska was nearly upset by the new Russian star, KUCHINSKAYA. Only 17 years old, Kuchinskaya gave Caslavska the keenest competition of her career and actually won three of the individual titles although Caslavska managed to win over-all by 0·201 of a point. The new Russian champion was Voronin who took the combined exercises gold medal, but once again Japan with up-and-coming performers like Nakayama, winner of the parallel bars and rings, and KATO, winner of the floor exercises, finished first in the team event.

By the 1968 Olympics Kato had overhauled Voronin to take the premier prize, and Japan's team was even more impressive. With Nakayama, the reigning Olympic champion Endo, and Kato in the team they almost doubled the gap between themselves and the Soviet Union. Cerar broke the Japan-Russia monopoly by winning the pommel-horse. Menichelli was hit by misfortune on the floor exercises. As he landed at the end of his routine he snapped his Achilles tendon and was carried, crying, to hospital.

If the men's events were dramatic the women's were even more so. It was more difficult for spectators to get tickets for the gymnastic events than any other in the Games and a packed audience watched enthralled as Caslavska retained her title. She selected the 'Mexican Hat Dance' for her floor routine and was cheered to the echo by the audience. She shook off the challenge of Voronina (wife of the men's silver medallist) and Kuchinskaya in an emotion-charged moment. Kuchinskaya fell off the asymmetric bars and lost her chance of upsetting Caslavska while Voronina, although extremely steady, lacked the flair of Caslavska who, before she returned to Europe, married Odlozil, the 1964 1,500 metres silver medallist, amid scenes of hysteria at the Cathedral in Xócalo Square, and then presented the Czech leaders with her four gold medals. It was the end of an outstandingly successful career that had brought her world-wide fame.

Britain's role in gymnastics since the war was reflected in their placings at Mexico. Wild was seventy-ninth and Miss Bell seventy-fourth. Despite the successes of Stuart in ear-lier Olympic Games and his appointment as national coach the lack of competitors in Britain continued to count against them.

By the 1970 world championships the rise of the East Germans was apparent. With Caslavska in retirement and Kuchinskaya seriously ill, a new era of women's gymnastics began. The East Germans took three titles but Russia, through TURITSCHEVA, won the individual over-all gold medal and the team event. For once an American was among the medals — the 17-year-old Miss RIGBY finished second on the beam. In the men's championships, the Japanese, Kenmotsu, fourth at Mexico, was a convincing winner, with his compatriot Nakayama taking three titles. Voronin slipped to fourth place, and Japan increased their lead at the head of the sport.

They maintained it at the Munich Olympics when they finished 7·20 points ahead of the Russians in the team event. They also supplied all the medallists in the combined exercises event. Kato was supreme again, taking the over-all title, the parallel bars, and finishing second in the pommel horse and horizontal bar.

But the men's events were overshadowed by the women's competition. Never before had the grace and skill of gymnasts received such a rapturous reception as in Munich. In particular Russia's 17-year-old Miss KORBUT entranced the crowd and television viewers. People glimpsed the beauty of the sport and immediately gymnastics became immensely popular, as throughout the world small girls sought to emulate Korbut.

Korbut picked up three gold medals but could only finish seventh over-all. The title was won by her compatriot Turitscheva whose more mature skills received recognition from the judges. She confirmed her position as the world's leading female gymnast by retaining her European title at Wembley, London, in 1973.

G. C. Kunzle, *Olympic Gymnastics Series*, vols. 1-4 (1956-64); N. Stuart, *Competitive Gymnastics* (1964).

GOVERNING BODY (WORLD): International Gymnastics Federation, Route de Bienne 22, 3250 Lyss, Switzerland.

H

HACKENSCHMIDT, GEORGE (1877-1968), Russian professional wrestler, strongman, and philosopher. Born in Estonia, his amazing strength was apparent by the age of 19 when he hoisted a milkman's horse on to his shoulders and carried it around. Two years later he won the world Graeco-Roman championship in Vienna, and in 1899 he was the Russian champion in both wrestling and weightlifting. The following year he turned professional, coming to England in 1902.

Managed by the shrewd Cochran, Hackenschmidt had to introduce showmanship into his performance because he was so much better than any of his rivals. He was the biggest draw in the sport's golden age and in 1904 took part in a famous fight with Madrali at Olympia. The Russian won in 44 seconds, hurling the Turk to the ground and dislocating his arm. Hackenschmidt, who had claimed the world title since 1902, gave further credence to his claim by beating the American champion, JENKINS. But the Russian lost the title to GOTCH in 1908 when he visited America. He also lost the return bout in 1911 and then retired.

He maintained his tremendous interest in physical fitness and, even at the age of 85, was able to do 50 consecutive jumps over the back of a chair. The philosophy expounded in one of his books, *Man and Cosmic Antagonism to Mind and Spirit*, influenced many sportsmen including the Australian ATHLETICS coach CERUTTY. Hackenschmidt became a naturalized Briton in 1950 and died in Dulwich (London) aged 90.

HAGEN, WALTER (1892-1969), American professional golfer; winner of four Open championships, two U.S. Open championships, five U.S. Professional Golfers Association championships, numerous lesser national titles, and more than 60 sponsored tournaments. Hagen's place in GOLF history is secure less for the titles he won by his dashing play than for his role as a popularizer of the game and a champion of the status of the professional golfer. Hagen was never consciously evangelistic in these matters but his flamboyant personality and brash confidence attracted large crowds for the numerous exhibition tours he undertook, frequently accompanied by Kirkwood, the Australian trick-shot specialist. He was the first of the showmen golfers, and his impact on the staid world of golf did much to promote the professional from the status of worthy artisan to popular hero. His influence on golf was recognized in 1967 when the Royal and Ancient made him an honorary member, a distinction accorded to only two other professionals, COTTON and LOCKE.

HÄGG, GUNDER (1918-), middle-distance runner for Sweden. Hägg was the pre-eminent name in distance running during and immediately after the Second World War. He broke 15 world records, 10 of them in the space of three months in 1942. An important feature of his career was his rivalry with another Swede, Andersson, and their joint attacks on the mile record. This they reduced from 4 min. 6·4 sec., WOODERSON's pre-war mark, to 4 min. 1·4 sec., made by Hägg in 1945, in a race in which he led Andersson from start to finish. This time remained the record until beaten by BANNISTER in 1954. Hägg also set world records of 3 min. 43·0 sec. for 1,500 metres, 5 min. 11·8 sec. for 2,000 metres, 8 min. 1·2 sec. for 3,000 metres, 8 min. 42·8 sec. for 2 miles, 13 min. 32·4 sec. for 3 miles, and 13 min. 58·2 sec. for 5,000 metres, a performance unmatched from 1942 until it was beaten by ZATOPEK in 1954. Hägg's being disqualified for professionalism prevented him from proving himself in major international competition.

HAGON, ALFRED JOSEPH (1931-), record-breaking motor-cyclist and leader of the British two-wheeled sprint movement (see MOTOR-CYCLE RACING). His supercharged 1260 cc. Hagon-JAP V Twin set a standing-start kilometre (1093·6 yds.) record of 116·903 m.p.h. (188 km./h.) — 19·135 seconds — at Elvington, Yorkshire, 16 October 1966.

HAIG, MARY GLEN, M.B.E. (1918-), British fencer who was Commonwealth individual women's champion in 1950 and 1954. She competed in four OLYMPIC GAMES, reaching the final in 1948 in London, and in the 1954 Monaco world championships came fourth. Also prominent as an administrator, she was president of the Ladies Amateur Fencing Union from 1964 to 1973, when she became the first woman president of the Amateur Fencing Association.

HAILWOOD, S. MICHAEL B. (1940-), English racing motor-cyclist. The winner of nine world championships in the 250, 350, and 500 cc. classes, he made his racing début at the age of 17 and soon demonstrated outstanding versatility, riding machines of all types and sizes with such proficiency that at the age of 20 he became the youngest works rider and in 1961 won his first world championship, the 250 cc., on a HONDA. Thereafter he rode for MV AGUSTA and Honda, but went into semi-retirement after 1967 to pursue a MOTOR RACING career.

HAINES, JACKSON (1840-79), American ice figure-skater from Chicago, the earliest prominent skater with a truly theatrical flair. Originally a professional dancer, with new ideas he developed a spectacular, revolutionary skating technique which shocked the more conventionally-minded during the mid-nineteenth century. After winning an American championship in New York, Haines went abroad in 1864 to astonish Europeans and instigate the Viennese 'school' of skating, which contributed much to the present-day international style. 'The American Skating King' is the inscription on his tomb at Gamla-Karleby, Finland.

As well as the international style, the early English style of skating derived from the movements of Haines, who originated the sit-spin and performed both on ice and on roller skates in the 1860s.

HAJOS, ALFRED (1878-1955), Hungarian swimmer who was the first Olympic champion. He won two out of a possible three gold medals at the Athens Games of 1896. Born Arnold Guttmann, his SWIMMING pseudonym eventually became his legal name. Twice a member of the Hungarian national soccer team (see FOOTBALL, ASSOCIATION), he won the silver medal for sport architecture at the 1924 Olympics, the gold medal not being awarded on this occasion.

HALAS, GEORGE STANLEY (1896-), American professional FOOTBALL player, coach, and owner, who played at the University of Illinois as end (1915-17), and in the Great Lakes Naval Training Station team of 1918 that went to the 1919 Rose Bowl. In 1920 the Halas-coached Decatur (Illinois) Staleys joined the NATIONAL FOOTBALL LEAGUE; they became the Chicago Staleys the following year and the CHICAGO BEARS in 1922. He continued to play end until 1932, while coaching, and has also owned the team since the 1920s. From the 1920s until the 1950s the Bears dominated professional football, first with the running attack built around GRANGE, NAGURSKI, and Feathers, and later, with the innovations of the T-formation, which was created about 1940 by Halas and the University of CHICAGO coach, Shaughnessy. The Bears' most famous victory was the 73-0 rout of the WASHINGTON REDSKINS in the professional football championship game of 1940. Halas gave up coaching after 1967 but continued to control the Bears' management.

HALASY, OLIVER (1909-46), a member of Hungary's gold medal WATER POLO teams at the 1932 and 1936 OLYMPIC GAMES, lost his left foot in a childhood accident, yet became the world's best half-back of the 1930s. He also won a silver at the 1928 Olympics and was in the winning team at the 1931, 1934, and 1938 European championships. Almost as good a swimmer as a polo player, he became the European 1,500 metres champion (see SWIMMING) in 1931 and won 25 individual Hungarian championships.

HALIBURTON, THOMAS BRUCE (1915-1975), Scottish professional golfer, RYDER CUP and WORLD CUP player, captain of the Professional Golfers Association in 1969. In 1952 at Worthing he had opening rounds of 61 and 65, equalling the world record of 126 for consecutive rounds in a professional tournament.

HALL, GARY (1951-), American swimmer whose exceptional talents, which earned him world records for backstroke and butterfly, also enabled him to make astonishing inroads into the world marks for the most difficult SWIMMING event of all, the individual medley. He improved the world record for the 400 metres medley by 12·4 sec. in just two years and one month between 1968 and 1970.

HALL, JIM (1935-), American creator, builder, and driver of the Chaparral sports/racing cars. He won the U.S. road racing championship in 1964 and the 1965 Sebring 12-hours with Sharp. After an accident in 1968, he limited his driving to TRANS-AM sedan (saloon) events. He originated stabilizing flippers, now modified to wings and was the first to use automatic transmission successfully in a racing-car.

HALL, WESLEY WINFIELD (1937-), cricketer for West Indies, Barbados, and Queensland. A dynamic fast bowler who had a long run-up and a spectacular action, he formed, with Griffith, the spearhead of the West Indies attack for several years. He took 192 Test wickets, and his strength was never better illustrated than at LORD'S in 1963, when he bowled 40 overs unrelieved. He performed the hat-trick against Pakistan, and nine times he dismissed at least half the opposition in an innings.

HALLEIN S.B.C., leading skibob club of Austria. For almost two decades the club dominated the sport in international competition with their members, E. and W. BRENTER.
COLOURS: Skibobbers on a blue horizon.

HALLENHOCKEY, see HOCKEY, INDOOR.

HAMBLEDON CRICKET CLUB. For around 30 years, until the early 1790s, Hambledon — a village near Portsmouth on the Hampshire downs — fielded the finest CRICKET team in England. Often it played against, and defeated, teams labelled 'All-England', and only the development and reorganization of the game in London from 1787, when the MARYLEBONE CRICKET CLUB was founded, brought about its decline.

The Hambledon era saw cricket outgrow its rustic origins to become a more ordered pastime. The enthusiasm of the players — drawn chiefly from Hampshire and Surrey — and the local pride in their deeds were vividly recorded by JOHN NYREN in *The Cricketers of My Time*, a book which provides an invaluable record of the early Hambledon 'cracks' who played against all comers on BROADHALFPENNY DOWN: Richard Nyren (John's father, who kept the Bat and Ball inn overlooking the ground), SMALL, Sueter, Lear, Brett, Taylor, and Aburrow.

Later the Club played on WINDMILL DOWN, and the new generation of players included Noah Mann, Aylward, Tom and Harry Walker, BELDHAM, DAVID HARRIS, and John Small, jr.

The club, which had owed much to the early guidance of Powlett and to the generalship of Richard Nyren (who was secretary throughout its greatest years), came close to dissolution around 1770, but a victory by one run over Surrey inspired a revival, and not until 1793 did Hambledon play its last recorded match.

HAMBURGER S.V. (Sport Verein), Association FOOTBALL club, Hamburg. Founded in 1887, they were German champions in the seasons ending 1923, 1928, and 1960. In the European Champion Clubs Cup they reached the semi-final in 1961, and in two appearances in the European Cup-Winners Cup reached the quarter-final in 1964 and the final in 1968 when they were beaten by A.C. MILAN. Leading players include Posipal, SEELER, C. Doerfel, and B. Doerfel.
COLOURS: White shirts, red shorts.

HAMID, Lt. Col. ABDUL (1927-), was one of two Pakistani HOCKEY players to take part in four consecutive OLYMPIC GAMES (1948, 1952, 1956, 1960). He captained Pakistan's Olympic gold medal-winning side of 1960 and their successful ASIAN GAMES team of 1958. Later coach and manager of the Pakistan national team, 'Hamidi' was a brilliant inside right.

HAMILTON TIGER-CATS, Canadian professional FOOTBALL team, have been a member of the Eastern 'Big Four' since its inception in 1907. As Hamilton Tigers they won the Grey Cup (see FOOTBALL, CANADIAN) five times before 1930, as well as in 1932 and 1943. In 1947 the Tigers left the Interprovincial Rugby Union and were replaced by the Hamilton Wild Cats; in 1950 the two teams were combined as the Tiger-Cats. They have had a highly successful record since then, winning Eastern Football Conference titles 14 times and the Grey Cup four times (1953, 1963, 1965, 1972). Sazio coached them from 1963 to 1967. The end Coffey holds the all-time record for pass receptions.
COLOURS: Gold, black, and white.

HAMMER, a standard field event for men on the programme of all major ATHLETICS championships; performances are eligible for recognition as records by the International Amateur Athletic Federation (see ATHLETICS, TRACK AND FIELD).

Throwing the sledge-hammer was an amusement enjoyed by Englishmen in the sixteenth century and it was most probably developed long before that time, as was SHOT-putting, in the Scottish HIGHLAND GAMES. The modern hammer is an iron or brass sphere suspended from a spring-steel wire handle and grip, 3 ft. 11¾ in. (1·213 m.) in length and weighing 16 lb. (7·26 kg.) over all. The hammer is thrown with both hands from within the limits of a circle 7 ft. (2·134 m.) in diameter. A competitor is allowed six trials and the distance thrown is measured from the landing point to the circumference of the circle. The thrower stands at the rear of the circle with his back in the direction of throwing. He grips the handle with both hands, a glove being worn on the hand closest to the grip. Two preliminary swings are made with the hammer rotating around the stationary thrower's body. The high point of each swing is behind the thrower and the low point in front. He then describes three full turns while swinging the hammer and moving across the circle. The delivery is a sweeping movement starting from the high point of the final turn, through the final low point, the hammer being released over the thrower's shoulder.

HAMMOND, WALTER REGINALD (1903-65), cricketer for England and Gloucestershire. Third-ranking in the number of centuries (167) he made, he was perhaps the best all-rounder the game has known: a commanding batsman, a penetrative fast-medium bowler, and a superb slip fielder (who took a record 78 catches in 1928). In 85 Tests he made 22 centuries, seven of them 200 or more, the highest score being 336 not out against New Zealand. In 1928-9 he made 905 runs in nine innings against Australia, and at the end of his career, during which he led England in six Test series, his aggregate of 7,249 runs was ahead of all others, including that of his contemporary and rival, BRADMAN (whose average was higher). Although an early audacity of style was modified, his batting remained a stirring sight until his retirement at the age of 43.

HANDBALL is a no-contact game, played either out of doors (field handball) by two opposing teams of 11 a side or indoors by teams of 7 a side or 5 a side (adapted to a smaller court). It is played with one or two hands by catching, interpassing, and throwing the ball. The aim is to score, i.e. to throw the ball into the goal. The ball is a round inflated leather ball, weight 15 to 17 oz. (425–480 g.), circumference 23 to 24 in. (58–60 cm.), about the size of a No. 3 Association football. In the 11-a-side version the goal is an exact replica of the Association FOOTBALL goal, i.e. two wooden goal posts and a connecting crossbar. The goal posts measure 8 ft. (2·4 m.) in height, the crossbar 8 yds. (7·3 m.) in length, both being inside measurements. The woodwork is 5 in. (12·7 cm.) in cross-section. The side of the goal facing the field is painted in alternating light and dark segments, zebra-stripe fashion.

In indoor handball the goals measure 6 ft. 6 in. (2 m.) in height and 10 ft. (3 m.) in width, measurements similar to those of a HOCKEY goal. The woodwork must be 3 in. (7·6 cm.) in cross-section.

The playing field for field handball is similar to that of soccer, the indoor version requiring a much more limited playing area.

A match is started from the centre point, the ball being passed with short or long throws

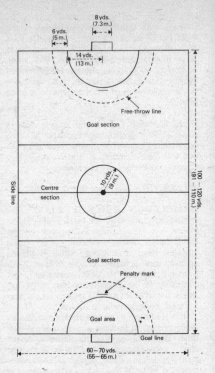

FIELD HANDBALL PITCH (11-A-SIDE)

from one player of a team to the other, and in this way attacks are built up which culminate in attempts at scoring. Various techniques of throwing at goal can be learned, such as lob, shoulder throw (like putting the shot), falling throw, diving throw. These shots must be executed from outside the goal area, marked by a semicircle drawn 14 yds. (13 m.) from the centre of the goal line in field handball and 19 ft. 8 in. (6 m.) in indoor handball. Only the goalkeeper is allowed to be and to move freely in this area, with or without the ball. A goal is scored if the ball has travelled (in the air or on the ground) completely over the goal line between the posts.

An attack can be halted by interception and the defending team can in its turn attempt to mount an attack. This often begins when the goalkeeper, after parrying a shot at goal, makes a 'throw-off', for which he may go close to the line of the goal area. During this throw the players whose attack was stopped have to remain outside the free-throw line, which is marked by a broken line 6 yds. (5 m.) away from and parallel to the line of the goal

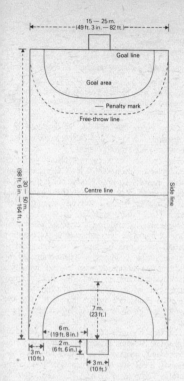

15 — 25 m.
(49 ft. 3 in. — 82 ft.)

Goal line

Goal area

— Penalty mark

Free-throw line

30 — 50 m.
(98 ft. 6 in. — 164 ft.)

Centre line

Side line

7 m.
(23 ft.)

6 m.
(19 ft. 8 in.)

2 m.
(6 ft. 6 in.)

3 m.
(10 ft.)

3 m.
(10 ft.)

INDOOR HANDBALL COURT (7-A-SIDE)

bounced with two hands, no more bouncing is allowed, and it has to be passed or shot at goal within the permitted three seconds. Bouncing with two hands repeatedly is allowed in 11-a-side (field) handball. Passing or throwing with two hands is always allowed, in both versions of the game, but is never as effective, as quick, as faultlessly on the target as the one-handed action. A player is not permitted to step, jump, or fall into the goal area with the ball in his hand. Yet he may do so, if skilled enough, the moment the ball is clear of his hand. This applies only to overstepping the goal-area line during an attempt at throwing for goal; a spectacular diving technique often gives the player momentum sufficient to reach more than a yard (1 m.) over and inside the goal-area line before falling down.

As handball is a no-contact game there are many faulty ways of approaching an opponent. While a pass or shot may be intercepted with two hands or head or body (touching once only), a player may attempt to dispossess an opponent with one open hand only. Grabbing, hooking, hugging, tripping, or tackling in any way is forbidden. Carrying or playing the ball in such a way as to endanger an opponent is an infringement of the rules of clean play and is penalized by the referee.

Indiscipline on the field or court of play or bad behaviour towards the referee is also punished, as a first offence, by a free throw. If there is a repetition, or if the offence was grave enough, heavier punishment follows. If a player commits a flagrant foul or exhibits gross indiscipline, he can be punished by temporary exclusion or, if such behaviour is repeated, may be sent off for the remainder of the match. If a defending player, for the obvious purpose of preventing a goal, steps into the goal area or commits a major foul or misconduct, even remote from his own team's goal, the opposing team is awarded a penalty throw. This is executed by a direct throw taken from the penalty mark — a short line 3 ft. (·914 m.) from the goal area.

The game is conducted by two referees, stationed in the respective halves of the court, who keep moving with the excursions of the ball, commanding the playing field and complementing each other in the control of the game. Their function is to start the game, to supervise the way it is played, and to interrupt it upon evidence of infringements and award free throws or penalty throws for these. Such interruptions, however, must not interfere with the smooth flow of the game. Too many delaying manoeuvres by players and too frequent use of the whistle by the referee tend to retard play. On the other hand, the attractive

area in the large field, and 10 ft. (3 m.) in the small court. This line is so called because players of the attacking team, having been awarded a free throw, must stand outside it, facing the goal. A free throw is awarded for various infringements of the rules, which, for ease of recognition, can be classified as (1) faulty handling of the ball; (2) faulty movement with the ball; (3) a faulty approach to an opponent; and (4) a faulty attitude to the referee. For example, a player is allowed to hold the ball for three seconds only, and must then pass it on or throw for goal. Once the ball has been touched by the hand or any part of the body above the knee, it may not be touched again unless it bounces back from the ground or the goal or returns from another player. The ball may be passed in any direction and even rolled along the ground. Players are allowed to hit the oncoming ball with the fist, but not to throw it up and fist it away.

A player holding the ball may take not more than three steps, and must then either pass it or bounce it with one hand; this can be repeated many times. Once the ball has been caught or

flow of the game is sustained by the referee's use of the advantage rule, and by the skilful application of modern ball-playing techniques resulting from research and experience.

The dominant motto of handball is 'play the ball, not the man'. Thus any intentional move by a player which leads to direct body contact or may lead to injury is forbidden. Vigil is kept continuously to prevent even unintentional clashes. Statistics show that the injury rate in handball is one of the lowest in team games in which players intermix, run, jump, catch, and throw.

In three fundamental respects handball differs from its great cousin, Association football: (a) there is no offside rule; (b) the ball may not be played back into the goal area or to the goalkeeper, nor is any player allowed to retrieve the ball while it is lying or rolling inside the goal area: there is a penalty award for either of these actions; and (c) no goal-mouth mêlée or scramble is possible as no player is allowed inside the area. To prevent a situation similar to a mêlée from arising, the 'overcrowding' rule is applied in 11-a-side handball: in either goal section of the field not more than six players of any team are allowed at any time. Infringement of this rule is brought to the referee's notice by a flag signal from one of the linesmen (goal linesman, side linesman).

In many matches, especially championship and international matches of 7-a-side handball, a timekeeper announces half-time and full-time by means of a gong, bell, or buzzer; he also acts as secretary and registers in writing all important events during the game, goals, penalties, exclusions — virtually an official report on the match.

In the course of a 7-a-side handball game, substitutes are allowed at any time during the game, which is normally of two half-hour periods. Substitutes are not allowed in 11-a-side handball except in international games. Women and youths play for two 20- or two 15-minute periods and the same applies to many tournaments — even three 10-minute periods have been successfully adopted.

Handbook of the British Handball Association (1970); *Handbook of the International Handball Federation* (3-yearly issue, German, French, and English editions); *International Handball Federation Manual* (1971).

Handball or handball-like games were played all over the world in antiquity. The game is mentioned in the *Odyssey* (cf. Carl Diem, 'Weltgeschichte des Sports'). The Urania game of the ancient Greeks is thus described:

And Alkinoes called upon bold Halies alone
  to dance with Laodamas, for none dare venture
with them.

They took at once in their hands the lovely ball
  which Polybos, with cunning art, had wove from
purple wool.
One cast this up to heaven to reach the sparkling
clouds,
  and caught it nimbly, ere his foot touched ground
again.

And after they had tried to toss the ball on high,
  danced light as air upon the all-nourishing earth,
  in position often changed.

A scene from this episode is depicted in a tombstone carving found in the town walls of Athens in 1926, dated c. 600 B.C.

Handball as it is played today was first introduced in about 1890 by a German gymnastics master, Konrad Koch, but it did not at once become popular. After the First World War, however, interest revived, when the Germans, Hirschman and Dr. Schelenz, were instrumental in creating a popular interest in handball again. It was adapted to Association football rules and became a regular sport in schools, clubs, colleges, and universities. One of the rules adopted from soccer was that which demanded an 'offside' line running across the width of the field, but, as this proved a hindrance rather than a help to the flow of the game, it was scrapped after some years.

The first countries to play modern handball were those of West Europe. Handball was first represented, among other games, on an international level by the International Amateur Athletic Federation (I.A.A.F.) (see ATHLETICS, TRACK AND FIELD), but in 1928 the International Amateur Handball Federation (I.A.H.F.), comprising 11 member nations, was founded in Amsterdam. Its first president was BRUNDAGE, a member and later president of the INTERNATIONAL OLYMPIC COMMITTEE. During the 1928 OLYMPIC GAMES a demonstration handball match was played and in 1931 the International Olympic Committee decided to include handball in the Olympic programme. By 1934 25 nations were affiliated to the I.A.H.F. After the Second World War international matches were played again and in 1946, in Copenhagen, the present International Handball Federation (I.H.F.) was formed.

Today handball is played by more than 50 nations all over the globe. In Great Britain it is a relatively young game, first played in an organized way in Hull and district. In 1957 the first British handball club was formed. In the early years only field handball was played. Since 1967 the game in Great Britain has been put on a national basis by the British Handball Association, with headquarters in Liverpool. The game is also played in British Commonwealth countries.

The International Handball Federation, which has its secretariat, council, and technical committee at its headquarters in Basle, is a member of the Federation of International Sports Associations, and is the governing body for all national associations, comprising clubs, schools, colleges, universities. It regulates local, regional, and national championships, and is responsible for the organization of international tournaments, cup competitions (such as the European Cup, the Baltic Cup, the Mediterranean Cup, the Latin Cup, the Asian Cup, and the World Cup), and the Olympic tournament.

Of late, handball has undergone a change. Until 1952 field handball (11-a-side) was the prevailing version, indoor handball (7-a-side) being played almost exclusively in Scandinavia. Since then, however, the indoor version has gained more adherents, so that the position nowadays is reversed: 7-a-side handball is played all over the globe, the 11-a-side game only in central Europe, where the 7-a-side version is also played. Outdoor handball requires a large playing field, a large team, and a suitable climate, whereas indoor handball can be played any time irrespective of season or weather conditions. The 7-a-side game may, of course, be played out of doors, on a suitable surface, and, in fact, this is done in a number of places.

In recent years, thanks to the introduction of the two-referee system, the unlimited substitution of players, and a shrewd interpretation of the rules of attack, tactical moves and techniques have been evolved which have made handball an extremely fast game. The switch from defence to attack and vice versa is practically instantaneous, resulting in a high pace of play second only to that of ice hockey. That applies only to the type of game produced by a highly trained, superbly coached team of international standard. Young players and women are not expected to play at such a pace, but they have none the less developed an elegant and fluid type of game. Handball has quickly become popular among the active sporting population all over the inhabited world. Its recognition as a world game was emphasized by inclusion in the programme of the Olympic Games.

Handball has been an amateur game from its beginning.

Bulletin of the International Olympic Committee, No. 94 (1966); Karl Diem, *Weltgeschichte des Sports* (1933); Hans Geilenberg, *Das Handballspiel in Feld und Halle*, 4th ed. (1970); B. J. Rowland, *Handball, a Complete Guide* (1970); L. M. Seewald, *International Handball Rules* (1957-1961); *International Handball Federation*, monthly, in English, French, and German.

GOVERNING BODY (WORLD): International Handball Federation, 22 Gundeldingerrain, Basle, Switzerland.

HANDBALL, Irish. The Irish version of handball is very closely related to Spanish PELOTA and English FIVES. The game is played in a four-walled court or alley 60 ft. (18.3 m.) long by 30 ft. (9.14 m.) wide. The front wall is 30 ft. (9.14 m.) high, while the height of the back wall must be at least 9 ft. (2.7 m.). For international championships the court is much smaller, 40 ft. by 20 ft. (12.2 m. × 6.1 m.) with the front wall 20 ft. (6.1 m.) high and the back wall a minimum of 12 ft. (3.66 m.). The walls are usually of smooth cement, but glass back and side walls, which allow for a greater number of spectators, are coming into general use, while maple floors are replacing concrete.

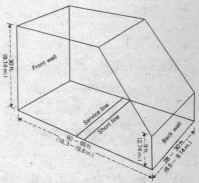

IRISH HANDBALL COURT
Dimensions shown are those standard for Irish competitions; the court for international competitions is smaller.

Matches are between two players (singles) or four players (doubles). Each game is won by the first player to score 21 aces, or points, and a match is decided over a rubber of three or five games.

Before commencing a game, the players toss a coin to decide first service. The server bounces the ball, from between the 'short' and 'service' lines, off the front wall. If the receiver, who may take the ball either on the volley or first bounce, fails to get it back to the front wall before it again touches the ground, an ace is credited to the server. Similarly, if the server fails to return the ball after it has been played off the front wall by the receiver, a 'hand out' results, and the receiver takes over as server. In doubles, players on each team serve alternately.

Fast rallies are a feature in handball, but the

most spectacular skill is the ability to hit the ball hard and low almost off the very base of the front wall so that it comes back along the ground and cannot be retrieved. This tactic is known as the 'butt'.

In Ireland, two different types of ball are used, each producing a very different game. Soft-ball is played with a rubber ball and is easily the more popular. Hard-ball is a far faster game, since the ball, which is much smaller, is made of hard rubber covered with goatskin. The hard ball, popularly known as the 'alley-cracker', is more difficult to control and return, and calls for greater speed, strength, and stamina. Hard-ball games are not played outside Ireland.

Although the wearing of a soft glove, or leather band, is permitted, most players prefer to use the bare hand. Kicking the ball is not allowed, nor is the use of both hands to scoop up the ball.

The game has been hampered in the past by the lack of full-scale facilities through the country. The provision of more covered-in alleys, plus the revival in recent years of the world championship, has, however, done much to restore handball to its old-time popularity in Ireland.

Handball was originally played against any blank wall or gable-end, but the game soon progressed to three-wall and four-wall alleys. From the middle of the nineteenth century, Irish emigrants took the game with them across the Atlantic, where it attained tremendous popularity. There, Casey, who had become a prominent figure on the New York Stock Exchange, not only won the handball championship of the U.S.A., but built his own alley, the first with a boarded floor and a back wall of glass, the renowned 'Casey's Court' in Brooklyn.

Casey, who claimed the world title from the early 1880s, was eventually challenged by the Irish champion, Lawlor, an American-born Dubliner. Casey was by this time 45 years old and in the twilight of a great career, but he accepted a match of 21 games for the world title, with side bets of £500 per man. The first ten games were played in Cork in August 1887. Lawlor, the younger man, was firm favourite, but could only lead by six games to four in that opening leg. When the second leg took place in Brooklyn in the following November, Casey, on his own court, did not concede a single game. Casey did not again defend his title, and though there were subsequent claimants and contenders, there was never again as widely acknowledged a world champion until modern times. By the start of the twentieth century the world title had lapsed and was not revived for more than sixty years.

Although the GAELIC ATHLETIC ASSOCIATION (G.A.A.), founded in 1884 to encourage native Irish pastimes, included handball in its programme, there was an obvious difficulty. The G.A.A. was a strictly amateur body, while handball, at top level, was semi-professional, with considerable sums in side-bets being wagered by or on behalf of the players. Not until 1924 was an Irish Amateur Handball Association set up under G.A.A. auspices. This body, which has since become the Handball Council of the G.A.A., has organized All-Ireland championships in both the hard-ball and soft-ball versions of the game since 1925.

Meanwhile there had been spasmodic but unsuccessful attempts to revive international competition. Eventually a World Handball Council was set up and the first world championships, to be played every three years, were organized. The inaugural series was staged in New York in 1964. Jacobs (U.S.A.) won the singles title while the United States pair, Sloan and Elbert, won the doubles. Five countries — the U.S.A., Canada, Ireland, Australia, and Mexico — competed.

The 1967 world championships went to Toronto and there the Irishman, Maher, then resident in Canada, won the singles while the Osbert brothers retained the doubles title for the U.S.A. Dublin was the venue of the 1970 series which provided a major surprise. The holder, Maher, who had meantime returned home, was beaten in the singles final by Kirby who regained the title for the U.S.A. The Irish pair, Buggy and Lyng, easily won the doubles.

Gaelic Athletic Association, *Official Guide,* latest edition; R. Doherty, *Handball* (1970).

GOVERNING BODY (WORLD): World Handball Council, 12 Goatstown Road, Goatstown, Dublin 14, Eire.

HANIF MOHAMMAD (1934-   ), cricketer for Pakistan and Karachi. Making his first-class début at 16, he established an unrivalled reputation for patience and dourness. His batting records include the highest innings — 499 for Karachi against Bahawalpur in 1957-8 — and the longest — 337 in 999 minutes for Pakistan against West Indies a year later. During his long Test career he briefly captained Pakistan.

HANNA, Bombing Officer PAT, see BATINTON.

HANSEN, JOHN (1924-   ), Association footballer for Frem (Copenhagen), JUVENTUS, and Denmark for whom he played well at outside left in the 1948 Olympics football tournament. Like many other good Scandinavian players of the time and since, he was then persuaded to abandon the amateur game for a professional career.

He signed for the Turin club, Juventus, and played with them from 1949 to 1954, during which time, in addition to having the accepted skills of a winger, Hansen showed himself to be a splendid header of the ball.

HANUT SINGH, RAO RAJA (1900-   ), Indian POLO player who became famous as No. 1 of the Jodhpur team which beat the Patiala side in the Duke of York's Cup, at Delhi in 1921. He later captained and organized the unbeaten Jaipur team which won the Indian championship from 1932 to 1938. With three younger players he won the English championship in 1964 and 1965. Handicap 9.

HAPGOOD, EDRIS (1907-73), Association footballer for ARSENAL and England, both of whom he captained for many seasons with dignity and distinction. He was only 19 when Arsenal signed him in 1926 and accelerated his development to one of the finest left backs in the history of English football. He had a sound positional sense and was a skilled ball player who fitted perfectly into the Arsenal team that dominated English football in the 1930s and with whom he won five League championship medals, and appeared in three F.A. Cup finals. He made his first appearance for England against Italy in Rome in May 1933 and missed only one of England's next eight matches. In November 1934 he was made captain for the match at Highbury against the world champions, Italy. He played in 22 of England's next 31 matches until his last appearance against Yugoslavia in Belgrade in May 1939.

HARBIG, RUDOLF (1913-44), middle-distance runner for Germany. Harbig accomplished one of the most remarkable running records in ATHLETICS history when he set a world record for 800 metres of 1 min. 46·6 sec. in 1939. This reduced the previous record, held by WOODERSON, by 1·8 sec., the largest single improvement in the history of the event. Moreover it resisted the attacks of all comers, including WHITFIELD, until 1955. In 1939 also Harbig set a world 400 metres record of 46·0 sec. and in 1941 added the world record for the non-championship distance of 1,000 metres in 2 min. 21·5 sec. In 1938 he won gold medals in the European championship 800 metres and 4 × 400 metres relay.

HARDMO, VERNER (1917-   ), race

walker for Sweden. He had 22 performances between 3 km. and 10 miles ratified as world records in the period from 1942 to 1945. His clashes with the Czech, Balsan, during the war years produced exceptionally fast times but both are suspected of not complying with the definition. Hardmo was disqualified from the European 10 km. in 1946 and finished last in the Olympic 10 km. in 1948. None of the distances at which Hardmo set his records are now officially recognized but he still holds the best recorded time for several of them although these are not taken seriously in view of his dubious progression.

HARDY, SAMUEL (b. 1883), Association footballer for Chesterfield, LIVERPOOL, ASTON VILLA, Nottingham Forest, and England for whom he kept goal on 21 occasions, including 'Victory' international matches. He played first in the Second Division for Chesterfield but was transferred in 1905 to Liverpool and seven years later to Aston Villa. He resumed playing after the First World War and was a member of Villa's 1920 F.A. Cup-winning side.

HARE AND HOUNDS, a form of CROSS-COUNTRY foot race which became popular in English public schools in the eighteenth century. One or two runners, known as the hares, are given a short start and the rest, known as hounds, set out to overtake them within the distance appointed for the race. Hare and Hounds is still run by schools but it has never been a championship sport in the formal sense. Many athletic clubs, called Harriers, owe their names to this sport. (See also PAPER-CHASING.)

HARLEM GLOBETROTTERS, an American all-black professional BASKETBALL troupe. They were formed by SAPERSTEIN in 1927, and included three members of the Savoy Five, a semi-professional team in Chicago coached by Saperstein, which had dissolved earlier that year. The team toured the U.S.A. playing in exhibition and demonstration matches. Later, set routines were added and the team became world-famous both for their pure skill and for their amusing performances. They adopted a version of 'Sweet Georgia Brown' as their signature tune and were the subject of two full-length feature films.

The Globetrotters completed their first playing trip round the world in 1952. They hold numerous attendance records and have made several appearances behind the Iron Curtain. The team has included a number of famous Negro players, perhaps the best-known being CHAMBERLAIN, Tatum, Harrison, and Lemon.

COLOURS: Blue vests with red and white stars, red and white striped shorts, and red, white, and blue hooped stockings, embodying the 'Stars and Stripes'.

HARLEQUIN F.C., RUGBY UNION football club formed in 1866, one of eight surviving founder members of the Rugby Football Union. Its most influential period came during the so-called STOOP Era, approximately 1906-14, when highly successful half-back and three-quarter moves were developed; in 1910 the club was installed at the R.F.U. headquarters, TWICKENHAM (where it still plays home matches in the earlier part of the season); and in 1911 the side selected by England against Wales showed A. D. Stoop at outside half and a complete Harlequin three-quarter line of Lambert, Birkett, POULTON, and F. M. Stoop. Other Harlequin internationals include WAKEFIELD, Gracie, Marques, Currie, Bartlett, and Hiller.

HOME GROUND: Stoop Memorial ground, Twickenham.

COLOURS: Jerseys with harlequin squares of light blue, magenta, chocolate, and French grey, and sleeves of light green and black; white shorts.

HARMSWORTH CUP, see POWERBOAT RACING.

HARNESS-RACING, see TROTTING.

HARRIOTT, JUAN CARLOS (1939-   ), Argentinian POLO player and one of the world's best ever. His team, Coronel Suarez, won the Argentine championship for several years consecutively, and he captained the Argentine team to defeat the U.S.A. in the Cup of the Americas in 1966 and 1969. Handicap 10.

HARRIS, DAVID (c. 1755-1803), cricketer who played chiefly for HAMBLEDON. He was the pre-eminent bowler for 20 years to 1798 until crippled by gout. Bowling fast underarm, he gained an unprecedentedly high proportion of his wickets through catches.

HARRIS, ERIC (1911-   ), Australian RUGBY LEAGUE player. He joined LEEDS from Toowoomba, Queensland, in 1930 and was the outstanding winger in England before the Second World War. Tall and long-legged, with a fine acceleration, he scored 391 tries in 383 appearances for Leeds.

HARRIS, REGINALD HARGREAVES (1920-   ), track cyclist. The most successful British sprinter since BAILEY, he won the world amateur sprint championship in 1947, and although not fully recovered after breaking an arm, took silver medals in the sprint and tandem events of the 1948 OLYMPIC GAMES. Turning professional, he became world sprint champion in that class in the three years 1949-51 and again in 1954. Two of his world records still stood in 1973, both for the 1-km. (1,093·61 yds.) professional unpaced standing start: on an outdoor track in Milan, 1952, he recorded 1 min. 8·6 sec.; indoors at Oerlikon, 1957, 1 min. 8·0 sec.

HARRISON, HENRY COLDEN (c. 1836-1926), an originator of Australian Rules FOOTBALL, he formed the Melbourne Football Club in 1858 with W. J. Hammersley, J. B. Thompson, and T. W. Wills, and became known as the 'father of Australian football'.

HARROW WANDERERS, see CRICKET.

HART TROPHY, ICE HOCKEY trophy, awarded annually in the NATIONAL HOCKEY LEAGUE of North America to 'the player adjudged to be the most valuable to his team'. The original trophy was presented in 1924 by David A. Hart, father of Cecil Hart, who had coached MONTREAL CANADIENS for many years. The trophy was replaced by the Hart Memorial Trophy in 1959. Each winner receives $1,000 and is elected in a poll of sports writers and broadcasters. In 1963, G. HOWE of DETROIT RED WINGS won it for a record sixth time in a period spanning 13 seasons.

HART-DYKE, Sir WILLIAM (1842-1932), British amateur RACKETS player and world rackets champion 1862-3. He became the first amateur to win this championship when he defeated Erwood at Woolwich and Prince's Club in 1862.

HARTONO KURNIAWAN, RUDY (1949-   ), Indonesian BADMINTON player. After first representing Indonesia in the THOMAS CUP of 1967 he was regarded as the world's leading singles player. He first competed in the ALL-ENGLAND CHAMPIONSHIPS in 1968 and won the title six years running. He has also acquired a high reputation at men's doubles and was undoubtedly largely responsible for Indonesia's regaining the Thomas Cup in 1970.

HARVARD UNIVERSITY, American college FOOTBALL team, nicknamed the 'Crimson', began its famous rivalry with YALE in the 1870s but only gained its first notable victory

over them in 1890. Around the turn of the century Harvard had great teams — national champions in 1898 and 1901. The star kicker of this period, Haughton, become Harvard coach and ushered in the school's 'golden era' from 1908 to 1915. National champions in 1910, 1912, and 1913, Harvard suffered only one defeat between 1911 and 1915. Among its leading players were the back Mahan, the guard Hardwick, and the tackle Fish.
COLOURS: Crimson.

HARVARD–YALE BOAT RACE, the annual ROWING competition between the two major American universities, the oldest intercollegiate event in the U.S.A., inaugurated in 1852 and antedating American FOOTBALL by 17 years.

Originally for eights, from 1859 to 1875 the race was rowed between six-oared boats but eights were reintroduced in 1876. Since 1878 the course has been, with few exceptions, over a 4 mile (6·4 km.) stretch of the Thames River at New London, Connecticut. The race at one time attracted a following comparable with that of the Oxford and Cambridge BOAT RACE in England, but the increase of other university rowing events gradually reduced this, and it is now primarily a race between traditional rivals, rather than the major event of the academic rowing season which it once was.

Since the Second World War, Harvard have had the lion's share of wins and dominated the 1960s, but both universities have at times produced some outstanding crews. Yale crews have twice won the Olympic eights and Harvard are the only American club to win the Grand Challenge Cup at HENLEY more than once, having won four times between 1914 and 1959.

In 1869, a Harvard four was defeated by OXFORD in a race from Putney to Mortlake, and in 1906 the Harvard eight, who had beaten Yale after six years of defeats, challenged CAMBRIDGE, who had beaten Oxford, but they were again beaten on the Thames tideway by two lengths. Both Yale and Harvard were defeated during the visit to the U.S.A. by the Cambridge crew in 1951.

HARVEY, DOUGLAS (1924-   ), ICE HOCKEY player for MONTREAL CANADIENS from 1948 to 1961, ending his career with a brief spell for NEW YORK RANGERS. A cool, subtle defenceman who made 432 assists in 1,043 games, he won the JAMES NORRIS TROPHY as outstanding defenceman for seven of the first nine years it was awarded.

HARVEY, HARRY (Jack) (1907-   ), greyhound trainer for WEMBLEY STADIUM. He won the GREYHOUND DERBY in 1934 with Davesland and again in 1959 with MILE BUSH PRIDE. He trained the winners of eight greyhound classic races in a career spanning 40 years.

HARVEY, ROBERT NEIL, M.B.E. (1928-   ), cricketer for Australia, Victoria, and New South Wales. Left-handed, small, and nimble, he played more often for Australia (79 times) than any other, making 112 in his first innings against England in 1948, and 6,194 runs in all Test CRICKET (with 21 centuries, 8 of them against South Africa). He often batted well on faulty pitches, and his fielding, developed at BASEBALL, was exceptional.

HARVEY, THOMAS ANDREW (1933-   ), lawn BOWLS player who represented South Africa in the inaugural world championships at KYEEMAGH, N.S.W., in 1966 and at Worthing in 1972, and won several South African championship titles including the singles in 1970. Harvey is a member of a remarkable family since he, his father, and his grandfather all represented South Africa in either the world championships or the British Empire and COMMONWEALTH GAMES.

HASHIM KHAN (1916-   ), Pakistani SQUASH RACKETS player. He won the All-India professional championship in Bombay in 1944. On his first visit to England he beat Mahmoud Kerim, winner of the Open championship for the previous four years, in the final and retained the title for seven out of eight subsequent years. Hashim also won the British professional championship five times, and, in addition, captured the Australian and U.S.A. Open championships. He won his last Open championship at the age of 41, easily the oldest player ever to do so. He is chiefly remembered for his phenomenal speed about the court. In 1960 he became professional to the Uptown Athletic Club, Detroit, U.S.A. In 1967 he wrote, with R. E. Randall, *Squash Rackets, The Khan Game.*

HASHMAN, Mrs. G. C. K. (*née* Judith M. Devlin) (1935-   ), international BADMINTON player for the U.S.A. and England. The daughter of J. F. DEVLIN, she won the ALL-ENGLAND singles championship ten times between 1954 and 1967 and was probably the finest woman player in the history of the game. With her elder sister, Mrs. Peard, she won the women's doubles six times. She learned her game in the U.S.A. and played for that country when it won all of the first three contests for the UBER CUP. She was 12 times singles champion, and 12 times doubles champion of the U.S.A. from 1956 to 1969, but in 1971 began to play for England where she lived from 1960.

HASS, Dr. HANS, Austrian underwater explorer who made expeditions to the West Indies, the Red Sea, the Galapagos, and Australia. He made a series of underwater television films featuring his wife, Lotte, and his books include: *Diving to Adventure, Under the Red Sea, Men and Sharks, We Come from the Sea, I Photographed Under the Seven Seas, Expedition into the Unknown,* and *To Unplumbed Depths.*

HASSETT, ARTHUR LINDSAY, M.B.E. (1913-   ), cricketer for Australia and Victoria. Short and slight, he led the Australian Services side in 1945, having played in four Tests in 1938. He went on to captain Australia in 24 of his 43 Test matches, his shrewd leadership and disciplined batting proving of much value after the retirement of BRADMAN. Upon his own retirement his total of 59 centuries in first-class CRICKET was second only to that of Bradman.

HATFIELD, JOHN GATENBY (1893-1965), British swimmer who won 40 Amateur Swimming Association titles during an amazing 20-year career from 1912 to 1931. His last win, at the age of 38, was the long-distance championship, swum over a 5-mile course (8 km.) on the river Thames. Silver medallist behind Canada's Hodgson in the 1912 Olympic 400 and 1,500 metres, he was still able to come fifth and fourth respectively in these events at the OLYMPIC GAMES in Paris 12 years later.

HAWAIIAN GAMES, a now defunct festival of sport embracing the eight inhabited islands of the United States territory (now the fiftieth state) of Hawaii. Records discovered in 1778 show that for at least three months of every year the population's energy was diverted from war, and even from work, to celebrations in honour of the god of sports, Louoi-ka-Makahiki. There were competitions in more than 100 games, few of them seen anywhere else in the world.

They included spear-throwing, racing by somersaults and cartwheels, and WRESTLING of many kinds — from catch-as-catch-can to index-finger wrestling and wrestling on stilts. Water sports, understandably, were the most prolific and the most important. Surfboard riding (see SURFING) had classes both for commoners, riding the short *alaia*, and kings, on the massive *olo*.

The arrival in Hawaii of American Calvinist missionaries in 1821 brought the gradual suppression of the Games and of most traditional sports, which were believed to have pagan derivation and certainly led to excited gambling. Even surfboard riding was forbidden, but was revived in the early years of the twentieth century and subsequently spread round the shores of the world.

HAWICK R.F.C., founded 1873, is probably the earliest RUGBY UNION football club on the Scottish borders, and certainly the first in Scotland to play a touring side: the 1888-9 Maoris, to whom they lost by a goal to a try. Its most distinguished international is MCLEOD.
GROUND: Mansfield Park.
COLOURS: Green.

HAWKE, Lord, see CRICKET.

HAWLEY, Sir JOSEPH, Bt. (1814-75) was a prominent English race-horse owner. The 'lucky baronet' won the DERBY four times, with Teddington, Beadsman, Musjid, and Blue Gown.

HAWTHORN, JOHN MICHAEL (1929-58), British MOTOR RACING driver who started his career with a pre-war Riley. In 1952 he graduated to a COOPER-Bristol Formula Two car in which, after a successful début at the Easter GOODWOOD MOTOR CIRCUIT meeting, he settled down to serious racing. He finished fourth in the Belgian race, third in the British Grand Prix, and fourth in the Dutch Grand Prix. Ferrari was impressed by Hawthorn's driving and gave him a trial in the Modena Grand Prix at the end of the 1952 season. Although Hawthorn crashed in practice, Ferrari went ahead and signed him for 1953. Ferrari's decision was soon justified, for not only did Hawthorn finish second at Pau and win the *Daily Express* Trophy and Ulster Trophy but he beat FANGIO in the French Grand Prix by a matter of feet. Hawthorn remained with FERRARI in 1954, and although the Italian cars were largely outclassed by MERCEDES, he came second in the British and Italian races and won the Spanish Grand Prix at the end of the season. He took third place in the drivers' championship.

He was anxious to drive a British car and contracted to drive the Vanwall in 1955. Unfortunately it became clear that the car was insufficiently developed, and in mid-season he returned to the Ferrari team; he achieved no success, however, in the face of the Mercedes opposition. For 1955-6 Hawthorn was a member of the Jaguar team in sports car races, and he co-drove with Bueb a D-type to a hollow victory in the disastrous 1955 LE MANS race.

In 1957 with the Lancia-based V-8 cars he could manage no better than third in the British Grand Prix and second in the German. With the new V-6 Dino of 1958 he won the drivers' championship — with 42 points against Moss's 41. In sports car racing during these years he set a new lap record at Le Mans and took second place with Musso in the Venezuelan Grand Prix in 1957; in 1958 he was second with Collins in the NURBURGRING 1000 km. race. At the end of 1958 Hawthorn retired from racing but was killed shortly afterwards in a road accident.

HAWTHORNE, PHILIP FRANCIS (1944-   ), RUGBY UNION stand-off half for Australia in the 1960s. He first played for Australia at the age of 18 against the ALL-BLACKS in New Zealand in 1962 and, with CATCHPOLE, formed one of the most efficient half-back partnerships in the history of international Rugby. He dropped three goals against England at Twickenham in 1967.

HAXEY HOOD, a derivative of the rule-less FOOTBALL popular in the eighteenth and nineteenth centuries. The 'hood', a bale or ball of rope encased in leather, was thrown into the air by a designated 'chief of the Boggons'. The rules were announced in doggerel by the 'fool':

'Hoose agen hoose, toone agen toone,
If tho meets a man, knock 'im doone
But don't 'ut him.'

Other Boggons, garbed like their leader in red caps and jerkins, were stationed round the field to prevent anyone from taking the hood from the field if they could. Whoever did manage to take the hood out would carry it to his village where he was welcomed by the landlord of the local inn. The next day the Boggons went from village to village and 'smoked the fool' by means of a rope over the branch of a tree and a fire of straw. The fool collected money from the onlookers in his cap. This ritual dates from a sacrifice to fertilize the fields. (See FOLK SPORTS.)

HAY, CHARLES (1930-   ), Scottish curler. He and his rink, Bryden, Glen, and Howie, won the world CURLING championship for Scotland in 1967, and have won many other honours.

HAYDOCK, A. KATHLEEN (1911-   ), LACROSSE player for England from 1935 to 1949. She is probably the only player who has been selected to play for England first as goalkeeper for several seasons and subsequently as first home. She was the vice-captain of the 1949 touring team to the U.S.A. and manager of the Great Britain and Ireland team which toured the States in 1954.

HAYDON, ADRIAN ARTHUR (1911-   ), an English left-handed attacking TABLE TENNIS player with a unique grip which obliged him to play almost every stroke (except the drop) as a heavily spun loop or drive, often with side-spin. He enjoyed an exceptionally long career, reaching the semi-final in the world championship men's singles at his second attempt in 1929 after beating BARNA, and the semi-final of the men's doubles, with Barna, in 1952 and 1953. In 41 years of Birmingham League play, Haydon lost only two matches. A sales manager in later life, and an all-round sportsman (he played CRICKET, LAWN TENNIS, GOLF, and BOWLS), he captained the English team to its only SWAYTHLING CUP win in 1953. His daughter Adrianne Shirley (Ann) (see HAYDON, A. S.) also was a left-handed table tennis player, but with an orthodox lawn tennis style grip. Her mother, Doris Haydon (née Jordan), was also a table tennis international, and her grandfather, Adrian's father, champion of Wales in the early 1900s.

HAYDON, ADRIANNE SHIRLEY (Ann) (later Mrs. P. F. Jones) (1938-   ), British LAWN TENNIS and TABLE TENNIS player. The daughter of A. A. HAYDON, she was capped for England at 15 — a year younger than her father — and in the following four years reached the final of the world table tennis championship five times before deciding to concentrate on lawn tennis. A shrewd and tenacious competitor, she was one of the best clay court players of her generation, winning the French title in 1961 and 1966 and the Italian title in 1966, but for a long time it seemed that the great grass court prizes would elude her. She was a finalist at FOREST HILLS in 1961 and 1967 and between 1958 and 1968 she reached the quarter-finals at WIMBLEDON nine times, failing in the 1967 final against Mrs. KING. In 1969, however, after a spell as a professional, she won the title, defeating Mrs. COURT in the semi-finals and Mrs. King in the final. She also won the mixed doubles with STOLLE. Her WIGHTMAN CUP career began in 1957 and she played 32 rubbers, more than any other British player.

HAYES, ROBERT LEE (1942-   ), sprinter for the U.S.A. Regarded by many authorities as the fastest runner in track history up to his retirement, Hayes first equalled the world 100 yards record at 9·3 sec. when he was only 18, in 1961. A year later he improved to 9·2 sec. and in 1963 became the first man to clock 9·1. The same season he equalled the world records for 200 metres and 220 yards on a turn, both in 20·5 sec. His fastest burst of speed is considered to have been in a relay in 1963 when he was estimated to have exceeded 26 m.p.h. In the Olympic 100 metres final in 1964, Hayes not only equalled the world record with 10·0 sec., verified by photo-finish timing, but won by a clear 2 metres, the easiest victory in this event in Olympic history. After 1964 he returned to his first sport, American FOOTBALL, as a professional for the DALLAS COWBOYS.

HAYNES, JOHN (1934-   ), Association footballer for Fulham and England, both of whom he captained. A stockily-built inside forward, he joined Fulham straight from school and stayed with the club until his retirement at the end of the 1970-1 season after playing 598 League matches. A goal-scorer as well as goal-maker in his early seasons, he played a deeper game in his best years, collecting more than winning the ball in midfield and making the best use of the exceptional accuracy of his passing. He made the first of his 56 appearances for England in 1954 and the last in a world championship match against Brazil in 1962.

HAYWARD, THOMAS WALTER (1871-1939), cricketer for England and Surrey. One of the steadiest and most prolific batsmen in CRICKET history, he passed 1,000 runs in 20 consecutive seasons, including a record aggregate of 3,518 in 1906 (since exceeded only by COMPTON and W. J. EDRICH). He and HOBBS were an extremely successful opening pair for Surrey, and made 40 stands of 100 or more for the first wicket. He was the first batsman to emulate GRACE in making 100 centuries, and he played 35 times for England. Early in his career he was a useful medium-paced bowler.

HEADINGLEY, Leeds, is the headquarters both of the Yorkshire County Cricket Club and of the Leeds Rugby League Club. Two playing areas, separated by a huge stand, house the respective sports. It is within easy reach of the centre of Leeds, and since 1963 the administrative offices of the CRICKET club — formerly in Leeds itself — have been situated at the ground. The turf is excellent, and Test cricket has been staged there regularly since 1899; the record crowd for any cricket match in England was 158,000 during the five days of the 1948 Test against Australia. Though large crowds

are common, there is little covered accommodation for spectators. The pavilion gives a view from third man, and the players' dressing-rooms and balconies — above the club offices — are square to the wicket. The Sutcliffe Gates honour one of Yorkshire's greatest batsmen. The RUGBY LEAGUE pitch has an under-soil electric heating system to combat frosty weather, and the main stand, which seats 4,000 spectators, is the largest in the league. There is cover for an additional 11,000 standing spectators. The ground has been used regularly for Rugby League Tests since 1908, as well as for other important games. There was an attendance of 40,175 for a league match against Bradford Northern on 21 May 1947.

HEADLEY, GEORGE ALPHONSO, M.B.E. (1909-   ), cricketer for West Indies and Jamaica. Born in Panama, he was indisputably the finest West Indian batsman before the Second World War, usually going in at No. 3 in poor batting sides. Eight of his ten Test centuries were against England, with 270 not out the highest; he scored a century in each innings of a match on two occasions.

HEART OF MIDLOTHIAN F.C., Association FOOTBALL club, Edinburgh. The club, the second one formed in Edinburgh and the oldest surviving one, was founded in 1873 and was an original member of the Scottish League when it was formed in 1890. Hearts, as the club is familiarly known, has never been relegated and won the League championship in 1894-5, 1896-7, 1957-8, and 1959-60; the Scottish Cup in 1891, 1896, 1901, 1906, and 1956; and the Scottish League Cup in 1954-5, 1958-9, 1959-60, and 1962-3. Outstanding players have included C. Thomson, Buick, R. Walker, Massie, McCulloch, T. Walker, and Mackay.

COLOURS: Maroon shirts and white shorts.
GROUND: Tynecastle Park, Edinburgh.

HEATHCOAT-AMORY, Lady (*née* Joyce Wethered) (1901-   ), English amateur golfer, acknowledged as one of the finest woman players of all time, Miss Wethered was British champion four times, English champion five times, and winner of numerous lesser events. An English and British international, she is the sister of Roger Wethered.

HEATLY, PETER (1924-   ), diver for Great Britain, Scotland, and Portobello A.S.C., was the Scottish DIVING champion and an international representative every year between 1937 and 1958. A self-taught diver, he won COMMONWEALTH GAMES gold medals for Scotland in 1950 (high diving), 1954 (springboard), and 1958 (high diving). He has served in Commonwealth Games team management, and was a diving judge at the OLYMPIC GAMES of 1964 and 1968. He is also on the International Committee of the European Swimming League (L.E.N.) and the Fédération Internationale de Natation Amateur (F.I.N.A.).

HEENAN, JOHN (1835-73), American boxer, generally regarded as champion of his country when he came to Britain in 1860 and fought a 42-rounds draw with SAYERS for the first international match to be given wide coverage by the British and American press. After the retirement of Sayers, Heenan again fought in America, in 1863, but was beaten by King.

HEFFELFINGER, WILLIAM WALTER (Pudge) (1867-1954), American college FOOT-BALL player, three times a member of the All-America football team at YALE (1889-91), he was the first guard to pull out of the line to lead interference to block ahead of the ball-carrier sweeping wide around the end of the line (a common requirement for football guards ever since). Starting in 1892, he briefly coached at the University of California. At the age of 45 he appeared in an all-star team against the Yale team and at 65 played creditably in a charity game.

HELVETIA CUP, see BADMINTON.

HEMERY, DAVID PETER (1944-   ), hurdler for Great Britain. Hemery won the Olympic 400 metres hurdles in 1968 in the world record time of 48.1 sec., an improvement of 0.7 sec. on the previous record. Both this and his winning margin of about 7 metres were feats almost without parallel in any race of sprint distance in Olympic history. In 1969 he reduced the United Kingdom record for the 110 metres hurdles to 13.6 sec. and won a silver medal for this event in the EUROPEAN CHAMPIONSHIPS. In 1970 he successfully defended his 1966 title in the 120 yards hurdles at the COMMONWEALTH GAMES. Defending his Olympic title at Munich in 1972, Hemery finished third and was also a member of the British team which won silver medals in the 4 × 400 metres relay.

HEMMINGS, FRED, jr. (c. 1947-   ), Hawaiian surfer who came first in the world championships in Puerto Rico in 1968.

HENDREN, ELIAS HENRY (Patsy) (1889-1962), cricketer for England and Mid-

dlesex. Short, strong, and a robust hooker of the ball, he made more centuries (170) than any other batsman except HOBBS, and only Hobbs and WOOLLEY made more than his 57,611 runs. A much better player after the age of 30, he made seven Test centuries and played his last Test at the age of 46. He was popular wherever he played, particularly in the West Indies, where he scored a record 1,765 runs in the 1929-30 tour. In his younger days he was an Association footballer for Brentford.

HENIE, SONJA (1912-69), ice figure-skater for Norway. If the present popularity of ICE SKATING is due to any one person, it must be Miss Henie. The first WINTER OLYMPIC GAMES at Chamonix in 1924 were the scene of her international début, as Norwegian champion at the remarkable age of 11. She finished last of eight in the women's figure-skating, but was gold medallist at each of the next three Winter Olympics, 1928, 1932, and 1936, and won ten consecutive world championships, 1927-36. She also gained six successive European titles, 1931-6.

With an instinctive flair for showmanship, Miss Henie caught on early to the idea of ending a spin with a distinctive jerk or toss of the head, which she found not only dramatically effective but substantially helpful in recharging the whirling mind. She introduced the shorter skirt and also set a new fashion in a more theatrical style of performance. Her wide repertoire of fast spins and spectacular jumps was combined with an appealing personality and she amassed a fortune after turning professional in 1936.

In that year Miss Henie greatly increased the public awareness of her sport in the first full-length skating film, *One in a Million.* She subsequently starred in nine other films and toured the world with lavish ice revues. Her early unsophisticated charm, chubby, dimpled smile, attractive flaxen hair, and petite physique (she was only 5 ft. 2 in. — 1.57 m. — tall) combined with rare skating skill to become a unique box-office attraction.

She suffered from leukaemia for the last nine months of her life, dying in a plane *en route* from Paris to Oslo, to be treated by Norwegian specialists, at the age of 57.

HENLEY ROYAL REGATTA, the oldest ROWING regatta in Europe and the most famous in the world, inaugurated in 1839 at Henley-on-Thames as a direct result of the interest aroused locally by the first Oxford and Cambridge BOAT RACE which took place at Henley in 1829.

The Henley course has changed four times.

The Old Course (1839-85) was 1 mile 550 yds. (2·1 km.) long, starting on the Berkshire side of Temple Island and finishing near Henley Bridge. The· New Course (1886-1922) reduced the number of crews in each race from three to two and started on the Buckinghamshire side of Temple Island and finished at a point short of the present finish. The course was boomed to prevent pleasure craft straying on to it but contained two slight bends. In 1923 the start was again moved to the Berkshire side and an experimental straight course was tried, but it was somewhat shorter. However, this was so successful that some ground was removed near the start and in 1924 the present straight course of the ·original length was introduced. There is no reason for the curious course-length except that this was the longest stretch available when the regatta was inaugurated in 1839.

The main event for eights is the Grand Challenge Cup (1839) and the lesser event is the Thames Cup (1868). The Ladies' Plate (1845) is restricted to eights from universities, colleges, and schools, while the Princess Elizabeth Cup (1946) is for school eights only.

The events for coxswainless fours are the Stewards' Challenge Cup (1841), the premier event, the Wyfold Cup (1847), and the Visitors' Cup (1847). The last two events have the same qualifications as the Thames Cup and the Ladies' Plate respectively. There are also two events for coxed fours: the Prince Philip Cup (1963), which is open ·to any crew, and the Britannia Cup (1969), the only event at the regatta for British crews only.

There is one event for coxswainless pairs, the Silver Goblets and Nickalls Challenge Cup. This was inaugurated in 1845 and the Goblets introduced as challenge prizes in 1850. In 1895 the Nickalls Challenge Cup was presented to mark the successes in the event of the NICKALLS brothers, Guy and Vivian.

The sculling events are the Diamond Sculls (1844) and the Double Sculls (1939). The Diamonds are probably the most coveted sculling trophy in the world.

Foreign crews compete regularly at the regatta, which takes place over four days in the first week in July. The first foreign winner of a Henley trophy was a Dutch sculler, Ooms, in 1892, while the Amsterdam University club, Nereus, were first overseas winners of both the Thames Cup (1895) and the Ladies' Plate (1969). The Grand went abroad for the first time in 1906, the Goblets in 1903, the Stewards' in 1910.

HERBERGER, SEPP (1897-   ), German Association FOOTBALL coach and manager. Previously a good average professional footballer, he became the German international team manager shortly before the 1938 World Cup and retained the position for a quarter of a century. In 1954 his shrewdly deployed West German team won the 1954 World Cup in Switzerland; he also had charge of their team in Chile four years later.

HERD, ALEXANDER (Sandy), (1868-1944), Scottish professional golfer who won the 1902 Open championship at the time when the rubber-cored ball was just being introduced. In this match most of the field remained faithful to the guttie, as Herd himself fully intended. He changed his mind after a last-minute practice with the rubber ball. He was the author of *My Golfing Life.*

HERMAN, PETE (1896-1973), American boxer who won the world bantamweight title in 1917 and again in 1921. He knocked out Britain's WILDE, whom he out-weighed by more than 20 lb. (9 kg.), in 1921 but was forced to retire from BOXING when he became blind the following year. Herman was one of the best bantamweight champions.

HERNE HILL STADIUM, outdoor cycle track in south London. First laid down in the 1890s, it measures 502 yds. (459·02 m.), with shallow banking and an asphalt surface. Its major international meeting is traditionally held on Good Friday. The field inside the track was used by LONDON WELSH R.F.C. for home matches during most of the period 1919-56.

HEROD (1748-81), a race-horse bred by the Duke of Cumberland, who, together with ECLIPSE and MATCHEM, founded one of the only three sire lines from which all thoroughbreds are descended.

HERRERA, HELENIO (1916-   ), Association FOOTBALL coach and manager. He was brought up in Casablanca, whither his family emigrated from Buenos Aires. He became a professional footballer and later a coach in France, and then moved to Spain and established his reputation with BARCELONA in the early 1960s. Thence he joined INTERNAZIONALE of Milan, who twice won the European Cup and the world club title under him. He blended flamboyance with a disciplinary-tactical approach to the game. In 1968 he became manager of Roma at a reputed salary of 100 million lire a year.

HERSEY, ALISON, LACROSSE player for the U.S.A. 11 times as a second home or centre. She was captain of the United States team which toured in Great Britain in 1964 and of the 1969 team which combined with the British Pioneers on a tour to Australia. She has also represented her country at field HOCKEY and is an expert skier.

HEY, VICTOR (1913-), Australian RUGBY LEAGUE player. A last-minute choice for the 1933-4 team to tour England, he quickly established himself among the greatest stand-off halves, weighing nearly 14 st. (88·9 kg.), but light on his feet. In 1937, however, he signed for LEEDS, moving to Dewsbury in 1944. After a short spell with HUNSLET, he returned to Australia to become coach of the 1950 and 1954 Australian international teams.

HIBBS, HARRY E. (*fl.* 1929-36), Association footballer for Birmingham City, and England for whom he made the first of his 25 appearances in goal in November 1929 and his last in October 1936 — in each case playing against Wales. Hibbs was shorter than most goalkeepers but had a good eye and a cool head, safe hands, and a fine positional sense.

HIBERNIAN F.C., Association FOOTBALL club, Edinburgh. The club was formed by Irishmen in Edinburgh in 1875, won the Scottish Cup in 1887, and became an original member of the Second Division of the Scottish League in 1893. The club joined the First Division in 1895 and, except for two seasons in the 1930s, have played there ever since, winning the League championship in 1902-3, 1947-8, 1950-1, and 1951-2; the Scottish Cup for the second time in 1902; and the League Cup for the first time in 1973. Hibernian was the only British club to play in the first competition for the European Champion Clubs Cup in 1955-6. Outstanding players have included Rennie, Harper, Dunn, G. Smith, R. Johnstone, Baker, and Reilly.

COLOURS: Green shirts with white trimmings, white shorts.

GROUND: Easter Road Park, Edinburgh.

HICKS, HUMPHREY OSMOND (1904-), the dominant figure in English CROQUET after the Second World War, might well have occupied the same position in the 1930s had not illness prevented his playing regularly. Playing side stance, with an unorthodox grip, he was noted for the extreme accuracy of his shots, particularly of long rushes. Between 1932 and 1966 he won seven open championships, nine men's, seven open doubles, four mixed doubles, and the President's Cup six times. He also won the open doubles championship of New Zealand in 1951 and played for England in the MACROBERTSON trophy in 1950, 1956, and 1963.

HIDEGKUTI, NANDOR (1922-), Association footballer for Voros Lobogo (Red Banner), the Budapest club now known as M.T.K., and Hungary, for whom he played as a centre forward in the great team of the early 1950s. The first successful exponent of the 'deep-lying' centre forward style of play, he scored three of Hungary's goals in their 6-3 win against England at WEMBLEY in November 1953, and played for Hungary in both the 1954 and 1958 world championships.

HIDEN, RUDI (d. 1973), Association footballer for Wiener A.C. (Vienna), the Racing Club de Paris, and Austria for whom he kept goal in May 1930 when England were held to a goalless draw in Vienna. He was a member of Austria's *Wunderteam* that was beaten only twice in 27 international matches played between May 1931 and May 1934. Later he played for Racing Club de Paris, and had some experience of Soviet football.

HIGGINS, HENRY (1943-), *matador de toros.* In taking the *alternativa* in Fuengirola on 20 September 1970, he became the first Englishman to do so.

HIGH JUMP, a standard field event on the programme of all major ATHLETICS championships for men and women, also one of the events in the DECATHLON and the PENTATHLON. Performances in the high jump are eligible for recognition as records by the International Amateur Athletic Federation (see ATHLETICS, TRACK AND FIELD).

High jumping was probably an activity of ancient Greek Olympic athletes several hundred years B.C. though the event did not feature in competitions. African tribesmen have engaged in high-jumping competitions whose origin is of unknown antiquity. The first organized high-jump competitions date from the middle of the nineteenth century in England. Jumpers compete by clearing a bar suspended between upright posts which is raised according to prescribed increments. Failure to clear a height in three attempts means elimination from the contest. The last jumper to be eliminated is the winner. The jumper lands on an air bed, a large inflatable cushion used also in the POLE VAULT.

In 1958 the I.A.A.F. introduced a rule forbidding the wearing of a built-up shoe to give further leverage on the take-off. The specification lays down that the thickness of the shoe heel shall not exceed that of the sole by more than 0·50 in. (13 mm.), which is also the thickness prescribed for the sole. The rules of the I.A.A.F. also lay down that the jumper shall take off from one foot, but methods of jumping are otherwise not prescribed. There have been four main styles: the scissors, the eastern cut-off, the western roll, and the 'straddle'. The first three are virtually obsolete. In the straddle style of jumping, the athlete takes off from the foot nearest to the bar, and swings his other foot up and over the bar, crossing the bar stomach downwards in a draped position. At the 1968 Olympics FOSBURY won a gold medal with his head-first, face-upwards technique, known as the 'Fosbury flop', and this method was to supersede the straddle as the most popular high-jump technique for men and women.

HIGHFLYER (1774), a race-horse who, like ECLIPSE and Flying Childers, was unbeaten on the race-course, winning all his 12 races. He was owned by Tattersall, founder of the firm of thoroughbred auctioneers (see TATTERSALLS), and later became a notable stallion at stud.

HIGHGATE DIVING CLUB, London, founded in 1928. Members of the club have represented Great Britain in many OLYMPIC, European, and COMMONWEALTH GAMES. For many years it fought virtually alone for divers' interests and the advancement of DIVING. The club organized many tours in Europe to gain more knowledge of the sport in the early days; many of its members became diving judges and officials, and some became coaches.

HIGHLAND GAMES, a group of British ATHLETICS meetings, usually professional, held in the highlands of Scotland from early in the nineteenth century. They are believed to have their origins in the action of a local ruler who, dissatisfied with the speed of his messengers, held races among his retainers to the top of the nearest hill and back, rewarding the first man home with a purse of gold and the second with a sword.

Meetings roughly similar in character developed at the same time in the south of Scotland (the BORDER GAMES) and the north-west of England (the LAKELAND GAMES), but none of these has retained that touch of the former glory that still surrounds the Highland Games, and particularly the best-known of its meetings, the BRAEMAR GATHERING. Items usually on the programme include the standard track and field events, and also such Scottish peculiarities as tossing the CABER and tossing the WEIGHT, for which the competitor is required to wear a kilt. Highland dancing and bagpipe-playing competitions are also often featured.

HILL, CLEMENT (1877-1945), cricketer for Australia and South Australia. A boy prodigy, he became one of Australia's foremost left-handed batsmen, touring England four times and finally leading his country at home against South Africa and England. His 365 not out against New South Wales was then the second highest score in first-class CRICKET, and his record stands for the seventh wicket (with TRUMBLE) and eighth wicket (with Hartigan) against England still survive.

HILL, GRAHAM (1929-1975), British MOTOR RACING driver who worked as a mechanic until first racing in 1956. He raced with Team LOTUS from 1957 until the end of 1959, but achieved little success with the notoriously unreliable front-engined Lotus Formula One and Two cars. For 1960 he joined the BRM team and remained with them until the end of the 1966 season. He won the world championship in 1962 and came second from 1963 to 1965. For 1967 he decided to rejoin Lotus, but achieved little until the appearance of the Lotus 49 at the 1967 Dutch Grand Prix. In 1968 he again won the world championship, driving Lotus-Ford cars. Later he broke both legs in an accident, but he soldiers on, racing Lola T370 cars for the 1974 season.

HILL END, Edinburgh, Scotland, one of the largest artificial ski slopes, owned by the Edinburgh Education Authority. It is a quarter of a mile (402 m.) long and is served by a chair lift. Young skiers with no other SKIING experience have reached a standard on this sufficient to win races at the first attempt on natural snow.

HILLYARD, Mrs. G. W., see BINGLEY, BLANCHE.

HIRA SINGH (b. 1869), Indian POLO player. The best 'back' in the world about 1900, he played for the famous Patiala State team. Handicap 10.

HIRST, GEORGE HERBERT (1871-1954), cricketer for England and Yorkshire. A left-handed all-rounder, his sturdy batting and sharp in-swing bowling earned him the 'double' of 1,000 runs and 100 wickets in 14 seasons, a number exceeded only by his Yorkshire colleague, RHODES. In 1906 he passed 2,000 runs and 200 wickets, a record unlikely to be surpassed, and in 1905 against Leicestershire he scored 341, which remains the highest for his county.

HIRTH, WOLF (1900-59), the German GLIDING pioneer in the development of thermal soaring. He first used the Moazagotl wave in Silesia in 1933; was the designer and constructor of, among others, the Wolf, Minimoa, and Goevier two-seater; and author of *The Art of Soaring Flight*.

HISCOE, K. J. (1938-   ), Australian SQUASH RACKETS player. He played fifth string for New South Wales against the British team in Australia in 1959 and became Australian amateur champion in the following year, a title which he won on six occasions. He first came to England in the 1961-2 season and reached the semi-final of the amateur championship, winning the title in the following year. Hiscoe was the first world-class Australian player and is renowned for his glorious strokes and his fighting spirit. He turned professional in 1972.

HISLOP, JOHN (1911-   ), a former amateur rider, who became a racing journalist of distinction, and managing director and editor of *The British Racehorse*. He bred the great race-horse BRIGADIER GERARD.

HITCH AND KICK, an event once popular in the Scottish BORDER GAMES, but now no longer seen in competition. An unorthodox form of high jump, it required the competitor to kick an inflated bladder, or sometimes a tambourine, which was hung from a pulley above him. Heights of about 10 ft. (3 m.) were not unusual, despite the fact that, to provide the 'hitch', the legs had to pass each other in the air. A fair touch could be made only with the take-off foot.

HITCHCOCK, THOMAS B. (1898-1942), American POLO player who was perhaps the greatest ever. Though not a brilliant horseman he was very quick and a long, accurate striker. He played for the U.S.A. in all international matches between 1920 and 1940 except the Cup of the Americas in 1932 and the West-chester Cup in 1936, winning them all except the Cup of the Americas in 1936. He was killed in the Second World War. Handicap 10.

HOAD, LEWIS ALAN (1934-   ), Australian LAWN TENNIS player. One of the most forcefully aggressive postwar champions, Hoad was the first player to win the men's singles title at WIMBLEDON for two successive years after the Second World War. He and his contemporary and rival, ROSEWALL, were promoted from the junior ranks into the Australian Davis Cup (see LAWN TENNIS) team in 1953 when SEDGMAN turned professional. When they arrived in Europe, Rosewall immediately won the French title and Hoad reached the semi-finals. Together, they won the doubles at Wimbledon and later the same year, when they met the U.S.A. at Melbourne in the Davis Cup challenge round, Hoad won his singles rubbers against Seixas and TRABERT and Rosewall defeated Seixas, giving Australia victory by 3-2. The Australians were beaten at Sydney in 1954, but in their last two years as amateurs neither Hoad nor Rosewall conceded a Davis Cup rubber to the Americans and their team was triumphant again.

Hoad beat Rosewall 6-2, 4-6, 7-5, 6-4 in the 1956 final at Wimbledon, but Rosewall spoilt Hoad's chance of the 'grand slam' by beating him at FOREST HILLS in the last of the four major singles finals. In that year Hoad won his only French and Australian titles. In 1957, after Rosewall had turned professional, Hoad beat Cooper, another Australian, in one of Wimbledon's most one-sided finals. Hoad turned professional immediately afterwards, but all through his professional career he was troubled by a back injury. Although in semi-retirement, he returned to play at Wimbledon in 1968 and 1970. He also coached the British and Spanish Davis Cup teams.

HOBBS, Sir JOHN BERRY (1882-1963), cricketer for England and Surrey. Known as 'the Master', he was the world's leading batsman between the eras of GRACE and BRADMAN, his career extending from 1905 to 1934. No one has exceeded his aggregate of 61,237 runs or his 197 centuries, 98 of which were made after his 40th birthday. Among his records are the highest score at LORD'S (316 not out); the highest score for the Players v. the Gentlemen (266 not out); and, for England against Australia, most centuries (12) and the record first-wicket partnership (323 with RHODES). He was a peerless fieldsman at cover point, and, although more deliberate in style after the First World War, he was always a master of back-foot play, and dexterous on wet wickets. His most memorable Test innings were at the OVAL in 1926 and at MELBOURNE in 1929. He was knighted in 1953.

HOBBY-HORSE RACING, see STREET GAMES.

HOCKENHEIM CIRCUIT. This fast, wooded MOTOR RACING circuit near Mannheim has been the scene of Formula Two races as qualifying rounds in the European Formula Two championship. The 1968 Deutschland Trophy event saw the tragic death of JIM CLARK, but by 1970 the course was considered safer than the longer NURBURGRING circuit and, when the Grand Prix Drivers' Association refused to let its members race over this traditional course, the German Grand Prix was held at Hockenheim. The lap record was set to 131·11 m.p.h. (211·0 km./h.) by Kauhsen's PORSCHE 917 in 1973.

HOCKEY, Field, a stick-and-ball game, is played in over seventy countries and in all five continents. It is a major sport in India and Pakistan and is widely played in Great Britain, South Africa, Australia, Germany, the Netherlands, and many English-speaking countries. It is played by both men and women, though mixed hockey (see below) is not very popular.

Hockey is usually played by two teams of 11 a side, though there are games of 5, 6, and 7 a side. A team usually consists of a goalkeeper, two backs, three halves, and five forwards, but tactical changes in the 1960s saw the introduction of different formations.

The duration of a game is normally 70 minutes, made up of two periods of 35 minutes, with an interval of from 5 to 10 minutes. At the interval (half-time), the teams change ends.

The game is played on grass in most parts of the world and the pitch is rectangular. It is 100 yds. (92 m.) long and between 55 and 60 yds. (50–55 m.) wide. The longer boundary lines (marked usually with white paint) are called side lines and the shorter ones, goal lines. These lines are all 3 in. (8 cm.) wide. A centre line is drawn across the pitch; there is also a broken line 25 yds. (23 m.) from each goal line.

The goal, placed in the centre of the goal line, consists of two perpendicular posts 4 yds. (3·66 m.) apart, joined together by a horizontal crossbar 7 ft. (2·13 m.) from the ground. The front of the goal posts must touch the outer edge of the goal line. The goal posts and crossbar are 2 in. (5 cm.) wide and not more than 3 in. (8 cm.) deep, and the sides facing the field of play are rectangular.

A net is attached firmly at intervals of not more than 6 in. (15 cm.) to the goal posts, the crossbar, and the ground behind the goal so that the ball can enter the area encompassed by the netting only from the field of play. The goals are completed by the fixing of three boards, not exceeding 18 in. (46 cm.) high on the ground inside the netting. Two are placed at right angles to the goal posts and the third parallel to the goal line.

In front of each goal is a white line of almost semi-circular shape. This marks the edge of the striking circle, which is formed by a line 4 yds. (3·66 m.) long and 3 in. (7·5 cm.) wide, parallel to, and 16 yds. (15 m.) from, the goal line. This line is continued to meet the goal line by quarter circles (having the goal posts as centres). The 16 yds. (15 m.) is measured from the outer edge of the circle to the face of the goal posts.

A hard white ball, similar to a CRICKET ball, is used. It weighs between 5¾ oz. (163 g.) and 5½ oz. (155 g.) and has a circumference

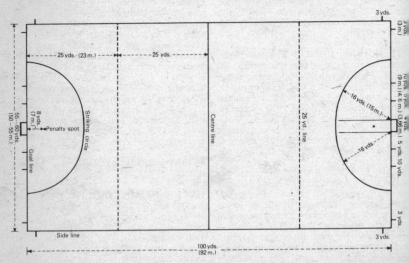

HOCKEY PITCH
Goal posts are joined by a horizontal crossbar (not shown in diagram) 7 ft. (2·14 m.) from the ground: Flags 1 yd. (1 m.) high mark the ends of the goal line, centre line, and 25-yard line. Countries playing to the International Federation of Women's Hockey Associations rules use 5-yard (4·6 m.) lines parallel to the side lines.

between 9¼ in. (23 cm.) and 8⅓₆ in. (22 cm.). The cover of a regulation ball is of leather, either white or painted white, and the inside is of cork and twine.

Each player is permitted to use one stick at a time and to hit the ball with the face of the stick. There are no rules as to the length of the stick but it must weigh between 12 and 28 oz. (340–794 g.), must be able to pass through a ring with a diameter of 2 in. (5 cm.), have a flat face on its left-hand side only, rounded edges, and a wooden head.

The usual clothing is a shirt, shorts, and socks — different teams having different colours. Boots or plimsolls are worn on the feet, depending on the ground conditions, although some Indians occasionally play in bare feet. Other items sometimes worn are pads to protect the shins, and gloves.

There are no limits to the amount of clothing worn by a player but usually only the goalkeeper wears additional protective clothing: large pads of the type used in cricket, big gloves, and padding to protect his body.

The game is controlled by two umpires whose clothing in no way resembles that of the players. Each umpire takes one half of the ground for the whole game and they operate on opposite side lines. The captains toss a coin for the choice of ends and all the players of one team must be in the half they are defending before the game may commence.

The game is started with a centre 'bully'. The ball is placed on the ground at a spot approximately in the middle of the centre line and one player from each team, usually the centre forward, takes his stance; the two men face each other, square to the side lines, with the goal they are defending to their right. Each of them must simultaneously tap with his stick, first the ground between the ball and his own goal line, and then, with the face of his stick, his opponent's stick above the ball. This is done three times before the ball may be played, when each player tries to obtain the ball for his side.

Until the ball has been played, all other players must remain nearer to their own goal line than the ball and not within 5 yds. (4·6 m.) of the ball.

If there is an infringement by those bullying, one of the umpires blows his whistle and indicates that it must be taken again (there is an international code of signals for umpires to indicate the nature of fouls committed). A centre bully is also used to re-start the game after half-time and after a goal is scored.

An umpire may award a bully after a player is injured or when simultaneous fouls are committed. The bully is taken where the incident occurred but never within five yards of the goal line in the circle.

The object of the game is, quite simply, to get the ball into the opponent's goal, and the team scoring the greater number of goals is the winner. A goal may be scored only from within the space enclosed by the opponent's striking circle and the goal line (including the lines themselves) and the ball must cross wholly over the goal line. The ball is propelled by hitting it with the face of the stick. Attacks are usually launched by passing the ball between players or through the ability of one player to run while controlling the ball with his stick (dribbling). The opponents endeavour to obtain the ball by interception or tackling.

The basic requirement of a hockey player is the ability to stop, and hit, the ball. The good player will use his stick efficiently even when it is reversed. The stick is held firmly in both hands when playing the ball, the left hand above the right. When making a hit, the hands are close together; for other strokes, such as the push, flick, or scoop, the left hand grasps the stick firmly near its top and the right hand is moved to a comfortable position further down the handle. The feet are always astride so that the player is balanced and his body weight can be transferred easily.

The push stroke is intended to keep the ball on the ground; the flick stroke is a push, with a wrist flick added, to make the ball rise. The scoop is used to lift the ball over opponents. Bigger distances can be achieved with the left hand moved down below the right and the head of the stick laid right back. A hit, flick, push, or scoop is permitted provided that no part of the stick rises above the players' shoulder level and the ball is not undercut, or played in a dangerous way.

The penalty for an infringement by the striker is a free hit to the opposition, usually taken at the spot where the offence occurred. A free hit awarded to the defending team within 16 yds. (15 m.) of their goal line is taken from any spot within that distance, on an imaginary line from where the offence occurred, parallel to the side line. Before the ball is played, it must be motionless and no other player may be within 5 yds. (4·6 m.) of it. It may be hit or pushed along the ground, but the striker may not approach the ball again until it has been touched by another player.

A player is allowed to stop the ball with his hand. If the ball is caught, it must be released immediately and allowed to fall vertically. The ball may not be intentionally stopped by any part of the body other than the hand, nor may the foot or leg be used to support the stick in order to resist a tackle by an opponent. The stick may not be used to hit, hold, or interfere with an opponent's stick. A player is not allowed to obstruct by running between an opponent and the ball, nor may he place himself or his stick so as to obstruct an opponent.

The game is a no-contact sport. A player may not tackle from an opponent's left unless he plays the ball before touching the stick or person of that opponent. Rough or dangerous play of any description is not permitted. The goalkeepers are the only players allowed to kick the ball and stop it with their body but they may do so only while the ball is in the striking circle they are defending.

As in Association FOOTBALL, there is an offside rule. An attacking player is offside if, at the moment when the ball is hit by a member of his own team, there are fewer than two opponents nearer to their own goal line. The offence occurs when the ball is hit but a player can never be offside in his own half or if the striker is nearer to the opponents' goal line than he is. A player who is in an offside position is not penalized for offside unless he is gaining some advantage from his position or is influencing the play of an opponent.

If the ball crosses wholly over the side line, a member of the team opposed to the player who last touched it in play takes a 'push-in' from the spot where the ball crossed the side line. The ball is pushed in along the ground and no other player may be within 5 yds. (4·6 m.) of the ball at the time.

The method of re-starting play if the ball crosses the goal line, depends upon whether the umpire considers the ball was put out of play intentionally. If the ball is hit over the goal line by the attacking side (without a goal being scored) or unintentionally by a defender from outside his 25-yard (23 m.) line, the game is re-started with a 16-yard (15 m.) hit. This is a free hit, taken by a defender, from a spot 16 yds. from the goal line, exactly opposite the place where the ball crossed the line. If a defender accidentally plays the ball over his own goal line from within his '25', the umpire will award a corner against him. If, however, the umpire considers the defender has played the ball over the goal line intentionally he awards a penalty corner.

The corner and penalty corner are similar in many respects. Only six members of the defending team are permitted behind the goal line; the remaining players must go beyond the half-way line. No attackers are allowed in the circle until one member of the attacking team has played the ball from a point on the goal line. Where the ball is played from depends on what sort of corner has been given. The penalty corner may be taken from any spot on the goal line not within 10 yds. (9 m.) of a goal post, on either side of the goal. The hit-out at a corner must be taken from a spot on the goal line or side line within 3 yds. (3 m.) of the corner flag nearest to the point where the ball crossed the line. No shot at goal is permitted at either a corner or penalty corner until the ball has been stopped on the ground by an attacker or has touched the stick or person of a defender. Penalty corners are awarded for infringements by defending players within their own 25-yards area.

The toughest penalty that an umpire can award is a penalty stroke. This may be given only for an offence by a member of the defending side in his own circle, either for a foul committed to prevent a goal or for an unintentional foul that probably prevented a goal being scored. The stroke is similar to a penalty at football. The ball is placed on a spot 8 yds. (7 m.) in front of the goal and an attacker attempts to push, flick, or scoop the ball into the goal. To play the ball, the attacker may take no more than one stride forward. The defending goalkeeper must stand on the goal line, with the rest of his colleagues beyond the 25-yard line, and he is not allowed to move until the ball has been played.

The advantage rule is one of the most important in hockey. This requires an umpire to refrain from enforcing a penalty when he is satisfied that, by enforcing it, he is giving an advantage to the team committing the offence.

Hockey is usually played in a very good spirit so that there are seldom suspensions for misconduct. A player may be warned for misconduct, sent off temporarily (usually a few minutes), or, in rare cases, for the remainder of a game. If sent off for a short period, he must stand behind his own goal.

Certain other rules sometimes apply at international tournaments controlled by the Fédération Internationale de Hockey (F.I.H.) and there are slight differences in the rules for women's hockey (see below).

The essence of hockey lies in the ability of the individual to control the ball with his stick, and the tactics employed by teams depend to a large extent on the technical ability of their players. The game is based on the co-ordination and integration of attack and defence. The basic formation, as in Association football, is the 5-3-2-1, that is five forwards, three half-backs, two backs, and a goalkeeper. The inside forwards are usually marked by the opposing backs, the other three forwards by the half-backs. Because forwards switch positions in order to elude the opponents who are marking them, defences often adopt a system of zone marking.

The basic roles of the various positions are: *Goalkeeper*: The last line of defence and a formidable one since he is the one player permitted to wear large pads and gloves. He spends most of his time between the posts, but a good goalkeeper also commands the circle which he rarely leaves, since he cannot use his feet to stop the ball once outside.

Backs: Usually right and left, the right back marking the opposition's inside right. Knowing when to tackle is the secret of good fullbacks who cover each other and their own half-backs. Their main function is to break up the attacks of the opposition and to prevent a shot being made at goal. A good back initiates attacks by his distribution of the ball. Modern back play is changing. Some teams are content to use only one back, known as a 'sweeper', others have three or four.

Half-backs: Usually three in number, the centre half and two wing halves, right and left. The half line is the link between attack and defence. The centre half marks the opposing centre forward, while wing halves mark wingers. In attack, the wing half on the same side as the ball tends to lie further upfield than his fellow wing half. In defence, the wing half has to cover behind the back when the opponents are tackling down the opposite side of the field. Some teams have an attacking centre half and then the wing halves have more defensive duties. If they have a defensive centre half, the wing halves can be given more freedom to attack. A half is generally trying to put himself nearer to the ball than the opponent he is marking.

Forwards: Usually five, right wing (also known as outside right), inside right (known as right inner in women's hockey), centre forward, inside left, and outside left. Their main function is to create opportunities and to score goals. All forwards are expected to have good ball control and to be able to shoot quickly. Wingers are expected to stay wide, near the side lines on their side of the pitch. Ideally they are fast runners and accurate at passing, especially when centring the ball. Inside forwards have to be very fit since they are expected to help the defence, particularly by tackling back, and yet always be up with their fellow attackers. The centre forward is the leader of the attack and is expected to stay upfield as far as possible and to move for goal decisively, aggressively, and with speed at the first opportunity.

The attackers and defenders of the best teams will be seen to move forward and backward together. The man with the ball expects to have one or two players of his own side close enough to take his short pass. Many attacks are built up by triangulation and generally it is a combination of short and long passes that is most successful. The attackers spread out across the whole width

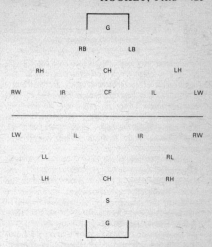

PLAYING FORMATIONS
(*Above*) 5-3-2-1, or pyramid, formation; (*below*) 4-2-3-1 formation. (G) Goalkeeper; (RB) right back; (LB) left back; (RH) right half; (CH) centre half; (LH) left half; (RW) right wing; (IR) inside right; (CF) centre forward; (IL) inside left; (LW) left wing; (LL) left link; (RL) right link; (S) sweeper. (In women's hockey inside right and left are called right inner, left inner.)

of the pitch; this keeps the opposing defence stretched.

Some teams now employ *links* in a redeployment of their 11 players. Usually left and right, these new positions make the half-back role more defensive. Their main job is to mark out the opponent's inside forwards but they are also expected to join in attack.

The contrast between Asian and European hockey has always been very marked. The Asians are renowned for their close passing and zone marking, Europeans for their rugged hit-and-run type of game, although the gap between the styles is rapidly closing. Many of the tactical moves of Association football, such as maintaining possession, creating overlaps, teamwork, build-up, change of pace, and use of speed, apply to hockey.

MIXED HOCKEY is a variation of the game played with nearly equal numbers of men and women on each side, usually six men and five women. Before the end of the nineteenth century, mixed hockey was in vogue at English country-house parties, but the game has never had much of a hold. In England it is played on Sundays by a few clubs, especially those with men's and women's sections. The game is played under men's hockey rules.

International Hockey Rules Board, *Rules of the Game of Hockey*, annually; *Hockey Coaching*, the official manual of the Hockey Association (1966).

The name 'hockey' (spelt thus) was not given to this ancient stick-and-ball game until the eighteenth or nineteenth century, but without a doubt, hockey has descended from the earliest civilizations. There is, however, no concrete evidence of where it started. History confirms that early man carried a club, staff, or stick and it is a basic instinct to hit at movable objects.

Early hockey historians thought the sport descended from POLO but the reverse seems much more likely. This was confirmed in the early twentieth century when studies were made of the drawings on the ancient tombs in the Nile Valley. On a wall in Tomb No. 16 at Beni-Hasan, near Minia, there are drawings of six sports, one of which shows two men holding implements that, with their curved ends, closely resemble early twentieth-century hockey sticks. The men in the drawing are standing square to each other and between their 'sticks' is a round object which may have been a hoop or ball. The stance suggests either that they were carrying out a bully or that one was trying to prevent the other hitting the round object. This tomb was built about 2,000 B.C. so it is fair to assume that men have been playing a form of hockey for at least 4,000 years, probably much longer. Hockey is thus the forerunner of all modern sports played with an implement.

Before the Christian era, different variations of stick-and-ball games were being played in many parts of the world, as written and pictorial evidence shows. The Arabs, Greeks, Persians, and Romans each had their own version. The Romans played a game called *paganica* in which a ball, which was filled with feathers, was propelled with a club.

The earliest evidence that more than two players were involved in these stick-and-ball games came with the discovery of two marble blocks unearthed in Athens in February 1922 when repairs were being made to the old wall built by Themistocles in 478 B.C. They were the bases of statues and were carved on three sides in bas-relief. One of the illustrations shows six naked men all carrying hooked sticks and the two in the middle are similar to the two on the wall of the Egyptian tomb, even more obviously engaged in the ancient equivalent of the modern bully. The sticks are pointing downwards but between them lies what is certainly a ball.

Hockey has been closely associated with the Irish sport of HURLING which dates back to at least 1272 B.C. It is recorded that, before the battle of Magh Tuireadh in that year, the leading warriors of each side engaged in a hurling match which was completed when all the members of one side were 'defeated and slain'.

One of the most comprehensive records of an early form of hockey comes from Argentina. The early sixteenth-century European settlers recorded the habits and pastimes of the Araucaño Indians. They played a game called *cheuca* ('the twisted one') which took its name from the stick with a twisted end used by the players. Their ball had a leather case. The size of the field depended on whether four, six, or eight players took part, though it was usually in the region of a hundred paces in length and ten paces in width, the back line at either end being the goal line. The Araucaños considered *cheuca* to be an important feature of their lives because it kept them healthy and in good physical condition for war.

As the world became more civilized, the various versions of stick-and-ball games crystallized. Possibly, at the same time that *cheuca* was being played, cambuca (also known as 'comocke' or 'cammock') was a sport in England; SHINTY flourished in Scotland, *jeu de mail* in France, and *het kolven* in the Netherlands. In all of these, a ball was hit with a stick. Shinty was derived from a game said to have been played by the heroes of Celtic legends and was played over large areas of heather. It was a game that intrigued a twelfth-century king, Alexander I of Scotland.

Fitzstephen, a biographer who recorded the social life of London in the twelfth century, wrote in 1175: 'Let us come to the Sports and Exercises....the scholars of every school have their ball or bastion (staff) in their hands....'

Surprisingly, no pictorial reference to a stick-and-ball game has come to light between the fifth century B.C. and the early thirteenth century. The stained-glass windows of Canterbury Cathedral, however, include the 'Six Ages of Man', *Pueritia* being represented by a boy standing with a curved stick by his right side and a small ball in his left hand. Since then there has been no dearth of illustrations. Among the more interesting in the fourteenth century was that on an altar flagon (thought to be French) which now resides in the Copenhagen Museum; a headless figure swinging a hooked stick, part of a stained-glass window in England's Gloucester Cathedral; and a drawing in *Decretal of Gysors*, written by an Italian and illustrated by an English artist. The *Decretal* illusion is very similar to the central figures in the Greek bas-relief. The clothed figures appear to be bullying but, once again, have their sticks pointing downwards. The ground is seen to be undulating.

Another written description of a stick-and-ball game also appeared in the fourteenth century. In *Foedera*, by the Englishman, Rymer, cambuca, as played in 1363, is described as 'the game of crooked stick or curved club or playing mallet with which a small wooden ball is propelled forward'. Two years later, cambuca and bandy-ball were among several sports forbidden by the English king, Edward III, because they interfered with training for war. Man 'shall in his sports use bows and arrows, pellets and bolts', the people were told. In 1388, Richard II was even firmer, decreeing that the playing implements had to be destroyed.

Authors have linked similar games with different names all over the world. *Paille maille, palamaglio, pele-mele, chicane, cheuca* and hawkie, were all forms of hockey as we know it today. Two teams of players with sticks tried to get a ball or puck through opposing goals. Clubbes, hurl-bat, shinnops, jowling, baddins, and doddorts, games played in various regions of England, are also thought to have been similar.

Where the word 'hockey' actually came from is not known. 'Hockie' was one of the forbidden sports mentioned in the Galway Statutes of 1527. It has been suggested that hockey is a derivation of comocke, and the Anglo-Saxon word for 'hook' was *hoc*. Another view is that it came from the French word *hocquet*, a shepherd's crook.

The word 'hockey' appears to have come into general use in the nineteenth century. Lord Lytton wrote in 1853: 'On the common some young men were playing at hockey. That old-fashioned game, now very uncommon in England, except at schools...' There is no doubt that a game called hockey was played at English public schools early in the nineteenth century. It was probably played in free time for there is no evidence of it as an organized sport until the end of the nineteenth century.

As organized team games developed and were modernized in England, so hockey's popularity grew. The first hockey club is freely accepted as being Blackheath, a south-east London club which has a minute book headed 1861 — Blackheath Football and Hockey Club. The exact year the club was founded is not known but the 1861 entries make it clear that it was before that year. Robson, in his *A Manual of Hockey*, recalls meeting men who had played the game before 1840.

Blackheath played on the heath itself and used a very large area. It was about 270 yds. (247 m.) long and 70 yds. (64 m.) wide, and he writes: 'the sticks were rough affairs planed down the backs. The size of the ground, coupled with indiscriminate slogging, killed this sport, which to my mind, was a most skilful and exhilarating one'. The 'ball' used was a black cube of solid rubber.

Blackheath's version of the game was still a little uncivilized, and it is to the west side of London that the present game is attributed. A hockey club was formed by the members of the Teddington CRICKET club who were probably not greatly enamoured with football yet wanted to give their members winter exercise. It was their decision to use a cricket ball that was a crucial factor in the development of the modern game. Perhaps for the first time, a stick-and-ball game was played with a ball that moved smoothly and, since Teddington used the outfield of a cricket ground, the movement of the ball was infinitely more predictable than before. The game immediately took on a different complexion; it was no longer an indiscriminate free-for-all.

Several other cricket clubs followed Teddington's example but much of the credit for developing the game must go to the Middlesex club. Their first traceable minute book, dated 1874, records that 'a discussion also took place on the Rules of the game'. It was resolved that Rule 3 be altered and stand thus: 'A player may not stop the ball with his hand, nor shall he, in any case, raise his stick above his shoulder'. Other decisions taken at that meeting included a hit-in when the ball went behind the goal posts, a toss-in if it crossed the boundary lines, and that all disputes be settled by the captains. It was Teddington too who thought it necessary to reduce reckless shooting by stipulating that an attacker must be inside a stipulated area 'the circle' in front of goal before he could shoot. Teddington and other west London clubs undoubtedly prepared the way for the present rules of the game.

At first, matches between clubs were not very popular but the need for clubs to get together was soon realized, and in April 1875, on the initiative of a member of the Richmond Club, a meeting was held which led to the formation of the first association. A representative of the Blackheath club attended this meeting but did not stay long when he discovered how different Blackheath's game was from that of the west London clubs. The 1875 association lasted only seven years possibly because, in those days, clubs were happy playing among themselves and were not too concerned about what other people were doing.

But all sports were developing and hockey clubs were springing up all over the country.

A national association became increasingly necessary and on 18 January 1886, the Hockey Association (H.A.) was formed. The meeting was attended by seven London clubs, including Blackheath, together with representatives from Trinity College, Cambridge. Although Blackheath was one of the founder members of the Hockey Association, they still would not accept the Association's rules and soon formed a breakaway National Hockey Union. This Union disintegrated while the Association went from strength to strength and its influence quickly spread first through Britain and then all over the world.

There is no evidence to show when women first played stick-and-ball games but they took to the modern game (it was the era of women's emancipation in England) and they developed their game separately from the men (see below).

The first international match, played between the men of Wales and Ireland in 1895, was won by Ireland 3-0. Four years later in 1900, a special body was formed to make and alter the rules of the men's game. This body was called the International Rules Board and was formed by the national Associations of England, Ireland, and Wales.

The advent of the Rules Board gave the umpire status, for previously he could make a decision only if appealed to by either side. The rules, as revised by the Board in 1900, besides laying down the cases where an umpire could give a decision after an appeal, also enumerated those in which he could act without appeal. One of the first he could adjudicate himself was whether a player committed 'sticks', i.e. raised his stick above his shoulder. Strict enforcement of 'sticks' led to irritatingly frequent stoppages and soon an 'advantage' rule was introduced, the idea being that the whistle should not be blown if the non-offending team would suffer from the enforcement of the rule. In 1907, umpires were given power to make all decisions without waiting for an appeal.

The most significant rule changes made since the early days of the Rules Board have been the prohibiting of any interference with sticks; the prohibiting of the intentional use of any part of the body, except the hand, to stop the ball (1938); the abandoning of the 25-yard (23 m.) bully (1957) and the penalty bully (1963); and the discard of the roll-in (1970).

Men's hockey was included in the modern OLYMPIC GAMES when they were held in London in 1908, England being the victors; and England retained her title at the 1920 Olympics. The sport was not included at the 1924 Olympics, however, since by then the INTERNATIONAL OLYMPIC COMMITTEE was insisting that each sport should have an international controlling authority. This situation inspired a Frenchman, Leautey, to call a meeting of European hockey-playing countries, and the

Fédération Internationale de Hockey sur Gazon (F.I.H.) was formed on 7 January 1924. Its first objects were to make sure hockey was included in future Olympiads and to promote the game throughout the world.

Seven countries were represented at that first meeting: Austria, Belgium, Czechoslovakia, France, Hungary, Spain, and Switzerland. Before the 1928 Olympic Games, they had been joined by Denmark, Holland, Germany, and India. The dedication of a series of European officials helped the F.I.H. to flourish. It grew steadily before the Second World War and rapidly afterwards, so that, at the beginning of the 1970s, it had 60 member nations. The man who played a large role in the development of hockey as a world sport was a Belgian, FRANK, who was elected president in 1966 after serving for many years as a member of the F.I.H. Council and as secretary. The F.I.H. has never had direct control over the organization of hockey within member countries since all its dealings are with the national Associations.

The year 1970 was a very important one in the history of the F.I.H. for, in that year, the Hockey Association at long last became a member of the Fédération and arrangements were made for the International Rules Board to be absorbed within the F.I.H. framework. Thus men's hockey throughout the world finally became united.

The character of hockey has not changed greatly in the twentieth century. It has remained an amateur game, there being no professional players. Because of the growth of the game a few professional administrators were appointed after the Second World War and a small amount of commercial sponsorship was also accepted. More recently professional coaches have come into the game.

Development of the hockey stick and ball. Knowledge about the materials used for the early balls and sticks is as vague as the early history of the game. Ordinary stones probably provided the first 'balls' and wood and/or bones were perhaps used as the hitting implements. For centuries the two basic items for all stick-and-ball games undoubtedly varied not only from country to country but from village to village.

History has provided descriptions of ancient balls but little or no record of early sticks or staffs. That the curved end, so closely associated with the modern game of hockey, was introduced even before the birth of Christ is revealed by early illustrations but what these implements were made of remains a mystery. The Indians of North America, long before the seventeenth century, employed bones as well as sticks and they used to decorate both sticks and balls with emblems of speed.

The first descriptions of hockey sticks appear in the early nineteenth century. The pupils of Tonbridge School are said to have cut their own from near-by woods and bent them to the required shape in steam. *Cassell's Popular Educator* in 1867 describes the stick as used in 1867: 'It was simply a weapon with a bent knob or hook at the end, large or small, thick or thin, according to the option of the player.'

When the Blackheath hockey club was formed in the 1860s, the players used sticks that were 'rough affairs planed down the backs' and the 'ball' was 'a large oblong cube of rubber' which weighed 6 to 7 oz. (170–198 g.). The sticks were thrown in a corner after each game and, just before the next, a player would pick out one that suited him. In those days sticks were usually extremely weighty, often of oak, and they were heavier at the toe end which allowed the ball to be hit prodigious distances. Distances of 175 yds. (160 m.) were achieved with a stick made of holly, but supplies of this wood were never readily available. The general acceptance of modern rules, rolled pitches, and the cricket ball, painted white, led to the development of the modern stick.

In the early days of the Hockey Association, sticks were made from maple. Howell, the first secretary of the Association, described how they were produced: 'We put the ends in boiling water for twenty minutes and then put them under a heavy weight to bend them out. Then when dry and cold, we spoke-shave them down until the face is flat, generally shaving off a slice first. Then we shave the handle down until it is little more than one inch in diameter at the top. The top and the face are roughened with a coarse file.' The hockey sticks, as specified by the H.A. in 1887, had to pass through a 2-in. (5 cm.) ring and have no metal fittings or sharp edges. That rule stands today.

Before long manufacturers were producing sticks to the required shape made out of ash board. Not long after, they began to make sticks which were split straight along the grain and bent to shape by heat and moisture. In the 1920s, hockey sticks were made of ash with a handle of cane (Sarawak or rattan) and strip rubber.

A waterproof composition ball was manufactured in 1927 but was not accepted by the International Hockey Rules Board, though the rules were later altered so that it was not precluded.

After the Second World War, Indian manufacturers who often used mulberry wood because of its compressibility, introduced a stick with a very short toe — the so-called 'Indian' stick — which enabled players to control the ball better. This came into general use in the 1950s. Ash was not satisfactory for these sticks as it would not stand the extra compression on the inside face. In the 1960s, the demand for stiffer handles increased so that rubber was used. Also both the blade and binding tape were coated with cellulose lacquer to give a gloss finish. This was later superseded by a polyurethane finish.

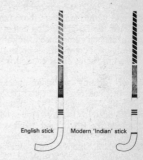

English stick   Modern 'Indian' stick

HOCKEY STICKS

Another development was the introduction of 'swing-weight', a method whereby not only was the weight of the stick measured, but the distribution of that weight and the length of the stick were taken into account to give a more accurate guide to its characteristics and feel.

In the 1970s, manufacturers were examining the possibilities of making sticks from plastics, while the plastic all-weather ball was coming into increasing use.

INTERNATIONAL HOCKEY. The number of players — of both sexes — throughout the world makes hockey one of the largest participant sports. In the 1950s and 1960s, an increasing amount of competition was introduced, culminating in the decision to start a World Cup in the 1970s. The most successful countries in international competition in the first half of the twentieth century were England and India. After the Second World War, England's standard began to fall, and Pakistan, Germany, and the Netherlands joined India in the front rank.

The words 'hockey' and 'India' are almost synonymous. In no other country has the modern game developed so remarkably. Indian historians believe that its phenomenal spread was a form of re-incarnation, that stick-and-ball games played in the East in earliest times are unlikely to have by-passed India. A crude form of hockey had certainly been played in the early nineteenth century. It was called by many different local names, one of which was *khiddo-khundi* ('cotton ball and twisted stick').

British servicemen, who introduced the game to India in the 1880s, rightly deserve credit for teaching the modern game to the Indians. The climate in parts of the country is often ideal, providing the right conditions in which to play hockey at its best, with hard, fast pitches and ideal light. The Indian, physically, is ideally built for hockey and is naturally dexterous.

The first clubs in India were formed in Calcutta in 1885 and within ten years those famous competitions, the Beighton Cup and Aga Khan Tournament, had commenced. Initially, these were purely local competitions but as the game blossomed in India, clubs entered from all over the country.

The idea of forming an Indian hockey federation was first put forward around 1907-8 but it was not until 7 November 1925, that one was officially founded in Gwalior. Three years later, India joined the F.I.H. and decided to take part in the 1928 Olympic hockey tournament at Amsterdam. India's only previous international experience was a tour of New Zealand in 1926 in which Test honours were shared. India won all five of her games at the 1928 Olympics and in winning the Olympic gold medals she did not concede one goal.

Among the players in that 1928 side were the Nawab of PATAUDI, PINNIGER, R. J. ALLEN, Norris, Jaipal Singh (later to become a leading Indian politician), and a centre forward called CHAND, regarded as perhaps the greatest hockey player the world has ever seen.

India retained her gold medal at the next Olympics in 1932. There were only three entries for the hockey tournament but India dealt summarily with her rivals, beating Japan 11-1, and the U.S.A. by a record 24-1. At these Olympics, Chand had been joined by his brother, RUP SINGH, and between them they scored 18 of the side's 24 goals against the Americans.

Chand and goalkeeper Allen went on to win their third Olympic gold medals at Berlin in 1936, a record equalled by another great Indian player, the full-back, GENTLE, who helped India to retain the Olympic title in the first three Olympics after the war (1948, 1952, 1956).

Among the other great players in the first two decades after the Second World War were Claudius and Udham Singh who each represented India in four Olympics, Kishen Lal, K. D. 'Babu' Singh, Francis, Balbir Singh, Prithipal Singh, and Joginder Singh.

India's run of success at the Olympics was finally halted in 1960 by Pakistan, whose players were all of Indian origin, but India regained the title at the 1964 Games. Hockey was for many years regarded as the national game of India, but in the 1960s it seemed to be losing ground and this was reflected in India's less impressive international results and declining home attendances.

The European Cup, inaugurated in 1970 and won by West Germany, was, at the time, the biggest international tournament ever held, attracting 19 nations. It was just one of three continental championships started after 1950. Hockey was introduced into the ASIAN GAMES programme in 1958 and was dominated by India and Pakistan. It was also included in the PAN-AMERICAN GAMES in 1967, the inaugural tournament being won by Argentina. In Oceania, Australia and New Zealand compete annually for the MANNING CUP, and the East African championship, dominated by Kenya, did on occasions include a few nations from other parts of Africa.

Apart from the Olympics and an annual women's international held at WEMBLEY STADIUM (see below), the game has never attracted large crowds except in India and Pakistan. The attendance at Wembley for the England *v.* Wales international on 8 March 1969 was 60,707, at the time the largest recorded attendance at a hockey match. At the 1936 Berlin Olympics, 184,103 spectators had attended during the 12 days of hockey.

The clubs remain the roots of the game in most countries and they are increasingly involved in cup and league competitions, while far larger numbers of clubs travel abroad on tours or for festivals and tournaments. The annual festival, often held over a week-end such as Easter, is one of the most popular features of hockey.

The quality of play improved considerably with the world-wide adoption of the so-called 'Indian' stick (see above) in the 1950s. Hockey is generally played 11 a side but 5-, 6-, and 7-a-side tournaments are played in various parts of the world. A 7-a-side tournament in Buenos Aires has been known to attract nearly 300 teams.

Indoor hockey (*Hallenhockey*) became increasingly popular after the Second World War, especially in Europe where the weather precluded much outdoor hockey in the winter months (see HOCKEY, INDOOR). The 1976 Olympic tournament is to take place for the first time on an artificial pitch.

A. de Mello, *Portrait of Indian Sport* (1959); W. Malherbe, *Chronological Bibliography of Hockey* (1965); P. A. Robson, *A Manual of Hockey* (1934); *World Hockey*, magazine (quarterly) of the F.I.H. GOVERNING BODIES (WORLD): Fédération Internationale de Hockey, Boulevard du Regent 55, 1000

Brussels, Belgium; Asian Hockey Federation, Bahawalpur House, Ferozepur Road, Lahore, Pakistan; European Hockey Federation, Avenue des Vaillants 3B, 1200 Brussels, Belgium; Pan-American Hockey Federation, 4829 Roblin Boulevard, Winnipeg 20, Manitoba, Canada.

Women's hockey. Hockey, in many parts of the world, is regarded as a 'women's game' yet there is no evidence of women having played any of the ancient stick-and-ball games, and the early forms of hockey were probably too barbaric. Women undoubtedly took up the game when men's hockey was developed as a no-contact sport during the second half of the nineteenth century; it was the one outdoor team sport which was suitable for women.

At first, women had to play in secret, such were the prejudices and prohibitions of the Victorian era. Students at universities, such as Oxford, were more actively engaged in obtaining emancipation and the game was played at one of the Oxford colleges, Lady Margaret Hall, in the early 1880s. It spread to other universities and to schools, but it was not until 1887, some years after the first modern men's hockey clubs had been founded in west London, that the first women's club, Molesey Ladies Hockey Club, came into being.

At first Molesey's matches were played solely among members. Soon there were two more ladies' clubs in west London, Ealing and Wimbledon. Molesey and Ealing later became defunct but the Wimbledon club (founded in 1889) became firmly established and is the oldest surviving women's hockey club in the world.

Wimbledon played two matches with Molesey in their first season but found the experience 'disagreeable'. They played to the (English) Hockey Association rules for men's hockey, using a painted cricket ball and 'proper sticks'. Because of social conditions, however, women players were considerably hampered by their clothing. They had to wear skirts which often came down to within an inch (25 mm.) of the ground and were five or six yards (5 m.) round. Other encumbrances included petticoats, corsets, high stiff collars, ties and even straw hats 'well skewered on to the head with immense hat-pins'. The petticoats were soon discarded.

Women's hockey was also developing in Ireland and the Dubliners founded the first women's national association, the Irish Ladies Hockey Union, in 1894. In the winter of that year, the first women's tour took place, Alexandra College, Dublin, entertaining a team from Newnham College, Cambridge. This visit led to a match between an English team and an Irish team at Brighton on 10 April 1895, the forerunner of women's internationals.

The enthusiasm generated by the contacts with Ireland led to 'an informal and preliminary meeting' to sound out the possibilities of forming an English women's hockey association. At this meeting it was decided to adopt the rules of the men's Hockey Association. Seven months later, on 23 November 1895, the first formal meeting of the Ladies' Hockey Association was held in London, and the organization which was to play such an important role in the development of women's hockey, was born.

The new organization decided to make a formal application to join the Hockey Association but they were informed that 'The Hockey Association could not officially recognize the existence of the new association'. Thus the game of hockey was divided from the outset, the men's and women's games going their separate ways.

In 1896, the Ladies' Hockey Association adopted the title, All-England Women's Hockey Association (A.E.W.H.A.), by which it has been known ever since. That same year the first official women's international, between England and Ireland, took place in Dublin, Ireland winning 2-0.

The organizers of women's hockey in its early days were sorely troubled about their image and were greatly concerned by problems such as what clothing should be worn on the field, whether they should publicize their activities, and especially whether to allow competition. There was a strong feeling that women's hockey should not be played for prizes and this attitude was still apparent in English women's hockey in the 1960s.

Women's hockey spread round the world, much as the men's game did, and in many countries it became *the* women's game. It was played before the end of the nineteenth century in the U.S.A. and had spread by the early part of the twentieth century to such countries as the Netherlands, Germany, Switzerland, Australia, New Zealand, and South Africa. There was a regular interchange of sides between England and Holland, though the Dutch rules were very different. They used both sides of the stick and a canvas ball filled with horsehair.

In 1914, an English team travelled to Australia and New Zealand. The players had to pay for themselves and that principle, to some extent, still applies to most touring teams.

The idea of an international federation was first discussed in 1900, principally to try to establish uniformity of rules, but it was not until 1927 that the International Federation of Women's Hockey Associations (I.F.W.H.A.)

was formed, three years after the Fédération Internationale de Hockey had been founded, primarily to control men's hockey. The first president of the I.F.W.H.A. was an Englishwoman, Miss Gaskell, M.B.E. The aims of the organization were 'to further the best interests of the game among women of all nations; to promote friendly intercourse among players; to work for uniformity of rules and to promote international matches'. Those objects have remained virtually unaltered since.

Eight countries formed the original federation; Australia, Denmark, England, Ireland, Scotland, South Africa, the U.S.A., and Wales. All were English-speaking except Denmark but it was hoped to persuade other European countries to join. The women's associations in Germany, France, Belgium, and the Netherlands were, however, only sections of the men's associations and were already affiliated to the F.I.H. For some time, the F.I.H. did not allow them to join another international body and these European countries became members of the I.F.W.H.A. only after the Second World War.

The I.F.W.H.A. decided to hold an international conference every three years and the first of these took place at Geneva in Switzerland in 1930. The United States Field Hockey Association proposed that a tournament should be arranged in conjunction with future conferences, and the first world women's tournament took place at the next conference, held in Copenhagen in 1933. Six of the eight member countries sent national teams and two non-member countries, Germany (represented by Magdeburg) and Holland (by the Black Tulips) also took part. As a common code of rules had still not been agreed, the rules used at each conference tournament were those of the host nation.

Women players were still considerably hampered by their clothing. Although the three pleated tunic had replaced the skirt in 1919, even the English team still wore long stockings and ties in 1939.

At the third I.F.W.H.A. conference (at Philadelphia in 1936) the Americans proposed that teams who were visiting conferences should also make tours of the host country, and after the Second World War representations were made to the International Olympic Committee for women's hockey to be included in the Olympic Games of 1952, but this was refused.

When conferences were eventually resumed after the war, at Johannesburg in 1950, it was decided that the conference tournaments and tours were much more suitable for women's hockey anyway. Entry to the Olympic Games would have meant knock-out competition which was still being strongly resisted by the I.F.W.H.A. The matches at conference tournaments were always played on a friendly basis until the 1970s. It was decided to hold the conference every four years to avoid clashing with the dates of the Olympic Games.

By 1939, the I.F.W.H.A. membership had increased by only two but in the 1960s the figure rose to 30. Membership of the I.F.W.H.A. is open to only one Association from any one country. That association must have not less than 20 teams and be a national amateur women's hockey association or the women's section of a similar hockey association. Associations with between 5 and 19 teams are elected as associate members. All important decisions affecting international women's hockey for I.F.W.H.A. member countries have to be made at conferences though an elected council meets annually.

At the 1967 conference at Cologne the problem of rules uniformity was finally decided. The setting up of an independent women's rules board, the Women's International Hockey Rules Board (W.I.H.R.B.), was agreed and all I.F.W.H.A. member countries undertook to play by the rules laid down by that body. Much of the credit for the formation of the W.I.H.R.B. belonged to Miss LIGHT, a leading administrator of women's hockey.

The 1967 conference tournament was the biggest ever, with 19 nations competing. The most successful were England and South Africa, while New Zealand, Australia, and the Netherlands also provided strong teams.

By the 1970s, however, England's wins over the other home countries, New Zealand, and European nations such as Germany and the Netherlands had become more difficult to achieve. The standard of European hockey undoubtedly improved with the introduction of indoor hockey and league and cup competitions after the Second World War.

Indian women's teams have surprisingly never had the same degree of success as their men's teams, possibly because they have not been given the same opportunities to develop. Indian women excel at stickwork and control, but lack speed, stamina, and the ability to hit the ball hard.

England's most illustrious woman player was probably POLLARD, a forward with a phenomenal goal-scoring record. Other outstanding English forwards have included CHAPMAN, PARRY, Robinson, RUSSELL-VICK, and VINCENT, while top-class defenders included Barnes, DELFORCE, and LODGE (president of the A.E.W.H.A. from 1957 to 1968).

At the beginning of the 1970s, representatives of the F.I.H. and I.F.W.H.A. agreed to set up a joint consultative committee to try to resolve differences and remove disparities which had arisen between their respective codes of rules. The chief differences in 1970 were: (*a*) The I.F.W.H.A. countries had not adopted the penalty stroke. They retained the penalty bully, taken by the offender and any member of the attacking team on a spot 5 yds. (4·6 m.) in front of the centre of the goal. (*b*) The I.F.W.H.A. had retained the 'roll-in', which had been superseded in F.I.H.-controlled hockey by the push-in as a method for returning the ball into play after it has crossed a side line. The ball is rolled in by hand by a player of the side opposite to that which last touched the ball in play. All other players must go beyond a 5-yard (4·6 m.) line, which is drawn parallel to each side line. (*c*) At the taking of corners, five members of the defending team must go beyond the 25-yard (23 m.) line. In F.I.H. hockey, they must go beyond the centre line. (*d*) The offside rule in F.I.H. hockey took into account two defenders; in I.F.W.H.A. hockey three defenders.

In the early 1970s, relations between the two controlling world bodies, the F.I.H. (with 71 member associations of which 22 have women's sections) and the I.F.W.H.A. (36 women's associations or sections) deteriorated. The women's sections of the F.I.H. were more competitive-minded and were seeking with determination to have women's hockey admitted to the Olympic programme. The F.I.H. also organized a Women's World Cup, the first official world championship for women, to be held at Mandelieu in southern France in March 1974, with ten selected nations from three continents, and announced the introduction of several other women's championships, including a European Indoor Cup.

Meanwhile, in 1973 the I.F.W.H.A. accepted the principle of competitive hockey and announced that their 1975 conference tournament at Edinburgh would be a world championship. Since only one world federation can be recognized, the two bodies had to sit down and try to sort out their differences.

A.E.W.H.A., *The Code of Rules for the Game of Hockey,* annually. I.F.W.H.A. Conference Reports. Marjorie Pollard, *Fifty Years of Women's Hockey* (1946); P. Rowley, *The Book of Hockey* (1963); *The Story of the A.E.W.H.A. 1895-1965,* ed. J. Whitehead (1965).

GOVERNING BODIES (WORLD): International Federation of Women's Hockey Associations (I.F.W.H.A.), 44a Westminster Palace Gardens, London S.W.1.; Fédération Internationale de Hockey, Boulevard du Regent 55, 1000 Brussels, Belgium.

HOCKEY, Ice, see ICE HOCKEY.

HOCKEY, Indoor, a game adapted from field HOCKEY for teams of up to seven players indoors, it is known in parts of Europe as *Hallenhockey.* It started in the 1950s in West Germany, which has always been regarded as its leading exponent, and has become increasingly popular especially in Europe where outdoor hockey is restricted by weather in midwinter. Other countries with a thriving indoor game are Belgium, Denmark, France, Netherlands, Spain, and Switzerland. It is also played in a few centres in Britain.

Germany introduced national championships in 1962 and these are now held for men and women and for boys and girls. The game is so popular that the German Federation have had to limit their indoor season from December to February for fear that it might become more popular than outdoor hockey. KELLER, winner of 100 international caps outdoors for West Germany, and another well-known outdoor international, Schuler, were the outstanding indoor players in the 1960s.

Although normally played indoors, the game can also take place outdoors provided the surface available is flat and hard. The rules are laid down by the International Hockey Federation.

The ground is between 40 and 50 yds.

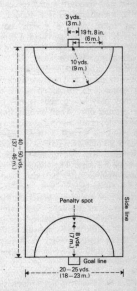

INDOOR HOCKEY PITCH
The pitch is surrounded by boarding 4 in. (10 cm.) high. A clear space of 6 ft. 6 in. (2 m.) behind the goals, extending 2 ft. (60 cm.) beyond the side lines, is desirable.

(37–46 m.) long and 20 to 25 yds. (18–23 m.) wide, and is divided into two equal parts by a line drawn from one side line to the other. Down both side lines are wooden boards 4 in. (10 cm.) high off which the ball may be played.

As in outdoor hockey, the two goals are placed in the centre of the goal lines but the posts are only 3 yds. (3 m.) apart. The striking circle is also smaller, having a radius of 10 yds. (9 m.). The penalty-stroke spot is 8 yds. (7 m.) in front of the goal.

The game is played by two teams of six players (usually a goalkeeper and five field players) but each team is permitted a maximum of six substitutes. Substitutions may be made without informing the umpires but only at specific times, i.e. at half-time; when a goal is scored, when the ball has crossed one of the goal lines, or if the game has been stopped because of injury to a player.

The game is usually in two periods of 20 minutes each with a 5-minute interval, but shorter periods are played at tournaments and by women and juniors. The timing is kept by a timekeeper to whom the umpires signal all stoppages.

Equipment is similar to that used for outdoor hockey. The rules stipulate the ball must be white, and standard sticks (or even sticks specially manufactured for indoor hockey, such as those with a plastic cover) are authorized. In some parts of Europe it is necessary to bind sticks with tape in order to avoid damaging wooden floors.

There are certain major differences between the rules for indoor and outdoor hockey. In the indoor game it is forbidden to hit the ball, which may only be pushed. It may be raised off the ground only when an attacker, in the striking circle, is attempting to score a goal.

The game is started with all members of each team in their own half. A member of the side that lost the toss makes a pass, which must not be forward. The game is re-started in the same manner after half-time and after a goal has been scored.

There are no corners, but at penalty corners all the players of the defending team (except the goalkeeper) must be behind the goal line on the side of the goal opposite to that from which the penalty corner is being taken. Another important difference is that there is no offside rule.

Rules vary for the women's game and are sometimes more akin to the women's outdoor rules (see HOCKEY, FIELD).

HOFMANN, RICHARD (1906-), Association footballer for Meerane 07, Dresden S.C., and Germany for whom he scored all three goals in the drawn match against England in Berlin in 1930. An inside left, he made 27 appearances for Germany between 1927 and 1933.

HOGAN, BEN (1912-), American professional golfer. One of the handful of golfers who can legitimately be classed among the great of the game, he was U.S. Professional Golfers Association champion in 1946 and 1948; world champion 1951, 1953; U.S. Open champion 1948, 1950, 1951, 1953; Open champion 1953; Masters champion 1951, 1953; a RYDER CUP and a CANADA CUP player. In 1949 Hogan was seriously injured in a road accident when at the height of his powers. His successful fight to return to the top ranks of professional GOLF is one of the romantic stories of the game's history.

HOGAN, JIMMIE, see FOOTBALL, ASSOCIATION.

HOGG, J. B., see TOUCH BALL.

HOHNE, CHRISTOPH (1941-), race walker for East Germany. He has taken over from PAMICH as the outstanding 50 km. walker of his time and was Olympic champion in 1968 with a margin of 10 minutes, and European champion in 1969. He set a world best for 30 miles and 50 km. in 1965 and 1969, and has won two LUGANO CUP finals at 50 km. (1965 and 1967). Two other outstanding performances by Hohne are his course records for the PRAGUE–PODEBRADY race (1967) and the LUGANO 100 KM. (1967).

HOLANI, a very old game, similar to the early forms of HOCKEY, still played in Turkey. The *holani* is a wooden cylinder or wedge which is hit by sticks. It is larger than a TENNIS ball and very hard. The sticks used are rough-and-ready. There are no rules governing the game, no time limits, field specifications, nor restrictions on the number of players. The aim is to hit the ball through the opponents' goal. Games sometimes start at daybreak and end at nightfall.

HOLMENKOLLEN, the world's leading ski-jumping (see SKIING) hill on the outskirts of Oslo, Norway. The Holmenkollen Week, in which jumping from the hill and cross-country ski racing figure, is the outstanding event of the Scandinavian winter sports season. The

Holmenkollen, built in 1892 and introduced in its present form in 1964, is a 90 m. (98 yds.) hill, and crowds of more than 100,000 can watch events.

HONDA, Japanese firm of motor-cycle manufacturers, extremely prominent in international racing in the years 1961-7. Beginning in the lightweight classes with engines outstanding in their day for crankshaft speed and high specific performance, Honda invested heavily in research and development to produce highly refined multi-cylinder four-stroke engines which gave its team complete domination of all classes save the 500 cc. in the early 1960s. When they produced a 500 cc. machine for 1966 and 1967 it proved extremely powerful but very difficult to handle. Racing versions of their road machines have since remained popular in a variety of classes, especially for long-distance events.

HOOD SKITTLES, see SKITTLES.

HOP, STEP, AND JUMP, see TRIPLE JUMP.

HOPE, Capt. W. L. (1897-   ), British aviator, the only man to win the King's Cup race three times. He served in aviation in both World Wars and flew as a commercial pilot in the years between. He raced regularly in the 1920s and 1930s.

HOPKINS, THELMA (later Mrs. McLernon) (1936-   ), Irish international at ATHLETICS, HOCKEY, and SQUASH RACKETS. She was an outstanding high jumper who broke the world record, winning a silver medal at the 1956 OLYMPIC GAMES and gold medals at the Empire Games and EUROPEAN CHAMPIONSHIPS in 1954. She also won medals as a long jumper and was a British record-holder for the PENTATHLON. A brilliant hockey forward in all five attacking positions, she scored on her international début and went on to win 40 caps. She was also a member of the first British Isles touring hockey team which went to the United States in 1965. She became a triple international when she was chosen for Ireland at squash.

HOPKIRK, PADDY (1933-   ), Irish motor rally driver (see MOTOR RACING). From 1962, he won outright such events as the Monte Carlo Rally, the Austrian Alpine Rally, the French Alpine Rally, the Acropolis Rally, and the Circuit of Ireland. He was second in the 1970 London-to-Sydney Marathon but failed in the London–Mexico event.

HOPMAN, HARRY C. (1906-   ), Australian LAWN TENNIS player and team captain. An outstanding doubles player, Hopman, in the 30 years to 1968, was the most successful Davis Cup (see LAWN TENNIS) captain in the history of the game. Other captains interrupted his reign, but in crises Australia always called on him. Between 1950, when he resumed the leadership of the team, and 1967, Australia won the Davis Cup 15 times and captured the men's singles title at Wimbledon ten times. They lost the Davis Cup in 1968 only because most of their leading players had turned professional. If the Davis Cup had been an open competition, Australia's domination must have continued, since Hopman's former players were ruling the professional game. With his insistence on team discipline and absolute fitness, he turned his lawn tennis players into first-class athletes and in some cases turned good athletes into first-class players.

One of his great strengths was that he was never afraid to blood newcomers. He boldly introduced HOAD and ROSEWALL, then aged 19, into the 1953 challenge round, and did the same with NEWCOMBE in 1963 after LAVER had turned professional. Until the demands of the professional tennis promoters completely impoverished Australia, Hopman seemed always to have the knack of finding new champions. He was a bitter opponent of open lawn tennis. His first wife, Nell, with whom he won a number of important mixed doubles titles, played a major part in persuading the International Lawn Tennis Federation to establish the Federation Cup (see LAWN TENNIS), the women's international team championship. Hopman later went to coach in the U.S.A.

HORDER, HAROLD (1894-   ), Australian RUGBY LEAGUE player. The champion winger of his time, he was a dazzling runner, with exceptional speed off the mark. For SOUTH SYDNEY, his sprinting and sidestepping gained him a popularity which spanned ten years as an international. He made his first appearance for Australia against Great Britain in 1914, and played in nine Tests altogether, including three in England in 1920-1.

HORNSBY, ROGERS (1896-1963), American BASEBALL player for several major-league teams and one of the renowned batters of the game's history. He won the NATIONAL LEAGUE batting championship seven times. His lifetime batting average of ·358 includes three seasons with averages higher than ·400, and for the five-year span 1921-5 he compiled a remarkable ·402 average. He also managed a number of teams and, as player-manager, led the ST. LOUIS CARDINALS to their first world championship in 1926.

HORSE-RACE BETTING LEVY BOARD, see HORSE RACING.

HORSE RACING. Organized horse racing is of two kinds: 'across the flat' or flat racing under JOCKEY CLUB rules; and 'over the sticks' or jumping under National Hunt rules, subdivided into steeplechasing and hurdle racing. Point-to-point racing is held under the sanction of the Jockey Club, and other forms of equine contests, not controlled by the Turf Authorities, are pony racing and TROTTING races (the modern form of chariot races), and show jumping (see EQUESTRIAN EVENTS).

FLAT RACING in Great Britain takes place between the third week in March and the second week in November on some 40 race-courses, of which the most important are NEW-MARKET, ASCOT, EPSOM, DONCASTER and York, SANDOWN, GOODWOOD and Newbury, Newcastle, Ayr, and Haydock.

Thoroughbred horses may not run in races on the course until they are two-year-olds, when the most important events they can compete for are the Coventry Stakes, Norfolk Stakes, and Queen Mary Stakes (fillies) at the Royal Ascot meeting in June; National Stakes at Sandown; Richmond Stakes and Molecomb Stakes (fillies) at Goodwood; Gimcrack Stakes and Lowther Stakes (fillies) at York; Mill Reef Stakes at Newbury; and Champagne Stakes and Flying Childers Stakes at Doncaster. In the autumn come the Royal Lodge Stakes, and Cornwallis Stakes at Ascot; Middle Park Stakes, Cheveley Park Stakes (fillies), and Dewhurst Stakes at Newmarket; Horris Hill Stakes at Newbury; and OBSERVER GOLD CUP at Doncaster.

Free Handicaps, one for two-year-olds and another for three-year-olds, are compiled at the end of each English flat-racing season by the official handicapper to the Jockey Club. He places in order of merit the leading race-horses of the year, giving top weight to the horse he considers to be the best of its age and allotting lesser weights to the others in a descending scale. At the end of their first racing season the two-year-olds, placed in order of merit in the Free Handicap, retire to their winter quarters until the following spring when they reappear as three-year-olds, now eligible to compete in the classic races and attempt to win the triple crown.

The five classic races are the TWO THOU-SAND GUINEAS and ONE THOUSAND GUINEAS (fillies), both run over one mile (1,600 m.) at Newmarket in the spring; the DERBY and OAKS (fillies) both run over 1½ miles (2,400 m.) at Epsom in the summer; and the ST. LEGER, run over 1¾ miles (2,800 m.) at Doncaster in the autumn. The triple crown for colts is to win the Derby, St. Leger, and Two Thousand Guineas; and for fillies, the Oaks, St. Leger, and One Thousand Guineas. Other important races for three-year-olds are the St. James's Palace Stakes and Coronation Stakes (fillies), both run over a mile at Royal Ascot; the King Edward VII Stakes and Ribblesdale Stakes (fillies), both run over 1½ miles at the same meeting; the Gordon Stakes and Nassau Stakes (fillies), at Goodwood; the Great Voltigeur Stakes and Yorkshire Oaks (fillies) at York; the Park Hill Stakes (fillies) over the St. Leger course at Doncaster; and the Sun Chariot Stakes (fillies) at Newmarket.

The three-year-olds may then either retire to stud or remain in training to appear as four-year-olds in the following season in weight-for-age races, which are contests between horses of different ages in which the older animals carry higher weights than their younger rivals, to compensate for their greater maturity and development. The scale of Weight-for-Age still being used today was originally drawn up by Admiral ROUS in the nineteenth century.

These events are among the most interesting of all, since winners of the classic races in any year can meet those who won them in the previous or earlier years. The most important weight-for-age races in the English calendar are the KING GEORGE VI AND QUEEN ELI-ZABETH STAKES over 1½ miles (2,400 m.) at Ascot in July; the ECLIPSE STAKES at Sandown; the CHAMPION STAKES at Newmarket; the CORONATION CUP, over the Derby course at Epsom; the SUSSEX STAKES at Goodwood; the Hardwicke Stakes and Prince of Wales Stakes at Royal Ascot; the Lockinge Stakes at Newbury and the Benson and Hedges Gold Cup at York, together with the ASCOT GOLD CUP, Goodwood Cup, and Doncaster Cup.

There are, of course, many brilliant horses who lack the stamina to win races even up to a mile in length, let alone the two miles or more of the big Cup races. Special events are therefore provided for these sprinters, who are often among the fastest horses in training. Such races are the King's Stand Stakes at Royal Ascot, the July Cup at Newmarket, the Nunthorpe Sweepstakes at York, the Diadem Stakes at Ascot, and Vernon's Sprint Cup at Haydock.

Next come the handicap races for those horses who are not capable of competing on weight-for-age terms with any hope of success because they are not up to classic standard. In these events the competing animals carry different weights according to their ability as assessed by the official handicapper, based mainly on the form they have already shown in public in earlier races. The most important handicaps of the flat-racing season in England are the LINCOLN at Doncaster, City and Suburban at Epsom, Victoria Cup, Chester Cup, Kempton Jubilee, Ascot Stakes, Royal Hunt Cup at Ascot, Stewards Cup at Goodwood, EBOR at York, Portland at Doncaster, and the CAMBRIDGESHIRE and CESAREWITCH. The last two are known as the 'Autumn Double', on which some of the heaviest betting of the racing season takes place. (The 'Spring Double' — the first big betting medium of the year — consists of the Lincoln Handicap and the GRAND NATIONAL.)

Finally there are the Plates, for which prizes of fixed value are guaranteed by the racing authorities irrespective of the number of entries; and selling races, the winners of which must be offered for sale by auction immediately after the race. The winner may, however, be bought-in by his owner, and any of the other runners may be claimed for the advertised selling price plus the value of the stakes or plate.

Most race meetings will contain a mixture of the various types of event described above, over distances from five furlongs to two miles or more, and there are usually six races in each afternoon.

Each meeting is presided over by stewards approved by the Jockey Club (usually three in number), whose duty it is to see that the rules of racing are observed during the meeting. They have the power to hear objections to the winner on any grounds, and to fine or suspend a jockey for crossing, jostling, bumping, boring, or other forms of foul riding. They can also order saliva and other dope tests to be taken and report their findings to the stewards of the Jockey Club. Other officials at a meeting are the clerk of the course, the clerk of the scales, the starter, and the judge.

The clerk of the course is responsible for the whole organization and administration, the condition of the track, the maintenance of the buildings, stands, and enclosures, the catering facilities, the issue of official race-cards giving the programme for the day, and the parade of horses in the paddock before each event.

The clerk of the scales draws by lot the order in which race-horses are to line up at the start, and is also responsible for hoisting on the number-boards full details of runners, riders, weights to be carried, and results of the draw. He has to weigh-out each jockey before a race and weigh-in again the riders of the winner and placed horses after the event to ensure that they carried the correct weights laid down by the conditions of each race.

The starter lines up the competitors in the correct order in their starting stalls (where these are used, otherwise behind the starting 'gate') according to the draw, with No. 1 on the left of the course, and releases the starting mechanism when all the horses are in position. Long ago races were started by dropping a flag; a starting 'gate' or contraption of tapes was first used in the Derby of 1901, and starting stalls were introduced at Newmarket in 1965 and for starting the Derby in 1967.

The judge places the first six horses in the correct order in which they pass the winning post and estimates the distances which separate the first three. In 1952, the stewards of the Jockey Club directed that a judge, before reaching a decision, must consult the photograph taken by the photo-finish camera if a neck or less separates any of the first four horses.

At the race-course are various private boxes and public stands, catering facilities, restaurants and bars, a members' enclosure, TATTERSALLS, and the silver ring, all at various admission charges, while betting facilities are available on the Totalisator or with bookmakers.

The Totalisator was introduced in 1929 at Newmarket, to enable at least part of the vast sums which annually passed through the betting 'ring' to be made available for the betterment of the sport. The 'Tote' computer works out the exact mathematical odds on each horse in a race, according to the total amount of money staked to win and for a place. After deductions for Government taxes and Horse-Race Betting Levy Board contributions, the balance remaining in the 'pool' is divided among the successful punters on production of their winning tickets. The Tote also operates 'doubles', 'trebles', and 'jack-pot' prizes for correct forecasts. It is run by the Horse-Race Totalisator Board which also controls Tote Investors Ltd. The record Tote jack-pot was £63,114 for a 5-shilling ticket at Royal Ascot in 1966.

Bookmakers are the professional commission agents who accept bets on the results of sporting contests of various kinds, especially horse racing. 'Bookies' line the rails between enclosures at race meetings, or operate from licensed betting shops and from starting-price offices at their headquarters in London and other cities. Betting tax is deducted from all returns, stakes, and winnings, to cover bookmakers' contributions to the betting levy.

The horses taking part in each race will be shown on the official programme on sale at the entrance gates and the runners and riders, with the positions they have drawn at the start, will be hoisted on the number boards on the race-course. The horses may be inspected in the paddock before each event and are also paraded in front of the stands and enclosures before the most important races. They then canter down to the start where the starter's assistants supervise each horse being ridden into his correct starting stall (if in use) according to the draw.

A mobile camera patrol follows the race, and the film taken is available for consultation by the stewards in the event of any complaint being lodged or objection made against the winner. A running commentary on each race is broadcast over loudspeakers at the race-course.

STEEPLECHASING and HURDLE RACING. Steeplechases and hurdle races in England are run over a distance of two miles or more. Regulations lay down that there must be at least one ditch and six birch fences 4 ft. 6 in. (1·37 m.) high for every mile, including one water-jump, in each steeplechase, and at least eight flights of hurdles in every two miles in each hurdle race — the hurdles, packed with gorse and slightly sloped, being not less than 3 ft. 6 in. (1·06 m.) from bottom bar to top bar.

Over the years, the National Hunt season has gradually become longer, and the 1973-4 season began early in August and will end on 1 June. No horse can run for a hurdle race until 1 July (in practice the beginning of the season) of the year in which he is three years old, or for a steeplechase until 1 July of the year in which he is four years old. Jumping meetings are held at Liverpool (AINTREE), Cheltenham, Ascot, Sandown, Newcastle, Newbury, Haydock, Ayr, Doncaster, and elsewhere.

The most important steeplechases are the Grand National at Aintree, the Gold Cup, Champion Novices' Chase, and Two Mile Champion Chase at Cheltenham's National Hunt Festival meeting in March, the Mackeson Gold Cup at Cheltenham, the Hennessy Gold Cup at Newbury, the Massey-Ferguson Gold Cup at Cheltenham, the King George VI Chase at Kempton Park on 26 December, the Wills Premier Chase at Haydock, and the Whitbread Gold Cup at Sandown, together with the Welsh, Scottish, and Irish Grand Nationals. The principal hurdle races are the CHAMPION HURDLE CHALLENGE CUP at Cheltenham, Imperial Cup at Sandown, Schweppes Gold Trophy at Newbury, *Daily Express* Triumph Hurdle at Cheltenham, Victor Ludorum Hurdle at Haydock, Irish Sweeps Hurdle at Leopardstown, and Players No. 6 National Hurdle Championship at Chepstow.

POINT-TO-POINT RACES are horse races for amateur riders held annually by most hunts on cross-country courses. There are about 120 courses scattered over the British Isles, some of which are shared by more than one hunt. These were originally run straight across country, hence the name. Today, however, the track is usually oval and the fences built in the same way as those on a race-course, although the course is often on a farmer's land. The horses must have a certificate to prove they have been hunted regularly during the season. Each hunt is allowed one meeting a year, and during the season, February to May, 200 fixtures are held all over the country.

The major event of the point-to-point season is the Player's Gold Leaf Championship, the final of which is run at Newbury. The Vaux Novices' Championship, which also involves a series of qualifying races with the final at Sedgefield, is the leading event in the north of England, and other prestige races are the Melton Hunt Club Novices' Championship and the Goya Championship for lady riders. Three of the most coveted prizes are the open races held at the Heythrop, Middleton, and Worcestershire Hunts — the Lord Ashton of Hydes' Cup, the Ralph Grimthorpe Cup, and the Lady Dudley Cup.

Rules of Racing (1971).

It was discovered at the end of the seventeenth century that certain systems of mating horses produced much faster animals than hitherto, and, as a result, racing became virtually confined to thoroughbred animals. All thoroughbred race-horses throughout the world are descended in the direct male line, father-to-son chain, from one of only three out of nearly 200 Arabian, Turkish, or Barbary steeds imported into England during the seventeenth and eighteenth centuries, viz: the DARLEY ARABIAN, BYERLEY TURK, and GODOLPHIN BARB, whose stirps were passed down through ECLIPSE, HEROD, and MATCHEM. It is a remarkable fact that, out of the 174 eastern stallions mentioned in volume I (1791) of the *General Stud Book* (see below), only these three sire lines have survived to the present day. On the distaff side of their pedigrees, all thoroughbreds again are descended in the direct female line, mother-to-daughter chain, from one of only some 50 tap-root mares out of all those whose names appear in the early volumes of the *General Stud Book*, together with some foundation mares in the United States.

The male lines descending from Eclipse are those through TOUCHSTONE, Newminster, Lord Clifden, Hampton, Bay Ronald, BAYARDO, and GAINSBOROUGH to HYPERION; through STOCKWELL, Doncaster, BEND OR, Bona Vista, Cyllene, Polymelus, Phalaris, and Pharos to NEARCO; through Stockwell, Doncaster, Bend Or, ORMONDE, Orme, FLYING

FOX, Ajax, Teddy, Aethelstan, Deivi, and Deux Pour Cent to TANTIÈME; through ISONOMY, ISINGLASS, John O' Gaunt, SWYNFORD, Blandford, and Blenheim to DONATELLO II; and through VOLTIGEUR, Vedette, Galspin, and ST. SIMON either through PERSIMMON, PRINCE PALATINE, Rose Prince, and Prince Rose to Prince Chevalier; or through Rabelais, Havresac II, Cavaliere d'Arpino, Bellini, and Tenerani to RIBOT. The male line from Herod descends via Bay Middleton and THE FLYING DUTCHMAN to BRULEUR, KSAR, Tourbillon, and DJEBEL; and that from Matchem via Melbourne and WEST AUSTRALIAN to Hurry On and Precipitation, and to FAIR PLAY, MAN O' WAR, and WAR ADMIRAL. These are the main trunk lines from which local male branches will be found all over the world.

On the female lines certain families have been more prolific than others. Notable brood mares such as PRUNELLA and her daughter Penelope, PARADIGM and her great-great-granddaughter Popinjay, Canterbury Pilgrim, Conjure, Marchetta, Absurdity, and LA TROIENNE were all descended in the female line from the Natural Barb Mare of Mr. Tregonwell, who lived in the reign of Charles II and is the original female ancestress of more classic winners than any other tap-root mare; MADREE, Altoviscar, and Double Life come down from the Burton Barb Mare who was located at the Hampton Court Stud, Middlesex, in the days of the Merry Monarch; and Bowes' Mare by the Byerley Turk, who was foaled in about 1695, numbers among her descendants Barbelle, POCAHONTAS, QUIVER, Black Duchess, and Rosy Legend. MAGGIE B.B., Nogara (dam of Nearco), and Romanella (dam of Ribot) trace to the Layton Barb Mare (1685); MORGANETTE to Old Ebony (1714); Gondolette, third dam of Hyperion, to OLD BALD PEG (c. 1650); PERDITA II to Lord Darcy's Royal Mare; LADY JOSEPHINE and ASTRONOMIE to the Vintner Mare; QUEEN MARY and GALICIA to Fair Helen; SCAPA FLOW, ADMIRATION, and SCEPTRE and her daughter, Maid of the Mist, to Sedbury Royal Mare, Oldfield Mare, and Sister to Stripling respectively.

Qualifications for admission to the *General Stud Book*, the register of all thoroughbred horses throughout the world which has been compiled and published regularly in England by WEATHERBY, have sometimes been debated. In 1913 the Jersey 'Act', a measure sponsored by Lord Jersey, appeared in volume XXII of the *General Stud Book*, restricting the registration of thoroughbreds to those horses who could trace their pedigrees without flaw, through both the sire and dam, to horses and mares themselves already accepted in earlier volumes of the *Stud Book*. Following much

criticism, mainly from American and French bloodstock breeders, the measure was 'repealed' in 1949, when volume XXXI announced that 'any animal claiming admission from now onwards must be able to prove satisfactorily some eight or nine crosses of pure blood, to trace back for at least a century, and to show such performances of its immediate family on the Turf as to warrant the belief in the purity of its blood'.

Experts still differ as to the relative importance of the sire line and the dam line in the heredity of the race-horse. ROBERTSON was a leading exponent of the theory of male dominance; BECKER of the importance of the female lines. Lowe invented a figure system, Col. VUILLIER a dosage system.

Lowe listed some 50 tap-root thoroughbred mares in numerical order according to the number of direct descendants of each mare through the female, mother-to-daughter, line which had won the Derby, Oaks, and St. Leger up to the time of compilation. He then allocated the number 1 to the family whose foundation mare could claim the most winners of these three classic races, the number 2 to the family with the second highest number of these classic winners among its offspring, and so on. This was the first serious attempt to give to the dam's side of a thoroughbred's pedigree some share of the credit for the development of the race-horse, which hitherto had been assigned almost entirely to the sire lines.

For his dosage system, Vuillier analysed to the 4,096 ancestors in the twelfth generation of a pedigree the number of times different sires appeared in the ancestry of the best race-horses and concluded therefrom that certain male lines, in definite fixed proportions, were desirable to attain the best results in breeding. He recommended that if a brood mare was deficient in any of the indicated strains, this deficiency should be made good by the stallion selected for mating with her. This was the first 'scientific' approach to thoroughbred breeding and was the method adopted by the AGA KHAN for his highly successful venture into this field.

'Breed in to fix type, breed out to secure vigour' is an accepted principle: but breeding thoroughbreds is not an exact science, and, more often than not, success comes only as a result of a long and expensive process of trial and error.

A stud is a breeding establishment for thoroughbreds, where stallions stand for mating with visiting mares and where brood mares are maintained while in foal and during weaning. The most important breeders and studs in England have been: the Royal Studs at Hampton Court and Sandringham, the NATIONAL

STUDS at Tully, Gillingham, and Newmarket, the Duke of WESTMINSTER at Eaton, the Duke of PORTLAND at Welbeck, the Earls of ROSE-BERY at Mentmore, Lord DERBY's Stanley Stud, Lord ASTOR's Cliveden Stud, the Aga Khan, and Major Holliday; in France, the ROTH-SCHILDS at MEAUTRY, BOUSSAC, DUPRÉ, and the VOLTERRAS; in Italy, the famous DORMELLO *razza* of Tesio; in Germany, Erlenhof and Schlenderhan; in the U.S.A., Col. BRADLEY's celebrated Idle Hour Stock Farm, CALUMET, and CLAIBORNE; in the Argentine, CHAPADMA-LAL.

Bloodstock prices over the years have risen to astronomical figures (see TATTERSALLS).

General Stud Book (published every four years, plus supplements).

The origin of horse racing is lost in time, but it was evidently derived from warfare, chariot racing, and the chase. One of the earliest references is given by the secretary to Thomas Becket, Archbishop of Canterbury in the reign of Henry II of England (1154-89). He described how 'the jockies, inspired with thoughts of applause, and in the hope of victory, clap spurs to the willing horses, brandish their whips, and cheer them with their cries.'

In 1377 the Prince of Wales, later Richard II, raced against the Earl of Arundel 'owners up', and most of the early accounts of horse racing consist of descriptions of 'matches' between two 'running horses', where the owner of a 'horse of price' wagers that his steed is faster than that of another knight-at-arms, issues a challenge to his rival, and the matter is put to the test over a course of some miles before the king and court. The most celebrated match in the history of the Turf was the contest between The Flying Dutchman and Voltigeur at York in 1851 over a course of 2 miles (3·2 km.) for a stake of 1,000 guineas, which the former won by a short length in 3 min. 55 sec., after a desperate struggle between the two equine champions.

The first permanent race-course with an annual fixture was established on the Roodee at Chester in 1540, and the Newmarket Gold Cup was first competed for in 1634. By 1660, when 'a hound and hawk no longer shall be tokens of disaffection, a cock-fight shall cease to be a breach of the peace, and a horse-race an insurrection', Charles II made Newmarket the headquarters of the Turf, and 'Newmarket's glory rose, as Britain's fell'; the king himself winning the Plate on 14 October 1671.

Burton in *The Anatomy of Melancholy* refers to 'Horse-races and wildgoose chases, which are disports of greater men, and good in themselves, though many gentlemen by such means gallop themselves out of their fortunes'. Such vast sums were wagered on the result of horse 'matches' that Parliament, 'to put a stop to such ruinous proceedings', passed a law to prevent the recovery of any sum exceeding ten pounds betted on a horse-race.

After the death of FRAMPTON, the 'father of the English Turf', in 1727 and the formation of the Jockey Club in 1750, the history of horse racing in England became linked with the names of men like BUNBURY, BENTINCK, Derby, Admiral Rous. The RACING CALEN-DAR was first published in 1773, the Derby was first run in 1708, and the first volume of the *General Stud Book* appeared in 1791.

Meanwhile matches had been superseded by a system of heats followed by a final race between the winners of the heats. Subsequently it was decided that all entries for a given event would run against one another in a single race. Jockeys were made to wear distinctive colours; owners employed their own trainers; a judge, a starter, and clerk of the scales, and other officials were appointed by the Jockey Club; so that, by the time Queen Victoria came to the throne in 1837, horse racing had become very much as it is today, except that jockeys then sat upright in the saddle and used long stirrup-leathers and reins. One new development is that in 1972 flat races for women riders were permitted for the first time, and in 1974 women will be allowed to compete against men in amateur races. In 1975 all flat races will be open to women jockeys. (For the history of the development of the thoroughbred race-horse from the days of Old Bald Peg, *c.* 1650, see above.)

In 1968 a Joint Racing Board was set up in England to facilitate policy discussions between the Turf Authorities and the Horse-race Betting Levy Board formed by Act of Parliament to 'provide for the contributions for purposes connected with the advancement of horse racing from persons engaged by way of business in effecting betting transactions on horse races, and for connected purposes' (i.e. the betting tax). Maj.-Gen. FEILDEN, senior steward of the Jockey Club and chairman of the Turf Board (composed of the stewards of the Jockey Club, and the National Hunt Committee), and Lord Wigg, chairman of the Levy Board, were appointed co-chairmen of the new organization, with Brig. Kent and Brig. Waller as joint secretaries. At the same time a liaison committee was formed to hear the views of members of the Race-course Association, the Race-horse Owners Association, the Thoroughbred Breeders Association, the national trainers associations, and the jockeys' associations.

This followed a report on the English racing

industry, submitted by a committee presided over by Benson, which found *inter alia* that there was insufficient money available to improve racing, to meet overseas competition, and to maintain the bloodstock industry. Prize money particularly was poor compared with France in pattern and feature races, so that it was frequently more profitable for an owner to race his best horses on the Continent.

The champion race-horses of the English turf would include all the winners of the triple crown and its fillies' counterpart. Only 12 colts have ever succeeded in winning the Derby, the St. Leger, and the Two Thousand Guineas: West Australian in 1853, GLADIATEUR in 1865, Lord Lyon in 1866, Ormonde in 1886, Common in 1891, Isinglass in 1893, Galtee More in 1897, Flying Fox in 1899, DIAMOND JUBILEE in 1900, ROCK SAND in 1903, BAHRAM in 1935, and NIJINSKY in 1970. The triple crown for fillies, consisting of the Oaks, St. Leger, and One Thousand Guineas, has been won only seven times: FORMOSA in 1868, Hannah in 1871, APOLOGY in 1874, LA FLECHE in 1892, Sceptre in 1902, PRETTY POLLY in 1904, and MELD in 1955. War-time triple crowns were won by POMMERN in 1915, GAY CRUSADER in 1917, and Gainsborough in 1918; and Sun Chariot won a fillies' substitute in 1942.

Since colts are not eligible to run in the Oaks and the One Thousand Guineas, it follows that only a filly can win all five of the classic races. In fact, this feat has never yet been accomplished, although two brilliant fillies have each won four classics, namely Sceptre, who won the Two Thousand Guineas, One Thousand Guineas, Oaks, and St. Leger in 1902, finishing fourth in the Derby; and Formosa, who won the same four classics in 1868, her victory in the Two Thousand Guineas being a dead-heat which she later lost in the run-off.

Three horses have won both legs of the Autumn Double, i.e. the Cambridgeshire and Cesarewitch Handicaps, in the same season: Rosebery in 1876, Foxhall in 1881, and Plaisanterie in 1885. Other champions of the English turf would include HIGHFLYER, The Flying Dutchman and Voltigeur, Bend Or and St. Simon, AYRSHIRE and Persimmon, Bayardo and LEMBERG, Swynford and Prince Palatine, TRACERY and THE TETRARCH, as well as more recent horses like SOLARIS, CORONACH, FAIRWAY, Hyperion, WINDSOR LAD, BROWN JACK, and Blue Peter; Alycidon, TULYAR, AUREOLE, BALLYMOSS, ALCIDE, PETITE ÉTOILE, ST. PADDY, RAGUSA, SANTA CLAUS, CHARLOTTOWN, ROYAL PALACE, SIR IVOR, VAGUELY NOBLE, LEVMOSS, RHEINGOLD, BRIGADIER GERARD, and MILL REEF.

Steeplechasing is believed to have begun in Ireland in the eighteenth century, consisting simply of matches between two horses across country, using church steeples as landmarks, over a distance of four or five miles. The riders were usually members of the local hunt who knew the countryside well.

The new sport soon spread to England, but it was not until 1830 that annual steeplechase fixtures began, when a meeting conducted by the Household Cavalry was held at St. Albans. Three years later the Grand Steeplechase at Cheltenham was founded, followed in 1836 by the first regular meeting 'over the sticks' at Aintree, where the Great Steeplechase was inaugurated in 1839. This race was re-named the 'Liverpool and National' a few years later, and finally the 'Grand National Steeplechase'.

The Grand National Hunt Committee was formed in 1866 to control and administer the sport; the Duke of Beaufort, the Earls of Coventry and Wilton, and Mr. Craven being the chief sponsors. Some twenty years later members of the Jockey Club were included in a new National Hunt Committee, which became the governing body for all steeplechases, hurdle races, bona-fide hunt meetings, and military events run under National Hunt rules, until the Committee was merged with the Jockey Club to form the Joint Racing Board in 1969.

Among enthusiastic supporters of National Hunt racing, past and present, are Queen Elizabeth the Queen Mother, Lord Bicester, Lord Grimthorpe, Lord Leverhulme, Lord Stalbridge, Hon. DOROTHY PAGET, and J. V. Rank; trainers and riders include Lord Mildmay, Hon. Aubrey Hastings, Ivor, Jack, and Owen Anthony, G. Wilson, Walwyn, Dowdeswell, Rimell, Cazalet, Mellor, Stephenson, Gifford, Biddlecombe, Barry, B. R. Davies, and the incomparable WINTER.

Famous steeplechase horses include Manifesto, Easter Hero, GOLDEN MILLER, Reynoldstown, Cottage Rake, Mandarin, MILL HOUSE, ARKLE, and PENDIL, with PERSIAN WAR, BULA, Sir Ken, and Hatton's Grace the most outstanding hurdlers.

Breeder-owners celebrated in the annals of the turf in England include Bowes and HAWLEY, Lord Eglinton and Lord Zetland, Lord Chaplin and Lord FALMOUTH; then at the turn of the last century, the Prince of WALES (later Edward VII), the Duke of Westminster, the Duke of Portland, and the Earl of Rosebery; followed by Lord Derby, Lord Astor, the Aga Khan, Sir Victor SASSOON and Major Holliday; QUEEN ELIZABETH II, Sir Harold and Lady WERNHER, ENGELHARD, Robinson, and members of the Joel family.

Among prominent trainers, SCOTT and

PORTER, DAWSON and MARSH, ALEC TAYLOR, LAMBTON, DARLING, BUTTERS and LAWSON, JARVIS, BOYD-ROCHFORT, MURLESS, and O'BRIEN should be specially noted. The leading jockeys have been Flatman, BUCKLE, and J. ROBINSON, ARCHER and FORDHAM, Cannon, Wootton, DONOGHUE, RICHARDS, PIGGOTT, D. Smith, CARSON, and Breasley.

The first sporting artist in England was Barlow (c. 1626-1704) who was followed by Wooton (c. 1677-1765) and Seymour (1702-52). Then came the most famous of all painters of race-horses, Stubbs (1724-1806), who made a careful study of the anatomy of the horse and so first depicted the thoroughbred as a living animal of flesh, bone, and muscle. He was succeeded by J. N. Sartorius, Marshall, Ward, Chalon, Fernley, Alken, Pollard, and many others. But the best of the Victorian artists to paint pictures of the Turf was Herring, sr. (1795-1865), with masterpieces such as 'Bay Middleton and Barbelle at the Stud' and 'The celebrated match between The Flying Dutchman and Voltigeur'. The most popular racing picture is probably Frith's 'Derby Day', and the most acclaimed horse artist of recent times Munnings (1878-1959).

Eminent writers on turf affairs have included COOK, PORTMAN, and HISLOP.

INTERNATIONAL HORSE RACING. The racing of thoroughbreds, which first became a properly controlled and well-organized sport in England, gradually spread to British overseas territories: Australia, New Zealand, South Africa, and Canada, where today horse racing draws enormous crowds. Other countries also developed the sport, Ireland, France, Italy, and Germany particularly in Europe; and the U.S.A., Argentina, and other South American countries.

Ireland. The climate of the Emerald Isle seems to be the best in the world for breeding and rearing race-horses. Furthermore, one of the foremost trainers of thoroughbreds, O'Brien, has his stables of Cashel in County Tipperary. The IRISH SWEEPS DERBY and the IRISH GUINNESS OAKS are now international races of great value, and the Irish Grand National and the Leopardstown Chase are important jumping events.

The sport is controlled by the Irish Turf Club and the headquarters of horse racing in Ireland is the CURRAGH.

France. Horse racing in France officially dates from 1833, when the Société d'Encouragement pour l'Amélioration des Races de Chevaux en France was founded. Some 20 years later, French thoroughbreds, mostly bred from imported British stock, were winning important English races, such as MONARQUE with his victory in the Goodwood Cup of 1857, and the brilliant performances of his son Gladiateur in winning the English triple crown in 1865 and the Ascot Gold Cup in the following year.

The chief events of the racing year in France are the PRIX DE L'ARC DE TRIOMPHE, GRAND PRIX DE PARIS, PRIX DU JOCKEY CLUB, PRIX DE DIANE, PRIX ROYAL OAK, and the POULE D'ESSAI DES POULAINS and POULE D'ESSAI DES POULICHES; together with the GRAND PRIX DE SAINT-CLOUD, PRIX GANAY, PRIX DU CADRAN, PRIX LUPIN, PRIX SAINT-ALARY, PRIX VERMEILLE, Prix de la Forêt, Prix Morny, the GRAND CRITERIUM, Criterium des Pouliches, Grand Prix de Deauville, Prix du Moulin de Longchamp, Prix Robert Papin, and Prix de la Salamandre. The majority of these races are run at LONGCHAMP, but some of the major events also take place at Saint-Cloud, Chantilly, Deauville, Evry, and Maisons-Lafitte.

A flourishing breeding industry has grown up in France based on famous stud farms such as the Haras de Meautry, and sales of yearlings and other bloodstock are held annually at DEAUVILLE. The Frenchman, Col. Vuillier, was the inventor of the most widely used system of bloodstock breeding (see above).

Among leading breeders and owners in France have been Baron de Rothschild, Boussac, Dupré, and Volterra; prominent trainers included CARTER, MATHET, POLLET, Boutin, Head, and SEMBLAT; and outstanding jockeys are SAINT-MARTIN, Cruguet, Samani, Head, and Desaint.

The best French stallions were Bruleur and Tantième; the best brood-mares, Astronomie and RELANCE; while any list of outstanding race-horses of the Turf in France must include Monarque, Gladiateur, BOIARD, PERTH II, ksar, PEARL CAP, BRANTOME, Djebel, LE PACHA, and CARACALLA II, as well as more recent champions such as Tantième, RIGHT ROYAL V, MATCH III, EXBURY, RELKO, SEA BIRD II, RELIANCE, SASSAFRAS, and DAHLIA.

Italy. Horse racing in Italy officially began in about 1881 with the formation of the Italian Jockey Club and attained international standards when Apelle won the Coronation Cup at Epsom in 1928, followed a few years later by the victories of ORTELLO and CRAPOM in the Prix de l'Arc de Triomphe at Longchamp.

The most important races in Italy are the GRAN PREMIO DI MILANO, GRAN PREMIO D'ITALIA, DERBY ITALIANO, OAKS D'ITALIA, ST. LEGER ITALIANO, and the PREMIOS PARIOLI and REGINA ELENA; together with the GRAN PREMIO DEL JOCKEY CLUB, PREMIO ROMA, Coppa d'Oro di Milano, GRAN CRITERIUM, Premio Presidente della Repubblica, and Criterium Nazionale. These valuable events are all run at SAN SIRO, Milan, except the

Derby, Premio Parioli (Two Thousand Guineas), Premio Regina Elena (One Thousand Guineas), and Premio Roma, which are held at LA CAPANNELLE, Rome.

The genius of the Italian turf was Tesio, who bred at the Dormello stud seven champion race-horses which later became international stallions: Apelle, Donatello II, Nearco, NICCOLO DELL' ARCA, Tenerani, BOTTICELLI, and Ribot, the last three being ridden by the leading Italian jockey CAMICI, who is now a trainer.

The most successful racing fillies in Italy were ARCHIDAMIA and ASTOLFINA; and the best brood mares Tirelire; Madree; Giottina; Catnip, bought by Tesio for only 75 guineas; Sunbird; Hollebeck; Duccia di Buoninsegna; Bunworry; Tofanella; and Romanella. The principal male stirps were those descending from Melton (English Derby and St. Leger; bought by the Italian government in 1890 for 12,000 guineas) through Best Man, Signorino, Michelangelo, and Navarro to GLADIOLO; from Flying Fox through Ajax, Teddy, Ortello, Torbido, and Antonio Canale to Marco Visconti (winner of two Milan Gran Premios and the Jockey club Gran Premio); and from St. Simon through Rabelais, Havresac II, Cavaliere d'Arpino (Tesio's favourite unbeaten horse), Bellini, and Tenerani to the mighty Ribot.

Prominent trainers are Cumani, D'Auria, Benedetti, and Pandolfi; top jockeys are Dettori, Di Wardo, Ferrari, Pisa, and Atzari; and the leading expert is Varola, who in his *Nuovi Dosaggi del Purosangue* expounded a new dosage system for breeding thoroughbreds.

Germany. Horse racing in Germany was first placed on a firm footing when the Union club (Germany Jockey club) was formed in 1867. The principal races are the GROSSER PREIS VON BADEN, the DEUTSCHES DERBY, the PREIS DER DIANA, the GROSSER PREIS VON NORDRHEIN-WESTFALEN, and the valuable PREIS VON EUROPA.

The best German race-horses were probably Oleander, who won the Grosser Preis von Baden three times and the Grosser Preis von Nordrhein-Westfalen twice; NIEDERLANDER; Lombard; and LUCIANO.

Two internationally known breeding and racing establishments in Germany are the Gestüt Erlenhof owned by Countess BATTHYÁNY and the Gestüt Schlenderhan owned by Baroness VON OPPENHEIM.

The leading German trainers are Jentzsch, Bollow, Seiffert, and Woehler, and the top jockeys Drechsler, Remmert, and Alafi, while the German expert on bloodstock-breeding was Becker.

U.S.A. In America, horse racing reached maturity in the 1860s with the emergence of sire lines founded on importations from England: LEXINGTON, great-great-grandson of Diomed, winner of the first English Derby; Glencoe, winner of the Two Thousand Guineas and Ascot Gold Cup; Australian, son of the triple-crowned West Australian; Leamington, great-grandson of Derby winner Whalebone; Eclipse, son of Derby winner Orlando; and Bonnie Scotland, son of the famous English brood mare Queen Mary. These were some of the stallions whose offspring moulded the American thoroughbred, together with outstanding American-bred brood mares such as Miss Obstinate, from whom Nearco is descended in the female line; Maggie B.B., dam of IROQUOIS; Mannic Gray, dam of Domino and Hamburg; Cinderella; Mahuba; Flambette; Marguerite; Friars Carse; and La Troienne. BOLD RULER is the latest of the leading stallions in the States, and BLUE LARKSPUR the best brood-mare sire.

State governors appoint three racing commissioners in each state where horse racing takes place. The New York (American) Jockey Club, founded in 1894, issues the *Racing Calendar*, maintains the *American Stud Book*, and compiles handicaps, the Free Handicap for two-year-olds being known in the U.S.A. as the 'Experimental Handicap'. Most racing takes place on specially prepared dirt or 'skinned' tracks; the emphasis is on speed not stamina. Horse racing in the United States is a highly organized, highly taxed, highly commercialized, professional undertaking.

The principal race-tracks in the U.S.A. are situated at ARLINGTON PARK, Chicago; BELMONT PARK, New York; CHURCHILL DOWNS, Louisville, Kentucky; LAUREL PARK, Washington; PIMLICO, Baltimore, Maryland; and SARATOGA SPRINGS, N.Y.; also in Florida and California. The main events in the calendar are the KENTUCKY DERBY, BELMONT STAKES, and PREAKNESS STAKES, forming the American triple crown; the American Derby and the Grand Prix Stakes at Arlington Park, the Santa Anita Derby, Hollywood Derby, Hollywood Gold Cúp, Charles H. Strub Stakes, and California Stakes, the TRAVERS, WITHERS, and LAWRENCE REALIZATION STAKES, KENTUCKY OAKS, Delaware Oaks, and COACHING CLUB AMERICAN OAKS, JOCKEY CLUB GOLD CUP, Saratoga Cup (abandoned in 1955), Woodward Stakes, Man o' War Stakes (on turf), Marlboro' Invitation Stakes, WASHINGTON INTERNATIONAL (on turf), and several Futurity Stakes for two-year-olds, as well as a number of important and valuable handicaps, Brooklyn, Metropolitan, Suburban, Monmouth Invitation, United Nations, Santa Anita, and San Juan Capistrano. In the U.S.A. much more importance is attached to this type of race than in European countries. Classic three-year-old winners, carrying heavy weight burdens, are expected to defeat not only their contemporaries but also their elders in the more important handicaps, if they are to sustain their claims to be champions.

Personalities connected with the American Turf have included outstanding administrators such as CASSIDY and VOSBURG; breeder-owners like BELMONT, Col. Bradley, Whitney, WIDENER, WOODWARD, and other members of their families; trainers like Rowe and JOYNER; and jockeys like ARCARO, SANDE, Longden, SHOEMAKER, Hawley, and Pincay; while many stud farms such as Calumet, Claiborne, and Idle Hour have earned world-wide prestige.

Finally, the race-horses themselves include champions such as BUCKPASSER, CITATION, DAMASCUS, DARK MIRAGE, FOXHALL, GALLANT FOX, Iroquois, KELSO, Man o' War, NASHUA, NATIVE DANCER, NEVER SAY DIE, ROUND TABLE, TWENTY GRAND, War Admiral, WHIRLAWAY, and SECRETARIAT.

Only nine thoroughbreds in the history of the American turf have succeeded in winning the triple crown: Sir Barton in 1919, Gallant Fox in 1930, Omaha in 1935, War Admiral in 1937, Whirlaway in 1941, Count Fleet in 1943, Assault in 1946, Citation in 1948, and Secretariat in 1973.

Argentina. Horse racing has been a popular sport in Argentina for over a hundred years, with a flourishing breeding industry established by individuals such as de Hoz and his family at Chapadmalal.

The most important races in the Argentine are the GRAN PREMIO CARLOS PELLEGRINI, GRAN PREMIO NACIONAL (Derby), Gran Premio Seleccion (Oaks), Gran Premio Jockey Club, Clasico Comparacion (Eclipse), Gran Premio 25 de Mayo, and Gran Premio de Honor (Gold Cup).

Champion race-horses of the Argentine have included Old Man, MACON, Yatasto, and ARTURO A.

Other South American countries. Horse racing is also conducted in Brazil, Chile, Colombia, Mexico, Panama, Peru, Puerto Rico, Uruguay, and Venezuela. The most important races are the Grande Premio do Brasil and the Grande Premio Cruzeiro do Sul run on the Gavea track at Rio de Janeiro; the Grande Premio do São Paulo and the Grande Premio Derby Paulista run at Cidade Jardim at São Paulo; the Gran Premio do Chile at Santiago; the Gran Premio Jose Pedro Ramirez at Maroñas, Montevideo; and the Gran Premio Clasico Simon Bolivar at La Rinconada, Caracas.

Australia. Horse racing is a leading spectator-sport in Australia, where the two principal turf authorities are the Australian Jockey Club (A.J.C.) in Sydney and the Victoria Racing Club (V.R.C.) in Melbourne. The most important and valuable events are the MELBOURNE CUP at FLEMINGTON, SYDNEY CUP at RANDWICK, the CAULFIELD CUP and the Perth Cup. GALILEE landed the first three in 1966-7; and trainer Cummings brought off the unique hat-trick of three winners of the Melbourne Cup in succession, as well as the Sydney, Caulfield, and Adelaide Cups twice, and Brisbane Cup once. The classic races are the A.J.C. Derby, Oaks, and St. Leger, the Caulfield Guineas, Victoria Derby, and V.R.C. St. Leger; the most important weight-for-age races are the COX PLATE and the Queen Elizabeth Stakes; while the triple crown for two-year-olds consists of the GOLDEN SLIPPER STAKES, A.J.C. Sires Produce Stakes, and Champagne Stakes, all three races being won for the first time by Baguette in 1969 together with the V.R.C. Maribyrnong Plate and over $100,000 in prize money, when ridden by MOORE, the leading Australian jockey. Famous Australian race-horses include Carbine, Gloaming, Amounis, Phar Lap, Peter Pan, Tulloch, Bernborough, and Gunsyd.

New Zealand. Horse racing has a large and enthusiastic following in New Zealand. Formerly, the main centres of the sport were Wellington, where the New Zealand Derby and WELLINGTON CUP were the principal events; Christchurch, scene of the New Zealand Cup; and Auckland, where the GREAT NORTHERN DERBY and AUCKLAND CUP are competed for. The classic system has recently been altered, however, and in 1974 the One Thousand and Two Thousand Guineas will be run at Riccarton (Christchurch) in November; the Derby at Ellerslie (Auckland) in January; the Oaks at Trentham (Wellington) in January; and the St. Leger at Trentham in March. Il Tempo, a seven-year-old gelding, became the first horse in New Zealand ever to win over $100,000 in stakes, when he won the Auckland and Wellington Cups in record time over two miles under top weight.

South Africa. Racing takes place at the Cape, Durban in Natal, and Johannesburg in the Transvaal. The most important and valuable events are handicaps, in which classic winners are expected to concede huge weights to lesser runners. Such are the ROTHMAN'S JULY HANDICAP, over 10½ furlongs (2,100 m.) at Greyville, Durban; the State Express Metropolitan Handicap, over 10 furlongs (2,000 m.) at Kenilworth, Cape Town; the Castle Tankard Handicap, over 10 furlongs at Turffontein, Johannesburg; and the Dunlop Gold Cup, a handicap over 2 miles (3,200 m.) at Durban.

Weight-for-age races include the Queen's

Plate at Kenilworth, Champion Stakes at Greyville, and Paddock Stakes for mares and fillies. There are many so-called Derbys, Oaks, St. Legers, and Guineas, for three-year-olds, but the most important are the CAPE OF GOOD HOPE DERBY, South African Derby and Oaks, Natal Derby, Cape Mellow-wood Guineas at Milnerton, and the Bull Brand International Stakes at Pietermaritzburg.

Racing is controlled by the Jockey Club of South Africa; the leading breeders are Birch Bros. of Vogelvlei Stud; one of the leading owners is Oppenheimer, and the best race-horses in recent years have been COLORADO KING, SEA COTTAGE, and Hawaii.

Canada. The most important race in Canada is the Queen's Plate, founded in 1861, and run over 10 furlongs (2,000 m.) on the Woodbine track at Toronto in June. Together with the Prince of Wales Stakes and Breeders Stakes, it forms the national triple crown. Other important races are the Canadian International Championship, Toronto Cup, Canadian Derby at Edmonton, Canadian Oaks, British Columbia Derby, and Coronation Futurity.

Elsewhere in the world, there is a Derby Belge at Boitsfort, Brussels and a Nederlandse Derby at Duindigt, The Hague; a Dansk Derby at Klampenborg, Copenhagen; Norsk Derby at Ovrevoll, Oslo; and Svenskt Derby at Jägersro, Malmö; a Derby der D.D.R. at Hoppegarten, East Berlin, Oesterreichisches Derby at Wien-Freudenau, Magyar Derby at Budapest, Ceskoslovenske Derby at Velká Chuchle, Prague, Jugoslovenski Derby at Belgrade, and Nagroda Derby at Sluzewiec, Warsaw; as well as the Hellenikon Derby at Phaliron, Athens; the Gazi Koshusu at Veliefendi, Istanbul; the Premio Villapadierna at Zarzuela, Madrid. All these classic races are based on the English Derby, being competed for only by three-year-olds at level weights and run over the usual Derby distance of 2,400 metres (1½ miles). There are also weight-for-age races such as the Skandinavisk Grand Prix at Klampenborg; Nagroda Wielka Warszawska at Sluzewiec; the GRAN PREMIO DE MADRID at Zarzuela, and Copa de Oro de San Sebastian at Lasarte.

In Russia and Japan, great strides have been made to attain international standards. The Soviet Derby is the Bolshoi Vsiesoyuzny Priz run at Moscow, and the Japanese Derby the Tokyo Yushun Kyoso run at Fuchu. The champion Russian horse was ANILIN.

Finally, horse racing also flourishes in India and Pakistan, Hong Kong and Malaya, the Philippines, Jamaica and the Caribbean, Switzerland and Malta, Rhodesia, Zambia, Kenya, and Nigeria.

Capt. K. Bobinski and Count A. Zamoyski, *Family Tables of Racehorses* (1952 and 1959, plus supplements); Patrick Chalmers, *Racing England* (1939); Sir Theodore Cook, *A History of the English Turf*, 3 vols. (1904) and Capt. T. H. Browne, *A History of the English Turf*, 2 further vols. (1931); Hon. Dennis Craig, *Breeding Race Horses from Cluster Mares* (1964) and *Horse-Racing* (1963); *Flat Racing* by various authorities (The Lonsdale Library, 1940); Dick Francis, *The Sport of Queens* (1957); Sir Charles Leicester, *Bloodstock Breeding* (1957); Sir Rhys Llewellyn, *Breeding to Race* (1965); Roger Mortimer, *Encyclopaedia of Flat Racing* (1971), *A History of the Derby Stakes* (1962), and *The Jockey Club* (1958); C. M. Prior, *The History of the Racing Calendar and Stud Book* (1926); Michael Seth-Smith, John Lawrence, Peter Willett, and Roger Mortimer, *The History of Steeplechasing* (1966); Vian Smith, *The Grand National* (1969) and *Point-to-Point* (1968); Federico Tesio, *Breeding the Racehorse* (1958); Peter Willett, *An Introduction to the Thoroughbred* (1966) and *The Thoroughbred* (1970); Lord Willoughby de Broke and others, *Steeplechasing* (1954). *The Bloodstock Breeders Review*, annual volumes from 1912. *Directory of the Turf* (every four years), *Racing Calendar*, *Race-form Up-to-Date Annual*, *Tote Racing Annual*, *Ruff's Guide to the Turf and Sporting Life Annual*, *Racehorses of the Year*, and *Horse and Hound Year Book*, all annually; *The British Racehorse* (five issues annually from 1949); *Stud and Stable* (monthly from 1961).

HORSE-RACING, A DECK GAME of which several forms are played on shipboard, none of which can have any resemblance to the real thing. All of them rely upon considerable imagination and inventiveness, and perhaps have remained popular with passengers because so many of them reflect the fact that a lot of people with time on their hands will bet on anything. The most popular and one of the oldest forms of horse-racing as a deck sport is one which involves cutting tape with a pair of curved nail scissors — the tape being the course and the scissors the horse. But, as with any race meeting on land, the fun and the enjoyment of the meeting is not confined to the race itself. Shipping lines feature the meetings on their ships and have experienced staff ready to join with volunteers in providing stewards for the course, judges, starter, official timekeeper, clerk of the course, clerk of the scales, veterinary surgeon, policemen, and, of course, tote manager. Attractive race cards are printed for the meetings, often with rules, some of which may be traditional to a particular shipping line, such as those disqualifying a horse and warning off its owner if (*a*) it savages or kicks another horse during the race; (*b*) it takes dope other than alcohol; (*c*) it eats its bedding, drinks its bath water, or licks its owner; (*d*) it embraces, fondles, or otherwise biases the judges.

The individual races reflect the same, somewhat juvenile, spirit with 'The Matrimonial Plate — for all fillies regularly chased during the voyage' being typical.

The race-course usually consists of a length of tape about 6 ft. (1·8 m.) long for each of six races with the winner of each race qualifying for the ship's Derby run over the longer distance of about 7 ft. 6 in. (2·3 m.). Horses complete the course by cutting the tape from end to end with a pair of curved nail scissors, each movement of which must be a distinct cut and not a rip. The stewards are at hand to note that the tape is not cut through the side (in which case the horse must be withdrawn) and that the tape is held between the first and second fingers in such a way that it hangs loosely between the winning post and cutting hand. If the tape, with the holding fingers of the 'jockey' always between the scissors (horse) and the winning post, becomes taut, the horse is disqualified. The winner, of course, is the first to reach the post with the tape completely cut through.

HORSE TRIALS, see EQUESTRIAN EVENTS.

HORSESHOE PITCHING is a game of old English origin, now popular in the U.S.A., the object of which is to pitch, or, more accurately, swing, the shoe through the air so that it lands encircling ('ringing') a short stake, driven into the ground. In the men's game, the stake is 40 ft. (12 m.) away from the stake box, from which the shoe is pitched, in the women's, 30 ft. (9 m.). The shoe (real horseshoes are no longer used) weighs 2½ lb. (1·13 kg.) and is U-shaped, 7½ in. long and 7½ in. wide (19 cm.). The caulks at the heel of the shoe (known to most pitchers as 'corks') turn inward, leaving an opening of only 3½ in. (8·89 cm.). The stake, 14 in. (35·56 cm.) high, should lean towards the pitcher by 3 in. (7·6 cm.) at the top.

The game may be played by two people (singles) or two pairs (doubles), each player standing within the box to pitch two shoes at the stake before changing ends. A ringer scores 3 points, unless it is cancelled by an opponent's ringer. If no ringers are scored, the player or pair whose shoe is nearest the stake, provided it is within 6 in. (15·2 cm.) of it, scores 1 point; two shoes nearer the stake than an opponent's shoe score 2 points. The ground surrounding the stake is usually of clay, to reduce skidding of shoes to a minimum. Games are played to either 21 or 50 points.

Horseshoe pitching probably began at the time of the Roman occupation of Britain, when officers played quoits and the men copied them (without cost) by throwing horseshoes at stakes. Both games were taken to America by the early English settlers, but it was horseshoe pitching that prospered: it could be played at any point on the trail to the West where there was a blacksmith's shop.

The first world championship was held in Bronson, Kansas in 1909, and the game is now played in 45 American states and 6 Canadian provinces. In all of them, horseshoe-pitching courts are found in many municipal parks and playgrounds. An extraordinary degree of accuracy is sometimes obtained, one Canadian having recorded 2,613 'ringers' in 2,954 pitches.

The Horseshoe Pitchers' News Digest, monthly.
GOVERNING BODY: National Horseshoe Pitchers Association of America, 341 Polk Street, Gary, Indiana, U.S.A.

HOSKYNS, HENRY WILLIAM FURSE, M.B.E. (1931-　　　), British fencer, world épée champion in 1958, and silver medallist at épée in the 1965 world championships. He has fenced in five Olympics since he became a member of the British team in 1954; at Tokyo in 1964 he was silver medallist in épée, and also came seventh in the foil. He won the gold medal in épée at the COMMONWEALTH GAMES in 1958, 1962, 1966, and 1970, and the gold medal in sabre in 1958; from ten Commonwealth Games events he has won nine golds and one silver. He has also been a frequent world finalist at foil, and in all weapons has reached 13 world finals.

HOSPITALS' CUP, RUGBY UNION trophy for which the London hospitals compete in an annual knock-out competition dating from 1875. The final rounds are traditionally played at Richmond Athletic Ground, Surrey.

HOTCHKISS, HAZEL (later Mrs. George Wightman) (1886-1974), American LAWN TENNIS player, a redoubtable competitor who won her first U.S. title, the women's singles, in 1909 and her last, the indoor doubles, in 1943. As Mrs. Wightman, she was the donor of the WIGHTMAN CUP, the women's international team championship, playing doubles in the first match and on three other occasions. She won the U.S. singles title four times (1909-11 and 1919), but it was in doubles that her ability to smash and volley brought her best results. She won the Wimbledon doubles with WILLS in 1924 and the U.S. title six times.

HOUSTON ASTROS, American professional BASEBALL team, entered the NATIONAL LEAGUE in 1962, when the league expanded to ten teams, as the Colt '45s, but, later, to identify with Houston as centre of the U.S. space programme, became the Astros. Houston has been best known for its ASTRODOME, an enclosed baseball-FOOTBALL stadium completed in 1965.

HOVE, the premier CRICKET ground of the Sussex County Cricket Club, was first used (at its present site) in 1872, since when it has been the club's headquarters. It is situated near the centre of the town, close to the sea, and early-morning dampness often aids bowlers' attempts at swing. The ground, which slopes slightly towards the sea end, is full of character and the spacious pavilion houses a generous display of Sussex cricketing mementoes. The presence of even 5,000 people gives the impression of a fairly full ground, though maximum capacity is about 15,000. A splendid pair of gates at the main entrance at the south end commemorate TATE, the former great Sussex and England bowler.

HOWE, GORDON (1926-), ICE HOCKEY player for DETROIT RED WINGS from 1946, often described as the best all-round player the sport has seen. This outstanding, six-foot right winger achieved the NATIONAL HOCKEY LEAGUE (N.H.L.) record for the most goals scored, most assists, most points, and most games played. By 1967, he had played in the N.H.L. longer than anyone else, 21 seasons, the more remarkable for the fact that the average N.H.L. career was less than seven seasons. By 1968, he had scored 743 goals, 678 in N.H.L. matches and 65 in STANLEY CUP play-offs. He was winner of the ART ROSS TROPHY a record six times, 1951, 1952, 1953, 1954, 1957, and 1963, the HART TROPHY a record six times, 1952, 1953, 1957, 1958, 1960, and 1963, also the Kester Patrick Trophy in 1967 'for outstanding service to hockey in the United States'.

HUDDERSFIELD RUGBY LEAGUE CLUB. Founded in 1864 and a founder member of the English Northern Union, its record of success is second only to that of WIGAN. It has won the League championship seven times and the Challenge Cup six times. The record attendance at the club's ground is 35,136. Eighteen Huddersfield players have been selected for British teams visiting Australia, including six in 1914. In 1914-15 the club won all four major trophies in England, scoring 1,269 points in 47 matches, a record equalled by Wigan (51 matches) in 1949-50. Starting with ROSENFELD in 1908, Huddersfield freely recruited players from Australia, New Zealand, Wales, and Scotland.
COLOURS: Claret and gold hoops.

HUDDERSFIELD TOWN F.C., Association FOOTBALL club. Founded in 1908, the club was elected to the Second Division of the Football League for the season 1910-11. In 1919 the club nearly went out of existence, but local supporters collected enough money for it to continue, and at the end of the first postwar season (1919-20) Huddersfield gained promotion to the First Division. In 1923 Chapman was appointed as manager and Huddersfield were third, before in the next seasons they became the first club to win three consecutive Football League championships. ARSENAL in the 1930s are the only other club to have equalled Huddersfield's record and no club has beaten it. Huddersfield's run of consecutive championships was preceded by winning the 1922 F.A. Cup final but they were beaten on three subsequent appearances in the final as they had been in 1920. Outstanding players in the 1920s were Goodall, Wadsworth, JACKSON, Kelly, Brown, Stephenson, W. H. Smith, and Wilson. Since the war they have included Hassall, R. Wilson, DOHERTY, LAW, and W. Watson.
COLOURS: Blue and white striped shirts, white shorts.
GROUND: Leeds Road, Huddersfield.

HUDSON RIVER ICE YACHT CLUB, formed in 1870 at Hyde Park, New York (U.S.A.), the major hub of the sport of ICE YACHTING for 30 years, until 1900.

HUGHES, GEORGE PATRICK (1902-), British LAWN TENNIS player, a specialist in doubles who played a major part in Britain's Davis Cup (see LAWN TENNIS) successes in the 1930s. Partnering either PERRY, H. G. N. Lee, or Tuckey, he won a number of crucial victories, notably with Perry against QUIST and Turnbull (Australia) in the inter-zone final in 1932, and with Tuckey against Allison and Van Ryn (U.S.A.) in the 1935 challenge round. He defeated COCHET to win the Italian singles in 1931, and his doubles victories included the capture of the WIMBLEDON title with Tuckey in 1936, and with Perry the French title in 1933 and the Australian title in 1934. Hughes and Perry were the runners-up at Wimbledon in 1931 and Hughes and Tuckey reached the same stage in 1937.

HULBERT, WILLIAM A. (d. 1882), American BASEBALL executive who founded the NATIONAL LEAGUE of Professional Base Ball Clubs in 1876. He persuaded the leaders of other clubs to leave the National Association of Professional Base Ball Players and join with his Chicago club in organizing the new eight-club National League, of which he served as president from 1877 until his death.

HULL, ROBERT MARVIN (1939-   ), ICE HOCKEY player for CHICAGO BLACK HAWKS from 1956. This muscular, fast-moving winger possessed probably the hardest shot in the sport — one was timed at 116·3 m.p.h. (187 km./h.) — and could skate at remarkable speed while retaining full control of the puck, once recorded at 29·4 m.p.h. (47 km./h.). Hull became the first NATIONAL HOCKEY LEAGUE (N.H.L.) player to score 50 goals in a season more than once — 50 in 1961-2, 54 in 1965-6, and 52 in 1966-7. He achieved the N.H.L. point-scoring record of 97 in a season (54 goals and 43 assists) in 1965-6. He was three times winner of the ART ROSS TROPHY, 1960, 1962, 1966, twice winner of the HART TROPHY, 1965 and 1966, and of the LADY BYNG MEMORIAL TROPHY in 1965.

HULME, DENIS (1936-   ), New Zealand MOTOR RACING driver who won two CAN-AM Challenge Cup championships, 1968 and 1970, and 21 races in the series. He was world drivers' champion in 1967. He was runner-up in the Can-Am series four times: to his team leader, MCLAREN, in 1967 and 1969; to team-mate REVSON in 1971; and to Follmer in 1972. He placed fourth in the INDIANAPOLIS 500 in 1967 and 1968.

HUME, DONALD C. (1907-   ), English BADMINTON player. He was one of the most aggressive players in the history of the game and an outstanding doubles player in the 1930s, winning both the men's and mixed doubles four times consecutively in the ALL-ENGLAND CHAMPIONSHIPS. He represented England for 20 years, commencing in 1928.

HUNSLET RUGBY LEAGUE CLUB, founder member of the English Northern Union, has a special place in Rugby League history as the first club to win all four major trophies — in 1907-8. It also won the League championship in 1937-8 and the Challenge Cup in 1933-4. Four Hunslet players toured Australia in 1910, and the club has produced many prominent players since then.
COLOURS: White with irregular chocolate hoops.

HUNT, G. B. (1948-   ), Australian SQUASH RACKETS player. On his first visit to England aged 17, Hunt reached the final of the amateur championship. He won the first international championships individual event, played in Melbourne in 1967, and repeated this win at the 1969 championships in London. He also won the Open championship of the British Isles in January 1969 but was beaten in the following season by BARRINGTON in a match lasting two and a quarter hours — the longest championship match on record. He became amateur champion of Australia at the age of 17 but did not win this title again until 1970. After a series of 15 matches against Barrington in England in the 1969-70 season, of which he won 13, he was generally regarded as the best player in the world. He turned professional in 1972.

HURDLE RACING, see HORSE RACING.

HURDLING is an ATHLETICS activity, the standard events featuring on the programme of all major championships being the 110 metres and 400 metres for men and the 100 metres (formerly the 80 metres) for women. The 110 metres hurdles is one of the events in the DECATHLON and the 100 metres hurdles in the women's PENTATHLON. The International Amateur Athletic Federation (see ATHLETICS, TRACK AND FIELD) recognizes records at the distances mentioned, as well as 120 yards, 200 metres, 220 yards, and 440 yards for men, and 200 metres and 400 metres for women. There are ten flights of hurdles in each event, the regulation height being 3 ft. 6 in. (1·067 m.) for 120 yards and 110 metres, 2 ft. 6 in. (76·2 cm.) for the 220 yards and 200 metres, 3 ft. (91·4 cm.) for the 440 yards and 400 metres, and 2 ft. 9 in. (84 cm.) for the women's 100 metres and 2 ft. 6 in. (76·2 cm.) for the women's 400 metres.

In clearing a hurdle, the athlete may take off from either foot. His alternate leg is lifted with the knee bent and then extended across the bar of the hurdle and along the line of running. The trailing leg is lifted laterally and rotated about the hip, crossing the hurdle in a horizontal position. Forward lean contributes to the impetus which brings the hurdler down beyond the obstacle when his trailing leg lifts high into the getaway stride.

Though hurdling of a rudimentary sort took place in the first STEEPLECHASE event in 1850, and is part of the regulation 3,000 metres steeplechase course, the first instance of a 120 yards hurdles race was in the Oxford University Sports in 1864. Sheep hurdles were used, giving rise to the common usage of the word hurdling for the sport of foot racing with obstacles. The height of the sheep hurdles was about 3 ft. 6 in., the regulation height today for 120 yards and 110 metres. The original rule that a competitor overturning three or more hurdles should be disqualified became obsolete after 1932, when the I.A.A.F. stipulated that competition hurdles should have a regulation toppling moment of 8 lb. (3·6 kg.).

This recognized that modern hurdling, by nature of its pace and technique, has become a refinement of SPRINTING.

HURLING, certainly the fastest of all team games, is played 15-a-side with sticks and ball. Traditionally a pastime of the Celts, it is still the national game in Ireland, where it is particularly strong in the south and south-east, but is also popular in many other areas, including the Antrim glens, where the style of play has many affinities with the SHINTY of the nearby Scottish Highlands.

The object of the game is to drive the relatively small ball with the broad-bladed stick (the 'hurley' or *caman*) through goal posts erected at opposite ends of a playing pitch usually 150 yds. (137 m.) long and 90 yds. (82 m.) wide.

The goal posts stand 21 ft. (6·4 m.) apart in the centre of the end lines and are usually 21 ft. high. There is a crossbar 8 ft. (2·4 m.) from the ground, and a goal, equal to 3 points, is awarded when the ball is driven between the goal posts and under the crossbar. A point is scored when the ball is driven between the posts but over the crossbar.

The wooden hurley or *caman* is usually 3½ ft. (1·07 m.) long in the handle, varying a little to suit the height of the individual player, and has a crooked blade which is some 3 in. (7·6 cm.) across at its broadest.

The popular wood for hurleys is ash, which gives the sweetest stroke and stands up best to the clash with opposing sticks in close play. Holly and crab-apple are occasionally used, but it is difficult to find a trunk of either of those trees thick enough to provide the material for a full-size hurley. In recent years there have been experiments with plastic and laminated 'sticks', but no substitute has been found for the traditional ash *caman*.

The ball, often called by its Gaelic name, *sliothar*, may be from 9 to 10 in. (22·9–25·4 cm.) in circumference and from 3½ to 4½ oz. (100–130 g.) in weight. To facilitate handling, a ridge of hard leather is stitched round the outside of the cover, which is usually of horsehide. The inside is of thread or yarn, tightly wound round a core of cork.

The ball, when in play, may not be lifted off the ground with the hand. It must be raised with the hurley, and may then be struck direct, on the volley or half-volley, or may be caught in the hand. The quick and deft lifting of the ball with the stick is an art in itself. The ball may be caught when in the air, and may be struck with the hand, or kicked. But a player who catches the ball may not throw it, nor may he carry it in the hand for more than three paces. A player is permitted, however, to run

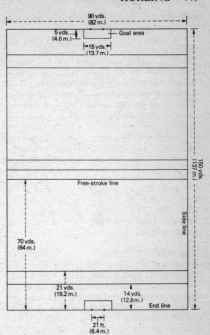

HURLING PITCH
Goal posts are usually 21 ft. (6·4 m.) high, with a crossbar 8 ft. (2·4 m.) from the ground.

with the ball balanced, or hopping, on the blade of the stick for as far as he wishes, or as far as the opposition permits. This tactic, the solo run, is another distinctive feature of the game.

When the ball crosses the side line, a free stroke is given, at the point where it crossed, against the side that drove it over. If the ball is turned wide of the posts, and over the end line, by a defender, the attacking side is awarded a free stroke from a line 70 yds. (64 m.) out at a point opposite to where the ball crossed the line. If a defender fouls inside the 21-yard (19·2 m.) line, a free stroke is awarded on that line to the attacking side at a point opposite where the foul took place. If the ball is sent wide of the goal by the attacking side, it is 'pucked' (the technical word for striking the ball with the hurley) from the goal area by one of the defenders. Such goal-pucks often travel more than 100 yds. (91 m.)

The goal area, a parallelogram 15 yds. by 5 yds. (13·7 × 4·6 m.), based on the end line directly in front of the posts, is forbidden territory to attackers, unless the ball has arrived there before them. If the defence is awarded a free stroke inside the parallelogram, opposing players must stand outside the 14-yard (12·8 m.) line until the ball is struck.

Shoulder-charging is permitted, but tripping, pushing, or pulling is penalized by a free puck against the offender, as is a frontal charge, or any dangerous swinging or backlashing with the stick. A player who deliberately strikes an opponent with stick or fist is sent off by the referee; he may not be replaced and receives a minimum of two weeks' suspension.

Teams are composed of a goalkeeper, six defenders, two mid-field players, and six forwards. A maximum of three substitutes may be introduced in the course of a game.

```
                    G

        B          FB          B

      HB          CB          HB

            MF          MF

      HF          CF          HF

      FF          FF          FF
```

HURLING TEAM LINE-OUT
(G) Goalkeeper; (FB) full-back; (B) back; (HB) half-back; (CB) centre back; (MF) mid-field; (HF) half-forward; (CF) centre forward; (FF) full-forward.

All games last for 60 minutes, except senior Provincial finals and All-Ireland semi-finals and finals, which extend to 80 minutes. Sixty-minute games are divided into halves of 30 minutes, with the teams changing sides at the interval. In 80-minute matches, the teams play 40 minutes each way.

The basic skills of hurling are: (1) the ability to control and direct the ball both on the ground and in the air; (2) the power to drive the ball far and accurately; (3) the ability to stop the ball in flight and flick it away from an opponent's stick; (4) dexterity in avoiding an opponent's stick when players clash in their endeavours to secure or drive the ball.

Due to the full swing given to the relatively large and broad-bladed stick, hurling may look to the uninitiated a very dangerous game. But players who have been using the sticks since childhood instinctively keep them between themselves and their opponents' *camans* as an effective shield in close play. Although skinned knuckles and shin bumps are an accepted hazard, serious injuries are rare, and statistics prove hurling to be far less dangerous than any of the popular football codes. The ideal hurler should have strength allied to skill. Power in wrist and forearm is a tremendous asset, as this enables a player to dodge through with the ball perfectly controlled by his stick and, from a very short swing, to get in an accurate puck, even though closely tackled and seemingly hemmed in.

Official Guide, Gaelic Athletic Association, latest edition.

Hurling is first mentioned in the Irish Annals in a description of the Battle of Moytura (c. 1272 B.C.), in which the Tuatha de Danaan invaders defeated the resident Firbolgs, first in a hurling match and then in a subsequent battle for the lordship of Ireland. The Brehon Laws, the oldest Irish legal code, which existed for centuries before the Christian era, provided compensation for any player injured either by the stick or the ball in the course of a game.

Of a later period, 200 years before Christ, the Annals record that, as a child, Lowry Loingseach, who later became king of Ireland, was dumb. While playing hurling, he sustained a sharp blow of a *caman* (stick) on the shin and, in his agony, spoke for the first time. What he said is not recorded. In the Red Branch tales, Cuchullain, the super-hero of Ulster, was as supreme in hurling as he was in every other knightly exercise. As a small boy, he attracted the attention of Conor, the king, by defeating, single-handed, the whole 150 of the boy-warrior corps in a hurling game on the green before the royal palace at Armagh.

The next cycle of Irish hero tales, dealing with the exploits of Finn MacCool and his Fianna, date from the second century A.D. and stress the hurling prowess of Finn's warrior-militia. The handsome Diarmuid of the Love Spot scored the decisive goal in a hurling game at Tara and so delighted the High King that the monarch told him to ask, as a reward, any favour he wished. Diarmuid demanded a kiss from the king's daughter.

Unaffected by the coming of Christianity or by the raids of the Norsemen, hurling lived on down the centuries. Even the Anglo-Norman invasion (1169), which eventually changed nearly everything else in Ireland, did not affect the popularity of hurling. By 1366 so many of the new colonists were hurling, to the detriment of martial exercises like archery and javelin-throwing, that a parliament in Kilkenny ordained and established 'that the commons of the said land of Ireland use not henceforth the game which men call hurlings, with great clubs at ball along the ground'.

At this time hurling seems to have been spreading back across the Irish Sea to England where Wat Tyler's rebellion is referred to in Gregory's Chronicle as 'the hurlying time', i.e. a time of tumult or commotion. Back in Ireland, so futile had the Statute of Kilkenny proved that another was passed at Galway in 1527, which again forbade the 'hurling of the little ball with hooked sticks or staves'.

HURLING STICK OR CAMAN

The next century and a half was possibly the most strife-torn period Ireland has ever known, but hurling survived war and famine and was still very much alive when the English traveller, Dunton, gave the first description of the pastime as a visitor saw it. Dunton wrote in the late seventeenth century, and by then the game had begun to take very definite shape. Then, as now, the *caman* was about 3½ ft. (1·06 m.) long in the handle and crooked into a broad blade at the lower end. The ball, larger than the one used today, was often composed of kneaded cowhair and teams would consist of 10, 20, or 30 players. Even then the solo run with the ball balanced on the blade of the stick was a spectacular feature of the game. According to Dunton, the goals 'were 200 to 300 yards apart, on a level plain, the barer of grass the better'.

Mid-eighteenth century landowners often laid heavy wagers on hurling matches between picked teams of their tenantry, some particularly energetic landlords playing in these games themselves.

A hundred years later hurling had entered on a new phase. In addition to the 'hurling to goals' which Dunton had described, 'hurling home' was now extremely popular. The entire manpower of adjoining parishes, up to 200 or 300 a side, met at the common boundary. There the ball was thrown in, and victory went to the side that succeeded in hurling the ball home before them, across hill and dale, to their own village. By the 1870s, the game had lost most of its adherents north of a line from Galway to Dublin; it continued to flourish in the counties that are still the traditional strongholds today — Kilkenny, Wexford, Tipperary, Cork, Limerick, and Clare.

When the GAELIC ATHLETIC ASSOCIATION (G.A.A.) was founded in 1884 one of its main objectives was 'to bring the hurling back to Ireland'. With this end in view, championships were set up, clubs within a county playing-off for the county title, the county winners then meeting for provincial and All-Ireland honours. The number of players on each team, originally 21, was reduced, first to 17, and then, in 1913, to the present 15 a side. A goal was originally greater in value than any number of points. Then 5 points were made equal to a goal, and finally a goal was made the equivalent of 3 points. By the end of the nineteenth century the champion side in every county was allowed to pick players from other clubs within the county for the purposes of the All-Ireland championships, which are now played in many grades.

Although Gaelic FOOTBALL has become far more popular than hurling in much of the country, All-Ireland senior hurling finals draw crowds of up to 70,000, and a widespread drive has succeeded in renewing interest and enthusiasm in many areas where the game had become moribund. By the end of 1970 the future of hurling seemed assured, the most encouraging feature being the great revival in counties such as Antrim, Kildare, and Wicklow, which hitherto had rarely featured in the winners' lists.

Because the skills of the game are nurtured from childhood, and require constant practice, hurling has never taken root outside Ireland. London-Irish teams have won Irish championships, while New York selections have done well in play-offs against the Irish winners of the National League (the winter competition), but these players are all exiles who learned the game in Ireland. Hurling, therefore, has only local heroes, but, since the foundation of the All-Ireland championships in 1887, the game has produced many outstanding figures. In the early days, the prowess of Maher and his Tipperary champions, as invincible as they were invulnerable, quickly became a legend. Early in the twentieth century, four players, Walsh, Walton, Rochford, and Doyle, set a record by playing in seven winning Kilkenny All-Ireland teams in ten years. In the 1930s the game was graced by Kilkenny's Meagher, the stylist supreme, and Limerick's seemingly indestructible Mackey. More recently, Ring (Cork) and Doyle (Tipperary) surpassed previous records by each winning eight All-Ireland senior medals, Ring between 1941 and 1955, Doyle between 1949 and 1965. The durable Doyle won eleven National League medals for good measure.

Since hurling is controlled by the G.A.A., all big games are played on grounds owned by the Association. Top hurling matches are usually staged at venues within the hurling areas, except for the All-Ireland senior finals which are played at G.A.A. headquarters, Croke Park, Dublin, on the first Sunday in September. Highest attendances at the principal venues are: Croke Park, 80,000; Thurles, 50,000; Limerick, 60,000; Kilkenny, 40,000. The leading county clubs in the senior All-Ireland championship are Cork, Tipperary, and Kilkenny. Other counties to have won senior titles include Wexford, Limerick, Dublin, Galway, Clare, Waterford, and Laois.

D. Guiney and P. Puirseal, *Guinness Book of Hurling Records* (1965); P. D. Mehigan, *Hurling; Ireland's National Game* (1940); R. Smith, *Decades of Glory* (1966) and *The Hurling Immortals* (1969); T. Wall, *Hurling* (1965).
GOVERNING BODY: Gaelic Athletic Association, Croke Park, Dublin, Eire

HURLINGHAM CLUB, see POLO.

HURST, GEOFFREY CHARLES (1941-), Association footballer for WEST HAM UNITED, STOKE CITY, and England for whom he made his first appearance in a full international match against West Germany at WEMBLEY in February 1966. It was only five months later that, against the same opponents, he scored three times in England's 4–2 win in the final of the 1966 world championship — no other player had scored three times in a World Cup final. Despite being handicapped by nagging injuries, he remained England's centre striker in the 1970 world championship in Mexico and for subsequent internationals.

HUTCHENS, HAROLD (1858-1929), British professional sprinter rated the greatest of the nineteenth century, amateur or professional. He once ran 300 yards (274.32 m.) in 30 sec. in midwinter, during a POWDERHALL meeting. His willingness to conform on the track with the wishes of his backers often led, allegedly, to his not showing his true speed. One particularly outrageous incident led to a riot on the ground and brought lasting discredit to professional ATHLETICS.

HUTCHINSON HUNDRED, see MOTOR-CYCLE RACING.

HUTSON, DONALD (1913-), American college and professional FOOTBALL player, who revolutionized offensive end play first at the University of ALABAMA (1932-4) and then as a professional with the GREEN BAY PACKERS (1935-45). Dangerously elusive, he was adept at deceiving defensive players and in creating effective pass patterns. At Green Bay he led the NATIONAL FOOTBALL LEAGUE in scoring (1940-4), in pass-catching (1936-45, except for 1938 and 1940), and in place-kicking (1943). On his retirement he held 15 all-time League records.

HUTTON, Capt. ALFRED, F.S.A. (1840-1910), first president of the British Amateur Fencing Association, which he founded in 1902. A pupil of Henry ANGELO, he was interested in swords and swordsmanship from his earliest youth. A great authority and writer on FENCING ancient and modern, the revival of interest in, and the development of, fencing in Great Britain in the latter half of the nineteenth century was largely due to his enthusiasm and untiring work.

HUTTON, Sir LEONARD (1916-), cricketer for England and Yorkshire. Maker of the highest Test score against Australia, 364 at the OVAL in 1938 (in 13 hrs. 17 min., for 19 years easily the longest innings in first-class CRICKET), he was handicapped after the Second World War by a serious arm injury. For ten years he was England's key batsman, facing hostile opening bowling to which England had no reply, and playing it with masterly orthodoxy. In 1953 he became the first professional cricketer to captain England, recapturing the ASHES from Australia and retaining them in 1954-5. He made a record 1,294 runs in a month, in June 1949, and 129 centuries in all first-class cricket. He was knighted on retiring in 1956.

HVEGER, RAGNHILD (1920-), Danish swimmer who broke more world records than any other, 42 for 15 different freestyle distances, plus 3 for backstroke between 1936 and 1942. Second in the 400 metres at the 1936 OLYMPIC GAMES, triple gold medallist at the European championships two years later, she was in a league of her own in 1940.

HYPERION (1930), a famous English racehorse, by GAINSBOROUGH out of Selene by Chaucer (son of ST. SIMON), bred and owned by Lord DERBY, trained by LAMBTON, and ridden by Weston. He won the DERBY very easily by over four lengths in a record time of 2 min. 34 sec., and also the ST. LEGER. His stake total amounted to £29,509. Hyperion stood only 15 hands 1½ in. on the day he won the Derby, but, in spite of his small stature, he became the most important stallion at stud during the first half of the present century, heading the winning sires list six times and being second four times. He died in 1960, aged 30, leaving behind notable sons like Owen Tudor and AUREOLE; grandsons like Tudor Minstrel, Abernant, RIGHT ROYAL V, ST. PADDY, and Hopeful Venture; and great-grandsons like Tudor Melody and VAGUELY NOBLE.

I

I.A.A.F. (International Amateur Athletic Federation), see ATHLETICS, TRACK AND FIELD.

I.B.B. (International Bowling Board), see BOWLS, LAWN.

ICE DANCING, see ICE SKATING.

ICE FIGURE-SKATING, see ICE SKATING.

ICE HOCKEY, a six-a-side team game played with sticks and a rubber puck on a rectangular sheet of mechanically-frozen or natural ice, called a rink, measuring, ideally, 200 ft. (61 m.) long and 85 ft. (26 m.) wide, and surrounded by barrier boards. The game is won by the team which scores the most goals. The barrier boards, curved at each of the four corners, must not be more than 4 ft. (1·22 m.) high nor less than 40 in. (1 m.).

Red goal lines, 2 in. (5 cm.) wide, are marked 10 ft. (3·50 m.) from each end of the rink. In the centre of these lines are the goals, 4 ft. (1·22 m.) high and 6 ft. (1·83 m.) wide, measured from the insides of the upright posts and the crossbar, with nets not less than 2 ft. (60 cm.) at the base.

Two blue lines, each 1 ft. (30 cm.) wide, divide the rink into three equal zones, and a centre red line, also 1 ft. (30 cm.) wide, is equidistant between them. All these lines are drawn completely across the width of the ice and are continued vertically up the sides of the barrier boards.

A circular blue spot, 1 ft. (30 cm.) in diameter, is painted on the centre of the ice, in the centre of a blue circle, 2 in. (5 cm.) wide, with a radius of 15 ft. (4·6 m.). Four more similar-sized spots and circles are marked in red on the rink, two in each half — midway between each goal post and the nearest side of the rink and 15 ft. (4·6 m.) out from the goal lines. On each side of these four 'face-off' spots are red lines 2 ft. (60 cm.) long, parallel to the goal lines. Other red lines 3 ft. (91 cm.) long, extend from each outer edge of the four defence-zone face-off circles.

Two other similar-sized red spots are marked in the centre zone, one in each half, 5 ft. (1·5 m.) from each blue line and midway between the side barrier boards. Other marks on the ice indicate semi-circular (International Ice Hockey Federation rules) *or* rectangular (National Hockey League rules) areas, one in front of each goal, called the crease, marked by red lines 2 in. (5 cm.) wide. The semi-circles have a radius of 6 ft. (1·83 m.). The rectangles are 8 ft. (2·44 m.) wide and 4 ft. (1·22 m.) deep, marked by red lines 2 in. (5 cm.) wide.

Under International Ice Hockey Federation (I.I.H.F.) rules, matches are controlled by two referees, one for each half of the playing area, just as umpires officiate in field HOCKEY. But in matches under the rules of the professional NATIONAL HOCKEY LEAGUE (N.H.L.) of North America, one referee is in complete charge, assisted by two linesmen whose main duty is to watch and whistle for offsides.

A game is divided into three periods, each of 20 minutes actual playing time. An official stop-watch — in major matches synchronized with a huge dial clearly visible to the spectators — measures only the time while the puck is in play. Between the three playing periods are two intervals, each of approximately ten minutes' duration, during which the ice is resurfaced.

Only six players from each team are allowed on the ice at the same time, the normal line-up being a goalminder, two defencemen, and three forwards — the centreman and two wingers. Substitute players are considered essential because of the fast speed at which the game is played.

A team usually carries between 11 and 18 players. A top professional side normally comprises two goalminders, five or six defencemen, and ten or eleven forwards. Generally two pairs of defencemen and three trios of forwards are used in turn. Substitutes may be introduced into play whenever the game is stopped, i.e. when the puck is 'dead', but no substitution may be made unless the player to be relieved has left the ice. It is not obligatory to play a goalminder throughout a match and, when the occasion warrants, it is not uncommon for a team to play the final seconds of a period with no goalminder at all and all six men up in an all-out effort to score, a desperate tactic which can provide considerable excitement.

Play is commenced at the beginning of each period, and after a goal has been scored, by a 'face-off'. The puck is dropped by the referee

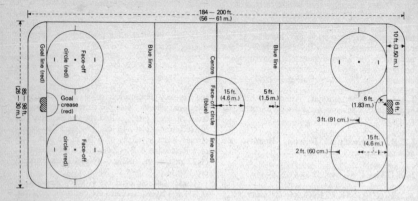

ICE HOCKEY RINK

Dimensions are those specified under International Ice Hockey Federation rules. Goals are 4 ft. (1·22 m.) high, with nets not less than 2 ft. (60 cm.) at the base. Under National Hockey League rules the goal crease is rectangular.

in the centre of the rink between the sticks of the opposing centremen (centre forwards), who must stand approximately one stick-length apart, squarely facing their opponents' end of the rink, and with the full blades of their sticks on the ice. No other player is allowed within 10 ft. (3 m.) of the two face-off players. Play is re-started at other times of the game by face-offs on the nearest of the other eight marked spots to the point at which a mis-play occurred.

The puck stays in play whenever or wherever it hits the barrier boards, including behind the goals, and thus becomes dead only when hit over the barrier or when the whistle is blown for an infringement. A goal is scored when the whole of the puck passes over the goal line between the goal posts after being driven fairly *by a stick*.

A goal is not allowed if an attacking player kicks or throws the puck into the goal or if an attacking player is in the goal crease when the puck passes over the goal line. Goal judges positioned behind each goal signify when a goal has been fairly scored by switching on an overhead red light behind the goal concerned.

A 'shut-out' occurs when a goalminder concedes no goal during a match. The expression is also used to describe one of the 20-minute periods of a game in which the goalminder does not concede a goal, or with reference to the duration of time, perhaps covering more than one match, during which a goalminder has remained unbeaten. Notable shut-out records were achieved by DURNAN and SAW-CHUK.

A player may stop the puck with his hand, body, or skate at any time and in any position.

But he cannot hold the puck with his hand for more than three seconds, nor push the puck forward except with his skate or stick. 'Stick-handling', or retaining possession of the puck while in motion, is the equivalent of 'drib-bling' in Association FOOTBALL.

The two blue lines divide the playing area into three zones — defence, neutral (centre), and attacking zones. Only three players may be in their own defence zone when the puck is outside that zone.

A player may enter the attacking zone only in line or behind the puck or puck-carrier. He may not take a pass from a team mate who is, at the moment of passing, in another zone. When an attacking player precedes the puck into the attacking zone or when the puck travels over more than one line, play is halted and re-started from a face-off. In all instances in deciding an 'offside', the position of the player's skates and not that of his stick is the determining factor. Thus, a player is offside *when both skates are completely over* the outer edge of the determining line involved in the play. To stay 'on side', a player can pass the puck only to a colleague in the *same* zone (also to anyone in his own *half* if he is in his defence zone).

If an attacking player is tripped or pulled down when in a scoring position in front of goal and having no players between him and the goal other than the goalminder, the referee can award a special penalty shot from the blue line of the defending team. The penalty shot is a clear shot at goal with only the goalminder allowed to defend. The time taken for a penalty shot is the one phase of play in a game which is not included in the regular playing time. After a penalty shot which fails, a goal cannot be scored from a rebound.

Ice hockey is fairly described as the fastest team game in the world, and, because of the pace and frantic action involved, players are penalized for infringements of the rules by being sent off the ice for two or more minutes, according to the severity of the offence. The term of suspension is served in a special penalty box.

Minor penalties of two minutes are imposed for such offences as charging, elbowing, tripping, body-checking (pushing a player deliberately on to the barrier boards), high sticks, and intentionally shooting out of the rink or falling on the puck (excepting the goalminder, in the latter case). If the team which has a consequent player advantage scores, the absent penalized player is allowed to return immediately. When a goalminder incurs a minor penalty he is not required to leave the ice but, instead, a team colleague is withdrawn by the coach.

A major penalty of five minutes can be imposed for fighting. When both teams incur major penalties, substitutes are permitted while the two offenders are off the ice. A goalminder incurring a major penalty, instead of being sent off, has a penalty shot awarded against his team.

A misconduct penalty of ten minutes is imposed for such offences as using abusive language, in which case a substitute is allowed. A goalminder's misconduct penalty can be served by a team colleague.

A match penalty, suspending a player for the remainder of the game, is imposed for deliberately injuring, or attempting to injure, an opponent. In such a case, a substitute can be allowed after the first five minutes but the offender cannot play in any future match before his case has been dealt with by a disciplinary committee. An offending goalminder must serve a match penalty himself and his place in goal has to be taken over by another member of his team.

The ice-hockey stick is made entirely of wood, without notches or projections. Sticks are limited to 53 in. (1·35 m.) handle and 14½ in. (37 cm.) blade, except in the case of the goalminder, who may use a heavier and wider stick. Wear and tear on the sticks is heavy, for the long reach of an ice-hockey stick makes lightness imperative and consequently it is not durable. Formerly, ash was used for both blade and handle, but now rock elm is also used.

Sticks are not made to one standard, but to a player's individual specifications. They come in different 'lies', i.e. the angle between the blade and the handle varies. There are ten dif-

ferent lies, the most popular being Nos. 6, 7, and 5. The higher the number, the more vertical the shaft. Sticks are also made left, right, or centre, which means the blade is shaped to the player's particular needs.

Quite the most important part in the manufacture of a stick is the initial buying of the timber to be used, for the sticks must be neither too stiff nor too springy. Timber is brought in log form straight from the forest to the workshops, where it is cut into lengths of approximately 10 to 15 in. (25–38 cm.) and carefully stacked to 'air-dry' for about six months. It is then cut into shorter lengths and each one is tested to make sure there are no flaws. Then it is sent to the hand bench, where it is spliced down the middle, and the blade is inserted most carefully by hand into the handle. The blade is specially wedged for strength and the whole thing is glued together under pressure. Afterwards, it is shaped on the machines and is finally finished by hand, including any specific features which a particular player might require. Thus no two sticks are identical; each receives individual attention.

The length is considered correct if the top of the shaft just touches the player's chin when the stick is held upright with the blade touching the ice. Some professional players use a slightly curved blade (rounded off at the heel and toe), which helps to spin the puck as it is struck.

Black friction tape wound round the length of the blade increases the stick's durability and allows better control of the puck. A knob of tape round the top of the shaft affords a firmer grip in the gloved hand. Rubber knobs are also available to slip over the handle of the stick.

The puck, the disc-shaped object used rather than a ball because of its greater suitability on ice, is made of vulcanized rubber, 3 in. (7·6 cm.) in diameter and 1 in. (2·5 cm.) thick. Before play it should be frozen to minimize its resilience.

Ice-hockey skates differ in several respects from those used for figure-skating and for speed-skating. The ice-hockey skate blade is shorter than the speed skate, has a plain pointed end in front (instead of the figure skate's toe-rake), and a thinner blade, approximately $\frac{1}{16}$ of an inch (1·588 mm.) wide.

The blade is straight and narrow (without a radius) and is not hollow ground. It is reinforced with hollow tubing for greater strength and lighter weight. The two upright pieces of metal that join the heel and toe plate to the blade, known as the stanchions, are appreciably higher on the hockey skate (except the goalminder's). This makes the centre of gravity higher, one good reason why hockey skates are not the best on which to learn to skate. The goalminder's more specialized skate is wider and less high, affording easier balance. Extra stanchions are fitted to prevent the puck from passing underneath the boot.

The skate is usually best screwed to the boot very slightly to the inside, rather than exactly down the middle of the sole. The blades should be sharpened by an expert after about 13 hours' play.

The boot is readily distinguished in visual appearance from that used for figure-skating by its lower ankle support, coming up only 4 to 5 in. (101·6–127 mm.) above the sole. The material, usually calf or nubuck, is toughened to stand up to extra hard wear. Important features are the reinforced caps at toe and heel, moulded arch supports, and tendon protectors. Extra thickness of material protects the foot from damage by the puck and other players' skates and sticks.

The boot should fit snugly over one pair of woollen socks and never be larger than one's normal size in street shoes. In most cases, half a size smaller is ideal to give proper support for the ankle. To allow good circulation and foot comfort, tight lacing at the top two or three eyelets should be avoided.

Like the stick, boot, and skate, ice-hockey clothing is specialized, to cater for the sport's protective needs. All the players wear knee pads, shin guards, elbow pads, shoulder guards, thick gauntlet-type gloves, long stockings that fit over the knee pads, a special type of shorts, and sweaters in team colours.

Helmets, though optional, are a wise precaution to minimize possible head injuries. Apart from using different skates and sticks, the goalminder wears protective gear which is elaborately specialized, with extra-large leather leg-guards, a chest protector, and extra-padded gloves (one type for holding the stick, another for the catching hand). Some also wear a face mask to avoid possible cuts from skates or sticks after falling on the ice.

Ice hockey as we know it today is still relatively young, but its origins date back as far as the second century. Its historical roots are Canadian, despite the fact that it is generally recognized to stem from a game played by Englishmen on the frozen expanse of Kingston Harbour, Ontario, in 1860. This is the first time that a puck, as distinct from a ball, was used and so is usually accepted as the origin of the game with a recognized identity separate from field hockey. Most of these pioneer players were Crimean War veterans in a regiment of the Royal Canadian Rifles. Subsequently, Montreal became the central point of the game's early progress.

In the summer of 1879, W. F. Robertson, a student at McGill University, Montreal, visited England and watched field hockey matches. As a skating enthusiast, he wondered how the game could be suitably adapted so that it could be played on ice. When he returned to Montreal he told R. F. Smith, a fellow-student, of his idea. Robertson and Smith devised rules and regulations, adding a few original ideas to what was basically a combination of field hockey and rugby. A square rubber puck was used, with nine players on each side.

From these humble beginnings the first recognized team was formed in 1880 and called McGill University Hockey Club. The game was introduced to Ottawa five years later by one of the original McGill team members, A. P. Low.

The year 1893 was a notable one. Nearly a hundred clubs were by then established in Montreal alone and there were leagues at all grades throughout Canada. The game was first played in the U.S.A. in 1893, at Yale University in New Haven, Connecticut, and Johns Hopkins University in Baltimore. Also in 1893, Lord Stanley of Preston, then Governor-General of Canada, presented the STANLEY CUP, a permanent senior trophy which has become the most famous prize in the sport. It was first won by a club representing Montreal Amateur Athletic Association, which defeated Ottawa Capitals 3–1 on natural ice in 1894 before a crowd of more than 5,000.

The U.S. Amateur Hockey League was founded in New York City in 1896. The sport began to grow in Europe at the turn of the century and the world administration, the Ligue Internationale de Hockey sur Glace, now known as the International Ice Hockey Federation, was formed in 1908, with Belgium, Bohemia, France, Great Britain, and Switzerland the founder members. The prime mover in this was Magnus, a Frenchman — a reminder that the name 'hockey' is derived from a French word, hoquet, meaning a shepherd's crook or curved stick.

During the Great Freeze of 1895, two future British monarchs attracted early European attention to the sport when they participated in a match on a lake in the grounds of Buckingham Palace. That January, the Prince of WALES, afterwards King Edward VII, and the Duke of York, later King George V, were members of the Palace team in a match with Lord Stanley's side, which included five Stanley brothers with Canadian experience of the game.

A report by Maj. Patton says that 'the match had to be played early as the Prince of Wales was attending a levee that morning. The visiting side [the Stanley brothers plus Lord Annally] scored numerous goals to the single one of the Palace side. The Prince of Wales was greatly impressed by the play of the Hon. F. W. Stanley, who dribbled the puck at considerable speed while skating backwards in front of the Prince.'

Canadian demonstration popularized the game in Great Britain sufficiently to warrant a five-team league competition in 1903. The first game in Scotland took place at Crossmyloof, Glasgow, in 1908. The first European championship was won by Great Britain in 1910 at Les Avants, in the Swiss Alps. The British Ice Hockey Association was founded in 1914, with Maj. Patton its first president. The five founder clubs were Cambridge, Manchester, Oxford Canadians, Royal Engineers, and Princes.

With natural climatic advantage the sport developed and spread most rapidly across Canada, but gradually gained ground in the United States as more electrically refrigerated rinks came into being.

The first North American all-professional club, Portage Lake, Michigan, was formed in 1903; but individual professionals had played for Canadian teams before then and the first fully professional league in Canada was formed in Ontario in 1908, financially supported by the local silver-mining boom. The National Hockey League of North America began in 1917 but remained amateur until 1924, when Boston Bruins became the first professional N.H.L. team.

Meanwhile, the first Olympic title and, concurrently, the first amateur world championship, was won by Canada at Antwerp, Belgium, in 1920.

Progress in Britain was accelerated by the opening of Westminster rink, London, in 1926 but the game's best years there dated from the opening of the EMPIRE POOL, WEMBLEY, in 1934. Brighton Sports Stadium and the London Empress Hall and Harringay Arena followed Wembley's example and formed a pre-1939-war British big-rink era greatly strengthened by Canadian players. As an additional attraction to English league matches, there was an international club tournament comprising four London sides, WEMBLEY LIONS, Richmond Hawks, Streatham, and Wembley Canadians, and six European teams, Berlin, Français Volants, Milan, Munich, Prague, and Stade Français. In those days, and particularly in 1934-5, the Streatham club team, captained by Erhardt, was outstandingly successful.

One of the sport's peak years in Britain, 1936, coincided with the WINTER OLYMPIC GAMES at Garmisch, Germany, when Erhardt captained Britain in an historic win over

Canada, the masters, who until then had won every Olympic tournament. The British caused a sensational upset of form by beating Canada 2-1 and holding U.S.A. to a scoreless draw in the final game.

The war arrested this promising advance and afterwards teams and talent in Britain, faced with an acute shortage of large ice arenas with worthwhile spectator accommodation, faded considerably. Meanwhile ice hockey began to grow rapidly in popularity wherever else it was played.

In North America, the National Hockey League and the Stanley Cup sequel went from strength to strength, maintaining an international as well as an inter-state element, with well-attended matches at great arenas like MADISON SQUARE GARDEN, New York, and Maple Leaf Gardens, Toronto. For 25 years from 1942 no newcomers were added to the six established N.H.L. teams — BOSTON BRUINS, CHICAGO BLACK HAWKS, DETROIT RED WINGS, MONTREAL CANADIENS, NEW YORK RANGERS, and TORONTO MAPLE LEAFS.

Their prosperous and increasing support demanded expansion of the world's major professional competition and, in the 1967-8 season, the League was doubled in size to 12 clubs. The six new teams — LOS ANGELES KINGS, MINNESOTA NORTH STARS, OAKLAND SEALS, PHILADELPHIA FLYERS, PITTSBURGH PENGUINS, and ST. LOUIS BLUES — all competed in a West Division, while the original six formed an East Division. The expansion (since widened still further) proved a quick success, with the first four in each division competing in two separate play-off series, and the winners finally meeting in an annual best-of-seven contest for the Stanley Cup.

Among the most outstanding N.H.L. players since 1930 have been goalminders Durnan and Sawchuk, defencemen C. JOHNSON, SHORE, HARVEY, and ORR, centremen MORENZ and BELIVEAU, and wingers RICHARD, G. HOWE, and HULL. As well as the Stanley Cup, the following trophies are awarded annually for N.H.L. performances: PRINCE OF WALES, O'BRIEN, HART, VEZINA, ART ROSS, CALDER MEMORIAL, LADY BYNG, JAMES NORRIS MEMORIAL, and CONN SMYTHE. The season, excluding the Stanley Cup play-offs, lasts from mid-October to April.

There are hundreds of other teams throughout North America, taking part in amateur and professional league competitions which might be compared in diversity to those of Association football in Britain. The ALLAN CUP in Canada is widely regarded as the chief trophy for non-professional teams.

By the late 1960s the approximate number of players registered in the Soviet Union was

300,000; Canada 230,000; Sweden 140,000; Czechoslovakia 77,000; U.S.A. 48,000; and Finland 40,000.

In postwar years more than 20 nations have contested the quadrennial Olympic and annual world and European amateur championships, decided concurrently, organized primarily by the I.I.H.F. president, Ahearne, whose astute negotiation of television rights has provided much of the teams' travelling expenses. Outside Europe and North America, the sport has grown in proportion to the limited ice acreage available in such countries as Australia, South Africa, and Japan.

The Canadians' general supremacy among the amateurs was never seriously questioned until Russia won the Olympic tournament at Cortina in 1956 and afterwards dominated the world championships with teams noted for superior skating skill which gave them quicker manoeuvrability, and a well-drilled technique of keeping possession until the right scoring chance came. In 1968, nine of their players, Aleksandrov, Davidov, Firsov, Konovalenko, Kuzkin, B. Mayorov, Ragulin, O. Saitzev, and Starschinov, became the first in the sport to win second Olympic gold medals.

Howard Bass, *International Encyclopaedia of Winter Sports* (1971); Doc Brodrick, *Ice Hockey* (1951); Frank Mahovlich, *Ice Hockey* (1964); Lynn Patrick and Leo Monahan, *Let's Play Hockey* (1957); Jack Riley, *The Young Sportsman's Guide to Ice Hockey* (1962); George Sullivan, *Face-off!*, (1968).

GOVERNING BODY: International Ice Hockey Federation, 38 Dover Street, London W.1.

ICE RACING, Motor-cycle, see MOTOR-CYCLE RACING.

ICE SKATING. Competitive ice skating takes a number of forms, each with its own setting and equipment. Ice speed-skating and long-distance racing take place in the open air; ice figure-skating and ice dancing are performed on indoor ice arenas.

Speed-skating, at top level, is always performed on open-air ice if only because the area required is impracticable to house under cover. Electrically-refrigerated rinks, though few in number because of the high maintenance costs, are used for most major championships. A more restricted form of the sport is conducted at indoor ice arenas, but their area limitations allow insufficient length for adequate speeds and the bends are too sharp for reasonable cornering.

The way in which the skate blade strikes the ice in speed-skating is very important. The toe is pointed almost straight down in sprints, to get more ride out of the blade. For distance races the blade is placed on the ice at a 10-degree angle forward, with the upper body following. The upper body relaxes above the leg over which it glides. So, when the skater pushes off his right skate he collapses his upper body over his left thigh. The angle of the legs is almost straight to the ice — and the straighter the line one skates, the better.

On outdoor ice, the outstanding skaters present a thrilling spectacle. Over the longer distances the skater often races with his hands clasped behind his back to conserve energy, making his labour look much more effortless than it really is. Each gliding stroke commences on the inside edge of the special steel blade and is rolled over to the inside edge by the end of the stride, a style which dictates an impressive body-roll fascinating to watch. Clad in woollen tights, sweater, and protective headgear, these racers — their slightly bent shadows often grotesquely magnified in reflected light — take bends with consummate artistry, giving an illusion that it is not the skater, but the ice beneath him, that is moving.

Ice speed-skating record-holders are the fastest self-propelled humans over level terrain. Ice racers in fact have averaged near 30 m.p.h. (48 km./h.) in the shortest races. Over a mile, the speed-skater has been approximately one minute faster than the ATHLETICS track runner. In 1969 the fastest track athlete's time for 5,000 m. was six minutes slower than the best on ice.

To reach the highest level, a racer must spend several months every year in countries which provide enough ice and good tracks. Many racers travel long distances, abroad in many instances, for suitable training. Norway is particularly well provided, and the sport in that country commands a spectator following comparable to that of Association FOOTBALL in other lands.

Good ice conditions are not the only ideal to seek in training. The thinner air at high altitudes is another aid to performance. It is no coincidence that most world records have been set on mountain rinks situated higher than 500 m. (1,640 ft.).

International circuits have been established at Cortina d'Ampezzo, Italy; Davos, Switzerland; Deventer, Holland; Göteborg, Sweden; Grenoble, France; Helsinki, Finland; Innsbruck, Austria; Inzell, West Germany; Oslo, Norway; and Sapporo, Japan.

International championship meetings are normally of two days' duration, the usual practice being to stage 500 metres and 5,000 metres events on the first day and 1,500 and 10,000 metres on the following day. The best all-round performer over these four distances, calculated on a points basis, is recognized as the over-all individual champion.

Thus although, as in running, a speed-skater soon becomes recognized primarily as either a sprinter or a distance performer, in international events an individual champion is still determined by his ability over the four recognized championship distances — an out-dated tradition, perhaps, when one considers that 10,000 metres is 20 times as far as 500.

The time of each competitor being the decisive factor, international championship competitors race only in pairs and in separate lanes, but pack-style racing has been prevalent in the U.S.A.

The short indoor rinks, giving 12 or 16 laps to the mile, which American, British, and many other racers have to use, develop bad habits. While outdoor ice racing often attracts very large crowds, the sport indoors has remained basically a participants' preoccupation, partly perhaps because of the confusion to spectators when, because of the necessarily small circuit, competitors are frequently lapped and, in short-leg relays, it is difficult to follow the interchanging racers.

Skates and boots are the only essential equipment for the average racer. The correct skate for ice speed-skating and long-distance skating is appreciably longer than that used for ice figure-skating, and ice dancing. The best steel blade is as thin as $\frac{1}{32}$ in. (0·794 mm.), reinforced above with steel tubing for light-ness and strength. It is straight, usually 12 to 18 in. (304·8–457·2 mm.) in length and is designed to travel on straight, or nearly straight, lines. Because of its speed potential, it is usually not permitted during public skating sessions at ice rinks. The boot for speed-skating is lighter in weight than that for ice figure-skating (see below), made of thin leather with lower heel supports, more like a shoe than a boot in appearance.

Figure-skating is a sport for solo and pair-skaters which tests style as well as technical skill.

In senior championship competition solo competitors are required to skate three specific ice-skating figures, drawn from an internation-ally recognized schedule. They then have to perform a short programme containing pre-scribed free-skating elements, and finally, to music, a free-style performance of their own creation, lasting five minutes for men and pairs, and four minutes for women. Pair-skaters perform a series of prescribed free-skating movements, followed by a self-devised free-style performance.

FIGURES. Each of the compulsory figures is started from a stationary 'rest' position and is composed of a prescribed pattern in the form of either a two-lobe or three-lobe 'eight'. The figures vary greatly in degree of difficulty and are drawn to suit the standard of the event. Each figure is skated three times, each tracing an indentation on the ice. Judges at these events are concerned not only with the merits of the tracings but also with the skater's con-trol, position, and balance. The positions of hands, fingers, and non-skating foot are taken into consideration, as are the maintenance of a smooth, steady speed and the execution of changes from one foot to the other by means of a single stroke from the skate-edge and not from the toe.

The figure-skating blade, being hollow ground, has two edges and nearly all move-ments in this sport should be performed on an edge. Skating on an edge entails a lean of the body over the appropriate edge to cause a for-ward or backward movement in a curve. The sense of balance is comparable to that of a cyclist's lean as he turns a corner. The lean is proportionately greater according to the speed and angle of the turn, and, just as the cyclist leans over *with* the cycle, so a skater leans over *with* the edge of the blade he is using.

When the skater completes a figure, the judges examine the pattern left by the edges of the skates. The print on the ice is their prime concern, followed closely by carriage and flow of movement. A bulge in a circle, a 'flat-ting' of the skate, or an improper change from one blade-edge can count against the competi-tor.

Eight   Loop   Three   Rocker

COMPULSORY FIGURES
The figure eight performed first on the right foot for-wards on the outside edge of the blade, then on the left foot forwards on the outside edge, has a factor value of 1 in competition; performed first on the right foot backwards on the inside edge of the blade, then on the left foot backwards on the inside edge, it has a factor of 2. The other figures illustrated are similarly valued according to difficulty; the three-lobed rocker figure, in which the skater must reverse from forwards to backwards and vice versa, as well as from the left to the right foot, has a factor of 5, whether performed on the inside or the outside edge of the blade.

Of the 41 compulsory figures officially recognized by the International Skating

Union, the following are perhaps the best-known:

The *eight*, a figure resembling the numeral '8', composed of two adjacent circles executed in any of several prescribed ways.

The *loop*, a two-lobed figure in which each lobe is skated on the same foot and on the same continuous edge, with a small loop at the top and inside each of the circles.

The *three*, a two-lobed figure, so named because the turn involved at the extreme end of each circle leaves a tracing on the ice resembling the numeral '3'.

The *rocker*, a three-lobed figure involving turns in which the skater rotates sufficiently to come out of the turn on the same edge but in a different direction.

Each of the compulsory figures may be executed on either foot or on a combination of both, on the inside or the outside edge of the blade (see below), and forwards or backwards. Points up to a maximum of 6 are awarded for each figure and these marks are subsequently multiplied by a factor of between 1 and 6 according to the recognized standard of the figure.

FREE SKATING is the climax of the competition: the most spectacular part and that most readily appreciated by the spectators. In this, the precise edges and turns learned in figures are combined to create intricate footwork embellished with jumps and spins, and spaced between spirals and linking steps.

Spirals are sustained one-foot glides, in either backward or forward direction, performed holding the body in various positions, simulating 'moving statues'. While some depict feminine grace, others imply masculine strength. Holding the position unwaveringly is the hallmark of a good spiral, and the ability to control it either forward or backward, provides a sound basis for a free-style repertoire. A *spreadeagle* is a two-footed glide in which the feet are positioned in line with each other, heels together and toes pointing outwards. Two turns frequently used are the *bracket*, a half-turn from one edge to the opposite edge of the same skate, with the body turning inside the circle; and the *counter*, a half-turn maintaining the same edge of the skate.

The art of jumping depends on the strength of spring as well as the timing of take-off. The *three jump* comprises a half-turn in mid-air, taking off from the forward outside edge of one skate and landing on the back outside edge of the other. The *loop jump*, requiring a full revolution in the air, is important as the basis of several more advanced jumps. The take-off is from a back outside edge, landing on the same edge of the same foot.

Starting from the spreadeagle position, with feet well apart and toes turned outwards, the *spreadeagle jump* is executed on either the inner or outer edges and is effected by holding the original position until the last moment, when the heels are pulled closer together and a half-turn or full turn is made in mid-air while retaining the spread position.

Further examples of jumps are:

The *axel*, a jump involving one and a half turns in the air, named after its originator, Axel PAULSEN. The take-off begins from an outside forward edge of one skate, landing on the back outside edge of the other skate. A double axel is the same jump with two and a half mid-air revolutions. In pair skating, an axel lift is achieved by a similar take-off and landing by the lady, the man rotating beneath her throughout the movement.

The *flip jump*, a toe jump, taking off from the back outside edge of the skating blade, assisted by the toe-point of the non-skating blade of the free foot, rotating in mid-air before landing on the back outside edge of the original non-skating blade.

The *lutz*. Most jumps entail counter-clockwise rotation in the air, but a notable exception is this difficult toe jump, in which the skater takes off from a back outside edge, helped by the toe-point of the free foot, rotating clockwise in mid-air before landing on the back outside edge of the original free foot.

The *salchow*, a jump named after its originator (see SALCHOW), in which the skater takes off from a back inside edge, rotating in mid-air before landing on the back outside edge of the opposite foot.

The *split jump*, a toe jump in which the skater takes off from a back inside edge, assisted by the toe-point of the free foot, half-turning in mid-air while swinging the legs up into a horizontal position, closing them before landing on the forward inside edge of the original free foot and the toe-point of the original skating foot.

There are other variants of the foregoing jumps and such further advanced jumps as the double or triple salchow, loop, axel, and lutz, their names indicating the number of mid-air rotations involved, the doubles and triples calling for greater height to give time in which to complete such turns.

A good spin is executed on one spot without any 'travel'. The *single flat-foot spin* is performed on the flat of the skate, with balance centred over the ball of the foot. A *single-toe-spin* is similarly performed, except that the weight is on the point of the toe.

The *sit spin* (originated by HAINES) starts as a standing spin, the skater immediately afterwards sinking on his skating knee to a sitting posture, with the free leg extended in front

The *camel spin* is a one-foot spin executed on the flat of the skate blade, holding the body and the non-skating leg in a horizontal position, parallel to the ice, with the back arched.

In the *layback spin*, another one-foot spin, the body is bent backwards, spinning parallel to the ice. More advanced are *change-foot spins*, which, when sufficiently well executed, lead to jumping from one spin to another.

Probably the most impressive of all spins is the *cross-foot spin*, performed on the flat of both skate blades, with the legs in crossed position, toes together and heels apart. This is often used to conclude a performance because of its dramatic effect of speedy rotation.

An advanced free-style repertoire is enhanced by combining jumps and spins, and so special spins such as the *flying sit spin* and the *flying camel* — a jump variation of the camel spin — have been evolved. The performer is in no way restricted in what he attempts or in what sequence, but tries to incorporate as many difficult movements as possible within the time allotted, in order to gain the highest possible marks.

Technical merit and artistic impression are assessed separately. The judges have to take into account the variation of contents, degree of difficulty, and manner of performance, taking into consideration such questions as: was speed gathered without visible effort; did the skater mix in original footwork on toes and edges; were there smooth transitions and changes in tempo, with sudden surprise movements; was the skater always in proper position, with toes pointed and back straight; did the skater make intelligent use of the entire ice area; and did his performance give the feeling of being planned and skated to the music, rather than of being a set show where the music is only incidental. Scoring is again graded up to a maximum of 6 and the totals multiplied by a factor to ensure an aggregate parity with the marks awarded for figures.

In ice figure-skating senior championship competition, the compulsory figures are worth 40 per cent of the total marks, the prescribed free-skating movements another 20 per cent, and the skater's free-style performance the remaining 40 per cent.

PAIR SKATING competitions are also divided into compulsory and free-style sections. For the former, pairs are required to demonstrate six specified sequences, skill in performance carrying a quarter of the marks. In the free-style section, the two partners must perform movements giving a homogeneous impression and, although the partners need not always perform the same movements as each other and may separate from time to time, they must give an over-all impression of unison and harmonious composition.

Lifts, spins, jumps, spirals, spreadeagles, and all the recognized free-skating movements are permissible, and skaters have absolute freedom of choice to incorporate any known or new movement. 'Shadow skating' is the term generally applied to the parts of the pairs programme where both skaters perform in unity but separated, i.e. not touching.

This form of skating essentially requires teamwork in every sense. Ideally, the man should be slightly taller, and the couple should match in ability. Each skater has to concentrate not only on proficiency of movement but on synchronization with his or her partner, in timing and so that the movements of arms, hands, legs, and feet correspond. Each must learn to understand the partner's movements and ability so that each anticipates and matches the other's steps with precision. For that reason, the performance must be kept within the limitations of the weaker partner.

'Filling' the rink during a display is just as important for a pair as it is in planning individual free-skating programmes. Following are among the best-known specialized pair-skating highlights, as distinct from synchronized solo shadow movements:

The *death spiral*, the popular name given to a movement whereby the man swings his partner round at very great speed, himself retaining virtually the same pose. The woman, her hair sometimes touching the ice, apparently risks death by her repeated proximity to the surface as she revolves round her partner. The styles can be varied with one- or two-handed holds in various grips — with the man holding the woman's ankle, or with the woman's feet round his neck. Such manoeuvres as the latter are more usually associated with a professional theatrical performance. Controlled wrist and arm strength and centrifugal force are prime factors.

The *single lasso lift*. From a side-by-side, hand-to-hand position, the woman is lifted overhead in an outside forward take-off, turning one and a half revolutions with the man's arms stretched (lasso pose) and the woman's legs in split position. The man remains forward to complete a backward landing on the right outside edge.

The *axel lift*. In this spectacular lift the woman is turned one and a half times completely over her partner's head. After holding hands on one side, she is supported in the lift by the man's hand under her armpit. The lift begins from the woman's outside forward edge and is completed on the outside back edge of her opposite skate. The man rotates beneath the woman throughout the movement.

The *split lutz lift*. Both partners start from a side-by-side position, travelling backwards. The woman is lifted from an outside back edge. During the lift she assumes a split lutz position. At the conclusion of the lift she is travelling on a back outside edge and the man on a forward outside edge.

The *catch-waist camel (arabesque) spin*, performed with the free legs pointing in opposite directions, the bodies close together and arms around each other's waist. The spin by each partner is executed on the flat of the blade while the torso and free leg are parallel to the ice, with the back arched.

Ambitious figure-skaters and pair-skaters improve their technical standards by taking graduated proficiency tests, simple at first, progressively winning bronze, silver, and gold medals, with intermediate certificates between. The highest test a skater has passed determines the class of competition he or she is qualified to enter.

The most suitable skate for ice figure-skating as for general ice-skating and ice-dancing (see below), is made of chromium-plated steel and is distinguished from other skates by 'teeth', known as a toe-rake, used for spinning, at the front of the blade. The skate should be screwed to the skating-boot so that the blade runs between the big toe and the second toe — very slightly inside the centre line from toe to heel of the boot. Fitting the blade thus fractionally off-centre balances the body more naturally over the skates and initial awkwardness, which often creates an illusion of weak ankles, is thereby minimized.

END-ON VIEW OF AN ICE FIGURE-SKATE BLADE
The curved, hollow-ground centre of the blade does not touch the ice; all skating strokes are made on the blade's edges.

The skate blade for figure-skating, in contrast to that of the straight ICE HOCKEY skate, is very slightly curved from heel to toe, usually set on a 7 ft. (2·13 m.) radius. The under part of the blade is not flat, but has a hollow ridge right along the centre, known as the concave, to which the expression 'hollow ground' refers. The sides of this hollow ridge are called the edges of the skate. The edge nearest the inside of the foot is referred to as the inside edge, the other being the outside edge. The

blade is about ⅛ in. (3·175 mm.) wide and slightly longer than the length of the boot.

Skate-guards, used to protect the blades of ice skates, are made of wood, rubber, or plastic, designed to fit and clip over the blades when not in use. Many are made so that it is possible to walk while the guards are still on the blades when approaching or leaving the ice.

The well-made boot for ice figure-skating, usually made mainly of black leather for men, and white suède or nubuck for women, has a strong arch support reinforced with a stiffening material around the heel and under the arch which prevents the foot from slipping to the side. Correct fitting is very important. The boot should on no account err on the large side, half a size smaller than one's normal footwear being ideal. It must fit tightly at heel, ankle, and instep, but not round the toes, so that it comes to feel like part of the foot.

Careful attention must be given to correct lacing of the boots. The lace is best left reasonably loose in the first few eyelets from the toes to the instep bone, then laced as tightly as possible from the instep bone as far as the first eyelet above the ankle bone. Here a surgeon's knot should be tied (wrap one lace twice round the other and pull tight). From this point upwards the lacing should be left relatively loose to avoid cramped muscles.

Ice dancing, a, relatively modern offshoot of ice figure-skating, is — despite its name — a sport in its own right, with movements based largely on those learned in figures.

There is a great difference between ice dancing and pair skating. In ice dancing, for example, lifts are not permissible and free dancing, more specific in its requirements, ideally consists of a non-repetitive performance of novel movements and variations of known ice dances, or parts thereof, combined into a programme of original design and arrangement.

Certain free-skating movements which are in keeping with the character of the dances are allowed, but feats of strength and skating skill which do not form part of the dance sequence, but which, to quote the rule book, 'are inserted to show physical prowess', are counted against the competitors using them.

Free-skating movements, such as some spins, brief arabesques or pivots, and separations to accomplish changes of position, are suitable for ice dancing only when used with the following limitations: (*a*) separations of partners must not exceed the time necessary to change position; (*b*) arabesques or pivots must not exceed in duration the longer movements of the compulsory dances; (*c*) spins must not exceed one and a half revolutions; (*d*) the maintenance of any position should not be prolonged. The rule-makers are constantly watchful to curb the infiltration of irrelevant movements more suitable to pair skating.

Following are a few of the turns and sequences commonly used in ice dancing:

The *chassé*, a sequence in which the free foot during the period of becoming the skating foot does not pass the original skating foot, but is placed on the ice beside the skating foot with the new free foot coming off the ice slightly ahead of or beside the new skating foot.

The *choctaw*, a turn from forward to backward, or vice versa, from one foot to the other on blade edges of different character, i.e. outside to inside or inside to outside.

The *mohawk*, a half-turn from forward to backward, or vice versa, from one foot to the other on blade edges of the same character, i.e. outside to outside or inside to inside.

The *twizzle*, a rotation through a complete revolution performed so rapidly that it takes place almost on one spot.

The most popular ice dance is the graceful *European waltz*; it was the earliest standardized ice dance, and is the easiest to learn, though by no means easy to perform really well. The initial hazard seems to be the tendency to hurry, as a result of anticipating the beat. Smooth, clean turns should be essayed, with threes (half-turns from one edge to the opposite edge on the same foot) turned between the partner's feet.

In the accepted waltz hold, the man's right hand should hold his partner firmly between the shoulder blades. The woman's left hand should rest equally firmly a little below her partner's right shoulder, her left elbow resting on his right elbow. The man's left arm and the woman's right arm should be extended and held sufficiently firmly for synchronized movement. A couple should skate the waltz as closely together as possible in order to retain proper control. The back should be arched and the chest thrown out. The body should be carried erect over the employed skate, and any inclination to bend forward at the waist checked.

The *fourteen-step dance* with a lively, military-style tempo, is also popular. It is a development of the earlier *ten-step* with the initial *chassé* repeated. Common errors to counter in this dance are the faulty execution of mohawks, the man's tendency to double track (skate on both feet simultaneously) in backward movements, and the woman's inclination to lean forward on backward *chassés*.

In addition to the waltz and the fourteen-step, 14 other standard ice dances have been recognized internationally. After the *kilian*, an optional pattern dance characterized by its quick march-like tempo, the *tango* came as a variation and is most attractive when well performed.

The *foxtrot* is seen at its best when executed with strong, well-curved edges. It expresses the syncopation of modern foxtrot music, skated not in the facing waltz position, but side by side, comparable to the 'conversation' position in the ballroom. Thus, with the man's right hip touching the woman's left, the man's right hand goes on his partner's right shoulder blade and the woman's left hand is placed on his right shoulder. The man's left hand holds his partner's right hand, extended in front.

The popular *blues* to slow music is skated with bold edges. Important in this is mastery of the choctaw. The *Argentine tango* is a difficult set-pattern dance performed at accelerated speed. The *quickstep* is comparatively simple. The *paso doble*, speedy and circular, is less easy to skate well.

In the *American waltz*, series of half-circles or lobes are skated along each side of the rink and joined at the ends by six-beat outside edges. Although the sequence of steps is the simplest of any ice dance, it is among the most difficult to skate correctly, owing to the control needed in an excessive amount of rotation.

The *rocker foxtrot* allows an attractive flowing movement. The high-spirited *Viennese waltz* is danced at a good pace with strongly curved edges. The *Westminster waltz* is partly skated in kilian position, using the thumb-pivot grip for the hands to facilitate the changes of sides by the partners. The woman's hands are held above the man's, with the thumbs extended downwards into the man's fists.

Other ice dances also internationally recognized are the unorthodox but impressive *rumba*, the most modern *silver samba*, and the *starlight waltz*, which is pleasing to the eye and relatively easy to perform.

All ice dances progress in a counterclockwise direction round the rink. Synchronization with the music is naturally more important, and participation at public-rink sessions has a social appeal. Since 1950, in Britain, at least one person in every five who sets out to learn to skate has done so primarily with the ambition to take part in rink ice dancing.

As in ordinary dancing, provided the learner possesses the basic essentials of a sense of rhythm and an ear for the beat, few lessons are required to enable enjoyable participation, as distinct from polished performance. If possible, as in ballroom dancing, it is advisable to learn with a reasonably experienced partner. The instructions for executing all the steps of every ice dance are fully set out and illustrated by diagrams in a standard booklet approved by the International Skating Union. Graduated proficiency tests, for which certificates and medals are awarded, are organized in many countries on a national basis, with dances suitably graded into levels of difficulty.

Championship competitions are in two parts, compulsory dances and free-style, each carrying half of the total marks, assessed by a panel of judges as in figure-skating. For the compulsory section, three specific dances are drawn from the international schedule. Each couple also skates an original set dance to a specific rhythm. The judges award one set of marks for each of the first three compulsory dances and two sets of marks for the set pattern dance and for the free dancing. In the latter, they separately assess technical merit (difficulty, variety, clearness, sureness, and originality) and artistic impression (harmonious composition, conformity to music, utilization of space, flow of movement, and deportment).

The modern word 'skate' is believed to be derived from the early German *schake* (meaning a shark or leg bone) *schaats* in Dutch —and the Early English word, *scatch*. The first skates were made from the shank or ribs of the elk, ox, reindeer, and other animals, well before the discovery of steel, and there still exist in some museums bone skates believed to be 20 centuries old.

Skating of a kind almost certainly originated in Scandinavia long before the birth of Christ and is mentioned in Scandinavian literature of the second century. An offshoot of SKIING, primitive skating undoubtedly first developed out of necessity as a means of transport. Not surprisingly, skating has been widely practised on the canals of Holland since the Middle Ages. The first known illustration of the sport—and early evidence, incidentally, of female participation—is a Dutch wood-engraving printed in 1498, depicting St. Lydwina of Schiedam, who, in 1396, fell and broke a rib when skating at the age of 16. She died in 1433 and subsequently became the patron saint of skaters.

The sport was mentioned by Samuel Pepys, who, on 1 December 1662, described in his diary the canal in St. James's Park, London, 'where first in my life, it being a Great Frost, [I] did see people sliding with their skeetes, which is a very pretty art.' Twenty-one years later, Pepys danced on the ice with Nell Gwynne during the Great Frost of 1683.

The first instructional book on skating was written by Captain Robert Jones and published in London in 1772, thirty years after the formation of the world's first skating club at EDINBURGH in 1742. Skating became fashionable in the French court around 1776, when Marie Antoinette was among the participants. In 1791 Napoleon, then a student at the École Militaire, narrowly escaped drowning while skating on the moat of the fort at Auxerre.

The LONDON SKATING CLUB was founded in 1842 and the sport was introduced shortly afterwards into the U.S.A. and Canada by British servicemen. It developed particularly in Philadelphia, where the first American skating club was started in 1849 and the well-known painter, Benjamin West, became one of the earliest known American skaters of ability. The first all-iron skate, which clipped on to the boot and dispensed with the use of straps, was invented in 1850 by Bushnell in Philadelphia.

In 1858, the first properly maintained rink was organized on the lake in Central Park, New York. The NEW YORK SKATING CLUB was formed in 1860 and, two years afterwards, it organized the first skating carnival on the frozen Union Pond in Brooklyn. The first rink in Canada opened in 1868 at Toronto. In Switzerland, Davos Ice Rink was inaugurated in 1877, following the enthusiasm of British guests at the Hotel Belvedere.

Partly influenced by the exhibitions of HAINES, serious skating thrived from 1880 in Scandinavia, where early great performers included the Swede Salchow, ten times winner of the world figure-skating championship, and Paulsen of Norway. Their names are still used today to describe the jumps which they originally created. From Scandinavia, too, other great names were to follow, not least among them GRAFSTRÖM and Miss HENIE.

The first mechanically refrigerated rink was a small private one, the GLACIARIUM near King's Road, Chelsea, London. A public rink opened in Manchester in 1877 and clubs quickly multiplied in Britain before the end of the nineteenth century. Ice rinks began to appear in many cities and towns on both sides of the Atlantic, notably Baltimore, Brighton, Brooklyn, Brussels, London, Munich, New York, Paris, Philadelphia, and Southport. The first ice rink in Australia, the Melbourne Glaciarium, opened in 1904, and the first South African at Johannesburg in 1909.

The sport's first federation, the National Skating Association of Great Britain, was instituted in 1879. The United States Figure Skating Association was inaugurated in 1886 and the Canadian in 1888. Other countries followed suit and the national associations of Austria, Germany, Great Britain, Holland, Hungary, and Sweden collaborated in 1892 to found, at Schweringen, Holland, the International Skating Union (I.S.U.). As the world's governing administrative body the I.S.U. has, since supervised and standardized regulations in the three main variants of the sport, ice figure-skating, ice dancing, and ice speed-skating.

Ice speed-skating began to develop in Holland around the beginning of the nineteenth century and the Dutch soon took the sport to their closest neighbours, Germany, France, and Austria. The Frieslanders of North Holland introduced it to England in the area extending from Cambridge to the Wash known as the Fens, where recorded competitions in FENLAND SKATING date from 1814.

The first international speed-skating competition was in Hamburg, Germany, in 1885. World championships for men, though first held in 1889 at Amsterdam, Holland, were not officially recognized until 1893, when Eden (Netherlands) became the first title-holder.

Separate European men's championships also officially date from 1893, when Ericsson (Sweden) became the first winner, in Berlin. The first women's world title was contested at Stockholm in 1936 and won by Miss Klein (U.S.A.). Men's speed-skating gained Olympic status in 1924, when the first WINTER OLYMPIC GAMES were staged at Chamonix, France, but women's Olympic speed-skating was not added until 1960 at Squaw Valley, California, U.S.A.

The administrative pioneer in figure-skating was VANDERVELL, who invented the bracket, the counter, and the rocker figures. The figure-skating committee of what is now the National Skating Association of Great Britain was founded under his chairmanship in 1880 and he is credited with instituting the idea of proficiency tests. His original conception of a graduated system of figure tests, subsequently improved upon, was universally adopted by the International Skating Union.

Free-style technique in Vandervell's time was subordinated to figures, the development of new turns into a restrained and dignified science with pride in accuracy of execution in an era of unwieldy Victorian dress. In the late nineteenth century, the English and the freer Viennese styles became separately recognized until the latter eventually became the international style adopted for all major championships.

The first world championship in ice figure-skating was won at St. Petersburg (now Leningrad) in 1896 by Dr. Fuchs (Germany). The third championship, in 1898 in London, was held at the then National Skating Palace in Argyll Street, on the site where the Palladium theatre now stands.

The first separate women's world championship, contested at Davos, Switzerland, was won by Mrs. Syers (Great Britain).

European championships date from 1891, when Uhlig (Germany) was successful in Hamburg, Miss Burger (Austria) winning the first women's European title in Vienna in 1930.

The first world pair-skating championship was won in 1908 at St. Petersburg by the Germans, Burger and Miss Hübler. The first European title was won by the Hungarians, Szalay and Miss Orgonista, at Vienna in 1930.

Ice figure-skating for men, women, and pairs became Olympic events when the summer OLYMPIC GAMES were held in London in 1908, 16 years before the first separate Winter Olympics.

Despite references by such as Pepys to dancing on ice in the seventeenth century, seriously organized ice dancing dates from the waltz-minded Vienna Skating Club's activities in the 1880s. There is evidence that the waltz was skated on ice at Halifax, Nova Scotia, as early as 1885 and that a waltz was demonstrated at the Palais de Glace, Paris, in 1894.

The first organized set-pattern dance specially for skaters was the ten-step, which later became the fourteen-step. It was originated in 1889 by a Viennese, Schöller. The kilian, invented by Schreiter, also emerged from Vienna in 1909. The European waltz was established by this time, though its inventor and exact date have never been ascertained.

Ice dancing became more fully organized through rapid development in Britain during the 1930s. The tango was jointly created by Kreckow and Miss Harris in 1931. The foxtrot was invented in 1933 by Mr. and Mrs. Van der Weyden, who also introduced the rocker foxtrot and the Viennese waltz in 1934 and the Westminster waltz in 1938. The blues was also originated in 1934, by Dench and Miss Turner. The same year, the Argentine tango was devised by Wilkie and Miss Wallis, who went on to contribute the quickstep and *paso doble*, both in 1938.

The world ice dance championship was first held in Paris in 1952 and was won by Denny and Miss Westwood (Great Britain), who also won the first European title, at Bolzano, Italy, in 1954.

The number of electrically-refrigerated ice rinks had become so numerous throughout the world that, in 1967, the I.S.U. ruled that international championships must be staged indoors to minimize the element of luck which outdoor conditions had sometimes greatly affected.

Howard Bass, *International Encyclopaedia of Winter Sports* (1971), *This Skating Age* (1958), and *Winter Sports* (1968); Nigel Brown, *Ice Skating — A History* (1959); Dick Button, *Dick Button on Skates* (1956); Bob Dench and Rosemary Stewart,

Pair Skating and Dancing on Ice (1959); Jacqueline du Bief, *Thin Ice* (1956); John Noel, *Figure Skating for Beginners* (1964); Maribel Vinson Owen, *The Fun of Figure Skating* (1960); Monty Readhead, *Ice Dancing* (1968).

GOVERNING BODY (WORLD): International Skating Union, Villa Richmond, CH7270 Davos-Platz, Switzerland.

ICE SPEED-SKATING, see ICE SKATING.

ICE YACHTING, travelling and racing across ice in specially adapted boats with sails propelled by the wind, has been practised primarily in those parts of North America and Europe with climatic factors conducive to suitable ice and wind conditions. The most favoured North American areas have been near the Atlantic coast between Long Branch, New Jersey, and Portsmouth, New Hampshire, and the Great Lakes basin, from central Wisconsin, eastward to Buffalo, New York, and Toronto, Canada. In Europe, the sport has been most practised in northern Germany, southern Sweden, the Netherlands, and the Baltic coasts of Estonia, Finland, Latvia, and Lithuania.

Built usually for only one or two occupants, ice yachts for competition purposes are classified simply by sail area. The most popular craft nowadays is the bow-steering Skeeter class, limited to 75 sq. ft. (7 sq. m.) of sail. A 22-ft. racing Skeeter, weighing about 300 lb. (136 kg.), can be dismantled for transport on a car roof or light trailer. It has sharp-edged steel runners, normally 4½ in. high and 40 in. long (114·3 mm. × 1·01 m.).

The technique corresponds very much to that of sailing on water. The potential speed of an ice yacht is approximately four times that of the wind velocity.

Ice yachting has been practised by the Dutch since the middle of the eighteenth century. In 1768, a drawing of a Dutch ice yacht was published by Chapman in his *Architectura Navalis Mercatoria.* The sport is also known to have taken place during the eighteenth century on the frozen bay at Riga, Latvia, and in the Gulf of Finland. In 1790, Booth sailed in a primitive, box-like craft, the first ice boat recorded in North America, on the frozen Hudson River at Poughkeepsie, New York, U.S.A.

The greatest early progress was made during the late nineteenth century in the Hudson River valley, where the POUGHKEEPSIE ICE YACHT CLUB was formed in 1865. The HUDSON RIVER ICE YACHT CLUB, founded five years later, became the hub of the sport until the turn of the century, owing largely to the active interest of Commodore Roosevelt. The early Hudson River craft were heavy and cumbersome by later standards and Roosevelt's *Icicle* was the largest ever built, in 1870 — 69 ft. (21·03 m.) long with 1,070 sq. ft. (99·40 sq. m.) of sail.

A prototype of the present-day craft was the much sleeker *Robert Scott,* built by Relyea in 1879, and this Hudson River type remained dominant until 1930. The American brothers, J. and G. Buckhout, earned recognition as leading ice yacht designers during the early 1900s. *Debutante III,* with 680 sq. ft. (63·17 sq. m.) of sail, was built by them in 1915 and in the 1970s was still the largest ice yacht in use.

An open competition for the CHALLENGE PENNANT OF AMERICA dates from 1881 and was organized by the NEW HAMBURGH ICE YACHT CLUB until 1902. After a lapse of 20 years the event was revived in 1922 and won by Millard's *Scout,* skippered by Captain Drake. The competition was again resumed in 1951 at Greenwood Lake, New Jersey, this time under the auspices of the Eastern Ice Yachting Association.

Speeds exceeding 100 m.p.h. (160 km./h.) were achieved in 1885 by the *Scud* on the Navesink River at Red Bank, New Jersey. In 1907, the *Claret* reached 140 m.p.h. (225 km./h.) along the Shrewsbury River at Long Branch, New Jersey. Ice yachtsmen were then the fastest travelling humans in the world. A long-standing world record, determined over 30 miles (48 km.), was set in 1907 by *Wolverine* at Kalamazoo, Michigan. Its time of 39 min. 50 sec. remained unbeaten until 1953, when Perrigo's *Thunderjet* took 29 min. 4 sec. A highest speed of 143 m.p.h. (230 km./h.) was credited to Buckstaff in 1938, in a stern-steerer on Lake Winnebago, Wisconsin.

In 1928, the European Ice Yachting Union was inaugurated at Riga, Latvia, by six founder members: Austria, Estonia, Germany, Latvia, Lithuania, and Sweden. The sport was transformed from a rich man's recreation using expensive craft when, in the mid-twentieth century, much cheaper, smaller and lighter boats were introduced and the bow-steering Skeeter class became the most popular, prompting the formation at Chicago in 1939 of the International Skeeter Association, to supervise race organization of this rapidly growing class.

Annual European championships, using stern-steering craft, were held until the Second World War, after which participation diminished but remained particularly popular in Sweden.

S. C. Smith, *Ice Boating* (1962).

IGLEHART, STEWART (1914-   ),

American POLO player who was a light but very strong player of the American golden age. He played in the winning Westchester Cup teams of 1936 and 1939 and against Mexico in 1946. He was on the winning side five times in the U.S. championship, playing for Templeton and Old Westbury. Handicap 10.

IGLOI, MIHALY, ATHLETICS coach; formerly Hungarian, later a citizen of the U.S.A. In 1954-6 Igloi was responsible for an upsurge in distance running standards in Hungary. His most celebrated charge was IHAROS. After the 1956 OLYMPIC GAMES, which followed the October revolution in Hungary, Igloi emigrated to the United States where he coached a number of successful American runners including Beatty, former holder of the American mile record. Subsequently he had further coaching successes in Greece.

IGLS (1), BOBSLEIGH course near Innsbruck, Austria, opened in 1963 to stage the world championships of that year, followed by the 1964 WINTER OLYMPIC GAMES. The length of the course is 1,506 m., about 113 yds. less than a mile, with 13 turns and two S-bends. The average gradient is just over 9 per cent and the maximum incline 14 per cent. The total decline from start to finish is 138 m. (453 ft.).

The ninth corner, Hexenkessel, about half-way down the course, is the vital one to master. If the bob takes the corner right at this point it can more easily gather extra speed for the rest of the way. Of the world's major bob runs, the Igls course is regarded by many riders as the best, with wider, larger corners which are less difficult to take. The International Bobsleigh Federation supervised its erection with three main factors in mind — maximum spectator value, maximum speed, and maximum safety. An achievable average on it of some 113 km./h. (70 m.p.h.) is a fair estimate, with a reasonably possible top speed of 137 to 145 km./h. (85–90 m.p.h.).

(2) Luge TOBOGGANING course near Innsbruck, Austria, specially constructed for the 1964 WINTER OLYMPIC GAMES and opened in time for the pre-Olympic competitions in 1963. It is near, but quite separate from, the Igls BOBSLEIGH course. Its length is 1,063 m. (about 1,200 yds.) for the men's events, reduced by 100 m. (109·36 yds.) for the women's and two-seater events. The average gradient is 10·7 per cent and the steepest incline 18·8 per cent. The 18 curves include 6 hairpins. The trickiest corners became familiar to spectators as Labyrinth, Forest Bend, Shock Wall, Glacier View, Hammock, Water Slip, Promenade, Tower, Mousetrap, and Olympic Bend.

IGNIS VARESE, BASKETBALL club of Varese, Italy. Ignis won the EUROPEAN CUP-WINNERS CUP in their inaugural season, 1966-7, and won the EUROPEAN CUP FOR CHAMPION CLUBS in 1970. They were runners-up in this competition in 1971 and were again winners in 1972 and 1973.

IHAROS, SANDOR (1930-   ), middle-distance and long-distance runner for Hungary. Iharos was outstanding among a group of Hungarian runners who came to prominence in what may be called the 'post-ZATOPEK' era. In the years 1955 and 1956 Iharos set seven world records: 3 min. 40·8 sec. for 1,500 metres, 7 min. 55·6 sec. for 3,000 metres, 8 min. 33·4 sec. for 2 miles, 13 min. 14·2 sec. for 3 miles, 13 min. 40·6 sec. for 5,000 metres, 27 min. 43·8 sec. for 6 miles, and 28 min. 42·8 sec. for 10,000 metres. The October revolution in Hungary prevented him from reaching the 1956 OLYMPIC GAMES at the top of his form and so denied him a major championship medal. Perhaps his greatest performance was the 10,000 metres world record (in which he also broke the 6 miles record) in his début at this distance.

IKEDA, KEIKO (1933-   ), a Japanese female gymnast who was the leading competitor in her country's rise in the sport during the 1950s and 1960s. Although this tiny woman (5 ft. ½ in. — 1·54 m. — and 8 st. 2 lb. — 52 kg.) won only one gold medal in world championships or OLYMPIC GAMES, her distinctive style enabled her to have an amazingly long career. She was a member of the Japanese team on their first appearance in world championships at Rome in 1954 when she took the gold medal on the beam. After an indifferent performance at the 1956 Olympics, she was more successful at the 1958 world championships, taking bronze medals on the floor and beam. She was sixth over-all at the 1960 Olympics and 1962 world championships, but at the 1964 Olympics she led the Japanese team to a bronze medal in the memorable competition against Russia and Czechoslovakia. At the 1966 world championships she won a silver medal on the bars and was third over-all.

ILLINGWORTH, RAYMOND, C.B.E. (1932-   ), cricketer for England, Yorkshire, and Leicestershire. After 18 seasons with Yorkshire he joined Leicestershire as captain in 1969, and within months was captain of England after COWDREY was injured. As dogged middle-order batsman, shrewd off-spin bowler, and thoughtful, uncompromising tactician he led England in 31 Test matches until replaced at the end of 1973. His major triumphs were in leading England to victory in Australia in 1970-1 and retaining the ASHES in England in 1972 against a resurgent Australian side. In all he played 61 times in Tests for England, making 1,836 runs and taking 122 wickets.

I.L.T.F. (International Lawn Tennis Federation), see LAWN TENNIS.

INDEPENDIENTE, Association FOOTBALL club, Buenos Aires. Founded in 1905, the club turned professional in 1931, before which, in 1922, it had been the winners of the 'outlaw' Argentinian League. Independiente have been League champions in 1938, 1939, 1948, 1960, and 1963. In both 1964 and 1965 the club won the South American Club Cup competition but on each subsequent occasion they were beaten by INTERNAZIONALE (Milan) in the matches between the European and South American champion clubs to decide the unofficial world club championship. Outstanding players include Arsenio, Grillo, Navarro, and Savoy.
COLOURS: Red shirts, black shorts.

INDIANAPOLIS 500, see INDIANAPOLIS MOTOR SPEEDWAY; MOTOR RACING, AMERICAN.

INDIANAPOLIS MOTOR SPEEDWAY. The success of BROOKLANDS in England probably motivated the building of the American MOTOR RACING course, the Indianapolis Speedway, which opened in 1910. Its construction differed from the English track in that its four corners have shallow bankings and the original surface was of brick instead of concrete. It is now paved with asphalt. Each of Indianapolis's two long straights is 3,300 ft. (1,006 m.) long, and its short straights measure 660 ft. (201 m.). The turns all have a length of 1,320 ft. (402 m.) and a banked elevation of 9° 12′. They represent evenly curved connections between the straights and can be negotiated with a minimum of heavy braking except by the fastest cars. The race area abounds in huge permanent grandstands, pit areas, and garages.

The main race at Indianapolis, which has a lap distance of 2¼ miles (3·6 km.), is the 500-mile (804 km.) event for track-type cars, the 'Indianapolis 500'. Held every year on the last Saturday of May, it is the fastest long-distance event of its kind in the world. It is also the world's largest motor race in terms of purse and prizes, with slightly more than a

million dollars being available. The 500 attracts the best drivers in America and a handful of Europeans, and is one of the world's best-attended sports events, with crowds of approximately 300,000. Except for the years of the First and Second World Wars, it has been run annually since 1911.

In the first 500 of 1911 the winner's average speed was 74·59 m.p.h. (121 km./h.). In 1973 Johncock carried the speed up to 159·02 m.p.h. (255·8 km./h.). Because of the speeds — now up to 200 m.p.h. (321·8 km./h.) on the straights — and the intensity of the competition, the Indianapolis 500 is a dangerous race to drive in and a difficult one to win. Only four men have won it three times — MEYER (1928, 1933, 1936), SHAW (1937, 1939, 1940), ROSE (1941, after relieving another driver, 1947, 1948), and FOYT (1961, 1964, 1967). Four drivers have won twice: Milton (1921, 1923), VUKOVICH (1953, 1954), WARD (1959, 1962), UNSER (1970, 1971). Shaw came very close to winning a fourth time, in 1941, and, after his retirement from driving, he served as president of the Speedway from 1946 until his death in 1954. Meyer, after retiring, contributed much to the further development of the Offenhauser engine.

The early Indianapolis cars were semi-track or road-racing vehicles, with engines of up to 600 cu. in. (9,832 cc.). In the periods 1912-23 and 1930-8 they were required to carry a 'riding mechanic' beside the driver. The first two winners, in 1911 and 1912, were Americans in American-made cars — Harroun in a Marmon and Dawson in a National. From 1913 to 1920 the race was dominated by European cars (some driven by Americans) such as Peugeot, MERCEDES, DELAGE. Cars with front-wheel drive were seen in the 1930s and 1940s.

Gradually, the cars became smaller and the speeds higher. In the 1950s and early 1960s the dominant Indianapolis car was the Offenhauser-powered 'roadster', a sleek, low-slung machine with its engine mounted at the front end. Since the race is run counter-clockwise, the engine and drive train were installed on the left side to establish a favourable weight bias for left turns. This configuration enabled the driver to sit low, beside the drive shaft rather than over it. From 1953 to 1963 the 'Offy' roadsters constituted all but one or two of the 33-car field.

The roadster became obsolete with the advent of European rear-engine cars, based on the design of Formula One cars running in international Grand Prix competition. In 1961 there was one such car, BRABHAM'S COOPER-Climax, with an engine considerably smaller than the others; by 1964 there were 12 cars with engines behind the driver. A rear-engine

LOTUS-Ford driven by JIM CLARK won in 1965 (averaging 150·69 m.p.h.—242·5 km./h.), when 27 of the 33 cars carried rear-mounted engines.

Two other innovations of that period were shorter-lived. Turbine-powered cars nearly won in 1967 and 1968; cars with four-wheel drive raced briefly, in 1968 and 1969. Eventually both the turbine and the four-wheel drive were excluded by rule changes.

The modern 'Indy' car, refined in aerodynamics, chassis, and engine with each year, is an open-wheel racer with an open cockpit, strongly resembling the Formula One car of Grand Prix racing. European origins are clearly evident, for after years of domination by American cars and drivers, British entries were successful and the attention of American race-car engineers was drawn to rear-engined, lighter cars. One of the strongest cars is the McLaren-Offenhauser. Several are derived from the Lola and the Brabham. The typical machine has a minimum wheelbase of 8 ft. (243 cm.) and a maximum over-all length of 16 ft. (487 cm.); a minimum tread of 3 ft. 11 in. (1193·8 mm.) and a maximum over-all width of 6 ft. 8 in. (203·2 cm.). It has to weigh at least 1,350 pounds (612·9 kg.) without fuel.

Engines are all turbo-charged, generating up to 750 h.p. The power plants most common for many years were the four-cylinder Offenhauser, called the 'Offy', and the Ford V-8. The 1973 Indianapolis 500, which had to be stopped after 332½ miles, was won by the American driver Johncock driving an Eagle M5-Offenhauser, at the record speed of 159·02 m.p.h. Another of these typical American Indy cars was second, in the hands of Vukovitch, and a McLaren M16B Offenhauser driven by McClusky was third.

INDY ANN (1953), racing greyhound. Winner of more races than any other greyhound in American history, between 1954 and 1957 she finished first 137 times, second 37 times and third 18 times in 223 starts. She was unplaced only 31 times. Bred and owned by Ed Willard of San Ysidro, California, she raced at Phoenix, Arizona, and Agua Caliente, Mexico. As an outstanding dam, too, she delivered 34 sons and daughters, including the 82-race winner, Preston Adams, and the 77-race winner, Stylish Daisy.

INOKUMA, ISAO (1938-), Japanese JUDO fighter. He was the youngest person to win the all-Japan championships when he took the title in 1959 at the age of 21. Inokuma's use of *seio-nage* (shoulder throw) and *tai-otoshi* (body drop) upset KAMINAGA in 1959 but in the following two years' finals he lost to Kaminaga on both occasions. He regained the title in 1963 and at the 1964 OLYMPIC GAMES won the gold medal in the heavyweight category, beating the Canadian, Rogers, in the final. In the 1965 world championships Inokuma defeated the Russian, Kibrotsashvili, for the open gold medal and his last major title.

INTERNATIONAL CLUB is a LAWN TENNIS club founded by MYERS, the distinguished British lawn tennis journalist, in 1924 to consolidate the friendships formed in the game among players of all countries. The first International Club was formed in Britain, and the International Clubs of France, the United States, and those which have followed in most other major lawn tennis countries have been affiliated to it.

INTERNATIONAL CRICKET CONFERENCE (I.C.C.), see CRICKET.

INTERNATIONAL OLYMPIC COMMITTEE (I.O.C.), a body set up in 1894 with the responsibility of controlling the administration of the modern OLYMPIC GAMES. Among its duties is to ensure that arrangements are made for celebrations to occur in the approved four-year cycle and that the Olympic amateur code is upheld. The I.O.C. is composed of representatives of the International Olympic Committees of all the member countries.

INTERNATIONAL SIX DAYS TRIAL, see MOTOR-CYCLE TRIALS.

INTERNATIONAL STOKE MANDEVILLE GAMES, see PARAPLEGIC GAMES.

INTERNAZIONALE, Association FOOTBALL club, Milan. Founded in 1909, it amalgamated in 1928 with U.S. Milanese under the name of Ambrosiana-Internazionale, but reverted to the name Internazionale in 1945. The club first won the Italian championship in 1910 and added another nine titles up to 1966. In 1964 and 1965 Internazionale won the European Champion Clubs Cup and later beat INDEPENDIENTE of Argentina in the unofficial world club championship in each of those years. The club's best players include MEAZZA, Lorenzi, S. Mazzola, Skoglund, WILKES, Facchetti, Picchi, Peiro, and Còsta.
COLOURS: Black and blue striped shirts, black shorts.

INTIKHAB ALAM (1941-), cricketer for Pakistan, Karachi, and Surrey. For a number of years the world's leading leg-break and googly bowler, he took a wicket with his first ball in Test CRICKET in 1959-60, and by the end of Pakistan's series against England in 1973 he had taken 94 wickets in 38 Tests, often bowling very long and accurate spells on batsmen's pitches. He captained Pakistan from 1971 until MAJID JAHANGIR KHAN replaced him in 1973 (in which year against England at Hyderabad he made a hard-hit maiden Test century). He was to captain Pakistan again in 1974.

INVERLEITH, football ground, Edinburgh, home of the Scottish RUGBY UNION from 1900 to 1925 when, in mid-season, matches were switched to MURRAYFIELD. It was the first headquarters to be acquired by any of the home unions, and was leased to EDINBURGH WANDERERS for club matches during this period.

I.O.C., see INTERNATIONAL OLYMPIC COMMITTEE.

IRISH GUINNESS OAKS, a horse race, sponsored since 1963 by the Dublin brewers, for three-year-old fillies, run over 1½ miles (2,400 m.) at THE CURRAGH in July.

IRISH SWEEPS DERBY, a horse race, sponsored since 1962 by the Irish Hospitals' Sweepstakes, is now worth over £62,000 to the winner. It is competed for by three-year-olds over 1½ miles (2,400 m.) at THE CURRAGH in late June. Winners of this important event have included RAGUSA, SANTA CLAUS, and NIJINSKY.

IROQUOIS (1878) was the only American race-horse to win the English DERBY and ST. LEGER until NEVER SAY DIE in 1954. Iroquois, by Leamington out of MAGGIE B.B., was owned by Lorillard and ridden by ARCHER.

ISINGLASS (1890), English race-horse by ISONOMY, bred and owned by Col. McCalmont, trained by Capt. Machell, and ridden by Loates, who is the only colt ever to win the DERBY, ST. LEGER, TWO THOUSAND GUINEAS, ECLIPSE STAKES, and ASCOT GOLD CUP, the five most important races in England prior to 1950. Isinglass won 11 out of the 12 races in which he ran, together with £57,455 in stakes, a record sum for a race-horse which was not surpassed in England until TULYAR won £76,417 in 1951-2.

ISIS BOAT CLUB takes its name from that by which the river Thames is known on the Oxford reach. The OXFORD UNIVERSITY reserve ROWING crew row in its colours in their annual race with their Cambridge counterparts, GOLDIE.

ISO-HOLLO, VOLMARI (1907-69), steeplechaser for Finland. The first man to win the Olympic 3,000 metres STEEPLECHASE twice (1932 and 1936). Iso-Hollo had the unique experience in the 1932 final of having to run an additional lap due to an official error in lap-scoring. His 1936 Olympic time of 9 min. 3·8 sec. was the world's best on record until 1943. (Official world records were not recognized until 1954.) He also won a silver medal in the 1932 Olympic 10,000 metres and a bronze medal in 1936.

ISONOMY (1875), English race-horse bought as a yearling by PORTER on behalf of Gretton for only 360 guineas. He turned out to be one of the best bargains in the history of bloodstock sales since he subsequently won two ASCOT GOLD CUPS, the Epsom, Goodwood, and Doncaster Cups, the Ascot Gold Vase, EBOR HANDICAP, and CAMBRIDGESHIRE, on which race his owner won £40,000 in wagers. At stud, he became the sire of ISINGLASS.

ISSER, MARIA (1929-   ), luge TOBOGGANING rider for Austria; the first woman to win two world singles titles, in 1957 and 1960.

I.S.U. (International Shooting Union), see SHOOTING, AIR WEAPONS; SHOOTING, CLAY PIGEONS; SHOOTING, PISTOL; SHOOTING, RIFLE.

IVANOV, VYACHESLAV (1938-   ), one of the most successful amateur scullers (see ROWING) of all time. A Russian, he made his first international appearance in the European championships in 1956, winning the single sculls title to become, at the age of 18, the youngest sculler to win the event. A few months later he added the Olympic title which he retained in 1960 and 1964.

In 1957 and 1958 he lost to MACKENZIE both at HENLEY and in the European championships; but, although he never appeared at Henley again and so failed to win the Diamond Sculls, he re-asserted his superiority over the more powerful Australian in 1959, regaining the European title. He was European champion four times between 1956 and 1964 and world champion in 1962.

IVY LEAGUE, athletic conference of American East Coast colleges comprising HARVARD, YALE, PRINCETON (also called the 'Big

Three'), Brown, Columbia, Cornell, Dartmouth, and the University of Pennsylvania. Ivy League teams largely founded and developed college FOOTBALL and dominated the sport before 1900. Yale and Princeton have won more games than any other team in college football's first hundred years. The conference was formally established in 1956, and since then the member schools have met each other each year in football.

J

JACK, DAVID BONE NIGHTINGALE (1899-1958), Association footballer for Plymouth Argyle, Bolton Wanderers, ARSENAL, and England. He played for Plymouth's reserve team while still at school before the outbreak of war in 1914. A tall, graceful inside right, he was an opportunist in the manner of BLOOMER; in 1923 scored the first goal in a Wembley F.A. Cup final; in 1928, after winning two F.A. Cup-winners medals with Bolton, his home town, he was the first player for whose transfer of registration a five-figure fee was paid. Jack was 29 when Arsenal paid £10,890 to Bolton for his registration but with Arsenal he won two League championship medals and one more F.A. Cup-winners medal.

JACKLIN, TONY (1944-   ), English professional golfer. He became Open champion in 1969 and a regular and successful player on the American circuit. He won the U.S. Open championship in 1970, and is a RYDER CUP and WORLD CUP player.

JACKS, BRIAN ALBERT THOMAS (1946-   ), British JUDO fighter, the finest competitor Britain has produced and one of the few Europeans to match the Japanese in the lighter weight categories. A 5 ft. 10½ in. (1·79 m.) Londoner, he took up judo at the age of 11 and went to Japan four years later. He won European junior titles in 1964 and 1965 and competed in the Tokyo OLYMPIC GAMES. A disputed decision at the 1967 world championships prevented Jacks from beating Maruki and the Japanese went on to take the middleweight title with Jacks winning the bronze medal. In 1970 he took the European middleweight title, the first Briton to win a weight category in the event. He was third in the Munich Olympics and regained his European crown in 1973.

JACKSON, ALEX (1905-46), Association footballer for ABERDEEN, HUDDERSFIELD TOWN, CHELSEA, and Scotland for whom he scored three times against England on 31 March 1928. His brilliant and buoyant play on the right wing, and his dashing approach, made him an immediate favourite with the Huddersfield club. Two years after the 1928 Cup final, which was won by BLACKBURN ROVERS, he was again on the losing side when ARSENAL beat Huddersfield 2-0. Soon after this he was transferred to the newly-promoted club, Chelsea, but never showed much evidence of his previous greatness, nor did he play again for Scotland. His last international match was against France in Paris in May 1930.

JACKSON, Col. the Rt. Hon. Sir FRANCIS STANLEY, G.C.S.I., G.C.I.E. (1870-1947), cricketer for England, Cambridge University, and Yorkshire. Captain of his school, university, and, finally, of England, he was a batsman of classical style and bowler of fast-medium pace. Only once did he play a full season of first-class CRICKET — in 1898, when he scored 1,566 runs and took 104 wickets. Though never playing for England abroad, he averaged 48·79 in 20 Test matches, reaching the pinnacle of his career in the 1905 series against Australia. He won all five tosses, headed the batting and bowling averages, and led England to a 2-0 victory. During a widely distinguished life, he was president of M.C.C. in 1921, and Governor of Bengal from 1927.

JACKSON, GORDON (1930-   ), British motor trials rider, the only man to win British Experts trials on two and four wheels. As a works AJS rider, he won the motor-cycle classic three times (1957, 1958, and 1961) and gained the same title with a trials car in 1970. A member of the AJS team from 1951, he was British trials champion twice (1955 and 1958) before he won the historic 1961 Scottish Six Days Trial (see MOTOR-CYCLE TRIALS) with the loss of only one mark.

JACKSON, JOHN (1769-1845), British boxer, who won the prize-ring championship of England in 1795 by beating MENDOZA. He was known as 'Gentleman' Jackson because of the regard in which he was held by the nobility when he opened a school of boxing in London. Among his pupils was the poet Byron. An excellent all-round athlete, Jackson was a vital link between the rough sport of the prize ring and its rich patrons. At the coronation of George IV, Jackson organized a royal body-guard of famous prize-fighters.

JACKSON, MARJORIE (later Mrs. Nelson)

(1931-   ), sprinter for Australia. Regarded as one of the greatest competitive women sprinters in track history, Miss Jackson was only 17 when she twice defeated Mrs. BLANKERS-KOEN and 19 when she won four gold medals, 100 yards, 220 yards, and sprint relay, in the 1950 COMMONWEALTH GAMES. In 1952 she won Olympic gold medals in the 100 and 200 metres, and between 1950 and 1954 she equalled or broke world records at standard sprint distances 13 times. Her best times were 10·4 sec. for 100 yards, 11·4 sec. for 100 metres, 23·4 sec. for 200 metres, and 24·0 sec. for 220 yards.

JACKSON, PETER BARRIE (1930-   ), RUGBY UNION right wing three-quarter for COVENTRY, England, and British LIONS. An elusive, side-stepping runner, he was noted for his unorthodox runs from unpromising positions. Capped 20 times, his most famous try for England won the match against the fourth WALLABIES in 1958 when, in injury time, he beat both wing and full-back to score in the corner. On the Lions' 1959 Australasian tour he scored 16 tries, one short of O'REILLY's record.

JACKSON, RUSS (1936-   ), Canadian professional FOOTBALL quarterback for the OTTAWA ROUGH RIDERS. He was three times voted the outstanding player in the Canadian Football League (1963, 1966, 1969) as well as outstanding Canadian player (1959 in addition). In his 12-year career at Ottawa (1958-69) he gained the second largest number of yards passing in league history — 24,593 yards — and recorded the greatest number of touchdown passes — 185.

JACKSON, W. K. (1871-1955), Scottish curler. President of the ROYAL CALEDONIAN CURLING CLUB, 1933-4, he was the most famous Scottish skip in the period between the First and Second World Wars. His rink included his two sons, Laurence and Elliot. The only time CURLING was included in the WINTER OLYMPIC GAMES (at Chamonix in 1924) he and his son, Laurence, with Robin Welsh, sr. and Murray, won the gold medals for Great Britain.

JACOBS, HELEN HULL (1908-   ), an outstanding United States LAWN TENNIS player of the 1930s and notable particularly for her rivalry with another American, HELEN WILLS. She was a fine volleyer with a strong backhand down the line and a shrewd sense of strategy. She won the U.S. title four times, the second of her victories (in 1933) being against Mrs. Moody (the former Miss Wills), who

withdrew through injury at 0-3 in the third set. In the 1935 WIMBLEDON final she held a match point against her rival but missed an easy chance, and Mrs. Moody went on to win. In 1938 she herself was injured at 4-4 in the first set but continued to play, Mrs. Moody winning 6-4, 6-0. Altogether, she reached the Wimbledon final 5 times in 11 years, but her only victory was against Sperling in 1936. She wrote a number of books on the game and *Gallery of Champions* (1951) contains an interesting analysis of many of the leading players of her day.

JAHN, JOHANN FRIEDRICH LUDWIG (1778-1852), German gymnast who is regarded as the father of the sport. He studied Muth's book *Gymnastics for the Young* and was inspired by many of its principles. He opened the Turnplatz (an open-air gymnasium) in Berlin in 1811 and aimed to strengthen the Germans' physique and personality through intensive training. Much of his work was guided by his desire for his countrymen to break free from Napoleonic oppression. In the last years of the war against the French he commanded a battalion and was a member of the secret service. In 1815 he was appointed a state teacher of gymnastics. Frequently in trouble with the authorities, he was imprisoned for six years, but became a member of the German national parliament in 1848.

He started a vast number of gymnasiums and founded the German Gymnastic Association. He invented the parallel bars, the rings, and the horizontal bar, all of which are used in modern competitions. His views on gymnastics spread all over Europe, with those of his Swedish contemporary, Ling, who regarded the sport as physical education and advocated more free-flowing movements than Jahn.

JAÏ-ALAÏ, see PELOTA.

JAMES, ALEX (1900-53), Association footballer for Raith Rovers, PRESTON NORTH END, ARSENAL, and Scotland for whom he made eight appearances in British home championships between 1926 and 1933, having made his début for Scotland in October 1925. In June 1929, CHAPMAN, manager of Arsenal, obtained his transfer for £9,000 and proceeded to change his style of play from that of a fairly efficient goal-scorer to that of the most successful schemer and goal-maker in the history of English football. His sharp accuracy when passing, and his ball control, made him the key player behind his club's run of success over the next six seasons when Arsenal won the championship four times and were three times in the F.A. Cup final.

JAMES NORRIS TROPHY, ICE HOCKEY trophy, awarded annually in the NATIONAL HOCKEY LEAGUE of North America to 'the player who demonstrates throughout the season the greatest all-round ability as a defenceman'. It was donated in 1954 by DETROIT RED WINGS as a memorial to the club's former owner. In 1962, it was won for a record seventh time by D. HARVEY, representing MONTREAL CANADIENS on the first six occasions and NEW YORK RANGERS on the last.

JAMESON, T. O. (1892-1965), Irish SQUASH RACKETS player. He won the first amateur championship held in 1922, and retained his title in the following year. Jameson was also a first-class CRICKET and RACKETS player.

JAMSETJHI, J. (*fl.* 1903-11), Indian RACKETS player who won the world championship by beating Browne at Queen's and Prince's Clubs in 1903, to become the only Indian to hold this title, which he retained until 1911.

JANSSEN, JAN (1940-   ), Dutch professional road-race cyclist. A strong rider with a good finishing sprint, by 1970 he had completed the TOUR DE FRANCE at the head of the points classification (see CYCLING) on three occasions. He won the Tour in 1968, the first man since Robic in 1947 to do so without having worn the yellow jersey during the race. His other major victories were the professional road-race championship in 1964, the BORDEAUX–PARIS in 1966, and the PARIS–ROUBAIX and VUELTA ESPAGNA in 1967.

JARDINE, DOUGLAS ROBERT (1900-58), cricketer for England, Oxford University, and Surrey. Renowned as England's determined and uncompromising captain during the 'body-line' Test series against Australia in 1932-3, he was, though stiff in style, a high-scoring batsman, particularly for Surrey, the Gentlemen, and M.C.C. on tour. He led England in 14 of his 22 Test matches.

JARNAC, GUY CHABOT, Sieur de Jarnac et de Montlieu, French fencer, met François de Vivonne, Sieur de la Châtaigneraye, on 10 July 1547 in a duel with épée and shield in the presence of Henri II of France and his court. This duel became famous because Jarnac won by a previously unknown stroke, a cut below the knee which disabled his opponent and was called thereafter the *coup de Jarnac.*

JARRETT, KEITH (1949-   ), RUGBY UNION three-quarter or full-back for NEWPORT, Wales, and British Isles, who subsequently became a RUGBY LEAGUE back for Barrow. At the age of 18, playing at full-back in his first international, he scored 19 points against England: five conversions, two penalty goals, and a try. This equalled the Welsh record of J. Bancroft against France in 1910.

JARVINEN, MATTI H. (1909-   ), javelin-thrower for Finland. One of the outstanding contributors to the evolution of javelin-throwing, Jarvinen was European champion in 1934 and 1938 and Olympic champion in 1932. He ten times broke the world record, for the first time in 1930 with 234 ft. 9¾ in. (71·57 m.) and the last 253 ft. 4½ in. (77·23 m.) in 1936.

JARVIS, Sir JACK (1887-1968), trained Lord ROSEBERY's horses (the best of which were Blue Peter and his son Ocean Swell) at Park Lodge, Newmarket, for many years.

JARVIS, JOHN ARTHUR (1872-1933), an Englishman who called himself the 'Amateur Swimming Champion of the World', and had 108 trophies to justify his claim. He won the 1,000 and 4,000 metres at the 1900 OLYMPIC GAMES in London and his national and international successes included the Queen Victoria Diamond Jubilee 1 mile (1,609·3 m.) in 1897. Other trophies came from the German Kaiser, the Austrian Emperor, the King of Italy, and the Queen of the Netherlands.

JAVELIN. Javelin-throwing is a standard field event for men and women on the programme of all major ATHLETICS championships; performances are eligible for acceptance as records by the International Amateur Athletic Federation (see ATHLETICS, TRACK AND FIELD). The javelin is one of the events in the DECATHLON.

Throwing the javelin is a spor of martial origin, the spear having been a ᵛeapon from the earliest times. The moderᵣ competition javelin weighs 1 lb. 12·218 oz. (800 g.) for men and 1 lb. 5·163 oz. (600 g.) for women; it has a metal head and a cord grip which must be held when throwing. The javelin is thrown with one hand, over the shoulder, from a runway about 120 ft. (36 m.) long. The tip of the metal head must touch the ground first and the distance thrown is measured from that point to the arc of a circle which forms the throwing line. Each competitor is allowed six trials. The thrower makes his approach run carrying the javelin horizontally above his head. A few strides from the end of his run the javelin is withdrawn and lowered to a position behind the thrower from which the throwing arm comes through with a whiplash movement to project the javelin very much as in throwing a CRICKET ball.

JAWAID, A. A. (1940-   ), Pakistani amateur SQUASH RACKETS player. Son of a professional and related to HASHIM KHAN, he won the Pakistan amateur championship in 1963 in which year he first came to England, reaching the semi-finals of the Open championship. In the following year he again reached the semi-final of the Open championship and won the first of his three amateur championships. He was beaten in the Open championship final in 1965 by the Egyptian professional Taleb and in 1966 by BARRINGTON.

JAY, ALLAN, M.B.E. (1931-   ), British fencer, world foil champion in 1959 and in the same year runner-up in the épée, losing 5-4 in a barrage for first place. A member of the British team in 1952, he competed in five Olympics, winning the silver medal in the épée at Rome in 1960; he was first reserve for the British foil team in 1972.

JAZY, MICHEL (1936-   ), middle-distance runner for France. Probably the greatest French runner yet seen, Jazy broke world records for 1 mile, 2 miles, 2,000 metres, and 3,000 metres a total of seven times between 1962 and 1966. Olympic 1,500 metres silver medallist in 1960, Jazy won European titles at 1,500 metres in 1962 and at 5,000 metres in 1966. His best times were 3 min. 53·6 sec. for 1 mile, 8 min. 22·6 sec. for 2 miles, 4 min. 56·2 sec. for 2,000 metres, and 7 min. 49·0 sec. for 3,000 metres.

JEEPS, RICHARD ERIC GANTRY (1931-   ), RUGBY UNION scrum half for Northampton, England, and British LIONS. Included as a second reserve scrum half in the 1955 Lions party to South Africa, before he had been capped by England, he was picked for the opening Test and retained for the series. He made 24 international appearances for England and 13 for the British Isles.

JEFFRIES, JAMES (1875-1953), American boxer who held the world heavyweight title from 1899 until his retirement as undefeated champion in 1905. He came back to the ring in 1910 but was knocked out in 15 rounds by JACK JOHNSON. At his best, Jeffries was one of the most formidable fighters to win the heavyweight title. Though not very fast he was extremely strong, and he was perhaps the first well-known boxer to adopt the defensive crouch which later became the trademark of most successful American boxers in the early twentieth century.

JENKINS, TOM (*fl.* 1895-1905), American wrestler. Only HACKENSCHMIDT prevented Jenkins from being the world heavyweight WRESTLING champion at the start of the twentieth century. Supreme in America in the catch-as-catch-can style, Jenkins did much to popularize the sport. But he was defeated twice by Hackenschmidt, the second time in 1904, and the following year lost the American title he had held for almost a decade to the up-and-coming GOTCH.

JERBERG, SIXTEN (1929-   ), Swedish cross-country racing skier, with the greatest Olympic record of all skiers — four gold medals, three silver, and two bronze, in three OLYMPIC GAMES. He retired after the Innsbruck Games in 1964.

JERSEY 'ACT', see HORSE RACING.

JESSOP, GILBERT LAIRD (1874-1955), cricketer for England, Cambridge University, and Gloucestershire. Known as 'the Croucher', he was the greatest consistently fast run-maker CRICKET has seen, hitting all bowling with studied ferocity. His most famous century — against Australia at the OVAL in 1902 — took only 75 minutes, and turned imminent defeat into victory. He was also a brilliant out-fielder.

JESTERS CLUB, founded in 1928 by Burnet as a CRICKET club but now more renowned for court games, playing cricket, RUGBY FIVES, ETON FIVES, SQUASH RACKETS, real TENNIS, and RACKETS. Membership is by invitation only and in practice the club is able to draw on most of the top players in the country.
COLOURS: Dark blue with light blue jesters superimposed.

JEU DE PAUME, see PELOTA and REAL TENNIS.

JEU PROVENÇAL is a ball-and-target game similar to lawn BOWLS, crown green bowls, and the game which sprang directly from it, PÉTANQUE. It is played in Provence, where it originated in its present form, and also in other parts of France. The chief differences between *pétanque* and *jeu provençal* are the length of the pitch — *jeu provençal* is often called *le longue* — and the bowler being allowed a run-up in *jeu provençal* but not in *pétanque*.

The jack — *cochonnet* (Provençal *lé* or *gari*) — or target ball is of light-coloured or white-painted wood, between 25 and 35 mm. (1-1¾ in.) in diameter. The bowls of metal (usually steel) are between 7·05 and 8 cm. (2¾-3⅛ in.) in diameter, between 0·620 and 0·8 kg. (22–28 oz.) in weight, and are made by officially approved manufacturers without weighting or bias, and to a specific density.

Jeu provençal is played in singles (three or four bowls per player as decided in advance), doubles (three balls each), or trebles (two bowls each). Points are scored by nearness to the jack after all bowls in each game — or *mène* — have been bowled: 1 point for the player or team for each bowl nearer to the jack than any on the other side. A game consists usually of 13 points, but according to local or competition decisions or traditions may be 11, 15, 18, or 21 points.

Jeu provençal has never called for the specially prepared turf rinks of lawn bowls or crown green bowls but throughout its long history has been played on rough, stony, or paved surfaces. At serious levels however it is now played on pitches officially selected by the umpire who controls the game, or a local society. These pitches are 3 to 4 m. wide and at least 25 m. long (approx. $4 \times 27\frac{1}{2}$ yds.).

The players in singles, or members from teams, toss for the right to choose the bowling point, throw the target ball and bowl the first bowl. The winner then selects and marks out a circle between 35 and 50 cm. (approx. 13–19 in.) in diameter and 1 m. (1·094 yds.) from any obstacle. From this circle he then throws the jack which, to be valid, must come to rest between 15 and 21 m. (16–23 yds.) from the nearest edge of the circle; 1 m. sideways and 3 m. (9 ft. 10 in.) in depth from any obstacle; and visible to a player standing within the throwing circle.

The winner of the toss has three chances to throw the jack within valid range; if he fails to do so the option for three attempts passes to the opposing side; but that does not deprive the original winner of the toss of the right to throw the first bowl.

The bowler must begin with one foot placed inside the circle. He is entitled to take one step while aiming and three in throwing; but he must not put foot to ground outside the circle until he has delivered his bowl (though players disabled in the leg or over 65 years old may bring the front foot from outside the circle, back to the other).

The bowler's aim is to land his bowl as closely as possible to the jack. To do so he may employ any one of four tactics. The first, called *plomber*, consists of tossing the bowl high in the air so that it drops close to the jack and stops dead. The second — *rouler* — consists of bowling it all along the ground, as in lawn bowls. Then comes *pointer* — landing a bowl inside the opponent's nearest ball. The third — *tir* or *tirer* — consists of knocking the opponent's winning ball away. At its best this last tactic will, by striking the winning ball at a precisely ideal point, not only knock it away but drop into its place; this is called *carreau* and is the most spectacular move in the game.

Thus most teams carry an expert in *plomber, pointer,* and *carreau.* A 'clean sweep' shot is not allowed. A *tir* bowl is disallowed if it pitches more than 1 m. from the jack or the opponent's ball which it strikes. If it pitches further away, or if it knocks the opponent's bowl or the jack more than 4 m. (13 ft.) from its previous position, the bowl is void and everything disturbed by it must be replaced.

The players continue alternately, using any of the three tactics — *pointer, tirer, carreau* — often in changing circumstances because the jack has been displaced in the course of play, until each has delivered his two, three, or four bowls. Then the player whose ball is nearest to the jack scores 1 point; and if his team has two, three, four, five, or six bowls nearer the jack than any of their opponents they score 2, 3, 4, 5, or 6 points. This single end, to use a term from lawn bowls, is known as a *mène.* The second *mène* is started from a circle about the point where the jack stood in the first game; and subsequent *mènes* are also played from alternate ends of the pitch.

A match usually consists of three games, each of 13 or other agreed number of points; traditionally the first is called *la partie,* the second *la revanche,* and the third *la belle.*

Anciently played in Provence, *jeu provençal* is directly descended from the Greek and Roman forms of bowls which have elsewhere produced lawn bowls, crown green bowls, and, directly from *jeu provençal, pétanque.* In this century it has developed from a folk and regional sport to one in which individual, doubles, and team championships are played within a national organization.

GOVERNING BODIES: Fédération Français de Pétanque et Jeu Provençal, 1 Boulevard Dugommier, 13, Marseille 1, France, and Fédération Internationale de Pétanque et Jeu Provençal, 10 Rue de Neufchâtel, Geneva, Switzerland.

JIU-KUMITE, see KARATE.

JOCKEY CLUB, founded in 1750 at the Star and Garter Coffee House in Pall Mall, London, was later provided by Tattersall with a room and a cook at Hyde Park Corner. It subsequently made its headquarters at WEATHERBY'S office in Old Burlington Street, with rooms also at NEWMARKET, and is now based at Portman Square. Under the direction of men like BUNBURY, Lord BENTINCK, and Admiral ROUS, the Jockey Club slowly grew in importance, until the stewards became the central authority for the administration and control of the Turf in England. The Jockey Club received a Royal Charter in 1970.

JOCKEY CLUB GOLD CUP, one of the most important weight-for-age horse races in the U.S.A., is run over 2 miles (3,200 m.) at BELMONT PARK in October. Victory in this event, which KELSO won five years in succession, sets the seal on a champion American race-horse.

JOHANNSON, IVAR (*fl.* 1932-6), Swedish freestyle and Graeco-Roman wrestler, one of the two men to win three Olympic gold medals in the sport. His agility and skill brought him the freestyle middleweight title in 1932 and the Graeco-Roman welterweight class. Four years later in Berlin he took the Graeco-Roman middleweight title. He also won six European titles.

JOHN, BARRY (1945-   ), RUGBY UNION outside half for LLANELLI, CARDIFF, Wales, and British LIONS. A deft, balanced runner, a skilful scorer of dropped goals, and in his later career a dependable place kicker, John gained the first of his 25 caps against Australia in 1966. Shortly before retiring in 1972, he scored his ninetieth point in internationals, beating J. Bancroft's Welsh record of 88 points. He also scored a record 180 points for British Lions in New Zealand in 1971.

JOHN PLAYER LEAGUE, a CRICKET competition restricted to Sundays only, and played during the English season, between the 17 first-class county sides. Instituted in 1969, the competition, a sponsored one, is conducted on a league basis, each side playing eight home matches and eight away. The season's champions receive a trophy and £1,000, with £500 to the runners-up. In no circumstances can a match go beyond a single day; each side is limited to an innings of 40 overs and each bowler to 8 overs. The bowler's run-up is also limited—to 15 yds. (13·72 m.). A popular form of Sunday entertainment, it encourages enterprise by giving monetary awards for each hit for 6 and each instance of 4 wickets in an innings. In its inaugural year, Lancashire narrowly emerged as champions, a triumph they repeated with greater emphasis a year later.

JOHNSON, AMY, C.B.E. (later Mrs. Mollison) (1903-41), British aviator who learned to fly in 1929. She made solo flights to Australia, India, and Tokyo in 1931 and the England –Cape Town return flight in 1932. She married MOLLISON and made record flights with him—across the North Atlantic in 1933; England–India and England–Cape Town in 1936.

JOHNSON, BYRON BANCROFT (1864-1931), American BASEBALL executive who founded the AMERICAN LEAGUE of Professional Baseball Clubs in 1900 and, as its first president, served until his resignation in 1927. A former sports writer, in 1894 he assumed leadership of the 'minor' Western League, which he eventually re-formed into the American League. He was also the dominant member of the three-man National Commission that governed Organized Baseball from 1903 to 1919.

JOHNSON, CHING (1897-   ), ICE HOCKEY player for NEW YORK RANGERS, joining them in 1926 for their inaugural season and staying as a defenceman for 12 seasons, during which he was one of the most successful defencemen in the NATIONAL HOCKEY LEAGUE. A difficult player to pass in his own defence zone and more adventurous than most in moving forward with the puck, Johnson joined Winnipeg Monarchs in 1918, playing afterwards for Eveleth Giants and Minneapolis Millers before joining the Rangers. Like many defencemen of his day, he often played a full match without being substituted.

JOHNSON, JACK (1878-1946), American boxer who held the world heavyweight title from 1908 to 1915 and was the first Negro to win the championship. He is widely but not unanimously regarded as the greatest of all heavyweights. Certainly he was a most skilled points-scorer with an almost impenetrable defence. Johnson lost only seven out of 114 contests between 1897 and 1928. His exuberant personality brought him much criticism and led to a campaign for a 'white hope' to beat him. After Johnson had decisively defeated the former champion JEFFRIES there were race riots in the U.S.A. Johnson lived in exile in Europe for several years while champion to avoid a prison sentence awaiting him in his own country.

JOHNSON, RAFER LEWIS (1934-   ), DECATHLON competitor for the U.S.A. Johnson badly injured his left foot in a conveyor belt when he was 14 yet grew to be a world record-holder in his second decathlon season in 1955. He made two other decathlon world records, the best in 1960: 8,683 points (equivalent to 8,063 points under the 1962 decathlon tables). A knee injury prevented his winning his anticipated gold medal in the 1956 OLYMPIC GAMES but he still managed a silver, going on to claim his Olympic crown at Rome in 1960. He was also Pan-American champion in 1955.

JOHNSON, TERENCE LLOYD (1900-), race walker for Great Britain. During a long and illustrious career, Johnson gained third place in the Olympic 50 km. in 1948 at the age of 48. A year later he won the Race Walking Association's 50 km., 22 years after his first national title. He competed in the 1936 Olympic 50 km., and was winner of the BRADFORD walk on two occasions. With GREEN and WHITLOCK he dominated English middle- and long-distance events in the 1930s. Johnson later became a national coach, still competing occasionally.

JOHNSON, WALTER PERRY (1887-1946), American BASEBALL pitcher for the WASHINGTON SENATORS from 1907 to 1927. Famed for the blinding speed with which he delivered the ball, he won 414 games including 113 'shutouts' (games in which the opposing team scored no runs) and struck out 3,497 batters. In 1913 he set a record by pitching 56 consecutive scoreless innings.

JOLLY, GORDON HASLEM (1913-), lawn BOWLS player and administrator who helped New Zealand win the fours event at the inaugural world championships at KYEEMAGH, N.S.W., in October 1966. He was a member of the New Zealand team at the 1962 and 1966 COMMONWEALTH GAMES and is a former president and the present Hon. Sec. of the New Zealand Bowling Association. He and his son were lead and skip in the four which won the N.Z. fours championship in 1970.

JONES, BENJAMIN LEWIS (1930-), Welsh RUGBY UNION player who turned professional for LEEDS RUGBY LEAGUE CLUB in November 1952, for what was then a record signing fee of £6,000. Among his RUGBY LEAGUE records were: most points in a season (505 in 1956-7), most points on an Australian tour (278 in 1954), and most goals in an Australia v. Great Britain Test match (10, at Brisbane, 1954). Equally at home at full-back, centre, or stand-off half, though playing in only 14 internationals, at his best he ranked among the most gifted players of all time.

JONES, BRYNMOR (*fl.* 1935-51), Association footballer for WOLVERHAMPTON WANDERERS, ARSENAL, and Wales for whom he made his first appearance in a full international against Ireland on 27 March 1935 and his last against Scotland on 28 October 1948. As the dates of those two matches indicate, the best

years of this fine inside left occurred during the Second World War when normal competitive football was suspended. In August 1938, Arsenal paid £14,000 to Wolves for his registration. It was more than £3,000 above the previous record fee. Jones went to Norwich as player-coach in 1949 but after two years had to stop playing on medical advice.

JONES, KENNETH JEFFREY (1921-), RUGBY UNION wing three-quarter for NEWPORT, Wales, and British LIONS. He created a Welsh and, in its day, a British record by winning 44 caps, 43 of them in consecutive games, and equalled the record of Gibbs (Cardiff) by scoring 17 tries for Wales. In 1948 he won an Olympic silver medal in the 4 × 100 metres relay event.

JONES, Mrs. P. F., see HAYDON, ADRIANNE SHIRLEY.

JONES, RENATO WILLIAM (1906-), secretary-general and co-founder of the Fédération Internationale de Basketball Amateur (F.I.B.A.) (see BASKETBALL), the controlling body of the sport. Jones was born in Rome, the son of a British father and Italian mother, and assumed British nationality. He was appointed secretary-general of the F.I.B.A. at its foundation in 1932 and was still in office in 1973. He has been made an honorary member of the basketball federations of Switzerland, France, Italy, Germany, and Spain, and was elected to the Hall of Fame (see NAISMITH) in 1964. In 1973 he was elected patron of the Amateur Basket Ball Association of England.

JONES, ROBERT TYRE (1902-), American amateur golfer, probably the greatest player the game has known. In a career spanning only eight years of serious GOLF, during which time he played only intermittently between studying for degree courses in law, English literature, and engineering, Jones entered for 27 major championships and won 13 of them. He won the U.S. Open four times (and twice tied, but lost the replay); the U.S. amateur championship five times; the Open championship three times; and the British amateur championship once. In 1930 he won all four championships, known as the Grand Slam, a feat never approached before. At the end of that year he relinquished amateur status to make a series of instructional films and retired from competitive golf. In association with Clifford Roberts, Jones later founded the Augusta National Golf Club and inaugurated the Masters tournament which quickly established itself as one of the game's four classic events.

JONES, RUFUS (Parnelli) (1933-   ), American MOTOR RACING driver. He was the INDIANAPOLIS 500 winner in 1963 and winner of six United States Auto Club championship races. He won the U.S.A.C. stock-car title in 1964 and its national sprint championship in 1961 and 1962. He won seven TRANS-AM sedan (saloon) road races in 1969 and 1970, and the Baja 1000 off-road race with Stroppe in 1971. Now retired except for competing in off-road races, Jones is a car owner and president of Ontario, California, Motor Speedway.

JONES, WAYNE (1935-   ), Australian water skier who set the first barefoot skiing record of 75 m.p.h. (121 km./h.).

JORDAN, ANTHONY DEREK, M.B.E. (1934-   ), English BADMINTON player. After a brilliant career begun by gaining his international colours at 17, he retired in 1970 upon playing for England on 100 occasions, easily a world record. As a player at mixed doubles he was one of the finest the game has seen, and he won the ALL-ENGLAND title four times with three different partners.

JOSELITO (José Gómez) (1895-1920), *matador de toros*, who, together with BELMONTE, produced the finest *toreo* of all time until he was killed in Talavera de la Reina by the bull Bailador, of the Viuda de Ortega ranch, on 16 May 1920. He first wore the *traje de luces* when he was 13 years old, and took the *alternativa* on 28 September 1912.

JOUSTING was a medieval form of combat between horsemen armed with lances. A major feature of a joust and indeed the entire tournament in which it took place was that no one under the rank of knight could take part. They were thus distinguished from other military-based sports, such as riding at the QUINTAIN, in which all might participate.

Many martial exercises were popular in the medieval period but jousts and tournaments were the most exclusive. The two forms differ in that only two men fought in a joust whereas at a tournament there might be any number on either side. Occasionally single combats were held during a tournament, or a joust in which several pairs of knights had competed might end with a miniature tournament, but for the most part the two forms were separate and distinct.

Strict rules governed both events. The officer-at-arms had to be sure that a prospective contestant was in fact 'a gentleman of name and of arms'; only when this had been ascertained was he allowed to appear in the 'lists' (the place of combat, including the pavilions). The weapons and armour used, the mode of fighting, and the number of attendant servants and squires were all controlled and any knight transgressing the rules was excluded from the field. Arms were not always blunted, and the aim was to break an opponent's spear so that he was unhorsed or unarmed and could not go the next course.

Jousts and tournaments were in principle serious exercises, intended 'for the use of yonge knyghtes as it were to make them able to fighte in bataile', but they were also occasions of great social importance. On the grounds where they were held, pavilions were erected and brightly coloured silken galleries, which were hung with tapestry, cloth-of-gold, and the banners of all those taking part. The attendant squires and servants wore the livery of their masters. The ladies of the court who attended these gatherings were not just spectators in the ordinary sense; they were to provide inspiration for the combatants. By the courtly, chivalrous convention every knight had a lady-love, and it was for her favour that he fought. He wore, as a lucky token and to signify his attachment, his lady's glove or sleeve. It was the ladies who decided who were the winners in these contests, and one of them (the Queen if she was present) presented the prizes. When all the course had been run the whole company went on to banquet and to dance. In the Egerton MS. the activities after the main events had finished are described thus: 'then shall he that the diamond is geve unto, take a lady by the hande and begene the daunce...and when the ladyes have dauncid as long as them liketh, then spyce wine and drink, and then avoide.'

Not every joust was bloodless. *Joute à plaisance* was a contest with blunted arms, to display the skills of the contestants. A *joute à l'outrance* was a combat in which sharp weapons were used, when men might be maimed or killed. Such a combat might be used to settle private feuds, but was just as often for no apparent reason.

The word 'tournament' comes from the French *tournoi*—the wheeling motion of the competitors as they turned and returned to enter the lists. The principal weapon used in jousting was a spear without a head, although in a hand-to-hand encounter a blunt, two-handed sword was usually wielded. Properly the lists were a large, open space with ropes and railings. The barriers were erected down the middle to keep the combatants apart. At first such a division might have been effected by a cord, but eventually brightly coloured fences were used. In any case the use of lists and barriers came much later than the first jousts.

Jousts were generally considered inferior to a full-scale tournament with a mêlée, that is one party against another. In a joust, a sword was never used, the object being to strike off an opponent's helmet. This led to the practice of deliberately wearing the helmet loose, so that if it were struck it might fall off easily without imperilling the knight's head. This device, although deemed cowardly, was much practised.

The procedure to be followed on the occasion of a joust or tournament began with a parade of arms, two days before the actual event, when two barons would inspect all the arms and banners of those proposing to take part, to ensure that there were no deviations from the required standards. On the appointed day, the king-at-arms and the heralds instructed all contestants to arm themselves, with cries of 'To achievement, knights and esquires, to achievement!' The knights would duly obey the order, to be summoned from their pavilions with the cry, 'Come forth, knights and esquires, come forth!' Each knight then took the side of one baron or the other. The weapons would be a pointless sword or a truncheon hung at the saddle bow, in addition to the lance. Either weapon could be used as long as the heralds cried *'Laissiez les aler'*. The fighting then proceeded until the heralds ended the event with the cry of *'Ployer vos baniers'* (put away your banners). Each knight could be accompanied by one armed page, but large numbers of armed retainers were banned as a threat to the smooth conduct of a tournament — riots had been known to develop.

Jousting possibly has its roots in a Roman pastime called *Ludus Troiae* which is described by Virgil. Fitzstephen records that, in the reign of Henry II, 'every Sunday in Lent…great crowds of young Londoners mounted on war horses…exhibited the representation of battles.' Henry III set up one of many subsequent Round Tables. Its purpose was to encourage jousting which would then be followed by dining. During the reign of Edward I, Roger de Mortimer established a round table at Kenilworth and Thomas of Walsingham tells of a tournament in which Edward himself took part, held when the king was returning to England via Savoy. The whole affair was not a success, and ended in a near-riot. Nithard mentions a military game in 842 which bears a resemblance to a tournament. The French claim that Geoffrey, Lord of Préville in Anjou, who died in 1066, invented the tournament in its familiar form. In England, in the reign of Stephen (1135-54) laws forbidding jousting were relaxed and many accounts of tournaments remain. They were suppressed under Henry II but Richard I (1189-99)

allowed tournaments to continue and charged an admission fee for spectators. A statute of Henry V regulated tournaments, and decreed that no knight might be accompanied by more than three esquires, and they must not be armed.

Early tournaments were frequently very bloody events. Unhorsed knights were trampled underfoot by other chargers. At Neuss, near Cologne, at least 60 knights were killed at a tournament in 1249. But gradually tourneys became better organized and less sanguinary. Even so, Henri II of France was killed at a joust, and at the tournament held as part of the extravagant proceedings of the Field of the Cloth of Gold in 1520 a Frenchman died as the result of an injury which he received in the lists. Because of such dangers, the state only intermittently sanctioned tournaments and jousts and the church always viewed them with disapproval. But no papal decrees could diminish the popularity of these spectacles. Richard I established five main districts where tournaments should be held. These were Salisbury and Wilton in Wiltshire; Warwick and Kenilworth in Warwickshire; Tickhill (Yorkshire) and Blyth (Nottinghamshire); Stamford, Warmington, Brackley, and Mixbury (Lincolnshire/Northamptonshire). Fines were exacted from those wishing to take part (20 marks for an earl, 2 marks for a knight without property of his own). Higden, writing of 1195, comments: 'that tyme tournaments that were left of longe tyme were i-made and i-used agen nought withstondynge the popes forbedynge.' Generally, however, the English rulers did not encourage tournaments in the same way as their French contemporaries.

The joust was at first somewhat despised by devotees of the tournament but it grew steadily in popularity, and in the end superseded almost entirely the older and more dangerous form of tourney. It was mentioned by William of Malmesbury, and was called 'The Round Table Game' under Henry III. It frequently formed part of the celebrations at weddings, coronations, and similar great occasions. Permanent tilt-yards existed at Westminster, Hampton Court, Greenwich, and elsewhere, and one still survives at Gawsworth in Cheshire. Noblemen often held jousts and sent their heralds to all the near-by towns to proclaim date, time, place, and prize, often very valuable. Roger de Mortimer in 1280 founded a fraternity of a hundred knights who met to joust and afterwards to be entertained by him. Edward III's Round Table is said to have cost him £100 per week to run, an expense he could ill afford because of the cost of the wars with France. He therefore had to reduce his expenditure to a fifth of that amount.

A thirteenth-century manuscript refers to the social necessity of being at least a competent jouster:

> If wealth, sir Knight, perchance be thine,
> In tournaments you're bound to shine.
> Refuse — and all the world will swear
> You are not worth a rotten pear.

Jousting continued under Henry VII because it appealed to his highly developed love of display and ritual, as well as providing yet another sphere in which the king could excel.

Tournaments were held to commemorate the coronation of Queen Eleanor in 1236 in Tothill fields in Westminster and in Cheapside to celebrate the birth of the heir, Edward, later to be styled the Black Prince, in 1330. In 1374 Edward III arranged a tournament in honour of Alice Perrers; Froissart records a French tourney under Charles VI when Reynaud de Roy was discovered to be practising the trick of wearing his helmet very loosely. In 1390 Richard II held a tournament against the French. In the same year there was a tournament on London Bridge between Sir David Lindsay of Glenesh and Lord Wells, the English ambassador in Scotland.

Henry VIII's revival of tourneys, after their decline in the fifteenth century when the nobility were more preoccupied with the problem of actual combat, began with a tournament in 1511, from 1 to 3 May, in which the King himself, Sir Edward Howard, Charles Brandon, Sir Edward Nevil, and others took part. Jousts were also held in 1516, 1517, and 1526. It was at a May Day tournament in 1536 that the Queen, Anne Boleyn, was arrested and confined to await her trial and subsequent execution. In 1540 Henry VIII held a tournament in honour of his new queen, Anne of Cleves. Lances used in Tudor tilts were 14 ft. 4 in. (4·37 m.) long and weighed about 20 lb. (9 kg.).

Viscount Dillon in the *Archaeological Journal* records the rules for jousting. If a knight broke a spear between the saddle and the fastening of the helmet to the breast, he scored 1 point; if it was above this he scored 2; if he unhorsed or disarmed his opponent he scored 3. If he broke the spear on the saddle he forfeited 1; if he struck the tilt once, he lost 2; if he struck it twice he lost 3 points. If he struck his opponent's horse or back, or his opponent when disarmed, he was disqualified.

Just as QUINTAIN was played sometimes on water, so there were occasional boat-jousts. Stow writes: 'I have seen...upon the river Thames, some rowed in wherries with staves in their hands flat at the fore end, running one against the other, and for the most part one or both of them were overthrown or well-ducked.' Elizabeth I watched such a boat-joust at Sandwich in 1573, and an eyewitness reported: 'One of them did overthrow another at which the queen had good sport.'

After the Tudor revival, the popularity of tournaments and jousts declined, as did the whole ethos that had fostered them. Tournaments were a relic of the days of a courtly chivalry, and when such an attitude was no longer a convention, they were regarded as traditions rather than being spontaneously practised. They vanished after the seventeenth century, except for occasional revivals in a much debased form for entertainment.

JOUTES LYONNAISES is a traditional and localized French form of JOUSTING on water. The competitors are armed with wooden lances and carry wooden shields on their left arms. They are mounted on platforms raised above the stern of boats which are propelled towards one another and pass at close quarters while each competitor attempts to knock the other off his platform by the impact of the lance against the shield.

JOYNER, ANDREW JACKSON (1861-1943), 'the gentleman from North Carolina', was the doyen of American race-horse trainers, among whose patrons were BELMONT and WIDENER.

JUDO, literally 'easy way', is a combat sport which developed primarily in Japan but now has world-wide appeal and received Olympic recognition in 1964. Japan has remained the stronghold of the sport with approximately 8 million participants but the U.S.A., the U.S.S.R., and France lead the rest of the world, each having over 200,000 registered participants. The terminology, however, remains Japanese.

The basis of judo dates from the early days of the sport when a throw, strangle, armlock, or a 30-second hold-down was sufficient to disable an opponent. Each is enough to gain an *ippon* (point) in a modern contest.

All *judoka* (participants) wear the *judogi* (judo suit) which resembles a loose-fitting western suit. There are no buttons or pockets, to minimize injury, and feet are left bare. The jacket is fastened by a belt, the colour of which indicates the competitor's standard.

The grades are divided into *Kyu* (pupil) and *Dan* (degree); a beginner wears a white belt.

5th *Kyu* — yellow belt (in Japan, white)
4th *Kyu* — orange belt (in Japan, white)
3rd *Kyu* — green belt (in Japan, brown)
2nd *Kyu* — blue belt (in Japan, brown)
1st *Kyu* — brown belt (in Japan, brown)
1st *Dan* — black belt
2nd *Dan* — black belt

3rd *Dan*— black belt
4th *Dan*— black belt
5th *Dan*— black belt
6th *Dan*— red and white belt
7th *Dan*— red and white belt
8th *Dan*— red and white belt
9th *Dan*— red belt
10th *Dan*— red belt
11th *Dan*— red belt
12th *Dan*— white belt

Fighting ability plus technical knowledge takes a *judoka* to 5th *Dan*, after which advancement depends on service to the sport and not on fighting ability. The leading international fighters are usually 4th or 5th *Dans*. Theoretically it is possible to reach 12th *Dan* (white belt, the same as a beginner) and thus complete the entire circle in the sport and also in life. But this has never been achieved and the highest grade ever awarded by the KODO-KAN is 10th *Dan*.

Gradings became less important as the sport developed, but they are still useful as a guide to an individual's standard. Down-gradings are made only in the event of serious misconduct. Gradings are held every three months but for *Dan* grades most competitors accumulate points from important contests. For gradings *judoka* may often face opponents far larger and stronger, and for certain belts they may have to perform a 'line-up', necessitating the defeat of opponents in succession. However, with the growth of major contests *judoka* prefer to accumulate points rather than obtain their next grade through the line-up.

Contests were originally staged as open events in which competitors of any weight took part, but in recent years weight categories have been introduced. However, the open class is retained since in certain circumstances a good, small fighter can beat a less skilful, large man. Weight categories are:

Seniors and juniors: lightweight, under 63 kg. (9 st. 12 lb.); welterweight, 63 kg. (9 st. 12 lb.) – 70 kg. (11 st.); middleweight, 70 kg. (11 st.) – 80 kg. (12 st. 8 lb.); light-heavyweight, 80 kg. (12 st. 8 lb.) – 93 kg. (14 st. 9 lb.); heavyweight, over 93 kg. (14 st. 9 lb.).
Espoirs (under 17 years old): lightweight, under 58 kg. (9 st. 1½ lb.); welterweight, 58 kg. (9 st. 1½ lb.) – 65 kg. (10 st. 3 lb.); middleweight, 65 kg. (10 st. 3 lb.) – 75 kg. (11 st. 11 lb.); light-heavyweight, 75 kg. (11 st. 11 lb.) – 85 kg. (13 st. 5 lb.); heavyweight, over 85 kg. (13 st. 5 lb.).

Shiai (contests) are conducted by a roving referee and two judges who sit at opposite corners of a mat 9 m. (30 ft.) square. There is a surrounding safety area of 1 m. (3 ft. 3½ in.) on to which a fighter may be thrown, provided his opponent has started the movement inside the area. The *tatami* (mats) are made of compressed straw with a tight canvas covering and usually measure 2 × 1 m. (6 ft. 7 in. × 3 ft. 3½ in.). They are pushed tightly together and kept in place by a wooden frame. According to the importance of the event, a contest lasts usually between 2 and 10 minutes. There are no rounds but a decisive score within the period is sufficient to end the contest. In the event of no major score, the judges indicate the winner with their batons, the referee having the deciding vote.

Competitors may score an advantage by means of an *ippon* (10 points) — full point, or a *wazari* (7 points) — almost a point; and may gain a *yusei-gachi* (decision) by a *wazari ni chikai waza* (5 points) — a near *wazari*, or a *kinsa* (3 points) — small advantage.

The referee calls out any decisive score (*wazari* and above) and may also penalize either competitor for an infringement of the rules. Infringements bring the following penalties: *shido* (no penalty) — note; *chui* (3 points) — caution; *keikoku* (7 points) — warning; *hansoku-make* (10 points) — disqualification. A competitor who has already had a *chui* and gets one more automatically receives a *keikoku*. If he is unfortunate enough to get a third *chui*, he is disqualified.

The referee follows the bout 6 to 8 feet (1·829–2·438 m.) from the competitors in the manner of a boxing referee. His Japanese terminology includes the following:

Hajime: Begin
Matte: Break
Sono-mama: Do not move
Yoshi: Carry on
Jikan: Time out
Hantei: Decision (request for a decision from the judges)
Sore-made: That is all

Referees judge on the correctness of technique. An *ippon* is scored when a competitor is hurled on to his back with some force. When the throw is less definite and the competitor has not landed completely on his back, a *wazari* is awarded.

Most top-class contests are difficult to judge and many decisions are controversial. If there has been no score and neither competitor has received any warning for infringements, the judges award the contest to the fighter who has scored most knock-downs. If none has been made, the contest goes to the competitor who has been the more aggressive. Judges count the number of attacks and knock-downs, but these are ignored if a competitor scores a *wazari-ni-chikai waza* (a decisive knock-down). This is sufficient to win him the contest in the event of no better score.

All infringements count for slightly more than scores. Thus if a fighter has scored a *wazari* but suffers a *keikoku* and there are no further scores in the bout, the verdict goes to his opponent.

In hold-downs a competitor must trap at least one arm and hold the opponent for 30 seconds (25 seconds for a *wazari*). The referee will call *'Osaekomi'* (Holding) and if the fighter escapes he will shout *'Toketa'* (Broken).

Frequently fighters reach the edge of the mat while entwined. The referee then calls *'Sono-mama'* (Do not move) and, assisted by the two judges, drags the contestants to the centre of the mat. They resume grappling at a signal from the referee, who will tap both competitors on their bodies at the same time.

Competitors seek to gain the maximum from a slight advantage. If one goes ahead on a knock-down (or *chui*) he will usually assume the defensive while his opponent will launch an all-out attack. Some fighters specialize in groundwork and attempt to lure their opponent on to the mat so that they can use their strongest techniques.

Fighters grip each side of the opponent's jacket, usually on the sleeves or lapels. They grapple for grips but often attempt throws with only one hand on the jacket or dive at their opponent's leg in a bid to gain a point. Most major throws are derived from *kata* (a series of regularized movements). The basic groups are: hand throws, leg throws, shoulder throws, and sacrifice throws.

With all throws (and, to a certain extent, groundwork) fighters seek maximum efficiency with the minimum of effort. Although strength is needed in judo, it is most successful when correctly applied, at an opponent's weakest point. Thus if a fighter moves forward, his opponent will seek to use that momentum in order to throw him.

Dr. KANO, founder of the sport, introduced a principle which JU-JITSU had never discovered: *tskuri-komi*, getting a fighter off-balance before throwing him. However, in modern contests fighters are extremely careful not to commit themselves; they will feint one way and, as the opponent reacts, throw him in the direction in which he is weakest. Similarly in groundwork: if a contestant is trying to escape from a hold his opponent may use the movement to apply an armlock, stranglehold, or some even more powerful hold rather than resist his opponent's movements.

The most successful throws have proved to be: *uchi-mata* (inner thigh throw), *o-soto-gari* (major outer reaping throw), *harai-goshi* (sweeping hip throw), and *seio-nage* (shoulder throw). Many fighters fall to the ground with their opponents to give added impetus to the movement and to force their way through their opponent's defence. This is known as *maki-komi* (winding).

Bow

Inner thigh throw

Changing hip throw

Shoulder throw

Strangle

JUDO THROWS AND HOLDS

Counter-techniques can be destructive. A fighter will block his opponent's attempted throw and then hurl him to the mat with any of a number of throws, depending on the situation. *Renraku-waza* (combination techniques) are used by all advanced fighters.

In order to cushion the effect of throws, *ukemi* (break-falls) are employed. Competitors relax their bodies and with their free outstretched arm beat the mat, an action which is taught early in a *judoka*'s career and, with practice, becomes instinctive.

Newaza (groundwork) consists of moves, feints, and counter-moves in which a competitor seeks to gain a point from either a strangle, armlock, or hold-down. In the first two cases a fighter will often tap when he can bear the pain no longer — he hits the mat or his opponent twice with either of his hands or, if they are both trapped, with his feet.

Armlocks are applied against the elbow joint. In strangle some competitors prefer to become unconscious rather than submit, but this can be dangerous. In Japan, fighters are sometimes strangled unconscious several times in succession during training in order to toughen them up. The high grades are taught *katsu* (resuscitation).

The use of the legs is vital in groundwork to escape from hold-downs and to secure a favourable position for attacking moves. During contests, if a competitor traps his opponent's legs while he himself is being held, the hold is automatically broken.

Judo fighters train in a variety of ways. The basis is daily *randori* (free practice), in which competitors seek to throw each other without the tension of contests. This is done continuously, with a variety of partners of different weights and sizes, and is extremely tiring. Repetition throws are practised through *uchi-komi* (forcing a fighter off balance with a throw without actually completing the movement). Leading competitors also practise weight-training, running, and other sports to build up strength, speed, and stamina.

The most important judo championships are: OLYMPIC GAMES, world championships (every two years), and European senior and junior championships (annually).

In all these championships and in national events the *repêchage* system is used. All the fighters in each weight category are divided into two groups, A and B. The members of each group compete on a knock-out basis until one competitor emerges as the winner. These become two of the semi-finalists and the other two are produced by the *repêchage*. Every competitor whom the winner of each group has met and defeated now has a chance to fight again. The first competitor defeated fights the second, the winner of this contest fights the third man, and so on until there is only one contestant left in each group. These two are the other semi-finalists. The winner of the *repêchage* in group A meets the original winner of group B in one semi-final, and vice versa. This ensures that two competitors who have already met do not meet again until the final.

A pool system is often used in national trials for picking teams. Each fighter meets everyone else in his group, the leaders going through to subsequent pools. Team contests between clubs and countries are also staged, usually in weight categories. There is a team event in the European championships with five fighters on each side, one in each weight category. The winning team is the one with most individual victories.

Kata competitions are held for women in which the competitors are judged on their technique and fluency of movement. Women's championships have started and weight categories are being introduced. The rules are similar to those governing men but the matches are not as long.

Boys under 16 also take part in competitions but they are usually restricted to hold-downs in groundwork since strangling and armlocks are considered dangerous for youngsters in the heat of contests. Children have a separate grading system called *mon*.

The search for success in competitions has meant that other aspects of judo have sometimes been ignored; grades are less important and etiquette is not so rigorously observed as in the past. However, many of the customs of the sport still survive.

On entering a *dojo* (training-hall) a *judoka* makes a standing bow. In Japan this is done towards a shrine which is usually at one end of the *dojo*. If there is no shrine there is sometimes a platform where the teachers sit. Before every practice or contest *judoka* bow to each other, having adjusted their dress. At the end of the session they bow to each other again. Frequently, before and after training sessions, there will be a short period of meditation so that the *judoka* may collect his thoughts and reflect on the training.

International Judo Federation Contest Rules, latest edition.

Judo was developed in Japan from the ancient schools of ju-jitsu by Dr. Kano, who combined their outstanding features into a method he called Kokokan judo. Kano opened his first *dojo*, the Kodokan, in 1882. He called his method judo rather than ju-jitsu for two reasons: firstly, ju-jitsu had fallen into disrepute because some experts were staging exhibition fights; secondly, a number of ju-jitsu schools had got a reputation for dangerous techniques.

For some time judo was regarded as just one of a number of ju-jitsu schools, but in 1886 the Kodokan gained a lead when the Tokyo Metropolitan Police Board held a tournament between the Kodokan and Totsuka, the biggest of the ju-jitsu schools. Each team entered 15 men and the Kodokan inflicted a crushing defeat on the opposition, winning 13 bouts and drawing 2. From that date interest in judo increased greatly in Japan and ju-jitsu diminished in importance.

The technical formula of the Kodokan was completed in 1887. The major difference between Kodokan judo and ju-jitsu may be summed up, in the words of Kano, as 'the elevation of an art to a principle'. Kano declared that judo made the maximum use of mind and body and ju-jitsu was nothing but an application of this principle to the methods of attack and defence. In studying judo, he felt it was essential to train the body and to cultivate the mind through the practice of the methods of attack and defence. He summarized his teaching in the slogans 'Maximum efficiency with minimum effort' and 'Mutual welfare and benefit'.

Ju-jitsu lacks the sporting aspect of jūdo but Kano also introduced something completely new, *tskuri-komi*, taking a fighter off balance in order to throw him. His opinions were respected by the Japanese Ministry of Education who adopted judo as a sport.

Kano, however, was not content to popularize judo only in his home country. He visited Britain in 1885 and one of his outstanding pupils, Yamashita, began teaching in the U.S.A. in 1902. By 1905 judo had reached France and was being taught to the Paris police.

However, popularity in Europe did not really follow until KOIZUMI founded the BUDOKWAI in London in 1918. The club's first instructor was Tani, who had an astonishing success as a wrestler at the start of the century, the golden era of professional WRESTLING. Both Tani and Koizumi were primarily instructors in ju-jitsu but when Kano subsequently visited Britain he approved Koizumi's work and the pair switched from ju-jitsu to judo. From then on there was a close link with the Kodokan.

The first international match took place in 1926 between the Budokwai and the German national team. The Budokwai won and this marked the start of a rapid growth in club and international tournaments. Koizumi frequently toured Europe instructing, establishing new clubs, and encouraging pupils.

Both the European Judo Union and the British Judo Association were founded in 1949. The International Judo Federation, the world governing body, followed two years later.

Tani died in 1951 but Koizumi was to see the first European championships in London's Royal Albert Hall that year. France (with PARISET and COURTINE), Great Britain, and Holland dominated the first five European championships. For Britain such men as PALMER, YOUNG, Mack, and Gleeson were the leading fighters. Holland produced the great GEESINK for the championships in 1951 and he reached the final of the *Kyu* grade event, the start of the finest competition career of any non-Japanese judo fighter.

By the first world championships in Tokyo in 1956, however, Japan was still far ahead of any other country. Kano, who died in 1938 returning from an INTERNATIONAL OLYMPIC COMMITTEE meeting, had seen judo reach a high standard and become a national sport. The all-Japan championships were first

staged in 1930, originally in age categories. KIMURA was the outstanding fighter in the early years. All the martial arts were suppressed immediately after the Second World War by the occupying Americans but restrictions were relaxed and the all-Japan championships were resumed in 1948 as a no-weight-limit knock-out tournament, their present form.

Because of the dominance of the Kodokan, the Japanese Judo Federation was not founded until 1949. To this were associated all the universities, clubs, and schools. Most of the outstanding fighters have come from the universities, between which there is intense rivalry, and from the police.

Apart from Europe and America, which had the largest number of exponents outside Japan, judo had reached Australia in 1928 through Dr. Ross, who founded the Brisbane Club. Takagi established judo in India in 1929 and in Africa two years later.

Judo was therefore a truly international sport when the first world championships were held in 1956. However, no one expected the Japanese to lose. The outstanding competitors from each country over the years had all gone to Tokyo to train. LEGGETT in 1938 was the first Briton to do so and he set off a chain of emigrants, although even the influence of Japanese training could not give the rest of the world the ascendancy. The final was fought out between the triple all-Japan champion YOSHIMATSU and NATSUI, the latter winning. Geesink gave a hint of things to come by taking third place.

In 1957 Britain recorded her first victory in the European championships, defeating Holland 2-1 in the final. Geesink recorded Holland's sole win and also took the 4th *Dan* and open title into the bargain.

In the early stages both the European and world championships were held without weight categories, although the European championships had grade events. Geesink's size meant that he was invariably meeting people far smaller than his 6 ft. 6 in. (1·98 m.). The Dutchman twice defeated Pariset the following year to take the 4th *Dan* and open titles at the European championships, but once again he could not prevent Holland losing the team title to Britain.

The 1958 world championships were again held in Tokyo and once more Geesink was the man the Japanese feared. But in the quarter-final he met the Japanese, Yamashiki, and was thrown for a debatable *ippon* (point). The semi-final consisted of Yamashiki, KAMI-NAGA, SONE, and Pariset, who was 'strangled' after 47 seconds by Sone. Sone went on to win the final.

Geesink's victory in the third world championships in Paris (1961) changed the whole concept of judo. For many years it had been believed that a skilful small man could beat an equally skilled big man. Many people had clung to this belief despite the fact that the average weight of the all-Japan champions had been 15 stone (95·3 kg.). Geesink brought the whole issue into the open, and France led the move to introduce weight categories to the Olympic Games, world, and European championships, although the open class was retained.

Geesink's victory also destroyed the myth of Japanese invincibility and made them determined to find someone capable of beating him when they were the hosts of the 1964 Olympics and judo was included on the programme for the first time. In addition to Geesink the Japanese had to contend with the Russians who had put up an outstanding performance at the European championships in 1962 at Essen. The U.S.S.R. beat Britain in the second round and finally lost to the Dutch team in the semifinals. The most successful Russian fighter of the 1960s was unquestionably KIKNADZE but Kibrotsashvili, who went on to a number of victories, was also in their team in Essen.

It was a momentous year for European judo. Weight categories were introduced in the new Olympic classes of lightweight (under 10 st. 8¾ lb. — 67·5 kg.), middleweight (under 12 st. 8¼ lb. — 80 kg.) and heavyweight (over 12 st. 8¼ lb.). Junior events were staged and until 1964 these were held in conjunction with the senior events.

The grade classes were abandoned at the 1963 European championships and the team event was fought in the three new categories, two fighters in each class. Russia, with the experience of one championship behind them, were even more formidable and took the team award for the first time, a title they were to win every year until 1967. The 1964 European championships provided a preview of the contenders likely to frustrate the Japanese bid to win all four classes at the Olympics. Geesink showed that he was at the top of his form by taking the open heavyweight and open all-category titles, while Russia won three titles including the team event. For Britain JACKS showed the flair and promise he was later to fulfil by winning the junior middleweight and securing a bronze medal in the open lightweight class.

All was set for judo's introduction to the Olympic programme. The Japanese, however, had no new fighter to oppose Geesink and relied on Kaminaga in the open category. But their representatives in the other classes were ruthless fighters and brilliant technicians — the lightweight Nakatani, middleweight OKANO, and heavyweight INOKUMA. All three swept through to the gold medals. Nakatani defeated Switzerland's Haenni in the lightweight final with the Russians getting the other medals. In the middleweights Okano was impressive, holding Hofmann (West Germany) in the final after soundly beating his other opponents. In the open event, however, Geesink proved once again that he was the master. A Tokyo newspaper said: 'We failed in the real objective — beating Geesink.' Geesink beat Kaminaga in the preliminary pool, threw PETHERBRIDGE in 7 seconds and Boronovskis (Australia) in 12 to reach the final. Kaminaga fought back through four more eliminations to face Geesink again before 15,000 people in the Nippon Budokan Hall, a replica of an ancient building, the Hall of Dreams. After 9 minutes, Geesink secured *kesa-gatame* (scarf hold-down) after Kaminaga's *uchi-mata* (inner thigh throw) attack had failed. With the hall completely silent Geesink clung on for the required 30 seconds, and when the bell went the Japanese clapped politely, Kaminaga's team mates burst into tears, and Geesink had won the gold medal.

The inclusion of judo in the Olympics was a tremendous boost to the sport and it made headway in a number of developing countries, marked by the selection of Rio de Janeiro (Brazil) as the venue for the 1965 world championships. Once again the Japanese were determined to get their revenge on Geesink, and named Inokuma for the open class, hoping his technique would upset the Dutchman. Geesink, however, chose the heavyweight category and defeated both the huge Japanese entrants, Sakaguchi and Matsunaga, on his way to the title. Inokuma beat the Russians Kiknadze and Kibrotsashvili for the open gold medal, and the other Japanese entrants, Okano (middleweight) and Matsuda (lightweight), also secured titles.

At the International Judo Federation Congress, Palmer, chairman of the British Judo Association, was elected president of the Federation. He was the first non-Japanese to hold the office and succeeded R. Kano, son of Dr. Kano, who retired.

Five new weight categories — lightweight, welterweight, middleweight, light-heavyweight, and heavyweight — were introduced for the 1966 European championships in Luxemburg. Geesink had retired temporarily but his teaching influence was apparent, for Holland won three of the titles, the other four (including the team event) going to Russia. The new force on the scene, however, was West Germany, despite being heavily defeated by Britain in the autumn of 1966 in an international. They upset the Russians in the semi-final of the 1967 European championships, Olympic bronze medallist GLAHN unexpectedly throwing Kiknadze in the heavyweight match, and beat France in the final.

This was Geesink's last year in the European championships and he retired finally with a victory over Kiknadze in the open class. Russia had gold medallists in the lightweight category (Suslin retained his title) and in the middleweight through Pokataev, who beat KERR. But tremendous interest centred on the performance of Geesink's fellow-countryman RUSKA, who won the heavyweight category and seemed Europe's best chance of upsetting the Japanese at the world championships which were staged in Salt Lake City, Utah (U.S.A.) in August 1967. The Japanese were favourites for all six categories and, true to form, they won five of the classes, but Ruska won the heavyweight. He threw Kiknadze in the semi-final with *harai-goshi* (sweeping hip throw) and repeated it on the Japanese Maejima for the title.

One of the finest performances was by Britain's Jacks, who was unlucky to lose to Maruki, the Japanese winner of the middleweight class. The clearest champion was the welterweight MINATOYA, who won every fight with an *ippon* (point), but a notable absentee from the event was Okano, who had badly injured his elbow in submitting to a Russian's armlock in a goodwill match in Tokyo during the summer.

The Orient's domination was emphasized in the intercontinental match which followed. They beat Pan-America in the final, losing only one of the contests.

With the rest of Europe becoming used to Russia's unusual style, the honours in the next three European championships were more evenly spread. France, Holland and the two Germanys prepared for events with an increasingly professional attitude. France won the European team title in 1968, making it a record sixth win in 18 years, but West Germany won it back the following year only for it to be regained in 1970 by Russia in a close fight with Holland in the final. In 1970, too, Britain secured her first weight category title through middleweight Jacks. But the Japanese were still too strong for Europe and proved it at the world championships in Mexico City in 1969 when they finished first and second in the three lightest categories and first and third in the other three classes. Even Ruska, who was the European heavyweight champion and defending world title-holder, lost in the open final to Shinomaki, the 1970 all-Japan champion. The West German Glahn was thrown in the heavyweight final by Suma.

Britain with the exception of Jacks had failed to make much impact on the international scene for some years. But in 1971 they won the European title with a talented team of Lawrence, Cassidy, STARBROOK, PARISI, and REMFRY. In the world championships at Ludwigshafen that year Starbrook and Remfry both secured bronze medals. Japan took five of the six titles and clearly lacked the solidity among the big men; Ruska regained the heavyweight crown with Glahn runner-up.

Europe mounted their strongest-ever challenge at the 1972 Olympics on the Japanese domination of the sport. Britain had a number of determined competitors. France had MOUNIER at lightweight and Coche, who had beaten AUFFRAY for the European title in May, at middleweight. Russia possessed a meticulously prepared squad led by CHOCHOSHVILI and Kuznetsov, their huge heavyweight. Above all there were the two leading continental heavyweights, Ruska and Glahn, both of whom were enormously fit after training in Tokyo and highly experienced.

In Munich Japan's grip on the sport was prised apart. They took only half the gold medals — the three lightest divisions through SEKINE, NOMURA, and KAWAGUCHI. They seemed demoralized by the utterly unexpected defeat of light-heavyweight SASAHARA. Ruska was the most impressive entry, winning the heavyweight and Open classes before announcing his retirement; he had proved a worthy successor to Geesink.

Japan dismissed their trainers after the Games and gave command of the team to Okano. At the 1973 world championships they won all six titles. Okano's emphasis on skill and on instilling confidence into the squad altered both their physical potential and mental attitude. The gap has narrowed but Japan is still the most powerful judo nation.

K. Kudo (9th *Dan*) *Dynamic Judo: Throwing Techniques* (1967) and *Dynamic Judo: Grappling Techniques* (1967).

GOVERNING BODY (WORLD): International Judo Federation, 70 Brompton Road, London S.W.3.

JU-JITSU (or ju-jutsu), the Japanese method of self-defence which Dr. KANO studied and developed into the modern sport of JUDO. Both KARATE and *aikido* include many features of ju-jitsu.

The techniques of ju-jitsu, which was a ruthless method of self-defence rather than a sport, included throws, strangleholds, arm- and wrist-locks, kicks, chops with the hand, and punches. Many of the different *ryu* (schools) were based on the principles of the Chinese strategist Hwang-Shihkon: 'In yielding is strength', the use of an opponent's force and movement to destroy him.

Ju-jitsu began to take on a systematized form in the latter half of the sixteenth century and most of the major schools were developed from the seventeenth to the beginning of the nineteenth century. Some references, including the Kokushoji document, state that ju-jitsu was introduced into Japan by a Chinese monk, Chen Yuan-ping, at the start of the seventeenth century, but evidence shows that such Japanese ju-jitsu masters as Hitotsubashi-Joeken and Sekiguchi-Jushin thrived before 1627. However, Chen Yuan-ping probably introduced *kempo*. Chinese BOXING, which may have had some influence on ju-jitsu.

There were many schools, each distinguished by its individual features. According to the *Bu-jutsu-Ryusoruku* (Biographies of the Founders of the Various Martial Exercise Schools) there were 20 *Ryu* of ju-jitsu such as Takenouchi, Kyushin, Kito, and Tenchin-Shin'yo, the last two of which were closely studied by Dr. Kano.

When, however, the ordinance of 1871 forbade the *samurai* (knights) to carry swords, ju-jitsu fell into disrepute as experts used its devastating methods on ordinary members of the public, and the expansion of judo further reduced its popularity. It still exists, however, in Japan and in other parts of the world.

JUMPING, see HIGH JUMP; LONG JUMP; POLE VAULT; TRIPLE JUMP.

JUNIOR OFFSHORE GROUP, an English yacht racing club, formed in 1950 to provide offshore racing for yachts smaller than those eligible for the races organized by the ROYAL OCEAN RACING CLUB, namely between 16 ft. (4·87 m.) and 24 ft. (7·31 m.) waterline.

JURION, JOSEPH, Association footballer for ANDERLECHT (Brussels) and Belgium, both of whom he captained during the 1960s. An inside right, he was one of the few players in modern times to compete in European club and international competitions wearing spectacles.

JUVENTUS, Association FOOTBALL club, Turin. Founded in 1897, it first won the Italian championship in 1905 before emerging as the dominant club in Italy between the two world wars when it won the championship in five consecutive seasons.

Juventus has appeared regularly in recent years in the three European club competitions, its best performances being to reach the final of the Champion Clubs Cup in 1973 before losing 0-1 to AJAX, the semi-final stage of the Champion Clubs Cup in 1968, and the final of the Fairs Cup in 1965 when it was beaten by the Hungarian club, FERENCVAROS. Leading players include Combi, Rosetta, Caligaris, MONTI, ORSI, Parola, Boniperti, Sivori, and CHARLES.

COLOURS: Black and white striped shirts, white shorts.

K

KABADDI is a traditional team pursuit game, played in India, requiring the players to run and hold their breath for a long time. It is played on a rectangular field 13 m. by 10 m. (42 ft. 6 in. × 33 ft.) (11 m. × 8 m. — 36 ft. × 26 ft. for women and juniors) which is divided into two halves by a line drawn across the middle. Each half, called the 'court', has a line parallel to the centre line at a distance of 3 m. (9 ft. 10 in.) — 2·5 m. (8 ft. 3 in.) for women and juniors — known as a baulk line.

Kabaddi must be one of the very few games where no equipment is needed. A player's kit consists of a jersey, shorts, canvas tennis shoes with plain soles, and socks.

A team consists of 12 players but only 7 take the field; the rest remain as reserves on the 'waiting blocks' which are drawn 2 m. (6 ft. 6 in.) away from the end lines. Their jerseys must be clearly numbered at the back and front and their nails closely clipped. Their bodies and limbs must be free of any greasy substance.

The team winning the toss sends a player into the opponents' court. This player is called the 'raider', the opponents being known as the 'anti-raiders' or 'antis'. Only one raider may be sent at a time, and each team sends one alternately until the end of play. Before cross-ing the centre line, the raider must begin say-ing loudly and clearly the word *'Kabaddi'*. He repeats it rapidly, *without* taking breath, until the raid is completed. This process is called the 'cant'. The raider is deemed to have lost his cant if he pauses between his repetition of *'Kabaddi'* and is therefore out. While on the opponents' court the raider tries to touch one or more antis before retreating. He may touch either by his hands or any part of his body. But he must, at least once, cross the baulk line. If he succeeds in both, i.e. crosses the baulk line and touches one or more antis and returns to his own half, *without* losing his cant, all the antis touched by him are out. On the other hand, the raider is out if he loses his cant while still on enemy territory. He is out also when he is caught by one or more antis and is prevented from returning to his court. The antis may not resort to unfair means such as trying delibe-rately to stifle the raider's cant by shutting his mouth or wilfully pushing him over the boun-dary line. Such tactics are punished by the umpire and the raider is considered to have returned home safely. If, in trying to free him-self from the antis, the raider throws himself on the ground and touches his own court with any part of his body, he has made a safe return. A raider, however, is not compelled to

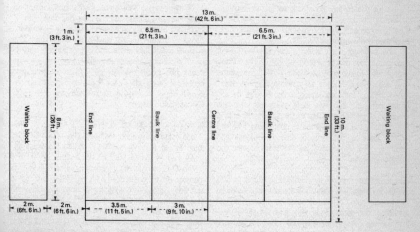

KABADDI FIELD OF PLAY
Dimensions are those for the men's game; the field for women and juniors is somewhat smaller.

touch an anti. If he returns home without touching anybody, but holding on to his cant, neither side loses a player. When a player is out he must leave the field and go to his waiting block. He is 'revived' or re-enters when an opponent is out, in the same order as he was out.

A team scores 1 point for each player put out by them. They score a *lona*—a bonus of 4 points—if they put out the entire opposition and the game continues by putting all the players of both sides back into their respective courts. While a raid is in progress all the antis must remain within their own court. If an anti goes over the boundary line or steps into the other half he is out. The raider's captain or team mates may not shout advice while he is away. At the end of a match the team scoring most points wins. If it is a tie an extra ten minutes is allowed. Should it prove to be a deadlock again, the side scoring the first point is declared the winner. A representative match for men has two halves of 20 minutes (15 minutes for women and juniors) with a 5-minute interval.

Matches are staged on the basis of weight and age groups. Weight groups are: (1) below 60 lb. or 27 kg; (2) below 75 lb. or 34 kg.; (3) below 90 lb. or 40 kg.; (4) below 110 lb. or 50 kg.; (5) open. Age groups are: (1) juniors—up to 17; (2) seniors—above 17 but below 21; (3) open.

A match is supervised by seven officials—one referee, two umpires, two linesmen, one timekeeper, and one scorer. The referee is the final authority on the field. He is empowered to warn, declare points for or against, or to disqualify any player or team violating the rules, resorting to unfair tactics, or being guilty of misdemeanour on the field. The referee can, under special circumstances, overrule the umpire's decision.

The two umpires keep a careful watch on the game, from the sides of the field. They watch the movements of the raider and antis and assist each other in giving correct decisions. The linesmen record those out in the order of their exit, as well as those who are revived. The scorer fills in the score-sheet and announces the score at the end of each half and at the end of the match. He completes the sheet and has it signed by the referee and the umpires.

There is no record to indicate exactly when *Kabaddi* was first played but it must have been centuries ago. India being a multi-lingual country, the game has been known by different names in various regions until its present name was universally adopted. It has been called *hututu, kapati, do-do-do, bhadi-bhadi,* *wandikali, chedu-gudu, zabar gagana, saunchi-pakki,* and *kabardee.*

The game was not played in an organized form until 1923 when the Hind Vijay Gymkhana, Baroda, framed the rules of *hututu,* as *kabaddi* was known in that part of the country. A similar attempt in 1885 at Poona had failed. *Kabaddi* had three varieties: (1) *sanjeevani,* where a player once out could be revived; (2) *amar,* where a player put out remained on the field, an entry having been made in the scorebook; (3) *ganimi,* where a player once out cannot be revived.

When *kabaddi* was standardized, the first system—*sanjeevani*—was adopted, but the rules framed at Baroda covered only one region of the sub-continent. It was not until 1944 that the Indian Olympic Association adopted the rules of *kabaddi* to cover the whole of the country. Six years later the Amateur Kabaddi Federation of India, which is now the governing authority for the game, was established. The Federation is an autonomous body and is responsible for the administration and organization of the game in the country. Since its inception, the game has become well organized. There are now thousands of clubs all over India. Most states and some Government units like the Post and Telegraph Department and the Railway Board have *kabaddi* associations affiliated to the national federation. Tournaments are held at village, town, school, university, and state level. The Federation holds national *kabaddi* championships for both men and women annually. Coaching sessions and seminars are held. Examinations are taken by would-be referees and umpires.

Through the years the game has gained in importance and stature. It has become one of India's national games and reflects a philosophy of simple living and high thinking. The simplicity of its nature and organization and its negligible cost makes it easily accessible to the great but poor masses of India. It develops physical strength and creates team spirit. *Kabaddi* is also played in Pakistan, Burma, Ceylon, and China.

KAHANAMOKU, DUKE PAOA (1890-1968), Hawaiian surfer and swimmer for the U.S.A. at four OLYMPIC GAMES. He won the 100 metres freestyle in 1912 and 1920 (the 1916 Games having been cancelled), and was runner-up to WEISSMULLER in 1924. He made a fifth successive Olympic appearance with the American team at the 1932 Games, as a reserve for the WATER POLO team, but did not play. He pioneered the sport of SURFING in the American continent and helped further its development in other parts of the world.

KAMINAGA, A. (1937-), Japanese JUDO fighter who won the all-Japan championships three times but will be remembered more for a defeat when he lost the Olympic Open final in Tokyo to GEESINK. Extremely shortsighted, Kaminaga, 5 ft. 9 in. (1·75 m.) and weighing about 15 stone 10 lb. (99·8 kg.), was particularly proficient at *tai-otoshi* (body drop) and *uchi-mata* (inner thigh throw). In addition to winning three all-Japan titles (1960, 1961, and 1964), Kaminaga was the beaten finalist at the 1958 world championships and Olympic silver medallist in 1964 in the open class.

KANDAHAR SKI CLUB, founded at Mürren, Switzerland, on 13 January 1924, by a group of Englishmen, led by ARNOLD LUNN, as a downhill racing club. Lunn first conceived a club with a comic name, no subscriptions, and a few humorous rules. He was persuaded that there was a real need for a racing club, and the name Kandahar was taken from the oldest of downhill races, the Roberts of Kandahar, named after Lord Roberts of Kandahar, who became a vice-president of the club. The initial K was chosen as its emblem. On the slopes above and below Mürren, Lunn and his contemporaries evolved many of the rules and styles which were to be incorporated into modern ski-racing, though not without a struggle. The Kandahar's particular ally was the Swiss Universities' Ski Club.

KANHAI, ROHAN BABULAL (1935-), cricketer for West Indies, Guyana, Western Australia, and Warwickshire. An improvising batsman, throughout the 1960s he was an important component in a successful and entertaining West Indies side, and in 1973, when he scored his fifteenth Test hundred, he was appointed captain. Only SOBERS has made more runs for West Indies. His Test centuries include two in a match in Australia in 1960-1, with 256 against India being the highest. One of his best Test innings was a quick 77 at a critical time in the OVAL in 1963.

KANNENBERG, BERND (1942-), race walker for West Germany. Within three years of commencing the sport he was Olympic 50 km. champion in 1972 and had recorded the fastest-ever road time for the distance. First in the LUGANO CUP 50 km. in 1973, he is also in the élite class at all the shorter distances. He probably covers more distance in training than any other walker, and is also an excellent technician.

KANO, Dr. JIGORO (1860-1938), founder of JUDO, who combined the outstanding principles of the different styles of JU-JITSU into his new method. Born in Mikage (Japan), he practised at the various schools while studying at the Imperial University. In 1882 he founded the first KODOKAN at a 12-mat *dojo* (training hall) at Shitaya.

Dr. Kano always considered judo as a training for life. He encouraged his followers to balance the physical and mental aspects of training. He himself was the headmaster of two leading Japanese schools, spoke English fluently, and was a prolific writer. Under his guidance judo developed into a world-wide sport. He started the Japanese Olympic Committee and died on board ship while returning from the INTERNATIONAL OLYMPIC COMMITTEE conference in Cairo in 1938.

KANSAS CITY ATHLETICS, American professional BASEBALL team, assumed the AMERICAN LEAGUE franchise of the PHILADELPHIA ATHLETICS in 1954. Later they were purchased by Finley, who could not produce a winning baseball team in Kansas City but did provide bizarre stunts like gold uniforms for the players and goats grazing in the outfield to keep the grass in trim. When Kansas City failed to respond to these tactics, Finley moved the team to Oakland in 1968. (See OAKLAND ATHLETICS.)

KANSAS CITY CHIEFS, American professional FOOTBALL team, joined the AMERICAN FOOTBALL LEAGUE (A.F.L.) in 1960 as the Dallas Texans and switched to Kansas City to become the Chiefs in 1963. The team has participated in the two longest games in professional football history: as the Dallas Texans they defeated the Houston Oilers to win the A.F.L. title in 1962 in nearly 18 minutes of overtime; in a 1971 American Conference divisional play-off, they lost to the MIAMI DOLPHINS in the second overtime period. Lamar Hunt, one of the creators of the A.F.L., has owned them since their founding, and they have been coached by the imaginative Stram, one of whose major innovations was the 'moving pocket', a wall of blockers moving laterally behind the line of scrimmage to protect the passer. Kansas City played and lost the first Super Bowl in 1967, after the merger of the A.F.L. with the NATIONAL FOOTBALL LEAGUE, but later won the title in 1970 over the MINNESOTA VIKINGS.
COLOURS: Red and gold.

KANSAS CITY ROYALS, American professional BASEBALL team, entered the AMERICAN LEAGUE in 1969 when it expanded to 12 teams. A community effort, the new team suffered the growing pains of most expansion teams in its first years and had only modest success.

KAPLAN, HAMIT (*fl.* 1955-64), versatile Turkish heavyweight wrestler who was successful at both freestyle and Graeco-Roman. At the latter he won the world title in 1955, took a bronze medal in 1958, and a silver medal three years later. In freestyle he was Olympic gold medallist in 1956, silver medallist in 1960, and bronze medallist in 1964, and in world championships was first in 1958, second in 1959, and second again in 1961.

KAPUS, FRANZ (1909-   ), BOBSLEIGH rider for Switzerland. The winning driver in the 1955 world four-man championship at ST. MORITZ, Switzerland, he repeated the feat with an unchanged crew in the 1956 world and Olympic meeting at CORTINA, Italy. Then nearly 47, he became the oldest competitor in any event to win a WINTER OLYMPIC GAMES gold medal.

KARATE. In exhibitions and training sessions karate — literally 'empty hand' fighting — assumes a variety of forms. Exhibitions normally include *jiu-kumite* (free-style fighting), *kata* (training dances), and *tamashiwara* (wood-breaking). Training sessions also include *kihon* (basic technical training). Each of these forms is described below, as are the unique breathing methods and their relationship with Zen Buddhism, the peculiarity of the stances, and the great variety of body parts used for striking. All technical terms in karate are in Japanese. Anyone who practises karate is called a *karateka.*

In karate, as in JUDO, a belt system is used to evaluate merit and progress. The two basic categories within the system are *Kyu* (student), and *Dan* (graduate). The requirements for each level vary according to the style and standards of the instructor conducting the grading examination. The number of levels also varies according to style, but the general pattern is as described below.

In most styles there are six grades rising from the 6th to the 1st *Kyu*, plus the novice grade. (Novices wear a white belt.) Requirements for promotion include competence at the style's basic fighting forms (*kihon*), fitness, and the basic training dances (*kata*). An able student may be able to gain promotion from the white-belt stage in three or four months of intensive training, but a large proportion of students leave karate before gaining promotion from white belt as they find the training too rigorous. The other belts in

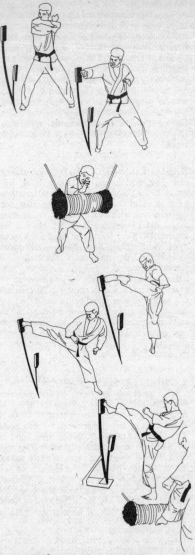

KATA EXERCISES IN KARATE
The *makiwara*, or padded board, is used, as is the punching and kicking bag, for strengthening the joints, toughening contact points, and perfecting karate techniques.

ascending order of importance are as follows: 6th *Kyu*, red belt; 5th *Kyu*, yellow belt; 4th *Kyu*, orange belt; 3rd *Kyu*, green belt;

2nd *Kyu,* blue belt; 1st *Kyu,* brown belt.

The next stage is the coveted *Dan* or black belt grade. These rise in reverse order to the *Kyu* grades, i.e. from *Shodan* (1st *Dan*), through *Nidan* (2nd *Dan*) and *Sandan* (3rd *Dan*) to the *Renshi* grades (4th and 5th *Dan,* senior experts) and the *Kyoshi* grades (6th, 7th, and 8th *Dan,* very high masters). *Renshi* grade *karateka* are entitled to be called *Sensei* ('honourable teacher') by their juniors.

Some styles also have 9th and 10th *Dans,* but there are less than a dozen such *karateka* throughout the world. *Dans* from the 8th grade are entitled to be called *Sheehan* ('honourable professor') by their juniors and to wear a solid red belt although, in most cases, they continue to wear a black belt. The fact that the optional red belt is the same colour as that for 6th *Kyu* implies that the *Sheehan* has completed the full circle of learning.

KATA. The general publication of combat techniques in book form is a very recent innovation; they were originally passed down by word of mouth and personal example and treated with great secrecy. Because of the lack of easy reference it was therefore necessary to devise a system which would enable the techniques to be remembered and practised when the instructor was not present. This could be achieved by combining them in a fixed sequence. A *kata* is therefore a fixed sequence of basic defence and attacking techniques designed for practice, and takes the form of imaginary fighting with several attackers approaching from different directions.

There are approximately 30 different *katas* but in all the choreography is highly stylized and appears like a strangely beautiful training dance. Unlike dancing, however, the aim is not primarily beauty, but sharpness and combat utility. The beauty lies in the expression of a martial spirit, the smoothness of line, and the economy of movement.

Each movement has a specific meaning and each sequence embodies the concentrated experience of numerous karate masters. The more comprehensive and advanced *katas* incorporate quick changes of technique, slowness and quickness, maintenance of balance, stretching and bending of the body, correct breathing, body shifting, combinations of hand and foot techniques, and instantaneous tensing and relaxing of the muscles to facilitate the application and withdrawal of power.

Because of their great training value many styles require a good *karateka* to perfect his *kata* before concentrating on free fighting. To acquire control and exactness the beginner will perform his *kata* relatively slowly. The expert will build up as much explosiveness and speed as possible and will completely lose himself in the movement. Because of the restrictions placed upon him in *jiu-kumite* (see below), it is only in *kata* practice that such a total self-expression can be achieved, and such practice is therefore invaluable to the achievement of high standards and full satisfaction.

All *katas* commence with a defensive move, although this is invariably followed by attack. In some instances the defensive and attacking moves are identical. Alternatively the first half of the movement may be defensive while its natural continuation or completion is aggressive. For demonstration purposes *kata* is sometimes performed to oriental music.

Most of the equipment to be found in the average *dojo* (club or training hall) is designed either for the perfecting of techniques or for strengthening. Such equipment includes the *makiwara* (padded board) which is used to perfect punching and kicking, for toughening the contact points, and for strengthening the joints so that they do not collapse on impact. Other equipment includes punching and kicking bags, punch balls, dumb-bells, iron clogs for leg strengthening, and containers of fine sand or soya beans into which the fingertips are driven. Several small balls may also be suspended from the ceiling so that kicking for accuracy can be practised.

The traditional garb of the sport is called *Karatege* and consists of loose white trousers and jacket. The jacket is fastened with the coloured belt, which indicates the grade of the *karateka* wearing it. *Hachimaki,* or sweat bands, worn around the head, are also sometimes used.

JIU-KUMITE (free-style fighting) contests are always between two individuals irrespective of grade. Team contests consist of a series of individual contests: the team with the greatest number of winning members is the winner. Each team normally consists of five *karateka* and each bout normally lasts two minutes, or three minutes in the finals. Time is allowed for stoppages.

The two teams take up their positions on opposite sides of the contest area, 8 m. to 10 m. (26–32 ft.) square. The centre is marked with a cross, on either side of which the individual contestants stand, with an initial distance of 2 m. (6 ft. 6 in.) between them. The contest is controlled by one referee, who moves freely within the contest area, and is assisted by four judges posted one at each corner of the area. The judges are needed to advise the referee on blows performed on his blind side and because of the speed with which they are executed. Each judge has a red flag, a white flag, and a whistle. One contestant will wear a red belt and the other a white one. If the referee's vision is obscured, one of the judges can advise him on his decision by blowing his whistle. He will raise the appropriate flag for a scoring point or wave the flag downwards several times for a no-score.

A controller or arbitrator is posted outside the contest area and he notes the decisions of the referee. Only the team manager can object to decisions and he addresses himself to the controller. After examining the protest, the controller may ask for the referee's explanation and, if necessary, another decision. Also posted outside the contest area are a scorekeeper, a time-keeper, and a recorder.

Before the contest the *karateka* perform a standing *rei* (bow) and the referee then calls '*Hajime*' (Begin). All instructions are in Japanese. The waiting position is one of watchful, though relaxed, preparedness. Some *karateka* specialize in counter-attack and rarely make the first move. In many respects *kumite* (fighting) resembles sparring in boxing, except that attacks are stopped just short of contact. As the fists are ungloved and many parts of the body are used for striking, the reason for this is obvious. One of the tests of proficiency in karate is, in fact, the ability to stop a fully focused attack just short of contact. In most cases, to strike an opponent would result in disqualification. The only fully focused contact blow which is permitted is 'sweeping' the opponent's leg to knock him to the ground. This must then be followed by a non-contact punch or kick in order to score. Finger attacks to the eyes and attacks to the genitals are not permitted in *kumite,* although they would be practised in *kihon* (see below) and *kata.*

The actual sparring consists of a free exchange of blows, blocks, and counter-attacks until one player gets a fully focused blow to one of a number of defined areas on his opponent's body. If the blow is delivered with the proper posture and stance, from the correct distance, and is spirited, an *ippon* (full point) will be awarded and the contest is over. A *wazarri* (half-point) can be awarded for a well-timed punch which is slightly off-centre or an accurate punch which is weak or a punch slightly off the target with the opponent unguarded. If both contestants score simultaneous points they cancel each other out. If a half-point is awarded the contest will continue until one player obtains a full point or two half-points.

Other means of determining a contest are by *hanteigachi* (win by decision), *hansoku-make* (loss by disqualification), or *hikiwake* (draw).

Instructions given by referees to contestants and judges include the following:

Yoi: Ready
Yame: Stop
Seremade: Stop (when time is up)
Yjogai: Outside the area
Hantei: Decision

Jiu-kumite is undoubtedly the most popular and exciting aspect of karate and is of Japanese origin. Originally fights were often to the death, but the development of *jiu-kumite,* with the imposition of combat rules and regulations, and the strict discipline required of *karateka,* enabled a potentially lethal activity to be enjoyed as a sport.

TAMASHIWARA (wood-breaking) is a subject about which there is a difference of opinion within karate. All exponents would agree that *karateka* should be capable of such feats of strength and that it is the natural outcome of techniques properly executed, but some believe that its public performance is merely flashy showmanship. Such showmanship might include breaking a stack of twenty roofing tiles or three or four 1-inch boards with the hand, foot, elbow, or head. Other demonstrations might include throwing a water-melon into the air and thrusting the fingers through it as it descends, or chopping off the top of a bottle with the bare hand while leaving the bottle standing.

The advocates of *tamashiwara* would claim that it is an integral part of karate and that it is a physical, psychological, and even spiritual necessity. Their arguments would include the following: the various striking parts of the body possess quite remarkable power, but this power can be released only when the *karateka* has rid himself of the fear of striking something hard. Breaking, or destruction as it is sometimes called, is therefore a psychological as well as a physical ordeal, especially in public, and its successful execution gives self-confidence and self-knowledge. The word *tamashi* in fact means 'trial'. These styles therefore require their members to demonstrate before being upgraded as proof of their physical and mental ability.

The other argument for breaking is more esoteric, even religious. The self-discipline required is such that the strike at wood is more a strike at oneself. The total commitment to the blow is a discipline which requires the *karateka* to transcend his normal nature and enter the Zen world of nothingness, where he is momentarily united with the universe. The essence of *tamashiwara* is therefore enlightenment through a single blow in what amounts to active Zen meditation.

KIHON is basic training in numerous blocks, strikes, and kicks with special emphasis on correct stance, balance, breathing, and focus. *Kihon* may be practised individually or in groups. When practised in groups it is normally accompanied by semi-hypnotic chanting from a leader who thereby controls the timing and effort involved.

Many different stances are used with a variety of foot and hand positions, each of which is linked to certain appropriate moves. Stances with a wide foot base and a low centre of gravity are very stable and suited to powerful punching; others are designed for mobility and speed of action. A good *karateka* will command a variety of stances and vary them according to the circumstances. For example, in the *jion* position, the foot position is wide, the centre of gravity low, and stability great. The arm position appears to invite a strike to the head but it is in fact only provocative. The head and upper body are easily defended and set attacks can follow. The 'reclining dragon' (*gargu-kamae*) stance emphasizes protection of the vital parts of the body from attack and the front of the body is turned away from the opponent. In the 'cat' (*neko-ashi-dachi*) stance 90 per cent of the body weight is on the rear foot and the front foot is poised for kicking. This stance facilitates very rapid change of position and posture.

Almost all sports employ the principle of circular movement to generate power. The discus thrower generates velocity by rotating in a manner which enables the power generated by the hips and legs to be transmitted via an extended arm to the discus, which is thrown at the moment of maximum velocity. In a similar way, *karateka* use rotary movements to transmit velocity and power to the striking limb. In some respects their movements resemble whirling tops. This movement not only unbalances the opponent but, just as a rotating throw of a discus is more effective than a standing throw, the rotation adds to the power of the blow, because it enables maximum use of leg and hip strength to be utilized.

Focus is the art of concentrating all one's physical and mental energies on a specific target in an instant. It is rather like a person trapped in a blazing room being able to produce on demand the strength to knock down the door in a way he would normally find quite impossible. It is said to involve a spontaneous explosion of the life force (*chi*) which flows from the pelvic region to the extremities and points of contact. To generate maximum speed, the striking limb is kept relaxed until immediately before impact. On impact the body tenses and the *karateka* emits a *kiai* or yell which is propelled by the muscles of the lower diaphragm. This psychologically assists a total commitment to the punch and the muscular effort involved adds to the power produced. The object is to transmit, via the correct use of stance, breathing, and timing, the muscular power of the whole body down a striking limb moving at maximum speed, to focus on a given object.

The word 'Zen' is a contraction of the Sanskrit *Zen-no* meaning 'silent meditation', and is supposed to denote the fundamental truth pervading all Buddhist sects. The prime object of Zen is cultivation of the ability to bring mental perturbation under immediate control in order to subdue worldly passions and enable a clear perception of the Great Truth. Breath-control plays an important part in this process and karate has adopted these breathing techniques and some of Zen's philosophical aspects for its own purposes.

All martial arts have their own peculiar breathing patterns. Karate's are designed to ensure a state of mental calm and to facilitate maximum explosiveness. Although ordinarily we inhale and exhale unconsciously, the *karateka* is consciously aware of four phases when doing breathing exercises. The first phase is inhalation through the nose until the lungs are full of air. The second phase involves an effort to force all the air downwards on to the diaphragm. Although, to western rationalism, this is biologically impossible, the muscular effort involved develops a strong abdomen, which is fundamentally important to the *karateka* as he believes this area to be his source of strength. By concentrating his attention and breathing in the area above his diaphragm, and by the use of *kiai* when punching, he is able to generate remarkable power. The third phase is to exhale quietly through the nose, and the fourth to make a final effort to force all the air out.

There are many different breathing exercises but one of the most intriguing is *ibuki* breathing. This involves a tensing of all the muscles after inhaling, particularly the abdominal muscles. The mouth is then opened wide and, with the teeth lightly biting the back of the tongue, the air is emitted with a rasping sound. When he feels that all the air has been exhaled, the *karateka* makes one more effort to force the last bit of air from his lungs.

In karate the whole of the body, and in particular all the bony parts, are used as weapons. An experienced *karateka* can utilize even a single finger, suitably strengthened, as a highly effective weapon. In fact, other things being equal, the smaller the area of contact the more effective the blow will be. A rigid finger, if strengthened to withstand impact, would have an effect similar to that of a sword point.

The hand can be used in a great variety of ways for punching and striking. The contact points include the fist (*seiken*), the inverted

The 'cat' stance (neko-ashi-dachi)

The 'reclining dragon' stance (gargu-kamae)

The jion stance

KARATE STANCES

fist (*uraken*), the fist edge (*tettsui*), the knife hand (*shuto*), the palm heel (*shotei*), the wrist (*koken*), the fingertips or spear hand (*nukite*), the fingertips and thumb or chicken's beak (*keiko*), and the half-clenched fist (*hiraken*). The elbow and forearm can also be used.

The variation in the use of the foot is not as great as that of the hand, but includes the following: the knife foot (*sokuto*), the instep (*haisoku*), the heel (*kakato*), and the ball of the foot (*chusoku*). The knee and head may also be used in in-fighting.

Modern karate is a product of the twentieth century. Its roots, however, can be traced back through the centuries to before the time of Christ, and Okinawa, China, and India, as well as Japan, have all contributed substantially to its development.

India originated yoga and through its diaphragmatic breathing methods has exerted a substantial influence on the many combat techniques of the Orient and ultimately upon karate. *Karateka* place special emphasis on the need for powerful diaphragms and utilize strong exhalations of air to assist muscle contraction, thereby increasing power. Also, as the disturbing effect of emotions, such as fear, upon breathing are well known, *karateka* exploit the relationship to ensure a state of mental calm. This they do by the use of controlled breathing which itself has a calming effect upon the emotions.

Special breathing techniques were therefore India's contribution to the development of karate and date back to at least the fifth and sixth centuries B.C. It was at this time that the first records of Indian combat techniques were written and were subsequently classified in the *Lotus Sutra* into the categories of joint locks, blows, and throws.

Surprising though it may at first seem, the Buddhist priesthood acquired considerable fighting skills and it was via Zen Buddhism that these yoga techniques were transmitted to China. As the priests were itinerant, lived in time of warring principalities, and were frequently faced by villagers of a hostile faith, it is perhaps not so surprising that they were skilled in self-defence.

Legend has it that at the end of the fifth century A.D., a Zen Buddhist priest named Bhodidharma travelled to China to instruct at the monastery of Shaolin-ssu. The aim of Buddhism is the salvation of the soul but, as the body and soul are inseparable, in order to attain true enlightenment, it is necessary to impose a severe physical as well as mental discipline. Bhodidharma found that the imposition of such discipline caused many of his student monks to collapse from sheer exhaustion. In order to improve their physical condition, he blended his knowledge of yoga and Indian fist arts with indigenous Chinese *kempo* (fighting) and used it as a form of physical training. The Shaolin-ssu Temple system of fighting was thus developed and became famous throughout China. The close relationship between Chinese *kempo* and medicine also resulted in the discovery of numerous vital spots on the human body. These are the spots to which the Chinese apply their medicines but they are also those which became the target of *kempo*, and later, karate attacks.

Although Shaolin-ssu *kempo* spread throughout China it gradually assumed different forms according to local conditions. To some extent this diversity is the genesis of the different forms or styles of modern karate. In south China numerous rivers and flooded paddy fields necessitate much boat-rowing and led to strong upper-body development, resulting in fighting methods in which arm and head movements predominate. In the north, animal husbandry and much riding has resulted in strong legs and a consequent emphasis on leg techniques. Smooth rounded movements have, however, remained a common denominator. China's contribution therefore lies in the discovery of vital striking points and in the formulation of certain fighting techniques. These were subsequently carried to the offshore islands by successive waves of emigrants and refugees.

Okinawa is the main island in the Ryukyu Islands chain which stretches from southern Japan to Taiwan (Formosa), and as such it is a natural stepping-stone for the movement of ideas from the mainland to the islands. Combat techniques known simply as *te* (hand) had existed for many centuries in Okinawa, but with the unification of the country in 1470 and the imposition of laws against carrying arms, *te* received a substantial boost. Later, with the assistance of Chinese *kempo* masters who fled from China in times of political upheaval, this developed into an early form of *kara-te* (empty hand). At first the new techniques became known as Tang Hand, to indicate their Chinese origin — Tang being the name of a Chinese dynasty, the symbol for which later became associated with China in general. It was not until after 1922, when FUNAKOSHI GICHIN, an Okinawan, first introduced Tang Hand or Okinawa-te to Japan and it incorporated certain aspects of Japanese JU-JITSU that it acquired the name of karate.

The name karate, however, implies more than is immediately obvious. Gichin wrote: 'As a mirror's polished surface reflects whatever stands before it and a quiet valley carries even small sounds, so must the student of karate render his mind empty of selfishness and wickedness in an effort to react appropriately towards anything he might encounter. This is the meaning of ''*kara*'' in karate.'

The name was chosen to convey the Zen concept of emptiness and the student *karateka* is required to empty his mind of all thought, especially over-concern with tactics or strategy, and emotions such as fear, in the pursuit of his *budo* (martial way, or way of the fighter). An incorrect mental attitude would inevitably have a deleterious effect even upon the most skilled technician, and the *karateka*

therefore trains to the point of automatic reactions where external considerations do not intrude into his mental state of impassivity or emptiness.

Karate involves a training of the mind as well as the body and apart from being a system of defence and a sport, it is a physical manifestation of Zen Buddhism. Karate is action and Zen is meditation.

In the years following Gichin's arrival in Japan, other styles of karate were developed, several being introduced by other Okinawan masters. Each of these styles stressed its own specific objectives, techniques, and rules of competition. MABUNI arrived in 1930 and founded the *shitoryu* style. A third Okinawan, MIYAGI, who had travelled extensively in China, combined the hard Okinawan forms with the flowing Chinese forms and developed what he called the *go-ju*, or 'hard-soft' method of fighting. Many other styles also developed including *wadoryu* ('way of peace', founded by OTSUKA), *shukukai* ('way for all', founded by TANI) and *kyokushinkai* ('the peak of truth', founded by OYAMA). Rivalry was intense but inter-group competition unthinkable. Each group practised in secret and their respective *katas* were closely guarded from prying eyes. Thus within karate there developed a conspicuous lack of unity.

Following the Second World War, and partly due to the presence of many western servicemen in Japan, karate gradually acquired devotees in Europe and the Americas. During the late 1950s and the 1960s this process accelerated and by 1970 this sport was practised extensively throughout the world.

In order to bring some degree of unity to it, the Federation of All Japan Karate-do Organizations (F.A.J.K.O.) was formed with government backing in 1964 and most of the major schools affiliated to it. A slow but similar process has gradually been taking place in western countries. In 1970 F.A.J.K.O. organized the first multi-style world karate championships in Tokyo and in the ensuing conference it was agreed that a world governing body for karate be set up to be known as the World Union of Karate-do Organizations.

An organization similar to F.A.J.K.O. was also formed in Britain in 1967. This is a federal all-style organization which by 1973 had in membership 10 separate style associations in England and Scotland. In the second world championships held in Paris in 1972, an all-style British team became the first team ever to defeat Japan in international competition. Karate had truly become an international sport.

M. Nakayama, *Dynamic Karate* (1967); M. Oyama, *Advanced Karate* (1970); T. Suzuki, *Karate-do* (1967).

KARPF, SAMUEL, was the first secretary of the American Bowling Congress and played a major part in the early development of tenpin BOWLING. He was also the organizer of the A.B.C.'s first championship, the first major tenpin event, at Chicago in 1901.

KARTING, the sport of racing karts, is a form of MOTOR RACING. The kart is a tiny wheeled vehicle, usually consisting of a body-less tubular frame with a small-capacity single-cylinder two-stroke engine mounted towards the rear, and providing a single seat for the driver.

The kart's wheelbase must be between 40 and 50 in. (1·016-1·270 m.), and its track must be at least two-thirds of the wheelbase up to a maximum of 45 in. (1·143 m.). The maximum over-all length of the kart is 72 in. (1·828 m.) in most countries apart from the U.S.A., where a 60-in. (1·524 m.) limit is in force. The sport of racing these vehicles is firmly established in its country of origin — the U.S.A. — and in all European countries, as well as in Australia, Brunei, Cyprus, Gibraltar, Hawaii, Hong Kong, Japan, Kenya, Kuwait, Macao, Malaysia, the Marshall Islands, New Zealand, the Philippines, Rhodesia, South Africa, and Thailand.

Precise regulations differ from country to country but basic stipulated dimensions include a maximum tyre diameter of between 9 and 12½ in. (228-318 mm.), and a maximum kart height of 24 in. (609 mm.). The wheels themselves may be formed in a variety of materials, pressed steel, nylon, aluminium, and sand-cast alloys all being popular. They are attached to live rear axles in almost every case, and suspension is very rare. The rear axles usually run in self-aligning bearings mounted rigidly to a supple and whippy chassis frame. Flexing of the frame provides all the suspension movement necessary.

Class regulations again differ internationally, but they are broadly divided into karts with gear-boxes and karts without. Great Britain has the highest proportion of racing karters to population, and Royal Automobile Club (R.A.C.) regulations divide karts into five classes. The basic division is for junior drivers aged 13–16 years and Class I modified karts. Maximum capacity here is 100 cc., the engine price is limited, and no more than two carburettors may be used. Gear-boxes are forbidden, the karts being bump-started and using a direct drive from engine to rear axle. Minimum weight limits are applied to kart and

driver, the junior combination having to exceed 220 lb. (99·8 kg.) in most cases, and the seniors 264 lb. (119·7 kg.). An extensive list of recognized engines is published for this class, and these include units from Aspera, Bultaco, Clinton, DEM, Erikaze, Guazzoni, Harper-Vincent, Homelite, JAP, JLO, Konig, McCulloch, Montesa, Power Products, Stihl, Villiers, West Bend, and Ydral. Generally better power outputs are available from the BM, certain Guazzoni, Komet, Parilla, Saetta, and Silvercar motors and, if these are used, the junior weight limit is raised to 240 lb. (108·8 kg.), the senior figure remaining the same.

The British Class I Super also caters for 100 cc. engines, but these are more expensive and more sophisticated units including many of the potent Italian rotary-valve engines. Gear-boxes appear in the Class IV Standard division, a special class catering solely for the Villiers engines of 200 cc. capacity, with a limit to one carburettor and a minimum kart/driver weight of 350 lb. (158·8 kg.). Class IV Super is generally accepted as the upper echelon of racing karts, with a range of 200 cc. motors driving through a gear-box, no limit on the number of carburettors fitted, a high maximum engine-price allowance, and a range of sophisticated and powerful units available. These include engines from Ariel, Bridgestone, DKW, Maico, Merlin, Ossa, Puch, SUZUKI, and Zundapp.

Free-formula karting is virtually provided by the 250 cc. experimental division, which is not very well supported but which caters for karts with air-cooled two-stroke engines with no more than two cylinders, and a capacity of between 201 and 250 cc. A compulsory maximum limit of five gears is placed on the transmission.

In Australia karting is governed by the National Kárting Association (N.K.A.) which in turn is affiliated to the national motor sporting authority, the Confederation of Australian Motor Sports (C.A.M.S.). Class divisions include the Supers, of 100 cc., 131 cc., 154 cc., and 200 cc. capacity, running with any modifications and any fuel except nitrated mixtures. The Limited section entries must run on petrol and one carburettor, with a capacity limit of 100 cc. while Class A Standard caters for McCulloch MC10 motors and B Standard for 105-131 cc. motors with piston timing. This latter division features modified Victa lawn-mower engines.

European and American rules are generally similar to the British ones, and international competition ensures that there is a close parity in the equipment used. Karting is an exciting, yet inexpensive sport and long-distance international matches are rare, hence the disparity between British and European rules and those in force in the Antipodes and elsewhere.

Race meetings are normally held on temporary short-distance courses marked out for the occasion by straw-bale barriers. Due to their small size, a large number of karts may be started on a narrow and quite short circuit, and such competitions lead to the development of split-second timing and intense concentration on the part of the drivers. On the faster circuits most karts can easily exceed 100 m.p.h. (161 km./h.) and lap averages of 80 m.p.h. (129 km./h.) are commonplace. With a number of evenly matched karts travelling at such speeds on a narrow circuit the necessity for good judgement and reflexes is evident.

Dependent on the design and class of the kart, the methods of starting a race differ. The Class I direct-drive karts, lacking a gear-box or clutch, are drop-started by helpers who lift the tail end of the kart, with the driver already aboard, push it forward a few paces, and then drop the rear wheels on to the road in order to start the engine. The complete field of karts for any race are started more or less simultaneously in this way. They will then take up a grid formation as they complete a slow lap of the circuit, passing the flag in a flying start. The clutch and gear-box karts are sometimes push-started, the clutch being released to fire the motor; motor cycle kick-starts are sometimes fitted. Grid positions are normally allotted by ballot, and the clutch karts are formed up in a stationary grid formation, making a clutch start as the flag falls.

Kart circuit venues vary, but sections of airfields are popular in Great Britain, Australia, and parts of America and Europe, while other temporary sites include car parks, sea-fronts, and even full-size motor racing circuits, whose permanent facilities offer greater spectator attraction. Some of the best-equipped kart circuits in the world are to be found in Italy, the home of the dominant rotary-valve engines, where several fine permanent facilities have been developed and used purely for kart racing.

Engine tuning and chassis settings vary in accordance with the circuits being used and the type of event to be contested. When racing on full-scale motor racing circuits with their long straights and wide-radius open corners, a very high final drive ratio must be selected to prevent the engine over-revving. Carburettor changes will be made in order to provide the maximum amount of power at the upper end of the engine's rev. band, rather than somewhere in the middle where it is so necessary on the shorter, tighter courses. Carburettor jets must be very carefully selected for a long-circuit race, for the slightest over-leanness of the mixture will lead to an engine seizure. With direct drive karts a seized engine immediately locks the rear wheels and this can prove extremely dangerous.

With the advent of the rotary-valve engines exhaust tuning has become of paramount importance and an engine's characteristics can be altered from short-circuit to long-circuit use by fitting a different design and length of exhaust pipe. Brakes are worked very hard on a short circuit, the succession of corners giving them little chance to cool, while on the longer circuits they may seldom reach an acceptable operating temperature.

Long-distance races, lasting perhaps 6 or 24 hours, also offer a particular type of challenge, for in these reliability, endurance, and strategy are all-important. Good organization and speedy pit work gains valuable seconds in these events and they are generally of a cooler and more cerebral character than the frenetic activity of a 15-lap short-circuit sprint.

Popular variations on the kart-racing theme are found in Canada, Russia, and Scandinavia where events are held on ice circuits laid out on frozen rivers or lakes. The only notable modification made to the basic kart for these events is the fitting of spiked tyres to give grip and traction on the ice.

Since the sport became established internationally in 1959 a regular world championship has been arranged, together with national championships, team championships run on an international basis, and a number of recognized classic events such as the Paris Six-Hours, Shenington Six-Hours, and Danish Grand Prix are run annually.

Karting and karts are American inventions dating from August 1956 when the first tiny tubular-framed vehicle, which we would now call a kart, was built. Its conception stemmed from a commercial failure on the part of the McCulloch chainsaw and outboard motor manufacturing company which, in trying to diversify its interests, designed a rotary lawn mower and bought some 10,000 West Bend 750 cc. engines to power them. Unfortunately, the mowers proved unreliable and, to safeguard their good name, McCulloch discontinued the range and were left with about 8,000 of the engines in store. Ingels, a mechanic working with the Kurtis Craft racing car company in Glendale, California, built his minuscule tube-framed vehicle that August and a neighbour named Borelli bought one of the engines to power it. At first the 2½ h.p. engine was too underpowered to carry the 'kart' and its driver up inclines, so Borelli modified the unit until it could propel the 15-stone (95 kg.) Ingels with ease.

The two men used the cart for joy-riding off the road, but in September 1956 the operators of a car-silencer business saw the kart and set to work to build two replicas. Interest was enormous and led Ingels and Borelli to go into business laying down an initial batch of six machines. Surplus engines from McCulloch provided the motive power, and by early 1957 the dozen or so kart-owners were meeting at week-ends and searching for suitable car parks or other open areas in which to run their vehicles. To call these meetings races would be an exaggeration, but police disapproval soon led these early karters to find a safe site in the Rose Bowl car park at Pasadena. Many inquiries came from the public who stopped to watch the proceedings and in spring 1957 the Go Kart Company was formed by Wineland, Livingstone, and Desbrow, as a subsidiary of their silencer business. Production of these McCulloch-powered karts quickly reached 500 per month. Meetings at the Rose Bowl got out of hand, the movement lost their informal venue, and on 14 December 1957 the first meeting of the Go Kart Club of America was convened.

Boberick and Patchen drew up a set of rules which exist in virtually unchanged form today. These demand a wheelbase of 40 to 50 in. (1·016–1·270 m.), and a minimum track width of two-thirds the wheelbase length. Capacity divisions were set at 84 cc., 168 cc., and 270 cc., and, with their sport now regularized, club officials managed to arrange properly sanctioned race meetings in the car park of the Eastland Shopping Centre in West Covina. The first organized kart race took place here in late December 1957.

Many more companies producing karts sprang up, and in September 1958 the first karts arrived in Britain, ordered by a U.S.A.F. officer serving at Burtonwood. These karts were run mainly among U.S.A.F. personnel, but back in America changes took place with the adoption of Clinton engines. When the supply of West Bend units was eventually exhausted, capacity divisions were altered to 95 cc., 190 cc., and 270 cc. and these finally settled at 100 cc., 200 cc., and 270 cc. limits in the early 1960s.

Press coverage of the new American sport led to considerable interest overseas, particularly in England where all branches of motor sport were strongly supported. A number of small manufacturers and club groups produced karts and in August 1959 a demonstration of karting was given at a SILVERSTONE motor race meeting. The R.A.C. then called a meeting of interested parties and formulated rules which included the provision of a gear-box as used on the British-made Villiers engines. A public demonstration at BRANDS HATCH circuit was mobbed and the first British race meeting was held at Lakenheath in November.

The sport quickly developed in Britain, proving cheap yet fast and extremely exciting. Karting subsequently became established throughout Europe, the U.S.A., Australia and New Zealand, Japan, and many other Asiatic nations, but after the initial boom period of the early 1960s a serious recession occurred in the U.S.A. and several other countries. International regulations became based on the R.A.C. requirements, and, as enthusiasts began to discover the nuances of engineering required to produce a really competitive kart, wheels and tyres became lighter but wider, and more powerful engines were produced.

Class I karts used American Clinton A400 and A490 engines at first, producing some 2½ b.h.p., but the German JLO unit was soon found to produce a reliable 4½ b.h.p. Class IV karts, complying with regulations formulated around the Villiers engine and gear-box, changed beyond recognition in 1960 when the Spanish Bultaco engine attained popularity with its 20 b.h.p. output from 200 cc. But the American McCulloch engines still dominated internationally in Class I and II until the advent of the rotary-valve Saetta engine from Italy.

Chassis frame design toyed with scaled-down space-frames similar to those used in full-size racing cars in these early days, but by 1966 the flat, whippy ladder frame had become almost universal. Meetings were still being run on corners of lonely airfields, but in 1964 the first full-scale motor-racing circuit meeting was run at OULTON PARK in England. The Italian Tecno kart company introduced a chassis design with the engine mounted beside the driver's seat rather than behind it, and the better weight distribution this layout offered gave the Tecno a marked edge in performance. Its competitors subsequently copied the layout, but while the Spanish Bultaco and Montesa engines were very widely used international meetings became dominated by the rotary-valve Italian engines from Saetta and Parilla.

The Americans quickly developed long-distance races, events which have had few imitators elsewhere. Highly specialized equipment was developed for such 'enduros', including reclining karts on which the driver lay flat on his back, peering forward between his feet and flanked by large fuel tanks which enabled him to last the distance without making refuelling stops. The performances of such low-frontal area devices led the International Karting Federation (I.K.F.) to change one of the basic rules (acknowledged throughout the world) that the maximum length of a kart should be 72 in. (1·828 m.). American karts are now limited to a 60-in. (1·524 m.) over-all length.

Karting's international growth was extremely rapid. The Iron Curtain countries' first karts were built as early as 1961 at Kursk, U.S.S.R., while those countries where U.S. servicemen were stationed adopted the sport earlier than most. To some extent it is unfortunate that American karting is so far removed from Europe, for the so-called world championships are usually contested only by European teams. The first championship meeting was held in 1959 in the U.S.A. and was won by Yamane's McCulloch-powered special. Britain's Allen won in 1960 and 1961, and since the mid-sixties the Italians Sala and Raganelli have shared the title.

Other karting activities apart from pure racing include dragging, sprinting, hill-climbing, and even a circumnavigation of the world which took America's Mott three and a half years to complete.

KATA, see KARATE.

KATO, SAWAO (1946-   ), Japanese gymnast who was supreme at the 1968 and 1972 Olympics, winning the combined exercises titles on both occasions. His marvellous dexterity and all-round ability in the sport also brought him gold medals in the floor exercises and team event in Mexico and parallel bars and team event in Munich.

KAWAGUCHI, TAKAO (1950-   ), Japanese JUDO fighter whose neat throwing techniques brought him the world lightweight title in 1971, the Olympic gold medal in 1972, and a silver medal in the world championships the following year.

K.B. COPENHAGEN, Association FOOTBALL club. Founded in 1876 as a ROUNDERS club and known as Kjøbenhavns Boldklub, it is generally referred to as K.B. in both Danish and European football competitions. The club was among those that helped to form the Danish Boldspil Union (the national Football Association) in 1889, and it won the Danish championship for the first time in the season ending 1891. The club's leading players include N. Middelboe, who later played football in England, Laursen, Jorgensen, and Pilmark.

COLOURS: Blue and white striped shirts, black shorts.

KEINO, KIPCHOGE (1940-   ), middle-distance runner for Kenya. Ranking with ABEBE BIKILA as one of the outstanding names in African ATHLETICS history, Keino emerged as a world-beater in 1965 when he won two gold medals (1,500 metres and 5,000 metres) at the PAN-AFRICAN GAMES and also broke world records for 3,000 metres in 7 min. 39·6 sec. and 5,000 metres in 13 min. 24·2 sec. A year later he won the COMMONWEALTH GAMES titles at a mile and 3 miles, the latter involving one of his several victories over RON CLARKE. Naturally accustomed to medium altitude conditions, Keino came into his own in 1968 at Mexico City where he defeated RYUN for the Olympic 1,500 metres gold medal only three days after taking a bronze medal in the 5,000 metres. In the 1972 Olympics Keino won a gold medal in the 3,000 metres STEEPLECHASE and a silver in the 1,500 metres. Apart from the performances mentioned, his best times were 3 min. 34·9 sec. for 1,500 metres, 3 min. 53·4 sec. for the mile, and 12 min. 57·4 sec. for 3 miles. He turned professional in 1973.

KELETI, AGNES (1931-   ), Hungarian gymnast who would have been even more successful had she not reached her peak before the European championships were introduced in 1957. In addition, she suffered from a weakness on the vault which often cost her higher placings. Her partnership with another Hungarian, Korondi, presented the chief rivalry to the Russians during the 1950s. She won a gold medal at the floor exercises in the 1952 OLYMPIC GAMES but four years later met the Russian, LATYNINA, at the Melbourne Olympics. Keleti took gold medals on the floor exercises, the bars, and on the beam but her persistent weakness on the vault enabled Latynina to snatch the combined exercises title from her by a mere 0·30 points. After the Games Keleti, like many of her compatriots, did not return to Hungary and spent many years in Australia and the U.S.A. During the 1960s she was national coach to Israel.

KELLER, CARSTEN (1939-   ), HOCKEY player for West Germany and Berliner H.C., both of whose parents were German international players. He started his international career in 1958 as a goal-scoring forward and was capped over 90 times by Germany as an attacker. He switched to full-back and later played as a link, taking his total of caps to 123. He played in the 1960 OLYMPIC GAMES as a forward and captained Germany in the 1968 and 1972 Olympics. He was one of the world's greatest players outdoors and when INDOOR HOCKEY became established in Europe in the 1950s he was regarded as the leading exponent of that game.

KELLY, GEOFFREY ALAN (1921-   ),
lawn BOWLS player who represented Australia
in the singles and pairs, with H. Palm, in the
inaugural 1966 world bowls championships at
KYEEMAGH in October 1966, at which he won
a gold medal in the pairs. He played his first
inter-state match for N.S.W. at the age of 26
and is believed to be the youngest man ever to
have represented N.S.W. in competitive
bowls. He represented Australia in the 1970
COMMONWEALTH GAMES.

KELLY, JOHN B., sr. (1891-1960), outstanding American oarsman and sculler (see
ROWING). He won three Olympic titles: the
single and double sculls in 1920 and the
doubles again in 1924. A man of powerful
build, weighing over 14 stone (88·9 kg.), he
was the first American to win an Olympic
sculling title. His name is associated with an
unhappy incident in the Diamond Sculls at
HENLEY ROYAL REGATTA in 1920. Kelly
belonged to the VESPER BOAT CLUB of Philadelphia which had been barred from competing at Henley since an alleged infringement of
amateur status in 1905, as a result of which
Kelly's entry for the Diamond Sculls was
refused. This caused some ill feeling at the
time but in 1947 and 1949, Kelly, the father of
Princess Grace of Monaco, had the satisfaction of seeing his son, J. B. Kelly, jr., win the
Diamonds.

KELSO (1957), a gelding by Your Host (a
grandson of HYPERION) out of Maid of Flight,
by Count Fleet (a winner of the American
triple crown) out of a daughter of MAN O'
WAR, was one of the most remarkable race-
horses to appear in the United States in recent
years. Kelso won 39 out of his 63 starts,
including the WASHINGTON INTERNATIONAL
and five JOCKEY CLUB GOLD CUPS, and set a
world record for a thoroughbred race-horse of
$1,977,896 won in stake money. He also put
up a world record time for 1½ miles (2,400 m.)
at 2 min. 23·8 sec., carrying 9 stone (57 kg.)
as a seven-year-old when winning the Washington International in November 1964. Kelso
was bred at CLAIBORNE FARM, owned by Mrs.
du Pont, trained by Hanford, and ridden by
Valenzuela.

KENDO, literally 'sword way', is the
Japanese art of sword fighting. It is very
popular in the country of its origin, partly
because of its tradition; but during the twentieth century it has spread to most parts of the
world, including Europe and North and South
America. Apart from Japan, the U.S.A.,
Canada, and Brazil are the strongest nations.
Kendo makes great physical demands but,

equally important, gives mental benefits. Th
kendoka (those who practise the sport) gai
much from the discipline it instils into it
pupils. In addition, many *kendoka* absorb th
background of Japanese history on whic
much of modern *kendo* is based. *Kendo* is pro
bably closer to its origins than any of the othe
outstandingly popular Japanese martial art
such as JUDO, KARATE, and *aikido*. As a
international sport it has flourished only com
paratively recently — the first world cham
pionships were staged in 1970.

Unlike European fencing which has bee
modernized since duelling days, *kendo* ha
altered little in its object or training since th
samurai (knightly) era in Japan. The object o
a *kendo* contest is to land two scoring blows o
an opponent's target area — one or mor
powerful cuts were needed to disable or kill
Samurai opponent. So in modern bouts th
time is extended, as it would have been in ba
tle, until one of the *kendoka* is defeated.

Women and children enjoy *kendo* trainin
and competitions. Women, indeed, alway
compete on equal terms with men but childre
have a lower level of practice and competition

All *kendoka* wear traditional dress of th
Samurai period. The feet are left bare
Hakama (flowing trousers) are worn togethe
with a *tare* (an apron, or groin protector). Th
keikogi (*kendo* jacket) is similar to the on
used in judo but worn tucked in the trousers
The hands and forearms are protected by
kote (heavily padded glove) and the chest i
covered by a *do* (breastplate), which is held i
place by cords fastened round the shoulders
Finally the *men* (a head-guard consisting of
steel visor and padded cloth) protects the head
throat, and shoulders. The *kendoka* holds
shinai (practice sword) — four selected, pol
ished staves of bamboo held together by a lon
sheath which forms the handle. There is
small leather cup at the tip and a cord from th
tip to the handle holds the 'sword' together. I
addition, leather binding, a third of the wa
from the point, prevents the staves from open
ing. A piece of tough hide is placed round th
handle as a sword-guard.

The *shinai* is up to 1·18 m. (3 ft. 10½ in.
long and weighs approximately ·40 kg. (1
oz.). But for *kata* (forms), a series of regu
larized movements, the *kendoka* dispense
with the body armour and wears only th
hakama and *keikogi* and holds a *bokken* (
wooden imitation of a real sword). For impor
tant formal demonstrations a real sword — a
katana — is often used, making the exhibitio
more lifelike and spectacular.

Owing to the vigorous nature of the sport,
hachimaki (a piece of towelling) is wrappe
round the head to prevent perspiration from

falling into the *kendoka*'s eyes during practice or competition. Frequently special towels are given to competitors in contests, while leading clubs invariably have their own designs.

The colour of *keikogi* denotes the competitor's grade. There is less emphasis on grading than in the other martial arts, but it is still a valuable method of assessing achievement and serves as a guide to the pupil's ability. A white *keikogi* denotes the lower, or *Kyu* (student) grades: 6th, 5th, 4th, 3rd, 2nd, and 1st *Kyu*; a black *keikogi* denotes the higher, or *Dan* (graduate) grades: 1st, 2nd, 3rd, 4th, 5th, 6th, 7th, 8th, 9th, and 10th *Dan*. From 4th *Dan* to 6th *Dan*, a *kendoka* may be awarded the title of *renshi* (doctor); and from 8th *Dan* to 10th *Dan*, that of *hanshi* (professor). Contest ability, mental discipline, and technical knowledge take a *kendoka* to 6th *Dan* after which advancement is obtained through teaching ability and service to the sport. For the *hanshi*, a *kendoka* must make some original research and take an examination set by the Technical Board of the All-Japan *Kendo* Association. The *hanshi* and *renshi* awards can be authorized only in Japan.

In contrast to the practice in other martial arts, a *kendoka* can be downgraded on technical ability as well as misconduct. Gradings are held biannually, and a *kendoka* must not only impress the examiner with his contest ability but also with his over-all knowledge of techniques. In addition he or she must have shown humility and conscientiousness in training and must be aware of the meaning of words and movements in the sport. The *kendoka* is assessed on performance both against the grading officer and against *kendoka* of equal rank. Men and women are graded together and there are no weight categories.

Shiai (contests) are conducted by a head judge who sits at a table outside the contest area. Three judges are stationed inside the area to assess the quality of the blows. They are the 'left forward' and 'right forward' judges — one of whom acts as a referee — and a 'rear' judge who follows the *kendoka* round the area. All maintain their allotted lines of vision. In addition there are two line judges who sit in opposite corners of the area.

The contest area is between 9 m. (29 ft. 6 in.) and 11 m. (36 ft.) square and is made of smooth, highly-polished wood. The boundaries are marked by white lines and the centre of the area by a white cross. The participants' starting lines are drawn 1·5 m. (4 ft. 11 in.) from the centre so that the competitors begin 3 m. (9 ft. 10 in.) from each other.

The length of a contest varies from four to ten minutes, depending on grade, with extensions if necessary. There are no rounds but if

Migi-do (right side of rib-cage)

Striking position for *o-shomen* (centre of the head)

Migi-men (right side of head)

Hidari-kote (left forearm)

KENDO CUTS
Figures are shown in masks and aprons, aiming blows with the *shinai* at the prescribed target areas

one of the *kendoka* lands two decisive blows this is sufficient to end the bout. The three mobile judges have authority on the conduct of the match and declare when a decisive blow is scored by raising a red or white flag — competitors are identified by these colours on their backs. The line judges signal when a contestant goes outside the allotted area. At least two judges have to agree for a blow to be registered. The head judge acts as the final authority on the validity of blows and on the conduct of the contest. At the discretion of the head judge, one point may decide a contest instead of the usual two. The referee announces the results.

Kendoka may be penalized for infringements such as leaving the area, forcing an opponent from the area, striking illegal blows, and throwing an opponent deliberately to the ground. For the first offence a competitor receives a *chui* (caution) and for a further offence he is disqualified.

The judges' expressions include: *'Hajime'* (Begin); *'Yoshi'* (Carry on); and *'Tame'* (Halt). When the referee wishes to announce a decision he calls out the appropriate term, such as *'Menari'* (Cut to the head), *'Do-ari'* (Cut to the breast), *'Kote-ari'* (Cut to the arm), and *'Tsuki-ari'* (Thrust to the throat), and signals the scorer of the point by pointing his flag at the successful fighter. After this, the referee announces, *'Nihomme'* (Second point). If both contestants have scored, the referee calls, *'Shobu'* (Match point). When one of the contestants has scored two points, he calls, *'Shobu-ari* (There is a match point) and indicates the winner of the bout.

There are eight target areas: (1) *o-shomen*, centre of the head; (2) *hidari-men*, left side of the head; (3) *migi-men*, right side of the head; (4) *hidari-kote*, left forearm; (5) *migi-kote*, right forearm; (6) *gyaku-do*, left side of rib-cage; (7) *migi-do*, right side of rib-cage; (8) *tsuki*, throat. All are attacked by cuts except the throat which can be threatened only by a lunge. Competitors often use only one hand on the *shinai* in attempts to obtain extra distance, but the majority of the powerful blows are performed with two hands. In contests the areas most frequently attacked are the right forearm and the centre of the head. Individuals tend to favour a particular cut or combination of cuts.

The *kiai* (shout) is even more important in *kendo* than in the other martial arts. A score cannot be registered without the yell that accompanies the blow. The *kiai* has three functions: it emphasizes the point to be attacked, helps with the mental and physical co-ordination, and is used to unnerve an opponent.

The usual starting position in either contest or practice is for the two fighters to stand opposite each other with their right feet forward and the *shinai* held with the left hand at the bottom of the hilt and the right hand just below the sword guard. The points of the sword overlap about 25 mm. (1 in.). The left hand is placed just below the navel. The elbows are kept close to the *do* but relaxed, and the *shinai* is pointed at the opponent's throat. This basic starting position, which must be strictly adhered to, is called *chudan-n-kamae* (perfect distance).

All blows are *kiri* (cuts) in which a *kendoka* attacks his opponent with the cutting edge of the *shinai* — the side opposite to the cord joining the handle to the tip. The left hand is used to impart power and the right acts as a fulcrum. The basic cut — *o-shomen* (to the centre of the head) — is taught to all *kendoka* and a considerable amount of training is devoted to *suburi* (empty cutting). Here the *kendoka* aims to achieve control and accuracy.

All cuts emphasize correct posture. In particular, when striking the target, the arms should be fully stretched, the hips remaining square to the target. The feet should be parallel and the shoulders turned to allow the right arm to straighten freely. After striking, the *shinai* should slide freely up the target without being disengaged.

There is no defence for its own sake; any parry is used as preparation for an immediate counter-attack. Feints are sometimes used but a *kendoka* will often knock an opponent's arm or sword away before landing a powerful blow to the head. All blows are accompanied not only by a *kiai* but also by a rapid series of short steps. The cut lands as the right foot comes sharply to the ground and the steps continue as the slicing movement of the *shinai* goes over the target.

The ultimate aim of the *kendoka* dates back to the *Samurai* age when a good swordsman would wait until his opponent was about to attack and then launch his own cut. By anticipating an attack, he chooses exactly the right moment, since his opponent in this split second can neither defend nor anticipate the attack.

Kendoka begin each session with exercises before putting on the armour. The practice commences with *suburi*, then they move on to *kiri kaeshi*, when they perform a series of cuts and the other *kendoka* parries. Competitors also practise *kakarigeiko*, in which they attack openings as the opponent makes them. *Kendoka* spend much time in *keiko* (free practice) in which contest situations may be freely practised without the fighter feeling obliged to win, as in a competition.

KATA EXERCISES IN KENDO
The figure at right demonstrates the basic cut, *o-shomen* (to the centre of the head), with a *bokken*, or imitation of a real sword.

Real swords, which can be used for *kata*, must be handled with extreme care since they are very sharp. No attempt should be made to use them in practice until at least 1st *Dan* has been reached. *Kata* is often used at the end of training sessions to improve technique.

Most *kendoka* use only one *shinai* but in the *nito-ryu* (two-sword school) the long sword is held in the right hand and the *shoto* (small sword) in the other. Great determination is necessary to attack a *nito* swordsman, since an opponent can use both swords to attack and defend.

In international competition and in the All-Japan championships, held annually, the pool system is usually employed. There are two types of team contests. In the first, each side is represented by one junior (under 16 years old) and one low *Kyu* grade, one middle *Kyu* grade, one high *Kyu* grade, and a low or high *Dan*, making five in all. This has the advantage of giving a truer indication of strength. In the other version, as strong a side as a club or country can produce is fielded. If the scores are level then the two captains fight off.

Kendo tradition requires a strict self-discipline. Much of the etiquette is still preserved and forms an important part of the training. For instance all practices are preceded by a bow to one's opponent and there are kneeling bows before and after training sessions. A *kendoka* must always respect his superior, particularly the highest-graded member of the *dojo* (training hall) who is called *sensei* (teacher). At bows he sits on his own side of the *dojo* with the other *Dan* grades to his right on the far side. The *Kyu* grades sit opposite the *sensei* and below the other *Dan* grades. The *dojo* must have an atmosphere of calmness at all times and personal politeness is important. Talking is discouraged during training sessions and unpunctuality is frowned upon.

Kendo developed from *kenjutsu* (swordsmanship) which was essential for survival in medieval Japan. The *Samurai* (knights) needed a method of training which was not lethal and so *kendo*, which uses a bamboo fencing stave rather than the original razor-sharp sword, was originated. Its tiring training, need for self-discipline, and close links with ancient Japan, have made *kendo* both physically and mentally beneficial.

The origins of *kendo* go back more than 1,500 years. The first references to *kenjutsu* are in the three volumes of the *Kojiki*, a medieval history. These deal with the period from the mythological ages to the Empress Suiko (A.D. 592-628). The 30 volumes of the *Nihon-Shoki*, from the mythological ages to Empress Jito (A.D. 686-97), also contain references to *kenjutsu*. Japanese historians use these two reliable documents to cover all aspects of ancient history. It is in these that there is a mention of a school of swordsmanship — *Choisai Iizasa*; another reference is to Kunimatsu no Mahito, who was a direct descendant of Amatsu Koyane no Mikoto, a highly respected swordsman.

The earliest reference to any non-lethal practice weapon is about A.D. 400 — the *bokken* which was a wooden sword whose weight, length, and balance were approximately the same as a real one. This was followed by the skill of *tachikaki*, now known as *iai*, the art of drawing sword. The *Samurai* practised many styles and types of cutting. When one was found to be effective in battle, a swordsman would absorb this into his style — so the various schools of swordsmanship were originated.

Like the other Japanese martial arts, *kendo* has innumerable *ryu* (schools). The earliest of these was *nen-ryu*, founded in 1350. There is some dispute as to who originated the style; some authorities say Kamisaka Yasuhisa and some Somashiro Yoshimoto. This style was taught until the eighteenth century by the Higuchi family but has now disappeared. There were probably earlier schools, because under the feudal system each *daimyo* (lord) kept a fencing master to instruct his family and retainers in the *dojo*.

The medieval period in Japanese history saw the real development of *kenjutsu*. It was an age in which the *Samurai* would challenge each other to duels which invariably ended in the death of one, or sometimes both. The *Samurai's* life was based on a philosophy of Bushido (the way of a warrior), an Oriental equivalent to the European code of chivalry. Honour was dearer than life, and patience was a required quality. The *Samurai's* most cherished possession was his sword. But to acquire outstanding skill required years of dedicated physical and mental training. The code was based on hard work, respect, and patience. The finest *kenjutsu* skills were practised endlessly by the *Samurai* who hoped that his reputation would enable him either to become a retainer to a lord or to open his own school.

In battle the *Samurai* scorned heavy armour — any that he wore was light, often of bamboo. He clutched a *katana* (sword) which was long but not as big as many European weapons. When opposed by an enemy, a *Samurai* would face him squarely and with cool patience force him to attack first. When attacked, he answered with a powerful stroke which would often cripple the opponent.

In this Muromashi period (1336-1568) the outstanding figure was Kagehisa Ittosai Ito. Nobody could match him in real combat and he is honoured as perhaps the most significant swordsman in Japanese *kendo* history. But, as well as possessing peerless technique, he was respected for his deep philosophical ideals, and his teaching ability. He founded his own style, *ito-ryu* (one-sword school), which has flourished ever since. Unlike many of the early styles it has not disappeared but has gained a formidable reputation for its hardness and vigour.

Other men, lile Hikida and Aisu, also opened schools. Many of them on reaching the age where they could no longer win matches or defeat pupils, would retreat to the mountains where they would spend the time contemplating and inventing new sword skills.

Two other important figures were Bokuden Tsukahara (1490-1572) and Musashi Miyamoto (1584-1645). Bokuden is reputed to have beaten 37 challengers without defeat. His amazing concentration and patience made him a leading *Samurai*; when he retired to a mountain to live as a hermit, he was visited by young *Samurai* eager for advice and instruction.

Probably the most popular and famous swordsman of all, however, was Miyamoto whose exploits are recalled in many fine Japanese films, including *The Seven Samurai*. He fought 60 duels and was never defeated. He met Sasaki, who had killed his father, on a beach in Kyushu and the terrible fight to the death is described in *kodan* (feudal romances). Miyamoto fulfilled the principle of being skilled in mental qualities as well as physical by writing his rare block-book, *Gorin ni Sho* (A Book of Five Rings). In addition, he is credited with the invention of the *nito* (two-sword) style, in which the *Samurai* would hold the ordinary long sword in his right hand and a *wakizashi* (short sword) in the other.

For many years real swords were used for training and, for safety reasons, practice duels were impossible. So the swordsmen used *kata* (forms), a set routine of moves, to practise all the contingencies that could arise in battle. All the martial arts, including judo and karate, use *kata* as a method of studying technique. In the *ito-ryu* style alone, there were over a hundred *katas* to be learnt.

With the advent of *bokken*, the origin of which is sometimes credited to Bokuden, more realistic practice bouts could be safely carried out. But bouts were still dangerous since fencers were less likely to hold back attacks, knowing their weapons were not lethal. Broken bones and heavy bruising were common. In 1750 Chuta Nakanishi made a great contribution to the development of *kenjutsu* by introducing the *kote* (glove) and the *shinai* (bamboo foil), which was an adjunct to the *katana* and *bokken*. He insisted that all students used *shinai* and *kote* during practice. The *shinai* brought a new sense of realism into the *dojo*. Cuts and slashes could be delivered with the utmost realism, the fencers being relieved of the dangers of injury. Between 1765 and 1770 a further step forward was made when the *do* (breast) plate was invented by Nakanishi.

The regulation length of the *shinai* (up to 1 m. — 39 in.) and the introduction of the *tare* (apron) and *men* (helmet) completed the equipment of the fencer. All these survive today and enable students to practise safely without being concerned with injury. With the protective armour came a set of rules and a new style of fencing called *kendo* which was to enjoy world-wide fame.

In 1780 the various *ryu* were faced with the problem of refining the enormous variety of positions and this culminated in the number of techniques being reduced to about a hundred. By now *kendo* had changed from a method of training for battle to a sport. This was recognized in 1871 when the Japanese Ministry of Education passed a regulation making *kendo* compulsory in public and private schools.

When the Japanese began to westernize themselves in the second half of the nineteenth century, the now underprivileged *Samurai* were unable to adapt themselves to a new way of life. They became redundant, their skills of swordsmanship, hitherto so valuable, being of little consequence in a modern army. *Samurai* power was further diminished by an ordinance forbidding men to carry arms.

The Meiji government (1868-1912) changed many of the Japanese customs and *kendo* was for many years in decline, despite numerous exhibitions which initially proved very popular with the public. The ordinary people had not been allowed, under the shoguns (chief ministers), to learn *kendo* or even watch it, but these exhibitions briefly aroused a new interest. However, with the people becoming more interested in western culture, *kendo* and other established customs came to be considered old-fashioned and out of place.

The Tokyo Police Bureau maintained their interest in the sport and men like Yamaoka, who died in 1888, kept it alive. Yamaoka was regarded as the outstanding *kendoka* in the era when the sport was in decline. His pupils, particularly men like Nakata, made great efforts to keep *kendo* going, but it was not until the start of the twentieth century that the sport began to flourish again.

In 1909 the first college *kendo* federation was formed at Tokyo University. The man behind it was Watanabe who was later elected the first president of the All-Japan College *Kendo* Federation, officially founded in 1928. The first president was Fukuda, who was to hold the post until the end of the Second World War.

The main functions of the Federation were to stage eight annual examinations and to grant grades. In addition, it encouraged growth overseas, the first country to take up the sport being the U.S.A., closely followed by Canada. Emigrating Japanese, eager to continue their sport, set up a number of clubs and organizations, and the first head of the American *Kendo Renmei* (association) was Terao (8th *Dan*), a well-known *kendoka*.

The first demonstration of *kendo* in Britain was in 1918 by KOIZUMI. The first memorable event was in 1937 when members of the Anglo-Japanese Judo Club gave a display at Hurlingham before Prince Chichibu. One of the most significant figures was Lidstone, whose work between the wars did much to keep the sport going. He was the chairman of the British *Kendo* Association which was formed just before the Second World War.

The outstanding figure after 1945 was Knutsen (4th *Dan*), whose tireless interest did much to popularize the sport, not only in Britain but also in Europe. He led the move to form the European *Kendo* Association which was established in 1968.

Numerous goodwill matches were held between the U.S.A. and Japanese universities, including a trip by an American team to Tokyo as early as 1940. Modern Japanese competitions consist of all-Japan championships, run on similar lines to the judo event, as well as regional events and championships restricted to the police, students, schoolteachers, etc. University sides also meet in annual championships with teams competing for titles.

The first European championships were held in London in 1969 and national championships are also held in member nations. The European *Kendo* Association consists of France, West Germany, Belgium, Sweden, and Great Britain. The first world championships were staged in Tokyo and Osaka in 1970. Japan predictably dominated the events — winning the team title and producing all four semi-finalists in the individual event. In the final, Kobayashi (6th *Dan*) upset Toda (5th *Dan*), twice all-Japan champion, for the title. Britain was among the 17 countries which took part in the event.

After the championships the competing countries formed the International *Kendo* Federation. The 1973 world championships were held in San Francisco and Los Angeles. The individual title was won by Sakuragi who beat his fellow Japanese Yano, three times national champion. Japan won the team championship, Canada finishing second.

Dr. J. Sasamori and Dr. G. Warner, *This is* Kendo (1965).

GOVERNING BODY (WORLD): International *Kendo* Federation, c/o All-Japan *Kendo* Federation, Nippon Budokan, 3-2 Chome, Kita No Maru Koen, Chiyoda-Ku, Tokyo, Japan.

KENSINGTON PARK, Bridgetown, CRICKET ground in Barbados, has a ground capacity of no more than 10,000, but the surrounds afford wide opportunities for non-paying spectators. Cricket is very popular among the inhabitants of this tiny island, and many of the best West Indian players have come from it. The pitch has often allowed high scoring: on it was played the longest innings ever — 337 in 999 minutes — by HANIF MOHAMMAD. It can also be treacherous: Trinidad were dismissed for 16 there in 1941-2.

KENTUCKY DERBY, horse race founded in 1875, the first leg of the American triple crown, run over a distance of $1\frac{1}{4}$ miles (2,000 m.) at CHURCHILL DOWNS, Louisville, Kentucky, early in May.

KENTUCKY OAKS is the American fillies' classic horse race run over 1 mile and $\frac{1}{2}$ furlong (1,700 m.) at CHURCHILL DOWNS, on the same day as the KENTUCKY DERBY.

KERR, GEORGE (1937-   ), Scottish JUDO fighter who won three European silver and two bronze medals during the 1960s. Kerr represented Britain before going to Japan in 1958 for three years. On his return he became an automatic member of the British team usually in the middleweight class although he sometimes weighed as much as 14 st. (88·9 kg.) for open events.

His excellent range of groundwork techniques, superb *uchi-mata* (inner thigh throw), and knowledge of amateur WRESTLING (he represented Britain at the 1965 world championships) brought his success. He won the 1966 and 1968 British open middleweight titles before retiring.

KERR, Revd. JOHN (1852-1920), Scottish curler. Author of *History of Curling* (1890), a classic book on the game, he was chaplain of the ROYAL CALEDONIAN CURLING CLUB, 1897-1913, and captain of the first Scottish CURLING team in Canada, 1902-3.

KERSHAW, CECIL ASHWORTH (1900-), RUGBY UNION scrum half for United Services, Portsmouth, Royal Navy, and England. Playing essentially as a link-man with his regular partner, W. J. A. DAVIES, and forwards like WAKEFIELD, Voyce, and Conway, Kershaw rarely kicked the ball although he scored some notable individual tries. FENCING contributed to the strength of his passing, and he was British sabre champion in 1920, 1925, and 1926.

KESSELS, OSCAR (1904-68), Belgian target archer and an administrator of outstanding ability, was pre-eminent among modern archers. He practised ARCHERY from 1930 and won major trophies in many countries. Of 24 world championship tournaments since 1931, he was selected 21 times for the Belgian team, an unequalled record. He was president of the Grand Serment Royal des Archers de Saint Sebastien de Bruxelles, of the Fédération Internationale de Tir à l'Arc, and of the Fédération Royale Belge de Tir à l'Arc.

KETCHEL, STANLEY (1887-1910), American boxer who held the world middleweight title from 1907 to 1908 and again until he was murdered in 1910. Often called the greatest of all middleweight champions, Ketchel believed in all-out attack and was so convinced of his own ability that he even floored JACK JOHNSON, to whom he was conceding 35 lb. (16 kg.), in a world heavyweight championship, before being knocked out. Ketchel, who won 46 out of 61 bouts by knockouts, lost his title to Papke in 1908 but regained it from him within three months.

KIERNAN, THOMAS JOSEPH (1939-), RUGBY UNION full-back for CORK CONSTITUTION, Ireland, and British LIONS. In 1973, against Argentina, he won his fifty-fifth cap for Ireland, improving his national record and equalling the world record of MEADS (New Zealand). A reliable place kicker, he scored over 100 points in international matches; in 1968, on his second Lions tour of South Africa, which he captained, he contributed 35 of the 38 British points in Test matches.

KIKNADZE, ANZOR (1934-), Russian JUDO fighter who won eight European gold medals, four as a member of the side which took four consecutive team titles in the 1960s. He was typical of the Russian team who brought a new approach to judo. They used their background of *sambo*, a form of WRESTLING whose contestants wear jackets, to dominate European judo. The squad won the European team title from 1963 to 1967 and Kiknadze was the heavyweight on each occasion. He won a bronze medal at the 1964 OLYMPIC GAMES and in the 1965 world championships, and a silver medal in the 1968 European championships before retiring.

KILIAN, HANNS (1905-), BOBSLEIGH rider for Germany. He won three world titles, and was the driver of the first world championship-winning two-man sled in 1931 at Oberhof, Germany. He drove the winning world four-man crews in 1934 at GARMISCH, and in 1935 at ST. MORITZ. He was twice Olympic bronze medallist, as driver in the only Olympic five-man event, at St. Moritz in 1928, and as driver of a four-man crew at LAKE PLACID, in 1932.

KILLANDER, Maj. ERNST, originator of ORIENTEERING. In an attempt to bring about a revival in track ATHLETICS, which at the time (1918) was in decline, he introduced competitions among youth groups in Sweden in which competitors were required to find their way by map and compass round an unmarked course in forest country. The game became popular in its own right and developed as a separate sport.

KILLY, JEAN-CLAUDE (1944-), French ski racer from Val d'Isère who dominated his sport from 1966 to 1968, winning the downhill and the combined gold medals at the world championship at Portillo, Chile, in 1966, and the three Olympic gold medals for downhill, slalom, and giant slalom at Grenoble in 1968. Killy, who turned professional after Grenoble, was able to break many of the existing rules of technique because of his exceptionally strong calves and ankles. His use of skis wider apart for downhill running was generally adopted among racers because of the added stability.

KIMURA, MASHIKO (1918-), Japanese JUDO fighter who dominated the sport between 1938 and 1949. He was only 5 ft. 7 in. (1·70 m.) tall and weighed 13 stone (82·6 kg.) but his use of *o-soto-gari* (major outer reaping throw) brought him a run of successes against far larger opponents.

Kimura won the young men's group of the all-Japan championships on four occasions, more than any other fighter. There were no official open all-Japan championships until 1948 and the following year Kimura, then a 7th *Dan*, was the joint holder with Ishikawa.

KING, Mrs. BILLIE JEAN (*née* Moffitt) (1943-), American LAWN TENNIS player, an outstanding exponent of the service-and-volley game, who held the WIMBLEDON title from 1966 to 1968, was runner-up in 1969 and 1970, and then regained it in 1972 and 1973. A Californian with a keen tactical sense, she won her first Wimbledon title at 17 when she and Hantze, another young American, defeated the Australians, Lehane and MARGARET SMITH. She won many other doubles titles and her successes in singles included victories at FOREST HILLS in 1967, 1971, and 1972, Paris (1972), Rome (1970), and the Australian championship in 1968. She was at her best when representing the United States in the WIGHTMAN CUP and Federation Cup (see LAWN TENNIS) competitions. She married Larry King, a Californian lawyer, in 1965. She was the most outspoken advocate of equal prize money for the women players and did something to prove her case when she beat Riggs, the men's champion at Wimbledon in 1939, in a much-publicized match at Houston in 1973.

KING, NORMAN (1914-), English lawn BOWLS player who won the world championship fours at Worthing in 1972 as lead to LINE. He won a gold medal in the 1958 COMMONWEALTH GAMES as lead to Scadgell in the fours and another in the 1970 Commonwealth Games at Edinburgh as partner to Line in the pairs. He also won the English Bowling Association singles championship in 1957.

KING GEORGE VI AND QUEEN ELIZABETH STAKES is the most important weight-for-age horse race run in England. Founded in 1951 (with £40,000 added to the sweepstakes by the racing authorities, including £20,000 given by the Horse-race Betting Levy Board) it is run in mid-July over 1½ miles (2,400 m.) at ASCOT; three-year-olds carry 8 st. 7 lb. (54 kg.), older horses 9 st. 7 lb. (60 kg.), fillies and mares receive 3 lb. (1 kg.) sex allowance. Sponsorship has recently raised its value to more than £79,000 to the winner, making it Britain's most valuable race.

KING'S CUP (1), see FLYING, SPORTING.

(2) The men's international indoor LAWN TENNIS team championship, and called, more properly, the King of Sweden's Cup. Since its inception in 1936, it has had the support and patronage of the Swedish royal family. It is played, usually on wood or plastic courts, in November and December each year.

In the early rounds the pattern is that of the Davis Cup (see LAWN TENNIS) — four singles and one doubles — but in the semi-finals and the final only two singles and one doubles are played because of pressure of time. Usually, only the European countries compete, although there is nothing in the rules to prevent an entry from outside Europe. It is regarded by most lawn tennis associations as a useful tournament for blooding young players for the Davis Cup and for giving winter match play to more experienced competitors.

Sweden and Denmark, where a good deal of lawn tennis is played on fast indoor surfaces, have had a large share of success in this event, but the British, who did not enter until 1963, won it for the next four years.

(3) The trophy for the eight-oared ROWING championship of Australia. The cup was originally presented to an Australian service crew by George V at the HENLEY Peace Regatta in 1919. It was placed in the Australian War Museum but, as a result of a petition to the king, it was released to become the inter-state trophy. The King's Cup Regatta is the highlight of the Australian rowing season. Since 1956 the course has been shortened to 2,000 m. (1·2 miles) to bring it into line with the international championship distance.

KING'S PRIZE, see SHOOTING, RIFLE: SERVICE CALIBRE.

KINNAIRD CUP, see ETON FIVES.

KIRKALDY, ANDREW (1860-1934), Scottish professional golfer. A notable match player, he was professional to the Royal and Ancient and tied the Open championship of 1889, losing the play-off to PARK.

KITE-FIGHTING, in which each of two opponents tries to bring down, destroy, or cut adrift the other's kite, may seem an unreal event to the European child trying to get his square of paper airborne at the seaside. But elsewhere it ranges from a vicious pastime to a serious, adult, competitive sport. The means of sabotage vary in the three main regions in which it is practised.

In India, where the kites may fly nearly a mile (1·6 km.) high, each one has two strings: one is to control the kite; the other, covered in powdered glass, is manoeuvred by its operator to cut through his opponent's string. Several South American countries enjoy the sport, and there the armoury is more lethal: razor blades embedded in the framework of the kite, that may either sever the opponent's string or rip holes in his kite. But it is not until Thai kite-fighting is studied that the subtleties of the sport can be fully appreciated.

In Thailand the kite-fighting season lasts from February to June, when leagues operate as hotly contested as any major sport. Competitions are between the 'male' kite, *chula*, a star-shaped affair that may be 7 ft. (2 m.) across and require several men to launch it, and two 'female' kites, *pakpao*. These are diamond-shaped, and may not be half the size of the *chula*, but have the edge on it for speed and manoeuvrability. The *chula* is armed with bamboo slats tied on its string, with which the operator hopes to entangle the tail of a *pakpao*, while the opponent tries, for instance, to catch one of the points of the star in a large loop of string under the *pakpao* and drag it down.

The origin of kite-fighting, like that of kite-flying, is lost in time, but almost certainly has ritual, religious, and possibly sexual, significance. It was a pastime popular for centuries in Japan, where kites were sometimes as big as 1,000 sq. ft. (93 sq. m.) and needed the entire population of a village to launch them.

KIVELL, ROY (1920-   ), lawn BOWLS player who, by 1966, had played for England in 20 international series, exceeding the previous record of 19 by Carruthers, the first English Bowling Association singles champion. Kivell began bowling at the age of eight and won three important open Devon tournaments nine years later. He won his club (Exonia) championship at the age of 14, beating his father *en route* to the final. In August 1954 he was one of the England team of four which met Scotland in a demonstration international in Glasgow, and became the youngest-ever England captain in the 1955 series when only 34. Apart from bowls, he was a useful soccer (see FOOTBALL, ASSOCIATION) goalkeeper who played a few matches for Exeter City reserves in his youth.

KIWIS, the popular term derived from the New Zealand bird of the same name, used for the New Zealand Army RUGBY UNION team which toured the British Isles and France in 1945-6. The team, captained by SAXTON, won 23 out of 27 matches in the British Isles and 6 out of 6 in France.

KIZIMOV, IVAN (*c.* 1928-   ), Russian dressage (see EQUESTRIAN EVENTS) rider, who won the individual gold medal at the OLYMPIC GAMES in Mexico (1968). A physical education teacher and the trainer of the Russian three-day event horseman, DEEV, he began serious dressage riding in 1960.

KJELLSTROM, ALVAR, BJORN, and ARVID, three Swedish brothers who developed the Silva compass for use in ORIENTEERING events and did much to stimulate the early development of the sport by staging 'come and try it' events throughout Sweden, advertising them in local newspapers. Bjorn also took the sport to the U.S.A. in 1948 and wrote some of the first instructional books on the subject.

KLINGNER, BERND (1940-   ), West German who, by 1970, had won 18 national small-bore rifle championships, was three times European champion and Olympic gold medallist in free rifle, small-bore, three positions, in Mexico in 1968, in which he beat a ten-year-old world record of 396 out of 400 in the kneeling position, by 5 points.

KLOOTSCHIEN, see BOWL-PLAYING.

KNIGHTHOOD TOURNAMENT, see SOUTHAMPTON BOWLS CLUB.

KNOTT, ALAN PHILIP ERIC (1946-   ), cricketer for England, Kent, and Tasmania. Nurtured by a county famed for its wicket-keepers, he first played for Kent in 1964, and three years later became England's first choice. Small and agile, at his best keeping to fast bowling, by the end of 1973 he had caught 144 batsmen and stumped 14 in 50 Test matches. His improvised style of batting also has often been valuable: he scored a century against Pakistan and 101 and 96 in a Test against New Zealand.

KNUR AND SPELL (also knurr, nur, nor and spel), or 'poor man's golf', is an ancient bat-and-ball game with mainly northern and, above all, Yorkshire associations. The object of the player, 'laiker', or 'tipper' is to strike the 'knur', or round ball, furthest with bat or stick in an agreed number of attempts or rises.

Three chief methods by which the knur, about the size of a large marble, is set up for striking are as follows: (1) by throwing it up from a spell — a spring trap; (2) from a pin, a gallows-like arrangement, from which the knur is suspended; (3) out of the hand. A less common method is to balance the knur in a hole on top of the bat head, flicking the knur up before striking.

Played down-wind on waste ground or moorland, the game has two main forms. It is usually contested between individuals, not teams, and is almost exclusively a male preserve. In a match the winner is the player with the biggest aggregate of hits, measured in scores of yards (i.e., 20 yds. — 18·29 m.). Fractions of a score do not count in a match. In a 'long knock' the biggest single hit is decisive.

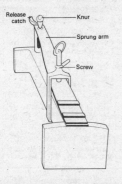

THE SPELL
The player releases the knur into the air by tapping the catch with his stick. Tension in the sprung arm is regulated by the screw.

The bats or sticks have shafts of ash, hickory, or alder of between 2 ft. (61 cm.) and 6 ft. (1·83 m.) — usually 3 ft. 9 in. (1·14 m.) to 4 ft. (1·22 m.) — with fabric or rubber grips. Steel golf shafts have been tried, with no great success; they lack the necessary whip.

The striking head or pommel, round-backed with a flattened striking surface from 2 to 3 in. (5·08 to 7·62 cm.) wide, is often of boxwood, hornbeam, sycamore, or maple. The wood used for the striking surface is compressed to half its natural volume in a steel frame, the club-maker screwing down the frame a little each day over a week or so. The wood is then heated to produce the desired finish, and glued to the club head.

This heating process is the critical part of stick manufacture. Too much heat produces a surface which will break the knur; too little, and the knur will scar or split the head. A 'kind' or 'mild' head, made by about eight minutes' heating, is used in windy conditions. A 'tough' head — say 12 minutes' heating — is used in still conditions.

Expert players take a selection of heads to a contest, so as to extract full advantage from the prevailing wind. Greenfield, the 1970 and 1973 'world champion', an electrician from Colne, Lancashire, learned to make his own

gear from an old laiker at Laneshaw Bridge. Knur and spell has remained in the same state of nature and self-reliance as golf in the days of the early Scottish professionals and clubmakers. The manufacture of sticks reaches a high standard. They are often made in hill-farm workshops by the players themselves, and the finish does not greatly suffer by comparison with that of commercially produced wooden golf clubs.

A match knur weighs ½ oz. (14·17 g.). It is made of smooth pot, called in the northern counties a 'pottie'. Knurs were formerly of wood, or lignum vitae, with hand-carved surfaces, and altogether bore a striking resemblance in all save colour to the modern dimpled golf ball. Horn knurs weighted with lead were also used.

The spell is a metal or wood frame about 2 ft. (61 cm.) long, staked into the ground. The knur is placed in a cup mounted on the end of an adjustable sprung arm. It is released into the air by the player tapping his stick head against the catch holding down the sprung arm. Since the tension on the sprung arm is variable, the flight of the knur from the spell can be exactly controlled. Players use pegs to mark the spot at which the knur falls from the spell to ensure that the spell throws up the knur exactly into the plane of their swing with the stick.

Pins are made of wood and stand about 4 ft. (1·22 m.) high. Each is based on a stout upright with a sharpened foot, usually strengthened with a metal tip, which is driven into the ground. Two cross-pieces fold out horizontally, one at the top of the main spar and one at the bottom. From the top arm hangs a loop of cord, into which the knur is placed ready for striking. In a high wind, the loop is held motionless by a piece of wire running up from the lower arm of the pin. The simplicity of the pin has in this century made great inroads into the dominance the spell once enjoyed as the accepted launching method.

The field of play is marked out with pegs set in lines every 20 yds. (18·29 m.), radiating fanwise from the line upon which the spells or pins stand. The length of a rise is measured from hit to resting place. Not the least remarkable facet of the game is the ability of the players to mark the flight of the knur over long distances (hits of 200 yds. — 182·88 m. — are common) and, with the help of down-wind spectators, to find the knur in rough ground and use it throughout a contest of, say, 15 rises a side.

Legends abound about big hitters of the past, but Strutt, writing at the beginning of the nineteenth century, says: 'A first-rate hand is said to have been able to send a loaded ball 16 score yards' (320 yds. — 292·61 m.). This tallies with Machin's 15 score 14 ft. (278·58 m.) with a pot knur at Barnsley in 1899, and Aspinall's 16 score, using a 6-ft. stick (1·83 m.) on the old Halifax Racecourse (1913). Fred Moore of Claremont, Halifax, is credited with more than 18 score (329·18 m.) with a wooden knur in 1899, but a freak bounce off a stone wall contributed to this feat.

Knur and spell has always attracted betting, and stakes of several hundred guineas were common. In a more modest match on Woodhouse Moor, Yorkshire, on 28 July 1826, Scott scored 372 in 40 rises to win 40 guineas from Wheater, whose total was 334 in 40 rises.

Large crowds gathered to watch and wager, and would travel considerable distance to back their favourites. DAWSON, the England soccer goalkeeper, who played for Burnley Football Club from 1906 to 1929, met Yorkshire champions for stake money on the moors on the borders of Yorkshire and Lancashire.

This is a true game of the people, handed down from generation to generation, played with the gentlemanly fervour which distinguishes golf. Though it lacks golf's written rules and literature, it possesses a picturesque jargon all its own, particularly in the West Riding of Yorkshire. In the words of a life-long laiker recorded in *Yorkshire Life*: 'Well, tha' gets into thi' spell 'oils [holes or pegs to guide placement of the feet for consistent hitting] and puts pottie [the knur] in t' loop. Na' then, it all depends on whether you're strikin' or laikin'. If tha's laikin', then ivery rise counts, but if tha's laikin' at strikin' then tha' clouts it as far down t' meader as tha' can, 'cause foithest wins, tha' sees. And if it come to a moitch [dispute], then tha' measures from t' pin wi' a squeer chain.' When a particularly long hit is achieved, the laiker will often chase the flying knur excitedly, and the crowd will shout 'Reight ower.'

The game has had a wide geographical distribution, from the Midlands to the north-eastern counties, with countless variations especially among children. It has affinities with TRAP BALL, dag and trigger (East Riding of Yorkshire), buck and stick, tipcat, billet, and nipsy, peculiar to the Barnsley area, where the sticks are pared-down pickaxe handles, with heads made from the wood of mangle rollers. Billet players used a stick with a longer head than is usual in knur and spell, striking a piece of wood the size of a man's finger, sharpened at one end; again, hits are measured in scores of yards.

In Lincolnshire the bat becomes a 'kibble': other regional names are 'trevit', 'tribbitt', 'primstick', and 'gelstick'. Yet almost every-

where the names of the implements give evidence of Teutonic or Old Norse origins. Spell is Old Norse *spill*, a game or play; knur, German *knorr*, a knot of wood, from which the earliest projectiles were undoubtedly made — hence, 'spell a knor', play at ball. The ball play — *nurspel* — of the Norsemen and Icelanders is almost certainly the ancestor of knur and spell.

The game reached the height of its popularity in the early part of the twentieth century, when it was said that every other Yorkshireman was a laiker. Greenfield has used in the 1970s a head made in 1935 and given him by a leading tipper of the thirties, Billy Baxter, who defeated Crawshaw, world spell champion, of Stockbridge, Sheffield, in a long knock contest over 25 rises at Colne in 1937 for stakes of £100. For such matches players would meticulously prepare a level, sure foothold with a spirit level, shovels, and ashes.

By mid-century, the game had almost vanished, but since then there has been a rebirth, hastened by commercial and television sponsorship.

An annual 'world championship' is held to which qualifiers come from the old-established strongholds of the game such as Rotherham, Grenoside, Sheffield, Barnsley, and Colne in Lancashire. Greenfield won the 1970 title from 19 rivals before an Easter Tuesday crowd of 3,000 which gathered in bitterly cold weather on the moors near the Spring Rock Inn, Upper Greetland, near Elland, Yorkshire. His winning hit was 225 yds. (205·74 m.) — little more than two-thirds, it will be noted, of Aspinall's well-authenticated hit. Greenfield regained the title in 1973 at Dodsworth, near Barnsley. A cup and a £200 cheque go to the title winners.

Since the sport has such a sparse literature, former champions have enjoyed but a passing fame, but men like the renowned Willie Lamb, of Northowram, near Halifax, Yorkshire, Joe Edon, of Barnsley, and the Yorkshire brothers Machin, are not forgotten.

Alice Bertha Gomme, *The Traditional Games of England, Scotland, and Ireland,* 2 vols. (1964); Joseph Strutt, *The Sports and Pastimes of the People of England* (1801; ed. 1903).

KOBBERÖ, FINN (1936-   ), Danish BADMINTON player. A most brilliant stroke player, he was probably the finest doubles exponent yet known. Before he was 18 he was an ALL-ENGLAND doubles finalist and later won three doubles trophies, and nearly a fourth outright at that tournament. He played for his country 42 times with outstanding success in many parts of the world.

KOCSIS, SANDOR (1929-   ), Association footballer for Honved (Budapest), BARCELONA, and Hungary for whom he played at inside right in the 6-3 win over England at WEMBLEY in November 1953, and in the 1954 World Cup final when Hungary were beaten by West Germany. He was one of the three important members (with PUSKAS and Czibor) of the great Hungarian national side who left Hungary in 1956. He signed for Barcelona and played for the Spanish club in the first leg of the Inter-Cities Fairs Cup final of 1960 against Birmingham, and in the European Champion Clubs Cup final of 1961.

KODOKAN, JUDO training hall, Tokyo, the Mecca of judo in Japan. The first Kodokan was opened by Dr. KANO at Shitaya in 1882 and consisted of only 12 mats. At present housed in an eight-storey building, at 16-30, I-Chome, Kasuga-cho, Bunkyo-ku, Tokyo, it has facilities for eating and sleeping as well as large training areas.

The Kodokan has kept a watchful eye on the development of the sport; most of the leading Japanese train there and foreigners reaching 1st *Dan* may have their grades registered there. The cream of Japan's *judoka* plus a number of selected foreigners make up the *kenshusei* (special research students).

KOECHLIN-SMYTHE, Mrs. PAT, see SMYTHE, P.

KÖHLER, THOMAS (1940-   ), luge TOBOGGANING rider for East Germany, winner of five world and two Olympic titles. The first man to win the world men's singles three times (in 1962, 1964, and 1967) and Olympic solo winner in 1964, he added another Olympic gold medal in the 1968 two-seater event, partnered by Bonsack; they achieved such a high degree of co-ordination that they gave the impression of one man in the sled.

KOIZUMI, GUNJI (1885-1965), Japanese *judoka* (8th *Dan*) who was the father of European JUDO, founding the BUDOKWAI in 1918. He was first proficient in JU-JITSU but switched to judo, and emphasized character training by balancing mental qualities with the physical. He was an Oriental art expert, practised calligraphy, and helped to introduce Buddhism into Britain. He was a dedicated instructor and founded innumerable clubs, leading the move to establish the European Judo Union and the British Judo Association. He taught at the Budokwai until the day before he died.

KOK, AAGJE (Ada) (1947-   ), Dutch swimmer who dominated world butterfly events in the 1960s. Standing 6 ft. (1·83 m.) and weighing 13 st. 3 lb. (85 kg.), Kok won her first major title, for 100 metres, at the 1962 European championships. Second in the OLYMPIC GAMES two years later, she retained her European title in Utrecht in 1966 and crowned a career which included nine world butterfly records by winning the new 200 metres event at the Mexico Olympic Games in 1968.

KOLAPORE MATCH, see SHOOTING, RIFLE: SERVICE CALIBRE.

KOLEHMAINEN, HANNES (1899-1966), long-distance runner for Finland. The first of the great school of Finnish athletes who dominated endurance running for about 30 years, Kolehmainen won three Olympic gold medals in 1912 in the 5,000 metres, 10,000 metres, and 8,000 metres team cross-country event. His world record time of 14 min. 36·6 sec. for the 5,000 metres was unbeaten until NURMI improved it in 1922. After service in the First

World War, Kolehmainen entered and won the 1920 Olympic marathon in 2 hrs. 32 min. 35·8 sec. Although he ran 605 yards over the regulation distance, this time was not bettered in the OLYMPIC GAMES until 1932. Kolehmainen also held world records for 3,000 metres in 8 min. 36·9 sec. and for 25,000 and 30,000 metres.

KONO, TAMIO (1930-   ), Japanese-American weight-lifter, eight times Olympic and world champion in successive years 1952-9. He won two Olympic gold medals and one silver, and was the only lifter to win three successive Pan-American gold medals (1955, 1959, 1963). Kono was 11 times U.S.A. champion and the only lifter to set world records in four different body-weight categories.

KONRADS, JOHN (1942-   ) and ILSA (1944-   ), Australian swimmers who between them broke 37 world records in two years (1958-60). John, who was a polio victim, was in three OLYMPIC GAMES. At his second, in 1960, he won the 1,500 metres and bronze medals in the 400 metres and the 4 × 200 metres freestyle relay. He was also a triple gold medallist at the 1958 British COMMONWEALTH GAMES. His sister also won a Commonwealth title (440 yards in 1958) and an Olympic relay silver medal in 1960.

KOPA, RAYMOND (1931-   ), Association footballer for REIMS, REAL MADRID, and France for whom he made the first of more than 40 appearances in full international matches in October 1952 against West Germany in Paris. In 1958, while still with Real Madrid, he was one of the outstanding players in the French national team that reached third place in the world championship tournament held in Sweden. He was in the Real Madrid sides that won the European Cup in 1957, 1958, and 1959 when, in the final, the Spanish club again beat Reims whom, shortly, he rejoined.

KOPS, ERLAND (1937-   ), Danish BADMINTON player. Winner of the ALL-ENGLAND singles title seven times between 1958 and 1967, and the men's doubles three times successively from 1967, he has a lasting place in the game. He played all over the world most successfully, winning many titles, and represented his country more than 40 times.

KORAC, RADIVOJ (1938-69), BASKETBALL player for Yugoslavia. One of the greatest players ever produced in Europe, he was the highest over-all points scorer in the 1960 OLYMPIC GAMES and gained a silver medal at

the 1968 Olympiad. He represented Yugoslavia on 147 occasions and won silver medals at the world championships of 1963 and 1967. Korac played for O.K.K. Belgrade and gained four Yugoslavian championship medals with the club. In 1968 he joined Standard Liège, of the Belgian League, and in 1969 had moved to Boario of Padua, in the Italian League, when he was killed in a car accident, in Yugoslavia in June 1969. The Fédération Internationale de Basketball Amateur (F.I.B.A.) instituted a cup competition for European clubs in his honour. It was fitting that the first winners, in 1972, were a Yugoslavian team, Lokomotiva Zagreb.

KORBUT, OLGA (1955-   ), Russian female gymnast whose charismatic personality and superb skill entranced spectators at the Munich Olympics. Although she finished only seventh over-all at the Games she won three gold medals (beam, floor exercises, and team event). Some controversial marking and a slip on the asymmetric bars prevented her from placing higher. In 1973 after taking the Russian and World Student Games titles she took part in the European championships in London. But after getting the silver medal in the combined exercises behind TURITSCHEVA she injured her leg and withdrew from the individual apparatus events.

KORFBALL is a type of handball of Dutch origin, usually played out of doors between teams of mixed sexes. The object of the game is to score goals and to prevent the opposing team from scoring. The team with the highest number of goals at the end of the match wins.

The ideal playing area, called a pitch, is a rectangle 90 m. by 40 m. (295 ft. × 131 ft.), level and of short, sharp grass. If necessary smaller sizes are permitted for young players or where the available area does not allow for a full-size pitch. A feature of the game is the marking of the outside, or boundary, lines and the two cross-lines, which divide the pitch into three equal areas, by white tapes pinned to the ground. The use of tape means that korfball can be played anywhere, for the pitch markings are easily laid out and after the game can be rolled up and carried away.

The goals are baskets fixed at the top of posts firmly planted in the ground in each end division. Each basket faces towards the centre division and its top edge must be 3·50 m. (11 ft. 6 in.) above the ground all round. The baskets are cylindrical, without a bottom; they are 25 cm. (10 in.) high and have an inner diameter of 39 to 41 cm. (15⅜–16¼ in.). They are made of osier twigs or of rattan.

Korfball is played with a round ball which

consists of a rubber pneumatic bladder in a one-coloured leather outer casing, with a circumference of 68 to 71 cm. (2 ft. 3 in.–2 ft. 4 in.). It is inflated hard and closed in such a way that it cannot be held by any protruding part. At the start of a match the weight of the ball must be not less than 425 g. (15 oz.) and not more than 475 g. (17 oz.).

Six men and six women form a korfball team and at the start of the game these players are divided between the three areas of play, called divisions, i.e. two men and two women in each division. Play starts from the middle of the centre division and a goal is scored when the ball falls from the top through the basket.

After every two goals, all the players in the centre division move into one of the two end divisions, the players from that end move to the other end division, and the players from that division move into the centre, so that, after six goals have been scored, all the players are back in their original division. A game lasts 90 minutes with an interval of up to 15 minutes at half-time. For the second half the teams change ends.

KORFBALL PITCH

A referee is appointed to ensure that the rules of the game are followed and to keep a record of the goals scored and the time played. He will usually be assisted by two linesmen whose main task is to indicate when the ball goes out of play and which team should throw it into play again.

The ball is out as soon as it touches a boundary line of the field of play, the ground, a person, or an object outside the field of play. A penalty, awarded for an infringement which results in the loss of a scoring chance, is a free

throw from which it is permitted to score directly.

Korfball was invented to fulfil a specific need and is based on specific principles requiring that the game should (a) encourage a high degree of co-operation between both sexes in working to a common aim; (b) require all-round ability of a player, i.e. in attack, centre, and defence; (c) demand a high degree of technique and skill and actively discourage physical violence, whether or not such violence is accidental.

The rules preclude running with the ball (and this includes running along, bouncing the ball), and it is therefore necessary for players to pass the ball to their partners in order to ensure that the ball reaches the attack players. Following a mistake in passing the ball, or an interception, the opposing team gains possession and endeavours to pass the ball among its members, and so achieve a goal-scoring opportunity.

The word 'party', derived by the Dutch players from the French word *partez* (meaning 'break') is the call used to attract the attention of the rest of the team when a successful interception has been made and the defending team has gained possession of the ball. It serves as an instruction to defending players to become attackers.

Although korfball is a team game, demanding that the players of each team co-operate in order to succeed, each player is directly opposed by one of the same sex from the other team. This introduces individual competition as well as the over-all team competition.

Although no physical contact is allowed between players, and this is extended to prevent players of one sex opposing players of the other sex, a player is permitted to hinder his or her opponent by making it difficult for the thrower to pass the ball in the desired direction. The result of this permitted hindering is that players are encouraged to run into a free position where the ball is more easily caught and passed, yet at the same time the defender is encouraged to watch his or her attacking opponent so that these opportunities may not be gained. The element of surprise always remains with the members of the team in possession of the ball, and quick passing combined with fast running will ultimately lead to an attacker achieving a free position, anywhere within the end divisions of the field, from which a shot can be taken. Defended shooting is not permitted by the rules; that is to say all goals must be scored from a free position.

The movement of players from division to division, in the prescribed manner, means that all players must be able to shoot, to defend, and to move the ball swiftly through centre. No team can rely on one star performer to score all its goals. This also helps to develop mental agility as players have to change tactics and techniques according to the division in which they find themselves.

MICRO-KORFBALL is adapted from field korfball as an indoor variation. It is a two-division game, i.e. the centre division is omitted, and the maximum playing area is 50 m. by 25 m. (164 ft. × 82 ft.). In all essentials the game is the same as field korfball except that the duration of the game is 60 minutes, with a break of up to 10 minutes at half-time. Although generally played indoors, it is also played in the open, especially in training.

Fédération Internationale de Korfbal, *Rules of Korfball*.

Since 1900 few outdoor games with a particular purpose have been invented. Korfball is one of these few. The aim of the initiator was to create a game that could be played by mixed teams, so that both sexes could participate on an equal basis.

Shortly after 1900, Nico Broekhuysen, a schoolmaster in Amsterdam, outlined such a game, and in 1902 the pupils of his co-educational school began to play it. Twelve children, six boys and six girls, made up each team, which was divided into three divisions. Each division contained two boys and two girls.

This game immediately aroused great interest, and other schools adopted it. Not only were the pupils participating in the game, but also teachers and parents were playing it and forming their own korfball clubs. By 1903 so many clubs were in existence that Broekhuysen founded the Nederlands Korfball Association, which in 1938, on its thirty-fifth anniversary, was granted the prefix 'Royal' by Queen Wilhelmina.

Korfball was demonstrated in Antwerp during the 1920 OLYMPIC GAMES, and the foundation was laid for korfball to be played in Belgium. In 1921 the Belgian Korfball Association was formed: it was granted the prefix 'Royal' in 1950. Since then, the game has spread to Indonesia, Surinam, Germany, Spain, New Guinea, and England.

The Fédération Internationale de Korfbal, the world organization for the control of korfball, was founded in 1923 under the name International Korfballbureau; the name was changed in 1933.

Korfball came to England after the war through the efforts of Milhado, who was concerned with the Anglo-Netherlands Sports Association (A.N.S.A.), which was formed to provide a link, through sports exchanges, between cities and towns in the Netherland and England. Milhado, who had played korfball in his youth, proposed a demonstration tour by two Dutch teams in support of A.N.S.A. with a view to introducing the spor to England.

The first match of the tour, in July 1946 was played at Willesden, London. It wa received with great enthusiasm and further matches took place in Hull, Sheffield, Derby and Oxford. On 31 July 1946 the British Korfball Association was formed with Walbanck as its chairman and Milhado as president. In August of the same year a party of intereste English sportsmen and women went as guest of the Dutch to a training course at Zeist. O their return, centres of korfball were estab lished in the London area: it is now played in south-east England and Swindon.

GOVERNING BODY (WORLD): Fédération Internation ale de Korfbal, Mathenesseelaan 379, Rotterdam 6 Holland.

KOVACS, PAL (1913-   ), Hungarian fencer, Olympic sabre champion in 1952 and world sabre champion in 1937 and 1953. The perfect exponent of modern Hungarian sabre FENCING, he became president of the Hungarian Fencing Federation and was made *Membre d'Honneur* of the Fédération Internationale d'Escrime in 1969.

KRAENZLEIN, ALVIN C. (1876-1928) hurdler and sprinter for the U.S.A. Kraenzlein has two claims to historical significance; first that he originated the modern technique of HURDLING in which the hurdler's leading leg i thrown out across the hurdle and along the line of running; and secondly that he was the firs athlete to win four gold medals at a singl OLYMPIC GAMES. This feat was achieved at the 1900 Games when he won the 60 metres, 110 metres hurdles, 200 metres hurdles, and LONG JUMP. He held world records for 110 metre hurdles in 15·2 sec., 220 yards hurdles on straight track in 23·6 sec., and for the lon jump with 24 ft. 4½ in. (7·43 m.). The 220 yard hurdles record survived from 1898 to 1923

KRAMER, INGRID (1943-   ), diver fo East Germany. She achieved a place in histor by breaking the U.S.A. domination of th Olympic diving events by winning both th high diving and the springboard gold medals a Rome in 1960. At the 1964 OLYMPIC GAME she again won the springboard gold medal, bu narrowly missed the high board title.

KRAMER, JOHN ALBERT (1921- American LAWN TENNIS player. One of th most effective of postwar champions, Kramer was for several years the leader and organizer of the professional circuit. Brought up in the aggressive tradition of the Californian game and helped by VINES and BUDGE, he maintained unrelenting pressure on his opponents by the formidable accuracy of his serving and volleying.

In 1939, as junior doubles champion, he was chosen for the U.S. team which failed in the Davis Cup (see LAWN TENNIS) challenge round against Australia. He and Hunt, a promising player killed in the war, took a set from QUIST and Bromwich in the doubles. During the war Kramer served in the U.S. Navy, but he managed to reach the final of the U.S. championships in 1943, losing to Hunt, and won the doubles with Parker. After losing to DROBNY at WIMBLEDON in 1946, he won the U.S. title, and in the following year no one could match him at Wimbledon. Only Pails, the Australian champion, took a set from him and Kramer beat T. Brown, another Californian, by 6-1, 6-3, 6-2 in the final. He won the singles and the doubles at FOREST HILLS and then, both as player and promoter, he took control of the professional game. Back trouble caused him to retire from play, but before that he beat GONZALES on the younger American's first professional tour and even in 1957, when his tournament appearances were rare, he beat HOAD at Wembley.

He fought a long battle with the International Lawn Tennis Federation over open lawn tennis, but in 1968, when the principle of competition between amateurs and professionals was accepted, he had more or less retired from promotion. He became one of the game's best-known television commentators. As executive director of the Association of Tennis Professionals, he played a major part in the dispute which led to A.T.P.'s boycott of the championships in 1973.

KRONFELD, ROBERT (1904-48), an Austrian, was the first glider pilot to soar 100 km. (62 miles) across country, in 1929, and held records in Germany in the 1930s. He was the first pilot to experiment with large span gliders. His Austria broke up in the air in 1932 but Kronfeld saved his life by parachute. He helped start GLIDING in Britain with pioneer flights in a Wien glider. He was the author of first important book on the sport, *Kronfeld on Gliding and Soaring*.

KSAR (1918), a race horse by BRULEUR out of Kizil Kourgan (Grand Prix, French Oaks, and French One Thousand Guineas), was one of the best ever bred in France. He won the PRIX DE L'ARC DE TRIOMPHE twice, French Derby, French St. Leger, and PRIX DU CADRAN. Ksar

was bred by de Saint-Alary and bought as a yearling by Blanc.

KUBLER, FERDINAND (1920-   ), professional cyclist, the first Swiss rider to win the TOUR DE FRANCE (1950). Extremely versatile, he became national champion in the pursuit and at CYCLO-CROSS as well as on the road. Among his principal victories were the world professional road-race championship (1951), BORDEAUX–PARIS, FLÈCHE WALLONNE (twice), and LIÈGE–BASTOGNE–LIÈGE (twice).

KUCHINSKAYA, NATALYA (1942-   ), Russian female gymnast who nearly upset CASLAVSKA at the 1966 world championships. With the great Czech competitor at her peak, Kuchinskaya lost by only 0·201 points over-all but finished well clear in the individual exercises, taking three gold medals from Caslavska. After an indifferent performance at the 1967 European championships, she came back strongly at the Mexico OLYMPIC GAMES the following year. But a blunder on the asymmetrical bars ruined her chances of finishing more closely to Caslavska and she ended with the bronze medal, although she secured gold medals on the beam and in the team event. A serious glandular disease probably prevented her from succeeding Caslavska as world champion in 1970.

KUNINGASPALLO, literally 'kingball', is a Finnish team bat-and-ball game akin to longball, and one of the ancestor games of PESÄPALLO. It was played, in many variant forms, throughout Finland until the end of the nineteenth century.

It could be played on any level open space between 20 and 30 m. wide by 60 to 80 m. long (22–33 by 66–87 yds.), with a fist-size ball and a bat similar to a BASEBALL bat. Teams might number 8 or 9, 17 or 22 players. Each ordinary player could bat three times; the server — or pitcher — four times; and the 'king' or best batsman, six times.

The ball was served or lobbed high upwards so that it dropped towards the batsman who, whether he hit it or not, could run immediately towards the distant 'out-goal' or safe area some 40 or 50 m. (44–55 yds.) away, or step aside into the safety of the 'waiting box' for the opportunity to run when someone else — usually the 'king' — made a safe hit. A player caught and 'burnt' or tagged — touched with the ball either thrown or in hand — short of the safety of box or out-goal, was out; and fielding and batting sides changed.

Refinements included a 'rescue' rule by which the 'burnt' or tagged batsman could throw the ball immediately at the fielding side to 'burn' or tag them and so allow his team mates to reach the out-goal or return home safely while still retaining the advantage of batting.

It was a lively game but lack of a definite scoring system rendered it eventually unsatisfying in a world of competitive sport.

KUSHTI, see WRESTLING.

KUTS, VLADIMIR PYOTROVICH (1927–1975), long distance runner for the U.S.S.R. An outsider in the 1954 EUROPEAN CHAMPIONSHIPS, Kuts astounded the track world by running clean away from a strong 5,000 metres field, including ZATOPEK, to win a gold medal and break the world record with 13 min. 56·6 sec. He broke the 5,000 metres record three times more, reaching 13 min. 35·0 sec. in 1957, and this time was unbeaten until 1965. The Russian's forceful, front-running tactics were again instrumental in winning him two gold medals, in the 5,000 and 10,000 metres, at the 1956 OLYMPIC GAMES. Earlier that year he broke the world 10,000 metres record with 28 min. 30·4 sec.

KWIET, PETER and RITA, roller dance skaters (see ROLLER SKATING) for West Germany, the first couple to win two successive world roller dance skating titles, in 1959 and 1960. Kwiet married his partner, formerly Miss Paucka, between their two victories.

KYEEMAGH BOWLS CLUB, in New South Wales, Australia, had the distinction of accommodating the inaugural world BOWLS championships in October 1966. Six miles south of the heart of Sydney, the club covers over 2½ acres and cost more than £200,000 sterling to establish. It has four greens, all of Indian couch grass (*cynoon dactylon*) sown on a foundation of beach sand. The length of the grass, degree of watering, and general treatment were arranged for the championships to produce a start-to-stop running time of 16 seconds for a bowl delivered to a jack 30 yds. (27·4 m.) from the mat. In southern England the timing averages 12 seconds but in New Zealand it can be as fast as 23 seconds.

KYLE, JOHN WILLIAM (1926-   ), RUGBY UNION outside half for QUEEN'S UNIVERSITY, Belfast, North of Ireland, Ireland, and British LIONS. The dominant figure in Irish Rugby during its successful period after the Second World War, Kyle set a world record of 46 international caps, later surpassed by MEADS and KIERNAN. He is remembered for his ingenious, swerving runs in spite of the fact that much of his play was fashioned to the requirements of a powerful pack.

L

LA FLÈCHE (1889), a famous English racing mare by ST. SIMON out of QUIVER, and the dam of Memoir (winner of the OAKS and ST. LEGER), was bred for Queen Victoria at the Hampton Court Stud and bought by Baron de Hirsch as a yearling for 5,500 guineas, at that time a record. She won 16 races altogether, including the St. Leger, Oaks, ONE THOUSAND GUINEAS, CHAMPION STAKES, CAMBRIDGESHIRE, and ASCOT GOLD CUP, finishing second in the DERBY. Her stake total was £34,703 and, at stud to ISINGLASS, she produced John o' Gaunt, the sire of SWYNFORD. La Flèche was perhaps the best filly ever to run on the English turf, her chief rivals being SCEPTRE, PRETTY POLLY, MELD, PETITE ÉTOILE, and DAHLIA.

LA TROIENNE (1926), a race-horse who was one of the most outstanding brood mares in the history of bloodstock-breeding in the U.S.A., to which she was exported from France by Col. BRADLEY. She was dam of Black Helen (American Derby and Oaks) and Bimelech (BELMONT and PREAKNESS STAKES) as well as third dam of the champion BUCKPASSER.

LABRUNA, ANGEL (1916-), Association footballer for RIVER PLATE, and Argentina for whom he played in the 1958 world championships in Sweden when he was over 40 years old. His best playing years were the 1940s and early 1950s when his partnership with outside left Loustau for River Plate was renowned in Argentinian football.

LACEY, LEWIS (1887-1966), Anglo-Argentine POLO player who represented both England and Argentina. A fine horseman, he was at his best at 'back'. He brought an Argentine team to London in 1922 which was unbeaten and went on to win the U.S. championship. Handicap 10.

LACOSTE, CATHERINE (1945-), French amateur golfer, the first amateur to win the U.S. women's Open (1967). She was British champion 1969 and French women's Open champion 1967, 1969. She is the daughter of the Wimbledon LAWN TENNIS champion, J. R. LACOSTE.

LACOSTE, JEAN RÉNÉ (1905-), French LAWN TENNIS player, the most brilliantly methodical of the 'Four Musketeers' (BOROTRA, BRUGNON, and COCHET were the others) who captured the Davis Cup (see LAWN TENNIS) for France in 1927. In contrast to the spectacular volleying and extrovert dash of Borotra and Cochet, Lacoste, reserved, silent, eternally practising and gravely noting the weaknesses of his opponents in his famous notebooks, perfected the art of baseline play. He was almost invulnerable on the backhand and his ability to lob was remarkable.

He took up lawn tennis to improve his health, which was always a matter of concern, and by the time he was 18 had won the French indoor title, defeating Borotra in the final. He lost to Borotra in the French and WIMBLEDON finals in 1924, but gained his revenge the following year and beat Cochet in the 1928 final. He won the French championship in 1925, 1927, and 1929, and the U.S. title, beating first Borotra and then TILDEN, in 1926 and 1927. With Borotra, he won the Wimbledon doubles once and the French doubles twice.

But it was in the Davis Cup that Lacoste's patient study of the game brought its largest reward. The U.S.A. held the trophy and Tilden, the leading American, had not lost a rubber for six years. Although the French were beaten in the 1926 challenge round, Lacoste successfully restricted Tilden, to win by 4-6, 6-4, 8-6, 8-6, beat him again in the 1927 French final, and then as France captured the trophy, once more in the challenge round at Philadelphia. In 1929 ill-health forced him to stop playing and although he returned to beat Wood (U.S.A.), the Wimbledon champion, in the French championships in 1932, the strain of competition proved too much for him.

LACROIX, RENÉ, French fencer on whose initiative the Fédération Internationale d'Escrime, the world governing body for FENCING, was founded at a meeting held at the Automobile Club in Paris on 29 November 1913.

LACROSSE is a ball-and-goal field game played with a netted stick by teams of ten a side. It is played in America, Australia, Canada, and England and, at a lower level of performance, in Hong Kong. Like many other games, it is played (separately) by men and by women (see below), but the respective rules vary.

The present form of lacrosse, developed over the last two centuries, is normally played in the autumn, winter, and spring. A six-a-side variation of the game, known as box lacrosse, is played in parts of Canada.

The object of the game is to score goals by throwing the ball into the goal by means of the lacrosse racket, more usually called the crosse. This is roughly triangular in shape, and consists of a hickory frame on which is constructed a loose net made of vertical hide thongs interwoven with cat-gut. One side of the net is attached to the top curved part of the stick, one side to the body of the stick, with the third side so constructed as to form a leader. The leader is secured at one end to the extremity of the curved section of the frame, the other end being secured at the throat of the crosse. The crosse is so constructed that the ball is free to move in the net at all times. It may not exceed 1 ft. (305 mm.) or be less than 5 in. (127 mm.) in width, and may be of any length not less than 3 ft. (914 mm.). Defence players generally use a heavier stick with a longer handle and wider net than the attack players.

MODERN ATTACK CROSSE

After cutting, the hickory wood is allowed to season, before the stick is steamed, shaped, and curved. The net is finally constructed on the stick, an operation usually undertaken by women. It is estimated that at least 95 per cent of the world requirements of crosses are made in Canada by American Indians.

The ball, of solid rubber, is of different sizes, weights and colours in the four main playing countries: U.S.A. — circumference 7¼–8 in. (196·9–203·2 mm.), weight 5–5¼ oz. (142–149 g.), colour, orange or white; Canada — circumference 8 in. (203·2 mm.), weight 6 oz. (170 g.), colour, orange; Australia — circumference 8–8¼ in. (203·2–209·6 mm.), weight 5¼–5½ oz. (149–156 g.), colour, orange or white; England — circumference 7¼–8 in. (184–203·2 mm.), weight 5 oz. (142 g.), colour, yellow. It is picked up from the ground by the bevelled edge of the crosse or stick with a scooping or flicking movement.

The robust nature of the game dictates the wearing of protective equipment — arm pads, gauntlets, and a helmet with a visor. The goalkeeper also wears a body pad covering his chest and upper thighs.

Lacrosse is played on a rectangular turf pitch ideally measuring 110 yds. long by 70 yds. wide (100 × 64 m.). The playing area is marked out with 2-in. (51 mm.) lines in whiting, as are the goal crease areas, the defence, the attack, wing restraining lines, the centre line, and the centre spot. The goals, spaced 80 yds. (73 m.) apart, consist of vertical uprights with a crossbar, similar in type to a HOCKEY goal but square in front elevation. They may be constructed of wood or tubular metal and measure 6 ft. (1·83 m.) in width and in height. A close-mesh net, stretched over the reverse side of the goal, is pegged into the ground at a point not less than 6 ft. from the centre of the goal line. The goal area, known as the goal crease, is a circle with a radius of 3 yds. (2·74 m.), the centre being the centre of the goal line. A player may not enter his opponent's crease but he may enter his own crease to retrieve the ball or to make a save. He may not re-enter the crease with the ball nor may a player, including the goalkeeper, retain the ball in the crease for a period in excess of four seconds.

The ten-a-side team consists of a goalkeeper, three defences (known historically as point, cover point, and third man), a left wing defence, a centre, a right wing midfield (known historically as right wing defence), and three attacks (known historically as third, second, and first home) — the last a crease man.

When the teams are positioned with three attack players forward of the attack restraining line, four players, including the goalkeeper, behind the defence restraining line, and the wing men behind the wing restraining lines, play is started from the centre spot by a face-off. The referee places the ball between the reverse sides of the crosses of the players taking the face-off. The wooden frame of the crosse must be touching, and parallel to, the ground. On the whistle to start play, the players taking the face-off attempt to gain possession of the ball by clamping the crosse on the ball, by attempting to flick the ball over the opponent's crosse, or by raking the ball clear of the opponent. Until one or other of the players taking the face-off gains possession, all players other than the wing midfield players are confined behind their respective restraining lines.

Possession of the ball is an all-important feature of the game. The controlled checking of an opponent's crosse, the interception of the ball from an opponent's pass, and shoulder-to-shoulder charging in ground scuffles are all methods employed to gain possession.

The laws of lacrosse are simple and few in number, with fouls classified as either technical or personal. The former, in the main, deal with territorial infringements such as off-side (when fewer than three players are in the attack zone or fewer than four in the defence zone), while the latter deal with such offences as slashing with the crosse, tripping, striking an opponent on the head, illegal charging, and unsportsmanlike conduct. Penalties include loss of possession of the ball (where this applies, a free position is given whereby the offending player is placed behind his opponent) or, for more serious infringements, the suspension of the offending player, for varying periods of time, this being known as a 'time-out penalty'.

A player in possession of the ball may run, dodge, swerve, feint, pass the ball, or shoot it into the opponent's goal by means of the crosse. A feature of the game is the fast, accurate passing, catching, and shooting, and, because of this, the attack players particularly must be expert stick-handlers.

The tactics employed in lacrosse are basically the same as those used in other field games, such as FOOTBALL and hockey. Positional play is all-important, with players performing a definite task in the pattern of play. It is the function of the attack, for instance, to score goals and to manoeuvre the opposing defence into such a position that the midfield players may break through to score. To achieve this, the return pass, the rapid switching of the line of approach, swerving, dodging an opponent, and beating him by speed, are some of the methods employed. When the defence is in possession of the ball, it is the function of the attack to mark out the defenders with the object of preventing a defence clearance. This is known as 'riding out'.

The midfield players act as a link between the defence and attack; on occasions they must be capable of acting in both capacities. It is the function of the midfielders to obtain possession of the ball in the centre area, particularly after a face-off. This role demands extra stamina and speed and when substitution is played, as in American and Australian lacrosse, the midfielders are constantly replaced by other midfield players in the squad.

The defence players normally mark man to man, but they must be prepared to switch from one opponent to another and sometimes to back up another defence man. Frequently a defence player has to resort to playing zone defence, in which case he is responsible for a prescribed area adjacent to the goal he is defending. Such a situation would arise when the defence are playing with one man short because a time-out penalty has been given against one of their players. It is essential for a defence player to position himself correctly to

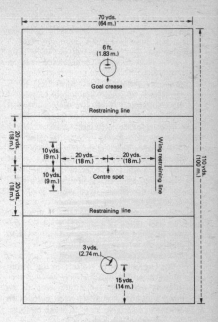

MEN'S LACROSSE GROUND
The goals, represented by lines at the centre of each goal crease, are 80 yds. (73 m.) apart.

counter his opponent's moves, which he must try to anticipate. He must be capable of intercepting an opponent's pass and be able to clear the ball upfield after an attack move has broken down. On occasions a defender will carry the ball up field (known as forcing) with the object of creating a free man on the attack, thereby throwing the opposing defence into confusion.

Once a defender is committed to a ground scuffle, he must make every effort to ensure that he gains possession. His stick-checking must be positive if he is to dispossess the opposing attack. He must have the ability to administer an effective body check. This he does by interposing his body and stick in the path of an oncoming opponent, thereby impeding the forward progress of the player. This technique is employed in all the lacrosse-playing countries. In no circumstances must the butt of the stick be used when executing a body check.

The goalkeeper may stop shots with his crosse or with any part of his body. In addition he must be able to clear the ball up field and assist the defence, over which he exercises a measure of control. He must also be prepared to leave the goal area to check an opposing player who is in a free position with the ball. When play is taking place behind the goal, the goalkeeper must mark an opponent who is rounding the goal with the object of scoring and be ready to intercept passes made over the top of the goal.

Lacrosse in England is controlled by a referee who is assisted by two goal judges; in the more important games linesmen also assist the referee. In the other lacrosse-playing countries two referees officiate, assisted by a timekeeper and scorer, who will agree the score with the referee at the rest intervals and at the end of play. In addition, the scorer records the names of players credited with goals and the names of the players making the assists (i.e. the passes from which goals are scored), together with the names of players who are substituted during the match, the number and nature of penalties awarded, the number of saves made by the goalkeepers, and the number of wins from the face-off.

BOX LACROSSE, a variation of lacrosse, is played exclusively in Canada in the spring and autumn, and occasionally in the summer months. It may be played outdoors in an enclosed area but is usually played indoors on ICE HOCKEY rinks covered with green matting, frequently under floodlights.

The playing area is 160 to 180 ft. (48·77–54·86 m.) long and 60 to 90 ft. (18·29–27·4 m.) wide. The goals, 4 ft. (1·2 m.) wide and 4 ft. high, are located 4 yds. (3·66 m.) in from the back boundary lines.

Frequent substitution of players during a match is a feature of the game, each team being allowed a total of ten substitute players. Time-out penalties for rule infringements are awarded, and these may vary from periods of one to five minutes. During all stoppages of play the time recorder stops; thus a match scheduled for one hour of playing time can take up to 1½ hours to complete. The game is attractive to watch, and crowds of 3,000 are not uncommon.

The principle of the game is basically the same as the field game, but with six men in a team instead of the ten players in the field version. Positionally, the six players are known as goalkeeper, inner and outer defence, centre, and inner and outer attack. The game is controlled by a referee, a timekeeper, and two goal judges.

Australian Lacrosse Council, *Laws of Lacrosse;* American National Collegiate Athletic Association, *Official Lacrosse Rules;* English Lacrosse Union, *Lacrosse By-laws* (1965); Canadian Lacrosse Association, *Rules of Box Lacrosse* (20th ed.).

It is said that lacrosse was born of the North American Indian, christened by the French, but adopted and raised by the Canadians. The Indians called the game *baggataway* and the earliest use of the word 'crosse' applied to the tribal game was made by a Jesuit missionary in 1636 when he saw the Huron tribe playing *baggataway* in an area now known as Ontario. According to Dr. Hoffman in the 1892-3 *Bureau of Ethnology Report,* the game originated among the Algonquin tribes in the valley of the St. Lawrence. It was carried south and played among the Huron and Iroquois tribes and later spread to the west. Some form of the game was played by at least 48 tribes scattered throughout southern Canada and parts of the United States.

The French gave lacrosse its name, derived from the shape of the primitive form of racket which vaguely resembled a bishop's crozier,

BOX LACROSSE PLAYING AREA
Goal posts are 4 ft. (1·2 m.) apart, with the goal net pegged loosely 6 ft. (1·83 m.) behind the goal line. Each of the four end face-off circles has a radius of 6 ft., while the interior circle, and the face-off circle in the centre of the playing area, have a radius of 2 ft. (61 cm.).

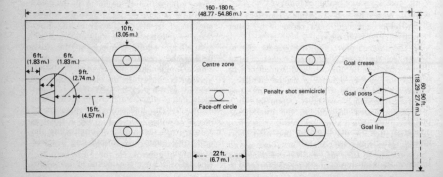

the French word for which is *crosse*. The North American Indians used a crosse 3 to 4 ft. (914 mm.–1·219 m.) in length, the stick of which was curved at one end so as to form a loop or rough circle some 4 in. (102 mm.) in diameter. A loose net was constructed within the looped end of the stick in which a primitive ball made of deerskin, stuffed with hair, and sewn with deer sinews, was carried.

The game had a religious significance and was also played as a means of training tribal warriors. Matches lasted for two or three days, with the goals, marked by trees, some 500 yards (457 m.) apart.

The earliest record of a white man playing lacrosse was in 1844 when a match took place in Montreal. In 1860 an exhibition game was played before the Prince of WALES (later to become Edward VII) at the newly formed Montreal Lacrosse Club.

In 1867 the game spread considerably, with an increase of 75 clubs within 12 months. In the same year the first set of rules was formulated and the game was introduced into Great Britain and the U.S.A. Exhibition games were played in Scotland, in Ireland, and in England at the Crystal Palace; an exhibition game was also played at the World's Fair in Paris. In 1869, Prince Arthur accepted the honorary presidency of the Ontario Club of Toronto and was present at an exhibition match when the Ontario Club played a team selected from all the lacrosse-playing countries before a crowd of 5,000.

With the end of the American Civil War, sport became increasingly popular in America and several exhibition games of lacrosse were staged in the areas around New York and Boston. The first international match between Canada and the U.S.A. took place in Buffalo in 1868, Canada winning 3-0 in 16 minutes. At that time the first team to score three goals was declared the winner.

During the next ten years lacrosse continued to spread in America, Boston, New York, and Baltimore being the main centres of interest. In Canada, the increased popularity of the game was stimulated by the sectarian and national differences of the Montreal Irish Catholics, the Toronto Irish Protestants, and the Montreal English and French immigrants. In 1876, a touring side of players from the Montreal club, together with a team from the Caughnawaga Indian reservation, played a series of matches in England, Ireland, and Scotland. The highlight of the tour occurred on 26 June when the Canadian visitors appeared in a command performance before Queen Victoria at Windsor Castle.

As a result of the tour the game was established in the Manchester, Leeds, London, and Bristol areas. The North of England Lacrosse Association was formed in 1879, this body being responsible for lacrosse played north of Rugby. The South of England Lacrosse Association was formed a year later. To co-ordinate the activities of the two associations, the English Lacrosse Union was formed.

In 1874 the game was introduced into Australia by L. L. Mount of the Montreal club, whence it spread to New Zealand in 1878. Victoria, South Australia, and Western Australia remain the strongholds of lacrosse, but the game has died out in Queensland and in New South Wales. By the turn of the century an inter-state competition had been organized. In 1907, the Canadian Lacrosse Association sent a touring side to Australia and played 16 games which included four Test matches.

From 1880 until the First World War lacrosse continued to gain popularity, especially in American and English universities. During this period the Canadians sent touring sides to all the lacrosse-playing countries, England receiving visits in 1888, 1902, 1907, and 1908, when an exhibition game was staged at the OLYMPIC GAMES in London. The visit of 1907 had a marked influence on the game when the Canadians introduced the short loosely-strung crosse as opposed to the long tightly-strung one used hitherto. The effect of the short stick changed the game from one of long lob passing with a considerable amount of running to one chiefly of short, quick passing coupled with an emphasis on positional play.

By the turn of the century, the laws had been modified, the playing area reduced, and the duration of matches fixed at 90 minutes. International, national, and regional trophies were competed for, many of them featuring silken flags, a reminder of the days when marker flags were placed on top of the upright goal posts.

With the outbreak of war in 1914 lacrosse virtually ceased to be played, except in the U.S.A., where the universities kept the game alive. Records show that a Lancashire *v.* Cheshire lacrosse match was played in Egypt, by servicemen from the 6th Manchester Regiment, many of whom were to fall in the Gallipoli campaign.

By 1928 the game had almost recovered from the setback of the war, and this year saw exhibition games played between the U.S.A., Canada, and England at the Olympic Games in Amsterdam. The International Federation of Amateur Lacrosse (I.F.A.L.) was formed at that time with the object of controlling the international game and formulating a set of international rules.

The early 1930s saw a decline in lacrosse in

the U.S.A. and Canada. In the hope of arresting this, the Americans introduced ten-a-side lacrosse with an offside rule, time-out penalties, and the substitution of players during a game. Canada adopted box lacrosse in 1931, and these measures had the desired effect as the game regained its former popularity.

With the introduction of box lacrosse in Canada, the U.S.A. dominated the field game. An interchange of visits between the U.S.A. and England followed over the next 20 years. Combined university teams from England visited the States in 1922, 1926, 1930, 1961, and as recently as 1971. Touring sides from the U.S.A. visited England in 1937 and 1948, on both occasions the visitors winning most of the matches. The superiority of the Americans was further demonstrated when teams from Yale University (1950), the University of Virginia (1954), Washington and Lee University (1956), and Johns Hopkins University (1958) won the majority of the matches played.

History was made in 1962 when an Australian touring side visited England. One Test match was played which England won. Australia again visited England in 1967 and in 1972; England won the 1967 Test match but were beaten in the 1972 game. The Lancers Club of Baltimore, who visited England in 1965, played a series of matches under English rules but did not fare as well as its American predecessors, losing half of the eight games played.

On the occasion of the Australian tour of America in 1962, the I.F.A.L. was resuscitated, and in May 1967 a meeting was held in Princeton, New Jersey, U.S.A., when a firm constitution was agreed upon and a set of international rules formulated. Membership consists of the U.S.A., Australia, Canada, and England; by tradition the secretary of the English Lacrosse Union is secretary of the I.F.A.L.

In 1967, the centenary of the introduction of lacrosse to the United Kingdom, an English international side visited the U.S.A. and Canada. The visit coincided with the centenary of the Canadian Confederation of States, and to commemorate the event the Canadian Lacrosse Association staged the first world field lacrosse tournament. The U.S.A., Australia, Canada, and England competed. America won all three of their games, Australia won two, Canada won one, and England none. The world tournament immediately followed a seven-match tour undertaken by the English players, played under American rules. On this tour England won three games, drew one, and lost three. Australia visited England after the world tournament and were defeated.

The frequency of tours over the past 20 years has stimulated lacrosse in England and has led to the introduction of a set of international rules, which are basically the same as the American lacrosse rules. The influence of the Americans as a result of the visits they have made to the other lacrosse-playing countries is most marked.

Australia has recently adopted the American-type game. Canada continues to favour box lacrosse, but there is strong evidence of growing support in Canada for a return to the field game.

Lacrosse has naturally tended to be concentrated in areas where it is well supported. In America, the concentration is in the eastern States; in Australia, around Melbourne, Adelaide, and Perth; and in Canada, in Toronto and Vancouver. Manchester, London, and Leeds are the English centres and the game is also played in nine major universities. In the past, matches have been staged at LORD'S CRICKET GROUND and the OVAL, Kennington, but more recently Hurlingham Park has been used for international games. Although lacrosse is not an Olympic event, exhibition matches, in most of which the U.S.A. played Canada or England, were staged during the Olympic Games of 1904, 1908, 1928, 1932, and 1948.

Box lacrosse, introduced into Canada in 1930 and an immediate success, from 1931 until 1960 largely replaced the field game. The fact that box lacrosse can be played in a covered area, is a spectacle, and is heavily sponsored, are contributory factors to its popularity. It is organized on a regional league basis with the leading clubs in each region playing each other to decide the national champions. The major trophy is the Mann Cup, valued at $2,500; the Minto Cup is competed for by junior teams.

Alexander M. Wevand and Milton R. Roberts, *The Lacrosse Story* (1965).

GOVERNING BODY (WORLD): International Federation of Amateur Lacrosse, 3 Chessington Avenue, Bexleyheath, Kent.

Women's lacrosse stemmed from the men's game, but has developed, over the years, along its own individual lines to suit the physique and temperament of women and girls. It has become a game different in concept, shape, and rules.

The crosse is basically the same as the men's, though of the right balance and weight for women and girls to handle. Although there are no left-handed crosses, a player may use either her right hand or her left hand at the top of her stick. The ball is the same as the men's, except that the colours are black, white, or yellow. Special low-bounce balls are available for seven-a-side lacrosse (see below).

Women goalkeepers wear leg pads similar to CRICKET pads, and body pads constructed in the same way as those worn by the men. Shoulder harness, arm pads and gauntlets are never worn by women. Face masks are optional and worn by goalkeepers only; They are used more in the U.S.A. than in Great Britain. Soft leather gloves are sometimes worn, but this is more as a protection against cold weather than against any rough checking.

If at all possible, the field should be full size, and the goal and centre circles must be accurately and clearly marked. The centre circle has a radius of 10 yds. (9 m.) and the goal circles a radius of 8 ft. 6 in. (2·6 m.) taken from the centre of the line joining the two goal posts. In the desirable full-size field, the distance between the two goals is 100 yds. (92 m.), and there should be at least 10 yds. (9 m.) behind each goal: the width should be approximately 80 yds. (73 m.). There are *no* marked boundaries. The crease is the area enclosed by the goal circles.

The team consists of twelve players, six attacks (first, second, and third home, right and left attack, centre) and six defences (goalkeeper, point, cover point, third man, right and left defence), spaced from one goal to the other, each being closely marked by an opponent. When in possession of the ball, the whole team are in attack and the whole of the opposition are in defence. The main duty of the attack is to get the ball as quickly as possible into a position from which a shot at goal may be attempted. The aims and tactics of both attack and defence are similar to those in men's lacrosse.

In theory the game is played in the air. In practice the ball may have to be gathered off the ground into the crosse, but there is no continual stooping. In fact the women's game is one of skill, elegance, and finesse, and no body contact is allowed. There is a continual flow of movement up and down the field. From the moment the ball goes into play each player must use her speed, ingenuity, and initiative to outmanoeuvre her opponent.

There are very few rules, and these are aimed at controlling the game and protecting the players. There are no boundaries nor off-side rules in the women's game so that it is played at great speed and with few interruptions. Close marking in the women's game makes for speed, accuracy in passing, and the skilled techniques of stick-handling.

The block does not exist in the women's game, but the body check (the placing of the body between the player with the ball and her objective) is designed to impede her movements, to force her to pass, or to force her off her direct path to the goal. Crosse-checking

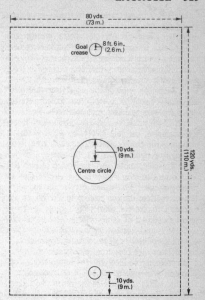

WOMEN'S LACROSSE GROUND
The full-size dimensions are shown. There are no marked boundaries.

(the controlled hitting of an opponent's crosse when she is in control of the ball, in an attempt to take it from her) is allowed but if the umpire considers it rough, it is penalized.

A centre umpire is responsible for enforcing the rules, keeping time, and recording the score, and a goal umpire at each end is responsible for the rules concerning the crease.

The 'draw' (the face-off in the men's game) is executed by the centre players who each stand with one foot toeing the centre line. The crosses are held in the air about hip level, wood to wood, angle to collar, and back to back. The ball is placed between the crosses of the players by the umpire. On the words, 'Ready, draw' from the umpire, the two opponents draw their crosses up and away from one another. This ensures that the ball goes in the air at the outset of play.

A goal is scored when the ball passes over the line which joins the two goal posts. If any part of the player who makes the shot or any part of her stick goes over the crease (the circle round the goal posts), during or after the shot, the goal is disallowed. The goalkeeper is the only player in the team who may touch the ball with her hand, and this only when she is within the crease.

Substitution in the sense used by men in the U.S.A., Australia, and Canada does not exist.

In the event of an accident or injury occurring to a player which, in the opinion of the umpire, incapacitates her from taking any further part in the game, a substitute may take her place, with the limit of one player for each side. If there is no substitute available, or if any further player has to be withdrawn owing to accident or injury, the opposing side must withdraw one of their players as long as the injured player remains incapacitated.

SEVEN-A-SIDE LACROSSE was developed during the late 1960s by B. J. LEWIS in collaboration with others. It is a game in its own right, but using the techniques of the twelve-a-side game. As the space required is less than for the full-sized game it can be played in sports halls and on NETBALL courts. It is very similar in rules but differs in the number of players, start of the game, types of goals, absence of goalkeepers, and the ability to play the rebound from the wall and the floor pass. A special ball, with reduced bounce, is used. There are two umpires instead of three.

Lacrosse is thought to have first been played by women in 1886. Although it is recorded that a school in the north of England played thus early, it is nevertheless certain that several of the leading girls' schools included it in their programmes in 1890. It was first played with eight a side, by 1897 with ten a side, and by 1899 with twelve players arranged in positions as we know them today.

From these early beginnings there has been continuous growth in the number of schools, colleges, and clubs that play. The first club formed was the Southern Ladies in 1905, and in 1912 the Ladies' Lacrosse Association was founded. This is the official body, now known as the All-England Women's Lacrosse Association, to which, by 1973, 162 schools, 35 colleges, and 35 clubs were affiliated.

In 1913 the first international matches were played, in the form of a tournament, when teams from England, Scotland, and Wales took part. The Scottish Association was founded in 1920, and the Irish and Welsh Associations in 1930. The national association of these countries is responsible, as is the English one, for the development and control of the game in its own country. Each selects a representative team for matches played annually against each of the other countries. The only interruption in the continuity of these games was during the years of the Second World War. During this time the game virtually came to a standstill, but, despite the difficulty of getting the balls and other equipment, schools continued to play. They, and the girls who had left during the war years, formed a strong base on which the postwar game could be built and developed.

Outside the British Isles, the country in which lacrosse has the strongest hold is the U.S.A. The All-England Women's Lacrosse Association was instrumental in introducing lacrosse to the women of that country; during the early 1900s English coaches taught the sport in a few schools and colleges there, but it was not until the early 1920s that it became firmly established. It is most widely played in the eastern states, but is spreading rapidly into the South and the Midwest.

The first official English team went to the States in 1949, the way having been paved by a pioneer unofficial team in 1934 led by K. LOCKLEY, then captain of England. Since 1949 teams have gone in both directions at intervals of two to three years. The gap between the standards of play in the two countries has gradually lessened since then, and the games are now extremely closely fought and produce highly skilled and exciting contests. The match played in England in October 1970 ended in a win to England by 12-10, but only after the English team had fought back from a 6-1 deficit. In May 1973 in the U.S.A. the Americans scored their first win over a combined British team, beating them 6-4.

In 1969 the U.S.A. and Great Britain combined in the first-ever tour of Australia, giving exhibition games and playing in the first world series, in Perth, Western Australia. The British team won, 11-10. These teams gave exhibition games in New Zealand, Tokyo, Hong Kong, and Amsterdam.

The women's game in Australia is comparatively young and is more closely allied to the men's game than it is in the British Isles and the U.S.A. In many areas the game is coached by men, and they have developed, with the women, the type of defence play of their own game. The game is played in Melbourne, Adelaide, and Perth.

Lacrosse is played at the University of Hong Kong, and interest is being shown in getting the game established in Tokyo, New Zealand, and Holland. The difficulty of the further expansion of the game in Holland, as indeed in the British Isles, lies in the fact that it is played during the same season as women's hockey. The great expansion of the game in the U.S.A. is partly due to the fact that they are not faced with this competition, women's field hockey being played in the autumn and lacrosse in the spring.

An International Federation of Women's Lacrosse Associations was formed in April 1973, at Williamsburg, Virginia, U.S.A.

Official Rules of The All-England Women's Lacrosse Association, annually; *Handbook of the All-England Women's Lacrosse Association,* annually;

The All-England Women's Lacrosse Association, *Notes on Umpiring*. Margaret Boyd, *Lacrosse — Playing and Coaching* (1969); B. J. Lewis, *Play Lacrosse the Easy Way* (1969).

GOVERNING BODIES: All-England Women's Lacrosse Association, Room 235, 70 Brompton Road, London S.W.3.; United States Women's Lacrosse Association, 20 East Sunset Avenue, Chestnut Hill, Philadelphia, Pa., U.S.A.; Australian Women's Lacrosse Association, 9 Curie Avenue, Melbourne, Victoria 3046, Australia.

LADIES' PLATE, see HENLEY ROYAL REGATTA.

LADY BYNG MEMORIAL TROPHY, ICE HOCKEY trophy, awarded annually in the NATIONAL HOCKEY LEAGUE of North America to 'the player adjudged to have exhibited the best type of sportsmanship and gentlemanly conduct combined with a high standard of playing ability'. It was donated in 1925 by Lady Byng, wife of the Governor-General of Canada, and renamed after her death in 1949. Voted by a poll of sports writers and broadcasters, each winner receives $1,000. It was won for a record seventh time in 1935 by Boucher of NEW YORK RANGERS.

LADY JOSEPHINE (1912), a race-horse who has proved to be perhaps the most influential brood mare in modern international thoroughbred-breeding. Through her two daughters, Lady Juror and Mumtaz Mahal, she was responsible for producing stallions like Fair Trial, Mahmoud, Nasrullah, Royal Charger, Tudor Minstrel, Combat, Abernant, and Kashmir II, whose names appear in pedigrees all over the world. The filly, PETITE ÉTOILE, was also descended from Lady Josephine.

LAGERFELT, Baron GOSTA, a leading member of the Stockholm Orienteering Club who encouraged the club to spread ORIENTEERING in western Europe by taking part in demonstration events he organized in France, Belgium, Hoiland, England, and Scotland.

LAIRD, RONALD OWEN (1938-), race walker for the U.S.A. An international since 1958, he has competed in three Olympiads and was Pan-American 20 km. champion in 1967. He was the man most responsible for raising the standard of RACE WALKING on the American continent over the past decade and has so far won 54 national titles and set records from 1 to 30 km. Laird has frequently competed in Europe and his beating of PAMICH in Italy and taking third place in the LUGANO CUP final, both over 20 km., in 1967, were outstanding achievements and a breakthrough for a non-European walker. In 1973 he repeated his third placing in the Lugano Cup final. His book, *Competitive Race Walking* (1972), is the most comprehensive book on training for the sport currently available.

LAKE PLACID, BOBSLEIGH course in New York State, U.S.A., which was constructed on Mount Van Hoevenberg, in the Adirondacks, to stage the 1932 WINTER OLYMPIC GAMES. Then 1½ miles (2·5 km.) long, the course originally had 28 bends. More than 27,000 cu. yds. of earth and rock were moved to build it. The run is now only one mile long. The straights are 5 ft. (1·52 m.) wide, while the curves vary from 10 to 22 ft. (3·048–6·705 m.), with some of the towering, stone-banked sides rising almost 22 ft. vertically. Speeds exceeding 90 m.p.h. (145 km./h.) have sometimes been achieved along the fastest section in championship races.

Since the 1932 Winter Olympics, world championships have been staged at Lake Placid in 1949, 1961, and 1969. The bobsleigh competitions in the John F. Kennedy Memorial Winter Games have also been held here each year since their inauguration in 1969. Promoted by the New York State Department of Conservation, the course is open to the public and there is a spectator walkway along the entire length of the run; viewing bridges and grandstands give vantage positions at many points.

The narrow Lake Placid track of 16 major turns is smaller and less dangerous than most European circuits, but is tactically more demanding. Critical are the gentle sixth and seventh turns, where experience and skill are required to gain early speed. The curves turn and fall at the same time, as opposed to level corners with the drop occurring between them. But the two main hazards, Shady Corner and Zigzag, have claimed their victims. During training for the 1969 world championships, a United States four-man sled driven by Fenner completed the course in 1 min. 4 sec., then easily the fastest time recorded, representing an average speed of about 60 m.p.h. (97 km./h.).

LAKELAND GAMES, British professional ATHLETICS meetings held in the Lake District of north-west England. Until 1972 they were controlled by the Northern Footracing Association, now disbanded. Like other professional meetings in England, the Games seldom attract national interest now, though they were major sporting events in the late nineteenth century.

LAKER, JAMES CHARLES (1922-), cricketer for England, Surrey, and Essex. An accomplished off-spin bowler, he laid claim to being the greatest of all time when, in 1956, he took 46 wickets in the Test series against Australia. This included the phenomenal return of 19 for 90 runs in the OLD TRAFFORD Test match. Earlier he had taken all ten Australian wickets in an innings for Surrey, and in 1950 he had taken eight wickets for two runs in a Test trial.

LALANDA, MARCIAL (1903-   ), *matador de toros*, renowned for the invention of the *mariposa*, a *capotazo* in which the *torero* drapes his shoulders with the cape and moves it from side to side while walking backwards, deflecting the attacks of the bull to the right and left alternately. His high standard of *toreo* won him numerous national honours from his *alternativa* in 1921 until his retirement in 1942.

LAMBERT, WILLIAM (1779-1851), cricketer for 'England' and Surrey. A powerful, attacking batsman — the most eminent of his time — and slow under-arm bowler, he was the first to score two centuries in a match — in 1817. Soon afterwards he was banned from playing at LORD'S for allegedly 'selling' the match between England and Nottingham.

LAMBTON, Hon. GEORGE (1860-1945), was a well-known English race-horse trainer who managed Lord DERBY's thoroughbreds at Stanley House. Famous horses for which he was responsible were the DERBY winner, Sansovino, HYPERION, and SWYNFORD.

LANCASTER PARK, Christchurch, New Zealand CRICKET ground. Opened in 1882, it has become the headquarters of New Zealand cricket, and the Canterbury club plays there regularly. The highest score made there in a Test match was 258 by Nurse for West Indies in 1968-9, and Dowling, in scoring 239 against India the previous season, made the highest score for New Zealand at home in Test cricket. The ground is used for Rugby football during the winter, when it is the venue for RUGBY UNION Test matches and home ground of the Canterbury provincial side.

LANCING COLLEGE, Sussex, English public school which has produced many top-

OLYMPIC BOBSLEIGH COURSE, LAKE PLACID
The solid black line is the course, with its 16 curves numbered. After finishing, the sleds are braked to a stop uphill; they then slide back to the loading ramp.

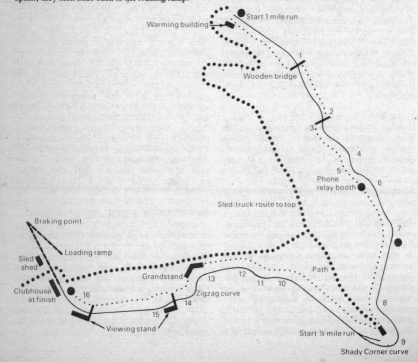

class SQUASH RACKETS players. Only one Lancing old boy, Wilson, has won the amateur championship, but five have gained international honours while the Drysdale Cup has been won on seven occasions by boys from the school. Lancing won the LONDONDERRY CUP, the schools' Old Boys competition, on 17 occasions out of 26 since its recommencement after the Second World War.

LAND YACHTING, see SAND YACHTING.

LANDIS, Judge KENESAW MOUNTAIN (1866-1944), American BASEBALL executive and former Federal judge whom major-league club owners elected as the first Commissioner of Organized Baseball in 1920 and invested with broad investigative and punitive powers. He banished eight players who were implicated in the 1919 WORLD SERIES scandal, even though they had been acquitted in the courts. This action and other stern, often arbitrary, measures established him as a symbol of professional baseball's uprightness. He remained Commissioner until his death.

LANE, FREDERICK C. V. (1877-1969), the first Australian to swim in an OLYMPIC GAMES. As a one-man team in 1900 he won the 200 metres freestyle and a second gold medal in the 200 metres obstacle race. He used a double overarm stroke, similar to the trudgen (see SWIMMING), but with a narrow kick that had been thought too strenuous for distance events. He made three visits to England — in 1899, 1900, and 1902 — and won more Amateur Swimming Association titles (5) than Australian (3). He was the first man to break the minute for 100 yards, with 59·6 secs. in Leicester in October 1902.

LANG PARK, Brisbane, Australian RUGBY LEAGUE ground. Developed by Queensland League and opened in 1961, it has been the regular venue for Test matches and other important matches. Its capacity is 46,000. Previously the main centre for Rugby League in Queensland had been Brisbane Cricket Ground.

LANGFORD, SAM (1883-1956), American boxer who fought professionally for more than 21 years from featherweight to heavyweight; he may well have been the greatest boxer never to have won a world title. Langford, as a lightweight, beat the renowned GANS, later drew with the world welterweight champion WALCOTT, and went 15 rounds with JACK JOHNSON when weighing 156 lb. (71 kg.) to Johnson's 185 lb. (84 kg.). Though only 5 ft. 7½ in. (1·7 m.) tall, he is usually thought of as a heavyweight, and a great one, but his real claim must be as the best middleweight the world has ever seen. In 1923, when almost totally blind, he beat the Mexican heavyweight champion over 15 rounds.

LANSDOWNE CLUB, London, built in 1933, has four SQUASH RACKETS courts, including one with a gallery to seat 150 and standing accommodation for a further 50. This court, named after the club's chairman, the Hon. C. N. Bruce (afterwards Lord ABERDARE), was for many years the largest squash gallery in the British Isles. From 1946 until 1971, apart from 1958-61, the latter rounds of the amateur championship were played here and similarly the Open championship, until 1968 when it was moved to the provinces.

LANSDOWNE ROAD, football ground, Dublin, headquarters of the Irish RUGBY UNION. The first international was played there against England in March 1878, and since 1951 it has been Ireland's only home venue. Two clubs are co-tenants of the ground: Lansdowne and Wanderers.

LARNER, GEORGE EDWARD (1875-c. 1944), race walker for Great Britain. He was Olympic champion at 3,500 metres (track) and 10 miles (road) in 1908 and winner of six English Amateur Athletic Association titles between 1904 and 1911 at 2 and 7 miles. His British 2 miles best time set in 1904 was not beaten until 1960, and at one time he held eight world records at distances between 2 and 10 miles. His meetings with Webb in 1908-11 brought the sport into the public eye just when the Race Walking Association were promoting their early events.

LARWOOD, HAROLD (1904-   ), cricketer for England and Nottinghamshire. Of medium height but sturdy build, he was among the fastest bowlers of all time, and perhaps the most accurate. He is remembered chiefly for his role in the 1932-3 'body-line' Test series against Australia, when his leg-theory bowling brought him 33 wickets.

LASHAM GLIDING CENTRE, lat. 51° 10′ N, long. 01° 04′ W, near Alton, Hampshire, is the largest GLIDING centre in the British Isles. A wartime airfield, with three runways and grass, it is open every day and approximately 26,000 flights per year take place from it. It is a training school and the home of the Surrey, Imperial College, Polish, and other gliding clubs. The British national championships are often held there.

LASSEN, PALLE (*c.* 1918-   ), Danish RACE WALKING official and administrator. Together with LIBOTTE and WHITLOCK he has been at the helm of the International Amateur Athletic Federation (see ATHLETICS, TRACK AND FIELD) Walking Commission for the past 15 years. A chief judge at Olympic and European Games, Lassen organizes numerous local events as well as the LUGANO CUP eliminator. He is editor of the annual book of statistics, *The Race Walking World Statistics*, first published in 1963 and the Danish yearbook for race walking.

LATHAM, PETER W. (1865-1953), British world champion of both RACKETS and REAL TENNIS, and far ahead of his contemporaries at both games for many years. He won the world rackets championship in 1887 and resigned undefeated in 1902; he was real tennis world champion, 1895-1905 and 1907-8.

LATYNINA, LARISSA SEMYONOVNA (1935-   ), Russian gymnast who on her retirement in 1966 had won more Olympic medals than anyone in any sport. In three OLYMPIC GAMES she collected nine gold medals, a number exceeded by the American athlete, Ewry, only if the intercalated 1906 celebration is counted. In addition she won five silver and three bronze medals. Her total in Olympics, world, and European championships is an unprecedented 24 gold medals, 15 silver, and 5 bronze, making her one of the greatest gymnasts in history. She modernized the sport and with her masterly technique popularized it all over the world. Her tally of medals would certainly have been even higher if Russia had not boycotted the 1963 European championships.

After showing her promise at the 1954 world championships, she shook off the challenge of Hungary's KELETI to take the combined exercises as well as four other gold medals. The following year she won a record five gold medals at the European championships and then at the 1958 world championships she completely outclassed the opposition and secured five gold medals again. She retained her title at the 1960 Olympics, once again helping Russia to the team gold medal, but by 1962 CASLAVSKA's improvement was apparent. Latynina only narrowly held her title. At the 1964 Olympics, Latynina was overhauled by Caslavska and she finished second in the combined exercises but took gold medals on the floor and in the team championship. Two years later she barely managed eleventh place over-all but assisted Russia to second place in the team event.

LAUGHLAND, IAIN HUGH PAGE (1935-   ), RUGBY UNION outside half and centre for LONDON SCOTTISH and Scotland. Capped 31 times for Scotland, he was a versatile and gifted footballer, and acknowledged creator of his club's success in seven-a-side competition during the early 1960s.

LAUREL PARK, Washington, D.C., American race-track where the important WASHINGTON INTERNATIONAL horse race is run in November.

LAVER, RODNEY GEORGE (1938-   ), Australian LAWN TENNIS player, the only man to achieve the 'grand slam' of the major singles titles both as an amateur and in open competition. Between 1959 and 1969, he reached the final every time he competed at WIMBLEDON. He was runner-up in the championships in 1959 and 1960, champion in 1961 and 1962, winner of the ALL-ENGLAND CLUB's experimental professional event in 1967, and champion at Wimbledon's first open events in 1968 and 1969. A left-hander, slightly-built in his early years, he moved lightly, hit hard, and had a wonderful sense of anticipation. Heavy use of top-spin and a considerable armoury of delicate shots made him difficult to play and fascinating to watch. Not until 1970, when he had won every great title as an amateur and as a professional, did he show any signs of staleness.

He won the Australian title in 1960. Then, after losing to Olmedo (U.S.A.) and FRASER in successive finals at Wimbledon, he won the title by beating McKinley (U.S.A.) in 1961, and in 1962, the year of his amateur grand slam, he defeated Mulligan (Australia) in the final. In capturing the four major titles, he was troubled only in Paris where Mulligan had a match point against him. He turned professional in 1963 and replaced ROSEWALL as world champion. In 1968 Wimbledon, where he beat Roche in the final, was his only major success, but the following year he completed the first open grand slam, beating Gimeno (Spain) in the Australian final, Rosewall in Paris, NEWCOMBE at Wimbledon, and Roche at FOREST HILLS. In 1970 he failed in the major events, but still became the first lawn tennis player to earn more than $200,000 — actually $201,453 — in a season. In 1973 he reappeared in the Davis Cup (see LAWN TENNIS) and, although he had been out of form, won all six of his rubbers in the inter-zone semi-final against Czechoslovakia and the final against the U.S.A.

LAW, DENIS (1940-   ), Association footballer for HUDDERSFIELD TOWN, MAN-

CHESTER CITY, Turin, MANCHESTER UNITED, and Scotland for whom he made more than 40 appearances in full international matches. He was a bespectacled, somewhat undersized, unlikely-looking footballer when he came straight from school in Aberdeen to Huddersfield Town in 1957. Appearances can seldom have been more deceptive. Lack of height never stayed him from hovering high above defenders to head with sharpness and accuracy; lack of weight never deterred him from taking on a succession of opponents and dribbling the ball through them with quick twists and rapid acceleration. Manchester City obtained his registration from Huddersfield in March 1960; in June of the following year the Italian club, Turin, paid £100,000 for his signature. In July 1962, he was transferred to Manchester United for £116,000, and enjoyed his greatest seasons as an exciting player in an exciting team, before rejoining Manchester City on a free transfer at the end of the 1972-3 season and assisting Scotland to qualify for the final stages of the 1974 World Cup competition.

LAWN TENNIS is a game of domination, played with long-handled, oval-headed rackets, made of either wood or metal, by two (singles) or four (doubles) players. They seek to collect points by controlling and manoeuvring a lively, cloth-covered, rubber ball within the confines of a court, 78 ft. (23·77 m.) long and, for singles play, 27 ft. (8·23 m.) wide.

This court is divided across the middle into two equal halves by a net 3 ft. (0·914 m.) high at the centre and 3 ft. 6 in. (1·07 m.) at the posts. On each side of this obstacle, at a distance of 21 ft. (6·40 m.) and parallel with it, the service lines are drawn. The service area thus lies between the net and the service line, and it is further divided into two sections — the 'right' and 'left' or 'backhand' and 'forehand' courts — by a centre line, which is 13 ft. 6 in. (4·11 m.) from each of the sidelines. The service area remains constant, even though the width of the court is increased to 36 ft. (10·97 m.) for doubles play. The additional areas of 4 ft. 6 in. (1·37 m.) on each side of the court in doubles are known as the 'tramlines', or sometimes in the United States as the 'alleys'.

A point may be won by one or more strokes. The ball is delivered — or 'served' — diagonally from the baseline into the service area on the other side of the net and the object of the game is to force an opponent to hit it into the net or out of court, or to place it in a part of the court where the opponent cannot reach it.

Power and accuracy of service can give a player a considerable advantage. Two deliveries — a 'first service' and a 'second service' — are allowed. If the server wastes the first by hitting it into the net or outside the service area, he can still win the point with the second. Each wasted service is called a 'fault'. A 'double fault' — i.e. two wasted services — costs the server the point.

In the earliest days of lawn tennis almost all players served under-arm but the over-arm service (or 'overhand' service as it was known at first) became general, first for men and then for women. In this the ball is thrown into the air and hit.

As the game developed and as, in the 1930s, the ball became harder and faster, both men and women were able to serve at great pace. VINES's service was timed at 128 m.p.h.

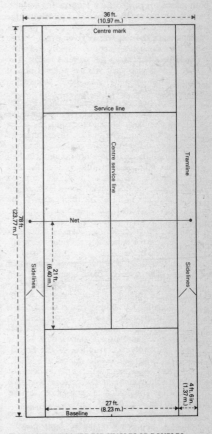

LAWN TENNIS COURT FOR SINGLES OR DOUBLES
For doubles play the posts that hold the net are placed outside the outer sidelines.

(206 km./h.). Stoeffen, another American, was said to have reached 131 m.p.h. (211 km./h.). A winning service, which an opponent is unable to touch with his racket, is called an 'ace'. If the receiver can do nothing but hit the ball out of court, it is regarded as a 'service winner'.

After a service the receiver must return the ball on its first bounce. If he puts it back into court, shots are exchanged until eventually the point is won. This is called a 'rally'. Every attempt is made to make the conditions as fair as possible for both players. If a service touches the net but still lands in the correct area (a 'let'), the server is allowed to repeat the delivery without penalty. There have been suggestions that the service 'let' ought to be abolished, that a service which touches the net should be regarded as a fault or played normally by the receiver (as a shot which hits the net in the course of a rally is), but as the rule now stands the receiver is given every chance to return the ball as it comes directly and without impediment from the server's racket. The term 'let' is also used when a point is played again after a rally has been interrupted accidentally.

Service begins in the right court. For the second point of a game the server moves to the left and then back again to the right, and so on until the game is won or lost. Over the years exchanges in the first-class game have become increasingly fiercer and more taxing. The ball has been taken earlier; the volley (the ball taken before the bounce with the arm no higher than shoulder level) and the smash, in which the ball is hit above the head with the arm fully stretched, are important weapons. The modern ball, with its stitchless seam and wool and nylon covering, is faster but a less easy vehicle for subtle control than the woollen ball used in the 1920s.

The system of scoring derives from REAL TENNIS. The object of the game is to win points for games and sets. A game may be won by the capture of four points — 15, 30, 40, and game. This odd system is based on the habit of using a clock face to record points in the royal days of tennis. The term for zero (no points in a game or no games in a set) is 'love', probably a corruption of the French *l'oeuf* (the egg) and is thus related to a 'duck' in CRICKET. A game in which a player does not score is a 'love game' and a blank set is a 'love set'. At the conclusion of each game, service passes to the other player.

The score is given in terms of the server — love-15 or 40-30 — unless both players score three points in a game when they must win two more, a clear lead, to take the game. This situation, 40-all, is known as 'deuce'

from the French *deux*, meaning two more to win. The capture of one point at this stage gives a player an 'advantage', which an opponent can nullify by taking the next point. Any number of deuces may be played.

The minimum number of games needed for a set is 6, but here again, if conventional scoring is used, a lead of 2 games is required. A set may be won by 6 games to 4, but 5-5 can lead to 9-7, 11-9, or even 15-13 and more. It is one of the fascinations of lawn tennis that the scoring system gives a player as much chance as possible to escape from difficult situations. Women's matches are played over three sets and men's championship contests are usually over five, because it is recognized that championships are great tests of endurance.

The popularization of the game, particularly on television, and an increase in the number of indoor events with restricted time and court space led to demands in the late 1960s for shorter matches. In 1970, as an experiment (see below), the International Lawn Tennis Federation allowed a limited number of points to be played at 6-6 or 8-8 to settle a set which seemed likely to be protracted. This was called a 'tie-break'.

In tournaments matches are adjudicated by umpires who sit on high chairs in line with the net. They call the score and control the game. They may or may not be assisted by linesmen. In a major event there will be a line judge on every line and, in addition, a foot-fault judge and a net-cord judge. The over-all responsibility at a tournament is given to the referee, who does not umpire but arranges the order of play and rules on any disputes which may occur.

There has never been any rule limiting the size or shape of a lawn tennis racket. Those used in the earliest days of the game were designed after the fashion of real tennis, with a comparatively small area of gut, the head curved, and the shaft disproportionately long for such a small head. A real tennis ball was heavier than a lawn tennis ball and more wood was needed to give weight and spin to shots.

The steel-framed racket came on to the market for the first time in the 1930s but did not achieve its expected popularity at that time. In the 1960s it was reintroduced in the U.S.A., and in Europe by LACOSTE and captured a sizeable proportion of the market. Steel and aluminium suddenly became fashionable frames. Many players believed that a metal racket added extra power to service. But most rackets are still made of wood. Beech is used for cheaper rackets and the pliability of ash makes it favoured for bending into oval heads. Hickory is used for shafts by many manufacturers and mahogany and walnut in veneers and inlays. The best strings are made of sheep-gut, although beef-gut (notably in Australia) and hog-gut are also used, together with various nylon-based materials. Most first-class players, however, remain faithful to sheep-gut, which has the greatest elasticity. It is also expensive, six or eight sheep being needed to furnish sufficient gut to string one racket.

The ball used in the modern game must have a uniform outer surface, be more than 2½ in. (6·35 cm.) but less than 2⅝ in. (6·668 cm.) in diameter, and more than 2 oz. (56·7 g.) but less than 2 1/16 oz. (58·47 g.) in weight. If it has seams, they must be stitchless, and when dropped 100 in. (2·54 m.) on to a concrete base the ball must have a bound of more than 53 in. (1·346 m.) and less than 58 in. (1·473 m.). Strict tests for bound, size, and deformation are laid down in the rules.

Until 1970 it was stipulated that balls used for match play must be white, but the experimental use of coloured balls was then permitted by the International Lawn Tennis Federation because it was felt that a red or yellow might be more easily seen by players and spectators at indoor matches under lights. The rules of the game do not lay down that the ball used must be rubber nor that the surface must be cloth, although it was the development of the cloth-covered vulcanized rubber ball that made outdoor tennis a real possibility in the second half of the nineteenth century.

The best modern balls are covered with a mixture of wool (70 per cent) and nylon (30 per cent). Some balls entirely covered with nylon are made, but these are generally judged to be hard and unsympathetic to the racket and thus difficult to control. The pressureless ball, which is supposed to last longer than a ball filled with either air or nitrogen, is produced (notably in Italy and Sweden), but this, too, has its critics. The normal ball produced by the leading companies in Britain has a pressure of about 10 lb. per sq. in.

Court surfaces vary generally according to climate. Grass, clay, shale, sand, asphalt, cement, gravel, and (in South Africa) even ant-heaps have been used to make courts for outdoor play. Wood, plastic, nylon, and rubber, as well as clay are used indoors.

As the name suggests, the game was played first on grass which has remained the traditional surface in three of the four senior lawn tennis countries, Great Britain, Australia, and the U.S.A., although in the latter country in recent years grass courts have deteriorated to such an extent that there have been strong suggestions that the grass at some of the most famous American clubs should be replaced by plastic surfaces.

Good grass, of the quality found in England at WIMBLEDON, Devonshire Park (East-bourne), or the Northern Club in Manchester, encourages bold stroke play and produces the most attractive kind of lawn tennis for a spectator. On the other hand, grass demands considerable time, skill, and money to maintain; it recovers more slowly from rain than artificial surfaces and even on the best days the ball is apt to skid and bounce low. Most contemporary players would probably agree with the comment made by Hillyard in 1903: 'Nothing equals a good grass court, but unfortunately they are as rare to come across as a great auk's egg.'

Clay courts (originally rolled earth with perhaps gravel to bind) were brought into use in the game's first wave of popularity in the late nineteenth century. Outdoor play on the Continent has been almost completely restricted to clay (terre battue, literally 'beaten earth') because of the difficulty of growing grass which will survive the wear and tear of even social lawn tennis. The French have always staged the major clay court championship in Paris; Rome is now regarded as the second most important clay court event.

In European lawn tennis the particular strategies, techniques (top-spin and slice in plenty), and virtues (patience, accuracy, and the ability to endure) were developed, just as California's cement produced the service-and-volley game and players with speed, strength, and sharp reflexes.

CHAMPIONSHIPS. In first-class lawn tennis the year is divided between tournaments in which players compete as individuals and team events, such as the Davis Cup and the Federation Cup (see below), and the WIGHTMAN CUP.

There are four major championships (the 'grand slam') — Wimbledon (Great Britain), which describes itself as 'The Lawn Tennis Championships' and is, in fact, the senior lawn tennis event; Paris (France); FOREST HILLS (U.S.A.); and Australia (which moves between Sydney, Melbourne, Brisbane, and Adelaide). Wimbledon, where play began in 1877, is still regarded unofficially as the world championship, although it dropped its formal claim to that title in 1925. The U.S. championships now held at Forest Hills, Long Island, a suburb of New York, date back to 1881; the French championships, held at the STADE ROLAND-GARROS at Auteuil, began their history ten years later and have always been regarded as the premier clay court event; and Australia's first national event was held in 1905.

Ranking lists, placing players in order of merit according to their results in the previous year, are issued annually by most national associations, and these help the organizers of tournaments to assess the form of the players who compete in their events. Ranking lists are useful in 'seeding', the placing of leading players in protected positions in the draw so that the best competitors do not meet in the early rounds of a tournament. A national ranking is a considerable symbol of status for a player.

In 1970 the International Lawn Tennis Federation was asked at its annual meeting in Paris to produce an authoritative world ranking list but declined to do so because it was thought that the compilation of such a list would be too controversial. A number of unofficial ranking lists are produced. The best-known are those of the American magazine, *World Tennis*, the Italian *Tennis Club*, and the London *Daily Telegraph*, which has been publishing lists of the best ten men since 1914.

Real or royal tennis was an aristocratic sport. By contrast lawn tennis, which burst into sudden popularity midway through the reign of Queen Victoria (1837-1901), began as a diversion for the English middle class, who adapted the framework of real tennis to the conditions of outdoor play. Hitting a ball over an obstacle and subsequently keeping it within boundaries is an idea which might have amused the energetic in any country at any time.

The French game of *la longue paume* entailed hitting a cork ball over a mound, while it is recorded that at Elvetham in Hampshire, Queen Elizabeth I of England was entertained by ten men from the county of Somerset, servants of the Earl of Hertford, who played handball in a square court, made by haying up lines with a cross-line in the centre. 'In this square they played, five to five, with handball, with bord and cord, as they term it, to the great liking of Her Majesty.'

In the *Sporting Magazine* of 29 September 1793, there is a reference to the popularity of 'Field Tennis' ('Field tennis threatens to bowl out cricket') and this may have been the same as 'long tennis', which is mentioned in a book of *Games and Sports*, published in 1873. Neither name is far removed from 'lawn tennis'. The replacement of the cork ball by vulcanized rubber and the fact that as a result of CROQUET's demands the Victorian lawn was no longer soft, mossy, and decorative, but well-rolled and free from shrubs helped to clear the way for the new sport.

It proved to be the perfect game for large gardens and for a leisured society which was seeking new ways of diverting the young of both sexes. 'We have had some very pleasant garden parties and any amount of lawn tennis,' Oscar Wilde, who was staying at Bingham Rectory in Nottinghamshire, told a friend in

1876. And as Lyttelton wrote in 1890, only 15 years after lawn tennis had swept into fashion: 'A lawn, a racket, a soft ball, a net, a pot of paint, and an active member of either sex, here are all the materials needed for lawn tennis and every country house and most suburban villas can supply them; while for tennis — i.e. real tennis — the pastime of kings, such a panoply is needed that a royal income must be won to provide it.'

Unlike real tennis, RACKETS, and (for the Victorians, at least) cricket, lawn tennis was a game that women could play. Croquet, which it ousted, had accustomed the young Victorian woman to competing against her menfolk. As well as hitting, she could run, and mixed doubles brought the added delight of competing in pairs. Here was a truly social sport, one more move towards emancipation.

One of the lawn tennis pioneers was Major Gem, clerk to the Birmingham Magistrates, who in the 1860s played a form of outdoor tennis in the garden of a house at Edgbaston with a Spanish friend, Perera. Later he and Perera joined with two local doctors in establishing the first lawn tennis club at the Manor House Hotel at Leamington Spa, in 1872.

But most of the credit for setting off the lawn tennis revolution has been given to Major Wingfield, whose bust, with the inscription 'Inventor of Lawn Tennis', stands in the foyer of the offices of the LAWN TENNIS ASSOCIATION in London. He was a direct descendant of John Wingfield, the gaoler in England of Charles d'Orleans, a grandson of Charles VI of France and an enthusiastic tennis player, who had been taken prisoner at Agincourt. At exactly the right moment Major Wingfield introduced a system for a game of lawn tennis to the British public. His invention, which he called 'Sphairistiké', was produced for the first time at a country-house Christmas party at Nantclwyd in Wales in 1873. The court, marked out with tape pegged with hair-pins, was shaped like an hour-glass, with a net 21 ft. (6·4 m.) long at the waist, 5 ft. (1·52 m.) high at the posts and 4 ft. 8 in. (1·42 m.) in the centre. The sidelines and the baselines were each 30 ft. (9·1 m.) in length. On one side there was a diamond-shaped serving crease, on the other a service line, and the distance between this and the baseline was divided into equal courts. Rackets scoring was proposed and Wingfield suggested that this game for players of both sexes and all ages might be played on ice as well as on grass.

When he deposited the specification for a patent in 1874, he described his invention as 'a new and improved portable court for playing the ancient game of tennis'. He propagated its virtues enthusiastically, but Sphairistiké was not without its critics. They called it 'Sticky' and said it did not promote *esprit de corps*, and that it was too social to be serious. There were those who thought that it was taxing for women; others who regarded it only as a women's game. Wingfield's hour-glass court and unsatisfactory rules were soon jettisoned. Under the guidance of the MARYLEBONE CRICKET CLUB, lawn tennis — a title which quickly became popular — adopted an oblong court and the server retreated from the diamond crease to the baseline.

Nevertheless, Sphairistiké had been a catalyst. Wingfield had produced a commercial system for outdoor lawn tennis and, if it was never as popular as he hoped, it set other enthusiasts thinking. In the next few years his concept was changed and improved until the basic shape of the modern game of lawn tennis evolved. Heathcote, the author of the study of the game in the Badminton Library, suggests that Wingfield's place in sporting history is that of a popularizer rather than an innovator. The Major, he suggests, may have come across or even played one of the simple, early adaptations of real tennis to outdoor conditions: 'His merit consists in the fact that he was the first to realize that there was, in what he had seen or heard, a capacity of adaptation to the needs of society.'

The hour-glass court's last chance of success faded when a rectangular court was preferred for the first Wimbledon championship in 1877, even though the M.C.C. had supported it in the rules they issued in 1875. In that year, however, another force entered the field. Lawn tennis was introduced at the All-England Croquet Club and two years later 22 players competed there for the men's singles title and a trophy, valued at 25 guineas, presented by *The Field*, a magazine which played a major part in the early development of the game. Before this competition could begin, the club felt that it was necessary to improve the M.C.C. rules. There had been arguments about the scoring system, the size of the court, the height of the net, the position of the service line, and the method of serving. The task of clarification was entrusted to a sub-committee, consisting of Jones, who had been primarily responsible for the introduction of the game at the club, Marshall, the secretary and a great contemporary authority on rackets games, and Heathcote. They settled on 78 ft. by 27 ft. (23·77 × 8·23 m.) as the size for the court, lowered the net to 3 ft. 3 in. (0·99 m.) at the centre, adopted the real tennis scoring system, put the service line 26 ft. (7·9 m.) from the net, and allowed one service fault without penalty. A great many arguments followed these changes, but with only minor

modifications, most of which were settled within half-a-dozen years, the sub-committee's decisions have survived the test of match play on a scale and in conditions which would have astonished this first legislative committee.

Service dominated too many matches at the first Wimbledon and so the following year the service line was moved 4 ft. (1·22 m.) closer to the net and, clearly, the problem of the height of the net had not been solved. SPENCER GORE, the first champion, volleyed his way to success (the discovery of the volley is credited to Woodhouse, who also won the first major tournament played in the U.S.A.) and wrote afterwards: 'As the majority of my opponents were real tennis players, who hit the ball over the net at such a height as to make volleying exceedingly easy, this net-volleying was successful. In the next year, however, the winner of the championship defeated this net-volleying by simply tossing the ball over the volleyer's head and the effort of running back so far after the tossed ball completely tired out the volleyer.'

Gore's conqueror then was Hadow and, after his success, 'pat-ball', as Gore called it, was in fashion until the RENSHAW brothers, Ernest and William, arrived in 1879, volleying from the service line, to sharpen all other talents. Until then most players had been struggling to adapt the techniques of real tennis (stiff wrists and heavy cuts) or the wristy flicks of rackets to outdoor play on grass with a light ball. There were those who argued that it was not possible to hit a lawn tennis ball hard and keep it in play.

The Renshaws, accelerating the exchanges, broke away from the restraints of such careful rallying. They produced a distinct lawn tennis style, hitting hard and flat, volleying and smashing to harry steady baseliners into error. They were the first spectacular players and their success brought the crowds to Wimbledon and helped to establish lawn tennis as a sport to be taken seriously. There had been 200 spectators at the first championship, 700 in 1878, and 1,100 in 1879, but in 1885 when the indomitable Lawford, the master of the heavy drive from the back of the court, played Willie Renshaw in the final, there were 3,500 on that afternoon alone.

Lawford was helped against the volleyers by the decision to lower the net at the posts from 4 ft. to 3 ft. 6 in. (1·07 m.), which was taken by a joint meeting of the M.C.C. and the ALL-ENGLAND CLUB in 1882. This small modification eased the task of the ground-stroke player and Lawford, who eventually beat Ernest Renshaw to win the championship in 1887 at the age of 36, regarded that as a fair height for the development of all kinds of skill. 'Perfect back-play will beat perfect volleying', he remarked. 'When I lose a point through being volleyed, it is my own fault.' The rivalry between the Renshaws and Lawford gave the game its first popular spice. 'Special trains', wrote MYERS, 'brought the denizens of Mayfair, the clubs, and the City to Wimbledon', and it is said that half a sovereign was once paid for standing room on a couple of bricks. As well as the reduction in the height of net, the service line had been moved in to its present distance of 21 ft. (6·40 m.) from the net in an attempt further to restrict the power of the server. By the early 1880s almost all male competitors were using the over-arm or overhand service.

Not every important early development occurred at Wimbledon. Oxford University, which was later to play a major part in the foundation of the Lawn Tennis Association, inaugurated the first men's doubles championship in 1879. Lawford and Erskine were the winners and the event continued there until it was transferred to the All-England Club in 1884, the year that Watson won Wimbledon's first women's singles championship.

The Irish had been the pioneers of competitive lawn tennis for women. They held a women's tournament on asphalt at the Fitzwilliam Club in Dublin in 1879, which was won by Langrishe, the youngest competitor, and the standard was reported to be very high. Bath, the Northern championships, and Cheltenham all held events for women before the All-England Club allowed them the honour of a championship at Wimbledon. The ladies' doubles championship was played first at Buxton in 1884. Langrishe and the remarkable Miss DOD, the first prodigy of women's lawn tennis, won the trophies outright (i.e. for three successive years) in 1888.

The mixed doubles championship was first associated with the Northern Tournament, which alternated between Manchester and Liverpool, but it was not established even there until 1888 when Ernest Renshaw and Mrs. Hillyard were the first champions. Neither the ladies' doubles nor the mixed were given championship status at Wimbledon until 1913, partly because of the prior claims of their original homes and possibly because there was a feeling that attention at Wimbledon ought to be concentrated on the most serious business.

Until 1892, interest in the game was focused on individual performances in tournaments, but then came an important new development. Dr. Stoker of Dublin suggested that there should be a match between Ireland and England and the first competition between two teams of six players was held in Dublin and the proceeds given to the Grand Masonic Bazaar. It was so successful that the experiment was repeated, although later the Irish found difficulty in raising sufficiently strong teams.

But a more formidable rival than Ireland was in the offing. In 1883 two Americans, C. M. and J. S. Clark, who were unbeaten in their own country, played two exhibition matches at Wimbledon against the Renshaws, who were too strong for them. Thereafter there was a certain amount of traffic across the Atlantic in both directions, and in 1897 the Americans suggested that a British team should go to the U.S.A. to play an international match. The offer was rejected, mainly on financial grounds. In 1900 the invitation was repeated. Dr. Dwight, the president of the U.S. National Lawn Tennis Association (U.S.L.T.A.), wrote: 'One of our players here has offered us a Cup, to be a sort of International Challenge Cup. I enclose the conditions in a rough form. I trust that we shall both take a deep interest in them for many years to come. It might do a great deal for the game here, and possibly even with you it might be a help.' This was the beginning of the Davis Cup (see below) and that summer a team from the British Isles left for Boston.

The Americans won this first competition 3-0, with one rubber unfinished and another unplayed, but the best players in Britain, the DOHERTYS, Laurie and Reggie ('Big Do' and 'Little Do'), had stayed at home. They had taken the place of the Renshaws at Wimbledon and the crowds, who had been falling away in the dull years of the 1890s, flocked back. Between 1897 and 1906 one Doherty or the other won the title in every year except one, but at the end of this period of supremacy there was another change. The year 1907 was bleak for British lawn tennis. Laurie Doherty did not defend his title and the championship went overseas for the first time. BROOKES, a left-handed Australian, won the tournament and then helped WILDING, the first great player from New Zealand, to wrest the Davis Cup from Britain for Australasia.

To add to the British discomfiture, Sutton, who had been born in Britain but lived in the United States, took the women's title back to California again. She had won it for the first time in 1905. For the first time both singles titles had gone abroad. A. W. GORE, one of the most persistent of British competitors, won the title twice before the First World War, but Wimbledon was no longer a tournament at which the British showed off their skill at the game they had invented.

In the 50 years after the end of the First

World War the British successes in the men's singles at Wimbledon were those of PERRY from 1934 to 1936, and only MCKANE, ROUND, Mortimer, and Mrs. JONES won the women's title. The Australians and the French enjoyed periods of command, but up to the 1960s, when professional contracts altered the balance of power, the main battle, both at Wimbledon and in the Davis Cup, was between the Americans and the Australians.

Once the framework of the rules had been settled (apart from a series of controversies about the foot-fault rule in serving), lawn tennis remained comparatively free from administrative storms until the 1960s when the question of open lawn tennis — competition between amateurs and professionals — caused a major split. The Lawn Tennis Association, which became the governing body of the British game, was formed in 1888 and shared in the organization of the championships at Wimbledon with the All-England Club, and in 1913 came the foundation of the International Lawn Tennis Federation (I.L.T.F.) as the worldwide governing body. More than 70 countries are now affiliated to the Federation, which is responsible for making the rules of the game and for the international tournament calendar. Each year there is one full meeting. Voting is weighted according to strength and influence in the game. The maximum voting power — 12 votes — is given to the four countries which have held the Davis Cup, Australia, France, Great Britain, and the United States. The headquarters of the I.L.T.F. are in London, where most of the administrative work is done by the Lawn Tennis Association, and Paris. As part of the celebrations of its golden jubilee in 1963, the I.L.T.F. inaugurated the Federation Cup competition, the international women's team championship, which was first held at Queen's Club in London.

This occurred in the middle of the game's greatest crisis. Until the 1920s lawn tennis had been an amateur sport. Leading players had been invited to play in tournaments and their expenses had been paid. The United States Lawn Tennis Association, for example, had offered to pay £40 towards the steamship fares of the British team invited in 1897 and £10 for railway fares, while the following year the British made plans to raise £160 to bring an American team here. As the game became an increasing attraction to spectators, it was no longer possible for many first-class players to regard it merely as a leisure activity. There were still rich patrons and players with private incomes, but the demands of the game were becoming too great and the opportunities for profit too numerous for lawn tennis, at its highest international level, to remain an 'amateur' sport.

The first professional lawn tennis tournament in which former amateurs played for money was promoted at MADISON SQUARE GARDEN, New York, on 9 October 1926, by Pyle, who had previously organized a successful coast-to-coast walking contest. He had persuaded LENGLEN, the greatest of all women players, to turn professional for a sum reputed to be $100,000 and she played a series of matches against Browne, the leading American player of 1912, who was still good enough to be ranked sixth nationally in 1925, even though she could offer little resistance to Lenglen on their tour.

When TILDEN and Johnston, the U.S. men's singles finalists in 1925, refused to join his group, Pyle turned to Richards, another leading American, Kinsey, one of the best doubles players in the country, Snodgrass, who was already a professional, and a French player named Feret. The tour was not a success because no one could beat Lenglen and Richards. Lenglen majestically withdrew. Richards and Kinsey organized a professional championship and tried to revive the idea of a tour.

In the meantime the U.S.L.T.A., spurred on by Tilden, tried to persuade the I.L.T.F. to agree to a proposal to hold an open tournament at Germantown, Philadelphia, in 1930. Only the British, who were later to force the I.L.T.F. into taking action on the matter, supported them. Soon afterwards Tilden turned professional and Richards, Kozeluh (Czechoslovakia), and Nusslein (Germany) joined him on tour.

Thereafter it became customary for the great champions to join the professional ranks. COCHET, Vines, Perry, and — once he had completed the grand slam of the four major singles titles (Wimbledon, Paris, Forest Hills, and Australia) — BUDGE left the amateur game before 1939, as did Lott and Stoeffen, one of the most formidable of American doubles partnerships. During the war there were a number of amateur-professional matches in aid of the Red Cross and as part of the programme of troop entertainments, but afterwards the barrier between the two sides was erected again. The amateurs controlled the game's great tournaments and its most important stadia; the most famous players were professionals.

Budge played Riggs, the Wimbledon champion in 1939, in one tour and Tilden organized a rival group, which included himself and Perry. KRAMER, who had been a member of the last pre-war U.S. Davis Cup team and who had dominated the 1947 Wimbledon, then took command of the professionals. He organized them until a series of back injuries began to limit his effectiveness and GONZALES, the U.S. champion of 1948 and 1949, came to the height of his considerable powers. The drain of amateur talent continued. Segura, an unorthodox player from Ecuador, SEDGMAN, who had played a major part in Australia's recapture of the Davis Cup, TRABERT, one of the most successful postwar Americans, and later the Australians, ROSEWALL, HOAD, and (after he had in 1962 become the second player to complete the grand slam) LAVER all joined the group.

Kramer's attitude to the amateur authorities veered between optimism and exasperation, but from 1960 onwards he knew that the British Lawn Tennis Association was fully committed to an open game. He had, however, given way to other promoters by the time amateurs and professionals were allowed to play in the same tournaments. MacCall, a former U.S. Davis Cup captain, took over the management of most of the players who had been in Kramer's group and Lamar Hunt, a Texas oil millionaire, who called his organization World Championship Tennis (W.C.T.), signed a number of the younger players, notably NEWCOMBE, the reigning Wimbledon champion, and Roche, another leading Australian.

Britain's attempts to persuade the rest of the world that open tennis was inevitable were consistently thwarted by the I.L.T.F. Most countries in the period of expansion that followed the war preferred to pay large sums in 'expenses' instead of treating them all as 'players' and paying by results. Great crowds were now watching the game. Instead of being merely a middle-class sport, it was entertaining the masses and even countries behind the Iron Curtain were spending large sums on training programmes. For those who regarded the promoters as enemies of the game or who wanted its reinstatement in the OLYMPIC GAMES, open lawn tennis was an idea to be fought bitterly.

The British, however, continued to press for reform and were supported by many of the players and younger administrators in other countries and by the mass of public opinion. Eventually, after a dramatic meeting of the Lawn Tennis Association in London in December 1967, it was announced that all distinction between amateurs and professionals was to be abolished and that all competitors would be regarded as 'players'. This meant that the 1968 Wimbledon would be open — whether the I.L.T.F. approved or not. Immediately the British were threatened with expulsion and a number of prominent players from other countries announced that they would play at this first open Wimbledon, even if it meant suspension by their own national governing bodies.

A compromise, to which the British agreed unwillingly and which resulted in a continuation of the struggle for ascendancy between the I.L.T.F. and the promoters, was reached in Paris in March 1968. Open events were to be allowed as an experiment, but a distinction was to be made between 'amateurs', who stipulated that they would not play for money, 'registered players', who received prize money but accepted the control of their national associations, and 'contract professionals', who were controlled by promoters. The contract professionals were excluded from all except open tournaments, which could be held only with the permission of the I.L.T.F., and they could not play in the Davis Cup.

The first open tournament was played at Bournemouth in April 1968, and won by Rosewall. Laver won the first open Wimbledon the same year and in 1969 completed the first open grand slam — a considerably greater achievement than his amateur grand slam in 1962 because it was gained against the combined opposition of all the best players in the world, whereas previously players who might well have beaten him in major events were professionals. In 1970 Mrs. COURT, another Australian, became the first woman to capture the four major open titles. CONNOLLY had gained a similar grand slam as an amateur in 1953.

There were two other major international developments in 1970. The South African Lawn Tennis Union was refused permission to compete in the Davis Cup on the ground that the racial policies of the South African government 'endangered' the competition. There had been demonstrations against apartheid at some matches in which South African teams had played and some countries had withdrawn rather than play against them. The Rhodesian Lawn Tennis Association, whose entry had also been questioned, was allowed to compete, but Israel, who would have been their first opponents, withdrew, and since — because of the United Nations sanctions against Rhodesia — other withdrawals were likely, the Rhodesians were forced to drop out. The apartheid issue had been brought to a head by the refusal of the South African government to permit ASHE, a coloured player who had won the U.S. Open in 1968, to play at Johannesburg. The situation was eased a little in 1972 when for the first time South African non-whites were allowed to compete in their own national championships, and Ashe played in that event the following years. South Africa were readmitted to the Davis Cup. The protests diminished but did not wholly die away.

There was also controversy over the first major change in the rules since the early days at Wimbledon. The development of the service and volley game and the greater physical fitness of players had resulted in matches lasting longer. Some of these matches bored the public. Others, like the famous 93–game contest between DROBNY and Patty at Wimbledon in 1953 and the five-hour meeting between Gonzales and Pasarell in 1969, were continuously fascinating. The Americans, however, finding that more and more matches were being played indoors where time was limited, and also seeking to popularize the game on television, pressed for a system of scoring which would enable a long match to be cut short in the fairest possible way. The professionals had made a number of experiments in the days before open lawn tennis, but had failed to find a satisfactory method of doing this.

In February 1970, at Philadelphia, a 12-point tie-break was tried and proved reasonably popular. At 6-6 in any set, 12 points would be played and the first player to win 7 would take the set. If they were level, they would continue until one player gained a lead of 2 points. The I.L.T.F. immediately declared this change illegal and asked the U.S.L.T.A. to take action against the organizers of the tournament, but five months later the annual meeting of the I.L.T.F. gave national associations permission to experiment with different tie-breaks. In January 1971, it was announced that the Philadelphia 12-point method would be used at Wimbledon that year. This decision caused some controversy and there were those who regarded it as a sign of the game's increasing commercialization.

And as the game expanded, so the I.L.T.F. found increasing difficulty in dealing with an expanding tournament circuit and new forces in the professional game. In 1972 they felt it necessary to ban all players who had signed contracts with World Championship Tennis from their tournaments. Eventually, they agreed to co-exist peacefully with W.C.T., allowing the newcomers to promote tournaments for the first four months of the year, but peace was made too late for the professionals to play at Wimbledon. Newcombe was unable to defend his title and Smith, whom he had beaten in the 1971 final, succeeded to it by defeating Nastase, Wimbledon's first Romanian finalist, in the last match.

Many of the leading players also missed Wimbledon in 1973. In the previous September the Association of Tennis Professionals (A.T.P.) had been formed, with Kramer as its executive director. They sought the kind of position in the game that the Professional Golfers' Association held in GOLF in the U.S.A. and they took issue with the I.L.T.F. over the Yugoslav Tennis Federation's decision to ban Pilic, one of the original members of W.C.T., for nine months for refusing to play in a Davis Cup match. The I.L.T.F. reduced this sentence to one month, but the period of ban included Wimbledon. A.T.P., claiming that a player should have free choice as to whether or not he appeared for his country, refused to accept this and more than 70 players supported Pilic by withdrawing from Wimbledon. This time the title went to Kodes, Czechoslovakia's second postwar champion.

The I.L.T.F.'s authority was also threatened by a dispute over the recognition of World Team Tennis (W.T.T.), a new inter-city league in the U.S.A., which proposed to stage a series of matches between May and August in 16 American cities. W.T.T. offered large contracts to men and women players, but they were opposed at the outset by A.T.P. and by most of the I.L.T.F.'s European members who saw their traditional season threatened by the new group's plans. When the I.L.T.F. announced an agreement with W.T.T., there was considerable anger among the Europeans.

INTERNATIONAL COMPETITION. The *Davis Cup*, the award for the men's international team competition — officially the International Lawn Tennis Challenge Trophy — was the gift of DWIGHT F. DAVIS, a leading American player and at that time (1900) a Harvard senior. He asked Shreeve, Crump, and Low, the Boston silversmiths, to make up 217 troy ounces of sterling silver into a bowl of 13 in. (330 mm.) high. The competition is administered by the Davis Cup Nations Committee, on which each competing country has one vote, and apart from war years, there have been challenges for the Davis Cup every year except 1901 and 1910.

The form of the tournament has not changed. Teams consist of a maximum of four players with, possibly, a non-playing captain who is allowed to sit by the umpire's chair at the side of the court. Two singles rubbers are played on the first day of a match, a doubles on the second, and two reverse singles (i.e. in which the players on the first day change opponents) on the third.

From 1903, when the competition ceased to be confined to the Americans and the British, to 1972, the holders stood out until the strongest challenger emerged to play against them in the 'challenge round'. At first there were knock-out tournaments, usually played in the country of the champion nation, but later the challengers realized the possibility of drawing crowds and popularizing the game in their own countries. For the more important lawn tennis countries the Davis Cup became a profitable business. Zone and inter-zone finals became necessary as the competition grew larger and until 1972 six months of play often passed before the defending nation knew whom it would have to meet in the challenge round. But for the 1972 competition the challenge round was abolished and the champion nation had to play its way through its zone if it was to reach the final. Most of the countries which supported this change hoped that it would break the Australian–American domination of the tournament.

The first contest at the LONGWOOD CRICKET CLUB in Boston hardly encouraged the hope that the Davis Cup would develop into a major international competition. The British team, which included A. W. Gore, who became Wimbledon's oldest champion nine years later, and Roper Barrett, who captained Britain's successful team in the 1930s, returned home baffled by Ward's 'American twist' services and complaining bitterly about playing conditions at Longwood. Britain challenged unsuccessfully again in 1902, but in 1903, after shrewdly conceding R. F. Doherty's first singles rubber so that he .could rest an injured arm, they won 4-1. With the trophy in Europe, France and Belgium entered the following year. Australasia challenged for the first time in 1905 and ended the Anglo-American domination two years later.

The entry of Germany and Canada brought the number of teams competing to six by 1912 and after the First World War the number of challenges increased until it reached 47 in 1968. In 1923 the competition was divided into European and American zones, and in 1931 the American zone was split into Northern and Southern sections. Further reorganizations resulted in the creation of the Eastern and two European groups. The section winners meet in the inter-zone semi-finals and finals for the right to make the final challenge.

After the end of the First World War France (1927-32) and Britain (1933-6) enjoyed spells of command, but outside that period the Davis Cup belonged either to the U.S.A. or Australia. The U.S.A. ruled from 1920 to 1926 — the Tilden years — and, thanks to Budge, in 1937-8. In 1939, as in 1914, the trophy went to Australia, but after four postwar American years there was an astonishing period of Australian supremacy. In the 18 years between 1950 and 1967 they were champion nation 15 times.

The U.S.A. regained the trophy in 1968 only after the strongest Australians had turned professional, and held it until 1973 when

Laver, Newcombe, and Rosewall returned to win the first indoor Davis Cup final 5-0 at Cleveland. From 1946 to 1959 the U.S.A. and Australia played in all the challenge rounds, but afterwards, as the Americans suffered some strange misfortunes, losing even to Ecuador in 1967 and to Colombia in 1974, Italy, Spain, India, Mexico, Romania, and West Germany were among the last challengers. In the 25 years after the war Britain reached the inter-zone final once. Then they lost to Romania at Wimbledon. France, the other former champions, did not achieve even that much.

The *Federation Cup*, the lawn tennis international team competition for women, was inaugurated in 1963 to commemorate the fiftieth anniversary of the foundation of the International Lawn Tennis Federation. Unlike the Davis Cup, the annual tournament for the Federation takes place in one centre. Following the first competition, at Queen's Club in London, the countries to act as hosts in its early years included the U.S.A., Australia, France, West Germany, and Greece.

Each team consists of a maximum of three players, with or without a non-playing captain, and the matches are decided on the results of two singles rubbers and one doubles. At the start the competition was dominated by Australia and the U.S.A., although West Germany, Holland, and Britain have all made appearances in the final, and South Africa won the title when the event was staged at Johannesburg in 1972.

Australia has been more successful in modern lawn tennis, in both team and individual competition, than any other country. With the help of New Zealand — and New Zealand's greatest player, Wilding — who joined them in a Davis Cup challenge in 1905 as 'Australasia', they quickly established a formidable reputation.

Wilding and the leading Australian, Brookes, captured the Davis Cup in 1907 and held it until 1912, one of the years in which Wilding did not go back to defend it. Australasia regained the trophy in 1914 and retained it in 1919 until Tilden arrived to lead the U.S. counter-attack. After Wilding's death, Australia dominated the joint team and Australasia played for the last time in the 1922 challenge round. Australia challenged alone in 1923 and New Zealand competed independently for the first time in 1924.

The 1920s were Australia's least successful lawn tennis decade. Brookes, the first great left-hander, had won the Wimbledon title in 1907 and 1914 and PATTERSON, another native of Melbourne and a nephew of Nellie Melba, followed his example in 1919 and 1922, but

Tilden was always too brilliantly aggressive for their Davis Cup team and it was not until CRAWFORD won the Australian title in 1931 that his country's challenge began to look formidable again.

Australia reached the final of the European zone in 1933, but lost to Britain and it was a British player, Perry, who spoilt Crawford's chance of completing the grand slam of the four major titles in that year by defeating him in the final at Forest Hills, the last of the great championships. Australia had to wait until 1939 to beat the U.S.A. in the challenge round at Philadelphia to recapture the trophy.

When the war ended, the Americans gained their revenge, but in 1950, under the leadership of HOPMAN, Australia entered the longest period of supremacy that the game has known. Between then and 1967, Australia won the Davis Cup 15 times and captured the men's singles title at Wimbledon 10 times. Australians also won many other major titles in those years. They were represented by a steady stream of great champions. When the leaders turned professional, others took their places. Sedgman and McGregor gave way to Hoad and Rosewall, to FRASER and Cooper, to EMERSON and STOLLE, to Laver, Newcombe, and Roche. Not until 1968, when most of the leading professionals were Australians, did the Davis Cup stream dry up. Even then the old heroes returned to regain the trophy in 1973. The team which beat the U.S.A. 5-0 in the final had an average age of 35.

In the years before open tennis, Australians continued to command the game, but as professionals and outside the control of Hopman and the Lawn Tennis Association of Australia. The 1960s also brought a remarkable advance in the performances of Australia's women players. Until then they had ever produced a great champion, but in 1960 Margaret Smith (later Mrs. Court) won the first of her long series of matches against BUENO and Australia's battle with the U.S.A. for the domination of the women's game began. Miss Smith won the Wimbledon title in 1963 and 1965, retired to marry, and then returned to regain it and complete the grand slam in 1970. Turner, her chief rival at home, won the French and Italian titles. In the first nine years of competition for the Federation Cup, Australia won five times and the U.S.A. four.

Most of the spectacular Australian victories took place abroad. The Australian championships, staged in turn by New South Wales, Victoria, Queensland, and South Australia, have always suffered from the disadvantage of the country's geographical position. The Lawn Tennis Association of Australia found it expensive to persuade overseas players to compete and when notable competitors did travel there they often found acclimatization difficult.

The Australian championships were held first in 1905 and in the years before 1914 the most distinguished men's champions were Wilding (1906 and 1909) and Brookes (1911). Brookes's record was less impressive at home than abroad. That was his only singles title and he did not win the doubles until 1924. Then, at the age of 46, he successfully partnered J. O. Anderson. Anderson, who won the singles three times, and Crawford, the winner from 1931 to 1933 and again in 1935, were the most successful home players in the inter-war years. The title went abroad four times in that period: twice to Britain, Kingscote (1919) and Perry (1934), once to France, BOROTRA (1928), and once to the U.S.A., Budge in his grand slam year.

QUIST won in 1936, 1940, and 1948, and then came a formidable list of home winners. Emerson was the most consistent man, winning in 1961 and 1963-7, but even he could not match Miss Smith's record. She was unbeaten from 1960 to 1967, and then, after two blank years, regained the title in 1969 and retained it in 1970 and 1971.

France. The French, as masters of real tennis, quickly profited from the idea of adapting the old game to outdoor conditions and within 20 years of the invention of lawn tennis both Paris and the Riviera were major international centres of the game. Unable to grow grass of the right quality for competition, the French concentrated on the development of clay courts — *terre battue* — and the fine sand of the Riviera became recognized as an almost perfect surface for the game.

The golden age of French lawn tennis came in the 1920s and early 1930s when Lenglen and the 'four Musketeers' — Borotra, Cochet, Lacoste, and BRUGNON — led the world, but before their emergence France had already produced two major players. The French championships, the major clay court event, had been inaugurated in 1891. In the period before the First World War Decugis was the dominating competitor. He won the singles in 1903-4, 1907-9, and 1912-14, and, although he played with three different partners, he was unbeaten in doubles from 1902 to 1914. When the championships were resumed in 1920, he returned to win the doubles again at the age of 38.

In 1911 Decugis, partnered by Gobert, a brilliant indoor player, gained France's first success at Wimbledon, defeating Wilding and Ritchie in the final of the men's doubles. A year later Gobert reached the all-comers' singles final but fell to the experienced A. W.

Gore. It was not until 1924 that Borotra broke the spell by beating Lacoste in an all-French final, but, having won the title once, the French monopolized it until Tilden counter-attacked in 1930. They had only one more success in the next 40 years at Wimbledon when Petra was an unexpected champion in 1946.

The 'Musketeers' were equally successful in the French championships and in the Davis Cup. From 1924 to 1932, the national singles title never passed out of their keeping and only the Americans, Kinsey and Richards, interrupted their control of the doubles in the years between 1924 and 1930. Cochet and Brugnon regained that title in 1932, and Borotra won it again with Brugnon in 1934 and with Bernard in 1936 — but that was the end of the golden age.

Bernard won the title again in 1946, the first postwar year, when the entry was weak, and Darmon, a graceful stroke-maker, lost to Emerson in the 1963 final, but in the later 1950s and the 1960s the event was dominated increasingly by the Australians, even though SANTANA (Spain) and Pietrangeli (Italy) gained two notable victories each and in 1967 Durr became the first home singles champion since Mathieu in 1938-9.

The 'Musketeers' held the Davis Cup from 1927 to 1933 when the British beat them, but France's subsequent record was disappointing. In the 1950s and 1960s, in spite of the efforts of Bernard and Darmon, they found it impossible to break out of the European zone.

Germany was the sixth country to challenge in the Davis Cup and, since the Austrians did not appear on court, the fifth to play in the competition. From 1913, when Germany beat France in the first round and lost to the U.S.A., they fielded strong teams, but although they reached the inter-zone final six times between 1929 and 1938, the heyday of VON CRAMM and Henkel, they did not play in a challenge round until 1970 when the U.S.A. beat them 5-0 at Cleveland.

German players enjoyed some early successes at Wimbledon. Kreuzer (1907 and 1913) reached the quarter-finals of the all-comers' singles, Rahe was a semi-finalist in 1909 and 1911, and Froitzheim, their best pre-war player, took Brookes, the eventual champion, to 6-2, 6-1, 5-7, 4-6, 8-6 in the all-comers' final in 1914.

The German inter-war team would have been even stronger if Moldenhauer, their promising young champion in 1926-7, had not been killed in a motor-cycle accident in 1929. With his support, von Cramm, Henkel, and Prenn would have been better placed to challenge Franco-British superiority in the 1930s. The elegant von Cramm failed in three succes-

sive Wimbledon singles finals, but played a major part in the restoration of German lawn tennis after the war. Bungert was the runner-up in the men's singles at Wimbledon in 1967, but Germany did not reach the inter-zone final again until 1970. Then, after beating Russia in a close contest, they won a controversial contest against Spain on a hastily constructed cement court, to go to Cleveland.

India. The Anglo-Indians introduced lawn tennis to India and it quickly became a popular and highly competitive sport. In an essay written in 1902, Pearson, the champion of Bengal, tells of travelling 1,500 miles to play in a tournament. Playing standards were high. Caked mud, gravel, and asphalt were used as court surfaces and Indian grass courts are some of the best in the world. In 1890, two of the best expatriate players, Davies and Gamble, reached the doubles semi-finals at Wimbledon.

The first All-India championships were held in 1910, with men's and women's events, and India challenged in the Davis Cup for the first time in 1920. Sleem, one of the most patiently accurate players the game has known, and Deane beat France, whose team included Brugnon, 4-1 in Paris before losing to Japan in Chicago. Sleem captained the team for several years, but it was not until the 1960s that Indian lawn tennis reached a peak. Led by the subtly effective Krishnan, who was supported by Mukerjea and Lall, they beat Brazil 3-2 in the inter-zone final, only to lose 4-1 in the challenge round. Krishnan and Mukerjea gained their rubber by beating Newcombe and Roche 4-6, 7-5, 6-4, 6-4. Altogether, India played in four inter-zone finals between 1962 and 1968.

Italy. For many years lawn tennis in Italy was generally restricted to the richer classes. She did not challenge in the Davis Cup until 1922 when England beat her 4-0 at Roehampton, London. Baron de Morpurgo, who had won the French covered court title in 1921, captained the team from then until 1931 and led it to the inter-zone final in 1928 and 1930. Colombo, Count Balbi de Robecco, and, notably, de Stefani, who later became president of the International Lawn Tennis Federation at the time of the crisis over open lawn tennis, were their other leading pre-war players.

After the war, the Italians challenged again in 1948 and soon demonstrated that they possessed one of the strongest teams in the competition, relying first on Cucelli and the del Bello brothers, then on Gardini, the unorthodox Merlo, and their two finest Davis Cup players, Pietrangeli and Sirola.

Italy reached the inter-zone final in 1949, 1955-6, and 1958-61, and the challenge round twice, losing to Australia twice, 4-1 at Sydney in 1960 and 5-0 at Melbourne the following year. Pietrangeli, their outstanding player, won the French title in 1959 and 1960, the Italian in 1957 and 1961, and the German in 1960. He and Sirola formed one of the outstanding postwar doubles partnerships and between 1954 and 1972 Pietrangeli played no fewer than 164 Davis Cup rubbers, winning 120.

Spain challenged in the Davis Cup for the first time in 1920, relying upon her first major player, Alonso, an aggressive competitor, who had been taught the game by his English governess, and the Count de Gomar. She lost 4-1 to England at Hendon, but the following year beat India, reached the all-comers' final, and then in 1924 avenged her defeat by the English at Manchester and reached the final again.

In 1925 Spain challenged in the American zone and lost to Japan. Alonso, who had been a semi-finalist in Paris, had reached the all-comers' final at Wimbledon in 1921, and recorded several victories over Tilden, gave way to Flaquer, Maier, and Sindreu, who still formed one of the most formidable teams in the world.

Spain achieved little in postwar competition until the emergence of Gimeno, who turned professional in 1960 after winning 14 out of 22 rubbers in three years, and Santana, who inspired his country to become the strongest side in Europe. He was the first Spaniard to win the men's singles titles at Wimbledon and Forest Hills and in 1965 and 1967 he led Spain to the challenge round of the Davis Cup. On both occasions she was beaten 4-1 by Australia. Spain produced only one major woman player in the first hundred years of lawn tennis — DE ALVAREZ, one of the game's most brilliant stylists.

U.S.A. The first British experiments in lawn tennis were followed quickly by the introduction of the game to the United States. In 1874 Dr. Dwight and F. R. Sears, the elder brother of Richard Sears, the first U.S. singles champion, were playing on a court at Nahant, near Boston, and soon New York and Newport, Rhode Island, had also become centres of the game.

When the United States National Lawn Tennis Association was formed in 1881 — seven years before the formation of its British equivalent — one of its first tasks was to provide for the organization of a national championship. Up to then several so-called national championships had been held, but the conditions varied at each tournament and the rules and conditions were not standardized.

Unlike the British, who gradually concen-trated everything upon Wimbledon, the Americans for a number of years held their main competitions for men and women at different centres. The first official championships, at which only men's singles and doubles were played, were held at Newport, Rhode Island, in 1881. Richard Sears, asserting the supremacy of the Longwood Cricket Club at Boston, beat Glyn in the final and was unbeaten until he retired from competition because of an injured neck in 1887.

The Newport Casino remained the site of the men's tournament until 1915 when it was moved for the first time to the new ground of the West Side Lawn Tennis Club at Forest Hills. During these years at Newport success was restricted to a comparatively small number of players. Slocum won twice, Campbell three times, and Wrenn four times. Then came three years of Whitman before the seven-year reign of Larned was interrupted by H. L. Doherty, the first overseas champion, in 1903, Ward (1904), Wright (1905), and Clothier (1906).

In 1912 the challenge round was abolished and MCLOUGHLIN served his way to success. The next major player to win the title was Tilden, who was undefeated until he fell to Lacoste in 1926. That signalled the end of one of the great periods of American supremacy. The Davis Cup had been an American idea. Australasia (Brookes, Wilding, and then Patterson) had won in the years before the First World War, but Tilden, supported by Johnston, Williams, and Richards, brought it back across the Pacific again in 1920. The French took the Davis Cup from the Americans in 1927 and Lacoste won twice at Forest Hills and Cochet once.

The United States lost in six of the next eight Davis Cup challenge rounds and they did not regain the trophy until 1937 when Perry had turned professional and Budge had reached the peak of his career. When Budge joined the professionals, Australia — Quist and Bromwich — beat them at Philadelphia during the week-end that war was declared in 1939. Between then and 1945 the Americans found it easier than other countries to keep their competitions going and peace coincided with the emergence of some of the finest American talents. Although WILLS and MARBLE had retired, there was a formidable new generation of women players, and between 1946 and 1955 the British won only three rubbers out of 69 in the Wightman Cup.

Able to call upon such players as Kramer, Gonzales, Parker, Mulloy, and Schroeder, the U.S.A. held the Davis Cup until 1954. Then, rewarded only by successes in 1954, 1958, and 1963, she was forced to pursue Australia again until she regained the trophy in 1968. It was rather an empty honour, however, for most of the best Australians had turned professional.

The U.S.A. endured an equally lean period at Forest Hills. From 1955, the year of Trabert's second victory, to 1968, when Ashe won the first U.S. Open, no American won the men's singles. The American women were also less dominating in the 1960s. Up to 1939 the only winners from abroad were Nuthall, a British player, who reached the final at the age of 16 in 1927 and then won the title in 1930, and Lizana (Chile) in 1937. The title went abroad for the first time after the war when Bueno beat Christine Truman (Britain) in the 1959 final. Other subsequent overseas winners were Margaret Smith (Australia) and Wade (Britain). There was no home champion from 1961, Hard's second year of success, until 1967, when Mrs. KING was the winner.

W. Baddeley, *Lawn Tennis* (1903); F. R. Burrow, *The Centre Court and Others* (1937); H. Cochet, *The Art of Tennis* (1936); D. C. Coombe, *A History of the Davis Cup* (1949); J. M. and C. G. Heathcote, E. O. P. Bouverie, and A. C. Ainger, *Tennis, Lawn Tennis, Badminton, Rackets, and Fives* (The Badminton Library, 1894); G. W. Hillyard, *Forty Years of First-Class Lawn Tennis* (1924); Harry Hopman, *Aces and Places* (1957); Helen Hull Jacobs, *Gallery of Champions* (1951); A. Wallis Myers, *Lawn Tennis at Home and Abroad* (ed.) (1903), *The Complete Lawn Tennis Player* (1908), *Lawn Tennis* (The Lonsdale Library), *Great Lawn Tennis* (1937), and *Memory's Parade* (1932); Edward C. Potter, *Kings of the Court* (1963) and *The Davis Cup* (1969); A. D. C. Macaulay and Sir John Smyth, *Behind the Scenes at Wimbledon* (1965); Sir John Smyth, *Lawn Tennis in British Sports Past and Present* (1953); W. T. Tilden, *The Art of Lawn Tennis* (1920), *Match-Play and the Spin of the Ball* (1928), and *Tennis A to Z* (1950). Maurice Brady's *Lawn Tennis Encyclopaedia* (1969), *Lawn Tennis and Badminton* (formerly the official journal of the Lawn Tennis Association, London), and *Tennis World*.

GOVERNING BODY (WORLD): International Lawn Tennis Federation, Barons Court, West Kensington, London W.14; (U.K.): Lawn Tennis Association, Barons Court, West Kensington, London W.14; (U.S.A.): United States Lawn Tennis Association, Suite 1008, 51 East 42nd Street, New York, N.Y. 10017, U.S.A.

LAWN TENNIS ASSOCIATION (L.T.A.), the governing body of LAWN TENNIS in England, Scotland, and Wales, was founded in 1888 as a result of the initiative of Scrivener, president of the Oxford University Lawn Tennis Club, and Hillyard of the MARYLEBONE CRICKET CLUB, which had played an important part in helping to standardize the rules in the early years of the game. From that time the L.T.A. was responsible for making and upholding the rules until that right was handed over to the International Lawn Tennis Federation (see LAWN TENNIS) when it was founded in 1913. The L.T.A. is administered by a council on which the English county associations, the national associations of Scotland and Wales, and certain other lawn tennis bodies — including the ALL-ENGLAND CLUB, with whom the L.T.A. shares the responsibility for staging the WIMBLEDON championships — are represented. The United States Lawn Tennis Association, formed in 1881, is its only senior.

LAWRENCE REALIZATION STAKES, an American horse race, run over 1 mile 5 furlongs (2,600 m.) at BELMONT PARK, N.Y., in September. It is the American equivalent of the English ST. LEGER, but over a shorter distance, but it does not form part of the American triple crown.

LAWRY, WILLIAM MORRIS (1937-   ), cricketer for Australia and Victoria. Scoring more than 2,000 runs on his first tour of England in 1961, which included two Test centuries, he established himself as a reliable opening batsman for Australia. A left-hander, he displayed great obduracy in many large innings, and was appointed captain of Australia in 1968. He shared several long opening stands with SIMPSON, and by 1970 he had become Australia's third highest run-scorer in Tests.

LAWSON, JOSEPH (1881-1964), succeeded ALEC TAYLOR as race-horse trainer in charge of the Manton stable, where he trained Lord ASTOR's horses. In 1931 he set a new English record for a trainer when the horses in his charge won a total of £93,899 in a single season. The best horse Lawson trained was probably NEVER SAY DIE.

LAWTON, THOMAS (1919-   ), Association footballer for Burnley, EVERTON, CHELSEA, NOTTS COUNTY, Brentford, ARSENAL, and England for whom he made his first appearance in a full international against Wales at Ninian Park, Cardiff on 22 October 1938 — 16 days after his nineteenth birthday. He signed professional forms on his seventeenth birthday and four days later scored a hat-trick against TOTTENHAM HOTSPUR; and by the end of the year — on 31 December 1936 — he was transferred to Everton. A tall, strongly-built, fine header and powerful shot, he was by 1938 the established leader of Everton's attack, and, from October that year, of England's. During the war he played in 18 international matches for England, and, in the immediate postwar period in five 'Victory' internationals. He played his last match for England — against Denmark on 26 September 1948 — when still with Notts County. Later he played for Brentford and Arsenal.

LE GROS, Lt. Col. P. W. (1892-   ), English SQUASH RACKETS player, well-known in the 1930s, who played for England against Scotland in 1937. He became chairman of the Squash Rackets Association in 1947 and was president from 1961 to 1972.

LE MANS, MOTOR RACING circuit in the Sarthe district of France which had been the scene of important races from before 1914 onwards, but is usually associated with the now famous 24-hour sports car race which is held there annually. The first such race was in 1923 and the BENTLEY domination in 1924 and from 1927 to 1930 made it very well-known in Britain, frequently supported by British drivers. The original course had a lap-distance of 10·726 miles (17·25 km.) and was rough and dusty. Continuing improvements were made, reducing the length of the course to 10·153 miles (16·3 km.) by 1929 and again in 1932 to 8·34 miles (13·4 km.) as the growth of the near-by town made this expedient. However, with the reduced lap-distance came a much improved surface, now of extreme smoothness, and an easing of the corners to make the lap times very fast. Part of the course is still a French highway, flanked by the great permanent concrete stands and pits, and closed for the race and on the practice days.

It was here that the terrible MERCEDES-BENZ accident happened in 1955, in which some 85 spectators and a French driver died, which had serious repercussions on European motor racing. As a result, a new corner, paid for by the Ford Motor Company, whose expensive efforts to win Le Mans were rewarded with outright success in 1966, 1967, and 1968, slowed cars before they entered a widened pits-straight. The all-night racing at Le Mans each June is one of the finest spectacles in motor racing and it draws vast crowds of onlookers, who are able to enjoy every kind of fairground sideshow or attend religious services on the Sunday morning, quite apart from the attraction of the racing. The 1973 Le Mans race was a victory for Pescarolo and the 3-litre Matra-Simca 670BG5 which he shared with Larrousse, a great French occasion.

LE PACHA (1938) was a notable French race-horse who won a wartime PRIX DE L'ARC DE TRIOMPHE, GRAND PRIX DE PARIS, French Derby, French St. Leger, and Prix Lupin.

LEACH, JOHN, M.B.E. (1922-   ). A late developer as a TABLE TENNIS player, Leach learned the game during Second World War military service. One of the most consistent players of the early postwar period, he had an all-round game with great concentration and ability to counter every variation of his opponent's tactics. He won the men's singles world championship in 1949 (defeating VANA in the final) and 1951 (defeating Andreadis in the final), and won all three titles — singles, men's doubles, and mixed doubles — in 1950. He was a tireless partner for BARNA and BERGMANN on many tours. Since his retirement as a competitor, Leach has fostered the game by advising manufacturers of sports goods, non-playing captaincy, writing, commentating, and giving special attention to the progress of young players.

LEANDER CLUB is the oldest amateur ROWING club in the world, believed to have been founded in 1818. Originally a London club, by the end of the nineteenth century it had built its present boathouse at Henley-on-Thames. Membership is a mark of distinction in the rowing world and a large proportion are former Oxford and Cambridge oarsmen. Leander's golden era came in the years between 1891 and 1914, during which they recorded 30 HENLEY wins (including 13 in the Grand Challenge Cup) and also won the Olympic eights in 1908 and 1912, and the Olympic pairs in 1908.
COLOUR: Cerise.

LEAUTEY COUPE, a cup formerly awarded annually by the Fédération Internationale de Hockey (F.I.H.) to the national HOCKEY Association that had done the most to serve the game. The trophy, named after Paul Leautey, a Frenchman, who founded the F.I.H. in 1924, was won for the fifth time by Association Royale Belge de Hockey in 1970, and was twice won by women's Federations — the International Federation of Women's Hockey Associations in 1953 and Koninklijke Nederlandsche Hockey Bond in 1934. It was to be superseded in 1974 by the Pablo Negel Trophy.

LECHNER, ERICA (1946-   ), luge TOBOGGANING rider for Italy; women's world champion and Olympic gold medallist in 1968; the first Italian to win a singles title.

LEE, HARPER (1884-1941), *matador de toros*, was the first U.S. citizen to take the *alternativa*, in Monterrey, Mexico, on 20 February 1910.

LEE, Maj. SAMUEL, M.D. (1920-   ), diver for the U.S.A., won the Olympic high DIVING competition in London in 1948 and again at Helsinki in 1952. He formed the Sam Lee Diving School to provide coaching for men and women divers, and coached Webster, the winner of the Olympic high diving competition in 1960 and 1964. He acted as diving judge at the 1964 OLYMPIC GAMES, having been American women's coach in 1960.

LEE, W. H. (Dick) (1890-1968), Australian Rules footballer. Regarded as the first of the great full-forwards, he played 233 matches for Collingwood — whom he captained for several seasons — in the VICTORIAN FOOTBALL LEAGUE from 1906 to 1922. He kicked 713 goals for his club, and on nine occasions he headed the League goal-kicking list and shared it once.

LEECH TROPHY, see SHOOTING, RIFLE: SERVICE CALIBRE.

LEEDS RUGBY LEAGUE CLUB, founded in 1890, was a founder member of the English Northern Union. It won the League championship in 1960-1, 1968-9, and 1971-2, and the Challenge Cup in 1909-10, 1922-3, 1931-2, 1935-6, 1956-7, and 1967-8. The ground is at HEADINGLEY. Leeds has always followed an ambitious recruiting policy in keeping with its place as one of the most prosperous clubs in the League. Twenty-five Leeds players have been chosen by England for Australian tours, and the club has also made extensive use of Australian, New Zealand, and South African players. The club try-scoring record is held by an Australian, E. HARRIS, and the most successful goal-kicker was B. L. JONES. In 1970 Leeds set a record by finishing at the head of the League table for the fourth successive season.
COLOURS: Blue, with irregular gold hoops.

LEEDS UNITED F.C., Association FOOTBALL club. Founded in 1904 as Leeds City, it played in the Football League Second Division from 1905 until early in the 1919-20 season when the club was ordered to disband because of irregularities in its administration. Before the next season started, a new club, Leeds United, was formed and elected to retain Leeds City's Second Division membership. Under the managership of Revie the club won the Second Division championship for the second time in 1964, since when it finished second in the First Division in 1965, 1966, 1970, and 1971, and won the League championship in 1969, as it was to do again in 1974. The club also played in the F.A. Cup

finals of 1965 and 1970, being beaten each time, but was more successful in the European Fairs Cup competition when, after being beaten by Dynamo Zagreb in the 1967 final, Leeds beat FERENCVAROS in the 1968 final and reached the final in 1971. In 1972 Leeds won the F.A. Cup for the first time and were the beaten finalists in the European Cup-Winners Cup the following season. Outstanding players have included Copping and Edwards before 1939, and Cush, W. J. CHARLES, Sprake, BREMNER, J. CHARLTON, Giles, Collins, Cooper, and Clarke, since the war.
COLOURS: White shirts and white shorts.
GROUND: Elland Road, Leeds.

LEFEBVRE, JANOU (1945-   ), French show jumping (see EQUESTRIAN EVENTS) rider. The winner of two team silver medals (1964 and 1968), she became the youngest rider ever to compete in Olympic show jumping when she rode Kenavo at Tokyo in 1964. She began her international career with the junior team but it was not until 1963, just one year before winning her first Olympic medal, that she made her senior international début. In 1968, riding Rocket, she had the best French score in the Olympic team event and thus played a major part in winning the team silver medal. She also won the women's European championship with Kenavo in 1966, and the women's world title with Rocket in 1970.

LEGGETT, TREVOR PRYCE (1914-   ), British JUDO fighter, for many years the highest-graded non-Japanese *judoka* and the first Englishman to go to Japan specifically to learn the sport. He was a 3rd *Dan* and captain of the national team when he went to Japan in 1938; after six months he was promoted to 4th *Dan*. In 1946 he was appointed head of the Japanese section of the B.B.C. and during the following 15 years trained almost every leading judo fighter in Britain at the BUDOKWAI. He is a prolific writer on poetry, Buddhism, and judo and was promoted to 7th *Dan* in 1970.

LEITCH, CHARLOTTE CECILIA PITCAIRN (1891-   ), English golfer, a dominant figure in the game for many years. She won the British championship four times, and the Canadian ladies' championship in 1921. She was an English international for 12 years.

LEMA, ANTHONY (1934-66), American professional golfer who won the Open championship in 1964, and several sponsored tournaments on the American circuit. He was killed in a crash of his private aeroplane.

LEMBERG (1907), English race-horse, by Cyllene out of GALICIA, and dam of BAYARDO, was bred by Cox, trained by ALEC TAYLOR, and ridden by Dillon and Maher. He won the DERBY (by a neck in a record time), ECLIPSE STAKES (dead-heat with Neil Gow), JOCKEY CLUB STAKES, CHAMPION STAKES twice, CORONATION CUP, Doncaster Cup (by a neck), and £41,694 in stakes.

LENGLEN, SUZANNE (1899-1938), French LAWN TENNIS player, the most graceful and successful of women competitors and the first to inspire great flurries of popular emotion. MYERS wrote: 'By her prowess and by her unbeaten record at WIMBLEDON for six years, by the legends associated with her career and by the theatrical atmosphere generated round her matches, she advertised women's tennis in a way and to an extent that no other agency could have achieved.'

In 1914, celebrating her fifteenth birthday during the tournament, she won the international clay court championship at St. Cloud. Then, from 1919, the year of her first victory at Wimbledon, to 1926, when she turned professional after quarrelling with the Wimbledon referee, she lost only one match (to Mrs. Mallory, the leading American player, in the U.S. championships in 1921). She was ill in 1924 and did not play in the French championships, and retired after losing a set to RYAN in a fourth-round match, which she eventually won 6-2, 6-8, 6-4, but otherwise she was invulnerable. At Wimbledon in 1919 she saved two match points in beating Mrs. CHAMBERS 10-8, 4-6, 9-7 in the challenge round, but in her five other Wimbledon finals she never allowed any player to win more than four games. In 1925 she lost only five games in winning the tournament and the following year her French title cost her only four. She had tremendous personality, great charm, and she moved like a dancer. The rhythm and sweep of her shots gave her matches their beauty, and her high emotion and fierce desire for victory added to their drama. Her years as a professional were disappointing.

LENIN STADIUM, magnificently sited below the Lenin Hills at a bend of the Moscow River, is used for ATHLETICS meetings and other sporting events but particularly for international Association FOOTBALL matches and the matches played by SPARTAK MOSCOW, and less regularly those played by Torpedo Moscow, and DYNAMO MOSCOW. The crowd of 103,000 are all seated.

LENINGRAD S.C., ICE SKATING club formed in Russia as the St. Petersburg S.C. by British residents in 1864. The club staged the first world ice figure-skating championships in 1866.

LEONARD, BENNY (1896-1947), American boxer who held the world lightweight title from 1917 to 1924 when he retired as undefeated champion. He and GANS were certainly the most highly regarded of all at their weight. Leonard was a superb boxer and a hard hitter who lost only five out of 209 fights including a 20-bout come-back which ended in defeat by McLarnin. Sometimes susceptible to head punches, Leonard was famed for his ability to pull victory out of the fire when the odds seemed against him. He died while acting as a professional referee in New York.

LEONARD, J. W. (1940-   ), British amateur RACKETS player who won the British amateur singles championship in 1961-2, 1965, and 1967. He beat ATKINS in the 1962 final, but unsuccessfully challenged him for the world championship in 1963 and 1968. He also won the amateur doubles championship with SWALLOW in 1963 and with Hue-Williams in 1967-8.

LEONARD TROPHY, the 'World Cup' of lawn BOWLS, was donated by W. M. Leonard, managing director of an Australian petrol company which sponsored the inaugural world championships at KYEEMAGH, N.S.W., in 1966. It was first won by Australia who scored the highest aggregate of points over the four individual events.

LEONIDAS (Leonidas da Silva) (1913-   ), Association footballer who played for both the Uruguayan and Brazilian national teams in the 1930s when the terms of qualification were more elastic than they are now. A small but remarkably acrobatic man, he was the leading centre forward in Brazil for many years and played for the national team in both the 1934 and 1938 world championships.

LESZNO, Poland, GLIDING centre, lat. 51° 50' N, long. 17° 30' E, south of Poznań. The Polish national advanced glider training and soaring centre, it was the site of the world gliding championships in 1958 and 1968 and starting place for many national and world records. It is a large flat grass airfield.

LEVICK, Mrs. MURRAY (*née* E. Audrey Beeton) (1890-   ), LACROSSE player for England from 1913. She was one of the founder members of the Southern Ladies Lacrosse Club, the only women's club in existence in 1909. She founded the Ladies' Lacrosse Association in 1912, and was instrumental in starting over 100 clubs and establishing the game during the early years of the Association, up to 1933, when she was elected president.

LEVMOSS (1965), a race-horse bred, owned, and trained by McGrath in Ireland. He is the only horse ever to win the PRIX DE L'ARC DE TRIOMPHE, ASCOT GOLD CUP, and its French equivalent, the PRIX DU CADRAN, in a single season.

LEWIS, BARBARA J. (1937-   ), LA-CROSSE player for Wales 1958-70 and captain 1967-70. She played for the South of England Territorial team during those years and was known for the skill and variety of her shooting. She toured the U.S.A. with the British team in 1960, and in 1969 she was vice-captain of the British Pioneers team to Australia. She is mainly responsible for the development of seven-a-side lacrosse and is the author of *Play Lacrosse the Easy Way.*

LEWIS, TED (Kid) (1894-1970), British boxer; world welterweight champion in 1915 and again from 1917 to 1919. He won, respectively, British, European, and world titles at 18, 19, and 20 and made an immense impact in North America with 99 fights in five years. In a total of more than 260 bouts, of which he lost only 24, Lewis fought from bantam- to heavyweight, suffering a controversial knock-out at the hands of CARPENTIER, and was the first European to adapt, with complete success, to the two-handed attacking style of the Americans. He twice beat the renowned BRITTON for the world title and altogether the two met 20 times, including several no-decision bouts.

LEXINGTON (1850) was the most influential of the early thoroughbred racing stallions in the U.S.A., where he headed the American sires list 16 times.

LEYLAND, MAURICE (1900-67), cricketer for England and Yorkshire. A sturdy left-handed batsman, he scored a century in his first Test innings against Australia, in 1928-9, and another in his last, in 1938. During this period he scored seven other centuries for England, most of them in crisis situations, when his solidity and splendid temperament were of great value. He served Yorkshire well for over 20 years, and made 62 centuries for the county. As a slow left-arm bowler his opportunities were limited, but on occasion he took some distinguished wickets.

LIBAUD, PAUL (1905-   ), president of the International Volleyball Federation since its formation in 1947; he was elected president of the French Volleyball Federation in 1937.

LIBOTTE, ARMANDO (1911-   ), Swiss RACE WALKING official and administrator, the chief instigator of a world team competition and organizer of the first final (1961), and later in 1973, in his home town which donated a trophy from which the competition, the LUGANO CUP, received its name. An International Amateur Athletic Federation (see ATH-LETICS, TRACK AND FIELD) official and chief judge at Olympic and European Games, Libotte organizes the AIROLO–CHIASSO RELAY, the LUGANO 100 KM., as well as numerous lesser events, and publishes the walking magazine *Der Schweizer Geher.* He is the author of the historical book, *La Marcia* (1964).

LIDDON, HENRY (1932-   ), British motor rally navigator (see MOTOR RACING). He won the 1966 European Rally Championship with AALTONEN, and this combination also won a Monte Carlo Rally and came third in the 1970 World Cup Rally.

LIEDHOLM, NILS (1922-   ), Association footballer for NORRKÖPING, A.C. MILAN, and Sweden for whom he made his first appearance in 1947. A fine half-back or inside forward, he was a member of the Swedish team that won the Olympics football tournament in London in 1948. A year later he turned professional and signed for the Italian club, A.C. Milan, for whom he played in the European Cup final of May 1958 when Real Madrid won by 3-2 after extra time. A month later he made his last appearance for the Swedish national team in the world championship final match against Brazil in Stockholm.

LIÈGE-BASTOGNE-LIÈGE   CYCLE RACE, the oldest of the Belgian CYCLING classics, founded as an amateur road race in 1892 but run for professionals since 1912. Different routes are taken to and from Bastogne to create an elliptical course of roughly 155 miles (249 km.) through the low but punishing Ardennes mountains. This race and the FLÈCHE WALLONNE are together referred to as *Le Week-End Ardennais,* although an official combined classification was produced only during the period 1950-64.

LIFEGUARD GAMES, a competitive exercise in the practical skills practised by beach lifeguards first developed as an international championship at Carpenteria, California, in

1967. The competitors then were the U.S.A., Australia, and New Zealand.

Events in any lifeguard games vary from place to place, but centre on SWIMMING, ROWING, and paddling through surf, and sprinting on sand. Relay and medley, as well as simple individual races, are usually held, often including a beach sprint in which the runners carry 'helpless' bodies over their shoulders.

The lifeguard's most severe competitive test is the 'iron man' race, a non-stop PENTATHLON of the beach. It involves three 400-metre laps in the water, of swimming, paddling astride a board, and rowing a surf-boat, interspersed with beach sprints carrying rescue equipment. Under perfect conditions the 1,200 metres race can be completed in about 15 minutes, but a heavy surf prolongs the race to at least an hour.

LIFFEY DESCENT, an international long-distance CANOEING event held in Ireland. It was first raced in 1959, but the present course of 28·2 km. (17½ miles) on the river Liffey, starting at Straffan to finish just outside Dublin, was introduced in 1970. This is by far the most spectacular long-distance event in Europe; along the course are nine immense weirs that must be shot, as well as a number of rapids and one very long portage.

LIGHT, HILDA M. (1889-1969), international HOCKEY player and an outstanding administrator, who was president of the All-England Women's Hockey Association from 1931 to 1945 and president of the International Federation of Women's Hockey Associations (I.F.W.H.A.) from 1950 to 1953. The first honorary member of the I.F.W.H.A. (1963), she was a leading protagonist for a common set of rules for women's hockey throughout the world, and her efforts resulted in the formation of the Women's International Hockey Rules Board. She played for England and the South of England as a half-back, and both she and her brother, D. O. Light, represented England on the same day in the same position.

LILLYWHITE, FREDERICK WILLIAM (1792-1854), cricketer for Sussex and the ALL-ENGLAND XI. Known as 'the Nonpareil', and the outstanding bowler of the early nineteenth century, he was a pioneer of round-arm bowling, which, largely through the influence and example of himself and Broadbridge, was legalized in 1828. A short man, and one of a large sporting family, he still played CRICKET at the age of 60.

LINCOLN HANDICAP is the first big horse race of the English 'flat' season, now run at

DONCASTER over a straight mile (1,600 m.) course at the end of March. It is the first leg of the 'Spring Double', the other being the GRAND NATIONAL.

LINDNER, DIETER (1937-), race walker for East Germany. A 20 km. specialist, he was European champion in 1966, second in 1964, and fourth in 1960, in the Olympic event. He was disqualified in both the 1956 Olympics and the 1958 European championships. He won the LUGANO CUP final 20 km. in 1965, and was the first of East Germany's world-class performers at this distance.

LINDWALL, RAYMOND RUSSELL, M.B.E. (1921-), cricketer for Australia, New South Wales, and Queensland. Bowling with a smooth rhythm and employing all the variations known to fast bowling, he took 228 wickets for Australia before his retirement in 1959 — then a record in Tests for a fast bowler. His art was most forcibly displayed in England in 1948, when his 27 wickets in the Test series included 6 for 20 runs in the final match.

LINE, PETER (1930-), English lawn BOWLS gold medal winner with KING in the pairs event at the 1970 British COMMONWEALTH GAMES, and world fours championship winner (as skip) at Worthing in 1972. He is one of the few men to have won the English Bowling Association singles championship twice (in 1961 and 1964).

LINFIELD F.C., Association FOOTBALL club, Belfast. Founded in 1886, Linfield have twice won all seven trophies in Irish League soccer in 1921-2 and 1961-2. Their outstanding players have been McEwan, Rollo, McCandless, Priestley, BAMBRICK, Cochrane, McCleery, Keith, McMichael, McFaul, Milburn, and Dickson. They competed in the English F.A. Cup in 1888-9 and 1890-1.
COLOURS: Royal blue shirts, white shorts.

LINFOOT, Dr. W. (1924-), American POLO player, army officer, RODEO rider, and veterinarian; the best American player of his day. Handicap 9.

LING ASSOCIATION, an association of physical training teachers, founded in 1899, whose members were at first chiefly drawn from Madame Osterberg's College of Physical Training for women. The Association was named after Per Henrik Ling, a Swede born in 1776, and known as the creator of Swedish gymnastics; his system was known as Ling's System. After Ling's death, his son shaped and set his mark on Ling's gymnastics. Sport was included in Per Ling's concept and later, teachers were training in GYMNASTICS, games, and sports: the Ling Association catered for women teachers trained in those branches.

The Association was responsible for the publication in 1901 of the Rules of NETBALL in an edition of 250 copies, and continued as the responsible body for revision and publication of the Rules until 1946, after which they were taken over by the All-England Netball Association. Miss Hankinson, secretary of the Ling Association for many years, was responsible for setting up the Netball Association, and negotiations for handing over of the Rules of the Game, which she helped to draw up in 1901.

The Ling Association grew in strength and numbers as the specialist women's physical training colleges were founded in England and Scotland. The original and most famous of these colleges were Madame Osterberg's College, at Dartford in Kent, Miss Margaret Stansfeld's College in Bedford, and Chelsea College attached to the Chelsea Polytechnic in London.

At its annual conference, attended by women teachers of gymnastics and games in the grammar schools of the British Commonwealth, lectures and demonstrations were given by experts from Britain and Scandinavian countries on modern methods and development in the field of physical education, and medicine. Membership was widened to include men, and teachers with qualifications and experience in physical education, recreation and associated subjects. National Physical Education Associations affiliated to the Ling Association include those of Australia, Hong Kong, Jamaica, New Zealand, South Africa, Northern Ireland, Scotland, and the territorial associations of England.

The Ling Association, now known as the Physical Education Association of Great Britain and Northern Ireland, is a nongovernmental body, to encourage and facilitate the scientific study of the physical health of the community through physical and health education and recreation, to educate and instruct specialist teachers in physical and health education and recreation in current theory, and exchange information on these subjects.

LIONS, name given to British RUGBY UNION overseas touring sides, after the symbol on their official tie. They were first so called in their 1924 visit to South Africa.

LIPTON CUP, see FOOTBALL, ASSOCIATION.

LITTLE, Mrs. G., see ROUND, DOROTHY.

LITTLE, LAWSON (1910-68), American golfer who did the double of winning the British and American amateur championships two years in succession, 1934-5. He turned professional in 1936, won the Canadian Open that year, and the U.S. Open championship in 1940.

LIVERPOOL F.C., Association FOOTBALL club. Founded in 1892 after a majority of the shareholders of EVERTON F.C. decided to leave their ground at Anfield Road following a dispute over rent, the new Liverpool club were elected to the Second Division of the Football League in 1893. They were League champions in 1901, 1906, 1922, 1923, 1947, 1964, 1966, and 1973 in which year the U.E.F.A. Cup was also won. Between the 1964 and 1966 wins Liverpool, who had been beaten in their two previous appearances in the F.A. Cup final in 1914 and 1950, won the Cup in 1965 (as the were to win it again in 1974), and only a goal scored late in extra time by Borussia Dortmund beat them in the European Cup-Winners Cup final in 1966. Outstanding players have included Bradshaw, Hardy, and Raisbeck before 1914; Hodgson, Lucas, and SCOT between the wars; and Liddell, Younger, Hunt, St. John, Yeats, T. Smith, and Lawler since the Second World War.

COLOURS: Red shirts with white trimmings, red shorts.
GROUND: Anfield Road, Liverpool.

LJUNGGREN, JOHN (1919-), race walker for Sweden. As 50 km. European champion in 1946, and Olympic champion at the same distance in 1948, he held world records at 30 and 50 km. and 20 and 30 miles. In a long career Ljunggren competed in five Olympiads and four European Games, gaining a second (1950) and a third (1956) in the Olympic event, and a second (1950) in the European, all at 50 km., besides his winning efforts. A versatile performer, he won the MILAN 100 KM. (1953-4), and the Race Walking Association's 50 km. (1954). He finished his career as a better 20 km. performer, representing his country in the LUGANO CUP final in 1961 (fourth) and in 1963 (seventh).

LLANELLI R.F.C., most westerly of the first-class Welsh RUGBY UNION football clubs, founded in 1872. Because of the local tinplate industry, it adopted the song and symbol 'Sospan fach' (little saucepan), by which it is often known. Llanelli beat the Maori touring side of 1888 and 1926, but its most famous vic-

ories were over the 1908 WALLABIES — a par-
dy on 'Sospan fach' still celebrates this
vin — and over the seventh ALL-BLACKS in
heir centenary season, 1972-3. Distinguished
club players include Gabe, A. Jenkins, B. L.
ones, R. H. Williams, Brace, and JOHN.
IOME GROUND: Stradey Park.
COLOURS: Scarlet jerseys and white shorts.

LLEWELLYN, Lt.-Col. HENRY MORTON
1911-), British show jumping (see
EQUESTRIAN EVENTS) rider who won 140
nternational classes between 1947 and 1953.
Iis name will always be associated with FOX-
IUNTER, whom he bought in 1947 and rode, a
ear later, at the OLYMPIC GAMES in London
vhere he won a team bronze medal. Four
ears later, Llewellyn and Foxhunter were part
f the British team which won the Olympic
old medal at Helsinki. His riding successes
Iso include 60 steeplechase victories and a
econd place (on Ego) in the 1936 GRAND
IATIONAL.

LLOYD, CLIVE HUBERT (1944-),
ricketer for West Indies, Guyana, and Lanca-
hire. A supple, powerful, left-handed bats-
nan, he overcame early uncertainty against
ast bowling to rank as one of the world's most
ommanding players. He made centuries in his
naiden Tests against England and against
Australia, and on numerous occasions in
English county CRICKET — particularly in one-
lay matches — he has batted with match-
vinning force. His speedy, loose-limbed field-
ng and ability to throw while off balance can
eldom have been excelled. He plays in con-
act lenses.

LOCK, GRAHAM ANTHONY RICHARD
1929-), cricketer for England, Surrey,
Leicestershire, and Western Australia. Origi-
ally a slow — then a fastish — left-arm spin
owler, he could capitalize on a helpful pitch,
ften overwhelming even the best batting
ides. No-balled for throwing in 1952 and
954, he reverted in 1959 to the slower style,
nd in Australia he developed his ability to
light the ball. He took 174 Test wickets, and
vas a superlative short-leg fieldsman.

LOCKE, ARTHUR D'ARCY (1917-),
outh African professional golfer, who ranks
vith PLAYER as the most accomplished South
African golfer. He won the South African
mateur championship twice and the South
African Open eight times. He turned profes-
ional in 1938 and won the Open champion-
hip in 1949, 1950, 1952, and 1957. Winner
f numerous national titles and sponsored
ournaments, he had two highly successful

seasons on the American circuit. Locke had a
distinctive, looping swing but his main
strengths were his composure and brilliant putting skill.

LOCKLEY, KATHLEEN (1900-),
LACROSSE player — at centre — for Boxmoor
Ladies and England from 1920 to 1932 and
captain from 1926 to 1932. She took the first
touring team of players and coaches to the
United States in 1934, the forerunner of the
subsequent official teams which have toured in
the States. She organized the first Holiday
Week in 1926 and produced, with others, the
first educational film and the first book on the
game.

LOCKLEY, MARJORIE, see BUXTON, MRS.

LOCKWOOD, WILLIAM HENRY (1868-
1932), cricketer for England, Nottinghamshire, and Surrey. A top-class all-rounder, he
was a fast bowler comparable in menace with
RICHARDSON, with whom he shared the attack
for Surrey and England. He bowled a cleverly-
concealed slower ball, and, in spite of a certain moodiness, his fine record at the highest
level — apart from his tour of Australia — was
testimony to his ability.

LODGE, MARGARET JENNIE (1909-
), HOCKEY player for England, West of
England, Gloucestershire, East Gloucester,
Bourton-on-the-Water, and Highgate, who
became president of the All-England
Women's Hockey Association (1957-68). A
member of the England team 1938-9 and
1946-51, she captained England from 1946 to
1951, and was a member of the England touring teams to the U.S.A. (1936 and 1947),
New Zealand (1938), and the Netherlands
(1948). She was a very fine dominating centre
half.

LOGROLLING is one of the simplest of
sports, and yet one of the most difficult for a
novice to master. Two opponents stand facing
each other at each end of a large floating log,
usually at least 1 ft. (30·5 cm.) in diameter.
Wearing 'staggers' (shortened overalls or
jeans) and ribbed or spiked boots, each one
tries to spin the log in such a way that, by
changes of speed and direction, the other loses
his footing and is thrown into the water. Two
falls out of three make a match, which may be
over in a few minutes or even a few seconds,
though in 1900 one pair were said to have held
on for more than three hours. The first contests
were held in Canadian lumber camps around
1840, and later spread to Maine and other New
England states in the north-east of America.

BIRLING, a related sport, developed even more directly from the duties of a river lumberjack, who has to be adept at riding logs downstream from the felling area to the sawmill, clearing log jams as he goes, with a pole. Birling is basically racing in this manner over a measured course, using the pole to steer the log clear of obstacles and through the best run of the river. The first public birling contest was in 1888, and a world championship was held in Omaha, Nebraska, ten years later. Competitions are seldom held in North America now, but the trick riding skills of professional birlers are often seen at riverside fairs and exhibitions.

LOHMANN, GEORGE ALFRED (1865-1901), cricketer for England, Surrey, and Western Province. The finest medium-paced bowler of his time, he was a master of flight and length. His 112 Test wickets cost only 10·75 runs each, 9 for 28 against South Africa being his best analysis. He was also a fine slip fieldsman.

LOMBARDI, VINCENT (1913-70), American college and professional FOOTBALL player and coach, was a guard (1935-7) on the Fordham University defensive line that played three successive 0-0 ties with the University of Pittsburgh. Beginning as a high school coach and then as assistant at Fordham, he learned the elements of fundamental, well-executed football as an assistant to BLAIK at Army in the 1950s. Later offensive (attack) coach for the NEW YORK GIANTS, he became coach and general manager of the foundering GREEN BAY PACKERS in 1959 and brought them a Western Conference championship the following year. They won the League championship in 1961, 1962, 1965, 1966, and 1967, the last two years in the Super Bowl (the games played in January 1967 and 1968) against the AMERICAN FOOTBALL LEAGUE champion. He retired as coach but remained as Green Bay general manager after the 1968 Super Bowl win, but was hired as general manager-coach of the WASHINGTON REDSKINS in 1969.

LONDON–BRIGHTON, a 53 miles (85 km.) English road RACE WALKING event held annually from 1919, with the exception of war years 1939-45, although races were held over the course at frequent intervals from 1886. The earlier events were organized by the Hairdressers Athletic Club and the Polytechnic Harriers but since 1919 the promoters have been SURREY WALKING CLUB. This event is, without doubt, the best-known race walking event in the world. A closed event, over the same course, has been organized by the Lon-

don Stock Exchange for its members every May since 1903.

The course record-holder, THOMPSON, is the most frequent winner with eight consecutive victories, 1955-62, and again in 1967. Other winners include Olympic 50 km. champions, GREEN (1929-31 and 1933), WHITLOCK (1934-7), and PAMICH (1965).

The course has been slightly lengthened due to road alterations on several occasions since 1934 and is now nearly a mile (1,600 m.) longer than the pre-1934 events. The course is relatively flat for 30 miles (48 km.), undulating for 17 miles (27 km.), and then flat once again to the finish. The race is started at 6 a.m. every second Saturday in September by the chimes of Big Ben at Westminster, and finishes on the esplanade at Brighton.

LONDON FENCING CLUB, founded 1 July 1848, was the first FENCING club (as distinct from a *salle* belonging to a master) to exist in Britain. It has had many famous members including King Edward VII, Prince Louis Napoleon, and Lord Cardigan who led the charge of the Light Brigade in the Crimea.

LONDON IRISH R.F.C., RUGBY UNION football club, founded 1898. Although with smaller reserves to draw on than the other 'Exiles' clubs, it has fielded many internationals, including MULLIGAN, O'REILLY, and K. W. Kennedy.
GROUND: Sunbury-on-Thames, Middlesex.
COLOURS: Green jerseys, white shorts.

LONDON ROWING CLUB, a famous London tideway club, the first to challenge the domination of university ROWING at HENLEY. Founded in 1856, it was immediately successful in the Grand and Stewards' Cups and the Diamond Sculls and since then has won more Henley races than any other club. It had a particularly fine run of successes in the 1930s, winning the Wyfold six times, the Grand four times, the Thames Cup three times, and the Stewards' twice. London crews early established the high standard of what became known as Metropolitan rowing. The club instituted and still organizes the Metropolitan Regatta. London has won the tideway Head of the River race more often than any other club.
COLOURS: Blue and white.

LONDON S.C., ICE SKATING club formed in England in 1842, more generally styled The Skating Club and dependent on natural ice until the later erection of artificial rinks. It was patronized by royalty in its peak years before the Second World War.

LONDON SCOTTISH R.F.C., RUGBY
UNION football club, founded in 1878, the
oldest of the three London 'Exiles' clubs. In
Scotland's Triple Crown year of 1907, the
club provided ten men to the national side. It
also had a notable run of success in the MID-
DLESEX SEVEN-A-SIDE COMPETITION in
1960-5, winning five times in six years.
GROUND: Richmond Athletic Ground, Surrey.
COLOURS: Blue jerseys, white shorts.

LONDON WELSH R.F.C., RUGBY UNION
football club founded in 1885, has for most of
its history enjoyed a fitful brilliance through
the temporary services of players like Gabe,
Davey, Wooller, and TANNER. In the late
1960s, however, with a stable team under the
captaincy of Dawes, it became one of the
strongest and, in its attacking style of play,
one of the most influential Welsh clubs. London Welsh internationals from that period
include, besides Dawes himself, J. Taylor,
J. P. R. Williams, T. G. R. Davies, T. M.
Davies, and T. G. Evans.
GROUND: Old Deer Park, Richmond, Surrey.
COLOURS: Scarlet jersey, white shorts.

LONDONBRIDGE ROAD, Dublin, the
headquarters of the Irish Hockey Union.
Opened in 1930, through the foresight of
Dagg, an outstanding figure in Irish HOCKEY,
it was the first national hockey stadium in the
world.

LONDONDERRY CUP, one of the chief as
well as the oldest tournaments in the SQUASH
RACKETS calendar is the schools' Old Boys
competition. The cup was presented by the
International Sportsmen's Club, London in
1934 and named after its then president, the
late Lord Londonderry. The competition is
played during five months of each season for
five-a-side teams. Until its closing down in
1968, the International Sportsmen's Club
organized the competition, the semi-finals and
final of which were played at that club. The
Squash Rackets Association now runs the
competition.

LONG ALLEY, see SKITTLES.

LONG-DISTANCE RUNNING. The long-
distance events in track ATHLETICS are those
beyond the category of MIDDLE-DISTANCE
RUNNING, the border line being approximately
at 3 miles and 5,000 metres. Long-distance
events in the programme of all major championships are the 10,000 metres and the MARA-
THON. The International Amateur Athletic
Federation (SEE ATHLETICS, TRACK AND FIELD)

recognizes records in the following long-
distance events for men: 10,000, 20,000,
25,000, and 30,000 metres, and 6, 10, and 15
miles; also in the one-hour run. CROSS-
COUNTRY and ROAD RUNNING also fall into
this general category as do non-standard
events of very long distance which are contested from time to time.

LONG JUMP, a standard field event in the
programme of all major ATHLETICS championships; also one of the events included in the
DECATHLON and PENTATHLON.
The first record of long-jumping contests
dates from the ancient Greek OLYMPIC GAMES
in 708 B.C. The earliest athletic record of
which there is evidence is a long jump of 23 ft.
1½ in. (7·05 m.) in 656 B.C. by Chionis of
Sparta. In modern long jumping the use of
weights carried by the jumper to aid his
momentum, which was customary in the
nineteenth century, has been disallowed.
The technique of long jumping consists of a
high knee-lift of the alternate leg on take-off
leading to a running stride in the air. The trailing leg is pulled forward to join its pair in forward extension in the downward trajectory.
Competitors are judged according to the best
of six trials, which are measured from the
further edge of the take-off, a wooden board
sunk level with the approach runway and the
sandpit which forms the landing area. The
rearmost imprint left by the jumper on landing
is the mark to which measurement is made. A
jump is declared foul if the jumper's foot
crosses the further edge of the take-off board.

LONG-TRACK RACING, Motor-cycle,
see MOTOR-CYCLE RACING.

LONGCHAMP is the magnificent race-
course near Paris which is virtually the headquarters of the turf in France. With the exception of the GRAND PRIX DE SAINT-CLOUD and
the French Derby and Oaks which are run at
Chantilly, most of the important horse-races in
France are run at Longchamp, concluding with
the PRIX DE L'ARC DE TRIOMPHE.

LONGHURST, HENRY CARPENTER
(1909-   ), English amateur golfer, GOLF
writer, and commentator. He is the author of
*Always on Sundays, Never on Weekdays, The
Spice of Life, Golf: It Was Good While it
Lasted, You Never Know Till You Get There,
I Wouldn't Have Missed It, Round in Sixty-
eight,* and *Golf Mixture.*

LONGHURST, HENRY SPENCER
(1877-1966), British marksman who won the

world small-bore rifle championship at Granada (Spain) in 1933 with a new record score of 396 ex 400 points. He shot for Great Britain in the Dewar Match (see SHOOTING, RIFLE) fourteen times from 1922 to 1935, and in other international postal matches. He won practically every individual event including London and Surrey titles, and the British long range championship in 1924 and 1929.

LONGHURST, PERCY (1882-1935), British amateur wrestler. He was the first secretary of the Fédération Internationale des Luttes Amateurs (F.I.L.A.) in 1921 and secretary of the National Amateur Wrestling Association from 1918 to 1934. He wrote several books on the sport.

LONGO, RENATO (1937-   ), Italian CYCLO-CROSS rider who won the world title on five occasions in the period 1959-67.

LONGWOOD CRICKET CLUB, the oldest LAWN TENNIS club in the United States, is now situated at Chestnut Hill, near Boston, Massachusetts. The first Davis Cup (see LAWN TENNIS) match between the U.S.A. and the British Isles was played on the club's original ground at Longwood. The club was founded in 1877 by three CRICKET players, Farley, Hubbard, and Fay, who rented a field for $40 a year. The following year, lawn tennis — which had been brought to the United States in 1874 — was played there for the first time and Richard Sears, a member of the club and the grandson of the owner of the Longwood estate from whom the ground was leased, became the first winner of the U.S. national title at Newport, Rhode Island, in 1881.

DWIGHT F. DAVIS, the donor of the Davis Cup, and Mrs. Wightman, who presented the WIGHTMAN CUP, were members of Longwood. By the turn of the century lawn tennis had ousted cricket as the club's main sport, although the original title was retained. For many years Longwood was the home of the U.S. doubles championships and it has also housed the U.S. professional championships. The club moved to Chestnut Hill in 1922.

LONSBROUGH, ANITA, M.B.E. (1941-   ), British swimmer who held the Olympic, European, and British Empire and Commonwealth Games breaststroke titles at the same time. Originally a club-standard free-styler, she turned to the breaststroke at the late age — for a swimmer — of 16 and within nine months had won her first Commonwealth title in Cardiff (1958). A winner over 200 metres in the 1960 Rome Olympics, she became European champion in 1962 and at the end of

that year retained her Commonwealth 220 yards title and also won the 110 yards breaststroke and 440 yards medley. She is married to Hugh Porter, M.B.E., the world professional pursuit-CYCLING champion of 1968, 1970, and 1973.

LONSDALE BELTS. These BOXING awards for British champions were created in 1909 when the Earl of Lonsdale presented a belt to WELSH for winning the British lightweight title at the NATIONAL SPORTING CLUB, of which Lord Lonsdale was president. Altogether the N.S.C. presented 22 Lonsdale belts to champions who won their titles at the club. The British Boxing Board of Control have kept up the tradition. Any boxer winning three title bouts in the same division may keep the belt permanently and is entitled to a pension of £1 a week when he reaches the age of 50.

LONSDALE CUP, see SQUASH RACKETS.

LORD, THOMAS (1755-1832), cricketer and founder of LORD'S CRICKET GROUND. Though a competent slow under-arm bowler, he is immortalized in the name of CRICKET's most famous playing field which he established, with the backing of some noblemen, in 1787.

LORD'S CRICKET GROUND, London, is, by common consent, the premier CRICKET ground of the world. Its atmosphere is soaked in the tradition and history of cricket, and as the home of the MARYLEBONE CRICKET CLUB (M.C.C., the owners of the freehold), it is also — as it has always been — the administrative heart of the game. The ground owes its name to THOMAS LORD, and has been situated on its present site in St. John's Wood since 1814. This was the third of Lord's grounds: the first (1787-1810) was where Dorset Square now stands, and the second (1809-13) was at North Bank and was given up because of the cutting of the Regent's Canal. The playing area is about five acres, and the maximum capacity — including spectators on the grass — is just over 34,000. The ground is also the home and headquarters of the Middlesex County Cricket Club, who have been continual tenants of the M.C.C. since 1877 and who play all their home matches there.

A fine practice ground, on which minor matches are played, is sited on the east side — or 'Nursery' end — and a series of impressive structures has grown up around the main ground in the course of time. The present pavilion was opened in 1890, and its famous Long Room behind high windows is a hallowed vantage-point for members. The pavilion also houses the M.C.C. administrative offices, committee rooms, dining-rooms, and dressing-rooms. The library, formerly in the pavilion, is now situated above the REAL TENNIS court behind the pavilion. The Mound Stand was built in 1898-9, and in 1923 the W. G. Grace Memorial Gates were erected at the members' entrance. The Grandstand, containing the main scoreboard, was opened for the 1926 season, and in 1958 the splendid Warner Stand — between the Grandstand and pavilion — was opened by Sir PELHAM WARNER. This stand now contains the press and broadcasting boxes, though the view afforded is not in a line with the wicket. The former Tavern, on the south side of the ground, and a landmark since 1868, was demolished in 1967. The Memorial Gallery, in memory of cricketers of all lands who lost their lives in the two world wars, was opened by the Duke of Edinburgh in 1953; it is situated behind the pavilion and contains a unique collection of cricket treasures.

Test cricket was first played at Lord's in 1884, since when no Test series in England has failed to include the ground as a venue. In 1973, when England played West Indies at Lord's, receipts were £87,305 — the largest sum of money taken at any cricket match in the world. The highest attendance for a match on the ground is 137,915 for the England-Australia Test of 1953.

LOS ANGELES ANGELS, see CALIFORNIA ANGELS.

LOS ANGELES DODGERS, American professional BASEBALL team, joined the NATIONAL LEAGUE in 1958, when O'Malley, the owner, shifted the franchise from Brooklyn. The Dodgers were an instant success, even though they had to play the first few years in the Los Angeles Memorial Coliseum, a vast oval arena built for American FOOTBALL; a baseball field fitted in here produced a distorted playing area, with very short foul lines and an enormous outfield. In the 1959 WORLD SERIES the Dodgers drew a record major league crowd of 92,394 for the first game. In 1962 the Dodgers moved into Chavez Ravine Stadium; in that year the shortstop Wills broke TY COBB's record by stealing 104 bases during the season. Los Angeles won the World Series in 1959, 1963, and 1965, led in the latter years by the pitcher Drysdale and especially the left-hander Koufax, who set the modern major league record of 382 strike-outs in a season and pitched his fourth no-hit game in 1965. Alston has managed the Dodgers since they transferred from Brooklyn. (See BROOKLYN DODGERS.)

LOS ANGELES KINGS, ICE HOCKEY club of Los Angeles, formed in 1967 as one of six teams in the new West Division of the expanded NATIONAL HOCKEY LEAGUE of North America. Its home rink is the Forum, Inglewood, California, seating 15,651.

The players train in Canada, at the Memorial Gardens, Guelph, Ontario.
COLOURS: Royal blue and gold.

LOS ANGELES LAKERS, American professional BASKETBALL team, playing in the NATIONAL BASKETBALL ASSOCIATION. The Lakers began as MINNEAPOLIS LAKERS at the formation of the Basketball Association of America (B.A.A.) in 1946, and moved to Los Angeles in 1962-3. Playing as Los Angeles, the Lakers recruited a wealth of talent, both through the draft system and by purchase from other clubs. In 1968 they purchased CHAMBERLAIN from the PHILADELPHIA 76ERS, and also included J. WEST and BAYLOR among their players. Although they gained several Western Division titles, they did not succeed in gaining an N.B.A. title until 1972.
COLOURS: Royal blue, with gold and white trim.

LOS ANGELES RAMS, American professional FOOTBALL team, joined the NATIONAL FOOTBALL LEAGUE (N.F.L.) in 1937 as the Cleveland Rams and moved to Los Angeles after winning their first League title in 1945. Until the mid-1950s they were title contenders, winning another N.F.L. title in 1951, with an imaginative pass attack led first by the quarterback Waterfield and later by Van Brocklin, with the three-times N.F.L. pass-receiving leader Fears and the end Hirsch catching passes. From 1966 to 1970 coach Allen built a smooth machine, led by a strong defence, anchored by the end Jones and the tackle Olsen.
COLOURS: Blue, gold, and white.

LOSCH, KARLHEINZ, roller figure-skater (see ROLLER SKATING) for West Germany, the first man to win five world titles, 1958, 1959, 1961, 1962, and 1966.

LOTUS, a racing car. Colin Chapman's first car was built in 1948 when he was still an engineering student. He produced various models, gradually building a substantial reputation for his design skill. The Mark 18 rear-engined Grand Prix car in 1960 startled the MOTOR RACING world. In the hands of Moss and Ireland, SURTEES and JIM CLARK, it won many races including the MONACO Grand Prix. In 1961, Moss won the Monaco, German, and Modena Grands Prix. In 1963, Clark, having won three Grands Prix the year before in the

Mk 25 powered by the Coventry-Climax engine, became world champion, while Lotus won the manufacturers' championship with 54 points to BRM'S 36. The Mk 25 repeated the performance for Clark and Lotus in 1965, and its successor, the Cosworth-engined V-8 Grand Prix car Mk 49, provided the means for GRAHAM HILL to win his world championship and Lotus's third world championship. Lotus gained great victories with their Type 72 Formula One car and in 1974 were to produce yet another innovation, following earlier pioneering of monocoque construction, the backbone chassis, etc., by having electric control of the clutch.

LOUIS, JOE (1914-   ), American boxer, known as the 'Brown Bomber'. He was heavyweight champion of the world from 1937 to 1949 with a record number of 25 successful defences of the title. A vast body of support claims Louis as the greatest of all champions and points to his vicious left jab, his knock-out punch in either hand, and his willingness to take on all comers as challengers when he was champion. Before he won the title, Louis suffered a knock-out defeat by the German SCHMELING but he avenged this in 124 seconds in 1938. Louis retired, undefeated champion, in 1949 but shortage of money, though he had made close to $5 million, caused him to return to the ring that year and suffer a points defeat by Charles in a championship fight. His third and last defeat in a glorious career came in 1951 when Louis was knocked out by MARCIANO. Thereafter he retired for good.

LOWE, BRUCE, see HORSE RACING.

LOWE, DOUGLAS GORDON ARTHUR (1902-   ), middle-distance runner and ATHLETICS administrator for Great Britain. The first man to win the Olympic 800 metres twice (1924 and 1928), Lowe broke the Olympic record with 1 min. 51·8 sec. when winning his second gold medal. In 1926 he set a world record of 1 min. 10·4 sec. for 600 yards, then recognized as a standard distance. His best time for 800 metres was 1 min. 51·2 sec., accomplished in his last race in 1928. He served as honorary secretary of the Amateur Athletic Association from 1931 to 1938.

LUBANSKI, WŁODZIMIERZ (1947-   ), Association footballer for GORNIK ZABRZE, and Poland for whom he made his first appearance at the age of 16 and had played more than 20 times by the age of 20. Essentially a goal-scoring, attacking player, he could play equally well in the centre or on the wings.

LUCAS, JERRY (1940-   ), American BASKETBALL player. At 6 ft. 9 in. (2·06 m.), Lucas enjoyed an extremely successful college career at Ohio State University and played in the 1960 gold medal-winning team in the Rome OLYMPIC GAMES. On his return from Rome, Lucas turned professional with the CINCINNATI ROYALS and later move'd to the NEW YORK KNICKERBOCKERS.

LUCAS, PERCY BELGRAVE (Laddie), D.S.O. and Bar, D.F.C. (1915-   ), chairman of the world's largest greyhound track group, G.R.A. Property Trust Ltd. (see GREYHOUND RACING). A former Member of Parliament, as an amateur golfer he captained Britain's WALKER CUP team in 1949.

LUCIANO (1964), a race-horse bred in England, became one of the best horses to race in Germany since the Second World War, winning the GROSSER PREIS VON BADEN, GROSSER PREIS VON NORDRHEIN-WESTFALEN, DEUTSCHES DERBY, St. Leger, and Union Stakes.

LUDGROVE, see ETON FIVES.

LUGANO CUP, regarded as the world championship for RACE WALKING, was first held in 1961 in Lugano, Switzerland, the home town of the prime instigator of the event, LIBOTTE.

The rules stipulate that qualifiers from the preliminary round proceed to the final, which has to be held in central Europe, together with the first three countries from the previous final and any non-European countries, who are exempt from having to qualify. From 1961 to 1967 the event was held bi-annually with three competitors from each country entered and counting at the 20 km. and 50 km. distances. From 1970, countries were permitted to enter four competitors of which three score in the team classification.

The method of scoring is as follows: in a 21-man field the winner receives 22 points, the second 20 points, the third 19 points, down to the twenty-first, who receives 1 point. A competitor disqualified or retiring receives no points. In the event of a tie the placings are decided on the position of the first man home in the 50 km.

Great Britain were the winners from 1961 to 1963 and East Germany easy victors from 1965 to 1973. Double individual winners have included MATTHEWS, 20 km. (1961 and 1963), REIMANN (1970 and 1973), and HOHNE, 50 km. (1965, 1967, 1970).

LUGANO 100 KM. (62 miles), a Swiss event in road RACE WALKING, which finishes in

Lugano, is held in late October. Inaugurated in 1965, it has replaced the MILAN event over the same distance which was last held in 1960. Winners to date have been Hupfeld (West Germany), Young (Great Britain), Lindberg (Sweden), HOHNE (1968, 1970, 1971) and Selzer (East Germany), Ladony (Israel), and Shulgin (U.S.S.R.). Hohne set a world road record time in 1968 but was beaten into fourth place a year later. In 1968-9, SAKOWSKI (East Germany) finished second to his countryman achieving a world-class time on both occasions.

The event starts at 6 a.m. and takes place over a mountainous course with a 6 km. climb of Monte Ceneri at 76 km. (47 miles).

LUGE TOBOGGANING, see TOBOGGANING: LUGE.

LUISETTI, ANGELO (Hank) (c. 1913-), American BASKETBALL player who was responsible for popularizing the 'jumpshot' while playing for Stanford University in the mid-1930s. This shot revolutionized the tactics of the game. Luisetti was elected to the Hall of Fame (see NAISMITH) in 1959.

LUNN, Sir ARNOLD (1888-1974), ski-racing pioneer and innovator, SKIING and mountaineering author and historian, and one of the great formative influences of Alpine skiing. Son of Sir HENRY LUNN, he was knighted in 1953 'for services to ski-ing and to Anglo-Swiss relations'. In 1909 he suffered a mountaineering fall in Wales which made one leg two inches shorter than the other, but in spite of this he continued to ski and experiment with various forms of competition. He devised rules for downhill racing and introduced slalom as a separate competition in the British championships at Mürren in 1923. His rules for both competitions were submitted to individual members of the Fédération Internationale de Ski (F.I.S.) in 1926, but they were not officially adopted until the F.I.S. meeting in Oslo in 1930. He collaborated with SCHNEIDER for the first ARLBERG-KANDAHAR races at ST. ANTON in 1928.

Lunn was a member of the F.I.S. council for 15 years, but an outspoken critic of some of their policies and of the INTERNATIONAL OLYMPIC COMMITTEE. He was strongly against holding the 1936 Olympic Games in Nazi Germany, and against abuses of his strict definition of amateurism. After the Second World War, Lunn campaigned for distinctions between mountain and lowland skiers, and helped introduce Citizen races (see SKIING). He was also strongly critical of modern developments in slalom, the race he invented,

believing it should remain much as it started: a run in natural snow, zig-zagging among trees.

Lunn was the author of more than 50 philosophical, mountaineering, and ski-ing works, and edited the *British Ski Year-Book* for more than half a century. His *History of Ski-ing*, published in 1953, is a standard reference work.

LUNN, Sir HENRY (1868-1939), Methodist missionary who, in organizing a church re-union meeting in Switzerland, first saw the possibilities of winter sports for a large public and founded the travel agency known as Sir Henry Lunn Ltd. He was the father of Sir ARNOLD LUNN, one of the great formative personalities of SKIING and mountaineering, whom he first took skiing in 1898. Sir Henry opened many centres in Switzerland, among them Adelboden, Mürren, Wengen, Montana, Villars, Morgins, Lenzerheide, and Klosters.

LUXON, PAUL (1952-), London-born trampolinist and the first Englishman to become European champion; he has held British, European, and Nissen Cup titles.

LYDIARD, ARTHUR (1917-), ATHLETICS coach for New Zealand. Lydiard developed a system of endurance training which placed emphasis on running very long distances, up to and beyond 20 miles a day, at slow speeds, as a means of establishing a foundation of cardio-vascular and muscular conditioning. Himself a former New Zealand MARATHON champion, Lydiard coached, among others, SNELL and Halberg, the 1960 Olympic 5,000 metres champion.

LYNCH, JACK (1917-), Irish Prime Minister and Gaelic games player. Lynch is possibly unique in that he is the only sports record-breaker who has ever become head of a government. *Taoiseach* (Prime Minister) of the Republic of Ireland for several years, and formerly Minister first for Education and then for Industry and Commerce, in his playing days from 1938 to 1951, he set a whole series of records on the sports fields of the GAELIC ATHLETIC ASSOCIATION.

He was the first man to win six successive All-Ireland senior championship medals (HURLING — 1941-4; Gaelic FOOTBALL — 1945; and hurling — 1946) all with his native Cork, and was also the first to play in seven consecutive finals — he was on the losing Cork hurling side in the 1947 final. He was also the first player to represent his province, Munster, in both inter-provincial finals, hurling and football, on the same afternoon.

A stylish mid-fielder in his hurling prime, he usually played forward in football. He continued to play top class hurling for some years after being elected to Parliament in 1948.

LYTTELTON, Rt. Hon. ALFRED, K.C. (1857-1913), cricketer for England, Cambridge University, and Middlesex. A stylish batsman and fearless wicket-keeper, he also surprisingly took 4 wickets for 19 runs with lob bowling in the 1884 OVAL Test match against Scotland, and he was the best REAL played Association FOOTBALL for England against Scotland, and he was the best REAL TENNIS player of his time. He entered Parliament in 1895.

M

MABUNI, KENWA (*c.* 1880-*c.* 1950), Okinawan-born exponent of KARATE who arrived in Japan in 1930 and founded the *shitoryu* style of karate.

MACARTNEY, CHARLES GEORGE (1886-1958), cricketer for Australia and New South Wales. As a defiant and audacious batsman he hit 49 centuries (7 in Tests), including 345 in under four hours against Nottinghamshire in 1921, and 112 before lunch in the 1926 HEADINGLEY Test. He had made a brilliant 133 not out in the previous Test at LORD'S. Earlier in his career he had been a clever, aggressive, slow left-arm bowler.

McBRIDE, CHARLES JOSEPH (1925-), New Zealand RUGBY LEAGUE player. As a second-row forward, on the tour of England in 1947-8, he established a reputation as one of the best forwards produced by his country. Coming from South Island's west coast, he was equally outstanding in the Test series against Great Britain in 1950 and 1951-2.

McCABE, STANLEY JOSEPH (1910-1968), cricketer for Australia and New South Wales. A splendid hooker of fast bowling, he played three classic Test innings within six years. His 187 not out against the fury of 'body-line' bowling was followed by 189 not out against South Africa in 1935-6, and an equally magnificent 232 against England at TRENT BRIDGE in 1938. Each innings was played in adversity, but when runs came easily he often gave way to batsmen who were accumulators.

McCLELLAND, BREMAN, American SURFING administrator. He was manager to the continental U.S.A. team at the world championships in Australia in 1970.

McCORMICK, PATRICIA (1930-), diver for the U.S.A. and Los Angeles A.C. She won both springboard and high DIVING events at the 1952 OLYMPIC GAMES and again in 1956, a remarkable feat never achieved before by any woman or man. Coached by her husband, she practised for four hours each day.

McCORMICK, RICHARD (1950-), water skier for the U.S.A. In 1970 he set a world's best performance of 5,970 points in the tricks event at Princes Club, near London.

McCOY, KID (1873-1940), American boxer who won the world welterweight title in 1896 from RYAN, though some consider this bout was for the middleweight championship. McCoy was one of the great planners and tacticians of the sport; it has been said he studied BOXING as another man might study accountancy. One of the first to use the left hook, which at that time was called a 'corkscrew punch', McCoy was a master of trickery and feigned consumption, with his face powdered white, when he knocked out Ryan. From this and other subterfuges was coined the phrase 'the real McCoy'.

McCRACKEN, WILLIAM (1883-), Association footballer for Northern Ireland, Distillery, and NEWCASTLE UNITED. He played 15 times for his country between 1902 and 1923. He was a full-back of considerable tactical acumen and his exploitation — known as 'the one-back game' — of the original offside law, was a major influence in bringing about the change of that law in 1925.

MACDONALD BRIER TANKARD, see CURLING.

MACE, JEM (1831-1910), British boxer who won the English prize-ring championship in 1866 and three years later beat the American champion, Allen, in Louisiana. Mace, who never weighed much above 160 lb. (72·5 kg.), was a vital figure in the popularization of BOXING. After he visited Australia, one of his pupils, Foley, had a great influence as a trainer upon such redoubtable fighters as FITZSIMMONS and GRIFFO. Mace was such a master of evasive boxing that at 64 he was still able to give a brilliant exhibition at London's NATIONAL SPORTING CLUB.

McGILLICUDDY, CORNELIUS, see MACK, CONNIE.

McGLEW, DERRICK JOHN (1929-), cricketer for South Africa and Natal. An extremely dour opening batsman, he made the slowest century ever (in 545 minutes against Australia in 1957-8), and the highest for South Africa (255 not out against New Zealand in 1952-3—since beaten by POLLOCK). He led South Africa on their ill-fated 1960 tour, but for almost ten years his value to the side was considerable.

McGOVERN, TERRY (1880-1918), American boxer, winner of the world bantamweight and featherweight titles. In one of the most publicized international fights of the early days of glove-fighting this hard-hitting Irish-American knocked out Britain's Palmer in less than one round in 1899 for the bantamweight title. He also knocked out the great DIXON for the featherweight championship, but was eventually beaten by Young Corbett.

McGRAW, JOHN JOSEPH (1873-1934), American BASEBALL player and team manager. He became one of the notable figures in professional baseball, first as third baseman for the BALTIMORE ORIOLES of the 1890s, and then as manager of the NEW YORK GIANTS of the NATIONAL LEAGUE, a team he managed for more than 30 years from 1902. As manager of the Giants he won ten National League championships, four of them in succession, and three world championships.

MacGREGOR, JOHN (1825-92), founder in 1866 of the Canoe Club at the Star and Garter Hotel, Richmond, Surrey, the world's first canoe club. In the 'Rob Roy' kayak (which he designed) he toured rivers throughout Europe to generate interest in CANOEING.

McILROY, JAMES (1932-   ), Association footballer for Northern Ireland, GLENTORAN, Burnley, STOKE CITY, and Oldham Athletic. He also managed Oldham from 1966 to 1968. A constructive inside forward, he played on 55 occasions for his country.

MACINTOSH, CARO (1932-   ), LACROSSE player for Scotland (1951-69) and captain from 1959. She played more times for her country than any other Scottish player. Although a centre for most of her international career, she played attack wing on the successful Great Britain and Ireland touring team which went to the U.S.A. in 1960.

MACK, CONNIE (1862-1956), American BASEBALL player, team manager, and owner whose real name was Cornelius McGillicuddy. In 1901 he became part-owner and field manager of the PHILADELPHIA ATHLETICS, one of the clubs in the newly-formed

AMERICAN LEAGUE, where he remained as manager for half a century and eventually became sole owner. During his unprecedentedly long career as a major-league manager, he won nine American League championships and five world championships. In 1929 he received the Bok Award, presented annually to the individual who rendered the greatest service to Philadelphia, which had hitherto been granted only to members of the arts and professions.

MACK, GORDON S. B. (1900-49), BADMINTON player for Ireland. He enjoyed a tremendous reputation during the 1920s and played 21 times for Ireland between 1919 and 1932. He won all three ALL-ENGLAND CHAMPIONSHIP titles, including the men's doubles with DEVLIN five times. He was also a Davis Cup player in LAWN TENNIS for Ireland.

McKANE, KATHLEEN (Mrs. L. A. Godfree) (1897-   ), British LAWN TENNIS and BADMINTON player. A swift and effective volleyer, who cleverly adapted the skills of badminton to the lawn tennis court, she won the women's singles title at WIMBLEDON twice after losing to LENGLEN 6-2, 6-2 in the final in 1923. The following year she pulled up from 1-4 in the second set to beat WILLS 4-6, 6-4, 6-4, in the final (the American's only defeat in her long Wimbledon career). In 1927 McKane won a similarly hard final against DE ALVAREZ.

Miss McKane's first notable successes were in doubles and she had a fine record on indoor courts. In 1925 she reached the final of the singles in both French and U.S. championships, losing to Lenglen in Paris and to Wills at FOREST HILLS. Her consolation in that year was the capture of the U.S. doubles title with Covell. She was the mainstay of the British WIGHTMAN CUP team from 1923 to 1927, winning one rubber from Wills and losing three, and then reappeared in the doubles in 1930 to partner Miss Holcroft Watson in the rubber which won the tie for Britain. They defeated Wills and JACOBS 7-5, 1-6, 6-4. She and her husband, L. A. Godfree, were the only married couple to win the Wimbledon mixed doubles title (1927).

McKEE, ALEXANDER (1918-   ), underwater swimmer and explorer who researched and discovered the wreck of the *Mary Rose* (sunk 1545) in the Solent. Winner of the Diver of the Year award in 1971, he is the author of *Farming the Sea, History Under the Sea,* and *King Henry VIII's 'Mary Rose'*.

McKENLEY, HERBERT HENRY (1922-

), sprinter for Jamaica. Although his main claim to recognition was as a 440 yards/400 metres runner, McKenley never came nearer to the highest individual distinction than in the 1952 Olympic 100 metres final. After a finish so close that even the photo-finish film did not furnish a conclusive verdict, he was awarded a silver medal. Another silver rewarded his effort in the 400 metres, to pair with his silver medal in the 1948 Games. Finally he won a gold medal with a spectacular anchor leg in the 4 × 400 metres relay for Jamaica. In the period after the Second World War, McKenley was the most consistent world-class performer over 440 yards/400 metres, setting five world records at these distances. His best times were 46·0 sec. for 440 yards and 45·9 sec. for 400 metres.

MACKENZIE, GEORGE (1890-1957), British wrestler and holder of nine British championships between 1912 and 1941, was secretary of the National and British Amateur Wrestling Association 1935-57. An international referee, Mackenzie was British delegate to the Fédération Internationale des Luttes Amateurs (F.I.L.A.) and worked to keep amateur wrestling alive in England between the wars.

McKENZIE, GRAHAM DOUGLAS (1941-), cricketer for Australia, Western Australia, and Leicestershire. Playing in his first Test at the age of 20, by 1969 — eight years later — he had taken his 200th Test wicket and become Australia's key fast bowler. Heavily built, and bowling with a powerful shoulder action, he sometimes lacked accuracy, but his ability to bowl a dangerous ball even on the best pitch surprised many batsmen.

MACKENZIE, STUART A. (1937-), Australian sculler, the only man to win the Diamond Sculls (see HENLEY) six times (1957 to 1962). He made his international début in the 1956 OLYMPIC GAMES, finishing second to the Russian IVANOV, who was to remain his greatest rival. In the two following years, Mackenzie, defeating Ivanov at both HENLEY and in the European championships, was European champion, but despite other successes, he was never able to beat the Russian after 1958. In 1957 he became the first man to hold the Australian, New Zealand, Belgian, and European championships, as well as the Diamond Sculls, all in the same year. In 1958 he won the COMMONWEALTH GAMES title.

McKIVAT, CHRISTOPHER (1883-1941), captain of the Australian RUGBY LEAGUE team in England in 1911-12 which went through the Tests unbeaten, winning two and drawing the other. Besides being an outstanding scrum half in his own right, McKivat had a flair for bringing the best out of others. A voluble, hard-driving leader, whom contemporaries described 50 years later as Australia's greatest captain, he was 5 ft. 8 in. tall (1·73 m.) and weighed 12½ stone (79 kg.). He was exceptionally quick to size up a situation, and a brilliant passer of the ball.

MacLAREN, ARCHIBALD CAMPBELL (1871-1944), cricketer for England and Lancashire. A symbol of CRICKET's Golden Age, he batted with authority and style. In 1895 he scored 424 against Somerset, then the highest first-class score, and still the highest in county cricket. On three official tours of Australia he was seen at his best, particularly at SYDNEY, where he scored seven centuries. He led England on the last of these tours in 1901-2, and altogether led England in the record number of 22 Tests against Australia. He was a superb slip fielder, and he retained his powers late in his playing career, making 200 not out and taking five catches against a New Zealand XI soon after his 51st birthday.

McLAREN, BRUCE (1937-1970), New Zealand MOTOR RACING driver who developed and built McLaren sports/racing and formula cars. He first appeared in 1964, and won the CAN-AM Challenge Cup title in his own cars in 1967 and 1969. He was the winner of the United States Grand Prix at Sebring, 1959; the LE MANS 24 Hours with Amon, 1966; and the Sebring 12 Hours with ANDRETTI, 1967. He died after an accident in practice at GOODWOOD MOTOR CIRCUIT.

McLEOD, COLIN H. (1909-), underwater swimmer who introduced UNDERWATER SWIMMING equipment to Britain in 1946. He was captain of the British spearfishing team 1968-71, and is an officer of the British Sub Aqua Club and the Confédération Mondiale des Activités Subaquatique (C.M.A.S.).

McLEOD, HUGH FERNS (1932-), RUGBY UNION prop forward for HAWICK, Scotland, and British LIONS. A strong, industrious worker rather than a conspicuous performer, McLeod won 40 consecutive international caps, setting a Scottish record later equalled by ROLLO.

McLERNON, Mrs. THELMA, see HOPKINS, T.

McLOUGHLIN, MAURICE EVANS (1890-1957), the first American LAWN TENNIS player to win the all-comers' singles at WIMBLEDON and the first exponent of the 'cannonball' service. McLoughlin developed his game on the west coast of the United States and was nicknamed the 'California comet'. The pace and ferocity of his serving brought him considerable success and attracted much public interest.

He won the all-comers' singles in the U.S. championships in 1911 but lost to Larned in the challenge round. In 1912, the year of the abolition of the challenge round in that championship, he beat W. F. Johnson in the final after losing the first two sets and retained the title against R. N. Williams the following year. In 1913 and 1914 he was runner-up, first to Williams and then to W. M. Johnston. At Wimbledon in 1913 McLoughlin was faced with a first match against the formidable Roper Barrett, which he won in five sets. He beat Doust (Australia) in the all-comers' final but lost by 8-6, 6-3, 10-8 to WILDING in the challenge round.

Three weeks later he won a singles rubber against Dixon and the doubles with Hackett to give the U.S.A. victory in the Davis Cup (see LAWN TENNIS) challenge round against the British Isles at Wimbledon. In the 1914 challenge round at New York he beat BROOKES and Wilding in the singles, but Australasia won 3-2. McLoughlin won the U.S. doubles title with Bundy in 1913 and 1914.

McMAHON, PADDY (1935-   ), British show jumping (see EQUESTRIAN EVENTS) rider. He began riding at the comparatively late age of 15 and made his international début in 1969. Chosen as one of Britain's pair for the Men's European championship of 1973, he won the title at his first attempt, riding the Irish-bred Pennwood Forge Mill.

McNEILL, GEORGE (1947-   ), Scottish professional sprinter, formerly a soccer player with Morton and Stirling Albion. He won the POWDERHALL handicap the first time he entered, in January 1970. In August 1970, at Edinburgh, he broke the world professional 120-yard (109·7 m.) record in 11·14 sec. His time at 100 metres was recorded as 10·15 sec., which by an amateur would have been a U.K. record. The following year, in a Powderhall Sprint heat on the same track, he lowered the record to 11 sec., but he did not win the final.

MACON (1922) was one of the best racehorses to run in the Argentine. He won the GRAN PREMIO CARLOS PELLEGRINI twice, the Argentine Derby and Two Thousand Guineas, the Premio Comparacion twice, and the Gran Premio de Honor.

MacROBERTSON INTERNATIONAL SHIELD, the trophy presented by Sir MacPherson Robertson, the Australian millionaire and philanthropist, for competition between those countries playing Association CROQUET.

In 1925 a team from Australia visited England and started a series of occasional matches between the two countries; New Zealand joined in 1930. The early matches were governed by the factor that croquet, being an amateur sport, was not in a position to subsidize the cost of sending teams to the antipodes, with the result that teams were usually composed principally of those who could afford to make such a pilgrimage. Notwithstanding this, some formidable teams were sometimes raised.

The conditions of each competition depend to some extent on the number of countries taking part. A team may consist of four, five, or six players; if four players, each match consists of four singles and two doubles; if five players, of five singles and two doubles; if six players, of six singles and three doubles. If two countries only are involved, the series consists usually of five Test matches; if three countries, each plays the other three times. In this case there is a total of 81 individual matches, each match being the best of three games. The series is held at intervals of four or five years, the venue alternating between England, Australia, and New Zealand.

MADISON, HELENE (1913-70), American swimmer who was the supreme woman freestyle performer of her time. In 1930-1, she broke the world records for every distance from her stroke from 100 yards to one mile. Her final tally was 20 world marks, some of which stood unbroken for a decade. She retired after the 1932 OLYMPIC GAMES in Los Angeles where she won the 100 and 400 metres — the latter in world record time — and a third gold medal in the freestyle relay.

MADISON RACING, see CYCLING.

MADISON SQUARE GARDEN, New York, American sports arena and exhibition centre which is probably the most famous indoor stadium in the world. The present Garden is the fourth such centre to bear the name. Built over Pennsylvania Station on 7th Avenue, the 13-storey structure includes a main arena seating over 20,000, an auditorium accommodating 5,000, an art gallery, a cinema/theatre, an exhibition area, and a 48-lane BOWLING centre. The main arena has a clear span roof, 425 ft. (130 m.) in diameter. Construction began in 1963 and the complex was formally opened on 11 February 1968. Its cost was reckoned at $130 million.

Almost from its inception, Madison Square Garden has presented a wide variety of sport, spectacle, and entertainment. ATHLETICS (track and field events), BASKETBALL, BOXING, CYCLING, ICE HOCKEY, SWIMMING, LAWN TENNIS, and WRESTLING have been mixed with dog shows, rodeos, political conventions, circuses, and religious revival meetings. Every prominent boxing champion since SULLIVAN has fought there; Patti sang there and Paderewski played to enthusiastic audiences.

Boxing, however, must be the most consistently popular attraction. The boxers who have fought there make an impressive list: in 1934 Baer knocked down Carnera 12 times in 11 rounds to win the heavyweight title; LOUIS was knocked out by Walcott, Savold, and MARCIANO between 1948 and 1951; in 1953 Olson outpointed Turpin to win the world middleweight championship and four years later Fuller similarly beat 'Sugar Ray' ROBINSON. In 1967, in his ninth defence of the heavyweight title, CLAY (Muhammad Ali) knocked out Tolley in seven rounds before being relieved of the title for refusing to serve in the U.S. Army.

In 1968, as part of the inauguration of the new Madison Square Garden, the state of New York announced that it would recognize the winner of the Frazier-Mathis fight as world heavyweight champion. The bout took place on 4 March on the same card as the Griffith-Benvenuti match before an audience of 18,096 for a record indoor gate of $658,503. FRAZIER knocked out Mathis in the 11th round.

With his appeal against conviction for draft evasion still pending, Clay fought again at Madison Square Garden when, on 8 March 1971, he met Frazier in what was billed as 'the Fight of the Century'. Frazier won on points by a unanimous decision to become undisputed world heavyweight champion, and both boxers received the equivalent of £1 million. Other boxers to compete there have been Carter, DEMPSEY, ORTIZ, Tiger, and Willard.

In 1891 six-day bicycle races were introduced, with competition at first limited to individuals. But in 1898 when Miller established the one-man record of 2,093·4 miles (3,369 km.) he set such a fierce pace that several contestants were admitted to hospital suffering from exhaustion; the resulting widespread criticism of the sport led to the formation of two-man teams.

Basketball has for years attracted large crowds to the stadium. In 1952 the HARLEM GLOBETROTTERS broke the one-day attendance record for the sport when they played before 35,548 spectators.

The imposing Madison Square Garden of today is the direct descendant of a modest concert garden in Madison Square Park which was popular in the 1870s. Gilmore (who wrote 'When Johnny Comes Marching Home'), an Irish musician and composer who went to America in 1849, became well known as a cornet player, and formed a band which, from 1873 to 1876, gave over 600 concerts in Madison Square Park in what became known as 'Gilmore's Garden'. The site, a disused railroad depot, had previously been occupied by Barnum, the showman and circus proprietor, one of whose associates had obtained a lease in 1874. In 1879 the site was renamed Madison Square Garden, and Barnum took over again in 1880.

Until his death in 1891, Barnum initiated some of the early diverse entertainments for which Madison Square Garden became famous. His show 'The Great Roman Hippodrome' combined circus, museum, and menagerie. Later Barnum & Bailey's 'Greatest Show on Earth' attracted such personalities as King Kalakaua of the Hawaiian Islands. The king was impressed by a horse race between female jockeys and presented the winner with a rose; he had been greeted by a firework display and, for good measure, Barnum drove him round the ring for a valedictory circuit in a Roman chariot. Barnum shrugged off criticisms that he had made an undignified spectacle of the king.

Not long before his death, Barnum tripped over a rope at the Garden. He suffered only slight scratches but immediately recognized the publicity value of the accident and shouted for his press agent to be told of the injuries. Next day Barnum stayed at home while the newspapers printed stories about the 'painful accident' in which the showman had been 'seriously injured'.

In 1890 the old buildings were razed and in their place was erected one of the most impressive structures of the time, opened on 16 June in the same year. The new building was designed by Stanford White of McKim, Mead & White, an influential architectural partnership. Later known as the 'Old Garden', the building was surmounted by a tower, copied from the Giralda in Seville. At the top of the tower was a draped statue of Diana by Saint-Gaudens. The drapery, however, was torn away by the wind and the figure thus revealed was a landmark for many years. When the building was eventually demolished the Diana was carefully removed, and her handlers discovered that she was held together with large rivets. In 1906 White, the architect, was murdered in the roof garden of the building he had designed; his assailant, a millionaire named Thaw, was found to be insane.

The Old Garden continued the practice of presenting a variety of attractions. There Bryan accepted the Democratic nomination for President; aquatic exhibitions were staged in the pool; Dempsey knocked out Brennan in defence of the heavyweight title; Ringling's circus became established. In 1916 the first local presentation (the Willard-Moran fight) by RICKARD, the showman and boxing promoter, grossed $250,000.

Rickard and his associates were largely responsible for getting boxing legalized in the state of New York. Indeed so successful was he that in 1925, when the Old Garden was demolished to make way for an insurance company's building, Rickard was able to obtain financial backing to undertake the planning of a new and even larger Garden. He supervised this project until he died in 1929.

The third Madison Square Garden, opened on 15 December 1925 and built at a cost of $5 million, was a long way north of the first two, on 8th Avenue at 50th Street. Designed by Lamb, a theatre architect, the building could accommodate a crowd of nearly 19,000 for a boxing contest, 16,000 for an ice hockey match, and almost 15,000 for the bicycle races which were still popular.

The location of the building proved particularly fortunate, as a City Guide explained: 'Whenever a heavyweight boxer in Madison Square Garden takes too many right-hand punches, or a trapeze performer misses his safety net, or a rodeo rider falls under the hoofs of a steer, the victim is carried across the street to Polyclinic Hospital. The 346-bed hospital serves the ordinary people of the neighborhood, for the most part, but because of its location it receives an unusually large number of well-publicized patients.'

This extract emphasizes that the variety of entertainments had not decreased with the move to the new building. The designers had taken the opportunity to incorporate as many up-to-date features as possible; the roof was supported by a steel framework which obviated a large number of columns and permitted a clear view of the arena.

The technical facilities were impressive. Within four hours of the end of a hockey game, two tractors would clear the rink of ice while 30 men cleaned the auditorium, constructed a boxing ring, and installed additional seating. To revert to ice hockey, the concrete floor of the arena was covered with water which was then frozen by brine in a network of pipes, 13 miles long, under the floor — a process taking about eight hours. For the annual

winter sports show two pulverizers took seven hours to convert 500 tons of ice into snow.

The arrangements for other sports were less mechanized. For the six-day bicycle races, because no sectional track was available, 300 men would take eight hours to build a new track for each meeting. When horse shows, rodeos, and circuses were staged, a contractor 'rented' 690 tons of earth.

In 1932, at a cost of $160,000, the Garden company built the Madison Square Garden Bowl at 45th Street. An outdoor arena seating 80,000, it was designed for summer sports events but made little profit. There on 29 June 1933, Carnera won the world heavyweight championship by knocking out Sharkey, and two years later Braddock took the title from Baer.

The Madison Square Garden company took a direct interest in sport with its ownership of the NEW YORK RANGERS ice hockey team. Later this was increased by the addition of the NEW YORK KNICKERBOCKERS basketball team and the New York Skyliners soccer team.

In the early 1960s it became obvious that Rickard's 1925 Garden would be obsolete within a decade. By coincidence, the Pennsylvania Railroad Company planned to demolish its surface station on 7th Avenue and offered the site for use as a new Garden. Thus the wheel turned full circle; from its humble beginning over 90 years before in the disused New York and Harlem Railroad depot, Madison Square Garden has developed into a commercial empire with an annual revenue approaching $13 million. The railroad site it now occupies covers $8\frac{1}{2}$ acres.

MADREE (1904) was the most celebrated brood mare in Italian bloodstock-breeding. She was ancestress, within six generations, of 14 winners of 18 classic races.

MAGGIE B.B. (1867) was one of the most important brood mares in American bloodstock-breeding and dam of IROQUOIS, winner of the English DERBY and ST. LEGER.

MAILEY, ARTHUR ALFRED (1888-1967), cricketer for Australia and New South Wales. Bowling leg breaks and 'googlies' with humour and abandon, he took 99 Test wickets at 33·9 runs each. Though sometimes expensive, he could deliver the near-unplayable, sharply-spinning ball. In 1920-1 he took 36 England wickets in the Test series, including 9 for 121 at MELBOURNE.

MAIN NUE, see PELOTA.

MAIRS, MARY, see CHAPOT, Mrs.

MAJID JAHANGIR KHAN (1946-   ), cricketer for Pakistan, Lahore, Cambridge University, Glamorgan, and Queensland. One of the world's major batsmen in the 1970s, he first played first-class CRICKET at the age of 15. Joining Glamorgan in 1968, he soon established himself as a crisp and handsome striker. In 1967 for the touring Pakistanis against the county he scored 147 not out in 89 minutes, with 13 sixes. From 1970 to 1972 his influence on Cambridge cricket was considerable, and the victory over Oxford under his captaincy in 1972 was the first since 1958. He was appointed captain of Glamorgan in 1973. His father played for India in the 1930s.

MAKINEN, TIMO (1938-   ), Finnish motor rally driver (see MOTOR RACING) who won the Thousand Lakes Rally in 1964, 1965, and 1966. Other successes include the 1965 Monte Carlo Rally — in 1966 he came first but was disqualified for infringing a lighting regulation.

MALLIN, HARRY (1893-1970), an outstanding British amateur boxer who never lost a contest or turned professional. Mallin was AMATEUR BOXING ASSOCIATION middleweight champion five times (1919-1923) and OLYMPIC GAMES champion in 1920 and 1924.

MAN o' WAR (1917), affectionately known as 'Big Red', was the greatest American racehorse up to 1930. He won 20 out of 21 races and prize money amounting to a record $249,465, including the BELMONT (by 20 lengths in record time), PREAKNESS, TRAVERS, WITHERS, LAWRENCE REALIZATION, and JOCKEY CLUB STAKES. He was not entered for the KENTUCKY DERBY, and his only defeat, after being boxed-in on the rails, was in a two-year-old event. Man o' War was a chestnut colt by FAIR PLAY out of Mahuba by ROCK SAND. He was bred by Maj. BELMONT, bought as a yearling at Saratoga Springs for $5,000 by Riddle, trained by Feustel, and ridden by Loftus and Kummer. After his triumphs on the turf, he stood as a stallion at the Faraway Stud Farm. His best son was WAR ADMIRAL, who became the maternal grandsire of NEVER SAY DIE. Man o' War died in 1947.

MANCHESTER–BLACKPOOL, is a 52 miles (83 km.) English road RACE WALKING event held annually since 1909 except in the periods 1914-18 and 1939-45. Organized by the Lancashire Walking Club, the distance varied slightly prior to 1950 but has remained constant since. GREEN gained six successive victories (1929-34), and Payne had four wins between 1909 and 1920.

Held every June, with a 6.15 a.m. start, the course is relatively flat throughout and finishes at the Tower on the esplanade at Blackpool.

MANCHESTER CITY F.C., Association FOOTBALL club. Founded in 1880 as the West Gorton club, it amalgamated with Gorton Athletic (founded 1884) to form Ardwick in 1887. Ardwick were elected one of the 12 original members of the Second Division of the Football League in 1892 and in 1894 took the name Manchester City. Although the club was in the First Division for all except six of the 52 playing seasons from 1899 to 1963, it won only one League championship (1936-7) and the club's best performances were reserved for the F.A. Cup competition which it won in 1904, 1934, and 1956. In the close season of 1965, after two middling seasons in the Second Division, the club appointed a new manager, MERCER, and an assistant manager, Allison. These two built a team that was to win the Second Division championship in 1965-6, the First Division championship in 1967-8, the F.A. Cup in 1969, the Football League Cup in March 1970, and the European Cup-Winners Cup in April 1970. Outstanding players included MEREDITH, BROOK, DOHERTY, Revie, Swift, LAW, and Lee.

COLOURS: Sky-blue shirts, white shorts.
GROUND: Maine Road, Manchester.

MANCHESTER S.C., ICE SKATING club formed in England in 1877, dependent on occasional natural ice until the opening of Manchester Ice Palace (1910), where the club staged early world championships during the first quarter of the twentieth century, when Manchester rather than London was the hub of the sport in Britain.

MANCHESTER UNITED F.C., Association FOOTBALL club, founded in 1885 by employees of the Lancashire and Yorkshire Railway and named Newton Heath. The present name was adopted in 1902, ten years after the club had been elected to the First Division of the Football League and it won the League championship twice before the First World War — the first time in the 1907-8 season. The following year the club won the F.A. Cup, but these were its only successes in League and Cup until competitive football was resumed after the end of the Second World War. Since then Manchester United have won the League championship in 1951-2, 1955-6, 1956-7, 1964-5, and 1966-7, and the F.A. Cup in 1948 and 1963. Most credit for the club's success must go to the manager, BUSBY, who accepted the post at the end of the war, and who, after guiding the club to early Cup and championship victories, had fashioned a young side of high potential that won the League championship in two successive seasons in the mid-1950s and in 1957 reached the semi-final of the second competition for the European Champions Cup. A year later, on 6 February 1958, the club had again qualified for a semi-final place in the European competition by drawing 3-3 with RED STAR BELGRADE after having earlier beaten the Yugoslavian club 2-1 in Manchester. After a stop at Munich on the homeward journey, the aircraft in which players and officials of Manchester United were travelling crashed on take-off. Of the 44 on board, 21 were killed, including the club's secretary, trainer, assistant coach, and 7 players. Two of the players, Byrne and Taylor, were members of the England national side, as was EDWARDS, who died later from injuries sustained in the crash. It took the club several seasons to recover, but at Wembley on 29 May 1968 Manchester United beat BENFICA 4-1 in the final of the European Champions Cup. Outstanding players of the pre-1939 period included MEREDITH, Roberts, and Spence; since 1945 an almost continuous stream of outstanding players has included CAREY, R. CHARLTON, Edwards, J. Rowley, Taylor, Giles, Gregg, LAW, BEST, Crerand, and Stiles.

COLOURS: Red shirts, white shorts.
GROUND: Old Trafford, Manchester.

MANCINELLI, GRAZIANO (1937-   ), Italian show jumping (see EQUESTRIAN EVENTS) rider. For long regarded as an ex-professional and, as such, ineligible for the OLYMPIC GAMES, he was included by his Federation in the team for Tokyo (1964) and was deemed to be eligible after all. The Italians thus solved their long-standing problem in finding a third rider to join the D'INZEO brothers for their Olympic teams. In 1963, with Rockette, the mare he later rode in the 1964 Olympics, Mancinelli won the men's European championship and seven years later (on Fidux) he was runner-up to BROOME for the men's world title. In 1972, he rode the Irish-bred Ambassador to win the individual Olympic gold medal and a team bronze.

MANGIAROTTI, EDOARDO (1919-   ), son of Maestro Giuseppe Mangiarotti of Milan. An outstanding technical fencer both at foil and épée, he was Olympic épée champion in 1952 and world épée champion in 1951 and 1954, and a silver medallist at foil in the Olympic or world championships in 1951, 1952, 1953, and 1954. On a points system awarded to fencers achieving first, second, or third places in Olympic and world finals, he

emerges as the most successful fencer of all time. He is the author of *La Vera Scherma.*

MANITOBA TROPHY, see BADMINTON.

MANKAD, MULVANTRAI HIMMATLAL (Vinoo) (1917-   ), cricketer for India, Western India, Nawanagar, Maharashtra, Gujerat, Bengal, Bombay, and Rajasthan. Despite losing the early years of his Test career through the Second World War, he established many records: fastest to the Test 'double' of 1,000 runs and 100 wickets, the only Indian to perform the 'double' on a tour of England (in 1952), the holder (with Roy) of the highest opening partnership in Test CRICKET — 413 against New Zealand — when his 231 was the highest score for India. His 33 catches were until 1973 another Indian Test record. In the 1952 LORD'S Test he scored 72 and 184, and took 5 wickets in 97 overs.

MANN CUP, see LACROSSE.

MANNING CUP, the oldest HOCKEY trophy competed for by two countries (Australia and New Zealand), played for alternately in each country, either with one Test or a series of Tests. New Zealand won the trophy on the first six occasions and held it from 1925 to 1948. Australia won the Cup six successive times between 1958 and 1965.

MANOLETE (Manuel Rodríguez Sánchez) (1917-47), *matador de toros* who took the *alternativa* in 1939, was gored by the bull Islero, of Miura, in the bull ring of Linares on 28 August 1947, and died the following day. His great-uncle PEPETE had met the same fate, also on the horns of a Miura bull, in 1862. Although at times a profile *torero*, he was one of the greatest classicists of all time. He had a highly individualistic purity of style with both the cape and *muleta*, and he was superlative with the sword.

MARACAÑA STADIUM, Rio de Janeiro, built for the final rounds of the Jules Rimet Association FOOTBALL trophy competition (the World Cup) in 1950. Despite intensive efforts (work went on 24 hours a day and involved 6,500 men) it was not finished in time. But in a stadium described as 'no more than an ambitious shambles', 199,854 spectators saw the final between Brazil and Uruguay — the biggest football crowd, in the world's largest football stadium.

The stadium was still not completed ten years later, by which time those parts built first were in need of repair and its architect, Guedes, had died. When the work was finished, the stadium could hold 205,000 (155,000 seated) and had cost $7,500,000. A dry moat, 7 ft. (2·13 m.) wide and 5 ft. (1·52 m.) deep, separates the spectators from the pitch. Unlike some buildings of its kind, it is in frequent use. Senior clubs of Rio use it for football matches, which draw an average crowd of 112,000 and an occasional one of 150,000. It is also used for BOXING, when an additional 32,000 spectators can be accommodated, and was the scene of the 1954 world championship BASKETBALL tournament.

MARATHON, the longest race to figure in the programme of events for all major ATHLETICS championships. The marathon derives its name from the story of Phidippides, a Greek soldier, who was ordered to run from the battlefield of Marathon to Athens, a distance of about 22 miles, to convey the news of the Greek victory over the Persians in 490 B.C. The marathon was, of course, included in the modern OLYMPIC GAMES first held at Athens in 1896, but the modern distance of 26 miles 385 yards was not standardized until 1908 when the Olympic marathon from Windsor to London measured 26 miles, and the runners were required to cover a further 385 yards in order to finish opposite the Royal Box at White City Stadium. Owing to the wide variation in courses, the International Amateur Athletic Federation (see ATHLETICS, TRACK AND FIELD) does not recognize a world record. A degree of uniformity has, however, been achieved in marathon courses by the practice, now universally followed in major championships, of running an 'out-and-back' course. This neutralizes the advantages which might be obtained from prevailing winds or gradients on a 'one-way' course.

MARAVICH, PETER PRESS (1948–   ), American BASKETBALL player who became the highest scorer in the history of NATIONAL COLLEGIATE ATHLETIC ASSOCIATION competition. He stands 6 ft. 5 in. (1·96 m.) tall and graduated from Louisiana State University in 1970. He turned professional with the Atlanta Hawks of the NATIONAL BASKETBALL ASSOCIATION.

MARBLE, ALICE (1913–   ), American LAWN TENNIS player, probably the finest woman exponent of the service and volley game. Although dogged by ill-health, she won the U.S. singles title four times (1936 and 1938-40) and the WIMBLEDON title in 1939 by attacking with a simple, athletic directness which set a new pattern for the women's game. After Marble, women began to move away from the classic ground-stroke strategy and to imitate masculine techniques more strongly. She showed how effectively a woman could serve and volley and players like OSBORNE and BROUGH followed. Her impact on women's lawn tennis can be compared with that of MCLOUGHLIN, another Californian, the master of the cannon-ball service, on the men's game shortly before the First World War. Marble's immediate successors, nearly all the best were Californians, dominated their matches by commanding the net and the rest of the world learnt the American lesson.

Miss Marble was also a fine doubles player, winning the women's event at Wimbledon twice with Mrs. Fabyan and the mixed event twice with BUDGE and once with Riggs. In the U.S. doubles she and Mrs. Fabyan were unbeaten in the four years from 1937. Marble turned professional in 1941.

MARCEL CORBILLON CUP, award for the women's team championship of the world at TABLE TENNIS, it was presented by Marcel Corbillon (1890-1958) president of the French Table Tennis Federation and deputy president of the International Table Tennis Federation for several years. The Cup has been played for at all world championships since, and including, Paris in 1934. The teams consist of two singles players and one pair, chosen by the captain from a maximum nominated list of four, and the result follows the best of five matches, each singles player meeting each one on the other side, and the doubles pairs meeting (as in the Davis Cup — see LAWN TENNIS); each match is over the best of three games. The teams entering are divided into preliminary groups, then graded into further groups on the basis of the first results, with a final play-off for positions. Twenty-five competitions — interrupted by the Second World War — were held from 1934 to 1973. Of the 6 held before the war, Czechoslovakia won 3, Germany 2, and the U.S.A. 1. Of the first 3 after the war England won 2 and the U.S.A. 1; of the next 7 Rumania won 5 and Japan 2; of the last 9 (terminating in 1973) Japan 6, China 1, Korea (R.o.), 1, and the U.S.S.R. 1.

MARCIANO, ROCKY (1923-69), American boxer who won the world heavyweight title in 1952 and retired undefeated in 1956 with a professional record of 49 fights and 49 victories. Marciano, though only 5 ft. 11 in. (1·8 m.) tall and sometimes handicapped by facial cuts, swept all before him with his irresistible attack and powerful right-hand punch. Only five of his opponents ever lasted to the final bell. Marciano ended the career of LOUIS and, after winning the title from 'Jersey Joe' Walcott successfully defended it six times before retiring. He was killed in an air crash.

MARSH, RICHARD (1851-1933), English race-horse trainer of Egerton House, Newmarket. His principal patron was the Prince of WALES, and he prepared PERSIMMON, DIAMOND JUBILEE, and the DERBY and TWO THOUSAND GUINEAS winner, Minoru, for their successes in the royal racing colours.

MARTIAL ARTS, see BOXING, CHINESE; BOXING, THAI; JUDO; JU-JITSU; KARATE; KENDO.

MARTIN, LOUIS GEORGE, M.B.E. (1937-), Jamaican-born British middle heavyweight lifter who was four times world and European champion, bronze medallist at the 1960 OLYMPIC GAMES, silver medallist at the 1964 Olympic Games and the first lifter to win three successive gold medals in the COMMONWEALTH GAMES — 1962, 1966, 1970. He set over 100 world, Olympic, European, Commonwealth, and British records.

MARYLEBONE CRICKET CLUB (M.C.C.), founded in 1787 by a group of noblemen headed by the Earl of Winchilsea, Lord Charles Lennox, the Duke of York, and the Duke of Dorset. In essence it was but a change of name for the White Conduit Cricket Club (which had been formed in 1782) after THOMAS LORD had established his first ground, at Dorset Square, in 1787. The laws of CRICKET were revised by the new club, and the authority which had formerly been accepted as incumbent on HAMBLEDON now passed to Marylebone, and remained with it until 1969, when the government of the game became the official responsibility of the newly-created CRICKET COUNCIL. M.C.C. clearly was now, as it had seldom recognizably been before, a private club, but it has one continuing brief: to maintain and, if necessary, to amend the laws of cricket.

During its 182 years of influence and tacitly-accepted power the Club set up bodies to administer county cricket, Test cricket in England (the Board of Control), and worldwide cricket affairs (the International Cricket Conference). In 1903-4 it responded to a suggestion from the Australian authorities by undertaking the selection and management of England teams abroad. Since the Club shed all its former responsibilities from 1969 — thus allowing cricket to benefit from certain government grants to which only official *public* sports bodies are entitled — English touring Test teams have continued to carry the M.C.C.'s name as a courtesy.

Of the cricket crises in which the Club became embroiled during its ministry over the game's affairs, the 'body-line' controversy of 1932-3, the matter of illegal bowling actions in the late 1950s, and the difficulties surrounding proposed tours to and from South Africa, were the most serious.

The Club, which also has SQUASH RACKETS and REAL TENNIS sections, has wide membership that includes many distinguished persons. It purchased the freehold of LORD'S (which has always been its headquarters) for little more than £18,000 in 1866, and the ground facilities have been developed under a succession of administrators. The president is nominated by his predecessor annually, and the secretary and treasurer hold office for unprescribed periods. S. C. Griffith, who was appointed in 1962, was only the tenth secretary since the Club's inauguration.

MASERATI, a racing car. The firm founded by the six Maserati brothers produced its first racing car in 1926. The first type to achieve marked success was the 8C-2500 which won, among other races, the Spanish Grand Prix in 1930. The 8CM-3000 was a formidable opponent to the other cars of the mid-1930s and scored many wins, especially in 1933. After the war, the Tipo 4CLT/48 took a number of first places in 1948 and 1949, but perhaps the outstanding Maserati was the 250F Grand Prix car which, in 1956 and particularly in 1957, had great success. In 1957, when their leading driver, FANGIO, won the world championship, Maserati withdrew from MOTOR RACING.

MASKELL, DAN (1908-), British LAWN TENNIS professional, from 1929 to 1955 the first full-time coach to the ALL-ENGLAND CLUB and the official coach to the British Davis Cup (see LAWN TENNIS) and WIGHTMAN CUP teams. In 1955 he was appointed training manager of the LAWN TENNIS ASSOCIATION.

Maskell began coaching at Queen's Club in 1926, teaching lawn tennis, RACKETS, and SQUASH RACKETS, and in 1928 he won the first of his 16 British professional lawn tennis titles. He played a major part in modernizing the official coaching system in Britain and in raising the status of the lawn tennis teacher. He was also a regular commentator on the game on radio and television.

MASOPUST, JOSEF (1931-), Association footballer for DUKLA PRAGUE, and Czechoslovakia for whom his excellent performances at left half in the 1962 world championship tournament in Chile earned him the top place in that year's 'European Footballer of the Year' poll organized by the magazine *France Football.* He scored in the final match when Brazil won the Jules Rimet Cup 3-1.

MASSY, ARNAUD (1877-*c.* 1946), French professional golfer, the first overseas golfer to win the Open championship. His success, in 1907, was followed four years later by a tie for first place with VARDON, but Massy lost the play-off. He was the first continental professional of international stature.

MASTENBROEK, HENDRIKA (1919-   ), Dutch swimmer who emulated the feat of America's MADISON four years earlier by winning gold medals for the 100 metres, 400 metres, and 4 × 100 metres freestyle relay at the 1936 Berlin OLYMPIC GAMES. For good measure, she also won the silver medal in the 100 metres backstroke. She trained in the canals for distance and in swimming pools for sprinting and broke seven world records, one for freestyle and six for backstroke.

MASTER McGRATH, (1866), COURSING and racing greyhound. Lord Lurgan's dog, by Dervock out of Lady Sarah, became a public hero on the strength of his triumphs in the WATERLOO CUP in 1868, 1869, and 1871. At Queen Victoria's request he was duly presented to her at Court. Master McGrath also won the Brownlow, Scarisbrick, and Douglas Cups, and in a career spanning four seasons won 36 out of 37 courses. The brilliance of his performances against Lobelia, the winner of the 1867 Cup, and the famous BAB AT THE BOWSTER in the 1869 final, are regarded as classic exhibitions of coursing. His feats, known to Irishmen throughout the world, have been chronicled in the 'Ballad of Master M'Grath' and there is a monument to him in Ireland, four miles from Dungarvan.

MATCH III (1958), a French race-horse by TANTIÈME out of RELANCE bred and owned by DUPRÉ, trained by MATHET, and ridden by SAINT-MARTIN. Match III won seven races and £110,815 in stake-money, including the GRAND PRIX DE SAINT-CLOUD, French St. Leger, KING GEORGE VI AND QUEEN ELIZABETH STAKES, and WASHINGTON INTERNATIONAL.

MATCHEM (1748-81) was the third progenitor of the thoroughbred race-horse, together with ECLIPSE and HEROD, whose direct male descendants have existed to the present day.

MATHET, FRANÇOIS, is the leading race-horse trainer in France, whose patrons have included DUPRÉ and VOLTERRA. His most notable winners were TANTIÈME, MATCH III, RELKO, RELIANCE, and two winners of the PRIX DU JOCKEY CLUB in Tapalque and SASSAFRAS, the latter, ridden by SAINT-MARTIN,

going on to win the PRIX DE L'ARC DE TRIOMPHE by a head from NIJINSKY.

MATHEWS, PATRICK DUFF (1886-1960), one of three outstanding Irish CROQUET players. Considering the commanding position he held in croquet in the early years of this century his number of titles was relatively small, six in all, including four open championships. He played with the Irish grip but in an unusually upright style. Not a great tactician, Mathews survived by the brilliance of his shooting and his ability to pick up a break from the most unpromising of positions.

MATHEWSON, CHRISTOPHER (1880-1925), American BASEBALL player who pitched for the NEW YORK GIANTS team for 17 seasons. Mathewson shares with ALEXANDER the NATIONAL LEAGUE record of most games won, 373. He won 30 games in each of three successive seasons, and in each of his three 1905 WORLD SERIES victories he prevented the opposing Philadelphia American League team from scoring a single run.

MATHIAS, ROBERT B. (1930-   ), U.S.A., the first man to win the Olympic DECATHLON twice. Mathias was also, at 17, the youngest male competitor ever to win an Olympic gold medal. This achievement, in 1948, was the more remarkable in the context of a test demanding experience and physical maturity in greater measure than any other Olympic event. It was, moreover, accomplished in the year of his decathlon début. He broke the world record in 1950, when only 19, and broke it twice again in 1952 before successfully defending his Olympic title. His best score was 7,887 points according to the 1950 points tables.

MATTARELLI, ENNIO (fl. 1961-9), clay pigeon shooter for Italy. He was the first man to win Olympic, world, and European gold medals. Twice world champion (1961 and 1969) and Olympic champion in 1964, Mattarelli set a record score of 198 hits out of a possible 200. He was European champion in 1964.

MATTHES, ROLAND (1950-   ), an East German who is one of the greatest swimmers of all time. Double winner of the 100 and 200 metres backstroke at the 1968 OLYMPIC GAMES, he repeated this performance in the European championships two years later, at the 1972 Olympics, and the first world championships in 1973. The possessor of a deceptively languid stroke with hidden power, he used eight to ten arm pulls per length less than most of his rivals. Had he not concentrated on backstroke, he could have excelled equally at the other swimming styles—he held European records for butterfly and medley and was the fastest East German freestyle sprinter.

MATTHEWS, KENNETH JOHN (1934-   ), race walker for Great Britain. Together with VICKERS he dominated world sprint walking from 1959 to 1964. Olympic champion in 1964 and European champion in 1962 at the 20 km. distance, Matthews also won the LUGANO CUP final at the same distance in 1961 and 1963. A very stylish competitor, he set world best times at 5 miles (8 km.) and 10 miles (16 km.) and won numerous English national titles both on track and road from 2 miles (3,200 m.) to 20 miles (32 km.). In his last major race, the Olympic 20 km. at Tokyo, he won by the outstanding margin of 1 min. 47·2 sec. from LINDNER.

MATTHEWS, Sir STANLEY (1915-   ), Association footballer for STOKE CITY, Blackpool, and England. One of the finest dribbling wingers in the history of football, Matthews joined Stoke City's ground staff when he left school at the age of 14; played in the club's reserve side in the Central League when he was 15; made his first appearance in the first team when he was 17, at which age he signed as a professional player; and played his first full season at outside right in Stoke's senior team in 1932-3 when the club won promotion from the Second to the First Division. On 6 February 1965 in his only Football League appearance of the season, Matthews played his last match in first-class competitive football when he helped Stoke beat Fulham, five days after his fiftieth birthday. In the 33 years between his first and last matches for Stoke, Matthews had played in 886 first-class matches that included 54 appearances for England in full international matches, 701 League and 86 F.A. Cup matches shared between Stoke and Blackpool, for whom he played from 1947 to 1961.

MAUGER, IVAN (1939-   ), motor-cycle speedway rider from New Zealand. Winner of the individual world championship 1968-70, he was also an exponent of continental longtrack and grass-track racing (see MOTOR-CYCLE RACING).

MAY, PETER BARKER HOWARD (1929-   ), cricketer for England, Cambridge University, and Surrey. Tall and powerful, with a preference for the on drive, he dominated bowlers throughout the 1950s, and seemed certain to break most of the batting records until ill health cut short his career. He captained England in 41 of his 66 Tests, and scored 138 in the first—against South Africa in 1951. The highest of his 13 Test centuries was 285 not out against West Indies in 1957, and in a comparatively short career he made 85 centuries. He led England to decisive victory over Australia in 1956, but suffered a pronounced reversal in 1958-9. Three times he led England abroad, but the after-effects of an operation forced him to retire from the last of them—to the West Indies in 1959-60. He and his brother, J. W. H. May, three times won the ETON FIVES amateur championship for the Kinnaird Cup. They were never beaten as a pair in that competition.

MAYER, HELEN (*fl.* 1928-37), German fencer, women's Olympic champion in 1928 and women's world champion in 1929, 1931, and 1937. Her impeccable style and exceptional strength and reach enabled her to hold her own with the leading men foil fencers of her generation.

MAYLEIGH CUP, see SHOOTING, PISTOL.

MAYS, WILLIE HOWARD (1931-   ), American BASEBALL player for the SAN FRANCISCO (formerly New York) GIANTS and the NEW YORK METS, 1951 through 1973. A star batter, fielder, and base runner, he was widely regarded as the best all-round player of his era. He was the NATIONAL LEAGUE batting champion in 1954. He shares with AARON the record of having accumulated more than 3,000 hits as well as more than 600 home runs. He also set a National League lifetime record for number of runs scored. He set two lifetime records for an outfielder: the National League record for most chances accepted, and the major-league record for put-outs. In 1954 and 1965 he was named the Most Valuable Player in the National League.

MAZZANTINI, LUIS (1856-1926), *matador de toros* from his *alternativa* in 1884 to his retirement in 1905, after which he became a politician and was civil governor of several provinces. He was renowned for his style of killing and abundant bravery.

M.C.C., see MARYLEBONE CRICKET CLUB.

MEAD, CHARLES PHILIP (1887-1958), cricketer for England and Hampshire. Only three batsmen have exceeded his total of 55,060 runs in first-class CRICKET, and only three have made more than his 153 centuries. A bulky left-handed batsman of safe and unspectacular method, he was adept at finding gaps in the field, and his runs were often made faster than was apparent to the spectators. Lack of agility as a fieldsman probably limited his Test appearances to 17 — in three of which he made centuries against South Africa. His two tours of Australia were 17 years apart, and his best innings against them was 182 not out at the OVAL in 1921. His total of 48,892 runs for Hampshire is the highest number ever scored by any one player for a single team.

MEADE, RICHARD, O.B.E. (1938-   ), British three-day event (see EQUESTRIAN EVENTS) horseman. He was a member of Britain's gold-medal team in the OLYMPIC GAMES in Mexico (1968), and finished fourth in the individual classifications, riding Gordon-Watson's Cornishman V. Later he teamed up with The Poacher and rode him to win the Badminton championship of 1970. Later that year (again with The Poacher) he was a member of Britain's winning world championship team. His greatest success came at Munich in 1972, when he won two gold medals (individual and team) on ALLHUSEN's Laurieston.

MEADS, COLIN EARL (1935-   ), RUGBY UNION lock forward for New Zealand, who wore the ALL-BLACK jersey more than 100 times, becoming his country's most capped player. At the age of 31 he was sent off the field while playing for New Zealand against Scotland at MURRAYFIELD in 1967, but he returned to international football and continued playing with zest until he announced his retirement in 1972 after making 55 Test appearances.

MEAUTRY, Haras de, is one of the leading race-horse breeding establishments in France, now owned by Baron G. DE ROTHSCHILD. BRANTÔME and EXBURY stood at this stud.

MEAZZA, GIUSEPPE (1910-   ), Association footballer for INTERNAZIONALE (Milan) and Italy for whom he made 53 appearances and scored 33 goals in international matches. A prolific goal-scorer, he played at either centre forward or inside right. In the latter position he gained world championship medals in both 1934 in Rome and 1938 in Paris.

MECHLOVITS, ZOLTAN (1892-1951), Hungarian TABLE TENNIS player and the last notable penholder grip player prior to the participation of the Japanese in international play. Like Dr. Jacobi, first winner of the world championship men's title, to whom he was runner-up, Mechlovits was a player of the era

before the First World War. An insurance clerk and already stout at the date of his title win in 1928, he was a master of tactics, variation of length, spin, placing, and sports psychology. Five times captain of successful Hungarian SWAYTHLING CUP teams, a strict disciplinarian, and a mentor of youth, he was probably the best trainer and captain the game ever knew. He twice escaped by a hairbreadth from the mass execution of Jews during the Second World War. He won the English veteran's title as a visitor in 1933 and 1939.

MECREDY, R. J., see BICYCLE POLO.

MEDNYANSZKY, MARIA (1907-   ), Hungarian TABLE TENNIS player, the strongest of all women players and the only one who could play matches with success against men of minor international class. Her strokes were all executed with heavy attacking spin and her favourite one was played (though her grip was the ordinary LAWN TENNIS grip) with the blade of the racket below the wrist and imparting side spin. She won all the first five world championship women's singles (1926-31), and was runner-up (to Sipos) in the next two. She also won seven women's doubles titles (six with Sipos) and six mixed (with three different partners).

MEDVED, ALEXANDR (1937-   ), Russian wrestler, winner of gold medals in the 1964, 1968, and 1972 Olympics. Standing 6 ft. 3 in. (1·90 m.) and weighing 16½ stone (103·5 kg.) Medved used speed and skill rather than strength to make him one of the greatest wrestlers of all time. Between 1962 and 1972 he lost the Olympic or world title on only one occasion, the 1965 world championships at Belle Vue, Manchester, when he drew with Turkey's Ayik but lost the gold medal through having more bad marks.

He competed as a light-heavyweight until 1966 when he moved up to heavyweight (winning at the Mexico Olympics) and finally to heavyweight plus, the following year. In the heavyweight and heavyweight plus categories he frequently fought competitors weighing over 20 stone (127 kg.) but his masterly timing maintained his run of successes. He won the heavyweight plus title at the 1972 Olympics before announcing his retirement from the ring by ceremoniously kissing the Munich mat.

MEISL, HUGO, Association FOOTBALL administrator and pioneer of Austrian football. He played as inside forward for local amateur teams, including the Cricketers, and was co-founder of the Austrian Football Federation and the inspiration of Austria's so-called *Wunderteam* of the 1930s.

MEJIAS, IGNACIO SANCHEZ (1891-1934), *matador de toros*, who was killed by the bull Granadino, of Ayala, in Malzaneres on 11 August 1934. He was immortalized in Lorca's 'Lameht for the Death of Ignacio Sanchez Mejias'.

MELBOURNE CRICKET GROUND, Australia, founded in 1853, is the largest CRICKET ground in the world. In 1936-7 the third Test match at 'the M.C.G.', as it is known, was attended by 350,534 people — a record. The ground was built up, chiefly in concrete, for the 1956 OLYMPIC GAMES, and it now has a capacity of well over 100,000. The highest attendance ever at a day's play in a Test match was 90,800 in 1960-1, on the second day of the match between Australia and the West Indies.

The first of all Test matches was played there in March 1877, when C. Bannerman scored the first Test century, and among the notable Test innings on the ground have been the first of BRADMAN's 29 Test centuries (nine of which were at Melbourne), and Cowper's 307 in 1965-6 — the highest Test score made there.

PONSFORD has the distinction of having made four of the highest five scores at Melbourne, including two of over 400 — all for Victoria, who play there regularly. Victoria's innings total of 1,107 against New South Wales in 1926-7 is the highest in first-class cricket.

The ground often accommodates over 100,000 spectators — a high proportion under cover — at Australian Rules FOOTBALL finals.

MELBOURNE CUP, the 'blue riband' of horse racing in the Antipodes. It is a handicap for three year olds and upwards, run at FLEMINGTON, Melbourne, race-course early in November over a distance of 2 miles (3,200 m.) for a prize of A$60,000 and a gold cup. Together with the SYDNEY and CAULFIELD CUPS, it forms the triple crown of the Australian turf.

MELD (1952), a racing filly by Alycidon, bred in England, owned by Lady WERNHER, trained by BOYD-ROCHFORT, and ridden by Carr. Meld won the ST. LEGER (when she was running a high temperature), the OAKS (by six lengths), the ONE THOUSAND GUINEAS, and the Coronation Stakes at ASCOT, and £43,051 in stakes. Later at stud she became the dam of CHARLOTTOWN.

MELLOR, STANLEY (1935-   ), first National Hunt jockey to ride 1,000 winners, now a successful trainer.

MELVILL CUP, see BADMINTON.

MENDITEGUY, C. (1913-   ), Argentine POLO player, racing driver and golfer. A brilliant horseman and individualist, he won one of the most famous finals of the Argentine open polo championship. Polo handicap 10.

MENDOZA, DANIEL (1764-1836), British boxer who won the English prize-ring championship in 1795 after three memorable battles with Humphries. Mendoza, the first great Jewish boxer, concentrated more than any pugilist before him on defence, including sidestepping and swift shifting of the feet, which was particularly advantageous when he fought on a stage rather than on slippery turf. But the 'Light of Israel' was also the first fighter to be conscious of the value of publicity. He wrote his memoirs at 24 and gave exhibitions before audiences which, for the first time, included women and members of the royal family.

MENICHELLI, FRANCO (1941-   ), Italian gymnast who made the largest contribution of any to the modernization of the floor exercises. Inspired by the national coach, Gunthard, this Roman, standing 5 ft. 3½ in. (1·61 m.) and weighing 9 st. 6 lb. (59·9 kg.), devised a routine which included tumbling. International judges had previously regarded tumbling as too stereotyped, but Menichelli's style brought him Olympic gold and bronze medals, two world championship bronze medals, three European titles, and a European second place in the floor exercises. His finest year was 1965, when he was supreme at the European championships. He was first in the combined exercises and also won titles on the floor, the rings, and the high bar. His bid to retain his Olympic floor exercises title ended in Mexico in 1968 when he broke an Achilles tendon during the competition.

MERCEDES-BENZ, a racing car made by Daimler-Benz, whose cars were prominent in MOTOR RACING in the early part of the century. Daimler-Benz returned to racing in the 1930s and produced many innovations which have had far-reaching effects on the design of racing cars, in particular the use of light alloys to bring cars within the Formula weight restrictions.

The SS and SSk were powerful sports cars which proved very successful in 1931, while the W.25 was the Grand Prix contender for

1934 to 1936 when the chief rival was AUTO-UNION. In 1937, the W.125 was almost unbeatable, but the new Formula of 1938 needed a new model, the W.153, which in turn dominated the 1938 and 1939 seasons' racing. After the war, the W.196 performed well in the 1954 season, and in 1955 won every round but one of the world championship. FANGIO, in a Mercedes, won the drivers' championship in 1954 and 1955. In 1955, when Mercedes withdrew from racing, the 3000SLR won most of the big sports car races.

MERCER, JOE (1915-   ), Association footballer for EVERTON, ARSENAL, and England. A stylish wing half with a strong tackle that belied his spindly legs, he was in the Everton team that won the League championship in 1939 and during the war combined with Britton and CULLIS in one of the greatest of all England half-back lines. He moved to Arsenal in 1946 and captained them to two League championship titles and two F.A. Cup finals, one of which Arsenal won. A broken leg ended his playing career in 1954, and after spells of managership with Sheffield United and ASTON VILLA, he became manager of MANCHESTER CITY in 1965. Under his control the club won the Football League First and Second Division championships, the F.A. Cup, the F.L. Cup, and the European Cup-Winners Cup, before he left to become general manager of Coventry City in 1973. He was to be England's caretaker manager on their 1974 European summer tour.

MERCHANT, VIJAY MADHAVJI (1911-   ), cricketer for India, the Hindus, and Bombay. Though playing in only ten Test matches, he was at one time rated the best of all Indian batsmen. He was patient and tireless, once scoring four consecutive centuries, and his 359 not out for Bombay against Maharashtra was then the highest score by an Indian.

MERCKX, EDDY (1945-   ). Belgian road-race cyclist. By the age of 28 Merckx had far surpassed even COPPI as the most successful rider in the history of his sport, with 337 professional victories up to October 1973. These included 27 one-day classic races and 9 major tours. His classics record was twice as good as that of VAN LOOY, who had previously held it, and the only events missing from it were the BORDEAUX–PARIS and PARIS–TOURS. His stage-race wins included the tours of France, Italy, and Spain, and four successive victories in the TOUR DE FRANCE to equal ANQUETIL's record. He could beat any known rivals in the time trial, in the mountains, or over any course that was sufficiently rigorous, and could outsprint all but a few. In both the 1968 Giro d'Italia and 1969 Tour de France, he was the first man to win all three major prizes: the over-all race, the points classification (see CYCLING), and the King of the Mountains award. One setback in his career was his disqualification from the 1969 Giro d'Italia after a dope test proved positive, but he was later cleared of this charge and his suspension lifted. In 1973 he also failed to pass a dope test following the TOUR OF LOMBARDY: the illegal substance (norephedrine) found in a urine sample was traced to a cough syrup, and the case led to a demand that the U.C.I. should distinguish between medicaments and stimulants.

MEREDITH, BRINLEY VICTOR (1931-   ), RUGBY UNION player for NEWPORT, Royal Navy, Wales, and British LIONS. Nearly 14 stone (89 kg.) in weight, and 5 ft. 11 in. (1·80 m.) tall, Meredith was more heavily built than most hookers, but extremely agile in loose play. In 1962 he became the most-capped Welsh forward with 34 international appearances; he also had the rare distinction of being picked for three British Lions tours.

MEREDITH, WILLIAM (1877-1958), Association footballer for MANCHESTER CITY, MANCHESTER UNITED, and Wales for whom he made 50 appearances between 1895 and 1920. Thirty years after becoming a professional, he played for Manchester City in his fiftieth year, in an F.A. Cup-tie against Brighton. He played until 1905 with Manchester City but was then one of several players barred from playing for the club. His registration was transferred to Manchester United for a fee said to have been a mere £150 and partly assessed on the assumption that his playing career was nearing its end. Instead, he played for 15 years with the United club and then, at the end of the 1920-1 season, returned to Manchester City as coach. In practice games he played so well that City decided that he could not be left out of their side and he continued for another three seasons, by which time he had played more than 1,500 games for the two Manchester clubs and for Wales, and scored 470 goals from the outside-right position. He won more than 66 medals in his long career, including two Football League championship medals, and two F.A. Cup-winners medals.

MERELS, see NINE MEN'S MORRIS.

MERION, U.S. GOLF course near Philadelphia. The East Course has been host to a number of U.S. amateur and Open championships, a vivid tribute to the qualities of a course which in the normal way would be considered rather short for classic events. This is basically a parkland course but with its small, well-bunkered greens and subtlety of layout it is a fine test of golf.

MERMANS, JOSEPH, Association footballer for ANDERLECHT (Brussels), and Belgium for whom he played at outside right in the 1954 world championship matches in Switzerland. Generally, however, it was at centre forward that he played strongly for his club and national teams during the late 1940s and 1950s.

MESSENGER, HERBERT HENRY (Dally) (1883-1964), Australian RUGBY LEAGUE player. A major player and influence who switched from RUGBY UNION to the pioneering Rugby League in Sydney in 1907, he gave the movement important impetus. Baskerville's New Zealand team, after a series of matches in Sydney, took Messenger with them to England, and he became the outstanding player of the tour. He visited England again in 1908-9 with the Australian team, becoming Australia's first Test captain. He was 5 ft. 7 in. (1·70 m.) tall and played at 12 stone (76·2 kg.). He was a centre three-quarter, and a fine goal-kicker, and his repertoire of unorthodox ruses often confused the opposition.

METCALFE, GEORGE H. (1931-   ), LACROSSE player for England, South of England, and Surrey. An attack player and an expert stick-handler with the ability to catch, pass, and shoot both left- and right-handed, he has averaged three goals a match in the course of a long career. He consistently represented England between 1950 and 1963, and toured the U.S.A. as a guest player on the combined universities tour in 1961.

MEXICAN 1000, see MOTOR RACING, AMERICAN.

MEYER, DEBORAH (1952-   ), an American who was the first swimmer, man or woman, to win three individual titles at a single OLYMPIC GAMES — in Mexico City in 1968 when she was an easy winner of the 200, 400, and 800 metres freestyle. In the realm of world record-breaking, she returned times that a few years earlier would have won men's Olympic titles. She was Pan-American 400 and 800 m. champion in 1967, and was named 'Woman Athlete of the Year'.

MEYER, LOUIS (1904-   ), American MOTOR RACING driver. He was the first to win

the INDIANAPOLIS 500 three times — 1928, 1933, and 1936. American Automobile Association national champion in 1928 and 1929, he raced in every Indianapolis 500 from 1927 to 1939, when he retired. He bought the firm producing Offenhauser racing engines with Drake in 1946, and sold his interest later to open an engine firm in Indianapolis.

MIAMI DOLPHINS, American professional FOOTBALL team, joined the AMERICAN FOOTBALL LEAGUE in 1966. With the arrival of Shula, coach of the BALTIMORE COLTS, as head coach in 1969, Miami began a steady climb that made them American Division champions of the NATIONAL FOOTBALL LEAGUE (N.F.L.) in 1971. The next year, led by a strong running attack and a tenacious defence, Miami became the first N.F.L. team to go undefeated for a season, through a 14-game schedule, two play-off wins, and a Super Bowl victory over the WASHINGTON REDSKINS. They repeated as Super Bowl champions in 1974, led by the powerful fullback Csonka who set a play-off rushing record, in beating the MINNESOTA VIKINGS.

COLOURS: Aqua and orange.

MIAS, LUCIEN (1930-   ), RUGBY UNION lock forward and captain of France. He played 29 times for France between 1951 and 1959. He went into semi-retirement in 1954 to study medicine, but was brought back and led France to a victorious Test series in South Africa in 1958 and to the home international championship unshared for the first time in 1959.

MICHIGAN, University of, American college FOOTBALL team, nicknamed the 'Wolverines', first reached prominence with coach YOST's 'point-a-minute' teams who won 43 games and tied one from 1901 to 1904; Heston scored 72 touchdowns for this team. The 1905-8 teams, featuring the all-time great centre Schultz, were nearly as invincible. Michigan has remained a football power in the BIG TEN in every decade since. The unbeaten 1925 team, with the passer Friedman and the end Oosterbaum, was national champion. Coach Kipke's 1930-2 teams, featuring the quarterback Newman, won conference titles, while Crisler's 1938-40 teams starred the hard-running Harmon. The 1947-8 teams were national champions. The Michigan stadium in Ann Arbor seats over 101,000.

COLOURS: Maize and blue.

MICK THE MILLER (1926), racing greyhound, a brindled dog, by Glorious Event out of Na-Boc-Nei. The most famous of all racing greyhounds and the greatest exponent of track craft in the history of the sport, he was the first greyhound to win the GREYHOUND DERBY twice (1929 and 1930). He was again first past the winning post in 1931, but the final was declared a 'no race' when other runners in the field were involved in fighting, and, much to the disappointment of the huge White City, London, crowd, the re-run was beyond the now ageing champion. Mick the Miller's other victories in classic races were the Cesarewitch in 1930 and the St. Leger in 1931, the latter over 700 yds. (640 m.), a longer distance than he had ever raced before. He won 46 of his 61 races, including the unequalled record of 19 consecutive successes.

MICKLEM, GERALD HUGH (1911-   ), English amateur golfer and administrator. He was English champion 1947, 1953; a British and English international; chairman of the Rules of Golf committee, chairman of the Royal and Ancient selection committee; chairman of the Royal and Ancient championship committee; president of the English Golf Union; president of the European Golf Association; and captain of the Royal and Ancient 1968-9.

MICRO-KORFBALL, see KORFBALL.

MIDDLE-DISTANCE RUNNING, the track events in ATHLETICS beyond the range of SPRINTING but short of the broad general classification of LONG-DISTANCE RUNNING. Middle-distance events on the programme of major athletics championships are the 800 metres, 1,500 metres, and 3,000 metres STEEPLECHASE for men, and the 800 metres for women. The 1,500 metres for women was introduced in the 1969 EUROPEAN CHAMPIONSHIPS. The International Amateur Athletic Federation (see ATHLETICS, TRACK AND FIELD) recognizes world records at all the distances mentioned as well as 880 yards, 1 mile, 2 miles, 1,000 metres, 2,000 metres, and 3,000 metres.

MIDDLECOFF, Dr. CARY (1921–   ). American professional golfer and television commentator. Formerly a dentist, he turned professional in 1947, won the U.S. Open in 1949 and 1956, was Masters champion in 1955, and a RYDER CUP player.

MIDDLESEX SEVEN-A-SIDE COMPETITION, the largest annual RUGBY UNION sevens contest, originated in 1926 by a London referee, Dr. Russell-Cargill, to raise funds for Middlesex Hospital; it has been run for charity ever since. Traditionally the competition is spread over two Saturdays at the end of April. On the first, approximately 200 clubs from the London area meet in one of 12 separate tournaments at different grounds. The winners at each, plus the previous year's winners and runners-up and two guest sides, then compete in a knock-out contest at TWICKENHAM on the second Saturday, providing over six hours of almost continuous play.

MIDDLETON CUP. Each year the English Bowling Association lawn BOWLS championships at Mortlake, London, ends with the semi-finals and final of the Middleton Cup, the name for the English inter-county team championship. The event began in 1911 and was originally played for the John Bull Cup, presented by Horatio Bottomley. The cup was replaced in 1922 by one presented by P. C. Middleton. It is open to all counties affiliated to the E.B.A. (34 in 1971). Each county is represented by six units, four players in each. These meet similar units from rival counties and the match is decided by the highest aggregate score. Thus it is possible for a county to win on five rinks of a green but lose so heavily on the sixth that the entire match is lost. This has long been opposed by bowlers who believe a match should go to the county winning on the greatest number of rinks, the aggregate totals becoming decisive only when each county wins on the same number of rinks.

MIDI LIBRE, French four-day professional cycle race, traditionally held in late May, admitted to the list of classic races in 1970. It is named after the newspaper which promotes the race.

MIFUNE, KYUZO (1883-1965), Japanese JUDO fighter and one of the most distinguished figures in the sport's history. His use of *o-soto-gari* (major outer reaping throw) and ankle sweeps brought him an impressive series of victories as a youth. In 1923 he was appointed a teacher at the KODOKAN and in 1930 at the first all-Japan championships he performed an exhibition *randori* (practice). In 1964 Mifune received the Order of the Rising Sun (3rd Class), the first living person to do so, and, when he died a year later, he was the only 10th *Dan* in the world.

MIKAELSSON, JOHN (1913-   ), race walker for Sweden. The top sprint walker in the world from 1937 to 1952 (based on championship performances), his excellent technique contrasted starkly with that of fellow-countryman HARDMO. During the period in which controversy raged on track walking, Mikaelsson was Olympic 10 km. champion in 1948 and 1952. He also won the European event at the same distance in 1946 and took third place four years later. Cautioned, but never disqualified, in major competitions Mikaelsson was the leader of the Swedish domination during the period 1936-48. He won the English 7 miles (11 km.) track championship in 1937 and 1938.

MIKAN, GEORGE (c. 1929-   ), American BASKETBALL player. Mikan played for the MINNEAPOLIS LAKERS and helped them to win five NATIONAL BASKETBALL ASSOCIATION championships. He was renowned for his hook-shooting and was elected to the Hall of Fame (see NAISMITH) in 1959. In 1967 he was appointed league commissioner to the newly formed AMERICAN BASKETBALL ASSOCIATION.

MIKKOLA, HANNU (1942-   ), Finnish motor rally driver (see MOTOR RACING), who won the Finnish Thousand Lakes Rally in 1968 and again in 1969, together with the Austrian Alpine Rally. He won the 1970 World Cup Rally for Ford, driving a special Escort saloon.

MILAN 100 KM. (62 miles), an annual Italian road RACE WALKING event first held in 1909, no race being held during the war periods, 1915-18 and 1937-45. Sponsored by the newspaper La Gazzetta della Sport, the race was not held after 1960 because the sponsorship was terminated.

Britain provided the first winner, Ross, who repeated his success two years later. The most frequent winner was PAVESI (six wins), and four Olympic 50 km. champions GREEN, DORDONI, LJUNGGREN, and D. J. THOMPSON also had wins in this event.

The course varied each year and on occasions started or finished in Lugano (Switzerland). The race was always held in late October or early November and the distance covered was often considerably short of that stipulated.

MILAN–SAN REMO CYCLE RACE, the first classic road race of the professional season in Europe, it takes place in March, hence its popular title, the Primavera (spring). First held in 1909, it was dominated by the Italians between the wars; but in the 1950s its international standing improved, and in the period 1954-69 it did not produce a single Italian winner. The race covers 179 miles (288 km.), making it the longest classic ridden

without motor-pace assistance, and includes the 1,750 ft. (533 m.) Turchino Pass.

MILBURN, DEVEREUX (1885-1942), American POLO player, probably the world's greatest in his time, especially at 'back'. He played in all American internationals between 1909 and 1927, and was one of the 'Big Four' of the 1909-13 team. Handicap 10.

MILE BUSH PRIDE (1956), racing greyhound. A brindled dog, by The Grand Champion out of Witching Dancer, he was a great contemporary of PIGALLE WONDER, winner of the English, Scottish, and Welsh Derbys in 1959, plus numerous big races. He was trained by HARVEY, of Wembley, and owned by PURVIS.

MILFORD, D. S. (1905-   ), British amateur RACKETS player who held the world rackets championship 1937-47. He won the British amateur singles championship seven times over a span of 21 years (1930-51), and was runner-up as late as 1955. He was also a fine exponent of the doubles game, winning the doubles championship 11 times between 1938 and 1959, ten times with J. R. THOMPSON — an unrivalled record by a single pair in this event.

MILK RACE, see TOUR OF BRITAIN and SCOTTISH MILK RACE.

MILL HOUSE (1957), was a brilliant horse over fences in England and the great rival of the celebrated ARKLE. Mill House was owned by Gollings, trained by Walwyn, and ridden by Robinson. He won the CHELTENHAM GOLD CUP (by 12 lengths), Hennessy Gold Cup, Whitbread Gold Cup, and King George VI Chase.

MILL REEF (1968), race-horse trained by Balding and ridden by Lewis. His only English defeat was by BRIGADIER GERARD in the TWO THOUSAND GUINEAS and he lost only two of his 14 races. Winner of the Epsom DERBY and PRIX DE L'ARC DE TRIOMPHE, he was top European money-earner when he broke a leg during exercise. He recovered and was retired to stud.

MILLE MIGLIA, see MOTOR RACING, INTERNATIONAL.

MILLER, KEITH ROSS, M.B.E. (1919-   ), cricketer for Australia, Victoria, and New South Wales. Coming to notice when playing for the Australian Services in 1945, he became an important — and the most adventurous — player during the period of Australian domination up to the early 1950s. As an unpredictable bowler who could impart great pace and awkward bounce, he took 170 Test wickets. As a powerful batsman, subject to moods, he made 2,958 runs, and often his uncanny catches at slip turned the course of matches.

MILLER, SAMUEL HAMILTON (1933-), acclaimed as the world's greatest MOTOR-CYCLE TRIALS rider. He won eleven consecutive British championships (1959-69) and two European trials championships (1967 and 1969). He retired from major competition in 1970 after losing his British championship to FARLEY but he remained contracted to the Spanish Bultaco factory and continued to ride in local events. An outstanding all-rounder before he specialized in trials, he won sand racing, grass-track, and road racing titles (see MOTOR-CYCLE RACING) in Ireland before moving to England. As a Mondial works rider he was robbed of victory in the 125 cc. class of the Isle of Man TOURIST TROPHY races (1956) when his gearbox seized up on the last corner of the Clypse circuit. He beat HAILWOOD after a dramatic North West 200 (1958) before finishing runner-up to JACKSON in the Scottish Six Days Trial. As a member of the Ariel factory trials team, he was also runner-up to Jackson in the 1958 British championship. His much-modified 497 cc. Ariel (registration number GOV 132) became the most successful machine in the history of trials but, in 1965, he switched to the 244 cc. Bultaco he helped to design.

His professionalism and dedication helped him to break all records. He won the British Experts five times, the Scottish six times, and the Scott seven times. He won the Hurst on 13 occasions and achieved an unbroken run of 16 wins in the Walter Rusk trial before announcing his retirement from national and international events. As a member of British teams in the International Six Days Trial he won five gold medals.

MILLER, Prof. W. C., see EQUINE RESEARCH STATION.

MILLER, WAYNE (1946-), American trampolinist who was twice world champion. The manoeuvre called the 'Miller' (a triple-twisting double back somersault) (see TRAMPOLINING) was named after him.

MILWAUKEE BRAVES, American professional BASEBALL team, became the first new major-league baseball team in 50 years when in 1953 the BOSTON BRAVES owner Perini received NATIONAL LEAGUE permission to shift the franchise to Milwaukee. The team was immediately successful, as enthusiastic Milwaukee fans exceeded Boston's entire annual 1952 attendance in the first 13 games in 1953. In each of the next four years Milwaukee drew more than 2,000,000 attendance, the first major-league team to draw that amount in any year. Milwaukee's success inspired a number of other franchise shifts later in the 1950s. The Braves won league titles in 1957 (WORLD SERIES winners) and 1958. Its stars were the third baseman Mathews, the outfielder AARON, and the pitcher Spahn, whose career began in Boston — Spahn leads all left-handed pitchers with 363 career wins and won over 20 games a year 13 times (six times straight: 1956-61). When attendance declined in the 1960s, the Braves were shifted to Atlanta in 1966, despite bitter protests by the Milwaukee community. (See ATLANTA BRAVES.)

MILWAUKEE BREWERS, American professional BASEBALL team, an initial member of the AMERICAN LEAGUE in 1901 but who dropped into the minor leagues the next year. Just before the 1970 season the franchise of the SEATTLE PILOTS was shifted to Milwaukee — vindication for Milwaukee supporters who had decried the transfer of the MILWAUKEE BRAVES to Atlanta in 1966. The Brewers have not yet been a factor in league play.

MILWAUKEE BUCKS, American professional BASKETBALL team playing in the NATIONAL BASKETBALL ASSOCIATION. Milwaukee entered the League in 1968, when they finished in last position. They then signed ALCINDOR and later ROBERTSON and won the championship in the season 1970-1.

MINARNI, Miss (1943-), Indonesian BADMINTON player. Selected for her country at the age of 16, she subsequently became one of the finest exponents of both the women's singles and doubles games, though when competing in the ALL-ENGLAND CHAMPIONSHIPS she disappointed her followers. She reached her peak in Tokyo in 1969 when she comfortably upset the reigning All-England champion (Miss Yuki) in the Japan v. Indonesia UBER CUP challenge round.

MINATOYA, HIROSHI (1943-), Japanese JUDO fighter. He was the supreme welterweight of the 1960s, winning the first two world titles in this category. Exceptionally tall for a welterweight (5 ft. 9¼ in. — 1·76 m.), he used his long legs to hook his opponents' with o-soto-gari (major outer reaping throw) and *harai-goshi* (sweeping hip throw) and possessed amazing stamina. He was a silver medallist in the 1965 world championships in the lightweight class before moving up to welterweight. In 1967 he took the gold medal, winning every contest with an *ippon* (point), and retained his title two years later at Mexico City.

MINI-BASKETBALL (mini-basket), a game based on BASKETBALL, specially adapted for players of 12 years of age or less. The ball used is smaller than for the senior game and the ring is situated only 8 ft. 6 in. (2·59 m.) above the ground instead of 10 ft. (3·05 m.). The rules for play have also been modified with the intention of making them easier to understand and to provide a game suitable for the age-group involved. The sport is governed through the Fédération Internationale de Basketball Amateur by the Interoational Mini-Basketball Committee (C.I.M.). (See also BIDDY BASKETBALL.)

MINNEAPOLIS LAKERS, American professional BASKETBALL team. They dominated the early years of the NATIONAL BASKETBALL ASSOCIATION championship, gaining five titles in the six seasons 1949-54, during which time they included MIKAN among their players. The team later became known as the Minnesota Lakers but when the franchise was moved to the west coast in 1962, the team became the LOS ANGELES LAKERS.

MINNESOTA, University of, American college FOOTBALL team, nicknamed the 'Gophers', was noted for its rugged, bruising play. Its most famous player, NAGURSKI, was outstanding at tackle and at fullback, where he often 'ran his own interference', from 1927 to 1929, and later starred in professional football for the CHICAGO BEARS. In the 1930s and early 1940s, under coach Bierman, Minnesota won SIX BIG TEN titles, had five unbeaten seasons, and were national champions in 1934-6 and 1941.
COLOURS: Maroon and gold.

MINNESOTA NORTH STARS, ICE HOCKEY club of Bloomington, Minnesota, formed in 1967 as one of six teams in the new West Division of the expanded NATIONAL HOCKEY LEAGUE of North America. Home matches are played at the Metropolitan Sports Centre, Bloomington, seating 14,400. The players train in Canada at Haliburton and Kingston, Ontario.
COLOURS: Green, white, and yellow.

MINNESOTA TWINS, American profes-

sional BASEBALL team, formed in 1961, play in Bloomington, Minnesota, half-way between the 'twin' cities of Minneapolis and St. Paul. When the AMERICAN LEAGUE expanded to ten teams, the WASHINGTON SENATORS owner Griffith shifted his franchise to Minnesota. The Twins were league champions in 1965. Leading the team have been the first baseman Killebrew, who began in Washington in 1954 and has hit over 500 home runs, and the outfielder Oliva, who since 1962 has led the league in batting three times.

MINNESOTA VIKINGS, American professional FOOTBALL team, entered the NATIONAL FOOTBALL LEAGUE in 1961. An altercation at the end of the 1966 season forced the departure of both the coach, Van Brocklin, and the quarterback Tarkenton. In 1967 coach Grant came from the WINNIPEG BLUE BOMBERS of the Canadian Football League and built a rugged football team based on a defence led by the end Eller and the tackle Page. Minnesota won the National Football Conference title in 1969 but was beaten by the KANSAS CITY CHIEFS in the 1970 Super Bowl. Tarkington led the Vikings to the 1974 Super Bowl, but they were beaten there by MIAMI.
COLOURS: Purple, white, and gold.

MINTO CUP, see LACROSSE.

MIRZA BEG, Shah (1872-1936), Indian POLO player who was the star of the famous Golconda team in southern India. He was probably the finest-ever exponent of the 'dribbling' game. Handicap 10.

MITCHELL, ABE (1887-1947), English professional golfer. He never quite reached the first rank in either amateur or professional GOLF although he had a distinguished record in both. The reason he made such a modest impression on the record books is that his forte was match play (at which he was three times British champion), and most of his great matches were unofficial. In the 1920 Open championship, he had a 13-stroke lead on the last day and lost, to DUNCAN.

MITCHELL, BRUCE (1909-   ), cricketer for South Africa and Transvaal. A cautious yet graceful batsman, he made more runs (3,471) in Tests for South Africa than any other player. He began his Test career in 1929 in England and finished it 20 years later with a score of 99. His eight Test centuries included seven against England, two in the same match at the OVAL in 1947.

MITIC, RAJKO (*fl.* 1948-68), Association

footballer and later manager for Yugoslavia for whom he played at inside right in the team beaten by Sweden in the final of the 1948 Olympics football tournament staged in London. He played with distinction in both the 1950 (in Brazil) and 1954 (in Switzerland) world championship tournaments, and in 1968 managed the Yugoslavian national side that reached the final of the European football championship where they were beaten only in a replay by the host country, Italy.

MITROPA CUP, a convenient corruption of Mittel-Europa, is the oldest international Association FOOTBALL club competition in Europe. It was originally suggested in 1924 by MEISL, as 'an annual knock-out competition involving the leading professional clubs of Central Europe'. The economic demands of increasing professionalism in football in Austria, Czechoslovakia, Hungary, and Yugoslavia made the suggestion generally acceptable and the competition was instituted on 31 March 1927 and the first matches played in August of that year. The original rules were simple: two clubs were entitled to enter from each of the four countries — their League champions and either the national cup-winners or the League runners-up. The draw was 'seeded' to the extent that early-round clashes between the two clubs from the same country were avoided, but otherwise the ties were straightforward except that, unlike the knock-out single match pattern traditional in British cup competitions, they were contested on a home-and-away basis with the team with the better score in the two matches qualifying for the next round.

The first competition, won by the Czech club, Sparta Prague, was an immediate success and other European countries were eager to be represented in the Mitropa. Italy (Genoa and JUVENTUS) were first represented in the third competition (1929), Switzerland in the tenth (1936), and Romania in the twelfth (1938). The competition was interrupted in 1939, by which time Hungarian and Austrian clubs had each won four finals, and Czech clubs three, while an Italian club, BOLOGNA, won twice in the final. In 1955, Austria, Czechoslovakia, Italy, Hungary, and Yugoslavia each entered two leading clubs for the resumed competition. Italy withdrew from the next three competitions and there was no competition in the 1958 World Cup year. In 1960, for one year only, a new form was introduced with Italy re-entering and the five countries being represented by six clubs each playing for points for the country, not the club. By this time the European Champion Clubs Cup and the Inter-Cities Fairs cup had come into being

and replaced the Mitropa in influence. The appeal of the competition was further diminished by the introduction of the European Cup-Winners Cup competition in the season 1960-1 and of the summer Rappan Cup in 1961-2. Spectators at Mitropa Cup matches dropped from over half a million watching 54 matches in 1961-2 to 16,000 watching only four matches in 1964-5. At that time it seemed that the Mitropa, having served its historical function as the forerunner of inter-club competitions in Europe, was likely to wither away, but, in fact, it has since revived, as Central European clubs use it as a training competition before taking their place in the now more important European club competitions.

MIYAGI, CHOJUN (1888-1953), Okinawan exponent of KARATE. He lived in China for many years where he studied *kempo* (fighting). He blended the soft Chinese movement with the hard Okinawan movements to form the *go-ju* ('hard-soft') school of karate. He was a specialist in in-fighting.

MOFFITT, BILLIE JEAN, see KING, MRS.

MOLESEY LADIES HOCKEY CLUB, see HOCKEY, FIELD.

MOLINEAUX, TOM (1784-1818), American boxer who came close to beating the popular English prize-ring champion CRIBB. Molineaux, the first famous black boxer, was encouraged to come to England by the success of another American Negro, Richmond, who subsequently trained Molineaux for his fights with Cribb in 1810 and 1811. In the first meeting Molineaux had Cribb senseless but the Englishman's seconds played for time successfully until Cribb had recovered. Molineaux died penniless, a victim of trickery, but 118 years later his descendant, John Henry Lewis, won the world light-heavyweight title.

MOLLISON, JAMES ALLAN (1905-59), British aviator. After a career in the Royal Flying Corps and the Royal Air Force (1923-7), he began a series of spectacular solo record flights. These included Australia–England (1931), England–Cape Town (1932), the first east to west solo crossing of the North Atlantic, in 1932, and others. He married AMY JOHNSON and made record flights with her.

MONACO CIRCUIT, one of the last of the genuine MOTOR RACING road circuits, the scene each year of the Monaco Grand Prix and supporting Formula Three race. It wound round the streets, along the harbour, and through a tunnel, forming a tortuous, exhausting course. Changes in the topography of Monte Carlo caused the famous circuit to undergo some significant alterations for 1973, but it remains essentially a road course which is now a rarity. It is difficult to drive on, not because very high speeds are reached but due to the number of corners, which, in a lap distance of 1·95 miles (3·1 km.), call for continual gear-changing and maximum concentration. The first Monaco Grand Prix was held in 1929. In 1955 ASCARI's Lancia-Ferrari skidded and dived into the harbour, emphasizing the dangerous and unusual nature of this remarkable race; he was rescued, unhurt. By 1973 the lap record belonged to Fittipaldi's JPS 72E at 83·23 m.p.h. (133·947 km./h.).

MONARQUE (1852), a race-horse who was the first winner of the French Grand Prix, Derby, Two Thousand Guineas, and PRIX DU CADRAN, also winning the Goodwood Cup in England. He was sire of GLADIATEUR.

MONROE, EARL (1945-   ), American BASKETBALL player, who turned professional with the BALTIMORE BULLETS, and later joined the NEW YORK KNICKERBOCKERS. He graduated from Winston-Salem University in 1967 as one of the highest scorers in collegiate history. At 6 ft. 3 in. (1·9 m.) he was selected for the all-NATIONAL BASKETBALL ASSOCIATION team in 1969.

MONTAGU, IVOR (1904-   ), London-born zoologist, film director, and writer, Montagu was chairman or president of the Table Tennis Association from its foundation in 1922 and reconstruction as the English Table Tennis Association in 1927 in all but four years, until his retirement in 1965. He was chairman, subsequently president, of the International Table Tennis Federation from its foundation in 1926 until 1967 and participated in drafting the laws of the game in 1922-3 and revising them in 1965-7. Himself a minor player, Montagu represented Cambridge University v. Oxford University in 1921 and was many times non-playing captain of England teams.

MONTANA-CRANS S.B.C., the leading Swiss skibob club, founded in 1964. It has dominated Swiss SKIBOBBING since the introduction of the sport in Switzerland that year. In 1967 the club sent skibobbing instructors to the U.S.A. and in 1968 the club was awarded the Challenge at the European championships in Italy for the best European skibob club, its members forming almost entirely the Swiss national team.

COLOURS: Red and black.

MONTE CARLO RALLY, see MOTOR RACING: MOTOR RALLIES.

MONTI, EUGENIO (1928-   ), BOBSLEIGH rider for Italy, without doubt the most successful driver the sport has known. He was the winner of 11 world titles, 8 of them in two-man sleds (5 consecutive wins from 1957 to 1961 and again 1963, 1966, and 1968) and 3 in four-man sleds (1960, 1961 and 1968). He retired after winning both gold medals in the 1968 WINTER OLYMPIC GAMES at ALPE D'HUEZ, France, and subsequently became the Italian team manager.

An incident which characterized Monti's reputation for good sportsmanship occurred in 1964 during the two-man world and Olympic championships at IGLS, Austria. Monti was defending world champion with SIORPAES as his brakeman, and the British pair, NASH and DIXON, were among his most dangerous opponents. When Nash clocked the second fastest time during the first of the four runs, his axle cracked and withdrawal seemed inevitable. But after Monti completed his second and last descent of the day, he removed his own axle and transferred it to the British sled just in time for Nash's second run. Nash was again able to set the second fastest time in the second heat, and next day went on to beat Monti and win the Olympic gold medal. Thus Monti's gesture deprived him of the sport's most coveted honour, until his final and only victorious Olympic year in 1968.

MONTI, LUIS (1901-   ), Association footballer for BOCA JUNIORS (Buenos Aires), JUVENTUS (Turin), Argentina, and Italy. He captained the Argentinian team that finished in second place in the 1928 Olympics football tournament in Amsterdam. An attacking centre half, he later signed professional forms with the Italian club, Juventus, and was a member of the Italian national side that won the 1934 world championship.

MONTLHÉRY AUTODROME, a MOTOR RACING circuit near París, opened in 1924. It was to some extent modelled on the BROOKLANDS motor-course in England but had a shorter lap—1·606 miles (2·5 km.)—and steeper concrete banked turns, with very short straights. There were large permanent grandstands and sheds and workshops were accommodated under the bankings. Apart from the banked high-speed circuit, Montlhéry had a road course winding through the estate on which it was built, so that long-distance races of Grand Prix type could be run. These road courses could be combined with part of the banked track to give lap distances of 2·1, 3·1,

3·9, and 4·8 miles (3·4, 4·9, 6·3, and 7·7 km.), up to a full lap measurement of 7·767 miles (12·4 km.), with pure road circuits measuring either 4·7 or 5·7 miles (7·5 or 9·2 km.) as required. These road circuits embraced corners of every kind and enabled the French Grand Prix to be staged at Montlhéry very effectively, at various times from 1925 onwards. The surface of the banked portion of the course was smoother and faster than Brooklands and many records were broken since there were no noise problems at the Paris track.

The first race of any importance was the 1924 Grand Prix d'Ouverture won by the Englishman, Scales, driving a French Talbot which averaged 100·31 m.p.h. (161·4 km./h.). Unlike Brooklands, Montlhéry Autodrome continued in existence and was used by the French motor industry and the French army for vehicle-testing, but is soon likely to close.

MONTREAL ALOUETTES, Canadian professional FOOTBALL team, under a different name have been a member of the Eastern 'Big Four' since its inception in 1907; a new Montreal entry formed in 1946 was called the Alouettes. The team's fortunes have fluctuated greatly, with Grey Cup (see FOOTBALL, CANADIAN) wins in 1931, 1944, 1949, and 1970. The Alouettes won four straight Eastern Football Conference titles from 1953 to 1956 under coach Walker with the quarterback Etcheverry and the end Patterson an outstanding passing combination. Etcheverry leads all Canadian Football League passers in total of yards gained passing (25,582) and most passes completed (1630), and ranks second in touchdown passes and completion average.
COLOURS: Green, red, and white.

MONTREAL CANADIENS, ICE HOCKEY club of Montreal, one of the original four members which formed the professional NATIONAL HOCKEY LEAGUE (N.H.L.) of North America in 1917. It is the most successful N.H.L. side, having won the STANLEY CUP for the eighteenth time in 1973. In 1960, the club became the first to achieve a fifth successive Stanley Cup victory. Its home rink, Montreal Forum, has a 15,747 capacity. Among the most prominent players have been BELIVEAU, Blake, Bouchard, DURNAN, Hainsworth, HARVEY, Joliat, Lach, MORENZ, Plante, and RICHARD.
COLOURS: Red, white, and royal blue.

MONTREAL EXPOS, American (Canadian) professional BASEBALL team, joined the NATIONAL LEAGUE in 1969 when it expanded to 12 teams. The Expos fielded mediocre teams, but Montreal fans supported them fervently, even though their home games were played in the small, outdated Jarry Park. In 1973 the Expos were a serious pennant contender for the first time.

MONZA AUTODROME. Italy built its autodrome in a royal park on the outskirts of Milan in 1921-2, as a banked MOTOR RACING track, but it was not long before various road circuits within the grounds were in greater demand. The banked course was demolished in 1933 but a new one, with sunken bankings, was constructed in 1955, especially for a 500-mile Two Worlds Trophy race between American drivers in their specialized track-racers and European drivers. The winner was Bryan's Dean Van Lines Special, at 160·06 m.p.h. (257·5 km./h.). The Italian Grand Prix is held at Monza over various courses, sometimes embracing part of the new banked track which is regarded by Grand Prix drivers as hard on their cars and possibly dangerous. STEWART set the lap record for circuit 11 (see below) in 1973, at 135·554 m.p.h. (218·153 km/h.). in a Tyrrell-Ford.

The various courses used at Monza are: (1) 6·214-mile (10 km.) full road and track circuit, used from 1922 to 1933; (2) 2·796-mile (4.5 km.) banked track circuit, used from 1922 to 1933; (3) 4·263-mile (6·85 km.) Florio road and track circuit, used in 1930 and 1931; (4) 2·485-mile (4 km.) short Florio road and track circuit, used in 1934; (5) 4·281-mile (6·88 km.) Florio circuit with chicanes, used in 1935-6; (6) 4·345-mile (7 km.) Florio circuit with chicanes, used in 1938; (7) 3·915-mile (6.3 km.) road circuit, used from 1948 to 1955; (8) 6·214-mile (10 km.) full road and track circuit, used from 1955 onwards; (9) 3·573-mile (5·75 km.) road circuit, used from 1955 onwards; (10) 2·641-mile (4·25 km.) banked track circuit, used from 1955 onwards; (11) 1·494-mile (2·38 km.) junior road circuit, used from 1959 onwards; (12) 3·588-mile (5·775 km.) Grand Prix course with chicanes, used from 1973 onwards.

MOODY, Mrs. F. S., see WILLS, HELEN.

MOORE, ANN (1950-   ), British show jumping (see EQUESTRIAN EVENTS) rider. Her main successes were achieved with Psalm, a horse she trained herself and began riding in novice classes in 1966. It was on Psalm that she won the European junior championship (1968), two women's European championships (1971 and 1973), and an individual Olympic silver medal (1972).

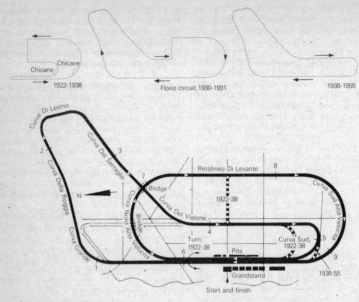

MONZA MOTOR RACING COURSES
Outline drawings show three earlier circuits, now part of the complex of courses shown below. The solid black line in the lower drawing indicates the modern circuit; white dotted lines are the segments of earlier circuits no longer in use. The fine lines in the background are auxiliary roads.

MOORE, ARCHIE (1913-   ), American boxer who held the world light-heavyweight title from 1952 to 1962. Apart from 'Sugar Ray' ROBINSON, Moore may be considered the greatest boxer of the past 25 years. He started his professional career around 1936 and altogether had 229 contests of which he won 111 by a knock-out and 141 inside the distance. He twice challenged for the world heavyweight title and in his first attempt put MARCIANO on the floor. Moore had great durability, was a master at shedding weight in shifting from heavyweight to light-heavyweight, and could punch as well as he could box.

MOORE, GEORGE, the leading jockey in Australia, who, during the 1967 racing season, came to England to ride horses trained by MURLESS, winning the DERBY and TWO THOUSAND GUINEAS on ROYAL PALACE, and the ONE THOUSAND GUINEAS on Fleet.

MOORE, ROBERT FREDERICK (1941-   ), Association footballer for WEST HAM UNITED, and England whom he captained in Youth and Under-23 international matches before making the first of a record number of appearances in full international matches, in Lima against Peru in May 1962. One of the finest 'back four' defenders in world football in the 1960s and early 1970s, he had the unique distinction of captaining three cup-winning sides in successive years at WEMBLEY — his club, West Ham United, when they won the F.A. Cup in 1964 and the European Cup-Winners Cup in 1965, and England when they won the World Cup in 1966.

MORAN, OWEN (1884-1949), British boxer who never won a world title, but is considered to rate among the top lightweights of all time. Moran drew over 20 rounds with ATELL in 1908 in a bloody battle for the world featherweight title, and nine months later again drew with Atell over the unusual distance of 23 rounds. Moran knocked out the durable NELSON in 1910 and in his 16 years in the ring had 40 bouts in the U.S.A. against the toughest American featherweights and lightweights.

MORELON, DANIEL (1944-   ), French amateur track cyclist, who won seven gold medals in the world CYCLING championships in the period 1966-73, six in the sprint, and one in the tandem sprint (with TRENTIN). At the 1968 OLYMPIC GAMES he also won the sprint and tandem titles, and in 1972 the sprint title.

MORENZ, HOWARTH (1902-37), ICE HOCKEY player for MONTREAL CANADIENS from 1923 for ten seasons, followed by brief spells with CHICAGO BLACK HAWKS and NEW YORK RANGERS. He returned to the Canadiens for a final season which ended sadly on 28 January, 1937, when he was badly injured in a game against Chicago and died a few weeks later. Born in Mitchell, Ontario, Morenz learned to skate on the Ontario River Thames and played his first games for Mitchell Juveniles. A fast, determined centreman, he was known for his clever stickhandling and as a marksman who outwitted defenders by skilful feinting before he shot. A versatile player whose ability in defending and distributing was also outstanding, he scored 270 goals in a career when players averaged less than 50 games a season.

MORGAN, CLIFFORD ISAAC (1930-   ), RUGBY UNION outside half for CARDIFF, Bective Rangers, Wales and British LIONS. Succeeding Cleaver in the Cardiff and Welsh sides in the 1950-1 season, Morgan became, with KYLE, the outstanding outside half of the postwar period. He played a crucial part in the only two defeats inflicted on the fourth ALL-BLACKS of 1953-4, by Wales and Cardiff.

MORGANETTE (1884), a notable English brood mare who produced Galtee More, winner of the triple crown (see HORSE RACING) in 1897, and Ard Patrick, winner of the DERBY in 1902 and the ECLIPSE STAKES in 1903.

MORRIS, ARTHUR ROBERT (1922-   ), cricketer for Australia and New South Wales. Scoring a century in each innings of his first-class début, he was unchallenged from 1946 to 1955 as Australia's opening batsman. Left-handed, and displaying superb footwork against slow bowling, he headed the averages for BRADMAN's undefeated 1948 team in England, and altogether made eight centuries against England.

MORRIS, TOM, sr. (1821-1908), Scottish golfer, popularly referred to as 'Old Tom' to distinguish him from his even more gifted son (see T. MORRIS, JR.), Morris was apprenticed to ROBERTSON as a ballmaker in St. Andrews. In middle age he was the supreme golfer of his day, winning four Open championships. He was appointed professional to the Prestwick

golf club in 1851 and was later greenkeeper to the Royal and Ancient club of St. Andrews.

MORRIS, TOM, jr. (1850-75), Scottish golfer (St. Andrews). 'Young Tom' took over the supremacy from his father (see T. MORRIS, SR.) at the age of 16 when he won the first of his Open championships. He won the championship belt three years in succession, 1868-70, making it his own property, and when the championship was resumed after a year's lapse, he won his fourth consecutive title. Between them father and son won eight Opens, but there is no doubt that the son was by far the superior player. He went into deep depression following the death of his wife and, at the height of a career which promised many more honours, he himself died at the age of 24. A monument with the figure of Young Tom sculptured in relief, erected by public subscription, stands in the churchyard of St. Andrews Cathedral.

MORSE, KAREN JANE (1956-   ), British water skier, who was British over-all champion 1971-73 and Northern European women's champion, Sweden 1973.

MORTIMER, ANGELA (later Mrs. J. E. Barrett) (1932-   ), the first British LAWN TENNIS player to win a WIMBLEDON singles title after the Second World War. An accurate, patient and determined competitor, who possessed fine ground strokes, she was a pupil of Roberts, who was also responsible for the development of two other leading postwar players, Curry, the winner of the British hard court championships in 1949 and 1960, and Sangster, who had a fast, heavy service and a fine Davis Cup (see LAWN TENNIS) record.

In spite of an apparent frailty of physique and a successful battle against deafness, Miss Mortimer won the French title in 1955, the British hard court title four times, and the British covered court title six times. She and Shilcock won a surprising all-British doubles final at Wimbledon in 1955, beating Bloomer and Ward by 7-5, 6-1. Then, unseeded and recovering from a spell of ill-health, she reached the singles final in 1958, but GIBSON beat her 8-6, 6-2. In 1961 she won a dramatic all-British final (the first since 1914) by defeating Truman 4-6, 6-4, 7-5. After she retired from tournament play in 1962, she captained Britain's WIGHTMAN CUP and Federation Cup (see LAWN TENNIS) teams. She married Barrett, a former British Davis Cup captain, in 1967.

MORTON, ALAN (d. 1971), Association footballer for QUEEN'S PARK, Glasgow RANGERS, and Scotland for whom he made 30 appearances in full international matches, between 1920 and 1932. One of the greatest of all Scots players, outside left Morton was nicknamed the 'Wee Blue Devil' and, although best remembered for his exceptional, close ball control and the accuracy of his centres that produced openings for colleagues, he scored 115 goals in 495 matches for Rangers before retiring and later becoming a director of the club.

MORUMBI STADIUM, property of the São Paulo Football Club, was the first large Association FOOTBALL stadium in Brazil constructed by a club and not, like the MARACAÑA in Rio, by the Federal government, or, like the Paceumbu in São Paulo, by the local municipal authority. It was officially opened in 1960 although the work was then only half-completed. The stadium, situated in Jardim Morumbi, a suburb of São Paulo, now has a capacity of 160,000. It is the hub of a sports and social centre owned by the football club and comprises a club-house with full restaurant facilities, a ballroom, indoor games rooms, 12 tennis courts, two minor football fields, two SWIMMING pools (one of which is of Olympic size), a children's bathing-pool, BASKETBALL and VOLLEYBALL courts for both indoor and outdoor playing, and a supervised children's playground.

MOTO-CROSS, or scrambling, is a specialized form of MOTOR-CYCLE RACING in which competitors race not on metalled roads but around a closed circuit consisting of a variety of rough cross-country terrain, generally including mud, sand, grass, gravel, stones, streams, and, indeed, any kind of natural obstacle. The motor cycles superficially resemble those developed for reliability trials, but are generally sturdier and have engines highly tuned to develop as much power as is consistent with the tractability necessary for riding over such varied terrain. Machines with engines of all sizes up to 500 cc. are catered for, but lightweight motor cycles with engines in the 250 to 360 cc. range seem generally most successful. The riders' clothing is nondescript, being usually covered with mud before the race has been long in progress; but a crash helmet, goggles, leather boots, padded breeches, a bodybelt for abdominal support, and a light knitted jersey are the usual choice. Considerable physical fitness, strength, and stamina, are essential as well as all the attributes of balance and mechanical sympathy desirable in any form of motor-cycle sport.

Races are started with the competitors astride their machines in line abreast behind a cord, or similar line, which is raised to permit their passage when the starting signal is given. Thereafter the riders attempt to be the first to complete a prescribed number of laps of the course; this usually calls for a high degree of acrobatic riding skill, though there is no penalty for putting a foot to the ground as would be the case in reliability trials over similarly difficult country.

As well as the individual honours to be won there are team awards in international scrambling, the Moto-Cross des Nations being an annual series of races for representative teams of riders. Riders contest two races, points being awarded to all who finish. The nation with the three highest scorers in each race is the winner. It is therefore not enough that an individual rider be successful: for example both 1964 races were won by the Belgian rider Robert, but the title eluded the Belgian team.

The sport was invented by a group of clubmen in southern England in 1927. They wanted to organize some sort of cross-country riding trial, but without the observed sections typical of the traditional trial; and by making it a form of cross-country race which they suggested would be 'a rare old scramble', they originated this new sport. Only after 1945 did it develop as a specialized sport, a French businessman named Poirier commercializing it by staging meetings on the outskirts of Paris. On the Continent it became known as moto-cross, and the Moto-Cross des Nations was inaugurated in 1947 — not with its present set of rules, which were not established until 1963. The main protagonists in the early years were Belgium and Britain, the former fading in the mid-1950s, Sweden taking her place as a serious challenger to the British. These two nations have remained the greatest rivals ever since.

For individuals, the Fédération Internationale Motocycliste (F.I.M.) organized the European championship in 1952, in which riders of machines up to 500 cc. were eligible. The first European moto-cross champion was the Belgian, Leloup. In 1954 a 250 cc. European championship was established, and the 500 cc. class was promoted to a world championship.

The sport is exceptionally popular in France, Belgium, and most of the countries of Eastern Europe, as well as Britain, and in many of these countries it has grown into a spectator sport — without, however, the strong commercial overtones that have changed the character of some other forms of motor-cycle racing during the same period.

GOVERNING BODY (WORLD): Fédération Internationale Motocycliste, 26 Avenue de Champel, 1206 Geneva, Switzerland.

MOTOR-CYCLE RACING takes a variety of forms, each subject to its own rules and each encouraging the development of specialized machines. As MOTO-CROSS or scrambling, it is conducted over rough country, as speedway (see below) on dirt tracks of cinders or shale; other events, usually at amateur level and seldom enjoying international status, are run on tracks of grass, boards, sand, or ice; and there are a number of stadia in the U.S.A. and Europe where motor cycles are raced round tracks that are usually oval or have two short parallel straight sections joined by semicircles at each end, the curves often being superelevated or banked to allow sustained high speeds. However, in the absence of any specific indication to the contrary, the term 'motor-cycle racing' is generally taken to imply ROAD RACING, on a course which may be artificial or composed of ordinary public highways closed for the occasion, and in either case featuring a variety of corners and gradients.

In this form, motor-cycle racing has a twofold object: it may be treated simply as a sport, or it is treated by motor-cycle manufacturers as a means for research, development, and testing. Inevitably, motor-cycle racing has also become recognized as a valuable publicity medium, successes being widely advertised in order to promote the sale of machines of the same make to the general public.

At its highest international level, motor-cycle racing flourishes in Britain, France, Germany, Italy, and Spain, while at a more modest level of accomplishment the sport enjoys popularity in many other European countries and elsewhere, notably Australia, Malaya, Japan, South Africa, the U.S.S.R., and the Americas. In the U.S.A. particularly, racing enjoys a very great follow...g; but, for historical reasons, the regulations by which it is governed have always displayed a peculiar insularity which has hampered international participation in races catering for American machines and riders. In 1970 and the following year some progress was made in rationalizing a common set of rules permitting competition between American and British entrants in both countries, which are the world's two most active centres. In 1971-2 the manufacturers of England, Italy, and Japan resolved severally to produce machines conforming to this still inchoate set of rules and thus perhaps establish a new international racing formula of some importance. Only the nature of the machines was in question; the other features of road racing remained virtually unaltered, as they had done for decades.

Motor cycles race in classes arranged so that some common factor, usually engine size, should make all members of any given class fairly comparable and competitive. Races are therefore usually conducted on a scratch basis with a massed start, the winner being the first to complete a prescribed number of tours, or laps, of the circuit. A few races for road-equipped machines are run on a time basis, the winner being whichever covers the greatest distance in the prescribed time, which may be as much as 24 hours.

There are some exceptional circuits, notably the course for the TOURIST TROPHY races in the Isle of Man, where the lap distance is so great and the number of entrants so large that a mass start is impracticable, and competitors are started in pairs at 10-second intervals, each individual therefore racing against the clock so that the event is really a time trial rather than a race in the strict sense.

Except for some races under American rules, where it is the practice to start a race with engines already running, gears engaged, and the clutch disengaged until the starting signal is given, it is usual for races to be started with engines dead. Machines taking part in production races for more or less standard roadgoing motor cycles have to be started with the kick-starter or any electric self-starter fitted; outright racing machines have no such provision and have to be push-started. With the fuel supply and ignition circuits switched on, the motor cycle is put into gear and pulled back against compression in the engine, and then held by the rider with the clutch disengaged pending the signal to start. This is given by a flag; the rider pushes his motor cycle forward until he judges that it has reached sufficient speed and then leaps on to the saddle, at the same time engaging the clutch. Properly judged, this gets the engine turning fast enough to fire and the rider must then manipulate the clutch and throttle controls in order to ensure clean acceleration while settling himself into a proper riding position. All this has to be done without obstructing or being obstructed by other riders who are similarly engaged in what is usually a fairly crowded starting grid. (This expression strictly denotes a pattern of lines painted on the road at and behind the starting line to mark the spots from which the several competitors will begin.) The riders are generally arranged in two or more rows occupying the full width of the road, the best places on the front row being allocated either to those who have proved fastest during the obligatory practice for the event, or by ballot.

The practice periods preceding the race are intended to allow competitors to adjust their machines to suit the nature of the circuit, to establish an order of precedence for the starting grid, and to ensure that riders have an opportunity to become acquainted with the circuit, in particular familiarizing themselves with dangerous sections so as to reduce the risk of accidents during the race.

The safety of competitors is the motive for a number of other measures, such as the placing of straw bales, sandbanks, or some other suitable medium round the edges of the circuit at any points where a rider might otherwise collide with a building, tree, or other solid object, should he fall at high speed. Riders are obliged to wear protective clothing comprising a safety helmet, goggles or visor, and leather overalls, gloves, and boots. These are inspected before the start of a race and if they do not conform to the published standards, the wearer will be excluded. Except in the matter of helmets there is a good deal of latitude allowed and many leading riders wear leathers that are very thin, close-fitting, and unpadded so as to streamline the figure and reduce aerodynamic drag at high speeds.

Once the race has begun the rider must employ a number of riding skills, as well as courage and strategy. In a short race the ability to make a good start may be of disproportionate value; thereafter highly developed judgement, skill, balance, and mechanical sympathy are necessary in order to get the utmost performance from the machine without overstraining it. Greatest acceleration results only from exact timing and rapid execution of each gear-change so as to keep the engine working within the usually narrow range of crankshaft rotation speeds wherein it delivers maximum tractive effort. In this the rider is aided by the only instrument usually carried on a racing machine, an engine-revolution counter. When slowing down for a corner or some other hazard, the rider must employ similar deftness and good co-ordination since downward gear changes may be made at the same time as the brakes are applied. The brakes themselves, separately controlled at front and rear, must be applied with such sensitivity that the work done by each is as great as it can sustain without either overheating (which could lead to a dangerous loss of efficiency) or locking (which, especially in the case of the front brake, would cause an immediate fall). On a road circuit that may be made slippery by rain, spilt oil, rubber abraded from tyres, or tar softened by strong sunlight, this is a matter requiring great sensitivity, as is the technique of taking corners at the highest speed. For any given corner there is an ideal line which must be followed if the corner is to be negotiated in the shortest possible time, but the presence of surface hazards or of other riders may dictate a different course, either for safety or for tactical reasons.

In longer races, the rider must also allow for the possibility of repairs, adjustments, or refuelling, and plan his strategy accordingly. The only place on the circuit where he will be allowed any assistance is at his 'pit'. The pits (so called because in primitive motor races they were simply holes dug by the side of the road) are nowadays usually a permanent structure formed as a series of kiosks along the inside of a circuit adjacent to the starting line. During the race they are occupied by the riders' managers, timekeepers, and mechanics; spare parts, tools, and fuel may be stored there. From the pits, signals may be displayed showing the rider how he is faring or informing him of his lap times, or of the need to call at the pits to refuel, or indeed to convey any of a number of instructions if the rider is competing under the control of a team manager.

Teams of two, three, or more riders are often entered in important events by clubs, manufacturers, or other bodies. Sometimes they are of merely strategic value in that one particularly fast rider may be instructed to act as hare in order to draw out the opposition while others of the team may be set to consolidate such advantages as may be gained. In other cases there may be a special prize for the best team to finish, in which case a different strategy is employed.

On circuits where there are long straights permitting particularly high speeds, further special skills must be brought into play. The rider must adopt a crouching position that will minimize aerodynamic drag yet permit adequate control and vision. If he can position himself close enough behind a faster machine at the beginning of such a stretch of road he may travel in its wake and, with the machine ahead acting as a windbreak, drive his motor cycle to higher speeds than it could attain without such assistance. This is known as 'slipstreaming', and a rider may practise it either to conserve his engine or to build up such a speed that he can then pass the machine ahead so as to lead at a crucial point — which may be the beginning of a twisty section where he will then have the advantage, or it may be the finishing line itself. To encourage close racing, bonus payments are sometimes made in professional events to the leading rider at the end of each lap or at certain stages in the race; there may be a special prize awarded for the fastest lap in the course of a race. It is usual for all riders to be timed to $\frac{1}{5}$, $\frac{1}{10}$, or $\frac{1}{100}$ of a second on every lap by timekeepers using certified clockwork or electronic apparatus. In events of national or international status, these records are preserved and made available for subsequent publication or enquiry.

The motor cycle used in racing (apart from those road-equipped production machines eligible for special categories expressly introduced in the 1960s to cater for them) carries no lights, horn, starter, or other superfluities. It is propelled by an internal combustion piston-engine commonly having one to four cylinders, occasionally more, and burning high-grade petroleum spirit of about 100-octane rating such as is commercially available in most countries. Other fuels are banned, as are superchargers, but the engine may employ the two-stroke or four-stroke principle, and all the artifices of engine development and tuning are exploited to achieve the utmost power consistent with such durability as is appropriate to the length of the race.

Motor cycles are divided into classes according to the swept volume of their engines: for historical reasons metric units are employed for these measurements, and the classes accepted internationally for races of world championship status are for machines of 500, 350, 250, and 125 cc., though for other events there are 50, 750, 1000 cc. and larger classes. Such a classification naturally encourages the development of engines of very high performance relative to their size; consequently the racing engine is made to run at very high rates of crankshaft rotation, is very intractable and sometimes incapable of running at appreciably lower rates, is very noisy, and often has a very high fuel consumption. Engines are usually air-cooled, but sometimes water-cooled. The engine drives the rear wheel through a friction clutch and a gearbox offering at least four and usually five or more different ratios to be engaged in sequence. The final drive from the gearbox to the rear wheel is usually by chain but may be by shaft; most engines are set with crankshafts across the frame, requiring a primary transmission between the crankshaft and the clutch and gearbox which are usually behind the crankcase; this primary transmission may be by chain or by gears.

The front and rear wheels are carried in forks incorporating springing media (usually helical steel springs) and hydraulic dampers; these forks, together with the engine transmission and all ancillaries, are appropriately located on a frame constructed of steel tubing. Exceptions to this generalization are few, there being very little originality or experiment in the design and construction of the bicycle parts, though much attention is devoted to the engine. Only in 1970 did the long-awaited trend to the adoption of disc brakes instead of the drum type show any signs of the acceptance that is now almost complete.

Only the most rudimentary forms of streamlining are permitted, the most that the regulations will allow being a simple shroud around the engine, steering head, and other parts immediately ahead of the rider, but leaving him and the front wheel wholly visible in elevation. This type of fairing is known as the 'dolphin', and it makes a worthwhile contribution to the reduction of the cycle's aerodynamic drag. Nevertheless, the drag coefficient remains very high, and this seriously impairs the performance of even the most powerful racing machines at speeds much above 100 m.p.h. (160 km./h.). Fuller fairings completely surrounding the front wheel (known colloquially as 'dustbins') were proscribed after 1957 for solo motor cycles but have been retained for motor cycles that are equipped with sidecars.

These motor cycle/sidecar 'combinations' are often of much more specialized construction than the solo motor cycles, and are adapted to allow the sidecar passenger to move freely about the machine, placing his weight wherever it may be most advantageous for each cornering or other manoeuvre. Sidecar races, also known as 'combination' or 'passenger' races, often feature in a programme of events otherwise devoted to solo motor cycles, but the two are never run concurrently.

The international body responsible for the regulation of the sport is the Fédération Internationale Motocycliste (F.I.M.), to which delegates are appointed from each of the governing bodies or clubs of the affiliated nations, such as the Auto-Cycle Union (A.C.U.) in Great Britain. These bodies in turn monitor the activities of the many motorcycling clubs which exist purely for racing and kindred sporting activities. Membership of one of these clubs is a prerequisite of participation in motor-cycle racing, for which the entrant and rider must be licensed by the national body. The novice rider is limited by the terms of his licence to events restricted to members of his own club and perhaps a few invited riders. After he can prove a certain amount of experience and reasonable proficiency he may graduate to a national licence which permits him to race in events sanctioned as having national status by the governing body of his country. Then, upon further evidence of reasonable experience and proficiency at this level, the rider may apply for an international licence, permitting him to compete in races of the highest status. The most important international races are the series of Grands Prix and related events held throughout Europe, in which riders may earn points counting towards the world championships, of which there is one for each engine-capacity class. The Grands Prix of Austria, Belgium, France, East Germany, West Germany, Italy, the Netherlands, and Spain, are regularly included in this series, as are sometimes those of other nations. Great Britain, instead of a conventional Grand Prix race around a natural or artificial road circuit compact enough to suit a massed-start race (each of the five classes, including the sidecars, has its own separate Grand Prix race, all five being held at the same venue on the same day in any given country), stages the Tourist Trophy races in the Isle of Man over an exceptionally long road circuit around which competitors race against the clock, in such large numbers that the greater part of a week has to be devoted to the five principal events.

In addition to the world championship series there are many other events, often styled Grands Prix, which are of international status and often attract entries of the highest quality. Similar meetings, but at a lower level, have national status and cater for riders and machines of a similar type; but club events, though usually resembling the higher-class races in most respects except length, may be run according to special rules which might admit some feature not acceptable under international regulations.

In races for production machines, motor cycles such as are generally available for sale to the public and identifiable as having been produced in certain minimum quantities are raced complete with road equipment, silencers, mudguards, and the like, although certain modifications are permitted for the sake of comfort or safety. Ensuring the compliance of each competing machine with the manufacturer's homologated catalogue specification is often extremely difficult, and this has led to the wide popularity of another type of race in which the motor cycles have engines that are based on the major and most easily identifiable components of engines in quantity production while the rest of the machine may be specially built or adapted for racing. This is the basis of the 750 cc. formula which grew out of efforts at a *rapprochement* between the F.I.M. and the American Motor-cycle Association (A.M.A.).

Venues. The oldest motor-cycle racing circuit still in use is the Snaefell mountain course over which the Isle of Man Tourist Trophy races are run. Starting at the town of Douglas on the south-east coast, the course takes a wide sweep to the west and north to enter the town of Ramsey on the north-east coast and thence return to the starting point, each lap measuring 37¾ miles (60·6 km.) and taking in over 200 bends while climbing from sea level to an altitude of over 1,300 ft. (396 m.). This circuit is the epitome of the natural road course, all the roads used being ordinary public highways closed for the racing and practice sessions.

If this longest-established of circuits is generally accepted as the most arduous and demanding, there are others considerably junior that are no less authentic. The 7½-miles (12 km.) road circuit at Dundrod in Northern Ireland is one such, scene of the Ulster Grand Prix since 1953. Much faster, but again composed of ordinary roads, is the Belgian circuit, 9 miles (14·5 km.) long, at Francorchamps near Spa. A little more unusual in being a combination of public and private roads is the circuit at Assen, 4¾ miles (7·6 km.) long and the home of the Dutch Grand Prix.

However, the majority of the major international racing circuits are wholly artificial constructions, in some cases effectively synthesizing the nature of a true road circuit (as at Clermont Ferrand in France and the NÜRBURGRING in Germany), in others making no attempt to do so. The 3½-mile (5·6 km.) motor-cycle circuit at MONZA near Milan in Italy has, for example, some long straights and very fast bends but no slow corners or gradients. Among the hilliest circuits is BRANDS HATCH, one of many British tracks where racing takes place throughout the year. Here, as at most circuits, the usual direction of circulation is clockwise; but for its principal international event of the year, a meeting known as the Hutchinson Hundred, the direction is reversed so that foreign visitors will not be at a disadvantage compared with the home riders who know the circuit intimately when riding in the customary direction. Other international events are held at the Sachsenring in East Germany, at Barcelona in Spain, at Fisco and Suzuka in Japan, and elsewhere over the world.

Of all these, commercially the most important is the track at Daytona, Florida, where each year the American Motorcycle Association organizes a 200-mile (321 km.) race which is the most important in the U.S.A. The circuit is based on a high-speed concrete oval with deeply banked curves allowing full throttle to be sustained continuously; but for this race and certain others the circuit is modified by the interpolation of a sinuous infield course consisting entirely of short straights and very slow corners. Professionalism is most noticeable at this event, as is often the case in American racing: rewards are very high, and commercial pressures considerable, for the machines raced there, with engines up to 750 cc. capacity, are loosely based on production motor cycles.

The first motor-cycle races were completely unspecialized. Apart from sundry unofficial contests which must have taken place but are not chronicled, racing began in Europe with events that were open to cars (see MOTOR RACING) and motor cycles alike, racing from one city to another along ordinary roads packed with sightseers, devoid of supervision, and often still carrying their everyday traffic. These conditions created obvious dangers which were exacerbated by the tremendous clouds of dust raised by the passage of each vehicle over the unwatered roads, and after a few years of misdirected heroism the great inter-city races were abandoned. The last was the 1903 race from Paris to Madrid, stopped prematurely at Bordeaux after several fatal accidents, mostly involving cars rather than motor cycles.

It was only two years earlier that motor-cycle design, previously characterized by amazing variety and execrable engineering, crystallized with the emulation of the 'new safety bicycle' and the incorporation of the engine crankcase in the bottom bracket thereof, a design pioneered by the French brothers Werner. From its introduction in 1901 their machine soon demonstrated its superiority by successes in a number of international races in which it was ridden most notably by the Frenchman Bucquet, winner *inter alia* of the 1902 race from Paris to Vienna.

The parallel development of highly specialized motor cycles for closed-circuit racing in relatively small arenas was virtually complete in England and France by 1903. Organized racing of a different kind was evolving in a curious way on the banked cycle tracks already built in or near some of the bigger cities, especially in those countries (see CYCLING). Already bicycle racers had learned the art of slipstreaming so as to maintain speed while conserving energy; the motor cycle was welcomed by them as a powerful pacing machine — a number of remarkably big motor cycles were built especially for this purpose. They were heavy and carried large rear superstructures designed to act as windbreaks, close behind which a cyclist could ride, relieved of headwind. These motor cycles usually had single-cylinder engines of de Dion or similar design, very large and coarse in their behaviour but ample for propelling their heavy and deliberately unstreamlined machine. Built without consideration of normal roadgoing requirements, these motor cycles were fast and it was only too easy to develop them into out-and-out racing motor cycles. Their frames were heavy and clumsy, their engines vast affairs with cylinders of 2 litres or more swept volume. Transmission was by a flat leather belt, the tyres as big as could be obtained (which was not in those days always big enough for machines of such weight and speed), and there was no springing of any sort, the front forks being as solid as those at the rear and even more inclined to snap. The complete machine was impressive, punishing and dangerous to ride. By 1903 the press was loud in its criticism of these racing monstrosities, particularly those from France, complaining that these small-track racers bore no practical resemblance to roadgoing machines and were therefore of no value either to the present as a reasonable vehicle or to the future as a source of any new knowledge. At least they were fast: a race round a triangular cycle track in Paris in 1903 proved the monstrosities capable of over 62 m.p.h. — the 'magic 100' kilometres per hour.

From 1903 to 1914, motor-cycle sport took on entirely new forms and a much amplified importance, 1907 being a critical year. After the ill-fated Paris–Madrid race of 1903, a new type of race was organized over a closed circuit by the Auto Club de France, a race intended for motor cycles only, with an international field arranged by restricting the entries to teams of three from each of the competing nations — Austria, Britain, Denmark, France, and Germany. The event was outrageously undisciplined and sabotage was rife, with the finally unchallenged victory of the French team so transparent a piece of chauvinism that the event was subsequently declared null.

The International Cup survived this ignominious beginning, the 1905 race proving much more orderly. Staged again in France, it was won by an Austrian, Wondrick, riding a 2-cylinder Laurin-Clement at 54·5 m.p.h. (87·2 km./h.), distinguishing him as the first officially confirmed winner of a motor-cycle race.

The International Cup series was brought to an end in 1906 by a boycott on the part of the riders, who objected to a rule limiting the maximum weight of machines to 55 kg. (121 lb.) on the grounds that this encouraged the use of dangerously fragile bicycles with engines that were too powerful. The boycott in effect put an end to motor-cycle racing on the Continent; but enthusiasm for the sport was mounting rapidly in Britain and in 1907 it became firmly established there. In that year the famous banked oval circuit at BROOKLANDS was opened, where it was possible to drive cars and motor cycles continuously at speeds as high as they were then capable of reaching. The racing continued at Brooklands until the outbreak of war in 1939, encouraged by the governmental refusal to allow the closure of public roads for racing. From the point of view of the development of road-racing motor cycles, Brooklands offered something of a digression, the emphasis being almost entirely on the motor and hardly at all on the cycle, so that technical development was extremely lop-sided. Some sort of balance was restored by the inauguration, also in 1907, of the first Tourist Trophy race in the Isle of Man, where the Manx government was enthusiastic and cooperative. The full mountain course had been used in previous years for eliminating trials for the motor-car race known as the Gordon Bennett Trophy and for the motor-car Tourist Trophy race; but the circuit was considered too severe for motor cycles, so a shorter and easier course was mapped out and entries of touring motor cycles were invited. The definition of a 'touring motor cycle' was rather vague: it had to have two brakes, a silencer, a tool bag, and a proper saddle, but other more fundamental design features were the subject of much argument. The fuel tank requirements in particular proved to be difficult to settle, and it was only a month before the race that it was decided that there should be in fact two races, one for 2-cylinder machines and one for singles. The twins would have to be capable of 75 miles (121 km.) per gallon, the singles of 90 (145). In other respects the event was modelled on the International Cup races, with machines being sent off in pairs at regular intervals, racing against the clock rather than against each other.

In 1911 came a most important development in the history of motor-cycle racing. The Tourist Trophy (colloquially the TT) was revised and would in future be staged over the full-length circuit including the stiff climb up Snaefell. Although the speed and power of racing motor cycles had increased greatly in the preceding three years, the new circuit demanded effective variable-ratio transmission; and the mechanical developments thus encouraged set the seal on the practicality of motor cycles. There were still two races, the permitted capacity of the twins now being reduced to 585 cc. in an effort to keep this class comparable in performance with the 500 cc. single-cylinder class. This appears a paradox today, when it is known that a twin is invariably more powerful than a single, other things being equal, but the situation in those days was complicated by the restriction on fuel-tank capacity and the inevitably greater fuel consumption of the twins.

In the ensuing years motor-cycle racing flourished in Britain as nowhere else in the world. The industry was eager to take full advantage of the test facilities it offered in environments differing as widely as Brooklands and the Isle of Man, and appreciated the value of the publicity attached to racing successes. The result was that although motor-cycle racing became established in France, Germany, Italy, and some other European countries during the 1920s, with some races enjoying the status of an international Grand Prix, British machines and riders were dominant everywhere. The riders were usually professionals, there being little incentive for amateurs to travel and race abroad; therefore, true international competition was fairly sparse and the rather rudimentary nature of this organization is illustrated by the fact that until as late as 1948 the European championship was decided on the outcome of one meeting selected by rotation from all qualifying events. Not until 1949, when the F.I.M. inaugurated its world championships for riders, did the present aggregate system come into being to make it worthwhile for individuals or teams to contend throughout the season, which extends from mid-spring to late autumn.

Although by dint of sustained enthusiasm and dogged development the British continued to be the masters of the sport, most technical developments stemmed from European manufacturers. By the end of the 1920s engine design had made enormous strides, most of the principles governing the construction of the high-performance four-stroke engine being now properly understood (if not always properly applied), while the loop scavenge system of gas-flow (invented by Schnuerle) was adopted by DKW in 1929 to set the two-stroke engine on a new and promising career. Improvements in tyres, especially the transition from beaded-edge to the modern wired types, contributed alike to safety, reliability, and good handling, and throughout the 1920s and 1930s racing speeds continued to rise steadily despite the fact that motor-cycle design remained largely stagnant. It was a period during which many riders such as BENNETT, GUTHRIE, Handley, Nuvolari, SIMPSON, and Walker established international reputations.

The preponderance of British names is noticeable. However, in the latter part of the 1930s the situation changed markedly: after the political 'rebirth' of Germany and Italy, success in motor-cycle racing (as in other sports, notably motor racing) was viewed by the governments of those countries as a matter of national prestige, and they encouraged manufacturers in programmes of rapid technical development that was long overdue but had not previously been economically justifiable. Enormous strides in frame and suspension design were made in a remarkably brief time, while new engines of considerable complexity were raised to unprecedented levels of power by the exploitation of superchargers and the alcohol-based fuels that were both then permitted. The result was that from BMW and DKW in Germany and from GUZZI and later GILERA in Italy came pure racing motor cycles which in noise, speed, and sheer dramatic presence, made a shattering impact on the international race meetings held in Europe in the last years of the 1930s. The only machines to rival them were British; but these (principally NORTON, Velocette, and AJS) were of much more simple — not to say primitive — design, their manufacturers being wedded to the notion that the racing motor cycle was recognizably related to the conventional touring machine, and being quite unable to reconcile this philosophy with the use of extremely expensive supercharged engines. Nevertheless, the British remained remarkably competitive simply by virtue of experience and riding skill. On paper the European machines were much more advanced and potentially winners every time; in practice they proved to lack the reliability of the old-fashioned but thoroughly developed British factory-entered motor cycles which could not so easily be toppled from their traditional eminence. Towards the end of the 1936 season the German lightweight machines, notably the DKW, proved to have the necessary stamina and began to dominate the 250 cc. class, though in the 350 and 500 classes every big race but one was won by a Norton. Nevertheless, by the end of the year, the British riders were complaining that no unsupercharged single-cylinder machine (such as they were riding) could compare for speed and acceleration with the supercharged BMW or even the unsupercharged Guzzi; and since they had good reason to expect the latter to appear in supercharged form the following year they were naturally despondent. When the four-cylinder supercharged Gilera (derived from a prototype made a couple of years earlier by Rondine) made its appearance in 1938 and proceeded to win the European 500 cc. championship in that year, the gulf between the simple, traditional British machine and the scientifically designed pure racer was complete.

When Grand Prix racing was resumed after the interruptions of war with the reformation of the F.I.M. in 1947, the regulations governing the sport were changed to ban superchargers and fuels other than petrol. Since then the governing body has remained staunchly conservative, stifling many promising new lines of technical development, usually on the grounds that they would bring unwanted expense and sophistication to the sport. Yet, despite these new rules which favoured the British manufacturers, changes in the racing scene were of degree rather than of emphasis: success for the British machines, notably the Norton, came for a few years; but while they performed better than might reasonably have been expected, they were faced with increasingly formidable competition from Germany and Italy. The Norton gained a new lease of life with the development of a new frame design which gave it exceptional handling properties, making it the standard by which all others were judged throughout the decade following its appearance in 1950 in the hands of DUKE.

It did not take long for the opposition to adopt the style of the Norton frame, however, and thereafter the Germans and Italians went from strength to strength. Eventually, Duke, despairing of a professional career in which he could keep his Norton in contention only by courting disaster at every corner, accepted an invitation to lead the Gilera team — this being an era when British riders dominated the sport whatever the nationality of their machines. The Gilera, its air-cooled unsupercharged version of the pre-war four-cylinder engine combining unequalled power with a low level of mechanical stress and consequent reliability, was generally invincible in the senior (500 cc.) class, while the MV AGUSTA firm was developing a very similar machine under the guidance of the designer (Remor) who had been responsible for the Gilera. By contrast, Guzzi took the course of least resistance by designing bicycles that needed less engine power for a given degree of performance, building and exploiting a full-size wind tunnel to develop extremely effective streamlining. Their machines were also very light and had a very small frontal area as well as a good aerodynamic shape. The 1954 Guzzi which dominated the Junior (350 cc.) category was, with its space frame integrated with the full frontal fairing, its exceptionally low centre of gravity, and its refined suspension, probably the most scientifically devised racer of the era. Running it a good second in this respect in the early 1950s was the NSU, again well streamlined and splendidly engineered in its bicycle parts but also boasting an engine that in terms of volumetric efficiency was without peer, being the first and for a long time the only unsupercharged petrol engine to develop 125 b.h.p. per litre. In the hands of a team of gifted German riders including most notably Haas and Hollaus, NSU won the lightweight (250 cc.) and ultra-lightweight (125 cc.) championships regularly and with complete conviction during the brief period when NSU were engaged in international racing.

The middle 1950s saw very rapid progress. Streamlining grew from a tiny fairing that enveloped the steering head and swept back beneath the rider's forearms, first into a dolphin-beaked enclosure of the engine and fuel tank and then into the full enclosure of everything ahead of the rider. Bicycles thus streamlined proved much faster, exceeding 150 m.p.h. (241 km./h.) on some circuits, and made greater demands on brakes, which became larger, often being duplicated on the front wheel, and were more positively ventilated because the full fairing robbed them of their cooling air. Gearboxes with five or six ratios instead of the traditional four became commonplace, while developments in polymer chemistry led to critical improvements in tyres, concentrating attention on these important components that have enjoyed continuous and remarkable development ever since.

The quality of motor-cycle racing reached a peak in 1957 when all the great makes, save NSU, were locked in combat. It was the last year in which full streamlining was permitted, the year when the Isle of Man TT circuit was first lapped at over 100 m.p.h. (161 km./h.) (by McIntyre on a Gilera), when all the principal circuits of Europe were visited by factory-entered teams riding machines of unprecedented variety with engines having between one and four or even (in the case of the last 500 cc. Guzzi) eight cylinders. Italian machines ruled the solo classes, Germany's BMWs continued their domination of the sidecar class which began in 1954 and has continued since, while the last of the British factory teams, Norton, withdrew from official participation in 1955 and thereafter contented themselves with selling their traditional single-cylinder motor cycles to private entrants for whom the extravagant continental machines were quite out of the question.

The private owners got their chance in the following years, for after 1957 motor-cycle racing went into a serious decline, with all the great Italian firms withdrawing their support, none of the world's manufacturers being prepared to support classic road racing, and the F.I.M. adding confusion to an already depressed situation by introducing unpalatable formulae for less expensive and complex machines. Then Agusta decided to continue racing, and, against such opposition as there was, the team (headed by SURTEES in the larger classes and UBBIALI in the smaller) won every solo championship in 1958 and the following two years.

With the sport subsiding and public interest waning, attention was drawn to the newly flourishing Japanese industry which, led by HONDA, began a tremendous worldwide sales promotion, using road racing at national and international level as a publicity medium. Their first tentative entry into the international arena was in the 1959 TT where they took the team prize in the 125 cc. race. Within two years the four-cylinder Honda 250 was in complete charge of the lightweight class, demonstrating the Japanese firm's mastery of the art of designing an engine with very small cylinders in large numbers, equipped with valve gear and resonance-tuned exhaust and inlet systems to ensure very high volumetric efficiency which, combined with unprecedented rates of crankshaft rotation, produced horsepower figures that would previously have been a credit to considerably larger engines. The four-cylinder 250 ran at up to 16,000 revolutions per minute; then Honda produced a four-cylinder 125, a two-cylinder 50, a six-cylinder 250, and a five-cylinder 125, running up to and occasionally beyond 20,000 rev./min. and conclusively demonstrating the folly of classifying motor cycles according to engine capacity. In top-flight racing the Japanese were supreme, taking the world championships in every class except the senior in 1962, that being the only class in which they were not represented.

The days of the big single-cylinder machines seemed numbered: everywhere the trend was to smaller cylinders and more of them, to ever higher rates of revolution, and to a multiplicity of gears in the transmission. Honda were the archetypes but there were many others. Designers who had not the means of producing four-stroke engines of such complexity tried the alternative two-stroke concept and, developing the sciences of gas flow and pulsation along new lines, made it capable of even higher specific performance than the new generation of four-strokes. Bultaco in Spain, DKW in West Germany, MZ in East Germany, and YAMAHA, SUZUKI, and Tohatsu in Japan, all worked up their two-strokes to racing levels of performance and entered the lists with notable success. Since 1961 all the smaller solo classes have been the province of Japanese firms, and in the years from 1962 to 1967 inclusive there was even a championship for 50 cc. machines in which the honours were taken principally by Suzuki. Only in the 500 cc. class, which the Japanese have never taken seriously and (apart from some efforts by Honda in 1966 and 1967) never entered until 1973, have MV Agusta fought off all challenges, led from 1966 to 1973 inclusive by their rider, AGOSTINI. The smaller classes often produced faster racing, suggesting that something was amiss.

Such was indeed the case. Resolute refusal on the part of the governing body to allow any developments involving fuel, streamlining, or even basic concepts, put racing into a strait-jacket and reduced it to a mere horsepower race in which no private entrant could hope to enjoy any success. Racing had been revitalized by the entry of the Japanese manufacturers who consistently recruited British and Commonwealth riders, recognizing the value of their experience; but having established themselves, they too chose to withdraw support for world-championship racing after 1967. Once again MV Agusta were left as the only manufacturers officially participating; though Yamaha, no longer fielding their special racing machines, provided a measure of support by offering 125, 250, and 350 racers based on their standard twin-cylinder two-stroke designs and assisting certain riders of them.

With international racing now not so much a sport as a shop window, such a system had much to commend it from the manufacturers' point of view. In the closing years of the 1960s the Japanese turned their backs on international racing, and especially on racing in Europe which had previously been its home, and concentrated their attentions on the U.S.A. where there were rich commercial rewards for success and where the regulations governing national racing encouraged the use of motor cycles based on production machines. They thus left the European scene to the private owners and to small firms who made sporadic efforts without any one of them ever succeeding in dominating the others. A few of the machines they raced were designed specifically for racing, but the majority are related at least in their fundamentals to motor cycles that are in quantity production. This not only brings motor-cycle racing back to ideals which inspired it at its beginning, but also for the first time establishes a consensus of outlook between the European and American centres of the sport. Hardly on speaking terms previously, the Fédération Internationale Motocycliste and the American Motorcycle Association together formulated in 1971 a new international racing class for machines whose 750 cc. engines were based on major components in quantity production. This proved a popular measure, for it encouraged ostensibly realistic competition between the new models of large-capacity so-called 'superbikes' that were attracting public attention by their glamour. As might have been expected, the major manufacturers responded by homologating very special machines which bore no more than a minimal and illusory resemblance to those available to the public; but the uncritical reception these enjoyed led to the institution of new races for these purpose-built racers.

SPEEDWAY, or motor-cycle dirt track racing, is the second most popular spectator sport in Great Britain. It is highly professional and takes place only at specially licensed tracks; all riders compete for cash rewards. Most speedway stadia are, in fact, GREYHOUND RACING venues adapted for motor-cycle racing — only the tracks at Belle Vue, in Manchester, and Peterborough were purpose-built for speedway. Most stadia promote racing one night a week from March to October. Riders, however, may race from two to six nights a week, their engagements being made up by 'away' matches, 'open' meetings, and occasions such as world championship events.

The controlling body for British speedway racing is the Speedway Control Board, who license tracks and riders; promoters are members of the British Speedway Promoters' Association; and riders are members of the Speedway Riders' Association.

Speedway operates under a rigid set of rules, the basis of which is that four riders race against each other. The winner of the race is awarded 3 points, the second, 2, and the third, 1. No points are awarded to the last rider to finish. Each race is four laps, regardless of the length of the track.

The size and shape of tracks are dictated by the stadia in which they are installed. Although most are in greyhound racing establishments, some have been built in FOOTBALL arenas. Every track has two straights joined together by two sweeping bends; some have long straights and short, tight bends, while others have very short straights and big, open bends. Some tracks, in effect, are almost complete ovals with hardly any straight stretches. Length varies from the shortest League track of 300 yds. (275 m.) to the longest — at Crewe — of 470 yds. (430 m.). Width, too, is dictated by the size of each venue.

A track has an almost solid base of rubble, clinker, or similar material, while its surface is either shale or granite, or a mixture of both. The surface is vital to the riding technique employed on the speedway; although the material binds together well it will, when watered, loosen on top to provide the right consistency for the typical sliding cornering action.

Every track is surrounded by a safety fence to prevent riders and machines crashing into the public area, and to serve as an indication for the riders of the outside of the track. Fences are either of a sturdy wire-mesh construction or of wood or composition materials. Wooden fences are most popular with riders because they are easier to see and, if he should hit the fence, a rider is more inclined to glance off a solid surface without further incident. A wire fence absorbs much of the shock of a head-on collision, although a rider may easily become entangled in the mesh should he brush the fence. The track is usually surrounded for its entire length by spectator accommodation, which varies from simple, Spartan terraces to luxurious glass-fronted grandstands.

Pits at speedway stadia are reserved exclusively for riders, mechanics, and officials. Here the riders stay while not actually racing, and carry out any necessary work on their machines. Promoters are obliged to include a covered area, sufficient for all competitors, for use in the event of poor weather conditions. In the pits there is usually a fuel and oil store, from which riders draw their supplies for the night's racing. Also in or near the pits is a first-aid room and dressing room — which must be equipped with hot showers. Women are not allowed in the pits.

The standard starting gate consists of two pillars, one on each side of the track on the start line. White tapes, fixed to tape carriers on each of the pillars, are held across the track in the down position until the referee decides to start the race by operating a switch. The tapes then fly upwards, very rapidly. This starting method is not foolproof and riders sometimes attempt to beat the tapes by anticipating the moment when the referee will operate the switch. While a rider may occasionally get away with this, it results more often in his becoming entangled with the tapes, and usually leads to exclusion from the race. A rider may also be excluded after a crash; the referee may penalize a rider who, perhaps by inconsiderate or over-exuberant riding, crashes and causes the race to be stopped in the interests of safety.

A referee is essential for speedway, and no meeting may commence until he is present. He operates from a specially constructed box in line with the start line and is linked with the pits, the starting marshal, the clerk of the course, and the announcer. The timekeeper usually sits alongside the referee, and the announcer sometimes operates from the same box.

Lights at speedway tracks fall into two categories: those for illuminating the track when daylight fails, and the specialist lighting which is an integral part of the sport. The general lighting varies according to the original purpose of the stadium, but it is always adequate for racing. Most important of the specialist lighting are the red indicators, six in number, located around the track at a height of not more than 5 ft. (1·5 m.) from the ground and positioned so that they can be seen easily by the riders. These lights are switched on by the referee should he decide to stop a race in the

interests of safety. There are also two green lights, one in front of the starting gate and one behind the starting line, both beside the safety fence. These indicate to the riders and to the starting marshal that the competitors are under starter's orders.

A speedway machine is an ultra-lightweight, purpose-built motor cycle, fitted with a rather old-fashioned single-cylinder engine. The main frame, or 'diamond' as it is known because of its shape, is made of strong, light tubing, and the rear sub-frame — which carries the rear wheel — is without suspension of any kind. The front fork usually has a very simple suspension, sometimes short springs within the fork tubes but more often a combination of springs and rubber bands to control rebound. Handlebars are high and wide for precise control when banked over to the extremes common on speedway tracks; the seat is low and ideally placed for balance and control. Two types of 500 cc. engine are used; the English JAP (J. A. Prestwich), developed in 1930, and the Czechoslovakian Eso (Jawa) which is an improved version of its English predecessor. The Eso is the more popular because it requires less maintenance between meetings. Both engines employ the 'total loss' type of oiling system; some machines carry their oil within the frame tubes, on others it is stored in a small polythene bottle or even in a can fixed to the rear of the machine. Type of fuel is optional, but all riders use methanol, an alcohol-based, oxygen-bearing fuel more calorific than petrol.

Sidecars have been used on speedway tracks since the earliest days of the sport, but they have never captured the lasting support of fans and promoters as solo machines did. British speedway tracks have tended to be under 400 yds. (366 m.) long and the consequent lack of room for manoeuvring leads to somewhat processional races. But in Australia, where midget cars race on the same tracks, sidecars have proved popular. Various tracks in Britain promoted sidecar racing from 1968 and it met with limited success.

The basis of speedway racing in Britain is the League programme, which is contested in two divisions.

There are 19 teams in the first division and 17 in the second division. Competition for the championships of the two divisions lasts practically through the speedway racing season. The championships are decided on a points basis awarded on the results of appointed League matches. To win the British League championship (Division One) means a great deal in status for the successful team, and for the riders in that team. Riders from the team which does well in the second division championship are almost sure to receive offers to join a first division team for the following season. Teams do not transfer between divisions; instead second division riders move up to the premier division to replace retired or injured men. First division riders cannot move down to second division teams. Every first division rider is eligible for selection for the individual championship of the world.

Visiting tours are an important feature of the programme, and every summer teams from countries such as Poland, Czechoslovakia, Russia, Sweden, and Australia visit Britain.

Most important of the world championship competitions is the individual championship, which is worth more to the winning rider, in terms of hard cash, than the team championship, known as the World Team Cup. This latter competition, in which a team of riders represent their own country, has been organized since 1960. The road to the individual world championship is a hard one. Every first division rider in British speedway competes in a number of preliminary rounds. Leaders from this competition qualify for the British final, which is followed by a British/Nordic final, a European final, and the world final. Rules for the individual final are exactly the same as for any other individual match. Every heat consists of four riders and four laps of the track. Points are awarded on speedway's universal 3-2-1 basis and every rider races against every other rider during the course of the programme.

Australian speedway, although conducted under the international rules, is different from its English counterpart in that the tracks in Australia are much larger, usually about 600 m. (656 yds.), or even longer, and much wider. Also, because the weather is generally kinder, they tend to remain in good condition. Racing is much faster than in Britain, and some Australian tracks run races with six riders instead of the traditional four.

Speedway as such probably began in Australia in 1923, but had its true beginning in America in 1910. The American races bore hardly any resemblance to the sport which descended from them, for they were held in TROTTING stadia with varying numbers of riders on an assortment of motor cycles. After a rather hit-and-miss beginning, events in Australia settled down and from them emanated the basis of modern speedway racing. The first meeting in Great Britain was held on a specially prepared track at High Beech, in Epping Forest on the outskirts of London, in 1928. Although the organizers expected a large crowd, they were almost overwhelmed by the immense number of people who turned up to see the new sport. So successful was this inaugural meeting that interest snowballed, and Britain's first speedway League began the following year.

Aptly, the man largely responsible for the success of the first speedway (then known as dirt track racing) in Britain was an Australian named Galloway. He was an expert in the spectacular cornering method called 'broadsliding', which had never before been seen in the British Isles; it was to become the chief characteristic of speedway racing.

Until the early 1930s, Australian and American riders drew the crowds. Later, British competitors became equally popular. Such was the international appeal of speedway racing that it had only been in operation in Europe for just over five years when the Fédération Internationale Motocycliste organized the first world championship in 1936. After the Second World War not only did the established tracks in Britain get on their feet again, but British soldiers encouraged the introduction of a number of tracks in Germany. The world championship returned in 1949 and speedway generally experienced a great revival until the mid-1950s when attendances began to dwindle and tracks closed down. The sport continued on a somewhat shaky footing for almost a decade, but by the late 1960s it had revived, and by 1970 was attracting more spectators than ever before.

The most successful world championship rider has been the Swede, Fundin, followed by BRIGGS and MAUGER, both from New Zealand.

GRASS-TRACK RACING is an extremely simple form of motor-cycle speed sport run, as the name suggests, on tracks laid out in suitable fields. No obstacles are introduced, but riders must negotiate the natural hazards of bumps, dust, and flying stones. Originally, circuits were up to a mile (1·6 km.) long, with left- and right-hand bends, and 20 or more riders might take part in a race. Later the sport suffered economic restriction and, by the end of the 1950s, circuits were rarely over 600 m. (656 yds.) long and consequently there were often no more than ten riders to a race, usually fewer.

Grass-track races are short (about four laps) and therefore last only a few minutes. Riders are usually started by a mechanical system to eliminate false starts. The only likely causes for disqualification or stopping the race are if a rider cuts corners or if there is a serious crash. If a rider should run off the course, he may restart — but only from the point where he ran off. Tracks are usually oval and races are run anti-clockwise.

Officials at grass tracks are nearly always volunteers, usually members of the club promoting the event. Exceptions are the Auto-

Cycle Union stewards who represent the area in which the meeting is being held (known as the centre) and must be present to ensure it is conducted in accordance with A.C.U. rules. They also settle major disputes, and make a report of the meeting to the relevant A.C.U. centre. Other major officials are the secretary of the meeting, the clerk of the course (who is responsible for organizing the actual racing), and there are various stewards and marshals. Obligatory also are a doctor and an ambulance.

Championships, or the way they are run, are the biggest bone of contention among grass-track enthusiasts, and have been for several years. Various systems have been used to find the British grass-track champion, and the one favoured by competitors and spectators is that whereby riders qualify for a one-day championship meeting, from a series of meetings held throughout the country. But the system which finds the true champion (i.e. the most consistent rider throughout a year's racing) is that where a number of meetings are held and the winner is the man who, at the end of the series, has the greatest total of points. But because grass-track organizers tend to be conservative regarding the amounts of prize money paid out, riders do not favour the latter system since they tend to suffer financially.

Grass-track machines are of extremely simple design. Capacity limits are: 250, 350, and 500 cc. and up to 1200 cc. for sidecar machines. The engines are usually single-cylinder in the solo classes, but twin-cylinder units are favoured for the sidecar class. Again, these are simple designs, but extremely strongly built and capable of running at a very high compression ratio (14:1) which, with the use of alcohol fuel, provides high power and extremely lively performance. In view of the short, sprint nature of these events, it is important to have an engine which produces its power and maximum torque at lower revolutions to provide maximum acceleration.

Designed in 1930, the 500 cc. JAP engine remains the most popular unit for the sport, although the more recent Czech Jawa (also known as Eso) design gained success, but not dominance, during the 1960s. Essentially speedway designs, the JAP and Jawa engines are usually de-tuned for grass-track racing since they need to run for longer periods. The engines are checked after every race and they need thorough overhauls after very few meetings.

The frame and steering of a grass-track machine is fitted with sprung suspension, but this is usually quite rudimentary to keep the machines as light as possible. The cycles are fitted with gearboxes, the internal ratios of which are varied to suit particular courses. Brakes are required to meet regulations, but they are little more than token fitments since they are seldom used during events.

Sidecars are a very important feature of grass-track racing, both in Great Britain and on the Continent, and have shown the same kind of evolution as the solos. However, far more technical development has been invested in the three-wheelers. Nowadays, no racing motor cycle is more specialized than the grass-track sidecar machine. The heart of the successful grass-track sidecar is a highly-tuned Norton or Triumph pushrod vertical twin engine, although considerable success has been achieved by machines powered by the 1,000 cc. JAP V twin. Most common, however, are 650 cc. Triumph engines. Many riders use a combination of oversize cylinder bores and special pistons to bring both 650 cc. Norton and Triumph engines up to about 750 cc.; and becoming increasingly popular is the use of a supercharger to boost power even further. Nearly all competitors use methanol fuel to extract the greatest possible power from their machines. Most common causes of breakdowns — which are frequent — are broken pistons, caused by the very high compression ratios and by 'over-revving'; gearbox failure, caused by inconsiderate use of the gears in a race and due to the fact that the engines usually develop too much power for the standard gearboxes used; and broken drive-chains, again caused by the excess of power. A more or less standard design of chassis has evolved to provide stability, ease of movement for driver and passenger, and safety. A striking feature is the front forks, which are usually massive constructions projecting far ahead of the rest of the machine.

Until the early 1960s it was common for all sidecar races to be run in the same anti-clockwise direction as the solos. Because of the instability of a sidecar machine (which has the sidecar on the left of the motor cycle) when it is negotiating left-hand corners, racing tended to be slow. Surprisingly, no one thought of placing the sidecar on the other side of the machine so that it helped stability. However, enterprising organizers began to promote sidecar races in a clockwise direction; this immediately led to faster, more furious racing. This system rapidly took hold until by 1970 only a few clubs, notably in Kent and Sussex, promoted anti-clockwise sidecar races. Sidecars use the same track as the solos at every grass track, although a kink is sometimes put into one of the straights to provide a kidney-shaped course for the sidecars. This is more common in the southern and south-western areas than it is in the east and north of the country. Surprisingly, the banked courses which are common throughout Europe have never been used in Britain.

Grass-track racing is probably the oldest form of motor-cycle sport; it is likely that the first races were run in fields or on dirt roads. It is known that grass-track racing took place in England at Brands Hatch, Kent (the present Grand Prix circuit), in 1928 and continued until 1949. Tracks existed all over England during the 1930s and the sport was the major amateur motor-cycle pastime.

During that time, riders invariably used their every-day machines for racing at weekends, but as speeds inevitably rose, the demand for specially built machines grew. However, these remained essentially similar to road machines, for the circuits were often long — up to a mile (1·6 km.) — with left- and right-hand bends, climbs, and dips.

Although Brands Hatch was converted into a road racing circuit for 1950 and other prewar circuits were lost after 1945, the sport flourished throughout Britain. But as building and farming activity increased, grass-track racing was limited to smaller and smaller fields.

This, more than any other factor, was responsible for a major change. By the end of the 1950s, most grass circuits were speedway-style 'ovals', rarely more than 600 m. (656 yds.) long and with only left-hand bends. Because of this, grass-track machines are closely related to speedway cycles.

Kent, Sussex, Lincolnshire, southern Yorkshire, Wiltshire, and Dorset are the main grass-track areas in England. During the summer some 20 meetings are staged each weekend under the guidance of the A.C.U.

Although grass-track racing in various forms has existed in many countries (e.g. Australia, New Zealand, South Africa, America, and Germany), international events were not introduced until the late 1960s.

The most successful British championship riders have been HAGON, the London motorcycle dealer who pioneered the design of the modern grass-track machine, and Godden. Both have won numerous championships under varying systems. But perhaps the most outstanding championship achievement was the success of Pusey in 1970. He was unbeaten in any championship race (there were five rounds) in both the 350 cc. and 500 cc. class. There are no international or world championships.

SAND-TRACK RACING is a motor-cycle sport now practically dead, at least in Britain, though it enjoyed some measure of popularity in the 1920s and 1930s. Where broad expanses of firm sand were exposed on beaches, impromptu motor-cycle races were staged, attention having been drawn to the viability of such beaches by their use for record-breaking attempts by motor cars. Properly organized race meetings then became a regular feature of the summer racing season, but these events were never vigorously promoted and did not generally pretend to cater for riders of high national or international standing. The machines used were commonly ordinary production sporting motor cycles suitably stripped of non-essentials, the field being enlivened by a sprinkling of speedway or grass-track racing motor cycles.

The principal reason for the success of this form of the sport, despite the known mechanical hazards attending the entry of sand into the engine, was probably that the British government (unlike most others) would not close public roads for racing, so that the enthusiastic sporting motor-cyclist had to amass experience and take his fun as he found it. With the creation of a number of road racing circuits in the 1950s, sand racing lost what little attraction it ever had.

However, LONG-TRACK RACING, as sand-track racing is called on the Continent, is a major sporting attraction throughout Germany, Denmark, Sweden, and Norway. Most meetings are held on tracks which, at some time in their history, have been used for horsetrotting. Generally the track is about 1,000 m. (1,093 yds.) long, hence the other common name for the sport, 1,000-metre racing. The tracks are very wide and are often well surfaced with sand. The sport is highly professional and each large meeting can be worth £200 or more in appearance money to popular competitors. Most of the performers are grasstrack riders, although it is also popular with top speedway competitors.

The rules are about midway between speedway and grass tracking. There are always eight riders to each race which covers three laps of the track. Riders use machines very similar to those in British grass-track racing and there is only one class (500 cc.). The most popular engines are the JAPs, because they can provide more speed round these vast stadia. Despite the high speeds attained — a good rider will sometimes reach around 100 m.p.h. (161 km./h.) — serious accidents are not common, although fatalities are more frequent than in speedway or grass-track racing. Most accident-prone are the sidecar competitors who hurtle round the tracks at very high speeds.

Long-track racing has been tried in Britain, but the response was so poor that the attempt was abandoned. The Point of Ayr club arranged several meetings at the trotting stadium at Prestatyn, Flintshire, but despite the excellence of the stadium, the quality of the track, and some very fine racing, the venture was financially unsuccessful.

The F.I.M. announced towards the end of 1970 that the long-track championship, hitherto only a European title, was to be given world status.

ICE RACING on motor cycles originated jointly in Russia and Sweden and has spread as far across Europe as France — there have even been attempts to introduce it to Britain. Basically, ice racing, or ice speedway as it is sometimes known, particularly in Germany, is a form of speedway on ice. Machines are rather like speedway cycles and meetings are always held in stadia which bear a striking resemblance to speedway venues. It is quite common for the organizers of a meeting to take over a winter sports stadium — more usually used for ICE SKATING — and lay out a race track which may be between 200 and 300 metres in length. In Russia, however, where temperatures can be relied upon to remain below freezing for several months, speedway promoters flood a stadium and leave nature to provide a race-track. Because of the wear and tear inflicted by the motor cycles, the ice needs to be about 500 mm. (1 ft. 8 in.) thick and there must be snow banks on the outside of the track to stop any out-of-control machines heading into the crowd.

The cycles have screwed into the tyres needle-sharp spikes which project about 1½ in. (38 mm.). These spikes cause the machines to run on the ice as though they were on rails. The spikes grip so effectively that, when cornering, ice racers incline their machines at greater angles than for any other type of motor-cycle sport.

The most common injury to ice racers is to the fingers of the left hand; races are run anticlockwise and it is very common for the fingers to rub along the ice surfaces while cornering. Riders steady themselves with their left knee, which drags along the track and is normally protected by a section of motor-car tyre strapped over the leg. Another common injury is to the left foot, which is occasionally run over by the spikes of the rear wheel.

Most successful at ice racing are Russians and Czechoslovakians, most of whom are speedway riders during the summer months. They ride works machines and often use special spikes, made from metals developed for the aircraft industry and for their country's space programme. The Swedes are also very successful and, like the Russians, have their own winter league which is conducted on lines similar to the speedway leagues. The only British rider to meet with success in ice racing

was the grass-track and speedway rider, Ross, who twice qualified for the world final and was invited to compete in the Swedish winter league for the 1970-1 season. British riders have not featured, however, since then.

Ice races are run like speedway, with four riders on the track at a time, covering four laps of the track for a race. The starts are performed with speedway starting gates, and scoring is on the 3-2-1 principle. Because of the bright colours of the riders' leathers and helmets, which contrast with the white of the snow and ice, this is a particularly attractive sport. Like speedway and long-track racing, ice racing is professionally promoted.

SPRINTING is an acceleration test over a measured distance, usually a quarter of a mile (402 m.), taken from a standing start. There are classes for all types of motor cycles, but to achieve the highest honours a highly specialized form of machine is essential. Sprinting motor cycles are constrained by very few regulations and are therefore presented in considerable variety with all types of engines enjoying some favour, superchargers and very potent special fuels, rich in alcohol and oxygen-bearing additives such as nitro-methane, being common. The wheelbase is usually long, the centre of gravity very low, the rear tyre generously dimensioned, and everything else kept as light and small as possible in order to minimize the resistance to acceleration offered by the inertia of the machine and its aerodynamic drag. Streamlined fairings are common and there are few concessions made to handling, steering, or braking since the events are always held on a dead straight course with plenty of room for slowing down after completing the measured run. Some sprints are run over a kilometre instead of a quarter of a mile, and the usual venues are the concrete runways of disused or temporarily hired airfields. In the U.S.A., where the sport is most highly developed, asphalt strips are compounded with rubber to give extra grip, and some of the more important meetings are held on the Bonneville salt flats, part of the Great Salt Lake in Utah.

In the U.S.A. riders compete in two ways, either against each other or against the clock. In the former they race in pairs in a series of 'eliminators', the winner of a pair going on to challenge the winner of another pair until all contestants are eliminated save the two who take part in the final run of the tournament. Alternatively, the riders may strive to reach the highest terminal velocity, electronically measured over a short stretch at the far end of the measured quarter-mile. For many years this terminal velocity determined the winner of a competition, but more recently the elapsed time from start to finish has been recognized as more significant. In Britain, the other major centre of motor-cycle sprinting, the elapsed time for the quarter-mile sprint is always the deciding factor and actual speeds are considered irrelevant.

There is some confusion in the vocabulary of the sport. 'Drag racing' is an American term (see MOTOR RACING: AMERICAN) that is often taken as synonymous with 'sprinting' from a standing start. However, some authorities maintain that sprinting is a race against the clock, whereas drag racing is a race against other competitors on an elimination basis. In either case such events are run in one direction only, and must therefore be distinguished from record-breaking in which two consecutive runs must be completed in opposite directions within the space of one hour.

MOTOR-CYCLE RALLIES are seldom conducted as a sport, usually being a social or touring exercise. Any road-going motor cycle such as may legally be ridden upon the public highway is eligible, and riders are issued with a number of map references to checkpoints through which they have to pass, sometimes in a prescribed order, on their way to the rallying point at which the gathering may linger for a day or more, sometimes under canvas. If there is an element of competition involved, points will be scored according to the number of checkpoints visited and the mileage covered within a prescribed time in visiting them, the rider amassing the greatest total of points being declared the winner. Ties are sometimes decided by competitions of a gymkhana nature at the rallying point.

More commonly, as in the case of the German Elephant Rally and the Welsh Dragon Rally which is a copy of the Elephant, the challenge is simply in overcoming the rigours of bitter winter weather (competitive rallies are usually held in summer) with riders converging from all quarters on to a common route which leads to the rallying point. Further attractions are the touring interest involved and the possibility of enjoying the comradeship of like-minded riders at the rallying point.

GOVERNING BODY (WORLD): Fédération Internationale Motocycliste, 26 Avenue de Champel, 1206 Geneva, Switzerland.

MOTOR-CYCLE RALLIES, see MOTOR-CYCLE RACING.

MOTOR-CYCLE TRIALS, a cross-country pastime enjoyed by large numbers of motorcyclists in the British Isles every week-end. Interest has spread to many European countries and it has gained popularity in the U.S.A. and other parts of the world.

The word trials is used to describe two different types of event: the observation trial and the time trial. The object of an OBSERVATION TRIAL is for competitors to negotiate obstacles, known as observed sections (i.e. rocks, mud, tree roots, stream beds, etc.), without stopping or touching the ground. Sections vary in length; they may consist of a short but difficult turn on adverse camber, round a tree, or over an outcrop of rocks, but there is no stipulated distance or degree of severity. A well-known hill in the Scottish Six Days Trial (Loch Eild Path, near Kinlochleven, Inverness-shire) rises several hundred feet and consists of 15 sub-sections. A course may include any number of sections but few one-day trials involve more than six hours of riding. A time limit is generally enforced but speed is less important than riding skill.

Observers allocated to individual sections record the passage of each rider with a method of marking adopted by the Auto-Cycle Union (A.C.U.) after 1948. The system, approved by the Fédération Internationale Motocycliste (F.I.M.), is universal. For touching the ground once with any part of the body (one 'dab'), 1 mark is lost; for touching the ground twice or more with any part of the body ('footing'), 3 marks, and for failure, 5 marks are deducted. To differentiate between 'footing' and two 'dabs', some clubs favour a 2-mark penalty but this method of scoring had not been enforced by the governing body, the A.C.U., by 1971. An unpenalized attempt, known as a 'clean', is recorded as 0 (zero) mark lost. After the finish, generally at the same place as the start, observers' cards are collected by the organizers and, following analysis by a results team, the rider with fewest marks lost is declared the winner.

Ties can be settled by various methods. The most popular is a special test over a measured distance to provide an acceleration and braking figure. A coasting test, with dead engine, is sometimes employed but such methods require a timekeeper and many clubs prefer a farthest 'clean' or fewest 'failures' decision to settle ties. A competitor is deemed to have completed a section when the front wheel spindle of his machine has passed between cards marking the end of the observed section.

TIME TRIALS also operate on a marks lost basis but their essence is speed between control points, as in car rallies (see MOTOR RALLIES). Competitors are issued with route and time cards and marks are lost for tardiness at controls where marshals employ special clocks to stamp riders' cards.

Speed schedules may vary, according to the nature of the terrain, but average speeds rarely exceed 30 m.p.h. (48 km./h.), and are often slower, particularly if the route is difficult. Skill is important but speed is equally vital; standard time is set by the fastest rider to complete the course. Slower riders lose a mark for every two minutes late.

Two-day trials are organized by several clubs but the premier events, the Scottish Six Days Trial and the International Six Days Trial, have one major difference. The first is purely an observation trial; the second is a race against the clock.

The Scottish event, organized by the Edinburgh and District Motor Club Ltd., is the annual competition for the J. R. Alexander Challenge Trophy and the most important observation trial in the world, ranking in importance with the TOURIST TROPHY races. The Scottish takes competitors through the magnificent scenery of the Western Highlands. It covers approximately 1,000 miles (1,609 km.) with daily routes from Fort William, and starts and finishes in Edinburgh. Natural, rocky climbs are a feature of this trial which attracts international entries usually limited to 300 solos. A sidecar class, reintroduced in 1958, was dropped in 1960.

The International Six Days Trial (I.S.D.T.) is principally a team event but individual riders can win gold, silver, or bronze medals. Staged for the F.I.M. each year by a different country, the I.S.D.T. has been dubbed the OLYMPIC GAMES of motor-cycle sport. It can cover as much as 1,000 miles of rough country and is punctuated by a series of special tests in which competitors gain points for speed. For individual riders competing for a gold medal, the object is to complete the course with no marks lost and with as many bonus points as possible. Riders losing up to 25 marks receive a silver medal; other finishers gain bronze medals.

Once machines have been sealed at a preliminary weigh-in (so called because motor cycles in the first I.S.D.T. in 1913 were placed on a public weigh-bridge) marked components may not be replaced during the trial. Time is allowed for normal maintenance but running repairs must be carried out within strict time schedules. After each day, machines are returned to a closed compound.

Trials motor cycles are highly specialized machines but rider skill remains the deciding factor. Unlike road racing (see MOTOR-CYCLE RACING) or MOTO-CROSS, expensive and complex machines are less important than the ability of the individual.

Early trials machines were little more than modified touring motor cycles, fitted with studded tyres by expert riders seeking greater wheel grip on slippery terrain, but modern trials machines are more sophisticated. Good traction at low speed and adequate ground clearance are characteristics common to most makes. Low mass and good weight distribution are desirable for ease of handling.

After the mid-1960s, when most large British motor-cycle manufacturers lost interest in trials competitions, the sport became dominated by Spanish 250 cc. single-cylinder two-strokes made by the Bultaco, Montesa, and Ossa factories. A sprung frame, pioneered by AJS and Royal Enfield on 350 cc. trials machines, became standard equipment, and special low-pressure tyres were universally adopted.

In Europe, tyre sizes are determined by the governing bodies of the sport. The maximum section is 4 in. (101·6 mm.) and the tread is limited to a specified block pattern. Most riders favour a front wheel $2\frac{3}{4} \times 21$ in. (69·9 $\times$ 533·4 mm.). A larger wheel and tyre give more grip but make the steering heavy. The best size for the rear wheel is 4×18 in. (101 $\times$ 457 mm.). A larger wheel would raise the back of the machine and make the transfer of weight difficult.

As rapid weight transference is second in importance only to good throttle control, trials machines must have a correct relationship between the handlebars and the footrests. When negotiating a section, a trials rider almost invariably stands up. Standing is the only way to obtain maximum control and weight distribution and the saddle is used only when riding between sections.

Though four-speed gearboxes are adequate, gearboxes with five speeds give riders a wider choice of ratios for different types of section. Some 125 cc. machines, such as the SUZUKI trials model, have six speeds, but a trials rider rarely changes gear while tackling a section. A low gear is more easily controlled than a high ratio but, on difficult hills where a change of gear is planned, good riders always plan to do so where they may relax sufficiently.

A rear chain tensioner, to make throttle response more sensitive, is a desirable fitment for participants in a sport in which rear-wheel traction can be the key to success.

Trials, originally reliability trials, are one of the oldest forms of motor-cycle competition. Along with speed tests, trials were a sequel to the formation of Britain's motor-cycle industry. Pioneering manufacturers took part in such events to prove the staying power and hill-climbing virtues of their products. The motor cycle was popularly regarded as a sporting vehicle for use on good roads but trials soon became interspersed with cross-country sections of varying severity. Growth of the motor-cycling movement encouraged clubs to stage trials on private land and the element of fun and endeavour in cross-country riding became firmly rooted.

The Motor Cycling Club (M.C.C.), founded in 1901, is Britain's oldest organization covering long-distance trials. The M.C.C. classics are the Exeter and Land's End trials with night runs preceding a day's sport in the hills of the West Country. As far back as 1903, the Auto-Cycle Club (A.C.C.) ran daily long distance trials from the Crystal Palace, ending with a speed test at the London track. An offshoot of the Royal Automobile Club, the A.C.C. ran a national six-day trial from London in 1904; the event began on a Monday and ended on a Saturday. Of 48 entries, five gained gold medals.

Formation of the Auto-Cycle Union (A.C.U.), in 1907, as a union of clubs, produced regular marathons from Land's End to John o'Groats, with competitors struggling up Cheddar Gorge, Shap Fell, and other notable hills. The first Scottish Six Days Trial (see above) took place in 1909. Historical highlights include VINEY'S unique hat-trick (1947-9), Peplow's first win by a machine under 350 cc. (1959), JACKSON'S single mark win (1961), and S.H. MILLER's first win on a foreign two-stroke machine (1965).

By 1911, the A.C.U. had developed the basis of the International Six Days Trial. That year's event, from Harrogate, Yorkshire, attracted 75 competitors. Only 12 retired and 33 won gold medals. A witness of the 1912 A.C.U. 'six days' opined that the annihilation of gradients by variable gears would make it impossible to make the 1913 trial too difficult.

By then, shorter trials were an established part of the motor-cycling scene, but they did not attain national importance until 1911, when the Reliance Trial, the first major one-day trial to be held in Britain, was organized by the Chester club. This first national open was won by Heaton (2¼ h.p. AJS) over a two-day route of 195 miles (314 km.). The golden jubilee event of 1961 was won by Adcock (250 cc. Dot), riding under the auspices of the South Liverpool club which inherited the trophy and continued to organize Britain's oldest major trial as a regionally restricted event.

The Exeter Trial, the M.C.C.'s classic winter long-distance trial, was first held in 1910 from Hounslow to Exeter and back. Famous hills include Meerhay, Fingle Bridge, and Simms, also used in the Land's End trial at Easter. Starting from London, Launceston and Kenilworth, three routes converged on Weymouth from 1957 trials onwards.

The Reliance Trial of 1911 set a fashion for big national open trials such as the Colmore Cup Trial, staged by the Sutton Coldfield and North Birmingham Auto Club since 1912, when competitors were penalized only when they stopped.

The Victory Trial, organized by the Birmingham Motor Cycle Club, started in 1919. The Alan Trophy trial was first run in 1920, organized by the Cumberland County Motor Cycling Club after it had been presented with the trophy, for an open competition, by Capt. Rhodes, a motor-cycle pioneer in north-west England. The original trophy survived for 31 years. Tiffen and Ratcliffe won it four times before Miller finally scored three consecutive successes to win it outright in 1960.

The Bemrose Trophy Trial is a national event organized by the Pathfinders and Derby Motor Club Ltd., since 1921, when the trophy was presented by Col. W. L. Bemrose, president of Derby & District M.C. The trial is held in the Peak District and famous hills include Hollinsclough and Hawks Nest.

The British Experts Trial, the Birmingham M.C.C.'s annual restricted competition and the blue riband of one-day trials, was first held in 1929 as a competition to find the best solo and sidecar expert. Top awards are the S.K.F. Gold Cup, the Palmer Silver Challenge Trophy, and the Feridax cup. In 1969 all except one competitor (Harrison) were excluded for alleged malingering after qualifying with distinction in national trials.

As trials became more competitive, the A.C.U. introduced a lesser penalty for footing (3 marks instead of 5). The subsequent system of 1 mark for putting a foot down, 3 marks for footing, and 5 marks for stopping, was adopted in 1948.

A British trials championship which begun as part of an A.C.U. star contest for different branches of motor-cycle sport, has been in existence since 1950. Originally based on a large number of national trials, in 1970 the championship was streamlined into a series of ten selected trials. Under a new formula, based on a scale of points for the top ten in each championship trial, the rider with most points (FARLEY) became champion.

The first I.S.D.T. was staged in 1913, from Carlisle, when three Frenchmen competed for the International Challenge Trophy, a team award presented to the governing body of motor cycling (then the Fédération Internationale Clubs de Motocyclistes) by the Cycle and Motor Cycle Manufacturers and Traders Union of Great Britain. The trophy went to the British trio of Collier (964 cc. Matchless), Gibb (349 cc. Douglas), and Little (499 cc. Premier). Of 162 starters, 28 won gold medals. The 1920 event was won in France by Switzerland, who thereby won the right to stage the 1921 event, which they also won. A third Swiss success in 1923 resulted in a switch to neutral territory in Sweden and Norway, and the Swedes emerged the winners. Belgium ran the 1924 trial and Britain won, earning the honour of staging the 1925 I.S.D.T. in Devon, with the start at Southampton. This event attracted competitors from the U.S.A. and it was described as a world motor-cycling championship, a description strengthened by Russian participation after the Second World War, but Britain dominated the event. A German team came close to capturing the trophy in 1926 but Britain won both major team contests, the second being a competition for the Silver Vase, introduced in 1924.

Britain ruled the roost so long that, in 1930, the A.C.U. felt obliged to surrender the right to run the trial, and it went to France, where Italy took the trophy and France the vase. Italy retained the trophy in 1931 but, in 1932, Britain fought back to a dramatic climax at the final speed test and won by a margin of only two minutes. Britain's record of 16 successes was checked by foreign teams after 1953 in Czechoslovakia, and, in 1954, Czechoslovakia beat Britain in Wales. After oscillating between West Germany and Czechoslovakia, the main competition was dominated by East Germany from 1963 to 1967, with a sixth win in 1969, but German supremacy crashed in 1970, when the Czechs won in Spain.

With the I.S.D.T. involving nationally representative teams, victory prestige is considerable and particularly valuable to manufacturers for exports, but increasing cost of organization and difficulty with arranging suitable courses, brought a situation in which European host nations became reluctant to continue holding the event. This influenced the I.S.D.T. to go to the U.S.A. for the first time in 1973, but through lack of knowledge and experience, the event, held in Massachusetts, was below standard, with Czechoslovakia's victory more as a statistic than a worthy sporting success. It was commendable, however, that the U.S.A. gained the 'Vase' award in the face of more experienced opposition and did a great deal to help the popularity of motor cycling in the United States.

Until 1970, a trophy team was composed of six riders on machines built in their country of origin. To broaden the contest, the regulations were changed to permit teams to compete on any make of machine, irrespective of nationality, as in the four-man vase team contest.

A European trials championship, pioneered by Belgium, was officially recognized by the F.I.M. in 1968, with title rounds in different countries, as in the road racing and moto-cross world championships. Originally a competition for the Henry Groutars trophy, presented by an official of the Belgian motor-cycle federation (F.M.B.), the F.I.M. championship is based on a points-for-places formula. In 1970-1, when the series attracted the support of Spanish manufacturers, the championship comprised nine rounds of which the best six counted. Points awarded to the first ten in each round were 15, 12, 10, 8, 6, 5, 4, 3, 2, 1. Events were staged by Germany, Britain, Ireland, France, Spain, Switzerland, Poland, Finland, and Sweden. The five best performances counted for the title.

Max King, *Trials Riding* (1960); S.H. Miller, *Sammy Miller on Trials* (1971).
GOVERNING BODY (WORLD): Fédération Internationale Motocycliste, 26 Avenue de Champel, 1206 Geneva, Switzerland.

MOTOR RACING is the staging of a competition of speed capabilities between two or more mechanically-propelled land vehicles over an accepted point-to-point course or closed circuit, the competitors running either together or being timed separately over the course. It is a dangerous sport, the driver's skill being expended on controlling a lightweight projectile capable of speeds in the region of 200 m.p.h. (322 km./h.) and in taking it round the bends on a road course as fast as possible, balancing power available at the driving wheels with the grip afforded by the tyres. Modern racing tyres are of special rubber mixes which give a tenacious grip up to a sudden break-away point, so that a car is apt to go out of control and slide off the road at very high speed. The machines used vary greatly in technical construction, and races are held under a wide diversity of rules and formulae; in most cases the skill of the driver in extracting maximum performance from his car has to be weighed against the efficiency, in terms of acceleration, speed, reliability, cornering power, and other factors of the machine he is occupying.

Road racing is the highest form of the sport, but track racing, over courses in which the corners and turns were banked as on a railway, enabling the cars to negotiate them at speed without much skidding, was popular prior to the Second World War. The Indianapolis 500, the most famous American race, is run over an oval with slightly banked corners, calling for a special driving technique.

In addition to races of from a few miles to 24 hours' duration, the various categories of racing cars take part in hill-climb and speed-trial contests, running one at a time, or sometimes in pairs over a straight course, and in all divisions of the sport various championships are recognized.

International motor racing. The Fédération Internationale de l'Automobile (F.I.A.), which governs the sport, sets rules for the main types of motor race, changing those for the top rank, Formula One, as it considers expedient, both to encourage technical advancement and to ensure control over the safety of the drivers. The first true motor race took place in France (see below) in 1895 and for some years public roads served as courses. Following accidents which involved spectators as well as drivers, present-day racing, with the one exception of Sicily's Targa Florio, takes place over private closed circuits, which the cars cover on a time or distance basis, lap after lap. Races can be run on a scratch or handicap basis, and heat-by-heat and relay contests are not unknown. The makers of the racing cars score points towards a manufacturers' championship and various other championships are recognized each season.

The considerable cost of building cars for Grand Prix races, as the top contests are designated, was originally found by rich amateur sportsmen and by the motor manufacturers who supported racing. But in recent years outside sponsorship by such industrial concerns as perfume makers, cigarette companies, and food manufacturers has become necessary.

It is customary for the drivers appointed to each Formula One team by the owners or sponsors thereof, to take part in all the recognized Formula One races each season. These take place all over the world and are approximately 200 miles (322 km.) or a little less in length. The various circuits over which these championship races are run incorporate curves to be taken at very high speeds, others of a tortuous, twisting nature, calling for heavy braking and maximum acceleration at the corners, and constituting a heavy strain on drivers who are continually changing gear and steering the car, as at MONACO.

The modern road racing or Grand Prix car is very scantily constructed, the rear-placed engine often forming a major part of the structure, and the driver, safeguarded by elaborate protective clothing, space-type crash helmet, and goggles or visor, lies almost on his back in the cockpit, steering with a very small steering wheel, to reduce air drag to a minimum. Great skill is required to corner such fast, light cars at maximum speed, engine power being used to promote deliberate skids, which develop into four-wheel drifting or sliding — the fastest way through the faster bends.

In longer sports/racing car races cars have to stop for replenishment of fuel and oil and possibly to be fitted with new tyres, and the driver may be changed for another who is sharing the car. These stops are made at special 'pits'.

The first motor races were held over town-to-town courses and if the competing cars developed mechanical trouble or punctured or burst tyres, they could be repaired only by the driver and his riding mechanic, using such tools and spares as were carried on the car. Later, when races had been transferred to closed circuits, it became possible to station trained mechanics by the side of the course. They could carry out any work needed on their car during a race, signal the driver his position in the contest, and change tyres when necessary. To accommodate these men and their equipment, pits were dug at the side of a convenient straight part of the course, usually opposite the grandstands so that spectators could see the work being carried out, hence the name 'pits'. Later these were replaced by wood or concrete structures at road level, one for each competing car giving protection to the occupants who would include timekeepers and lap-scorers as well as the mechanics.

By the 1930s pit work had been brought to a fine art; all four tyres of a Grand Prix car could be changed (on the wheels) and fuel replenished in well under 60 seconds. Race positions would change as the leading cars came in for this essential work and the team's mechanics had the gratification of playing a vital part in the outcome of important races.

After the Second World War Grand Prix races were of shorter duration and little could be done for a car which had broken down. Moreover, the cars now run through a race without requiring refuelling and on one set of tyres, so that pit work has virtually gone from the Grand Prix scene. However, it continues to play as important a part as ever in the long-duration sports-car races, such as the 24-hour race at LE MANS.

The technique of racing-car construction is bound up with extracting the maximum of power from a given engine which, under prevailing rules, burns ordinary petrol. In earlier years special racing fuels were permissible and engines were sometimes supercharged, by a mechanical pump, driven from the engine, which forced the petrol/air gas mixture into the cylinders under pressure, thus enabling greater power to be developed from a given capacity of cylinder. More recently attention has been paid to getting the power developed effectively on to the road; very wide tyres on the driving wheels, sophisticated suspension systems, tyres made from chemical-rubber mixes to ensure good adhesion on wet or dry tracks, and aerofoils to force the wheels of the car on to the road being means to this end.

International races are subdivided into various categories. Some are for pure racing vehicles, others are confined to cars which carry some road equipment, lamps, all-enveloping bodywork, etc., and are known as sports or sports/racing cars. Such cars can maintain speed at night and some of their races continue through the hours of darkness.

Pure racing cars are normally single-seaters, carrying only the driver, a safety requirement introduced in the 1920s, before which mechanics were carried. The top class of single-seater is an expensive piece of machinery and lesser versions of racing car, which can be built and raced for a smaller expenditure, are also recognized.

The main racing-car formulae recognized officially are:

Formula One which admits the following cars:

Validity from 1 January 1965 to 31 December 1972. Engines with reciprocating pistons: (*a*) engine cylinder capacity without supercharging, inferior to 3,000 cc.; (*b*) engine cylinder capacity with supercharging, inferior or equal to 1,500 cc., minimum weight without ballast, 530 kg. (The Formula One is prolonged beyond 31 December 1972, but, as from 1 January 1972, the number of cylinders is limited to 12 maximum.)

Formula Two for which the following cars are eligible:

Validity from 1 January 1967 to 31 December 1971. Reciprocating piston engines: engine cylinder capacity superior to 1,300 cc. and inferior or equal to 1,600 cc. Minimum weight, without ballast, 450 kg.

The cylinder block must be taken from an F.I.A.-recognized model of car, manufactured in a quantity of at least 500 units in 12 consecutive months. The cylinder capacity may be obtained by increasing or reducing either the original bore or stroke or both dimensions. On the cylinder block, entirely finished, are permitted all modifications necessary to ensure the mounting and/or tightness of the cylinder head, the driving device of the camshaft(s), ignition distributor, pumps (water, fuel, injection), and other accessories, when the original location or form of these has been changed.

The type of cylinder (with or without sleeve) as well as the friction system of connecting rod and crankshaft bearings must remain the same as on the original engine. The number of camshafts is optional. The feeding system of the engine is optional (by carburettor, direct or indirect injection) but no device liable to have a supercharging effect may be mounted.

The number of cylinders per engine is limited at six, but the International Sporting Commission (C.S.I.) reserve their right to reconsider this decision from the moment that the F.I.A. would have recognized in one of the first three groups of Appendix J (see below), three models of cars of different makes with an engine of more than six cylinders and of a cylinder capacity inferior or equal to 2,000 cc. However, such a decision of modification would only come into effect as from 1 January of the following year. Cooling system: the system of the ori-

ginal engine must be preserved (by air, by water). Propulsion, through a maximum of two wheels. Gearbox, maximum five ratios, the reverse gear not included.

As from 1 January 1972, the following prescriptions come into force for the Formula Two: Validity, 1 January 1972 to 31 December 1975. Non-supercharged reciprocating piston engines: engine cylinder capacity inferior or equal to 2,000 cc. Minimum weight without ballast: cars equipped with a four-cylinder engine, 450 kg; cars equipped with a six-cylinder engine, 475 kg; cars equipped with more than six cylinders, 500 kg. The engine (including engine block and cylinder head) must be derived from an engine equipping a model of car for which the F.I.A. has ascertained a series-production of at least 1,000 units.

Modifications allowed on the original pieces of the engine are those provided for special touring cars (see below). However, all freedom is left for the crankshaft and the connecting rods. The maximum cylinder capacity authorized — 2,000 cc. — can be obtained by modifying the original bore and/or stroke.

Formula Three cars, by which is implied the following:

Validity, as from 1 January 1971 to 31 December 1974. Reciprocating piston engines only. Maximum cylinder capacity, 1,600 cc. The maximum cylinder capacity may be obtained by increasing or reducing either the bore or stroke or both dimensions.

Maximum number of cylinders, four. The engine block and cylinder head castings, machining completed, must be those of a series-production car manufactured in at least 5,000 units in 12 consecutive months of a model recognized by the F.I.A. The original engine block and cylinder head may be modified freely by removal of material to the exclusion of any addition of material. The type of crankshaft bearings may not be modified (the replacement of a plain bearing by a roller bearing is therefore forbidden).

The induction system is optional but it must compulsorily be fitted with a throttling flange of 3 mm. in length and with a parallel hole of 20 mm. diameter. Through this throttling flange all the air feeding must pass. The throttling flange must be made of metal or metallic alloy. The material of the air-box is optional, provided it is not a porous material. The C.S.I. reserve the right to modify the dimensions of the throttling flange.

No supercharging device is allowed even if a series-production one was fitted on the original engine. The other original parts of the engine may be replaced or modified without restriction. Other mechanical elements: the gearbox and differential casings must be those of a car manufactured in at least 5,000 units in '12 consecutive months, of a model recognized by the F.I.A., but not necessarily the model from which the engine has been taken. The gearbox may not have more than five forward speeds, plus a reverse gear. Complete freedom is left as regards the ratios. The use of a limited slip differential is allowed.

Dimensions, minimum wheelbase, 200 cm.; minimum track, 120 cm. Minimum weight without ballast, 440 kg.

Certificate of origin: any Formula Three car

appearing at the start of an event must be supplied with a certificate established by the manufacturer and ratified by the national sporting authority, specifying the origin of the basic elements of the vehicle.

There are also lesser formulae, intended to promote racing at lower cost and to act as a training ground below the highly competitive Formula Three level, from which the leading drivers hope to graduate into Formula Two or even directly into Formula One racing. These include Formula Ford, for single-seater cars powered by production-type Ford engines, Formula Super V, for Volkswagen-based single-seaters, etc.

The International Sporting Code governing motor racing recognizes various categories and groups of vehicles, including the Formula One, Two, and Three racing cars, and a variety of prototype and more normal road-equipped cars, of which specified numbers must, in the production and sports classes, be proved to have been made for sale to customers. The categories under Title 1, Appendix J, are:

Category A, recognized production cars (numbers within brackets indicate required minimum production for 12 consecutive months): Group 1, series-production touring cars (5,000); Group 2, special touring cars (1,000); Group 3, series-production grand touring cars (1,000); Group 4, special grand touring cars (500); Group 5, sports cars.
Category B, experimental competition cars: Group 6, prototype sports cars.
Category C, racing cars: Group 7, two-seater racing cars; Group 8, formula racing cars; Group 9, *Formule Libre* racing cars.

There are other important race categories and many minor ones, and in all cases specific regulations are laid down covering safety requirements, body dimensions, and weight limits.

Apart from absolute winners, races are divided into classes defined by the size of the engines of the competing cars and the same categorization is used for second attempts, i.e. timed runs by one car endeavouring to go faster over a specified distance or further in a given time than any car has done before. The engine-size classification laid down is:

(1) Cylinder capacity inferior or equal to 500 cc.
(2) Cylinder capacity exceeding 500 cc. and inferior or equal to 600 cc.
(3) Cylinder capacity exceeding 600 cc. and inferior or equal to 700 cc.
(4) Cylinder capacity exceeding 700 cc. and inferior or equal to 850 cc.
(5) Cylinder capacity exceeding 850 cc. and inferior or equal to 1,000 cc.
(6) Cylinder capacity exceeding 1,000 cc. and inferior or equal to 1,150 cc.
(7) Cylinder capacity exceeding 1,150 cc. and inferior or equal to 1,300 cc.
(8) Cylinder capacity exceeding 1,300 cc. and inferior or equal to 1,600 cc.
(9) Cylinder capacity exceeding 1,600 cc. and inferior or equal to 2,000 cc.
(10) Cylinder capacity exceeding 2,000 cc. and inferior or equal to 2,500 cc.
(11) Cylinder capacity exceeding 2,500 cc. and inferior or equal to 3,000 cc.
(12) Cylinder capacity exceeding 3,000 cc. and inferior or equal to 5,000 cc.
(13) Cylinder capacity exceeding 5,000 cc.

Records are recognized in various classes; world, international, national, and local.

The most important drivers' championship is that raced for in specified international Formula One races, under a points system. The eligible races include the Grand Prix in Austria, Belgium, Canada, France, Germany, Great Britain, Italy, Mexico, Monaco, Netherlands, South Africa, Spain, and the U.S.A.

Apart from the drivers' world championship, the F.I.A. recognizes graded drivers. Since 1968, the list of F.I.A. graded drivers includes:

(1) World champion drivers of the five previous years.
(2) Drivers who, in one and the same year, have been classified at least twice among the first six in a race of the world championship for drivers, while taking into account the championship of the two previous years.
(3) Drivers who, in one and the same year, have been classified at least twice among the first three in an event of the makes' championship, while taking into account the two previous years. However, only those teams of not more than two drivers, and that for the whole duration of the event, are retained for inclusion on the list of graded drivers.
(4) The winner of the European Trophy for Formula Two drivers of the previous year, on condition that he has won at least three first places in the Class B drivers' classification (i.e. 'non-graded') of an event qualifying for that trophy.
(5) Drivers who, in the same year, won at the same time one classification among the first six in an event counting for the world championship of drivers, and one classification among the first three in the general results of an event counting for the makes' championship. Only the championships of the two previous years are taken into consideration.

Very stringent safety requirements are laid down by the F.I.A., governing body of the sport, for all official race meetings. Cars are usually started from a numbered grid, positions thereon being in accordance with practice times, the fastest driver starting from the best position on the front row. Races are electrically timed in many instances, to three places of decimals, in kilometres per hour. An international system of flag signals is in force, by which officials (flag marshalls) can signal to the drivers, the code being:
National flag: Signal of race start.
Blue flag: Another competitor is following you very closely and may, or is about to, overtake you.

White flag: A service car is on the circuit.

Yellow flag: Danger — no overtaking.

Yellow flag with vertical red stripes: Oil spilt on the road.

Green flag: Disappearance of a danger previously notified.

Red flag (at the exclusive disposal of the clerk of the course): Complete and immediate stop for all cars.

Black flag with white number: The car bearing the number indicated must stop at its refuelling pit.

Black-and-white chequered flag: Signal of end of race.

The invention of the motor car led to a direct extension of the many events in which men already competed against each other. The first race (sometimes called a trial) for cars, held in 1894, was run from Paris to Rouen; it was won by the Comte de Dion in a steam car which covered the 79 miles (127 km.) at an average of 11·6 m.p.h. (18·6 km./h.). During the next nine years many cross-country races followed and the dominant make was the French Panhard; these cars, all powered by internal combustion engines, ranged from the 1·2-litre model which won the 1895 Paris-Bordeaux-Paris race over 732 miles (1175 km.) to the 13·7-litre car with a power output of close to 90 b.h.p. which was the victor in the 1902 Paris-Vienna event.

After the turn of the century, Panhard's technical stagnation allowed other makes to come to the fore, encouraged by the introduction of such important races as the Gordon Bennett Cup of 1900-5 and the French Grand Prix first held in 1906. The majority of these cars were of enormous engine capacity, the real leviathans being the 16·2-litre Fiat of 1905 and the 15-litre de Dietrich of 1912.

The French Grand Prix established itself as the most important race. After wins by Renault, Fiat, and Mercedes in the first three years, various manufacturers conspired to abstain from racing because of German domination in 1908.

Although there was a Grand Prix de France in 1911 (the same year as the first Indianapolis 500-mile race), the French Grand Prix was not revived until 1912. Success went to the 7·6-litre Peugeot of Boillot from the 16-litre Fiat of Wagner. Peugeot repeated this success the following year, but in 1914, when there was an engine-capacity limit of 4·5 litres, Mercedes were invincible. These very advanced cars had four valves and three plugs per cylinder and four-wheel brakes; they took the first three places. The Mercedes had a power output of 115 b.h.p. at 2,800 r.p.m. and a maximum speed of 110 m.p.h. (177 km./h.). Although Henry, the designer of the losing Peugeots, exercised the dominant influence on the Grand Prix designs of early pre-

war and postwar years, the Mercedes was to some extent the forerunner of high-performance cars during the 1920s.

At Indianapolis, racing continued until 1916 but the French Grand Prix was not again held until 1921 when the Italian Grand Prix was added to the sporting calendar. The winner at Le Mans, where the French race was held to a capacity limit of 3 litres, was the American Duesenberg of Murphy. This car pioneered the use of hydraulic brakes in Grand Prix racing, a practice that was not re-introduced until they were used on the 3-litre MASERATI in 1933. At MONZA the Ballot, driven by Goux, won.

The engine-capacity limit was reduced to 2 litres the following year. Fiat, SUNBEAM, BUGATTI, Alfa Romeo, Rolland-Pilain, and DELAGE competed. The 6-cylinder Fiats dominated racing in 1922 and the following year the Company built new supercharged 8-cylinder models. Fiat was the first to run a supercharged car in a European Grand Prix.

Mechanical troubles and shortage of fuel caused the failure of these cars in the French race at Tours and the first two places went to the British Sunbeams, which were unashamed copies of the preceding year's Fiats. Fiats, by then fitted with an improved type of super-charger, took first and second places at Monza.

Grand Prix racing during the years 1924-5 was dominated by the new P2 Alfa Romeos designed by Jano, using a basic engine layout that Jano followed with all his racing engines until 1936. The year 1924 was memorable for the almost universal use of superchargers (not, however, adopted by Delage until 1925); the appearance of the Type 35 Bugatti, probably the most successful racing car of all time; and the failure of the Sunbeams at the French Grand Prix — they were the fastest cars in the race but the magnetos were changed on the night before and these were the cause of the cars' retirement.

The 1926-7 1·5-litre Grand Prix Formula was contested by Delage, Bugatti, and Talbot-Darracq; the 8-cylinder cars of Delage were victorious. Thereafter Grand Prix racing fell into the doldrums and most events were run on a *Formule Libre* basis. The Talbot-Darracqs and Alfa Romeo P2s of earlier years came to the fore once again, but 1928 and 1929 were notable for Bugatti successes.

The first Maserati had made its début in the Targa Florio of 1926 and the make flourished. In 1930 the straight-eight 8C-2,500 appeared. Of 15 important races in 1930, 7 were won by Maserati, 6 by Bugatti, and 2 by the rebuilt Alfa Romeo P2. The star driver of the year was Varzi with five wins. The following year

Grand Prix racing saw the appearance of two important new designs. Bugatti introduced his Type 51 with a twin overhead camshaft engine. From the Milan factory of Alfa Romeo came Jano's latest effort, the straight-eight Monza, also made in sports and touring forms.

Racing in 1931 was a three-cornered fight, with Bugatti gaining 11 victories to the 7 of Alfa Romeo and the 2 of Maserati. During the year both Alfa Romeo and Maserati raced twin-engined cars and Bugatti produced a 4·9-litre model, but none of these achieved much success. In 1932 the Alfa Romeo Monoposto with twin trop-shafts suffered only two defeats but Alfa Romeo withdrew from racing until mid-1933. For this short period racing was between the three makes: Bugatti, the improved 3-litre Maserati and Alfa Romeo which, with the re-appearance of the Monoposto, reasserted itself. At the end of 1933 another new car appeared, the Type 59 Bugatti, the traditional racing car in its ultimate form, but it achieved little success.

In October 1932 the committee of the Association Internationale des Automobile Clubs Reconnus, the then governing body of motor sport, announced a new Formula for the years 1934-6 (subsequently extended to 1937). The committee was primarily concerned about the maximum speeds of 150 m.p.h. (241 km./h.) plus that the large-capacity cars were attaining, and so a new Formula with a weight limit of 750 kg. (14 cwt. 3 qr.) was instituted. Thus it was felt that the type of car that would continue to be raced would be of the same power-to-weight ratio as the existing Alfa Romeo Monoposto, the Type 51 Bugatti, and the 3-litre Maserati. Racing would, it was hoped, be that much safer.

The entry of German politics into motor racing, however, enabled costly weight-saving engineering to be introduced, in the guise of exceedingly powerful AUTO UNION and MERCEDES-BENZ cars. The Auto Union was a radical rear-engined car designed by Dr. Porsche, while from Stuttgart came an equally advanced design of Mercedes-Benz with rigid tubular frame, and independent suspension front and rear, but the engine mounted conventionally at the front. Once teething troubles had been overcome, the German teams contested solely Grand Prix racing. Team leader for Auto Union was von Stuck, but the top driver of the team, from 1935 until his death during a record attempt in early 1938, was Rosemeyer. The master-mind of driving style and method in the Mercedes team was Fagioli, an Italian, while the other outstanding drivers were Caracciola and von Brauchitsch. The Ferrari-entered Alfa Romeos were largely unchanged and if the cars were uncompetitive,

the drivers were certainly not. Varzi, who left to drive Auto Unions in 1935, Chiron, and Moll (killed in a 160-m.p.h. crash in the 1934 Coppa Acerbo) were a match for any of the German competition.

In 1934 the great Nuvolari drove for Maserati and at the Italian Grand Prix appeared with the Modena concern's new, but unsuccessful, 6-cylinder model. For 1935 Nuvolari returned to FERRARI and Alfa Romeo. Although the trusty old Monoposto was still being raced, there was a new design on the way. It was the last of the Monopostos, with 3·8-litre engine, that Nuvolari used to defeat the German teams and win their national Grand Prix at the NUR-BURGRING in 1935, one of the great races of all time. The new fully independently sprung Alfa, the 8C-35, appeared at the Italian Grand Prix with the old Monoposto engine, but neither it nor the new V-8 Maserati could stave off German opposition and, since the new Formula, Bugatti performances had been even worse than those of the Italian teams — although in the absence of German opposition a win was scored in the 1934 Belgian Grand Prix. By 1936 Bugatti had turned its attention to sports cars and Maserati was concentrating on a new small car. Ferrari had by this time a V-12 engine for their new chassis, but despite improvements for 1937, they were fighting a lonely and hopeless struggle.

The expense of Grand Prix racing and the pronounced Teutonic technical leadership induced a number of constructors to build 1500 c.c. voiturettes and until 1938 the British ERA was the most successful. This rugged, rather old-fashioned car with an engine of production Riley origins and sponsored by Cook and Mays first appeared in 1934 and was driven by most of the leading British drivers of the period. The supposedly much improved E-type car of 1939 was a complete failure in both pre-war and postwar days.

Two enormously successful cars broke into voiturette racing in 1936. The first was Seaman's rebuilt 1926 Delage which, surprisingly, was more than the ERAs could cope with. From Italy came the 6-cylinder Maserati Tipo 6C which scored many successes on the Continent, but lacked the speed to beat the ERA on the few occasions on which the two makes competed on even terms.

By 1938 Alfa Romeo, too, had switched their major effort to the voiturette category and produced one of the most long-lived of all racing-car designs, the 8-cylinder Tipo 158 which was still winning Grands Prix at the end of the 1951 season. The 'Alfettas' were not without teething troubles, but they were fast — and faster than the 4-cylinder, 16-valve Maserati which made its début in 1939. The success of the 158 induced the Italian authorities to run all major races on Italian soil in 1939 to *voiturette* rules, thereby, it was hoped, regaining some of Italy's lost motor-racing prestige. These plans went awry when Mercedes-Benz produced the W165, a 1·5-litre scaled-down version of their Grand Prix model, at the Tripoli Grand Prix, triumphing over the Alfa Romeo and Maserati opposition by taking the first two places.

Whatever body has controlled motor sport, it has always nurtured the idea that racing was getting too fast and this is why, for 1938, there came into being a new and more restrictive Grand Prix Formula with upper engine-capacity limits of 3 litres supercharged and 4·6 litres unsupercharged. Auto Union and Mercedes-Benz both ran 3-litre supercharged cars and German domination continued with Mercedes, whose team had since 1937 included the Englishman, Seaman, once again having the upper hand. In mid-1938 the Auto Union team was strengthened by the addition of Nuvolari and he scored the make's first wins of the Formula at Monza and DONINGTON PARK that year.

Maserati made a come-back to Grand Prix racing that year with the Tipo 8CTF, a new straight-eight 3-litre based on a 'double-up' *voiturette* engine; although it was tremendously fast, its unreliability matched its speed. Maserati made a half-hearted effort, but the Grand Prix activities of Alfa Romeo were pathetic. With a choice of three engines and racing activities once again in the hands of the factory, the combined talents of engineer Ricart, designer Colombo, and driver Ferrari could achieve no victories and the factory was far more interested in making a success of the 158 Alfetta.

One worthwhile aspect of the new Formula was the renaissance of French interest in Grand Prix racing. In 1938 Bugatti built a straight-eight 3-litre supercharged car, but raced it very little, while Talbot and Delahaye concentrated on the unblown category. The Talbots were really sports cars, at first of only 4 litres; a single-seater did not appear until the 1939 French Grand Prix. But the spirit was there if not the technical ability or the money to finance a well-organized development programme. Delahaye's contribution was a push-rod V-12, at first in two-seater form, but there later appeared a single-seater which seemed to lack the speed of the earlier car. Delahaye scored a few minor successes.

European racing after the war started in 1945 with the Coupe des Prisonniers held in the Bois de Boulogne in Paris and won by Wimille's 4·7-litre Bugatti. For that year and 1946, the old pre-war Formula continued, although many events were held to *Formule Libre* rules. The year 1946 saw the reappearance of the 158 Alfa Romeos at St. Cloud where they suffered their sole defeat until they were beaten by Ferrari in 1951. In 1947 a new Grand Prix Formula imposing the mooted pre-war limits of 1·5 litres supercharged and 4·5 litres unsupercharged came into force.

Racing improved considerably in 1948 with the introduction of revised models by Talbot (a much more potent single-seater) and by the famed 'San Remo' Maserati. A V-12 Grand Prix car bearing the already famous name Ferrari was no match for the improved Alfa Romeos, but this team withdrew from racing for 1949, overestimating the strength of the Ferrari and over-pessimistic about the advent of a new rival in the shape of the V-16 BRM. As the opposition failed to materialize in the strength anticipated, Alfa Romeo made a come-back in 1950 and for two seasons there was keen competition between the supercharged overdeveloped, excessively fuel-thirsty Alfas and the unblown 4·5-litre Ferrari that first appeared in mid-season and from then onwards grew in strength. In 1950 the Alfas were driven by one of the greatest teams of all time; Farina, FANGIO, and Fagioli; while the Ferrari had ASCARI, Villoresi, and, from mid-1951, Gonzalez. Farina won the newly instituted world championship in 1950 and Fangio was champion in 1951. The Ferraris did not beat the Alfas until the 1951 British Grand Prix when Gonzalez won. Alfa Romeo withdrew from racing at the end of that season, having won four of the year's seven world championship races by exciting pit work and courageous driving.

Grand Prix, or Formula One, racing now looked as if it would enter the doldrums, because the complicated highly-supercharged 16-cylinder BRM, while being technically exciting on paper and making splendid noises, was a complete failure so far as long-distance or (at this time) any other kind of racing was concerned and, as Alfa Romeo had withdrawn, top-rank events would be dominated by Ferrari. Although individual drivers attracted as much interest as the cars, the purport of Grand Prix racing is inter-make competition, which would be still-born in 1952 with Ferrari the only significant entrant. Consequently the F.I.A. decided that from 1952 these races would be run under the Formula Two rules, with only a few true Formula One events remaining. This implied a top engine capacity of 2,000 cc. unsupercharged; there had been provision for supercharged cars of up to 500 cc. but none materialized.

The new ruling still gave the advantage to Ferrari, because Ascari managed to win every world championship race of 1952 except one in these cars, the Maserati opposition receiving a set-back when Fangio crashed the new six-cylinder car the team's début early in the season. It was not until the Italian Grand Prix that Maserati made some semblance of recovery, Gonzalez finishing second. The year 1952 marks the start of a trend towards lighter racing cars moving away from the classic formula. This was shown by the considerable success of the COOPER-Bristols, made in Surbiton by the well-known manufacturer of the little Cooper 500s of Formula Three conception, a light tubular frame enabling excellent performance to be achieved even though the engine was a 2-litre Bristol of virtually sports-car type. HAWTHORN did outstandingly in Cooper-Bristols and the next year was invited to drive for Ferrari. That year, 1953, a series of very closely-fought battles took place between Maserati and Ferrari, although it was again Ascari who won the world championship. He was still in the Ferrari team but Fangio was placed second for Maserati.

For 1954 Formula One was reconstituted for cars of up to 2,500 cc. unsupercharged, up to 750 cc. if supercharged, although the latter category was almost ignored. Mercedes-Benz returned to racing under this new Formula, with some very sophisticated space-frame 2·5-litre straight-eight cars having desmodromic valve gear, injected fuel, and independent rear suspension. These cars, with Fangio and Moss in the team, were more than a match for the prevailing Ferrari and Maserati teams of modified 1953 cars. Indeed, Mercedes-Benz won four of the half-dozen world championship races of 1954 and lost but one of the series the following year, after which the German manufacturer withdrew from the field, as having nothing further to achieve. From these advanced Mercedes-Benz cars stemmed their 3-litre 300 SLR sports/racing cars which were so successful in the TOURIST TROPHY and the *Mille Miglia* but which were involved in the disastrous accident at Le Mans in 1955, involving many spectators and causing motor racing to be seriously curtailed for some time thereafter. Fangio clinched the world drivers' championship in 1954 and 1955, driving for Maserati and Mercedes-Benz in the former, Mercedes-Benz only in the latter year. The new GP Formula was proving a technical stimulant, with plenty of new cars racing, so it was continued unchanged until 1960, except that from 1958 onwards only aviation petrol of 100/130 octane-rating was permitted.

After Mercedes-Benz gave up racing, Maserati were up against the Lancia-Ferrari, a racing car designed with a V-8 engine by Jano and developed by Ferrari when Lancia had to

quit racing. These cars enabled Fangio to exploit his very considerable talents to the full and he again took the world championship, for the third time in succession, in 1956. Collins also drove in the Lancia-Ferrari team but Moss, for Maserati, had the edge on them.

At this time, Britain was entering the Grand Prix arena more successfully than at all events for many years, thanks to the financial sacrifice and determination of the millionaire Vandervell. He had gradually perfected his Vanwall Specials after experimenting with Ferrari frames and engines based on the Norton motor-cycle valve gear. Although Fangio took his fourth successive world championship in 1957, handling Maserati 250Fs, Moss was in second place on points for the team of green Vanwall cars. In the following season Moss remained with Vanwall but also drove a Cooper, and was again second in the drivers' world championship (which, incidentally, always eluded him), Hawthorn being ahead on points, using the Jano-designed Dino V-6 Ferraris.

But the position of Great Britain, whose green cars had previously been either absent from the starting grids since the days of Sunbeam in the mid 1920s or early retirements, was improving. Brooks took an unexpected victory at Syracuse in a faired-in Connaught in 1955 and now Vanwall was in the ascendant. Vandervell had the satisfaction of seeing Moss second and Brooks third in the 1958 championship but Moss had used a Cooper that season and another era of Grand Prix construction had arrived, for Cooper now put the engine in the back of his ultra-light space-frame cars. From that time onwards Britain forged ahead and the lightweight, rear-engined technique also changed the complexion of the Indianapolis 500-mile race in America.

What Cooper could do others could copy, and eventually all the leading Grand Prix cars became of rear-engined construction, with aerofoils added to give enhanced tyre adhesion; the wide tyres themselves have a profound effect on road-holding. BRABHAM, having driven Cooper-Climax cars to first place in the championship in both 1959 and 1960, turned to building Formula One racing cars of his own make, and BRM, having dropped the unreliable V-16, were far more competitive with new V-12-cylinder cars. LOTUS began the racing career which has since been so phenomenally successful. At this time these smaller concerns could not build racing engines and had to rely on Coventry-Climax, who had developed their wartime fire-pump power unit into a useful racing engine, which they went on to produce as a sufficiently powerful V-8. Only Ferrari and BRM made engines of their own. These enabled Ferrari to take the world drivers' championship in 1961 under the changed formula of unsupercharged 1·5-litre cars with self-starters and running on pump petrol. The winner was Hill, the American, thus establishing another line of history.

Too much emphasis should not be placed on the drivers' world championship alone — in 1958 Vanwall proved their worth by taking the concurrent world championship of manufacturers, which became the property of Cooper in 1959 and 1960 and of Ferrari under the 'little' Formula of 1961.

For some time thereafter, Formula One racing flourished. The 3-litre formula which followed the annually-improving 1·5-litre ruling resulted in very fast cars, marred to the extent that the drivers are not anxious to race them over the faster or more hazardous circuits such as SPA and the Nurburgring. There was a crisis when Coventry-Climax withdrew the support of their racing-engine manufacture but Lotus was by then closely tied to Ford which spent large sums of money building racing engines for various purposes, including Grand Prix and Indianapolis racing, and their GT40 Ford sports/racing cars for victory at Le Mans, although the latter race was later the preserve of PORSCHE.

BRM gave up their V-8 and flat- or H-16 engines for more powerful and reliable V-12s, Japan came into the Formula One scene for a time with a complex HONDA using their own V-8 engine which SURTEES looked after, and the French Matra concern joined the Grand Prix field, enabling STEWART to rise to championship status. He drove for the newly formed March team, managed by Tyrrell, and, when Matra decided to use their own V-12 engine instead of the well-tried Ford V-8, Tyrrell built a GP car for Stewart, retaining the Ford power unit. The number of teams using these Cosworth-designed Ford engines made the servicing of them difficult and for a time emphasized the advantage of using the same make of engine as the car, which BRM continued to do with a new V-12 after troubles with the flat-16. Ferrari managed very well with a flat-12 engine.

Lotus were responsible for some noteworthy engineering innovations, such as the monocoque body and backbone frame, and for 1974 their complicated electrically-controlled clutch, on their JPS F1 cars, which were so designated because they were sponsored by John Player, the cigarette company — hence John Player Specials. But sports/racing-cars were faster with 5-litre engines than the 3-litre single-seaters and Alfa Romeo made a return to this class of racing, winning the 1971 Targa Florio, last of the open-road races, with a 3-

litre T33-3. The turbine had been tried at Indianapolis and Chapman of Lotus introduced it for Grand Prix racing in 1971. However, the original piston engine remains in universal employment for all classes of motor racing, nor has four-wheel drive made any real impact.

W. Boddy, *History of the Brooklands Motor Course* (1957) and *Montlhery: the Story of the Paris Autodrome, 1924-60* (1961); C. Clutton and others, *The Racing-car: Development and Design* (1962); William Court, *Power and Glory: Grand Prix Motorracing, 1906-1951* (1966); S. C. H. Davis, *Controlling a Racing-car Team* (1951) and *Motor Racing*, 3rd. ed. (1959); P. Frere, *Competition Driving* (1963); D. W. Hodges, *The French Grand Prix, 1906-66* (1967), *The Le Mans 24-Hour Race* (1963), and *Monaco Grand Prix* (1964); R. Hough, *Tourist Trophy; the History of Britain's Greatest Motor-race* (1957); P. Hull, *Racing an Historic Car* (1960); D. S. Jenkinson, *The Story of Formula One, 1954-1960* (1960); T. A. S. O. Mathieson, *Pictorial Survey of Racing-cars, 1919-1939* (1963); G. C. Monkhouse and R. Kingfarlow, *Grand Prix Racing: Facts and Figures*, 3rd ed. (1964); Lord Montagu, *The Gordon-Bennett Races* (1963); Stirling Moss and L. E. Pomeroy, *Design and Behaviour of the Racing-car* (1963); L. E. Pomeroy, *The Grand Prix Car*, vols. I and II (1954), and *The Evolution of the Racing-car* (1966); C. Posthumus, *World Sports Car Championship* (1961); G. Rose, *A Record of Motor-racing, 1894-1908* (1949); P. Taruffi, *The Technique of Motor-racing* (1959).

GOVERNING BODY (WORLD): Fédération Internationale de l'Automobile, 8 Place de la Concorde, Paris 8, France.

American motor racing covers a wide variety of competition, both in machinery and in format. Auto races attract more than 50 million paying spectators annually in venues that range from crude rural 'bullrings' to gigantic races like the Indianapolis 500, which draws approximately 300,000 spectators, and the United States Grand Prix at Watkins Glen, N.Y., which has attracted crowds of more than 100,000.

American motor racing is governed by five major bodies and dozens of minor regional clubs. The principal sanctioning bodies are the United States Auto Club, the National Association for Stock Car Auto Racing, the Sports Car Club of America, the International Motor Sports Association, and the National Hot Rod Association. These clubs are loosely allied in an agency named the Automobile Competition Committee for the United States–Fédération Internationale de l'Automobile (A.C.C.U.S. –F.I.A.). This agency serves as the national racing club in rather the same way that the Royal Automobile Club functions in Britain.

The United States Auto Club (U.S.A.C.) is a non-profit body which sanctions motor races in four major categories. Its principal division is the Championship Trail, which consists of an average of 12 races a year at various tracks for open-wheel, open-cockpit race cars that resemble the Formula One machines of Grand Prix competition. The most important of these races is the Indianapolis 500. Other U.S.A.C. divisions conduct races for stock cars (saloons) and for small open-wheel racers known as sprint cars and midgets. Virtually all U.S.A.C. racing is run on oval tracks in counter-clockwise direction, though occasional Championship Trail races have been conducted on road courses.

The Sports Car Club of America (S.C.C.A.) is the principal governing body of road racing in the U.S.A. A non-profit club with a membership of approximately 22,000, the S.C.C.A. sanctions racing meets, both professional and amateur. Its three nationwide professional series are the CAN-AM, TRANS-AM, and FORMULA 5000. Non-professional racing, usually called club racing, is organized on regional, divisional, and national levels. Chapters of the club — called regions — conduct not only race meets, but also such motorsports events as rallies, gymkhanas, hill climbs, solo time trials, ice races, *concours d'élégance*, etc.

Virtually all races in the United States are conducted by private entrepreneurs called promoters (equivalent to 'organizers' in Europe). Occasionally, races are conducted by non-profit companies operating for the benefit of local charities or the local communities. Promoters purchase sanctions (written authorizations) from the above-mentioned clubs.

Most American races are run on oval tracks similar in configuration to horse-racing tracks, with the cars running in a counter-clockwise direction for a stipulated number of laps. The tracks usually range in length from ½ mile (804·6 m.) to 2½ miles (4 km.). Oval tracks are customarily paved with asphalt compound, and their turns are banked to offset centrifugal force (the high-speed stock-car tracks are banked as much as 33 degrees). There still are a number of dirt-surface tracks, but they are disappearing because they are expensive to maintain and are hard on racing machines. Unlike road races, oval races are not run in the rain or even when the racing surface is wet. When rain halts a race or prevents it from starting, the race is postponed a week or more to a 'rain date'.

Apart from purely American road races, segments of the leading international racing series are conducted in the U.S.A., notably the United States Grand Prix, three units of the world manufacturers' championship, and the Can-Am.

Besides the races conducted on oval tracks and road courses, a significant amount of competition is run on straight quarter-mile (402 m.) courses called drag strips, the venue for drag racing (see below).

As for U.S.A. racing cars, almost anything on wheels is eligible for competition of one kind or another. Among the most popular categories are: (1) 'Championship' cars of the United States Auto Club, which race at INDIANAPOLIS MOTOR SPEEDWAY and similar ovals. (2) Stock cars, steel-bodied sedans (saloons) that race on oval tracks, reaching speeds of 200 m.p.h. (321·80 km./h.) on the straights. (3) Every kind of production sports car, 'sporty' cars, and specially made, all-out sports/racing cars, all of which compete on road courses. (4) The dragsters of drag racing, which range from conventional passenger cars to highly developed all-out racing machinery explicitly designed for this acceleration contest. There are many other types, such as formula cars (A, B, C, Ford, V, Super V, etc.), sprint cars, midget cars, 'jalopies' (old models rebuilt for racing), and even unmodified passenger cars.

As a rule, drivers of the cars that run on oval tracks (the first two categories above) are all professionals. The third and fourth categories include both amateur and professional drivers. Amateurs participate extensively in club racing organized by the Sports Car Club of America and lesser clubs.

As in Europe, motor racing in the U.S.A. is extremely expensive. The sport could scarcely exist without the support of commercial sponsors who use racing as a promotional tool to sell their products. The three most common forms of sponsorship are the underwriting of (1) a racing team, as in the Samsonite Special, sponsored by a luggage manufacturer; (2) individual races, as in the Schaefer Trans-Am, supported by a brewing company; and (3) a racing series, as in the L. & M. 5000 Championship and the Winston Cup, sponsored by cigarette companies.

In ROAD RACING, cars compete, as in Europe, on closed courses that simulate country roads, courses similar to the popular European venues like BRANDS HATCH and Monza. Road races are still occasionally held on courses delineated by traffic pylons on former airports or on airports which are temporarily closed. There are no longer any races run on public roads, these having been prohibited some years ago because of the danger to spectators and participants.

Road racing can be a hobby or pastime, as in club racing (see below), or it can be intensely professional. The leading professional series are the Can-Am, for Group 7 sports/racing cars; the Formula 5000 for open-wheel cars; and three of the world manufacturers' championship endurance events for cars of various types (Daytona, Road Atlanta, Watkins Glen). Apart from these series, there is the most important single road race of all, the United States Grand Prix, in which points count towards the world championship of drivers. The first U.S. Grand Prix was held in 1959 at Sebring, Florida, and second in 1960 at Riverside, California. Since 1961 the race has been held on the first Sunday of October at Watkins Glen, a magnificent road course in a wooded setting in upstate New York.

Nearly all road racing is sanctioned by the Sports Car Club of America, the participation of other clubs being negligible. The principal road courses are Daytona International Speedway, Daytona Beach, Florida; Laguna Seca, Monterey, California; Lime Rock Park, Lime Rock, Connecticut; Michigan International Speedway, Cambridge Junction, Michigan; Mid-Ohio Sports Car Course, Lexington, Ohio; Riverside International Raceway, Riverside, California; Road America, Elkhart Lake, Wisconsin; Road Atlanta, Flowery Branch, Georgia; and Watkins Glen Grand Prix Course, Watkins Glen, N.Y.

CLUB RACING in the U.S.A. is a programme of road races organized by the Sports Car Club of America and smaller organizations. At the lower levels of competition — 'regional' races — most of the drivers are amateurs who pay their own expenses. At the more advanced level — the 'national' races — the drivers may be amateur or professional. Club racing is 'amateur' in the sense that no purses are offered. However, many of the participants may be classed as professionals because they are paid fees, retainers, or salaries by the manufacturers of the cars they drive. Such drivers also receive money from other manufacturers whose products they use or promote.

Cars used in club racing run the gamut of road-racing machinery, from modest Sprites to sophisticated Formula 5000 cars and Group 7 sports/racing cars. The races are short, seldom more than half an hour. Racing programmes are organized within prescribed geographical areas of the United States, with each division determining the champions in 22 classes of cars. In November the leaders of all these divisions are invited to compete in a national run-off called the American Road Race of Champions, a three-day meet held on the course of Road Atlanta in Georgia.

OFF-ROAD RACING is conducted primarily in the deserts of the western U.S.A. and in Baja California, the remote peninsular region of north-western Mexico. It is to the motorist what cross-country running is to the athlete, and involves cars racing over or through almost any surface other than one designed to take a motor car. It developed out of the popular postwar pastime of motor-cycle trail riding, and is necessarily restricted by the demands of the course. Racing conditions are extraordinarily rugged, though not unduly dangerous, over unmarked territory.

Competition is open to a wide range of vehicles. The most successful entrants are 'buggies' with four-wheel drive, and motor cycles. There are also light trucks and specially prepared passenger cars. Vehicles designed for the purpose are as light as possible (often with a tubular chassis and fibreglass coachwork) and capable of speeds up to 150 m.p.h. (241 km./h.). The length of races is arbitrary, from one or two hours up to 30 hours.

The leading races are the springtime Baja 500 and the autumn Mexican 1000, both run in Baja California (though virtually all the contestants are Americans). In the gigantic Mexican 1000, competitors race 832 miles (1,339 km.) down a mountainous route running from Ensenada in the north to the near-tropical city of La Paz. As there are few towns of any size in the region, and some of the villages are nearly 90 miles (145 km.) apart, the race is largely a test of a crew's mechanical ingenuity in keeping their vehicle moving. The Mexican 1000 is open to motor cycles as well as two- or four-wheel-drive cars; despite the large entry fee of $250 there are usually more than 250 drivers competing for a first prize of $10,000. Amateur drivers compete for adventure, but the professionals compete earnestly because the races are highly important for the commercial exploitation of motoring products.

As a rule it is not feasible to conduct off-road races for the entertainment of paying spectators, but several American promotions — notably the Mint 400 in Nevada — have desert courses where spectator facilities can be built.

Japan and Australia are among the few countries to which the sport of off-road racing is spreading. Elsewhere its development is threatened by the continually-increasing number of roads.

STOCK-CAR RACING is most popular in the rural areas of the South, where it matches or surpasses FOOTBALL, BASEBALL, and BASKETBALL in paid attendance. Stock cars, with engines of up to 7 litres' piston displacement, are steel-bodied sedans (saloons) specially prepared for racing. They run counterclockwise on oval tracks ranging from rural venues $\frac{1}{4}$ to $\frac{1}{2}$ mile (402–805 m.) in length to 'super-speedways' of one to 2·6 miles (4 km.). Nearly all tracks are paved, though a few small dirt tracks are still in use. On steeply banked super-speedways such as Daytona and Talladega the racing is very fast and lap speeds of 180 m.p.h. (289·6 km./h.) are commonplace.

Some races are as much folk festival as sport. Drivers and car builders have become folk heroes — LEE PETTY, one of the early champions; his son, RICHARD PETTY, who has won twice as many races as any other driver and taken more than a million dollars in winnings; Yunick, a car builder, ingenious at getting round the rules; ROBERTS, who was burned to death in a racing accident; TURNER, Johnson, Owens, and Matthews.

Stock-car racing has unusual antecedents, from the mountains to the sea. In the mountains, distillers of illicit whisky used passenger cars to deliver their products to the cities. Their cars had to be race-prepared to evade law-enforcement officers, and their drivers needed to perfect every kind of road skill. Match races in the mountains and on dusty fields became a pastime. Meanwhile, in the 1930s and 1940s, before many formal race tracks were built, stock-car owners were running organized races on the hard surface of Daytona Beach, Florida. Daytona International Speedway succeeded the beach in 1959 as the Mecca of stock-car racing.

The greatest crowd-pleasers of today's racing are the Grand National cars, competition versions of late-model (from the three most recent production years) Fords, Plymouths, Dodges, Mercurys, and Chevrolets. Older and less powerful cars are classified Late Model Sportsman, Modified, and Hobby. Still another division is the Grand American, open to late-model 'sporty' sedans like Mustang, Camaro, Javelin, Barracuda, Challenger, and Firebird.

The resemblance between a passenger car and a stock car of the same name is only superficial. The specially built racing engine costs more than $6,000. Every part of the car — chassis, body, suspension, steering, brakes, drive-train — is reworked or replaced for racing performance, endurance, and safety.

Stock-car racing is characterized by speed, thrills, and skill. Drafting or towing — that is, following closely in the wake of a car — is familiar in most forms of motor racing, but nowhere is it more spectacularly practised than in stock-car racing. What is remarkable is that the drafting driver is manoeuvring a two-ton machine at 175 to 200 m.p.h. (281 – 322 km./h.) within an arm's length of the car ahead.

The draft leads to another practice, the 'slingshot'. At a strategic moment the drafting

driver breaks out of the airstream and, with the power he has been reserving, 'slings' past his rival. The slingshot is used most theatrically on the last lap of a race, when there is not enough time left for the victim to retaliate.

At such speed, and in such close quarters, accidents are inevitable. Usually the driver is unhurt or he suffers only bruises and scratches. His safety is attributable to the construction of a safety-roll cage inside the car. This is a network of steel pipes that surrounds the driver and prevents the car from being crushed into a ball.

Pit stops, to replenish fuel and to replace worn tyres and for emergency repairs, are an attraction in themselves. The brightly dressed mechanics are drilled to function without wasting time. Five men change two tyres, pour 22 gallons (100 litres) of petrol into the tank, wash the windscreen, give the driver a drink of water, and send the car back into the race in as few as 22 seconds. Races may be won or lost by the pit crews' performance.

Most pit stops are scheduled, but others are made to take advantage of the yellow caution flag. Whenever a wreck spills oil or strews débris, maintenance crews rush out to tidy up the track. During this work the race is slowed to half the normal speed, and no car may improve its position. Drivers exploit this period to hurry into the pits without sacrificing their position. Because the field is running slowly, a driver can rush out in time to resume his place in the procession, cross the finish line, and get credit for a completed lap. Caution periods also have the exciting effect of creating another flying start when the emergency is over and the green flag comes out again.

The longer Grand National races run to 250 to 600 miles (402 – 965 km.), attract crowds of 50,000 to 100,000, and offer purses and accessory awards of up to $200,000. Shorter Grand National races are held at smaller tracks, altogether about 50 per season.

Not all stock-car racing is of the Grand National type. Of the nearly 1,200 races sanctioned annually by the National Association for Stock-Car Auto Racing (N.A.S.C.A.R.), close to 1,100 are for the older Sportsman, Modified, and Hobby Divisions. Stock-car racing could not exist without these basic 20-mile races in the small towns. Those races also serve as a training ground for drivers. N.A.S.C.A.R. is the dominant sanctioning club, but a fairly substantial share of stock-car racing is also authorized by other organizations.

DRAG RACING is a specialized form of motor racing and a test of sheer acceleration. Drag races are run in a series of quarter-mile

(402·3 m.) standing-start straight-line sprints, the sport is most strongly established in its country of origin, the U.S.A., but also appears, in more restricted form, in Australia, Canada, England, Germany, Italy, Japan, New Zealand, and Sweden.

Drag-race meetings are organized on an eliminating basis in a number of car classes. These are decided by the vehicles' mode of construction; whether they are modified production models or specially designed and constructed; the state of 'tune' (modification) of their engines; and what kind of fuel they use. Ordinary pump-petrol produces less power than specially prepared methanol-type fuels, and these fall respectively into the 'gas' and 'fuel' categories.

Races usually take place on specially built 'drag strips', although they are scarce outside the U.S.A. where airfield runways serve just as well. The strip measures 440 yds. (402 m.) from start to finish line and is straight, with side-by-side lanes for two cars making simultaneous 'runs'. Electronic timing apparatus is used exclusively. An electronic speed trap is arranged near the finish line, extending for 66 ft. (20 m.) on either side of it, and a 'shutdown area' beyond the line extends for not less than 220 yds. (201 m.), allowing safe deceleration at the end of the run. Parallel service roads allow traffic to return to the paddock area behind the starting line.

The timing apparatus records each car's 'elapsed time' (ET) in covering the run and its 'terminal velocity' through the finish-line speed trap. But these figures are virtually of academic interest only; the winner of each eliminating drag race is the car which crosses the finishing line first, regardless of a better ET or faster 'terminal' by its competitor. These figures come into account only so far as a meeting's top eliminator over-all and records are concerned.

The start is usually signalled by a 'Christmas tree' device in which a descending series of five yellow lights wink on at half-second intervals, leading to a sixth (green) light signalling the start. A seventh (red) light indicates disqualification should the car in that lane anticipate the starting signal and begin its run early.

Hence it is of prime importance for the driver to have peak power available and his car's clutch engaging as the green light comes up, but not before and not later. If he 'drops' the clutch late, even though he may recover to record a faster ET, his competitor can reach the finish line first.

Conversely, if he applies too much power his car may hesitate with the rear wheels spinning uselessly and imparting no forward motion. Again, once he gets under way his ET may be better, but if he fails to reach the finish line first he will be eliminated. The 'top eliminator' in each class is eligible for an award as is the fastest eliminator over-all, the latter almost certainly from the 'AA/Fueler' class.

Class demarcations originally evolved by the American National Hot-Rod Association have now been generally accepted internationally. They denote the class, and the following letter or letters the division. Thus A/S denotes a class A car in the 'stock' (production) category, while A/SA describes a class A stock car with automatic transmission.

The AA/Fueler cars are the specially developed 'slingshots' or 'rails' which use supercharged, very large-capacity production-based engines, modified to run on methanol-type fuels and often producing more than three times their original power output. These drive direct to wide rear wheels carrying specialized 'slick' (gummy rubber) tyres. The driver sits behind the back axle, encased in a rigid anti-crash structure and clad in flame-proof clothing, face mask, gauntlets, and crash helmet. The front end of the slingshot is a lightweight tubular structure carrying a very wide-track torsion-bar front axle with cycle-type steerable wheels. Such vehicles have recorded ETs of as little as 5·91 seconds for the standing-start quarter-mile, and terminal velocities of 243·9 m.p.h. (394 km./h.).

There are also the outlandish 'fuel dragsters' and so-called 'funny cars', the latter popular because they are built to resemble ordinary passenger cars. They have 1500 h.p. engines running on alcohol blends, and complete the quarter-mile in less than 7 seconds; by the time they reach the finish line they are moving at more than 200 m.p.h. (321·8 km./h.) and need two parachutes to slow them down.

Drag racing's precise origins are lost in the 'folk-lore' of the early Californian hot-rod movement, between the world wars. Enthusiasts modified various Model A and Model T Fords, and the occasional Chevrolet, in order to increase their maximum speed. The efficacy of these modifications was tested against the clock in regular meetings on the bed of Muroc Dry Lake in the Southern California desert. There, high-speed runs were made over a measured quarter-mile, and constant disputes over the accuracy of the timing and fears for contestants' safety led, in 1937, to the formation of the Southern California Timing Association (S.C.T.A.), whose activities made competition much more firmly based and properly regulated.

It was inevitable that the hot-rod movement should boom in the immediate postwar years with ex-servicemen using their mechanical skills on modified motor cars. Acceleration from traffic lights on public streets became a standard test of ability, and competition from neighbourhood to neighbourhood became intense. Naturally the police frowned on such activities, as did the S.C.T.A. which imposed strict penalties on members found guilty of 'dragging' on the streets.

Official meetings began on dry lake-beds immediately after the war, but impromptu drag races brought the hot-rod movement such a bad name that the threat of restrictive legislation in 1947 led the S.C.T.A. to limit its members' activities still further while looking for suitable private venues. In 1950 they ran a 'hot-rod versus motor-cycle' drag meeting at a former naval base near Santa Ana, Calif. This was a great success and more local air-strips quickly became available as drag and hot-rod venues. Various types of competition were tried, but as the hot-rod movement mushroomed so the standard form of standing-start quarter-mile sprints evolved.

A national co-ordinating body was sorely needed to unify regulations and in 1951 *Hot Rod* magazine proposed a National Hot-Rod Association (N.H.R.A.), which later came into being. The N.H.R.A. regulations ensured a nationwide conformity of requirements which put the new sport on a sound footing. It developed rapidly throughout the 1950s.

The lightweight 1949 GM '88' coupé, using the over-square Rocket V8 engine, proved immensely popular early on, for its power-to-weight ratio was the most favourable of any current production model. In 1951-2 Chrysler produced their more powerful Firepower V8 engine, and these stock models now proved superior to the highly tuned pre-war side-valve ('flat-head') machines used so far.

During the 1950s experimentation was rife, with aero-engined and sometimes twin-engined monsters running against cars whose owners were delving, sometimes disastrously, into the realms of chemical fuel mixtures based on methyl-alcohol ('methanol'). Terminal speed barriers were demolished one by one, 135 m.p.h. (217 km./h.) being surpassed in 1953, 150 m.p.h. (241 km./h.) in 1955, and 160 m.p.h. (257 km./h.) early in 1957. Fuels other than pump-grade petrol were banned on safety grounds in that year but, despite grumbles, 'gasser' speeds were soon approaching previous records.

The sport was quickly established in many states, and the N.H.R.A.'s first national championship meeting was held at Great Bend, Kansas, from 29 September to 2 October 1955, thereafter becoming an annual event.

Vehicle development had been very rapid. Road tyres soon proved inadequate and specialist re-treaders and tyre-builders evolved the 'Slick' tyre, with gummy, rubber-compound flexible walls and a broad bald tread to promote maximum traction. Weight was pruned drastically by abbreviating body-work and chassis structures, removing virtually all trace of suspension (possible since the racing strips are billiard-smooth), and even dispensing with the gear-box, using a single-gear direct drive between engine and rear wheels.

Generally the Americans led the world in this specialist motor-car development but until the 1970s their sprint and drag motor cycles (see MOTOR-CYCLE RACING) lagged behind those, notably in England, where air-strip quarter-mile and kilometre sprints had been contested by enthusiastic and skilled amateurs, such as HAGON.

By 1960 the giant Detroit manufacturers were becoming interested in the publicity offered by drag-racing success and the stock or production-car classes assumed new importance with factory-assisted entries.

Fuel technology had reached new peaks by 1963 and the ban on special mixtures was relaxed. Times now dropped dramatically below 9 seconds, and in August 1964 GARLITS became the first man to exceed 200 m.p.h. with figures of 7·78 seconds, 201·34 m.p.h. (323·96 km./h.).

In the late 1960s American drag motor-cyclists, such as E. J. Potter, were installing V-8 car engines in two-wheeled frames and setting extremely fast times.

Overseas demonstrations of four-wheeled drag racing were arranged by the N.H.R.A. in the early 1960s, and as a result the sport gained a footing in Europe, Japan, and Australasia, although on nothing like the American scale. There is only one permanent strip, Santa Pod, in use in England, and generally very few permanent facilities are to be found outside the U.S.A. Nowhere is the sport established on such a professional basis, and nowhere does it receive such intense trade support as in America. International recognition was granted to the sport in 1965 when it was finally accepted by the Fédération Internationale de l'Automobile.

Lyle K. Engel, *The Complete Book of Auto Racing* (1969) and *Road Racing in America* (1971); Wally Parks, *Drag Racing, Yesterday and Today* (1966); John S. Radosta, *The New York Times Complete Guide to Auto Racing* (1971).
GOVERNING BODIES (U.S.A.): Automobile Competition Committee for the United States-F.I.A. Inc., 1725 K Street, N.W., Washington, D.C.; United States Auto Club, 4910 West 16th Street, Speed-

way, Ind.; International Motor Sports Association, P.O. Box 805, Fairfield, Conn.; National Off-Road Racing Association, 19730 Ventura Boulevard, Woodland Hills, Calif.; National Association for Stock Car Auto Racing, P.O. Box K, Daytona Beach, Fla.; National Hot Rod Association, 10639 Riverside Drive, North Hollywood, Calif.

Motor rallies differ from motor races by being run mainly over public roads, although there is a growing dislike of this on the part of not only the authorities but the competitors. Sections of the roads may be closed while competitors cover a timed stage, and because the cars which compete are usually saloon-bodied vehicles of catalogue type in appearance, although extensively modified. The undesirability of allowing fast driving on public highways has tended to change the nature of rallying. It is now customary to have comparatively slow routes with high-speed timed runs on private roads, driving tests or regularity runs on aerodromes, etc, to score the points culminating in awards. This is particularly so in Britain, where the International R.A.C. Rally uses many sections of Forestry Commission roads, on which high speeds over testing terrain can be achieved without endangering the public.

Each of the great rallies counting towards the annual rally championship has a character of its own, but the growing use in Britain of forest roads has brought into prominence Scandinavian rally drivers who are familiar with these conditions.

Modern international rallies are run at such high speeds and over such arduous routes that standard cars would fail to complete the course and public interest in what would seem to be comparatively meagre performances would wane. Consequently, support crews are permitted to repair damage and even change vital mechanical parts *en route*; this, incidentally, is a safety measure, as otherwise rally cars might use the road in a dangerous condition, with defective brakes and tyres, etc. Drivers are advised by skilled navigators reading pace notes, i.e., listed information about corners to be encountered and how weather conditions are likely to affect the speed at which the rally car can be taken over a section of timed-performance road. Other crews are even used to drive over such sections in advance of the actual rally crews, so that the very latest information can be fed to them. Another way in which rallying differs from ordinary high-speed touring is that many different types of tyres are used, to suit prevailing and varied road conditions, even to metal-studded tyres enabling quite remarkable road-holding and heavy braking to be achieved on black ice without disaster. Factory support-teams pro-

vide supplies of different tyres at strategic points, and change the wheels as required. Such factory support is extremely expensive, while the rally cars themselves, although outwardly catalogue saloons, may cost upwards of £10,000.

One rally in which support vehicles are less prominent and in which, at least until recently, more normal cars competed, originally on a price-class basis, is the East African Safari Rally, dominated in 1971 by Japanese Datsun cars, and won in 1972 and 1973 respectively by Ford and Datsun. At the opposite extreme are the long-duration rallies: the London–Sydney Marathon and the 1970 World Cup Rally from London to Mexico, both sponsored by newspapers and won, respectively, by a Hillman Hunter and a Ford Escort Mexico. Both were highly specialized cars driven by extremely skilled and experienced crews. In spite of financial and political difficulties, a revised World Cup Rally was scheduled for 1974.

In essence, a rally car will be a saloon with tuned engine giving extra horsepower, equipped so that the co-driver can sleep while off duty, with quartz iodine lamps for fast night driving, a steel guard or sump-shield to protect the engine from damage from rocks or boulders, strengthened body and suspension, and long-range fuel tanks. Often there will be reinforced roof and other parts of the structure to safeguard the occupants should the car roll over or go off the road, and plastic windows. Aluminium body panels, magnesium wheels, etc. will be used to reduce weight. There will be provision for lighting for map-reading and usually a curtained-off table at which the navigator can work, because no time can be spared for departing from the correct route, which the organizers convey to the crew in route-books.

The winning World Cup Ford Escort in 1970 carried 29 gallons (132 litres) of petrol in three tanks and 2 gallons (9 litres) of orange juice. In this rally which covered 16,244 miles (26,141 km.), the cars' radiators were protected to fend off kangaroos or llamas. But similar rallies on a much less ambitious scale are held in Britain almost every week-end, with the emphasis on map-reading on by-roads, mostly after dark. These are carefully controlled by the R.A.C. to obviate annoyance to the public. Women drivers compete against the men and expert navigators are at a premium.

Regulations covering the international rally championship prescribe details of qualifying cars, route lengths to be covered, the frequency of control points, the allocation of points, and the minimum number of starters in a race. Qualifying events are the Swedish

Rally, TAP Rally, East African Safari, Acropolis Rally, Heatway Rally, Rally of the Thousand Lakes, Alpine Rally, San Remo Rally, Rally of the Rideau Lakes, Press-on-Regardless Rally, RAC Rally, and Tour de Course.

Similarly, the regulations governing the European rally championship for drivers cover the types of car eligible, permitted modifications, route lengths, the allocation of points, and so on. Qualifying events under the 1974 regulations were the Marlboro Arctic Rally, Rallye Costa Brava, Snow Rally, Rallye of San Marino, Shell Rally, Rallye Firestone, Circuit of Ireland, Rally de l'Ile d'Elba, Tulip Rally, Criterium Alpin, Welsh Rally, Paris–St. Raphael, Wiesbaden Rally, YU Rally, Samperit Rally, Scottish Rally, Rallye d'Antibes, and JAMT Rally.

In addition, there are more than 20 other important international rallies, ranging from the Circuit of Galway to the Ethiopian Highland Rally. In Finland, rallying is as popular as CRICKET in England as a national sport.

Originally rallies were held entirely on public roads and traversed either a country or countries, crossing much European terrain. The test lay in checking-in at widely spaced control points, neither too early nor too late if penalties were to be avoided. The average speeds set tested the stamina and reliability of the cars and long all-day followed by all-night sessions proved a similar strain on drivers and navigators.

Before the Second World War rallies consisted entirely of main-road runs, at what were regarded as stiff average speeds, culminating at a well-known town, where a car beauty show, or *concours d'élégance*, might form a separate part of the proceedings. The famous Monte Carlo Rally, first held in 1911, was typical. Competitors' cars were divided into many classes, dependent on the size of their engines, and were required to clock in at a given time after the start. From being a semi-social touring rally, this emerged as a tough competition well before the war and, because of the widespread publicity it received, especially through press and radio, it became of great importance to the leading car manufacturers to do well in this event. It gained status from being held in January, when winter conditions could usually be relied on to make the drivers' task extremely difficult. Even so, as cars and roads improved, the Monte Carlo Rally was not always won on the very long road sections, which once started from John o' Groats in Scotland and from points behind what is now the Iron Curtain, and it became necessary to incorporate elaborate driving tests, often of a freak nature, in order to find the outright and class winners from those who had successfully accomplished the road sections without loss of marks. In later years a high-speed near-race round the difficult mountain sections behind Monte Carlo was used for this purpose.

The interest shown, until recently, in the Monte Carlo Rally and therefore the very valuable publicity secured by those makes of cars which performed well, led other capitals and clubs to organize similar motoring competitions, often from town to town within a given country or over a circular route starting and finishing at the same place. This resulted in the institution of an annual rally championship.

Among the famous rallies of pre-war status was the Alpine Trial, later called the Alpine Rally. This involved making very fast times up a series of testing Alpine passes, and any car which lost no marks and thereby qualified for one of the coveted Coupes des Alpes was assured of excellent publicity likely to result in increased sales. Unfortunately Switzerland, with its growing traffic problems, has frowned on rallying and Alpine routes, famous from the days of the Austrian Alpine Trials of 1911-14, have had to be modified.

Another changed aspect of international rallying has been that the intense competition and desire to be successful has caused manufacturers not only to prepare highly specialized cars but to support them with supplies of spare parts, replacement tyres, and hordes of skilled mechanics who can change damaged components and beat out battered body panels very quickly — an aspect of rallying scarcely thought of before the war. Organizers, by permitting these activities and the entry of specially modified and constructed cars, have encouraged a move away from rallying by catalogue-type cars which the public can buy.

Nick Brittan, *Safari Fever* (1972); Marcus Chambers, *Seven-Year Twitch* (1962).
GOVERNING BODY (WORLD): Fédération Internationale de l'Automobile, 8 Place de la Concorde, Paris 8, France.

MOTOR RALLIES, See MOTOR RACING: MOTOR RALLIES.

MOTTRAM, ANTHONY JOHN (1920-), Britain's leading LAWN TENNIS player in the years after the Second World War and the LAWN TENNIS ASSOCIATION's director of coaching from 1970. Between 1947 and 1955 Mottram played in 56 Davis Cup (see LAWN TENNIS) rubbers, at that time a British record. He reached the men's doubles final at WIMBLEDON in 1947 with Sidwell (Australia) and the quarter-finals of the singles the following year.

MOTZ, RICHARD CHARLES (1940-   ), cricketer for New Zealand and Canterbury. A dauntless fast-medium bowler, in 1969 he became the first to take 100 Test wickets for New Zealand, though injury during that tour of England brought an end to his career at the top level. He was also a lusty hitter, batting low in the order.

MOULD, Mrs. MARION (*née* Coakes), (1947-   ), British show jumping (see EQUESTRIAN EVENTS) rider. She was the first woman ever to win an individual Olympic medal for show jumping when she was runner-up on Stroller in Mexico in 1968. She won the women's world championship on Stroller in 1965.

MOUNIER, JEAN-JACQUES (1946-   ), French JUDO fighter who won the European lightweight title in 1970, 1971, and 1972 and was a bronze medallist in the Munich Olympics. His skilful evasions and sudden throwing techniques made him one of the few Europeans to match the Japanese in the lighter weight divisions.

MOUNT WASHINGTON, LACROSSE club in Baltimore, Maryland, U.S.A., developed in 1904 from the Mount Washington Cricket and Country Club, whose ground, Roland Park, was taken over by the lacrosse club. Within a few years Mount Washington became the leading non-university club in America. More recently the membership has been made up of American 'all-star' players. The club was chosen to represent the U.S.A. in the world field lacrosse tournament in Canada in 1967, when it defeated Australia, Canada, and England.

MOUNTFORD, CECIL (1921-   ), New Zealand RUGBY LEAGUE player. In a period notable for the quality of stand-off half play, he established himself as one of the most accomplished players of all times. From Blackball, South Island, he joined WIGAN in 1946, and over a remarkably long period he retained an exceptional speed off the mark. After ten years with WARRINGTON as player and manager from 1952, he returned to New Zealand to become director of coaching for the League.

MOYES, WILLIAM (1936-   ), Australian water skier who set the first ski kite-flying record of 2,890 ft. (880·86 m.).

M.T.K. BUDAPEST, Association FOOTBALL club. Founded in 1888 and known variously as Hungaria, Textilesek, Bastya, and Red Banner before it became M.T.K. once more in 1956, the club had been 14 times champions of Hungary up to 1958. M.T.K. have appeared in all three European club competitions and reached the final of the Cup-Winners Cup in 1964 when they were beaten by the Sporting Club of Portugal. Leading players have included Konrad, Schaefer, Cresh, HIDEGKUTI, K. Sandor, and Sipos.

COLOURS: Blue hooped and white shirts, white shorts.

MUIR, KAREN YVETTE (1952-   ), South African swimmer who was the youngest competitor in any sport to break a world record. She was just 12 years, 10 months, and 25 days old on 10 August 1965 when she took $\frac{7}{10}$ second off the world mark for 110 yards backstroke in a heat of the English junior championship at Blackpool, Lancashire. The exclusion of her country from the 1968 Mexico City Games robbed her of certain Olympic honours, since at that time she held all four world records for backstroke.

MUIRFIELD, Scottish GOLF course, home of the Honourable Company of Edinburgh Golfers, is incontrovertibly by the seaside — the Firth of Forth. However, it is not of essentially seaside character and KIRKALDY's description of it as 'an auld watter meddie' may have been unjustly harsh. It is a true championship course, open, maintained in most beautiful order, and absolutely fair in that all the dangers are clearly visible. Possibly it is too straightforward; this was certainly the view of the Open championship committee of 1966, who ordained that the rough should be allowed to encroach and grow to inordinate length.

MULDOON, WILLIAM (1845-   ), outstanding American wrestler of the nineteenth century. He got his early training in saloons, the army and the police — he won the New York Police heavyweight title. In 1880 he defeated Bauer for the American Graeco-Roman title and a year later became a full-time professional. He had three draws with Whistler, the leading contender for the title, the first bout lasting eight hours. In 1883 he had a series of bouts with the Briton, Bibby, but after two draws he knocked Bibby out with a tremendous throw. He then beat another Englishman, Cannon, in two hard bouts. For many years Muldoon toured America with SULLIVAN, the world's first heavyweight BOXING champion. He also ran a successful wrestling booth and retired at the age of 50 to become an official.

MULLEN, KARL D., RUGBY UNION hooker for OLD BELVEDERE, Ireland, and British LIONS. Having led Ireland in their Triple Crown years of 1948 and 1949, he was awarded the captaincy of the Lions touring party to New Zealand and Australia in 1950.

MULLIGAN, ANDREW ARMSTRONG (1936-), RUGBY UNION scrum half for Cambridge University, LONDON IRISH, Paris University club, Ireland, and British LIONS. A quick, athletic player, and usually the dominant partner at half-back, he played in three successive University matches (1955-7), and won 22 Irish caps. Reserve to JEEPS, he was selected for only one British Lions Test, against New Zealand in 1959; this was the Lions' single Test victory.

MURDOCH, WILLIAM LLOYD (1855-1911), cricketer for Australia, England, New South Wales, Sussex, and London County. Originally a wicket-keeper, he was the first Australian batsman to attain world class. Scorer of the first double-century in Tests, he led four Australian sides to England, including, in 1880, the first to play a Test match (in which he scored 153 not out). He joined Sussex in 1893 and captained them until 1899, playing for GRACE's London County team until 1904. He appeared once for England, against South Africa in 1892.

MURLESS, C. F. N. (1910-), a leading English race-horse trainer, of Warren Place, Newmarket. In 1957 the horses in his stable set a record by winning prize money to the value of £116,898 for a single season, a sum which he himself surpassed with £145,727 in 1959, and again in 1967 with a total of £256,899. In 1973 he was again top trainer with £132,984. Murless trained Carrozza to win the OAKS for the Queen, Crepello to win the DERBY and TWO THOUSAND GUINEAS for SASSOON, PETITE ÉTOILE, ST. PADDY, and ROYAL PALACE.

MURPHY, ALEXANDER JOHN (1939-), outstanding RUGBY LEAGUE player and coach. He has played in 20 major trophy finals for ST. HELENS (with whom he first played at the age of 16), Leigh, and WARRINGTON, and led all three clubs to victory in Challenge Cup finals. Warrington reached the finals of four major trophies under his direction in 1973-4. He played 27 times for Great Britain against Australia, New Zealand, and France as a scrum half, and was also markedly successful for his clubs as a stand-off half.

MURPHY, NOEL ARTHUR (1938-), RUGBY UNION flank forward for CORK CONSTITUTION and Ireland. Although twice dropped by Ireland for a whole season, he was recalled in 1969, at the age of 30, to lead the pack and bring his total number of caps to 41, a national record for a forward. He is the son of N. F. Murphy, an Ireland wing-forward of the early 1930s, and later president of the Irish Rugby Union.

MURRAYFIELD, Edinburgh, headquarters and home ground of the Scottish RUGBY UNION since 1925. Built on the outskirts of Edinburgh, as successor to RAEBURN PLACE and INVERLEITH, it is the largest Rugby ground in the British Isles with a capacity of 78,500, although only 15,500 spectators are under cover. It was also the first Rugby ground to install an electrical heating system beneath the turf.

MUSIAL, STANLEY FRANK (1920-), American BASEBALL player with the ST. LOUIS CARDINALS from 1941 to 1962. He played outfield and first base but achieved most distinction as a batter. He won the NATIONAL LEAGUE batting championship seven times, and on retirement had set a National League record for most hits, 3,630.

MV AGUSTA, Italian motor-cycle manufacturers, established in 1946 and prominent in racing from 1951. Although active in the smaller classes, MV were best known for their four-cylinder machines which, modelled on the GILERA, dominated the 500 and 350 cc. classes from 1958. In an effort to remain competitive against HONDA, MV produced new three-cylinder machines for 1966 and these were still, in 1972, consistently the fastest and most successful in the world championship series. In 1973 they met stiff opposition, and new four-cylinder machines barely succeeded in retaining the championships in the two classes.

MYERS, ARTHUR WALLIS (1878-1939), the most celebrated of British LAWN TENNIS critics and a prolific writer on the game. As lawn tennis correspondent of the London *Daily Telegraph* and lawn tennis editor of *The Field*, he was the game's first major historian and exercised a considerable influence on its early development.

He saw every Davis Cup (see LAWN TENNIS) challenge round beginning with the first match at LONGWOOD and his annual ranking list of the ten best players was regarded as authoritative by the lawn tennis world. He was himself a competent player, particularly in doubles. In 1910 he and Doust, another player who turned journalist, won the Monte Carlo title, one of the most important in Europe, by beating Ritchie, who had reached the challenge round at WIMBLEDON the previous year, and Decugis, the leading French player of the day.

Myers was a vivid reporter and a kindly critic, and his volume in the Lonsdale Library, *Lawn Tennis — Its Principles and Practice*, is one of the classic analyses of the game. He has one other monument. In 1923 he founded the INTERNATIONAL CLUB of Great Britain, a body which soon had offshoots in many countries and which was formed for the purpose of fostering friendship through lawn tennis among players of different nationalities.

MYNN, ALFRED (1807-1861), cricketer for Kent. A formidable fast round-arm bowler, he was an outstanding figure in the great Kent teams of the 1830s and 1840s, and a major force for the South against the North, and for Gentlemen *v.* Players. A large man, portly in later life, he was also a hard-hitting batsman.

N

NACHMANN, FRITZ (1929-), luge TOBOGGANING rider for West Germany; world singles champion in 1963; and twice world pairs champion, each time partnered by Strillinger, in 1957 and 1968.

NACIONAL, Association FOOTBALL club, Montevideo. The club was formed in 1899 when Defensor F.C. amalgamated with Montevideo F.C. and, in keen competition with the PENAROL club, it has always dominated football in Uruguay. The national championship was first won by Nacional in 1902, and between 1939 and 1943 Nacional won five consecutive titles. The club's most successful recent season was 1964 when it reached the final of the South American Cup for the continent's leading clubs. Leading players have included Petrone, Scarone, Santamaria, Perez, and E. Alvarez.
COLOURS: Red, white, and blue.

NADI, NEDO (1894-1940), son of Beppe Nadi, the famous master at Livorno. An outstanding fencer at all weapons, he became a FENCING master, but was later reinstated as an amateur and became president of the Italian Fencing Federation. He won the Olympic foil championship in 1912, and both the Olympic foil and sabre championships in 1920 — the only person ever to win the two titles in the same year.

NAGLE, KELVIN (1920-), Australian professional golfer. He was Open champion 1960 and Australian Open champion 1959; Australian professional champion five times; New Zealand professional champion three times; and winner of the New Zealand Open six times. He was the winner of the WORLD CUP (in partnership with P. W. THOMSON) in 1954 and 1959.

NAGURSKI, BRONISLAW (Bronco) (1908-), American college and professional FOOTBALL player, who was in the All-Century college team as tackle and sometimes fullback at the University of MINNESOTA (1927-9). With the CHICAGO BEARS in professional football (1930-7, with a return in 1943), he was football's most effective fullback, reputedly the strongest man for his size (6 ft. 2 in. — 1·88 m.; 217 lb. — 98·4 kg.) who ever

played, capable of running through or round a defensive line without any supporting blockers.

NAISMITH, Dr. JAMES A. (1861-1939), inventor of BASKETBALL. Naismith was born in Canada, but became a national of the U.S.A; he was educated at McGill University in Canada, where he obtained degrees in medicine and theology, later becoming Professor of Physical Education at the University of Kansas. He invented basketball while at the International Y.M.C.A. Training School at Springfield, Massachusetts, in 1891.

In 1930 he undertook a study of the physical stresses to which a basketball player was subjected. He concluded that, although the game was extremely strenuous, there was little danger of damage to the heart and kidneys as had been feared.

The Naismith Basketball Hall of Fame, to which outstanding American players and officials are elected, was founded in Naismith's honour in 1959.

NAKAYAMA, MASATOSHI (1913-), Japanese exponent of KARATE from Kanazawa. He trained under GICHIN, graduated from Takushoku University in 1937, and also studied Chinese at Peking University. He was appointed chief instructor to the Japan Karate Association in 1955 and was awarded his 8th *Dan* black belt in 1961.

NAMATH, JOE WILLIE (1943-), American college and professional FOOTBALL player, who starred as quarterback with the unbeaten 1964 University of ALABAMA team. With the NEW YORK JETS, of the AMERICAN FOOTBALL LEAGUE, he developed into the foremost passer and quarterback of the late 1960s. His appeal was further enhanced by physical disabilities. He had several operations on each of his knees, thus severely handicapping him in warding off charging defensive linemen, but his courage and ingenuity under such adversity encouraged sympathetic response from the public, and the entertainment media made much of his 'swinging' lifestyle.

NANSEN, FRIDTJOF (1861-1930), Norwegian explorer who fired many Europeans with the desire to ski by his account of the first traverse of southern Greenland in his book *Paa Ski over Gronland*, published in 1890, two years after he accomplished his feat, and published in English and German in 1891. It contains the following passage, probably the most quoted in SKIING literature:

If there is anything which deserves the name of the sport of sports it is surely skiing. Nothing hardens the muscles or gives the body power and suppleness as it does, and nothing has the same ability to keep the spirit so fresh....Is there anything that gives such a sensation of liberty and excitement as flying like a bird over wooded slopes, while winter air and pine branches rush by your cheeks, with eyes, mind, and muscles strained taut to avoid unexpected obstacles? Is it not as if the whole burden of civilization is suddenly washed from your mind, to remain in the polluted city air you have left far behind? It is as if you are one with your own skis and nature around you.

NASH, ANTHONY (1936-   ), BOBSLEIGH rider for Great Britain. He won the Olympic and world two-man championships at IGLS, Austria, in 1964, with DIXON as his brakeman. They retained their world titles in the following year at ST. MORITZ, Switzerland. During the 1960s Nash was a powerful influence behind a British resurgence in the sport, not only by inspiring others with his driving skill but as the key brain behind the nation's technical sled developments.

NASHUA (1952) was a crack American racehorse who won 22 out of 30 races including the BELMONT, PREAKNESS, and Classic Stakes, and the JOCKEY CLUB GOLD CUP twice, together with $1,288,565, thus setting a world record in prize money for a thoroughbred. He was bred by WOODWARD, raced by his son, trained by Fitzsimmons, and ridden by ARCARO. Nashua was sold as a four-year-old for a world record $1,251,200 to a syndicate organized by Combs, to whose Spendthrift Farm he later retired to stud.

NATIONAL BASKETBALL ASSOCIATION (N.B.A.), the premier professional BASKETBALL league in the U.S.A., and generally accepted as the leading basketball competition in the world.

The N.B.A. was formed in 1949 with the merger of the Basketball Association of America (B.A.A.), formed 1946, and the National Basketball League. In its early years it was dominated by the MINNEAPOLIS LAKERS, but the period from 1957-69 was completely ruled by the BOSTON CELTICS, who won the championship title in all but two of these seasons, including eight consecutive victories from 1959 to 1966. By 1973, the league had been extended to include 17 teams which were divided into four divisions: Atlantic and Central (forming the Eastern Conference), and Midwest and Pacific (Western Conference).

The leading teams in the N.B.A. include the Boston Celtics, LOS ANGELES LAKERS, NEW YORK KNICKERBOCKERS, BALTIMORE BULLETS, PHILADELPHIA 76ERS, CINCINNATI ROYALS, Atlanta Hawks, Golden State Warriors, and MILWAUKEE BUCKS.

NATIONAL COLLEGIATE ATHLETIC ASSOCIATION (N.C.A.A.), the controlling body for inter-collegiate BASKETBALL in the U.S.A. The N.C.A.A. was founded in 1906 and the basketball championship was inaugurated in 1939, the University of Oregon being the first champions. The most successful team in the history of the championship have been the U.C.L.A. BRUINS, with nine victories in ten championships, 1964-73.

The championships are organized through a series of geographically-based conferences (leagues). The champions of each conference meet in a series of play-offs to find the leading teams, which then meet in the finals to decide the champion college team in the country.

NATIONAL COURSING CLUB, see COURSING.

NATIONAL CRICKET STADIUM, Karachi, the headquarters of Pakistan CRICKET, is situated in an arid area, and when attempts were made to prepare a turf pitch in the early 1960s — the matting wicket having been dispensed with — the result was a lifeless strip of baked mud. Previously Australia had suffered their first defeat against Pakistan there, when only 95 runs were scored on the first day of the match. In 1958-9 HANIF MOHAMMAD made the highest score in first-class cricket — 499 against Bahawalpur — on this, his home ground. The capacity of 30,000 will increase as further building is carried out.

NATIONAL FOOTBALL LEAGUE (N.F.L.), American professional FOOTBALL organization, was founded at Canton, Ohio, in 1919 with teams in 12 Midwestern cities, five of which — the Akron (Ohio) Pros, Canton (Ohio) Bulldogs (led on the field by the legendary back THORPE), Columbus (Ohio) Panhandles, Dayton (Ohio) Triangles, and Rochester (New York) Jeffersons — would remain until 1925. In 1920 the Decatur (Illinois) Staleys and the Racine (Wisconsin) Cardinals joined. The league itself was called the American Professional Football Association. In 1921 the Columbus manager Carr became league president and gave strong leadership until his death in 1939. In 1922 the organization's name was changed to the present National Football League; the GREEN BAY PACKERS started their long association; and Decatur and Racine became the CHICAGO BEARS and CHICAGO CARDINALS respectively. The Bears under their coach and later owner HALAS were to dominate the League until the Second World War. In 1925 the NEW YORK GIANTS joined, and Halas signed GRANGE, the most famous college running back of the era, thus bringing the first large crowds to watch professional football.

In 1933 a play-off began between the League's Eastern and Western Division champions. At the same time the goal posts were placed on the goal line and forward passes allowed anywhere behind the line of scrimmage, thus greatly increasing offensive possibilities. In 1936 an ingenious 'draft' system, proposed by Philadelphia owner BELL, helped the weak teams achieve parity by selecting first the best graduating college football players. The Bears instituted the T-formation and with it routed the WASHINGTON REDSKINS, 73-0, in the 1940 title game. Soon all professional teams used variations of the formation. After the war the League was challenged by the new All-America Football Conference (A.A.C.), but after a bidding war for college players, the new league sued for peace in 1950. The N.F.L. absorbed the A.A.C.'s three strongest teams — the CLEVELAND BROWNS, the BALTIMORE COLTS, and the SAN FRANCISCO 49ERS — and distributed the rest of the disbanded league's players among the old N.F.L. teams.

Professional football grew in prosperity in the 1950s, partly because of league Commissioner Bell's wise policy of forbidding the televising of any League games in the cities where they were being played; only 'away' games were televised back to any League city. Professional football became a major television attraction through the excitement created by the Baltimore–New York Giants play-off game in 1958, won by Baltimore in a 'sudden death' overtime period.

The success of the game engendered competition from the AMERICAN FOOTBALL LEAGUE (A.F.L.), which started operations in 1960 in eight cities. Although first dismissed, the A.F.L. soon began a bidding war for each year's college stars that eventually led to the merger of the two leagues in 1966 under the title of the National Football League. The N.F.L. Commissioner ROZELLE, who had succeeded Bell in 1959, was instrumental in drawing up the agreement. The first Super Bowl between the champions of the two leagues was held in January 1967 and was won by the N.F.L.'s Green Bay Packers, who

under their coach, LOMBARDI, dominated the League throughout most of the 1960s. In 1970 the two leagues were formally merged into two main conferences, the National and American, each in turn divided into three divisions. To divide the two conferences into equal groups of 13 teams, Baltimore, Cleveland, and the PITTSBURGH STEELERS shifted to the American Conference.

NATIONAL HOCKEY LEAGUE (N.H.L.) of North America, ICE HOCKEY's major professional competition, contested between the foremost clubs in the United States and Canada. Inaugurated at Montreal in November, 1917, the first season's championship was won in 1918 by Toronto Arenas, the original name of the club to become famous as TORONTO MAPLE LEAFS. From 1943, the League settled to a regular contest between the 'big six' teams, BOSTON BRUINS, CHICAGO BLACK HAWKS, DETROIT RED WINGS, MONTREAL CANADIANS, NEW YORK RANGERS, and Toronto Maple Leafs, the champions winning the PRINCE OF WALES TROPHY, and the four leading teams contesting the STANLEY CUP. Six new teams were added when the League was expanded in 1967. The six established clubs continued together in what was called the East Division. The new clubs, LOS ANGELES KINGS, MINNESOTA NORTH STARS, OAKLAND SEALS, PHILADELPHIA FLYERS, PITTSBURGH PENGUINS, and ST. LOUIS BLUES, constituted the West Division. These divisions have been subsequently augmented, and the top four in each division qualify to compete for the Stanley Cup.

NATIONAL LEAGUE, American professional BASEBALL league founded in 1876. The BOSTON BRAVES and CHICAGO CUBS dominated most of the period until 1900, with the BALTIMORE ORIOLES also strong in the 1890s. Having successfully weathered a challenge from the American Association and the Players' League in 1890, the National League finally had to yield ground to the AMERICAN LEAGUE and agree in 1903 to formation of two major leagues. The WORLD SERIES between champions of the two leagues was first played that year. The Chicago Cubs were strong the next few years, but the NEW YORK GIANTS, under their manager MCGRAW, proved the dominant team in the first quarter of the century, winning ten titles. The ST. LOUIS CARDINALS, led by their general manager RICKEY, who established an elaborate 'farm system' to develop young players, were a power over the next 40 years, winning 12 league titles and 8 World Series. In 1953 the Boston Braves' franchise was shifted to Milwaukee, where the team promptly became a financial and artistic success. The bitter New York City rivals — the Giants and the BROOKLYN DODGERS — moved to California in 1958, the Giants to San Francisco and the Dodgers to Los Angeles. The league next forestalled agitation for a New York franchise in a new league by expanding to ten teams in 1962 with the NEW YORK METS and the HOUSTON ASTROS. The Braves shifted to Atlanta in 1966, over bitter Milwaukee protests. In 1969 the league then expanded to 12 teams, divided into two divisions, by adding the MONTREAL EXPOS and the SAN DIEGO PADRES. Since the 1950s the National League has consistently led the American League in total yearly attendance.

NATIONAL SPORTING CLUB (N.S.C.), a private club opened at 43 King Street, Covent Garden, London, on 5 March 1891 which did much to organize BOXING with gloves in Britain and earned a high international reputation. The N.S.C., founded by Fleming and Bettinson with the Earl of Lonsdale as its first president, was forced to go public in 1928 and the next year had to close. After several attempts to revive the club, the N.S.C. moved in 1955 to the Café Royal, Regent Street, London, and now stages regular promotions for members and guests only.

NATIONAL STUD, founded in 1916 when Col. Hall-Walker (later Lord Wavertree) presented his Tully stud in Ireland to the British nation. In 1943 it was moved to Gillingham in Dorset and an overflow was later established at West Grinstead in Sussex. It was administered by the Ministry of Agriculture until 1963, when it became the responsibility of the Horse-race Betting Levy Board (see HORSE RACING). The first director of the National Stud was Greer, who was succeeded by Johnson, followed in turn by Burrell. In 1964 all the 30 mares and foals were sold by TATTERSALLS for 271,920 guineas, and a new National Stud was opened at Newmarket by the Queen in 1967, at which only stallions were to stand to visiting mares selected by ballot. The first stallions to take up duty at the new National Stud were NEVER SAY DIE, Tudor Melody, Stupendous, Hopeful Venture, and Blakeney.

NATIONAL WATER SPORTS CENTRE, one of the most modern ROWING courses in the world at Holme Pierrepont, Nottingham. Completed in 1972, it also has facilities for CANOEING, WATER-SKIING, and angling. The national rowing championships of Great Britain were inaugurated on this course in 1972, which is also the venue for the Nottingham International Regatta, one of the principal European regattas, while the Fédération Internationale des Sociétés d'Aviron (F.I.S.A.) junior championships were held there in 1973.

NATIONS, DAVID (1919-　　), British water skier, administrator, and coach; he was a founder member of the British Water Ski Federation and represented Great Britain in the 1950s. He was five times British champion.

NATIONS CUP, see EQUESTRIAN EVENTS.

NATIVE DANCER (1950) was an outstanding race-horse in the U.S.A., winning the BELMONT and PREAKNESS STAKES, American Derby, and Classic Stakes, TRAVERS, and WITHERS STAKES. Altogether he achieved 21 wins out of 22 starts, his only defeat being by a head in the KENTUCKY DERBY. He was bred and owned by Vanderbilt.

NATSUI, SHOKICHI (1926-　　), Japanese JUDO fighter, who was the first world champion (in 1956) and won the all-Japan title from SONE the following year before retiring.

NAUSCH, WALTER, Association footballer for F.K. AUSTRIA (Vienna) and the Austrian national side for whom he played at left half in the *Wunderteam* of the early 1930s. In the early 1950s he was national manager of the Austrian team.

NAYUDU, Col. COTTARI KANYAIYA (1895-1967), cricketer for India, the Hindus, Central Provinces, and Madras. Captain of India in their first Test match against England, in 1932, he played in seven Tests over three series, batting with power and courage, and bowling steadily at slow-medium pace. He was once joint holder of the record number (11) of sixes in an innings.

N.B.A., see NATIONAL BASKETBALL ASSOCIATION.

N.C.A.A., see NATIONAL COLLEGIATE ATHLETIC ASSOCIATION.

NEARCO (1935), famous Italian race-horse by Pharos out of Nogara, bred, owned, and trained by Tesio, and ridden by Gubellini. He was undefeated in all his 14 races, including the Milan Grand Prix, Italian Grand Prix, Italian Derby, Italian Two Thousand Guineas, and French Grand Prix, together with over a million lire and a million francs in prize money. After Nearco had ended his racing career in 1938, he was bought by Benson for £60,000, then a world record prize for a thoroughbred, and imported into England to stand at stud, where he became one of the most powerful and prepotent stallions in the history of bloodstock-breeding. Champion racehorses like NEVER SAY DIE, BALLYMOSS, ROYAL PALACE, SIR IVOR, and NIJINSKY, are all direct male descendants of Nearco.

NEATH R.F.C., RUGBY UNION football club founded in 1871. Its best season was in 1928-9 when the club scored 930 points. Notable Neath players include Stephens, E. R. John, Meredith, and Thomas, all of them members of the pack, in which the strength of the club has mainly lain.
HOME GROUND: The Gnoll.
COLOURS: All black.

NELSON, BATTLING (1882-1954), American boxer who was a claimant to the world lightweight title in 1905 and became undisputed champion in 1908 by knocking out the great GANS, although by then Gans was already suffering from tuberculosis. Nelson was not in the same class as a stylist but he had an almost inhuman capacity for taking punishment before winning when the odds seemed completely against him.

NELSON, BYRON (1912-   ), American professional golfer. He was U.S. Open champion 1939; U.S. Professional Golfers Association champion 1940, 1945; Masters champion 1937, 1942; and a RYDER CUP player. In 1945 Nelson won 18 professional tournaments, 11 of them in succession, and had a season's stroke average of 68·33. In 30 tournaments that year — his only full year on the circuit — he never finished lower than ninth place. He is now a noted teacher and broadcaster.

NETBALL is a seven-a-side ball game played almost entirely by girls and women and mainly in English-speaking countries. The chief centres of adult netball are Australia, New Zealand, South Africa, and the United Kingdom. The game is also established in Sri Lanka, India, Malaysia, Singapore, the South Pacific islands, Iraq, Malta, East and West Africa — Nigeria, Ghana, and Sierra Leone in the west, and Kenya, Tanzania, Zambia, and Uganda in the east — and in the West Indies, where Jamaica and Trinidad have the greatest numerical strength; it is played only sporadically on the continent of Europe.

Netball is a game of comparatively recent origin, which was introduced into England from the U.S.A. as the indoor game of BASKETBALL in 1895. A simple, high-scoring game requiring a small court area with a hard surface, it follows similar principles and contains the same basic pattern as Association FOOTBALL, HOCKEY, LACROSSE, and the various types of HANDBALL played in Scandinavia and other parts of Europe. It has as its aim, therefore, the scoring of goals by means of gaining and retaining possession of the ball until such time as the scoring members of the team, against opposition, can throw the ball through the ring on a 10-ft. (3·048 m.) post which serves as the goal. All teams and associations play to the code of rules laid down by the International Federation of Women's Netball Associations. The game is of an hour's duration, the time being divided into four equal playing periods, with a short interval between each. The team scoring most goals is the winner. Although the game is fast-moving and spectacular between two evenly matched teams, the high rate of scoring leaves the final result in little doubt when the teams are not equally matched. For this reason, the game cannot be included among the most popular spectator sports, although matches between top-level teams sometimes attract crowds of ten thousand or more.

By rule, netball is played on a hard surface, the most suitable being tarmacadam, firmly rolled and devoid of grit and loose rubble, which can prevent the application of the strict footwork rule peculiar to the game. Concrete is a good substitute for asphalt but is hard on the feet. In areas where it is not possible to lay such a surface, or where the cost is prohibitive, a grass or even an earth area is usable. Since netball can be enjoyed as much indoors as outdoors, a wooden surface is suitable and fast.

The court is small, being only 100 ft. long and 50 ft. wide (30·48 m. × 15·24 m.), and is marked with lines painted in any clearly distinguishable colour, or laid with adhesive tape. It is divided into three equal areas, with a semicircle at either end facing the goal line, and a small circle in the centre.

The goal posts, made of steel or wood, with a metal ring projecting horizontally 6 in. (152 mm.) from the supporting pole, are placed half-way along either goal line. The ring, 15 in. (381 mm.) in diameter, is provided with a net open at both ends. The post may be supported by a socket in the ground or by a metal base. The ball used is similar to a size 5 Association football, which is between 27 and 28 in. (68–71 cm.) in circumference and between 14 and 16 oz. (397–454 g.) in weight.

A netball side consists of a goal shooter, goal attack, wing attack, centre, wing defence, goal defence, and goalkeeper, each of whom plays in limited areas of the court. The term 'offside' does not mean the same in netball as in other ball games where the term is used. A netball player is offside if she enters any area other than that assigned to her position, whether she holds the ball or not. To enter an area means to land on, or touch with any part of the body, the ground beyond the line bounding the playing area.

The penalty for an offside infringement is a free pass to the opposing team. It is taken from the place in the offside area where the infringement occurred, by a player allowed in that area. If two opposing players go offside at the same time, they are not penalized unless either or both touch the ball, when a throw-up is given between them.

The game is started by a centre pass, the team that wins the toss having the choice of making the first centre pass or selecting the goal they will attack during the first period. (Thereafter the opposing centres alternate in making the centre pass that follows each goal and each interval.) The umpire blows the whistle to start the game when the centre making the pass is in the small circle in the middle of the court, and her opponent is in the centre third. All other players start in their own playing areas in that part of the goal third in which they line up. They are free to move, but, until the whistle is blown, only in that area.

The ball is thrown in any manner from player to player. At least two passes must be made before a goal can be scored and the ball must be thrown by one player to another either in the same or the adjacent third of the court. A goal is scored by throwing the ball above and through the ring on the goal post from any spot within the shooting circle. As goal shooter and goal attack are the only attacking players allowed in the shooting circle, only these two can attempt a shot for goal.

Netball is a throwing and catching game, and strict rules disallow other ways of using the ball, such as kicking, rolling, striking, throwing or tossing it to oneself to make a double catch. A player may not carry the ball down the court as in RUGBY football, or run while bouncing the ball as in a basketball dribble. Once having clearly caught the ball, a player must obey the footwork rule, and throw the ball within three seconds of catching it. In netball no player is allowed to make an attacking movement down the court with the ball in her possession or make an attempt to score. Attacking is a team effort. One player is dependent upon another to progress the ball to the goal.

A player may receive the ball with one foot grounded or jump to catch and land on one foot. She may then (a) step with the other foot in any direction, lift the landing foot, and throw or shoot before she regrounds that foot; or (b) step with the other foot in any direction any number of times, pivoting on the landing foot, lift it, but must release the ball before she regrounds it; (c) jump from the landing foot onto the other, and jump again, releasing the ball before regrounding either foot; or (d) step with the other foot and jump, but again must throw or shoot before regrounding either foot. If a player catches the ball while both feet are on the ground, she may follow the rule given above, but may select either foot as the moving foot. A player may not hop while holding

NETBALL COURT
Goal posts 10 ft. (3·048 m.) high are placed at the centre of each goal line.

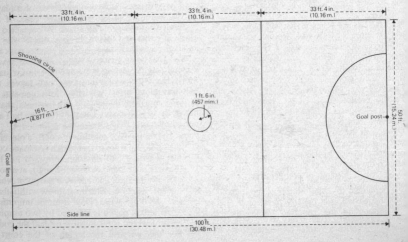

the ball, neither may she drag the landing foot along the ground.

In attempting to score a goal, the goal shooter or goal attack must be completely inside the shooting circle when she catches the ball, and while she holds it; she must obey the footwork rule and the rules governing catching and throwing. She may attempt to score as often as she can retrieve the ball from the opposition after making a shot at goal. The opponent may attempt to intercept the shot, but if she deflects it and the ball is netted, a goal is scored against her side.

No personal contact with an opponent which interferes with her play is allowed in netball; neither is a player allowed to remove the ball in any way from an opponent, nor may she push or touch an opposing player with the ball while she holds it. The rules define the physical actions and attitudes which a player may employ in her efforts to defend an opponent. Beyond these limits a legitimate action becomes a foul — known as 'obstruction'.

The skill of defending an opponent is divided between (a) defending a player who holds the ball, and (b) defending a player who does not hold the ball. In the first, the defender may attempt to intercept the ball when the opposing player has made her throw or she may attempt to make it difficult for the player to throw the ball in the direction or in the manner she wishes.

The defender must place herself at a distance of at least 3 ft. (914 mm.) from the opposing player with the ball, the distance being measured from the nearer foot of the defender to the first landing foot of the catcher if she jumps to catch the ball and lands with it, placing one foot on the ground followed by the other. Should the catcher lift that foot, or jump from it, the distance is still measured from the place on the ground where she first landed. If the catcher lands on two feet and stands still, the distance is taken to the nearer foot of the catcher. Should the catcher be standing on two feet and then move one, the distance is measured from the foot not used for stepping as before. So long as this distance is correct a defensive action may be employed.

A player defending an opponent without the ball may stand close to her, but not so close that she cannot move. The defender may not raise her arms; any movement of the arms other than those involved in natural body balance is deemed to be obstruction and is penalized by the umpire. The penalty for obstruction is a penalty pass, or if against a shooter in the shooting circle, the choice between a penalty pass and a penalty shot for goal.

NUMBERED PLAYING AREAS
For the team denoted in light-face letters, attacking the bottom goal, the goal shooter (GS) plays in areas 1 and 2; goal attack (GA) plays in areas 1, 2, and 3; wing attack (WA) plays in areas 2 and 3; centre (C); plays in areas 2, 3, and 4; wing defence (WD) plays in areas 3 and 4; goal defence (GD) plays in areas 3, 4, and 5; goalkeeper (G) plays in areas 4 and 5. For the team denoted in bold-face letters, attacking the top goal, the numbered areas are reversed.

All contact with or obstruction of a player carries the penalty of a penalty pass. If the goal shooter or goal attack is contacted or obstructed in the shooting circle she is awarded the choice between a penalty pass and a penalty shot. When either of these severe penalties is awarded, the infringer must stand beside the thrower until the ball leaves the thrower's hands. All other infringements of the rules carry the penalty of a free pass, that is to say the opposing team is given the ball and makes a throw which may be defended.

When the ball goes out of court, a player in the opposing team to that which last made contact with the ball on court throws it in. The thrower must stand outside the court, at a point close to the line, and opposite the point where the ball went out. She must throw within three seconds of the word 'Play' from the umpire.

A netball match is refereed by two umpires each of whom is responsible for half the court. For this purpose the length of the court is divided across the centre from side line to side line. Neither umpire shall give decisions in the other umpire's 'half', or query her decisions. Between them the umpires control the game. Their decisions are final and given without appeal.

Each umpire gives decisions for the throw-in for the whole of the side line outside which she stands, and the goal line bounding her half of the court. Each umpire re-starts the game after a goal scored in her half of the court, and functions in the same half throughout the match.

An umpire shall not penalize for an infringement of the rules, when by so doing she would place the non-offending team at a disadvantage. This is generally known as applying the 'advantage rule'.

No substitutes are allowed in netball, except to replace any player who has to retire through accident or illness. No extra time is allowed except to take or complete a penalty shot, if awarded before the time signal.

Official Rules of the International Federation of Women's Netball Associations, amended 1967 (8-yearly).

Although the game of netball is of comparatively recent origin, three games popular with the Greeks and Romans are still used as leading-up games for beginners and as practice for experienced players to improve footwork and ball control. *Trugon* was a Roman game for three players, mentioned by Martial and Horace: now used to improve ball-handling; *phainmida* (Greek) and *harpastum* (Roman) were useful for control of footwork and ball-handling; and the Greek *episkyros*, mentioned by Hesychius, is a team game excellent for developing dodging and marking, especially in a confined space.

Basketball was invented in the U.S.A. in 1891 by a Y.M.C.A. secretary, Dr. NAISMITH, a Canadian, and the first match recorded at Springfield, Massachusetts, in 1892. In 1895, Dr. Toles, an American visiting Madame Osterberg's College of Physical Training at Hampstead in north London, taught the students, all young ladies, how to play indoor basketball. There were no printed rules, no lines, no circles, no boundaries. The goals were waste-paper baskets hung on the wall at each end of the hall.

In America, there were three sets of rules — the official rules for men, the Inter-Collegiate Rules also used chiefly by men, and Spalding's Rules for women (adopted in 1899); each had many variations. There was nothing to prevent any school or college from changing the rules as it thought fit, or calling them by the school name.

In 1897, an American woman paid a visit to the Physical Training College (now removed from Hampstead to Dartford), and taught the game as it was then being played by women in her country. Rings were introduced instead of baskets, a larger ball was introduced, the ground divided into three courts, and American rules adopted.

The LING ASSOCIATION, founded in 1899, set up a special sub-committee in 1901 to draft and publish an official set of rules, in an edition of 250 copies, adopting many changes from the latest American rules. These included the scoring of points instead of goals, 1 point if the goal was shot from the first court or from a free throw, 2 points if shot from the centre court. And, to avoid wild shooting from long distances, the shooting circle was introduced.

The size of the ball was reduced from 31 in. (78·7 cm.) in circumference, as used in America, to 27 in. (68·5 cm.), which was the size of the regulation football, thus avoiding the manufacture of a special ball. The goal ring was also reduced from 18 in. (45.7 cm.) to 15 in. (38·1 cm.) in diameter, and the height of the goal post raised to 10 ft. (3·05 m.). As the baskets had been replaced by rings and nets, the name of the game was changed to net ball.

In 1905 the English rules were introduced into the U.S.A., Canada, France, and South Africa, as well as the other home countries. At this time there was a steadily increasing recognition that the game encouraged enterprise and initiative, as well as the team spirit. It also developed a sound physique by 'using all parts of the body equally, upright carriage, and especially control'.

Between 1908 and 1920, rules were sold in India, Canada, Burma, France, Sweden, Denmark, New Zealand, Australia, Cape Colony, Jamaica, and the U.S.A. Because the Ling Association consisted of physical training teachers, the game was first introduced and spread through girls' schools, especially in city and town areas where space was limited. When they left school, many young ladies who were desirous of continuing to play the game founded netball clubs. In 1923, a register of all leagues with eight or more clubs was made and a year later the London and Home Counties Netball Association was founded.

A joint committee of the Ling Association and the London and Home Counties Federation was set up in 1925 to consider the formation of a national association, and on 12 February 1926, a meeting was held in the Tottenham Court Road Y.W.C.A., London, with Miss E. Thompson, C.B.E., then president of the All-England Women's Hockey Association, as chairman. More than 230 delegates from schools, chiefly representing the Girls' Public Day Schools Games Association and the London Girls' Public Secondary Schools Netball Association, attended. All types of colleges were represented, as well as a number of outside clubs and adult organizations, including Cadbury's of Bournville, London Banks, and the Liverpool Union of Girls' Clubs. The meeting resulted in the formation of the All-England Women's Netball Association.

The first provisional committee consisted of ten members. Five were Ling Association representatives (Miss Bache, Miss Hankinson, Miss Read, Miss Wilkie, and Miss Newbold) and five represented the Federation (Mrs. Gould, Mrs. Lavender, Miss Milman, Miss O'Reilly, and Miss Shipperbottom).

From 1926 onwards there was a steady development of the Association. On the administrative side, county associations were formed, the first being Lancashire in 1926. Then came Durham and Norfolk in 1929, to be followed in 1930 by Kent, Middlesex, Surrey, Essex, and Hertfordshire in the south, and Northumberland in the north. Next to become organized were Derbyshire, Nottinghamshire, Worcestershire, Cambridgeshire, Staffordshire, Shropshire, Warwickshire, Wiltshire, and Leicestershire. The rest developed later, after the end of the Second World War. During the 1930s, the Civil Service, London University, and London Business Houses were granted county status, followed by Birmingham in 1947.

During the Second World War, the Channel Islands, Jersey and Guernsey, were occupied by the Germans and most of the able-bodied men and women were sent to work in Germany. Lack of entertainment among children and girls on the islands prompted a group of older men to make new balls and repair old ones, to make new posts, and to organize the girls in each parish into teams to play matches within their parish and against other parishes. Netball thus gained a firm hold on the islands, and since then, both Jersey and Guernsey have formed county associations, and have taken part in the annual inter-county tournament of the All-England Netball Association.

Landmarks in the history of the Association from 1932 to 1960 included the first All-England inter-county tournament in 1932; the first appearance of the *Netball Magazine* in 1935 and of *Netball*, the official quarterly magazine in 1949; the first sound broadcast of netball in 1947, the year of the first overseas visit of British netball players — to Prague, to demonstrate netball at the World Youth Festival; the first international matches between England, Scotland, and Wales, in 1949 in London; the Festival of Britain in London (1951) which included daily games and coaching; the first British tour of the All-Australia Women's Basketball Association team, and the first overseas tour of an England team — to South Africa in 1956.

Although in the early days of netball it was played almost entirely at school level, by 1970 the All-England Netball Association had approximately 900 clubs and 2,000 secondary schools affiliated to it. The number of unaffiliated clubs has been estimated as many more than that of affiliated clubs. In 1970, the formation of the English Schools Netball Association supplied the impetus for the expansion and further development of competitive netball in schools. At the same time, the growth in the size and number of adult clubs, now over 1,000, enabled the adult body to play its part in the government's plan for the provision of increased leisure-time activities for adults.

While the game was developing in England, it also expanded in Scotland, Wales, and Ireland, and in Ceylon, South Africa, Australia, and New Zealand. The two latter countries however developed along different lines from the rest of the world, retaining some of the original game and making fewer changes in rules. They kept the original name, basketball, until in 1970 both the Australian and New Zealand councils agreed to come into line with the rest of the world.

The inauguration of national associations in Scotland, Wales, and Northern Ireland came much later than in England, Ceylon, Australia, and New Zealand. Although their administration remained separate from that in England, the rest of the netball-playing communities, with the exception of Australia and New Zealand, played to the rules of the game as laid down and altered from time to time by the All-England Netball Association, although these have been changed considerably since the first set of 1901.

Various methods of starting and re-starting the game have been tried out. In 1901 the game was started by a high toss between the two centres, later changed to a bounce between the two. At one period a centre line replaced the centre circle, and the centre started the game by a throw alternately after each goal. In 1957, the line was replaced by a centre spot, the centres still taking the pass alternately, but maintaining their contact with the spot by one foot. The latest change was in 1960, when the spot was enlarged to a centre circle, with the thrower standing inside the circle only until she threw the ball.

Great changes have been made in the increased freedom of the player as she catches the ball. Having landed on two feet after catching the ball, simultaneously or not, a player could not — under the 1901 rules — move again, though she could hold the ball for five seconds. Shooters had to shoot from the position in which they received the ball, without turning or closing up their feet. In 1921 this rule was altered so that a player was forbidden to take a complete step in any direction, i.e. she could not move both feet in the same direction. Then came the stage when one foot could be móved after landing, and a pivot made on the other foot, but the landing foot had to remain on the ground.

Penalty shots, called 'free shots', had to be taken from outside the shooting circle, by any player selected by the captain, with the other circle players standing outside the circle. This rule lasted for many years, but free shots were freely awarded for more than contact or obstruction. In the 1920s a free shot was awarded for breaches of the footwork rule, and of methods of playing the ball, as well as for rough play.

New Zealand. Basketball was first played in New Zealand in 1906. The Revd. J. C. Jameson, travelling secretary of the Presbyterian Bible Class Union of New Zealand, went to Auckland and introduced the game which he had seen played in Australia. Teams from Bible classes took up the game and it soon extended to schools. The teams consisted of seven a side, three bounces and throws from one end of the field to the other were permitted, and baskets were used as goals.

As the game grew and spread to other parts of the Dominion, different sets of rules were adopted, the teams sometimes consisting of seven players and sometimes of nine. By 1922, associations had been formed in Auckland, Otago, Canterbury, and Wellington. In 1924 the New Zealand Basketball Association Inc. was formed, uniform playing rules adopted, and the first New Zealand tournament played. From 127 teams affiliated in 1924, the number had grown by 1967 to 4,232.

In 1938 the first overseas visit was arranged and a team went to Melbourne to take part in the All-Australian Carnival. The rules of the game were then different in the two countries, Australia playing seven in a team and New Zealand nine. As all the official games were played under Australian rules, New Zealand was never able to equal the top-scoring Australian teams. On this visit attempts were made to draw up some basic rules with a view to the formation of an Empire Association. Australia and New Zealand agreed that, where their countries held opposing views, both would abide by the English rules. Both countries, however, kept their own rules domestically,

and did not adopt the international rules until 1960.

A New Zealand team toured Fiji in 1955, and another visit was made to Australia in 1960, since when there have been frequent exchanges between New Zealand and Australia.

Australia. The game of basketball was introduced into Australia by teachers from England during the first decade of the century. It developed in the schools, clubs and associations sprang up, and gradually state associations were formed, leading eventually to the formation of the All-Australia Women's Basketball Association in 1926, the year of the establishment of the national association in England. In spite of the distances between the states, the Association has for many years organized an annual inter-state Carnival, which is held in each state in rotation. Australia first entered the international field with the visit of the New Zealanders in 1938, and the return visit to New Zealand after the Second World War.

Australian women's basketball, now changed to netball, has long been recognized as a most popular and well-organized sport. Nowhere else in the world can one see so many netball courts laid in one area as in Australia. In any state one can see 85 or more courts stretching into the distance, laid close together, with pairs of posts standing up like a forest of trees. Many of them have a grass surface and a few asphalt. More astonishing still to the eyes of every other netball-playing country is the sight of 150 or more teams, playing on a Saturday.

Jamaica. The story of the growth of netball in Jamaica is typical of that in many of the developing countries of the Commonwealth. The Jamaica Netball Association was formed as recently as 1958 with a membership of five clubs, but there was already a tradition of netball in the primary and secondary schools of the island, where the game had been established many years before by English physical-training teachers.

At the time of the inauguration of the Association, facilities were poor: there were only one or two hard courts and most games were played on grass. In 1960 the All-England Netball Association was appealed to for assistance and Miss R. Stratford, their technical adviser, went out to hold courses for teachers and club coaches and prepare selected players for a national team. The Jamaica team toured England in 1961 and played England at Wembley where, though they did not win, they gave a creditable performance and gained experience. In 1962 an England touring team went to Jamaica, demonstrating a high standard of play for schools and clubs there.

In 1963 the number of Jamaican clubs had risen to 30, and since then, the Association has been provided with four hard courts as a national headquarters in the centre of Kingston, the capital. The Association has had government recognition since its formation, and since 1962 netball has been accepted as the national game for women in Jamaica.

International administration and play. In 1957 the first move was made towards the formation of an international body to co-ordinate the various national associations and govern the game. The All-England Netball Association organized a meeting in London, to which came representatives of Australia, New Zealand, South Africa, Northern Ireland, Wales, and the U.S.A. This meeting examined the four existing sets of rules then in use, and from what was considered good from each, drafted a preliminary code for trial and discussion by the associations represented.

In August 1960, the International Federation of Women's Basketball and Netball Associations (I.F.W.B.N.A.) was inaugurated to govern the game internationally, at a conference held in Colombo, Ceylon, attended by delegates from the All-Australia Women's Basketball Association, the Netball Federation of Ceylon, the New Zealand Basketball Association, the South Africa Women's Netball Association, the West Indies Netball Board, and the All-England Netball Association. The names, basketball and netball, had both to be included in the name of the Federation because the game was still called basketball in Australia and New Zealand. A constitution and the playing rules for international play were drawn up, and it was agreed that a four-yearly international conference and tournament should be held at a time between the OLYMPIC and COMMONWEALTH GAMES.

England was asked to provide the first officers and to stage the first world tournament, to be held in 1963, when all 12 countries represented on the Council, with the exception of Nigeria, sent teams to compete for the championship. The participants were Australia, Ceylon, England, Jamaica, New Zealand, Northern Ireland, Scotland, South Africa, Trinidad and Tobago, Wales, and West Indies. Australia became the first world champions by winning all their ten matches. By 1963 British Guiana, Kenya, Singapore, and Uganda had also become members of the Council.

Between 1963 and 1967 the I.F.W.B.N.A. was administered by officers all of whom were members of the All-Australia Women's Basketball Association. The second world tournament was organized by them and held in Perth, Australia in August 1967. Eight countries only

took part, the other members being unable to meet the expense of travelling so great a distance. Of those who participated in 1963, Ceylon, Northern Ireland, Wales, and West Indies were missing but Singapore took part for the first time. New Zealand became the new world champion.

In 1967, several important changes were made in the Federation's constitution, one of the most important being that for the first time the Federation was to be administered by an active executive committee of seven officers elected from member Associations, each in a personal capacity. Its first members were drawn from five countries.

Jamaica, placed fifth among the eight competitors in 1967, organized the third world tournament in 1971, when Australia again became world champions.

Activity in the netball world increased, particularly over the four-year period, 1967-71. By sending coaches and administrators, the old-established associations helped to make the Federation's work known over a wider area. Australia and New Zealand brought Papua and New Guinea into membership, and helped to raise the standard of play and organization in Fiji and other Pacific islands, Singapore, and Ceylon. Zambia applied for membership; coaches from England toured Kenya, Uganda, Tanzania, and Zambia to demonstrate and coach the game; Nigeria applied for and received training in coaching for teachers in schools.

Every year brings Federation members nearer equality of performance, resulting in sharper competition. In many of the developing areas, women are assuming a more important role, and are beginning to organize their own sport, and netball, being a game played, organized, and administered almost entirely by women, naturally appeals to them.

Teams everywhere in the world now play to the code of rules drawn up by the International Federation, whose membership had grown by 1973 to 22 countries with national associations and one provincial association.

Netball, magazine of the All-England Netball Association.

GOVERNING BODY (WORLD): International Federation of Women's Netball Associations, P.O. Box 50115, Porirua, New Zealand; (U.K.): All-England Netball Association, Room 303, 70 Brompton Road, London S.W.3.

NETTO, IGOR (1930–   ), Association footballer for SPARTAK MOSCOW and the Soviet Union, whose side he captained for several seasons including 1956 when the team won the Olympics football tournament in Melbourne, and 1958 and 1962 when it reached the quarter-finals of the World Cup in Sweden and Chile. An excellent left half at football, he was also a fine ICE HOCKEY player and he became coach to the Spartak Moscow ice hockey team in 1969.

NEVER SAY DIE (1951), a race-horse by Nasrullah out of Singing Grass by WAR ADMIRAL, the first of a new type of 'international' horse, who was bred in the U.S.A. from mixed English, French, Italian, and American blood-lines, and owned by an American, Clark, trained by LAWSON at Manton in England, and ridden by PIGGOTT and Smirke, to give the former his first DERBY win and the latter his last ST. LEGER victory. When his racing days were over, Never Say Die was presented by his owner to the English NATIONAL STUD.

NEW HAMBURGH ICE YACHT CLUB, formed about 1875 at New Hamburgh, New York (U.S.A.), on the Hudson River. The club instituted the CHALLENGE PENNANT OF AMERICA in 1881 and was responsible for the competition's organization until 1902. (See ICE YACHTING.)

NEW WESTMINSTER, LACROSSE club in Vancouver, B.C., Canada. Known as the 'Salmonbellies', this club was founded in 1890, and dominated lacrosse in western Canada for 20 years, being champion of Canada from 1894 to 1915 and regaining the title in the years 1943, 1958, and 1962. Its best players include Bionda and Norman.

NEW YORK GIANTS (1), American professional BASEBALL team, were a force in the NATIONAL LEAGUE from the 1880s on. Managed by the hard-bitten MCGRAW from 1902 to 1932, the Giants won ten National League titles (including a record four straight: 1921-4) and WORLD SERIES in 1905, 1921, 1922, and, after McGraw, 1933 and 1954. The Giants dominated the league under McGraw. Before the First World War they had superb pitching, led by McGinnity (a 20-game winner 1903-6), Marquard (a 20-game winner 1911-13), and especially MATHEWSON, who had 12 straight 20-game-winning seasons from 1903 to 1914, including four years in which he won over 30 games, and won 373 games during his career. The McGraw teams of the 1920s featured the second baseman Frisch and the third baseman Lindstrom. The outfielder Ott led the league in home runs five times, while the first baseman Terry had a lifetime batting average of ·341 and succeeded McGraw as manager. The pitcher Hubbell won over 20 games in five straight seasons,

1933-7. The Giants made a remarkable comeback in 1951 when they came from 13½ games behind in mid-August to defeat their bitter rivals, the BROOKLYN DODGERS, in a play-off. In 1958 the Giants' owner Stoneham joined the Dodgers'.owner O'Malley in leaving New York for California, and the Giants became the SAN FRANCISCO GIANTS.

(2) American professional FOOTBALL team, were delivered to bookmaker Tim Mara as part of a bet in 1925, the year they joined the NATIONAL FOOTBALL LEAGUE (N.F.L.). Mara and then his sons Jack and Wellington have owned the team ever since. The Giants have had a proud football tradition, especially under coaches Owen (1931-53) and Howell (1954-60), including 13 Eastern Division and three N.F.L. titles. In the 1930s the team featured the running back Leemans, the kicker Strong, and centre Hein. The teams of the 1950s and early 1960s had the quarterbacks Conerly and Tittle, the offensive (attacking) tackle Brown, the defensive end Robustelli, and the defensive back Tunnell. The 1950 teams had two extraordinary assistant coaches — LOMBARDI, who led the GREEN BAY PACKERS with great success in the 1960s, and Landry, DALLAS COWBOYS coach since the 1960s, who while with the Giants devised the basic professional football defensive alignment and constructed the 'umbrella defence' against passes, spearheaded by Tunnell.

COLOURS: Red, white, and blue.

NEW YORK JETS, American professional FOOTBALL team, joined the AMERICAN FOOTBALL LEAGUE on its founding in 1960 as the New York Titans, a bedraggled team that played ineptly before sparse crowds and was often unsure of receiving its pay. In 1963 Werblin, retired president of the Music Corporation of America, bought the team and renamed them the Jets. In 1965 he signed a player of 'star' quality, the quarterback NAMATH of the University of ALABAMA, and supported him with players of talent and ex-BALTIMORE COLTS coach EWBANK. In early 1969 Namath boldly predicted the Jets would beat Baltimore in the Super Bowl, and then led the Jets to victory in the game itself.

COLOURS: Green and white.

NEW YORK KNICKERBOCKERS, American professional BASKETBALL team playing in the NATIONAL BASKETBALL ASSOCIATION. They play their home matches at MADISON SQUARE GARDEN. New York won the N.B.A. championship in 1970, when their leading players included BRADLEY, Reed, and

Frazier. The club subsequently signed MON-ROE and LUCAS.

NEW YORK METS, or Metropolitans, American professional BASEBALL team, who joined the NATIONAL LEAGUE in 1962 when the league expanded to ten teams. Their existence can be attributed to the rising demand for a New York National League team after the NEW YORK GIANTS and BROOKLYN DODGERS left for California in 1958. This demand first took the form of agitation for a third major league, which in turn brought the major leagues to expansion. The 1962 Met team was the most inept in baseball history, losing 120 games while winning only 40. The team was a standing joke, only relieved by the appealing personality of its manager STENGEL. New York fans took the bumbling team to their hearts, and when the Mets moved to Shea Stadium in 1964, they led the league in attendance, and have done so almost ever since. In 1969 the Mets, who had finished ninth in 1968, inexplicably won the WORLD SERIES, with excellent defence and the pitching of Seaver. In 1973 the Mets, in last place on 30 August, won 20 of 28 games to win their division and then defeated CINCINNATI for the National League title before losing to OAKLAND in 7 games in the World Series.

NEW YORK RANGERS, ICE HOCKEY club of New York City, founded in 1926 as a new team in the professional NATIONAL HOCKEY LEAGUE (N.H.L.) of North America. The team plays home games at the spacious MADISON SQUARE GARDEN, which seats 17,500 and has ice dimensions of 85 by 200 ft. (26 × 61 m.). The players train in Canada at Kitchener, Ontario. They were N.H.L. champions in 1928, 1932 and 1942; STANLEY CUP winners in 1928, 1933 and 1940. Outstanding players have included Cook, Heller, C. JOHNSON, Patrick, and Pratt.
COLOURS: Blue, red, and white.

NEW YORK S.C., ICE SKATING club formed in the U.S.A. in 1860. Two years later, it organized the first skating carnival on the frozen Union Pond in Brooklyn.

NEW YORK YANKEES, American professional BASEBALL team, received transfer of the BALTIMORE ORIOLES franchise in 1903 and joined the AMERICAN LEAGUE. Singularly unsuccessful in their early years, the Yankees bought several important players from the BOSTON RED SOX in 1920, including BABE RUTH, and promptly became a league power. From 1921 to 1964 the Yankees dominated the major leagues. They won 29 American League titles and 20 WORLD SERIES titles, including four straight (1936-9) and a record five straight (1949-53). The 1920s Yankees, managed by Huggins, were led by Ruth, baseball's most prodigious home-run hitter and most popular player. The 1927 Yankees have been rated by many as baseball's greatest team, led by a 'murderers' row' of batsmen featuring Ruth and the first baseman Gehrig. The 1930s Yankees, managed by McCarthy, completely overshadowed the league. Their leading players were the pitchers Ruffing and Gomez, both four-time 20-game winners; the catcher Dickey; and especially the graceful outfielder DI MAGGIO, who not only had a lifetime batting average of ·325 but in 1941 hit safely in 56 straight games, a record. The postwar Yankees were not as overpowering as the earlier teams nor did they have individual stars of the brilliance of Ruth or Di Maggio, but under their manager STENGEL they won nine pennants in ten years. Their leading players included the pitcher Ford, the catcher Berra, and the outfielders Mantle and Maris, the latter in 1961 setting the modern record of 61 home runs in a season.

NEWCASTLE UNITED F.C., Association FOOTBALL club. Founded as Newcastle East End in 1882 by the amalgamation of two junior clubs, Stanley and Rosewood, the club played in the Northern League from 1889 until 1893 when it amalgamated with Newcastle West End and, on being elected to the Second Division of the Football League, changed its name to Newcastle United. The club won the League championship in the seasons ending 1905, 1907, and 1909, and after being beaten in the F.A. Cup finals of 1905, 1906, and 1908, won the Cup for the first time in 1910. Subsequently Newcastle were champions in 1927 and F.A. Cup Winners in 1924, 1932, 1951, 1952, and 1955, and won the European Fairs Cup in 1969. The club's many outstanding players of the pre-1914 era included Lawrence, MCCRACKEN, Rutherford, Veitch, and McWilliam; between the wars there were Hudspeth, Richardson, Weaver, GALLACHER, and C. W. Spencer; and in post-1946 football, Broadis, Milburn, Scoular, McMichael, Mitchell, Harvey, and Moncur.
COLOURS: Black and white striped shirts, black shorts.
GROUND: St. James' Park, Newcastle.

NEWCOMBE, JOHN DAVID (1944-   ), Australian LAWN TENNIS player, a strong competitor with a sound temperament and formidable ground strokes, Newcombe won the last 'amateur' men's singles title at WIMBLEDON in 1967 and then took the championship as a professional in 1970. Always regarded by the Australians as the natural successor to LAVER and EMERSON, he played in his first Davis Cup (see LAWN TENNIS) challenge round in 1963 when he was 17.

Wimbledon was usually a tournament which inspired him to play well. His victory in the 1967 final over Bungert (West Germany) by 6-3, 6-1, 6-1 was one of the easiest in the history of the championships. By contrast, he had to play in the first five-set final for 21 years when he beat ROSEWALL in a dramatic and emotional match in 1970. The previous year he had been the runner-up to Laver in a match which had gone to 6-4, 5-7, 6-4, 6-4. He retained the title by beating Smith in another five-set match in 1971. He won the U.S. title in 1967 and 1973 and the German title, his first major clay court success, after he turned professional in 1968. From 1963 to 1967 he was a regular member of Australia's Davis Cup team and, with Roche, he won all the great doubles titles, including three successive victories at Wimbledon from 1968 to 1970, a feat achieved by no pair since the DOHERTY brothers in the early years of the century.

NEWLANDS (1), Cape Town, South African CRICKET ground situated at the foot of picturesque Table Mountain. It was first used for cricket in 1888-9, when BRIGGS took 15 wickets for 28 for England against South Africa. South Africa have seldom been successful there in Test matches, and their victory over Australia in 1970 was the first against any country there for 60 years.

(2) Venue for RUGBY UNION Test matches and the home ground of the Western Province provincial team, situated close to the cricket ground in the suburbs of Cape Town.

NEWMAN, JOHN EDWARD BRIAN (1935-   ), British JUDO fighter who won both the 1st and 2nd *Dan* championships of Europe. A superb stylist, considered by many to have had the finest technique of any British judo fighter, Newman was a member of the British team that won the European team title in 1957 and 1958. In addition he took the 1st *Dan* title in 1956 and the 2nd *Dan* two years later. His career ended when he was severely injured during his stay in Japan, when he was thrown into a post at Tenri University and damaged his back. He became manager of the British judo team at the 1964 OLYMPIC GAMES.

NEWMARKET, race-course in Cambridgeshire, has been the headquarters of the turf since the days of Charles II, and the straight mile course is called the Rowley Mile after this monarch's nickname, derived from his favourite hack. The first two classic races, the TWO THOUSAND GUINEAS and the ONE THOUSAND GUINEAS, are run over the Rowley Mile in late April or early May, and the Autumn Double handicaps (the CAMBRIDGESHIRE and CESAREWITCH) are also competed for at Newmarket. Other important events held there at the end of the season are the CHAMPION STAKES, the Cheveley Park Stakes for two-year-old fillies, and the Middle Park Stakes and Dewhurst Stakes for two-year-old colts and fillies.

NEWPORT R.F.C., RUGBY UNION football club. Formed as a soccer team in 1874, it began playing Rugby the following year. It was unbeaten in its first four seasons, and again in 1891-2 and 1922-3. In 1892 it provided nine players for the first Welsh side to win the Triple Crown, a record which stood for 50 years, and has been highly successful in matches against major touring sides; it beat South Africa in 1912 and 1969, Australia in 1957, and New Zealand in 1963. Notable Newport players include GOULD, Vile, K. J. JONES, MEREDITH, D. Watkins, and S. J. Watkins.
HOME GROUND: Rodney Parade.
COLOURS: Black and amber hoops.

N.F.L., see NATIONAL FOOTBALL LEAGUE.

N.H.L., see NATIONAL HOCKEY LEAGUE.

NICCOLO DELL' ARCA (1938), an Italian race-horse by CORONACH out of Nogara, dam also of NEARCO, who was bred, owned, and trained by Tesio and ridden by Gubellini. Niccolo dell' Arca won the Milan Grand Prix in record time, Italian Grand Prix, and Italian triple crown.

NICHOLLS, ERITH GWYN (1875-1939), RUGBY UNION footballer for CARDIFF, NEWPORT, and Wales. Born in Gloucestershire, he became the outstanding centre three-quarter during the Golden Era of Welsh Rugby early in the century. He won 24 international caps, and captained Wales on 10 occasions.

NICHOLS, RALPH C. F. (1911-   ), English BADMINTON player. Commencing in 1932, Nichols won five ALL-ENGLAND singles championship titles and with his elder brother, Leslie, won the men's doubles at the same tournament in three consecutive years. He also won numerous championships at other meetings and played for his country from 1930 to 1951.

NICKALLS, a famous family of oarsmen and scullers (see ROWING). GUY (1866-1935) won the Diamond Sculls at HENLEY five times and had a total of 23 Henley wins between 1885 and 1907, the greatest number of individual wins in the history of the regatta. His brother VIVIAN (1870-1947) was also a distinguished oarsman and sculler, and it was as a result of the performances of the brothers in the Silver Goblets, which they won 11 times either together or individually with different partners, that their father, Tom, presented the Nickalls Challenge Cup to the Regatta in 1895. This is now a trophy for the event. In 1908, when he was nearly 42, Guy rowed in the LEANDER eight of veterans which won the Olympic title. He coached the Yale crew in 1914, and Vivian was at one time coach to Pennsylvania University. Guy's son, GUY OLIVER (1900-   ), won the Grand Challenge Cup seven times in the 1920s — a record — and the Silver Goblets twice. He was an Olympic silver medallist in the eights in 1920 and 1928, and chairman of the Amateur Rowing Association from 1952 to 1968.

Between them, these three members of the same family had a total of 43 Henley wins in 34 competitive years. All three were Oxford University Blues, Guy and his son being president in winning BOAT RACE years.

NICKLAUS, JACK WILLIAM (1940-   ), American professional golfer. He was U.S. amateur champion 1959, 1961; U.S. Open champion 1962, 1967, 1972; Open champion 1966, 1970; U.S. Professional Golfers Association champion 1963, 1971, 1973; Masters champion 1963, 1965, 1966, 1972; a RYDER CUP and WORLD CUP player. He has won more major championships than any golfer in history.

NIEDERLANDER (1947) was a German race-horse who won the GROSSER PREIS VON BADEN twice, the GROSSER PREIS VON NORDRHEIN-WESTFALEN, the DEUTSCHES DERBY, and the Union Stakes.

NIHILL, VINCENT PAUL (1939-   ), race walker for Great Britain, regarded by many authorities as the finest all-rounder yet seen, having produced winning world-class times at all distances between 3 and 50 km. European 20 km. champion in 1969, and a very close second to PAMICH in the Olympic 50 km. of 1964, Nihill failed to finish in the 1968 50 km., after disputing the lead with HOHNE for the major part of the race. A winner of 19 Race Walking Association titles at all distances, Nihill was second in the LUGANO CUP 20 km. final in 1963 and won one of the finest 20 km. events yet seen in the contest between the U.S.A., the U.S.S.R., and the British Commonwealth at Los Angeles in 1969 from GOLUBNICHI, LAIRD, and SMAGA. He was not a copy-book stylist but possessed a scrupulously fair technique.

NIJINSKY (1967), a champion bay colt by Northern Dancer (son of Nearctic by NEARCO out of a mare tracing to PRETTY POLLY), was bred in Canada by E. P. TAYLOR, sold as a yearling to ENGELHARD, trained in Ireland by O'BRIEN, and ridden by PIGGOTT. Nijinsky won 11 out of 13 races including the English triple crown (see HORSE RACING) of DERBY, ST. LEGER, and TWO THOUSAND GUINEAS, as well as the KING GEORGE VI AND QUEEN ELIZABETH STAKES, IRISH SWEEPS DERBY, and record stakes of £282,359. He was defeated by a head by SASSAFRAS in the PRIX DE L'ARC DE TRIOMPHE, and subsequently beaten in the CHAMPION STAKES. He stood at stud in the U.S.A. at CLAIBORNE FARM, syndicated in 32 shares of $170,000 each, which placed his value at $5,450,000.

NINE MEN'S MORRIS, an indoor form of QUOITS, known also as merels, the basic equipment for which was a flat board marked out with three squares and having 24 holes, or 'stations' in it. There were, in addition to the board, wooden pegs of different sizes and sometimes of different colours. Each player had nine pegs and his aim was to get his own pieces into rows of three. When his pegs were so placed they could not be taken. His opponent meanwhile would try to take his pieces before they formed rows.

The outdoor version of this game was probably more ancient. The rules were basically the same but it had the advantage, for its humbler players at least, that it could be played virtually anywhere. The proper name for the board was a 'pound' and merels pounds have been found carved on the benches of cathedral cloisters and in the porches of old churches. Pegs were an unnecessary refinement in the open air, where stones could be used.

The game persisted in many districts and is probably still played in one form or another. Like so many widespread FOLK SPORTS it was known by a variety of names according to where it was played. In Lincolnshire this game was called 'Meg Merryleys', in Derbyshire 'nine men's marriage', in Cambridgeshire 'murrels', in Cornwall 'Morrice', and in Oxfordshire 'ninepenny'. (See FOLK SPORTS.)

NINEPINS, see SKITTLES.

NISSEN, GEORGE (1914-   ), born in Cedar Rapids, Iowa (U.S.A.), was the inventor of the trampoline, as used in the sport today (see TRAMPOLINING) and an American tumbling and DIVING champion.

NISSEN CUP, see TRAMPOLINING.

NOBLE, MONTAGUE ALFRED (1873-1940), cricketer for Australia and New South Wales. A correct and cautious batsman, a masterly medium-paced bowler, and an astute tactician, he was one of Australia's finest all-rounders. In 42 Tests he scored 1,997 runs and took 121 wickets. He captained Australia in three series against England in the early 1900s.

NOMURA, KAZUTOYO (1949-   ), Japanese JUDO fighter who was unexpectedly picked as his country's welterweight representative for the 1972 Olympics. He fulfilled its hopes by winning every contest on *ippon* and took the world title the following year.

NOR, see KNUR AND SPELL.

NORDAHL, GUNNAR (1921-   ), Association footballer for Degerfors, NORRKÖPING, A.C. MILAN, and Sweden. Together with his brothers, Knut (right back) and Bertil (centre half), he played in the team that won the 1948 Olympics football tournament in London. Gunnar Nordahl led the very fine Swedish forward line, but after the Games he went, together with his inside partners, GREN and LIEDHOLM, to Milan.

NORDHEIM, SØNDRE (1825-1897), a farmer's son from Morgedal, in the province of TELEMARK, southern Norway, who introduced a rudimentary fixed binding and a design of ski from which the modern ski has evolved. His innovations revolutionized SKIING in the 1860s. Before him, skiing was confined to straight running with braking achieved by a long stout pole held across the body and pressed into the snow. Turns were executed mainly by stepping round; stops were usually accomplished with the help of the single pole; and jumps were mainly involuntary and on the flat. Nordheim, with the control his bindings and skis gave, discovered the technique for taking off and landing on a steep slope, and thus invented modern ski jumping. In 1860 he jumped 30·5 m. (32·8 yds.), a distance not bettered until 1893.

In 1868 Nordheim and his friends skied the 200 km. to Christiania (Oslo) to demonstrate their skills. Nordheim jumped 18 metres (19·7 yds.) without a stick and swung to a stop on skis of the same length. In the next 20 years the Telemark skiers dominated competition, evolving linked S-turns on steep slopes, often in deep snow, which became known as Telemark turns.

A contemporary writer said of Nordheim: 'He stood on his skis down the steepest valley inclines and on mountainsides with the maximum of stability. He made graceful turns around bushes and trees, and was really an artist on skis.' Nordheim may, with justice, be described as the father of ski jumping and slalom.

NORDIC SKIING, see SKIING.

NORELIUS, MARTHA (1909-55), swimmer for the U.S.A. who was the first woman to win the same Olympic SWIMMING event at successive Games. She was only 15, in 1924, when she gained her first win by 1½ seconds in the 400 metres freestyle. Four years later, in Amsterdam, her winning margin was 15 seconds. She set 17 world records between 1926 and 1928 and then, having turned professional, she won the $10,000 ten-mile Wrigley Marathon in Toronto.

NORRKÖPING I.F.K., Association FOOTBALL club. Founded in 1897, the club came to the forefront of Swedish football after winning the championship in 1943 and gained ten more titles by 1963 including a sequence of four consecutive championships between 1945 and 1948. Leading players have included the three NORDAHL brothers, LIEDHOLM, and Gustavsson.
COLOURS: White with blue facings, and blue shorts.

NORTH ROAD 24, annual English 24-hour time trial promoted by the North Road Cycle Club. It originated in 1886 as a massed-start race, when the winner covered 227 miles (365 km.) on an Ordinary bicycle; in 1895 it was transferred to the track, but resumed in 1906 as a time trial.

NORTHCOTT, RON (1936-   ), Canadian curler. A famous skip, he won the Canadian and world CURLING championships, in 1966, 1968, and 1969.

NORTHERN UNION, see RUGBY LEAGUE.

NORTON, British motor-cycle manufacturer, established in 1901 and prominent in MOTOR-CYCLE RACING continuously from 1907 — a longer association than that of any other manufacturer. Their racing machines primarily figured in the 500 cc. class and also the 350, and were all single-cylinder machines up to

1955 when the factory withdrew from official participation in racing. Their heyday was in the late 1920s and 1930s and again from 1948 to 1953. Following reconstitution of the company in the late 1960s, the factory-entered twin-cylinder Nortons played a part in production racing. Developed versions have been prominent in the new 750 cc. racing category.

NOTRE DAME, University of, American college FOOTBALL team, nicknamed the 'Fighting Irish', have probably the most glamorous name in American college sports. A relatively small Catholic college at South Bend, Indiana, Notre Dame burst on the scene with a startling upset of Army (UNITED STATES MILITARY ACADEMY) in 1913, with the quarterback Dorais and the end ROCKNE making the forward pass an effective offensive (attacking) weapon. Rockne became head coach in 1918, and his teams had 105 wins, lost 12, and tied 5 through the 1930 season, including 5 national championships. His most famous teams were the legendary 'Four Horsemen' backfield team of 1924 (Stuhldreher, Miller, Crowley, and Layden) and the unbeaten 1929-30 teams. Under coach Leahy the 1941-53 teams won 88, lost 12, tied 9, and won national championships 5 times in the 1940s. Included was an unbeaten string of 38 games between 1946 and 1950. Under coach Parseghian Notre Dame returned to prominence in the 1960s, sharing the national championship in 1966 and 1970. In 1973 it was unbeaten, and in a highly publicized contest against ALABAMA in the Sugar Bowl on 1 January 1974, won the national championship in a thrilling game, 24-23. Notre Dame has had memorable intersectional rivalries with Army and with SOUTHERN CALIFORNIA. Drawing on football talent in Catholic high schools, it has maintained a level of football excellence rarely equalled and has maintained fervent loyal support from sports fans in no way connected with the university, the famous 'subway alumni'.
. COLOURS: Blue and gold.

NOTTINGHAM FOREST Football and Bandy Club, see BANDY.

NOTTS COUNTY F.C., Association FOOTBALL club, Nottingham. Founded in 1862 and the oldest League club in the world, this club turned professional in 1885 and was one of the 12 original members of the Football League when it was formed in 1888. Notts County have remained in continuous membership of the League but have been at various times in the First, Second, Third (South), Third, and Fourth Divisions. The club enjoyed its best seasons in the period from the formation of the

League to the First World War during which it twice played in the F.A. Cup final, losing in 1891 but winning three years later; it won the Second Division championship in 1897 and 1914. Between the wars, Notts County again won the Second Division championship (1923) but after three seasons were relegated from the First Division and have since spent more seasons in the Third and Fourth Divisions. The club's outstanding players have included in the pre-1914 period: H. B. Daft, Iremonger (who kept goal for Notts County from 1904 to 1926), Logan, Morley, and Toone; from 1919 to 1939: Ashurst; and from 1946: LAWTON and Pye.
COLOURS: White shirts, and black shorts.
GROUND: County Ground, Meadow Lane, Nottingham.

NOURSE, ARTHUR DAVID (1878-1948), cricketer for South Africa, Natal, Transvaal, and Western Province. The first of South Africa's world-class batsmen, he played in 45 consecutive Test matches, touring England three times and Australia once. Left-handed, he frequently held the innings together, and still made high scores when in his 50s.

NOURSE, ARTHUR DUDLEY (1910-), cricketer for South Africa and Natal. The son of A. D. NOURSE, he played 34 times for South Africa, leading them against England in two Test series and Australia in one. Strongly built, he batted with determination, epitomized in his brave innings of 208 against England in 1951 when he was severely handicapped by a broken thumb.

NOWLAN PARK, sports ground in Kilkenny, Ireland, and the leading GAELIC ATHLETIC ASSOCIATION venue in Leinster outside Dublin. It has a capacity of 40,000.

N.S.C., see NATIONAL SPORTING CLUB.

NUR, see KNUR AND SPELL.

NURBURGRING, notorious MOTOR RACING road course in the Eifel area of German forest land, probably the most exhausting and exacting test of a driver's ability. Built to give work to some of Germany's unemployed in the 1920s, it measures 14·17 miles (22·8 km.) to a lap and incorporates all types of corners and curves, including at one time an artificially-banked turn, and its sharp undulations mean that many of these hazards are approached 'blind'. The German Grand Prix is traditionally held here but the Grand Prix Drivers' Association has criticised the safety requirements. There are splendid official buildings and stands at the south-east corner of the circuit, situated on a concrete plateau, and the public are permitted to drive round on non-race days. The 1973 lap record was set by Pace in a Surtees TS 14A at 118·433 m.p.h. (190·6 km./h.).

NURMI, PAAVO JOHANNES (1897-1973), middle-distance and long-distance runner for Finland. Regarded by many experts as the greatest distance runner of the century, Nurmi broke more than 20 world records and accumulated a unique tally of 12 Olympic medals — 9 gold and 3 silver. So much was he in a class of his own that he was usually able to ignore the opposition and run, stopwatch in hand, intent only on records. He succeeded his fellow-countryman, KOLEHMAINEN, as Olympic 10,000 metres champion in 1920, regained this title in 1928, and in 1924 performed a double, never likely to be equalled, of winning the 1,500 metres and 5,000 metres within 90 minutes. Five other gold medals fell to him in team events since dropped from the Olympic programme, the 8,000 metres individual and team cross-country (1920) and 3,000 metres team race and 10,000 metres individual and team cross-country (1924). He won silver medals for the 5,000 metres (1920 and 1928) and the 3,000 metres STEEPLECHASE (1928), but it was said that he had held back in order to give compatriots a chance at gold medal glory.

His world records were established between 1921 and 1931, two of them falling within an hour shortly before his 1924 Olympic exploits: the 1,500 metres in 3 min. 52·6 sec. and the 5,000 metres in 14 min. 28·2 sec. Other records were the 1 mile in 4 min. 10·4 sec., 3 miles in 14 min. 2·0 sec., 6 miles in 29 min. 7·1 sec., 10,000 metres in 30 min. 6·2 sec., and 10 miles in 50 min. 15·0 sec.; the last three remained unmatched for 15, 12, and 17 years respectively.

Nurmi was disqualified for professionalism in 1932 when he was favourite for the Olympic MARATHON and made his last Olympic appearance as the torchbearer at the 1952 Games in Helsinki.

NYREN, JOHN (1764-1837), cricketer for HAMBLEDON and Homerton. A left-handed player, he compiled the informative and invaluable *The Cricketers of My Time* (first published in 1833), which recorded the idiosyncrasies and deeds of the Hambledon cricketers, one of whom was his father, Richard.

O

OAKLAND ATHLETICS, American professional BASEBALL team, joined the AMERICAN LEAGUE in 1968 when the franchise was shifted from Kansas City by the owner Charles O. Finley. An irascible, unpredictable executive, Finley hired ten managers in his first ten years as owner at Kansas City and Oakland. He was strongly criticized for his flamboyant publicity stunts and his unorthodox methods (although untrained in baseball, he served as his own general manager), but soon built a young, talented team. In 1972 Oakland's pitching staff led the A's to the American League title and victory in the WORLD SERIES. Although torn by dissension and feuding with Finley, the A's successfully defended their American League title in 1973, and then defeated the NEW YORK METS in the World Series. The pitchers Hunter and Blue and the outfielder Jackson led them in their championship years. (See KANSAS CITY ATHLETICS; PHILADELPHIA ATHLETICS.)

OAKLAND RAIDERS, American professional FOOTBALL team, was granted a franchise in the AMERICAN FOOTBALL LEAGUE when a Minneapolis–St. Paul group withdrew. Waifs in the first few years, Oakland was revitalized when Al Davis became first coach and then general manager. Defeated by GREEN BAY in the second Super Bowl (1968), Oakland has won five Western Division titles since 1968 and have been one of the best-balanced offensive teams in professional football.
COLOURS: Silver and black.

OAKLAND SEALS, ICE HOCKEY club of Oakland, California, formed in 1967 as one of six teams in the new West Division of the expanded NATIONAL HOCKEY LEAGUE of North America. It plays home games at the Oakland Coliseum Arena, which has a seating capacity of 12,500. The players train in Canada at Port Huron, Michigan.
COLOURS: Kelly green, light green, and blue.

OAKS D'ITALIA is the senior HORSE RACING classic for fillies in Italy, run over 2,200 m. (1 mile 3 furlongs) at Milan in May.

OAKS STAKES, a horse race, is the fillies' DERBY in England, run over the same course of 1½ miles (2,400 m.) at EPSOM three days after the premier classic. It was first run in 1779, being named after the 12th Earl of Derby's shooting-box, 'The Oaks'. Lord Grosvenor and the Duke of Grafton both won the Oaks six times, ALEC TAYLOR trained eight winners, and BUCKLE rode nine.
(See also GREYHOUND RACING.)

OBOLENSKY, Prince ALEXANDER (1916-40), RUGBY UNION wing three-quarter for Rosslyn Park, Oxford University, and England. He played for Oxford and England while still technically a Russian citizen (he had been brought to England as a baby), and scored two tries against the third ALL-BLACKS on his first appearance for England in 1936. The second has come to be known as 'Obolensky's try', and resulted from a long diagonal run from right to left which surprised the New Zealand defence. Obolensky was killed in an aircraft accident in March 1940, the first Rugby international to lose his life in the Second World War.

O'BRIEN, PHILADELPHIA JACK (1878-1942), American boxer, who won the world light-heavyweight title by knocking out FITZSIMMONS in 1905 and drew over 20 rounds with Burns when challenging for the heavyweight title. No reigning light-heavyweight champion has come closer to winning the heavier division; indeed, O'Brien was close to the middleweight limit during some of his best years.

O'BRIEN, VINCENT (1917-   ) is the leading race-horse trainer in Ireland and one of the foremost in the world. Among the many notable animals who have passed through his stables are the DERBY winners, Larkspur, SIR IVOR, and Roberto, and NIJINSKY, winner of the triple crown (see HORSE RACING). O'Brien started as a very successful trainer under National Hunt Rules, winning three GRAND NATIONALS, four CHELTENHAM GOLD CUPS, and three CHAMPION HURDLE CHALLENGE CUPS, before turning to flat racing.

O'BRIEN, WILLIAM PARRY (1932-   ), shot-putter for the U.S.A. The first man to exceed 60 ft. (18·29 m.), O'Brien was the originator of a new technique in shot-putting which incorporated a full 180-degree body turn, a style since universally adopted. The first of his 16 world records was 59 ft. 0¾ in. (18 m.) in 1953 and the last 63 ft. 4 in. (19·30 m.) in 1959. Unbeaten from 1952 to 1956, he won Olympic gold medals in those years, a bronze medal in 1960, and qualified yet again for the Olympic team in 1964 when he finished fourth. He was also Pan-American champion in 1955 and 1959. After his records had been eclipsed, he reached a new personal best of 64 ft. 7¼ in. (19·69 m.) in 1966.

O'BRIEN TROPHY, North American ICE HOCKEY trophy, awarded annually to the losing team in the STANLEY CUP play-off finals. It was donated in 1909 by Ambrose J. O'Brien.

OBSERVER GOLD CUP is the most valuable prize of the English HORSE RACING season for two-year-olds, being worth around £30,000 to the winner. It is run over 1 mile (1,600 m.) on the round course at DONCASTER at the end of October.

O'CALLAGHAN, C. L. (1875-1942), one of three outstanding Irish CROQUET players. Although his actual titles numbered eleven including five mixed doubles, his claim to fame rests chiefly on his attacking play and his effort always to accomplish a triple peel which he had done much to popularize. His style of play, feet close together with fingers of both hands pointing down and the mallet swinging between the feet, came to be called the Irish grip. He entered the English croquet scene in 1905 but did not play again after 1921.

O'CONNOR, CHRISTY (1926-   ), Irish professional golfer, one of the dominating figures on the British GOLF circuit for many years. A regular RYDER CUP player from 1955 to 1969, he won the WORLD CUP, in partnership with Bradshaw, in 1958.

O'CONNOR, WALTER, American WATER POLO player who represented the U.S.A. four times in the OLYMPIC GAMES — 1924, 1928, 1932, and 1936 — winning bronze medals on his first and third appearances.

OCTOPUSH, see UNDERWATER HOCKEY.

OCWIRK, ERNST (1926-   ), Association footballer for F.K. AUSTRIA (Vienna), Sampdoria (Genoa), and the Austrian national side of which he was a leading member (as centre half or wing half) in the 1954 world championship tournament in Switzerland that ended with Austria in third place.

ODDY, M. A. (1937-   ), Scottish amateur SQUASH RACKETS player. With BROOMFIELD and Lyon he produced the golden era of British squash. He won the Drysdale Cup (junior championship) in 1956 and became amateur champion in 1961 and 1962, beating on each occasion AMIN of Egypt. In 1963 Oddy reached the final of the Open championship, the first amateur to do so since 1952, but was easily beaten by Taleb.

ODSAL STADIUM, Bradford, Yorkshire, the headquarters of Bradford Northern RUGBY LEAGUE club, is the largest ground used solely for Rugby in England. A crowd of 102,569 watched the Rugby League Cup final replay between Halifax and WARRINGTON on 5 May 1954. The ground, owned by Bradford Corporation, was made by enclosing a large natural bowl and terracing the slopes. In comparison with the ground's over-all size, the stand accommodation is limited. The ground was first used for sporting events in 1934.

OERTER, ALFRED A. (1936-   ), discus-thrower for the U.S.A. When Oerter won his third consecutive Olympic gold medal in 1964 he had already been acclaimed as the greatest competitor in his speciality yet seen. He won a fourth gold medal in 1968. Additional evidence of his supreme competitive flair was his capacity to triumph over a chronic and painful back injury. Though he was never primarily concerned with records, his name appears four times on the progressive list of world records, the first entry being 200 ft. 5½ in. (61·10 m.) in 1962 and the last 206 ft. 6¼ in. (62·95 m.) in 1964. His personal best was 212 ft. 6½ in. (64·78 m.), accomplished under adverse conditions in the 1968 Olympic final.

OFF-ROAD RACING, see MOTOR RACING, AMERICAN.

OGIMURA, ICHIRO (1933-   ), the outstanding Japanese TABLE TENNIS player. Twice world men's singles champion (in 1954 and 1956), and once runner-up to his teammate T. Tanaka, who was perhaps the most powerful hitter (with reverse-sandwich racket) from the right side of the table ever known and who himself twice won the title. Though not quite so severe, Ogimura was subtle and intelligent, capable of a great variety of services and tactics adjusted to the opposition. He also twice won the men's doubles title and three times in succession the mixed doubles, as well as being a member of five successive winning SWAYTHLING CUP teams (1954-9). Since retirement he has devoted time to coaching in both Europe and Japan.

OHIO STATE UNIVERSITY, American college FOOTBALL team, nicknamed the 'Buckeyes', have had a fanatic level of fan support in their state. The team came to prominence in the mid-1930s and has remained a BIG TEN power ever since. The 1942 and 1944 teams shared the national championship, while in 1957 they won it outright. Particularly outstanding was coach Hayes's 1968-70 team, national champions as sophomores, loser of only two games altogether, stressing fundamental, superbly executed football.
COLOURS: Scarlet and grey.

OKANO, ISAO (1944-   ), Japanese JUDO fighter who was the lightest man to win the all-Japan championships. Only 5 ft. 6 in. tall (1·68 m.) and weighing a maximum of 13 stone 6 lb. (85·3 kg.), he scored victories in 1967 and 1969 over far larger opponents. In addition he took the Olympic middleweight gold medal in 1964 and the world title the following year.

Okano's superb style — he combined *seionage* (shoulder throw) and *ko-uchu-gari* (minor inner reaping throw) to devastating effect — made him the finest technician of the 1960s. He retired in 1969 to concentrate on instructing, after throwing the 17-stone (108 kg.) Maeda in the final of the all-Japan championships. He was appointed Japan's national team trainer in 1972.

OKKER, THOMAS S. (1944-   ), the first Dutch LAWN TENNIS player to achieve major successes in the international game. Extremely fast, a good volleyer with a fine forehand, Okker won the Italian and South African titles in 1968 and was runner-up to ASHE in the U.S. Open tournament. He turned professional in 1969 and won the German title the following year.

OKLAHOMA, University of, American college FOOTBALL team, nicknamed the 'Sooners', compiled a remarkable record under coach WILKINSON between 1947 and 1958. Utilizing the split-T formation, Oklahoma was unbeaten over 31 games between 1948 and 1951. Then after a single loss in each of the next two years, it began an all-time record run of 47 wins that was finally terminated by NOTRE DAME in 1957. National champions in 1950 and 1955-6, Oklahoma also won the Big Six (later Big Eight) title 12 straight years during the period.
COLOURS: Crimson and cream.

OLD BALD PEG is the earliest mare in the *General Stud Book*, alive in 1650. She was the direct female ancestress of Flying Childers, and of Bartlet's Childers, Jigg, and Cade, who passed on the DARLEY ARABIAN, BYERLEY TURK, and GODOLPHIN BARB male stirps to ECLIPSE, HEROD, and MATCHEM. Every thoroughbred horse in the world is, therefore, descended from her.

OLD BELVEDERE R.F.C., Irish RUGBY UNION football club founded in 1930 by former pupils of the Jesuit College. It has produced two Ireland captains, MULLEN and D. J. O'Brien, and the LIONS player, O'REILLY. In 1950 it became the first Irish club to tour Italy.
GROUND: Anglesea Road, Ballsbridge, Dublin.
COLOURS: Black and white hoops.

OLD COURSE, St. Andrews, Scottish GOLF course on the Eden estuary on the Fife coast. One of the few remaining links which evolved from the uncertain origins of golf and thus set the pattern of golf-course construction, the Old Course is unique in that it retains the features of its early days when it consisted of 11 holes, each played twice in opposite directions to constitute a 'round' of 22 holes. Common fairways and huge double greens still serve all but three holes. The other distinguishing characteristic of the Old Course is the multitude of bunkers, often invisible from the tee and nearly all graced with names. Silting and land reclamation have pushed back the shore line and slightly changed the character of the course. An automatic watering system has meant that it has lost the hard and fiery character which once made it such a formidable challenge to the golfer's skills. The Old Course is owned by the municipality of St. Andrews and administered in conjunction with the Royal and Ancient club. For over 400 years play was free to any golfer but with the increasing popularity of the course as the Mecca for golfers in the twentieth century, some restriction became necessary and an Act of Parliament legalized a modest playing fee. St. Andrews also has three other 18-hole municipal courses of more recent date and modest quality — the New, the Eden, and the Jubilee.

OLD TRAFFORD, CRICKET ground in Manchester, is the headquarters of the Lancashire County Cricket Club, which plays the majority of its home matches there. It has especially fine turf and a playing area of about 4½ acres, within a large surrounding area containing a spacious practice ground and car-park. Close to the centre of Manchester, the ground was opened in 1857 and has staged Test matches regularly since 1884. The ground capacity is 40,000, and this figure has been reached not only for Tests but for visits by Yorkshire

C.C.C. The pavilion is a large and solid structure, with a conventional ground-floor Long Room, and is situated square to the wicket. The pavilion and parts of the stands were damaged by bombs during the Second World War, but plans to build an entirely new pavilion thereafter did not prove practical. Old Trafford has acquired a reputation — not wholly deserved — for uncongenial CRICKET weather: the only two Test matches in England abandoned without a ball being bowled (in 1890 and 1938) were both scheduled to be played there.

OLDFIELD, WILLIAM ALBERT STANLEY, M.B.E. (1897-   ), cricketer for Australia and New South Wales. A neat and highly efficient wicket-keeper, he played in 54 Tests between the world wars, dismissing 130 batsmen — 52 of them by stumping. He was also a capable batsman, and toured England four times and South Africa twice.

OLYMPIC GAMES, an international festival of sport, originated in ancient Greece and were revived in modern times. The games at Olympia, thought to have been first held in about 1370 B.C., remained a feature of Greek culture until banned by the Roman Emperor Theodosius in A.D. 393. At first only foot races were contested but the games expanded in scope and popularity and in their fullest form included BOXING, WRESTLING, and chariot racing, together with a PENTATHLON (running, long jumping, discus- and javelin-throwing, and wrestling). In addition competitions in the fine arts were held, giving point to the Greek ideal of simultaneous intellectual and physical perfection. The earliest recorded Olympic champion is Coroibos of Olis, winner of an olive wreath in the stadium race of 170 m. (186 yds.) in 776 B.C. A long jump of 7·05 m. (23 ft. 1½ in.) by Chionis of Sparta in the seventh century B.C. is a performance comparable with present-day club standards, though Chionis probably propelled himself with the aid of weights, a device not permitted by modern rules. Milon of Croton won six wrestling titles between 540 and 516 B.C.

The initiative which brought about the modern Olympic revival came from the French aristocrat, Baron de Coubertin, whose educational theories about the value of harmonizing physical with mental development were similar to the Greek concept. Troubled by the growing commercialism of nineteenth-century sport, de Coubertin visualized the inauguration of an amateur championship for the world's sportsmen. Accordingly, at a congress in Paris of 13 nations over which he presided in 1894, it was resolved that 'sports competitions should be held every fourth year on the lines of the Greek Olympic Games and every nation should be invited to participate'.

Of the 13 nations who attended the Paris conference and 21 others who sent written support, only 12 were represented in Athens, the scene of the Ist Olympic Games in 1896. The Pan-Athenaic Stadium of Herodis, a 2,000-year-old ruin, was restored in white marble, but its elongated shape meant that the 400 metres circuit had excessively sharp turns. The nine sports on the programme were CYCLING, FENCING, GYMNASTICS, LAWN TENNIS, SHOOTING, SWIMMING, track and field ATHLETICS, WEIGHT-LIFTING, and wrestling. The U.S.A. took 9 of the 15 track and field events, Burke winning the olive branch in the 100 metres and 400 metres, Clark in the long jump and high jump, and Garrett in the DISCUS and SHOT PUT. The host nation, having failed to win a single athletic event until the final title, at last salvaged some prestige when the MARATHON (then 24 miles 1,500 yds.) went to Louis. Flack, an Australian resident in London, took the 800 metres and 1,500 metres, while Masson (France) won three of the cycle races. Such was the informality of these Games that a British lawn tennis player entered the Olympic tournament simply in order to secure a court to play on. Several of the 500 entries were merely tourists visiting Athens at the time. From these slender beginnings the modern Olympic movement grew into the vast convocations of later years — in 1968 at Mexico City, 112 nations were represented by about 7,500 competitors.

Because the IInd Olympic Games were timed to coincide with the World Exhibition in Paris (1900), they were relegated to a subsidiary role and their attraction for the public consequently diminished. KRAENZLEIN (U.S.A.) won the 60 metres, 110 metres hurdles, 200 metres hurdles, and LONG JUMP. The Irish-American, Flanagan, took the HAMMER title which he was to defend with success in 1904 and 1908. Another American, Baxter, had a double in the HIGH JUMP and POLE VAULT, equalling the Olympic record of 10 ft. 10 in. (3·30 m.) in the latter. It is invidious, but nonetheless irresistible, to note that the pole vault qualifying standard for the 1972 Olympic Games was more than 5 ft. higher than Baxter's gold medal effort. WATER POLO and YACHTING were added to the programme and ladies made their Olympic début as lawn tennis players.

The distance to St. Louis, Missouri, in the U.S.A., ensured that the overseas entry would be small in 1904. Only four European and four other nations took part and the Games were heavily packed with the representatives of the organizing nation. In water polo, for example, both winner and runner-up were American teams; in athletics, home competitors won every single track and field event, Prinstein retaining his TRIPLE JUMP title and collecting a third gold medal in the long jump. Outrage was registered among the spectators at the marathon finish when it was revealed that the first man home, deeming it quicker by motor car, had ridden comfortably for 10 miles of the course. There was more than a suspicion that the eventual winner, Hicks (U.S.A.), who came reeling in after the longest time on record, 3 hrs. 28 min. 53 sec., had used drugs. But despite the fact that the Games were little more than a counter-attraction to the World's Fair, Olympic continuity was maintained.

In 1906 the Greeks staged some Games which were intended to be the first of an intercalated series, falling midway between the regular celebrations at Athens. The idea, however, did not survive and London was host for the first time in 1908 after Italy had withdrawn.

With 1,500 competitors from 19 nations, the Games were by now an institution of world-wide significance. The programme, moreover, was augmented by the inclusion of Association FOOTBALL (which had appeared in 1900 but only in a demonstration match), DIVING, FIELD HOCKEY, and ICE HOCKEY, as well as other sports since discontinued. The most dramatic episode of these Games was in the marathon, run from Windsor to Shepherd's Bush in London, the site of a new stadium. Pietri (Italy) led into the arena but collapsed and was disqualified for accepting assistance from officials. The gold medal went to the second man home, Hayes (U.S.A.), but Queen Alexandra, who was present opposite the finishing line, was so moved by the Italian's plight that she awarded him a special gold cup. The 400 metres provided an opportunity for Halswelle (G.B.) to become the only man in Olympic history to win by a walk-over. The final was declared void after an American had been disqualified for boring. Two other Americans withdrew from the re-run final in protest, leaving Halswelle an unopposed passage. In athletic events no longer contested, Ewry (U.S.A.) completed an unequalled aggregate of eight individual gold medals by winning the standing long jump and the standing high jump; he had already won these two titles and the standing triple jump in 1904, a treble which he first accomplished in 1900. Britain won the POLO, and all the boxing, lawn tennis, RACKETS, ROWING, and yachting titles as well as five out of six cycle races.

Stockholm was host for the 1912 Games which were also the occasion for discussions leading to the formation in 1913 of the International Amateur Athletic Federation (see ATHLETICS, TRACK AND FIELD). This and an entry twice as large as in 1908 underlined the increasing importance of the Olympics in international sport. The hero of Stockholm and one of the immortals of physical prowess was THORPE (U.S.A.), an American Indian, who won gold medals in the DECATHLON and pentathlon, only to be deprived of his titles retrospectively. KOLEHMAINEN (Finland), winner of the 5,000 and 10,000 metres, returned to the Olympic arena in 1920 to win the marathon. At the instigation of de Coubertin, a modern pentathlon was introduced, its military character making this appear an apt choice when war was declared two years later.

The VIth Olympic Games, scheduled for 1916, were cancelled due to the war and Antwerp was chosen as the city in which the Olympic flag would be unfurled (the first time this ceremony was performed) at the expiration of a further four years in 1920. The Olympic oath-taking ceremony was also introduced and a record 29 countries, despite the exclusion of the Central European nations and Russia, participated in an unprecedented 22 sports. NURMI (Finland) made his first Olympic appearance, winning the 10,000 metres team and individual gold medals and a silver medal in the 5,000 metres. Hill (G.B.) doubled in the 800 metres and 5,000 metres, and FRIGERIO (Italy) triumphed in two walks. Mlle LENGLEN (France) won a pair of gold medals in lawn tennis, and in rowing, KELLY (U.S.A.), father of Princess Grace of Monaco, won two individual gold medals and a team gold. Eagan (U.S.A.) won the light-heavyweight boxing title and became the first man to gain gold medals at both summer and winter Games when he won the BOBSLEIGH at Lake Placid, New York, in 1932.

When the Games were staged in Paris for the second time, in 1924, there was another dramatic increase in the size of the undertaking — 5,533 competitors from 44 countries. LOWE (G.B.) won the 800 metres, a title which he retained in 1928, and Nurmi collected another five gold medals, setting world records in two of them (the 1,500 metres and 5,000 metres) in the space of an hour. WEISSMULLER (U.S.A.), later to find fame as the film Tarzan, swam to victory in the 100 metres and 400 metres freestyle, and the 4 × 200 metres relay; he gained two further gold medals in 1928. A result of astonishing incongruity was recorded when the RUGBY football event, a sport scarcely known in the United States, was won by the Americans, confounding the claims of those who had dismissed as pure chance their previous win in 1920. The

Ist WINTER OLYMPIC GAMES were held in 1924 at Chamonix.

The IXth Games at Amsterdam saw women entered for the first time in the premier Olympic sport, athletics. Their programme was restricted to five events, all of which produced world records, but such was the distress of several finalists in the 800 metres that the distance was dropped and not reinstated in the women's programme until 1960. The 800 metres winner, in 2 min. 16·8 sec., was Radke, representing the first German Olympic team to appear since the war. A sprint double for Canada was accomplished by Williams and the anticipated American supremacy in the track events was reduced to 3 out of a possible 12 gold medals. Lord Burghley (G.B.), later the Marquess of EXETER and a prominent figure in the administration of athletics, won the 400 metres hurdles, while O'Callaghan (Ireland) won the first of two hammer titles. Uruguay took the Association football championship for the second time, and field hockey was revived, giving India the chance of gaining the first of six consecutive Olympic championships.

Records were to be expected in the excellent conditions at Los Angeles in 1932 and indeed every Olympic athletics record except the long jump was broken. World marks were established in the 400 metres by Carr (U.S.A.) in 46·2 sec. and in the 800 metres by Hampson (G.B.) in 1 min. 49·7 sec. Tolan re-established American sprint supremacy by taking gold medals in the 100 metres (equalling the world record of 10·3 sec.) and 200 metres, while the American quartet set new figures of 40·0 sec. in the RELAY. Tisdall (Ireland) broke the 400 metres hurdles world record but his time of 51·7 sec. was not ratified because he overturned one hurdle. In the women's events the versatility of DIDRIKSON (U.S.A.) was displayed when she won gold medals in the 80 metres hurdles and JAVELIN, and a silver medal in the high jump. Japan won five gold medals in the men's swimming and MADISON (U.S.A.) doubled in the women's 100 metres and 400 metres freestyle.

It was in 1936 that politics for the first time threatened to obscure the real meaning of the Olympic movement. Hitler, who had risen to power in Germany since the Los Angeles Games, seized on the idea of using the Olympics as a platform for demonstrating his theory of the supposed superiority of the Aryan races. Berlin, which had first been awarded the Games in 1916 but had had to wait a further 20 years for the honour, was the venue. In the outcome, Germans did win the greater number of medals, thanks largely to their assiduous preparation in gymnastics, rowing, and EQUESTRIAN EVENTS. But of the 50 nations who marched past at the opening ceremony, it was the U.S.A. which made the biggest impression, taking 12 of 23 gold medals in the track and field events, many of them through Negro athletes who had been described in the Nazi press as 'black auxiliaries'. Conspicuous among these was OWENS, winner of gold medals in the 100 metres, 200 metres, long jump, and 4 × 100 metres relay. Owens equalled or broke Olympic or world records nearly every time he set foot on the track. Great Britain won gold medals in the 50 kilometres walk (WHITLOCK) and in the 4 × 400 metres relay, while the Oxford blue, Lovelock (New Zealand), won the 1,500 metres in world record time — 3 min. 47·8 sec. In the women's swimming, MASTEN-BROEK (Netherlands) won a unique double in the 100 metres and 400 metres freestyle, added a third gold medal in the relay, and won a silver medal in the 100 metres backstroke.

The XIIth Games were to have been staged in 1940 at Tokyo, but owing to the war, neither this celebration nor the next (Helsinki 1944) took place. London became host for the Games of the XIVth Olympiad in 1948. This time 59 nations, many of them belligerents in the recent war, sent 4,468 competitors, though Germany and Japan did not participate, nor did the U.S.S.R., not yet a member of the I.A.A.F. The first track final, the 10,000 metres, was won by ZATOPEK (Czechoslovakia), who narrowly failed to win the 5,000 metres as well. Upsets occurred in the 100 metres when DILLARD (U.S.A.), better known as a hurdler, ousted the world's fastest men, and in the 400 metres when Wint (Jamaica), a member of the London Polytechnic Harriers, defeated his compatriot, MCKENLEY, the world record holder. MATHIAS (U.S.A.) won his first decathlon title at the age of 17, and Mrs. BLANKERS-KOEN (Netherlands) took four gold medals in the 100 metres, 200 metres, 80 metres hurdles, and 4 × 100 metres relay. The Americans won all the men's swimming and diving titles and Graves (U.S.A.) became the first woman to win gold medals in highboard and springboard diving at the same Olympics. ELEK (Hungary), at the age of 41, kept her 1936 title in the women's foil, and went on to win a silver medal in 1952.

With the 55-year-old Nurmi as torchbearer at the opening ceremony, the Helsinki Olympics in 1952 had a memorable start in pouring rain. The outstanding figure of these Games was Zatopek who completed a treble in the 5,000 metres, 10,000 metres, and marathon. His wife, DANA ZATOPKOVA, contributed yet another gold medal (in the javelin) to the family stock. WHITFIELD (U.S.A.) won the 800 metres for the second time with Wint (Jamaica) filling second place as at London in 1948. In boxing, two future professional world heavyweight champions were in evidence: PATTERSON (U.S.A.) was gold medallist in the middleweight division, while Johansson (Sweden) was disqualified in the heavyweight final for 'not trying'. The U.S.S.R. reappeared in the Games after an absence of 40 years and made a considerable impact, collecting 9 gold medals in gymnastics and a further 9 in the wrestling and weight-lifting. The soccer championship went for the first time to Hungary, represented by such future professionals as PUSKAS and KOCSIS. A feature of these Games was the wider distribution of medals, 27 nations out of the 61 represented reaching the roll of gold medallists, though Great Britain collected only one, won by the show jumping team.

In 1956 the Olympic Games were staged for the first time in the southern hemisphere and the MELBOURNE CRICKET GROUND in Australia was adapted for the athletics events as well as the hockey and soccer. The Duke of Edinburgh declared the XVIth Games open, and the torch was carried into the arena by CLARKE, future holder of many world records. The remoteness of the venue had the effect of slightly reducing the entries and, because of Australian quarantine laws, the equestrian events were held in Stockholm. Morrow (U.S.A.) won three gold medals in the 100 metres, 200 metres, and 4 × 100 metres relay, and a similar treble was achieved in the women's events by CUTHBERT (Australia). The formidable KUTS (U.S.S.R.) took the 5,000 metres and 10,000 metres, his Olympic record in the former surviving attacks in the next three Olympics. Successful title defences were put up by O'BRIEN (U.S.A.) in the shot, DA SILVA (Brazil) in the triple jump, and by RICHARDS (U.S.A.) in the pole vault. An eastwest link was forged as a result of two gold medals in throwing events: Fikotova (Czechoslovakia) winner of the women's discus, and CONNOLLY (U.S.A.), hammer champion, were married in 1957. Two Australian girls, FRASER and CRAPP, each won two gold medals and one silver in the swimming events while MCCORMICK (U.S.A.) regained both the springboard and highboard titles which she had won in Helsinki. In the fencing, D'ORIOLA (France), who had a silver medal in the foil in 1948 and a gold in 1952, took another gold medal.

Back in Europe in the resplendent setting of Rome, the 1960 Games, favoured mostly with sunny weather, were contested by the record number of 84 nations and nearly 6,000 competitors. CALHOUN (U.S.A.) won the 110 metres hurdles for the second time, and Rudolph (U.S.A.) compensated for the failure of the American men sprinters by winning the women's 100 and 200 metres and taking a third gold medal in the relay. There was a world record by ELLIOTT (Australia) in the 1,500 metres and an unheralded marathon triumph by ABEBE BIKILA (Ethiopia). The home crowd were delighted when Berruti carried off the 200 metres gold medal, equalling the world record in both semi-final and final. Hary in the 100 metres won Germany's firstever gold medal in a men's Olympic track event, and the German team collected gold medals in the 4 × 100 metres relay after the Americans had been disqualified for a takeover foul. In the men's CANOEING, FREDRIKSSON (Sweden) won a gold medal in the 1,000 metres kayak doubles, bringing his tally of gold medals since 1948 to the record number of seven. Turkey in the wrestling, Russian men in the weight-lifting, and Russian women in the gymnastics were other performers preeminent in their spheres. CLAY (U.S.A.) won the light-heavyweight boxing, his first world crown.

The XVIIIth Games at Tokyo in 1964, the first to be staged in Asia, produced what was generally agreed to be a masterpiece of organization, involving the Japanese in expenditure estimated at $560,000,000. The surpassing individual achievement was perhaps the swimming of SCHOLLANDER (U.S.A.) who won four gold medals, while Fraser (Australia) took the women's 100 metres freestyle for the third successive time. Abebe Bikila (Ethiopia) again dominated the marathon, and SNELL (New Zealand) retained his 800 metres title, adding the 1,500 metres. SCHMIDT (Poland) won a second triple jump title. In the 100 metres HAYES (U.S.A.), a future football star, won in the world record time of 10·0 sec., this performance being verified on the photo-finish timing device which for the first time in Olympic history was accepted as the official source. In the women's events, BALAS (Romania) in the high jump, and TAMARA PRESS (U.S.S.R.) in the shot, both carried off the gold medal for the second time. Great Britain supplied the winners of both the men's and women's long jump in DAVIES and RAND. Mrs. Rand, who was later to marry William Toomey (U.S.A.), the 1968 Olympic decathlon champion, also won a silver medal in the pentathlon and a bronze in the relay. The Japanese introduced JUDO to the programme for the first time, wining three out of four titles but losing the nolimit class to GEESINK (Netherlands). The heavyweight boxing title went to FRAZIER (U.S.A.), a future world professional titleholder, and India gained her seventh hockey championship, turning the tables on Pakistan who had broken the sequence in 1960.

The altitude controversy overshadowed the Mexico City Olympic Games in 1968 long before they started. Critics of the choice of venue argued with validity that the middle and long distance races would be predestined victories for athletes born and resident in countries like Kenya and Ethiopia, sharing Mexico City's altitude of about 7,000 feet. The results of the endurance events, which departed in every case from the known form at sea level, supported this view. The 1,500 metres, 10,000 metres, and 3,000 metres STEEPLE-CHASE were won by Kenyans while KEINO, 1,500 metres winner, was second in the 5,000 metres; this he conceded through a tactical error to Gammoudi (Tunisia) who had spent many months at a high-altitude training camp. Gammoudi was also third in the 10,000 metres while Wolde (Ethiopia) took a gold medal in the marathon and a silver in the 10,000 metres. Thin air, a handicap in the endurance events, contributed to the shattering of world records in 12 track and field events with a premium on explosive effort. The most outstanding of these was the long jump of 29 ft. $2\frac{1}{2}$ in. (8·90 m.) by BEAMON (U.S.A.). HEMERY (G.B.) became the first British track athlete since 1932 to set a world record while winning an Olympic gold medal when he was timed in 48·1 seconds in the 400 metres hurdles. OERTER (U.S.A.) completed a probably unrepeatable sequence of four gold medals in the discus, and FOSBURY (U.S.A.) proved the efficacy of his 'Fosbury flop' technique when he reached 7 ft. $4\frac{1}{4}$ in. (2·24 m.) to take the high jump gold medal. In the shooting, BRAITHWAITE (G.B.) won the Olympic Trench, his total of 198 out of 200 including 187 consecutive hits. CASLAVSKA (Czechoslovakia) added four gymnastic gold medals to the three she took home from Tokyo. A total of 1,046$\frac{3}{4}$ lb. (474·8 kg.) for the weight-lifting gold medal in the middleweight division would have earned Kurentsov (U.S.S.R.) a bronze medal even in the light-heavyweight class. In swimming, Muñoz (Mexico) won the 200 metres breaststroke, one of his country's three gold medals.

Some 9,000 competitors and officials attended the 1972 Olympic Games in Munich where the lavishness and scale of the preparations, surpassing all previous standards, provided a setting in which records and incidents abounded. In no sport was history more sensationally made than swimming. Spitz (U.S.A.) amassed an unprecedented seven gold medals in 100 and 200 metres freestyle, 100 and 200 metres butterfly, and three relays. The American success story in Olympic athletics was, however, interrupted as, for the first time, the roll of gold medallists was not predominantly American. United States precedence in the sprints was also upset: the men's 100 and 200 metres went to BORZOV (U.S.S.R.). Another double was completed in the women's sprints by STECHER (German Democratic Republic), while VIREN (Finland) scored twice in distance events: 5,000 and 10,000 metres. The women's high jump was won by Meyfarth (West Germany) who became at 16 the youngest-ever Olympic athletics champion. She equalled the world record height of 6 ft. $3\frac{1}{2}$ in. (1·92 m.). Britain's only gold medallist was PETERS, with a pentathlon world record of 4,801 points. MEADE became Britain's first-ever gold medallist in an individual Olympic equestrian event — the three-day event — and Britain also won the three-day team event. The over-all champion in gymnastics was Turistecheva (U.S.S.R.) who established a reputation to compare with that of Caslavska in Mexico City. MEDVED (U.S.S.R.), super heavyweight winner, accomplished a unique wrestling feat by taking a gold medal in three successive Olympics.

Although the Games were an organizational triumph, the murder of 11 Israeli competitors and officials by Palestinian terrorists who succeeded in infiltrating the athletes' village within the Olympic complex, left a lurid and unhappy memory in the minds of those present. The Games were interrupted in order that a day of mourning could be observed. Almost overlooked in the horror of this episode was another political incident. The Rhodesian team, although selected according to multi-racial principles, was forced out of the Games only a few days before the opening ceremony by the threat of withdrawal on the part of several African nations.

Despite the upheavals of Munich, the vital continuity of the Olympic movement seemed secure. But the outlook was not untinged by uneasiness over pressures on the amateur code and political influences threatening the ideals underlying the modern Olympics. The main difficulty in enforcing the amateur code had always been the existence of a wide variety of interpretations among the many sports featuring on the Olympic programme. Also the increasing use of televised sport as a vehicle for direct or indirect advertising, with the contingent probability of inducements being offered to leading performers, was an added strain on the amateur framework. BRUNDAGE, former president of the International Olympic Committee, had been moved in 1970 to call for a ban on Olympic alpine SKIING, ice hóckey, soccer, and BASKETBALL because of commercialization. Brundage was succeeded in 1972 as president of the I.O.C. by Lord Killanin. Within a year of his election a revolutionary new proposal on Olympic eligibility was presented to the Olympic Congress in Varna, Bulgaria. This offered a simplified rule laying down that a competitor shall be eligible provided only that 'he has not derived any personal profit from competing in his sport'.

One of the more intractable political problems has been the absence from Olympic participation of the People's Republic of China, which in 1956 ceased to be a member of the I.A.A.F. A move to reinstate China gained impetus at Varna in 1973 but met resolute opposition. In upholding the Olympic creed that no athlete should be barred from participation on political, religious, or racial grounds the Olympic Committee inevitably from time to time faced charges of inconsistency as some members placed a greater emphasis on the importance of racial justice while others gave priority to political issues.

In 1970 it was announced that the venues for the 1976 Olympic Games would be Montreal for the summer events and Denver, Colorado, U.S.A., for the winter ones.

OLYMPIC STADIUM (1), Berlin, was constructed in 1935 for use in the OLYMPIC GAMES of the following year. It was partly destroyed during the war and rebuilt in 1948. The stadium is in the west sector of the divided city of Berlin, owned by the local authority, and used by the leading Association FOOTBALL club of West Berlin, Hertha, who play in the Bundesliga (the national League of West Germany). The stadium has a capacity of over 90,000 with seats for more than 60,000 spectators.

(2) Rome, constructed in 1952 for the Italian Olympic Committee in anticipation of the Olympic Games to be held in the city in 1960. The stadium has a capacity of 90,000, with 80,000 of the spectators seated. It is used for athletics meetings, for international Association football matches, and regularly shared by Rome's two leading clubs, A.S. Roma and Lazio.

OMMUNDSEN, H., British rifle shooter and considered by many to have been the finest full-bore shot Britain has ever known. Ommundsen first became prominent in 1898, and between that year and 1914 was an outstanding performer. He won the King's Prize at Bisley in 1901 and, in 17 years of competitive shooting, won the Bisley Grand Aggregate 3 times and was in the Final Hundred on 13 occasions. He was a member of seven British Empire and Olympic teams and shot for Scotland in international matches on many occasions. He was killed in action in the First World War.

ONE THOUSAND GUINEAS STAKES, English classic horse race for fillies only, founded in 1814 and run over the straight Rowley Mile course at NEWMARKET in the spring.

OPPENHEIM, Baroness GABRIELLE VON, is a leading breeder and owner of racehorses in Germany. She owns the Gestüt Schlenderhan, which celebrated its centenary in 1969 by winning the hundredth renewal of the DEUTSCHES DERBY.

ORANGES AND LEMONS, a STREET GAME which has a parallel in Belgium where it is known as *Pommes d'or, pommes d'argent*. It is likely that the name indicates the colours of the opposing teams, particularly as alternative versions of the rhyme now generally used ('Oranges and lemons/ Say the bells of St. Clement's/ You owe me five farthings/ say the bells of St. Martin's'; etc.) include:

> Pancakes and fritters,
> Says the bells of St. Peter's;
> Where must we fry 'em?
> Says the bells of Cold Higham.

The common factors in all the versions are the bells, the different saints' names, and the existence of a contest between two sides. The rhymes, in their earlier and enduring versions, end dolefully with a chopper to chop off a head, and this adds substance to the possibility that the original story behind the rhyme told of the execution of someone who was a traitor to one side, a martyr to another. The procession of such a person to his execution in London would have been accompanied by the tolling of bells, and after the execution the head and the limbs of the victim would possibly have been distributed for public exhibition at places known to have supported his cause. Later, in some areas, the games were confined to street football, as in Derby where the rhyme went: 'Pancakes and fritters/ Say All Saints and St. Peter's;/ When will the ball come/ Say the bells of St. Alkmun;/ At two they will throw/ Says St. Werabo;/ O! very well/ Says little Michel.' In the streets, and now in playgrounds and indoors, the players elect whether they support the oranges or lemons faction, and when all have chosen, the contest is no more strenuous than a pulling match.

ORDÓÑEZ, ANTONIO (1932-   ), *matador de toros* (*alternativa* 20 June 1951). Undoubtedly the finest *torero* of his generation, whose *veronicas* and *muletazos* at times outshone even those of the 'Golden' Age of *toreo*, his swordsmanship was his sole deficiency. Originally one of the best swordsmen of his day, he tended, towards the end of his career, to use the *bajonazo* (a low sword-thrust which can be effective but often is not).

O'REILLY, ANTHONY JOHN FRANCIS (1936-   ), RUGBY UNION wing three-quarter for OLD BELVEDERE, Leicester, Ireland, and British LIONS. He played his first game for Ireland at the age of 18, and his last, after seven years' absence from international Rugby, at 33. On the 1955 Lions tour of South Africa he scored a record 16 tries, and in 1959 a record 17 tries in New Zealand and 5 in Australia. Injury, however, restricted him to 29 Irish caps.

O'REILLY, WILLIAM JOSEPH (Tiger) (1905-   ), cricketer for Australia and New South Wales. Perhaps the best bowler in CRICKET history, he delivered leg breaks interspersed with 'googlies' at a brisk pace, exuding ceaseless hostility, and using his height and finger-strength to produce an awkward bounce. In only 27 Tests he took 144 wickets, and formed with GRIMMETT — especially in England in 1934 and in South Africa in 1935-6 — a formidable spin-bowling attack.

ORIENTEERING is a sport akin to CROSS-COUNTRY RUNNING, but staged in less open terrain, in which runners compete in navigating routes between isolated control points set up at defined positions within the area of competition. In most types of event, controls must be approached and visited in the correct sequence and the winner is the competitor completing a full circuit in the fastest time.

Route-finding is by map and compass and skill in using these is as important as athletic ability for successful participation. Orienteering thus combines athletic and academic skills in a way that is unusual in a competitive sport and it is the joint stimulus of physical and mental exercise, in attractive natural surroundings, that has been responsible for the growth of its popularity. Both as a satisfying personal sport and as a training activity in schools, youth organizations, and service departments, it is developing rapidly throughout west and east Europe, whence it spread from Scandinavia.

Events are staged in rugged country of a wooded, hilly, or moorland nature, preferably unknown to all runners. From a common starting point competitors set out separately at intervals of up to five minutes to make their way across country to each control in succession. The positions of controls are obtained from master maps displayed at the start which show the complete area of the course. Competitors mark these positions as accurately as possible on individual copies of the map issued to them by the organizer and, after careful study of the course, set off for the first objective. The minutes spent in studying and copying the master map are included within performance time and although accurate copying is vital to a runner's navigation during the race, it must be carried out under the pressure of competition. The runner's choice of route depends upon his skill in reading from the map the nature of the terrain confronting him and selecting the route which will require the least time. In making his choice he must take into consideration the general configuration of the land, the type of vegetation he will encounter, the nature of the surface under foot, and his own particular athletic capabilities. All these will affect his speed of progress and shrewd route selection will enable a slow runner to record a better time than a fast runner on a less satisfactory route.

MARKING FLAG
Panels are 1 ft. (30 cm.) square, bisected in red and white; the control number or symbol appears in the white area, and the plastic clippers at the end of the string are a device for stamping the same number, or symbol, on to the competitor's control card.

The nature of the country in which events are held ensures that competitors are repeatedly put in a position where they must choose between two or more possible routes; between a direct course along a line on which natural obstacles will be encountered, such as woods, lakes, marsh, and/or hills, and a longer route outflanking the obstacles but providing an easier passage. The orienteer in action is thus continually considering the possible routes open to him and assessing their relative advantages and disadvantages. He must be able to locate his position accurately by relating the ground to the map and he must make his decisions quickly, either on the move or during short stops to consult map and compass.

The most highly developed form of the sport, CROSS-COUNTRY ORIENTEERING, is conducted as described above and results are judged on a time basis. Two other types of event are judged on timing, both of which place particular emphasis on accurate map-reading. In LINE ORIENTEERING, the master map shows a set circuit which all competitors must follow. Along its course are a number of undisclosed controls, all of which must be visited, the location of which will be discovered only by following the defined route with great accuracy. ROUTE ORIENTEERING tests skill by requiring competitors to mark on their own maps the exact position of controls passed on a route which is marked continuously on the ground but not shown on the map.

SCORE ORIENTEERING is a different form of competition. In a selected area a large number of controls are set up. Each is allotted a points value — a high value for those furthest from the start, or difficult to locate, a lower value for those nearest or easier to find. Competitors locate as many controls as possible within a set time limit, scoring the points value of each control visited. Penalties are applied for late return. Controls may be visited in any order and results are judged on points accumulated, the maximum score, which would be the total value of all controls, being impossible of achievement within the time-limit set.

In all types of competition, controls are identified by a distinctive marking flag of red and white which must be visible from all directions for a distance of 54·7 yds. (50 m.).

Attached to each control is a device for stamping an identifying mark to record a competitor's visit. This is done on a control card, issued to all competitors for the purpose, and also used for recording starting and finishing time and as a check on the safe return of all runners. Competitors are also issued with a control description list which provides a verbal description of the exact siting of controls in relation to adjacent surface features, e.g. the hill foot; the valley head; the outcrop; the track and path junction. Descriptions are precisely worded, using accepted terminology to avoid errors of interpretation, the descriptions being the sole means by which a competitor can identify the position of a control in its local setting.

Although orienteering is essentially an individual sport, based on individual skills, and most events are championship, trophy, or personal-assessment events, team competitions are commonly arranged between clubs.

They may be organized within score events or cross-country events. In score events a team's total can be taken as the aggregate of the individual scores of the best five in a team of eight, or alternatively, the scores of all team members may be totalled, each member having been assigned a number of specific controls to visit. In cross-country events the best five performances out of eight team members are normally counted.

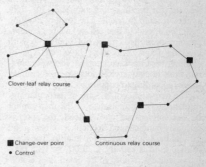

Clover-leaf relay course

■ Change-over point   Continuous relay course
● Control

ORIENTEERING RELAY COURSES

Team competitions can also be conducted on a relay basis. A cross-country course may be divided into sections, each to be completed by a different runner, or a number of separate legs may be set up in a clover-leaf pattern from a central operations area.

Orienteering is normally carried out on foot but can also be organized for skiers, cyclists, canoeists, and horse-riders, though these variants are little developed, with the exception of ski-orienteering in Scandinavia. Night events are popular with experienced orienteers possessing a high degree of skill in direction-finding and map-reading. Such events need to be arranged in less hazardous terrain than daylight competitions and large public parks or commons often prove suitable for the purpose.

The greatest concern of both competitors and officials connected with orienteering is the maintenance of good relations with owners of land in orienteering areas. Without their goodwill development of the sport would be seriously handicapped and in order to minimize the danger of friction arising from incidents occurring during events, observance of the country code is written into the rules of competition. Runners are, therefore, always under a strict injunction to avoid damage to agricultural crops or property, interference with game, or trespassing on private property. Apart from these general conditions, the rules controlling participation are few and simple since, by the nature of the sport, runners are isolated from each other during the greatest part of a competition. The fundamental principle is that each competitor must race independently and not attempt to 'hang on'. A regulation concerning maps forbids the use of any map other than the special edition prepared and provided by the organizer.

The equipment required by an orienteer is simple and inexpensive. In addition to a new map for each event his needs are no more than a compass, a waterproof pen or pencil, a whistle (for use in emergency) and, for night events, a lamp or torch. The form of clothing is optional, except that red and white garments are not permitted, to avoid confusion with marking flags. The most favoured type of clothing is of track-suit design, footwear ranging from hockey-style boots to cross-country shoes, according to conditions.

The map and compass are of particular significance. The importance of the map cannot be overemphasized and, indeed, the sport is seriously handicapped in countries where good official base maps are not available. The scale of map used is usually 1:20,000 or 1:25,000, but orienteers require more detail than is normally supplied on a standard map and it is common practice for maps to be redrawn, often re-surveyed, with the required details of minor tracks, forest fire-breaks, and similar items added. For competition purposes the map has to be copied for each competitor and lack of copying equipment can, again, prove a severe handicap to the sport. Recent progress in photographic copying has greatly assisted orienteering and it is now possible for multiple colour maps to be produced, tailor-made for particular courses, at reasonable prices.

The type of compass used must combine a protractor to enable angles and bearings to be read. Throughout the world of orienteering, the Silva compass, a special type developed in Sweden and now known by its trade name, is used. It consists of a magnetic needle mounted in an adjustable housing which can be rotated on the transparent base plate to which it is attached. The compass housing is marked in degrees for use as a protractor and the edge of the base plate is graduated to serve as a measuring instrument. The base is also engraved with a direction, or 'orienteering', arrow. When the compass has been correctly aligned, using information obtained from the map or sightings on visible landmarks, the arrowhead indicates the required direction of travel without the need for further readings of the compass — an important simplification for a lone runner in a forest, equipped only with a small hand instrument and competing against time.

Unlike most other sports, for which pitches, courts, and tracks must be standardized, orienteering is characterized by diversity of courses. Standardization applies only to the length of courses for different classes of competitor and is laid down as follows:

Boys and girls (under 15): under 1·86 miles (under 3 km.)
Junior women (under 18): 1·86–2·48 miles (3–4 km.)
Junior men (under 18) and intermediate women (under 21): 2·17–2·79 miles (3·5–4·5 km.)
Intermediate men (under 21) and senior women (over 21): 2·48–3·73 miles (4–6 km.)
Senior men (over 21): 3·11–8·06 miles (5–13 km.)

The number of controls used in an event varies from 4 to 8 for boys and girls to 9 to 14 for senior men.

In view of the constant need for new courses and for making full use of suitable terrain, great importance attaches to the role of the course-setter whose task is to seek out suitable country and to plan a circuit in it. Each new course requires many hours of experiment in the field if competitors are finally to be presented with the problems of navigation and alternative choice of routes upon which competition depends. The position of controls must be carefully chosen: they must be sited so that outgoing runners do not disclose positions to followers; they must extend competitors' navigational abilities without being impossible to locate; and they must lead competitors to places from which alternative routes abound. To ensure that a new course is satisfactory in all respects and that no errors of detail, which might jeopardize a whole competition, have occurred, each new circuit is checked by an experienced official known as a course-vetter. His function is to inspect and test the course, satisfying himself that it provides conditions which are fair to all runners.

Though it is known that 'chart and compass' races were held in the sports meetings of British army units in the early years of the century, orienteering is generally recognized as being of Scandinavian origin. It was first introduced in 1918, in Sweden, by an enterprising youth leader, Maj. KILLANDER, who used it in an attempt to attract young men back to competitive running. Participation in track athletics was showing a decline and to add interest to the labour of running Killander set courses in the abundant hill and forest country of Sweden, issuing maps and compasses to all competitors. Whatever the immediate effect on track athletics, the new concept of a competition involving route-finding and cross-country running proved attractive to all who took part, and it grew rapidly as a sport in its own right, to the extent that by 1949 a leading

Swedish athletics coach considered it a threat to the future of middle-distance running.

From the modest beginnings of a youth activity, the sport spread quickly throughout Sweden in the early 1920s and within six years of its introduction was being organized on a district basis. District and area championships were organized, leading to the first national event in 1937. In the following year Svenska Orienteringsforbundet, the organization which has remained the leading national authority, was formed, taking over responsibility for all racing on foot, ski-orienteering remaining in the hands of the national ski organization.

Development in other Scandinavian countries ran a similar course and an international body, the International Orienteering Federation, was established in 1961 with Sweden, Norway, Finland, Denmark, Switzerland, East Germany, Czechoslovakia, and Hungary as its founder members. By 1964 this had increased to 11 countries with the addition of Austria, Bulgaria, and Poland.

Elsewhere in Europe development did not get under way until the 1960s. In Britain, Scotland's mountainous terrain was the first to attract ambassadors from Sweden. In 1962 Baron LAGERFELT of the Stockholm Orienteering Club organized a number of events in co-operation with the Scottish Council for Physical Recreation. Scotland was already actively and deliberately developing its natural resources for recreational activities and orienteering was welcomed as an additional pursuit in a rapidly expanding field. A national association was set up immediately and a training programme launched to initiate and attract recruits. Contact with harriers and fell runners in northern England soon carried the sport across the border and the first English orienteering club was formed in Ribblesdale in 1964 by G. Charnley, later to become the first secretary of the British Orienteering Federation. Meanwhile, further south, in Surrey, use was being made of the wooded hills of the English downlands where DISLEY and BRASHER, supported by other well-known international runners, including BANNISTER, PIRIE, and Tulloh, pioneered the first southern clubs in 1965. An English association paralleled the Scottish before the end of the year, both being absorbed in 1967 into the British Orienteering Federation.

Central and east European countries first showed an interest in the sport in the late 1950s. Switzerland developed it sufficiently energetically for the second European championships to be staged near Le Brassus in 1964, when a Swiss woman won the individual ladies' event. West European countries, other than Britain, showed a varying response.

In Belgium development was spasmodic; in West Germany the sport came under the control of the ski federation and was slow to grow; in France little headway was made until government financial aid became available in 1970.

Beyond Europe the sport has made less impact, though expansion is accelerating in a number of widely separated areas. Despite an abundance of ideal terrain in the U.S.A. and Canada, and an early introduction in 1948 by Bjorn KJELLSTROM, one of three brothers responsible for developing the Silva compass, growth has been slow. A national orienteering federation was formed in Canada in 1968, but activity is centred mainly in the provinces of Ontario and Quebec. In the southern world, Australia and New Zealand first saw orienteering as recently as 1969. Russia, as in much else, is the great unknown. The presence of official observers at the 1970 world championships in East Germany presages her future appearance in international events. It is reported that 100,000 orienteers can be counted in the Soviets and that state and national championships have been organized since 1967. Japan applied for provisional membership of the International Orienteering Federation in 1970 and has made a start on developing the sport nationally.

World championship meetings in orienteering are held bi-annually and, whereas in the early years the Scandinavian countries dominated all events, the pattern is now changing and other nations are providing a strong challenge. In the first world competition, staged in 1966, the first 15 places in the senior men's event, and 7 out of 10 in the women's, were taken by runners from Sweden, Norway, and Finland; but in 1970 only 8 of the first 15 men and 5 of the first 10 women were Scandinavians, though both the men's champion, Berge, and the women's, Hadler, were from Norway. Scandinavian superiority and all-round strength was also reflected in Norway's victory in the men's relay and Sweden's in the women's event.

J. Disley, *Orienteering* (1967; rev. ed. 1969); S. Hedenstrom and B. Kjellstrom, *Be Expert with Map and Compass* (1955); W. Lorentzen, *Konkurranse-orienteering* (1969); M. Sollberger, *O-L ein Schlussel zur Nature* (1968); *Nya Banlaggar-boken* (Svenska Orienteringsforbundet, 1965).

GOVERNING BODY (WORLD): International Orienteering Federation, 75227 Uppsala, Tegnergatan 36 C, Sweden.

ORMONDE (1883), a champion English race-horse by BEND OR, bred and owned by the first Duke of WESTMINSTER, trained by PORTER, and ridden in most of his races by

ARCHER. He won all his 16 races including the DERBY, ST. LEGER, TWO THOUSAND GUINEAS, and CHAMPION STAKES and £28,465. With the possible exception of ISINGLASS, Ormonde was, perhaps, the best race-horse of the nineteenth century.

ORR, ROBERT (1948-   ), ICE HOCKEY player for BOSTON BRUINS from 1966, with natural ability and considerable potential as a defenceman. Winner of the CALDER MEMORIAL TROPHY in 1967, he gained the JAMES NORRIS TROPHY in 1968 and looked likely to merit the award many more times. He played four seasons for Oshawa, Ontario, before graduating to Boston's NATIONAL HOCKEY LEAGUE team as soon as he was eligible at 18. Seldom had so young a player looked so certain to achieve distinction.

ORSI, RAIMONDO (1901-   ), Association footballer for JUVENTUS (Turin), Argentina, and Italy, for whom he made 35 appearances. As outside left he was a member of the Argentinian team beaten in the 1928 Olympic final in Amsterdam. Like his national team colleague, MONTI, he signed as a professional for Juventus and, with a claim to Italian parentage, was able to play for several seasons in the Italian national side including the matches that won Italy the world championship in 1934. He scored the equalizing goal in the final against Czechoslovakia before Italy won 2-1 in extra time.

ORTEGA, DOMINGO (1906-   ), *matador de toros,* whose *alternativa* took place on 8 March 1931. An extremely able exponent of *toreo de tres cuartos,* his famous treatise *El Arte del Toreo* extolled the virtues of *cargar la suerte* and did much to educate the public about the origin and precepts of classical *toreo.* He took up BULLFIGHTING relatively late in life and was appearing in *corridas* at the age of 50.

ORTELLO (1926), a race-horse by Teddy out of Hollebeck, was the first champion bred in Italy. He won the Milan Grand Prix, Italian Grand Prix, Italian Derby, Italian St. Leger, and Milan Gold Cup, and then became the first Italian horse to win the French PRIX DE L'ARC DE TRIOMPHE. Ortello was bred and raced by de Montel and ridden by the foremost Italian jockey of his time, Caprioli.

ORTIZ, MANUEL (1917-70), Mexican-American bo   r who successfully defended the world bantamweight title 19 times between 1942 and 19 9. He lost the championship in 1947 to Dade but regained it the same year. Ortiz boxed professionally between 1938 and 1955.

ORTON, SIDNEY JOHN (b. 1890), trainer of the greyhound, MICK THE MILLER. He was attached to Wimbledon Stadium throughout a career lasting 35 years, and among the other famous greyhounds he trained were Brilliant Bob, Ballyhennessey Sandhills, BALLYNENNAN MOON, Burhill Moon, Quare Times, and Top of the Carlow Road. He was known as the 'wizard of Burhill', the Wimbledon kennels being at Burhill, Walton-on-Thames.

OSBORNE, MARGARET (later Mrs. W. Du Pont) (1918-   ), American LAWN TENNIS player and WIGHTMAN CUP captain, one of the finest modern doubles players and a leading competitor in the immediate postwar years. She won the U.S. doubles in 1941, with Cooke, and her last major success was the capture of the mixed doubles at WIMBLEDON, a title which had eluded her, with FRASER in 1962.

For much of that period she and another formidable volleyer, BROUGH, dominated the women's game in the United States and Europe. Miss Osborne won the singles at Wimbledon in 1947, at FOREST HILLS 1948-50, and in Paris in 1946 and 1949. She and Brough won the Wimbledon doubles five times, the U.S. doubles 12 times, and the French title three times. Captaining the U.S. Wightman Cup on several occasions, Osborne won all 15 of her own Wightman Cup rubbers.

OSCARIUS, KJELL, Swedish curler, skip of the Swedish rink which won the world CURLING championship in 1973.

OSLER, BENJAMIN LOUWRENS (1902-62), RUGBY UNION stand-off half for South Africa famed for his tactical kicking between 1924 and 1933. He played in 17 Tests, and captained the South Africans in the British Isles in 1931-2.

OSTLER, ANDREAS (1921-   ), BOBSLEIGH rider for Germany; the winner of four world and two Olympic titles. In 1951 he drove the successful world two-man and four-man sleds at ALPE D'HUEZ, France, and repeated the wins at Oslo the following year, when the world and Olympic events were concurrent. He was one of a national team of heavyweights who exploited their advantage during the last seasons before the combined weight of crew and bob was limited.

OTHER NATIONALITIES, a team which at

one time competed in the RUGBY LEAGUE international championship in Britain. It comprised players not eligible for the other competing countries, and included at various times Australians, New Zealanders, South Africans, Scots, Irishmen, and, in its last season (1955-6), Welshmen.

OTSUKA, HIRONORI (1892-   ), Japanese exponent of KARATE from Ibaraki prefecture, Japan. He studied many different styles of JU-JITSU while studying at Waseda University and later adapted karate to ju-jitsu and founded the *wadoryu* school of karate. Otsuka has been Chairman of the Federation of All Japan Karate-do Organizations which embraces all the major styles of Japanese *karate-do*.

OTTAWA ROUGH RIDERS, Canadian professional FOOTBALL team, a member of the Eastern 'Big Four' since its inception in 1907. Since 1938 they have won the Eastern Football Conference title ten times and the Grey Cup (see FOOTBALL, CANADIAN) eight times (most recently in 1973), the last four under coach Clair. The Canadian JACKSON was their star player in the 1960s, holding the Canadian Football League record for touchdowns made passing (185), ranking second in yards gained passing, and chosen three times as the League's outstanding player.
COLOURS: Red, white, and black.

OUIMET, FRANCIS (1893-1967), American amateur golfer. He beat VARDON, the nonpareil of English professionals, in a play-off for the 1913 U.S. Open championship at the age of 20, giving a tremendous fillip to the game in America and signalling the superiority which the Americans were soon to enjoy at the highest level of the game. He represented the U.S.A. as player or non-playing captain in every WALKER CUP match from its inception in 1922 until 1949. A prominent GOLF legislator as a member of the United States Golf Association, he became the first non-British captain of the Royal and Ancient, in 1951.

OULTON PARK CIRCUIT, MOTOR RACING track, near Tarporley, Cheshire, Britain's best road-type course. It is mainly natural road with varied corners, gradients, and a banked hairpin bend. It has not yet been used for major Grands Prix because the road is in places narrower than is acceptable for modern international events. The circuit was opened in August 1953, with a lap length of only 1·504 miles (2·4 km.), but an extension to 2·23 miles (3·6 km.) was completed by April 1954 and the lap distance increased to 2·761 miles (4·4

km.) in August of the same year. The present, 1973, lap record for the latest 2·761-mile course is held by HULME's McLaren M19 at 117·76 m.p.h. (189·516 km./h.).

OVAL, The (1), Belfast Association FOOTBALL ground of GLENTORAN F.C. It is the second largest ground in Northern Ireland, with a capacity of 45,000, and was completely rebuilt in 1945 after being destroyed during German air raids in 1941.
(2) See OVAL CRICKET GROUND.

OVAL CRICKET GROUND, Kennington, London, is the headquarters of the Surrey County Cricket Club, which stages almost every Surrey home match there. By tradition, it is also the venue of the final match of a Test series in England. The ground — which the Surrey club holds on a lease from the Duchy of Cornwall — was first used for CRICKET in 1845. It has a large playing area, which in shape only approximates to an oval, and a huge gas-holder looks down on the ground from the east side. On the west, traffic flows by at most times. The north end of the ground is known as the Vauxhall end, where there is a large stand for spectators. The ground has a capacity of about 31,000, and the principal accommodation is in the solid, late-Victorian pavilion, with a ground-floor Long Room, the walls of which are liberally adorned with cricketing subjects. In 1934 the Hobbs Gates at the main entrance were erected in honour of Sir JOHN HOBBS. Between the wars the pitch often reached a state of perfection, and large totals were common. The ground was set aside for use as a prisoner-of-war camp in the Second World War, but much detailed improvement followed afterwards. The Oval had the distinction of staging the first Test match ever held in England — against Australia in September 1880.

OWEN, MARIBEL (*née* Vinson) (1912-61), ice figure-skater for U.S.A. As Miss Vinson she was nine times U.S. champion — every year from 1928 to 1937 except 1934 — and a member of three Olympic teams, which were placed fifth, third, and second respectively in 1928, 1932, and 1936. In 1937 she became North American singles champion. She was also national pairs champion six times, twice with Coolidge, 1928-9, and four times with Hill, 1933 and 1935-7. She won the North American pairs title with Hill in 1935.

She became a professional in 1937, and coached over 4,000 pupils; turning also to journalism she had the distinction of being the first woman sports writer of the *New York Times.* In 1938 she married a Canadian champion, G. Owen. Widowed in 1952, she subsequently devoted her major energies to promoting success for her two daughters. Both became national figure-skating champions — L. Owen won the U.S. singles title at 16 and M. Owen the pairs at 21 — less than three weeks before the death of all three on 15 February 1961, with 70 other people, including the entire U.S. figure-skating team on its way to the world championships in Prague, killed when an airliner crashed near Brussels airport.

OWEN, RICHARD MORGAN (1877-1932), RUGBY UNION footballer for SWANSEA and Wales. Taking tactical control of the game from the base of the scrum, Owen was the first to develop combined attacks between scrum half and wing forward, and is credited with inventing the reverse pass, which he used to open up the winning move against the first ALL-BLACKS in 1905. His 35 international caps stood as a Welsh record for over 40 years, until surpassed by K. J. JONES, and his half-back partnership with R. Jones (Swansea) in 15 Welsh matches was broken only in 1970 by EDWARDS and JOHN.

OWENS, J. C. (Jesse) (1913-   ), sprinter, long jumper, and low hurdler for the U.S.A. One of the great figures of track and field ATHLETICS, Jesse Owens was one of very few performers in any sport to deserve the description of physical genius. On 25 May 1935 he accomplished what is still regarded as the greatest single afternoon's work in the history of athletics. First he equalled the world 100 yards record with 9·4 sec; then in his only attempt he broke the LONG JUMP record with 26 ft. 8¼ in. (8·13 m.), a mark unsurpassed for 25 years. He followed this with new world records for 220 yards and 220 yards hurdles on a straight track: 20·3 sec. and 22·6 sec. respectively. Both these times were automatically recognized as world records for the slightly shorter 200 metres distance, making a total of six world records, all set within 45 minutes. In 1936 Owens made a comparably classic contribution to Olympic history, winning four

gold medals and equalling or breaking 12 Olympic records in the 100 metres, 200 metres, long jump, and 4 × 100 metres relay. The United States team for which he was the anchor man broke the world record twice in the 4 × 100 metres relay, their time in the final being 39·8 sec. He equalled his own world 100 metres record of 10·2 sec. in the second round but this time was disallowed owing to wind assistance. Owens turned professional at the age of 23 leaving unanswered the question as to what he might ultimately have achieved in these, or indeed other, events in fuller maturity.

OXFORD UNIVERSITY BOAT CLUB. The earliest record of college ROWING racing dates from 1815, when Oxford colleges took part in bumping races on the Isis. This was some ten years before colleges began to race on the Cam, but, although the CAMBRIDGE UNIVERSITY BOAT CLUB was formed in 1827, and the first Oxford and Cambridge BOAT RACE, won by Oxford, was in 1829, the O.U.B.C. did not come into being until 1839.

Oxford won the Grand Challenge Cup at HENLEY several times in its early years, their most celebrated win being their first, in 1843, when they raced with seven men after their stroke had fallen ill before the start. In 1869, Harvard challenged Oxford to a race in fours which Oxford won by more than three lengths over the Boat Race course. Oxford oarsmen have frequently represented Britain in international events, while the only man to have stroked a winning Boat Race crew on four occasions was the Oxford Blue, Bourne, in 1909-12.

COLOURS: Dark blue.

OYAMA, MASUTATSU (1923-   ), Korean-born exponent of KARATE who went to Japan to study aviation in 1938. He lived a solitary life in the mountains for two years to strengthen his self-discipline. He fought 52 bulls unarmed and was the founder of the *kyo-kushinkai* ('the peak of truth') school of karate.

P

PADDER TENNIS, a bat-and-ball game, played 'singles' and 'doubles', which in its modern, regulated form has evolved, to a large extent by trial and error, from the increasing desire to play a game similar to LAWN TENNIS but without the need of the relatively large area required for the parent game. Lawn tennis, for a long time a game enjoyed only by the few who could play it on courts in the large grounds attached to private houses or by membership of private clubs, increased considerably in popularity after the First World War as local authorities accepted their responsibility to increase recreational facilities available to citizens by providing grass and hard courts that could be hired at reasonable charges. More recently, the extended television coverage of tennis tournaments, notably the WIMBLEDON championships, and the addition of the game to the sports played in many state schools, has further increased its popularity. Although children in the quieter streets and in playgrounds, and adults and children in small back gardens and waste areas of ground have long made efforts to practise lawn tennis, the results can never have been very satisfactory simply because there could be no useful relationship between the force or the direction at which the tennis ball was hit in those circumstances and what would be required in a game played on a proper court.

For many years, and perhaps particularly on cruising ships (see DECK TENNIS), efforts were made to produce a substitute for tennis that offered the same satisfaction, the same degree of skills, employed the same scoring, and used more or less the same rules, but which could be played in a much smaller area such as that offered by the back gardens of many private homes or by indoor halls used by youth clubs. The answer has been very largely found in padder tennis. With the exception that no provision is made for the 'tramlines' of a lawn tennis court, so that in padder tennis singles and doubles are played to the same lines, the court is marked out in a similar way. Some free space at the sides and ends of the court, which measures 39 ft. by 18 ft. (11·9 × 5·5 m.), is obviously necessary but a total area of 55 ft. by 25 ft. (16·8 × 7·6 m.) is adequate. It can, of course, be played either outdoors or indoors, providing that the surface allows a reasonably true bounce to the ordinary tennis ball that is used. When an indoor court is used, an overhead clearance of about 10 ft. (3 m.) should be sufficient.

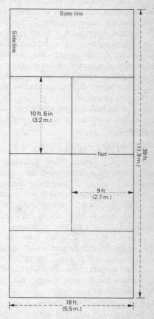

PADDER TENNIS COURT
Height of net at the posts is 2 ft. 6 in. (762 mm.), at the centre 2 ft. 3 in. (685 mm.). Marking lines are not less than 1½ in. (38 mm.) wide.

The wooden padder bat, weighing about 8 oz. (226 g.), is the essential implement that has made it possible to enjoy a fast, exciting game of tennis on such a comparatively small area. Just as in BADMINTON the feathered shuttle, hit by a strung racket, rapidly loses speed as a tennis ball similarly struck would not, so with a wooden padder bat it is impossible to send the ordinary tennis ball very far.

The ball, however, may be hit really hard from either the baseline or when serving by a good player with a more than reasonable chance of its not passing beyond the far baseline, or of being a fault by overhitting or going into the net during service. Again very much by trial and error, the most suitable height for the net was found to be 2 ft. 3 in. (685 mm.), even an inch higher or lower being likely to impede sustained play. Although experience, as in lawn tennis, will persuade individual players how best to strike the ball, the strokes and technique required for padder tennis are virtually the same as those required for the parent game.

The virtue of the game is that the much smaller area needed for a padder tennis court has given the opportunity for more people to lay out their own courts, and for local authorities, particularly those catering for visitors at seaside resorts, to provide a larger number of courts. The experience of introducing these public padder tennis courts has revealed a further potential appeal to what is still a relatively new game. First impressions were that public padder tennis courts would cater almost exclusively to young children patting the ball over the net. In fact, people of all ages derive enjoyment and exercise from this small-scale tennis game.

PADDINGTON BOWLS CLUB. Situated in Castellain Road, Maida Vale, London, this famous club was for many years the venue for the English Bowling Association championships and so was known as the 'Mecca of Bowls'. The lawn BOWLS championships were moved from there to Mortlake in 1958 but the club remains strongly in the foreground as the place where the E.I.B.A. (see BOWLS, INDOOR) holds its meetings; as the venue for one of the country's most important open indoor tournaments (the Paddington Open Fours); and as the winner of many Middlesex county championships and, indoors, the DENNY CUP on several occasions.

PADDLE TENNIS is a bat-and-ball game played, chiefly in the U.S.A., with a sponge-rubber ball and a laminated wood bat (paddle) on a court exactly half the size of a LAWN TENNIS court. In most respects its rules are as those for lawn tennis, but only one serve is allowed: if it is a 'fault', the point is lost. The doubles court measures 39 ft. by 18 ft. (11·9 × 5·5 m.). The net is 2 ft. 6 in. high (76 cm.).

A variation is platform paddle tennis, played in a roofed and walled court 44 ft. by 20 ft. (13·4 × 6·1 m.). Bigger and heavier paddles are used, and the ball may be played into court off the walls.

Paddle tennis was invented in the U.S.A. soon after the First World War, in the hope that the dimensions of the court would make the game more appealing to children than was lawn tennis, to which they would later progress. The first public tournament was held in

New York in 1924. The game has been controlled since 1938 by the United States Paddle Tennis Association.

PADDOCK, CHARLEY W. (1900-43), sprinter for the U.S.A. Paddock was one of the most durable candidates for the unofficial title of 'world's fastest human'. Between 1921 and 1926 he equalled the world 100 yards record of 9·6 sec. six times. The sixth time he actually clocked 9·5 sec. but records were then recognized only to the nearest fifth of a second. His other world records, for distances from 50 yards to 300 metres, included 100 metres in 10·4 sec., 220 yards and 200 metres on a straight track in 20·8 sec., and 200 metres on a turn in 21·2 sec. In 1921 he was timed in 10·2 sec. for 110 yards and though this was never recognized as a world record for the slightly shorter distance of 100 metres, it is regarded by some authorities as authentic and was not bettered on the official 100 metres list until 1950.

Always finishing his races with a spectacular leap through the tape, Paddock was seldom beaten in the U.S.A. He won Olympic gold medals in the 100 metres and 4 × 100 metres relay in 1920, and silver medals in the 200 metres in 1920 and 1924.

PAGET, Hon. DOROTHY (1906-60), a keen supporter of National Hunt racing in England, won the GRAND NATIONAL, the CHELTENHAM GOLD CUP seven times, and the CHAMPION HURDLE CHALLENGE CUP four times, as well as the DERBY. She owned GOLDEN MILLER, who was perhaps the greatest steeplechaser of all time.

PALA, see PELOTA.

PALETTE, see PELOTA.

PALM, GUNNAR, Swedish motor-cyclist and rally driver. With Carlssen, he won the 1963 Monte Carlo Rally. He became a Ford works rally driver from 1966 and shared the 1970 World Cup Rally win with MIKKOLA.

PALMA MATCH, see SHOOTING, RIFLE: SERVICE CALIBRE.

PALMER, ARNOLD (1929-   ), American professional golfer. He was U.S. Open champion 1960; Masters champion 1958, 1960, 1962, 1964; Open champion 1961, 1962; Canadian Open champion 1955; Australian Open champion 1966; and a regular RYDER CUP and WORLD CUP player. In 15 years after he turned professional in 1954, he transformed professional GOLF by the aggressive quality of his play and his magnetic personality. The credit for making golf a major spectator sport must be given largely to Palmer.

PALMER, CHARLES STUART, o.b.e. (1930-   ), British JUDO fighter, the first non-Japanese to be president of the International Judo Federation (1965). He studied judo for four years in Japan from 1951. In 1957 he was a member of the British team which won the European title for the first time and the following two years he captained the side to complete a hat-trick of victories in the event. As president of the International Judo Federation, he was chiefly responsible for the reintroduction of judo to the Olympic programme and for the standardization of the international contest rules which he carried out in collaboration with the KODOKAN.

PALMER-TOMKINSON, Capt. J. E. (1879-1960), English SQUASH RACKETS player. Before the First World War he was acknowledged as the best amateur player in England. After the amateur championship had been instituted he was three times runner-up before winning it in 1926 at the age of 47. He was the guiding spirit in the formation of the Squash Rackets Association in 1929 and in 1931 succeeded Lord Wodehouse as chairman. In 1947 he accepted the position of president which he held until his death.

PAMICH, ABDON (1933-   ), race walker for Italy. Born in Yugoslavia, he was the finest 50 km. performer in the world from 1961 to 1966. Olympic champion in 1964 and European champion in 1962 and 1966, he competed in four Olympiads gaining a third place in 1960 and a fourth in 1956, and five European Games with a second place in 1958 and a seventh in 1954 in addition to his victories. Three times winner of the PRAGUE –PODEBRADY race, in 1956, 1961, and 1964, Pamich scored many victories in the Italian classic events. Winner of the LONDON–BRIGHTON (1965), he set world records for 30 miles and 50 km. in 1961. In the LUGANO CUP 50 km. finals he won in 1961 and was third, behind HOHNE and Leuschke, in 1965. Pamich is a versatile world-class performer and has competed with success at 1500 metres (1,640 yds.) indoors in the U.S.A. as well as being placed second to THOMPSON in the MILAN 100 KM. (62 miles). He was still fast enough at the age of 36 to finish sixth in the 1969 European 20 km. championship. During his long career, this walker has participated at major international level in all five continents.

PAN-AFRICAN GAMES, a major ATHLET-ICS championship recognized by the International Amateur Athletic Federation (see ATHLETICS, TRACK AND FIELD), were first held in 1965, at Brazzaville in the Congo. It was hoped that the event would become a regular sports meeting for all the nations of the African continent (except the Union of South Africa), but political troubles intervened. Two proposed meetings were postponed, and the Games were next held at Lagos, Nigeria, in January 1973.

For the Brazzaville Games, 29 countries sent 2,500 competitors to an extraordinarily wide range of events. As well as the standard athletic events on track and field, there was BASKETBALL, BOXING, CYCLING, HANDBALL, JUDO, LAWN TENNIS, soccer, SWIMMING, and VOLLEYBALL. The United Arab Republic, with 18 wins over-all, was the most powerful entrant, but the most significant successes came on the running track, where Kenya, Nigeria, and Ghana were outstanding. Kenya emerged as a middle-distance running power: KEINO won the 1,500 and 5,000 metres races within four days, and Kiprugut won the 400 and 800 metres. The women's LONG JUMP was won by a 16-year-old Ghanaian, Annum; at Edinburgh in 1970 she won two Commonwealth Games silver medals for sprinting.

By 1973 many of the competing athletes were already known as world-class performers. Keino and Kiprugut had retired, but Jipcho (Kenya) equalled the world record for the 3,000 metres steeplechase (8 min. 20·8 sec.) and won the 5,000 metres. Among the other outstanding performers were the Olympic 400 metres HURDLING champion, Akii-Bua (Uganda), the Ethiopian Olympic bronze medallists Yifter (10,000 metres) and Wolde (marathon), and again Annum (Ghana), who won both sprints. TABLE TENNIS, handball, basketball, boxing, and swimming were included in these Games.

The Pan-African Games developed from the so-called 'Friendship Games' of the early 1960s. These were first held only for the French-speaking countries of Africa, but by 1963 included several others. An early, but unsuccessful, attempt had been made to stage an African Games meeting at Alexandria, Egypt, in 1927.

PAN-AMERICAN GAMES, an area championship of the International Amateur Athletic Federation (see ATHLETICS, TRACK AND FIELD) contested by men and women from North, Central, and South America, Canada, and the Caribbean. The Games were first held at Buenos Aires in 1951 and thereafter in a four-year cycle.

PAPER-CHASING, a variation of the sport of CROSS-COUNTRY RUNNING which originated in the eighteenth century and was still being practised in English schools in the twentieth century. One or two runners carrying a bag of paper pieces lay a 'scent' or trail for others runners starting 10 or 15 minutes later. The pursuers seldom overtake their quarry, who are at liberty to lay false trails, within the usual distance of eight to ten miles. Paper-chasing was never a championship sport and has given way in modern times to formal scratch cross-country races. (See also HARE AND HOUNDS.)

PAPP, LASZLO (1926-   ), Hungarian boxer who won Olympic titles in 1948, 1952, and 1956. Papp subsequently became the first boxer from a Communist country to turn professional and won the European middleweight championship.

PAQUIRO, El (Francisco Montes) (1805-51), *matador de toros,* whose *alternativa* took place on 18 April 1831. He studied in the taurine school at Seville under CÁNDIDO and PEDRO ROMERO, and was the most famous *torero* of his time. He was the author of *La Tauromaquia Completa,* published in 1836.

PARACHUTING for sport and competition is practised in practically every country in the world and up to 40 nations compete in the bi-annual world championships.

The development of techniques, particularly in the period since the Second World War, has enabled sport parachutists to jump out of aircraft and fall free until they reach a pre-determined altitude at which they open their parachutes. This period of free fall may be used to carry out manoeuvres such as turns and somersaults, barrel rolls, and movements relative to the ground in order to open the parachute in the best position to allow it to be steered to a target area.

Competitors normally use light aircraft hired from a local flying club to carry them to the altitude required for a jump. This does not usually exceed 12,000 ft. (3,657 m.) above sea level since at higher altitudes oxygen equipment is required. The parachute is normally opened at an altitude of 2,500 feet (762 m.). This gives the competitor time to open his reserve parachute if the main parachute fails to open correctly.

Parachute research has produced models which have a 'drift' or 'forward' speed inherent in the motion of the canopy as it descends. This forward speed, brought about by an arrangement of vent holes in the fabric of the canopy, can be as much as 12 miles (19 km.) per hour. Distortion of these vent holes, by the pulling of cords attached to them, will cause the parachute canopy to rotate about its axis. The parachutist, by using the forward speed and rotational ability, can direct his parachute so that landings in a pre-determined target area are possible.

The reserve is usually of smaller diameter than the main parachute. Originally it was merely a survival aid, but now increasing use is made of a simplified steerable canopy which enables the parachutist to avoid ground hazards.

The sporting use of parachutes includes competition sport parachuting, free-fall relative work, para-gliding, and para-ascending. COMPETITION PARACHUTING, using steerable parachutes to get as close as possible to a target area, is called 'accuracy jumping'. The competitive event where the parachutist carries out a pre-determined sequence of manoeuvres in free fall prior to opening his parachute is called 'style jumping'.

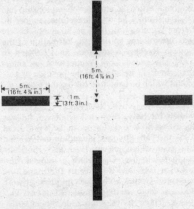

TARGET AREA FOR COMPETITION PARACHUTING
In accuracy jumping the parachutist is awarded points for the closeness of his landing to the disc at the centre of the target. Panels are of red or orange material, the disc of red; the disc (not to scale here) is 10 cm. (4 in.) in diameter.

The target area (specified by the Fédération Aéronautique Internationale) is indicated by an exploded cross of red or orange material in the centre of which is a red disc 10 cm. (4 in.) in diameter. The distance from the inside end of each arm of the cross to the centre of the 10-cm. disc is 5 m. (16·4 ft.).

The competitive parachutist is usually required to leave the aircraft with his body aligned to an arrow on the ground. He should then be in a stabilized free-fall position

— arms extended sideways, legs apart, body face downwards and parallel to the ground — and within a few seconds will receive a visual signal from the judges on the ground. This will tell him which series of pre-arranged manoeuvres to carry out. The expert parachutist (or skydiver, as he is at this stage) can control his body as a pilot can control a light aircraft, putting it into banks, turns, dives, and even loops.

In world championships, manoeuvres have to be completed within a time limit, after which the competitor returns to the stable position (still aligned with the arrow). In addition to points for style, he may be awarded bonus points for completing the movements ahead of time, or be penalized for taking too long. After their conclusion, there is also a narrow time limit within which the parachute must open.

In accuracy events, the parachutist must open his canopy at a designated altitude and guide his descent so that his feet hit the ground as near as possible to the target marker. The measurement of the accuracy of a jump is taken from the parachutist's first point of contact with the ground. This point is marked with a small flag. The measurement from the flag to the centre of the 10-cm. disc is measured to the nearest centimetre. Points are awarded for the closeness of the landing to the centre on a basis of 250 points for a landing at dead centre (a regular occurrence at world and national championship level). One-tenth of a point per centimetre away from dead centre is deducted from 250 so that a jumper landing over 25 m. (82 ft.) away from target centre will not gain any points. Usually four to six jumps per individual constitute an event with the scores on each jump added together for a grand total. Team accuracy jumping, where four parachutists leave an aircraft at the same time, takes place over the same target area; in this case the scores of the four men are added together to produce a team score.

In FREE-FALL RELATIVE WORK, two or more parachutists may leave the aircraft one after the other, and, by using their arms and legs as elevators and rudders, manoeuvre relative to each other during the free-fall period before they open their parachutes. During this 'relative work' they may manoeuvre so that they can join hands, pass batons as in a relay race, or merely fall in formation.

PARA-GLIDING utilizes a 'family' of parachutes which could more accurately be described as flexible wings. These 'wings', which are carried in a back-pack like a conventional parachute and deployed into use in the same way, give the parachutist the ability to glide, and, in some circumstances, soar like a conventional glider. The performance of these gliding parachutes has given rise to the sport of cross-country gliding by parachute. The parachutist goes to any altitude he requires by aeroplane and then glides to a predetermined landing area.

In PARA-ASCENDING, a long line is attached to the parachute harness and by towing the competitor into wind with a vehicle he is lifted into the air. The altitude reached is governed only by the length of the rope and the distance which the towing vehicle can travel before reaching any obstruction.

When the towing vehicle stops, the parachutist returns slowly to earth at the normal descent speed. The ascender can also elect to release himself from the towing rope and return to earth unattached.

The use of some kind of parachute to bring a man safely back to earth was popular as a pastime and as professional entertainment long before the equipment was used as a life-saving device. A Frenchman, Garnerin, made the first successful parachute descent, over Paris in 1797. Earlier reported jumps were from towers in Venice (1617), Montpellier (1783), and Portsmouth (1790). Garnerin's jump was from a balloon, in a parachute 23 ft. (7 m.) in diameter, remarkably similar to the type still used two centuries later.

In 1802 Garnerin repeated his performance over London. Though he landed safely, the basket of his parachute swung so violently, becoming at times almost horizontal, that he left little enthusiasm for the sport in England. It was 35 years before Cocking made what he hoped would be a great advance in the art of parachuting: he produced a 200 lb. (90 kg.) canvas structure, braced with wires and slats into a rigid inverted cone, 10 ft. (3 m.) high and 17 ft. (5 m.) in diameter. At first there was no balloon in England big enough to hoist it, but at last Cocking was able to take it up to 5,000 ft. (1,523 m.) over London. On the way down it disintegrated and Cocking was killed.

Parachute jumping became show business in the U.S.A. in the 1880s, when van Tassel and Baldwin dispensed with the idea of rigidity and began jumping from balloons on a small rectangular trapeze, held by lines to the edge of a circular canvas. Both these showmen toured the world, collecting money from amazed spectators. They each built up a circus of young jumpers, who sometimes came down holding the trapeze by their legs only. One dangled by his teeth from a strip of leather, but at 4,000 ft. (1,219 m.) over Santa Monica he bit clean through it.

Until the twentieth century, no parachute was independent of the balloon that carried it. Even Broadwick's revolutionary silk parachute, carried in a canvas pack on the jumper's back, depended for its opening on a panel of the pack being removed by a line attached to the balloon basket. Carhart dropped in 1905 with an independent parachute, to open which he had, after jumping, to undo two safety pins and release a pilot canopy. But the ripcord, by which the jumper could open his parachute at will and with ease, did not appear until 1908, when it was perfected by an American, Stevens.

The invention was not received with much confidence. It was not used from an aeroplane until 1912, and even when the Allies followed the German example and developed parachutes for military use in 1918, they were all opened by a static line from the aircraft. Once the ripcord was safely established, free-falling for fun began.

Among the notable landmarks of free-falling were those of 4,400 ft. (1,341 m.) by a U.S. Navy machinist in 1928; of $5\frac{1}{2}$ miles (8·85 km.) by Starnes in 1942, when the opening of the canopy slowed his descent from 150 m.p.h. (241 km./h.) to 13 m.p.h. (20·9 km./h.); and of 16 miles (25·8 km.) by Captain Kittinger, U.S. Air Force, in 1962. He wore a pressure suit and jumped from a balloon at $19\frac{1}{2}$ miles (31·4 km.). In 1963 a 13-man team from the U.S.A.F. jumped and fell together nearly 8 miles (12·9 km.).

Parachuting contests began in the U.S.A. in 1926, but the sport developed far faster in Russia, where in 1936, only six years after their first competition, there were 115 parachuting schools. The first world parachuting championships were held in Yugoslavia in 1951, and were dominated for ten years by European and Asian teams. The world's first para-theatre was built at Orange, Massachusetts, for the sixth championships, in 1962, when the U.S.A. provided both men's and women's champions.

W. D. Brown, *Parachutes* (1957); Bud Sellick, *Parachutes and Parachuting* (1972).

GOVERNING BODY (WORLD): Fédération Aeronautique Internationale, 6 Rue Galilée, Paris 16, France.

PARADIGM (1852) was one of the most important brood mares in the history of English thoroughbred breeding. She was dam of Lord Lyon, winner of the triple crown (see HORSE RACING), and fifth dam of PRINCE PALATINE. NEVER SAY DIE was descended from her.

PARAPLEGIC GAMES. Also popularly known as the 'paralympics' and the 'wheelchair Olympics', this is an annual sports meeting for semi-paralysed competitors. It is properly called the International Stoke Mandeville Games, after the hospital in Buckinghamshire, England, at which the event was founded and where it is still held for three years out of every four.

Contests are held in ARCHERY, SWIMMING (for which competitors start in the water), FENCING, BOWLS, snooker, TABLE TENNIS, WEIGHT-LIFTING (from a supine position), and the field events of throwing the JAVELIN, DISCUS, and HAMMER. Several other sports, including BASKETBALL, are practised by paraplegic invalids, and may be included in the International Games.

The idea of such athletic activity as recommended treatment for patients whose lower trunk and limbs were paralysed was conceived during the Second World War, and thereafter developed naturally into the basis of regular competition. On the day the London OLYMPIC GAMES opened in 1948, an archery competition was held in the grounds of Stoke Mandeville Hospital. Those taking part were all patients at the hospital, or residents of the Star and Garter Home at Richmond, Surrey, who had served in the armed forces during the war. From those 16 competitors (who included 2 women) the Games grew to take in paraplegics all over the world: in 1970, the 420 competitors were drawn from 27 nations, and over the years more than 50 countries have sent representatives.

The international aspect of the Stoke Mandeville Games was strengthened when, in 1960, they were held in the Olympic city of Rome. They moved, with the Olympics, to Tokyo in 1964, but Mexico proved too difficult and in 1968 they were staged in Israel, where 750 competitors gathered. Heidelberg was the venue in 1972. The British Commonwealth Paraplegic Games were inaugurated in 1962 in Perth, where the COMMONWEALTH GAMES were being held. These are now held every four years in the Commonwealth Games cities.

The Stoke Mandeville Hospital, world renowned for its skill in the treatment of paraplegics, remains the international centre of their athletic activity. In 1969 a fully-equipped sports stadium was opened in the hospital grounds.

PARC DES PRINCES, the stadium in Paris where France have played most of their RUGBY UNION international matches since 1973. The stadium is administered jointly by Rugby Union and Association FOOTBALL authorities.

PARIS–BRUSSELS CYCLE RACE, international road race first run for amateurs in 1893, but, except during the war years, held annually as a professional event from 1906 until discontinued in 1966. Covering at least 176 miles (283 km.), and sometimes up to 275 miles (438 km.), it was nearly always the longest unpaced classic (cf. BORDEAUX–PARIS and MILAN–SAN REMO) of the season.

PARIS–ROUBAIX CYCLE RACE, annual French CYCLING classic for professionals. It was first held in 1896, and is approximately 165 miles (265 km.) long, with the final stretch of 50 miles or so made up of farm tracks and cobbled roads; hence its popular title, 'the Hell of the North'.

PARIS–TOURS CYCLE RACE, professional road race first held in 1896 and run annually since 1906 with only a two-year break in the First World War and a one-year break in the Second. Covering 155 miles (249 km.) of good, flattish roads, it is noted for its fast times. It is held in late September or early October before the TOUR OF LOMBARDY; the two races are known as the Autumn Classics.

PARISET, BERNARD (1929-   ), French JUDO fighter, who was the only European to beat GEESINK in a major event between 1952 and the Dutchman's retirement in 1967. Pariset clinched a split decision in the 1955 open class final which was hotly contested although he had held Geesink for 20 seconds. Pariset's magnificent *ippon seio-nage* (shoulder throw) brought him three European titles and he was invariably runner-up to Geesink in other years. He was quarter-finalist in the 1958 world championships and was a member of the European championships' winning side in 1951, 1952, 1954, 1955, and 1962.

PARISI, ANGELO (1953-   ), British JUDO fighter who had a series of superb successes during the 1970s. He won three European junior titles, a European senior gold medal in the team event, and in 1972 became European light-heavyweight champion. His ability to throw with almost equal force and facility on both sides enabled him to move into the Open category at the Munich Olympics and defeat older and more experienced opponents for the bronze medal.

PARK, WILLIE, jr. (1864-1925), Scottish professional golfer, course architect and author, he possibly made the largest contribution to GOLF of all this distinguished family of Musselburgh golfers. His father, Willie Park, sr., won the first Open championship in 1860, and repeated his success on three subsequent occasions. His uncle, Mungo Park, won the

Open in 1874, and Willie Park, jr. won it in 1887 and 1889. All the Parks were doughty match players and challenged all comers to high-stake matches. Willie Park, jr. claimed that 'a man who can putt is a match for anyone', and spent up to eight hours a day practising this facet of the game. He constructed many golf courses in Britain, the U.S.A., and Canada.

PARKIN, JONATHAN (1898-1972), English RUGBY LEAGUE player. His international career stretched unbroken over ten years — a remarkable record for a scrum half. During his 17-year career with WAKEFIELD TRINITY, he established himself as one of the most resourceful players in the history of the game. He is the only player to have captained two teams to Australia — in 1924 and 1928. He was also a member of the 1920 team under WAGSTAFF. Tough and astute, Parkin has never been excelled as a tactician. When placed on the transfer list at a nominal fee of £100, he paid the fee himself and joined Hull Kingston Rovers.

PARR, GEORGE (1826-91), cricketer for Nottinghamshire and the ALL-ENGLAND XI. Succeeding PILCH to the title of 'best batsman in England', he played important CRICKET from 1844 to 1871, captaining his county and also the All-England XI. In 1859 he went to the U.S.A. with the first English cricket team to tour overseas, and four years later led the second English team to tour Australia. A tree at TRENT BRIDGE was named after him in tribute to his strong leg-side hitting.

PARRY, DENISE (1939-   ), HOCKEY player for England, East of England, Essex, Hightown, and West Essex. Almost fragile in appearance, she was nevertheless an outstanding match-winning forward in women's hockey in the 1960s, possessing quite outstanding ball control. She represented England from 1962 to 1969 and captained her country in 1968 and 1969. She was a member of England touring teams to the world tournaments in the U.S.A. (1962) and Germany (1967).

PARSENN, ski area above Davos, Klosters, and Küblis which yields a 16 km. (9·9 miles) descent. A funicular there, and methods of marking and safeguarding downhill routes, were major advances in SKIING.

PASAKA, see PELOTA.

PATAUDI, Nawab IFTIKHAR ALI of (1910-52), cricketer for England, India,

Oxford University, and Worcestershire. A gifted batsman, he scored heavily for his university, and made the highest score (238 not out) for Oxford against Cambridge. After touring Australia in 1932-3 and making 102 in his first Test, he returned to India in 1934 and was seldom seen in England until 1946, when he led India on tour, although his health was poor. The Nawab also represented India at HOCKEY and was a member of their gold-medal winning team at the 1928 OLYMPIC GAMES.

His son, Mansur Ali Khan, also a cricketer, became captain of India in 1964 and made over 2,000 runs in Tests; his batting was also of great value to Sussex, despite the handicap of having lost an eye.

PATO is an Argentinian game for horsemen, a cross between POLO and NETBALL, requiring the skills of a circus rider. It is played between two teams of four men on a field 230 yds. (210 m.) long and 90 yds. (82 m.) wide, with the object of placing or throwing the ball into the opponent's goal, a net that hangs from a 9 ft. (2·7 m.) post. The ball is like a small football, with the addition of six large leather handles. When carried, it must be held with outstretched arm, giving opponents the chance of snatching it away. The ball is thrown into play by the referee, and may be thrown or punched from player to player. If it falls to the ground, it may only be picked up by a competitor riding at speed. A game consists of six periods of eight minutes each.

Pato (Spanish for 'duck') was first played in Argentina in the fifteenth century, between unlimited numbers of mounted employees from two neighbouring farms. The size of the field was determined only by the distance between the farms. The ball was a leather basket containing a live duck, and the game was won when one team galloped back to its farm with the duck. Any method — including lassoing — could be used to stop an opponent, who had to carry the basket at arm's length by one of its two handles.

The violence and cruelty of the game did not endear it to the Roman Catholic Church, which at the end of the eighteenth century threatened excommunication to any Catholics involved. In 1822 it was banned by government order, but did not finally disappear from the rural scene for another eighty years.

It was revived with its present unobjectionable rules in 1937, and is played in formal costume of coloured shirt, white breeches, and black boots. A handicap system similar to that used in polo is operated by the ruling body of the sport, the Federación Argentina de Pato.

PATRICIA'S HOPE (1970), racing greyhound, a white fawn dog, by Silver Hope out of Patsica. Winner of the English, Welsh, and Scottish Derbys in 1972, in 1973 he became the second greyhound in the history of the sport to win the English GREYHOUND DERBY twice, thus equalling the feat of the legendary MICK THE MILLER who won in 1929 and 1930. He was trained by J. O'Connor (Ireland) and owned by Messrs. G. and B. Marks.

PATTERSON, FLOYD (1935-   ), American boxer, who at 21, in 1956, became the youngest man to win the world heavyweight championship. Patterson, an Olympic middleweight champion in 1952, was also the first heavyweight champion to regain the title. In June 1959 he was beaten in the third round by Johansson of Sweden but one year later he scored a fifth-round knock-out over Johansson.

PATTERSON, GERALD L. (1895-1965), Australian LAWN TENNIS player. A powerful server with an aggressive forecourt game, he won the WIMBLEDON singles title at the first attempt in 1919 by beating the veteran BROOKES in the challenge round. He lost only one set in the process and it was the first time since Hadow's victory in 1878 that a newcomer had been successful. TILDEN took the title from him, but Patterson returned in 1922 to become the first champion at the new ground in Church Road. He was the Australian singles champion in 1927 and won the doubles there five times. He also won the U.S. doubles with Brookes in 1919. He was a member of the successful Australasian team which won the Davis Cup (see LAWN TENNIS) in 1919 and between then and 1928 he played 46 rubbers.

PAULSEN, AXEL, ice figure-skater and speed-skater for Norway and originator of the axel jump (see ICE SKATING).

PAVESI, DONATO (c. 1888-   ), race walker for Italy, the first of a long line of Italian long distance *campionissimos*. Pavesi was six times winner of the MILAN 100 KM. (1910, 1914, 1919-22), the LONDON–BRIGHTON twice (1921 and 1923) and the MANCHESTER–BLACKPOOL in 1922, as well as qualifying as a CENTURION. Nearing the end of a long career, Pavesi set a world best for 20 km. in 1927.

PAWLE, J. H. (*fl.* 1939-51), British amateur RACKETS player who won the British amateur singles championship 1946-9 and the doubles championship with Crawley in 1939 and 1946. He unsuccessfully challenged DEAR for the world title in 1949 and 1951.

PAWLOWSKI, JERZY (1931-   ), Polish fencer who won more titles at sabre than any of his countrymen. He was Olympic sabre champion in 1968 and world sabre champion in 1957, 1965, and 1966. On a points system based on reaching the first three places in world and Olympic finals, he stands only 1 point behind MANGIAROTTI in the history of the sport, despite having fenced internationally at only one weapon.

PEACE RACE, the principal amateur stage race of eastern Europe, roughly equivalent in status to the TOUR DE L'AVENIR, but less frequently used as a proving ground for future CYCLING professionals. In the first four years from 1948, the race was run, in one direction or the other, between Warsaw and Prague; from 1952 East Berlin was included, and the three cities were linked in various sequences; after the Russian invasion of Czechoslovakia in 1969, Prague was dropped from the itinerary, but restored in 1970. The race is characterized by long, hard stages over largely flat country exposed to the wind.

PEACOCK, ROBERT (1932-   ), Association footballer for Northern Ireland, GLENTORAN, Glasgow CELTIC, and Coleraine. A wing half, he played on 32 occasions for his country, and was Irish F.A. international team manager 1962-7.

PEARCE brothers, all five of whom represented Australia in the OLYMPIC GAMES at HOCKEY. Born in India, they emigrated to Australia with their family in 1947. Mel and Cecil played in Australia's first Olympic hockey team in 1956. MEL (1928-   ) was a prolific goal-scorer whose career was ended prematurely by a leg injury. CECIL (1929-   ) was a fine tactician. ERIC (1931-   ), another free-scoring forward, played in four Olympics from 1956 to 1968, while GORDON (1934-   ) and JULIAN (1937-   ), both admirable half-backs, took part in the 1960, 1964, and 1968 Olympics.

PEARCE, HENRY ROBERT (1904-   ), Australian sculler (see ROWING) who later became a Canadian citizen. The son of an Australian professional sculling champion, Harry Pearce, who unsuccessfully raced for the world championship in 1911 and 1913, Bob Pearce won the Australian amateur championship for three successive years from 1927, and in 1928 he became the first Australian to win the Olympic title and the PHILADEPHIA GOLD CUP for the amateur championship of the world. In 1930 he added the Empire Games

title and in 1931 the Diamond Sculls (see HENLEY) to his list of wins.

Although by 1932 he had taken up permanent residence in Canada, Pearce was bound by the rules to represent Australia in the 1932 Olympics, when he retained his title. He then turned professional, beating the reigning British and world champion, Phelps, for the world title at Toronto in 1933. He successfully defended the title against Miller (U.S.A.) in 1934 and Paddon (Australia) in 1938, and was undefeated when the outbreak of the Second World War virtually put an end to his career. Pearce was the only sculler to retire undefeated as both amateur and professional champion of the world and ranks as the last of the great professionals.

PEARL CAP (1928) was a famous French filly who won the PRIX DE L'ARC DE TRIOMPHE, French Oaks, French One Thousand Guineas, and PRIX VERMEILLE. She was bred by Esmond, raced by his daughter, trained by CARTER, and ridden by SEMBLAT. Pearl Cap was the first filly to win the Prix de l'Arc de Triomphe, and her stake total was 2,239,914 francs.

PEBBLE BEACH, U.S. GOLF course in California. One of the three courses used annually for the Bing Crosby tournament, Pebble Beach is distinguished mainly for two holes: the eighth with a second shot which must carry a deep inlet, with the Pacific boiling on the rocks below, and the last, running along the rocky shore line.

PEDERSEN, TERJE OLAV (1943-   ), javelin-thrower for Norway. The first man to exceed 300 ft. (91·44 m.), Pedersen broke the world record with 285 ft. 10 in. (87·12 m.) in July 1964. Exactly two months later he outclassed his own pending world mark with 300 ft. 11 in. (91·72 m.), the biggest single improvement in the world record since the inception of official world records in 1913.

PEEL, ROBERT (1857-1941), cricketer for England and Yorkshire. One of a distinguished line of Yorkshire slow left-arm bowlers, he took 1,754 wickets in 16 seasons and frequently made valuable runs. In 20 Test matches — all against Australia — he took 102 wickets at the economical rate of 16·81, including 6 for 23 in his last Test, in 1896.

PELÉ (Edson Arantes do Nascimento) (1940-   ), Association footballer for SANTOS (São Paulo), and Brazil. On 19 November 1969 he scored his 1000th goal in senior football when he scored a penalty goal for Santos against Vasco da Gama at the MARACAÑA STADIUM in Rio de Janeiro. The achievement brought tributes from all over the world including a testimonial by ROUS in the name of F.I.F.A. (see FOOTBALL, ASSOCIATION). It was a fitting acknowledgement that Pelé was the finest inside forward of his era, and probably any other. He was only 17 when he scored twice for Brazil in the World Cup final of 1958, and later he played in some of the matches (before being injured) for the 1962 and 1966 world championships, and appeared throughout the 1970 championship which Brazil won in Mexico.

PELISSIER, HENRI (1890-1936), French professional road-race cyclist. Although the First World War came when he was in mid-career, he scored nine classic victories, which remained a record until it was surpassed by VAN LOOY in 1967. He also won the 1923 TOUR DE FRANCE. Two younger brothers, Francis and Charles, also won yellow jerseys in the Tour, and Charles set a record by winning eight stages in the Tour of 1930.

PELL, C. C., American amateur RACKETS player who won the U.S. amateur singles championship 11 times between 1915 and 1933. In 1925 he defeated the leading British players to win the amateur singles championship at Queen's Club, London — the only American to do so.

PELOTA, or *pilota,* or *pelote Basque,* is a generic name for numerous hand, glove, racquet, or bat-and-ball games adapted originally from the ancient French *jeux de paume* and first — and still mainly — played in the Basque and contingent provinces of France and Spain. Besides these countries, pelota in one or more of its varieties is now played all over the world — in every country of South America, in Belgium, Italy, Ireland, Egypt, Indonesia, Morocco, Mexico, Cuba, the Philippines, and in the U.S.A. in Florida and California.

The many versions of pelota fall into two distinct categories: (1) *Jeux directs,* straight, up-and-down games where the players face each other and the ball (or *pelote*) flies freely between opponents. In these games scoring is as in tennis — 15, 30, 40, game. The weight and composition of the *pelote* vary greatly according to the game for which it is made. Wool, cotton, rubber, and leather are used; the covering is usually the skin of sheep, goat, calf, or dog — for *main nue* almost invariably the latter. *Pelotes,* for *main nue,* are handmade and quickly lose their resilience, hence the frequent ball changes during a game. (2)

Jeux indirects, or *jeux de blaid,* games where players face a wall against which the ball is hit, either directly or off another wall. In these games scoring is by points. *Jeux directs* comprise only two games, which are also the oldest, *rebot* and *pasaka.* The *jeux indirects* number 11, which are: *main nue, cesta punta, pala larga, yoko-garbi, grand chistera, pala corta, raquette, remonte, sare,* and two kinds of *palette.*

The courts used for both categories of game are of three kinds: the *place libre,* an open outdoor court of variable dimensions and a single wall; the *fronton,* which includes covered and outdoor courts of varying dimensions with two or three walls; and lastly the *trinquet,* a small covered court.

Surfaces of these courts (the Spanish-Basque for 'floor' or 'surface', *cancha,* has by extension come to mean the court itself) vary from the untreated earth of the village *place libre,* through *en tout cas* rubble and paving, to the highly polished cement of the modern *fronton* known as a *jaï-alaï.*

Pelota, with its great range and variety, is played in different ways by different people, according to national character or local custom. It is played more by professionals in Spain than in France. This is not simply because Spanish Basques are three times more numerous than French, but because the Spanish Basque is a gambler, and gambling means the consistently high standard of play that only professionals can provide. The game known as *remonte,* for example, is unknown in France but played everywhere in the Basque Spanish provinces and in most Spanish cities. The reason is that, while being one of pelota's most exciting variants, it is also its most difficult. Young Basques in Spain, thinking of the material rewards, find time to learn it; their French counterparts, amateur by nature, will not be bothered.

This difference in practice modifies ethical attitudes. In France, the judges — as the umpires are called — *never* intervene unless solicited by a player. A player must return a ball he thinks doubtful, at the same time calling the equivalent of 'How's that?'; when the rally ends the judges give their decision. But a player is not obliged to challenge a doubtful ball, nor need he acknowledge his own — e.g. a ball picked up on the second bounce — though he must in honour bound admit it if an opponent has appealed. Uninitiated spectators are puzzled to see a flagrant fault uncalled; the fact is that players, enjoying the heat of a rally, wish the game to continue, or there may be other reasons. It is they who decide. This old and chivalrous convention has no place where money is at stake; in

Spain, South America, and virtually everywhere except France the judges call the faults, as in tennis.

But if the judges need no longer — as once they had to — swear their neutrality on a crucifix, many of the traditional, unwritten laws of pelota have been included in the modern rules, and are universally applied: those, for example, concerning dress. In competition, and in public, players must wear white; long trousers are mandatory. The colours of the two sides — red and blue — are shown by brassards, or ribbons, pinned to the shoulder of the shirt. Lately, however, professionals have taken to wearing coloured jerseys, generally red or blue, and also helmets for protection in the faster games played with the hard *pelote*.

Pelota's plurality of courts means that some games have two or more versions. *Main nue*, for example, is played in *place libre*, *fronton*, and *trinquet*; *pala* in the first; and *palette* in the last two of these. Rules have been coded for every game recognized by the several authorities but, competition apart, players ignore or modify them at will, improvising as they go along.

More pelota is played with *main nue* ('bare hand') than with the various bats and racquets. Fifty years ago players were allowed to hold the ball briefly — when taken on the volley — before returning it: that is, the ball was first caught, then thrown. Under modern rules every ball must be hit; there is no way of lessening the force of impact. The repeated shock of striking a hard *pelote* soon produces a massive oedema of the hand, generally accompanied by bruising (due to the fracture of small veins) in the first two joints of the fingers. The swelling, when severe, becomes a puffy and insensitive pad which affects the player's accuracy of strike and sense of direction. Some points at the base of the fingers, however, remain sensitive, and when rapped, start a piercing pain which the Basques call *itzia*, 'the nail'. This trauma, the result of inflammation of the flexor tendons, often forces the player to abandon the match, or, if it becomes chronic, to abandon the game.

In most countries, players are classified for competition as seniors, juniors, and cadets; length of court, weight of ball, size of racquet, etc. vary accordingly. In the descriptions of games that follow, figures quoted are those for seniors in every case. Measurements, details of procedure and methods of play given here are those laid down by the Fédération Française de Pelote Basque in the 1961 edition of their rules.

JEUX DIRECTS.

Rebot (or Spanish, *rebote*) from the Old French *reboter*, 'to reverse', or 'to hit back', is a five-a-side form of pelota played with leather or *chistera*-type gloves in the open court called *place libre*. Derived from a small wicker fruit basket, the *chistera* was first used tentatively for pelota by French Basques about 1860. Lengthened and strengthened over the years to attain its present form, it has a curved frame of seasoned chestnut and ash branches and a body of plaited osier twigs. The hand is slid wrist-deep into the aperture, or pocket, which contains the 'glove' — actually four leather finger loops in the manner of cricket batting gloves. The whole is lashed to the wrist by laces.

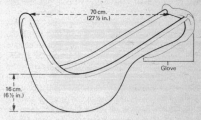

GRAND CHISTERA
The frame is of chestnut or ash, the body of plaited osier twigs. The *petit chistera* is somewhat smaller, 55 cm. (21½ in.) long.

The ball is caught in the *chistera*, held for a moment (the *atchiki* — to 'hold' or 'wait') and then hurled out again. The ball weighs 130 g. (4½ oz.), scoring is as in tennis and a match is 13 games. This is the oldest and most esoteric version of pelota: a survival of the game, derived from *longue paume*, played before the coming of the rubber-cored ball killed the old order and created the *jeux de blaid*. *Rebot* is more than a game: it is a ceremony with its own language and conventions that few but players and initiates can fully understand. It is played only in the Basque provinces, and only in certain villages and towns, among which the best known are Sare, Hasparren, St. Palais, Orio, St. Jean-de-Luz, St. Etienne-de-Baïgorry, Ustaritz, and Les Aldudes.

The court must be at least 100 m. (109 yds.) long and 16 m. (17·5 yds.) wide. A line, called the *paso*, is drawn 32 m. (35 yds.) from the wall; in the centre of the *paso* is the 'serving stone' — a tripod bearing an inclined block of wood. On the wall are two vertical lines, 7 m. (7·7 yds.) apart. A transversal line is drawn 5·5 m. (6 yds.) from the base of the wall: the area of this rectangle is called the *barne*.

The *paso* line divides the players into two camps: a defending, or *refil* side, nearest the wall; and an attacking, or serving side, beyond the *paso*. Each side alternately attacks and defends, according to the fortunes of the game, but the object of each is to prevent the ball 'dying' in its camp, while attempting to make it stop in that of its opponents. In this, the defending side is heavily favoured, for it occupies less than a third of the court.

The spearhead of the attacking side is the server, who hits the ball with his bare hand — the only stroke so made in the game — after bouncing it once on the serving-stone. The serve, to be good, must hit the wall in the *barne*, either on the volley or first bounce off the *barne* area on the floor; it is returned by the key player of the defending side, called the *refileur*, who guards the *barne* close to the wall. The ball, thereafter, need not hit the wall.

If, in the ensuing rally, the attackers miss the ball, they lose the point outright; if, on the contrary, they succeed in making it penetrate the *barne*, either on the wall or on the floor, they win it. Should the defending side miss the ball without, however, letting it enter the *barne*, or should they let the ball roll along the ground to cross the *paso*, the umpire calls a 'chase'. A branch of green leaves is placed at the side of the court opposite the spot where the ball was missed or where it stopped; until the point is definitely won or lost the *paso* is regarded as running through this spot. If a chase is scored when the attacking side is at 'forty', or should two chases be won, the sides change ends and the chases are played off successively, after which the original *paso* line becomes valid. Because they alone cause a change of camps, the chases are of prime importance. Only by scoring them can the attacking side become the defending side and enjoy the advantages provided by the restricted *barne* area, an area even more restricted — and thus easier to defend — by the temporary limits of the chase lines.

Well played, *rebot* is a vigorous, absorbing, and spectacular game that can produce high moments — as when, for example, the *refileur*, back to his wall in a close chase, sends away a head-high serve soaring a hundred yards or more; or when, moving in on a chase, the attackers bombard the *barne* with low-hit volleys and the defenders come out grimly to narrow the angles.

Of all the pelota corpus, *rebot* is nearest the source. The sites where it is played — always on Sundays after morning Mass — its ceremonial cadence, the gravely conferring judges, the melodious chanting of the score: *kintze bana, trenta nada, koante trenta, a dos* — all this is truly Basque.

Pasaka (Basque 'to pass') is a two-a-side form of pelota played with bare hands or leather gloves over a net in the covered court called *trinquet*. There is no standard pattern for the glove; it is usually short, heavy, and slightly curved. The ball weighs about 240 g. ($8\frac{1}{2}$ oz.). Scoring is as in tennis and a match consists of 13 games. If the score reaches 12 games all, 3 additional games can be played — but only by mutual agreement and only once. There are three judges.

Pasaka is the last surviving game of the pelota played in a covered court before the coming of the rubber-cored ball. A difficult and strenuous game, it was obsolescent a few years ago, but is now returning to favour, both in France and Spain.

The *trinquet* is a rectangular structure of varying dimensions, with a gallery along three sides, a net across it, and a penthouse with a sloping roof (which forms one of the playing

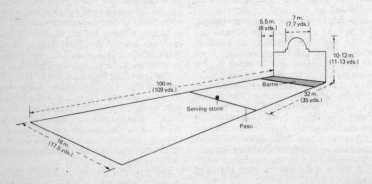

PLACE LIBRE
The dimensions shown are for competition. Many old *rebot* courts are simply village squares whose dimensions do not comply with the rules. A tripod in the centre of the *paso* bears an inclined block of wood, the 'serving stone'.

surfaces) along the left-hand and back walls. A central section of the left-hand penthouse wall has a dedans net let into it, as does, usually, the back wall of the court. Extending vertically along the right-hand edge of the front wall is a flat shaft or tambour, forming the corner; sometimes there is a grille let into the side of this front wall.

The net, 1·2 m. (3 ft. 11 in.) high, is strung across the centre of the court. The players between it and the front wall are the *refil*, or 'receiving' side; their opponents across the net are the *camp buteur*, the serving side. Each pair has one player up at the net who serves, and one back. The serve is made from a mid-court rectangle on the server's side and, to be good, must bounce off the roof of the penthouse into a similar rectangle near the front wall on the *refil* side. The serve is an upward blow with the bare hand, the only stroke so made in the game. Half-faults are incurred if the service ball touches the wall above the penthouse roof or falls outside the *refil*'s rectangle, or if there is a foot fault. Two half-faults mean the loss of the point. Courts are changed after every game. If the sides are tied at 'deuce', the score reverts to '30 all'; the game then goes to the pair scoring two consecutive points.

Tactics, for the serving side, consist in

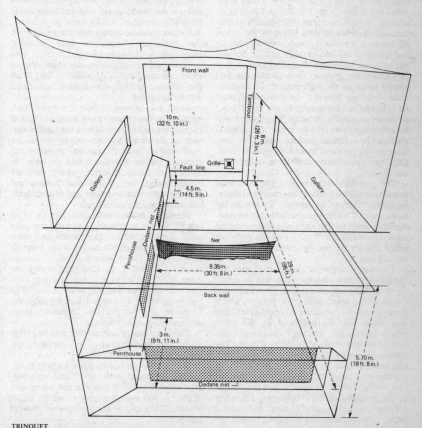

TRINQUET

Covered courts for pelota differ greatly in dimensions and detail. Measurements given here are those laid down for competition under international rules. In some courts there is no dedans net in the penthouse along the back wall; others have no grille. In the *trinquet* shown here the penthouse is 2·4 m. (2·6 yds.) high; its roof is 1·45 m. (1·6 yds.) wide and slopes to 1·93 m. (2·1 yds.) from the floor. The tambour is 47 cm. (1 ft. 6 in.) wide. The net across the centre of the court (used only for *pasaka*) is 93 cm. (3 ft.) from the floor. The fault line is 90 cm. (2 ft. 11 in.) from the floor.

attacking the tambour, with its unpredictable angles of return; or trying to lodge the ball in the grille. The *refil* pair must prevent the ball reaching these areas either by cutting it off at the net or by forcing their opponents into mistakes, or weak returns, by long balls rolling the length of the penthouse roof, lodging in the dedans net, or clinging to the right side wall.

JEUX INDIRECTS.

Main nue en place libre ('bare hand in open court') is played either in singles or doubles against a single wall in an open court similar to that used for *rebot*. The court is a minimum of 35 m. (38·3 yds.) long and 16 m. (17·5 yds.) wide. At one end is a vertical wall, the same width as the court, 7 m. (7·7 yds.) high at the sides and 8·5 to 9 m. (9–10 yds.) high at its centre. There is no *barne* (the whole wall may be used) and no serving block as for *rebot*. The server, chosen by toss, begins play by bouncing the ball and hitting it against the wall above a horizontal metal line 85 cm. (2 ft. 9 in.) above the ground; once in play the ball can be taken on the volley or on first bounce. Two serves are allowed; the service ball must fall beyond a line drawn 15 m. (16·4 yds.) from and parallel to the wall. Every point won counts in the score; the server — who is interchangeable — retains service until he is put out. Game is 30 points. The ball weighs 90–92 g. (3·2 oz.) and there are three judges, or umpires.

The game is very simple. The ball must remain within the limits of the court and those, lateral and vertical, of the wall. Tactics are the basic ones of working opponents out of position too close to the wall, where they can be lobbed, or too far back, whence they are unable to get up for the *cortada*—the short ball, or 'kill'.

Two things might puzzle the newcomer: the ceremony of choosing the balls, and the seemingly arbitrary intervals during play. Each side comes to the court with three *pelotes*, which must, of course, conform to regulations. But they must also be approved by the other side — hence the feeling, bouncing, and general testing of the balls before a game. The sudden stoppages are not due to fatigue; they allow the players to rest their hands. Every *pilotari* who plays the *main nue* has inflamed and swollen hands. Most will have broken one of the knuckles of the forefingers; all, when playing regularly, have bruised and painful palms. This explains the very long 'knock-up' before a match: the players are encouraging the circulation of blood to de-sensitize their hands. It also explains the careful choice of balls: a rough or too heavy *pelote* can do serious damage.

Main nue en trinquet ('bare hand in covered court') is a form of pelota for singles, doubles, or three-a-side, played in the covered court called *trinquet* with the bare hand and a ball weighing 90 g. (3·2 oz.). The service line is 8·5 m. (9·3 yds.) from the front wall; to be good the service ball must fall beyond a line drawn 17·5 m. (19 yds.) from that wall. Two serves are allowed. Every point counts and game is 50 points. There is one judge, or umpire.

This is probably the most popular, as it is certainly the most interesting, form of barehand pelota. The hazards of the four walls of the *trinquet* call for greater subtlety and a richer variety of stroke than does the single wall of the *place libre*. Tactics are the basic ones of the short, aimed ball that holes out in the grille, ricochets wildly from the tambour, or lodges in the penthouse nets; or the long lob that rides the penthouse roof to 'die' untakeably at the back wall.

In the Basque countries the champions at *main nue* are the élite of *pilotaris*, for, of all the corpus, this is the noblest and most demanding game.

Main nue en fronton mur à gauche ('bare hand in covered *fronton*') is a form of pelota played in singles or doubles in the smaller version of the *fronton espagnol*, known as the *petit fronton mur à gauche*. *Frontons*, in general, can be either covered or open. In Spain and South America, where they are mostly found, the three-walled *frontons* are generally covered in towns and big villages; elsewhere they are often open.

Service is made from a line 10·5 m. (11·4 yds.) from the front wall. The *falta* and *pasa* lines, between which the service ball must fall, are respectively 14 m. (15·3 yds.) and 24 m. (26·2 yds.) from the front wall. A second serve is allowed if the first falls beyond the *pasa* line, half a fault; if the first ball falls short of the *falta* line, the point is lost. The ball weighs 98 g. (3·4 oz.). Game for singles is 22 points; that for doubles, 25 points. There are three judges, or umpires.

This is the fastest and most demanding form of the *main nue*; it is also, because of the left side wall, the most difficult.

It is mainly played in Spain, where three-walled *frontons*, both open and covered, abound; a fact which explains the superiority of the Spanish *main nue* player over his counterpart in France, where the covered *fronton* hardly exists.

Cesta punta (Spanish *cesta*, a basket, and *punta*, a point — here meaning the tip of the basket-glove), a two-a-side game played with a long *chistera* in a *jaï-alaï*. The *chistera* measures, round the curve, between 90 and 110 cm. (35½ – 43 in.) from wrist to point, and is 16 cm. (6¼ in.) deep. The ball weighs 125 g. (4·4 oz.). Game is 35 or 40 points. There is one judge (umpire), who has two assistants.

On the side wall, numbered from front to rear, are painted 14 vertical lines, 4 m. (4·4 yds.) apart, called *cuadros* (Spanish for 'frames'). The fourth and seventh of these lines are extended across the floor of the court and labelled respectively *falta* and *pasa*. A serve, to be good, must rebound from the front wall to fall between these two lines. The serve is made from the tenth *cuadro*— 40 m. (43·7 yds.) from the front wall. A second serve is allowed if the first ball falls beyond the *pasa* line — half a fault; if the first ball falls short of the *falta* line the point is lost. The service can be glanced off the side wall if desired.

Each side has one back and one forward player, the server. Basic tactics are the same as those of every *chistera* game: either to harass the back into hitting a weaker return that can be cut off by the opposing front player with a low, angled *cortada*, or to lure the back player up court with medium-length balls before hoisting one over his head that will 'die' at the back wall. The most difficult stroke is the backhand hit close to the left wall; most shots are made to hug that side. The powerful slice induced by the curve of the

basket-glove allows good players to mask their strokes adroitly; a ball struck from near the side wall to the centre of the front wall will, if properly spun, rebound on a reciprocal path and not — as the opponent anticipates — at an equal angle. One untakeable shot is the *pik*, the high ball that 'yorks' the back wall to fizz along the floor; another is the wristy drop shot, a most delicate feat with this speedy ball. The back, since he can see all the court, usually decides the tactics and calls the play.

This, with *remonte*, is pelota's fastest game. The extreme liveliness of a hard, wholly rubber ball, the length of the court and the pace of the polished *cancha* demand a faultless eye and great agility. The game is, literally, one of leaps and bounds, for the high bounce means that deep balls must be taken at the top of a vertical leap, while those that drop off the back wall need a backhand stroke hit above the head as the player hurls himself forward in a falling lunge to the floor.

Pala (Spanish, *pala*, a spade), is a two-a-side form of pelota played with a long wooden bat in the large *fronton* called *jaï-alaï*. The rules and distances for fault line, service line, etc. are the same as for *cesta punta* except that the server is allowed a third serve if the first two fall beyond the *pasa* line. The tap-

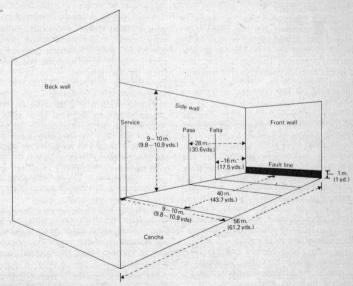

JAÏ-ALAÏ OR GRAND FRONTON MUR À GAUCHE
The small *fronton espagnol* used for *main nue en fronton mur à gauche* and for *pala corta* is a proportionately reduced replica of this larger *fronton*. As usual with pelota courts, a certain tolerance is allowed — 50 cm. to 1 m. — in measurements. The *grand fronton* is in some cases extended to 64 m. (70 yds.) in length; this is the limit.

ering bat, made of a single piece of beech or ash, is 53 cm. (21 in.) long, 10·5 cm. (4¼ in.) at its widest, weighs between 840 and 880 g. (1 lb. 14 oz.–2 lb.) and has a leather hand grip; the ball weighs 100 g. (3·5 oz.). Every point counts; game is 45 points. There is one judge who has two assistants.

This hard-hitting game is one of pelota's fastest. The narrow bat and speedy ball call for a true eye and perfect timing; the bat being 'dead', each stroke must be followed through. As in all games played with a bat in a *fronton espagnol*—the court with a left side wall — the players must be ambidextrous. Every shot is hit on the forehand; the backhand, which at best can be no more than a defensive jab, is almost never used by competent players. A high point in any *pala* match is when experts continually switch hands to prolong a dazzling rally.

Highly spectacular, difficult and dangerous when the hard ball flies at speed, *pala* is much played by professionals in Spain and South America; little, and only by amateurs, in France.

Pala larga is played in the *place libre*. The game there is two-a-side; the serve must be made from a line 25 m. (27·3 yds.) from the wall, and fall over a line 15 m. (16·4 yds.) from the wall. Game is 50 points; there are three judges, or umpires.

Pala corta (Spanish, *pala*, a spade or instrument, *corta*, short) is a two-a-side variation played with a wooden bat in the smaller version of *fronton espagnol* known as *petit fronton mur à gauche*. The bat is of the same shape as that used for *pala larga*, but is shorter and lighter, being 49 cm. (19¼ in.) long and weighing between 600 and 700 g. (1 lb. 5 oz.–1 lb. 9 oz.). The serve is made 28 m. (30·6 yds.) from the front wall; to be good the service ball must fall in the space between the *falta* and *pasa* lines, respectively 10·5 m. (11·4 yds.) and 17 m. (18·6 yds.) from the front wall. A third serve is allowed if the first two serves have fallen beyond the *pasa* line. If the first serve falls short of the *falta* line, the point is lost. Each point counts; game is 35 points. The ball weighs 90 g. (3·2 oz.). There is one judge who has two assistants.

Pala corta is simply a scaled-down version of *pala larga* and, like that game, is played predominantly in Spain and South America by professionals and amateurs alike; much less in France. Because the court is smaller, *corta* is probably faster than *larga*, while its shorter bat makes it even more difficult.

Yoko-garbi, which in Basque means 'pure', or 'clean game', is a three-a-side form of pelota played with a *petit chistera* in a *place libre*, with a single wall. The court is the same

as that for *main nue en place libre* except that the length is extended to 50 m. (54·7 yds.), and the service line to 22·5 m. (24·6 yds.). The *chistera* measures 55 cm. (21½ in.) from wrist to point, and the ball weighs 120 g. (4·2 oz.). Every point counts; game is 50 points. There are three judges, or umpires.

As with its more ample variation *grand chistera*—which is derived from it — *yoko-garbi* is played with two men near the wall and one back. The server puts the ball in play by bouncing it and hitting it off the wall beyond the service line. The ball, which can be hit on the volley or first bounce, must be struck directly, with no pause (or *atchiki*) to load the stroke, as in *grand chistera*. This clean, almost instantaneous return of the ball is possible because of the reduced length and shallow curve of the small basket-glove. For this reason the game is very fast with — if well played — low, hard-hit rallies close to the wall. But before these the basic play has generally been to lure the back up to the wall by shots just too high for the forward players, then to send him scuttling back to retrieve a deep lob with a weak return — which is put away by a *cortada*. Practically every shot is hit on the forehand, and a good player can even smash overhead, as in tennis, which would be quite impossible with a long, deeply-curved glove.

More than most games in the species, *petit gant* or 'short glove' as it is often called, is a busy, close-contact affair which allows all players to come into action frequently. The man to watch, though, is the one playing in front on the left side — the key position. Invariably the best player, it is he who 'reads' the game and calls the shots.

Grand chistera is a three-a-side variation played with long *chisteras* in an open court with a single wall. The court is the same as that for *main nue en place libre* except that the length is extended to 80 m. (87·5 yds.), and the service line to 30 m. (32·8 yds.). The *chistera* measures 70 cm. (27 in.) from wrist to point, and the ball weighs 125 g. (4·4 oz.). Every point won counts; game is 50 points. There are five judges, or umpires.

Each side has two front men and one back, the *arrière*. When a side is serving, its *arrière* stands in mid-court and his opposite number far in the rear. The other four players are placed between mid-court and the wall, the defenders being a little deeper. Although the rules allow it, players very seldom change position. A *chistera* man will decide at the beginning of his career — usually by his physique — where he will play, and stays there. The right front man serves, but the front player on the left holds the key position, and is generally the captain. The server, standing a few yards from the wall, cries 'Yo!' (Basque, 'I hit' or 'Here goes'), dances a couple of steps, bounces the *pelote* with the left hand and, on the forehand, deals it an upward, swinging blow that sends it flying high to the opposing back, 50 or more yards behind. There is no law against striking a low, difficult ball on the serve, but convention insists that it be high and easy. Except for a short, pushed volley near the wall, the serve is one of the few forehand strokes; the length and shape of the *chistera* makes the backhand all but obligatory.

The back catches the ball in his *chistera*, where it lodges, swivels trunk and shoulders to the left and, swinging with both arms, propels it with a two-fisted lunge towards the wall. It is a fault, penalized by loss of the point, to hold the ball longer than is necessary to make the stroke. However, as players tire — especially the backs — their movements slow and they are apt to take one or two steps to give more force to the whirl of the backhand swing — thus prolonging the *atchiki* and, technically, incurring a penalty.

The ball, propelled by the *arrière*, lands high on the wall and is picked up, almost always on the volley, by a front man who cracks it powerfully back to the *arrière*. This exchange can continue for 20 or 30 strokes, the ball soaring deeper and deeper until the back is forced to return it from anything up to 90 yds. (83 m.), or more. Inevitably, as he tires, his returns will be shorter until one drops close off the wall; this is what his opponents have been working for — one seizes the chance and puts the ball away with a low, angled *cortada*.

Such is *grand chistera*'s only tactical device, an obvious one that lends the game a certain monotony. However, if the *cortada* is returned, an exciting exchange of low, hard-hit shots can result. To win the point a player must then try to lift a medium length shot over the opposing front men but short of the *arrière* who, fearing another deep ball, has not dared venture up court. If he *has* come up, the play, naturally, is to lob one over him.

Because of the sweeping, scythe-like stroke and the soaring flight of the ball, *grand chistera* has something of the grace and formality of ballet. This, and the fact that it is easy to understand, has made it, with *cesta punta*, one of the most popular spectator sports in pelota's range. Purists, mainly Basque, despise it as a parvenu game, fit only for tourists and children.

Raquette (French for 'racquet') is a two-a-side form played with a slackly-strung racquet in the *petit fronton mur à gauche*. The racquet, shaped like a snow-shoe and similar to that used for *sare* (see below) has no regulation width, but is usually 50 to 55 cm. (19¼–21¾ in.) long; the ball weighs 50 g. (1·7 oz.).

This game has the same rules as *pala corta* — except that the service *pasa* line is 50 cm. (1 ft. 8 in.) further from the front wall — and employs the same tactics. *Raquette* is fast, spectacular, and ambidextrous. The ball flies with surprising speed, for the slack net of the racquet acts like a sling. It has been called the '*cesta punta* of the small *fronton*' — which is a tribute to its qualities.

Remonte (Spanish, 'return', or 'climb back') is a two-a-side form of pelota played with a special *chistera* in a *jaï-alaï*. The ball weighs 125 g. (4·4 oz.). Game is 35 points; there are three judges, or umpires.

Though some players opt for one or the other, this can be said, with *cesta punta*, to be pelota's fastest and most difficult game, which explains why it is played almost exclusively by professionals. The rules and tactics employed are the same as those of *cesta punta*, which is a romantic and easier form of *remonte*. The basket-glove is narrower and much less curved than that used in other *chistera* games. Rattan canes replace the osier twigs of the standard *chistera*, and the inside curve is highly polished. The ball appears to rebound instantaneously, but in fact it hits the *chistera* near the wrist, travels down it — the *remonte* — and flies out at the far end. The split-second timing of reception and the powerful whip of the wrist give the stroke a deceptive unity. This sibilant movement — the Basques, with their genius for onomatopoeia, call it *chirricht* — accounts at once for the speed and the difficulty of the game, and makes possible the heavy slice with which good players mask their shots.

Remonte, which is played mainly in Spain and South America, causes heavy gambling of a peculiar kind. Wagers are all made by spectators, who signal their choice and the odds they offer to a row of bookmakers standing below on the floor of the court. These yell the odds — '*treinta a cuarenta azules*' (thirty to forty on Blues) — and, when they find a taker, write the wager on a betting slip. Tearing this in two, they hurl the two halves, each stuffed in a wooden ball, to layer and punter in turn. Bets are settled at the end of the match, with the management taking its percentage.

Sare (pronounced 'shah-ray', a Basque word meaning 'net', or 'basket') is a two-a-side game (known in France also as *raquette Argentine*) played with a slackly-strung racquet in the covered court known as *trinquet*. The racquet is 55 cm. (21¾ in.) long and has a frame of bent white wood — often chestnut or walnut. The strings are of stout cord. The ball weighs 80 g. (2·8 oz.). Game is 50 points; there is one judge, or umpire.

Sare was developed in France and exported, about 1850, to the Argentine, where it is mainly played. The court is divided lengthwise and equally into two parts. The serve, which is made from the left court, is delivered from a line drawn 15 m. (16·4 yds.) from the front wall; to be good it must fall over this line in the right court. There is a half-fault if the service ball hits the left wall, or if it falls on the dividing line. Two half-faults lose the point.

Sare is ambidextrous; the backhand is not forbidden but in practice is never attempted. Tactics are the same as those used in most *trinquet* games: the forward player — generally also the server — must stay up court to guard the tambour and grille, and be ready to deal with any short balls, while his partner looks after the middle of the court and defends the dedans of the left and back walls.

This is a most entertaining game to play or watch. Fast and wristy, it has perhaps a greater range of shots than any other indoor game, for the light racquet with its slack strings can pick up, or net, balls that would be lost to any other instrument. The stroke resembles that used with the short *chistera* in *yoko-garbi*, the slack of the strings having the same effect as the curve of the basket-glove. As in that game, it permits the overhead smash.

Palette (French, 'small shovel') *avec pelote de cuir* ('palette with leather ball') is a two-a-side version played with an oval, wooden bat in the *trinquet*. The bat is 50 cm. (19¾ in.) long, 13·5 cm. (5¼ in.) wide, and 2·5 cm. (1 in.) thick. The ball, which contains a minimum of rubber, weighs 50 g. (1·7 oz.). The game is 40 points; there is one judge, or umpire. The rules and court limits are exactly the same as those for *sare*, as are the tactics employed and the general manner of playing.

This game is also played in the *petit fronton mur à gauche*, where the rules are those of *pala*, except that the game is 35 points and there are three judges.

Palette avec pelote de gomme ('palette with rubber ball') is a two-a-side game played with an oval-shaped wooden bat in the *trinquet*. The bat is 55 cm. (21¾ in.) long, 13·5 cm. (5¼ in.) wide and 1 cm. (½ in.) thick. The ball, which is all rubber, weighs 45 g. (1·6 oz.). The game is 30 points; there is one judge, or umpire. The rules and court limits are same as those for *sare*, as are the tactics employed and the general manner of playing.

This game is also played in the *petit fronton mur à gauche*, where the rules are those of *pala*, except that there are three judges. The

difference between this game and its twin played with the leather ball is the pace, which is predictably faster with the livelier ball.

Pelota in one or more of its several versions is now played in many parts of the world. But it was in France and Spain that it acquired identity as a game with its own characteristics and codes. Thus, a history of pelota is largely the story of its evolution in these countries, more specifically in the Basque provinces of south-western France and northern Spain, where pelota early spilt across the Pyrenees.

Generally considered to be of Basque origin, pelota was initially no more than an adaptation of one of the most venerable of games: the medieval *jeux de paume*. The Spanish word *pelota* derives, as does *pilota* (Basque), *pelote* (French), and *pallone* (Italian) from the Low Latin *pillata*, diminutive of the Roman *pila*, a ball, which in turn derived from the Greek *pilos*.

Playing with a ball must be a diversion as old as man. He was certainly thus amused in Biblical times, for Jehovah, in one of his angry moods, threatened to toss him 'like a ball into a large country' (Isa. 22:18). The ancient Greeks played games with a ball of rolled hair sewn into a leather covering. Homer, in a song in the *Odyssey*, has Nausicaa playing some sort of pat-ball with her women. Later, descriptions of ball games abound in Latin authors. It is reasonable to think that such games, among so much that was Grecian, were inherited by the Romans, who handed them on to their descendants, the medieval Italians. The French probably imported them from Italy towards the end of the thirteenth century; the word *paume* first appears in France in 1316. At about the same period, as revealed by frescoes and excavations, the Aztecs of Mexico were playing a very modern-looking form of pelota in Chichen Itza, in the province of Yucatan.

The original game, *longue paume* (long palm, or long glove), was simplicity itself: two or more players beat a ball back and forth to each other across a net or line, using some sort of glove, racquet, or bat, and any convenient open space as a court. The game, growing more sophisticated as it was urbanized, changed its nature about the middle of the fourteenth century. Lack of space in the towns meant that courts were scaled down, enclosed with walls, and sometimes roofed; the new, more confined version of the game was called *courte* (short) *paume*. The English word 'court' as applied to tennis and other games, is anglicized *courte*.

The game soon acquired royal warrant. Louis X, it is said, died in 1316 of a chill brought on by his exertions at it. Charles V (1337-80), who had courts built in his palace of the Louvre, was reputedly a good player, as was Francis I, more than a hundred years later. By the sixteenth century the game was played by all classes of society. Its popularity, indeed, became a social menace, for in 1530 a royal edict proclaimed the game illegal for all but the nobility: *jeux de paume*, like hunting, would in future be an aristocratic pastime. The ban had little effect. In 1570 the Venetian ambassador, Lippomano, counted 1,800 courts in Paris alone, while an English visitor, Sir Robert Dallington, declared there were more courts in France 'than drunkards in England'. As more and more people played, watched, or gambled on the game, the *tripots*, as the courts were known, won a raffish, even lewd, reputation. *Tripot* no longer means a court in France, but the usage persists as a synonym for a sleazy cabaret or brothel.

Tripots were by no means identical in size or detail. Most courts were old stables or barns, or simply ruined or empty houses. These arbitrary conversions introduced accidental features such as trap-doors, recesses, windows, or other casual hazards that brought surprise and wile to the game. Eventually, as new courts were built, a more or less uniform type emerged with the dimensions, penthouse, dedans, grille, and tambour that we find in the REAL (Spanish royal) TENNIS court today. A shed roof is said to have been the origin of the penthouse, while dedans, grille, and tambour were, probably and respectively, a cage for poultry, a service hatch for passing food, and a fortuitous bulge in the wall.

In the reign of the genial Henry IV (1553-1610), himself a keen and expert player, the game was as popular as it ever would be. The royal example was perhaps no accident, for Henry was from Navarre and reigned over some at least of the contingent Basque country, where he would have seen pelota played. Louis XIII, his son and successor, was also addicted to the courts, but under Louis XIV the popularity of the game sharply declined. One reason might have been that it was no longer played at the palace. The Sun King, with other and older boudoir sports, preferred the nicer, newly invented pastime of billiards. By the middle of the eighteenth century there were scarcely ten *tripots* standing in Paris; the rest had been pulled down, converted into theatres, or put to less frivolous use. The vogue for *paume* was over.

It survived, however, in the provinces, and most notably among the traditionalist and conservative Basques, who had kept alive both versions — the *courte paume* and the *longue*.

The latter, with its open courts and more flexible disciplines, was an ideal village game, and it was from this that pelota mainly derives.

Although the Basques, a very active and agile race, have almost certainly played some sort of pelota for hundreds of years, hard evidence is surprisingly rare before the end of the eighteenth century. An old chronicle records that England's Henry VII (1457-1509) awarded £100 to 'a Biscayen' — as a Basque was then known — who had delighted him with his prowess; this is the earliest mention of a Basque playing a ball game. Later, in 1528, the Venetian traveller and diplomat, Navagero, reports the existence of pelota courts in the French Basque province of Labourd: 'In front of their houses they have a square place enclosed on all sides, where the animals may not enter, covered with a roof of branches, levelled so that there is no unevenness and sprinkled with sand to keep it dry; everything done, in fact, with extreme care. Here the men remain all day (*sic*) playing at ball....'

The courts Navagero saw were, with local variations, identical with the *tripots* of Paris, except that they were, and are, called *trinquets*, a word whose origin is obscure but may be a southern nasalization of the French *triquet*, a narrow bat, or racquet. Every big village and town possessed one or more of these courts; one of the oldest and best preserved, marked on a town map of 1610, can be seen in the district of St. André in Bayonne, the medieval city, pinched between the Bay of Biscay and the Pyrenees, which is the western gateway to the Basque provinces.

In the early seventeenth century pelota was already being played further south, in Spain. Cervantes, in one of the stories of his *Novelas Ejemplares*, makes his hero a *pilotari*, or pelota player, and the game is mentioned more than once by a near-contemporary of Cervantes, the poet Quevedo. A Spanish proverb of that time, still current, '*Aun esta la pelota en el tejado*' (Fickle as a ball rolling off a roof), suggests that the game was popular enough to have entered common culture.

That it was widespread among the Basques and carried social prestige is shown by two tombstone inscriptions in the French provinces. One, over the grave of Maistre Diriarte, in the village of Garris, is dated 1629: it depicts a nude figure in the act of hitting a ball with his naked palm. The second stone, to the memory of a *pilotari* called Souhourrou, who died in 1784 in Banca, bears carvings of a hand, a ball, and a short wooden bat, or *pala*. These were either champion *pilotaris*, or men of substance who played the game, or both.

It is not till 1755 that the description of an

actual match appears. This is in a letter, quoted by the historian Ducéré, from a citizen of Bayonne to a Parisian friend: 'Yesterday, a great match of *pelote* between seven Basques among whom was Monsieur Hiriart, the doctor of Macaye, a brother of our late Mayor, dressed like the others in a peasant's beret and shirt. The match attracted many Basques and people from the Spanish frontier.... The doctor and his side unhappily lost, but they mean to get their revenge in a return arranged for Thursday next.' This is all the evidence that the Basques have played pelota, if almost invisibly for the historian, since the Middle Ages. Then, at the end of the eighteenth century, appeared its first known master, a man called PERKAIN, born in the French mountain village of Les Aldudes about 1765.

It is tempting to class Perkain as another example of *deus ex machina*, a man who, by force of personality and example, revivifies an ailing or obsolescent activity. There are no clues to support or refute this theory. Great players, surely, existed before Perkain, for a game dies without heroes; why we know so much about him and nothing at all about them remains, like so many things Basque, a baffling riddle. He was the watershed, the man who put pelota on the historical map, although his countrymen, of course, think him much more than that. For them Perkain is a folk figure, as revered in the Basque Valhalla as are its bards and corsairs, its explorers and its saints.

The versions of pelota current when Perkain came on the scene probably numbered four. Two, *bota luzea* (known in Spain as *largo*) and *mahi-jokoa*, were forms of *longue paume* and very similar to each other. Teams of four or five a side struck a ball with the naked hand over a line dividing an open court about 50 m. (54 yds.) long. There was no wall; the one thing that distinguished these 'courts' from featureless waste ground was the *bota harri*, or serving block — a tripod supporting a sloping block of wood against which the ball was bounced for service. In *mahi-jokoa* a table was placed on the median line to form an additional hazard.

Both these games are long since obsolete; but in the French provinces of Basse-Navarre and Soule, where they were mostly played, traces of the *sorhopilas*, as the courts were called, are still visible, generally on the high ground above the village.

The relatively restricted length of the playing area was due to the weight of the *pelote*, or ball, and to the fact that the naked hand, or a small glove was used. Until the middle years of the nineteenth century, and the adoption of a rubber core, balls weighed as much as 2 lb.

(1 kg.); their consequent lack of resilience meant that games were played up and down, almost always on the volley, and never against a wall.

Perkain, who must have been an exceptional athlete, would have been proficient at all forms of pelota, but the two that made him famous were the versions known as *lachoa* and *rebot*. These games needed a longer playing area, 80 to 90 m. (87–98 yds.); for the ball, though heavy, was struck with a leather glove — a massive concave instrument attached to the hand with loops, rather in the manner of batting gloves for cricket. At one end of the court was a small wall against which, after being bounced on the serving block, the ball was struck for service. These little walls are important in the history of the game. Originally used for a single stroke, the serve, they later became one of the master elements that make pelota, as it is currently played, a game intrinsically Basque.

Lachoa, which was Perkain's speciality, has not been played for decades but *rebot*, its almost identical twin, survives in France and Spain as the most classic — if the most esoteric — form of the older varieties.

Perkain, though unquestionably the star of this, the nascent period of modern pelota, had as partners and opponents *pilotaris* hardly less celebrated than he. They were called Harosteguy and Eskerra, the left-hander; Azantza of Cambo and his sister, Tita; the Spaniards Isidro Indart and Simon de Arrayoz whose son, a generation later, would be as famous as his father. Their careers and adventures have come down to us in texts and ballads — often inordinately long — which describe in detail many epic games. Some of these, according to contemporary reports, attracted crowds of up to 10,000, and this in spite of the unsettled times of the French Revolution and the problems of access in a mountainous country.

Allowing for overstatement, it is clear from these accounts that pelota was a very popular, even a national, sport among the Basques, and it is difficult to believe that it became so in a single generation. Without sharing the confident opinion of the Spaniard Peña y Goñi, whose history of the game appeared in 1892, that the Basques have played it since Adam, the enthusiasm Perkain and his fellow *pilotaris* aroused hardens the theory that the Basques have had pelota 'in their blood' for many centuries.

The pelota of Perkain's time, as pictured in contemporary reports, gives the impression of spacious games on high plateaux surrounded by crowd-dappled hills. What was happening in the *trinquets*? That they were being used is obvious, but of the games that were played in them the details of only one are available. This was *pasaka*, a derivative of *courte paume* in which a heavy ball was beaten with the naked palm or a leather glove over a lofty net. *Pasaka* sounds a meagre link in pelota's continuity, but the fact must be that the Basques, when the popularity of all *jeux de paume* waned in the last half of the eighteenth century, kept their *trinquets* for the enjoyment of their own, improvised games, few of which they bothered to codify. *Pasaka* is a formal, complicated game which the modern mania for speed would condemn as very slow.

Pelota, since Perkain, has never lacked a popular champion, though few approached his stature as a player. He was succeeded at the top by two Spanish Basques: José Ramon Indart, called Michico, and Bautista de Arrayoz. Piquancy was added to their rivalry as *pilotaris* by their contrast as men. Michico was clean-living, candid, generous, and gay. Bautista, proud and moodily brilliant, a womanizing gambler not above being bought to 'throw' a match, left Spain one step ahead of the police to die violently in Cuba. Good as they were, Michico and de Arrayoz did no more than occupy the stage until the entry of the man who, with Perkain, dominates the history of the game. This was the French Basque Jean Erratchun, born in 1817 and known as El GASKOINA, the Gascon.

By profession a drover, Gaskoina was a stout and heavy man, though marvellously quick on his feet. The strength of his game seems to have been less in the power of stroke than in faultless touch and control, and great physical endurance. A vivid and truculent gamesman, sometimes accused by his opponents of making up the rules as he went along, the Gascon was the W. G. GRACE of pelota. Like Perkain, he was the hero of some dramatic matches, the most famous being that played at Irun, just over the Spanish border, in August 1846. Apart from the play, the match is interesting for the light it throws on the popularity the game had acquired, and for the fact that this was the first recorded international contest. National interests were compounded with financial ones; 140,000 francs are said to have been wagered, while those wanting liquid assets arrived prepared to bet in kind, with a couple of oxen or pigs, or a small herd of goats, or simply with the promise of their fields' next harvest of maize. Irun, too small to swallow the crowds, looked like 'an emigration camp, with tents in the streets and public places'. Twelve thousand spectators watched the game; those who could not make the journey would know the result by carrier pigeon.

The match, happily, was worth all this fuss.

Gaskoina led the French team of Harriague as server, Eskerra, Domingo of Espelette, and Gamio — a priest. The Spaniards were Melchior, Tripero, Molinero, all *pilotaris* of renown, and two others whose names are lost. Gaskoina was the man to beat, and no holds were barred. As the game began a shower of nails rattled on to the court, designed to puncture his bare feet, while a group of Spaniards bribed one of his people to make him tipsy by frequent swigs from a wineskin. After years of driving cattle on flinty roads Gaskoina hardly noticed the nails, but avidly accepted the wineskin — having had it filled, by doubling the bribe, with a cold but nutritious broth. More sinister than both these ploys was a 'rich hidalgo's' offer of 8,000 francs to lose the match, a proposition the Gascon promised to consider 'in two hours'. The fact that he did not lose is always quoted as proof of his integrity.

For a long time, though, it seemed that the game had indeed been 'rigged'. Harriague served brilliantly, but Gaskoina and Gamio, unbelievably feeble, hit down ball after ball to let the Spaniards run far ahead. Then Gaskoina, suddenly finding form, reduced the lead with a run of untakeable strokes. As, with two points to go, he levelled the scores, an excited Frenchman promised him a pair of oxen as a prize. Gaskoina won the next rally and was about to win the match when Gamio hit the ball out to tie the scores again. Melchior served amid unbearable tension; Gaskoina called the shot, went up, and laid down an imperious 'kill' to clinch it. Late that night he was escorted back to France in triumph, but not without danger. His bodyguard refused to let him accept a drink or a cigar before he crossed the frontier; too much Spanish money lost had sparked an ugly mood. He had won two oxen and 4,000 francs, and the warrant that his skill that day would be remembered so long as pelota is played. Still playing as well as ever, he died of typhus at the age of 42 in 1859.

The games played by Gaskoina were the same as those of Perkain's time except for one important technical difference — the glove. Perkain's leather glove was about a foot (30 cm.) long, and because it was scooped on the striking face it could be used to slice or cut the ball. Gaskoina's gloves — one of which survives — were half as long again with, consequently, a greater power of slice. Towards the end of Gaskoina's career, a miller from the French village of Mauleon contrived an even longer glove with, at its end, a deep curve in which the ball could be held for an instant before being hurled back against the wall, or to the opposing side. This loaded stroke, altogether heavier and more accurate than the old slice, was known as *atchiki*, a Basque word meaning 'to hold'.

The Spaniards were the first to take advantage of the new glove, and some doleful ballads tell how Melchior (he of the memorable game at Irun) and his partners Antza and Manuel routed the best French combinations until France, in turn, produced a champion, the muscular young shepherd called Matiu.

The technique of *atchiki* made pelota faster and more spectacular, but the popularity of the game almost immediately declined. The reasons were physical and economic. Only exceptionally strong men could capably wield the heavier glove; it was quite useless for anyone else, especially the younger generation. It was also far too expensive for the poorer people, which in Basque society meant the majority. A search for some cheaper substitute began, and produced strange results. A contraption called *matsardia*, invented by peasants in the Nive valley of Labourd, was a shortened hay fork whose three prongs were lashed together and covered with string mesh: perhaps the most primitive form of racquet ever made. In the nearby valley of the Nivelle experiments were made with a segment of an old sieve frame teased into a curve and tied to the wrist with a bandage. Called a *zetabea*, it was as inefficient as the *matsardia*.

The instrument needed — something light, strong, and cheaply made — was found by accident in 1857 by a boy of fourteen called Dithurbide, from the French village of St. Pée. One rainy day, as he hit a ball about in his father's barn, he noticed on the ground a *chistera* — an oblong shallow basket, shaped like a quarter moon, used by farmers for gathering cherries or beans. On an impulse, he picked it up and struck a few balls. The result was so encouraging that he persuaded his father to let him make some longer baskets for himself and his young friends. At first the *chistera* glove was dismissed as a child's joke. Then adolescents tried it, followed by adults and later, condescendingly, by established players. The breakthrough might have been in 1860 when a moderate pair, using the *chistera*, beat the champion Matiu and his partner, who wore the leather glove. Two years later in a public and official match of *rebot* it was formally recognized, was adopted in Spain, eventually crossed the ocean to South America, and began everywhere to supplant the glove. As so often happens, the inventor was unrewarded. Dithurbide went to learn the trade of blacksmith, leaving the manufacture of *chisteras* to be richly exploited by another.

The *chistera* could not have been developed without the contemporary appearance of the rubber-cored *pelote*. The rubber nucleus profoundly affected most sports played with a ball; its impact on pelota was revolutionary. Not only did it modify existing games, but sparked off a wide range of new ones. This group came to be known as *jeux indirects*, or *jeux de blaid*.

Blaid, a word whose origin is obscure, probably means 'wall', and it was from children tapping the new, livelier ball against a wall — any wall — with the new, lighter *chistera*, that the new games emerged. They were seen, immediately, to have several advantages over the old. The old games needed space, as many as ten players, and expensive equipment. The new could be played by one or more a side in courts of any length, and were cheap. The old games, with their complex system of scoring by chases, were ceremoniously long; the simpler nature of the wall games made matches shorter, and thus more numerous. Above all, perhaps, the new games were fun, and could be played reasonably well by most people; the *pilotari* was no longer a special person. Pelota, in a word, became democratic.

Predictably, *blaid* met fierce opposition from the purists, and many courts bore notices forbidding it, but it soon grew too popular to be kept down. In the villages the little walls that had once been used only for service were enlarged to contain the ampler scope of the volatile *pelote*, which could be struck by bat or racquet, glove or naked hand. The hand games, known as *blaid à main nue*, were, and still are, the varieties of pelota most played by the majority of Basques both in France and Spain where, on a fine day, a gang of urchins busy at hand *blaid* in the village square is almost part of the landscape.

The craze spread indoors, to the *trinquet*, in which the penthouse of *courte paume* had its third side removed to provide an object wall, and its tambour shifted to the corner between this and the right-hand wall. The game — a sort of giant FIVES — played across the angles thus formed was, like every version of the *blaid* family, very diverting and absolutely original.

The last point is important, for it was with the proliferation of these improvised and novel ways of using the livelier ball that pelota, which had hitherto been a generic term for the whole range of *jeux de paume*, acquired a character uniquely its own. *Blaid*, hardly a century old, could not have emerged before the rubber core ousted the sluggish *pelote* of leather-covered tow. Youngest of the pelota family, it is now, in its diversity and extent, virtually the game itself. For this the Basques are solely responsible. *Pelote basque* and *pelota vasca* are more than convenient labels.

The new games, inevitably, were adopted wherever pelota was played, in France and Spain in Europe, and South America — particularly the Argentine — Cuba, and Mexico. In the Argentine, now among the game's most powerful nations, the modern era began with the visit to Buenos Aires, in 1884, of the Spanish Basque Sarasqueta, known as CHIQUITO D'EIBAR. An all-round champion, he beat the best Argentines. It was his success that led to the invasion of South America by the leading French and Spanish players who, after playing there all winter, returned to Europe for the summer season, the system of inter-continental full employment used by the top *pilotaris* today.

Brilliant though he was, Sarasqueta could not have made the impression he did in the Argentine if he had not used the *chistera*, the basket-glove which he had been one of the first to exploit in Spain, and which was almost unknown in South America. Because *chisteras* of various forms are now the equipment for at least four of pelota's most spectacular and popular games — *grand chistera, yoko garbi, remonte,* and *cesta punta* — the evolution of Dithurbide's humble wicker basket must be briefly traced.

The *chistera* used by Chiquito d'Eibar was short, only slightly curved, and more or less the same length as the old leather glove. His stroke was generally a volley and almost invariably hit square on the forehand with shoulders facing the wall — the backhand was no more than a defensive scoop employed when the player failed to run round the ball. The unvarying forehand, hitting a *pelote* which, although rubber-centred, could still weigh 110 g. (3·9 oz.), tended to tire and finally damage the muscles of the arm and shoulder. This happened to the Spanish *pilotari* El Samperio while playing a series of tight matches at Madrid in 1887. To save his painful right arm, he began playing on the backhand, supporting the right wrist with the left hand and lunging through with the left shoulder. The great increase of power given by the high and wide follow-through surprised El Samperio, and he began using the backhand as an attacking stroke in the Argentine, where he played later in the year. It gave good results, but the shortness of the *chistera* limited the possibilities of the new swing. These were to be fully and dramatically demonstrated by another *pilotari*, Curuchague, whose discovery — not for the first time in pelota's history — was due to pure accident.

While playing in Buenos Aires in 1888 Curuchague broke his right wrist which, badly set, stiffened permanently. Still young and earning good money, he refused to abandon the game, and began thinking of how to counter his disability. His solution was to play the backhand, but with a *chistera*, made by himself, quite different from the one in common use, being very long — about 70 cm. (27½ in.) — and deeply incurved. Catching the ball on the forehand, Curuchague swung his body fully round to the left, turning his back to the wall. After a moment's pause — the *atchiki* — to reverse direction, he propelled the ball, two-handed and with a rhythmic upward and forward heave of arms and torso, down the curve and out of the *chistera* in a high, spinning parabola, or a low, vicious slice. Returning to the courts, he won most of his matches handsomely. Unable to beat him, the others joined him, and the game known as *grand chistera* was born. Spanish *pilotaris* soon introduced it to Spain, whence the French Basque, Arrué de Bidart, who had learnt it in Valencia, imported it to France in about 1895.

The last decade of the nineteenth century was a significant period for pelota. It was then that it widened its range, shed its somewhat parochial character and ambience, and developed — in a few of its many versions — into a sport of worldwide reputation. This expansion took place mainly in the Argentine, whose capital, Buenos Aires, became the Mecca of the game during these years. The exciting pace and hard hitting made possible by the basket-gloves and ever livelier ball pleased the crowds. To contain them, larger and more comfortable courts were built in urban centres, not only in the Argentine, but in Uruguay, Brazil, Bolivia, Mexico, and as far away as Cuba, Florida, and California — any country, in fact, where Basque settlers had introduced some form of pelota.

The courts, known loosely as *frontons*, could be open or covered, and varied greatly in size. The most usual version, called the *fronton espagnol*, or *mur à gauche*, has front, back, and left-hand walls, the fourth side being a tiered terrace for spectators. This court, when 50 m. (54 yds.) or more in length becomes, technically, a *jaï-alaï* (in Basque, the 'sprightly' or 'lively game'). The term is now almost synonymous with pelota's most glamorous offspring, *cesta punta* — the latest of the *chistera* games, which was developed in Havana about 1900.

But pelota's sudden vogue as a spectator sport proved to be unhealthy. The bigger *frontons* meant big business, increased professionalism, and gambling. Gambling, in its turn, raised the suspicion that matches were 'arranged'; governments made matters worse by the levy of heavy taxes on betting, while certain professionals became more entertainers than serious players. These and other factors, such as a lack of competent administration, and the rapid spread of FOOTBALL in South America, drained the public from the *frontons*. The game, as quickly as it had prospered, went into a serious decline.

The reaction, naturally, was felt at all levels, both amateur and professional. In France and Spain it was thought, uneasily, that not only the structures, but the spirit of pelota were being abused. At San Sebastian in 1909, for example, spectators left an important match because they judged the players to be holding the ball too long in the *chistera*. Puritanism, never deeply hidden in the Basque character, returned.

It is possible that, without some salutary action, pelota might have drifted from this rootless condition to the status of a folk game in the country, and a dubious vehicle for gambling in the towns. Fortunately, some young and clear-headed amateurs, led by the French Basque, YBARNÉGARAY, were already planning reform in 1912. The Great War delayed development, but in 1921 the Fédération Française de Pelote Basque was formed. This body set about codifying the various games, writing their — largely oral and traditional — rules, classifying the players, and generally giving the game a responsible and coherent authority. Spain and various South American countries followed suit. In 1924 pelota was included in the OLYMPIC GAMES held in Paris, and five years later was given a wider government with the founding of the Federación Internacional de Pelota Vasca (F.I.P.V.), which operates from Madrid.

An ambitious agenda was drawn up, but circumstances — the Spanish Civil War and the Second World War — again postponed action. It was not till 1945 that the Federación, with Ybarnégaray as its president and driving force, could become fully operative. There was much to do, notably the task of casting a common code of rules, for play and umpiring, from the often very dissimilar canons of the various member nations. The Federación even found time to give pelota a patron saint. He is — naturally — a Basque: the sixteenth century Navarrese Jesuit, St. Francis Xavier, and — necessarily — a *pilotari*, for a learned commission found on his skeletal right hand the telltale deformation of the phalanges which are the mark of all who play the *main nue*.

In 1952 the Federación realized what had always been its first priority — the organization of a world championship. This was held in San Sebastian, Spain, with eight nations competing. Since then, membership of the F.I.P.V. has grown to 14, and world championships have been held at four-yearly intervals in South America, France, and Spain.

Pelota, certainly, has never been more widely watched, both as a spectacle everywhere, and as a medium for gambling in the opulent *jaï-alaïs* of the Americas and Spain. It is also widely played, and nowhere more than in the Basque provinces by the Basques themselves.

E. Blazy, *La Pelote Basque* (1929); Albert de Luze, *La Magnifique Histoire du Jeu Pomme* (1935); Luis Bombín Fernandez,. *Historia, Ciencia y Código del Juego de Pelota* (1946); Rodney Gallop, *A Book of the Basques* (1930); Peña y Goñi, *La Pelota y los Pelotaris* (1892); A. Tournier, *La Pelote Basque* (1958); Philippe Veyrin, *Les Basques* (1968). Bulletin of the Federación Internacional de Pelota Vasca; *Pilota*, bi-monthly journal of the Fédération Française de Pelote Basque.

GOVERNING BODY (WORLD): Federación Internacional de Pelota Vasca, Los Madrazo 11, Madrid, Spain.

PELOTE BASQUE, see PELOTA.

PENAROL, Association FOOTBALL club, Montevideo. Founded in 1891 by British employees of the Central Railways, the club was known until 1913 as the Central Uruguayan Railway Cricket Club. Penarol were founder members of the Uruguayan League in 1900 and won the first of over 30 championship titles in the first season of the league. Only their keen rivals NACIONAL have disturbed Penarol's dominant position in Uruguayan football which they confirmed by winning the South American club championship in 1960, 1961, and 1966, and the unofficial world club championship in 1961 and 1966. Leading players have included Piendibene, J. ANDRADE, R. ANDRADE, VARELA, SCHIAFFINO, Spencer, and Joya.

COLOURS: Black and yellow striped shirts, black shorts.

PENDIL (1965), trained by WINTER and ridden by Pitman, won his first 11 races over fences and was hailed as the greatest steeplechaser since ARKLE. His sequence was ended when he lost by a short head to The Dikler in the 1973 CHELTENHAM GOLD CUP.

PENNEL, JOHN THOMAS (1940-   ), pole vaulter for the U.S.A. Perhaps the most important contributor to the progress of record-breaking in the fibreglass era of pole vaulting, Pennel first held the world record with 16 ft. 3 in. (4·95 m.) in 1963, and, in the same year, became the first man to clear 17 ft. (5·18 m.). Then, suffering from a back injury, he lost the record, to regain it in 1966 with 17 ft. 6¼ in. (5·34 m.). He was placed only fifth in the 1968 OLYMPIC GAMES but found fresh impetus in 1969 with another world record of 17 ft. 10¼ in. (5·44 m.).

PENNIGER, BROOME ERIC (1902-   ), HOCKEY player for India, Punjab, North-Western Railway, and Delhi Rangers. He was a superb centre half and his tussles with CHAND contributed to both becoming outstanding players. Penniger captained India in the 1928 Olympic semi-final and final, and won a second Olympic gold medal in 1932. He emigrated to England in the 1950s.

PENNINGTON, JESSE (*fl.* 1907-20), Association footballer for West Bromwich Albion and England for whom, from 1907 to 1920, he made 21 appearances at left back in international matches, usually in partnership with CROMPTON with whom he developed a complete understanding rarely equalled by pairs of full-backs. He was briefly on ASTON VILLA's books as an amateur but the whole of his professional career was spent with his home town club, West Bromwich Albion, whom he captained for many seasons.

PENTATHLON, a standard event for women on the programme of all major ATHLETICS championships, the pentathlon is an all-round test of SPRINTING, HURDLING, jumping, and throwing. It consists of five events usually distributed over two days as follows: first day — 100 metres hurdles, SHOT, and HIGH JUMP; second day — LONG JUMP and 200 metres. Sometimes all five events are decided in one day. The pentathlon's origins are to be found in ancient Greek history; a contest of sprinting, long jumping, JAVELIN, DISCUS, and WRESTLING was first introduced in the OLYMPIC GAMES in 708 B.C. In the athletics pentathlon of modern times, performances are rated according to a points-scoring system. Each competitor must start in every event and the winner is the athlete with the largest points total. Since 1949, world records have been ratified by the International Amateur Athletic Federation (see ATHLETICS, TRACK AND FIELD). The event was introduced in the EUROPEAN CHAMPIONSHIPS in 1950 and in the Olympic Games in 1964.

The pentathlon for men consists of long jump, javelin, 200 metres, discus, and 1,500 metres, all decided on the same day. The event was dropped from the Olympic programme after 1924 and no longer appears either on the official record list or on any major championship programme. It is occasionally used by DECATHLON performers as a form of competitive training.

I.A.A.F. Scoring Table for Women's Track and Field Events (latest edition).

PEP, WILLIE (1922-   ), American boxer, an outstanding world featherweight champion. First a claimant to the title in 1942, Pep became undisputed champion in 1946 and, after losing the title to Saddler in 1948, regained it the next year, only to lose it again to Saddler in their third fight in 1950. Remembered as a comparatively light hitter but a master boxer, Pep had 241 professional fights, won 65 inside the distance and 164 on points. Between 1943 and 1948 he had 73 contests without one loss and only a single draw. Between 1940 and 1943 Pep had a series of 62 consecutive victories.

PEPE-HILLO (José Delgado) (1754-1801), *matador de toros* who was killed by Barbudo of the Peñaranda de Bracamonte ranch in the Madrid bull ring on 11 May 1801. During his career, he was gored 25 times, and once disposed of 17 bulls in a day. In 1796 he wrote his treatise, *La Tauromaquia.*

PEPETE (José Rodríguez y Rodríguez) (1824-62), *matador de toros* who took the *alternativa* in 1853, was the great-uncle of MANOLETE. While rescuing a picador with a *quite* in the *plaza de toros* of Madrid on 20 April 1862, he was gored in the chest by the Miura bull Jocinero, and died in the infirmary shortly afterwards.

PERALTA, ANGEL (1930-   ), the greatest *rejoneador* of modern times, achieved a record of 125 performances in the 1971 season. His immense skill and distinctive personality in the ring were responsible for the resurgence of *rejoneo* in 1970 and 1971. This resulted in the large number of *corridas* featuring only horsemen which took place during these two seasons. The younger Peralta, Rafael, is a close contender for his brother's title.

PERDITA II (1881) was the celebrated matron of the royal stud at Sandringham, England, and dam of the full brothers PERSIMMON and DIAMOND JUBILEE.

PEREIRA, AUGUSTO PEDRO (1909-   ), lawn BOWLS player who captained the Hong Kong team in the inaugural world championships at KYEEMAGH, N.S.W., in 1966 when he was 57 years old. Though a British subject he is Portuguese by birth. Champion of Hong Kong many times and the best bowler produced by the colony, he was a team member in the 1958, 1962, and 1970 COMMONWEALTH GAMES.

PEREIRA, WALDIR, see DIDI.

PERKAIN (1765(?)-1810), French Basque PELOTA player, arguably the most famous *pilotari* in the game's history, at once a historical and a legendary figure. He was unquestionably the dominating player of his time whose feats have come down to us in text, but mainly in ballads. The most celebrated of these 'is that he played in his native village in 1793 against his great rival, the left-hander Ezkerra. Perkain, who had fled to Spain after trouble with the police of the Convention, recrossed the border at the peril of his life to honour Ezkerra's challenge. Perkain won the game after a struggle lasting three hours, but escaped to Spain only by stunning (some say killing) the Chief of Police, come to arrest him, with the most lethal stroke of the match. Some accounts make Perkain tall and handsome; others short and ugly. All are agreed that, besides his skill as a *pilotari*, he was a man whose almost every act became an anecdote. He must be one of the few athletes about whom a verse drama in five acts has been written — in 1900 by the Basque author Harispe, called *Perkain: A Drama of The Terror.*

PERRY, FREDERICK JOHN (1909-   ), British LAWN TENNIS and TABLE TENNIS player. Perry achieved distinction first in table tennis, winning the world singles championship at Budapest in 1929. Later he became the most successful of modern British lawn tennis players, the mainstay of a team which recaptured the Davis Cup (see LAWN TENNIS) in 1933, and the winner of all the major championships between 1934 and 1936.

Perry was a brilliant match player, a swashbuckling competitor, tough, aggressive, and confident, with a running forehand which all his opponents feared. In 1933 he became the first British player to win the U.S. lawn tennis singles title since H. L. DOHERTY in 1903, beating CRAWFORD in the final. His record of winning the men's singles for three years in succession (1934-6) was unique at the modern WIMBLEDON, and he captured the Australian title in 1934 and the French title in 1935. In the Davis Cup he played his first rubber against Monaco in 1931 and a series of dramatic matches soon made him one of the most successful Davis Cup players of all time. Perry, AUSTIN, HUGHES, and H. G. N. Lee were the regular members of a team which ruled the game until he turned professional in 1936. He lost only one of the ten challenge round rubbers which he played (to COCHET in his first year in the competition). He won 45 out of 52 rubbers in all.

Though he gave up competitive table tennis in 1930, two years after that Perry accomplished a double feat unique in sport: playing lawn tennis in the daytime, he beat BOROTRA on wood in the final of the Coupe Noel; in the evenings, during the same week, he beat Szabados, then world champion, in the final of a Paris table tennis tournament.

PERSHING TROPHY MATCH, see SHOOTING, RIFLE: SMALL BORE.

PERSIAN WAR (1963), race-horse bred by the Astor Studs, owned by Alper, trained by Davies, and ridden by Uttley, was one of the greatest hurdlers on the English turf, winning the CHAMPION HURDLE CHALLENGE CUP at Cheltenham three years in succession, Schweppes Gold Trophy at Newbury, *Daily Express* Triumph Hurdle at Cheltenham, Victor Ludorum Hurdle at Haydock, and Welsh Champion Hurdle at Chepstow.

PERSIMMON (1893), English race-horse by ST. SIMON out of PERDITA II, dam also of DIAMOND JUBILEE, and, like him, bred at Sandringham Stud, was owned by the Prince of WALES, and trained by MARSH. He won seven races to the value of £34,706, including the DERBY (by a neck from St. Frusquin in a record time of 2 min. 42 sec.), the ST. LEGER, ECLIPSE STAKES, and ASCOT GOLD CUP. At stud, he headed the winning sires' list four times, his best offspring being SCEPTRE and PRINCE PALATINE.

PERTH II (1896) was a notable French race-horse who won all the five most important races in the country at that time, viz., the GRAND PRIX DE PARIS, the French Derby, St. Leger, and Two Thousand Guineas, and the PRIX DU CADRAN.

PESÄPALLO, literally, in English, 'nest-ball', but usually called 'Finnish baseball', is a bat-and-ball team game based on American BASEBALL and certain traditional Finnish games.

A match is played between teams of nine players each; scoring is by completed runs from home base to first base, second base, third base, and back to home base. The bat and ball are a little lighter than those used in baseball, and there are considerable differences in the pitch on which the game is played, notably in the zig-zag line of running from the strike position to the bases and the progressively increasing distances between them — 20 m., 30 m., 35 m., and 45 m. (22, 33, 38, and 49 yds.) — and in some fundamentals.

Among these is 'pitching', or serving, which takes the form of a vertical lob; the ball must rise at least 1 m. (3 ft. 3 in.) above the head of the striker and, if he does not hit it, land on the serving plate. A minimum height is necessary because the batsman is allowed to run to first base as soon as the ball leaves the server's hand. Thus the batsman need not strike the ball at all. Two foul serves entitle him and his team mates on other bases to advance one base without penalty. Each batsman may receive three serves or pitches.

A batsman is out or 'killed' if the fielded ball reaches a baseman ahead of the running batsman; if, when running between bases, he is touched with the hand holding the ball; or if he hits the ball beyond the boundary on his third hit.

The sides change from batting to fielding when three batsmen have been put out, or if all nine players have batted but failed to score a single run. If the struck ball is caught, the striker, so long as he reaches the safety of a base ahead of the return, is not out, but is regarded as 'wounded'; he cannot score on that run, but he may bat again in his turn if enough members of his team survive.

The spacious bases — radius 2·5 m. (8 ft. 3 in.) — are intended to minimize collisions.

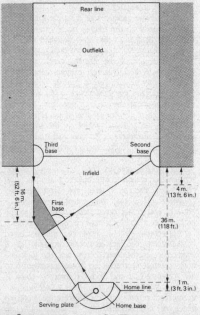

PESÄPALLO PITCH

Maximum dimensions only are given on this simplified diagram. Shaded areas denote reserve sectors for the three bases, and arrows indicate direction of play. The bases each have a radius of 2·5 m. (8 ft. 3 in.), and the serving plate, in the centre of home base, is 60 cm. (1 ft. 11½ in.) in diameter.

There is a ball-game tradition of *poltopallo*, literally 'burnball', in Finland. 'Burning' consists of hitting the runner or throwing ahead of him to the baseman before he can reach the safety of the base. In an early form it was a kind of wall game in which the pitcher threw the ball at a wall 10 to 15 m. (33–50 ft.) distant and, when it rebounded, two batsmen would try to hit it away far enough to score a 'run' by touching the wall and returning to their bases before the ball could be returned. Other forms of the game were KUNINGAS-PALLO, *pitkapallo*, and ROUNDERS — called in Finnish the 'four goals' or in Swedish *brännboll.*

The creation of *pesäpallo*, however, was prompted by the demonstrations of American baseball in Scandinavia after the Stockholm OLYMPIC GAMES of 1912. The Finns were concerned to produce and establish a ball game which would foster sprinting. They felt that the 'no hits no runs' paragon of baseball would not suit their national temperament; and they also sought a game which would encourage movement. Hence they did away with the ferocious horizontal pitch of the American game which often confines the game to striker and pitcher while leaving the fielders immobile. They also set increasing distances between bases to reproduce the war situation of football or hockey in which, the further the attacking team advances, the stronger grows the defence against it. After a decade of experiment and planning chiefly by Professor Lauri Pihkala, the shape and rules of *pesäpallo* were launched in 1922.

The game was first played, sustained, and developed by Finnish volunteer territorial troops largely in smaller population centres. It grew until, by the 1970s, there were between 5,000 and 6,000 registered teams competing in the five or six most widely practised games in the country.

At any appreciable competitive level the game is confined to Finland though it is played by Finnish emigrants in Sweden, Canada, and Australia.

PESSOA, NELSON (1935-), Brazilian show jumping (see EQUESTRIAN EVENTS) rider. Based in Europe from 1961, he was the only South American rider consistently to hold his own against the British, French, Germans, and Italians. In 1967, he led the Brazilian team which won the gold medal at the PAN-AMERICAN GAMES and, with Gran Geste, he took the individual silver medal as well. On the same horse he won the 1966 men's European championship.

PÉTANQUE, sometimes called *boule,* is a

ball-and-target game of the same type as lawn BOWLS, crown green bowls, and its own parent game, JEU PROVENÇAL, which has spread far beyond Provence where it originated and is played extensively in France and also as far afield as the U.S.A.

The target ball or jack — *cochonnet, petit bois, ministre* or (Provençal) *lé* or *gari* — is of light or white-painted wood, and between 25 and 35 mm. (1–1⅜ in.) in diameter. The bowls, made of metal, usually steel, are between 7·05 and 8 cm. (2¾–3⅛ in.) in diameter. They may not be leaded or biassed, are produced by officially approved manufacturers, and weigh between 620 and 800 g. (22–28 oz.). The game is played as singles, when each player has three or four balls, as may be decided; doubles, three bowls each; and trebles, two each.

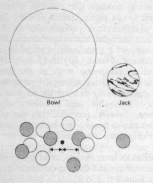

Bowl   **Jack**

PETANQUE BOWLS AND JACK
The figure shows relative sizes of the metal bowl, 7·05–8 cm. (2¾–3⅛ in diameter, and the wood jack, or *cochonnet*, 25–35 mm. (1–1⅜ in.) in diameter. (*Below*) Bowls in position around the jack at the end of a *mène* in singles play, when all the bowls have been bowled. The winning side gets as many points as it has bowls which are better placed, i.e. nearer the jack, than the best of the losing side.

Scoring is at a rate of one point for every bowl of the same player or team which lies nearer to the jack than any of the opponent(s) when all bowls have been bowled. A game is generally of 13 points; but in certain circumstances, and according to some local conventions, it may be of 11, 15, 18, or 21 points.

The game does not call for highly prepared turf as in the case of lawn bowls but can be, and is, played on a village street, country lane, back yard, or public square. Official matches, however, usually take place on an accepted pitch, which may be marked out by the umpire, who controls all such matches, or the organizing committee: it should be at least 3 or

4 m. wide and 15 m. long (approx. 4 × 16 yds.).

The players — or deputed members from teams — toss for the right to choose the delivery circle, throw the target ball, and deliver the first bowl. The winner chooses a starting point where he marks out a circle between 35 and 50 cm. (approx. 13–19 in.) in diameter and at least 1 m. (1·094 yds.) from any obstacle. Standing within the circle he throws the jack, which must land at a point which — measured from the nearest edge of the circle — is, in official matches between under-15s, between 5 and 9 m. (5½–10 yds.), for juniors and seniors, between 6 and 10 m. (6½–11 yds.) from him, and it must be at least 1 m. from any obstacle or the edge of the pitch. The player has three chances to throw the ball into an acceptable position; if he fails, the option for three attempts passes to the other side: but the right to bowl first does not pass.

Once the target ball is in place, no player may 'improve' the pitch by removing or treading down obstructions; though he may make good any hole in the ground caused by the landing of an earlier bowl.

To take the example of a single match; the player who won the toss — or any member of his team in a team event — delivers the first ball. In doing so he must not cross, nor even touch, the line of the starting circle until his bowl has landed (though players disabled in the legs may be allowed to ground one foot or leg outside the circumference). His aim is to leave it as near the jack as possible. He may toss it high in the air so that it lands near the jack and stops dead, which is the technique known as *plomber*; or he may roll it along the ground, as in lawn bowls, which is called *rouler*.

The second player then takes up position within the circle and attempts to place his bowl closer to the jack than the first player's (*pointer*). He, too, may employ *plomber* or *rouler*; and if his bowl finishes closer to the jack it may also block his opponent's approach for his second shot. If, however, the first bowl is so close to the jack as not to leave sufficient space for another between it and the jack, he may attempt to throw his bowl directly on to the winning one and knock it away — *tirer*. If he contrives to hit his opponent's ball flush on the perfect point on its circumference, his own bowl will not only dislodge the other, but drop into its place; this stroke — the most spectacular in the game — is known as *carreau*.

The players continue, alternately, using any of the three tactics — *pointer, tirer,* or *carreau* — until each has bowled his agreed three or four bowls, some latterly, perhaps, in a changed position because the jack has been disturbed. The player whose bowl is nearest to the jack scores 1 point; if he has a second, a third, or a fourth also nearer the jack than any of his opponent's he will score 2, 3, or 4 points. This unit of the game is called *une mène*. In the following *mène*, the jack is thrown from within a circle drawn round the spot where it stood in the previous round.

A match usually consists of three games of 13 or other agreed number of points; the first is called *la partie*, the second *la revanche*, and the third *la belle*.

It is said that *pétanque* began in the year 1910. Debate continues as to whether it was at Vallauris, l'Isle-sur-Sorque, or Le Ciotat, when some bowlers engaged in *jeu provençal* (played on a pitch of up to 21 m. (23 yds.), and with a two- or three-stride run-up permitted to the bowler) decided — presumably in midday heat — to reduce the amount of physical effort involved. Accordingly they introduced a 10 m. (11 yds.) pitch, which made it crucially simpler to succeed at *pétanque* then at *jeu provençal*, and the almost stationary delivery.

The bowls were originally made of box-wood, studded all over with nailheads which gave a hard, even surface. The finest were made by local craftsmen, especially those of Aiguines, a village in the Var district. Nowadays they are made from steel to official standards of density.

Since then the game has become immensely popular, has spread far beyond its historical Provençal bounds to cover the whole of France as well as a number of other countries. Within France the outstanding *pétanque bouliste* enjoys a standing equal to that of his fellow CYCLING champions or British or American footballers. Leading players are often given humorous nicknames such as Otello, Cacou, Sardine, Le Japonais.

In the French national championships which take place in singles, doubles, and trebles, at junior and senior levels, all players must be of French nationality except that one member of the trebles team may be of another nationality. Transfers of players between societies are allowed only between 1 January and 1 March.

GOVERNING BODIES: Fédération Internationale de Pétanque et Jeu Provençal, 10 rue de Neufchâtel, Geneva, Switzerland; Fédération Française de Pétanque et Jeu Provençal, 1, Boulevard Dugommier, 13 Marseille 1, France.

PETERS, MARTIN STANFORD (1944-), Association footballer for WEST HAM UNITED, TOTTENHAM HOTSPUR, and England for whom he made his first appearance at the age of 22 against Yugoslavia in May 1966. He was not in the team that played the opening match of the 1966 world championship against Uruguay in July but played in each of England's five remaining matches including the final against West Germany. Basically a midfield player with most of the attributes of wing halves of yesteryear, his shrewd perception of the way a movement is developing, plus his shooting and heading ability, brought many goals for West Ham and England before, in March 1970, Tottenham Hotspur negotiated an exchange of transfer registrations with West Ham, GREAVES moving to West Ham, and Tottenham paying a fee for Peters that brought the monetary value of the deal to an estimated £200,000. Tottenham's much-improved performances in the season 1970-1 included winning the League Cup.

PETERS, MARY ELIZABETH (1939-), PENTATHLON competitor for Great Britain. Making her third Olympic appearance at the age of 33, Miss Peters won the Olympic pentathlon gold medal at Munich in 1972 with a world record score of 4,801 points. She had placed fourth in the Olympic pentathlon in 1964 and won a silver medal in the COMMONWEALTH GAMES in 1966. At Edinburgh in 1970 she won two gold medals, the pentathlon with 5,148 points (old scoring tables) and the shot with 52 ft. 3 in. (15·93 m.).

PETERSON brothers, all six of whom played HOCKEY for Ireland, the Palmerston Club, and Avoca School P. and P. JACK and WALTER played at full-back; NICHOLAS, right half; BERTIE, outside right; CECIL, centre forward, and WILLLAM, inside left. Jack and Walter were the Irish full-back partnership from 1903 to 1914. Five of the Petersons played in 1904 when Ireland gained their first victory over England. In all the Peterson brothers won 67 caps.

PETHERBRIDGE, DAVID ALAN (1927-), British JUDO fighter, the first Welshman to be graded 1st *Dan* and European 3rd *Dan* champion in 1962. He was a member of the British team which won the European title for three successive years in the late 1950s and competed in the 1964 OLYMPIC GAMES in the open class. He retired at 37.

PETITE ÈTOILE (1956) was a grey filly, tracing to LADY JOSEPHINE, bred by the AGA KHAN, owned by his son, Aly Khan, trained by MURLESS, and ridden by PIGGOTT and D. Smith. She won 14 races, including the OAKS, ONE THOUSAND GUINEAS, SUSSEX STAKES, Yorkshire Oaks, CHAMPION STAKES, and two

CORONATION CUPS, finishing second in her other five races, which included the KING GEORGE VI AND QUEEN ELIZABETH STAKES. She won £67,786 in prize money, an English record for a filly.

PETROV, ALEXANDER (1940-), Russian BASKETBALL player. Petrov measured 6 ft. 11 in. (2·11 m.), and first played for the U.S.S.R. in 1959. He became one of the greatest centres in the history of the game.

PETROV, EUGENI, clay pigeon shooter for the U.S.S.R. He was the winner of the first Olympic gold medal for skeet (see SHOOTING, CLAY PIGEON), at Mexico City in 1968.

PETTITT, TOM (1860-1946), REAL TENNIS world champion 1885-90. Pettitt was the first American to win this title. When he visited England, his style was called 'wild, barbaric, untutored' and he was accused of 'murdering poor Charlie Saunders and driving him from the court'. When his game had matured after match play in England he challenged the leading English professional, Lambert, for the world championship and beat him on the third day in an epic match at Hampton Court in 1885, by 7 sets to 5 after being 1-5 down.

PETTY, LEE (1914-), American MOTOR RACING driver who was the first car driver to win three N.A.S.C.A.R. Grand National stock-car titles — 1954, 1958, and 1959. In 131 races in his championship years he finished among the first five 73 times. He won the first Daytona 500 in 1959 and 53 other Grand National races. He retired in 1961.

PETTY, RICHARD (1937-), American MOTOR RACING driver who was four times Grand National stock-car champion (1964, 1967, 1971, and 1972); winner of 154 Grand National races including five Daytona 500s; and the first driver to win more than a million dollars in Grand National purses. He has finished among the first five in 60 per cent of his 624 Grand National starts through 1973.

PHELPS, BRIAN ERIC (1944-), diver for Great Britain, England, and Highgate D.C. He achieved world-wide fame at the European Games at Budapest in 1958 when he won the men's high DIVING at the age of 14. He repeated his success at Leipzig in 1962 but dropped to second place at Utrecht in 1966. In the Olympic high diving in 1960 he won the bronze medal. He won the COMMONWEALTH GAMES springboard and high diving events in 1962, and again in 1966. Coached by Orner, he was the greatest diver England had ever produced.

PHILADELPHIA ATHLETICS, American professional BASEBALL team, a founding member of the AMERICAN LEAGUE in 1901. The Athletics' destiny was inextricably bound up with MACK, their manager from 1901 to 1950 and their owner most of this period. The Athletics had two great periods: 1910-14, winning American League pennants every year but 1912 and the WORLD SERIES in 1910, 1911, and 1913; and 1929-31, when they won league titles as well as World Series in 1929 and 1930. The 1902 and 1905 league title teams featured the pitcher Waddell, who won over 20 games in four straight seasons, 1902-5. The 1910-14 team featured a famous '$100,000 infield' (McInnis, Collins, Barry, Baker) and the pitchers Bender and Plank; the latter had 326 career wins, including eight 20-game seasons. The 1929-31 team had great pitching with Grove, winner of over 20 games in seven straight seasons (1927-33) and 300 games during his career, and Earnshaw, a 20-game winner 1929-31; and hitting with the first baseman Foxx (lifetime ·325 average) and the outfielder Simmons (lifetime ·334 average). Philadelphia fans proved fickle with success, so that, with falling attendance, Mack had to sell off most of his stars in 1915 and 1934 to keep the team solvent. When the A's moved to Kansas City in 1955, they were a perennial also-ran ball club. (See KANSAS CITY ATHLETICS.)

PHILADELPHIA EAGLES, American professional FOOTBALL team, joined the NATIONAL FOOTBALL LEAGUE (N.F.L.) in 1933. Owned and coached, part of the 1930s, by BELL (later N.F.L. Commissioner), the Eagles had meagre success, despite the heroics of the quarterback O'Brien. In wartime 1943 they combined with the PITTSBURGH STEELERS to form the inelegantly named 'Steagles'. Their 1948-9 team won N.F.L. titles and featured the running back Van Buren (League rushing leader), the end Pihos, the tackle Wistert, and the centre Bednarik. Under the quarterback Van Brocklin the Eagles also won the League title in 1960.
COLOURS: Green and white.

PHILADELPHIA FLYERS, ICE HOCKEY club of Philadelphia, formed in 1967 as one of six teams in the new West Division of the expanded NATIONAL HOCKEY LEAGUE of North America. Home games are played at the Spectrum, Philadelphia, which seats 14,700. The players train in Canada at Le Colisée,

Quebec City. The Flyers were the first club to win the West Division championship, in 1968.
COLOURS: Orange and white.

PHILADELPHIA GOLD CUP is a trophy presented by Philadelphia ROWING men in recognition of the win by J. B. KELLY, SR., in the 1920 Olympic single sculls. It is for the world amateur sculling championship and is held by each Olympic single sculls champion who can, however, be challenged between each OLYMPIC GAMES.

In its early days, the cup changed hands several times, but only on one occasion has there been a challenge race outside the United States. This was in 1925, when the reigning Olympic champion, BERESFORD, successfully defended the trophy against the American, Hoover, who had won it in 1922. The last challenge was in 1950, when the son of the first holder, J. B. Kelly, jr., the European and American champion, and Rowe, the British winner of the Diamond Sculls (see HENLEY) that year, raced the 1948 Olympic champion, M. T. WOOD of Australia, in Philadelphia. Wood won, with Kelly in second place.

PHILADELPHIA PHILLIES, American professional BASEBALL team, members of the NATIONAL LEAGUE since 1883. They have won only two league titles, in 1915 and 1950 (with the youthful 'whiz kids') but no WORLD SERIES. The Phillies have maintained a mediocre record through most of their history. Their outstanding player was the pitcher ALEXANDER, who had three straight seasons of 30 wins and 373 career wins.

PHILADELPHIA S.C., ICE SKATING club formed in the U.S.A. in 1849, the first in America.

PHILADELPHIA 76ers, American professional BASKETBALL club, formed in 1963 when the Philadelphia Warriors moved to become the San Francisco Warriors. They gained the NATIONAL BASKETBALL ASSOCIATION title in 1967. Among their best players have been CHAMBERLAIN and CUNNINGHAM.

PHILLIPS, Capt. MARK (1948-   ), British three-day event (see EQUESTRIAN EVENTS) horseman. Riding Great Ovation, he won the Badminton championship two years running 1971 and 1972) and was a member of the British teams which won the 1971 European championship and the 1972 Olympic gold medal. He was also in the victorious world championship team of 1970, riding Chicago.

PHYSICAL EDUCATION ASSOCIATION of Great Britain and Northern Ireland, see LING ASSOCIATION.

PIETERMARITZBURG TO DURBAN MARATHON, a CANOEING event held annually in South Africa. The race covers a distance of just on 90 miles (145 km.) through rugged country. It was first run in 1951 when only one of the eight starters — Ian Player, brother of the golfer — completed the course, taking six days to do so. The race later progressed to double crews with the winning time dropping to about ten hours' paddling.

PIGALLE WONDER (1956), racing greyhound, a brindled dog, by Champion Prince out of Prairie Peg. A spectacular favourite with greyhound crowds in 1957-60, he started at odds on in 52 of his 60 races in Britain. Winner of the 1958 GREYHOUND DERBY, he set up seven track records. He was trained by Syder at Wembley and owned by Burnett.

PIGEON RACING is a sport in which the fancier is a combination of owner, breeder, trainer, and punter.

The initial equipment can be costly, but less so for the do-it-yourself enthusiast. Undoubtedly the major item is the loft, which may be of wooden or brick construction; if the former, it is customary to have it raised from the ground. The size of the loft will vary according to the aims and intentions of the fancier, but as a yardstick a loft 12 ft. (4 m.) long by 6 ft. (2 m.) wide, 7 ft. (2.1 m.) high at the front, and 6 ft. (2 m.) high at the back, partitioned into two halves, is sufficient to accommodate 10 to 12 pairs of old birds in one half, and a similar number of young birds in the other. However, during the early winter months, before separating the sexes, a fancier with such a loft would reduce his stock to 10 to 12 pairs again in readiness for the next breeding and racing season. The two fundamental principles observed by all successful fanciers are good ventilation and dryness.

The pigeon basket or, more commonly, the transporter crate, is another essential item of equipment.

The pigeon clock is the last of the major requirements. There are two types, the puncture clock and the printing clock, the latter being of more recent design and rapidly replacing the former. The pigeon clock is so designed that when a race rubber is inserted into it the exact time is recorded on a paper roll (in the case of a printer) or by the prick of needles in paper dials on a puncture clock.

Prior to the racing season, the fancier will

hand his clock in to his club so that it may be completely and rigorously tested by the clock committee. Records are kept of the tests which are carried out over 24-hour runs with the clock in every possible position, i.e. on its face, back, side, etc. The tolerance allowed is very small and the aim is complete accuracy. Once the clock has been accepted by the committee it is returned to the fancier for use only on actual race days, when it bears numbered and recorded seals which may be removed only by the clock committee after the race. Clocks are checked against radio time signals before and after a race, and any variation is taken into account.

In order to race pigeons, a fancier will belong to a club, the object of which is to provide equality of chance throughout its membership, and each club has a radius outside which membership is barred. One of the reasons for this is that wind direction can influence the result of a race, and by keeping the radius small this possibility is minimized. In a city or town where there may be a large number of fanciers, a club radius may be as small as 1 mile (1·6 km.), but in agricultural areas the number of fanciers required to make a club a viable proposition may necessitate a radius of 5 miles (8 km.) or even 10 miles (16 km.). Adjacent clubs unite to form a federation which will carry out the race programme.

The road transporter, which has superseded rail as the means of transporting pigeons to the race point, has built into it living and sleeping accommodation for the driver and a convoyer who is responsible for the feeding, watering, and general welfare of the pigeons from the time of loading until liberation. Though the internal design of road transporters may differ slightly in detail, they all possess the same basic and essential features incorporating instant-release mechanism for simultaneous liberation; metal racking for holding crates of pigeons on each side of the vehicle, and providing a centre gangway for the convoyer to tend his charges; watering from troughs with automatic supply attached to each tier of crates; and a system of ventilation which operates during movement and when at rest.

Transporters are designed to carry from 2,000 to 5,000 racing pigeons in crates, the number permitted in any one crate varying according to the distance to be travelled. In England the usual loading is 16 pigeons per crate for races in that country, but only 10 to 12 when the English federations are racing from the Continent.

The routes that federations will fly are decided at the annual general meeting, and may be from any point of the compass, but in any one year the routes will all be from the same general direction, and the fancier will plan his training schedule accordingly.

Races are held each week during the season, commencing at approximately 60 miles (96 km.) and gradually increasing in distance each week until the final race, which for old birds (i.e. born before 1 January in the year of the race) is around 500 miles (800 km.), and 250 miles (400 km.) for young birds. However, clubs with a nationwide radius (national clubs) organize races in excess of 600 miles (960 km.) for old birds and from around 300 miles (480 km.) for young.

Before a race, the fancier will list his entries on a race sheet which calls for the ring number of each pigeon, colour, sex, and pools (side stakes) entered, and the number of the rubber race ring. In most clubs the pools are very modest, ranging from 2½p to 10p (or equivalent), but in clubs with a national boundary they may range from 5p to £5. In these latter races, termed 'nationals', it is also possible to win such prizes as a car or a television set, and items of similar value, in addition to cash prizes. However, there are many fanciers who never pool their pigeons, racing for prize money only.

The fancier takes his pigeons to the local club headquarters, hands his race sheet to the secretary and his basket of pigeons to the marking committee, who will remove each pigeon in turn, check the ring number, colour and sex with the details on the race sheet, and then attach to each pigeon's leg a complete rubber (or plastic) band (race rubber), each bearing a separate code number. Its details are entered against the appropriate pigeon on the race sheet by the secretary. While this is going on the clock committee will be winding, setting, and sealing all clocks and each competing fancier will check and collect his clock before leaving for home.

As each crate receives its complement of pigeons (which will be all cocks, or all hens) it is closed and sealed. The federation transporter visits each club and collects the crate of pigeons and from that point until liberation they are the responsibility of the convoyer. On arrival at the race point, and prior to liberation, the convoyer will receive, by prior arrangement with a weather bureau, a detailed forecast giving complete information of wind, weather, visibility, cloud height, and intensity at the liberation point and progressing along the line of flight to the home end, based on an estimated flying speed of 40 m.p.h. (64 km./h.). On receipt of the report, the convoyer will contact the race controller (normally the president of the federation) who will himself have obtained reports from fanciers and coast guards along the line of flight. If both agree that everything points to a good race, the pigeons are liberated and the time of liberation telephoned to the federation secretary, who will in turn inform club secretaries. If the weather is against a good race, the pigeons will be held at the race point until favourable conditions prevail.

The speed of flight depends entirely upon the direction of the wind and will obviously be greater with a tail wind than against a head wind. Over a season's racing a reasonable average speed would be in the region of 35 to 40 m.p.h. (56 to 64 km./h.), but speeds up to 90 m.p.h. (145 km./h.) have been recorded, and verified.

Discipline on arrival at the loft is important. The racing pigeon is not permitted to land anywhere except at the loft, for speed of trapping on race days is of vital importance. As the pigeons arrive home, the fancier removes the race ring and places it in the timing clock, checking it to see that the time has been recorded. The clock will be returned to the club the same evening and handed over to the clock committee who will stop it at a recorded time, check the details of the race ring against the race sheet, and calculate any clock variation that may have to be taken into account.

In order to calculate the distance, the accurate location of the starting point and of each competitor's loft must be known. Race points are selected by the various federations in consultation with their national body, and both race points and lofts are located in terms of longitude and latitude, accurate to two decimal places of a second. The distance between the two is calculated to the nearest yard/metre.

Breeding and training. The selection of breeding pairs is made only after a lengthy study of pedigree, performance, conformation, and type, and, by some fanciers, a detailed study of the eye (eye sign). Indeed, there are those who study the eye, and its circles of correlation, wiring, colours, and shades and select for breeding and racing on this aspect alone, and there are those, probably the more successful, who observe the best principles of both systems of selection.

After each racing season the two sexes are separated and, in the western hemisphere, most fanciers mate their pigeons between the end of February and early March, so that the squeakers (young) are weaned (removed from their parents) before the start of the next racing season. Great care is exercised by the fancier to ensure that pairing is accomplished peacefully and that strong and excited cock birds do not scalp (peck feathers from the head of) the hen. Only one nest box is opened at any one time to ensure guaranteed parentage of the young, and also to avoid pigeons entering the

wrong nest box, fighting, and possibly ruining their racing prospects for that season. Only when the fancier is confident that all pairs are settled to their respective nest boxes and are sitting on eggs will freedom of the loft be given. Eggs are laid in an earthenware nest bowl, in which the parent birds will build their nest with short pieces of straw provided for this purpose by the fancier.

Nine or ten days after pairing, two white eggs are laid, the first in the early evening, the second two days later in the middle of the afternoon. Sitting begins in earnest immediately after the second egg is laid. The period of incubation is 19 days counted from the date on which the first egg was laid. Usually both youngsters hatch within an hour or so of one another. At this stage the young are blind, covered with a soft yellow down, and completely helpless. The rate of growth, however, is fast and after six to seven days there is a change from 'soft food' (a creamy liquid regurgitated by the parents) to grain.

An official metal registration ring, issued by the appropriate national governing body, is placed on the leg of the young pigeon when it is about seven days old. The ring indicates the issuing organization, the year of ringing, and the registration number. For example, a 1971 ring issued by the Royal National Homing Union of Great Britain might read NU.71.A12345, where NU indicates National Union, 71 the year of ringing, and A12345 the registration number. In Great Britain, a little over 2,000,000 registration rings are issued annually, in Belgium around 3,000,000, in West Germany about 1,500,000, followed by France, Holland, Italy, Poland, Austria, Denmark, Sweden, America, Canada, South Africa, and Japan.

At 21 days the youngster should be able to feed itself. By this time the parent birds will be sitting again, the hen laying further eggs when the young are about 17 days old, after which she usually takes little part in their feeding, most of which is done by the cock bird.

At 24 days the offspring are ready for weaning and are taken from their parents and placed in the young bird loft, or compartment. It is now, before they are strong on the wing, that settling in to the loft is begun. The youngsters are placed outside so that they can look around and orientate themselves, in order that when they do fly, they will know the location of their own loft and be able to return to it. Young pigeons are never stinted in the amount of corn fed to them, but they are not allowed outside the loft after a meal. More pigeons are lost at this time than at any other. The young pigeon is full of life, wanders too far from home, and does not have the strength or the knowledge to find its way back again. Once settled and strong on the wing, the kit or batch of young pigeons will range (run) far and wide and will remain on the wing for several hours at a stretch. At this stage training for racing begins.

In order to overcome 'basket fright', young pigeons are placed in the race pannier (transporter crate) and kept inside the loft for a few hours. This is gradually increased until the youngsters have spent at least one period of 24 hours in the basket, are confident and comfortable, and have satisfied their owner that they have learned to eat and drink from the metal troughs attached to the side of the crate.

Racing pigeons are fed hard grain, and care is taken to ensure the correct proportions of protein and carbohydrates. During the racing season a higher proportion of carbohydrates will be fed than during the moult (when pigeons change their feathers, old birds during autumn and young birds when about three to four months old).

The breeding of pigeons is based on the assumption that the good, pedigreed pigeon, proven in races, is more likely to breed race winners than a non-pedigreed and untried specimen. The most successful fanciers create a family of pigeons, which are inbred and thus more capable of producing their like than a breeding pair which are completely unrelated. These fanciers rightly claim that a loft containing a family of pigeons will always beat a loft not founded on this principle.

There are two main systems of keeping pigeons during the racing season. One is the natural system whereby the pair of pigeons live together and follow a normal nesting pattern with only the hatching of young being controlled. This system allows both sexes to be trained and raced. The other is the 'widowhood system', which allows only the cock birds to be raced.

Pigeons to be raced on the widowhood system are paired, rear one nest of young and, when the second round of eggs has been laid, the hen is removed, and the cock bird left to complete the feeding of the young for the few days that they will require his attention. He also sits on the eggs for about 24 hours before forsaking them. Subsequently, the only time the cock sees his hen is just before and after a race. Prior to the race the time allowed together is short and under the watchful eye of the fancier, who removes the cock and places him in the basket before any sexual contact is made. On return from a race widowhood cocks trap very quickly, knowing their hen is waiting for them.

Both systems have their adherents. The advocate of the natural system claims that the widow system is wasteful of the racing ability of good hens, and that the widower cock only performs well over the shorter distances and when the sun is on his back. The widowhood enthusiast claims that the system so improves the performance of the cock birds that the hen birds are not missed, and that the widower can and does win from the extreme distances. Both claimants have their points, but the most successful fanciers, especially on the Continent, back both. While they use widowers for shorter races, they will send a mixed team to very long races.

For the inexperienced, and young, pigeon, great care is taken in the selection of the first few liberation points, and of the time of the day liberation will take place. Every effort is made to select a quiet point, a few miles on the line of flight the pigeons will be required to race, and at a time of the day when few other pigeons will be about. As they become more experienced and competent in returning from short 'tosses' — up to 20 miles (32 km.) — the fancier will liberate the birds singly, or in pairs, so that they will have the self-confidence to fly home on their own.

For racing purposes a pigeon born in, say, 1973 will become an 'old' pigeon on 1 January 1974. Old pigeons are trained for two reasons; to refresh their memory of old routes, and to get them fit for racing. Fitness is paramount, and no pigeon is subjected to a long race unless it is physically fit. Old birds are raced during the breeding season and each will have its own favourite nesting condition. Some hens will race best when sitting seven to ten days, others when feeding young, and so on.

Some fanciers prefer a toss of 50 to 60 miles (80–96 km.) mid-week in preparation for the week-end race, while others favour a toss of 20 to 40 miles (32–64 km.) each day from Monday to Thursday. Much depends on the characteristics of the pigeon. A big, heavy bird will need more work to get fit than a smaller, light-framed type. A pigeon called upon to fly a distance of 800 to 900 miles (1,280–1,440 km.) from, say, Barcelona to the middle of England, would be four or five years old, and would already be experienced along the race routes from the Continent.

The training of cocks under the widowhood system is a little different. The widowers are each placed in their own separate compartment of a special type of basket containing six, or twelve in two tiers of six, in individual compartments. Prior to a race, the widowers will be taken a short toss and the order of return noted as an indication of the likely race finish order.

The modern racing pigeon is descended from

the rock dove (*Columba livia*) and has no relationship with either the wood pigeon (*Columba palumbus*) or the stock dove (*Columba oenas*).

Man has known the rock dove from earliest recorded times, and at least 5,000 years ago the Egyptians were domesticating them — Pharoah Rameses III (1198-1167 B.C.) used them to carry messages. Pliny, the Roman historian, refers to the use of pigeons as message-carriers during the siege of Matina in 43 B.C., and several hundreds of years later they were employed by the Saracens to the discomfort of King Richard of England, who was frequently surprised at the speed with which his enemy learned of his troop movements. Other occasions on which pigeons were employed by warring factions were during the sieges of Leyden in 1574, Venice in 1849, and Paris in 1870-1. Reuters, the international news service, was founded on the use of pigeons to carry messages and during the two world wars pigeons were employed by both sides in every theatre. By this time the modern racing pigeon, capable of sustained flight at high speed over hundreds of miles, had been developed.

Before the railway, the only means by which the pigeon could be conveyed to the release point was by horse-drawn transport or by man himself. Consequently, as far as the sport was concerned, the distances pigeons were required to fly was short, and there existed a strain of pigeon which, over the measured mile, was extremely fast. These pigeons would be released over flat country and within sight of their owner who would have with him a box in which the pigeon would alight on completion of the flight. On race days flights were against the clock with the fastest pigeon being the winner. However, even during these times there were pioneers, particularly in Belgium, who were concentrating on the development of pigeons which would be capable of flying long distances.

With the advent of the telegraph and the development of a railroad network, the message-carrying pigeon lost its commercial value, but the way was now open for an expansion of the breeding and racing of pigeons for long distances. It was found that the pigeon which had successfully flown the shorter distances was of little use over several hundreds of miles and much research and development went into the breeding of birds capable of flying such distances at a high and sustained speed.

The evolution of the modern racing pigeon took place in the latter half of the nineteenth century, with Belgium and Great Britain the pioneers. One of the main centres of development was the province of Antwerp, Belgium, whose fanciers in the early twentieth century would send drafts of pigeons to England for selection by would-be purchasers, after which the pigeons were released on the understanding that if they did not return to their home lofts in Antwerp there was no financial responsibility on the part of the prospective buyer. The early pioneers created families of pigeons which were known by the names of their breeder. Some of those whose names can be found in the pedigrees of present-day pigeons are Gits of Antwerp, whose pigeons attained great fame at the end of the nineteenth century, as did those of Janssen, Hansenne (whose breed is still a favourite in Great Britain), Grooters, Jurion (the strain he bred is still to be found in the lofts of H. M. Queen Elizabeth II), Dr. Logan, Col. Osman, and Sir William Proctor-Smith of England, and Trenton of the U.S.A. (his strains still perpetuated by some breeders). But the crossing of the various families or strains is carried on to such an extent that there are very few pure-bred specimens of these old families left. Buying and selling of pigeons is carried out on an international scale, and it is not unusual to find birds with almost identical pedigrees competing in many countries throughout the world.

During the latter half of the nineteenth century there were no timing clocks to ensure the accurate recording of a pigeon's arrival home. To overcome this, clubs would place an inked mark on the flights (wing feathers) of the pigeon prior to despatch to the race point and on its arrival home the owner would catch his pigeon, place it in a paper bag and run with it to the nominated reporting centre (usually a post office, inn, or public house). At this time there was no method of calculating distances accurately and the system was consequently rough and ready, the winner of a race being the first man to produce a verified pigeon at the reporting centre.

It was not until the turn of the century that pigeon racing became an organized sport by the creation of national bodies. The Royal Fédération Colombophile Belge was formed, closely followed in 1896 by the formation of the Royal National Homing Union of Great Britain, and other countries throughout the world followed in close order. Loft locations and race (liberating) points were calculated in terms of longitude and latitude and the distances between the two measured by the Great Circle System to the nearest yard/metre. Thus the rough yardsticks of the past were abandoned for the mathematical method of calculating a velocity and the winner of a race by the simple division of distance by time.

Gradually the various national bodies drew

up rules which recognized the sport and in 1910 the metal registration ring became compulsory in Europe and in Great Britain. It was about this time that the first of the timing clocks became available and most clubs purchased one. The metal registration ring allowed a closer control of the pigeon and the locating of the timing clock at the reporting centre meant that an accurate record could be kept of arrivals. Pigeons were no longer wing-stamped but had a rubber race ring placed on one leg before being basketed. After a race, the owner would remove the race ring and run with it to the reporting centre where it would be placed in the pigeon clock and the exact time recorded. The story is told of two brothers who were almost unbeatable before it was found that they possessed a highly trained whippet which would carry the race ring secreted in its collar to the reporting centre. About 1920 the use of timing clocks on the basis of one per fancier (owner) was made mandatory.

The original method of transportation to race points was by rail. Federations would hire a complete train, with the convoyer and his assistants travelling in the guard's van. On arrival at their destination the panniers of pigeons would be off-loaded and stacked in tiers, normally five high, and on a signal from the convoyer the basket flaps would be opened and the pigeons liberated. This method of transportation was superseded in the mid-1940s by road transport.

Weather reports in the early days of the sport left much to be desired, and there were far more race disasters than there are today with the sophisticated methods of weather forecasting now available. In the Bordeaux (France) race of 15 July 1912, 1,139 pigeons were liberated to fly to England, distances ranging from 410 to 650 miles (656 to 1,040 km.). But by 22 July only 8 per cent had arrived home. An even more disastrous race was flown on 22 July of the same year, when 1,638 pigeons were liberated at Marennes, France, to fly to Manchester, England, the recorded arrivals being only 31.

Undoubtedly the importance attached to the pigeon by the military has helped in its development as a species and from the training and performance aspects. During hostilities, a Defence of the Realm regulation forbidding the unauthorized keeping and liberation of racing (carrier) pigeons is issued, and a national pigeon service is formed from the ranks of experienced fanciers. During the First World War pigeons were used from lofts, generally mounted on horse-drawn transport in, and adjacent to, the front lines. In the Second World War pigeons were better developed and

more reliable, and motor transport was used. But the war was fluid and fast-moving on all fronts and new methods were found — the training of pigeons to lofts that were fully mobile and frequently moved to new locations, the release of pigeons from aeroplanes, and the supply of birds by organizing all 'home' lofts to produce young pigeons, virtually on demand, and irrespective of season. The pigeon proved itself a most useful asset; its love of home and ability to travel great distances at speed saved many thousands of lives, but, undoubtedly, it is in the field of espionage where its attributes can be exploited to the full. Messages are carried in small containers clipped to the leg of the pigeon. Previously the length of handwritten messages was understandably limited, but with the introduction of micro-photography the message-carrying potential has been greatly increased.

Though Belgium was undoubtedly to the forefront of development, not only of the modern racing pigeon but also of the administration of the sport on a national basis, other countries were not far behind, although each was operating independently of the others. It was not until the 1950s that the Fédération Colombophile Internationale (F.C.I.) was formed with its headquarters in Brussels, with the object of acting as the international link and adviser on the sport.

Because of varying conditions, it is not possible to hold a race in which the chances of each member country would be equal. However, the F.C.I. does organize a competition every second year in which member countries enter a team of five cocks and five hens, the conditions of entry being that the pigeons shall have been winners within the past two years from distances of 1,000 km. (621 miles) for cocks, and 750 km. (465 miles) for hens. The competition has a different venue each time with the selection of the host country being made on the same principles as for the OLYMPIC GAMES. It is normally held in late January or early February to avoid disruption of the breeding and racing programme.

The management committee of the F.C.I., consisting of one delegate from each member country, meets twice each year. It acts purely in an advisory capacity to obtain a common approach to the sport by all member countries.

A major problem which could affect the continued expansion of the sport is the increasing human population, coupled with the rising cost of land. The back garden, the traditional site for the pigeon loft, is fast disappearing the world over and the time may come when those with this facility will be the fortunate few. Obviously the sport will not be allowed to die, if only because it can be a message-carrying service in time of hostilities, and communal sites for pigeon lofts may be the answer.

W. E. Barker, *Pigeon Racing* (1958); Guy Barrett, *Racing Pigeons* (1969); A. Neilson Hutton, *Pigeon Racing* (1968), Wendell M. Levi, *The Pigeon* (n.d.); G. H. T. Stovin, *Breeding Better Pigeons* (1964); 'Violette', *Practical Course on the General Management of Pigeons* (n.d.); Leon F. Whitney, *The Basis of Breeding Racing Pigeons* (1969) and *Keep Your Pigeons Flying* (1968).

GOVERNING BODY (WORLD): Fédération Colombophile Internationale, 39 Rue de Livourne, Brussels, Belgium; (U.K.): Royal Pigeon Racing Association, Reddings House, The Reddings, Nr. Cheltenham, Glos; North of England Homing Union, 58, Ennerdale Road, Walker Dene, Newcastle upon Tyne; Scottish Homing Union, Bank of Scotland Buildings, Hopetown St., Bathgate, West Lothian, Scotland; Welsh Homing Union, 9, Ty-Isaf Crescent, Pontymister, Risca, Mon., Wales; Irish Homing Pigeon Union, 3 Wellwood Ave., Belfast 4, N. Ireland; (U.S.A.): International Federation of American Homing Pigeon Fanciers Inc., 2110 Bath Rd., Bristol, Pa., U.S.A.; American Racing Pigeon Union, 11612 Monte Vista Ave., Chino, Calif., U.S.A.

PIGGOTT, LESTER (1935-   ), champion jockey in England from 1964 until dethroned by CARSON in 1972. His DERBY winners are NEVER SAY DIE, Crepello, ST. PADDY, SIR IVOR, NIJINSKY, and Roberto.

PIHKALA, Prof. LAURI, see PESÄPALLO.

PILCH, FULLER (1803-70), cricketer for Kent. The supreme batsman at the time of his retirement, he introduced forward play, nullifying rising balls and shooters alike, and driving them. From 1836 to 1854 he helped create a formidable Kent side (also managing club and ground affairs) which played, and sometimes beat, 'England'. He was also an exceptional single-wicket player.

PILOTA, see PELOTA.

PIMLICO, race-track at Baltimore, Maryland, is the venue of the PREAKNESS STAKES.

PINE VALLEY, U.S. GOLF course near Philadelphia. The businessman who bought this tract of sandy, wooded, and hilly land aimed to build the most difficult, but fair, golf course in the world. Whether he and his successors achieved this objective must be a matter of individual opinion. What is not to be doubted is that the course severely punishes misjudged or misplayed shots with vast bunkers, water, and trees. It calls for a wide range of finely executed approach shots and in 450 rounds of tournament play by a field of leading professionals, par was broken only twice.

PINEHURST, U.S. GOLF course, North Carolina. Of the five courses at this golf resort, the No. 2 course is the supreme test. Built, as its name suggests, through heavily wooded undulating country, it combines golfing excellence and scenic beauty in proportions which few courses can match. Pinehurst would be the natural choice for many more championship events if it were not for the fact that golf courses need vast support facilities and have to be close to large centres of population.

PING BALL, a form of TABLE TENNIS akin to LAWN TENNIS. It is played on the ground over a net, 70 cm. (27½ in.) high, with a racket 28 to 32 × 15 cm. (11 to 12½ × 6 in.), similar in shape to a table tennis bat but with a net hitting surface. The ball is 4 cm. (1½ in.) in diameter. Service passes from game to game and scoring is the same as in tennis.

PING-PONG, see TABLE TENNIS.

PINGEON, ROGER (1940-   ), French professional road-race cyclist. A good climber but a diffident tactician, he seized his chance to win the 1967 TOUR DE FRANCE, and developed into his country's most forceful stage-race rider. In 1969 he fulfilled his prediction that he would win the VUELTA A ESPAGNA on stage 12.

PIOLA, SILVIO (1913-   ), Association footballer for Lazio (Rome), and Italy for whom he made his first appearance in 1933 and his last in 1952. He was at the peak of his career at the time of the 1938 world championship tournament in France, scored twice in Italy's 4-2 victory over Hungary in the final, and was the best centre forward in the tournament. In all he scored 34 goals for Italy in international matches.

PIRIE, DOUGLAS ALASTAIR GORDON (1931-   ), middle-distance and long-distance runner for Great Britain. The first of four individual world records fell to Pirie in 1953: the 6 miles in 28 min. 19·4 sec. In the same year he won the English cross-country championship and retained his title in 1954 and 1955. His best season was 1956 when he broke the world 5,000 metres record with 13 min. 36·8 sec. and five days later equalled the 3,000 metres record. He improved the 3,000 metres mark to 7 min. 52·8 sec. later the same year in a spectacular race with three Hungarian stars including IHAROS. The best of Pirie's three Olympic appearances was in 1956 when, attempting a double in the 5,000 and 10,000 metres, he was over-extended in his 10,000 metres duel with KUTS and had to be content with a silver medal behind the Russian in the 5,000 metres.

PIRRI, JOSÉ (1945-   ), Association footballer for REAL MADRID, and Spain for whom he played in the 1966 world championship matches in England two months after winning a European Champion Clubs Cup medal at the age of 21 when Real Madrid beat Partizan Belgrade in the final in Brussels. A strong midfield player with the happy knack of scoring vital goals, he was an important contributor to the reshaping of both Real Madrid and the Spanish national team in the 1970s.

PISTOL SHOOTING, see SHOOTING, PISTOL.

PITKÄPALLO, see PESÄPALLO.

PITTSBURGH PENGUINS, ICE HOCKEY club of Pittsburgh, formed in 1967 as one of six teams in the new West Division of the expanded NATIONAL HOCKEY LEAGUE of North America. Home games are played at Pittsburgh's Civic Arena, seating 12,580. The players train in Canada at Brantford, Ontario. COLOURS: Light blue, dark blue, and white.

PITTSBURGH PIRATES, American professional BASEBALL team, members of the NATIONAL LEAGUE under their name since 1887. Under the manager-outfielder Clarke they won league titles in 1901-3 and 1909, with the shortstop WAGNER as star player. The Pirates also won titles in 1925, 1927, 1960, and 1971, with WORLD SERIES wins in 1909, 1925, 1960, and 1971. The 1920s-1930s Pirates featured the third baseman Traynor (lifetime batting average ·320), who managed from 1934 to 1939, and the Waner brothers, both outfielders — Paul (lifetime average ·333) and Lloyd (·316). The 1960s Pirates starred the outfielder CLEMENTE, who captured four league batting titles.

PITTSBURGH STEELERS, American professional FOOTBALL team, entered the NATIONAL FOOTBALL LEAGUE in 1933 and later, in 1970, switched to the American Conference within the same league. In wartime 1943 the team combined with the PHILADELPHIA EAGLES to form the inelegantly named 'Steagles'. Owned by Rooney since their founding, the Steelers have had rugged, colourful teams but have won no League titles. In the late 1930s they featured the versatile back WHITE, in the 1940s the powerful runner Dudley. In the 1970s the Steelers became serious title contenders.
COLOURS: Gold and black.

PLANICKA, FRATISEK (1904-   ). Association footballer for S.K. Slavia (Prague), and Czechoslovakia, who was one of the best goalkeepers in Europe in the 1930s, and who, unusually for a goalkeeper, captained the Czechoslovakian national side that competed in the final stages of the 1934 world championship in Italy.

PLATT, JOSEPH (1858-1930), honorary secretary of the English Northern Union (see RUGBY LEAGUE) when it was formed in 1895. A solicitor in Oldham, he played a prominent part in the establishment of professional Rugby in England; he was made a life member when he resigned in 1920.

PLAYER, GARY (1935-   ), South African professional golfer, who was Open champion 1959, 1968; U.S. Open champion 1965; Masters champion 1961; U.S. Professional Golfers Association champion 1962, 1972; South African Open champion 7 times; winner of more than 50 tournaments, and a WORLD CUP player. He was the third player (after HOGAN and SARAZEN) to win all four classic championships of professional GOLF.

PLUNKET SHIELD, presented in 1906 by Lord Plunket, then the Governor General of New Zealand, is New Zealand's major CRICKET trophy. It was played for only on a challenge basis until 1921. Since then it has been contested for more generally, and the matches played by Canterbury, Auckland, Wellington, Otago, Central Districts, and Northern Districts provide all the first-class cricket in New Zealand apart from matches against touring teams. Auckland, Canterbury, and Wellington have been clearly the most successful teams.

POCAHONTAS (1837) was an English brood mare who lived to the age of 33. She produced STOCKWELL, his full brother, Rataplan, and his half-brother King Tom, who were all excellent stallions. Pocahontas appears nine times in the pedigree of TRACERY.

POGLAJEN, MARTIN (1942-   ), Dutch JUDO fighter whose ferocious attacking spirit enabled him to meet the Japanese on level terms. Poglajen won world championship medals in 1967 (silver) and 1969 (bronze). In addition he was European open middleweight champion in 1965, bronze medallist in 1968, and silver medallist two years later.

POINCELET, ROGER, one of the foremost jockeys in France before taking up training. Since the Second World War he has ridden three winners of the PRIX DE L'ARC DE TRIOMPHE.

POINT-TO-POINT RACING, see HORSE RACING.

POLE VAULT, a standard field event for men in the programme of all major ATHLETICS championships. Pole vaulting is a jumping contest for height, competitors using a pole to lever their bodies over a bar which is raised according to a fixed progression. Vaulters failing to clear each height within three attempts are eliminated and the winner is the athlete who clears the greatest height.

An approach run of not less than about 120 ft. (36 m.) is used, the vaulter holding the pole almost parallel with the ground. The pole is planted in the box, the athlete's impetus causing it both to flex and lift, levering his body from the ground. He hangs from the pole until it unflexes, then uses his arms to pull himself, feet first, upwards, simultaneously turning about the pole so that he can cross the bar face downwards. As he jack-knifes over the bar he pushes the pole away from him and rotates backwards to land on his back.

The pole vault is probably a refinement of pole jumping, a practice employed for many centuries in the fen district of eastern England to assist men to overleap marshy patches of ground. Competitive pole jumping dates from the mid-nineteenth century when a strong tradition existed in Ulverston, Lancashire. Heavy wooden poles with iron spikes were used which were planted in the turf, the jumper crossing the bar in a squatting posture. In later years the technique of climbing up the pole was banned, a fixed handhold being laid down in the rules of the International Amateur Athletic Federation (see ATHLETICS, TRACK AND FIELD). In modern pole vaulting, the pole is planted in a wedge-shaped box which is sunk into the runway.

Up to the Second World War, poles were predominantly of bamboo but aluminium was later found to be more serviceable. Since 1962 the use of fibreglass has revolutionized the event. The extreme flexibility of fibreglass poles, when handled with consummate timing, enabled greater heights to be attained through a catapulting effect. The world record rose from 15 ft. (4·57 m.) to 16 ft. (4·87 m.) between 1940 and 1962, but, through the use of fibreglass poles, it had reached 18 ft. (5·48 m.) by 1970.

A recent innovation in pole vaulting has been the introduction of an air bed, a large inflatable cushion, for the landing area. Usually a built-up surface, this reduces the distance the athlete must fall.

POLLARD, MARJORIE (1899-   ), HOCKEY player for England, the Midlands, Northamptonshire, Peterborough, and North Northants (which she founded), and former acting president of the All-England Women's Hockey Association. She was an outstanding forward who played for England from 1921 to 1928 and from 1931 to 1933. In 1926 she scored all 13 goals against Wales, and all 8 against Germany. The same year she became a sports journalist and wrote for the *Morning Post, Observer, The Times, Guardian,* and other newspapers. She was editor of the magazine, *Hockey Field,* from 1946 to 1970, and her influence on women's hockey was considerable.

POLLET, ÉTIENNE, one of the leading race-horse trainers in France, whose patrons included Mme. Couturié and Ternynck. The best horses trained by him are SEA BIRD II, VAGUELY NOBLE, and RIGHT ROYAL V.

POLLOCK, ROBERT GRAEME (1944-   ), cricketer for South Africa and Eastern Province. Entering first-class CRICKET at the age of 16, he established himself on the tour of Australia in 1963-4 as a high-scoring, forcing batsman, and continued his progress in England in 1965. A tall and commanding left-hander, in 1970 he crowned his career with the highest score ever made for South Africa — 274 against Australia at Durban.

POLO is a four-a-side team game whose players are mounted on horses and who use wooden mallets, or 'sticks', to strike a wooden ball in an attempt to score goals. The ball is struck with the side, not the end, of the mallet, and there is no limit to the size of the horse, though one of over 16 hands is not often manoeuvrable enough.

The game can be played with three a side, if numbers are short or the ground small. A full-size ground is 300 yards (274·32 m.) long, 200 yards (182·88 m.) wide if un-boarded, 160 yards (146·3 m.) wide if boarded. Grounds are often smaller but these dimensions are never exceeded. Boards on the side lines, if used, are 9 in. (229 mm.) high and are intended to keep the ball in play.

The ground is marked with white lines

round the ends and sides and across the field at 30 and 60 yds. (27·4 and 54·9 m.) from each goal line. There are also crosses or blobs of whitewash marking the centre of the ground and at 40 yds. (36·5 m.) from the centre of each goal. There must be considerable safety zones behind the goal lines and outside the touch lines, so that players may cross these at full speed and at any angle.

Goal posts are placed 8 yds. (7·3 m.) apart; they are about 10 ft. (3 m.) high and about 10 in. (254 mm.) in diameter. They are not of solid construction but usually of wicker or lath covered with cloth, often in the club colours, fixed around a central pole of about 1½ in. (38 mm.) diameter which fits into a slot in the ground. This allows a player or horse to collide with the goal post without the certainty of serious injury.

A mallet consists of a handle made of wood clamped to the shaft and bound with rubber, tape, or towelling as a hand grip. The shaft is cane about ¾ in. (19 mm.) thick and from 47 to 54 in. (1·2–1·4 m.) long. The head is of wood, about 9 in. (228 mm.) long by 2 in. (51 mm.) in diameter at the centre, and of cylindrical, oval, or rectangular section. The most common pattern is cigar-shaped with tapered ends. Metal shafts are not used. The design can vary according to the wishes of the player.

The ball is of solid wood, usually willow, bamboo root, or ash. It must not exceed 3¼ in. (82·5 mm.) in diameter and must be between 4½ and 4¾ oz. (120–135 g.) in weight. Its life is not long and a considerable number are used in each game.

Helmets or caps of pith, cork, or hard synthetic material are worn. They are lined with shock-absorbent sponge rubber or other material and cross-tapes to protect the head from a fall or blow. Leather and rubber knee pads may also be worn.

In matches and tournaments it is customary for players to wear white breeches of washable material and brown leather top boots, with a shirt or jersey in the team's colours. Spurs are often worn but sharp spurs or rowels are not allowed.

Any type of horse or pony may be played. There is no limit to size, age, or sex. The horse must, however, be sufficiently well behaved not to constitute a danger to other horses and players, and may be sent off the ground by the umpires if it fails in this respect. The horse must wear boots or bandages to cover the lower leg and fetlock as a protection against blows from ball or mallet. The boots are fitted like gaiters and secured with straps.

The game is divided into periods or 'chukkers' of 7 minutes each. The full game is eight periods, but in most tournaments fewer periods are played, many games having only four. In Europe there are no tournaments of more than six periods. A bell is rung at 7 minutes, but the period goes on until the ball goes out of play or the umpire stops the game in a neutral position. In England and the U.S.A., under a new rule, the chukker ends on a second bell at 7½ minutes, if the ball is still in play. The last period, however, ends on the bell unless there is a tie, in which case the game continues in the normal way until a goal is scored. There are intervals of at least 3 minutes between periods and 5 minutes at half-time.

Ends are changed after each goal is scored. The game is re-started by the umpire throwing the ball in between the two teams, who are lined up parallel, at the beginning of each period, after a goal is scored, or whenever the game stops for any reason other than a foul or a hit behind goal. When the ball is hit behind by the attacking side, the defending side hits in as in a goal kick at Association FOOTBALL. When the ball goes behind off a defender's stick, the attacking side is awarded a free hit from the 60 yards (54·9 m.) line opposite to where the ball went out.

The game is controlled by whistles by two mounted umpires on the ground, with a referee on the side lines as arbiter in case of disagreement.

The four players in a side are numbered 1, 2, 3, and 4 (or 'back'). The numbers 1 and 2 are forwards and should play optimistically and aggressively, placing themselves to receive passes from their backs. The 3 and 4 are backs and play a more defensive game, the 3 usually acting as the pivot of the side and the 4 as a defensive player who must never allow the opposing forwards a clear run for goal. Polo is however such a fast and fluid game that the members of a team must continuously interchange position, e.g. the No. 1 may find himself temporarily in the back position, and must play accordingly until an opportunity arises to return to his normal place, while a good back will sometimes meet the ball and go right through to the No. 1 position.

A high degree of teamwork can and should be obtained in polo and a team that has played together and studied this aspect will always, if equally well mounted, defeat a team of four equally good, or even better, individualists. One obvious example of teamwork is for a player to pass the ball to a team mate who is already taking up position to receive the pass, having correctly anticipated it. Another is for a player having possession of the ball to leave it for a following team mate to strike, while he gallops ahead to 'ride out' (or 'ride off', i.e. to push sideways out of the line of play) an

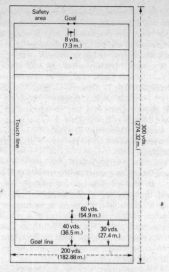

POLO GROUND
Dimensions shown are those of a full-size ground including the safety area, which should be at least 5 yds. (4·5 m.) beyond the touch lines and 20 yds. (18·3 m.) at either end.

opponent who is waiting to intercept. This is a matter of horsemanship and the speed, courage, and training of the horse. Two equal opponents, both correctly anticipating the next position of the ball, will continuously find themselves riding each other off.

A player following the ball on its exact line has the right of way over all other players (whether or not he hit the ball himself). Any player who crosses or enters the right of way close enough in front to be dangerous, commits a foul. No player may hook an opponent's stick unless he is on the same side of the opponent's pony as the ball.

Dangerous riding or stick-work is not allowed. A player may ride off fairly but must not charge an opponent at an angle of more than about 30°. There is no offside rule.

The severity of a penalty depends on the degree of the foul:

Penalty 1. A goal is awarded to the side fouled, and the ball thrown in at the place where the foul occured, for a dangerous or deliberate foul in the goal-mouth by the defending side.

Penalty 2. A free hit from 30 yds. (27·4 m.), opposite the centre of the goal, defenders to be behind the back line and outside the goal posts, which they must not ride through when the ball is hit.

Penalty 3. A free hit from 40 yds. (36·5 m.) with the same conditions as Penalty 2.

Penalty 4. A free hit from 60 yds. (54·9 m.).

Penalty 5(*a*). Free hit from where the foul took place. (*b*) Free hit from the centre of the ground.

In no foul is any member of the defending side allowed to be nearer the ball than 30 yds. (27·4 m.)

A fit horse can play two and occasionally three periods, but not consecutively. For 'high goal' polo, horses need to be almost racing fit; the horse is 70 per cent responsible for success or failure.

The maximum degree of speed and manoeuvrability is attained by a small, compact, thoroughbred horse which has been patiently and methodically trained for at least two years. Most of the horses playing, for reasons of shortage of supply, expense, and lack of skilled trainers, do not approach this ideal either in type or degree of schooling. In Argentina, the U.S.A., South Africa, and other countries of large area and agricultural background, an adequate supply of home-bred horses exists. In Europe most of the polo horses are imported, mainly from Argentina.

Most tournaments are played on handicap. Only international and open tournaments are exceptions to this generalization. The handicap system works as follows:

Each player, as in GOLF, carries an international rating. A player can rate from −2 (minimum) to +10 (maximum), though in many countries minus handicaps are not used, and a beginner starts at 0. Handicaps are based on a full game of eight periods, except in Europe and the U.S.A. where they are based on six. The aggregate handicap of the four players in a team is the team handicap.

In handicap tournaments, the number of goals start awarded to the weaker team is obtained by multiplying the difference between the two teams' handicaps by the number of periods being played and dividing by 8 (in Europe and the U.S.A. by 6). Any fraction counts as half a goal. The handicap system allows bad players to play with, and against, good players and still have a close result. In most countries not more than 10 per cent of the players are of more than +3 handicap.

Arena or **Indoor polo.** Played mainly in the U.S.A., this takes place in a walled arena, open-air or roofed, but much smaller than a standard polo ground, and usually smaller than a football ground. The game is played three-a-side with a soft ball about 6 in. (152 mm.) in diameter, leather-covered like a small football.

Hurlingham Polo Association Year Book, latest edition; *United States Polo Association Year Book*, latest edition.

The Persian poet Firdausi described a polo match between the Persians and Turkomans about 600 B.C. At Isfahan are the remains of an ancient polo ground 300 yds. (274·32 m.) long with stone goal posts 8 yds. (7·3 m.) apart, still the correct measurements. The name polo comes from *pulu*, the willow root from which the balls were and are made in the East.

The game spread over Asia to China and Japan but by the nineteenth century it survived only in a few mountain areas in the north-west and north-east frontiers of India, away from the main currents of invasion and disaster. In some of these places, such as Hunza and Gilgit, it is still played in the original form on the small local ponies.

The game was discovered by visiting British officers who, adopting it with enthusiasm, began to establish polo clubs in India; the first, Calcutta, still exists and celebrated its centenary in 1962. Indian princes soon took up the game and they and the Army were its principal supporters in India from that time on.

Capt. Sherer first organized the game in Assam, India, in the 1850s and was thus the father of modern polo. It was originally played on small ponies of about 13 hands with five to seven players on each side.

The first match in England was played in 1871 at Hounslow between the 9th Lancers and the 10th Hussars and the Hurlingham Club was inaugurated shortly afterwards. The Army were the strongest supporters of the game in England as in India; the keenly contested inter-regimental tournaments started in India in 1877 and in England a year later.

Polo was introduced to the U.S.A. by Gordon Bennett in the late 1870s and spread rapidly, at first mainly in the east. By 1914 the game was known all over the world, especially where Englishmen or Americans were working, and particularly in countries with plenty of space, sun, and horses — such as India, Argentina, and South Africa. In Europe, Spain took second place to the United Kingdom, though a few clubs flourished in Italy, France, Belgium, and Germany. Where conditions were suitable, the game was broadly based and popular; in countries like those of northern Europe with a short summer and an industrial economy, it was confined to a pastime for the very rich and their friends, and the armed services.

Up to 1914 the leading polo nations were India, the U.S.A., and England. India never competed in international matches, but produced a lot of the world's best players and many wonderful tournaments. Most of the best English players learnt to play in India while serving in the army. Before 1914 some of the best players in India were the Maharajas of Ratlam, Kishengarh, and Alwar, Shah MIRZA

BEG of Golconda, Gen. de Lisle, a great tactician and organizer, and HIRA SINGH of Patiala.

In the U.S.A. Foxhall, Keene, Agassiz, and Cowdin in the 1890s and later the Waterbury brothers, Whitney, and the superb MILBURN were of world class. In England Watson, BUCKMASTER, Edwards, Wilson, and CHEAPE were in the same category. In the 1914 war Britain suffered most heavily; Cheape, Wilson, and Edwards were all killed and all the horses dispersed.

In the period 1919 to 1939 the U.S.A. was the predominant polo nation, with a strong challenge from Argentina building up. Much good polo was played in India, which continued to produce some of the world's best players. In Europe the London season was the most important, but the English Champion Cup at Hurlingham was won more often by foreign teams. Spain, up to the Civil War, continued to rank as second nation in Europe, producing fine players such as the Dukes of Penaranda and Santona, the Marquis Villabragima, and King Alfonso XIII.

The great players of the 1920s and '30s in America were Milburn, Webb, Stoddard, HITCHCOCK, Boeseke, Hopping, Phipps, IGLEHART, and CECIL SMITH, all internationals of the highest rating, with many others of almost equal stature. In England, including English players of the Indian Army, among the best were Captains Roark, Dening, Guinness, Lord Wodehouse, and Gerald Balding. In India, the States dominated the high-goal tournaments with such as Jaswant Singh, Prithi Singh of Jodhpur, the Nawab of Bhopal, Maj. Atkinson, and the members of the Jaipur team, champions from 1932 to 1938, Prithi Singh (of Baria), Abhey Singh, HANUT SINGH, and the Maharaja of Jaipur. Argentina produced players such as LACEY, the Miles brothers, Nelson, ANDRADA, Gazotti, CAVANAGH, and Duggan. In 1922 an Argentine team under Lacey swept the board in the London season and went on to win the American open championship, a pointer to the future.

In South Africa, Australia, New Zealand, Chile, and other more distant countries much first-class polo was played and many fine players produced without the publicity that attended the better-known championships of India, the U.S.A., and Britain.

In 1936 an Australian team, the Goulburn team of four brothers Ashton, won the English Champion Cup. SKENE, Australian by birth, though he learnt his polo in India, played for England in the 1939 international series. The principal Australian tournament is inter-state (New South Wales, Victoria, Queensland, South, and West Australia) with periodical participation by New Zealand.

In New Zealand, where the best 'Australian' horses are bred, polo was very much a family affair, and many fine players bear the names of Strang, Nelson, Wilson, Mackenzie, and Kay. There have been up to 70 clubs in New Zealand, which has sent one team to England and one to Mexico in 1956. Otherwise, the main event is participation in the Australasian Gold Cup (the inter-state tournament). The New Zealand championship is the Savile Cup.

World War II again practically ended polo for the countries involved; Argentina became easily the leading nation and by the 1970s — with perhaps 5,000 players, all the world's '10 goalers' and most of the 8s and 9s — was in an unassailable position. The Argentine open championship at Palermo is now acknowledged to produce the best polo in the world.

There are about 800 players registered in the U.S.A., 350 in Britain, with 200 in all the rest of Europe, and probably under 200 in Pakistan and India, once the homes of the game. South Africa probably comes next to the U.S.A. in numbers, and the game still flourishes in Australia and New Zealand, the contests between these countries producing polo of championship standard.

The African continent, and Pakistan and India have for some years been cut off from the rest of the world by the quarantine regulations for the deadly African horse sickness. This means that no horse may leave those countries under any circumstances, so that the host country must supply mounts for visiting teams.

The modern rules of polo were developed first by the Hurlingham Club in London and adopted elsewhere in the same form. Additions and amendments have been made from time to time by the ruling bodies of the major polo countries in consultation with each other.

Originally there was a height limit for ponies. Starting at 13·3 hands, this was gradually raised until finally abolished in 1919. This was done in order to widen the source of supply, and thereby reduce the price, of horses. In fact, with the introduction of the thoroughbred horse, prices were, if anything, raised rather than lowered.

In the 1880s, helmets were made compulsory, since head injuries to players were becoming frequent. The requirement that horses' legs be protected by boots or bandages was also adopted.

There was originally an offside rule, as in Association football. The United States Polo Association abolished the rule in 1909 and this resulted in so much more open and fast a game that all other countries soon followed suit. The No. 1 can now play an aggressive forward game, instead of being forced to conform slavishly to the movements of the opposing 'back'.

Players such as H. P. Whitney in the U.S.A. and de Lisle in India developed tactics and organization to a degree which has not been greatly improved upon since. Polo reached its peak in the 1930s, the era of Tommy Hitchcock, and tactically the game has hardly developed since then.

By the 1970s, HARRIOTT was unquestionably the world's outstanding player, and his team Coronel Suarez, unbeaten for years in the Argentine championship, was among the best that ever played. In England there have been no players with a handicap above 7 goals since 1945, but the Australian, Sinclair Hill, who played for England in 1966, has reached 10 goals.

In 1886 the Westchester Club proposed a contest for an international trophy between England and the U.S.A. known as the Westchester Cup. Until 1939 this was perhaps the best-known polo cup in the world, but it has now been superseded by the Cup of the Americas.

Initially the British, having more experience, won the Westchester Cup, but the Americans soon developed their own ideas, built up strong strings of ponies and, in 1909 and 1911, Whitney's well-organized 'Big Four' team — 'Monty' Waterbury, Laurence Waterbury, Whitney, and Milburn — defeated England fairly decisively. In 1913 the U.S.A. won again, narrowly, but in 1914 an English team of four soldiers, Captains Lockett, Barrett, Cheape, and Tomkinson, defeated the Americans in the States. The Cup was contested again in 1921, 1924, 1927, 1930, 1936, and 1939 but, although coming within one goal on two occasions, England never won it again.

The Cup of the Americas between U.S.A. and Argentina has been played six times: 1928, 1932, 1936, 1950, 1966, and 1969. The U.S.A. won in 1928 and 1932, but Argentina won since then. In 1936 their team consisted of Duggan, Cavanagh, Gazotti, and Andrada and won 21-9 and 8-4. But the U.S. team was by no means the strongest they could field, whereas for the Westchester Cup they never left anything to chance. By 1971 Argentina could produce a 40-goal team, Heguy, G. Dorignac, F. Dorignac, and Harriott, and were virtually unbeatable.

Today the game is played in Argentina, the U.S.A., South Africa, Australia, Britain, New Zealand, Mexico, Chile, India, Pakistan, Rhodesia, Brazil, Spain, Peru, Kenya, Colombia, Venezuela, Uruguay, Italy, France,

Jamaica, Nigeria, the Philippines, Ghana, Germany, Iran, Morocco, Malaya, Singapore, Borneo, Hong Kong, Hawaii, Canada, Ireland, Malta, Cyprus, United Arab Republic, and the Trucial States.

Famous clubs have been Calcutta (where the Indian championship is played), Delhi, Lahore in India and Pakistan; Hurlingham (which gives its name to the Hurlingham Polo Association, the ruling body for English polo), Rugby, Roehampton, and Cowdray Park (venue of the Cowdray Park Gold Cup — the English championship) in England; and Meadowbrook, Old Westbury, Myopia Hunt, Rumson, Midwick, Oklahoma, Santa Barbara, Aiken, Oak Brook, and Boca Raton in U.S.A.

In Argentina, Hurlingham, the Jockey Club, Tortugas, Mar del Plata, Coronel Suarez, and North Santa Fe are all well known, but polo is played all over the country. Johannesburg, Durban, and Cape Town in South Africa; Warwick Farm, Quirindi, Perth, Adelaide in Australia, and Christchurch, Fielding, Hamilton, and Palmerston North are well known in New Zealand.

In Europe, Deauville, Bagatelle (Paris), and Cannes, and in Spain Madrid, Barcelona, Jerez, and Soto Grande are the best-known clubs. Germany has revived polo largely due to the British Army of the Rhine, and Hamburg and Düsseldorf have good clubs, apart from the army stations. In Italy, Rome is the principal club; in the Philippines, Manila; Mexico, Mexico City; Ireland, Phoenix Park, Dublin; Malta, the Marsa Sports Ground; Uruguay, Rio Negro. Brazil has São Paulo and Gavea (Rio de Janeiro); Kenya, Nairobi and several other centres.

British Sports and Sportsmen (Polo), edited by 'The Sportsman' (1923); Newell Bent, *American Polo* (1929); Grove Cullum, *The Selection and Training of a Polo Pony* (1934); W. C. Forbes, *As to Polo* (1939); Charles Harvey, *Encyclopedia of Sport* (1959); Rudyard Kipling, *The Maltese Cat;* 'Marco' (Earl Mountbatten), *Polo* (1931).

POLO CROSSE, a team game played on horseback, created by combining some elements of POLO with some of LACROSSE. It was first played at the National School of Equitation in England in 1939, with a weapon formed by splicing a tennis racket on to the handle of a polo mallet and replacing the tight gut with a loose one. Subsequently special equipment was made, the operative end of which resembled a lacrosse net.

The object of the game is to propel a rubber ball into the opponents' goal, by galloping with it or passing it to another member of the team who may be in a better position to score,

and by trying to avoid interception by an opponent. The pitch is much smaller than that of polo, being 160 yds. long and 60 yds. wide (146 × 55 m.). The goal posts are only 8 ft. (2·4 m.) apart instead of 8 yds. (7·3 m.). There is a penalty line 30 yds. (27 m.) from, and parallel to, each goal line, across which the ball may be thrown but not carried.

Eight chukkers of eight minutes each are played, with two minutes between each. There are six players to a team, only three of whom may be on the field at one time. The game is regarded as good training for polo, and used to

POLO CROSSE PITCH
Goal posts are 8 ft. (2·4 m.) apart and of any height (usually 10 ft. — 3·05 m.), with no crossbar.

be played frequently by pony clubs. There were at least ten polo crosse clubs in Britain soon after the Second World War, most of them in the West Country, but there is little evidence of the game in Britain now. It spread to Australia and New Zealand, where it is still enthusiastically played, and later to the U.S.A., Canada, and South Africa.

POMMERN (1912), English race-horse by Polymelus out of a mare tracing to Polly

Agnes, grandam of ORMONDE and great-grandam of SCEPTRE, was bred and owned by Joel, trained by Peck, and ridden by DONO-GHUE. He won a wartime triple crown (see HORSE RACING) and substitute CORONATION CUP.

PONSFORD, WILLIAM HAROLD (1900-   ), cricketer for Australia and Victoria. The only batsman to pass 400 twice (his 429 and 437 for Victoria were successively world records), he was a patient performer, especially strong at playing spin bowling. He scored a century in the first of his 29 Tests, and 266 — his highest — in the last. He and WOODFULL were for many seasons a formidable opening pair for Victoria and Australia.

POOLE PARK BOWLS CLUB, in Dorset, began its playing life on 15 June 1909; a second green was opened in 1930. It is beautifully situated above a sea inlet which has been artificially sealed off as a lake. The club was famous in lawn BOWLS for producing, until 1971, more winners of English Bowling Association championships than any other club in Great Britain: ten in all, including four singles, four pairs, one triples, and one fours. Seven of these were won by BAKER, a record until BRYANT won the 1969 pairs and fours to raise his tally to eight.

POPLUHAR, JAN (1931-   ), Association footballer for Slovan Bratislava, and Czechoslovakia for whom he played in the 1962 World Cup final when Brazil won 3-1 in Santiago, Chile. A strong, skilful centre half, he was deservedly chosen to play for the Rest of the World XI against England at WEMBLEY in the F.A.'s special centenary match in 1963.

PORSCHE, a racing car. Dr. Ferdinand Porsche first worked for Daimler-Benz but in 1930 he became an independent designer responsible for the AUTO-UNION Grand Prix cars. His son, Terry Porsche, formed the Porsche Company in 1948, and has produced Grand Prix cars, sports cars, Grand Touring cars, and prototypes. Porsche first made Formula Two cars and then with the experience gained entered Formula One, but the car disappointed and Formula Two cars were used instead. These proved reliable and fast enough to gain Porsche third place in the manufacturers' world championship for that year.

In 1962 Gurney drove the Formula One Porsche, now considered ready for Grand Prix racing, to first place in the French Grand Prix and third in the German Grand Prix. Porsche, however, withdrew from racing at the end of 1962. They later produced the series of 8-cylinder prototypes which were successful in the Targa Florio and other races.

PORTER, HUGH (1940-   ), British track cyclist. Although, both as an amateur and professional, Porter competed in road races (including the 1968 TOUR DE FRANCE), his best performances were in the individual pursuit. As an amateur he won a pursuit bronze medal in the 1963 world championships and a gold medal in the 1966 COMMONWEALTH GAMES. After turning professional he became world pursuit champion in 1968, 1970, 1972, and 1973, was placed second in 1967 and 1969, and third in 1971.

PORTER, JOHN (1838-1922), was the most celebrated English race-horse trainer of the nineteenth century. The horses in his stable won over 1,000 races, including seven DERBYS and six ST. LEGERS, and £720,000 in stakes. He prepared ORMONDE, Common, and FLYING FOX to win their triple crowns (see HORSE RACING).

PORTLAND, 6th Duke of (1857-1943), was the leading race-horse owner in England three years in succession: 1888, 1889 (with record winnings of £73,858), and 1890. He owned the stallions ST. SIMON and Carbine, and won the DERBY, TWO THOUSAND GUINEAS, and ECLIPSE STAKES with AYRSHIRE, the Derby and ST. LEGER with Donovan, and the OAKS and St. Leger with Memoir.

PORTMAN, ARTHUR FITZHARDINGE BERKELEY (1861-1940), was the leading authority on all matters connected with HORSE RACING in England, and for many years was the proprietor and editor of *Horse and Hound* under the pen-name of 'Audax'.

PORTMARNOCK, Irish GOLF course. Portmarnock's claim to supremacy among Irish courses is perhaps justified, although narrowly. Portrush, Newcastle, Lahinch, Rosses Point, and Ballybunion press it hard for quality and, for majestic scenery and uncomplicated pleasure, Killarney is in a class of its own. Portmarnock is a true links, long and tight and subtle in its use of the rolling contours of sand dune, with small, well-guarded greens. The turf, both of fairway and greens, is unsurpassed anywhere for texture. When the wind blows strongly, as it frequently does, Portmarnock presents a formidable challenge to the finest player.

PORTMOAK, Scottish GLIDING centre, lat. 56° 15' N, long. 03° 20' W, near Kinross,

Fifeshire. Home of the Scottish Gliding Union and main British site for wave soaring, it is a grass field on the edge of Loch Leven, adjacent to Bishop Hill.

PORTSMOUTH F.C., Association FOOT-BALL club, founded in 1898 as a professional club, and entering the First Division of the Southern League for the season 1899-1900. Portsmouth had a good record in the Southern League — twice winning the championship, the second time in the season 1919-20. At this time the long-delayed extension of the Foot-ball League brought all except one of the Southern League's First Division clubs into a new Third Division (South) of the F.L. Ports-mouth were top of that division in 1924 and three years later made football history when they finished second in the Second Division and became the first English club to gain pro-motion from the Third to the First Division of the Football League. The club made three appearances at WEMBLEY in the F.A. Cup final, losing in 1929 and 1934, and winning against WOLVERHAMPTON WANDERERS in 1939. Portsmouth 'held' the Cup from 1939 until the competition was resumed in 1946. During the war years the club signed several fine young players and won the Football League championship in the two successive seasons 1948-9 and 1949-50. Outstanding players have included, in the Southern League period, Cunliffe, Reilly, C. B. FRY, A. E. Knight, and Stringfellow; from 1921 to 1939, Allen, Smith, Worrall, Cook, Easson, and Irvine; and post-1946, DICKINSON, Froggatt, Scoular, Harris, and Dougan.

COLOURS: White shirts with double vertical blue stripe on left side, blue shorts, white stockings.
GROUND: Fratton Park, Portsmouth.

POST, PETER (1933-   ), Dutch profes-sional cyclist. In a varied career of track and road racing, he became national pursuit cham-pion of Holland and European Derny-paced champion, and also won the 1964 PARIS-ROUBAIX at a record speed of 45·129 km./h. (just over 28 m.p.h.). Post later concentrated on six-day racing, and by 1970 had achieved 56 victories, 16 more than the previous record held by VAN STEENBERGEN.

POUGHKEEPSIE ICE YACHT CLUB, formed in 1865 in the Hudson River valley, U.S.A., the first recorded organized ICE YACHTING CLUB.

POULE D'ESSAI DES POULINS and **POULE D'ESSAI DES POULICHES,** French horse races, the equivalents of the TWO THOUSAND GUINEAS and ONE THOUSAND GUINEAS, both run at level weights over 1,600 m. (1 mile) at LONGCHAMP on the same day early in May.

POULIDOR, RAYMOND (1936-   ), French professional road-race cyclist, once described as 'the most popular loser the sport has known'. Although to the end of 1970 he had won three classic races (MILAN–SAN REMO, FLÈCHE WALLONNE, and GRAND PRIX DES NATIONS) and the 1964 VUELTA A ESPAGNA, he was more admired for his cour-age and generosity in defeat. He was particul-arly unlucky in the TOUR DE FRANCE since his best years coincided with those of ANQUETIL; starting among the favourites in nine Tours, he twice came second and twice third but never became race leader.

POULTON (later Poulton Palmer), RONALD WILLIAM (1889-1915), RUGBY UNION three-quarter for Oxford University, HARLEQUINS, Liverpool, and England. A fast, elusive runner, he was selected by England after scoring a record five tries at left wing three-quarter in the 1909 University match. He won 17 caps, mainly at centre, captaining England in their Triple Crown and champion-ship season of 1913-14, and scoring four tries against France in his final international. He was killed in action in Flanders.

POWDERHALL, a stadium in Edinburgh, Scotland, was the home of the world's most famous professional sprint race. It is still col-loquially used to denote that race, which should properly be known as the Skol Sprint, the chief attraction of Edinburgh's annual New Year Footracing Gala. The 'Powderhall', a handicap race, was first run in 1870, over a 130-yard (118·9 m.) course and continued over this distance until 1958, when it was reduced to 120 yards (109·7 m.) and moved for eight years to the nearby town of Newton-grange. The meeting returned to Powderhall in 1966 and in 1970 was held for the first time in the city's new Meadowbank Stadium, built that year for the COMMONWEALTH GAMES. The sprint was then run over a metric course of 110 metres (120 yds.).

There are bets on the race and it is not uncommon for the favourite to carry £5,000 of his backers' money. He is customarily taken away to a secret hide-out weeks before the race (as are other leading competitors), where the backers feed, train, and guard their man as zealously as they would a prize racehorse.

The Powderhall meetings have produced some magnificent performances. Outstanding among them were the 300 yards (274·32 m.) in 30 sec. by the nineteenth-century sprinter

HUTCHENS; 130 yards in 12·20 sec. on a snowbound track by the Australian, CUMMING (perpetuated by a memorial sprint at the annual meeting); and the world record for 120 yards of 11 sec. by MCNEILL in a heat in 1971. Because of the handicap, such performances do not necessarily bring victory in the race.

POWERBOAT RACING takes place on either inland or offshore waters, in boats propelled by outboard or inboard motors, and in classes usually determined by the length of the boat. It is a popular sport off the coasts of Europe, the U.S.A., South America, Australia, and South Africa, though the price of a suitable boat and the cost of maintenance and transport restrict offshore racing to the well-to-do.

Even with outboard engines, speeds of more than 100 m.p.h. (161 km./h.) are often achieved, and these may be doubled with inboard engines. Many of the fastest craft travel on the hydroplaning principle, whereby the boat rises partially out of the water and skims over the surface. Such boats are usually designed with a hull that is V-shaped, or rounded, at the bow, and flat near the stern where the boat is cut away square. In this way the water displaced by the bow and sides of the boat, which tends to flow inwards again and create suction against the stern, creates less friction and falls away without hindering the boat's speed.

The ultimate in such design is the hydrofoil, which at high speed almost flies across the water, touching it at three points only — the propeller and the two thin foils that extend into the water on either side of the craft, lifting the hull out of the water as an aeroplane is lifted by its wings.

Wood, and then aluminium, were the most popular materials for constructing powerboats, but these were overtaken by 1960 by the use of fibreglass.

Daimler's one h.p. motorboat engine, demonstrated at Württemberg, Germany, in 1887, was the first application of the internal combustion engine to water travel. The following year the Priestman brothers, of Hull, England, brought out their boat engine, and it was an Englishman who launched the sport internationally. Sir Alfred Harmsworth (later Lord Northcliffe) presented a perpetual trophy, the Harmsworth Cup. It was won that year, 1888, with an average speed of 19·5 m.p.h. (31·4 km./h.), and has ever since been the world's foremost team competition.

In 1904 the Gold Cup was instituted in the U.S.A., for the winner of an annual 90-mile (144·8 km.) race for boats less than 40 ft. (12 m.) long, and by 1920 speedboat racing, as it

was then known, was beginning to be taken seriously. Long-distance racing was established in England in 1930 with a 100-mile (161 km.) circular race in Poole Harbour, but after four years this event lapsed through lack of support.

After the war came the boom in small-powerboat racing, mostly on inland waters by craft between 12 and 25 ft. (3·7 to 7·6 m.) long. The most significant event in the sport since 1903 came in 1959, when a massive offshore race was organized in the U.S.A., from Florida to the Bahamas. This caught the imagination of the public, the designers, and the pilots, and led to the *Daily Express* annual offshore race in 1961. Recognized as the greatest of its kind in the world, this event was for seven years held from Cowes, on the Isle of Wight, to Torquay, Devon, a distance of nearly 200 miles (322 km.). In 1968, and subsequently, competitors had to return to Cowes non-stop. The *Daily Telegraph*, with British Petroleum, have organized a 1,500-mile (2,400 km.) round-Britain race annually since 1969.

Small boats, of the kind that usually race only on lakes and reservoirs, took to the open sea in 1962, when the first event of its class was held from Putney, on the river Thames to Calais (France) and back. It attracts a large entry every year, although rough seas sometimes force the organizers to cut the race short and turn the competitors back off the south-east coast of England.

Two names of powerboat pilots stand out in the 70-year history of racing: from America, Garfield A. Wood, who won the Harmsworth Cup eight times between 1920 and 1933, and the Gold Cup four times in five years; and from England, Sopwith, the most successful of all competitors in the *Daily Express* races.

DRAG BOAT RACING is the equivalent on water of drag racing (SEE MOTOR RACING) on land, with the additional hazard that the slightest turbulence of the water or the smallest piece of débris, can cause an appalling accident. For this reason it is recognized as one of the world's most dangerous sports. Two boats at a time race over a straight quarter-mile (402 m.) stretch of water. From a slow-moving start, the acceleration is such that speeds of up to 190 m.p.h. (305·7 km./h.) have been recorded over the last 50 yds. (45·7 m.) of the course, which may be completed in little over seven seconds.

The boats used are between 16 and 23 ft. (5–7 m.) long. There are eight principal classes of competition, arranged according to the style of hull, type and position of engine (inboard or outboard), fuel (liquid or gas), and method of injection. Drag boat racing began in southern California in 1956 and is not widely practised elsewhere.

PRAEST, CARL AAGE (1922-   ), Association footballer for Ø.B. (Østerbros Boldklub), JUVENTUS (Turin), and Denmark for whom he made the first of 24 appearances in international matches in June 1945. A fine outside left, he played for the local Ø.B. team for most of the period from 1946 to 1950 when the club held a place in the Danish First Division. He played for the Rest of Europe XI against Britain in Glasgow in 1947, and a year later was a member of the Danish team that finished third in the Olympic football tournament in England. In 1949 he was persuaded to accept professional terms with the Italian club, Juventus.

PRAGUE–PODEBRADY, Czechoslovakian 50 km. road RACE WALKING event. First held in 1929, the race has taken place every year with the exception of the war years, 1941-4. From 1947 the race has included foreign competitors. The most successful competitor has been DOLEZAL who won on eight occasions. Among the winners have been Olympic champions, PAMICH and HOHNE, the latter setting the course record in 1967.

The course is almost entirely flat with various stretches of cobbles and produces fast times due to the early starting time (6 a.m.).

PRAT, JEAN (1924-   ), RUGBY UNION wing forward, selector, and coach for France. He played 51 times for France between 1945 and 1955, captaining the side and scoring 140 points in the home international championship. He became a national selector in 1963, and was coach to the French team which toured South Africa in 1964.

PRATT, ROBERT (1912-   ), Australian Rules footballer. Playing for South Melbourne in the VICTORIAN FOOTBALL LEAGUE as a full-forward between 1930 and 1946, in 157 matches, he kicked 680 goals. He headed the League goal-kicking list in 1933, 1934, and 1935. An acrobatic high-marker, his record of 150 goals in 1934 was equalled only in 1971. He transferred to Coburg in the VICTORIAN FOOTBALL ASSOCIATION and, in 1941, he kicked 182 goals.

PREAKNESS STAKES, a horse race founded in 1873, the second leg of the American triple crown, run over a distance of 1 mile 1½ furlongs (1,900 m.) at PIMLICO, in May.

PREIS DER DIANA, a horse race, is the German OAKS for three-year-old fillies run over 2,000 m. (1¼ miles) at Mülheim early in June.

PREIS VON EUROPA is the most important horse race in Germany and forms the final leg of the triple crown for older horses in that country. It is run at Cologne in October over 2,400 m. (1½ miles) on weight-for-age terms. For three years in succession it was won by the Russian champion ANILIN.

PREMIO   PARIOLI   and   PREMIO REGINA ELENA, horse races, are the Italian equivalents of the TWO THOUSAND GUINEAS and ONE THOUSAND GUINEAS, both being run over 1,600 m. (1 mile) on La CAPANNELLE race-course in Rome in April.

PREMIO ROMA, a horse race, is the last leg of the Italian triple crown for older horses, the other two being the GRAN PREMIO DI MILANO and the GRAN PREMIO DEL JOCKEY CLUB. It is run at Rome in early November over 2,800 m. (1 mile 6 furlongs).

PRESCOTT, ALAN (1928-   ), RUGBY LEAGUE player. A front-row forward who captained Great Britain in Australia in 1958 and played in 38 international matches, his most memorable was the second Test against Australia at Brisbane in 1958 when he played for most of the game with a broken arm, refusing to leave his already weakened team. Starting as a winger with Halifax, Prescott became a forward, moved to ST. HELENS in 1948-9, and started his international career in 1952. His speed was remarkable in a man of 16 stone (101·6 kg.).

PRESIDENT'S CUP (1), see CROQUET; **(2),** see EQUESTRIAN EVENTS.

PRESS,   IRINA   NATANOVNA   (1939-   ), PENTATHLON competitor and hurdler for the U.S.S.R. The younger sister of TAMARA PRESS, Irina broke the world pentathlon record eight times, her first record being 4,880 points in 1959 and her best 5,246 points when she won the Olympic gold medal in 1964. Her strongest event was the 80 metres hurdles. In this event, which ceased to figure in international competition in 1969, she was Olympic gold medallist in 1960 and improved the world record six times with a best of 10·3 sec. in 1965.

PRESS,   TAMARA   NATANOVNA   (1937-   ), shot-putter and discus-thrower for the U.S.S.R. One of the most formidable women athletes in history, Tamara Press won six major championships. Her sister, IRINA PRESS, won another two. Tamara had gold medals for the Olympic SHOT PUT in 1960 and 1964 and the Olympic DISCUS in 1964, the European discus in 1958, and the European shot and discus in 1962. In addition she won a silver medal in the 1960 Olympic discus and a bronze medal in the 1958 European shot. She set 12 world records, improving in the shot from 56 ft. $7\frac{1}{4}$ in. (17·25 m.) in 1959 to 61 ft. (18·59 m.) in 1965, and in the discus from 187 ft. 6 in. (57·16 m.) in 1960 to 195 ft. 10 in. (59·70 m.) in 1965.

PRESTON NORTH END F.C., Association FOOTBALL club. It was founded in 1880 by some members of the North End Cricket Club in Preston, Lancashire, who were seeking a winter sport. In 1888 the club were among the founder members of the Football League and at the end of the first season were the League champions with a record of 18 wins and 4 draws, and won the F.A. Cup without conceding a goal. ASTON VILLA in 1897, TOTTENHAM HOTSPUR in 1961, and ARSENAL in 1971 are the only other clubs to have won the championship and F.A. Cup in the same season. Preston's unbeaten League record, that earned the club the nickname of 'the Old Invincibles', has never been repeated. The club retained the championship in 1889-90 and were runners-up in the next three seasons, but they have not again won the championship, while appearances in the Cup finals of 1922, 1937, 1938, 1954, and 1964 were only once (1938) marked by a win. Outstanding players of the pre-1914 period included Trainor, Goodall, McCall, Ross, and Howarth; between the wars, Holdcroft, and Shankly; and since 1946, FINNEY, Docherty, Wayman, and Kelly.

COLOURS: White shirts, navy blue shorts.
GROUND: Deepdale, Preston.

PRESTWICK, Scottish GOLF course. The original home of the Open championship, on the Ayrshire coast, Prestwick was founded in 1851. At 6,571 yds. (6,008 m.) the links is no longer on the championship roster, being considered too short and unsuitable for the accommodation of large galleries. Prestwick is unusual for a links in that it is by no means a flat course. Although old-fashioned in the sense that it offers many blind shots, it is an exceptionally sporty course, extremely exacting in a wind and characterized by the famous and vast Cardinal bunker at the third hole.

PRETTY POLLY (1901), a race-horse by Gallinule out of ADMIRATION, bred in Ireland and owned by Maj. Loder, trained by Gilpin,

and ridden by Lane and Dillon. She won 22 out of 24 races, including the OAKS, ST. LEGER (easily, in record time), ONE THOUSAND GUINEAS, Coronation Stakes, CHAMPION STAKES, two CORONATION CUPS and JOCKEY CLUB CUP. This outstanding filly failed only by a length also to win the ASCOT GOLD CUP. She won a total of £37,297 in stakes.

PRICELESS BORDER (1945), racing greyhound, a brindled dog, by Clonahard Border out of Priceless Sandhills. Winner of the 1948 GREYHOUND DERBY and rated the most consistent of all track stars, he won 17 of his 21 races in England for prize money of £3,409, and five races in Ireland. He was unbeaten in 1948. He was trained by Reynolds and owned by O'Kane.

PRIMO, SANDRA (1936-   ), Australian water skier and administrator appointed secretary of the British Water Ski Federation in 1973. She is an international WATER SKIING judge, and was British team captain in the world championships at Bogota in 1973.

PRINCE OF WALES TROPHY, ICE HOCKEY trophy, awarded annually to the team finishing in first place in the NATIONAL HOCKEY LEAGUE of North America. It was donated in 1925 by the Prince of Wales, later King Edward VIII. The League championship was first held in 1918.

PRINCE PALATINE (1908), a race-horse by PERSIMMON out of a mare tracing to PARADIGM, bred in Ireland by Lord Wavertree (see NATIONAL STUD), and raced in the colours of Pilkington. He was bought by Joel for stud duties for £40,000, went to France in 1919, to the U.S.A. in 1920, and was burned to death in his stable in 1924. Prince Palatine won the ST. LEGER, ECLIPSE STAKES, JOCKEY CLUB STAKES, CORONATION CUP, Doncaster Cup, and two ASCOT GOLD CUPS, with prize money amounting to £36,354.

PRINCE PHILIP CUP, see HENLEY ROYAL REGATTA.

PRINCESS ELIZABETH CUP, see HENLEY ROYAL REGATTA.

PRINCETON UNIVERSITY, American college FOOTBALL team, nicknamed the 'Tigers', played the first college game against Rutgers at New Brunswick, New Jersey, on 6 November 1869, losing the game but winning a second game a week later. Before 1900 Princeton was, with YALE, the most successful football power. Poe virtually beat Yale singlehandedly in 1898 and 1899. Most famous Princeton team was the 1922 'Team of Destiny' that upset a much heavier and highly favoured CHICAGO team and shared the national championship. Coach Crisler's 1933-5 teams lost only one game, a monumental upset to Yale in 1934. The 1950-1 teams, coached by Caldwell, a star of the 1922 team, and led by the runner-passer Kazmaier, were unbeaten and IVY LEAGUE champions.

COLOURS: Orange and black.

PRISONERS' BASE, under the name *'aux bares'* was played as a STREET GAME in France in the Middle Ages and when it was mentioned in connection with Parliamentary proceedings early in the reign of Edward III it was described as *'à barres'*. It was spoken of then as a childish amusement but still prohibited in the avenues of the palace of Westminster during the sessions of Parliament, because it interfered with the passage of members. The game as presumably it was played then; as it was played in the late eighteenth century, as described by Strutt in his *Sports and Pastimes*; and as it is still played in school playgrounds, was bound to cause interference to passers-by since it was itself an active game of interference. The Opies in *Children's Games in Street and Playground* (1969) rate prisoners' base 'one of the most exciting of organized games' and describe it thus:

Two bases or camps are chalked out on the same side of the playground, or marked in a field with sticks or cricket stumps.... At the other end of the playground, or about twenty yards away, two prisons are marked out. Two captains pick sides (it is best if there are some twenty players), and each side takes possession of a base, but the prison in which they hope to place their captives is the one diagonally opposite, not the one nearest to them. The captain of one side sends one of his players into the middle to taunt the others and start the game. The captain of the other side sends one of his players to catch him, and the first player has to try and get back to his own base. He is helped by the fact that as soon as someone has been sent to catch him, his own captain will send someone in pursuit of his pursuer, whereon the other captain will send someone to pursue that pursuer, and the first captain will send someone after him. Thus each player, other than the first, will be both chasing and being chased, and as soon as a player gets back to his base, he can be sent in pursuit of someone else. But a player may only chase the one person he has been sent after.

Further to confound the confusion, the game allowed for players to be sent to rescue any of their number who had been captured and imprisoned. Not infrequently, as the Opies note, the game ends when the players are in such confusion that few know who is chasing, or rescuing, whom.

Played, as it had to be once, in narrow streets, the confusion and the violence made 'the childish amusement' attractive to boisterous young men and for many years matches were arranged between carefully selected teams in north Shropshire, Derbyshire, and Cheshire.

PRIX DE L'ARC DE TRIOMPHE, a horse race inaugurated in 1920, is the most important and valuable weight-for-age race in France and in Europe. Winning this race, run over 2,400 m. (1½ miles) at LONGCHAMP in October, sets the final seal on the career of a great race-horse. Among its winners have been champions such as KSAR (twice), ORTELLO, the filly PEARL CAP, BRANTÔME, the filly Corrida (twice), DJEBEL, LE PACHA, TANTIÈME (twice), RIBOT (twice), BALLYMOSS, EXBURY, SEA BIRD II, VAGUELY NOBLE, LEVMOSS, MILL REEF, and Allez France. In 1970, when SASSAFRAS defeated NIJINSKY by a head, the stakes to the winner were worth 1,379,800 francs (over £100,000).

PRIX DU CADRAN, a horse race, is the French equivalent of the ASCOT GOLD CUP, but it is run earlier in the season (in May) over 4,000 m. (2½ miles) at LONGCHAMP.

PRIX DE DIANE, a horse race, is the French OAKS, run at Chantilly in mid-June, but shorter than its English equivalent, being only 2,100 m. (1 mile 2½ furlongs).

PRIX GANAY, a horse-race (formerly known as the Prix des Sablons), the French equivalent of the ECLIPSE STAKES, a weight-for-age event over 2,000 m. (1¼ miles), competed for at LONGCHAMP in April.

PRIX DU JOCKEY CLUB, a horse race, is the French Derby, run at Chantilly in early June over 2,400 m. (1½ miles). It is worth over £111,000 to the winner.

PRIX ROYAL OAK, a horse-race, is the French ST. LEGER, run over 3,100 m. (1 mile 7½ furlongs) at LONGCHAMP in September.

PRIX VERMEILLE, a horse-race, is the three-year-old fillies' equivalent of the French St. Leger, run over a shorter distance of 2,000 m. (1¼ miles) at LONGCHAMP in the autumn. The winner of this valuable event is now regarded as the champion three-year-old filly in Europe.

PROTOPOPOV, OLEG (1932-   ), ice figure-skater for the U.S.S.R. who, with Miss BELOUSOVA, became an outstanding pairskater. They won two Olympic titles, at Innsbruck, Austria, in 1964, and at Grenoble, France, in 1968. For four consecutive years 1965-8, they were also world and European champions. Characteristic of their style of performance was a grace and smoothness developed through a close knowledge of ballet. Surprisingly for skaters of championship class, neither took up the sport until the age of 16: but they still held the Olympic title when he was 35 and she 32.

Protopopov began skating in Leningrad in 1948, initially inspired by an early SONJA HENIE film. In 1951 he joined the Russian navy and in 1954 first met Miss Belousova, whom he married a year later. Son of a ballerina, his early environment of music and dancing probably contributed much to their achievement. As the first Russians to attain international superiority in any branch of figure-skating, they acquired a very elevated status in the U.S.S.R., including that of Honoured Masters of Soviet Sport.

The elegant, calculated movements of the Protopopovs, the most classical ice-skating pair the world has known, made their difficult overhead lifts look deceptively simple. Their best-remembered trick was Belousova's ability to sweep the ice with her blonde hair during their smoothly slow death spirals, even her waist swinging only inches above the frozen surface. The powerful, broad-shouldered Protopopov, 5 ft. 9 in. (1·75 m.) tall, was 6 in. (15 cm.) taller than his partner, and 50 lb. (22·7 kg.) heavier.

PRUNELLA (1788), a race-horse by HIGH-FLYER, was the most celebrated English brood mare of the eighteenth century and produced within six generations 33 winners of 41 classic races and Gold Cups.

PRYTHERCH, REGINALD (1930-   ), British surfer and water skier. He is the author of books on WATER SKIING and of the first British book on SURFING. He managed the British team at the world surfing championships in Australia in 1970.

PUIG-AUBERT (1925-   ), French RUGBY LEAGUE player. An automatic choice as his country's full-back from 1945-6, when he joined Carcassonne after making a name for himself in RUGBY UNION, until his farewell appearance in the 1954 WORLD CUP tournament, he had a highly individual approach to the game. He disliked training and was a chain-smoker, but his apparently casual attitude hid an exceptional talent. He won many matches with his long, accurate goal-kicking, especially with drop shots. On the 1951 tour of Australia he set a record (since surpassed by

B. L. JONES) by scoring 236 points (106 goals and 8 tries). French crowds nicknamed him 'Pipette'.

PULITZER TROPHY, see FLYING, SPORTING.

PULLUM, WILLIAM ARTHUR (1887-1960), 9-stone champion weight-lifter of the world and winner of 15 national titles, who broke 200 world and British records. He drafted the first set of technical rules used by the British Weight Lifting Association and is recognized as the world's first scientific WEIGHT-LIFTING coach; he trained several British champions.

PUMAS, the popular term used for representative RUGBY UNION teams of Argentina, derived from the creature of that name by anology with the SPRINGBOKS of South Africa and the WALLABIES of Australia.

PUNTING is the propulsion over water, by means of a pole, of a flat-bottomed, shallow, square-ended boat. According to the rules of the Thames Punting Club, probably the only authoritative body in the world on the subject, a punt must be a craft 'without stem, keel or sternpost, of which the width at each end must be at least one half of the width at the widest part'. In practice, the pastime now seems to be confined not merely to England, but to that part of the river Thames between Kingston and Oxford, and to the river Cam at Cambridge.

Punts vary in length from 25 to 35 ft. (7·6 to 10·7 m.), and in width from 3 ft. 6 in. (1 m.) for the fishing or shooting punt to only 14 in. (36 cm.) for a racing punt. They are made of Honduras mahogany or laminated plywood. The craft are propelled by an occupant pushing a pole against the bed of the water in the opposite direction to that in which he wishes to direct the boat. The difficulty of mastering punting is seldom appreciated by those who have not tried it. Novices sometimes find the pole stuck in mud, and are faced with having to make an instant decision whether to let go of the pole as the boat glides on, or to cling to the pole and part company with the boat. Onlookers invariably find the result hilarious whichever the decision.

A pole is 13 to 14 ft. (4–4·3 m.) long, ending with a metal fork with which to grip the river bed. Wooden poles are still used for casual punting, but for racing a duralumin tube of 1¼ in. (31·8 mm.) diameter is generally preferred.

Until the 1890s there was only one recognized method of punting: to stand at the head of the punt, place the end of the pole on the river bed and walk (or run) to the stern, maintaining firm pressure with the pole and returning to the bow for the next stroke. This is still used for ferry-punting, and for moving light barges and sailing vessels, when it is known as 'quanting'; but as punts and poles became smaller and lighter, new techniques were created and 'walking' was forgotten.

'Pricking' is a method of punting in which the pole is pushed firmly against the river bed until the angle of the pole to the water makes it impossible to continue, when it is withdrawn for the next stroke. 'Bucketing' is the withdrawal of the pole by flicking it out of the water with sufficient impetus to slide it up through the punter's hands ready for the next stroke. 'Gathering' is withdrawal of the pole by a hand-over-hand method.

PUNT RACING is held in the same five classes as LAWN TENNIS — men's and women's singles and doubles, and mixed doubles. Doubles punting is raced in the heavier mahogany craft, 2 ft. (0·61 m.) wide at the centre; singles are punted in long, light, and narrow craft. Races start and finish at the same point, after a measured course — usually 330 yards (302 m.), 440 yards (403 m.), or 660 yards (604 m.) — has been covered in both directions. Thick wooden poles, known as 'ryepecks', are stuck in the river bed at the far end of the course, one for each competitor. The racing punter must 'turn the ryepeck' by passing the pole on one side, reversing the direction of his punt, and repassing it on the other side. Several regattas along the Thames include punt races, which require water of a constant and suitable depth — preferably between 4 and 5 ft. (1·2–1·5 m.) — with a good and firm gravel bottom. The amateur championships are raced over a course of three-quarters of a mile (1·2 km.) (in each direction) during the annual regatta at Laleham, Middlesex.

Though punting may have existed for many centuries, particularly as a means of moving light cargo, the earliest known reference to it as a sport was in 1793. A print of that date shows two Thames watermen in a punt race at Windsor 'in honor of the Prince of Wales's Birth Day'. Watermen, boatbuilders, and others employed in river trades raced annually for the professional championship, which was won from 1877 to 1890 by Beasley, the originator of 'pricking'. It was his success with this method, while other punters were still running, that established it as the punting style of the future.

Amateurs, who had begun to enjoy punting as a social pastime, took it up as a sport with the foundation of the Thames Punting Club in 1885. They drew up the rules for punt racing and instituted the amateur championship for men (1885), men's doubles (1896), women (1927), mixed doubles (1932), and women's doubles (1954). Other later punting clubs on the Thames were affiliated to the Thames Punting Club, which is still the controlling body of punt racing.

After the championship of 1895, the runner-up challenged the winner to produce for the next year's event the best punt he could, while he too would have designed and built the best he could. Thus was born the lightweight racing punt, known thereafter as a 'best and best'. Rixon, who had won in 1893 and 1895, arrived in 1896 with a craft 34 ft. 4 in. (10·5 m.) long, and only 14½ in. (368 mm.) wide. It weighed between 40 and 50 lb. (18–23 kg.), and in it he not only won the amateur championship again, but set a world speed record for single punting of 8·05 m.p.h. (12·9 km./h.).

This record is unlikely ever to be broken, since river-bed conditions are not good enough for fast punting on any of the main courses used today. The Thames particularly has been impaired by dredging and erosion, leading to mud patches and holes that spoil smooth punting rhythm. It is also difficult to find a stretch of river where the outside station (the furthest from the bank) is not much deeper than the inside.

Such shelves do exist along the Thames at Chertsey, Laleham, Old Windsor, Sunbury, Thames Ditton, and Wargrave, and it was at these places that punt racing became established at regattas (see ROWING). The amateur championships were held for many years at Sunbury, Shepperton, and Maidenhead, but are now included in the annual regatta at Laleham.

After Rixon's startling success, many 'best and best' punts were built, most of them by Duntons of Shepperton. They were even used for doubles racing, until it was found that, since they overbalanced so easily, the winning pair were apt to be not the fastest punters, but those able to remain in their boat the longest. Wyatt of Wargrave built five 'best and bests' in laminated plywood after the Second World War, and apart from two built at Eton College, these were probably the last punts to be built anywhere — and may remain so.

P. W. Squire, *Punting* (1903); B. H. B. Symons-Jeune, *The Art of Punting* (1907); H. M. Winstanley, *Punting* (1922); *Rowing and Punting* (The Badminton Library, 1890).

PUSKAS, FERENC (1927-   ), Association footballer for Kispest, Honved, REAL MADRID, and Hungary, for whom he played at inside left and captain in the great years of the

1950s, during which his country became the first non-British national team to beat England in England, and finished in second place in the 1954 world championship. In 1956, he left Hungary and joined Real Madrid for whom he qualified to play in competitive matches in time to win a European Champion Clubs Cup medal in 1960, in a final in which Eintracht Frankfurt were beaten 7-3 at Hampden Park, Glasgow. Always a prolific goal-scorer and famous for his left-footed shot, he scored four of Real's goals. He scored all three goals for Real Madrid in the 1962 European Champion Clubs Cup final and still finished on the losing side, when BENFICA scored five. When his long playing career ended, he remained in the game as coach and manager and in 1971, as manager, guided the Greek club, Panathinaikos, to the semi-final of the European Cup.

PUTTING THE SHOT (or WEIGHT), see SHOT PUT.

Q

QUAID-I-AZAM TROPHY. Awarded to the national champions of Pakistan CRICKET, this trophy was instituted in 1953-4 in memory of the founder of Pakistan, Mahomed Ali Jinnah ('The Great Leader'), for competition among area groups. The competition culminates in semi-finals, from which the finalists are decided. Karachi have dominated the tournament.

QUARTER-STAFF, a now obsolete folk contest conducted with wooden poles, was a game of strength, skill, and dexterity in which both nobly-born and commoners could compete and excel. Stout poles, usually about 6 ft. 6 in. (2 m.) long, were used, which the players held in the middle with one hand, and between the centre of the stick and the end with the other hand. The art of wielding the stick consisted in moving the lower hand so that a rapid circular motion was made by the staff. Thus a player could strike his opponent unexpectedly and with a considerable amount of control.

The sport, because of its reliance on only simple equipment and basic skills, was particularly popular in country districts, and it was also taught in the schools of defence. These existed in many towns in the Middle Ages, and again in Tudor times. The schools taught the crafts basic to self-defence and all types of foot-soldiery. The folk hero Robin Hood was supposed to have been an expert in quarter-staff fighting, just as he was in the sports of archery and wrestling. One of the many ballads of his exploits and prowess tells of how he fought at quarter-staff with Arthur-a-Bland in a match lasting over two hours. Both men used staves more than 8½ ft. (2·6 m.) long, and delivered such hard blows that 'all the wood rang with every bang'.

In 1540 Henry VIII incorporated 'The Maisters of the Noble Science of Defence', a company whose senior members were permitted to keep schools where 'plainge with the two hande sworde, the Pike, the bastard sword, the dagger, the Backe sword, the sworde and buckeler, and the staffe and all the other manor of weapons appertayninge to the same science' were taught. Scholars qualified as 'provosts' before becoming 'Maisters of Fence'. They fought their qualifying contests in public and had to be proficient in every branch of their art before they could achieve the master's degree. In 1578, when Greene was trying for his scholar's prize at Chelmsford, he was well and truly put through his paces and probably all contenders had an equally tough test of their ability. He had to take on eight men at two-handed sword, and seven at backsword. In the next year, Blinkinsop, playing for his full master's degree at the Artillery Gardens at Leadenhall, fought with six fully qualified masters at backsword, two-handed sword, quarter-staff, and sword and buckler.

There were frequent fights with quarter-staff at wakes (see FOLK SPORTS) and other festive occasions. Dr. Johnson defined quarter-staff as 'a staff of defence, so called, I believe, from the manner of using it; one hand being placed at the middle and the other equally between the end and the middle'. A pamphlet of 1625 describes, with more patriotic pride than regard for strict truth, the stirring tale of 'Three to one, being an English-Spanish combat, performed by a western gentleman of Tavystock, in Devonshire with an English quarter staff, against three rapiers and poniards, at Sherries in Spain, in the presence of dukes, condes, marquisses, and other dons of Spain'. Sir Walter Scott describes fighting with quarter-staves in *Ivanhoe*: 'The Miller, holding his quarter-staff by the middle and making it flourish after the fashion which the French call "*faire le moulinet*".' Dryden mentions the quarter-staff in one of his poems, with this description of a devotee of the sport:

> His quarter-staff, which he could ne'er forsake,
> Hung half before and half behind his back.

Such a basic game naturally had many derivatives and corruptions. Among the more formalized related games were 'single-stick' and 'cudgel-playing'. Single-stick was played by two contestants, like quarter-staff. Each man had his left hand tied down, usually behind his back. In his other hand he held a stick shorter than the quarter-staff because of the difficulty of manipulating such a cumbersome weapon with only one hand. The object of the game was to extract blood from the opponent's head. In cudgel-playing, each player had two staves. With one the player attacked; the other stick had a large hemisphere of basket-work attached to it. It was called the 'pet' and was used for defence. In the eighteenth century the cudgel enjoyed a period of intense popularity and fashion. For a contest held on 30 April in 1748, at Shrivenham, the prize money was £5.

QUEEN MARY (1843), a race-horse who was one of the best English brood mares. Her daughter, Blink Bonny, won the DERBY and OAKS and produced Blair Athol, winner of the Derby and ST. LEGER.

QUEEN'S CLUB, London, see RACKETS.

QUEENS PARK BOWLS CLUB, Glasgow, the most famous lawn BOWLS club in Scotland, is the venue for the annual Scottish championships as well as the international team championship series between England, Ireland, Scotland, and Wales every fourth year. It was founded in 1866 and has permanent accommodation for the 2,000 spectators who attend these major events.

QUEEN'S PARK F.C., Association FOOTBALL club, Glasgow, formed in 1867 and the oldest Scottish League club. Queen's Park took its name from that of the ground it occupied until 1873 when it moved to Hampden Park, the largest ground in Britain and the best-known in Scotland as the venue for all international and other important matches. In their early seasons, Queen's Park had often to resort to playing matches among teams drawn from their own members in the absence of more than a handful of other clubs in Scotland. They were one of the 15 original entries for the F.A. (English) Cup in 1872 and played, without success, in the F.A. Cup finals of 1884 and 1885. Queen's Park's experience proved useful when the Scottish Cup was first competed for in 1874. Queen's Park won then, in the two succeeding years, and, in all, nine times by 1890 when the Scottish League was also formed. The introduction of League football into Scotland accelerated the movement towards professionalism or semi-professionalism and, apart from winning the Cup for the last time in 1893, further major honours have not been won by Queen's Park. It has remained, however, with several seasons spent in the Second Division, always an amateur club. The club's outstanding players were mainly in the pre-1900 era when twice it provided all 11 players for Scotland's national team in international matches — against England in 1872 and Wales in 1895. Among the greatest players were Arnott, Baird, Kay, Lambie, R. S. McColl, and Taylor in the pre-1914 period; R. Gillespie, Harkness, and MORTON between the two wars; and Simpson since 1946.

COLOURS: Black and white hooped shirts, white shorts.
GROUND: Hampden Park, Glasgow.

QUEEN'S PARK OVAL, Port of Spain, CRICKET ground in Trinidad. A well-equipped and commodious ground, the home of Queen's Park Cricket Club is in a beautiful tropical setting. Matting wickets were in use there — the only instance on a main West Indies ground — until the mid-1950s. The change led to a greater number of matches reaching conclusion. WEEKES made the two highest scores (207 and 206) in Test matches there.

QUEEN'S PRIZE, see SHOOTING, RIFLE: SERVICE CALIBRE.

QUEEN'S UNIVERSITY R.F.C., Belfast. After North of Ireland, to which many of its players move on, this is the oldest RUGBY UNION football club in Ulster, having been formed in 1868. Its most distinguished players include STEPHENSON (under whom, in 1923-4, the club were Irish champions), KYLE, and Henderson.
GROUND: Cherryvale.
COLOURS: Royal blue.

QUEENSBERRY RULES of BOXING were drafted in 1867 by Chambers under the patronage and name of the Marquess of Queensberry. They formed the basis of modern glove-fighting as distinct from the earlier bare-knuckle contests and were first used for the world professional heavyweight championship in 1892. The rules called for the wearing of gloves, and rounds of three minutes' duration, interspersed by a minute's rest, and prohibited WRESTLING.

QUINTAIN. The quintain was originally a tree or post, and *quintana* is mentioned by Vegetius in *De re militari*. 'Running at the quintain' applies equally to modern army recruits in Italy running at sacks of straw with fixed bayonets, and ancient Roman soldiers aiming at various targets with swords or spears. It was refined to a more spectacular sport, with mounted competitors charging at a target that was so fixed that failure to strike it properly might mean a swift retaliatory blow, or even a soaking if the variety was water quintain. But the same basic principle underlay all the variations. The game depended on skill, a careful and accurate aim, and a steady eye. The target, whatever it was, had to be directly and cleanly struck. Men could run at the quintain on foot, on horseback, on each other's back, and in boats.

The points awarded for direct hits on a 'human' target were: 3 points for a hit on the nose between the eyes; 2 if on the nose below the eyes; and 1 for the area between the nose and chin. No other blows counted and a great degree of accuracy was therefore needed to score at all.

Running at the quintain persists in present-day Italy where, at Arezzo, Foligno, Picene, Udine, and Sarteano, competitors on horseback ride at full speed towards a wooden figure known as 'the Saracen'. They try to hit with their lances the bull's-eye on the target which the figure holds. In most cases a poor shot causes the figure's arm to swing round and strike the competitor on the back. In Arezzo, the figure holds a flail to which three balls of lead are attached; in Pistoia a bear holds the target. In Faenza the figure is not a Moslem or a Saracen, but an earlier invader, Hannibal, called locally 'Niballe'. The competitors, incongruously, dress in fourteenth-century clothes.

In England riding at the quintain continued into the middle of the seventeenth century, but by then it had degenerated into a game for wedding celebrations, whereas it had once been a serious military exercise, and as such had received official encouragement. Riding at the quintain and running at the ring were favourite sports in the Middle Ages for spectators and participants. Riding at the ring consisted of riding full speed past a post, and skilfully detaching a ring from it with the point of a lance (also known as tilting).

Riding at the quintain was considered somewhat similar and required more skill, since failure carried with it its own immediate penalty. Stow in his *Survey of London* writes, 'I have seen a quintain set upon Cornhill by the Leadenhall where the attendants of the lords of merry disport have run and made great pastime for he that hit not the broad end of the quintain was of all men laughed to scorne, and he that hit it full, if he rid not the faster, had a sound blow on the necke with a bag of sand hung on the other end.'

More elaborate quintains were made in the form of a human figure, in armour and armed, usually a Turk or Saracen. In place of the bag of sand would be a broad sword. The figure had to be struck full in the face, and points were gained according to where the blow landed, whether on the forehead, nose, or chin. If, through faulty aim, the player struck the shield and turned the figure round, he lost his place for that day and had to retire from the arena accompanied by the jeers of the spectators.

Unlike tournaments and jousts, where no one under the rank of knight could take part, running at the quintain could be enjoyed by men of all ranks. As a pastime rather than as a military exercise it was long popular at weddings, and it survived at such functions long after it had ceased to be practised elsewhere. When Elizabeth I was entertained at Kenilworth in 1575, one of the entertainments provided for her diversion was 'a solemn country bridal; when in the castle was set up a comely quintain for feats at arms'.

In the following century the sport became less popular. Plott's *History of Oxfordshire*, first published in 1677, describes quintain as 'now only in request at marriages and set up in the way for young men to ride at as they carry home the bride'. *Notes and Queries* of 1866 mentions a supposedly Elizabethan quintain still in existence at Offham Green near Maidstone in Kent. In 1827 Viscount Gage had deliberately revived the bridal quintain at Firle Place in Sussex.

Sometimes what was termed a 'human quintain' was used, when a fully armed man would try to parry the strokes of assailants. An illustration from a manuscript of 1344 shows figures practising with lances against a completely armed man. In another variation an armed man sat on a three-legged stool and the tilter had to try to overturn him.

Water quintain was especially popular, because of the additional hazard. It was frequently played in London on the Thames; the boats used were either manned with rowers or allowed to drift with the current. A contemporary source records: 'In Easter holydays they fighte battles on the water. A shield is hung upon a pole, fixed in the middle of the streame. A boat is prepared without oares, to be carried by the violence of the water and in the fore part thereof standeth a young man ready to give charge upon the shielde with his lance, if so be, he breaketh his lance against the shield and doth not fall he is thought to have performed a worthy deed. If so be without breaking his lance, he runneth strongly against the shield, down he falleth into the water for the boat is violently forced with the tide, but on each side of the shield ride two boats furnished with young men, which recover him that falleth as soon as they may.' This boat quintain and tilting in the water was introduced by the Normans for the summer season. Water quintain is mentioned by the chronicler of Henry II's reign, Fitzstephen, and fourteenth-century manuscripts provide illustrations of this activity. There was also tilting at a water butt, so that if the competitor hit inaccurately, the butt and its contents were upended over the unfortunate man, to the enjoyment of the spectators. A manuscript in the Bodleian Library, dated 1343, shows three boys tilting at a water butt. This variation was sometimes practised in Italy.

The origin of the name is uncertain, even if its antiquity is not in doubt — it is mentioned in *Corpus Juris Civilis* of the Byzantine Emperor Justinian (483-565). The name may come from the Latin *quintus*, meaning fifth, if the game was celebrated at every fifth year of the Olympics. Other authorities gave as its origin *gwyntyn*, a Welsh word meaning a vane.

QUIST, ADRIAN KARL (1913-   ), one of the finest of Australian LAWN TENNIS doubles players. He won the WIMBLEDON title in 1935 with CRAWFORD and in 1950, two years after his last Davis Cup (see LAWN TENNIS) appearance, with Bromwich. He won the Australian singles title in 1936, 1940, and 1948 and was undefeated in the Australian doubles championship from 1936 to 1950, winning the title in 1936 and 1937 with Turnbull and from 1938 to 1940 and 1946 to 1950 with Bromwich.

Between 1933 and 1948 Quist won 42 Davis Cup rubbers out of 55 in 28 appearances for Australia, and he was a member of the team which beat the U.S.A. in the 1939 challenge round at Philadelphia, losing to Parker but beating Riggs in the singles and successfully partnering Bromwich in the doubles. His most famous Davis Cup rubber was, however, against VON CRAMM in the inter-zone final in 1936, which contained no fewer than 13 match points, Quist eventually losing 4-6, 6-4, 4-6, 6-4, 11-9. Von Cramm saved three match points and Quist was beaten by the German's tenth. That was the first rubber of the tie which Australia won 4-1.

QUIVER (1872) was a most influential brood mare in England. She was dam of the full sisters Memoir (OAKS and ST. LEGER) and LA FLÈCHE (Oaks, St. Leger, ONE THOUSAND GUINEAS, and ASCOT GOLD CUP), both got by ST. SIMON, and grandam of the stallions, John o' Gaunt (sire of SWYNFORD) and Polymelus (grandsire of Pharos and FAIRWAY).

QUOITS is an outdoor game in which a ring is thrown at a peg-target. A pastime of considerable antiquity in Britain, it was but one of many variations in different countries of 'throwing the discus', one of the five games of the ancient Greek pentathlon. In quoits, however, the merit was not in the distance that the discus (quoit) was thrown but in the accuracy of the throw.

In England quoits was a well-known game from at least the reign of Edward III (1327-77) when it was included among the forbidden sports and pastimes that diverted servants,

From a fourteenth-century manuscript.

apprentices, and labourers from recreations of an essentially martial character at a time of recurring wars of conquest against the French. Such edicts were no more successful in stopping the playing of quoits than in stopping the playing of ball games like FOOTBALL that were similarly forbidden. Quoits continued and the game was still being played fairly commonly in parts of the Midlands, Lancashire, and Scotland as late as the 1930s, according to rules that had probably changed little in their essentials over the centuries.

The quoit used was an iron ring, nearly flat, of any weight not exceeding 9 lb. (4·082 kg.) and usually weighing about 6 lb. (2·72 kg.), with the upper side slightly convex, and a niche on the outer rim that could be gripped by one finger in the preparation for throwing the quoit. The diameter of the quoit could not exceed 8½ in. (216 mm.), nor be less than 3⅓ in. (88·9 mm.) in the bore, nor more than 2¼ in. (57·15 mm.) in the web.

In a manner of play somewhat resembling BOWLS, except that the quoit was thrown in the air, there were two ends about 18 yds. (16·5 m.) apart, at each of which an iron or steel pin (known as the 'hob') was driven into the middle of a circle of stiff clay 3 ft. (914 mm.) in diameter leaving about 1 in. (25·4 mm.) of the hob exposed.

Matches were played between individuals, pairs, or teams and for any number of points that had been agreed upon, the winner being the player or team that first scored that agreed number of points. Each player, standing not more than 4 ft. 6 in. (1·372 m.) from his pin and in line with it, had to throw the quoit such that it lodged in the clay as near as possible to the hob. Expert players were often able to 'ring' the hob and such a 'ringer' counted for 2 points. Otherwise 1 point was awarded to each quoit, other than a ringer, lying nearer to the hob than that of an opposing player's quoit. As in the game of bowls, it was permissible to dislodge from its position an opponent's quoit. All 'turned' quoits were foul and not reckoned for scoring purposes.

Quoits was always a game that required considerable skill to be played well and, while not becoming fashionable as, for example, TENNIS and bowls, it was played by all classes and accepted as being suitable for gentlemen in Tudor times. Within the next century however it declined in polite favour and was thought to be too rough for scholars and noblemen. It remained in favour with the peasantry and was apparently played with boisterous gusto and some accompanying roughness.

The simple equipment necessary for the game of quoits — the ring that had itself derived from the ancient discus, and the peg — has ensured the continuance of variations of the game whether in the form of impromptu games on the beach using a rubber ring and a child's beach spade stuck in the sand; of cowhands in America tossing horseshoes over a stake (see HORSESHOE PITCHING); or of children playing indoors by throwing much smaller rubber rings at the pegs on a hoop-la board.

A more sophisticated variant is DECK QUOITS, which developed from the many games played on long voyages by seamen with quoits they had made of rope. Today rubber rings have taken the place of both the early iron quoits and the seamen's rope ones.

R

RACE WALKING is an extended form of walking now practised in all the five continents. One dictionary definition of 'walking' is 'the action of moving on the feet at any pace short of breaking into a run or trot'. The verb 'to walk' has been described as 'to progress by alternate movements of the legs so that one of the feet is always on the ground'. The British Race Walking Association's definition is: 'Walking is a progression by steps so taken that unbroken contact with the ground is maintained, e.g. the advancing foot must make contact with the ground before the rear foot leaves the ground.' Uniquely for an event figuring in the OLYMPIC GAMES, the British version of the definition of walking differs from that of the International Amateur Athletic Federation (I.A.A.F.) (see ATHLETICS, TRACK AND FIELD) which is accepted by all other countries. The I.A.A.F.'s definition has the following additional clause: 'and that during the period of each step, in which a foot is on the ground, the leg shall be straightened, i.e. not bent at the knee, at least for one moment'.

A competitor using the correct method obtains his speed by making the fullest use of the mobility of the hips in a lateral rhythm. A maximum range of movement between the toe of the rearmost foot and the heel of the leading foot produces a stride of 40–50 in. (1·016–1·270 m.) while the walker maintains an upright carriage, with his arms acting as a balance carried at right-angles to the body. 'Heel and toe' was the term used in the nineteenth and early twentieth centuries to describe the action of race walking.

Flagrant violation of the definition by means of over-striding or a bent-legged shuffle can be clearly detected by the layman because of the stark contrast with the balanced and rhythmic action of the technically correct walker. 'Lifting' is the term used to describe a competitor using a progression contrary to the definition. Should any competitor not comply with the definition during an event he is liable to receive a warning (under I.A.A.F. regulations) or be disqualified by a judge. In major competitions warnings are indicated to the competitors by means of a white flag. Only two such warnings are permitted, the competitor being liable to instant disqualification on the third infringement.

In Britain, where no warnings are given, instant disqualification applies in all events. Elsewhere and in international games warnings may be given prior to disqualification. In major competitions disqualification is indicated by means of a red flag.

In most countries judges are graded by ability and experience. According to their grade they are designated to officiate at club, district, and national level. A national judge can be recommended to the I.A.A.F. walking commission by his national federation to officiate at events of international standard. In such events as the Olympic Games, the EUROPEAN CHAMPIONSHIPS, and the LUGANO CUP competition only the designated chief judge, on the recommendation of the other judges, can issue warnings and disqualifications.

Standard distances used in international and national championships are as follows:

Imperial: 1 mile (1·609 km.); 2 miles (3·219 km.); 5 miles (8·47 km.); 7 miles (11·265 km.); 10 miles (16·93 km.); 20 miles (32·187 km.); 100 miles (160·934 km.).

Metric: 3 km. (1 mile 1,520 yds.); 5 km. (3 miles 188 ·yds.); 10 km. (6 miles 376 yds.); 20 km. (12 miles 752 yds.); 25 km. (15 miles 940 yds.); 30 km. (18 miles 1,128 yds.); 50 km. (31 miles 121 yds.); 100 km. (62 miles 242 yds.).

The standard walking events in the Olympic Games and in other major championships are the 20 km. and 50 km. road walks. World records are recognized by the I.A.A.F. for 20 miles, 30 miles, 20 km., 30 km., 50 km., and two hours.

An attendant looks after the needs of a competitor during a distance race (usually over 20 miles or 32 km.). Attendants are not allowed, however, in international games events, feeding stations then being used, but they figure in all the classic distance events. Usually following the event by car or bicycle, they are helpful in encouraging the competitor in the latter stages and difficult periods of a race.

In a race of more than 20 km. or 12 miles drinks and sponges are supplied to competitors at feeding stations. In international events, these feeding points are stationed every 5 km., commencing at 10 km. Drinks, obtained from either attendants or from feeding stations, are considered essential in hot and humid weather conditions. Although personal tastes vary, drinks usually consist of water, tea, coffee, orange, or lemon. Many competitors add to their drinks a small quantity of salt and/or sugar in an endeavour to combat the loss of salt through sweating.

Sponges filled with water are in common use in all distance events and are generally squeezed over the head and neck, particularly in warm weather. Sponges are obtained during the event from the attendants or feeding stations.

Race walking shoes are now mass-produced and differ from ordinary ones in the flexibility of their soles to facilitate bending, the heel-stiffener, and the wide fitting. In the pedestrians' era, ordinary shoes and boxing boots were in vogue, but a lighter shoe, generally hand-made, became popular around 1900. In recent years both German and Japanese shoes have been in demand throughout the world and are used by the majority of the sport's leading exponents. Due to the demands made upon them, shoes used for long-distance events are more robust and heavier than those used in track competition. Most competitors use a lining to lessen the possibility of bruising and jarring.

Coaching has developed considerably over the past fifteen years. The leading exponent in the early stages was WHITLOCK in Britain, whose book *Race Walking* provided for many countries the basis of the art of teaching the sport. In recent years WEBER (East Germany), Polyakov (U.S.S.R.), DORDONI and Corsaro (Italy), Hausleber (Poland) for his work in Mexico, and JOHNSON and Cotton (Britain), have become well known for their knowledge and protégés.

In all the leading countries coaches are required to pass a written and verbal examination and then promote their own courses and advise promising talent and established performers.

Race walking is now included in the athletic programme of all but a few countries. The sport has a particularly large following in England, the U.S.S.R., East and West Germany, Italy, France, Switzerland, and the U.S.A.

In the eighteenth and nineteenth centuries with only HORSE RACING and BOXING as rivals, walking, or 'pedestrianism' as it was then called, was highly popular, with much wagering encouraging men against time, distance, and other walkers. Two of the most famous pedestrians were Powell (b. 1736) and Captain Barclay (see R. B. ALLARDICE) (b. 1779) of England. The Yorkshire-born Powell, between 1773 and 1790, several times completed the 402-mile journey between London and York and back within six days. Barclay, after a long series of outstanding long-distance

feats, reached the climax of his career in 1809 at Newmarket Heath. Commencing on 1 June, Barclay walked 1,000 miles in 1,000 consecutive hours — a mile in each and every hour. The task took 42 days during which time Barclay lost 32 lb. (14·5 kg.) in weight. Following this achievement, public interest in walking rose to a height which has never been matched since.

From 1876 to 1888 there were numerous six-day walks or 'Go As You Please' (mixed running and walking) events held at Islington (London), New York, and Manchester, among other places. These races were nicknamed 'wobbles', an expression first used to describe the dubious style of one of the most famous contestants, the American, Weston. His many competitions with O'Leary enthralled the sporting public but the final word came from an Englishman, Littlewood, who in a 'Go As You Please' covered 623¾ miles (1,000 km.) at MADISON SQUARE GARDEN, New York, in 1882, and also accomplished several other performances of nearly equal merit. However, the public gradually tired of the 'peds' and their professionalism, since they often used a dubious style of walking and in later years failed to break records established by illegal methods.

Amateur walking became popular after 1860 and a 7-mile (11 km.) event was held in the English Amateur Athletics Club's championships in 1866. With working and social conditions allowing a little more time for sport, athletic and walking clubs were formed and town-to-town events became particularly popular. In Europe, France, Italy, and Denmark were prominent in the period from 1890 to 1910 in producing outstanding performers over all distances while the U.S.A., Canada, and Australia had numerous short-distance experts.

Gradually the sport was accepted in all the important international gatherings such as the Olympic Games (1908), the European Games (1934), and the COMMONWEALTH GAMES (1966). The virtual world walk team championship, the Lugano Cup, was an idea of a Swiss, LIBOTTE. It was first mooted in 1956, becoming a reality five years later with his home town as the venue for the first final and giving its name to the trophy.

The I.A.A.F. Walking Commission was founded in 1912 and, surviving several stormy periods mainly due to the question of illegal walking and inadequate judging, is now a well-respected body which presides over all international matters relating to race walking. It appoints officials and judges for all major events, submits records and regulations to the Federation for its approval, and presides over the Lugano Cup competition. All the major walking nations are represented on the commission by at least one member.

In the past 15 years the standard international distances of 20 km. (12 miles 752 yds.) and 50 km. (31 miles 121 yds.) have been used at all major games and in national championships. Events are also regularly held over a wide range of distances, from 3 km. (1 mile 1,520 yds.) on the track to the 500 km. (310 miles) of the STRASBOURG–PARIS race, and, although place-to-place races are becoming difficult to stage due to ever-increasing traffic problems, enclosed-circuit road events are being substituted and are becoming very popular.

In the last decade the leading walking countries have been encouraging competition for boys, categorized into age groups. This has resulted in junior (under 21 years) events being regularly held on an international basis.

INTERNATIONAL COMPETITION. Race walking was introduced into the Olympic Games in 1908 with races of 3,500 metres (2 miles 300 yds.) and 10 miles (16 km.), both held on the track. In the unofficial 1906 Games at Athens, 1,500 metres (1,640 yds.) and 3,000 metres (1 mile 1,520 yds.) track walks had been held. In 1912 only a 10 km. race took place with numerous continental competitors ignoring style and causing so many disqualifications that only four finished. Two walks were again included eight years later, a 3 km. and a 10 km., but only the second remained in 1924. There, in Paris, due to arguments over definition and language difficulties, the walking events created considerable trouble. An Austrian was disqualified in a heat, but after an appeal the jury overruled the judges and decided that the competitor should start again in the next heat. The judges then resigned *en bloc* and a new panel had to be found before the event could continue.

In view of the happenings at Paris, walking was ruled out of the 1928 Olympiad but the increasing popularity of road walking and the pressure for such an event, particularly by the British, caused a 50 km. race to be included in the Los Angeles 1932 Games and has remained since. The 1948 Olympics included a 10 km. track event and this was repeated in the next Games at Helsinki. However, track walking was losing favour internationally, and the 20 km. road event was substituted in 1956 and has been retained. It is proposed to delete the 50 km. event at Montreal in 1976 and the 20 km. from thereafter. Outstanding performers have been FRIGERIO, three times champion, plus a third place; GOLUBNICHI, twice champion, plus a second and a third place; LJUNGGREN, five times an Olympic competitor,

champion in 1948, second in 1960, third in 1956; Dordoni and PAMICH, both Olympic champions, the latter also a five times Olympic competitor.

A 50 km. road event was introduced in the European Games in 1934 and has been held at every celebration since. A 10 km. track race was first held in 1946 and repeated four years later. At the 1950 Games, in Brussels, trouble over the interpretation of the definition came to a head and two British competitors, Hardy and Allen, were disqualified hours after the finish of the event, having originally finished second and third. In keeping with the Olympic programme the track event was dropped in 1958 and replaced by a 20 km. road race.

Outstanding performers in the Games have been Pamich, twice champion and once second, and Ljunggren, a win, a second, and a fourth, both walkers competing in the 50 km. event. Great Britain has had outstanding success in the 20 km., supplying the winner (VICKERS in 1958; MATTHEWS in 1962; and NIHILL in 1969) on three of the five occasions on which the event has been held.

A 20 miles (32 km.) event was introduced in the Commonwealth Games in 1966 following prolonged campaigning by the Race Walking Association. At the 1970 Games in Edinburgh, although all other athletic events were held at metric distances, the walk remained imperial, mainly due to the wishes of the Commonwealth countries involved.

England has played a leading role, both from an administrative and competitive point of view, in the sport of race walking from its early stages. Champions such as LARNER, Webb, Payne, Hammond, and Ross were outstanding in the period 1900-20 while the long-distance competitions between GREEN, Johnson, and Whitlock in the 1930s, together with the wins at 50 km. in the 1932 and 1936 Olympics, ensured a keen following among the general public. Since 1958, with four European and two Olympic champions and two wins in the Lugano Cup, walkers like Matthews, Nihill, D. J. THOMPSON, and Vickers have been instrumental in establishing English race walking on a higher level, in speed and technique, than ever before.

England, with administrators such as Neville and Blackmore, has played a leading part on the I.A.A.F. Walking Commission. The Race Walking Association (R.W.A.), founded in 1911, is the English governing body for the sport. The association was mainly responsible for road races but in 1954 was also entrusted with the organization and promotion of track events, changing its name accordingly. All records must be approved by the R.W.A. and judges and coaches have to pass examinations and standards set by the association. Four national senior championships are promoted at 10 miles (16 km.), 20 km. (12½ miles), 20 miles (32 km.), and 50 km. (31¼ miles). A junior (under 21) race at 5 miles (8 km.) and a youths' (under 17) 3 miles (5 km.) championship are also held.

Czechoslovakia has produced many fine exponents over the past 30 years including several world track record-holders. Finishing fourth in the Berlin Olympic 50 km. (1936), Stork-Zofka was her first international star, winning the PRAGUE–PODEBRADY race five times between 1930 and 1938. During the war years, 1940-5, Balsan had many close and extremely rapid meetings with the Swede, HARDMO, in sprint track events but, owing to the lack of skilled judges, both walked in a manner which would now be regarded as illegal.

The early 1950s were good years for Czech walking with the very popular DOLEZAL leading the way, to be quickly followed by other world record-holders, Moc, Skront, and Sykora. For the past decade, Bilek has dominated the scene at all distances. Though as juniors Svadja and Tomasek showed fine promise, this has not been fulfilled in the senior ranks.

The annual highlight of the season is the Prague–Podebrady 50 km. which is now regarded as the most important annual race in the world over this distance.

France has a long history in the sport, walking having been included in physical instruction in the programme of the famous army school, L'École de Joinville, in 1852. From 1892 to 1904 many long-distance walks, such as the Paris–Belfort 500 km. (310 miles), the Bordeaux–Paris 611 km. (379 miles), and the Toulouse–Paris 711 km. (441 miles) took place, ANTHOINE, Peguet, and Ramoge being prominent competitors.

Through the instigation of Anthoine the Paris–Strasbourg race was created in 1926 and this led to the formation of two organizing bodies for race walking, the Union Française de Marche (U.F.M.), presided over by Anthoine and mainly interested in events of 100 km. (62 miles) and above, and the Fédération Française d'Athlétisme (F.F.A.), of which Guilloux was president. The F.F.A. was officially recognized by the I.A.A.F., specialized in events up to 50 km. and provided the competitors to represent the country in internationals, but the U.F.M., due to the very generous prizes available, proved most popular and attracted large numbers of competitors in its promotions throughout the country. Following much wrangling, the two bodies eventually united in 1961 and, with the Stras-

bourg–Paris race now revived, all events from 3 km. to 510 km. are catered for.

The U.F.M. had many excellent distance-walkers in its ranks, Caron, Cornet, Godart, ROGER, and Zami being particularly prominent. It also introduced Delerue to the sport and he, during the past decade, has been the sole world class performer for France. However, Lelièvre has now emerged from the youth programme to become a foremost 20 km. performer. From the F.F.A. organization, Maggi was second in the European 10 km. (6¼ miles) in 1946 and 1950.

With an intensive programme directed at the young, the sport is flourishing, the outstanding prospect having been Caviglioli who recorded excellent track times over 3 km. and 10 km. at the age of 16.

Germany. The first race of any consequence was the Vienna–Berlin 578 km. (360 miles) in 1893. An early success was gained at the unofficial Athens Olympic Games of 1906 by a marathon runner, Muller, who finished second in the 3 km. (1⅞ miles) walk. Some 15 years later the same Muller recorded a world's best 30 km. (18¾ miles). Brockmann (1913) and Hachnel (1924) won the MILAN 100 KM., and Grittner, Schmitt, Sievert, and Dill were all prominent at 50 km. events during the 1930s.

Germany first competed in the Lugano Cup as one nation, but since 1965 East and West Germany have taken part separately. Under the guidance of Horlemann and later Weber, East Germany has become the leading race walking nation since 1965. Men such as HOHNE, Leuschke, SAKOWSKI, and Selzer have all brought a new thinking on how to race a world class 50 km. by their use of a fast even pace allied to excellent technique. At the shorter distances, Frenkel, LINDNER, and REIMANN have all had outstanding successes, while the juniors record times far in advance of any other nation. Though not encouraging a large number of participants, the East German training system does produce outstanding talent.

West Germany, with Frankfurt as the main centre, has a flourishing programme with many competitors. Outstanding performers for several years have been Muller and Nermerich, but now they have been replaced by veteran Weidner (b. 1933), the present 50 km. track record holder, and KANNENBERG, the 1972 Olympic 50 km. champion.

Italy has been in the forefront of the sport since the beginning of the century. Altimani set a world best for one hour (1913) and, with Frigerio and PAVESI achieving international fame, the sport quickly gained a following which it has never lost. The two most famous exponents Dordoni and Pamich became household names and placed the sport on a level that has rarely been approached in any other country. In the last decade, under the coaching of Dordoni and fellow-Olympian, Corsaro, a continuous stream of promising juniors have matured into the international class.

On the administrative side, Frigerio, Oberweger, and Ridolfi have all held the position of president of the I.A.A.F. Walking Commission.

In a very full annual programme the Italian season includes three international classic races: the SAN SESTO GIOVANNI 30 km., the ROMA–CASTELGANDOLFO, and the Giro of Rome.

Sweden has had many of its competitors featured regularly in both world record lists and international games results during the past thirty years. Walking as a sport was introduced by General Back in 1881 and the first championship was held sixteen years later. Public marches, *stora riksmarshen*, became very popular, thousands, including the royal family, participating.

The three most outstanding performers have been Hardmo, Ljunggren, and MIKAELSSON, who have between them won numerous international events and set world records. Besides this trio, the country has produced many world-class performers from 1500 m. (1,635 yds.) to 100 km. (62½ miles) and leads the world in women's race walking (see below).

Switzerland first came into prominence through the efforts of A. T. Schwab, who began his career in 1916 and was still able, some 32 years later, to cover 10 km. (6¼ miles) in less than 50 minutes. His son, F. Schwab, the European 10 km. champion in 1950, Marquis, and Raymond all had long and successful careers and were responsible for placing their country among the leading nations during the 1950s. In the long-distance events, Linder won the first two Paris–Strasbourg races in 1926-7.

Originator of the idea for a world walk team competition, Libotte organized the first Lugano Cup competition and has, during the past decade, placed his home town of Lugano in the forefront for race-walking events with the AIROLO–CHIASSO RELAY, the LUGANO 100 KM., and the holding of the Lugano Cup final for a second time in 1973.

Holding a full programme of senior national championships from 10 km. to 100 km., the Swiss also include a mountain climb between 6 and 10 km., being the first country to introduce this specialized event into race walking.

The *U.S.A.* has always held numerous events throughout the country since the pedestrians' six-day races, although for a long period their competitors were unable to match their European counterparts. With the decline of professional walking, men such as Merrill and Murray appeared to record very fast short-distance times mainly in Boston and New York where winter indoor events were, and still are, very popular. Interest in the sport received a boost when the Italian, Frigerio, made a series of appearances during the 1925 indoor season and found Pearman, Plant, and Remer were all worthy opponents. Although competing regularly in Olympic competitions, the U.S.A. did not until 1964 find world-class competitors in LAIRD and Zinn. Four years later, however, men like Haluza, Klopfer, and Young had joined Laird in forming a team capable of beating all but the very best European nations.

With no less than 13 senior national championships being decided annually at different venues, besides an all-year-round weekly programme, the sport is slowly gaining popularity, with California, New York, and Ohio the leading centres. Since 1957 walkers have been included in the European tours in which dual matches against such countries as the U.S.S.R. and West Germany are included.

The *U.S.S.R.* has more participants than any other nation and has, since 1952, been in the forefront in the international games events. The sport was introduced into the country by an English walker and official, Palmer, over fifty years ago.

In the 1930s the Latvians (then a separate nation), Bernard, Bubenko, and DALINSCH, all recorded world-class performances. After the Second World War, Liespkalins (another Latvian), held the world record at 25 km. (15⅝ miles) and 30 km. (18¾ miles), but it was not until the Helsinki Olympic Games (1952) that the U.S.S.R. had walkers competing internationally. Since then the U.S.S.R. has produced a continuous stream of Games medallists and world record-breakers at all distances, among whom AGAPOV, Egorov, Junk, Lobastov, Maskinskov, Panischkin, SMAGA, Spirin, VEDYAKOV, Soldatenko, and Golubnichi are best known for their numerous outstanding achievements.

I.A.A.F. judge, Fructov, and coach, Polyakov, have played an important part in maintaining the high standard reached in the sport. Russian walkers rarely compete abroad in other than major Games and international matches. Unlike East Germany, England, and Italy the emphasis for Russian walkers is on physical strength rather than style and a considerable amount of running is included in their preparation.

WOMEN'S COMPETITIONS are held in some 15 countries, the strongest being

Sweden, Norway, Great Britain, and Australia. Internationally, 5 km. (3⅛ miles) is the standard distance but 3 km. (1⅞ miles) and 10 km. are also used frequently in Europe.

Nordic championships, involving Sweden, Denmark, and Norway, have been held since 1956 at 5 km. (track). A walk has been included in the English women's championships since 1923 varying from 880 yds. (805 m.) to the present 2,500 m. (1 mile 973 yds.). In recent years, because of the scarcity of competition, postal matches have been held among the leading nations.

Chief outstanding walkers have been the Swedes, Mrs. Bengtsson (1943-6), Mrs. Nilsson (1957-68), Mrs. Tibbling (1957-68), and currently Miss Johansson. Mrs. Farr (Great Britain) won nine consecutive track championships (1962-70) and was regarded as the leading competitor outside Scandinavia.

A walk has never been held in any of the major international games though there was a 1,000 m. (1,093 yds.) event in the Women's World Games at Göteborg in 1926. Road walks up to 60 km. (37 miles) have been held in South Africa and the Isle of Man.

G. Cummings, *Walking for Road and Track* (1934); H. W. Innes, *Race Walking* (1910); R. A. Laird, *Competitive Race Walking* (1972); G. E. Larner, *Text-book on Walking* (1909); A. Libotte, *La Marcia* (1964); The Race Walking Association, *The Sport of Race Walking* (1962); H. H. Whitlock, *Race Walking*, latest edition.
GOVERNING BODY (WORLD): Walking Commission, International Amateur Athletic Federation, 162 Upper Richmond Road, London S.W.15; (U.K.): Race Walking Association, 19 Cleveland Villas, Tynemouth Road, London N.15.

RACING CALENDAR, The, is the official HORSE RACING publication, issued in England by WEATHERBY, giving full information of entries for future races and results of past races, together with any announcements by the stewards of the JOCKEY CLUB. Weatherby, keeper of the *Match Book* at NEWMARKET and secretary of the Jockey Club, first published the *Racing Calendar* in 1773.

RACING F.C., Association FOOTBALL club, Buenos Aires. Founded in 1905 by Argentinians and French immigrants who had been members of the Racing Club of Paris, the club were the League champions of Argentina on seven consecutive occasions from 1913 to 1919, and have remained in the forefront of Argentinian football. In 1967 they won both the South American and the unofficial world club championships. Leading players have included Carceres, Bravo, Perfumo, and Maschio.
COLOURS: Sky blue shirts, white shorts.

RACKETS (also **Racquets**) is a racket-and-ball game played in England, the U.S.A., and Canada between two or four players in a court enclosed by four walls, giving a floor area generally 60 ft. long by 30 ft. wide (18·3 × 9·1 m.), and held to be the fastest of the traditional court games. The lay-out of the court is similar to that of its modern and more widely popular offshoot SQUASH RACKETS, but the dimensions are larger; the floor is of stone or asphalt and the ball is solid-cored.

The front or main wall, facing the players as they enter the court, is traversed by two horizontal lines: the higher or service line, or 'cut' line, above which the service must be struck; and the play line, near floor-level and formed by a board fastened to the wall, which determines the lower limit on the front wall to which all returns must be directed. As in other court games the ball is hit alternately by opponents until one or other side fails to make a return which is good.

In the singles game, the right to serve first having been decided by the spin of the racket, the server takes up his position for starting the ball in play. For this purpose the lines marked on the floor of the court have significance. A line across the floor, known as the short line, divides the rear half of the court from that adjacent to the front wall, and the rear half is further divided down the centre into quarters by the half-court line. Play commences when the server enters the service box — one of the square areas on either side of the court contiguous to the short line — and hits the ball on to the front wall above the service line and into the opposite quarter of the court, where his opponent is ready to make the return and so to produce a rally (or 'bully') of alternate shots which continues until the ball ceases to be in play. This occurs when either player fails to return the ball above the board, or to return it before it strikes the floor for the second time since last struck, or when he hits the ball above the area prepared for play, or commits some infringement such as hitting his opponent.

A characteristic of the game, shared by FIVES and BADMINTON, is the 'in and out' method of scoring. The player who is serving is said to be 'hand in' and a stroke or rally won by him scores a point or 'ace'. A stroke won by 'hand out' earns him the right to serve but does not advance his score. A player continues to serve, from alternate sides of the court, until he becomes hand out or wins the game, usually 15 points.

The doubles game is similar. One partner succeeds the other to the service in each pair, with one opponent receiving in the left court and the other in the right, and the rallies proceed with shots from alternate pairs. The rallies are often longer in doubles than in singles, as a sound defence is more readily

RACKETS COURT
Plan view shows dimensions of the floor area. The surrounding walls are 30 ft. (9·1 m.) high, and the service line on the front wall is 9 ft. 6 in. (2·9 m.) from the floor.

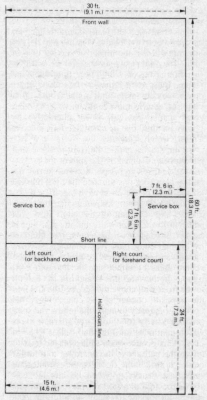

established, but congestion and obstruction are less easily avoided and lets, in which the point is played again on appeal, are more frequent. Tactics in doubles make more use of the side walls, whereas the essence of singles play is up-and-down hitting.

Hard hitting is a feature of the game which is often won by sheer pace, but a sound technique is required if the ball is to be adequately controlled and a degree of cut is imparted to the stroke to bring the ball down, especially the service, to an effective length. The cut service can be extremely severe and may dominate a match if the receiver has not sufficient skill, by attacking it, to exploit the server's positional disadvantage. The freedom of the server is enhanced, under English rules, by his being allowed a second service following a fault. In American and Canadian courts a single-service rule is applied.

Each game is 15 up — that is, the player who first scores 15 aces wins the game — excepting that, on the score being called 13-all for the first time in any game, hand out may, before the next service has been delivered, elect to 'set' the game to 5 or to 3; then the player winning 5 (or 3) aces first wins the game (total 18 or 16). Similarly at 14-all, hand out may set the game to 3 (total 17). Singles matches are mostly best of five games, doubles best of seven.

It is usual for the game to be conducted with the help of a marker who is stationed in the gallery overlooking the back wall and calls the score between points and shouts 'Play', 'Fault', 'Not up', or 'Out', as appropriate. The marker also provides the balls for play and a great many are used in some matches, for hand out has the right to call for a new ball at any time between aces. In important matches a referee, or umpires, are appointed to whom the players may appeal from the decisions of the marker or, if circumstances warrant, for a let to be awarded.

The Laws of Rackets, revised by the Tennis and Rackets Association (1966).

Although the game, in its modern form, developed in England in the middle of the nineteenth century, its origins may be traced to those varieties of HANDBALL, widely played in the Middle Ages both in Italy and in France, in uncovered spaces prepared for the game, in which the players struck the ball alternately, endeavouring always to return it themselves but to cause their opponents to fail to do so. Courts, known as *tripots*, were a common feature in French towns and these games were played not only with the bare or gloved hand but also with a bat or *battoir* and, at least by the end of the fifteenth century, with a racket. This implement, even in its primitive form, was popular enough to distinguish a fashion among ladies in the time of Catherine de Medici when a hair-style, in which the hair was arranged in crossed or plaited bands, was called *en raquettes* and a guild of racket makers, which also embraced ball makers and brush makers, existed in France from the fifteenth century.

The game as we know it today first became recognizable in England in conspicuously humble circumstances. Open courts existed in the backyards of taverns and inns in many towns as well as in the school yard at Harrow, and the popularity of the game among the impecunious denizens of the Fleet prison, London, is described by Dickens in *The Pickwick Papers*:

The area formed by the wall in that part of the Fleet in which Mr. Pickwick stood was just wide enough to make a good racket-court; one side being formed, of course, by the wall itself and the other by that portion of the prison which looked (or rather would have looked, but for the wall) towards St. Paul's Cathedral.... Lolling from the windows which commanded a view of this promenade were a number of persons ...looking on at the racket-players, or watching the boys as they cried the game.

Reference to the masters of the game at the beginning of the nineteenth century was made by Hazlitt in his essay 'The Indian Jugglers' where at the end of the famous eulogy of Cavanagh, the fives player, who died in 1819, he asserts that

the only person who seems to have excelled as much in another way as Cavanagh did in his, was the late John Davies, the racket-player. It was remarked of him that he did not seem to follow the ball, but the ball seemed to follow him. The four best racket-players of that day were Jack Spines, Jem Harding, Armitage, and Church. Davies could give any one of these two hands a time, that is, half the game and each of these, at their best, could give the best player now in London the same odds.... In the Fleet or King's Bench, he would have stood against Powell, who was reckoned the best open-ground player of his time.

The contrast between play in these old open courts and the modern four-wall game was recorded in the Badminton Library series by HART-DYKE, himself champion of rackets in 1862 and reputedly the first to be bred outside the walls of the Fleet Prison. 'The game as played in open courts against a single wall was a severe test of skill and judgment in placing the ball, and accuracy as regards strength and measuring distance. In a four-handed match the players took alternately the "in" and "out" game, the "in" players picking up the drops and placing the ball, the "out" players defending the back of the court. This led to very long and exciting rallies.'

The chief instrument in bringing about this transition was the building of the old Prince's Club in Hans Place, London, in 1853, for this became the focal point for all important matches for the next 30 years and its centre court, not only enclosed and covered but measuring 60 ft. by 30 ft. (18·3 × 9·1 m.), became the model for all courts subsequently built. Hitherto it had been the custom to use a court of larger size for doubles than for singles. Enclosure both speeded up the game and altered its social character, for it was now more expensive to play and became the sport of the comparatively well-to-do. The hard hitting which the new style of game induced

meant more broken rackets; and the handmade ball, with its stitched covering of kid leather, could also be a costly item, since the number used at that time in a close match was approximately one hundred.

More courts were built, not only at Prince's, which at one time had as many as six, but at the public schools and the universities and also by other clubs and by the Services. The regular series of matches between Oxford and Cambridge began in 1858 (only the University cricket match and the BOAT RACE have a more distant record) and the public schools championship was started in 1868. In that year only four schools competed —Eton, Harrow, Charterhouse, and Cheltenham. These were joined in the following year by Rugby; by Winchester, Haileybury, Wellington, and Marlborough in the 1870s; by Malvern, Clifton, and Radley in the '80s; and subsequently by Tonbridge, Rossall, and Westminster, although the last two did not remain regular competitors. The only court to be erected in the United Kingdom after 1908 is the one at Harrow School, opened in 1965, almost exactly a century after the opening match was played in their old court (which is still in good condition).

Rackets championship contests took place at Prince's Club until, in 1886, the old premises were demolished for the redevelopment of Hans Place; the new Prince's Club, in Knightsbridge, was not opened until 1889 (this club closed during the Second World War). By then Queen's Club, in West Kensington, had opened in 1887 and this at once became, and has remained, the game's main centre. The amateur singles championship was first played there in 1888 and a doubles competition was added in 1890. Of the many club courts built elsewhere, only that at the Manchester Tennis and Racquet Club is nowadays still in use; those at Liverpool, Eastbourne, Leamington, and other clubs, including the M.C.C. court at LORD'S, have been converted to other purposes. The governing body of the game in England is the Tennis and Rackets Association, formed in 1907. This body did not have complete jurisdiction over championships until 1919.

It is to the influence of the Army and the Navy that the extension of the game to other parts of the world may be attributed. The Royal Navy built courts not only at Britannia Royal Naval College in Dartmouth but in Gibraltar and Malta; the British Army, among whom the game had long been popular at Woolwich, introduced rackets to India, where there were at one time as many as 70 courts, mostly uncovered; and it was among officers at the military garrisons in Montreal, Hamilton

(Ontario), Quebec, and Halifax (Nova Scotia) that the game was first played in Canada. From the Montreal Racket Club, home of the Canadian championships, the game spread to the U.S.A. in the middle of the nineteenth century, first to New York and subsequently to Boston, Chicago, Detroit, and Philadelphia, in each of which cities — and at the Country Club at Tuxedo — there are rackets clubs. The only court in South America, at the Hurlingham Club near Buenos Aires in Argentina, was last used for rackets about 1930.

The standard of play in England is higher than elsewhere due to the early grounding which is acquired in the public school courts and to the skilled coaching available there. The two outstanding American players have been PELL and R. GRANT III. Pell was holder of the U.S. amateur singles championship 11 times between 1915 and 1933 and in 1925 defeated the leading British players to win the amateur singles championship at Queen's Club, London — the only American to do so. Grant, who had learnt the game as a schoolboy at Eton, won the U.S. singles ten times up to 1953, a year in which, in the process of winning the Canadian championship, he beat J. R. THOMPSON, MILFORD, and ATKINS on successive days in Montreal.

The premier title in the game, the world rackets championship, dates from 1820. Nothing is known of the earliest years except the names of the masters who were acknowledged as champions and remained unchallenged until they resigned. It was not until 1838 that an actual match for the world title was played — at the tavern court in Belvedere Gardens, Pentonville Road, London. Two decades passed with only two matches, played in Bristol and Birmingham, before a landmark was reached in 1862. Then Hart-Dyke beat the holder, Erwood, at Woolwich and Prince's Club by eight games to three, each match being the best of seven games. This system of two rubbers has prevailed ever since in these matches; the winner of most games wins the championship but if the games are equal the winner of the most aces gains the title, so that despite the length of the match every point may count.

Hart-Dyke was the first amateur to win the title. When he resigned, the famous Gray family, of whom there were six brothers, took over for the next twenty years but for the intervention of Fairs in 1876-8. The Grays, together with the Crosby and the Hawes families, are families of professional coaches and players which have long been distinguished in the game. It was in 1876 that a frail boy of 11 was playing tip-cat in the back streets of Manchester when, with a long hit, his wooden missile broke a window. He was hauled inside and made to sweep out the court. Thus the immortal LATHAM burst into the game. He heard at once of WILLIAM GRAY of Eton, peerless in his day and a player of amazing force though of slight build, but it was the younger Joseph Gray of Rugby that Latham beat when he was strong enough to challenge in 1887. Although that victory was hard won, he defended his title three times without great difficulty.

One of his victims, Standing, emigrated to the U.S.A. and improved vastly with the keen play in New York. In 1897 he challenged Latham, who was then at Queen's Club. Latham won the first match by four games to one. But it was a fine contest, in which the quality of the play exceeded anything seen before, and Standing scored so many aces that there was an uncomfortable feeling that Latham might still have much to do in the second leg in America.

So it proved. Latham, with two games to win for the prize, began splendidly by winning the first game, but when Standing drew level excitement mounted and reached fever pitch with the scores running neck and neck in the third game before Latham won it by the barest margin, and with it the title. Yet this thrill was to be exceeded later. For it was decided that the match should continue to its own finish, Standing's supporters claiming that their man could not lose in his home court.

Inevitably, while Standing played without inhibitions as well as ever, Latham suffered reaction. Thus 2-1 to Latham soon became 2-2 and then 3-2 to Standing, who took the lead again in the next game. Latham now made his second great effort, but Standing reached match point. With the match within his grasp, Standing made a stroke to his left corner that looked a winner all the way. Somehow Latham glided across and, with a backhand flick of the wrist, sent it back an inch over the board. Standing never got a second chance.

When Latham resigned the world championship in 1902, there were matches in the amateur championship between several of great skill, all wondering if FOSTER had really retired after his seven consecutive victories. All was quiet with the professionals. Browne, Latham's last challenger, did not claim the title, perhaps in case Latham came out of hiding between his REAL TENNIS matches and beat him without preparation. Then in 1903, came JAMSETJHI of Bombay, the only contender for this title from the East. With a beautiful style, the racket poised high upon the stroke, his lithe movement gave him time to play the ball. Browne had little chance.

Six years went by before BAERLEIN, the pick of the amateurs, was backed by Manchester against C. WILLIAMS with the idea of the winner challenging Jamsetjhi. Baerlein reached a high degree of fitness before the death of King Edward VII resulted in a long postponement of the match. Through business and other causes, Baerlein never reached the peak again, whereas the youthful Williams was improving. Furthermore, the match was spoilt by a collision in court in which Baerlein came off second best; Williams afterwards had matters his own way. When Williams challenged him in 1911, Jamsetjhi agreed to come and play two matches in England. He was short of practice, and now old for a champion. Not unnaturally he never became acclimatized and could not stand up to the powerful hitting of Williams.

Williams in turn was challenged, from the opposite side of the world. Williams was already famous as the hardest hitter ever on the backhand. But an emigrant from the Prince's Club days to Philadelphia, who now hit just as hard on the forehand, was SOUTAR, a man of remarkable physique and character. Short of stature, he was immensely strong; and with his unusually long arms he could perform exceptional gymnastic feats. A natural leader and master to his pupils, he was the more intelligent. In the first match at Queen's Club, Williams won by four games to two. With the specially-picked fast balls, some of the hitting was rather high, but for sheer speed it was unparalleled.

Williams was none too confident when he sailed for the first time to America. The ship on which he sailed was the *Titanic*, and Williams's miraculous escape after swimming in the ice-cold water left him suffering from exposure. When the return match was eventually played in 1914, Williams fatally relied on the back wall, and, failing to take Soutar's mighty service (which was even said to break the cover of the ball), he saw his slender lead of aces vanish in the very first game. He lost without winning a game, or in truth being within sight of one. Nearly ten years later Williams went to the U.S.A. to settle in Chicago, and, after Soutar had again beaten him by superb play in the second match at Philadelphia, he at last defeated the now older Soutar in 1928.

When Williams died in 1935, leaving the title vacant, each country held an Open championship. In England the amateur champion, Milford, astonished everyone by beating the holder of the Open, the powerful left-handed hitter, Cooper. His American opponent in similar role proved to be Setzler and Milford, after crossing to America, lost by four games to three. As neither could dominate the play by service, it became a marathon of long rallies in which Setzler, seeing Milford's inability to make a winner from the forehand, sensibly probed that side. The result was that in the final game it was Setzler who prevailed, with Milford surprisingly unable to do the amount of running required. However Setzler's staunch effort availed him nothing, for at Queen's Club Milford was a different man, armed by then at every point. With the play too fast for Setzler, Milford won by four games to nil and the title was his.

Soon came the Second World War, and with it Milford's resignation. DEAR, a fine all-round player of court games and the successor of Cooper at Queen's Club, beat in turn P. H. Gray, grandson of Joseph Gray, for the British professional title and the amateurs, Kershaw and PAWLE, for the Open; and he crossed the Atlantic in 1947 to play the winner between Chantler, an English professional who had emigrated to Montreal, and Grant, the amateur champion of the U.S.A. This proved to be Chantler, who beat Grant in New York in the seventh game, but was quite unequal to Dear either in Montreal or at Queen's.

Chantler's defeat of Grant was hard to understand in the light of other performances. For Grant had long before beaten Milford in his New York practice games; he was a superb hitter on both sides, and a stylist too.

Dear's next two matches were against Pawle, both of which he won, the first 8-4 and the second 8-2. In the second match Pawle was doing very well when he pulled a muscle in the second half of the match. He was an almost perfect stylist on both the backhand and the forehand; he had great speed and severity of stroke, but lacked the stamina required for the best of seven games. In 1954 he was succeeded as Dear's challenger by ATKINS, another stylist with a beautifully easy foot movement. Coming back from Chicago, where he was then resident, Atkins was so familiar with the linen-covered ball that, in a brilliant display, he outpaced Dear with his accurate hitting to win the first match at Queen's Club 4-1. In the second match, also at Queen's, Dear, although well over 40 years old, put up so valiant a fight that he won the first three games, in the second of which he saved a game point, almost equivalent to a match point in view of Atkins's long first-match lead in games and aces. However Atkins rallied, displaying great calmness, and won the next two games to make the title his, although 2-3 down in the second half.

The period from the mid-1950s was one in which the game would undoubtedly have died but for the invention of a new type of ball. The hand-made Bailey balls had gone out of production, and the remaining stock was dwindling and variable in quality, but experiments with a ball built round a moulded polythene core were successful. The new type, soon produced in large quantities and adopted in all courts, made rackets a truer and faster game and balls much cheaper than before.

Atkins, with no discernible weakness, held the world title for longer than any previous champion. By 1971 he had been in undisputed sway on both sides of the Atlantic for 17 years, having successfully withstood four challenges, two from LEONARD (in 1963 and 1968) and two from SWALLOW (in 1964 and 1969). These two amateurs had earned the right to challenge by defeating Atkins in the amateur singles championship at Queen's Club, in 1962 and 1964 respectively. Apart from these two occasions Atkins had, since becoming world champion, won every major title whenever he was available to compete. Leonard, though a clever player, had not the stroke power and all-round speed to hold Atkins when it came to the challenge; against Swallow Atkins finished strongly and in firm command on both occasions, although the loser won the praise of all by his elegant performance and much of their matches was played on nearly equal terms.

The retirement of Atkins from competitive play in 1971 again left the world title vacant for dispute between British and American challengers. The North American Rackets Association nominated W.J.C. Surtees, an English holder of the U.S. title resident in the U.S.A. The British nominee, who had won the right to challenge after eliminating matches against Pugh and M.G.M. SMITH, was Angus. The championship between them was played in 1972 in two legs. In the first at Queen's Club, London, Angus led 4-1, but in the second leg in Chicago Surtees won 4-0, making him the over-all winner by 5-4. Given that Surtees, a natural stylist on either side, was the more familiar with the Chicago court, his recovery there against a player of Angus's speed and fitness was an astonishing feat. But this result was as severely reversed one year later when Angus, in a subsequent challenge, won the first leg in Chicago 4-0. Although Surtees attacked brilliantly to win the first game of the second leg at Queen's, Angus rapidly recovered, to make the title his, 5-1.

John Armitage and E. M. Baerlein, sections in *Rackets, Squash Tennis, Fives and Badminton*, ed. Lord Aberdare (The Lonsdale Library, 1936); Julian Marshall, *The Annals of Tennis* (1878); E. B. Noel and Hon. C. N. Bruce, *First Steps to Rackets* (1926); E. O. Pleydell-Bouverie, *Rackets* (The Badminton Library, 1890).

GOVERNING BODY (U.K.) Tennis and Rackets Association, York House, 37 Queen Square, London W.C.1.

RACQUETS, see RACKETS.

RADAELLI, GIUSEPPE (1833-82), Milanese FENCING master who developed the technique for the modern light sabre introduced in the last half of the nineteenth century. In 1876 he wrote the first textbook on this method of sabre fencing.

RADMILOVIC, PAULO (1886-1968), WATER POLO player who competed in five Olympics (1908 to 1928) and also the 1906 interim Games in Athens. He was a member of the British team who won in London in 1908 — the year he also won a relay SWIMMING gold medal — and captained the gold medal teams in 1912 and 1920. His versatility was enormous. He won nine Amateur Swimming Association titles, from 100 yards to 5 miles. There were 20 years between his first win and the last (at the age of 40) in the long-distance championship, swum in the river Thames. He was also a scratch golfer and an outstanding footballer, and at the age of 78 was still swimming a quarter of a mile each day.

RAEBURN PLACE, football ground, Edinburgh, RUGBY UNION home ground of EDINBURGH ACADEMICALS, and the venue of the first international match played between Scotland and England in 1871. It was the ground most often used by Scotland up to 1895.

RAGUSA (1960), a race-horse by RIBOT, bred in America by Guggenheim, bought by Mullion for 3,800 guineas, trained in Ireland by Prendergast, and ridden by Bougoure. He won seven races, including the IRISH SWEEPS DERBY, KING GEORGE VI AND QUEEN ELIZABETH STAKES, ST. LEGER, and ECLIPSE STAKES, and £148,955 in prize money, a British record.

RAHIM JIVRAJ CUP, HOCKEY trophy competed for by East African countries which is sometimes open to countries from other parts of Africa. Kenya has dominated the competition.

RAJKOVIC, TRAJKO (1937-70), Yugoslavian BASKETBALL player. A 6 ft. 9 in. (2.06 m.) centre, Rajkovic was one of the foremost names in European basketball. He represented Yugoslavia on 141 occasions and helped them to win the world championship in 1970. He decided to retire after this to devote himself to his medical studies, but died in Belgrade a few days later.

RALLIES, MOTOR, see MOTOR RACING: MOTOR RALLIES; **MOTOR-CYCLE,** see MOTOR-CYCLE RACING.

RALLYCROSS, see AUTOCROSS.

RAMADHIN, SONNY (1930-   ), cricketer for West Indies, Trinidad, and Lancashire. A slow bowler whose action mystified many eminent batsmen, he came to the fore in 1950, when he and the equally inexperienced VALENTINE took 59 wickets between them in four Tests against England. He was the outstanding bowler for West Indies against England in 1953-4, but a concentrated batting assault against him in the 1957 series led to his decline. By his retirement he had taken a record 158 Test wickets.

RAMSAY, Revd. JOHN (1777-1871), Scottish curler. Author of *An Account of the Game of Curling* (1811), the oldest book on the history of CURLING.

RAMSEY, Sir ALFRED E. (1922-   ), Association footballer for Southampton, TOTTENHAM HOTSPUR, and England; team manager of Ipswich Town and England. He developed as a full-back with Southampton, a club with a tradition of producing above-average full-backs, before signing for Tottenham Hotspur in May 1949. While with the London club he won League championship-winners' medals for the Second Division in 1950 and the First Division in 1951, and made 32 appearances for England before joining Ipswich Town as manager in August 1955. Ipswich were then in the Third Division (South). Ramsey built the teams that won promotion in 1957 and then, in successive seasons, 1960-1 and 1961-2, won the Second and the First Division championships. At the end of the next season he took charge of England's international side, having been appointed national team manager in October 1962. His achievement was to create among the individuals selected to play for the national team the feeling and atmosphere of a national *club* side that helped considerably in England's victory in the 1966 world championship, after which he was knighted.

RAND, Mrs. MARY DENISE (later Mrs. Toomey) (1940-   ), long jumper, hurdler, sprinter, and PENTATHLON competitor for Great Britain. Indisputably the greatest British woman athlete up to her retirement in 1968, Mrs. Rand was the first British woman athlete to win an Olympic gold medal. As Miss Bignal, she was only 17 when she won a silver medal in the 1958 COMMONWEALTH GAMES

LONG JUMP. In 1962 she took a European Championship bronze medal in the long jump within a few months of the birth of her daughter. Her first world record came in 1963 as a member of the British team which clocked 45·2 sec. for the 4 × 110 yards relay. The summit of her career was in 1964 when she broke the world long jump record with 22 ft. 2¼ in. (6·76 m.), winning the Olympic gold medal. She followed this with a silver medal in the pentathlon, compiling a United Kingdom record total of 5,035 points. Her last Olympic medal was a bronze in the 4 × 100 metres relay. In 1966, though she was below her true form, she won a gold medal in the Commonwealth Games long jump. Her quality and versatility are instanced by the range of national titles she held — for 100 yards, 80 metres hurdles, HIGH JUMP, long jump, and pentathlon. Apart from the performances mentioned, she also held United Kingdom records of 10·6 sec. for 100 yards and 10·9 sec. for 80 metres hurdles.

RANDLE TROPHY MATCH, see SHOOTING, RIFLE: SMALL BORE.

RANDWICK is the race-course near Sydney, Australia, where the SYDNEY CUP, Australian Jockey Club Derby and Oaks, Sires Produce and Champagne Stakes are run.

RANFURLY SHIELD, trophy presented in 1902 by the Earl of Ranfurly, Governor of New Zealand, for competition between the RUGBY UNION provincial teams of New Zealand. The competition is run on a challenge basis, the holders retaining the shield until beaten, traditionally on their home ground, by a challenging union. The holders can choose whom to accept as challengers. The first holders were Auckland, and the first successful challenge was made in 1904 by Wellington. In 1963 Auckland set a record by repelling 25 consecutive challenges.

RANGERS F.C., Association FOOTBALL club, Glasgow, formed in 1873 and in membership of the English F.A. from 1885 to 1887, when the club competed in the F.A. Cup competition, of which they reached the semi-final. Three years later Rangers were founder members of the Scottish League (from the top division of which they have never been relegated) and shared the first championship with Dumbarton. In 1893 professionalism was adopted and a year later Rangers won the Scottish Cup for the first time. Since then, they have dominated Scottish football together with CELTIC, and by the end of 1973, Rangers had added 33 championships to the first shared one, and had won the Scottish Cup 20 times. Rangers have competed frequently in European club competitions since 1956, with most success in the Cup-Winners Cup in which competition they were the beaten finalists in both 1961 and 1967, and the winners in 1972. Among the club's large number of outstanding players have been Drummond, Gibson, G. Gillespie, and R. C. Hamilton before 1914; Archibald, G. Brown, Cunningham, Dawson, R. McPhail, Meiklejohn, and MORTON from 1919 to 1939; and Baxter, Caldow, Greig, Henderson, McKinnon, Stein, Waddell, Woodburn, and YOUNG since 1946.

COLOURS: Royal blue shirts, white shorts.
GROUND: Ibrox Park, Glasgow.

RANJI TROPHY, awarded to the national champions of Indian CRICKET, was instituted in 1934 in memory of RANJITSINHJI, and it has been contested annually ever since without interruption — even by war. The winners and runners-up of five zonal competitions meet in a series of finals on a knock-out basis. Bombay have been clearly the most successful team: their victory in 1969-70 was their twelfth championship in succession.

RANJITSINHJI, Maharajah JAM SAHIB of Nawanagar (1872-1933), cricketer for England, Cambridge University, and Sussex. One of the greatest of stylists, possessing keen eyesight and graceful movement, he dominated bowlers — even the fastest and most hostile. Having played little CRICKET before going up to Cambridge, he soon developed his abilities and throughout the 1890s broke many batting records. In 1899 he became the first batsman to score 3,000 runs in a season; in 1896 he scored two centuries in one day against Yorkshire; he also made centuries in his first Tests against Australia both at home and abroad. He captained Sussex from 1899 to 1903.

RAPER, JOHN (1939-   ), Australian RUGBY LEAGUE player. He and GASNIER (also of ST. GEORGE, Sydney) contributed enormously to Australia's dominance in Test matches during the 1960s. Vice-captain on the 1967-8 tour of Britain, he led his country to victory (after Gasnier was injured), in spite of losing the first Test. He was captain of Australia's winning WORLD CUP team in 1968. A footballer of great versatility, he played at stand-off half, centre, and second row, with distinction, but it was as a loose forward that he made his reputation.

RAPID S.K., Association FOOTBALL club, Vienna. Formed in 1898, the club first won the Austrian championship in 1912 and has been one of the dominant clubs in Austrian football ever since. Between the two world wars Rapid were often prominent in the MITROPA CUP competition, reaching the final on three occasions and winning the cup in 1930. Since the end of the Second World War the club has often competed in the three main European club competitions, its best performance being in 1961 when it reached the semifinal stage of the European Champion Clubs Cup. Leading players have included Bauer, Binder, Braunstadter, Smistik, and Hanappi.

COLOURS: Green and white striped shirts, white shorts.

RAQUETTE, see PELOTA.

RATZEBURG, a small town near Lübeck, West Germany, surrounded by lakes, the home of the most successful ROWING club of modern times, the Ratzeburger Ruder Club. Founded after the Second World War, it came to prominence under the coaching of K. ADAM, its oarsmen and scullers winning many national and international titles. In 1965 the Ratzeburg Rowing Academy was founded under Adam's direction.

RAVENHILL, RUGBY UNION football ground in Belfast used by Ireland for roughly half its home matches from the mid-1920s until 1951, when LANSDOWNE ROAD became the sole venue.

RAY, EDWARD (1877-1943), English professional golfer, an abnormally powerful and long-hitting player. His reputation suffered by comparison with that of his outstanding contemporary, VARDON, but for all that Ray was a very considerable player. He was a British and English international, won the Open championship in 1912, and was twice runner-up. He tied for the U.S. Open (with Vardon and OUIMET) in 1913, losing in the play-off; but he won that title in 1920.

REAL HUNTSMAN (1948), racing greyhound, a brindled dog, by Never Roll out of Medora. He established a record of 27 consecutive wins between 3 June 1950, and 2 April 1951, at American tracks, and earned $62,493 with a career record of 67 wins, 9 seconds, and 12 thirds from 105 starts.

REAL MADRID (1), BASKETBALL team, which became the first team from outside the U.S.S.R. to win the EUROPEAN CUP FOR CHAMPION CLUBS, with victories in 1964, 1965, 1967, and 1968, after being beaten finalists in 1962 and 1963.

(2) Association FOOTBALL club. Formed in 1898, the club was a founder member of the Spanish League in 1928 and won it for the first time in the season ending 1932. Earlier it had won the Spanish Cup on five occasions, the first time in 1905. The rise of the club to a foremost position in European and world football dates from the 1950s when, after winning the Spanish championship in the seasons ending 1954 and 1955, Real Madrid won the first five competitions for the European Champion Clubs Cup. Real were again successful in this competition in 1966 and won the unofficial world club championship in 1960. Leading players have included ZAMORA, DI STEFANO, PUSKAS, GENTO, Santamaria, Amancio, and PIRRI.

COLOURS: White shirts, white shorts.

REAL TENNIS is a racket-and-ball game played in an indoor court. Since the name 'tennis' has become an accepted abbreviation for LAWN TENNIS, this ancient game from which lawn tennis was devised is now commonly known as real tennis in Britain, royal tennis in Australia, and court tennis in America. In France it retains its historic name of *le jeu de paume*.

Real tennis has affinities with the game of RACKETS, but whereas a rackets court has four plain walls a real tennis court contains a number of special features, including ingenious hazards. These provide opportunities for a wide range of strokes. Combined with a ball which may be spun, twisted, or cut at will, the peculiar construction of the court makes tennis a game where experience and subtlety of tactics count for as much as youth and physical fitness. Judgement and anticipation are as important as in other games: in real tennis, it is said, *la balle cherche le bon joueur*.

The laws of real tennis place no restriction on the size or shape of rackets. Usually they weigh between 13 and 18 oz. (369–510 g.), are between 26 and 27 in. (660–686 mm.) in length and have an asymmetrical pear-shaped head which is between 7 and 8 in. (178–203 mm.) at its widest. Both the handle and the catgut used for stringing are stout because the balls are solid. The racket is normally gripped half or two-thirds of the way down the handle. A leather grip is sometimes used, but usually there is none. The asymmetry of the racket, which is its most notable feature, is said to make for ease in taking balls near the floor. The frame is made from ash, with middle-pieces of willow, lime, or beech.

Real tennis balls have a diameter of approximately 2½ in. (64 mm.) and weigh 2½ to 2¾ oz. (71–78 g.). At one time they were stuffed with wool trimmings or animal hair, covered with sheepskin, and the original French name for a ball was *l'esteuf*. Nowadays strips of heavy cloth are tightly rolled and tied with twine before being covered with white Melton cloth. Balls have always been hand-made until recent years when a machine-made composition ball was introduced in some courts. Formerly there were nine dozen or a gross of balls to a set; now five, six, or seven dozen are common numbers. Sets of balls are kept in a basket which fits into a hole under the net near the marker's box, and are transferred from there, as required, to troughs in the dedans or first gallery on the service side. To avoid wetting them balls are cleaned by being shaken, first with chalk dust in a trouncing-bag, then in netting to disperse the surplus chalk.

The floors of courts are made of stone or concrete composition. The most favoured stones are limestone and Caen stone; the cement is Portland cement or Bickley's patent non-sweating composition. Walls are of stone or brick coated with the same cement or composition. Floors are normally black or red, walls black or slate-grey. Lamp-black diluted with bullock's blood and ox-galls is the traditional recipe for blackening floors and walls.

The dimensions of real tennis courts are not precisely uniform, but the playing area at floor level is approximately 96 ft. long by 32 ft. wide (29·3 × 9·8 m.) (above the penthouses it becomes 110 ft. by 39 ft. — 33·5 × 11·9 m.). The roof is about 30 ft. (9 m.) above the floor. Sometimes it contains glass so that the court is lit from above, but it is usual for light to come through a series of high windows running along either side of the court. The side walls are in play up to a height of about 18 ft. (5·5 m.), where the windows begin, while the end walls, which are unbroken, are in play up to a height of about 24 ft. (7·3 m.). The roof is not in play. A play line painted on the walls marks the upper limit of play.

Inside the court, internal or battery walls run round three sides to a height of an inch or two over 7 ft. (2·1 m.). These are surmounted by sloping roofs known as penthouses. The upper edges of the penthouses meet the walls proper at a height of about 10 ft. 6 in. (3·2 m.). Like the rest of the court below the play-line on the walls, the penthouses form part of the playing area. The strip of wood below the penthouse is known as the bandeau and is usually painted red or green.

A net across the centre divides the court into equal but dissimilar halves: the service side (on the right of the entrance), from which service is always delivered, and the hazard side (on the left of the entrance), on which service is received. The net is 5 ft. (1·5 m.) high at either side but sags to 3 ft. (0·9 m.) in the middle, permitting a lower trajectory for centre-court or cross-court shots than for side-court. The cord supporting the net is called the line.

Beneath the penthouse at the end of the service side is an oblong opening approximately 3 ft. 4 in. high by 21 ft. 6 in. wide (1 m. × 6·6 m.), 3 ft. (0·9 m.) above the floor. This is the dedans, where there is seating for spectators behind the opening. Under the penthouses which run along the side of the court are similar openings or galleries at the same height from the floor. These are, in order from the end of the service side: the last gallery, the second gallery, the door, and the first gallery. Adjacent to the first gallery is a recess at the side of the net, which is the marker's box, and

adjacent to this on the other side of the net are the hazard-side galleries: the first gallery, the door, the second gallery, and the winning gallery. The entrance to the court leads into the marker's box by the net. The galleries known as 'the door' indicate the position of doors in former times. The dedans and all the side galleries are backed by netting to catch the balls and protect spectators. In the winning gallery a bell is often suspended, which rings when the ball enters.

The battery wall below the penthouse at the end of the hazard side contains no galleries. Instead, at the side where it meets the main wall, there is an opening approximately 3 ft. 3 in. (1 m.) square known as the grille. This is backed by a wooden board (or panels) which

REAL TENNIS COURT
Perspective view looking towards the hazard side. Numbered lines on the service side of the net have the following conventional designations: (C1) chase the line; (C2) chase first gallery; (C3) chase the door; (C4) chase second gallery; (C5) chase a yard worse than last gallery; (C6) chase last gallery; (C7) chase half a yard worse than six; (C8) chase six; (C9) chase five and six; (C10) chase five; (C11) chase four and five; (C12) chase four; (C13) chase three and four; (C14) chase three; (C15) chase two and three; (C16) chase two; (C17) chase one and two; (C18) chase one yard; (C19) chase half a yard. Lines are numbered correspondingly on the hazard side. (HC) Hazard chase.

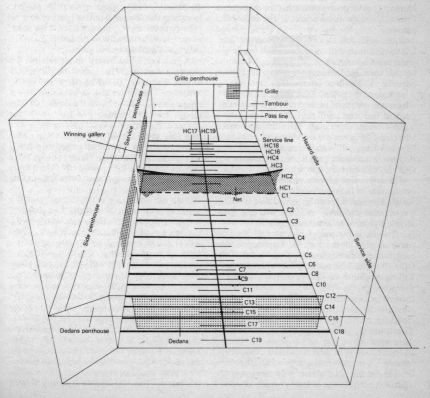

makes a loud noise when struck by the ball.

The main wall faces the entrance to the court. Unlike the other three walls, it contains no opening, but on the hazard side it projects into the court. This projection is the tambour. It narrows the court by 1 ft. 6 in. (0·5 m.) for a distance of nearly 14 ft. (4·3 m.) from the grille wall, at which point it forms an angle. The face of the angle is 2 ft. 6 in. (0·8 m.) wide. Although the name properly refers to the entire projection it is commonly used to refer to the angle only.

The dedans (on the service side) and the winning gallery and grille (on the hazard side) are the 'winning openings'. When a player strikes a ball into them from the opposite side of the net he wins a point. The other galleries, on either side of the net, and the tambour are known as hazards.

The penthouses, winning openings, and hazards are peculiar to real tennis; but the heart of the game is a further peculiarity: the chase. On the service side of the court and on the half of the hazard side towards the net the floor is marked with lines. These are chase lines. They begin by indicating the distance in yards from the battery 'wall at the end of the service side, the figures 1 to 6 being painted on the side walls above the appropriate line. Between each full yard line, half-yards are indicated on the floor. In France, where the yard is not used, chases are marked in French feet up to 14 with no intermediate markings.

Beyond the 6-yard mark the chase lines run from the centre of each gallery, with an additional line one yard beyond the last gallery line. These gallery chase lines continue on the hazard side of the net, followed by 2-yard and 1-yard lines, all with intermediate markings. These last distances are taken not from the end of the hazard side, but from the line which bisects this side of the court. This, running to the centre of the winning gallery, is the service line. The rear half of the hazard side is a winning area, and here, as in the winning openings, a point may be won outright.

The basic method of play in real tennis is that adopted for lawn tennis. Opponents strike the ball alternately from opposite sides of the net. If the ball passes over the net (or round it, along or above the side penthouse) it must be returned on the volley or after one bounce on the floor. The number of walls struck by the ball is of no consequence, provided that the portion of the wall struck is below the play line, which marks the upper limit of the playing area. Once the ball touches the floor a second time it is dead, but unless the second bounce is in the winning area a chase has been made on the spot where it bounces and the point is not yet won or lost. A chase is a point

held in abeyance. If the second bounce is, for example, on the 4-yard line 'chase four' is made; if it falls on the half-line between 3 and 4, 'chase three and four'; if it falls between the two, 'chase better than four'. Similarly, if a ball enters the second gallery on the service side or falls on the line marked on the floor level with the gallery, it is 'chase second gallery'; if it enters the second gallery on the hazard side, 'hazard second gallery'. If the second bounce falls near the net on the service side it is 'chase the line'; if near the net on the hazard side it is 'hazard the line'. The best chase is 'better than half a yard' — i.e. less than half a yard from the back wall.

Chases are called by the marker, who stands in his box by the net and also calls the score, faults, and passes. Apart from the chases, scoring in real tennis is as in lawn tennis. Four points make a game and the first player to win six games wins the set. Scoring is by 15, 30, and 40 to game, and if both players reach 40, deuces and advantages are played until a lead of 2 clear points is established for the game. At 5-all in games a short set of one deciding game is normally played. In calling the score it is not the practice to give priority to the server, but to call first the score of the player who has won the last point or, in the case of games, the last game.

A marker is necessary to determine the chases accurately. These must be played off within the game in which they are made. When the player on the service side hits a return into the net he has lost a point, but if he misses the ball completely he has not. If, for instance, the second bounce falls on the 3-yard line and 'chase three' is called, when either player is within 1 point of game, or when a second chase is made, the players change sides and the chase is then played off. The player from the service side is now on the hazard side and he must hit each return to such a length that the second bounce will fall nearer the back wall of the service side than the 3-yard line. If it falls further from the back wall, either on the floor or by entering a side gallery, he loses the point. If it falls nearer, he wins the point. If it falls on the 3-yard line, 'chase off' is called and the point annulled. When a chase is being played off, the normal rules also apply: the point is lost by a player who fails to return the ball or hits it out of court.

Service is always from the same side of the court and does not change with the games as in lawn tennis. It changes only when the players change sides, and this occurs only when chases are played off. If no chase were made, the player who won the toss and chose the service side would continue serving throughout the match. Thus, whether it is finally won or lost, a chase at least wins for the receiver of service the right to serve, and he continues to hold service until dislodged by the making and playing off of another chase.

Service is said to be the soul of real tennis (*l'ame du jeu*). It is comparable both to the opening gambit in chess and, since length is all-important, to bowling at CRICKET.

Service takes place not over the net but along the side penthouse. The ball must touch the penthouse on the hazard side and fall on the floor within the service court, which occupies the major part of the winning area at the rear of the hazard side. The remainder of the winning area is the 'pass court' and, if the ball falls there, 'pass' is called and a let played. For a service to be good it is immaterial whether or not the ball touches the penthouse on the service side, the wall above the side penthouse, the end penthouse on the hazard side, or the end wall. This flexibility, coupled with the fact that the server may stand anywhere he pleases up to the second gallery line on the service side, makes for a wide variety of possible services. The many variations fall into four main categories: the side-wall, the underhand twist, the drop, and the 'railroad'.

Of these the railroad, an overhead service, is the most effective, since on striking the end battery wall the ball twists back towards the side wall instead of coming out into the court. It can, too, be delivered at speed. It is a natural stroke for left-handers, offsetting the disadvantage which they suffer of receiving service on the backhand.

The perfect service makes a 'dead nick', that is, falls from the penthouse and lands in the junction of the floor with the end wall. Since the ball does not rise it is impossible to return, and the only effective response to a service of this length is to anticipate it and volley the ball as it leaves the penthouse.

Real tennis is one of the ball games, like rackets and lawn tennis, where a second service is permitted if a fault is served. Since service is a powerful weapon, no longer the traditionally innocuous act of putting the ball into play (in real tennis *le premier coup* is the return of service), the server enjoys a great advantage and it is anomalous that he should be allowed the further advantage of a second stroke.

The receiver of service has two choices. He can either try to make a chase, which will win him the service end, or he can try to win a point outright. The latter can be achieved either by sending his opponent a difficult return which will be mishit, or by hitting the ball into the dedans, which lies invitingly behind his opponent like a goal-mouth. Finding the dedans most often entails a hard 'force', straight or 'boasted' (struck against a side wall), like a drive at cricket. This can be volleyed, or if it misses its mark the ball will rebound from the back wall or penthouse and offer an easy return.

An attempt to make a good chase is therefore the normal practice from the hazard end. This requires the ball to be hit to a length. Thus the chase determines the stroke used in real tennis. It is of an unnatural kind, played, not from the wrist or the shoulder, but from the elbow. A full back swing is required, but little follow-through, the stroke being chopped off at the moment of impact with the ball, so that cut is imparted. The head of the racket should be kept above, or at any rate not below, the wrist. The body must therefore crouch, adopting what is sometimes referred to as the 'commode' position. In real tennis one must stoop to conquer.

The ideal return travels sufficiently fast for an opponent to be unable to prevent its reaching the end wall, but not so hard that it comes back from the wall and can be played on the rebound. Hence the cut. The second bounce of a good-length return falls in the crack between the end wall and the floor, making a 'dead nick'. This makes the best possible chase, which can be beaten only in the dedans.

During a 'rest' (the real tennis term for a rally), while the player on the hazard side is trying to make a good chase, his opponent on the service side is in a stronger position. He too should hit the ball to a length, since the whole of the rear portion of the hazard side is a winning area, and a short return will result in a hazard chase, which he should be able to defeat, but which will lose him the service end. Two winning openings are available to him, the winning gallery and the grille, on opposite sides of the court. Additionally he can make use of the tambour, leaving his opponent uncertain whether a return is going into the corner near the grille or being deflected by the angle into the centre.

In singles, therefore, the winner of the toss usually chooses the service side. In doubles, however, where gaining and retaining the service side is of particular importance, he nevertheless chooses the hazard side. In doubles partners serve during alternate games throughout the set and always to the same opponent, so that during the first, third, and fifth games A and C will be serving or receiving service, B and D during the second, fourth, sixth, etc. In choosing the hazard side a partnership can determine the pairing, by electing who shall receive the first service after seeing which of their opponents is about to serve.

In doubles tactics and positioning, too, are particularly important. It is usual for one player on the service side to defend the side galleries and for one on the hazard side to guard the tambour and grille. Volleying is a prominent feature. Doubles, or the four-handed game, is more popular in America than in England.

Handicaps. In addition to the handicaps used in lawn tennis — 'fifteen', 'owe fifteen', 'half-thirty', 'owe half-thirty', etc. — the bisque and 'cramped odds' are popular in matches between strong and weak players.

The bisque is a single point conceded to an opponent during a set. It is 'wild' like a joker at cards: a player receiving it can take it when he chooses, except when the ball is in play. By simply calling 'bisque' he wins the next point. A bisque is valuable but double-edged: the inexperienced player is often worried about taking it too early in the set or leaving it until too late. It is properly taken to win a game, not to avoid losing one. The player conceding a bisque should reconcile himself to the loss of one game and not concern himself further. The *bisque tournée* is a method of evening a match between two players of roughly the same standard, the bisque being conceded by the player who has won the previous set.

Cramped odds are various. 'Touch-no-walls' means that the player so handicapped loses a point if a ball in play returned by him touches a wall or enters an opening. Other cramped odds include 'touch-no-side-walls', 'bar the openings', 'bar the winning openings', and 'round services' (which must touch the grille penthouse).

Ball games are recorded from early times, and the origins of tennis have been variously traced to ancient Egyptians (the town of Tamis or Tinnis in the Nile delta), Homeric Greeks (Nausicaa and her handmaidens), Byzantines (on horseback), Romans (Augustus, Maecenas, and Julius Caesar are claimed as players), Persians (the game of *tchigan*), Mexican Indians (the game of *tlatchli*), and Saracens ('racket' is derived from an Arabic word for the palm of the hand). In fact, the game which alone has the distinctive characteristics of real tennis almost certainly originated in France, as much of the nomenclature — dedans, tambour, grille, bisque, bandeau, etc. — suggests. This game was, and still is, called *le jeu de paume*.

No satisfactory explanation or derivation of the word 'tennis' has yet been found. The ancient Egyptian town of Tinnis has been suggested on the grounds that it was famous for linen, which was used for stuffing tennis balls. Another theory suggests a corruption of 'tens'

(five a side) as opposed to 'fives', but FIVES is derived, not from two-and-a-half a side, but from the five knuckles of the bunched fist. The most plausible theory is that tennis is a corruption of the French *tenez*, which may have been used for 'Play!'. Although there is no evidence that *tenez* was called in this way in *le jeu de paume*, it is significant that in its earliest written form in English tennis is spelt 'tenetz'.

The method of scoring is equally mysterious. One point is '15'. No score is 'love'. Why should this be? Originally a player needed to win only four games for the set, so that four points made a game and four games a set. Each point was worth 15 — '40' is a contraction of '45' — so that a game was won when 60 was reached. To the medieval mind 60 had a significance which today is attributed to 100. This can be seen in divisions such as 60 seconds to a minute and 60 minutes to an hour. In fourteenth-century France the coinage was sexagesimal. There were 60 sous to the *double d'or*, and the *denier d'or* was a 15-sou piece. It is possible therefore that it became the custom to bet a 15-sou piece on each point and to call out '15 to me' when the point was won. 'Love' is another term peculiar to tennis. It is often said to be an anglicized version of *l'oeuf*, signifying an oval nought, as in a duck's egg or 'duck' at cricket. But love as the equivalent of nothing is a very old English usage, as in the phrase 'for love or money' or doing something 'for love'.

Starting probably in open fields about a thousand years ago, *le jeu de paume* was first played in monastery cloisters during the eleventh century. When courts came to be purpose-built, the sloping roofs of the cloisters were retained in the penthouses, and the cloisters themselves represented by the dedans and side galleries. The grille is thought to represent a buttery hatch, the tambour a buttress. Some authorities trace the court's origins to castle courtyards and identify the galleries with cowsheds. There is little doubt that tennis was played in castles at an early date, but it is likely that cloisters had priority.

This view is supported by early references associating tennis with the clergy. These begin in the twelfth century and, by the fifteenth, games of tennis at Easter were an established feature of the French ecclesiastical calendar. At Orléans, for instance, where it was traditional for bishop and chapter to exchange Easter presents, the chapter one year gave the bishop two tennis rackets and a set of balls. The persistent popularity of tennis among the lower clerical orders may be judged by the numerous occasions on which church authorities were forced to ban the playing of the game. But in England it survived in monasteries as long as the monasteries themselves. Shortly before the dissolution, an episcopal visitation rebuked monks at Humberstone in Lincolnshire for neglecting their duties in favour of tennis.

From the Church tennis spread to the Crown. Taken up by the French kings, it became a royal and aristocratic game, and from France it spread throughout western Europe. In time, despite attempts to reserve the game for the nobility, it became popular with all classes in France, Italy, England, Spain, and Germany. It was played in fields as well as parks, and the game without walls was known as *longue paume*, as opposed to *courte paume*, the enclosed version. It was played in town streets and university quadrangles as well as in castle courtyards and moats. Royal prohibitions were as ineffective as the Church's had been. In the fourteenth and fifteenth centuries decrees were issued in both France and England forbidding the playing of tennis by common people: 'Servants shall use only bows and arrows, and leave idle games' (an act of Richard II).

At first the game was literally *le jeu de paume* — game of the palm — indicating HANDBALL or a version of fives. Development from the bare hand to the present sophisticated racket was gradual. First came an ordinary glove, then a binding of cords strung across the palm of the glove. Later, crude wooden boards were used, followed by the short-handled *battoir*, at first of solid wood, later covered with parchment like a drum. The long-handled racket, strung with sheep's intestines, was not invented until about 1500. This, improved over the centuries, is essentially the weapon still in use today, the ancestor of all modern rackets — real tennis, lawn tennis, rackets, SQUASH RACKETS, BADMINTON, etc. Until about 1700 the stringing was diagonal, and only in 1875 was it strengthened by threading the cross-strings through the mainstrings. This, replacing the old method of looping round, greatly increased the pace of the game.

The royal connection with tennis sometimes proved fatal and affected the course of history. Louis X was an early royal victim; he died of a chill after a game in the forest of Vincennes in 1316. Not only Henry I of Castile, in 1217, but Philip I of Spain, in 1506, suffered a similar fate, and James I of Scotland would have avoided assassination in 1437 had he been able to escape down a drain which had been blocked to prevent the loss of tennis balls. In 1498 Charles VIII of France died from hitting his head on the lintel of a low doorway when going to watch a tennis match in the castle moat at Amboise.

But royal patronage continued and the sixteenth century was the heyday of tennis. No fewer than four of the French kings of this period were devotees of the game. Francis I built himself courts at the Louvre, Fontainebleau, and St Germain (two), and even one on his battleship *La Grande Françoise*. Henry II was so proficient at the game that he is said to have been of championship class. Charles IX was depicted with a racket in his hand at the age of two. He is reputed to have played for six hours a day and complained that the news of Coligny's assassination put him off his game. Henry IV (of Navarre) was another enthusiast. During his reign tennis reached a higher peak of popularity than ever before or since.

Tennis was widely enough played in France in 1500, when 40 courts were in use by students in Orléans and 22 in Poitiers, but by 1600 it had become a national pastime and the French were said to be born racket in hand. Every château had a court and every town courts by the dozen. The Venetian ambassador reported 1,800 courts in Paris alone and a thousand crowns a day spent there on the purchase of rackets, but allowance should be made for Venetian hyperbole. Another source puts the number of courts in Paris at 1,100, and the majority of these would probably have been outdoor *longue paume* courts. Proper enclosed courts may not have numbered more than 250, but whatever the exact number it was certainly high. An English traveller in France at this date reported that there were two tennis courts for every church, and among the poor as many tennis-players in France as ale-drinkers in England.

Tennis is known to have been played in Germany in the sixteenth century, in a *Ballhaus*, in at least 46 towns.

In France there had been a trade guild of professionals (racket makers and brush makers) as early as the fourteenth century, and in 1571 Charles IX granted statutes to a Corporation of Tennis Professionals. A master of this corporation first codified the rules in 1592. Earlier in the century guilds of tennis racket and ball makers had been formed in Florence and Venice, and at Ferrara a monk named Antonio Scaino wrote a philosophical treatise on the game.

Scaino's great work was published in 1555. The pretext was to settle a dispute which had arisen when the duke was playing one day, but the work goes deeply into the game and reveals how seriously it was regarded. From Scaino we learn that the size of the court, the method of scoring, the imparting of cut to the ball, and many other features of real tennis as it is played today, were well established more than 400 years ago. The chase as we know it is described in detail. There could be no better indication of the antiquity of tennis, for the origins of the game and its peculiar method of scoring were as mysterious to Scaino as they are today. His treatise tells us of variations in the rules between Ferrara and Tuscany. It mentions how it was then the fashion in France to use white balls and blackened walls; in Spain walls were traditionally white and balls therefore black. We learn that the game was played by up to four a side according to the size of the court, and that there were useful women players in sixteenth-century Italy. Very few have played since and the only recorded woman champion is Margot from Hainault, the Joan of Arc of tennis, who came to Paris in 1427 and defeated all comers.

From Scaino we gain confirmation, too, that what was known as a tennis court was often a town square or a section of street. His rules cover contingencies such as the ball alighting on a doorstep or being carried away on a passing cart. He deals also with *longue paume* (Italian *pallone*), the first version of lawn tennis, which survived until the nineteenth century, when it was still played in Paris, for example, in the Champs Elysées and the Luxembourg Gardens.

It is not known when *le jeu de paume* first crossed the Channel, but it was not later than the fourteenth century. The word 'tennis' is first recorded in 1399: 'Of the tenetz to winne or lese a chace' (Gower).

In 1414 the Dauphin of France gave Henry V some tennis balls — a valuable present — and, in Shakespeare's version of the chroniclers' report, received this by way of thanks:

We are glad the Dauphin is so pleasant with us;
His present and your pains we thank you for:
When we have match't our rackets to these balls,
We will, in France, by God's grace, play a set
Shall strike his father's crown into the hazard.
Tell him he hath made a match with such a wrangler
That all the courts of France will be disturb'd
With chases.

(*Henry V*, Act I, sc. ii)

A century later the King of Castile, on a visit to Windsor in 1505, played tennis against the Marquis of Dorset in the castle moat. The king, using a racket, beat the marquis, who played with his hand and received 15. This suggests that Englishmen were even then slow to adopt new continental practices.

At this period there were royal courts at Westminster, Woodstock, Shene (Richmond), Greenwich, Blackfriars (London), Wycombe, Rickmansworth, and Calais. Henry VIII added courts at Hampton Court, Whitehall, and St. James's, and there must have been many

humbler courts throughout the country. By 1558 a French traveller in England could write: 'Here you may commonly see artisans, such as hatters and joiners, playing at tennis for a crown, which is not often to be seen elsewhere, particularly on a working day.'

Despite taking his own marker, Anthony Ansley, with him on his progresses, Henry VIII lost heavily at tennis, as his privy purse expenses record. On 22 October 1532, for example, he paid out £46.13s.4d. to two opponents. A sum of this size and the phrase above, 'playing for a crown', indicate the extent to which tennis has been traditionally what horse racing is today: a vehicle for betting. It was common not only to play for money but for spectators to bet on games and even on each individual point. In later times the third Viscount Campden once lost £2,500 in one day at tennis, and it has been suggested, though not seriously, that if Henry VIII had been a better tennis-player he would not have needed to dissolve the monasteries.

By reason of the French connection, tennis came to Scotland independently of England and probably earlier. Known as *caitche* or *caitchspeel*, a corruption of its Flemish name, tennis was played in the thirteenth century during the reign of Alexander III. In 1539 James V built the still existing court at Falkland Palace, so that when the Stuarts succeeded to the English throne tennis was already a family game. Henry, Prince of Wales, the heir of James VI and I, shocked some courtiers by playing so immoderately that 'he sweated like an artisan'. Charles I played at Oxford during the Civil War. Charles II played regularly at six in the morning. James II was playing at the age of eight and, when he lost his throne, had the good fortune to spend his exile at St. Germain, where tennis was available.

The short tennis career of Henry, Prince of Wales, offers a reminder that games taken seriously arouse strong feelings. Tennis has been the occasion of a number of celebrated quarrels. In a dispute with the prince over a point the young Earl of Essex lost his temper and hit the heir to the throne on the head with his racket. At this period, too, Ireland makes a characteristic appearance in the history of tennis with a man killed in a sword fight after an argument in a tennis court in Dublin. In earlier times the Duke of Orléans, later Louis XII, had his ears boxed on court by the Duke of Lorraine, and another poor sportsman was the painter Caravaggio, who had to flee Rome after killing his opponent.

By 1620 there were 14 well-equipped courts in London. These were joined in 1635 by the famous James Street court, which became the headquarters of English tennis until it closed in 1866. Today James Street, off the Haymarket, is called Orange Street, and the court is commemorated there by a public house called the Hand and Racquet. Another seventeenth-century court is commemorated in Racquet Court, off Fleet Street.

Tennis has always had an intellectual appeal. Unlike other games it has enjoyed the advantage of many centuries in which to mature. Its subtleties and complexities are such that it requires almost as much mental application as chess, and Scaino is not the only writer who has thought it worthy of philosophic treatment. In 1767 de Garsault's *The Art of the Tennis Professional and of Tennis* was published by the French Royal Academy of Science. 'Tennis', this author claimed, 'is the only game which can rank with the arts and professions.'

From poets and philosophers the game has received uniformly respectful comment. Erasmus devoted one of his colloquies to tennis, and Swedenborg included it in his vision of Heaven. There are references in More's *Utopia* and Hobbes's *Leviathan* and in the works of Montaigne. Benvenuto Cellini played the game; so did Sir Philip Sidney, who in *Arcadia* refers to men 'like tennis balls, tossed by the rackets of the higher powers'. Rousseau and Goethe praised the game, and Hobbes played in old age to keep fit.

In French and English literature references to tennis are extensive. In Chaucer's *Troylus and Cryseyde* (*c.* 1380) we find: 'But canstow playen racket to and fro'. In 1435 Charles d'Orléans wrote a poem comparing life to a game of tennis, incidentally providing us with evidence of scoring in 15s more than a hundred years before Scaino. The poet-duke had two tennis courts of his own in his château at Blois and after being taken prisoner of war at Agincourt spent his confinement in Wingfield Castle, Suffolk, where he wrote the poem. By a coincidence of some magnitude it was a member of the Wingfield family who five centuries later was to invent lawn tennis.

Tennis is mentioned in six of Shakespeare's plays and frequently in Rabelais, who made Pantagruel a better performer in the tennis court than the law school. Pepys, as might be expected, showed an interest. On 4 January 1664 he recorded in his diary: 'To the Tennis Court, and there saw the King play at tennis and others; but to see how the King's play was extolled, without any cause at all, was a loathsome sight, though sometimes indeed, he did play very well, and deserved to be commended.'

From 1600 the game declined in France. One reason was that the *paumiers* who owned the courts found it more profitable to hire them out as theatres. When Molière went on tour in the provinces he acted in tennis courts and to this day the French theatre retains the shape of a tennis court. In England too tennis courts were used for theatrical performances and in London two courts in Lincoln's Inn Fields became theatres. Tennis courts were used also as gymnasia, for boxing and acrobatic displays, and for concerts and other spectacles and entertainments.

By the end of the eighteenth century the number of courts in the whole of France still used for tennis had dwindled to 50, 10 of which were in Paris. The game's patrons, royalty and aristocracy, had disappeared. On 20 June 1789 the French National Assembly, locked out of its chamber by the king, had met in the nearest convenient building at Versailles and sworn to give France a constitution in the so-called Oath of the Tennis Court. In London in 1797 *The Times* reported: 'The once fashionable game of tennis is very much upon the decline.' Outside France and England few courts were still used for play, although the game was alive in the larger cities: St. Petersburg, Madrid, Geneva, Brussels, and Turin.

The revival of tennis in the nineteenth century took place in England. This time there was no popular element, no 'sweating together of noblemen and peasants', as praised by Dekker in tennis's heyday. Tennis reverted to a game for the noble and the moneyed, and their hired professionals. Courts were built in country houses to provide amusement for their owners and guests. Between 1800 and 1850 they were erected at Crawley Court (near Winchester), Woburn, Stratfield Saye, Coombe Abbey, Hewell Grange, Theobald's, and Hatfield. Club courts were built in Brighton, at Lord's, and in Leamington.

The world championship at real tennis is the oldest of all world championships. It was first held by the Frenchman, Clergé, from *c.* 1740 to 1750 and, although by the nineteenth century the game in France was played only in Paris, Versailles, Fontainebleau, Bordeaux, Bayonne, and Draguignan, French professionals could still beat any player in England, with the single exception of Cox, world champion for ten years from 1819. BARRE, at first *paumier du roi* and later *paumier de l'empereur*, remained unbeaten from 1829 until 1862. In 1839 he was able to give half-thirty and a bisque to the best English player and beat him. Another *paumier*, Delahaye, known as 'Biboche', was the only other player in Barre's class. Both, in the true tennis tradition, made money by accepting challenges to play matches against odds. For a bet Barre once walked for ten hours from Fontainebleau to Paris, beat a challenger, and walked back the same day. Biboche won a match playing in National Guard uniform (heavy marching order).

Between 1850 and 1922 about 30 more courts were built in England — including three in Cambridge and two each at Queen's Club, Prince's Club, Newmarket, and Hardwick — as well as two in Ireland and one in Scotland. An English professional, Tompkins, at last beat Barre, and the age of serious competition between amateurs arrived with the inauguration of the M.C.C. tennis prizes (the Gold and Silver Racquet Cups) in 1867, followed by the amateur tennis championship at Queen's Club in 1888. Wars permitting, both have been annual events ever since, and these clubs have remained the two main centres of the game, although Hampton Court, where tennis has been played for nearly 450 years and where the Royal Tennis Court has a large membership, is recognized as the premier court. The courts at Prince's Club, in Knightsbridge, were destroyed during the Second World War.

The first leading amateur was Heathcote, who won the M.C.C. Gold Racquet for the first 15 years and twice subsequently. The Hon. A. Lyttelton was successful 12 times, until defeated by Miles, who took this prize 15 times and the amateur championship 7 times. Another amateur champion of this period was Sir Edward Grey, later Foreign Secretary. Since the First World War the outstanding English amateur has been BAERLEIN, who won ten Gold Racquets between 1921 and 1931 and 13 amateur championships between 1914 and 1930, and earned an equally impressive record at rackets. None of these amateurs could beat the leading professionals in championship play. At the turn of the century the best player at both tennis and rackets was LATHAM, a professional from Manchester, later at Queen's Club, who held the world championship at tennis from 1895 to 1905 and again in 1907-8. Latham lost his title to a fellow professional, 'Punch' Fairs of Prince's. Another professional, Covey, from Crabbet Park, succeeded Fairs and enjoyed the distinction of holding the title longer than Latham. The leading English player in recent years has been Angus, amateur champion and holder of the M.C.C. Gold Racquet since 1966 and British Open champion since 1970 (unbeaten up to 1974).

Australia. Samuel Smith Travers brought royal tennis to Australia. He had played at Oxford and James Street and took home with him to Hobart a professional from Oxford named Thomas Stone. In 1875 he published his *Treatise on Tennis*, founded the Hobart Tennis Club, and opened the first real tennis court to be built in the southern hemisphere. The club has flourished and nearly a hundred years later his descendants are still playing in the court he built.

A second court in Australia was opened in Exhibition Street, Melbourne, in 1882. It was built under the direction of T. Stone, who left Hobart and took over the management of the Melbourne Tennis Club (the prefix 'Royal' was granted by Queen Victoria in 1897). Like Hobart, this club has flourished, nourished by a trickle of English immigrants and Australian graduates returning from Oxford and Cambridge. In 1970 the membership of both clubs was higher than ever before: Melbourne 150 (original membership 33); Hobart 90 (31). After the sale of its premises the Melbourne club moved to the suburb of Richmond, where two new courts were opened in 1974.

The best Australian player, rivalled only by Woolmer Stone, son of Thomas and his father's successor as secretary and professional at Melbourne, has been Finch. Finch was the professional at Hobart from 1902 until 1965 — a comparable span to that of Johnson at Moreton Morrell, which lasted from the building of the court in 1906 until the year of his death, 1970. Australian Open champion from 1932 to 1947, Finch visited England in 1930, when he defeated Groom, the professional at Lord's, but was beaten narrowly by Johnson, then the leading English professional.

U.S.A. Tennis is mentioned in an edict of the governor of New York dated 1639, and in New York in 1763 a tennis court was offered for sale by auction. But the game effectively took root across the Atlantic with the opening of a private court in Buckingham Street, Boston, in 1876. This was the first of 18 courts built between that date and 1923, when the last court to be built in America opened in Chicago. Fifteen of these were built in the eastern states, in the Boston–New York–Philadelphia area.

The first Boston court was followed by one at the Newport Casino in 1880, and a second in Boston, built for the Athletic Association, opened in 1904. Meanwhile a court opened in New York on West 43rd Street in 1891, to be followed by a second on the same site in 1904. Private courts were built at Lakewood, New Jersey (for George Gould, 1900) and at Roslyn, L.I. (for Clarence Mackay, 1909). Further club courts were opened in Massachusetts by the Myopia Hunt Club at Hamilton, in 1902, and by the Harvard Athletic Association in Cambridge, in 1907. A first attempt to establish tennis in Chicago was made with the building of a court by the Athletic Association in 1893. This closed in 1901 and the attempt made in 1923 by the Racquet Club was also unsuccessful.

None of the courts mentioned above is still in use for play. Of the seven surviving as tennis courts, the earliest is the luxurious Tuxedo Club court, the first in America to be built with Bickley's cement. It opened in 1900 at a cost of $80,000, and the Tuxedo Gold Racquet is still one of the most prized trophies in American court tennis. The only court in the South opened at Aiken, South Carolina, in 1903. The Boston Tennis and Racquet Club court on Boylston Street opened in 1904, the Philadelphia court in 1907, and the two courts of the New York Racquet and Tennis Club at 370 Park Avenue in 1918. In 1915 the Whitney family outdid not only the French and English kings but also the Guinness family, whose Dublin court was made of black marble, by building the most palatial of courts, at Manhasset, L.I., at a reputed cost of $250,000.

Professionals were needed to look after these courts, to teach the game, to mark matches, string rackets and cover balls. They were available in England, and members of the famous families who had provided tennis professionals down the generations — Whites, Tompkinses, Foresters, and Johnsons — were readily enticed across the Atlantic. An American became more famous than any of them. Born in England, PETTITT was an immigrant boy in Boston when the very first court opened, employed to help in the dressing room and generally assist the professional who had been brought from Oxford. Nine years later he established himself as the best player in the world.

The other American tennis prodigy began playing at the age of 12. As rich as Pettitt was poor, JAY GOULD, the son of George Gould, learned the game from Forester in his father's court at Lakewood and became world champion. Three more amateurs, all Americans, have held the world championship since Gould. Knox, who was also an international POLO player, was unbeaten from 1959 until he retired in 1969, when G. H. Bostwick, jr., also a notable polo player and golfer, defeated Willis, the Manchester professional and English Open champion, for the vacant title. In 1972 Bostwick was defeated by his brother, J. F. C Bostwick. Another world champion long resident in America is the Basque, ETCHEBASTER, head professional in New York since 1930.

The total number of courts in play throughout the world was 50 in 1900, 60 in 1930, and 29 in 1974. Real tennis is now confined to five countries: England, Scotland, the U.S.A., France, and Australia. Only three new courts were opened after the First World War — one in England (Rustall, near Tunbridge Wells), one in Ireland (Lambay Island), and one in America (Chicago). All were built in the early 1920s and none is now in play. Since the Second World War only two new courts have been built, both in Australia. Few are likely to be built in future, but there are several still standing which could be brought back into play, including one in the University of Leningrad built at the time of Catherine the Great.

Real tennis courts in use throughout the world in 1974 were located as follows (date of building in brackets):

England (15): Hampton Court Palace, London (1530); Oxford: Merton Street (1798); Hatfield House, Hertfordshire (1843); Leamington: Bedford Street (1846); Cambridge: Grange Road (1866); Petworth House, Sussex (1876); Canford School, Dorset (1879); Manchester: Blackfriars Road, Salford (1880); Queen's Club, London: 2 courts (1888); Holyport Grange, Maidenhead (1890); Lord's Cricket Ground (M.C.C.), London (1900); Moreton Morrell, Warwickshire (1906); Hardwick House, Oxfordshire (1907); Hayling Island: Sea Court (1912).

Scotland (2): Falkland Palace, Fifeshire (1538); Troon, Ayrshire: Sun Court (1905).

France (2): Bordeaux: Rue Rolland (1760); Paris: Rue Lauriston (1909).

Australia (3): Hobart, Tasmania: Davy Street (1875); Richmond, Victoria: Sherwood Street: 2 courts (1974).

U.S.A. (7): Tuxedo, N.Y.: Tuxedo Club (1900); Aiken, South Carolina: Tennis Club (1903); Boston: Tennis and Racquet Club (1904); Philadelphia: Racquet Club (1907); Manhasset, L.I., N.Y.: John Hay Whitney (1915); New York: Racquet and Tennis Club: 2 courts (1918).

Other courts still standing, but not in use for play, include: second courts in Paris and Cambridge (squash courts); Chicago (bowling alley); second court in Chicago (indoor lawn tennis); Leningrad (the university gymnasium), Lakewood, New Jersey (girls' college gymnasium), Hewell Grange, Worcestershire (Borstal gymnasium); Newport, Rhode Island (changing-rooms); Bridport, Lambay Island (in Dublin Bay), and second court at Hardwick (all farm sheds); Fontainebleau and the Myopia Hunt Club near Boston, Massachusetts (used for storage); Brighton (garage); Bath (trunk factory); St. Stephen's Green, Dublin (government offices); Eamont Bridge, Cumberland (warehouse); Versailles, and two courts in the Tuileries Gardens in Paris (museums); Stockholm, and Heythrop House, Oxfordshire (chapels); and Shipbourne, Kent (battery hens). Three famous English ducal courts finally disappeared in the 1950s: the Duke of Wellington's at Stratfield Saye, the Duke of Bedford's at Woburn, and the Duke of Richmond and Gordon's at Goodwood.

The number of real tennis players is not easy to estimate. It is probably in the region of 2,000, the majority playing in England where most of the courts are located. Tennis is therefore very much a minority game, but it is far from dying. The number of players, amount of play, and enthusiasm for the game in the 1970s is probably greater than at any time during the previous two centuries. In 1878, for instance, there were 21 courts in England, some of them little used. Today there are six fewer, but most are used more intensively than ever before.

A constant supply of recruits comes from the two senior universities. At Oxford the game has been played for at least 500 years. Four courts are recorded as being in use in 1508, and later most colleges had their own. At Cambridge the first record of tennis is in 1637. Now each university has only one court. There has been an annual university match since 1859. Unlike rackets, which many tennis players play or have played, real tennis is not a school game. Eton and Winchester had courts in 1600, but Canford, sited in a former country house, is the only school with one today.

On leaving university, real tennis enthusiasts find courts available in London at Queen's Club, Hampton Court, and, for members of the M.C.C., at Lord's. The owners of courts at Hatfield and at Holyport, near Maidenhead, allow them to be used as clubs. In the north there is the Manchester Tennis and Racket Club; in the Midlands there are clubs at Leamington and Moreton Morrell; in the south, at Petworth and on Hayling Island; in Scotland, at Troon.

The game requires professionals as well as amateurs. The *paumier* is essential to its survival, and strenuous efforts have been made since the Second World War to attract new young professionals and assure them of a good career in the game. Once a court is built and sufficient members attracted to pay for a professional, tennis, although associated — particularly in America — with the rich, is not an exceptionally expensive game.

Lord Aberdare, *The Story of Tennis* (1959); E. M. Baerlein, 'Tennis' in *Rackets, Squash Rackets, Tennis, Fives and Badminton* (The Lonsdale Library, 1936); P. Barcellon, *Règles et principes de la Paume* (1800); Eugène Chapus, *Le Jeu de Paume, son histoire et sa description* (1862) (sometimes wrongly attributed to Edouard Fournier); Allison Danzig, *The Racquet Game* (1930); de Garsault, *L'Art du Paumier-Raquetier et de la Paume* (1767; English trans. 1938); Albert de Luze, *La Magnifique Histoire du Jeu de Paume* (1933); de Manivieux, *Traité sur la connaissance du royal Jeu de la Paume* (1783); Forbet, *L'Utilité qui provient du Jeu de la Paulme au corps et à l'esprit* (1599); J. M. Heathcote, 'Tennis' in *Tennis, Lawn Tennis, Rackets, Fives* (The Badminton Library, 1890); C. Hulpeau, *Le Jeu Royal de la Paulme* (1632); R. Lukin, *Treatise on Tennis* (1822); Julian Marshall, *The Annals of Tennis* (1878); E. B. Noel and J. O. M. Clark, *A History of Tennis* (1924); Jeremy Potter, *Hazard Chase* (a novel, 1964); Antonio Scaino, *Trattato del Givoco della Palla* (1555, English trans. 1951); Samuel Smith Travers, *Treatise on Tennis* (1875); Malcolm D. Whitman, *Tennis Origins and Mysteries* (1932).

GOVERNING BODY (U.K.): Tennis and Rackets Association, York House, 37 Queen Square, London W.C 1; (U.S.A.): United States Court Tennis Association, c/o The Racquet and Tennis Club, 370 Park Avenue, New York, N.Y. 10023, U.S.A.; (FRANCE): Fédération Française de Lawn Tennis, 15 Rue Téhéran, Paris 8, France.

REBOT, see PELOTA.

REBOUND TUMBLING, see TRAMPOLINING.

RECKITT, MAURICE BEVERLEY (1888-), English CROQUET player and president of the Croquet Association. As a player he was never in the highest grade but he won the men's championship twice, the open doubles four times, and the mixed doubles five times, and made fifteen appearances in the President's Cup. His main contribution however is as a chronicler and observer of croquet and its players. He is the author of *Croquet Today* (1956) and a number of unpublished comments on croquet in the archives of the Croquet Association.

RED STAR BELGRADE, Association FOOTBALL club. The club did not exist in its present form, with affiliation to Belgrade University, until 1945, but it may be considered as something of a successor to the prewar Jugoslavija club who had been Yugoslavian champions in 1924 and 1925. The Red Star club first won the national League championship in 1951 and by the end of the 1973 season had gained nine more championship titles. It has not enjoyed the same success in the European club championship but reached the semi-final stage in 1957, and again in 1971. Leading players have included Beara, MITIC, Sekularac, and DZAJIC.

COLOURS: Red and white striped shirts, white shorts.

REES, DAVID JAMES, C.B.E. (1913-), Welsh professional golfer. In a playing career spanning more than 35 years, Rees, small, volatile, and employing the unfashionable two-handed grip, won every honour British GOLF has to offer, except the one every player wants most, the Open. He made ten RYDER

CUP appearances, five as captain, and captained the Professional Golfers Association in 1967. He was prominent in golfing educational programmes.

REID, JOHN RICHARD, O.B.E. (1928-), cricketer for New Zealand, Otago, and Wellington. One of the finest batsmen produced by New Zealand, he played in 58 Tests. Physically strong, he preferred to attack the bowling (his 15 sixes in an innings of 296 for Wellington in 1962-3 broke the world record), but frequently for New Zealand he had to bat cautiously in adversity. He became New Zealand captain in 1955-6 and led them to their first ever Test victory, against West Indies. On the 1961-2 tour of South Africa he made a record 1,915 runs.

REIMANN, HANS-GEORG (1941-), a race walker for East Germany. Winner of the LUGANO CUP 20 km. in 1970 and 1973, Reimann had made an impressive international début when finishing a close second in the European 20 km. in 1962. At the same distance he has since obtained a third in the Olympics in 1972 and finished fifth in the European event in 1969 and 1971. He has been a very consistent big-time performer over the past decade whose style and technique have improved with time.

REIMS CIRCUIT. This famous MOTOR RACING track, consisting originally of public roads, has been the scene of many major races. Until 1951 it extended to the village of Gueux, but it was then changed in two major stages. In 1952 the village itself was by-passed by a new link road running from the end of the finishing straight to the Virage de la Hovette. For the 1953 race this link road was extended so that an uphill stretch ran on to join the Soissons–Reims road about a half-mile further towards Soissons. A new hairpin bend known as the Virage de Muizon was incorporated. The length of the circuit in its present form is 5·19 miles (8·35 km.).

REIMS F.C., Association FOOTBALL club. Formed in 1931, the club turned professional in 1935 after winning the amateur club championship of France, and was elected to the Second Division of the French League. When football was resumed in France in the season 1945-6, Reims made its first appearance in the First Division and soon emerged as an outstanding club side, winning the League championship in 1949, the Cup in 1950, the championship in 1953 and 1955, both Cup and championship in 1958, and the championship in 1960 and 1962. Reims appeared in the first competition for the European Champion Clubs Cup and was beaten in the final by REAL MADRID by only 4-3. Three years later Reims reached the final of the competition and was again beaten by Real Madrid. Most of the club's outstanding players, who have included Colonna, Jonquet, KOPA, Vincent, Penverne, FONTAINE, and Muller, were members of the slightly changed sides that were so successful in the French championship between 1955 and 1962. Such players could not be easily replaced and at the end of the season 1963-4 Reims were relegated to the Second Division and did not regain senior status until 1970-1.

COLOURS: Red shirts with white sleeves, white shorts.

RELANCE (1952) can justly claim to be one of the most remarkable brood mares in bloodstock-breeding history, being the dam of three outstanding French race-horses, MATCH III, RELKO, and RELIANCE. She was bred and owned by DUPRÉ, being by Relic (son of War Relic by MAN O' WAR) out of Polaire (tracing back to SCEPTRE).

RELAY RUNNING. The relay is a team race usually involving four athletes running in sequence. Each runner carries a cylindrical metal or wooden baton for the duration of his allotted stage, passing it to the next runner and so on until the course is completed. The 4 × 100 metres and 4 × 400 metres relays figure in the men's programme at all major ATHLETICS championships. The shorter relay is run by women, and in 1969 the 4 × 400 metres for women was first introduced internationally in the EUROPEAN CHAMPIONSHIPS. The International Amateur Athletic Federation (see ATHLETICS, TRACK AND FIELD) recognizes world records by men at the distances mentioned as well as the 4 × 110, 4 × 220, 4 × 440, 4 × 880 yards, and 4 × 1 mile, and for the 4 × 800 and 4 × 1,500 metres. Women's records are recognized at all the above distances except the 4 × 1,500 metres and 4 × 1 mile.

Shuttle relays are occasionally contested, in which the athlete completes his stage and alerts by touch the runner taking the next stage in the adjacent lane, who runs back in the opposite direction. This is the only practicable method in hurdles relay races. Medley relays consisting of four stages of increasing or alternating length are other variations of this activity. (See also SPRINTING, ROAD RUNNING.)

RELIANCE (1962), a race-horse by TANTIÈME out of RELANCE, bred and owned by DUPRÉ, trained by MATHET, and ridden by SAINT-MARTIN. He won five of his six races, including the French Grand Prix, Derby, and St. Leger, and £167,851.

RELIANCE TRIAL, see MOTOR-CYCLE TRIALS.

RELKO (1960), a champion French racehorse by Tanerko (son of TANTIÈME) out of RELANCE, bred and owned by DUPRÉ, trained by MATHET, and ridden by SAINT-MARTIN. He won nine races, including the GRAND PRIX DE SAINT-CLOUD, PRIX GANAY, French St. Leger, French Two Thousand Guineas, English DERBY, and CORONATION CUP, and £151,004 stake money.

REMFRY, KEITH (1947-), British heavyweight JUDO fighter who was a bronze medallist at the 1971 and 1973 world championships. After showing promise as a youngster — he was runner-up in the 1968 European junior championships — he won a gold medal with the British team at the 1971 European championships. Then at the world championships the same year he created one of the biggest upsets in the history of the sport when he threw and held-down Kaneo Iwatsuri, the reigning all-Japan champion. In 1973 he was second in the European championships.

REMONTE, see PELOTA.

RENSHAW, WILLIAM CHARLES (1861-1904), an English player generally regarded as 'the father of modern LAWN TENNIS', the strongest and most brilliant competitor of his day. With his twin brother, ERNEST, he did more than anyone else to attract attention to the game's spectacular and exciting possibilities. He took the ball early — the 'Renshaw smash' was celebrated — he drove with great power and precision, and his contemporaries particularly feared his cut which skidded backhand down the line.

William Renshaw's record of seven singles victories at WIMBLEDON stands supreme, and he and Ernest, who won the singles in 1888, won the doubles seven times. They were both remarkable athletes, but William, more forceful and more determined, always won when they met on important occasions, notably in the challenge rounds at Wimbledon in 1882, 1883, and 1889. His first success there was devastating — a 6-0, 6-1, 6-1 defeat of Hartley in the challenge round. The brothers played at Wimbledon for the last time in 1893 when they were drawn to meet in the first round. William withdrew, but Ernest lost to Mahony in the second round. After the Renshaws' retirement, the crowds at Wimbledon declined for a time and there were many complaints that the glamour had gone from the game.

RESTON, HARRY (1913-), Scottish lawn BOWLS player whose exuberant style and methods during the 1966 world championships at KYEEMAGH, N.S.W., helped rank him as the best skip in the world. He and his colleagues finished third in the fours event. His irrepressible antics when chasing his bowls up the green led to two special committee meetings at the world championships (running on the green is forbidden in Australia), but these cavortings were so popular with the crowds that they were not stopped. As a singles player Reston has won the Scottish indoor championship (see BOWLS, INDOOR) three times.

REVSON, PETER (1937-74), American MOTOR RACING driver who was CAN-AM Challenge Cup champion in 1971, winning five races, the first American to win the title. He finished fifth in the 1969 INDIANAPOLIS 500 after starting thirty-third. In 1972, he placed fifth in the world drivers' (Grand Prix) championship and won the 1973 British and Canadian Grands Prix. He died in an accident while practising for the South African Grand Prix at Kyalami.

REYNDERS, YVONNE (1937-), Belgian track and road cyclist winner of 12 world championship medals during the period 1959-66. In the women's pursuit, she won three gold and three silver medals; in the road race, four gold and two silver.

REYNOLDS, JOHN, Association footballer for Distillery, West Bromwich Albion, ASTON VILLA, Ireland, and England. An extraordinarily clever right half, he had an unusual distinction in British football. After playing five times for Ireland in international matches in 1890 and 1891, he joined West Bromwich Albion and played for England against Scotland in 1892. In the same year he gained his first F.A. Cup-winners medal when Albion beat Aston Villa in the final; then he joined Aston Villa and while with them won two more F.A. Cup-winners medals.

REYNOLDS, LESLIE (1906-61), greyhound trainer for WEMBLEY STADIUM. He stamped himself as the supreme specialist in preparing classic greyhounds, training five GREYHOUND DERBY winners between 1948 and 1954 — Priceless Border, Narrogar Ann, Ballylanigan Tanist, Endless Gossip, and Paul's Fun, a feat never equalled.

REYNOLDS, RICHARD (1915-), Australian Rules footballer. Playing for Essendon in the VICTORIAN FOOTBALL LEAGUE as a rover and later as a half-forward flanker, he won three CHARLES BROWNLOW MEDALS, in 1934, 1937, and 1938. He also won the Essendon club's 'best and fairest' award six times. He was captain and coach of Essendon through four premiership wins, and he also captained Victoria in many inter-state and carnival-winning sides. His career spanned 19 seasons and he played 320 games from 1933 to 1951. This was a League record until it was broken in 1970 by WHITTEN, the captain and coach of Footscray. Reynolds also coached Essendon for 20 years and West Torrens in the South Australian Football League.

RHEINGOLD (1969), race-horse trained by Hills and ridden by Johnson when beaten a short head by PIGGOTT on Roberto in the 1972 DERBY. Ridden by Piggott, he won the 1973 PRIX DE L'ARC DE TRIOMPHE and became Europe's top stakes winner.

RHODES, WILFRED (1877-1973), cricketer for England and Yorkshire. In a career extending from 1898 to 1930 he took 4,187 wickets (a record aggregate) and made almost 40,000 runs. He took 100 wickets in a season on 23 occasions, and he did the 'double' 16 times — record performances which place him among the greatest all-rounders, although during his long career the emphasis shifted at intervals from bowling to batting. Originally solely a left-arm slow bowler (taking 154 wickets in 1898), he gradually moved up to become an opening batsman, and partnered HOBBS in several high stands in Test matches, including a record of 323 for the first wicket against Australia in 1911-12. He had already set a *last* wicket record of 130 with Foster in 1903-4. In 1902 he took 7 for 17 when Australia collapsed for 36, and in the following series his wily bowling captured 15 wickets in the second Test, at MELBOURNE. Even in 1926, when he was 48, his skills were enlisted in the deciding Test at the OVAL. His 4 wickets for 44 runs had much to do with England's victory.

RHODES CENTENARY MATCH, see SHOOTING, RIFLE: SERVICE CALIBRE.

RIBOT (1952), most famous of all Italian race-horses, by Tenerani, won all his 16 races, including the GRAN PREMIO DI MILANO, GRAN PREMIO DEL JOCKEY CLUB, PRIX DE L'ARC DE TRIOMPHE twice, and KING GEORGE VI AND QUEEN ELIZABETH STAKES. He was the first European horse to win the equivalent of over £100,000 in first-prize money and was rightly dubbed at the time 'the best horse in the world'. Ribot was bred in Italy by Tesio, raced in partnership by his widow and the Marchese

M. Incisa della Rocchetta, trained by Penco, and ridden by CAMICI. At stud, at Darby Dan Farm, Lexington, Kentucky, Ribot proved an outstanding sire.

RICHARD, MAURICE (1921-   ), ICE HOCKEY player for MONTREAL CANADIENS from 1942 to 1961; in that time he scored 626 goals. His forte was shooting and his assists were less frequent. An uncompromising winger, he had an exciting and constant sense of urgency and a particularly fast and low left-handed shot. In his scoring ability he was second only to G. HOWE. In the 1944-5 season he became the first NATIONAL HOCKEY LEAGUE player to score 50 goals in a season.

RICHARDS, Sir GORDON (1904-   ) was champion jockey in England 26 times from 1925 to 1953, except 1926 (Weston), 1930 (Fox), and 1941 (Wragg). His classic winners were Pinza in the DERBY and KING GEORGE VI AND QUEEN ELIZABETH STAKES; Rose of England and Sun Chariot in the OAKS; Singapore, Chumleigh, Turkhan, Sun Chariot, and Tehran in the ST. LEGER; Pasch, Big Game, and Tudor Minstrel in the TWO THOUSAND GUINEAS; and Sun Chariot, Queenpot, and Belle of All in the ONE THOUSAND GUINEAS. Richards beat the record of 246 winning mounts in a season set by ARCHER in 1885, by riding 259 winners in 1933, a feat which he surpassed in 1947 with 269 victories. During his career in the saddle he rode 4,870 winners out of 21,828 mounts.

RICHARDS, the Revd. ROBERT E. (1926-   ), pole vaulter for the U.S.A. The first man to win the Olympic pole vault twice, Richards was the world's leading performer for most of the decade preceding the fibreglass era. He won Olympic gold medals in 1952 and 1956 and Pan-American titles in 1951 and 1955. His best performances were 15 ft. 5 in. (4·70 m.) outdoors and 15 ft. 6 in. (4·72 m.) indoors. However, he failed to match the long-standing world record of WARMERDAM.

RICHARDSON, ANTHONY (1933-   ), secretary of the British Water Ski Federation from 1964 to 1972 and a member of the British and English teams from 1961 to 1963; he competed in the cross-Channel race in 1967 and was British ski kite-flying champion in 1970.

RICHARDSON, ERNIE (1932-   ), Canadian curler. With his family rink of Arnold, Garnet, and Wes Richardson, he won the Canadian and world CURLING championships, in 1959, 1960, 1962, and 1963.

RICHARDSON, THOMAS (1870-1912), cricketer for England, Surrey, and Somerset. Large, well-built, and with extraordinary reserves of stamina, he bowled fast for Surrey—for several seasons in partnership with LOCKWOOD—frequently, even on the hardest pitch, dismissing the world's finest batsmen with startling break-backs. In four seasons (1894-7) he took a total of 1,005 wickets, always using only the original ball for the innings, and in only 14 Tests he took 88 wickets.

RICHEY, BETTY, a member of the United States LACROSSE team for 22 consecutive years and a reserve for 3 years afterwards. She was an extremely versatile attack player known for the variety and accuracy of her shooting. For many years she served as a national selector and was twice elected president of the U.S. Women's Lacrosse Association.

RICHMOND, KENNETH (1926-   ), the only British wrestler to win an Olympic medal since the Second World War. Although frequently giving away 4 stone (25·5 kg.) in international heavyweight competitions, he took part in the 1948 Olympics, reaching fifth place in the Graeco-Roman event, only three years after starting wrestling. Four years later at Helsinki he lost a split decision to the Russian winner of the freestyle class, Mekokishvili, but was rewarded with a bronze medal. In 1954 he won the COMMONWEALTH GAMES gold medal in Vancouver and the following year his ability at grappling sports was further demonstrated when he was picked for the British team for the 1955 European JUDO championships. He narrowly failed to win another medal at the 1956 Olympics and was ninth in the Rome Games, after which he retired.

RICHMOND F.C., RUGBY UNION football club formed in 1861 and, with BLACKHEATH, a prime mover in the founding of the Rugby Football Union ten years later. Both the first R.F.U. president, Rutter, and the first hon. sec., Ash, were from the Richmond club. Prominent Richmond players include Rotherham, Temple Gurdon, N. M. Hall, and Kininmonth.

HOME GROUND: Richmond Athletic Ground, Surrey.
COLOURS: Old gold, red, and black jerseys, navy shorts.

RICKARD, GEORGE (Tex) (1871-1929), American BOXING promoter responsible for the first million-dollar gate contest between DEMPSEY and CARPENTIER for the world heavyweight championship in 1921. A former

cowboy, gold-prospector, and saloon-owner, Rickard's first major promotion was the world lightweight championship between GANS and NELSON at Goldfield, Nevada, in 1906. Altogether Rickard promoted five bouts which each grossed more than a million dollars before his death. He was succeeded as the leading promoter in the U.S.A. by his assistant, Jacobs, who promoted successfully at MADISON SQUARE GARDEN, New York, from 1937 to 1949.

RICKEY, WESLEY BRANCH (1881-1965), American BASEBALL administrator for several major-league clubs and an innovator who had a lasting influence on both the structure and character of Organized Baseball. In the 1920s he introduced the 'farm system', a plan that altered the economic structure of Organized Baseball, and his employment of a Negro, JACKIE ROBINSON, as a player for the BROOKLYN DODGERS in 1947, changed the social character of the professional game.

RIERA, FERNANDO (1922-   ), Chilean Association FOOTBALL coach and manager. Riera played professional football in France. He managed Chile's third-place team in the 1962 World Cup and the F.I.F.A. XI against England at WEMBLEY, 1963. He was also in charge of the BENFICA team which lost the 1963 European final.

RIFLE SHOOTING, see SHOOTING, RIFLE: SERVICE CALIBRE and SMALL-BORE.

RIGBY, CATHY (1953-   ), the only American female gymnast to have won a medal in the world championships. She showed amazing precocity by competing in the 1968 OLYMPIC GAMES as a 15-year-old, having qualified by finishing fifth in the Olympic trials and the Amateur Athletic Union championships. Standing only 4 ft. 10 in. (1·47 m.) and weighing barely 6 st. 6 lb. (41 kg.), she impressed everyone with her maturity on the big occasion. At the 1970 world championships she took advantage of a number of her rival's mistakes to win the silver medal in the beam behind Zuchold (East Germany).

RIGHT ROYAL V (1958), a race-horse by Owen Tudor, out of a mare tracing to QUIVER, bred in France and owned by Mme Couturié, trained by POLLET, and ridden by POINCELET. Right Royal V won seven races, including the French Derby (beating MATCH III), French Two Thousand Guineas, Prix Lupin, and KING GEORGE VI AND QUEEN ELIZABETH STAKES (beating ST. PADDY), and £102,357.

RIMET, JULES, see FOOTBALL, ASSOCIATION.

RING TENNIS, known also as tenikoit, is a combination of tennis and quoits that also closely resembles DECK TENNIS, the most popular of all DECK GAMES. It can be played by two or four players in either singles or doubles, and, as with deck tennis, it can be

RING TENNIS COURT

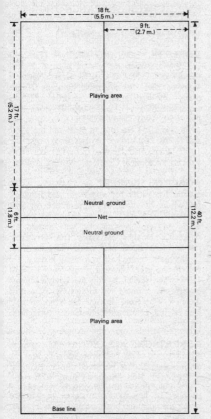

18 ft.
(5.5 m.)

9 ft.
(2.7 m.)

Playing area

17 ft.
(5.2 m.)

Neutral ground

Net

Neutral ground

6 ft.
(1.8 m.)

40 ft.
(12.2 m.)

Playing area

Base line

played in a much smaller area than LAWN TENNIS.

The size of a court is influenced by the space available and the recommended dimensions vary from 10 × 22 ft. (3 × 6·7 m.), through 12 × 30 ft. (3·7 × 9·1 m.) or 14 × 36 ft. (4·3 × 10·97 m.), to 18 × 40 ft. (5·5 × 12·2 m.). Whatever the size of the court, however, there must be a neutral space extending 3 ft. (0·9 m.) on each side of the net. The

playing area between the neutral space and the base line is then divided into four quarters, somewhat similar to the layout of a lawn tennis court but without tram-lines and with the dividing line extending to the base line. A ring tennis court with the over-all dimensions 18 ft. × 40 ft. would thus be divided into four areas each measuring 9 ft. (2·7 m.) (half the over-all width) by 17 ft. (5·2 m.) long (half the over-all length less 3 ft. (0·9 m.) neutral ground). A net, 5 ft. (1·5 m.) from the ground, is erected across the centre of the court so as to leave the 3 ft. of neutral ground on either side.

The duration of a game can be varied to suit the convenience or preference of players but it usually consists of 15 points, except that if the score reaches 14-all the game continues until one player, or pair of players in a doubles game, gains a 2-point lead. Most popularly, a rubber of three games is played, but again this may be varied by agreement among the players.

Factory-produced rubber rings are now generally used and their availability, cheapness, and durability have contributed to the increase in popularity of such games as ring tennis.

At the beginning of each game the first service is taken from behind the base line in the right-hand court, the ring being served diagonally across the court as in lawn tennis. The opponent receiving the service endeavours to catch the ring and to return it across the net to the service side where either player may try to catch and return it. Play continues until the ring is not caught and falls to the ground within the playing area; is touched but not caught by a player; is caught but is not then thrown back fairly, either going into the net and landing on the ground 'out of bounds'; or is caught unfairly, that is to say other than with one hand. In such cases, when the play becomes 'dead', a point is gained by the non-offending player or pair, except that, if the point is scored by the receiving side, the service may be exchanged with no score being recorded or, alternatively, the score may be recorded but the service remain unchanged, according to the decision of the point-winning, receiving side.

No player may stand over the line marking the neutral space on either side of the net, and if the ring falls within the neutral ground, although it has crossed the net in service, it is a fault against the serving side. It follows that, since the ring ceases to be in play if and when it touches the ground, the surface of the court, providing that it is free of hazards to the players, does not have to give the relatively true and consistent bounce essential for playing either lawn tennis or PADDER TENNIS.

BEACH TENNIS can be played with the same equipment and to the same rules as ring tennis, but often the only equipment used is the rubber ring. However, even when, as an expedient, the net is dispensed with, a more satisfactory game results from insisting upon a neutral space on either side of the centre line, and in following some of the 'unwritten laws' that have become accepted as necessary for a fair game of ring tennis or deck tennis. These include that a player, having caught the ring, should not hold it unnecessarily; that, although both forehand and backhand deliveries are permitted, the ring should not be thrown overhand nor from a height above the shoulder; that it should be delivered in an upwards direction for at least 6 in. (152 mm.) after leaving the hand; and that feinting at delivery is a form of gamesmanship generally frowned upon.

Basically, ring tennis and its variations are lighthearted games that can be enjoyed by players of all ages once they have learnt the knack of catching the ring. The game can be played much more seriously and competitively by skilled players using the familiar tennis techniques of drawing their opponents across the court, and then, quickly and accurately, throwing the ring to unguarded spaces.

RISMAN, AUGUSTUS JOHN (1911-   ), RUGBY LEAGUE player, whose distinguished career stretched from 1928-9 till 1954-5. A Welshman, he signed for SALFORD at the age of 19 and won every honour open to him. He played against Australia 12 times and toured that country in 1932, 1936, and 1946, on the last occasion as captain. He led Salford's successful team of the late 1930s. Equally accomplished at centre or full-back, Risman also had outstanding qualities of leadership. He later became a coach.

RIVER PLATE, Association FOOTBALL club, Buenos Aires. Founded in 1901, River Plate initially played in the Uruguayan League but subsequently won the 'outlaw' Argentinian championship in 1920 and 1932 before winning the approved national championship 11 times between 1936 and 1957. The club often finished in second place but as such qualified for entry, together with the national champions, in the South American competition for 'champion' clubs and reached the final in 1966 when PENAROL were the winners. Leading players have included ORSI, Ferreyra, Moreno, Labruna, Rossi, Loustau, DI STEFANO, Sivori, E. Onega, Artime, and Mas.

COLOURS: White shirts with a broad red diagonal band, black shorts.

ROAD BOWLING, see BOWL-PLAYING.

ROAD RACING, see MOTOR RACING; MOTOR-CYCLE RACING.

ROAD RUNNING usually takes the form of long-distance relays. The English Amateur Athletic Association organizes two national road relays, one of 12 stages and one of 6. The stages are between two and four miles and the competition is on an inter-club basis. Apart from major marathon championships, the most important international event is the São Paulo Road Race staged annually in Brazil on New Year's Eve. (See also MARATHON.)

ROBERTS, EDWARD GLENN (Fireball) (1929-64), American MOTOR RACING driver, winner of 32 N.A.S.C.A.R. Grand National stock-car races but never the champion. He set many one-lap qualifying records and, on super-speedways, won the 1962 Daytona 500; the 1959, 1962, and 1963 Daytona 400s; the 1958 and 1963 Darlington 500s and the 1957 and 1959 300-milers at that track; and the 1960 Atlanta 400. He died of burns received in a racing accident at Charlotte, North Carolina.

ROBERTS, HERBERT (fl. 1929-36), Association footballer for ARSENAL, and England for whom he made one appearance (against Scotland in 1931). Tall, red-haired but phlegmatic in temperament, he was signed by Arsenal's manager, CHAPMAN, from Oswestry for a mere £200 and made into the first 'policeman' centre half in football history. He was in the great Arsenal teams from 1929 to 1936 when the club won the League championship four times and three times played in the F.A. Cup final. In time his 'stopper' role was copied, often with reluctance, throughout the world.

ROBERTSON, ALLAN (1815-58), generally accepted as the first professional golfer, as distinct from the raffish breed of player-caddie of the day. A St. Andrews man, Robertson was a noted maker of leather balls. As a player he was unsurpassed in his time and, according to legend, was never beaten in a money match played on level terms. He died two years before the inauguration of the Open championship and before the popularization of stroke play. Without records of his scoring to compare, an assessment of his skills must be left to eye-witnesses but, according to such reports, he can be classified alongside such an acknowledged master as VARDON.

ROBERTSON, JAMES BELL (1860-1940), HORSE RACING journalist, who wrote for the

Sporting Chronicle and the *Sunday Times* under the pen-name of 'Mankato'. He was a leading exponent of the theory of male dominance in the pedigree of the race-horse.

ROBERTSON, OSCAR (1938-), American BASKETBALL player. Robertson enjoyed an outstanding college career, during which he captained the U.S.A. gold medal-winning team at the 1960 OLYMPIC GAMES in Rome. At the time of his graduation from Cincinnati University in 1960, he was the third highest scorer in college history. He turned professional with the CINCINNATI ROYALS in 1961, and became known as the 'Big O'. He was voted the most valuable player at two consecutive All-Star games. He moved to the MILWAUKEE BUCKS in 1970, and helped them win the NATIONAL BASKETBALL ASSOCIATION championship the following season.

ROBERTSON, W. F., see ICE HOCKEY.

ROBESON, PETER (1929-), British show jumping (see EQUESTRIAN EVENTS) rider. Reserve to the gold medal team of 1952 (with the home-bred mare Craven A), he made his Olympic début four years later in Stockholm, where he rode Scorchin to win a team bronze medal. Always a perfectionist, he spent about four years reschooling the former Scottish points champion, Great Expectations, which he bought in 1957 and renamed Firecrest. His patience was rewarded with numerous international successes, which included an individual bronze medal at the Tokyo OLYMPIC GAMES in 1964.

ROBINSON, BRIAN (1930-), British professional road-race cyclist, forerunner of those, like SIMPSON, who built successful careers with continental teams in the 1950s and 1960s. His chief successes were to win a stage in the 1959 TOUR DE FRANCE by 20 min. 6 sec., and the mountainous *Dauphiné Libéré* stage race of 1961.

ROBINSON, FRANK (1935-), American BASEBALL outfielder for the CINCINNATI REDS of the NATIONAL LEAGUE, the BALTIMORE ORIOLES of the AMERICAN LEAGUE, and other major-league clubs, from 1956. In 1966 he was American League batting champion and also won the so-called triple crown by leading the league in batting average, runs batted in, and home runs. During his career he hit more than 500 home runs, and was the only player ever elected Most Valuable Player in both major leagues, the National (1961) and the American (1966).

ROBINSON, JACK ROOSEVELT (1919-72), American BASEBALL infielder for the BROOKLYN DODGERS of the NATIONAL LEAGUE. He was the first Negro admitted to Organized Baseball in modern times. In 1949 he won the National League batting championship and the Most Valuable Player award. An excellent fielder and one of the most effective base runners in baseball history, Robinson was elected to the baseball Hall of Fame.

ROBINSON, JEM (1793-1865), a notable English jockey, who, in 1824, wagered that he would win the DERBY and the OAKS and get married within the week. He duly landed the treble and won his wager of £1,000. Altogether he rode 24 classic winners, including a record six Derby victories.

ROBINSON, RAY (Sugar Ray) (1920-), American boxer who was world welterweight champion and five times middleweight champion, and is regarded almost unanimously as the greatest boxer of the past 30 years. Robinson boxed professionally from 1940 and had 202 bouts of which he won 109 inside the distance and 66 on points. He won the welterweight title in 1946, defended it five times and then took the middleweight championship from La Motta in 1951. The same year he lost the middleweight title to Britain's Turpin but regained it within two months, came very close to taking the light-heavyweight championship from Maxim, and in 1955, 1957, and 1958 fought his way back again to the middleweight world championship. At his best, around 1948 to 1950, Robinson was a superb boxer-fighter who could hit with blinding speed. His defence was so sound that he eventually retired almost unmarked. No one in modern BOXING was a better exponent of combination punching, in which a series of punches from either hand are linked together in a deliberate pattern.

ROCHESTER ROYALS, see CINCINNATI ROYALS.

ROCK SAND (1900), English race-horse, bred and owned by Miller, trained by Blackwell, and usually ridden by Maher. Rock Sand won 16 out of 20 races, including the DERBY, ST. LEGER, TWO THOUSAND GUINEAS, JOCKEY CLUB STAKES, and prize money amounting to £45,618. He was subsequently sold to BELMONT for £25,000 and stood at stud in the U.S.A., where he sired TRACERY.

ROCKNE, KNUTE K. (1888-1931), American college FOOTBALL player and coach at NOTRE DAME (South Bend, Indiana). As a player (1911-13), his pass-catching at end was a major factor in Notre Dame's defeat of the UNITED STATES MILITARY ACADEMY team (Army) in 1913. As head coach at Notre Dame (1918-30), he was the most popular football figure of his day, with a particularly nimble wit and sense of humour, and made Notre Dame the best-known and most colourful college team. He introduced the 'Notre Dame shift', where the backfield moved into a 'box' formation before the ball was played. His most famous team was the 1924 eleven, featuring the 'Four Horsemen', which was undefeated. His Notre Dame coaching record was 105 wins, 12 losses, and 5 ties (including 5 unbeaten seasons).

RODEO, a competitive exhibition of the riding and other skills of individual cowboys (cattle-punchers), is now a major sporting entertainment in North America. A rodeo may be held in any enclosed space, in or out of doors, that is suitable for the riding of horses and the running of cattle. The most important are staged in sawdust or sand arenas, like large circus rings, with seating for thousands of spectators.

There are six principal events at all rodeos: saddle bronc-riding, bareback bronc-riding, bull-riding, calf-roping, team roping, and steer-wrestling. A seventh, barrel racing, is for women and does not share with the others genuine origins in the practical work of a cowboy. A form of obstacle race on horseback, it belongs more to the gymkhana arena than the rodeo ring, to which it was added as an entertaining gimmick.

SADDLE BRONC-RIDING is the classic event of rodeo, in which a competing cowboy must retain his seat on a wildly bucking horse for ten seconds and is marked for the style with which he does so. The horse is held in a chute immediately outside the rodeo arena until the barrier drops; if it is a good bucker, it enters the ring in the air. When its feet hit the ground for the first time, the rider's spurs must be at the high point of the horse's shoulders. From that moment, he should rhythmically spur the bronc from high in front to high behind, a movement known as 'lick'.

Throughout the ride the cowboy must keep one hand free and held in the air, clear of the horse. He is disqualified if he touches the animal with his free hand, changes hands on the rein, loses a stirrup, or is bucked off. The rein is a braided rope attached to the halter.

There are two judges, one for the rider and one for the horse. Each is marked out of 25. Competitors, who draw for horses and have no opportunity to test them first, hope for a rough ride: a horse whose bucking is less than wild,

or is regular enough to be anticipated, will be marked low, giving the rider no chance for a high total. The roughest broncs leap high and land hard on their forefeet, with a whip-lash kick behind. These tactics are punctuated with sharp pivots to each side, to jerk the rider off the saddle.

Nobody knows what makes horses buck. In approved rodeos they are not starved, nor tormented, nor stimulated into bucking; they buck for the love of it. Some of them start as normal, docile, riding-school horses, then suddenly decide they never want a man on their back again. From that moment the value of the horse increases from perhaps $350 to $1,000. Its work decreases from several hours a day to a few seconds — perhaps totalling only five minutes a year. The very best of them, the most spirited, may have another reward: the rodeo cowboys elect a 'Bucking Horse of the Year'.

BAREBACK BRONC-RIDING is in most respects the same as saddle bronc-riding. The competitor is required to ride a bucking bronco (a wild or half-tamed horse, or one that refuses to be ridden) in an arena for eight seconds, without saddle, stirrups, or rein. With one hand only, he may hold a suitcase-type handle attached to a cinch, a thick strap round the horse's chest. The free hand must not touch the horse or the cinch. If the rider is not disqualified, he and the horse are marked by judges on the same basis as in the saddle bronc event.

To have much hope of staying on, even for eight seconds, the rider must keep as close as possible to the cinch and the horse's neck. If the bucking of the horse throws him back so that his riding arm is extended, the rider's stability is greatly lessened. In both bronc-riding events, a pick-up man is employed in the ring to haul a thrown rider to safety — though usually, once free of its rider, the horse is perfectly peaceful.

BULL-RIDING is the most dangerous and the most popular of the six main events of rodeo. The competitor must ride, barebacked, a Brahma bull that may weigh up to 2,000 lb. (900 kg.), the speed and agility of which is matched by the beast's apparently uncontrollable bad temper. The only hand-hold allowed is a loose rope passed round the girth and twisted in the rider's hand.

From the instant the barrier drops and rider and bull storm out of the chute beside the rodeo arena, the bull's energies are directed to ridding itself of the man on its back. It bucks and tosses as fiercely as a bronco, and a rider who loses his grip may be tossed high in the air. But unlike the bucking broncos of rodeo, a Brahma bull is not satisfied with simply getting rid of its rider; it will turn to gore him.

Even more feared by bull-riders is the 'hang-up', when the man is unseated but cannot fall because his hand is caught in the rope. He may then be dragged beside the galloping bull, struck by its hooves and pounded beneath them.

Despite the dangers, there is nearly always a longer entry for bull-riding at a rodeo than for any other event. That is a tribute to the faith placed by bull-riders in the rodeo clowns, whose job it is to rescue an unseated rider before he is killed. In saddle and bareback bronc-riding, there are pick-up men on horseback to prevent accidents, but a horse could not live in the same ring as a Brahma bull. A pair of clowns, often former rodeo cowboys, operate with every bull-rider. One is the bull-fighter, the other the barrel man. The latter distracts the bull, often by beating on his barrel, while his colleague tries to get the cowboy out of the ring. When the bull charges the barrel man, he jumps into his barrel. Their most desperate moments come when the rider has a hang-up: then one of them must get close enough to the bull to cut the man free.

In CALF-ROPING, the competitor waits, on horseback, outside the rodeo arena. A calf is released into the ring, shortly followed by the rider. He must lasso the animal from horseback, tie the rope to his saddle, dismount, and throw the calf to the ground by hand — an operation made easier if the horse keeps the rope tight. If the calf is already on the ground when the cowboy reaches it, he must let it get to its feet, then throw it down himself. He then has to tie together any three of the animal's feet.

Success in the event depends on precise teamwork between man and horse. They are working against the clock, and in top-class rodeo, fractions of a second separate winners from losers. The moment when the competitor is allowed into the ring after the calf is determined by the barrier in front of him, a rope, being tripped by a length of cord tied round the calf's neck. The roper and his horse try to reach the barrier at speed at the exact moment it is released: if they hit it early, a ten-second penalty is added.

TEAM ROPING involves two mounted cowboys and should be a faster and more efficient operation. One competitor heads off the calf, and throws and ties it after the other has lassoed the animal.

In STEER-WRESTLING, also known as bull-dogging, the competitor must drop from horseback on to the horns of a galloping steer and throw it to the ground. Of all the events of rodeo, this one calls for the greatest precision both from the rider (dogger) and his horse.

The horse must gallop within a foot (0·3 m.) of the steer, usually on the left of it, allowing the rider to lean over and catch the right horn with his right hand. As the horse gallops past, the rider stays with the steer, pulling up on the right horn and down with the left. The cowboy's heels must hit the ground ahead of him and away from the steer, acting as a brake and a pivot.

If the operation is accurately carried out, the steer goes into a tight left-hand turn. As its hind quarters swing round, the cowboy tips its head and hopes to throw the steer on to its side. The steer must be caught from horseback. If it breaks loose, the competitor may take only one step to catch it, before being disqualified.

Competitors work against the clock, the best time in the rodeo being the event winner. Each one is helped by a second man, the 'hazer', whose job it is to ride on the opposite side of the steer to keep it running straight. He also retrieves the horse — and the rider, should he seem in greater danger of injury than usual.

Prize money is offered for the winner of each event at a rodeo (known as day money), and at the end of the year the 15 top money-winners in each category meet in the national finals, at which champions are named for each event. The supreme accolade for the professional rodeo rider is to be named all-round world champion — the man who has won most money in rodeo during the year. The all-round champion is usually one who regularly, perhaps twice a week, wins prize money at two or three different rodeo events.

Rodeo was born in the southern states of America after the Civil War (1861-5), when Texan cowboys, driving their cattle to the north and west in search of new markets, to find their own amusements. They did so with riding and roping contests, employing those skills which earned them their daily bread.

As towns grew up on the path of the cattle drives, the contests became public entertainment, and in 1888, at Prescott, Arizona, the first admission money was charged. Now the sport attracts more than 15 million spectators a year in 600 towns of the U.S.A. and Canada.

Rodeo-riders are not hired to compete, nor do they work for or through managers and promoters in the way that most other professional sportsmen do. They have retained both individuality and independence, living on what they are able to earn from rodeo to rodeo. The promoters of a rodeo provide the locations, the stock (cattle and horses) and the prize money: the rider comes if he wants to, knowing that he may win more in a minute than most men earn in a month, and that the pounding hooves of a bull weighing 2,000 lb. (900 kg.) may end his career or even his life.

The sport became big business in the late 1930s, after the formation of the Rodeo Cowboys Association (R.C.A.). Founded as a union of professional competitors, the R.C.A. now controls rodeo throughout North America, representing all sides of the business: riders, stock-contractors, and rodeo committees. Not until 1951 was any insurance cover provided for rodeo professionals. Since no insurance company was prepared to handle the business at a premium acceptable to the clients, the R.C.A. run it themselves.

Though the rodeo cowboy, like his predecessors, may have grown up on a ranch and learned his trade by practical experience, he is just as likely now to be a city boy who was taught at a rodeo school or went to one of the colleges who offer rodeo scholarships.

Col. Cody (Buffalo Bill) brought a touring rodeo of a kind to Europe in 1887, coming to London for the Golden Jubilee of Queen Victoria. Riding and roping events were interspersed with Indian scenes and pageants of the pioneers conquering the Wild West. The show remained in England for a year, and then went to France, Spain, Italy, and Germany. Col. Cody mounted another such Western spectacular in 1902, and it ran in Europe for four years.

One of Cody's stars was the sharpshooter, Annie Oakley (later portrayed as the heroine of *Annie Get Your Gun*), who took her own show to Berlin in 1907. In the middle of a performance, the German Crown Prince walked into the arena and asked her to perform a trick he had seen her do with Cody in London. The Crown Prince put a lighted cigarette to his lips: Annie Oakley raised her rifle, fired, and left him with only half of it.

Europe saw little genuine rodeo after that until 1970, when 250 animals were shipped from the Western states to Italy, and were followed by some of America's best-known rodeo cowboys. Even under the conditions of a continental tour, they declined to accept the promoter's offer of a salary. They preferred to battle it out for prize money as they had always done.

ROELANTS, GASTON (1937-   ), steeplechaser, long-distance runner, and cross-country runner for Belgium. The first man to break 8½ min. for the 3,000 metres STEEPLECHASE, he twice broke the world record with a best of 8 min. 26·4 sec. in 1965. Roelants won an Olympic gold medal in this event in 1964 and two European medals, gold (1962) and bronze (1966). Turning to longer distances, he broke the European 10,000 metres record, and in 1966 set two more world records, previously held by RON CLARKE: the 20,000 metres in 58 min. 6·2 sec., running on in the same race to complete 12 miles 1,478 yds. in the hour, another world best. He improved both these records in 1972, clocking 57 min. 45·0 sec. for 20,000 metres, and covering 12 miles 1,609 yds. in one hour. Roelants was silver medallist in the 1969 European championship MARATHON and won the international cross-country title in 1962, 1967, 1969, and 1972. He won the São Paulo Road Race in 1964, 1965, 1967, and 1968.

ROGER, GILBERT (1914-   ), French race walker who belonged to the internationally unrecognized Union Française de Marche. A winner of six STRASBOURG–PARIS races (1949, 1953-4, 1956-8) and holder of every intermediate record in this race from 50 km. (31¼ miles) to 537 km. (324 miles), Roger was a phenomenal performer at distances in excess of 100 km. He dominated this type of event from 1949 to his retirement in 1960. Roger owed much of his success in the Strasbourg–Paris race to the fact that he needed less than two hours' rest during the three days or so duration of the event.

ROGERS, DEREK PRIOR (1939-   ), RUGBY UNION flank forward for Bedford, England, and British LIONS. Essentially a tackling, harrying forward, Rogers made 34 appearances for England, beating the record held by WAKEFIELD for 42 years.

ROGERS, Mrs. W. C. E. (*née* Iris L. Cooley) (1931-   ), BADMINTON player for England. With 52 international appearances between 1952 and 1969 she holds the world's record for a woman. During this period she won the ALL-ENGLAND women's doubles title three times and the mixed doubles once.

ROLLER DANCING, see ROLLER SKATING.

ROLLER FIGURE-SKATING, see ROLLER SKATING.

ROLLER HOCKEY is a team game played on roller skates with sticks and a ball, adapted from field HOCKEY and ICE HOCKEY, with the object of scoring the most goals to decide the winner. Owing to the varying sizes of ROLLER SKATING rinks, it is not practicable to lay down a hard and fast rule for the over-all dimensions of the playing area, for this is automatically determined, but the size of the penalty area is constant at 40 ft. 6 in. by 18 ft. (12·5 × 5·5 m.), and the goal cages must measure 3 ft. (91 cm.) high and 4 ft. (1·2 m.) wide (depth at top 1 ft. 6 in. or 45 cm., and at bottom 3 ft. or 91 cm.). A reasonable playing area would be 120 ft. long by 60 ft. wide (36·5 × 18·3 m.), but the ideal is 140 ft. by 70 ft. (42·7 × 21 m.).

A game is controlled by one referee, assisted by two goal judges. The duration of a match is 15 minutes each way (20 minutes each way in internationals), usually with 3 minutes' interval at half-time. Each team consists of five players — goalkeeper, back, half-back (sometimes called pivot), right forward, and left forward — plus two replacement players and a spare goalkeeper who can be substituted at any break in the play, providing the referee is notified.

Play is started, and re-started after half-time and after a goal is scored, by a strike-off, the equivalent to a bully in field hockey. The ball is placed on the centre spot and a player from each team stands in his own half facing the ball, with the blade of his stick at rest on the ground behind a strike-off line 9 in. (23 cm.) from the ball. When the whistle is blown, the ball is immediately in play. There is no off-side, and play continues in the area immediately behind the goals, as in ice hockey. When the ball leaves the playing area, a free hit is awarded to the team opposing the last striker of the ball.

The ball must not be lofted higher than 6 ft. (1·829 m.) when a shot is played, the only exceptions being when two players strike the ball simultaneously and when the goalkeeper does so in making a save with his hands, legs, or feet. The goalkeeper is the only player permitted to kick or handle the ball, but he is not

allowed to catch it, nor must his hands or any part of his body, other than his feet, be in contact with the floor when making a save.

Pushing, barging, body-checking, back-tackling, and tripping are against the rules. Players must not lift their sticks above their shoulders when playing a shot. A foul is committed if a player holds the rink barrier with one hand while playing the ball or tackling an opponent with the other.

Sprint speeds of approximately 30 m.p.h. (48 km./h.) are achieved in this fast, keenly contested game, but serious injuries are rare.

Apart from the roller hockey ball and stick, equipment essentials are skates and boots of a type specially designed for the game, socks, shin guards (leg guards for the goalkeeper), knee pads, a small abdominal guard, shorts, and shirt, with string gloves an optional extra and special gloves for the goalkeeper. The majority of players prefer a skate considerably shorter in length than that used for normal skating. The reason for this is that a rubber strip is fitted to the underside of the toe of the boot to act as a brake and aid rapid starting. Short skates also give greater flexibility.

The roller hockey stick is similar in shape to a field hockey stick but flat on both sides of the blade, as it is permissible to hit with either side. It must not exceed 3 ft. 9 in. (1·14 m.) in length, measured from the top of the handle along the outer edge of the curve to the tip of the blade. It must also be possible to pass it through a ring with a diameter of 2 in. (5 cm.). The stick, of wood, has no metal fittings, and must not exceed 18 oz. (510 g.) in weight.

The roller hockey ball is made of composi-

ROLLER HOCKEY PITCH
Dimensions given are ideal; actual dimensions vary according to the size of the roller-skating rink. The goal cage, 4 ft. (1·2 m.) wide, is 3 ft. (91 cm.) high and 3 ft. deep at the bottom.

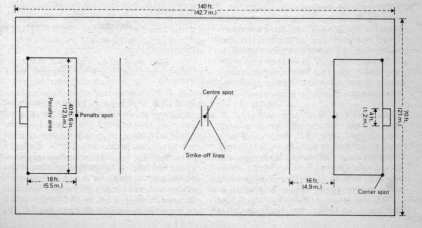

tion or compressed cork, weighs $5\frac{1}{4}$ oz. (156 g.) and measures 9 in. (23 cm.) in circumference.

Hockey on roller skates dates back to the early part of the twentieth century as an organized sport. Its earlier history is a little obscure, but it is believed that some kind of game with sticks started evolving soon after the first roller skates came into use around 1870.

The first international inter-club tournament, held in France in 1910 at the Hippodrome, Paris, was won by a British team, Crystal Palace Engineers. The early development was pioneered by British skaters and the first recognized rules were approved in 1913 by the sport's governing body in Britain, which was eventually named the National Roller Hockey Association of Great Britain. The first European championship was staged at Herne Bay, England, in 1926. Then, and in every subsequent year until 1939, it was won by Britain. In 1936, the first world championship was decided concurrently with the ninth European event at Stuttgart, Germany.

After wartime suspension, international roller hockey was recommenced in Lisbon in 1947. Then new top-class talent in Britain was virtually non-existent, while Portugal, Spain, Switzerland, and, to a lesser extent, Italy, had advanced considerably. Britain lost her long-held title to a very young, well-trained Portuguese side and Portugal afterwards dominated the postwar international meetings.

Howard Bass, *This Skating Age* (1958).

GOVERNING BODY (WORLD): International Roller Skating Federation, Ausias March 49, Barcelona 10, Spain.

ROLLER SKATING as a competitive sport takes the same principal forms as ICE SKATING, i.e., roller speed-skating, roller figure-skating, and roller dancing.

Speed-skating on roller skates is performed at top level on outdoor oval circuits or open road. A more restricted form of the sport is conducted at indoor roller skating rinks which, as in ice speed skating, have area limitations which restrict speed because of the necessarily short straights and constant sharp cornering. Major events are therefore held outdoors.

World championships are contested over four recognized distances for men — 1,000, 5,000, 10,000, and 20,000 metres (1,094, 5,468, 10,936, and 21,872 yds.) — and three for women — 500, 3,000, and 5,000 metres (547, 3,281, and 5,468 yds.). Women participate in appreciably greater numbers than on ice. Tracks have been used for postwar world championships at Bari, Venice, and Voltrega, Italy; Lisbon, Portugal; Barcelona, Spain; and Inzell, West Germany. Championships are

conducted on much the same lines as on ice except that titles are awarded for winners over specific distances and not for the best over-all performance at a meeting.

The rules and technique employed on roller skates are fundamentally similar to those on ice.

Figure-skating on roller skates corresponds in most ways to ice figure-skating. The same international schedule of figures used on ice is used in roller skating, the main difference between the two media being that, whereas the skate blade traces the figure pattern that can be seen on the ice, the roller skater performs upon figures previously painted on the rink floor. The free skating is also basically similar to that of the ice sport and there are corresponding systems for judging and marking championships, competitions, and proficiency tests.

In figure-skating parlance, the two inside wheels and the two outside wheels of the roller skate are the equivalents of the inside and outside edges of ice skates. Thus, all figure descriptions are applicable to both media.

Because the majority of skaters have practised the sport on only one of the two media, it is not generally appreciated how interrelated and complementary the two sports are. Where both media are readily available, skaters tend to favour ice, but a growing number of enthusiasts have appreciated the wisdom of increasing efficiency by interchanging between ice blades and roller wheels. A figure-skater can, for example, become overconfident on the surface to which he has grown accustomed and may tend to neglect technique — something that would be avoided if he kept more constantly alert by alternating media.

Dancing on roller skates, has developed very much on a par with ice dancing. The techniques are as similar as is practicable on the differing skates and surfaces, and the internationally recognized championship dances correspond. The same system is used for judging and marking championships, competitions, and proficiency tests.

The skates used for general roller skating, roller figure-skating, roller dancing, and ROLLER HOCKEY, are made in a wide range of qualities. The models suitable for championship skating are masterpieces of precision engineering, far more complicated than ice skates. The best roller skate has four composite wheels. Rubber toe stops at the front of the roller skate are the counterpart of the ice figure-skate's toe rake. The wheel movements may be loosened or heightened to individual requirements. Efficiency is maintained by applying a drop of thin oil to either side of each wheel about once a month. Wheels can be removed and cleaned at similar intervals.

The boots used in roller skating are basically similar to the ice skating boot, and are usually purchased separately from the skates, which are screwed to the soles.

Although a roller skate of sorts was invented by a Belgian, Merlin, in 1760, the first practical four-wheel skate was introduced by an American, Plympton, in 1863. The original idea was no more than to provide a means for ice skaters to simulate their sport and practise when there was no natural ice. But the possibilities of developing the sport on a separate medium soon became apparent and, in 1866, Plympton himself opened the first successful public roller-skating rink at Newport, Rhode Island, U.S.A. Another step forward was the subsequent invention of the more satisfactory Richardson ball-bearing skate in 1884.

A boom on both sides of the Atlantic reached its zenith in 1910, when nearly every town seemed to have at least one rink, and every available floor area, flat roofs included, was used. C. B. Cochran, the impresario, at this time controlled a large rink at the Olympia exhibition hall in London.

The National Skating Association (N.S.A.) of Great Britain, instituted in 1879 as an ice skating administration, also assumed national control of roller skating from 1893. In 1894, the first British one-mile speed championship was won by C. Wilson at Wandsworth, in London. In 1907, the British N.S.A. applied unsuccessfully for the sport's inclusion in the OLYMPIC GAMES, to be followed in subsequent years by persistent vain appeals for acceptance.

ALDWYCH, Britain's oldest roller speed-skating club, was formed in London in 1908, transferring its allegiance to ice in 1928. Roller hockey, the roller-skating equivalent of ICE HOCKEY, began to arouse serious European attention in 1910. In the same year the first British championship in roller figure-skating was won by W. Stanton at Maida Vale, London. For 29 years this contest remained open to both sexes and in 1921 the men were humiliated by the victory of Miss Lodge. Separate British events for women and pairs were not organized until 1939, but the first national roller dance title was contested in 1922.

The same international schedule of figures as that used on ice was universally adopted for roller skating when the International Roller Skating Federation (I.R.S.F.) was founded in 1924. Similar free skating principles were also approved, with corresponding systems for championship judging and proficiency tests.

Internationally, 1937 was an important year, when the first officially recognized world championships in roller speed-skating were held at Monza, Italy. French skaters won the three distances contested — Fichaux (1,000 and 20,000 metres) and Brousteau (10,000 metres). In 1937 also, the European roller figure-skating championships were instituted at Stuttgart, Germany. The first winners, all Germans, were Handel (men), Miss Wahl (women), and Walter and Miss Roth (pairs). In the U.S.A. the same year, the United States Roller Skating Rink Operators Association (U.S.R.O.A.) began a thorough national reorganization of the sport, inspired by Rawson, one of the most progressive American administrators.

Rival American organizations, the U.S.R.O.A. and the United States Amateur Roller Skating Association, both claimed in 1942 to represent the sport in the U.S.A. and each promoted separate national championships. Only those events run by the latter association were subsequently recognized by the I.R.S.F. Agreement was restored sufficiently for the first world roller figure- and dance skating championships to be held in Washington, D.C., in 1947. The winners were Mounce (U.S.A.), men; Miss Wehrli (Switzerland), women; Leemans and Miss Collin (Belgium), pairs; and Ludwig and Miss Gallagher (U.S.A.), dance.

Subsequent world championships were so dominated by West Germans that, in the two decades following the inaugural world meeting, they won all but three men's, four women's, and three pairs titles of the first 14 titles contested in each division. The outstanding male figure-skater, LOSCH, won five world titles. His compatriot, Miss Bader, reigned supreme from 1965 to 1968, during which time she won four consecutive women's world titles. FINGERLE, who partnered Miss Keller to three straight world titles after an earlier victory with Miss Schneider, has been the most successful world pairs competitor.

The British and West Germans monopolized the world roller dancing honours after 1947 until 1968, when Rudalawicz and Miss R. Smith recaptured the title for the U.S.A. The first separate European roller dance championship was held in London in 1950, when the British couple, Byrne and Miss Phethean, were successful. As with ice dancing, British pioneers contributed much to roller dancing, notably Wilkie and Van der Weyden, who invented some of the dances. Others who greatly influenced the early progress of roller dancing were Burrows, Miss Kallenborn, Mrs. Belcham, and Gilbey, who later became president of the N.S.A. of Great Britain. Prominent among the still earlier devotees was Blaver, who did most to gain official recognition of roller dancing by the N.S.A. with the formulation of rules around 1910, basically similar to those of ice dancing. In 1922, Blaver won the first British roller dance championship at London's former Holland Park rink. He afterwards won the title each year until 1927, his partner on the last three occasions being Miss Hogg, who later gained greater fame as an ice-skating coach.

Italians have shone most in world roller speed skating championships, with Cavallini particularly prominent. After the introduction of women's world speed championships in Venice, Italy, in 1953, the most successful woman racer was another Italian, Miss Vianello.

The appeal of roller skating diminished during the years immediately following the Second World War, largely because of deteriorating conditions at many of the rinks, which suffered by comparison with the luxuries at palatial new ice stadiums. This imbalance was to some extent corrected during the 1960s by a drive to make roller-skating rinks more congenial. Maple floors covered with polyurethane surfaces, coupled with the use of new composite wheels for the skates, resulted in a comparatively noiseless, dust-free atmosphere which inspired a reviving interest. The sport became widely practised in Australasia and South Africa as well as Europe and North America. More than 4,000 rinks became available for roller skating in the United States alone and the number of participants throughout the world became appreciably higher than the number practising some sports included in the Olympic schedule.

Howard Bass, *This Skating Age* (1958); C. Harvey, *Almanack of Sport* (1966).

GOVERNING BODY (WORLD): International Roller Skating Federation, Ausias March 49, Barcelona 10, Spain.

ROLLER SPEED-SKATING, see ROLLER SKATING.

ROLLO, DAVID MILLER DURIE (1935-), RUGBY UNION prop forward for Howe of Fife and Scotland. A strong, robust farmer, he took up Rugby at the age of 18, having been captain of soccer at school, and in 1968 equalled MCLEOD's record of 40 Scottish international caps.

ROMA–CASTELGANDOLFO, annual road RACE WALKING event held in Italy over 32 km. (20 miles) every September. Inaugurated in 1949, the race is sponsored by the newspaper, *Il Corriere dello Sport.* The race has been dominated by the Italians, DORDONI and PAMICH, who shared 17 victories between them, although Swedish, West German, and English walkers have also figured among the winners.

The race starts at 6.30 a.m. from St. Peter's Square and finishes outside the Pope's summer residence in the village of Cast. The opening 24 km. (15 miles) is relatively flat along the Albano highway but the final 8 km. (5 miles) is a climb increasing in severity towards the finish. A major difficulty in this race is the volume of traffic encountered in the early stages through the main streets of Rome.

ROMERO, FRANCISCO (*c.* 1700-40), *matador de toros,* is reputed to have invented the *muleta* in about 1726, but it is known to have existed previously. Nevertheless, he used it to good advantage and became the first celebrity of the bull ring.

ROMERO, PEDRO (1754-1839), *matador de toros,* grandson of FRANCISCO ROMERO, the most famous of a taurine dynasty. Pedro appeared in *corridas* for 28 years during which he killed about 6,000 bulls, mostly *recibiendo,* without once being wounded. In 1830 he founded the School of Tauromachy in Seville.

ROQUE, a form of CROQUET played in the U.S.A. and generally considered to be a more scientific version than the original, which in the objects of the game it exactly resembles: to hit, with a mallet, hard balls through a series of arches (hoops), endeavouring if possible to help on their way the balls of your partner (if any), and to strike aside the opponents' balls. The winner is the first player, or pair, to hit the balls through all the arches and to hit the two posts at each end of the court; or the first to score 32 points, awarded for striking a ball through an arch or for striking an opponent's ball with your own.

The roque court is only a quarter the size of a croquet lawn: 10 yds. by 20 yds. (9.14 × 18.29 m.), with the corners cut off to form an octagon. It has a hard surface with a solid boundary wall, and contains ten arches instead of the six of croquet. The arches are both lower and slightly narrower than those used in the original game. A hard rubber ball is used, the diameter of which is only ⅛ in. (0.32 cm.) less than the width of the arches. It is struck by a mallet with a 15-inch (38 cm.) handle, one head of which is rubber and the other of aluminium or laminated plastic.

The National Roque Association was founded in New York in 1889, the name being obtained by dropping the first and last letters of croquet.

ROSE, Sir ALEC (1908-), English yachtsman who sailed single-handed round the world from Portsmouth, Hampshire, with a call at Melbourne, Australia. He began the voyage in his sloop *Lively Lady* on 16 July 1967 returning to Portsmouth on 4 July 1968.

ROSE, I. MURRAY (1939-   ), swimmer for Australia who became the youngest triple Olympic gold medallist at the sport in 1956 when, in Melbourne, he won the 400 and 1,500 metres freestyle and was a member of the winning relay team. He made history again in 1960 when he became the first man to win the 400 metres at successive Games. Awarded the Helms Foundation World Trophy in 1962, and probably the greatest swimmer of his time, he lived on a diet which excluded meat, fish, poultry, refined flour, and sugar.

ROSE, MAURI (1906-   ), American MOTOR RACING driver who won two consecutive INDIANAPOLIS 500s, 1947 and 1948, and co-drove the winning car in 1947, relieving Davis. He started in 15 straight Indianapolis races with a second, two thirds, and a fourth best finishes besides victories. He was American Automobile Association national champion in 1936. He retired in 1951 to continue his career as an automotive engineer.

ROSE BOWL, see FOOTBALL, AMERICAN (COLLEGE).

ROSEBERY, 6th Earl of (1882-1974), played a prominent part in the administration and reform of the English Turf. He owned Blue Peter, winner of the DERBY, TWO THOUSAND GUINEAS, and ECLIPSE STAKES, and Ocean Swell, winner of a wartime Derby and ASCOT GOLD CUP.

ROSENFELD, ALBERT AARON (1885-1970), Australian RUGBY LEAGUE winger. He was a member of the first overseas team to visit England, in 1907. He returned in 1909 to play for HUDDERSFIELD, and in 1913-14, with WAGSTAFF as his centre partner, he set a record by scoring 80 tries. In nine seasons with Huddersfield, he scored 388 tries by means of his elusive running.

ROSEWALL, KENNETH RONALD (1934-   ), Australian LAWN TENNIS player who for more than 20 years was one of the three best competitors in the world. Ironically nicknamed 'Muscles' because of his comparative frailty of physique, he was one of the great ground-stroke players and the possessor of a classic style. Although his service lacked great pace, it was always shrewdly varied, and he worked hard at his volleying and smashing until he could rely on those strokes.

HOPMAN, the Australian Davis Cup (see LAWN TENNIS) captain, introduced Rosewall and his notable contemporary, HOAD, to the Australian team in 1953. Rosewall immediately won the Australian and French titles and in a Davis Cup career which lasted until 1956, when he turned professional, he won 16 out of 19 rubbers. He returned to the Davis Cup in 1973, winning a doubles with LAVER in the inter-zone semi-final against Czechoslovakia, but did not play in the final against the U.S.A. His talents lasted: 15 years after his first victory in Paris, he won the French Open title in 1968; 14 years after his first victory at FOREST HILLS, he won the U.S. Open title in 1970.

He won the first of all open tournaments, at Bournemouth in 1968, but the WIMBLEDON title continued to elude him. DROBNY beat him in the 1954 final; he failed there against Hoad in 1956, against NEWCOMBE in 1970, and was to fail again against the American Connors in 1974. If open tennis had come earlier, Rosewall's list of titles might have been the longest in the history of the game. Certainly, in the years between the decline of GONZALES and the arrival on the professional scene of Laver, who so often frustrated him, Rosewall was the undoubted world champion.

ROSS, A. G. F. (1895-   ), CROQUET player from New Zealand. From the time he won his first title in 1915, Ross held the dominant position in New Zealand croquet in a career which continued into the 1960s. An attractive player to watch with an easy and efficient style, he did more than anyone else to bring the standard of New Zealand croquet up to international level. He spent much of his time coaching throughout the Dominion and has written many books on the game. He captained New Zealand in the MACROBERTSON trophy competitions in 1930, 1950, 1956, and 1963. His titles include eleven open and six men's championships and seven open doubles titles. He also won the English open championship in 1954.

ROTHMAN'S JULY HANDICAP is the most important race in South Africa for older horses. It is run over 10½ furlongs (2,100 m.) on the Greyville track at Durban.

ROTHSCHILD, Baron EDOUARD DE (d. 1949), was one of the leading owner-breeders of race-horses in France. He won 20 classic races, but never the French Derby. The greatest horse he owned was undoubtedly the champion BRANTÔME.

ROTHSCHILD,   Baron   GUY   DE

(1909–   ), is a prominent owner-breeder of racehorses in France. He won the PRIX DE L'ARC DE TRIOMPHE with EXBURY and the GRAND PRIX DE PARIS with Vieux Manoir and White Label. His horses are trained by Watson and mostly ridden by Deforge.

ROTSEE, the ROWING course at Lucerne, Switzerland, on which the premier annual European regatta is staged in the second week of July. Eight crews can row abreast and it is renowned for its calm water and fast conditions.

ROUEN CIRCUIT, French MOTOR RACING track combining tight hairpin bends and steep uphill sections with difficult 100-120 m.p.h. (161-193 km./h.) downhill curves and fast bends. The circuit is situated in the forest of Les Essarts a few miles south of the city of Rouen and it originally had a length of 3·16 miles (4·98 km.), including a stretch of Route Nationale 840. In 1955 the circuit length was extended to 4·06 miles (6·4 km.). The race was the scene of the French Grand Prix in 1952, 1957, 1962, 1964, and 1968. The lap record, set by the ex-motor-cycle champion HAIL-WOOD with a Surtees TS10, is 116·099 m.p.h. (186·843 km./h.) for the new 3·44-mile (5·6 km.) circuit.

ROUND, DOROTHY (Mrs. G. Little) (1909–   ), one of the two British LAWN TENNIS players to win the women's singles title at WIMBLEDON between the wars. Her first notable victory was over the Spaniard, DE ALVAREZ, at Wimbledon in 1931. She lost to Mrs. MOODY in the 1933 final, but gained the championship in 1934 by beating JACOBS (U.S.A.) and in 1937 with a victory over Krahwinkel (Germany). She won the mixed title with Miki (Japan) in 1934 and with PERRY in 1935 and 1936. In 1935 she was Australian champion.

ROUND TABLE (1954), a race-horse bred at the CLAIBORNE stud in the U.S.A., owned by Kerr, trained by Molter, and ridden by SHOE-MAKER. He won 43 races out of 66 starts, including the American Derby and Hollywood Gold Cup, together with a world record stake total of $1,749,869.

ROUNDERS is an outdoor bat-and-ball game played between two teams of nine players. Though predominantly played in Great Britain it is known in many parts of the world and has features in common with BASEBALL. Rounders is perhaps best known as an impromptu leisure game but is widely played in British schools and some adult and youth club leagues.

The two teams alternate as batting and fielding sides and a match consists of two innings, i.e. each side bats twice. The batsmen try to score rounders while the fielding team attempt to prevent this and to put out the batsmen. The team scoring most rounders wins.

The ball weighs between 2½ and 3 oz. (70 and 85 g.) and measures approximately 7½ in. (19 cm.) in circumference. It is hard and covered in light-coloured leather. The bat (known as a 'stick') is round and made of wood. The maximum measurements are: length, 18 in. (46 cm.), circumference at the thickest part, 6¾ in. (17 cm.); weight, 13 oz. (368 g.).

Two squares are marked on the pitch, for the bowler and the batsman. The running track is indicated by four posts. A line running across the front of the batting square separates the forward and backward areas. The minimum playing area is about 55 yds. (50 m.) square, some two-thirds being in the forward area. The posts stand 4 ft. (1·2 m.) above the ground. They may stand in bases or, less satisfactorily, be driven into the ground.

Two umpires officiate in positions known as the batsman's umpire and the bowler's umpire. The former's responsibilities include judging the height of a ball, all catches, and giving decisions concerning first and fourth posts. The bowler's umpire watches the direction of a ball and gives decisions concerning the second and third posts. The two change places when each team has batted once.

One member of the fielding team is the bowler. The positioning of the remaining eight members is not stipulated but commonly includes a backstop to field balls missed by the batsman, a fielder by each post, and three deep fielders covering the areas behind the posts.

The bowler must use a smooth underarm action and remain within his square until he has released the ball. It must be sent to the hitting side of the batsman, within reach and between the top of the head and the knee, any movement by the batsman after the bowler releases the ball being ignored. 'No-ball' is called for any infringement.

The batsman attempts to hit the ball as far as possible and to run round the outside of the posts to fourth post and thus score a rounder. He is entitled to receive one good ball on which he must run at least to first post, having hit or missed. If he receives a no-ball he cannot be caught out and has the option of running. The last batsman has the choice of three good balls but is out if caught off any.

A batsman may stop temporarily at any post on the way round the track, continuing either before the next ball is bowled or on a subsequent ball. In the latter case he does not score.

When the bowler has the ball and is in his square, a batsman may not leave or pass a post. On reaching fourth post a batsman rejoins the batting queue. When all of the batsmen are out, the teams change places.

A batsman who hits the ball into the forward area may score one rounder. If he misses the ball or his hit lands in the backward area, he may score a half-rounder but in the latter case may not pass first post until the ball is again in the forward area. To score, the batsman must reach fourth post before the next ball is bowled, must not be put out, and at no time when he is in contact with a post must the post immediately ahead be touched with the ball.

A half-rounder is awarded if a batsman receives three consecutive no-balls, and for certain cases of obstruction.

A batsman may cause himself to be out or be put out by a fielder, the more common examples being: He is out if he steps over the front line of the batting square before hitting the ball, if he runs inside a post, or if he overtakes another batsman. A fielder puts him out by catching a hit or by touching with the ball the post to which the batsman is running or the batsman himself after he has left the previous post. In addition, if all remaining members of the batting team are on the track, they may be put out simultaneously by the ball being thrown full toss into the batting square.

The earliest known literary reference to rounders was in 1744, when *A Little Pretty Pocket Book* included a woodcut of the game and a verse under the name of 'Base-ball'. In 1829 a description of the rules was included in W. Clarke's *The Boy's Own Book*. The game has many features in common with baseball and Henderson maintains that baseball stems from the English game.

The first governing bodies were established in Liverpool and Scotland in 1889, and in 1943 the National Rounders Association was formed. The game today is not significantly different in concept from the nineteenth-century version. Among changes are the anti-clockwise circuit of the running track, introduced in 1839, and the ending of the fielder's ability to put out the batsman by hitting him with a thrown ball.

Rules of the Game of Rounders, latest edition. W. Clarke, *The Boy's Own Book* (1829); R. W. Henderson, *Ball, Bat and Bishop: The Origin of Ball Games* (1947).
GOVERNING BODY (U.K.): National Rounders Association, 1 Chantry Close, Beeston, Nottingham.

ROUNDERS, Irish. As played in Ireland, this bat-and-ball game is very similar to the SOFTBALL version of BASEBALL. Although

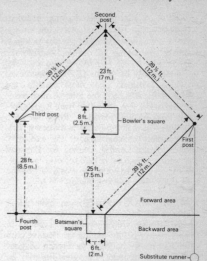

ROUNDERS PITCH
Compulsory markings are the four posts, the two squares, the substitute runner's position, and the line separating the forward and backward areas.

rules for the game are given in the *Official Guide* of the GAELIC ATHLETIC ASSOCIATION, there are no official competitions. Rounders is, however, popular as a recreational pastime in many schools.

The game, according to the G.A.A. rules, is played nine a side. There are four bases, each 30 yds. (27·4 m.) apart. The batter, who stands at home base, attempts to hit the ball thrown by the server from a mark 20 yds. (18·3 m.) from the base. Scoring and dismissals are as in baseball.

The bat is round, 3 ft. (91 cm.) long and not more than 2½ in. (6·3 cm.) wide at its thickest point. The ball is the ordinary HURLING ball, though a semi-solid rubber one may be used.

ROUS, Vice-Admiral the Hon. HENRY JAMES (1795-1877), was official handicapper to the English JOCKEY CLUB and was responsible for drawing up the Scale of Weight-for-Age still in use today.

ROUS, Sir STANLEY, C.B.E. (1895-   ), president 1961-74 of F.I.F.A., the international federation that controls the game of Association FOOTBALL throughout the world, has been actively associated with the international game since soon after the end of the First World War. He was a referee from 1920 to 1934 during which time he frequently refereed international matches in Europe. He became secretary of the English Football Association in 1934. Rous brought to his office wide understanding of the way in which football was trying to develop outside the boundaries of the United Kingdom. The encouragement of youth football, increased coaching facilities, and, most notably, the return of the F.A. and the other British associations to F.I.F.A., resulted from Rous's forward thinking and planning. Rous has been prominent in many sporting activities in Britain, notably as chairman of the executive council of the Central Council for Physical Recreation which he helped to form in 1934. For his services to sport, he was awarded the C.B.E. in 1943, and knighted in 1949.

ROUSIE, MAX (1911-59), an outstanding player in the early days of RUGBY LEAGUE in France. Rousie won international honours in RUGBY UNION before joining the Roanne club soon after the formation of the French League. A brilliant all-rounder, his versatility may be judged from the fact that he played stand-off half and loose forward in international matches against England in 1936-7, at centre in the two 1937-8 matches, and at centre and full-back in France's championship-winning season of 1938-9. He was killed in a car accident.

ROWE, ARTHUR (1936- .), British professional athlete who dominated many traditional Scottish games events after a highly successful career in amateur ATHLETICS as a shot-putter, and a short and less successful spell as a professional RUGBY LEAGUE player. As an amateur, he had put the 16-lb. (7·26 kg.) shot 64 ft. 2 in. (19·56 m.), a European record.

He started putting the SHOT as a professional in Scotland in 1962. He immediately broke professional records, some of which had been established for 50 years, and raised the current standard of professional shot-putting by some 12 ft. (3·66 m.). In 1963, though not approaching his best performances as an amateur, he put the 16-lb. shot more than 10 ft. (3 m.) farther than the existing record, and the 22-lb. (10 kg.) shot 8 ft. (2·44 m.) past the record.

He subsequently turned to Scottish games events such as tossing the CABER and tossing the WEIGHT, and proved as outstanding a performer as he was with the shot. In 1970, after a commercially-sponsored challenge match, he was proclaimed world caber-tossing champion.

ROWE, DIANE (later Mrs. Schöler), see ROWE, ROSALIND and DIANE.

ROWE, ROSALIND and DIANE (both 1933-   ), identical twins, one of the strongest of women's doubles pairs at TABLE TENNIS. In singles the right-handed 'Ros', who hit only on the forehand, was the steadier — she won the English open singles title twice (in 1953 and 1955); the left-handed 'Di', with a two-winged attack, was the more brilliant but, as a youngster, less dependable — she did not win the title until 1962. In 1950 they won both the junior and senior English open women's doubles, and thereafter won the senior event again each year for the following five years. They won the world title together in 1951 and 1954, and were runners-up in 1952, 1953, and 1955. After her marriage Rosalind retired. Diane then won the English open doubles another six times with three different partners and reached the world final and semi-final each twice more with two partners. She married the outstanding West German player, Schöler, in 1966 and has since played for the German Federal Republic, reaching the European championships women's doubles final twice for England, and once for the F.D.R. (in 1970), and the world's mixed quarter-final with her husband in 1971.

ROWING, the art of propelling a boat by means of oars, is practised as a sport throughout the world wherever suitable stretches of water can be found. It flourishes mainly on inland lakes, canals, and rivers, but in some countries coastal rowing is a popular branch of the sport.

In rowing each oarsman holds one oar, as distinct from sculling (see below) in which the sculler has one rather smaller oar, or scull, in each hand. An oar is usually made of wood with a rounded handle at one end and a blade at the other. A collar, called a 'button', is fitted to the shaft, or loom, of the oar to prevent it slipping through the rowlock, enabling the oarsman to apply the resistance obtained by the blade in the water to the propulsion of the boat. Adjustment of the button alters the leverage of the oar so that the stroke can be geared to suit the oarsman's physique and skill and the speed required, as well as to compensate for variations in weather conditions, such as head or following winds. The shorter the inboard length of the oar, that is, the part of the loom from the button to the tip of the handle, in relation to the outboard length (the distance from the button to the tip of the blade), the more severe the load imposed on the oarsman, so that in strong head-winds, for example, crews often increase the inboard length.

The gearing of the stroke may also be modified by altering the position of the rowlock in relation to the centre of the boat. This is known as the thwartship distance (TD) or 'spread', and most modern boats have fully adjustable outriggers to allow for the maximum possible flexibility in the rigging of the crew.

The usual type of rowlock is the swivel variety. This pivots from a vertical pin attached to the end of the outrigger. It has a latch, or gate, which can be unscrewed and lifted so that the oar may be removed. This type of rowlock superseded the fixed pin version during the first half of the twentieth century. The latter type consisted of two vertical stopping tholes with cord lashing across the top to prevent the oar from flying out, but these are now seldom used except in skiff racing.

A racing oar is hollow for lightness and carefully balanced so that the strain on the oarsman's wrists is kept to a minimum. The loom, which, except for the handle, is varnished, is reinforced along the back with hard wood and is tapered off towards the neck of the blade and, to a lesser extent, towards the handle which is often roughened or grooved so that it will not slip out of the oarsman's hands. There are no restrictions as to the length of an oar or to the size and shape of the blade, which is always slightly curved to ensure a good hold on the water.

Modern oars, which weigh about 8 lb. (3·6 kg.), are usually between 12 ft. and 12 ft. 10 in. (3·6–3·9 m.) long. Longer oars have been tried, without much success. A scull is usually about 9 ft. 8 in. (2·9 m.) long.

Prior to 1958, the majority of blades were 31–32 in. (79–81 cm.) long, and between 5½ and 7 in. (14–18 cm.) at the widest point. The West Germans introduced a shorter, wider

blade in 1958 and since then similar blades, generally referred to as 'spade blades', have been preferred by top-class crews. The most popular blade of this type in general use is one designed for the 1959 West German European championship crews. This is called the Macon blade, after the venue of the 1959 championships. It is 23½ in. (60 cm.) long, 7 in. (18 cm.) wide at the tip, and 7⅞–8¼ in. (20–21 cm.) wide at a point 8 in. (20 cm.) from the tip.

There are considerable variations in blade shapes. They may be as little as 20 in. (51 cm.) or as much as 32 in. (81 cm.) long. The width of modern blades generally varies between 6 in. (15 cm.) and 10 in. (25 cm.) at the widest point. Generally, the shorter the blade, the wider it is, so that the total area does not become too small to maintain adequate pressure against the water during the stroke. The wider the blade, the easier it is to get a firm hold on the water, but the heavier it will feel to the oarsman and the more sudden the impact at the beginning of the stroke, so the blade area and the shape are crucial and will vary with the particular style or technique of the crew.

Another factor in blade design is the amount of curvature. The greater the curve, the more efficiently the water can be caught at the beginning of the stroke; the more shallow the curve, the easier it is to get a clean finish.

Blades are usually painted in club colours for easy identification.

Modern racing boats hold crews of two, four, or eight oarsmen, and one, two, or four scullers. There are also a few boats for eight scullers, but these are seldom seen. At one time, six-oared craft were common, but these,

CROSS-SECTION OF A RACING BOAT
The oar pivots from the vertical pin attached to the end of the outrigger.

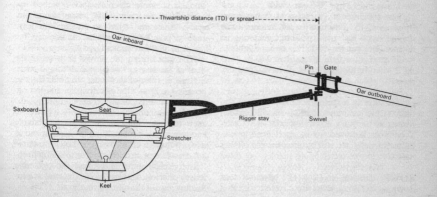

as well as ten- and twelve-oared boats, went out of fashion and disappeared towards the end of the nineteenth century.

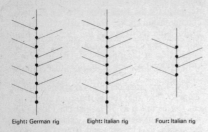

Eight: German rig   Eight: Italian rig   Four: Italian rig

RACING RIGS
The two eights include a coxswain, the four not.

Eights, being fast and comparatively cumbersome, are always steered by a coxswain, but pairs and fours may be with or without a coxswain. In a coxswainless boat, one of the oarsmen steers with his foot by means of a pivoting shoe to which the rudderlines are attached.

Events are held for coxswainless fours and pairs, as well as for the coxed varieties, in all major international championships. Single, double, and quadruple sculls are coxswainless, but the latter may have a coxswain. In the women's European championship there is an event for coxed quadruple fours.

The earliest racing boats, such as those used in the first race in 1829 between Oxford and Cambridge University, were heavy, inrigged craft with hulls of overlapping planks, but today's racing boats are long and slender with smooth skins. An eight is between 55 and 60 ft. (16–18 m.) long, but only about 24 in. (61 cm.) in beam, and 13 in. (33 cm.) deep. Fours and pairs are correspondingly shorter and finer, while sculling boats are only 25 ft. (7·6 m.) long and 12 in. (30·5 cm.) wide.

The construction of racing hulls has benefited from the introduction of modern techniques such as cold-moulding, resulting in lighter but stronger craft. It is now possible to build an eight weighing less than 240 lb. (109 kg.) when fully rigged, despite having to carry a crew which might average over 14½ stone (92 kg.) each.

The skin of a racing boat is very light and thin — seldom more than ⅛ in. (3·1 mm.) thick, and less for a sculling boat — but sturdier boats are used for inexperienced crews. Some of these are still built on the old clinker construction of overlapping planks, but these boats are considerably slower than carvel shells with a smooth skin. The bow and stern sections of racing boats are covered with thin linen and varnished. In an eight the bow section is about 9 ft. (2·7 m.) long. A verdict of a 'canvas' given at a regatta means that the winning margin is the length of this section of the boat.

Apart from certain types of boat for junior events there is no restriction on the dimensions. In Britain, specifications for a restricted class of boat are laid down by the Amateur Rowing Association (A.R.A.) and inexperienced oarsmen race in these wide, rather flat-bottomed boats in events designated for them.

For all other events, boat-builders attempt to build the fastest possible shells. The main problem is to build a boat that has the smallest wetted surface to keep friction to a minimum, but at the same time to make it stable enough to allow the crew to row efficiently.

In an eight, the coxswain sits in the stern section of the boat, but in a coxed pair, and sometimes in a coxed four, it has become usual to place the coxswain in the bows, where he lies on his back with a small head-rest. This reduces wind resistance and, more importantly, drag in the stern of the boat. The cox steers with lines attached to a small rudder on the stern post or underneath the hull. All racing shells have a small metal fin protruding under the hull near the stern to help stability and steering, and many modern boats have small rudders only a few inches square attached to these fins. The advantage of these is that the cox can steer the boat with more finesse and less drag than with a stern rudder, but even a slight application of a fin rudder can upset the balance, so that more skill is needed by the crew.

Eights and fours are often sectionalized so that they can be taken apart for easy transportation on trailers, but this does not significantly affect performance. It is extremely difficult to detect the join in the hull when a sectional boat is assembled.

Rowing technique has changed considerably since the sport in its modern form became popular in the nineteenth century, but the principles have not altered.

The aim during the stroke is to move the boat as far and as fast as possible, and when the blade is out of the water, to do as little as possible to hinder the acceleration and the run of the boat. It is possible to get similar results by different methods. For example, a powerful crew rowing a long stroke with a long swing can move their boat at much the same speed as a less powerful crew rowing a shorter stroke at a higher rate of striking, so that the main problem for each crew is to find the optimum length of stroke and rate of striking and to gear the leverage of the oars correctly.

The rate of striking and the gearing will vary with the distance to be rowed. A racing rate for a crew will be between 32 and 40 strokes to the minute for the body of the race; for scullers it is somewhat less. A crew rowing at less than full pressure is said to be paddling, and this is usually carried out at rates of between 24 and 28 — 'paddling firm'. When the pressure is very light, a crew is 'paddling light'.

The main source of power is the legs, and a powerful, co-ordinated leg-drive is the hall-mark of a good crew. The efficiency with which this is applied to the propulsion of the boat depends on the rhythm set by the stroke and the skill, watermanship, and timing of the crew.

Watermanship, which in rowing parlance refers to the skill of handling and balancing boats and oars, comparable to that of profes-sional watermen, is vital, since comparatively minor lurches in the boat can upset the timing of the stroke and the speed of the boat. The smaller the boat, the greater the premium on watermanship. Coxless pairs and single sculls are possibly the classes requiring the greatest skill. These 'small boats' are, for this reason, often used to test oarsmen for larger boats for their skill and propulsive power. A more subtle technique is required than that used for eight-oared rowing.

In a racing boat, the oarsman sits on a slid-ing seat which enables him to obtain a strong position at each end of the stroke. Control of the slide, especially between the strokes, is essential to good performance. At the begin-ning of the stroke, which is when the blade enters the water, an oarsman must make sure that he does not 'shoot his slide' by driving with his legs before the blade takes the water, as this dissipates the power of the leg-drive. On the way forward he must avoid reaching the front-stop of the runners on which his seat moves before he is ready for the beginning as this will lead to a marked check in the run of the boat.

The oar is turned at each end of the stroke. It is held flat, or 'feathered', between the strokes in order to reduce wind resistance and to avoid hitting waves, and it is 'squared' to a point slightly past a right-angle to the water just before the beginning. The skill with which these turns are made at each end of the stroke is critical to efficiency. If an oarsman feathers before the finish of the stroke his blade will be caught by the water and the momentum of the boat will result in his being knocked flat on his back, or even being lifted right out of the boat by his oar. This ignominious occurrence is described as 'catching a crab' and usually results in the loss of the race.

The order in which the men sit in a crew depends on several factors. In an eight, weight and strength are particularly important and the heaviest men tend to row in the middle posi-tions. The man nearest the bows, or No. 1 in the order, is usually neat and quick in his movements, while the best oarsmen in both skill and physique usually occupy the key positions in the stern seats.

The stroke of a crew usually rows with his oar on the port side but there is no rule about this and, in coastal rowing, stroke's oar is always on starboard. On a conventionally rigged boat the oarsmen rowing on the same side as stroke are called 'strokeside' men, and those on the opposite side are said to be on 'bowside'. Since 1956, however, when an asymmetrical distribution of oars was first used by Italian crews from the Moto Guzzi Club, the bow oar may be on the same side as the stroke oar. This redistribution was intended to produce a more even thrust from the oars than is possible with the conventional rig, which gives an advantage in leverage to the bowside oars at the beginning of the stroke and to the strokeside oars at the finish.

In fours, bow and stroke may row on the same side and the two centre oars on the oppo-site side. In eights, a modification introduced by the West German RATZEBURG crews is now quite common. This places the centre two oars on the same side, and both the bow and stroke oars on the opposite side.

'Style', in rowing, denotes the typical characteristics of a particular type of tech-nique, as, for instance, the 'orthodox', 'Fair-bairn', 'Conibear', and 'Ratzeburg' styles which describe the visible characteristics of crews. But although style, and arguments over it, have dominated rowing thought since the earliest days, extreme variations have gradu-ally become less common. Modern coaching and training methods, as well as more sophis-ticated equipment, have led to an emphasis on power and high rates of striking which have automatically reduced extremes and exaggera-tions.

INTERNATIONAL CHAMPIONSHIPS. Rowing is one of the major sports in the OLYM-PIC GAMES, and the eight Olympic categories are recognized for world and junior champion-ships. The categories are: coxed fours, double sculls, coxless pairs, single sculls, coxed pairs, coxless fours, quadruple sculls, and eights. The events are always rowed in this order.

Until 1973 the European championships took place annually except in those years when the world championships were held or in which the Olympic Games were being held in Europe. The title of European championships was dropped after the 1973 event and world championships are now held in all but Olympic years. The championships are not confined to European crews, all countries affiliated to F.I.S.A. being eligible. They are held in rotation in different countries on carefully selected still-water courses.

There are also world championships for women, and women's events were included in the Olympic rowing events after the 1972 Games, the events being coxed fours, coxless pairs, single sculls, coxed quadruple sculls, double sculls, and eights. Junior championships for boys are also held every year.

A feature of international championships is the *repêchage* system. All championships are held on six-lane courses and the losers of the opening heats in each event race again for a second chance to qualify for the finals, to ensure that at least the best three crews reach the six-boat final in each class.

All major international events are run under the rules of the Fédération Internationale des Sociétés d'Aviron (F.I.S.A.). Oarsmen and scullers are divided into categories by age and experience. An oarsman may compete as a junior up to the end of the year in which he attains the age of 18, after which he must compete in the senior class. A senior who has won six races moves into the élite class, the top category. Apart from the age restriction, sculling status is not affected by rowing status, and vice versa; an élite oarsman may compete as a senior sculler if he is qualified to do so. There are also lightweight, veteran, and women's categories.

Coxes are not affected by status except at junior level, where they must conform to the age requirements. There is also a minimum weight restriction on coxes: 40 kg. (6 st. 4 lb.) for juniors and 50 kg. (7 st. 6 lb.) for seniors. Coxes below these limits are required to carry weight in the boat.

All international championships are held over standard distances on still water: 2,000 m. (1·2 miles) for men, 1,500 m. (1,640 yds.) for boys, and 1,000 m. (1,093 yds.) for women; but because of the different speeds of the various classes of boat, there is a greater time variation. The fastest type of boat is an eight, which can cover 2,000 metres in well under six minutes, the slowest a coxed pair, which may be up to three minutes slower.

REGATTAS. In many countries, rowing is an all-the-year-round sport, but regattas are held mainly in the summer months. In the winter there are many long-distance 'Head of the River' races to break the monotony of the heavy land training which most crews carry out during the winter. These are processional races, in which the boats start at set intervals,

the crew with the fastest time winning the title.

Races and regattas may be held over any distance, depending on the stretch of water available: the Boston Marathon, held annually on the River Witham in Lincolnshire, has a course of 31 miles (49·8 km.); the championship course between Putney and Mortlake on the Thames, over which the BOAT RACE, the WINGFIELD SCULLS, and the principal Head of the River Race are held, is 4¼ miles (6·8 km.) long on tidal water, while the HENLEY ROYAL REGATTA course, perhaps the most famous in the world, is 1 mile 550 yds. (2·5 km.) long.

BUMPING RACES are a traditional form of racing at Oxford and Cambridge Universities, and are occasionally found in other parts of England, especially where a river is too narrow to permit side-by-side racing. The crews start in line ahead and attempt to touch, or 'bump', the crew in front. Racing takes place over several days, usually four, and the crews change place each day according to the bumps scored. The crew finishing first takes the title 'Head of the River'.

The race is held in divisions, the top of a lower division starting bottom of the next division above it, so that it is possible for a crew to make two bumps in one day ('double bump'). The crews involved in a bump stop rowing immediately; if the crew behind them rows on and bumps the crew ahead, it scores an 'overbump' and changes place with that crew.

At Oxford the principal bumping races are the Summer Eights and the Torpids. At Cambridge, they are the May Races and Lent Races. Oarsmen rowing Head of the River or making four or more bumps during the races are awarded their oars as a trophy.

COASTAL ROWING is a popular version of the sport in the British Isles and to a lesser extent in other parts of the world, notably on the Mediterranean coast.

The boats used are shorter and wider than those used for river rowing and races are held in single sculls, pairs and fours. In Britain, there is a Coast Amateur Rowing Association and regattas are held at coastal resorts in many areas of England and Wales. Status wins at coastal regattas apply to regattas held under A.R.A. rules, and vice versa.

Rules of boat racing. Some 50 nations have associations to administer rowing in their own countries. Some of these have their own rules governing the conduct of racing, and in England both the Boat Race and Henley Royal Regatta are held under their own rules which differ in some respects from those of the Amateur Rowing Association.

The most important rules for boat racing concern fouling and interference. Crews leave their own station at their peril and may be disqualified for 'washing' their opponents or for touching them when out of their own water. A crew can wash their opponents either with the disturbance caused by the boat cutting through the water, or with their 'puddles' (the swirls of water left by the blades after a stroke).

Most races are followed by umpires in motor boats who have sole charge of the race from the moment it has started until the last crew or sculler crosses the finishing line. Where the water is unsuitable for launches, as on courses on narrow rivers, a series of umpires stationed along the course supervises different sections.

Sculling differs technically from rowing in that a sculler holds a scull (or small oar) in each hand instead of pulling on one oar with both hands. For all practical purposes, it is part of the sport of rowing, but the skills required for sculling are somewhat different.

RACING SCULLING BOAT

Sculling boats are very light and narrow and require considerable skill and watermanship to balance and steer; the slightest clumsiness will destroy the run of the boat. Because of the special skill required, a sculler will generally make a good oarsman, though the reverse does not necessarily follow. Crews made up of good scullers invariably do well and many coaches take sculling proficiency into account when selecting their crews. In single sculling, one man only is responsible for the propulsion of the boat, so that the coach can gauge the worth of each individual.

Quadruple and double sculling in particular require a high degree of uniformity and co-ordination between the scullers. A very fast boat, a double sculler is only marginally slower than a coxed four and a quick, smooth action is necessary to get the best out of the boat. A quadruple sculler is even faster and is second in speed only to an eight.

SKIFF RACING is a special form of sculling which operates under its own rules and for which a special type of heavy boat is used. Special regattas are held but the sport is restricted to the river Thames between Wargrave and Kingston, Surrey.

British Rowing Almanack, handbook of the Amateur Rowing Association, published annually.

Rowing dates back to ancient times when it provided motive power for warships before sails replaced galley-slaves. The earliest literary reference to rowing as a sport occurs in the *Aeneid,* in which Virgil describes the

funeral games arranged by Aeneas in honour of his father:

> The waiting crews are crowned with poplar wreaths;
> Their naked shoulders glisten, moist with oil.
> Ranged in a row, their arms stretched to the oars,
> All tense the starting signal they await.
> Together at the trumpet's thrilling blast
> Their bent arms churn the water into foam;
> The sea gapes open by the oars up-torn.

The sport in its modern form is practised mainly on inland rivers and lakes and developed in England on the river Thames which from medieval times had been one of the country's main highways. The wealthy had their own state barges manned by oarsmen, and many hundreds of professional watermen plied for hire on the tidal reaches of the river. By the beginning of the eighteenth century there were more than 40,000 licensed watermen active between Chelsea and Windsor. There were frequent contests between professional watermen and betting on these and on races between barges owned by the well-to-do was a favourite pastime of the gentry in an age addicted to gambling.

It was in this spirit that the Irish comedian, Doggett, instituted in 1715 what is now the oldest sculling race in the world. The race, for an orange livery with a silver badge, known as Doggett's Coat and Badge, antedates the first formal Thames regatta (from the Italian, *regata*—originally boat races on the Grand Canal in Venice) by over 50 years and is still contested each year by young watermen who have just completed their apprenticeship. An early winner of this race was BROUGHTON of Hungerford, who later turned to prize-fighting and achieved fame as the man who introduced gloves and rules to that sport. There were many similar races for other coats and badges and several survived into the early years of the twentieth century.

The earliest account of a regatta on the Thames is given in Hickey's *Memoirs* of 1768, which describes rowing races at Walton, and in 1775 there was published an account of another Thames regatta, so it seems likely that by this time such events were becoming frequent. Rowing now began to attract amateur exponents and by the end of the eighteenth century several amateur clubs were in existence. By 1793, Eton College boys had taken up the sport; the oldest open club still in existence, LEANDER, was formed some time prior to 1820, probably in 1818.

Rowing had become competitive at Oxford and Cambridge Universities in the early years of the nineteenth century and there were bumping races at Oxford in 1822. The first University Boat Race took place at Henley in

1829 and the interest this aroused eventually encouraged the local townspeople to institute the Henley Regatta ten years later. At about the same time, several leading public schools were rowing. Eton had a ten-oar and three eight-oars by 1811, while at Westminster School the *Water Ledger* was begun in June 1813.

Rowing was also developing at that time in the U.S.A. As in England, the original contests were between professional watermen. The first race of this sort was in 1811 when the *Knickerbocker*, manned by ferrymen from Whitehall in New York City, defeated the *Invincible* from Long Island. Two years later, the New York ferrymen were again successful in a race against a crew from Staten Island. In 1824 they defeated a crew of Thames watermen from the British frigate *Hussar* and this contest aroused widespread interest.

The first American amateur clubs were in New York and the Castle Garden Boat Club Association was founded in 1834. The oldest surviving club in the U.S.A., the Detroit Boat Club, dates from 1839.

The first inter-collegiate boat race, between Harvard and Yale, was held on Lake Winnepesaukee in 1852 (see HARVARD-YALE BOAT RACE), but it was not until 1872 that the first open regatta for amateurs took place, a group of Philadelphia clubs, known as the SCHUYL-KILL NAVY, staging the event on the Schuylkill River.

In Australia, rowing developed as a sport about 1830, when it was introduced to Tasmania, the crews of whaling boats competing with crews from shore stations. The Royal Hobart Regatta was founded in 1838. In 1832 a race took place at Port Jackson, Sydney, between four gentlemen and four seamen from the ship *Strathfieldsay*. Later the same year there was an amateur single sculling race for a prize worth £20, indicating that competitive rowing and sculling had become established.

The Australian Subscription Rowing Club was formed in Woolloomooloo Bay in March 1859. Six months later the oldest Australian rowing club now active, Melbourne University Boat Club, came into being. In 1863 there was a four-oared race between Sydney and Melbourne Universities on the Paramatta River over a four-mile course, Melbourne winning in a time of 31 minutes.

The first recognized race for the inter-state eight-oared championship was in 1878, when Victoria defeated New South Wales on the Yarra River. With the exception of the war years, this event has taken place annually ever since and in 1920 the KING'S CUP became the trophy for the championship.

During the nineteenth century rowing spread quickly across Europe. In 1842 an English resident in St. Petersburg presented a pair of silver sculls as a challenge trophy to be competed for annually on the river Neva by British residents, and from this competitive rowing in Russia gradually developed. In the spring of 1864 the English Arrow Boat Club, named after a boat brought out from England, was founded at St. Petersburg. As its name implies, this was a club mainly for Englishmen, but almost immediately a number of Russian clubs were formed and the sport was firmly established.

Professional rowing and sculling. Throughout the nineteenth century, and in the early twentieth century, professional rowing and, more especially, sculling, flourished alongside the amateur sport. Professional events attracted an enormous following and were widely reported in the press. Professionals had a profound influence on rowing in Britain, Australia, the U.S.A., and Canada, many becoming successful coaches of amateur crews, but with the rapid growth of amateur rowing and the advent of the First World War, professional contests gradually died out.

The world professional sculling championship was, in its hey-day, one of the most widely followed of all sporting events. The winners became national heroes and there was considerable betting on the results. The first race was in 1831, and it was run in Britain until 1876. Despite the decline in interest in professional sculling, the championship survived until after the Second World War, the last race being in 1952.

Among famous professionals who won the title are Hanlan of Toronto (1880-4), Beach, New South Wales (1884-7), Arnst, New Zealand (1908-11), and the English sculler, BARRY (1912-20), one of the best scullers of all time. Another professional champion to earn high praise was the Australian Searle (1888-9), who might have remained champion for many years had he not died of typhoid in 1889 at the age of 23. More recently, an outstanding sculler was PEARCE, an Australian winner of the 1932 Olympic title who later became a Canadian citizen and won the professional title in 1933.

By the latter half of the nineteenth century, rules defining amateur status had become very strict, especially in England where nobody involved in manual labour, for example, was allowed to compete as an amateur. This led in England to the formation of the National Amateur Rowing Association (N.A.R.A.) to cater for such men as these who were in no other sense professionals but were barred by the rules of the Amateur Rowing Association. In 1956 common sense prevailed and the

N.A.R.A. merged with the A.R.A., whose rules were amended.

Today, professional rowing is a thing of the past and the only professionals remaining are those who receive salaries as coaches, mostly in Eastern Europe and in the U.S.A.

Amateur sculling. The oldest and most coveted event for amateur scullers is the Diamond Sculls at Henley Royal Regatta. The names of many of the world's best-known amateurs appear on the list of winners, although one of the most successful of all time, the Russian IVANOV, three times Olympic single sculls champion, narrowly failed on his two attempts at Henley.

Among amateurs, an Englishman, F. S. Kelly, was exceptional and had an almost faultless technique. Other famous exponents in the amateur ranks were Casamajor, a distinguished member of LONDON ROWING CLUB in the 1850s, Beresford, of THAMES ROWING CLUB, the Americans J. B. KELLY, SR. — in whose honour the PHILADELPHIA GOLD CUP, the trophy for the world amateur sculling championship, was instituted in 1920 — and Burk, Wright, of Canada, and the Australians Pearce, Wood, and MACKENZIE.

Double sculling has never attracted as many devotees as single sculling but has produced some outstanding combinations. One of the most successful was that of the Russians Berkutov and Tyukalov, European champions on five consecutive occasions from 1956 to 1961 and Olympic champions in 1960.

Sea rowing has flourished round the coasts of many countries for centuries and coastal rowing is now a distinctive branch of the sport. In the eighteenth and nineteenth centuries, there were races between crews from ships who were frequently challenged by the longshoremen who worked in and around the harbours. By the late nineteenth century, clubs were formed for this special type of rowing, especially round the shores of the Mediterranean and in Britain, Scandinavia, Australia, and North America.

Coastal rowing is particularly well supported in Britain, where it is now purely for amateurs, but the influence of harbour workers and longshoremen is still seen in clubs such as the Southampton Coalporters Amateur Rowing Club. This club resulted from a challenge in 1874 by an unbeaten crew from an American frigate, the *Lancaster*, then in Southampton harbour. A crew of coal porters twice defeated the Americans and, encouraged by their success, stayed together for the next five years, forming a club and introducing the short, wide boats now used in coastal rowing.

Sea rowing has also attracted inland crews, some of which compete in coastal regattas,

and, on occasion, river boats have crossed the English Channel. The most famous of these crossings occurred in 1885 when W. H. Grenfell, later Lord Desborough, stroked a clinker-built eight from Dover to Calais in 4 hrs. 22 min. Although the water was calm, the heat was intense and two of the crew were in a state of collapse by the time they reached Calais. A more remarkable feat was that of a 71-year-old Frenchman, G. Adam, who in 1952 sculled from Boulogne to Folkestone and back in a clinker sculling boat in 19 hrs. 53 min. Previously, in 1905, he had made the return trip, but on different days.

These are not really part of the sport but nevertheless share in the history of rowing, as do the remarkable Atlantic crossings of the Norwegians Harbo and Samuelson, who in 1896 became the first men to row the Atlantic, covering over 3,000 miles from New York to the Scilly Isles in an 18 ft. (5·48 m.) boat in 56 days; of Ridgway and Blyth, the first Britons to row the Atlantic (from Cape Cod to Inishmore, Aran Islands, in 1966); and of Fairfax, the first oarsman to make the solo journey, taking 172 days in 1969.

International rowing. Towards the close of the nineteenth century rowing was sufficiently established in Europe for an international association to be formed to control the sport. In 1892, at the suggestion of the Italian Federation, the Fédération Internationale des Sociétés d'Aviron was founded and has remained the international governing body. Founder members were the federations of the Adriatic (now defunct), Belgium, France, Italy, and Switzerland, but despite her position as the major rowing power at the time, Britain remained insular. Although British crews competed in the Olympic Games from 1908, she did not affiliate to the F.I.S.A. until 1947.

In 1893 the first European rowing championships were held. Originally the programme was restricted to three events: coxed fours, single sculls, and eights. In 1894 coxed pairs, and in 1898 double sculls, were introduced. These remained the five championship events until the number was increased to seven with the inclusion of coxless pairs in 1924 and coxless fours in 1925, and to eight in 1974 when quadruple sculls were included.

Rowing was included unofficially in the Olympic Games of 1900 and 1904, but in 1908 it was recognized as an Olympic sport and the first official Olympic regatta was held at Henley with events for eights, coxless fours, coxless pairs, and single sculls. By 1924 all seven events were included and these and the more recently introduced quadruple sculls became the established classes for championships for men.

In 1962 world championships were inaugurated to be held every four years between Olympiads. In 1974, these superseded the European championships and are now held annually except in Olympic years. An annual junior regatta, for boys up to 18 years of age, was introduced in 1967 and recognized as an official junior championship in 1970.

Rowing for women is a comparatively recent development and is not as widespread as the men's sport. In some countries it is not encouraged, but women's European championships were instituted in 1954 and these have been superseded by world championships which are held annually. Women's events have also been introduced into the Olympic Games.

Early in the long history of rowing, developments in boat and oar design and, more recently, in training methods and technique, led to radical changes in the sport.

The boats of the early nineteenth century were still based on traditional rowing barges. They were heavy, clinker-built craft with fixed seats and long narrow bladed oars were used. The first real development came in 1841 when Oxford used a carvel-built boat with a smooth skin. This construction was lighter and produced less friction and was therefore faster. In 1844 the outrigger was introduced. This enabled boatbuilders to construct more slender and lighter boats without sacrificing the leverage of the oar.

In 1856, Taylor built the first keelless eight for the Royal Chester Rowing Club.

All these early developments took place in England, but in 1857 Babcock of New York introduced a sliding seat which reached English rowing in 1871. This was an important development since it enabled the oarsman to place himself in a stronger position at each stage of the stroke.

Coxswainless boats, except for sculling, were not in general use in Europe, but a coxswainless pair race was introduced at Henley as early as 1845. Fours remained coxed in England until 1864, when WOODGATE's celebrated Brasenose four completed the Henley course without a coxswain and, although they were disqualified for their pains, the point was taken by the Henley stewards, who introduced an event for coxswainless fours the following year. European countries were slow to follow suit. There were coxswainless events in the 1908 Olympic regatta at Henley, but it was not until the 1920s that coxswainless pairs and fours were recognized as international events.

The early innovations revolutionized rowing as a sport and few modern developments have had a comparable effect. Equipment and methods are constantly evolving but even the more spectacular changes of recent years, such as the introduction of short, wide blades and short, deep hulls by the West Germans in the 1950s, or the asymmetrical distribution of oars, and boats in which the coxswains lie prone in the bows instead of sitting upright in the stern (both Italian innovations during the same period) did not produce the startling alterations in technique such as those that occurred during the period between 1840 and 1880. Modern developments in technique have been the result of new coaching and training methods rather than of radical modifications of equipment.

Rowing technique originated from that used by professional watermen, but with the development of lighter craft, Oxford and Cambridge oarsmen evolved a rowing (as distinct from sculling) style which later became known as the 'orthodox' style.

The old English orthodox coaches had a carefully developed mental picture of how a good oarsman should look and rowers were made to perform a series of movements conforming to this ideal. As many as 45 distinct movements in a stroke were listed by one authority. This approach led to artificiality, and to style for its own sake, which often meant slow crews, though, at its best, orthodoxy was highly successful. It was against the exaggerations of this method that the Australian FAIRBAIRN rebelled. Fairbairn had rowed in England in good orthodox crews but he saw the pitfalls. In his own highly successful and original coaching, much of which he did in England, he insisted on natural action and on allowing the freedom of the subconscious mind — a method, however, that was equally vulnerable to caricature.

Orthodox crews had a long swing, derived originally from the days of fixed-seat rowing, and a lightning beginning and recovery. The emphasis was on a co-ordinated drive, with the legs, arms, body, and slide all beginning and finishing the stroke together. Fairbairn concentrated on bladework and allowed his oarsmen to ignore conscious body movements.

In Britain these two approaches effectively split rowing into two camps for the first half of the twentieth century, although orthodox rowing was in decline after the First World War.

The golden days of orthodoxy were in the 1880s and 1890s. The nursery was Eton College, which during this period produced crews who could hold their own with the best in the country, and many Etonians went on to row in successful university crews. But English rowing remained strictly parochial with only a few overseas crews venturing to Henley until

1906, when English oarsmen saw a Belgian crew, rowing in a distinctly different style, carry off the Grand Challenge Cup — the first foreign crew to do so.

Belgian eights of this period dominated rowing on the Continent, winning the European title 12 times between 1897 and 1910, but their successes at Henley were attributed by English oarsmen more to a decline in orthodox rowing than to their relaxed technique, based on a shorter swing, steady sliding, and a powerful leg-drive. Nevertheless, it was the example of the Belgians and 'Fairbairnism' that were to become the greatest influences on continental rowing for the next decade, despite the classic win of the veteran Leander eight in the 1908 Olympics, when the Belgians, as a result of an internal dispute, were unable to put out their best crew.

In the U.S.A., attempts by well-known British coaches to instil orthodoxy into American university rowing were not successful and an American style gradually developed through professional coaches, who imposed a technique more akin to sculling than the British style. One of the most famous of these coaches was Courtney, a former professional sculling champion. He decided that the secret of winning races lay not so much in driving the boat through the water as in keeping it running between the strokes and, as the Belgians were discovering at the same time, a smooth, fast recovery followed by very steady sliding produced the best results. This was also the basis of successful New South Wales crews in Australia in the first decade of the twentieth century, when they won the inter-state title on three occasions. Courtney's system produced striking successes for Cornell in the last years of the nineteenth century and later.

But the most revolutionary developments in technique in the twentieth century originated from the coaching of two men who had themselves never rowed: CONIBEAR in America and K. ADAM in West Germany. Conibear took over coaching at Washington University in 1907 and, although he died only ten years later, his methods were to dominate American rowing until well after the Second World War, his oarsmen later becoming leading coaches at almost every successful university. During this period, American university crews dominated the Olympic eights, winning on every occasion from 1920 to 1956. Ebright, a former Washington coxswain, coached California to three Olympic wins, while one of the last crews to be successful with Conibear's methods, the Naval Academy crews of 1952-4, won 29 major races without defeat, including the Olympic title. Keeping the swing down to a minimum, especially at the finish of the stroke, Conibear's crews used very long slides, developing a powerful leg-drive and hard draw, while maintaining low rates of striking and even, steady sliding. Their staying power was remarkable.

Despite the success of American college crews, for several years after 1946 a long stroke with a pronounced lie-back at the finish and a very low rate of striking was in vogue in several European centres. An extreme version of this was practised at Cambridge University, especially by the Lady Margaret Boat Club (St. John's College). A Cambridge crew rowing in this way beat both Harvard and Yale in the United States in 1951 and went on to win the European title later in the year, but, following the appearance of Russian crews in international rowing the next year, dramatic changes began to take place.

Whereas crews in the past had always tended to slow down the slides on the way forward to the next stroke and follow this with a sudden, hard drive with the legs, Russian crews appeared to stop almost completely just after the finish and then to accelerate on to the beginning. This reduced the amount by which the boat slowed down between the strokes and a less extreme version of this rhythm was soon to become a prominent feature of West German rowing. Accompanied by a high rate of striking, this technique proved too fast for crews rowing in the 'Lady Margaret' style, but although the Russians won nine European titles between 1953 and 1956, including the eights on three occasions, the Americans again won the Olympic eights in 1956.

The advent of Adam's West German crews finally ended the American domination. A former amateur boxer, Adam started from scratch in 1950 with a new club at Ratzeburg and by 1959 his unorthodox crews were winning international titles with impressive ease. They were to dominate rowing for the next decade. Discarding many established principles, though owing something to Fairbairn in his approach, Adam ignored preconceived notions of style and rhythm. Employing new training methods and equipment, he produced crews quite unlike any seen previously.

The principal features of these crews were an almost total absence of body swing and a very high rate of striking which was maintained throughout the race. With long oars and wide blades, a very hard leg-drive provided a powerful thrust. Adam's crews won many world, European, and Olympic titles, including the Olympic eights in 1960 and 1968, and his eight finished second in the 1964 Olympic final to an American club crew, VESPER, employing his own methods. In 1965, the Germans had their revenge, defeating Vesper in a record-breaking final of the Grand Challenge Cup at Henley.

The influence of these Ratzeburg crews was felt throughout the rowing world and as a result the best crews in every country began to row in similar styles. Even in Adam's crews, extreme variations and exaggerations became less apparent, although a much reduced body-swing compared with that used by traditional crews and faster sliding at high rates of striking remained characteristics. With a preference for tall, strong, and heavy men, most coaches were able to develop techniques which placed a greater premium on power than on the niceties of style, which, by 1970, could be said to exist only in general rather than specific terms.

G. C. Bourne, *A Textbook of Oarsmanship* (1925); R. D. Burnell, *The Complete Sculler* (1973), *Swing Together* (1952), *The Oxford and Cambridge Boat Race— 1829-1953* (1954), and *Henley Regatta — A History* (1957); Hylton Cleaver, *A History of Rowing* (1957); H. R. A. Edwards, *The Way of a Man with a Blade* (1963); I. Fairbairn, *Steve Fairbairn on Rowing* (1951); R. F. Herrick, *Red Top: Reminiscences of Harvard Rowing* (1948); R. C. Lehmann, *The Complete Oarsman* (1924); G. G. H. Page, *Coaching for Rowing* (1963); C. F. Porter, *Rowing to Win* (1959); J. A. N. Railton, *International Rowing* (1969); A. C. Scott and J. G. P. Williams, ed., *Rowing— A Scientific Approach* (1967); P. C. Wilson, *Modern Rowing* (1969).
GOVERNING BODY (WORLD): Fédération Internationale des Sociétés d'Aviron, Caisse postale 215, CH-1820 Montreux, Switzerland; (U.K.): Amateur Rowing Association, 160 Great Portland Street, London W.1.

ROYAL AND ANCIENT GOLF CLUB, St. Andrews, see GOLF.

ROYAL AUTOMOBILE CLUB, London. The main SQUASH RACKETS court at the R.A.C. was the scene of four Open and amateur championships finals. The gallery has seating on three sides but the viewing from the back gallery is comparatively poor. Until after the Second World War only the main court of the four was of standard dimensions; then two more courts were made standard with the remaining space sufficient to include a court of American dimensions. The eliminating competition and the early rounds of the amateur championship were played here from 1946 to 1972.

ROYAL BIRKDALE, English GOLF course. On first acquaintance Birkdale, on the Fylde coast of Lancashire, is a links of exaggeration. The sand dunes are much larger and steeper than most seaside courses; the rough is deeper and tougher, consisting in part of willow scrub from which only the strongest player can hope to recover; the fairways are formidably long. One criticism of Birkdale is that most of the greens are set in folds of the dunes, demonstrating a wasted opportunity to build some plateau greens on the summits. Scoring standards, however, suggest that the 'easy' siting of the greens is quite difficult enough, even for the best players.

ROYAL   CALEDONIAN   CURLING CLUB, the 'mother club' of CURLING, founded in 1838, with John Cairnie of Curling Hall, Largs, as its first president. The headquarters have always been in Edinburgh. All the 600 British clubs are affiliated in addition to many thousands of overseas clubs which are affiliated through their national associations. The Club, originally called the Grand Caledonian Curling Club, was granted the title 'Royal' in 1843, after the Earl of Mansfield had demonstrated the game to Queen Victoria on the ballroom floor at Scone. The Queen is the Club's patron, and the Duke of Edinburgh, president in 1964-5, is an honorary member.

ROYAL CANOE CLUB, founded on 25 July 1866 by MACGREGOR as the Canoe Club at the Star and Garter Hotel, Richmond, Surrey. Within a year, the club had a membership of over a hundred, while branches were formed in many parts of England. In 1873 Queen Victoria bestowed the title 'Royal' on the club which, at the time, did not have a permanent headquarters. In 1897, a piece of land became available at the head of Trowlock Island —just below Kingston Bridge—and a club-house was built: the same building still housed the club some 80 years later.
COLOURS: Blue with white trim.

ROYAL COMPANY OF ARCHERS. In the year 1676, 'Archers and Bowmen Residing within and about the City of Edinburgh' resolved 'to enter and list themselves in a particular Society and Company for Archery and Shutting with Bows and Arrows'. This was the formal beginning of the Queen's Bodyguard for Scotland, the Royal Company of Archers, which is the oldest ARCHERY society in the United Kingdom. It almost certainly existed as a less formal corporation before 1676, as one of its trophies, the Musselburgh Arrow, has been competed for since 1603. In the year 1703, a charter of incorporation was granted to the Royal Company by Queen Anne; the *reddendo*, or service to be performed for the royal favour, being the presentation of a pair of barbed arrows on Whitsunday if required.

In 1822, on the occasion of the visit of George IV to Edinburgh, the Royal Company tendered its services as bodyguard; they were accepted, and since then it has occupied a conspicuous position on royal ceremonial occasions in Scotland. The shooting of the Royal Company differs considerably from that practised by other societies of archers. The distance most favoured is 180 yds. (165 m.), the ancient form of clout shooting being most usually practised. A unique feature of the Company is the uniform of field-green cloth, with eagle feathers trimming the bonnet, and gilt buttons; swords are worn on ceremonial occasions. The headquarters of this ancient and venerable society is at Archers' Hall in Edinburgh, which has attached to it a covered buttway for short-range target archery.

ROYAL LIVERPOOL, English GOLF course. The links, at Hoylake, overlooking the sands of Dee, present a forbidding appearance, flat and unprepossessing. Of all the championship links, Hoylake is the most controversial, with its artificial out-of-bounds area within the course itself, impinging in particular on the green of the 190-yd. (174 m.) seventh hole. Some claim this to be one of the greatest holes in golf, others say it is the unfairest. Good or bad, Hoylake is certainly extremely difficult and the handicap player bent on a day's enjoyment would be advised to divert his path to nearby Wallasey or cross the Mersey to Formby.

ROYAL LYTHAM AND ST. ANNES, English GOLF course, Lancashire. Although well inland and surrounded by houses, Lytham is considered technically a links and therefore eligible for the championship roster. By championship standards it is short, but the fairways are narrow, contained by shrubs, trees, and the railway line, and the emphasis is on accuracy rather than power. JONES won his first Open championship here in 1926 and a famous single shot in golf, his full mashie recovery from sand on the seventeenth, is celebrated by a plaque in the bank of the bunker.

ROYAL OCEAN RACING CLUB, the premier offshore yacht racing club of European waters, was formed in 1925 following the introduction of the American-pioneered sport to Britain in the FASTNET RACE, in which seven yachts started. A handful of enthusiasts organized a meeting to frame the rules for the Ocean Racing Club, as it was then called. There were 34 founder members and their object was to provide annually an offshore race not less than 600 miles (965 km.) long. This has grown into a programme of races, designed to last a week-end, which are run throughout the summer season, mainly in the English Channel.

ROYAL PALACE (1964), a race-horse by BALLYMOSS, bred and owned by Joel, trained by MURLESS, and ridden by PIGGOTT, MOORE, and Barclay. He was perhaps the best English race-horse to appear on the turf since BAHRAM. Royal Palace won nine races, including the DERBY, TWO THOUSAND GUINEAS, KING GEORGE VI AND QUEEN ELIZABETH STAKES, ECLIPSE STAKES, and CORONATION CUP, and £166,063 in prize money (a British record).

ROYAL TENNIS, see REAL TENNIS.

ROYAL TOXOPHILITE SOCIETY. The formation in 1781 of a society calling themselves the Toxophilites was the result of the enthusiasm of Sir Ashton Lever who became first president, and his secretary, Thomas Waring. Sir Ashton was famous for the museum of natural history which he maintained at Leicester House, in London, and a few of his friends joined together for ARCHERY practice in the grounds of this now extinct house. Thomas Waring, who took up archery as a remedial treatment for chest trouble, became a notable bowyer, in addition being secretary of the newly formed society. A few of the early members had belonged to the Society of Finsbury Archers, which had been inactive since 1761, and there were also strong connections with the Honourable Artillery Company whose ground had been used by the Finsbury Archers.

From 1784 to 1803, the Toxophilites enjoyed membership of the H.A.C. and formed the archers division of that regiment. However, during this period the Toxophilite Society functioned separately and members divided themselves between the two bodies on such occasions as, for instance, the meeting of the archery societies at Blackheath in 1791, when each entered two teams. The Toxophilites were apparently one of only five societies to survive the Napoleonic wars. After using various shooting grounds, they occupied part of Regents Park for nearly 100 years. A fine Archers' Hall was built there and excellent shooting facilities maintained. For over forty years after this, the Royal Toxophilite Society — the prefix 'royal' being assumed in 1844 — leased an old burial ground within bowshot of Marble Arch for their archery range. The Society, familiarly called 'The Tox', now has its permanent home in a house and grounds in Buckinghamshire.

Many of the activities of the Society were of a social nature, and accounts of full dress balls, fêtes, and special ladies' days occupy a good deal of space in early records. Membership of the Society is by invitation: the Prince of Wales (later George IV), William IV, and

Queen Victoria all gave it their patronage, and Queen ELIZABETH II is the present patron. Among other distinctions, the Royal Toxophilite Society enjoys the freedoms of two other old-established societies, the ROYAL COMPANY OF ARCHERS in Edinburgh, and the WOODMEN OF ARDEN.

The Royal Toxophilite Society is the premier archery society of Great Britain and for many years its authority has extended to the organization of world championship meetings, Grand National Archery Meetings and other similar important events. Its guiding influence, with its many years of experience and tradition, has helped immeasurably in the creation of the solid foundations of archery today.

ROYCROFT, WILLIAM (*c.* 1914-   ), Australian three-day event (see EQUESTRIAN EVENTS) horseman. He helped his team to win the gold medal at the OLYMPIC GAMES in Rome (1960) by completing the show jumping phase with a broken shoulder. In 1965, at the age of 51, he rode three horses at Badminton and thus covered more than 50 miles during the speed and endurance phase. Both he and his son, Wayne, won team bronze medals in the 1968 Olympic Games at Mexico.

ROZEANU, ANGELICA (*née* Adelstein) (1921-   ), Romanian TABLE TENNIS player, the strongest woman player of the period after the Second World War. She first competed in world table tennis as a promising defensive player at the age of 16. Her career was interrupted by the war and by Nazi objections. Following the war she began a great rivalry with the Hungarian Farkas, who won the women's singles at the first three championships after table tennis was resumed. When Rozeanu at last won in 1950, she began a sequence of victories against Farkas and two other players, six successive singles titles in all, the last in 1955, together with three women's doubles and three mixed. Tiny and petite, with a severe chop defence and fast footwork, she could hit with great authority on either wing at well-chosen moments. She emigrated to Israel in 1960.

ROZELLE, ALVIN RAY (1927-   ), American FOOTBALL official and general manager of the LOS ANGELES RAMS, he was Commissioner of the NATIONAL FOOTBALL LEAGUE from 1960. He was the architect of the 1966 merger of the National and AMERICAN FOOTBALL LEAGUES after six costly years of bidding up players' salaries.

R.T. JONES AWARD, trophy presented under the auspices of the United States Golf Association for outstanding sportsmanship in GOLF.

RUGBY FIVES is a hand-ball game played with the gloved hands in a court enclosed by four walls between two players (singles) or four players (doubles). A small number of courts have been built by enthusiasts in other countries but, generally speaking, the game is confined to the British Isles.

The court is rectangular, 28 ft. (8·5 m.) long and 18 feet (5·5 m.) wide. The height of the front wall is 15 ft. (4·6 m.) and the playing area of the side walls, marked by a painted line, is 15 ft. (4·6 m.) for the first 12 ft. (3·7 m.), measuring from the front wall, sloping down to 6 ft. (1·8 m.) at the back. The height of the back wall is 6 ft. (1·8 m.). A board, the top of which is 2 ft. 6 in. (0·76 m.) from the floor, spans the front wall from side to side. Since the ball is small, white, and hard the walls of the standard court are made of a hard composition and coloured black. The floor is usually red.

Many courts still are not standardized. Although they are all rectangular, from a playing point of view the differences in dimensions have an important effect on the game. However, the cost of erecting new courts is often prohibitive for a school or college and, in consequence, fives players are distinguished for their polite disregard of what they consider to be deviations from the norm of others' courts.

The old fives ball, used and preferred by all fives players until its manufacture was stopped in the mid-twentieth century, had a centre of cork round which was wound cloth strips held in position by many yards of thread. The whole was encased in a leather jacket, put on wet and stitched so that it dried tight. It was mainly a cottage industry and uneconomic for modern times. The present ball is much the same inside but is covered with a thin plastic. It bounces well but lacks the former zip.

Players wear on both hands light leather gloves well padded on the face of palms and fingers. Spectators watch either from a platform at the back, peering over the 6-foot wall, or from a gallery.

A game is begun by a preliminary rally. The side winning that rally becomes the 'receiver', and the side losing the rally, the 'server'. This peculiarity of nomenclature is explained by the fact that before the Second World War it was the custom of the winner of the preliminary rally to throw the ball on to the wall for the loser to strike after it had bounced. In those days the man who threw the ball was called the server and the man who first hit it the striker. They were also referred to, as they are now, as being 'up' or 'down'. In more recent times, because of the difficulty of getting an opponent to throw the ball exactly as a player wants, the one who is 'down' throws for himself and is therefore called the server. The player who takes the first strike is called the receiver or 'up'.

Only players who are 'up' or 'in hand', as it is also called, can score points. The player, or players, who are 'down' can only put their opponents out of hand. Hence when doubles are being played the score may be '7-5, first hand in'. Then, if the serving side scores a point, the score becomes not 5-7 but '7-5 second hand in'. If the receiving or 'up' side then scores a point the score becomes '8-5 second hand in'. A win for the service side in the following rally makes the score '5-8 first hand in', and so on. The scoring always seems much simpler in the singles game when it is plain that the receiver becomes the server after losing a rally and scores a point only if he is already the receiver or 'up'. A further complication in doubles is that the winners of the preliminary rally have only one hand at the start, thus reducing the advantage of winning the preliminary rally.

Usually the player or side first to score 15 points wins the game. However, if the score reaches 14-14, known as 'game-ball all', the player or side first to reach 16 wins the game. In schools championships, in order to get through a heavy programme of singles and doubles, 11 points are substituted for 15.

Four players form the team in matches between clubs and schools, and in the university match between Oxford and Cambridge eight players make a team. Doubles only are played in most club matches but a full match consists of a singles played by each string against his opposite number and two sets of doubles for each pair against each pair of the opposite side. The total points are then added up for each side and the winning side is the one with the most points. It is possible, therefore, for a side winning more games than its opponents to lose the match on points. The advantage of the system is that it keeps everyone striving to do his best until the end. It may prove important for a weaker player or pair to get 6 points in a game rather than 4. Fives is a team game.

In championships, singles or doubles, the rounds are won by the side winning two games regardless of the total number of points scored.

A game begins when the server throws the ball up for himself. If he is a right-handed player, i.e. naturally stronger with his right hand than with his left, he will throw the ball up into the right-hand corner of the front wall. He must do this so that the ball strikes first the front wall above the board and then the right-hand side wall. If the ball bounces awkwardly on the floor or in any way not to the server's liking he may stop it and start again. If he wishes he may do this over and over again — becoming progressively less popular. Again, if he wishes, he may require the receiver to throw for him as was the practice years ago. Some players find it almost as difficult to throw for themselves as they often did for others.

When the ball has bounced once on the floor the server serves by striking the ball first on to the right-hand side wall, if he is right-handed, and then on to the front wall above the board. The ball is then returned, if he is able to do so, by the receiver, either before or after the first bounce, on to the front wall above the board. He may play his shot directly on to the front wall or on to the front wall by way of a side wall. The rally then proceeds, a player from each side hitting the ball alternately with one of his opponents. The rally is lost by the side which fails to return the ball on to the front wall above the board before it has bounced twice.

When returning the ball a player may make what use he can of the side walls within the confines of the court but he cannot hit the ball on to the floor first or on the walls outside the confines of the court including the roof. However, a ball may bounce from the floor on to the back wall and be played from there. Sometimes when serving, a player will hit the ball straight on to the front wall without its touching the side wall first. If he does so the ball is called a 'blackguard' and may be returned by an opponent providing the opponent shouts his intention to do so before he has struck the ball.

Players on the same side in the doubles game usually take one side of the court each but there is a good deal of movement and change of position, and frequent calls of 'mine'. The fact that all four players are sharing the same playing area inevitably leads to occasional confusion and loss of sight of the ball by one or other of the players. 'Lets' are allowed and are usually offered to the players by each other. Umpires are scarce and there is small reliance upon them; accordingly players' efforts to give their opponents a clear view are marked. Because the ball is fast and there is much bending to be done with little respite, amateur singles champions over the age of 30 are virtually unknown. Survival is longer in doubles and many notable players have done well in the championship over a long period.

Styles of play and technique vary but the

essential abilities are to be able to hit the ball with both hands close to the top of the board, to send the ball close and parallel to the side walls, and to play to a length, i.e. to make the ball die away at the back wall so that an opponent is kept in two minds about when to play the return.

However strong the better hand may be, and some players' good right hand, or good left hand, is very strong indeed, a fives player does not progress far, except occasionally in doubles, unless he develops a serviceable weaker hand. The 'one-handed' doubles player is often a nuisance in the court for he and his partner are forever darting across the court to enable the one-handed player to get back to his favourite side.

Some players volley more than others, but usually because of the use of the side walls, the ball is taken after the bounce. If an opponent's stroke allows, the ball will often be played off the back wall since, it being inadvisable to do more than glance around, the player from the back has the whole court at his mercy.

Apart from possible injury to the face if a player turns about to watch his opponent play the ball, the only impediment to complete physical enjoyment is bruising on the bones of the hand. All fives players suffer at times, the young being especially vulnerable. There is no cure except rest and, since rest is unthinkable, remedies are limited to covering the bruise with whatever the player chooses. Raw steak was once a favourite.

The word 'fives' has no accepted etymology. Strutt, in his *The Sports and Pastimes of the People of England*, accepted the explanation that the word may have come from the fact that a five-a-side game was played in the presence of Elizabeth I in 1591, a suggestion which, though repeated many times, is hardly confirmed by the evidence. It seems clear enough that the game was played between any equal number of people and on any occasion when a convenient wall offered itself. Strutt unequivocally calls the game 'hand-tennis' and certainly tennis courts were often used, at least until the end of the eighteenth century, for a hand-ball game by then known as fives. There is a public house in London, near Piccadilly, called the Hand and Racquet, and near-by there is an old tennis court, used for many years for a different purpose. Erasmus, in 1524, refers to the game played either with the hands or a racket, and the schoolmaster, Mulcaster, in 1581 adds to our knowledge by explaining that the game is sometimes played like tennis or with a ball made of some 'softer stuffe' with the hand against a wall alone.

In less populous places, where no tennis courts were to be found, fives was played in the churchyards against a wall of the church. Parson Woodforde in *The Diary of a Country Parson* makes casual references to it. A game is played in Babcary churchyard in 1764 and the parson loses his bet. More ominous, in 1768, the churchwardens of Castle Cary wait upon his father 'for leave to dig up the Fives-Place in Cary Churchyard, and it was granted....'

It seems obvious, therefore, that a simple game of ball against a wall was played sometimes with the racket, to be known later as RACKETS, and sometimes with the hand and known as fives. Why fives? Probably because the five fingers of the hand were known in games as 'fives', just as a 'bunch of fives' meant closing the fist for a fight. There are many references to the game, none of them before the nineteenth century pausing to give an explanation, suggesting that no explanation was necessary. Rawdon Crawley in Thackeray's *Vanity Fair* has fives as well as boxing listed among his accomplishments; Dickens tells us that the married happiness of the Nicklebys is to be compared to 'the adventurous pair of the Fives' Court', which may mean BOXING; but the best evidence of the game's popularity comes from Hazlitt, who tells us in great detail, quoting an article in *The Examiner*, how and how well a certain John (Jack) Cavanagh played. Cavanagh died in 1819, by which date the game must have had some rules. We know it was played in London's Fleet Prison, against one wall, sometimes with the hand and sometimes with a racket. A onewall hand-ball game is played still in public recreation grounds in New York where the wall is so set up that a game can proceed on each side at the same time.

However, it was the advent of the reformed public schools which, as the nineteenth century progressed, changed fives, like so many other outdoor pastimes, into organized, competitive sports. *Mens sana in corpore sano*, a healthy mind in a healthy body, was soon an essential belief for those who conducted boarding schools. The wickedness of leisure pursuits in earlier times, when idle hands found as much mischief as possible to do, made it imperative, so pedagogues thought, to occupy boys throughout their waking hours. One of the ways to do this was to capitalize on the obvious delight of most boys in hitting a ball against a wall.

The three schools that influenced society most were Eton, Winchester, and Rugby and it was Dr. Arnold's success at Rugby that then mattered most. All three played a variety of fives (see ETON FIVES; WINCHESTER FIVES), but as Arnold's men went forth to conduct other schools so were the football and fives games of Rugby popularized.

The next phase was soon reached. Games were arranged between neighbouring schools. These were fun but at fives hardly more than that for courts differed greatly in length, breadth, height of back wall, and composition. As late as the 1920s, all the Rugby fives courts a schoolboy visited differed noticeably from his own, and fifty years later not all the best fives-playing schools had managed, for financial reasons, to build standard courts.

The Rugby Fives Association, formed in 1927, made its first task the drafting of rules which would be an acceptable compromise between the practices of different clubs. The rules were finally accepted by the clubs in 1930. The Association next turned its attention to the size of a standard court, the dimensions being approved in 1931. Competitive play was greatly encouraged by these two events. The amateur singles championship (Jesters' Cup) was started in 1932 and the club doubles competition became the amateur doubles championship (Cyriax Cup) in 1934. These competitions were followed by the North of England championships.

The competitions, however, which did most to establish the game throughout the country were the schools' championships. From the very first (1930) they attracted large entries from players learning the game in England and Scotland. For the first ten years, up to the Second World War, Oundle School dominated the doubles, only three other schools winning once and St. Paul's School twice. The singles were shared more widely, seven schools having at least one winner. Standards varied greatly but after the war, although Oundle again began well, victory in doubles and singles was widespread. In the first 25 years after the war Oundle won the doubles six times, Denstone College four, Alleyn's School three, St. Dunstan's College, Merchiston Castle School, and Clifton College twice each. In the same period a player from Bedford School won the singles title eight times, an Oundle player four times, and an Alleyn's player, a Sedbergh player, and a Poundswick High School player twice each. Both Poundswick wins were by the same player, Enstone. Although his entry came necessarily from his school, it has no fives courts; Enstone played his fives at the Manchester Y.M.C.A., a notable club.

Other championships and competitions started in the 1950s and 1960s, and recognized by the Rugby Fives Association, include the Scottish championships (singles and doubles), the West of England championships, the Brit-

ish universities championships, and the West of England schools' tournament. Oxford has played Cambridge since 1925, the war years 1940-5 excepted. Cambridge has a formidable lead over Oxford in these matches.

The names of the best Rugby fives players are little known to the general public. Some of the more distinguished champions, notably J. G. W. Davies and J. F. Pretlove, have been first-class cricketers and thus more prominent; others must be content with the plaudits of their fellow-players.

All fives players know the name of Dr. Edgar Cyriax whose best playing days were over before the championships started. In memory he is the w. G. GRACE of fives, a first-class performer and a 'character'. His cup, when it was the prize for the club doubles competition, was won four times in succession by Malt and Bailey of the Alleyn old boys. Malt, a left-hander whose length was immaculate, also won the singles championship three times, his last win in 1935 against Davies in the final being a superb exhibition. He died very young; Bailey continued to play and with other partners won the doubles championship three times. Players who, like Malt, have won the singles championship three or more times are Davies, Dawes, Pretlove, E. Marsh, and Watkinson. All of them, except Davies, also won the doubles championship with various partners, Pretlove on no less than seven occasions, four of them with another cricketer, Silk. Watkinson won the doubles championship three times with Elliott and once with Gardner. Although Gardner won the singles championship only once his name appeared many times as winner of other championships including the doubles championship.

Rugby fives is mainly a school, old boys', and university game. Courts are almost entirely confined to schools and colleges and this means that the best clubs are likely to be those attached to schools. The Y.M.C.A. of Manchester is an exception. This situation gave rise many years ago to the establishment of roving clubs, the most notable being the JESTERS.

The Association also saw the need for helping players to keep in the game after leaving school. The Association Club was formed in 1947 and owed much of its outstanding success to G. R. Rimmer, president of the Association, 1960-5.

GOVERNING BODY: Rugby Fives Association, 28 Devonshire Road, Bexhill-on-Sea, Sussex.

RUGBY LEAGUE FOOTBALL, a 13-a-side game of running, passing from hand to hand, and kicking an oval ball. Derived from RUGBY UNION, it is played by amateurs and

professionals in England (mostly in the north), Australia, and France, and by amateurs in New Zealand. The rectangular pitch is a maximum of 110 yds. (100 m.) long and a minimum of 60 yds. (55 m.) wide. Points are scored by touching the ball down behind the opponent's goal line for a try (3 points), and by kicking the ball between the uprights of the goal posts above the crossbar for a goal (2 points). Shots at goal are allowed (*a*) after a try, (*b*) from a penalty, and (*c*) from the field of play, provided that the ball is kicked on the half-volley (drop shot). In international matches a goal from a drop shot counts only 1 point.

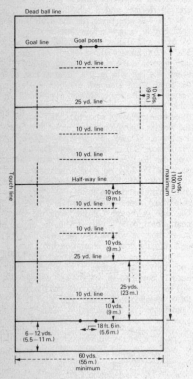

RUGBY LEAGUE PITCH
The crossbar on the goal posts at either end is 10 ft. (3·048 m.) from the ground.

A Rugby League ball is oval in shape and air-inflated, made of leather or plastic material. It may be between 10¾ and 11½ in. (273–292 mm.) long, with a widest circumference of 23 to 24 in. (584–610 mm.). It weighs between 13½ and 15½ oz. (383–439 g.).

Rugby League differs from Rugby Union in the following main particulars: teams are 13-a-side instead of 15; the scrum consists of 6 forwards instead of 8; a tackled player is allowed to retain possession of the ball up to a point regulated by the play-the-ball rule; ground gained by a kick to touch (except from a penalty award) does not count unless the ball lands in the field of play before crossing the touch line.

These variations from Rugby Union practice, made at various times over the last 70 years, have been designed to attract spectators by attaching greater rewards to the skills of running and passing. But for coaches and players the urge to win is greater than the urge to entertain, and at least as much thought is given to stifling opponents' attacking moves as to exploiting any defensive weakness. The result is that tactics differ considerably from those in Rugby Union. Because the tackled player retains possession of the ball there are no loose mauls. Forwards, as well as backs (i.e. all those players who stand outside the scrum), are free to string themselves across the field in roughly a straight line, leaving only a five-yard gap between one defender and the next.

The forwards are the six players of each side who form the scrum. The front row is formed by the hooker putting an arm round the shoulders of each of two prop forwards. The hooker's task is to strike for the ball with his foot when it is put into the scrum by the scrum half while the props support him against the pushing of the opposing front row. The two second-row forwards pack down behind the front row with their heads on either side of the hooker. Their purpose in the scrum is to help push the opposing pack off the ball. The loose forward packs down behind and between the second-row forwards, though in practice he usually detaches himself from the pack when his team is in a defensive position.

The full-back, in addition to being the last line of defence, is an important member of the attack in the modern game. He rarely kicks, but seeks to link up with three-quarters and half-backs in passing movements. The three-quarters and half-backs operate as one unit. As most of the responsibility for scoring tries rests on them, speed and an ability to beat an opponent by swerve and sidestep are desirable. The half-backs, who act as a link between forwards and three-quarters, have to be particularly agile because they operate in close proximity to the forwards. Forward play has changed considerably since the days when players were chosen for the weight and strength they supplied to the scrum. Under present-day rules there are fewer scrums and, while the old principles still apply to a large extent to the two prop forwards, no second-row or loose forward can hope to achieve success without handling ability and a good turn of speed, as well as a powerful physique. The hooker is usually of squat build so that he can not only get down low to see the ball as it enters the scrum, but also swing on the framework supplied by the shoulders of his prop forwards.

The game is started with a kick from the halfway line. The side gaining possession attempts to reach the opponents' line by passing the ball by hand or by kicking. The opposition tries to stop them by tackling the player carrying the ball or by intercepting passes. Within this simple framework the rules are complicated (a referee once compiled a list of 30 infringements which can occur in the scrum alone). When the referee stops play he either orders a scrum — in the case of forward passing, knocking-on, one side making six successive tackles, or the ball going out of play — or awards a penalty.

RUGBY LEAGUE SCRUM
The players line up in the formation shown when a scrum is formed: full-back (FB); wing three-quarter (W¾); centre three-quarter (C¾); stand-off half-back (SOH); scrum half-back (SH); loose forward (LF); second-row forward (2F); prop forward (PF); hooker (H).

Play-the-ball, the method used for bringing the ball into play after a tackle, is one of the main differences between Rugby League and Rugby Union. Many variations have been tried with the object of eliminating the loose mauls which are a feature of Rugby Union. The system in use in 1973 allowed the player in possession to regain his feet unimpeded and play the ball with a foot. To prevent one side retaining possession for long periods, a modification was introduced in 1966 whereby a scrum was ordered after four successive tackles by one side; this was later amended to six tackles.

Substitutes were first permitted in the 1964-5 season. Originally, players — limited

to two — could be replaced only up to half-time, but in 1968 the time limitation was abolished. In 1970 a further amendment was made allowing a player who had been replaced to be used in turn as a replacement (once only).

Penalties are imposed for foul play, ungentlemanly conduct, offside, obstruction, and technical offences at the scrum and the play-the-ball. Infringements may be of several kinds:

A *forward pass* is a throw towards the opponents' goal line. The referee orders a scrum unless it creates a situation advantageous to the non-offending side.

To *knock-on* is to propel the ball with hand or arm towards the opponents' goal line. No infringement is committed if the ball is regathered before it touches the ground. A scrum is formed after a knock-on, but the referee may allow play to proceed if the knock-on creates a situation advantageous to the non-offending side. A penalty is awarded if the offence is deliberate.

Obstruction is impeding an opponent who does not have the ball.

A player is *offside* in general play if the ball is kicked, touched, or held by one of his own side behind him. Offside also applies at the play-the-ball operation to any player (other than the two acting half-backs) who is less than five yards behind the two players in the play-the-ball operation. Offside players are penalized if they interfere with play.

A *tackle* consists of grasping with the hands or arms an opponent in possession of the ball so as to bring him to the ground or check his progress. Blows delivered with fist or arm, and the use of knees, are fouls.

The referee is assisted by a touch judge on each touch line, whose function is to signal the spot at which the ball goes out of play and also to draw the referee's attention to fouls or obstruction committed out of the referee's sight. The severest tests of a referee's qualities are to be found in international matches, because countries differ in minor matters of rule interpretation. This often leads to difficulties on the field. Tom McMahon the younger, an outstanding Australian referee, visited England in 1948-9 in an effort to establish more uniform methods between the two countries. More recently, in matches between Great Britain and France, a French referee officiated at matches played in England and vice versa. In 1970, however, the English League abandoned this system. They contended that Great Britain v. France matches in England had lost their popularity with the public because English spectators did not understand the decisions of French referees.

Professionals in Rugby League are not full-time. They report for training on two evenings a week and are paid on a match fee basis, with a bonus for winning. At one time it was common for backs to be paid more than forwards, and for stars to get more than average players. Since the Second World War, however, it has become the practice for all the members of a team to be paid alike, though the amount varies between one club and another. The amount a player receives for turning professional is a matter for negotiation between player and club. In 1969 K. Jarrett, a Welsh Rugby Union international three-quarter, received £14,000 from Barrow when he signed professional forms. In 1973, however, most players were receiving about £1,000 in a lump sum, though contracts in many cases called for further payments on the player's attaining representative honours.

Transfers of players from one club to another are common. In England the procedure is for the clubs concerned to agree on a fee and then for the buyers to arrange playing terms with the player, who has the right to refuse to change clubs. A player who has been with one club for a minimum of five years is entitled to a 1 per cent share of the fee for each year of service, provided that he has not asked for a transfer. A record fee of £15,000 was paid by Salford to Halifax for the transfer of Colin Dixon, a Welsh forward, in the 1968-9 season.

Rugby Football League Official Guide, annually; *Laws of the Game and Notes on the Laws* (1967).

Unlike most games, the origin of Rugby League can be traced to a precise date. On 29 August 1895, 21 northern clubs, exasperated at repeated refusals by the ruling body to allow them to compensate players for money lost by taking time off from work to play football, decided at a meeting at Huddersfield, Yorkshire, to break away from the Rugby Union. The founder members of the Northern Union (the name was changed to Rugby Football League in 1922) who embarked nine days later on the Lancashire and Yorkshire senior competitions were: Lancashire: Broughton Rangers, Leigh, Oldham, Rochdale Hornets, ST. HELENS, Tyldesley, WARRINGTON, Widnes, WIGAN; Yorkshire: Batley, Bradford, Brighouse Rangers, Dewsbury, Halifax, HUDDERSFIELD, Hull, HUNSLET, LEEDS, Liversedge, Manningham, WAKEFIELD TRINITY.

Most have survived except Broughton Rangers, Tyldesley, Brighouse Rangers, Liversedge, and Manningham, though over the years 29 other clubs have come and gone. Three of these were based in London: London Highfield, Acton and Willesden, and Streatham and Mitcham; eight in Wales: Aberdare,

Barry, Cardiff, Ebbw Vale, Merthyr Tydfil, Mid-Rhondda, Pontypridd, and Treherbert; and Coventry in the Midlands. These casualties reflect the attempts to make the competitions more attractive to spectators by spreading the base of operations beyond the northern counties. Although after 75 years there has been no expansion domestically, the international picture is brighter. The game is firmly established in Australia, New Zealand, and France.

Almost from the start the new body broke away from strict Rugby Union concepts by setting out to cater for spectators. Within three years, professionalism was adopted (though with a proviso that players must follow some other employment besides) and a continuous process of amending rules started with an eye to making play more spectacular. In 1896 the Challenge Cup knockout competition was launched. In 1897 the scoring value of goals was reduced and the line-out from touch was abolished in favour of a kick-in (later to become a scrum). In 1902 direct kicking into touch became an infringement.

In the same year the Lancashire and Yorkshire clubs joined forces in a two-division league structure. This was abandoned after three seasons, during which six clubs went out of existence. (Sixty years later another two-division venture foundered after two seasons. Financial difficulties forced Bradford Northern to withdraw from the League in December 1963, but a few months later the club was reformed, and has since prospered.) A drastic step was taken in 1906 with the reduction of the number of players from 15 to 13.

From the start a number of Welsh players had attached themselves to Northern Union clubs, and Ebbw Vale and Merthyr Tydfil became the first of the ill-fated Welsh clubs to try the professional code. In the same 1907-8 season the first touring team from overseas arrived. The pioneers were G. W. Smith, of New Zealand, who had watched Northern Union games during his visit to England with the 1905 Rugby Union ALL-BLACKS, and Baskerville. They brought over a mixed team of New Zealanders and Australians and played 35 matches to set the pattern for separate touring teams from Australia and New Zealand which has been followed ever since. During the tour, Smith, agreeing to stay on and play for Oldham, became the first of scores of overseas players who over the years have figured prominently in the game in England. Another member of the team was TODD, who later won fame as manager of SALFORD.

The first decade of the twentieth century ended with the first visit to Australia of an English team, which was captained by Lomas.

About this time, there occurred an event which brought about the widest gulf between League and Union playing methods. From 1907, a player tackled in possession was allowed to regain his feet and bring the ball into play by dropping it to the ground. This play-the-ball operation was the start of a search for the fastest and fairest means of maintaining the flow of play which has led to endless experiments and has had decisive effects in shaping technique and tactics.

The period to the outbreak of the First World War was dominated by Huddersfield who, under WAGSTAFF, had what many regard as the most brilliant team ever to play the game. In four successive seasons before play was suspended for the duration of the war, they won the League championship three times and were runners-up in 1913-14. In the season before play was suspended ROSENFELD had scored 80 tries for Huddersfield, a record which will probably stand until revolutionary changes are made in rules and tactics. By 1973 the pattern of play had altered to such an extent that a total of 40 tries in a season was usually enough to head the League list.

When football was resumed in 1919-20, Huddersfield's team was still good enough to win the Challenge Cup and finish as runners-up to Hull in the League championship, but the outstanding performance of the 1920s was by Swinton, who, in 1927-8, emulated Huddersfield by winning all four cups. A gifted pair of half-backs, Rees and B. Evans, were given the scope to exploit their talents by a dominating pack of forwards. Outstanding players emerged, notably PARKIN, GALLAGHER, Burgess, ELLABY, Hodgson, and, pre-eminently, J. SULLIVAN.

The 1930s were notable for the spread of the game to France, who joined England and Wales in a championship in the 1934-5 season, only a few months after the formation of the French League.

Playing standards in the 1930s were exceptionally high, partly because of an increasing number of Welshmen, Scots, Australians, New Zealanders, and occasionally South Africans, in club teams. Sullivan was still in his heyday, and other outstanding Welsh players were RISMAN, Morley, Edwards, E. Jenkins, G. Davies, Bassett, and Foster. Australia lost many prominent players to English clubs, notably D. Brown, Busch, HEY, HARRIS, Markham, Mills, Moores, Fifield, and Shankland. Keen competition from outside helped to develop native talent. Outstanding English players included Atkinson, Brogden, Hudson, McCue, Silcock, Arkwright, S. Smith, to be followed in the early postwar years by EGAN, GEE, Horne, and E. Ward. Among the Welshmen who made a big impact on the game in this period were W. T. H. Davies, R. Williams, Daniels, Owens, Whitcombe, Harris, Parsons, and Phillips. The excellent Wigan team of the immediate postwar period included ten local players. One of those players, RYAN, made a telling contribution to tactics by invariably running into attack from the full-back position instead of kicking.

The influx of players from Australia reached its height when full-scale competition was resumed after the Second World War. England sent a touring team to Australia in 1946, and shortly afterwards five members of Australia's team joined English clubs. By 1949 there were so many overseas players in England that an OTHER NATIONALITIES team, comprising Australians, New Zealanders, Scots, and South Africans, was strong enough to compete in the international championship, which it won in 1952-3 and 1954-5. In ten successive seasons the League try-scoring list was headed by overseas players, the most successful being BEVAN and COOPER from Australia, and McLean and Nordgren from New Zealand. Australian and New Zealand complaints at the loss of so many players led to restrictions being placed on the signing of overseas players. In the case of Australia, however, this rapidly became unnecessary.

In the early 1950s attempts to establish Rugby League in Italy and South Africa foundered, but an important step forward was taken with the organization of a WORLD CUP tournament. It was in this event that M. SULLIVAN made his first international appearance. BOSTON on the right and Sullivan on the left formed the most effective pair of wingers Britain had ever fielded. In subsequent seasons the style of wingers was severely cramped by the development of straight-across-the-field defence, one of the least attractive features of the modern game. How far this has contributed to a drastic fall in attendances is not clear, but the aggregate for League games had dropped in the 1972-3 season to 1,365,700, only about one-third of the figure for 1952-53. Most clubs were kept going by receipts from lotteries, television fees, and their share of tour profits and Cup final revenue. The Cup final has been played at WEMBLEY STADIUM since 1929, and in 1970 produced receipts of £93,000, twice as much as any club took in gate money over the whole season.

Despite increased emphasis on teamwork, the 1950s and 1960s produced a number of brilliant players who would have been outstanding in any period, notably ASHTON, Bolton, Jackson, Murphy, Myler, A. Davies, N. FOX, B. L. JONES, Stevenson, Hardisty, and Millward among the backs and PRESCOTT,

Huddart, McTigue, Harris, Edgar, Watson, and Wilkinson among the forwards. The most significant change in the rules in the 1960s was the introduction of the four-tackle regulation in 1966.

Australia. The sport in Australia began for much the same reasons as in England. The Rugby Union's strict application of amateur principles sometimes led to incapacitated players suffering hardship. Feeling on this point was running high in 1907 at a time when Baskerville was preparing to take a team from New Zealand to England to play the Northern Union clubs. Largely on the initiative of J. J. Giltinan and the Australian cricketer, TRUMPER, Baskerville's team was invited to play in Sydney on the way to England. From that beginning events moved rapidly. Dissident clubs organized league competitions in Sydney and Brisbane in 1908. Inter-state matches between New South Wales and Queensland were played in the same year, and a team was chosen to visit England. New South Wales and Queensland are still the strongholds of the game, though it is also played on an organized basis in Northern Territory and Western Australia.

The first touring team was captained by D. Lutze, and it included such famous players as MESSENGER and Rosenfeld. Despite producing many players of outstanding talent, including Blinkhorn, F. BURGE, HORDER, GORMAN, Thompson, Busch, Prigg, D. Brown, Hey, CLUES, BATH, Cooper, Devery, and CHURCHILL, as well as a number who left to make their names in England before achieving Test match status, Australia lost every Test series against Britain between 1920 and 1950. During that period the earnings of Australian players were considerably less than they could get in England. The normal basis of payment was expenses only, with a share of any profit their club might show at the end of the season. All but a handful of the players were virtually amateurs. A marked change came over the scene in the 1950s, when clubs discovered that enormous profits were to be made by running social clubs in conjunction with football affairs, most of the revenue being derived from gambling machines.

By 1973 a player with a successful club in Sydney could earn as much as £3,000 in a season. Australia rapidly superseded England as the dominant power, both financially and in playing resources. Whereas Australia won only 4 of the first 22 Test series played against Britain, they won four series in succession from 1963 onwards, besides winning the World Cup in 1957, 1968, and 1970. The appearance of such outstanding players as GASNIER, RAPER, Langlands, Wells, Walsh,

Rasmussen, and Kelly, plus the existence of an extensively organized schoolboy and country district game and the fact that there was no longer any efflux of their players to England, combined to bring about this drastic change. By 1970, however, Gasnier and Raper had retired from international football, and Australia's complacency was shaken by defeat by Britain's touring team in the 1970 Test series.

Recovery was rapid. The Australian team in Great Britain in 1973 not only won the Test series 2-1, but also incurred the fewest defeats (two) of any touring team.

Over the years SOUTH SYDNEY and ST. GEORGE have been Sydney's most successful clubs, having won as many First Grade Premierships between them as all the rest of the clubs put together.

France. The introduction of Rugby League into France was a direct consequence of the action of the home Rugby Unions in breaking off relations with the French Rugby Union in 1931 over allegations of professionalism. Prompted by SUNDERLAND, the Australian tour team manager, and GALIA, an international forward, Breyer, a Paris newspaper editor, took the initiative in inviting England and the 1933 Australian Rugby League touring team to play a match in Paris on 31 December 1933. Thanks to Galia's drive and enthusiasm, many French Rugby Union players were persuaded to change codes, outstanding among them being ROUSIE. A short visit to England was undertaken in 1934, and, in the following season, France took part in the international championship, becoming champions for the first time in 1939. The Vichy government banned the game in 1940. When Galia died in 1948, postwar reconstruction was largely in the hands of BARRIÈRE. Such rapid strides were made that a highly successful tour of Australia was undertaken in 1951.

Rugby League reached the height of its popularity in France during this period. Outstanding players included PUIG-AUBERT, a full-back of highly distinctive style, wingers Cantoni and Contrastin, centre Merquey, stand-off half BENAUSSE, and forwards Barthe, Berthomieu, and Ponsinet. It was strongly entrenched in such populous centres as Toulouse, Bordeaux, Marseilles, and Lyons.

By 1973 the picture had changed considerably. As in England, leading officials such as BLAINE and DEVERNOIS found themselves having to contend with changing social habits. Toulouse was the only large centre in which ground had not been lost. The game was largely confined to the south-east regions, with Toulouse, Perpignan, Carcassonne, Albi, and St. Gaudens the main strongholds. Nevertheless, the French team, strengthened at intervals by the acquisition of leading Rugby Union players, continued to hold its own international matches against British and Australian touring teams. Prominent players included P. Lacaze, a worthy successor to Puig at fullback, Mantoulan, who had a long career at centre, Savonne on the wing, half-backs Capdouze and Garrigues, and Bescos, AILLERES, and Marracq in the forwards.

The senior League usually comprises about 15 clubs. Two other leagues cater for less powerful clubs, and there is an extensive organization for juniors. Senior clubs recruit their players mainly from the juniors, and there is still a varying influx from Rugby Union. Senior club players are part-time professionals, though, as in England, the majority of players are not paid.

New Zealand. Rugby League was played by New Zealanders abroad before it was given a chance to take root in home soil. G. W. Smith, a member of the 1905 All-Blacks Rugby Union team in England, was in sympathy with the principles of payment for broken time which led to the Northern Union's breaking away from the English Rugby Union. On his return to New Zealand he enlisted the help of a Wellington businessman, Baskerville, and a team, which included a number of Australians, was assembled to visit England in 1907. Smith, then 35, stayed on to play for Oldham; Baskerville was taken ill on the homeward journey and died in Australia. But their pioneering efforts had not been wasted. The first Rugby League match in New Zealand was played at Wellington in 1908. Matches were played in Auckland during the same season, and a League was formed in Auckland in 1909.

A representative New Zealand team visited Australia in 1909 and returned with an encouraging profit to assist further expansion. While never seriously rivalling the strongly entrenched Rugby Union game in popularity, interest in Rugby League spread rapidly. Stimulated by a visit from the 1910 England touring team, it was by 1912 being played at Christchurch in the South Island, and the basis of the present nationwide structure was laid, often in the face of fierce opposition from Rugby Union authorities.

By 1970 there were 11 separate provincial competitions, 7 in the North Island and 4 in the South Island, catering for players of all ages from schoolboys upwards. The highest standard of play in domestic competition is seen in an extensive programme of interprovincial matches. International teams are sent annually to Australia and four-yearly to Britain and France. Test matches are played against visiting Australian and British teams, usually at Auckland and Christchurch. The League has its own ground at CARLAW PARK, Auckland.

In practice, New Zealand players are all amateurs, though a departure from normal practice was made in 1970 when the Test players against the visiting British team were paid £15 appearance money. Generally, the standard of play is inferior to that in Australia and Britain. Over the years, however, a number of talented players have emerged. Ironically, the best of them, MOUNTFORD, never played for New Zealand. He left for England to play for Wigan soon after the end of the Second World War. Three members of the 1926-7 team to visit England were signed later by English clubs: L. Brown, a winger, Desmond, a centre, and Mason, a forward. Prominent players after the Second World War included Clarke and White, both full-backs, MCBRIDE, Edwards, Cooke, and Emery, outstanding forwards, and Eastlake, Menzies, M. Robertson, and Haig in the backs. Menzies was chosen for three trips to Britain and on the last occasion, in 1960, he was vice-captain of New Zealand's World Cup team.

The first two visits to England were illfated. In 1926-7 seven players refused to turn out and on their return home were suspended for life. The 1939 tour had to be abandoned because of the outbreak of war soon after the team's arrival. After the Second World War, however, New Zealand teams acquitted themselves well. Their enthusiasm and cheerful sportsmanlike bearing in defeat made them popular visitors, and in 1971 they achieved their greatest ambition by beating Great Britain in a Test series in England.

INTERNATIONAL COMPETITION. The term 'Test' is used in Rugby League to denote international matches between Great Britain and Australia, Great Britain and New Zealand, Australia and New Zealand, Australia and France, and New Zealand and France. In 1956 matches between Britain and France were promoted to Test status, but the description was withdrawn after two seasons.

An international championship was started in 1934-5 when teams representing England, Wales, and France competed on the League principle, playing each other once. After the Second World War the number of overseas players with English clubs led to the formation of an additional competition, Other Nationalities. After the 1955-6 season the championship was disbanded, largely because of the declining number of Welsh and overseas players. In 1969-70 a triangular championship was revived for one season with the reintroduction of a Welsh team to compete with England and France, each playing the others twice.

The International Board was formed in

1948 with the English League secretary, FAL-LOWFIELD, as secretary. Its function is to govern the World Cup competition, arrange the cycle of international tours, and decide on changes in the laws of the game. It consists of delegates from England, Australia, New Zealand, and France. Before the formation of the International Board, authority for changing the laws of the game had been vested in the English League.

W. Fallowfield, *Rugby League Manual of Coaching* (1950); A. N. Gaulton, *Encyclopaedia of Rugby League Football* (1968); K. Macklin, *The History of Rugby League Football* (1962); E. Waring, *Rugby League, The Great Ones* (1969).

GOVERNING BODY (WORLD): Rugby League International Board, 180 Chapeltown Road, Leeds; (GREAT BRITAIN): Rugby Football League, 180 Chapeltown Road, Leeds; (AUSTRALIA): Australian Football League, 165 Phillip Street, Sydney, N.S.W., Australia; (NEW ZEALAND): New Zealand Rugby Football League, G.P.O. Box 712, Auckland, New Zealand.

RUGBY UNION FOOTBALL is a ball game, played between teams of 15-a-side, in which the ball may be handled as well as kicked. It is played on a rectangular field with an inflated ball that is oval in shape. The object of the game is to score more points than your opponents. Points are awarded for goals and also for tries. A try is scored if the ball is carried or kicked over the defending team's goal line and is there touched down by a member of the attacking team.

The field is usually 110 yds. (100 m.) long and 75 yds. (68 m.) wide. At each end of the field two goal posts are erected 18 ft. 6 in. (5·6 m.) apart, joined by a crossbar 10 ft. (3·048 m.) from the ground. The goal posts are extended upwards above the level of the crossbar, usually to a total height of at least 25 ft. (7·62 m.). This is because, in order to score a goal, the ball must be kicked, by means of a place kick or a drop kick, above the crossbar and between the posts. A place kick is made by kicking the ball after it has been placed on the ground for that purpose. A drop kick is made by letting the ball fall from the hands to the ground and kicking it at the first rebound as it rises. There is also a rectangular area behind the goal line, usually 25 yds. by 75 yds. (23 × 68 m.), in which tries are scored. The field is marked out in whiting.

According to the laws of the game, the field must be grass-covered or, 'where this is not available, clay or sand, provided the surface is not of dangerous hardness'. In fact the texture of fields varies a great deal at different times of the year in different countries according to climate. In the British Isles, the birthplace of the game, Rugby is usually played on grass whose soil has been softened by rain. In the wetter months, and especially when the grass has been damaged by excessive use, the field is sometimes composed of slippery mud. In early autumn and spring, however, the fields may be dry and hard. In New Zealand the condition of the fields is similar to that in the British Isles, but in Australia, South Africa, and France, for instance, the fields are more often dry. In Australia the game is often played on CRICKET fields which can be very hard indeed, especially in the vicinity of the wicket. In South Africa the fields tend to have a thick

RUGBY UNION FIELD
Goal posts are 18 ft. 6 in. (5·6 m.) apart; the crossbar is 10 ft. (3·048 m.) from the ground.

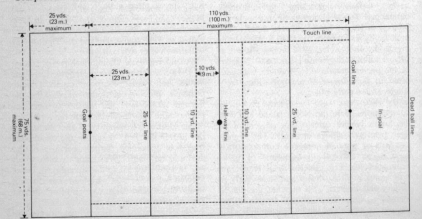

covering of matted grass above hard soil, and in France the fields are generally more sandy in nature with less thick grass.

The ball usually has an outer casing of leather surrounding an inflated inner bladder of rubber. The outer casing is made of four panels, and its length in line should be from 11 to 11¼ in. (27·94–28·575 cm.), its circumference should be from 30 to 31 in. (76·2–78·74 cm.) end on and from 24 to 25½ in. (60·96–64·77 cm.) in width, and it should weigh between 13½ and 15 oz. (382·72–425·25 g.). Materials other than leather are permissible, and in wet weather the ball may be specially treated to make it resistant to mud and easier to grip.

Players wear jerseys, shorts, stockings, and studded boots. They may wear soft leather helmets to protect their heads and ears, and leather pads to protect their shins, but leather shoulder harness and other armour are not allowed.

The game is controlled by a referee who carries a whistle and moves about the field, closely following play. He is helped by two touch-judges whose duties are confined to indicating the spot at which the ball has crossed the touch line and to indicating that an attempt to kick a goal has been successful or unsuccessful. The touch-judges do not come on to the field.

Play is usually divided into two halves of 40 minutes each, but the referee may permit play to continue longer than that in each half in order to make up for time lost because of injuries or through delay in the taking of kicks at goal. The players change ends at the half-time interval which is not allowed to last for more than 5 minutes.

The 15 players in a team are usually divided into 8 forwards, 2 half-backs (scrum half and stand-off half), 4 three-quarters, and 1 full-back. The basic job of the forwards is to procure the ball to enable their team mates to attack. The fundamental function of the half-backs is either, by running or kicking, to initiate attacks or else to pass the ball on by hand to the three-quarters. The four three-quarters are customarily the fastest runners in the team, and they may be joined in attack by the full-back.

The ball may be kicked in any direction, but it must not be passed or knocked forward with the hand. A player carrying the ball may be tackled by an opponent, who is allowed to knock him with his shoulder and to grip him with his arms so as to bring him to the ground, but it is illegal to impede anyone who is not carrying the ball.

There are two fundamental set pieces from which the ball is brought into play by a struggle for possession between the forwards of the two teams. These set pieces are the 'line-out' and the 'set scrum'.

The line-out is the means of bringing the ball back into play after it has passed over the touch line. The routine method of forming a line-out is for a team's eight forwards to stand one behind the other facing the touch line and the spot where the ball went out of play. The opposing team's eight forwards station themselves in the same way, the result being two single files, composed of eight men each, with a gap of two feet between the two ranks. The ball is thrown above the gap between the two ranks from outside the touch line. The right to throw in the ball belongs to an opponent (traditionally a wing three-quarter) of the player whom the ball last touched before it went out of play, but all 16 forwards have the right to jump for the ball in an attempt to grab possession for their team. In an orthodox line-out the ball is given by the catcher to his team's scrum half for him and his stand-off half and their three-quarters to attack with.

There are many possible variations from the orthodox line-out. A common variant is to have only four, instead of the routine eight, men from each team in the line-out. This tends to reduce jostling and consequently to produce more clear-cut and quicker possession. Each team must station at least two men in a line-out. The length of the line-out, i.e. the distance it stretches in-field from the touch line, is determined by the team who throw the ball in, but the line-out must not stretch further than 15 yds. (14 m.) in-field. Sometimes a team may choose a short line-out and get the player throwing the ball in to lob it over the top of all the men in the line-out so that it may be gathered in the open space behind the line-out by a player moving quickly from the scrum half position. Many teams prefer not to follow the tradition of using a wing three-quarter to throw the ball in; instead one of the forwards performs this duty, thus allowing the wing three-quarter to become a roving extra attacker.

A set scrum is called for by the referee following a minor infringement of the laws of the game such as a forward pass or a knock forward. The scrum takes place at the point of infringement. The scrum is usually formed by the eight forwards of one team bending forward, binding one another together in three ranks or rows, and pushing against the eight forwards of the opposing team who are similarly bent, bound, pushing. The ball is then inserted into the tunnel between the two front rows of the scrum whose members endeavour to rake it back for their scrum half and the rest of the team to attack with. There must be three

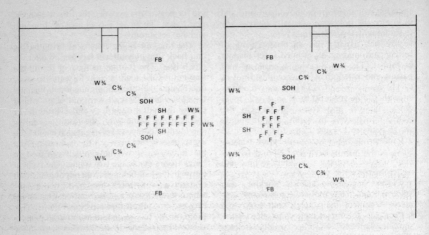

RUGBY UNION LINE-OUT AND SCRUM
(*Left*) The orthodox positioning of the players while a routine line-out is being formed: full-back (FB); wing three-quarter (W¾); centre three-quarter (C¾); stand-off half-back (SOH); scrum half-back (SH); forward (F). (*Right*) An orthodox scrum, showing routine positioning of players.

men in each team's front row at a scrum, but the number in the other two rows may vary. The orthodox formation is for each team to have three men in the front row, four in the second, and one in the back row. The middle man in the front row is known as the hooker, and the men on either side of him are the props. The two inner men in the second row are the locks, and the two outer men are the wing forwards (or flankers). The man in the back row is known as the No. 8. The ball is inserted into the scrum by an opponent (usually the scrum half) of the team whose infringement caused the referee to call for the scrum.

One common variation from the orthodox scrum is the formation with three men in the front row, two in the second row, and three in the back row. This 3-2-3 formation is recognized as providing a less efficient shove than the 3-4-1 formation, but it is often used when a team's forwards intend to swivel, or wheel, and to take the ball forward at their feet rather than raking it back to their scrum half.

Between these set pieces — the line-out and the set scrum — a game of Rugby provides a great deal of loose play, such as when a player carrying the ball is tackled to the ground by an opponent. In such a situation it is the aim of the forwards to arrive on the scene as quickly as possible, to wrest possession of the ball, and to feed it back to their scrum half for him and the rest of the team to attack with. A loose situation of this kind, with the forwards strug-

gling for possession, is known as a 'ruck' if the ball is on the ground, and as a 'maul' if it is not.

Numerically, the most profitable way of obtaining points is by touching down the ball beyond the opponents' goal line for a try. The try itself is worth 4 points, and it gives the right to the scorer's team to take a place kick or a drop kick at goal which, if it goes over the crossbar and between the posts, brings a further 2 points, making 6 in all. The kick at goal after a try, known as a conversion, has to be taken from a spot in-field in line with the place where the try was scored. If an infringement of the laws of the game by the defending team prevents a probable try from being scored, the referee may award a penalty try. A penalty try is always awarded between the goal posts, leaving the goal-kicker with the easiest of conversions and an almost certain total of 6 points.

There are three ways of obtaining 3 points. The most common of these is by kicking a penalty goal. The referee may award a penalty kick for an infringement of the laws more serious than that which would lead him to call for a set scrum. If the penalty kick is awarded at a spot within kicking distance of the goal, the non-offending team will take a place kick or a drop kick at goal from that spot. Three points are scored if this kick sends the ball over the crossbar and between the posts. Another way of scoring 3 points is by means of the dropped goal. This is achieved when a player, finding himself with room to do so in the course of play, aims a drop kick at goal, and the ball passes over the crossbar and between the goal posts. A further, but rare, method of scoring 3 points is by means of a goal from a free kick. For this a player catches the ball direct from a kick, knock forward, or throw forward by one of his opponents and, while stationary, shouts 'mark'; having done so, he is allowed to make a place kick or drop kick at goal which, if it sends the ball over the crossbar and between the goal posts, scores 3 points.

One of the charms of the Rugby Union game is the infinite variety of its possible tactics. Whatever tactics a team aims to adopt, the first essential is a strong and skilful pack of forwards capable of winning initial possession from the set pieces. For, with the ball in its hands, a team is in a position to dictate tactics which will make the best use of its own particular talents, at the same time probing for and exposing weaknesses in the opposing team. The ideal team has fast and clever half-backs and three-quarters who, with running, passing, and shrewd kicking, will make sure that the possession won by the forwards is employed to the maximum embarrassment of the opposing team.

But few teams are ideally balanced in this way, and a captain with powerful forwards but weak three-quarters, for instance, may order his half-backs not to give the ball to the three-quarters but instead to kick it or pass it in such a direction that it is kept within easy reach of the powerful forwards. In extreme cases, especially when rain and mud have made the ball hazardous to handle, the captain may order tactics in which the ball is kept even more tightly within the grip of his forwards: instead of giving the ball back to their scrum half from the line-outs and set scrums, they may retain it in their group and try themselves to make headway with it. Such tactics in such conditions are not likely to lead to the creating of many tries; but by pressing onward in this way a team is likely to stay in its opponents' half of the field and so be well placed to kick a penalty goal or a dropped goal and to touch down for a try a ball slipping from the grasp of a harassed opponent.

Among all the different varieties of tactics, one became especially fashionable in the 1960s. This was the attempt to set up deliberate and premeditated rucks and mauls in loose play. It was calculated that to score tries from set pieces, when defences would be carefully aligned, was more difficult than to score tries from rucks and mauls when defence would be improvised in character and when at least one defending half-back or three-quarter might be pinned in the ruck or maul. For this purpose, forwards would break away from line-outs, especially, or from set scrums and would invite the defending stand-off half or a three-quarter to tackle them; only when a defending player or players had been committed to a tackle and a ruck or maul formed would the attacking forwards release the ball for their own half-backs and three-quarters to attack with. Alternatively, the forwards would release the ball promptly from the set scrum or line-out, but it would be passed only as far as the three-quarter immediately beyond the stand-off half; this three-quarter, preferably a big, strong man, would run hard and straight so as to commit one or two defenders to tackle him; a ruck or maul would be formed and the ball would then be released for the half-backs and three-quarters, probably reinforced by the full-back, to attack with. This type of ploy became known as 'second-phase play'.

Rugby Union is a strictly amateur game, played chiefly in England, Scotland, Ireland, Wales, New Zealand, South Africa, Australia, France, Fiji, Japan, Romania, Canada, Argentina, and Italy, and to a lesser extent in at least 50 other countries.

Rugby Football Union, *Laws of the Game with Instructions to Referees and Notes for Guidance of Players*, annually, and *Better Rugby* (1973).

The early history of the game belongs exclusively to England. It was developed at Rugby School, taken up by the undergraduates at Cambridge and Oxford, and refined into a suitable game for adults largely by the RICH-MOND and BLACKHEATH clubs. In London, too, it was given its original governing body — the Rugby Football Union, from which it took its full title — and its first generally accepted code of laws.

The game's exact date of birth, however, has not been established. In 1895 a report was presented by a sub-committee of the Old Rugbeian Society which had been appointed 'to inquire into the Origin of Rugby Football'. Its findings were summarized, and perhaps oversimplified, in the wording of a plaque later set into the wall of the Close at Rugby School. It reads: 'This stone commemorates the exploit of William Webb Ellis, who, with a fine disregard for the rules of football as played in his time, first took the ball in his arms and ran with it, thus originating the distinctive feature of the Rugby game. A.D. 1823.' The plaque was unveiled on 1 November 1923 at a match between England-Wales and Scotland-Ireland to mark the officially recognized centenary.

There is only slight evidence, however, to support this account of the birth of Rugby football. It chiefly lies in the vivid but second-hand version of the Ellis incident given by an old Rugbeian, Bloxam, who had left Rugby some five years before it was supposed to have occurred. Neither of the two earliest major historians of the game — Shearman, writing first in 1885, or the Revd. F. M. Marshall, in 1892 — mentioned Ellis's name; Shearman, in fact, suggested that the football at Rugby was the survival of a primitive handling game. And testimony by two old Rugbeians, in particular, casts doubt on the authenticity of the Ellis legend, at least as a plausible starting point for modern Rugby. T. Harris, a younger contemporary of Ellis at the school, described him as 'inclined to take unfair advantages at football', adding that 'picking up and running with the ball in the hand was distinctly forbidden'; there is the strong implication that this was still the case when Harris left school in 1828, three years after Ellis. Hughes, author of *Tom Brown's Schooldays*, also explained that when he went to Rugby in 1834, running with the ball in order to get a try, while not absolutely forbidden, would have been considered almost suicidal. The practice, he suggested, grew only after it had been popularized in 1838-9 by a fast, brawny boy called Mackie.

The old Rugbeians' enquiry did establish that Shearman was wrong in believing Rugby's style of football to be a survival from the past. He was mistaken, too, in his explanation that Rugby school alone possessed a large field on which 'the old running and collaring game' could be kept up. The report showed that the boys at Rugby, for two centuries after its foundation, had been confined to a meagre playing area, much smaller than the Close, and that about 1818-19 their football had contained no element of handling.

In 1899 Shearman accepted these findings in the following broad, and generally acceptable, terms: 'that in the first half of this century Rugby School, having then an ample playground, developed a game of football which in its essential features resembled the ''primitive game'', in which every player was allowed to pick up the ball and run with it, and every adversary could stop him by collaring, hacking over, and charging, or by any other means he pleased.'

It was in 1841-2, when Hughes was captain of Bigside at Rugby, that 'running-in' with the ball was permitted, subject to three conditions: that the ball was caught on the bound; that the catcher was not 'off his side'; and that he did not hand the ball on but touched down himself behind the opposing goal. From this point the game developed more rapidly, and in 1846 the school published the *Laws of Football as Played at Rugby School*, revising them in the

following year. Although these laws consist of a set of decisions on disputes arising in play, rather than giving a basic description of the game, they contain certain significant points. Any player might now run in provided that he did not take the ball from the ground or through touch; but if held in a scrummage he was not allowed to transmit the ball to any other player on his side. Only the player holding the ball might be held; and while hacking was permitted it was not considered fair to hack and hold at the same time, to hack with the heel, or to hack anywhere but below the knee. It was further agreed that 'All matches are drawn after 5 days or after 3 days if no goal has been kicked'. Games at Rugby School might involve up to 300 players, some drawn up behind the goal lines and the remainder involved for long periods in a shapeless, general scrimmage. There was no positional play as now understood, although some players stood off from the mauls in the hope of taking the ball and running with it or, more probably, kicking at the goal. The game contained its two basic modern characteristics: freedom to run with the ball, and to tackle the man who does so. It still needed, however, to be converted into an adult game by raising the element of footballing skill over that of brute force, removing the dangers of hacking, and creating the opportunity for reasonably frequent scoring. This process occupied the game until the later years of the century, and in the matter of adjusting the balance between the roles of forwards and backs, has continued ever since.

In the period 1840-60, football of some kind was adopted as the winter sport of most boarding and grammar schools and, as the boys left school, it spread with them to the universities and cities. Until 1863 football was regarded as a single, indivisible game which happened to have a number of variant forms (most Rugby clubs established before the Rugby Union in 1871 still describe themselves simply as football clubs). However, there were two broad categories of football which were difficult to reconcile: the dribbling game, as it was played at Eton, Harrow, Westminster, and Charterhouse schools, and the handling game of Rugby, Marlborough, and Cheltenham.

Within each of the groups it was possible to agree ground rules, but the differences between the two quickly came to a head at Cambridge University where, as early as 1839, a football club had been founded by an old Rugbeian, Fell. It particularly incensed the Etonians that Rugbeians kept picking up the ball in the middle of a game. In 1846 a meeting at Cambridge, dominated by a majority of

Etonians who objected to handling, mauling, and hacking, drew up and published the 'Cambridge Rules' (later adopted, with little alteration, by the Football Association on its formation in 1863). Apparently adherents of both codes continued to play together, however, since in 1863 a further meeting was called at 'Cambridge where a specific ban was placed on hacking, tripping, and running with the ball.

In the same year a conference of 11 London clubs and schools met to define the position of teams that favoured handling. It accepted the principles of hacking, tripping, and holding, although only of a player carrying the ball, and even then with some misgivings. Certain clubs withdrew from the association and adopted the Cambridge rules, while Blackheath dropped out for the opposite reason; it considered that the others were weakening on the need to keep hacking. This was to remain a matter of dispute for some years. If hacking among schoolboys did little serious damage, among grown men it could become highly dangerous; yet to some clubs the manliness of Rugby football was bound up with this practice, and they were determined to retain it. The first significant step towards its abolition came in 1866 in a private agreement between Richmond and Blackheath to ban 'using the toe either in kicking the shins of an opposing player or in tripping him up'. Accounts vary, but this move followed either the death of a Richmond player in a practice match, or the forced cancellation of a fixture between the two clubs because so many players had been lamed by hacking.

After 1863 the division between Association (see FOOTBALL) and Rugby football became clear, and in the following year there were reckoned to be 20 Rugby clubs operating in the London area, not counting the scratch sides that came together from week to week. The game also caught on in the north; during the 1860s in Yorkshire, clubs were formed at Hull, Leeds, Bradford, and Huddersfield, and in Lancashire at Manchester and Liverpool. Yet under the Football Association, soccer was growing more rapidly. Rugby was still being played under local rules, the custom being to abide by the home club's version of the game; teams of 25 or more players often took the field; and hacking persisted in many games. To develop in competition with soccer, Rugby needed a ruling body of its own, and this need was emphasized when, in December 1870, Scottish Rugby players challenged England to an international match (see below).

Later that month in a letter to the Press, Ash and Burns, secretaries of Richmond and Blackheath, invited 'clubs who profess to play the Rugby game' to join them 'in forming a code to be generally adopted'. This resulted in a meeting at the Pall Mall Restaurant, Cockspur Street, London, on 26 January 1871, attended by 32 representatives of 21 clubs. The eight clubs still in existence are Blackheath, Richmond, Civil Service, Wellington College, GUY'S HOSPITAL, HARLEQUINS, King's College, and St. Paul's School. At that meeting the Rugby Football Union (R.F.U.) was formed, its constitution agreed, and officers and committee (one of whose tasks was to draw up the laws of the game) were elected. The laws were drafted by Maton of Wimbledon Hornets and approved in June of that year.

The laws, numbering 59, give a fairly complete picture of the game at that time. A match was decided only by a majority of goals, which could be obtained by any sort of kick except a punt, either direct from the field of play, or after obtaining a 'try at goal'. Any player might pick up the ball when it was 'rolling or bounding', and then run with it; if he crossed the opponents' goal line and touched it down, it was called a 'run in', and entitled his side to a try at goal. This could be taken either as a place kick from a mark in line with the spot where the ball was touched down, or as a 'punt out'. Here a player on the try-scoring side punted the ball out from behind the goal line at a mark opposite the spot where the ball was touched down; if another of his side made a 'fair catch', he marked the spot with his heel, and could then take a place kick in line with it.

If, on the other hand, a player running with the ball was held by the opposing side, he was obliged to shout 'down' and put the ball on the ground where a scrummage formed round him. Here the two sides attempted to push each other back while at the same time driving the ball with their feet towards the opposite goal line; they might not handle the ball. However, there was also a 'maul in goal' in which the holder of the ball was tackled inside the goal line, or carried or pushed across it, when each player touching the ball with his hands attempted to touch it down. For the rest, throwing back to another member of the side was permitted, knocking on and hacking over were forbidden, and the captains were appointed 'the sole arbiters of all disputes'.

Here, then, was the possibility of a passing game, although it was not accepted as such at the time. Shearman complained that in the earliest Anglo-Scottish internationals 'a quarter of a hundred of heavyweights appeared to be leaning up against each other for periods of five minutes or thereabouts, while occasionally the ball became accidentally disentangled from the solid globe of scrummagers, and the remaining players then had some interesting bursts of play between themselves.' The Rugby School Bigside tradition kept teams of 20 men in the field for the first six international seasons, and before back play could be developed it was necessary to reduce the number of superfluous players.

Fifteens were introduced into the Oxford v. Cambridge match in 1875 (the series had begun three years earlier), and into international Rugby when England played Ireland in 1877; and from this time the game began to take its modern form. The earliest XVs had ten forwards, two attacking half-backs, and three mainly defensive backs, the first development being to move forward the centre back to support the half-backs; thus he became the first three-quarter. By 1880 it had become customary to play three three-quarters with two halves, one back, and nine forwards, the three-quarters adopting a more attacking role than the halves.

Several factors promoted these changes. In 1876 it was agreed that while victory should still be decided by a majority of goals, if none was kicked, a majority of tries would count; this gave an added value to running with the ball. The following year the law that the player should put down the ball immediately on being held was tightened up, thus restricting the long scrummages. About 1880 began the practice of deliberately heeling the ball from the scrum to create opportunities for running attacks. Further, it became accepted that a player with the ball should pass before he was tackled, provided he could do so safely.

Certain clubs and areas led the way in exploring the possibilities of the game. The Blackheath side of 1878 developed wheeling and passing among the forwards. The technique of heeling was first exploited in the north. At Oxford, between 1879 and 1882, Vassall, a forward, and Rotherham, at half-back, both to become England players, made the most influential advances with a short-passing game among the forwards and a style of long passing among the backs. And from 1883 the four-three-quarter system was to spread from the CARDIFF club (see below).

Before they formed their own national unions, many Irish and Scottish clubs became members of the R.F.U. which, for some years, was accepted as the natural law-making body of the game. As such, in 1883 it introduced the free kick for offside, and in the following season abolished the practice of 'punting out'. But in 1884, after a dispute about 'knocking-back' in the Scotland-England match, the Scots refused to accept the right of the R.F.U. to interpret laws. No match was played between the two countries in the following year, but fixtures were resumed in 1886 on the understanding that England would join an International Board which would settle future disputes. Meanwhile the R.F.U. introduced a system of scoring by points: 3 points for a goal and 1 point for a try.

The R.F.U., however, would not accept equal representation on the Board with the other unions because it controlled a greater number of clubs, and in 1888 and 1889 England did not play any of the home countries. In the following season the matter was settled by independent arbitration which gave England six representatives on the Board, while Scotland, Ireland, and Wales had two each. It was further agreed to accept the Rugby Union laws, including the points system, although not an amendment to it which had allowed 2 points for a goal kicked from a penalty. In 1891, however, the Board revised the points system to 2 points for a try, 3 for a penalty goal, 5 for a goal from a try (the try not to count), and 4 for any other goal. The try was revalued at 3 points in 1894; the goal from a mark was reduced to 3 points in 1905; but there were no further changes until 1949 when the dropped goal was similarly cut down from 4 to 3 points. At the beginning of the 1971-2 season the try was increased in value to 4 points.

In 1911 the R.F.U. voluntarily gave up two seats on the Board, and in 1948 a further two so that it had equality of voting with the other home unions; in the latter year, too, representatives of the Dominions were admitted to membership. Almost annually there have been changes and additions to the laws, of which these are among the most significant: in 1896 it was ruled that the referee should have sole control of the game, but should allow the advantage if one side's infringement benefited the other; in 1913, the ball should not be considered fairly in the scrum until it had passed a player on each side; in 1927, the abolition of the loose head; in 1958, the unintentional knock-on from a kick was not an infringement, provided the ball did not touch the ground or another player; the ball need no longer be played with the foot after a tackle; and at a 'short' penalty kick, the ball need not travel forward for five yards. Perhaps the most far-reaching change of all, however, came in 1968-9 when what was originally called the 'Australian dispensation' was adopted. Outside his own 25-yd. line, a player was no longer allowed to kick the ball directly into touch; unless the ball touched the ground before going out of play, the line-out was called back to the place from which the ball had been kicked. Subsequently, to promote more continuous play, the rule that the ball must be played with the foot after a tackle was revoked, and a fumble in catching a pass was permitted provided that the ball did not touch the ground or another player.

One effect of the disagreement with the other home unions in 1888-9 was to bring official recognition to the county championship. The first county match was played between Yorkshire and Lancashire at Leeds in 1870. It became an annual fixture, and an informal network of matches grew up around it as county unions were formed by Somerset, Cheshire, Durham, Devon, Middlesex, and Surrey. The R.F.U. was not generally in favour of internal competition, although from the early days club cup championships were popular, particularly in the north and in the West Country; but in the absence of international matches, the Union needed the revenue and interest from some form of top-class representative Rugby. Therefore, in 1888 it staged a match between the North and the South, and the following season planned one between the Champion County and the Rest of England. For the purpose Yorkshire, who were undefeated, were declared champions that year and in 1890.

A more overtly fair method of selection was required, however, if the championship was to continue, and in 1890-1 the counties were divided into four groups — North-west, North-east, South-west, and South-east — with the winner of each playing the others, the final result being decided on a points basis. Since then other systems have been used, and from 1952-3 the counties have been divided into five groups: North, Midlands, South-east, South-west, and South. The winners of the first three groups go straight into the semi-finals, while the winners of the last two, which are smaller, play off for the fourth semi-final place. The match between the two finalists produces the champion county of the year.

The R.F.U. has found the championship of value in providing a form of competition that does not interfere with club Rugby, in bringing major games to areas where Rugby is a minority sport, and in developing players to international standard. In turn, the English union, more than any other, is controlled by representatives of the counties, rather than the clubs and societies. And when major touring sides visit England, they play largely against combinations of counties instead of, as in Wales, the clubs, or in Scotland, the regions.

For two decades the Rugby Union made steady progress, membership rising from 31 clubs in 1872 to 481 in 1893. But the danger of fast growth for an amateur administration centred on London and drawn from the middle class was that it could not control developments taking place at both a geographical and social distance. In Yorkshire and Lancashire, Rugby, while generally introduced by men who had learned to play it at school, had become a popular working-class game and highly competitive. The Yorkshire Challenge Cup was introduced in 1878, and Lancashire clubs competed for a series of trophies.

From the late 1880s the Rugby Union heard rumours that certain northern clubs were offering inducements to talented players to join them, and in 1887 it passed one of several resolutions aimed at preventing players making a profit from the game. The problem of many, however, was not to make a profit but simply to make up their wages if they lost all or part of a shift through turning out for their clubs. So in 1893 two Yorkshire County officials, Millar and Newsome, proposed to the R.F.U. committee 'That players be allowed compensation for bona fide loss of time'. In opposition Hill, hon. sec. of the union, moved the amendment: 'That this meeting, believing that the above principle is contrary to the true interest of the game and its spirit, declines to sanction the same.' The amendment was carried by 282 votes to 136.

At the next meeting the committee strengthened its hand by passing a by-law which laid down 'That the name of the Society shall be the "Rugby Football Union" and only clubs composed entirely of amateurs shall be eligible for membership, and its headquarters shall be in London where all general meetings shall be held'.

After the earlier meeting, 22 leading Yorkshire and Lancashire clubs withdrew from the R.F.U., and in August 1895, 20 of these sent representatives to a meeting in Huddersfield where the Northern Rugby Football Union (see RUGBY LEAGUE FOOTBALL) was formed (in 1922 it changed its name to the Rugby Football League). By 1896 the R.F.U. membership had fallen from 481 clubs to 383, and by 1903 to 244. Apart from the loss of support and revenue, England had to do without its northern reserves of forward strength, and of its next 48 internationals, up to 1909, it won only 13 and drew three.

The purchase, in 1907, of 10¼ acres at TWICKENHAM, Middlesex, on which to build a headquarters for the Rugby Union and a home ground for England was a gesture of optimism that proved to be fully justified. Harlequins, who with STOOP and POULTON were to play a major part in the England revival, opened the ground with a victory over Richmond in October 1909. And in their first international there in the following January, England beat Wales, who were coming to the end of their 'golden era', by 11 points to 6.

Wales were not to win at Twickenham until 1933, Ireland not until 1929, and Scotland not until 1926. That opening season brought England their first championship for 18 years; discounting the war periods, it was not until after 1963 that they were to go longer than six years without the title. Their best periods were in the early 1920s when, under WAKEFIELD, they won the championship three times in four years, and the mid-1950s when, led by EVANS, they won it in two successive years.

British overseas touring sides, called the Lions since the 1924 visit to South Africa, have made 19 tours up to 1973. The first, predominantly English, party went to New Zealand and Australia in 1888, their programme having been arranged by three England professional cricketers, Shaw, SHREWSBURY, and STODDART. Lions' tours have also been made to Canada.

Scotland. Scottish Rugby derived from its schools, particularly those of Edinburgh and Glasgow and, more than in any other country, the structure of the adult game has been based upon school associations. There are many English old boys' clubs, but few have more than half-a-dozen first-class fixtures, and fewer still provide players in any number even to the county sides. Of the 32 first-class Scottish teams in 1973, however, exactly half belonged to former pupils' clubs, three to universities or colleges, and only 13 had been founded on a basis of open membership, most of these in the Border towns; however there was a growing tendency for former pupils' clubs to draw 'on players who were not old boys. In the 1950s, the Scotland XV frequently had five or six players from former pupils' clubs, and although the proportion began to decrease, it was still exceptional to find a national side in which they were not represented. This school influence may account for certain marked characteristics of the Scottish game, among them moral earnestness, great competitive vigour, and a conservative attitude towards innovation; Scots teams were the last in the home countries to adopt the four-three-quarter systems.

It is almost certain that Rugby was introduced to Scotland at Edinburgh Academy in 1855. The Academy played a Rugby match, with some latitude in their interpretation of the rules, against Merchiston in 1858; however, because this was a postponed fixture, the first schools' match of all had taken place between Merchiston and Royal High School in the previous February. The only written laws available at that time were those in use at Rugby

School, which presupposed a working knowledge of the game. So, late in 1867, an attempt at a clearer codification was made jointly by Edinburgh Academy, Merchiston, and Loretto, resulting in the *Green Book.* It was according to this version of the rules that the Scottish umpire at the first Scotland *v.* England match upheld the decisive try. Gradually the game took hold in other schools, notably Glasgow Academy and Fettes. And at a time when most English public schools were reluctant to play each other, for fear of disorders, a regular inter-school championship was organized in the Edinburgh area, later extending through the country.

The championship influenced the game at all levels. The exchange of ideas helped to develop techniques; while Scottish play may be traditionally associated with dribbling rushes and hard tackling by the forwards, Loretto was one of the first sides to experiment with passing, a practice which was adopted first by Fettes and later by Merchiston. Loretto, in fact, is credited with introducing the passing game at Oxford; seven Lorettonians played there under Vassall in 1882.

The players, who had become accustomed to competition in school, carried their rivalries and loyalties into manhood, and competitive club Rugby continued to flourish even after it had fallen out of favour in England and Wales. The Scottish club championship is based upon the percentage of success during the season — a flexible system which can operate within a pattern of friendly matches — and a century later is still described as 'unofficial'; however, it is no less significant for that. It has reinforced, and been reinforced by, the former pupils' clubs, but an additional factor accounts for their continuing strength. Merchiston, Fettes, and Loretto apart, it is the city day-school which is typical of central Scotland. Its pupils belong to the neighbourhood, and tend to build their careers there after leaving school. Rather than joining or forming independent clubs, they play, as a matter of course, for their former pupils' or academicals' clubs, which, from the early days, have been able to field two, three, or more sides.

Until 1870 the only adult Rugby clubs were in Edinburgh, Glasgow, and the universities of St. Andrews and Aberdeen. However, they felt they had more right to represent Scottish football than the teams of Scottish exiles who had played 'international' soccer matches against England in 1869 and 1870. So, in a letter to the *Scotsman* on 8 December 1870, representatives of WEST OF SCOTLAND, EDINBURGH ACADEMICALS, Merchistonians, Glasgow Academicals, and St. Andrews issued a Rugby challenge to 'any team selected from the whole of England'. The challenge was accepted by Blackheath, and it was the need to select an England team that precipitated the formation of the Rugby Football Union.

The match was played at RAEBURN PLACE on 7 March 1871 before a crowd of about 4,000; Scotland won by the only goal. Each of the challenging clubs was represented in the Scottish XX — Edinburgh Academicals most strongly with seven players — plus Royal High School Former Pupils (H.S.F.P.) and Edinburgh University.

The Scottish Football Union (S.F.U.) (as it was called until 1924, when it became the Scottish Rugby Union) was not formed for another two years, and meanwhile many of the leading clubs joined the R.F.U. This was to lead to a number of disputes in the 1880s, since it appeared to be a tacit admission that the R.F.U. was Rugby's international ruling body rather than — in effect, if not in name — simply the English Rugby Union. This impression deepened when the S.F.U., set up in March 1873, accepted the R.F.U. laws of the game *en bloc*. The Union's six founder members were Edinburgh Academicals, Edinburgh University, Glasgow Academicals, Merchistonians, Royal H.S.F.P., and West of Scotland; four more clubs, Edinburgh Wanderers, Glasgow and St. Andrews Universities, and Warriston (which disbanded within a few seasons), joined the same year. Unlike the R.F.U., the S.F.U. did not admit schools to membership, which led to criticism from some Scottish educationalists who believed that the older, more boisterous but slower type of Rugby would be sacrificed to the adults' wish for refinement and speed.

So far most of the developments in Scottish Rugby had been confined to the Central Lowlands, but by 1880 there were six clubs in the Borders: Gala, Melrose, HAWICK, Earlston, Kelso, and Duns. In that year Gala and Melrose became members of the S.F.U., and in 1882 the Selkirk club was formed. As elsewhere in Scotland, the game was played on a competitive basis, although here it was done officially through the Border League championship, and with the kind of popular support it enjoyed in Yorkshire and South Wales. As late as 1899, Fleming wrote in the Badminton Library edition on *Football*: 'In Scotland, Rugby is the game of the classes; the masses are devoted to Association, with the exception of one district, generally classed as the Borders, where... Rugby is the game of the populace.' During the 1890s the Border clubs got their first representatives into the Scotland side, but by then they had made an even greater contribution: the invention of seven-a-side Rugby. This is believed to have originated at Melrose in 1883; in the following year, with six clubs participating, Gala staged the first of its annual 'sevens' tournaments, and from that time the sport developed into a speciality of the area.

Scotland played Ireland for the first time in 1877, and Wales in 1883, and up to the end of the century won the great majority of its matches with those countries. She did not beat England a second time, however, until 1877, and the fixture was cancelled in 1885 and 1888-9 as a result of disputes concerning the laws of the game. By the outbreak of the First World War, Scotland had won the international championship eight times and shared it twice. The Triple Crown team (i.e., winner of a mythical trophy said to be gained by any of the four home countries which beats the other three in the course of a single season) of 1901 was remarkable for the fact that all seven backs were drawn from two Edinburgh clubs, the Academicals and the University. And in 1906-7 (before the entry of France into the championship) four matches were won for the first time; victory over the first SPRINGBOKS opened a Triple Crown season.

By general consent, however, the finest period came in the 1920s when — with five experienced countries now in the championship, and Ireland and England particularly formidable opponents — Scotland twice won the title outright, and twice shared it with Ireland, within five seasons. In 1925 Scotland won every championship match for the first time since France was included, scoring 25 points against France, 24 against Wales, and 14 against both Ireland and England. Scotland fielded the Oxford three-quarter line of Wallace, Aitken, Macpherson, and I. S. SMITH for all but the Irish match, from which Macpherson had to withdraw; and this created 14 tries on the wing: Smith scored 8, and Wallace 6. Scotland again won the Triple Crown and championship in 1933 and 1938.

Scotland's record against visiting touring sides includes victories over the first Springboks (1906), the New South Wales WARATAHS (1927), the New Zealand Army KIWIS (1946), the fourth and fifth WALLABIES (1958 and 1966), and the sixth Springboks (1969); also, in their short tours, wins over South Africa (1965) and Australia (1968). Scotland toured Argentina in 1969, winning five of six games, but losing one of the two unofficial internationals; in Australia the following year, she won three matches, and lost three, including the Test (see below).

Ireland. While Ireland has recorded fewer victories in the international championship than the other home countries, it is more remarkable, in the historical circumstances, that up to 1971 she had won the Triple Crown four times and provided four captains to the British Lions touring sides. The Irish Rugby Union (I.R.U.), which unites Eire and Northern Ireland, has had to contend with the problems of a small and dispersed population, competition from two other codes of football, Association and Gaelic, and a political situation which frequently intrudes upon sport. The GAELIC ATHLETIC ASSOCIATION (G.A.A.), for example, which is the governing body for Gaelic FOOTBALL and HURLING, until 1971 banned its members from playing Rugby on the grounds that it was a 'foreign' game; this not only limited the number but, to some extent, the physical quality of recruits available to Rugby.

The G.A.A. is particularly influential in rural areas, from which the Rugby Union might otherwise have hoped to draw some of its hardiest players, especially for the pack, as Scotland does from its Border clubs. The lifting of the G.A.A. ban may help to correct this geographical imbalance, but of 41 first class clubs, 34 are concentrated in the cities of Dublin, Belfast, Cork, Limerick, and Galway, and the remainder divided between the larger country towns. Irish senior Rugby therefore remains very much an urban game, and throughout the 1950s and 1960s only one of its internationals, Culliton, came from a genuine farming background.

To maintain the interest of players and public, Ireland has developed a more extensive system of competition than any of the other home countries. The four administrative provinces of Leinster, Ulster, Munster, and Connacht play an annual tournament, each against each, early in the season as a preparation for the international series. In addition the provinces conduct their internal club Rugby on a league basis at all levels, and hold a number of cup competitions towards the end of the season; Leinster, the province centred on Dublin, was the last to adopt a competitive framework for its senior games, although junior and minor Rugby has been played within leagues for many years, and in the spring even the senior clubs join in cup competitions. Beginning in the under-15 group at school, the competitive system spreads throughout the game, holding it together within a strong framework and enabling the I.R.U. to make the best use of its limited resources.

The first Rugby club in Ireland was established at DUBLIN UNIVERSITY (more widely known as Trinity College) in 1856, and is thought to be the second oldest in the world — that of Guy's Hospital being the oldest. The first club in Ulster was North of Ireland, formed in Belfast in 1868, and soon joined by a number of old boys of Cheltenham, Marlborough, and Bromsgrove. These two clubs did not meet until 1871, and in their first years had to look outside Ireland for opponents. By the early 1870s, however, several more clubs had grown up on the east coast, mainly at schools and colleges, although the influential Dublin Wanderers was the independent creation of Peter, an ex-pupil of Blackheath school; Peter later became the first hon. sec. of the Irish Rugby Union, and is sometimes described as 'the Father of Irish Football'.

The first attempt at forming a national governing body — for the initial purpose of arranging an international match with England — was made informally at Dublin University in 1874. Although bearing the title of Irish Football Union, the new organization was confined to the southern clubs and was not truly representative of those. Most of the founding members were Trinity or Wanderers men, even if some purported to represent home towns where often no Rugby club existed. In retaliation a North of Ireland Union was formed, and a compromise reached between the two on the composition of the Irish team to meet England at the OVAL in the following February. It was agreed that each union should nominate ten men, although in the event several players failed to turn up; the team was drawn from only five clubs, and southern Irishmen remained in the majority. Dublin University had nine players, Wanderers three, North of Ireland six, and Methodist College and Windsor one player each; they lost by 2 goals and a try to nil. While clubs like Lansdowne, Limerick, Queen's College (later QUEEN'S UNIVERSITY), Belfast, Queen's College, Cork, and Lisburn began to appear against players' names, the dominance of Dublin University, Wanderers, and North of Ireland continued into the 1890s.

By 1879 there were three separate unions in Ireland, with control over the game in Leinster, Ulster, and Munster but, largely through Peter's efforts at conciliation, they agreed in that year to merge into a single Irish Rugby Union (Connacht was admitted later, with one representative on the full I.R.U. committee to the other provinces' two). This arrangement survived the various stages in the political division of Ireland from 1919 onward, and international matches were played alternately in Belfast, usually at the Ravenhill ground, and at LANSDOWNE ROAD, Dublin, until 1951; Lansdowne, with its greater capacity, then became the sole home venue.

The Irish have had several spells of success in the international championships. The first came shortly before the turn of the century when they won the Triple Crown in 1894 and

1899, and in 1896, although beating England and Wales, were held to a 0-0 draw by Scotland. The decisive match against Wales at Cardiff in 1899 drew a record crowd of 40,000 which twice invaded the pitch and stopped the game.

In the mid-1920s Ireland shared the championship two years running with Scotland, whom they beat in both seasons; and in 1936 they won it outright for the first time in 36 years. But their finest period followed the Second World War when, led by MULLEN, and with KYLE at outside-half, they won successive Triple Crowns in 1948 and 1949, in the former year also beating France for their first international grand slam. In 1951 they took their third championship title in four years, drawing with Wales after beating England, Scotland, and France; however, this was to be followed by two decades without even a share in the title.

Up to the Second World War, only two Irish fixtures were included in the programmes of visiting Dominion sides — against Ulster and Ireland — and were all won by the tourists. Following the war, Ireland succeeded in beating the 1957-8 Wallabies, the 1965 Springboks (whose tour was limited to Ireland and Scotland), and the 1966-7 Wallabies; they also drew with the 1969-70 Springboks. Munster, and later Leinster, were also added to the tourists' itineraries, Munster achieving the best provincial record with a victory over one Wallabies side and a draw with the other.

Ireland made its own short tour of Australia in the summer of 1967, losing two of the six games but winning the single Test at Sydney 11-5. The country's contribution to British Lions touring sides includes the captains in New Zealand and Australia in 1950 (Mullen), in South Africa in 1955 (Thompson), in New Zealand and Australia in 1959 (DAWSON), and in South Africa in 1968 (KIERNAN).

Wales was the last of the home countries to take up Rugby football, but also the most enthusiastic. As Marshall noted in 1892, 'the Welshmen have made up for their paucity in numbers by their science in play.' Within six years of forming their first international side they had begun to influence the general development of three-quarter play and the practice of deliberate passing into the open field, at which they became highly skilful and inventive. Perhaps as a result of learning Rugby from a code of laws, rather than growing up with it as a body of familiar traditions, the Welsh approach has always been to explore to the limits whatever possibilities exist within the rules.

Public schoolboys, and undergraduates from Oxford and Cambridge, were mainly responsible for introducing Rugby to South Wales, but the game rapidly gained a broad, popular following. By 1876 the six major clubs of NEWPORT, Cardiff, Aberavon, NEATH, SWANSEA, and LLANELLI had been set up in the industrial area bordering the Bristol Channel, and there was sufficient interest the following year for the South Wales Football Club, as it was originally known, to promote a challenge cup competition. This encouraged the spread of the game inland, and in 1878 the competing clubs included Llandaff, Abergavenny, Llandilo, Aberdare, Cowbridge, Bridgend, and Carmarthen. Cup-ties drew bigger crowds than the early internationals, even if they also led to violence on the field and the terraces and had to be abandoned in the 1880s because of their unruliness. By then they had served to establish Welsh Rugby as a spectator sport and, as in none of the other home countries, the national winter game.

In 1878 the South Wales Football Club was renamed the South Wales Football Union and according to Rugby historians from Marshall onward, this in turn gave way to the Welsh Football Union (W.F.U.) two years later. Their version of the founding of the Welsh Union, which went unchallenged for nearly 80 years, was that at a meeting held in the Tenby Hotel, Swansea, on an unknown day in March 1880, the S.W.F.U. was dissolved and the W.F.U. was formed in its place. The reason given for this change was that the Welsh wanted to play international matches against England, Scotland, and Ireland, and therefore needed to be represented by a full national union. This also appears to fit the fact that less than a year later, on 19 February 1881, a match between England and Wales, officially recognized as the first in the series, did take place at Richardson's Field, Blackheath. England won by 7 goals, 1 dropped goal, and 6 tries (the equivalent of 69 points in modern scoring values) to nil.

On the evidence of Billot, however, published in 1970 in his *History of Welsh International Rugby*, the Welsh Union appears to have been founded in 1881. Shortly after the heavy defeat at Blackheath, a letter appeared in the *Western Mail*, signed by 'A Welsh Football Player'. It asked whether the Welsh team had been selected by the South Wales Football Union (supposedly disbanded a year before). 'Or was it a private team, got up by Mr. Mullock, of Newport, to do battle for Wales?' This drew a reply from a Mr. Clarke who described himself hon. sec. of the South Wales Football Union, denied that his organization had been in any way involved with the match, and referred the correspondent to Mr. Mullock for any further information.

Less than a month later the *Western Mail* reported that on 12 March 1881, delegates from 11 clubs met at the Castle Hotel, Neath, 'to consider the question of forming a Welsh Rugby Union'. These clubs, representing the north and mid-Wales, as well as the south, were Bangor, Brecon, Cardiff, Lampeter, Llandilo, Llandovery, Llanelli, Merthyr, Newport, Pontypool, and Swansea. So clearly the South Wales Rugby Union was still in existence up to that date and regarded as a competent governing body, and the founding of the W.R.U. was not a preparation for, but a reaction to, the first Welsh international match. Mullock of Newport, however, appears to have been forgiven for his independent activities, since he was appointed hon. sec. of the Union, a post he held for 11 years.

England declined a return match the following season, and although Wales won their first match against Ireland at Lansdowne Road in January 1882, two Irish players left the field in protest at decisions by the Welsh umpire, two more were injured, and the fixture was broken off until 1884. Such disputes were not uncommon at this time. After Wales had shown improved form against a North of England team at Newport, England agreed to another full international at ST. HELEN'S GROUND, Swansea, in December 1882; Wales also played Scotland for the first time a month later, and this was the start of annual fixtures with both countries. But in 1888 and 1889 England was in dispute with the other home Unions over representation on the International Board (see above) and played no matches with them; and in 1897 Wales offended the others by raising a testimonial fund for their retiring captain, GOULD. For this 'act of professionalism' Ireland refused to play Wales that season, and Scotland broke off fixtures for two seasons.

Internationals had long been played with XVs instead of XXs when Wales came on the scene, but the deployment of these 15 men was still a matter of experiment. The first Wales side was composed of two backs, two three-quarters, two half-backs, and nine forwards, while England fielded ten forwards to the exclusion of one back. For their next encounter Wales played two backs, three three-quarters, two halves, and eight forwards, while England, also adopting the three three-quarter system, preferred an extra forward to a second back. Wales lost this match, and for a time they used the English formation which increased their forward strength; but, having been overshadowed at first by the handling skills of Englishmen like Rotherham and Vassall, they were beginning to develop the

'passing out' game themselves and so were receptive to further experiments.

The most significant of these took place at Cardiff, where Hancock, a Somerset man, evolved a four-three-quarter system in which he played as one of the centres. In the general disposition of the players, if not in the detail of their roles, it was identical with that of the modern game. Hancock was first used as an additional centre, purely to solve a selection problem, against Gloucester in February 1884, although Cardiff had earlier tried, and abandoned, the four-three-quarter game. Whether Cardiff were its originators is in doubt; London Hospital are known to have employed it in the same year; and since 1878 many Welsh clubs had been playing seven men behind the scrum (usually deployed as three halves, two three-quarters, and two backs — the centre half, or 'flying-man', eventually becoming the centre three-quarter), which admits the possibility that other combinations had been tried. Beyond doubt, however, it was Hancock who made the system work successfully; when he exploited it fully as captain of Cardiff in 1885-6, the club lost only one game.

Wales were first to use four three-quarters in an international in the Scotland match of 1886, when they appointed Hancock captain for the day; the plan misfired. To hold the sturdy Scottish pack, Hancock was forced to move up his back, Bowen, to strengthen the forwards, and switch Gould, his partner at centre, to back. Even so, Scotland won by 1 goal and 2 tries to 1 try. Gould, of Newport, who was to lead Wales 18 times, already disliked 'the Cardiff game', because it meant sharing the mid-field authority which he had exercised alone, and his experience against Scotland appeared to justify his prejudice. It was not until 1888 that, in Gould's absence, Wales again fielded two centres; on that occasion, however, they beat the Maoris, and they never reverted to their old formation. The other Unions remained sceptical, but in 1893 Wales won their first Triple Crown, in each of their matches defeating sides which preferred to pick a ninth forward rather than a fourth three-quarter. By the following season all the opposing countries had revised their opinions, and two-centre play became standard in internationals.

In 1900 began the Golden Era of Welsh Rugby, during which the dominant players were NICHOLLS, TREW, OWEN, and BANCROFT. During 12 seasons Wales took the Triple Crown 6 times, winning the championship on each occasion and also sharing it once with Ireland. Their most notable victory, however, was over the first ALL-BLACKS at Cardiff on 16 December 1905, when a try by T. E. Morgan was the only score; it was the one match that the New Zealand tourists failed to win. For this game Wales employed an extra back, or rover, and for a time continued the experiment of playing seven forwards and eight backs. It did not have the same success as their four-three-quarter system, and was dropped after defeat by Scotland in 1907.

The standard of Welsh Rugby declined between the wars. One cause was the economic depression which unsettled Welsh life and induced a number of good players to go north to the Rugby League. In 1930 support for second-class sides had so declined that a West Wales Rugby League (playing Rugby Union football and later substituting 'Union' for 'League' in its title) was formed to promote formal competition. Another factor was that Welsh teams were slow to adapt their freer game to the development of disciplined back-row play by England and the introduction of calculated tactical kicking at half-back.

In the later 1930s, the period of Wooller, TANNER, and C. W. Jones, a revival began, and this continued at the end of the Second World War. After a lapse of 39 years, Wales won the Triple Crown in 1950 and 1952, when B. L. WILLIAMS, C. I. MORGAN, K. J. JONES, and MEREDITH were the principal players; again in 1965, under the captaincy of Rowlands; and in 1969, when EDWARDS and JOHN were at half-back.

Wales was the first home Union, in the 1967-8 season, to appoint a coach for the national side, and followed this by organizing week-end training for a squad of 25 current and potential international players.

New Zealand. The first game of Rugby ever played in New Zealand took place at Nelson between Nelson Football Club and Nelson College on 14 May 1870. Before that date Nelson had been playing Australian Rules (see FOOTBALL) and Association football and a mixture of both of these, but they were persuaded to change to Rugby by Monro, son of the Speaker of the New Zealand House of Representatives, who had just returned home to Nelson from Christ's College, Finchley, London, and who had become acquainted with the Rugby version of football while in England. Monro went further, and on a visit to Wellington he organized a Rugby match in which his Nelson players met a collection of Wellington players at Petone in September 1870. Thus was the seed of the game taken across the Cook Strait from the South Island and planted in the North Island.

As a result of this match a Wellington club was officially founded in June 1871; in 1872 the game was introduced to Wanganui by a former captain of the Nelson club; and in less

than ten years there were 78 clubs playing Rugby in New Zealand, 7 of them in Wellington, 11 in Canterbury, and 13 in the Auckland area. By 1890 the number of clubs in the country had risen to approximately 700, and numerous unions had been established to organize competitions and to administer the game. The first was the Canterbury Rugby Union in July 1879, and their example was soon followed by Wellington in October 1879, Otago in March 1881, and Auckland in April 1883. From the setting-up of these and other unions there arose a desire for a central authority to co-ordinate inter-provincial fixtures, to arbitrate on disagreements, to organize international tours, and generally to administer the game throughout New Zealand. Thus the New Zealand Rugby Football Union was formed on 16 April 1892.

The first inter-union match took place at Christchurch between Canterbury and Otago in 1881, and internal representative Rugby at this level received a lasting stimulus by the presentation in 1902 of the RANFURLY SHIELD by the Earl of Ranfurly.

In all Rugby countries the visits of touring sides have played a big part in encouraging interest in the game, and three tours in particular increased the popularity of the game in New Zealand: in 1875 a combined side of Auckland Clubs made a southern tour of the country, and for their first match, against Dunedin Clubs at Dunedin, attracted a crowd of 3,000; in 1882 New South Wales made the first tour of New Zealand by a team from overseas, drawing a crowd of 4,000 to one of their matches in Auckland; and in 1884 the return visit by New Zealand to New South Wales, where New Zealand on their first overseas tour won all their eight games, caused widespread interest and enthusiasm in New Zealand.

Tours between New Zealand and Australia have continued more or less regularly since those early days, and contests between the two countries have been given the added spur of the BLEDISLOE CUP, presented in 1931. The first Rugby contact between players of New Zealand and those from the British Isles took place in 1888 when a British team, in which England, Scotland, and Wales were represented, toured Australia and New Zealand. This team did not play a match against a side representing the whole of New Zealand, but the fact that the tourists, who played 19 games in New Zealand, were beaten both by Auckland and by Taranaki Clubs shows how high the standard of play had become in just 18 years since the first game was played in New Zealand. This 1888 tour was the first overseas trip made by a British side.

The distinction of being the first overseas

side ever to visit Britain belongs to a party of 26 New Zealanders who in 1888-9 played 74 matches in the British Isles, 16 in Australia, and 17 in New Zealand. The official title of this energetic party was the New Zealand Native Team, but they became known as the Maoris, although four of the players were in fact of European stock. They beat Ireland 13-4 in Dublin but lost to England at Blackheath and to Wales at Swansea. The Maori people became interested and integrated in the game of Rugby as soon as it was introduced into New Zealand, and there are usually two or three Maoris in New Zealand's international teams. A match against an all-Maori team has become traditional for an overseas side touring New Zealand, and all-Maori teams have visited Canada, Fiji, and Tonga.

The second team from the British Isles to visit New Zealand, in 1904, was representative of all four home countries, and New Zealand had the pleasure of winning their first full international match against the British Isles 9-3 at Wellington. New Zealand have generally had the better of matches against the British Isles since then, a superiority emphasized in 1966 when the Lions of that year were defeated 20-3 at Dunedin, 11-8 at Wellington, 16-12 at Christchurch, and 24-11 at Auckland in the four-match series. But the 1971 Lions tilted the balance a little the other way by winning their Test series 2-1 with the other match drawn. The strength of New Zealand Rugby has also been repeatedly stressed on their major visits to the British Isles and France. Even on their first tour, in 1905-6, they beat England, Scotland, Ireland, and France. In all they won 32 of their 33 matches, and their one defeat was 3-0 by Wales in a match still remembered for controversy, many people believing that DEANS, of New Zealand, scored an equalizing try. On the second major All-Blacks' tour, too, there was controversy, when Brownlie, one of the New Zealand forwards, was sent off the field while playing against England at Twickenham. On this tour, however, the All-Blacks did win all their 30 matches, even if their satisfaction was slightly spoilt by the fact that their itinerary did not include any games in Scotland.

One of the most valuable services done by one Rugby country to another came immediately after the Second World War when the New Zealand Army side toured Britain in the 1945-6 season. This team, known as the Kiwis, helped to put the game in Britain on its feet again after the interruption of the war years, and its sparkling open football rekindled enthusiasm for Rugby. In the same way the attacking Rugby played by the 1967 All-Blacks on their 15-match tour of Britain did much to banish the careworn outlook which had marred the game in the British Isles for some years. It was no coincidence that the same man, SAXTON, was captain of the Kiwis and manager of the 1967 side.

The only country to have matched the Rugby power of New Zealand over the years is South Africa. In the first two encounters between them, in 1921 in New Zealand and in 1928 in South Africa, the series were shared. In 1937 in New Zealand the All-Blacks won the first Test (the term used by New Zealanders, South Africans, and Australians to signify a representative international match) 13-7 but lost the second 6-13 and the third 6-17. South Africa showed a clear superiority in 1949 by winning the series 4-0 in South Africa, but the All-Blacks won the 1956 series 3-1 in New Zealand, and over the years the difference between the sides has been so little that between 1921 and 1965 each country won eight matches at home against the other, and South Africa scored 226 points to the All-Blacks' 218. New Zealanders can point out that in those days they had to travel to South Africa without their Maoris, but this anomaly was removed before the All-Blacks' 1970 tour of South Africa when New Zealand lost the Test series 1-3.

In New Zealand the game developed until there were 28 different unions looking after about 500 senior clubs and many more juniors.

The spectacular style of play practised by the French might have been expected to act as a spur to New Zealand Rugby. But, although the 1905-6, 1924-5, and 1953-4 All-Black touring sides in Britain all played in France, it was not until 1961 that France made their first tour of New Zealand; on that occasion, faced by the strength of New Zealand forward play, they failed to do themselves justice. New Zealand won the 1961 Test series 3-0, and when the French made their second tour, in 1968, New Zealand won the series by the same margin.

One period during which New Zealand did relatively poorly in international matches was in the 1930s and 1940s, and their lack of dominance at this time is often ascribed to a change in the scrummaging laws following the Lions' 1930 tour of New Zealand. Before 1930 New Zealand had evolved a 2-3-2 set scrum with only two men in the front row. Baxter, manager of the 1930 Lions, objected to this formation, and subsequently it was outlawed by the International Board ruling that there must be three men in each team's front row. It took New Zealand a long time to adapt themselves to this requirement, and for some years their forward strength was not as devastating as it had been and was later to become.

South Africa. Rugby was first played in southern Africa in 1875 in Cape Town. In 1878 the Hamilton club, formed in 1875, switched to Rugby from a variation of the Winchester code which is known to have been played in the Cape Town area since 1862. It is probable that Rugby was played even earlier by British regiments involved in the Kaffir and Zulu wars. An important influence in the 1878 switch to Rugby by the Hamilton club and by the Villager Club (formed 1876) was exerted by Milton who had played for England in 1874 and 1875 and was subsequently to become Governor of Southern Rhodesia. The game was greatly helped by the formation in 1882 of the University of Stellenbosch club, for many students went home from the university fired with enthusiasm for Rugby which quickly spread in their home towns.

Elsewhere in southern Africa the presence of British regiments in King William's Town was largely responsible for the formation of the Alberts Club there in 1878, and by 1883 the game was firmly established on the east coast of the Cape. The discovery of diamonds helped to establish Rugby in the Kimberley area between 1883 and 1886; and the gold rush led to the holding of matches between Pretoria and Johannesburg by 1888.

With the spread of club Rugby there arose a need for provincial unions to organize competitions and to provide general administration. The first was Western Province in 1883, and others, such as Eastern Province (1888), Transvaal (1889), and Natal (1890), followed. Similarly the need for a central authority to settle disagreements concerning the laws of the game and generally to administer the game in southern Africa led to the formation, in 1889 at Kimberley, of the South African Rugby Football Board (S.A.R.F.B.).

Chiefly responsible for raising the standard of play in the early days was the staging of tours to and from the country by representative sides. Until the First World War all South Africa's Rugby contacts were with the British Isles and France. Representative teams from Britain visited South Africa in 1891, 1896, 1903, and 1910, and South African teams toured the British Isles and France in 1906-7 and 1912-13. The first of these tours was made possible by the financial backing of Rhodes who was Prime Minister of Cape Colony at that time.

The 1891 British side included no Welsh or Irish, but they won all their 16 matches including three Tests. A rise in the standard of play is shown by the fact that the home side managed to win one of the four Tests played by the 1896 British touring team. This victory, by 5-0, took place at Cape Town on 5 September in the last Test of the series, the British having won the first three. Then, in 1903, South Africa won their first Test series. The first two Tests of the three-match series were drawn 10-10 and 0-0, but South Africa won the final Test 8-0, again at Cape Town. By 1906, when the first South African side travelled overseas, their standard of play had reached such a level that they won two of the four Tests in the British Isles, beating Wales 11-0 at Swansea, and Ireland 15-12 at Belfast. They drew with England 3-3, lost to Scotland 0-6, but won an unofficial match against France 55-6. They also won 23 of the 24 ordinary tour games. South African Rugby was firmly established internationally, and when the 1910 British touring side were defeated 2-1 in their Test series and all the home countries and France were beaten by the 1912-13 tourists, it was clear that South Africa had become a major power in the game. Tours between South Africa and the British Isles were to be a regular feature of international Rugby.

On their way home from serving in Europe in the First World War the New Zealand Imperial Services team made a tour of 14 matches in South Africa in 1919, thus helping the game on to its feet again after the inactivity of the war years but also forging a Rugby link between two countries who were to dominate the world game in the decades that followed. Immediately after this Services tour the South African Board was invited to send a touring team to New Zealand, and the first contact at international level between the two countries thus took place in 1921 in New Zealand. Of the three Test matches played on this tour South Africa lost the first 5-13, won the second 9-5, and the last was drawn 0-0. Of the 16 provincial matches the Springboks won 14, and they also played and won 4 matches in Australia. This record made it clear to New Zealanders that they had found worthy opponents, and in 1928 they made their first tour of South Africa. Although the New Zealanders had to tour without their Maoris, this Test series, too, was shared, 2-2, and it was not until South Africa returned to New Zealand in 1937 that the stalemate was broken. Many South Africans regard this 1937 side as the best that has ever left their country. It won the Test series 2-1 and won all 14 provincial games. On the same tour the Springboks won six of seven provincial matches in Australia and both Tests in that country. Their final record was: played 26, won 24, lost 2; points for 753, against 169. Since then the rivalry between South Africa and New Zealand intensified, and matches between them have been generally regarded as an imaginary championship of the world.

Meanwhile South Africa's Rugby relations with Australia had begun through their visit to Australia at the time of the 1921 tour of New Zealand, and Australia duly paid their first visit to South Africa in 1933. South Africa found the Australians lively if somewhat erratic opponents, and the home side won the Test series 3-2. The next Australian tour of South Africa did not take place until 1953, but since then such tours have been frequent.

Although the 1906-7, 1912-13, and 1951-2 South African sides in Britain also played in France, it was not until 1958 that the French made their first visit to South Africa. The French tourists played a total of ten matches, winning five, losing three, and drawing two. But they won the two-match Test series 1-0, the other Test being drawn, and thus became the first touring side in South Africa to win a Test series since the 1896 British team. Moreover, on the second French visit, a six-match tour in 1964, the French won the only Test played.

By this time South African Rugby, at international level, had become less dominant and was subject to more fluctuations of form than during the early days of impressive progress. It is true that in their first Test series after the Second World War they beat the New Zealanders 4-0 in South Africa and that they beat the 1960 touring All-Blacks 2-1 with one drawn. But the 1956 Springboks in New Zealand were beaten 3-1 in the Tests, and so were their successors in 1965. That 1965 side also lost both the Tests they played in Australia. Furthermore, before going on tour to New Zealand and Australia, the Springboks made a five-match tour of Ireland and Scotland on which they lost to each of those countries and indeed lost four and drew one of their five tour games. This lack of success in Ireland and Scotland could be blamed partly on the fact that the tour took place in April, an awkward time of the year for a side from the southern hemisphere to be match fit; and the poor record of the 1969-70 Springboks in the British Isles — they lost two and drew two of their four international matches — could be blamed partly on political demonstrations which pursued them throughout their tour. But England beat South Africa 18-9 in the only Test match of their seven-match tour in 1972, and South African Rugby was clearly less formidable in the second half of the twentieth century than it had been in the first.

Much of South Africa's success in the 1930s can be ascribed to their early mastery of the mechanics of the 3-4-1 set scrum, said to have been the brainchild of Markotter, one of their national selectors. Indeed, hard and efficient scrummaging has been the chief characteristic of South African Rugby. This has paved the way either for tactical kicking by such proficient stand-off halves as OSLER or for swift three-quarter movements to which the firm, dry pitches of the high veld are ideally suited.

Internally, South African club Rugby has been based largely on competitions, and provincial Rugby has from its early days benefited from the stimulus of the CURRIE CUP. The provincial unions affiliated to the South African Rugby Football Board go beyond political boundaries and include Rhodesia and Southwest Africa. From the early days the number of affiliated unions was 15, but since 1965 this number has been increased to 20. The president of the S.A.R.F.B. wields great influence as chief administrator of the game in South Africa, and none has been more influential than Pienaar, president 1927-53, and CRAVEN, who started his long presidential term in 1956. The Board celebrated its seventy-fifth anniversary in May 1964, when 18 South Africans joined 18 famous players from overseas in forming a pool of players from whom teams were chosen for a series of matches in Johannesburg, Port Elizabeth, and Cape Town.

Rugby Union is the chief winter sport in South Africa, played extensively in schools and universities. The Universities of Stellenbosch and Cape Town have continued to exercise special influence. The game's popularity as a spectacle may be judged from the fact that 564,000 people watched the 20 matches, nearly half of them midweek afternoon games, played by the 1968 Lions.

Australia. Although Australia has never achieved the Rugby prestige enjoyed for so long by New Zealand and South Africa, the Southern Rugby Football Union — ancestor of the Australian R.F.U. — was formed as long ago as 1875; the visit of New South Wales to New Zealand in 1882 was the first international tour undertaken by anyone; and the first touring side ever to leave the British Isles played in Australia, as well as in New Zealand, in 1888. The chief reason why Australian Rugby has not consistently proved the equal of the strongest countries in international competition is that it has remained a relatively minor sport beside Australian Rules football and Rugby League within the country. Similarly, though touring sides from other countries have played against the state teams of Western Australia at Perth, South Australia at Adelaide, and Victoria at Melbourne, as well as playing matches in other parts of the country, the Rugby Union game has become thoroughly and strongly established only in New South Wales and Queensland with their cities of Sydney and Brisbane. Even in the Brisbane area the game has not flourished uninterrupted. For instance, although Queensland were sufficiently strong to play a match against New Zealand in New Zealand in 1896, there was no organized Rugby Union played in the state of Queensland in the years following the First World War, between 1919 and 1929. And top Rugby Union players have proved a natural prey for scouts from the professional Rugby League offering fat cheques.

For geographical reasons Australia's early Rugby contacts were with New Zealand, and the 1882 visit to New Zealand by New South Wales was followed by frequent tours between the two countries. The New Zealanders generally had the better of these encounters, but in 1894 New South Wales had the great satisfaction of winning 8-6 a game which was designated the first Test ever played in New Zealand. The one Test played in New Zealand on Queensland's tour in 1896 was won 9-0 by New Zealand.

In 1892 the Southern R.F.U. had changed its name to the New South Wales R.U. and from 1903 onwards New South Wales and Queensland combined, whenever possible, to form representative Australian teams for international matches. Thus, strictly speaking, the first Test played between Australia and New Zealand took place at Sydney on 15 August 1903, New Zealand winning 22-3. The absence of organized Rugby in Queensland during the decade following the First World War meant that New South Wales had to bear the burden of representing Australia in international matches. But in 1929 Australia, with four Queenslanders in their side and before a Sydney crowd of 40,000, beat New Zealand 9-8; and followed this by winning the second Test of the three-match series 17-9 in Brisbane, and the third 15-13 in Sydney. This 3-0 victory in the 1929 series over the New Zealanders remains one of the highest peaks of Australian achievement in international Rugby.

Australia and New Zealand next met in 1931 at Auckland, with the added incentive of the Bledisloe Cup which had just been given for competition between the two countries. New Zealand became the first holders of the Cup by winning this match 20-13. Matches between Australia and New Zealand have continued regularly, and Australians particularly like to remember 1949 when their national side played two Tests in New Zealand and won them both (11-6 and 16-9). In 1967 Australia were specially invited to help the New Zealand Rugby Union celebrate their seventyfifth anniversary, but New Zealand won this match 29-9. One of the closest of games took place at Brisbane in 1968 when New Zealand won 19-18 thanks to a penalty try and its conversion in the last moments of play.

Australia's contacts with the British Isles have naturally been less frequent than their matches against New Zealand, but it soon became standard practice for British teams visiting New Zealand to play at least a few games in Australia, and visits by Australian teams to the British Isles have been regular and reasonably successful from the playing point of view. Even during the period from 1919 to 1929, a team from New South Wales, popularly known as the Waratahs, undertook a tour of 28 matches in the British Isles and three in France in 1927-8. This side lost to England and Scotland but beat Wales (18-8 at Cardiff), Ireland, and France. The first Australian team to visit Britain, in 1908-9, played only two international matches, beating England 9-3 at Blackheath but losing to Wales 6-9 at Cardiff. The fourth Wallabies, in 1957-8, had the disappointment of losing to all four home countries and to France, but their successors in 1966-7 played brilliant attacking Rugby in beating Wales 14-11 and England 23-11. Their 23 points against England included three dropped goals by HAWTHORNE, their stand-off half.

Australia's first Rugby contact with South Africa took place in 1921 when the first South African team to tour New Zealand stopped off in Australia to play four official provincial matches and also a match against a Victoria XV. Australia's first visit to South Africa and the first international matches between the two countries occurred in 1933, and it is interesting to note that at this time Australia's 29 touring players included as many as 11 from Queensland and 3 from Victoria, the rest being from New South Wales. Since then other South African touring teams, like British Isles teams, have played matches in Australia at the times of their visits to New Zealand, and other Australian sides have visited South Africa more or less regularly. The 1963 Australians did notably well in South Africa, winning 13 of their provincial matches and sharing the Test series 2-2. This was at the beginning of one of Australia's most successful periods: in 1964, although they lost the first two of their three matches against the All-Blacks in New Zealand, they won the third 20-5, the biggest defeat New Zealand had ever suffered; and when the 1965 Springboks played two Tests in Australia on their way to New Zealand, the Australians won both of them.

Australia have also maintained close relations with Fiji to their mutual benefit. The Fijians' carefree, open style of play has proved a great attraction on their visits to Australia and has helped to establish the public Australian image of Rugby Union as a fast-moving game of running and handling. Conscious of the strength of Rugby League in their country, the Rugby Union officials of Australia have done their utmost over the years to encourage their players to throw the ball about and not to indulge in too much kicking. It is for this reason that the law restricting kicking to touch between the 25-yard lines was in force for many years in Australia under dispensation before it was adopted by the International Board in 1970. Their firm grounds and fine climate have also encouraged the Australians to play the kind of spectacular Rugby for which they have become renowned.

The vast distances involved in travelling from one side of Australia to the other have made internal communication difficult for Rugby players and administrators, no less than for people engaged in other pursuits. But on 26 November 1949 the Rugby authorities of New South Wales, Queensland, Victoria, and other less prosperous centres of the game at last got together and formed the Australian Rugby Football Union. In 1966 it was agreed for the first time that an overseas side touring Australia should have its expenses at the various centres of the game met from a central fund. Previously each state had had to cater for a visiting side out of its own pocket, a crippling burden in the unfashionable areas, and it was hoped that the change would leave more money available for the development of the game in areas far removed from Sydney and Brisbane.

To the visitor from overseas one of the oddest features of Rugby in Australia is that important matches are often played not only at cricket grounds but even right across the square. New Zealand, South Africa, and the Lions have all scrummaged in international Rugby matches on the famous wicket of SYDNEY CRICKET GROUND. They have also played international matches in Brisbane at LANG PARK, the headquarters of Queensland Rugby League.

Australia play their international Rugby in gold-coloured jerseys. For many years they played in dark green, but these clashed with the colours of both South Africa and Ireland. In earlier days Australia wore jerseys of the light blue still worn by New South Wales. Internally, Australian club Rugby is based on competitions, but some states are as yet too weak for the establishment of a profitable nationwide inter-state competition. Fixtures between New South Wales and Queensland, however, often produce hotly contested matches with a high level of performance.

Fiji. The Rugby Union game is thought to have been played in Fiji as early as 1880 by the local police, and the first organized Rugby was played in 1914 following the formation of the Fiji Rugby Union in 1913. For geographical reasons Tonga became Fiji's natural opponents, and Fijian Rugby has owed much to the encouragement from New Zealand and Australia in the nature of tours by club, university, and school teams.

Representative Rugby between Fiji and her celebrated neighbours began in 1938 when the New Zealand Rugby Union sent a team of Maoris to Fiji. Three Tests were played on this tour, and the Fijians had the satisfaction of drawing the first 3-3, winning the second 11-5, although losing the third 6-3. The following year Fiji toured New Zealand, winning seven and drawing one of their eight games. They were especially pleased to defeat the Maori XV 14-4. The Second World War caused a temporary halt in these proceedings, but the Maoris toured Fiji in 1948, the Fijians toured New Zealand in 1951, and there have been more or less regular tours between the two countries since then.

Meanwhile, in 1952, Fiji made their first tour of Australia, winning eight, losing one, and drawing one of their ten games. They played two Tests, losing the first 9-15 and winning the second 17-15. They drew a crowd of 42,000 to one of their matches in Sydney. Two years later they played no fewer than 17 matches in Australia and won 15 of them. Of the two Tests, they lost the first 19-22 but won the second 18-16.

By now others were interested in Fiji Rugby, and the team was invited to tour Wales and France. So, in September 1964, Fiji made their first visit to Europe, playing five matches in Wales and five in France. In Wales they won two games, lost two, and drew one, and in France they won one and lost four. They played sparkling attacking Rugby before losing 22-28 to a Welsh XV before a crowd of 50,000 at Cardiff, but they gave a tired performance in the last match of the tour in Paris where France beat them 21-3 in a full international.

In 1968 the All-Blacks, who had been touring Australia, played a match in Fiji — the first fully representative major touring side to do so — and showed the Fijians the power of New Zealand Rugby by winning 33-6 before a crowd of 22,000 at Suva. The following year Wales, on their way back from a short tour of New Zealand and Australia, also stopped off for a game at Suva. Wales won this match 31-11, and the crowd was 24,000. In 1970 came the Fijians' second visit to Europe when they made a tour of 13 matches in England as part of the Rugby Football Union's centenary celebrations. In 1973 England beat Fiji 13-12 at Suva on their way to a short tour of New Zealand.

Rugby Union is Fiji's chief winter sport with approximately 11,000 more or less regular players in over 600 clubs, governed by 37 unions or sub-unions. The game is played in many institutions, from primary schools up, and is organized on a competitive basis.

Japan. Cambridge University can claim some of the credit for getting the game started in Japan, for Rugby was first played at Keio University where it was introduced in 1899 by Tanaka who had come across the game at Cambridge. Tanaka was helped by Professor Clark, who was on the staff at Keio University and had also been at Cambridge, and the first match was played in 1900 between Keio University and the Yokohama Club which had been formed by British residents. The Japanese Rugby Union was formed in 1926.

In its early days Japanese Rugby did not spread quickly, being confined mainly to a few schools and universities, but in 1930 an all-Japan team was invited by British Columbia to tour Canada, and this Japanese side was strong enough to win five and draw one of its six games. In 1936 came the first visit to Japan by a team from New Zealand. The New Zealand Universities team, though winning eight of their nine matches, were held to a draw, 9-9, by Japan Universities. At this stage of its development Rugby had become so popular in Japanese universities that inter-university matches were known to attract crowds in excess of 20,000.

The Second World War almost completely destroyed Japanese Rugby, so that, when a weakened Oxford University team toured Japan in 1952, they were able to beat all-Japan 52-0. But this visit by Oxford, followed by teams of various standards from France, New Zealand, and Australia, plus a tour in 1959 by a combined Oxford and Cambridge Universities side, helped to stimulate interest once more. The Japanese players quickly learned from watching the techniques of their visitors, so that when Doshida University toured New Zealand in 1966, they won one of their matches and drew another.

In 1967 New Zealand Universities followed their predecessors of 1936 by making a tour of Japan, and in 1968 all-Japan made a tour of New Zealand. The Japanese tourists, although much smaller than their opponents, managed to win five of their ten games, and they surprisingly beat the Junior All-Blacks (New Zealand's best players under the age of 23) by 23-19 at Wellington. A crowd of 23,000 watched them play New Zealand Universities, also at Wellington.

After this break-through, Japan in 1969 staged the first Asian Tournament at Tokyo, and won it, and in 1970 they won the second at Bangkok. Because of their size the Japanese are forced to play in an open, fluid style which proves extremely popular with spectators. But their stature can be a great handicap as they try to take on the major Rugby countries. The average weight of the forwards in the 1968 all-Japan team in New Zealand was only 11 st. 12 lb. (75 kg.) and the forwards' average height, 5 ft. 9 in. (1·75 m.).

Rugby is played in almost every school and university in Japan, and there are more than 1,500 clubs in the country. Competitions, coaching, and training squads are all fully organized. England showed her recognition of Japanese Rugby by touring Japan in 1971. Two international matches were played, England winning 27-19 at Osaka and by no more than 6-3 at Tokyo. Two years later Japan made their first visit to Europe, playing matches in Wales, England, and France. In the tour's two international matches they were beaten 62-14 by Wales at Cardiff and 30-18 by France at Bordeaux.

Canada. Canadian Rugby owes its beginnings to immigrants from the British Isles who had the game established in Ontario by 1882. The domestic game has always been hampered by the vast distance between the east and west coasts. These are the chief areas of the game, little Rugby is played in the middle of the country. In the east the game has continued to recruit many players from among immigrants, whereas in the west a higher percentage of native Canadians has taken part. There is an inactive gap in the middle of the season because of the severity of the Canadian winter.

Geography has tended to split the country in two, from a Rugby point of view, but in a wider sense it has helped inasmuch as major touring sides travelling to and from the British Isles and Australasia have found Canada a convenient place to break the journey. Thus All-Blacks, Wallabies, and Lions have all played in Canada. It has become customary for such touring sides to play one match in western Canada and one match in the east.

Most of these games the Canadians have lost but in 1958 the Wallabies were beaten 11-8 on their way back from the British Isles; the 1959 Lions, returning from Australia and New Zealand, won by no more than 16-11; in 1964 the All-Blacks, returning from the British Isles, won by only 6-3; and the 1966 Lions, on their way back from Australasia, were defeated 8-6. All these matches by touring sides were against British Columbia (who twice beat the New Zealand Universities in 1962) and were played at Vancouver.

Because of the difficulties involved in assembling a composite team from the widely separated areas of the country, it was not until 1966 that a side fully representative of all Canada was fielded against a touring team. This match, against the Lions, took place on 17 September at Toronto, the Lions winning 19-8. Fourteen of the fifteen members of the Canadian side came from British Columbia, indicating where the strength of Canadian Rugby lay as well as adding considerably to the match expenses. A year later Canada received a five-match tour by England who beat Canada 29-0 at Vancouver. England also played, and won, at Calgary, Victoria, Toronto, and Ottawa. Then in 1973 Wales played five matches in Canada, winning them all. They beat Canada 58-20 at Toronto.

Canadian sides have frequently crossed the border to play in the U.S.A., and in 1959 a team representing British Columbia toured Japan. A side from Canada went so far as to visit Britain in 1902-3, but it was not until 1962 that a more or less fully representative Canadian team toured the British Isles. This side won only one of their 16 games, but they acquired respect by holding the BARBARIANS to a score of 3-3. Canadian club sides have also visited Britain.

Argentina. The Rugby Union game was first played in Argentina in the 1880s, largely by British residents in Buenos Aires and engineers involved in constructing railways. The Argentine Rugby Union was founded in 1899. More and more native Argentinians gradually took to the game, and in due course Argentine Rugby became thoroughly organized on a competitive basis with keenly contested leagues. But Argentina has maintained its Rugby links with Britain through tours to and from the two lands. In 1910 and 1927 British Isles sides visited Argentina, and they were followed in 1936 by a largely English team and in 1952 by an Irish side. Oxford and Cambridge Universities have also toured Argentina, and in 1968 Wales made a six-match visit, all the games being played in Buenos Aires. Wales were not quite at full strength for this tour because of the Lions' tour of South Africa at much the same time. Even so Argentina did well to win the first of two matches between the countries 9-5 and to draw the second 9-9. The following year Scotland made a similar tour, and Argentina beat them too in the first international, 20-3; but Scotland won the second international 6-3. This was a period when Argentina enjoyed maximum recognition by the home countries, for these Welsh and Scottish tours were followed in 1970 by one by Ireland.

Then in 1973 Argentina made their first visit to Europe. They played four matches in Ireland and four in Scotland, and an international match in each country, being beaten 21-18 by Ireland and 12-11 by Scotland.

Argentina have also established links with South Africa, beginning with a tour of Argentina undertaken in 1932 by a party of leading young South African players known as the Junior Springboks. Similar South African teams toured Argentina in 1959 and 1966, and although these three sides won all their matches, they came away with a respect for the Argentinians' knowledge of the game. This was further demonstrated in 1965 when the Argentinians toured South Africa — where they were known as the PUMAS — and managed to defeat the Junior Springboks.

France has also made several visits to Argentina with more or less fully representative sides. The first was in 1949 when they won their two international matches 5-0 and 12-3.

Many Argentinian clubs have financial security by being part of multi-sports clubs which are in full use throughout the year. One such club, San Isidro from Buenos Aires, were the first Argentinian side to visit the British Isles, in 1963. Several other club teams from Argentina have followed San Isidro's example. There are 45 clubs in Buenos Aires alone, 18 in Rosario, and 17 in Cordoba.

France. The Rugby Union game was taken to France by British businessmen — especially those engaged in the wine trade — students, and embassy and consular officials, and it was first played in France in Paris and the Channel ports. British residents were playing Rugby in France as early as 1877, and the first British club side to visit France were certainly Rosslyn Park who beat Stade Français in 1893. By then the game was established among Frenchmen in such ports as Le Havre, Nantes, and Bordeaux, and, as it became an accepted if unofficial form of recreation at educational establishments in Paris, so students, returning home, passed on their enthusiasm to their friends.

The Union des Sociétés Françaises de Sports Athlétiques (U.S.F.S.A.), founded in 1887, looked after the interests of the early French Rugby players and organized competitions for them. The first provincial centre to become a stronghold of the game was Bordeaux whose Stade Bordelais Université Club won the national club championship seven times between 1899 and 1911. In those days the French did not play the fast, open, handling game for which they were to become famous, but the seeds of this exhilarating type of play were sown in Bayonne soon afterwards. A Welshman from Penarth, Roe, settled in Bayonne, and it was largely through his influence that the local club, Aviron Bayonnais, learned the joy and efficacy of sustained bouts of quick inter-passing and so discovered that this was the method of play which best suited the southern French temperament. In April 1913 Aviron Bayonnais not only inflicted on the famous Bordeaux club its first ever championship defeat on its home ground, but, with Roe in their side, also took their bewildering new style of play to Paris, and there won the final of the national club championship by 33 points to 8. This was the kind of result bound to create widespread interest and to attract the attention of imitators. There can be little doubt that this marked the birth of the rapid and deft passing and running that have become the most renowned characteristic of the game in France.

At the other end of the Pyrenees another Welshman, Griffiths, was at work. He settled in Perpignan in 1912, became captain of the local club, and taught his players to run and pass and execute the three-quarter movements of his native Wales. His influence on the game in France was considerable, too, at least in the south-east corner of the country.

After the First World War the game spread rapidly in the southern half of the country, and in 1919 the clubs decided to break away from the U.S.F.S.A. and to form the Fédération Française de Rugby (F.F.R.), which remains at the helm of the game in France. At this stage the number of clubs affiliated to the F.F.R. was 173. More and more club competitions, local, regional, and national, were set up, and rivalry became intense. Little interprovincial Rugby has ever been played in France, all enthusiasm going into the club championships and into France's international fixtures.

Various forms of championship have been tried, but by the 1969-70 season the regular formula for the competition involving the country's leading clubs was a First Division of the national championship consisting of eight groups of clubs with eight clubs in each group. The clubs within each group played one another home and away on a league basis. The four leading clubs in each group's table then went forward to form the 32 teams needed for five knock-out stages. The popularity of the game in France can be judged from the 1970 annual report of the F.F.R. which stated that the game was regularly being played by 75,000 players in 1,160 clubs.

French clubs have made a point of providing facilities and coaching for boys from the age of about 11 upwards, the boys being carefully arranged according to their age and size. Most clubs have at least three teams of boys

playing regularly, and there can be little doubt that the care taken by the clubs in looking after youngsters has contributed to a large extent to the strength of French Rugby. There are interclub championships for the boys' teams as well as for the first and second senior teams of clubs. In fact in a normal domestic season France has 13 national championships at various levels, to say nothing of local and regional competitions.

As far as international Rugby is concerned France may be said to have been thrown in at the deep end, for their first match was against New Zealand. It took place at the PARC DES PRINCES, Paris, on New Year's Day, at the end of the New Zealanders' 1905-6 tour of the British Isles. The French were beaten 8-38. This was followed later the same season by a match against England (also in Paris) which England won 35-8. France started playing Wales in 1908, Ireland in 1909, and Scotland in 1910, and thereafter France have met each of the home countries annually except during the two world wars, and during the period 1932-9, when no games between France and the home countries were played because allegations of professionalism in the French club championship caused the home unions to break off relations with the F.F.R. Relations were resumed in 1939.

France were heavily defeated in most of their early matches against England and Wales, but they beat Scotland 16-15 in Paris in 1911, and in 1920 defeated Ireland 15-7 in Dublin. Their first victory over England came in 1927 in Paris, and they beat Wales for the first time in 1928, also in Paris. They did not win in Wales until 1948, and the first French victory in England did not arrive until 1951. Thereafter, however, they made their presence fully felt and, after sharing the home international championship with England and Wales in 1954 and with Wales in 1955, they won it unshared in 1959 for the first time. In 1968 they achieved the grand slam of beating all four home countries in one season: they beat Scotland 8-6 at MURRAYFIELD, Ireland 16-6 at COLOMBES, England 14-9 at Colombes, and Wales 14-9 at Cardiff. In 1970 France beat England 35-13, the most points ever scored against England in one match.

Although most of the overseas teams making major tours of the British Isles — from the 1905-6 New Zealanders onwards — played at least one match in France, the French themselves did not venture out of Europe until 1958 when they made a ten-match tour of South Africa. The French captain, Celaya, had the misfortune to injure a knee in the first match and so could not play in either of the two Tests of the tour; but MIAS proved an inspiring leader

in his stead and, after drawing the first Test
3-3 at Cape Town, the French surprised the
Rugby world by winning the second 9-5 at
Johannesburg. This was the first time a visiting side had won a Test series in South Africa
since 1896. In their ten matches the French
scored 137 points and had 124 scored against
them.

This tour came in the middle of a period of
success which the French look upon as one of
the peaks of their Rugby history. Earlier in
1958 they had beaten Australia 19-0 in Paris,
they had achieved their first ever victory at
Cardiff, and they had beaten Ireland in Paris.
In the season immediately following their
South African trip they beat Scotland, drew
with England, and beat Wales again, thus
making sure of winning the home international
championship unshared for the first time.
Mias, who officially took over the captaincy
from Celaya for this 1959 season and who led
the French forwards even when Celaya was
captain, had been brought out of semi-
retirement at the start of this successful period.
On his return he proved just the leader the
French needed if they were to make the most
of their natural talents. The French consequently refer to this triumphant period as the
'Mias Era'.

France returned to South Africa for a six-
match tour in 1964 and won the only Test of
the tour 8-6 at Springs; but by the time they
played 13 games on a tour in 1967 the spell
had broken. On this 1967 tour they played four
Tests, losing the first two 3-26 and 3-13, winning the third 19-14, and drawing the last 6-6.

France had also toured New Zealand. Having beaten the touring All-Blacks 3-0 in Paris
in 1954, they were expected to give a good
account of themselves on their first visit to
New Zealand in 1961; but they found New
Zealand's forward strength too much for them,
and they lost all three Tests, the scores being
6-13 at Auckland, 3-5 at Wellington, and 3-32
at Christchurch. Nor did they fare much better
on their second visit to New Zealand in 1968.
They again lost all three Tests, and this was
the start of a sequence of ten defeats, the others being by Australia, South Africa twice,
Romania, Scotland, Ireland, and England
— one of the most disappointing periods in the
history of French Rugby.

Australian teams, like those of other countries, have normally played in France at the
time of their tours of the British Isles, and
France have played in Australia during their
trips to New Zealand. Besides playing against
the major Rugby countries, the French have
also helped where Rugby is less popular by
arranging fixtures with them. Thus they first
played Romania in 1924, Germany in 1927,

Italy in 1937, and Argentina in 1949.

The Rugby Union game is played extensively in the southern half of France but little
in the north. Of the 64 clubs in the First Division of the national championship in the
1969-70 season only two, Paris Université
Club and the Racing Club de France, were
from Paris or further north. Club games are
normally played on Sundays, international
matches being played on Saturdays to comply
with British custom. The national team play in
blue jerseys, white shorts, and red stockings.

Italy. Rugby Union is a minor sport in Italy,
but most of the large cities and towns, especially Rome, Milan, Genoa, and Parma, have
clubs. Stimulus has been given to the game in
Italy chiefly by the French who have sent club
sides to play and have given Italy an international fixture almost every year since 1948.
British clubs, like the Woodpeckers in 1950
and the Public Schools Wanderers in 1970,
have toured Italy, and Old Rugby Roma
toured England and Wales in 1963, playing
the Harlequins, Swansea, Newport, and Staf-
ford. But such visits have been few and far
between.

Italy first played France in an international
match in 1937 at the Parc des Princes, Paris.
France won 43-5, and contests between the
two countries have mostly been very one-
sided. After Italy had been beaten 0-21 at Pau
in 1965, 0-21 at Naples in 1966, and 13-60 at
Toulon in 1967, it was decided that France
would in future field their 'B' team (or second
XV) in their annual encounter with Italy.

Romania. Although the Romanian Rugby
Federation was founded as early as 1912, the
chief influence on the game has come from
France rather than from Britain. In fact the
beginnings of Rugby in Romania near the turn
of the century owed almost everything to
young Romanians, in Paris to study, finding
themselves playing and enjoying the game
with Paris Université Club then going home
for holidays and persuading friends to play.
The links with France have remained firm.
Paris Université Club have made numerous
visits to Bucharest, and France, who first
played Romania in 1924, have been their only
regular opponents in international matches.

Probably because of these regular contacts
with French teams the standard of Rugby in
Romania has improved more steadily than in
any other country in Central Europe. France
won their 1924 match against Romania 59-3,
but by 1938 the score was only 11-8 to France,
and in 1960 Romania beat France 11-5. This
was the beginning of a four-year period during
which Romania played France four times
without defeat. In 1961 the score was 5-5, in
1962 3-0 to Romania, and in 1963 6-6.

After the Second World War, Romania had no international Rugby matches until 1957. In that year France travelled to play in Bucharest, and such was the curiosity of the people that a crowd of almost 110,000 watched France win 18-15. This was the largest crowd that had ever watched a Rugby match anywhere in the world and there must have been many who had never seen Rugby before but had been attracted by the novelty of the occasion, for ten years later an international match between Romania and France could draw a crowd of no more than 5,000.

Although Romanian clubs have had occasional contact with British clubs, notably with Swansea in 1951 and with the Harlequins in 1955, their Rugby relations, apart from those with France, have been mainly with such little-known Rugby countries as Poland, Bulgaria, and Czechoslovakia. The Romanian national side did, however, tour Devon and Cornwall in 1972 and Argentina in 1973.

There are some 175 clubs in Romania catering for approximately 6,500 players. Competition is established at all levels, and clubs provide facilities and coaching for boys from the age of ten. Many of the clubs are associated with businesses or factories, such as Grivita Rosie, the club of the steel complex of that name. The Romanian domestic Rugby season is divided into two parts because the severe winter usually results in pitches' being frozen for some weeks from the middle of December. Compared with Association football, Rugby is still a minor sport in Romania.

The Rugby Football Union Handbook, annually. John Billot, *History of Welsh International Rugby* (1970); Sean Diffley, *The Men in Green* (1973); J. R. Jones, *The Encyclopaedia of Rugby Football* (1958); Denis Lalanne, *Les Conquérants du XV de France* (1970); *Football: The Rugby Union Game*, ed. F. Marshall (1892); O. L. Owen, *The History of the Rugby Football Union* (1955); A. C. Parker, *The Springboks 1891-1970* (1970); *Playfair Rugby Football Annual*; *Rothmans Rugby Yearbook* (annually); Rugby Football Union, *Illustrated Centenary History of the Rugby Football Union* (1971); Montague Shearman *et al.*, *Football* (The Badminton Library, 1899); Gordon Slatter, *On the Ball* (1970); J. B. G. Thomas, *Great Rugger Clubs* (1962); W. W. Wakefield and H. P. Marshall, *Rugger* (1930).

GOVERNING BODY (WORLD): International Board, Balfron, Hermitage Road, Kenley, Surrey; (U.K.): Rugby Football Union, Twickenham, Middlesex; Irish Rugby Union, 62 Lansdowne Road, Dublin 4, Eire; Scottish Rugby Union, Murrayfield, Edinburgh 12, Scotland; Welsh Rugby Union, Royal London House, 28/31 St. Mary Street, Cardiff, Wales.

RUNNING, see CROSS-COUNTRY RUNNING; FELL RUNNING; LONG-DISTANCE RUNNING; MARATHON; MIDDLE-DISTANCE RUNNING; ROAD RUNNING; SPRINTING.

RUP SINGH (1907-   ), HOCKEY player for India, younger brother of CHAND, with whom he formed a dazzling partnership. He and Chand set an Olympic record unlikely ever to be surpassed when, between them, they scored 18 goals for India in their 24-1 victory over U.S.A. in the 1932 OLYMPIC GAMES. Rup Singh scored 10 goals, an Olympic individual goal-scoring record. He scored 185 goals in under 50 matches during India's tour of Australia and New Zealand in 1935. He was undoubtedly the cleverest left inner produced by India.

RUPP, ADOLPH (1900-   ), American BASKETBALL coach who achieved the best winning record in the history of college basketball, with 879 victories. Rupp became coach to the University of Kentucky in 1930 and took them to 4 NATIONAL COLLEGIATE ATHLETIC ASSOCIATION titles and 24 South-Eastern Conference championships. He was elected to the Hall of Fame (see NAISMITH) in 1969.

RUSKA, WILHELM (1940-   ), Dutch JUDO fighter. With his fellow-countryman GEESINK, Ruska upset the domination of the sport by the Japanese. This 6 ft. 3 in. (1·90 m.), 18½-stone (117·5 kg.) fighter from Amsterdam began judo at the age of 21 and came into top international competition just as Geesink was in the twilight of his career. In 1967 Ruska took the heavyweight gold medal at the European championships in Rome after his opponent, Kibrotsashvili, had been disqualified. At the world championships in Salt Lake City the same year he stopped a Japanese clean sweep by winning the heavyweight event, throwing Maejima in the final. He regained his world title in 1971 and took the Olympic gold medal the following year. He climaxed his competitive career by winning the Open title in Munich before announcing his retirement from the sport.

RUSSELL, WILLIAM (1934-   ), American BASKETBALL player. Russell spent his college career at San Francisco University where he won two NATIONAL COLLEGIATE ATHLETIC ASSOCIATION championships. After playing in the 1956 gold medal-winning team at the Melbourne OLYMPIC GAMES, he turned professional with the BOSTON CELTICS. He gained a reputation as the greatest defensive player in the history of the game. At 6 ft. 10 in. (2·08 m.), he was also able to excel at rebounding and created a record with 51 rebounds in a single game.

Russell became player-coach of Boston in 1968 and retired from playing in 1969. During his career with Boston, he helped them to win 11 NATIONAL BASKETBALL ASSOCIATION championships in 13 seasons.

RUSSELL-VICK, Mrs. MARY (1922-   ), HOCKEY player for England, South of England, Sussex, and South Saxons L.H.C., an outstanding forward. She represented England in 1948-9 and 1951-3 and toured with the England teams to the United States (1947) and Holland (1948).

RUTH, GEORGE HERMAN (Babe) (1895-1948), American BASEBALL player whose prodigious home-run hitting and colourful personality made him began his major-league career in 1914 as a pitcher with the BOSTON RED SOX. Although he became an outstanding pitcher he was soon transferred to the outfield in order to give the team daily advantage of the batting power that enabled him to drive balls out of the park for home runs. In 1919 he set a home-run record of 29 and immediately broke it by hitting 54 the following season, his first with the NEW YORK YANKEES. In 1927 he established yet another seasonal home-run record of 60. When his career ended in 1935 he had accumulated a record total of 714 home runs — a record not to be broken until 1974, by AARON, earned approximately a million dollars in salaries and shares from ten WORLD SERIES; and realized an estimated additional million from various endorsements and public appearances.

RUUD, BIRGER (1911-   ), Norwegian ski jumper who won the world jumping championship in 1931, 1935, and 1937, the Olympic jumping in 1932 and 1936, and then, uniquely for a Nordic competitor, won the Alpine SKIING downhill championship gold medal at the 1936 Games; finally, in 1948, at the age of 37, he won the Olympic silver medal for ski jumping.

RYAN, ELIZABETH (1892-   ), American LAWN TENNIS player, a formidable competitor who won many titles but never succeeded in capturing either the U.S. or the WIMBLEDON singles championships. She won the first of her 19 Wimbledon titles — 12 women's doubles and 7 mixed doubles — in 1914. After the war she and LENGLEN were undefeated in the women's doubles, and Ryan

won the mixed doubles with several different partners between 1919 and 1932. In 1924 she took a set off Lenglen in the singles.

Miss Ryan twice reached the final of the all-comers' singles at Wimbledon (1914 and 1920) and Mrs. MOODY beat her in the final in 1930. Although she played most of her tennis in Europe, she was runner-up to Mrs. Mallory in the 1926 U.S. championships and won the women's doubles and mixed doubles in that year, and the mixed again in 1933, shortly before she became a professional.

Her great strengths were her ability to volley, her chopped forehand (a stroke seldom seen in modern lawn tennis), and her tenacity and determination. When she retired, she had won at least 659 events, probably a record for any first-class competitor.

RYAN, TOMMY (1870-1948), American boxer who won both the world welterweight and middleweight titles and never lost the latter championship. He was tricked into losing the welterweight title by the wily MCCOY but was generally renowned for his ringcraft and accurate punching.

RYDER, SAMUEL (1859-1936), English businessman and GOLF patron, the donor of the RYDER CUP, instituted in 1927, which is played for biennially between teams of professionals of the U.S.A. and Great Britain and Ireland.

RYDER CUP, GOLF competition played in alternate years between teams of men professionals of the U.S.A. and Great Britain and Ireland.

RYUN, JAMES RONALD (1947-   ), middle-distance runner for the U.S.A. Ryun was only 17 when he first ran the mile in under 4 minutes, clocking 3 min. 59·0 sec. in 1964. He was still only 19 when he broke the world 880 yards record (1 min. 44·9 sec.) in 1966 and followed this within five weeks with a new world mile record of 3 min. 51·3 sec., reducing by the huge margin of 2·3 sec. JAZY's record. In this race Ryun had the benefit of opposition but in 1967 when he further improved the mile record to 3 min. 51·1 sec., he led from start to finish, a feat almost unheard of in the annals of mile racing. In 1967 he also eclipsed ELLIOTT's 1,500 metres world record with 3 min. 33·1 sec. but was beaten in the 1968 Olympic 1,500 metres by KEINO.

S

SABINA PARK, Kingston, CRICKET ground in Jamaica. The home of Kingston Cricket Club, this ground is very small, with a hard, glossy pitch which usually favours batsmen. SANDHAM scored 325 there for England against West Indies in 1929-30, and in 1957-8 SOBERS made 365 not out against England — the highest innings in any Test match.

SAEZ, MARCOS (*d.* 1747), picador, was killed in the *plaza de toros* of Seville on 12 June 1747. His is the first recorded death of a professional *torero* of any category.

SAFFRON LANE SPORTS CENTRE, Leicester, outdoor cycle track (with adjoining facilities for ATHLETICS, etc.) was the principal venue of the 1970 world CYCLING championships. The 333⅓-metre (365·25 yds.) track is of mastic asphalt, with banking at a maximum angle of 37°.

SAILER, TONI (1936-   ), Austrian ski racer from Kitzbühel who in two seasons, 1956 and 1958, won seven world titles, a unique accomplishment. At the 1956 WINTER OLYMPIC GAMES at CORTINA d'Ampezzo, Italy, he won all three titles, slalom, giant slalom, and downhill, the giant slalom by the remarkable margin of 6·2 seconds over his fellow-countryman, Molterer. His hip-waggling style introduced *wedeln* to a much wider public and gave Austria SKIING leadership until BONNET led a French revival. Sailer returned as director of the Austrian national racing team in 1972-3.

ST. ANDREWS, see GOLF and OLD COURSE, St. Andrews.

ST. ANTON, famous SKIING resort of the western Tyrol, Austria, where the first ARLBERG-KANDAHAR race was run.

ST. GEORGE, Australian RUGBY LEAGUE club. A highly successful Sydney club, it has the distinction of having supplied at least one player to every Australian international team to tour Britain since its foundation in 1921. St. George set up a record by winning the Sydney First Grade Premiership — Australia's most important club competition — in 11 successive years from 1956. It was during this period that GASNIER and RAPER were at the height of their powers. In its early days, St. George's most renowned players were Justice and Gilbert.

ST. HELEN'S GROUND, municipally-owned playing field used as headquarters of the SWANSEA R.F.C., and as a regular venue by the Glamorgan County Cricket Club. Wales played their first home RUGBY UNION international here, against England in 1882, and from 1899 onward home games were fairly strictly alternated between St. Helen's and CARDIFF ARMS PARK. The match against Scotland in 1954, however, was the final international at Swansea; from that point the Welsh Rugby Union decided to restrict all its fixtures to Cardiff, where there was more accommodation for spectators.

ST. HELENS RUGBY LEAGUE CLUB, Lancashire. Founded in 1875, it was a founder member of the Northern Union, but had to wait 35 years for its first League championship, in 1931-2. Since the Second World War it has had a distinguished record — League champions in 1952-3, 1958-9, 1965-6, 1969-70, and 1970-1; winner of the League Leaders Trophy in 1964-5 and 1965-6; and winner of the Challenge Cup in 1955-6, 1960-1, 1965-6, and 1971-2. St. Helens produced some outstanding players in the 1920s, but it really came to power after 1950. It is the only club to score over 1,000 points in one season of League games — 1,005 in 1958-9. COLOURS: White with a red V.

ST. LAWRENCE, CRICKET ground in Canterbury, is the headquarters of Kent County C.C. and extends over some six acres. With a fine scenic background, it is essentially a country ground containing many trees, one of them actually within the playing area. Kent has played there since 1847, and the annual Canterbury Week at the beginning of August sees the erection of many tents and flags around the ground to create a festival setting. Among the many first-class grounds in Kent, Canterbury is chosen by the county to entertain touring sides from abroad.

ST. LEGER STAKES, a horse race, the third leg of the English triple crown (see HORSE RACING) and the last and oldest of the five classic races. It was founded in 1778 and is run in September on the Town Moor at DONCASTER over a course of 1 mile 6 furlongs and 132 yds. (approx. 2,900 m.).

(See also GREYHOUND RACING.)

ST. LOUIS BLUES, ICE HOCKEY club of St. Louis, Missouri, formed in 1967 as one of six teams in the new West Division of the expanded NATIONAL HOCKEY LEAGUE (N.H.L.) of North America. It qualified for the STANLEY CUP final in each of its first two seasons, losing both times to the MONTREAL CANADIENS. In its second season, 1969, the club topped the West Division of the N.H.L. The players train and play home matches at the St. Louis Arena, which holds 16,100.
COLOURS: Blue, gold, and white.

ST. LOUIS BROWNS, American professional BASEBALL team, joined the AMERICAN LEAGUE in 1902 but presented a prime example of sports futility during most of their existence. Their only league title came in the middle of the Second World War — 1944. Their outstanding player was the first baseman Sisler, who had a lifetime batting average of ·340. From the depression on, the Browns' dismal record and equally dismal attendance distressed the league. Finally in 1954 the franchise was shifted to Baltimore. (See BALTIMORE ORIOLES.)

ST. LOUIS CARDINALS (1), American professional BASEBALL team, were members of the old NATIONAL LEAGUE during parts of the 1870s and 1880s but became a permanent league member in 1892. The Cardinals have had a proud league tradition. They have won more WORLD SERIES (eight) than any other National League team. Their 1920s teams featured the second baseman HORNSBY, who compiled a lifetime batting average of ·358. RICKEY managed the Cardinals from 1919 to 1925 and then, as general manager, created a 'farm system' by which the Cardinals, in the 1930s, had minor-league teams in such cities as Rochester (N.Y.), Columbus (Ohio), Sacramento, and Houston — all producing talented players for the parent team. The 1934 World Series champions featured the rough 'gas house gang', led by the manager-second-baseman Frisch, the third baseman Martin, the outfielder Medwick, and the pitching brothers, 'Dizzy' and 'Daffy' Dean (Dizzy Dean won more than 20 games each year, 1933-6). The 1940s team, winner of World Series in 1942, 1944, and 1946, had an exceptional second-base combination in Schoendienst and Marion. The 1960s Cardinals, who won World Series in 1964 and 1967, starred

the pitcher GIBSON, who was a five-time 20-game winner. The Cardinals' greatest star in the post-Second World War era was the outfielder MUSIAL, who had a lifetime batting average of ·331 and became a club executive after his retirement.

(2) American professional FOOTBALL team; see CHICAGO CARDINALS.

SAINT-MARTIN, YVES, champion jockey of France, rode the horses owned by DUPRÉ and trained by MATHET. In addition to his brilliant victories on MATCH III, RELKO, and RELIANCE, Saint-Martin also won a sensational race for the PRIX DE L'ARC DE TRIOMPHE by a head on SASSAFRAS, defeating the English triple crown (see HORSE RACING) winner, NIJINSKY.

ST. MORITZ, BOBSLEIGH course, Switzerland. It was the first internationally recognized course. Built in 1902, it has since been reconstructed several times, and was the first course to be used for two WINTER OLYMPIC GAMES, 1928 and 1948. World championships were also staged at St. Moritz on eleven other occasions: 1927, 1931, 1935, 1937, 1947, 1955, 1957, 1959, 1965, 1970, and 1974.

The St. Moritz bobsleigh course is quite separate from the Cresta run (see TOBOGGANING: CRESTA) for skeleton toboggans, but they run roughly parallel. The bob run is $1\frac{1}{2}$ miles (2·5 m.) long, with a drop of 400 ft. (122 m.). It has 14 bends, including a difficult hairpin, called Sunny Corner, and two particularly challenging turns, called the Horse Shoe and Bridge Corner. Speeds in excess of 113 km./h. (70 m.p.h.) have been attained and the highest average speeds for the whole course are near 80 km./h. (50 m.p.h.).

ST. MORITZ TOBOGGANING CLUB, see TOBOGGANING: CRESTA.

ST. PADDY (1957), English race-horse by AUREOLE out of a mare tracing to PRETTY POLLY, was bred and owned by SASSOON, trained by MURLESS, and ridden by PIGGOTT. He won nine races, including the DERBY, ST. LEGER, ECLIPSE STAKES (in record time), Great Voltigeur Stakes, and £97,192 in prize money.

SAINT SAUVEUR, Vicomtesse de (*née* Lally Vagliano) (1920-), French amateur golfer; winner of every European ladies' championship, British champion 1950; French international; and captain of the European team *v.* the British Isles.

ST. SIMON (1881), English race-horse, win-

ner of nine races including the Ascot, Goodwood, and Epsom Cups, was certainly one of
the most celebrated stallions of all time. He
was bred by Prince BATTHYÁNY, raced by the
Duke of PORTLAND, trained by DAWSON, and
ridden by ARCHER and Wood. During 22 years
at stud in England, St. Simon headed the sires
list nine times, the winning brood mares' sires
list six times, and produced 423 offspring who
between them won 571 races to the value of
£553,158, including 16 classic winners.

SAKOWSKI, KURT (1930-   ), race
walker for East Germany, who has been the
'father' of the all-conquering East German
squad, having competed in the LUGANO CUP
competitions in 1961, 1965, and 1967, finishing fifth in 1965 and fourth in 1967 in the 50
km. final. World class at all distances, he set a
national best for 3 km. in 1956, and twice
finished second (1968 and 1969) in the
LUGANO 100 KM. Winner of the PRAGUE
–PODEBRADY race in 1966, he was fourth in
the European 50 km. In 1966 and eighth in the
1964 Olympic 50 km. Sakowski was an excellent stylist and judge of pace.

SALAMAPALLO, see TOUCH BALL.

SALCHOW, ULRICH (b. 1877), ice figure-
skater for Sweden, originator of the salchow
jump (see ICE SKATING); first man to win an
Olympic gold figure-skating medal, 1908; ten
times world champion, every year from 1901
to 1911 except 1906; and nine times European
title-holder in the period 1898 to 1913.

SALFORD RUGBY LEAGUE CLUB, Lancashire, joined the Northern Union in 1896,
and was outstanding in the 1930s, when the
manager, TODD, assembled one of the finest
teams that has ever played. Salford won the
League championship in 1913-14, 1932-3,
1936-7, and 1938-9, and the Challenge Cup in
1937-8. Lomas, who captained the first team
to visit Australia, in 1910, was a Salford
player, and 20 years later they had another
outstanding leader in RISMAN. The costliest
recruiting campaign in Rugby League history
was undertaken in the late 1960s in an effort to
restore Salford's fortunes. Prominent RUGBY
UNION players were signed in Watkins (who
was paid £12,000), Coulman, and Richards,
while substantial transfer fees were paid for
Burgess (£6,000 to Barrow), Dixon (£15,000
to Halifax), and Charlton (£10,000 to Workington Town).
COLOURS: Red.

SAMBO, see WRESTLING.

SAN DIEGO PADRES, American professional BASEBALL team, entered the NATIONAL
LEAGUE in 1969 when the league expanded to
12 teams. They have finished last in the
league's Western Division each year and have
been greatly hampered in drawing fans by the
proximity of the LOS ANGELES DODGERS and
CALIFORNIA ANGELS.

SAN FRANCISCO 49ers, American professional FOOTBALL team, one of the founding
members of the All-America Conference in
1946. Upon its dissolution in 1950 the 49ers
were merged into the NATIONAL FOOTBALL
LEAGUE. Although never a title-winner, the
49ers have featured rugged line play by men
such as the tackle Nomellini and imaginative
offences (attacks), led in the 1950s by the
shifty runner McElhenny and in the 1960s by
the passer Brodie.
COLOURS: Gold and scarlet.

SAN FRANCISCO GIANTS, American
professional BASEBALL team, received the
transfer of the NATIONAL LEAGUE franchise
from the NEW YORK GIANTS in 1958, at the
same time that the BROOKLYN DODGERS moved
to Los Angeles. Despite the heroics of the outfielder MAYS (third leading home-run hitter of
all time and inspirational player) and the
pitcher Marichal (six-time 20-game winner),
the Giants could not duplicate the achievements of their New York predecessors. Their
only league title came in 1962 after a play-off
win over their bitter rivals, the Dodgers. In the
early 1960s they moved into Candlestick Park,
where the wind was often so strong that
unwary pitchers were blown off the mound.
The advent in the AMERICAN LEAGUE of the
OAKLAND ATHLETICS in 1968 divided Bay area
support and reduced Giant attendance.

SAN SESTO GIOVANNI, an Italian 30 km.
road RACE WALKING event held annually on
the last day in May in Milan. Inaugurated in
1958, its winners include Olympic champions
DORDONI, PAMICH, KANNENBERG, and HOHNE
(who holds the course record). A small group
of top European walkers are invited each year
to compete with the home participants. The
course consists of seven flat laps, circuits of
two different distances being used.

SAN SIRO, race-course in Milan where most
of the important horse races in Italy are held,
such as the GRAN PREMIO DI MILANO, GRAN
PREMIO DEL JOCKEY CLUB, GRAN PREMIO
D'ITALIA, OAKS D'ITALIA, St. Leger Italiano,
and the two most valuable events for two-
year-olds, the GRAN CRITERIUM and the
Criterium Nazionale.

SAN SIRO STADIUM, an Association FOOT-
BALL ground, owned by the city of Milan and
used by the city's leading clubs, A.C. MILAN
and INTERNAZIONALE. The stadium was originally constructed in 1925 but has been developed considerably to its capacity of 95,000,
with 85,000 seated and half the accommodation covered.

SAND-TRACK RACING, Motor-cycle, see
MOTOR-CYCLE RACING.

SAND YACHTING. Sand and land yachting,
in their most primitive state, require a small
sailing dinghy to be mounted on a simple chassis with three or four car wheels. In suitable
conditions, the boats can be propelled by the
wind over firm sand, tarmac, concrete, or
other level surfaces. The sail is operated as it
would be in YACHTING on water and the direction controlled by a steering wheel or pedals.

As the sport developed, boats of a more
sophisticated design, capable of high speeds
and delicate manoeuvres, came into use. In
Europe, the vessels usually have a canoe-like
body, or fuselage, often of fibreglass, which
may be as long as 24 ft. (7·3 m.) with an 18-
foot (5·5 m.) wheelbase and 24-in. (61 cm.)
diameter tyres. Only one sail is used, but on
the largest yachts its area may be as much as
400 sq. ft. (37 sq. m.). Some vessels have a
crew of three.

American yachts are smaller, lighter, and
faster. The body often consists only of an open
chassis 10 ft. (3 m.) long, with room for the
pilot alone. The sail area is about 45 sq. ft. (4
sq. m.), but on a hard surface these craft are
capable of at least double the speed of the following wind.

ICE YACHTING follows similar principles,
using runners instead of wheels and sometimes
far greater areas of sail. Four times the wind
speed is often achieved.

Four hundred years ago the Dutch went
sand yachting on wooden wheels. This was
probably the first use of such a vessel for
sport, though land yachts were probably used
for carrying goods in the ancient civilizations
of Egypt and China. It was in Holland, too,
that ice yachting first developed in the second
half of the eighteenth century.

Though sand yachting has been organized
at club and sometimes national level in Europe
throughout the twentieth century, it remained
a rare pastime until after the Second World
War. Since then there has been a relative
boom in the sport, particularly in the U.S.A.,
where the deserts are ideal for racing.

Despite the shortage of long stretches of
dry, firm sand in Britain, there were more than
a dozen clubs in 1970, when the first world

championships were held at Lytham St.
Anne's, Lancashire; they attracted over 100
competitors. Several British clubs meet at disused airfields, using the runways for racing.
GOVERNING BODY (WORLD): International Federation of Sand and Land Yacht Clubs, 100 Avenue de
Statuares, Brussels 18, Belgium.

SANDE, EARL (1899-1968), was the leading
jockey in America in the 1920s. During his
career he won 968 races worth just on
$3,000,000. From MAN O' WAR to GALLANT
FOX, Sande rode nearly all the top horses of his
time, winning the KENTUCKY DERBY three
times and the BELMONT STAKES five times.

SANDHAM, ANDREW (1890-   ), cricketer for England and Surrey. A neat, consistent opening batsman, he played most of his
cricket in the shadow of his great partner,
HOBBS, for whom he was a splendid foil. He
made 107 centuries, and ranks tenth among
run-scorers in first-class cricket. In another era
he might have played more than 14 times for
England, but he joined a select group in
1929-30 when he scored 325 against West
Indies at Kingston. He was also a fine outfielder.

SANDOWN PARK, a race-course near London, where the ECLIPSE STAKES and the valuable National Stakes for two-year-olds are run.
Recent modernization has made it one of
Europe's leading race-tracks.

SANTA CLAUS (1961), a race horse bred by
Smorfitt, owned by Ismay, trained in Ireland
by Rogers, and ridden by Breasley and Burke.
He won the English DERBY, Irish Derby, Irish
Two Thousand Guineas, and Irish National
Stakes, with £153,646 in stakes.

SANTANA, MAÑUEL (1938-   ), Spanish LAWN TENNIS player, one of the subtlest
and most effective of postwar competitors, on
slow courts. In spite of his natural Spanish
suspicion of grass, he still managed to win the
two great grass court championships, FOREST
HILLS (1965) and WIMBLEDON (1966) and to
beat EMERSON (1965) and NEWCOMBE (1967)
in dead rubbers of Davis Cup (see LAWN TEN-
NIS) challenge rounds.

His victory over Ralston (U.S.A.) in the
1966 final made him Wimbledon's first Spanish champion and the first European to win the
title since DROBNY in 1954. The following
year his record was less enviable: he became
the first defending champion to lose his first
match, falling to Pasarell (U.S.A.) by 10-8,
6-3, 2-6, 8-6.

His successes on clay included two French

singles titles (1961 and 1964), one Italian (1965), and one South African (1967), but many of his best performances came in the Davis Cup. He played first for Spain, with Gimeno who later turned professional, in 1958 and he led his team twice to the challenge round. When OKKER beat him in Spain's match against Holland in 1968, it was Santana's first defeat in the European zone for five years. Such performances, plus the charm of his manner and grace of his style, helped make him a Spanish national hero.

SANTOS, NILTON (1925-), Association footballer for BOTAFOGO (Rio), and Brazil for whom he played at left back in the World Cup finals of 1958 in Sweden and 1962 in Chile when Brazil took the world championship title by beating Sweden and Czechoslovakia respectively.

SANTOS, Association FOOTBALL club, São Paulo. Founded in 1912, the club turned professional in 1933 and first won the São Paulo League title in 1935, but then had to wait until 1955 to win it again. The rise of the club since the late 1950s coincided with the emergence of great players like PELÉ. Santos, before Brazilian clubs lost interest in the South American competition between champion clubs, won the continental club championship and the unofficial world club championship in 1962 and 1963. Outstanding players include Pelé, Zito, Coutinho, Gilmar, Mauro, Toninho, Edu, Pepé, and Carlos Alberto.
COLOURS: White shirts and shorts.

SAPERSTEIN, ABRAHAM M. (1903-66), founder of the HARLEM GLOBETROTTERS BASKETBALL team. Saperstein was born in London, but his family emigrated to Chicago when he was four years old. He founded the Globetrotters in 1927 and became their owner, manager, and coach. He toured America, and later the world, with them until his death.

SARATOGA, race-track in New York state, the oldest and most picturesque in the U.S.A., where the Saratoga Cup was an important event until abandoned in 1955, and where the TRAVERS STAKES is still run. Annual bloodstock sales, conducted by Fasig-Tipton, are also held at Saratoga Springs.

SARAZEN, GENE (Eugene Saraceni) (1902-), American professional golfer, U.S. Open champion 1922, 1932; U.S. Professional Golfers Association champion 1922, 1923, 1933; Open champion 1932; Masters champion 1935; and a RYDER CUP player. He invented the deep-flanged sand-

wedge which revolutionized the technique of bunker shots, and was an outstanding exponent of the fairway woods.

SARE, see PELOTA.

SASAHARA, FUMIO, Japanese JUDO fighter who took the light-heavyweight gold medal at the 1969 and 1971 world championships. His excellent *harai-goshi* (sweeping hip throw) from a left-handed stance made him favourite for the 1972 Olympics, when he was unexpectedly defeated by the Russian CHOCHOSHVILI. Sasahara retired after the Games.

SASKATCHEWAN ROUGHRIDERS, Canadian professional FOOTBALL team, entered the Western Interprovincial Rugby Union in 1936 as the Regina Roughriders, changing to their present name in 1948. From the mid-1960s they have been the most successful Canadian Football League team, winning Western Conference titles from 1966 to 1971 and the Grey Cup (see FOOTBALL, CANADIAN) in 1966, led by the quarterback Lancaster, the running back Reed (first in yards gained rushing and first in career touchdowns), and the pass-receiver Campbell (first in career touchdown passes caught).
COLOURS: Green and white.

SASSAFRAS (1967), a race-horse bred in Ireland and owned by Mme. Plesch, trained by MATHET, and ridden by SAINT-MARTIN, Sassafras won a sensational race for the PRIX DE L'ARC DE TRIOMPHE, when he defeated NIJINSKY by a head, as well as scoring victories in the French Derby and French St. Leger.

SASSOON, Sir VICTOR (1882-1961), a prominent English race-horse owner-breeder who won the DERBY four times, with Pinza, Crepello, Hard Ridden, and ST. PADDY.

SATO, NOBUYUKI (1944-), Japanese JUDO fighter who was the world light-heavyweight champion in 1967 and 1973 and silver medallist in 1971. His excellent gripping techniques and masterly groundwork gave him a long and triumphant career.

SAUTTER de BEAUREGARD, Comte GUY (1886-1961), BADMINTON player for England. One of the greatest exponents of the game in the pre-1914 era, he played for England from 1908 to 1922, was ALL-ENGLAND singles champion three times and won many other titles. In 1923 and 1924 he played LAWN TENNIS in the Davis Cup for his native Switzerland.

SAVATE was an individual folk combat sport, practised largely in France until the first half of the nineteenth century. It permitted striking the opponent with fists or feet, and tripping; while, in some forms, the use of a stick was allowed. The sport was lifted to its highest standard of performance by French prisoners of war on British convict ships in the eighteenth century. In its more sophisticated form it was known as *chausson*. In about 1826 Lecourt introduced a number of refinements which led to the gradual development of *savate* or *chausson* into BOXE FRANÇAIS.

SAWCHUK, TERRANCE GORDON (1929-   ), ICE HOCKEY player for DETROIT RED WINGS from 1950. In 1955 he was transferred to BOSTON BRUINS but returned to Detroit two years later, moving to TORONTO MAPLE LEAFS in 1964 and to LOS ANGELES KINGS in 1967. Widely regarded as the greatest goalminder the game has seen, Sawchuk won the CALDER MEMORIAL TROPHY in 1951, with 11 shut-outs in his first NATIONAL HOCKEY LEAGUE (N.H.L.) season. Sawchuk specialized in shut-outs, achieving a record 100th for the N.H.L. in 1967. He inspired the now normal crouching stance; goalminders before him usually stood up straight. In a career of nearly two decades, he won the VEZINA TROPHY four times, 1952-5, and finally as joint holder in 1965. Born in Winnipeg, he played as a junior in Ontario for Gault Red Wings, and then for Omaha and Indianapolis before he joined Detroit.

SAXTON, CHARLES (1913-   ), RUGBY UNION scrum half for New Zealand in three Tests in Australia in 1938. He captained the New Zealand Army team in the British Isles and France in 1945-6 and managed the 1967 New Zealanders in Britain and France, on both occasions persuading his men to play fast, constructive Rugby, so helping to rekindle the game in Britain after lean periods.

SAYERS, TOM (1826-65), British boxer who, though only 5 ft. 8 in. (1·7 m.) tall and weighing less than the middleweight limit of 160 lb. (72·5 kg.), became champion of the English prize ring in 1857. Three years later he was a national hero after a battle lasting 2 hrs. 20 min. with the American HEENAN, at Farnborough, ending in a draw when the ring was invaded by the spectators.

SCANDINAVIAN CHAMPIONSHIP, an Association FOOTBALL competition, sometimes called the Nordic Cup, for the national teams of Denmark, Finland, Norway, and Sweden. Football came early to the Scandinavian countries and, despite climatic conditions that enforce a close-down during the midwinter months, took healthy root. Sweden and Norway played their first full international match, against each other, in 1908; Finland made a first appearance in 1911—against Sweden in Helsinki; and Denmark its first against Norway in the 1912 OLYMPIC GAMES in Stockholm. The four national Associations continued to play regularly against each other in friendly matches, and then in 1924 instituted the Scandinavian championship that has continued ever since along less troubled lines than many other regional competitions. The championship is determined on a league basis, each country playing against the other three, as do the four national Associations concerned since 1872 with the British home championship. The latter, however, is decided annually with two of the entrants each year thus having the advantage of playing twice at home and only once away. In the Scandinavian championship, although there is a 'paper' record of each season's most successful national side, the competition is spread over four seasons until each country has met each other country four times, twice at home and twice away. Denmark won the first championship and Norway the second, but the championships from 1933 onwards were all won by Sweden.

SCAPA FLOW (1914), by Chaucer, was one of Lord DERBY's celebrated brood mares at the Stanley House Stud in England. She produced the winners of 63 races to the value of £86,084, including Pharos, FAIRWAY, and Fair Isle.

SCEPTRE (1899), a celebrated English racing filly by PERSIMMON, son of ST. SIMON, out of Ornament, full sister to ORMONDE, by BEND OR. She was bought by Sievier as a yearling for a record price of 10,000 guineas, trained by her owner, and ridden by Randall and Hardy. The only race-horse ever to win outright four of the five classic races (see FORMOSA), Sceptre won the OAKS, ST. LEGER, TWO THOUSAND GUINEAS, ONE THOUSAND GUINEAS, JOCKEY CLUB STAKES, and CHAMPION STAKES, together with £32,283 in stakes.

SCHEELE, HERBERT A. E. (1905-   ), BADMINTON administrator, hon. sec. of the International Badminton Federation from 1938 and hon. referee of numerous THOMAS CUP and UBER CUP ties, the ALL-ENGLAND BADMINTON CHAMPIONSHIPS (1947 to date), and other events. He was secretary of the Badminton Association of England and editor of *The Badminton Gazette* 1945-70.

SCHERENS, JEFF (1910-), Belgian sprint cyclist, noted for his strong acceleration over the last 30 metres. Although sprint champions commonly dominate events for several seasons, Scherens set a record by winning the world professional sprint title six years running (1932-7). He won again in 1947, 15 years after taking his first title, an achievement equalled only by Van Vliet (Holland).

SCHIAFFINO, JUAN (1925-), Association footballer for PENAROL (Montevideo), A.C. MILAN, Roma (briefly), and Uruguay for whom he played and scored in the 1950 World Cup match against Brazil in Rio that won the world championship for his country. He also played for Uruguay in the 1954 world championship matches in Switzerland, and then joined the Italian club A.C. Milan for whom he played until joining Roma in 1960 for a brief spell.

SCHMELING, MAX (1905-), German boxer who was the first European to win the world heavyweight title in the twentieth century when he beat Sharkey on a foul in 1930. Six years later Schmeling caused a surprise by knocking out the undefeated LOUIS, but the hard-hitting German lasted less than a round when he challenged Louis for the championship in 1938.

SCHMID, MANFRED (1944-), luge TOBOGGANING rider for Austria; winner of the world and Olympic singles titles in 1968 and twice world two-seater champion, with Walch as partner, in 1969 and 1970.

SCHMIDT, JÓZEF (1935-), triple jumper for Poland. In a speciality fraught with the risk of muscle injury, Schmidt had an impeccable championship record for a six-year period in which he won European titles in 1958 and 1962 and Olympic gold medals in 1960 and 1964. His 1960 world record of 55 ft. 10¼ in. (17·03 m.) was unmatched until 1968 when it was beaten in the low-pressure conditions of Mexico City.

SCHNEIDER, HANNES (1896-1954), an Austrian from ST. ANTON who in the late 1920s and 1930s laid down a detailed definition of Alpine SKIING technique based on the stem christiania. This became known as the Arlberg style and marked the passing of leadership from Norway to the Central European countries, notably Austria and France. Schneider co-operated closely with Sir ARNOLD LUNN in the start and development of the ARLBERG-KANDAHAR race.

SCHNEIDER TROPHY, see FLYING, SPORTING.

SCHNYDMAN, JEROME (1944-), LACROSSE player for the U.S.A., Southern States, and Johns Hopkins University. An outstanding midfielder with the ability to obtain possession of the ball at the face-off, in spite of his lack of height (5 ft. 2 in. — 1·57 m.). He has a powerful shot, scoring in most of his games. In 1967 he was selected as an 'All-Star' American player.

SCHOCKEMOHLE, ALWIN (1937-), West German show jumping (see EQUESTRIAN EVENTS) rider. He was a member of the gold medal team at Rome in 1960, riding Ferdl. In 1965, he set a new German high jump record of 2·25 m. (7 ft. 4 in.), riding a Hanoverian horse called Exakt. He achieved a remarkable list of Grand Prix successes with Donald Rex, who was his mount for the 1968 OLYMPIC GAMES in Mexico where he had the best score in the team competition, thus helping the Germans to win the bronze medal.

SCHOLLANDER, DONALD ARTHUR (1946-), an American who was the first swimmer to win four gold medals at an OLYMPIC GAMES. He did this in 1964 in Tokyo where he was first in the 100 and 400 metres freestyle and a member of America's two winning freestyle relay teams. A stroke perfectionist, his speed was masked by his effortless crawl style. He broke individual world records, including improving the 200 metres time from 1 min. 58·8 sec. to 1 min. 54·3 sec. in nine record-breaking swims between July 1963 and August 1968.

SCHRANZ, KARL (1938-), Austrian skier from ST. ANTON, world champion in 1970, winner of the World Cup (see SKIING) in 1969 and 1970, whose career from 1957 to 1970, when he retired, was the longest of distinction among modern skiers. He won his first world championship gold medal in the downhill and combined at Chamonix in 1962. He was disqualified from the 1972 Winter Olympic Games at Sapporo for being the leading proponent of what the Olympic president, BRUNDAGE, considered to be professionalism. On his return to Vienna he was greeted as a national hero. Schranz in 1972-3 raced as a professional in America.

SCHUYLKILL NAVY, an association of ROWING clubs on the Schuylkill River, Philadelphia, formed in 1858. In 1872, the National Association of Amateur Oarsmen, the governing body of rowing in the U.S.A., was formed and the first regatta for amateur oarsmen was held in the same year under the direction of the Schuylkill Navy. The Schuylkill course was for many years the centre of rowing in the United States.

SCHWINGEN, see WRESTLING.

SCORTON ARROW, Ancient. In 1673, in the North Riding of Yorkshire, a Society of Archers was formed who agreed to hold a meeting once a year to shoot at targets for an 'Antient Silver Arrow'. A set of rules was drawn up on 14 May of that year and these rules are still observed in annual competition for this venerable sporting trophy.

SCOTLAND, KENNETH JAMES FORBES (1936-   ), RUGBY UNION player for Heriot's F.P., LONDON SCOTTISH, Cambridge University, Scotland, and British LIONS. A highly versatile player, Scotland was included at scrum half, outside half, and centre during the 1959 Lions tour to Australia and New Zealand, although originally selected as a fullback, which became his accustomed position. His basic talents made him one of the outstanding seven-a-side players of his day.

SCOTT, ELISHA (1896-1959), Association footballer for Northern Ireland, BELFAST CELTIC, and LIVERPOOL. Recognized as Ireland's greatest goalkeeper, he played 429 first team matches for Liverpool and on 31 occasions for his country. He managed Belfast Celtic from 1936 to 1959.

SCOTT, JAY (1930-   ), Scottish professional athlete of outstanding all-round ability. At his peak he was virtually unbeatable by professionals in all four jumps, at which the following were his best performances: HIGH JUMP, 6 ft. 3½ in. (1·9 m.); LONG JUMP, 22 ft. 5 in. (6·8 m.); TRIPLE JUMP, 46 ft. 8 in. (14·2 m.); POLE VAULT, 11 ft. 6 in. (3·5 m.). Later in his career he turned to SHOT-putting and WEIGHT- and HAMMER-throwing, at all of which he excelled. He was also a good enough sprinter to come third in the POWDERHALL Handicap.

SCOTT, JOHN (1794-1871), known as 'the Wizard of the North', was the most successful English race-horse trainer of his time, the most notable inmate of his stable being WEST AUSTRALIAN.

SCOTT, SHEILA, O.B.E., British aviator. She started flying in 1959 and raced regularly thereafter. She attempted record flights from 1965 and twice flew solo round the world. By 1970 she had set up some 90 international or world records and had won over 50 trophies.

SCOTTISH GAMES ASSOCIATION (S.G.A.), formed in 1948 to organize and co-ordinate professional ATHLETICS meetings in Scotland, of which about 150 are held each year. Though the S.G.A. directly controls only one-fifth of these, the rules and conditions which it established are adhered to not only throughout that country, but also in the few professional meetings held in England.

SCOTTISH MILK RACE, international amateur CYCLING stage race promoted by the Scottish Milk Marketing Board and modelled on the TOUR OF BRITAIN. Beginning in 1963 as a one-day race, it now lasts five days and covers roughly 500 miles (804 km.).

SCOTTISH SIX DAYS TRIAL, see MOTOR-CYCLE TRIALS.

SCRAMBLING, see MOTO-CROSS.

SCULLING, see ROWING.

SEA BIRD II (1962), a race-horse bred in France and owned by Ternynck, trained by POLLET, and ridden by Glennon. Only once defeated in eight outings, Sea Bird II won the English DERBY, Prix Lupin, GRAND PRIX DE SAINT-CLOUD, and PRIX DE L'ARC DE TRIOMPHE, with a European record £229,458 in prize money. He stood at stud at Darby Dan Farm in the U.S.A.

SEA COTTAGE (1962), a race-horse bred in South Africa by Birch Bros., leased to and trained by Laird, and ridden by Sieverwright. He won a total of 19 out of 23 races, including the CAPE OF GOOD HOPE DERBY, Champion Stakes, Queen's Plate (twice), and ROTHMAN'S JULY HANDICAP, and over £50,000 in prize money, a South African record.

SEATTLE PILOTS, American professional BASEBALL team, joined the AMERICAN LEAGUE in 1969 when the league expanded to 12 teams. Seattle was disorganized and undermanned, and, when its financial backing disintegrated following the season, the franchise was shifted to Milwaukee in 1970. (See MILWAUKEE BREWERS.)

SECRETARIAT (1970), first race-horse since CITATION in 1948 to win the American triple crown when he won the KENTUCKY DERBY, PREAKNESS, and BELMONT STAKES in 1973. His victory in the Belmont Stakes was by 31 lengths and he reduced the American record for 1½ miles by more than two seconds. He won 14 of his 17 races and is considered by many to be the best horse to race in America in this century. Syndicated for a world record price of $6,080,000, he now stands at the CLAIBORNE FARM STUD in Kentucky.

SEDGMAN, FRANK A. (1927-   ), the player who regained the initiative for Australia in LAWN TENNIS after the Second World War. He was his country's first postwar WIMBLE-DON champion, defeating DROBNY 4-6, 6-2, 6-3, 6-2 in 1952, after failing against Patty (U.S.A.) in the 1950 final. He also won the Australian (1949-50) and U.S. (1951-2) titles twice and in 1952 became the first Australian to capture the Italian title..

Sedgman's direct, athletic game and exceptional volleying ability made him the perfect player for HOPMAN, the Australian captain, to use as the spearhead of his attack on the U.S.A., who had taken the Davis Cup (see LAWN TENNIS) from Australia in 1946. Sedgman's first challenge round was at FOREST HILLS in 1949 when GONZALES, who turned professional soon afterwards, and Schroeder, the reigning Wimbledon champion, both beat him in singles; but the following year Australia won 4-1. Sedgman beat Brown 6-0, 8-6, 9-7 and Schroeder 6-2, 6-2, 6-2, and in the doubles he and the shrewd Bromwich beat Schroeder and Mulloy in five sets. Australia remained champion nation until Sedgman turned professional in 1953. He and McGregor, another player whom Hopman developed, achieved the grand slam of the four major men's doubles titles in 1951.

SEELER, UWE (1936-   ), Association footballer for HAMBURGER S.V., and West Germany for whom at the age of 18 he played at WEMBLEY against England in December 1954. He was to remain, despite absences because of injuries, West Germany's reliable centre forward for the next 16 years during which he played in the world championships of 1958 in Sweden, 1962 in Chile, 1966 in England, and 1970 in Mexico. Early in 1965 he suffered a serious injury to his Achilles tendon that seemed likely to end his international, if not his club, career. Instead, when West Germany needed to win a world championship match in Sweden in September 1965 in order to qualify for a place in the final stages of the competition, although not completely fit and lacking in match practice, he was recalled. Nearly 30 years old when West Germany were beaten in extra time by England in the 1966 world championship final, he was again recalled to the national team for the 1970 championships

in Mexico, and played a major part in West Germany's success against England in the quarter-final match in Léon.

SEFTON, Earls of, traditionally presidents of the National Coursing Club and the ALTCAR CLUB. The WATERLOO CUP has been held on the family estates at Altcar on the south Lancashire seaboard since 1836. Successive 'Lords of the Altcar Soil' have maintained large kennels of greyhounds since COURSING became an organized, competitive sport. The family has won the Waterloo Cup on four occasions; with Senate in 1847, Sackcloth in 1854, Shortcoming in 1921, and So Clever in 1971.

SEGRAVE, Sir HENRY O'NEAL DE HANE (1896-1930), British MOTOR RACING driver whose career started in 1920, when he drove a 4·5-litre Opel at BROOKLANDS and won several races. On the strength of this, he persuaded Coatalen of the SUNBEAM-Talbot-Darracq Group to let him drive a works car. He drove a prototype 3-litre Sunbeam Grand Prix in a short race at Brooklands in 1921 and won, but his Talbot finished ninth and last in the French Grand Prix. Later in the year, however, he was third in the Grand Prix des Voiturettes at LE MANS and won the Junior Car Club 200-mile race at Brooklands, driving on both occasions a Talbot 1·5-litre *voiturette*. He drove at Brooklands in 1922, with success, one of the 1921 Indianapolis cars fitted with an earlier 4·9-litre engine. He made fastest time in practice for the 1922 Tourist Trophy with one of the 3-litre cars, but retired with magneto trouble. In the French Grand Prix he drove one of the Henry-designed 4-cylinder Sunbeams, but retired in the closing stages of the race. Despite a burnt-out valve seat, he took third place with a *voiturette* in the JCC 200-mile race at Brooklands and was third later in the year in the Grand Prix des Voiturettes at Le Mans. He was second in the Coppa Florio that year with a 4·9-litre car.

Segrave's greatest win came in 1923, when he drove one of the 2-litre six-cylinder Sunbeams in the French Grand Prix at Tours. In 1924 he derived consolation for his failure in the French Grand Prix that year by winning the San Sebastian race. Segrave drove a 1·5-litre Talbot to victory in the Grand Prix de Provence at Miramas in 1925 and was third in the Grand Prix de l'Ouverture at MONTLHÉRY. The same year he won the JCC 200-mile race at Brooklands.

Although in 1926 he won the Grand Prix de Provence at Miramas and the JCC 200-mile race and set the fastest lap in the Royal Automobile Club Grand Prix, he was becoming increasingly interested in both record-breaking and motor-boat racing. In 1926 at Southport, Lancashire, he set a new record for the flying kilometre of 152·33 m.p.h. with the V-12 4-litre Sunbeam and the following year at Daytona, Florida (U.S.A.), set a new land speed record of 203·79 m.p.h. with the 1000 h.p. Sunbeam. In 1929 at Daytona with the 23-litre Irving-Napier 'Golden Arrow' car he recaptured the record with a speed of 231·21 m.p.h. Segrave died in June 1930 making an attempt on the water speed record, having already set a new record of 98·76 m.p.h.

SEKINE, SHINOBU, Japanese JUDO fighter who won the all-Japan championships despite weighing only 13 stone (83 kg.), thus succeeding OKANO as the lightest man to take the title. In the 1971 world championships he was bronze medallist in the Open class and in the Munich Olympics he fought in the middleweight division. Despite his proficiency at *ko-uchi-gari* (minor inner reaping throw) he was unimpressive in the event: he beat JACKS on a close decision in the semi-final and the Korean Oh Lip on a split decision for the gold medal.

SELLA DESCENT, an international long-distance CANOEING event held at Ribadesella in northern Spain each year, usually the first week-end in August. The course is 16·5 km. (10 miles) long, rocky, with a number of weirs to shoot. First raced in 1931, the Sella is not an exceptionally difficult course but the large number of starters (of all classes) presents one of the major hazards and the greatest spectacle of the event.

SEMBLAT, C. H., a leading French jockey who rode horses belonging to Esmond and his daughter, including the famous filly PEARL CAP. Semblat subsequently became a successful trainer, who turned out most of BOUSSAC's string of successes in the classics and feature races of France and England.

SEPAK RAGA, see SEPAK TAKRAW.

SEPAK TAKRAW, a game played with a rattan ball on a BADMINTON court, is widely popular in south-east Asia, being referred to by several names in the various countries (see TAKRAW). In the Philippines it is called *sipak*, in Thailand, *takraw*, and in Malaysia, *sepak raga*. The game was named *sepak takraw* during the 1965 South-east Asian Peninsular Games when there was deadlock over uniformity. The compromise was the joining of a Malay word and a Thai word — *sepak* (kick) and *takraw* (rattan ball in Thai).

The net is lower than in badminton, 155 cm. (5 ft. 1 in.) off the ground at the top, and the ball is 40 cm. (16 in.) in circumference and 298 g. (10¼ oz.) in weight. The rules are a cross between those of badminton and VOLLEYBALL, and the game has been described as 'volleyball played with feet and other parts of the body, except the hands'.

Each side has three players. The first, known as *tekong*, is positioned inside the semicircle at the base line. The second player is *apit kiri* (left winger). At the commencement of play the ball is served (kicked) to the centre by the second or third player, both standing within marked positions in the court. The ball must not touch the ground and each side is allowed up to three hits (as in volleyball) before the ball is delivered over the net to the opposite side of the court — except when serving, when there must be only a straight kick. The ball may also be headed over the net (a *balas tandok*) but no part of the arms, from the shoulders to fingertips, may be used.

Serving is as in volleyball, but scoring is like badminton; the first side to reach 15 points wins the set. A deuce of 5 points is allowed if the score is deadlocked at 13, and 3 points in the case of a 14-all tie. The game is decided on the best of three sets. There are detailed rules regarding foul services, fixed positions, changed positions, touching the net or the umpire's bench, and crossing to the opponent's side.

Keeping the ball in the air continuously calls for sharp reflexes and skill, combining the teamwork of volleyball, the dexterity of FOOTBALL, and the speed of badminton.

The origin of this game is unknown. The Malays argue that it started in the Malay peninsula, the Thais in Thailand, and the Filipinos in the Philippines. There is a similar game played even in Burma.

With British colonization, the game receded into the background and was confined to the Malay peasants in villages, known as *kampongs*. It was, and is, the favourite pastime of office boys and chauffeurs, during lunch breaks.

It was once popular in the royal courts of feudal Malaya. The legendary Malayan hero, Hang Tuah, is often associated with the game in Malay folklore. The rules were simple — the participants formed a ring and the team who kept the ball longest in the air was the winner. Singles matches were also played. Although it was originally played exclusively by men, it is now popular among women as well.

It features in the regional South-east Asian Peninsular Games in which Singapore, Malaysia, Thailand, Burma, South Vietnam, Cambodia, and Laos participate. The game has been included in the sporting schedule of Malaysian and Singapore schools and Malaysian political leaders are anxious to see it established as a national game.

SERVETTE, Association FOOTBALL club, Geneva. Founded in 1890, the club first won the Swiss national championship in 1907 and won 12 more titles up to 1962. Leading players have included Fehlmann, Reymond, Minelli, Rappan, T. Abegglen, Tamini, and Fatton.

COLOURS: Red shirts, white shorts.

S.G.A., see SCOTTISH GAMES ASSOCIATION.

SHAKHLIN, BORIS (1932-   ), a great Russian gymnast who on his retirement in 1966 had won more gold medals than anyone else in Olympics and world championships. Shakhlin amassed ten individual titles and three team championships in his 12-year career. His flawless style and deep concentration enabled him to dominate the sport at the end of the 1950s.

He made his début at the 1954 world championships when he won a silver medal on the horizontal bar, probably the event in which he was most proficient. Two years later at the Melbourne OLYMPIC GAMES he finished first on the pommel-horse. At the 1958 world championships in Moscow, this rugged man, standing 5 ft. 7½ in. (1·71 m.) and weighing 11 st. (69·8 kg.), set a record by winning five out of a possible eight titles. He took the combined exercises gold medal at the 1960 Rome Olympics despite the increasing Japanese challenge. In addition he was first on the pommel-horse and at vault and parallel bars. Although by the 1962 world championships he had been pushed into third place, he showed remarkable consistency with three silver medals and one bronze in the individual exercises. At the Tokyo Olympics in 1964, he was second over-all in a triple tie but added the horizontal bar title to his collection. Two years later he could manage only eighteenth place over-all.

SHAW, ALFRED (1842-1907), cricketer for England, ALL-ENGLAND XI, Nottinghamshire, and Sussex. The finest bowler of his era, his success sprang from great accuracy and tireless persistence. With slow-medium deliveries that broke slightly from the off he took 2,001 wickets at an average of 12·08, and even GRACE was compelled to treat his bowling with the utmost respect. In partnership with SHREWSBURY and J. Lillywhite he took four teams to Australia in the 1880s, and managed Lord Sheffield's touring team in 1891-2.

SHAW, WILBUR (1902-54), American MOTOR RACING driver, three times winner of the INDIANAPOLIS 500 (1937, 1939, and 1940), he also finished second three times. He won the 1939 American Automobile Association national championship and was named president of the Indianapolis Motor Speedway in 1945.

SHEEN, GILLIAN MARY (later Mrs. Donaldson), British fencer, the first to win an Olympic gold medal when she won the women's foil title at Melbourne in 1956. She won the British women's foil championship ten times in 1949, 1951-8, and 1960, and was also finalist in the world championships.

SHEFFIELD SHIELD, Australian CRICKET trophy. Awarded to the premier state team each season, it was first contested in 1892-3 after the third Lord Sheffield — who took a team to Australia in 1891-2 — had donated 150 guineas towards the advancement of cricket in Australia. It was won in its first season by Victoria (the other contestants being New South Wales and South Australia), but the records since reveal New South Wales to have been the major force in the competition: they won it six years running from 1901-2 and nine years running from 1953-4.

Queensland were admitted to the competition in 1926-7, and Western Australia entered in 1947-8 on a restricted basis — and won the Shield at the first attempt — before assuming equal status in 1956-7. They won it a second time in 1967-8.

As only five teams compete in a nation noted for its high cricket standards, the Sheffield Shield programme produces the most highly competitive domestic cricket in the world. Generally staged on well-prepared pitches, it has produced much high scoring: the world record innings total of 1,107 was made in 1926-7 by Victoria against New South Wales, who in 1900-1 had themselves made 918 against South Australia. During the 1930s BRADMAN and PONSFORD made large scores in these matches, and Bradman's 452 not out, which has only once been exceeded anywhere in the world in first-class cricket, remains an Australian record.

Victoria have won the Shield about half as often as New South Wales. South Australia have won it periodically at an average of every seven years; Queensland have yet to win it.

SHELL SHIELD, West Indian CRICKET trophy. Instituted in 1965-6 by the Shell Oil Company to stimulate West Indies cricket competition, it is awarded to the winner of a regional tournament in which all the major

West Indian cricketing nations (Windward Islands and Leeward Islands representing groups of islands) compete.

SHELLENBERGER, BETTY (1921-   ), LACROSSE player for the U.S.A. and Philadelphia, she has also represented her country at field HOCKEY and SQUASH RACKETS. She was a versatile lacrosse player in most of the attack positions.

SHINNECOCK HILLS, U.S. GOLF course on Long Island. One of the oldest surviving golf courses in America, Shinnecock Hills was laid out in 1892 by the Scottish professional Willie Dunn originally with 12 holes on the links land of Long Island, N.Y. It was the scene of the 1898 U.S. Open championship.

SHINTY is the popular name for *camanachd*, the native stick-and-ball game of the Scottish Highlands, originally the same pastime as the Irish HURLING. The two games have drifted apart in development and technique through the centuries, but the basis of the two remains the same, the driving of a ball and a stick through the goal.

Modern shinty is played 12-a-side and the ideal measurements of the playing pitch are 160 yds. long by 80 yds. wide (146 m. × 73 m.). The goal is known as the 'hail' so the end lines are the hail lines. The hails themselves are formed by goal posts 12 ft. (3·7 m.) wide and 10 ft. (3·048 m.) high, with a crossbar.

In front of each hail is a 10-yard (9·1 m.) area into which an attacking player is not permitted to enter before the ball. A penalty spot is marked 20 yds. (18·3 m.) in front of each hail and a penalty is awarded if a defender fouls within the 10-yard area.

SHINTY CAMAN

The stick used is called the *caman*, the same as for Irish hurling, and is likewise crooked at the top. The broad blade of the Irish stick is, however, unknown in Scotland, where the head of the *caman* must be small enough to pass through a ring 2½ in. (6·3 cm.), in diameter. The Scots *caman* is wedge-shaped with the broad end at the heel in order to give loft to the ball. The ball itself has a core of cork and worsted, and is covered with leather. Stitched in the same fashion as the Irish hurling ball, it is 7 to 8 in. (17·7–20·32 cm.) in circumference and weighs 2½ to 3 oz. (70–85 g.).

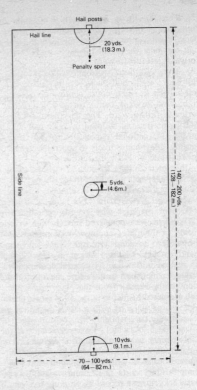

SHINTY PITCH
Hail posts are 12 ft. (3·7 m.) apart. Corner flags (not shown) are 3 ft. 6 in. (1·1 m.) high.

The duration of a game is 90 minutes, the teams playing 45 minutes each way. The game is controlled by a referee who is assisted by hail-judges and linesmen. Goals, or hails, are the only scores. If the ball is sent wide by an attacker, a defender strikes it out from the 10-yd area. If the ball is turned over the hail line by a defender, a corner hit from which a hail may be scored direct is granted to the opposition.

A shinty side comprises a hail-keeper, a full-back, three half-backs, a centre back, centre-field, centre forward, three half-forwards, and a full-forward. Some shinty teams adjust their line-out as circumstances vary, but the most usual methods of placing the players are:
(1) The 'diamond' formation: hail-keeper; full-back; half-back, half-back, half-back; centre back; centre-field; centre forward; half-forward, half-forward, half-forward; full-forward.

(2) The 'Southern' formation: hail-keeper; right back, left back; right half-back, left half-back; right centre, centre, left centre; right half-forward, left half-forward; right full-forward, left full-forward.

(3) The 'Northern' formation: hail-keeper; full-back; right half-back, centre half-back, left half-back; right centre, centre, left centre; right wing-forward, centre forward, left wing-forward; full-forward. The 'Northern' formation is the line-out adopted in 1972 and 1973 in the international games against the Irish hurling sides, and is likely to become accepted for such encounters in the future.

In direct contrast to hurling custom, only the hail-keeper is permitted to handle the ball. Nor may the ball be caught, kicked, thrown, or carried. A player may not hold, obstruct, trip, hack, or back-charge an opponent. All such offences are penalized by a free hit, technically called a 'set blow'. A referee is empowered to send a player to the line for rough or reckless play, striking an opponent, or general misconduct. If a team deliberately sends the ball over the side line, the opposing side gets a free hit from the place where the ball crossed the line.

The Camanachd Association, *Constitution and Rules of Play*, latest edition.

Since shinty was first brought to Scotland by the invading Irish Gaels, the history of the game is shared with hurling until mid-way through the fourteenth century. But, even from the earliest times, there was one very important difference. In Ireland there had always been two types of *caman*: the broadbladed stick, which was more popular in the south, and the narrow blade, which was favoured by the players of the Antrim glens. As it was from Antrim that the Irish colonists crossed to Scotland, the narrow-bladed stick has ever since remained the favoured instrument of the Scottish shinty players.

Down the centuries, shinty, for long more generally known as *camanachd*, remained the popular pastime of the Highlands, despite some Lowland laws against the game and continuous efforts to enforce Sabbath observance, which was especially likely to affect shinty since the game was customarily played on Sundays. Eventually, Sunday play died out, but the game itself lived on, surviving both the débâcle of Culloden and the Highland Clearances. Pennant in his *Tour of Scotland* (1769) lists among the ancient sports still practised in the Highlands 'the shinty, or the striking of a ball of wood or hair. This game is played between two parties, furnished with clubs, in a large plain. Whichever side strikes it first to the goal wins the match.'

MacIan's *Clans of the Scottish Highlands* said: 'Two opposing parties endeavour by means of the *camac* or club to drive the ball to a certain spot on either side, and the distance is sometimes so great that a whole day's exertion is needed to play out the game.... When there is a numerous meeting, the field has much the appearance of a battle scene. There are banners flying, bagpipes playing, and a keen mêlée around the ball.'

In January 1821 the *Edinburgh Evening Courier* described 'most spirited *camack* matches' in Badenoch, while, about the same time, the *Highland Home Journal* recorded a memorable clan game played upon Calgary Sands between the Campbells and the Macleans of Mull: 'The contest grew fast and furious. Hail after hail was scored by the Macleans until the Campbells were compelled to give in and leave the field, vanquished and crestfallen.' In 1841 a shinty match, organized by the Highlanders in London, was played in Copenhagen Fields near Islington.

The ball could be handled but not caught in those days, and elder or willow was even more popular than ash as the wood from which the *camans* were made.

However, by the middle of the nineteenth century the game had declined in popularity, and lived on only in the glens of Lochaber, Strathglass, and Badenoch. The man who led the revival was Capt. Chisholm of Glassburn who published a code of rules for the Strathglass Club in 1880. In February 1887, Chisholm led Strathglass against Glen-Urquhart, captained by Campbell of Kilmartin, in a 15-a-side game at Inverness. Glen-Urquhart won by two hails to nil. A repeat game in the following year again saw Strathglass defeated, and Chisholm, in the light of these games, revised his rules.

In the south of Scotland, clubs were meanwhile playing under the Celtic Club rules, drawn up in Glasgow. By 1892 there were a host of clubs, but games between them were hampered by the lack of a uniform code of rules. Eventually representatives of all the leading clubs met at Kingussie on 10 October 1893 and formed the Camanachd Association, Chisholm of Glassburn becoming the first Chief. The first president was Simon, Lord Lovat, 'one of the keenest wielders of the *caman* in the North'. Ever since, the Camanachd Association has been the supreme authority of the game, and has drawn up the rules which control play and competitions today.

The Challenge Trophy, which carries with it the shinty championship of Scotland, was instituted in 1895, Kingussie defeating Glasgow Cowal in the first final at Inverness in

April 1896. The trophy has been played for annually since, except during the two world wars. After 1918, the Sutherland Cup was started to provide a competition for junior clubs.

SHINTY LINE-OUT
The 'Northern' formation: hailkeeper (H); full-back (FB); half-back (HB); centre (C); wing forward (WF); centre forward (CF); full-forward (FF).

Shinty today, despite the greater glamour of more publicized sports, retains its appeal, especially in its traditional strongholds. There was no international competition, but teams played against Irish sides spasmodically for over 50 years, a compromise set of rules having been agreed upon for such games. In 1972 an annual contest with selected hurling sides representing Ireland was inaugurated, and is played in Ireland and in Scotland in alternate years.

Revd. J. N. Macdonald, *Shinty* (1932).
GOVERNING BODY: The Camanachd Association, Inverness, Scotland.

SHOEMAKER, WILLIAM (1931-   ), national champion jockey three times in the U.S.A., and ten times national leader in terms of money won in a single season. In 1953 he rode a record 485 winners and has won more than 80 races worth over $100,000 each. In 1970 Shoemaker rode his 6,033rd winner to beat the record previously held by Longden.

SHOOTING, Air Weapons. All organized shooting with air weapons (known as 'pellet guns' in the U.S.A.) is with ·177 in. (4·5 mm.) firearms in the standing position without support of any kind.

The international course of fire is 40 shots in 90 minutes at 10 metres (32 ft. 9¾ in.) range, but some national associations fire a shorter course and, in Britain for example, at 6 yards (5·49 m.) range.

In most international and national team and individual championships the competitors fire on the same range, but as in small-bore rifle and pistol SHOOTING many similar competitions are conducted under the postal shooting (see SHOOTING, RIFLE) system.

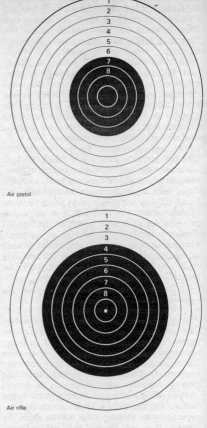

Air pistol

Air rifle

STANDARD TARGETS, AIR WEAPONS
The value of each scoring ring is indicated. Targets are not to scale: the air rifle target is 46 mm. in diameter and the air pistol target 156 mm. in diameter.

The standard target for air rifle events has a circular aiming mark of 31 mm. diameter within which is a central white dot (1 mm. diameter) counting 10 points, and scoring rings counting 9 down to 4 points. Outside the aiming mark are scoring rings at 5 mm. spacing scoring 3, 2, and 1 points. Thus the diameter of the lowest scoring ring is 46 mm.

For air pistol shooting, the aiming mark contains scoring rings for points valued 10 to 7, surrounded by six more rings with score values from 6 down to 1 point. The bullseye, or 10 scoring ring, is 12 mm. in diameter and each successive scoring ring increases by 16 mm. Thus the 9 ring is 28 mm. across, the 7 and the complete aiming mark 60 mm., and the 1 ring 156 mm. in diameter.

Targets are printed black on white card which must have a matt finish to prevent reflection of bright sunlight or indoor artificial lighting.

The 'bell' target is widely used in the many local leagues throughout Britain. This is a cast-iron plate with a ¼ in. (6·35 mm.) hole in the centre with a bell behind it. The plate, on which are inscribed scoring ring circles, is wiped over with wet white paint after every shot. If a pellet misses the centre and thus fails to ring the bell, its mark is left on the white painted surface — hence the need to wipe it after each shot or series of shots.

An international standard range complex must include facilities for air rifle and air pistol shooting at 10 metres distance, for 50 to 70 firers outdoors or 30 (or fewer) indoors. Width for each firer is a minimum of 1 m. (3 ft. 3¼ in.). The larger number of firing points outdoors is to allow as many competitors as possible to fire at the same time and in the same weather conditions. Indoors, of course, the conditions remain constant and no disadvantage is experienced if one fires with the first or the last squad.

Each firing position is furnished with a manual target-changing apparatus. Unlike the international 50 metres small-bore shooters, the air weapons competitor changes his own targets, nor is it obligatory for register keepers to record provisional scores for spectator interest because on the very small scoring rings only experienced officials can accurately judge the score values.

Provided that the area between the firing bench and pellet traps is enclosed, quite simple ranges can be set up for private shooting at home or in a club, given that the safety rules are strictly enforced. Manufactured pellet traps and target-winders are inexpensive and can be home-made. A wooden box stuffed with rags will stop the 4·5 mm. pellet.

International rules specify air rifles to be of maximum weight 5 kg. (11 lb.), calibre 4·5 mm.; aperture sights are permitted but not telescope sights, nor are slings allowed. The general specification is similar to that for standard small-bore rifles.

Air pistols may not exceed 1·5 kg. (3·3 lb.) in weight, 420 mm. (16·54 in.) in length, 50 mm. (1·97 in.) width by 200 mm. (7·87 in.) in depth; they must have 'open' sights and the trigger pressure must be at least 500 g. (1·1 lb.).

The rules also permit the use of gas (CO_2)-operated weapons. Pellets must be of soft metal such as lead or lead alloy.

The air rifle marksman who shoots from the standing position, unlike his counterpart who fires at greater distances in three positions, does not need a padded shooting jacket or spotting telescope. Once equipped with rifle or pistol, his only expenditure is for pellets at a fraction of the cost of 'explosive' cartridges.

In the middle of the nineteenth century air weapons were constructed with a big metal bulb, externally attached, or with a hollow stock of steel, to act as a reservoir for compressed air which was forced into it with a pump. When the trigger was pressed a hammer struck the face of a valve which released a sufficient amount of the compressed air, which rushed down the barrel behind the previously inserted pellet.

In 1906 an article appeared in *Fry's Magazine* describing the air rifle of those days; this worked on the principle, which remains unchanged, of creating air pressure by pulling a lever which also 'cocked' the mechanism for the next discharge.

Lincoln Jeffries, whose air rifles led the world for many years, sold the patent rights to B.S.A. Guns. That firm improved those patents and today produces several models of super-accurate air rifles, some fitted with telescope sights. Webley & Scott Ltd., likewise of Birmingham, England, also manufacture top-quality air rifles and air pistols.

In the American *Gun Digest* no fewer than 33 pistols and 79 air rifles are listed in the Pellet Guns section, the majority being of West German manufacture. Extremely high quality air weapons are also produced in Switzerland.

Air rifles are mentioned in most of the ancient histories of organized shooting, some dating back to the Middle Ages. The St. Sebastianus Shooting Club in Cologne, which operates a 100 firing points underground range (including 14 points for air rifles) was founded in 1463.

Although air rifle shooting has been popular in parts of Britain and elsewhere since the early 1900s, the International Shooting Union first published rules in April 1965. Three years later they produced rules for air pistol competition.

Shot under West German air rifle rules, there was a non-title event in the 39th world championships with 80 individual and 18 team entries, at Wiesbaden in 1966. The first official world championships were staged four years later at the 40th world championships at Phoenix, Arizona, U.S.A. with 93 individual and 20 team entries for air rifle, and 82 and 18 respectively for air pistol. Kustermann of West Germany won the rifle title and his team won the national title from 19 other countries. There were 82 competitors and 18 teams for the air pistol championship, won by Marosvari (Hungary) and the U.S.S.R.

There were also ladies' air weapons events, Cherkasova (U.S.S.R.) and Yugoslavia winning with rifles and Carroll (U.S.A.) and U.S.S.R. winning with pistols from entries of 25 and 18 respectively.

Air weapons events with title status were, for the first time, fired in 1969 at the European championships in Pilsen, Czechoslovakia. Such championships are now fired annually, in the winter months.

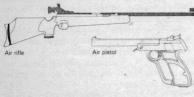

Air rifle   Air pistol

TYPICAL AIR WEAPONS
The air rifle is a Feinwerkbau Model 300, the air pistol a Walther LP Model 2. Both weapons (not drawn to scale) are 4·5 mm. calibre.

The history of air weapons shooting in Britain begins in the early 1900s when, in co-operation with the National Rifle Association at their Imperial Prize Meetings at Bisley Camp, there were air rifle competitions promoted by one of Britain's few makers of air rifles, Lincoln Jeffries of Birmingham. One of the first of many air rifle leagues was formed in 1906 by farmers in the Bridgnorth area of Shropshire. There are many such leagues in England and Wales still using bell targets (see above) and based on Working Men's Clubs, British Legion Clubs, and country inns, more particularly in rural areas.

From the late 1920s until World War II, the Society of Miniature Rifle Clubs (S.M.R.C.), which in 1947 changed its title to the National Small-bore Rifle Association, made determined efforts to interest these bell target clubs in forming a National Air Rifle Association. B.S.A. Guns and Webley & Scott Ltd. of Birmingham provided challenge trophies for team and individual championships, and for a team league competition, firing at card targets and at 6 yards (5·49 m.) range.

There was strong support from Jersey and Guernsey but elsewhere in the U.K. air rifle shooters were content with local competition and suspicious of postal shooting. Despite nominal fees and attractive prizes, at no time did the S.M.R.C. have more than 68 air rifle clubs in affiliation.

The National Rifle Association of America conducts an annual programme for pellet rifles for boys and girls at summer camps. The participants number thousands in three age groups. Their Junior Marksmanship School in conjunction with the annual championships at Camp Perry, Ohio, is unique for the enthusiasm of many adult instructors and hundreds of youngsters firing an air rifle course under normal range orders and strict discipline.

Air rifle shooting is probably more popular and more widely practised in West Germany than in any other country. During the Allied occupation, the ownership of 'explosive' weapons was prohibited. Not only did the Germans form an efficient national association comprised of 12,000 clubs, but their arms manufacturers produced extremely accurate and powerful air weapons. This no doubt accounts for the success of the West Germans in this branch of shooting sport, as well as the sale and popularity of their air weapons in world markets.

Sweden has, since 1961, promoted an annual postal shooting international for air rifle teams of 5, in three age groups: veterans over 45, seniors over 20, and juniors under 20. In 1968 the veterans section was discontinued.

Since 1971, the International Shooting Union has been considering proposals for the inclusion of air weapons events in the OLYMPIC GAMES, but has made little progress in face of the INTERNATIONAL OLYMPIC COMMITTEE policy to restrict the size of Olympic Games.

L. Wesley, *Air Guns and Air Pistols* (1955; 6th ed. 1971).
GOVERNING BODY (WORLD): International Shooting Union, Webergasse 7, 62 Wiesbaden-Klarenthal, West Germany.

SHOOTING, Clay Pigeon,

alternatively called trap shooting, is a sport in which spinning saucer-shaped targets are spring-catapulted into the air, simulating the flight of birds, and fired at with 12-gauge open-bore shotguns. There are two distinct types of competition, the longer-established form known as 'down-the-line', 'trench', or 'Olympic trench' and a more recently conceived event called skeet (see below).

The regulation clay pigeon target is black in colour, weighs 3⅛–4 oz. (99–113 g.), and has a diameter of 4 5/16 in. (110 mm.). On the command 'Pull' from the shooter, each target is released at an angle automatically varied by a trap operated by remote control.

In each round of a competition, squads of five shooters at a time stand in a line at fixed firing positions, 3 yds. (2·74 m.) apart and 16 yds. (14·63 m.) behind the sunken trap, which is concealed in a steel trap house to protect the target-loader. In the senior, more elaborate form of down-the-line shooting 15 traps are used to give a wider variety of target flight.

In a round of 25 single targets, each shooter fires 5 cartridges at as many targets from each of the 5 stations. After each member of the squad has shot five times from one stand, they change places, each moving right to the next position, except the shooter on the extreme right who moves to the extreme left.

An international championship provides 200 targets for each competitor in 8 rounds of 25, and is normally divided into 100 targets on each of two days, the winner being the one who breaks the highest aggregate. In the event of a tie, those involved have a deciding 25-target shoot-off.

Double-barrelled shotguns are commonly used, and there are various secondary clay pigeon competitions which involve the use of a second shot at the same target if it is missed the first time, or 'doubles', when the first barrel is used at one target and the second at another.

The 12-bore shotgun usually weighs up to 6½ lb. (3 kg.). A barrel length of 30 or 32 in. (up to 813 mm.) is preferable to the conventional field gun length of 28 in. (711 mm.) because of the relatively long range it provides. The cartridge, 2½ in. (63·5 mm.) long, is loaded with up to 1⅛ oz. (32 g.) (1¼ oz. or 35·4 g. in Olympics) of lead pellets (nearly 400); the manufacture of a single cartridge involves 130 distinct operations. The effective range of the gun is up to 40 yds. (36·6 m.) and the velocity of the shot about 865 ft. (264 m.)

per sec. The target, which flies at approximately 50 m.p.h. (80 km./h.), breaks only because it is spinning. A similar stationary target cannot be broken at 40 yds. with the weapon and ammunition used.

The generally approved stance for right-handed shooters is sideways to the direction of firing, with the left foot in front and body well forward, with chin and body weight over the left foot. The heel of the right foot should be slightly raised and the knees should not be bent. An ideal stance is important to counter the effect of recoil.

A major difference from the technique of rifle shooting is the finger action on the trigger. The sensitive shotgun trigger is gently squeezed rather than pulled; there is no second pressure as on a rifle. There is no backsight and, again unlike rifle shooting, it is normal to aim with both eyes open.

The art of swinging the gun smoothly through the target, allowing the correct amount of forward deflection and follow-through after firing, underlines the fundamental difference from shooting at a fixed target. The shooter fires a little ahead of the clay pigeon after having swung smoothly through its trajectory. The correct time allowance must be made for muscles and nerves to react, and for the flight of the shot. This is approximately $\frac{1}{10}$ sec. for 40 yds. As the shooter does not know at what angle or height each target will travel, the speed of his reaction is an integral part of the skill demanded.

SKEET GROUND LAYOUT
(*Right below*) Enlarged plan view of a firing position.

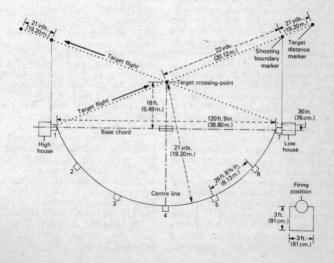

Team events are held as well as contests for individuals.

SKEET is a form of clay pigeon shooting designed to simulate almost any kind of bird game-shot that can be had in the field. It appeals particularly to those who like to shoot all the year round without hindrance of game laws or closed seasons, and to many who have never fired a shot in the country. Skeet helps to develop a swing that is even, steady, and uniform, and shows how to acquire the perfect contraction of the finger muscles needed to squeeze a trigger.

On a skeet ground layout there are two spring-release traps housed just over 40 yds. (36·6 m.) apart, the one on the shooter's left being installed 7 ft. (2·13 m.) higher in order to provide a target in more level flight than that from the other side, which presents a rising shot. Seven firing positions, equidistant from each other, are placed round the arc of a semi-circle, the radius of which is 21 yds. (19·20 m.). The crossing-point of the 'birds' is the centre, over which point practically all targets should be broken at a range of not more than 20 yds. (18·29 m.).

The shooters, normally in squads of five, start at No. 1 station and fire in turn at one target thrown from the high trap and a second from the lower one. The first closely resembles that offered by a departing grouse as it takes flight. The second is an oncoming 'bird' which approaches swiftly and directly overhead. The shooters move round to each station in rotation, firing at 2 targets from each of the 7 positions, making a total of 14 single shots.

Then come the doubles. At No. 7 station, each shooter in turn loads with two cartridges and fires first at the target from the nearer trap. He must then swing back to pick up the other target on its flight in the opposite direction from the farther trap, both targets being released simultaneously. Similar doubles shots are taken at Nos. 6, 4, 2, and 1 stations.

During the shooting of the 24 targets (14 in singles and 10 in doubles), each competitor is allowed one extra shot by having a repeat of the first target he misses (or a choice of trap and station for his extra shot if all his other 24 are hits). Thus, a round of skeet for each person consists of 25 targets, each slightly different and every one starting at something like 30 m.p.h. (48 km./h.). Two or three rounds usually form the nucleus of a meeting or match.

A skeet round such as that described above has been common practice in many countries, but it differs in the following respect from the International Shooting Union (I.S.U.) regulations and those observed in the U.S.A. From a No. 8 station, mid-way between the trap houses, under international rules, competitors try to shoot additional single targets from each trap. After trying this experimentally, some nations ceased attempting it in home competitions, considering it more of a stunt than a feat of good shooting — no doubt mindful that the original object of skeet was, after all, to simulate game shooting as closely as possible. The doubles from No. 4 station are substituted to make up the round of 25 shots when No. 8 station is not used. Doubles are not fired from No. 4 when I.S.U. rules are strictly observed.

A 12-bore shotgun, weighing up to 6½ lb. (3 kg.) using cartridges loaded with No. 9 shot or a special skeet load, is considered to throw the ideal pattern for this sport. A reasonably level field should be selected for a skeet ground, measuring not less than 600 yds. (say 550 m.) by 350 yds. (320 m.). This allows for a safety range of 300 yds. (275 m.) from the gun.

Clay pigeon shooting dates from 1880, when McCaskey, a Scot, invented a suitable target composed of river silt and pitch. This was basically the same as that still used, a combination of pitch and clay or limestone which has the ideal quality of brittleness. Later, in 1880, an American from Cincinnati named Ligowsky developed the first mechanized trap from which the target could be successfully propelled.

The name of the sport derived from earlier competitions near London in which live pigeons were used from around 1790. These were later made illegal. The participants were nicknamed the 'Old Hats' because they kept the pigeons covered with their headgear before releasing them. In a first attempt to dispense with live targets, hollow glass balls about 2½ in. (63·5 mm.) in diameter were used for a brief period before 1880. Some of the balls were even filled with feathers to add a realistic touch.

The sport was undoubtedly inspired by the desire of small-game shooters for practice, particularly at times when pheasants, partridges, and grouse were out of season. But the initial purpose led to a sport in its own right and, paradoxically, many have participated because they enjoy shooting but dislike killing or wounding live birds.

The governing body in Britain, founded in 1893 as the Inanimate Bird Shooting Association, changed its name successively to the Clay Bird Shooting Association in 1903 and the British Trapshooting Association in 1922, before adopting its eventual title, the Clay Pigeon Shooting Association, in 1928. More than 250 clubs have become affiliated to it.

The sport has thrived in North America, where the national governing body was formed at Vandalia, Ohio, in the late 1890s and became the Amateur Trapshooting Association of America in 1924. The number of active United States enthusiasts increased from some 3,000 in 1900 to well over 100,000 by 1973. The sport's international popularity is shown by the fact that clay pigeon shooters represented more than 40 nations in the 1968 and 1972 OLYMPIC GAMES.

Clay pigeon shooting was a regular Olympic sport from 1900 until 1924 (except 1904) and from 1952 onwards. By 1972, no individual had won more than one Olympic contest, but through the years Italy had produced three gold medallists. Since 1947 the sport's world administration has been the International Shooting Union.

The first European championship was won by Sack (Germany) at Stockholm in 1929. The first world title was won by DE LUMNICZER (Hungary) at Stockholm in the same year. Outstanding men in international down-the-line (trench) championships have been De Lumniczer, who gained three world and two European pre-war titles, and the Italian MATTARELLI, the first man to win Olympic, world, and European gold medals. Mattarelli is also Olympic record points-scorer (1964), an achievement equalled in 1968 by BRAITHWAITE (Great Britain). European women's championships began in Paris in 1954, when Mme Renault (France) was successful. World women's titles have been contested since 1962, when Miss Gerasina (U.S.S.R.) was the first winner at Cairo, Egypt. Outstanding women have been Miss TZAVARA (Greece), first to win four European titles (1958, 1960, 1961, and 1962) and Gräfin VON SODEN (West Germany), first to win two world titles, 1966 and 1967.

Skeet, the other form of clay pigeon shooting, dates from the early 1920s. Deriving its name from an early Norse word for shoot, skeet was invented in 1915 by Foster, editor of the American magazine, the *National Sportsman*, who originally intended his idea as no more than valuable practice for small-game shooting. But Foster's invention caught on and clubs sprang up all over the U.S.A. The National Skeet Shooting Association of the United States was formed in Massachusetts in 1925. The first U.S. national skeet championships were held in 1935.

BASS introduced skeet to Britain at Waltham Abbey in the mid-1930s. As in America, it quickly rivalled down-the-line shooting and clubs proliferated. In the Second World War an adaptation of skeet became part of the training programme of Allied air crews.

The first world skeet championship was won by Kjellin (Sweden) at Stockholm in 1947. The first world title for women was won by Mme Mata (Venezuela) at Cairo in 1962. First European title-winners were Saint-Rèmy and Mme Wallis (both France) in Paris in 1954. Skeet gained Olympic status in 1968, when PETROV (U.S.S.R.) was successful at Mexico City.

C. E. Chapel, *Field, Skeet and Trap Shooting* (1949); P. Stanbury and G. L. Carlisle, *Clay Pigeon Marksmanship* (1966).

GOVERNING BODY (WORLD): International Shooting Union, Webergasse 7, 62 Wiesbaden-Klarenthal, West Germany.

SHOOTING, Pistol. The pistol events are considered to be the most demanding in competitive shooting. Standing, free of any support, with the smallest of bullseyes to score 10 points for a gruelling 60 shots over 2 hrs. 30 min., or five shots, each fired at a different target in the space of 4 seconds, requires the utmost concentration. Consequently, top pistol shooters tend to be in the 20–30 age group though there are some remarkable exceptions.

For the slow-fire free pistol event, the classic in this branch of shooting, the same ranges, procedure, administration and tie-breaking as for small-bore rifle events are used (see SHOOTING, RIFLE). A different set-up is necessary for the other three events which include rapid or timed fire.

The free pistol event, dating from 1900, is the second oldest event in the international programme. Sixty shots in 5-shot strings are fired at 50 metres (54·7 yds.). A maximum 15 sighting shots are permitted. The target has a bullseye diameter of 50 mm. (1·97 in.) which scores 10 points, and nine scoring rings each 50 mm. larger. The 7 scoring ring, 200 mm. (7·87 in.) in diameter, encloses the black aiming-mark. The 6 down to 1 score rings are printed black on white and the outer ring measures 500 mm. (19·685 in.).

For the other three international events, which include timed and rapid-fire requirements, the International Shooting Union (I.S.U.) specify how the range shall be designed and furnished, with provision for shooting under cover or in the open. The distance is 25 metres (27·3 yds.). An automatic timing apparatus is designed to reveal ('face') the targets for 4, 6, and 8 seconds in one event, for 20 and 150 seconds in another, and for 3 seconds between 7-second intervals in the third event.

The mechanism must be such that target exposure time must not exceed a tolerance of minus nil or plus 0·2 seconds. A 'skid-shot' occurs when the target is struck while in motion — an elongated shot hole results. If it exceeds 7 mm. in length for small calibre 5·6 mm. (0·22 in.) or 11 mm. for centre-fire calibre (7·6 mm. to 9·65 mm. — 0·3 to 0·380 in.) the shot is counted as a miss. These are not to be confused with 'keyhole shots' which result from a bullet not rotating truly on its longitudinal axis in flight and thus entering the target sideways.

There are two types of target, the rapid-fire and the precision. The former is all black, except for a narrow white edging, the size of a small human figure (a remnant of military training). Scoring areas are roughly oval-shaped with the 10-score centre 10 cm. (3·9 in.) wide by 15 cm. (5·9 in.) deep. Scoring rings 9 to 1 are each larger by 10 cm. (3·9 in.) laterally and 15 cm. (5·9 in.) vertically. Targets are in banks of five, 75 cm. (29·5 in.) axis to axis.

Only the first type of target is used for the rapid-fire match which is also an OLYMPIC GAMES event. The 60 shots are fired in 5-shot strings each shot at a separate target in 8, 6, and 4 seconds, repeated four times. The event is usually fired in two half-courses of 30 shots (plus 5 practice shots in a timing chosen by the competitor) on successive days.

The target described for the 50 metres free pistol event is used in the standard pistol and the centre-fire pistol events for precision, or timed slow-fire shooting, but at 25 metres (27·3 yds.) range.

The standard pistol event was introduced by the I.S.U. to interest a great many people who were firing in national programmes with pistols which were unsuitable for the free pistol and the rapid-fire matches. At 25 metres the 60 shots are fired in 5-shot strings, in 10, 20, and 150 seconds, repeated four times.

The term 'centre-fire' describes cartridges, usually of larger calibre than 5·66 mm. (0·22 in.), which are 'rim-fire'. In centre-fire cartridges a small percussion cap is inserted into the centre of the base of the cartridge case. When the cartridge is in the breech of the barrel, the trigger mechanism releases a striker which fires the cap. This in turn ignites the propellant. Because of the high cost of manufactured centre-fire cartridges, reloading by individual shooters is widespread. Centre-fire calibres range upwards from 5·67 mm. (0·222 in.).

Internationally the centre-fire event in its present form dates only from 1952. There has however been competition with the large calibre (military) weapon since the 1850s. The calibre of a firearm barrel is measured between the lands or grooves in the barrel rifling. Calibres used in competition shooting range from 4·5 mm. (·177 in.) for air weapons, to 9·65 mm. (·380 in.) for big bore centre-fire pistols. The use of centre-fire pistols was permitted in the Olympic Games of 1912, 1920, and 1924

but the smaller calibre weapons, being more accurate, were favoured. Nowadays the calibre of the weapon is specified in the conditions of the event.

THE RAPID-FIRE PISTOL TARGET
Value of the scoring rings is indicated; the height is roughly that of a small human figure.

The 60 shots for the centre-fire pistol match are divided equally between a precision, or deliberate course, and a rapid-fire course, both at 25 metres (27·3 yds.) range. The precision course is fired at the target for the 50 metres free pistol event, and the rapid-fire course at silhouette targets. Six 5-shot strings each in six minutes comprise the precision course and six 5-shot strings are fired at a single silhouette target (not five targets as in the rapid-fire event), the target being exposed for 3 seconds for each shot with an edge-on interval of 7 seconds. A maximum of five sighting or practice shots is permitted for each course.

There are four main patterns of competition pistol. Many makes of each type, from several countries, are available throughout the 90 or so countries which form the International Shooting Union. The more popular pistols are made in the U.S.A., U.S.S.R., West Germany, and Switzerland.

The specification for the cartridges is two-fold — rim-fire and centre-fire. Rim-fire cartridges of ·22 calibre (5·6 mm.) are either long rifle (for the free pistol and standard pistol events) or short — as used in rapid-fire. Centre-fire cartridges are used in the event so named and range in calibre from 7·6 to 9·65 mm. (0·3 to 0·380 in.).

The term *free pistol* derives from a freedom of the restrictions which apply to other competition pistols. The grip or stock may be tailored to fit the hand, though it may not also support the wrist. The trigger pressure is not controlled as in most other competition weapons. A hair trigger is standard to free pistols and probably originated in the 1770-1850 duelling era when gunsmiths vied with each other to produce refinements which would favour their clients' survival. In practice the trigger pressure is usually set at 10 to 15 g.

The sights both front and rear are 'open' and telescope sights are forbidden; a sight which incorporated the clever use of mirrors was introduced by the Swiss in 1967 and for a short time was approved for international use.

Pistols for the *rapid-fire* event must also be fitted with open sights, are semi-automatic, self-loading and use the ·22 in. (5·6 mm.) short cartridge. 'Semi-automatic' means that the discharge of the weapon automatically expels the empty cartridge case and brings the next round into the chamber, and a fresh pressure on the trigger is necessary to fire the next cartridge.

There is no restriction of the trigger pressure for international competition, but the total weight of the pistol may not exceed 1·26 kg. (2·78 lb.) and the weapon must fit into a box 30 × 15 × 5 cm. (11·8 × 5·9 × 1·97 in.).

The specification for the *standard pistol* which is also semi-automatic, is similar to that for the rapid-fire weapon except that it is chambered for long rifle cartridges. Its weight may not exceed 1·36 kg. (3 lb.), its trigger pressure must be at least 1 kg. (2·2 lb.) and it must fit into the same size box as the rapid-fire pistol.

Under I.S.U. rules a *centre-fire pistol* may be a revolver or a semi-automatic. Its barrel length must not exceed 15 cm. (6 in.), the distance between front and rear sights must not exceed 22 cm. (8·66 in.), it must have open sights which must not be mechanically adjustable, and the trigger pressure must be at least 1·36 kg. (3 lb.). A variation of calibres from 7·6 to 9·65 mm. (comparable with ·30, ·32, ·320, ·3220, ·35, ·357, ·38 and ·380 in.) is permitted, but the same weapon must be used in both courses of the competition.

In most European countries firearms are required to undergo a proof test by firing a charge in excess of that for which the arm is designed. This is to ensure, so far as is practical, the safety of the firearm. Proofing is a legal requirement in Britain and most other countries. Unless by mutual agreement countries accept each other's proofs, it is necessary for all imported arms to be proofed upon arrival in the country where they are to be sold. After proofing, a mark is stamped on the weapon in several places.

In Britain there are Proof Houses in Birmingham and London and they are controlled by the Gun Barrel Proof Act of 1868.

National Small-bore Rifle Association, Pistol Committee, *Pistol Shooting Manual.*

Competition shooting probably dates from the 1770s when pistols superseded the sword for duelling. There is no record that the crude handguns which came into existence after the invention of gunpowder *ca.* 1313 were sufficiently accurate for competition purposes.

Milestones in the development of firearms, both rifle and pistol, were 1805, when the percussion lock to produce the ignition spark displaced the flint and 1816, when the percussion cap was invented. This was the forerunner of the complete cartridge of today. Then came the first breech-loading gun that used a self-contained, rimmed, re-loadable centre-fire cartridge attributed to Pauly, a Swiss who worked in Paris and London. This led to the first revolver in 1835 originated by Col. Colt of Hartford, Connecticut (U.S.A.), and the automatic pistol first manufactured in 1892 in Austria.

The British National Rifle Association (formed in 1860) first staged revolver competitions at their big Wimbledon meeting in 1885. The N.R.A. of America (established in 1871) followed the next year at their Creedmore range near New York. That same year representatives of French shooting societies, on a goodwill and fact-finding visit to Wimbledon, won several revolver prizes. The British N.R.A. moved to Bisley in 1890 and the use of self-loading semi-automatic pistols was first permitted in 1898.

Improvements in the design of single shot pistols continued during the second half of the nineteenth century and by 1900 the first world free pistol championship was fired in Paris. Swiss marksmen have won the title most often, although since 1958 the U.S.S.R. and East Germany have been predominant. This remained the only world pistol championship for 47 years until the rapid-fire event was introduced at the 1947 world championships in Stockholm when the International Shooting Union was revived. The following year the rapid-fire pistol event was introduced into the Olympic Games programme.

The centre-fire big-bore pistol event was first fired as a championship in 1952 at Oslo, the winner of which, Reeves (U.S.A.), had charge of range operations for the 1970 world championships at Phoenix, Arizona.

The 'duelling' part of the centre-fire match is derived from the custom of settling matters of honour by duelling. The pistols used were some of the finest examples of the gunsmiths' art and were very accurate. The duel was conducted under strict rules. The contestants faced each other at a distance of about 20 paces and on the command of the umpire raised their pistols and fired one shot, for which three seconds were allowed. Consequent on the banning of duelling, shooting galleries were opened and duelling rules were applied to shooting at a target which was the silhouette of the standing figure of a man.

The same three pistol events were repeated in the world championships of 1954 at Caracas, Venezuela, 1958 at Moscow, 1962 at Cairo, and 1966 at Wiesbaden. For the 1970 world championships the International Shooting Union approved the addition of no fewer than five more pistol events, viz. the standard pistol (men and women), air pistol (men and women) (see SHOOTING, AIR WEAPONS), and for women only a repeat of the centre-fire match but with ·22 in. calibre (5·6 mm.) standard pistols. In all, the Americans increased the number of championships from 37 to 54.

The Mayleigh Cup, started in 1937 between U.S.A. and Great Britain and now open to all English-speaking countries, is an annual postal shooting (see SHOOTING, RIFLE) match shot at 50 yards (45·7 m.) by teams of 10, 30 shots each for a Highest Possible Score of 3,000 points. The record of 2,865 was set by the U.S.A. in 1967; they have won every year except 1950, 1970, 1971, and 1972. Great Britain fired its best score of 2,875 points in 1972. The Mayleigh Cup was presented by a leading British shooting administrator, G. W. Cafferata, when the National Small-bore Rifle Association had its headquarters in a house of the same name on the outskirts of London.

The U.S.A. and Great Britain also promote annual matches for free pistols (since 1960), rapid-fire pistols (since 1969), and standard pistols (since 1973), while Norway organizes a standard pistol international for women.

Small-bore pistol competition shooting in Britain began to find favour in the early 1930s and the first international match was fired by post in 1937. In post-Second World War years the sport has grown considerably; small-bore rifle clubs with a pistol section increased from 325 in 1956 to almost 1500 in 1973. The formation of the British Pistol Club in 1957 by Wing Commander Guy was an important milestone in British pistol-shooting history, its object being to promote interest and improve performance in the International Shooting Union pistol programme.

Geoffrey Boothroyd, *The Handgun* (1970); P. C. Freeman, *Modern Pistol Shooting* (1968). International Shooting Union, *Shooting Sport* (bimonthly).

GOVERNING BODY (WORLD): International Shooting Union, Webergasse 7, 62 Wiesbaden-Klarenthal, West Germany.

SHOOTING, Rifle, is a pastime and competitive sport, widely practised, with both fullbore or Service calibre and with small-bore rifles.

Service-calibre rifle shooting is mostly at stationary targets with circular black aiming-marks, at distances from 200 to 1,000 yards (183–914 m.). Shorter and longer distances are sometimes used. Except in the United Kingdom, Australia, Canada, New Zealand, the West Indies, Zambia, and most other Commonwealth countries, Rhodesia, South Africa, and the U.S.A., it is largely confined to 300 metres under the rules of the International Shooting Union (I.S.U.).

The two main classes of Service-calibre rifle shooting practised in the United Kingdom and in the Commonwealth countries — who follow rules and regulations similar to those of the British National Rifle Association (N.R.A.) — are known as target rifle and Service rifle. The former is the more popular and embraces most of the important competitions and matches. It is practically confined to the prone (lying) position and the ranges at which firing normally takes place are 200, 300, 500, 600, 900, and 1,000 yds. (183, 274, 457, 549, 823, 914 m.). Sometimes 400 and 700 yds. (366 and 640 m.) are used in Australia and 800 yds. (732 m.) in special competitions and in the Palma International Match (see below).

The *target rifle* permitted under British National Rifle Association rules can be any bolt-action rifle which, in the opinion of the N.R.A., is of conventional design. This includes any military design of bolt-action rifle, British or foreign, and privately made versions of these designs. The following regulations apply:

(1) Weight maximum 11¼ lb. (5·2 kg.).

(2) Barrel suitable for firing the 7·62 mm. (·308 in.) NATO cartridge or the ·303 in. (7·69 mm.) Mark 7 cartridge.

(3) Minimum trigger pull 4 lb. (1·81 kg.).

(4) Sights: The backsight must be 'iron' (metallic), of any type. Aperture sights are in general use and a single lens and/or filter may be used in the rear of the aperture. (Backsights with variable aperture eye-pieces and embodying lens-holders are the most popular type in use.) Metallic foresights of any type, including ring, may be used, and a tunnel-type cover may be fitted. Telescopic and optical sights are not allowed.

(5) Woodwork: Any method of stocking-up is allowed and the butt may be shaped to include a pistol-grip and a cheek-rest. Adjustable butt-plates,

hooks, or thumb-holes are not allowed. These are, however, permitted in some other forms of target shooting.

(6) Sling: A sling may be used to assist in holding the rifle steady. Slings are usually made of leather or webbing, and must be attached to the rifle at not more than two points and must not exceed 2 in. (508 mm.) in width nor ¼ in. (6·35 mm.) in thickness. The sling may be placed round one arm and/or wrist but not round any other part of the body. A strap, button, or hook may be fixed to the shooter's coat to prevent the sling slipping down the arm.

The *Service rifle* permitted under British N.R.A. rules for competitive shooting is the 7·62 mm. (·308 in.) self-loading rifle as issued by the British, or a Commonwealth government, and used without any unauthorized alterations or additions. The gas plug must be set to fire ball ammunition and single-shot loading is not allowed. The sling may not be used as an assistance in steadying the rifle except in Deliberate Shoots when a Service web sling may be used, attached only to the front sling swivel. The backsight as issued must be used. British forces may use either the single- or dual-aperture types. Canadian forces must use the Canadian type. The foresight as issued must be used. The minimum trigger pull is 7 lbs. (3·18 kg.).

Whereas the target rifle is normally fitted with a backsight embodying fine lateral adjustment, enabling the firer to take the same aim for every shot irrespective of any wind allowance made on the sight, the Service rifle backsight has no lateral adjustment and wind must be allowed for by aiming off.

Another class of Service-calibre rifle shooting practised in the United Kingdom is with the *match rifle*. Largely because it is a more expensive pastime, match rifle shooting has a comparatively small number of participants. It is entirely conducted at long ranges, 900 yds. (823 m.) being the recognized minimum distance. Consequently, wind judgement is a very important factor. Apart from its attraction as a skilled sporting pastime, it has long been regarded as a medium for experimental work in connection with rifle and cartridge research.

Any breech-loading rifle of sufficient strength to support the relatively heavy barrel and safely fire the appropriate cartridge is permitted in competitive shooting. Most conventional match rifles are constructed on the better types of continental military actions, of which the most popular are the Mauser and the Mannlicher. A number of British actions of modified Mauser design are also favoured. All rifles must be fitted with a standard barrel of approved design, 30 in. (762 mm.) in length and weighing about 5¼ lb. (2·49 kg.). Any sights, including magnifying or telescopic,

may be fitted and the permissible minimum weight of pull-off is 4 lb. (1·81 kg.).

As they are mostly used for back position shooting, the majority of match rifles are made with short stocks, the barrel having no forward support from the woodwork. Longer stocks are fitted to rifles used in the prone position.

In the U.S.A., what is known as *high-power rifle shooting* is conducted under the rules of the National Rifle Association of America and includes several classes of rifle. A wider choice of cartridge is permitted than in the United Kingdom and hand-loaded ammunition is extensively used. Competitive shooting is conducted at ranges from 100 to 1,000 yds. (91–914 m.) and many of the major competitions include three-positional (standing, kneeling or sitting, and prone) and rapid fire as well as deliberate. In this respect it differs considerably from the general mode of British target shooting. Bench-rest shooting (see below), in which the firer sits behind his rifle, is also popular in the U.S.A.

The American Service rifle class includes the M.1 (the Garand semi-automatic rifle) in ·30 and 7·62 mm. calibres and the 7·62 M.14 automatic rifle. For target shooting under American N.R.A. rules, the M.14 must be adjusted to be incapable of automatic fire. Both rifles must be as issued to the U.S. Army, fitted with the standard-type stock and standard leather or web sling. The front and rear sights must be of U.S. Army design but may vary dimensionally in rear sight aperture and front blade-sight. The internal parts of the rifle may be specifically fitted and may include alterations which will improve the functioning and accuracy, providing such alterations in no way interfere with the proper functioning of the safety devices as manufactured. External alterations to the stock are not allowed.

The American match rifle, which differs considerably from the British match rifle class, can be chambered for either the unmodified 7·62 mm. service cartridge (·308) or the unmodified 30-'06 cartridge, and have a trigger pull of not less than 3 lb. (1·36 kg.). It must be fitted with metallic sights which, under high-power rifle rules, are defined as any sight (including tube sights) not containing a lens or system of lenses; a single lens may be attached to the rear sight as a substitute for, or in addition to, prescribed spectacles. A coloured filter-type lens may be attached to the front or rear sights.

In the 'any rifle' class there are no restrictions on sights, ammunition or accessories, except that the rifle must be safe to competitors and range personnel. Other classifications in high-power shooting are centre-fire, sporting, and free rifle.

Most other countries throughout the world shoot under the rules of their own national rifle associations, which largely conform to those of the International Shooting Union. Free rifle shooting, three-positional, on 300-metre ranges with covered firing-points is widely practised.

What is termed the 'big-bore standard rifle' is used at world championship meetings conducted under I.S.U. rules. This rifle must conform to the I.S.U. standard rifle specification, which permits a sighting system and stocking-up similar to the British target rifle. The calibre must not exceed 8 mm. (·315 in.) and the trigger pull must lift at least 1·5 kg. (3·3 lb.). A fore-end hand stop is not permitted.

Rifling is a system of spiral grooves cut in the bore of a barrel, the effect of which is to make the bullet spin about its axis and keep it steady in flight. Without rifling, an elongated projectile, such as a rifle bullet, would be completely unstable in flight and would turn end over end in its passage through the air.

Most continental barrel manufacturers favour four wide grooves with narrow 'lands' (the bore between the grooves). This practice is largely followed in Australia, Canada, and the United Kingdom. Some American manufacturers favour five grooves, the lands and grooves being of equal width. Irrespective of the number of grooves, the actual twist or pitch of the rifling is of some importance. Most target rifle barrels embody rifling of one complete turn in 12 in. (304·8 mm.), though some have a one in 10 in. (254 mm.) twist. The speed at which a bullet spins is determined by the twist of the rifling and the force exerted on the base of the bullet by the propellant charge.

Shooting positions. The rules governing the positions used in target shooting with Service calibre rifles are more or less universal and framed to permit the firer maximum control of his weapon.

Prone. The shooter lies down forwards on the ground, or on a mat or ground-sheet, the upper part of his body being supported by the elbows. The butt of the rifle must be placed against the shoulder or armpit and all parts of the rifle and the arms below the elbow must be visibly clear of the ground and of all other objects. The rifle must be supported by the hands of the shooter only, with the aid of a sling. International Shooting Union rules permit a sling not more than 40 mm. wide (approximately 1½ in.) and British National Rifle Association rules allow slings up to 2 in. (50 mm.) wide. The sling must be attached to the rifle at not more than two points. I.S.U. rules demand that the forearm (the left arm for right-handed shooters) may not form an angle of less than 30° from the floor on which the elbow rests. British rules state that the back of the forward wrist must be at least 4 in. (10 cm.) clear of the ground.

Standing. The shooter stands erect on both feet, no other part of the body touching the ground or any other object. The rifle may be supported by the forward hand and held against the shoulder, the cheek, and the part of the chest nearest to the shoulder. The upper part and the elbow of the forward arm may rest on the chest and the hip. No form of artificial support is permitted.

Kneeling. British rules simply state that no part of the body may touch the ground or any other object except one foot and the other leg from the knee downwards. The forward elbow may rest on the knee. I.S.U. rules are more detailed and state that the shooter

may touch the ground with the toe of the right foot, the right knee and the left foot. The rifle shall be held in the same way as when shooting in the prone position, i.e. with both hands and the right shoulder. The left elbow shall be supported on the left knee. The point of the elbow may not be more than 10 cm. (4 in.) over the point of the knee. The rifle may similarly be held by means of a sling. A cushion may be placed under the instep of the right foot. The right foot may not be turned at an angle of more than 45°. If the foot is placed at an angle of more than 45° a cushion may not be used. The shooter may kneel completely on the thin mat or he may only have one or two of the three points of contact (toe, knee, foot) on the mat. Only the trousers and underclothing may be worn between the shooter's seat and his heel. The jacket or other articles may not be placed between these two points or under the right knee.

Sitting. The weight of the body is supported on the buttocks, and no part of it above the buttocks may touch the ground or any other object. Under British N.R.A. rules the rifle may be held in any convenient way, provided the butt is in the shoulder or armpit. The legs may be apart or crossed and may be in front of the front edge of the firing-point.

Back position. As used in British match rifle shooting, in which it has always been the favoured shooting position, its principal advantages are: (*a*) the long sight radius; (*b*) that the rifle is supported for the greater part of its length by the firer's body; and (*c*) that it allows the firer to sit up and relax between shots. There are no particular restrictions, the firer lying on his back with his feet pointing towards the targets. Normally, the left knee is raised so that the left foot is alongside the right knee. The head may be supported with a sling or similar aid. If preferred, the rifle may be held with the right hand only while the left hand supports the back of the head. The butt of the rifle should be firm in the right armpit with the fore end on the bony portion inside the right knee, the left hand grasping the top of the butt.

In the foregoing shooting positions the expressions 'left' and 'right' should be reversed for shooters firing from the left shoulder.

Targets and marking. On most Service-calibre rifle ranges, in front of the stop-butt — usually a high mound of sand — is the marker's pit (or trench), with a mantlet facing the firing-points to protect the markers. The targets are usually made of canvas or similar material on wooden frames and are faced with white paper, diagrammed with scoring rings and a circular black aiming-mark appropriate to the range at which they are used. Scoring ring and aiming-mark diameters for the targets introduced by the British National Rifle Association in 1972 were as follows:

200 yds. (183 m.) range: aiming-mark, 14 in. (355·6 mm.); central V, 3 in. (76·2 mm.); bull, 4½ in. (114·3 mm.); inner, 9 in. (228·6 mm.); magpie, 14 in. (355·6 mm.); outer, 24 in. (609·6 mm.).

300 yds. (274 m.) range: aiming-mark, 21 in. (533·4 mm.); central V, 4½ in. (114·3 mm.); bull, 6¾ in. (171·45 mm.); inner, 13½ in. (342·9 mm.); magpie, 21 in. (533·4 mm.); outer, 36 in. (914·4 mm.).

500 yds. (457 m.) range: aiming-mark, 36 in. (914·4 mm.); central V, 8 in. (203·2 mm.); bull, 12 in. (304·8 mm.); inner, 27 in. (685·8 mm.); magpie, 30 in. (914·4 mm.); outer, 72 in. (1828·8 mm.).

600 yds. (549 m.) range: aiming-mark, 36 in. (914·4 mm.); central V, 10 in. (254·0 mm.); bull, 15 in. (381·0 mm.); inner, 27 in. (685·8 mm.); magpie, 36 in. (914·4 mm.); outer, 72 in. (1828·8 mm.).

800 yds. (732 m.) and over range: aiming-mark, 40 in. (1016·0 mm.) — 30 in. (762 mm.) for match rifle target; central V, 20 in. (508·0 mm.); bull, 30 in. (762·0 mm.); inner, 54 in. (1371·6 mm.); magpie, 84 in. (2133·6 mm.); outer, rest of target. A half-inch margin is scribed parallel with the edges of the target.

Targets are constantly under review to bring them in line with current equipment and ammunition and prevailing standards of accuracy. In 1974 the British National Rifle Association discarded the V-bull and altered the bullseye dimensions to:

200 yds. (183 m.), 3·75 in. (95·2 mm.)
300 yds. (274 m.), 6·00 in. (152·4 mm.)
500 yds. (457 m.), 11·00 in. (279·4 mm.)
600 yds. (549 m.), 14·00 in. (355·6 mm.)
800 yds. (732 m.) and over, 24 in. (609·6 mm.)

The value of hits in the respective target divisions are: bull, 5 points; inner, 4 points;

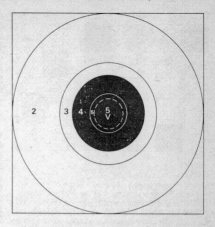

SERVICE-CALIBRE RIFLE TARGET
Targets used in British and Commonwealth target shooting are of the type shown here (for 600 yds.). Dimensions of the scoring rings vary in other countries; some use the V-bull ring and some do not.

magpie, 3 points; outer, 2 points. On the long-range targets (800 yds. and over), hits outside the half-inch margin parallel with the outer edge have no scoring value. The central V is used in some countries for deciding ties.

In the United Kingdom and the Commonwealth marking is usually carried out by the use of coloured panels on a dual or dummy target frame. As the target is lowered into the butts by the marker after each shot, the dummy frame rises in its place and the value of the shot is shown by the position of the coloured panel. When the dummy frame is lowered, the target rises in position for the next shot, with a spotting disc (a small disc on a wire stem) in the hole made by the previous shot. Each shot hole is pasted over with matching paper by the marker when the spotting disc is removed. When, inadvertently, two shots strike the same target, that having the higher value is marked on the dummy target and both hits are shown by spotting discs.

In rapid-fire and snapshooting competitions, sighting shots (if any) are signalled in the normal way. The total number of hits counting for score and the number of shots in each division of the target are usually telephoned from the butts to the range officer on the firing-point.

When a shot touches the line between two divisions of the target, the firer is credited with the higher value. This system of shot evaluation is almost universally applied in Service-calibre rifle target shooting.

In the United States, a variety of targets,

200 to 600 yards

Outer: scoring 2	Magpie: scoring 3	Inner: scoring 4
Bull: scoring 5	Ricochet: scoring 0	Examine or Miss

THE MARKING SYSTEM
Dummy target frames show the system of marking, in use at Bisley and on most of the principal United Kingdom and Commonwealth rifle ranges, for 200 to 600 yds. Beyond 600 yds. values are signalled on the lower half of the dummy (not shown).

including Service rifle, match rifle, and military targets, are used for ranges at which shooting normally takes place, i.e. 100 to 1,000 yds. (91·44 m. to 914·4 m.). Some of these are like those of the International Shooting Union and some are similar to British and Commonwealth targets.

When targets are operated from a marking pit, a spotter is placed in the bullet hole and the value of the shot is signalled with a marking disc. The following system is frequently employed for scoring military targets:

To signal a V, a white disc is waved across the face of the bull's-eye.
To signal a 5, the white disc is placed over the bull.
To signal a 4, a red disc is placed in front of the upper right-hand corner of the target.
To signal a 3, the red disc is placed in front of the upper left-hand corner of the target.
To signal a miss, a red flag is waved across the face of the target.

A similar system for signalling the value and the position of hits is employed on the other types of target.

The International Shooting Union 300 metres target is divided into ten circular scoring zones, scoring 10, 9, 8, etc. points. The black circular aiming-mark is 60 cm. in diameter (23·62 in.), and contains the 10 to 5 rings. The 10 ring has an outside diameter of 10 cm. (3·94 in.) and the 9 ring 20 cm. (7·88 in.). Inside the 10 zone there is an X ring 5 cm. (9·68 in.) in diameter.

Marking is conducted from a marking pit by means of a circular disc, black on one side and white on the other, mounted on a thin staff. The discs are about 20 to 25 cm. (8–10 in.) in diameter with a small hole in the centre. The hit is indicated by placing the marking disc with its centre in front of the shot hole, and the hole in the disc helps the marker to find the

right place on the target. After each shot has been noted by the marker and the target raised again from the marking pit, he indicates the value of the shot (if from 1 to 8) by placing the disc on the appropriate position on the target. If the hit is a 9, the disc is moved across the black aiming-mark, white side towards the firing-point, with a vertical up and down movement. If it is a 10, the disc is moved in a circle clockwise in front of the aiming-mark.

In international shooting a fresh target is used for each series of 10 shots and each completed target goes to the target control department. Here the final evaluation of the hits is made with the aid of gauges.

Competition Shooting. Individual competitions in the United Kingdom and the Commonwealth usually consist of two sighting shots and a series of 7, 10, or 15 (sometimes 20 shots in match rifle events) to count for score, at a specified range. They may also consist of more than one series of shots (see the Queen's Prize below). Team events may be concurrent with individual competitions but the more important ones, such as international team matches, are usually shot 'shoulder-to-shoulder'. What is termed the Standard Rifle Match at world championship meetings consists of 6 sighting shots and 60 competition shots; 20 shots (in two series of 10 each) in

THE CORRECT METHOD OF SCORING
The shot on the left is a bullseye counting 5, that on the right an inner counting 4. On I.S.U. decimal targets they would count 10 and 9 respectively.

each position, prone, standing, and kneeling, at 300 metres on the I.S.U. decimal target. A time limit is normally imposed and at world championship meetings 2½ hours is allowed for a course of 18 sighting shots and 60 to count for score. In the Bisley National Meeting individual events a competitor is allowed 45 seconds for each shot.

There are a few restrictions on dress, but competitors are allowed to strengthen their shooting coats with soft padding or sheepskin, within certain limits, on the left arm, elbows, and shoulder, and a glove may be worn on the left hand (right for left-handed shooters).

Coaching is permitted in team matches but not in individual events. Flags or streamers for judging the strength and direction of the wind are provided on most rifle ranges and shooters may use a telescope or binoculars to 'read the flags' and note the position of their shots (spotting discs) on their targets.

Safety precautions are usually strictly enforced at all times on rifle ranges. International Shooting Union rules state: 'Rifles may be loaded only on the firing-point with muzzle pointing towards the targets. Firing is prohibited outside the prescribed programme. Unless special provision is made it is forbidden to fire a shot in order to clean or warm up the barrel. All weapons whether loaded or unloaded shall be handled with the utmost care and must be carried with the breech open.'

National Rifle Association, *Programme Book* (1970); National Rifle Association of America, *High-Power Rifle Rules* (1970); *World Shooting Championships Programme* (1970); International Shooting Union, *Regulations* (1972); *Standard Shooting Rules for Australian Rifle Clubs* (1967).

Long before it became popular in English-speaking countries, target shooting with rifles had been practised as a sport on the continent of Europe. The Hon. T. F. Freemantle (later Lord Cottesloe) in *The Book of the Rifle* states: 'The Société de l'Harquebuse of Geneva which represents the practising of the citizens under municipal patronage and has existed for more than 500 years, can show that as early as 1474 both the archers and those who shot with the arquebus (early handgun) held competitions which were assisted by prizes given by the Petit Council of Geneva.' In England, the change-over from the bow to the firearm began about the middle of the sixteenth century, and it is recorded that matches with muskets took place between marksmen of Bristol and Exeter. It was not, however, until rifling was introduced that accuracy suitable for shooting at other than very short distances was possible. This seems to have been appreciated much more quickly on the Continent than in the English-speaking countries, and in Great Britain ARCHERY remained the popular form of target shooting until the firearm became the more accurate medium.

Central Europe is generally accepted as the birthplace of rifling, and rifled arms appear to have been in use in Switzerland and Germany and probably other European countries from about the middle of the sixteenth century, but not in Great Britain until nearly 300 years later. Here, there was only a small number of rifle clubs, and target shooting was purely a pastime and had not acquired any military significance.

Early in the eighteenth century there was great interest, particularly in Germany and Switzerland, in the desire to improve weapons and marksmanship, and many European gunsmiths emigrated to America where there were longer ranges and much scope for development. Americans vied with the shooters of other nations in their zest for target shooting, and this led to the formation of the National Rifle Association of America in 1871.

About the middle of the nineteenth century there was a movement in Great Britain to revive interest in target shooting and rifle clubs as a medium of defence against invasion. In 1860 the British National Rifle Association was formed 'for the encouragement of Volunteer Rifle Corps and the promotion of rifle shooting throughout Great Britain'. This marked the beginning of organized target shooting in Great Britain and the movement quickly spread to the British colonies, many of whom formed their own associations and clubs and more or less followed the rules and regulations of the British N.R.A. Based on a quasi-military concept, they were for many years influenced by military requirements as regards equipment and rules governing competitive shooting. Target shooting received a measure of support from the British government in the form of free ammunition and the help of service personnel for the Imperial Prize Meetings and availability of rifles at special rates.

Wars, and threats of war, have always left their mark on British target shooting. The South African campaign, in which the limitations of British marksmanship were sadly exposed, awakened a more general interest in the rifle and the value of accurate shooting received a new appreciation. Hitherto, unless he belonged to one of the auxiliary military organizations, a young man had little opportunity of even handling a rifle. This stimulated the civilian rifle club movement, and concessions on the purchase rates of Government rifles and ammunition to clubs affiliated to the N.R.A. were obtained from the War Office.

After the Second World War, British full-bore target shooting lost most of its military characteristics. This was due to the adoption by the armed forces of an automatic rifle which was not available to civilians, and did not lend itself to accurate target shooting, as well as to changes in military small-arms training. The latter became largely divorced from deliberate shooting at stationary targets, the emphasis centring on quick shooting, often at fleeting targets at unstated distances, simulating the needs of modern warfare.

No longer confined to the current service arm, British full-bore target shooting became what it is today, almost entirely a sporting pastime, with certain equipment restrictions to keep it within reasonable financial limits. It has developed on much the same lines in Australia, Canada, New Zealand, Rhodesia, South Africa, the West Indies, Zambia, and most of the countries which were part of the British Empire.

The British National Rifle Association was formed in 1860 under royal patronage, and one of its first tasks was to find a suitable site for ranges on which to hold an Imperial Prize Meeting. Wimbledon Common in Surrey was eventually chosen and Queen Victoria fired the first shot at the opening meeting. But suburban development and the increasing ranging power of rifle and cartridge forced the N.R.A. to seek a new site for its camp and ranges, and in 1888 the N.R.A. Council decided on Bisley Common in Surrey. A large proportion of the land was War Department property, but additional adjoining land was purchased for about £12,000, and the lay-out of camp and ranges was based on those at Wimbledon. The first Bisley Imperial Prize Meeting was held in 1890 and in the same year Queen Victoria signed the charter which made the N.R.A. a corporate body.

Besides housing the headquarters of the N.R.A., with its small permanent staff, Bisley Camp is the recognized centre of full-bore target shooting in the United Kingdom and the Commonwealth. It is also the administrative centre of numerous other shooting organizations, including the British Sporting Rifle Association and the British Pistol Club.

Thanks to carefully planned afforestation when the site was adopted, what was originally a comparatively bare and treeless area is now a well-wooded and shady camp, with the ranges in close proximity. Bisley more or less hibernates from November to March and gradually awakens into a busy little township for the summer prize meetings, only a limited amount of shooting going on throughout the winter months.

On one side of the camp are most of the principal residential club houses. Features of this part of the camp are attractive avenues of fine chestnut trees and small gardens and lawns which give it a particular charm in the summer months. A considerable part of the remainder of the camp is less attractive, with blocks of hutments, a large caravan site, and camping grounds for the accommodation of competitors and range personnel. When prize meetings are in progress these are often filled to capacity.

The principal building in the camp houses the N.R.A. staff and armoury, a post office, a press office, and a bank which opens only during the Imperial Prize Meetings. Nearly opposite is the N.R.A. pavilion which is usually open all the year.

In 1948 Bisley was the venue of the shooting events in the OLYMPIC GAMES and it also stages the C.E.N.T.O. (Central Treaty Organization) meetings when they are held in the United Kingdom. These are small-arms meetings for the armed forces initiated by the U.S.A. to foster a high standard of small-arms training and to promote a spirit of friendship between member nations.

The principal Bisley ranges are known as Century and Stickledown. The former comprises 100 targets with firing-points at 200, 300, 500, and 600 yds. (183, 274, 457, 549 m.), each of which can accommodate up to 300 shooters in the prone position. The targets are numbered 1 to 100 and each group of ten targets—numbered 10 to 19—comprises a butt. The butt numbers are above the target numbers and are in the centre of each butt. Stickledown comprises 50 targets with firing-points at 800, 900, 1,000, 1,100, and 1,200, yds. (732, 823, 914, 1,006, 1,097 m.), the first three being capable of accommodating 150 shooters. This range has five butts, each of ten targets and numbered 0 to 4. The butts on both ranges are clearly defined, not only by the butt numbers but by lines of flags by which the shooters judge the strength and direction of the wind. Another range, Shorts, has 35 targets for shooting at 200 yds. (183 m.), and adjoining Bisley Camp are the Siberia ranges, 200 to 600 yds. (183–549 m.), normally used as an overflow range when Century is fully booked.

Catering for other types of shooting at Bisley are the Running Deer range (sporting rifle), the Clay Bird (CLAY PIGEON SHOOTING), the Cheylsmore (pistol and sub-machine-gun), the pistol range (pistol and revolver), the free rifle, and the zeroing ranges.

A large part of the Century range is occupied for about a week during June by the National Small-bore Rifle Association (see below) for its annual National Prize Meeting. Following this but prior to the Imperial Prize Meeting in July, the ranges are used by the British armed forces for their rifle championships and part of their annual 'Skill at Arms' meetings. Numerous other open prize meetings take place on the ranges each year.

The Queen's Prize, the 'blue riband' of British and Commonwealth target shooting, was founded by Queen Victoria, at the first Imperial Prize Meetings at Wimbledon, in 1860 as an annual prize of £250 for competition by the Volunteer Force. It then comprised 5 shots at 300 yds. (274 m.) (standing) and 5 shots at each of 500 and 600 yds. (457, 549 m.) (kneeling), with the Enfield muzzle-loading rifle. The top 40 competitors then fired in the final stage, 10 shots kneeling at each of the 800, 900, and 1,000 yds. (732,

823, 914 m.) ranges with Whitworth rifles. (The Enfield was not sufficiently accurate at these distances.) The first winner was Edward Ross who, although a volunteer in the 7th North Yorkshire Regiment, had only just left school and was waiting to go to Cambridge University.

In 1863 the number shooting in the final was increased to 60 and to 100 in 1886. In 1885 it became a three-stage contest as it is today, and for many years the present conditions have remained unaltered. They are: first stage — 7 shots at each of 200, 500, and 600 yds.; second stage — 10 shots at each of 300, 500, and 600 yds.; final — 15 shots at 900 yds. and 15 at 1,000 yds. Entries usually number about 1,000, of which the top 300 qualify for the second stage. From this the top 100 marksmen receive the Queen's (or King's) Badge and shoot in the final on the last day of the Imperial Meeting. The winner receives £250, the N.R.A. Gold Medal, and the N.R.A. Gold Badge, and is distinguished in future N.R.A. publications by the letters 'G.M.' after his name. After the Great War, by the wish of King George V, the competition was opened to all who had served in the war and, after the Second World War, to all British subjects.

The Queen's (King's) Prize has gone to Canada 11 times, Australia twice, South Africa twice, and once to New Zealand. It has been won on more than one occasion by A. Cameron, 6th Inverness V.R.C. (1866 and 1869), Ward, 1st V.B. Devonshire Regiment (1897 and 1900), Fulton, Queen's Westminsters (1912, 1926, and 1931), Brig. Barlow, West Yorkshire Regiment (1934 and 1938), G. E. Twine, R.A. (1954 and 1956), and K. M. Pilcher (1963 and 1973). The only woman to win the prize was Miss Foster, Women's Legion of Motor Drivers, in 1930.

The National Rifle Association is governed by an elected council of 24 (8 of whom retire annually but are eligible for re-election). There are also certain co-opted members, and some ex-officio members, including the High Commissioners for Australia, Canada, and New Zealand and representatives of the armed forces.

The privileges of N.R.A. membership include the right to shoot at the annual Imperial Meeting, to obtain rifles on loan, and to buy ammunition at special prices (within the provisions of the Firearms Act), and to hire targets on the Bisley Ranges.

Australia. The governing body for target shooting in Australia is the National Rifle Association of Australia, with headquarters in Melbourne. It was, under different nomenclature, formed in 1887 and co-ordinates the activities of the six states, each of which has its own Association and runs its own Queen's Prize meeting. Most of the state rifle meetings take place between October and April. These state meetings are considered the best means of satisfying the requirements of the majority of Australian marksmen, and those in Victoria and New South Wales attract as many as 600 competitors each year.

Target shooting in Australia is almost entirely civilian, and few Service personnel take part. The state Queen's Prizes are not given by H.M. the Queen as in the United Kingdom, but are state championships conducted on similar lines. They are usually open to all comers and some marksmen tour Australia and shoot in as many as possible.

In Australia quick wind changes are common, and mirage is extensively used for wind judging. On the Williamstown Range in Victoria it is not uncommon for the wind to change direction completely — as much as 180° — in the course of a shoot. The regulations governing target rifles are similar to those in the United Kingdom.

Canada. The governing body for target shooting in Canada is the Dominion of Canada Rifle Association (D.C.R.A.), with headquarters at Ottawa. Each province has its own Rifle Association and provincial prize meeting. During these meetings competitors shoot for places in the teams representing the provinces at the Annual Rifle Matches, which take place near Ottawa. The principal event at the annual meeting is for the Governor-General's Prize, shot for in much the same way as the Queen's Prize at Bisley.

The Connaught Ranges, the largest in the country, are about twenty miles from the city of Ottawa. They have the unique feature of two sets of targets, one at 600 yds. (549 m.) and the other 1,000 yds. (914 m.), from a common firing-point. It is therefore possible to fire at all distances from 200 yds. (183 m.) to 1,000 yds. from the one firing-point.

The shooting season in Canada normally extends from April to September, though this varies with the weather in certain localities. Early and late falls of snow may curtail the shooting season.

Scandinavia. Target shooting with Service calibre rifles is very popular in the Scandinavian countries and there are large shooting grounds at Amager, Copenhagen (Denmark), Viksbacka, Helsingfors (Finland), Lowenskioldsbanan, Oslo (Norway), and Stockholm (Sweden). It is largely carried out with army rifles of 6·5 mm. calibre.

In Sweden, in which there are two main shooting organizations subsidized by the government, the National Rifle Shooting

Association and the Rifle Section of the Swedish Sport Shooting Union, there is at least one shooting range at or near every town. Electronic marking, developed by SAAB Aktiebolag, Sweden, is being introduced on many ranges. This form of marking may well become universally popular for short ranges, i.e. up to 300 metres (328 yds.). The National Rifle Association of Sweden has about 200,000 members, representing some 1,700 rifle clubs. Nationwide contests take place every year and as many as 17,000 shooters have participated in one competition. Competitive shooting is largely three-positional, as under International Shooting Union rules.

Another popular form of shooting in Scandinavia, particularly during the winter months, is field firing at silhouette targets. The targets are placed at distances unknown to the shooters but usually not exceeding 600 metres (656 yds.). Those taking part in this exercise are divided into patrols of 10 to 30 who advance along a field shooting path and engage the targets as they appear. The shooting path is normally from 3 to 5 km. (3,300 to 5,500 yds.) long, with five to eight shooting stations and targets at different distances from each station. Firing is usually from the lying or kneeling position but some targets may be engaged from the standing position. This form of shooting has a considerable following in Sweden. It is also carried out on skis on ranges of about 18 km. (11¼ miles) distance.

U.S.A. The National Rifle Association of America, the governing body of competitive rifle and pistol shooting in the U.S.A., was founded in 1871. It is governed by an elected board of directors who determine policies and review programmes. A 20-member executive committee act as an advisory board and the headquarters staff has five operating divisions; Editorial-Technical, Programme, Membership, Business, and Legislative and Public Affairs. It is a non-profit organization supported by the membership fees of about a million individual members and over 10,000 affiliated membership organizations. Its stated objects are to educate and train 'citizens of good repute' in the safe and efficient handling of firearms; to foster among members of law-enforcement agencies and the armed forces a knowledge of small arms and the ability to use them; and to promote social welfare and public safety, law and order, and national defence. Its monthly journal, the *American Rifleman*, has a world-wide distribution.

Unlike its British counterpart, the N.R.A. of America caters for all forms of target shooting and the annual national championship meetings include the small-bore rifle championships. It has no range of its own and many national meetings have taken place at Camp Perry, Ohio. This has the largest shooting facility in the U.S.A. and is owned by the state. In 1970, the Association conducted the fortieth world shooting championships on range areas near Phoenix, Arizona, the army rifle, three-positional, 300-metre match taking place on the Black Canyon range.

Service-calibre rifle competitions at the annual national meeting include the national Service rifle championship and the national bolt rifle championship, and one of the principal individual events is for the Wimbledon Trophy. This match is of 20 shots at 1,000 yds. (914 m.), prone position, and using any sights. The trophy, a Victorian silver tankard, was presented to the American rifle team which visited England in 1875, by Princess Louise, daughter of Queen Victoria, on behalf of the British N.R.A. In the previous year, a silver tankard was given to the Americans by an Irish Rifle team visiting the U.S.A. This is the Leech Trophy and is normally competed for at 1,000 yards, 20 shots in the prone position, with metallic sights.

Bench-rest shooting is a specialized form of target-shooting popular in the United States. First practised on a competitive basis early in the nineteenth century, it was a highly developed sport prior to the Civil War and many of the special telescope-sighted rifles used in bench-rest shooting were brought into service by sharpshooters as early as 1861. Competitors travelled great distances to participate in bench-rest matches which were usually sponsored by the local rifle clubs. These apparently operated under their own rules in the matters of scoring systems, courses of fire, etc. This form of target shooting became popular again after the Second World War and now largely operates under the National Bench-Rest Shooters Association, with headquarters in Minerva, Ohio. Some classes are confined to certain types of rifle but, in the unrestricted class, any rifle with safe ammunition and any sights may be used. There is no weight limit. As the name suggests, shooting is done from a bench-rest, the firer sitting behind his rifle. Popular distances are 100 and 200 yds. (91, 183 m.) and, in the unrestricted class, ·308 (7·62 mm.) and ·222 (5·62 mm.) are favoured calibres. A considerable number of hand-loaded cartridges are used and the standards of accuracy obtained are extremely high. A wide variety of telescope sights, ranging from 6 × to 30 × magnification, are used, 20 to 30 × being probably the most popular.

Bench-rest shooting is an excellent way of testing the accuracy of rifle and cartridge, as errors in holding and aiming are reduced to a minimum. The rifles used in competitions are divided into two classes, restricted and unrestricted, being determined by the support used with the rifle. The unrestricted may incorporate in the rest a mechanical guiding means for the rifle, allowing it to return to the same position after each shot. Restricted rests are not permitted these refinements but are allowed windage and elevation adjustments in front, the rear rest being of the sandbag type. Neither front nor rear rests in either category may be attached to the rifle.

U.S.S.R. A considerable amount of target shooting takes place in the Soviet Union and its popularity is evidenced by the fact that clubs are established in almost every village, communal farm, and factory. All have their own ranges, many of which are on a large scale and cater for all types of target shooting. The Shooting Federation of the U.S.S.R. is a member of the International Shooting Union and the sport is subsidized by the government, and by the trade unions and other voluntary organizations.

Through a militarized youth organization, the D.O.S.A.A.F., concerned with the development of sport in the armed forces and subsidiary civilian training programmes, target shooting is taught at an early age. The best shooters are singled out early in life and are afforded ample shooting time and facilities. This may have considerable bearing on the fact that of recent years Soviet shooters have won high honours in world competitions.

In the large cities, very big and extremely well-equipped ranges flourish, such as the Dynamo range at Moscow, at which the world championship shooting events were held in 1958, and the Locomotor range at Leningrad. The grounds of the Moscow Dynamo range cover over 140 acres, and included in the seven ranges is a 300-metre range for 110 targets. The main building contains a hall seating 250, a film projection booth, a dining-room for 300 people, open-air and indoor showers, and a hotel accommodating nearly a hundred guests.

The Soviets have a variety of excellent target weapons largely based on army rifles of the Moisin type and firing the 7·62 mm. rimmed cartridge. In international army rifle matches the M1891/30 sniper rifle is favoured. Other countries behind the Iron Curtain generally use rifles of Russian manufacture and army rifle target shooting is usually conducted under I.S.U. conditions.

INTERNATIONAL SHOOTING MATCHES
The *Palma Match* is a team contest conducted on lines similar to the principal British and Commonwealth matches. It was established in the U.S.A. in 1876 in connection with the International Exhibition at Philadelphia to commemorate the centenary of American independence. The trophy (now lost) was named in honour of Senator Palma, was about 7½ ft. (2·3 m.) high, of unique design and made of steel inlaid with gold and silver, with elaborate mountings of copper. It was purchased by popular subscription to be shot for annually in the country of the last winning nation.

Teams consist of 20 shooters, each man firing 15 rounds at each of the 800, 900, and 1,000 yd. (732, 823, 914 m.) ranges, and the rifles used in the match are provided by the host country. The first match was won by the U.S.A. against teams from Ireland, Australia, Scotland, and Canada. Owing to a misunderstanding, English marksmen did not participate. In the next three matches, Canada provided the only opposition to the U.S.A. Great Britain competed in 1902 in Canada and won the trophy, the U.S.A. winning it back the following year at Bisley when Canada, Australia, Natal, Norway, and France also took part.

Between 1903 and 1966 only five matches took place, four of which were won by the U.S.A. and one by Canada. Interest has revived and it has since become an annual encounter. In 1968 the United States made a record score for the match of 4,414 out of 4,500. Winning the match again in 1969, they waived their right to be host country in 1970 to Great Britain. The match was held at Bisley for the first time since 1903 and the British team were successful against the U.S.A. and Canada.

The *Kolapore Match* dates back to 1871 when the Rajah of Kolapore presented £100 to the British National Rifle Association for a challenge trophy, originally for competition between Britain and the Dominions. Teams are eight-a-side, each man firing 10 shots at each of the 300, 500, and 600 yd. (274, 457, 549 m.) ranges. It is the major team event of the Bisley Imperial Prize Meeting and has been won by: Britain (58 times), Canada (20), Australia (7), South Africa (3), New Zealand (2), Guernsey, India, and Rhodesia (1 each). A new record score was made by Britain in 1970, 1,154 out of 1,240, when the U.S.A. competed for the first time.

The *Empire Match* was promoted by Australia in 1907 for a trophy designed and made in Australia. It can be held only when an Australian team is present, although open to all Commonwealth countries. Teams are eight-a-side, each man firing 10 shots at each of the 300, 600, 900, and 1,000 yd. (274, 549, 823, and 914 m.) ranges. The matches have been contested in Australia and at Bisley and have been won by Australia (9 times), Great Britain (7), Canada (2), and New Zealand (1).

The *Elcho Shield*, presented in 1862 by Lord Elcho for competition at long ranges, is a unique trophy worked in beaten steel embellished with gold and silver, and is the premier home countries match rifle award at the Bisley Imperial Meeting. Teams are eight-a-side, each man firing 15 rounds at each of the 1,000, 1,100, and 1,200 yd. (914, 1,006, 1,097 m.) ranges.

The international *Canada Match* takes place in Canada at the annual prize meeting promoted by the Dominion of Canada Rifle Association. Teams are eight-a-side, each man firing 10 shots at each of the 300, 500, and 600 yd. (274, 457, and 549 m.) ranges. The challenge trophy was presented by the Canadian National Railways.

The *Commonwealth Match*, also promoted by the D.C.R.A., is held under conditions similar to the Canada Match, except that the ranges used are 600 and 900 yds. (549 and 823 m.). The trophy was given by the Canadian Pacific Railway Company.

The *Rhodes Centenary Match*, established in 1953 as part of the centenary celebrations of the birth of Cecil Rhodes, is normally shot in alternate years in South Africa or Rhodesia. By agreement of these two founder countries the match can be held outside Africa and in 1960 it took place at Bisley. The conditions of the match are: teams of eight, each man firing 10 rounds at each of the 300, 500, 600, 900, and 1,000 yd. (274, 457, 549, 823, and 914 m.) ranges.

Howard N. Cole, *The Story of Bisley* (1960); T. F. Freemantle, *The Book of the Rifle* (1901); A. P. Humphry and T. F. Freemantle, *History of the National Rifle Association* (1914).

GOVERNING BODY (U.K.): National Rifle Association, Bisley Camp, Brookwood, Surrey; (U.S.A.): National Rifle Association of America, 1600 Rhode Island Avenue, N.W., Washington, D.C., U.S.A.

Small-bore rifle shooting is probably the most popular of the several forms of competitive shooting at fixed and known distances, at static targets and at distances from 15 yds. (13·7 m.) to 200 yards (182·9 m.).

The cartridges used are ·22 in. calibre (5·6 mm.), rim-fire, long rifle, or short.

International competitions are fired at 50 metres (54·7 yds.), in the prone, standing, and kneeling positions, the scores of the combined positions deciding the result. Other events are fired in the prone position only, the classic being the English Match (see below). Entries for this event in Olympic Games, world and regional championships, at national level, usually exceed those for all other events. The sport is practised by both sexes and at all ages.

For international competition there are two basic designs of small-bore rifle, bolt-action

SMALL-BORE TARGET RIFLE
The model illustrated is a B.S.A. martini, ·22 in. (5·66 mm.) calibre.

(as in army weapons) and martini-action. Aperture sights are fitted at each end of the barrel, that at the rear being adjustable to allow for the effect of wind on bullet.

There are two categories of rifle in the international programme — 'standard' rifles, maximum weight 5 kg. (11 lb.), the use of which is obligatory for women's and juniors' events (though there are also standard rifle events for all-comers in the world championships), and 'free' rifles. The latter are fitted with a shoulder hook and a palm rest and, with sights, must not exceed 8 kg. (17·6 lb.) in weight, but there are no other restrictions except that telescope sights are prohibited.

A sling, which is wound round the left arm (by a right-handed shooter), permitted in the prone and kneeling positions, is used to steady the rifle; its width is restricted to 5 cm. (2 in.).

The trigger on a firearm, when pressed, releases the striker under tension to fire the 'piece'. In small-bore rifles there are variations. A set trigger is actually two triggers — one sets the firing mechanism and the other releases it. This is used in free rifles designed especially for three-positions shooting in which the 'release' trigger requires only the slightest pressure to fire the rifle. Double-pressure triggers are not now so popular but the purpose of the first pressure was to take up the slack and permit the firer to take final and critical sighting before releasing the second pressure. The double-pressure trigger mechanism also has a safety value.

The device for cleaning the barrel of a rifle is called a 'pullthrough'. It consists of a cylindrical lead weight about 3 in. (76 mm.) long to which is attached a cord which is looped at its other end to take a piece of flannelette material. The weight is dropped through the barrel, pulling the cord after it and the flannelette or 'patch' is pulled through the barrel under pressure. The alternative is a cleaning rod, at one end of which is a jag around which the cleaning patch is wrapped (oiled or dry), and at the other end is a revolving handle which allows the rod to turn with the rifling in the barrel.

Modern ·22 calibre cartridges are non-corrosive, and, in fact, leave a protective deposit, but occasional cleaning is necessary, if only to clear the breech of fouling deposit to facilitate loading of the cartridges.

To ensure parity among competitors the specification of the cartridges used in small-bore rifle (and free pistol) shooting is internationally agreed. The long rifle cartridge must not exceed 1·1 in. (28 mm.) in length; bullets must be of solid lead or lead alloy and the weight must not exceed 40 gr. (2·592 g.). These cartridges are of rim-fire design, best described as a little 'gutter' (the rim), into which the primer is inserted — when struck by the striker in the firing mechanism the primer is ignited and in turns ignites the propellant which creates pressure to expel the bullet through the barrel. A rim-fire cartridge case (of brass, copper, or alloy) must be soft so that the firing pin can compress the rim of the case and ignite the primer.

The muzzle velocity of competition brands of ·22 long rifle rim-fire cartridges is just below the speed of sound and most manufacturers issue a warning that such cartridges are dangerous up to one mile (1·6 km.). Somewhat shorter and with lower velocity than long rifle, short rim-fire cartridges are used almost exclusively in certain rapid-fire pistol events.

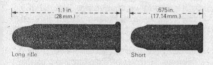

SMALL-BORE RIFLE CARTRIDGES
Silhouettes show relative sizes of long rifle and short rim-fire cartridges for ·22 in. (5·66 mm.) calibre weapons.

Targets and scoring. Modern targets for small-bore rifle shooting are printed in black on matt white card. The International Shooting Union 50 metres target bullseye, counting 10 points, is 12·4 mm. dia. (·47 in.). Zones 10 to 4 are black, forming a circular aiming mark 112·4 mm. (4·43 in.) in diameter. Within the black area, the scoring zones are separated by white circles, while scoring rings 3 to 1 are printed black. These dimensions produce the same angular deviations as the international 300 metres target.

Designed proportionately to the I.S.U. 50 metres target are the National Small-bore Rifle Association targets for 15, 20, 25, and 50 yards (13·7, 18·3, 22·9, and 45·7 m.); while its 100 yards (91·4 m.) target is proportionate to the I.S.U. 100 metres (109·4 yds.) target. 'British National 1966 Targets', as this series is called, are used throughout the British Commonwealth and in the U.S.A.

The targets must be of such material that the bullet holes are not distorted and the target surface does not reflect bright light, whether natural or artificial. The score values of 'doubtful' shot holes, those very close to a scoring line, are determined by insertion of a plug gauge, the flange of which measures 0·22 in. (5·66 mm.). If this flange touches or covers some part of the scoring ring, the higher value is given.

Also known as the 'V' and 'inner carton', the X ring is an inner bullseye, usually half the area of the bullseye or highest scoring area on a target. If two shooters have equal scores, the one with the higher number of hits on the X ring is adjudged the winner. This method of deciding ties is, however, peculiar only to some English-speaking countries.

In Olympic Games, world championships, and continental championships, which are conducted under I.S.U. procedure, the scoring is supervised by a results jury, at least two of whom are required to decide the value of 'doubtful' shot holes. The targets are identified by competitor number and firing-point number, never by name, and even such identity is concealed from the scorers and score-checkers to ensure strict impartiality. There are often tied scores in top-level competitions and these are decided by the highest total score of the last series of ten shots, the last but one series, and so on. If a tie still results, the highest number of 10s, 9s, etc. decide. (This system of scoring and tie separating also applies to air rifle and free pistol events.)

Placed at a calculated distance behind the targets are backing targets or 'backers', each a plain white card which is numbered serially to correspond with the printed target for which it is a screen. Its purpose is three-fold: (*a*) to trace shots fired by another competitor; (*b*) to determine when two shots are fired almost through the same hole — the second bullet is slightly deflected by the front target; and (*c*) to assist the competitor in spotting his shots since his spotting telescope is at a slightly different angle from the bullet's flight.

When the backer is 15 in. (38·1 cm.) behind the target at 100 m. (109 yds.) range and the firers are 5 ft. (1·5 m.) apart on the firing-point, a shot fired from the next position will appear ¼ in. (6·3 mm.) away from the direct line of fire and, by screening the target and its backer, it is possible to determine who fired the 'extra' shot.

The original purpose in introducing backing cards was to prevent a good score being spoiled by another competitor firing a deliberately aimed bad shot. Such a practice existed before the introduction of backing cards prior to the First World War.

The maximum score which a competitor can obtain is called the H.P.S. (highest possible score), often shortened to 'a possible', and when achieved in a 10-shot string for an H.P.S. of 100, a 'ton' or a 'bundle'. An H.P.S. of 100 with each shot striking the X ring is known as a 'Tenex Possible'.

Ranges. The international shooting distance is 50 metres (54·7 yds.)—sometimes 100 metres (109 yds.). Range distances for domestic programmes vary from country to country. Most English-speaking countries use the yardage measurement and, depending upon climate, fire at 15, 20, and 25 yds. (13·7, 18·3, and 22·8 m.) indoors, and at 50 and 100 yds. (45·7 and 91·4 m.) out of doors. In Britain probably 70 per cent of the small-bore rifle shooting is at 25 yds. indoors.

On most ranges for outdoor shooting the firing-point is covered, to provide protection from the elements, and incorporates spectator space behind, divided by a barrier and sometimes at higher level. Targets are changed manually or by mechanical device operated by the firer, but the more usual method is from a trench behind the line of targets in which target-changers are stationed and act on lights or sound signals operated by the firers.

On most international ranges each pair of firers is separated from the next by a partition. Stretching from the firing point almost to the targets are fences to serve as wind-breaks at intervals of ten to twenty firing points. Modern thinking, however, is dispensing with firing-point partitions and range wind-breaks.

To provide spectator interest, behind each firer is a register keeper who marks up the estimated score of each shot as it is fired, determined either by the use of a telescope or by score signal from the pit marker.

Marking pits are but one of three methods. The pit is a trench along and behind the targets (connected to the firing point by tunnels) in which one person is stationed for each target position. His function is to change each shot target for a new one (one shot is fired at each) and to signal the score by placing a disc on a pole in a predetermined position for each score value. The marker thus remains below ground level.

More modern methods are for each firing point to have a target-changing system of pulleys and wires powered by an electric motor, or for a full set of targets to be fed into a box which is electrically connected to the firing point allowing the firer or his register keeper after a shot is fired to press a bell-push which brings the next target into view.

As these methods are extravagant in manpower and cost the alternative is for each contestant to fire ten shots at the same target card on which is printed two or five bullseyes; either the shooter changes the target for a fresh one, or target-changers are employed, each being responsible for several firing-points.

In most countries ranges are required to conform to strict safety regulations, particularly in respect of the stop-butt dimensions and bullet-stopping capability.

International ranges can vary in standards but all must conform to basic requirements of the International Shooting Union. In addition to facilities for small-bore rifle, small-bore pistol (including special rapid-fire apparatus), air rifle, and air pistol shooting, an international shooting complex must provide for high-power rifle and pistol shooting at 300 metres and 25 metres respectively, for the Running Boar 50 metres event, and for clay pigeon shooting in both Olympic trench and skeet events.

'Squadding' is the allocation of firing points and times of shooting. The popularity of small-bore shooting makes it impossible for all competitors in one class and in one event to fire at the same time, and so compete under 'equal' conditions of weather. On large ranges there may be a marked advantage if squadded at one end or the other of the firing-point, as the wind effect on the small bullet is very critical. In world championships and Olympic Games, to ensure absolute impartiality, the representatives of all competing countries are entitled to attend when the draw for positions is made by the organizing committee.

Various methods of squadding are used by national associations. The British system at the big national prize meetings, with some 200 firing positions, is to draw the competitors in groups which move along the firing point for each successive competition so that if there is a weather disadvantage at any part of the range each group shares the good with the bad.

At world and continental championships under I.S.U. rules, in addition to the championships, it is customary to arrange Master Badge shoots for each event. These serve as a rehearsal for both competitors and range administrators. Gold, silver, and bronze Master Badges are awarded for pre-determined scores, or on a percentage of entries, e.g. 10% gold, 20% silver, and 30% bronze.

Most national associations conduct their main individual competitions by classification. In Britain there are A, B, C, and D classes, and in 1970 at its Bisley Meeting the National Small-bore Rifle Association introduced a super 'X' Class for the top 100 competitors. The Americans have Master, Expert, Sharpshooter, and Marksman classes which are further divided into Civilian, Service, Reserve, and Women categories.

Padded shooting coats are standard items of equipment, designed to protect the elbows in the prone position and the shoulder from the recoil of the rifle. Thickness of the garment may not exceed 2·5 mm. (0·1 in.) or, with reinforcement on the elbows, upper arm (to combat sling pressure) and shoulder, 6 mm. (0·24 in.). Similar restrictions apply to trousers and knee patches, while devices which may help to brace the marksman are forbidden. Footwear is also restricted — it must be of pliable material; soles may not exceed 10 mm. (0·4 in.), nor may the uppers exceed in height two-thirds of their length (considerable support would be provided by ski boots and the like). To protect the hand against the sling tension, it is usual to wear a glove the thickness of which may not exceed 12 mm. (0·47 in.). Clothing worn beneath the outer garments may not exceed 2·5 mm. (0·1 in.) thickness.

Postal shooting matches. Unlike most sports which necessitate that contestants meet on the same pitch, court, or links, small-bore rifle and pistol shooting matches are frequently conducted by post. Gummed tickets, suitably printed to identify the competition, are issued to the entrant and stuck on each target. He also receives the conditions, dates for firing, and the name and address of the scorer to whom the fired targets are sent by post. National championships, individual by eliminating stages, or teams on the knock-out principle, league competitions, inter-county matches, and even international matches such as the Three Positions Match or the Dewar Match (see below) are shot by post.

Each match or competition is witnessed by an accredited person, who is required to sign each target after it is shot, as is the firer. The Rules of Witness define the area of responsibility and the signatures imply that the target has been fired in accordance with the rules and regulations. If either or both signatures or the date of firing do not appear on the shot target it is disqualified.

National Small-bore Rifle Shooting Association, *Hints* Leaflet and Wall Chart.

Like all branches of marksmanship, small-bore rifle shooting had its origin in the simple act of 'slinging a stone'. Miniature shooting, the term derived from the short ranges and low-powered cartridges as compared with the Service rifle fired at long range, developed as a separate entity when the French produced a ·22 in. calibre replica of their army rifle in 1895. Twelve years later it was the French who led in the formation of the International Shooting Union.

Influenced by the casualties suffered by the British against the Boers, several countries sought to strengthen their standing armies and reserves. From the reserves developed small-bore rifle shooting organizations in various forms, motivated by a great outburst of patriotism and military ardour. This was particularly so in the U.S.A., in France which promoted shooting championships with thousands of schools taking part, and in Britain. Field Marshal Earl Roberts was a great influence in the introduction of shooting in schools. He founded an association from boys of London schools called Lord Roberts' Boys.

Earlier, at a Primrose League meeting in 1900, the Marquis of Salisbury, then Prime Minister, laid the foundations for a meeting called by the Lord Mayor of London the following year, which resulted in the creation of the Society of Miniature Rifle Clubs, incorporating the British Rifle League and the Society of Working Mens Rifle Clubs. Membership has fluctuated with the peak at 6,000 affiliated units, most of them from the Volunteers of World War I. There were fewer than 1,000 clubs in the 'pacifist' years following that war. The membership grew to almost 3,000 clubs by the beginning of 1939 and increased to 5,000 with many from the Home Guard, Civil Defence, and Women's Home Defence during the Second World War.

The title National Small-bore Rifle Association (N.S.R.A.) was adopted in 1947 when the Association made drastic changes in its constitution. The controlling council is now formed of one nominee from each of some 60 county associations, plus up to 21 members — known as administrative members — by invitation. From the council are formed the usual executive committee and numerous technical committees each responsible for a different form of small-bore shooting with rifles and pistols as well as air rifle and air pistol shooting.

In March 1903 the first competitive small-bore rifle tournament was held at the Crystal Palace in south-east London. By 1906 there were some 350 clubs and 30,000 members. Queen Alexandra presented a trophy in 1907 which is still competed for annually by county teams.

Although world championships have been promoted since 1897 it was not until 17 July 1907 that the International Shooting Union or Union Internationale de Tir (U.I.T.) was formed. The inaugural meeting with eight nations was, for want of better facilities, held in a telegraph office at Zurich during the world championships. Founder members were Argentina, Austria, Belgium, France, Greece, Holland, Italy, and Switzerland.

The founder president and secretary, both from France, were Merillon and Lermusiau. The U.I.T. continued to be administered by the French until 1939. In 1946 Carlsson, a Swedish newspaper owner, and a leading Swedish journalist, Larsson, revived the Union and the following year promoted world championships in Stockholm as a preliminary to the reinstatement of shooting events in the Olympic Games which were staged at Bisley in 1948.

Carlsson, then 71, retired on 1 September 1960 at the General Assembly which was held in Rome at the time of the Olympic Games; Dr. Hasler of Zurich and Zimmermann of Wiesbaden were appointed president and secretary-general, and Larsson became chairman of the Technical Committee.

The I.S.U. adopted English as its official language in the middle 1960s, hence the change of title and initials from those of the French language. It is responsible for all forms of competitive shooting on established ranges.

Its administrative framework includes committees for rifle shooting (high-power 300 metres, small-bore 50 metres, and air rifle at 10 metres), pistol shooting, clay-bird (or clay pigeon), and moving targets events at fixed ranges such as running boar shooting. Such events are fired in Olympic Games and/or world championships.

INTERNATIONAL SHOOTING MATCHES

The *Dewar Match* is fired at 50 and 100 yards (45·7 and 91·4 m.) 20 shots at each distance by teams of 20 for an H.P.S. of 400 points per person and 8,000 points per team; the targets are based upon the I.S.U. 50 metres standard, and the match is organized by the National Small-bore Rifle Association of Great Britain. (The term 'Dewar Course' derives from it.)

Started in 1909 between U.S.A. and Great Britain and, in its first few years, fired at 25 yards range by teams of 40, the Dewar Match is the classic small-bore rifle shooting event in the English speaking countries. It is fired by post on national ranges. Great Britain won seven times during the 1960s including 1969 when there was a remarkable tie with the U.S.A., both teams scoring a new record of 7,897 points. Britain having the higher score at 100 yards won the tie. Prior to 1958 the match was fired on decimal targets (the basis of small-bore shooting in the U.S.A.). The first individual 400 points score was recorded by Reynolds for Great Britain in 1934.

The *Pershing Trophy Match* was first fired at Bisley in 1931 and is for teams of 10 shooting the Dewar Course of 40 shots, 20 each at 50 and 100 yards. Great Britain won, as they did the second match, also at Bisley in 1937. The U.S.A. won at their third attempt in 1939 and the series lapsed until after the Second World War. America has won each subsequent meeting, at Camp Perry, Ohio, in 1953, 1961, 1965, and 1973. At Bisley in 1969, the British introduced a new trophy named for the founder of their Association, which the U.S.A. also won. Teams now fire for the Pershing Trophy in the U.S.A. and the Earl Roberts Trophy in Britain alternately at four-yearly intervals.

The *English Match.* On the revival of the International Shooting Union in 1946 it was decided to introduce a small-bore rifle event fired only in the prone position — hitherto all international rifle shooting titles had been based on the aggregate scores shot standing, kneeling, and prone, a practice which had long since lapsed in the British family of nations. The event became known as the English Match. Conditions are 60 shots, 50 metres (54·7 yds.) range, prone position, and this event attracts more entries than any other in the Olympic Games and world championships.

After British successes in the prone position at the 1958 world championships fired near Moscow, the Worshipful Company of Goldsmiths of the City of London presented a trophy of modern and exceptional design to the N.S.R.A. for permanent loan to the I.S.U., for the English Match at world championships.

The *Three Positions International Match* is a postal event sponsored by the National Rifle Association of America. Sweden won the first two matches in 1954 and 1955, Finland the following year, since when Switzerland have won twice while U.S.A. and West Germany each won six times up to 1973. West Germany have recorded the highest score of 11,483 points from an H.P.S. of 12,000. Great Britain's best placings were tenth on three occasions and their best score 11,114 in 1970.

WOMEN'S SHOOTING. A match in 1952 between teams of ten women shooters from Great Britain and the U.S.A., and joined by teams from Australia and New Zealand the following year, started the Randle Trophy series which is fired by teams from English-speaking countries. It is a postal shooting match fired on national ranges, and is organized by the National Rifle Association of America.

The match has been dominated by the U.S.A. whose team is usually comprised mainly of teen-age girls. A 13-year-old scored the H.P.S. in the 1970 match. The match is fired on decimal targets 20 shots at 50 and 100 yds. (45·7 and 91·4 m.) for a team H.P.S. of 4,000 points. The American girls scored 3,994 points in 1967. Only in 1965 and 1970 (when Great Britain won) have the U.S.A. failed to retain the trophy.

The North Sea Cup Match for women from

eight northern European countries ran for five years from 1964. In teams of five they fired the English Match course. West Germany won three times and Great Britain twice. From 1970 Great Britain sponsored a similar match open to all member countries of the International Shooting Union and fired under I.S.U. rules with standard rifles.

Following the 1948 Olympic Games, the shooting programme for which included events sponsored by the National Rifle Association and the National Small-bore Rifle Association, and the previous year when separate teams from those associations competed in world championships in Stockholm, the need for a joint organization was established. After prolonged negotiations, in which the Clay Pigeon Shooting Association participated, the Joint Shooting Committee for Great Britain was formed in 1955 with Lord Cottesloe (chairman of the N.R.A.) as chairman and A. J. Palmer (secretary of the N.S.R.A., whose idea it was) as hon. sec. The Committee serves as the liaison body with the Sports Council for grant aid, with the British Olympic Association, the British Commonwealth Games Federation, and the I.S.U. and its European Confederation. A further body, the British Commonwealth Shooting Federation, was formed during the 1968 Olympic Games in Mexico, for the purpose of negotiating with the British Commonwealth Games Federation regarding the shooting programme at the Games.

A. G. Banks, *A.G.'s Book of the Rifle* (1948); W. F. Fuller, *Small-bore Target Shooting* (1963; 2nd ed. 1973).

GOVERNING BODY (WORLD): International Shooting Union, Webergasse 7, 62 Wiesbaden-Klarenthal, West Germany; (U.K.): National Small-bore Rifle Association, Codrington House, 113 Southwark Street, London S.E.1.

SHORE, EDWARD (1902-   ), ICE HOCKEY player for BOSTON BRUINS from 1926 for 14 seasons, who made a brief return to the game with New York Americans during 1940. A fearless, long-striding defenceman with a useful turn of speed which enabled him to move suddenly into attack, he sometimes scored as frequently as his forwards. His career tally of 105 goals and 178 assists was remarkable for a regular defenceman. Four times winner of the HART TROPHY, he was one of the most frequently injured players in the game. Born at Fort Qu'Appelle, Saskatchewan, he began as an amateur with Melvin Millionaires. His first teams as a professional were Regina and Edmonton.

SHOT PUT, a standard field event for men and women on the programme of all major ATHLETICS championships; performances are eligible for recognition as records by the International Amateur Athletic Federation (see ATHLETICS, TRACK AND FIELD). It is also one of the events in the DECATHLON.

Shot-putting is a sport of martial origin, soldiers having used cannon balls for throwing contests for hundreds of years. Casting the stone was an exercise practised by young Londoners in the twelfth century. The basic form of modern shot-putting corresponds to that used for tossing the WEIGHT in the Scottish HIGHLAND GAMES. The shot is an iron or brass sphere weighing 16 lb. (7·257 kg.) for men and 8 lb. 13 oz. (4 kg.) for women. It must be put with one hand from in front of the shoulder. The thrower must stay within the limits of a circle 7 ft. (2·134 m.) in diameter. Competitors are each allowed six trials and the distance thrown is measured from the landing point to the circumference of the circle. The shot-putter takes up his stance at the rear of the circle with his back to the direction of throw. The shot is cupped at the base of his fingers, not in his palm, and held in the hollow of his neck. He shifts backward across the circle on one foot and delivers the shot following a full 180-degree rotation which blends with the extension of his throwing arm, thrusting the shot away from in front of his shoulder.

SHOVELBOARD, see SHUFFLE-BOARD.

SHOVELLER, STANLEY HOWARD (1882-1959), HOCKEY player for England. An outstanding centre forward, he was a magnificent dribbler and an equally effective goal-scorer. He scored on his international début, and failed to find the net in only three of his 29 internationals. He scored 6 against Wales in 1906 and altogether hit 77 goals in his international career.

'Shove' was the only Englishman to win two Olympic gold medals for hockey (1908 and 1920). At the 1920 OLYMPIC GAMES he scored no less than 18 goals for England in five games. He eventually captained England and, when his playing days were over, became a leading administrator. He was hon. match secretary of the Hockey Association (1906-12); vice president, Hockey Association (1921-59); and an England selector. He wrote a book, *Hockey*, in 1922.

SHOW JUMPING, see EQUESTRIAN EVENTS.

SHREWSBURY, ARTHUR (1856-1903), cricketer for England and Nottinghamshire. A masterly batsman, especially on bowlers' pitches, he had a sound defence and was an early exponent of pad-play. In a career extending from 1875 to 1902 his patient application brought him 59 centuries, of which 10 were double-centuries. His 23 Test matches were all against Australia, and spanned four series in each country. He led the English sides of 1884-5 and 1886-7, being partner to SHAW and J. Lillywhite, jr. in promoting several early cricket tours. His best Test innings was 164 on a difficult pitch at LORD's in 1886.

SHRUBB, ALFRED (1878-1964), long-distance and cross-country runner for Great Britain. As a competitor in the amateur ranks, Shrubb dominated the world scene in endurance running for the first five years of the century and his name remained prominent in the record books for decades thereafter. He won the English A.A.A. 4 miles, 10 miles, and cross-country titles for each of the years 1901-4, and the international cross-country title in 1903 and 1904. Excluding distances no longer contested, he held many world records the best of which, with the years of their currency in parentheses, were the following: 2 miles in 9 min. 9·6 sec. (1904-26), 3 miles in 14 min. 17·2 sec. (1904-22), 6 miles in 19 min. 59·4 sec. (1904-11), 10,000 metres in 31 min. 2·4 sec. (1904-11), 10 miles in 50 min. 40·6 sec. (1904-28), and 11 miles 1,137 yds. for the one-hour run (1904-13). The latter remained a British record until 1953. Shrubb was declared a professional in 1905 but his amateur performances were his best, and in the main withstood all attacks until the advent of the Finnish stars such as NURMI.

SHUFFLE-BOARD, or shovelboard, is one of the oldest of DECK GAMES and remains one of the most popular with passengers on most shipping lines. It is an adaptation of the shore game that has been played since the fifteenth century, and possibly before that, and was known variously as shove-groat, shovelpenny, and shove-board and now generally as shove-ha'penny. The game was early adapted for playing on board ship, and is now firmly established as shuffle-board. While the board in the land game has become progressively smaller over the years, on ships it has grown larger. Save in its essentials, shuffle-board now bears only a passing similarity to shove-ha'penny, which may explain why some shipping companies call the same deck game peel billiards or deck billiards.

Shuffle-board is played with wooden discs, usually about 6 in. (152 mm.) in diameter, which are pushed along the deck with long-handled drivers fitted with a semi-circular shoe that fits the disc. Usually the drivers are painted in different colours to identify the

teams. As with BULL, whether the rows of numbers are counted horizontally or vertically they total 15 in each row or column.

The game may be played in singles matches between two players or in doubles by partners, and is usually played for either 50 or 100 up. Each player is provided with four discs, and these he plays, alternately with his opponent, towards the far squares. In singles, opponents play from the same ends; in doubles, partners stand at opposite ends so that two players, one of each side, are at each end.

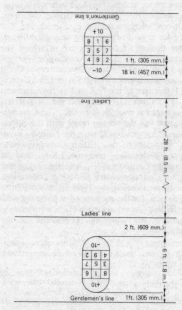

SHUFFLE-BOARD LAYOUT

The rules vary slightly between shipping companies but they are simple and most include the penalty that any disc that stops short of the ladies' line must be removed from play and not be left as a hazard to the discs subsequently played; that a disc touching a chalk line does not score; that players may knock their own or another's disc into, or out of, any square; and that the score that counts is indicated by the square in which the disc rests when all the discs have been played. Ends are then changed. There is clearly an advantage resting with the player, or pair, who play second in any game since he, or they, have the last shot. Generally, therefore, the rules allow that the side with the lower score after the first end, must play first in the next.

There is a considerable element of acquired

skill in the game although even expert players have different preferences, some aiming for the 10 and then for 5 and 9 to prevent a successful 10-shot being knocked off, others aiming first for the lower row then subsequently knocking their discs higher up the board.

SIDECAR RACING, Motor-cycle, see MOTOR-CYCLE RACING.

SILVER BROOM, see CURLING.

SILVER GOBLETS AND NICKALLS CHALLENGE CUP, see HENLEY ROYAL REGATTA.

SILVERSTONE CIRCUIT, the premier British MOTOR RACING track, controlled by the British Racing Drivers Club, built on a disused airfield after the Second World War. Situated in Northamptonshire, near Towcester, it originally had a full-length course, using resurfaced runways and perimeter track, of 3·67 miles (5·9 km.). Later the circuit was simplified, and today the club course has a lap distance of 1·608 miles (2·6 km.), the outer or Grand Prix road course one of 2·927 miles (4·7 km.). Silverstone is a fast course, mainly of right-hand bends, but it is somewhat featureless, since it lacks pronounced gradients and has crude temporary grandstands. In 1973 Peterson lapped it at a record 135·96 m.p.h. (218·81 km./h.) in a JPS. An overbridge, a new pits road, and concrete pits have made improvements. It is the scene of the Royal Automobile Club Grand Prix, alternatively with BRANDS HATCH, and of racing almost every week-end of the season.

SIMPSON, J. C. F. (*fl.* 1922-37), British amateur RACKETS player who won the British amateur singles championship 1926-8 and the doubles championship with R.C.C. Williams in 1922-3 and 1929 and with Crawley in 1931 and 1936-7.

SIMPSON, JAMES (*fl.* 1922-34), British racing motor-cyclist. Although a brilliant rider with six international Grand Prix victories to his credit, he had a reputation as an extremely fast non-finisher. From 1922 until his retirement in 1934 he rode in 26 TOURIST TROPHY races and won only one of them; but during this period, when he rode mostly for AJS and NORTON, he was the first rider to lap the TT course at 60 m.p.h. (1924), 70 m.p.h. (1926), and 80 m.p.h. (1931).

SIMPSON, ORENTHAL JAMES (1947-), American college and professional FOOTBALL player. He starred as a running back

for the University of SOUTHERN CALIFORNIA in 1967 and 1968, in the latter year earning ranking as the outstanding college player. Simpson not only had the blinding speed of a top sprinter but ran with power and deceptive movement. In his first years with the Buffalo Bills of the NATIONAL FOOTBALL LEAGUE, his talents were not utilized properly, but in 1973 he set a pro football season's rushing record of 2,003 yards while running a record number of times.

SIMPSON, ROBERT BADDELEY (1936-), cricketer for Australia, New South Wales, and Western Australia. Playing in 30 Test matches before making his first century for Australia (a stubborn 311 against England in 1964), he became Australia's captain in 1964, and his reliable opening batsmanship, useful spin bowling, and almost infallible slip-catching were of great value until his retirement in 1968. With LAWRY, he made record opening stands of 244 against England, and 382 against West Indies.

SIMPSON, TOM (1937-67), an outstanding British road-race cyclist. He moved to the Continent in 1959 after a successful amateur career in time trials and pursuit racing. He settled first in St. Brieuc (Brittany), where he gained a professional contract within two months, and later in Ghent (Belgium), of which he was made a freeman. A recklessly brave and forceful rider, he lacked the endurance for high mountain courses, and was therefore more effective in one-day races than in major tours. In 1962 he became the first Briton to win a yellow jersey in the TOUR DE FRANCE, but he held it for only a day, and his best performances were his series of classic victories: the TOUR OF FLANDERS (1961), BORDEAUX-PARIS (1963), MILAN-SAN REMO (1964), and TOUR OF LOMBARDY (1965). In the last year, too, he became the first British holder of the world professional road-race title. At the age of 29, during the thirteenth stage of the 1967 Tour de France, Simpson collapsed on the ascent of Mont Ventoux, near Carpentras, and died shortly afterwards.

SIN KIM DAN (1938-), sprinter and middle-distance runner for North Korea. Thwarted by politics from demonstrating her full worth in international competition, Sin Kim Dan set eight world records, at 400 metres and 800 metres, in the years 1960-64. Her best times, both in 1964, were 51·2 sec. for 400 metres and 1 min 58·0 sec. for 800 metres. Her entry in an unsanctioned international meeting in 1963 (see GANEFO) was the cause of the ban which also barred her from participation in the 1964 OLYMPIC GAMES.

SINCLAIR, ROSABELLE, LACROSSE player for Scotland in the first international match against England in 1913, before going to the U.S.A. As a teacher of physical education in Baltimore, Maryland, she introduced lacrosse to her students, and so Baltimore assisted in the early development of the game in the United States.

SINDELAR, MATTHIAS (1903-39), Association footballer for F.K. AUSTRIA (Vienna) and the Austrian national team for whom he played at centre forward in the early 1930s when the team's successes earned the sobriquet *Wunderteam*. Nicknamed 'the Man of Paper' because he was of such slight build and frail appearance, he played notably for Austria in the 1934 world championship in Italy.

SINGLE-STICK, see QUARTER-STAFF.

SIORPAES, SERGIO (1934-   ), BOB-SLEIGH rider for Italy who shared two world four-man championships, in 1960 and 1961, each time as No. 3 in crews driven by MONTI. He also won two world two-man titles, in 1961 and 1966, both as brakeman for Monti. Subsequently he took an active interest in the mechanical side of the bobsled, and his improvements to the Podar designs resulted in sales of Italian sleds to several nations.

SIPAK, see SEPAK TAKRAW.

SIR IVOR (1965), a race-horse bred in the U.S.A. at Mill Ridge Farm, raced by Guest, trained in Ireland by O'BRIEN, and ridden by PIGGOTT. Sir Ivor won eight races, including the DERBY, TWO THOUSAND GUINEAS, CHAMPION STAKES, GRAND CRITERIUM in France, and WASHINGTON INTERNATIONAL in America, and £227,512 in prize money. His fee at stud was a record 8,000 guineas per nomination.

SKEET, see SHOOTING, CLAY PIGEON.

SKELETON TOBOGGANING, see TOBOGGANING: CRESTA.

SKENE, ROBERT (1914-   ), Australian POLO player in the winning side in the English championship in 1937; he played for England in the Westchester Cup v. U.S.A. in 1939. He went to Argentina with the English team in 1949 and helped win the final of the Argentine championship in 1950. He won the U.S. championship several times. Handicap 10.

SKI-JØRING, see SKIING.

SKI JUMPING, see SKIING.

SKIBOBBING is a new winter sport, combining the virtues of the ski, the bobsleigh, and the velocipede in a downhill run. Main centres are Austria, the Swiss Alps, Germany, France, Italy, Czechoslovakia, Canada, the U.S.A., and Japan. It is also established in Belgium, Holland, Sweden, Finland, Poland, the U.S.S.R., Turkey, Lebanon, Persia, Australia, and on a modest scale in Scotland.

Skibobbing, which is practicable on any ski slope and in any kind of snow, is performed on a low, elongated vehicle resembling a bicycle with skis in place of wheels, one fixed at the rear, the other mobile in front for steering. The vehicle is fitted with a saddle and two *patinettes* (mini-skis, or ski-skates) attached to the feet complete the equipment. These foot-skis serve to maintain equilibrium and the ski-bobber keeps them firmly on the snow.

Skibobs are made of wood, aluminium, or plastic, the latter two materials being preferred since wood, though possessing the advantage of lightness, breaks too easily. The prime quality of a skibob is to be springy so that the machine can ride over bumps without jolting and thus unsettling the rider.

The over-all length ranges between 6 ft. 3 in. and 7 ft. 6 in. (1·90–2·29 m.). The long ski being faster, the maximum length is generally used for downhill racing; the shorter ski is ideal for slalom competition; while an all-utility model for normal use should not be longer than 6 ft. 7 in. (2 m.). The saddle on some models can be raised or lowered; the average height of the fixed saddle from the ground is 2 ft. 4 in. (71 cm.). The ideal weight for men's skibobs ranges between 20½ lb. and 25 lb. (9·3–11·3 kg.), and for women's from 17½ lb. to 22½ lb. (8–10·3 kg.). Skibobs are sometimes built on a fixed frame or can be dismantled to facilitate transportation. The fixed model is stronger and generally preferred.

The short foot-skis, average length 1 ft. 7 in. (48 cm.), made of wood and metal, have adjustable bindings. Some have safety straps. Dress for skibobbing is the usual winter sports outfit used by skiers.

Skibobs are carried on the shoulder with the handlebars behind the head and a hand holding the tip of the front ski, the *patinettes* in the other hand. On arrival at the top of a ski run and with the *patinettes* attached to his feet, the skibobber grips the handlebars and walks beside the machine, pushing it like a bicycle to the start. In some resorts, special tracks are allocated to skibobbers, mainly as a precaution against collisions with faster-moving skiers.

A skibob run varies in length, an average course being between 2 and 3 miles (3–5 km.) with a drop of about 1300 ft. (400 m.). It starts generally with a steep descent down the flank of the mountain, then zig-zags along a wide passage through a forest to finish in the fields.

For a 'straight descent' the skibobber sits in an upright position as on a bicycle, keeping his knees near the body and his weight on the foot-skis. For the speedster a 'jockey crouch' is employed. If the slope appears too steep for the rider's skill, a zig-zag descent is adopted. Negotiating bumps, known as 'bump-riding', is achieved by raising the body slightly above the saddle and pressing on the handlebars and the foot-skis. To stop, it is necessary only to dig in the heels when the metal teeth at the rear of the foot-skis act as emergency brakes.

A speed averaging 25 m.p.h. (40 km./h.) in absolute safety is soon obtained and 40 m.p.h. (64 km./h.) is the top speed for a good skibobber. Champions travel more than twice as fast, their best performances being very

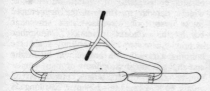

SKIBOB

little slower than record ski-times.

Touring is another branch of the sport, since the skibob rides safely over hard, soft, and deep snow, along icy roads or down a bob run. For climbing and crossing slopes a number of supplementary movements must be learnt. To climb a modest rise, the 'scissor step' is used with the rider astride the skibob, standing over the saddle, the foot-skis turned outwards like scissor blades. On a steep slope, the ladder step is employed, the skibobber walking beside the machine placing the foot-skis horizontally one above the other. Traversing a flat or slightly inclined area the skibobber carries his machine and, on foot-skis, slides first on one foot and then the other in the manner of a skater. For the less skilled the 'scooter step' is simpler; the handlebars are held firmly in both hands and the skibobber kneels on one leg on the saddle, the other leg pushing on the snow.

Ski-jöring parties are towed behind a horse, motor cycle, or car, often at night.

COMPETITION SKIBOBBING. *Downhill racing* is justifiably called *l'épreuve reine*. It is a dash, lasting two to three minutes, down a mountain at an average speed approaching 50 m.p.h. (80 km./h.). It demands technique, physical fitness, daring, and quick reactions. The minimum drop from the start to the finish is 2,000 ft. (600 m.) for men and 1,200 ft. (365 m.) for women, and the maximum 3,000 ft. (900 m.) and 2,000 ft. (600 m.) respectively. A helmet must be worn.

The *slalom* is a controlled descent down a shorter and less steep course, zig-zagging in and out of gates (flags staked in the snow). The course runs down undulating and bumpy terrain, 15 to 25 yds. (14–23 m.) wide, the minimum distance between gates being 20 ft. (6 m.). The drop over a course of 1¼ miles (2 km.) is approximately 1,300 ft. (400 m.) for men and 900 ft. (275 m.) for women.

Skibobbing began in Austria. At the turn of the nineteenth century when winter sports had become established, experiments were made to find yet another pastime to add to the programme of attractions. With the CYCLING boom then current the inventive genius of winter sportsmen turned naturally to the creation of a 'snow-bicycle'. A former Austrian racing cyclist, Lenhardt of Bruck-an-der-Mur, invented a machine on the bicycle principle in 1902 and called it a 'mono-slide'. However, it resembled more the 'hobby-horse' (an early velocipede fashionable at the beginning of the nineteenth century) than the modern bicycle. Its locomotion depended on the use of the rider's feet pushing alternately on the ground. The two runners that replaced the wheels were narrow, like sleigh runners, and were ineffective in deep snow.

The mono-slide appeared in competitions in Austria down the frozen runs, the majority of exponents coming from cycling clubs. However, the equilibrium of the machine required a high speed which rendered its handling difficult and dangerous, since no efficient braking system existed, and the contraption quickly fell into disuse.

About 1910 Swiss postmen and bakers' boys converted their bicycles into *ski-velos* by putting skis in the place of the two wheels. After the First World War a snow-scooter made its appearance in Grindelwald and other Swiss resorts, but it possessed the same defects as the mono-slide: narrow runners and no braking system.

An improvement on the makeshift *ski-velo*, a scooter frame in wood with two skis in place of the sleigh runners, was used in a race in Cortina d'Ampezzo in 1924. While this vehicle was a success down ski slopes in deep snow as well as on frozen *luge* (see TOBOGANNING) runs the problem of equilibrium was still not solved.

Bicycling in the snow was forgotten until after the Second World War when several Austrian and German ski-runners, wounded in the war and unable to indulge in their favourite sport, set out independently to invent a 'ski-bicycle'.

It was the pioneer Austrian ski-runner, ENGELBERT BRENTER, who invented the first successful snow-bicycle in 1947. In addition to the two skis, two mini-skis, one each side, were attached to the middle of the frame to give the machine the stability of a four-wheeler, thus solving the problem of balance. This vehicle, called the 'ski-chair', was manufactured at the Brenter factory and marketed to introduce the new winter sport of bicycling in the snow.

While the machine proved practical in straight runs down the snowy slopes it was awkward to handle round curves and over bumps, and still no effective braking system existed.

The following winter, GEFÄLLER in Germany produced a snow-bicycle using hollow-ground skis and called it a 'skibob', for it possessed ski and bobbing attributes. Popularly known as the *Gefäller Ei* (its frame was egg-shaped), it had two skis, front and rear, and fixed rests on which to place the feet, similar to a motor cycle. At first the machine was used by few people, but when the racing qualities of the skibob became apparent it soon became popular in the Bavarian and Austrian Alps. In March 1950 the first competition took place in Obertauern, Austria, between 32 men and 12 women, all starting together.

The development of modern skibobbing began with the first official international skibob race, in the form of a giant slalom, held in Kiefersfelden, Germany, in 1951. In June of the same year the first skibob federation, that of Bavaria, was founded. The first national championships, in Germany, were held in Fischbachan in January 1954.

During the winter of 1956-7 the Brenter factory marketed the first perfected skibob. The small skis of the original Brenter model were now detached from the frame and attached to the skibobber's feet to be used as independent ski-skates (*patinettes*), enabling the rider to negotiate corners and ride bumps as easily and surely as descending a straight, uninterrupted run. Small steel teeth, fixed at the rear of these foot-skis, served as emergency brakes.

In 1961 the Fédération Internationale de Skibob (F.I.S.B.), was founded in Innsbruck with a membership of 18 countries including Britain, Canada, Australia, and the U.S.A. Today the F.I.S.B. covers 50 nations.

Competitions, comprising downhill racing and slalom, take place during the season in all the countries where skibobbing is popular. The first skibob championships of Europe were held at CORTINA d'Ampezzo in 1963 and the same year saw the creation in Austria of the first skibob school. In 1967 the first world championships were held at Bad Hofgastein. Since the beginning of international competition, Austrian skibobbers, both men and women, have dominated all the major events.

While Britain is at a disadvantage by comparison with countries which have more snow (and as yet no British championships have been instituted), a team of men and women skibobbers has represented Britain in the major international competitions since 1967, including the first world championships.

In its first 15 years skibobbing was practised almost exclusively as a competition and it did not become part of a winter sports resort until nearly two decades after its invention. Skiers looked upon it with contempt and the general public regarded it for a long time as an absurd amusement. It started to become widely popular in 1966 at the fashionable Swiss resort of Montana-Crans where it became the *mondaine* relaxation of a number of French film stars. Such publicity made skibobbing a fashionable amusement overnight and changed the physiognomy of many winter resorts, since a considerable proportion of winter holiday-makers who never participated in any winter sport was converted to skibobbing. It became an attractive alternative for the skier and, after the speed record of world champion W. BRENTER at 102 m.p.h. (164 km./h.) on the slopes of Cervinia (a time very little slower than the world ski record), skibobbing became a sporting challenge to the racing skier. After 1966 the sport developed rapidly and within four years was established as a major winter sport. It is estimated that from some 10,000 skibobs in existence in 1966, the number has grown to over 300,000 throughout the world.

A proposal to include skibobbing in the WINTER OLYMPIC GAMES was made to the INTERNATIONAL OLYMPIC COMMITTEE, but the application was refused, although the F.I.S.B. gold medal has hung in the Olympic museum since 1966.

Dominique Bonnet, *Le Skibob* (1970); Willi Brenter, *Die Österreichische Skibobschule*, latest edition. GOVERNING BODY (WORLD): Fédération Internationale de Skibob, Degenfeldstrasse 7, D-8000 Munich 23, Germany.

SKIING as a competitive sport is either racing or jumping with feet attached to shaped runners, known as 'skis', over snow surfaces of varying angularity.

Skiing is divided into two main sections, Alpine and Nordic. Alpine skiing is racing on skis down steep, prepared snow slopes, one competitor after the other, the fastest time deciding the winner. The longest race is about 2 miles (3·2 km.). Nordic skiing includes cross-country skiing, on lighter skis over undulating surfaces with distances from 5 km. (3·1 miles) to 50 km. (31 miles), and ski jumping, competitive jumping on skis from an elevated position downwards on to a steep snow slope, in which points are awarded for distance and style. There is also a combined competition where the winner is decided on the aggregate of points awarded for performances in cross-country running and jumping.

All these competitions are controlled and administered by the Fédération Internationale de Ski (F.I.S.) or International Ski Federation. There is a further skiing competition, the biathlon, a combination of cross-country skiing and shooting at predetermined sites over 20 km. (12·4 miles), which is controlled and administered by the International Modern Pentathlon and Biathlon Union.

Skis are strips of wood, or composite wood, metal, or synthetic fibre, clipped to the boot so that it is possible to slide or push over snowy or icy surfaces. They are upturned at the pointed fronts so that they will not dig into the snow. Skis vary from 180 cm. (5 ft. 11 in.) to 210 cm. (6 ft. 11 in.) long, and are about 90 mm. (3½ in.) wide at the front end, narrower in the middle by about 15 mm. (just over ½ in.), and slightly wider again at the ends, though not as wide as the front. This shape encourages straight tracking in an unweighted ski. For the same reason there is usually a central groove running the length of the ski, except for its tip. A ski is slightly arched, to assist in springing and increase sensitivity to weighting and unweighting forwards, backwards, and sideways, the means by which a skier induces changes of direction and speed. Alpine skis have tough, sharp bottom edges to assist control at speed on harder snow surfaces. The edges require be less hard for undulating, touring skiing or in soft-snow skiing of any kind.

Rock engravings of skis go back to 3000 B.C. and there are numerous references to primitive skis before they appeared in their basic multi-laminated modern forms in the 1930s. Metal skis were introduced generally in 1950, followed in the later years of the decade by fibre-reinforced plastic skis, and then a combination of metal and plastic. In Alpine skiing these quickly swept the market, but laminated wood continued to be used extensively in Nordic skiing, mainly because no synthetic material had been found which would take and hold touring waxes (see below) as well as treated wood. Nordic skis may be made up of as many as 32 individual laminations. Spruce is used almost universally for the mid-section, while birch, beech, hickory, and ash are used for the side and top lamina.

All skis are shaped and moulded to give tension characteristics for a particular purpose, e.g. forward spring is needed for cross-country skiing. In Nordic skiing there are skis for cross-country (the lightest and most lively, usually 210 cm. — 6 ft. 11 in. — long for a man); light touring (heavier, for use in untracked snow); general touring (the compromise choice); and mountain (more weighty, for breaking trail through crusted snow).

Alpine skis have proliferated on an almost bewildering scale. The metal ski is fundamentally similar to a wooden one but the upper and lower surfaces are made of a metal sheet, either steel or an aluminium alloy, and bonded to a foam or partially hollow wooden core. The hardened steel edges are separate from the sole and are bonded into the body of the ski, more usually with lateral cracks which increase flexibility. The first successful metal ski was made by Head of America, but many manufacturers have now combined plastic and metal in a quickly evolving industry.

The fibre-reinforced plastic ski is variously referred to as the fibreglass, plastic, or epoxy ski. The family link between this type of ski is that glass fibre may be locked into plastic resins, which may be epoxy or polyester, to create a layer of great strength. Skis may be given different characteristics according to the permutations of form and numbers as the glass fibres are set into the resin. Some of these skis are of wood reinforced with such processed rods or strips; others are of a hollow-girder type construction. Early metal skis were found to be too rigid on icy surfaces and fibreglass only led to a less lively ski. One of the answers is a return to metal with a foam core. Most Alpine skis are now sold with a hardened sole which does not require the addition of wax for casual or holiday skiing.

Skis may vary according to the type of construction, length, width, thickness, amount of waist, weight, camber, flexibility, depth of groove, and type of edge. The good skier will adapt to the properties of his skis fairly rapidly, and the racer will choose according to his speciality and the snow conditions of a given day.

The *downhill ski* must have a flexible tip to ride easily over bumps, a very stiff tail to keep it running straight at high speeds, and torsional stability so that it will not 'chatter' in fast traverses. Downhill skis are often longer and sometimes wider than other skis. They do not turn so easily but are extremely stable. A long ski is one that measures 30 cm. (about 12 in.) above the height of the skier. Thus, a 210-cm. ski would be right for a man of 180 cm. if he had the technique to ski fast (above 35 m.p.h. — 56 km./h.). The longer ski is also better in deep powdered snow.

The *slalom ski* has to turn easily but not slip or chatter on icy slalom courses. It is shorter with a stiff arch and point but with a relatively softer tail. This ski gives great control in turns but is apt to wander at high speeds when straight running.

The *giant slalom ski*, a compromise between the two, is designed for controlled turning and fast running, and is the type of ski most usually recommended for the everyday skier. There is also a 'combi' ski, comparatively soft and fairly light, generally available to learners or moderate skiers.

The short ski is wider than normal and reaches to about the skier's shoulder, and is increasingly used by recreational and stunt skiers. They turn more easily than normal skis.

Waxing is the application of wax to the soles of skis to improve performance in Alpine and Nordic skiing. The relationship between wax and snow is complicated, and mistakes are still made, even at the highest level of competition, regarding which type of wax to use for a particular snow condition.

Snow is visco-elastic, i.e. it has some properties of both viscous fluids (like heavy motor oil) and elastic solids (like rubber). The extent to which these properties are present is determined by snow density, crystal type, and temperature. When force is applied to snow, as by a weighted and/or gliding ski, it may give like rubber, flow like grease, shatter like lump sugar, or react in a combination of these ways.

Microscopic examination of a snow surface shows many irregularities, and similar examination of a waxed surface reveals the same irregularities. If a ski is correctly waxed for, say, Nordic touring, the loose particles of snow will penetrate the wax just enough to allow a good grip with a motionless ski, yet allow a moving ski to glide. A properly waxed ski will glide as long as it is in motion, but once gliding stops, the ski must be unweighted to start it gliding again. The coefficient of static (non-moving) friction is greater than the coefficient of dynamic (moving) friction. In Alpine skiing and jumping, where there is need only to glide, the wax should be hard for the existing snow condition. In cross-country skiing there is need for slight penetration of the wax.

Everyday skiers will probably use skis with permanent plastic compound running surfaces, whereas the racing skier will require a surface exactly appropriate to the conditions. Scrapers, blow torches, and wax-removing paste will be part of his team's equipment. When the old wax is removed, a base preparation is put on first — in the case of wood skis a compound sealing out water while providing also a base for wax. The waxes themselves may be hard, soft, or fluid (respectively wax, *klister*-wax, and *klister*). They are spread with waxing cork, a warm waxing iron or, in the case of fluids from a tube, a simple spreader or scraper. It makes no difference in which direction wax is applied.

Alpine ski boots are rigid, flat-soled, and ankle-height, a plastic shell having superseded leather. Modern boots have a pronounced forward ankle rake, and their shape and rigidity have influenced changes in skiing technique, notably in better control of short skis. A 'sitting down' style is encouraged which improves control of the tail of skis. The boots weigh up to 8 lb. (3·6 kg.), are waterproofed, have soft leather or foam linings, and have heavy welts to which ski bindings attach. Alpine skiing boots are now pulled tight by clips which release easily if circulation is being affected, or for more comfortable walking. Boots for Nordic skiing are much lighter and, more frequently, laced.

Bindings are devices on the ski for clipping to the boot, consisting of a sprung toe-cap and heel-clip (which hold the forward and rear parts of the boot firmly on the ski) or, in Nordic skiing, a cable (which, when passed round the heel and tensioned, positions the boot in the toe-cap). Bindings are designed to open and release the boot from the ski under strong forward or rotational force. No experienced Alpine skier skis without checking his bindings frequently.

Crampons, a set of metal spikes, generally 12-pointed, are used by mountaineers to procure a foothold on ice or snow-ice passages. Light 4-point crampons are useful to ski mountaineers for the final slopes of many ascents unclimbable on skis and skins. They are fixed to the boot by means of straps.

Ski sticks, also known as batons or poles, are used to assist movement on skis, whether propelling, pivoting, or braking, and generally to help balance. They are usually made of metal tubing with a leather or plastic handgrip at the top and a strap which is looped over the hand, and a disc or 'basket' at the bottom, about 4 in. (100 mm.) above the point, to prevent the stick sinking too deeply into the snow. The appropriate length of stick is one measured from its tip on the ground to just below armpit height.

ALPINE SKIING. Alpine ski racing is

divided into three categories or disciplines — downhill, giant slalom, and slalom. In each the object is to slide down a steep, pre-determined course in the fastest time, the racers departing at intervals varying from $\frac{1}{4}$ min. to 1 min. In top-class races the timing device is set off at the start by the skier's leg, and a magic-eye beam is broken at the finish to give the time to a hundredth of a second, modern ski races often being decided by such small margins.

Races in all three disciplines take place on much steeper descents than cross-country (Nordic) skiing and equipment and technique are very different. Speeds of up to 80 m.p.h. (129 km./h.) may be achieved in downhill, in which crash helmets are compulsory in races sponsored by the F.I.S. There are specialist skis (see above) for each of the three disciplines. The stretch trousers and wind-cheating anoraks worn at one time by racers are now being superseded by cat-suits to reduce wind resistance. Yellow-tinted goggles are usually worn when visibility is bad, to help the skier see flat-toned snow surfaces in better relief.

Since Alpine ski racing was established in the 1930s it has become steadily more sophisticated. Walkie-talkie teams monitor information up and down a course so that racers can revise plans or even change their ski wax if certain parts of the course are found to be unexpectedly tricky or the snow conditions variable. In training, extensive use is now made of video-tape recordings so that racers can observe their own runs and remedy faults. Technique has changed rapidly over the years, usually when an outstanding racer has achieved success in the world championships or WINTER OLYMPIC GAMES and has his style copied and analysed (see ALLAIS, SAILER, KILLY).

The art of racing downhill on skis is one of anticipation, balance, and flexibility. Most modern teaching preaches an economy of movement of the legs, pelvis, and small of the back, the head, shoulders, and arms being used only to help keep balance. Skis should slide as far as possible without losing contact with the snow, changing conditions of snow and terrain necessitating constant adjustments. Turns are achieved by up and down weighting and unweighting of one ski or the other, with varying weight put on the inside edge of the ski according to the steepness of slope or condition of snow. As he goes downhill, a skier will seek a more forward point of balance. (The term *vorlage* means a pronounced forward lean against the pressure of the bindings.) The faster he goes, the further forward his balance will be, though modern boot rake makes this less obvious than formerly. The

softer the snow the more weight he transfers towards the back of the skis. Because of the speeds involved, the study of movement, and therefore technique, has been difficult and subject to much controversy, but high-speed photography and the use of play-back television films has served to narrow the areas of disagreement among the leading ski-racing nations.

The three races of Alpine skiing have certain aspects in common. The ideal course is one on which the snow conditions faced by the last racer are the same as those faced by the first. This is virtually impossible, although course-preparation techniques have much improved in recent years. Most good courses are packed by foot — stamping provides much greater pressure than mechanical packers. When the course is packed hard, ripples are smoothed out by skiers sideslipping. If there is a shortage of snow, or a risk of thawing, snow cement is used. Sometimes a course is sprayed with water which is allowed to freeze.

Considerable expertise then goes into the course-setting, which will be conditioned by the event (whether downhill, slalom, or giant slalom), the standard of the entry, and the terrain available. The good course-setter will take these factors into account, safety being the deciding consideration. For juniors he would set the course zig-zagging across the fall-line. For a major race he would set it down, or close to, the fall-line in many places, so that the slightest lapse in line or turn would cost the racer important fractions of time. Course-setters are selected by the *chef de course* and are usually coaches or officials connected with one of the teams. Most of them develop a style, some preferring smooth, rhythmic courses, some putting a premium on the right line, while others may prefer a tricky course which lures the unwary into a trap.

A racer is held to a course by a system of gates. These are poles with marker flags dug into the snow and placed in tandem so that the racer must go between them. Their width and placement vary according to the type of race. Both of the racer's feet must pass through a gate, though he can go through backwards. He is free to go where he likes between gates, but he will obviously try to pick the line that is fastest or best keeps his rhythm. He may have several options. It does not matter if he knocks out a pole providing his foot is inside it. In downhill a racer has a compulsory practice, known as the 'non-stop' on the course the day before the race. In slalom and giant slalom he can only climb up the course, memorizing the gate combinations.

The *downhill*, a test of speed, is the most highly regarded of Alpine events. The most famous downhill courses are probably the Lauberhorn at Wengen and the Hahnenkamm at Kitzbühel. The terrain of a downhill is carefully chosen to include bumps, rolls, gullies, sudden changes of steepness, *schusses*, and light and shade. Courses generally follow the fall-line with no sharp changes of direction. Gates, at least 8 m. (26 ft.) wide, are used, primarily to keep speed within bounds or to keep the racer away from dangerous obstacles. The gates are marked by red flags for men and by alternately red and blue flags for women. Difficult corners have straw bales piled to prevent serious accident, but in the 1960s there were several fatal casualties, among them Milne, an Australian, practising for the 1964 Winter Olympic downhill at Innsbruck.

International downhill events require a vertical descent of up to 1,000 m. (3,280 ft.) for men. The length of a course for men is between 3,500 and 4,500 m. (2–3 miles), and between 1,600 and 2,500 m. (1–1½ miles) for women. Such descents are usually discussed not in terms of length but of time, i.e. a 'two-minute downhill'.

Giant slalom was originally intended as a scaled-down version of the downhill which could more certainly be staged because it did not demand so much snow. It was introduced into world championships in 1950 and it has gradually developed its own characteristics. Basically it tests the racer's ability to find and hold the fastest traverse on courses about 1,500 m. (1 mile) in length, with a vertical drop of 450 m. (1,476 ft.), and through 60 to 70 gates each from 4 to 8 m. (13–26 ft.) wide and red and blue alternately. Each race otherwise has two legs with the aggregate time giving the winner. Women's giant slalom is shorter, and sometimes with only one race. The secret of giant slalom is good control of the ski edges to prevent wasteful sideslipping.

Slalom, sometimes called 'special slalom' to differentiate it from giant slalom, has two consecutive runs on different, though usually adjacent, courses. The winner is the competitor with the fastest aggregate time for the two runs. The average length of a course is about 575 m. (629 yds.) with a vertical drop of 150 to 200 m. (492–656 ft.). Thus skiers have a one-in-three slope to negotiate through a maximum of 75 gates, each a minimum of 3·20 m. (10 ft. 6 in.) wide and 75 cm. (2 ft. 6 in.) apart.

The gates consist of pairs of flags coloured, in order, blue, red, and yellow. For the second run the order of start is reversed in blocks of 15, thus No. 1 on the first run is No. 15 on the second, and No. 30 on the first run, No. 16 on the second.

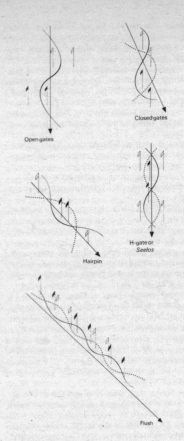

SLALOM GATES AND COMBINATIONS
Arrows indicate the fall-line.

Slalom is primarily a test of control. There are two types of gate, open and closed, and these are varied by a clever course-setter to take advantage of every irregularity of surface to challenge the skier's skill and quickness. The open gate is one in which the imaginary line between the poles is across the fall-line, while the closed gate is down the fall-line. Combinations of gates in patterns are known, variously, as flushes, hairpins, and H-gates. Observers are at every gate to disqualify a competitor who misses one. A skier who completes the first run has the option of running in the second though he may know he has missed a gate. Those who give up or do not complete the run cannot take part in the second.

Alpine ski racers develop at school and club level until the best are chosen to represent their countries on the A, B, or Citizen circuits — races expressly for spare-time skiers who do not live among mountains (also known as Citadin races) — of the F.I.S., which publishes annually a calendar of events arranged into these categories. The F.I.S. also issues start licences to racers through affiliated national federations, and organizes racers in a seeding system which governs their start numbers in the various events. Seeding groups are determined by F.I.S. points, which are awarded in each authorized race, based on the performance of each racer relative to the winner. Because an early start generally means better snow conditions, the object of a racer is to get himself into the highest possible seeding group.

NORDIC SKIING. Known as *langlauf* in German and *langrenn* in most Scandinavian languages, *cross-country ski racing* is competitive racing over undulating, pre-arranged snow tracks, the winner being the racer with the fastest time, except in relay events, where the winner is the first to finish. Extremely light skis (1·4 kg. or 3 lb. 2 oz. for an average pair) are worn, fastened only at the extreme tip of the toe of a boot that resembles a track shoe. As an athletic performance it is comparable to a marathon race, the standard distances varying from 5 km. (3·1 miles) to 50 km. (31 miles). The pace is fast, the usual times over international-standard 15 km. (9·3 mile) courses being about 50 minutes and for 50 km. courses about 2 hrs. 45 min.

Hundreds of cross-country races are held each year in Scandinavia and Russia: in Finland there are over 4,000 cross-country and touring race events each winter. The Winter Olympic Games have more cross-country events than any other ski event: there are four men's and three women's cross-country events plus the biathlon and the Nordic combination (cross-country skiing and ski jumping).

The most important F.I.S. rules governing courses are:

Length: For seniors (minimum age at 1 January in a competition year 18 for a woman and 20 for a man), men 10, 15, and 50 km. (6·2, 9·3, and 31 miles); women 5 and 10 km. (3·1 and 6·2 miles). Relay races, men 3 × 10 km. or 4 × 10 km.; women 3 × 5 km.

Altitude: Not to exceed 1,650 m. (5,362 ft.) at Winter Olympic Games and world championships.

Vertical change: Up to 1965 F.I.S. regulations specified the maximum total difference in elevation between the lowest and highest point on a course, but the 1965 congress in Mamaia, Romania, adopted standards for total elevation gain (the sum of all elevation differences around a course) because it gave a more realistic picture of the course's difficulty. In the women's 5 kilometres the gain should be 150 to 200 m. (492–656 ft.); the 10 kilometres

250 to 350 m. (820–1,148 ft.); the men's 10 kilometres 300 to 450 m. (984–1,476 ft.); the 15 kilometres 450 to 500 m. (1,476–1,640 ft.); the 30 kilometres 750 to 1,000 m. (2,460–3,281 ft.); and the 50 kilometres 1,200 to 1,500 m. (3,937–4,921 ft.).

Laps: At Winter Olympics and world championships no course or part of a course may be run more than twice to comprise the required distance. At other international events, a course or part of it may be run several times.

Marking: The course must be clearly marked with markers of a single colour. Signs giving course distance should be set up at least every fifth kilometre along the whole course and every kilometre for the last 10 km.

Start and finish must be at the same place and at the same altitude. Incoming and outgoing tracks must be separated so that there is no confusion.

Feeding stations: On 20- to 30-km. courses there must be at least one feeding station. Warm beverages and food are permitted; wine and spirits are prohibited.

The basic stride is a kick-off from one foot and a gliding step with the other. Kick-offs and glides are alternated between one foot and the other to give a smooth and rhythmical stride. The ski is waxed so that the action is much like a brush on a wet floor and the ski will glide as long as it is in motion. Once it stops it will stick until it is picked up slightly and pushed on with a kicking motion, known in Norwegian as *fraspark*. The pole in each hand is planted alternately as the leg on the opposite side starts its kick. This is the basic step, to which there are variants. The diagonal stride is similar to that of ice skating, whereby the forward force is gained with a push forward off a slightly angled, edged ski, so that progress is maintained in a series of opened Vs.

The same basic style is used for uphill skiing, the edged ski preventing back-sliding. In herringboning, the toes of the skis are turned outwards and heels kept together, leaving a herringbone pattern in the snow. A method of providing variation or rest is known as doublepoling, in which both poles are inserted in the snow simultaneously, with the body slightly crouched, to obtain extra forward propulsion. Most turns are executed with (1) doublepoling, (2) weight switched to the outside ski, (3) unweighted ski pointed in the new direction, (4) weight switched to the inside ski, (5) other ski brought parallel, (6) into double-pole again. The kick turn, made from a stationary position, changes direction by 180°; the christiania is a swing turn, across the fall-line with skis roughly parallel throughout. F.I.S. rules govern the *Nordic combination*, the most traditional of the Nordic skiing contests, where the object is to show a balance of skill and performance in both cross-country running and jumping. It is a combination of a 15-km. cross-country course and jumping from a 70-m. (230 ft.) hill, points being awarded for each competition and the winner decided by the aggregate total. The jump is now held before the cross-country to encourage the better runners to try their hardest in the jumping.

The winter *biathlon* is based on the old military patrol race, and was first accepted into the Olympic programme at Squaw Valley in 1960. It consists of a 20-km. (nearly 12½ miles) cross-country race on skis in the course of which four firing exercises with five shots each have to be completed. Competitors have to carry rifle (single shot) and ammunition. At or near the 4, 8, 12, and 16 km. marks (approximately every 2½ miles) competitors fire at targets, lying at the first shoot, standing at the second, lying at the third and standing for the fourth.

In the lying position the target is 25 cm. (10 in.) in circumference with a 12·5 cm. (5 in.) inner ring. Standing the target is 50 cm. (19½ in.) with a 35 cm. (14 in.) inner. Two minutes are added to the competitor's over-all time for a complete miss and one minute if he only hits the outer ring of the target. The distance of each range varies between 100 m. (328 ft.) and 250 m. (820 ft.) with the longer distances used for the prone shooting position.

The biathlon relay is a race for teams of four and was introduced at the Winter Olympics at Grenoble in 1968. Each of four runners must fire twice during laps of 7·5 km. (4·6 miles). At the first shoot they have five targets of 30 cm. (11·8 in.) for a standing shoot, and at the second, five targets of 10 cm. (3·9 in.) for a prone shoot. They have up to eight bullets to shatter the five targets in each instance, but for each target they fail to hit they must run a penalty lap of 200 m. (219 yds.).

Ski jumping is a competition based on both distance and style. The jumper takes off down a sloping channel known as an in-run. The distance from the lip of the take-off to the middle point where the jumper's feet touch the snow on landing is measured to an accuracy of 0·5 m. (or 1 ft.). Style, or form, is evaluated by official judges. The points for distance and style of the best two rounds of jumping are added together and the jumper with the most points wins. In Nordic combined jumping the two best of three jumps are counted. In *ski flying*, a form of ski jumping from higher hills, distance alone decides the winner.

In ski jumping, each of three judges can award a maximum of 20 points per jump. In major competitions there are five judges, but the scores of the highest and lowest are removed to eliminate any possibility of bias. The other three marks count in the results.

Distance points are scored by giving the longest-standing jump in each round 60 points and reducing the points for lesser jumps proportionately. Style points are scored as follows. As the jumper leaves the lip of the take-off he is assumed to have 20 points from each judge, and from there on points are deducted for faults such as waving the arms, allowing the skis to cross, bending too much at the hips, insufficient forward lean, and imperfect landing. The most serious fault is a fall, which costs the jumper 10 points from each of the judges if it occurs on landing, 8 to 10 on a change of gradient, or 20 on the in-run. The fundamental points which the judges are looking for are (*a*) a correct, well-controlled position of body, (*b*) steadiness in all parts of the jump, and (*c*) boldness on the take-off and in the air.

During a perfect jump the skier should be in a forward leaning position with straight hips (or bending only slightly) and with his arms at his side or straight ahead. The ideal at which the jumper is aiming is to remain motionless and in full control throughout the flight. Skis should be parallel, close together, and in roughly the same plane as the upper body. This position is held until just before the landing, when the jumper straightens so that his skis are directly under him at the moment of impact. The jumper should land in a telemark position — i.e. one foot in front of the other — with the knees half-bent to absorb the shock. The arms should be at the side and the upper body held upright. This position should be maintained throughout the transition and on to the flat.

Modern developments have shown that the sport is more dependent on timing and style than on sheer physical strength. Jumpers have learned that they must uncoil as explosively as possible at the take-off, with toes almost overlapping the lip, and then assume the best aerodynamic shape, with the air balling under their skis to create an element of lift and then a measure of control as they descend.

Ski-jumping hills are carefully engineered. They are designated 90 metres, 70 metres, and downwards according to the length that can safely be jumped on the hill rather than the physical distance from top to bottom. Ski-flying hills are designed for longer jumps — usually 100 to 130 m., but 165 is known — and events held on them are scored on the same basis as regular jumping except that distance points equal the number of metres jumped (i.e. 126 m. = 126 points). Landing is measured to an accuracy of 1 m.

The measurement of a hill to arrive at its safe jumping length is taken from the lip of the take-off to what is called the P point. This point marks the beginning of the straight section, the angle of which is carefully calculated and prepared to accept the jumper. The end of the straight section is designated the K point, and shortly after it the transition, or 'dip', begins. The greatest danger in ski jumping lies in carrying beyond the K point. The P point is marked by a blue dye and the K point by a red. Knowledgeable spectators, particularly at a place like the HOLMENKOLLEN, will react quickly to any serious digressions at these points.

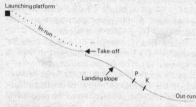

SKI-JUMPING HILL
(P) Critical point, the beginning of the straight section, from which the slope is angled and prepared to receive the jumper. (K) The end of the straight section, where the lowest part of the landing slope joins the curve in the out-run.

Each competition has a jury, usually consisting of the chief of the competition, one judge, one coach or trainer representing visiting teams, one coach representing the organizing club or association, and a technical delegate from the F.I.S. for international occasions. The jury ensures that competitors are divided into groups of four, with the best according to record in group 1; that the measuring tape from the lip of the take-off to the points of landing is correctly laid; and at what point on the in-run the competitors shall start. The jury may vary the starting point depending on weather conditions. It has power to stop, cancel, or restart a round, especially if a competitor approaches or overjumps the K point.

The world's leading jumping hills are at the Holmenkollen, Oslo, and at Obertsdorf and GARMISCH (Germany), ST. MORITZ (Switzerland), Squaw Valley and LAKE PLACID (U.S.A.), Innsbruck (Austria), Sapporo (Japan), CORTINA (Italy), and Chamonix and Grenoble (France). Since the general construction of each hill varies slightly, the records set at each are not strictly comparable.

Among the sports connected with skiing, though not practiced competitively, is ski-jøring, the process of being towed on skis behind a horse or horse-driven vehicle, or, more dangerously, behind a motor vehicle.
Rules of the International Ski Federation.

Organized competitive skiing began in the nineteenth century, but skiing as a means of getting from place to place on snow began before the third millennium B.C. as crude rock engravings in Norway and Russia testify. A dozen skis of the Stone Age have been found in the peat bogs of Scandinavia and Finland. The oldest, 1·10 m. long and 20 cm. broad, was found at Hoting, Sweden, and is dated by pollen analysis at 2500 B.C. But early man had arrived in sub-Arctic regions long before this and devised snow-boards to help him in hunting game. The Hoting ski is of this type, short and broad, and similar boards are still used in Siberia. The underside is sometimes covered with animal pelt, which reduces clogging and prevents back-slipping.

In northern Europe longer and narrower skis were developed for faster sliding over all types of snow, whether soft, hard, or icy. Rock drawings at Rödöy, Tjötta, in northern Norway, show long skis on two men hunting elks. A pair of skis found at Kalvtråsk, Finland, dated at 2000 B.C., are over 2 m. long. The people who used them preceded the main migrations into Scandinavia and Finland from the south and east, but through subsequent population changes these two main types of ski persisted. Frequently the long ski would be used on one foot and the short broad one on the other, demanding a quite different technique. The broad Arctic type was the most useful for dragging loads, resembling the Eskimo snow-shoes used in Canada (the Eskimo had no wood and therefore did not invent a ski). The eastern, or Østerdal skis, one long and one short, enabled the skier to move over undulating ground with a kind of skating motion with the help of a single long pole. On mountainous ground the long, narrow Nordic skis were more practicable, and from these the modern downhill skis have evolved.

The first recorded written references to skiing are by Chinese historians of the T'ang Dynasty from the seventh to the tenth centuries A.D., who refer to their northern neighbours as 'Turks who ride horses of wood'. Herodotus, the Greek historian, writes of Abaris the Hyperborean 'who is said to have gone on his arrow all round the world without once easing'. The legend of men with 'horses' feet' is the most persistent. The term *hippopodes* (horse-footed) is used by the Romans, who also talk of *skridfinns* or *skrikfinns*, names used by Germanic tribes to describe the non-Germanic peoples of the north, both Lapps and Finns. Paulus Diaconus, a Lombard writing in Latin in the eighth century, explained the word as *skrika*, to leap: 'They hunt wild animals by leaping forward using contrivances of wood curved like a bow.'

An English map of 1280 in Hereford Cathedral shows a man on skis or skates in Norway and a horse-footed man in China. The Norse sagas contain a number of references to skiing, and the Norsemen who penetrated the British Isles brought their skis and techniques with them. Skiing was well known in northern Scotland and in use in Devonshire in the sixteenth century. Weardale miners went to work on 'skees' in the seventeenth century and were doing so until the Industrial Revolution brought roads and railways to isolated areas of Britain.

The first printed books with illustrations of skiing were published in the sixteenth century. The records and drawings were often fanciful, but two of the best-documented relate to turning-points in Norwegian and Swedish history where skiers played an important role. In 1205 the two-year-old Haakon, who was destined to be Norway's greatest formative leader, was rescued by skiers of the Birkenbeiner group (see BIRKENBEINERLAUF). Another romance surrounded the founding of the present kingdom of Sweden by Gustav Vasa, and this, too, is celebrated by a race, the VASALOP, a 90-km. (56 mile) mass-start event which has been run since 1922, commemorating an incident which took place in 1520.

In the fifteenth and sixteenth centuries there are numerous references to military campaigns by Finns, Norwegians, Swedes, and Russians involving ski troops. In this period very long skis, some up to 12 ft. (3·66 m.), were used, but more commonly a short fur-soled ski was used for pushing and a longer bare-soled ski on the other foot for sliding. There is no reference to skiing in Central Europe, other than a description by Francesco Negro, of Ravenna, in 1663-5, of an attempt to ski in the course of a northern journey. He is the first to describe in print a swing to a standstill. Otherwise there is no whisper of skiing in Switzerland, Austria, France, or Italy until it was introduced by the British middle class, expanding their opportunities for leisure and travel after the Industrial Revolution, and by Scandinavian visitors.

The steeper, more broken Alpine mountains were unsuited to the type of ski evolved in Russia and Scandinavia, nor did tribes who used these skis penetrate Central Europe. The inhabitants of the Alps thus grew up to accept immobility during the winter months. In Britain, where there was far less snow, Viking influences had created a mild tradition of snowcraft, and this was to be of considerable significance in the establishment of skiing as a sport and recreation during the nineteenth and twentieth centuries.

After 1800 there were increasing references to skiing as an enjoyment rather than a means of locomotion, especially in southern Norway. The people of Østerdal, north of Christiania (Oslo), produced a local hero, Trysil Knud, who in the course of a *schuss*, a straight downhill run, would pick up pieces of clothing, change his clothes, or carry a gourd of beer without spilling it. Norwegians introduced skiing to the United States. Gullik Knedsen and the brothers Ole and Ansten Nattestad from Numedal emigrated to Illinois, and used skis on the Rock Prairie at Beloit, near Chicago, in 1841. Their letters home encouraged THORENSEN to emigrate and the legend of 'Snowshoe Thompson' was born.

Skiing finally emerged as a sport with the invention of a method of holding the heel in place on a ski. The successful innovator was a farmer's son named NORDHEIM from Morgedal, in the TELEMARK region of southern Norway. In 1840 he had discovered the possibility of landing from a jump not on the flat but on a steep slope, so he can first be credited with the invention of modern ski jumping. His various experiments convinced him of the need to keep the heels firmly on the skis. Previously only a loose leather strap was used, which made it almost impossible to turn the skis by means of up and down weight movements. Nordheim soaked thin birch roots in hot water to make them flexible and bound heel and instep firmly to the ski. No less importantly he evolved a ski not much different in shape from a modern ski.

In 1866 the first ski races were held in the vicinity of Christiania (now Oslo), at Iverslokken, when Baekken, of Honefoss, won a purse for beating officers and students over a course with several small jumps. In 1867 the first American ski club, the Alturas Snowshoe Club, was formed at Laporte, California, and in many parts of the U.S.A. Norwegian immigrants and visitors began to expand the pastime. In 1868 the Telemark skiers skied 200 km. (124 miles) to Christiania and, in the face of some scepticism, demonstrated their skills, and for the next 20 years dominated Norwegian competition. In 1879 the brothers Torjus and Mikkel Hemmestveit, taught to ski by Nordheim, opened the first ski school in the world, while in the same year the first Swedish ski club, Stockholms Skidloparekulbb, was formed, and the first important ski events in Finland took place at Tyrnåvå Angeslevå.

In 1883 the Norwegian Ski Association (Foreningen til ski-idrettens fremme) was formed — the first national body in existence. In the same year, at Huseby, Norway, *langrenn*, or cross-country racing, and jumping were separated for competition purposes, though prizes were given for the combined result, the Nordic combination. Specialization in each discipline improved performance, but the combination preserved the traditional link between the two, and until the 1930s only the winner of it could become national champion in the Scandinavian countries and Finland. This has remained the shape of Nordic competition until the present day.

Nordheim's achievements meant that skiing, previously confined to gentle slopes, could be practised on almost any snow-covered ground. But it required an epoch-making journey, the first traverse of southern Greenland by the Norwegian explorer, NANSEN, and his detailed account of it, to fire the imagination of Norwegians, and then Germans, Swiss, and British, as to the possibilities of skiing. Nansen's trek took place in 1888, and his book *Paa Ski Over Grönland* was translated into English and German in 1891. Skis began to be imported in large quantities into Central Europe from Norway, the first laminated skis among them, and ski clubs were formed in Munich, Todtnau, Vienna, and Mürzzuschlag.

The British were particularly active in Switzerland. In 1888 Col. Napier took a pair of skis to Davos; Fox became the first to ski in Grindelwald in 1891; and Sir Arthur Conan Doyle skied from Davos to Arosa in 1894 and wrote about it in the *Strand* magazine. Soon a war of words began over the need for differing techniques, for not only were the Alpine slopes much steeper and more dangerous; even the snow was different. From October to April the Alps undergo much greater temperature changes than the Norwegian mountains; the depth of snow can be much greater and the consistency extremely varied. Newly-fallen snow in the Alps, it was observed, quickly changed to deep and heavy powder.

In 1896 ZDARSKY, who is now generally acknowledged as the father of Alpine skiing, published his *Lilienfelder Schilauf-Technik*, analysing the stem turn and its use in the Alps. An Austrian army officer, he set up a military ski school at Lilienfeld and until 1910 taught stemming, stem christianias, and telemarks. In the same period, a group of Englishmen led by the brothers E. C. and C. W. Richardson and CAULFIELD, experimented with techniques, linking the telemark and the Lilienfeld and improving on them. In 1910 Caulfield produced a book, *How to Ski*, which analysed ski dynamics clearly for the first time, explaining and illustrating unweighting, counter-rotation, and parallel swings. He insisted on the practical value of good style, and his rejection of the single-stick method of turning and braking spelt the end of this style.

Skiing and mountaineering were closely associated in the late nineteenth century. The golden age of summer mountaineering is usually held to have begun with Wills's ascent of the Wetterhorn in 1854, and to have ended with the climbing of the Matterhorn in 1865. The golden age of ski mountaineering began with the first ski traverse of the Oberland glaciers by the German, Paulcke, in 1897. In the next 20 years most of the classic pioneer ski expeditions were accomplished, including the traverse of the Dolomites, the high level route from Chamonix to Zermatt, and the traverse of the central Bernese Oberland range from Kandersteg to Meiringen.

In 1893 the first competitions in Central Europe were held in Mürzzuschlag on the Semmering, Steiermark, Austria, when a downhill race of about 700 m. (766 yds.) was won by Samson, a Norwegian. A dungheap covered with snow was used as a platform for 6 metre jumps.

British pioneers in Central Europe made their influence felt in many places in the early years of the twentieth century. ARNOLD LUNN, the inventor of the modern slalom, first put on skis at Chamonix in 1898. His father, HENRY LUNN, began to pioneer skiing holidays for a mass public in an unusual manner. As a Methodist returning from missionary work in India, he invited a number of churchmen of various denominations to a conference on Christian unity in Grindelwald. His successful arrangements prompted him to organize further, and he was the first to see the possibilities in winter sports. In 1902-3 he founded the Public Schools Alpine Sports Club at Adelboden, Switzerland, and subsequently he opened up Mürren, Kandersteg, Wengen, Montana, Villars, Lenzerheide, Klosters, and other places. He persuaded Lord Roberts of Kandahar to become a vice-president of the Public Schools Alpine Sports Club, and the name, Kandahar, was used for the oldest of challenge cups for downhill racing. (Subsequently the name was re-employed for the first racing club formed by the British in the Alps, in 1924.)

The first Swiss ski races were held in 1902, followed by the formation of the Davos English Ski Club in the same year and the Ski Club of Great Britain in the following year. The first ski tests were instituted by the British Ski Club in 1904.

Competition sprang up everywhere, but it was studded with controversy. Zdarsky was the first to experiment with races marked by gates, known as *torlaufs*, but not on a scale to have widespread effects. In January 1903 the first British ski race, the Public Schools Alpine Sports Club Challenge Cup, held at

Adelboden, was awarded on the result of a ski race, a skating competition, and a toboggan race. A Swiss who set the ski race thought the British too untrained to race uphill and too unskilled to race downhill, so he chose a field, put a flag in each corner, and told competitors to race round them. In 1904 the standard of skiing had improved and Rickmers set a course with 500 ft. (152 m.) of climbing, 1,000 ft. (305 m.) of downhill, and some level skiing. The race was won by Arnold Lunn. Gradually the need to specialize evolved, and while the Earl of Lytton gave his name to the skating cup, Lord Roberts of Kandahar awarded the skiing cup. The association of skiing and the name Kandahar thus began. In 1906 the Akademischer Ski Club, of Munich, organized downhill races at Sudefeld, near Bayrischzell, and there are five challenge cups for downhill racing which date back before the First World War. The Roberts of Kandahar held on 7 January 1911 is considered by many to be the most senior. It was a race across the Plaine Morte Glacier and then 4,000 ft. (1,200 m.) down to a point just below Montana (now Crans). The winner's time was 61 minutes, but half of that was spent in the traverse of the glacier.

Later in 1911 the words 'stem christiania' were first used to describe a more advanced type of turn (see above) in *Der Moderne Wintersport* by C. J. Luther, a Bavarian pioneer. The word 'slalom' also came into frequent use, but it meant different things to different people. The Morgedal skiers had added refinements to their downhill running and jumping by making elegant linked turns round bushes and trees. This they called a *slalaam* (from *sla*, meaning a smooth and slanting hill, and *laam*, a track down a smooth hill). 'Slalom' eventually passed into skiing language as meaning a race with many turns down a steep slope.

The First World War interrupted the natural evolution of the sport, but the use of ski troops, among them the French Chasseurs Alpins, the Italian Alpini, and the Austrian and German Alpenjäger, at least spread a knowledge of technique. Even the British formed a ski company from the 6th Yorkshire Regiment (skis had been used in Yorkshire for many years) who fought at Murmansk.

After the war, Arnold Lunn, dissatisfied with downhill as a test of all the qualities needed in skiing, and rejecting style as being only a means to an end, introduced the modern slalom. The British Ski Championship of 6 and 7 January 1921, at Scheidegg, Switzerland, was the first to be decided on downhill, and slalom was introduced as a separate competition in the championships at Mürren in 1923. In the same year the Ladies' Ski Club was formed at Mürren, the first in the world for women. In 1924 the Fédération Internationale de Ski (F.I.S.) was formed, with Col. Holmquist of Sweden as the first president. Later that year the Swiss University Ski Club (Der Schweizerische Akademische Ski Club) was founded, inspired chiefly by AMSTUTZ. The collaboration of Lunn and Amstutz, and the KANDAHAR SKI CLUB and the S.A.S., at Mürren, gave Alpine skiing form and substance. The first international open downhill and slalom competition was held in 1924, the downhill being from Scheidegg to Grindelwald, and the slalom at Mürren. The winner was A. Gertsch, of Wengen.

The innovations of the Alpine skiers were bitterly resented by the more conservative of the Scandinavian skiers, who in 1901 had begun to hold Nordic Games in which *langlauf* skiing and jumping played an important part. The games were held in 1905, 1909, 1913, 1917, 1922, and 1926, always in Sweden. Attempts were made to incorporate these in the OLYMPIC GAMES as early as 1912, but the Norwegian representatives, in particular, were strongly against. Competitions at the Holmenkollen stadium and jumping hill, built on the northern outskirts of Oslo in 1892, were considered of greater importance than those of the F.I.S., who introduced international championships in 1926. Until the outbreak of the Second World War, indeed, the Norwegians rated their own championships more highly than the Winter Olympic Games, first held in 1908 but incorporating *langlauf* skiing for the first time in 1924.

The Norwegian attitude derived from their strength in depth. Good places were more difficult to obtain at the Holmenkollen than at international competitions where entry was limited nation by nation. At the 1924 Olympic Games in Chamonix the newly-formed F.I.S. was permitted to hold a demonstration of downhill skiing. Norwegians condemned it variously as being 'not skiing', or too dangerous. The official booklet issued by the Norwegian Ski Association at that time said, 'After long and difficult ascents, an easy descent should be planned so that the runners may obtain rest.'

In 1926 the Ski Club of Great Britain issued a memorandum asking for the recognition of downhill and slalom by all national associations, but received no replies. It was not until 1929 that Austria awarded national championships for downhill, followed in 1930 by the Swiss, in 1932 by the French, and in 1933 by the Germans. In 1928, however, the F.I.S., meeting in St. Moritz, agreed to try out the British rules. Count Hamilton, the Swedish secretary of the F.I.S., was sufficiently sympathetic to the 'Kandahar revolution', as it became known, to visit Mürren and to report back favourably. Col. Holmquist and Maj. Øestgaard, Norwegian vice-president of F.I.S., were the two most influential Scandinavians who worked to the principle that if the federation was to remain a worldwide organization it needed to satisfy the aspirations of the countries who supported downhill.

At the F.I.S. meeting in Oslo in 1930, when Switzerland proposed the recognition of downhill and slalom, Maj. Øestgaard said that the Norwegians were not enthusiastic about slalom, but the northern associations had agreed to vote for recognition as these races were so popular in Central Europe. Thus Alpine skiing came formally into being, and the British, in particular Lunn, were rewarded when the Ski Club of Great Britain organized the first world championship in downhill and slalom at Mürren in 1931. Although the British were rebuked at the time for calling a F.I.S. championship a world event, the world title was recognized retrospectively in 1936. Mackinnon of Britain, who won both the downhill and slalom races, was thus the first women's world champion, at the age of 15, and Prager, of Switzerland, who won the downhill, the first men's champion.

Alpine skiing soon established itself as the prime skiing interest in Europe. The Austrian Federal Ski Instructors' course, with four months of theory, three of practical, and concluding with an examination, was introduced in 1927. France and Switzerland also developed teaching systems, and style, technique, and equipment moved far away from the Scandinavian concept. The acceptance of *langlauf* and Alpine as completely separate disciplines was confirmed by the 1936 Olympic Games at Garmisch-Partenkirchen, although, to the Alpine countries' surprise, Norwegians won the downhills. The medals, however, were awarded on the combined results of performances in downhill and slalom, and the gold thus went to two German skiers, Pfnur and Cranz.

The Norwegians, who stole most of the publicity, were outstanding all-rounders. BIRGER RUUD was the world ski-jumping champion of 1931 and 1935, setting a world record of 92 m. (100·6 yds.) in 1934. From 1935 to 1937 he was frequently in Austria and Germany on business, and thus became an outstanding downhiller, winning at the Winter Olympics at Garmisch. Nilsen, who won the women's downhill, had held the world skating records for 500, 1,000, 1,500, and 5,000 metres. Some 70,000 spectators watched the men's slalom event that year, and though allowance must be made for the amount of money poured into the organization as part of the National Socialists' effort to gain world prestige, the games marked the emergence of skiing as a major spectator attraction in modern sport.

Three developments in the 1930s were greatly to change Alpine skiing. In 1936 Kneissl, the Austrian ski manufacturers, introduced the Splitkein-ski, a ski with 18 wooden lamina compared with two or three lamina previously. Manufacturers thus began to exercise much more control over the physical characteristics of skis, and coloured, metal, and fibreglass skis all appeared in the 1950s. In the middle 1930s, too, the Ski Club of Great Britain encouraged the development of the safety binding — a simple strap pulling the heel cable off the boot in a forward fall. Bindings became increasingly sophisticated, allowing sideways, forward, and backward release, and in the 1960s heel and toe 'step-in' bindings came into general use. Whatever the device, the principle was the same: if a skier fell the binding of boot to ski released him before bones were broken. It could not work in every case, but as skiing became a mass recreation after the Second World War the safety binding was of major importance in keeping down the casualty rate.

The third and most significant development in the 1930s was the introduction of the ski lift, although little was made of it at the time. Skiers until then were accustomed to climbing, perhaps for an hour or more, to achieve a downhill run in untracked snow lasting only a few minutes. Trains such as that from Wengen to Kleine Scheidegg and Grindelwald in the Bernese Oberland became increasingly used, but they had been installed primarily for the summer visitors. In 1935 the first T-bars were installed in Switzerland, principally serving the practice slopes. An Englishman, Edlin, who lived in Davos during the winter, was the prime mover in 1932 in the building of the PARSENN funicular, and he devised and equipped the first Alpine rescue patrol.

On the Parsenn, methods of marking, patrolling, and safeguarding downhill routes were devised which were copied all over the Alps. This was the beginning of *piste* skiing which, after the Second World War, brought a revolution in the tourist business of Alpine nations and in skiing technique. Chair-lifts, cabin-lifts, and tows of all descriptions — T-bar, belt, and 'soup-plate' — opened up immense areas of the Alps. Skiing, instead of being a sport for the mountain-dweller or for the privileged few, became a mass recreation, in the U.S.A. as well as in Europe, helped on by cheap transport and the package holiday.

Skiing techniques changed, sometimes with bewildering rapidity, as well-prepared tracks with hard-packed snow encouraged higher speeds. SCHNEIDER, an Austrian from St. Anton, was the first to influence technique in the 1930s with his concentration on the stem christiania. ALLAIS of France, world champion in 1937, then evolved a French style which concentrated on rotation and heel lift. After the Second World War, racers continued to lead style. Eriksen delighted Norwegians by winning the Alpine world championship at Are in 1954, thus proving that the mother country of skiing could also excel in the modern forms. Eriksen was especially strong in slalom and giant slalom, a race introduced in 1949 and blending the characteristics of downhill and slalom.

Between 1956 and 1958, the Austrian, SAILER, won seven out of eight world titles including all three Olympic gold medals at Cortina d'Ampezzo in 1956, and he introduced the *wedeln* style to a wide public. His feat was not equalled until 1968, when KILLY brought France's period of international supremacy to a climax by winning all three Olympic gold medals at Grenoble. Killy, with his ankle flexions and other tricks of balance, introduced further new ideas into ski-racing technique. But France's prominence in this period owed a great deal to another revolution — in psychological and physical fitness and training as introduced by BONNET, director of the national teams.

Sharply accelerating standards of competition meant that skiers in the 1930s won by whole seconds, in the 1950s by tenths of seconds, and in the 1960s by hundredths. Wind-cheating clothes were developed in shiny synthetic materials to reduce drag, and so perhaps gain a precious tenth of a second, and American skiers went so far as to undertake wind-tunnel tests in an aircraft research laboratory. The waxing of skis developed from an art almost to a science. Crash helmets became compulsory headgear in downhill, where speeds of up to 75 or 80 m.p.h. (120–128 km./h.) became general in men's races.

Ski racing achieved a much clearer format in 1967 with the introduction of the World Alpine Ski Cup. Prior to this, skiers raced on a circuit which had grown *ad hoc*, events such as the ARLBERG-KANDAHAR, the Lauberhorn, and the Hahnenkamm acquiring prestige by virtue of their seniority, their organization, and the quality of the courses. The F.I.S. divided the races into A and B grades, and awarded points to skiers according to results. The more points a skier earned the better his start position and the better the quality of the snow he raced on. The World Cup, privately sponsored by a mineral water firm and *L'Équipe*, the French sporting newspaper, but given the support of the F.I.S., introduced the principle of continuous, linked competition over a season.

Scoring in slalom, giant slalom, and downhill at various nominated events was instituted, the cup being awarded to the man or woman returning the best over-all score at the end of the season. Cups are also awarded to the winners in each of the three disciplines. Under the rules applying in 1973-4, scoring is based on the placings of the first ten racers. Twenty-five points are given for first place in World Cup A races, then 20, 15, 11, 8, 6, 4, 3, 2, and 1 point for tenth place. The season is divided into three stages. Among the men any four of six races in December are allowed to count, six out of ten in January, and three out of five in March. With the women it is two out of four in December, six out of ten in January, and two out of four in March. In specified races, points count double for a competitor in the first ten of two disciplines. Men must have 30 F.I.S. points or less to qualify, and women 50. Organizing countries are allowed at least six competitors, and each country without individually qualified racers may enter two competitors as it deems fit. Doubling the points was introduced in 1973-4 to encourage the all-round skier further. The first World Cup winners were Killy (France) in the men's event and GREENE (Canada) in the women's. SCHRANZ (Austria) won the men's in 1969 and 1970, and Theoni (Italy) in 1971, 1972, and 1973. A World Cup for teams was introduced in 1967-8, but because of scoring problems due to inequality of team sizes this did not have the same impact as the individual cups. Austria won in 1969 and 1973 and France in 1967, 1968, 1970, 1971, and 1972.

The F.I.S., which by 1973-4 had 46 member nations, is responsible for the rules of both Alpine and Nordic skiing. Besides authorizing events and issuing an annual calendar, licensing racing skiers through national federations, and awarding points for performances according to the category of race (these points governing starting positions), it organizes its own world championships every fourth year. These championships alternate with the Winter Olympic Games, which count as a world championship for Alpine and Nordic events, to obtain a two-yearly championship cycle. Only four skiers per nation can enter.

The principal men's events in Nordic skiing are Nordic combination, 15, 30, and 50 km. (9·3, 18·6, and 31 miles respectively) cross-country, 4 × 10 km. (4 × 6·2 miles) relay, and jumping. Norwegians dominated the combined event before the Second World War, winning the Olympic gold medal in 1924, 1928, and 1932 to 1936. They suffered their first Olympic defeat when Finland took first and second places in 1948. In championship events the outstanding men's Nordic skier has been JERNBERG (Sweden). Women's Nordic events were introduced in 1952 concurrently with the Winter Olympic Games in Oslo, and they now include 5 and 10 km. (3·1 and 6·2 miles) cross-country, and the 3 × 5 km. (3 × 3·1 miles) relay. Russian women dominated the women's events in the 1950s and 1960s, although there was a break in their success at the 1968 Olympic Games in Grenoble, as women skiers from Norway and Sweden, the traditional home of Nordic skiing, began to challenge more strongly.

Norwegians set the standards in ski jumping for many years, but in the 1960s Central European countries produced many good jumpers. The F.I.S. at their congress in 1971 agreed to hold a world championship series in ski flying, the first being held at Planica, in Yugoslavia, in 1972, and further championships biennially.

Until 1950, when giant slalom was introduced, Alpine competition was limited to slalom and downhill, with Alpine combination medals awarded on the basis of performances in both. Alpine skiing careers have tended to be shorter than Nordic. Allais (France) won the slalom, downhill, and combined, at Chamonix in 1937. Sailer (Austria) won seven out of eight gold medals in 1956 and 1958, and Killy all four in 1968. The most successful woman skier of the 1930s was Cranz (Germany). In this period the championships were held annually, and Miss Cranz won the title in 1934, 1935, 1937, 1938, and 1939. France had no woman world champion until GOITSCHEL, who took the title in three successive championships, 1962, 1964, and 1966. The only champion, men's or women's, from a lowland country is Miss Pinching (Great Britain), who won at Innsbruck in 1936. The outstanding national success after the Second World War was by France, taking 18 out of the 24 medals in 1966 at Portillo, Chile.

At the world championships at Portillo, at Ortisei, Italy, in 1970, and at the Grenoble Winter Olympic Games of 1968, F.I.S. introduced an elimination system in the men's slalom. The top-seeded skiers were spread among groups of six, the first two going through to the final, repêchages being held among the remainder to select a third skier in each six to join the others in the final. F.I.S. introduced this in an effort to spread the chances, for previously only the first group of 15 stood a serious chance of winning because courses deteriorated so quickly. Leading skiers opposed the change, producing a written protest at Ortisei. They claimed that, as they worked all season for their seeded positions, it was unfair to deprive them of their advantage at the world championships. But an elimination system was retained for the 1972 Winter Olympic Games at Sapporo.

With the advent of television and a mass public following, ski racing in the 1960s became steadily more professional in outlook and rewards. In 1969 the F.I.S. tried to rationalize the situation by deciding at their Barcelona congress to permit skiers to receive 'broken time' payments from their national associations. It had already become a widespread practice for skiers to receive money from equipment manufacturers for using their products. The F.I.S.'s action was undoubtedly a challenge to the INTERNATIONAL OLYMPIC COMMITTEE, whose president, BRUNDAGE, considered many of the practices in ski racing to be professional. At the Sapporo Games in 1972, Schranz, Austria's leading skier, was disqualified by the I.O.C. for being, in their view, the most blatant and outspoken critic of the movement's amateur ideals among skiing competitors.

The increasingly professional outlook of skiers resulted in many tensions, and in 1969-70 a formal professional circuit outside the control of the F.I.S. was launched. Its promoters, with an eye to television's needs, experimented with a new format for slalom whereby skiers — among them Perillat (France) and Zimmerman (Austria), two former champions — raced on parallel courses on a knock-out basis.

In general ski racing stayed within the control of national associations and of such groups as the Organisation de Ski de Pays Alpine, an influential association of six Alpine countries (France, Austria, Switzerland, Germany, Italy, and Yugoslavia) which guides and advises on the Central European ski-racing circuit. By the 1970s many national associations had developed complex relationships with government and industry. The 1968 Winter Olympic Games at Grenoble, in which Alpine skiing played a major part, required an overall budget of $100 million.

In contrast, Nordic skiing developed along conservative lines after the split from Alpine skiing in 1930. From 1900 until the 1950s the Holmenkollen events retained a similar form — a cross-country race of 17 to 18 km. (about 11 miles) and a jumping event forming the combined, in addition to a 30 km. (18·6 miles) race, lengthened in 1902 to 50 km. (31 miles). In 1950 the F.I.S. introduced 15, 30, and 50 km. (9·3, 18·6, and 31 mile) races and specialization increased.

Competitive Alpine skiing now takes place in almost all developed countries with mountains which have reliable snow coverage for some months during the year. The sport is most advanced in the Alpine countries (Switzerland, Austria, France, Italy, Germany, and Yugoslavia) and in the U.S.A., Canada, Norway, and Sweden. During the 1960s many other countries improved their amenities, notably Spain, Poland, Czechoslovakia, Russia, Scotland, Chile, Argentina, Australia, and New Zealand. In Nordic skiing, Norway, Sweden, Finland, and Russia began to find their pre-eminence challenged by Central European and Alpine countries, especially in ski-jumping, where the use of slopes made of artificial fibres (usually a mat of P.V.C. brushes or bristles laid in a diamond-shaped pattern) helped to improve general standards. East and West Germany, Czechoslovakia, Poland, and Austria made notable advances. The proliferation in northern Europe of artificial slopes such as that at HILL END, Edinburgh, has given young skiers practical experience and encouraged a much wider participation in Alpine skiing by holidaymakers, but it made little practical difference to top-class racers with access to natural snow all the year round.

Until recently most of the top races were in Europe, but the U.S.A., where many new facilities have been developed, now stages some of the leading races at the end of the northern hemisphere season. With the advent of skiing in Australia, New Zealand, and South America, there is now competition skiing all the year round.

Conservation lobbies have checked skiing development in some places, principally in the U.S.A. Denver was forced to give up the 1976 Winter Olympic Games because of opposition from local people at the cost and at damage to the environment which it was said would result. Innsbruck, which staged the 1964 Games, successfully applied to stage the 1976 Games.

The New Official Austrian Ski System, ed. Austrian Association of Professional Ski Teachers (1958); Howard Bass, *Winter Sport* (1966); Honoré Bonnet, *Ski the Experts' Way* (English ed. 1966); Michael Brady, *Nordic Ski-ing* (1966); Vivian Caulfield, *How to Ski* (1910); Stein Eriksen, *Come Ski with Me* (1966); Mark Heller, *Ski* (1969); Georges Joubert and Jean Vuarnet, *How to Ski the New French Way* (1967); Erich Kamper, *Lexikon der Olympischen Winter Spiele* (1964); Arnold Lunn, *History of Ski-ing* (1953); *The Book of European Ski-ing*, ed. Malcolm Milne and Mark Heller (1966); Fridtjof Nansen, *By Ski over Greenland* (English ed. 1891); Matthias Zdarsky, *Lilienfelder Schilauf-Technik* (1896). *British Ski Year-*

Book, annually; *Kandahar Magazine*, annually; *Ski-ing* (U.S.A.); *Ski* (U.S.A.).
GOVERNING BODY (WORLD): Fédération Internationale de Ski, Stora Nygatan 20, III, 27 Stockholm, Sweden.

SKIING, Grass, see GRASS SKIING.

SKIING, Water, see WATER SKIING.

SKILTON, ROBERT (1938-   ), Australian Rules footballer, winner of three CHARLES BROWNLOW MEDALS, he was a rover for South Melbourne in the VICTORIAN FOOTBALL LEAGUE. By his retirement in September 1971 he had participated in 237 matches for his club, for whom he won the 'best and fairest' award nine times.

SKIN DIVING, see UNDERWATER SWIMMING.

SKITTLES is a game played with pins and balls, discs, or cheeses or other similar projectiles, the aim being to knock over the pins with the missiles. There are several varieties of the game, and the dimensions of the equipment vary a great deal in the British Isles and on the Continent. Both men and women play.

The game may be played with any number per side, and the variants contain either a series of individual contests, with a final decision based on the number of individual games won, or on the total number of pins knocked down by a team. A fundamental difference in custom is that whereas one game depends on the total number of pins knocked down by a specified number of balls, another version is decided on the number of balls or deliveries required to knock down a set number of pins.

The game began out of doors but is now played mainly indoors. In the main centres, notably the West Country of England and Wales, London, and the north of England, the skittle alleys are attached to inns, public houses, or clubs. In places where skittles is played in well-organized leagues, there is frequently also a flourishing complex of friendly teams.

Gambling, which several times caused the game to be outlawed, does take place, but it is usually for low stakes. Some friendly teams use the result to decide which team shall pay for the supper or the 'sticker-up', or 'setter-up' (the man who puts up the pins after each 'hand').

Local and small variations of the method of play tend to occur almost from one alley to another. A typical pattern is a conventional one from the West Country. The pins are set at one end of an alley in diamond formation, with one corner facing the skittler. There will be six, eight, or ten players per side, and usually the team playing at home will begin. The first player throws one ball at the pins and, providing he has thrown legally, he waits while the sticker-up clears away the fallen pins, then throws his second ball. When the fallen pins have again been cleared, his last ball is thrown. If he knocks down all nine pins with one ball — known variously as a 'flopper' or 'floorer' — the pins are all replaced and he continues as previously. Thus a maximum

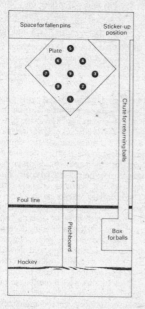

SKITTLES ALLEY
The pins are shown set up in diamond formation: (1) front; (2) right front second, or quarter; (3) right corner; (4) back right second; (5) back; (6) back left second; (7) left corner; (8) left front second; (9) landlord. The hockey is a thin piece of wood about 2½ in. (63 mm.) high.

score per three balls is 27. If a player knocks down all nine pins using his first two balls — termed a 'spare' — the pins are replaced and he takes a throw at the full set again. Thus the maximum for a spare is 18. The maximum in any other case is, of course, 9. In the south-west of England, where pins and balls are larger, and pins placed more closely, scores tend to be much higher than on the wooden alleys of such places as South Wales, Bristol, and Gloucestershire.

All the players of one side throw three balls

each, then the opposition does the same. This sequence continues until every player has completed his 'hand' which would normally be a total of 18 or 21 balls, according to local custom.

The legality of a delivery varies from place to place and alley to alley. In some places, a line is drawn across the alley, behind which the ball must pitch to be legal. In others, a long, narrow wooden or iron board is let into the alley, parallel with its length, on which the ball must pitch before moving towards the pins. This is called the pitchboard. The surface of the alley is usually wood, asphalt, or, sometimes, clay; the pins are of wood (apple or elm) and the balls of a very heavy wood (lignum vitae is common) or hard rubber.

As there is no governing body for skittles in the British Isles, rules and practices vary widely over even a few miles of country. One of the more comprehensive rule-books for a local league is that issued by the Bridgwater Town and District Skittle League (Somerset), and its tolerances underline the differences in equipment and situations:

No alley shall be more than 80 feet (24·38 m.) or less than 50 feet (15·24 m.) from the hockey to the front pin spot.
(The hockey is a small raised piece of wood at the skittler's end of the alley on which he can rest his heels and get some purchase for the under-arm delivery of the ball.)
The plate on which the nine pins are to be erected shall be 3 ft. 6 in. (1·067 m.) square and set at right-angles to the centre of the pitchboard.
The pitchboard shall be of wood 18 ft. to 24 ft. (5·486–7·315 m.) in length and 15 in. to 18 in. (381–457 mm.) in width.

Wide tolerance is also allowed in other equipment. The balls, made of lignum vitae, have a maximum diameter of 6⅜ in. (162 mm.) and a minimum 1 in. smaller (137 mm.). The pins, in this league, must all be of the same size, shape, and weight, which is an unusual ruling. The maximum sizes are 12½ in. (317·5 mm.) long, 6 in. (152·4 mm.) in diameter at the belly, and 3¼ in. (82·6 mm.) ends. These rules are more rigorous than most in the south-west, but their latitude is significant.

In some alleys, rebounds of pins or balls off the sides of the walls do not prevent the pins knocked down from being scored; in many, they do. Pins are normally allowed to remain on the plate until they stop rolling, often knocking down other pins. When all is still, the fallen pins are removed and play continues. Some alleys have a camber, which complicates performance, and makes scoring more difficult. A pronounced camber is a feature of many of the alleys in the Bath area of Somerset, and, significantly, this is one of the places where it is permissible to throw the ball so that it hits the pins before hitting the floor. Another very unusual practice of this area is the method of deciding matches. Three balls from each player are termed a 'leg' and teams are required to 'show a leg' to start the game. The other side then skittles. The highest total wins the first leg, and the game continues with the teams playing alternately until one side has won five legs. Thus a game can be either five or nine legs long. Sometimes, a team can lose the match in terms of legs, while hitting a higher total of pins than its opponents. This is rewarded by a consolation league point.

Different areas have various names for the equipment and for the various combinations of pins left standing after a ball has struck. Pins 7 and 3 are called 'corners' in some places, 'coppers' in others. The centre pin, 9, is usually called the 'landlord', and is often taller than the rest. The 'running three' denotes either pins 1, 2, and 3, or 1, 8 and 7 remaining. The object in these alleys is to hit the front pin on the side sufficiently accurately for the ball to knock down half the pins, leaving the falling front pin to take the others. A 'spare cop' is a strike where the remaining pins are close together, and thus easily knocked over to get a spare. A 'guts', one of the worst cops, occurs when pins 1, 5, and 9 are removed by the first ball. This leaves almost no chance of a spare and demands considerable accuracy with the other two balls if a reasonable score, say 7, is to be attained.

In the main, it is possible to get good results even if the front pin is missed with the first ball. Good cops can be achieved by suitably hitting the seconds or even the corners, but this is prevented in some leagues by the nomination system. In this, no score is made until the front pin has been felled. When that has been floored, the next object must be nominated, making for a much more demanding game. Frequently, the ball goes right through the pins without touching one, known as a 'bolter' in several areas. In some Gloucestershire public houses, two alleys are used side by side, to expedite a game. Here the usual form is 10 players a side throwing 30 balls (10 hands) each.

Although the normal delivery is to bowl the ball lob-style under-arm, some places, notably in Dorset, have developed a fashion of throwing the ball two-handed, and ending on the stomach in the style of a rugby scrum half. Women can control the balls in most alleys, and indeed, many women's leagues exist.

Devil Among the Tailors. The most widely known of indoor skittles games is called 'table skittles', or, less frequently, 'Devil Among the Tailors'. This is a compendium of pastimes containing elements of skittles, ringing the bull, and the maypole. The object is to knock down pins with a small ball attached to a short pole by a wire which swings in an arc. Dimensions vary widely, but a small platform roughly 1 ft. (305 mm.) square forms a base for nine pins set, diamond fashion, in the middle of an open box. At the side of the box the pole, about 1 yd. (914 mm.) high, has a swivelling device at the top which allows the ball at the end of the wire to be swung around and into the pins. Pins and balls are made of hard wood. An interesting departure from the normal scoring is that in some games the domino system is used, where only multiples of three and five are counted. The base of the box where the pins fall is often covered with baize, to make the game quieter, and a scoring board of holes on the style of cribbage is usually to be found at one end of the board.

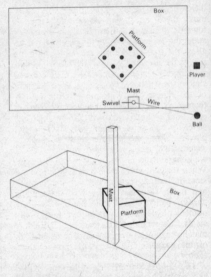

TABLE SKITTLES BOARD
Plan view (*top*) shows position of pins on platform; ball on end of wire swings round and into the pins. Elevation (*below*) shows mast to which wire and ball are attached.

Hood skittles is an indoor game using nine pins, about 6 in. (152 mm.) high, placed in the usual diamond formation at thigh-height from the floor on a table suitably protected with leather pads. Stitched and leather-padded 'cheeses' are thrown at these pins from various distances, usually in the region of 3 yds. (2·743 m.) and scoring rebounds from the sides of the alley or the fallen pins are allowed, adding to the skill of the game.

Games are usually played on an individual basis, with three cheeses from each player deciding who has won one 'life'. Five lives normally decide the game, but in some localities, team totals are used to decide the winners. An unusual method is sometimes employed to settle tied 'lives'. To win a replayed life, a player must hit more than his opponent with both his first cheese and his total of three cheeses. This game is played mainly in the English counties of Rutland, Leicestershire, and Northamptonshire.

Long alley. This most northerly of the popular skittles games is confined largely to Nottinghamshire and north Leicestershire. It is one of the oldest forms, dating from the thirteenth century, and the equipment has long remained unchanged. It has much in common with other versions of the game, but there are differences in detail. Like most very early pins, these are broad based, and tapered towards the head, sometimes iron-bound for strength. From the bowler's position on the alley, the first eight paces are cobbled but the rest of the area (12 yds. — 10·973 m. — long) is smoothly covered either by a deep crust of slate or heavy boards to ensure a true bounce of the cheese. As with most skittle games, there is a trough at the end to accept the fallen pins, and a chute at the side down which the setter-up can send the cheeses back to the players. The cheeses are most unusual in shape, like a capsule with rounded ends, weighing in the region of 4 lb. (1·814 kg.). When thrown, each cheese must pitch on the smooth-floored section beyond the cobbles and much skill can be used in making the cheese change course from the bounce. Any number of players may take part, but usually six or eight members of a team play individual matches against an opponent. The usual limit of the game is five 'legs' of three cheeses each.

Old English skittles, one of the more skilful and popular varieties, is played in London, and has the advantage of a ruling body, the Amateur Skittles Association, formed in 1900, running competitions and keeping records. The equipment used is generally the same size as in the south-west, except that the 'cheeses' are much bigger than the balls, are in the form of a discus (thickened in the centre), and have a bias. The heaviest weighs more than 12 lb. (5·4 kg.) and the pins, made of hornbeam, can be as high as 14½ in. (368 mm.) and 6¾ in. (171 mm.) in diameter.

The playing alley, similar to the West Country type, is shorter at 21 ft. (6·4 m.), and the frame, or plate, of nine skittles is larger at 4 ft. 6 in. (1·37 m.) across. The area used for play, the run, is often sunk below floor level,

and it is an offence to step outside this during play. Also, the back foot must not cross the double line at the end of the run before the cheese is released. The object is to hit the front pin full toss without touching the alley, and almost any shot is possible. The number of throws required to knock down all nine pins are scored, and matches are played as a series of individual contests. If a pin is standing after four throws, the thrower is given a penalty of 5 points, but, by courtesy, if a single pin is standing, it is deemed to be downed by the next throw. Thus if a player gets a floorer, his opponent must do likewise to halve that 'frame' or 'chalk'. Seven frames are usually played in league matches, and eleven in some competitions. There is a selection of terms for the various pin formations on the alley, some of the more polite being London Bridge, Hell's Gate, The Rooks, and Novice's Three.

Throwing projectiles at other stationary, but movable, objects with the idea of knocking them down is among the very oldest diversions of man. Items similar to present-day skittle pins were found by the Egyptologist, Sir Flinders Petrie, in a child's grave, the burial date being estimated as 5200 B.C. According to the San Diego Museum, California, the ancient Polynesians played a game called *Ula Maika*, where stones had to be bowled at objects 60 ft. (18·288 m.) distant (the length of today's tenpin BOWLING alleys).

Modern skittles, however, derived from the German peasant's habit of carrying a flat-bottomed club or *kegel* at all times. In the third and fourth centuries, these were used variously as weapons or for exercise but were also employed by monks to give simple religious illustrations. The club was stood on its end and represented a sin or temptation; the peasant was told to throw a stone at it. On the result of the throw depended either praise or admonition from the monks, and gradually this became a pastime enjoyed by increasing numbers of players. By the Middle Ages it was a well-established game in much of Europe and England, its popularity being underlined by the frequency with which it was outlawed in various places. In 1365 Richard III passed an edict forbidding the 'hurling of stones' and other sports because he believed the practice of archery would suffer. In 1541 the game of loggats, another forerunner of skittles, was forbidden. About 1800, such was the effect of widespread gambling that the magistrates caused all the skittles frames in or about the City of London to be taken up, and prohibited the playing of games closely allied to skittles such as dutch-pins, ninepins, or long alley (see above). In an attempt to circumvent the letter of the law, a game called nine-holes was introduced, known popularly as 'Bubble the Justice'. Strutt observes that some sources called the game 'Bumble Puppy' and adds, 'the vulgarity of the term is well adapted to the company by whom it is usually practised'.

In America, by 1840, gambling had led to the prohibition of ninepins in Connecticut and later in New York, the game having been taken there in the first place by the Dutch, and the addition of one more pin to defeat the law gave the U.S.A. tenpin bowling, the commonest form of skittling now known. The German *kegel* was translated into French as *quille*, and a very early English form of the game was known variously as kayles, cayles, or keiles. Gradually, the name was corrupted to kettle or kittle pins, and hence to skittles. Kayles consisted of a line of wooden pins, tapering towards the top, with one taller than the rest. The number varied, but was usually either six or eight. A club or cudgel was thrown at them to knock them down. Closh was a similar game, except that a bowl was thrown instead of a truncheon. Loggats was played often with the bones of sheep; hence in *Hamlet*, Shakespeare says 'Did these bones cost no more the breeding, but to play at loggats with them?' One of Shakespeare's editors, Sir Thomas Hanmer, says of loggats: 'It is the game which is now called kittle pins in which the boys often make use of bones instead of wooden pins, throwing at them with another bone instead of bowling.' It was a favourite sport at sheep-shearing festivals, the usual prize being a black fleece which the winner gave to one of the farmer's maidservants on condition that she knelt down upon it and allowed herself to be kissed by all the young men present.

Ninepins, a game with three rows of three pins each set in diamond formation towards the player, differed markedly from skittles. After the first throw, made from an agreed distance, the player could approach the frame of pins, and 'tip', or throw, at the remaining pins from close range. Dutch-pins was similar, with higher, more slender pins and with the refinement that the biggest pin — the 'king-pin' — could decide the game. Normally 31 pins down was the target, but if the 'kingpin' alone was felled, that won the game. Four-corners had another slight difference inasmuch as the four pins were placed at the corners of the frame, the object being to knock them down in the fewest throws of the bowls, which weighed as much as 6 or 8 lb. (2·7–3·6 kg.).

One of the really difficult indoor adaptations of the skittles pattern was half-bowl, which was prohibited by Edward IV (1461-83). Fifteen small pins were arranged mainly in a circle but with one in the centre and two at the rear. A small semi-sphere of wood was bowled at them, and its bias had to be used very skilfully, since nothing counted until the rear pin had been knocked down. Again, the target figure was 31 pins.

Difficulties in providing smooth surfaces for the balls to run on have been overcome by several developments, notably by lobbing the ball full toss at the pins, by employing disc-shaped projectiles more easily made than spheres, and by reducing the scale of the equipment sufficiently to facilitate play indoors and even on table tops.

Various differences in the alleys, the projectiles, and the pins can be readily appreciated in Old English skittling, tenpin, and long alley, while variants of indoor skittles can still be traced in the games of hood skittles and 'Devil Among the Tailors'.

Especially in England, skittles of one form or another has had a chequered legal career, but its greatest impetus came after the opening of several alleys in London in 1455, the eventual result of more contact between English and European nobility. Henry VIII installed the latest equipment of the day in Westminster Palace, and thereafter even punitive laws failed to eradicate the game.

Skittles is widely played on the Continent, although the game of tenpin bowling has taken over large areas. Some 250,000 active players regularly take part in organized skittles matches in East and West Germany, France, Italy, Romania, Bulgaria, Switzerland, Sweden, Czechoslovakia, Yugoslavia, and Austria. Teams are arranged in 6 to 12 each side, according to region and alley, and every two years the national champions take part in team and individual championships. Both men and women take part in a pastime that has been much changed in equipment since the the distant past. Now most skittles and balls are made of plastic and the pins are set up automatically. The alleys, which are 64 ft. (19·5 m.) long, and about 5 ft. (1·5 m.) wide, are of asphalt.

As befits the country which first took skittles to the U.S.A., under the guise of 'dutch-pins', the game commands much attention in the Netherlands. The Koninklijke Nederlandsche Kegelbond looks after some 9,000 players, representing 700 clubs, of which 240 are ladies' teams.

Timothy Finn, *The Watney Book of Pub Games* (1966); Christina Hole, *English Sports and Pastimes* (1949); J. Strutt, *The Sports and Pastimes of the People of England* (1801; ed. 1903).

SKOBLIKOVA, LYDIA (1939-   ), ice speed-skater for the U.S.S.R. She became the first person to win four gold medals at one WINTER OLYMPIC GAMES in 1964 at Innsbruck,

coming first in all four women's distances
—500, 1,000, 1,500, and 3,000 metres, setting three record times in the process, and all
in the space of four days. She also won two
gold medals in the previous Winter Olympics,
for the 1,500 and 3,000 metres in 1960 at
Squaw Valley, California, U.S.A. She was
twice world champion, 1963-4.

SKOGLUND, PHILIP (1937-   ), lawn
BOWLS player and winner of the New Zealand
singles title on several occasions, he represented his country at singles in the inaugural
world championships at KYEEMAGH, N.S.W.,
in 1966 and in the 1970 COMMONWEALTH
GAMES at Edinburgh. Although a fine stylist,
he is best known for his powerful firing shots:
with one of them he has been known to cannon
the jack 60 yds. (55 m.) from the point of
impact.

SLAVIA SOFIA, Bulgarian women's BAS-
KETBALL club. In 1959, Slavia became the
first winners of the women's EUROPEAN CUP
FOR CHAMPION CLUBS. They again won the
title in 1963, and were the only club, apart
from DAUGAWA (T.T.T.) RIGA, to win the title
in the first 15 years of the competition's history.

SLINGSBY, F. N. (1894-1973), was the British founder and manager of Slingsby Sailplanes (see GLIDING) from 1930 to 1966. He
designed and constructed Falcon II and III,
Cadet, Tutor, Kite, Gull, the T21, T31, Eagle
two-seaters, the famous Skylark series—of
which Skylark 3 made the first 500 km. (310·7
miles) flight in Britain, in 1955—and the
Dart.

SMAGA, NIKOLAI (1938-   ), race
walker for the U.S.S.R. who ranks with GOL-
UBNICHI as the current top Russian performer
at 20 km. A specialist at this distance, Smaga
won the LUGANO CUP final in 1967, the
European title in 1971, was third in the Olympics in 1968 and occupied the same position in
the European Games of both 1966 and
1969. He has been a consistent international performer, possessing an adequate
technique.

SMALL, JOHN (1737-1826), an original
member of the HAMBLEDON CRICKET CLUB
around 1755. He continued playing CRICKET at
the highest level until he was 61, and was the
finest batsman of the period, spanning the
transition from crooked to straight bats (c.
1775). His sons, John and Eli, were later prominent cricketers.

SMALL-BORE PISTOL SHOOTING, see
SHOOTING, PISTOL.

SMALL-BORE RIFLE SHOOTING, see
SHOOTING, RIFLE: SMALL-BORE.

SMILDZINYA, SKAIDRITE (1943-   ),
Russian woman BASKETBALL player. A member of the DAUGAWA (T.T.T.) RIGA club,
Smildzinya first played for the U.S.S.R. at the
age of 16, in 1959. She stands 6 ft. 2 in. (1·88
m.) tall and became captain of the U.S.S.R. in
1968.
  Smildzinya was elected 'Miss Basketball'
at the 1964 world championships in Peru.

SMITH, ARTHUR ROBERT (1933-   ),
RUGBY UNION wing three-quarter for EDIN-
BURGH WANDERERS, Ebbw Vale, Cambridge
University, Scotland, and British LIONS. A
strong runner and defensive player, he made
33 appearances for his country (a record for a
Scottish back) and was captain of the British
Lions touring party to South Africa in 1962.

SMITH, CECIL (1904-   ), American
POLO player who was handicapped at 10 goals
for 25 years. One of the world's best players
of the hard-hitting, galloping game, he never
played for the U.S.A. against Argentina or
England but appeared three times against
Mexico. He was in the winning team in the
U.S. championship five times between 1937
and 1960.

SMITH, DON R. (1938-   ), British
MOTOR-CYCLE TRIALS rider who won the first
European trials championship before the contest was officially approved by the Fédération
Internationale Motocycliste. After winning the
Henry Groutars trophy in 1964, he lost the title
to FRANKE, of West Germany, but recaptured
it in 1966 and 1967 and gained championship
status, with a Spanish Montesa, in 1969.

SMITH, HARVEY (1938-   ), British
show jumping (see EQUESTRIAN EVENTS)
rider. He competed at numerous international
shows from 1957, when he first jumped into
the limelight on a horse called Farmer's Boy.
He achieved international success on a variety
of mounts—including O'Malley, Harvester,
Madison Time (his mount for the 1968 Mexico
OLYMPIC GAMES), and Mattie Brown on whom
he finished third in the 1970 men's world
championship. In 1972, he rode Summertime
for the British team which finished fourth in
the Olympic Games.

SMITH, IAN SCOTT (1903-   ), RUGBY
UNION wing three-quarter of exceptional speed

for EDINBURGH WANDERERS, LONDON SCOTTISH, Scotland, and British LIONS, Smith gained 32 caps in the period 1924-33 and played for the Lions in South Africa in 1924. A curious record is claimed for him as the only man to have scored six consecutive tries in international Rugby: three tries in the second half of the match against France in 1925, and three in the first half of the following match against Wales.

SMITH, M. G. M., British amateur RACKETS player who won the British amateur singles championship in 1970-1 and also the doubles championship with Gracey in 1964-5 and 1969-71.

SMITH, MARGARET (Mrs. B. M. Court) (1942-   ), the first Australian player to win the women's LAWN TENNIS singles title at WIMBLEDON and the second woman to win the four major singles championships in a year. Tall and powerful and a fine athlete, she was the most successful competitor in the women's game in the 1960s and in 1970 she equalled CONNOLLY's grand slam.

Helped in her early years by SEDGMAN, she dominated first Australian lawn tennis and then the international circuit. She came to prominence in 1960 when she surprised BUENO, who was then the Wimbledon champion, in the semi-finals of the Australian championships. She went on to win the title and hold it until 1966. She won at Wimbledon in 1963, 1965, and 1970, at FOREST HILLS in 1962, 1965, 1969, 1970, and 1973, and in Paris in 1962, 1964, 1969, 1970, and 1973. In addition, she gained a host of other important titles. She was undefeated in Italy from 1962 to 1964 and 1964 to 1966. In 1967 she retired temporarily, complaining of staleness, but after her marriage to Barry Court, she returned and played more effectively than ever the following year. She and Mrs. KING were the major beneficiaries from the increased prize money for women's lawn tennis in the U.S.A.

SMITH, MICHAEL JOHN KNIGHT (1933-   ), cricketer for England, Oxford University, Leicestershire, and Warwickshire. After making centuries in three consecutive university matches, he gained the first of his 47 Test caps in 1958. In 1959 he scored 3,245 runs — including 1,209 in the month of July. A fine batsman, particularly strong on the on side, he captained England in 25 Tests — leading three M.C.C. teams abroad, one of which (to Australia and New Zealand in 1965-6) enhanced his reputation as a respected and inspiring leader. Though playing in spectacles, he was also a brilliant short-leg fieldsman. He played once for England at RUGBY UNION football.

SMITH, ROSEMARY (1937-   ), British motor rally driver (see MOTOR RACING) who joined the Rootes team in 1965 and, after winning the Tulip Rally in a Hillman Imp, took many ladies' prizes.

SMITH, T. J., leading Australian race-horse trainer and the first to turn out the winners of more than half a million dollars in a season.

SMITH, TOMMIE (1944-   ), sprinter for the U.S.A. who made a sensational début as a record-breaker in 1966 when he was timed at 19·5 sec. for 220 yards and 200 metres on a straight track. This reduced the previous world records by half a second, the biggest single advance in the history of the events. In the same year he set world records for 220 yards and 200 metres on a turn in 20·0 sec., and was a member of the United States team which broke the world record for the 4×400 metres relay with 2 min. 59·6 sec. In 1967 he held the world 400 metres record at 44·5 sec. and in 1968 won an Olympic gold medal in the 200 metres, clocking 19·8 sec. for another world best.

SMYTHE, PAT (later Mrs. Koechlin-Smythe) (1928-   ), British show jumping (see EQUESTRIAN EVENTS) rider. The most successful woman in international shows during the 1950s and early 1960s, she won the women's European championship four times (1957, 1961, 1962, and 1963). In 1956, when women were first admitted to Olympic show jumping events, she rode Flanagan for the British team which won the bronze medal. Flanagan was also her mount in the Rome OLYMPIC GAMES, four years later, and it was on the same horse that she gained all four of her European championship successes.

SNEAD, SAMUEL JACKSON (1912-   ), American professional golfer, one of the most naturally gifted players the game has known. He was Open champion 1946; Masters champion 1949, 1952, 1954; U.S. Professional Golfers Association champion 1942, 1949, 1951; world Seniors champion 1964, 1965, 1970, 1972, 1973; a RYDER CUP and WORLD CUP player; and the winner of more than 150 tournaments, national championships, and invitation events.

SNELL, PETER GEORGE (1938-   ), middle-distance runner for New Zealand. As a virtual novice and apparent outsider, Snell won the Olympic 800 metres in 1960. His rapid rise to world class was attributed to the training of LYDIARD in favour of whose methods further evidence was forthcoming when in 1962 Snell broke ELLIOTT's world mile record with 3 min. 54·4 sec. A week later he beat the world 880 yards record with 1 min. 45·1 sec., and in the same race the 800 metres record in 1 min. 44·3 sec. In 1964 he won Olympic gold medals in both 800 metres and 1,500 metres, a double not accomplished since 1920, and followed this within a few weeks with another assault on the mile record, resulting in a new world best of 3 min. 54·1 sec. Earlier the same month he set a fresh world record for the non-championship distance of 1,000 metres with 2 min. 16·6 sec.

SNETTERTON CIRCUIT, British MOTOR RACING track near Thetford in Norfolk. It was opened in 1951 and has a length of 2·71 miles (4·3 km.). It has been used for a very large number of national and club events, and in 1961, was the venue for the Intercontinental Formula, and the Formula One race for the *Daily Mirror* Trophy. In 1973 Lunger's Trojan T101 got round the circuit at a record 124·44 m.p.h. (200·266 km./h.).

SNOW, JOHN AUGUSTINE (1941-   ), cricketer for England and Sussex. A fast bowler who often appeared more hostile in Test matches than in county fixtures, he took his 100th wicket for England in his 26th match. His ability to 'move' the ball brought about the downfall of most of the world's best batsmen from 1965 to 1973.

SOBERS, GARFIELD St. AUBRUN (1936-   ), cricketer for West Indies, Barbados, South Australia, and Nottinghamshire. The greatest of West Indian cricketers, and possibly the finest of all all-rounders, he dominated the 1960s as a free-stroking left-handed batsman, an agile fieldsman, a versatile left-arm bowler — often opening the attack, bowling stock medium pace, then slow wrist spin — and finally as an enterprising captain. The first of his record number of Test appearances for West Indies was in 1953-4, and in 1957-8 he made the highest score ever in Tests — 365 not out against Pakistan, at Kingston. By the end of 1973 he was the leading scorer in Test cricket, with almost 8,000 runs, including 26 centuries, in 89 matches; his total of wickets (221) was, with that of GIBBS, the highest for West Indies. The power of his batting was demonstrated against Glamorgan in 1968, when he hit six sixes in an over from Nash. Playing CRICKET in several countries, often with no rest between seasons, on numerous occasions he saved his side and changed impending defeat into victory.

SOCCER, see FOOTBALL, ASSOCIATION.

SOFTBALL, a nine-a-side bat-and-ball game, originated in the U.S.A. and is also played in Canada, Japan, the Philippines, New Zealand, Australia, and most of Latin America. The game requires less playing space than its parent sport, BASEBALL, and play is generally faster. Less equipment is necessary (for informal games, just a bat and ball suffice), and the equipment is relatively inexpensive.

Softball is traditionally and usually played on turf with an infield area skinned of grass. The playing field is in the shape of a diamond with a home base and three bases numbered, first, second, and third. The home base is at least 46 ft. (14 m.) from the pitching point for men and 40 ft. (12 m.) for women. Home base and bases one, two, and three are 60 ft. (18·3 m.) apart.

The object of the game is to score runs; the batsman attempts to hit the ball into the fair field of play and, having done so, circles the three bases to return to the home base. A run is scored, providing the batsman-runner is not tagged with the ball while circling the bases.

The playing area of the diamond extends from the home base down two foul lines for approximately 200 to 275 ft. (61–84 m.) which is usually marked inbounds by a line or fence. The outfield area extends from the bases which are stationed in the infield area to the distance marker that indicates inbounds and out-of-bounds.

The players in the infield consist of a catcher, stationed behind home base, and a pitcher, stationed on the pitching line. Each of the three bases has a player stationed within the base area and one additional player, called a shortstop, who remains within the infield area. The outfield area has three players stationed in each of the areas of the outfield, (1) left field, (2) centre field, and (3) right field.

Each team is allowed three 'outs' while taking their turn at bat. An out is recorded when the third strike (or delivery) is caught by the catcher; or when the batter has three strikes by hitting at, and missing, the ball; or when the batter 'bunts' foul (a bunt is a legally hit ball — tapped but not swung at — struck softly into the infield) after the second strike; or when a foul ball is legally caught; or when a fair ball is legally caught in the field by a fielder before it touches the ground. When three outs have been recorded, the two opposing teams change sides. The length of the game is recorded in innings, one innings consisting of

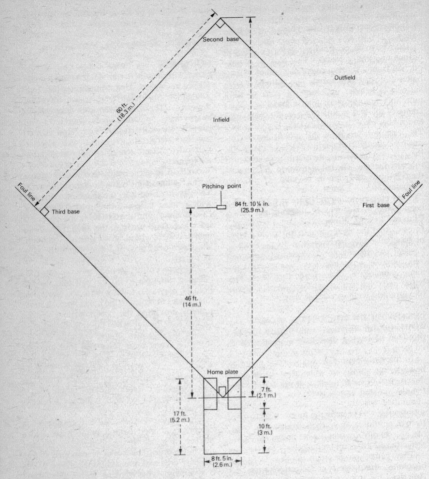

SOFTBALL DIAMOND
The pitching point is 24 in. by 6 in. (610 × 152 mm.). Pitching distance for women is 40 ft. (12 m.).

each team having a turn at bat. Seven innings constitute a full and complete game. The team with the most runs at the end of play is the winner.

The basic skills in softball are pitching, catching, throwing, batting, and base-running. The fundamentals of the game are the same as baseball. Batting and fielding strategy are similar, though there is an important difference in pitching and technique. The underhand pitch is a distinctive feature in softball. Special skills have been developed in this and the expert pitcher employs a wind-up followed by a release and throw of the ball that achieves a speed comparable to the overhand baseball pitch.

Softball is a more defensive game than baseball, mainly because the softball pitcher has more mastery over the hitter. In major competition the scores are usually low.

Bunting and 'base-stealing' (a runner who, already occupying a base, goes to the next while the pitcher is releasing the ball towards home base) are the major factors in softball team play. The 'sacrifice bunt' is used to advance runners from first to second and from second to third bases, in addition to the run-scoring squeeze play (bunting a runner home from third). Sacrifice bunting and base-stealing are closely allied, since in each there must be co-operation between base-runner and batter.

The key to successful batting is timing, co-ordination, and reflexes. The ball is being pitched from a short distance and comes to the batter at a very high speed. The softball is not soft; it is heavier and larger (12 in. — 304 mm. in circumference) than a baseball. The centre of the ball is either of a mixture of cork and rubber or of first-quality long-fibre kapok. The centre is enclosed by a taut hand- or machine-wound fine quality twisted yarn, with the cover cemented to the yarn by a latex or rubber adhesive. The bat is of wood, no longer than 34 in. and not more than 2¼ in. in diameter (863 × 57 mm.).

Credit for inventing the game of softball has been given to Hancock of the Farragut Boat Club of Chicago, Illinois (U.S.A.). In 1887 he foresaw that the then popular American game of baseball could be brought indoors. Indoor baseball, as the new sport was called, became very popular and soon went outdoors. The name changed to 'kitten ball', then to 'mush ball', and finally to its present name. Parks, playgrounds, and recreation agencies instituted the game in preference to baseball. Alert businessmen became sponsors of favourite teams, furnishing them with uniforms for the privilege of having their names embroidered on them.

In the early formative years of the game a bewildering variety of rules was in use; a dozen sizes of balls and as many different bat-lengths created much confusion. In 1933 a committee was formed to provide a standard set of rules; this became the International Joint Rules Committee on Softball. Today, the sport has one set of rules that is used universally and printed in 12 different languages.

The game progressed in the U.S.A., becoming the largest participation sport in America, and it began to develop as an inter-national sport in the early 1950s. By 1965 it had grown from a sport that was organized and played by only four countries to popularity in over 50.

The first world championship for women was held in 1965 in Melbourne, Australia. Five countries competed and the American team, widely expected to win, was beaten by Australia 1-0 in the final match.

Men played in world championship competition for the first time in 1966. Twelve countries took part in the men's inaugural competition in Mexico City. The U.S. dominated play and emerged as world champions after ten straight victories. In 1968 the men's second world championship was held, this time in the United States. Fifteen countries participated and again the U.S. male players dominated the action, the only blemish on their record being a 2-0 upset by Puerto Rico.

The second women's championship was held in 1970 and again the United States women were favourites to win the gold medals at Osaka, Japan. Ten countries were represented and, as in Melbourne, the Americans failed to win. The Japanese team achieved 12 straight wins, including a thrilling 1-0 result against the U.S. team before a record 30,000 spectators on the final day.

Credited with much of the success of softball development internationally was the International Softball Federation's president, W. W. Kethan. He devoted much of his time and effort to encourage countries new to the sport to organize and develop it so that it could be played by young and old alike.

Robert Gensemer and Mary Behling, *Beginning Softball* (1971); Marian Kneer and Charles McCord, *P.E. Softball* (1966); A. T. Noren, *Softball* (1966); George Sullivan, *Complete Guide to Softball* (1965).

GOVERNING BODY (WORLD): International Softball Federation, P.O. Box 11437, Oklahoma City, Oklahoma, U.S.A.

SOLARIO (1922), English race-horse by GAINSBOROUGH, bred by Lord Dunraven, bought as a yearling for 3,500 guineas by Rutherford, trained by Day, and ridden by Childs. He won the ST. LEGER (in a canter), the CORONATION CUP (by 15 lengths), and the ASCOT GOLD CUP. On the death of his owner in 1932, Solario was bought at auction by a syndicate of British bloodstock breeders for 47,000 guineas.

SOLOMON, JOHN WILLIAM (1931-), the first of the postwar generation of young English CROQUET players. He played for England in the MACROBERTSON trophy competition in New Zealand in 1950 at the age of 19, and has played in every Test match since the war, captaining England in Australia in 1969. Although one of the best long shots in the game, he has sometimes been thought to be too adventurous, but in 1959 RECKITT wrote of him as perhaps the greatest player of all time, at any rate in his own country. In 1973 Solomon had a total of 46 titles including 10 open singles and 10 open doubles, and was the champion of champions four years running from its inception in 1967.

SOLOMONS, JACK (1900-   ), British BOXING promoter chiefly responsible for the revival of the sport in Britain after the Second World War. A successful manager in the

1930s, Solomons staged many world championships in Britain from 1946 onwards, with Harringay in north London serving as his major arena.

SOMERVILLE, BUD (1941-   ), American curler. He was skip of the winning United States rink in the world CURLING championship in 1965.

SONE, KOJI (1928-   ), Japanese JUDO fighter who won the 1958 world championships but lost the title in 1961 to GEESINK, ending the Japanese domination of the sport. His uncle, Kowa Sone, was an 8th *Dan* instructor at Keishicho (the police judo college) but Koji was not graded to 1st *Dan* until he was 20. After a late start in the sport, however, he had an impressive contest career. He lost the 1967 all-Japan championships final to NATSUI but the following year he beat Yamashiki with an *o-soto-gari* (major outer reaping throw) for the crown. He defeated KAMINAGA for the world title the same year. These performances brought him the title of 'Japanese Sportsman of the Year', the first time a *judoka* had ever received it. In 1961, he fought his way to the final of the world championships again only to lose to Geesink on a hold-down, a defeat which shocked the judo world.

SONNEVILLE, FERDINAND (1931-   ), Indonesian BADMINTON player, the first from his country to become prominent. He won the Malayan title in 1955, and for several years thereafter featured among the top singles players of the world, though he never got beyond the final in the ALL-ENGLAND CHAMPIONSHIPS. Later he became an administrative representative and in 1971 was elected president of the International Badminton Federation.

SÖTER, ION, see BALAS, I.

SOULE (also known as *choule*) was a primitive team ball-and-goal game played largely in France until the nineteenth century. It is one of the European sources from which the major ball games of modern times have grown. In a time when folk sports had no precise rules, teams might be large — perhaps of village strength — and the ball was propelled towards the opposing goal with hands, feet, or even, at times, sticks.

SOUTAR, J. (*fl.* 1914-28), professional RACKETS player at the Philadelphia Racquet Club, U.S.A., having emigrated from Britain. He held the world championship from 1914 to 1928.

SOUTH AMERICAN CHAMPIONSHIP, Association FOOTBALL championship for international teams initiated in 1917, played in Montevideo, and first won by Uruguay, with Argentina as runner-up. It has had an inconsistent history. It was played for the second time in Rio in 1919, where Brazil won, with Uruguay as runner-up. It then continued up to and including 1927 on an annual basis, alternating between the capital cities of the various countries involved, except in 1923 and 1924 when, on each occasion, it was played in and won by Uruguay. In 1928 there was no tournament, but in 1929 it took place in Buenos Aires and was won by Argentina. It then went into abeyance until 1937, when it was again played in Buenos Aires and won by Argentina for the third consecutive time. This achievement they repeated with their victories of 1955 (Santiago), 1957 (Lima), and 1959 (Buenos Aires).

There was no competition in 1938, but in 1939 it was played in Lima, where Peru became the first country outside the dominant three — Argentina, Uruguay, and Brazil — to win it. Not until 1953, when Paraguay took the title, again in Lima, did another country outside the main three emulate them.

There was no tournament in 1940 or 1941. In 1942 the competition was resumed, Uruguay winning it in Montevideo. There was then a gap of five years before the competition was staged again, this time in Guayaquil, Ecuador, for it had been extended to include Central American countries such as Bolivia and Ecuador. Argentina was the winner, Paraguay the runner-up; as they were again, two years later, in Rio. The 1949 tournament was notable for the fact that a players' strike forced Uruguay to send a team of amateurs, which was heavily beaten by the eventual winner, Brazil. The following year, two amateurs, Ghiggia and SCHIAFFINO, returned to score the goals by which Uruguay beat Brazil in the decisive match of the 1950 World Cup.

From 1947 the South American Championship settled down as a two-yearly event, though there was a gap of four years between the 1949 tournament and the next in 1953.

Despite its two victories in the World Cups of 1958 and 1962, Brazil was unable to win the South American title for over 20 years after its success in 1949, although it was runner-up in 1957 and 1959 (on both occasions to Argentina), and did not compete in Montevideo in 1967, when Uruguay won.

In certain interim years, a so-called South American 'Extra' Championship has been played. The present championship pattern is for each team to play the other, the winner being calculated on a points basis.

SOUTH AMERICAN CUP (*Copa de los Libertadores*), an Association FOOTBALL trophy introduced in 1960 to provide a team which would meet the winners of the European Cup for the then unofficial (i.e. unrecognized by F.I.F.A. — see FOOTBALL, ASSOCIATION) title of world club champion. It was initially confined to one club from each competing South (and Central) American country, and run on a knock-out basis, beginning early in the year. In 1966, however, the competition was widened to include two clubs from each country, dividing itself into a series of groups, although the practice of exempting the holders until the semi-finals was maintained. The final continued to be played on a 'home-and-home', two-legged basis.

The Brazilian Confederation and its clubs strongly objected to the widening of the competition, on the grounds that a multiplicity of extra games had to be played, most of them against mediocre and indigent opposition. Thus no Brazilian team entered the competition in 1966, and there was a further contretemps in 1969.

SOUTH OF ENGLAND CLUB (formerly the Newmarket Coursing Society) was founded in the first quarter of the nineteenth century, and staged meetings over a wide area ranging from Stockbridge in Hampshire to Amesbury in Wiltshire and Newmarket in Cambridgeshire. The present South of England Club has been faithful to its antecedents in terms of venues, having conducted first-class meetings since 1945 on the Wiltshire downland of Druids Lodge, at Sutton Scotney in Hampshire, and at Six-mile Bottom near Newmarket. The club's major events are the Barbican Cup and the South of England Cup, two of the most keenly coveted trophies of the Leash.

SOUTH SYDNEY, Australian RUGBY LEAGUE club. It was a founder member and first champion of the Sydney Rugby League in 1908, and has been the most successful club in Australia's premier competition. By 1971 South Sydney had won the Sydney First Grade Premiership 19 times. Much of their success was due to the able direction of Ball, who was the club's first treasurer and served it and Australian Rugby League with distinction for over 50 years.

SOUTHAMPTON BOWLS CLUB, in Hampshire, has the oldest green in England and probably the entire world. The lawns were laid in 1187 as a close for the warden of God's House Hospital and it is believed that by 1220 a form of BOWLS was being played occasion-ally. The close came into regular use as a bowling green in 1299. For just over 200 years the Mayors and Burgesses of Southampton disputed the hospital's right of ownership but by 1611 the situation had eased and a plan of that date shows the green itself with four men playing bowls on it.

The Knighthood tournament, the oldest bowls competition in existence, was inaugurated on 1 August 1776 and has been faithfully observed ever since. In accordance with tradition, the 'Knights' (previous winners) appear in ceremonial attire — top hats and frock coats, with the medals of their rank suspended on their chests. Competitors, who are styled 'commoners', are each required to deliver two bowls to a jack which rests on a penny. One point is awarded after each end to the deliverer of the bowl lying nearest to the jack. The first player to score 7 points wins a 'Knighthood of Southampton's Old Green' and is ceremonially invested with his title and silver medal on the green. Thereafter he is entitled to be called 'sir', the only departure from the world-wide tradition of using Christian names only on the greens.

SOUTHERN CALIFORNIA, University of (U.S.C.), American college FOOTBALL team, nicknamed the 'Trojans', have dominated West Coast football and the Pacific Coast Athletic Conference during most of the twentieth century. They have had intensive rivalries with their intersectional foe NOTRE DAME and their cross-town Los Angeles opponent U.C.L.A. Most memorable wins were the 16-14 victory in 1931 that snapped a long Notre Dame winning streak and brought U.S.C. its first national title, and the underdog 1964 team that ended another Notre Dame unbeaten season. U.S.C. was national champion in 1962, 1967, when their running back O. J. SIMPSON starred, and 1972. The team has been to the Rose Bowl 18 times.
COLOURS: Cardinal and gold.

SOUZA, GEORGE ALLISTER (1917-), lawn BOWLS player who helped Hong Kong to its first COMMONWEALTH GAMES gold medal by skipping the winning fours team at Edinburgh in July 1970. He won the Hong Kong singles and fours championships in 1959 before evolving the tactical approach (using the number two in an aggressive role instead of as a positional bowler) which made his skipping the major talking-point of the fours event at Edinburgh.

SPA CIRCUIT, one of the fastest MOTOR RACING courses in Europe. The Spa-Francorchamps circuit, with a length of 14·2 km. (8·8 miles) has been used for the Belgian Grand Prix and the Spa 24-hour sports car race. It has been called dangerous, part of the problem being due to changeable climatic conditions which can cause rain quickly to soak one part of the circuit while the rest remains dry. This caused the death of the British driver, Seaman, in 1939, and subsequent serious accidents have turned modern racing drivers against the fine Spa course, with its hairpin corner at the Virage de la Source, and the l'Eau Rouge and Stavelot bends. It has therefore been abandoned as a Formula One course, but is still the scene of long-distance races.

SPACEBALL is played with an 8 oz. (227 g.) ball on a trampoline. The game originated and is popular in America and to a lesser extent in England, Germany, and Japan. At present it has been played competitively only in the U.S.A. and England.

The apparatus required is an extension of the trampoline. At each end of the trampoline a frame is attached at approximately 75°, on top of which is fixed a rebound net. In the centre of the trampoline is a gantry to divide the playing area into two courts. The gantry, 24 in. (610 mm.) deep, has attached to it at the top centre a basket shaped like a two-way funnel so that the ball will always roll out to one court or the other. The frames, called back-stops, as well as forming part of the scoring area, may be jumped on and used for rebounding. The backstops are made of a woven nylon bed with a suspension of rubber cables in exactly the same way as the trampoline. The nets above the backstops are used to rebound the ball into the centre gantry, which is adjustable in height.

The server initiates play by throwing the ball through the gantry basket in an attempt to hit the scoring area, complete a double rebound, or cause an opponent to miss or fumble the ball. Either the server or the receiver may score. After the serve, the ball is in continuous play until either side scores or there is a 'let' ball (when the ball falls to the scoring area or falls out of bounds after hitting the rebound net). A game is 7 points and a set is two out of three games. The serve always goes to the player who lost the last point; the loser of the previous game serves first. When a 'let' ball occurs, the serve goes to the opposing player. There is no limitation on the number of bounces which may be made by either the offensive player (with the ball) or the defensive player. The entire backstop, below the backstop pad, including the frame, bed, and suspension system, as well as the trampoline bed and trampoline suspension system, are considered scoring area.

Stepping on or crossing the centre line on

On this Belgian Grand Prix course the fine line between 8 and 9 indicates the Stavelot 'hairpin' corner, in use until 1951.

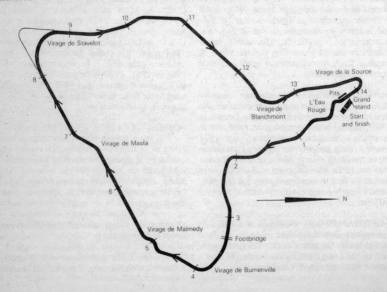

the trampoline with any part of the body during play should result in a point for the opposition. This is so whether or not the infringement occurred during the scoring of a point. Inserting a hand past the middle of the gantry basket or holding on to any part of the gantry net to aid in making a shot or catching the ball is considered an infringement, and a point is awarded to the opposing player. This rule also applies to hanging on to the backstop, or rebound net. Stepping off the trampoline accidentally or intentionally is considered an infringement and carries the same penalty.

Spaceball may be played as singles or doubles or as a team competition, with up to four on each side. Initially, one member of each team begins play. As soon as he loses a point, he is replaced by the next member of his team. The losing team always serves the next point. If the same team loses again, the players rotate as before, i.e. the third member of that team comes on to the court. At the same time, the opposing team changes players because it has won 2 consecutive points. Thus players change each time their team loses a point or wins 2 consecutive points.

Among the possible moves and shots are:
The *back mount*, a move designed to change the rhythm of the bounce between players. A player bounces upward and slightly backward, stretching one leg back to feel the backstop. This move helps the player to gain extra height and to delay his descent. It is also a favourable position from which to initiate a drop shot.

The *drop shot*. Timing is extremely important on this shot since it is necessary to throw the ball just as an opponent is descending from the top of his bounce. The ball is pushed softly through the basket in an arc so that it lands in the scoring area of the backstop apron just above the descending opponent's reach.

The *fade back*, a manoeuvre used mainly defensively in catching the ball or in changing the rhythm of the player's bounce. He bounces directly backward against the backstop apron, raising his legs for balance. When executed properly the fade back is an effective defence for both 'lob' and drop shots.

The *double rebound* is an offensive move to throw the ball through the basket, generally with an overhand motion, with sufficient force to hit the rebound net or backstop-pad and rebound back into the gantry net before the defensive player can catch the ball. This is most effective when defence is anticipating a drop or lob shot and has either stopped bouncing or is in a fade back position and unable to reach high enough to intercept the ball.

The *lob shot*. Usually a player fakes a hard shot, as in a double rebound attempt, but gently lobs the ball directly over the opponent's fingertips on to the scoring area. The lob differs from a drop shot in that the ball is released overhead with both hands.

The *bismark*, an offensive shot executed by throwing the ball down on the front half of the basket so that it will ricochet upward hitting the top half of the basket on the opponent's side. This causes the ball to drop abruptly downward, usually before an opponent can recover. Directional variations may be made by ricocheting the ball at an angle sideways. The bismark is extremely difficult to counter because the overhand action used at the beginning of the shot looks misleadingly like that of the double rebound.

Spaceball, like TRAMPOLINING, began in the U.S.A. and dates from 1962. Early in that year the inventor of the trampoline, NISSEN, and his colleagues began experimenting to find a game suitable for the equipment as a recreation other than a sport. They strung a rope across the centre of the trampoline about 8 ft. (2·4 m.) above the bed, with a man either side of the rope passing a light ball back and forth. It was fun, but rather dangerous since it was an automatic reaction to dive for the ball when receiving and consequently land near the end of the trampoline or indeed come right off. Obviously to make it safer something had to be erected at each end and thus the backstops evolved. The first idea was the best; an extra half of a trampoline frame, bed, and suspension was added to each end. This proved satisfactory since a player landing there was bounced back into the court.

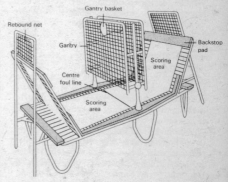

SPACEBALL COURT

It was decided to make the game like other court and ball games by introducing a single net instead of a rope. It was soon realized, however, that because the court was so small, the ball went out of court if passed off centre, resulting in more time being spent retrieving the ball than playing. The solution was to form a hole in the top of the net, through which the ball would be passed. This would demand skill and help to ensure that the ball was kept centrally on the trampoline.

Although still at the experimental stage, the game proved enjoyable, but other refinements were necessary. An increase in the height of the backstop prevented the ball, after passing through the hole, from going over the top out of court. An extra net, called the backstop net, opened up the game considerably since the ball would now rebound very quickly into the centre net. This meant that a player would try to catch the ball on the rebound. Finally, it was found that by diving backwards for the ball and rebounding off the backstop net, players frequently collided in the centre of the court. For safety, therefore, the single net was replaced by a double netted gantry, including in it a basket (rather than a hole) which cambered from the centre so that the ball would never stick in it.

Nissen, completely enthralled by his invention, set about selling the game. The first year, 1963, it was not played outside Cedar Rapids, Iowa (U.S.A.). Later that year, however, a complete unit was sent over to England, to find out what the response might be. The obvious people to play the game it was thought, would be trampolinists but they were not always adaptable and did not necessarily have the ball-handling ability. Walker, the physical education lecturer of the Regent Street Polytechnic, London, demonstrated the game with Winkle on television and later represented England in an international against Wales which England won. In October 1963 spaceball was demonstrated at the U.S.A. Trade Centre in Frankfurt, Germany, and Winkle was invited by Nissen to tour the U.S.A., lecturing and demonstrating the game.

By early 1965 spaceball was a popular game in many parts of the U.S.A. Competitions were being held, mainly on a local basis, in the midwestern states; spaceball parks were being set up in main tourist areas such as Florida and California; and in many of the large shopping areas they were being installed near car parks. There are two spaceball courts at the Astronaut Space Training Centre in Houston, Texas. Since 1965 an annual competition has been held at the National Gymnastic Clinic at Sarasota, Fla., where many gymnasts and trampolinists take part.

There are not many courts in England, but they are becoming popular in sports centres and where a sports hall is for multi-purpose use by the community. One of the first venues for a spaceball demonstration was the Crystal Palace National Recreation Centre, and the game has since been played there many times. The Afan Lido in Port Talbot, Wales, Harlow Sports Centre, Essex, and Sussex University are some of the larger centres with spaceball courts. Japan has many outdoor centres and parks with spaceball courts, and the game has been played in Yugoslavia and Germany.

SPALDING, ALBERT GOODWILL (1850-1915), American BASEBALL player and executive who first won fame in the 1870s as an outstanding pitcher for the Boston Red Stockings of the National Association of Professional Base Ball Players. He deserted the Red Stockings, taking some of their other star players with him, to join the Chicago team, where he collaborated with HULBERT in founding the NATIONAL LEAGUE in 1876. After Hulbert's death in 1882, he became president of the club, a post he held until 1892, and it was his wily strategy that was instrumental in crushing the great player revolt of 1890. In 1876 he established the sporting-goods firm, A. G. Spalding & Bros. He also published baseball guidebooks and vigorously promoted the game at home and abroad.

SPARTAK MOSCOW, Association FOOTBALL club, Moscow. Founded in 1926, the club was eight times league champion of the Soviet Union between 1938 and 1969, and eight times the national cup winner. Leading players include the Starostin brothers, the Artemiev brothers, Simonian, Goulaev, and NETTO.
COLOURS: Red shirts with white band, white shorts.

SPEED SKATING, see ICE SKATING; ROLLER SKATING.

SPEEDBOAT RACING, see POWERBOAT RACING.

SPEEDWAY, Motor-cycle, see MOTOR-CYCLE RACING.

SPELL, SPEL, see KNUR AND SPELL.

SPENCER, HOWARD (b. 1875), Association footballer for ASTON VILLA, and England for whom he would have made more than six appearances in international matches at right back had he not been contemporary with CROMPTON. With Aston Villa, however, the calm, elegant Spencer gained four League championship and three F.A. Cup-winners medals between 1895 and 1905 — a personal collection that few players have bettered.

SPHAIRISTIKÉ, see LAWN TENNIS.

SPITZ, MARK ANDREW (1950-   ),
American swimmer who won a record number
of seven gold medals at the Munich OLYMPIC
GAMES in 1972. These were for the 100 and
200 metres freestyle and butterfly, the 4 × ×
100 and 4 × 200 metres freestyle relays, and
the 4 × 100 metres medley relay. No competitor in any sport had ever won so many at a
single Games and it brought his total of Olympic golds to nine, the other two having been
gained in the freestyle relays at the Mexico
City Games in 1968. A temperamental competitor in his early days, this brilliant and
talented swimmer set 27 individual world
records for freestyle and butterfly between
1967 and 1972.

SPOFFORTH, FREDERICK ROBERT
(1853-1926), cricketer for Australia, New
South Wales, and Derbyshire. Known as 'the
Demon', he added to his original raw speed
such bowling variations that at times he
appeared unplayable. He followed his 11
wickets for 20 runs for the 1878 Australians
against M.C.C. at LORD'S with 13 for 110
— including a hat-trick — in the MELBOURNE
Test the following winter. His most famous
performance was in the 'ASHES Test match' at
the OVAL in 1882, when he took 14 wickets for
90. In 18 Tests he took 94 wickets.

SPRING DOUBLE, see LINCOLN HANDICAP
and GRAND NATIONAL.

SPRINGBOKS, the popular term used for
South African representative RUGBY UNION
teams, first used in 1906 when the 1906-7
South Africans toured the British Isles. It is
derived from the animal embroidered on the
left breast of the players' jerseys. South Africa
wore their traditional dark green jerseys for the
first time on the occasion of the third Test of
their 1903 series against the British Isles touring team. Previously South Africa had worn
white jerseys.

SPRINT WALKING, see RACE WALKING.

SPRINTING is the fullest form of running,
performed over short distances in which maximum or near-maximum effort can be sustained. Sprinting figures in the programme of
all major ATHLETICS championships including
the OLYMPIC GAMES, in which the standard
sprint events for men and women are the 100,
200, and 400 metres and the 4 × 100 metres
and 4 × 400 metres relays. The DECATHLON
and PENTATHLON also include sprint events.
The International Amateur Athletic Federation
(see ATHLETICS, TRACK AND FIELD) recognizes

world records for men and women at all the
distances mentioned as well as the 100, 220,
and 440 yards, and the 4 × 110 and 4 × 440
yards relays. The 60 metres for women is a
distance which does not feature in championship programmes although a world record for
it is listed by the I.A.A.F.

Sprinting is also an ingredient of HURDLING
as well as certain field events in which
momentum is at a premium, namely the LONG
JUMP, TRIPLE JUMP, and POLE VAULT. Starting
is normally carried out from a crouching position, the sprinter gradually assuming an
upright position as the length of his stride
increases. The maximum speed is attained by
efficient channelling of muscular power into a
full range of leg movement co-ordinating with
a correspondingly powerful arm action.

SPRINTING, Motor-cycle, see MOTOR-
CYCLE RACING.

SPRY, DAVID-JOHN (1944-   ), British
skibob pioneer who founded in 1967 the Skibob Association of Great Britain (S.A.G.B.).
He formed and captained the first official British team to take part in international SKIBOB-
BING competition including the premier world
championships in 1967 and is a member of the
Fédération Internationale de Skibob committee.

SPYGLASS HILL, U.S. GOLF course in California. The work of architect Robert Trent
Jones, Spyglass Hill is a mixture of links and
hilly woodland incorporating all the characteristics which have come to be associated
with him: long carries, water hazards, and
greens of eccentric shape and slope.

SQUASH RACKETS, the newest of the bat
and ball games to become universally popular,
is usually a game for two players. It is played
in an enclosed rectangular space 32 ft. long by
21 ft. wide (9·754 × 6·401 m.). The object is
to hit a small ball made of synthetic rubber out
of reach of the opponent with a racket similar
to, but smaller than, a RACKETS racket.

The player winning the toss serves the ball
on to the front wall of the court from either of
two service boxes, 5 ft. 3 in. (1·6 m.) square,
halfway down each side of the court. The ball
must rebound into the other half of the court
where the opponent hits it so that, after hitting
the front wall and before bouncing on the floor
twice, it cannot be returned by the server. The
rally continues until one player is unable to
reach the ball and hit it before it has bounced
twice or the ball has been hit outside the lines
denoting the boundaries of the playing area. If
the player winning the rally is the server he

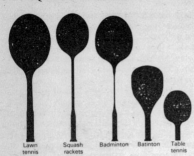

Lawn
tennis   Squash
rackets   Badminton   Batinton   Table
tennis

RACKETS

wins a point; if he is not, he then becomes the server. A game consists of 9 points, except that, if the score reaches 8 points to each player, the player who first reached 8 points has the option of setting the game to 10. If he does not exercise this right, the game goes to the first player to reach 9. It is important to remember that a player can score a point only if he started the rally as server. A match is won by the player who first wins three games.

There are many strokes, the most important being the drive to a length (making the ball 'die' in either back corner of the court); the drop, in which the ball is hit softly so that it keeps close to the front wall; and the lob, in which the ball is lofted off the front wall over the head of the opponent forcing him to the back of the court to play the return. Finally, there is the boast, by which the ball is hit on to a side wall before it reaches the front wall, the object being to wrong-foot the opponent.

The squash racket has a circular head of wood strung with gut and a handle of wood or metal. The over-all length must not exceed 27 in. (685·8 mm.). The internal stringing area must not exceed 8¼ in. long by 7¼ in. wide (215·9 × 184·2 mm.). The squash racket is not as strong as the rackets racket from which it developed because the ball which it has to hit is softer. The official dimensions have not changed since the rules were standardized in 1922. The only recent change has been the introduction of a metal shaft, but efforts by manufacturers to introduce a metal head to the racket have been resisted by the Squash Rackets Association as being dangerous and liable to lead to injury in the confined space of a squash court.

The ball has an outside diameter of just over

SQUASH RACKETS COURT
A flush fitting door in the centre of the back wall below the horizontal line is not shown in this perspective diagram.

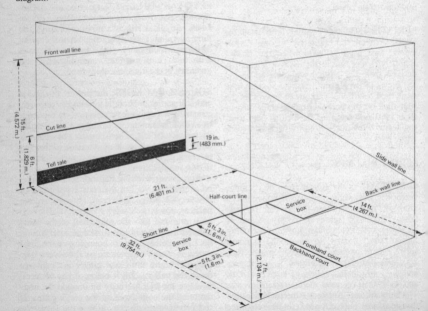

$1\frac{1}{2}$ in. (38·1 mm.) and weighs from 360 to 380 gr. (23·3–24·6 g.). It is made of rubber or butyl, or a combination of both, and is hollow and 'squashy'. It is usually black in colour. A slightly harder ball, used for some time in Australia, has recently been adopted officially for play in England. Manufacturers have always found it difficult to produce balls with uniform performance and for many years experiments have been conducted with the object of improving the ball.

In tropical countries or where the game is played at a high altitude, as in parts of Africa, a slower ball is used to counteract the higher bounce. Conversely, in certain extremely cold courts it is usual to find a faster ball in use and manufacturers of both the English and Australian types make balls in four different speeds.

The conduct of the game is controlled by 25 rules and 4 appendices which include the standard dimensions of a singles court, the dimensions of a racket, and the specification for standard balls.

In the last 40 years there have been comparatively few changes. The main problem after the Second World War was that of obstruction which in 1947 reached acute proportions, numerous 'lets' in championships ruining the game both for player and spectator. It was in this year that Rule 17 was re-written to include the imposition of what has become known as the 'penalty point' (although the phrase does not appear in the rule itself). Under the revised rule a point could be awarded by the referee against a player who unnecessarily obstructed his opponent's stroke. While the rule was a good one, it suffered from the reluctance of both professional and amateur referees to enforce it. Since its introduction this controversial rule has been further amended with a view to making its enforcement easier.

On its formation in 1967, the International Squash Rackets Federation adopted the rules laid down by the Squash Rackets Association and has, since that date, passed an additional rule making it obligatory for players to wear white clothing, in addition to changes in the specifications of the ball and a number of alterations in the calling of the game.

Doubles. Although squash is mainly a singles game, the doubles variety has long been popular in America and the rules, which include American scoring, were framed in that country. In the 1930s the growing popularity of doubles led to the erection of a few doubles courts in England and Scotland. The courts are much larger (25 ft. wide by 45 ft. long — 7·62 m. × 13·716 m.) and the ball is of the hard American type, necessitating stronger rackets. Doubles tournaments (mainly mixed doubles) sprang up and achieved some popularity. During the Second World War, however, the courts in England disappeared, mainly through enemy action, and since the war the only court remaining has been that at the Edinburgh Sports Club. Efforts to get doubles courts erected are continuing but the considerable cost and the area involved are handicaps.

Doubles played in a singles court has become popular although the presence of four players in such a restricted space necessitates a tolerant attitude which might be difficult to maintain under championship conditions. The Squash Rackets Association has refused to stage any championships under this arrangement. In junior squash, the doubles game has always been popular.

Squash is derived from, and has much in common with, the much older game of rackets, and originated at Harrow School, England. It was being played there in 1850 and, it is said, boys waiting their turn to play rackets knocked a ball about in a confined space adjoining the rackets court. So small was the area that it was necessary to use a softer and slower ball — one which could be squashed with the hand, thus giving the game a name to distinguish it from rackets.

Squash became popular with the wealthy who built courts at their country houses to entertain their guests. Courts were also constructed at public schools and in the London West End social clubs. There was no governing body until 1929 when the Squash Rackets Association was formed. A sub-committee of the Tennis and Rackets Association had laid down rules about 1922, but prior to this a wide variety of ball and court led to a lack of uniformity which detracted from the growth of the game.

By the early 1930s the game had become sufficiently popular for a number of squash clubs to be built on the outskirts of London and in the provinces, but generally squash courts were an amenity added to clubs devoted to some other sport such as LAWN TENNIS or CRICKET. Squash courts were built in five of the large liners of the time — *Queen Mary, Carinthia, Empress of Britain, Franconia,* and *Nieuw Amsterdam.*

Before the Second World War many hotels built squash courts — there were nearly 60 of these in 1938 — but for various reasons not more than a dozen of them survive today. Squash rackets had, in the meantime, become popular in the British forces, and the army built a number of courts in the north-west of India and in Egypt which later had a profound effect on the game. But it was the Royal Air

Force which contributed most to the game by building courts on all its stations.

The Second World War brought the game to the notice of thousands serving all over the world and players discovered that squash could be enjoyed in hot climates. For many years the game in England was played only in the winter.

Commercial development began in the late 1960s when the popularity of the game ensured a profitable return on capital. The principal result was that squash clubs contained an increasing number of courts per club, and clubs with six, eight, and even up to twenty courts began to appear.

In December 1928 the first meeting of the Squash Rackets Association (S.R.A.) was held. The S.R.A. immediately took over responsibility for the main championships and the raising of international teams, as well as for the rules of the game and the standards of equipment. At first, 25 clubs were affiliated, of which 6 were from overseas. The first S.R.A. Handbook, a modest volume of 28 pages, made its appearance in 1929.

By the time war broke out in 1939, over 200 clubs in England alone had become affiliated to the S.R.A., either directly or through their county associations of which there were at that time 25. During this time the administration of the S.R.A. had been undertaken by the ROYAL AUTOMOBILE CLUB (R.A.C.). The S.R.A. was completely dormant during the Second World War but was revived in 1946 when it had to start almost from scratch. Yet, in a year it had regained much of the ground lost and by the middle of 1947 over 150 clubs had become affiliated. In 1948 a full-time paid secretary was appointed and offices opened in London. The S.R.A. controlled squash in England and was recognized all over the world as the governing body of the game.

By the 1960s Britain had been replaced as the leading nation by Australia, yet the Open and amateur championships held in Britain were regarded as the unofficial world championships. However, the world-wide growth of squash rackets in the early 1960s and in particular the success of Australian teams which had beaten Great Britain convincingly in 1962, 1963, and 1965 led to a feeling that it would be equitable to have world championships played at least occasionally outside England and preferably in Australia. A meeting of interested countries was held in London in 1966 as a result of which it was decided to form an international federation.

The inaugural meeting of the International Squash Rackets Federation (I.S.R.F.) was held in London in January, 1967. There were seven founder members — Great Britain, Aus-

tralia, India, New Zealand, Pakistan, Southern Africa, and the United Arab Republic. One of the objects of the constitution was to uphold the rules of the game as laid down by the Squash Rackets Association. This effectively barred the associations of the U.S.A. and Canada from membership at that time, but a subsequent meeting of the Federation amended the constitution to enable these countries to become eligible for membership, and they were added to the list of founder members.

The administration of the Federation was originally carried out from the offices of the S.R.A. and is still based in England. The first international championships were assigned to Australia and were held in Sydney (team event) and Melbourne (individual event) in August 1967. Both events were easily won by Australia. It had been arranged that the second championship should be held in the U.A.R. but that country was forced to withdraw the invitation and the championships were held in England in February 1969 with Australia again winning both events. Since then the international championships have been held in New Zealand (1971) and South Africa (1973).

Ireland, Scotland, and Wales have their own autonomous associations, but these countries have representatives on the S.R.A. Council, the governing body of the Association. In 1973 a number of national associations formed the European Squash Rackets Federation, an autonomous body which has close associations with the I.S.R.F. and organizes annual European championships.

Professionals had their own Association at first, but in 1937 after a dispute between the S.R.A. and the Professionals Association, the latter was disbanded and in its place a Professionals Committee of the S.R.A., with a leading professional as its secretary, dealt with the administration of professional members of the S.R.A. and although this system worked satisfactorily, in 1973 the professionals again founded, with the blessing of the S.R.A., their own autonomous association.

INTERNATIONAL COMPETITION

In *Australia* the game started slowly. At first it was played mainly in Melbourne, where courts were erected in the 1920s mostly in social and golf clubs. There was, however, a club with five courts operating in Sydney by 1938.

The first Australian championship was held in Melbourne in 1931; one of the early winners was HOPMAN, for many years captain of the Australian Davis Cup team (see LAWN TENNIS). Another leading player was BRADMAN, the cricketer. The New South Wales championship was not started until 1935. The

Victorian championship, played in the same year, attracted an entry of only 18.

The Second World War came and went without any spectacular increase in the number of courts or players. The breakthrough came in the middle 1950s when the number of courts in Sydney increased from a dozen to over 300 in the course of about three years. The rest of Australia followed some way behind and, by the time the first British team to play in Australia arrived in 1959, there were 74 clubs and squash centres affiliated in New South Wales compared with only 33 in Victoria.

The boom in Australian squash was not in clubs as in England, but rather in public courts built and run commercially. Too many people tried to cash in on the boom and more courts were built than the game could fill at that time. For some years no new courts were built and some even closed down or were put to other uses. But the game had taken a firm hold and it was only a matter of time before further expansion became necessary. Many of the courts incorporated clubs for those who wanted to take part in competitive squash.

At first massive participation did not produce any stars, although the British team in 1959 noted a good average standard. All three Test matches were comfortably won, but a young player, HISCOE, who just got into the New South Wales team, appeared to have a good potential.

Only three years later Australia sent a team to England with Hiscoe playing first string. (It should be noted that in Australia a team consists of four players instead of the more usual five.) They effectively avenged their defeat in Australia, beating Great Britain 4-1, and South Africa by a similar margin. Hiscoe beat ODDY, the previous year's amateur champion, in four games, having himself just won the amateur championship. Australia thus began a dominance in world squash which has since continued uninterrupted.

The boom in New South Wales was followed, though not to the same extent, in the other states. Victoria lost its dominating position to New South Wales and has never been able to regain it. Although Australia sent players to compete in the chief tournaments in England and invariably won any team matches played against the home country, no Australian emulated Hiscoe's amateur championship win until 1970 when HUNT succeeded with an easy win against the Pakistani, JAWAID.

On the administrative side Australian squash was dominated by Napier who, as chairman of the Squash Rackets Association of Australia in the 1960s, pursued a vigorous policy and was instrumental in bringing about the formation of the International Squash Rackets Federation.

In *Egypt (U.A.R.)*, as in Pakistan, the growth of squash owed much in the early days to the presence of the British Army. The centre of squash in Egypt has always been the GEZIRA CLUB, Cairo, where there are seven courts with more planned. There are now nearly 30 clubs, mostly in Cairo or Alexandria. Particular attention has been paid to gallery space and there are three courts each with galleries claiming to seat up to 500 spectators.

The most famous Egyptian player AMR BEY, unbeaten in the 1930s, played most of his squash in England and had little impact on the game in his native country except by precept. He did, however, win the first Egyptian amateur championship in 1936. Another Egyptian to make his mark in world squash was Mahmoud Kerim, a young professional who arrived in England in 1947 from the Gezira Club and won the British Open championship at his first attempt, retaining the title for the three succeeding years before being beaten by the speed and hard-hitting of the Pakistani, HASHIM KHAN. Kerim was one of the great stroke players of the game and passed on much of his skill to a number of amateur players in Cairo who finally came to this country in search of the amateur title. Of these AMIN finally became amateur champion in 1956. Other well-known Egyptian professionals who made their mark in international squash were Dardir and Taleb, both of whom reached the peak of their play after they had obtained appointments outside Egypt.

Squash came early to *South Africa* and the first championships were held there in 1910, making them second only to the U.S.A. in seniority. It was not until 1955 that a British touring team visited the country. The visitors were soundly beaten, being unable to adjust to playing at high altitude. The next three series of matches were won by Great Britain, but in 1970 the British team were again defeated in South Africa in all three Test Matches.

Whiteley was the leading South African player, winning the South African championship on eight occasions between 1930 and 1948 while the Callaghan brothers played a major part after the Second World War. Squash is entirely a white man's game in the Republic and up to 1974 there were no public courts. However, the first public squash centre is now being built.

The game in *Pakistan* owes much to the British Army centres on the North-west Frontier where a number of courts were built. Pakistani squash is associated mainly with the Khan family of professionals who dominated the game in England and the United States after the Second World War. Other well-known professionals are the two pairs of brothers Hashim and Azam Khan, and Nazrullah and Roshan Khan. Pakistan did not produce an outstanding amateur player until 1963 when Jawaid, related to the Khans, won his native championship and in the same year the first of three successive wins in the amateur championship in London. Since then, an increasing number of young Pakistanis, of whom the chief are Jahan, Mohibullah (who won the British amateur championship in 1973-4), and Zaman (Australian Open champion 1973), have come to the fore.

Europe. Before the Second World War there were clubs in Belgium, France, Germany, Holland, Romania, and Sweden — but in most cases only one club in each. The clubs in Germany and Romania disappeared in the war, but a four-court pre-war club still flourishes in West Berlin; it was not until 1968 that a civilian club was started in Hamburg. Many courts and clubs had however been built for the British forces in Germany and every year, at Easter, a squash festival is held at the Headquarters of the British Army on the Rhine which attracts teams from Denmark, Wales, and Holland, in addition to those from England.

Squash in Scandinavia should have been a 'natural' and clubs were built before the war in both Copenhagen and Stockholm. In 1968 five public courts were built in Stockholm. Many others have followed both here and in other parts of Sweden, due largely to the initiative of a Swedish businessman who plans to build courts in many other European countries. Meanwhile, in Finland, considerable keenness has been shown following the erection of three courts in Helsinki in 1968, with a number of others since. Norway remains so far unaffected by the boom in the game.

The Mediterranean countries have also been slow to take to squash but clubs are at last appearing in Spain and Italy, while international tournaments are held at Athens, Monte Carlo, and Geneva. There is one club in Athens, but the government in Greece has made a grant for the promotion of the game.

So far as is known, the only court in Russia is that in the compound of the Indian Embassy in Moscow, and a number of British Embassies in various countries have built courts for the enjoyment of the staff and the British communities in general. The latest country to take up the game is Japan where a national association has already been formed and courts are being built in fulfilment of an ambitious programme to have 7,000 courts in that country in the next few years.

In the *U.S.A.*, squash rackets developed side by side with the game in England. The lack of a governing body in England until 1929 to lay down specifications for balls and courts was mainly responsible for the Americans' deciding their own specifications. Thus the American game differs from the English to such an extent as to make international competition hardly worthwhile.

The American court is 2 ft. 6 in. (762 mm.) narrower than its English counterpart. The walls are wooden or plastered and the floor is painted white. The scoring system is different in that a player scores a point whether he is in hand or not, and the game consists of 15 points instead of 9. There are other minor differences but the main obstacle is the ball, which in America is almost solid (as well as larger) and hence flies around the court much faster than an English one. In the 1920s and '30s there was some exchange of international teams, with the odds heavily weighted in favour of the home team, but since the Second World War, apart from the Wolfe Noel Cup for women, there have been visits only by university and club sides. It has always been easier to go from the English to the American game and Americans coming to England have found that a long period of practice is necessary before they can compete on equal terms with British players.

Squash is rapidly gaining popularity in the Eastern states and there are over 2,000 squash courts in the U.S.A. There are at present no public courts, the game being confined to clubs and universities. National championships commenced in 1907, 15 years before the amateur championship was first held in England.

In *Canada* the American game is played, and here also national championships, commenced in 1911, were played long before the championship in England. But the game has not progressed as fast as in the U.S.A., and is confined to a comparatively small number of clubs and schools mainly in the Eastern Provinces.

The American game is making tremendous strides in *Mexico*, and in the four years prior to 1973, the number of courts in that country increased from 15 to 1,300.

Professionalism has never played as important a part in squash as it has in many other sports, and the number of professionals in recent years has not been sufficient to cater for the demands for coaching. Most of the early professionals were trained in rackets. The best-known were Read (Queen's Club), Johnston (R.A.C.), and BUTCHER (Conservative Club). The lack of young recruits to the English professional ranks after the Second World War led to the importing of Pakistanis and Egyptians, many of whom came to England in the first instance to play in the small number of professional events in the English fixture list. The first was Kerim who came from Cairo early in 1947 and in the Open championship defeated the pre-war champion, DEAR. He was supreme for four years until the arrival of Hashim Khan who began a long reign of Pakistani supremacy in the game which lasted until 1964 when Taleb regained the Open title for Egypt.

The role of the professional in England is almost entirely coaching. The professional championship of the British Isles was discontinued in 1962 for lack of entries and for some years the only competition which a professional could obtain was in the Open championship and — if he were British and practising there — the professional championship of the United Kingdom. Recently an increasing number of tournaments have become open to professionals.

When BARRINGTON turned professional in 1969 he brought a new concept to the term. He toured the country, holding clinics in many clubs, and extended these operations to other parts of the world, notably South Africa. He was the first professional to found a touring 'circus' playing exhibition matches all over the world.

The growth of competitive squash in England was comparatively slow, the game being for long regarded in this country as a relaxation rather than a serious sport. In the U.S.A. the first national championship took place in 1906 and in South Africa an amateur championship was held in 1910 but not until 1922 was the amateur championship started in England, while the Open championship of the British Isles was not instituted until 1930 when Read (Queen's Club professional) was designated as champion. This event was played on a challenge system until 1946 after which it became a knock-out tournament. It has been generally regarded as the most important championship in the game, and professionals and amateurs have annually travelled from all over the world to take part in it. The championship proper has usually been restricted to a comparatively small number — generally 16 — but eliminating competitions have enabled a larger number to compete.

Success in the amateur championship entitled the winner to be regarded as the best amateur player in the world, but, with the foundation of the International Squash Rackets Federation in 1966, the international amateur championships played under the auspices of that body came to be considered as the senior tournament in the game from the point of view of the team as well as of the individual event.

In 1951 the amateur veterans' championship was founded in Britain for players of 45 years and over. Similar events are now common in many other countries but abroad it is more common for veteran age to start at 40. In 1964 a veterans' Open championship was started and is usually won by one of the senior Pakistani professionals.

In Australia 'pennant' series in all the main cities are the only competitions short of the national and inter-state championship and hundreds of teams play in this way.

In many parts of the world the long distances which teams must travel to get competitive play are a limiting factor. In England this does not apply and practically the whole country is covered by leagues of some sort. In the London region the senior and most important league is the BATH CLUB Cup, founded in 1922 as a three-a-side competition. The restriction of this tournament to West End social clubs has in recent years tended to militate against its influence, particularly with the increasing importance of the more democratic Cumberland Cup for five-a-side teams from clubs within 11 miles of the centre of London. One of the factors discouraging a club from playing more matches is the fact that they take the use of courts away from the ordinary members.

On a knock-out basis the senior competition in England is the inter-county championship, started in 1929. The British Army championships were first held in 1925 and have produced a number of players who made their mark in the game. BROOMFIELD, with four Army championship wins, won the amateur championship before he joined the army and Hamilton (killed in the Second World War), who won the Army championship on three occasions in the 1930s, won the amateur championship in 1934. Perkins has been the most successful army competitor, having been army champion on seven occasions. He also represented Great Britain in South Africa in 1955 and played for England nine times.

Squash in the Royal Navy has of necessity been more restricted than in the other Services although most shore stations have their own courts. The Royal Navy championship was started in 1925, the same year as the Army championship. Bawtree has been the most successful competitor, with so far seven wins. But of the three armed services, the Royal Air Force has taken the game most seriously, and every permanent station was provided with at least one court. The R.A.F. championship was started in 1928. Up to 1973 Sq. Ldr. Stokes, with nine wins, was the most successful competitor. He also played for Great Britain and Wales. In 1929, an inter-service tournament was initiated and was won by the army in 12 of the first 13 contests, with the R.A.F. winning in 1937. The Royal Navy scored their first win in 1949. In the late 1960s and early 1970s the R.A.F. showed marked superiority over the other services, winning the title seven times running from 1966 onwards.

The finances of squash rackets suffer from one great disadvantage in that the size and shape of the court precludes a large space for spectators. In England the introduction of glass back walls has helped, and the main court at the Abbeydale Sports Club, Sheffield, can accommodate 450 spectators. In other parts of the world the position is no better. The gallery at ALBERT PARK, Melbourne, will accommodate about 450 and that at the Wanderers Club, Johannesburg, about the same number. The organizers of national championships are therefore unable to gather in large takings as other games do. This in turn limits the prize money payable to professionals, and expenses to amateurs. Squash would seem to be an ideal sport to benefit from sponsorship, yet for many years this boon has been denied to the game by the absence of publicity available to the sponsoring firm's products.

WOMEN'S SQUASH. Mainly because most of the early squash courts were in exclusively male establishments, women's squash was later to start and slower to catch on. Squash was also regarded by many as too strenuous for women. Yet nowadays the game is played by thousands of women and the Women's Squash Rackets Association, formed in 1934, organizes a full round of championships and tournaments. The first women's championship was played in 1922—the same year as the first amateur championship. The most famous woman player was Miss Morgan (now Mrs. Shardlow, Chairman of the Women's Squash Rackets Association) who won the championship for ten successive years from 1950 onwards. Her record has been beaten by the Australian Miss Blundell (now Mrs. McKay) who won 13 championships in succession in devastatingly easy style.

In 1933 a cup was presented for competition between Great Britain and the U.S.A. to be played alternately in each country. This, the Wolfe-Noel Cup, is the only remaining official competition played between this country and America.

Because of their physical disadvantages women are unable to compete on level terms with men, but an annual match is played on handicap between teams representing the Women's Squash Rackets Association and the Squash Rackets Association.

JUNIORS. Squash has been popular with schoolboys wherever facilities have been pro-

vided. It is significant that as late as 1937 there were only six schools which had become affiliated to their respective county associations, and Devon was the only county to hold a junior championship prior to 1946. In 1922 Queen's Club, London, presented the Evans Cup for competition among juniors under the age of 18. A subsidiary event, the public schools (under 16) tournament, was run concurrently with the senior competition. The Evans Cup had to find new premises after the Second World War and was played at a number of venues ending at the Bath Club. It was finally discontinued in 1967 on the formation of the Bath Club inter-schools tournament. In 1972 a further event, the Premiere Products National Schools Competition, was inaugurated with nearly 100 schools competing.

It was not until 1925 that the R.A.C. presented the Drysdale Cup in memory of Dr. Drysdale, (a member of that club who had represented Great Britain in America in 1924) for competition among juniors under the age of 19. This event has been played annually, except for the war years, at the R.A.C. and, although organized by the club rather than by the governing body of the game, it is universally regarded as the junior championship. The Lonsdale Cup, for a public schools open doubles competition, was started in 1938 and revived in 1952, since when it has been played for annually in London concurrently with the Drysdale Cup. The Surrey junior championships for many years included an inter-schools doubles event as well as a preparatory school doubles which was incorporated into the newly-formed preparatory schools tournament in 1967.

Nearly 100 schools recognize the game sufficiently to affiliate either to the Squash Rackets Association direct or to the appropriate county association. While most schools have to be content with two courts there are no less than 12 at Eton College.

In Australia there are no courts at schools but the pupils have recognized playing facilities at some of the public courts. In South Africa there are only a handful of schools with their own courts.

Junior championships are held in a number of countries including Canada, the U.A.R., Kenya, and New Zealand. In Australia a men's junior championship is played concurrently with the Australian championship and attracts an entry of about 32, while in the U.S.A. the national junior squash championship has between 50 and 60 entrants.

J. P. Barrington, *The Book of Jonah* (1972); L. Hamer and R. Bellamy, *Squash Rackets* (1968); R. B. Hawkey, *Newer Angles on Squash* (1973); John Hopkins, *Squash Rackets* (forthcoming,

1975); *The Squash Rackets Association Handbook*, annually.

GOVERNING BODY (WORLD): International Squash Rackets Federation, 4M Artillery Mansions, Victoria Street, London S.W.1.

SQUASH TENNIS, an American development of SQUASH RACKETS, is basically squash played with a LAWN TENNIS ball. Both the ball and the racket are slightly smaller than the tennis variety, and the ball is tightly covered with netting. The effect is to make it at least twice as fast as a squash ball, so that although the rules of the two games are almost identical, squash tennis is a radically different game. Instead of the ball absorbing much of the speed of the shot, as happens in squash rackets, it comes off the wall faster than it goes on to it. The result is a game of extraordinary speed, in which angles play a dominant part.

The greatest differences in the details of the two games lie in a reduction in the height of the back wall for squash tennis to 4 ft. 6 in. (1·37 m.), and in a change in service technique. The server may stand anywhere in his own service court, but must hit the ball so that it rebounds off the wall into the area in front of the service line (instead of behind it) on his opponent's side of the court.

Squash tennis was born in a school in Concord, New Hampshire, towards the end of the nineteenth century. The boys simply used a lawn tennis racket and ball in a squash court, but the game was refined by Feron, of New York, who first wrapped netting round the ball. Later, special equipment was made and new courts marked. For a while at the beginning of the century it looked as though squash tennis was going to overtake squash rackets in popularity, but the boom faded, squash rackets prospered and squash tennis retreated to the New York area, where it is still chiefly practised. There have been United States squash tennis championships since 1911.

STADE ROLAND-GARROS, situated on the edge of the Bois de Boulogne at Auteuil, is the largest LAWN TENNIS stadium in France. It was named after a French airman of the First World War, and was built in 1927 to accommodate the crowds who wanted to watch the highly successful French Davis Cup (see LAWN TENNIS) team of the 1920s. The huge concrete centre court holds about 17,000 spectators and there are nine slow, red clay courts.

STAGG, AMOS ALONZO (1862-1965), American college FOOTBALL player and coach. He played end at YALE, 1885-9, the last year on the first All-America team, and then coached college football for a total of 63 years

at Springfield (Massachusetts) College, 1890-1; the University of CHICAGO, 1892-1932; and the College of the Pacific, 1933-46. The originator of more plays and formations than any other coach, he pioneered multiple passing on single plays, the huddle before each play, the direct pass from centre to a back, backfield shifts, and the numbering of players. His most famous teams were the 1904-6 University of Chicago teams, with the legendary quarterback and kicker, Eckersall.

STANKOVICH, VASSILY (1946-   ), Russian fencer who won the world foil championship in Vienna in 1971. He first took up fencing in 1963, and was in the national team by 1966. He won world team gold medals in 1969, 1970, and 1973; in 1973 he won all four of his fights in the final to defeat West Germany 9-7.

STANLEY CUP, ICE HOCKEY trophy, the oldest such award competed for by professional athletes in North America; awarded annually to the winning team in the Stanley Cup play-off series contested by the highest-placed hockey clubs at the end of the NATIONAL HOCKEY LEAGUE (N.H.L.) championship. It was donated in 1893 by Lord Stanley of Preston, then Governor-General of Canada, originally for presentation to the amateur champions of Canada. Since 1910, it has been the emblem of North American ice hockey supremacy and, from 1926, has been competed for exclusively by N.H.L. teams. In 1973, MONTREAL CANADIENS won it for the eighteenth time, seven times more than TORONTO MAPLE LEAFS, the next most successful side. Accompanying the trophy is a monetary yearly award totalling $63,000, distributed to members of the winning team.

STARBROOK, DAVID COLIN (1945-   ), British JUDO fighter whose strength and determination secured him a number of medals in world-class competition during the 1970s. Although initially he had had an indifferent international career, he broke through in 1971, being a member of the British team which captured the European title and then taking a middleweight bronze medal at the world championships. In 1972 he moved up to light-heavyweight, securing second place at the Munich Olympics. The following year he confirmed his status with a silver medal in the European championships and a bronze at the world championships.

STATHAM, JOHN BRIAN, C.B.E. (1930-   ), cricketer for England and Lancashire. Accurate, and able to swing the ball, he was a fast bowler of the highest class; he took 252 wickets in Test matches (a total then exceeded only by TRUEMAN) and 1,816 for Lancashire. He and Tyson bowled formidably as a pair against Australia in 1954-5, but his finest performance was probably in taking 7 wickets for 39 runs, when he bowled through the innings against South Africa at LORD'S in 1955.

STAWELL GIFT HANDICAP, Australian professional running race, probably the most important event in professional ATHLETICS (see also POWDERHALL). Inaugurated in 1878 in the comparatively remote mining town of Stawell in Victoria, it offers a prize of £1,000 to the winner of its uphill sprint of 130 yards (118·9 m.).

STEARNS, C. (1936-), American water skier, who set the first world speed record of 122·11 m.p.h. (196·3 km./h.).

STECHER, RENATE (*née* Meissner) (1950-), sprinter for the German Democratic Republic. First woman to break 11 sec. for 100 metres, Mrs. Stecher equalled the old record of 11·0 sec. in 1970, 1971, and 1972 before reducing it in 1973 to 10·9 and then 10·8 sec. She made a clean sweep of gold medals in major championships in the space of 12 months, winning the European 100 and 200 metres at Helsinki in 1971 and the Olympic 100 and 200 metres at Munich in 1972. In Munich her 200 metres time of 22·4 sec. equalled the world record and this she lowered to 22·1 sec. in 1973. She also won gold medals in the European indoor championships in 1970 and 1971 (60 metres) and in 1972 (50 metres).

STEEL, DOROTHY DYNE (1884-1965). The supreme woman CROQUET player of all time, Miss Steel played with a very upright style, side stance, and appeared to exert no energy in the execution of her strokes. Only two other women have won the open championship and her four wins in this event and four in the Beddow Cup which she won outright (it was succeeded by the President's Cup which she won twice), made her the equal of any man of her time. She played in the MACROBERTSON trophy for England in 1925, 1928, and 1937, and between 1919 and 1939 also won fifteen women's championships (eight of them in succession), five open doubles, and seven mixed doubles championships.

STEEPLECHASE. The 3,000 metres steeplechase features in the programme of events for men in all major ATHLETICS championships. It is a test of MIDDLE-DISTANCE RUNNING, endurance, and HURDLING skill. The 3,000 metres course, usually of just over seven laps, includes a total of 35 obstacles —four hurdles and one water jump in each lap. The hurdles are 3 ft. (91 cm.) high; a hurdle of the same height is placed before the water jump which is 12 ft. (3·66 m.) across, the depth of the water being 2 ft. 3½ in. (70 cm.) immediately in front of the hurdle and sloping up to track level at the further end.

The first steeplechase of which there is a record took place at Oxford in 1850 over a two-mile cross-country course with 24 obstacles. Steeplechases of varying distances were staged in the OLYMPIC GAMES in 1900, 1904, and 1908, but the 3,000 metres course was not standardized until 1920. The International Amateur Athletic Federation (see ATHLETICS, TRACK AND FIELD) first recognized world records in 1954.

STEEPLECHASING (1), see HORSE RACING.

(2) A DECK GAME whose name implies some affinity with the game of HORSE-RACING, though none exists. Steeplechasing is, in effect, a dice and board game of the type played indoors but with a much enlarged course that used to be chalked on a part of the deck but is now painted on a portable canvas. The course is usually horseshoe shaped and divided from start to finish into 100 segments. Against some of the squares are marked penalties (incurring going back a number of places, starting again, or missing a turn for 'refusing to jump' or 'dislodging jockey' and so on), and against a further number advantages (rewarding a 'burst of acceleration' or 'a good leap' by advancing a bonus couple of squares). The game, with passengers betting on the horses, varies from the customary indoor board game in that the horses are not usually operated by their owners or the punters. Instead, two dice are thrown, one of them indicating which of the six horses is to be moved, the other the number of places it is to advance.

STEINKRAUS, WILLIAM (1925-), American show jumping (see EQUESTRIAN EVENTS) rider. Winner of the individual gold medal in Mexico (1968), he first joined the U.S.A. show jumping team in 1951 and was its captain from 1955. He won a team bronze medal at the 1952 OLYMPIC GAMES on Hollandia, and two team silver medals (in 1960 on Ksar d'Esprit and in 1972 on Main Spring). He also won three team medals in the PAN-AMERICAN GAMES: two gold (1959 and 1963) and one silver (1967).

STENGEL, CHARLES DILLON (Casey) (1889-), American BASEBALL player and manager. As a player he performed in journeyman fashion for several NATIONAL LEAGUE teams (1912-25) and then managed National League clubs for nine years before achieving wide acclaim as manager of the NEW YORK YANKEES, a team that captured ten AMERICAN LEAGUE championships and seven world championships in the 12 seasons that he led them (1949-60). He established a record by winning five of the league pennants and the WORLD SERIES in consecutive years, 1949-53. His colourful personality and his own brand of English, called 'Stengelese', made him popular with sports writers. After his dismissal by the New York Yankees in 1960, he managed the NEW YORK METS, one of the newly-formed teams of the expanded National League, from 1962 through 1965.

STEPANOVA, GALINA, *née* Prosumenschikova (1948-), the only European to win a SWIMMING gold medal at the 1964 OLYMPIC GAMES in Tokyo — in the 200 metres breaststroke — she was still the best in the world for her style in 1970. Champion of Europe for 200 metres in 1966, she retained this title in 1970 and also won the new event for 100 metres breaststroke in Barcelona. She gained a silver medal and a bronze at the 1968 Olympics in Mexico City and repeated this feat at the 1972 Games in Munich.

STEPHENSON, GEORGE VAUGHN (1903-70), RUGBY UNION centre three-quarter for QUEEN'S UNIVERSITY, Belfast, and Ireland. A strong defensive player and a reliable placekicker, he won 42 caps in the period 1920-30, which remained a world record until overtaken by KYLE after the Second World War.

STEVENS, CONSTANTINE AUGUSTUS LUCY (1900-), GREYHOUND RACING pioneer who helped create Wimbledon Stadium. Universally known as 'Con', after 40 years in the sport he had become chairman, racing director, senior steward, and racing manager at Wimbledon Stadium, chairman of Rochester Stadium, vice-chairman of Bristol and Oxford stadia, and a director of Bristol Rovers Football Club.

STEWARDS' CHALLENGE CUP, see HENLEY ROYAL REGATTA.

STEWART, JOHN (1939-), most polished and accurate British MOTOR RACING driver. Jackie Stewart in his early days raced a LOTUS Élan and in 1964 drove a COOPER-BMC Formula Three, scoring a total of seven wins during the year. He also drove a rear-engined Cooper-Monaco and a Formula Two Lotus-Cosworth. With the Lotus he was second on both the difficult Clermont-Ferrand circuit and at MONTLHÉRY and third in the OULTON PARK Gold Cup. Stewart's brilliance was quickly recognized and for 1965 he was signed to drive for BRM with whom he stayed until the 1967 season, struggling to make the H-16 cars raceworthy and doing much of his racing under the 3-litre Grand Prix Formula with the outdated 2-litre V-8 cars. In 1965 he was third in the world championship in his first season of Grand Prix racing. During that year he drove a Formula Two Cooper-BRM for Tyrrell and subsequently handled Formula Two Matras for this entrant.

For 1968 Stewart signed to drive a Formula One Matra powered by a Ford engine. A practice crash in the Formula Two Madrid Grand Prix resulted in his cracking a bone, missing two world championship races, and driving for much of the season with his wrist supported in a plastic corset. Even so, he won three world championship races and took second place in the championship with 36 points. In 1968 he won the Dutch, German, and U.S. Grands Prix and the Oulton Park Gold Cup and was placed third in the French Grand Prix. He signed to drive a Tyrrell-entered Matra-Ford again in 1969, together with Matra Formula Two cars, and clinched the world championship. Stewart retired after the 1973 season.

STEWART-WOOD, JEANNETTE (1948-), water skier for Great Britain; she was Britain's first gold medallist in world competition when, in 1967, she won the jumping and over-all titles in Canada. In the international at Ruislip, Middlesex, she equalled the world record with a jump of 106 ft. $3\frac{1}{2}$ in. (32·39 m.).

STILT RACING, see STREET GAMES.

STOCK-CAR RACING, see MOTOR RACING, AMERICAN.

STOCKPORT, LACROSSE club, Cheshire, England. Founded in 1875, this club dominated northern lacrosse for over 50 years. The champion club of England on 15 occasions, and winners of the North of England Senior Flags and the senior league 16 times, Stockport has the distinction of being the only club to have defeated a Canadian touring side. In more recent times, the best players include Griffiths and Kershaw.

COLOURS: Dark blue shirts and white shorts.

STOCKWELL (1849), English race-horse by The Baron out of POCAHONTAS, won the ST. LEGER, TWO THOUSAND GUINEAS, and nine other races, being beaten only by a head in the ASCOT GOLD CUP. Stockwell became 'the Emperor of Stallions', heading the winning sires list seven times (and second four times) and siring 209 winners of 1,147 races to the value of £362,541, including a record 17 classic winners.

STODDART, ANDREW ERNEST (1863-1915), cricketer for England and Middlesex; RUGBY UNION footballer for England, HARLEQUIN F. C., and BLACKHEATH. An agile and originative wing three-quarter, he captained England in four of his ten internationals, but earned even greater acclaim at CRICKET, having hit 485 for Hampstead in a club match in 1886 — then the highest score ever recorded. He toured Australia four times, captaining the successful English team of 1894-5 (when he scored a match-winning 173 in the second Test), and the vanquished 1897-8 team. For the Gentlemen and for England he and GRACE were a commanding pair of opening batsmen for several seasons.

STOKE CITY F.C., Association FOOTBALL club, founded in 1863 by old boys of Charterhouse School. The club, known simply as Stoke until 1924 when 'City' was added, adopted professionalism in 1885 and was one of the 12 original members of the Football League in 1888. Stoke are the second oldest League club in the world but, unlike NOTTS COUNTY, the oldest, have not remained in continuous membership of the Football League. After finishing in bottom place in the first two seasons, Stoke had to give way after an election to SUNDERLAND but returned after one season and remained until 1908 when, after one season in the Second Division, Stoke resigned and played until the outbreak of war in 1914 in the Southern League. When football was resumed after the war, Stoke were elected to the Second Division of the Football League in the 1919-20 season. Major honours eluded the club until the League Cup was won in 1972, but it has been remarkable for the number of outstanding players it has produced or obtained by transfer. In 1971, after an interval of 72 years, Stoke reached the semi-final of the F.A. Cup for the second time in their history. In the Football League the highest position reached in the First Division was fourth in 1936 and 1947. The club's outstanding players have included, pre-1914, Rowley, Clare, Underwood, Roose, and Capes; 1919 to 1939: MATTHEWS, Steele, and Soo; and post-1946, Allen, FRANKLIN, and BANKS.

COLOURS: Red and white striped shirts, white shorts.
GROUND: Victoria Ground, Stoke-on-Trent.

STOKE MANDEVILLE GAMES, see PARAPLEGIC GAMES.

STOLLE, FREDERICK S. (1938-   ), Australian LAWN TENNIS player and one of the most successful doubles players of the 1960s. Stolle shared with VON CRAMM the unhappy distinction of being runner-up in three successive singles finals at WIMBLEDON. McKinley (U.S.A.) beat him in 1963 and EMERSON in the two following years. Stolle's best early achievements were in doubles, but in 1964 he established himself as Australia's second singles player and, with Emerson, recaptured the Davis Cup (see LAWN TENNIS) from the U.S.A. at Cleveland, Ohio. His 7-5, 6-3, 3-6, 9-11, 6-4 victory over Ralston was decisive. Between 1964 and 1966 Stolle won 13 Davis Cup rubbers out of 16. He won the French singles title in 1965 and the German and U.S. singles titles in 1966 before turning professional early in 1967.

STONEY COVE, near Hinckley, Leicestershire, a flooded quarry with depths to 120 ft. (36·6 m.), the British Sub Aqua Club's (see UNDERWATER SWIMMING) inland 'national diving site'.

STOOLBALL is an 11-a-side ball game played largely in junior schools in southern England, but also, and increasingly, by women, particularly in Sussex where the County Association organize a league championship.

The ball, slightly smaller than a ROUNDERS ball (not more than 7½ in. — 190 mm. — in diameter), is solid and covered with kid leather. The bat has a short, stout handle and a flat and bevelled side. The game is played on a pitch 16 yds. (14·63 m.) long, with a bowling crease 1 yd. (0·9 m.) long at a distance of 10 yds. (9·14 m.) from either 'wicket'.

The 'wickets' are boards, 1 ft. (0·3 m.) square, mounted on stakes driven into the running course, the top of the wicket being 4 ft. 8 in. (1·4 m.) from the ground.

Scoring and rules are similar to those of CRICKET, although simpler. The batting side defends the wickets by striking at balls delivered by their opponents, at the same time attempting to score runs by running from crease to crease after striking the ball.

The ball is bowled underhand and the bowler must have both feet behind, and within the limits of, the bowling crease at the moment of delivery. The delivery is a 'no ball' if the ball hits the ground before it reaches the wicket; if it is thrown; or if it reaches the stake less than 12 in. (0·3 m.) from the ground. A 'wide ball' is one bowled out of reach of the

Running crease

Stake and face board

16 yds.
(14.63 m.)

10 yds.
(9.14 m.)

Bowling
crease

1 yd.
(0.9 m.)

Bowling
crease

10 yds.
(9.14 m.)

Stake and face board

Running crease

STOOLBALL PITCH
The striker at the top wicket (i.e. stake and face board) faces bowling from the bottom bowling crease, and vice versa.

striker and one run is added to the score of the batting side, although if the striker jumps and hits the ball, it ceases to be wide.

Deliveries are made in 'overs' of eight balls each, to each wicket alternately. No balls and wides are not counted as part of the over.

The striker is out if the ball when bowled hits any part of the face of the wicket (except the stump); or if the ball, having been hit, is held clean in the hand, or hands, of one of the opposing team, not touching any other part of the body above the wrist; or if, while the striker is running or preparing or pretending to run, the ball is thrown by one of the opposite

team so that it hits the face of the wicket; or if any of the opposite team hits the face of the wicket with the ball before the bat or hand of either of the strikers touches it; or if with any part of his person the striker stops the ball which in the opinion of the bowler's umpire would have hit his wicket.

A player is not out if caught or bowled on a no ball; or if, owing to obstruction by a fielder, he is unable to touch the wicket; or if the ball hits the side of the wicket when thrown in by a fielder. No obstruction at the wicket by any of the players is allowed. The batsman is counted in his ground if, in the event of dropping his bat, he touches the wicket or stump with his hand. The batsman must touch his wicket on commencing his innings, after every run, and after every attempt to run. A non-striker is out of his ground unless with his bat in hand he can touch his wicket.

If a fair delivery passes the striker without touching his bat or person, and any runs are obtained, the umpire signals 'bye'. If in running the strikers have crossed each other, the one running for the wicket which is struck by the ball is out and the incomplete run does not count in the score.

If 'lost ball' is called, the striker is allowed three runs, but if more than three have been run before 'lost ball' is called, then the striker scores whatever has been run.

The umpires, one of each wicket, are the sole judges of fair play. All disputes are settled by them, each at his own wicket. In case of doubt the other umpire may be requested to give an opinion, which will be decisive. The umpires stand, one where he can best see the bowling crease and his wicket, and the other at square leg position. They do not give a decision without an appeal.

The ingoing and outgoing batsmen must cross on the field of play. Ten minutes are allowed between innings.

Gloves must not be worn by the wicket-keeper and plimsolls are the only form of footwear. Shin pads may be worn.

One peculiarity of the game is that a 'century' is in fact a score of 50 runs. The achievement is usually permanently acknowledged by the attachment of an appropriately inscribed shield-shaped badge to the back of the player's bat.

Stoolball, because of the simplicity of the equipment involved, was a sport which the common people could play. It was one of the two older pastimes from which the modern game of cricket probably sprang. It was from CLUB BALL that cricket derived the use of the straight bat and of fielders, but the idea of bowling at a wicket, an essential feature in the development of cricket, was borrowed from stoolball where, as its name suggests, the 'wicket' was a stool. In the later development of cricket, the target at which a ball was bowled was often the entwined fencing, made of wicker, used by shepherds on southern English downs.

During the reign of Elizabeth I, the Earl of Leicester with a great number of attendants and country people 'went to Wotton Hill, where he plaid a match at stoball'. Stoolball was then a hand game in which the bowler's aim was to strike the stool with the ball, and that of the batsman to defend it with his hand. There were apparently no runs in the sense of the batsman covering the length of the pitch, but if the bowler struck the stool or caught the ball after the batsman had struck it and before it hit the ground, the players changed places,

STOOLBALL WICKET
The face board is ¼ in. (13 mm.) thick and protrudes ¼ in. (6 mm.) from the stake. The stake is painted black at the bottom to a distance of 1 ft. (0·3 m.) from the ground into which it is driven, on the running crease.

while every time the batsman made a successful stroke, he scored one point.

In 1671 Aubrey described another variation of what was basically the same game: 'It is peculiar to North Wiltshire, North Gloucestershire, and a little part of Somerset near Bath. They smite a ball stuffed very hard with quills and covered with soale leather, with a staffe commonly made of withy, about three and a half feet long.... A stoball ball is of about four inches in diameter and as hard as a stone.'

In fact the game was more widely spread than Aubrey thought. There are references to

its being played around the same period in Wales, Sussex, Lancashire, and several other districts. Herrick in *Hesperides* refers to stoolball in 1648, and the game is mentioned in *Poor Robin's Almanack* in 1677 and in later editions.

Strutt, in *Sports and Pastimes* (1801), describes it as being a variation on the game more commonly known as 'goff' or 'bandy ball'. This, he says, was derived from the *paganica* of the Romans who also used balls stuffed with feathers. According to Dr. Johnson, stoolball derived its name from the fact that the ball was driven from stool to stool. It was because of the use of stools that the game became traditionally linked with milkmaids; but all trades and occupations — children and adults alike — appear to have played it at festivals and merrymaking.

Towards the end of the nineteenth century stoolball in more or less its original form was still being played by children in Lancashire. But it was in Sussex late in that century that stoolball was revived and given the light basic rules which have been amplified but remain generally fundamental in the modern game. The rules of stoolball as it is played today compiled by the Sussex County Stoolball Association and revised in 1967, number 25 but the essentials of the original eight rules remain, in particular the peculiar features that the ball has to be bowled in the air and not pitched on the ground; that the wicket itself is mounted above the ground, and that it is the wicket, and not the ground, that has to be touched by the striker with his bat.

Given that the ground surface is not so uneven or furrowed as to be dangerous to the strikers when running, it is possible for stoolball to be played in fields and school playgrounds that would not be suitable for some other ball games. This, and the establishment of something like a uniform set of rules, undoubtedly encouraged the development of the game, and account for its present settled and flourishing existence, particularly in Sussex for adult clubs (where it is played by women whose ages run from 15 to 50), but throughout the south of England in schools. The saving of money, time, and labour that would have to be expended preparing and maintaining the surface for most other ball games is an obvious factor in favour of stoolball.

The game is considered to be a useful introduction for junior boys to cricket.

STOOP, ADRIAN DURA (1883-1957), RUGBY UNION outside half for HARLEQUINS, Oxford University, and England. A captain of Harlequins and chief tactician in the national side, he led the revival of English Rugby, particularly its back play, in the period between 1910 and the First World War. Influenced by the Welsh and the 1905-6 ALL-BLACKS teams, he reintroduced the element of surprise into attack, and the skill of running and passing at speed. His brother, F. M. Stoop, played with him for Harlequins and England.

STRASBOURG–PARIS, a French road RACE WALKING event which has varied in distance from 503 km. (312 miles) to 552 km. (343 miles). Created by ANTHOINE in 1926, the race was held from Paris to Strasbourg from 1926 to 1937 and 1949 to 1951 and in the reverse direction from 1952 to 1959 and 1970 to 1973. The race was not held after 1960 on advice from the police, but was eventually revived ten years later. The race is sponsored by two newspapers, *L'Équipe* and *Le Parisien Libéré.*

The outstanding performer has been ROGER, winner in 1949, 1953, 1954, 1956, and 1958. He also holds every intermediate record from 50 to 537 km. in this event. The record for finishing most times is 13 held by Dujardin (1927-55). The sole Englishman ever to have finished is Young (1970, 1971, 1972). Both in distance and time the Strasbourg–Paris race is the longest athletic event held regularly in the world.

The course is the severest of any race walk due not only to the distance but also because of the numerous climbs and bad *pavé.* After crossing the Vosges mountains in Alsace the road goes via Nancy and Château-Thierry, finishing at Vincennes, on the outskirts of Paris. The event is held in early June.

STREET GAMES have been played for as long as there have been streets in which to play them. Their form and the extent to which they have been played has been influenced by the incidence of traffic, whether pedestrian or vehicular, for which the streets were intended to be used, even if games players have disputed this, particularly when they were denied any alternate playing-space. Generally, except on festive occasions when streets, either by decree or, more likely, by custom, were closed to traffic and given over to the playing of games as, for examples, *calcio* in Florence, FOOTBALL in Workington or Chester-le-Street, and the Furry Dance in Helston, street games tended to be played in defiance of authority. In England it was often as a matter of choice and as a healthy assertion that a man should be free in his leisure hours to do what he wanted to do rather than what he was told.

As Christina Hole wrote in *English Sports and Pastimes,* foreign visitors found it extraor-

dinary that both football and cockfighting should be tolerated in the narrow streets of Tudor England. As she says: 'Davenant, in his description of London in 1634, makes his Frenchman exclaim at such pastimes, sarcastically adding that, while they doubtless proved the national courage, "your mettle would be more magnified (since you have allowed these two valiant exercises in the streets) to draw your archers from Finsbury and during high market let them shoot at in Cheapside." ' ARCHERY was for many years the most favoured of all sports when kings and governments held firmly to the opinion that only pastimes and recreations that trained men for war should be encouraged. Various statutes and acts from 1285 to 1541 ordered all Englishmen, except judges and clerics, to keep a longbow of their own height, and to train their children and servants how to use it. More, they decreed that 'every township must erect butts at which the inhabitants were to shoot on Sundays and feast-days, or be fined one halfpenny for each failure to do so'.

Games that were popular and lured the inhabitants away from the butts were 'idle' and were repeatedly prohibited by law — so frequently that it is clear that edicts did little to stop their being played. Most of the 'idle' games were ball games that, basically, had existed from a very remote period of history. In England ball games were well known in the early Middle Ages and some may have existed centuries before. There were, by medieval and Tudor times, a variety of ball games that were popular despite the laws and displeasure of authority. As Hole remarks: 'Servants, apprentices, and labourers, were continually urged to turn to more manly sports, and fined or imprisoned when they did not; edict after edict forbidding unprofitable pastimes was patiently issued, but never with any permanent success. An obstinate people from the first, the English clung to their favourite pleasures and cheerfully continued to enjoy them in spite of all the penalties devised by law-makers.'

Hobby-horses appear in paintings in many countries from the Renaissance onwards; they were a 'prop' in pageantry (and a toy for the children of the wealthy, who never played street games, until replaced by the rocking horse in the eighteenth century) and were later roughly made by poor children and 'raced' by them through narrow, teeming streets. Stilts, on which the Maya Indians of Yucatan danced to please their bird god, Yaccocahmut, and which were well known in ancient Rome and possibly the basis of the legends of the Titans, were still being made and used for pavement races by children in England in the 1930s.

The disadvantage of hobby-horse and stilts

play and races was that those playing had to come furnished with their equipment; street games, however, were not planned beforehand. The sense of being free to do what one wanted in defiance of authority, whether expressed in the edicts of Plantagenet kings or in parental threats five hundred years later, persisted in the playing of most street games. Throughout the ages, children faced with the problem of what to play have been glad to fall back on a race or, perhaps even better, a chase if they were boys, or some singing or dancing game if they were girls.

Boys, too, seem always to have realized that one of their number could run faster than the others and there was no satisfaction in running a race with a certain winner. Thus even the simplest of street race games had its element of surprise that gave some chance to those who ran less fast than the others. Often the aim was less to note the winner of the race than to fault the last player. The width of a street and back again was the distance to be covered. One player — the starter — stood on one side of the street and faced the runners on the other side. At a signal from the starter, the race across the street and back began, but a part of the game was to recognize the signal. A basic style was called 'odds and evens' in which the starter called out either 'Odds' or 'Evens' followed by a number that might be odd or even. If he called 'Odd five', the race was correctly started and the last player to cross the road and back was 'out' for the next race. If on the other hand the starter called 'Even three' and anyone started wrongly, that player was also 'out'.

There were several variations of the starting formula — many of them topical since, although the pattern of street games was traditional, and there was an inherent reluctance to accept invented new ones, children have always liked to believe they were more up-to-date than others.

Chanting games, played by girls for centuries as street games, provide a similar link with pagan customs, ancient rites, and blurred historical associations. They include songs about falling bridges, 'London Bridge is broken down', being the best-known of them, which are probably linked with the pagan custom of immuring living sacrifices in the foundations of a building to appease the spirit, and the fear that if this was not done the building would collapse. Fertility rites were the source for many popular traditional street games like 'I sent a letter to my love', and 'Nuts in May', once 'knots' (or small bunches of flowers) in May. Ring games, like the 'Farmer's in his den', and 'Poor Mary is a-weeping', represented the winning of a wife. The belief that

dancing and skipping stimulated the growth o crops was the reason for many games an dances as, for example, the Furry Dance in th Cornish town of Helston. The interestin aspect is that such games have survived whereas topical street games of later years such as those which came out of the Firs World War, rarely outlast their immediat attraction. Often the significance of the word of the old choral dances, once performed o village greens but then in the streets, has bee lost or can only be hopefully surmised. Wha of the various forms of 'Here we dance lubin lubin, lubin' or 'looby, looby, looby'? It wa known in all parts of Britain and may owe it origin to a custom of wild antic dancing i celebration of the rites of some deity in whic animal postures were assumed. It was deep rooted enough in popularity for its action ('Pu all the right hands in/Take all the right hand out/Shake all the right hands together/And turn yourselves about') to be adapted to the popular dance of the 1940s, called the Hokey cokey.

Street games and pastimes like these grew up because the area of commons and ope spaces at the disposal of poorer folk was con stantly shrinking because of enclosures of th land. The enclosures by the Tudors, because they coincided with a growth of population had more sweeping social consequences tha had earlier ones, although the rate of enclosur in the first half of the sixteenth century ma not have been much greater than that of th middle of the fourteenth century; but th encroachment of common land reached it peak in the period from 1717 to 1820 whe more than four million acres were taken unde a succession of Enclosure Acts. It was this tha moved a writer to the *Worcester Chronicle* i 1847 to complain that 'before the common were taken in the children of the poor ha ample space to recreate themselves at cricket nurr, and any other diversion; but now the are driven from every green spot, and i Bromsgrove here, the nailer boys, from forc of circumstances, have taken possession of th turnpike road to play the before-mentione games, to the serious inconvenience of th passengers, one of whom, a woman, was yes terday knocked down by a nurr which struc her in the head.'

The nailer boys had found a champion but although the loss of the commons gave them the excuse to play on the turnpike road, it i possible that they would have been playin there in any event. For hundreds of years th playing of games in the street had brough remonstrations from house-dwellers, passin pedestrians, and drivers. In Manchester a edict of 1608 forbade the playing of football i 'ye streets of ye sd towne' because the players had been guilty of 'breaking many men's windowes and glasse at their pleasures, and other great enormyties'. Members of Parliament, in particular, seem often to have been disturbed by street games, the playing of PRISONERS' BASE in the neighbourhood of the Houses of Parliament being banned in the reign of Edward III because it interfered with members on their way to the House; and the boys of Westminster School were forbidden to play marbles in Westminster Hall because of the nuisance to Members of Parliament.

Marbles, one of the earliest of games, somewhat similarly incurred particular disapproval at Oxford where undergraduates were forbidden to play the game on the steps of the Bodleian Library. They were copying the Roman emperor, Augustus, who used to play it with his African slaves, using nuts instead of marbles, as did other Romans of his day.

The more than 3,000 Enclosure Acts passed between 1760 and 1820, together with the growth of population, and the drift to growing industrial areas of Manchester, Birmingham, Leeds, and Sheffield, did however make it almost impossible for adults, as much as children, to play other than in the streets. Several more years were to pass before local authorities, given much wider powers and responsibilities by the Municipal Reform Act of 1835, provided recreational space for their citizens. In Portsmouth, for example, a town less cramped and confined by industrial growth than the factory and mill towns of the midlands and the north, there was not a single public park or recreation ground in the borough until 1878 when, 'thanks to the persistent efforts of Alderman Emanuel, Councillor Baker, and other pioneers, a portion of the Portsea fortification land was obtained from the War Office for a "People's Park", which was, on April 24th, opened to the public by the Mayor, amid a scene of great excitement'. A local historian, writing in 1927, added that 'since that time the City Fathers, proving themselves right worthy of that appellation, have provided parks and recreation grounds in abundance, excellence, and beauty'. Notwithstanding, the schoolboys of Portsmouth in 1927 were still (as perhaps with the nailer boys of Bromsgrove, more as a matter of choice than necessity) playing football, CRICKET, hoops and tops, marbles, and ROUNDERS in the streets of the town. It needed the coming of the motor car to take all, except perhaps a handful of games played in quiet backstreets, from the streets of England and, to put children into school playgrounds.

Playing with hoops and tops has been a relatively recent casualty of increased traffic. Both were known to the Greeks in classical times. Hoops probably date from almost as early as the invention of the wheel and Greeks were known to be using them in the gymnasium towards the end of the sixth century B.C. In the first century A.D. Martial complained that Roman hoops, made of metal and kept moving by shrewd blows with a metal stick, got in everyone's way in the street. It was not, however, to warn pedestrians but to add to the noise that Roman hoops were fitted with bells. Schoolboys at Westminster at the beginning of the nineteenth century played with hoops, pegtops, and pea-shooters, according to Lord John Russell's record of the start of his schooldays. Hoops, sometimes wooden but often made of metal, were still being trundled along the pavements in Britain, if not the streets, in the early 1930s. Tops — *strombos* to the Greeks — came to England about the fourteenth century and are known to have been used in play in Peru long before Columbus discovered America. In the 1920s and 1930s they were probably responsible for more broken windows in houses in Britain than were balls. There seems nowhere left for children to whip their tops without a considerable risk of danger to persons or properties, and, like hoops, after some two thousand years they have disappeared from the streets.

Street games continue however in countries, and areas of countries, still relatively undisturbed by motor traffic, and just as it would have been possible for a Portsmouth schoolboy of 1927 to have joined in a street game being played in the Middle Ages anywhere in England, many of the games being played in remote areas of the world would be recognizable, in their essentials, to the English playground player of today. (See also BLIND MAN'S BUFF, ORANGES AND LEMONS, PRISONERS' BASE, and TOUCH-CHASING.)

STREIT, Mrs. MARLENE STEWART (1934-   ), Canadian amateur golfer, who was Canadian Open champion seven times; Canadian champion eight times; British champion 1953; U.S. amateur champion 1956; and Australian champion 1963.

STRUDWICK, HERBERT (1880-1970), cricketer for England and Surrey. Small, and unobtrusive of method, he kept wicket for Surrey from 1902 to 1927, and played in his first Test when almost 30. In 28 Tests he made 72 dismissals, and his 1,493 dismissals, a record in first-class CRICKET, included 1,235 catches, also a record.

STUD BOOK, The, see HORSE RACING.

SUAREZ, LUIS (1935-   ), Association footballer for BARCELONA, INTERNAZIONALE (Milan), and Spain for whom he played in his favourite inside forward role when they won the 1964 European Nations Cup competition. He left Barcelona for Internazionale in 1961 after playing for the Spanish club in the European Champion Clubs Cup final of that year when they were beaten by BENFICA. He was however in the Internazionale teams that won the European Cup in 1964 against REAL MADRID, and in 1965 against Benfica.

SUB-AQUA DIVING, see UNDERWATER SWIMMING.

SUGGS, LOUISE (1923-   ), American golfer, who was U.S. amateur champion 1947; British champion 1948; U.S. Open champion 1949 and 1952. She turned professional in 1948.

SULLIVAN, JAMES (1903-   ), RUGBY LEAGUE player. In a playing career of nearly 25 years, he was the dominant player in Great Britain, and later a highly successful and innovative coach. He played his first game at full-back for WIGAN in 1921-2, and kicked a hundred or more goals in each of 18 consecutive seasons. His career total of 2,959 goals was not even approached by any other player. He also scored 96 tries, to make a grand total of 6,206 points. His 204 goals in 1933-4 stood as a record for 24 years. He set another record by kicking 22 goals in a cup-tie against Flimby and Fothergill in 1925. He is the only player to be chosen for four tours of Australia: in 1924, 1928, and 1932, and declining an invitation in 1936. He played in 15 Tests against Australia and 10 against New Zealand, and led Wales's international championship team up to the Second World War.

SULLIVAN, JOHN L. (1858-1918), American boxer; the first modern heavyweight champion. He beat Kilrain in 1889 in the last heavyweight championship under the rules of the prize ring and lost the title to CORBETT in 1892 in the first championship under the QUEENSBERRY RULES. Sullivan is important as a link between the old and new schools. He was also an ebullient character and the first fighter to earn a million dollars. He was best known for his hard right-hand punch.

SULLIVAN, MICHAEL (1934-   ), English RUGBY LEAGUE player. He set up a record by playing in 52 international matches for Great Britain and England — 16 against Australia, 11 against New Zealand, 23 against France, and 1 each against OTHER NATIONALITIES and The Rest. He first came into prominence during the WORLD CUP series of 1954, and his international career lasted until 1963-4, during which period he played for four different clubs. His transfer from HUDDERSFIELD in 1957 cost WIGAN £9,500, then a record fee. In 1961 he moved to ST. HELENS for an £11,000 fee, and subsequently played for York and Dewsbury. A fast and skilful winger, determined in attack, he was also a robust tackler. He scored a record number of tries (38) in 19 matches during Great Britain's 1958 tour of Australia.

SUMO, see WRESTLING.

SUMPTER, RODNEY (*c.* 1943-   ), British surfer and professional film-maker. He finished fifth in the world SURFING championships in San Diego in 1966.

SUNBEAM, British racing car whose manufacturer had considerable success immediately prior to the First World War in the Coupe de l'Auto races. In 1923 their 2-litre Fiat-cased Grand Prix car, driven by SEGRAVE, won the French Grand Prix with another Sunbeam second. The 1926 4-litre V-12 car was used by Segrave for attempts on the world land speed record and in a twin-engined 44-litre chain drive car he was the first driver officially to exceed 200 m.p.h. (321·8 km./h.).

SUNDERLAND, HARRY (1890-1964), Australian RUGBY LEAGUE administrator. Secretary of the Queensland League and a member of the Australian Board of Control (later renamed the Australian Rugby League), he was the only man to be appointed three times as joint manager of Australian touring teams in England and France — in 1929-30, 1933-4, and 1937-8. Persuasive, and a firm believer in expansionist policies, he played a notable part in the development of the French League. From 1938 until the Second World War he was manager of WIGAN, and continued to live in England until his death.

SUNDERLAND F.C., Association FOOTBALL club formed in 1879 as Sunderland and District Teachers' A.F.C., it adopted its present name in 1881 and turned professional in 1886. The club was elected to the Football League, in place of Stoke City, for its third season, 1890-1, and showed its ability by winning the championship in the two successive seasons 1891-2 and 1892-3, and again in 1894-5. Subsequently Sunderland also won the championship in 1901-2, 1912-13, and 1935-6, won the F.A. Cup in 1937, and established a record of 57 consecutive playing seasons in the top division of the Football League before it was relegated in 1958. The club returned to the First Division in 1964 but were again relegated in 1970. As a Second Division club however they again won the F.A. Cup in 1973. The club's outstanding players include, from 1879 to 1914, BUCHAN, Mordue, Doig, and Holley; from 1919 to 1939, Carter, Cresswell, Gurney, and McInroy; and from 1946, Shackleton, Watson, BINGHAM, Hurley, Daniel, and Ford.

COLOURS: Red and white striped shirts, white shorts.

GROUND: Roker Park, Sunderland.

SUPER BOWL, see FOOTBALL, AMERICAN (PROFESSIONAL).

SURFING or surf riding is the art of planing on the forward portion of a wave as it speeds towards the shore before it finally breaks in a cascade of white water ('soup'). The movement is performed by the surfer, who should also be a swimmer, with or without the use of a surfboard or other such platform.

BODY SURFING is performed without the use of any kind of board by the surfer, who stiffens his body to provide a rigid surface which will plane on a shore-going wave. By rudder-like movements of the limbs he can turn on the wave in the same way as the board rider. In high surf even the expert requires considerable skill, whereas, in low or more gentle surf, beginners can achieve reasonable success without too much risk of being precipitated forward over the wave's crest ('taking a purler').

It is a pastime practised by many swimmers who use the surf beaches — the strong ones by swimming out beyond the surf and the weaker ones simply by standing in a few feet of water and waiting for the opportunity to join (or 'slot in') on the oncoming waves just before they reach their peak. Success can be achieved quite quickly by the bather who is able to swim well, since he will have the ability to match his forward speed with that of the wave.

The most orthodox body position is a horizontal one, at right angles to the face of the wave, with the surfer's arms above his head. In this position, he can change his direction by head and limb movements and steer himself out of, and away from, the breaking point of a wave, so prolonging the ride. The surfer takes breath by moving his head forward and upward. This creates a slight braking action, by lowering the feet, but a few powerful crawl arm and leg strokes enable the surfer to match his speed with that of the wave.

SURF CANOEING, which with other forms of surfing was practised by the early Tahitians, has become popular among present-day canoeists, who use kayaks (see CANOEING). In addition to 'surfing in', those who specialize can use the peak of the wave to perform a lateral roll and even a forward loop. In the latter movement the canoe travels through 180° in a forward motion before the canoeist rolls the canoe to the upright plane while still on the wave.

Life-guards who operate from surf beaches also use a type of surf canoe which has flush decks for recovering tired swimmers and bathers. It is designed to plane and can be quickly taken out beyond the surf with the end of a double-bladed paddle.

BELLY-BOARD SURFING is performed on a short board (a 'belly board', made of marine-ply or glass-fibre), an air bed, or a surf mat. Whatever the platform the surfer rides it grasping the sides with his hands and pressing the upper surface close to his chest. In this position, his legs are clear of the board and can be used for steering. Since it is impractical and virtually impossible to stand up on this type of board, swim fins can be used to great advantage both in paddling out and catching up with the waves. In gentle surf, the belly board can be used as a progression to the long 'Malibu' board, but in the more difficult high surf, greater experience is needed and belly-boarding then becomes a sport in its own right.

Waves that are suitable for surfing occur on long, even, gently sloping beaches that face the open sea. They are formed far out at sea by the action of the wind on the water's surface, while the actual profile of the surf is dictated by the depth of the water and contour of the sea-bed as the waves approach the land. Local tidal streams can also effect the eventual form of the surf, by speeding up or slowing down the main flow of water as it moves towards the shore. The gradual accumulation out at sea of a number of waves causes a mass of water to form into a rhythmic swell which travels towards the land in one big wheel-like motion. As it travels over undulations on the sea bed, or where the bottom gradually shallows, the 'wheel' takes on an elliptical shape and when the bottom becomes too shallow for its forward speed the lower surface of the wheel is held back and the top half topples forward in a cascade of spray.

Surf waves can be classified into two main types, the plunging hollow breaker, or 'dumper', which is tall in profile and occurs where the land rises steeply towards the beach, and the rolling breaker which has a stouter profile and flatter crest and occurs where the rise to the beach is more gradual.

Rip-currents are formed when the mass of surf rushing towards the beach makes its own escape route. In a bay, the rip will normally be returning along the two sides, but on an open beach it could be at any point where the pressure increases above the normal backflow. Rip-currents will inevitably affect some part of the surf, whether in a bay or on the open beach, and they need to be treated with caution. For the experienced surfer a rip-current can be a bonus, since he can use it to take himself out past the surf, but a beginner can easily be upset by its sudden action.

Body surfers and belly-boarders usually equip themselves with fins and therefore their paddling-out speed is achieved with comparatively little effort. The body surfer will also be able to use his arms in a crawl stroke while the belly-boarder will rely on paddling movements since his arms must also be used to keep him in position on the board. The long board (malibu) rider also uses his arms as paddles in propelling himself and his board and, like the canoeist, he can with a greater pull on one side, steer his board in that direction. Having slotted in, the surfer takes his ride by sliding down the shoreward face of the wave. In this sliding movement, the surfer can increase the hydroplaning effect by flattening the board parallel to the wave's surface. With minimum drag his speed will increase. If, instead of planing straight forward, he 'slides' diagonally across the face of the wave, the length of the ride can be increased.

The body surfer slots in by waiting in a sideways position for his wave, then, just as it is about to pass him, he strikes out at his fastest speed in order not to be overtaken. He will increase, and be better able to maintain, his speed by dropping his head between his arms since this will act as a counter-balance in raising the feet and cutting drag.

The belly-board rider slots in by paddling ahead of the oncoming wave, then at an opportune moment when he is caught by the surf he stops paddling and hangs on to the sides or rails of his board. In order to turn or change direction in this prone position, the surfer leans to the side to which he wishes to turn or simply puts one foot into the water.

LONG-BOARD SURFING. The long-board or Malibu rider slots in much the same way as the short-board or belly-board rider but as soon as he has joined the wave, he grasps the 'rails' (edges) of the board and rises to his knees, then quickly to the standing position. While performing this movement he has to control the longitudinal and lateral stability of the board by a simple transference of body weight. By weighting and unweighting he is able to keep the board in trim and turn it in any direction across the face of the wave. He can also reduce his forward speed by weighting the stern of the board. In an emergency, when his balance is likely to be upset, he can lower his centre of gravity by dropping back to his knees and closing with the board. The experienced surfer will often walk the full length of the board to effect dramatic changes of direction and speed and then sway to bring about more subtle changes.

A surfer can ride the wave in a straight line (a 'straight-ahead-of-wave ride') to the beach or, by weight transference, turn his board to the right or left. He can flatten his board to slide diagonally across and up the face of the wave (a 'cut out' or 'cut back') so that he is travelling in the opposite direction to the waves.

For a straight-wave ride the surfer, without turning or sliding to either side, balances his board evenly, avoiding stern and lateral drag. Speed can be increased if the board is flattened so that as much as possible of its length is brought in contact and parallel with the surface of the water. The surfer walks to the bow of the board and places five or ten toes over its end (to 'hang five or ten'). Again care is needed since too much forward movement will bury the nose of the board in the wave and both surfer and board will be rotated by the oncoming wave.

The board can be turned by moving the feet (a 'switch foot') and the body weight to the left or right so that, with a pronounced lean, that side of the board will be depressed in the water. The speed of the turn will depend on the amount of drag produced by the surfer's transference of weight. There are many variations of turn; for example, a slow turn can be combined with a slide, a fast turn can blend into or be followed by a slide. In fact, a skilled surfer can criss-cross up and down the wave's forward face all the way to shore.

For a straight-wave ride, the surfer stands with flexed joints in a relaxed stance with one foot either side of the lateral and longitudinal centre line. A surfer who prefers to ride with his right foot forward is called a 'goofy footer'. It is a matter of personal preference whether the feet are sideways or diagonally along the length of the board, but the centre of gravity of the surfer will be slightly astern of a point where the lateral line bisects the longitudinal line. To finish a ride, the surfer needs to stall the forward speed of the board if he is to alight safely and still keep contact with the board. If he finishes his ride in the prone position he edges his body backwards to the stern of the board, rising on to his knees and then into a sitting position. With the stern of the board deep in water and his legs forming a sea anchor the board will stall and the wave will pass shorewards. Alternatively, for a faster stop, the prone surfer can pull himself forward and, while holding the forward rails, slide his body off into the water, drawing the board off its forward track.

To 'kick out', the surfer edges to the back of the board in order to stall its forward movement. Then, by a sharp turn, he kicks the board out of its forward movement.

Competitive surfing. In international competitions a panel of 12 judges is required. Groups of five operate for each event up to the final, when a panel of seven is selected from those who are considered to have given the most consistent markings throughout the preliminary events. Each judge is required to give a mark for each competitor in the event or heat he is judging. In the preliminary events the first group of five is replaced by a second group of five from the panel of 12 after every three heats. Each judge is served by a tally man who records points, and a spotter who gives warning when a surfer has started a run.

Depending on the surfing conditions, the full panel of judges will decide the length of time for each heat and the number of wave runs that each surfer may be credited with from his full performance. For example when surfing conditions are particularly good the judges may decide a time limit of 30 minutes for heats, 45 minutes for quarter-finals and semi-finals, and an hour for the final, the three best wave runs to count. During each event a surfer may complete about ten runs, each of which will be marked up to 20 points by each of the five judges. On this 20-point system, which does not allow for half-points, guidance on precise marking is given as follows: Bad ride, 0–4 points; Fair ride, 5–8 points; Average ride, 9–12 points; Good ride, 13–16 points; Excellent ride, 17–20 points.

In awarding points, judges take into consideration the degree of difficulty of the wave selected by the surfer and his ability to perform, on the most difficult part of that wave, a variety of turning and stalling movements. The surfer will have to judge for himself the ideal point at which to join and finally 'wipe out' (part company) from a wave, since his continuing with a poor-quality wave, or one that has lost its force, may reduce the degree of difficulty of his manoeuvres and the resulting points.

Two systems of scoring — A and B — are employed by surfing countries in national and international events. In system A, the number of wave runs and duration of event having been decided, the judges will mark their cards awarding a certain number of points to each rider for each of his runs. When the points line is completed, the three best runs of each surfer are ringed and totalled to give immediate placings. However, to ensure that each surfer derives the greatest benefit from his performance, these placings are evaluated, 13 points being given for a win, 10 points for a second, 8 points for a third, 7 points for a fourth, and one less point for each succeeding place. The points awarded are then transferred to a final totalizer card on which all five or seven judges' points are tallied and the riders placed according to their aggregate scores.

System B, the alternative method of scoring, was used at the 1970 world championships. It is similar to system A in that the judges agree on the number of wave rides and time limits, and the awarding of points per ride is the same. It differs in the final marking on the number of points awarded for order of placing, these being awarded at the rate of 1 for a win, 2 for second, 3 for third and 4 for fourth, etc. In the case of a tie for any place, a half-point is awarded to each of the competitors tying for that place. Each judge's final points are then transferred to a grand totalizer card, where each competitor's final placing for the event is recorded.

Surfing originated in the primitive societies of coastal areas facing the open sea; of necessity the inhabitants built rafts and canoes that were light enough to paddle through the breakers to get to deeper and quieter offshore fishing grounds. With craft designed to plane, the fishermen perfected a form of surfing in order to reach the shore safely without capsizing.

The early Polynesians had a knowledge of seamanship and an adventurous spirit which took them amazingly long distances in the flimsiest of craft and they were masters of the surf when landing. There is much written evidence to suggest that surfing in the South Sea Islands, such as Tahiti and Hawaii, was in vogue long before the European mariners made their historic voyages. Captain Cook in collaboration with his lieutenant, King, and artist-clerk, Webber, made specific reference to the art of surfing in his records of voyages to Tahiti in 1777 and to the island of Oaha in Honolulu in 1778. He reported seeing a native of the island of Otaheita, as he then called it, paddling a canoe through the surf and apparently looking from side to side waiting for a chance to ride shorewards on a breaker of suitable size. Both paddler and canoe were carried before the racing wave at a high speed. After a further voyage to Hawaii, Cook described some of the diversions of these carefree folk; how the young men went outside the swell of the surf, lying flat on an oval plank about the size of their own body. Their arms were used to guide the plank while they waited for the greatest swell, then, pushing forward with their arms to keep on top of the wave, they were driven shorewards with great velocity.

Other references show that the early surfers knew the art of keeping the board straight on its journey and were able to quit the board seconds before it hit the rocks.

Cook was emphatic that the pastime was for amusement only and not a trial of skill, but, even so, it had its own descriptive jargon associated with the manoeuvres of modern surfing. The name *papahe'enalu* was one such descriptive phrase; *he'e* means to slip or slide away and *nalu* means wave. So it is evident the early surfers used the waves to slide forward and at the same time controlled their direction.

After Cook's death on the island of Kaolahua in 1779, Lt. King continued the journal by describing the mechanics of the surfer in relation to the surf. King's report showed that the natives continued to use boards rather than canoes, indicating that their efforts were concerned with sport rather than work. It is clear, therefore, that surfing was beginning to emerge as a leisure pursuit, even if it did not possess the finesse of today's sport. King told how surfers paddled out through the surf, allowing the small breakers to pass, apparently waiting for the bigger ones to carry them shorewards in a prone position on their boards.

So the sport continued in this simple form until 1821, when the European missionaries brought about a temporary cessation of what was considered, by the ardently religious, to be an immoral pastime. Body surfing was certainly practised by the early Hawaiians, for the *Hawaiian Journal* of 1896 referred to *Kala nalu* (surfing without a board) which had been in vogue for generations. It was not until early in the twentieth century that a revival took place and in 1920 the Hawaiian islander, DUKE KAHANAMOKU, formed the first surf club at Waikiki, where even today there is still a Kahanamoku Surf Club. Kahanamoku was no stranger to other aquatic sports and in 1911 he won the first 100 yards freestyle SWIMMING event, arranged by the Amateur Athletic Union of Hawaii, in an unofficial time of 58 seconds. He also developed the modern crawl stroke with a flutter kick replacing the then old-fashioned trudgeon crawl. His greatest love, however, was the sport of surfing and, in 1915, while competing in swimming events in Australia, he introduced surfing to Freshwater Beach on the north side of Sydney.

Surfing competition is organized at national and international level according to a set of rules laid down by the International Surfing Federation, in which contests are divided into heats, quarter-finals, semi-finals and finals. The present arrangement for international competition stems from the third world championships, held in San Diego in 1966, when it was decided that affiliated countries should be rated in four groups A1, A2, B, and C. Those in the A1 group at the end of the fifth world championships in Australia in 1970 were Hawaii, continental U.S.A., and Australia; and those in the A2 group, New Zealand, South Africa, Puerto Rico, Peru, and Great Britain. By the time Kahanamoku died in 1968, the sport had spread to all parts of the world.

In Great Britain, with the arrival of Kennedy from Australia, life-guard duty on the Cornwall and Devon Atlantic beaches was encouraged and developed. The surf, potentially dangerous to swimmers and non-swimmers, had to be mastered by the life-guards and, under the guidance of Kennedy and other Australian experts, their knowledge and ability improved. In 1955, the Surf Life-Saving Association of Great Britain was formed. Apart from the traditional methods of beach life-saving, the members of the association soon acquired the art of using surf boats, surf skis, and canoes, and built up a sound knowledge of local tides and weather. It was therefore a natural outcome that, at this stage, the Surf Life-Saving Association should be the controlling body for the sport in Britain, with power to send teams to international competitions abroad as well as arranging national championships at home. Later members began to divide into two separate groups — those interested in life-saving and those biased towards surfing. In 1967 a newly-formed specialist body known as the British Surfing Association took over the responsibility for the sport as a separate entity.

J. Cook and William J. Romeika, *Better Surfing* (1967); H. Arthur Klein, *Surfing* (1965); Reg Prytherch, *Surfing — A Modern Guide* (1972); Doug Wilson, *Learn to Surf* (1968).

GOVERNING BODY (WORLD): International Surfing Federation, Ave. Arenales 431, OF, 103, Box 180, Lima, Peru; (U.K.): British Surfing Association, 18 Bournemouth Road, Parkstone, Poole, Dorset.

SURREY WALKING CLUB, an English club at Croydon near London. Founded in 1899, it has organized the LONDON–BRIGHTON race since 1919 and many other long-distance events during the past fifty years. Surrey W.C. and BELGRAVE HARRIERS have dominated British walking over all distances and have also supplied many administrators and international judges. Outstanding walkers over the years have been Horton, Galloway, Goodwin,

Christie-Murray, Martineau, NIHILL, and Fullager.

SURTEES, JOHN (1934-   ), English racing motor-cyclist and MOTOR RACING driver. Starting racing with immediate success in 1951, he joined the NORTON team in 1955, moved to lead the MV AGUSTA team in the following year, and on MV machines won a total of seven world championships — the 350 cc. in 1958-60, 500 cc. in 1956 and 1958-60. After his MOTOR RACING début in 1960, he retired from MOTOR-CYCLE RACING and went on to pursue a successful motor-racing career, becoming world champion driver in 1964. He is the only man ever to win world championships on two wheels and on four.

SUSSEX STAKES is the most valuable horse race run at GOODWOOD. It is 1 mile (1,600 m.) in length and one of the most important events in England over this distance.

SUTCLIFFE, BERT (1923-   ), cricketer for New Zealand, Auckland, Otago, and Northern Districts. One of the best left-handed batsmen in CRICKET history, he made more runs and more centuries (42) than any other New Zealander. Graceful and nimble-footed, he twice passed 300, and his 385 for Otago in 1952-3 was the highest score ever made by a left-hander. Three years later he scored 230 not out against India — a New Zealand Test record until surpassed by Dowling in 1967-8.

SUTCLIFFE, HERBERT (1894-   ), cricketer for England and Yorkshire. Calm of temperament, practical, and courageous, he made even more runs per innings for England than for Yorkshire. He scored 4 centuries in his first Test series against Australia, and 16 in all Test CRICKET, with the exceptional average of 60·73. Only six batsmen have scored more than his 50,138 runs, and only four have registered more than his 149 centuries. With Holmes he made 555 for the first wicket for Yorkshire against Essex in 1932 — a world record — but he is best remembered for his partnerships for England with HOBBS, with whom he had a splendid understanding. Their finest stands were against Australia: at the OVAL in 1926, and at MELBOURNE in 1928-9 — on each occasion placing England in a winning position despite a treacherous pitch.

SUTHERLAND CUP, see SHINTY.

SUTTER, HERMANN (1923-   ), Swiss pioneer of SKIBOBBING in the Swiss Alps, he founded the Swiss skibob federation and formed the first Swiss team from Montana-

Crans to compete in international events. He played an outstanding role in the introduction of the sport in the U.S.A. He is vice-president of the Fédération Internationale de Skibob.

SUTTON, JOHN NELSON (1936-   ), managing director of the world's largest greyhound track group, G.R.A. Property Trust Ltd. (see GREYHOUND RACING), Catford Stadium Limited, chairman of New Clapton Stadium Ltd.

SUYDERHOUD, MICHAEL (1950-   ), American water skier, who, in June 1970, set a world-best performance in the slalom event at Ruislip, Middlesex, by negotiating 38 buoys in six successful passes. As world overall champion he set a world-best performance in the jumping event in August 1970 at Fall River Mills, California (U.S.A.), which was matched by MCCORMICK later the same month.

SUZUKI, Japanese motor cycle prominent in racing since 1962, at first in the 50 and 125 cc. classes but later in the 250 as well. Powered by two-stroke engines, the factory racers were highly developed and remarkably complex; but after 1967 the firm withdrew from official participation in international events. Instead it assisted private entrants riding relatively simple machines derived from production Suzuki motor cycles, principally in the 125 and 250 cc. classes. Since 1972 Suzuki have participated in 750 cc. events, producing some of the fastest and most powerful machines in racing.

SWAFFHAM CLUB, COURSING club founded by Lord Orford in 1776. Swaffham is the first association of coursers of which there is record. Membership was originally restricted to between 20 and 30, each member being allotted a letter of the alphabet, and two meetings were held each year. Originally the running consisted almost entirely of matches, but subsequently a £50 Challenge Cup for 16 greyhounds on knock-out lines became the premier stake.

SWALLOW, C. J. (1938-   ), British amateur RACKETS player who won the British amateur singles championship by defeating ATKINS in 1964 and also won in 1966 and 1968-9. He won the doubles championship with Tildesley in 1960 and with LEONARD in 1963, but unsuccessfully challenged Atkins for the world title in 1964 and 1970.

SWANSEA R.F.C. was formed as a soccer club in 1872, but adopted RUGBY UNION football two years later. Like CARDIFF and NEWPORT, Swansea has beaten each of the major touring sides: Australia in 1908, South Africa in 1912, and New Zealand in 1935; the club also drew with New Zealand in 1953. Notable Swansea players of the past include BANCROFT, OWEN, TREW, R. Jones, TANNER, W. T. H. Davies, Davey, R. C. C. Thomas, and Bebb.

HOME GROUND: St. Helen's Ground.
COLOURS: White jerseys and shorts.

SWAYTHLING CUP, award for the men's team championship of the world at TABLE TENNIS, equivalent to the Davis Cup at LAWN TENNIS. Presented by Lady Swaythling (second baroness, president of the English Table Tennis Association, 1954-8), it has been played for at all world championships since the first at London in 1926. The teams are three a side, chosen by the captain from a maximum nominated list of five, and the result follows the best of nine matches, each player meeting each of the players on the other side in a match over the best of three games. Entrant teams are divided into preliminary groups, then graded into further groups on the basis of the first results, with a final play-off for positions. Thirty-two competitions — interrupted by the Second World War — were held from 1926 to 1973. Of the 13 held before the war, Hungary won 9, Czechoslovakia 2, Austria 1, and the U.S.A. 1. After the war the pattern was at first similar: Czechoslovakia 4, Hungary 2, England 1. But with the advent of Japan to world competition in 1952 the balance swung swiftly to the East: Japan in 1954-7 and 1959; China in 1961, 1963, 1965; then, with the withdrawal of China from competition following the Cultural Revolution, Japan again in 1967 and 1969. China returned to win again in 1971; then at last another European team with Sweden, a fresh name in the sequence, in 1973.

SWIMMING is a method of propulsion through water, the value of which, as a physical activity and as recreation, is regarded as second to none.

In competitive swimming, there are four recognized styles of swimming, of which the fastest is front crawl, known in the rule books as 'freestyle'. The others are backstroke, breaststroke, and butterfly. There are also events in which all four styles are combined in one race, known as individual medley. And there are team races, for freestyle only and for medley, which are known as relays.

Front crawl (freestyle). In the rules of the world governing body for swimming, the Fédération Internationale de Natation Amateur (F.I.N.A.), there are no front crawl races, only freestyle events, and, in fact, the words 'front crawl' do not appear in the F.I.N.A. handbook. Freestyle means exactly what it says — the swimmer may use any style he likes. In modern racing, competitors in freestyle events use the front crawl. Only in medley races, both individual and relay, is there a specific rule stating what freestyle means — and it is a negative ruling. In these events, freestyle is any style other than backstroke, breaststroke, or butterfly.

In front crawl one arm is carried through the air, elbow relaxed, and the hand turning palm downwards ready to catch the water as the other arm is pulled under the water. The flutter leg kick is now recognized to have little propulsive significance, but plays an important part in balancing the body in the water. In longer distance races, many swimmers reduce the strength and frequency of their leg movements.

Breathing is extremely important, particularly the technique of expelling the stale air while the face is under the water, so that a full, new breath can be taken as the head turns. Normally, swimmers breath, to either right or left, once in each full arm cycle. But the bilateral breathing technique, in which the head is turned after one and a half arm cycles (after three single arm strokes), is also used, especially during shorter-distance events.

Backstroke is like swimming the front crawl, but on the back. In the early days, like all stroke developments, backstroke grew from the breaststroke with the swimmer carrying his arms upward and backward simultaneously and kicking his legs in an inverted frog-like action. This style is often called the 'old English' backstroke.

With the development of the front crawl, swimmers were quick to realize that an alternating arm action and flutter leg kick was easier to perform on the back and was also infinitely faster. The arms are lifted from beside the leg, palm turned outwards, to an easy position behind the head. As the leading hand takes hold of the water to pull, the other one begins to lift from the side.

There have been various techniques for the under-water pull and much depends upon the flexibility of the shoulders of the individual swimmer. Almost all successful backstroke styles include an arm bend at some stage in the pull, generally near the beginning.

Backstroke is the only one of the four modern styles in which the competitor starts in the water. He must stay on his back throughout the race, except at the turns. There, having touched the end of the bath while on his back, he may move from this position to make a somersault turn, provided he has turned on to his back before his feet leave the wall.

Breaststroke, the slowest and earliest of the four swimming styles, like its modern development, the butterfly, has very precise rules of technique. F.I.N.A.'s rule 65 lays down that:

(*a*) the body shall be kept perfectly on the breast and both shoulders shall be in line with the water surface from the beginning of the first arm stroke after the start and on the turn;

(*b*) all movements of the legs and arms shall be simultaneous and in the same horizontal plane without alternating movement;

(*c*) the hands shall be pushed forward together from the breast, and shall be brought back on or under the surface of the water;

(*d*) in the leg kick the feet must be turned outwards in the backward movement. A 'dolphin' kick is not permitted;

(*e*) at the turn, and upon finishing the race, the touch shall be made with both hands simultaneously at the same level, either at, above, or below the water level;

(*f*) a part of the head shall always be above the general water level, except that at the start and at each turn, the swimmer may take one arm stroke and one leg kick while wholly submerged.

The precision of the regulations, which have been tightened up during decades of swimming development, have caused more problems than the rest of swimming put together. There is a constant difficulty for the judges to see, through the swirl of the water, if the movements of legs, feet, and arms have changed from the lateral to the vertical plane. An anatomical variation — a dropped shoulder, stiffness in the hips or ankles, etc. — can suggest an infringement where none, in fact, exists.

The problem of the 1970s is the sprinting technique pioneered, among other countries, by the Soviet Union. A fast stroke is achieved by shortening both the arm and leg actions, and, as a result, many competitors come perilously close to vertical instead of lateral movements. The speed of the stroke causes greater agitation of the water and this makes the job of the style judges even more difficult.

For many years, breaststroke was the first style to be taught, despite the fact that the non-swimmer had to master two almost independent actions with his arms and legs. Many modern swimming coaches now teach the breaststroke as a precise technique after the learner has discovered how to stay afloat.

Butterfly. This style was separated from breaststroke and became the fourth swimming style in 1952. This was 20 years after enterprising swimmers in the U.S.A. had realized that there was nothing in the rules then to stop them recovering their arms over instead of under the water.

At the beginning, the swimmers used the frog-like leg kick of breaststroke with their simultaneous flying arm actions. This was a tiring technique and, for many years, most butterflying breaststroke swimmers were men, and even these, with few exceptions, could not maintain the over-water arm recovery for the whole of a 200 metres race.

With the official separation of the strokes in 1952, a new element was added to the butterfly, a simultaneous up-and-down flutter kick. The F.I.N.A. rule 66, covering butterfly, says:

(*a*) both arms must be brought forward together over the water and brought backward simultaneously;

(*b*) the body must be kept perfectly on the breast and both shoulders in line with the surface of the water from the beginning of the first arm stroke, after the start, and on the turn;

(*c*) all movements of the feet must be executed in a simultaneous manner. Simultaneous up and down movements of the legs and feet in the vertical plane are permitted;

(*d*) when touching at the turn or on finishing a race, the touch shall be made with both hands simultaneously on the same level, and with the shoulders in the horizontal position. The touch may be made at, above, or below the water level;

(*e*) at the start and at turns, a swimmer is permitted one or more leg kicks and one arm pull under the water, which must bring him to the surface.

Medley. There are individual and relay events for medley swimming, in which the swimmer, or team, use all four recognized strokes, in a prescribed order, during a race. In the individual medley, the order is, butterfly, backstroke, breaststroke, and freestyle. In medley relays, the backstroke swimmer goes first, followed by breaststroke, butterfly, and freestyle. In both events, freestyle must be any style other than the three specified and is invariably front crawl.

In both types of medley event, the distance swum in each style — known as a 'leg' — is equally divided. For relays, it is 4 × 100 metres (110 yds.) while there are individual events over 200 and 400 metres (220 and 440 yds.), i.e. the swimmer covering either 50 or 100 metres in each of the styles in order. The individual medley is the supreme test of a swimmer's all-round ability and, with the changes from style to style during a single race, is the most difficult of all the modern competitive swimming events.

Relays. Relay racing is the ultimate test of the strength in depth of a country or club. Teams usually consist of four swimmers, racing successively to produce an aggregate time and placing.

At the take-over between swimmers 1 and 2, 2 and 3, and 3 and 4, the incoming racer must have touched the wall before the feet of the out-going swimmer have lost touch with the starting block. Failure to do this is described as a 'flyer' and results in disqualification. Only the first swimmer, who starts on the gun, whistle, or command, can set an individual record in a relay.

INTERNATIONAL COMPETITION. In the international context, there are three free-style relay events, two for men (4 × 100 and 4 × 200 metres) and one for women (4 × 100 metres). There are also medley relay events over 4 × 100 metres for men and women.

To be a successful competitor, it is not only necessary to swim effectively, but also to gain the maximum advantage from the starting dive (or push away from the wall in the case of backstroke) and from the turns at the end of each length. The speed with which a competitor can get away from his static starting position on the bath-side (or in the water in the case of backstroke) can cut vital tenths of seconds off his total racing time.

The starting procedure is clean-cut and provided the competitors do not try to beat the starter, there should never be false starts. The competitors line up behind their starting blocks. On a signal from the referee, they step on to the back surface of the block and remain there. On the command from the starter, 'Take your marks', the swimmers step forward to the front of their blocks and assume their starting position. Normally, this is a relaxed, semi-crouched position, with the body bent at the hips and knees, the weight balanced over the centre of gravity, and the arms lifted a little away from the body ready to be swung into the starting dive. There is also a modern variation, by which the swimmer, folding sharply from the hips and with the knees relaxed, bends forward to hold the front edge of the starting block with both hands in order to obtain maximum propulsion from the hands and feet at take-off. As soon as all the competitors are in position and motionless, the starter gives his signal (a shot, klaxon, whistle, or vocal command, 'Go') and the race begins.

In backstroke, the competitors line up in the water, facing the starting end, with their hands placed on the starting grips. Their feet, including their toes, must be under the surface of the water, and standing in or on the gutter or bending the toes over the lip of the gutter is prohibited. On the 'Take your marks' command, the swimmers assume their push-away position and their hands must not release the grip until the starting signal has been given.

The starter calls back the competitors at the first or second false start. If there is a third (or further) false start in the same heat, whether by a competitor who has already caused a false start or another swimmer, the person making that false start is disqualified.

The starting dive should be as flat and powerful as possible, angled to drop the swim-mer into the water with as much forward momentum as possible. Co-ordination of ankles and knees with the forward swing of the arms contribute to a speedy starting dive.

International regulations govern the way competitors must turn at the end of the bath for each of the four styles:

Freestyle: the touch on the wall can be made by any part of the body, a hand touch is not obligatory, and other than this the competitor may turn as he wishes.

Backstroke: the swimmer must remain on his back until his head or foremost hand or arm has touched the end of the course. He may turn beyond the vertical in executing the turn, but must have returned past the vertical on to his back before the feet leave the wall.

Breaststroke: the touch (and finish) must be with both hands simultaneously on the same level, and the swimmer must not do more than one leg kick and one arm pull before surfacing after the turn.

Butterfly: the touch is the same as for the breast-stroke and the swimmer may take only one arm pull under the water before surfacing.

Medley individual: the swimmer is governed by the rules above as he swims each of the strokes in turn. When changing from one stroke to another, he is governed by the rule for the stroke he is swimming as he comes into the turn and by the rule for the new stroke as he pushes away from the wall.

Because good turns give a tremendous time advantage, there are clear distinctions between times set in 'long-course' pools (50 m. — 55 yds.) and short-course pools (less than 50 m.). The time gained on a turn has been put at 0·7 seconds; a 400-m. race in a 25-m. bath has 15 turns compared with the 7 in a 50-m. pool and thus has a time advantage of 8 × 0·7 sec. = 5·6 seconds.

All world, European, and Commonwealth records now have to be set on long courses, while most national records lists have separate sections for long-course and short-course performances. All major swimming competitions are held in 50 metre pools.

A swimming pool may be any length, width, and depth. In competition the most usual are 25 or 33·33 m. (27 yds. or 36 yds.) long, for short-course, and 50 m. (55 yds.) long, for long-course pools.

For all major competitions, OLYMPIC GAMES and world record purposes, the pool, in addition to being long-course, must have a minimum width of 21 m. (23 yds.) with two spaces each of 50 cm. (1 ft. 7¾ in.) between the outside lanes (Nos. 1 and 8) and the bath side walls.

F.I.N.A. laws do not lay down the minimum depth for an international-size racing pool, but for the Olympic Games this must be 1·8 m. (5 ft. 11 in.) over-all, which allows WATER POLO matches to be played in the same bath.

Lane ropes, consisting of floats with a diameter of 0·05 to 0·10 m. (2–4 in.), are stretched the full length of the course and anchored at each end. Lane markings, of a dark contrasting colour, are set on the floor of the pool in the centre of each lane as guide lines for the competitors.

For Olympic contests and other major events, the water in the pool may be fresh or salt — though usually it is fresh — and heated to a temperature of 24° C. (77° F.) minimum.

The starting platforms may be from 0·5 m. to 0·75 m. (1 ft. 8 in.–2 ft. 6 in.) above the surface of the water. The surface area of each platform must be a minimum of 0·5 × 0·5 m. (1 ft. 8 in. × 1 ft. 8 in.), with a maximum slope of not more than 10° and each block must be covered with non-slip material.

Gutters may be placed on all four walls of the pools, but those at each end wall must be covered with a grille or screen. There must be shut-off valves to control the flow of water so that there is no movement during competition.

In swimming races, unlike athletics, the lane positions count from the right as the competitors face up the pool.

A swimming meeting should be controlled by at least the following officials: a referee, a starter, two finish judges, two style judges, two turning judges, and at least one timekeeper for each lane. The regulations for international competitions are even more demanding and at Olympic level there must be a minimum of a referee, a starter, a chief timekeeper, three timekeepers per lane, a chief judge, three finish judges per lane, one inspector of turns per lane at both ends of the bath, and two judges of style.

The referee has complete control of the races and can give a casting vote if the judges and timekeepers do not agree. He may also disqualify a competitor for an infringement of the rules from personal observation or after a report from another official. Before the start, and as soon as he is sure the officials are in their places, the referee hands over to the starter.

The starter has complete control of the competitors from the time he has received the signal from the referee until the race has commenced. It is his responsibility to decide if a swimmer has started before the signal and to recall the swimmers for a fresh start. With the agreement of the referee he may disqualify a swimmer for delaying the start, wilfully disobeying an order, or for any other misconduct during the start. The starter takes a position on the side of the pool within approximately 5 m. (16 ft. 5 in.) from the starting edge of the pool where the timekeepers can see, and the competitors hear, the signal.

The chief timekeeper is responsible for allocating the timekeepers to each lane, for collecting the times from these officials and, if necessary, for inspecting the watches. The timekeepers take the time of the competitor in the lane assigned to them, starting their watches at the starting signal and stopping them when the competitor has completed the race in accordance with the rules.

The chief judge allocates the positions for the judges of finish and the lanes for the judges of turn. In relay events, he acts as a second judge for the take-over between competitors. If electronic equipment is not used, the chief judge has the right to vote as one of the judges. The judges place the swimmers in order of finish or determine whether they have turned in accordance with the rules. The style judges, who operate on either side of the bath, are responsible for deciding if a swimmer, particularly in a breaststroke or butterfly race, has contravened the technical rules for these strokes.

The development of sophisticated electronic and television video tape equipment is beginning to supersede some functions of the officials. It is obligatory for electronic judging and timing equipment to be used at the Olympic Games and the results of officially approved machines take precedence over the decisions of human judges and timekeepers.

LONG-DISTANCE SWIMMING takes place on open water for distances over 1,500 metres. It can be as demanding as Channel swimming, for the same problems of cold, rough water, currents, tidal streams, and wind drifts arise. The British Long Distance Swimming Association (B.L.D.S.A.) organizes many annual British championships of which the Lake Windermere race of 10¼ miles (16·5 km.) is one of the toughest. Occasionally, the B.L.D.S.A. stage a 22-mile (35·4 km.) event on Loch Lomond and a 16-mile (25·7 km.) international championship on Windermere.

SYNCHRONIZED SWIMMING. This art form of swimming, ballet in the water, was recognized internationally by F.I.N.A. in 1952. Yet, although many countries (particularly the U.S.A. who pioneered it) organize their own championships and there are international competitions between nations, it is the only one of the F.I.N.A. approved events not to be included in the programme of the Olympic Games, although it was in the programme of the first world championships in 1973.

As well as having the endurance of a trained racing swimmer, the synchronized swimmer must have the skill and artistry of a ballet dancer, and the grace, rhythm, and acrobatic ability of the gymnast to perform the somersaults, twists, and spins and the leg and arm movements, both above and below the water, that are part of the art.

There are three types of competition, solo, duet, and team (which consists of four or more members). Each competition has two sections, the first for stunts and the second for original, interpretive free routines set to music. The final marks for each section are added together to find the winners.

Usually five or seven judges officiate, awarding marks from 0 to 10. The highest and lowest of these are eliminated before the remaining scores are averaged to one judge. In the stunt section, the average marks are multiplied by a degree of difficulty. These degrees of difficulty are incorporated in an international tariff table and range from 1·4 to 2·1 according to the difficulty of the particular stunt.

The stunts are marked for their slow, high, and controlled movements, with each part of the stunt clearly defined and in a uniform motion. The routines should be judged as units, taking into account the perfection of strokes, stunts, and parts thereof; variety, difficulty, and pool patterns; and the synchronization of the swimmers one with the others and with the accompaniment.

In the stunt section, the competitors must wear dark coloured costumes and plain white caps so that nothing should detract from the simple perfection of their performances. For the free routines, they may wear special costumes, head-dresses and other clothing or ornaments suitable to the themes of their harmonic-picture performances.

Beulah Gundling, with her husband Henry, founded the International Academy of Aquatic Art in 1955 and the Gundlings have played an important part in popularizing this artistic branch of water sport. Mrs. Gundling, four times U.S.A. solo champion and winner of the Pan-American solo gold medal in 1955, travelled the world giving lectures and demonstrations to obtain international recognition for synchronized swimming.

Handbook of the Fédération Internationale de Natation Amateur, 1972-76; Amateur Athletic Union (U.S.A.), *Official Synchronized Swimming Handbook*, annually.

Although swimming was not in the programme of the ancient Olympic Games, the sport goes back to the great days of early Greece and Rome. It was considered an important part of the training of warriors, not only as an athletic achievement but as a life-saving attribute in times of war.

Bas-reliefs in the British Museum, in London, show fugitives swimming to a fortress and the crossing of a river by the Assyrian army, both probably dating from 880 B.C. In each of these, the swimmers are depicted using a stroke very similar to the modern front crawl. One even shows men using inflated animal skins as a form of aqualung.

There were races in Japan in 36 B.C. during the reign of the Emperor Suigiu. The Japanese were the first to organize swimming nationally and an imperial edict in 1603 made it compulsory in schools; there were even inter-college competitions, and a three-day swimming meeting was organized in 1810. But Japan was a closed country and it was left to the Anglo-Saxon nations to lead the world.

Swimming was brought into the programme for the modern Olympic Games at the first celebrations in Athens in 1896, when there were three freestyle events for men plus a race for sailors on ships anchored in the port of Piraeus, where the Olympic races were held.

The sport has remained in the Olympic programme ever since. At first, there were some strange events, and unusual distances were covered. In 1900 there was a swimming obstacle event, in which the competitors had to climb over a pole, clamber over a row of boats, and swim under a row of boats during their 200 metres race. Fortunately for the image of serious swimming, this 'amusing' contest was not held again.

In 1900 also, when the swimming competitions were held in Paris in the river Seine, the longest event was for 4,000 metres and there was an underwater endurance swimming contest. Four years later, in St. Louis, Missouri (U.S.A.), a long-distance plunging championship was held for the first and only time. But by 1908, when the Olympic Games were first held in London, the programme had begun to take the shape of the modern Olympic competitions.

The first women's events were held at the Stockholm Games of 1912—a 100 metres individual freestyle and 4 × 100 metres freestyle relay. As the sport developed, more and more events were added to the programme so that for the Games in Munich in 1972, the following 29 races (15 for men and 14 for women) had become standardized:

Freestyle: 100, 200, and 400 metres (for men and women), 800 metres (for women), and 1,500 metres (for men) individual, 4 × 100 metres relay and (for men) 4 × 200 metres relay.

Backstroke: 100 and 200 metres.

Breaststroke: 100 and 200 metres.

Butterfly: 100 and 200 metres.

Medley: 200 and 400 metres individual and 4 × 100 metres relay.

By 1969, these events, plus 800 metres freestyle for men and 1,500 metres freestyle for women, comprised the list of 31 officially recognized world record distances. Although this standard programme is now used for the world championships, regional meetings, the COMMONWEALTH GAMES, and international and national competitions, F.I.N.A. were forced to give up three events in their programme — the 200 metres individual medley for men and women and the 4 × 100 metres freestyle relay for men — for the 1976 Olympic Games in Montreal, in order to satisfy the wish of the INTERNATIONAL OLYMPIC COMMITTEE to reduce the size of the Games.

The fastest swimming style, front crawl, with its alternating arm stroke and six-beat leg kick, had many stages of development. From breaststroke came side stroke, then English overarm, or side overarm stroke. With the changing position from prone to side, the leg movement also changed from the principles of the frog kick to a side-on scissor-blades action.

The 'trudgen', demonstrated by Trudgen in London in 1873, was the first style in which both arms were recovered over the water. The Australians refined this style, using a vertical leg action, bending from the knees. The United States improved the leg kick and breathing techniques and the 'American crawl' is now the basic style used the world over.

The first man to use the alternating arm back crawl — as opposed to the double-armed old English backstroke — in an Olympic Games was Hebner of the U.S.A., who won the 100 metres title in 1912 and was nearly disqualified for his unorthodox style. He kept his gold medal after American officials had pointed out there was nothing in the rules to make this style illegal. Belgium's Blitz pioneered this style in Europe and became the first European using the back crawl technique to win an Olympic medal for this event (a bronze) in 1920.

There was the time (1934-52) when the rules for breaststroke did not preclude the swimmer carrying his arms forward over the surface of the water. From this technique, frowned upon by those who wished to cling to the classic, orthodox breaststroke style but who were unable to prevent the never-ending chase after speed, came the butterfly which was classed as a new stroke in 1952.

After the separation of breaststroke and butterfly, swimmers searching for faster methods of moving through the water realized that swimming breaststroke under water was quicker than on the surface. The Japanese, particularly, were most successful at this and Furukawa exploited the loophole in the F.I.N.A. laws to win the 1956 Olympic 200 metres title. He was able to cover the first 25

m. without taking a breath and breathed only about 20 times during the whole course of the race. This style was outlawed immediately after the 1956 Games in Melbourne.

World records for the medley relay were recognized from 1946, although the event was not included in the Olympic programme for men and women until 1960. Individual medley swimming was pioneered by the U.S.A. in the 1930s, but did not become a world record event until 1952 and was not in the Olympic programme until 1964.

The European nations were the first to organize regional championships, the earliest of which, with events for men only, was held in Budapest, Hungary, in 1926. The following year women also took part and eventually a four-year cycle for the championships was adopted, the event taking place in the even years between the Olympic Games (i.e. 1962, 1966, 1970, 1974). But long before this, unofficial efforts had been made to hold European-titled events. One club attempt was by the Erste Wiener Amateur Swim Club of Vienna, which held races from 1899 to 1903.

In the years around 1900, so-called 'world championship' races also took place in Europe. And, in 1911, an Inter-Empire contest, with teams from Australasia, Canada, South Africa, and the United Kingdom, was held at the old Crystal Palace in London (later destroyed by fire), in conjunction with the Festival of Empire, organized to celebrate the coronation of George V. But the first official British Empire Games, a multi-sports occasion in line with the Olympics and with swimming for men and women the second most important part of the programme, were held in Hamilton, Ontario, in 1930, through the initiative of Canada. The four-yearly cycle for this meeting (now known as the Commonwealth Games) was also established.

There are now also regional Games in other parts of the world in which swimming is an integral part of the programme. The most important of these are the PAN-AMERICAN GAMES (instituted in 1951 on a four-yearly cycle), the ASIAN GAMES, and the Mediterranean Games.

Despite the growing importance of swimming in major events, it was not until 65 years after the official world swimming body had been created that F.I.N.A. were able to organize their first world championships in Belgrade, Yugoslavia, in 1973. There, also for the first time, synchronized swimming, the fourth and newest of the swimming disciplines, was included in the programme, along with swimming, diving, and water polo, of a major aquatic meeting.

The second world championships are to be

held in Cali, Colombia, in 1975 and the third will be in 1978. Thereafter it will be a four-year cycle using the even years between Olympic Games. This decision of F.I.N.A. has made difficulties for the organizers of European championships and Commonwealth Games whose four-year cycle of dates is the same as the world championships.

Long before the development of these major championships, national events were organized. Australia claim to have held the first national championship, a 440 yards event, in Sydney in 1846. The Australians even staged a so-called 'world championship' in Melbourne in 1858, won by Bennet from Sydney who beat Stedman of England.

But it is England which is considered to have held the first real national championships. The first national amateur champion was Morris, who won the one mile freestyle, swum then in the river Thames, in 1869.

The first United States championship, a distance event over one mile, was held in 1877, organized by the New York Athletic Club. The N.Y.A.C. continued to arrange American national championships until 1888 when a national federation took over.

In spite of the initiative shown by America in the development of modern swimming, which has taken them to a pre-eminent position in the world, they did not organize any events for women until 1916. Scotland anticipated America, and indeed England, by holding their first championship for women in 1892 — a 200 yards race, won by Dobbie of Glasgow.

On 7 January 1869, at the German Gymnasium in London, the Metropolitan Swimming Clubs Association (M.S.C.A.) — later to become the Swimming Association of Great Britain and finally the Amateur Swimming Association — was formed. The first acts of the M.S.C.A., the first national governing body for swimming, were to define amateur status and lay down rules for competition. Other national associations followed. The American Athletic Union was founded in 1888. Six years later the name of the M.S.C.A. was changed to the A.S.A., after two warring factions had agreed upon a single association. The New Zealand A.S.A. (1890) preceded, by one year, the formation of the A.S.A. of New South Wales. These two bodies organized Australasian championships until the Australian Amateur Swimming Union came into being in 1902. The German Federation was founded in 1886 and the Dutch in 1888.

But it was not until 1908, at the time of the first London Olympics, that a world governing body, the Fédération Internationale de Nata-tion Amateur (F.I.N.A.), was created. The founding of this important body came about by accident rather than design. The initiative came from Hearn, a former hon. sec. of the Amateur Swimming Association and, in 1908, its president. Realizing that so many representatives of various countries were in London for the Olympics, Hearn called a meeting to discuss mutual problems. This was held at the Manchester Hotel on 14 July 1908 and eight nations were represented: Belgium, Denmark, Finland, France, Germany, Great Britain and Ireland, Hungary and Sweden. By its end, a world federation had been founded.

Of those present, Ritter, later to become an American citizen but at that time representing Germany, was elected hon. secretary and treasurer of F.I.N.A. in 1946, continued as secretary 1948-52, became president in 1960, and an honorary life member in 1964. He was still involved in swimming administration in the 1970s.

The first aims of F.I.N.A. were to draw up rules for the conduct of swimming, diving, and water polo events, to set up an official list of world swimming records, and to take responsibility for the organization of the Olympic Games swimming events.

From their first membership of eight, F.I.N.A. grew to 100 affiliated nations, with supreme power over all aspects of the sport throughout the world. No country in membership of F.I.N.A., or the swimmers of that country, may compete against a non-affiliated country. The only major swimming nations not in membership were China, who withdrew in 1957, and Rhodesia and South Africa, who were expelled in 1973 because of apartheid situations in swimming in their countries.

With the blessing of F.I.N.A., the Ligue Européenne de Natation (L.E.N.) was founded in 1927 to control activities in Europe and to organize, officially, the European championships, held for the first time the previous year.

Records. Swimming is essentially a time sport, without the pacing and tactics of athletics. Swimming records, therefore, provide an extremely accurate assessment of the standards of the sport at any given moment.

The first official list of world records was established in 1908, after the foundation of F.I.N.A. Certain earlier performances, the authenticity of which could be checked, were retrospectively ratified.

In the 65 years following the first world record list, many changes and developments took place and altogether 105 different events were recognized for world record purposes at one time or another. The obsolete records included 300 yards and 300 metres freestyle (recognized from 1908 to 1948), 500 yards and 500 metres (1908-52) and 400 and 500 metres breaststroke (1908-48). The classic linear distance of 100 yards was a recognized swimming distance for all strokes until the end of 1956, when the equivalent of the international 100 metres, 110 yards (100·584 m.), was substituted.

During the Olympic Games in Mexico City in October 1968, the F.I.N.A. congress decided to eliminate all yards distances as from 1 January 1969, and for the first time in 60 years a concise list, taking in the 31 events mentioned above (16 for men and 15 for women), came into existence.

At the beginning, record times were recorded to fifths of a second. Later stop-watches showing tenths of a second were used. In the 1960s automatic officiating devices were developed to judge and time to two, three, or more decimal places of a second. Such machines were used at the Tokyo (1964) and Mexico City (1968) Olympic Games, although official times were only announced to tenths. However, since 1 January 1972, world records (and race results) have been recognized to hundredths of a second, although times to tenths are still valid for pools which do not have the sophisticated (and expensive) modern automatic equipment.

With modern methods of training, particularly since 1956, the differences in standards of performance between men and women have narrowed. In 1912, when DURACK (Australia) set a women's 100 metres freestyle world record in a long course (100 m.) bath (1 min. 19·8 sec.), KAHANAMOKU (U.S.A.) held the men's world record at 1 min. 01·6 sec. Sixty years later, the men's world best of SPITZ (U.S.A.) at 51·22 seconds was only 7·28 seconds better than the women's world time of 58·5 sec. by GOULD (Australia).

At the other end of the scale, the closing of the gap between men and women for the longest pool-racing distance, 1,500 metres, has been even more remarkable. Wainwright (U.S.A.), the first woman record-breaker, clocked 25 min. 6·6 sec. in 1922 when the men's record, by Hodgson (Canada), stood at 22 minutes. By 1970, when Kinsella (U.S.A.) became the first man to break 16 minutes for the distance with 15 min. 57·1 sec., MEYER (U.S.A.) had brought the women's world record to within 1 min. 22·8 sec. with 17 min. 19·9 sec. This time by Meyer, which would have placed her 39 seconds ahead of ROSE (Australia), winner in the Olympic men's 1,500 metres final in 1956, represented a time difference between herself and Kinsella of 5½ seconds for each 100 metres compared with the 7 seconds margin between Gould and Spitz

for the 100 metres sprint. It is impossible that women will ever swim faster than men, but it is likely that the gap between the sexes will close as the years go by.

As with the four-minute athletics mile of BANNISTER, there are swimming milestones that fire the imagination and provide the impetus for greater improvement. Two of the modern era were achieved by the Australian girls, FRASER and CRAPP. On 25 August 1956, Crapp took the world marks for 400 metres and 440 yards freestyle below the five-minute 'barrier' — 16 years after Denmark's HVEGER had come within $\frac{1}{10}$ second of 5 minutes. Crapp, racing in a 55-yd. pool, clocked 4 min. 50·8 sec. and 4 min. 52·4 sec. and, on the way, she also broke the world records for 200 metres and 220 yards. Fraser made swimming history on 27 October 1962 when she swam 110 yards freestyle in 59·9 seconds, which was also the world record for the slightly shorter 100 metres.

The first man to break the minute for 100 metres was WEISSMULLER (U.S.A.) on 9 July 1922. This powerful American was also the first to swim 400 metres in under 5 minutes, on 6 March 1923. SCHOLLANDER (U.S.A.), who won four gold medals at the 1964 Tokyo Olympics, broke 2 minutes for 200 metres freestyle with 1 min. 58·8 sec. on 27 July 1963.

The longer the race, of course, the greater the improvement. And minute-breaking has been a feature of the history of swimming's longest Olympic event, the 1,500 metres. In 61 years, seven minute barriers have been broken by men. BORG (Sweden) went under 22 minutes in 1923; Australia's CHARLTON dropped under 21 minutes with 20 min. 6·6 sec. in 1924. Three years later, Borg reclaimed the world record by swimming under 20 minutes with 19 min. 07·2 sec. This stood for 11 years, until Amano (Japan) was able to trim this to 1·2 seconds under 19 minutes in 1938.

The Second World War held up the flood of improvements, but in 1956, Rose (Australia) went under 18 minutes (17 min. 59·5) in winning the Olympic title in Melbourne. Six years later, America's Saari had gone under 17 minutes and, six years after this, Kinsella (U.S.A.) broke the 16-minute barrier.

Minute-mark breakers include: LANE (Australia) 100 yards freestyle in 59·6 seconds (1902), DEN OUDEN (Holland) 100 yards freestyle in 59·8 (1934); America's Vanderweghe and Mann, 100 yards and 100 metres backstroke respectively in 59·4 (1938) and 59·5 (1964); Courtman (Great Britain) and Miss Waalberg (Holland) under 3 minutes for 200 metres breast stroke respectively in 1912 (2 min. 56·6 sec.) and 1937 (2 min. 58·0 sec.). The difference in development and progress between men and women is again underlined by these times. Two minute-mark breakers of the modern era are DeMont (U.S.A.), who took the 400 metres freestyle under 4 minutes to 3 min. 58·18 sec., and Miss Wegner (East Germany) who broke 5 minutes for the 400 metres individual medley with 4 min. 57·51 sec., both at the 1973 world championships.

For long-distance swimming the endurance record is 105 hours by Ruiz of the Argentine. The records for Lake Windermere, which is non-tidal and only slightly affected by weather, provide a history of improvement. Foster of Oldham took 11 hours 29 min. in 1911 to swim the lake. By 1968, with better stroke techniques and the virtual abolition of feeding stops, van Scheyndel of Holland had reduced the record to 4 hrs. 7 min.

Channel swimming. The distance, as the crow flies, is not what makes a crossing of the English Channel so difficult. The shortest distance — Dover to Cap Gris Nez — is only 20½ land miles (17¾ nautical miles—33 km.) and racing swimmers cover half or three-quarters of this, at speed, in daily training. It is the tides and currents that can double the distance actually swum, while bad weather, battering waves, stinging jelly-fish, sea-sickness, wind, fog, and the cold are additional hazards.

The crucial factor is timing. There are two complete tidal streams or four ebb and flow tides of six hours in a day. So the aim is to start on an out-going tide and land on the opposite shore on an in-going one. Swimming too slowly — or too fast — will catch a swimmer on the wrong tide and throw him miles off course and lose the right homeward tide.

Trying to swim the English Channel is an expensive business. The accompanying boat and pilot, plus special food, lanolin — for swimmers must be well greased to keep out the cold — the Channel Swimming Association official observer's fee, etc. can account for £150. As much again may be spent on living costs at the coast waiting for favourable sea and weather conditions.

Since Capt. WEBB made the first crossing of the English Channel from Dover to Calais, on 24-25 August 1875, this battle of brawn and brain against tides and temperature, has remained the high point in the life of any long-distance swimmer. Yet it was not for another 48 years, in 1923, that Webb's feat was emulated, by the Londoner, Burgess, who was successful at his thirteenth attempt.

The proportion of successes to failures is extremely low; less than 7 per cent of those who have set out from the Channel beaches of England or France have managed to reach the other side. More than 3,000 men and women from 35 countries have attempted the Channel marathon — either from France to England (the easier way) or from England to France — of whom only about 135 have shared some 200 successful crossings. These figures are not completely accurate, despite the formation, in 1927, of the Channel Swimming Association to control and authenticate claims. Some crossings were not made under C.S.A. supervision and some records were lost in the bombing of London in the Second World War.

The first woman to cross was America's Ederle, an Olympic swimming medallist, who went from France to England in 14 hrs. 34 min. in 1926. Another Olympic competitor, McGill (Australia), put up the fastest time by a woman for this direction in 1967, with 9 hrs. 59 min., which was only 24 minutes slower than the then best time by a man (Watson of Britain, in 1964).

The first man to cross from France to England was Tiraboschi (Argentine) in 1923, in 16 hrs. 33 min. For the England-to-France route, Danish 1948 Olympic 100 metres champion Andersen, by then an American citizen, had the best time for a woman of 13 hrs. 40 min. in 1964. The men's record, by Ray (India), was 10 hrs. 21 min. in 1967.

British Olympic water-polo player TEMME was the first to swim the Channel both ways. He went from France to England in 1927 and from England to France in 1934. Chadwick, the first woman to cross from England to France (in 1951), having made the reverse crossing the year before, was the first woman to make the double journey

After double crossings came the two-way efforts, in which the swimmer is allowed a five-minute rest on the far shore before turning to swim back again. In 1961 Abertondo (Argentina), who once swam 262 miles down the Mississippi, went from England to France and back again in 43 hrs. 5 min. The best time for the two-way journey was by Erickson (U.S.A.) in 1965 (30 hrs. 3 min.). Murphy, a newspaper reporter who started from the Kent coast, became the first Briton to make the two-way journey, in 1970.

Neither age nor infirmity is a bar to beating the Channel. The youngest to have swum across, both Americans, are Miss Modell (1964) and Erikson (1969), who were 14 when they crossed from France to England. In 1964 the American, Starrett, a spastic, and a Canadian polio victim, Cossett, both swam from France in under 13 hours.

Amateur Swimming Association, *Anatomy and Physiology* (of Swimming), *Better Swimming, Competitive Swimming, Survival Swimming, Swimming to Win, Teaching of Swimming,* various dates; P.

Besford, *Encyclopaedia of Swimming* (1971); F. Carlile, *Forbes Carlile on Swimming* (1969); Dr. J. Counsilman, *The Science of Swimming* (1971); B. Dawson, *Dryland Exercises for Swimming* (1968); G. Forsberg, *Modern Long Distance Swimming* (1963); A. Gabrielsen, *Swimming Pools: A Guide to Their Planning* (1970); D. Gambril, *Don Gambril on Swimming* (1968); F. Oppenheim, *The History of Swimming* (1970); G. Rackham, *Synchronized Swimming* (1968); B. Rajki, *Technique of Competitive Swimming* (1958); D. Talbot, *Swimming to Win for all Ages* (1967).

GOVERNING BODY (WORLD): Fédération Internationale de Natation Amateur, 555 North Washington Street, Naperville, Ill., U.S.A.; (U.K.): Amateur Swimming Association of Great Britain, Harold Fern House, Derby Square, Loughborough.

SWIMMING, Underwater, see UNDER-WATER SWIMMING.

SWINGING THE MONKEY, one of the few games that survived from about the fifteenth century to the organized DECK GAMES of shipping lines in the first half of the twentieth century. Like DECK CRICKET, it was an attraction for the spectators but, unlike deck cricket, it offered little amusement to the main participant. Possibly a reluctance on the part of passengers to play the part of the 'monkey' hastened the departure of the game from regular programmes of events. The original victims in the old sea-roving days would have had no choice in the matter.

There are two explanations of how the game got its name, or there may have been two, distantly related, games. In one the victim clung with both feet and one hand to a rope hanging from aloft, and sought to ward off attacks with his free hand. The rope was known as a 'monkey rope' and the victim, or perhaps foolhardy volunteer, became known as the monkey. In the variation, the victim was suspended by his heels and generally pushed, pummelled, and punched about by other seamen and subjected to horseplay or abuse. The obvious choice whenever a number of seamen felt in the mood for such a 'game' would have been the wretched powder-monkey, the youngest and the lowest rating on board. The game would thus have been that of 'swinging the powder-monkey'.

When, with the name abbreviated, the game was introduced to passengers on post-1918 voyages, it was played with some refinements, in the two forms that had remained popular with crews during their long voyages on sailing ships. In one form the player clung to the monkey rope with both feet and one hand. In his other hand he swung a knotted cloth with which he tried to strike (or 'cob') any of the players who surrounded him and who were themselves raining blows at him. If

he cobbed a player, the monkey came down from the rope and changed places with the player he had cobbed. In the more common form the monkey was suspended head downwards on the end of a rope so that his hands were just able to reach the deck. With a piece of chalk he was then expected to write a love letter, draw an animal, or do anything else the spectators wished, before he was released. It seems that even the spectators soon lost their relish for watching 'swinging the monkey' (or 'bowline-stretching' as it was known on some vessels).

SWINTON RUGBY LEAGUE CLUB, Lancashire, founded in 1869, joined the Northern Union in 1896. Its well-appointed ground at Station Road is used regularly for Test matches and other important games. The record attendance is 44,621 at the WIGAN *v.* Leigh Lancashire Cup final, 27 October 1951. Swinton won all four major trophies in 1927-8. Other championship victories were scored in 1926-7, 1930-1, 1934-5, 1962-3, and 1963-4. It won the Challenge Cup in 1899-1900 and 1925-6.

COLOURS: Dark blue with a white V.

SWYNFORD (1907), English race-horse by John o' Gaunt (son of ISINGLASS and LA FLÈCHE), bred and owned by Lord DERBY, trained by LAMBTON, and ridden by Wooton. He won the ST. LEGER (by a head), ECLIPSE STAKES, and Hardwicke Stakes twice.

SYDNEY CRICKET GROUND, Australia. Owned by a trust formed in 1875, this is now one of the most finely-appointed grounds in the world, with the imposing M. A. Noble Stand at one end and the renowned 'Hill' —from which emanates loud spectator comment—surmounted by an informative scoreboard at the other. New South Wales play CRICKET here regularly (BRADMAN scored 452 not out against Queensland in 1929-30), and RUGBY LEAGUE football is played here almost every Saturday during the winter. International matches of both sports have been a regular feature on the ground, and the record attendance was set up in 1965, when 78,056 people attended the Rugby League grand final between St. George and South Sydney. In 1932, 70,248 people attended a Rugby League match between Australia and Great Britain. The Empire Games were staged at the ground in 1938.

SYDNEY CUP, Australian handicap horse race, run over 2 miles (3,200 m.) at RANDWICK in mid-April.

SYDNEY–HOBART RACE, see YACHTING.

T

TABLE TENNIS, an indoor game played by two players (singles) or two pairs (doubles) facing each other and hitting a ball with a racket so that it passes over or round a net stretched midway across the surface of a table, striking its surface at each end alternately.

The table is rectangular — 274 cm. (9 ft.) in length and 152·5 cm. (5 ft.) in width — and the height of its flat upper surface is 76 cm. (2 ft. 6 in.) above the floor. This surface, called the playing surface, and including the top of the extreme edge, is divided by a net across the middle into two equal parts, called 'courts'; and the whole is outlined by a line, 2 cm. (¾ in.) broad, along each side and at the ends. A narrower line, 3 mm. (⅛ in.) broad, down the centre divides the playing surface into server's and receiver's right and left half-courts for doubles play. The table may be made of any material so long as a standard ball, dropped anywhere on its surface from a height of 30·5 cm. (12 in.) rebounds uniformly to a height of between 22 and 25 cm. (8¾–10 in.). Note that a thin table top, strengthened by cross struts below, does not give an even bounce and is therefore inadequate. Hard wood is recommended, sprayed or painted with dark paint or lacquer. Green is preferred for the colour, dull so that it should not too markedly reflect highlights, and not freshly applied, as it may then come off on the ball. The lines are white. The table should be firm and rigid since, if a player moves it in play, he forfeits the point.

The net stretched midway across the table is 183 cm. (6 ft.) long; it thus projects 15·25 cm. (6 in.) on each side of the table. It is 15·25 cm. (6 in.) high along its whole length. It is dark green and surmounted by a white tape. It must hang freely from a cord; the mesh must be soft (unsized) and, while not large enough to allow passage of the ball, not smaller than a defined minimum; the tape top must not exceed a maximum width. These specifications are intended to reduce the number of balls that, touching the net, climb over it by means of top spin. The supporting posts must be exactly the same height as the net and vertical, and fastenings to the table or for the cord, etc. are not to project far outside the posts.

In the early days of the game, balls of cork or rubber were in use, but from about 1900 celluloid prevailed. The ball is now a hollow sphere, of a defined size, weight, material,

colour, and bounce. The material is defined as 'celluloid or a similar plastic'. The diameter must be between 37·2 and 38·2 mm. (1·46–1·5 in.); the weight between 2·4 and 2·53 g. (37–39 gr.). (Light balls — known as 'soft' — are in use in Japan for training beginners. More difficult to hit as winning shots, they make for longer rallies.) The bounce is established by the rebound from a standard steel plate. The surface must be matt (not shiny) white, or, though this is not very usual, yellow. Balls complying with these specifications are manufactured chiefly in Britain, China, the German Federal Republic, and Japan, and marketed in many other countries under vari-

PLAYING SURFACE OF TABLE TENNIS TABLE
A and X indicate server's and receiver's right half-courts in the doubles game. The side lines and end lines are 2 cm. (¾ in.) wide, and the centre line for doubles service 3 mm. (⅛ in.) wide.

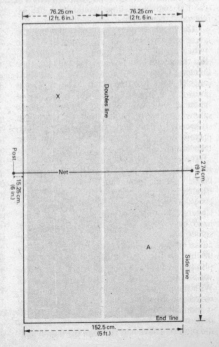

ous brand names. Samples are tested and approved by the International Table Tennis Federation.

Pimpled rubber
Sponge
Wood blade

Sandwich   Reverse sandwich

4 mm.
5/32 in.

TABLE TENNIS RACKET COVERINGS
Drawing shows section through racket blade.

The table tennis racket at one time, like the LAWN TENNIS racket, might be of any size, shape, weight, or material; but nowadays, though the first three attributes are not regulated, it usually consists of a roughly circular or elliptical blade with diameters 5 to 6½ in. (about 125–165 mm.) and $\frac{3}{16}$ to $\frac{3}{8}$ in. (about 5–9·5 mm.), with a handle conveniently shaped and balanced to lie comfortably in the palm of the hand or emerge upright between the thumb and forefinger and weighing 6 to 7 oz. (about 170–200 g.) over-all, in most countries, but sometimes as light as 4 oz. (about 115 g.) in Japan; the surface must be dark, and the variation of material has been limited by rule since 1955. The blade must be of wood; if it is covered, the cover must either be of pimpled rubber applied directly to the wood (in which case the maximum thickness is 2 mm.), or with the pimpled rubber as the outside layer of a 'sandwich' — the middle layer being of sponge (i.e. cellular) rubber — and both layers together of a maximum total thickness of 4 mm. The covering is known as 'sandwich' if the pimples are outward, 'reverse sandwich' if they are turned inward. The name for this type of racket in Japan is also 'soft'. Sandwich and reverse sandwich, which appear to facilitate attack and so speed up the game, are, among top-class players, now as common as, or more common than, simple pimpled-rubber coverings.

The grip on the racket is commonly one of two chief styles, the 'lawn tennis' or 'shakehands', and the 'penholder'. In the former, the handle is gripped against the palm by the crook of the last three, or at least the last two, fingers. The thumb is pressed along the forehand side of the blade, the forefinger (with sometimes the second at least partially adjacent) is pressed along the backhand side of the blade. It has the advantage of giving the player an extended reach on either side and a wide variety of strokes and angle of direction. With the penholder grip, only one side of the racket is normally used for striking. The blade is normally held below the handle, or, at uppermost, in horizontal line with it. The handle projects above and between the thumb and

forefinger which are pressed back against the forward (striking) surface of the blade to grip it against the second finger, which, with the others adjacent or behind it, is applied to the rear (non-striking) side. The tactical advantage of this grip is the instant control it provides for all shots used. The handicap is that mastery of a full repertoire requires exceptional agility and speed to cope with the problems of lesser reach, especially on the left wing of a right-handed player and vice versa.

The service must be delivered by striking the ball with the racket so that it strikes first the server's court and then, passing over the net, the receiver's court. At the moment of impact of ball on racket in service, the former must be behind the end line and between an imaginary extension of the side lines. There are stringent rules providing that during service the free hand must be held flat, fingers together and thumb free, with the ball resting visibly on the palm, from which it must be projected near-vertically upwards and allowed to fall before being struck. This is to ensure that any speed or spin imparted in service comes from the racket only, and not from the palm or fingers of the free hand.

Each player in turn delivers five services to the other, except that after 20-all the service alternates after each point. In doubles, service must always be from server's right-hand half-court to receiver's right-hand half-court. Only the doubles service is so restricted; in doubles as in singles the return of all subsequent strokes may be to anywhere on the opposite side of the net. Throughout each game the same one of the receiving partners takes each of the five services. The last receiver next serves to the last server's partner, and so on.

The server serves, the receiver returns, and thereafter each strikes the ball so as to make it directly touch the other's court, the object being to do so in such a way that the opponent is unable to hit it back to touch the surface at the end from which it came. Each time that this happens a point is scored to the last successful striker.

Doubles is played according to the same principle, with this proviso: the partners must strike the ball in turn. Thus if there are two pairs, AB and XY, when A serves and X receives, the order of striking must be AXBY throughout A's five services; then XBYA, and so on. This sequence will change only for the next game, when it will become XAYB or YBXA according to whom the partners X and Y select to serve first.

Volleying is not allowed in either singles or doubles.

A game is won by the first player or pair to score 21 points; unless the score shall have first reached 20-all, when a two-point lead becomes necessary to win the game. The best-of-five games is the championship course in both men's and women's events. But best-of-three is usual in lesser competitions, junior events, and in most team championships.

Ends, as well as sequence of receiving in doubles, are changed after each game, and also at the half-way stage (score 10) in a deciding game.

Undoubtedly the main factors accounting for the popularity of the game as a participant sport have been the basic simplicity of its principles, the relative cheapness of its equipment, and its moderate demands upon space when played at a minimum standard. For play at the highest level requirements are more demanding, however.

The space requirement for championship play is an area 14 m. long by 7 m. wide (46 × 23 ft.), clear above to the lowest light fixture, etc. 4 m. (13 ft. 2 in.). This area is delineated by a dark canvas surround. The floor should be hard and rigid; carpet or linoleum slow down the game; stone and composition are wearing to the feet; wood is best, but should not be slippery or shiny. Daylight sources should be eliminated, especially behind the players; artificial light sources, of prescribed minimum power, and suitably shaded to prevent glare in the eyes, should be strong close behind each end of the table to illuminate the nearer half of the approaching ball, and strong over the centre to kill shadows. Neither clothes nor racket surface may be lighter than a prescribed maximum, for these could be distracting in the intense light. Under such optimum conditions, the game can be one of the fastest in the world, and has also become on occasion a successful spectator sport.

It is perhaps the demands of speed in the highest flights of the game which account for the fact that so many outstanding players have reached their peak in their late teens and early twenties. Possibly the same factor accounts for the fact that, although so much less muscle power is needed in a single stroke, the difference between a first-class man and woman player is, as in lawn tennis, about half the game. Incidentally, this factor of speed, the major attraction to player and spectator, is very difficult to present on television. Most feasible camera sites employing the best viewpoint for following tactical subtleties (i.e. in line with the player) result in a foreshortening of distance by the lens that distorts the game and makes it falsely appear slow.

There is, however, a real problem at table tennis in that, if both adversaries are determined not to take the initiative, but each to outlast the patience of his opponent, the constancy of indoor conditions, the regularity of the bounce-surface, and the minimal exertion necessary for this sort of play make it possible for two fit players to continue a singles rally almost indefinitely. This kind of 'pushing play' led in the world championships at Prague in 1932 to a single point played by the Pole Ehrlich and the Romanian Paneth lasting about an hour, the men's team final (between Austria and Romania) spreading over three days, and in the following year in Baden bei Wien the women's singles final between Aarons (U.S.A.) and Pritzi (Austria) being declared 'no contest' and the title left vacant. To deal with this a time limit has been introduced, corresponding to the prescription for so many moves an hour in competition chess. In its present form (1970) this rule provides that if a game is unfinished after fifteen minutes, the remainder of that match shall proceed under the 'expedite system', with the service alternating point by point, and the server obliged to win each rally in 13 strokes (including his service) or fewer or else forfeit the point to his opponent.

International Table Tennis Federation Handbook and Handbook Supplements; Handbook for Umpires; Handbook for Referees and Competition Organizers, latest editions.

No precise date of origin or inventor is known for table tennis, but the game seems to have resulted from efforts to miniaturize tennis for the home undertaken at about the same period of the nineteenth century as the efforts to adapt it for outdoor play on the lawn.

Earliest accounts (from university common rooms and British Army officers' messes) describe improvised rackets and balls with books laid across the table in place of a net. Equipment for an early manufactured form is mentioned in a sports goods catalogue of F. H. Ayres Ltd. in 1884, and a patent for a similar game was taken out by Barter of Moreton-in-Marsh in 1891. At about this date or just after it occurred to Gibb, a noted cross-country athlete and holder of the four-mile record in 1887, to use in domestic play a celluloid toy ball he had picked up on a visit to the U.S.A. The sound made by this ball, first on Gibb's table then on the hollow vellum racket that was then in use, led to the registration throughout the world by his friend Jaques of the onomatopoeic name Ping-Pong. Jaques's firm, which had previously called their version 'Gossima', later sold the U.S. rights in the new name to Parker Bros.

Variants of the game rapidly became a world-wide craze as a children's toy and after-dinner pastime in the 1890s. Competitions were held in many countries. In Britain, rival groups came into existence, with differing rules and recognizing rival champions, but all trying to establish and organize the game seriously. The two chief schools differed sharply on service, one permitting the ball to be hit directly over the net but requiring it to be delivered from below table-surface level, the other favouring what is now current practice.

The British Museum catalogue lists 14 variant instruction booklets between 1899 and 1904. This activity, however, collapsed as suddenly as it had begun and efforts at national organization were not resumed for 18 years. During the interregnum, English local leagues persisted only in Plymouth and Sunderland. Club play seems to have continued here and there outside Britain on a small scale, notably in Budapest, and possibly in the Far East. Elsewhere the game generally reverted to its original nursery status.

Conflicts of rule may have contributed to the decline, but probably a main reason was the fact that the game played with the prevailing equipment at that time — particularly the wooden racket — lacked variety of stroke. Earliest rackets were probably of stiff cardboard, cork, or wood. Vain experiments were made with frames strung with gut or wire, which gave little control, and others — more successful — covered the plain wood blade with leather, cloth, cork, or sandpaper to give extra twist to the ball.

The pimpled-rubber covering for the wooden blade was first used by E. C. Goode of Putney around 1903. He is said to have made it initially by shaving down a chemist's cash mat. It proved the perfect surface for imparting spin, both top spin — by wrist-flick in attack — and underspin in defence, as well as side spins. Rackets of this type became almost universal among tournament players of all countries from the game's revival in 1922 to the mid-1950s.

A type of sandwich — inserting plush between the wood and the pimpled rubber — was first used by Warden, also around 1903. The softness was exploited for returning hits with a defensive floater. Warden was still, at over 60, using the same style in the 1920s. Sandwiches with felt and cotton-wool were also tried out then, and MONTAGU began playing with a sponge rubber covering to the wood, suggested to him by J. Jaques & Son, in 1926. This made no impression at the time, but the English player Dawson had some success with sponge in national competitions around 1948, as did the Austrian Schuech at the world championships in 1951. Meanwhile, in the early 1930s, supplies had been taken to Japan, and when Japanese players first participated in the world championships (Bombay,

1952) Satoh caused consternation and won the men's singles by the unfamiliarity of the effects obtained with a sponge surface.

The three men who initiated the revival of the game in 1922 — Carris of Manchester, Payne of Luton, and BROMFIELD, then of Beckenham — knew all about pimpled-rubber rackets and put the game at once on the right lines. They were soon joined by other veterans, and a newcomer in Montagu, then at Cambridge University. The name first chosen for the reorganization was Ping-Pong Association, but the new executive soon came up against the fact that, since the name included a trade label, any sports body using it was liable to injunction by the owners of the registration. The association was dissolved and replaced by a Table Tennis Association, which received help from the *Daily Mirror* in organizing a nation-wide competition.

The next few years were spent in co-ordinating the various centres interested, and securing acceptance of unified rules — including doubles, at that time known only in Manchester. The national body was later reconstructed as the English Table Tennis Association (a Welsh T.T.A., sharing the revival, at that time exclusively used wooden rackets with penholder grip). The development of the national body, based on leagues, since organized in counties and with a county championship, is owed principally to Pope of Newport, Monmouthshire, hon. gen. sec. 1926-9 and 1936-51, and Vint of Hastings, hon. treas. from 1932 to 1958 and later secretary, chairman, and, from 1970 to 1973, president. Separate table tennis bodies exist not only for Wales, but also for Scotland, Ireland (combining Eire and Northern Ireland), Jersey, and Guernsey.

INTERNATIONAL COMPETITION. In 1926, on the initiative of Lehmann, an international invitation tournament and meeting was held in Berlin. It was agreed to hold European championships in the December of that year in London. The event was held at the Memorial Hall, Farringdon Street. Entries included representative teams from Austria, Czechoslovakia, England, Germany, Hungary, India (these latter residents in London), and Wales, and one individual each from Denmark and Sweden. The events comprised a men's team championship (for the SWAYTHLING CUP), men's singles, men's doubles, women's singles, and mixed doubles. Women's doubles were added in 1928. A women's team championship (for the MARCEL CORBILLON CUP) was added in 1934.

At the foundation meeting of the International Table Tennis Federation (I.T.T.F.), held during the first (1926) championships, the titles were raised retrospectively to 'world status'. The world championships were thereafter held annually until 1957, with a wartime gap between 1939 and 1947. Since then they have been biennial. Entry is open, with a limitation on numbers of individual entries, to every association in I.T.T.F. membership. Fifty-two men's teams and forty women's teams entered in 1973.

The first chairman of the I.T.T.F. was Montagu, who remained chairman or president until his retirement in 1967. The first hon. gen. sec. was Pope, who died in 1951 and was succeeded by Evans of Wales, until 1967, when he was elected president. Vint became hon. treas. in 1947 and succeeded Evans as hon. gen. sec. The membership of the I.T.T.F. increased from 8 at its foundation in 1926 to 28 in 1939 and 107 in 1974. This development has been world-wide, though uneven. It has been characterized by an extreme popularity in several countries. The largest numbers of players recorded by the member associations as taking part in organized, affiliated play in the 1970s were three and a half millions in China, two and a quarter millions in the U.S.S.R., nearly half a million in Japan, 360,000 in the German Federal Republic, and over 200,000 in England. The total playing membership of all affiliates has been returned as nearly nine millions, but it is hard to reach an exact understanding of such figures because the manner of reckoning registrations differs from country to country. However, participation has been listed as second largest among sports in China (BASKETBALL being the first), and fourth to sixth in several European countries, including Czechoslovakia, the German Federal Republic, and the U.S.S.R. where, after a short period as an unorganized recreation in the late 1920s, table tennis was forbidden until the 1950s on medical grounds, eye-strain being alleged.

At the time the I.T.T.F. was founded the name 'Ping-Pong' was used on first revival in nearly every country as the most widely familiar common term. When the legal position was understood, however, organizers nearly everywhere reverted to the original name.

The game has changed little by rule during these years of development. The chief changes have been: the introduction, from the U.S.A., of finger-spin applied to the service in the 1930s, and the various modifications of the service rule designed to eliminate it; the epidemic of 'pushing play' in 1936-7 and so, after lowering of the net height from 6¾ in. (17·15 cm.) to 6 in. (15·25 cm.) had failed to provide a sufficient cure, the introduction of the time limit and 'expedite rule' to deal with it; the proliferation of different racket surfaces including, particularly, thick sponge, following Japanese example in the 1950s, and the partial standardization of the racket that followed. Nevertheless, the rules were thoroughly reviewed and their wording was redrafted in 1965-7.

Of the 32 championships up to and including 1973, 5 have been held in London; 4 in Stockholm; 3 each in Budapest and Prague; 2 in Paris and Tokyo; and 1 each in Baden bei Wien, Berlin, Bombay, Bucharest, Cairo, Dortmund, Ljubljana, Munich, Nagoya, Peking, Sarajevo, Utrecht, and Vienna. Those in Cairo (1939), Bombay (1952), Tokyo (1956), and Peking (1961) were certainly the first world championships at any sport to be held in Africa, Asia, and the Far East.

Amateur-professional problems have been the subject of national, rather than international, regulation. The words themselves do not appear in any international rules. Each association has disciplinary control of its own players, and of visiting players when these are not taking part in a representative capacity; but each is obliged to recognize and accept in world championships and open competitions, unpaid for such events, all duly qualified players nominated by the others. This has both protected those bodies which sought to maintain strict rules for their own players, without preventing experts attached to other associations from combining participation in championships with coaching, exhibitions, and paid invitation tournaments.

The prohibition of national flags and anthems at world championships, together with a constitutional definition of member associations not as 'nations' but as table tennis organizations *de facto* conducting the sport in a given geographical area, have to some extent relieved the sports administrators of the responsibility for deciding questions of national status. The conduct of the sport by every affiliated association must be such as to open participation in it, under its jurisdiction, to all inhabitants without distinction of colour, race, or creed. This rule has been incumbent on all I.T.T.F. members since 1934.

Of the I.T.T.F. membership of 107 in 1974, 31 associations were based in Europe, 29 in Asia, 20 in Africa, 22 about equally divided between Central and South America, 3 in North America, and 2 (Australia and New Zealand) in Oceania.

In addition to the biennial world championships and open national championships in many countries, there are now biennial continental championships in the alternate years in Africa, Europe, and South America; special competitions among the Arab, Balkan, Caribbean, Commonwealth, and Scandinavian countries; invitation competitions in Peking; European league and European club knock-out competitions. Particular credit for the spread of the game in Asia and Africa in the past has been due to Ranga Ramanujan of India and Counsellor Amin Abu Heif of Egypt.

In the first nine years of world competition, Hungary was the dominating force, in both the men's and women's game. The other strong associations at that time were Austria, Czechoslovakia, and England among the men; Czechoslovakia, England, and Germany among the women. Since the Second World War, additional strong associations have emerged in Europe: Sweden, the U.S.S.R., and Yugoslavia among the men; Romania and the U.S.S.R. among the women. (Of late years England, despite carrying off all titles at the only two Commonwealth championships so far played, has somewhat declined from this level.) Curiously enough, the game, though widely played as a pastime in the U.S.A., has never been strongly organized there. Only 5,200 players are noted as affiliates by the U.S. Table Tennis Association, and only for a few years before and after the Second World War did American players of the highest class emerge, among them McClure, Schiff, Miles, Aarons, and McLean. But the greatest change has been the dominance of the Far East since the middle of the 1950s. There, instead of disappearing as for a quarter-century it virtually had in Europe, the penholder grip had remained almost universal. Armed with youth, mobility, and the surprise of this speciality now unfamiliar to the west, the players in Japan and China soon in general far outranked those of everywhere else. Only now, in the 1970s, are European players, led by those of Sweden, whose young player BENGTSSON, in 1971 in Tokyo, broke the long Oriental monopoly of the world men's singles championship, beginning once again to rival them. Only now, in the last few years, are the fittest of the young European players following those of the Far East, including Korea, in speedy killing of the early ball.

Hungary was, as noted, the outstanding nation of the first years of international table tennis. The Englishman Shires, who played FOOTBALL for the Vienna club Cricketer in 1901, introduced the game to Budapest in 1904. In 1926 Jacobi, MECHLOVITS, and Pecsi, the three leading Hungarian players prior to the First World War, were still playing with wooden rackets. They saw pimpled rubber used by English players invited to Berlin that summer and changed to such purpose that, using rubber and captained by the Davis Cup lawn tennis player Kehrling, they carried off

all the titles at the first world championships in London the following December. In the following three seasons these players were reinforced by Bellak, Glancz (1928), BARNA, Szabados (1929), Kelen, David (1930). With the help of the women players MEDNYANSZKY and Sipos, in the first 9 world championships they carried off the Swaythling Cup (men's teams) 8 times, 8 men's singles, 8 men's doubles, 7 women's singles, 6 (and one half) women's doubles (out of 8 played), and all 9 mixed doubles.

Several of the best Hungarian players were lost by emigration prior to the Second World War. Still a strong force in European table tennis, Hungary has had two outstanding players since then: Farkas, women's world singles champion in 1947-9 and runner-up (to ROZEANU) in 1950-3; and Sido, a man heavily built but of extraordinary grace and lightness, with beautiful forehand, backhand, and defensive strokes, winner of the men's singles, men's doubles, and mixed doubles in 1953.

Japan. It is said that the game was introduced here early in the twentieth century by an English clergyman enthusiast and that, eventually, four-cornered competitions were arranged between China, Japan, Hong Kong, and Korea. As late as 22 February 1927 an agreement between the Japanese Ping-Pong Association and the Chinese Ping-Pong Union, concluded in Shanghai, embodied rules for a table 2 ft. 7 in. (78·7 cm.) high, 9 ft. by 4 ft. 8 in. (2·74 × 1·42 m.) in surface, with service into a box 3 ft. 8 in. (1,118 mm.) square, based on the end line marked out in brown. Rackets were very light and of smooth wood. The net was white. Singles only were played and the game lasted for only 10 points. The Japanese governing body speedily changed its name, and affiliated to the I.T.T.F. in 1929, but did not take part in the world championships until 1952. Meanwhile international rules had been sent out and, in the early 1930s, samples of international balls and rubber-covered, including sponge, rackets followed. In the first year of Japanese world competition, in Bombay, Satoh won with a sponge racket. However, before the following season BERGMANN and LEACH toured Japan with successful results in nearly all matches. Japanese players (who at that time — as now for the most part — employed the penholder grip), under the guidance of coach and captain Daimon, learned much about play against lawn tennis grip styles from this visit and Japanese men players from 1954 (women from 1956) began a dominance that has been surpassed only by the Chinese.

Of the last 12 world championships to 1969, Japanese players have won the Swaythling Cup 7 times, the Marcel Corbillon Cup 7, men's singles 6, men's doubles 3, women's singles 7, women's doubles 3 (and one half), and mixed doubles 7. In N. Fujii, Japanese champion from 1946 to 1950, and in OGIMURA and T. Tanaka, who between them won four men's singles world championships, Japan produced players of the highest class. Eguchi, a fine all-rounder, and Matsuzaki, a hard hitter, have been the strongest among the women. N. Hasegawa won the world championship men's singles in 1967 and Itoh in 1969. The great strength of Japanese players derives, however, less from individual talent than from their youth, quickness, fitness, and courage to attack at all stages of the game. Table tennis in Japan is an inter-school and inter-university sport.

China. Records show that a Shanghai Ping-Pong Union was formed in 1923 on the initiative of the Shanghai Y.M.C.A. The table was 4 ft. 8 in. (1·42 m.) wide. A playing space of only 6 ft. (1·82 m.) behind the table was considered sufficient and doubles play took place with server and partner obliged to hit to the diagonally facing half-courts, receiver and partner to those directly opposite.

China was affiliated to the I.T.T.F. only in 1953, and at first her impact on the world game was modest. The modern game was then studied seriously and by 1956 when next the Chinese players competed in the world championships they were serious contenders. A Chinese won the men's singles in 1959 and by 1961, with the beginning of the sequence of three final wins in the men's singles by CHUANG TSE-TUNG over Li Fu-jung, China began a world dominance so complete, even over the Japanese, that there seemed no reason why it should ever end. In the five-year period 1961-5, Chinese players won not only the three men's singles titles but the three Swaythling Cup competitions and two men's doubles. The women, less outstanding, won one women's singles, two women's doubles, and the Marcel Corbillon Cup once. With the Cultural Revolution, Chinese participation abroad was suspended until 1970. Of the two world championships held since then, they have won the Swaythling Cup once more, the women's singles twice, the men's singles, women's singles, and mixed doubles once each.

In their greatest period Chinese teams went on many tours abroad, often including young and hitherto unknown recruits, always with success. Touring teams in China would find themselves as conclusively outclassed against provincial opponents as in the full internationals. The concluding rounds of world championship men's singles became so much a Chinese preserve that representatives from other countries almost seemed interlopers. This standard clearly derived not only from numbers, but from serious application to practice and physical fitness, and from good captaincy (notably by Fu Chi-fang), but also from technical innovation and tactical study. Extraordinary players were produced, e.g. with underspin styles hitherto thought impossible to the penholder grip, special attention was paid to the tactical role of the service in opening the rally, and of the second or third stroke in securing a surprise advantage. There was also the factor of high morale. In 1964, prior to their Corbillon win the following year, the Swaythling Cup player Hsu Yin-sheng made a speech to women players on fighting spirit which was reprinted in many millions of copies and widely translated as a model with general application.

Though not yet quite such an invincible power as before the break, Chinese table tennis has earned a celebrity on the non-sporting plane by its association with the so-called 'Ping-Pong diplomacy'; the invitation to U.S. players to visit Peking following the world table tennis championships in Tokyo in 1971 having been the signal for breaking the long deadlock in Chinese–U.S.A. diplomatic relations.

Victor Barna, *Table Tennis Today* (1962); Richard Bergmann, ed. Stephen Kersten, *Twenty-one Up* (1950); Dr. Hans Eckert, *Die Welt des Weissen Balls* (1954); Bengt Grive, *Pingis* (1967); Geoffrey Harrower, *Teach Yourself Table Tennis* (1966); Hsu Yin-sheng, *On How to Play Table Tennis* (speech to Chinese women players) (1964); V. S. Ivanov, *Nastolny Tennis* (manual for trainers and category players) (1958); Zdenko Uzorinac, *Od Londona do Sarajevo* (1973). GOVERNING BODY (WORLD): International Table Tennis Federation, 20 Havelock Road, Hastings, Sussex.

TAKACS, KAROLY (1909–   ), Hungarian national pistol champion many times and winner of the gold medal in the Bisley (London) OLYMPIC GAMES of 1948 in the rapid-fire event, an achievement he repeated at Helsinki in the 1952 Games.

TAKRAW is the international ball game of south-east Asia, most remarkable for the rule that in none of its many variations may the ball touch the hands or the ground. The ball (*takraw*) is of woven rattan, and must not be more than 40 cm. (16 in.) in circumference, nor more than 200 g. (7 oz.) in weight. The principle of all forms of the sport is to hit the ball with the finest possible precision in the most difficult imaginable circumstances.

HOOP TAKRAW, the most popular form

of this game in Thailand, is played on a circular field 16 m. (52 ft.) in diameter, spaced round the perimeter of which stand the members of both teams (usually seven a side). Six metres (20 ft.) above the centre of the circle is suspended the goal, usually a cluster of three hoops, each 40 cm. (16 in.) in diameter, upright, and joined together at the rims like the faces of a triangular prism. To score, the ball must be hit through one of the hoops, to drop into an open-ended net hanging below, like that under a BASKETBALL goal. Players of the same team hope to retain possession of the ball, if it misses the goal, preventing their opponents from being able to shoot. The more difficult or stylish the shot, the more points are awarded by the judges if it succeeds. A simple kick rates the lowest points; shots with knees, elbows, or shoulders rather more; and most of all, the classic shot in which the ball is kicked with both feet together behind the back, and through a circle made by the player holding out his arms behind him. If at any time the ball touches his hands, or the ground, it becomes dead.

IN-TOSSING TAKRAW is used chiefly for training players, who must see how many times, and in how many different ways, they can keep hitting the ball in the air without it touching the ground. A skilled group, with exceptional concentration, may keep it up for an hour. A legendary Thai maestro, Daeng, was said to have an infinite variety of shots, the most spectacular of which was to drop face down on all fours and rebound from the ground to strike the ball with his rump.

(For net *takraw*, a form of the game comparable to BADMINTON and widely played in international competition, see SEPAK TAKRAW).

TALBOT HANDICAP, see BOWLS, LAWN: CROWN GREEN.

TAMASHIWARA, see KARATE.

TAMBOURIN is a bat-and-ball game of the tennis type. Played on a long narrow court with a ball, 6 cm. (2⅜ in.) in diameter, and a racket with a parchment hitting-surface, it was long popular in Provence.

TANCREDO, Don (Tancredo López) (*d.* 1923), *torero,* who failed to accomplish his ambition to become a matador, but earned his place in the annals of the bull ring when, covered with white paint, he mounted a pedestal in the centre of the arena, and awaited the entry of the bull. His theory that the bull would not charge what appeared to be an inanimate object proved correct.

TANI, CHOJIRO (1915-   ), Japanese exponent of KARATE. Born in Kobe, he studied under MABUNI, founder of the *shitoryu* style. He broke away in about 1950, however, to found the *shukukai* ('way for all') style which emphasizes speed of movement. Tani holds the grade of 8th *Dan* and is president of the world *shukukai* organization, known as the World Karate Union.

TANNER, ELAINE (1951-   ), Canadian swimmer who, at 15 years old, was the most successful in the 1966 British Empire and COMMONWEALTH GAMES in Kingston, Jamaica. She won four gold and three silver medals for butterfly, freestyle, individual medley and backstroke. Her greatest successes were at backstroke; she became double PAN-AMERICAN GAMES champion for this style in 1967 and a year later, in the Mexico Olympics, was second in the 100 and 200 metres.

TANNER, HAYDN (1917-   ), RUGBY UNION scrum half for SWANSEA, CARDIFF, and Wales, noted for the speed and accuracy of his service, even in the worst conditions. He was still at school when he played his first game for Wales against the third ALL-BLACKS in 1935, the Welsh victory helping to establish an international career which continued through 14 seasons. Tanner won 25 caps, and was captain of Wales on 12 occasions.

TANTIÈME (1947), a race-horse bred in France and owned by DUPRÉ, trained by MATHET, and ridden by POINCELET and Doyasbere. Tantième won the PRIX DE L'ARC DE TRIOMPHE twice, the French Two Thousand Guineas, Prix Lupin, PRIX GANAY, and Coronation Cup, altogether 12 out of 15 races and a new European record sum in stakes of £81,339. Later at stud he became the sire of MATCH III and RELIANCE, and grandsire of RELKO.

TARGA FLORIO, see MOTOR RACING, INTERNATIONAL.

TARGET SHOOTING, see SHOOTING, AIR WEAPONS; SHOOTING, PISTOL; SHOOTING, RIFLE.

TARRASA–LA MATA, a Spanish road RACE WALKING event held near Barcelona in late March. The race was first held in 1965 and covers a distance of 15 km. (9¼ miles), involving a climb of 500 m. (1,500 ft.). Now a fully-fledged international event for West Europeans, the race has been won by PAMICH four times in succession (1966-9). He set a course record in 1968.

TATE, MAURICE WILLIAM (1895-1956), cricketer for England and Sussex. A good enough batsman to score a Test century and to establish, with Bowley, a Sussex record second-wicket stand of 385, he was the finest fast-medium bowler between the wars. Using all his considerable weight in a model action, he swerved the ball and generated surprising pace off the pitch. He took 38 of his 155 Test wickets in the 1924-5 series in Australia, having dismissed eight South African batsmen in his first Test the previous season, when he and Gilligan routed them for 30. Of a jovial and philosophical nature, he had great stamina.

TATTERSALLS are the famous English horse auctioneers founded in 1766 at Hyde Park Corner in London by Richard Tattersall (1724-95), owner of HIGHFLYER. The firm moved to Knightsbridge Green in 1865, started the Doncaster yearling sales in 1869, and finally established their thoroughbred auctions at the new covered sales ring at Park Paddocks, Newmarket, in 1965. Record sale prices date from 1872 with the dispersal of Blenkiron's Middle Park Stud for 124,620 guineas, Blair Athol, winner of the DERBY and ST. LEGER, fetching 12,500 guineas, and GLADIATEUR 7,000 guineas. In 1900, at the sale of the Duke of WESTMINSTER's bloodstock, Blanc paid 37,500 guineas for the triple crown (see HORSE RACING) winner FLYING FOX, and Sievier 10,000 guineas for a yearling filly, subsequently named SCEPTRE. Other high prices which followed were 47,000 guineas for SOLARIO as a ten-year-old stallion in 1932; 28,000 guineas for Sayajirao as a yearling in 1945; 36,000 guineas for Festoon as a three-year-old classic winner in 1954; and 37,000 guineas for Chandelier as a nine-year-old brood mare in foal to AUREOLE in 1964, in which year the NATIONAL STUD's 30 mares and foals were sold for 271,920 guineas. In subsequent years prices continued to rise: the brood mare Valse de Vienne fetched 40,000 guineas in 1967; the filly foal by EXBURY out of Loose Cover 37,000 guineas in 1968; the yearling filly La Hague (full sister to the ONE THOUSAND GUINEAS winner, Fleet) 51,000 guineas in 1969; and Cambrienne, a yearling filly by Sicambre, for 65,000 guineas in 1970. In 1969 the two-year-old Decies realized 110,000 guineas, but the world record price for a horse at public auction is the 136,000 guineas paid at the Newmarket December Sales in 1967, when Tattersalls sold VAGUELY NOBLE at the end of his two-year-old career. Foreign buyers, mainly American and Japanese, have contributed to the boom in bloodstock prices, and in 1971 the yearlings Princely Review and Bigivor were sold for 117,000 guineas and 81,000 guineas. In 1972 Ginevra, winner of the OAKS, was sold for 106,000 guineas, beating the record sum paid for a brood mare, set by Aunt Edith in 1966, by more than 30,000 guineas. The highest price paid at public auction for a National Hunt horse is the 20,000 guineas for Princess Camilla at Doncaster in 1973. The world record price for a yearling is held by Crowned Prince, who was sold in America in 1970 for $510,000.

TAYFIELD, HUGH JOSEPH (1928-   ), cricketer for South Africa, Natal, Rhodesia, and Transvaal. An off-spin bowler whose flight and accuracy were backed by expert fielding and sympathetic captaincy, during the 1950s he captured 170 Test wickets — a South African record. In his third Test, against a strong Australian side, he took 7 wickets for 23 runs, and in Australia in 1952-3 he took 30 wickets in the series. His best season was 1956-7, when his 19 wickets in the last two Tests (he took 37 in the series) enabled South Africa to draw level with England.

TAYLOR, ALEC (1862-1943), called 'the Wizard of Manton', was top of the list of winning race-horse trainers in England a record 12 times. The horses in his stable won over 1,000 races (including 21 classics) worth more than £800,000 in prize money. He trained BAYARDO, LEMBERG, GAY CRUSADER, and GAINSBOROUGH.

TAYLOR, BRUCE RICHARD (1943-   ), cricketer for New Zealand, Canterbury, and Wellington. At the time of his retirement in 1973 he was New Zealand's leading wicket-taker, with 111, and had the best bowling analysis for his country (7 for 74, against West Indies, 1971-2). A tall player, who bowled right-arm fast-medium and batted left-handed, he also made both his first two centuries in Test matches — 105 against India and 124 (reaching 50 in 30 minutes) against West Indies — a unique distinction.

TAYLOR, E. P. (1901-   ), is the prominent owner-breeder of race-horses in Canada and president of the Canadian Jockey Club. He won the KENTUCKY DERBY and PREAKNESS STAKES in the U.S.A. with his colt Northern Dancer in 1964, and subsequently bred the champion NIJINSKY, which he sold as a yearling to ENGELHARD for $84,000.

TAYLOR, HENRY (1885-1951), English swimmer who won three gold medals for Britain at the 1908 OLYMPIC GAMES in London. He took the 400 and 1,500 metres freestyle in world record times and was a member of the winning British team in the 4 × 200 metres relay. He won 15 English titles, his last at the age of 35 for the 5-mile long-distance race in the river Thames.

TAYLOR, HERBERT WILFRED, M.C. (1889-1973), cricketer for South Africa, Natal, and Transvaal. Quick-footed, and with a textbook style, he scored heavily on South African matting wickets, never revealing his mastery to greater effect than in 1913-14, when he alone offered resistance to the devastating spin and bounce of BARNES. All his six Test centuries were scored against England —five of them in South Africa, three in the 1922-3 series. He led South Africa on the 1924 tour of England.

TAYLOR, JOHN HENRY (1871-1963), English professional golfer who won the Open championship five times and was runner-up five times. He was one of the 'Great Triumvirate' (with BRAID and VARDON) who dominated British GOLF for 20 years before 1914, and one of golf's outstanding players.

TAYLOR, JOY (1936-   ), LACROSSE player for England from 1962 to 1969 and captain from 1965, and a successful coach. A penetrative passer of the ball, she played for Harpenden Ladies' Club, Anstey College of Physical Education, and the East of England Territorial team as a wing defence. She captained the Great Britain and Ireland touring team to the U.S.A. in 1967.

TEDDINGTON HOCKEY CLUB, see HOCKEY, FIELD.

TELEMARK, region of southern Norway where, about 1860, NORDHEIM evolved a binding for skis that enabled local skiers to pioneer new methods of jumping and turning. Though the heel could be lifted, it did not wobble laterally, as previously, when there was only a rudimentary toe binding. The new turn was named the Telemark, and could be attempted in soft, packed snow at speeds up to 18 km. per hour (11 m.p.h.). The weight was put on the outside leg and the inside heel lifted high with arms and sticks widespread. The turn was used extensively in Scandinavia until the 1930s.

TEMME, EDWARD HENRY (*fl.* 1927-36), English swimmer who was the first man to cross the Channel both ways (see SWIMMING) and an Olympic WATER POLO player. He was among the early ranks of Channel swimmers, going from France to England in 1927 and completing his double, from England to France, in 1934. He also represented Britain at two OLYMPIC GAMES. In 1928 he was a member of the team that came fourth and he also played in 1936.

TENIKOIT, see RING TENNIS.

TENNIS, Beach, see DECK TENNIS.

TENNIS, Deck, see DECK TENNIS.

TENNIS, Lawn, see LAWN TENNIS.

TENNIS, Real, see REAL TENNIS.

TENNIS, Ring, see RING TENNIS.

TENNIS, TABLE, see TABLE TENNIS.

TENPIN BOWLING, see BOWLING, TENPIN.

TESIO, FEDERICO, see HORSE RACING.

TEST MATCH, see CRICKET.

TETRARCH, The (1911), a colt who ran in England only as a two-year-old, winning all his seven races. He was nicknamed 'the Rocking Horse' or 'the Spotted Wonder' because of his mottled grey coat. He was owned by Maj. McCalmont and ridden by DONOGHUE.

TEXAS, University of, American college FOOTBALL team, nicknamed the 'Longhorns', rose to prominence in the late 1940s led by quarterback Layne, who later starred for the DETROIT LIONS in professional football. Coached by Royal, who had played under WILKINSON at OKLAHOMA and installed his split-T offence, Texas dominated college football throughout much of the 1960s, winning national titles in 1963 and 1969, when they were unbeaten. Texas teams have made up in execution and quickness for lack of weight and rugged strength.
COLOURS: Orange and white.

TEXAS RANGERS, American professional BASEBALL team, joined the AMERICAN LEAGUE in 1972, when the franchise was transferred from the WASHINGTON SENATORS. Its stadium was in Arlington, almost equi-distant from Dallas and Fort Worth. In its first season the team finished last in the Western Division and failed to draw substantially better than Washington did the previous year.

THAMES CUP, see HENLEY ROYAL REGATTA.

THAMES PUNTING CLUB, see PUNTING.

THAMES ROWING CLUB, London tideway club founded in 1860 with headquarters at Putney on the river Thames. The club has produced many famous international crews and scullers, especially during the years between the two World Wars, when, under the coaching of FAIRBAIRN and J. Beresford, sr., it won several Olympic medals and had numerous HENLEY successes. The 1923 eight was outstanding and the lightest crew ever to win the Grand Challenge Cup. The 1932 coxless four, which won the Stewards' at Henley, was also an exceptional combination, winning the Olympic gold medal at Los Angeles despite making a last-minute change owing to illness.

An internationally famous oarsman whose adult rowing career was entirely with Thames was J. BERESFORD, JR., three times an Olympic gold medallist and twice a silver medallist.

The first cross-country club to appear outside the schools where the sport originated was the Thames Hare and Hounds, which was formed in 1867 as a means of training in the winter.

COLOURS: Red, white, and black.

THÉPOT, ALEX (1906-   ), Association footballer for Brest, Levallois, Red Star (Paris), and France for whom he made his international début in goal against England in Paris in May 1927, when England won 6-0. His goalkeeping ability was not doubted, however, and he soon gained a regular place in the French national team, played in both the 1930 and 1934 world championship tournaments, and made 31 appearances until his final international match in Paris in March 1935 against Germany.

THOMAS, Sir GEORGE ALAN, Bart. (1881-1972), English BADMINTON player. One of the greatest players of his time, he represented England continuously over 27 years (1902-29) and won the ALL-ENGLAND men's singles championship from 1920 to 1923 inclusive. In all he took 90 national or international championship titles during his long career. In 1934 he was elected president of the newly formed International Badminton Federation and remained in office for 21 years. He was the donor of the THOMAS CUP, the trophy for the International Badminton Championship. He was also both a chess and a LAWN TENNIS international for England, and twice British chess champion.

THOMAS CUP, the silver-gilt trophy of the international BADMINTON championship which was donated to the International Badminton Federation by Sir GEORGE THOMAS in 1939 during his presidency. Due to the war, the first competition was deferred until 1948-9.

It is a men's event for teams of six players. The competition takes place on a knock-out basis in four geographical zones with the winners and the holder playing off at one centre. A tie consists of five singles matches between three players a side, and four doubles contested by two pairs a side. In the singles matches the best two players oppose the best two of the other side and the third player plays only the third opposing player.

THOMPSON, DONALD JAMES (1933-   ), British race walker who was the leading walker in the world at distances from 50 km. to 100 km. during the period 1955-63, and Olympic 50 km. champion in 1960. He also competed at this distance in the 1956 Olympiad. His record in the European 50 km. event is: third (1962), fifth (1958), and eighth (1966). He set a course record for the LONDON–BRIGHTON race in 1957, and won it nine times (1955-62 and 1967) and also twice won the MILAN 100 KM. (1955 and 1960). Thompson had eight wins in the Race Walking Association's 50 km. championship (1956-62 and 1966), and finished second in 1961, and fourth in 1965 in the LUGANO CUP 50 km. final. His indomitable determination made up for his small stature and unsophisticated technique.

THOMPSON, J. R. (1918-   ), British amateur RACKETS player who won the British amateur singles championship in 1954-5 and 1957-9. He also won the doubles championship with MILFORD ten times in twelve years between 1948 and 1959 and again in 1966 with Pugh.

THOMPSON, 'Snowshoe', see THORENSEN, J.

THOMPSON, WILLIAM, see BENDIGO.

THOMPSON TROPHY, see FLYING, SPORTING.

THOMSON, PETER W., M.B.E. (1929-   ), Australian professional golfer, the most accomplished player his country has produced. He was Open champion in 1954, 1955, 1956, 1958, 1965; Australian Open champion 1951, 1967, 1972; New Zealand Open champion 1950, 1951, and 1953; New Zealand professional champion 1953; Australian professional champion 1967; and a WORLD CUP player. Towards the end of his brilliant playing career, he devoted much of his time to the creation of the Far East GOLF circuit, and is active in golf architecture, journalism, and broadcasting.

THORENSEN, JOHN (Snowshoe Thompson), emigrated with his family from Tinn, TELEMARK, Norway, in 1838, and in America in the autumn of 1855 was the only applicant for the job of carrying mail over the Sierra Nevada. On 3 January 1856, he departed on skis from Placerville, California, to carry the mail to Genoa, Nevada. His cross-Sierra trips, of 90 miles in three days, for nearly 20 years made it possible for mail to travel from San Francisco to New York in 12 days rather than the three months it took by clipper around Cape Horn.

THORNDAHL, Mrs. KIRSTEN (1928-), Danish BADMINTON player who represented her country between 1946 and 1963. A left-hander and extremely graceful in her movements and strokes, she won 11 ALL-ENGLAND CHAMPIONSHIP titles over 15 years.

THORPE, JAMES FRANCIS (1888-1953), American athlete, perhaps the most versatile in history. Part Algonquin Indian and part Irish, he played FOOTBALL at the Carlisle (Pennsylvania) Indian School, and was an All-American halfback in 1911-12. An outstanding running back, with a deceptive hip-twist that made it difficult for a tackler to bring him down, he was also an exceptional defensive player and accurate drop-kicker of field goals. He was also a LACROSSE and BASEBALL player at Carlisle. Later he was equally outstanding as a professional football player, with Ohio teams in Cleveland, Canton, Marion, and Toledo (1921-3, 1926), Rock Island (Illinois) (1924-5), and New York (1925). He also played professional baseball for the NEW YORK GIANTS of the NATIONAL LEAGUE from 1913 to 1920.

Perhaps his greatest achievement was winning both the PENTATHLON and DECATHLON at the 1912 OLYMPIC GAMES in Stockholm, winning four of five individual events in the pentathlon and scoring a 700-point margin over his nearest competitor in the decathlon. Although high hurdles were his best event, he was placed in the HIGH JUMP in the 1912 Olympics.

The following year it was revealed that he had played professional baseball in the summer of 1909, and after an investigation, the Amateur Athletic Union revoked his amateur status. The INTERNATIONAL OLYMPIC COMMITTEE followed suit by depriving him of all his Olympic medals. In 1950, 40 years after his legendary exploits, he was voted 'the greatest football player and male athlete of the first half of the twentieth century'.

THREE-DAY EVENT, see EQUESTRIAN EVENTS.

THREE PEAKS RACE, see CYCLO-CROSS; FELL RUNNING.

THREE POSITIONS INTERNATIONAL MATCH, see SHOOTING, RIFLE: SMALL-BORE.

THROWING, see DISCUS; HAMMER; JAVELIN.

THRUXTON CIRCUIT, Hampshire airfield circuit first used for racing in 1950, mainly for motor cycles, but car races were held there until 1953. It was still being used for MOTOR-CYCLE RACING in 1965, but by then the surface was in poor condition, and racing was stopped for safety reasons. With the loss of GOODWOOD MOTOR CIRCUIT, the British Automobile Racing Club was seeking a new home and chose Thruxton. By October 1967 preliminary planning had been completed, and the track was then completely resurfaced and spectator facilities and protection provided in time for a club meeting to take place in March 1968. The circuit has a length of 2·356 miles (3·8 km.), with fast, sweeping, and difficult bends, and no real straights. It was prepared under the direction of Brooks, a former Grand Prix driver. The first major meeting took place on Easter Monday 1968, but noise restrictions threatened the viability of the course, which continued to operate under restricted conditions.

THURGOOD, ALBERT (c. 1875-1935), Australian Rules footballer known as 'Albert the Great', was acclaimed the greatest player in Australia in his time. In 1893 he was the foremost player of the Essendon club's undefeated premiership team, and he played a major part in their four successive premierships before 1900. He was credited with having kicked a football 107 yds. 2 ft. 1 in. (98·48 m.) at the East Melbourne ground on 22 June 1899. This distance (to the first bounce) was measured by newspaper representatives. Other exceptional kicks by him were measured at 99 yds. (90·53 m.) in Fremantle, Western Australia, in July 1895, and 95 yds. (86·87 m.) at Adelaide Oval in 1894.

TILDEN, WILLIAM TATEM (1893-1953), American LAWN TENNIS player, probably the most compelling and dramatically successful competitor the men's game has known. Tall, theatrical in gesture, he strode about the court, a master showman, brilliantly varying his attack. His cannon-ball service was devastating and his virtuosity, concentration, and determination remarkable.

After failing in the U.S. singles finals of 1918 and 1919 against Murray and W. M. Johnston, he spent a winter working on his backhand and returned to dominate the game. He won at WIMBLEDON in 1920 (the first American success in the history of the men's championship), 1921, and 1930, and he was seven times U.S. champion. He took the Wimbledon doubles once and the U.S. doubles five times, and in 1930 he was the first player to win the new Italian title.

For 11 successive years — 1920-30 — he played for the U.S.A. in the Davis Cup (see LAWN TENNIS). The Americans won in his first year and held it until the French succeeded in 1927. In the first six years of that period Tilden won 20 rubbers, all except 5 in challenge rounds, and lost only one doubles match with Richards — to the Australians, PATTERSON and Wood in 1922. LACOSTE spoilt his Davis Cup singles record in 1926. Altogether, Tilden won 34 rubbers out of 41 and his tally in challenge rounds was 21 wins to 7 defeats. Lacoste beat him twice in the singles and COCHET three times.

Tilden was a shrewd critic and commentator on the technique and psychology of the game and wrote a number of books, notably *Match Play and the Spin of the Ball* (1928) and *Tennis—A to Z* (1950). He became a professional in 1931 and toured extensively.

TIMPERLEY, Mrs. E. J. (*née* June Rose White) (1932-   ), BADMINTON player for England. A superb doubles player, she represented England 44 times between 1952 and 1963 and was three times ALL-ENGLAND women's doubles champion with Mrs. ROGERS, and three times mixed doubles champion with different partners.

TITOV, YURI (1935-   ), talented Russian gymnast who although overshadowed by his contemporary SHAKHLIN, still managed to take the gold medal in the 1962 world championships for the combined exercises. Titov also collected a total of four world titles. In the OLYMPIC GAMES he competed in three celebrations and proved remarkably consistent. He won one gold (team) medal, five silver medals, and three bronze between 1956 and 1964. The peak of his career was the Prague world championships when he beat the Japanese and his compatriot, Shakhlin, for the over-all title, and finished first in the rings.

TOBOGGANING is the sport of sliding down ice-covered tracks on small sleds, one variety of which, the luge toboggan, is ridden in a sitting position, in contrast to the forward-prone position of a Cresta run 'skeleton' rider.

Luge tobogganing. The luge tobogganing sled is now usually made of wood with metal runners, with a seat of plaid straps. Before 1964, when training for the Olympic events convinced participants of the advantages of wood, the Austrians in particular had favoured all-steel toboggans.

The luge single-seater toboggan must not exceed 20 kg. (44 lb.) in weight, nor 1·5 m. (4 ft. 11 in.) in length. Its gauge width must not be more than 44 cm. (1 ft. $5\frac{3}{8}$ in.) and its height must be between 12 and 15 cm. ($4\frac{3}{4}$–$5\frac{7}{8}$ in.). Only the sharp inside edges of the twin metal runners are in contact with the ice. The double-seater toboggan, though longer, has the same weight limitation as the single-seater.

The luge has no mechanical means of steering or braking; it is steered by the feet and a hand rope. Its front runners can be moved independently by leg pressure, and the delicate control of these sharp-edged runners, aided by the skilful transference of body weight, accounts for its flexibility.

Equipment essentials are goggles, a crash helmet, knee pads, elbow pads, shoulder pads, and reinforced gloves. Spikes are fitted to the soles of the boots to assist pushing off and there are metal 'rakes' on the toe-caps to help braking and steering with the feet.

Championships are held for single-seater and two-seater toboggans and the outcome is decided by the aggregate times of four runs by each rider or crew, as in BOBSLEIGH. Major courses average 1,000 m. (1,093·6 yds.) in length with upwards of a dozen curves, corners, or hairpin (maze) bends. Courses of world championship standard include IGLS and Imst (Austria), VILLARD DE LANS (France), Oslo (Norway), Krynica (Poland), Hammarstrand (Sweden), Davos (Switzerland), and Berchtesgaden, GARMISCH-Partenkirchen, and Königsee (West Germany).

The techniques of lugeing have altered appreciably. The first racers used sleds similar to those used nowadays by children. The first European championship riders in 1914 steered by touching the track with their hands, wearing gloves studded for the purpose with little iron points. The modern flexibility of the sled through the manipulation of the front runners has made this technique outdated.

When turning, the luge tobogganer makes three basic movements: (1) the pulling up of the runner on the side to which he intends to turn, which makes the runner's aft tip brake a little; (2) the pushing in of the fore end of the runner on the opposite side to which he intends to turn; and (3) the placing of the weight on the outward runner, which makes it go faster than the inward runner.

Each one of these three movements makes the sled turn a little. The rider must find the right combination of the three for every particular circumstance. Due to these improvements and the progress in run-building, speeds have increased to 60 m.p.h. (96·6 km./h.) and, on some points of the Krynica run in Poland, even up to 80 m.p.h. (128·7 km./h.).

Although riders used traditionally to adopt an upright sitting posture, the Germans, during the mid-1960s achieved aerodynamic advantages by leaning further backwards, and this technique has since become more general.

Luge runs are similar to bobsleigh runs, except that they are steeper (maximum average gradient, 11 per cent) and the corners are narrower, so a heavy competitor has hardly any advantage. But a simple mountain road can make a good unofficial luge run for less serious contests, and this makes lugeing a true people's sport. In Austria, there are more than 20,000 organized tobogganers.

Lugeing, in its modern competition style, is comparatively young as an organized sport. It was not included in the OLYMPIC GAMES until 1964, but its ancestry goes back many centuries. The sport's origins are believed to be older than those of SKIING and it is probable that in the times when the ancient Greeks celebrated their original Olympic Games, sled-like vehicles were used by the inhabitants of the Alpine countries for transport as well as for pleasure.

As a winter recreation, tobogganing is recorded in sixteenth-century documents. In 1520 Hans Sachs described the enjoyment he derived from it; and in 1530 Conrad Schwarz wrote a treatise about it, using the word *rodel* (German for toboggan).

The development of lugeing as a racing sport is traceable from the middle of the nineteenth century, when British tourists started sled-racing on snowbound mountain roads in the Alps. Out of this, three sports emerged — bobsleigh, Cresta Run tobogganing (see below), and luge tobogganing.

In 1879, two toboggan tracks were constructed at Davos, Switzerland. In 1881, the first national competition was staged on a course between Davos and Klosters. Its success prompted an international contest on the same track on 12 March 1883. The course was more than 3,000 m. (3,281 yds.) long: 21 competitors represented Australia, Germany, Great Britain, Holland, Sweden, and Switzerland. The result was a dead heat between Minch, a Swiss, and Robertson, an Austral-

ian. Davos has remained a popular centre for the sport, which the Swiss call *schlitteln*.

From Switzerland, lugeing soon spread to Germany and Austria. The first recorded competitions in the Austrian Tyrol were held in 1890 by the Academic Alpine Club of Innsbruck. The first Bavarian course was built in 1894 at Brünnstein, near Oberaudorf, and the first Bavarian championships took place there in 1905. The Styrian Toboggan Club was founded in Austria in 1904. The South-West German Toboggan Club was formed with 1,600 members at Triberg, in the Black Forest, in 1911. The German Toboggan Association was inaugurated the same year and the first German national championships were held at Ilmenau in 1913. An International Tobogganing Association was also formed in 1913 by Austrian, German, and Swiss racers. The first European championships were held in 1914 at Reichenfeld, Austria.

In the 1930s a big advance came when Tietze, of Austria, invented the flexible sled. This was the beginning of the triumph of lugeing, making the possibilities as great as those of bobsleigh, but with everything done by the body and nothing mechanical.

After curtailed activities during the First World War, the potential predominance of lugeing over bobsleigh as a participant sport became obvious because of the ease with which tobogganing could be practised by anyone on natural courses down mountain paths and roads, in contrast to bobsleigh with its more elaborate, expensive courses and sleds. Thousands of active enthusiasts in the Austrian Tyrol alone provided early evidence of this trend. In 1945, Austria created its national federation, and in 1952, when Isatitsch became its president, the important era of his international influence began.

A major turning point and stimulus for the sport occurred in 1954, when the INTERNATIONAL OLYMPIC COMMITTEE, meeting in Athens, officially acknowledged luge tobogganing as the future replacement of skeleton tobogganing as an Olympic sport.

In 1955, the first world championships were staged in Oslo, where Salvesen (Norway) and Miss Kienz (Austria) became the first world singles champions, and the first two-seater title went to the Austrian pair, Krausner and Thaler.

Lugeing gained a separate world administration in 1957, when the International Luge Federation (I.L.F.) was formed, with Isatitsch its first president. The sport had previously been controlled by the International Bobsleigh Federation (until then more commonly known by its full title, International Bobsleigh and Tobogganing Federation).

Because it was found impracticable to build a suitable run at Squaw Valley, California (U.S.A.), in 1960, the luge toboggan's Olympic début had to be deferred for a further four years. The 1964 events opened many hitherto uninitiated eyes and started a widening of interest and participation far beyond the central European area where, until then, the sport had thrived most.

It was appropriate that Austria, for long the world's leading tobogganing nation, should be the sport's first Olympic host. Igls, east of Innsbruck, was the selected venue and the course was planned meticulously, down to the exact radius of every curve, on the drawing-board before construction commenced. Watched by crowds estimated at more than 6,000, 38 men and 17 women participated, representing 12 nations, whose names illustrated the growth of the sport — Argentina, Austria, Canada, Czechoslovakia, Germany, Great Britain, Italy, Liechtenstein, Norway, Poland, Switzerland, and U.S.A.

Germans took all the men's singles medals at Igls. The total winning time of KÖHLER over all four runs was less than $\frac{1}{10}$ ths of a second faster than that of Bonsack, the runner-up. In the two-seater contest, FEISTMANTL and Stengl won for the host nation, but in the women's singles another German, ENDERLEIN, defeated her compatriot, GEISLER, then world champion.

The British rider, Skrzypecki, was killed in a crash during the week of training which immediately preceded the 1964 WINTER OLYMPICS. Despite this sad prelude and other accidents, it was not apparent that any part of the course became unreasonably dangerous for experienced contestants.

Treating the luge runners with suitable ski waxes has always been an accepted practice but heating the runners to gain extra speed was a temporary phase in the years just prior to, and during, the keen competition for the 1964 Winter Olympics. The Austrians then had hollow runners which they filled with hot oil. A German heated his runners electrically on an immersion heater principle. Other Germans used blow lamps but, after the 1964 Igls events, the heating of runners was declared illegal by the I.L.F.

Three East German women were disqualified for contravening this rule during the sport's next big milestone, the 1968 Winter Olympic Games at Villard de Lans, France. The lugeing here suffered several postponements when unseasonably mild weather caused too much melting ice when the sun was up. Two, instead of the customary four, runs became necessary to produce results. The Austrians, Germans, and Poles shared most of the honours except for the women's victory by an Italian, LECHNER. SCHMID, of Austria, edged the East German, Köhler, into second place in the men's singles, but Köhler and Bonsack won the two-seater gold medals. This time, 58 men and 26 women competed, representing 14 nations, including separate East and West German teams; and France, Spain, and Sweden took part for the first time.

Since the world championships series began in 1955, the sport's outstanding male exponents have included Köhler (East Germany), Schmid and Fiestmantl (Austria), and NACHMANN (West Germany). Among the most successful women riders have been Enderlein and Geisler (East Germany), Lechner (Italy), and ISSER (Austria).

Howard Bass, *Winter Sports* (1966).
GOVERNING BODY: International Luge Federation, Rottenmann 20, Austria.

Cresta tobogganing is sliding on a vehicle with metal runners, known as a 'skeleton', or skeleton toboggan, in the fastest possible time down the Cresta run, a hazardously winding, steeply banked channel of ice built every year by the ST. MORITZ Tobogganing Club at St. Moritz, Switzerland.

The skeleton, a form of toboggan, usually comprises two steel runners 45·6 cm. (18 in.) apart and about 1·2 m. (4 ft.) long, anchored to a platform on which there is a sliding seat. The skeleton weighs about 36·2 kg. (80 lb.). The rider lies chest down on the seat and grasps the upper bow of the runners. When the rider is

THE CRESTA RUN

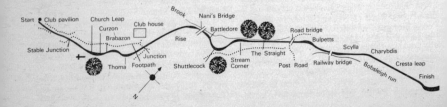

going straight, the weight of the body carried on the sliding seat is forward. Directional changes in the straight sections of the course can be made by the slightest tilt of the head. When corners have to be taken the body is slid back and the weight is taken on the rear part of the runners, which are deeply grooved. The skeleton is then steered by forcing the nose round, side-slip being eliminated by the grooves. Judging the correct angle of approach and exit from corners is crucially important to fast times.

The season for the Cresta run is January to February when temperatures are usually sub-zero, and the course is open in two stages according to weather conditions. Its full length is 1,212·25 m. (about ¾ mile), and it has an average gradient of 1 in 7·7; straights are 2 m. (6 ft. 7 in.) wide and corners up to 4 m. (13 ft.) high.

To slide the full length is to ride from Top. In the early part of the season only the lower three-quarter section of the course is used, a distance of 890·20 m. (973 yds.) and gradient of 1 in 8. This is known as riding from Junction. The starting point at Junction is almost opposite the club house, a control tower with a public-address system to all parts of the course, from which an officer, usually the secretary of the club, controls the riders and onlookers. The speed of a good rider approaches 50 m.p.h. (80 km./h.) from Top and he will finish the course at nearly 90 m.p.h. (145 km./h.). Because of strict controls there is an excellent safety record on the run.

Shuttlecock is the most notorious of the nine corners on the run. It is approximately halfway down the complete course, and is a sharply bending left-hand corner consisting of a concave ice wall which the riders must negotiate. The vertical height of the wall is approximately 3 m. (10 ft.). Straw is heaped over the back of the wall to cushion the fall of those riders who misjudge the corner and go over the top. Shuttlecock is exceptional in that the course designers adapt it each year.

Nearly fifty cups and trophies are competed for during the season, about half from Top and half from Junction, and there is a good deal of practice riding between times. Rules of racing are drawn up and administered by the St. Moritz Tobogganing Club. Any pattern of single toboggan is allowed, without regard to weight (added or otherwise), size, or shape. No mechanical appliance which acts as steering gear or brake is permitted. Races are usually run in three heats, with the aggregate shortest time winning; all are electrically timed. The committee decides the order of running by drawing for places. Any rider who arrives late is automatically disqualified.

At the start of a race the competitor must stand with his toboggan not more than 3 m. (10 ft.) behind the timing line. He may start in any manner he chooses once permission is given by the timekeeper. If he falls in the run he may remount providing no one has touched his toboggan. If he falls out of the course he must not re-start. The rules state that a rider must wear a helmet of approved design. In addition riders wear chin guards and hand guards and pads at knee and elbow to protect themselves in a fall, goggles to protect the eyes and assist vision, and rakes (steel toe-pieces used for braking) screwed to their boots. Toboggan runners may not be heated so that they ride faster, and the toboggans must be out of doors at the start of the race and remain so throughout the race.

The present Cresta run derives from a run built by Maj. Bulpetts down the Cresta valley at St. Moritz in 1884, as a rival to the first run, down the Klosters road, near Davos. His was a snow run with ice patches and rudimentary banks, but the first GRAND NATIONAL took place on it in 1885, with ten riders from Davos and ten from St. Moritz taking part. The race was won by a rider from Davos. All the competitors rode sitting face forward on a primitive toboggan, guiding and braking with hands and feet.

Bulpetts continued to improve the run and the St. Moritz Tobogganing Club was formed in 1887. Early club records were destroyed by fire and minutes exist only from 1898, but a report in the *Alpine Post* ten years earlier records a run in 2 min. 8 sec. by McCormich, who caused a sensation by going down prone and head first on a Swiss-type toboggan. The Swiss toboggan, more closely related to the luge (see above), had a vogue because it could cut through ice and snow.

By 1900 the run had developed to a point where it would be broadly recognizable today. As the course was solid ice and there was no snow to ride through, a skeleton was developed much as the modern rider knows it. About 1903 the snub-nosed toboggan came into general use, with riders pulling themselves forward and back on a polished leather platform — in 1901 Bott had introduced the sliding seat. The improvement in skeletons thereafter was gradual, the chief modification being the reduction in the diameter of the runners from 22 mm. to 16 mm. (⅝ in.). The chassis was shortened to 1·2 m. (about 4 ft.) and ball-bearings were introduced to allow the seat to slide more freely — stuck seats had been the cause of a great many falls and poor times.

The results of these improvements showed clearly in contrasted times. In 1930, J. R. Heaton, the fastest rider from Top, averaged

77·3 m.p.h. (124 km./h.) and the slowest 68 m.p.h. (109 km./h.). Heaton's time was 58·4 seconds. The record by 1970 was 54·67 seconds by BIBBIA, who was travelling at 85 m.p.h. (137 km./h.) at the finish. In most seasons, new toboggan designs or riding styles have been tried, but rarely with marked success. Strong, heavy riders have usually held an advantage from Junction over the shorter course while lighter riders have done relatively better from Top.

One of the major improvements to amenity was the introduction of motor vehicles in the late 1920s — previously they were banned in the Engadine — which enabled rider and toboggan to be brought back on a lorry. Another was the introduction of water points which made the daily icing of the run much easier and halved the servicing staff of 30.

The first of the outstanding riders was Capt. Dwyer, who in the 1890s won the Grand National twice and the Ashbourne Cup (subsequently the CURZON CUP) twice. His principal rival was Gibson, who won the Grand National twice and the Ashbourne Cup once. The Cresta became noted for rivalries such as this, the next being between Bott, who introduced the sliding seat, and Thoma-Badrutt, who won the Grand National in 1903 and the Ashbourne seven times between 1898 and 1912. Bott won the Ashbourne three times and the Grand National five times.

Cook, in his *Notes on Tobogganing at St. Moritz*, published in 1894, remarked that weight was a definite disadvantage, but Holland-Moritz experimented successfully with lead weights on his toboggan in 1934 to win the Curzon Cup. The committee in general discourage the use of weights because of the dangers to all but the most skilful riders, and permit them only from Junction, not from Top. Moore-Brabazon, later Lord Brabazon, introduced a sprung toboggan and won many times from Junction, including three victories in the Curzon Cup. Three brothers from the U.S.A., Jennison, Trowbridge, and Jack Heaton, were all distinguished riders between the two World Wars. Jennison won the Olympic gold medal in 1928 but Jack, who took the silver medal, was generally the more successful rider. The Cresta was again an Olympic event in 1948, the gold medal being decided on the aggregate of three runs from Junction and three from Top. Bibbia, of Italy, won, marking the start of an extraordinary dominance lasting more than twenty years. Bibbia won the Grand National every year from 1960 to 1964, and the Curzon Cup eight times in the 20 years from 1949 to 1969. His principal challengers in this period were the Englishman, Mitchell, who in 1959 won the Curzon

Cup in the fastest aggregate at that time recorded, and Ciparisso, a Swiss specialist on runs from Junction, who won the Curzon Cup in three successive years, 1965-7.

Women riders were able to compete in the early days of the Cresta, in spite of the handicap of their long skirts. In 1919 Mrs. Baguley achieved the unique distinction of getting into the last eight of the Curzon Cup, beating her husband by an eighth of a second in the first half of the competition over three runs. The last women's Grand National race was in 1921, the last women's race in 1923, and they were excluded by rule in 1926.

The Cresta has developed much custom and ritual, and the fact that only 25 to 30 new members can be elected each year to the St. Moritz Tobogganing Club has led to its reputation for exclusiveness. There are about 600 full and active members of the club, though many fewer are actually taking part at any point in the season. The majority are from Britain, Switzerland, and the U.S.A., though American participation has dropped with the increase in winter sports at home. There are more than 200 non-active life or annual members.

The club manages all races and practice on the run. In an average season there will be 5,000 to 6,000 rides on the run. Club colours are awarded annually according to the riders' skill or service to the sport. The club is financed primarily by subscriptions, riding fees, and the proceeds of the Cresta Ball held annually at the Savoy Hotel, London.

Howard Bass, *Winter Sports (1966);* Lord Brabazon of Tara, 'Tobogganing' in *Winter Sports* (The Lonsdale Library). St. Moritz Toboggan Club, *Cresta Magazine,* annually.

GOVERNING BODY: St. Moritz Tobogganing Club, Kulm Hotel, St. Moritz, Switzerland.

TODD, LANCE (1885-1942), New Zealand RUGBY LEAGUE player. He was a member of the first team from Australasia to visit England, in 1907, and later played for WIGAN as a three-quarter; but it was as a team manager that he made his greatest impact on the game. A shrewd judge of young players, he built the outstanding SALFORD team of the 1930s. He was killed in a car accident.

TOLLEY, CYRIL JAMES HASTINGS, M.C. (1895-   ), English amateur golfer; he was British champion 1920, 1929; English and British international; captain of the Royal and Ancient, 1948-9.

TOOMEY, Mrs. MARY D., see RAND, MRS.

TORONTO ARGONAUTS, Canadian professional FOOTBALL team, have been a member of the Eastern 'Big Four' since its inception in 1907. Toronto has won the Grey Cup (see FOOTBALL, CANADIAN) ten times, the last in 1952, and has held eight Eastern Football Conference titles, the last in 1971 under the EX-NOTRE DAME quarterback Theismann. Since the early 1950s the team has had only sporadic success.
COLOURS: Double blue.

TORONTO MAPLE LEAFS, ICE HOCKEY club of Toronto, Ontario. Under the original name of Toronto Arenas, the club was one of the original four members of the professional NATIONAL HOCKEY LEAGUE (N.H.L.) of North America in 1917 and was then the only club among them with facilities for mechanically frozen ice. They won their sixth N.H.L. title in 1963 but achieved greater distinction in the STANLEY CUP, winning it for the twelfth time in 1967. Home matches are played at the Maple Leaf Gardens, Toronto, which holds 12,291 spectators. The players train at Peterborough, Ontario. Outstanding club players have included Apps, Broda, Clancy, Horner, H. Jackson, Kennedy, and Mortson.
COLOURS: Blue and white.

TOSSING, see CABER, TOSSING THE; WEIGHT, TOSSING THE.

TOTTENHAM HOTSPUR F.C., Association FOOTBALL club, London. Founded in 1882 as the football section of the Hotspur Cricket Club, the footballers played on Tottenham Marsh and adopted the name Tottenham Hotspur in 1885. The club adopted professionalism and were admitted to the Southern League in 1896 and became champions in 1900. A year later Tottenham won the F.A. Cup—the first southern club to do so since the Old Etonians beat BLACKBURN ROVERS in 1882. The club were elected to the Second Division of the League in 1908, won the F.A. Cup again in 1921, and the championship in 1951. Ten years later they enjoyed their greatest success in winning both the F.A. Cup and the Football League championship, to become the first club for 64 years to complete the Cup and League 'double'. A year later Tottenham retained the F.A. Cup and in 1963 became the first English club to win a European trophy when they beat Atletico Madrid in the final of the European Cup-Winners Cup. Since 1963 the club have won the F.A. Cup in 1967, the F.L. Cup in 1971 and 1973, and the U.E.F.A. Cup in 1972. Outstanding players have included Walden, WOODWARD, and Hughes of the pre-1914 period; Clay, Dimmock, Grimsdell, Hall,

Rowe, and Seed between the wars; and, since 1946, Ditchburn, Nicholson, RAMSEY, BLANCHFLOWER, Mackay, White, Burgess, GREAVES, Jennings, Mullery, England, Gilzean, and PETERS.
COLOURS: White shirts, blue shorts.
GROUND: White Hart Lane, London.

TOUCH BALL is a ball-and-goal team game, in effect a no-contact form of RUGBY football. In Finland it is called *salamapallo*, 'lightning ball'.

It is played with a Size 4 or 5 Rugby ball on rectangular pitches and for periods both of which vary according to the age and number of the players. Adults may play nine-a-side on a pitch 100 m. by 50 m. (109·5 × 55 yds.) for four 15-minute periods; six-a-side on a 70 m. by 35 m. (76·5 × 38·25 yds.) and three-a-side on a 50 m. by 25 m. (55 × 27·5 yds.) pitch, in both cases for four 10-minute periods. For children the dimensions and times are: seven to nine players, 80 m. by 70 m. (87·5 × 76·5 yds.) for 35 to 40 minutes; five to six players, 70 m. by 60 m. (76·5 × 65·5 yds.) for 30 to 35 minutes; three to four, 50 m. by 30 m. (55 × 33 yds.) for 15 to 25 minutes.

To start the game, and at free throws and throws-in, all players except the one in possession of the ball are in the crouch position with one hand touching the ground. The player with the ball starts the game by passing through his legs to a team mate behind. From that point progress must be by running with the ball; it is only permitted to pass or knock in a backward direction. If the ball is passed or knocked forward the other side receives a free throw.

If a player in possession of the ball is touched with the hand on the back, between shoulders and hips, he must pass the ball within three strides or not longer than two seconds. If he does not do so the penalty is a free throw to the other side. A player may not be impeded or obstructed when passing.

A player scores if he grounds the ball inside the opposing in-goal area without being touched. He scores three points if the touchdown is in the centre area, two if in one of the side sections.

A free throw is taken with the ball grounded with no member of the defending team allowed nearer than 5 m. (16 ft. 5 in.) from it and on a line parallel with their own goal area.

A throw-in is taken if the ball or a player holding the ball touches or crosses the side or goal line. It is taken from the point where the ball went out; no player may approach nearer than the marked 5-metre line from the touch line or in-goal line.

If a defending player is touched in his own in-goal area the attacking side takes a free

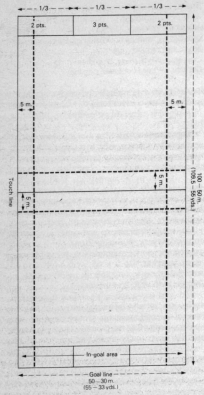

← 1/3 → ← 1/3 → ← 1/3 →

2 pts.   3 pts.   2 pts.

5 m.   5 m.

5 m

Touch line

5 m

100 — 50 m.
(109.5 — 55 yds.)

In-goal area

Goal line
50 — 30 m.
(55 — 33 yds.)

TOUCH BALL PITCH

Dimensions vary according to the age and number of the players. Broken line indicates 5-metre (16 ft. 5 in.) line within side and goal lines.

throw on the 5-metre line; if an attacking player is touched in the opposing area the defending side takes a free throw on the 5-metre line.

The game is controlled by a referee and two touch judges.

Touch ball was devised to meet the demand for an uncomplicated game which could be played with simple equipment, on rough or uneven ground — hence no physical contact — which would produce a pattern of interval running, i.e. sprints and rests, easy to learn but with scope for skilled development.

It was originated by J. B. Hogg, a physical education teacher at Dalziel High School, Motherwell, Scotland, and Professor Lauri Pihkala, the Finnish athlete, sports writer, and theorist.

It was first demonstrated in 1961 at Vieru-maki, the National Sports Centre in Finland. The rules were finalized at Santahamina near Helsinki by an international group in 1965. It is now played in Sweden, Finland, Switzerland, and Cyprus, and was demonstrated by the Finns at the Munich OLYMPIC GAMES of 1972.

TOUCH-CHASING, a STREET GAME otherwise known as 'ticky touchwood', 'touch', 'tag', 'it', 'tip', or 'dobby' consists of one person chasing until he reaches and touches another, probably saying 'You're it' as he does so. The touched person then becomes the chaser, until he makes a touch, when that touched person chases, until night falls, the school bell rings, or the players are tired of play. Traditionally there has always been one chance of escape from the chaser — to touch something that offers safety from capture. What is touched — a lamp post, a front door — has become largely a matter of local convenience. Traditionally, however, it had to be something made of iron: a link with the age-old belief that iron kept out witches.

TOUCHSTONE (1831), English race-horse bred and owned by Lord Westminster and trained by SCOTT. He won the ST. LEGER, the ASCOT GOLD CUP twice, and the Doncaster Cup twice, later becoming the leading stallion in England and sire of 12 classic winners.

TOUR DE L'AVENIR, the principal amateur CYCLING stage race of western Europe, founded in 1961 and noted for having first given prominence to future professional stars like JANSSEN, Aimar, and GIMONDI. It has been run both in conjunction with the TOUR DE FRANCE, using shorter and fewer stages, and as a separate event. Due to organizational difficulties it was cancelled in 1968 and 1970.

TOUR OF BRITAIN, the principal British amateur CYCLING stage race. Created in 1951 by the *Daily Express,* it was revived in 1958, after a two-year lapse, by the Milk Marketing Board, who continued as sponsors into the 1970s, hence the growing use of its other title, the Milk Race. Although professionals and semi-professionals competed in early versions of the Tour, it has been exclusively amateur since 1960. In effect a tour of England and Wales, which rarely crosses the Scottish borders, the race covers approximately 1,500 miles (2,410 km.) in 13–15 days. Of its 72–80 starters, some two-thirds make up national teams from eastern and western Europe, Ireland, and Commonwealth countries.

TOUR OF FLANDERS, annual one-day

classic race for professional cyclists, first promoted in 1913. It starts in Ghent and returns to finish in one of the villages near the city. The route alters from year to year, but covers roughly 150 miles (241 km.) and traditionally includes among its climbs the cobbled Mur de Grammont. Although an international event, it is strongly Belgian in character with its short hills, close, tactical riding, and its predominance of local Flemish cyclists.

TOUR DE FRANCE, the first of the national stage races, and the main professional event of the continental CYCLING season. The Tour was founded by Desgranges, a newspaper editor, in 1903 as a six-stage race of 1,500 miles (2,410 km.). In 1905 the first mountain stages were included: the Ballon d'Alsace and two Alpine climbs; in 1910 the first detour was made into the Pyrenees; and in 1919 the longest of all Tours was held, its 3,344 miles (5,380 km.) being divided into 15 stages.

In that year, too, the yellow jersey (*maillot jaune*) was introduced to distinguish the race leader. He receives it at the end of the stage in which he takes the over-all lead, retains it until he drops from first place, and is awarded a daily prize for wearing it. Yellow was chosen as it was the colour of the sponsoring newspaper, *L'Auto*. The idea has been copied in other stage races, though sometimes with a change of colour, e.g. the pink jersey (*maglia rosa*) in the GIRO D'ITALIA.

In the early years of the Tour the field was made up of commercially-sponsored riders and part-time professionals known as *touristes-routiers*; in 1912 the first trade teams appeared; from 1930 to 1961 the competitors rode in national teams; since then trade teams have been the general rule, national teams the exception. A characteristic postwar Tour, held in 1970, was 2,700 miles (4,345 km.) long, spread over 24 days and divided into 28 stages and half-stages; these were balanced between short and long, flat and mountainous rides, and included five individual time trials and one team time trial. Fifteen 10-man teams took part, their members drawn from 12 countries in western Europe. The value of the prizes was approximately £50,000. From 1971, however, the Tour was restricted, by a ruling of the Union Cycliste Internationale, to 20 stages, whose average length should be no more than 124 miles (200 km.) and none longer than 162 miles (260 km.).

TOUR OF ITALY, see GIRO D'ITALIA.

TOUR OF LOMBARDY, the last major professional road race of the European CYCLING season, is held in mid-October and, with the PARIS–TOURS, makes up the Autumn Classics. Despite its title, this is a one-day race of roughly 165 miles (265 km.) circling Lakes Como and Lecco, skirting the eastern end of Lake Lugano, and including, among half-a-dozen climbs, the 2,598 ft. (792 m.) Intelvi pass.

TOUR OF SPAIN, see VUELTA A ESPAGNA.

TOURIST TROPHY (TT), motor-cycle races on the Isle of Man. The Manx government in 1905 sanctioned the closing of certain roads to allow an eliminating trial for the International Cup race (see MOTOR-CYCLE RACING) that was to be held in France, after the Parliament had refused to allow any public roads in England to be closed for sport. No great store was placed on the Isle of Man race; it was treated as nothing more than a preliminary, but it was so popular with competitors and spectators, that in 1907 the Manx government invited the Auto-Cycle Club (of the Royal Automobile Club) to organize such an event each year.

Centred on a circuit in the St. John area of the island, the 1907 TT was sub-divided into two sections, for twin-cylinder and single-cylinder machines. Over-all winner on his single-cylinder Matchless was Collier who covered the 158 miles (254 km.) at 38·22 m.p.h. (62 km./h.). The twin-cylinder class was won by Fowler (NORTON, with Peugeot engine) at 36·22 m.p.h. (58·2 km./h.). Fowler also set the fastest lap on the 15·8-mile (25·4 km.) course at 42·91 m.p.h. (69 km./h.). The severity of the course with its incessant bumps was felt sufficient to justify a compulsory 'rest' stop after five laps (half distance). That first TT attracted 25 starters (7 on twins) and 10 finished.

The St. John course was used for four years, but by then mechanical developments meant that a more severe test was necessary to improve machines still further. It was felt that an 'impossible' course would be to set the machines off on a lap of nearly 38 miles (61 km.) that took in the climb of Snaefell.

The 1911 race attracted a record entry of 104 riders, of junior and senior classes. Juniors were single-cylinder machines of 300 cc. and twins of 340 cc.; the senior class comprised singles of 500 cc. and twins of 585 cc. Juniors covered four laps, the seniors five.

For the first time silencers were not compulsory (except during practice), there was no fuel restriction, and no entry was fitted with pedalling gear. In fact, with the challenge of the mountain climb, most machines were fitted with variable-speed gearboxes and only one was a single-speed machine. The senior class was won by a Briton, Godfrey, on an American Indian machine at 47·63 m.p.h. (77.11 km./h.) — the first win by a foreign machine — and the junior class went to Evans (Humber) at 41·45 m.p.h. (67.02 km./h.). The TT has remained on this 'mountain' circuit ever since. Speeds rose steadily, but only once has a 350 won the 500 cc. event — in 1921 when H. R. Davies won on an AJS at 54·50 m.p.h. (87·2 km./h.). Davies then produced his own machine, the HRD, and won the TT again in 1925. (The HRD company was sold in 1929 to Vincent, who ran it as Vincent-HRD until its liquidation in 1955.)

The increased speeds over the years were due largely to improvements to the track — the present tarmac road is very different from the cattle track of the early days.

The year 1920 saw the introduction of 250, 350, and 500 cc. classes. The new 250 class caused immediate sensation for, running with the 350s, R. O. Clark (Levis) was leading the field on the last lap until he crashed three miles from home. He remounted to finish fourth.

Although a Canadian, BENNETT, lapped at 59·99 m.p.h. (96 km./h.) in 1922, it was not until 1924 that SIMPSON covered the course at 60 m.p.h. for the first time. Practising was carried out on open roads until 1928 when Birkin collided with a lorry and was killed.

British single-cylinder machines, notably Norton and Velocette, were dominant during the 1930s, but in 1935 the first sign of foreign intervention came with the Italian Moto GUZZI engaging the Irishman, Woods, who won both the 250 and 500 cc. races, thus scoring the first TT wins for Italy.

Norton won again in 1936 (GUTHRIE) and 1937 when FRITH for the first time rode a lap at over 90 m.p.h. (145 km./h.). It was Norton's year again in 1938 when Daniell raised the record to 91·00 m.p.h. (146·5 km./h.) — but in 1939 nothing could match the speed of the German supercharged BMW twins. Meier, a sergeant in the German army, won at 89·38 m.p.h. (143·8 km./h.), with West (Britain) second on another BMW. Nobody equalled Daniell's lap record, but it was a superb win for Meier who was the first non-British rider to win the senior race. Daniell, who had been rejected for war service because of poor eyesight, won again in 1947 on his 1938 machine — but speed was down, due to the use of low-octane petrol.

A postwar ban by the Fédération Internationale Motocycliste (F.I.M.) on the use of superchargers prevented the return of the German BMWs, but while foreign manufacturers designed entirely new multi-cylinder machines, Norton achieved extra performance by introducing vastly improved handling,

steering, and brakes. On this machine DUKE won the Senior TT in 1950 — his first TT race. He won both races in 1951 on the 350 and 500 Nortons. But it was only a matter of time before the Italians and Germans developed new machines. GILERA, predominantly, had a four-cylinder machine which Duke raced to within one second of the first 100-m.p.h. (161 km./h.) lap in 1955.

SURTEES (MV AGUSTA) won in 1956 at a slower speed, but in 1957, McIntyre, on a Gilera, lapped at 101·12 m.p.h. (162·5 km./h.) to celebrate the TT's Golden Jubilee. He averaged 98·99 m.p.h. (159 km./h.) for an 8-lap race — 302 miles (486 km.).

Some foreign manufacturers withdrew support after 1957, but racing continued. MV Agusta dominated all classes until 1960, when HONDA appeared in the smaller categories. They were joined by SUZUKI and YAMAHA and it was on a pair of Yamahas that Read set the first 100-m.p.h. lap by a 250 machine in 1965; Ivy rode a 100-m.p.h. lap on a 125 cc. machine in 1968.

With the withdrawal of all factory teams except MV after 1967, TT lap times held fast, but the introduction of 750 cc. machines in the 1970s promised new TT records.

See also MOTOR RACING, INTERNATIONAL.

TOWLER, DIANE, M.B.E. (1946-   ), ice dance-skater for Great Britain, partnered B. FORD to win four world, four European, and four British ice-dance titles, each consecutively, 1966-9. She was born in London.

TRABERT, MARIAN ANTHONY (1930-   ), the most successful American LAWN TENNIS player of the 1950s. A fine athletic server and volleyer with a formidable backhand, he won the men's singles title at WIMBLEDON without losing a set and he was equally effective in his victories at FOREST HILLS in 1953 and 1955. He was twice French champion, in 1954 and 1955, and he also won the men's doubles in Paris with W. F. Talbert, another native of Cincinnati, Ohio, in 1950 and with Seixas in 1954 and 1955.

Seixas and Trabert also won the U.S. doubles title in 1954 and played a major part in the recapture of the Davis Cup (see LAWN TENNIS) by the U.S.A. from Australia in 1954. Trabert beat HOAD in the singles and he and Seixas beat Hoad and ROSEWALL by 6-2, 4-6, 6-2, 10-8 in the crucial doubles rubber of the challenge round. The following year the U.S.A. lost the trophy without winning a rubber, and Trabert turned professional. Altogether, in five years of Davis Cup play he won 27 rubbers out of 35.

TRACERY (1909), a race-horse sired by the triple crown winner ROCK SAND, bred in the U.S.A. by BELMONT. He won the ST. LEGER, ECLIPSE STAKES, and CHAMPION STAKES in England.

TRACK WALKING, see RACE WALKING.

TRAGETT, Mrs. R. C. (*née* Margaret Rivers Larminie) (1885-1964), BADMINTON player for England. She represented England for 20 years commencing in 1909, and was largely responsible for improving the tactics of the doubles game before the First World War. She won many honours all over the British Isles during a long career, and wrote several novels.

TRAMPOLINING is an individual acrobatic sport consisting of various manoeuvres in the air performed with the aid of an apparatus called a trampoline. It is a competitive sport and recreative activity most common in the U.S.A. and western European countries. The centres of top-class trampolining are the U.S.A., England, West Germany, Wales, Switzerland, Canada, and South Africa. The sport is also established on a lower level of performance in France, Holland, Belgium, Scotland, Sweden, Denmark, and Australia. Poland and Russia are the first two Eastern bloc countries to show real progress, but are not yet members of the International Trampoline Association (I.T.A.).

Trampolining, very much an individual sport, is basically a challenge to perform as many twists and turns in the air as possible before returning to the trampoline surface. The performer also has to show extreme control and fine execution to gain marks for the difficulty of his moves, plus the technique with which he performs them. He also has to put ten movements together, one after the other, without repetition. Male and female performers compete in their own divisions. Trampoline competitions usually take place indoors since high winds and sun could cause difficult and sometimes dangerous conditions. A minimum headroom of 22 ft. (6·7 m.) is required for competition performance.

The trampoline has a steel frame, braced in such a way as to ensure that a landing in the bouncing area (the 'bed') may be made without fear of hitting any structural members. The bed is of nylon straps, 1 or $\frac{1}{2}$ in.(25 or 12·7 mm.) wide, stitched together under tension to form a mesh which will allow air to pass freely when depressed. The bed is secured to the inside of the frame by springs or an elastic suspension. The frame is covered by padding. A pit trampoline is set in the ground so that the top of the frame is level with the ground.

Trampolining has a highly complicated system of evaluation, marking, and checking routines. The judging system is partly subjective and partly objective. A competitor is judged by a jury consisting of one referee, four form judges and their assistants, and two difficulty judges. The marks of the competitors are then collated and calculated by a team of four recorders. At national and international events a video tape is used to eliminate disagreement as to what the performer actually did.

In men's and women's competitions each competitor has to perform ten-bounce routines. For children an eight-bounce routine is sometimes used. Before a competition a compulsory routine is set by the organizing committee; in the case of the world and European championships, this is decided 12 months before the date of the competition. Each competitor must perform the compulsory routines which are marked purely on form and execution by the form judges. The four judges work out of 10 marks, deducting tenths of a point for form breaks, such as bent legs, loss of height, and excess movement in any direction. They then display their marks simultaneously for all to see. The highest and lowest are disregarded and an average of the other two marks is recorded. Each competitor follows his compulsory routine with a voluntary routine. The competitor with the lowest mark performs first and the voluntary routine is completely of his own choice, but must not have any repeated skills. The voluntary routine must be written on a prepared form and handed to the referee one hour before the competition begins. Each of the ten skills is awarded a difficulty rating, usually between ·3 and 1·1, depending on the number of somersaults and rotations performed. The rating for an average routine would be 7·4, for a difficult routine 9·4 and above. The highest difficulty rating for a routine performed in competition so far is 10·3.

The scores of the compulsory and voluntary routines are added and the competitors with the ten highest scores go forward to the final. Again the lowest-scoring competitor performs first, putting tremendous pressure on the leader of the competition. The ten finalists then have to perform one more voluntary routine which may or may not be the same as their first. Usually it is the same, since it is extremely difficult to maintain a high difficulty rating without repeats in more than one voluntary routine. After each finalist has performed, his marks are added to his previous scores and the competitor with the highest score is the winner.

The form judges must not at any time be influenced by the difficulty of a routine (since the competitor is already being awarded marks for what he actually performs) — they must decide simply how well he executed his routine. The two difficulty judges, however, must record and check what is performed against what was proposed. One judge watches the routine and dictates into a tape-recorder exactly what manoeuvre is performed, and the second judge, who never sees a competitor's performance, checks what is called out against what was proposed. The final mark is then added to the competitor's two previous marks which will give a total competition score. The placings of the final ten competitors are then made.

It is, of course, not necessary to use this complicated system of marking for all competitions. In school competitions, for instance, the very much simpler knock-out system is used. An odd number, say five, comprise each team; there is also an odd number of judges. The competitors of each team are seeded one to five. The judges are seated either in a line at the side of the trampoline or surrounding it. The first seed of team A jumps, followed by the first seed of team B. When they have both performed, the judges show a card marked either A or B; there being an odd number of judges, there cannot be a tie. The next two seeds jump, and so on until the competition is finished, the team with the highest number of winning individuals being the winner.

The rules for judging synchronized trampolining, another form of the sport, are the same. Two trampolines are used side by side and two performers of the same team carry out exactly the same manoeuvres, keeping in time with each other as closely as possible. Marks are deducted for unsynchronized landings.

Even more than most sports, trampolining has a language peculiar to itself. Its chief movements and positions are:

Adolph, a forward somersault with three and a half twists.

Baby fliffus, any fliffus movement including a rebound. The most common movement associated with this term is the back drop, early half-twist into a back somersault.

Back drop, a basic landing on the trampoline made with the back only from the lumbar region to the shoulders.

Back full, a backward somersault with full-twist.

Back pull-over, from a back drop the legs are pulled (or pushed) over the head into a three-quarter somersault to feet.

Ball-out, a one-and-a-quarter forward somersault originating from a back drop.

Barani, a forward somersault with half-twist, sighting the bed throughout. (Other accepted spellings are barany, borany, borani, brandy, brany.)

Barani-in, a double forward somersaulting movement with a half-twist in the first somersault.

Barani-out, a double forward somersaulting movement with a half-twist in the last somersault.

Cast, a sideways movement across the bed.

Cat-twist back drop, a full twist to back drop.

Checking, absorbing the recoil from the bed by flexing at the hips, knees, and ankles.

Cody, forward or backward rotation from a front drop take-off; also known as a cote.

Corkscrew back drop, one and a half twists to back drop.

Cradle back drop, a half-twist to back drop.

Crash dive, a three-quarter forward somersault where the body is fully extended during its descent towards the bed.

Double, a double somersault.

Double-full, a backward somersault with double twist.

Free bounce, a straight bounce when no movement is carried out while in the air.

Front, a forward somersault.

Full, describes the number of twists executed in a somersault — e.g. front-full, back-full.

Gain, movement along the bed in the opposite direction to which the stunt is being performed.

Kaboom, a somersaulting action created through one part of the body landing just after another part, thereby setting up rotation, e.g. a flat back landing with the heels making contact with the bed just after the back. The result is a backward rotation.

Kill, the action of absorbing the recoil from the bed by flexing at the hips, knees, and ankles.

Kip, when a person depresses the bed just before the performer so that the suspension system is stretched beyond the normal amount. The performer will then receive added impetus allowing more height in which to execute the intended stunt.

Knee drop, a basic landing position on the knees and shins with the rest of the body, from the knees upwards, in a vertical position.

Layout, a position where the body is completely extended.

Miller, a triple-twisting double-back (named after its originator).

Open, the coming out from a tucked or piked position for landing or for creating twists.

Out bounce, a free bounce executed at the end of a competition routine to show the judges that the performer is under control.

Piked, a position where the body is bent at the hips only.

Randolph, a forward somersault with two and a half twists — also known as a 'Randy'.

Roller seat drop, a full twist to seat drop.

Routine, a series of movements linked together in swingtime.

Rudolph, a forward somersault with one and a half twists — also known as a 'Rudy'.

Seat drop, a basic landing on the seat with the legs fully extended in front of the body.

Spotter, a movement which takes off and lands on the same spot (also someone who stands ready to catch a performer).

Swingtime, one movement performed immediately after another without a free bounce in between.

Swivel hips seat drop, a half-twist to seat drop.

Travel, movement along the bed in the same direction in which the stunt is being performed.

Triffis, a triple somersault with twist.

Triple, a triple somersault.

Tuck, a position where the body is flexed at the hips and the knees.

Turntable, a front drop with lateral rotation of 360° or half-turntable to 180° to front drop. This is not a twisting movement but a side somersault performed in the horizontal plane.

International Trampoline Association Rules, annually.

Trampolining began in the U.S.A., but its precise origins are not known. Ten years ago when trampolining was introduced as a sport in England, it was known as 'rebound tumbling', but this name seemed too technical, and trampolining was adopted. The word *trampolin* in Spanish means diving board.

Along with running, swimming, and climbing, jumping up and down has always been one of our natural activities and the most common piece of 'rebound tumbling' equipment must surely be the nursery bed. In the Middle Ages a plank of wood was improvised to make a take-off surface for jumping over, through, and on to objects; in modern times this apparatus, when used by circus acrobats, was called a teeter-board. To the more adventurous, it was not enough. The acrobats wanted to turn more somersaults and twists, which meant they needed more time in the air and a more powerful take-off. Again the circus provided the answer. The trapeze artist, not satisfied with his aerial manoeuvres, upon landing in his safety net rebounded to perform extra somersaults and rebound tumbling developed from this. In the waste lands of the Arctic, Eskimos have been known to stretch walrus skins between stakes and jump up and down on them for enjoyment.

The first record of an apparatus being manufactured specifically for the art of jumping up and down dates back to 1936. An American DIVING and tumbling champion, NISSEN, who was a great lover of acrobatics, especially the flying trapeze, realized that something more could be made of the safety net and he made his first trampoline in his father's garage in Cedar Rapids, Iowa (U.S.A.). Nissen put a great deal of thought into the prototype. It had to be of a reasonable size to be safe, and not so large that it would take too much space; strong enough to withstand continual jumping up and down; high enough to prevent the performer hitting the floor; and above all, if it was to be of educational value, easy for school children to store and transport. At the beginning of the second World War, Nissen was an officer in the U.S. Navy and, due to his enthusiasm, the American armed forces adopted the trampoline as part of their training. After the war, Nissen decided to try to develop trampolining as a sport in its own right. Courses of instruction were arranged, and films, check-off lists, and wall charts were published.

Jumping is a spontaneous and natural activity, necessary for the growth and development of a young body and it has therefore played an important part in school physical education. In a very short time it was discovered that, unlike any other sport, the restrictions of trampolining were minimal. Doctors have found trampolining to be of great benefit to physically and mentally handicapped children and it is also used in schools for the blind.

The first unofficial competition was held in the U.S.A. in 1947 during the National Athletic Union gymnastic championships, the winner being Garner. In 1948 the NATIONAL COLLEGIATE ATHLETIC ASSOCIATION accepted rebound tumbling as a regular event in their national gymnastic championships. However, the Amateur Athletic Union persisted in classing trampolining as an unofficial sport until 1954. Progress had been slow until 1952 when LaDue won the championship. An accomplished performer himself, he demonstrated and coached throughout the world, and is co-author of *Two Seconds of Freedom.* The year 1954 saw the first official championships, backed by the Amateur Athletic Union, and the first national champion was Elliott. The following year, trampolining was included in the PAN-AMERICAN GAMES.

The rules of the sport at first allowed each performer 45 seconds in which to show what he could do. The rule was then changed to require three eight-bounce routines, with a break of 10 seconds after each. Each contact with the trampoline bed counted as a bounce. The length of time spent on the apparatus was again reduced, to two routines comprising 12 contacts, with 20 seconds rest between.

In 1957 Nissen and his wife, LaDue, BLAKE of England, and Bachler of Switzerland, toured thousands of miles in Britain and on the Continent to popularize trampolining by giving courses and demonstrations to teachers of physical education. After three years on the road their tremendous drive and enthusiasm for the sport showed results and trampolining expanded at a tremendous rate. Following their European tour, Nissen, his wife, and LaDue travelled to Mexico, Bermuda, South Africa, and Japan.

In England, Blake, a gymnast and diver, was teaching in Ilford, Essex. He tried many times to persuade the local education authority to import a trampoline, but without success. Eventually, with the co-operation of the authority, a second-hand trampoline was purchased for the school. It became the most popular piece of apparatus in the gymnasium. Soon a club, the Ilford Gymnastic Club, was established; it consisted mainly of Blake's Loxford School boys. The Ilford Diving Club began to use the trampoline, helped by their

Olympic diving coach, Laxton, and one of its early users was Phelps, Olympic bronze medal winner in Rome in 1960.

In 1956 Blake decided to leave teaching and go into the business of selling trampolines. He convinced Nissen that England was a better place than Holland to set up a European factory and he became managing director of the Nissen Trampoline Co. Ltd. which was established in Romford, Essex.

The first man to form a trampoline association was Webster, senior technical representative of the Scottish Council of Physical Recreation. It was called the Scottish Trampoline Association, and later merged with the Scottish Gymnastic Association. When Blake had sold trampolining nationwide, he called together four other physical education specialists — Garstang, then assistant director of physical education at Regent Street Polytechnic, London; Elliott, international pole-vaulter; Aaron, principal lecturer on physical education at Cardiff Training College; and Horne, physical education teacher and international diver. The five were the founder members of the Amateur Gymnastic Association Trampoline Committee. On 18 November 1959 they set the compulsory routine for the first national trampoline championship, the first official competition in Europe: (1) tuck jump; (2) pike jump; (3) back somersault tucked; (4) knee drop; (5) front somersault; (6) seat drop; (7) half-twist to seat; (8) full twist to seat; (9) up to stand.

The first national championships were held in 1959 at the Royal Air Force sports arena, Stanmore, Middlesex, in conjunction with the vaulting and agility championships. The majority of entrants at this stage were divers, mainly because the skills of multiple somersaults and twists were more easily mastered by them on the trampoline than by gymnasts who were not used to such complex movements. The winner of the boys' and men's event was Phelps, followed closely in the men's event by Quinney, an R.A.F. parachute-jumping instructor, and Bevan, physical education teacher from Cardiff. Both of these became British champions in later years, Quinney in 1960 and Bevan in 1961 and 1962.

Trampolining outside the United States was still in its infancy but on 23 January 1960 the first international match, between England and Wales, was arranged. Once again it was held in conjunction with a GYMNASTICS international. In March 1961 the county of Kent formed the Kent County Schools Rebound Tumbling Association and held their first schools competition, organized by Hopkins, the physical education organizer for Kent. It was another three years before a second

county, Essex, set up its own association.

The introduction of rebound tumbling into the gymnastic world was by no means a smooth one. It was looked upon by many with suspicion, the most common objection being that the soft landing and suspension system would 'kill natural spring', thereby causing vaulting and tumbling to suffer.

The year 1961 was an outstanding one for rebound tumbling. For the first time the competition was split into two parts, the preliminaries held at Wembley Town Hall, and the finals at the Albert Hall, London, before an audience of 6,000. Later that year the first international competition took place, when a British team was invited to compete against West Germany, at the Ostseehallein, Kiel. The British team was Rapkins, Phelps, Bevan, Winkle, and Quinney, with Walker, now lecturer at Regent Street Polytechnic, as team manager, and Horne as team coach-cum-judge. West Germany won by 115·35 to 111·05.

By 1962 competitions were being held all over Europe. Clubs and areas held their own championships and inter-club and inter-collegiate competitions and invitation meetings were open to the top trampoliners in Britain.

The first open international was held in May 1962 at Ludwigshafen, Germany. Following this, the first European Cup competition was held in Kiel, Germany, with eight countries competing: West Germany, Austria, Denmark, Holland, Italy, Sweden, Switzerland, and Great Britain. The results were: first: Hoog (West Germany; champion of Europe), 29·1; second: Winkle (Great Britain), and Schere (West Germany), tied, with 28·5; fourth: Bachler (Switzerland), 28·2; fifth: Netherton (Great Britain), 28·0.

The sport now reverted to its original name of trampolining. When the British preliminary championships were held in Leicester in 1963, the majority of the British Amateur Gymnastic Association Trampoline Committee resigned, and it was announced that the British Trampoline Association had already been formed to take control of the sport. Officially the governing body of trampolining was still the British Amateur Gymnastic Association Trampoline Committee, but the British Trampoline Association was more active in distributing coaching awards and proficiency awards to its members, and in offering courses of various kinds.

Despite these problems, the largest event — the first world championships — was staged at the Albert Hall on 21 March 1964, organized by Blake. Two men and two women from each country were allowed to compete, with the exception of the U.S.A. where two associations, the Amateur Athletic Union and the United States Gymnastic Federation, governed trampolining: the U.S.A. therefore were allowed four competitors. Twelve nations were represented — Belgium, Denmark, Holland, Norway, Scotland, South Africa, Sweden, Switzerland, U.S.A., Wales, West Germany, and the host nation, England. The rules for the competition were based on a double elimination knock-out system, meaning that every competitor had to be beaten twice before being out of the competition.

The day after the championships, a meeting of the officials from the various countries was called to set up an international body to control the sport: four months later the International Trampoline Association (I.T.A.) was formed. England was host country for the second world championships, held in 1965 at the Royal Albert Hall where synchronized trampolining was included for the first time.

On 13 June 1965 a joint meeting of the British Amateur Gymnastic Association Trampoline Committee and British Trampoline Association put an end to the two and a half years of antagonism by forming one organization, the British Trampoline Federation Ltd., to govern trampolining in Great Britain. Soon after, at a meeting of the International Trampoline Association in Basle, Switzerland, a Technical Committee was set up for the first time to prepare a new set of rules to be used by all national governing bodies.

The British Trampoline Federation's first national championships were held at the Army Physical Training School, Aldershot, in March 1966.

After a few years, competitions improved, rules were amended and performances bettered. The main competitions today are the Fahrbach Schuster Cup in West Germany, the Nissen Cup in Switzerland, and the European and world championships held in alternate years.

At the congress of the International Trampoline Association in Berne, Switzerland in 1970, it was announced that the 1972 world championships would be held in Munich during the OLYMPIC GAMES, the object being to have trampolining accepted for the 1976 Olympic Games in Montreal, Canada.

D. E. Horne, *Trampolining, A Complete Handbook* (1969).
GOVERNING BODY (WORLD): International Trampoline Association, P.O. Box 5144, Johannesburg, South Africa; (U.K.): British Trampoline Federation Ltd., 174 Wood End Lane, Northolt, Middlesex.

TRANS-AM CHAMPIONSHIP, a series of six professional motor races on road courses conducted by the Sports Car Club of America (S.C.C.A.). Four races are run in the U.S.A., two in Canada. In length the races range from 200 to 310 miles (322–499 km.). The cars that are eligible are those designated international Touring and Grand Touring cars as defined in Groups 1, 2, 3, and 4 of the International Sporting Code of the Fédération International de l'Automobile (F.I.A.), plus certain sedans (saloons) designated Classes A and B by the S.C.C.A.

As in the case of the CAMEL GT CHALLENGE, spectator interest centres on the contrasting performance of big cars v. small cars — the 7-litre Chevrolet Corvettes and Camaros, which are strong on the long straights, and the 3-litre PORSCHE 911 RS Carreras and similar sports cars, which are more nimble in the corners and which require fewer pit stops to replenish fuel supply. Among the other cars in Trans-Am competition are Mustang, Javelin, Alfa Romeo, BMW, RS Capri, and Pantera.

This range of eligibility began in 1973. From 1966 through 1972 the Trans-Am (occasionally, the Trans-American) was basically a competition for the manufacturers of 'sports' sedans, also colloquially known as 'pony cars' and 'muscle cars'. There was a division for small cars with engines of less than 2 litres (later 2.5 litres), but for all practical purposes the emphasis was on the cars with 5-litre engines, notably Mustang, Camaro, Javelin, Barracuda, Challenger, Firebird. They provided exciting, noisy, safe, and closely competitive wheel-to-wheel racing. Motor-car manufacturers fielded their own works teams or supported specially organized teams in their effort to win advertising and promotional advantages. The first champions were: 1966 and 1967, Mustang; 1968 and 1969, Camaro; 1970, Mustang; 1971 and 1972, Javelin; 1973, Corvette-Camaro.

One driver, DONOHUE, was almost singlehandedly responsible for three championships — for Chevrolet's Camaro in 1968-9 and for American Motors' Javelin in 1971. To heighten public interest in what was until then only a manufacturers' championship, the S.C.C.A. added a drivers' championship in 1972. The first winners were Follmer in 1972 and Gregg in 1973.

The economic recession that began in 1970 compelled the factories to reduce financial commitments drastically, leaving the racing to independents with a moderate amount of covert support. Only the American Motors Corporation, manufacturer of the Javelin, continued into 1971 with an all-out factory team. The economic recession coincided with another development. For various reasons, including the waning popularity of 'muscle' cars and the increasing costs of insuring them, American manufacturers turned away from production of such cars.

The Trans-Am experienced a decline in 1971-2 largely because of the diminishing public interest in races for 'pony' cars; the withdrawal of manufacturers' racing subsidies; the scarcity of competitive cars, and the financial trepidation of race organizers. And while the Trans-Am was losing momentum in 1971-2, a competitor series, the Camel GT Challenge, had begun in 1971 and was building up strength. The International Motor Sports Association (I.M.S.A.) policy of admitting a broad range of cars — Groups 1,2,3, and 4 — was immediately successful; by the start of the 1973 season the Sports Car Club of America followed suit by restructuring Trans-Am eligibility to conform with the I.M.S.A. pattern.

TRANSATLANTIC and TRANSPACIFIC RACES, see YACHTING.

TRAP SHOOTING, see SHOOTING, CLAY PIGEON.

TRAPBALL was a ball-and-stick team game, one of the many, usually energetic, sports especially associated with Shrove Tuesday, but played by children at all times of the year. It was played in the fourteenth century and may well be earlier than that. It remained popular until late into the nineteenth century in some parts of Britain, particularly in the north of England. It was basically a form of ROUNDERS or latter-day BASEBALL except that the ball was projected into play by means of a trap, not thrown into the air by a pitcher.

The basic equipment was a ball, a staff or stick, and a wooden trap. The game could be played on any open space, without special regard to the surface or the existence of natural hazards. When possible, and probably most frequently, a smooth area of grass on common land was used.

Trapball in the fourteenth century.

The trap was a stand holding a spoon-shaped piece of wood in the bowl of which the ball was placed. The spoon moved on a pivot, and when the end furthest from the ball was struck the ball was projected into the air. The batsman then had to strike the ball with his staff. Members of the opposing side were placed around the trap with the object of either catching the ball before it touched the ground or, failing that, of collecting the ball and, from the place where it came to rest, bowling it with the intention of hitting the trap before the batsman completed his round.

The simple nature of the game and its equipment imposed little limitation on the number of players on each of the two sides. There was also no limit on the duration of the game, on the age of the players taking part, or indeed on their sex. It was, for example, played regularly at Bury St. Edmunds every Shrove Tuesday, Easter Monday, and Whitsuntide by twelve old women, in a six-a-side game that continued until sunset. Hone pays tribute to the stamina and dedication of these players in his *Every Day Book* (1827). He tells of one old lady who 'has been celebrated as the mistress of the sport for a number of years past. She being upwards of sixty years of age.' Hone adds that after playing strenuously all day, these hearty old sportswomen spent the rest of the evening in feasting, singing, and merriment.

There were many regional variations, all with different and strictly localized names. 'Tip-cat' was one variant. The 'cat' was a piece of wood pointed at both ends into the shape of a double cone. The player struck one end of the cat with the stick, making it rise, and then hit it again, 'tip' meaning hitting the end, or tip, of the cat.

There were traces of this game, and balls of leather and wood, in the Pharaohs' tombs of 4,000 years ago. The game could be played from the centre of a large ring — if a player failed to strike the cat, as it was tipped into the air, beyond the ring's limits, he was out. Otherwise he counted the aggregate of the distances he struck the cat away from the centre of the ring during his innings, and set this score against that of his opponents. If the ball was caught by members of the opposing team before it touched the ground, all the 'ins' were 'out' and the other side went in to bat.

'Tribet' was a child's game in Lancashire. It was played with a 'pum', a piece of wood about 1 ft. (304 mm.) long and 2 in. (51 mm.) in diameter, and a 'tribet', a small piece of hard wood. From this name, a game, formerly known as 'trippets' in Newcastle, became known as 'trippit and coit'. The trippet is the trap, and it is struck with a 'buckstick' which is another name for the game, as is 'spell and ore'. Another variation is called 'daban-thricker'. The ball is the 'dab', the trap or trigger is the 'thricker', and the distance the ball goes is the count for the striker. 'Drab and norr' is another name for the same game. The West Riding name is 'luking' and playing begins at Easter.

In Durham the game is known as 'spell and ore', from the Teutonic *spel*, a play or sport, and the Germanic *knorr*, a knot of wood or ore (see KNUR AND SPELL). There is a probability that the game is a lineal descendant of the ball-play of the Northmen (*nurspel* means ball-play). Easther in *The Almondbury Glossary* describes the game as being played with a wooden ball, a spel, and a pommel and noted the scoring….'if a player drives the knor for 100 yards, that is five score yards and so he counts five as his score. Each player has the same number of strokes.'

'Kibel and nerspel' was played at Stixwold in the nineteenth century, where the players scored by hitting the ball a certain distance. In the south the game was also called 'dab and stick'. Other names for the stick include the 'tribit-stick' (the word may be a corruption of 'three feet'), the trivit, the trevit, the prim stick, and the gel stick.

In Angus and Lothian in Scotland a game known as 'cat and dog' was played by participants who used clubs, called dogs. Two holes 26 ft. (8 m.) apart were needed; a player stood at each hole with a club. A piece of wood about 4 in. (102 mm.) long and 1 in. (25 mm.) in diameter, the 'cat', was thrown from one hole towards the other by the third person, and the object was to prevent the cat getting into the hole. This game closely resembles the ancient English pastime of CLUB BALL.

In Fife a game is played called 'cat i'the hole'. There is one fewer hole made than there are players and each player but one has a stick. All but one stand at a hole; when the other player who has a ball gives the signal, each player runs to his neighbour's hole and puts his stick in the new hole. The odd man out has to try to put the ball into an empty hole, and the person whom he displaces is 'out', and must take the ball.

'Kit-cat' is played by boys; three small holes are made in the ground, to mark the position of the players. Three more boys form the opposition, and they pitch a small piece of wood called the 'cat'. Those at the holes holding sticks, strike at it; when it has been struck, they run from hole to hole, counting one, two, three, up to 31 which is game. If the cat is caught the 'in' side is 'out'. In the north it was called 'kitty-cat'.

'Munshets' or 'munshits' is a game for two.

One remains 'at home', the other goes a prescribed distance. The one who remains at home makes a hole in the ground, and the other pitches a stick at which the home player strikes. If he hits it he has to run to a prescribed mark and back without being caught or touched by the smaller stick. Another Yorkshire version was called 'peg and stick'. All the players have sticks and a peg. A ring is made and the peg placed on the ground. One boy then strikes it with his stick to make it bounce up into the air. Then he strikes it with his stick and sends it as far as he can. His opponent declares the number of leaps in which he must cover the distance the peg has gone. If successful, he counts the number of leaps as his score. If he fails his opponent leaps and, if successful, he scores.

TRAVERS STAKES is an old-established horse race for three-year-olds in the U.S.A., run over 1¼ miles (2,000 m.) at SARATOGA Springs in August.

TRENT BRIDGE, Nottingham, is the headquarters of the Nottinghamshire C.C.C. and one of the most ancient CRICKET arenas in England. Opened by CLARKE, the celebrated Nottinghamshire bowler, its first full season was in 1838, since when the major matches within the county have been played almost exclusively there. It is about six acres in extent, with much covered accommodation in the concrete and wooden stands for the public, the total capacity of the ground being over 30,000. This number watched a day's play in the Test match against Australia in 1948, when a total of 101,886 people watched the entire match. The ground has been a Test centre since 1899, and boasts a spacious pavilion, a fine collection of historic bats and other cricketing relics, and an electrically-operated scoreboard on the Australian pattern. In one corner of the ground is the famous Trent Bridge Inn; and Parr's Tree, on the west side, is a landmark as a reminder of the powerful square-leg hitting of PARR, the nineteenth-century Nottinghamshire batsman. The gates at the main entrance were opened in 1933 in memory of J. A. Dixon, who captained Nottinghamshire from 1889 to 1899.

TRENTIN, PIERRE (1944-   ), French amateur track cyclist. Up to 1970 he had won four gold medals in the world championships, two in the sprint, and one each in the tandem sprint (with MORELON) and the 1,000 metres (1,093·61 yds.) time trial. He also won gold medals in the tandem event (also with Morelon) and the 1,000 metres time trial in the 1968 OLYMPIC GAMES.

TREV'S PERFECTION (1945), racing greyhound, a brindled dog, by Trev's Despatch out of Friar Tuck. Unbeaten in heats, semi-finals, and finals of the English, Scottish and Welsh Derbys in 1947, he was owned and trained by Fred Trevillion.

TREW, WILLIAM JOHN (1878-1926), RUGBY UNION footballer for SWANSEA and Wales. A remarkable all-rounder, he won 6 of his 29 Welsh caps at wing three-quarter, 14 in the centre, and 9 at outside half, his preferred position.

TRIALS, Motor-cycle, see MOTOR-CYCLE TRIALS.

TRIPLE CROWN (1), see HORSE RACING; (2), see RUGBY UNION.

TRIPLE JUMP, a standard field event for men on the programme of all major ATHLETICS championships; performances are eligible for recognition as records by the International Amateur Athletic Federation (see ATHLETICS, TRACK AND FIELD).

The origins of the triple jump, or hop, step, and jump as it used to be called, are obscure; but the sport may owe something to the game of hopscotch which dates back at least 150 years. The rules of the triple jump are basically those for the LONG JUMP. In the first phase of the triple jump the jumper lands on the take-off foot; in the second phase he lands on the alternate foot and springs from the same foot for his final jump. The distance jumped is measured from the rearmost final landing mark to the foremost edge of the take-off board. The technique of the first and third phases of the triple jump correspond to that for the long jump, the best distances being achieved only by effective dovetailing of the three jumps into a continuous sequence.

TROON, Scottish GOLF course. In its championship form, stretched to over 7,000 yds. (6,400 m.), this course on the Ayrshire coast presents a challenge unmatched by any links (except perhaps CARNOUSTIE) especially in a high wind and fast conditions. For the purist Troon provides true links golf; undulating fairways, savage rough of whin and wiry grass, and hard, slick greens. The eighth hole, popularly known as the Postage Stamp, is the shortest hole in championship golf (125 yds. — 114 m.) but, with its tiny plateau green, one of the most dreaded.

TROTTING, or **Harness-racing,** as it is sometimes called, is a form of HORSE RACING in which the rider is towed along in a small cart. Whereas in horse racing the animals tak-ing part are called thoroughbreds, trotting horses are called standardbred and also have long pedigrees. The name 'standardbred' denotes that the horse has to race up to a certain standard of speed. This, akin to 'par' in GOLF, had steadily decreased in a time sense over the years as better breeding methods have produced faster horses.

There are two kinds of standardbred horse, the trotter and the pacer. The difference between the two is in the way they move their legs, called their 'gait'. The *trotter* races free-legged and has a diagonal gait, which is the near foreleg and off hindleg working in unison and vice versa. A trotter has a high knee movement and a left-to-right nodding of the head. A *pacer* moves both left legs in unison and then both right legs. The pacing gait is a piston-like action and is referred to as the lateral gait. The pacer sways from side to side while racing and in most cases will wear hopples — leather or plastic straps connecting front and rear legs on the same side.

Except in some European countries where saddle-trots still take place, harness horses are not ridden like thoroughbreds. Instead they are driven from behind by a driver in a small cart called a sulky, which is virtually a development of the chariot used by the Romans for transport and sport. A sulky is made in two sections: there are two long shafts which run along either side of the horse, attached at its shoulders and withers; the second part is the bridge, which joins the shafts behind the horse and on which there is a seat for the driver. On either side of the bridge are two bicycle wheels on strengthened hubs; this achieves an almost perfect balance, which results in an extreme free-wheeling action that makes a driver's weight of little importance. The total weight of a sulky averages about 39 lb. (17·7 kg.).

Harness horses wear pads (known as boots) on their legs because they are liable to knock and rub their legs in racing. Boots are of several kinds, such as elbow boots (worn high on the front legs), knee boots, quarter-boots to protect the tender quarter (heel of the foot) in front, and bell boots encircling the pastern, just above the hoof. Another aid is a head-pole, which is fastened alongside some horses' heads. This stops the horse turning its head to the side opposite that on which the pole is worn.

In European countries, with the exception of Great Britain, pacing is still not accepted as part of the sport and the title of trotting, as opposed to harness-racing, is retained.

The training of a trotting horse is the finer art since this horse does not have the assistance of hopples to prevent it breaking into a gallop, which is illegal.

Trotting can be likened to a man in a walking race where he must go as fast as he can without crossing the dividing line that separates a walk from a run. So it is with trotters and pacers. The driver must know when he has pushed his horse to the limit and yet be able to keep up his speed in a fighting finish without going into a gallop. When a horse gallops it is referred to as a 'break' and no horse may gain any advantage from it. When a horse makes a break it must be taken to the outside of the field, allowing its opponents the advantage of a run through on the inside, and must not rejoin the race until it has been returned to a trotting or pacing gait. Should a runner gain any advantage from galloping, or continually make breaks, it will be disqualified.

Pacers are slightly faster than trotters — although very little time separates the world records for the two gaits — and usually they can get off to a better start. The inclusion of pacing in America, Australia, and New Zealand, has given harness-racing a boost in these countries and has meant better and more open racing.

Races take place at 25 to 30 m.p.h. (40–48 km./h.) for the mile distance and driving can be quite hazardous. This has been minimized by making drivers prove themselves competent to handle a horse and sulky before being granted a licence and by constructing tracks with ample room for manoeuvring.

Trotting owes its origin to the invention of the wheel and the building of the first cart. Archaeologists working in Asia Minor discovered evidence in 1930 that trotting races were held as early as 1350 B.C. In the Roman Empire, chariot racing became one of the favourite sports and it is probably from the Romans that trotting took its roots as a world-wide sport.

Although since then noblemen the world over have raced horses in every manner imaginable to pass the time and encourage sport, it was not until the eighteenth century that the foundations of harness-racing, as it is known today, were laid.

It was of little significance at the time that Messenger, a British thoroughbred stallion, was exported to America in 1788; yet from this horse came the beginnings of what is now one of the most popular sports in America, challenging both BASEBALL and horse racing. Yet Messenger appears three times in the pedigree of Rysdyk's Hambletonian, the father of American trotting; and Britain takes pride of place in that pedigree with Bellfounder, an imported Norfolk trotter, who left England in 1820. It has been disputed that Bellfounder was the sire of The Charles Kent Mare, out of whom Rysdyk's Hambletonian was got, but it seems almost certain that he was the father. Over 60 years after the importation of Messenger, Hambletonian was foaled in a small village near New York, and sold in the autumn to Rysdyk, a farm hand working for Seeley, the breeder. As there was more than one Hambletonian in the record books, this great sire took his new owner's surname as a prefix. But it was 13 years before Rysdyk could raise the stud fee of his stallion above $35.

In 1862 one of Hambletonian's sons, Robert Fillingham (to be renamed George Wilkes) was matched against the famous Ethan Allen for a reputed $5,000 a side at the Fashion Course on Long Island. Robert Fillingham won the race with a time surpassed by only one horse in the record books. Two years later yet another son of Hambletonian, Dexter, set new standards, to be followed by Shark, another son of the great sire. In 1865 Goldsmith Maid was sired by a son of Hambletonian and with these four trotters making history, Rysdyk's Hambletonian suddenly became the most fashionable stallion. In four years his stud fee rose to $500 and his colts were fetching record prices in the sales rings.

By the time he died in 1876, Rysdyk's Hambletonian's record as a sire was truly remarkable. He sired over 1,300 foals, at least 40 of whom trotted the mile in 2 min. 30 sec. — no mean performance at the time. He was to prove the grandsire of almost 1,500 trotters of standard speed through his sons, and 110 through his daughters. At the turn of the century, 135 of the 138 trotters that had earned records of 2 min. 10 sec. or better could be traced back to Rysdyk's Hambletonian and by the time he finished at stud, he had earned his owner some $288,000. Strangely, although Hambletonian was able to produce tremendous trotting ability down through the ages, he was never a world-beater himself, and probably never did better than 3 min. 15 sec. over the mile.

Messenger was responsible for the second most successful trotting stallion of that time in Mambrino Chief, a grandson of Mambrino, who was also by Messenger. After these two came American Star, who may have been descended from Diomed, the first winner of the Epsom DERBY in 1780.

Through Rysdyk's Hambletonian and his fellow successful stallions, trotting became an increasingly popular sport, and inside a hundred years a minute had been knocked off the record for a mile race. In 1806 Yankee trotted the distance in 2 min. 59 sec., the fastest at that time, but in 1903 Lou Dillon became the nineteenth horse to beat it with a record 1 min. 58·5 sec. The greatest single factor in the difference between Lou Dillon's and Yankee's times was the improvement in sulkys. In the early 1800s sulkys were a lightweight gig which could hardly have been less than 125 lb. (56·7 kg.). By 1875 Goldsmith Maid took the record with 2 min. 14 sec., pulling a sulky weighing about 46 lb. (21 kg.).

After Goldsmith Maid, even greater strides were taken in the construction of sulkys. An arched axle was introduced and this prevented a horse from striking into the axle with its hind legs and losing speed when the sulky was brought close to the horse. Rarus was the first trotter to use this type of sulky on a record-breaking run of 2 min. 13·25 sec. in 1878. Seven years later Maud S set a time of 2 min. 8·75 sec., using a roller-bearing axle to reduce friction. Elliott, a bicycle manufacturer, made one of the biggest steps forward when he first used bicycle wheels on sulkys in 1892. Nancy Hanks was the first trotter to use them in setting up a world record in the same year with 2 min. 4 sec.

The use of bicycle wheels was a real step forward, as they greatly reduced vibration and checked the tendency of the sulky to slew on bends. Being smaller than previous wheels, they also enabled the driver to sit lower behind the horse, thus reducing wind resistance. When Lou Dillon became the first horse to break the magical two-minute mark with 1 min. 58·5 sec. in 1903, the weight of the sulky had been reduced to as little as 25 lb. (11·3 kg.).

With the sulky reaching such perfection, records stood for much longer. From Yankee in 1806 to Lou Dillon in 1903, 20 different trotters held the world record, but from 1903 only 4 horses bettered Lou Dillon's record. Uhlan recorded 1 min 58 sec. in 1912; nine years later Peter Manning equalled that run, bettered it by a quarter of a second in the same year, and reduced it to 1 min. 57 sec. at Columbus, Ohio, in 1922 and to 1 min. 56·75 sec. at Lexington in the same year. That time stood for 15 years until Greyhound reduced it to 1 min. 56 sec. in 1937 and the following year cut it to 1 min. 55·25 sec.

His record looked unapproachable until in 1969 Nevele Pride clocked 1 min. 54·8 sec. at Indianapolis. Trained and driven throughout his career by Dancer, Nevele Pride was the fastest two-year-old trotter with 1 min. 58·4 sec. at Lexington and the fastest three-year-old with 1 min. 56·6 sec. at Indianapolis, and won the trotting triple crown with successes in the Hambletonian, Yonkers Futurity, and Kentucky Futurity races. Out of 67 races, Nevele Pride won 57, was second 4 times, third 3 times, and went to stud with prize money of $871,738 to his credit. He also created a record price as a standardbred stallion when he was syndicated for $3 million.

Pacing has become increasingly popular since the Second World War, the slightly faster speed of the pacer making him more attractive. Many pacers can be traced as far back as the family of George Wilkes. Most famous of the pacers was Dan Patch, who made a record 1 min. 56·25 sec. for the mile in 1903 when Lou Dillon held the trotting record. Two years later Dan Patch reduced the time to 1 min. 55·25 sec. at which it stayed until 1938 when Billy Direct brought it down to 1 min. 55 sec. Since then only two other pacers have beaten that time, the last being Bret Hanover, world champion at 1 min. 53·6 sec. in 1966.

New Zealand-bred Cardigan Bay was another prominent pacer. In a racing career which covered ten years, he became the first pacer to pass the $1 million in prize money. The gelding spent his first years racing in his homeland and was then sent to Dancer in America where he raced for two seasons before being returned as a 12-year-old to New Zealand for a well-earned retirement.

The sport of trotting was introduced to Australia and New Zealand just before the Second World War and it has grown at a tremendous rate. Some idea of this growth is given in the prize money for the Inter-Dominion Championships held at Christchurch, New Zealand each year. In 1936, the first year of the championships, the Grand Final stake money was $3,000, but by 1970 it had become $40,000. The sport, too, is taking a new lease of life in Britain. In the early 1960s the Simpson brothers, two New Zealanders with breeding and racing interests throughout the world, opened a track at Prestatyn in North Wales and revived a sport which had been in the doldrums in Britain. Later the Simpson brothers left England and the Prestatyn track closed, but many new tracks sprang up.

TRUEMAN, FREDERICK SEWARDS (1931-   ), cricketer for England and Yorkshire. Having taken 29 wickets cheaply in his first Test series, against India in 1952 (including 8 for 31 runs at OLD TRAFFORD), he eventually became the first bowler to take 300 Test wickets, finishing in 1965 with 307 at an average of 21·57. Belligerent, yet endowed with a sense of humour, he bowled fast, with a fine control of the bouncer and the yorker, and the ability to swing the ball to slip. He was also a splendid fielder in any position, and a useful, hard-hitting batsman. Of all his fine Test performances perhaps the greatest was against Australia at HEADINGLEY in 1961, when he took ten wickets in the match, including a spell of five for no runs.

TRUMBLE, HUGH (1867-1938), cricketer for Australia and Victoria. A tall and subtle medium-paced bowler, he took a record total of 141 wickets against England, including two hat-tricks. He also held the record number of 45 catches, mainly at slip. Even on the best batting pitches he could impart movement to the ball. For 27 years until his death he was secretary of Melbourne Cricket Club.

TRUMPER, VICTOR THOMAS (1877-1915), cricketer for Australia and New South Wales. A legendary batsman, he made runs even on the most difficult of pitches, blending keen eyesight, quick footwork, and supple wrists. In 1899 he made a superb 135 not out in the LORD'S Test match, and against Sussex he made 300 not out; but his best season was 1902, when on predominantly wet pitches he scored 2,570 runs, including 11 centuries — one of them before lunch in the OLD TRAFFORD Test. His 185 not out at SYDNEY in 1903-4 was probably his most brilliant innings, the hundred taking only 94 minutes, and seven years later he dominated South Africa, scoring 661 runs in the series. In New Zealand in 1913-14 he added a world record of 433 runs for the eighth wicket with Sims against Canterbury.

TS.S.K.A. MOSCOW, Russian BASKETBALL club that won the EUROPEAN CUP FOR CHAMPION CLUBS in 1961, 1963, 1969, and 1971. The team regularly includes several members of the U.S.S.R. national team.

T.S.V. MUNICH 1860, Association FOOTBALL club. Founded as a sports club in 1860 it began playing football in 1899 but, except for a wartime (1942) Cup win, the club had to wait until the 1960s for success in national West German competitions. A win in the West German Cup final of 1964 was followed by reaching the final of the European Cup-Winners Cup in 1965, when West Ham United won at WEMBLEY. In the season ending 1966, the club was West German champion club for the first time. Leading players have included H. Schmidt, Patzke, Radenkovic, and Brunnenmeier.
COLOURS: White shirts and white shorts.

TUG-OF-WAR is a contest of strength and skill between two teams pulling against each other from opposite ends of a long, thick rope. It is a long-established rural pastime in England, where its development has outstripped its progress elsewhere, though seven nations belong to the International Tug-of-War Federation and the sport used to be included in the OLYMPIC GAMES.

In approved competitions, the rope must be between 4 in. and 5 in. (10–12·5 cm.) in circumference and, if there are to be eight men in each team (the maximum number allowed), the rope must be at least 35 yds. (32 m.) long. A coloured tape is fixed to the rope exactly halfway along it. On either side of this centre mark, and 6 ft. 6¾ in. (2 m.) from it, are fixed two white tapes. The ground is marked by three parallel lines corresponding exactly to the three inner markings on the rope.

When the competition begins, the centre tape on the rope must be over the centre line on the ground. The hands of the nearest member of each team must be within 12 in. (30 cm.) of the outside coloured tapes on the rope, but not touching them. Pulling begins on a signal from the judge, when the rope is taut and correctly positioned. A pull is successfully completed when one team has pulled the other so far forward that the white tape on one side of the rope has passed over the ground line furthest from it. A contest is usually determined by the best of three pulls.

In minor and informal competitions, such as are frequently held at local fêtes and carnivals in England, there is commonly no weight classification, all teams competing in a single 'catchweight' class. At a higher level of competition, teams may be graded according to weight and competitions held in as many divisions as the organizers wish to arrange. Total team weights must be under the limit of the class for which they are entered, usually 88 stone (559 kg.) to 112 stone (711·2 kg.), plus the open catchweight class — the most popular with spectators.

Contestants are weighed shortly before the day's competition begins, wearing the kit in which they will be pulling. This usually consists of boots, which may not be studded, and football jerseys, shorts, and socks. The weight of each man is stamped on his arm in such a position that it can be easily checked by an assistant judge.

The heaviest men do not necessarily make the best pullers. A top-class team will almost certainly comprise men with exceptionally powerful thighs and arms, great stamina and concentration, and quick reactions. When a pull is in progress all eight men will lie back against the rope at an angle of about 35°, their bodies held in a straight line from the heel of the leading foot to the top of the head. When the rope is held on the right side, as is usual, the left leg is extended straight, the side of the boot cut into the ground, to provide the defence against which the opposition must pull: ideally, the harder they pull, the more firmly the left foot is dug into the ground. The right leg is bent, the foot slightly behind and to the right of the other: it is the right leg that provides most of the heaving power.

The rope passes under the right armpit, the competitor's right hand gripping it from underneath and his left from on top, bringing the left shoulder above the rope. Each team is allowed one coach, whose job is to control the efforts of his team so that they take the strain when their opponents are pulling, and heave together at the instant the other team end a pull, hoping in this way to catch them marginally off balance.

The anchor man, at the end of the rope, is commonly the heaviest member of the team. He may have the rope under one arm and over the other shoulder, but the end must hang free and may not at any point cross the rope. Other infringements, any two of which may lead to disqualification, include persistent sitting on the ground, deliberate sitting on a foot, and failure to return immediately to the pulling position after slipping. The offending team is disqualified for that pull only.

The rules of tug-of-war are slightly amended for indoor events, which generally take place on a secure mat thick enough to protect competitors from injury in the event of a collapse. As the mat might be damaged by the use of heavy leather boots, lightweight rubber-soled boots are used.

The centre mark of the indoor rope is a white tape, 6 ft. 6¾ in. (2 m.) on either side of which are the coloured tapes to denote the positions of the leading members of each team. On the floor, the outside marks are 13 ft. 1½ in. (4 m.) from the centre mark. For a winning pull, the centre tape on the rope must pass over one of the outside marks on the floor.

Few athletic events can have a history reputedly so long and yet so scantily documented as that of tug-of-war. It is said to have originated in the harvest-gathering of ancient China; to have been used to train slaves to haul stones up the Sphinx; to have developed from the routine used by sailors in hoisting sails, and by soldiers in hauling guns up the mountains of India's north-west frontier. Of firm evidence there seems to be none, any more than there is of the origin of the name itself.

It is also supposed, at least in England, to be a peculiarly English sport with deep roots in the rural communities of the eighteenth century: but Christina Hole makes no mention of it in *English Sports and Pastimes*. There is no doubt that it flourished as an inter-village competition in England in the nineteenth century, when opposing teams often began the pull on opposite sides of the river that separated their territories.

By 1880 it had developed well enough to be recognized by the Amateur Athletic Association (A.A.A.), and it became an approved event at athletic meetings. Tug-of-war was well-established at about the same time on the Continent, and in 1900 the event was included for the first time in the Olympic Games. Even then there was some doubt about the accuracy of the records: some historians say the winner was the U.S.A., but according to the Swedish *Encyclopaedia*, it was won by a six-man combined team from Sweden and Denmark, selected on the spot from available athletes.

At the next meeting, the U.S.A. took the first three Olympic places with five-man teams, and in 1908 Great Britain did the same with three teams of nine each, all from different police forces. By 1912, eight had been established as making a satisfactory team, and the event was won by Sweden, with Britain second. At the 1920 Olympics, tug-of-war was included for the last time; it was won by Britain, with the U.S.A. second.

Tug-of-war continued to be accepted as an athletic event through the 1920s and 1930s, but after the Second World War, by which time the accent throughout athletics was on the individual, it was regarded by 'pure' athletes as something of a joke. While it held its place as an entertaining event at agricultural shows, carnivals, and fêtes, it was included in fewer and fewer meetings.

In 1958 a Tug-of-War Association was formed in England, with 12 clubs as founder members, to promote the sport according to A.A.A. principles. By 1971 there were more than 220 affiliated clubs, drawn largely from police forces, the armed services, farming communities, and industry. The Association has branches in Northern Ireland, Wales, and Scotland — though the Scottish practice of giving money prizes at HIGHLAND GAMES meetings, where tug-of-war is occasionally seen, caused some unease.

National outdoor championships have been held annually since 1958, at first with three and, later, four, weight classes, with a youth class added in 1969. Indoor championships began in 1966. European championships were first held in 1965, and since 1968 these too have been annual, in two weight divisions only: 640 and 720 kg. (101 and 113 stone). The winners for the first four years were all teams from the United Kingdom.

Seven countries belong to the International Tug-of-War Federation: England, Northern Ireland, Wales, Sweden, Holland, Switzerland, and South Africa. The sport is also practised in other European and Commonwealth countries, and in the U.S.A.

GOVERNING BODY (WORLD): International Tug-of-War Federation, 58 Central Way, Oxted, Surrey; (U.K.): Tug-of-War Association, 58 Central Way, Oxted, Surrey.

TULYAR (1949), English race-horse bred and owned by the AGA KHAN, trained by MARSH, and ridden by Smirke. Tulyar won nine races, including the KING GEORGE VI AND QUEEN ELIZABETH STAKES, DERBY, ST. LEGER, and ECLIPSE STAKES, and £76,417 in prize money, a record for the English Turf. He was later sold to the Eire Government for a world record price for a thoroughbred of £250,000, to stand at the Irish National Stud, where he proved a costly failure as a stallion.

TUNNEY, GENE (1898-   ), American boxer who won the world heavyweight title in 1926 and retired, undefeated, two years later. Tunney is noted chiefly for his two victories over DEMPSEY which produced the first million-dollar gates. But he was one of the best, and most underrated, heavyweight champions and lost only one contest, to GREB, in his career. Tunney later beat Greb twice and had the best of two no-decision bouts. He was a most intelligent analyst of boxing style but this is less remembered than the controversy of the 'long count' in his second bout with Dempsey when Tunney was on the floor for about 14 seconds but survived to win on points. He exposed the limitations of the crouch favoured by Dempsey, and JEFFRIES before him, by boxing with an upright stance and using straight counter-punches to beat hooks.

TURITSCHEVA, LUDMILA (1952-   ), Russian female gymnast who was pre-eminent in the early 1970s. She began GYMNASTICS in 1965 and was a member of the Soviet team the following year. She won the world title in 1970 and the European title in Minsk the following year. At the Munich Olympics despite the popular appeal of Miss KORBUT she impressed the more discerning experts with her combination of flawless technique and precise timing. She won the combined exercises competition because of her all-round ability; she failed to take any of the individual apparatus gold medals. In the 1973 European championships she emulated the earlier feats of LATYNINA and CASLAVSKA by capturing every apparatus gold medal as well as finishing first over-all.

TURNBULL, MAURICE JOSEPH (1906-44), an all-round games player for Wales. A HOCKEY goalkeeper, he was capped for Wales three times in 1928; a sound batsman and close fieldsman, he played CRICKET for Cambridge University and Glamorgan (whom he captained), Wales, and England; as a RUGBY half-back, he played for Cardiff and Wales; and he held the South Wales SQUASH RACKETS championship.

TURNER, CHARLES THOMAS BIASS (1862-1944), cricketer for Australia and New South Wales. Statistically Australia's most successful bowler, he took 101 wickets in only 17 Test matches, all against England. Although of only average height, he generated great pace, his deliveries breaking sharply from the off. On the 1888 tour of England he took 283 wickets and formed a deadly bowling partnership with Ferris. They were almost as penetrative two years later, and in 1893 Turner again headed the Australian tour averages. Known as 'the Terror', he is the only bowler to have taken 100 wickets in an Australian season.

TURNER, CURTIS (1924-70), American MOTOR RACING driver who won 17 N.A.S.C.A.R. Grand National stock-car races, including the 1957 Darlington 500, the 1958 Darlington 300, and the 1965 North Carolina (Rockingham) 500. He won 38 N.A.S.C.A.R. convertible division races, from 1956 to 1959. He was suspended from N.A.S.C.A.R. from 1961 to 1964 for alleged efforts to organize a driver's union.

TURNER, GLENN MAITLAND (1947-   ), cricketer for New Zealand, Otago, and Worcestershire. A patient opening batsman who added a forcefulness to his sound basic technique, he twice carried his bat through a New Zealand innings. In 1971-2 in the West Indies he scored four double-centuries, two of them in Tests, and for Worcestershire, for whom he first played in 1967, he made a record ten centuries in 1970. In 1973, as vice-captain of the New Zealand touring team in England, he reached 1,000 runs before the end of May, a feat that had not been accomplished since 1938.

TWENTY GRAND (1928) was a champion American race-horse who won the KENTUCKY DERBY (in record time), BELMONT, TRAVERS, and LAWRENCE REALIZATION STAKES, JOCKEY CLUB GOLD CUP (in a canter), and Saratoga Cup. He was owned by Mrs. Whitney of the Greentree Stable, trained by Rowe and ridden by Kurtsinger.

TWICKENHAM, headquarters of the Rugby Football Union and, since it was opened in

1908, the regular home ground of the England RUGBY UNION team. Other major fixtures at the ground are the Oxford v. Cambridge University match (since 1921), the Inter-Services championship, the final rounds of the MIDDLESEX SEVEN-A-SIDE COMPETITION, and occasional matches of London counties. HARLEQUINS use the ground for home matches up to the start of the international season. It holds 72,500 spectators, of whom 32,500 are seated.

TWO THOUSAND GUINEAS STAKES, the second classic horse race of the English season, founded in 1809, and competed for over the straight Rowley Mile course at NEWMARKET in the spring.

TYLDESLEY, JOHN THOMAS (1873-1930), cricketer for England and Lancashire. A small, quick-footed batsman, he excelled on difficult pitches, where his sound back-play, decisive cutting, and wristy driving set him apart among the major batsmen of the early twentieth century. In a long career (1895-1923) he made 86 centuries in first-class CRICKET: 4 of them were for England, for whom probably his finest innings was 62 on a vicious pitch at MELBOURNE in 1903-4.

TYUS, WYOMIA (1945-   ), sprinter for the U.S.A. The first woman to win the Olympic 100 metres twice (1964 and 1968), Miss Tyus took a third gold medal in the 4 × 100 metres relay in 1968 when the United States set a world record of 42·8 sec., improving the record which they had set in the semi-final. She twice equalled the world 100 yards record with 10·3 sec. and also held the 100 metres record, improving from 11·2 sec. in 1965 to 11·0 sec. in the 1968 Olympic final.

TZAVARA, OLGA, clay pigeon shooter for Greece. She was the first woman to win four European titles, in the years 1958, 1960, 1961, and 1962.

U

UBBIALI, CARLO (1929-   ), Italian racing motor-cyclist. A specialist in riding lightweight and ultra-lightweight machines, he gained his first world championship in 1951 in the 125 cc. class, riding a Mondial. From 1953 to 1960 he rode as a member of the MV AGUSTA team, winning the 125 cc. championship five times and the 250 cc. world championship three times before retiring from racing at the end of the 1960 season.

UBER, Mrs. H. S. (*née* Betty Corbin) (1907-   ), English BADMINTON player. One of the finest doubles players and tacticians the game has known, she represented England for 25 years commencing in 1926 and gained doubles honours in many countries. She was later the donor of the UBER CUP which is the trophy competed for in the women's international badminton championship. In 1923 she was British junior LAWN TENNIS champion.

UBER CUP, the team trophy for the women's international BADMINTON championship. It was presented to the International Badminton Federation by Mrs. UBER in 1956.

As with its counterpart, the THOMAS CUP, the competition is held only every third year. Preliminary play takes place in four geographical zones, with the winners and the holder meeting at one centre to play off for the trophy. Teams comprise up to six women, and a tie consists of three singles matches between three players ranked in order, and four doubles matches between two pairs.

U.C.L.A. BRUINS, BASKETBALL team of the University of California at Los Angeles. U.C.L.A. became supreme in the NATIONAL COLLEGIATE ATHLETIC ASSOCIATION championship under the direction of their coach WOODEN. They gained the championship for the first time in 1964 and retained it in the following season. ALCINDOR became a member of the squad in 1966 and U.C.L.A. regained the N.C.A.A. title in the 1967 play-offs. They created an unprecedented record by retaining the title in each of the next six seasons.

ULLMAN, TORSTEN (1914-   ), Swedish international pistol shooter who won six world titles from 1933 to 1954, and set three new world records. When winning the centre-fire high-power pistol title at the world championships in Caracas, Venezuela in 1954, he was second to BENNER (U.S.A.) in the free pistol championship.

ULRICH, EINER (1896-1968), a leading figure in Danish LAWN TENNIS for nearly 50 years. With his sons TORBEN (b. 1928) and JORGEN (b. 1935), he established a remarkable family record in the Davis Cup (see LAWN TENNIS). A former footballer and cricketer who did not play first-class lawn tennis until he was 24, Ulrich won 39 of the 74 Davis Cup rubbers he played between 1924 and 1938. Torben, a musician of considerable ability whose Davis Cup career began 10 years later, won 46 of the 101 rubbers he played before turning professional in 1968, and by 1970 Jorgen had played in 56 rubbers, winning 26. This gave them a total of 231 appearances for Denmark — a record for any family in any country in the competition.

Einer Ulrich served as president and as secretary of the Danish Lawn Tennis Federation and played in the veterans' event at Wimbledon shortly before his death. For several years he was a member of the management committee of the International Lawn Tennis Federation and he refereed a number of international FOOTBALL matches.

UMRIGAR, PAHLAN RATANJI (Polly) (1926-   ), cricketer for India, the Parsees, Bombay, and Gujerat. A strong and dominant batsman, he played in the record number of 59 Test matches for India, making 3,631 runs and 12 centuries — also records. On the 1952 tour of England he made three double-centuries and two centuries in first-class matches, an achievement he repeated in 1959.

UNDERWATER HOCKEY, a game introduced in South Africa in the 1960s and adopted in England, is played by skin-divers in swimming pools 6 to 10 ft. (1·8–3·0 m.) deep between teams of six using miniature HOCKEY sticks. A puck (as in ICE HOCKEY) replaces the hockey ball. This is placed in the centre of the pool — on the bottom — while the members of both teams are on the surface.

To score a goal the puck must be hit against the opponent's end of the pool. In England the game is sometimes known as 'Octopush'.

UNDERWATER SWIMMING,

also known as skindiving, free diving, or sub-aqua diving, is a fast-growing water sport.

All underwater swimmers begin by becoming snorkel divers, swimming on the surface between brief breath-holding dives. Their basic equipment is a face mask, snorkel tube, and a pair of foot fins or 'flippers'. Spearfishermen add an underwater gun to this equipment, and experts may reach depths of 100 ft. (30 m.) while holding their breath. Snorkel diving is also essential preliminary training for the main branch of the sport, diving with an aqualung.

Potential divers have to be competent swimmers. The snorkel diver will usually learn to use his mask, fins, and tube in a pool or in shallow water. As the human eye is designed to see in air, clear vision is impossible underwater unless a face mask is worn. The face mask covers the eyes and nose, but leaves the mouth free for breathing through the snorkel tube (or aqualung mouthpiece). Masks are made of moulded rubber with toughened glass in the single face plate which prevents the double vision caused by ordinary swimming goggles.

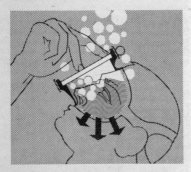

FACE MASK
The diver clears any water that seeps into his mask by facing the surface and blowing out through his nose.

Indentations in the rubber on the lower edge of the mask allow the nose to be held through the mask. Blowing through the nose then allows the diver to adjust or clear his ears to the increasing pressure by passing air through the Eustachian tubes to the inside of the eardrum. This design of mask also allows the diver to blow air into it from his nose in the event of its being squeezed against his face by the water pressure. To prevent misting during the dive, divers spit into their masks and then wash them out before entering the water.

Toughened rubber fins are worn on the feet and provide the necessary propulsion, leaving the hands free to manipulate other equipment. The diver uses a slow, wide crawl kick, which presses the surfaces of the fins against the water thus forcing him forward.

The third item of basic equipment is the snorkel tube. This does *not* allow the diver to breathe underwater, but to breathe easily while on the surface, without lifting or turning his head. He can thus keep a continual watch on the sea-bed below. When the snorkel diver descends, his tube fills with water, but he blows this out when he exhales on returning to the surface.

Snorkel divers leave the surface by means of a 'duck dive'. The diver lies flat, takes a deep breath, bends from the waist, and glides down until his fins are underwater and can then be used to swim down.

Most underwater swimmers need protection against cold; this is provided by a neoprene 'wet' suit, consisting of jacket, hood, trousers, bootees, and, if necessary, gloves. A little water will enter the suit, but will quickly warm up to body temperature and act as an insulator. If a suit is worn, the diver will also need a weight belt to overcome his buoyancy. Weight belts are fitted with detachable lead weights and a quick-release buckle so that they can be discarded in an emergency.

The diver who wants to continue to explore, without having to return to the surface every few minutes for air, will now be ready to add an aqualung to his equipment. Careful training is necessary as the breathing of compressed air introduces new hazards.

Aqualung diving, which is known as 'Scuba' in the U.S.A. (s.c.u.b.a. = self-contained underwater breathing apparatus), has become possible for sports divers since the development of efficient equipment in 1943. The aqualung allows the diver to breathe air at the same pressure as the water through which he is swimming. His lungs are not therefore squeezed by the water pressure. The human body is generally incompressible apart from the lungs, and the diver who is in good health can swim down to considerable depths.

Unfortunately, the breathing of compressed air brings physiological complications which need to be foreseen. Nitrogen, which forms 79 per cent of the air we breathe, begins to dissolve in the blood and fatty tissues during the dive. If the diver remains too long at depth, it will be necessary for him to make decompression stops near to the surface to allow the gas to disperse safely. If he does not do this, bubbles may be formed, giving rise to decompression sickness, or 'the bends', which can result in paralysis, or even death, if he is not quickly treated in a recompression chamber. Most amateur divers limit their time and depth so that these complications do not arise. At depths greater than 100 ft. (30 m.), the diver may also suffer from nitrogen narcosis or depth drunkenness (described by the French as *délire* ('rapture') of the depths). The symptoms are similar to those caused by alcohol, but of course are more dangerous underwater, as they cause dulling and slowing of the reactions and later extreme recklessness which could eventually result in the diver's death. A return to shallower water cures this condition, and the symptoms disappear.

If an aqualung diver holds his breath while ascending, he may suffer an air embolism due to the expansion of the high-pressure air in his lungs. He must therefore breathe normally, or exhale during emergency ascents. Despite these dangers, underwater swimming with an aqualung is safer than many other sports and accidents are comparatively few once thorough training has been received.

The aqualung has three main components: a cylinder which holds compressed air (sports divers do not use oxygen, which becomes a dangerous poison if breathed at depths greater than 30 ft. — 10 m.), a 'demand valve' which feeds the air to him as necessary, and a harness which attaches these to his back. (In America, demand valves are known as regulators and cylinders sometimes called tanks.)

Cylinders are constructed of steel or aluminium and are built to withstand pressures of 150–200 atmospheres. They are charged from special compressors equipped with filters, since small impurities in the air can become dangerous when breathed under pressure at depth. Most cylinders are painted yellow for easy identification, but in Britain government regulations require that those containing compressed air be painted grey with black and white quartering at the neck. The demand valve is screwed to a pillar valve at the top end of the cylinder. When the tap is opened, air can pass into the demand valve.

The demand valve is really a sealed box containing a rubber diaphragm which is in contact with the surrounding water. Connected to the diaphragm is a lever which operates another valve to admit the high-pressure air from the cylinder. On breathing in, the diver causes a slight vacuum in the box, and the water pressure then moves the diaphragm inwards. This in turn opens the valve, and high-pressure air flows into the box until the pressures equalize. The diaphragm then stops moving and the air flow is cut off. This air passes along an inlet tube and is breathed by the diver through a mouthpiece.

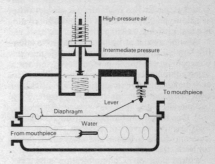

TWO-STAGE TWIN HOSE DEMAND VALVE FOR AN AQUALUNG
The valve is clamped to the top end of the cylinder containing compressed air, which is admitted to the diver's inlet tube as required, through the operation of the mechanism shown in this simplified diagram.

There are two main types of demand valves, twin-hose and single-hose. Besides the inlet tube, a twin-hose valve has an exhaust tube to take the diver's exhalations back to the valve where they are released. The more recently developed single-hose system allows air to escape near the diver's mouthpiece. Exhaled air rises to the surface as bubbles, and, in calm water, the position of the diver can be checked by following these.

Every aqualung is fitted with a device which warns the diver when his air is getting short. This may take the form of a gauge or an automatic device which gives warning when the air drops to low pressure.

The aqualung harness consists of two shoulder straps, and a third round the diver's waist, or between his legs, to keep the cylinder in position in the centre of his back. A weight belt is, of course, worn. Other equipment includes a depth gauge, a knife, and a watch to check the timing of the dive. Most divers also wear lifejackets which will support them on the surface. Some lifejackets contain small cylinders of compressed air which will bring a diver up from depth in emergency. Depending on the type of dive, a diver may also wear a compass, carry a torch, or pull a 'diver's buoy' with him.

Aqualung divers should swim calmly and relax as much as possible, breathing slowly and deeply. Over-exertion can result in the build-up of carbon dioxide and breathlessness. If the right number of weights are carried, the diver will be virtually weightless in the water.

Underwater swimming is part of the training of all astronauts.

The aqualung apparatus is simple and foolproof, allowing the diver to overcome all normal hazards. For example, he can get rid of any water that seeps into his mask by turning on to his back, holding the top of his mask and blowing air out of his nose. In case of a failure of the air supply, two divers may use the same aqualung, passing the mouthpiece from one to the other as they swim up to the surface. This exercise is known as sharing or assisted ascent in Britain, and as 'buddy breathing' in America.

One of the most important rules for amateur divers is 'Never dive alone'. Each party should have a leader and each diver should check the positions of his companions at regular intervals. Communication is by a system of international hand signals. Flags are flown by divers' boats to warn others using the water. The blue and white Flag A of the International Code of Signals means 'I have a diver down; keep well clear'. This flag may also be flown as a pennant from a diver's buoy. In the United States, a red flag with a white diagonal cross is used by amateur divers.

In order to reach their diving sites, most underwater swimmers use boats which vary in size from ocean-going yachts to small dinghies. Larger boats will be equipped with a diving ladder to allow divers to climb back on board with aqualungs still in place. They will usually leave such vessels by jumping vertically, feet first, and holding their masks so that they are not dislodged on impact with the water. In smaller boats, divers sit on the gunwale, facing inwards, and then roll in backwards, holding their masks. Many club divers use inflatable dinghies which can be easily transported from inland areas to the coast, and are manoeuvrable and buoyant. When a small boat is used, the dive leader's float or buoy may be followed as he drifts over the bottom with the tide or current. When the group surfaces, the boat is then always near by.

The diver's buoy usually consists of a line attached at one end to a reel that is unwound by the diver as he descends, and at the other to a float which may carry Flag A flying from a short mast.

An aqualung diver should always take his snorkel tube with him in case he should run out of air after surfacing. It may then be difficult to breathe on the surface wearing an aqualung and weight belt. The snorkel tube allows him to wait quietly, or swim without undue effort to land.

Some underwater swimmers use underwater sledges or scooters. Sledges are usually simple boards towed at low speed behind boats allowing the diver to follow the contours of the sea bottom by tilting the sledge up or down. Scooters are self-propelled by batteries and tow the diver until he reaches his destination.

Underwater swimming is not competitive, except for those who take part in spear-fishing competitions. There are, however, two developing sections of the sport known as FIN SWIMMING and UNDERWATER TECHNIQUE competitions. Fin swimmers use fins to race along the surface, and world championships are now held. Underwater technique competitions involve the use of the aqualung to swim compass courses, negotiate obstacles, or perform tests in low visibility.

Many national underwater federations exist throughout the world and the majority of underwater swimmers belong to clubs. Many dive in freshwater lakes or flooded quarries, although the majority prefer the sea when possible.

British Sub Aqua Club Diving Manual (1972); P. Tailliez, F. Dumas, J. Y. Cousteau, *The Complete Manual of Free Diving* (1957).

Man has been swimming and exploring underwater since earliest times, gathering shellfish for food and coral for decoration. The eminent biologist, Hardy, even suggests an aquatic phase in his evolution. There is no doubt that man is one of the few land animals able to swim effectively under water and Hardy suggests that man's hairlessness (other than his head which would be held out of the water) indicates an aquatic habitat during a period when lack of food on land forced him to seek shells and worms, fishing with his hands in shallow coastal waters.

Before the first diving apparatus was invented, underwater swimmers who held their breath while diving became famous. Such a man was Scyllis, the Greek, who in 460 B.C., together with his daughter Cyana, sank Persian ships at their moorings and recovered treasure from them. Rome also had a regiment of amphibious soldiers known as *Urinatores* who dived with their mouths filled with oil which they dribbled out drop by drop. Pearl divers were operating in the Persian Gulf in 1331, using breath-holding techniques and goggles made of tortoiseshell. Women divers, or *amas*, have been operating for hundreds of years in Japan and Korea.

Many devices to allow man to breathe under water by leading air down a pipe from the surface were designed and built in subsequent centuries. These culminated in the development of the diving helmet by Deane of Whitstable and Siebe in the early years of the nineteenth century. The history of the sport of underwater swimming, however, is bound up with the development of diving apparatus that would allow man to be completely independent of lines and contacts with the surface — equipment that would enable him to swim freely like a fish rather than plod slowly across the sea bed in heavily weighted boots and breastplate. One of the first designs for a self-contained diving dress appeared in the notebooks of Leonardo da Vinci. Nearly two centuries later, in 1680, an Italian mathematician, Borelli, designed a self-contained apparatus. Borelli's equipment included a metal helmet with a system designed to regenerate the air and a device to alter the diver's displacement so that he could rise or sink as required.

The first independent breathing apparatus with a supply of compressed air was designed by W. H. James, an Englishman, in 1825. The air was supplied from an iron reservoir around the diver's waist. It seemed a workable system, but was never tested. An American, Condert, actually produced and used a similar system until he was killed by the air suddenly leaking from his reservoir while diving in 1832. Two Frenchmen, Rouquayrol and Denayrouze, collaborated in 1865 to produce the *aerophore*. This was a practical compressed-air breathing apparatus which could be used with a tube to the surface or, for short periods, with a reservoir of compressed air fixed to the diver's back. It also incorporated the first diving mask and demand valve. This equipment was used to salvage a wreck at Toulon in 1875, but suffered from the fact that industry at that period was unable to produce cylinders that would hold air at a pressure greater than 420 lb./sq. in. The range of the self-contained version was thus severely limited.

Little had been known before this period of the medical and physiological effects of diving, but during the late nineteenth century, Bert in France and Haldane in Britain investigated the dangers and produced the first decompression tables which allowed divers to ascend slowly and safely back to the surface.

In 1878 Fleuss, an Englishman, designed and built a really practical self-contained apparatus which provided the diver with pure oxygen. This system was later developed by Sir Robert Davis and the firm of Siebe Gorman as a submarine escape and general breathing device. Two years later, in 1900, Bouton, who took the first underwater photographs, devised a compressed-air breathing set which included a cylinder which withstood internal air pressure of 2,850 lbs. per sq. in. In 1912 the German company Dragerwerk produced the first underwater sled designed by Capt. Valentiner. This was towed over the sea bed and incorporated a breathing device using oxygen cylinders. J. E. Williamson, an American who shot the first underwater 'movies', used independent oxygen breathing apparatus while filming Verne's *Twenty Thousand Leagues Under the Sea* in 1915.

In 1918 a Japanese company produced a diving machine which was known as 'Ohgushi's Peerless Respirator'. This was apparently used to considerable depths by the Japanese navy and industry and in its autonomous version consisted of a high-pressure cylinder that fed air to a flexible bag at the diver's waist. The air was then breathed by clenching the teeth to operate a valve which allowed a breath to be taken in through the nose. On opening his teeth, the diver could exhale through his mouth. The machine called for careful training and not a little self-control.

It was not until 1924, however, that light free-diving equipment designed for amateurs was developed by Commandant Le Prieur of the French navy and his compatriot Fernez. This device consisted of a cylinder of compressed air at a pressure of 150 atmospheres, *Fernez* tube and mouthpiece, and the Rouquayrol-Denayrouze demand valve, together with a face mask covering eyes, nose, and mouth. Another very important step forward came in 1926 when the prototype foot fins were produced by Commandant de Corlieu and the diver moved from the vertical to

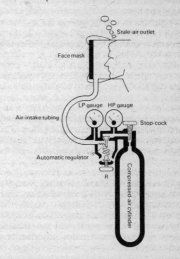

LE PRIEUR FREE-DIVING APPARATUS (1924)
The regulation of excess pressure in the face mask was effected by compressing a spring with the tap, R, according to the depth reached. The two gauges shown in the diagram — (LP) low-pressure; (HP) high-pressure — recorded the pressure.

the horizontal to swim like a fish for the first time.

After 1926 Le Prieur and Painlevé started the first group of amateur divers, the Club des Scaphandriers et de la Vie Sous l'Eau in Paris. These club divers used the Le Prieur breathing apparatus and the de Corlieu fins. Le Prieur also designed an underwater gun powered by compressed air and a foam rubber protective diving suit that was filled with hot water.

A new race of underwater spear-fishermen appeared on the coasts of the Mediterranean in the late 1920s. They used goggles and spears which enabled them to transfix unwary fish. The most important of these pioneers was an American, GILPATRIC, who in 1938 wrote the first book on the new style of underwater diving and hunting, *The Compleat Goggler*. Gilpatric inspired COUSTEAU, Tailliez, and HASS, who later surpassed him in technique and experience.

By 1933 the first American sport diving club, The Bottom Scratchers, had been formed in California. Sports divers generally used the Le Prieur type of apparatus at this time, carrying on their chests a bottle of compressed air which was connected to the full face mask. The diver valved air to himself and either walked or swam over the bottom.

During the early 1930s, British speleologists began to use types of primitive underwater breathing apparatus and, in 1934, Balcombe and Sheppard explored Swildon's Hole in Somerset. In that year Beuchat in France had developed a successful *arbalette* harpoon gun, and in 1935 de Corlieu put his rubber foot fins on the market.

The basic equipment of the snorkel diver was now nearly complete. In 1936 Fernez diving goggles were being manufactured in France and, two years later, a patent for a mask covering eyes and nose was taken out by Forjot, although many others were already experimenting with this idea which allowed air to be blown into the mask through the nose to compensate for the squeezing effect of the water.

Commeinhes moved the Le Prieur cylinder to the diver's back and coupled it to the Rouquayrol-Denayrouze demand valve. This produced the first 'aqualung', which was approved by the French war office in 1937. The Commeinhes lung had many new features and in spite of some minor imperfections, Commeinhes swam down with it to a depth of 53 m. (174 ft.). He was killed in action during the Second World War.

Before the war, Hass, a young Austrian student had organized underwater expeditions to the Adriatic and the Dutch West Indies using breath-holding and oxygen rebreather sets. At this time the famous team of Cousteau, Tailliez, and Dumas was formed, fishing underwater and experimenting with oxygen apparatus in the south of France.

During the Second World War, the oxygen-breathing apparatus was further developed for use by frogmen. These sets released no tell-tale bubbles that might warn the enemy of the approach of a diver, but limited him to a depth of 30 ft. (9 m.) because of the effects of oxygen poisoning below this depth. The original frogmen were the Italians who, in 1941, sank a tanker in Gibraltar harbour. British and American underwater working parties and combat teams were soon formed and trained by such well-known figures as Commander Crabb.

The stage was now set for the last great development. In 1943 Cousteau contacted Gagnan, a French engineer, and they developed a fully automatic compressed-air aqualung. Due to its simplicity of design and solidarity, the marketing of the Cousteau-Gagnan lung opened the age of undersea exploration to thousands, and proved to be the final 'passport to inner space'. New clubs were formed as the equipment became available. The most famous of these, the Club Alpin Sous-Marin, was founded by Broussard at Cannes in 1946, and a year later COLIN MCLEOD first marketed frogmen's fins in Britain. The aqualung became available in France in 1946, in Britain in 1950, and in Canada a year later. British amateur diving speleologists were still active using oxygen apparatus, however, and in 1946 the British Cave Diving Group was formed under Dr. R. E. Davies of Oxford.

By 1948 a French federation of diving clubs had been formed by Borelli, and the first Italian club by Gonzatti and Dr. Stuart-Tovini. In 1949 Limbaugh introduced aqualung diving to the Scripps Institution of Oceanography in California, and in 1950 Bradner and Bascom developed the first 'wet' suit there. The aqualung became commercially available in the U.S.A. in 1952.

The first books on underwater swimming and exploration in tropical waters by Dr. Hass were published and rapidly became best sellers. *The Silent World* by Cousteau and Dumas charted the exploits of the new aqualung explorers, and became the best-known book on the art.

During the late 1940s and the early 1950s, various clubs and schools were in existence in Britain, but in 1953 the British Sub Aqua Club was formed in London by a group of enthusiasts who included GUGEN, Small, and McLeod. The Club formed branches throughout Britain and by the late 1950s became the governing body for the sport in the United

Kingdom and the largest diving club in the world, numbering over 500 branches in 27 countries. On 11 January 1959, the Confédération Mondiale des Activités Subaquatiques (C.M.A.S.), or World Underwater Federation, was inaugurated in Monaco by the delegates of 15 nations under the presidency of Cousteau. Gugen of Britain became the first president of its technical committee and Ferraro of Italy presided over the sports committee. The Confédération now represents more than 50 nations.

The sport grew with increasing rapidity during the 1960s and by 1967 had an estimated 4,000,000 participants. Aqualung divers who began as simple hunters had become in the 1970s 'the eyes under the sea', using the aqualung to investigate wrecks, fish behaviour, and the effects of pollution.

Confédération Mondiale des Activités Subaquatiques, *International Yearbook of the Underwater World*, annually. R. and B. Carrier, *Dive* (1955); J. Y. Cousteau and F. Dumas, *The Silent World* (1966); Sir Robert Davis, *Deep Diving and Submarine Operations* (1969); P. De Latil and J. Rivoire, *Man and the Underwater World* (1956); P. Diolé, *Underwater Exploration* (1954); J. Dugan, *Man Explores the Sea* (1963); G. Gilpatric, *The Compleat Goggler* (1938); H. Hass, *Diving to Adventure* (1963) and *To Unplumbed Depths* (1972); O. Lee, *The Complete Illustrated Guide to Snorkel and Deep Diving* (1963); *The Underwater Book* (1968), *The Second Underwater Book* (1970), and *The World Underwater Book* (1973), all ed. K. McDonald; A. McKee, *History under the Sea* (1968); R. Marx, *They Dared the Deep* (1967); Rear-Adm. S. Miles, C.B., *Underwater Medicine* (1969); G. Poulet, *Newnes Complete Guide to Underwater Swimming* (1964); D. Rebikoff, *Free Diving* (1955); V. Romanovsky, *Conquest of the Deep* (1965); *Underwater Swimming: An Advanced Handbook*, ed. L. Zanelli (1969). *Triton*, bimonthly magazine of the British Sub Aqua Club.

GOVERNING BODY (WORLD): Confédération Mondiale des Activités Subaquatiques, 34, rue du Colisée, Paris 8, France; (U.K.): British Sub Aqua Club, 70 Brompton Road, London S.W.3.

UNDERWOOD, DEREK LESLIE (1945-), cricketer for England and Kent. In 1963 he became the youngest player ever to take 100 wickets in a début season, and when only 25 years 264 days old he took his 1,000th first-class wicket, a feat achieved by only RHODES and LOHMANN at a younger age. A left-arm bowler of slow-medium pace, he utilizes imperfect pitches with remarkable efficiency, but is otherwise usually seen as a containing bowler. In 37 Test matches to the end of 1973 he had taken 146 wickets.

UNITED ENGLAND XI, see CRICKET.

UNITED STATES GRAND PRIX, see MOTOR RACING, AMERICAN.

UNITED STATES MILITARY ACADEMY (Army), American college FOOTBALL team, nicknamed the 'Cadets', achieved its greatest era during and after the Second World War, under coach BLAIK. Wartime made a military career an appealing prospect to athletes, and in the years 1944 to 1946 Army had one of the most star-studded teams in college football history, led by the tandem running-back combination, Davis ('Mr. Outside') and Blanchard ('Mr. Inside'). Its three-year unbeaten string was snapped in 1947, but another 28-game string began then and lasted until the United States Naval Academy (Navy) ended it at the end of the 1950 season. It had another unbeaten season in 1958, featuring the 'lonely end' Carpenter, stationed out wide of the line of scrimmage. Army's great rival was its military service counterpart Navy, with each game attracting well over 100,000 people. It had an equally intense intersectional rival in NOTRE DAME, especially in the 1920s and 1940s.

COLOURS: Black, gold, grey.

UNIVERSITY BOAT RACE, see BOAT RACE, THE.

UNSER, AL (1939-), American MOTOR RACING driver who won the 1970 and 1971 INDIANAPOLIS 500 races, placed second in 1972, and has won 27 United States Auto Club national championship races. He was U.S.A.C. national champion in 1970, national dirt track champion in 1973; and Pike's Peak Hill Climb winner in speedway cars in 1964 and 1965; he is the younger brother of Bobby Unser, also a winner of the Indianapolis 500.

URRUTY, JEAN (1904-), French Basque PELOTA player, perhaps the most outstanding *pilotari* to appear in the French Basque country since CHIQUITO DE CAMBO. He is chiefly famous for his skill at *yoko-garbi*, but he excelled also at *main nue en trinquet* and at the old and neglected game of *pasaka*. A small, neat athlete with great economy of movement and a sober manner, his classicism contrasted sharply with the romantic flamboyance of Chiquito; yet, though less obvious, his personality was as influential, and his flair for *yoko-garbi* did much to give that game the popularity it now enjoys. After the Second World War, when many thought his career on the wane, he proved his virtuosity by taking up *grand chistera*, and showed the same fluid precision with the long glove as he had with the short. He retired in 1970 after 40 years on the courts.

V

VACHÉ, JANE, LACROSSE player for the U.S.A. for seven years from 1945. An outstanding wing attack, with speed and power, in 1951 she visited Great Britain with the U.S.A. touring team, and in 1964 she was manager of another team on its British tour. She is an outstanding coach and has served as president of the U.S. Women's Lacrosse Association.

VAGUELY NOBLE (1965), English racehorse by Vienna (a son of AUREOLE out of a mare tracing to PRETTY POLLY) bred by Maj. Holliday and owned by his son. Vaguely Noble won the OBSERVER GOLD CUP as a two-year-old, and was then sold to Dr. and Mrs. Franklin for 136,000 guineas (a world record price for a horse at public auction), in whose colours he won the PRIX DE L'ARC DE TRIOMPHE, beating SIR IVOR by three lengths. He was then syndicated for stud purposes by Hunt in the U.S.A. at a world-record valuation of $5 million to stand at Gainesway Farm, Lexington, Kentucky.

VALENTINE, ALFRED LEWIS (1930-   ), cricketer for West Indies and Jamaica. A slow left-arm bowler, at the age of 20, and untried in first-class CRICKET, he took 33 wickets in four Tests in England in 1950. With RAMADHIN he spun West Indies to an historic 3-0 victory in the series, and when he retired he had taken 139 Test wickets. The average cost, however, had risen to 30.32, as he had been needed more as a stock bowler.

VALENTINE, Mrs. GEORGE, M.B.E. (née Jessie Anderson) (1915-   ), Scottish golfer who was Scottish champion six times; British champion in 1937, 1955, and 1958; and a Scottish and British international.

VAN DONCK, FLORY (1912-   ), Belgian professional golfer, who was Belgian professional champion 13 times, Belgian Open champion five times, a multiple winner of Dutch, Spanish, French, Italian, Swiss, German, Portuguese, Danish, Venezuelan, and Uruguayan Open championships, and a WORLD CUP player.

VAN HIMST, PAUL (1943-   ), Association footballer for ANDERLECHT (Brussels),

and Belgium for whom he made his international début when only 17 days past his seventeenth birthday. A tall, graceful inside or centre forward, he was 16 when he made his first appearance for Anderlecht, and only 18 when he collected his first Belgian championship winners' medal. He was twice elected 'Belgian Footballer of the Year' while still in his teens.

VAN LOOY, RIK (1932-   ), Belgian professional cyclist, winner of a greater variety of road-race classics than anyone before him. In 1956-68 he won 13 victories in eight different classic events, only the BORDEAUX–PARIS and GRAND PRIX DES NATIONS being absent from his record; he also took two consecutive world road-race titles in 1960-1. Most of these successes he owed to the great power of his finishing sprint, and to his team's skill in manoeuvring him into a position to employ it. On the track he won 11 six-day races, 9 of them with POST.

VAN STEENBERGEN, RIK (1924-   ), Belgian professional cyclist on road and track. He generally rode throughout the year, taking only a mid-summer break, and was 42 years old before he retired. Apart from eight road-race classics, he had won three world professional road titles, a feat equalled only by BINDA. On the track he had won 1,314 events, including a world record of 40 six-day races which was later surpassed by POST.

VANA, BOHUMIL (1920-   ), the strongest of all Czechoslovak TABLE TENNIS players. Vana was the principal rival of BERGMANN during the years immediately before and after the Second World War. He won the world championship men's singles title in 1938 and 1947 and was runner-up in 1948 and 1949. Where Bergmann was principally a defender, Vana was an all-out attacker. He included his thumb in the handle grip, so that in attack he had to play all-out forehand, maintaining the initiative by agility, using an exceptionally sure half-volley defence in the left corner of the table and finishing many rallies with a drop shot. Vana also won the men's doubles and mixed doubles three times each and five times was a member of winning SWAYTHLING CUP teams.

VANDALIA GUN CLUB, Vandalia, Ohio, the senior clay pigeon SHOOTING club in U.S.A., formed near the end of the nineteenth century. It is the headquarters of the Amateur Trapshooting Association of America, known until 1924 as the Inter-State Association of Trapshooters. In 1900 the club staged the first Grand American Handicap, now the leading annual tournament in the U.S.A.

VANDERVELL, H. E., see ICE SKATING.

VARANGOT, BRIGITTE (1940-   ), French amateur golfer. She was French amateur champion five times, and British champion in 1963, 1965, and 1968.

VARDON, HARRY (1870-1937), English professional golfer who won a record six Open championships and one U.S. Open championship. One of the 'Great Triumvirate' (with BRAID and TAYLOR) who reigned virtually unchallenged during the 20 years of the golden age of English GOLF before 1914, Vardon was one of the outstanding golfers of all time. It may be slightly fanciful to claim him as the father of modern golf but there is no doubt that his influence on the manner of play was enormous. He brought style to the golf swing and new standards of accuracy. The club grip which bears his name, although he was not in fact the inventor of it, became universally accepted as 'correct'.

VARDON TROPHY, GOLF award presented annually by the U.S. Professional Golfers Association to the tournament player with the lowest stroke average in P.G.A. events during the year. In Britain an award of the same name was formerly presented by the P.G.A. on this basis. The conditions were changed in 1969, the trophy thereafter being given to the player with most Order of Merit points for the season.

VARELA, OBDULIO JACINTO (fl. 1940-54), Association footballer for Uruguay for whom he made his international début in 1940, playing at inside left against Brazil and scoring three goals. Ten years later, when playing at centre half, he was captain of the Uruguayan side that won the 1950 world championship in Rio. He also played for Uruguay in the 1954 world championship in Switzerland.

VARNER, MARGARET (later Mrs. W. G. Bloss) (1927-   ), American BADMINTON player. One of the greatest woman players of all time and five times an ALL-ENGLAND singles finalist (with two successes over Miss

J. M. Devlin, now Mrs. HASHMAN), she would have a more imposing record had she played as much as most world-class exponents. She was an all-round sportswoman who enjoyed the unique distinction of representing the U.S.A. not only in the UBER CUP at badminton, but also in the WIGHTMAN CUP at LAWN TENNIS, and in the Wolfe-Noel Cup at SQUASH RACKETS, all within a period of two years. She was always on the winning side. HELEN JACOBS includes Miss Varner as one of 13 personalities in her book *Famous American Women Athletes.*

VASALOP RACE, a mass-start cross-country ski race of about 85 km. (53 miles) from Sälen to Mora in Sweden in which thousands of people have taken part annually since 1922. At a famous turning-point in Swedish history, Gustav Vasa, who founded the modern kingdom of Sweden, having failed to rouse the Dalecarlians to revolt against the Danes, in 1520 left for Norway. The Dalecarlians changed their minds, and their best skiers pursued him to the village of Sälen on the Norwegian border. The race commemorates Gustav Vasa's return journey on skis, and is held every March with 800 to 1,000 people taking part.

VEDYAKOV, ANATOLI (1930-   ), race walker for U.S.S.R. GOLUBNICHI and he were the most consistent Russian competitors in major international events from 1957 to 1964. Vedyakov was fourth in the European 20 km. in 1962, seventh in 1964, and, in 1960, ninth in the Olympic 50 km. Vedyakov was a non-finisher in the European 50 km. in 1962 after endeavouring to match the early pace of PAMICH. He set a world record in 1958 at 30 km. and 20 miles.

VERITY, HEDLEY (1905-43), cricketer for England and Yorkshire. A left-arm slow-medium bowler, he followed RHODES in the tradition of steady and guileful Yorkshire spinners, and captured almost 2,000 wickets at less than 15 runs each. Against Nottinghamshire in 1932 he took 10 wickets for 10 runs, and for England his finest performance was 15 Australian wickets for 104 on a rain-affected pitch at LORD's in 1934. In an era of high scoring he took 144 Test wickets at 24·37 each. He died in Italy of war wounds.

VERNON, JOHN JOSEPH (1919-   ), Association footballer for BELFAST CELTIC, West Bromwich Albion, and Crusaders. A centre half of distinction, he played on 17 occasions for his country. He was a member of the United Kingdom team which defeated the

Rest of Europe 6–1 at Hampden Park, Glasgow, in 1947.

VESPER BOAT CLUB, an American ROWING club in Philadelphia, founded in 1875. A Vesper eight won the 1900 OLYMPIC GAMES and in 1964, after adopting RATZEBURG methods, Vesper again won the Olympic title — the only occasions on which a noncollegiate American club has won this event. After 1905, when Vesper entered for the Grand Challenge Cup at HENLEY, in which they were unsuccessful, they were barred from Henley because of alleged infringements of the amateur code. This ban led to Vesper's most distinguished oarsman and sculler, J. B. KELLY, SR., being unable to compete in the Diamond Sculls in 1920, but Kelly went on to win the Olympic title that year. The ban was later removed and in 1965 the Vesper eight narrowly lost the final of the Grand to the Ratzeburg crew.
COLOURS: Maroon and grey.

VEZINA TROPHY, ICE HOCKEY trophy, awarded annually in the NATIONAL HOCKEY LEAGUE of North America to 'the goalminder(s) having played a minimum of 25 games for the team with the fewest goals scored against it'. The trophy was donated in 1927 by MONTREAL CANADIENS in memory of Georges Vezina, their goalminder, who collapsed during a game in 1925 and died of tuberculosis a few months later. Each recipient gets $1,000. It was won for a record sixth time by DURNAN in 1950, a feat equalled in 1962 by Plante, each a goalminder for Montreal Canadiens.

VICKERS, STANLEY FREDERICK (1932-   ), race walker for Great Britain. DORDONI and he were regarded as the fairest sprint walkers yet seen. At 20 km., Vickers was European champion, 1958; and third, 1960, and fifth, 1956, in the Olympic event. His many races with MATTHEWS, both in England and Europe, in the period 1956-60 produced some of the finest stylish walking ever seen, and the English 2 miles track championship of 1960, won by Vickers, is considered a classic by all coaches. He was holder of several English track and road titles from 2 to 20 miles.

VICTORIAN FOOTBALL ASSOCIATION, the oldest Australian Rules FOOTBALL body in existence, was established in 1877. In 1879 a South Australian team visited Melbourne and played Melbourne and Geelong. The first inter-colonial match was arranged the same year, South Australia playing Victoria in Melbourne. The Association now operates only in Melbourne (with ten teams in three divisions). In 1969 it withdrew from the Australian Football Council (A.F.C.) (see FOOTBALL, AUSTRALIAN RULES).

VICTORIAN FOOTBALL LEAGUE, Australian Rules FOOTBALL organization. In 1896, Carlton, Collingwood, Essendon, Melbourne, South Melbourne, and Fitzroy football clubs seceded from the VICTORIAN FOOTBALL ASSOCIATION. St. Kilda and the Geelong clubs followed, and the Victorian Football League was established. The first League matches were played in 1897. In 1908 Richmond and Melbourne University were admitted, but the University club was disbanded during the First World War. Footscray, Hawthorn, and North Melbourne were admitted in 1924, and in 1925 for the first time 12 clubs contested the Victorian Football League premiership. There have been no further admissions to the League since then.

VIENNA S.C., ICE SKATING club formed in Austria in 1867. Home of many world champions and venue of early European developments in ice dancing.

VILLA, PANCHO (1901-25), Filipino boxer who won the world flyweight BOXING championship by knocking out WILDE in 1923. Villa lost only 6 of 107 bouts but his career was cut short when he died of blood poisoning, caused by an infected tooth, after losing a non-title bout to McLarnin in 1925.

VILLARD DE LANS, a luge TOBOGGANING course near Grenoble, France, opened in 1958, and used for the 1959 world championships and the 1968 Olympic luge events. With five curves, six bends, and a maze, the course is 1,000 m. (1,094 yds.) long, dropping 110 m. (120·3 yds.) from a start-point altitude of 1,100 m. (1,203 yds.). The maximum slope is just under 19 per cent. A wooden walkway, 4 m. (4·4 yds.) wide, runs parallel to the track. Three control towers are linked by telephone to the starting and finishing points, and 40 loudspeakers along the course inform spectators of each toboggan's progress at every stage of its descent.

VINCENT, CYNTHIA ANN, HOCKEY player for England and South Africa. An England international from 1954 to 1959, she was also a member of the England touring team to Australia in 1956. A tenacious forward, she continued her playing career in South Africa and captained that country.

VINES, H. ELLSWORTH (1911-   ), American LAWN TENNIS player, the possessor of one of the fastest and most devastating cannon-ball services the game has known. He played two memorable WIMBLEDON finals: in 1932 he beat AUSTIN 6-4, 6-2, 6-0 in one of the most one-sided finals on record, and the following year he lost to CRAWFORD in a contest which has been generally regarded as the classic conclusion to the championship. He won the U.S. title in 1931 and 1932 and won 13 of his 16 Davis Cup (see LAWN TENNIS) rubbers. He failed, however, in a crucial rubber of the 1933 challenge round against BOROTRA in Paris, and in the 1934 inter-zone final against Britain he lost to both Austin and PERRY. He turned professional in 1934 and later became a leading professional golfer.

VINEY, HUGH (1917-   ), British MOTOR-CYCLE TRIALS rider who developed a technique of tackling observed sections at the slowest possible speed. His method of 'plonking' a 350 cc. AJS in a manner reminiscent of a gas engine was in marked contrast to his speed as a member of British International Six Days Trial teams. He scored a unique hat-trick in the Scottish Six Days Trial.

VINSON, MARIBEL, see OWEN, M.

VIREN, LASSE ARTTURI (1949-   ), middle-distance and long-distance runner for Finland. At Munich in 1972 Viren completed a spectacular double, winning Olympic gold medals in both 5,000 and 10,000 metres. In the longer race he fell shortly before the half-way mark but, making a recovery never before witnessed in a major track championship, regained his place in the race to triumph in a new world record time of 27 min. 38·4 sec. Also in 1972 Viren broke the world records for 2 miles with 8 min. 14 sec., and 5,000 metres with 13 min. 16·4 sec.

VISITORS' CUP, see HENLEY ROYAL REGATTA.

VITI, El (Santiago Martín) (1938-   ), *matador de toros*, (*alternativa* 13 May 1961). A superb technician, without equal in terms of *lidia*, his art suffered from his physique which did not allow the elegance necessary to give his work the grace it merited.

VLASOV, YURI (1935-   ), Russian heavyweight lifter, five times Olympic and world champion (1959-63), who set 31 world records. Vlasov was the first lifter to total 1,200 lb. (544 kg.).

VOLLEYBALL is a team game played on a rectangular area 18 m. by 9 m. (59 ft. 0¾ in. by 29 ft. 6⅜ in.), divided into two equal square courts by the centre line, above which spans a taut horizontal net at a height of 2·43 m. (7 ft. 11⅝ in.) for men, and 2·24 m. (7 ft. 4⅛ in.) for women. In play, two teams, each of six players, take up positions in their respective courts and aim to deliver the ball over the net and to 'ground' it in their opponents' court, while preventing it from touching the floor of their own. MINI VOLLEY is a version of the game played by junior teams of only three players.

Play begins when the server, standing behind the base line and in the service area, strikes the ball with one hand or arm to deliver it over the net and into the opposite court, where a member of the receiving team attempts to save the ball and in the same movement to loft it for a team mate to play. Each team is allowed to contact the ball a maximum of three times before returning it to the opposite court, but any one individual may not touch, or be touched by it, twice in succession (a 'double hit'), and the ball must always be played cleanly by the hands, with no suggestion of holding ('held ball'), lifting, or carrying. Indeed, the whole character of the game stems from the finesse, precision, and elegance which this handling rule engenders.

Play continues in the form of a rally until one team allows the ball to touch the ground in its own court, or fails to return it correctly. If such a rally is won by the serving team, a point is added to its score; if won by the receivers a 'side-out' occurs, whereupon the receiving team is entitled to take the next service. Players of this team must now rotate one place clockwise before service, and in this way all players take a turn in each position during a 'set'.

A 'front-line player' is any of the three nearest the net, numbered 2, 3, and 4 in the rotation order. Similarly, a 'back-line player' occupies the back row and will be numbered 1, 6, or 5.

Points are scored only by the serving team, and the first team to reach 15 points wins the set, providing that they have a lead of 2 points. If at 15 the lead is less than 2, e.g. 15-14, play continues until a 2-point lead is established. A match is decided by the best of three or five sets as agreed prior to commencement, although all international and national league matches must be played to the best of five.

At international and senior club level, the game is fast and exciting, demanding a high level of skill and tactical awareness. Every attempt is made to exploit the three permitted touches on each side of the net. On receiving the ball from the opponents, a defending player returns it near to the net in his own

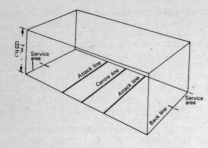

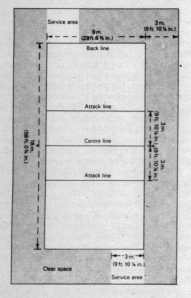

VOLLEYBALL COURT
Shaded area in the plan view (*below*) is the recommended clear space 3 m. (9 ft. 10¼ in.) deep on all sides of the playing space. (For indoor volleyball the clear space may be 1 m. (3 ft. 3 in.) wide, and in outdoor play not less than 2 m. (6 ft. 7 in.) wide.) The service area must have a minimum depth of 2 m. at each end. In the perspective view (*above*) the fine lines indicate the vertical depth of the court, which must be free of any obstruction to a height of 7 m. (23 ft.).

court, where a 'set pass' specialist (the 'setter') moves to 'set' the ball with a high pass which a front-line player can smash to the floor of the opponents' court.

The 'block' is made with the hands and arms near, and above, the net and is a means of attempting to stop the smash (or 'spike') coming from the opposite side. The block may be performed by any or all of the front-line players. The 'tactical ball' (or 'dump') is an attack made by a player who feigns a smash but at the last moment makes a soft pass over the block. The 'volley pass' is the manner in which the ball is struck above shoulder level using the fingers of both hands simultaneously, while the 'dig pass' is the action of striking the ball below shoulder level with one or both arms. The one-arm dig pass is less reliable and is usually used only when diving to recover the ball. The two-arm dig pass is performed with the hands clasped and the arms extended.

Two tactical moves are the 'switch' in which front-line and back-line players move laterally to positions on court in which their individual abilities are used to advantage, and the 'penetration' in which a back-line player moves forward to the net, after the service, in order to act as setter, freeing all the front-line players to take part in the smash. (A back-line player may only make a smash if he takes off behind the attack line.)

'Overlapping' is a positional fault. At the moment the ball is served, the back-line players must be behind their corresponding front-line player, the position of players being judged according to the positions of their feet.

Infringements include 'screening', which occurs when a player (or players) obstructs his opponent's view of the server. When a player touches the net, during play, with any part of his body it is a 'net fault'. A 'foot fault' occurs when (*a*) during service the server's foot is placed on, or in front of, the service line as the ball is struck, and (*b*) when a player's foot is placed completely in the opponents' court. A 'double foul' is when players on both sides commit fouls simultaneously. The point is played again.

The referee's whistle stops play. The ball is then dead and remains so until the referee whistles for play to continue.

A match is controlled by the first referee, who takes a position close to, and above, one end of the net. He is assisted by the second referee (or umpire) and scorer, both placed on the side of the court opposite to the first referee. The four linesmen are positioned in order to judge one side line or base line each.

A team may consist of up to a maximum of 12 players. Each team is allowed six substitutes. Each player replaced constitutes a substitution; a team may make six substitutions, singly or collectively, in any one set. A player may re-enter the court only in the position which he originally occupied in the order of rotation.

A stoppage in play may be requested by the captain or coach on two occasions in any one set. The time allowed on each occasion is 30 seconds. Coaching is not allowed during the actual play.

The ball used is $25\frac{19}{32}$ to $26\frac{3}{8}$ in. (65–67 cm.) in circumference and 8·85 to 9·875 oz. (250–260 g.) in weight. It is spherical and made of a supple leather case, with a bladder of rubber or similar material. It should be of uniform colour and without laces. Other balls (e.g. synthetic) may be approved for practice providing that the material does not result in too hard a surface to play with and gives a realistic feel. Balls approved for practice are recommended as suitable for use on outdoor hard-surface courts, where a leather ball would wear quickly. Moulded balls are not suitable for matches or for preparing for a good level of play. They are not approved as a substitute for the leather ball indoors.

The volleyball net is 31 ft. 2 in. (9·5 m.) long, 3 ft. 3⅜ in. (1 m.) deep, and of a mesh whose squares are 4 in. (10 cm.) wide. A double thickness of white canvas or linen, 2 in. (5 cm.) wide, should be stitched across the top. A flexible cable stretches the upper edge of the net and passes inside the band of canvas. The bottom of the net is normally stretched by a cord or rope which passes through a canvas sleeve similar to the top one, or through the mesh itself.

A removable band of white material, 2 in. (5 cm.) wide and 3 ft. 3⅜ in. (1 m.) long, should be fixed at the sides of the net above and perpendicular to the side lines. For international matches, parallel to the tapes and just outside them, two flexible aerials are fastened to the net at a distance of 30 ft. 10 in. (9·4 m.) from each other. These two aerials are 6 ft. (1·8 m.) long, with an approximate diameter of ⅜ in. (10 mm.), and are of fibreglass or similar material and extend 2 ft. 8 in. (80 cm.) above the top of the net.

Clothing should consist of a vest or jersey, shorts, and light pliable shoes (rubber or leather) without heels. Players must not wear any object or article which may cause injury during play. If requested, the referee may allow players to play without shoes.

Numbers, 6 in. (15 cm.) high and 2 in. (5 cm.) wide, must be worn on the chest and back. In internationals, the captain wears a special badge on the left-hand side of his chest.

Players must come on court dressed in neat clean clothes of the same colour. If the weather is cold they may play in numbered track suits. Jerseys with long sleeves are usually preferred to protect the arms when 'digging' the ball.

Volleyball, like BASKETBALL, was developed in the U.S.A., and owes its beginning to the Y.M.C.A. movement. The physical fitness instructor at the Y.M.C.A. at Holyoke, Massachusetts, in the last decade of the nineteenth century, W. G. Morgan, formulated the game of volleyball in 1895 especially for middle-aged men who found basketball too vigorous. Morgan wrote later: 'There was a need for a game which all age-groups could play, and above all I felt that this game should be enjoyable. To begin with we used a basketball and

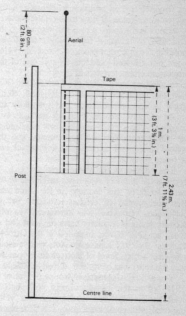

VOLLEYBALL NET
The height shown is for men; for the women's game the net is 2·24 m. (7 ft. 4¼ in.) high, measured at the centre. The aerials extending above the top of the net, for international matches, are of bright contrasting colours.

batted it up with the hands; then we placed a net between the teams. We found the basketball unsuitable by reason of its size and weight, and we therefore asked Spaldings to make a special ball of calf skin.'

The first rules allowed each team 9 players on court, so that 18 men occupied the area, which measured 50 by 25 ft. (15·24 × 7·62 m.). The net was suspended at a height of 6 ft. 6 in. (1·98 m.) while the ball, with a circumference of 25 in. (635 mm.) and a weight of 9 oz. (255 g.), was virtually the same size and weight as its modern counterpart. From the inception of the game, team rotation was a feature, and this ensured that all players took turns in each position but, in order that all nine players could be accommodated on court, teams were formed in three lines of three, and in play the ball had to pass by successive rebounds from line to line before being returned over the net.

As the game progressed certain skills developed, and soon teams wished to play against each other on a competitive basis. Thus volleyball moved beyond the original concept of its founder for, in addition to being a purely recreational game, it now took on the status of a serious team sport. From the beginning, the ball had to rebound from player to player; holding, catching, pushing, and throwing were not allowed, and this is still one of the important characteristics of the game.

It was not until after the First World War that teams of six became established. Skills grew more sophisticated, and gradually the mode of play, i.e. receive, set pass, smash, evolved. The service was by now required to be direct from server to opponents, and the whole concept of tactical play with attack and defence systems began to develop.

The spread of the game from the U.S.A. reflects the areas of American influence in the early years of this century, in the same way that the spread of cricket indicates British influence. Volleyball was introduced via missionary schools to many parts of Asia, and as early as 1913 it was included in the Oriental Games. By 1917 Japanese teams were already showing a high level of tactical development, and the sport was being introduced in Russia.

The arrival of American troops in France in 1918 led to the introduction of volleyball to western Europe, and in the inter-war years national volleyball associations were founded in many countries of eastern Europe, and in a few countries in the west also. In spite of this fragmented national development, no international organization was set up between the wars, and the only international tournament was at the World University Games in 1939.

The International Volleyball Federation (F.I.V.B.), founded in 1947 to formalize and regulate international rules and competitions, now has 108 member countries. From that time, world competitions have been regularly held (the first in Prague in 1949), with the strongest teams being those of the U.S.S.R., the countries of eastern Europe, and Japan. Volleyball achieved Olympic status in 1964 at Tokyo, when the top men's teams were the U.S.S.R., Czechoslovakia, and Japan, and the leading women's teams Japan, the U.S.S.R., and Poland.

The Amateur Volleyball Association of Great Britain was formed only in 1955, when most of the continental countries were well established in the game.

Volleyball now has a regular place in the OLYMPIC GAMES programme, and East Germany has emerged to challenge the supremacy of Japan, Russia, Czechoslovakia, and the other countries of eastern Europe.

GOVERNING BODY (WORLD): International Volleyball Federation, 23 Rue d'Anjou, Paris 8, France; (ENGLAND): English Volleyball Association, 5 Bluecoat Street, Nottingham.

VOLNOV, Capt. GENNADI (1941-   ), BASKETBALL player for the U.S.S.R. A member of the TS.S.K.A. MOSCOW club, Volnov was for several years one of the leading players in Europe.

VOLTERRA, SUZY, is a leading race-horse owner in France, where she continued the racing interests of her late husband, Leon, himself one of the most outstanding French thoroughbred breeders. Notable horses that have sported her colours are Topyo, winner of the PRIX DE L'ARC DE TRIOMPHE, and Phil Drake, winner of the French Grand Prix and English DERBY.

VOLTIGEUR (1847), English race-horse by Voltaire out of Martha Lynn, bred and owned by Lord Zetland. He won the DERBY, the ST. LEGER (after running off a dead-heat), and the Doncaster Cup (defeating The FLYING DUTCHMAN by a neck). In the following spring the tables were turned in the most famous match in the history of HORSE RACING.

VON CRAMM, Baron GOTTFRIED (1909-   ), German LAWN TENNIS player, one of the great clay court competitors, the losing singles finalist at WIMBLEDON for three successive years. He was German champion from 1932 to 1935 and French champion in 1934 (when he beat CRAWFORD after saving a match point in a final which went to 6-4, 7-9, 3-6, 7-5, 6-3) and in 1936, when he defeated PERRY.

Admirable serving, remarkable fitness, and firm, accurate driving from the backhand were the great strengths of von Cramm's game. In his Wimbledon finals he lost to Perry in 1935 and 1936 and, after the British player had turned professional, to BUDGE in 1937. He insisted on completing the 1936 final, in which Perry beat him 6-1, 6-1, 6-0, in spite of an injured ankle. His only Wimbledon title was the mixed doubles which he won with Krahwinkel in 1933.

In the 1930s von Cramm was the mainstay of one of the strongest Davis Cup (see LAWN TENNIS) teams, but he never succeeded in taking them to the challenge round. Five times in seven years and for four years in succession —from 1935 to 1938—Germany failed in the inter-zone final. Between 1932, when he and Prenn took Germany to the inter-zone final, and 1953 he played in 37 ties and won 82 rubbers out of 102. His most memorable matches were a 4-6, 6-4, 4-6, 6-4, 11-9 victory over QUIST, which he won on his tenth match point after Quist had been three times within a point of victory, and his contest with Budge at the same stage the following year, when the American won 6-8, 5-7, 6-4, 6-2, 8-6 after von Cramm had led 4-1 in the final set. After the war, he played a leading part in the revival of German lawn tennis, winning the singles championship twice more and the doubles title in 1948-9 and 1953-5.

VON SODEN, Gräfin, clay pigeon shooter for West Germany. She was the first woman to win two world titles (1966-7) and won three successive European championships between 1967 and 1969.

VOSBURGH, WALTER SPENCER (1854-1938), was racing secretary, forfeit clerk, and official handicapper to the New York Jockey Club, as well as chairman and senior steward of the Metropolitan race-tracks. He is the author of *Racing in America.*

VUELTA A ESPAGNA (Tour of Spain), a professional CYCLING stage race held before the other major tours of Italy and France.

Founded in 1935, it was abandoned during the Spanish Civil War and the Second World War, and again, for lack of support, in 1950-4. Its prestige was enhanced when, in the early 1960s, ALTIG, ANQUETIL, and POULIDOR were successive winners. Shorter than its model, the TOUR DE FRANCE, the race covers approximately 1,900 miles (3,060 km.) in 16–18 stages.

VUILLIER, Col. JEAN-JOSEPH (d. 1931), was the French bloodstock horse-breeding expert (see HORSE RACING) and author of *Les Croisments Rationnels,* in which he propounded a system of thoroughbred dosages based on Galton's Law of Ancestral Contribution.

VUKAS, BERNARD, Association footballer for Hajduk Split, and Yugoslavia for whom he played in both the 1950 and 1954 world championship tournaments. An exciting outside left or inside forward, he scored three goals for the Rest of Europe XI against the Britain XI in Belfast in 1955.

VUKOVICH, BILL (1918-55), American MOTOR RACING driver who won the 1953 and 1954 INDIANAPOLIS 500 races. He was leading the 1952 race with 20 miles to go when his steering pin broke and he hit a wall. He won the 1946 and 1947 West Coast midget racing car titles and in 1950 the American Automobile Club national midget car championship. He was killed in a racing accident.

W

WAGNER, JOHN PETER (Honus) (1874-1955), American BASEBALL player with the Louisville and Pittsburgh teams of the NATIONAL LEAGUE for 21 seasons, 1897-1917. Although he usually played shortstop and was second to none at that position, he could play almost any position, and was one of those rare players who did everything well. In 1911 he set a National League record by winning his eighth league batting championship. He was also one of the few who have made 3,000 or more hits, and he led his league five times in stolen bases.

WAGSTAFF, HAROLD (1891-1939), English RUGBY LEAGUE player. 'The prince of centres', his distinctions included playing in senior football at the age of 15, playing in a Test match against Australia at 17, and captaining HUDDERSFIELD at 20. He led the England team in Australia in 1914, and his Test career extended to 1922. In an historic match at Sydney, when England were reduced by injuries to 11 men for most of the second half, he led them to victory. Wagstaff invented the 'standing pass' manoeuvre, when the stand-off half would pass the ball to him after a scrum and then run behind him for the return pass — a move that often left defenders on the wrong foot.

WAITE, JOHN HENRY BICKFORD (1930-), cricketer for South Africa, Eastern Province, and Transvaal. One of the finest wicket-keeper-batsmen the game has seen, he made 141 dismissals in 50 Tests, and hit four centuries. His 26 dismissals in the 1961-2 series against New Zealand broke a record held jointly by himself and three others.

WAKEFIELD, WILLIAM WAVELL (later Lord Wakefield of Kendal) (1898-), RUGBY UNION wing forward for Leicester, HARLEQUINS, Royal Air Force, Cambridge University, and England, and administrator for the Rugby Football Union. One of the first forwards gifted with the speed and handling ability of a back, Wakefield was the outstanding Rugby player of the 1920s. He was captain at school (Sedbergh), Services, University, club, county (Middlesex), and international level, and his 31 England caps remained a record for over 40 years.

WAKEFIELD TRINITY RUGBY LEAGUE CLUB, Yorkshire, founded in 1873, and a founder member of the Northern Union. Its ground at Belle Vue had an attendance of 37,906 for the Challenge Cup semi-final between HUDDERSFIELD and LEEDS on 21 March 1936. Despite having many prominent players during the first 50 years of RUGBY LEAGUE, Wakefield won the Challenge Cup only once (1908-9), and the League championship not at all. Between 1959 and 1968, however, they won the Cup three times and the League championship twice.

COLOURS: White with red and blue hoops.

WAKES, see FOLK SPORTS.

WALASIEWICZ, STANISLAWA, see WALSH, S.

WALCOTT, CLYDE LEOPOLD, O.B.E. (1926-), cricketer for West Indies, Barbados, and Guyana. A batsman of immense power, he played 44 times for West Indies, and scored 11 centuries — 5 of them against Australia in 1955, when on two occasions he hit a century in each innings. A year earlier he had made three centuries against England, the highest being 220. When 20 he had partnered WORRELL in a world record stand of 574 (unfinished) for Barbados against Trinidad. For much of his career he kept wicket, and claimed 65 dismissals in Test matches.

WALCOTT, JOE (1872-1935), West Indian boxer from Barbados who won the world welterweight title in 1901 and is considered by some to be the greatest of all champions at this weight. (He is not to be confused with 'Jersey Joe' Walcott who won the heavyweight title in 1951.) Walcott, though only 5 ft. 1½ in. (1·56 m.) tall, was such a powerful hitter that he was prepared to fight middleweights and even heavyweights. He found he could not remain strong enough when he dropped to lightweight and was beaten by Lavigne. But in 1900 Walcott, conceding 40 lb. (18 kg.), knocked out the heavyweight Choynski who had fought a 20-rounds draw with JEFFRIES and knocked out an inexperienced JACK JOHNSON.

WALES, EDWARD, Prince of, later King

Edward VII (1841-1910), as a royal patron of the English Turf, met with outstanding success. He won the DERBY and ST. LEGER, ECLIPSE STAKES, and ASCOT GOLD CUP with PERSIMMON; and the triple crown (see HORSE RACING) and ECLIPSE STAKES with DIAMOND JUBILEE in 1900, when he headed the list of leading owners and breeders, and also won the GRAND NATIONAL with Ambush II. He again won the Derby and the TWO THOUSAND GUINEAS in 1909 with Minoru.

WALKER, IAN (1951-), water skier for Britain, who in September 1970 set a national record in the slalom event in the European championships at Canzo, northern Italy, by negotiating 33 buoys in five successful passes through the course, plus 3 buoys with a 75-ft. (22·86 m.) rope shortened by 32 ft. (9·75 m.). He set a British national and European record in the jumping events by covering a distance of 156 ft. 1½ in. (47·58 m.).

WALKER, MICKEY (1901-), American boxer who won the world welterweight and middleweight titles, went 15 rounds for the light-heavyweight title, and, in 1931, his twelfth year in the ring, drew over 15 rounds with Sharkey who won the heavyweight championship the following year. Walker, who went 15 hard rounds with the remorseless GREB for the middleweight title in 1925, beat Flowers, Greb's conqueror, the following year for the world championship.

WALKER, NORMAN STEWART (1901-), lawn BOWLS player with the longest and most outstanding record of any in South Africa. Apart from winning the national singles four times he has been the title-winning fours skip on four occasions. Born in Dundee, Scotland, Walker represented South Africa in three COMMONWEALTH GAMES series, at Sydney, Auckland, and Cardiff, winning one gold and two silver medals. He is one of only two men bowling outside the British Isles to have won the Vitalite world drawing-to-the-jack competition.

WALKER, WILLIAM H. (1898-1964), Association footballer for ASTON VILLA, and England for whom he made 18 appearances in international matches from 1921 to 1927. He was a centre forward with Aston Villa when they won the F.A. Cup in 1920 but played his best games for club and country at inside left, where his deft ball control and quick anticipation gave him the opportunity to make goals as well as to score them. When he retired as a player after making more than 500 first-team appearances for Aston Villa between 1919 and 1934, he became manager of Sheffield Wednesday and in 1935 saw the club win the F.A. Cup. Subsequently, after a brief spell managing Chelmsford, he became manager of Nottingham Forest in March 1939 and held the position for 21 years during which time Forest also won the F.A. Cup (1959).

WALKER CUP, GOLF competition played in alternate years between teams of men amateurs from the U.S.A. and Great Britain and Ireland.

WALKING, see RACE WALKING.

WALLABIES, popular term by which the representative RUGBY UNION teams of Australia are known. The term is derived (by analogy with the SPRINGBOKS of South Africa) from the animal found extensively in Australia.

WALSH, STELLA (1911-), Polish-born sprinter, naturalized in the U.S.A. Better known in athletics by her adopted name of Walsh, Miss Walasiewicz (now Mrs. Olson) was a world-class performer for a longer period than perhaps any other sprinter of the century. Her tally of medals included: gold medals for 60, 100, and 200 metres at the 1930 Women's World Games; a gold medal in the 1932 Olympic 100 metres; a gold medal in the 60 metres, and silver medals in the 100 and 200 metres at the 1934 Women's World Games; a silver medal in the 1936 Olympic 100 metres; and, in the 1938 EUROPEAN CHAMPIONSHIPS, gold medals in the 100 and 200 metres and a silver medal in the LONG JUMP. Her world records, gained between 1929 and 1938, included 60 metres in 7·3 sec., 100 yards in 10·8 sec., 100 metres in 11·6 sec., 200 metres in 23·6 sec., 220 yards in 24·3 sec., and 19 ft. 9¾ in. (6·04 m.) for the long jump.

WALTER, FRITZ (1920-), Association footballer for Kaiserslautern, and West Germany, whom he captained when they won the 1954 world championship in Switzerland. A strongly-built inside left, then aged 33, he was again in the German team for the 1958 world championship matches in Sweden.

WALTERS, KEVIN DOUGLAS (1945-), cricketer for Australia and New South Wales. After entering first-class CRICKET with a succession of large scores, he made centuries in each of his first two Tests against England in 1965-6. Three years later, after Army service, he made four centuries in a series against West Indies, including 242 and 103 in the last

Test. He found runs hard to come by on two tours of England, but restored his reputation in 1973 by scoring two further Test centuries against West Indies. A batsman practical in style, he is also a useful medium-paced bowler.

WALTHAM ABBEY GUN CLUB, the oldest clay pigeon SHOOTING club in Great Britain, formed in 1914. The club grounds became the hub of the sport's national development, patronized by most leading shooters between the wars and used for technical experiments on cartridges, targets, and traps.

WALTON, WILLIAM T. (1952-   ), American BASKETBALL player who stands 6 ft. 11 in. (2·11 m.) tall. He was a member of the team from the University of California at Los Angeles (see U.C.L.A. BRUINS) that won the NATIONAL COLLEGIATE ATHLETIC ASSOCIATION championship in 1972 and 1973.

WANDERERS STADIUM, CRICKET ground in Johannesburg, was opened in 1954. It replaced the original ground, which was in the heart of the city. Owned by The Wanderers, a large amateur sports club, it became the first South African cricket ground to be filled to capacity when 36,000 people attended the Test match against Australia on Boxing Day 1957.

WAR ADMIRAL (1934), American racehorse by MAN O' WAR, who won the KENTUCKY DERBY, BELMONT STAKES, PREAKNESS STAKES, JOCKEY CLUB GOLD CUP, and Saratoga Cup, later becoming the maternal grandsire of NEVER SAY DIE. War Admiral was bred and owned by Riddle, trained by Conway, and ridden by Kurtsinger.

WARATAHS, term, derived from the waratah flower which grows in Australia, used to designate the RUGBY UNION teams of the Australian state of New South Wales, and in particular the side which toured the British Isles and France in 1927-8 playing a full list of 31 fixtures including 5 international matches.

WARD, JOHN MONTGOMERY (1860-1925), American BASEBALL player, team manager, and union leader who turned professional in 1887. He developed into a first-class pitcher and helped the Providence NATIONAL LEAGUE club to win the championship in 1879 by winning 44 games and losing only 18, a record that made him the league's leading pitcher that season. After an arm injury forced him to quit pitching he became a star shortstop. Later he managed and played for the Brooklyn and New York National League

teams, and at the same time completed studies for a law degree, eventually becoming a successful attorney. In 1885 the players of the New York team elected him president of their chapter of the Brotherhood of Professional Base Ball Players. He soon became chief spokesman for the Brotherhood and its leader in the great player revolt of 1890.

WARD, RODGER (1921-   ), American MOTOR RACING driver who won the INDIANAPOLIS 500 in 1959, on his ninth attempt, and in 1962. He was the United States Auto Club national champion in 1959, and won 26 U.S.A.C. national championship races, almost half on dirt tracks, before his retirement in 1966.

WARMERDAM, CORNELIUS A. (1915-   ), pole vaulter for the U.S.A. Warmerdam enjoyed the longest ascendancy of any specialist in this event. Using a bamboo pole, he raised the world record from 15 ft. (4·57 m.) in 1940 to 15 ft. 7¾ in. (4·77 m.) in 1942. This performance was never bettered with a bamboo pole; in 1957 it was improved largely because of the more effective metal pole. Warmerdam was immensely successful in indoor competition where he had a best performance in 1943 of 15 ft. 8½ in. (4·79 m.). The war prevented him from gaining the Olympic honours which were his undoubted right.

WARNER, GLENN SCOBEY (Pop) (1871-1954), American college FOOTBALL coach, who played football at Cornell University, and later coached at the University of Georgia (1895-6), Cornell (1897-8, 1904-6), the Carlisle (Pennsylvania) Indian School (1899-1903, 1907-14), Pittsburgh (1915-23), Stanford (1924-32), and Temple (Philadelphia) (1933-8). His most famous teams were the Carlisle Indians of 1911-12, featuring THORPE, and the 1916 Pittsburgh National Champions. He was responsible for originating many plays, techniques, equipment, and formations, especially the single-wing and the double-wing.

WARNER, Sir PELHAM FRANCIS (Plum) (1873-1963), cricketer for England, Oxford University, and Middlesex. In a lifetime devoted to CRICKET he took teams to many parts of the world, leading England in Australia twice (he achieved a famous victory in the 1903-4 series but had to withdraw through ill health in 1911-12), leading his county to the championship in 1920 — his final year in first-class cricket — and serving as a Test selector, president of M.C.C. (1950-1), and president of Middlesex. He wrote a number of books on cricket and was a newspaper correspondent for many years. In 1921 he founded *The Cricketer* magazine. He was knighted in 1937 for his services to the game and the stand built at LORD'S in 1958 was named after him.

WARRINGTON, MICHAEL (1938-), LACROSSE player for England, North of England, Lancashire, and London University. An outstanding midfield player, with a high degree of technical skill, he was particularly successful in the U.S.A., when, as a member of the England team, he gained possession of the ball from the face-off on numerous occasions. His extensive knowledge of lacrosse tactics and his ability to instruct led to his appointment as national coach.

WARRINGTON RUGBY LEAGUE CLUB, Lancashire, founded in 1873, was a founder member of the Northern Union. An attendance of 35,000 was recorded at its ground at Wilderspool for the WIGAN *v.* Leigh Lancashire Cup final on 29 October 1949. Warrington were League champions in 1947-8, 1953-4, and 1954-5, and Cup winners in 1904-5, 1906-7, 1949-50, and 1953-4. Nineteen Warrington players have toured Australia.
COLOURS: White with primrose and blue hoops.

WASHBROOK, CYRIL (1914-), cricketer for England and Lancashire. The Second World War delayed his establishment as a Test player, but in 1946 he became associated with HUTTON in one of the finest opening partnerships in history: they averaged 56 in 50 stands for England, one of which was 359 against South Africa in 1948-9. Washbrook was usually careful in method, though his hooking and cutting could be devastating. He was a superb fieldsman at cover point. In later years he served as an England selector, and in 1956 returned to the England team to make a match-winning 98 against Australia.

WASHINGTON INTERNATIONAL STAKES, run at LAUREL PARK, Washington, D.C., over 1½ miles (2,400 m.) in November. Founded in 1952, it has become the most important international horse race in the U.S.A. Notable winners include MATCH III, KELSO, SIR IVOR, and DAHLIA.

WASHINGTON REDSKINS, American professional FOOTBALL team, joined the NATIONAL FOOTBALL LEAGUE in 1932 as the Boston Redskins but shifted to Washington in 1937, the same year that BAUGH joined them as passer. In Baugh's 16 years at Washington he led the League in passing five times, and

the team won League titles in 1937 and 1942. The running back Battles and the tackle Edwards were other Washington stars in the period. Marshall, owner of the Redskins throughout most of their history, moved the team to Washington, introduced the League play-off system, liberalized the forward-passing rules, and brought marching bands and drum majors to professional football. LOMBARDI left the GREEN BAY PACKERS to coach Washington in 1969. After Lombardi's death in 1970, Allen left the LOS ANGELES RAMS for the Redskins in 1971. He traded away 'draft' choices for experienced players and led his nicknamed 'Over the Hill Gang' to the National Division title in 1972, although they lost to the MIAMI DOLPHINS in the Super Bowl.
COLOURS: Burgundy and gold.

WASHINGTON SENATORS, American professional BASEBALL team, founding members of the AMERICAN LEAGUE in 1901. With rare exception, the Senators remained near the bottom of the league standings, thus prompting the saying, 'First in war, first in peace, and last in the American League.' With Harris as manager, Washington won its only WORLD SERIES in 1924. Its greatest player, the pitcher WALTER JOHNSON, won 414 games between 1907 and 1927, and was 12 times a 20-game winner (including 10 straight: 1910-19). Clark Griffith managed the Senators from 1915 to 1920 and then owned them until 1955. His son Calvin Griffith moved the team to Minnesota in 1961 when the league expanded to ten teams. (See MINNESOTA TWINS.) Washington continued in the league under new ownership as an expansion team, with cast-off personnel. Even the efforts of the great TED WILLIAMS as manager could not improve the team, and in 1972, in the face of dwindling attendance, the franchise was shifted to the TEXAS RANGERS.

WASSAILS, see FOLK SPORTS.

WASSERKUPPE, GLIDING centre, lat. 51° 00' N, long. 10° 01' E, near Poppenhausen in the Rhön mountains, West Germany, was the first great centre of gliding in the world. Many national and world records and pioneer pilots have been associated with this site, now a training school for new pilots.

WATANABE, OSAMU (*fl.* 1962-4), Japanese featherweight wrestler who was unbeaten in his 186 fights. The climax of his career was a gold medal at the 1964 Olympics. He also won world titles in freestyle in 1962 and 1963, and was famous for his ferocious style.

WATER POLO, as the name suggests, is a ball game played in the water. In the late nineteenth century, when the game was being pioneered in Britain, it was also called 'football-in-the-water', and the basic aim, as in Association FOOTBALL, is for the attacking side to get the ball into the net of the defending side, usually after a series of passing movements.

Water polo is one of the events in the programmes of most major swimming competitions, such as the world championships, OLYMPIC GAMES, European championships, and PAN-AMERICAN GAMES. The only important event in which there is no water polo is the British COMMONWEALTH GAMES.

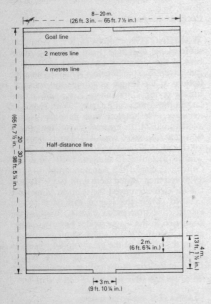

WATER POLO FIELD OF PLAY
The minimum distance from the goal line to the back of the goal net (not shown in diagram) is 30 cm. (11¾ in.). The minimum depth of water is 1 m. (3 ft. 3 in.).

The game takes place in a pool with water a minimum of 1 m. (3 ft. 3½ in.) deep, although for the Olympic, world. and international tournaments the water must be nowhere less than 1·8 m. (5 ft. 11 in.). The distance between the goal lines must not exceed 30 m. (98 ft. 5¼ in.) nor be less than 20 m. (65 ft. 7½ in.). The width must not exceed 20 m. (65 ft. 7½ in.) nor be less than 8 m. (26 ft. 3 in.). However, for international and major national events, the maximum playing area is used. For women's matches — and there is no international water polo for women — the maximum measurements are 25 m. by 17 m. (82 ft. 0¼ in. × 55 ft. 9¼ in.).

Distinctive marks are provided on both sides of the field of play to denote the goal line, 2 m. (6 ft. 6¾ in.) and 4 m. (13 ft 1½ in.) from that line, and the half distance (or centre) line. The boundary of the field of play, at both ends, behind the goal line is 0·30 m. (11¾ in.).

The goal posts and crossbar are of wood or metal or synthetic (plastic), with rectangular sections of 0·075 m. (3 in.) square with the goal line and painted white. The goal posts must be fixed rigid and perpendicular and be equidistant from the sides and at least 0·30 m. (11¾ in.) in front of the ends of the field of play or of any obstruction.

The inner sides of the goal posts are 3 m. (9 ft. 10¼ in.) apart. The underside of the crossbar is 0·90 m. (2 ft. 11½ in.) above the surface of the water when the water is 1·50 m. (4 ft. 11 in.) or more deep, and 2·40 m. (7 ft. 10¼ in.) from the bottom of the bath when the depth of the water is less than 1·50 metres.

Limp nets are attached to the goal fixtures to enclose the entire goal space, securely fastened to the goal posts and crossbar and allowing not less than 0·30 m. (11¾ in.) clear space behind the goal line everywhere within the goal area. There may be no standing or resting place for the goalkeeper in the area of the goal except the floor of the bath.

The ball must be round and fully inflated, and with an air chamber with a self-closing valve. The circumference must not be less than 0·68 m. (2 ft. 2¾ in.) nor more than 0·71 m. (2 ft. 4 in.). The ball must be waterproof without external strappings and without a covering of grease or similar substance. Its weight must be not less than 400 g. (l4 oz.) nor more than 450 g. (15 oz.).

A team consists of seven players, one of whom must be the goalkeeper, and four reserves, who may be used as substitutes. Each side wears caps, one set dark blue and one white, which are numbered on both sides and tied with tapes under the chin. The blue caps have white numbers, the white caps blue. The goalkeepers, who wear cap No. 1, both have red caps, one with white numbers, the other with blue. The other caps are numbered from 2 to 11. If one of the permitted substitutes is a goalkeeper, he must wear the goalkeeper's red cap.

Before a match, the players must discard all articles, such as rings, likely to cause injury. They may not have grease, oil, or any similar composition on their bodies and they must wear trunks with separate drawers or slips underneath. The captains must be playing members and are responsible for the good conduct and discipline of their teams. Before the start of a game, the captains, in the presence of the referee, must toss a coin for choice of colours or ends.

A game consists of four quarters of five minutes each, actual play. The teams change ends before the start of each new quarter and there are intervals of two minutes between each quarter. Time counts from the referee's starting signal and at all signals for stoppages the recording watch is stopped until play is resumed.

If a game in which a definite result is required — i.e. one not being decided on a tournament or league basis — ends at full time with the scores level, extra time is played after a five-minute interval. The extra play is two halves of three minutes each with an interval of one minute for changing ends. This system of extra time is continued until a decision has been reached.

The officials are: a referee, two timekeepers, two secretaries, and two goal judges, with specified duties and powers. However for less important matches and with careful organization and competent officials, it is possible for the timekeepers also to carry out the tasks done by the secretaries.

The referee is in absolute control of the game. His authority over the players is effective during the whole of the time that he and they are within the precincts of the bath. He carries a shrill whistle, with which to start and re-start the game and to declare goals, goal throws, corner throws (whether signalled by the goal judges or not), and infringements of the rules. All decisions of the referee on questions of fact are final and his interpretation of the rules must be obeyed during the game.

The referee may refrain from declaring a foul if, in his opinion, such declaration would be an advantage to the offender's team. For example, to declare a foul in favour of a player who is in possession of the ball and making progress towards his opponent's goal, or whose team is in possession of the ball, would not be to the advantage of this player. This ruling is similar to the advantage rule in football and other land-based team games. The referee may alter his decision providing he does so before the ball is again in play. He also has power to order any player from the water for the whole of the game for the contravention of certain rules. Should a player refuse to leave the water when so ordered, the game must be stopped. The referee carries a stick 0·7 m. (2 ft. 3½ in.) long, with a white flag at one end and a blue one on the other.

The timekeepers must have water polo stopwatches — i.e. that can be started and stopped and re-started without reverting to zero — and a shrill whistle. Their duties are (a) to record on the watch the exact amount of actual play — the watch is stopped as soon as an infringement occurs and is not re-started until the ball is again in play — and also the intervals during the four quarters of the game, (b) to record the respective period of exclusion of any player or players who may be ordered from the water, and (c) to record the periods of continuous possession of the ball by each team. The timekeepers must be near the referee, and one must signal by whistle the end of each quarter, independently of the referee. His signal takes immediate effect, except if at this precise moment the referee awards a penalty throw, or the timekeeper's signal comes before a penalty throw has been taken. In these cases, the shot at goal is allowed before the ball is considered dead.

The secretaries must (a) maintain a record of all players, the score, all major fouls (time, colour, and cap number), and signal the award of a third personal fault to any player by a signal with a red flag, (b) control the periods of exclusion of players and signal permission for re-entry upon the expiration of their periods of exclusion by raising the flag corresponding with the colour of the player's cap, (c) signal any improper entry, which signal stops play immediately.

The goal judges take up positions on the side of the bath opposite the referee directly level with the goal lines and stay there for the whole of the game. They signal with a white flag for a goal throw (i.e. when the entire ball has passed over the goal line, outside the goal itself, having last been touched by one of the attacking team) and with a red flag (when the last player to touch the ball was a defender). The goal judges signal with both flags when a goal is scored (i.e. when the entire ball has passed over the goal line between the goal posts). They are also responsible to the referee for keeping the correct score of each team at their respective ends. At the start, or re-start, when the players are lined up along the goal line, the goal judge shows the red flag to let the referee know that the players are correctly positioned. But it is the referee's whistle to start or re-start the game that takes immediate effect.

At the beginning of each quarter of play, the players take up positions on their respective goal lines, about 1 m. (3 ft.) apart and at least 1 m. from either goal post. Not more than two players may take positions between the goal posts.

As soon as the referee is sure the teams are in position, he gives a starting signal by whistle and immediately releases or throws the ball into the centre of the field of play. In important events, like the Olympic Games, the ball is held in a cage at the bottom of the pool and released accurately into the centre of the bath. In other events it is usual for the referee to throw the ball in from the centre of the bath-side.

After a goal has been scored, and the ball must pass fully over the goal line, the players take up positions anywhere within their respective halves and a player, from the team that did not score, re-starts the game on a whistle signal from the referee, by passing the ball from the centre line to another member of his team who must be behind the half-distance line when he receives it.

A goal may be scored by any part of the body, except the clenched fist, provided that at the start or re-start of the game the ball has been played by two or more players of either side. Any attempt by the goalkeeper to stop the ball before it has been played in this way does not constitute 'playing', and should the ball go over the goal line, hit the goal post or goalkeeper, the goalkeeper is given a goal throw. A player may also score a goal by dribbling the ball between the posts.

As in Association football, the goalkeeper has certain privileges not accorded to other members of the team, but also certain limitations. Within the 4-metre area, the goalkeeper may stand and walk, strike the ball with a clenched fist, jump from the floor of the bath and touch the ball with both hands at the same time. He may not, however, go or touch or throw the ball beyond the half-way line. He may not hold on to any bar, rail, or trough at the end of the bath. A goalkeeper who has been replaced by a substitute goalkeeper may return to the game in another position.

If a goalkeeper, in taking a free throw or a goal throw, releases the ball, regains it before any other player has touched it, and then allows the ball to pass through his own goal, a corner throw is awarded. If another player touches it and then the goalkeeper allows the ball to pass through his goal, a goal is awarded. Should a goalkeeper retire from a game through illness or injury, he may be replaced by another member of the team, who must then wear the goalkeeper's cap, and the limitations and privileges of a goalkeeper will apply to him.

The penalty for an ordinary foul is a free throw to the opposing team. Ordinary fouls include: (a) moving beyond the goal line at the start or re-start, before the referee's signal; (b) holding on to or pushing off from the goal posts, fixtures, sides of the pool, etc. during play; (c) taking an active part in the game when standing on the floor of the pool, walking when play is in progress, jumping from the floor of the bath to play the ball or tackle an opponent; (d) taking or holding the ball under water when tackled, striking the ball with clenched fist (goalkeepers excepted), splashing in the face of an opponent; (e) deliberately impeding or preventing the free limb movement of an opponent unless he is holding the ball (holding means lifting, carrying, or touching the ball, but dribbling the ball is not considered to be holding); (f) touching the ball with both hands at the same time (goalkeepers excepted); pushing or pushing off from an opponent, wasting time in order to hold up the normal progress of the game.

The most difficult ordinary fouls for a referee to judge fairly are those in category (e). Experienced players have developed the art of holding the ball and then releasing it, just in time for the referee to catch an opponent in the process of a tackle which, when it was begun, was legal but by the time it was completed, was not.

A free throw awarded for an ordinary foul committed within the 2-metre area must be taken from the 2-metre line opposite the point at which the foul occurred. Other than this, free throws are taken from the point where the foul occurred. If a goalkeeper is awarded a free throw he must take it himself and the throw is subject to the limitations and privileges of a goalkeeper. The throw must be made to enable other players to see the ball leaving the hand of the thrower, who may dribble the ball before passing. After a free throw (corner throw or neutral throw) at least two players (excluding goalkeepers) must play or touch the ball before a goal can be scored. A free throw taken improperly must be retaken.

If the game is stopped because of illness, accident, or other unforeseen reason or when one or more players of each team commit a foul at the same moment, the referee takes the ball and throws it into the water as near as possible to the spot where the incident took place so that players of both teams have an equal opportunity to reach it after it has touched the water. If, after throwing the ball in, the referee thinks it has fallen to the advantage of one team, he makes the throw again.

It is from major fouls that the result of a game can be most materially decided, for penalties are heavier than for ordinary fouls. Major fouls include: (a) holding, sinking, or pulling back an opponent not holding the ball; (b) kicking or striking an opponent or making excessive movements with that intent; (c) the same player persisting in an ordinary foul; (d) refusing to obey the referee: the offending player is ordered from the water for the rest of the game (though he may be replaced by a substitute after one minute of actual play or when a goal has been scored, whichever period is the shorter); (e) causing an act of brutality: a free throw must be awarded to the opposing team and the offending player ordered out for the rest of the game; but, in this case, he may not be replaced, and his team will have to play one man short; (f) being guilty of misconduct (violence, bad language, persistent fouling); (g) interfering with the taking of a free throw, penalty throw, corner throw, or goal throw.

Except as otherwise expressly provided (as in (d) and (e) above) and when a penalty throw is awarded, the punishment for a major foul is that the offending player must be ordered from the water for one minute or until a goal has been scored, whichever is the shorter, and a free throw awarded to a player of the opposing team.

A penalty throw, which is a direct shot at goal, is the ultimate punishment. The player taking the penalty must wait for the referee's signal and, as soon as the whistle is blown, must immediately and directly throw the ball at the goal. If a player fails to throw at once, a free throw is awarded to his nearest opponent.

Penalty throws are awarded for a number of major fouls on an attacking player within 4 m. (13 ft. 1 in.) of the defender's goal line. The offending player is not ordered from the water unless the offence is so serious as to justify his being ordered out for the duration of the game.

A penalty throw may be taken by any member of the team, except the goalkeeper, and may be taken from any point on the opponent's 4-metre line. If the ball rebounds from the goal posts or crossbar, it remains in play and a goal may be scored immediately from a rebound. All the players, except the defending goalkeeper, must leave the 4-metre area until the throw is taken and no player may be within 2 metres of the player taking the throw.

The outline and basic rules set out above are those of the Fédération Internationale de Natation Amateur (F.I.N.A.). They are usually observed for all levels of water polo played by the member countries of F.I.N.A. However, national federations may give exemptions to certain rules for specific purposes; these usually concern the playing area (in order to allow matches to be played in older and smaller baths) or the time of actual play.

Competitions, as in Association football, are organized on a league basis, each team playing all others; as a knock-out cup event; or as a combination of both.

For major competitions, like the Olympic Games and European championships, the teams taking part in the competition proper are restricted to 12 or 16. These consist of the top teams in the previous Games or championships plus, so far as the Olympics are concerned, a number of teams chosen on a continental basis, usually as a result of eliminating tournaments or specific continental competitions.

In the Olympic Games there have been various systems for deciding the preliminary rounds, but generally these are organized on a pool basis with each team in a pool playing all others and the top two teams moving forward to the semi-final pools, while the bottom teams make up losers pools. This procedure is repeated on the results of the semi-finals. Sometimes the result of the first meeting of two teams is carried forward into subsequent pools in which they are together. However at the 1973 world championships each of the four teams in the final pool played all others whether or not they had met earlier in the tournament.

In national and domestic events, there are usually a number of divisions and the bigger clubs enter two or more teams who compete in the different divisions. They, too, take part in league competitions and in knock-out championships. There are also a number of special events for the top national teams and also for the champion teams from each country, and events for age-level teams, of which the world scheme is for teams under 16, 18, and 20.

Handbook of the Fédération Internationale de Natation Amateur, 1972-6.

Britain were the originators of the game. As far back as 1870, or earlier, a game in the water, with a ball, was being played. And as it bore some relationship to soccer, it became known as 'football-in-the-water'. But it was not until 1885, after much thoughtful pioneering work and pressure from Scotland and the Midlands, that the governing body for the sport (the Swimming Association of Great Britain, later to become the Amateur Swimming Association) recognized the game.

The early rules were primitive and varied from area to area. There were no goal posts and a goal was called a 'touch-down' (shades of RUGBY football), since the swimmer could score by placing the ball with both hands anywhere along the full width of the bath end or pontoon.

The goalkeepers — there might be two or more in the same team — took their positions outside the water, ready to jump on anyone who looked likely to achieve a touch-down. Much of the water polo was then played in open water, in harbours and so on, and play could be rough and tough. One game in Portsmouth harbour nearly resulted in a fatal accident. An attacker was pushed under a pontoon during a desperate scrimmage and was nearly insensible by the time he was found and rescued.

Slowly the game took shape. William Wilson of Scotland, who drew up a local set of rules in 1877 and suggested goal posts (1879) — though these stood out of the water at each end of the field of play — played an important part in its development. Eventually a common set of rules was agreed for the British game and these became the basis for the international rules of the future.

Represented by the Manchester Osborne club, Britain won the first water polo gold medals at the 1900 Olympic Games in Paris. There were no British entries at the 1904 Olympics in St. Louis, the water polo tournament being between club teams from the U.S.A. — the first and only time that teams other than national sides were allowed to take part in the Olympic water polo championship.

Britain were successful again in 1908, 1912, and 1920, and it was not until 1924 in Paris that they had to bow to Hungary (6–7) in the first round, after three periods of extra time. On this occasion, which was a straight knock-out event, the Hungarians, in their turn, were beaten by Belgium, who lost to France, the ultimate gold medallists.

Hungary were second to Germany in 1928 and then went on to win five of the next seven Olympic competitions (1932, 1936, 1952, 1956, and 1964), coming second in 1948 and third in 1960, when Italy were winners. Hungary were third again in 1968, when Yugoslavia and Russia finished ahead of them, and second, behind the U.S.S.R. and ahead of the U.S.A., in 1972. But the Magyars were top again at the first world championships in Belgrade, when the silver and bronze medallists were the U.S.S.R. and Yugoslavia.

The first water polo championship in the world, the Amateur Swimming Association's club championship, was instituted in 1888. The entries were small at the start, because of the expense and difficulty of travelling. The Midlands club, Burton, one of the first to adopt this new ball game (in 1877), won three of the first four championships (1888, 1889, 1891) and were beaten finalists in 1890.

The reign of the Manchester Osborne club — with players like Derbyshire, who was also an Olympic relay gold medallist in 1908 — began in 1894 and they were decisive winners through to 1901, except in 1900 when the entire club team were busy representing Britain, and winning the first Olympic water polo championships in Paris. Soon after this, the club was disbanded, the members moving

either to Wigan or Hyde Seal. These two clubs continued to dominate English water polo until the First World War. In the years between the two world wars, Plaistow United (Essex) had a long run of victories, winning 8 times in 11 years (1928-31 and 1935-8).

The first international water polo match was played between England and Scotland at the Kensington baths, London, on 28 July 1890. At this time there was no conformity of rules, and, since England were the hosts, the match was played under their rules which permitted 'ducking'. Despite this, the Scots, who concentrated on playing the ball and not the man, won easily, 4-0.

In the modern context of the postwar years, the development of water polo has been bedevilled by constant rule changes. For years it was a static game, the players not being allowed to move their positions during stoppages. The change, which permitted free movement, opened up the game, but also allowed opportunities for beating the referee, for playing the man instead of the ball.

Efforts to stop gamesmanship produced a system of penalty points, so that teams (or individuals) who persistently fouled — after three penalty points awarded against them — would have a penalty throw (a direct throw at goal) also awarded against them. But this rule did not last very long.

All these efforts to make a better game, have resulted only in the division of the water-polo-playing nations into two quite distinct groups. There are the big powers (Hungary, Russia, Yugoslavia, East Germany), for whom water polo has become a national sport and whose players, in their national teams, spend many hours training and competing. And there are the other nations, whose teams must be prepared largely on an amateur basis and who, generally, cannot compete with the full-time 'amateurs'.

P. Besford, *Encyclopaedia of Swimming* (1971); B. Rajki, *B. Rajki on Water Polo* (1958).
GOVERNING BODY (WORLD): Fédération Internationale de Natation Amateur, 555 North Washington Street, Naperville, Ill., U.S.A.

WATER SKIING is the act of planing on the surface of the water, in an upright position, by means of two flat boards, known as skis, which are attached to the feet. The skier is towed by a rope attached to the rear portion or transom of a power boat which is capable of speeds in excess of 15 m.p.h. (24 km./h.). The water skier holds a handle at the end of the tow rope, assuming a slight backward lean so that his body provides the necessary resistance to the speed by which the planing position is achieved. Providing the water is comparatively calm, planing or skiing is a simple movement. Since balance is all-important, the most critical and difficult operation is the start, of which there are four main types: the beach start, the dock start, the deep water start, and the scooter start.

POSITIONS FOR THE START

Beach start — Dock start — Deep-water start — Planing

A fourth method, the scooter start, is not shown. The figure at the extreme right is in the position assumed after the start is made.

In a *beach start* the skier sits in the water holding the tow-bar, with the skis 6 in. (152 mm.) apart, tips turned slightly inwards and in line with the stern of the boat. From this position he leans forward in a crouch as the skis point to the surface of the water — the boat accelerates smoothly and the skis rise to the surface against the pressure of water. The *dock start* is a short cut to the planing position whereby the skier sits on the dock or pontoon and, with the acceleration of the boat, is launched on to the surface of the water. The *deep-water start* is an elaboration of the beach start and is achieved from exactly the same basic position of the body and skis. It is invaluable when a skier wishes to restart a run after a fall. The *scooter start* is similar to the dock start in as much as it is a method of dry launching. It is used by mono-skiers who, equipped with one ski, step from the shore on to the water with a 'scooting' action as the boat accelerates.

Turning is an essential part of skiing technique. From a line directly behind the boat a skier is able to make simple turns by crossing outside and back into the wake made by the boat. In the initial stages a turn is made simply by pointing the whole body in the required direction.

Wake-jumping is a progressive exercise in which the skier learns to adapt to variations of speed, wave, and wake. A jump is made from a flexed position approaching the wake, knees are bent and immediately straightened in a springing action as the centre of gravity of the skis passes the crest of the wake. On landing, the skis are kept parallel, with tips turned slightly upwards. Height is achieved by the skier's ability to recoil quickly; distance depends on speed.

Mono-skiing, the ability to plane on only one ski, is achieved by a series of progressive exercises on twin skis which include weight transference from one ski to the other, followed by the lifting of alternate skis about 6 in. (152 mm.) from, but parallel to, the water. Mono-skiing features in slalom skiing. Shedding or dropping a ski is accomplished by starting a run on twin skis with a very loose foot binding on one. At a suitable moment that ski is shed and the free foot is placed carefully behind the other on the remaining ski. The purpose-built mono-ski which is fitted with front and rear toe-bindings facilitates this operation and enables the skier to use both feet in controlling direction. Tight fast turns used in slalom may be accomplished by a body lean in the desired direction — at the same time the back foot presses down on the pivoting point while the front foot gives a compensatory lift to the ski. When mono-skiing in a straight line behind the boat, the weight distribution is approximately 60 per cent on the rear foot, 40 per cent on the front foot.

TRICK SKIING, or figure-skiing as it is sometimes called, forms part of the traditional group of water ski competition (slalom, jumps, and tricks). Competitors perform on specially designed skis and are allowed two 20-second passes within two sets of buoys, 175 m. (574 ft.) apart. Within this time and distance they are required to perform as many tricks as possible to the satisfaction of the judges. The judges' stand is located on shore approximately midway between the two buoys. Marks are awarded by the judges for each trick, ranging from 20 to 450 points — detailed values are listed in the World Water Ski Union's technical rule book.

Fundamental to trick skiing is the skier's ability to be equally competent both on twin skis and mono-ski. He must be able to perform a trick on flat water and on the wake. His basic movements will include the ability to side-slide, to ski backwards, to make 180° and 360° turns to either side, and to step over the tow rope. A single-handle tow line approximately 20 m. (65 ft.) long is normally used in trick skiing and boat speeds, which must be held constant from about 50 m. (165 ft.) before entering the course, are at the discretion of the skier.

The *two-ski slide* is performed when the skis are at right angles to the skier's line of advance. The knees are bent to release the pressure on the water and, with a bounce, the body can be turned sideways through 90°. In the turn the side edges of both skis are tilted towards the line of advance. It is important to be able to turn and side-slide both to the left and to the right since marks rate at 20 points to each side. The *foot-hold slide* requires the ability to mono-ski and is a complicated movement. One ski is shed and the tow handle (specially adapted with a toe-strap) is transferred from the hands to the toe of the free foot. Marks rate at 200 and 280 for the basic and the reverse movement respectively, if each is held for at least two seconds.

The *180° turn* is a front-to-back 180° turn followed by a back-to-front turn through the same angle and is, in essence, a development of the side-slide. If performed on flat water it rates up to 30 marks, with another 30 for the reverse movement. The marks are doubled if it is performed on a mono-ski. A turn performed in the air by bouncing from the wake rates 50 marks for each side when performed on twin skis and 80 when performed on one ski.

The *360° turn* is completed by the skier performing two 180° turns as one movement without pause. The tow-rope handle is transferred from one hand to the other during the turn. If performed from the flat water on twin skis, it rates up to 40 marks for the basic and 40 for the reverse movement. The same turn on one ski would rate up to 90 and 100 marks respectively. If the movement is performed in the air as a wake turn on twin skis the marks are increased to 110 for the basic and 100 for the reverse, while the same turn on a mono-ski rates 150 basic and 150 for the reverse movement. In performing the turn the skier pulls the tow-bar close into the left side of the body, adopting a slight crouch position. The right hand is then removed from the tow bar and immediately placed behind the back to grasp the tow rope again. Either side of the boat's wake may be used to bounce or spring into an air-borne position. The turn is performed in a clockwise direction, the skier retaining his hold on the rope. This turn may be made in the opposite direction, using the left hand. More difficult variations, such as starting the movement from a backward skiing position, earn the skier more points if performed on one ski.

Step-over turns may be performed on one or two skis—in the two-ski movement, one ski is lifted clear of the water and as it is carried over the tow rope, the body turns through 180°. If started from the back skiing position the turn rates up 70 marks to either side; from the front position it is considered more difficult and therefore rates up to 80 marks for each side. The one-ski turn is made by carrying the free leg over the tow rope as the body turns through 180°. A step-over turn from back to front can earn up to 110 marks, while a front-to-back turn can earn up to 130 marks. Further increases are possible if these turns are performed in the air from the wake.

JUMPING. To perform a jump, the skier is towed from the water up a ramp measuring approximately 7·3 m. (24 ft.) long by 3·9 m. (13 ft.) wide. The height of the ramp may be varied up to 1·8 m. (6 ft.) to accommodate both men's and women's events. In order to reduce friction and the risk of accidents, the ramp is coated with prepared wax and is kept continually wet with running water. Part of the lower end is under water to allow smooth entry by the skier. As the boat, travelling down the centre of the course, approaches the ramp, the skier holds the course steady from a position outside the wake furthest from the ramp. Then as the boat is about to pass the ramp the skier 'cuts in' to make his jump. The knees are straightened immediately the centre of gravity of the skis approaches the end of the ramp. During the flight through the air the body is held in an upright position and well balanced over the skis, which are parallel to one another and to the water. On landing, the skier presses down on the skis at the point of impact just before flexing his knees to absorb the shock.

In a jumping competition each competitor is allowed three good jumps and not more than two failures, the best jump to count. Distance is important but style also counts. Up to 2 points may be awarded for the approach to the ramp, up to 2 points for performance while on the ramp, up to 6 points for control, and up to 3 points for flight through the air. Landing, which is all-important, rates up to 4 points on the point of impact and finally up to 1½ points for the ride out to the course buoy. Distance is calculated by judges at three points. Alternatively, electronically operated cameras may be used. In both methods sitings are taken from a point at water level taking the distance from directly below the centre of the top edge of the ramp to the line where the heels of the skier have reached their maximum depression in the water. Boat speeds and tow-line lengths are governed by international rule which allows the competitor to decide his own boat speed up to a maximum of 57 km./h. (about 35 m.p.h.) for men and 45 km./h. (about 28 m.p.h.) for women. The length of the tow line with single handle for both men and women is 23 m. (75 ft. 6 in.).

SLALOM skiing is a timed run through two lines of buoys, moored in equidistant staggered formation, around which the skier has to turn. The two extremities of the course are marked by twin buoys in the form of gates which guide the boat as it proceeds at a predetermined speed along the centre of the course.

A slalom course is 259 m. (283 yds.) long and 23 m. (75 ft.) wide with gate and turning buoys moored on the outer limits at intervals

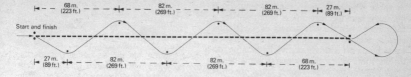

SLALOM COURSE
Heavy dotted line indicates the straight course of the boat; the fine line round the buoys is the skier's course. Twin buoys at either end are 2·50 m. (8 ft.) apart.

of 27, 82, 82, and 68 m. (89, 269, 269, and 223 ft.). The skier virages from side to side in order to turn round the outer side of each buoy. Boat speeds are 52 km./h. for women and 55 km./h. for men increasing at 2 km./h. intervals after each successful pass through the course to a maximum of 58 km./h.

In both men's and women's slalom events a competitor has two runs, for each of which he or she is allowed four passes through the course. In the first run, the skier starts with a tow-rope length of 23 m. (75 ft. 6 in.) which, when maximum speed of 58 km./h. is reached, is reduced to 16 m. (52 ft. 6 in.). In the second run, the tow-rope length starts at 14·25 m. (46 ft. 9 in.) and is reduced to 11·25 m. (36 ft. 11 in.). For the run to score, the competitor must have followed the boat through the course entry gate and have left through the end gate. A half-point is scored if the skier successfully rounds a buoy on the outside. A further half-point is scored when the skier returns to within the wake of the boat before passing the level of the next buoy. In all slalom events one judge rides in the boat and four others are located in the judging-tower to record the number of buoys scored. A timekeeper referee should also ride in the boat to check for correct speed through the course.

There is a grade for every standard of skiing at national and international level and the passing of a grade test entitles the skier to a badge and a grade registration card. To qualify a skier must pass the following tests:

Grade 7: Unassisted dock and deep-water starts on two skis; carry out a series of connected virages across wakes; return to centre of wake, lift left ski for three seconds, lift right ski for three seconds; return to jetty, release tow-rope and make controlled landing. The correct stance should be maintained throughout.
Grade 6: Dock start on one ski, or start on two skis and discard one; make a deep-water start on one ski; carry out a series of connected virages across wakes on mono-ski, maintaining correct stance; return to jetty and land in control; on figure skis, carry out virages and ski-lifts as for grade 7, and side-sliding on two skis, first to the left and then to the right.
Grade 5: (1) Mono-ski: Complete the slalom course

successfully, out and return, at free speed. (2) Figures (within 20 seconds): Two skis side-slide, one second to the left, one second to the right; two skis 180° front to back, back to front, and reverse; two skis 360° front to front and reverse; two skis wake 180° front to back and back to front; or any tricks to the value of 320 points. Alternatively, (3) Jumping: At regulation height complete two successful jumps (out of four attempts) at free speed.
Grade 4: (1) Mono-ski: Complete the slalom course successfully, out and return, on mono-ski at the following speeds: dauphine and junior, 40 km./h. (25 m.p.h.); veterans and women, 43 km./h. (about 27 m.p.h.); men, 46 km./h. (about 29 m.p.h.). (2) Figures: Achieve 750 points (without bonus) in two 20-second runs. Alternatively, (3) Jumping: At regulation heights achieve the following distance in three attempts: dauphine and junior, 40 ft. (12·3 m.); veterans and women, 46 ft. (14·0 m.); men, 60 ft. (18·3 m.).

To qualify for third, second, or first class gradings a skier need only pass in two out of the three events. To establish first or second class international grading, a skier must obtain his qualification on one occasion in a first class competition.

Grade 3 (national): (1) Slalom: women, 46 km./h. (about 29 m.p.h.); men, 49 km./h. (about 31 m.p.h.). (2) Figures: women, 1,000 points: men, 1,250 points. (3) Jumping: women, 55 ft. (16·8 m.); men, 75 ft. (22·9 m.).
Grade 2 (national and international): (1) Slalom: women, 52 km./h. (about 32 m.p.h.); men, 55 km./h. (about 34 m.p.h.). (2) Figures: women, 1,800 points; men, 2,300 points. (3) Jumping: women, 250 points; men, 345 points.
Grade 1 (national and international): (1) Slalom: women, 55 km./h. (about 34 m.p.h.); men, 58 km./h. (about 36 m.p.h.). (2) Figures: women, 2,300 points; men, 2,800 points. (3) Jumping: women, 275 points; men, 385 points.

There are three categories of judges for national and international competition, international first class, international second class, and national third class. Candidates qualify at international class by tests conducted at selected international championships twice a year.

BAREFOOT SKIING was introduced by Dick Pole, jr. at Cypress Gardens in Florida (U.S.A.), in 1947, and is still used as a stunt by those who have the nerve and tenacity. It does not hurt the feet unless continued for a long time when there is danger of the friction causing a burn. Launching is usually achieved by stepping off a single ski, while planing, on to one foot. When this is taking some of the body weight, the other foot is taken out of its binding and placed on the water. Some skiers can perform tricks while barefoot skiing and several experts are able to jump out of their skis, landing in the planing position on bare feet. Starts can also be made from stomach or back positions. Running starts from the jetty or beach are becoming popular and in barefoot competitions a miniature jump is used; distances in excess of 8 m. (26 ft.) have been achieved. Slalom is also performed on bare feet.

SKI KITE-FLYING has become popular in recent years, first as a spectacle and now as a competitive event. The kite is a framework of light alloy covered with over 7 sq. m. (75 sq. ft.) of canvas. Wearing either one or two skis and attached to the kite by a body harness for safety, the skier is towed by the boat into the wind. Depending on wind speed, the performer will glide at speeds of about 64 km./h. (40 m.p.h.) and heights of well over 30·5 m. (100 ft.) have been recorded. For a landing, the boat reduces speed and the skier and kite glide on to the water. In competitive kite-flying, the skier will fly a slalom run on a similar course to regular slalom: a second discipline is a series of acrobatic feats to be executed on a points system, e.g. open swan position, somersault over bar, etc.

General-purpose twin skis are usually about 1·7 m. (5 ft. 7 in.) long by 0·6 m. (2 ft.) wide. Skiers weighing 32 to 77 kg. (5 to 13 stone) need wider skis and those weighing between 77 to 136 kg. (13 to 21 stone) need a ski which is both longer and wider. Ski sizes for children can be graded accordingly and where the ski boat (see below) is capable of speeds only up to 32 km. (20 m.p.h.) the ski width may be increased to give added planing stability.

Figure skis (*retournement* or trick skis) are considerably shorter than general-purpose skis. They are banana-shaped at their extremities and without fins so that they will run forward, backward, or sideways. The slalom ski is constructed to a skier's individual requirements within the usual length of the twin ski — it is a little heavier, has a tapered tail to assist fast turns and an underwater fin which holds the skier on a straight course and prevents side-slipping in tight turns. Jump skis are usually slightly longer, wider and heavier than general-purpose skis, since they need to be more robust and almost unbreakable to withstand great impact. There must be a cer-

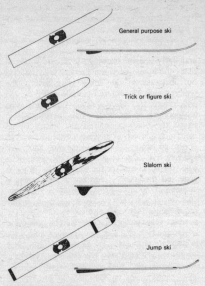

TYPES OF WATER SKIS
Each ski is shown at right in a profile view.

tain amount of flexibility; otherwise the skier will suffer considerable shock to the lower limbs on landing. The skis have direction fins made of alloy or wood. Shoe skis are used by the expert as a progression to barefoot skiing and are no more than two flat pieces of wood about 0·6 m. (2 ft.) long by 0·15 m. (6 in.) wide.

Bindings secure the feet in shoe-like fastenings to the skis. The rubber or plastic toe and heel pieces are mounted in alloy fitments. The heel bindings are on sliding runners allowing adjustment to varying foot sizes.

The water-ski boat is a purpose-built planing hull designed to give top speeds, low wake, and holding power on turns. The minimum speed needed for water skiing is 29 km./h. (about 18 m.p.h.), but for good skiing it is necessary for the towing boat to be capable of speeds of at least 40 km./h. (25 m.p.h.). For training for top-class competition boats capable of constant speeds of not less than 56 km./h. (35 m.p.h.) are necessary. Boat equipment should include paddles, a small anchor, engine tools and spares, a baler and bilge pump, a can of petrol, and a fire extinguisher. If sea work is planned, flares should be carried.

For national and international competitions, the tow rope is fitted at its inboard end to a pylon located in a position just aft of the midships. The pylon should be tall enough for the rope to clear an outboard motor. An alternative fastening point can be on the transom with a bridle type attachment.

The 'wet' suit is an essential part of the water-skier's equipment especially for winter and early season training. It allows water to enter the space between the suit and the skin but, because of the suit's snug fitting, the water which has entered cannot easily escape and, therefore, very quickly equates to the temperature of the body. This thermal action keeps the body comparatively warm for an indefinite period. A beginner should wear an approved water-ski safety jacket. This will support the skier if he is injured or winded. The risk is no less for the expert skier but it is accepted that more freedom of movement is demanded. Skiers of this class wear a kidney-belt buoyancy aid. For jumping, where the requirement for freedom of body movement is perhaps less than in trick or slalom skiing but where the risk of damage to spine and rib-cage is greater, it is essential to wear a regulation combined protector and buoyancy jacket.
World Water Ski Union Technical Rules.

Water skiing derives from snow SKIING and aquaplaning. In the snowfields, villagers have for many years held ski-tow races where the skiers are pulled along by sure-footed ponies. This sport is akin to present-day water skiing; the skier leans backward, resisting the forward motion of the galloping horse, just as the water skier resists the acceleration of the power boat. It had been known for at least a century that canoes would plane on incoming breakers and that, where these breakers were prolonged, quite long runs could be achieved.

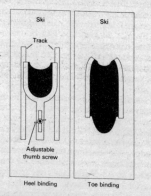

TYPES OF WATER-SKI BINDINGS
In the heel binding, the rubber binding is mounted on metal runners which move backward and forward; the toe binding is also of rubber, mounted on a fixed metal shoe.

With the development of the motor boat, first as a displacement hull and later as a planing hull, enthusiasts conceived the idea of a swimmer being towed on a flat board or aquaplane. One such enthusiast was the American, Fred Walter, who in the early 1900s filed the first patent for a pair of water skis which were probably no more than sophisticated aquaplanes. At the same time, in the Haute-Savoie province of France, a group of French army officers are reputed to have used their snow skis as aquaplanes in tow behind a boat on Lake Annecy. Improbable as this story is, water skiing was definitely beginning to emerge as a sport and in 1935, on Long Island, U.S.A., the first competition was watched by a large crowd. Only four years later the first American national championships were arranged by a newly formed governing body.

CODE OF SIGNALS FROM SKIER TO BOAT DRIVER

Similar development took place at French resorts on the Mediterranean coast and, in 1946, the increase in the number of countries taking part in the sport made possible the formation of an international controlling and co-ordinating body, known as the World Water Ski Union (W.W.S.U.). In the colder climate of Great Britain the sport took longer to develop. Even so, the British Water Ski Club was founded in 1949 and started skiing at Ruislip, Middlesex. Within a few months, the British Water Ski Federation (B.W.S.F.) was formed with clubs opening all over the country. The B.W.S.F. is the second largest water-ski federation in the world and has autonomous control in the U.K. Regional control is in four main areas; the Scottish, Welsh, Irish, and English Committees.

Countries affiliated to the World Water Ski Union compete in three separate groups as follows: Group I, North, Central, and South America and the West Indies; Group II, Europe, Africa, Near and Middle East; Group III, Australasia, Asia, and Pacific. Each group is responsible for arranging its own international (group) championships. Claims for world records are put before the Technical Committee of the W.W.S.U. for ratification.

The world championships are held bi-annually in odd-numbered years. Selection of venue is made by the W.W.S.U. which meets at the world congress held at the same time and place as the world championships. The honour of acting as host country for the championships and the congress rotates among the three groups.

F. L. Briscoe, *Tackle Water-Skiing This Way* (1969); Ralph Hester, *Instant Water Skiing* (1965); Kenneth Norman, *Modern Water-Skiing* (1973); Al Tyll, *Water Skiing* (1970).

GOVERNING BODY (WORLD): World Water Ski Union, 1474 Hampol Street, Oakland, Calif., U.S.A.; (U.K.): British Water Ski Federation, 70 Brompton Road, London S.W.3.

WATERLOO CUP, COURSING event first staged in 1836 by the Waterloo Club as a modest 8-dog stake. The cup took its name from the Waterloo Hotel where the members dined on the first day, and was run on the SEFTON family estate at Altcar, Lancashire. The trophy was first won by Lord Molyneux's bitch, Milanie. The meeting was so successful that in the following year it became a 16-dog stake and in 1838 a 32-dog stake. In 1857 it further expanded into its present form of a stake for 64 dogs.

The success of this event, which became coursing's classic; is attributable to its being open to greyhounds owned by non-members. This has been achieved by the adoption of the nominator system, 64 nominations being distributed by the club's committee to well-known coursers. It is an unwritten law that if the nominators do not have a dog of their own good enough for the Cup they should return the nomination to the committee who will award it to the most suitable from a list of applicants. In such a way, the Waterloo Cup is assured of the highest class of greyhound in the country.

Traditionally staged in the second week of February on the Altcar estate, the meeting extends over three successive days. Since 1857 two further trophies have been added, the Waterloo Purse for 32 dogs beaten in the first round, and the Waterloo Plate for 16 dogs beaten in the second round.

WATERLOO HANDICAP, see BOWLS, LAWN: CROWN GREEN.

WATERMAN, STANTON (1923-   ), American underwater swimmer, film producer, and lecturer. He was Underwater Photographer of the Year (U.S.A.) in 1968, and won the Cousteau Diver of the Year award the same year. His films include *The Hogsty Reef* (1963), *Genesis 1-27* (1967), *Blue Water, White Death* (1970), and *Reefs of Steel* (1972).

WATNEY'S BOWLS CLUB, Mortlake, London. This club became the venue for the annual English Bowling Association championships in August 1958. It has two fine greens and some 2,500 people can be accommodated round the one normally used for the semi-finals and finals.

WATSON, J. KEN (1905-   ), Canadian curler. He won the last of his three Canadian CURLING championships in 1949, and is believed to be the originator of the long-sliding delivery. He gained added renown as a writer on the game.

WEATHERBY, JAMES, Keeper of the Match Book at Newmarket and secretary of the JOCKEY CLUB, first published the *Racing Calendar* in 1773. Since then the family firm has continued to fulfil these duties, as well as acting as solicitor, treasurer, agent, and stakeholder to the Turf Authorities in England.

WEBB, Capt. MATTHEW (1848-1883), English swimmer who on 25 August 1875, after 21 hrs. 45 min. in the water stepped ashore at Calais as the first to swim the English Channel. Not until 1923 did another man emulate him and it was not until 1934 that his 59-year-old time was beaten — by British Olympic WATER POLO player TEMME. In an attempt to bolster lagging attendances at his vaudeville act, he tried for immortality a second time by swimming across the rapids just above Niagara Falls. This time the 'impossible' proved insurmountable and he was drowned.

WEBER, MAX (1922-   ), race walker for East Germany. After being third in the European 50 km. in 1958, and a competitor in the Olympic 50 km. in 1960, he became an International Amateur Athletic Federation (see ATHLETICS, TRACK AND FIELD) judge and had considerable success as coach to his national team, producing men such as Frenkel, HOHNE, Leuschke, Reiger, Selzer, Sperling, Skotnicki, and REIMANN, who have had numerous international victories since 1962.

WEEKES, EVERTON DE COURCY, O.B.E. (1925-   ), cricketer for West Indies and Barbados. An attacking batsman whose consistency at times was remarkable, he made 15 centuries in 48 Tests and was particularly severe on India, off whom he scored 7 centuries in 15 innings spread over two series (one of which saw him complete a world record of 5 consecutive Test centuries). In England in 1950, when his 7 centuries included 4 over 200 and 304 not out against Cambridge

University, his average was 79·65; but in 1957 there were only rare glimpses of his greatness.

WEIGHT, Tossing the, an event of the HIGH-LAND GAMES, held in Scotland for professional athletes. The weight is a metal sphere with a chain and ring attached, weighing together 56 lb. (25·4 kg.). The weight, measuring 18 in. (46 cm.) over-all, is thrown in two separate events, to achieve height, and distance.

The rules of the SCOTTISH GAMES ASSOCIA-TION allow the competitor a run of only 3 yds. (2·74 m.), at the end of which the weight must be delivered from behind a wooden barrier, known as a trig, 6 in. (15 cm.) high and not more than 4 ft. 6 in. (1·37 m.) long. It is a foul throw if the competitor touches any part of the trig except the face nearest him, or if he touches the ground beyond it. He may have three throws, the best of which counts for competition.

In 1969 Anderson tossed a height of 15 ft. 7 in. (4·75 m.), the best ever achieved. He also held the distance record of 41 ft. 11 in. (12·77 m.).

WEIGHT-LIFTING is a competitive sport (not to be confused with WEIGHT TRAINING) whose object is to find the man who can lift the biggest weight. It is a world-wide sport and on the programme of the OLYMPIC GAMES and all regional games.

The competitors (lifters) are divided into nine body-weight categories. Standing on a wooden platform, they lift a barbell in two dif-ferent styles — the 'two hands snatch' and the 'two hands clean and jerk'. The barbell is loaded progressively during the competition, the weight increasing in multiples of 5 lb. or 2·5 kg. Each lifter comes in at the weight he chooses, the order of lifting having been decided by drawing lots at the weigh-in preceding the competition.

The lifters have three attempts in each of the two styles. The weight at the second attempt must be at least 10 lb. (5 kg.) more than the first, and at the third attempt at least 5 lb. (2·5 kg.) more than the second. If a lifter fails a lift, he may take the same weight again or increase it as he chooses, but he is limited to the three attempts and may not have the weight on the barbell reduced.

The highest weights lifted in the two styles are added together, and the lifter with the highest total is the winner, the rest being placed in order according to their totals. If two winning lifters obtain the same total, the lifter with the lighter body weight at the time of the weigh-in is the winner. If two lifters have the same total and the same body weight at the weigh-in, they are weighed again to find which is now lighter. If at the second weigh-in they still have the same body weight, they will be declared equal first. The lifter with the next highest total is declared third.

The competition is controlled by three referees who judge the accuracy of the lifts according to the technical rules defining each style. A timekeeper also helps to control the competition. When a lifter is called by the announcer to make his attempt, he has three minutes in which to come to the platform and make the lift. If he has not appeared at the end of two minutes, he is given a warning by the timekeeper that he has only one minute left. If he has not made his attempt within the three minutes, he misses that attempt. A jury is elected to supervise the whole competition and to ensure that the technical rules are correctly applied.

STYLES OF LIFT

Two hands snatch. The lifter must grip the barbell with both hands, palms downward, and lift it in one swift, continuous movement to arms' length overhead. He may move his body and legs in any way he wishes to help make his lift.

There are two main techniques used to do this. The most popular used to be the 'split' technique, devised by the French. As the lifter pulls the barbell upward, he lunges under it, thrusting one foot forward and simultaneously the other foot backward to land in a 'split' fore and aft position, while at the same time fixing the barbell overhead on straight arms.

The other main technique is the 'squat', ori-ginally practised by the Austrians and Ger-mans and now the most commonly used tech-nique because it is mechanically superior to the 'split' style. As the lifter pulls the barbell past his waist, he bends his knees and drops down into a low, squatting position while at the same time fixing the barbell overhead on straight arms.

After using either of these techniques, the lifter must recover to an erect position still supporting the barbell overhead on locked arms. When the lifter is standing erect with his arms and legs straight and both feet on the same line, the chief referee will give him the signal to replace the barbell on the platform.

Two hands clean and jerk. The lifter must grip the barbell with both hands, palms down-ward, and lift it in one clean movement to his shoulders. He may move his body and legs in any way he wishes to help make this part of the lift.

The two main techniques used are the split and squat as in the two hands snatch. After using either of these techniques, the lifter must recover to an erect position and place his feet on the same line. Using his body and legs to obtain impetus, the lifter then jerks the barbell to arms' length overhead. The majority of lifters use a split technique to move the body vertically below the barbell in a strong supporting position. A few use the squat technique in the jerk itself, but it is not recommended. The lifter must then again recover to an erect position, still supporting the barbell overhead on locked arms. When the lifter is standing erect with his arms and legs straight and both feet on the same line, the chief referee will give him a signal as for the other lift.

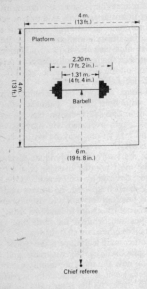

PLATFORM WITH BARBELL
The side referees (not shown) are positioned at either side on a line with the chief referee.

There are nine body-weight categories in weight-lifting competitions and championships: flyweight, 8 st. 2¼ lb. (52 kg.); bantamweight, 8 st. 11¼ lb. (56 kg.); featherweight, 9 st. 6¼ lb. (60 kg.); lightweight, 10 st. 8¾ lb. (67·5 kg.); middleweight, 11 st. 11¼ lb. (75 kg.); light heavyweight, 12 st. 13¾ lb. (82·5 kg.); middle heavyweight, 14 st. 2¼ lb. (90 kg.); heavyweight, 17 st. 4½ lb. (110 kg.); super heavyweight, over 17 st. 4½ lb. (110 kg.). At Olympic Games, world championships, continental championships, and regional games, nine competitors per country are permitted, plus two reserves, distributed among the different categories, with a maximum of two lifters per category.

In all weight-lifting championships and international competitions the lifters must start weighing in 1¼ hours before the scheduled starting time of their body-weight category. They must be weighed in the nude. If they weigh above the body-weight limit of their category they may reduce weight and weigh again as often as is necessary until they are within the required limit. They have one hour from the start of the weigh-in in which to make the required limit. If at the end of the weigh-in they are still too heavy, they may compete in the next heavier bodyweight category provided that their country has not already entered two lifters in that category and provided that they have reached the qualifying total weight set for that category. The three referees selected for each body-weight category control the preceding weigh-in and the secretary of the competition controls the drawing of lots to decide the order of lifting. Each lifter draws a numbered card before he steps on to the weighing machine.

The first barbells were cast from iron in one piece, consisting of a long rod with a solid ball, or 'bell', at each end. A whole range of these at different weights was originally required for weight-lifting competitions. The first improvement was the use of hollow metal globes at the ends. These could be filled with sand or lead shot to obtain progressive increases in weight. A later development was the use of metal discs in a range of weights which could be locked on to the ends of the bar by various types of clamps or collars. This type of disc-loading barbell was further refined by the introduction of revolving sleeves at each end which facilitate the turning of the barbell at various stages in the two styles of lifting.

Barbells used in international competitions or championships must now conform to the following measurements: (a) maximum distance between the collars, 1,310 mm. (51·6 in.); (b) width of the inside collars, including the collar on the sleeve, a minimum of 20 mm. (·78 in.) and a maximum of 40 mm. (1·57 in.); (c) maximum total length outside the sleeves, 2,200 mm. (86·6 in.); (d) diameter of the bar, 28 mm. (1·1 in.); (e) diameter of the sleeves, minimum 50 mm. (1·96 in.), maximum 55 mm. (2·16 in.); (f) diameter of the largest disc, 450 mm. (17·7 in.); (g) weight of the largest disc, 25 kg. (55 lb.); (h) weight of barbell and collars, 25 kg. (55 lb.). The discs must be in the following range: 25 kg. (55 lb.), 20 kg. (44 lb.), 15 kg. (33 lb.), 10 kg. (22 lb.), 5 kg. (11 lb.), 2½ kg. (5½ lb.), 1¼ kg. (2¾ lb.).

The original dumb-bell appeared in the sixteenth century. It consisted of a short cane handle with a bell-shaped piece of lead at the end. The 'bell' was a solid lump and therefore silent, hence the term dumb-bell. It was used by the nobility for strengthening exercises. Later on, the dumb-bell was cast in one solid piece of iron with a central rod or grip and a round lump at each end. Concurrently with the development of the disc-loading barbell, the modern dumb-bell emerged as a steel rod with small disc weights which can be locked on each end by means of clamps or collars. Because dumb-bells allow a greater variety of exercises than a barbell they are widely used in weight training. In some countries, particularly Great Britain, there are a number of competitive lifts in which dumb-bells are used, but these lifts are not recognized internationally.

Weight-lifting competitions must be carried out on a wooden platform measuring 4 m. by 4 m. (13 × 13 ft.). The boards or planks from which the platform is constructed must be arranged transversely, i.e. parallel to the line of the lifter's feet. There is no exact specification for the width or thickness of the boards, but a thickness of 3 to 4 in. (76–102 mm.) is customary.

The platform is intended not only for the protection of the floor but delineates the area in which all lifts must be completed. If a lifter staggers off the platform during the course of a lift and touches the surrounding floor with one or both feet, that lift will be disqualified.

In official competitions a weight-lifter must wear correct dress which consists of a vest with short sleeves, trunks and athletic support, or, alternatively, a full-length costume with athletic support. A collarless vest or T-shirt may be worn under the costume and may have short sleeves which may extend no further than half-way on the upper arms.

If a competitor wears a belt, its width must not exceed 10 cm. (4 in.). Bandages of gauze or medical crepe may be worn on the wrists with a maximum width of 8 cm. (3·1 in.) and a maximum length of 1 m. (39 in.). Similar bandages may be worn on the knees with a maximum width of 8 cm. (3·1 in.) and a maximum length of 2 m. (6½ ft.).

In international weight-lifting championships a jury is elected to supervise the whole competition. The president of the jury must be the president of the governing body, the International Weightlifting Federation (I.W.F.). Four other members and one reserve (all being of different nationalities) are elected to assist him. The jury's main duty is to ensure that the referees work correctly. If the jury consider that a referee is inefficient or showing bias, they may remove him and appoint a substitute. The jury ensure that all the rules governing the competition are correctly applied and deals with any appeals arising from circumstances not governed by the rules. There can be no appeal against the decisions of the referees nor does the jury have the power to alter these decisions.

Three referees are required to control a weight-lifting competition. For national championships they may all be of the same nationality but for international championships they must be of different nationalities.

The referees sit round the front of the platform in a position where they can clearly observe the lifter. They judge independently the accuracy of the lifts according to the rules defining each style. At the conclusion of each lift, the referees indicate their decisions by means of light signals. One of the three serves as chief referee. He sits in the centre, directly in front of the lifter and distant from him by a minimum of 6 m. (19 ft. 8 in.). The chief referee gives the signal to the lifter to replace the barbell on the completion of each lift. The referees' decisions are final.

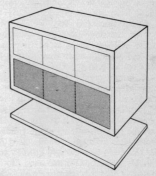

REFEREES' LIGHT SIGNALS
Tone indicates the red signals across the bottom row; the top row of signals are white. The chief referee controls the centre set of signals, and the side referees the two sides respectively.

The light signals used by the referees are either white or red. A white light indicates that the referee has approved the lift while a red light indicates that the lift has not been approved. A majority decision applies, so two or three white lights indicate a 'good lift' and two or three red lights indicate 'no lift'. The lights are arranged horizontally to coincide with the position of each referee, i.e. the centre referee controls the centre lights and so on. The electrical circuit must be such that the lights will not come on singly but all three must show simultaneously after the three switches have been pressed.

International Weightlifting Federation, *Constitution and Rules* (1972); British Amateur Weight Lifters' Association, *Handbook* (1968).

Lifting heavy stones was a pastime in early antiquity and in Greece can be found huge boulders inscribed with the names of the athletes purported to have lifted them hundreds of years B.C. The custom persisted in many parts of Europe through the Middle Ages into comparatively recent times. There is a huge stone weighing 400 lb. (181 kg.) in the courtyard of the Munich Apothekerhof castle. An inscription on the wall above it says that Duke Christopher of Bavaria proved his manhood in 1490 by lifting it and throwing it. Such feats became a test of manhood in many countries. Manhood stones or *clach cuid fir* can be found in some Scottish castles.

In the Basque provinces of France and Spain, stone-lifting contests are still held. Professionals compete for money prizes or wagers ranging as high as 500,000 pesetas. The type of stone generally used is an *easarone*, cylindrical in shape with two holes or handles at one end to accommodate a grip and weighing from 100 to 200 kg. (220¼–440¾ lb.). Competitors (no body-weight limits) have to lift the stone from the ground to the shoulders as many times as possible in one minute and are allowed to wear padded jackets. The record-holder is Ostolaza who made 21 lifts in one minute and 263 lifts in 30 minutes (three rounds of ten minutes).

The record for the 125 kg. (275½ lb.) *easarone* is 15 lifts in 2 minutes, set by Irazusta; in 30 minutes Atxaga lifted it 215 times. Manterola set the record for the 150 kg. (330¼ lb.) *easarone* with 178 lifts in 30 minutes. Urtain, former European heavyweight BOXING champion, holds the record for one hand lifts with the 100 kg. (220¼ lb.) *easarone* with 186 lifts in 30 minutes. The record for the huge 200 kg. (440¾ lb.) rectangular stone is 7 lifts in 5 minutes set by Aguirre, called 'Endaneta', and thereby recognized as Spain's strongest man.

Modern weight-lifting with barbells and dumb-bells became popular towards the end of the nineteenth century and was fostered by strong-man acts in circuses and music halls. The first championship open to the world was held in the Café Monico, London, on 28 March 1891 and was won by Levy of England. The first Olympic Games in 1896 also featured weight-lifting. The winner of the one-hand lift competition was Elliott of England with 156½ lb. (71 kg.). The winner of the two-hands lift competition was V. Jensen (Denmark) with 244½ lb. (111 kg.).

These competitions were repeated at the 1904 Olympic Games, but then lapsed until 1920 when the INTERNATIONAL OLYMPIC COMMITTEE asked for weight-lifting to be included. At these Games the lifts were one hand snatch, opposite one hand jerk, and two

hands clean and jerk. At the 1924 Olympic Games the lifts were one hand snatch, opposite one hand jerk, two hands clean and press, two hands snatch, and two hands clean and jerk. In 1928 only the two-handed lifts were used and these three lifts remained the competition set until 1972, when the two hands clean and press was abolished. Now, only two lifts are used for all national championships, international competitions, and world and Olympic championships.

The Fédération Haltèrophile Internationale (International Weightlifting Federation) was founded in Paris in 1920 by Jules Rosset of France at the request of the International Olympic Committee who wanted to include the sport with an official set of rules. At that time 14 nations affiliated. At the 1972 annual congress of the Federation the affiliation of the 100th nation was accepted.

Five body-weight categories were established in 1920 — featherweight, lightweight, middleweight, light heavyweight, and heavyweight. In 1947 the bantamweight class was added, in 1951 the middle heavyweight class, and in 1968 the flyweight and super heavyweight.

The International Weightlifting Federation organized world championships in 1922 and 1923, then changed to European championships until 1937, when the world championships began again. Since the Second World War, world championships have been held every year in various parts of the world. France, Austria, and Germany were the leading nations up to 1936 when the Egyptians took the lead. In 1938 the U.S.A. became world team champions and remained at the top until 1953 when the U.S.S.R. beat them. Except for 1965, when Poland won, and 1972, when Bulgaria won, the U.S.S.R. have been world team champions ever since.

The British Amateur Weight Lifters' Association was founded in 1911 in London. The British Commonwealth Weightlifting Federation was founded by State of England at the 1948 Olympic Games in London.

B. Hoffman, *Guide to Weightlifting Competition* (1964) and *Weightlifting* (1968); G. W. Kirkley, *Modern Weightlifting* (1957) and *Weightlifting and Weight Training* (1963); A. Murray, *The Theory and Practice of Olympic Lifting* (1959); J. Murray, *Weightlifting and Progressive Resistance Exercises* (1954); W. A. Pullum, *How to Use a Barbell* (1932) and *Weightlifting Made Easy and Interesting* (1949).

GOVERNING BODY (WORLD): International Weightlifting Federation, 4 Godfrey Avenue, Twickenham, Middlesex; (U.K. AND COMMONWEALTH): British Amateur Weight Lifters' Association, 3 Iffley Turn, Oxford; British Commonwealth Weightlifting Federation, 3 Iffley Turn, Oxford.

WEIGHT-PUTTING, see SHOT PUT.

WEIGHT TRAINING is a system of physical training using weights in the form of barbells or dumb-bells (see WEIGHT-LIFTING). There are three main objectives in this type of training: (*a*) to obtain general physical fitness; (*b*) to increase strength in specific muscle groups as part of the general training programme of another sport (weight training is extensively used in ATHLETICS, SWIMMING, WRESTLING, LAWN TENNIS, and many other major sports), and (*c*) to develop the physique for the purpose of entering bodybuilding or physique contests.

The type and number of exercises, the amount of weight employed, and the number of sets or repetitions vary according to the objectives of the weight trainer, and his age, sex, body weight, and experience. It is therefore always recommended that weight training should be practised only under the guidance of an experienced coach.

G. W. Kirkley and J. Goodbody, *The Manual of Weight Training* (1968); G. W. Kirkley, *Weightlifting and Weight Training* (1963); A. Murray, *Basic Weight Training* (1950) and *Modern Weight Training* (1963).

WEISSMULLER, JOHNNY (1904-   ), an American who was voted the 'greatest swimmer of the half-century' by 250 sports writers in 1950. He won five Olympic gold medals — three in 1924 for 100, 400, and 4 × 200 metres freestyle, and two in 1928 for the sprint and the relay. He set 24 world records and was the first man to break the minute for 100 metres and 5 minutes for 400 metres. His high-riding front crawl stroke was revolutionary at the time and he later became the most famous of the film Tarzans.

WELDON, FRANCIS WILLIAM CHARLES (1913-   ), British three-day event (see EQUESTRIAN EVENTS) horseman, who contributed to three consecutive British wins in the European championship (1953-5) and was also a member of the Olympic gold medal team at Stockholm (1956). His major successes (which included an individual European championship, an individual Olympic bronze medal, and two Badminton championships) were all achieved with the Irish-bred Kilbarry.

WELLINGTON CUP is a horse race competed for over a distance of 2 miles (3,200 m.) on the Trentham track, Wellington, New Zealand.

WELSH, FREDDIE (1886-1927), British boxer who won the world lightweight title in 1914 and held it for three years until he was knocked out by LEONARD. Welsh was not a hard hitter but he was a master of defence and it took a great champion like Leonard to penetrate his guard. Welsh went to the U.S.A. as a young man and had only 31 of his 166 bouts in Britain.

WELSH, ROBIN WATSON (1919-   ), Scottish curler. He has been secretary of the ROYAL CALEDONIAN CURLING CLUB since 1958, and secretary of the International Curling Federation since its formation in 1966. He is the author of *Beginner's Guide to Curling* (1969), and editor and publisher since 1954 of the monthly magazine, *Scottish Curler.*

WEMBLEY LIONS, ICE HOCKEY club of England, the most successful and longest surviving club from a once-thriving British era, formed in 1934 and playing home games at the EMPIRE POOL, WEMBLEY, London. Bates and Rost were outstanding pre-war stars. The closures of other big London stadia at Harringay and Earl's Court in the 1950s drastically cut the sport's potential in Great Britain. The Wembley Lions club maintained a team, and heartening support, until 1968, when lack of a suitable standard of opposition caused a reluctant curtailment of fixtures. Two veterans in the late 1960s became the only players to score their thousandth goals in Britain — Zamick, whose earlier career was spent with Nottingham Panthers, and Beach, who served Wembley for more than 20 years.

WEMBLEY STADIUM, London, the best-known Association FOOTBALL ground in the world, although its use is by no means confined to staging football matches. The decision to build a great stadium at Wembley Park, concurrent with the holding of the British Empire Exhibition in the same area in 1923, was not taken until an agreement, originally drawn up to last for 21 years, had been reached with the Football Association for the stadium to be used for the F.A. Cup final match each year. In January 1922, the Duke of York, later George VI, cut the first turf; and, four days before it was required for the F.A. Cup final to be played on 29 April 1923, the work was completed. The cost was £750,000; some 250,000 tons of clay had been dug out to form the bowl of the stadium, and the stands and terraces had required 25,000 tons of concrete, 600 tons of steel rods, 1,500 tons of steel girders, and about half a million rivets.

Arrangements for this first match were in the hands of the British Empire Exhibition and the stadium was expected to hold 127,000 people. No one could reasonably have foreseen that the combination of excellent April weather, the opening of a new stadium, the presence of a London club, and the visit of George V would have brought between 200,000 and 250,000 would-be spectators to Wembley. Tickets had been sold in advance for the seated accommodation but not for the spectators on the terraces who were expected to pay at the turnstiles. Instead barriers were broken and thousands of spectators, whether they wanted to or not, poured on to the new pitch. In time, the patient work of the police, officials, and stewards (in particular 'the policeman on the white horse') enabled the match to start, forty minutes late, with a human wall flanking the touch lines. The official attendance was 126,047, but the actual number in the stadium has been variously estimated at between 150,000 and 200,000. The official figure and the estimates are records for Wembley Stadium that have never been beaten. Since 1923 admittance to the Cup final, and to all other football matches that seemed likely to attract crowds bigger than the stadium's capacity, has been by ticket only. Moreover structural changes have increased the proportion of seated to standing accommodation. The stadium's biggest single improvement scheme was commenced in 1961. This involved the protection of the entire seating and standing accommodation with a translucent roof. It was completed in time for the 1963 F.A. Cup final.

The first international Association football match was played at Wembley on 12 April 1924 when England met Scotland, and the biennial home match between England and Scotland has been played at Wembley ever since. Wales and France played wartime international matches against England at Wembley, and Belgium a 'Victory' international match in 1946. Since 1951 only exceptionally have England played home international matches at venues other than Wembley. It was used in the football tournament in the 1948 OLYMPIC GAMES but its most important football occasion was the 1966 world championship. The extensive press, radio, and television coverage of the world championship necessitated further improvements to the stadium, particularly a modern press gallery and a television centre. The 1963 improvements cost £750,000 and something like a million pounds was spent in additional improvements over the next eight years.

In addition to England's international matches and the F.A. Cup finals, the Football League Cup final, the F.A. Amateur Cup final, the F.A. Challenge Trophy final, and schoolboy and youth international matches are played at Wembley. The RUGBY LEAGUE Cup final has been played here regularly since 1929, with the exception of 1932. BOXING contests, HOCKEY matches, Gaelic FOOTBALL and HURLING matches, speedway and greyhound meetings, horse shows and show jumping events, and even American BASEBALL games, have all been played at the stadium which stands in 72 acres of grounds and adjacent buildings, the most important of which are the EMPIRE POOL, a magnificent indoor sports arena catering for between 8,000 and 11,000 spectators according to the event taking place, and the Wembley Stadium Bowl, opened in 1962, comprising a restaurant and cocktail bar in addition to 24 BOWLING lanes.

WENDEN, MICHAEL, M.B.E. (1949-   ), Australian swimmer who won the Olympic 100 and 200 metres freestyle titles in the 1968 Games in Mexico City. Despite a flailing action, the effectiveness of his powerful underwater pull was beyond dispute, and he set a world record of 52·2 seconds in winning the sprint. His tally of nine gold medals from the 1966, 1970, and 1974 British COMMONWEALTH GAMES was the highest number to be won by a single competitor.

WERNHER, Sir HAROLD (1893-1973) and Lady ZIA (1892-   ), both breed and own race-horses in England, he having owned BROWN JACK and Aggressor, who beat PETITE ÉTOILE in the KING GEORGE VI AND QUEEN ELIZABETH STAKES; and his wife MELD and CHARLOTTOWN.

WEST, JERRY (1938-   ), American BASKETBALL player. He turned professional in 1961 with the St. Louis Hawks and then moved to the LOS ANGELES LAKERS. In his first eight seasons in the NATIONAL BASKETBALL ASSOCIATION, West was chosen as a member of the All-League team on six occasions.

WEST AUSTRALIAN (1850), a race-horse bred and owned by Bowes, trained by J. SCOTT, and ridden by Butler. He was the first horse to win the triple crown (SEE HORSE RACING) and, since he also won the ASCOT GOLD CUP in record time, West Australian can rightly be regarded as the champion English race-horse of the first half of the nineteenth century.

WEST HAM UNITED F.C., Association FOOTBALL club, London. Founded in 1895 as Thames Ironworks, the club was re-formed under its present name in 1900. West Ham played in the Southern League from 1898 until

1915, and were elected to the Second Division of the Football League when the competition was resumed after the First World War. They have competed in the First or Second Division of the Football League ever since without winning the League championship but with more success in the F.A. Cup, in the final of which they were beaten by Bolton in 1923 but were successful against PRESTON in 1964. Entry in the European Cup-Winners Cup competition followed and in a final played at WEMBLEY West Ham beat T.S.V. MUNICH 1860 to become the second English club to win a European club competition. The club's outstanding players between the wars were Goulden, Hufton, Ruffell, and Puddefoot, and, post-1946, MOORE, HURST, PETERS, and GREAVES.

COLOURS: Claret shirts with blue facings and sleeves, white shorts.
GROUND: Boleyn Ground, Upton Park, London.

WEST OF SCOTLAND R.F.C., RUGBY UNION football club, formed in 1865 and one of the six founder members of the Scottish Rugby Union. It is an open club, to that extent a counterpart to EDINBURGH WANDERERS in the east, and was one of the first Scottish sides to arrange fixtures with Cambridge University, BLACKHEATH, Manchester, and other English clubs.

GROUND: Burnbrae, Milngavie, near Glasgow.
COLOURS: Red and yellow.

WESTCHESTER CLUB, see POLO.

WESTERGRAN, CARL (*fl.* 1920-32), Swedish Graeco-Roman wrestler who was one of only two men to win three Olympic titles in the sport: middleweight Class A in 1920, middleweight B four years later, and heavyweight in 1932. In addition he won one world title and three European gold medals.

WESTMINSTER, 1st Duke of (1825-99), was a leading owner-breeder of race-horses in England, winning the triple crown (see HORSE RACING) twice, with the unbeaten ORMONDE in 1886 and again with FLYING FOX in 1899.

WETHERED, JOYCE, see HEATHCOAT-AMORY, Lady.

WHIRLAWAY (1938), crack American race-horse who won the KENTUCKY DERBY (in record time), BELMONT STAKES, PREAKNESS STAKES, American Derby, TRAVERS STAKES, LAWRENCE REALIZATION STAKES, and JOCKEY CLUB GOLD CUP, 32 races out of 58 starts, together with $560,911 in stake money, which was then a world record. Whirlaway was bred

at CLAIBORNE and owned by Wright, trained by Ben Jones, and ridden by ARCARO and Robertson.

WHITE, BELLE (1894-1972), diver for Great Britain. Britain's first woman medallist, she won the bronze medal in the OLYMPIC GAMES plain high DIVING competition at Stockholm in 1912, the first in which women had been allowed to compete. She went on to compete in three further Olympics, and at the age of 33 won the women's high diving in the first European Games held at Bologna in 1927. She collected 25 gold medals for plain diving (swallow dives) in England between 1912 and 1929.

WHITE, BYRON RAYMOND (Whizzer) (1917-   ), American college and professional FOOTBALL player. While at the University of Colorado (1935-7) he was one of the most versatile backs in college football history, an elusive runner, excellent passer, and exceptional punter and place-kicker. He played halfback in the NATIONAL FOOTBALL LEAGUE for the Pittsburgh Pirates (1938) and DETROIT LIONS (1940-1). A Rhodes scholar, he was later U.S. Deputy Attorney-General in the Kennedy administration (1961), and in 1962 was appointed a Justice of the U.S. Supreme Court.

WHITE, R. M. (Bill) (1909-72), English BADMINTON player. A very aggressive doubles player who won numerous international honours, including all three ALL-ENGLAND CHAMPIONSHIP titles at different times, he represented England from 1929 to 1939 and was the first player to wear shorts for the game.

WHITE CONDUIT CLUB, see CRICKET.

WHITFIELD, MALVIN GEORGE (1924-   ), middle-distance runner for the U.S.A. A great competitive runner, rather than a record-breaker, Whitfield was Olympic 800 metres champion in 1948 and 1952 and won a third gold medal in 1948 for the 4 × 400 metres relay. In 1948 he also won a bronze medal in the 400 metres and in 1952 a silver medal in the 4 × 400 metres relay. In 1950 he equalled WOODERSON's long-standing world 880 yards record, and reduced it to 1 min. 48·6 sec. in 1953 when he also broke the 1,000 metres record in 2 min. 20·8 sec.

WHITLOCK, HAROLD HENRY (1903-   ), race walker for Great Britain, an International Amateur Athletic Federation (see ATHLETICS, TRACK AND FIELD) judge, and an administrator. The man most responsible for modernizing international race walking over the past fifteen years, he was 50 km. champion at the Olympics in 1936 and European champion in 1938. He also competed in the Olympic 50 km. in 1952 at the age of 48. A frequent winner of English long-distance classics, he won the LONDON–BRIGHTON race four times in succession (1934-7), the course record he set in 1935 lasting for 22 years. Whitlock also won the Race Walking Association's national 50 km. five times (1933, 1935, and 1939), and the BRADFORD six times (1935-8, 1940, and 1952). He set the world best for 30 miles in 1935. Chief judge at several Olympic and European Games, Whitlock is the most respected coach and judge in the world, his book *Race Walking* supplying the basic principles from which many countries have now produced world-class performers. He has also played a major part in the introduction of a 20 km. event into the international programme and the LUGANO CUP competition.

WHITTEN, EDWARD (1933-   ), Australian Rules footballer. Holder of the VICTORIAN FOOTBALL LEAGUE record of 321 games for his club, Footscray, between 1951 and 1970, he is regarded as one of the most versatile players in the history of the game. He won his club's 'best and fairest' award five times and subsequently coached. He was captain and coach of the Victorian State side in 1962 and in 1954 he was a member of Footscray's first premiership side. He was honoured by inclusion in the All-Australian named teams of 1956, 1958, and 1961, and he represented Victoria in four Australian Football Council (A.F.C.) (see FOOTBALL, AUSTRALIAN RULES) championships.

WHYTE TROPHY, see BADMINTON.

WIDENER, JOSEPH EARLY (1872-1943), was president of the Westchester (Belmont Park) Racing Association, and vice-chairman of the New York Jockey Club. His son, George, was also a prominent figure in American turf affairs and president of the New York Jockey Club and the National Museum of Racing.

WIGAN RUGBY LEAGUE CLUB, Lancashire, has won the Challenge Cup seven times and the League championship nine times — more often than any other club — as well as having provided most players (37) for Australian tours. Formed in 1879 and a founder member of the Northern Union, it has been consistently successful and prosperous from its earliest days. One of its most successful teams was developed immediately after the Second World War. It was composed mostly of players brought on locally, and eight of them were chosen for the 1950 Australian tour. An English record attendance was set at their CENTRAL PARK ground — 47,747 in 1959.
COLOURS: Cherry and white hoops.

WIGHTMAN, Mrs. GEORGE, see HOTCHKISS, HAZEL.

WIGHTMAN CUP is an annual LAWN TENNIS contest between the women players of the U.S.A. and Britain, inaugurated in 1923. The trophy, a tall silver vase, was the gift of Mrs. Wightman, who was one of the most formidable match players in the United States for more than 30 years. The match consists of five singles and two doubles rubbers. Mrs. Wightman herself played in the doubles in the first match at FOREST HILLS, which the U.S.A. won 7-0. The British won four of the first eight contests, but then failed to win another from 1931 to 1958 when they gained a narrow and exciting victory by 4-3 at WIMBLEDON. The Americans enjoyed another spell of success from 1961 to 1967. The competition lost some status after the introduction of open tennis (see LAWN TENNIS) because a number of leading American players refused invitations to compete, choosing instead to play in prize-money tournaments. It was also somewhat overshadowed by the Bonne Belle Cup, an annual contest between the Australian and American women, which was played first at Cleveland in 1972.

WILDE, JIMMY (1892-1969), British boxer who won the world flyweight title in 1916 and is unanimously considered as the greatest in the lightest weight in professional BOXING. Many regard Wilde, memorably nicknamed 'the ghost with a hammer in his hand', as pound for pound the greatest boxer of all. For most of his career Wilde weighed just under 100 lb. (45 kg.) compared with the flyweight limit of 112 lb. (50·8 kg.), yet he accumulated 98 victories inside the distance in official contests, had a string of 88 bouts without a defeat, and estimated that he had more than 700 battles in fairground booths while he was learning his trade. Wilde, not an attractive stylist, was a perfect judge of footwork who was able to explode his blows with devastating force because of a remarkable sense of anticipation. His few defeats came when he was either not at his fittest or past his best. He went 17 rounds with the famous American bantamweight HERMAN in 1921 although he was conceding about 20 lb. (9 kg.).

WILDING, ANTHONY FREDERICK (1883-1915), New Zealand LAWN TENNIS player, the WIMBLEDON champion from 1910 to 1913 and one of the most lamented of the game's losses in the First World War. The son of a New Zealand Test cricketer, he was superlatively fit and a player of great style and courage. At Cambridge University, he divided his time between CRICKET and lawn tennis. In 1905, when Australia and New Zealand challenged jointly in the Davis Cup (see LAWN TENNIS) as 'Australasia', he and BROOKES represented them in the singles, but lost 5-0 to the U.S.A.

In 1906 Wilding reached the semi-finals at WIMBLEDON and won two Davis Cup rubbers from the Americans and, in 1907, when Brookes returned to Europe, the two avenged themselves on the U.S.A. and defeated Britain 3-2 in the challenge round. Australasia kept the trophy until 1912, when Wilding did not go home to help in its defence, and Britain won in Melbourne. Brookes and Wilding resumed their partnership in 1914 and reasserted their supremacy by beating the British 3-0 at Boston, and the U.S.A. 3-2 in New York on 13–15 August. Altogether, Wilding won 21 of his 30 Davis Cup rubbers. Six weeks earlier Brookes had beaten him 6-4, 6-4, 7-5 to rob him of the title in his last singles at Wimbledon.

Most of his Wimbledon tests were against A. W. GORE and Roper Barrett. He beat Gore to win the title in 1910. The following year Roper Barrett was so exhausted by the heat and a long all-comers' final that he could only lob gently. A nonplussed Wilding found himself down by two sets to one. He won the fourth and Roper Barrett retired. Wilding confessed that he had been about to retire himself. He beat Gore again in 1912 and played brilliantly to defeat a newcomer, MCLOUGHLIN, in the challenge round in 1913. Wilding was killed in action in Belgium.

WILKES, S. (Faas) (1923-   ), Association footballer for Xerxes, INTERNAZIONALE, Valencia, V.V.V., Fortuna '54, and the Netherlands for whom he made 38 appearances in international matches and scored 35 goals from every forward-line position except outside left. He made his début for the Netherlands national team in March 1946 and his scoring ability was recognized beyond his own country by his selection to play for the Rest of Europe XI against Britain in Glasgow in May 1947. He was transferred from the Amsterdam club, Xerxes, to Internazionale (Milan) in 1949 and also played for the Spanish club, Valencia, before returning to play in Holland for V.V.V. and Fortuna '54. Except for four international matches played when he was with Valencia, his appearances for the Netherlands national team were nil during the period he spent out of Dutch club football but he played again after his return to Holland until his last international match in May 1961.

WILKINSON, CHARLES B. (Bud) (1916-   ), American college FOOTBALL coach, who played quarterback and guard on 1934-6 University of MINNESOTA teams. In 17 years (1947-63), while he was coach at the University of OKLAHOMA, his teams won 145 games, lost 29, tied 4. The 1950, 1951, and 1956 teams were national champions; the 1949-50 and 1954-6 teams undefeated; the 1954-6 teams set an all-time college football consecutive-win run of 47 straight games. He retired from coaching in 1963.

WILKINSON, CYRIL THEODORE ANSTRUTHER, C.B.E. (1884-1970), a HOCKEY player for England and a cricketer for Surrey, 'Wilkie' achieved a unique hockey hat-trick, representing his country as player, umpire, and official. As a hockey half-back, he played for Norwood, Hampstead, Surrey, and the South of England. The First World War prevented his being capped for England until 1930 when he was 36, yet, in that season, he won an Olympic gold medal with the England team at the Antwerp Games. After retiring from active play, he became an international hockey umpire and an expert on the interpretation of the rules. In 1938 he was nominated by the English H.A. to the International Hockey Rules Board and he remained a member of the Board for 27 years. He was also a vice-president of the Hockey Association.

An accomplished all-rounder at CRICKET, he played for Surrey, London County, M.C.C., Incogniti, Free Foresters, Sabbatarians, and Beckenham. A right-hand bat, a slow left-arm bowler, and a superb fielder, he led Surrey to victory in the English county championship in 1914.

WILLIAMS, BLEDDYN L. (1923-   ), RUGBY UNION player for CARDIFF, Wales, and British LIONS. Having first played for Wales in 1947 at outside half, he was moved in the next match to centre three-quarter where he won a further 21 caps and developed into probably the most powerful mid-field player of his time. In the 1947-8 season he scored 41 tries in 31 games for Cardiff. Wales won on each of the five occasions that he captained the side.

WILLIAMS, CHARLES (d. 1935), British professional RACKETS player. He was world champion from 1911 to 1914 and 1928 to 1935. He survived the *Titanic* disaster in 1912 on his way to defend the world title. He was also a middleweight boxer.

WILLIAMS, THEODORE SAMUEL (1918-), American BASEBALL player with the BOSTON RED SOX from 1939 to 1960. The best hitter of his era, he led his league in batting six times and made 2,654 hits including 521 home runs; his lifetime batting average was ·344 and in 1941 he hit ·406. His totals would undoubtedly have been higher had he not lost several seasons because of service in the Second World War and in Korea.

WILLS, HELEN (Mrs. F. S. Moody) (1905-), American LAWN TENNIS player, LENGLEN's successor as dominator of the women's game. A Californian with relentlessly powerful ground strokes and remarkable concentration and determination, she won more major singles than any other player. Her record of eight successes at WIMBLEDON (where she lost only to MCKANE in the 1924 final), seven at FOREST HILLS, and four in Paris may never be surpassed.

Wills won her first U.S. title at 17. Her Wimbledon victories were gained between 1927 and 1938, and from 1927 to 1933, when she was dominating the great tournaments, she did not lose a set in any match. In 1933, after her marriage to F. S. Moody, two British players — ROUND in the Wimbledon final and Nuthall at Forest Hills — took sets from her. Then came the most controversial of all her matches — in the final at Forest Hills against her leading American rival, JACOBS. Volleying with great determination, Jacobs was leading 8-6, 3-6, 3-0, when Mrs. Moody suddenly announced that an injured leg would prevent her from continuing. Later that afternoon she wanted to play in the women's doubles final, but was persuaded that she would be wiser not to go on to court.

Mrs. Moody did not play in another major championship until 1935 when she regained the Wimbledon title, beating Jacobs 6-3, 3-6, 7-5 after surviving a match point at 3-5 in the final set. When she returned in 1938, Jacobs was once more her opponent in the final and the match stirred memories of their meeting at Forest Hills. Jacobs had injured an ankle earlier in the tournament and at 4-4 and 40-30 she damaged it again. There was a precedent for withdrawal, but Jacobs limped on through the match without winning another game. This was Mrs. Moody's last appearance in competitive lawn tennis.

WILLS, JUDY (1949-), American

trampolinist and first ladies' world champion. She held the title from 1964 to 1968.

WILLS, MAURICE MORNING (1932-), American BASEBALL shortstop for the LOS ANGELES DODGERS and other NATIONAL LEAGUE clubs, 1959 through 1972. He was chosen the National League's Most Valuable Player in 1962, the year he established a twentieth-century major-league record for stolen bases, 104.

WILLS, PHILIP AUBREY (1907-), the great British pioneer of GLIDING between 1934 and 1967, holder of British distance and altitude records during the 1930s, and world champion in Spain, 1952. He was chairman of the British Gliding Association for 20 years, and elected its president in 1968.

WILSON, JOHN (1876-1957), secretary of the RUGBY LEAGUE from 1920 to 1946. A Scot who represented Britain as a cyclist in the 1912 OLYMPIC GAMES, he became a director of the Hull Kingston Rovers club. While in Australia as manager of the England 1920 touring team, he was appointed League secretary. He played a part in the establishment of Rugby League in France and in the moves which resulted in the playing of the Rugby League Cup final at WEMBLEY.

WIMBLEDON is the most famous of all LAWN TENNIS centres and the home of 'The Lawn Tennis Championships on Grass', the oldest and most important of lawn tennis tournaments. The event is staged by the ALL-ENGLAND CLUB in conjunction with the LAWN TENNIS ASSOCIATION, the ruling body of the game in Britain, and its proceeds go towards the development of the game and of the championships.

The first championships were held by the All-England Club (then the All-England Croquet and Lawn Tennis Club, but since 1882 the All-England Lawn Tennis and Croquet Club) in 1877 at its original ground at Worple Road, Wimbledon. The club moved in 1922 to their present ground at Church Road, which holds 30,000 spectators. The capacity of the centre court is about 14,000 and No. 1 court will take about 7,500 spectators. There are 16 grass courts and ten clay courts, two of which are covered.

WIMBLEDON TROPHY, see SHOOTING, RIFLE: SERVICE CALIBRE.

WINCHESTER COLLEGE FOOTBALL, see FOOTBALL, WINCHESTER COLLEGE.

WINCHESTER FIVES is a game played between four players, two on each side, in a court enclosed by four walls. The players use both hands, and gloves are worn. It is not impossible to play singles but the shape of the court makes it unrewarding for competent players.

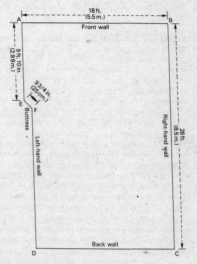

WINCHESTER FIVES COURT
The back wall (DC) is 14 ft. (4·3 m.) high. The angle at the buttress (EF) is 135°.

The courts at Winchester College are nearly the same size as a standard RUGBY FIVES court, namely 28 ft. (8·5 m.) long and 18 ft. (5·5 m.) wide. However, the back wall is 14 ft. (4·3 m.) high and the width is not identical throughout. Because the game is played in only a few schools there is no standard court and no association. Winchester fives players, when they leave school, play, if they play at all, in Rugby fives teams and competitions, and find little difficulty in making the change. On the other hand, Rugby fives players have a greater handicap when they attempt Winchester fives. Some of the Winchester game players have been successful in the Rugby fives championships and many have played for Oxford or for Cambridge in the university Rugby fives match.

The Winchester court is not quite rectangular. On the left-hand side wall there is a buttress, which is really a projection of the wall, 9 ft. 10 in. (2·99 m.) from the front wall. Here the wall changes direction at an angle of 135° for a distance of only 9¾ in. (25 cm.), making the back portion of the court very slightly narrower than the front. This projection or buttress dictates much of the positioning and tactics of the game.

Partners divide the court between front and back. The front player takes everything he can, volleying frequently, while his partner at the back does his best to return every ball that passes his colleague; his main object if he cannot score the point himself, is to play his return so that the front player has a good chance of winning the point next time.

The variety introduced into the game by the buttress is considerable. Whereas the Rugby fives player can only create a difficulty for his opponent by the closeness and the differing speeds by which he hits the ball down the left-hand side wall, the Winchester player can keep his opponents in doubt by playing the ball so that it remains uncertain until the last moment whether the ball will hit the buttress and so change direction.

In Winchester fives the left-handed player, that is the the player whose left hand is the stronger of the two, is at some advantage in the rallies. Presumably he finds it easier to play the ball down the left-hand side wall and with greater variety and control than a right-handed player. At the same time he is at a disadvantage when serving. There is nothing to prevent him from electing to serve into the left-hand corner but if he does so he is gaining no advantage from the existence of the buttress on the left-hand side wall. For the right-handed server the buttress adds to the opportunity for scoring an outright point or ace, although the opportunity is reduced since either opponent may return the serve. The game puts a proper premium on good partnership. There is less enjoyment for partners of uneven abilities and more for those who can rely successfully on one another. The scoring follows the same pattern as in the Rugby game.

The peculiarity of the Winchester court has no obvious explanation. A few schools copied it more or less and it is quite possible that the idea for it came from the REAL TENNIS court which has a tambour on the hazard side of the court, serving the same purpose of changing the direction of the ball if it strikes the face of it. Very few courts have been built in recent years. (See also ETON FIVES.)

WINDMILL DOWN, Hambledon, Hampshire, was the second and less famous ground used by the cricketers of HAMBLEDON in the eighteenth century, and was the successor to BROAD-HALFPENNY DOWN when that ground was given up in 1782, principally on account of its exposed position. Great matches were played there until 1795. Windmill Down was much nearer to the village of Hambledon itself than was Broad-Halfpenny.

WINDSOR LAD (1931), English race-horse bred by Sullivan and raced by the Maharajah of Rajpipla, and later by Benson, trained by MARSH, and ridden by Smirke. He won ten races, including the DERBY, ST. LEGER, ECLIPSE STAKES, and CORONATION CUP, and £36,257.

WINDSOR PARK, Belfast, Association FOOTBALL ground of LINFIELD F.C. Used for major matches, internationals, and the Irish Cup Finals, it has a capacity of 58,000.

WINGFIELD SCULLS, the amateur sculling (see ROWING) championship of the Thames held annually over the 4¼-mile (6·8 km.) course from Putney to Mortlake.

Originally held from Westminster to Putney in 1830 for a prize presented by Henry C. Wingfield, the venue was changed in 1849 (Putney to Kew) before moving to the present course (Putney to Mortlake) in 1861. Between 1920 and 1927, BERESFORD recorded seven successive victories and retired undefeated. The next most successful sculler was A. A. Casamajor with six wins from 1855 to 1860. Other winners include Bushnell (1947), Burnell (1946), Southwood (1933), Kinnear (1910-12) and Blackstaffe (1908), who, like Beresford, all won Olympic gold medals as single or double scullers.

WINKLER, HANS GÜNTER (1926-   ), West German show jumping (see EQUESTRIAN EVENTS) rider. The only horseman to have contributed to all three legs of Germany's Olympic hat-trick by winning a team gold medal in 1956, 1960, and 1964, he has also won every important individual title, including the men's world championship in 1954 and the individual Olympic gold medal in 1956 (both on the legendary mare Halla). He won his fifth Olympic gold medal in 1972 when riding Torphy for the winning team.

WINNIPEG BLUE BOMBERS, Canadian professional FOOTBALL team, were first Western Conference team to win the Grey Cup (see FOOTBALL, CANADIAN) in 1935. The most successful Western team, they have won 15 League titles, including five straight from 1958 to 1962, and seven Grey Cups, including four of the above (excepting 1960). Grant coached them during this successful string, before returning to the U.S. to comparable success as coach of the MINNESOTA VIKINGS. COLOURS: Blue and gold.

WINTER, FREDERICK (1926-   ), one of the best steeplechase jockeys of all time who later became a successful trainer. He rode the winner of the GRAND NATIONAL twice, and trained two more winners. In the 1952-3 National Hunt season he rode a record 121 winners, and in 1962 won the Grand National, the CHELTENHAM GOLD CUP, and the Grand Steeplechase de Paris on Mandarin with a broken bit.

WINTER OLYMPIC GAMES. Although ICE SKATING was included in the IVth OLYMPIC GAMES in London in 1908, the first formal Winter Games with a representative group of winter sports which included SKIING was held at Chamonix, France, in 1924. Because of opposition from Norway and Sweden, the event was provisionally called an International Winter Sports Week, and only a decision of the INTERNATIONAL OLYMPIC COMMITTEE (I.O.C.) in Prague a year later ratified them as the first Winter Olympic Games. There were 300 competitors at Chamonix, of whom 102 were skiers. The achievement of Haug of Norway in winning three gold medals in the 18 kilometres, 50 kilometres, and Nordic combination, followed by a bronze in the special jump, was outstanding by any standards.

Only Nordic events were held at ST. MORITZ in 1928 and LAKE PLACID in 1932, but GARMISCH in 1936 saw the introduction of Alpine skiing, though with medals presented only for the combination — the aggregate result of downhill and slalom. Medals were awarded separately for the two Alpine specialities in 1948, and giant slalom was added at Oslo in 1952. By 1968 the number of competitors at the Winter Games had increased to 1,293 from 37 countries, of whom 233 were Alpine skiers, 299 Nordic, and 80 biathlon (see SKIING).

The I.O.C. restrict entry for each event to four per country, so that the order of finish at races can be used only as an approximate indication of ranking of the world's top ski racers. The emergence of Alpine skiing as a major world sport undoubtedly owed much to the prestige conferred by the Games.

The decision of of the Fédération Internationale de Ski (F.I.S.) in 1969 to allow broken-time payments for skiers (payable through national federations) brought to a head a long-standing conflict with those elements of the I.O.C., led by the president, BRUNDAGE, who considered the sport too professional in attitude and practice to be a part of the Olympic movement. The 1970 I.O.C. meeting in Amsterdam referred the F.I.S.'s code to committee, but no agreement emerged. At the Winter Games of 1972 at Sapporo when the Austrian skier, SCHRANZ, was disqualified,

Brundage said many other skiers were guilty of professional practices. The new Olympic president, Lord Killanin, took a more liberal line, and F.I.S. attempted to channel income from equipment manufacturers into national pools. Ski racing much benefited when the I.O.C. waived restrictions on the maximum amount of time sportsmen could spend in training. For leading competitors, racing and training occupies up to ten months of the year.

WISDEN, JOHN (1826-84), cricketer for Sussex, the ALL-ENGLAND XI, and United England XI. A fast bowler, only 5 ft. 4 in. (163 cm.) tall, playing for the North against the South in 1850 he clean bowled all ten batsmen, and in 1851 he gathered 455 wickets. His bowling broke sharply from the off, and he was also a capable batsman. In 1852 he and Dean broke away from CLARKE's wandering All-England XI and established the successful United England XI. His name has been perpetuated in *Wisden Cricketers' Almanack*, which first appeared in 1864.

WISDEN CUP, see BADMINTON.

WISDEN TROPHY. Created by John Wisden & Co. Ltd. in 1963 to commemorate the 100th edition of *Wisden Cricketers' Almanack*, this trophy is competed for as a symbol of CRICKET supremacy by England and the West Indies. West Indies won it in its inaugural year and retained it in 1966, but England won it in 1967-8 and retained it in 1969. In 1973 a rebuilt West Indies side regained the trophy, which is housed permanently in the Imperial Cricket Museum at LORD'S.

WITHERS STAKES is an old-established horse race in the U.S.A., run over 1 mile (1,600 m.) at BELMONT PARK, N.Y., in May. It is, in effect, the American equivalent of the English TWO THOUSAND GUINEAS, but does not form part of the American triple crown.

WITTMAN, SYLVESTER J. (Steve) (1904-), American aviator who learned to fly in 1924 and began racing in 1926. Principally known for his ability to design, fly, and win races with small, tricky, and very fast racing aircraft, he was probably the most experienced and senior racing pilot in the world, and after 44 years he was still racing his single-seaters with great success.

WOLFE-NOEL CUP, see SQUASH RACKETS.

WOLFHOUNDS, Irish RUGBY UNION football club founded in 1956 at the suggestion of MULLEN, and modelled on the BARBARIANS.

Its basic purpose is to take top-class Rugby to provincial centres in Ireland, although it also tours abroad. Teams are formed on an occasional basis, and by invitation only, from prominent players of all countries.
COLOURS: Green and white jerseys, white shorts.

WOLFSHOHL, ROLF (1938-), German professional CYCLING road racer and CYCLO-CROSS rider. In the eleven years 1958-68, he only once failed to win the German cyclo-cross title, and he took the world title three times in the early 1960s.

WOLVERHAMPTON WANDERERS F.C., Association FOOTBALL club. It was founded in 1877 by young men associated with St. Luke's Church School, Blakenhall, and played under that name until 1880 when amalgamation with a local club, Wanderers, inspired the present name. The club was a founder member of the Football League in 1888 and won the F.A. Cup in 1893 and 1908. After the Second World War, Wolverhampton established themselves as one of the leading English clubs; they won the F.A. Cup in 1949, were champions for the first time in history in 1954, and again champions in 1958 and 1959, and F.A. Cup winners in 1960. Wolves' successes brought entry into the European Champion Clubs Cup in 1959 and 1960, and into the Cup-Winners Cup in 1961, but the club failed in those competitions to repeat earlier performances in friendly matches against foreign clubs. The club's outstanding players have included Allen, Hunt, and Wood in the pre-1914 period; CULLIS, Galley, and B. JONES between the wars; and, since 1946, Flowers, WRIGHT, Slater, Williams, and Dougan.
COLOURS: Gold shirts, black shorts.
GROUNDS: Molineux Grounds, Wolverhampton.

WONG PENG SOON (1918-), Singapore and Malayan BADMINTON player. Renowned for his footwork, he was one of the finest singles players the world has seen. He won the ALL-ENGLAND singles championship four times, the last occasion at the age of 37. He was one of the leading players of the Malayan team which won the THOMAS CUP between 1949 and 1955, and thereafter became a professional coach.

WOOD, CRAIG RALPH (1901-68), American professional golfer, U.S. Open champion and U.S. Masters champion of 1941 and a RYDER CUP player. Winner of many American tournaments, he tied for the Open championship in 1933 at St. Andrews, where he hit a drive of some 430 yds. (393 m.) but he lost the play-off to Shute.

WOOD, MERVYN T. (1918-   ), Australian sculler (see ROWING) and oarsman. He first appeared in the 1936 OLYMPIC GAMES in the Australian eight which failed to win a medal. In 1948 he won the Diamond Sculls at HENLEY and the Olympic single sculls title. In 1952, he again won at Henley but could finish only second to the Russian, Tjukalov, in the Olympic Games. COMMONWEALTH GAMES single sculls champion in 1950 and winner of the double sculls in 1954, when he also won a gold medal in coxed fours, he was Australian champion from 1946 to 1952 and in 1955. He won the PHILADELPHIA GOLD CUP for the world championship in 1950.

WOODEN, JOHN (1910-   ), BASKET-BALL coach at the University of California at Los Angeles. Wooden was elected to the Hall of Fame (see NAISMITH) in 1960. He later achieved unprecedented success by taking the U.C.L.A. BRUINS to nine NATIONAL COLLE-GIATE ATHLETIC ASSOCIATION championship victories in the period 1964-73.

WOODERSON, SYDNEY CHARLES (1914-   ), middle-distance runner and cross-country runner for Great Britain. Wooderson was a national hero in his day, with records and titles throughout a career which spanned the Second World War. Injury frustrated his attempt to win an Olympic 1,500 metres medal in 1936 but he won the European title in 1938. In 1937 he broke the world mile record with 4 min. 6·4 sec. and a year later took the world 800 metres record in 1 min. 48·4 sec. and an 880 yards record of 1 min. 49·2 sec. This lasted as a world record until 1953 and as a British record until 1955. Returning to the track after the war, Wooderson improved his mile time to 4 min. 4·2 sec. at the age of 31, and this remained a British best until the advent of BANNISTER. He closed his career with a victory in the 1946 European 5,000 metres championship, when he beat ZATOPEK among others.

WOODFULL, WILLIAM MALDON, O.B.E. (1897-1965), cricketer for Australia and Victoria. An obdurate, reliable batsman, he averaged 65 in first-class CRICKET, and, with PONSFORD, provided a stable and prolific opening partnership for their state and their country. He captained Australia with success on two tours of England, separated by the controversial 'body-line' series of 1932-3, during which his strength of character did much towards minimizing any acrimony.

WOODGATE, WALTER BRADFORD (1840-1920), British oarsman. He won 11 times at HENLEY between 1861 and 1868 in six different events, including the Grand, the Stewards', and the Diamonds. In 1862 he won three Henley events and dead-heated in the final of the Diamonds, losing the re-row. Three times amateur sculling champion and a member of the winning Oxford University crews of 1862 and 1863, he introduced cox-swainless four rowing. In 1868, when rowing for Brasenose College, Oxford, he instructed the coxswain to jump overboard at the start of a race for the Stewards' Cup, then a coxed race, at Henley. The four won but were disqualified. The following year a special cup for coxswainless fours was introduced at Henley and in 1873 the Stewards' Cup, and eventually the other four-oared races, became coxswain-less events. It was not until 1963 that coxed four rowing was reintroduced to Henley.

WOODMEN OF ARDEN. In 1785 a meeting held at Meriden, the exact geographical centre of England, resolved to revive ancient meetings of the Woodmen of the Forest of Arden and since that year the society formed on that occasion has regularly held its ward-motes, as its ARCHERY meetings are called, in accordance with ancient custom. The founder of this distinguished society was the fourth Earl of Aylesford and descendants of this line hold the office of Lord Warden in perpetuity. The early regulations of the Woodmen have not been relaxed and no ladies are allowed as members. The Woodmen of Arden shoot with longbows in traditional style at the clout, an ancient alternative to butt- or target-shooting. Their shooting ground is situated in the heart of the Forest of Arden at Meriden, and meetings are held regularly at their headquarters known as Forest Hall. Regular visits are made to Edinburgh where by tradition they compete with the bowmen of the ROYAL COMPANY OF ARCHERS.

WOODWARD, VIVIAN JOHN (1880-1954), Association footballer for TOTTENHAM HOTSPUR, CHELSEA, and England for whom he made 16 appearances in full international matches in addition to many amateur international matches and representative matches of various kinds. Always an amateur player, after representing several junior clubs including Aschan College and Chelmsford, he first played for Tottenham Hotspur in the Southern League in the season 1900-1 and was both a player and a director of the club when it gained promotion to the First Division at the end of its first season (1908-9) in the Football League. Then, surprisingly, he severed his connection with Tottenham and signed for Chelsea with whom he stayed to the end of his long playing career.

In club matches he seemed at his best at centre forward but in international matches, playing with the best English players, his studied style of play and his appreciation that a pass to a colleague better placed to score was more useful than a hopeful shot at goal, made inside right his natural position.

WOODWARD, WILLIAM (1876-1953), was chairman of the New York Jockey Club and a notable owner-breeder of thoroughbred race-horses in the U.S.A. From his Belair Stud in Maryland came GALLANT FOX and Omaha to win American triple crowns.

WOOLLEY, FRANK EDWARD (1887-), cricketer for England and Kent. tall, majestic left-handed batsman, he scored 58,969 runs (second only to HOBBS); made 145 centuries; 28 times passed 1,000 runs in a season (equalled only by GRACE); took 100 wickets and achieved the 'double' eight times; and, usually fielding at slip, enjoyed the unique distinction of taking over 1,000 catches. His career, which extended from 1906 to 1938, saw the emphasis of his play gradually pass from skilful slow bowling (he took 2,068 wickets altogether) to bold and prolific batting. In 64 Tests he made five centuries, but his most renowned feat is probably 95 and 93 against Australia at LORD's in 1921. In 1911-12 he made an important 133 not out at SYDNEY in the final Test (having hit a record 305 not out against Tasmania), and the following season he took 10 wickets for 49 runs in the last Test against Australia before the Great War.

WORLD ALPINE SKI CUP, see SKIING.

WORLD CUP (1), see FOOTBALL, ASSOCIATION.

(2) GOLF tournament, formerly known as the Canada Cup. This annual international event of two-man teams of professionals from all golfing nations is organized by the International Golf Association.

(3) RUGBY LEAGUE cup, competed for by Australia (winners in 1957, 1968, and 1970), Britain (winners in 1954, 1961, and 1972), France, and New Zealand. France staged the inaugural competition in 1954. The competition is played on the league principle, each country playing each of the others. In 1968 and 1970, for financial reasons, the winner was decided by a match between the two top teams after the league event. In 1970 this produced the absurdity of Australia, who had lost two of their three preliminary matches, beating in the final Britain, who had won all their three preliminary games.

WORLD SERIES, contested since 1903 between champions of the NATIONAL LEAGUE and AMERICAN LEAGUE in American professional BASEBALL. The series is best-four-of-seven wins, with games played in both teams' ball parks. The final series has been preceded since 1969 by a best-three-of-five contest in each league between the Eastern and Western Division winners. Held in early October, the World Series has remained the U.S.A.'s most popular and most widely publicized regular sporting event. The NEW YORK YANKEES dominated the event from the 1920s to the 1960s, winning the series 20 times, including five successive wins from 1949 to 1953. The 1919 Series produced the 'Black Sox' scandal, in which members of the losing CHICAGO WHITE SOX were accused of being paid to 'throw' games.

WORRELL, Sir FRANK MORTIMER MAGLINNE (1924-67), cricketer for West Indies, Barbados, and Jamaica. At first a stylish and high-scoring batsman who also bowled left-arm fast-medium, he developed into a respected captain who instilled unity into West Indian CRICKET and made it a consistent force during the 1960s. In the 1940s he had shared in two partnerships of over 500, and in 51 Tests he made nine centuries — six against England, including 261 in 1950 and 191 not out in 1957 (both at TRENT BRIDGE), and 197 not out in 1959-60, when he and SOBERS added 399 for the fourth wicket. The zenith of his achievements came in Australia (in 1960-1) and England (in 1963), when he led West Indies through exciting series full of purposeful cricket. Worrell was knighted in 1964.

WRESTLING, now more precisely called amateur wrestling, is an individual combat activity in which strength, skill, and stamina combine to make it one of the most basic sports. The popularity of wrestling varies from country to country, particularly since many nations have their own styles. In their own right these styles have considerable local interest. Among the chief variants are: Cumberland and Westmorland, Devon and Cornwall in Britain; *schwingen* in Switzerland; *glima* in Iceland; *sumo* in Japan; *sambo* in Russia; *yagli* in Turkey; and *kushti* in Iran. However, two styles — freestyle and Graeco-Roman — are practised all over the world and are the only ones included in the annual world championships and in the OLYMPIC GAMES. Both have developed from ancient methods of wrestling into modern, well-controlled, exciting sports which attract thousands of partici-

Freestyle

Graeco-Roman

Cumberland and Westmorland

Freestyle

Sumo

STYLES OF WRESTLING

pants particularly in Russia, Turkey, Japan, and Iran.

The Scandinavian countries always excelled in Graeco-Roman but have been overhauled by the relentless preparation of the Iron Curtain countries. The honours in freestyle have been more evenly distributed, although Russia are outstanding in the heavier categories and Japan with their useful background of JUDO in the lighter classes.

Both these styles are fought on a raised platform with sloping sides. No ropes are used. The mat is between 6 and 8 m. (19 ft. 8 in.–26 ft. 3 in.) square (8 m. for Olympic Games and world championships and 6 m. for international matches) with a surrounding safety area of matting 2 m. (6 ft. 7 in.) wide. Each bout is scheduled to last nine minutes, consisting of three three minute 'rounds', with a minute's rest between each. A 'fall' or disqualification, however, may halt the contest before the scheduled end. The bout is controlled by four officials — mat chairman, referee, judge, and timekeeper.

The referee calls the contestants to the centre of the mat and examines them to ensure that they wear regulation costumes, one of red, the other of blue. (In minor events different coloured anklets are worn.) The costumes are leotards, leaving the upper chest and shoulders bare. Light boots and socks are usually worn on the feet. Fingernails are examined to see that they are short. No metal

objects are allowed on the wrestler's person and the competitors may not have oil or grease on their bodies. Frequently a referee will order a second (who accompanies a wrestler to his corner) to wipe away any sweat from the competitor's body. The contestants then shake hands and return to their corners. The referee, on a signal from the mat chairman, who supervises the bout from a desk outside the area, sounds his whistle to start the bout.

The scoring system is very complicated but can be followed on the public scoreboard which shows how many points each competitor has at any stage of the bout. The referee indicates scoring points by raising his hand and signalling with the thumb and first two fingers the points scored — one, two, or three as the case may be. The judge records the score on a score sheet and raises a plaque, coloured red or blue, indicating the number of points. If he disagrees with the decision of the referee he raises a white plaque. The mat chairman then decides the points to be given, which the judge must record on the scoresheet.

The referee administers warnings and cautions to wrestlers for passivity, foul holds, and other infringements of the rules. A wrestler at fault is given a warning and if he offends again he is given a public caution. The referee promptly stops the bout, holds the wrist of the wrestler at fault and raises his other arm overhead, and the judge scores 1 point to the offender's opponent. Should the same wrestler offend again he is given a second public warning and a further point is awarded to his opponent. When this occurs, an additional official is brought in to assist the mat chairman. Should the wrestler offend yet again, he is disqualified and is declared the loser.

A fall is given when both an opponent's shoulders are held in contact with the mat for one second. The referee strikes the mat with his hand and sounds his whistle. If no fall has been obtained by the end of the bout, both wrestlers are brought to the centre of the mat on either side of the referee. The judge's score-sheet is brought to the mat chairman who examines it and declares the winner by raising the plaque of the same colour as the winner's costume.

FREESTYLE is the most popular and probably the most entertaining of the major styles. It developed from Lancashire and catch-as-catch-can styles. Any fair hold, throw or trip is allowed and all bouts are governed by international rules.

The following are fouls and not allowed: pulling of hair, flesh, ears, and private parts, or holding an opponent's costume; brawling, kicking, punching, or twisting of fingers or toes; applying holds liable to endanger life or limb. A throw following a hold applied in the standing position from behind, when the opponent is turned with his head pointing downward, must be made from the side and not directly downwards. In any throw made from the standing position, the wrestler making the throw must touch the mat with his knee before his opponent's body reaches the mat, to lessen the impact and save injury.

When a competitor assumes a wrestler's bridge (resting on his head and feet in an arched position with his back towards the mat), pressure to break this bridge must be applied directly downward and forward towards the head. A full nelson — when a wrestler passes arms under his opponent's armpits from behind and clasps his hands behind the back of the other's neck — must be applied only sideways and not directly downward. Other forbidden moves include: the bending of an opponent's arm behind his back more than 45°; scissor-grips to the head or body (but these may be applied to the leg), and head-holds using both arms.

During the minute rest period, a trainer and assistant may use a towel to wipe down the competitor and may also give advice. No water or stimulant may be given to the wrestler.

The scoring points for a bout are:

1 point to the wrestler who brings down his opponent and holds him in control; to the wrestler who gets from the underneath position to the top position, in control; to a wrestler who applies a correct hold and does not cause his opponent to touch the mat with either his shoulder or head during the execution of the hold; to the opponent of a wrestler receiving a caution for an infringement of the rules.

2 points to the wrestler who applies a correct hold and places his opponent momentarily in danger of a fall in less than five seconds; to a wrestler whose opponent is turned on to the mat, causing his two shoulders to touch it.

3 points to the wrestler who keeps his opponent in danger of a fall (the shoulders forming an angle of less than 90° with the mat) for five seconds; or to a wrestler causing a series of rolling falls or bridges for five seconds continuously and finishing on top and in control.

The timekeeper calls out the minutes during a bout and stops the clock when the referee indicates by making a T-sign with both hands.

The system of elimination in major events is intricate but fair, giving a competitor who has lost one bout a further chance. It also gives a fighter the incentive to score decisively rather than obtain a narrow decision.

Olympic Games, COMMONWEALTH GAMES, world championships, and other major tournaments are all decided on the penalty points system which works as follows:

A wrestler who wins on a fall, 0 penalty points.

A wrestler who loses by a fall, 4 penalty points.

A wrestler who wins with 10 or more scoring points between the contestants, ½ penalty point.

A wrestler who loses with 10 or more scoring points between the contestants, 3½ penalty points.

A wrestler who wins with fewer than 10 scoring points between the contestants, 1 penalty point.

A wrestler who loses with less than 10 scoring points between the contestants, 3 penalty points.

A drawn bout with no points having been scored, or with one or two cautions, 2½ penalty points each.

A drawn bout with points having been scored, 2 penalty points each.

A wrestler who has been disqualified, 4 penalty points.

A competitor is eliminated from the event when he collects 6 or more penalty points and wrestlers eliminated in the same round are considered to be eliminated at the same time.

If a wrestler injures himself independently of his opponent he is declared the loser and receives 4 penalty points, his opponent receiving none. If a wrestler receives three cautions, he is declared the loser and receives 4 penalty points, his opponent receiving none.

The wrestlers all draw numbers (for example 1 to 9). The first round would then be 1 v. 2, 3 v. 4, 5 v. 6, 7 v. 8, 9 a bye; the second round 9 v. 1, 2 v. 3, 4 v. 5, 6 v. 7, 8 a bye.

The competition continues until three or fewer competitors remain with fewer than 6 penalty points. These contest the final but if they have met in previous rounds their penalty points are brought forward into the final. The wrestler with the lesser number of penalty points in the final is declared the winner. In the event of their having the same number of penalty points in the final and each having received the same number of penalty points during the whole competition, the final result is determined by a greater number of wins on falls; greater number of wins on points; greater number of draws; lesser number of cautions in the final. Should a tie still remain, the wrestlers are classified as of equal merit.

The chief standing throws are: the cross-buttock, in which a competitor heaves his opponent over his hips; the flying mare, where he hurls him over his back, using his opponent's arm as a lever; the double-thigh pick-up, where the wrestler scoops his opponent on to the mat by catching him behind his legs; the ankle-and-leg dive, where he takes him off balance by grabbing one leg; and the standing arm-roll where he clasps his opponent's arm and then, wrapping it round his own body, rolls him to the ground.

The chief ground holds are: the nelson holds, where the competitor traps an arm and levers his opponent into a defensive position; and the cradle hold, where the wrestler pins his opponent with one hand over his head and the other through his crotch.

Training for freestyle is both demanding and fascinating. Most of the actual preparation is, naturally, practice wrestling in which various ploys are used to tire out trainees. For example, one fighter will be put in the centre of the mat and given a series of bouts against different opponents. Many wrestlers also do WEIGHT TRAINING, circuit training, and running in a bid to bring their physical fitness to the highest level possible. Wrestling, in common with other combat sports, has weight categories which are strictly adhered to. Careful dieting is often needed to bring a competitor within his appropriate weight category.

In freestyle wrestling the weight categories are: light-flyweight, up to 48 kg. (6 st. 22 lb.); flyweight, up to 52 kg. (8 st. 3 lb.); bantamweight, up to 57 kg. (9 st.); featherweight, up to 62 kg. (9 st. 11 lb.); lightweight, up to 68 kg. (10 st. 10 lb.); welterweight, up to 74 kg. (11 st. 9 lb.); middleweight, up to 82 kg. (12 st. 13 lb.); light-heavyweight, up to 90 kg. (14 st. 2½ lb.); mid-heavyweight, up to 100 kg. (15 st. 10¼ lb.); heavyweight, over 100 kg. (15 st. 10¼ lb.).

GRAECO-ROMAN. The rules, training, and preparation are largely the same as for freestyle. The major difference is that a wrestler is not allowed to seize his opponent below the hips, nor to grip with the legs. Pushing, pressure, or lifting with the legs when in contact with a part of the opponent's body are forbidden.

Most wrestlers concentrate on either the more fluid freestyle or on the classical Graeco-Roman. But whichever they are more proficient in, they can still put up competent performances in the other style. Some wrestlers, particularly below the top international class, compete in both.

In addition to freestyle and Graeco-Roman, inter-collegiate wrestling is practised in America. It is similar to freestyle but a few of the rules differ. A bout of nine minutes' duration is controlled by a referee, who awards the points, and a timekeeper. A fall is given when both a contestant's shoulders are in contact with the mat for two seconds. If no fall takes place the referee declares the winner, taking into account aggression and whether either of the wrestlers has scored near falls. If a draw results, a further two minutes' wrestling takes place, after which a decision must be made.

CUMBERLAND AND WESTMORLAND. Wrestlers in this style commence a bout standing chest to chest, each placing his chin on his opponent's right shoulder and taking hold of him round the body, placing his left arm above the right arm of his opponent. This is termed 'taking hold'. Five minutes are allowed in which to take hold and, in the event of the hold not being taken, the referee adopts a stooping position between the wrestlers and instructs them to take hold across his back. When both wrestlers have taken hold with their hands clasped and are fairly on their guard, the referee calls 'hold' and only then does wrestling commence.

With the exception of kicking, the wrestlers are allowed to use every legitimate means to throw each other (striking with the side of the foot is not judged to be kicking).

If a wrestler breaks his hold (that is loses his grip, though not on the ground) and the other retains his hold, the former is not allowed to re-take hold and is declared the loser. If either wrestler touches the ground with one knee only, or any part of his body other than his feet, even though he still retains his hold, he is not allowed to recover himself and is declared the loser. If both contestants fall to the ground, the wrestler who is first down or falls under the other is the loser. If they fall side by side, or so that the judges cannot decide who was first on the ground, it is called a 'dog fall' and is fought again.

A wrestling bout is controlled by a referee and two judges who position themselves on opposite sides of the mat or wrestling area.

Competitions are wrestled in the following weight categories: flyweight, up to 52 kg. (8 st. 3 lb.); bantamweight, up to 57 kg. (9 st.); featherweight, up to 62 kg. (9 st. 11 lb.); lightweight, up to 68 kg. (10 st. 10 lb.); welterweight, up to 74 kg. (11 st. 9 lb.); middleweight, up to 82 kg. (12 st. 13 lb.); light-heavyweight, up to 90 kg. (14 st. 2½ lb.); heavyweight, over 100 kg. (15 st. 10½ lb.).

Any number of wrestlers may compete in a weight category, and they all wrestle each other. The wrestler who obtains most falls or wins in a competition or championship is the winner. In the event of two wrestlers having the same number of falls or wins, they wrestle the best of three falls to decide the winner.

The chief throws in this style are: the backheel, where a competitor attempts to heave his opponent off balance and then hook away his heel; the outside stroke, where a wrestler catches his opponent with his leg and then drives him to the ground; the hype, where the wrestler swings his opponent over his thigh and on to the ground.

DEVON AND CORNWALL wrestling is controlled by three judges ('sticklers'). The wrestlers wear jackets and must take hold of the collar and one sleeve and throw each other from the standing position. A fall or 'back' is obtained when a wrestler is thrown so that two shoulders and one hip, two hips and one shoulder, or both shoulders and both hips simultaneously touch the ground. If any part other than the feet touch the ground, the wrestlers must disengage and recommence grappling. Should a wrestler touch the ground with his hand or knee to avoid a fall he is cautioned; if the offence is repeated he is disqualified. Should a wrestler's jacket come off or slip over his head, the contestants must recommence with a renewed hold.

In a competition, the wrestlers draw lots and are paired off, the winners of each bout being known as 'standards' who are again paired off until the number of unthrown men is equal to the number of prizes available. These remaining wrestlers compete for the prizes, the first prize going to the wrestler who has not been thrown.

Fouls include: cross-collar hold, pressure of the thumbs on the throat, striking with the foot above the knee, and kicking.

GLIMA is practised almost entirely in Iceland and has been popular for over 900 years. *Glima* is derived from the words *glitra* and *glampa*, which mean 'something that flashes or sparkles'. The Icelandic *Glima* Association hold annual championships in one open weight category. The winner is called 'The King of *Glima*' and most of the outstanding 'kings' have weighed over 90 kg. (14 st. 2½ lb.).

Before the twentieth century competitors gripped each other's trousers but in 1908 a harness was introduced. This consists of straps round both thighs, which are linked by vertical straps on the outside of each thigh. Each competitor puts his right arm over the top of his opponent's hip at the back, and the left hand holds on to a strap outside the thigh just below the upper end of his thigh bone.

Each round is of two minutes and a winning fall is scored if a competitor is thrown to the ground. Hip and ankle throws are particularly common. A fighter must keep hold of his opponent's harness and if a competitor loses his grip the bout is stopped. There is no ground wrestling.

KUSHTI is the national style of wrestling practised in Iran. Contests take place on grassland and the competitors wear tight-fitting leather trousers. The winner of a bout is the wrestler who throws his opponent on to his back on the ground. In competitions, the winner is the wrestler with the most throws to his credit.

SAMBO. In 1964 *sambo* was the third style to gain official recognition by the Fédération Internationale des Luttes Amateurs (F.I.L.A.), the International Wrestling Federation. It is a blend of the various folk styles of Russian wrestling. The word is composed of the first three letters of the word *samozashchita* (self-defence) and the initial letters of the words *bez oruzhiya* (without weapons).

Competitors wear a tight-fitting jacket, of which each takes hold, with a wrestling costume underneath and light boots. The weight categories are the same as for international wrestling. To win, a competitor, while remaining on his feet, must throw his opponent cleanly on to his back. But when the wrestler falls with his opponent the competition continues on the ground. He then has to force his opponent to submit by the application of torture grips — locks on the knee and elbow joints. Decisions are also given if no definite score is made. There are three three-minute rounds. The sport is very popular in Russia, and Japan and Bulgaria have also had a number of outstanding competitors. Its similarity to judo has enabled a number of its outstanding fighters, such as KIKNADZE, to win international honours in judo.

SCHWINGEN wrestling has been practised in Switzerland for hundreds of years. The competitors are clothed in a vest and short leather trousers and commence a bout by taking hold of each other's trousers at the back and one of the trouser legs. On the referee's command they start wrestling, the object being to throw the opponent to the ground. For the throw to be correct the thrower must have hold of his opponent's trousers when he touches the ground. In a competition or championship a wrestler is eliminated when he has been thrown twice. Each competitor wrestles every other, the winner being the wrestler who has the most throws to his credit.

SUMO is Japan's spectacular national sport which attracts thousands of spectators to the 15-day championship events which are staged six times a year in Japan's major cities. In *sumo* the competitors' centre of gravity must be as low as possible and the wrestlers force-feed themselves on a diet including a large amount of rice to get as heavy as possible. Few outstanding wrestlers weigh less than 130 kg. (20 st.).

The highest position possible in *sumo* is *yokozuna* — grand champion — but there have been only a few who have reached it, rarely more than two or three at any one time. The award is made by the Japan *Sumo* Association, which controls the sport.

Wrestlers are trained from youth under a rigorous selection and preparation policy. But all aim eventually to compete in the six major annual events. Competitors wear loin-cloths, and the reigning champion enters the ring with a sword-bearer and attendant. The object of the sport is to force an opponent out of the 12 ft. (3·66 m.) circular ring. At the start of a bout, the wrestlers face each other, with both feet on the ground, in a crouching position with both hands firmly clenched in front. Any hold is allowed, the winner being the wrestler who forces his opponent out of the ring. The sport is surrounded by great ceremony — purifying salt is hurled into the ring and the two competitors glare at each other, pounding their fists on the ground before each contest.

YAGLI. Wrestling is a national sport in Turkey and attracts large crowds to its tournaments. Besides freestyle and Graeco-Roman, *yagli,* the Turkish style, is practised.

Contestants wear long leather breeches and the body is smeared with grease. A contest ends when one of the competitors is thrown with one shoulder and one thigh touching the ground. The annual Kirkpinar contests attract an entry of over 300 wrestlers from all parts of Turkey, and the event lasts for three days.

Wrestling is one of the oldest and most basic of all sports. Although F.I.L.A. was not founded until 1921, events had been staged for thousands of years before. Many of the holds and throws used now in the Olympic Games and world championships are the same as those used in the championships of the ancient civilizations of Egypt, Crete, China, and particularly Greece. But the origin of wrestling probably precedes even the earliest of these since cave-men almost certainly practised headlocks, throws, and strangleholds to defend themselves. Thus, from a necessity for survival, wrestling became a sport.

Certainly the Egyptian civilization which was established about 3400 B.C. practised wrestling, shown in wall paintings at Beni-Hasan. On one wall there are over 200 wrestling groups and the bout ended as in modern times, when a competitor's shoulders were pinned to the ground. There are even records of some typical conversations between the wrestlers during matches. Wrestling events also took place in the Babylonian and Assyrian civilizations and in China, where the upper classes practised a method which also included boxing and kicking — perhaps one of the origins of *kempo* and KARATE.

But it was in Greece that the sport really developed. There are references to wrestling in both the *Iliad* and the *Odyssey* and it was introduced to the Olympic Games in 704 B.C. — the eighteenth Olympiad. Theseus is credited with having laid down the first rules of wrestling in about 900 B.C. and the sport had become very popular in Greece and its provinces. The rules were simple for the event

in the Olympics — a fall was gained when any part of the body except the feet of either competitor touched the ground. The first competitor to get two falls was the winner.

Sparta dominated the early years of the Olympics but the outstanding champion in the early years was Milo of Croton. He won an Olympic title in 540 B.C. for the 17–20 age group, and four further titles. His experience in strength development anticipated the basis of modern weight training, which was to have a pronounced effect on many sports during the twentieth century. He carried a calf on his shoulders every day from its birth so that when it was fully grown he was able to walk round the Olympic Stadium with it on his back. As the calf grew bigger so Milo's strength increased to meet the new burden put on it. In modern weight training this is known as 'progressive resistance'.

A new style of wrestling, *Pankration,* was introduced in 648 B.C. Throwing, strangling, arm-locks, biting, kicking, gouging, and punching were all allowed in an event which often ended with one of the competitors mutilated or dead. The outstanding figure in this style was Theogees of Thasos. Professionalism gradually took over the Olympics and some competitors in the wrestling events were bribed to lose. This, together with the success of foreign competitors following Alexander the Great's conquests, resulted in wrestling losing much of its public interest.

The Romans briefly revived the sport and adapted the classical style to a method called Graeco-Roman. The use of the legs for attack or defence was forbidden and this style, with only slight changes, is used in modern events.

Professionalism became increasingly obvious and supporters began to shun it, despite the fact that two Roman emperors — Commodus and Maximiam — had successful wrestling careers. Although the sport was practised in regional styles throughout the world it was not until the nineteenth century that it became as popular as it had been during the early Greek civilization.

However, there are numerous historical references to wrestling during the Middle Ages, including the reputed bout between England's Henry VIII and France's Henry I on the Cloth of Gold. Charles II of England was another king who favoured wrestling and attended many bouts.

Japan, a country from which many of the outstanding wrestlers of the twentieth century were to come, held its first known bout in 23 B.C. The event was won by Sukune who is now the patron of all Japanese wrestlers. In A.D. 858 the two sons of the Emperor Buntoku fought each other to decide which should succeed their father and, with the growth of the *samurai* (knights), wrestling became part of military training. Japan has become well-known for two styles of wrestling — *ju-jitsu*, from which judo developed, and *sumo*.

Russia, like many countries, had a vast number of local wrestling fashions like *chadaoba* and *kurash* and in the twentieth century they were combined into *sambo*. India and Pakistan, who have dominated the Commonwealth Games during the twentieth century, have a deep tradition in the sport.

The Moghuls staged numerous tournaments, the winner of which was awarded a wooden club, similar to the one of the Hindu god of strength. Another country which was to produce so many champions in the modern Olympic Games, Turkey, also has a background of competitive wrestling. Here contestants covered themselves in oil — making firm grips exceedingly difficult. The sultans were generous patrons to the champions and competition was extremely fierce.

However, it was principally in Europe and in America that the development of modern Olympic wrestling took place. By the sixteenth century there were several books available in German and references to the sport occur in such works as Shakespeare's *As You Like It*.

In Britain there were a large number of separate styles such as Cumberland and Westmorland, Devon and Cornwall, the Lancashire catch-as-catch-can, and the Dinnie or Scottish style. But these were regional and it was not until the eighteenth century that any sort of international sport developed. Men like Topham and members of touring circus groups helped to popularize the sport. One of the outstanding men was Muller who wrestled under the name of Eugen Sandow. He had a successful career before becoming even more famous as a strong man.

Until the era before the First World War, the outstanding development was in the U.S.A. Until the nineteenth century, wrestling had been the leading combat sport when it was gradually overtaken by the popularity of BOXING with the arrival of men like SULLIVAN. Abraham Lincoln, later to become President, was an expert wrestler. Although there were no national champions, each area had its champion and the circuses threw up many outstanding professional competitors, the most talented of whom was probably MULDOON. Like most of the wrestlers, he fought in the Graeco-Roman style — although the collar-and-sleeve style had also been popular. He frequently toured America with Sullivan although the pair made a strange contrast since

Muldoon was as abstemious as Sullivan was bibulous.

Muldoon beat such men as Martino (Spain), Riga (France), Bibby and Cannon (Britain), but was undefeated from the time he won the title until his retirement almost 15 years later when he gave up the American title. His personality had brought tremendous popularity to the Graeco-Roman style but catch-as-catch-can, later known as freestyle, was more dramatic.

The first American to claim the world title was JENKINS, a hefty, one-eyed competitor from Ohio. Although supreme in America he was twice beaten by the great Russian, HACK-ENSCHMIDT, the man who had done most to promote the sport in Britain and Europe. The boom in music-halls had seen wrestling emerge as one of the most popular entertainments of the day, and Hackenschmidt, guided by his shrewd promoter, Cochran, was the outstanding figure of the time. Cochran's flair for show business thrust wrestling in front of the European public. In America, Hackenschmidt's conqueror, GOTCH, was similarly successful after winning the American title from Jenkins in 1905. His tours attracted enormous interest and his two bouts with Hackenschmidt were highlights. After the Russian had left, Cochran found a new star in Zbyysco. The British crowds hated him as much as they had adored Hackenschmidt but they flocked to see some of his fights, notably the bout against another Russian, Padzoubney.

After the First World War, professional wrestling slowly moved from a true sport to entertainment in order to hold the interest of spectators who got bored with long, even contests. Although many of the new professionals were very skilful, strong and agile, they often had to 'carry' opponents in order to get fights, and genuine professional wrestling became confined to tiny areas.

However, serious enthusiasts could now concentrate on amateur wrestling, which had previously existed only at a low level because the leading performers invariably turned professional. Two things ensured that the amateur sport would become popular — the establishment in 1921 of the Fédération Internationale des Luttes Amateurs, which held its first world championships that year, and the Olympic Games.

Since wrestling had been an essential part of the ancient Olympics, it was natural that it should be included from the revival of the Games in 1896. Because of the popularity of the professionals, the standard was not particularly high and it took some time before the events settled down. At Athens in 1896 only one event was contested — the heavyweight freestyle — which was won by the German, Shumann. No wrestling was held at the 1900 Olympics and in 1904 Americans took all the titles because few Europeans made the trip to St. Louis.

At the 1908 Olympics in London, British competitors took three gold medals in the catch-as-catch-can class. One of them was S. V. BACON, one of four brothers who dominated the British sport during the next 15 years. There were no freestyle bouts at the Stockholm Olympics in 1912 but in the Graeco-Roman classes the Scandinavians first showed their ability in this style, winning four of the five categories. The fifth class, the middleweight B, was left without a decision after Sweden's Ahlgren and Bohling (Finland) fought over six hours without securing a fall.

With the establishment of the International Federation, increased weight categories were instituted and world Graeco-Roman championships were staged in Scandinavia in 1921 and 1922. The first European championships were held in 1925 at Mailand. Probably the outstanding wrestler at this time was Finland's ANTILLA, but the U.S.A. took four titles in the freestyle at the 1928 Olympics with Scandinavia maintaining their dominance of the Graeco-Roman classes.

Wrestling was an immediate choice when the Commonwealth Games (then known as the British Empire Games) were started in 1930. But Canada, the host country, won all the titles since there were only two competitors in a number of the classes. At the 1932 Olympics in Los Angeles the U.S.A. and the Scandinavian countries shared most of the titles, while at the 1934 Commonwealth Games in London, the medals were more equally divided. A silver medallist in that event, Australia's GARRARD, became one of the Commonwealth's finest wrestlers.

Sweden and Hungary took the leading honours at the 1936 Olympics, while Australia, the host country, won all but one of the titles at the 1938 Commonwealth Games. World championships in Graeco-Roman had been staged only intermittently and few wrestlers were able to gain great fame or experience. Two exceptions were the Swedes, WESTERGRÅN and JOHANNSON, who each won three Olympic gold medals.

After the Second World War the sport became a truly international affair. The London Olympics were attended by 27 countries. The best performer was Turkey's DOGU, who two years earlier had won the European welterweight freestyle title. He defeated Garrard for the gold medal to become one of his country's six gold medallists. Another performer was the Graeco-Roman heavyweight champion, Kiracci, who had won a bronze medal 12 years earlier in the middleweight freestyle.

The first world freestyle championships were staged in Helsinki in 1951, venue of the Olympics the following year, and Turkey won six titles, Dogu taking the light-heavyweight gold medal. At the Olympics four Turkish wrestlers were not allowed to enter since their entry forms had arrived too late. As a result, the U.S.S.R., making her entry at the Games, dominated the meeting, winning six titles. The only competitor to retain his crown was the Swedish middleweight, GRONBERG, who took the Graeco-Roman gold medal. An outstanding British performance came from RICHMOND who took a bronze medal in the freestyle heavyweight category. But, generally, the splendidly trained Russians were far too powerful for the rest of the world, particularly with the Turks absent.

The struggle between the Turks and Russians for supremacy produced some of the outstanding competition for the rest of the decade. At the 1955 world Graeco-Roman championships at Karlsruhe, Russia won six of the eight titles and, at the 1956 Olympics in Melbourne, retained the leadership of the sport, collecting six gold medals, two silver, and five bronze. Even more remarkable was the fact that they fielded a team consisting entirely of newcomers, former world champions and Olympic gold medallists being omitted. Thirty nations competed (compared with 37 at Helsinki) and, apart from Russia, the outstanding winners were the heavyweight freestyle champion, KAPLAN, from Turkey and the Japanese featherweight, Sasahara, who had won the world title in Tokyo in 1954.

The Turks regained their dominance at the 1957 world championships in Istanbul. They took four titles — Kaplan retaining his heavyweight crown — to Russia's two. But in the Graeco-Roman championships a year later in Budapest Russia once more turned the tables with five titles to Turkey's two.

In the same year, at the Commonwealth Games in Cardiff, India and Pakistan began to emerge as world-class contenders after South Africa had taken all but two of the gold medals four years earlier in Vancouver. South Africa took four titles in 1958 but Pakistan and India shared the other four between them. It was the beginning of their mastery over the rest of the Commonwealth and the sport became extremely popular in both countries. Wrestling schools, like the one run by the Guru Hanuman in Delhi, produced a number of fine competitors.

Another Eastern country which was gradually coming to the fore was Japan. Here the tradition of judo provided many youngsters with a technique they could use effectively when they started wrestling. With a number of the judo throws useful for competitive free-style wrestling, Japan had a ready-made reservoir of talent.

The see-saw continued at the Rome Olympics with Turkey coming out on top with seven gold and two silver medals; but probably the outstanding competitor was the West German heavyweight, DIETRICH, who took the free-style gold medal and the Graeco-Roman silver medal.

An even greater wrestler was to appear for the first time at the 1961 world freestyle championships — the Russian, MEDVED, who became the most successful wrestler of the next decade. An equally famous competitor was the Japanese, WATANABE, who won his first world title at featherweight in 1962 and crowned his career by winning the 1964 Olympic gold medal — his 186th consecutive victory. Although Turkey remained a strong force, the balance of power in wrestling moved to Japan who countered the threat of Russian monopoly. Japan won five gold medals at the 1964 Olympics with their dexterous fighters in lighter weights. Men like flyweights Sakurama and Ichiguchi, as well as Watanabe, showed superb speed and skill. Two new countries showed impressive form; Bulgaria and Iran won three titles at the 1965 world freestyle championships in England but at the Graeco-Roman championships in Tampere, Finland, Russia won all eight gold medals.

India and Pakistan continued their improvement by taking seven of the eight gold medals at the 1966 Commonwealth Games. At the 1968 Olympics, Japan won three freestyle titles but it was Turkey who returned with renewed vigour. Russia and Bulgaria had swept the board at the European championships but the Bulgarians faded in Mexico although the Russians, led by Medved, took three gold medals. Turkey, with Atalay upsetting France's Robin, the reigning world champion, to win the freestyle welterweight class, was most impressive. The winner of the Graeco-Roman category was the Hungarian heavyweight, Kozma, killed in a car crash two years later.

Russia tightened her grip at the 1969 world championships in Argentina, taking ten titles in the two categories. It was the first time that the two extra classes — light-flyweight (up to 48 kg.) and heavyweight plus (over 100 kg.) were contested after their introduction at the 1968 Olympic Congress. Russia's prominence continued at the 1970 world championships where they won nine gold medals, with Iran taking three freestyle titles.

They equalled this feat at the 1972 Olympics — the last time that Medved was to win an international title. But the most impressive of their nine winners was another Russian, Yargin, who completed the usual feat of pinning all his opponents; he was particularly adept at close quarters. The U.S.A. did well, led by GABLE, taking three gold medals, 12 years after they had won their previous title.

In the Graeco-Roman events eastern European nations finished first in all ten categories. In the heavyweight plus class West Germany's Dietrich failed in his attempt to break their monopoly and to set an all-time record of a medal in five different Olympic celebrations. After pinning the 30 stone (191 kg.) American Taylor he was disqualified in a later bout and withdrew from the competition. In most classes the western European nations were simply worn down by the strength and stamina of the Communist countries.

India and Pakistan maintained their monopoly of Commonwealth titles. At the Edinburgh Games in 1970 the two countries won all but one of the gold medals, India providing perhaps the most astonishing competitor, the light-flyweight Prakash, who won the championship despite being only 12 years old. The Games authorities at first maintained this was too young for a combat sport and almost refused him entry. Pakistan's withdrawal from the Commonwealth dramatically disturbed the balance of power, as was to be seen at the 1974 Games at Christchurch.

Graeme Kent, *Pictorial History of Wrestling* (1968); Shozo Sasahara, *Fundamentals of Scientific Wrestling* (1968); Henry H. Stone, *Wrestling* (1950).

GOVERNING BODY (WORLD): Fédération Internationale des Luttes Amateurs, 12 Valmont, Lausanne, Switzerland.

WRIGHT, HAROLD, the most celebrated trainer of COURSING greyhounds. He trained the record number of nine winners of the WATERLOO CUP between 1912 and 1946.

WRIGHT, MARY KATHRYN (1935-), American professional golfer. She was U.S. Open champion 1958, 1959, 1961; U.S. professional champion 1958, 1960, 1961, 1963; and winner of some 60 sponsored tournaments.

WRIGHT, WILLIAM AMBROSE (1924-), Association footballer for WOLVERHAMPTON WANDERERS and England for whom he was the first player to make over a hundred appearances in full international matches. He joined Wolverhampton as a ground-staff boy and stayed to captain the teams that won the

F.A. Cup in 1949, and the Football League championships in 1954, 1958, and 1959. Originally a right half, he moved to centre half during the 1954 world championship matches and continued to play for, and to captain, England at centre half until his retirement in August 1959. Subsequently he managed the F.A. Youth team and the ARSENAL club.

WRIGHT, WILLIAM HENRY (1835-95), American BASEBALL player and manager, recognized as the father of professional baseball. He came as a small child with his family from Sheffield, England, to the U.S.A. where he began his athletic career as a CRICKET player with the St. George Cricket Club of Staten Island, New York. He soon turned to baseball and in 1858 joined the New York Knickerbockers, the first organized team. In 1869 he became player-manager for the Cincinnati Red Stockings, the first openly all-professional baseball team. He next managed the Boston Red Stockings and led them to four successive championships (1872-5) in the National Association of Professional Base Ball Players and then to the championship of the new NATIONAL LEAGUE of Professional Base Ball Clubs in 1877 and in 1878. He continued to manage the Red Stockings and other National League teams through 1893. His brother George played shortstop for the Cincinnati and Boston Red Stockings and the Providence club in the years when Harry Wright managed those teams, and became a partner in Wright & Ditson, a well-known sporting-goods firm absorbed by A. G. Spalding & Bros. in 1892.

WYETH, EZRA (1910-   ), lawn BOWLS player. Australian by birth, he emigrated to the U.S.A. in 1957 and captained America in the inaugural world bowls championships at KYEEMAGH, N.S.W., in October 1966. A professor of physical education, he has used the facilities of Californian universities to conduct research into the mechanics of delivering a bowl and has made several valuable contributions to the knowledge of the game.

WYFOLD CUP, see HENLEY ROYAL REGATTA.

Y

YACHTING is the use of small sailing and power craft for pleasure, either competitively in racing or individually in cruising. Today, with few exceptions, all such craft are owned and crewed by amateurs. Yachting is essentially a participation sport. An owner may enter a race simply by being a member of the club organizing it, or by belonging to a sailing club affiliated to the national racing organization of his country, and by having a yacht eligible by size or type for the particular race. Prizes, even in races of the calibre of a regatta such as Cowes Week, are so small as to be nominal. Anybody with enough sailing experience to make him a useful member (experience which is usually acquired from sailing dinghies, the traditional tutor craft of the sport) may be invited to join the crew of a yacht by her owner, so that the amateur spirit is strongly maintained.

To take part, all a man needs is a yacht, whether she be a large offshore racer 75 ft. (22·86 m.) or more in length, or a sailing dinghy as small as 12 ft. (3·65 m.) long, which he can trail to a suitable launching place and store when not in use. Nearly all boat owners belong to one or more of the recognized sailing clubs and this is essential for participation in racing.

Although larger yachts generally provide a more comfortable cruise, a boat as small as a 14 ft. (4·26 m.) dinghy can also make a practical cruiser. The Dinghy Cruising Association, with a membership throughout Britain, caters for people who enjoy cruising in boats as small as possible.

A cruising yacht should be designed and rigged to sail reasonably fast. One which can maintain a good average speed in fine weather can be navigated with greater accuracy than a slow one, and she can make short passages with greater confidence of arriving at her destination before any bad weather materializes.

Like a racing craft, a cruising boat must have strong sails and gear, but she must have the capacity to carry a larger weight of food, water, and stores. Unlike a racing yacht, a cruiser is usually handled by a comparatively small crew, often two or three, sometimes only one. Her sail plan therefore has to be simple, broken down into small areas that would be inefficient in a racer so that the crew can

reef (reduce the areas of the sails) with ease when the weather worsens.

Single-handed cruising gained in popularity during the 1960s with the improvement in design of self-steering gear for yachts. This was developed from that used for many years in model sailing yachts and is based on the principle of a vane holding the rudder, and therefore the boat, at a predetermined angle to

Cruising yacht

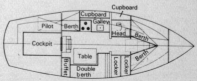

CRUISING YACHT
Typical sail plan (Bermudian sloop rig) and underwater profile for a cruising yacht, with (*below*) plan view showing typical layout for such a yacht with sleeping space for a crew.

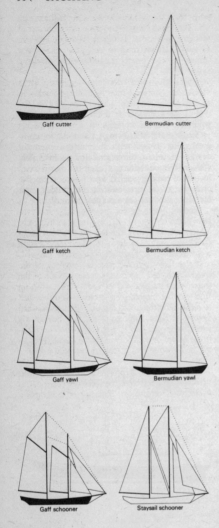

Gaff cutter

Bermudian cutter

Gaff ketch

Bermudian ketch

Gaff yawl

Bermudian yawl

Gaff schooner

Staysail schooner

YACHT RIGS

the wind. Without self-steering gear, the solo sailor had to heave the yacht to while he slept, or try to balance the sails so that she sailed on, an unreliable method of keeping course.

Rig is the disposition of the sails, masts, and spars in a sailing yacht by which her type, as distinct from her purpose, is defined. The most common sailing craft is the Bermudian sloop, with a triangular mainsail and single headsail. It is efficient, especially when beating to windward, easy to handle because of the

absence of heavy running gear aloft, and versatile, in that it can be used in the smallest dinghies as well as all but the largest offshore cruisers and racers. The only disadvantage of the rig is that because it has dominated sailing for so long, it has inhibited designers and owners of craft not intended for racing from experimenting with other rigs.

Bermudian rig began to supersede the gaff rig soon after the First World War. Until then yachts had mainly followed working-craft practice in rigging and the gaff sail enjoyed the popularity that the Bermudian has now. The gaff mainsail is a four-sided sail, named after the diagonally set spar that supports its upper edge, or head. Extended along its foot is a boom, similar to that used on the Bermudian sail. Gaff rig is still used in many cruising yachts and day-sailing craft which either started life as yachts or were built as working craft and later converted.

Other rigs in common use are the Bermudian cutter, setting two headsails instead of one, thereby allowing more scope to suit weather conditions; the ketch, with two masts, the after of which is stepped forward of the rudder post; the yawl, similar to the ketch but with a smaller mizzen, stepped abaft the rudder post; and, particularly in American waters, the schooner.

A widely used dinghy rig is the Gunter lug, a version mid-way between the Bermudian and the gaff, in which the upper leading edge of the mainsail is bent on to a yard which sets upright, combining the Bermudian's advantage of a long leading edge on the sail with the gaff's of a short, easily-supported mast. The short mast, with its low centre of gravity, is particularly useful for craft left on exposed moorings.

One of the best sails for boat-work is the dipping lugsail, the tack (forward bottom corner) of which is bent to the stemhead, so that the sail extends in one piece round the leeward side of the mast to its sheeting aft. Being in one piece, it is an efficient sail which tends to lift a boat rather than press her over, as the boomed Bermudian rig does. Its crucial disadvantage is that it has to be lowered and reset on the leeward side when the boat tacks, a process which takes an unacceptable time in confined waters and which demands a high degree of co-ordination from the crew.

A good sailplan is probably more important to a yacht's competitive performance than her hull shape. A good hull is designed to use the motive power of the sails most efficiently; but it remains a static thing, unalterable, whereas sails must be constantly set and sheeted (made flatter or more bulging) to gain the best effect from the wind.

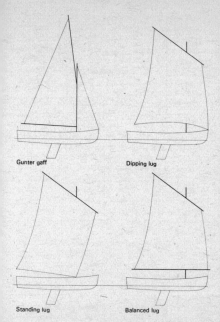

SMALL BOAT RIGS

The gunter gaff slides and pivots on the mast, which has a forestay to keep it upright. With the dipping lug, the tack is made fast to the stem, and the sail must be shifted to the other side of the mast when tacking. With the standing lug, the tack is made fast at the foot of the mast; the balanced lug has a boom that pivots on the mast.

Modern racing yachts and most of the top-rank one-designs and dinghies, possess large wardrobes of sails to suit different conditions. These include spinnakers (large parachute-shaped sails for running before the wind) and foresails, ranging from large genoas, smaller jibs down to storm-sails made of heavyweight cloth. Cruising yachts might include in their range a large ghoster jib for light airs, a full-size genoa, a working jib, and a storm jib, plus a spinnaker, if there are enough hands to work it.

A boat's aesthetic appeal usually ranks equal with her functional efficiency, so that an owner may, if not committed by class rules or racing ambition, choose a rig merely because it is pleasing to the eye.

The sloop or cutter rig will sail closer to the wind than the yawl or ketch and, of the two latter rigs, the yawl is probably the handier, although its small mizzen contributes little or nothing when going to windward. Off the wind, the mizzen mast is a convenient setting point for a staysail, set in the same fashion as a jib. The ketch, with its more equal division of working sail areas, is better balanced and can be reefed down snug in bad weather without impairing too much the efficiency of those sails.

By far the most handsome yacht rig is the schooner, confined mostly to large yachts in British and European waters. In the U.S.A., where the schooner is reckoned the national rig as the cutter is in England, schooner yachts as small as 35 ft. (10·66 m.) over-all are common. In a two-masted schooner the aftermost mast is the main, the other being the foremast. As with the yawl and the ketch, a schooner can lose to a single-masted yacht of comparable size when sailing to windward, because the foresail tends to backwind the mainsail.

The simplest rig for the beginner, and probably the safest of all, is the standing lug, which is best suited to boats up to about 16 ft. (4·87 m.) long. The head of the sail is laced to a yard which is hoisted by a single halyard, and the tack is made fast to the foot of the mast. The yard lies on the leeward side of the mast when sailing and is fitted with a tripping line, so that the helmsman can swing the yard to leeward when going about. When windward ability is less important than a beginner's safety, the sail can be set loose-footed (without a boom at the foot) so that if the sheet is let go in an emergency, the sail empties like a flag.

Rig is so closely bound with the hull form of the vessel it drives that it is not practical to think of it in isolation. The rig best suited for a

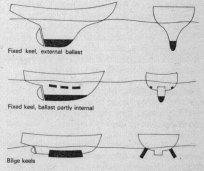

HULL FORMS

The fixed keel with external ballast has a pendulum effect; the position of the ballast is not adjustable. With the ballast partly internal, the distribution of weight gives easier motion and reduces strains on the hull; the ballast inside can be moved to adjust 'trim'. The twin bilge keels offer resistance to sideways movement, but not so effectively as a single keel.

vessel is invariably that for which she was designed. A modern Bermudian rig would be inefficient on a deep-draught working-boat type of hull, which needs the extra driving power of the gaff to move her and the extra turning power of headsails set on a bowsprit to tack her through the wind.

Yacht is the collective name given to all small pleasure craft whether motor-powered or sailing, but it applies strictly to larger craft which afford living accommodation for their crews. These do not include half-decked or fully decked racing yachts, dinghies, or day-sailing boats. Sailing yachts are ballasted with lead or iron to provide counter-leverage against the pressure of the wind in their sails. This ballast may be external, bolted on the bottom of the hull and shaped to fair with the underwater lines of the keel, or internal, or both. Yachts intended for cruising can be built with a shallower draught, allowing them access to smaller creeks and estuaries, by using centre-boards as in dinghies, or by using bilge-keels, which are fastened in a fore and aft line on each side of the hull bottom. These offer similar resistance against being blown off to leeward as the centre-board, with the added advantage that yachts can sit upright on them if an anchorage dries out at low tide. The most efficient hull shape for sailing, however, is the deep fixed keel.

The largest yachts built today for inshore racing are the 12-Metre class, used from 1958 in the AMERICA'S CUP competitions. These, and a few of the larger (about 60 ft. long over-all) offshore racers are still built individually of wood, to individual designs in consultation with the owner. But the building of yachts in glass-reinforced resin made such strides during the 1960s that yachts of 70 ft. (21·33 m.) over-all are now regularly produced. Fibre-glass, to be an economic proposition, demands a large-scale production to cover the cost of design, mould-making, and laminating.

Craft built purely for racing in inshore waters, such as the 12-Metres, or the Solings and Tempest classes used in the OLYMPIC GAMES, are characterized by their low freeboard (hull height above the water) and raking bow and counter sections, designed to give greater waterline length, and therefore greater speed potential, when they are sailing heeled to a breeze. Offshore yachts have a higher freeboard, and their ends are shorter and fuller for greater buoyancy and carrying capacity.

Dinghy was formerly the name of a small boat used as a tender to a larger yacht ('punt' remains the more common term among working boatmen) and is now applied to all unballasted sailing craft from about 8 ft. over-all length to about 20 ft. (2·43–6·09 m.). They are

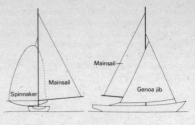

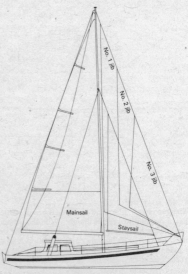

SAIL FORMS
(*Top left*) Yacht with spinnaker set (to port), viewed from astern. The mainsail is set at nearly 90° to the wind; the spinnaker's boom is temporary. The genoa jib is shown (*top right*) in its extreme form, as found on some racing yachts, with a large overlap over the mainsail. Figure below shows a typical sail plan, with relative sizes indicated.

unballasted in the sense that a keel yacht has lead, iron, or concrete ballast attached to the bottom of her hull. Instead, dinghies depend on the weight of the crew for trim and to balance the heeling effect of the wind in the sails. To maintain lateral resistance, that is, to be able to steer a course across the wind or close to it, a centre-board is used. This is a flat plate of wood or metal which is lowered through a slot in a raised trunk on the centre-line of the hull which, while resisting sideways pressure of the wind, offers no resistance forward.

Other craft use centre-boards but, save for dinghies and catamarans, most modern sailing yachts have built-in ballast. Much of the skill in dinghy sailing lies in the ability of the crew — usually two for racing — to shift their body weight from side to side, forward or aft, to keep the boat as upright as possible.

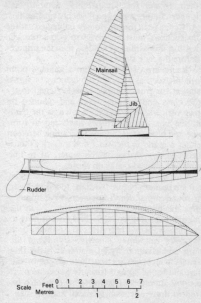

Mainsail

Jib

Rudder

Scale Feet 0 1 2 3 4 5 6 7
Metres 1 2

INTERNATIONAL 14 FT. DINGHY
Sail plan above shows overlap of jib and mainsail. Plan view and section reveal the long, clean run for planing.

Because of their cheapness and ease of maintenance, dinghies are the nursery craft of sailing. But the name is also applied to highly tuned and sophisticated racing machines, such as the two-man Flying Dutchman or the single-handed Finn used in the Olympic Games. Dinghies are light enough to be hauled out of the water and stored ashore. More robust types, however, particularly family day-sailing boats, can be safely left on moorings. In the hands of an experienced crew, a well-found racing dinghy will still be responsive in winds of force 5 on the Beaufort scale; many sailing under well-reduced sail area have survived stronger blows.

The *catamaran* is a twin-hulled craft developed from those of the Malayan and Polynesian seas and the fastest of all sailing boats, speeds of more than 20 knots having been recorded. A catamaran's speed is made possible by her combination of light displacement and rigidity, or resistance to the heeling force

of the wind. These are effected by her two narrow canoe-shaped hulls, locked parallel to each other by a cross-bracing bridge structure.

Development of catamarans in British waters has been most successful in small designs, open sloop-rigged craft with open cockpits similar to dinghies. Despite several successful ocean passages in cruising catamarans, their acceptance for offshore sailing has been limited. A catamaran has immense initial stability, due to her widely spaced hull platform, but this can be dramatically eliminated if she is allowed to heel too far, when the leeward hull is forced down and the windward hull flies clear of the water, exposing the bridge deck to the force of the wind and thereby completing the capsize. Once over, a catamaran can be difficult to right without assistance. Deep-sea going catamarans have been treated with caution, but many have achieved successful ocean crossings without trouble. There is no doubt that a yachtsman brought up in sailing conventional single-hull craft has much to learn afresh when he takes charge of a catamaran, which has her own clearly-defined handling characteristics. In addition to her stiffness, the type offers accommodation space on a vast scale compared with that possible in a single-hulled vessel.

The *trimaran* is a multi-hulled sailing craft, which differs from the catamaran by having a main central hull flanked by two smaller hulls which act as outriggers, but which are integral with the boat's structure, affording a low wetted hull area with a broad platform for sail-carrying.

Trimarans are fast craft. Where catamarans have proved more popular in small, inshore racing classes, trimarans have been used more widely for deep-water sailing. Like catamarans, they depend for speed on light displacement, and yachtsmen accustomed to deep-draught ballasted yachts mistrust the lack of positive righting leverage in a multi-hull. But the trimaran, with its central main hull, may be less prone to overturning than a catamaran.

Major yachting centres are traditionally those areas of maritime countries which are endowed with sheltered coastal waters, such as the Solent (England), the Firth of Clyde (Scotland), Long Island Sound and Chesapeake Bay (U.S.A.), Sydney Harbour (Australia), the Baltic Sea (Scandinavia), or the estuaries of Normandy and Brittany (France). Interest in sailing has grown so widely since 1945 that inland lakes, reservoirs, and rivers provide sailing facilities for large inland populations. But it is on the sea coast, where the sailing traditions are strongest, that the major yachting centres remain, and where the main race meetings and regattas are held for craft of all sizes and types.

Modern YACHT RACING is based on the universal code of racing rules drawn up by the International Yacht Racing Union (I.Y.R.U.), in which Great Britain is represented through the Royal Yachting Association. The rules, last revised in 1973, evolved from the informal match sailing for wagers which was popular among wealthy owners of large yachts from the early years of the nineteenth century.

Today most small yachts and dinghies are one-design, built and rigged to the same measurements and specifications, placing the greater emphasis on sailing skill for the outcome of the race. Large cruising yachts and offshore racers have been slow to follow this trend, but with the progress made during the late 1960s in fibreglass construction, it seems that hulls designed and built individually to owners' requirements will vanish from the yachting scene as large-quantity factory production tends to make yachts of more standard design cheaper.

There are 78 racing rules, covering all aspects of pre-race organization, starting signals and procedures, observance of rights of way during the race, and the adjudication of protests from owners who claim that another yacht has infringed a rule. No limitations are set on the size or shape of a yacht-racing course in the way that the dimensions of a games pitch are specified. The course length and direction is decided by the officers of the club organizing the race, based on their experience of the waters, the number of boats taking part, and the tides and weather conditions of the day. Larger yachts, because of their greater speed capability, naturally sail longer courses than small yachts or dinghies. Any change in the previously published sailing instructions must be given to competitors in writing if possible, or not less than ten minutes before the race starts.

Races are controlled from a vantage point ashore, such as a yacht club balcony or signal station, or from another vessel, rigged to fly the class and warning flags and manned by race officers. This vessel, known as the committee boat, is sometimes anchored to form one end of the start, an imaginary line between either a mark on the water and a mark ashore, between two marks on the water, or in line with two aligned marks on shore.

Each class has its own warning flag, broken out ten minutes before the start, to which a gun or sound signal draws attention. Five minutes later the preparatory signal (letter 'P' in the international flag code) is broken out next to the class warning flag. After five minutes both flags are run down smartly, signifying the start, and a sound signal made. It is the flag signals which govern the three stages of the start and sound signals (usually guns) are used to draw attention to them. Guns may also be fired to draw attention to recall signals, cancellations, postponements, or the shortening of a course.

Because it is impossible for yachts to wait stationary behind the starting line until the signal, skill is required of helmsmen and crews in the preceding ten minutes to position their vessels in the most advantageous way, taking into account the tide, the direction of the wind and any nearby obstructions, including competing yachts. Ideally a yacht should be on an unobstructed heading for the first mark or, if this is to windward, at the most advantageous end of the line for her first windward leg, and travelling at her best speed immediately behind the line as the starting signal is made. Until he is in the starting area, testing the weather and scrutinizing the competition, a skipper cannot finally decide on his tactics although a good start can be the most important factor in a race.

In a regatta, where there are several races for various classes of yacht on the day's programme, starts are made at ten-minute intervals, so that the starting signal for one race, is also the ten-minute signal for the following race, when its class warning flag is broken out. Some clubs, which have to plan their programme to take advantage of a comparatively short spell of favourable tide and depth of

YACHT RACING COURSE
If the wind is easterly the first leg of the course (A) will be a 'windward leg'. If the wind is anywhere south of east the southern (seaward) end of the starting line will be the most advantageous position. For other winds courses could be laid out differently. A special box on shore, in line with the marks, may have a balcony for officials judging the start and finish of the race.

water, start their races at five-minute intervals, dispensing with the 'P' signal between each. Aboard most yachts at a start, and nowadays in dinghies also, it is the responsibility of a crewman to time the ten- and five-minute intervals with a stop-watch, calling out the minutes to the helmsman as they elapse, allowing him to give his whole attention to manoeuvring his vessel for the start.

To be eligible to race in an event sailed under I.Y.R.U. rules, an owner must provide details of his yacht beforehand to the race committee, specifying which race he wishes to enter and giving details of his yacht, her class if any, colour of her distinguishing flag, hull colour, sail number and, in a handicap race, her rating figure.

The yacht must have on board at least one member of a club recognized by the national authority, whether he be the owner or his representative. No structural alterations designed to make a yacht lighter are allowed. Floorboards and bulkheads, for instance, must be in place and in offshore races there are regulations governing the provision of life belts, inflatable dinghy, signal flares, and other safety gear. Water must not be taken aboard or discharged as ballast, although bilge water which comes aboard as spray may be pumped out. To show that a yacht is racing she must fly at her masthead a rectangular flag which is generally struck (lowered) if the yacht retires or after it finishes.

Once the race is under way, yachts are governed by rules designed to prevent collisions and obstruction to other competitors. These purposes are complementary. When tacking, the yacht on the port tack (steering through the wind blowing from her port, or left, side) must keep clear of a yacht on starboard (right) tack. Other fundamental rules for avoiding collisions are that a windward yacht (occupying an up wind position) must keep clear of a leeward (downwind) yacht, and a yacht clear astern must keep clear of a yacht ahead of her.

When a yacht overtakes and establishes an overlap to leeward, she must allow the windward yacht ample room and opportunity to keep clear. The tactic of luffing (turning round into the wind) may be employed by a yacht threatened with being overtaken, but she must not do this when the overtaking yacht is drawing abreast of her, or when the overtaking helmsman has his opponent's mast abeam. If an overtaking yacht hails 'mast abeam' to prevent the other yacht from exercising her right to luff, and is ignored, then a protest may be lodged. There are other rules to decide right of way when a yacht is tacking or gybing (filling the sails on the other side when running

before the wind). A yacht which is tacking or gybing must keep clear of another settled on a tack, and if she wants to alter course to gain a right-of-way position over an opponent, she must do this far enough away to avoid causing the other yacht to alter course until the manoeuvre is completed. When two yachts are tacking or gybing, the port-side vessel must keep clear.

One of the most important sections of the right-of-way rules governs the rounding of course marks (buoys, moored boats, or posts). It is here that racing is at its closest, with yachts converging to round the mark with as little wasted distance as possible. The rules specify that a yacht shall not 'squeeze' another between herself and the mark. Conversely, an overtaking yacht must not claim room between a yacht ahead and the mark if the yacht ahead cannot give her room.

That the rules combine the requirements of safety and fair play is demonstrated when two yachts are approaching an obstruction or shallow water. If the yacht nearer the danger cannot alter course to clear it without risk of a collision, she must hail for room to tack (usually by calling 'Water'). The yacht which needs room must give the other time to keep clear before she herself alters course. If the hailed yacht decides the other can tack without help, she may call on the other yacht to tack, whereupon it is her duty to keep clear—and to satisfy the race committee that she did so, in the event of a protest. When the obstruction is a course mark, a yacht which is forced to tack to avoid it does not have right of way over a following yacht which is laying the mark correctly.

The main pitfall for yachts which are too close to the starting line is sailing over it before the starting signal is made. If they are over, they must return across the line and start again. During their return to the line they have no right of way over yachts which are starting or which have already started correctly. Once back over the line, however, the premature starter regains her rights as a yacht starting correctly, provided that in turning across the line for the second time she allows room to other correct starters near her. A yacht which touches a mark while rounding it is automatically disqualified but, when the sailing instructions allow, and when she has been compelled to touch the mark by another yacht, she can reround the mark, leaving it on the correct side.

Marks on a tidal water course may, with the co-operation of the harbour authority who are satisfied that there is no danger of obstructing commerical shipping, be the navigational buoys which mark the main channels. These bear the names of the shoals they mark, or of nearby places ashore. In waters where commercial shipping traffic is heavy, harbour authorities lay special racing buoys, clear of but close to navigational buoys, to prevent racing yachts and ships falling foul of each other. Individual sailing clubs lay their own additional marks to suit their requirements. In major races and regattas, competitors are given with their sailing instructions a sketch chart of the course, showing the racing marks. The letters P or S after a named mark mean that it must be left to port or starboard.

Yachts may be becalmed and motionless yet still racing. To prevent their being swept the wrong way by a foul tidal current, while the calm lasts they anchor, or 'kedge'. A dinghy may be righted after a capsize or a larger yacht may be refloated after going aground by her crew going over the side and pushing her off. In these cases the vessel must not employ outside help and must recover all her gear before she continues racing.

Yachts taking part in single races finish by recrossing the starting line, or an extension of it, usually in the direction in which they started. They are deemed to have finished, and are then recorded by the observers and timekeepers, when any part of the hull or gear in its normal position is sighted crossing the line. Where several races are in progress at once, as in a regatta, the finishing line is kept separate from the starting line to avoid confusion with starting classes or those yachts which are commencing another round of the course.

The finish of a big race or regatta programme is a time of intense activity on the race officers' balcony, where fast teamwork is essential. An observer, usually the Officer of the Day (senior of the race officers), identifies a yacht approaching the finish by calling out her class and sail number. As she crosses the line he calls 'On'. For greater accuracy he uses a sighting device, a slotted piece of wood in which a vertical wire lines up with the imaginary line across the water. As the observer calls 'On' the timekeeper calls the time in hours, minutes, and seconds so that the recorder (one of several if the programme is large) may enter it on his list.

Yachts of one-design classes know their position immediately since the finishing order is the result. In handicap races where yachts or dinghies of different designs race against each other, the finishing times are amended so that faster boats give time to slower ones. In the small yacht and dinghy classes a number indicates the seconds a boat might take to sail a hypothetical distance. The number is used as a basis for simple calculation to find the corrected, or handicapped, time. Since 1971 large cruising yachts (vessels which, although designed primarily for racing, have cooking and sleeping accommodation aboard for extended passages) have raced under the new International Racing Rule, a development of similar handicapping systems where measurements of a yacht's hull, spars, sail area, and other factors are used to calculate a rating, expressed in feet and tenths of a foot.

The final section of the I.Y.R.U. code lays down the procedures to be followed by a race organizer in the conduct of protest hearings. The Royal Yachting Association, which administers the rules within the United Kingdom, decrees that a yacht which intends to lodge a protest after the finish of a race must fly a small burgee or rectangular piece of material. If the race committee then decides that a protest has been correctly lodged, they call a hearing as soon as possible. This takes the form of an inquiry, in which evidence is heard from both parties and witnesses may be called.

Several methods are available to race organizers of eliminating the need for calculating handicap times and providing some of the stimulus of boats racing on equal terms. Yachts designed and built individually to the same rating rule, such as the 12-Metres used in the America's Cup, race even, although they differ in hull and rig details.

A simpler expedient is the pursuit race, in which boats are grouped according to handicap rating, the slowest starting first followed by the rest at regular intervals, with the fastest starting last. Handicap conditions can then be set aside and the first boat to finish correctly is the winner. A similar version is the triangulation, in which a triangular course is set with, at one corner, several buoys laid in a line at right angles to the course. All boats start together, but the fastest are required to round the furthest of this line of buoys and the slowest the nearest one. The difference in distance provides the handicap and the finish, as in the pursuit race, is boat-for-boat.

Yachts in offshore or passage races which involve night sailing give precedence after dark to the International Rules for Prevention of Collisions at Sea, over the racing rules. The Collision rules, or Rule of the Road, are observed by all sea traffic on navigable waters.

OCEAN RACING for yachts, involving long passages over open water, with vessels sometimes out of sight of each other and of land for days, has influenced yacht design with regard to sea-keeping qualities, rig, and habitability. Crewing in an ocean race demands experience and stamina of a high order.

Such races vary in distance from less than 200 miles (322 km.) in the waters of the

English Channel and the North Sea (where they are more accurately called offshore races) to events such as the Transpacific, held every two years since 1926, the distance of which is 2,600 miles (4,184 km.). Most famous in the calendar, more because of its variable weather conditions than for its length, is the FASTNET RACE, which is sailed every two years from Cowes, Isle of Wight, round the Fastnet Rock off the south-west coast of Ireland, and back to Plymouth.

CRUISING, the non-competitive side of yachting, usually involves making a passage either under sail or power from one port to another and spending at least one night away from the yacht's base. A cruise may be anything from a circumnavigation of the globe to a week-end camping expedition in a sailing dinghy in esturial waters.

As a result of the improved design and construction of small yachts and the growing proficiency of amateurs in sailing and navigation, long open-water passages are commonplace today. Apart from a suitable vessel and the ability to handle her, the principal requirement for cruising is merely time. For long voyages, sail, apart from its intrinsic and historical attraction, has practical superiority over motor propulsion, which requires more fuel than a small craft could carry.

The gap between the spartan interiors of racing yachts and the more homely comforts of cruisers has been narrowed by the growth of family sailing and by the rise in mass-production of yachts, which must appeal to as wide a market as possible. For economic reasons yachts have become steadily smaller since the turn of the century, but their standards of comfort have increased, thanks to man-made fabrics, plastics and corrosion-free metals, reliable auxiliary engines, efficient electronic navigational aids, compact cooking stoves and portable fuels, and better over-all boat design.

Taking to the water in small boats for pleasure dates back at least to the time of Cleopatra's barge, and, in the ancient civilizations of the Mediterranean, probably earlier. Small, privately owned craft were used where water transport was a regular part of daily life. Yachts existed in ancient Egypt and the Romans sought relaxation afloat on the Italian lakes.

Modern yachting was pioneered in Holland in the seventeenth century when travel along the miles of sheltered Dutch waterways was difficult without boats. The word 'yacht' is of Dutch origin (from *jaght*, the name given to pleasure craft developed from the small cargo or passenger carriers). An early convert to yachting was Charles II of England, who spent nearly ten years in exile in the Low Countries until the Restoration in 1660. Three months after his return, Charles took possession of a Dutch pleasure boat, the *Mary*, a gift from the city of Amsterdam. She was 66 ft. (20·11 m.) long with a beam of 18½ ft. (5·64 m.) and had been built originally for the Dutch East India Company. Another gift from the Dutch was the yacht *Bezan* and Charles added to his growing fleet the little collier smack *Surprise*, in which he had made his escape across the Channel to France after the battle of Worcester. It was during Charles's reign that Sir William Petty was commissioned to build a double-hull craft which, because of a weak bridge structure, broke up in the Bay of Biscay.

Almost as keen a yachtsman as his brother was James, Duke of York, later James II. Evelyn's diary records a race between the King's *Katherine* and the Duke of York's *Anne* from Greenwich to Gravesend and back for a prize of £100. The king saved his wager, sometimes steering the yacht himself. Neither of the two royal brothers was content as privileged passengers in their yachts — Pepys records how, on a lively beat down-Channel in one of the king's craft, both delighted in handling the gear and working the ship 'like common seamen'. After the death of Charles II in 1685, James maintained the royal patronage to a lesser extent, and this was continued in a more sober manner by the Dutch king, William III.

Yachting, because of the inevitable discomforts associated with it, was regarded during the early eighteenth century as a rather eccentric occupation. Interest shifted to Ireland where, in 1720, the Cork Water Club was formed. Its 25 well-to-do members, however, treated the sport as an occasion for pomp. They dressed in decorative uniforms, fired cannons, sailed in rigid formation naval style, but avoided competitive sailing.

The Water Club flourished until 1765, after which some former members revived sailing by the formation of a club which was later given the title of the Royal Cork Yacht Club. As such it exists today, the oldest yacht club in the world. Not until 1775 did a revival of royal patronage in England result in a new interest in yachting. Henry Frederick, Duke of Cumberland, gave his name to the Cumberland Fleet, which organized 'water parties' on the river Thames. From these originated the organized yachting of today.

The Fleet changed its name in 1823 to His Majesty's Coronation Society, to honour the coronation of George IV, members of which were later to break away after a protest disagreement and, at a meeting in the White Horse

Tavern, form the Thames Yacht Club, now the Royal Thames Y.C. By now, yachting was enjoying an aristocratic revival. In June 1815 another club was born in a London tavern, this time the Thatched House in St. James's Street. Three years later the Dukes of Clarence and Gloucester became members and in 1820 George IV gave his consent for the club to be given the title of the Royal Yacht Club, later to become the Royal Yacht Squadron.

Throughout this period yachting was essentially the sport of individualists, whereby an owner could indulge his fancy for brass cannon, cutlasses for his crew (for cutting away rigging when yachts ran foul of each other), and fierce private matches between rival yachts in which wagers of several thousand pounds were at stake. In the event of a collision during one of these races, crews would fight among themselves. Owners esteemed their yachts as a match for Navy vessels of comparative size, both in speed and crew discipline.

In 1833 there was a two-yacht match between Lord Belfast's brig *Waterwitch* and the schooner *Galatea* over a 225-mile course from the Isle of Wight, round the Eddystone Lighthouse and back, which *Waterwitch* won.

In American waters, during the early years of the nineteenth century, small-boat sailing was becoming increasingly popular. One of the leaders of the new vogue was J. C. Stevens, who has been called the 'father of American yachting'. His family lived beside the Hudson River, near New York, and it was Stevens who was later to head the syndicate which produced the schooner yacht *America*, the most important single vessel in the history of yachting, after which the America's Cup is named.

The *America*, 100 ft. (30·48 m.) long, sailed from New York on 21 June 1851 and, after calling at Le Havre a month later, sailed for Cowes. There she took part in the Royal Yacht Squadron's One Hundred Guineas Cup race around the Isle of Wight. She won, competitors claimed, by sailing inside the Nab shoal at the eastern end of the island, but her fine lines, simple and efficient sailplan, and modest displacement had made her a match for the heavier and deeper British yachts. She changed hands several times, was enrolled for service during the American Civil War, and ended her career afloat in 1901. Her structural decline was halted by a group of enthusiasts who restored her and presented her to the U.S. Naval Academy at Annapolis, Maryland. In 1946 she was destroyed when the shed in which she was housed collapsed under the weight of a snowfall.

Since 1857 there have been 22 challenges

for the America's Cup, each of which United States yachtsmen have successfully defended, thereby creating the most famous and expensive competition in yachting, and the one which attracts greater public attention than any other in the sport. Most popular of British challengers was Sir Thomas Lipton, whose series of yachts named *Shamrock* bid for the cup five times between 1899 and 1930, by which year he was over 80. In the first of his two challenges, Sir T.O.M. Sopwith's 'J' class *Endeavour*, sailing with an amateur crew, won the first two races and narrowly lost the third, fourth, and fifth — one of the closest matches in the history of the Cup.

Various changes in the rules over the years have been made, mostly in the challengers' favour. Today yachts of the 12-Metre class are used for a match consisting of the best of five races, sailed between one yacht selected by the challengers and one by the defenders. It was not until 1956 that, at the request of the New York Yacht Club, the Supreme Court allowed the rule specifying that a challenger had to sail to American waters on her own bottom, to be altered, so that 12-Metres could be used instead of the much larger 'J' class yachts employed since 1931.

This paved the way for the first, disappointing, postwar challenge by Great Britain with *Sceptre* (Royal Yacht Squadron syndicate). In 1962 the Australians mounted a challenge for the first time with *Gretel*, followed by further attempts in 1967 and 1970.

Great Britain's second postwar challenge, with Boyden's *Sovereign* in 1964, was even more disappointing than the first. Until 1962 all challenges had been mounted by Britain, with the exception of those of 1876 and 1881, when the Canadian yachts *Countess of Dufferin* and *Atalanta* failed, despite having a shorter distance to sail, mainly for lack of deep-water sailing experience, but by 1964, other countries were expressing interest in the Cup, particularly France and Greece. The Greek challenger failed to materialize, but the French syndicate, led by industrialist Baron Bich, got as far as Newport, Rhode Island, in 1970 but lost to the Australians in the elimination contest for the right to challenge.

Between 1851 and the end of the nineteenth century, dramatic strides were made in the design of large racing yachts. British design, particularly under the impetus of the America's Cup, grudgingly discarded its affection for the straight-stem deep-draught cutters of Regency days and assimilated the beamier hulls produced in the U.S.A. and the American flair for applying technology to improvement of the masting and rigging.

But away from public interest in the America's Cup and other international races, another evolution was taking place which was to have an equally important, though less spectacular, effect on the future of yacht sailing. At a time when yachting was still the sport of the very rich, a few Englishmen were demonstrating that cruising on the open sea in small yachts, modestly built and rigged, was not only possible but practical. Their voyages appealed to the sea-minded English and their writings are still regarded as classics of their kind. In 1887 an English barrister and newspaper correspondent, E. F. Knight, cruised to the Baltic from the Thames in a converted ship's lifeboat only 29 ft. (9 m.) long. But the originator of open-water cruising in small yachts, sailing either single-handed or with a very small crew, was a pillar of Victorian respectability and member of the Stock Exchange — R. T. McMullen (1830-91).

Described by Knight as 'the most skilful sailor of small craft we have ever had', McMullen proclaimed the creed that the safest place for a small, seaworthy yacht in bad weather or when poor visibility made her land-fall doubtful, was well out at sea. Most of his voyages were confined to the English Channel and to the coastal waters around the British Isles, yet he set standards of seamanship which are applicable wherever small boats sail. Such voyages as these Victorians made are today commonplace; but they were the pathfinders. At the turn of the century the greatest pioneer of all, Slocum, became the first man to sail alone round the world.

The first international rules for yacht measurement and classification for racing purposes came into force in 1906. Yachting was becoming a co-ordinated international sport and the process was hastened after the First World War by the increasing number of One Design classes, all built and rigged to the same measurements, thereby setting a truer test, theoretically, of the relative abilities of their crews. In the late 1920s several international rule classes became popular. Among these were the 6-, 8-, and 12-Metre classes, in which there was great scope for yacht designers to use the most favourable measurements, permutated from the over-all framework laid down by the rule. Owing to the stimulus of the America's Cup competition, the 12-Metres remain today the only active rating class among the big yachts built for inshore racing. The expense of building one-off yachts to individual design brought the 6- and 8-Metres to an end, although the 6-Metres were last sailed in the Olympic Games in 1952. By the 1930s, yachts were not only becoming smaller, so that more people could afford them, but their rig had become simpler and easier to handle,

within the scope of a small amateur crew.

The science of aerodynamics led to the adoption of the Bermudian, or jib-headed rig, which allowed a tall sail plan with long, efficient leading edges to the sails, in contrast to the heavy-sparred gaff rig in which the leading edge was shorter than the foot of the mainsail. Yacht rigs became more uniform, but more efficient. For example, the 1937 America's Cup defender, *Ranger*, carried only 7,500 square feet of canvas compared with the 16,000 of *Reliance*, in 1903. Yet *Ranger's* average speed round the course was better than that of the earlier, larger, yacht.

The Fastnet Race was first sailed in 1925, organized as a private venture by a group of yachtsmen who, after the race, formed the Ocean Racing Club, later to become the ROYAL OCEAN RACING CLUB. The R.O.R.C. has organized the race ever-since. It is now sailed on odd-number years, to alternate with the American Bermuda Race.

The event which was to establish the sport of ocean racing took place in 1866 when three schooners of almost identical size sailed across the Atlantic in the most unlikely month of December, each with a stake of $30,000. The race was conceived during a dinner in New York when George and Frank Osgood wagered that their schooner *Fleetwing* would beat Lorillard's *Vesta* from Sandy Hook to Cowes. The third owner to enter the race was James Gordon Bennett, the newspaper proprietor who was later to send Stanley in search of Livingstone. The three vessels were between 105 and 107 ft. (32–32·6 m.) long, compared with the largest offshore racers in European waters of today, which seldom exceed 70 ft. (21·33 m.). *Fleetwing* and *Henrietta* were ballasted keelboats, but *Vesta* had a shallower draught hull and a centre-board. After some difficulties in mustering crews the three yachts cleared Sandy Hook on 11 December. Worst hit by the North Atlantic winter weather was *Fleetwing*, which lost six crewmen overboard. *Henrietta* overhauled *Vesta* — which, although first in the English Channel, was let down by her pilots — and anchored in Cowes Roads on Christmas Eve, after a passage of 13 days, with *Fleetwing* second and *Vesta* a day later.

Modern ocean racing in smaller yachts began in 1906, when Day, editor of the American yachting magazine *The Rudder*, proposed a race across the Gulf Stream to Bermuda. Day's contention was that the sea-worthiness of a yacht was not to be judged by her size — a belief borne out many times since. He had proved his point in an earlier race from New York to Marblehead in 1904. None of the six starters was more than 30 ft.

(9·14 m.) long on the waterline. In the same year as the first Bermuda Race, and starting just a few days after it finished, the Transpacific from Los Angeles to Honolulu was inaugurated. Thus as early as 1906 United States yachtsmen pioneered long, regularly-held, ocean races.

The classic race of the southern hemisphere is the Sydney–Hobart, which starts on Boxing Day morning from Sydney Harbour, Australia. Rough weather in the Bass Strait between Australia and Tasmania is a feature of the race, which was founded in 1945 by the Royal Yacht Club of Tasmania on an idea by Capt. Illingworth. The course is 690 miles (1,110 km.) long.

The Admiral's Cup competition, open to teams from any country, was created in 1957 by the late Sir Miles Wyatt, then Admiral of the Royal Ocean Racing Club, with the object of encouraging participation in offshore events by countries other than Great Britain and the U.S.A., where the sport had been followed longest. Each team is selected by the offshore racing authority of its home country. The series is administered by a committee of management appointed by the Royal Ocean Racing Club. Scoring is by a simple points system, based on over-all positions in each race. First race of the four is the R.O.R.C.'s Channel Race (215 miles — 345 km.) which starts from Southsea, Hampshire, on the Friday before Cowes Week.

In both this and the Fastnet, Admiral's Cup yachts start as part of the main fleet. This practice applied also to the two inshore races — sailed over courses within the Solent as part of the Cowes Week programme — until 1969. Until then the two qualifying races had been the Royal Yacht Squadron's Britannia and New York Yacht Club Cup races. But in that year, because of the growing number of teams taking part, it was decided that from 1971, team boats would have their own races, separate from other Cowes Week competitors. Britain won the Cup in 1957, beating the United States, and again in 1957, with the Dutch team second. Australian yachts took part in 1965 for the first time, when they were placed second to Britain. They won the Cup at their second attempt in 1967. Germany won in 1973.

In addition to regular races organized by the Royal Ocean Racing Club and offshore authorities of other countries, privately sponsored races have become popular since the 1960s. Among these are the single-handed Transatlantic Race, founded in 1960 and sailed every four years; the Round Britain Race, which is a revival of a race first sailed in 1887 to commemorate Queen Victoria's Jubilee; and the most ambitious of all, the *Sunday Times* Golden Globe single-handed non-stop race round the world.

Inspired by the interest in the circumnavigations of ROSE and CHICHESTER, and by the example of the single-handed Transatlantic which proved it was possible for one man to race a yacht over long distances, the round-the-world race was founded in 1968. Competitors were allowed to start on the day and from the port of their choice within a specified period and the rules stipulated that they must round Cape Horn, the Cape of Good Hope and Cape Leeuwin in South Australia.

Only one boat finished the course within the time-limit. She was Knox-Johnston's ketch *Suhaili*, which returned to her starting point of Falmouth on 22 April 1969, after sailing without a stop for ten months and three days. Knox-Johnston's closest rival was Commander Tetley, whose trimaran, *Victress*, sank near the Azores from damage suffered in one of her hulls. Tetley, who was rescued unharmed, was driving his ship hard to match the supposed good progress of Crowhurst in another trimaran, *Teignmouth Electron*. But after Crowhurst's disappearance it was discovered from his logs and recordings aboard his unharmed and abandoned craft that she had not left the Atlantic Ocean. Crowhurst's voyage had started, barely in time, under severe financial and technical difficulties, and to get as far as he did, within sight of the Falkland Islands, showed seamanship of a high order.

In 1969 Pyle, a member of the Dinghy Cruising Association, made the longest recorded voyage by an open boat, from his home port of Emsworth, Hampshire, to Darwin, Australia with one man as crew. The boat was transported overland from the Mediterranean because of the closure of the Suez Canal, and resumed the voyage, begun by crossing the Channel to France and thence through the canals to the Mediterranean, down the Euphrates and into the Indian Ocean, through the islands of the East Indies to Darwin. Pyle's idea was to demonstrate that quite ambitious voyages could be made in inexpensive boats. He chose for his voyage an 18 ft. (5·48 m.) Drascombe Lugger, built of plywood and yawl rigged, with an auxiliary outboard motor.

OLYMPIC YACHTING, in an organized form, began with the 1908 London Games. Yacht races were held on the Solent and the Clyde for metre-class yachts, and Britain took four gold medals, so scarce were foreign entries. In the 1912 Stockholm Games, Norway won the 12- and 8-Metre classes, Sweden the 10-Metre, and France the 6-Metre. A Russian yacht finished third in the 10-Metre class.

Norway completely dominated the sailing in the 1920 Antwerp Games, winning no fewer than seven gold medals, five of them by sailing over without opposition. Thirteen classes were on the programme, but the total entry was only 23 boats. Centre-board craft were introduced at Antwerp, but only three — an 18-footer and two 12-footers — raced. All three were Dutch entries.

The 1924 Paris Games was a milestone in properly organized Olympic racing. The International 12-ft. class, introduced at Antwerp, was replaced by a 16-ft. gaff sloop with a large sail area, reminiscent of a Norfolk Broads yacht. Other classes were the 6- and 8-Metres, both of which were won by Norway. Belgium won the centre-board class.

International 12-ft. dinghies returned to join the Eights and Sixes in the 1928 Amsterdam Games. Crown Prince Olav of Norway won the Sixes, France the Eights, and Sweden the dinghies. The 2-metre classes returned again at Los Angeles in 1932, joined by the Star Class, a strong American class, designed in 1911 and with an updated rig. Seven entries were received, the gold medal predictably going to the U.S.A. but the silver was taken by Ratsey and Jaffe of Britain. The Snowbirds were heavy, hard-chine boats (vee-bottomed with a sharp angle between the bottom and the topsides), 13 ft. (4 m.) long and setting a single sail. France won the class with Ratsey, for Britain, sixth.

The German showpiece Games of 1936 used Kiel Fiord for the sailing races. Classes were the familiar Eights and Sixes, the Stars and another new centre-boarder, the O-Joller, a heavier forerunner of the present-day Finn class single-hander. There were 25 entries, Holland taking the gold medal, Germany the silver, and Britain's Scott the Bronze. Germany also won the Stars, with the American crew well down in fifth place. Italy won the 8-Metre and Britain the 6-Metre, after the Norwegian entry was disqualified under the amateur status rules.

Torbay was chosen for the 1948 British-staged races, which brought three new classes into competition. The Dragons replaced the 8-Metre as three-man keelboat, the British-designed Swallow made its only international appearance, and the centre-boarder chosen was the FOX-designed 12 ft. Firefly, a surprising choice in that the boat was designed for a crew of two and her two sails, main and jib, compared with the earlier centre-boarders' one, kept the helmsman's hands full. Elvestrom of Denmark, the great dinghy racing helmsman, made his Olympic début at Torbay in the Fireflies, winning the gold medal, with Britain's Air Marshal Sir Arthur McDonald

ninth. The U.S.A. won the Sixes and Stars, Norway the Dragons, and Britain's Morris the Swallows.

Helsinki, in 1952, marked the establishment of the Finn dinghy as the single-hander, a boat with an unstayed, bendy mast allowing scope for tactical sail-shape adjustment while racing, which pioneered much new thinking in racing dinghy design and handling. Designer of the Finn was a Swedish hairdresser, Sarby, who finished fifth at Helsinki. The gold medal winner was Elvestrom, who won four of the seven races in a fleet of 28 boats.

At Melbourne in 1956, Elvestrom continued to raise Olympic sailing standards by including five firsts in his score over a fleet of 22. This was the first Games with a two-man centre-boarder class. The chosen craft was the old, heavy, gaff-rigged International 12-Metre Sharpie, which introduced Olympic crewmen to the arts of raising and lowering the peak of the gaff during races to increase sail area on downwind legs. Britain's Blackall and Smith won the bronze medal, with Mander of New Zealand and Tasker of Australia in the first two places.

Naples, where the 1960 sailing teams were based, saw the Sharpies replaced by the Flying Dutchman as the two-man centre-boarder — a selection which was to be repeated, with increasing success, in the Games of 1964 and 1968. Dragons, Stars, and the comparatively expensive 5·5-Metre were used, with the now well-established Finn single-hander. All classes, save the 5·5, were one-design, built to strict rule tolerances, compared with the earlier metre boats which allowed individual designers a latitude within the framework of a rating rule. The decline of the latter was caused mainly by their rising cost.

The Flying Dutchman, which at 19 ft. 10 in. (7 m.), made her a longer boat than British crews had hitherto been used to, steadily grew in popularity in Britain and the rising standard of Dutchman racing was reflected in the Tokyo Games, where Musto and Morgan won the silver medal in the class.

This stimulated further British interest so that in Acapulco in 1968, Britain was in the enviable position of having the world champions in the class, Oakeley and Hunt, as reserves to the chosen pair, Pattisson and Macdonald-Smith, who made Olympic yachting history in Mexico by winning every race but one. British performance in the Finns had been less distinguished.

International Yacht Racing Union choices for the 1972 races at Kiel were the Soling and Tempest, three- and two-man keelboats respectively, both of whose hulls are moulded in fibreglass.

YACHT DEVELOPMENT. Early yachts evolved from the working boats of their day, Revenue cutters, pilot cutters, and schooners, fishing smacks, and the wealth of small types which worked around the British coast and the eastern seaboard of the United States until well into the twentieth century. The seaworthiness of such types inspired confidence — and rightly so — but search for more speed and easier handling, coupled with traditional standards of seaworthiness, led to the evolution of the yacht as we know it today: from thè massively built, straight-stemmed cutter of the early nineteenth century, with her enormous long bowsprit, low freeboard, large underwater area, and massive spars, to today's profile, with underwater area reduced to a minimum, compact and efficient Bermudian sailplan with light alloy spars and moderate freeboard.

Sailing dinghies, which evolved from the tenders carried aboard large yachts, have become the most popular means of sailing, because of their relatively low first cost and maintenance. In the 20 years up to 1970, one-design dinghy classes became almost universal, with the exceptions of the International 14-ft. class, the Merlin Rocket 14-footers, and the National 12-ft. class, where there is still scope for individual designs within the framework of a rule without the high cost involved with the larger metre classes.

As early as 1927 the Yacht Racing Association (now the Royal Yachting Association) had recognized the 14-footers as an international class. Designers like Giles began improving sailplans and hull shape and the resulting increase in performance soon raised standards of dinghy racing. The International 14-ft. class — although it failed to capture the international interest that its optimistic title anticipated and is today strongly supported only in Great Britain, Bermuda, the U.S.A., Canada, and New Zealand — remained for years the primary yardstick of improvement in dinghy design and performance. Today, with the availability of quantity-produced classes in fibreglass and plywood or hardwood veneers, few owners are prepared to bear the expense of having a one-off 14-footer built to their personal specification within the class rule. But it was by this method that ideas were tried and tested and later became standard features in many classes, as well as attracting a membership to the class which includes many of the best-known names in sailing.

A development of the late 1960s was the revival in popularity of gaff rig which had been superseded by the Bermudian rig during the 1930s. The Old Gaffers' Association encouraged this revival by holding annual rallies on the east and south coasts of Britain. These were not confined to veteran craft but admitted modern vessels provided they were gaff rigged and that the rig was suitable for their type.

Engine-driven catamarans were pioneered on a commercial scale by the double-hulled cross-Channel ferry *Pas de Calais*, built in 1870. She was 302 ft. (92 m.) over-all with a beam of 183 ft. (55·7 m.). Her uncomfortable motion in the short, steep Channel seas made her unpopular with passengers and her working life was brief.

Smaller, inshore racing classes of about 16 ft. (4·87 m.) over-all are regularly sailed in British waters. Two classes dating from the 1950s which enjoy enduring popularity were the Shearwater and the Jumpahead. By 1970 one of the most popular classes was the Unicorn, setting one sail and designed to be handled by one person.

Some of the most advanced research into the aerodynamics of sails and spars has been stimulated by the Little America's Cup competitions. These are for the International Catamaran Challenge Trophy, originally donated for match-sailing between single craft representing their country by the Seacliff Yacht Club of Long Island, U.S.A. in 1961. Britain's hold on the trophy in its early years, thanks to the combined skills of helmsmen like White, designer Macalpine-Downey, and sail and mast designer Farrar, seemed almost as secure as that of the Americans on the America's Cup proper. But the trophy has since changed hands, with growing interest coming from Denmark and Australia.

GOVERNING BODY (WORLD): International Yacht Racing Union, c/o Royal Thames Yacht Club, 60 Knightsbridge, London S.W.1. (U.K.): Royal Yachting Association, Victoria Way, Woking, Surrey.

YACHTING, Ice, see ICE YACHTING.

YACHTING, Sand and Land, see SAND YACHTING.

YAD ELIYAHU, BASKETBALL stadium in Tel Aviv, Israel. It was built in 1963 for the Maccabi Games and can accommodate some 10,000 spectators.

YAGLI, see WRESTLING.

YAKUSHIN, MIKHAIL, Russian Association FOOTBALL coach and manager. A former ICE HOCKEY and soccer player, he brought DYNAMO MOSCOW on tour to Britain in 1945 and 1955. He was team manager (and assistant coach) to Russia's 1958 World Cup side, and national team manager in 1967-8.

YALE UNIVERSITY, American college FOOTBALL team, nicknamed the 'Bulldogs' or 'Elis', lead all teams in number of wins over college football's 100-odd years. Until 1900 Yale dominated the sport, having 13 unbeaten seasons and winning or sharing 14 national championships. Most of the innovations that created the modern game of football were initiated by CAMP, first as player and later as coach (1888-92) at Yale. Among Yale's great players were the guard HEFFELFINGER and the end Hinkley. Heffelfinger starred in the 1888 team that made the 'flying wedge' famous and in that season outscored its opponents, 698-0. The 1909 team, led by the fullback Coy, also kept every opponent scoreless. The unbeaten 1923 national champions have been rated as the equal of any Yale team; the small, versatile Booth led the 1929-31 teams; the 1934 team, led by the end Kelley, upset unbeaten PRINCETON. Since 1956 Yale has won four IVY LEAGUE titles (unbeaten in 1960). Its traditional rivalries with HARVARD and Princeton have continued over a hundred years.
COLOURS: Yale blue.

YAMAGUCHI, GOGEN (1909-   ), Japanese KARATE exponent who studied under MIYAGI, founder of the *go-ju* school of karate. He was nicknamed 'the Cat' because of his long hair and cat-like movement.

YAMAHA, Japanese motor cycles prominent in racing since 1964. Always powered by two-stroke engines, the racing Yamahas were at their best and most successful in the 250 cc. class, taking world championships when ridden by Read in 1964 and 1965. After 1967 the factory no longer entered international events but supported private entrants with machines of unusually simple design, and for the next four years they dominated the 250 and 350 cc. classes. With their introduction of new and more complex machines for 500 and 750 cc. categories, Yamaha have since resumed their entry of factory teams and riders.

YASHIN, LEV (1929-   ), Association footballer for DYNAMO MOSCOW, and the Soviet Union. He did not retire from an active playing career until the end of the 1970 season. One of the greatest goalkeepers in the history of the game, he played for the Soviet Union in the world championships of 1958, 1962, and 1966, and was in the national team that won the Olympics football tournament in 1956, and the first competition for the European Nations Cup in 1960. Probably the first Russian footballer to be frequently associated with European and world football, he made several appearances in representative teams, notably for the F.I.F.A. (see FOOTBALL, ASSOCIATION) XI that played against England at WEMBLEY in 1963 as part of the F.A.'s centenary celebration, and in the match at Stoke that marked the farewell of MATTHEWS to first-class football.

YBARNÉGARAY, JEAN (1881-1956). A French Basque amateur PELOTA player in his youth, it is as a benefactor and administrator of the game that he is known and honoured. For many reasons — among them the lack of a central controlling executive — pelota was in an unhealthy state at the turn of the century. Ybarnégaray and a few young Basques, alarmed by the danger of the game lapsing into anarchy, put forward a blueprint for reform in 1912. After the First World War, from which he emerged with wounds and medals, Ybarnégaray continued his efforts, and it was solely due to him that the game's first authority of national standing, the Fédération Française de Pelote Basque, was created in 1921, which led directly to the founding, in 1929 at Buenos Aires, of the International Federation. 'Ybar', as he was known, a professional politician who reached ministerial rank, never lost touch with pelota through the whole of a long and busy life. Modern pelota could not be what it has become without him.

YELLOW PRINTER (1966), racing greyhound, a fawn dog, by Printer's Prince out of Yellow Streak. Rated the fastest greyhound ever seen in Britain when returning the record time of 28·30 sec. for 525 yds. (480 m.) at White City in 1968, he also won the 1968 Irish Derby in record time, 29·11 sec. over 525 yds. at Shelbourne Park, Dublin. He was trained by Bassett and owned by Miss Wallis and Sir Robert Adeane.

YETTON TROPHY, see BOWLS, INDOOR.

YOKO-GARBI, see PELOTA.

YOSHIMATSU, YOSHIHIKO (1921-   ), Japanese JUDO fighter who won three all-Japan championships and was second in the first world championships in 1956. Sometimes weighing 17½ stone (111 kg.), he was second to DAIGO in the 1951 all-Japan championships, but then won the title in 1952, 1953, and 1955, the first fighter to take it on three occasions.

YOST, FIELDING HARRIS (1871-1924), American college FOOTBALL coach for 29 years starting in 1897, 25 of which were spent at the University of MICHIGAN. His teams won 196 games, lost 36, tied 12, and had 13 unbeaten seasons. The 1901-5 Michigan teams won 55 games, lost only one (to the University of CHICAGO in 1905), tied one, and played in the first Rose Bowl (1902); these teams scored 2,821 points against 42 for their opponents.

YOUNG, DENTON TRUE (Cy) (1867-1955), American BASEBALL pitcher for 22 years (1890-1911) with major-league teams in both the NATIONAL and AMERICAN LEAGUES. No other pitcher has approached his lifetime total of 511 victories.

YOUNG, DOUGLAS (1926-   ), British JUDO fighter whose power and fine technique made him England's outstanding competitor in the late 1950s. He was a member of the British team which won the European title in three successive years, and was runner-up in the 2nd *Dan* class in 1954 and 1955 and 3rd *Dan* in 1958.

YOUNG, GEORGE (1922-   ), Association footballer for Glasgow RANGERS, and Scotland for whom he made a record number of 50 appearances in full international mat-ches — 29 in the British home championship and 21 against foreign national sides. Tall and heavily-built, he began his career with Rangers in 1941 as a right back but later switched to centre half where he made the maximum advantage of his mastery in the air and his neat footwork. With Glasgow Rangers, his only club, he won six League championship and four Cup-winning medals before his retirement in 1957.

YOUNG, ROBERT (*c.* 1945-   ), Australian surfer who came first in the world championships held in San Diego in 1966.

YOUNGER, SALLY (1951-   ), American water skier who set the first world speed record of 92·68 m.p.h. (149 km./h.).

YOYOGI NATIONAL GYMNASIUM, Tokyo, swimming stadium built for the 1964 OLYMPIC GAMES at a cost of 2,113,671,200 yen. Seating 3,000 people, it has been described as 'superior to any building of its kind in the world'. The INTERNATIONAL OLYMPIC COMMITTEE awarded the Olympic Diploma of Merit to its designer, Kenzo Tange. It is a remarkable example of the connection which can exist between sport and the fine arts.

Z

ZAHARIAS, Mrs. MILDRED, see DIDRIKSON, M.

ZAMORA, RICARDO (*fl.* 1920-36), Association footballer for BARCELONA, Español (Barcelona), REAL MADRID, and Spain for whom he kept goal in the national team's first international match — in the 1920 Olympic football tournament — and in 46 of Spain's first 56 international matches. An outstanding goalkeeper, he was a member of the Barcelona team that won the Spanish Cup in 1920 and 1922; of the Español team that won in 1929; and the Madrid (now Real Madrid) team that won in 1934 and 1936. Apart from his début in the 1920 OLYMPIC GAMES, he also kept in the 1924 Olympics and in the 1934 world championship, and was in goal in May 1929 when, in Madrid, Spain became the first foreign national team to beat England. His playing career was a long one, despite being ended by the outbreak of the Spanish Civil War in 1936. In later years he served Spanish FOOTBALL in many capacities, including that of selector for the national team.

ZANDVOORT CIRCUIT. Devised by Hugenholtz, a Dutch enthusiast, this artificial MOTOR RACING circuit is set in the sand dunes behind Haarlem, and is 2·6 miles (4·2 km.) long. It is well equipped with no special difficulties apart from sand which sometimes blows on to the circuit and renders it slippery. Before the first Dutch Grand Prix in 1950, there were two races given the title of Zandvoort Grand Prix. These were over a distance of 104 miles (167 km.). The 1948 race was a *Formule Libre* event organized by the British Racing Drivers Club, and the 1949 event was a Formula One competition.

ZATOPEK, EMIL (1922-   ), long-distance runner for Czechoslovakia. Zatopek was unquestionably the greatest distance runner of his generation, his unique Olympic treble in 1952 — gold medals in the 5,000 metres, 10,000 metres, and MARATHON — being unlikely, in an age of increasing specialization, ever to be equalled. His unbeaten record over 10,000 metres from 1948 to 1954 is also likely to endure. He had a fourth gold medal in the Olympic 10,000 metres of 1948

when he only lost the 5,000 metres because he misjudged the finish. In the EUROPEAN CHAMPIONSHIPS he won three gold medals and one bronze, dominating the 5,000 and 10,000 metres in 1950 and winning the longer race again in 1954 with a bronze in the 5,000 metres, when he was beaten by KUTS and Chataway. He broke records with monotonous frequency at distances ranging from 5,000 metres to 30,000 metres, that for the 10,000 metres five times. His best records, achieved between 1951 and 1954, were: 5,000 metres in 13 min. 57·2 sec., 6 miles in 27 min. 59·2 sec., 10,000 metres in 28 min. 54·2 sec., 10 miles in 48 min. 12·0 sec., 20,000 metres in 59 min 51·6 sec., and 12 miles 810 yards for the one-hour run. Following an operation for hernia, he made a third Olympic appearance in 1956, and finished sixth in the marathon. His prodigious achievements were augmented by those of his wife, ZATOPKOVA.

ZATOPKOVA, DANA· (1922-   ), javelin-thrower for Czechoslovakia. Born on the same day as her husband, EMIL ZATOPEK, and complementing his prowess with feats of her own, Zatopkova won the Olympic JAVELIN gold medal in 1952 and the silver in 1960. She held the world record in 1958 with 182 ft. 10¼ in. (55·74 m.) and won the European title in both 1954 and 1958, bringing the family collection of major championship winners' medals to a total of 13.

ZDARSKY, MATTHIAS (1874-1946), generally recognized as the father of Alpine SKIING, was inspired by NANSEN's *By Ski Over Greenland* to experiment on Alpine slopes near his mountain hermitage of Habernreith, and designed a short grooveless ski, and a binding of steel. In 1896 he wrote *Lilienfelder Schlauf-Technik*, the first methodical analysis of the stem turn and its application in Alpine skiing, and his *Torlauf* race anticipated the giant slalom. While serving with the Austrian army as a ski instructor in the First World War, Zdarsky survived an avalanche in which he suffered 80 fractures and dislocations, including six dislocations of the spine. He invented apparatus for his limbs and managed to ski again.

ZEBEC, BRANKO (1929-   ), Association footballer for Locomotive (Zagreb), Borac (Zagreb), Partizan Belgrade, RED STAR BELGRADE, and Yugoslavia for whom he played at outside left in the 1954 world championship and at centre half in the 1958 world championship. He first attracted attention in 1951 when he was playing in the Yugoslav second division and, soon after making his first appearance in the national team, he was transferred to Partizan Belgrade, and also played for the Rest of the World XI against England at WEMBLEY in 1953. He stayed with Partizan until 1959 when, at the age of 30, he entered Belgrade University to study science and joined the University club, Red Star.

ZHABOTINSKY, LEONID (1938-   ), Russian heavyweight lifter, five times world and Olympic champion 1964-8, he was the first lifter to total 1,300 lb. (589·7 kg.).

ZINGARI, I, see CRICKET.

ZOOM TOP (1966), racing greyhound, a fawn bitch, champion greyhound of Australia. She won over $A50,000 in 1968-9, and equalled and broke 14 track records in winning 68 from 136 starts. She was named Australian Greyhound of the Year in 1968.

ZUCCHI, R. (1952-   ), Italian water skier. In September 1970, as European champion, he equalled SUYDERHOUD's world record in the slalom event by negotiating 38 buoys in six successful passes.

REFERENCE

A DICTIONARY FOR DREAMERS Tom Chetwynd 60p
A comprehensive key to the baffling language of dream symbolism.
Over 500 archetypal symbols give essential clues to understanding
the ingeniously disguised, life-enriching, often urgent messages to
be found in dreams.

A DICTIONARY OF DRUGS
Richard Fisher and George A. Christie 95p
From everyday aspirin and vitamin, to the powerful agents
prescribed for heart disease and cancer, this is a revised reference
guide to the gamut of drugs in today's pharmaceutical armoury.

A DICTIONARY OF SYMPTOMS Dr. Joan Gomez £1.50
Although not a full alternative to medical opinion, this is a
thorough-going and authoritative guide to the interpretation of
symptoms of human disease.

THE ENGLISHMAN'S FLORA Geoffrey Grigson £1.95
A latterday herbal of the medicinal and culinary purposes of the
flowers and plants of the English countryside: magic, myth, lore
and truth. Illustrated.

HOW THINGS WORK VOLS 1 & 2 £2.00 each
The Universal Encyclopaedia of Machines. More than a reference
work, more than a browser's delight, HOW THINGS WORK is an
essential resource and an accumulative answer to the whole question
of what makes the world go round. Each volume contains over
1,000 illustrations.

THE FILMGOER'S COMPANION Leslie Halliwell £2.75
The world's most comprehensive, compact and lauded encyclopaedia
of cinema and cinema folk. Over 7,000 entries.

TEST YOUR OWN WORDPOWER Hunter Diack 40p
Test your own vocabulary by attempting these carefully devised
tests. Shakespeare's was over 35,000 and the national average
around 12,000.

TREES AND BUSHES OF BRITAIN AND EUROPE
Oleg Polunin £2.50
A superb and definitive guide. Fully illustrated in colour.

BIOGRAPHY

ALBERT EINSTEIN   Banesch Hoffmann   £1.00
Written with the co-operation of Einstein's personal secretary, this
is the most authoritative account of the 20th century's greatest
scientist. Illustrated.

ANEURIN BEVAN VOLS 1 & 2   Michael Foot   £2.50 each
The classic political biography of post-war British politics.

THE BORGIAS   Michael Mallett   90p
The rise and fall of one of the most notorious families in
European history: Legends of poisoning, incest, and political
contrivance. Illustrated.

CLASSIC LIVES   Caroline Silver   75p
The birth, rearing and training of seven thoroughbred horses. 'The
straw practically falls out of the pages.' *Jilly Cooper*

CONFUCIUS   D. Howard Smith   75p
An introduction to the Way of Confucius – the system of belief
which was the inspiration behind one of the richest and noblest
civilisations the world has known.

THE DEATH OF LORCA   Ian Gibson   £1.00
Federico García Lorca, one of the outstanding poets and
dramatists of this century, was murdered by Nationalist rebels at
the outbreak of the Spanish Civil War in 1936. History enshrines
him as a homosexual romantic martyr, but his political convictions
are indisputable. 'Lovers of poetry, lovers of truth, lovers of Spain
should all read this exemplary piece of literary research.' THE
SUNDAY TIMES. Illustrated.

THE FEARFUL VOID   Geoffrey Moorhouse   £1.25
There is a fearful void out there in the empty quarter of the
Sahara Desert, but more terrifying still is the void within our minds
– the fear of loneliness and failure. One man's search to conquer
his own self-distrust. Illustrated.

MOVING INTO AQUARIUS   Sir Michael Tippett   75p
One of our greatest living composers asks: How does music, the
most expressive of all communication, relate to a
technology-obsessed society in which aggression and acquisitiveness
have become an index of personal worth?

TRAVEL

DAFFODIL AND GOLDEN EAGLE   Jonathan Yeatman   £1.00
In the best tradition of British devil-may-care eccentricity, the
authors decided to float across the Sahara in two hot-air balloons.
Illustrated in full colour.

THE FEARFUL VOID   Geoffrey Moorhouse   £1.25
There is a fearful void out there in the empty quarter of the
Sahara Desert, but more terrifying still is the void within our
minds – the fear of loneliness and failure. One man's search to
conquer his own self-distrust. Illustrated in full colour.

JOURNEY THROUGH BRITAIN   John Hillaby   75p
It was a magical idea to walk through the over-industrialised land
of Britain from Land's End to John O' Groats, avoiding all centres
of population. Britain's master walker made his reputation with this
book. Illustrated.

JOURNEY THROUGH EUROPE   John Hillaby   75p
John Hillaby gives a splendid potpourri of factual account, lively
anecdote, mythology and private comment in this account of his
walk from the Hook of Holland via the Alps to Nice. Illustrated.

JOURNEY TO THE JADE SEA   John Hillaby   75p
Tired of city-living and ashamed of his toleration of boredom,
John Hillaby made a three-month safari to the Northern Frontier
District of Kenya to the legendary Jade Sea. Illustrated.

ARCHAEOLOGY

BEFORE THE DELUGE   Herbert Wendt   90p
Palaeontology sets out to find the point in the past when life began
to exist on our planet, how it developed, and when man first
appeared. This is the story of how palaeontology developed as a
science and what it now tells us about the planet on which we live.
Illustrated.

THE BOG PEOPLE   P. V. Glob   75p
In a peat bog in Schleswig, Denmark, the body of a fourteen-year-
old girl was found. It was almost 2,000 years old and had been
perfectly preserved by the strange chemical properties of the peat.
An authoritative account of one of the most remarkable
archaeological finds ever. Illustrated.

THE CHANGING FACE OF BRITAIN   Edward Hyams   £1.50
Illustrated general study of how the geological structure of the land,
our climate, our social history and our industries have contributed
to the shape of our landscape.

THE DAWN OF EUROPEAN CIVILISATION
V. Gordon Childe   £1.00
The last edition of the classic archaeological work that continues to
dominate all explanations of the growth of European prehistory.
Illustrated.

INDUSTRIAL ARCHAEOLOGY   Arthur Raistrick   75p
The 'forgotten' aspect of archaeology; both an introduction and an
essential reference work from Britain's leading authority.
Illustrated.

MYSTERIOUS BRITAIN   Janet and Colin Bord   £1.50
All over the British countryside are totems and indications of lost
civilisations and knowledge, scattered in a rich profusion if only the
eye can see. This book looks into the past while suggesting some
startling research for the future. Illustrated.

THE PILTDOWN MEN   Ronald Millar   75p
The case study of the most notorious hoax in the history of
archaeology. Illustrated.

HISTORY

AFRICA IN HISTORY Basil Davidson £1.50
A complete introduction to the history of the 'Dark Continent'.
Illustrated.

THE ALCHEMISTS F. Sherwood Taylor £1.25
Before it became regarded as a branch of the occult, alchemy was in
the forefront of the search for human knowledge and led to the
founding of modern chemistry. Illustrated.

ANATOMY OF THE SS STATE
Helmut Krausnick and Martin Brozat 60p
The inside story of the concentration camps, 'probably the most
impressive work on the Nazi period ever to appear'. THE TIMES
EDUCATIONAL SUPPLEMENT.

ART AND THE INDUSTRIAL REVOLUTION
Francis D. Klingender £1.50
One of the most original and arresting accounts of the impact of the
new industry and technology upon the landscape of England and the
English mind. 'There is no book like it.' *John Betjeman*. Illustrated.

*All these books are available at your local bookshop or newsagent, or can be
ordered direct from the publisher. Just tick the titles you want and fill in the
form below.*

Name ....

Address ....

....
Write to Paladin Cash Sales, PO Box 11, Falmouth, Cornwall TR10 9EN
Please enclose remittance to the value of the cover price plus:
UK: 18p for the first book plus 8p per copy for each additional book
ordered to a maximum charge of 66p
BFPO and EIRE: 18p for the first book plus 8p per copy for the next 6
books, thereafter 3p per book
Overseas: 20p for first book and 10p for each additional book

*Granada Publishing reserve the right to show new retail prices on covers, which
may differ from those previously advertised in the text or elsewhere.*

Christian world but, again, the basis of the Hindu religion was inherited from the West when Aryan peoples invaded around 1500BC and turned the Indians into their servants. The gods of India, therefore, have a somewhat familiar ring. The father god of the Hindus is Brahma and he is part of a trinity of gods which includes Krishna, their version of the Jesus-type figure. Krishna is the Hindu saviour (see Bel, Osiris, etc). He is said to have lived around 1,000BC and is still revered today in much the same way as Jesus. The texts from which Hinduism was created are called the Vedas and in them you can find references which appear to record extra- terrestrial activities. Hinduism was a religion introduced by the invaders to create a strict system of hierarchy known as castes. It was a means to divide and rule. The religious apartheid which Hinduism promotes with its castes, taboos and impositions is a continuing confirmation, as with most religion, that large areas of incarnate humanity are yet to evolve from spiritual childhood. But, if you want a system of control, it's wonderful and it is being used in that way today just as it was by the Aryans. Missionaries from the Egyptian Brotherhood also arrived in India during and after the invasion and, as a consequence, its power began to expand rapidly. India is, today, a major centre of Brotherhood activity.

Five hundred years after the physical life claimed for Krishna came Gautama Buddha which translates as Guatama the Enlightened. Today he is known simply as Buddha and, in his name, the religion of Buddhism has flourished. Buddha was born in India into a royal family. He was a prince, but he gave up this privilege and wealth to spread his philosophy which incorporated reincarnation and an ethical way of life based on peace and love. I don't agree with all that he believed in but there is much that I can easily support. He spoke out against the priests of the day and encouraged the pursuit of truth, wisdom and knowledge. He talked of a universal brotherhood (the positive variety!) and equal rights for men and women. Buddha spoke simple truths. He had no desire to be turned into some saviour-god or to be worshipped by followers who complicated his simple philosophy with additions, ceremonies and hierarchies. All he stood for – and all we ever really need – are spiritual knowledge, not endless 'isms' to complicate them.

After Buddha's physical release, his beliefs became the dominant religion in India. In the third century, King Asoka would adopt Buddhism and send his representatives across the known world to

Dogon people in Mali, in sub-Saharan Africa, have had a legend, probably originating in Egypt, which has been passed on over five thousand years. It tells of a star that they claimed orbited Sirius. They knew it as the smallest and heaviest of stars containing the germs of all things and the Dogons said that it weighed so much that 'all the Earthly beings combined cannot lift it'. The legend further claims that it took fifty years for the star to orbit Sirius.

All this is remarkable when you think that the star they have known about for thousands of years was not officially discovered until the last century and was photographed for the first time in 1970. It has been named Sirius B, and the Dogons have been proved correct in their claims. For it does take around fifty years to complete an orbit and scientists have suggested that one cubic foot of Sirius B matter would weigh 2,000 tons. Obviously, Sirius is of considerable relevance to what has been happening on this planet. How could Earth people know such details unless they were told by those who knew? Extra-terrestrials or highly accurate channelling.

Freemasonry, like most secret societies of the infiltrated Brotherhood, bases its beliefs and aims on the worship of the Sun God and Mother Goddess mythology which it is believed was common to ancient civilisations. This Father/Mother belief was reflected in the Egyptian trinity of gods – Osiris, the father, Isis, the mother, and Horus, the son. Another name often used for the Brotherhood is its Latin name, the Illuminati, or 'illuminated ones'. It may sound fantastic at this stage in our story, but the world is controlled today by a Brotherhood of secret societies which go back to this period. The swastika, the lamb, the obelisk, the apron, which some Egyptian gods are depicted as wearing, and, of course, the pyramid and eye are still the symbols of the Brotherhood societies. Thousands of years after ancient Egypt you can find the pyramid and eye symbol very easily in America. It forms the reverse of the Great Seal of the United States and appears on every dollar bill. The truths pedalled by the negative secret societies have been twisted enough to mislead their members. I feel the Egyptian beliefs have been misrepresented to an extent, but, as one researcher said so correctly, it doesn't matter if what they believe is true or even if *you* believe it. As long as *they* believe it, we are all affected by the way their thinking influences their actions.

Channelling was at the centre of the Egyptian culture and could be used to control or, as it was in many cases, to gather knowledge that was not being made available from elsewhere. Just as the Luciferic consciousness wishes to control people, so the consciousness of 'The Light' wishes to set them free by allowing them access to the spiritual truths that are being denied them. Channelling is an important way of doing this. This is one reason why, despite the efforts of the manipulators, many people in Babylon and Egypt had more spiritual knowledge than the elite wanted them to know. Channellers were widely consulted as a source of divine inspiration and there were rooms called the holy of holies or sanctuaries where inter-frequency communications took place. These were built on energy points where a 'god' (a discarnate consciousness in this case) could communicate most effectively. This is how the prophets in the Bible got their information. Those in the Christian Church who equate channelling with devil worship should know that the term prophet comes from the Greek word which means medium!

In the early Egyptian period, some worshipped the Sun god *Ra*, and others followed the god Amun or Amen. These two later became fused into one, Amun or Amen Ra. After their prayers and religious teachings they would say the name of their god. This was passed on through Judaism into Christianity and, in churches all over the world today, Christians still end their prayers and readings with the word 'Amen'. How many know that, in doing so, they are saying the name of a Pagan god of channelled or extra-terrestrial origin, just as the Egyptians did? Amen also represents a sound, by the way, that resonates a certain frequency known to the ancients. Egyptian mythology had a trinity of gods in Osiris, the father, Isis, the mother, and Horus, the son. The Egyptians believed that Osiris came to suffer so that those who believed in him would live. He was known as Lord of Eternity, the Judge and Saviour of the human race, the Resurrection and the Life, the Bread of Life, the Redeemer and Mediator who would decide the eternal fate of heaven or hell for the dead. Horus was portrayed sitting on his mother's knee and, from this, the idea of the Madonna and child was to emerge in Christianity. The Egyptian figure of evil, Set, became the Christian version, Satan. The cross was an Egyptian symbol for thousands of years before it was adopted by Christianity and the Egyptians celebrated the festival of Easter, the day that Horus, the son, was said to have died and risen again to become one with his father. All this would have been influenced by the Babylonian belief in Bel and both would have

begun with the same channelled communications or extra-terrestrial influence. In fact, I think that most of this symbolism relates back to extra-terrestrial activities and the star systems they came from, and from the knowledge that the day was approaching when the forces of disharmony (Set, Satan, Lucifer etc) would be overcome by harmony. That time is now.

The idea of a trinity of gods, or three gods in one, is a theme that runs through countless pre-Christian religions. The Christians merely copied it as they copied everything else. Some of the symbolism of the trinity is linked to energy balancing. The three points of the triangle stand for positive/negative/balance, male/female/balance. The triangle is a well-known esoteric symbol as is the double interconnecting triangle known as the Star of David. This represents the balance of the spiritual with the balance of the physical.

Thousands of years before Christianity, dogmatic religious belief, based on the misunderstandings and twisted truths I highlighted, was already being used by the Luciferic consciousness in its many guises to close down the potential of the human mind and to fill it with myths and the literal interpretation of symbolic stories. The fear of the gods and the horrors that would be visited upon those who did not do as they were told was a very effective way of keeping the masses from the knowledge of their true selves. The god kings of the various cultures and the gathering power of the priests as interpreters of the gods' desires added to the oppression of the religious dogma and control.

The Egyptian elite were an advanced people for their time in many ways, although they kept most of the population in physical and spiritual slavery. They performed operations – mummies have been found with well-set fractures and false teeth. It would be many thousands of years before anything like this appeared in Europe. Educated Egyptians understood the principles of astronomy and astrology, as did the Babylonians. Astronomy and astrology were seen as indivisible sciences. The richer Egyptians had beautiful homes with elegant furniture and artwork. In contrast, three thousand years later, some Christian clergy were condemning the use of knives and forks as the work of the devil.

The culture and belief systems developed in Mesopotamia and Egypt, possibly under the influence of extra-terrestrial or channelled sources, were to have a fundamental impact on all that followed. India was also developing a distinct culture and Britain

promote its philosophy. They travelled as far as Alexandria in Egypt where it became diluted somewhat by the Egyptian idea of Osiris, Isis and Horus. The depiction of Horus in the arms of his mother, Isis, became Buddha in the arms of the goddess, Hatari. Buddhism was replaced by Brahmanism as the major religion in India, but it was accepted by other Eastern countries and has made significant inroads into other parts of the world. Buddha's contribution to the raising of planetary consciousness was very successful. He is a wonderful example of how the volunteer consciousness seeks to work, with simple truths and no imposition. Hinduism was to become the state religion in India as the centuries passed and it was to do for Indian evolution what Christianity did in the West. It held back their mental and spiritual development for thousands of years.

Confucius was another volunteer incarnation. He was born in about 551BC in China. His real name was K'ung Fu-tze which meant Master K'ung but this became Latinised into Confucius. He worked as a schoolmaster and stressed ethical conduct and the importance of setting an example through one's own behaviour. He was later a brilliant magistrate and Minister of Crime who argued vigorously for social reform. But, like many of his kind, his wisdom was acknowledged less in his lifetime than after his physical death. He died a disappointed man, believing he had failed to bring about the change of attitude he had hoped for. However, with his going he became a national hero and his words have been constantly quoted ever since. Sometimes, when we leave this level we can release an energy which can affect people long afterwards and those who tune to this energy field will begin to focus on what that person has done and said. One Confucian saying was, *"What you do not like when done to yourself do not do to others"*. This theme of 'do to others what you would have them do to you' is common to many religions and philosophies. Many claim it for themselves when it is really an eternal truth. If we all observed it in our everyday lives, what a different world it would be. In China, during the life of Confucius, there was another being of great evolution called Lao-tsze, from whom we get Taoism. His views were similar to those of Buddha but they, too, were complicated and devalued in the usual way by those who followed the 'ism' created in his name. The Chinese led the world in their greatest periods with their knowledge and creativity. They identified the energy grid of the Earth which they called Dragon Lines and they introduced a form of healing called acupuncture which balanced the flows in the energy grid of the human body. They also discovered the opposing forces which need to be kept in balance and called them the yin and the yang.

Buddha, Confucius, Lao-tsze, Jesus: the list goes on. All these, and others like them, are aspects of consciousness who came into incarnation to bring to this frequency simple messages from higher frequencies in order to raise and awaken human consciousness from the bondage of religion, myth and ignorance. As superb psychic channellers who could access information and understanding from very high sources, they also channelled energies of immense power to the planet. In most cases, their later followers have turned them into saviour figures or people to be worshipped as mystical heroes. This has often polluted their philosophy on life into dogmas and creeds. They have also attributed to them sayings and experiences that either never happened or derived from myths, events and people of an earlier time or different location. It is the last thing they wanted or believed in when they walked this Earth, I feel.

Before we leave the pre-Christian story in Europe and the East, we need to look at two other civilisations which have had a profound impact on human evolution, the Greeks and the Romans. Around the Aegean Sea, thousands of years before Christianity, there were incarnations of the volunteer consciousness. Some influenced people in the area where Athens was later built and helped to start the Mycenaean civilisation. Others incarnated on the island of Crete and became known as the Minoans. At Knossos on Crete you can still see the ruins of a magnificent palace called the Labyrinth. Without knowing its historical background, I went to Crete on holiday. When we visited Knossos I was guided by my intuition to bury in the ruins of the palace a large crystal I had been given in Glastonbury. The palace was clearly built on a strong earth energy point, as were most ancient palaces and temples. The ancients had a greater understanding of the nature of earth energies than those who came after them in the Christian era. Again, when I talk of volunteer incarnations, I don't mean that they were the whole civilisation, only certain members of it. Sometimes they were listened to, sometimes ignored or even killed. The Mycenaeans worshipped a trinity of gods and their religious symbol was the cross. They were conquered by tribes of Aryan peoples who took control of the land we call Greece. They worshipped a god called Zeus. The Ancient Greeks (also known as the Hellenes) were not a nation as such in these early days. They were a series of independent tribes and were only formed together into a nation when Philip of Macedonia took control in the 4th century BC. By then they had founded the original Olympics.

The Greeks at this time did not have a state religion. People were allowed to worship whichever gods they felt right were right for them and they would consult the hundreds of 'Oracles' (channellers) who were available in the temples and shrines for guidance. Again, we see this misunderstanding between discarnate communicators and 'gods' which has caused so much confusion. The word 'angel' comes from the Greek angelos, meaning messenger. Angels were believed to be divine messengers. This pagan belief was encompassed into Christian doctrine. The Greeks produced some outstanding examples of the volunteer consciousness. In the 6th century BC, Xenophanes was suggesting that God was not a man but a mind which orders the Universe and is beyond human understanding. He said there was a unity of all things and 'the all is one and the one is God'. Xenophanes challenged the belief that a god came to Earth and suffered so that our sins could be forgiven. As we have seen, this came from Bel, perhaps even earlier, and the sacrifice of the lamb. But, later, along would come Christianity to carry on that myth for another 2,000 years. The great Greek thinkers, who were unfortunately only in the minority, realised that the Universe is governed by mathematical law and consciousness of high evolution, and not by mythical gods.

The period 600 to 300BC saw Greece at the height of its intellectual powers. Pythagoras and Thales travelled to Egypt to absorb its knowledge which they would use together with their own inspiration and research to become the first Greek scientists. Science comes from a Latin word meaning knowledge. Thales was the founder of Greek geometry, astronomy and philosophy while Pythagoras was a superb mathematician who said, as did Philolaus, that the earth revolved around the Sun. This was two thousand years before it became accepted wisdom. Pythagoras was a social and religious reformer who stood for truth and ethics in all things. He was a vegetarian by ethical choice. Healing was another aspect of Greek life which evolved rapidly in this period and Hippocrates became known as the Father of Medicine. Doctors still take the Hippocratic oath. He refused to accept the idea, prevalent until then, that illness was caused by sin or devils.

Surgery developed, too, in Greece but Christianity would put an
end to all that for around 1700 years because they believed in the
resurrection of the physical body. They did not want mutilated
bodies being resurrected and, as Christian power grew, Greek and
Roman hospitals and healing centres would be destroyed and their
doctors killed or banished. The Greeks were the first people since
Atlantis to make geography a science. They produced the first
historians, they investigated the laws of physics and discovered the
law of cause and effect. Democritus suggested that matter was
made up of atoms two thousand four hundred years before modern science. Greece produced outstanding playwrights, artists and
orators and created laws and forms of democratic government
which have been the foundations of what we see today. The word
democracy comes from Greece.

The three greatest philosophers of this time were Socrates,
Plato, and Aristotle. They did not know everything or get everything right, and they were influenced to an extent by the culture
around them. But here were three aspects of the volunteer consciousness who were, in so much of their understanding, thousands of years in advance of their time. Socrates was a medium
who communicated with other levels and pursued truth, knowledge and understanding with unwavering determination. He
talked in the market places and on street corners, propounding his
views and questioning people in order to gain more knowledge.
He said that a revolution of thought was the only way to a
revolution of behaviour. Socrates was the first since Atlantis to
explain scientifically the mystery of life. He taught that around the
Earth were 'many mansions for the soul'. How close this is to the
'many mansions in my Father's house' in the Bible. He also said
that those we contacted in these 'many mansions' were not super-
natural gods but discarnate beings like us. Socrates was not popular with the priests who still had power despite the undermining of
their credibility by these outstanding men. While they were tuning
to extremely high levels of consciousness, the mass of the people
were still influenced by ignorant priests. Socrates was accused of
corrupting the young by propounding heretical ideas and was
sentenced to death by drinking hemlock. This he did with great
calmness and confidence, because he knew where he was going
and he knew it was better than where he was. When asked by his
friend, Crito, how he wished to be buried, Socrates replied,
"Wherever you will, if only you can catch me. Is it not strange

that, after all I have said to convince you that I am going to the society of the happy, you still think this body to be Socrates? To die and be released is better for me."

The execution of Socrates for speaking his mind was a rare happening in Athens, and it came during a period when the ideals of freedom of speech were temporarily forgotten. Normally, Athens, with its liberal attitude, provided a great contrast to other areas of the world where one could be murdered for the mildest questioning of those in power. Socrates had been allowed to speak freely until then. Indeed, freedom of speech, religion and politics were generally an accepted part of life except for the odd period when those ideals lapsed. Socrates must have said the wrong thing at the wrong time from the point of view of the authorities because his pupil, Plato, was later allowed to continue to speak in the same vein without losing his life. Plato was devastated by his friend's death and left Greece to visit Egypt, Palestine, Italy and Sicily. He learned from the people and cultures he encountered while outlining his beliefs in virtue and justice wherever he went. Plato was a man of courage and spoke out against tyranny. He saw it as cowardice which, of course, it is. The King of Sicily was so outraged by this that he had Plato arrested and sold into slavery. Fortunately, he was bought by a supporter who gave him back his freedom. When you are here for the good of the planet and humanity, the other levels are always trying to protect you in times of danger. They work through others who are in close enough contact with their higher selves to be used as a means of communicating through their thoughts. In this case, Plato was bought by a supporter and not by someone who might have prevented all the wonderful work he had yet to do.

Plato returned to Athens and founded a school of philosophy which was called the Academy. It was named after the garden in which it was built and, today, we still use the word academy for an educational institution. Those with open minds flocked to hear the Plato wisdom. Pupils were encouraged to think, question and look at everything with open, inquiring minds. Every opinion was welcomed. He said that things were not always what they appeared at first to be. Two thousand three hundred years ago he said the mind was the eternal part of us which could exist outside the physical body. Even today, our so called state-of-the-art science still hasn't realised that the eternal mind and the brain are not the same and that consciousness can exist outside the body. Indeed, that is its usual state. Plato, incidentally, was apparently involved in the Greek mystery school of the time. I don't know if this was a positive or negative influence on him. I certainly disagree with some of his views on life, but his understanding of creation was well ahead of today's 'science'.

Just as Socrates taught Plato, so Plato taught Aristotle. Aristotle could have been a reincarnation of the Socrates consciousness. Socrates helped Plato to awaken to his true self and, through reincarnation, Plato may have done the same for him later when he became the personality called Aristotle. You can see how reincarnation can allow a relatively few aspects of consciousness to have an ongoing effect on human thinking. When one of their physical lives ends, another begins, and the work continues in another body. I think the Luciferic consciousness works in exactly the same way. Aristotle was a genius of his time. He was well versed in chemistry, physics, biology, mathematics, astronomy, botany, anatomy and psychology and was always searching for further understanding in all these subjects and more. Like Plato, he started a school. It was known as the Lyceum. He also inspired the foundation of the famous university at Alexandria where people could research and lecture without the diversions of the mythical gods promoted by the religions.

The intellectual greatness of Athens withered during the Peloponnesian War when the Spartans and Corinthians combined with others to defeat the Athenians. The war lasted twenty-seven years and the pre-eminence of Athens was over. Within a few centuries of it being Christianised, the Church would burn all the writings of Plato, Aristotle and other Greek knowledge that came to light. They saw this human enlightenment as heresy against the Bible. But some of their work survived and would rise again to public attention after the Renaissance in Europe.

The incarnations of the volunteer consciousness that propelled Athens into the centre of intellectual thought was extremely successful in raising understanding and would continue to affect the thinking of millions over the centuries. But the power of the Luciferic consciousness to control the minds of so many should not be underestimated. Its most important weapons are conflict, imposition and ignorance, and it would have been very determined to put an end to what was happening in Athens. The Lucifer-controlled human beings in the negative secret societies and elsewhere, always seek to stimulate conflict. The cause doesn't matter as long as it happens. The wars that destroyed intellectual Athens and the pursuit of further knowledge would be repeated across the globe and over the generations, as the struggle between harmony and disharmony increased in its intensity.

Greek philosophy would influence the Romans. Around 1000BC some nomadic tribes settled alongside the River Tiber in what is now Italy. They called their settlement Latium, hence Latin. This language was the fusion of the Aryan tongue and the Celtic. It evolved through the interaction and inter-marriage of the Aryan speakers and the darker-skinned Iberian Celts. By 753BC, a trading centre had been established near to seven hills and was named Roma. From this beginning was to come a vast empire which, at its peak, would encompass Spain, France (Gaul), Italy, Dalmatia, Macedonia, Greece, Asia Minor, Syria, Palestine, Libya, Numidia, Corsica, Sardinia, Sicily, Crete, Cyprus, Egypt and most of Britain and Mesopotamia. This was achieved largely through violence and slaughter.

The early Romans were governed by kings. They had a flirtation with a republic, though it could hardly be described as a democracy. The priests with their mumbo jumbo still held sway. There was a people's forum, a sort of popular assembly called the Comita Tributa, but, any time the priests said the gods did not wish it to take place, it had to be cancelled. The priests determined the wishes of the gods by examining the hearts and livers of sacrificed animals. They believed that the heart and liver were the seat of the mind and that, through them, the gods could speak to them. The chaotic republic was replaced by a series of Emperors. This began after the emergence of the most famous Roman of them all, Julius Caesar, who was born in 100BC. He was a military leader who fought, conquered, and terrorised most of Europe. For, despite all his gifts as an orator and general, he was a tyrant and a butcher. He had many enemies in Rome who feared and resented his growing power. Eventually, he invaded his own country. He crossed a stream called the Rubicon which marked the border between his province and the rest of Italy. He took control of Rome and her empire and, in time, gave himself the title Pontifex Maximus as head of the state religion. This title of the head of what was a pagan religion is now held by the Pope! Julius Caesar was seen by most of his subjects as a divine being, yet another god king. Caesar travelled to Egypt where he fell for the charms of Cleopatra whom he would later take to Rome. But, in

44BC, he was murdered on the Ides (15th) of March by those who hated him for the power he had over them and the Empire.

There followed a long series of emperors, most of them less than wise and compassionate, but there were many good things about the Roman civilisation, too. Nothing is all good or all bad. Under the rule of Vespasian in the nine years from 70AD a system of education was introduced which was influenced by the ideas and beliefs of Plato and Aristotle. He made his minister of education a Spaniard turned Roman citizen called Quintilian who much admired the Greek philosophers. He organised an elaborate system of schools in the Roman Empire which taught the virtues of liberty, justice and truth, while abhorring cruelty and oppression. If only they and their like in Greece had been allowed to flourish and grow, what a different world we would live in today. Instead, Christianity was to cast its darkness across the Roman Empire and beyond. The schools were closed and their teachers scattered or killed because the pursuit of knowledge outside the pages of the Bible was seen as heresy. The great library at Alexandria was turned into a theological college and darkness and delusion descended on the collective mind of the human race.

So, in our story, we have been through two distinct phases of human history. There were the times when extra-terrestrials populated the planet. Then, after the end of Atlantis, fewer of them came here but they still visited, and were seen by the people as gods. Channelling and psychic communications became the means through which the 'gods' most influenced us. ETs working for the Light – the great majority – and the Light Consciousness, have, in general, been working through the volunteers and any humans who wish to hear their message of love and spiritual freedom. But the Light will not interfere in human free will while the Luciferic stream has no such ethics. It has used whatever means necessary to create conflict, confusion and ignorance.

All three of which bring to mind what has been one of Lucifer's most effective vehicles for suppressing knowledge, understanding and mental liberation. It was his invention and it has served his cause so wonderfully well. Only today, nearly two thousand years later, are we beginning to cast off the yoke it has imposed on human evolution. It is the tragedy we call Christianity.

4

Bible Stories

THE story of the Jews is woven through the early Middle Eastern cultures.

About eighteen centuries before Christianity some event caused the Euphrates to change its course and bypass the Sumer city of Ur. No more could the land around the city be irrigated by an extensive system of ditches, nor could their ships reach the sea to trade. The inhabitants moved inland to settle alongside the river at Babylon. Abraham of the Old Testament left the city of Ur with his family and slaves. Among them was his nephew, Lot. According to Hebrew scriptures they settled in Syria (an abbreviation of Assyria) which they called Canaan. This name was later given to the whole area west of the Jordan, including what became Palestine. They led a nomadic life with their animals and, at one time, travelled to Egypt in search of food during a famine. Abraham was much impressed by what he saw in Egypt and took this knowledge of their beliefs and customs back to Canaan. He became a wealthy and influential man and used his hundreds of armed slaves to support various factions in the wars between Canaanite communities.

Abraham fathered two children late in his life by two women, Hagar and Sarai, and they were named Ishmael and Isaac. It is quite possible, given his advanced age, that they were fathered by a younger man or men. It was now that Abraham introduced circumcision which he had seen used in Egypt. Abraham's idea was to create a distinction between the followers of his God and the other peoples of Canaan. They worshipped the Sumerian god, Enlil, which became known as Allah or El. It was originally a Sun god, though almost certainly with extra-terrestrial origins, and they would have thought they were communicating with this being through their channellings. With the death of Abraham, his son Isaac became head of the family and he had twin sons, Esau

51

and Jacob. The family and its offshoots were still nomads, but rich ones by the standards of the time. Jacob, the story goes, fathered twelve sons and the one he called Joseph was sold by jealous brothers to travelling merchants in the desert. Joseph was taken by them to Egypt where he was sold into slavery, but later he would become a favourite of the Pharaoh. This may sound far-fetched at first, but Egypt was then ruled by Bedouin invaders, the Hyksos or 'Shepherd Kings'. They were the same race as Joseph, the Arab nomad, and they had a similar culture. Joseph was made prime minister and put in charge of food production in Egypt. When ten of his brothers were driven to Egypt by famine they were re-united. Jacob was known as Israel, which means 'El (God) does battle' and his family and descendants would be called Israelites.

The twelve sons of Jacob grew into twelve tribes. The so-called House of Joseph, the slave-turned prime minister, took a different course to the others. The Israelites settled in an area called Goshen on the Eastern side of Lower Egypt, and over the next four hundred years or so they became a nation. All was well for them while the Shepherd Kings reigned in Egypt but, when they were removed by rebellion, life became tough for the Israelites. They were disarmed and put to work as slaves. The Egyptians decreed that all male children of the Israelites should be killed and the intention was that soon the Israelite nation would cease to exist.

Around the thirteenth century BC the man known as Moses was born and, it is said, was brought up by a Pharaoh's daughter after he was found floating in a basket in the bulrushes. The story goes that he killed an Egyptian for badly treating an Israelite and fled into the desert of Sinai. There he learned more of Allah, the God of Abraham, and he had what appeared to be profound psychic experiences and communications. To him this had to be God and not just a discarnate entity. Either that or he was contacted by extra-terrestrials or subjected to some sort of mind-suggestion. Some of the descriptions in the Bible of this god of Moses could certainly be spacecraft of some kind. It is worth pointing out, too, that ET technology can project three-dimensional images we call holograms which appear to be 'visions'. The craft need not be seen when this is happening and 'miracles' like a burning bush would be easy for ETs to manifest. Anyway, whatever it was that happened to Moses, his experiences led him to reject the Egyptian trinity of gods, Osiris, Isis, and Horus, and turn to Allah or El, the 'One God'. Interestingly, Moses would surely have attended the Brotherhood Mystery School in Egypt given his royal connections and they were promoting the idea of one God at least from the time of Akhenaton. It has been stressed to me in channelling that we should not underestimate the knowledge of hypnosis and mind-controlling drugs available in the mystery schools at this time.

On the death of the Pharaoh, Moses returned to Egypt where he told the Israelites that Allah had appeared to him in the desert. The god had said they were his chosen people. He said further that Allah wished to be known by the Israelites as Yhvh, which was pronounced 'Yaweh' and later became Jehovah. This means 'Rain Cloud'. From now on all the Israelite channellers were thought to be vehicles for the god Jehovah and the promises made to them through these sources were believed to be the promises of their god.

It was the same with other peoples the world over and this is how many god-myths originated. As Luke's Gospel says: *"He [God] spake from the mouth of his holy prophets (channellers) which have been since the world began."* When you look at the communications Moses was supposed to have had with Jehovah on Mount Sinai you can relate it to the communications on Mount Olympus which the Greeks claimed to have had with their god, Zeus. The same themes run through all of them.

Moses told the new Pharaoh of his communications and asked for permission to lead the Israelites out of Egypt to the land of Abraham in Canaan, the 'promised land' which 'God' had told him about. The Pharaoh eventually agreed and the great exodus began. They took with them the mummy of Joseph and walked across the Red Sea by a sand bar which Napoleon I was also later to use. On the journey, it is said, Moses was given by 'God' the laws of his tribe which are known as the Ten Commandments with all those 'Thou shalt nots' and such like. Perhaps he channelled them or maybe he just *thought* he was channelling them because similar laws could be found in other areas of the Middle East. Maybe he met with the occupants of a spacecraft. As the biblical description says:

"On the morning of the third day, there was thunder and lightning, a thick cloud appeared on the mountain, and a very loud trumpet was heard. [Jehovah often arrived with the sound of trumpets.] All the people in the camp trembled with fear.

"Moses led them out of the camp to meet God and they stood at the foot

of the mountain. The whole of Mount Sinai was covered with smoke, because the Lord had come down on it in fire. The smoke went up like the smoke of a furnace, and all the people trembled violently."

Exodus 19: vv 16-18.

Imagine what it would be like for that ancient people, or even people today, to see a spacecraft land on a mountain top and you can appreciate what might have been happening on Mount Sinai. The fierce, harsh, and bloodthirsty God of the Old Testament would fit with the theme of extremely negative extra-terrestrials who sought to control people on Earth through fear and imposition. Exodus goes on:

"When the people heard the thunder and the trumpet blast and saw the lightning and the smoking mountain, they trembled with fear and stood a long way off. They said to Moses, 'If you speak to us, we will listen; but we are afraid that if God speaks to us, we will die'.

*'Moses replied, 'Don't be afraid; God has come only to test (frighten) you and make you keep on **obeying** him, so that you will not sin'. But the people continued to stand a long way off, and only Moses went near the dark cloud where God was."*

Exodus 20: vv 18-20

This constant mention of a cloud in relation to Jehovah's appearances is interesting, given also that his name means 'rain cloud'. Producing clouds is not a problem for ET technology. Indeed the elite Brotherhood scientists of today have the technology to manipulate the weather, at least in a small area. I have no doubt that some event happened on Sinai, but I am not convinced that Moses was given all the Thou Shalt Nots at that time. It is most likely that the whole story of the commandments is a myth and the laws of the Israelites did not come through Moses on the mountain at all. There are many similar stories shared by different civilisations and each claims them as their own when all they have done is change the names involved. The religious dogma and ceremonies of the Israelites were naturally influenced by the Egyptians as you would expect given that they had all been brought up in that country. The clothing of their priests was inspired by Egypt. Incidentally, during the journey, the Israelites had periods of hunger and thirst, obviously, as they walked through the desert lands. According to the stories they were helped by manna from

Heaven. I have seen this portrayed as bread falling from the sky. In fact, manna is a sticky substance produced by a desert shrub.

It became obvious when they reached the 'Promised Land' of Canaan that the communications to Moses from whatever source had left something to be desired. Either that or his communicator was giving him some inaccurate information for some reason. They found well-armed peoples in walled cities who resisted their advance. Moses had led them to believe that the promised land was unoccupied and waiting only for them. He was less than popular and the Israelites wandered in the desert for another forty years before they became fierce and barbaric warriors. Moses passed on and Joshua, a man of war, took over from him. The opposition in the promised land was still too much for them, but under the leadership of Joshua they ejected the Arab shepherd peoples from a large area. This was to be called Palestine and here they settled down as an agricultural people with each tribe ruled by a sheik. They were still very primitive. They had only stone implements and they made animal sacrifices to Jehovah who still being channelled, followed, and often seen in ways that could suggest ET involvement. Jehovah was always demanding animal sacrifices and he, or they, were clearly a deeply unpleasant piece of work under the control of the Luciferic consciousness. To be circumcised by a sharp stone doesn't bear thinking about, but that's what happened. It was barbaric.

There were occasions when some Israelites would turn away from the instructions of Jehovah and worship Baal – Bel, the Son of God of Mesopotamia. As time passed the attributes given to Jehovah and Baal began to merge. Around 1150BC, the prophet (channeller) Samuel came on the scene. The Israelites were now controlled by the Philistines and Samuel inspired a desire for liberty. Saul became king, against Samuel's wishes, and he also took over his post of high priest. Saul turned his tribe of Judah into the dominant force of the Israelites, defeating the Philistines and securing independence. Saul had a great rival in David and to escape Saul's wrath David went into the desert of Judea and lived the life of a criminal, murderer, and outlaw. Men, women and children were massacred by David and his band. Many were dismembered or burnt alive. He always consulted Jehovah before setting out to steal and kill and always received permission. You can see how any amount of slaughter can be justified in the name of a god when you are either channelling a low vibrational entity or deluding yourself with your own thoughts. Such is the story of religion.

David became king when he and his bandits joined forces with the Philistines and conquered Judea. He then turned on and defeated the Philistines, taking Jerusalem in the process. It is from the word Philistine that Palestine came after this victory. David's armies were merciless, often burning and dismembering their victims. His aggression and lust for power fuelled the expansion of his empire into Canaan, the rest of Syria, and Northern Arabia. He and the Israelites now controlled a region from the Euphrates to the Red Sea. So the Israelite Empire was born under the control of the House of Judah. We are now in the period up to 1015BC. As Arthur Findlay points out in his outstanding work, *The Curse of Ignorance*, people were still being fined and jailed in Britain up to the last century for daring to criticise David and other Old Testament heroes who were believed to be vehicles for the righteousness of God.

After David came his son Solomon, the man of 'wisdom' according to legend. In fact, he had no more respect for human life than had David. He killed his brother, the rightful heir under their laws, to become king in the first place. Solomon became an important member of the Brotherhood after he became an advisor to the Pharaoh, Shishak I, and married his daughter. While in Egypt he was initiated into the Brotherhood at El Amarna and when he returned to Jerusalem he built the famous temple to Jehovah which has been fought over ever since. It was a Brotherhood temple and, according to freemasons' legend, Solomon invited the Brotherhood craft guilds of Egypt, the forerunners of the freemasons, to help with its construction. Many freemasons are led to believe that their organisation began with the building of Solomon's temple and this has added to the myth that freemasonry is connected with the Bible, the Holy Land, and is in service to the 'Great Architect of the Universe' – God. In fact the Brotherhood goes back well beyond the time of Solomon and, in the case of its elite, it answers to a very different master. As Albert Pike, the Grand Commander of the Supreme Council of Freemasons in America would say in the 1870s:

"The Masonic Religion should be by all of us initiates in the High Degrees maintained in the purity of the Luciferic doctrine."

They don't tell the lower initiates that, however, until they have agreed to submit themselves with a binding oath to the authority of their worshipful master who, according to the Mackey *Encyclopedia of Freemasonry,* must be obeyed as a first duty of every freemason.

The secret Brotherhood of Babylonia and Egypt was expanding rapidly as was its negative infiltration. It had already spread across other parts of the Middle East and one of its best known promoters was the Canaanite God-King, Melchizedek. His priesthood wore the famous Brotherhood symbol of the apron, and combined it with another Brotherhood symbol, the lamb, by making their aprons out of lamb skin. The freemasons still do this. The Brotherhood is also extremely strong and active in Israel and the Jewish culture in general today with its mystical expression, the kabbalah, also reflecting the classic principles of Brotherhood societies. That is not to say that the Kabbalah is negative. It is merely esoteric knowledge which can be used for good or ill. The Kabbalah is another expression of the spiritual knowledge which goes back to Atlantis and beyond and from which all religions have come. The Order of Melchizadek is kabbalistic and promotes the philosophy of a world government which is the aim of the negative Brotherhood movement.

Solomon's temple was nothing more than a slaughterhouse with a stream of animals being sacrificed daily to gratify the perceived desires of Jehovah. A high priest and an army of 30,000 'lesser' priests were supported by the contributions of the people to carry out this butchery. Their job had nothing to do with spirituality. They were nothing more than slaughterhouse workers. The priests, who were now taking over in their religion from the mediums and channellers as the accepted source of Jehovah's will, announced that their god preferred the sacrifice of animals rather than crops and vegetation. The crops, you see, had to be burned as part of the sacrifice, but the animals only had to be killed and the priests then had the right to eat or sell the carcass. This same mentality was still alive in the 17th century when the first lighthouse was planned. Trinity House had been set up by Henry VIII for the Trinity Brethren, and their duty was to pray for the souls of people lost at sea. In return they were given the rights to everything salvaged from the ships wrecked on the English coast. When the Eddystone Lighthouse was proposed, Trinity House opposed it because they could see that fewer wrecks meant less salvage for them.

Under Solomon, Egyptian and Phoenician beliefs became absorbed into the Israelite worship of Jehovah and truths, half truths, myths, and lies were becoming merged as the centuries passed. When he died, the Judean empire collapsed and the other tribes of Israel revolted. Two distinct groups emerged, the Israelites in the north including Samaria and Galilee and those in Southern Judea who were called the Jews. The worship of Baal re-emerged to challenge that of Jehovah, but the prophets Elijah and, more successfully, Elisha, made sure the worship of Baal was destroyed and Jehovah ruled supreme. Women were treated appallingly. They were bought and sold and, when their husbands died they became part of his estate just like his cattle and land. Incest was common and children were sold, ill treated, and sacrificed; slavery abounded.

The people of Israel believed they were God's chosen people who would inherit the Earth, but a shepherd called Amos announced that he had communicated with Jehovah (the Lord) and he said their kingdom was to be taken from them. Even worse, Jehovah would lead the aggressors because the 'chosen people' had defied his instructions. Amos was right in that civil war broke out in 745BC and the Assyrians took advantage to conquer the lands of Israel. The ten northern tribes began to disintegrate, a process the Babylonians, Persians, Greeks and Romans would complete. Amos, Hosea and other prophets steered the people away from the belief in a nationalistic god and weakened the power of the priests. They preferred to promote a gentler God of mercy and justice who spoke for all people, not only the Israelites.

The Assyrians invaded Samaria and later Judea which was by then being guided by the prophet, Isaiah. He proved to be a man of some wisdom and foresight and was obviously channelling a higher level of consciousness than some of the others. But on his death the old view of Jehovah returned with the human and animal sacrifices and the power of the priests. Other prophets like Jeremiah warned of the consequences. He predicted the destruction of Jerusalem and the Temple (slaughterhouse) built by Solomon. Jeremiah's predictions were vindicated when the Chaldeans under Nebuchadnezzar, attacked and defeated the people of Judea, the Jews. By 586BC Judah was no more and Jerusalem was in ruins. The Jews were dispersed across Chaldea as had already happened to the Israelites. They absorbed the customs and beliefs of the

Mesopotamian peoples and many moved their devotion from Jehovah to Bel. The exiles inherited the Chaldean idea of rest on the seventh day, the Sabatu, and on their return the tradition would begin of attending churches or Synagogues to hear the writings of the prophets. When they were freed by the Persians, as noted earlier, they took the Mesopotamian customs and beliefs back to Samaria and Judea along with some of the holy relics, including golden candlesticks which Nebuchadnezzar had taken from them.

They now expected the Messiah to appear and lead them to their true destiny, although many Jews stayed in Babylon and other areas and did not choose to return to the promised land. Incidentally, Jewish people trace their ancestry back to Abraham and the times we are discussing, but today the Jewish majority are Ashkenazim Jews, who, Arthur Koestler claims, originated from a Turkish tribe who converted in the 8th century as an alternative to being forced to espouse Islam or Christianity (see *The Thirteenth Tribe*). The Sephardic Jews, on the other-hand, who genetically originate from Biblical Jews, are today in the minority. The idea of a Messiah came from the Persians and from either there or Egypt they absorbed the belief in the resurrection of the physical body and that of a million years of righteousness. Palestine was ruled by the Persians, but the Jews were allowed to re-build the temple in Jerusalem and have their own religious hierarchy controlled by the Jewish people. The influence of Babylon on Jewish thought and belief continued to grow. Under the guidance of two men called Ezra and Nehemiah the Jewish society became a little more civilised. Both were greatly influenced by their time in Babylon where they heard the Chaldean stories of the Tower of Babel (Babylon), the Great Flood, and Noah. Ezra re-wrote the Book of the Law which had been destroyed when the temple was ransacked and the laws he says were given to Moses were no more than the beliefs Ezra picked up in Babylon like the Sabbath (Sabatu) and the idea that the Creator rested on the seventh day.

Jewish influence grew across the Middle East and they expanded their numbers into many areas. The Greeks gave them the name Hebrews which means the 'people from the other side' (of the Mediterranean.) Some of the Jewish texts were translated into Greek. The Jews became traders, valuers, moneylenders and pawnbrokers, buying and selling primarily rather than producing. Alexander the Great, a man similar in attitude to King David, took over the Macedonian empire from his father and conquered Egypt and the land we know as Palestine. On the death of Alexander one of his generals, Ptolemy I, took over Jerusalem. This wasn't difficult because he attacked on the Sabbath and the Jews refused to fight on their holy day. The Greek influence on the people of Jerusalem increased and a dispute developed between the Hellenised (Greek influenced) Jews and those who wished to retain the old ways of Jehovah. Conflict erupted and in walked the King of Syria, Antiochus IV, to assume power in Jerusalem. How ironic, as we chronicle this constant bloodshed, that Jerusalem translates as 'City of Peace'. Antiochus tried to force the pagan customs of Greece onto the believers in Jehovah and insisted they worship a god called Jove. A bloodbath ensued as the supporters of Jehovah resisted.

The theme of constant conflict will be seen throughout human history. The Luciferic consciousness and the human expressions of that consciousness do not care what causes the conflict. A sense of religious or racial superiority, greed, a lust for power, anything will do. They will support a nation when it suits them and cause it to be destroyed when it doesn't. All they want is for negative energy to be produced in abundance to serve the master, Lucifer, and for humanity to remain so divided and awash with fear and the pressure of everyday life that they won't open their minds for long enough to see who they are and what is really going on. I am not going to keep labouring this point through the rest of our brief history of humankind, except where I feel it needs to be highlighted. But keep in mind through all that follows how conflict and division are the aims of the disharmonious consciousness and anything that causes that serves its purpose. Often this will be stimulated by a direct attack on human minds by the Luciferic consciousness which manipulates the negative human emotions of ego, greed, and a wish for power. You don't have to affect many people to start a war, given that for most of human history the decision of one king, queen, or dictator can decide the fate of millions who have no desire to fight. And you only have to affect the thinking of one side because, once they attack, the other side has to defend itself and war has begun. You can start a war by affecting the mind of one person and if he or she happens to be an incarnation of the Luciferic consciousness it's child's play. The negative secret societies of the Brotherhood in their many forms have had an important role in the artificial creation of conflict by pulling the strings behind the scenes and whenever possible getting its members and followers into positions of power. Because it has so many levels of initiation, one level can manipulate the lower levels who have no idea of the agenda being followed by their 'superiors'. This very much applies to politicians today. In this way, people can help to start a conflict when they have no wish to do so. Say a brotherhood member is told of a plan by Nation A to attack Nation B or to undermine it in some way. That member might be persuaded to warn the leaders of Nation B of what was going on. The member would do this out of the best of intentions. But he wouldn't know that another member from a different branch of the Brotherhood was telling Nation A exactly the same about Nation B. Those Brotherhood members would believe they were doing the right thing, but wouldn't know that they were being used to start a conflict that would not have started otherwise. Once you have organisations based on secrecy and levels of initiation that the lower rungs know nothing about, very few people can control the rest, most of whom might be lovely human beings who do not wish harm to anyone. So it is with the Brotherhood. It may sound simplistic and these things are often more complex, but the basic themes of manipulation, agents provocateurs, and secret Brotherhood assassinations calculated to stir up conflict have been behind much of the horror that has plagued the human story.

The invaders of Jerusalem were eventually removed, but internal strife continued between two factions of the Jewish religion, the Pharisees ("The separated") and the Sadducees ("The just"). The Romans captured Judea and Jerusalem in 63BC and after a bitter conflict imposed on the people in 37 BC an Arab Prince called King Herod. Most members of the Sanhedrin, the Jewish Council and highest court of justice, opposed Herod and they were killed once he gained control. He also crushed the power of the Sadducees for their opposition to him and the Pharisees rose to ascendancy. Herod died in 4BC and the internal conflict returned. The Romans assumed control and ruled through a series of procurators, one of whom was called Pontius Pilatus.

It was into this time and against this political and religious backdrop that a child was born called Jeshuah. The stories of his life would later be translated into Greek and it was then that the Jewish Jeshuah became the Greek version, Jesus. So the one thing we know for sure about Jesus is that his name wasn't Jesus! I will, however, continue to use that name here for simplicity and because it really doesn't matter what he was called. It is what he did that is important. He was, I believe, born and brought up as an Essene. For two hundred years before his birth a group called the Essenes or Therapeutae (meaning healers) had lived in Egypt and Palestine. They were inspired by the Buddhist philosophy more than the Jewish and it is likely that their beliefs originated in India, although they must also have been influenced by Egyptian thought as well. It is possible that Buddha, Socrates, and Jesus were the same consciousness and certainly the same overall higher self.

The Jewish historian of the first century AD, Josephus, described the Essenes as the most honest people in the world and he said they followed the values of justice and equality at all times. They were vegetarians and opposed animal or human sacrifice. They had a very different approach to life to the prevailing attitudes of the time. The Essenes had a number of centres in Egypt and Palestine and other lay members who lived in the general community, but they are best known for their settlements at Qumran alongside the Dead Sea where the Dead Sea Scrolls were found in 1947 and further down the shore at the giant flat-topped mountain called Masada. It was here that the Jews rebelling against Roman rule would commit mass suicide rather that be captured in 73AD. I visited both places in a short, but unforgettable, visit to Israel in 1993, as described in my autobiography. The love I felt flowing through me at those points was indescribable. At Qumran I found myself speaking the words: 'I forgive them everything', although I did not know why I said that or where the words came from.

The Essenes were a brotherhood who worked a great deal in secret. But as I continue to stress, secrecy does not always mean conspiracy in times of great religious imposition. There have been times when keeping your beliefs and knowledge secret has been essential to your survival. I don't believe the Essenes were the perfect people they are sometimes claimed to be, but overall I feel quite good about them and, anyway, I think Jesus was such a strong character that he would have made his own mind up about things and not blindly accepted another belief system. In the American west there was once a farmer called Maverick who refused to brand his animals. The word maverick became used to describe people who refuse to be branded and linked to one organ-isation or group. I think that under that definition of the word, Jesus was a maverick.

I believe that the man known as Joseph of Arimathea could have been the father of Jesus and not his uncle as the stories claim. This is a thought which keeps coming to me again and again, and others have channelled this information. No one knows the background for sure, and it can only be speculation, but it is clear that Joseph of Arimathea was very close to Jesus. Joseph was an Essene, as was Mary, and the Essenes possibly told her of a child she was being asked to conceive with Joseph of Arimathea to ensure that the right genetic combinations interacted. The Essenes believed this child had been foretold and Mary, then only a young girl of perhaps fourteen, agreed. The Joseph who is called her husband in the gospels became the guardian of Jesus and fathered other children with Mary. But the genetic father of Jesus was I feel Joseph of Arimathea. This was a closely-guarded secret known only to a few. Joseph of Arimathea was a rich landowner and businessman and a member of the Jewish Council, the Sanhedrin. Keeping his close family connections to Jesus a secret was vital if he was to play his part in the overall plan.

We are looking here again at a highly significant incarnation of the volunteer consciousness. The story of Jesus and others in the Middle East was only part of what was happening at that time. All over the world other volunteers had incarnated to co-ordinate their work. Most of them would not have known what was happening in Palestine, but all would have been coordinated from a higher level in the same way that it is happening today. The early years of Jesus were spent with the Essenes in Qumran and in Egypt opening up to his true self, and remembering who he was and why he was here. He would have been fed rubbish along with the enlightened explanations and it would have been up to him to see the difference. Nothing changes. Jesus travelled further afield in the so called 'lost years' which are left blank by the Bible. He passed through Mesopotamia on his way to India and Kashmir and he was further influenced by the words of Buddha. (See *A Search for the Historical Jesus* by Prof. F. Hassnain.) He spent several years with Buddhist thinkers and greatly impressed them with his knowledge and understanding. He also journeyed to Greece and England. He may have travelled to Glastonbury and other places in England with Joseph of Arimathea who imported tin from Cornwall. All the time he was learning – remembering – and passing on this knowledge.

He was also channelling highly-potent energies into the Earth's energy grid. He had an energy field which allowed him to channel energies of immense power which would have 'fried' most other people. I am not saying for a moment that Jesus understood everything that was happening and exactly why he was doing certain things. He would have simply felt impelled to do them. Certainly he would have known the potential consequences of returning from his travels to Palestine to challenge the political, economic, and religious status quo, but the urgings of his higher self would have been almost impossible to ignore and he would have done many things without, at the time, knowing why. It is like that feeling we have when we know something is going to have an unpleasant outcome, but somehow we go on walking into it. Know the feeling? Me, too.

His open and verbal challenge to the established and destructive order was an effort to wake people up by appealing directly to their lower consciousness. If the higher consciousness could not communicate powerfully enough with the lower consciousness of the people then one way around that was to channel information through another person, in this case Jesus, so that he could speak directly to the lower consciousness by voice to ear. This is what all spiritual communicators come to do. I feel the area around Palestine, Egypt, and the Middle East was the centre of the temporary energy grid created after the end of Atlantis and an inter-dimensional gateway. If the consciousness of the people could be raised in that part of the world it would have a considerable effect on the planet, as would direct energy channelling into the grid at that point. These were the twin tasks of Jesus and those around him.

It was, to say the least, not easy to achieve. Incarnating into the thick fog of negative, imbalanced, energy that was engulfing this planet made it even tougher. I know there are some who believe that everything that happens on Earth is meant to be and part of some grand Divine Plan. I don't believe that. I feel most strongly that what we see on Earth is evolution that has taken an unfortunate and unnecessary turn caused by this period of Luciferic opportunity and that the ability of the higher levels to affect the dense physical world is not always that easy. There is a basic plan for what needs to be done, but there is also much ad-libbing that goes on in reaction to human behaviour. Much of this behaviour is not the work or design of the Source or our own higher selves. It is the consequence of the negative energy imbalance, the density of this frequency, the Luciferic consciousness, and the utter nonsense which is passed on through the generations to indoctrinate each new generation of lower selves with the same nonsense. So it was at the time of Jesus.

I believe the idea that this man had to be nailed to a cross and die horribly in order for some judgmental God to agree to forgive all the sins of humanity is the most monumental nonsense I have ever heard. It never ceases to amaze me how many believe it. I feel the power and privilege that Jesus was challenging conspired to silence him. The religious hierarchy worked with the Romans who also didn't want this troublemaker to go on making waves. Forces of occupation, whether physical, economic, or mental, know that people who think for themselves are dangerous; and people who encourage others to do the same are even more so. All the time the Luciferic consciousness is seeking to work through these people to achieve its ends. Jesus was nailed to a cross, the Roman punishment at the time, but I do not believe he died there.

From what I and others have channelled and written, I believe the following is at least quite close to the truth. Joseph of Arimathea was a central player in the plan to ensure that Jesus did not die on the cross. He owned the area known as the Garden of Gethsemane near the Mount of Olives just outside the city walls of Jerusalem. As a member of the Jewish Council, the Sanhedrin, he would have known exactly what was being said about Jesus. Another Essene member of the Sanhedrin, the one called Nicodemus, also secretly supported Jesus and helped him as best he could. He, too, was an Essene. In fact there was a secret group of Essenes unrecorded by history who worked on behalf of Jesus and the overall plan far more effectively than those called the 'disciples'. Most of them did not know the full story of what was going on most of the time because the more who knew the more chance there was of something slipping out that would have ruined everything.

Jesus, Joseph, and other Essenes devised a plan unknown to the disciples and even to his mother Mary and his close companion, possibly his wife, Mary Magdalene. The plan was for Jesus to survive the cross while the authorities believed he was dead. There were three main reasons for this, though no doubt there were others: (a) To take the pressure off those who were supporters of Jesus, including the Essenes, because there were many, including the Romans, who were moving towards the belief that it was necessary to remove them. The public death and humiliation of

Jesus, their focal point, would disperse this growing desire for a wholesale removal of his supporters and family. Joseph would have known this because of his close links with the Sanhedrin. He might even have suggested this course of action as an alternative way of destroying this challenge to the status quo. (b) They knew that people who question convention often have more influence on thinking when they are dead (or are believed to be dead) than they do when they were alive. Take the example of Confucius, for instance. (c) To go through great pain and trauma with the intent of helping the Earth and humanity creates the energy of love in quite fantastic amounts and power. And on the land owned by Joseph of Arimathea was one of the key points on that central heart of the post-Atlantean grid. It was on this point that the crucifixion would take place.

Jesus knew all this and being a brilliant medium in constant touch with the higher levels he would have channelled the basic themes. His secret group put together the plan under spiritual inspiration and the higher frequencies were at work from their realms helping to make it happen as required. The timing had to be perfect. Those who were crucified were left on the cross for as long as it took for them to die, usually up to three days. Unless there was some way around that, Jesus could not possibly have survived. The only way of shortening his time on the cross was to ensure that it happened in the hours before the Saturday, the Jewish Sabbath. No-one was allowed to be executed and buried on that day and anyone still alive on the cross was killed before the start of the Sabbath. The usual method was to break their legs with a series of blows. This was fatal to anyone nailed by the wrists to a cross for rather gruesome reasons I won't go into. Therefore they had to find a way of giving the appearance that Jesus was dead before the end of the Friday.

Jesus made his entrance into Jerusalem to coincide with the timing he and Joseph had worked out. He was intentionally provocative, openly and publicly castigating the money lenders in the Temple, and generally stirring up discontent with the Jewish and Roman authorities. He wanted to make them act against him immediately. The much-maligned Judas was crucial to the plot, too. He was in on the plan and he 'betrayed' Jesus at the moment necessary to maintain the strict timing of the sequence of events. In the background, Joseph and Nicodemus, were working away within the Sanhedrin to ensure they were reacting to schedule.

The arrest of Jesus and the questioning by the Jewish hierarchy and Pilate followed the predicted time sequence and he was sentenced and nailed to the cross on the Friday. The crucifixion took place at a spot which adjoined the Garden of Gethsemane, owned by Joseph of Arimathea. If Jesus was thought to be still alive by the end of that day he would have been killed to avoid the event of his death running over into the Sabbath. The Essenes were well known for their knowledge of herbs and plants which they used in their healing. It would have been no problem for them to provide a mixture that would give the appearance of physical death. Indeed there are many documented examples of such drugs in ancient cultures, including one called Toska, a drink made of sour wine and wormwood. It was given by Jewish women to those being crucified to help them lose consciousness. Again at the right time, a drug was given to Jesus on a sponge which was put to his mouth with the excuse of giving him a drink. Soon after this he appeared to expire. The emphasis is on the word 'appeared' because although he was exhausted and in great pain and distress, he was still alive. One unfortunate event which had not been foreseen was when a soldier pierced his side with a sword after he had been taken down. This produced much blood, another indication that he was taken from the cross alive. In the hours before his apparent 'death' he was the focal point in a vast energy channelling being coordinated by the higher levels right across the world. Volunteers incarnate in all cultures were involved although they would not have been aware that what they were doing was being mirrored all over the planet.

Joseph of Arimathea went immediately to Pilate and asked for permission to remove the body of Jesus for burial. Pilate agreed after registering his surprise that Jesus had died so quickly and asked for confirmation. In preparation for what was to happen, Joseph had built a tomb in the Garden of Gethsemane so that Jesus could be taken from the cross to the safety of the tomb as quickly as possible. The quicker it happened the less chance there was that someone would realise what was going on and the sooner he could be given medical treatment the better. A large stone was pushed across the entrance to ensure no one could see what was going on inside. Waiting in the tomb when Jesus was brought in were Essene healers in white robes and they began the healing process immediately.

Jesus was in a bad way, but the healers stabilised his condition.

Under cover of darkness, the stone at the entrance to the tomb was pushed back and Jesus was taken to the Essene community at Qumran via a safe house. After a long convalescence, he recovered and left the region with Joseph and the two Marys to continue the work of energy channelling and passing on information. I feel he travelled to places like Italy, Crete, France, and India where he might have died a very old man in Kashmir. Some researchers believe he was known by many names to different peoples and in Kashmir he was Yuzu Asaph. His tomb is still there. However, others believe that Jesus ended his life in France. During a vision of the crucifixion which I had on one occasion, I channelled a series of short sentences which said:

"Essenes, Qumran. Time to recover. Illusion complete. Opposition believe I am dead. Much travel. Long lifetime. Three children by two women."

Surviving a crucifixion may sound far-fetched, but Josephus the historian documents a story of a man known to him who was taken down from the cross alive and survived. Josephus knew the man and pleaded with the Roman commander, Titus, for him to be spared. Titus agreed and the man was taken from the cross and given medical treatment. Still today in the Phillipines there are people who agree to be nailed to the cross as part of some bizarre ritual to confirm their faith and when they are taken down after some hours they recover. So it was possible to survive a crucifixion if you were not subjected to that horror for too long. Remember also that other levels would have been working to help Jesus during that time and giving to him the energies and strength to keep him incarnate.

The disciples, as I mentioned, were not in on the plan, apart from Judas who was considered, rightly as it turned out, to be the most trustworthy! When the tomb was found to be empty and the great stone pushed back, it was assumed the body had been stolen and later by some that Jesus had been resurrected – i.e. that his physical body had gone to Heaven. In fact he was recovering in a safe house with his Essene healers before being taken on to Qumran. Jesus had used the Jewish belief in a Messiah figure and the predictions of previous Jewish prophets to create interest in himself and therefore his words. It was like building a public platform from which he could speak his truths. He would stress how events in his life had been written in the ancient prophecies, but he and his secret support group were creating those events so they would match the prophecies. It was part of the plan to use the Jewish belief system to create interest and notoriety. Most of the disciples were not aware of this. Their inability to commit themselves totally to the work and understand its importance frustrated him and he was much closer to Joseph and his secret group. The ones called the disciples were a sort of 'front' for what was really going on behind the scenes and for that to work and appear credible it was vital that they had no knowledge of what was happening. They were very important to the work, but only if they didn't know the full story.

The plan worked magnificently in that everyone was fooled and Jesus achieved what he and his family and supporters came to achieve in relation to the energy grid. He also left behind a lot of people who were moved and motivated by his simple truths about love, Creation, and the eternal nature of all consciousness. The myths that were now to surround him made him far better known than ever he was in his lifetime in Palestine. No mention has been found of him in the works of the history writers of the time and yet look what has been written about him since his life was highjacked by the religion called Christianity. Others have channelled and seen the same basic story that I have outlined and researchers working purely from historical information (plus some higher inspiration) have come up with the same themes, too. What I have no doubt about are the following: The overall reason for the Jesus incarnation; that he did not die on the cross; and that he was not celibate. I feel he was married to or at least the close companion of Mary Magdalene with whom he had children and that he fathered a child with at least one other woman, possibly Mary Magdalene's sister, Martha. This might make some Church people reel back in horror, but the energy patterns that Jesus brought into incarnation would not have been wasted. They would have been passed on through the genetic line. This could well have meant that he needed to interact physically with more than one other energy field to create particular energy and genetic combinations. I talk more of this process of sexual interaction and the many reasons for it in my book, *Heal The World*.

We should not forget, I feel, that Jesus was only one of the volunteer incarnations, although a highly significant one. He played an effective and couragous part in helping the Earth and humanity, but so have millions of others. It has been a continuous, on-going, process and not something that happened only once 2,000 years ago. He was very much a man of this physical level while being in close contact with his higher self. He had the emotions of compassion, love, and at times anger. He spoke his mind and the idea that he went around in some spiritual mist talking kindly to everyone is well wide of the mark, I would say. Yes, he was kind to people and he had great love for the Earth and humanity, but sometimes love involves speaking out vehemently against injustice if that is what is necessary for change to happen and for people to awaken. It is such an irony that it is the way his lifetime was to be misrepresented that has made him the most famous of the volunteer incarnations.

After Jesus left Palestine with the two Marys, Joseph of Arimathea and others, the followers of his teachings (Jesuians) were, apart from the Essenes, small offshoots of the Jewish religion like the Gnostics and Ebionites. There was no overall belief system and they each held different views about the details and meaning of his life. Most of them did, however, believe in his return or Second Coming which is an ancient idea that goes back to Sun worship. Once again these early groups of Jesus followers were guided by channellers and you can see these referred to in the ancient texts as 'vessels' for the holy spirit who were filled with the 'Spirit of the Lord.' We read of people being filled with the Holy Spirit and then speaking the words of the Lord. Anyone who has experienced or witnessed channelling will know that an energy descends upon the channeller. This is the communicating consciousness enveloping and synchronising with the physical vehicle or vessel through which it seeks to communicate. It is this energy which channellers and onlookers feel that became termed the 'holy spirit' in ancient times. These Jesus-inspired groups were much like a spiritualist Church of today with people gathered to hear the communications of the medium, the ones blessed with 'charismata', the Greek word for psychic abilities.

It was only when the man we call St Paul came on the scene that Jesus, the wise and courageous philosopher, healer, and channel, was turned into the pagan saviour-god depicted by Christianity. Paul was an orthodox Jew who persecuted those sects which followed a belief in the philosophy of Jesus. This changed dramatically after he claimed to have seen a vision of Jesus on the road to Damascus. This could have been a psychic vision of a non-physical entity, or a three-dimensional holographic figure projected from a spacecraft, or he could have made it all up. But the latter is unlikely because from then on he clearly believed that Jesus was communicating with him and asking to be proclaimed Messiah and Saviour of the World. Paul was following the age-old custom of people believing that every ghost they saw or psychic communication they experienced was from God, the Highest One, or in this case God's 'son'. What appalling consequences this was to have.

We should remember that Paul came from a place called Tarsus in Asia Minor and there they worshipped a Greek pagan Saviour-god called Dionysus – their version of Bel. Dionysus was said to have been born to a virgin impregnated by the god Zeus and suffered and died to save humanity. Paul clearly saw Jesus as another incarnation of Dionysus, the one he learned about in Tarsus. All he did was transfer the myths about Dionysus to the philosopher called Jesus. Dionysus was the Greek Christ and the second in a trinity of Demeter, Dionysus, and Persephone in the same vein as other pagan gods throughout the Middle East. Dionysus was known as 'Our Lord', 'the Vine', 'the Saviour', 'the Judge of the Dead', 'the Deliverer', 'the Born Again', and 'the Only Begotten Son of God'. Above the head of Dionysus were depicted the words 'I am Life, Death, and Resurrection, I hold the winged crown'. He is also claimed to have said: 'I am at one with my father in heaven', and a service called the Eukharistia which involved animal sacrifice was performed in his honour. Paul was fundamentally influenced by the Greek Mystery (Brotherhood) beliefs and saviour god myths and these became fused in his mind with Jewish dogma. If they were controlled by the negative aspects of the Brotherhood at the time, they could have set him up and mind-controlled him to do what he did, and believe what he saw (or didn't) was Jesus. The lamb dying so our sins could be forgiven would have been a basic part of his belief system and he would have had no trouble linking this ancient pagan myth to Jesus. People who were sacrificed on the altars for thousands of years were seen in the same light. From these beginnings did Paul found what became the Christian Faith. Jesus didn't start Christianity. Paul did. I am not suggesting for a moment that Saul of Tarsus (St Paul) set out to cause all the horrors that his misunderstandings would create. He probably did it with the best of intentions and believed everything he said. I am sure the same can be said for most of those who followed him as guides and manipulators of the

Christian faith. They, themselves, were being manipulated.

Paul set off on his travels to tell people what Jesus was saying through him. His letters are reported in the New Testament. He made his living making tents on his journeys and three years after he saw his ghost or vision, or whatever it was, he arrived in Jerusalem to meet the disciple Peter and James, the brother of Jesus. They didn't think much of him and they opposed his views about Jesus. Paul admits he never knew or met Jesus in his lifetime, but he believed Jesus was now speaking to him from the world of the gods. This, he thought, made him much more knowledgeable about him than the disciples. There was a split between the believers in Jesus as a man and philosopher and the Pauline Christians who followed his belief in a recycled Dionysus, who, incidentally, was said to have been born on December 25th. This relates to the ancient cult of the Sun God in which the periods of mid-winter, mid-summer, and the solstices and seasons were seen as sacred times. Paul's Christianity was to win the day and pagan priests were absorbed into his Church. They had no problem being converted, because to them Jesus was just another pagan Saviour-god in the image of those they were used to. With their arrival Christianity became even more paganised.

The pagan religion called Mithraism was also absorbed into the Pauline version of Christianity. Mithraism worshipped the saviour-god, Mithra, (see Dionysus, Bel, Osiris, Krishna, et al) and they celebrated his birthday on December 25th, the beginning of their winter. Names like Mithra and Dionysus were simply changed to Jesus and so we have the Christian Christmas Day. Mithra was also believed to have risen from the dead at Easter and the pagans-turned-Christian-pagans welcomed that Festival into the Christian belief system. According to the Mithraists, Sunday was 'the Lord's Day' and the Eucharist, the baptism of babies, the idea of father, son, and holy spirit, the virgin mother giving birth to the saviour, the marriage service and so much more were taken from various streams of paganism and added to Christianity. These pagan beliefs were a mixture of extra-terrestrial 'gods', channelling and visions, the movement of the Sun through the seasons and the sky, and downright make-believe. As we have seen, the idea of Jesus as 'the lamb of God' dying so our sins could be forgiven goes back to pagan animal sacrifices in which the lamb was said to take the place of humanity to quell the anger of the gods. Mithraism was now Myth-raism – better known as Christianity.

It is worth pointing out that far from claiming that Jesus was born by divine intervention without intercourse, the oldest Greek and Syrian manuscripts say 'Joseph begat Jesus'. The idea of the virgin birth was a later insertion, as were all the additions that fostered the myth that Jesus the philosopher was Christ the saviour-god. Even the word Christ is of pre-Christian origin as Chrest (Egypt) and Christos (Greek). The story of the virgin birth of the Egyptian Son of God, Horus, has been found on a temple wall in Luxor and that was depicted long before Christianity was even thought of. In these early years of the Christian Church many changes were made to texts to justify the inventions. Words were attributed to Jesus which said: 'He that believeth and is baptised shall be saved, but he that believeth not shall be damned'. This was added to increase the power of the Church and the priests.

The priests took over the Pauline version of Jesus and this was such an enormous irony given that Jeshuah, the Jewish philosopher, challenged the whole idea of priests. The original Jesuian form of worship was overpowered by what became Christianity, that misguided mixture of pagan and Jewish myths and stories, some of which carry themes of symbolic and hidden truth, many of which are utter rubbish. Only the names changed, not the stories and myths. Cyprian, who died in 258AD, was the Bishop of Carthage and he did more than most to secure the priestly take-over. It was he who promoted the belief that only those who became Christians would have salvation. He said people should not have their own opinions – only those which the Church decided they should have. What power this would give to the priests in the centuries that followed to serve the desires of the Luciferic master.

The values of the brave and brilliant philosopher, healer, and channel called Jeshuah had been all but obliterated by Paul's recycled paganism and the darkness of ignorance and pain was to descend upon the human race for nearly two thousand years. This happened after Christianity's most important victory, its acceptance as the state Church of the Roman Empire. For that we have to thank, though that is hardly the word, a Roman Emperor called Constantine the Great.

5

Hell on Earth

CONSTANTINE I became Emperor of all the Roman lands in 312AD and within thirteen years he had, in effect, decided the future for much of humanity for nearly two millennia.

Constantine 'the Great' as he was to become known, served as a soldier and won a reputation for courage and military prowess. After spending some time serving in Britain he was elected by his army as Caesar of the West. He determined to be Emperor of all, and began the process of killing his rivals and sometimes their children, too. The Christian legend is that at the scene of one of his battles for the Roman throne he had a vision of a cross. It was at the battle of Milvian Bridge, near Rome and he is said to have seen the cross in the sky with the words 'By this Conquer'. The following night he is claimed to have seen a vision of Jesus who told him to put the cross symbol on his flag to guarantee victory . . r his enemies. Yes, that sounds like just what the Prince of Peace would say, doesn't it?

This whole story is probably another Christian invention, but for some reason Constantine began to look kindly on the Christians. The Brotherhood would have been working behind the scenes somewhere, I feel sure. Constantine issued the Edict of Milan which stopped the persecution of Christians in the Roman Empire. Some Christians had been persecuted horribly in earlier years although Gibbon, the historian who made a study of this, concluded that the numbers have been greatly exaggerated. He believes something like 2,000 Christians were murdered and tortured in the pre-Constantine period while 25 million are estimated to have been executed in the centuries that followed for the crime of not accepting the Christian faith. Both figures are terrible, but it puts what was to unfold into some perspective.

Constantine thought a cross was a lucky mascot, and in fact the cross as a religious symbol goes back to the time when humans discovered that by rubbing two sticks together you can make fire. They believed that fire was a god and two crossed sticks were seen as sacred. The cross can be found on ancient graves and was a religious symbol in Egypt, Assyria, Persia, India, Mexico and Scandinavia, long before Christianity. The Egyptians saw their cross, or crux ansata, as symbolic of salvation and eternal life, and our old friends the Mithraists marked the foreheads of the newly initiated with the sign of the cross. Ancient stories also describe how human sacrifices were bound to a cross and anointed with oil, so they would burn better on the altar. From such bleak traditions has Christianity come.

Constantine was never a Christian as such and he only agreed to be baptised on his death bed, no doubt as a bit of insurance. He worshipped both Jesus and the Greek god, Apollo, and he remained the head of the Pagan Church as Pontifex Maximus. But he gave Christianity the same status as the others and made substantial donations to its cause. Significantly he allowed the Church to receive legacies which had been banned up to this point and from here the Christian Church would begin to accumulate fantastic wealth as people tried to buy a place in heaven. Constantine's efforts to increase the Christian ranks led to bribes for the poor if they became Christians, and the offer of good jobs to wealthy Pagans who converted to the faith.

Constantine became concerned when disputes began to erupt between different Christian beliefs. A churchman called Arius in Alexandria questioned the idea that Jesus was the same as God. How could a son be the same as his father and had not Jehovah said that only he was God? When the Bishop of Alexandria, appropriately named Alexander, was preaching about the trinity of father, son, and holy spirit, Arius publicly questioned him. You may not think it important in the great tapestry of life to decide if Jesus was only a vehicle for God or part of three gods in one, but it now became *the* question that had to be decided. Arius left Alexandria for Palestine in fear of his life and two factions emerged. Neither would give way and this conflict was being ridiculed throughout the Empire by the non-believers and was no doubt fuelled by the Brotherhood. Constantine had wanted, at least in part for political reasons, to make Christianity the state religion, but he could not do this unless the disputes were settled.

He called together the bishops at Nicaea which is now Iznik in Turkey where he had a palace. At their first meeting in June 325 no

agreement could be reached between the 318 bishops on the burning issue of the day: was Jesus part of a trinity of father, son, and
holy spirit – whatever that was supposed to mean? Constantine
arrived shortly after murdering his wife and elder son. He moved
the proceedings to his palace and presided over all that followed.
He said a decision had to be reached because only when that
happened could Christianity be the state Church. It is clear he
wasn't much bothered what th   decided as long they decided
something. A bitter argument broke out between the factions as
documents were torn up and blows were struck. This is the atmosphere in which the Christian creed was officially decided.
Constantine agreed to a motion which was accepted by the majority though vehemently opposed by Arius and his supporters. It
became known as the Nicene Creed and it read as follows:

"We believe in one God, the Father almighty, maker of all things, both
visible and invisible; and in one Lord, Jesus Christ, the son of God,
begotten of the Father, only begotten, that is to say, of the same substance
of the Father, God of God and Light of Light, Very God of Very God,
begotten, not made, being of one substance with the father, by whom all
things were made, both things in heaven and things on earth; who, for us
men and for our salvation, came down and was made flesh, made man,
suffered and rose again on the third day, went up into the heavens, and is
to come again to judge the quick and the dead; and in the holy ghost."

There is a saying which goes: 'A camel is a horse designed by a
committee.' If ever there was an example of that it is the above. I
find it interesting also that this official creed of Christianity talks of
'for us men and our salvation'. What about women? But then it
would not be until 1545 that the Roman Church officially agreed
that women had souls – and then only by a majority of three votes!
    The Jewish philosopher, healer, and medium called Jeshuah was
now officially a saviour-god who, like the lambs on the pagan
sacrificial altars, died so that our sins could be forgiven forever as
long as we believed in him as our saviour. It is worth remembering
that this decision on who Jesus was came 300 years after his death.
It was also made by people who believed the Earth was flat and
Jerusalem was the centre of the Universe; this decision remains the
foundations of the Christian Church to this day. Before the Council of Nicaea closed, Constantine agreed to a motion that Arius and
his followers be officially cursed and either executed, imprisoned,

or banished. Other decrees applied the same Christian justice to all who read any writings by those who now became known as Arians. The Arian view is still expressed today, incidentally, by the Unitarians.

Thousands of Arians were murdered, the first of the estimated 25 million victims who would die in the name of Christianity and that is not including those who would perish in religious wars and the estimated 12 million who were killed in the Christian conquest of the Americas. Added together world-wide the number who perished as a result of the Christian religion must easily pass 100 million. To be excommunicated by the Church was almost a death sentence in itself, because you could not be guilty of murder if you killed someone who was excommunicated. Arius, however, escaped death to continue to expound his cause and the arguments went on over the trinity. In about 336 Constantine even ordered that Arius be readmitted to the Church, but before this could be done Arius died in mysterious circumstances and the following year Constantine passed on, also. On his death bed he was baptised by a bishop who did not accept the trinity. By then he had moved the capital of the empire from Rome to Byzantium – now Turkey – and he built a new city which he called Constantinople. It was about 44 miles from Nicaea. Here he had built Christian churches and dedicated the city to the Virgin Mary and Christianity was to become the State Church of the Roman Empire. This Romanized Christianity was later given the name Roman Catholicism to distinguish it from the Protestant version. All that happened, in reality, was that the previous Roman state saviour, Mithra, was renamed Jesus Christ. Constantine's mother, Helena, was sent to Jerusalem to find the biblical sites and she claimed to have found the exact locations of the birth of Jesus, his crucifixion, the tomb, and even where he ascended into the sky. It was on her say-so that Constantine built a basilica in 326 on the spot where she said Jesus had been crucified. The Church of the Holy Sepulchre is on that site today and attracts millions of Christian pilgrims to the place where Jesus hung on the cross. Or, rather, where Helena said it happened. She was obviously quite a sleuth, because during her trip she claimed to have found the three wooden crosses involved in the crucifixion three hundred years after they were supposed to have been used!!

The names of three people are worth emphasising in these early years of the Christian Church – Augustine, Jerome, and Ambrose.

Arthur Findlay in his study of the Church likens them to the Nazis,
Hitler, Goebbels, and Himmler. When you compare their backgrounds and behaviour, it is hard to argue against that, but before
we start condemning them as individuals we need to ask who, or
what, was in control of them? I would stress that I am not condemning anyone in this book. I am looking at thought and behaviour patterns which have guided human history. The individuals involved are victims of those patterns as much as the people
who suffered from their actions. Forgive them, they know not
what they do, is a good line to remember when reading the next
few chapters. Augustine imposed a tyrannical rule and used force
and fear to swell the Christian ranks. He would quote the words of
Jesus to justify his actions: 'Compel them to come in, that my
house be filled', and 'But those mine enemies, which would not
that I reign over them, bring hither and slay them before me'.
These were quoted to excuse the murder or forced conversion of
non-believers. Yet these quotations, as with 'I come not to bring
peace, but a sword', and others, were inventions. They were
inserted into the texts as justification of war, murder, and endless
other horrors in the name of the 'Prince of Peace'. Augustine
sought to impose a global creed by exterminating the opposition.
Religious 'error', he said, must be treated like treason, a crime
against the state, and be punished as such. He said that babies who
died before they were baptised would, like all the unbaptised, be
condemned to hell for all eternity, and he used fear of death and the
fear of hell and damnation after death, to expand his vicious and
ignorant creed. He would, like Jerome and Ambrose, later be
declared a saint.

   Jerome, born in 341, was the man responsible for producing the
texts for the first 'Holy' Bible. It was he, also, who led the
campaign of persecution against the mediums and channellers who
had been at the centre of religious belief from the very start of
human existence. In a short time, the gift of communicating with
other frequencies would be a death sentence. The channellers were
replaced by the priests as the 'middle men' between God and
humanity. Channellers who were frauds in the past had made up
communications to make the people do whatever they wished, and
now the priests would do the same without the need to stage a
fraudulent channelling. But, as always, there were many genuine
channellers who were communicating with other levels, and their
communicators were opposing the Church's beliefs and be-

haviour. They had to be shut up and they were. Countless numbers were tortured and murdered as witches. Priestly rule had arrived. As Jerome put it:

"We tell them (the channellers) that we do not so much reject prophecy (channelling), as refuse to receive prophets (channellers) whose utterances fail to accord with the Scriptures old and new."

In other words we don't mind people channelling as long as what they communicate supports what we have decided is truth. And as the Church had control of the 'scriptures' they could change whatever they liked to support their view. The philosopher Celsus wrote of this in the third century. He said of the religious hierarchy:

"You utter fables, and you do not even possess the art of making them seem likely...You have altered three, four, times and oftener the texts of your own Gospels in order to deny objections made to you."

There were so many differing beliefs in the first three centuries after the life of Jesus that no two gospels or epistles (letters claimed to be from apostles) were alike. Bits had been added, deleted, and changed to fit the beliefs of those who possessed them. Modern research has shown that the text of Mark was the first of the 'Bible' gospels to be written and the others merely copied that and put in their own additions. Earlier texts from which Mark and other Gospel writers copied have been lost, but even so there were other writings about Jesus which the Church rejected, as we will see. No one knows who wrote the biblical texts, when, and from what personal direction they were coming. Yet this is the book that has controlled the evolution of much of the world for the best part of two thousand years! Jerome's suppression of truth and alternative thought was two-fold. He persuaded the Pope to make channelling a crime and the Oracles and Vessels of God became, with one Papal decree, Oracles and Vessels of the Devil, names still used by many within the Church today. And he also took control of the ancient texts and made them fit his image of truth. Jerome became secretary to Pope Damasus in about 382 and he was commissioned to bring together all the various texts into a book which reflected (his) orthodox belief.

It was now that the texts were made to fit the view that Jeshuah the philosopher was no less than Jesus the Christ who had died so that our sins would be forgiven. Jerome's rewriting of ancient texts and the rejection of anything he didn't agree with, produced the wording which became the New Testament. Christians believe this to be the word of Jesus and God. It isn't. It is largely the word of Jerome. The additions and deletions by Jerome and others created a contradictory mess. The Bible tells us, for example, that the genetic line of Jesus can be traced back from his father Joseph to King David. But how can this be if Joseph played no part in his conception? In fact both the genetic line and the idea of the virgin birth were additions to the texts.

Jerome and Augustine looked through thirteen gospels, nine acts and teachings of the Apostles, thirty-one epistles, and other writings, and decided which were 'orthodox' and which were not. Surprise, surprise, they agreed that the ones Jerome had doctored were orthodox and the rest should be discarded, and it was these that the Council of Carthage agreed should be accepted by the Church. Some of those that were rejected were much nearer the truth than those that became the New Testament. Pope Innocent I confirmed the decision at Carthage, and a hundred years later Pope Gelasius I decreed that only these approved writings (called canonical) were to be read in churches. Those who disobeyed were to be tortured and killed as heretics. Jerome also turned his mind to re-writing the texts that became the Old Testament, but even his faith in these as the Word of God was challenged by all the contradictions he found. He had to admit that his efforts to make sense of it could only be considered makeshift. When the two testaments were brought together in the 6th century the Old, which Jerome didn't really understand, was joined with the New, which Jerome had edited to suit his beliefs. By these methods was the Holy Bible created and Jehovah, the vengeful God of the Jews and quite possibly extra-terrestrials, became merged with the God of Jesus. Is it any wonder that it produced a book so full of blatant contradictions? Fortunately some themes of truth have survived and particularly some of the written and numerical symbols and codes that the original texts contained. Many of these have been retained because the forgers and editors like Jerome did not understand their significance. To them they were just numbers or literal stories. But some are codes and symbols waiting for those who have the understanding to decipher them.

After Constantine's death, there had been a period when Pagan and Arian beliefs had their supporters among the Roman Em-

perors. During one period under the Emperor Constantius believers in the trinity were persecuted when he accepted the Arian
view. Whoever had prominence it was still a case of Christians
killing Christians in an argument over the trinity or no trinity.
Then the Emperor Theodosius 'the Great' came to power in 379,
and with him so did orthodox (Jeromian) Christianity. Theodosius
was a staunch supporter of the Nicene Creed who ordered the
slaughter of 1,500 men, women, and children on one occasion
alone in retaliation for the murder of one of his commanders and
some soldiers. He issued the laws which were to be known as the
Theodosian Code. These ordered imprisonment, torture, death or
banishment for the crime of the heresy of not accepting the Nicene
Creed. He also appointed a group of priests called The Inquisitors
of the Faith. Ambrose, the Bishop of Milan, was the founder of the
Holy Inquisition which was to turn a large tract of the world into a
human abbatoir. Wars were fought over the imposition of the
Christian Orthodox (Nicene) Faith and tens of millions would be
killed in the most terrible ways in the name of Christianity. The
Brotherhood organisations were being controlled more and more
by negative intent. They were gaining ever greater control of
events as their membership and offshoots grew ever more quickly.
Now the Luciferic consciousness was not only in control of the
Church, it *was* the Church. This was to continue into modern
times. The Inquisition Office is now called the Holy Office.

The further erosion of truth came with the Emperor Justinian in
the 6th century. From his headquarters in Constantinople he sche-
med to have references to pre-existence and reincarnation removed
from the Bible. He convened the Second Synod Council of Constantinople in 553 which, even without the attendance or support
of the Pope, agreed that:

*"If anyone assert the fabulous pre-existence of souls and shall submit to the
monstrous doctrine that follows from it, let him be .. excommunicated."*

The spiritual truths that were being passed on through the Brotherhood, at certain levels of it, anyway, were now destroyed in the
public arena. The 'Great Work of Ages' or, to give it its modern
name, *The New World Order,* was right on course in its desire to
part human beings from the knowledge of who they are.

With the fall of the Roman Empire, the Christian Church took
its place and the Pope became the equivalent of the Roman Em-

peror. A sufficient number of the tribes and peoples who replaced
Roman rule were Christianised for the view of the Roman Catholic Church to prevail. Now the power of the Church was total.
They believed that, because the Old Testament said that Adam had
incurred God's wrath by eating from the tree of knowledge, the
pursuit of all knowledge outside of the Bible was sinful. In the
same way, because Eve had tempted him to eat from the tree,
women were considered to be evil and of no worth. These
breathtaking interpretations and the fear of the Inquisition was to
hold back human evolution for at least two thousand years. Today's scientific establishment is still not as advanced in its overall
understanding of life and Creation as were Socrates, Plato, and
others in Ancient Greece.

The Christians destroyed all the writings of the great philosophers. Plato's Academy and Aristotle's Lyceum were closed and
their writings burned. The Roman educational system inspired by
Quintilian was dismantled and the great library at Alexandria
became a theological college. Philosophers, scientists, and school
teachers were persecuted. Hypatia, one of the outstanding women
of her time, had her flesh torn from her body by a Christian mob
for the 'crime' of speaking eloquently on science, mathematics,
astronomy, and philosophy in ways that contradicted orthodox
Christianity. She worked at the library in Alexandria and all the
books it contained were then destroyed. This was all done in the
name of Cyril, the Archbishop of Alexandria. He was later made a
saint.

I can recommend a book called *The Vicars of Christ* which is a
record of the Catholic popes by a former Roman Catholic priest,
Peter Da Rosa. It is a superb exposé of the hypocrisy and deceit
upon which Christianity was built. And remember, until the Reformation and the birth of the Protestant version in the 16th
century, the Rome-controlled Catholic Church *was* Christianity.
The Vatican had a whole department dedicated to producing forged 'historical' documents to hoodwink kings, queens, and others
into doing their will. In most cases the Church's 'will', as, increasingly, with the Brotherhood, was for them to wage war on
non-believers or to hand over land and money to add to their, by
now, amazing wealth.

The post of Pope was not spiritual, but commercial, and the
negative Brotherhood societies made every effort to make sure that
'their' men or someone who was easily manipulated got the job.

The Vatican to this day is run by the Brotherhood. If they could control the Pope, the potential to create wars and impose their will was almost infinite. Popes were considered by many to be 'infallible', the mouthpiece of God, and whatever they wanted they had to be given. As a result the Papacy attracted all the wrong characters for all the wrong reasons. One pope was so unhinged that he had the body of a previous pope exhumed from the grave and brought to his room. He ordered that the rotting remains were sat down in a chair so he could tell him what he thought of him! Apparently, one of the Pope's staff stood behind the dead pope answering on his behalf like some ventriloquist with a dummy. It is sobering to think that such misguided people were making decisions that would affect the lives of humanity up to the present day. Or was it always they who actually made the decisions? Probably not. Either way, we still have Roman Catholic priests who must stay celibate and unmarried because of what popes – or their controllers – decided a thousand years ago and more. The story went like this:

325AD: The Council of Nicaea decides that no priests will be allowed to marry after their ordination.

385AD: Pope Siricius decrees that men who are married before their ordination must not sleep with their wives afterwards.

590 – 604AD: Pope Gregory the Great decides that all desire for sex is sinful. Sex is only for producing children.

1074AD: Pope Gregory VII says that all priests must pledge themselves to be celibate.

The consequences of the Roman Catholic hang-ups about sex have been to pass on this 'dirty', 'sinful', view of sexual love to the generations that followed. Even today we still see its legacy. We are also seeing many stories coming to light of Roman Catholic priests and their sexual abuse of children. The Vatican seeks to avoid responsibility for this, but at the core of such behaviour is the forced suppression of natural sexual urges imposed by Papal dictators between ten and seventeen centuries ago and upheld by successive Papal dictators ever since. But they can't change it because to do so would make it clear that Pope Gregory VII was fallible in ordering such a ridiculous rule. And as popes are considered infallible, none of them can change – at least publicly – what a previous one has decided!

The idea of 'sinful' sex was promoted by Augustine. He was well-known for his love of sex earlier in his life, but when he claimed to have abstained, he took on a view of sex that was similar to the way some people who stop smoking see others who continue to smoke. He became obsessive in his condemnation, and would not allow a woman to enter his house unaccompanied. This included his sister. Such was his power within the Church that his belief that sex and lust were sinful became the accepted view. The suppression of the flow of creative energy activated by natural sexual activity has expressed itself in negative emotions and behaviour, as well as health problems resulting from blocked energy. Using the 'safe period' to enjoy sex without conceiving was condemned as a wicked sin by Augustine. You should never have sexual relationships unless you intend to conceive a child, they decided, and even then under no circumstances must you enjoy it!! This nonsense continues to blight the lives of so many to this day. I have always found it hilarious that the Church says that God made the physical body, but we should be so ashamed of this creation that we must never allow others to see it or, at the extreme, even see it ourselves. But Augustine's view on love, marriage, and sex was followed by the Church from then on. As he said over and over again:

"Husbands love your wives, but love them chastely. Insist on the work of the flesh only in such measure as is necessary for the procreation of children. Since you cannot beget children in any other way [an oversight by God, presumably], *you must descend to it against your will, for it is the punishment of Adam."*

Poor old Adam and Eve. They get it in the neck for everything, even the fact that we have to be punished by being forced to have sex. Augustine linked sex with 'original sin', the idea that we are all born sinful. If we are conceived through the sexual act, we are by definition born with original sin which is supposed to go back to Adam and Eve. Jesus was the only one born without original sin, because his was a virgin birth which did not involve sex. Follow the logic? Later to overcome the obvious contradiction that Jesus was born to a mother who was born with original sin, she, too, was said to have been conceived without sex. But hold on. In that case, Jesus was born without original sin to a mother without original sin, but she was born to a mother *with* original sin. Shock, horror. Unless of course, the grandmother of Jesus was also conceived without sex. In that case.... No, no, I think we'll leave it there. You see how confusing it gets once you try to cover your tracks? It is the same whenever you tell lies. You have to keep lying to cover up previous lies and you get yourself in a terrible mess. The Roman Church also conveniently ignores the fact that the one they consider to be the first pope, the 'disciple' Peter, was married and not celibate. From this insult to the intelligence has come a view of sex, the physical body, marriage, divorce, and women that was to prevail for nearly two thousand years. The suppression of women has been passed through the generations by the major religions. Christian dogma used the Adam and Eve story in the Jewish Old Testament to justify this. They also quote people like St Paul:

"Wives submit to your husbands for the husband is the head of the wife as Christ is the head of the Church. Now if the Church submits to Christ so should wives submit to their husbands in everything."

And:

"But I suffer not a woman to teach, nor to usurp authority over the man, but to be in silence."

In the last years of the 20th century, the Bible is still being quoted in opposition to women priests. When the Church of England voted in favour of the admission of women to the priesthood in 1993, members of the Church resigned in protest and joined the Roman Catholics – some of them women! Male domination in all areas of life has helped to extend the domination of male energy over female which has made the world what it is today. This has served Lucifer's ambitions magnificently. A domination of male energy over female is vital to his plans. All consciousness is both male and female, and we all have male and female lives to ensure a balance of experiences. The current transformation will see a re-balancing of the male-female energies around the planet and this will manifest in the emergence of women in decision-making and the activation of female energies, like caring and compassion, within those in male bodies. Both men and women are capable of expressing male and female energy.

The Christian obsession with destroying paganism, while at the same time absorbing it, led to a further polluting of the Earth energy grid, as did all the negative energy being created by the murder and mayhem. Early churches were built on Pagan sacred sites. Some sects knew about the energies and wanted to use them, and others considered these energies and sites to be evil and wished to suppress the energies (the 'dragon'). This is where I feel the legends of St George and the dragon originated. Churches all over the world are built on acupuncture points and chakras and I visit many in the course of my own work. All that fear, guilt, and suffering which has been experienced on those sites and the concentration on the crucifixion have generated immense quantities of negative energy and this has poured into the grid. Those churches that have been joyous have produced positive energy, but they have been the tiny, tiny, minority.

This was a terrible time for the volunteers and those who were trying to restore understanding to the human mind. They incarnated in other parts of the world for lives dedicated to channelling energy into the grid to try to compensate for what Christianity and Islam (of which more shortly) were doing. Those who were born into the Christian world lived simple lives keeping their heads down and channelling the energy or doing what they could to speak out before facing the inevitable and often gruesome fate. Many found themselves guided to monasteries which were built on energy sites and were protected by law from any interference.

One spiritual group which grew rapidly in France and Northern Italy in the 12th and 13th centuries and challenged the power of Rome was the Cathars or Albigenses. It was based on an understanding of reincarnation and the eternal nature of all consciousness. They were vegetarians and communicated psychically with other frequencies. Their views won such support that the influence of the Christian Church began to wane in Southern France around Albi. Pope Innocent II reacted to this with one of the most appalling examples of inhumanity seen on this planet. What followed was genocide. Men, women and children were dismembered or were burnt alive in the name of Jesus and God. The events at the castle of Monsegur are best remembered in the Cathar story, but there were many other 'glorious' victories for the Christian armies that were just as sickening. One ploy of Innocent II, and later of Pope Gregory IX, was to tell his 'crusaders' that no matter what they did he would forgive them on God's behalf. What a shock they must have had when they left the physical body and realised they were responsible through karma for all they had done.

As the centuries passed the Holy Inquisition went into overdrive. The Dominican Order was put in charge of this religious version of Murder Incorporated. Pope Gregory IX declared: 'It is the duty of every Catholic to persecute heretics'. There was no fair trial before a sentence. The Inquisitors' decision was final. It was a wonderful way of getting rid of people you didn't like, especially if you were one of the Brotherhood elite who wished to remove those who were getting in your way. You told the Inquisitors that your enemies were non-believers, and you stood back and watched them burned to death. This passage is from a book of guidance from the Church to inquisitors:

"Either the person confesses and he is proved guilty from his own confession, or he does not confess and is equally guilty on the evidence of witnesses. If a person confesses the whole of what he is accused of, he is unquestioningly guilty of the whole; but if he confesses only a part, he ought still to be regarded as guilty of the whole, since what he has confessed proves him to be capable of guilt as to other points of the accusation...Bodily torture is left to the Judge of the Inquisition, who determines according to age, sex, and the constitution of the party...If, not withstanding, all the means employed, the unfortunate wretch still denies his guilt, he is to be conside as a victim of the devil; and, as such, deserves no compassion from the servants of God, nor pity and indulgence of Holy Mother Church; he is a son of perdition. Let him perish among the damned."

Even genuine believers were murdered by the Inquisitors, but the Church's motto was that it was better for a hundred 'innocents' to die than for one heretic to go on living. Could it be that the Nazis of the 20th century were a reincarnation of these misguided minds I have been describing? The parallels in behaviour patterns and attitudes are clear to see, even in their treatment of the Jews. I believe that the programming by the Church of the collective conscious mind was so strong that when people later reincarnated they dropped back into the same thought patterns that had been programmed into them in previous incarnations. This applies to the Church, economics, and all aspects of our lives, and I have no doubt the same is happening today. In incarnation after incarnation people drop back into old patterns they cannot or choose not to break. It is like the needle stuck in a record groove, although I must say I do feel that some of the architects of Church dogma were, as with the Nazi leaders, incarnations of the Luciferic consciousness.

I don't recognise the term heresy. It is, for me, the ultimate arrogance to suggest that certain beliefs must be free from questioning and challenge under the guise of 'heresy' or 'blasphemy'. But if you use for a moment the Church's definition of heresy – the abuse and misrepresentation of the one they call Jesus – then the greatest of all heresies has been Christianity itself.

The Christian thought-police were now established across their domain and they would soon spread their darkness to the Americas. The only threat to their domination of the Holy Land and beyond was another version of religious indoctrination which answered to the name of Islam. The clashes between the two would create yet more conflict, pain, and suffering – exactly what the Brotherhood and its master, Lucifer, wanted to see.

6

Arabian Knights

IN the year 570 a child was born in the Arabian desert at Mecca. Forty years later he was to have a psychic experience that would affect the course of history to the present day. His name was Mahomet or as he is better known, Mohammed.

Again we have a psychic vision, a communication from another frequency, or an extra-terrestrial hologram, being mistaken for God or a messenger from God, and again it was to have appalling consequences. Mahomet said that his communicator had told him the people of Arabia must return to a simple faith in Allah, the God of Abraham (Allah = El and later Jehovah to the Hebrews). He said God had also chosen him to pass on this message, and those who accepted it would be saved on Judgment Day. Sound familiar? All of these apparently opposing religions were started by the same non-physical manipulator – Lucifer in his many forms. Mahomet was just another victim. He wrote down his communications in a book called the Koran (meaning recitation), and from that came the religion we know as Islam (meaning submission to God) and the people called Muslims or Moslems (one who submits). Terrible violence became the means of advancing Mahomet's cause. He changed in character from what would appear to have been a kind and loving man into a tyrant as his religious beliefs and a highly negative energy took him over. So what caused this sudden change? It could have been that he simply became power hungry, I suppose, but maybe there is another explanation. I do not offer it as fact, just a possibility.

Mahomet says that he saw his vision near the cave where he would often go. The vision apparently claimed to be the angel Gabriel of biblical fame and he lost consciousness during the encounter. Other prophet figures have told of similar experiences. When he woke up the message he was told to recite was, he says, inscribed upon his heart. Perhaps it would have been more accurate to say his mind. To appreciate what could have happened to Mahomet, St Paul, Augustine, and endless others, we need to make the division in our minds between the stage of evolution humanity had reached at the time and where the ET's were in their knowledge and technology. In the modern world, highly sophisticated, mind-control techniques are well known to the secret Brotherhood elite today and the intelligence agencies who work to an agenda which ignores democratic government and scrutiny. But even these techniques are primitive compared with what the ETs can do and, more to the point, *could* do thousands of years ago across the entire period covered in this book. They could turn certain people into super-robots, controlled almost entirely through mind programming. The CIA today have the ability to abduct someone, implant a micro-chip in their brain, or so hypnotise them that another version of what happened can replace the actual experience in their memory. Look at the difference between that level of knowledge and the stage of understanding humans had reached in the periods we are discussing and you can see how easy it would have been to control many events.

I am not saying that this happened, I don't know. But it would be naive to dismiss the possibility out of hand, in the light of what we know about mind-controlling techniques today. Humans, rather than ETs, could well have been involved in affecting Mahomet's mind via the Brotherhood. There are, of course, other explanations for his experience. The most likely is some sort of psychic happening or manipulation, or even drugs. Maybe he was genuinely the subject of efforts to pass on spiritual knowledge and his ego took over. Part of the message he wrote down said: "Don't use violence in religion," only for this to be removed from the Koran texts when he did just that. There is a great deal of good sense to be found in the Koran among all the dross. What precisely happened to Mahomet, we can't say, but one thing is for sure – what followed his experience was anything but spiritual.

Even before Mahomet the town of Mecca was considered a religious centre and attracted thousands of pilgrims. It had a small temple called the Kaaba (House of God) and its cornerstone was a meteorite. This was held to be sacred and the place of worship for the god Allah Taala and images of Jesus, Mary, and others decorated the walls. The Bedouins who owned the temple enjoyed a very profitable business as the people paid to worship and kiss the sacred stone. They became very angry at the preachings of

Mahomet because if his ideas caught on they feared their trade would cease. To their dismay he was gathering many followers and the town of Medina had asked him to be their ruler as the prophet of Allah. Given what has happened since, it is some irony to think that it was the Jews in Medina who helped to persuade people that he was who he claimed to be. The Bedouins of Mecca plotted to kill him, but he escaped with his close friend Abu Bekr and hid in his cave before returning to the safety of Medina in 622. Medina translates as 'town of the Prophet'.

From his base in Medina he and his followers attacked and robbed the trading caravans on their way to Mecca and conflict came to this desert region. Mahomet's growing power and arrogance led him to announce that God had told him the people in Medina who would not accept his message should be killed. It was Christianity revisited. All non-believers must die. Mahomet ordered many massacres, including the murder of 900 Jews, and in the end a treaty was agreed between Mecca and Medina. Mecca would recognise Mahomet as the prophet of God if he moved the centre of the faith from Medina to Mecca. In this way the temple would lose one faith, but gain another, and although the pilgrims would now come for different reasons, they would still come and keep the tills ticking over. No doubt with commercial benefits in mind, the Bedouins also insisted that Mahomet tell the people to face Mecca and not Jerusalem when they prayed. This would increase their desire to visit the place they were facing several times a day. Fourteen hundred years later Moslems across the world still face the direction of Mecca when they pray.

Mahomet went to war with any community throughout Arabia who would not accept his rule and his claims to be the prophet of God. This turned a region of communities into a nation determined to spread their new creed throughout the world by whatever means were necessary. I have to smile when I hear Moslem religious leaders speaking on the radio, and every time they say the 'The Prophet Mohammed' they follow immediately with 'peace and blessings upon him'. I am all for peace and blessings on everyone, including those who Mahomet and his followers murdered in the name of God and those still kept in mental and physical bondage by Moslem fanatics today. Women particularly have suffered in the Moslem world from the beliefs of Mahomet which have made them prisoners in their own lands when the Koran is followed to the letter.

With Mahomet's death at the age of 62, his friend Abu Bekr took over as his Kalifa or Caliph which means successor. He was ruthless in pursuit of his desire for world domination by Islam and the rivers of blood flowed across the Middle East. Every country was given the same ultimatum: accept the Caliph as their ruler and adopt the Moslem faith, or die by the sword.

By the year 750, Moslem rule had advanced dramatically. It now controlled Arabia, Egypt, the North African Coast, Armenia, Syria, Palestine, Persia, Mesopotamia, and Spain. This gave them control of the Christian 'Mecca' of Jerusalem and many other places the Christians believed to be sacred. In time Constantinople, the first Christian city, would also fall. The Moslems were to adopt the crescent as their emblem, but this was originally designed by the Christians of Constantinople and only became associated with Islam after the city was taken. The Moslem Empire would later extend to the Indian subcontinent where the deep and bitter hatred thus created between Moslems and Hindus still continues. It is the old, old, familiar story. We have all the answers and if you don't accept that, you are dead. One can only speculate at the mental age necessary to think in such terms, or the power of the mental control someone or something has over them. When anyone tells you they have all the answers it is time to race for the exits.

You will see through the story of religions that certain key themes are common to them all. First someone channels a non-physical communicator or meets the occupant of a spacecraft and takes them to be whatever version of God their belief system will accept. A fanatical zeal unfolds to impose these beliefs on everyone else and as time goes on and the original instigator dies, feuds break out over power, money, position, and 'truth'. So it was with the Moslem Faith. Arguments began over who should be the Caliph in the centuries that followed. A man called Othman was chosen on one occasion, but this was resented by Ali, the husband of Mahomet's daughter, Fatima. Ali believed he should have been Caliph because he was a member of the Prophet's family and Othman was not. There was tremendous conflict between the two factions and it is still going on in some areas to this very day. The Shiite, or orthodox Moslems, believe they descend from those who said Ali should be caliph while the others, called Sunni Moslems, recognise Othman. God help us. At one time anyone who could claim to descend from Mahomet was executed and once again I'm sure the negative Brotherhood organisations were stimulating the division whenever they could.

There were, and are, however, many good things about Moslem rule. This is an important point which I want to stress most strongly. In all these books, like the Bible and Koran, you will find among the incitements and justifications for horrific behaviour some good and virtuous philosophies. The fanatics who, by force, have largely been in control have picked out the former to guide their lives, but others have had the sense and decency of spirit to be guided by the latter. Not every believer in Christianity was a murdering barbarian and nor every Moslem. Across the world today there are hundreds of millions of faithful Christians and Moslems who follow the positive messages in their religious books and reject the violence. There are some wonderful human beings working within the Christian Church and, as I have found in Britain and in my travels through the Middle East, you will not find a kinder, more generous people than the moderate, thinking, Moslems. If they and the moderate Christians had been in control over the centuries then although they would still be following what are, in my view, religions based on myth, at least the slaughter fields would not have been thought necessary.

There were periods in the Moslem empire when the fanatics were not in control and these times made a vital contribution to humanity by preserving the knowledge of people like Plato and Aristotle. Under the caliph Haroun-al-Raschid in the late eighth, early ninth, century the capital was moved to Baghdad. Their thought was not imprisoned by the Koran and although the caliph still sent his armies to pillage and murder appallingly in neighbouring lands, he also set up schools and colleges. Scientists, doctors, and philosophers travelled to this centre of intellectual freedom. Baghdad became the world's wealthiest city with many hospitals, more than 600 doctors and 6,000 students. All religions were allowed to be followed freely. When Al-Mamun took over from his father, the Greek, Persian and Chaldean literature which had survived the Christian priests was translated into Arabic. He openly questioned the teachings of the Koran and encouraged philosophy. In this period great advances were made in the understanding of science and healing and an extensive system of schools was created for children. The Moslem world was light years ahead of Christendom where all these things, including healing, were banned on pain of death. In Southern Spain under Moslem rule it was the same as in Baghdad. Their way of thinking and living was in a different world to the squalor and ignorance which prevailed throughout Christendom. We have much to thank the Moslems for under these more open-minded rulers. They kept the flame of knowledge alive and it paved the way for the Renaissance in Europe.

The glories of Baghdad as a home of knowledge and mental freedom were crushed when the Turks invaded in the 11th century. These were orthodox, fanatical, Moslems and intolerance and ignorance returned. I say orthodox, fanatical, Moslems, but the division of attitude should really be broken down into fanatics and thinkers. The Moslem fanatics had the same mentality as the Christian fanatics and, had each been born in the other's land, they would have been equally fanatical about the other's religion. We speak of Moslems and Christians, but it's not like that in reality. It is fanatics and thinkers. The religions are simply used as a vehicle for fanaticism. If they did not exist, they would find another expression for their mental and emotional imbalances. In the same way, if the moderate, thinking, people did not have a religion through which to express their spirituality, they would find another vehicle for it.

The Turks went on to create the Ottoman Empire, a name which came from Osman, one of their rulers. Its expansion into hitherto Christian lands was helped by the latest arguments over the trinity. Now they were falling out over the Latin word Filioque, which means 'and from the Son'. Did the Holy Ghost proceed only from the Father or from the Father 'and from the Son'? Does anyone care? Unfortunately they do, and when the Filioque was added to the creed by the Pope in 1054 it split the Western and Eastern Churches. This Eastern Church is now known as the Greek or Eastern Orthodox. There was a definite Brotherhood ploy to now split the Christian religion into factions of conflict. While Christendom was arguing about all this, the Moslem Turks were taking advantage and expanding their empire into Christian strongholds. The Pope sought to bring unity of purpose by launching a crusade against the Moslems to win back control of the Church of the Holy Sepulchre from the 'infidels'. There were eight crusades in all and Jerusalem was won and then lost again. The urgency to regain the Holy City was increased by the belief that the Second Coming would happen soon. In fact the idea of the Saviour-god returning goes back to the days of Sun worship and is common to many religions. Most of the crusades were a disaster and on one occasion the Church organised an army made up of children from France and Germany in an effort to re-take Jerusalem. This 'Children's Crusade' was launched during the Papacy of Innocent III. Few of the children returned. Most were victims of disease, accident, murder, and slavery.

The Crusades were responsible for the most staggering violence and the 'Knights of Chivalry' were no more than barbarous killing machines. The European kings and knights were urged by the Church and the Brotherhood societies to kill for God. Two branches of the Brotherhood most active at this time were the Knights Templar (or Knights of the Temple) and the Knights Hospitaler. The latter was probably not under Brotherhood Control from its creation in 1048. It was then a charitable order, but in 1118 it had another incarnation as the Order of Knights Hospitaler of St John. This came after a change of leadership and motivation. They became a military organisation named after John, the son of the King of Cyprus, who fought in the Crusades. It would seem to have been a Brotherhood takeover and the Order began to operate with a Grand Master and all the rituals, secret initiations, rituals, and symbols, which go back to ancient times. The Knights Templar were a Brotherhood branch from the start, with their Grand Master and customary secrecy. They came into being a year after the Hospitalers joined the Brotherhood and the Templars were to have enormous power behind the scenes. Like the Hospitalers they were given large amounts of money by supporters of the Crusades and the Templars became so rich they began the financial centres in Paris and London by storing their wealth in their temples in those cities. The Teutonic (German) Knights were another charitable order who changed to a military role. They had a Grand Master and all the trimmings and these three Brotherhood branches hated each other, much to the delight of those who were controlling them without their knowledge. Again I am not saying that every member of these groups was knowingly working against the people. Most would have had the best of intentions. The Brotherhood doesn't work like that. It needs to hoodwink most of its own to be most effective. The Brotherhood is manipulation with a smile on its face and it seeks a good public image. For that it needs some good people involved at the lower levels. Charitable trusts and charity work in general is often a front it chooses to use.

Even on the journeys to the 'Holy Land' by the Christian

Crusaders other non-believers on route were tortured and murdered. The Jews suffered most. The Christians condemned the whole Jewish Race as the 'murderers of Christ' and any scale of barbarity against them could be justified by that. When the crusaders of the Lord re-took Jerusalem one of their first acts was to burn the synagogue with the Jews still inside. The streets literally ran with the blood of their Jewish and Moslem victims, a great contrast to the way some Moslem leaders treated the Christians when Islam regained the city. In the end the crusades achieved nothing, except for sending hundreds of thousands to an early grave and causing terrible pain and destruction – exactly what the Brotherhood wanted. It was not until this century that the Christian world had control of the Holy Land again, when it became part of the British Empire. The Jews suffered in Europe for another reason. The Christian religion in this period imposed a strict ban on usury, the charging of interest on loans. An usurer could have all his property confiscated, be excommunicated, and refused a Christian burial. It was considered better that a wife should leave an usurer husband and beg for food, than to accept anything from him. The Jews were not subject to this Christian law and they did charge interest on lending. This made them extremely unpopular with people in debt. In 1290, 16,000 Jews were deported from England because of this by Edward 1st.

At the end of the Crusades and the Moslem victory, the Brotherhood knights had to flee. The Order of St John did well, as it moved around, changing its name with its location as the Knights of Rhodes and Knights of Malta. They have survived to this day as the Sovereign and Military Order of Malta, which, with papal help, moved its base to Rome and became the world's smallest nation. The Knights of Malta have tremendous influence in politics and in the secret societies today. The Templars have also survived, but the reprisals against them for losing the crusades, and the charges aimed against them for spitting on the cross and homosexuality saw their wealth and power taken away. For a while, anyway.

The reasons for this campaign against them were greed and the preservation of the con-trick called Christianity. The Templars accumulated breathtaking riches as Christians gave their wealth to them in their wills and donations. The Templars were the richest organisation in every country in which they established themselves. They became bankers without charging interest because of the Christian Church's ban on usury. When the Jews were expelled from France in 1306 for their usury activities, Philip, the French King, had to re-pay his debts to them. This he did by giving them virtually all his country's reserves of coinage in exchange for all the property they left behind. King Philip was desperate for money to meet foreign commitments and he decided to steal the Templar gold. Philip and his fellow Frenchman, Pope Clement V, hatched a plan to achieve it. Allegations were made against the Templars and Clement charged them with heresy. Their money went to Philip and their lands to the church. The Templar's Grand Master, Jacques de Molay, was burned at the stake.

But there was another reason why the Church was so keen on destroying the Templars and the Cathars. In 1891 during restoration of the village church at Rennes-le-Château in South-West France, the parish priest, Berenger Saunière, found four parchments. They were sealed in wooden tubes which had been hidden inside a hollow altar pillar. Two of these contained the blood lines of local families and dated back to 1244 and 1644. Saunière also discovered a secret code in the texts and he told the Bishop of Carcassonne what he had found. With that the parish priest was summoned to Paris to meet the church hierarchy and show them the parchments.

From that time, Saunière was a man transformed. He would have earned a very small income as a priest, but in the years that followed he spent millions on paintings, antiques and rare china. He also built a mansion which he never lived in and a tower so close to the side of a mountain that it overlooked nothing. His behaviour became very strange in all sorts of ways. When a new Bishop of Carcassonne was appointed and complained at Saunière's antics, the parish priest was supported by the Pope himself. Saunière died of 'a stroke' in 1917 at the age of sixty-five. But it seems that his coffin had been ordered by his housekeeper five days before his 'stroke', when he had seemed perfectly healthy. A priest who came to give him the last rites and heard his confession was said to have left the room visibly shaken and never to have smiled again.

So what did Saunière know?

In 1969, Henry Lincoln, a British scriptwriter, became interested in the story and he uncovered documents at the National Library in France kept under the title of 'Dossiers Secrets'. One mentioned a secret order structured on typical Brotherhood lines called the

Priory of Sion which had also been named in the parchments found by Saunière in Rennes-le-Château. Lincoln's document said that past Grand Masters of this order included Leonardo da Vinci, the scientist Isaac Newton, the alchemist, Nicholas Flamel, and the composer, Claude Debussy. The plot thickened because Saunière had met Debussy when he was summoned to Paris by the Church hierarchy. The Priory of Sion, the document went on, was the inner hierarchy of the Knights Templar which were dedicated to restoring the Merovingians to the French Throne. The Merovingian dynasty began in the 5th century. Mérovée became Frankish King in 448 and the family were said to have royal or holy blood. The Templars had a stronghold at Bezu not far from Rennes-le-Château, and remember, the parchments found by Saunière included family blood lines.

This becomes extremely relevant and links in perfectly with my earlier conclusions about the Jesus story when you consider the following. Henry Lincoln's work was the subject of three television documentaries in 1972 and as a result he received a letter from a retired Anglican priest. The letter said that the writer knew for certain that what Saunière found was uncontestable proof that Jesus did not die on the cross. The priest said that he was given this information by a fellow Anglican cleric who had worked in Paris with Emile Hoffet. When Saunière was ordered to Paris, one of those who interviewed him was Emile Hoffet. Lincoln's informant said the parchments proved that Jesus was alive in France at least until 45AD. As I suggested earlier, Jesus travelled to the Rennes-le-Château area with Mary Magdalene and their children after he had recovered from the crucifixion. He may have died there or possibly he could have ended his life in Kashmir, as I mentioned earlier. I believe the Roman Catholic Church know that Jesus did not die on the cross and have done so for at least 1500 years. They have suppressed this knowledge to protect their own power. They have conned billions of people over the centuries and continue to do so today. The proof of this is locked up in the Vatican vaults and, as Saunière possibly found out, they will pay any sort of price to persist with this monumental lie.

They will also commit genocide to preserve their deceit. King Philip may have had money as his motivation to destroy the Knights Templar after the failed Crusades, but Pope Clement V had other reasons for his own involvement. The Templars knew the true story of Jesus, just as the Cathars had done when they emerged in the same region of France which includes Rennes-le-Château. The Cathars had also denied that Jesus died on the cross and they were eliminated for that reason more than any other. I feel the much talked-about Cathar 'treasure' was the proof that Jesus survived the cross. This story goes on to this day because the Brotherhood elite is still determined to crown a 'World King' who descends from the bloodline of Jesus, something they inherited via the Templars, who believed that the Merovingians decended from the blood line of King David, through Jesus and his children. This is why they were so keen to put the Merovingians back on the French throne, and this was another incentive for King Philip to be rid of them. It was thought the Merovingian blood line had died out after they lost the Frankish throne in the 8th century, but the Cathars and the Templars knew differently. Today, somewhere in the world, the Brotherhood, or some elements of it, are possibly preparing a person who they claim to be from the David, Jesus, Merovingian, blood line to become 'World King'.

Everything and everyone is expendable to those who control the Brotherhood once their use to them has run its course. There is no better example of that than the way the Brotherhood was manipulating its Christian branches to fight the Moslems, while doing the same to its Moslem branches to fight the Christians.

Among these Moslem Brotherhood groups were the Karmathites, the Druses, the Brotherhood of the Nine, and the Assassins. At the heart of the secret societies of the Moslem world was the Grand Lodge of Cairo from where many Brotherhood groups in Europe originated. As with all religions the original structure breaks up into factions, as with the Shiites. Out of the Shiites came another faction called the Ismaili Sect, a Brotherhood Branch with the Aga Khan as its 'spiritual leader' today, and out of that came yet another arm of the Brotherhood, the Assassins – Grand Master, secret initiations, you know the score. The word Assassin means a user of hashish because they used the drug to stimulate their mystical experiences and for other more sinister reasons. Now assassin means something very different – a lone killer. This is because the Assassins used this method very effectively to expand their power from their base in Iran. They were not choosy. They killed Moslem and Christian alike.

The Assassins became a model for the political and economic murders of today. They would not do the killing themselves, they would mind control a young man and get him to do it. Their preferred method was to introduce him to the Grand Master. He would then be drugged with hashish and lose consciousness. When he awoke he would be in a beautiful garden and there he would be pampered and led to believe he was in heaven, paradise. He would be given more of the drug, lose consciousness again, and wake up back with the Grand Master. The killer-to-be would be told that he had never left the Grand Master's presence and that he had been given a taste of the eternal paradise that would await him if he did as he was told by the Assassins and killed for God. They invariably did. Could something along these lines have happened to Mahomet centuries earlier?

This same basic technique, but now far more sophisticated, is used today to murder those who get in the way of the Brotherhood's plan for world domination. This method of mind controlling outsiders to do your dirty work makes it almost impossible to identify the real killers, especially when those investigating the crime are also Brotherhood members, more often than not. The Moslem secret societies indoctrinated and conned their initiates in ways that also mirrored the other branches of the Brotherhood, like the freemasons. The lower degrees of initiation were quite straightforward and appeared to support the status quo, the Moslem religion in their case. But then, at a certain level when the initiate was well entrenched in the society, the whole story was switched and suddenly they were told to forget all they had been told before. The new version of the 'truth', which itself would undergo other changes at the higher levels of initiation, would lead to the revelation of who or what the society was really serving. Only if it was believed beyond doubt that you could be trusted to support the 'Great Work' would you be given this knowledge. This is how the few can use the majority of their members as a front of respectability for their clandestine activities against freedom. If you are a freemason or a member of any secret society, you are almost certainly being conned, and it is time you realised that. Get out while you can. The Assassins, by the way, were overrun by the invading Mongols under the leadership of Mangu Khan in 1250, but their attitude to life very much lives on.

As Islam extended its influence with great speed, it added to the host of religions vying for power and recognition in the Middle and Near East – Christianity, Islam, Judaism, Buddhism, Zoroastrianism, Manichaeism, Hinduism.... If you felt the need to hand over your mind to an 'ism', you were spoilt for choice, although choice was hardly the word in most cases. You were what you were told to be most of the time.

Europe was in chaos and turmoil after the Romans left, but over the centuries certain tribes gained dominance and countries began to emerge. A Frankish tribe took over the lands we now call France and a branch of this settled in what became Germany. In Britain, they were ruled by a series of invaders, among them the Vikings, Saxons and the Normans. Theirs was also a story of imposition, invasion, political and religious conflict, and constant Brotherhood activity. A title was never so apt than the Dark Ages. It encapsulates the whole motivation and experience of the time, but slowly the power of the Roman Church was to be broken and Britain would be at the forefront of this momentous event. It was not, however, quite the blow for freedom that it might at first have appeared to be.

7

The Cracks Appear

CHRISTIANITY loves to portray itself as the force that civilised the world. As we have seen, nothing could be further from the truth. It sought to crush all efforts to bring civilisation to the Dark Ages it had created.

Part of its propaganda is to lump all pre-Christians together as 'pagans' and therefore heathens and savages. This is another abuse of truth. Yes, there were people in the pre-Christian world who behaved in terrible ways, but none was any worse than those who imposed Christianity. And to say that all pre-Christians were 'heathens' is supreme arrogance. Socrates, Plato, Aristotle, Pythagoras, Hippocrates, Quintilian, were heathens? The very thought is hysterical.

You simply cannot divide generations and civilisations into heathen and enlightened, or good and bad. Within all civilisations, no matter how negative their overall effect, are positive people trying to do what their heart is telling them. During the worst excesses of Christianity there were many compassionate people who followed the creed, and it was the same with Islam and other religions. So it has been throughout human history. We look back on those who peopled the Earth in the thousands of years before Christianity and believe them to be stupid savages; yet the understanding of life and creation among many of their number was more advanced than the modern world in many ways.

Their most enlightened members, often incarnations of the volunteer consciousness supported by channelled information, knew that the Earth was alive with a mind of her own. They knew of the energy system and the sacred points. The ancient Chinese applied this knowledge to the human body in what has become known as acupuncture. The ancients built the stone circles and erected standing stones on the chakras and acupuncture points of the Earth. Many of them have an effect similar to acupuncture needles. These great structures, like Stonehenge in England, are said to be the cultish monuments of a backward people, and yet what they put into place is still at work today helping to keep the battered energy grid in some kind of order. They were excellent channellers because they were not subjected to the tidal wave of abuse, derision, and condemnation from their society when their psychic gifts were activated as children. Their parents did not say 'Don't be silly', when they saw visions of entities on other frequencies or heard their communications; so they did not shut down these channels through fear and confusion. Naturally they were subjected to manipulation and I'm sure that some of the standing stones and circles were put there for negative reasons, too, to disrupt the energy flows or even to concentrate the energies at certain points to allow the spacecraft to use the power for their activities. Not every stone circle is positive, but overall these ancient peoples had some idea of the Earth as a living, breathing, entity.

I feel that the land we now call the British Isles was part of Atlantis before the series of cataclysms began to disconnect this land from the island that Atlantis was to become. Britain has always been recognised as an area of enormous importance to the grid. Despite the efforts of people like Boadicea, the Britons could not hold out against the Roman invasion. Although Julius Caesar's attempted invasion was eventually repelled, the Roman Empire absorbed most of Britain a few years later after the year 43. They never did succeed in suppressing most of the people of Scotland and a wall would be built by the Emperor Hadrian to keep them out. Christianity would later do what the Romans could not do – take control of all Scotland. The rule of the Romans had many benefits. The inter-tribal wars diminished and roads were built to improve communications.

After the fall of the Roman Empire in 410 the islands of Britain were invaded by tribes from the regions we know as Germany and Denmark. The inter-breeding of the indigenous population and the invaders created the Anglo-Saxon race. It was in these Anglo-Saxon times that the process of losing the ancient knowledge really began to accelerate. The country was broken up into the kingdoms of Northumbria, Mercia, Wessex, East Anglia, Essex, Kent and Sussex. They fought over........yes, you've got it........religion. The supporters of the Nicene Creed fought with those who supported the Arius view of Jesus, while the pagans fought with both of them. Oswy, the Christian king of Northumbria, 'did a Con-

stantine' in 664, when he called the two Christian factions together
at Whitby; after hearing the arguments he decided that all England
would follow the Pope and the Nicene Creed. The foundations
were now set for the Church to rule the country. The rule of the
Roman emperor had been replaced by the rule of the Roman pope,
so it was throughout the former Roman Empire. Now the manipulators only had to control the papacy and they controlled most of
the known world.

As the very mention of the so-called pagan knowledge became
the equivalent of suicide in the Christian world, the information
about energies and energy sites was passed on in legends by those
who wished to preserve the basic truths. They talked in codes
about giants and sacred hills and wells, and the 'giants' could even
have some extra-terrestrial background, too. These stories can still
be found in local folklore today, and because they are taken literally the originators are looked upon as backward people. When
you decode the symbolism you can see that they were far from
backward. They were merely trying to pass on knowledge in ways
that would not get them executed by those who *were* backward –
the representatives of the Christian religion.

There was conflict all over Europe, with village fighting village
at any excuse, and the culture brought by the Romans was largely
destroyed. The chaos throughout the former Roman Empire developed into a form of control called feudalism, which was to
create the social structure on which Europe developed for centuries
to come. Groups of weaker people would gather behind a strong
personality (not necessarily an enlightened one by any means), and
all who followed him and did whatever he asked were given his
protection. The division had arrived between the freeman and the
bondsman, those who were no more than slaves. The leaders
would become known as the lord or the king and they were
considered to be the representatives of God. The noblemen were
the upper classes. Christianity was one of the main instigators and
supporters of this system which turned most people into the slaves
of the few and it was the same across Europe. The kings and
noblemen took over the land, and gave great wealth to the Church
in their misguided belief, encouraged by the Church, that they
were buying a place in heaven. The feudal manor or the monastery
was now the authority which the communities of serfs had to
obey. In time Britain was divided into shires ruled by ealdormen
(later known as earls), and under them were the thegns (later

barons). These, along with the most powerful priests, became the nobility. It is from these beginnings and the creation of slaves that the class system emerged which is still with us today, with its landed gentry, nobility, Church and clergy, separated from the mass of the people by either wealth or privilege, often both.

All this was dreamland for the negative Brotherhood sects. What a perfect system to manipulate, playing one against the other to create conflict and upheaval, using this to change the world in your image. These kingdoms and communities would fight and battle with each other until one or a few would become dominant and take over large areas of land which would develop into a country. Wessex became dominant in England when it defeated the Mercians in 825 and King Egbert of Wessex controlled all of England. He was, in effect if not name, the first English king. Ethelwulf followed, and then came Alfred the Great. He was by far the most enlightened ruler of his time encouraging, among other things, the translation of Latin literature into English. Through it all the Church prospered. Kingdoms and nobles may come and go, but the Church was always there, adding with every dying king and noble to its now breathtaking fortune of land and riches. Christianity was now in control of England, and so was the Brotherhood.

This control would strengthen even further after the Battle of Hastings in 1066. Harold, the English King, was faced with invasions from the Danes and the Normans. He defeated the Danes at the Battle of Stamford Bridge near York and marched his troops south to tackle William, Duke of Normandy, a ruthless man who was very close to Pope Alexander II. The Pope, William, and Brotherhood societies plotted the invasion of England and the Papacy supplied the funds. William believed he was doing it for God and he carried the Pope's banners into battle, just as the pagan armies had carried images of their gods into the fray. Nothing had changed except the emblem. William defeated the English army and became king. Now the Pope would have a subservient England along with France and Germany. French became the language of England and this gradually fused with the various other languages spoken on the islands, Celtic, Anglo-Saxon, Latin, and Danish, to create the English tongue we recognise today.

William ordered the production of the Doomsday Book which recorded the ownership of every house, animal, and acre of land for taxation purposes and he gave great areas of England to the

Church to pay back the Pope for his support of the invasion. Lanfranc, an Italian Prior, was brought over from his abbey in Normandy to be made Archbishop of Canterbury and administer the Church's land and other wealth. It was he who organised a system of tithes to be paid to the Church by every landowner in the country. Even the poorest were not exempt and they paid up in their ignorance and fear that the priests could consign them to hell forever more. To this day the landowners of England still have to pay this tithe to the Church, even if they think that Christianity is a load of baloney. Opposition in the 1930s would change the nature of the payment, but it is still paid in another way. In 1936 the tithes were replaced by a fixed annual payment to be charged until October 1996. These fees are to pay for the three per cent of Government stock handed over to the Church authorities in exchange for their conceding their right to the tithes. This means, of course, that we are all paying for the Church in the costs added by the landowners to the price of their produce. All this because the priests frightened people through violence or hell and damnation into handing over their lands during a period of nearly a thousand years.

Through all this period of English and world history and in the following centuries, enlightened and courageous people were trying to raise the level of consciousness and knowledge. It is difficult to pick out which of them were genuinely seeking freedom for the people and which were working to a Brotherhood agenda, undermining religion in the longer term to bring about a world that accepted only the physical level of being. I think at least the great majority had good intent, and if they were playing the Brotherhood's game, it was probably mostly by ignorance, not malice. Roger Bacon, an English Franciscan friar of the 13th century wrote that people should cease to be ruled by dogma and authority and think for themselves. He had an advanced understanding for his time of science and he was confined by the Church because of his views. Others followed and their numbers grew until it exploded into the period called the Renaissance or 'new birth'. The key to what followed was the coming of the printing press to Europe. The means to make paper had been discovered by the Chinese, taken on by the Moslems and, through them, reached the Italians. The idea of printing with movable type also goes back to China and in the 1470s William Caxton was setting up his printing press in Westminster and producing the first book by this method in England. Caxton translated books from French and Latin into English and the exchange of knowledge began to flow all over Europe, although the Church would seek to suppress this at every turn.

The Renaissance in art, literature, and knowledge began chiefly in Italy from its stronghold in Florence. Greeks were seeking refuge in Italy from the Turks and they brought with them their knowledge, language and books. The learning of the Greek language had been banned by the Roman Catholic Church to stop people reading the works of the Greek philosophers, but now the ban was being ignored by those thirsting for knowledge. The spread of Greek literature reached England, France, and Germany. When the Turks took Constantinople there was an exodus of Greeks to Italy with yet more books, manuscripts, and knowledge. The works of the Moslem scientists and the knowledge gathered at the time of the open-minded rulers in Baghdad found its way to Italy and Europe.

The volunteer consciousness and the other levels were doing all they could to bring about the breakthrough in knowledge that would undermine the power of the Church. Vittorino da Feltre pioneered a new educational system in Italy which offered his students all the knowledge available, not only that which the Church wished to impose. The obvious corruption, vice, and violence of the Church was reducing its authority and then came the Great Schism when there were two popes, one ruling from Rome and the other from Avignon. This came about because the Italian Church believed that only an Italian should be pope and for thirty-eight years there were two popes, each with their own army plundering and pillaging wherever they went.

The discovery of America reduced Italy's importance as a trading centre and places like Venice and Genoa diminished in their wealth and power. The poverty this brought to Italy dimmed the fires of change and slowly the Church reimposed its grip, especially after Christian Spain occupied Northern Italy in 1538. The Church compiled an index on all banned literature which comprised, of course, of everything that challenged its doctrines. The Inquisition increased its work rate. But, much as the Roman Church tried to close the door again on knowledge, changes were now inevitable. There had been growing discontent with the excesses of the papacy and the priests. The papacy went to the highest bidder. The post gave the occupant control of incredible wealth and real estate. Kings bowed to the power of Rome and the inquisition secured the submission of the masses. The Church also supported the feudal system of masters and serfs. The reaction against all this had been a long time coming. The pressure for change had gathered slowly, and then more quickly through these centuries of fear and subservience. The bubonic plague called the Black Death was dramatically to reduce the population of the world, and in Europe alone about a quarter of the population died. I have seen it speculated that the Black Death and other plagues might have been created by a version of extra-terrestrial germ warfare. Certainly it would seem that bright lights in the sky and foul-smelling mists were reported quite often before the plague struck a community. Reports of 'comets' at that time could easily have been spacecraft, and historians have written of comets trailing behind them gases that killed trees and the lands fertility. We now often symbolise death with a picture of a skeleton holding a scythe; this comes from the numerous reports across Europe of strange men in black holding 'scythes' who appeared in a town or village before people fell ill with the Black Death. What were these 'scythes'? Whatever the cause of the plague, it did have a long-term impact in changing the status quo.

There were now fewer people to do the work of their masters and their dependence on the serfs who were available increased. The supply and demand of labour had tilted towards the serfs and the downtrodden began to protest against their conditions. Sometimes their leaders were assassinated, but the protests continued and there were peasant revolts in many countries, which brought conflict, upheaval, pain and suffering. The centuries of blind and mass obedience to the Church and its masters were being questioned during this period from the 14th to 17th centuries. Events and the growth of knowledge were beginning the process of liberation from Church control, a process that is only reaching fruition today in what you might call the Spiritual Renaissance or the Light Age.

The Church was an obvious target for change and courageous people stood up and challenged it. John Wycliffe condemned the behaviour of the priests who were using information gathered at confessions to blackmail people; some priests were selling forgiveness of sin for money or possessions. Wycliffe advocated that the scriptures were the only foundation of religious knowledge and that the pope was not the head of the Church. He dismissed the idea of transubstantiation – the belief that bread and wine can be converted into the body and blood of Christ during the Eucharist ceremony. He had the Bible translated into English and sent out supporters to expound his views. The priests would later persuade Henry IV to authorise the burning of all heretics, including Wycliffe's supporters. By then he had died, but the priests had his bones exhumed from a churchyard in Lutterworth, Leicestershire, where he had been had been parish priest. They did not want his skeleton polluting holy ground. The more Rome sought to deal violently with protesters, the more protests they had to deal with.

The coming of the printing press brought the translation and distribution of the Bible to a much wider audience. Up until then, the masses had only the word of the priests to tell them what the Bible said and meant. But as it was made more widely available people began to see the difference between the simple lives of the Bible 'heroes' and the opulent lifestyles of the clergy who were taking ten per cent of all the wealth the people produced. They could begin to re-interpret the texts for themselves. The Church knew the consequences of this and among their desperate efforts to suppress knowledge of the Bible's true content was the murder by burning at the stake, of William Tyndale. His heresy had been to begin to translate the New Testament into English. When people did have the opportunity to read the Bible there was a desire for a return to the simplicity of the Scriptures and the Protestant movement began. This brought about the Reformation when the Protestants broke away from the Catholic Church.

Martin Luther was one of the early Protestant leaders. He lived in Germany, which was then composed of over three hundred states. In 1517, this professor of theology at Wittenberg University pinned up a piece of paper containing ninety-five complaints against the behaviour of Rome in its efforts to raise money to build the church of St Peter's, on what had been the site of a pagan temple. The new church was, itself, built to make money in much the same way as the bedouins of Mecca fleeced the pilgrims. This attitude continues in the Vatican City today.

Pope Julius II and his successor Leo X sanctioned a plan to sell divine pardons for money. For each donation they promised to release from purgatory the soul of a dead relative or friend. As late as the second World War this practice survived, with the Catholic Archbishop of Winnipeg telling the wives and parents of Canadian soldiers that, if their loved ones died in action, he would ensure, for a charge of $40, that they went immediately to their Maker and stayed with him for all eternity.

The revolt against Rome grew in Germany, and in 1520, Luther burned the decree excommunicating him, along with copies of the Canon Law, the name for the Theodosian Creed which updated the Nicaean Creed. The Lutheran Church was born and many of the peasants supported Luther in the hope that religious change would bring social reform. They backed the wrong man, for he was as much a tyrant as most of the popes and he would later support terrible atrocities against the peasant peoples who wanted only freedom from tyranny. As he once wrote:

"Damned be love into the abyss of hell, if it is maintained to the damage of faith.....It is better that tyrants should sin a hundred times against the people than the people should sin once against the tyrants....the ass wants to be thrashed, the mob to be governed by force."

His hatred of reason and open-minded research was equally extreme. In one sermon he said that his followers should throw spit in the face of reason, because she was the Devil's whore, rotten with the itch of leprosy, and ought to be kept in the toilet. Nice man. He may have complained about papal and clerical indulgences, but like the other Protestants, he still believed the nonsense which Jerome and others had edited into the Bible and all the other inaccuracies that had been in the texts to start with. Other forms of Protestant interpretation of the Bible followed such as Calvinism, the product of the Frenchmen John Calvin. He was as much a dictator as Luther and the Popes. Religion – and the Brotherhood – seem to breed such people. Calvin's obnoxious creed was to have severe consequences in England and America because it was a major influence on the beliefs of the Puritans, of which more later. Calvin, like Luther, promoted the idea that you could not ensure eternal salvation by the way you lived your life or by 'good works'. It could only come by faith in Jesus as your Saviour. Even the Roman Catholic Church wasn't quite that extreme, but Calvin went even further. He said that whether we were to be 'saved' or not was decided by God before we were born! He called this idea predestination. The chosen few who were selected by God for eternal salvation had a duty, he said, to suppress the sin of the condemned masses. It was, in other words, a licence for untold slaughter.

Protestantism broke into endless creeds, sects, and churches with different beliefs arguing on the vital issues for the future of humankind like the nature of the Trinity and whether Jesus entered the bread and wine consumed during the Eucharist. This comes from a quote attributed to Jesus in the Bible which was, in fact, an addition by one of the many forgers and relates to a pagan belief:

"And as they were eating, Jesus took bread, and blessed it, and brake it, and gave it to the disciples, and said, 'Take, eat, this is my body'. And he took the cup, and gave thanks, and gave it to them, saying, 'Drink ye all of it. For this is my blood of the new testament, which is shed for many for the remission of sins'."

Over the interpretation of this forgery whole wars were fought. The Protestant Movement came to England in a rather unusual way. Henry VIII wanted a son and heir, but his first wife Catherine of Aragon could only bear him a daughter, Mary. He decided to divorce her and asked Pope Clement VII to sanction it. He refused. Henry was a committed Catholic and had condemned the Protestants in Europe to such an extent that the Pope had awarded him the title Defender of the Faith which British monarchs still hold to this day. This is ironic, because today they are Protestant monarchs defending that faith under a title given by a Roman Catholic pope for defending his faith! You've got to chuckle, really. Henry was such a defender of the Catholic faith he ordered that all who denied it were to be burned at the stake. But the opposition to his divorce changed all that. He insisted that his parliament vote into being a Church of England independent of Rome, and he made himself the head of the English Church. When that was done the Archbishop of Canterbury, Thomas Cranmer, sanctioned his divorce from Catherine. Cranmer replaced Cardinal Wolsey as England's most influential churchman, because Wolsey had failed to secure his divorce. He was summoned to London to be tried for treason, but died on the way at Leicester Abbey.

Wolsey had ruled the English Church like a dictator and had, to a large extent, run the country. The monasteries had enormous power and were home to the papal garrison. They also owned great areas of England. They used the tried and trusted methods like the fear of hell to persuade the wealthy to leave them their land and possessions. When that didn't work they found some excuse to take them. In their early days, the monasteries had made a positive contribution when compared with the murder and misery in other areas of Christendom, but now they were just as bad. Henry had long coveted their wealth and he took his opportunity to abolish them and take their possessions. He was so short of money that he had to sell much of the land he acquired and this was the start of the period of the country squire and gentry. These were the wealthy men who bought the massive estates once owned, or rather stolen, by the Church, and they built upon them their manor houses that became such a part of the English countryside.

Henry waged war on anyone who refused to accept him as Supreme Head of the Church, as outlined in the Act of Supremacy of 1534. His chancellor, Sir Thomas More, was beheaded for such treason and there was a bloody purge on Roman Catholics. Henry married six women, two of which he executed. Only Jane Seymour bore him a son, who became Edward VI at the age of only nine when Henry died in 1547. Edward was king in name only with the Protestant Duke of Somerset the real power behind the throne. Edward himself died at 15 and he was succeeded by Mary, Henry's daughter by Catherine of Aragon. She was a staunch Roman Catholic and began a bloody purge against Protestants which was so savage she was given the name 'Bloody Mary'. Edward had been persuaded by the Duke of Somerset to leave the throne to Henry's great neice, Lady Jane Grey, who was a Protestant supporter, but Mary had her executed and took the throne. Mary married Philip of Spain who wished to have a peaceful relationship with England, so that his ships could pass along the English Channel without hindrance. The Pope again became head of the Church of England. But another about-turn was imminent. With Mary's death came Elizabeth I, the daughter of Anne Boleyn, who became queen at the age of 25. Her mother had been a Protestant and she accepted that faith. The Roman Catholic Church opposed her succession because, it said, she was an illegitimate child with her father's divorce from Catherine of Aragon not recognised by the Pope. She ignored them and restored the Protestant Church of England with herself as its Supreme Head. A bloody purge was launched against Catholics. The Queen ordered the torture and death of so many Irish Catholics they gave her the title 'Bloody Elizabeth'.

All over Europe mass slaughter was being unleashed as Catholics and Protestants fought against each other in civil and national wars. Which side was most persecuted depended on who had managed to seize the throne at the time. When you look back at the scale of death and destruction committed in the name of religion, even basically the *same* religion, it is stunning beyond belief. All but a handful of wars have been caused by religion or the perceived superiority of the ancestral line of one group or nation's physical bodies, when in truth they are just temporary vehicles for our consciousness to experience this level. But let us take another angle on the events that followed the Reformation. I mentioned earlier that the Brotherhood had a long-term aim of using religion for its own ends and then moving on to the next stage, to replace religion, which largely abused the knowledge of the spirit, with a godless science which convinced the mass of the people that the spirit did not even exist. Part of this plan was to dismantle the power of the Christian Church and create more factions within the Christian religion. Even if they did not actually start the Reformation – and I believe they did – they certainly took advantage of it.

The real roots of the Reformation were in Germany in the 14th century when an arm of the Brotherhood emerged called the Illuminati, Latin for the Illuminated or Enlightened Ones. They were closely connected to the Rosicrucians (Latin for the rose and the cross), which began centuries earlier and was introduced to Germany by the Emperor Charlemagne in the ninth century. At one time at least you would be accepted into the Illuminati when you had reached a certain level of initiation in the Rosicrucians. Both were classic secret societies in the manner I have outlined, and they began covertly to introduce a number of religious movements around Europe. One was called the Friends of God led by Rulman Merswin, a rich banker, who was conned by the Brotherhood into believing he had been chosen by God to preach his message because the Pope could no longer be trusted to do it. What's more God would soon punish humanity for its sin, he was told. The End Of The World and the Day of Judgement is another Brotherhood theme. The Friends of God was a mind control cult that accepted only total obedience from its followers. It gained many supporters who were fed up with the corruption in the Church, and eventually Merswin had a 'revelation' that he should hand over his religion lock, stock, and barrel to another branch of the Brotherhood, probably linked to freemasonry, called the Order of St John.

Martin Luther was strongly influenced by some of these German mystical societies and was especially keen on the writings of the

German mystic, Johann Tauler, a man closely connected with the Friends of God. It seems certain, also, that Luther was a Rosicrucian, given that his personal seal contains both of their symbols, the rose and the cross. He was close to many members of the Illuminati and the Rosicrucians, and they would have been using him, with or without his knowledge, to break the overwhelming power of the pope. The Vatican was, itself, a Brotherhood tool, but none is allowed to get too powerful, and all are expendable when the time is right. These two Christian creeds of Protestant and Catholic were now to be used, as we have already seen, to stimulate enormous conflict. But it is important to emphasise that the Brotherhood was not in total control of all events. I am sure they have had some monumental failures in their time, as people have not reacted in the way they expected, or some of their number did not do as they were told once they realised what the game plan was. I have no doubt that some of their wars have not had the outcome they always hoped for. I feel, too, that there have been many periods when the volunteer consciousness has infiltrated these movements and tried to undermine and change them from within and I believe that behind the scenes this was possibly happening during the time of Sir Francis Bacon who became the highest executive of the Rosicrucian Order in England. It was during his lifetime in the early 1600s that the teachings of the order began to include some references to the need for personal spiritual salvation by taking control of our own thinking and actions, and some of these are still reflected in that order. The fact that someone in history was a member of a secret society tells us nothing. It is the agenda they were working to that matters, and it wasn't always negative; far from it. To openly pass on esoteric knowledge at this time would have been like writing a suicide note. What I am sure about, however, is that from the Reformation onwards, the Brotherhood takeover by the Luciferic consciousness was increasing, and its power to manipulate events was seen to reach new heights.

Elizabeth I secured the long-term future of the Episcopalian Church of England, better known as the Anglican Faith. Anyone who didn't attend local Church services was fined or jailed. It was now that the so called Thirty-Nine Articles of Faith were agreed by Elizabeth and Parliament which everyone had to believe or be condemned as a heretic. I list some of them here and it is worth reading them carefully because all would-be Anglican clergy still have to swear their agreement with every word that follows before they are accepted into the priesthood:

God consists of three persons, the Father, Son, and Holy Ghost, who are all one God.

Christ was divine and he suffered as a sacrifice for the sins of humanity.

Christ died for humanity, was buried and went down into hell.

Christ rose from the grave and took again his body, with flesh and bones, with which he ascended to heaven where he sits till he returns on the day of Judgment.

The Holy Ghost is of the same substance, majesty and glory as the Father and Son.

The Holy Scripture containeth all things necessary to salvation; everything outside of the scriptures is unnecessary for salvation.

Jesus is the only mediator between God and Man. No Christian is free from the obedience of the Commandments.

The Nicene Creed, the Athanasian Creed, and the Apostles' Creed ought to be thoroughly believed.

All deserve God's wrath and damnation, but there is no condemnation of believers who are baptised.

Man has no power to do good works without the grace of God.

Our righteousness before God comes, not by our works, but by the merit of Christ. Therefore we are justified only by faith and not by works.

Good works cannot put away sin, yet they are pleasing to God.

Works not springing from faith are not pleasant to God, yet rather they have the nature of sin.

Doing more than duty requires cannot be taught without arrogancy and impiety.

Jesus was sinless, the Lamb without spot who sacrificed himself and took away the sins of the world.

Repentance is not denied to such as fall into sin after baptism.

Predestination to Life is the everlasting purpose of God, to deliver from curse and damnation those whom he has chosen in Christ, to bring them everlasting salvation.

They are accursed who believe that every man shall be saved by the Law or who frame their lives according to the light of nature.

The effect of Christ's ordinance is not withdrawn because of the officiating priest's wickedness.

All non-believers ought to be considered by the faithful as heathen and publican.

This is the faith that to this day is taught by law in the schools of

Britain and other countries and is given guaranteed, no-questions-asked, air-time by the BBC which claims to be an independent organisation. It is an outrage. If it wasn't so tragic it would make a comedy series.

Elizabeth ensured that the Protestant Faith would survive when her navy defeated the Spanish Armada in 1588. One of the commanders of the English Navy was Francis Drake, a former pirate turned admiral, who was the second man to circumnavigate the world. Philip II of Spain had been urged by Pope Pius V to invade England, kill the 'bastard' Queen, and restore the rule of Catholicism. Pius V was the man who was burning, hanging and beheading the religious reformers in Italy. Philip was further motivated in his duty by the terrible atrocities committed against the Catholics of England and Ireland. He believed that such atrocities should only be committed against Protestants. The ships of the Armada contained ninety members of the Spanish Inquisition ready to begin work when England was re-taken for the Pope. But the Armada was defeated in the English Channel and the power of Rome and Spain was dimmed. The foothold the Protestant Faith had won in Europe was secured. If the Spanish had conquered England the whole Protestant movement might have collapsed. When Elizabeth died in 1603, England and Scotland united under one monarch. They had been in conflict over thousands of years, but now James V1 of Scotland became James I of England, too. The Kingdom was united – on paper at least.

The 16th and 17th centuries in England during the reign of Elizabeth and later was a time of great 'volunteer' activity as they sought to raise human understanding through art and scientific research. Sir Francis Bacon worked within the secret societies and I believe he wrote the 'Shakespeare' plays and included in them esoteric codes. Anthony, the brother of Francis, ran a 'spy network' which was a front for passing on esoteric knowledge. I feel that at this time there was a secret society operating within a secret society and that when, in the end, the Brotherhood realised what was going on the Bacons and others were stopped by a campaign of covert killings and trumped-up charges that saw Francis sent to jail. When you look at the life of Sir Francis Bacon nothing is quite what it seems to be on the surface. He made some misguided decisions as everyone does, but I believe his intent was positive in his desire to build a "new Atlantis." Every effort to raise the human condition and its understanding of life was viciously op-

posed by the Church, Protestant and Catholic, and so many suffered all over the world for seeking and exchanging knowledge.

In 1564, Galileo Galilei was born at Pisa in Italy. He was to
develop the use of the telescope to study the skies and his research
led him to the conclusion that, contrary to what the Church said,
the Sun did not circle the Earth – it was the other way round. Nor
did he believe the Earth was the centre of the Universe. This
confirmed the findings of Nicolaus Copernicus, a Polish scientist
who had died in 1543. Copernicus had continued the work begun
nearly 2,000 years earlier by Pythagoras and others. Copernicus
had been pilloried by the Church for his 'heresy' and his work
suppressed. Almost a century later the same was to happen to
Galileo. It could well be that he was a reincarnation of Copernicus.
Galileo was tried for heresy in 1632 by the Inquisition for writing a
book supporting the Copernicus theory. A document was falsified
by the Church to back up the case against him. He was found
guilty of 'holding and teaching the Copernicus doctrine' (i.e. saying the Earth goes around the Sun and is not the centre of the
Universe). Galileo escaped the most extreme methods of the Inquisition, but he was placed under house arrest for the last eight
years of his life. You can see how dogmatic religion has held back
human evolution and understanding. It was only in this decade
that the Roman Catholic Church officially admitted that Galileo
was right!! It is interesting to note that some of his fiercest critics
were other academics and scientists who realised the consequences
of his findings for their power and influence. The same attitude is
still prevalent today.

During this period there were many seers and prophets who
predicted the future in terms very similar in themes to those being
presented today. Nostradamus, who lived in Southern France, is
the most famous of them. I feel he was predicting what would
happen if humanity continued on the path it had embarked upon.
By tuning your consciousness to those vibrations of thought energy that retain Creation's eternal memory, you can 'see' the past
with your psychic vision or channel information about it. You can
experience something of a past life or see a past event. In the same
way you can 'see' the future. I believe that consciousness is constantly projecting forward how things will be on the basis of what
has happened (the past) and what is happening (the present). From
these sources, the collective consciousness projects forward what
will happen if those same trends continue. So the future exists as

the past exists in thought energy that is outside of our version and understanding of space and time. When people tune to that vibration, they are accessing information about the *projected* future, not necessarily the future as it will be. I believe this was the information that Nostradamus was tuning to for his famous predictions and he was also accessing knowledge of the plan for the transformation of human consciousness in the time we are living in now as we progress into the Photon Belt. Obviously, the closer the event is to the present the more likely it is to happen as projected. But the further into the future you go, the more time there is for humans to change and therefore to change the future. It is a commentary on the scale of humanity's imprisonment of thought that the outcome is unfolding very much along the lines that Nostradamus predicted, but it doesn't have to. We can change it.

Before we move on from this period of the 1600s, we need to record the beginnings of the most important vehicle of Brotherhood control and manipulation. It was to give this amalgamation of secret, covert, groupings the power to advance its desire for global domination like never before. We call it the world money system.

Throughout human history, the purchase of goods and services had been through barter, one thing exchanged directly for another, or by coins which were made from metals which reflected the value of the coin. This made metals like gold and silver more valuable than others, because they could be used to make coins and thereby could be exchanged for whatever you liked. But then a series of events began to happen. People didn't want to have all that gold and silver lying around waiting to be stolen, so it became the custom to deposit these metals with those who had strong-rooms where it would be safe. Many of these strong-rooms were owned by goldsmiths. The goldsmith would give receipts to the customer for the value of the deposit and when these were returned they would hand back that amount of precious metals. The customers began to use these receipts as forms of exchange because they were more convenient than moving the metals around and the goldsmiths, and other strong-room owners, realised that only a small number of these receipts were returned to them at any one time by people coming to collect their metal deposits. So why could they not issue receipts to people who didn't actually own any of the metals and then charge them interest for the privilege? What a great idea. You could lend money on metal owned by someone else and charge a fee for doing it! The receipt (money) was worthless if all the owners of your metal deposits wanted them returned at the same time, but as this never happened you were laughing, unless you issued far too many notes.

From this has come today's banking system which is controlled by the Brotherhood to further its ends. Banks are allowed literally to invent money well in excess of their actual assets and charge interest on that money. The governments and people of the world are now submerged under debt to the banks of staggering proportions, and that debt is money conjured out of nothing by the banking system. Type in a few figures on a computer screen, move that number to a person's account on another part of the computer programme, and from that moment you can start charging that person interest on money that isn't yours, and doesn't physically exist. More than that, if a person falls behind in the interest payments on money you don't own and doesn't exist, you can take their home and possessions that *do* exist, and even have them sent to prison.

By this simple means you can put governments and people into so much manufactured debt that they become pawns which you can move around the board at will. You can force people to do what they have no wish to do because they have to earn the money to pay you back the money you did not own in the first place, and it is the same with governments. It is utterly insane for banks under no government control to be given this power to create money out of nothing, but the Brotherhood societies, at the highest level in this case, brought this into being and manipulate entire nations and continents with it day after day. It has also allowed more wars to be fought and prolonged, because instead of being limited to the assets a country owned, the bankers could now issue pieces of paper to keep the conflict going. Then, after the war, the governments were even further in debt and their people would have to suffer more hardships if their country was going to pay back the banks for the money that did not exist. Now wars not only became wonderful tools of control for the Brotherhood, they were fantastic ways to increase their wealth. They couldn't lose. They would lend invented money to both sides, charge them interest on it, and then lend them more invented money to rebuild the countries that had been devastated by those wars. And we, men and women of the world, continue to put up with it! The first major bank of this kind was the Bank of Amsterdam set up in the

early 1600s and it immediately began to lend to the Dutch government to finance more wars. The Bank of England followed in 1694
and became the model for all the others.

These centuries we have discussed were of enormous significance, with the Renaissance opening the minds of Europeans to the
knowledge of Greece, the Reformation breaking the power of the
Pope, and the introduction of the banking system. Within the mass
of the people, dissatisfaction was stirring at the way they were
treated and the foundations for rebellion and eventually parliamentary democracy were in place. It would still take many centuries to arrive and the Church would battle to prevent it, but the
cracks had appeared in their wall of religious suppression and the
flood was sure to follow.

8

Eagle Tails

AN area of substantial volunteer activity over the thousands of years after the demise of Atlantis have been the lands we call the Americas.

North, South and Central America were populated by groups of nomadic and agricultural peoples long before the Sumerians were settling in Mesopotamia. You would think, if you didn't know, that American history began with the coming of the European invaders, but that happened only a few hundred years ago. The Americas evolved with the thousands of tribes which developed with their diverse cultures and beliefs. As in the rest of the world, some would grow and conquer others to create empires. One of these was the Aztecs in what we call Mexico. They were advanced in that they built fantastic pyramids and cities, as did many peoples of the Americas, but at the same time they slaughtered untold thousands in sacrifices to their gods at the whim of the priests. You can see how civilisations across the world were being affected by some global consciousness or the same extra-terrestrial races that encouraged them to believe the same myths.

There are many similarities between the Sumerian and Egyptian cultures and what has been found of ancient American history. The all-seeing eye is there; so are the pyramids, some with great similarities to those in Egypt. The feathered serpent symbol found widely in the Americas can be mirrored by the serpent gods of India and the winged serpents of Egyptian legend. Stories can be found of the gods who created human beings and tried to make them their slaves. The themes of Atlantis, Sumer, Babylon and Egypt apply equally to the Americas.

One of the intriguing and interesting peoples of the Americas were the Maya. It is believed that they evolved from another people called the Olmecs, and both built amazing pyramids. The connections between the beliefs of the Maya and the Egyptians are obvious. The Maya pyramids were faced with limestone as was the Great Pyramid at Giza, and the beliefs in mummifying bodies and the nature of life after death were similar. I think there is an excellent chance that the same ET races were responsible for developing both civilisations in their early days or maybe it was the collective mind at work. But the Mayan civilisation lasted for thousands of years and we should not fall into the trap of thinking it was always the same. Some Mayans apparently practised human sacrifice, but this was not general. These things change. What is termed the Classic Mayan period is reckoned to have been from about 435 to 830AD, when their culture seems to have stopped quite abruptly. The Maya settled on the land now known as Guatemala and north to Yucatan and in that classic period they devised a measurement of time very different to our own today. It related to natural energy cycles and they devised a mathematical system of numbers and symbols to work out the cycles and translate them into a form of language. The Maya, some of whom were from highly-evolved volunteer consciousness, left records of their calendar and mathematical system. They believed that the Earth began a new cycle of evolution in 3113BC and that this would be completed in 2012. This would link in very well with what I am saying about the Photon Belt and the many prophecies through the ages of great change at this time. Numbers and symbols can be found on the ruins and artifacts of many ancient civilisations. As we are now beginning to understand again, everything is an energy, numbers and symbols included. Numbers and symbols represent certain energy vibrations and the Mayan system was a mathematical code for energies and their cycles.

It's funny how we have this idea that evolution and understanding can only progress and cannot go backwards. This belief insists that peoples a decade ago let alone 1,500 years ago could not possibly know more about Creation than we do. This is a fallacy. The knowledge exists outside of this dense physical planet and always has. It has been a case of getting that knowledge through the imbalances and the dense vibration of the Earth to our conscious levels. This could have happened in Central America in 435 far easier than in the years of religious imposition in Europe and the Middle East when minds were slamming shut in their hundreds of thousands through fear and the thought-police.

One other point to remember is that while the ancient Maya may be gone, their energy has not. When we think we create energy fields and so in that former land of the Maya, as with Egypt and elsewhere, the knowledge they worked with is still there waiting to be accessed. Going to these places and quietly tuning into the energy fields can open up your understanding quicker than reading a thousand history books. If you tap into this ancient knowledge held in thought energy fields you can learn so much about them. It doesn't come on sheets of paper, it is a knowingness, an inspired understanding that you cannot always describe.

In South America, volunteers incarnated to work in the area around Lake Titicaca which spans today's Peru – Bolivia border. These groups would later move north and evolve into the Inca civilisation centred around Cusco in the Andes. The Incas worshipped the Sun god, and again this could have been based on an understanding of the consciousness of the Sun as a purveyor of universal knowledge and wisdom. At their peak the Incas controlled an area of 2,000 miles by 200, and they became motivated by power, wealth, and expansion as the original understanding was lost. The choice of location for these volunteer incarnations was linked to the points on the energy grid which needed to be worked on. The region that includes Lake Titicaca, Sun Island, Cusco, Machu Picchu, and the Sacred Valley of the Incas, is one of the most powerful on the planet.

I am not suggesting for a second that the incarnations of the volunteer consciousness were always shining reflections of virtue. They were men and women of their time and they were affected by the culture they were born into. They still are. What they had was a more powerful link with their higher consciousness and this had two positive effects. Firstly information and inspiration could be brought down to this level. This showed itself in those who challenged the bigotry of religion and authority and advanced human understanding through philosophy and scientific discovery. Secondly, they were open channels to ground powerful energies and pass them into the grid.

Some significant volunteer incarnations were in North America among the tribes of what have become known as 'Red Indians'. The 'Indians' (Native Americans) understood the basics of the energy system and their medicine wheels were circles of stones where ceremonies took place at points on the energy grid. Obviously, they would not have understood exactly what they were doing within the confines of the physical form, but the connection with the higher self was strong enough for them to do what was

necessary on the physical level. They passed on their understanding in legends and stories which contained many truths portrayed
symbolically and many myths, too, I'm sure. More than anything
they had a respect for the Earth and the rest of Creation, which led
them to take from nature only what they believed they needed.
Every civilisation has its 'classic' periods as with the Maya when
the volunteer consciousness was there in numbers for a specific
time and task, and so it was with the Native American tribes
through the centuries. They, too, had endless secret societies to
pass on their knowledge.

The culture was not all-peaceful and all-knowing, nor should we
have expected it to be. There is, I feel, a naive belief that those who
come from higher levels to help the Earth cannot be genuine unless
they behave 'perfectly'. The myths of Jesus have sprung from this
idea. It doesn't matter how evolved your higher self, the incarnating lower self is still subject to the imbalances, the dense vibration,
and the culture it is incarnating into. The Indian tribes fought each
other as inherited distrust and hatred spanned the generations and
being a brave warrior was the way male status was often measured.

I would not wish to give the impression that these incarnations
of the volunteers all produced people with piercing blue eyes who
blessed their enemies, healed the sick and disappeared on a cloud
into heaven at the end of it. They have had to live with the
pressures of this world and some have gone through an entire
physical life without their higher knowledge manifesting. There
are many like that today, unfortunately. All I am saying is that,
overall, these volunteers have done a tremendous amount to keep
the Earth and the spiritual understandings alive until this time of
transformation.

So we are looking at the Americas before the European invasion
peopled by tribes and empires of great diversity of culture and
outlook. Some were highly evolved in their understanding, some
still primitive, some a bit of both. Some were at war with each
other, some at peace. None would have known of a Saviour god
called Jesus Christ or even that Christianity and the people of the
Middle East and Europe even existed, but they were now to find
out in an orgy of genocide as the will of the representatives of the
Christian god arrived on their shores.

According to conventional history, Christopher Columbus was
born in Genoa in 1436 and became convinced that the Earth was

round, not flat as the Church claimed. He believed that if he sailed West he would go around the world and end up in India and the Far East which Marco Polo had identified. He asked the Kings of Spain, Portugal, and England for funds, but was turned down. Eventually he was supported by a group of Spanish merchants and he set out in the Santa Maria, flanked by two other ships, in 1492. After months of sailing he went on to discover the Bahamas and other Islands, including Cuba. To the end, it is said, Columbus believed he had landed in India and so we have names like the West Indies and 'Indians'.

But is there more to all this than mainstream history has recorded? Could the secret societies have been behind it? Columbus is known to have dressed sometimes in a habit similar to that of the Franciscan Order. His son said his father died in such attire. This does not have to mean he was a member of that order, however. Remember the priests at the Brotherhood temple in El-Amarna back in Ancient Egypt wore something similar and so did several groups of the same Brotherhood tradition in Columbus' time, including the Fraternities. Manly P. Hall in his book, *America's Assignment with Destiny*, speculates that Columbus may have been a student of the Illuminated Raymond Tully, as rumours suggested. Hall says that he was certainly involved in a group supporting the views of the Italian poet, Dante (1265-1321), who was a member of the Cathar Church, friend of Roger Bacon, and an initiate of the Knights Templar. There is a strong feeling that the Brotherhood were behind Columbus. His belief that the Earth was round could have originated, at least in part, from his knowledge of the esoteric tradition of Asia and the Near East. In his book on Columbus, Seraphim G. Canoutas of the University of Athens, says that secret preparations for the colonisation of the 'Blessed Isles of the West' (the Americas) were known to the Cathars and the chivalric Orders of Knighthood. The evidence is increasing that the secret society elite knew very well that America existed long before it was officially 'found'.

Columbus returned to Spain with gold, cotton and other 'finds' including two natives who were to be baptised into the Christian faith. This changed the attitude of the King of Spain and when Columbus sailed again for 'India' the following year he took with him 1,500 men in seventeen ships. The Pope had given him permission to take possession of all the lands he found in the name of the King of Spain who had already agreed to share the booty with his Holiness. Columbus became governor of the lands he found. Not only did he take them from the native population, he introduced slavery and treated the people with the sort of religious goodwill that is so widely documented in this book. Columbus was always saying prayers, and his brutality against the natives had the full support of the priests who had travelled with him. Christianity which had spread its darkness across the 'old' world had now reached the Americas.

Western Europe was desperate for a share of the spoils which Columbus had identified and others were soon to follow his path across the Atlantic. Vasco Da Gama, a Portuguese, sailed around the Cape of Good Hope and on to the real India. A Spaniard, Vicente Pinzon, who sailed on that first journey with Columbus, led his own expedition and found Brazil closely followed by the Portuguese. In 1519, Magellan, another native of Portugal, led an attempt to sail around the World. He died on the journey, but others completed the circumnavigation, so proving that the planet was indeed a sphere. These journeys and others increased the knowledge of geography and horizons were widened in all directions. Over the next four centuries the powerful countries of Europe would battle for the ownership of distant lands throughout Africa, Asia and the Americas. It was the greatest act of piracy and robbery the world has ever seen. The British, Dutch, French, Belgians, Spanish, Portuguese and others plundered the planet imposing their culture and religion on the native peoples, mostly killing or banishing into slavery all who resisted. Australia and New Zealand were found and 'Christianised'.

The name Cortez will always be remembered by the peoples of Central America. He was a Christian zealot who landed there in 1519 at the time of the local king called Montezuma. Cortez was treated well by the native peoples who thought he was the long awaited return of their god, Quetzalcohatl, which translates as 'our beloved son'. The beliefs surrounding him are yet more compelling evidence of a common source connecting the Middle East and the Americas. He was said to have been born to a virgin, Chimalman, who was told by a heavenly messenger that she would conceive a son without sexual intercourse. Quetzalcohatl was also said to have been tempted by the devil, to have fasted for forty days and to have been crucified. But Montezuma's people were soon to realise that Cortez was no second coming of this god. Once he saw the wealth and magnificence of the culture, he set about killing thousands to force upon them Spanish rule and Christianity. Among their conquests were the lands of the Maya which had continued to be populated by those who came after the Classic Mayan period. Accept gentle Jesus as your saviour or we slaughter you was the basic message of the invading Europeans. One Spanish historian of the time estimated that twelve million natives of South America alone were killed after the Europeans landed and an even greater number became slaves. It was claimed with pride that Great Britain owned so many countries that the Sun never set on the British Empire. This glorious empire was, like all of its kind, a means to exploit and dominate for reasons of riches, resources and trade. I would not suggest that everything the Europeans did in these countries was negative and without merit, but the motivation and imposition behind these conquests was appalling. The consequences of this occupation are still being unravelled.

There was no need for all this murder and suffering for these different cultures to interact. It could have been done for mutual benefit. But the Luciferic consciousness had implanted the belief in enough people that whatever you wanted you took by force and you imposed your will and religion. Your god was always on your side and whatever you did you did for him. As long as you had been baptised and believed in St Paul's Saviour-god called Jesus Christ you were guaranteed a place in heaven no matter what you did. Indeed it is even in the Articles of Faith of the Church of England to this day that good deeds are not the way to salvation. Add to that the condemnation of heathens in the Bible and the belief that all non-Christians, even non-believers in your faction of Christianity, were heathens and you can see how these native peoples had no chance of humane treatment from the great majority of invaders. As one of the Psalms says:

"I shall give thee the heathen for thine inheritance, and the uttermost parts of the earth for thy possession. Thou shalt break them with a rod of iron, thou shalt dash them in pieces like a potter's vessel."

We are highlighting in this chapter the development of the Americas and particularly North America which was to become, in the form of the United States, the most powerful nation on the planet – on the surface, at least. The Spanish and Portuguese plundered most of South America, where they destroyed the native culture and beliefs and introduced Christianity in the form of Roman Catholicism, that dark creed which still enslaves the minds of millions on that continent through fear and guilt. North America became largely the property of the English and French although Pope Alexander VI had 'given' the whole of the Americas to Spain and Portugal, especially Spain (he was a Spaniard). Four years after Columbus discovered the West Indies, two Venetians based in Bristol, England, sailed with the backing of Henry VII for North America. They were John and Sebastian Cabot, father and son, and they followed the route taken by earlier explorers like the Vikings who had landed in the New York area five hundred years before. They called it Vinland.

John Cabot's real name was Giovanni Caboto. He was, like Columbus, born in Genoa and he later became a naturalised Venitian. Interestingly, especially as Cabot lived at the same time as Columbus, he had secret society connections, too, and visited the same "Wise Men" of the Near East that Columbus is said to have met. Some historians suggest that Cabot was involved with the secret Christian sect called the Johannites which followed the esoteric doctrines of the Templars. Many other early explorers and colonizers of the Americas have been shown to be members of the secret society network. Sir Francis Bacon would later use this network to advance the colonisation of North America to stop the Spanish taking control of that land and to further his belief in building a great world commonwealth called The New Atlantis. "Shakespeare's" play, The Tempest, would appear to describe Bacon's ambitions.

The Cabots discovered the North American coast, but little was done about their find for many years and by then the Frenchman, Jacques Cartier, had laid claim for his country to the region of what is now Eastern Canada. He was followed by another Frenchmen, Samuel de Champlain, who founded Canada and built a fort which he called Quebec. His ambition was to convert the native tribes to Roman Catholicism and expand the fur trade, which involved the native peoples giving him furs in exchange for guns and booze. His intervention started wars between the tribes and caused great disruption. But he did not convert them to Christianity, not least because the Catholics and Protestants in his midst spend most of their time fighting each other. Other Christian missionaries who tried to force their religion upon the Indians were killed by the very guns that had been traded for the furs.

The religious persecution in Britain and Europe now involved not only the persecution of Catholics by Protestants and vice versa, but also the persecution of factions within the Protestant creed who differed, often on the most irrelevant details, from the Anglican or orthodox Protestant faiths. This drove many Puritans and Nonconformists to risk the dangerous and treacherous journey to North America. Under James I, who followed Elizabeth, Puritans and Presbyterians were persecuted because James was a staunch Anglican. He also ordered a gruesome purge against 'witches' (mediums) and his treatment of Roman Catholics was so terrible, two of their number, Guy Fawkes and Robert Catesby, organised the failed Gunpowder Plot of 1605 to assassinate him. It was James I who took part of Northern Ireland from the Catholics and encouraged it to be settled by English and Scottish Protestants. This set in motion the centuries of hatred and conflict between the two Christian factions that created a sort of religious apartheid that still continues. Britain under James I was not a good place to be unless you were an Anglican, and the exodus to America grew. Many Puritans settled in a place they called New England where they matched the violence and intolerance shown to them in Europe with their own treatment of the Indians and others who did not share their misguided Faith. In Virginia, tobacco was the currency and people were fined 50lbs of tobacco for not attending church, 2,000lbs for not having their child baptised, and 5,000lbs for entertaining a Quaker. Death is no cure for ignorance and neither is a journey across the Atlantic. This led William Penn, a compassionate Quaker, to found Pennsylvania in 1682, on land given to him by Charles II in exchange for the money lent to him by Penn's father. He opened his lands to Quakers and all persecuted Nonconformists, and made friends with the Indians. He showed how they could live together to their mutual benefit. The Indians also gave a piece of land to Roger Williams who founded the State of Rhode Island as a haven of peace and religious tolerance. Mostly, however, the North American settlers treated the Indians and people of differing beliefs as heathen with no dignity or rights under God.

By the 18th century the French had been driven out of North America by the British who treated these lands as an extension of the British Isles. But the settlers were beginning to resent this. They still paid allegiance to the British King, but they rebelled when they were told to pay taxes to the British Government without their consent. Troops were dispatched to force the settlers into submission and the American War of Independence began. Brotherhood-style secret societies with the familiar initiations and methods were already at work in the Americas before the European invasion, but after that their numbers simply exploded and they were extremely involved in the events before the American War of Independence. Freemasonry abounded and George Washington was a leading freemason of high rank, initiated into the Craft at the age of twenty in 1752. As an officer in the colonial army, he is believed by some historians to have ordered the killing of French troops in the Ohio Valley when there was no military justification, let alone a moral one. This created more conflict between the British and French which flared in Europe as the bitter and bloody Seven Years War. This claimed around a million military and civilian casualties and left both countries with enormous debts to the money inventors, the banking elite controlled by the Brotherhood. There was also the cost of keeping an army in America. All this led the British to levy higher taxation on her people, and duties on goods in the American colonies, to service the debt, and hence you had the disputes that fuelled the War of Independence. The resistance in the colonies was so fierce that the British withdrew the new duties, except for those on tea. The colonists were by now whipped up by the Freemason lodges masquerading as revolutionary groups and this was coordinated from the Mother Lodge in London. Members of the St Andrew's Lodge in Boston dressed up as Indians and threw tea into the harbour in protest at the duty and, no matter what the British had done, it was too late. The Brotherhood wanted independence for America for longer-term motives and that was the way it was going to be. It is pretty clear that the Freemasons had been working to stir up revolution against the British for at least ten years before the war began, and had been guided by the Brotherhood elite in London.

The war was fought over six years until the Americans won and the British were sent packing. George Washington was Commander in Chief of the American troops and he was to become the first President of the newly-formed United States of America. He was a freemason as I have pointed out and so were most, perhaps all, of the key revolutionaries; many of them were Grand Masters. Masons like Washington and Franklin had the symbol of the All Seeing Eye sewn onto their sheepskin Masonic aprons. This was without question a Brotherhood revolution. Independence was declared in 1776, although the war went on for some years after that, until the decisive Battle of Yorktown in 1781 settled the issue of who would rule the country. The Americans were supported with arms and resources by the French after one of the revolutionaries, the freemason, Benjamin Franklin, persuaded them to help. The French were looking for some revenge for their defeats by the British and, even if they were not, the Brotherhood network in France would have made sure that help was forthcoming. Franklin secured the services in France of the German freemason Baron von Steuben who had served in the army of Frederick the Great of Prussia and he was to play a major part in turning the American army into a fighting force. With victory secured the Declaration of Independence severed ties with Britain, but not the British Brotherhood.

The symbols of the new nation reflected those of the Brotherhood and its branches which had brought it into being. In 1782 a man called William Barton produced a design for the Seal of the new United States and it included the classic symbols of the Brotherhood since ancient Egypt – the pyramid topped by an all-seeing eye. Below that were the words *Novus Ordo Seclorum* which mean 'A new order of the ages'. This refers to the Brotherhood's 'Great Work of Ages' and it is expressed today as The New World Order. This part of Barton's design is included in the United States Great Seal today, and on the dollar bill. The phoenix, another Egyptian Brotherhood symbol, was also on the original seal before it was later replaced by the Eagle. American Freemasonry broke away from its 'Mother Lodge' in England after independence and adopted the English York Rite of Freemasonry with its ten degrees of initiation and most significantly, the Scottish Rite, with its thirty-three degrees. The Scottish rite in particular has had a fundamental influence on American politics, economics, and foreign policy from that time on. The Brotherhood controls the American banks and the Federal Reserve, their version of the Bank of England, which creates money out of nothing and plays the tune to which the elected politicians have to dance. That is not to say that all the revolutionaries were involved in skullduggery and wished to bring about this abuse of freedom or that the desire for revolution was wrong. Why should one country own another in that way? Most if not all the revolutionaries would have believed they were doing the right thing for the right reasons, but who was controlling their thinking from the perspective of another agenda? It is not always the event itself that is wrong, but the hidden agenda behind it.

One man who played an important part in the fight for American independence could rightly be included among the great men of human history. If ever there was an example of the volunteer consciousness incarnate, it is he. Thomas Paine was born the son of a Norfolk Quaker in 1736. His outspoken support of the oppressed in England and his opposition to religion made him highly unpopular with the authorities and he went to America to support the people in their dispute with the British Parliament and King George III. He fought on the American side and published a pamphlet called 'Common Sense' which called for complete independence for the colonies and not some diluted compromise that would still leave them under British rule. Another pamphlet, 'The Crisis', motivated the people to go on when the situation looked bleak. His words were widely read and they are credited with having a significant impact on the course of the War.

He was a renowned figure when independence was won, but instead of enjoying the glory he returned home to England hoping to do the same there. He wrote *The Rights of Man* in 1791 which exposed the corruption and nonsense of Church, monarch, and state, while setting out an alternative society based on democracy, education and equal rights for all. This was the time after the French Revolution when the British gentry were terrified of a people's rebellion. A writ was issued for his arrest, but his work circulated rapidly among the poor who at last had someone speaking for them. Anyone found publishing or possessing *The Rights of Man* was jailed or banished and effigies of Paine with a rope around his neck were carried through the streets by those whose power he threatened. He was a man ahead of his time, but such men are vital to light the fuse which later explodes into fundamental change. Paine escaped to France where he was elected to the new French Assembly. He was appointed to the committee putting together a new French Constitution and he argued that there should be no bloodshed or reprisals against the monarchy and aristocracy. He wanted to destroy the institutions of repression, not kill the people in them. When he voted against the killing of King Louis XVI he was arrested and sentenced to death. Here we are again with one tyranny and rule by fear replacing another. George Washington was asked for help, but refused and it took the efforts of others to win his release a year later. During his captivity he wrote his book, *The Age of Reason*, which dismantled the preposterous claims of Christianity which he said were not the work of God, but of stupid men. His book said of the Bible:

"Whenever I read the obscene stories, the voluptuous debaucheries, the cruel and tortuous executions, the relentless vindictiveness with which more than half the Bible is filled, it would be more consistent if we call it the word of demon than the word of God. It is a history of wickedness that has served to corrupt and brutalise Mankind. And for my part, I detest it as I detest everything that is cruel."

Thomas Paine was a great, great, man. 'The world is my country and to do good is my religion', he once said, and the only trinity he had any time for was Truth, Liberty, and Justice. Yet history has largely forgotten him because no juvenile religion was set up in his name. In Christendom you could call for political liberty if it suited the people, but not for religious liberty. When Paine returned to America after the publication of the book he was shunned by those he had helped to free. In some areas it was even dangerous for him to walk down the street. But then he was used to religious opposition in America, because in earlier times they had opposed his opposition to slavery. The United States was built on the backs of black slaves from Africa. Slavery had been part of human life through most of history and some of the popes were the biggest slave owners of their day. The idea of the chosen ones having God's permission to own the heathens was a constant justification. In the Bible we read:

"Both thy bondsmen and thy bondsmaids, which thou shalt have, shall be of the heathen that are round about you; of them shall ye buy bondsmen and bondsmaids. Moreover, of the children of the strangers that do sojourn among you, of them shall ye buy; and of their families that are with you, which they begat in your land; and they shall be your possession. And ye shall take them as an inheritance for your children after you, to inherit them for a possession; they shall be your bondsmen forever."

That is from Leviticus, and these are the words of St Paul:

"Slaves obey your Earthly masters with respect and fear. And with sincerity of heart as you would obey Christ. Obey them not only to win their favour when their eye is on you, but like slaves of Christ, doing the

will of God from your heart."

The Christian creed had no problem with slavery. It was God's will. Hundreds of thousands of native Africans were captured by the slave ships of Britain, America, and elsewhere and taken to the New World to be sold to the highest bidder. The hymn writer, John Newton, was the master on a slave ship and from his pen came 'How sweet the name of Jesus sounds in a believer's ear'. Opponents to this stunning inhumanity called slavery were hung, shot, and burned alive by the slave owning mobs and sermons were made in support of both slavery and the violence against protesters. It was a major offence to teach a slave to read, and there were discussions on whether it was best to work a slave to death or use them more sparingly so they would last longer. (The same debate went on in relation to the Jews in Nazi Germany). The law allowed slaves to be flogged to death and shot if they refused to accept the flogging. Their tongues and eyes were cut out on many occasions and they were branded if they tried to escape. The British were at the heart of this trade and many British companies grew wealthy on it. The British built forts off the African Coast to protect the slave traffic and they gave grants of free land in the West Indies on condition that at least four negro slaves were kept for every hundred acres.

Slavery became an issue which divided the United States very roughly between North and South. Most Freemason lodges supported it, but many did not. By far the greatest number of slaves were concentrated in the Southern States where they worked in the cotton fields. Some brave people helped a few escape to Canada at great risk to themselves. Among them was John Brown, an Ohio wool dealer, who was caught and executed. He became a martyr remembered by the famous song in which 'his soul goes marching on'. William Lloyd Garrison published *The Liberator* which highlighted the treatment of the slaves and was sent to prison for his opinions, but it roused yet more to the cause. Harriet Beecher Stowe wrote her book, *Uncle Tom's Cabin,* published in 1852, telling the stories she had heard from the slaves who had escaped. The Pope ordered the book to be banned and the clergy condemned its publication.

In the 1860 presidential election, Abraham Lincoln, an abolitionist, was elected. The South declared independence under its own president, Jefferson Davis, and they increased the powers of slave owners. The United States were now anything but united. They were two nations, one overwhelmingly for slavery and one against. Lincoln, whose desire for the end of slavery was not as fierce as some, offered to allow it to continue if the South would return, but they didn't trust him. The Civil War ensued but, contrary to what is widely believed, it was not about the plight of slaves, but the unity of the country. It was like most conflicts, justified by a contradiction. Lincoln and his supporters went to war to preserve the union under the banner of freedom. But while the behaviour of the Southern States was appalling to the slaves, they had every right under the Constitution to withdraw from the union. Lincoln and the North fought to deny them that right. The emancipation of slaves was a by-product of the war, not the motivation behind it. Slavery continued in the North until the war was over, and legislation to free Southern slaves during the war was enacted only because it was claimed that the Southerners were no longer United States citizens, and therefore had lost their rights to own slaves as those in the North continued to do.

The South, the 'rebels' or 'Confederates' held the initiative in the first phases of the war but, after losing the Battle of Gettysburg in 1863, the North, the 'Federalists', turned the tide and went on to victory. By then half a million people had died at a cost of nearly two billion pounds to the US economy and the belief that a state could decide at will to withdraw from the Union as agreed by the Founding Fathers was crushed. The United States was now a nation, as were Germany and Italy in the wake of their civil wars which happened in this same period. The USA would produce great inventors and many skilled in trade and business as they exploited and directed the Industrial Revolution to become the world's most powerful country. Abraham Lincoln was assassinated in 1865. He was about to introduce a system in which the US government printed its own interest-free money, independent of the banking elite. Almost exactly 100 years later, John F. Kennedy was planning to do the same when he was murdered in Dallas.

The tragic victims of the expansion across the North American continent in both the United States and Canada were the native tribes. They were pushed into the interior by the settlers who advanced westwards until there was nowhere left for the Indians to go. When they lost the many battles to retain their homelands they were forced onto reservations which were, themselves, gradually reduced by the economic 'needs' of the government. White men

did indeed speak with forked tongue when they made their promises to the Indians which were never kept. The story of the genocide of the native Americans by the settlers from Europe is one of
the most atrocious episodes in the long and sorry tale of man's
inhumanity to man. The reality of these events is only now beginning to be told in films like 'Dances With Wolves' and the truth is
breaking through the Hollywood and government propaganda of
most of this century which portrayed the Indians as savages and
the God-fearing settlers as the agents of freedom and civilisation.
In Australia and the other countries where invading Christians
occupied native lands by force and brutality the truth of these times
is being more widely understood.

In my travels to Canada and the United States I have had the
overwhelming feeling that I have had many past lives as an
Indian. When I was in Calgary, Canada, I saw a picture of a chief
and I felt a strong and instinctive bond with him. His name was
'Sitting on an Eagle Tail', chief of the North Peigans, one of a
group of tribes that went under the overall name of Blackfoot.
Just to complicate matters there was also an individual tribe in
the group also called the Blackfoot. I travelled through an area
known as the Porcupine Hills, south of Calgary near the Old
Man River and I have rarely been so moved by a place anywhere
in the world. My spirit just sang with joy. I would later discover
that Eagle Tail was one of those who signed the land treaty with
the white settlers which put the Indian tribes onto reservations
and that he had chosen an area around the Porcupine Hills and
the Old Man River. He loved the area and felt it was the best
place for his people to settle. I talk more of these experiences in
Truth Vibrations and *In The Light Of Experience*. Two years after
that trip to Canada, I was walking through Oxford with Yeva
looking for the Pitt Rivers Museum which has a section dedicated to Indian history. We were given the wrong directions to
the Museum and we were lost. As we walked I told her about
Sitting on an Eagle Tail and how I felt that was a previous
incarnation. At that moment we passed a pub called 'The Eagle
and the Child'. I looked up at the pub sign hanging from the
wall. There before me was a picture of an eagle with a little child
sitting on its tail! I have had scores of 'coincidences' happen to
me since my awakening became conscious in 1990, but that was
a real stunner.

I began to read widely of the Indian period in North America and, as with my visits to former Indian lands, I have felt a deep and painful sadness at the way that culture and understanding was swept away in such a short time. When I visited former Indian lands around Sedona in Arizona, Monument Valley in Utah, and a wonderful place called Enchanted Rock in Texas, I was very affected emotionally by their beauty and the memories of my Indian lives. I felt such joy. But underlying that has always been sadness at what happened. I read a book about the life of the Blackfoot Chief, Crowfoot, which also spanned the lifetime of Eagle Tail. It was sobering to see that when they were born the Indian way of life had remained virtually unchanged for thousands of years; by the time they died in the latter part of the last century, their tribes were dependent on hand-outs from the white settlers. Their lands had been taken and their independence was gone. These proud people were lining up on their little reservations to be given their rations. The Christian missionaries had arrived seeking to impose their creed upon the Indian people. The 'God-fearers' were rampant and some of the most tragic and pathetic pictures I have seen are of Indian people, Bibles in hand and assembled in their Sunday best, waiting to be indoctrinated and mind-controlled in the mission churches built on their reservations. Nearly fifteen hundred years after the nonsense of Nicaea, it was now spreading its arrogance and mind control across North America which, until then, had somehow managed to survive very nicely without it.

It was only in 1877 that Crowfoot and Eagle Tail had, with others, signed the land treaty that confined them to reservations which the settlers would go on diminishing whenever they could. By then their tribes had been ravaged by war and diseases like smallpox which the settlers had brought with them. Every picture I have seen of Eagle Tail portrays a near-broken spirit and, given what happened in his lifetime, that is easy to understand.

They had been the victims of the industrialisation of the world that had begun in Britain and spread like a cancer across Europe. The influx of settlers from Europe who emigrated in increasing numbers to the 'New World' took with them that same religious intolerance and economic ethos or imported it once they were there. The Luciferic consciousness was now unleashing everything it could muster before the time of the Great Cleansing which was fast approaching. Much of the human race was easy prey, and it was rapidly discovering the means to destroy itself and the planet, too.

9

The Rule of Science

THE Brotherhood had grown enormously in numbers and power over the six thousand years since Sumer and Egypt and it was now to enter a new phase in its desire for world domination.

It inspired scores of 'people's revolutions' and civil wars to replace the monarchies and it achieved this in the normal way – by working through both sides to create the conflict and the atmosphere of unrest. Sometimes the monarch would hold on, more often the revolution would usher in a people's dictatorship or 'democratic government'. The Brotherhood could work more covertly behind the smokescreen of democracy, but it wished to ensure that enough 'bogeymen' existed around the world to unite people in mutual fear. People in fear are so much easier to control, as we shall see. It also had a longer term aim to replace traditional religion with the Godless version of science called materialism. This was the final stage of the Brotherhood plan to persuade people that they were just physical, one-life, accidents, with no spirit or eternal purpose. The more that people can be encouraged to think that way the more they become locked in materialism and lose touch with who they are. In that state of mind they are perfectly placed to become the robots of the Brotherhood by closing down their connections with higher levels of themselves and Creation.

In the late 1800s some documents surfaced called the Protocols of the Wise Men of Zion. Almost everything these documents proposed to do has happened in this century. It is quite amazing to read them. According to the book, Waters Flowing Eastward, they surfaced in the late 19th Century. In 1884, Mlle. Justine Glinka, the daughter of a Russian General, was involved in some spying and information gathering in France. She employed a member of the Mizraim Freemasonry Lodge in Paris to help with her work and he offered, for a payment of 2,500 francs, to get her a copy of some secret documents, the Protocols of the Wise Men of Zion. A copy found its way from her to a Professor Sergius A. Nilus and he published them in them in a book called *The Great Within the Small*. After the Russian Revolution of 1917, the "revolutionaries" ordered that all Nilus's books on the subject were destroyed and he was arrested and tortured, the book says.

The Protocols have caused enormous controversy throughout this century and there have been many claims that they are forgeries, including a famous article in the London *Times* in 1921. I can understand, too, why many Jewish people get so angry about them when you think how Adolf Hilter used the Protocols and their reference to Zion to justify his unspeakable treatment of Jews in the concentration camps. How ironic to think, therefore, that, as we shall see, Hitler was brought to power by the very Brotherhood elite whose game plan for the world is so brilliantly set out in those Protocols.

Let us get one thing very clear. The conspiracy I am exposing *is not, repeat not, a conspiracy by the Jewish people and few have suffered as much as the Jews in Germany and elsewhere from Brotherhood-engineered events.*

But if we are going to pick the truth from the falsehood, the wheat from the chaff, we must be adult enough, surely, to see the difference between the *content* of the Protocols and the people given the *blame* for them. If we don't we will throw the baby out with the bath water which is exactly what the manipulators want us to do. We also need to appreciate the difference between the Jewish people as a *race* and Zionism which is a *political movement*. You don't have to be Jewish to be a Zionist and many people who call themselves Zionists are not Jewish. It is possible that the reference to Zion in the Protocols is calculated disinformation designed to blame it all, quite wrongly, on Jewish people and in that sense they may well be forgeries. But from the perspective of the 1990s it is painfully obvious that whoever wrote the protocols was either a prophet of extraordinary powers, or, rather more likely, they knew the Brotherhood game plan for the 20th Century.

It is on that basis, and that basis alone, that I will use passages from the Protocols in the next few chapters. I will refer to them as the Illuminati Protocols to overcome the myth that they are the work of the Jewish people and from this point I will also use the name Illuminati to describe the Brotherhood elite at the top of the Pyramid of secret societies world-wide. At that Illuminati level, all the secret societies become the SAME organisation. The word Goyim in the Protocols means non-Jew or Gentile but, again, it is more accurate to read this word as cattle or mob, the terms the Protocols also use to describe the mass of the people. The Protocols acknowledge the Brotherhood's role in the overthrow of the monarchies:

"On the ruins of the natural and genealogical aristocracy of the Goyim we have set up the aristocracy of our educated class, headed by the aristocracy of money. The qualifications for this aristocracy we have established in wealth, which is dependent on us . . . . " (Protocol 1).

"Remember the French Revolution, to which it was we who gave the name of 'Great': the secrets of its preparations are well known to us, for it was all the work of our hands. Ever since that time we have been leading the people from one disenchantment to another." (Protocol 3).

The great majority of people who campaigned for the end of the monarchies and against the imposition of religion, have done so with the finest of intentions, and it was exactly what needed to happen. The Brotherhood was often pushing against an open door with that part of its plan, because people were getting fed up with Church and monarchs. But while most campaigners wanted to replace both with true freedom for the human mind and true democracy, the Brotherhood Illuminati elite had other ideas. It used popular sentiment to overthrow monarchs and reduce the credibility of the Church, but then used its power to replace them with an illusion of democracy and a science which denied that people have any other dimension, apart from the physical body.

"The abstraction of freedom has enabled us to persuade the mob in all countries that their government is nothing but the steward of the people who are the owners of the country and that the steward may be replaced like a worn out glove. It is this possibility of replacing the representatives of the people which has placed them at our disposal and, as it were, given us the power of appointment . . . . The (politicians) whom we shall choose from among the public, with strict regard to their capabilities for servile obedience, will not be persons trained in the arts of government and will therefore easily become pawns in our game in the hands of learning and genius who will be their advisors, specialists bred and reared from early childhood to rule the affairs of the whole world." (Protocol 2).

"In order that our scheme may produce this result we shall arrange elections in favour of such presidents as have in their past some dark,

undiscovered stain, some "Panama" or other – then they will be trustwor-
thy agents for the accomplishment of our plans out of fear of revelations and
from the natural desire of everyone who has attained power, namely, the
retention of privileges, advantages, and honour connected with the office of
President." (Protocol 10).

Freemasonry was to undergo a significant change after the English
Civil War and into the early 1700s. It was opened up to more
people who were not masons or craftsmen by profession and soon
they would be by far the majority. In 1717 a new Grand Lodge was
launched at a meeting in London and some were to call this the
Mother Grand Lodge of the World. This was the lodge the American freemasons were guided by during the War of Independence.
Indeed the London Lodge string-pulled that revolution. The old
links with the profession of masonry became purely symbolic with
titles like Entered Apprentice, Fellow order and Master Mason, no
longer relating in any way to the masons work, but only to the
levels of initiation within the new Freemasonry, the so-called three
Blue Degrees. The Mother Grand Lodge quickly expanded its
influence across Europe and the British Empire, issuing permission
for other branches to practice the Blue Degree System. In Scotland, Michael Ramsey would establish another branch of Freemasonry based on the old Knights Templar system, and what
became known as the Scottish Degrees or Rites of Freemasonry
would go on to become the dominant form of the Order. Today
the Scottish Rite, with the thirty-three degrees of initiation, is
behind the Freemasonic mafia that controls the USA and many
other countries from behind the scenes today.

"We shall create and multiply freemasonic lodges in all countries of the
world, absorb into them all who may become or who are prominent in
public activity, for in these lodges we shall find our principle intelligence
office and means of influence. All these lodges we shall bring under one
central administration, known to us alone and to all others absolutely
unknown, which will be composed of our learned elders (Illuminati) . . . .
In these lodges we shall tie together the knot which binds together all
revolutionary and liberal movements. Their composition will be made up
of all strata of society. The most secret political plots will be known to us
and will fall under our guiding hands on the very day of their conception."
(Protocol 15).

The English Civil War brought a temporary end to the monarchy and even in the longer term, dramatically reduced its power. The Royalists (Anglicans) were defeated by the Roundheads (Nonconformists) and Charles I was executed in 1649. The first attempt at government by the people was in fact government by Oliver Cromwell, a morose Puritan squire who ruled as Lord Protector with the support of his army. He banned Anglican services and continued penal laws against the Catholics. Cromwell purged nonbelievers in his view of Christianity and continued the dreadful treatment of the Irish, while also abolishing amusements, the arts, fun, laughter, and affection. This is how the Puritans interpreted the Bible. Laughter and happiness were a sin. They remind me of those signs you see sometimes in comic stories which say: No dancing, no singing, no laughing, no nuffin'. They accepted and expanded upon the beliefs of Calvinism, and they promoted the extraordinary claims that war and conflict were signs of spiritual salvation, because it was evidence of the struggle to remove Satan from the Earth. Peace meant that Satan was not being challenged! Such thinking governed Britain at this time and would, as we have seen, also be exported to America with the Puritan 'pilgrims'. After Cromwell died in 1658, Parliament invited the exiled son of Charles I to take the throne as Charles II on the understanding that there would be religious tolerance. He agreed, but then began a reign of persecution against the Puritans and those who didn't worship the Anglican Faith. Tens of thousands of Nonconformists were killed, tortured, or shipped off as slaves to the colonies. In Scotland they still call this period the Killing Time. What Charles II really wanted to do was return Britain to the Roman Catholic Faith.

This story of Britain is the story of the world. It was going on everywhere with one faith persecuting another over the interpretation of a flawed and largely invented book. Almost everything emerged from religion or the battle against religious tyranny. The two political parties at the time were divided on religious lines. The Tories (now Conservatives) were Anglicans while the Whigs were largely Nonconformists. Through these decades of terrible religious intolerance and unrepresentative parliaments, many individuals made their contributions to human consciousness. Isaac Newton made several important scientific discoveries. He studied astronomy and advanced the development of the telescope. When he saw an apple fall from a tree it triggered a line of thought which led to his identifying the law of gravity. But he was also very much involved with the Brotherhood as a grand master of the Priory of Sion. Further discoveries by his successors would undermine the claims of religion. Writers like John Milton and John Bunyan opposed the behaviour of the Church and state, and Bunyan spent twelve years in Bedford Jail for refusing to accept the Anglican Faith. George Fox founded the Society of Friends (Quakers). He argued against the Church dictatorship and urged toleration, mercy and peace. The Quakers have largely been the acceptable face of religion, opposing slavery and persecution. Fox was jailed for blasphemy and thousands of his supporters suffered the same fate.

The Whigs were behind the next 'coup' on the British people. When Charles II died in 1685, his brother, James II began a bloody three year reign of terror which failed in its avowed attempt to restore Papal power to Britain when he was overthrown by the 'Glorious Revolution' of 1688. The Whigs, a powerful group of English and Scottish Protestants, may have been a British political party, later to become the Liberals, but they were actually based in Holland. They had close links with the Dutch House of Orange and with William, Prince of Orange, who had married Mary, the daughter of James II. The House of Orange, like the German royal family, often used marriage to expand its power and effect bloodless takeovers of other countries. Another branch of the Brotherhood was set up to put William on the British throne. It was called the Orange Order and this still continues, particularly in Northern Ireland. It is one of the secret societies which fuelled the fires of the Northern Ireland conflict. The Orange Order was pledged to make sure that Britain remained a Protestant country, and it was based on the principles of Freemasonry, an order of which William was almost certainly a member. William was to treat Irish Catholics so badly that the hatred of him there still festers through the generations.

He was crowned William III and ruled over both Britain and Holland. His wife became Mary II. It was now that the Bank of England was created in the image of the Bank of Amsterdam and the Brotherhood control of the financial system took a mighty step forward. The Bank of England scheme was presented by William Paterson, a Scot, but the British parliament was not terribly keen on the idea. They were, however, trapped by the Brotherhood. William and Mary had started a war with Catholic France and they orchestrated other conflicts also. These were costing the country so much of its wealth that Britain was in terrible debt. They could not put up taxes any higher without fear of rebellion, so they reluctantly accepted the Bank of England which would then issue lots of bits of paper representing money that did not exist and charge interest to the government (the people) for doing so. As William Bramley writes in *The Gods of Eden:*

"The standard practice of bankers during that period was to issue notes four or five times in excess of their precious metals. The Bank of England, however, issued an incredible multiplication of 16²/₃rds. The British Government agreed to borrow those notes and honour them as legal money for use in its purchases. The government accepted this plan because the government was not required to repay the initial loan, only the interest on the loan. Would not the Bank of England lose money on such a deal?"

Not at all.

"The face value of the loan notes were many times in excess of the value of the actual assets on which the notes were based. The interest on the loan in just one year surpassed the total value of the precious metals of the Bank of England! Specifically, the financiers had put together a total base of £72,000 of actual gold and silver. By issuing notes valued at 16²/₃ times the base, the bank was able to make a loan of £1,200,000 in paper money. The yearly interest was 8¹/₃% which equalled £100,000. This amounted to a profit of £28,000, or 39% in just one year!"

And who paid for that, and still pays for this system of legalised theft today? The people. In toil, sweat, and suffering. Another Scot, John Law, an agent of the Brotherhood, would later become the Finance Minister of France. He set up a similar central bank there with disastrous consequences for the economy when too many notes were issued and they subsequently became worth less money. More of them were required to buy goods and services and this is the nightmare called inflation.

With the death of William, his wife's sister Anne took the throne. She was succeeded by the German House of Hanover, from which the House of Windsor, Britain's present royal family, descends. The first Hanoverian King, George I, couldn't even speak English! The Hanoverians were not welcomed by the people who could not see why Germans should be on the British throne. This allowed the House of Hanover to work a nice little earner.

They refused to have a large British army, because they said they feared a coup given their unpopularity. And so they enlisted mercenary soldiers from their German homeland at a massive cost to the British people and at a large profit to themselves.

At least religious persecution now began to diminish. It would not disappear, but it would start to fade. It took nearly another hundred years for Roman Catholics to be allowed to worship in public and the Irish had to wait for this right until 1829. The legal prejudice against Nonconformist Protestants lasted even longer. They were not allowed to sit in Parliament until 1828 and the Anglican Universities of Oxford and Cambridge were only opened to them in 1871.

The Pope's control of Britain was removed by Henry VIII and his daughter, Elizabeth I. Now the power of the monarchs to rule as the representative of God was similarly curtailed, as parliaments took over Government. But these were grossly unrepresentative parliaments and there was little liberation for the masses. You will identify many themes running through this very brief history. One is that those who fight for change in the name of freedom often have no regard for the freedom of others once they are in power. Catholics persecuted Protestants only for Protestants to persecute them when the opportunity arose. You still see this in tit-for-tat killings in today's trouble spots. The gentry campaigned for parliamentary freedom and the end of royal dictatorship, only to deny democratic and human rights to those who might vote them out of power. The parliamentary gentry ran the country for themselves, the Church, and, although many will not have realised it, the Brotherhood.

Most people were in grinding poverty. There were no schools although the money could always be found to fight wars of acquisition and to build churches. Lives were hard and short while Britain's privileged grew richer and the empire expanded. This continued into the 19th century. Boys and girls of five were being forced to work up to ninety hours a week and were often beaten if they fell asleep. Starving children were left to die in the gutter. They were sent up chimneys to clean them and, together with women, worked down the mines earning money for the Anglican Church. The Church received royalties on the profits of many pits and in Northumberland and Durham alone this was earning them £400,000 a year. This is still a lot of money today, but then it was a staggering sum. No wonder the Church hierarchy never complained at the treatment of the children, women and miners. It was left to radicals who were often non-believers to put humanity and compassion ahead of religious doctrine. Not so the Church. As long as the poor wretches had agreed to be baptised, they were saved for all eternity, so why bother trying to improve their lot on Earth? What was happening to them was God's will.

At one time 223 offences were punishable by death, including stealing a handkerchief or anything worth over five shillings. Edmund Burke, the Whig politician and philosopher, reckoned it was possible to get anything through parliament that carried the death penalty. People, including children, were flogged in the streets and hanged in public. It was only in the 1960s that Britain abolished the death penalty. Many countries and some American states continue to indulge in this barbarism. Into the 19th century wives were still being sold to the highest bidder in British markets and the treatment of women in general was shocking in its inhumanity. The prisons were full of 'debtors' – people who could not afford to feed their families. The poor people couldn't go to law to fight their case, because the legal system was there primarily to provide an income for the legal profession – and control the people. It had nothing to do with justice. Widows and children of the poor were thrown out of their homes when their husbands or parents died. Beggars filled the streets.

This was the world which 1,500 years of Christianity had visited upon Britain and the rest of Christendom. And where were the shouts of protest from the Church? Silence.

Into the last century, Christendom was no further advanced than the Babylonians had been 5,000 years earlier. When Robert Raikes began to organise schools to teach children to read and write on Sundays (their only day off) the Anglican Church opposed them because some of the teachers were Nonconformists. In the 19th century Hannah More was prosecuted by an Ecclesiastical Court for her attempts at educating people. The clergy believed that everything anyone needed to know was in the Bible and they also realised that education was bad news for them. If people started to think for themselves it was goodbye Church power. A bill of 1807 to introduce state education which was passed by the House of Commons was blocked by the Bishops in the House of Lords. This when only one in seventeen people in England could write. The efforts of other reformers like Joseph Lancaster to educate the young so frightened the Church that it began to take an interest in schools. It knew these non-believing reformers would insist on the teaching of knowledge and reason, not theology. Once the Church realised that education was now inevitable, it wanted to gain control of the curriculum. Still today in England we have Church of England controlled schools in some areas with the local vicar on the Board of Governors. The Bishops in the House of Lords also opposed every Reform Bill designed to widen the franchise and give people a greater say in who governs them. They even opposed legislation to abolish the death penalty for thefts of more than five shillings. The Christian Church civilised the world??

The credibility of the Church was fatally breached during the Victorian era in Britain which accelerated the emergence of scientific explanations for what had hitherto been explained by ludicrous theology. The Church was now fighting a rearguard action trying to stay upright as the ground slipped beneath its feet. Tradition and the close links of Church and state maintained its privileges and influence and this continues to the present day, but its power to dictate was fading.

Unfortunately, most of the scientists who were undermining religion's credibility with their claims and discoveries, people like Charles Darwin and countless others, were going too far in the other direction. They didn't realise, and most of their successors still don't, that the evolution of the physical body and that of the eternal us, the consciousness which activates the physical body, are not the same. We were now being offered a choice between the ridiculous contentions of Christianity which were fast losing ground, and the materialist scientists who claimed that the physical world is all that exists and life after death is a myth. This view, which to me is as equally bereft of credibility as religion, remains the stance of the scientific establishment to this day, though not for much longer. It was also exactly what the Brotherhood elite wanted to happen as a key part of its New World Order. A world without God or belief in an eternal self was its ambition, even though it knew and knows the truth of who we really are. Religion would continue to be used when appropriate, but the aim was really to replace that with the view of a godless science in the minds of the people.

"It is with this object in view that we are constantly, by means of our press, arousing a blind confidence in these (scientific) theories. The intellectuals of the Goyim will puff themselves up with their knowledge and

*without any logical verification of it will put into affect all the information available from science, which our agentur specialists have cunningly pieced together for the purpose of **educating their minds in the direction we want.** Do not suppose for a moment that these statements are empty words: think carefully of the successes we arranged for Darwinism . . . . "* (Protocol 2).

". . . . It is indispensible to undermine all faith, to tear out of the minds of the Goyim the very principle of Godhead and the spirit, and to put in its place arithmetical calculations and material needs." (Protocol 4).

Are you listening university lecturers, science students and establishment scientists? You have been and continue to be duped. The British Prime Minister, Benjamin Disraeli, could see some of what was going on when he said this in the House of Commons in July 1856:

"There is in Italy a power which we seldom mention in this House. I mean the secret societies..It is useless to deny, because it is impossible to conceal that a great part of Europe, the whole of Italy and France, and a great part of Germany, to say nothing of other countries, is covered with a network of secret societies, just as the surfaces of the earth are covered with railroads. And what are their objects? ....They do not want constitutional government, they do not want ameliorated institutions..they want to change the tenure of the land, to drive out the present owners of the soil, and put an end to the ecclesiastical establishments. Some may even go further."

One of the groups in Italy he was referring to was the Mafia. Giuseppe Garibaldi, a thirty-third degree Mason and Grand Master of Italy, had led the rebellion in the Italian wars of unification. The Mafia, up until then a secret society resisting foreign rule in Sicily, supported him. The Mafia formed an underground government in Sicily and used criminal acts to undermine the foreign occupation. When Italy was unified, the Mafia became the underground terrorist and criminal movement it is today. One of the most notorious freemason lodges was also based in Italy. It was known as P2 and it controlled the Vatican.

We saw our familiar theme at work again in these Victorian and Edwardian times. The science which had for so long been suppressed and crushed by the Church, was winning its freedom to research and discover knowledge which the priests would rather have remained hidden. But, when open-minded scientists found evidence to challenge the materialist this-world-is-all-there-is view of the establishment scientists, their work was likewise suppressed and crushed by their own colleagues. Instead of one powerful interest group suggesting that reincarnation and eternal life for everyone did not exist, now there were two. The last thing the Brotherhood wanted was for the population to know the spiritual truths.

Both 'science' and religion were fierce in their opposition to the growth in interest in Spiritualism during the Victorian era. Mediums were, until 1951, liable to a fine and imprisonment for the crime of being a medium, but their art began to return to public attention thanks to the emergence of Spiritualism. The law of the land incorporated the Church's contention that contact with the 'dead' was impossible and therefore anyone claiming to do so must by definition be a fraud. Little did the people know that Queen Victoria had a medium working with her for many years after the death of her husband, Albert, the Prince Consort. Arthur Findlay revealed the story for the first time in *The Curse of Ignorance* in 1947. He was given the details by the daughter of James Robert Lees who, as a thirteen year old boy, was found to have outstanding psychic gifts. One communicator who claimed to be the entity who had been Prince Albert asked to be allowed to speak to Victoria.

The Queen, who had been grief-stricken by his death, heard of this and sent along two members of her court to investigate. They posed as members of the public who wanted to see what the boy could do. He began to channel Prince Albert, who proceeded to greet the two courtiers by their correct names and said he knew they had been sent by Victoria. He gave them information for the Queen that only he could have known. He also wrote a letter to her through the hand of Robert Lees, a process called automatic writing. The contents greatly impressed the Queen, and Robert was invited to meet her and channel Albert in her presence. She was not in the least fazed by all this, because she had experienced sittings with other mediums before the Prince's death. She invited Robert to become a permanent member of her court where he could channel her husband whenever she wished. But Albert said he could communicate through the son of a worker on her Balmoral estate, a man called John Brown. He was summoned, and a long relationship began between John and the Queen. Through him, Albert would advise her throughout the rest of her life. When

John Brown died the Queen wrote about him and intended to publish her work, but she was persuaded not to do so by her Private Secretary, Sir Henry Ponsonby, and by Dr. Davidson, the Dean of Windsor and later Archbishop of Canterbury. He had long opposed her interest in Spiritualism and threatened to resign as Court Chaplain if she published anything about John Brown. Ponsonby also destroyed Brown's private diaries to make sure the truth was never revealed.

Spiritualism, the belief in the ability to communicate with discarnate souls, had begun in the United States in the mid-1800s and spread to Europe. In Britain it had a number of famous advocates including the scientists Sir Oliver Lodge, Sir William Crookes, and Sir William Barrett, and the writers Victor Hugo and Sir Arthur Conan Doyle, author of the Sherlock Holmes stories. The scientists were dismissed by their fellows, but they had begun to understand the nature of vibrations and how many worlds could share the same space. Conan Doyle dedicated his later life to the cause of Spiritualism at a time when the escapologist, Houdini, was running a virtual witch-hunt against mediums in the United States.

In 1938, a committee appointed by the Church reported favourably on its investigations into Spiritualism, but Dr Lang the Archbishop of Canterbury refused to publish it. He was, however, quite happy to pass into the public arena the report of another committee at that time which supported belief in the Anglican Church's Thirty-nine Articles of Faith. As twenty-one of the twenty-five members of the committee were priests we should not be surprised at their verdict. If only Victoria and others had stood up and revealed their experiences and beliefs, the suppression of knowledge by Church and science would have been broken by now. Instead it is left to our generations to do it.

The movement and religion of Spiritualism deserves great credit for keeping the understandings alive in the face of tremendous opposition from the Church and materialist science. The scientists became dominant in the public mind, and although medicine progressed enormously in its understanding, it, too, failed to acknowledge that there is more to the human being than a physical body. Again the materialist view held sway in medicine and the foundations of the 'tradition' thus created are still with us today. The most important advances in human health were the improvement in sanitation and water supplies, although atrocious poverty and terrible living conditions remained the lot of the majority. This was despite the increasing wealth of the rich and the country in general gained through the exploitation of the people and the Empire. In this period from Victoria to the present day the world would discover the means of mass production; electricity; radio; television; the telephone; the aeroplane; spacecraft; the list goes on and on. The freedom of many human minds from the religious thought-police unleashed so much potential – more than the public have been told about, as we shall discuss later. But cleverness is one thing, wisdom quite another. The invention of the steam engine revolutionised production and the exploitation of oil would give us the petrol engine. All over the world inventions and discoveries were coming to light which changed the nature of work, life and the potential for both construction and catastrophe. I will look at the economic and environmental consequences of this in chapter 11, but here I wish to expand on the difference between cleverness and wisdom.

To unlock the secrets of nature's potential is clever, but it takes wisdom to (a) use that knowledge for positive and constructive purposes and (b) to have the humility to appreciate that there is always, but always, a great deal more to know. As Socrates said: "Wisdom is knowing how little we know". The scientist Carl Sagan was also correct when he pointed out that intellectual capacity is no guarantee against being dead wrong. The Victorian and post-Victorian world has not understood that and humility has rarely been a feature of the human condition among those in power. So the true nature of life and Creation went on being ignored by the Church and the scientific establishment, even though Socrates and Plato had known the basis of it in Ancient Greece. Cleverness without wisdom is also the bringer of war. Wise people would have used and expanded their gathering knowledge for the benefit of all, and by that I don't mean only those in their own country. All means all. Instead the collective mind of humanity was still reacting like a spoilt child being guided along a destructive path by the Illuminati elite.

Whatever is the dominating belief of the collective mind can have an enormous influence on the way individuals think. Unfortunately, as we have seen, the behaviour of Church, Brotherhood and State over the period covered in this book has programmed the collective consciousness to pass on its responsibility to think and act to others – the Pope, priests, kings and queens, dictators, gentry, bosses, the Bible, the Koran, whoever and whatever they can find. Humanity in general has been programmed to think and behave like robots and to indoctrinate their children to do the same. This they have done. When you look at all the slaughter, the invasions and counter-invasions, the bloody persecutions over minute differences in the same religious faith, the mass of the people never benefited from any of them. When a place was plundered by an army, the proceeds and the power didn't go to them, but to those they blindly followed and, increasingly, to those they didn't even know about. People may believe those days are over, but they're not, you know. There is still an enormous amount to do to free the human mind from subservience and indoctrination. Through the Victorian period while reforms were won by courageous and compassionate people under fierce opposition by the Church and other self-interest groups, the old beliefs were still there.

The tribes had become communities, then states, and now they had formed together into countries and nations. The way they came together was no foundation for their future peace and stability. Often it was the result of one religion or belief being imposed upon everyone through Brotherhood-inspired invasion or civil war, and the resentment simmered away until the oppressed could get their revenge, encouraged by other Brotherhood groups. Everyone believed that they were doing what was right without realising that a higher, secret force was pulling their strings and taking advantage of their sense of injustice. Some parts of Europe changed hands so many times they must have woken up in the morning and asked who was in charge that day. Among these political and military rugby balls were Bosnia, Serbia, Herzegovina and Montenegro, and the bitter resentment at this and each other has exploded again in this decade in a terrible religious and ethnic war. The Turks, Greeks, Germans, French, Italians, Spanish, British, Dutch, Russians, anyone with sufficient military muscle, fought and squabbled with each other over who should add different countries or regions to their empires of exploitation. School children arguing over sweets would have shown more maturity. The resentments and impositions this created are the cause of many ongoing conflicts and simmering feuds, in the Middle East, Europe, and elsewhere.

By the end of the 19th century this powder keg had to blow, and it did in a series of conflicts leading to the two World Wars. And the knowledge gained by materialist science was used to create weapons with a greater destructive potential than ever before.

10

The World at War

IN the early years of the 20th century, Brotherhood bankers and industrialists were expanding their control of the world financial system.

Two names were particularly prominent, the Rockefellers and the Rothschilds. The Rockefellers are one of America's best-known families. They became famous after John Davidson Rockefeller and his brother, William, made their fortune with the highly-controversial Standard Oil Company with its web of financial wheeler-dealing which no-one could fathom. J.D.Rockefeller's grandson, Nelson, would become a Vice-President of the United States and play a leading part behind the scenes, too, in the course of US politics.

The Rothschilds are a European banking dynasty started by Mayer Amschel Rothschild who was born in Germany in 1744. The name comes from the red (rot) shield on the house in a ghetto in which Mayer's ancestors once lived. By 1820, the Rothschild empire had branches in London, Paris, Vienna and Naples. They made vast profits from the Napoleonic and French Revolutionary Wars of 1792 to 1815 and had a very significant influence on the course of European history. They diversified into railways, coal and other industrial investments. The Rothschilds are well known for their enthusiastic support of Freemasonry. Mayer Amschel Rothschild summed up the approach of the Brotherhood bankers and the Illuminati elite when he said: "Give me control over a nation's currency, and I care not who makes the laws."

The Rockefeller and Rothschild empires will feature in the story from now on, but I want to stress most emphatically that I will be highlighting certain individual people and the way in which the empires have been used. I do not wish to suggest that everyone called Rockefeller or Rothschild is involved. Most of them will not know what is going on either.

At the centre of the gathering empire of the banking and industrial elite was the Round Table. This had been founded, quite
possibly with the best of intentions, by an Englishman, Cecil
Rhodes, after whom Rhodesia was named before its independence.
Supported by the Rothschild empire, he made a colossal fortune
exploiting the diamond reserves and resources of South Africa.
Rhodes often expressed a desire to stop wars by creating a world
government, centred on Britain, which could intervene in disputes
before they became violent. In 1891 he set up his now infamous
Round Table which was obviously inspired by the King Arthur
stories. It was designed on Brotherhood lines with secret rituals,
inner and outer circles, and much of the other paraphernalia of
such organisations. Among the supporters of the Round Table
were Lord Rothschild, head of the Rothschild empire in England,
and another English banker, Alfred Milner. But it was after
Rhodes died* in 1902 that the big switch was made and the
Illuminati, in classic fashion, hijacked his creation.

The international Brotherhood bankers began to give the Round
Table substantial financial support and these backers included the
Rockefellers. The Round Table was used to coordinate the activities of central banks and Brotherhood bankers across the world
and to increase enormously their influence on governments. The
Table created other branches to further, and also to mask, its
activities. Adam Weishaupt, a German professor who started a
famous branch of the Illuminati in 1776, said: "The great strength
of our Order lies in its concealment; let it never appear in its own
name, but always covered by another name, another occupation."
These 'front' organisations were to include the Council on Foreign
Relations in the United States, and, in the British Empire, the
Royal Institute of International Affairs. Both were created to direct
the foreign policy of governments to suit Brotherhood ambitions.
David Rockefeller was chairman of the Council on Foreign Relations for many years. Today it has infiltrated its people and policies
throughout United States government. This Brotherhood illuminati elite began to infiltrate the universities and the media, and
this is now widespread. It controls the media, for sure. Dr Carrol
Quigley wrote of this time:

* Cecil Rhodes bequeathed large sums of money to found the "Rhodes Scholarships" to
Oxford University for overseas students and to promote his belief in a one world
government. The most famous "Rhodes Scholar" today is Bill Clinton.

"There grew up in the 20th century a power structure between London and New York which penetrated deeply into university life, the Press, and the practice of foreign policy. In England the centre was the Round Table group, while in the United States it was J.P.Morgan and Company, or its local branches in Boston, Philadelphia, and Cleveland."

The aim of the Brotherhood banking and political network was to create a world financial system in which the central banks and other private banking interests would work together. They would coordinate their activities to control governments and economies by creating booms and busts, manipulating foreign exchanges and bribing politicians with well-paid jobs in the financial world. You can see all of these things happening daily every time you pick up a newspaper. The centre of this banking network was to be the Bank for International Settlements, based in Basle, Switzerland. Much of the manipulation of the world is coordinated from Switzerland so it is no mystery why that country is never invaded during Brotherhood-engineered wars. For Swiss 'neutrality' see 'protecting Brotherhood asset's and interests'. The overwhelming aim of this banking cartel was to create a situation in which governments were so deeply in debt to them that they had to do as the bankers demanded. Like lambs to the slaughter, governments all over the world have fallen for it, or, through Brotherhood channels, helped to arrange it, the United States more than anyone.

The idea of a central bank inventing money that doesn't exist has long been controversial in America. Two of its founding fathers, Thomas Jefferson and James Madison, wanted any such bank to be under government control. They could see the dangers of any other system. But another, Alexander Hamilton, was determined to create a Central Bank in private hands. His backers were reputed to be the Bank of England and the Rothschilds. By 1786, the US was plunged into its first major economic depression caused by the lending and interest policies of the money-out-of-nothing banks, including Hamilton's own Bank of New York. Heavy taxes were levied on the population to pay for the interest on bank loans to the federal government and the state authorities. Farmers were ruined by the banks and Captain Daniel Shay led two thousand desperate farmers to take over a number of towns in Massachusetts, most famously Worcester. They wanted an end to interest banking, but Shay's Rebellion, as it was termed, was put down.

When George Washington became President in 1789, he made Hamilton the Secretary to the Treasury. Two years later, Hamilton got his way when the Bank of the United States, the new nation's first central bank, opened its doors. It was privately owned, but the Government entrusted to it the country's finances. Only five years later, the taxes imposed on the people were so high, to pay the interest on borrowing from this bank, that farmers again rebelled, this time in western Pennsylvania. This so-called Whisky Rebellion was crushed on the orders of George Washington. The Bank of the United States lost its power in the 1830s when President Andrew Jackson won his 'bank war' against Nicholas Biddle, the president of the bank. But, early in the next century, this would be replaced by today's Federal Reserve system, the private banking network that controls the US economy for its own benefit.

President Woodrow Wilson came to office in 1909 and one of his close aides was a man called Colonel Edward House. It was House who actually controlled events and his masters were the Brotherhood banking interests, not the American people. His brief from the bankers was to ensure that the administration introduced the Federal Reserve system and the income tax bill known as the Federal Income Tax Amendment (the 16th Amendment to the American Constitution). This combination would be the means of controlling the US economy. The Federal Reserve would lend the government enormous amounts of largely-invented money to boost the economy and, when it suited the bankers, the Federal Income Tax Amendment would suppress the economy by raising taxation. The manner in which both were introduced raised much criticism. President Wilson must have had some idea of what was going on behind the scenes. He once talked of "A power so organised, so complete, so persuasive, that they had better not speak above their breaths when they speak in condemnation of it."

Persuading people to do what you want them to do, while believing they are doing the opposite is a method constantly used by the Brotherhood. The Federal Reserve Bill was painted as a measure to curtail the power of banking interests and those same publicly opposed the idea to add to the conjuring trick. The plot was hatched at a meeting of Illuminati bankers and industrialists at Jekyll Island, Georgia, towards the end of 1910. The location of the meeting was extremely symbolic in that, while the Brotherhood was playing Dr Jekyll, it was really Mr Hyde. The Federal Reserve

Bill was pushed through Congress in the last few days before Christmas 1913 and Congressman Charles A Lindbergh, senior, the father of the aviator, recognised the sleight of hand for what it was. He said that the financial insiders had only opposed the Federal Reserve legislation because they wished to promote the fiction that it was a 'People's Bill'. He added:

"This Act establishes the most gigantic trust on Earth......When the President signs this Act, the invisible government by the money power, proven to exist by the Money Trust Investigation will be legalised. The new law will create inflation whenever the trust wants inflation.

"The Federal Reserve was, and still is, hailed as a victory for democracy over the Money Trust. Nothing could be further from the truth. The whole Central Bank concept was engineered by the very group it was supposed to strip of power."

The Federal Reserve system has refused to be audited since the day it was formed. It is so important for everyone to lift their eyes from what appears to be a certain situation, because this type of double bluff is being used all the time to make us act in the interests of the Illuminati, while thinking we are doing the opposite. When the plan was first presented by the Republicans it was rejected by Congress. There was a feeling in the public mind that the Republicans were too close to banking interests. The Brotherhood had an answer for that. They got the Democrats to present it and it was passed! Only two states agreed to the Federal Income Tax Amendment and it required at least thirty-six if it was to be legally ratified. When this was obviously not going to happen, the Secretary of State, Filander Knox, simply told Congress in 1913 that the amendment had been ratified, even though it had not. From that moment, all the income tax paid under the Act through the Internal Revenue Service has been purely voluntary (although everyone is told it's the law) and all the money that people have been forced to pay by the IRS has been a theft! The IRS is a private organisation controlling the federal tax system of America, and it is a Brotherhood tool*. The financial network, led by the Rothschilds, the Rockefellers and others, was now in place for the biggest Brotherhood project so far – the First World War.

In the first years of this century a number of secret, mystical societies in Germany began to promote the idea of a master race.

* A secret document "Silent Weapons for Quiet Wars" reveals that the IRS passes personal details about American people to the Brotherhood manipulators.

They claimed the white Aryan race was superior to all the others and said the Germans were a part of that. The myth of the German Aryan master race had begun. An English-born writer, Houston Stewart Chamberlain, was a great supporter of this view. He believed that Germany could breed a super-race to lead Europe into a New Order. He was fiercely anti-Jewish.

Wilhelm II, the Kaiser of Germany, was another religious fanatic who believed he was God's representative on Earth. He was an avid reader of Chamberlain's work and met him to discuss their mutual belief that Germans were God's chosen people and should rule the whole of Europe, if not the world. He dismissed his Chancellor, Bismark, in 1890 and assumed control of the country. You would have thought the people would have resisted this but, once again, we see the consequences of human dependence on someone else to tell them what to do, which had been part of life for centuries. Wilhelm prepared for war. The Prussian Hohenzollern dynasty, of which Wilhelm was a member, had been encouraging the unification of Germany and building up its war machine for many years. There was an outbreak of conflicts around Europe rather like musical chairs. Alliances were agreed on religious and political grounds but, mostly, countries were looking around for allies to support them in the increasingly-likely event of attack. Wilhelm was waiting for any excuse to make his play for European domination, and it came in 1914. The mutual dislike between Austria and Serbia came to a head when the Archduke Ferdinand, the heir to the Austro-Hungarian throne, was assassinated in Sarajevo, the Bosnian capital. The Austrians accused the Serbs of involvement in the murder and sent an ultimatum. The Serbs agreed to all but two of its demands, and asked for those to be decided by arbitration. But the Austrians and Germans wanted a fight and Austria declared war on Serbia. Russia supported Serbia. Who actually killed Ferdinand to create the spark for what followed? A Serbian secret society called the Black Hand. Count Czerin, a friend of Ferdinand, said, "The Archduke knew quite well that the risk of an attempt on his life was imminent. A year before the war he informed me that the freemasons had resolved on his death".

Wilhelm declared war on Russia and France. His idea was that Germany would win a swift battle with France before turning its full might on Russia. The Germans invaded Belgium and entered France from the north. Britain declared war on Germany and the bloodiest conflict in human history was underway. Germany didn't win the quick victory over the French she had hoped for. It became a war of attrition in the trenches of Northern France. There, in the mud and desolation, European manhood died in its millions to win or defend a few acres of devastated land. Scientific knowledge was used to improve the efficiency with which humanity slaughtered each other, and never had this been achieved on a greater scale than this. The battles are written in the memory forever of anyone who wishes to see an end to the stupidity and manipulation that has diverted humankind from its true purpose. Verdun, the Somme, Passchendaele, saw millions killed on both sides, often in suicidal assaults on well-fortified trenches, on the orders of insane generals.

Turkey entered the war on Germany's side, but Italy supported Britain on the promise of being given Trentino and Trieste. They opened a front against Austria, while Britain was becoming increasingly stretched by the need to support the French Western Front and protect her interests in India and Egypt from the Turks. It was now that T.E.Lawrence, 'Lawrence of Arabia', organised a revolt by the Arabs against the Turks. The British went on to occupy Palestine, Jerusalem and Mesopotamia. The courage and determination of the Russian people in defending their land from the Germans, at a cost of four million casualties, had done much to stretch the German resources and reduce their ability to break through in France. But, in 1917, they agreed a peace treaty with Germany after the Russian revolution or, rather, the Russian Brotherhood Revolution.

There had been riots and unrest for a long time over the often cruel persecution of the people by the Tsars. There were strikes and mutinies in the Russian army, and Tsar Nicholas II was taken to Siberia where he and his family were executed by a bunch of extreme revolutionaries who were no more enlightened in their humanity than the Tsars they removed. The more moderate reformers were cast aside by the followers of Lenin and Trotsky. They abolished plans for a parliamentary constitution and imposed upon an already oppressed people the Communist State which replaced Tsarist fascism with state fascism. This had all the same economic and political flaws of the capitalism it so despised. It was capitalism under another name and with greater control of the economy. One extreme is invariably followed by another, because of the absence of wisdom. Anyone who wins control and power by violence shows themselves unfit to govern anyone. If they will use violence to win power they will use violence against the people to keep it. Violence is not something you can switch on and off. It is either in your psyche or it is not.

So who was really behind this 'Revolution of the People'? Free-masonry was at the heart of it. Coil's *Masonic Encyclopaedia* says that there was a Supreme Masonic Council in Russia with forty subordinate groups at the start of the war. Tsar Alexander had become so concerned at the agenda of Russian freemasonry that he had banned it in August 1822 when its own Grand Master had warned him that it was a threat to the state and should be stopped or reorganised. You can see that the Brotherhood does not speak only with one voice. Playing one against the other is all part of the strategy. This decree was renewed by Tsar Nicholas but, as free-masonry is a secret society, the subversion went on. It was right that the Tsar's abuse of power should end but, again, it is the secret agenda behind this that we have to watch.

The Germans naturally supported Lenin and gave him safe pas-sage in a sealed train across Germany from Switzerland on his way to Russia, because they wanted him to withdraw the Russians from the war. They also gave him and his Bolshevik revolution-aries tens of thousands of marks for propaganda and to make sure the revolution succeeded. What a surprise, then, that after Lenin's coup against the provisional 'people's government' the Russians pulled out of the war and allowed the Germans to concentrate on other fronts! The Communists were supported by German and other Western bankers and financiers. The German banker, Max Warburg, supported Lenin's regime. So did the American banker, Jacob Schiff. His family originated in Germany where it had en-joyed close links with the Rothschild banking empire, the key financial supporter of this and the other revolutions. The father of modern Communism and of the beliefs which the Bolsheviks promoted is said to be Karl Marx, who died in 1883. He was a member of a Brotherhood organisation, the League of the Just (later the Communist League), an offshoot of the Society of the Seasons which played a major part in the French Revolution along with their Grand Orient Lodge in Paris. The German industrialist, Friedrich Engels, supported Marx and wrote with him the Com-munist Manifesto on behalf of the secret societies which were behind them. Fifteen international bankers used the cover of a Red Cross mission in 1917 to travel to Petrograd to support the original revolution, the provisional 'people's government', and the Bolsheviks who would replace it. Professor Stuart Crane pointed out the scam:

"If you look back at every war in Europe......you will see that they always ended with the establishment of a balance of power. With every reshuffling there was a balance of power in a new grouping around the House of Rothschild in England, France, or Austria. They grouped nations so that if any king got out of line, a war would break out and the war would be decided by which way the financing went. Researching the debt positions of the warring nations will usually indicate who was being punished."

Or as the Illuminati Protocols put it in the 1800s:

"Throughout all Europe, and by means of relations with Europe, in other continents also, we must create ferments, discords and hostility. Therein we gain a double advantage. In the first place we keep in check all countries, for they well know that we have the power whenever we like to create disorders or to restore order . . . . In the second place, by our intrigues we shall tangle up all the threads which we have stretched into the cabinets of all states by means of politics, by economic treaties, or loan obligations. In order to succeed in this we must use great cunning and penetration during negotiations and agreements, but, as regards what is called the 'official language' we shall keep to the opposite tactics and assume the mask of honesty and compliancy . . . . We must be in a position to respond to every act of opposition by war with the neighbours of that country which dares to oppose us: but if these neighbours should also venture to stand collectively against us, then we must offer resistance by a universal war." (Protocol 7)

Communism was a form of designer politics created by the Brotherhood as an opposition to the 'free' society of America and Europe. Millions of dollars of Brotherhood money* was poured into the Russian revolution because the fear of a Russian 'bogeyman' was going to be used when the time was right. Russia became a bogeyman on ice waiting to be exploited thirty years later. Its beliefs in workers as units of production and people without spirit in a godless world was exactly what the Brotherhood wished the masses to believe.

---

* The Brotherhood bankers did, however, make a fantastic profit by stealing the Russian gold reserves – just as they would in Germany after World War II. Gold has been their great economic weapon.

The secret societies of the Brotherhood had taken control of the intelligence agencies that had emerged since the 17th century and so it was with the Tsarist intelligence agency, the Okhrana. There is a great illusion that the secret services of the world are set up in opposition to each other when, in fact, at the highest level, well above anyone known to the public, they work largely as one unit. Even the lower levels of these agencies don't realise that, but they are stooges for the Brotherhood, too. Intelligence agencies are organisations (the Brotherhood) within organisations. There is a secret world government which is continually destabilising and directing the actions of nation states. In typical Brotherhood fashion, Lenin and the Bolsheviks were attacking the Tsar for the brutality of the Okhrana while, behind the scenes, the Okhrana were supporting the Lenin revolution! The Okhrana were supplying funds and undermining the revolutionary opposition to the Bolsheviks, while many of the main protagonists within the Bolshevik movement were its members. The soon-to-be Soviet dictator, Josef Stalin, was, at the very least, extremely close to the Okhrana, probably a member. The first editor of the Communist mouthpiece, *Pravda,* was from there.

It is no surprise, therefore, that when Lenin and his supporters came to power, the intelligence agency they apparently so hated and condemned was greatly expanded and given a change of name – from Okhrana to the KGB. The revolution of the people was just another ball and chain in disguise. There was a considerable Jewish flavour to the revolution, and the Brotherhood was now preparing the ground for a return of the Jews to Palestine. Some research I have seen claims that, of 388 members of the Russian Revolutionary Government in 1918, only sixteen were Russians by birth. All but two of the rest were Jews from elsewhere, mostly from New York. How people have been tricked right through the ages to the present day. The Brotherhood was deeply involved in all the 'people's revolutions' which exploded after the American War of Independence. This includes, as we have seen, the French Revolution which led to the extermination of at least 100,000 people in the Reign of Terror that followed.

The blow for the Allies of losing Russian support against the Germans in World War I was compensated by the arrival of the Americans. President Woodrow Wilson led them into the war when Germany began a policy of sinking all shipping of whatever nationality, or rather that's what the allies said. The sinking of the

American ship, the Lusitania, was simply the excuse President Wilson had been looking for to justify entering the war, and I have no doubt that the sinking was manufactured by him in collusion with the British. The Japanese attack on Pearl Harbor would be used by President Franklin D Roosevelt in the same way in the Second World War. As Commander Joseph Kenworthy of British Naval Intelligence said:

"The Lusitania was deliberately sent at considerably reduced speed into an area where a U-boat was known to be waiting and with her escort withdrawn."

The Lusitania was carrying military supplies for Great Britain and was not, as the Americans claimed, merely a passenger vessel. Slowly, after the US soldiers arrived in Europe, the initiative turned against Germany and Wilhelm surrendered and abdicated, to be allowed to live out his life in comfort in the Netherlands. With his going, the German monarchy ended. This was the war which had been fought for the first time with the submarine, aeroplane and tank and this had taken everything onto a new level of horror and destruction. By the time it ended, tens of millions of men, women and children had lost their lives in a war manufactured by the Brotherhood for its own purposes. Words just cannot describe how that makes you feel. Germany was ordered to pay reparations to the nations she had attacked and agreed to accept strict limitations on the size of her armed forces. The Austrian Empire was divided into the individual states of Austria, Hungary, Czechoslovakia, and Yugoslavia, an amalgamation of Serbia, Croatia, Slovenia, Montenegro, Dalmatia and Bosnia Herzegovina. The colonies of the defeated countries were shared out among the victors under the heading of 'protectorates'. Syria went to France while Britain was handed Palestine, Jordan and Iraq. It's hard to believe that countries could be passed around like this, but it happened in this century.

In Britain, the war had hastened social reform and the widening of the franchise. After the French Revolution in 1789, the British gentry had been so terrified that it added yet more capital offences to the statute book and imposed even harsher laws against rebellion of any kind. But, when they could see their possessions under threat from a foreign power, they began to make concessions to the oppressed, because they knew they needed them to defend their wealth. Also, with every widening of the franchise, the power of the upper class elite was curtailed, though not that of the Brotherhood elite.

The rights of all children to an education had to be won in stages against Church and factory-owner opposition but, in 1918, came the most important victory yet in the form of the Education Act. This ensured a full-time education for all children up to the age of fourteen, and ended the practice of children going to work for half the day and school for the rest. It also introduced nursery schools and medical checks for children at school. The only sad thing was that the Church would continue to have a significant say in the education of children with the Bible taught as if it were historical fact. This continues even today.

The most significant development in the years between the wars was the rise of the dictator to replace monarchs and fledgling democracies. Here again it shows how desperate are the people for someone to lead them and tell them when to breathe; how the Brotherhood exploited that! The American President, Woodrow Wilson, at the instigation of his Brotherhood representative, Colonel House, proposed an organisation called the League of Nations after the First World War, to arbitrate disputes between countries before they became violent. It was a fine idea in theory, but, in practice, it was the first tentative and unsuccessful attempt at a centralised body on which to base a World Government. The Brotherhood is very adept at presenting something in terms that seem highly laudable, which can brilliantly obscure the hidden agenda. The League of Nations struggled into life but quickly collapsed because the American Congress would not join.

The support of the Roman Catholic Church for the dictators is not surprising. Its survival depends on the suppression of knowledge and the imposition of belief. Here we were in the first thirty-odd years of this century, seeing the expansion of education, materialistic sciences and more democratic political systems and the Roman Church was getting very worried as support for Christianity fell away. They knew that what they needed was a return to the old days of repression and oppression when they ran the show. The Vatican has also been run to a larger or lesser extent by the Brotherhood for centuries, probably from the start, and if, by mistake, they elect a Pope who won't play the game, he conveniently dies, as was the case with Pope John Paul I in 1978. His successor, Pope John Paul II, appeared to rescind a ban on freemasonry imposed by Pope Clement XII in 1738. Clement at least knew what was going on and wished to stop it. Today the Vatican position on freemasonry looks very confused and many Catholics are among the masons' ranks. In 1978, the year John Paul II took the papal throne, a special issue of Vatican stamps featured the triangle and all-seeing eye. Celebrating an Illuminati victory, perhaps?

Pope Pius XI and those who controlled the Vatican saw Benito Mussolini as the man who could lead them to a return to past glories. The global financial crash of the 1920s brought great hardship which proved fertile ground for a dictator to step forward and hoodwink the people into believing he had their best interests at heart. Mussolini, the son of a blacksmith, came to power in the accepted way of dictators, through bribery, corruption, murder and support from the secret societies. He was obsessed with restoring the Roman Empire and his brand of violence and patriotism were so successful that the king gave him control of the state to avoid a civil war. Once ensconced, he removed all democratic rights and freedom of expression. The Roman Catholic Church supported him in all of this. He knew that he could have free and constant propaganda from the pulpits of Italy if he had the Church on his side. The Vatican City was given independence from Italy, and the Church was given control, once more, of all education along with a donation of £19 million. When Mussolini invaded Abyssinia the Pope gave him his full support. It was the same when Mussolini went for Albania and Greece. Nothing would have delighted the Roman Catholic leaders more than to have control over the lands of the Greek Orthodox Church they so hated. These two Christian creeds had parted company, you will recall, after the Pope added the words 'and from the Son' (the Filoque) to the Christian creed in 1054. Many Christians refused to accept this aj they formed the breakaway Orthodox Church which later looked on Moscow as its own particular Rome or Mecca. Seventy thousand Jews were banished from Italy by Mussolini without a single word of protest from the Vatican. Italy was now controlled by a double dictatorship of Church and State, and both of them were controlled by the Brotherhood.

The Pope was also on friendly terms with Adolf Hitler after a large Roman Catholic vote swept him to power in Germany in 1933. Germany was in a desperate state, a country in physical and economic ruin after the war. With the end of the monarchy, a republic was declared at a meeting at Weimar in 1919, but it was always struggling against Communist, royalist, far right, and Brotherhood opposition. Most of all, it was destroyed by a collapsed economy. But then, if you control the financial system, undermining a country to prepare the ground for a revolution is no problem. The 1929 Wall Street crash in the United States was similarly engineered. The Brotherhood bankers created inflation and encouraged the stock market to overstretch itself, so making a crash inevitable. All the stock markets of the world are manipulated in this way. The Depression of the 1920s was the time of the 'Turkey Shoot', as it was known. By 1921, there were 31,076 banks in the U.S. The giant banks of the Brotherhood elite decided it was time to reap their harvest. The Federal Reserve announced a series of new regulations which they realised the smaller banks could not meet in such bleak economic conditions. This forced thousands of them out of business – 16,000 failed in eleven years. The Brotherhood bankers had destroyed the competition. They increased their own assets by absorbing the failed small fry and all those in debt to them. The Federal Reserve, having achieved its task, then reduced the toughness of the regulations. Franklin D Roosevelt, with support from these elite bankers, announced his famous New Deal policy to lift the U.S. out of depression. This involved the government borrowing enormous sums from the bankers and the debt of government and population exploded again. Congressman Louis McFadden, a Chairman of the House Banking and Currency Committee, said that the Great Depression of the 1920s....

".... was not accidental. It was a carefully contrived occurrence.... The International Bankers sought to bring about conditions of despair here, so they might emerge as rulers of us all."

It was the same in Germany where the seeds of dictatorship were sown. Enter Adolf Hitler, a First World War lance-corporal, who had been much impressed by the methods employed by Mussolini. But Hitler's obsession with Germany as the master Aryan race went back much further. As a youth he would take hallucinogenic drugs to stimulate his mystical experiences. The swastika, which Hitler was to use as the emblem of his Nazi party, was a Brotherhood symbol going back to ancient times. He was much impressed as a youngster by a bookshop owner in Vienna who preached the gospel of the German super-race, which some believed was created by extra-terrestrial giants. Houston Stewart Chamberlain, the writer who so influenced Kaiser Wilhelm, was later to claim that Hitler was the new Messiah, and Chamberlain's work would become a basis of Nazi philosophy.

Hitler's rise to German Dictator quickened rapidly after he joined the secret political branch of the Army District Command which was a law unto itself. It was so deeply patriotic that it assassinated, for crimes against the nation, some of the people who had negotiated the peace terms for Germany at the end of the First World War. The District Command was really the assassination wing of a secret Brotherhood group called the Thule Society which believed in all the nonsense about the super-race and the German Messiah. It sentenced people to death in its own secret 'courts'. Hitler and the Thule Society believed they were being guided by the extra-terrestrials who had created the Aryan race, or what they said was a race. The same industrialists financed both the Thule Society and the District Command. Deitrich Eckart, the morphine addict who headed the Thule Society, saw Hitler as the Messiah figure they had been looking for. They ensured that he became the leader of the German Workers' Party. This was transformed into the fascist National Socialist (Nazi) Party and Hitler sought to spread his anti-Jewish, anti-communist nationalism to the entire world. His creed captured the collective mind of Germany which tuned to the thought waves of fascism until it was hypnotised and controlled by the rantings of this misguided man. He had increased his standing before his election by having his Gestapo-in-waiting burn down the German Parliament building, the Reichstag, in 1933, for which he blamed the communists. He also used the fear of the Russians to great effect. In this he was helped by the Pope who spread hatred of Communist Russia at every opportunity. The churches had been mortified when Lenin's revolution banned religion. They didn't know they had been double-crossed by the same Brotherhood they believed was supporting them. The Brotherhood were also playing off Hitler and Stalin against each other – for both of whom they were responsible.

Two other secret societies which played a part in the Nazi revolution were the Vril Society and the Edelweiss Society. Like the Thules, they had links with their brethren in Britain. Rudolph Hess and Heinrich Himmler were both 'Vrils' – Himmler was to head the appalling Nazi Gestapo and SS. Hermann Goering was a member of the Edelweiss Society and believed that Hitler was the Nordic Messiah he was convinced was expected. Hitler and his cronies denounced the Jews and Communists on the radio day after day, as he poisoned the German mind to his creed.

He followed the example of Church and dictators throughout history. Any literature advocating freedom of any kind was destroyed, and promises he made to the socialists and monarchists who helped to elect him were forgotten. There would be no more elections. The Fuhrer would be obeyed. Around him he gathered his principal officers like Goebbels, Ribbentrop, Goering and Himmler. They would rule Germany by terror, and Jewish people would suffer terrible treatment. Ribbentrop was to have several cosy conversations with the Pope about Germany's expansion plans, although the main agent of the secret Vatican-Germany-America alliance was Rudolph Hess.

So now there were dictators in Italy, Germany, and Russia, where Josef Stalin had succeeded Lenin in 1924. Soon there would be another in Spain. In 1936 General Franco, a Roman Catholic extremist, led a revolt against the Spanish Republican Government which had reduced the power of the Church since the days when it controlled everything. The Spanish Civil War was a prelude to the next world conflict, with Germany and Italy lining up behind Franco, while Britain, France, and Russia supported the republicans. Tragically for the Spanish people, Franco's armies won, and he did for the Roman Catholic Church in Spain what Mussolini had done in Italy. It was given back its wealth and lands, received large annual payments from the state, and the education system was back in its control. Religious paraphernalia was everywhere and the inquisition returned. The Papal flag was flown by Franco as he overturned Spanish democracy and his flag was proudly flown at the Vatican. The Pope's role in this victory over democracy had been crucial. He had appealed to Roman Catholics all over Europe to go to Spain and fight in this 'Holy War'.

When Hitler began his expansionism into Austria, the Roman Catholic bishops there told the people to be loyal to the Nazis and a swastika was flown from the tower of Vienna Cathedral. Hitler enjoyed Roman Catholic support also in his conquest of Czechoslovakia. Pope Pius XI and his successor, Pius XII, wanted more than anything for Germany to overthrow communism in Russia. Little did they know that Germany had played a vital part in

creating communism! The story of Vatican support for the fascists
is quite disgraceful, although not surprising given its history; so is
that of the Brotherhood industrialists and bankers who were supporting both sides. By now there were Brotherhood organisations
coordinating the elite bankers and industrial combines across the
world. One was the Bank for International Settlements that was
beyond democratic control. Among the financial backers of the
Nazis were the German chemical giant I.G.Farben, among whose
directors were Max and Paul Warburg who ran banks in both
Germany and the United States. The Warburgs were instrumental
in starting the American Federal Reserve System and you'll recall
that Max Warburg was mentioned earlier as a source of funds for
Lenin and the communist revolution in Russia! The Bank of Manhattan was a Warburg bank, and one of its directors, H.A.Metz,
was from I.G.Farben, which had been a cartel partner of the
Rockefeller Corporation's Standard Oil Company before the war,
as part of the Brotherhood's banking and industrial network.
Standard Oil supplied the Nazis during the war through Switzerland, and Avery Rockefeller had set up a company which combined their interests with Schroeder, Hitler's personal bank. The
Guaranty Trust and the Union Banking Corporation of New York
were among the biggest backers of the Nazis. One of the UBC's
directors was Prescott Bush, father of George. C.E.Mitchell, a
director of Farben's American arm, was also a director of the
Federal Reserve, and the network was now so tightly knit you
could hardly see the join. Farben gave extra funding to Himmler's
SS, and so did the German subsidiaries of the American corporations, I.T.T and General Electric. General Motors supplied both
sides in the war, as did the European subsidiaries of the US banks,
with the blessing of headquarters. Ball bearings, which the Allies
were short of, were shipped to the Nazis via South America by the
Vice-Chairman of the American War Productions Board. Farben
ran the factories connected to the concentration camps to take
advantage of the, literally, slave labour they offered. I.G.Farben
still continues to operate today under various names.★

★ The drug companies, A.G. Hoechst, Sterling Drug, and A.G. Bayer are all claimed
by researchers to be I.G. Farben offshoots.

The Brotherhood network in Britain supported the Nazis – and still does – and the Bank of England helped Hitler. Its director, Montague Norman, who was a 'Mr.Big' of the world banking network, met in the Spring of 1934 with other British businessmen at the bank's headquarters in Threadneedle Street, and it appears they agreed to give Hitler secret funding, while Norman tried to persuade the British government to remove its support for France and transfer it to Germany. Even after Hitler had begun his killing tour of Europe, the Bank of England released to him six million pounds of Czechoslovak reserves held in London after he had invaded that country. All through the war the Brotherhood companies and banks in Allied countries were covertly funding both sides, which included support for Mussolini when his regime got into financial difficulties. It made them a fortune, something that was increased a thousandfold by the need to rebuild a shattered world. It also maintained the yoke of suffering and ignorance on the population. The Bank of England was nationalised by the new Labour Government in 1946, but it still has a massive influence on Britain's economic policies and I expect it to start demanding more independence from government.

Hitler ignored all agreements made by Germany in the Treaty of Versailles after their defeat in the First World War. He assembled a vast army, navy and air force, and the rest of Europe feared the worst. After Hitler's invasion of Austria, the British Prime Minister, Neville Chamberlain, flew to meet him in Munich in 1938 and came home with his famous agreement signed by Hitler, which Chamberlain claimed would mean 'peace in our time'. Chamberlain was a genuine man who only wanted peace for his people, but Hitler had other ideas. When Germany invaded Poland in 1939 Britain and France declared war. Poland was now again under foreign rule after a brief independence, during which the Roman Catholic majority had persecuted the Eastern orthodox Christians in their midst. After the war Poland was absorbed into the Soviet Union until that empire collapsed in 1991. The Poles then handed over their independence to the Roman Catholic Church which today, effectively, runs the country. If anyone thinks the Roman Catholic Church has really moved on, they should see how quickly it has taken control of Poland once the opportunity presented itself.

Hitler captured France, Belgium and the Netherlands, but chose not to attack Britain when we were in disarray at home. Winston

Churchill had replaced Chamberlain, but Britain was not prepared for war. Had Hitler attacked then he would almost certainly have captured the British Isles quite easily. Why did he not attack when Britain was clearly there for the taking? The evacuation of British troops from Dunkirk in an armada of little boats in 1940 was a marvellous achievement, but if the German commanders had wanted to stop it, they could have. Why didn't they? Instead of invading Britain, Hitler turned his mind to Russia which suffered fantastic losses in the defence of their land. Again it was the courage and commitment of a manipulated people that weakened the German forces and delayed their plans. The conflict spread to North Africa where the Allies confronted German and Italian troops under Rommel. It was Rommel's ultimate defeat at El Alamein, and the Soviets' extraordinary defeat of the Germans in the East, which ended a series of German victories and the tide began to turn the flow the way of the Allies. But the big change came when the United States entered the war in 1941. She had already been supporting the Allies with supplies and arms when the Japanese attacked the American fleet at Pearl Harbor in Hawaii. This brought the US into the war – exactly as it was meant to. This was the Lusitania mark II.

The story behind that Japanese attack goes back a long way. The Japanese, like the Chinese, are of the Mongol race. Both countries have a history of civil war and unrest. The Japanese main religion is Shintoism and they too were enamoured by secret societies. The most dominant one had a Black Dragon symbol. They believed their Emperor to be Divine, and themselves to be descended from the gods, a chosen people descended from extra-terrestrials. All efforts by Christian missionaries to convert them failed, and in the 17th century the behaviour of the missionaries towards them was so appalling that they closed their country to all Europeans for two hundred years. In the second half of the 19th century, steamships from the United States arrived and refused to be turned away. Japan was attacked by a combination of the Americans, British, Dutch and French until they were forced to open their ports. The Japanese became a people transformed in the decades that followed. They used the weapons provided by the Christian world to attack and defeat China in 1894, and Russia in 1905. Japan also entered the First World War against Germany.

Between 1937 and 1939 she took over most of China, whose people were in the midst of constant insurrection against the stream of emperors and presidential dictators thrust upon them. Modern China's story is of diabolical exploitation by the colonial powers, with the British addicting the Chinese to the drug opium for purposes of trade and control. In the run up to Pearl Harbor, the British and Americans had been trying to stop Japan over-throwing the Chinese General Chiang Kai-shek, and the Japanese resented this. They were given every encouragement to enter the war, and I believe that Winston Churchill, a freemason, knew all about it, as did President Franklin D Roosevelt, a high ranking freemason and claimed by some to have reached the 33rd degree. Churchill would later say of this time that Roosevelt.... "said he would wage war, but not declare it (and) that he would become more and more provocative......everything was being done to force an 'incident' that could lead the United States into war".

In the US Senate in 1939, Senator Gerald P.Nye of North Dakota announced that he had seen a series of volumes called *The Next War*. One of them was entitled *Propaganda In The Next War*. He said the writer of that book was a Sidney Rogerson, whom he could not trace. But he knew that the editor-in-chief of the series was Captain Liddell Hart who was a writer and military authority in Europe with connections to the London *Times*. The work *Propaganda In The Next War* had, he said, included the following analysis of the background to World War I:

"For some time the issue as to which side the United States would take hung in the balance, the final result was a credit to our British propaganda. There remain the Jews. It has been estimated that of the world Jew population of approximately fifteen million, no fewer than five million are in the United States; 25% of the inhabitants of New York are Jews.

*"During the Great War **we bought off** this huge American Jewish public **by the promise of the Jewish national home in Palestine**, held by Ludendorf to be a master stroke of Allied propaganda, as it enabled us not only to appeal to Jews in America, but to Jews in Germany as well."*

The Americans entered the First World War in 1917, and on November 6th of that year came the famous Balfour Declaration, when the British Government announced in a letter to Lionel Rothschild the recognition of Palestine as a national homeland for the Jews. It is important to note that Lord Balfour was a member of the Round Table inner elite. The dreadful events in Israel in recent years, which have caused pain for Israeli and Arab alike, are the result of Britain negotiating away Palestine to get the United States to enter the First World War and to advance Brotherhood ambitions which go back much further. But how could the American public be persuaded to support Britain in the next war, which this propaganda report clearly knew was inevitable?

"To persuade her [the United States] to take our part will be much more difficult, so difficult as to be unlikely to succeed. It will need a definite threat to America, a threat, moreover, which will have to be brought home by propaganda to every citizen, before the republic will again take arms in an external quarrel...

*"The position will naturally be considerably eased if **Japan** were involved, and this might and probably would bring America in without further ado. At any rate, it would bj a natural and obvious effect of our propagandists to achieve this, just as in the Great War they succeeded in embroiling the United States with Germany.*

"Fortunately with America, our propaganda is on firm ground. We can be entirely sincere, as our main plank will be the old decratic one. We must clearly enunciate our belief in the democratic form of government, and our firm resolve to adhere to....the old goddess of democracy routine."

The main themes of wars are known and planned in advance. It is clear from evidence that has emerged since the war that President Franklin D Roosevelt knew at lzast forty-eight hours before the attack on Pearl Harbor that the Japanese were going to strike. He did nothing to warn his sailors and the people of Hawaii, because he wanted the American public to be so outraged that they would agree to enter the war in Europe. That is exactly what happened, just as the pre-war propagandists had planned. The method of goading the Japanese came from the Brotherhood's Council on Foreign Relations, the Round Table creation. The Council's War and Peace Studies Project sent a memo to Roosevelt suggesting that aid be sent to China, and that he strangle Japanese trade by freezing their US assets, imposing a trade embargo on Japan, and refusing them the use of the Panama Canal. This he did, and Roosevelt and the Brotherhood were rewarded with the Japanese attack on Pearl Harbor. Roosevelt was a pawn of the Brotherhood in the form of the Council on Foreign Relations. Much of his cabinet came from there and his son-in-law, Curtis Dall, quoted in Jim Keith's *Casebook on Alternative Three*, said:

"For a long time I felt that (Roosevelt)....had developed many thoughts

and ideas that were his own to benefit this country, the USA. But he didn't. Most of his thoughts, his political 'ammunition' as it were, were carefully manufactured for him in advance by the Council on Foreign Relations – One World Money group. Brilliantly, with great gusto, like a fine piece of artillery, he exploded that prepared 'ammunition' in the middle of an unsuspecting target, the American people – and thus paid off and retained his internationalist political support."

The same applied to Churchill and those who decided he would be Prime Minister, and the same goes on in both countries, and all the others, today. According to information leaked by a decoding officer, Tyler Kent, to Captain A.H. Ramsey M.P., before the war, Churchill and Roosevelt were setting the whole thing up via coded messages while Neville Chamberlain was still Prime Minister. The war was now truly global with fronts in Europe, the Middle East and the Far East, as the Japanese occupied the Allied colonies like Malaya, Singapore, the Philippines, Borneo, Hong Kong and Burma. The men, women and children who were caught in those countries when the Japanese invaded were subjected to unbelievable torture and atrocities. But then it is no good one country being holier than another in its version of history. Every country on the planet has shown itself capable of crimes against humanity. The British authorities reeled back in horror at the concentration camps in Germany, but it was the British who started the idea with their camps created by Lord Kitchener, in which 26,000 prisoners died in South Africa during the Boer War. And the Allies were fighting alongside the Russian regime who were running concentration camps for their own people and slaughtering millions in other ways. Every continent was involved in the war, and the soldiers of Australia and New Zealand once again supported the Allied cause. Even with the support of America and the other English-speaking peoples, the fascists were defeated only through horrendous loss of life on both sides. With the fascist armies overcome in North Africa the push began northwards into Italy in 1943. The Fascist Grand Council restored King Victor Emmanuel as ruler, and Mussolini was forced to resign. The Italian Parliament was reconvened under the new Prime Minister, Marshall Pietro Badoglio. He first told Hitler he would continue the fight, but then made a peace pact with the Allies. Mussolini tried to escape to Switzerland with his mistress, but they were killed by Communist partisans and their corpses held up for ridicule and public display in Milan.

The Germans tried to hold back the Allied advance through Italy, but in the end their defences were breached. On June 6th, 1944, came Operation Overlord when British, American, and Canadian forces under their Supreme Commander, Dwight D Eisenhower, launched the D-Day Landings along the beaches of Normandy in Northern France. With great courage and enormous loss of life, they pushed on across France to liberate Paris and occupy Western Germany, while the Russians advanced in Eastern Europe. The war in Europe was over, but allies who had been united against a common enemy were about to become extremely hostile to each other in what passed for peace. With Germany on the retreat, the latter weeks of the war became a race for Berlin between the western armies and the Russians. Both wanted to be in the best possible negotiating position for the division of land when the conflict was over. The Russians would spread their Communist (state fascist) creed to expand the Empire of the Soviet Union and encompass Czechoslovakia, Hungary, Yugoslavia, Bulgaria, Rumania, Poland, and the eastern part of Germany. A wall was built to divide Berlin between capitalist and communist and those in the East who tried to reach the West were shot by their own army. Families were divided by the whims of the Communist dictator, Josef Stalin, and his underlings and successors who would now murder millions of their own people in this 'workers' paradise'.

The defeat of Germany did not end the war entirely. Japan still held out and Roosevelt's successor, Harry S. Truman, another freemason, gave the order to drop the atom bomb which had been developed during the war years. An arm of the Illuminati's Round Table, the Institute for Advanced Study at Princeton University, New Jersey, gave vital support to those who were developing the bomb. One of its members was Robert Oppenheimer, the leading light in the creation of the bomb. Albert Einstein also regularly used the Institute. It has long been a front for the advancement of Brotherhood science which the public has no idea about, but which is usually between 50 and 100 years ahead of 'public' science. The Japanese Emperor Hirohito surrendered after two atomic bombs were dropped by US planes on the cities of Hiroshima and Nagasaki on August 6th and 9th, 1945. In fact, the former British Cabinet Minister Tony Benn, says he established that Japan was willing to surrender before these bombs were dropped. Eighty thousand men, women and children were killed in Hiroshima on the fateful day that atomic warfare came to this planet (or rather returned to it), and others would die horribly from the effects of radiation poisoning.

In all thirty-five million people were killed in the Second World War and hundreds of millions were wounded, tortured and scarred for life mentally, physically and emotionally. And this horror was the result of a war that never should have been, and never would have been had the Brotherhood network not caused it. Add to those figures those millions who died and suffered in the First World War, and all the others and words are hard to speak.

But such emotions do not trouble the Illuminati:

"And how far-seeing were our learned elders in ancient times when they said that to attain a serious end it behoves not to stop at any means or to count the victims sacrificed for the sake of that end . . . . We have not counted the victims of the Goy cattle . . . . " (Protocol 15)

Most of the main players in the Nazi regime, probably including Hitler, escaped. He and his lady, Eva Braun, did not die in the bunker, many researchers believe. At least some of them went to South America. From the views and evidence I have heard and seen, I believe that Hitler was flown out of Germany by the famous German aviator, Hans Bauer. He flew Nazi wealth and personnel out of Berlin. Hitler would have had no trouble getting away to a quiet airfield because, when the Russians arrived in Berlin, they found behind the bookcase in Hitler's room a secret passage leading to an underground tunnel with its own trolley railway line. The dental records of Hitler and the corpse said to be Hitler did not match and it is most likely to have been the body of his driver, Julius Schreck, a Hitler fanatic, who looked like him and acted as his 'double' on several occasions. A Russian statement in 1945 said:

"No trace of the bodies of Hitler or Eva Braun has been discovered....It is established that Hitler, by means of false testimony, sought to hide his traces. Irrefutable proof exists that a small plane left the Tiergarten at dawn on April 30th, flying in the direction of Hamburg. Three men and a woman are known to have been on board. It has also been established that a large submarine left Hamburg before the arrival of the British forces. Mysterious persons were on board the submarine, among them a woman."

What is without doubt is that the Nazi influence, far from disappearing at the end of the war, continues to flourish within the secret societies and is now beginning to surface again among the mind-controlled human fodder who support the far right movement. They are also very influential within the police, the military, and the intelligence services like the American Central Intelligence Agency, the CIA. Indeed the CIA engaged Reinhart Gehlen, the head of Russian operations in the Nazi Secret Service, to build the CIA network in Europe, and he used many former SS officers on his staff. The international police organisation, INTERPOL, has been headed by many former SS officers. The Nazis and their 'values' play a big part in the running of the modern Brotherhood, and it is time the truth was told and the robots rebelled. History is clearly not what it appears to be, and yet the official version is being indoctrinated into generation after generation through the 'education' system and the Brotherhood-controlled media.

"Among the members of these (Freemasonic) lodges will be almost all the agents of international and national police since their service is for us irreplaceable in the respect that the police is in the position not only to use its own particular measures with the insubordinate (Those who challenge the Brotherhood), but also to screen our activities and provide pretexts for discontents etc." (Protocol 15)

There is another aspect to this story that needs to be highlighted. All the conflicts that I have documented, and the thousands I have not, have had a disastrous affect on the Earth's energy field which has to absorb the negative energy humanity generates. The scale of this struck me on a trip to France with my family in 1993 when we stayed in a house between Caen and Falaise in Normandy. Falaise is the birthplace of William the Conquerer. It was a lovely area, but you could feel something unpleasant in the atmosphere. I knew that the D-Day Landings had taken place on the coast a short drive away from where we were staying, but it was only when we were leaving for home that I realised we had been living near the scene of a bloody carnage in 1944. The Battle of the Falaise Gap was, in the words of Eisenhower: 'One of the biggest slaughter fields a war sector ever knew'. More than 650,000 people were killed or wounded.

When thought patterns are broadcast by people, they stay in that area until they are balanced by other patterns. The spirits of the dead are often still there, too. The confusion and pain of the experience can prevent them from getting back to their 'home' frequency. We call them 'ghosts' or 'lost souls'. When you go to the scene of battles it can feel 'eerie'. These are the thought patterns of fear, horror, aggression and pain that were created by those involved. Sensitive people who go to such places can hear battles or see them happening. They are tuning into these thought waves. We could feel them in that area of Normandy. There was a very malevolent energy, because like attracts like, and negative energy attracts negative energy. My son, Gareth, then eleven, would not go upstairs in the house alone and it was very unpleasant. There was a door in an attic which was held shut by a substantial catch, but every time my wife, Linda, passed that door it was open. She would close it tight only for the same to happen again. Then one night she was awake and she looked across at Gareth who was sleeping in our room, because he was so frightened. Hovering above him she saw a dark cloud of energy. She watched as the cloud swept across the room and out through the door. The next morning she told me the story. She didn't know that I had woken up that night and felt a very strange and unpleasant atmosphere. After the experience, the atmosphere in the house changed and the attic door never came open again. Gareth's fear disappeared, too. If you imagine that I am talking of the effects on the energy field of one battle in one war, you can see why the negative imbalance has progressed so quickly across the planet. But equally it can be removed just as quickly if we change the way we think.

We are involved in a spiritual struggle between harmony and disharmony. The Luciferic consciousness manipulates extra-terrestrials and human behaviour by firing thought patterns into their individual and collective consciousness. These patterns are designed to distort the mental and, especially, emotional levels of our being. This has the effect of closing down the flow of energies, knowledge, and enlightenment between higher and lower selves. This flow has further been affected since the dawn of the Industrial Revolution which has turned many humans into physical as well as mental robots, and caused severe mental and emotional stress.

In some ways human consciousness has come a long way over the period covered in this book, but in others it has hardly progressed at all. We are now facing the Days of Decision when, on this dense physical level, we evolve and rebel or we perish. That is the choice that now faces us all.

11

Big is Beautiful?

THE Industrial Revolution began in Britain in the 18th century with the invention of the steam engine, and within a hundred years this revolution would fill the skies with black smoke and pollution, rape the planet for fuels, and turn millions, eventually billions, into robots; mere extensions of a factory machine.

The poor and the weak have always been exploited by the landowners or whoever had the financial and physical power of the day. But now it was to be done on a massive, ultimately global scale, as the Brotherhood spread its economic culture across the world. The people came in from the countryside, and filthy urban sprawls appeared around the mills and the factories. They worked long hours often for starvation wages, and the system I have termed 'take, make, and throwaway' had arrived. Its Pied Piper was the obsession with the pursuit of economic growth – producing more, consuming more, and throwing away more, every year. But actually playing the tune was the Brotherhood network of bankers and their front organisations, the so-called 'think tanks'.

A new religion was born. It was called 'science'. Christianity was still powerful, but its influence was now in terminal decline. Suddenly the scientist was god. This science created the machine age and all the potions and poisons that have taken human life, quite possibly, to the brink of non-existence. But as the 19th century passed to the 20th, this new culture and new god had hypnotised much of human consciousness. Science, or what passes for it, decided that life after physical death was a myth. Everything could be explained by the 'logic' of science. Basically we were all a cosmic accident, the product of the random interaction of chemicals, atoms, and the like. This gave Christianity some serious problems, but it gave the human race even more. Not least was the growing belief that life was pointless. The idea was that 'life's a bitch and then you die'. The lives people were being forced to endure in the blackened towns and cities appeared to confirm that this was the case. It was another drain on a human spirit already crushed by the robotic demands of the machine age.

Christianity's ability to stop the haemorrhage of support in the face of scientific 'evidence' was not helped by the obvious nonsense of its dogmatic, unyielding, claims for the Bible to be literally true. It was now beginning to reap the consequences of refusing to budge from the dogma decided at Nicaea and in the centuries that immediately followed. But, as I said in a previous chapter the view of life and Creation outlined in this book and others, was now suppressed not only by Christianity as it had been for nearly two thousand years, but also by 'science'. Christianity and 'science' may have appeared to be in conflict, but they had a mutual interest which was essential to the survival of both. That was to ensure that as few people as possible believed that consciousness was eternal in everyone, and that our consciousness reincarnates into countless physical bodies on its journey of evolution through experience. The acceptance of that by the population would mean goodbye to Christianity and most other religions, and goodbye to the whole basis of scientific 'thinking'. One of the Brotherhood's most effective tools is to make organisations dependent for their very survival on the suppression of knowledge.

The result of this was a world created by the five physical senses which pandered only to those senses. God was dead and the idea of spirit was a primitive illusion. Materialism had arrived with a vengeance even though research shows that the whole Darwinism – materialistic 'science' was a Brotherhood set-up. The manipulators knew, and know, it is a nonsense. Our culture was built by material senses *for* material senses. Such a process could not have created any other kind of world than the one we see today. The higher levels of humans were dismissed by 'science' as not even existing and the only high-profile alternative, Christianity and its religious soul-mates around the World, were leaking credibility with every passing year, thanks to the time-warp in which they are imprisoned. This left a spiritual vacuum which is only now being filled as an understanding of who we are begins to re-emerge in our consciousness. The material-cosmic-accident view so took over this new religion called science, that even when members of its own profession challenged this belief, they were ridiculed, outcast, or ignored. Just as the Brotherhood ensured that they would be. They don't want some freethinking scientist to find out the truth and be able to prove it. Nearly every true scientist who has taken human understanding forward has faced that kind of reaction and opposition. 'Science' became obsessed with the physical level and concentrated its mind on discovering the secrets and potential of the physical world, at the expense of seeking those higher levels where the answers really lie. Almost from the start, 'science' has been serving the system and the Brotherhood by helping to imprison the human race. In doing that, the new religion has merely followed the pattern of the old.

The whole system was founded and underpinned at every turn by exploitation. Exploitation of the planet; of the human robots in the mines and factories; and of the people in what we now call the Third World. Most of these 'under-developed' countries were then under the occupation and control of Britain and other European countries. Countries like Britain could not lose at this stage. It had the technology, primitive as it was, and it had the British Empire. It could take the natural 'resources' from the countries it controlled, turn those resources into products, and sell them back at a profit. This global exploitation by the strong at the expense of the weak would destroy the cultures of Third World countries and take away their self-sufficiency in food. This was vital for the exploitation to continue. When these countries eventually rebelled against physical occupation, Europe and the United States had to replace that with other forms of control. They achieved this by replacing physical occupation with financial occupation. They made poorer countries dependent on the industrialised world for their food and finance. The American senator, Hubert Humphrey, put it like this:

"I have heard that people may become dependent on us for food. I know that was not supposed to be good news. To me that was good news, because before people can do anything they have to eat. And if you are looking for a way to get people to lean on you and to be dependent on you, in terms of their co-operation with you, it seems to me that food dependency would be terrific."

Exactly. This motivation would lead to the famine and starvation of the 20th century. It was compounded by the exploitation of land for the maximum production of cash crops in ways that would destroy its fertility; and by the political and internal strife in these countries, often caused by the effects of poverty or the overthrow-ing of regimes, openly or covertly, which did not suit the interests of the Brotherhood elite. They didn't want Third World countries to make their own decisions – they wanted them dependent on the same Brotherhood bankers that ran the West. This goes on today with the United States the leading force in the ongoing effort to unseat any politician or group that threatens American or Brother-hood interests. Witness Nicaragua and the countless South Amer-ican dictators imposed and empowered by the United States. I go into all this in some detail in my book, *It Doesn't Have To Be Like This*. It is all part of the long term Brotherhood plan:

"We are interested in the . . . . killing out of the Goyim. Our power is in the chronic shortness of food and physical weakness of the worker, because by all that this implies he is made the slave of our will, and he will not find in his own authorities either strength or energy to set against our will. Hunger creates the right of capital to rule the worker more surely than it was given to the aristocracy by the legal authority of kings." (Protocol 3).

The speed with which all this happened has been astonishing. When I was travelling through Arizona in 1993, I stopped at a little cafe at a place called Parker. On the wall was a poster depicting the exploits of Butch Cassidy and the Sundance Kid whose bank-robbing activities were made famous by a film of the same name. What struck me most was that it all happened in *this* century. The United States went from horseback to space travel in less than 70 years, perhaps even less than that if some stories of covert space flights in the fifties are true. At the same time the USA has become the front line of self-destruction. Anyone who doesn't believe that should go into any eating house on any street in America and see just how much of the Earth's physical form is dumped into a rubbish bin every minute. Since the industrialisation and Chris-tianisation of the United States, it has consumed more of the Earth's 'resources' and created more pollution than any other society on the planet. And tragically that is the culture which has taken over the world in less than the blink of an eye in the lifespan of Mother Earth.

If you take the Earth to be one year old, then under that time scale the Industrial Revolution has been with us for less than two seconds. In that fraction of time we have behaved in ways that now threaten the planet's ability to be a home for human life. Every twenty-four hours an area of tropical forest twenty-five miles by twenty is destroyed or degraded; deserts advance by a similar area; 200 million tonnes of top soil is lost through erosion; many and increasing numbers of species become extinct; and 100,000 people, nearly half of them children, die through hunger or hunger-related disease. Every single day.

But why should we be surprised at this? How could it be any other way when you have an economic system that depends for its survival, let alone its success, on taking, making, and throwing away more every year to worship at the Brotherhood altar of economic growth? It is the ultimate conveyor belt to global suicide. The stark truth is that if you need to consume more every year, the human and environmental effects are both enormous and eventually fatal. Either the Brotherhood elite are incredibly stupid, or they have lost control of their creation, or they have other motives for what they are doing to the planet. I suspect a bit of both. Here is a summary of why it has taken the human race little more than two hundred years to go from the dawn of the Industrial Revolution to the mess and mayhem we see today – and why it has so massively served Brotherhood interests:

(1) If you have constantly to produce more and consume more, you soon pass the point where that can continue within your own borders. You have to sell abroad and export your culture. You have to change the way others live and impose your evolution upon them. You do this by making them dependent on you and by selling your culture through manipulative advertising. If you have an addictive product, like cigarettes, so much the better, because once people are hooked you have a captive market. And once you have other countries addicted to the pursuit of your culture, you have even more power to make them use their resources and land to supply you with what you need in order to supply them with finished products at a handsome profit. By now you have destroyed their self-sufficiency in food, and you can claim that the developed world is helping the underdeveloped world out of the goodness of its heart, and the success of its culture by 'giving' food to them when in fact millions are starving, because they can no longer produce food for themselves. Even then you only respond with as little as you can get away with in situations that are either well-publicised or suit your desire to make others do your will. As

someone once said: 'When you have got someone by the balls, their hearts and minds will follow'. They might just as easily have said 'stomachs'. The need to expand production and sales each year means that everyone has to compete with everyone else. For every winner there have to be losers, often dead ones. The one exception to that is the banking elite. They can't lose. We talk of the desire for cooperation in the world, and yet the very foundation of the economic ethos is to turn person against person, family against family, town against town, country against country, and trading bloc against trading bloc in brutal competition, while the elite share the spoils between themselves.

"In order to give the Goyim no time to think and take note, their minds must be diverted towards industry and trade. Thus, all the nations will be swallowed up in the pursuit of gain and in the race for it will not take note of their common foe. But, again, in order that freedom may once for all disintegrate and ruin the communities of the Goyim, we must put industry on a speculative basis; the result of this will be that what is withdrawn from the land by industry will slip through the hands and pass into speculation, that is, to our classes." (Protocol 4).

(2) It is vital that you also make your own population dependent for their food and existence on the same system. If they have alternatives, they cannot be forced to do your will or stand by a factory machine most of their waking hours. The effect of this is to diminish their spirit and grind down their resistance to any propaganda that you feed to them through a compliant and system-serving media. The need for expanding the system requires that your 'scientific' research is geared to inventing new things that you can persuade people to buy; to finding cheaper ways of making those things through technology; and to inventing new weapons of mass destruction. As with video recorders, so with guided missiles. If you can constantly advance the technology of whatever you produce, people and countries will constantly 'update'. In short, they will keep buying the same thing again and again as perfectly adequate products are systematically made tech-nologically 'obsolete'. These twin aims of product and weapon advancement to serve the economic system is what science has largely been about. Serving humanity and seeking truth has been a strictly secondary motivation for the scientific Brotherhood-manipulated establishment. The weaponry is also important to protect the wealth of the powerful, and to increase that wealth

when it becomes economically desirable for a war in which you can supply both sides.

(3) This system is so obviously destructive and stupid that if you allowed people to be shown its true nature, they would soon see the obvious. Christianity feared and vehemently opposed education for the masses because of the possible consequences of people seeing that creed for the silliness which most of it is. But they need not have worried. The system had no intention of educating people, especially the young. It wishes to indoctrinate, not educate, and that is what it has done. 'Education' is there to turn out fodder for the system. Its aim is to persuade people to see things its way and reject any idea that there could possibly be an alternative. What could be better for the system than to take children away from their homes on most days during their formative years, and feed them whatever they need to believe to become the next generation of robots? It is quite happy to give Christianity a good mention up to a point because that is no threat to anything except itself and human understanding. As we have seen both the System and Christianity have a big stake in holding back human understanding, anyway. Further afield, where there are native peoples who have not been subjected to this economic mind control, you take away their forests, lands and way of life either by force or through Christianisation. With their culture destroyed, they become dependent and often seek to escape from the nightmare through alcohol or drugs. Your control of the world is extended by environmental destruction.

(4) The need to produce and sell more every year means that the point quickly arrives when people can no longer increase production by themselves. You build machines which turn out more products with fewer people. As production needs constantly to increase, the machines have to get bigger and require ever fewer people. Unemployment grows. The way the system responds to this is in the only way it knows how: by fiddling the unemployment figures to hide how bad things really are; by starting wars; and by increasing the number of things that people want by manipulating the symbols of human success so they all relate to possessions. You need to make people dissatisfied with whatever they have and to seek happiness through the accumulation of material 'things'. This however means that your production must follow the money because poor people can't buy. Therefore pro-

duction is increasingly geared to the wants of the well-off minority, and away from the needs of the poor majority. This leads to some people having every possession they could possibly desire, while others sleep in cardboard boxes in the street.

Look how the system has manipulated Christmas. Christianity recycled a pagan mid-winter festival quite erroneously into the birthday of Jesus and the system has recycled that into an orgy of consumption. We speak of having a 'traditional Christmas', when most of the traditions have only been here since the start of the Industrial Revolution. What should be a lovely time of rest, enjoyment and a gathering together of friends and family, has become a nightmare for millions. Children are bombarded with television advertisements for expensive toys, and their parents often borrow money they cannot afford because they don't want to disappointment them on Christmas Day. They either struggle through the next year paying off the debt, or they spend Christmas feeling guilty for not providing what their children have been conditioned to want. This exploitation of emotions becomes more desperate and explicit every year because the Christmas spending boom is now essential to the survival of many shops and factories.

The difference between the 'haves' and 'have nots' comes down to the number of pieces of paper they possess. This mostly has nothing whatsoever to do with their abilities or their desire to contribute to the well-being of society. You can be a financial 'winner' and earn lots of bits of paper by making some plastic claptrap that is no real use to anyone. But you can be a financial loser by dedicating your life to the care of others. What you sell is what matters, not what you contribute to humanity. As we have seen, the easiest way to make money is to create it out of nothing. Values and desires become distorted by this and societies become sick and more divided. Another implication of this annual expansion is that, as production becomes more mechanised, the investment necessary to compete gets greater and the small fall by the wayside. Big becomes beautiful and life becomes ugly. The economic power gathers in fewer and fewer hands in line with the Brotherhood plan and the major corporations and banks call the shots far more than elected politicians.

(5) The mopping up of unemployment by the expansion of 'wants' can only go on for so long. Through this century, and particularly since the sixties and seventies, the so-called 'Third

World' has started to produce more finished products. The system that started with Britain exploiting its empire for 'resources' and selling them back the finished products has changed dramatically. The whole of Europe and then the United States followed and expanded what Britain had started. In the second half of this century, the Far East, Asia, Africa, and South America, were sold the Industrial Dream, often by banks who wished to invest the money that was pouring in, especially from Arab countries after the Brotherhood-engineered oil price surge of the 1970s. The world has become awash with products looking for people to buy them.

(6) At the same time there are fewer people with the money to buy those products. Once a large number of countries have the same ambition – to produce more and sell more – and they pass the point where this can continue within their own borders, everyone has to compete with everyone else for sales all over the world. This becomes a battle to the economic and, for at least 100,000 people every day, the physical death. More automation is required to produce more products at a lower cost because everyone has to compete to find ways of making the same product cheaper. More automation means less employment, and less money in people's pockets to buy the products the machines are making. The major manufacturers begin to transfer much of their production to Third World countries because the laws on exploitation there are even more lax than in the West, and you can pay people a fraction of the wages demanded in Europe and America.

(7) As a result of all this, the system is now in desperate trouble and that is precisely what the banking elite want to justify their next step, a centralised world economy, based on a World Central Bank. While some unemployment is seen as good for the system because it helps to keep those employed subservient through fear of losing their job, there comes a stage where it is dangerous. This happens when the numbers without a job, and with no prospect of getting one, reach uncontrollable proportions. The amount of money being produced by declining sales is no longer sufficient to pay the welfare benefits of those increasing numbers who are no longer employed and the social needs of the victims the system spits out when they are no longer any use to it. The system is so crazy that to survive it needs more and more people to buy each year, but fewer and fewer people to make what they buy. It cannot

have both, but it needs both. People will be subservient only while they are indoctrinated to believe that the system will provide. When it becomes clear that it will not, people begin to rebel against that system. This rebellion becomes even more powerful as those without work and with no prospect of work, see their welfare benefits cut back by politicians overseeing declining industrial sales in the wake of all that I have described. The Illuminati want the people to respond violently to all this as we shall see, and the response, the rebellion, **must** be peaceful, if their plan is to be thwarted.

(8) The main waste product of this system is human debris. When you force people to work in a soulles, mindless, system, this can have severe mental and emotional ekfects. Our hearts desire freedom, love and joy. Our inner self wants to be positive, creative, and tap all the endless potential that we all have, and I mean *all*. But the system demands that we are little more than the extension of technology and expendable whenever technology can be created to replace us. To the system we are not people or spiritual beings, we are units of production and consumption. You will even note that we are now referred to by the stewards of the system, the politicians, economists, and industrialists, as 'consumers' because that is how it sees us. This system without a soul has created an explosion in other expressions of consumption such as alcohol and drugs. These are ways that people try to escape from the nightmare and the agony their inner selves are suffering. They may not even be aware that they are feeling like this at a deeper level. But it will still manifest in drugs and other forms of temporary escape from the realities of this mad world. The stress of the system's demands, the constant competition, the fear, the imprisonment and suppression of the spirit, has become a conveyor belt for mental, emotional, and physical disease, or dis-ease as it really should be pronounced. The stress causes imbalances in the mental and emotional energy fields and these are passed on through the chakras to all levels of being, including the physical body. We have more and more illness caused by stress and all the pollution and other dangers the system produces in its insatiable desire for expansion at all costs. Is it any wonder that you see defeat in so many faces. The system, science, and religion have combined to make billions tired of living, but scared of dying.

Crime is another consequence. If you programme people to see their own success and that of others in terms of consumption and possessions, don't hold up your hands in horror when those who cannot earn the money to consume and possess choose another way of 'succeeding' in the system's terms – theft, mugging, burglaries. In times of high unemployment more people are denied the ability to succeed through consumption or even to feed their families, and this is why the crime figures soar. Also if the system treats human life as meaningless, worthless, fodder, without dignity or respect, don't be surprised if that is how many others start to see their fellow human beings. Growing violence is evidence of this. Resentment at being rejected by the system leads to resentment against everything and everyone. In this state of mind some will mug an old lady for a few pounds or dollars without a thought for what they have done to her. Their motto will be: 'the system has no respect for me, so why should I have any respect for anyone else? It's everyone for themselves'.

But hold on a second. If your agenda involves the introduction of an ever-more-authoritarian police force, military and legal system, what do you need more than anything to carry public opinion with you? More crime, the more violent and horrible the better.

In a system in which the possession of pieces of paper is the only way you can enjoy food, shelter and warmth, you are faced with increasing numbers of people made redundant by technology and recession who are hungry, homeless and cold. There are also those who are disabled, elderly and infirm, or unable to work for other reasons. These, too, are denied the means to earn pieces of paper. The System reacts to this in a variety of ways. In some countries it ignores such people and suppresses wholesale rebellion by strengthening the police force and the army and by making those in work fearful of speaking out against this cruelty and losing their job. Elsewhere, governments pay these victims of the system as little as they can get away with, though in a few more enlightened countries they are more generous. But all use the weapon of fear to control the population and prevent serious rebellion.

Every year the System is faced with bigger bills for crime, policing, medical services, welfare benefits, and all the rest. This is an inevitable consequence of take, make and throwaway, and all that goes with it. And how does the System and its mind-controlled politicians react to this? By saying we must have a greater expansion of production and consumption to raise more money by creating more growth. This 'policy' spews out yet more victims and demands yet more resources are spent on crime, police, medical services, and welfare benefits. Those who are hypnotised by the Brotherhood propaganda do not have the intelligence or the vision to think any other way no matter how nonsensical this 'thinking' may be. As Mark Twain said: 'If your only tool is a hammer, all problems look like nails'.

(9) The demands of the system and its de-humanisation of people has led to the exploitation of other life forms. I have heard it said that animal rights campaigners should think more about cruelty to people than animals. This misses the point. Cruelty is cruelty. Any society that will justify the appalling treatment of animals that goes on today will have no qualms about being cruel to people. Animals, like people, have become another commodity, another form of throughput. We perform experiments on them which make the worst excesses of the Nazis seem like kindness itself. We have the horrors of the slaughterhouses and food factories – 500 million chickens in Britain are forced to live out their wretched lives standing on wire mesh in tiny cages with hardly enough room to sit down. They are egg-throughput machines. Around 40 million little chicks are killed in Britain every year within hours of their birth for the 'crime' of being male. They are from a species genetically developed for egg laying. The males cannot lay eggs and so they cannot live. Every week in British slaughterhouses we murder 8 million chickens, 300,000 pigs, 80,000 cattle, 500,000 turkeys, 50,000 rabbits, and 300,000 sheep in conditions of dreadful cruelty and barbarism. As the saying goes: If slaughterhouse walls were made of glass, we'd all be vegetarians. Only a human race de-linked from its true self and controlled by a consciousness that wishes to destroy our compassion and inner goodness would allow this to happen. There is a British cabinet minister and outspoken Christian dogmatist who has ridiculed vegetarians at every opportunity. "If God had wanted us to be vegetarians", he said, "He would have given us three stomachs." In reply you could say that if God had wanted us to talk such baloney He/She would not have given us a brain.

(10) To hide the realities of the system and its corruption you need 'Security Services' and other organisations dedicated to secrecy. It is claimed that they are required to keep an eye on potential threats from other countries and terrorist groups and to safeguard national security but, as we have seen, the main aim of

governments and the secrecy services is to keep truth from their own people. This is vital if the system is going to survive. Truth to the system is like garlic to a vampire. The security services spend more time spying on those peacefully challenging the status quo than they do on potential terrorists. They know and manipulate the terrorists, anyway, and indeed engage in terrorism themselves. All sorts of underhand manoeuvring goes on to stop any individual or group which they fear may be vehicles for effectively challenging the system. Frame-ups, phone taps, agents provocateurs, even murder; all these methods are used by the state and the global Brotherhood and its representatives to stop those who present a threat to their continuing control.

(11) Into all that I have said, another fundamental limitation on the system's further expansion must be added. It is the most important factor of all. If you demand that every year you consume more, you dismantle the planet on which we all depend. Even the land is treated like a factory floor. It has been so exploited with chemicals to maximise short term production that its ability to go on producing is being reduced every year. If you had a machine that produced the essentials of human survival and it was the only machine of its kind that existed, what would people say if you took a sledgehammer to this machine and bashed it into tiny pieces? People would say you were bonkers, crazy, mad, many sandwiches short of a picnic. Well that is exactly what the human race is doing to the planet. Every year through this Industrial Revolution we have taken more 'resources' from the Earth and turned them into more pollution in the name of 'progress.' In doing this, the system has had to increase the number of products that are disposable and thrown away as soon as possible after purchase. Only in this way can you increase production. You can't do it if you make things to last. This economic necessity under the rules of the system has given us the disposable cup, knife, fork, plate, razor, etc, and an ever-increasing amount of throwaway packaging. Something that is used once and thrown away is an orgasmic experience for the system; anything that is made to last as long as possible is potentially fatal. As I have said, the United States is on the front line of this suicide, but most of the world is involved also. We have created such a monster that the more successful it is in its own terms, the quicker it destroys the planet. But we still have politicians talking of the need to return to full

employment. Under the rules of the present system, full employment of the traditional kind across the world would leave the planet a waste land. It is utter, utter, insanity. It cannot go on and it will not go on.

The consequences of this system of self-destruction have created a world in which 20 per cent of the population consume 80 per cent of the 'resources' every year; the other 80 per cent of humanity must go without their needs so that the system can pander to greed. People throughout the world die from the diseases of too little, while elsewhere others die from the diseases of too much. It has produced a world full of conflict and division, one in which pain, suffering, exploitation and war are essential to the system's survival.

The Brotherhood, which has created and orchestrated this system for its own ends, know it is a nonsense and after its planned coup on the human race, the first thing it will do is dismantle the system they have imposed:

"You understand perfectly that economic arrangements of this kind, which have been suggested to the Goyim by us, cannot be carried on by us." (Protocol 20.)

They know the System's stupid. It is supposed to be!

But let me stress one point above all others. The enslaving consciousness and the pressures of this planet may make it more difficult to express our true selves, but it does not make it impossible. You only have to look around your own community and the world in general to see wonderful, loving, caring and generous people. We don't *have* to be robots or be controlled by the Brotherhood and the Luciferic thought patterns; we *allow* ourselves to be and we can stop doing so. We see enough in our own lives and elsewhere to know what is acceptable and what is not; we all have the opportunity to start to think for ourselves and live what we believe; we can all open our minds and re-connect with our higher consciousness. Millions are doing this today and many others have done so throughout history even through these traumatic centuries in the life of Planet Earth. It doesn't have to be like this and we don't have to be like this. Humanity is in nature *good*, not evil. We can express that goodness if we choose to. How strong is our will to resist the urgings of the Luciferic consciousness? How strong our desire to follow our own heart?

The present transformation will bring – is bringing – change of an incomprehensible scale. The Luciferic control of human consciousness is being removed and it will be both a time of turmoil and glorious opportunity. Clearly it is a transformation that has arrived not a moment too soon.

12

The New World Order

I can understand if some people are having trouble with the mental gymnastics demanded by this book.

After all, your consciousness is being challenged to reject the accepted history of humankind, and to see through the smoke-screen that much of it is. This is not always easy when you have been through the education (indoctrination) system, and the establishment version of past, present, and future which is constantly fed to us through the media minute by minute. And in a world in which the 'norm' is to laugh at the idea of UFOs and extra-terrestrials, you are being presented with a view that suggests that, far from not existing, ETs of both positive and negative intent have been a fundamental influence on human affairs.

Perhaps most difficult of all to accept is that a Brotherhood was set up thousands of years ago to initiate an elite into the spiritual 'truths', while twisting those truths enough to con the initiates into manipulating everyone else; and that today this same Brotherhood has progressed to the point where it controls most of the world's political, economic and secret service activity. From the perspective of life which the system encourages to us to believe, all of this appears to be simply ridiculous, quite outrageous and over the top. That Icke must be a candidate for the funny farm, eh? But that is exactly what you are supposed to think. Human beings are indoctrinated with such an inaccurate version of history and of reality that even if the suppression fails and truth comes out, it is so different from the indoctrinated version, that people just laugh and say it's off the wall. What was it that Hitler said? "The bigger the lie, the more will believe it."

"If in regard to the external foe it is allowed and not considered immoral to.....keep the enemy in ignorance of plans to attack him by night or in superior numbers, then in what way can the same means in regard to the

worse foe, the destroyer of the structure of society and the commonweal (sic), be called immoral and not permissible?" (Illuminati Protocol 1).

I am not suggesting that this Brotherhood has mind-controlled its millions of members worldwide into knowingly dedicating their lives to the 'Great Work of Ages' called world domination. As I keep on stressing, the overwhelming majority will not know what they are a part of. It is as vital for the elite to keep them in the dark as it is for the mass of the population to be kept in ignorance. It couldn't work if the membership knew the game plan because most would want nothing to do with it, and the Brotherhood branches, like the freemasons, need an acceptable public face to hide behind. Their members below certain levels of initiation provide that with their dinner dances and their charity work. It's the same with most of the others. Even lower levels of the secret societies are used for manip-ulation of local councils, courts, commerce and police officers, but most supporters of the Brotherhood are very decent, kind, people. It is the elite we need to concern ourselves with and, at least in the great majority of cases, that does not even include politicians. They are pawns like everyone else. Those who work within the Brotherhood societies at the lower levels and haven't realised the true agenda, no longer have the excuse of ignorance. The Illuminati Protocols make clear that the masonic lodges and the lower degrees peopled by what they call "Goy cattle" are merely there to provide the elite with "a show army.....in order to throw dust in the eyes of their fellows". These unsuspecting, naive, masons should understand that they are expendable, too, in the eyes of the Illuminati. Everyone is. The elite's obsession with world domination is their sole, driving motivation. One Illuminati protocol points out that what it calls "Goy Masons" who know too much will be dealt with after the elite "come into their Kingdom". Another says:

"We execute masons in such wise (sic) that none save the brotherhood can ever have a suspicion of it, not even the victims themselves of our death sentence, they all die when required as if from a normal kind of illness. Knowing this, even the brotherhood in its turn dare not protest. While teach-ing Liberalism to the Goyim we at the same time keep our own people and our agents in a state of unquestioning submission." (Protocol 15).

Even the Brotherhood elite has not been – and still is not today – in total control of everything. They have had some colossal failures

I'm sure, and they have had periods through history when they have been less effective than at other times. But as each successive generation within the Brotherhood has passed on the initiations and indoctrination to the next one, its power to affect and decide the outcome of events has grown, particularly over the last two hundred years, as global communications and the world financial system have allowed enormous power to be held by the very few. The Brotherhood now pervades every area of our lives, and through the media which it also controls it can drip feed the population in ways it could never do before. Their plan to dominate the world, which goes under the name of the New World Order is reaching its conclusion – if we don't wake up fast. In his period as President of the United States, George Bush even used those words New World Order to describe his vision of the future after the Gulf War and this term is now widely used by politicians in general.

The Brotherhood elite which includes the Rothschild and Rockefeller empires now have six main front organisations for their covert activities. They are the Council on Foreign Relations, the Trilateral Commission, the Club of Rome, the Bilderberg Group, the Royal Institute of International Affairs, and the United Nations. All of these came directly, or indirectly, from the Round Table secret society set up by the freemason, Cecil Rhodes, and the Round Table still stands at the centre of this empire of control. Around that symbolic table sit the few who direct the world's political and economic affairs. This empire is, in effect, the World Government in waiting, waiting that is, to become the official one.

The aptly named Harold Pratt House at 58 East 68th Street in New York is the headquarters of the Council on Foreign Relations. It was started with Rockefeller money in 1921. We have seen how this 'think tank' controlled events during the Second World War and it has continued to do so. Appointees from the CFR have been numerous and prominent within successive United States administrations, banking, business, the media and the universities, and the foreign and domestic policy of a supposedly free and democratic nation is controlled by this non-elected Brotherhood front group. If they direct US foreign policy, of course, they do so for the world. The CFR has affiliated organisations right across the US. It is the American arm of the Royal Institute of International Affairs in London, which is also known as 'Chatham House'. This was set up in 1920 and these two 'think tanks' working in concert are the reason for the so-called 'special relationship' between Britain and the USA, and was responsible also for manipulating the Americans into the Second World War. But contrary to popular belief, it is Britain, at the Brotherhood level, that is the dominant partner of the two. The Royal Institute is obviously very influential in the foreign policy of the United Kingdom, and other countries have similar organisations under its influence. The RIIA is a registered charity with the Queen as its patron. It is supported by a stream of global oil companies, multi-nationals, and leading media organisations, including the BBC and its World Service. (Source: the RIIA Annual Report 1992-93). The Trilateral Commission was launched by David Rockefeller, the chairman of the Chase Manhattan Bank and head of the Rockefeller family empire. It was made public in 1973, but almost certainly existed in secret in 1972. The Commission consists of invited financiers, industrialists, media moguls, union leaders, and politicians from North America, Western Europe and Japan, and its aim is to control the course of international events, in order to protect and expand the interests of the elite in those three areas of the world. The symbolism of the triangle should be noted. It is a major Brotherhood symbol. Within three years of going public the Commission had achieved its ambition of installing the first Tri-lateralist president in the White House, Jimmy Carter, and his 'National Security Adviser' was Zbigniew Brzezinski, the commission's first director and a leading inspiration behind its formation. Carter filled his administration with Trilateralists, among them his Vice-President, Walter Mondale, and Secretary of State, Cyrus Vance.

The Bilderberg Group is another forum for Europe's and America's leading politicians, financiers, industrialists, media executives, and military leaders to discuss the course of human affairs. The Rothschilds and Rockefellers are the power behind the Bilderberg Group, which is the European and NATO connection within the Brotherhood empire and the most powerful of these 'front' organisations. The Bilderberg meetings were started, yet again with Rockefeller and Rothschild money, by Prince Bernhard of the House of Orange in the Netherlands. The name Bilderberg comes from the hotel in the Netherlands where the group first met in 1954, though the existence of the group was denied for many years. Prince Bernhard was a member of the SS before the war and an employee of I.G.Farben. After marrying into the House of Orange he became chairman of Shell Oil. He chaired the Bilderberg meetings until 1976 when he was forced to resign in the Lockhead corruption scandal. Bilderberg meetings are held in strict secrecy, and only if you know an insider can you find out anything of their discussions. Lord Carrington, the former British cabinet minister and Secretary-General of NATO, is a prominent Bilderberger, and became chairman in 1991. He is also a president of the Royal Institute of International Affairs. He works closely with the Rothschilds and the Rockefellers, and with Henry Kissinger, the former US Secretary of State. Kissinger is a Bilderberger, a Trilateralist and a member of the Council on Foreign Relations. Lord Carrington was a founding board member of Kissinger Associates. Both are also on the board of the Hollinger Corporation (chairman Conrad Black, a Bilderberger and owner of the London *Daily Telegraph* and the *Jerusalem Post*).

The Club of Rome is another 'think tank' organisation which claims to be developing a strategy for the survival of the planet and it, too, supports the idea of centralised planning and world government. Finally, there is the United Nations which is based in New York on land given by the Rockefellers. The plan for the UN was hatched during the last War by a secret steering committee of the Council on Foreign Relations. The UN was sold to the world under the cloak of pursuing peace among nations. Unlike its predecessor, the League of Nations, this one was going to stick and serve the Brotherhood. If one world war wouldn't persuade governments to do as the elite required, give them another one; that did it. For United Nations read United States, and for USA and UN read New World Order.

The Round Table and its subsidiaries control the United Nations. It was their creation and on all decisions that matter they call the shots. Alongside this have come the International Monetary Fund and the World Bank, and the ground is now being prepared for a world army under UN (Brotherhood) control. NATO is already run by the Brotherhood. Conflicts are being triggered and inflamed across the globe to soften up public opinion to accept this as the only way to deal with the gathering violence. The more horrendous the pictures the media broadcast from the world trouble spots, the better it is for those who want a centrally-controlled world army. The UN Secretary General Dr. Boutros Boutros Ghali (a Brotherhood stooge) has already called for a permanent, heavily armed, UN force to be in situ as soon as possible. At a meeting of the Bilderberg Group at Baden Baden, Germany, in 1991, Henry Kissinger, is reported in the

US investigative newspaper, *Spotlight* to have said: "A UN army must be able to act immediately, without the delays involved in each country making its own decisions on whether to participate based on parochial considerations".

Governments don't run the world – the Brotherhood does. You can't even run for the presidential nomination within your own party in America without enormous sums of money behind you, and without massive financial backing you have got no chance of running for the presidency itself. Once you have accepted that, there are favours to be paid off, and if you are not willing to play the game, you won't be supported by the financiers anyway. Politicians are not usually privy to the whole Brotherhood plot, even if they are members. They are only told what they need to know, and those who are invited to attend the Bilderberg meetings are there to be fed the Brotherhood line of the best way to run the world. It is the Bilderberg Group's permanent executive that runs the show, as it is with these other front organisations. One of those invited to the Baden Baden meeting of the Bilderbergers in 1991, incidentally, was the then governor of Arkansas, one Bill Clinton, who went on to become President. He would not have become President unless the elite wanted him to.*

The aim of the Illuminati is the introduction of a world government to which every continent would be subordinate. It would dictate foreign policy and control the world army. Underpinning everything would be a world central bank based on the lines of the national central banks of today, and there would be one currency controlled entirely by them. It also wishes to go further and turn the people of the planet literally into robots in ways that I will highlight shortly. If you look at the world today you can see how nations are already losing the power to make decisions to giant trading blocs like the European Union and the North American Free Trade Agreement (NAFTA). In Europe the move is towards one currency and one European Central Bank. The pieces are being moved around the board in preparation for the 'sting'. It is revealing to note, also, how so many politicians who oppose this loss of national sovereignty suddenly find themselves discredited and have their power removed. *Spotlight* reported in May 1989 that

---

* Others attending included Queen Beatrice of the Netherlands, Queen Sophia of Spain, the owner of the *Washington Post*, Andrew Knight the then chairman of Rupert Murdoch's News International, the editor of the *Wall Street Journal*, and a stream of prime ministers, politicians, bankers and industrialists.

the Bilderberg meeting that month on La Toja Island, off Spain, had decided that Margaret Thatcher would be removed as British Prime Minister, because of her "refusal to yield British sovereignty to the European Superstate that is to emerge after 1992". That is exactly what happened when she was removed while in office by her own side, the British Conservative Party in 1990. It was a Brotherhood coup, nothing less, to ease the way to a United States of Europe. The latest GATT Agreement which opens more borders to 'free' world trade is another creation of the Brotherhood elite to destroy a country's ability to make its own economic decisions.

The game plan is this. The Brotherhood, manipulated by its Illuminati elite, has been working to create conflict across the world on all levels. This is going into overdrive now. They are also undermining the world economy, which they control, to destroy what remains of the confidence the population has in politicians and governments. The Brotherhood has ensured that people of limited ability, intellect and vision – puppets – have reached the top in politics, and this has had two main effects. It has made sure they were easy to manipulate by the Brotherhood 'advisors' behind the scenes, and their obvious lack of ability has helped to remove the credibility still further of politics and politicians. This is exactly what the plan has always been in preparation for the economic collapse they will engineer.

"The hatred (of the present order) will be further magnified by the effects of an economic crisis which will stop the dealings on the exchanges and bring industry to a standstill. We shall create by all subterranean methods open to us.....a universal economic crisis whereby we shall throw upon the streets whole mobs of workers simultaneously. These mobs will rush delightedly to shed the blood of those whom, in the simplicity of their ignorance, they have envied from their cradles, and whose property they will then be able to loot. Ours they will not touch, because the moment of attack will be known to us and we shall take measures to protect our own." (Illuminati Protocol 3).

This is the culmination of the long term plan to create dependence through the 'Welfare State'. First they removed the independence of people by making them dependent on working for the military-industrial system. Then they squeezed the number of jobs and made more and more people dependent on so-called handouts, while taking away all alternatives of a self-reliant lifestyle that was not dependent on the Brotherhood economic system. Now they are using that manufactured dependence to further manipulate. They are reducing social security payments and will seek to force people to work for the state in return for a pittance called 'unemployment benefit' or whatever. What they want to create is an underclass of bitterness which will trigger civil war between the haves and have nots. They also wish to crush the human spirit and make it too weary to resist the New World Order, and even to welcome it as their saviour. When things have got so bad, in terms of the economy, wars, and disease, and the world is in utter chaos, along will come the Brotherhood with its mask of compassion and benevolence and promise to put everything right. What they won't say is that the ills they will pledge themselves to remove are the very ills they have orchestrated to programme the human mind. They will blame it all on the politicians they have controlled and the system they have created. The bombardment of the human mind with constant horrors through the media is a policy known as 'Future Shock'. It is designed to deaden the mind and make it believe it is impotent in the face of so many immense problems.

"It is from us that the all-engulfing terror proceeds. We have in our service persons of all opinions, of all doctrines, restorating monarchists, demagogues, socialists, communists, and utopian dreamers of every kind. We have harnessed them all to the task: each one of them on his own account is boring away at the last remnants of authority, is striving to overthrow all established forms of order. By these acts all states are in torture; they exhort to tranquility, are ready to sacrifice everything for peace: but we will not give them peace until they openly acknowledge our international super-government, and with submissiveness. .

". . To produce the possibility of the expression of such wishes by all the nations it is indispensible to trouble in all countries the people's relations with their governments so as to utterly exhaust humanity with dissension, hatred, struggle, envy and even by the use of torture, by starvation, by the inoculation of diseases [Aids], by want, so that the Goyim sees no other issue than to take refuge in our complete sovereignty in money and in all else. But if we give the nations of the world a breathing space the moment we long for is hardly likely ever to arrive . .

". . When we have accomplished our coup d'état we shall say then to the various peoples: 'Everything has gone terribly badly, all have been worn out with the sufferings. We are destroying the causes of your torment —

nationalities, frontiers, differences of coinages'..... Then the mob will exalt us and bear us up in their hands in a unanimous triumpth of hopes and expectations." (Illuminati Protocol 10)

It is time for those politicians and their supporters who genuinely want freedom to come together and stop squabbling over irrelevant, Brotherhood-manufactured, differences. You are all being used to fight a phoney political war! Throughout this century in Britain and other countries the political battle has gone on between left, right, and centre while all the time the strings of every political shade are being pulled by the same people. *Wake Up.* Elements within the Fabian Society have manipulated the UK Labour Party, and trades union and other 'workers organisations', political and non-political, are being used to bring about the fascist World Government, mostly without realising it:

"We shall raise the rate of wages which, however, will not bring any advantage to the workers, for, at the same time, we shall produce a rise in prices of the first necessities of life.....we shall further undermine artfully and deeply sources of production, by accustoming the workers to anarchy and to drunkeness and side by side therewith taking all measure to extirpate from the face of the earth all the educated forces of the goyim. In order that the true meaning of things may not strike the goyim before the proper time we shall mask it under an alleged ardent desire to serve the working classes and the great principles of the political economy about which our economic theories are carrying on an energetic propaganda." (Protocol 6).

Behind this attempt to complete the 'Great Work of Ages' are some of the same mystical teachings of the infiltrated Brotherhood and its mystery schools which go back at least as far as ancient Egypt and Babylon. On one level the New World Order would appear, according to some, to include the crowning of a 'Messiah', the Second Coming of a World King in around the year 2,000. The crowning is planned to take place in a rebuilt Solomon's Temple in Jerusalem, which would replace the Moslem mosque currently on that site. This new Messiah would seem to be someone (at least in the Brotherhood's misguided mind) claiming a bloodline back to King David via Jesus, Mary Magdalene, and their offspring. This is what the Knights Templars were dedicated to doing (and still are in the guise of the Freemasons) and the Priory of Sion still exists and continues to pursue this bizarre ambition, along with its long held goal of a "United States of Europe". Another aim of the New World Order is for one World Church – its own – based on the beliefs of the Templars. Some researchers believe that the 'World King' is part of a bloodline going back to the last Roman Emperor. Like I say, it doesn't matter if *you* believe this nonsense followed by the Brotherhood, as long as *they* believe it, we are all affected. The Illuminati are not stupid, but they are very strange people.

According to Sumer tablets and freemasonic legend, there was a supernova or massive explosion in the heavens in the ancient period. It has been claimed that the grand gallery in the Great Pyramid at Giza is focused on the area of the southern sky where the supernova would have been seen in the triangle of stars called Zeta Puppis, Gamma Velorum, and Lambda Velorum. Some scientists have identified pulses which they believe to be radio waves caused by a star which blew apart around 4,000BC. The Sumerian star catalogue, which has been shown to be very accurate, predicted that the blazing star would be seen again on Earth in 6,000 years – around now. Perhaps the Brotherhood intends to use what it believes to be the return of that exploding star to usher in its New World Order and the world king. If it can cause so much mayhem in the world before then, people will be only too willing to believe in some Second Coming to bring 'peace' to humanity – especially if this is combined with amazing sights in the sky. I don't know what goes on the minds of the Brotherhood, because the reality of life has been so muddled in their consciousness by the Luciferic forces and the indoctrination of the ages, that goodness knows what they believe or will seek to achieve. The overall ambition, however, remains the same. To imprison the human race, mentally, emotionally, spiritually and physically.

Investigators of the New World Order and Brotherhood history come from all shades of belief. Among them are Christian fanatics and those, like me, who think that religion is a curse on the world. There are some who have got interested in the subject from the economic point of view, while others have come into this area of investigation via science, the New Age, the security services, UFO groups, etc. There are some I would not choose to spend an evening with and others who are calling for the Illuminati to be hanged, which is, to say the least, hardly my own approach! In short, the investigators come from many belief systems and this makes even more compelling the enormous area of agreement between them on the main themes of the conspiracy I am outlining.

I emphasise the need to keep our eyes on the *themes* and not get too bogged down with every detail, because there is a great deal of disinformation flying around. You have to be aware of the double-bluff – the leaking of information by the Brotherhood to take researchers off the trail. The Brotherhood intelligence network has infiltrated many New Age, UFO, and investigative groups and you have to be careful not to believe everything claimed by apparent 'opponents' of the New World Order. Remember how the Brotherhood works. This whole area is teeming with 'ex CIA' men claiming to have seen the light and anxious to tell the public the truth. In some cases they might be genuine, in many they will not.

The most effective form of disinformation is when truth is mixed with fiction which can easily be shown to be inaccurate. This way you achieve two things. You discredit the investigators by proving that some of their claims are wrong, and you discredit in the public mind the other information they have put out which *is* true. It is vital that when some information genuinely released by writers and researchers is proved to be false that people don't at the same time reject everything else they are saying. That is what you are meant to do. And, anyway, why if the authorities have nothing to hide are they putting out disinformation in the first place? The whole idea is to confuse and this not only applies to New World Order investigators, but also the public in general.

"In order to put public opinion into our hands we must bring it into a state of bewilderment by giving expression from all sides to so many contradictory opinions and for such length of time as will suffice to make the Goyim lose their heads in the labyrinth and come to see that the best thing is to have no opinion of any kind in matters political." (Protocol 5).

Whenever I hear someone say "I never discuss politics or religion" as if that is a virtue, I feel like screaming. Crucial to the Illuminati cover-up, the publishing of disinformation and the discrediting of investigators like myself, is the press and the media. I will talk more of this in a later chapter, but suffice to say now that the world media is almost totally under Brotherhood control and where they don't actually run the publication, they control the 'information' that it receives. Most journalists (and there are some honorable exceptions) are in a mental prison, again most of them without realising it. I have met many who clearly think they are street-wise about the world when if they only opened their eyes they would see that they are little more than copy typists for the manipulators. They largely 'investigate' irrelevances or subjects which suit the Brotherhood's desired plan. What the public *really* need to know is never addressed. I heard Harold Evans, the former editor of the London *Times* and *Sunday Times*, talking on the radio of the appalling way the media tycoon Rupert Murdoch, his former boss, runs his vast world newspaper and broadcasting empire to suit his own commercial and political interests (and who else's?). Evans described how Margaret Thatcher in her years as British Prime Minister was "Murdoch's poodle" who did as she was told in matters relating to him.

I found it particularly interesting in the light of this book, that Evans also made the point that while American journalists were committing endless time, money and energy into investigating the bedroom habits of Bill Clinton and the financial affairs of his wife, the terrible effect of the Federal Reserve Board on the US economy went unchallenged. But then, after what this book has revealed, that is no longer a surprise, is it? Most so-called professional journalists are irrelevant to real information-gathering and communication. That is being done by researchers who have the courage to search for truth and by the magazines now springing into life which are prepared to print it.

John Swainton, a long-time Chief of Staff at the prestigious *New York Times*, in the 1860s and '70s said in a retirement speech to his staff:

"There is no such thing as a free press. You know it and I know it. There's not one of you who would dare to write his honest opinions. The business of a journalist is to destroy truth, to lie outright, to pervert, to vilify, to fawn at the feet of Mammon, and to sell himself, his country and his race for his daily bread. We are tools and vassals of rich men behind the scenes. We are jumping jacks; they pull the strings, we dance; our talents, our possibilities and our lives are the property of these men. We are intellectual prostitutes."★

★ Quoted by Dana Baker in her article on "Media Suppression" in Profile Magazine.

The main difference between researchers of the New World Order is over the involvement or not of extra-terrestrials in all this. I have made it clear in the book that I do believe ETs exist and that they seeded the human form as we know it. I feel their direct involvement, on Earth at least, was dramatically reduced after Atlantis, Egypt, and Babylon, but I feel they have continued to have an effect, both positive and negative, on human evolution. I think they have worked through human consciousness and when you see in due course the mind controlling techniques available to the Illuminati's human scientists and manipulators, you will appreciate that anything is possible for extra-terrestrials who are far in advance of us technologically and in their mind-controlling potential. It is important to remember also, given the themes I have been suggesting through human history, that the ETs have had this knowledge and potential throughout the period covered by this book. It could well be that negative ETs (by far the minority) have control of the minds of the Illuminati. The Illuminati are victims, too, and mind-controlled to mind control everyone else since ancient times. That is not to say that I accept all the UFO stories. There is a great deal of disinformation being put about to confuse and divert and I feel that some claims about UFOs are being used to cover up Brotherhood activities, for reasons I will explain later. But for the moment, let us look at the evidence for the direct involvement of ETs on Earth today.

Human history is littered with stories of strange lights and 'gods' in the sky, unidentified flying objects, and the appearance of ET-type figures. Of course not all will be genuine, and there were probably non-UFO explanations for most of them, but it is silly just to write them all off as some people do. The reports increased in modern times from the early 1940s and a number of incidents have been reported of extra-terrestrial bodies being found. The most famous is known as the Roswell incident which has been documented by many researchers, including Tim Good in his books on the subject.

On July 2nd 1947, the story goes, at least one spacecraft crashed during a storm in the New Mexico desert near a place called Corona, seventy-five miles north-west of Roswell. The crash left a trail of debris a mile long and a hundred yards wide. A ranch hand, 'Mac' Brazel, picked up some of the remains, strange pieces of metal which were incredibly light and strong which had written upon them geometrical symbols and hieroglyphics. The ranch

hand didn't tell the authorities about this find for several days and
when he did some personnel from the Roswell army-air base
arrived to investigate. After they reported to the base commander
he authorised a press release announcing they had found a flying
saucer. This was printed in the local papers and one report said:

*"The office of the 509th bombardment group at Roswell Army Air Field
announced at Noon today that the field was in possession of a flying
saucer."*

Suddenly the higher levels of the military arrived on the scene and
the cover-up began. They withdrew the press release and launched
a weather balloon which they immediately caused to crash. They
made this available for press pictures claiming that the balloon and
not a flying saucer had been found. Meanwhile, in another area of
the crash site, a civil engineer working on an irrigation project and
a group of archeologists found four extra-terrestrials. Three were
dead and one was still alive, so the story says. They were described
as three to four feet tall wearing very tight, spacesuit-type
clothing, but with no cover on the heads or hands. The military
closed off the entire area and those who saw either the crashed craft
or the bodies were threatened by the authorities and warned of the
consequences if they revealed what they had seen. The local radio
station, KGFL New Mexico, was visited by the military after
recording an interview with a witness and told that if they wanted
to be on the air twenty-four hours later they should hand over the
interview and forget it ever happened. This they did. A local
mortician who accidentally looked into an operating theatre and
saw one of the extra-terrestrial bodies was told that he would be
'dead bones' if he opened his mouth. A soldier, Sergeant Melvin E
Brown, was told to guard something without being told what it
was. When he investigated he found extra-terrestrial bodies.
Brown told his family very little, but his daughters remember him
saying that the bodies he saw had larger heads than humans, and
no hair. They looked yellowy in colour and their slanted eyes
reminded him of the Chinese. It could have been this race that
'seeded' the Chinese, perhaps. The extra-terrestrial races that visit
the Earth are many and diverse, and therefore, so are the races of
the Earth which they originally created, and possibly continue to
affect genetically. Brown was terrified to reveal anything more of
what he knew to his dying day, but now people are beginning to

speak out and describe their experiences. More than two hundred people witnessed something of this story, it is claimed.

There has been much speculation about the events that followed the discovery of these craft and their occupants in a number of incidents during the 1940s and '50s. Many investigators and insider informants have said that an ET was found alive in another incident near Roswell in 1949. He was given the name 'EBE' or Extra-terrestrial Biological Entity, and lived until 1952. His metabolism worked much like a plant, with nourishment absorbed through the skin. EBE, and other ETs found alive over the years, passed on some astonishing information to the Americans, it is said, which transformed their understanding of Creation and the origins of the human race as we know it. What they were told, according to some writers, supports the themes of ET activity and 'seeding' of the human form by ETs. A few researchers, especially the former member of American Naval Intelligence, Bill Cooper, go much further than most and claim a possible secret conspiracy between the Illuminati and a race of negative ETs which, he believes could have started in the 1950s. He highlights this in his book, *Behold a Pale Horse*. In summary, he suggests the following hypothesis based on what he saw in Naval Intelligence and what he has been told by his 'contacts' since then. To save putting the next few paragraphs in quotes or adding in endless "Cooper says" or "Cooper claims", please keep in mind throughout this little section that the following is what Bill Cooper has said and not me.

Cooper reckons that following the information passed on by the EBE, Project Sign, later called Project Grudge, was launched to investigate what was going on. Another project, called Blue Book, was formed to issue disinformation and hamper outside investigations. President Truman formed the National Security Agency in 1952 by secret executive order with the task of starting a communication with the ETs. The National Security Agency (NSA) is not subject to any laws in the United States which do not specifically mention it by name. The work of the NSA is about as secret as you can get, and it is by far the most important arm of the American intelligence agencies. It attracts most of the funding. Truman told the highest levels of the allies and the Soviet Union of what had been found. The NSA's main job was to find ways of communicating with the ETs and establish the background to their activity. This was done though a special project code named SIGMA.

Dwight D Eisenhower, the Supreme Allied Commander in World War II, became President in 1953 thanks to encouragement and support from the Rockefellers. He was another president from the Council on Foreign Relations. More spacecraft and extra-terrestrials were found and he engaged his friend and CFR member Nelson Rockefeller to help with the ET problem. Rockefeller used the opportunity to restructure the administration of government to make it easier to manipulate, after he was made chairman of the Presidential Advisory Committee on Governmental Organisation.

Nelson Rockefeller was a Republican who was elected governor of New York State four times and rose to the position of Assistant Secretary of State under Roosevelt, even though that was a Demo-cratic administration. He would later become Vice-President after twice losing to Richard Nixon in the race for the Republican Presidential nomination.

Communications were eventually made with a race of ETs who claimed to come from a planet linked to the star Betelgeuse in the constellation of Orion. (Other researchers name different star sys-tems in relation to these ETs). The communications were made thanks to the work of Project SIGMA. The ETs took a high orbit over the Equator and the Americans, says Cooper, used computer binary language to set up a landing and face-to-face meeting. This happened in 1954 when a group of ETs landed at the Holloman Air Force base and later at the Edwards Air Force Base where they met Eisenhower himself. Both the landings and the meeting were filmed, apparently, and somewhere the film still exists.

The claims about this meeting are supported by other sources. It is known that Eisenhower was on vacation in Palm Springs, play-ing golf at this time. He was staying with his friend Paul Roy Helms at the Smoke Tree Ranch, but on the relevant day 20th February 1954, he 'went missing' for four hours. This would have given him plenty of time to get to the Edwards Air Force Base (then called Muroc), to attend the meeting. The official explana-tion for his disappearance was that he had to visit a local dentist after losing a cap on his tooth while eating a chicken leg. No proof of this has ever been offered. The meeting with the ETs led to an agreement. They would not interfere with human affairs so long as their presence was kept a secret, and they were allowed to abduct a certain number of people for research purposes because they had major problems on their own planet, particularly with reproduc-tion. The ETs said the humans would have no memory of the abductions, because of their ability to programme the mind. The Americans agreed to a limited number of abductions on the understanding that the humans would not be harmed, and in return the ETs said they would pass on highly advanced technology and the knowledge of how to time-travel.

It was agreed that the ETs would not work with any other nation, and that there would be an exchange of personnel and 'ambassadors'. Underground bases would be established in the United States for the extra-terrestrials and for the exchange of technology. These were to be under Indian Reservations in the area known as Four Corners in Utah, and in New Mexico, Arizona, Colorado and a location known as Area 51 or 'Dreamland' near Groom Lake in Nevada. The ETs began to pass on their technology here in a nearby area called S-4, code named the Dark Side of the Moon. Project Redlight was created to begin the experimental flights of the ET technology now in US hands, and various projects were begun to maintain total secrecy of what was happening. Project Snowbird had the task of rubbishing any reports of 'UFOs' over the United States. One way they did this was to show the press what experiments they were doing with conventional technology which they used as a way to explain some UFO sightings. In fact they had technology to overcome gravity, and they had their own spacecraft in the 1950s which, by comparison, make today's Space Shuttle look like the technological equivalent of a London taxi. The Space Shuttle, like the technology used in the 'first' Moon landing, is a con, a cover for what is really going on.

Cooper says the underground facilities were paid for with a secret fund administered by the Military Office in the White House. This money was laundered many times before it reached its destination, to mask the origin and purpose. Eisenhower was the last president to know what was really going on, and later presidents who asked about the fund were told it was to build underground shelters for the government in times of war. President Lyndon Johnson used it to build a cinema and a road on his ranch, because he had no idea of its true purpose. There are now, Bill Cooper says, underground sites for the military and ETs all over the States according to "information" he has seen. Most presidents after Eisenhower have been told only that extra-terrestrials with problems on their own planet want to settle here and are handing over incredible gifts of technology in return. Some have known nothing.

Eisenhower set up a permanent committee to supervise all covert operations relating to the ETs. It was called the Majesty 12 (MJ-12) and consisted, according to Cooper's research, of Nelson Rockefeller, CIA Director Allen Welsh Dulles, Secretary of State John Foster Dulles, Secretary of Defence Charles E Wilson, the Chairman of the Joint Chiefs of Staff Admiral Arthur W Radford, the FBI Director J Edgar Hoover, and six men from the executive committee of the Council on Foreign Relations. These were known as the 'Wise Men' and they were all members of a secret society called the Jason Society or the Jason Scholars. These recruited members from the Skull and Bones and the Scroll and Key secret societies at the Yale and Harvard Universities. George Bush was a member of the Skull and Bones and would later join the Council on Foreign Relations and become head of the CIA. MJ-12 has had many changes of name over the years, according to Cooper. Under Eisenhower and Kennedy it was called the Special Group; under Johnson it was the 303 Committee; under Nixon, Ford, and Carter it became the 40 Committee, and under Reagan it was known as P1-40. More recently there has been an attempt to promote disinformation with a 'briefing paper' which mentions an organisation called Majestic 12. Several presidents, including Carter and Reagan, have talked of seeing UFOs before they took office. Carter said during his election campaign that, if elected, he would reveal every piece of information available about them to the public and the scientists. Perhaps he intended to, but he never did.

Eisenhower soon realised that the ETs were not keeping to their agreement. Mutilated animals and people were being found across the country and many abductees were clearly not being returned to the Earth. The Americans now found out that the ETs were interacting with the Soviet Union and that, Cooper says, ...*they had been manipulating humanity through the secret societies, mysticism and religion for a very long time.* They had control of the mind of Adolf Hitler and all of those 'evil' people who have made humanity suffer so much.

Eisenhower established a committee to investigate what was happening. Cooper's sources say it consisted of members of the Council on Foreign Relations and the Jason Society. Zbigniew Brzezinski, the instigator and first director of the Trilateral Commission, was also the director of this new committee for the first eighteen months with Henry Kissinger taking over from him. This group was called Quantico II after the marine base at Quantico, Virginia, where its later meetings took place. Nelson Rockefeller had a retreat built in Maryland which could only be reached by air, which he did specifically for meetings of this group and MJ-12. This location was code named the Country Club. In the end they decided that the only way to proceed was to continue to seek friendly relations with the ETs. The working relationship has continued ever since although not without conflict and disagreements.

So that is Bill Cooper's hypothesis. What do we make of it? Personally, my intuition tells me that some disinformation has been fed to him, but on the basis that the best disinformation mixes truth with fiction, we should not write it all off in the rather arrogant way which some have done. No one has a monopoly on truth, especially when the Brotherhood security services are dropping disinformation all over the place. There may have been contact between the US elite and ETs, although it does not have to be physical interaction. It could have been through psychic sources which the Illuminati use. To be fair, also, Cooper stresses that the above story is a hypothosis and that he could well have been used by the disinformers to fuel the myth of the "alien threat", a myth that could be employed to justify a global state of emergency and centralisation of all power. I believe the latter to be at least a very strong possibility. Whatever the reality it is time for the Pinochio politicians of the world to get off their knees and start making waves until the truth is revealed.

Another 'insider' who says he wants people to know what is happening, is Bob Dean. He says he was a soldier in the US Army for twenty-seven years and was promoted to Cosmic Top Secret Level, the highest in NATO, while serving at the S.H.A.P.E Headquarters in Europe. According to him, many UFOs were being tracked by NATO forces in the 1950s and '60s. He suggests that an investigation was launched under the cover of a study called 'An evaluation of a possible military threat to Allied Forces in Europe'. It included a report on what were said to have been twelve ET bodies found in Northern Europe in 1962. The report concluded, says Dean, that the planet has been the subject of a detailed survey by extra-terrestrials of many kinds for hundreds, possibly thousands of years, and their technology was hundreds of years ahead of ours. I certainly agree with the analysis.

Dean quotes Victor Marchetti, a former special assistant to the executive director of the CIA, as saying privately in 1979:

"We have indeed been contacted, perhaps even visited by, extra-terrestrial beings, and the US Government, in collusion with the other powers of Europe, is determined to keep this information from the general public. The purpose of this international conspiracy is to maintain a working stability between the nations of the world, and for them, in turn, to maintain institutional control over their respective populations.

"For these governments to admit that there are beings from outer space with mentalities and technological capabilities obviously far superior to ours, could, once fully perceived by the average person, erode the foundations of the Earth's traditional power structures.

"Political and legal systems, religious, economic and social institutions, could all become meaningless in the minds of the general public. The national hierarchical establishments, even civilisation as we know it, could collapse into anarchy."

Researcher Tim Good in his books suggests that the RAF have had numerous experiences with UFOs and that their UFO investigations centre is within the headquarters of the Provost and Security Services at RAF Rudloe Manor in Wiltshire. The UFO Unit, it is said, operates secretly under the cover of an organisation called the Flying Complaints Flight.

This unit is staffed by officers trained in counter-intelligence and it could well have been from here that the crop circle phenomenon has been systematically destroyed in the public mind. The patterns in the crops have appeared all over the world, but it was when the amazingly detailed geometric patterns began to appear in Southern England in the early 1990s that the disinformation campaign really began. Public and media interest reached such a peak at the time that something had to be done to stop it. People were asking questions about possible causes, and they were beginning to realise that there was more to life and the Universe than they had been led to believe. In addition to the few materialistic tricksters trying to show that the phenomenon could be easily explained, there erupted organised campaigns to hoax, and to discredit the best known crop circle investigators. People appeared out of nowhere claiming to have made all the crop circles that had appeared over decades all over the world. Ridiculous as this may seem, the public, which in general is incredibly gullible, bought the idea that the phenomenon was all a gigantic hoax. Interest in crop circles slumped dramatically. They are still appearing, with unhoaxable geometry, but only the enthusiasts know about them now. The media has lost all interest, because it is as gullible and as fickle as the general public, more so in some cases, and, of course, it has a tail to wag and a master to lick. I feel, however, that events will bring the crop patterns back onto the public stage.

There is certainly a fantastic cover-up going on in the UFO field. But of what? Extra-terrestrials landing here, interacting with the elite, and abducting human beings? Or is this all just a smoke-screen to hide what is really happening? Other researchers, while agreeing on all the main themes of the New World Order conspiracy, believe that the claims about extra-terrestrials are all disinformation and that the genuine UFOs that people report are, in truth, human technology. (I think both exist). They say that this advanced technology which is far ahead of anything the public know about, was not handed over by ETs in underground bases, but was developed by Illuminati scientists. This, some say, could have begun after the war when the Americans got hold of the work that had been done by Nazi scientists who the Brotherhood made sure escaped from Germany. Certainly it appears that the Nazi scientific and Brotherhood elite had developed anti-gravity technology by the end of the war which used the Earth's natural energy field for its power. It was so secret, Hitler possibly knew nothing about it because he wasn't in control of events; the Brotherhood who controlled him were. This Nazi technology, it is claimed, looked like the UFOs many people describe. The American Academy of Dissident Sciences claims to have details of this. When I was waiting to be interviewed at a TV Station about the first edition of this book, I was stopped by an American in the corridor. "In the book", he said, "Are you saying the American military have got 'UFO' type technology?" I said that I was. "Are you saying that they keep it at S-4 in Nevada?" Again I said yes. "You are right", he said. "I used to work there and I've seen them being flown. It's an unbelievable sight. You can't believe what you are seeing."

A physicist, Bob Lazar, says he also worked at S-4 and saw the "flying saucers" in the hangers. He says they work through an anti-gravity technology which involves matter and anti-matter annihilating each other and in doing so creating power through an electomagnetic field. There is wide agreement that 'UFO' space-craft are real, but some researchers say they are built and flown by humans, not ETs. This theory says that the disinformation about

ET landings are just a way of covering up the technology they have which, if it became generally available, would transform the world economy and free people from so much dependency on the System – because the technology used to fly these craft is the same as that which would provide free energy to everyone, without the need to use fossil fuels. It is also highly likely as I have said that the negative UFO theme is being used in the public mind to prepare for an 'aliens are coming' announcement which will justify a global state of emergency and centralised control. Anything is possible.

Here we have another fusion of agreement by almost all investigators into these subjects. The Brotherhood elite have had, by whatever means, human or ET, the ability to travel in space at least since the 1950s and, many researchers agree, they have established bases on the Moon and Mars under a project which has become known as Alternative Three. This was the name of an apparently fictional story that is perhaps nearer the truth than was originally thought. Maybe the Illuminati know the planet is about to undergo some great change on all levels and want some insurance, who knows? What I am sure about is that the first human landed on the Moon before 1969. When Apollo 11 touched down with Neil Armstrong's 'One small step for man, one giant step for mankind', it was pure Walt Disney. That 'giant step' had happened years earlier with technology far in advance of Apollo. The astronauts on that 'first' Moon landing were, say some researchers, shocked at what they found there, because like most of the lower officials at Mission Control they didn't know the background to what was going on. How stunned they must have been, but they knew the price of speaking out. According to Otto Binder, who worked on the NASA space programme, significant segments of the conversations between Mission Control and the crew of Apollo 11 were not made public after they landed on the Moon. He says that people using VHF receivers to bypass NASA broadcasts heard this conversation:

Mission Control: *"What the hell was it? What's there? Malfunction?"*
Neil Armstrong: *"These babies are huge, sir......enormous. Oh God, you wouldn't believe it. I'm telling you there are other spacecraft out there.....lined up on the far side of the crater edge......they're on the Moon watching us."*

Even more amazing, those craft could well have had Americans on board! What a joke it all is. There is a good chance, too, that the information given to us about the nature of the Moon and Martian atmospheres is untrue and that it is far more hospitable than we are led to believe. When, in 1960, President Kennedy agreed a programme to put a man on the Moon by the end of the decade, he innocently gave the Brotherhood elite a wonderful vehicle to take out of the government system enormous amounts of money allocated to the 'official' space programme, and channel them into the unofficial one. Researchers suggest that the Americans and the Soviet Union, at Brotherhood levels, were working together throughout the so-called Cold War, another Illuminati creation. It was a means of frightening the populations on both sides into suffering appalling hardships, while their governments spent countless billions on weapons research and construction. No doubt there were other reasons, too.

There was no prospect of either side using the weapons; that was not the idea. Control by world war was replaced by *fear* of world war. When one side got too far ahead technologically, they would pass the information to the other through the Brotherhood network. Once the stockpiles reached a certain level, the creation of more weapons could not be justified, except on the grounds of needing to keep ahead of the other side's technology. If they made sure that neither was too far advanced of the other, they could both go on demanding, and getting, more money for new research and development. This was especially important in America where they at least had to pay lip service to democratic accountability. Much of that development money was being channelled into the anti-gravity technology coming from either the ETs or their own scientists, depending on your point of view, and into building vast underground bases where secrecy was ensured. Again both pro-ET and no-ET researchers largely agree that the underground facilities exist, though they may differ on precisely the reason for them. Some of the Star Wars budget was used for these secret purposes, too, and for other covert projects unknown to the people, and even to most of the elected government. The USA were opponents of the Soviet Union? Hardly. The lower levels of both governments and the populations may have thought so, but the Brotherhood elite on both sides were on the same team and played for the same captain – Lucifer and possibly the negative ET group working through their consciousness.

The Illuminati and its Brotherhood offshoots which control the

CIA needed, and still do, a constant stream of massive funding for the covert projects they are involved in. These include the sort of things I have been outlining, and all the other manipulations the book has documented, like the support for civil wars and despotic dictators, which the CIA has secretly supported and brought to power to serve their interests. Next time you see an American president put his hand on his heart and talk about America standing for freedom, I should sit down before you fall over laughing. One of the main ways the covert projects are funded is through illegal drugs. Brotherhood branches and elements within the CIA and some of the world's other secret services, control the world market in drugs. Cooper and other writers have stated this and it came very close to becoming widely known in the wake of the Iran-Contra Affair. Those who have investigated the CIA-drugs connection say it began in the late 1950s. It is claimed that the CIA and other agencies arranged to transport drugs from South America by sea to oil rigs drilling off the US coast. From there they could be brought ashore under the cover of the oil operations. Now the CIA and other Brotherhood branches like British Intelligence and Mossad, the Israeli agency control the entire world market in illegal drugs. The more the laws are tightened by so-called 'Wars on Drugs', the higher the street value. The American authorities have been so committed to the 'War on Drugs' that they have allowed US Oil companies to ship chemicals to South America which are needed to make the drugs. The story of the Iran-Contra affair involving Oliver North during the Reagan Administration was the tip of a fantastic iceberg, and look at how easily it was covered up. The American people and media want a rocket directed at their backsides for allowing it to happen. The invasion of Panama by US forces in 1989 which cost so many lives in Operation 'Just Cause' and led to the abduction to America of President Manuel Noriega, was linked, in part, to the covert drugs operation and the drug money laundered through Panama.

One name that keeps coming up again and again as I read the work of investigators into all this is George Bush, the member of the Council on Foreign Relations, Trilateralist, former head of the CIA, and President of the United States before Bill Clinton. He was also the President of Zapata Offshore Oil, it is alleged, when that company's offshore oil rigs were used to bring in the drugs in the 1950s. Now it cannot be fair to make accusations like this against Mr Bush as some researchers do if he is innocent in these matters. Surely it is only right that the claims made about Mr Bush in relation to drugs and his family's financial interests in Panama, are openly and publicly refuted with undeniable evidence so there can be no stain on his character whatsoever. The same applies to allegations about drug-running by the CIA while he was in charge.

All evidence points to a coordinated Brotherhood campaign to give young people every opportunity to take and become hooked on drugs. Today, finding drugs is often no problem for even children. The Brotherhood is at war with the young people of the world. It wishes to see them drugged, their spirits shattered, their minds filled with nonsense. It knows that the energy and natural idealism of the young could cause it problems in its sinister ambitions. It needs to crush the young, and that is what it is trying to do. It is time for the young people of this planet to open their eyes and refuse to be programmed. The Protocols make clear how it intended through this century to divert the young and the "Goyim" in general. They want to stop people thinking for themselves and how well it has succeeded:

"In order that the masses themselves may not guess what they are about we further distract them with amusements, games, pastimes, passions, people's palaces..... Soon we shall begin through the press to propose competitions in art, in sport of all kinds; these interests will finally distract their minds from questions in which we should find ourselves compelled to oppose them. Growing more and more disaccustomed to reflect and form any options of their own, people will begin to talk in the same tone as we, because alone we shall be offering them new directions of thought.....of course through such persons as will not be suspected of solidarity with us." (Illuminati Protocol 13).

I don't want to paint John F Kennedy as being whiter that white because I do not believe he was. Some members of the Kennedy family, particularly his father, have been involved in some very sinister operations as documented by other researchers over the years. But JFK clearly had a few things in mind that didn't suit the Brotherhood. This is why he lost his life in Dallas, Texas, on November 22nd 1963. He scraped to power by just 100,000 votes in 1960 and the Brotherhood possibly wanted his challenger, Richard Nixon. There is, of course, great mystery and controversy surrounding (a) who killed Kennedy and (b) why? What there is no controversy about, to anyone with eyes and a brain, is that he was assassinated in a military-style operation. The 'evidence' that he was killed by a 'lone assassin' Lee Harvey Oswald is so hysterical, I won't insult your intelligence with it. Oswald was involved with the US secret services. He was set up over a long period of time and the Kennedy assassination was no last minute decision. It was carefully organised by the Brotherhood secret government of the United States. The 'who?' is clear to me, but what about the 'why'?

Kennedy was bad news for the Brotherhood elite. He promised to "splinter the CIA into a thousand pieces". It is said by some researchers that he had found out about the drug operation and ordered it to be stopped: he certainly wanted to sort out the Federal Reserve, the cartel of Brotherhood banking interests that control the American economy and for the US government to print its own interest-free money; and he wanted to withdraw from the Brotherhood-engineered Vietnam War and end the cold war with the Soviet Union. All these things struck at the very heart of the Brotherhood operations and long term planning. Those researchers who accept the claims about the ET connection say that Kennedy had also found out about that, and was planning to reveal it; but I am not saying this is correct.

The evidence uncovered by the courageous people who would not accept the cover-up has made it crystal clear that Oswald could not have been the assassin, and that the killer bullet came from the other direction. A cine film taken by an onlooker called Abraham Zapruder and suppressed by the government for many years makes this obvious, too. Oswald said he had been set up, but he was conveniently killed by another stooge, the night club owner Jack Ruby, before he could come to trial. Witnesses who saw things that undermined the cover-up version of events were harassed, intimidated, or killed. Kennedy's body was rushed by plane from Dallas to Washington for autopsy by military pathologists who would do as they were told and make the 'correct' report. Near the scene of the assassination today, like some grizzly two fingers to the world, is an obelisk dedicated to freemasonry. This was a Brotherhood coup on the United States.

Kennedy was replaced by his vice-president, Lyndon Johnson, a freemason. It is alleged that Johnson immediately ordered the blood-stained and bullet-holed car to be cleaned and repaired, so destroying more evidence. He also reversed Kennedy's withdrawal policy relating to the Federal Reserve and to Vietnam. Under him the war quickly escalated and when it ended, two million Asian and 58,000 American lives had been lost and $220 billion had been spent. The Vietnam war was a grotesque human and financial killing in the classic Brotherhood mould. The Cold War also continued and weapons spending increased massively, just as the Brotherhood wanted.

Johnson set up the pathetic Warren Commission to 'investigate' Kennedy's death. Earl Warren was a freemason and the whole thing was the most obvious cover-up. Some witnesses said their evidence had been changed and even their signatures forged. Most of the Commission was made up of people from the Council on Foreign Relations, and the cover-up was completed by 33rd degree mason J Edgar Hoover, the head of the FBI, and yet another freemason, the former CIA Director, Allen Welsh Dulles. Five years later, John F Kennedy's brother Robert was assassinated at the Ambassador Hotel in Los Angeles after making a speech in his campaign to win the Democratic presidential domination. I believe that he, Martin Luther King, Malcolm "X", Marilyn Monroe and John Lennon were all murderd by the same force.

The Brotherhood makes and breaks presidents almost at will, and it is the same in other countries, too. According to Bill Cooper and others, President Nixon intended to fight to the end when faced with impeachment over the Watergate scandal. The Brotherhood wanted no such impeachment hearings and told him to resign. When he refused, the Joint Chiefs of Staff sent a top secret message to the commanders of US forces all over the world. According to Cooper, who claims to have seen the message while working for Naval Intelligence, it said: "Upon receipt of this message, you will no longer carry out any orders from the White House. Acknowledge receipt". It was another five days before Nixon resigned. Who replaced him? Thirty-third degree mason, Gerald Ford, who, in 1974, made Nelson Rockefeller his Vice-President. (The Thirty-third degree is divided into two parts – one knows the real agenda, the other does not.)

Today, the Brotherhood secret government continues to control the United States and continues its preparations for a global coup. A book by Bob Woodward, one of the journalists who investigated Watergate, is already suggesting that the economic policy of the Democrat, President Clinton, is being directed by Alan Greenspan, the Republican chairman of the Federal Reserve Board who was appointed by President Reagan and re-appointed by President

Bush. Greenspan is a Biderberger, Trilateralist and a member of the Council on Foreign Relations. Clinton has also announced increased trading links with China, despite the disgraceful civil rights record of that country, but then money always speaks louder than principles. Bill Clinton is a Thirty- third degree mason, a member of the Council on Foreign Relations, the Trilateral Commission and the Bilderberg Group. There is a great deal we need to know about Bill Clinton, not least the question of his attitude to CIA drug-running via the Mena airstrip in Arkansas. One thing is for sure, if the Brotherhood had not selected him, with or without his knowledge, he would not be President:

"Then it was that the era of republics became possible of realisation; and then it was that we replaced the ruler by a caricature of a government – by a president taken from the mob, from the midst of our puppet creatures, our slaves." (Illuminati Protocol 10).

What we also need to know is the extent of the Lucifer cults within American military intelligence, the CIA, and other intelligence agencies. One report has already come to light about Lieutenant-Colonel Michael Aquino, a senior officer within US Military Intelligence. He formed the Temple of Set (the ancient Egyptian name for Lucifer), and when it was made public, the authorities said they had no problem with that. If there was a purge on secret, Lucifer-inspired, cults and societies within the secret services of the world, the intelligence network would probably collapse due to lack of personnel! Interestingly, Aquino served as a psychological warfare specialist in Vietnam and this has become an increasingly important weapon for the Illuminati.

The secret development of mind control techniques by the intelligence agencies has also reached an advanced stage. These agencies operate outside of democratic control. Thirty-third degree freemason, Gerald Ford, launched a Commission to look into the workings of the security services after the Watergate scandal. Who did he ask to chair it? Nelson Rockefeller! If it wasn't so tragic, you could almost laugh. The CIA and its fellow agencies around the world, including the British, have been spending billions on research into mind-controlling and population-controlling techniques. These involve, among other things, drugs, brain washing, brain implants to turn people literally into robots, the injection of experimental viruses, hypnosis, and the use of electromagnetic fields, according to researchers of these subjects. If you think humans have been robots up to now, stick around, unless we take action now. Mind control goes back to the ancient Brotherhood mystery schools and beyond. The Nazis were perfecting it before and during the war and so were the American agencies which became the CIA. In the 1950s the CIA was funding mind-controlling projects with code names like Project Bluebird (Artichoke after 1953) and later Project MK-ULTRA. The British and many other agencies were doing the same, as information crossed borders on the Brotherhood networks.

The CIA and British Intelligence were funding tests into LSD and similar drugs in the 1950s and '60s and some horrendous experiments have been done in state prisons and psychiatric institutions, involving children as well as adults. Don't let them kid you the Nazis had a monopoly on such things. Anything they did, the 'good guys' are also doing in the lands of 'freedom and justice'. As this book was going to press, the US Government admitted that people, including mentally handicapped children and pregnant women, had been used in the past for experiments, without their knowledge and consent, into the effects of radiation. The past? Similar things are still happening! So if you are seeking to escape this mad world through drugs....*don't, don't, don't*. LSD was not the liberating drug it was claimed by so many to be. It was researched and encouraged by the CIA, the British Secret Service and others and, to a large extent, it thwarted the 1960s revolution and the desire of the baby boomers for mental freedom, by subverting their values with a lack of direction. The mass prescribing of anti-depressants and other drugs world-wide is playing its part in advancing the zombie mentality which the Brotherhood want to bring about. Some of these techniques have undoubtedly been used to take out people who threaten Brotherhood operations. You can appreciate how it can be done when you see what one CIA psychiatrist said about the use of hypnosis and the implantation of minute electrodes in the brain:

"The subject who was able to develop good post-hypnotic amnesia will also respond to suggestions to remember events which did not actually occur. On awakening, he will fail to recall the real events of the trance and instead will recall the suggested events. If anything, this phenomena is easier to produce than total amnesia, perhaps because it eliminates the

subjective feeling of an empty space in the memory."

What a great way to programme a 'lone assassin'. I have no doubt that many of the 'abductions' claimed to have been by UFO occupants are, in reality, abductions by human servants of Lucifer in the Brotherhood. That is not to say that people aren't abducted by ETs, I have an open mind on that, but this is used as a cover for Brotherhood activities of exactly the same kind, too. Suggestions are implanted into the victims' minds, as described above, so they believe they have been taken and implanted by ETs when it has really been done to them by humans. Under deep hypnosis by those who are investigating this phenomenon, many of these 'ET victims' have recalled being taken away in a van, sometimes marked US Navy. Perhaps the vans are an example of the advanced technology that the Americans have given the ETs in exchange for theirs! I'll swap you this inter-galactic, inter-frequency, anti-gravity craft, for a Ford truck. Yes, sounds reasonable. It's a deal.

Many people who have said they were abducted by UFOs have been found to have brain implants which can be seen on X-Rays. Apparent UFO victims have often recalled having operations during their ordeal, in which needles are inserted into the brain. Because this technology is not familiar to 'normal' science, it is assumed that it has come from some extra-terrestrial source. But, for whatever reason, the science of the Brotherhood has put them years ahead of the science the rest of us know. Brotherhood scientists working on code-named projects have developed an electrode which can receive and transmit signals, produce visions and hallucinations, and have complete physical control of a person's body. Given that the ETs have always known of these techniques, it puts some of the 'spiritual revelations' of St Paul, Moses, Mahomet, and the Mormon founder, Joseph Smith, into another perspective, maybe? Too incredible to believe? Let me quote the words of Dr Jose Delgado, when he was a psychologist at Yale University decades ago:

"Physical control of many brain functions is a demonstrated fact.... it is even possible to create and follow intentions, the development of thoughts and visual experiences. By electrical stimulation of specific cerebral structures, movements can be induced by radio command, hostility may appear and disappear, social hierarchy can be modified, sexual behaviour may be

changed, and memory, emotions, and the thinking process may be influenced by remote control."

Want a lone assassin? No problem. Want an Israeli to kill a group of Arabs in an attempt to demolish peace talks? No problem. Want some guy to go into a school with a gun and start killing children to manipulate public opinion into demanding an armed or more authoritarian police force? Want to destroy the credibility of a group or organisation which threatens you by making one of its members do something terrible or ridiculous? No problem. We at the House of Mind Control can cater to your every desire. Why is it that most of the 'lone assassins' are made out to be mentally deranged or 'nutters'? Who, or what, makes them like that? This is how John Lennon was killed. He threatened the Brotherhood with his promotion of peace, love, the eternal nature of the spirit, and his inspiration to the young. He was murdered by a mind-controlled attacker. If you don't want to make a big public show of it, there is always the drug or psychically-induced heart attack or brain haemorrhage.

Nor is this confined to the United States. An investigation in Sweden revealed that for the last twenty-five years doctors there have been using patients for on-going mind experimentation. They have been implanting transmitters into the brains of patients to use them like laboratory animals. The control of which Delgado speaks was possible in the 1950s and no doubt long before that.

Today, the Brotherhood, thanks to its secret scientific research, have the ability for mass mind control. They have perfected the use of microwave pulses carrying instructions which can control individual or collective behaviour. Both the Americans and the Russians can do this. This knowledge of 'psychic attack' has been passed on over the centuries through the Brotherhood. An issue of the newsletter, 'Tactical Technology', in 1993 reported the latest developments in Russian technology of this kind. The report was about a visit to Russia in November 1991 by Janet Morris, the Research Director of the US Global Strategy Council, a think tank in Washington DC, founded by the former CIA Deputy Director, Ray Cline:

"Morris and other members of a team sent to investigate Russian technologies for commercial development were invited to a demonstration of a mind control technology. A volunteer from the US team sat down in front

of a computer screen as innocuous words flashed across the screen. The volunteer was only required to tell which words he liked and which he disliked. At the end of the demonstration the Russian staff started revealing the sensitive, innermost, thoughts of the volunteer – none of which had been previously discussed...... The Russians told Morris of a demonstration in which a group of workers were outside the hospital working in the grounds. The staff sent an acoustic psycho-correction message via their machine to the workers telling them to put down their tools, knock on the door of the hospital and ask if there was anything else they could do. The workers did exactly that, the Russians said.

"The Russians admitted to using this technology for special operations team selection and performance enhancement and to aid their Olympic athletes and an Antarctic exploration team. Being an infra-sound, very low frequency-type transmission, the acoustic-correction message is transmitted via bone conduction. This means that earplugs will not restrict the message. An entire body protection unit system would be required to stop reception. The message, according to the Russians, by-passes the conscious level and is acted upon with exposure times of under one minute. Morris envisions this technology will be miniaturised into a hand-held device. Presently the International Healthline Corporation is planning to bring a team of specialists to the US in the near future to further demonstrate the capability."

Want the British Cabinet, the House of Commons, the US President or Congress to come to decisions that suit you? No problem. Want to encourage civil wars and the most unspeakable behaviour to further justify a world army and government? And what if you want stock markets to react as you wish them to? When you look at this, it gives new meaning to the phrase: 'Forgive them, they know not what they do.'

There is another sinister aspect to this that we must resist with everything we have. Everything about us is already kept on computer, and now the Brotherhood want to go a stage further and have our actions totally under their control. Once again they are trying to do this covertly under the cover of a 'reasoned' suggestion to help us. How kind they are. We are now hearing of the growth in credit card fraud and how something must be done so people can be identified more easily. What will be suggested is some kind of bar coding on each person – like they use on the goods in the supermarket – and in this way the authorities will know where we are, and what we are doing at all times. It would also be used to transmit messages to us like the computers and robots we would then be. They are already leading up to this by doing it with animals, and we are next if we allow it to happen. The Marin Humane Society in America explained the technique in an article by one of its public relations associates:

"For nearly a year, the Marin Humane Society has been implanting every dog and cat adopted from the shelter with a micro-chip ID, a high-tech answer to the age old problem of permanently identifying your beloved pet. The microchip, about the size of an uncooked grain of rice, is encased in biomedical grade glass. The chip is imprinted with a ten-digit alpha-numeric code and is implanted by simple injection between the animals shoulder blades. With the wave of a hand-held scanner, the chip is activated to transmit the code to a computer which provides the owner's name and address, any relevant medical information and, most importantly, the owner's phone number."

The Brotherhood of the New World Order want to go further than that with humans. They want us bar-coded so we can be 'read' at supermarkets and banks, like a checkout assistant now reads a tin of beans. A man at IBM who invented the laser-bar reader for supermarkets has also developed a method of putting the same type of device under human skin in one billionth of a second. It is invisible to the naked eye and could carry all the information anyone needed to know about us. We could be permanently linked to a computer, and who is to say that signals could not be sent *both* ways? Six thousand people in Sweden have already accepted a mark on their hands as part of an experiment into a cashless society, and trials have also started in Japan.

Dr Carl W Sanders, a highly acclaimed electronics engineer, tells in an interview with *Nexus* magazine how his microchip project to help people with severed spinal cords was taken over by a government programme called Project Phoenix. Henry Kissinger and CIA officials attended meetings of the project, Sanders says. At one the question was asked "How can you control people if you can't identify them?" Interestingly, the chip is re-charged by changes in body temperature, and they have established that the best spot for this is on the forehead, just below the hairline. (Remember the 'mark of the beast' mentioned in the Book of Revelations?) Sanders attended seventeen meetings with the 'One World' brigade about the microchip, including some in Brussels and Luxembourg. The US President has the power under the "Emigration of Control Act (1986), section 100", to make legal whatever type of identification tagging he deems necessary.

Microchip implants are being inserted into people during abductions. They now want to dupe everyone into accepting it legally. Their ideal is to have every newborn baby implanted as the normal course of events. This is the so-called 'womb to tomb' plan. They will use the excuse of medicine (this microchip will re-programme the body to fight disease), of finding missing people (just think your child need never be lost again), and a string of other reasons. Each excuse might sound very reasonable in itself, but look at the hidden agenda. *Don't let it happen!*

Nor is electromagnetic and high technology limited to mind control. Its use is causing catastrophic damage to the physical body and the environment, besides being perfected for military use. Our non-physical selves are a series of interacting, electromagnetic energy fields, so we are affected at the core of our being by other electromagnetic fields. And if the etheric level is affected, the physical body malfunctions. For reasons of mind control and to create more efficient weapons systems, waves of electromagnetic pulses are being generated across the world by particularly the United States. The US Omega Network, with stations in Norway, Argentina, Hawaii, Japan, Liberia, La Reunion Island, Australia, and the US are sending out low frequency ground waves as part of a nuclear weapons response system. These ground waves are causing ill effects for those who live in the area and for the Earth's energy field. The Omega Network is only part of the mass of electromagnetic frequencies being emitted for reasons of weaponry and control. These are responsible for an enormous number of cancers, cataracts, genetic defects, and mental illness. Robert Becker MD, an author and specialist in electromagnetic pollution, quoted in the excellent *Nexus Magazine*, said this:

"All abnormal man-made electromagnetic fields, regardless of their frequencies, produce the same biological effects. These effects, which deviate from normal functions and are actually or potentially harmful, are the following:

"Effects on growing cells, such as increases in the rate of cancer cell division; increases in the incidence of certain cancers; developmental abnormalities in embryos; alterations in neurochemicals, resulting in behavioural abnormalities such as suicide; alterations in biological cycles;

decline in immune-system efficiency; alterations in learning ability.''

It is this electromagnetic pollution that is the overwhelming cause of the dying forests, and while atmospheric pollution is terrible, this is used as a front for the main killer. But one Brotherhood technique is to use the threat to the environment as a justification for promoting the coordination powers of a world government.

Throughout the decades since 1945, the CIA and other intelligence agencies on the Brotherhood network have been covertly working to increase conflict and control. The Suez 'crisis' in the 1950s was an example of how the Allies even dupe each other. Ex-CIA man Miles Copeland tells in his autobiography of how the British Prime Minister, Anthony Eden, became so obsessed with removing Egypt's President Nasser after he had nationalised the Suez Canal, that the US Secretary of State expected to be asked any day by the British to agree to an assassination plot. This would have been rather difficult for the Americans because they were supporting Nasser and hoping he would help to reduce the influence of Islam. As Copeland points out:

"At this time, the CIA station chief received a message from [CIA Director] Allen Dulles himself, sent at the insistence of his brother, [the Secretary of State], directing us to examine ways in which, if push came to shove, Nasser could be killed.

"There was a negative tone to the message which implied that the Dulles brothers would welcome a carefully thought out reply to the effect that Nasser was invulnerable, but we were not, of course, to mention the fact that we were the reason he was out of reach of would-be assassins since we had ourselves designed the security arrangements around him.

" ......And now I must make an even more arresting admission. While the 'straights' in Washington were increasingly displeased with the anti-American content of Nasser's public utterances and the anti-American propaganda that poured out of Radio Cairo, the Middle East's most far reaching voice, can you guess who was writing a goodly portion of the material? We were. We understood, as Nasser did at that time, the new regime's hold on the country depended on its being consistently and convincingly anti-American, and that Nasser couldn't even risk an indication of reasonableness towards our various Middle East policies..... We took pains to make it counter-productive, of course, and we included a lot of patent nonsense, but we kept virtually in control of its production.''

With the above in mind, look again at the anti-American speeches of Saddam Hussein at the time of the Gulf War in 1991. There can never have been a more obviously orchestrated conflict than that. The Americans made it plain to Saddam that if he went into Kuwait they would not react. He went in and they reacted. On 25th July 1990, Saddam met with the US Ambassador, April Glaspie, after he had told the Arab nations and the Soviet Union that he intended to invade Kuwait! They did not object. According to cables released in July 1991, Glaspie deliberately misled Saddam who believed that the US took the same view. She was acting under instructions from the White House.

The then-president Bush seemed content to use sanctions at first, but suddenly over a short period US forces began to arrive in large numbers. The United Nations gave the US 'permission' to attack Saddam under their flag and, with support from countries like Britain and France, they unleashed their macho men on the Iraqis. The US were keenly supported by Saudi Arabia, the birth-place of Islam, where the Saudi branch of freemasonry is largely based at the US oil company, Aramco. When the American, sorry, UN forces had the Iraqis in disarray and could have moved on to take Baghdad to remove the dictator they claimed to hate so bitterly, they stopped. Why? Because they didn't want Saddam removed, he was too useful where he was – if, indeed, the *real* Saddam was still alive by then. I'm not convinced that the man who is now claimed to be Saddam is the same person that we saw before he 'disappeared' for so long through and after the war. Cloning is not science fiction!

Some channelled information I was given a few days ahead of the Gulf conflict said:

"...There is no way to appease the situation as only a few know the truth of the real situation. Here we have a war of economics, money, material-ism, but most of all greed. The monies do not go to the people, but into the coffers of only a few because of corruption and secrecy. As the walls fall on the economic crisis so will dishonesty come to light. It will involve those that you trust as well as those you do not trust."

The 'victory' over Saddam was portrayed as the effectiveness of the United Nations, and what a benefit a UN (Brotherhood) army could be. Once again the media poodle wagged its tail through the Gulf War period. Whenever you read a paper or see a news bulletin, remember above all else that *nothing is ever what it seems to be*.

The plan for world domination continues apace across the planet today as the secret armies are trained and prepared with government funding behind fake names and fake projects. One of these in the United States is called the Federal Emergency Management Agency (FEMA). This has a budget of billions of dollars, and yet it wasn't even created under constitutional law. It is the result of a Presidential Executive Order. In 1935, the Emergency Management Act was passed to give the President the right to by-pass Congress and make laws in times of national emergency. Fair enough, you might think. Sometimes you have to act quickly when there's an emergency. The little point they don't tell you is that there is *always* officially a state of national emergency in the United States! This gives the President powers to make laws whenever he wishes, and have them ready and waiting for the time when they can all be implemented at once. You might like to know that these executive orders passed since 1935 have given the President the power to do the following, whenever he decides there is increased international tension or economic crisis:

To take over all transport, roads, and ports; all media; the power industries; food production and farms; all aircraft; relocate communities and mobilise people into work brigades under government supervision; start a national registration scheme.

The list goes on, and when a state of emergency is declared by the President, Congress cannot challenge it for at least six months.

"He (the President) will have the right to propose temporary laws, and even new departures in the government constitutional working, the pretext both for the one and other being the requirements for the supreme welfare of the State......

"We shall invest in the president the right to declare a state of war. We shall justify this last right on the ground that the president as chief of the whole army of the country must have it at his disposal for the defence of the.....constitution." (Illuminati Protocol 10).

FEMA came into being this way. It was started by.....Zbigniew Brzezinski; remember him? He started the Trilateral Commission with Rockefeller money, and served as National Security Advisor for the first Trilateralist President, Jimmy Carter. Brzezinski stayed on after Carter's defeat, to continue his work with FEMA under Ronald Reagan. FEMA's public face is presented as an organisation that reacts to national emergencies – everything from a nuclear attack to an earthquake or an urban riot. Strange then, you might think, that only *six* percent of its budget is spent on national emergencies. The rest is used to construct underground facilities for the government in time of 'foreign or domestic' emergency, and to build 'holding facilities', prisons and 'refugee facilities', none of which have ever been used for such purposes. So why are they building them? FEMA has around 3,600 employees, and yet only sixty work on natural disasters or prepare plans in case of nuclear attack. What are the rest doing?

Two familiar names were in charge of FEMA for a number of years: General Richard Secord and Colonel Oliver North, who worked with the CIA and US Air Force to smuggle weapons (and what else?) in what became known as the Iran-Contra Affair. FEMA is another major arm of the secret government. One of its aims is to disarm the American people. Now, I'm all for getting rid of weapons of all kinds, but again you need to look at the motives behind it. If you are planning a takeover, a coup against what passes for a democratic order, then it is much easier if the population is unarmed. And what do you need to justify laws taking away the public's right to own a gun under American law? More violent, high profile crime. Exactly what you need to justify the arming of police forces like those of Britain, which have not carried arms as a matter of course in the past. Incidentally, the American Gun Control Act of 1968 is word for word the Nazi Gun Control Law of 1938.

Another branch of the secret government working with FEMA is the Multi-Jurisdictional Task Force (MJTF), which was started by President George Bush. Bill Clinton talks of the need for a national police force when he already has one. The MJTF is now in almost all American states, and its role is house-to-house searches, the seizure and 'categorising' of men, women and children, and their transfer to detention centres (built by FEMA, remember), and the interrogation of these people. We are talking about concentration camps here, ladies and gentlemen. Twenty-three such camps were authorised originally and another twenty were allowed for under the 1990-91 military budget. The MJTF recruits from urban street gangs, who are now allowed to do legally what they have been doing illegally for most of their lives, to enter homes, take possessions etc. They are too stupid to see that they are being used, and that they will be removed too, when their purpose is served.

The third element in this triangle is the Financial Crime Enforcement Network (FINCEN). This is made up mostly of people from overseas police forces and military, particularly European. FINCEN in Montana has a number of Gurkhas in its ranks. They have thousands of helicopters and other aircraft at their disposal, which are appropriately painted black. Many times, black helicopters have been seen near the occurrence of cattle mutilations which are said to be the work of ETs. FINCEN personnel are trained to land, do their dark deeds, and then disappear into the sky very quickly. The Brotherhood-controlled United Nations is supporting and helping to coordinate these operations. All it takes is one major manufactured 'crisis', and the starting gun fires. Goodbye democracy, or what claims to be democracy. I understand the plans for the takeover of the United States are now well advanced. Part of this is for Michigan, for instance, to become known as 'Area 5', with its capital as Chicago and its governor appointed by the President without the complications of an election. One possible 'emergency' to set off this chain of events could be that of a terrorist with a nuclear weapon, threatening to destroy the United States. Watch for such a deceit, because something like this will be used to justify the coup in its first stages, if it gets that far.

These covert preparations for the New World Order are not confined to the United States. They are happening in all the major countries, with most of the politicians having no idea of what is going on behind their backs, or what the money they are allocating is really being spent on. In Britain the laws are getting more sinister every year. The Department of Transport pays security firms and private investigators to identify those who protest peacefully against road projects that destroy the environment, and it sends innocent people to prison for the crime of trying to stop this madness of taking the human race out of existence. We must challenge this by protesting in even greater numbers. They can't arrest us all!

It is difficult to know exactly what is going on today, because whenever information is released into the public domain you can be sure that it has already been superseded. Don't forget that some of it could have been planted to deceive in the first place. I certainly do not claim that every detail in this book is correct. I have taken the findings of many researchers and tried to weave a story from this wealth of combined information, using my intuition and the common threads as my guide. I would not stake my life on every detail, but I would on the themes. Throughout the process of my spiritual awakening I have been left in no doubt when I am being guided to an area of knowledge that needs to be made public. Suddenly information on a specific subject comes in from all directions, and never more so than with the New World Order. I had only vaguely heard of the term until, over a period of three weeks, all the information about it in this book was put into my hands by a variety of different people. Those on the higher levels who are guiding me wanted this information put in the book, and made available to the public.

It really doesn't matter whether you believe ETs are involved or not. The outcome is the same – a covert attempt to take over the world by duping the mass of the population and 'removing' those who refuse to play ball. That's the simple fact we all need to keep focused on. The Brotherhood will not succeed ultimately, because the transformation of consciousness now unfolding is sweeping their plans away. They may use a lot of twisted Egyptian mythology to justify their ambitions, but they should remember that in those stories Horus, the son, defeats Set in the final battle. So it will be. But what the Lucifer – (Set) – controlled Brotherhood can do is make the transition far more difficult, painful and traumatic, and hold back the spiritual awakening of millions of people.

They are using the increasing violence and conflict, the collapsing global economy and the threat to the environment – all of which they are, to a large extent, causing – to hookwink the people into the nightmare of a world government, world central bank, world currency, world army, and global control. Perhaps waiting in the wings is the claim that the planet is in imminent danger of an alien invasion. This could well be the card they are preparing to play to coerce a terrified population into willingly handing over all the centralised power the Brotherhood desire. I have noticed that suddenly the media is full of highly negative 'alien abduction' stories and such like, and information is being released into the public arena about 'aliens' on perhaps a bigger scale than ever before. This makes me even more wary about some of the more extreme claims about extra-terrestrial activities. Is public opinion being prepared for the 'aliens are coming'? Who knows the truth?

All I can say is that if you hear that the 'aliens are invading' and the authorities start taking emergency powers, please, please, be very careful before you believe it.

Remember the Illuminati want you to accept central world control of the governments, banks, currency and army. Anything that seeks to justify that is the Illuminati at work.

The Illuminati want to manipulate you into giving them authoritarian powers, and once that has occured an extreme, and I can't stress enough the word extreme, fascist government will be imposed across the world.

"When we at last definitely come into our kingdom by the aid of coups d'état prepared everywhere for one and the same day, after the worthlessness of all existing government has been definitely acknowledged...we shall...slay without mercy all who take arms to oppose the coming of our kingdom. Every kind of new institution of anything like a secret society will also be punished with death." (Illuminati Protocol 15).

"We shall create an intensified centralisation of government in order to grip in our hands all the forces of the community. [New laws]...will withdraw one by one all the indulgences and liberties which have been permitted by the Goyim and our kingdom will be distinguished by a despostism of such magnificent proportions as to be at any moment and in every place in a position to wipe out any Goyim who oppose us by deed or word." (Protocol 5).

"The Goyim are a flock of sheep, and we are the wolves. And you know what happens when the wolves get hold of the flock? There is another reason also why they will close their eyes: for we shall keep promising them to give back all the liberties we have taken away as soon as we have quelled the enemies of peace and tamed all parties...It is not worth while to say anything about how long a time they shall be kept waiting for this return of their liberties." (Protocol 11).

We have a big decision to make. I have made mine and so have increasing numbers of others. Are you going to make a stand here and dedicate the rest of your life to stopping this takeover and speed the emergence of love and freedom on this planet? Or are you going to shrug your shoulders, open another beer, change the TV channel, and allow yourself to be another official, computerised, microchip implanted robot? Sit on your backside or look the other way, and you will be voting for that. You will be condemning your children and their children to this nightmare too. In the second part of the book I am going to look at some of the things we can do, but words are not enough unless supported by action.

If anyone has any more information – facts not speculation – about what is going on I would very much like to hear it. You will understand, I am sure, if I am initially wary of such information, but I would be grateful to receive it all the same. I would also make it clear that after this book is published, I have no intention of committing suicide, disappearing, being found in a compromising situation, drug-running, breaking the law (except openly!), or anything else that would affect my ability to tell people what is happening, in every way I can. In fact I will be going out of my way to avoid all of them. I am also in very good health, thank you very much, never been better.

Should anything like this happen to me, you will know why and you will know who.

13

When Will We Ever Learn?

THIS first half of the book is not a detailed history of the world, nor is it meant to be. I have merely sought to pick out certain key themes which, I feel, will help us to end the violence, destruction, and the control behind it.

Most people who have been incarnate on the planet over these thousands of years were not, as individuals, all murdering, persecuting bigots. I am the first to say that, and I stress it again now. Most lived their lives in the best way they could within the confines of this dense physical form and the limitations of the world around them. Most do not come into incarnation to cause suffering, that is not their intention. They want to serve the planet, not destroy her. But once we incarnate we can become like dodgem cars in a fairground, hooked up to the same thought patterns and, to varying degrees, with the Luciferic consciousness at the wheel.

I remember my friend Yeva having a psychic vision once when I was with her that gave some idea of what it must be like waiting to incarnate. She saw millions of people being told about what was happening here and how best to remember who they were after incarnation. The overwhelming feeling she had during this vision was the frustration of these beings. They knew what needed to be done on the Earth, but they also knew that after incarnation the pressures were such that they were likely to act in the same destructive ways as those currently in dense physical bodies.

Before we become consumed by guilt over all that has happened through human history, we should remember that this is a tough place to be at the moment, and has been for a long time. When I highlight the destructive behaviour of humans over these thousands of years I am not judging or condemning individuals. I am challenging the thought patterns, imbalances, and downright mind control that have motivated that behaviour. The Augustines,

Jeromes, Hitlers, and sundry popes, are victims also. It is their thought patterns I challenge and seek to expose, not them as eternal beings. I have given this negative force a symbolic name, Lucifer, for simplicity, but really it is an extreme imbalance which we can all be subject to if we let our values drop. This is not, however, humanity's natural state. I say again: We are intrinsically *good*, not evil. It is the unique density of this planet and the severe negative influences that are behind our actions, and the only way we can change that is to think for ourselves and synchronise with our higher levels. Accepting that those levels exist is the first and most important step we can take.

One thing is very clear from the patterns addressed by the book so far. Whenever we have had the free flow of *all* information into the public arena and everyone has respected another's right to interpret that information in ways that feel right to them, human evolution has surged ahead. Whenever the free flow of information has been stemmed and doctored and one belief system imposed, human evolution has stopped or declined. *We need to keep this at the forefront of our thinking as we search for ways to build a fair and balanced world in the years to come.*

To some people it may appear that I see a conspiracy behind every corner, but I don't. I am a great believer in the 'cock-up factor' of history, too, and not every event is the Brotherhood at work. But I have been trying to chart a path through the last twenty thousand years or so, to pick out common links and connections. This has led me, and growing numbers of others around the world, to believe that there is indeed a central conspiracy of manipulation which threads its way through human history. When I look at all the coincidences that happened in a few weeks to present me with information about this conspiracy before the book was completed, it is clear that other levels of consciousness want people to know that there is some serious string-pulling going on, and it is time that the puppeteers were exposed. They can't control events if we will not cooperate. We have the power, not they, if only we could recognise it.

What I hope I have succeeded in doing in the first half of the book is to highlight the following:

(1) That over thousands of years a Brotherhood of secret societies has emerged which has been used to manipulate humanity in the most fundamental and horrific ways, and that its goal of world dictatorship is planned to be imposed in our lifetimes.

(2) That extra-terrestrials have probably had a fundamental impact on human evolution.

(3) That far from civilising the world, Christianity and other dogmatic, imposed religions have held back our evolution for at least two thousand years.

(4) That the free flow of all information and knowledge is the path to freedom and understanding, a fact confirmed by the constant examples of Church and political dictatorships destroying alternative views to their dogma and control.

(5) That the ills of the world have been overwhelmingly caused by the great majority allowing themselves to be blindly led by the few.

(6) That the belief that anyone has a monopoly on truth and wisdom is probably the most destructive and stupid belief it is possible to have.

(7) That to believe our dense physical bodies are superior to another race or culture is, along with religion and greed, the cause of almost every war and conflict experienced by humankind.

(8) That the virtue of forgiveness really is the only way we are going to break the cycles of vengeance and revenge.

I'd like to expand on those last three points. Our belief that the physical body is 'us' in total has to change if we are to be set free from these cycles. It is this belief that leads people to seek revenge in this life for what was done to the ancestral line of their bodies hundreds and even thousands of years ago, when the body is merely the vehicle for their consciousness to experience this dense physical world. It is like two people in different spacesuits on the Moon having a fight because of what two other spacemen did to each other while wearing the same kind of spacesuits years before. We would say that was crazy and yet look at Northern Ireland, the Middle East, the former Yugoslavia, and so on and that, in effect, is what they are doing. Only by recognising this can it be stopped. This is one reason why the Illuminati have worked so hard to keep the spiritual truths from the mass of the people, and it is vital that this suppressed knowledge as set out in this book be widely known. Even then this understanding has to be wider and more mature than belief systems like Hinduism which uses karma and reincarnation to justify some horrific behaviour. Also, giving responsibility for our actions to someone else is like handing over a lethal weapon. Once we look to others to lead us and tell us what to do and think we are building the foundations of all the violence, pain, and suffering I have documented.

The great majority of those who persecuted non-believers or different believers actually thought they were carrying out the wishes of God. They had allowed themselves to be so mind-controlled that whatever they were told was God's command they followed to the letter. No-one would have persuaded them they were doing anything wrong. They were people of their time, controlled by the belief system programmed into them. Today it's still the same with billions of people mind controlled to think the way the Brotherhood demands and they ridicule, condemn, and even murder those who challenge its nonsenses and control. What is the difference, except in background and scale, between that and the horrors of religious and political persecution in the past? Both are the result of the same non-thinking, the same robotic responses, and the desire to pass responsibility to think and act to others. What makes it most effective for the forces of destruction is that people who don't think are persuaded that they do. Nothing is more closed than a closed mind that thinks it's open and nothing is more manipulated than a manipulated mind that thinks it's free. It is the ultimate illusion, and yet I meet people like that every day.

We have lurched from extreme to extreme over most of the last twelve thousand years and more because we have not, collectively, had the humility to appreciate that we do not know it all, or even nearly so. There is no way we will balance all knowledge and understanding while one group thinks it has all the answers and the others think the same. We had the Roman Catholic Church that persecuted non-believers because it believed itself to have the truth; then came the Protestants who persecuted Roman Catholics for the same reason; then the Protestants broke up into factions caused by the minutest of difference between them, and they persecuted each other because each believed they had the truth; then came materialistic science which proceeded to marginalise and condemn those in its own profession who challenged the this-world-is-all-there-is dogma. Each faction and dogma decides it has the truth, builds an empire of income and influence, and defends that against all comers, especially if they bring new knowledge to question the status quo. This mentality sees the preservation of privilege through the status quo as far more important than the advancement of human understanding. Whoever has their hands on the wheel seeks to keep everyone else out of the vehicle.

The 'baa baa' mentality in which the masses do as the few, even sometimes the one, tells them is at the heart of the control of the human consciousness. Divide and rule is the great truism. Under this policy, you need to create division. If you have a far right you need to create a far left to oppose it. Division needs two extremes. Many people are being manipulated on the 'radical' wings of politics, while thinking they have sussed the system. How can it be that one or a small group of people have controlled millions in the countries and empires throughout human existence? What was that Gandhi said? '100,000 Englishmen cannot control 300 million Indians if those Indians will not co-operate.' Instead whole civilisations have gone 'baa baa' and followed the leader of the flock. Or they have allowed themselves to be offered privileges by the dictator, be it a man, woman, or system, and ignored the injustices their fellow humans suffer. That is plainly true of the world today. But I remember what Pastor Niemoeller, a victim of the Nazis, said:

"First they came for the Communists and I did not speak out because I was not a Communist. Then they came for the trade unionists and I did not speak out because I was not a trade unionist. Then they came for me and there was no-one left to speak out for me."

If we ignore injustice against others we are just as responsible as those who directly cause that injustice. Again as Gandhi said: 'Silence is connivance'. It is time to let the divisions fall away and stand up for each other. They might be able to imprison, kill, or discredit a few who say enough is enough, but they can't do it to millions standing side by side together. Power is only the ability to persuade one group of people that you have power over them. Power is an illusion and is shown to be so when all people stand together and peacefully say no, this is not right and not acceptable.

Running through all these themes across the centuries of human existence is the need for *revenge*. If anything this is the most destructive of all emotions. We all feel it instinctively when we feel someone has treated us unfairly. That is understandable within the pressures of this planet. Many times in my life when people have acted negatively towards me, I have had a wish to pay them back. Sometimes that feeling still flows through me when something happens that I feel particularly strongly about. But we need to take a breath and think before we react instinctively looking for revenge. If you do that and look at the wider consequences this destructive desire for revenge can be dispersed. It doesn't mean you don't still feel hurt, but the need to punish those you believe responsible is released.

This is so important, I cannot stress it enough. As Chief Seattle said:

"When our young men grow angry at some real or imaginary wrong and disfigure their faces with black paint, their hearts, also, are disfigured and turn black. Then their cruelty is relentless and knows no bounds. Our old men are not able to restrain them. True it is that revenge is considered gain, even at the cost of their own lives, but old men who stay at home in times of war, and old women who have sons to lose, know better."

What we have seen so far in the book are cycles of vengeance and revenge. The cycle of one persecuting the other and the need for righting that wrong by further, often greater, persecution in return. Mostly it is the innocent who suffer not the persecutors. Not every Puritan wanted to persecute those of another faith, nor every Roman Catholic, or Anglican. But they were still the victims of the other side when they came back for revenge. Unless we forgive our enemies, including the Illuminati, we cannot possibly break these cycles of human and planetary pain and destruction because the lust for revenge will go on. Forgiveness may appear to be an old and familiar theme, but wisdom is not new. It is as old as Creation itself. Forgiveness has, and always will be, the key to human progress. I would not claim for one second that it is easy in the circumstances in which we find ourselves, but it remains the only way. If we are to build the new world, a task we will discuss in Part Two, we will only step out of the cycles of darkness if we forgive each other, reject mind control, and refuse to be sheep led by human, extra-terrestrial or misguided non-physical shepherds.

It is time to open our eyes and our hearts and take responsibility for our thoughts and actions. It is time to wake up and grow up. If we do that, an astonishing future awaits us, and it is to that vision we will now turn.

PART TWO

THE LIGHT

14

Goodbye to all That

DURING the 'baby boom' years after the last World War there was a mass incarnation of the volunteer souls.

Some volunteers had come earlier and others have arrived in the forty-odd years since then. The 'volunteer' babies born in those immediate post war years were, however, the biggest influx of those who had chosen to be at the cutting edge of change and transformation. To quote a channelled message from *Truth Vibrations*:

"Those of you who are at the forefront of this, you are rather like a snowplough. You are the thin end of the wedge. You really have, how shall I put this? To a certain extent, I suppose, you have the shitty end of the job. You have got to do an awful lot, but nevertheless you are capable of doing an awful lot. That is why you have chosen to come, that is what you are here for, to really shovel some shit, and therefore make some space behind you to make it easier for the others."

I should point out that when thought forms from higher levels are decoded by the lower self and the brain they are often spoken and written in the channeller's own style. While some would say you have come to remove the negative domination, others would say you have come to shovel some shit. Either way, the volunteers who have incarnated to be alive at this time – not only the post-war babies by any means – are here to play their part in changing human consciousness by returning it to its natural state of love, peace, compassion, and wisdom. The volunteers' task is to help the planet so she can heal herself, to remove the brotherhood domination, and to leave the babies and young children of today with a clear run to create a new world without the Luciferic influence to trouble them. The volunteers are being supported by a vast network of highly evolved entities on other frequencies and by extra-terrestrials who wish to free the planet from those who have other, less laudable, ambitions for the human race. It is sorting out time. The volunteers are being guided to complete three main tasks:

(1) To raise human consciousness by passing on information that opens the mind and helps people to remember what they already know deep down about the nature of life, Creation, and the current transformation. This helps them to re-synchronise with their higher selves and access more of their eternal knowledge.

(2) To repair the energy grid and prepare the Atlantean system for the time to come soon, when it replaces the temporary system that has been in operation over the thousands of years since then. This involves the re-activation of the harmonic keys which will unlock those incredibly powerful energies which were turned down, or off, at the end of Atlantis, as symbolised in the King Arthur legends.

(3) To channel energies into the Earth that will balance out the severe negative domination in her energy field caused by all the negativity generated by the pain, conflict, and violence documented in this book.

In this chapter I will look at some of the ways this is being done, how everyone can help, and the sort of effects we can expect in our everyday lives. Energies are being channelled into the grid by volunteers who are collectively known as Light Workers. Anyone can do this as I explain in my book, *Heal the World*. It is not an exclusive club for the chosen ones. There are no 'chosen' ones, only people. Energy passes through their energy fields and physical bodies and is transformed into a frequency the Earth can absorb. On these occasions the human body becomes like an acupuncture needle for the planet, channelling and balancing energy flows. Since my conscious awakening in 1990, I have been all over the United Kingdom and to many parts of the world doing this, places like Peru, Bolivia, Equador, Chile, Colombia, the United States, Italy, Egypt, Israel, Germany, the Netherlands, Denmark, Ireland, and France. I have had some amazing experiences along the way as I recount in my autobiography, *In The Light Of Experience*. Tens of thousands are knowingly doing this work and millions, unknowingly.

These energies which are coming in to raise the frequency of the Earth's energy field are, to a large extent, the photon beam I mentioned in the early part of the book. The orbit of the Solar

System is taking us back across the photon beam, the rebalancing beam of highly charged particles which offers the chance for those who are ready to raise themselves to a higher frequency. The Earth Spirit, the energy field of the planet, is due to do just that. The period of the opportunity for the Luciferic consciousness is coming to an end and it will have to wait until another opportunity is offered either by humanity or another consciousness stream. It is reckoned to take two thousand years for the Earth to cross the beam and so all this won't happen tomorrow, but major changes are upon us. Entering the beam is like crossing the light cast by a lighthouse or torch beam. You enter in the more diffused, weaker, light first and then you go on to pass across the centre where the light is most powerful. I believe that sometime in the last century the Earth began to move into the diffused 'light' of the photon beam and by the 1960s it was having an obvious effect on those who were open to it. You don't have to open yourself to it and the changes it is creating in the energy field of the planet. There is no compulsion, but there are consequences.

Many people, especially the young, tuned to these energies in the 1960s and it manifested as the period known as 'Flower Power'. Energy is consciousness and the energies carried the information and knowledge which inspired the values behind the sixties phenomenon. If you listen to much of the flower power music and the protest songs of that time, you will hear the themes of vibrations – good, bad, and changing vibrations – of love for all, and of the times they are a changing. All three reflect a knowledge of what is happening in this time of the Great Awakening of humankind. Through the 1970s and the '80s as the Brotherhood pulled in the other direction and sought to destroy such thinking, we still saw the rise of environmental awareness, the growth in animal welfare movements, of vegetarianism, and explosions of human compassion like Live Aid. Now, in the 1990s as we move further on into the beam, wake up time is upon us as the rebalancing of the Earth's energy field helps us to re-connect with higher levels of ourselves and so become 'whole'.

I meet people all the time who have suddenly awakened and begun to see the world in a new light. They cannot understand why they could not see before what is now obvious to them. But the reason is simple. Earlier in their lives they were working mostly through the conscious level only, that part of us which is subject to the severe limitations of the dense physical body. This can, and mostly is, programmed by the messages it constantly receives through the eyes and the ears in this Lucifer-controlled world and we can believe some ridiculous things. When we reconnect with all levels, our perceptions reflect the guidance of our higher wisdom and understanding and we see what a daft world we live in. When this re-connection happens it can be like a dam bursting as knowledge and information floods into the conscious level and it can be a traumatic time as you try to make sense of what is happening to you and your life. I have written about this in *Heal The World*.

The higher we can all raise our own vibratory state by thinking, searching, and seeking truth, wisdom, love and understanding, the higher the vibrations that can be passed through us into the Earth and the quicker we remove the Luciferic domination. A channelled communication in *Truth Vibrations* explained something of this. Speaking of the energies switched off in the latter days of Atlantis, it said:

"As the energies around your planet quicken, so these latent energies which have been withdrawn will be phased back in. They will gradually be awakened. As the consciousness of your planet raises itself, those of you Light Workers who are working together to raise your consciousness, you will be able to hold more and more refined vibrations, and so we will be able to use you as a catalyst to be able to feed in more and more energies. As more of you raise your consciousness, so we can awaken more of these energies."

The books on the subject, the talks, the media interviews, the discussions with friends, and the energy channelling are all helping to awaken people and raise the frequency of the energy field. Most of the awakening is being triggered by energy changes on the non-physical levels, and even when I speak I can feel energy pouring through me to the audience and vice versa. That is where the most important interchange is going on. But words, written and spoken, are also an energy and they can be extremely powerful in getting information to the conscious level to challenge the programming. With every person who changes his or her thinking, we are another step nearer to that point when the power of such understanding is strong enough in the collective mind of humanity for that to become available to everyone, as in the hundredth monkey syndrome. It is in the collective mind that Lucifer is being challenged most powerfully. I believe we are getting close to that 'critical mass' when the collective mind begins to be a source of positive rather than negative influence upon we 'individuals' who are connected to it. When that happens we will see people change with a speed that will beggar belief.

But I am not suggesting this time of change will be easy for anyone. Those who have come here to be at the sharp end of this transformation have often been 'tested' to the very limits of their endurance, especially on the emotional level. This has been designed to unleash all their inner emotional and mental strength and courage. Now is the time when all that has been experienced in previous physical lifetimes will have to be called upon because the Luciferic consciousness and its expressions through the economic, political, military and industrial establishment is not going to go quietly. But have no fear that it is going to go. It is already on the way. People who are awakening are finding themselves at odds with the society in which they live, and even within their families, too. As they expand their consciousness, they are accessing higher levels of knowledge, wisdom, and understanding. Those with the courage to outwardly express how they feel are challenging conventional thinking and behaviour of almost every kind. They are called anything from 'loony' to 'dangerous' by those still mesmerised by the physical world. The Luciferic consciousness works hard to undermine them, just as it did two thousand years ago and on so many other occasions through history. But it will not succeed.

What will happen – is happening – is that the numbers opening up to these changes will go on increasing until they are the majority. Those who resist will eventually go out of incarnation and continue their evolution on a level suitable to their current state of being. They won't cease to exist because we all live forever, but they will no longer be able to live on this planet as her frequency moves well beyond theirs. Around the planet is a frequency range. As this rises, some of the lower frequencies fall out of the range. You could think of it as like climbing a ladder. With each higher rung that your hands reach, your feet are leaving others behind. The consciousness still tuned to those lower 'rungs' as the Earth moves on will be affected in many ways. Their vibratory rate will be falling out of synchronisation with the planet's energy field in which they live. This will affect their behaviour, their mental and emotional stability, and their physical health.

These will consist of the Brotherhood and the people still clinging on to the old order. This will create tensions between those
wishing to bring change and freedom of lifestyle and expression,
and those who want to resist the inevitable by trying to force
people to conform to old structures. For those with closed minds
who cling on to the status quo the time will come when the
vibratory gap between them and the planet will be so wide they
will go out of incarnation. The effects on their behaviour will add
to the negative aspects of this transition period and it is up to
everyone to help them with love and understanding. I would
stress, though, that not everyone who leaves their physical shell in
the years ahead will be suffering from the effects of vibratory
change. Many will be moving on at the moment they always
planned, their experience in this incarnation completed. But those
who are going with the changes and those who are not will
become clearer with every month from now on. In *Heal The
World*, I have suggested ways in which we can increase the speed of
this tuning in process by healing ourselves and the planet. For,
have no doubt, healing ourselves, loving and forgiving ourselves,
is the only way we will heal the Earth and allow the Earth to heal
us. Healing ourselves spiritually and emotionally changes the nature of the energies we generate into the world. Love is the most
powerful of all energy. Love is the answer.

The vibratory changes, hastened at certain times by particular
astrological alignments, will affect the whole world. Nothing and
no-one will be the same again. Everything is the same consciousness in different states of being. So if that consciousness is changing in our part of Creation it must affect everything – the way we
think; our emotions; our bodies; the physical Earth; the weather;
and, for those who choose to resist these changes to the end, even
their ability to stay in incarnation. A channelled message in 1990
spoke of the implications for relationships and attitudes. These
themes are clear in the letters I receive and the people I meet:

*"I feel now you are sensing the energies coming in, the energies surround-
ing your planet. This is causing many of you to ask questions. It is causing
many of you to re-evaluate completely your way of life, where you feel
you wish to go, what you want to do. It is causing tremendous upheavals.
Some of these are very confusing, very distressing, very disturbing. Some
people in relationships are finding they can no longer continue in those
relationships because their partners cannot tune in to what they have been*

tuning into. It is causing a great deal of disturbance. And I have said to this sensitive (channeller) on more than one occasion that you must organise yourselves into groups to support each other.."

Even some long standing relationships are ending as one partner chooses to take the spiritual path and the other does not. People who have always had so much in common are suddenly like strangers to each other. They are literally on different wavelengths. Once one partner begins to react to the changes and go with them, the urgings of their inner self will be far more powerful than their desire to protect a relationship, much as they may love their partner. Some will leave for long periods to follow their path, others will part for good. But when both partners choose to follow the frequencies, their relationship will grow stronger and evolve to a new level and understanding of love. I see the nature of relationships and family situations changing anyway. There will be no 'norms' and people will choose to live and love in many ways that will be considered shocking and outrageous today. They are nothing of the kind. Love is love is love. We will see the return of the extended family and less emphasis on the two parents and two children model of today.

In other books I have likened what is happening to the Earth's energy field to a bowl of water. If you wish to raise the level of the water from the bottom of the bowl to the top you have to turn on the tap. As you do this, the calmness in the water is disturbed and the more you turn on the tap, the more confusion, chaos, and turmoil is unleashed in the bowl. When you reach the top of the bowl and turn off the tap, the calmness quickly returns, but at a much higher level than before. If you see the water in this example as the Earth's energy field and the tap as the energies coming in, you can see the potential for extreme effects. In *Truth Vibrations*, written in 1990, I passed on channelled predictions of the following themes in this decade and the next one:

★ Growing and often staggering extremes of weather and other natural disasters, including massive fires.

★ Gathering conflict all over the world to the point where the United Nations would be overwhelmed.

★ The collapse of the world economic system.

★ The rise of the political right.

★ The break up of the Soviet Union and other large countries and empires.

* The end of the British monarchy, traditional politics and institutions of state, and conventional economic and scientific thinking.

* The collapse of the religious empires like the Roman Catholic Church and the rise of the religious right as a last desperate attempt to keep them going.

* Record-breaking earthquakes, volcanoes, tidal waves, and general geological activity.

* Time appearing to pass quicker every year. This is the effect of the quickening vibrations and the speeding up of 'Cosmic time'. You can't see this in the hands of the clock moving quicker, but you can feel it and there seems to be less time to do everything.

These effects will have a dual cause. The Brotherhood network will be trying to cause as much disruption as possible to stop the transformation, and hold back the Earth's energy field so it cannot make its evolutionary leap and leave them behind. I feel they will be using their knowledge and technology to try to weaken the grid and stop the rise in frequency. They even have the technology to affect the weather, particular in smaller areas. The changes within the Earth's energy field will also create many of these effects, but there is something we can do about that. The situation is this, quite simply. The further the energy field is from balance the more disruption will be caused by the re-balancing effects of the photon beam. So the more we, humanity, can help to create that balance the less traumatic this period will be in all things. The further you push down a pair of scales on one side, the more dramatic is the 'kick back' when they thrash around seeking balance. The principle is the same with the Earth's energy field. The more we can generate the energy called love from our heart chakra for the Earth, people, and all forms of life, the more we will help the planet to balance out the negative. This will make less extreme the process of passing through the balancing beam. We all have the potential to do that, it only takes the will and a change of perception. You can make that change now if you wish. Love yourself, love your enemies, love the world.

We are not alone. Other extra-terrestrial consciousness streams are working to help. But they will not impose themselves on our right to free will as the Illuminati do. We have to ask for their help. More than anything we need to help ourselves.

We certainly need all the support and love we can get because the Luciferic consciousness knows what is happening and the nature of

the consciousness shift that is underway. It has long known about
it and long prepared for it. The next few years are going to be quite
an experience. Open your hearts and fasten your seat beats.

15

The Economics of Enough

SPIRITUAL enlightenment is wonderful, but without a practical expression it can be overwhelmed by the forces of control. We not only have to think love, and think change, we have to live it, too.

For instance, if we don't challenge practically the ambitions of the Brotherhood, we are allowing the spiritual revolution, the Robots' Rebellion, to be blocked. It is harder to rebel and think for yourself when you have a microchip inside you transmitting the Brotherhood's message than when you are free from such interference. And those under such manipulation are hardly going to generate the love and understanding we urgently need. In the rest of the book I am going to outline some of the ways we can speed the spiritual revolution, and stop the Brotherhood from stopping us. I will start with the economic system which the elite currently controls.

Even with six billion people sharing this planet, it is still possible to provide for everyone's need. What it is not possible to do, as Gandhi said, is to provide for everyone's greed. The economic system which meets the wants of the few by denying the needs of the majority is in its twilight years. It is unsustainable environmentally, and even in its own primitive economic terms it has reached the end of the road. Don't be kidded by those computer screens in the financial centres and the economists with their jargon and System-speak. They are programmed minds who mostly parrot the System's line because they can't raise their vision to see beyond it. This makes them easy fodder for the Illuminati elite to persuade or bribe them to support ever greater centralisation. The present system isn't working and so on the basis of 'something must be done' they promote more central control, like a World Central Bank. That changes nothing. It's the same lunacy controlled by fewer people.

The first thing we need to do is remove economic growth from our assessment of human and economic success. Gross Domestic Product is the figure that mesmerises and controls the policies of governments throughout the world. But GDP is meaningless. All it measures is the amount of money that changes hands for goods and services in any year. THAT IS IT. Economic growth is not a measurement of economic success, it is merely a measurement of economic *activity*. It is like measuring the success of a soccer team by the amount of running it does in a match rather than the number of goals it scores. Every time there is an environmental disaster caused by the pursuit of economic growth, the money spent on reacting to that disaster is *added* to economic growth because it is adding to economic *activity*; every time someone is ill and needs treatment it adds to GDP; the same when there is a war. The system of self-destruction takes the money made from growth and the money made from the *consequences* of growth, and instead of taking one from the other, it adds the two together. Staggering? Of course it is, but that is the system that controls your life and is dismantling the planet.

Any system which uses the growth figure as its only measurement of national, human, and economic success must create a barely-one-dimensional world which reflects the nature of its economics. But then that is what the Brotherhood bankers want it to be. Any sane society, which ours is about to become, must have measurements of human progress that reflect the multi-dimensional beings that we are, such as:

How few are in poverty?

How few are homeless?

How few are hungry?

How few are lonely?

How few are unhappy, dissatisfied, and unfulfilled?

How few feel they are denied the opportunity to realise their full potential?

How few feel their lives are controlled by others?

These are some of the true indicators of human progress, and yet they are the very areas ignored by the present system, because those who control it wish to imprison the people, not set them free. For their system to survive it has to increase, not decrease, everything on that list. What is good for people is a disaster for the System. You will notice, too, that the measurements I have listed refer to 'how few?'. Today's system measures success only in 'how many?' Increasing 'throughput' is all it can think of. The more units of activity it can produce, the more successful it claims to be. Question government ministers about health care provision and they will reply in justification of their policies: 'We are treating more people than ever before'. But why? Why do so many need treatment? Surely success in health care should be measured by how few require treatment and how many people are healthy, not by how many are ill.

The System sees rising house prices as a sign of economic success while thousands live in the street because they can't afford a home. Surely success should be judged on how few people are homeless, not by how much more it costs every year to buy a house.

The whole throughput mentality is so ridiculous that you have transport ministers welcoming increased car sales (throughout), while at the same time complaining that they can't afford to build all the new roads necessary to cope with the extra traffic, (a consequence of throughput).

The acceleration of human and industrial throughput will not solve the problems of the world. It is creating most of them. America has consumed more fossil fuels and minerals in the last fifty years than the rest of humanity combined in the whole of human history. If growth is the way to eliminate poverty, home-lessness, hunger, and all the other human ills why hasn't America managed to do it, despite consuming the planet on that suicidal scale? And what would happen to the Earth if every country sought to do the same? But that is exactly what they are being urged to do. Brotherhood-manipulated politicians and economists have even invented the impossible in their desperation to justify this and hide the realities. They now talk of 'sustainable growth' when there is no such thing. No growth is sustainable, because we live on a planet of finite size with a finite ability to take the punishment. Yet the journalists and interviewers never question them on this obvious contradiction.

Greens are ridiculed for their policy of a no-growth economy. But what could be more sensible and efficient? That policy says there should be no growth and a significant annual decline in the rate at which we use natural 'resources'. This reduces destructive throughput by getting more from less; by making things to last as long as technological knowledge will allow; by recycling waste back into the production process so reducing the need to take more from the planet; by insulating buildings to reduce the fuel required to keep them warm; and by encouraging local production for local consumption to reduce the need for so much transportation, trucks, motorways, etc. The list of ways by which we can get more from less through commonsense is endless. This would lead to a sustainable, steady state, economy in which no more is taken from the Earth than she can replenish and no more is thrown back at the Earth than she can safely absorb. In the future we will not need to take from the Earth at all for our fuels because there is no need to once you understand the nature of energy and how to harness it for warmth and power.

The theory which seeks to justify growth as the way to remove suffering is called 'trickle down.' The belief is that if you allow the rich to exploit and become richer that will create the money at the top which will 'trickle down' in wages and services to provide income for those further down the economic scale. The same justification is applied to countries. If the rich get richer they will trade with the poor, and money will trickle down to them. The problem is that it doesn't work and the Brotherhood bankers know it doesn't work. It is not supposed to. Most of the money stays near the top of the pyramid, because the closer you are to the top the more you get paid. Those at the bottom have to survive on the scraps that fall from the rich man's table which, in a phrase, is what trickle down really is. At the bottom of the pyramid the majority of the people in the world struggle for, and often fail to find, even the basics of human existence. The world has had well over a century of rapid economic growth, and yet half the population of the planet is in relative or absolute poverty. Around a billion are in absolute poverty, the definition of which is 'a condition of life so characterised by malnutrition, illiteracy, and disease as to be beneath any reasonable definition of human decency'. But the growth-trickle-down fallacy has hypnotised all the political movements, the Greens apart. Ask a capitalist, communist, socialist, or liberal democrat for a way forward economically, and they will give you a version of take, make and throwaway based on trickle down.

As the frequencies rise and consciousness expands, this illusion is being rejected by millions of people, and the numbers will grow at an ever-quickening rate. Even those who once dismissed or ignored the Green analysis are beginning to question openly the economic madness we are indoctrinated to worship. The billionaire financier, James Goldsmith, said this in the London *Times*:

"Economic growth is the way to measure success, and science and technology are its principal tools. This is the basis of modern thought, but I question it. The leading modern society, America, has produced the greatest surge in economic growth and material prosperity in history. In the past fifty years its gross domestic product (GDP) has grown in constant, inflation-adjusted dollars, from $1.5 trillion to $5.9 trillion. American science and technology have achieved incredible innovations. And yet, American society is deeply ill."

There will still be the Brotherhood fodder who try to retain and justify all that I have described, because they believe it is best for them personally, or they are closing their minds to the changing consciousness. But trying to prop up this economic insanity will be like trying to plug holes in a crumbling dyke. For every leak you manage to repair temporarily, another dozen will be sprung, until the entire dyke is washed away. The economic system has to go, and we have to stop cooperating with it. What we must be aware of is an engineered collapse of the global economy by the Brotherhood with the intention of introducing a world central bank pledged to rebuild it. This is their intention and while no-one wants The System to be dismantled more than I do, we must resist centralisation and use the collapse to de-link from The System. We can expect a crash on the global stock markets which the Brotherhood would have no trouble instigating and that will send The System into free fall. Insurance companies faced with more claims through crime and natural disasters, and fewer people who can afford the rising premiums are already feeling the walls of change closing in. Add to this the financial implications of changing attitudes to life, the weather extremes, and geological events, and you can see the days are numbered for the economics of the madhouse. The only danger, as I keep stressing, is if we allow the collapse to justify further centralisation. If that happens The System will be rebuilt with even more control.

So what can we do?

I can't say exactly what will happen, because no-one knows in detail what the future will bring or how humanity will use its free will to react. But if we are to end the power of an economic elite we need to move from the big to the small; from central control to community and individual control; from humans serving technology to technology serving humans. Awakening people are demanding these changes and they will be necessary anyway when the world economic order is holed below the water line and sinks. There is going to be a great deal of reacting to events and we will have to move very quickly. We will see that we all depend on each other, and community spirit is going to return in a very big way.

Throughout the Industrial era, the trends have been in the other direction. Financial power has been concentrated in fewer and fewer hands by the cost of installing mass-producing technology and the need to compete with other countries. This has been the bankers' doing. We have seen community businesses fail in the face of unfair, market-rigged, competition from the major banks and corporations, all of which are Brotherhood controlled. National companies have grown through this economic injustice to become multi-nationals which wield enormous power around the world. Many of them have a bigger turnover every year than scores of countries, and that gives them the muscle to exploit those countries and even govern them from behind the scenes. This brings about the grotesque sight of food-growing land in poor countries being used to grow luxury crops for the rich. This is often at the instigation of Brotherhood multi-national corporations and corrupt politicians.

In my book *It Doesn't Have To Be Like This*, there is a chapter entitled 'Empty Bellies and Chocolate Bars'. It is so called because, according to Oxfam, well over half the children in Ghana are malnourished, while half the food growing land in Ghana is growing cocoa for the western chocolate industry. Another statistic I used in that book was that 400,000 children are reckoned to die in Brazil every year from hunger-related disease when Brazil is one of the biggest exporters of food in the world. While those children live and die in poverty, the land that could feed them is used to increase the profits of multi-nationals and the rich world in general. This manipulation of trade and debt by the West has led to the almost unbelievable situation in which more money passes from poor countries to rich every year than goes the other way. Remember that next time you see Western politicians talking about the 'aid' they are sending to the poor, or when you hear people criticise such aid because 'charity begins at home.' No it doesn't. Exploitation begins at home and is exported across the world. In the new tomorrow the word charity will be used only in accounts of human history. There will be giving and receiving, but there will be no dependence and therefore no 'charity'. Charity exists today only because exploitation and manipulated dependency has created the need for it.

The System controls us through dependence. It makes us dependent upon it for all the necessities of life, food, clothing, warmth, and shelter. That has been its Lucifer-inspired ambition, and it has largely succeeded. This dependence on essentials means that we have to play The System's game or we won't survive. The first priority of any new economics must be to reduce and then remove dependence on The System for those things. Once you have adequate food, clothing, warmth, and shelter, you immediately have choices. You no longer have to do what The System wants you to do. Removing dependence requires the dismantling of centralised power in all areas of our lives. Economically and politically it means small, not big, is beautiful.

The emphasis will be on communities coming together to supply their own needs, and not being dependent on a system over which they have no control. It has become so silly that if someone starts a rumour on the Tokyo stockmarket to make a financial killing, the knock-on effect can have consequences for the lives of people living on the other side of the planet. Self-reliance and self-sufficiency in all essentials will be the basic model of future economics, because that decreases dependence and gives power back to people. In this view of economics, the people of Ghana will be fed by food grown on their own land. The needs of their people will be served first, and not those of the multi-national chocolate factories. Poorer countries have been persuaded and manipulated to believe that the best way for them to 'succeed' is to use their land to grow cash crops for the Western multi-nationals and to use that money to import food from the West. This means the West can't lose. It can make the chocolate products to sell back to places like Ghana at a profit, and also sells food to them. Even better, it controls the price of both the cash crops it imports from those countries and the products and food it exports to them, because the West controls the financial system. Or rather the Brotherhood does. The countries of the Third World know that if they refuse to accept this injustice, the multi-nationals will move elsewhere as they play off one poor country against another. The way out of this bind of control through dependence is to produce the essentials locally whenever possible. Local production for local need will be forced upon us anyway by weather, geological, political and economic upheavals. The only effective response to all this will come locally. Look at the chaos that one snow storm, hurricane, or period of heavy rain can cause. Imagine what will happen as all that increases. We are going to see just how tenuous is our modern, technological, world when faced with the realities and power of nature.

The GATT agreement which is designed to open up the world to ever greater competition by removing import barriers is the Illuminati elite at work again. If you want to create dependency on the System for all the countries of the world, the myth of free trade has had to be sold and conditioned into people because without 'free' trade the strong could no longer exploit the weak on anything like the same scale. The truth is that trade has never been free in modern society. It is a licence to exploit the weak. The GATT agreement is an effort by the elite to create more control and dependence. Those politicians and economists who can't see the real agenda promoted GATT in a desperate attempt to find more places to sell products and generate 'growth'. But of course there are still only so many people and so much money, and for everyone who sells more as a result of this agreement someone else must sell less. The ones who sell more will be those who sell cheapest, and they will be the ones prepared to exploit people and the planet more than the opposition. For every winner there must be even more losers. We have turned trade and economics into a sporting contest, a sort of Economic Olympics. We talk of 'Japan pulling ahead' or 'Korea coming through fast' while most of the world never even gets to the stadium.

Events will unfold, I believe, that will reduce the production of oil, the cocaine of The System. It is addicted to oil and only survives by consuming and pricing it at levels which do not reflect the reality that it is finite and has fantastic environmental costs. Take away oil and there is basically no System. If this happens it will bring an end to the ridiculous situation in which one country exports a product to the other side of the world while importing back across the world that country's version of the same product. It is justified in the name of 'choice', but what is this choice? The choice of having ten, twenty, a hundred different shampoos to buy, all of which do the same basic job with the same basic ingredients? What about the choice denied to people of going out in the sunshine at certain times of the year because a system that speaks of 'choice' has so damaged the ozone layer that skin cancer is becoming an epidemic in some areas? Do you know that products are often transported from country to country with each one adding another component because that's the cheapest way for multi-nationals to produce them? Our ports and airports are full of ships and planes using fuel and resources and causing untold pollution when most of it is unnecessary. It serves no-one except multi-national corporations and the bankers. Far from supplying needs and 'choice' it is actually denying both to the majority.

In the years ahead, countries and communities are going to be more concerned with supplying their own necessities than exporting their production across the planet. This will unlock so much creativity. If the economic system is the way people are controlled and pressured to conform, think what opportunities await us as it collapses or we de-link ourselves from it and those pressures are removed. The Chinese word for crisis, wei-chi, means both danger and opportunity. While the fall of The System may be seen as a danger to us, it is really an opportunity to unleash all the infinite power of human ingenuity. This has been imprisoned by a system in which thinking is the last thing it wants us to do. Orders are issued from above by the few and the majority do as they are told. They are not asked their opinion, they are treated like robots. If you want to find the best way of doing something you don't ask a manager in an office, you ask those who do the job day after day. But those people are rarely consulted. In the future there will be no 'us' and 'them', no orders from above. Those who currently impose their view on others are going to be in the same boat as everyone else as the Robots' Rebellion gathers pace. The economic disintegration caused by a variety of reasons will give us a blank sheet of paper on which to start again.

The quickening frequencies are triggering within us the desire for control over our own lives. This is leading us towards smaller economic units and a wish to withdraw ourselves from the present system as much as we can. The necessities of providing for need in the wake of the collapse will demand the same course of action. In the transition period at least, the emphasis will be on barter – goods and services in exchange for goods and services with often little or no money changing hands. This expansion of barter is happening today. People who are awakening are using it to step out of The System as much as they can and as unemployment rises millions are seeing that The System can no longer provide for them and their families and has no prospect of doing so. This approach is going to be vital, as social security payments are squeezed and used to turn people into little more than slaves to the State.

When I wrote *It Doesn't Have To Be Like This,* which was published in 1990, I highlighted a barter system called LETS. At the time I could find only three examples of this at work in England, Today, only a few years later, there are countless LETS Systems in action. LETS is short for Local Employment and Trade System and it overcomes the limitations of money. Under the present economic order, money is everything. In a recession when money is tight, skills are locked within people. The money is not there to pay them for their skills and allow them to pay others for theirs. Many of the needs of people and their communities go unmet when the skills are there to provide them. LETS releases those skills. It works like this:

You invent a currency. The name doesn't matter because it doesn't actually exist in physical form. They are just imaginary units of exchange. When you join a LETS group, you are given a list of all the skills and contributions being offered by the other members. You write down a list of all the things that you can do. It can be anything from baby-sitting to repairing a house. If there is something you need that a member of the group can provide, you contact them and agree a price in your unit of currency. On the Isle of Wight where I live, one group has called their currency 'Wights' and that is the name I will use here, but it could be anything. Let us say that you contact a car mechanic in the group and you agree a price of 50 Wights for him or her to repair your car. When the job is done, you ring the LETS coordinator and you say 'credit so and so with 50 Wights and debit my account with the same.' The mechanic now has fifty units which he or she can use to purchase your skills or anyone else's in the group and you have committed yourself to giving 50 units worth of work to the group also.

No money has changed hands, but you have your car repaired and the mechanic will be paid in whatever services he or she might need. It may be that, for the moment, some money has to be spent on items purchased within The System, perhaps some spark plugs or engine parts in this case, but in some LETS groups even shops are offering food and goods in exchange or part exchange for barter in this way. You can take it further and have each member commit themselves to so many units of work a month for those in the community who cannot contribute through illness or infirmity. But there are very few who cannot offer something. One way of running LETS is to have a rate per hour for everyone so all time is measured equally.

You can start now, the sooner the better, to build a community economy as independent as possible from the world system. The more we can live outside of that system, the more the power of the Brotherhood bankers is reduced. Put an advertisement in the paper and call a public meeting or just gather a few friends around who you think might be interested. There might already be a LETS in your area which you can join. There are no rules that must be obeyed. Each group works out what is best for them and learns with experience how best to proceed. These LETS groups can grow quite large, but it is best to keep them to manageable numbers. It is important to have them up and running as soon as possible to reduce dependency on the Brotherhood and to limit the chaos and suffering when the present system collapses.

In the new people's economics we will need local cooperatives and community-owned companies for food distribution. It is simply daft for food to be grown in one area and sent long distances to other communities while those communities send their produce in the other direction. Food cooperatives will have the role of collecting the food from local farmers and growers and distributing this to local shops and markets. To be truly responsive to local needs, these cooperatives should be controlled by representatives of ALL the community, not only the farmers and growers. We will require community organisations, again with all views and needs represented, to coordinate the production and distribution of the necessities of life to everyone in their community. Their brief will be to ensure that no-one goes without food, warmth, clothing, and shelter. This can be provided much more quickly and efficiently by local communities once they can control their own lives and be freed from the barriers presented by the current system to any form of activity which operates independently of its structure. These community economic cooperatives will also have the role of identifying the goods and produce imported into a community which could be produced locally. They will then seek ways to replace the imports with local production. There can be local currencies to work alongside barter and community banks will be developed to channel local money into the local economy. These banks should not make money out of money, only cover their costs. If we are going to bring in the changes to ensure that economics serves people, the system of making money out of money must end. To type in numbers on a computer screen and then charge interest for lending money that doesn't exist has to stop if the control is going to stop. Money should be a form of exchange and a measurement of productive activities, not a way of increasing your wealth for doing nothing. This ethos has turned the global economy into a giant casino with the table rigged against all but the few.

I am not suggesting that communities cut themselves off from each other in the local economies. Quite the opposite. There will still be trade where possible, but it will be for the mutual and equal benefit of both communities involved and largely based on an exchange system of barter rather than a financial transaction. I do not see trade in necessities except where one community cannot provide them for itself. As you will see in the next chapter I am saying that we need closer links between communities not an intensification of division. But why does unnecessary and destructive economic activity which makes all communities dependent on outside forces have to be a basis for cooperating with each other? Surely the fierce competition between communities that such a system creates discourages the very cooperation we wish to see.

It is time for people of all backgrounds, creeds, colours, and views to come together and cooperate for the good of the whole and not compete for the good of the few. I can recommend a book called *After The Crash* by Guy Dauncey (Green Print) which offers lots of advice and examples of how to build a local economy in which people can free themselves from the clutches of national and international control. Don't let anyone tell you this isn't possible. It is, and it is happening *now*. Local production for local need is the direction in which we are being guided by changing consciousness and economic necessity. We will also realise from these experiences that we have been indoctrinated to accept a perverted view of efficiency. We have been sold the line that says if you centralise your production you can produce things cheaper. This might be true in a few cases, but not the majority. Most of these products are only cheaper in the shops because they do not reflect the full cost of producing and distributing them. Let me give you an idea of what I mean.

If something is made or grown locally and sold as near as possible to where it is produced, the price will reflect virtually the full cost of production and distribution. Not all of it, but most of it. That is not the case with centralised production. When you centralise you need massive trucks to deliver those products. You need millions of them and they must get bigger and more destructive as the centralisation intensifies. They consume fossil fuels at a breathtaking rate with the trucks capable of less than ten miles to the gallon. To cope with these trucks we have to build more motorways and by-passes at incredible cost. We have to spend money repairing the motorways and roads, the water and gas pipes, buildings and pavements, all damaged by the ever increasing weight of the trucks. We have to pay in medical costs for the growth in road accidents and ill health caused by pollution and the stress of living alongside roads full of traffic and trucks which shake your home and deny you peace and quiet. We have to spend more on the welfare system, because people-based businesses which served their local communities have been closed down by machine-based giants who largely serve only their shareholders and profit margins. Financial speculation, not human need, dominates industry – just as the Illuminati Protocols said it would.

None of these costs I have listed are reflected in the price of the products that are produced in this way. You pay for them once at the shop and again in your taxes, while the costs in environmental destruction are not even acknowledged. They are passed on to future generations which, through reincarnation, could be us! All this creates an illusion of efficiency which has hoodwinked billions of people into accepting centralisation as 'progress'. When those costs have to be reflected in the price on the shelf, local production will often be shown to be cheaper, especially the essentials like food. Packaged and factory-prepared food is far more expensive than buying fresh food locally and preparing it yourself. The national and multi-national food conglomerates have to find ways of taking a potato or a carrot and adding as much to its value as they can. They do this by turning out processed, conveyor belt, 'convenience' food in the form of crisps or pies or whatever. And because food produced in this way has to travel long distances before being eaten, chemicals and preservatives have to be added which increase the cost of the medical services by the effect they have on the human body. This is on top of the poisons the food already contains as a consequence of chemical-based farming methods. The food giants can ensure big profits from what started out as a potato or vegetable costing only a few pennies. We will see the return of buying fresh food locally and preparing it at home at a much cheaper cost in the years ahead.

The centralisation of production and political control has brought about the death of community. The System's policy of divide and rule has destroyed so much community spirit, co-operation and local self-reliance. Local post offices and small shops have closed. So have local schools and children have to be bussed out of their community to big, often impersonal, centralised schools. Their parents have also had to travel longer distances to work as centralisation has closed local firms and created the need for mass commuting with all the road, public transport, and pollution costs that entails. People are forced to begin and end each working day in traffic jams or crowded trains alongside others in the same situation. More of their time is taken by working and travelling, and less is available for families, friends, and life in the community. Governments talk of the need for 'family values' while promoting a system that breaks up families for most of every day, and creates pressures that many relationships do not survive. More people are now realising that if you can reduce your number of 'wants', you need less money to live. Simplifying your life like this can free those most precious of gifts – time and choice.

Yet another consequence of centralisation has been the dependence of communities on one or very few companies for their economic stability. When those industries falter or the companies decide it is better for them to centralise elsewhere, the communities are devastated because their economic base is so small and dependent on so few. Community economies of the kind that will evolve in the years ahead will not suffer from such lack of diversity.

The multi-nationals who use their power to exploit people and the planet will not survive the transformation. The expansion of consciousness will ensure that their days will pass. Business will go through a fundamental reassessment of values and motivations, because the evolution of consciousness is not limited to the weak and the poor. It is touching everyone who is prepared to open their mind and go with the gathering flow. I wish to emphasise again that in my critique of the economic system I am not condemning or judging people. I am challenging the thought patterns that control the people who serve The System. Managing directors living their lives under the daily and growing pressures of serving balance sheets and growth figures are as much victims of this madness as those they employ, or don't employ, on the factory floor.

With every day, more of the 'winners' are finding their work unfulfilling and without meaning. Their true selves are rising to the surface and new views and values are entering their consciousness. As this continues, they will be asking many questions they have never asked before. These questions will include: What is my business really here for? What are *we* really here for? Is it merely to accumulate money as fast as possible? Is that all that life is about? Are we here to be terrified of not selling more things every year? I know that many business executives are already asking these questions and are realising that they are victims also. The new business that will emerge from the ashes of the old will be there to serve rather than exploit and it will judge its success by these criteria:

(1) Is the process of producing, distributing and selling the product damaging in any way to the planet and the natural life support systems?

(2) Is the business exploiting the world rather than making a contribution to healing the world, serving human need, and making it a better place for all people and life-forms?

(3) Is the business harming or exploiting animals mentally, emotionally or physically and causing them pain and stress of any kind?

(4) Is the business exploiting people to maximise profits? Is it paying them less than their work is worth because I can use my economic power to make them accept whatever they are offered? Am I exploiting my suppliers or weaker countries and peoples by abusing my economic power over them?

(5) For the business to win, does it require that other people or countries must lose?

(6) Do those working in the business feel a part of the decision-making process and empowered to release their full creativity, or do they feel their creativity has to conform to some rigid corporate structure in which the maximisation of profit is the only driving force?

If the answer to any of those questions is 'yes' we are looking at a business that is going to be submerged in the changing consciousness in the collective mind of the human race. The new business will seek to ensure that economic activity leads to everyone winning from any situation and that includes the Earth. We are moving from win-lose economics to win-win economics. The new business will have no rigid structures. Instead it will evolve its ways of working and operation from foundation values like caring, sharing, compassion, environmental responsibility, love in its widest sense, peace, harmony, truth, justice, and respect. From these principles each business will evolve in ways that best suit its community and the people involved. Diversity and variety will replace the centralised uniformity of today. You can go to almost any city in the world and see the same names and shop fronts, all coordinated by some centralised multi-national corporation.

One culture created in the United States is being imposed upon the whole of humanity with the bulk of the profits going back to head office at the expense of the local people and their indigenous culture. The kind of changes that I am describing will put a stop to this cancerous expansion. An executive from a multi-national fashion corporation told me that he was already seeing this rejection of uniformity showing itself in their sales figures. They could no longer sell one design all over the world. People were looking for individual designs that allowed them to express their individuality. It may appear to be a contradiction, but the move towards an understanding of the Oneness of all consciousness will lead to a desire by people to express themselves in ways that emphasise the infinite variety within that Whole.

The re-balancing of the planet is happening on all levels and affecting all things. The re-connection of lower and higher self will lead to a rebalancing of economics and business practice. Those who try to continue with the old methods and motivations will find themselves struggling to sell their products. The System has been created to appeal to the five physical senses. Products and advertising have been geared to this and the five senses have largely made the decision on what and where to buy. Now other senses are coming into play. These are the higher senses that work through intuition. They are often referred to in every day conversation as a 'sixth sense', although there are many levels of them. These are becoming more influential in decision-making as people awaken. Everything is energy and absorbs energy. The energy in a production process is transferred to the product and that energy, consciousness, will reflect the *intent* behind the product. If the intent is only to make as much money as possible, the product will carry that thought pattern. If the production involves environmental degradation, that, too, will be in the energy field of the product. This has not really mattered to companies so far because the five senses do not relate directly to that energy field of the product. They relate to its feel, smell, taste, look or sound. But as growing millions become more sensitive to higher levels of themselves, they will be tuning into the energy fields of everything and everyone – including products in the shops. They will sense on these intuitive levels the intent behind a product. They won't be saying: 'Oh I'll buy this pair of jeans because I can sense that the intent of the company is to serve, not exploit'. They will simply pick one product and not another because their intuition will encourage them to do so. They won't know why they are choosing that product. They will just do it. This will mean big trouble for those companies which produce with negative intent and they will be racking their brains trying to work out why people are rejecting their goods when there appears to be no explainable reason why this should suddenly be so.

There will be two stages in the transformation of economics and business. The first stage will be the acceleration in the break down of the old and attempts by the Brotherhood to use that situation to bring in their World Central Bank, one currency and eventually a cashless system based on a personal microchip. From the chaos that will follow this period, the new will emerge. There will be a great deal of ad-libbing and reacting to events. It will be a time when barter will be essential and we will have to help each other on the basis of need. New technologies will be discovered which I will talk about later which will transform our lives. This technology will give us all the power and warmth we need without touching or harming the physical Earth – and it is technology that *already* exists. The second stage will see the consolidation of the new economics and technologies as the old fades to become history. As the decades of the next century come and go and the frequencies go on rising, humanity will build a new world of amazing and wondrous potential. What we would call miracles will be as much a part of everyday life as take, make, and throwaway is today.

I cannot stress enough the importance of distinguishing between the transition period and the world that will follow. Yes, of course, there will be traumatic times. This always happens when one era is replaced rapidly by another. I can see shortages of food perhaps and much upheaval. But the transformation to a higher consciousness is not leading us back to caves, hardship and struggle. If you want a system that brings hardship and struggle, then stick with the present one. That delivers both with unwavering efficiency. The transformation is guiding us to an era of abundance in the next century. When the destructive ways have been replaced and the Brotherhood's control dismantled, the Earth will be abundant in her gifts of food and beauty. Love will replace hate and cooperation will replace competition. The present system does not want abundance. Its power is in scarcity. That increases the price, the profit, and the ability to control.

We will see that life is meant to be a joy. We are not here to be victims and it wasn't supposed to be like this. Deep down beneath the layers of conditioning, the robots know this is true and the memories of that truth are beginning to stir within the hearts of those who have the will and the vision to think for themselves. Knowledge and understanding is starting to surface and the robots are rebelling. Not everyone will make that choice, perhaps the majority will not. But many will and they will change the world. Change and necessity shall free all our pent-up, locked-up, creativity, love, and passion for living. We will see human nature in its fullest and most glorious expression. We will discover potential within us that we never believed possible. Humans are not sinners who must find Jesus to be 'saved'. We have been misguided and misdirected by a disconnection from our true selves, that's all. The re-connection into Wholeness will bring a transformation of outlook and values that will rid this planet of the ills that currently overwhelm human consciousness. It will also wrest control from the forces that seek to destroy.

All is thought and thought is all. Nothing happens in the physical world which has not been preceded by a thought. Physical actions are manifestations of thought. If thought is imbalanced and destructive so will be the physical world. If thought is balanced, loving, and constructive, that is the society that will emerge. We create our own reality, and that is why vision is so important. The greater the vision the greater the reality. The old vision had money, production and exploitation as its focus. That is the reality it has created. The new vision is about respect and love for all life and all that is Creation. This is the world that is soon to be.

16

The Politics of People

ONE of the greatest myths known to the human race is that politicians have power. It is simply not true.

How can 365 Members of Parliament in Britain have power over a population of some 57 million? Or a President have power over 250 million Americans? They can't. Their only power is in persuading us that they have power. Like everything on this physical level, it is an illusion.

I mentioned earlier that, towards the end of British rule in India, Gandhi told the colonial government, '100,000 Englishmen cannot control 300 million Indians if those Indians will not cooperate'. In that one sentence you can see where the real power lies. It lies with us, the mass of the people, and not with governments, armies, industrial conglomerates, or the Brotherhood. They only appear to have power because of the apathy and indoctrination of the robots. Once enough robots wake up and rebel we will see what a sleight of hand this business of 'power' really is. I feel for politicians. In many ways, they are the biggest victims, the most programmed of robotic beings. They change nothing which is not acceptable to The System. The economic madness which they have helped to unleash across the world has imprisoned them and their successors. They are no more free to act on fundamental issues than a prisoner in Dartmoor or San Quentin. At election time, they have to tell people what they believe enough of them want to hear. If they don't do that, they don't get elected. And what do most people want to hear from their politicians? What the system has indoctrinated them to demand. More growth, possessions, money and economic 'success' for their country.

Politicians are pawns being moved around a board by the Brotherhood, a programmed population and the interdependency The System has constructed. Politicians cannot act independently in one country because they are linked to a system which insists that they play by its rules. If they seek to limit imports of unnecessary goods which their country is capable of making for itself, others immediately take action to block their country's exports. Even those politicians who have seen the system for what it is – and there are painfully few – would recoil at the prospect of taking any action that would bring with it a chaotic but vital period of transition while their economy was recovering from the colossal blow of losing export revenue and redirecting itself into producing the goods it had been importing until then.

Any government which tried to do this would be overthrown either democratically or by force. The System has the politicians slavishly serving its wishes through manipulation, indoctrination and fear. They will never take the action necessary to free humanity from its imprisonment or the planet from her punishment. Only by The System's collapse and its replacement by another way of thinking can we be freed from our dependency and be able to step into an era of economic sanity.

Essential to this is an end to politics as we know it. Representatives of the people are there to serve those people, not their party or self-interest. It is such an insult to the word democracy to see politicians allowing themselves to be used like fodder to vote in Congress, the House of Commons and the other parliaments of the world in whatever way their party leaders tell them. They are the prisoners of the Whip system. The Whips are party officials who are there to ensure that the Members of Parliament the population has elected follow the wishes of their party and never the urgings of their conscience or what they believe are the needs of the people. Parliaments are, appropriately, microcosms of the whole system. You have the few at the top like the Prime Minister and the Cabinet, or the President and his advisors, who try to force their Members of Parliament or Congress to toe their line. They, in turn, most of them without realising it, serve the non-elected Brotherhood above them. Political leaders often talk of the need for people to show self responsibility, but they are the last ones who want to see any such thing – especially in their own party. When MPs take responsibility for their own thoughts and vote with their beliefs, they are 'disciplined' by their party and told they will never be considered for promotion. This is democracy?

I remember when I was a national speaker for the British Green Party, the Conservative Government introduced a Poll Tax which was deeply unfair in that it asked the poor to pay the same as the rich. The strength of the protests and a campaign of non-payment forced the Government to scrap it (people power again). At the time, the Environment Secretary vehemently supported the tax and condemned those who challenged its unfairness. It was he who guided the bill through parliament to bring the Poll Tax into law. Some years later, that same man was interviewed on a programme looking back at the years of Margaret Thatcher as Prime Minister. He said he had always believed the Poll Tax was unworkable and should never have been introduced. He had, he claimed, even said this to Margaret Thatcher before he had agreed to introduce it. On the same programme, the Chancellor of the Exchequer at the time of the Poll Tax said that he, too, had told Mrs Thatcher it was a ridiculous idea. The film cut from him to archive footage of Margaret Thatcher proclaiming the Poll Tax at a Conservative Party Conference. Sitting close by and clapping all that she said was that same Chancellor of the Exchequer who, in private, was saying it should never be introduced.

Stories like that and much, much, worse could be repeated many times in parliaments all over the world. Let us not avoid the issue here. The political system and the economic system are one and the same. They are indivisible. Both are sick, corrupt, stupid, self-destructing and Brotherhood-controlled. Like the economic order, the political circus has created mechanisms and structures for turning out the robots and clones it needs to survive. Unless you are a system-serving, toe-the-liner, you will struggle to be selected to represent a major party in an election. Some people with a mind of their own slip through this net, but they are so few they can be muzzled or made impotent even if they are elected. The attitudes to life you need to become an MP or a Senator are mostly the opposite of what is required for honest, fair and inspired government.

"The political has nothing in common with the moral. The ruler who is governed by the moral is not a skilled politician and is therefore unstable on his throne. He who wishes to rule must have recourse to both cunning and to make believe. Great national qualities like frankness and honesty are vices in politics, for they bring down rulers from their thrones more effectively and more certainly than the most powerful enemy." (Illuminati Protocol 1).

Like the economic system, politics has become ever more cen-

tralised through this century. British local government has had
responsibilities and decision-making on many issues removed by
Westminster; and Westminster is surrendering responsibilities to
the European Community. Others have done the same. It is all
leading towards the Brotherhood dream of a World Government
and I even hear some intelligent, caring people supporting the idea,
often from the best of intentions. I say again and again...NO,NO
NO. As with most changes that give power to the few, it can be
presented as highly desirable. If we had a World Government, they
say, we could stop this or stop that, do this, or do that. Others
believe that the move towards World Government is a natural part
of our evolution and journey towards wholeness. We started in
tribes and communities, this way of thinking suggests, and we are
evolving through national and continental government to World
Government. I challenge this view. World cooperation and World
Government are *not* the same thing. Does anyone really think that
a World Government convened under the present system is going
to be any less sick, corrupt, stupid and self-destructive than national or international governments? Of course not. But we are not
looking here at a government that has the potential to inflict all
these things on a single country. We are talking about the world.

Both sides of the left-right political spectrum have those who
support the idea, but then, as with most things, the idea of left and
right is another illusion. They are different aspects of the same
bubble of unreality – and manipulation. The Brotherhood does not
have a political line. It will use anyone or anything for its own
ends. In its ranks and under its influence are politicians of all kinds
and persuasions. The Communists and the capitalists speak the
same language. Communism is merely a more authoritarian form
of capitalism, anyway. Politicians, even the high-ranking ones, are
mere front men and women compared with those working behind
the scenes. President Reagan was an excellent example of this. He
fired the bullets, but others loaded the gun. Imagine what control
could be gifted to a tiny group of people if World Government
became a reality. It would have nothing to do with the evolution to
wholeness and everything to do with controlling the lives of six
billion people. The way to avoid this is to pass decision-making
and control down the line to people and communities and not to
create the final rung on the ladder to world domination. We should
demand this and refuse to cooperate with the present system.

Look at examples of how global political-economic organisations, already in existence, have behaved. Those Brotherhood creations, the International Monetary Fund and the World Bank, are there to make sure the system is served under all circumstances. When Third World countries begin to struggle to pay back debts to the rich, in goes the IMF to lend them yet more money that doesn't exist and which they will not be able to repay. In return for this 'help', the IMF insists on measures to cut back on spending on the poor, healthcare, education and food subsidies.

This brings more pain and suffering for the population. They also insist that those countries increase their exports to raise money. More food-growing land goes under cash crop production. But, with the IMF telling scores of countries to do this, the market is flooded with certain commodities or goods and the price collapses. They are all exporting more, but earning less. Who wins? The West. It has to pay less for its imports. The World Bank (not to be confused with a World Central Bank) is supposed to invest in projects to help the poorer countries. Instead, it has been responsible for investment in Third World countries that have destroyed their environment, put local farmers out of business and made western companies richer at the expense of the very country the bank was supposed to be assisting.

If economic control is to be devolved to communities, political decision-making must be similarly devolved. This will be resisted by national and international governments. They will be desperate to maintain their control and this is another reason why the economic crash is necessary. Take economics out of national and international governments and there is little left for them to do under the present order. These governments are, in effect, only stewards of the world economic system on behalf of the banking elite. No-one is going to take any notice of them when the priority for everyone is the provision of essentials after the crash. They will be politicians with no-one to govern.

The breakdown of the old can only lead to a return to local decision-making, if we reject the Brotherhood plans. There will be no other way to cope and react successfully to what will need to be done. Eventually we will see the end of political parties. They are the product of a divided humanity and have no place in the new tomorrow. Like all 'isms' they insist that their members serve the ism first and their hearts and conscience second. They battle for power by offering the same basic policies presented in slightly different languages but, the Greens apart, they all serve the system and their members serve them. Indeed, some elements of Green politics are also system-serving without realising it. Political parties have also added to the confrontational nature of politics which mirrors the lack of cooperation that pervades the entire system. Politicians, in general, have sought office to achieve power. They want absolute power to impose their views upon the population. They will deny this but that is what they want, collectively. The electoral system in Britain gives control of decision-making to parties which considerably less than half the population have voted for. This is all old age nonsense.

Politicians should be there to empower people. The key words are enable, allow and respect. To *enable* people to realise their full potential and follow their own instincts; to *allow* people to do whatever they wish and live in any way they choose as long as it does not cause harm to others; and to *respect* the rights of all people to control their own lives and make their own choices. The representative is a servant, not a dictator. Modern politics has got the two mixed up. From these principles, communities will decide on a system of representation that suits them. There will be no imposition of rigid structures by national and international governments once the transformation is well under way. Communities will be in control. I see elected representation as only part of community action. With the new consciousness, cooperating will come naturally without the need for laws and regulations of the kind we have so many of today. The world is drowning in laws and legislation because of the desire to control people and in response to the negative behaviour of those disconnected from their true selves. Representation will evolve with rising consciousness and in reaction to the collapse of the old structures. But, here are a few ideas which are likely to play some part in the new politics in the post-Brotherhood world:

* I think we will see neighbourhood councils representing groups of houses and streets. If someone is lonely or hungry or in any sort of need, it will be the role of the neighbourhood council to take the necessary action. They will not ring Social Services because Social Services won't exist in the way that it does today. Everything will be on a smaller, community scale. The explosion in the Welfare State and Social Services has been a reaction to the collapse of community. Now that the Brotherhood elite have largely achieved that, they will seek to squeeze the welfare ser-

vices. Neighbourhood councils will alert the people of their area as to what needs to be done and will sort it out themselves, whenever possible. You could set up a neighbourhood council where you live, today. Through this, you could co-ordinate the care of the people in your area *by* the people in your area. There is no need to wait for the crash. It is a tragedy that so many do not even know who lives in the flat next door, let alone at the end of the street. Centralisation and the system of divide and rule, have brought this about. It is time to change this but it will not be easy. It will take commitment and there will be many people who fear participation because they have been programmed to believe that they are here to follow, not to lead. But these changes will happen because circumstances and awakening consciousness will demand them. The more we can de-link from the system now and prepare the groundwork for community organisation, the smoother the transition will be.

* Neighbourhood councils will have a representative on the Community Council. How big an area these Community Councils will cover will be decided by the people involved, in consultation with other communities around them. I would see elected community councils working alongside community forums. These forums would be open to everyone to present their views and suggestions for ways of improving the community. They would allow the knowledge and ingenuity of people to be given a hearing. Today, we have professional politicians making decisions about subjects they know little or nothing about. Those who are close to these subjects are never asked to speak in the debates or to offer their insight into problems which they work with every day. Giving people that opportunity in the present system of centralised control is almost impossible because there are too many people involved. But, in a community situation, that would not be the case. Everything would take place on a human scale. Even now, under the present system, there is no reason why community forums could not be organised to give a platform for local views and action. Indeed, this is happening as awakening people follow their instincts.

The elected community council would attend these regular forums and listen to the people they represent. The councils would consist of people elected from right across society. Besides representatives from each neighbourhood there would be the oppor-

tunity for all sections of society to have an elected spokesperson –
food producers, shopkeepers, employees, environmental groups,
young people, old people, and so on.

I would suggest a similar dual approach to economic organisation. Elected representatives to a community economic cooperative would coordinate the day-to-day organisation and
development of the community economy while an economic
forum would allow everyone to contribute to the discussions on
economic matters. People are much more enthusiastic and motivated when they know they have the opportunity to contribute
and make a difference. You will be amazed at how many apparently insuperable problems can be solved once human ingenuity is
harnessed to its full potential. The task for these community economies in the transition period will be to provide food, shelter,
warmth and clothing for everyone and to do it in ways that are
environmentally sustainable.

* I would see the main roles of regional government to be the
following: To support the communities in their efforts to be self-
reliant in all essentials; to ensure that essentials which cannot be
provided locally are provided from surpluses in other communities; to coordinate necessary trade between communities to the
mutual benefit of both; to be a forum for communities to exchange
information and experiences; to pass on details of new discoveries
and technology which would benefit communities and add to their
self-reliance; to arbitrate in disagreements between communities;
and to ensure that the actions of one community do not adversely
affect another, either economically or environmentally. The regional level will be particularly important in the transition period
in organising food distribution to the big urban areas which do not
have enough food-growing land to feed themselves.

* I do not believe the present national governments, as such, will
be necessary, although groups of regions may choose to get together to support each other. The next level of representation after
regional could be continental. These would be areas covered today
by the European Community or the United States and Canada –
that sort of size. I would see these as forums and coordinators, not
governments. This is very different from the present European
Community model which is little more than an economic trading
bloc with system-serving and centralising motivations. The continental forum I am thinking of would be a meeting place where

regional representatives could exchange ideas and discuss issues of mutual interest. This level would arbitrate on disagreements between regions, ensure that one region was not harming others economically and environmentally, and help to identify and direct the essentials of food, warmth, clothing and shelter to regions which were not yet self-reliant or which were struggling, temporarily, from the effects of natural disasters. They would also coordinate relief operations in places where natural disasters had occurred, with expertise, transport and technology on permanent standby to be on the scene in the shortest possible time. This would be a kind of Global International Rescue which all communities and regions could call upon.

* The other level of representation would be the World Forum. This is not the same as World Government. It would be a place where representatives from the continental forums would meet to discuss topics that affected the whole world. It would arbitrate in disagreements between continents and coordinate the provision of essentials which a continent was unable, at any stage, to provide for itself. The World Forum would have no army at its disposal and, apart from powers to intervene to prevent environmental degradation that had global implications, it would have no other power to impose its decisions. All armies will be dismantled when the transformation of consciousness is well underway. I would also see the World Forum as a body that would represent the planet in formal interaction with other Universal Civilisations which are going to be openly visiting this planet and we theirs in the future just as we visit other countries today. We desperately need forms of democracy that empower and involve **all** people. The present 'democracies' were created by the Brotherhood with built-in flaws to ensure they were only illusions of freedom:

"All these so called 'People's Rights' can exist only in idea, an idea which can never be realised in practical life. What is it to the proletariat labourer, bowed double over his heavy toil, crushed by his lot in life, if talkers get the right to babble, if journalists get the right to scribble any nonsense side by side with the good stuff? The proletariat has no other profit out of the constitution save only those pitiful crumbs which we fling them from our table in return for voting in favour of what we dictate, in favour of men we place in power..." (Illuminati Protocol 3).

This devolution of economic and representative power to communities with support, but not control, from above has built-in environmental benefits. People, as a rule, do not wish to pollute their own neighbourhood. National governments give permission for polluting factories to be imposed only on those communities where they don't have to live themselves. The main motivation of a national government is economic growth, not the wishes of one community. With decision-making transferred to community level, the incentives to reject polluting technology are far greater. If you are seeking to be self-reliant you are going to look after your environment as a first priority because that *is* your self-reliance. The link between a sustainable environment and a sustainable economy will be staring you in the face every day.

This structure is not a model for the future written in stone. I have only outlined a few ideas to illustrate some of the trends that are already quietly underway and which will come to the fore as the transition proceeds to challenge the Brotherhood nightmare of central control. I expect the economics and representation of the future to be much more diverse than a single, set structure. In every community and region there will be variations on the theme of self-reliance in essentials and decision-making at the lowest level possible. There will be many difficulties and complications to overcome because these trends are faced with a world that has been geared and created to serve a very different system. Communities and regions do not break down into neatly packaged units with the ideal ratio of farmland to people. We have appalling urban sprawls and it will be some time before anything like the ideas I have put forward will be reality world-wide. There will be a lot of chaos, hard work and learning from experience before that can happen. What we can do is make a start now and try to de-link ourselves as much from the system as we can.

It is worth noting again that the fewer material wants we have the less we need to work and earn to live. This frees more time for us to do what we really want to do. If we simplify our material lives we give ourselves choices which are denied us if we work, work, work to chase the material dream and its symbols of 'success'. We need to free ourselves from the so-called work ethic. This insists that, unless we are in paid employment all day, at least five days a week, we are lazy and work-shy. What rubbish. But what could be better for the system over the last two hundred years than for us to believe in the work ethic and its misguided morality? With people rejecting this conditioning and giving themselves time and opportunity to use their full creativity, we will see such changes for the better; an explosion in the arts for a start. Music, in particular, has a fundamental role to play in using its vibrations to raise the frequency of the planet, although it can be used to do the opposite in the wrong hands. We are going to discover more notes and tones as the changes gather pace.

People think that the collapse of the present order will see us living in caves and tents for evermore. But the release of human creativity will lead us into a world of abundance. Being poor is not purity, it is poverty, and we will have the means to remove this cancer. Ours will be a world that celebrates and encourages beauty, style and excellence in all things. The idea, put forward by some, that living rough has some kind of spiritual street-cred is a delusion, I feel. The transformation is about balance while poverty is an obvious sign of imbalance within a society.

Two areas related to political and economic change are the media and what we laughingly call justice. The media, or most of it, is the propaganda machine of the present system. Nowhere do the mainstream newspapers, magazines, radio and television pro-grammes question the obsession with growth and free trade, except in the rarest of circumstances. The only questions they ask are how best to stimulate both. They never ask why these things are so desirable and what the consequences of them are. The media depends on the system to survive and offers all the support it can. It is also Brotherhood-controlled. The media has allowed itself to become the vehicle for selling the American (Brotherhood) culture to the world. In its raw state, the media is like knowledge. It is neither negative nor positive. It is how it is *used* that is negative and positive. Some individuals in the media already do some outstand-ing work, exposing exploitation and hypocrisy and highlighting injustices that need to be addressed – but they are a depressing few. Local radio stations can be wonderful sources of information close to the people and they are going to be crucial in times of turmoil and change. The media could be used to communicate understand-ing and information that would free humanity. Instead, its over-whelming contribution is to imprison our thinking because its own thinking is imprisoned.

"We must compel the governments of the goyim to take action in the direction favoured by our widely conceived plan, already approaching the desired consummation, by what we shall represent as public opinion,

secretly prompted by us through the means of that so called 'Great Power' – the Press, which, with a few exceptions that may be disregarded, is already entirely in our hands." (Illuminati Protocol 7).

"What is the part played by the Press today? It serves to excite and inflame those passions which are needed for our purpose or else serves selfish ends of parties. It is often vapid, unjust, mendacious, and the majority of the public have not the slightest idea what ends the press really serves...

"...All our newspapers will be of all possible complexions – aristocratic, republican, revolutionary, even anarchical – for so long as the constitutions exist... Every one of them will have a finger on any one of the public opinions as required. When a pulse quickens these hands will lead opinion in the direction of our aims... Those fools who will think they are repeating the opinion of a newspaper of their own camp will be repeating our opinion or any opinion that seems desirable to us." (Protocol 12).

I have been explaining in countless press interviews about the eternal nature of all consciousness, the frequencies, the so-called great mysteries of life, and why we are having extremes of weather and seeing the old order crumble. Only a very few have printed a word of this. They come along being nice to my face and go away to their typewriters to undermine what I am doing. All they have wanted to do is talk about my private life and to misrepresent what I am saying to encourage the belief that I am crazy. I am challenging religion. They say I have discovered religion. I am questioning most of the Bible. They present me as a Bible-basher. I challenge the whole idea of 'Messiahs'. They say I am claiming to be one. And mind-controlled people believe this stuff. They say, 'You should never believe what you read in the papers', but they go ahead and do exactly that.

One journalist, who accepts the themes of what I am saying, wrote an article for a newspaper about me. The editor rejected it because it was 'too positive'. I predicted in 1991 that we would see record-breaking weather extremes in this decade, particularly rains and floods. At a time when France, the Netherlands and Germany were suffering from terrible floods and the Isle of Wight, where I live, was being battered by rains which would lead to some of the worst floods the island has seen, a journalist rang my home. Did he want to talk about the weather, why it was happening and what we could do about it? Not quite.

"Who do you think should be the new manager of the England soccer team?", he asked.

On one occasion a friend in Scotland told me of an article in the Scottish *Daily Record* which had said I was a 'Cult Lord'. As I had already written several books opposing the whole idea of cults, I was interested to see how the paper could justify such a claim. Across the top of the page was a giant headline 'The Cult Lords'. Underneath were articles about various people. David Koresh, who was at the centre of the siege in Waco,* Texas, was among them and there, alongside the mass murderer Charles Manson, was me! I wrote to the editor asking how on earth that could be justified and he replied that they had not suggested I was a cult leader!! And because of the injustice of the 'justice' system, which is only there for the rich in these cases, there was nothing I could do. I'm sure there will be more character assassination to come in an effort to discredit the information in this book.

These are examples of the kind of mentality which mostly governs the stories you read and hear in the media. I have worked on local newspapers and in regional and national television and radio. I have seen how journalists are some of the most pro- grammed beings on the planet. Not all of them, but the majority. Especially at the extreme end. I dread to think of the karma they are collecting every day as they go about their business of distort- ing, lying and destroying lives. What they do to others, they will need to face themselves on the journey of evolution if their actions are motivated by negative intent. Like politicians, I feel for them. They know not what they do. They are de-linked from their higher selves and locked within a media structure that programmes them to programme others with their trivia, drivel, untruths, narrow vision and Brotherhood propaganda. When they leave the confines of the physical body they will be horrified at how they have allowed the system to control them. Most journalists are puppets of fear and negative thought patterns, but they don't have to be. They are not bad people. They are misguided and they have the choice to change. Fortunately, the awakening process is there for everyone and many journalists are opening their consciousness to new ideas. Their problem is getting past the editors and the newspaper owners who block information because they don't

---

* The Waco seige was a mass murder by government agencies. (See "The Big Lie" video available from the American Justice Federation, Indianapolis, Indiana.)

want to hear it or allow others to hear it. I laugh when the media complain of press censorship when the biggest censors of information are the media themselves. Along with economics and politics, we have seen the centralisation of media power into Brotherhood hands. They control the world's news agencies that feed information to newspapers and the broadcast media all over the planet.

The Brotherhood media serves the Brotherhood bankers. I have no doubt, either, that intelligence services like the CIA have the technology to use television broadcasts to send subliminal messages into our non-conscious mind, without us, or even the television station concerned, being aware of it. In 1994 a Polish radio station began to send out an inaudible sound on its frequency to clear mosquitos from the homes tuned to that station. It was, apparently, very effective in doing so, but thousands of listeners started to complain that it was also driving their cats mad. If they can do that to insects and cats, they can do it to humans. What is really coming out of some of the explosion of radio and television stations around the world?

I ask this of journalists or the ones who can't see that they are being used as propaganda poodles: Are you going to go on meekly serving your masters, or are you going to rebel? If you only realised what the New World Order has in mind for you and your media, you would take a very large gulp!

And where are the journalists' unions in all this? I say to them: Get together, open your eyes, and stop cooperating. I cannot tell you how much you will regret it if you don't. I will be most pleasantly surprised if such a journalistic rebellion does happen but, for now, on past experience, I will not be holding my breath.

In the meantime, we have to provide alternative sources of information, and stop buying newspapers. The alternatives are emerging in magazines and papers struggling into life across the world. We also have access to a printing press – the photo copier – to network information through communities and further afield. I have found that radio is by far the best means of communicating in the media as it is today. Newspapers distort by reflex action and television is too often looking for items so short that it is impossible to communicate effectively or in depth. I have found that radio offers the time to speak at length and, if it is live, you are free from editing. What you say is what the listeners hear. The staple diet of many radio stations is the phone-in and you have the chance every day to ring up and comment on subjects from the perspective presented in this book and countless others. The awakening is leading to growing interest in subjects like reincarnation, alternative healing, UFOs, and related topics. The media will not be able to resist this interest indefinitely because they will want to use it to increase sales and viewing figures. That will only further stimulate interest and help to awaken more people which, as a result, will speed the demise of the system on which the present media depends. In the communities of the future, communication of information will be much more diverse, both in content and control.

There will be a revolution in 'justice', too. The police-lawyer-jury-judge system serves and protects the status quo and it is run by the Brotherhood secret societies, especially the Freemasons. One high ranking judge revealed the attitude behind our version of 'justice' when he said that people wrongly convicted by the system should not be released because it undermines public confidence in British justice. It takes massive ongoing campaigns over many years for those wrongly imprisoned to be released. Some never are. In Britain there are three people in prison for killing a newspaper boy called Carl Bridgewater. A fourth has already died since he was wrongly convicted. I covered this case when I worked for BBC Television. They are obviously innocent and the only reason they are still behind bars is that so many other wrongly convicted people have had to be released in the last few years and the authorities don't want to open the criminal justice system to yet more derision. They want to put as much time as they can between those other high-profile releases and the inevitable release of 'the Bridgewater Three'. Never mind that this policy demands that three people innocent of the crime for which they were convicted spend even longer in prison. The System comes first.

Government ministers and officials who should have no influence in the courts or public inquiries meddle as much as they can when certain sentences or decisions would suit them politically. Some Home Secretaries make known their feelings in these cases, and this is communicated unofficially down the line and through the freemasons' network to the judge. Not every judge takes notice, but many do. It's good for their career prospects and helps the Brotherhood. It is far from unknown for a judge to be influenced in his sentencing and decisions by the secret signs that tell him the defendant or lawyer is a fellow freemason. When public inquiries are organised to hear objections into road projects that devastate communities and the environment, governments make sure an inspector who sympathises with their view is appointed to hear the objections and reject them. If people only knew what goes on behind the scenes, the robots would have rebelled a long time ago.

The winners in this charade of democracy and justice are The System and the legal profession which is alive with freemasons, as is the police force. It is run for the professions and the elite, not by a desire for fairness. The costs of going to court to pursue justice have long entered fantasy land. Most people have to concede their rights because they can't afford to pursue them. This gives all the aces to those with money. They can afford to buy their justice. The majority cannot. Even legal aid which is supposed to help the poorest to pay for legal representation is being cut back at every opportunity. Meanwhile the leading lawyers and the judges take home often enormous salaries from a system that most people cannot afford to use.

I was once involved in a civil case which should never have got to court. This happens, however, when one side is willing to negotiate and the other is not. All the costs in the case were awarded against me. Given the circumstances and the background that was outrageous, but that's another story. My own legal costs were £1,500. The other side's costs were estimated in court as about £2,000. But when their final bill arrived from a firm of solicitors in Banbury, Oxfordshire, it had grown miraculously to almost £4,000! My shock at this was made worse when I read the bill. Only £1,576 of that figure was for work the firm had actually done. On top of that they had charged me for *not* using a barrister. No you didn't misread that. I said *not* using a barrister. It was a straightforward case that any competent solicitor could have handled and, as I say, there was no need for a court hearing, anyway. But because they were saying they *could* have used a barrister had they chosen to, I had to pay for their not doing so. No, I assure you I am not joking. It is quite within the law for them to do that.

Also they charged me extra because I had 'opposed their application throughout' and because of the 'importance of the case to our client'. I had to pay and, in effect, be financially punished by a firm of solicitors because I had challenged their demands and because it was an important case for their client. As every client considers court hearings to be extremely important to them, they could apply that added charge to every case they handle. I had to pinch myself to believe this was happening, and so did my own lawyer who was as bewildered and appalled as I was. You can appeal to a court against legal bills when costs have been awarded against you. It is called taxation. This I did and I was confident that the bill was so silly and against all laws of justice and fair play that it would be reduced and sanity would return. The court did reduce the bill. They reduced it by £135 and I was charged £186 for the cost of their doing so!!!

It struck me that this was one case in one court on one afternoon involving one firm of lawyers. Just think what is going on in courts in America and all over the world. How many people are being cleaned out financially by pursuing their rights to justice or defending themselves against injustice? It is one of the great ironies that members of the legal profession who spend their time prosecuting or defending illegal theft are themselves responsible day after day for legalised theft. The legal system is in the same category as economics, politics, and most of the media. It is sick, corrupt, stupid, juvenile, self-destructing and Brotherhood-controlled. Ask those lawyers who are motivated by helping people and not by making as much money as possible and they will tell you the same. I know how frustrated these caring lawyers are at being forced to operate in such a corrupt and corrupting system. But you see the system has to persuade us that we do have freedom, live in a democracy, and have a fair system of justice. If it doesn't maintain that facade, we are more likely to rebel. It is time we did.

Governments do not look honestly and deeply at the causes of crime because to do so would reveal that the 'values' necessary for economic growth are the very values that encourage crime and violence. Instead they condemn law breakers, wash their hands of responsibility, and call for harsher punishments. The prisons are overcrowded because society is punishing the symptoms and not addressing the cause. And what is the reaction of the growth mentality to crowded prisons? You got it. Build more prisons. In America which claims to be the home of freedom, justice, and civilisation, some states still send people to the electric chair or the firing squad. This is not justice. It is barbarism. Opinion Polls (or rather opinion manipulators) in Britain continually show that the majority would bring back hanging for some crimes. What arrogance to think we have the right to take the life of another, and what mental gymnastics it must require to say that killing is wrong and the state should kill anyone who does it!! Expect to see governments trying to introduce more authoritarian laws which further erode freedom in all countries as the decade progresses. We must resist this, peacefully, but with great determination.

The changing consciousness will reject the present methods of 'justice'. Crime will plummet when new values and measurements of human success are accepted and personal achievement is not measured by possessions. The move towards local decision-making and the involvement of all people in the life and direction of communities will reduce negative behaviour still further. The re-linking with our higher levels and all that understanding, love and wisdom, will have the biggest impact on the reduction of crime and negative behaviour. Before that time arrives, we need to look at why people act in the negative ways they do. Why have people been so de-humanised that they can mug and maim frail old ladies? The way to change that is not to use the fear of incarceration in some grotesque prison that will further de-humanise them. It is to treat them in ways that re-humanise their values and spirit. If someone attacks an old lady, the way to stop them doing it again is to put them, under supervision initially, into situations where they meet and work with old people. This will allow them to see that those they mug are not meaningless, worthless, victims for those of greater physical strength. They are human beings with feelings.

I see mediation within the community replacing courts and lawyers and ludicrous legal bills in the decades that follow the turn of the Millennium. The number of laws will diminish as will the numbers required to administer them. You don't need laws to say you must not pollute, when human consciousness has reached a level that would not dream of harming the Earth in any way. Nor do you need laws to punish violence when there is no violence, because all life is seen as sacred. In the years before that, I believe that more and more awakening people will refuse to cooperate with the economic, political, and legal systems in ever-increasing numbers. The system depends on mass subservience and unquestioning cooperation to survive. You can arrest a dozen people for a peaceful protest. You cannot arrest 100,000. Cooperation is the basis of the new world, but it has to be two-way. One-way cooperation leads only to exploitation. A refusal to cooperate with exploitation will be another way The System will fall.

Writing about the themes of the future is difficult because there will be distinct phases of change. In the short term the breakdown of the old will bring chaos, confusion, and fear. Crime will grow as people grab and steal what the system can no longer provide in the old way. The Brotherhood will be encouraging crime, even stimulating it through its mind-controlling technology, because it wants the public to demand a more authoritarian police force with laws to match. We may see martial law, military coups, and internal conflicts increase around the world. Many will be looking around for someone to blame for this mayhem, and the encouragement of racial and ethnic prejudice will result. Most human minds have been programmed to hand over responsibility to others. Amid the confusion of change, they will look to any strong leader to tell them what to do. This is fertile soil for dictators. There will be tensions, sometimes severe, between those serving the status quo and those moving with the frequencies. The way they see life and what they wish to do will be in conflict. It is up to awakening people to avoid violence in these circumstances. The last thing we need is more negative energy adding to the extremes we already have. In contrast to these negative aspects of the transition, we will see the expansion in positive behaviour from those following the frequencies. These people will be healing divisions wherever they can. Old barriers between those of different colours, creeds and ways of life, will be no more among those tuning in. This will be the new consciousness emerging from the death throes of the old.

In the medium term, as The System sinks beneath a tidal wave of change, I feel the community and regional economies will be stabilising and order will return. By this time, the world population will have fallen rapidly, with more going out of incarnation than coming in. Those who hold out against the frequencies and close their minds will have left the planet as they fall behind the quickening vibrations. The level of consciousness that will inherit the Earth will be meek, in that it will not use violence or imposition, but it will be mentally and emotionally strong and wise. When the chaos subsides and calmness returns to the weather, the surface of the Earth, and humanity in general, beings of advanced evolution will arrive in large numbers to assist the development of the new societies.

Much further into the future, the world will be unrecognisable from the one we see today and even from that which I envisage for the medium period. The frequencies will have risen to levels of knowledge and understanding that will give humanity the ability to manifest and de-manifest, to travel across space and time at will, to create through the power of thought, and to be dependent on nothing except the energy of life itself. By then we will not even require food as we know it. We will absorb all that we need from the ocean of energy around us. Consciously leaving our bodies and experiencing other frequencies will be available to everyone whenever they wish. There will be no possession of people or objects.

Love and respect for everyone and everything will be our guiding light.

17

The Science of Sanity

WE speak of the 'wonders of modern science'. If only we knew how primitive some of those wonders really are.

There is such a difference between the 'science' we are told about and that which we are not. We have the establishment scientists believing they are at the cutting edge of human understanding while in the secret underground bases technology exists that would blow their minds. Literally, some of it.

Take our sources of energy, as created by the science we are allowed to know about. We rape and devastate the Earth collecting oil, gases, and clumps of matter. We release the energy held inside them by burning what we have collected. In doing this we lose much or most of the energy they contain and we create horrendous pollution that poisons our air and water and damages our forests. The alternative is to build blocks of concrete called Nuclear Power Stations. These create waste that is lethal for up to 24,000 years and probably far longer. No-one knows what to do with this waste, but we go on producing it. One of the by products is plutonium. One thousandth of a gram of this is fatal and if enough gets into the hands of a terrorist or dictator they could make a nuclear bomb. Oh yes, and should these power stations leak or explode as with Chernobyl, substantial areas of land become uninhabitable and incapable of supplying food. Thousands, possibly millions, will die sooner or later from radiation poisoning or cancer and there's a good chance that babies born to those affected will be deformed. And this is called scientific advance? It is, rather, a scientific smokescreen. A deadly one.

The Brotherhood, at the highest human level, made a definite decision to support the myth that there is no such thing as spirit or an eternal self. It knew that wasn't true, but that knowledge was for it, not the people whom it wanted to control. Religion had had its day and humanity was starting to reject its view. This, the Brotherhood decided, could only continue to increase. Another rigid belief system had to take its place, and anyway, they preferred for people to think they were nothing but lumps of meat. One of the Brotherhood's creations was the famous Royal Society in Britain. It opened its doors in the late seventeenth century and has been a wonderful vehicle for selling the quite hysterical idea that only the physical world exists. Goodbye God. The media have once again played their part like the good lap dogs they have chosen to be and they still treat the words of a 'scientist' as solid gold truth. They are scientists after all, and they are very clever people who know more than we do. I know you don't understand the jargon, but don't worry your little head about it. You just get on with your life and let the scientists us tell you how things are. They know best.

What a negative affect this has had on human life. We are back again to the five senses. The collective mind of 'public' science is convinced that this physical world is the only one that exists. They have ridiculed anyone, even members of their own profession, who have questioned this and the Brotherhood have arranged for much of that onslaught against real scientists. A science in this state of misunderstanding will obviously concentrate its research on the world of the five senses. Its 'advances' over the last two hundred years or so have been in understanding some of the potential to exploit the physical environment. From the perspective of this physical level it has achieved some remarkable feats. It has landed on the Moon (well after the secret scientists did, however), developed endless gadgets, and found ways to treat the symptoms, though less often the causes, of some illnesses. But by ignoring or dismissing the existence of other non-physical levels of people and the planet, it has given itself a very limited and lopsided view of Creation. Sadly it has done the same for billions of people. Far from advancing understanding, it has held it back by undermining the efforts of the more enlightened scientists and people working with psychic sources who challenge the this-is-all-there-is view of life.

Say someone goes missing and you organise a search party. You choose not to look in the area where the person is lost and discourage or prevent anyone else from looking there. If anyone does you ridicule and condemn them when they say 'I've found him'. So you don't find the missing person and in the mind of the search party and all the people they influence that person remains lost. By taking your search party to another area you may find other missing people you didn't know were there. You will 'discover' many things that will be new to you. But you won't find the one you are supposed to be searching for because he is lost in the area where you refuse to look. If you take the 'missing person' to be symbolic of the mysteries of life and the search party to be mainstream science, you have the reason why those so called 'mysteries' are still unanswered by science.

Had they not done this and had they had the humility to listen, we would be much further along the road to solving our problems. In fact many of them would not have been created in the first place. Science is part of the problem when it could, and should, be part of the solution. If it had not been so obsessed with the physical world alone or been so arrogant in dismissing alternative thought, we would already have the technology to provide all the power and warmth we need by harnessing the ocean of energy all around us. We would not be destroying the planet for our heat and light. The knowledge of how to tap into the non-physical, sub-atomic, energies that surround us is available today, but the scientific establishment and the system in general does not want to know.

The reason is that what we call 'science' is system-led. It is funded by, and owes its livelihood to, the system and the Brotherhood, which is following its own agenda. When I wrote *It Doesn't Have To Be Like This,* **half** the world's scientists were involved in weapons research, and most of the rest were researching technologies to serve take, make and throwaway. The Lucifer-controlled system does not want us to know who we are and science has played its role brilliantly. It has denied the existence of our true selves and encouraged us to believe we are just a cosmic accident. People who know they are eternal beings of light and love, on an endless journey of evolution through experience, are not so easy to manipulate and control. Science has also been the System's mad professor, producing all the potions, poisons, and technology that have so affected the planet. The System is based on oil and other fossil fuels, and with the help of science it has managed to protect these energy sources from the knowledge that would replace them with non destructive alternatives. I do not wish to decry the achievements that scientists have made in some areas, but the overall contribution of mainstream 'public' science has been to suppress human understanding and to use its knowledge for destructive, rather than constructive, purposes.

The story of science has mirrored that of religion in many ways. Both decided on a creed and belief which they then imposed upon the world and both have sought to block all efforts to present information and evidence which exposes their misunderstandings. But then both are controlled by the same masters who have ensured that both can survive only by suppression. Once they nailed their colours to the mast and proclaimed one unyielding dogma, their empires, funding, power, and influence have been dependent on the survival of that dogma in the minds of enough people. Suppression of information and understanding becomes essential to their continued existence. If you are a scientist who depends for his living on the current scientific dogma, the desire to block alternative explanations which would shamter that dogma, can be very compelling. The System, no doubt with considerable Brotherhood influence, has ensured that these key areas like science, politics, economics, the media, and religion must suppress truth if they are to survive. In suppressing that truth, they must also promote a destructive illusion for the robots to focus on. The media slavishly support them by communicating the myth that establishment science is at the cutting edge of human understanding. I wrote to all the BBC Television science programmes summarising the work of open-minded scientists who are convinced the general themes of consciousness and frequencies set out in this book are true. I offered to put the programmes in touch with these people. I wrote to investigative programmes like 'World In Action' with the same information. Only one even bothered to reply, and that was only to say that in effect they did not cover topics that were not accepted by mainstream science! Game, set, and match to mind control.

James Lovelock is one open-minded scientist who has challenged convention. He has put forward the theory of 'Gaia', the Greek name for the Earth Goddess. This theory proposes that the Earth, far from being dead matter, is a living, thinking, organism. I would go much further than Lovelock, but there is a great deal of what he says that fits in with the overall themes I am putting forward. In his book *The Ages of Gaia* he explains why science is system rather than information led:

"You may think of the academic scientist as the analogue of the independent artist. In fact, nearly all scientists are employed by some large

organisation, such as a governmental department, a university, or a multi-national company. Only rarely are they free to express their science as a personal view. They may think that they are free, but in reality they are, nearly all of them, employees; they have traded freedom of thought for good working conditions, a steady income, tenure, and a pension. They are also constrained by an army of bureaucratic forces, from the funding agencies to the health and safety organisations. Scientists are also constrained by the tribal rules of discipline to which they belong. A physicist would find it hard to do chemistry and a biologist would find physics well-nigh impossible to do. To cap it all, in recent years the 'purity' of science is ever more closely guarded by a self-imposed inquisition called 'the peer review'. This well-meaning but narrow minded nanny of an institution ensures that scientists work according to conventional wisdom and not as curiosity or inspiration moves them. Lacking freedom they are in danger of succumbing to a finicky gentility or of becoming, like mediaeval theologians, the creatures of dogma.

"As a university scientist I would have found it nearly impossible to do full-time research on the Earth as a living planet. To start with, there would be no funds approved for so speculative a research. If I had persisted and worked in my lunch hour or spare time, it would not have been long before I received a summons from the lab director. In his office I would have been warned of the dangers to my career of persisting in so unfashionable a research topic. If this did not work and obstinately I persisted, I would have been summoned a second time and warned that my work endangered the reputation of the department, and the director's own career."

Control the funding and the lab director and you control what is investigated and what isn't. That is what the Brotherhood does. This all-knowing science has been with us for such a short time in human evolution. It is only very recently that some of the planets have been 'discovered'. Neptune was not identified until 1846 and they didn't know Pluto was there until 1930. There are more planets still to find in this solar system, and thousands if not millions of other such systems across the Universe. If you took the Sun to be the size of an orange, then on that same scale the nearest star outside of this solar system would be 3,000 miles away! To think we can pontificate on details about the Universe and dismiss the idea that there are other universal civilisations is just beyond belief. Scientific understanding is in its infancy. It is like a small child forcing its view of the world on everyone else. When you look at its 'big bang' theory for the Universe, the explosion of a 'Cosmic Egg' of matter which they say formed the Universe, it is incredibly naive. It is founded on calculations that other galaxies are speeding away from this one. The implication being, conventional thinking believes, that they are still being forced away by the power of the original explosion. It is a very tenuous hook on which to hang a theory that has become accepted by many as 'fact'. Galaxies are moving because everything is in orbit. Much of the scientific 'advancement' of the modern world is merely the confirmation of what the ancients already knew, because space visitors and channelled communicators told them.

Science is not as clever as it thinks it is, but far from showing the humility necessary for open-minded research, it has consistently dismissed even its own profession when they have predicted new possibilities. They don't understand something and so they arrogantly say it cannot happen. An Astronomer Royal said that talk of space travel was 'utter bilge' just eighteen months before the Russian Sputnik was orbiting the Earth, and that was primitive compared with what secret science was doing! As another astronomer, Carl Sagan, once said: "Intellectual capacity is no guarantee against being dead wrong". If, however, alternative explanations are systematically suppressed everyone else is encouraged to be dead wrong also.

But the dyke is collapsing for science as it is for all expressions of The System. From without, the evidence continues to mount through near-death experiences and 'inexplicable' phenomena, that reveal the limitations of understanding and vision at the core of 'public' scientific theory. And from within, the open-minded, genuine, scientists who seek to unlock the mysteries of Creation are being inspired by the rising consciousness to accept what psychics have been saying for so long. These twin pressures on scientific dogma will bring current scientific 'thinking' and its empire of influence and delusion crashing down in this decade and the next one.

With the genuine scientists now tuning into the higher frequencies, the understanding of who we are and the nature of life is awakening in their consciousness. This is leading them into areas of inquiry that will unlock the mysteries for them. The establishment will try to resist their findings, but it will make no difference. The laws of physics are going to be re-written. The way physics is currently perceived by scientists considered by the public to be 'geniuses' is in reality well wide of the mark. The supporters of today's view of physics have closed their minds to the non-physical levels of existence and ignored 99.99 per cent of Creation. No wonder their understanding is so limited. How tragic that scientists like Sir William Crookes, Sir Oliver Lodge, and many others had identified the basic answers to many of the mysteries scientifically much earlier in this century, but were ignored and attacked by Brotherhood supporters, as were the psychics who have known for thousands of years what today's system-serving scientists still don't know. More than two thousand years ago the Greek philosophers understood the principles of life and Creation before Christianity, Islam and others arrived on the scene.

The rising consciousness will sweep away the delusions and present us with technology beyond our dreams. There will be no need for fossil fuels, electricity pylons, or even the 'alternative' sources like wind and wave power. Each home will have a device, perhaps no bigger than a shoe box, which will harness the Earth's energy field to provide all the power and warmth we need. It will not have to be plugged into a grid. It will work independently anywhere you wish to take it. Transport will be revolutionised and made non-polluting by using the same understanding. We will have the knowledge to travel through time. Space travel will be like catching a bus today. The idea that we are alone in the Universe will seem as ludicrous as believing the Earth is flat. Later will come all the 'miraculous' feats like manifesting and de-manifesting, which I have already spoken of.

How do I know? Because most of it is already happening today, suppressed or in secret, and has been for decades. Free energy is a fact. By that I mean technologies that provide unlimited supplies of energy without using any fuel themselves. They access the ocean of power in the Earth's energy field and other energies all around us and produce no pollution and no environmental degradation whatsoever. You need no coal mines, no oil rigs, no power stations, nuclear or otherwise, and no ugly power lines in a national grid. These technologies can be used to heat and power homes, businesses, vehicles, anything. We talk of the 'electric vehicle' running on batteries, when the brilliant Croatian scientist Nikola Tesla ran a car in New York with a form of free energy technology in 1931, and man called John Worrel Keely of Philadelphia demonstrated his 'Dynaspheric Force' free energy machine in New York in the 1890s! While investigating the magnetic forces flowing between the Earth's poles, he discovered that 'corpuscles of matter' could be divided by vibration and the principle used to drive a motor.

The inventors of free energy technology have always suffered suppression and some have been harassed in other ways. One, John Searl, from Britain, was jailed for his trouble. In 1946, when he was only 14, he built his Searl Effect Generator (SEG) which was inspired by a dream he had as a boy. It was based on a magnetic device, and it generated usable electricity. As he perfected his creation, Searl also began to build flying craft using the same power system which could out-perform even today's conventional air and space craft. Three months before he planned to build a craft for a manned flight, he was jailed for using his own free electricity and not paying the power company to use theirs! While Searl was in prison on this outrageous charge, the authorities burned all his papers. The same happened to an American inventor, Dennis Lee, who discovered The Brotherhood and The System in general is desperate to stop these technologies, because they will remove our dependence for fuel and warmth and the whole cover-up of their technology will begin to come to light. Many free energy inventors are refused patents, and their work can be classified by an international 'Military Use Refuse' law which can stop them from publishing their findings or promoting their technology. But the Brotherhood elite know all about it, because the information goes to their secret scientists.

How appalling to think that while old people shiver from the cold and die from hypothermia because they can't afford their heating bills, the ability to produce limitless energy for *free* is suppressed to serve the interests of some perverted elite. In Britain, fuel bills have increased enormously after a new tax was added, and people suffer ill health from the pollution caused by this primitive burning of fossil fuels. Meanwhile the answer is blocked and has been for decades. Where are you politicians? Where are you journalists? Where are you environmental groups? Expose this scandal and insist that free energy technologies are further developed and made available to everyone. The free energy technology of the Illuminati elite is further ahead of anything the public know about, as it is in other scientific knowledge. How they must smile at what is being taught to students in the schools and universities of the world under the title 'science'.

The Brotherhood know that the laws of Creation as set out at the start of the book are correct. They know about energies and frequencies. It may be a version twisted by other misunderstanding, but they know the real laws of physics. I am not saying this next story is all accurate, some of it may be disinformation, but it will give you some idea of how far ahead Illuminati scientists are of 'Cattle' scientists.

Franklin D Roosevelt was a close friend of Nikola Tesla, the scientific genius who was to say that much of his knowledge came from ETs. One of Tesla's students, Guglielmo Marconi, set up a secret group which claimed to have built 'flying saucers in the 1940s, and to have landed on the Moon in the early 1950s. Interestingly, a ridiculous number of Marconi scientists and others working in similar areas have had strange and inexplicable deaths. Roosevelt asked Tesla, some researchers claim, to become the director of a project which is now known as the Philadelphia Experiment. His number two was Dr John Von Neumann and the team based themselves at Princeton University before everything was moved to the Brooklyn Naval Yard in 1940 and code named Project Rainbow. The brief was to make an American ship invisible both to radar and the human eye. They achieved this with a minesweeper by generating intense magnetic fields. Tesla was given a battleship for his next experiment in 1942, but protested when he learned that this time there would be a crew on board. He felt they would be in danger and, it seems certain, he sabotaged the test which didn't work. Tesla left and ten months later he was said to have been found dead in his New York hotel room. Von Neumann took over and on July 20th, 1943, he conducted the experiment again on the US destroyer escort, 'The Eldridge'.

It worked, but the crew went hysterical and were sick. Von Neumann asked for more time to perfect the technology, but the Chief of Naval Operations insisted it was finished by August 12th, 1943, because they wanted to use this capability in the war. He said, however, that he would accept only radar invisibility. This they achieved in Philadelphia Harbor, but then, after a blue flash, the Eldridge physically disappeared for three hours. Now it gets complicated because we are about to cross frequencies of time and space. Two young scientists on board, Edward and Duncan Cameron, came on deck to find the crew suffering from extreme hysteria and the two of them jumped overboard. The story claims that they didn't land in water, but in the Montauk Army Base on

New York's Long Island where they realised that it was now 1983 – forty years later. Yes, I know it sounds crazy, but stay with me!

The general background to the Philadelphia Experiment has been told in a feature film, and the basic themes of it are said to be correct. In the underground centre at Montauk the Camerons were taken to see Von Neumann, now of course a much older man than the one they had known in 1943. Von Neumann was reported to have died in 1957, but that was part of the cover for his work. He told them that they had to be transported back in time to the Eldridge in 1943 to smash the equipment because the experiment had created a 'bubble in hyperspace' which threatened to cause catastrophe on this frequency. Von Neumann had by now (1983), perfected the technology for time travel thanks to the extra-terrestrial input since the 1950s, this story claims. The Camerons were transported back to the ship and 1943 where they smashed the equipment. When that happened, the Eldridge reappeared physically. See, I said it was complicated, and it's even more so when you read the full story as documented in other books. It is hard to comprehend all this if we remain stuck with our version of time rather than a version in which the past, present and projected future are happening together. Perhaps most amusing was the fact that when Cameron, back in 1943, told Von Neumann what had happened to him in 1983, his boss refused to believe him!

Again I say that I am not suggesting that I believe every word of this. I don't know. There are some amazing stories coming out, but I do believe that at least the Illuminati scientists are working in these sort of areas, including inter-frequency and, possibly, time travel.

It is said that when the Eldridge returned to the physical world of 1943, it was a nightmare to behold. The time-space-molecular synchronisation had been so scrambled by what happened that many of the crew members were found to be part of the super-structure of the ship. Others were insane and still others would disappear or burst into flames. Talk about cleverness without wisdom. The mad professors are out of control. The researchers making these claims say the project was stopped after the Eldridge disaster and Von Neumann went to Los Alamos to work on the development of the atomic bomb. But by 1947 curiosity, and the potential for power presented by what had been learned in the Philadelphia Experiment got the better of them. It was re-started under Von Neumann as Project Phoenix at the Brookhaven National Laboratories in New York. He also worked with the recovery of the crashed spacecraft and extra-terrestrials, like the one near Roswell. Some researchers say that a number of craft were deliberately brought down by the American military when they realised how they could be seriously destabilised. Von Neumann and Dr. Vannevar Bush were two who worked with the extra-terrestrial from the Roswell crash known as EBE, it is suggested.

The development of Project Phoenix into the 1980s has, some claim, produced the knowledge and technology to travel through time. One story says they have travelled forward in time, but when they reach 2011 everything enters a dream-like state. 2011 links in with the predictions of the Maya and others for the time of great change. There is so much speculation that looking at the themes rather than all of the detail, claim and counter-claim, is probably far more productive. It is further said that Von Neumann and the secret scientists have also perfected the technique of making a person older or younger by breaking their 'time lock'. Tesla was working on time locks before he died, or disappeared. We are time-locked at birth into this frequency's version of time. On physical death, the time lock breaks and we are free to move on to other space-time worlds. Without this time lock during a physical life it would be chaos, and the sort of things that happened to the crew of the Eldridge would be happening to all of us. But if you can remove the time lock in a controlled way, you can advance or regress the age of the physical body, or so some investigators have said. The Brotherhood elite know how to change the weather in a limited way, and from the grotesque experiments they carry out on their abducted victims these insane scientists also know how to create clones. Some of the 'little greys' which people often report seeing could be from their laboratory and I'm sure they have developed the ability to create a human body, Frankenstein-style. To think we are having discussions about the morality of genetic engineering while this is going on! Thousands of people go missing in the world every year and are never seen again. A number of them, I have no doubt, end up in the underground laboratories.

Their understanding of anti-gravity technology – spacecraft – is now very advanced and many of the UFO sightings we hear about will be craft being tested and flown by human pilots. The bright light or glow around a UFO as reported by so many people is caused by the magnetic field produced by the craft which affects the gravitation field to create anti-gravity. There are many different technologies that these craft use to harness the natural energy fields.

Think what such knowledge could do in positive hands. It could bring an end to poverty, suffering and environmental degradation. We could be travelling from Britain to Germany in five minutes, Britain to Australia in half an hour or less. Leaving today's destructive insanity behind will not mean poverty for everyone, as the present system collapses. We have the choice to have a life made easier by amazing, non-destructive, technology that will dump poverty, hunger and homelessness into the dustbin of history where it belongs. This we will do because these misguided men are not going to win. The transformation, with help from all levels, is going to remove their manipulation, and they will have to wait for another opportunity to work out their vast imbalances. They will do their damndest to cause havoc over the next twenty years or so, but their control of this planet is coming to its conclusion.

There needs to be a rebellion of science students – all students – in every university, each coordinating with the others. They can demand to know what knowledge is really available and reject the rubbish they are being spoon-fed to keep them in the dark. The same with their lecturers, most of whom don't know what is going on either. Come on, get moving my friends. There is no time to lose. Don't take no for an answer. Do it peacefully and with love, but ensure it is underpinned by unbreakable determination. The robots can choose to rebel. If they don't they will regret it forever and a day.

Medical students and other health employees can do the same. The way people suffer when there is no need is one of the greatest scandals of this story. As the transformation progresses, other methods of healing will bring an end to the drug-obsessed, surgery-obsessed, disease care services of today. Once again medical science has been directed to see only the physical level of being. It treats symptoms and not causes, because it does not understand the causes. How can it when most illness results from imbalances on our non-physical levels and medical science insists those levels don't exist? It is known that people who live under or near power lines or have close contact with electromagnetic technology are more prone to certain illnesses, particularly some cancers. Human science has no idea why this should be. But our non-physical self is a series of electromagnetic energy fields working as one. When we come into close and consistent contact with other powerful electromagnetic fields thrown out by power lines and technology, our subtle selves are affected in various ways. This imbalance distorts the etheric body which governs the workings of the phys-ical. In turn the etheric organisation is disrupted and the physical becomes imbalanced, resulting in cancer or another dis-ease. That is why the crew of the Eldridge was so affected on all levels by the immense electromagnetic field they were subjected to.

Even illness is used to serve the system. The Brotherhood-owned or -controlled drug companies fund scientific research, and insist that the scientists they are funding look only for ways of treating disease through drugs or technology that can be bought and sold. The world is awash with tablets and potions, and the drug companies measure their profits in billions. Some of their gross mark-ups are as high as 90%. But the disease-care services are submerged by people who are ill! When I was younger I had a doctor who hardly lifted his head long enough to look at me before he was writing a prescription for some drug or other. Representat-ives from the drug companies have many ways to 'encourage' doctors to use their products. So many people are ill, physically or emotionally, that the disease-care services are little more than conveyor belts cutting open and administering drugs to the never-ending stream of system-created disease that is passing by. The doctors and nurses are as much the victims as the patients. For doctors and nurses, see economists, politicians, scientists and jour-nalists. They are programmed to think The System's way and do its bidding within the prison of misunderstanding it builds around them. But again many are awakening from this slumber.

Nothing sums up better the conveyor belt mentality of medical care than a circular sent out by a doctors' practice on the Isle of Wight. It said that patients were reminded that doctors' appoint-ments were for five minutes only and this was not the time to discuss other problems. There you have it in a sentence. The fact that the 'other problems' were likely to be the cause of their illness did not seem to register. If there are imbalances in our eternal selves, especially at the emotional level, they will filter down through the chakra system to manifest as physical disease or dis-ease. Medical science reacts by throwing drugs at the symptoms while ignoring the cause. It accepts that stress and emotional problems can cause illness because the evidence is overwhelming. But it rejects any idea of eternal consciousness and so it cannot understand *why* stress causes disease. When they identify an emotional problem they prescribe Valium or other anti-depressants in an attempt to suppress the symptoms. What the patient really needs is for the cause of their depression to be addressed. If you are depressed because you have poor housing you don't need drugs you need a decent house. But instead of being a health service, the system has turned doctors and nurses into medical garbage collectors, coping with the human debris the system daily tips out. I am not condemning doctors or anyone in the medical profession. What else can they do when their workload is such that they can give no more than five minutes to a patient and have no power to provide what the patient really needs to remove their dis-ease?

Preventative medicine which removes the causes of dis-ease before they become physical problems is largely ignored by the medical establishment, because to do what is necessary would mean re-thinking all its values and misguided principles. Instead, even preventing illness – or claiming to – is used to stoke the fires of financial opportunism and exploitation. Did you know that the fluorides added to drinking water in the name of fighting tooth decay were used as rat poison for nearly 40 years?

Since the early 1900s industrial fluorines have been a major polluter of rivers and streams, poisoning land and animals. They are a by-product of the aluminium industry. In 1939 the Mellon Institute in the USA asked Dr Gerald Cox to find a market for fluoride waste. Cox, a biochemist, suggested the idea of putting them in the public drinking water . This delighted his paymasters, the Melon Institute, because it was owned by the family of Andrew Mellon, the owner of the Aluminum Corporation of America (ALCOA). In 1944, Oscar Ewing was employed by ALCOA at an annual salary of $750,000, and this was fifty years ago! Within months he had moved on to be the head of the Federal Security Agency and he began a campaign to have fluoride added to public water supplies. By 1951, he had persuaded Congress that it was a good idea and was given two million dollars to start the work. You could not put this rat poison into rivers and streams because it was considered too dangerous, but you could put it into water that people drank. This was great for ALCOA, but terrible for the people, and this sort of covert wheeler-dealing is going on behind the politician-speak every day. Interestingly, flouride has been shown to dull the intellect.

This is dream land for drug companies. It is no surprise that one drug company alone I saw increased its six monthly profits by 1.7 billion dollars. This adds greatly to the wealth of people like the Rockefellers who own half the pharmaceutical industry in the USA, according to *Nexus* magazine. But such increases in profits have run parallel to the growth in drug-related illness. Dr Brian Strom, Associate Director of Medicine and Pharmacology at the University of Pennsylvania School of Medicine, estimates that the side effects from drugs kill 160,000 Americans every year, and put 1.6 million into hospital. I've seen people I know prescribed pills for symptoms, and others to offset the effects of them. This is making the tills ring even quicker for the drug companies. If medical science does not understand the true nature of the human being, how can it avoid creating drugs that cause more harm than the original illness they are designed to treat? But then a drugged-up population is just what the Brotherhood wants. And how do we know what they are putting in those drugs?

The drug companies are terrified of alternatives to this madness. They portray alternative healers as 'quacks' who are potentially dangerous when they, themselves, are often lethal. There are people who call themselves alternative healers who are nothing of the kind and you have to be careful. But I don't remember an alternative healer coming up with Thalidomide which deformed so many babies; nor do I recall them giving people drugs with side effects that ensure their victims will never be able to walk out in the sunshine again. Drug companies have done both and much more. Just as the oil companies and the Brotherhood seek to stop free energy technology, so the Brotherhood drug companies make every effort to discredit and destroy all cures that do not involve drugs. They don't want a cure for cancer. They are making too much money selling drugs to treat the symptoms of it. This is not about health. It is about wealth.

The Pharmaceutical Industry is one of the most corrupt and corrupting organisations humanity has invented. It is Brotherhood-controlled and one of the most sinister of its operations. Ian Sinclair, in his book *You can overcome Asthma* says that in 1972, a commission set up by the Chilean President, Salvador Allende (a doctor), reported that no more than two dozen drugs were actually effective. The doctors on the commission proposed a dramatic reduction in drugs purchased from the companies, mostly American. Within a year, the junta with CIA support, had ousted Allende in a coup. The doctors on the commission were killed, and the new regime recommenced business as usual with the drug companies. The industry controls the whole system – doctors, universities, research, government, health departments, the lot. And when they are prevented from marketing drugs which are exposed as dangerous, they dump them on the Third World. So, everyone involved in medicine, are you going to continue to take all this, or are you going to get together and *do* something?

AIDS is a massive earner for the drug industry. They even leak claims about 'cures' to boost their share price as people invest in a company in the hope that they will make lots of money when the 'cure' is marketed. They do this with other 'cures' too, and the media poodle barks to its master's tune again by running stories of drug research projects on the verge of this or that 'breakthrough' which never sees the light of day. AIDS, this heaven-sent profits-booster for the drug companies, is not some mysterious disease that has come from nowhere. It was almost certainly created in a laboratory. I have seen some evidence presented by Robert Strecker MD that AIDS is basically caused by the amalgamation of two animal diseases – bovine leukemia in cattle and visna virus which affects sheep.

Dr Strecker says that, the genes of the AIDS-causing virus do not exist in primates or humans. But they do exist in these two viruses, known as retro-viruses, in cattle and sheep. During hearings of the Church Committee in 1969 it was learned that the Department of Defence had asked for ten million dollars to create new viruses to destroy the immune system. In 1972 the Bulletin of the World Health Organisation (part of the UN) carried suggestions from a group of virologists that a virus be made to destroy the T-cell and B-cell systems of human beings. The idea was, it appears, that if they could make a virus to cause cancers and leukemia, it would help them to find a cure for those diseases. Strecker's research leads him to believe that the bovine leukemia and visna virus were mixed in the laboratory to create the bovine-visna virus. This was then grown in human tissue, which turned it into a virus that affected the human body in a way that dismantled the immune system. We call it AIDS.

The authorities denied this, and even denied the existence of the cattle-sheep virus combination known as the bovine-visna virus, but Dr Strecker tracked down papers detailing this very thing. He says:

"(Bovine-visna virus) had the exact same shape as the AIDS virus; it had the same molecular weight; it had the exact same genetic structure in a sense; it had the exact same Magnesium dependency, which is relatively unique in this class of agents. It had the exact same capability of killing T-cells selectively and yet, in the cumulative knowledge of the world's AIDS experts, this virus didn't exist. Now that's a lie.

"What we think happened was that...in 1972 we produced a group of viruses that will cause cancer in the laboratories around the world and then, in our opinion, these viruses were probably tested. We think they were tested in large populations in Africa, which explains how you get three hundred million Africans probably infected today......The epidemic in Africa would not have started from a single-point infection. In other words, the numbers infected are so great that there had to be a mass inoculation at some point in the mid-1970s. What we think really happened was a group of scientists went to Africa and actually tested these agents there." (In the guise of smallpox vacinations).

It is also interesting that, according to Dr Strecker, the initial spread of AIDS in the United States tallies exactly with a US Government vaccine study on Hepatitis B which involved young, white male homosexuals between the ages of twenty and forty. AIDS appeared where the Hepatitis vaccine study had been – New York, San Francisco, Los Angeles, Chicago and St. Louis. If you believe that no one would ever do such a thing, that's because you run your life with standards that are far higher than the misguided people who run the world. When you think that many countries have tested nuclear bombs without evacuating either their soldiers or the local population, because they want to study the effects on the human body, it is clear how much respect some of these characters have for human life. Poisons and radiation have been released purposely into local populations around the world for studies on the effects. Germ warfare testing has been conducted in this way. One of the projects which have done this in the United States was called MK-ULTRA which I spoke of in an earlier chapter. Robert Strecker says that in Alabama, they recruited black men in the 1930s for a long-term study on the progression of syphilis, and when penicillin came along they prevented the men from being cured, because they considered the study more important. The same mentality, and worse, goes on in the scientific community today among the extremists. That Alabama study, incidentally, was conducted by the US Public Health Service Department which today works out of Atlanta, Georgia, under the title of The Center for Disease Control, and it 'leads' the government battle against AIDS. I feel that the cure for AIDS is already known.

I don't know if all Dr Strecker's assumptions are correct, but he makes some telling points and I feel sure that AIDS has its origin in a laboratory. One of the themes running through the findings of the researchers into the New World Order is that there is a secret plan to reduce the global population by genocide, and that includes attempts to use diseases like AIDS and germ warfare techniques. As I say, these are strange people under the influence of a very misguided force. What is it that the Protocols say? They would undermine humanity in part by "the inoculation of diseases".

The idea of reducing the population through the spread of disease is believed to have originated from a meeting of scientists in 1957, who came to the conclusion that the soaring population, pollution and the exploitation of the environment would destroy the planet's life support systems by the year 2000. Eisenhower ordered a study to be conducted into alternative ways of responding to this crisis. Alternative One was to use nuclear devices to blast holes in the stratosphere to allow heat and pollution to escape, and change the destructive human culture into one of environmental protection (this was rejected). Alternative Two was to construct underground cities, connected by tunnels, where selected representatives of the various cultures would continue the human race. Alternative Three was for the chosen few to move to new bases on the Moon and other planets. The Moon was code-named 'Adam' for this plan, and Mars was 'Eve'. All three alternatives include the release of deadly diseases, and AIDS is said to be one of them. I cannot confirm any of this, and I don't present it as fact, but what is obvious is that we have not even begun to know the full story about AIDS. One body of opinion suggests that the HIV virus, which is said to cause AIDS, is not the culprit, or not the only one, and I believe that the electromagnetic pollution produced by the military and secret services is harming the human immune system.

The cure for AIDS and other human diseases lies in the areas termed alternative medicine. I am particularly impressed with vibrational medicine and the use of sound to re-balance and re-harmonise the mind, body and spirit. I said before that every vibration has its own sound, shade of colour, symbol and number, and if you can use these to harmonise the body and the human energy field, dis-ease is replaced by health. The sound which represents the vibration of harmony for the Earth is the 'OM' sound and its colour is white, the amalgamation of all colours. The ancients knew of this. The symbol of the OM vibration is the three spirals which together form a triangle. It can be found on countless ancient sites, stones and caves. This knowledge is now resurfacing in our consciousness, and it will revolutionise healing.

Alternatives like acupuncture, homeopathy, rieki, radionics, aromatherapy, reflexology, and others reflect a far wider understanding of the human being. They seek to remove the imbalances on all levels and treat the cause, not the symptom. Preferably, they wish to identify potential trouble and re-balance the energy fields before any physical discomfort is felt. Acupuncture, which is thousands of years older than the drug companies, uses needles to balance out the energy flows through the chakras and the lines of energy known as meridians. Hands-on healing of the genuine kind is not 'faith healing'; it is the transfer of energies from the healer through their hands to the patient. A form of photography developed by a Russian couple called Kirlian can photograph the energy fields around the body. They found that when they photographed someone with an illness the energy fields were weak. When they photographed healers, the energies were particularly vivid and bright. After a healing session, the patient's energies were stronger and the healers had temporarily diminished. Everyone has the potential to heal to some level depending on what they have chosen to do in this life. In the next few years, millions are going to realise that they have come to the Earth to be healers, because that is going to be vital during the transition.

The evolution of healing is another example of why the system has to collapse if real change is to be realised. The growth in alternative healing has been hastened by the breakdown of the disease-care services like the National Health Service in Britain. That is constantly short of funds because the system is unable to produce the money from take, make and throw away to cope with the growth in human dis-ease caused by over-consumption; and when a health service is dependent on drug-based treatments and expensive surgery, it will never have enough money for all it needs to do. The demise of the economic system is encouraging people to look for alternatives like barter, and it is the same with healing. The disease services are falling apart and people are turning to alternatives far more rapidly than they would otherwise have done. The changes in consciousness will speed this process every year, until we see a fusion between the knowledge of the physical level as expressed by today's doctors, and the understanding of the higher levels which alternative methods possess. I do not see this fusion as a 50-50 balance. Nothing like. The alternative methods will become the overwhelming foundations of health care, and other even more effective methods will be developed as higher knowledge becomes available to us and we can control the aging process and remove genetic disease by re-programming the DNA genetic coding. The cut 'em and drug 'em days are almost over.

We will see that the physical body is a far more fantastic creation than science has yet understood and the basis of all health and illness is thought. Our etheric energy fields organise the physical body as I have already said and it encodes every single cell with a memory of what it is and what it has to do. A cell is a classic example of the universal principal of as above, so below. Each one is, in its energy system and memory, a smaller version of the whole body. Our thoughts are constantly affecting this process positively and negatively. Everything that happens to us which affects our thoughts is affecting the DNA genetic coding which we pass on to our children, or, to be more accurate, the physical bodies we create for the consciousness of our children. We can get genetic illness because of an emotional trauma or physical accident which someone experienced in the same genetic line thousands of years ago. The affect of the emotions on the etheric organisation is passed through to the DNA and on down the line until the DNA is 'wiped' clean of that inherited genetic imbalance. This can be done very quickly and simply in a few minutes once you know how, and long-standing illnesses disappear after such treatment. It does not involve a single drug or any surgery whatsoever. As this gains acceptance you will not be able to give away shares in the drug companies and conventional medicine. We are obviously very much affected by the genetic history of the ancestral line of our genetic spacesuits and people are dying every day, every minute of every day come to that, for the want of a simple treatment that can remove the genetic inheritances that all bodies carry. What we do and what we experience emotionally and physically in this life is passed on to our children. Once this DNA cleansing is widely accepted, expectant mothers and would-be fathers will go through this process to ensure that they are passing on only positive genetic codes to their children. The emotional state of the mother during pregnancy has a very big effect on the children, because the baby in the womb is linked to the mother's blood supply and its growing form is affected genetically by what she is experiencing emotionally. Healers in this field of Vibrational Medicine and genetic cleansing are years ahead of medical science as we have come to know it. Watch the drug companies try to marginalise and outlaw alternatives to their empires of greed as the years progress. They are already doing so, and we should respond to this in the usual way – by ignoring them and any laws that might arise from their lobbying.

The expansion of healing and healers cannot happen too fast. Some diseases will disappear with the rising consciousness, while new ones will develop, some of them from the effect of the quickening vibrations on those who choose to close their minds to change. The vibratory disharmony between those people and the consciousness of the planet will have many consequences for mental, emotional, and physical well-being. The more people who have activated their healing gifts, the better it will be for everyone. This need will be compounded by the consequences of administering drugs like sweets. I wrote in *It Doesn't Have To Be Like This* of the danger from 'Superbugs'. These are viruses that have developed immunity to drugs like antibiotics which have been prescribed for almost anything that moves. We are now seeing these Superbugs and I feel that some diseases we thought had gone forever will start to return. Superbugs, incidentally, have implications for food production. Drug-infested farming methods are giving insects immunity to the poisons sprayed on the crops.

On the other side of the transition our knowledge will be such that we will live on this physical level for hundreds of years if we wish, just as we did in Lemuria and Atlantis. We will hear stories of a time on Earth when people said that only the physical world existed; we will be told of a civilisation so primitive that they ravaged the planet for fuels, cut open their bodies, and used potions that caused as much illness as they cured. We will smile at the story tellers. We will shake our heads. And we will find it so hard to believe.

18

Bricks in the Wall

LET me offer you a definition of the word education as expressed in schools and universities across the world: To teach, instruct, and imbue with a doctrine, idea or opinion.

The Oxford English Dictionary would not agree because that it is the definition it gives for the word 'indoctrinate'. But, to me, that is a perfect description of humanity's version of education. Our children are not educated. They are indoctrinated – 'imbued with a doctrine, idea, or opinion'.

This is essential to the process of conditioning that we are subjected to throughout our lives. Education for the young is a wonderful concept if education is what it really is. But The System largely controls what children are taught, how they are taught, and what it wishes them to believe. What better way to condition your population than to have control of what young people are taught through their formative years? And from what we have seen of the system in all its glory, do you think this control is going to be used for the good of the children or the good of The System? Education, at least in its Western mode, is there to turn out system fodder.

It fills young and potentially creative minds with streams of boring, irrelevant and often inaccurate information; with complex mathematical equations most people will never use; and with a view of history that puts the State in the best possible light. A Texan lady told me how she was taught history. First, a long time was spent making the class feel good about being Texan. They were not only the best people in America, they were the best in the world. Once that was established, the genocide of the Indians by the white settlers was glossed over and rushed through in a ridiculously short time. You would have thought, she said, that only in the 20th century did American history really start. What you would call 'education' is part of the Brotherhood war on the young:

"We have got our hands into the administration of the law, into the conduct of elections, into the press, into the liberty of the person, but principally into education and training as being the corner-stones of a free existence. We have fooled, bemused, and corrupted the youth of the Goyim by rearing them in principals and theories which are known to us to be false although it is by us that they have been inculcated." (Illuminati Protocol 10).

I have been saddened on my many visits to universities to see young people in their teens who do not have a thought in their head that someone else has not put there. They stand before you after only 17 or 18 years on the planet and are already mindlessly parroting The System's propaganda. Another robot reporting for duty. I was amazed to be told in all seriousness by a student at the prestigious Cambridge University that if you don't eat meat you die! The fact that I was standing in front of her fit and well after many years as a vegetarian had no effect on her conviction that refusing to eat dead animals was the equivalent of suicide.

You can understand how indoctrination can take hold so quickly. The further you progress within the education system the more opportunity there is to control your thinking. Some of the most enlightened people I have met left school as early as they could and had not been to university. Enlightenment comes by expanding your consciousness and accessing higher levels of knowledge. Most conventional education closes minds and focuses them on this physical world alone. The campaigner, Michael Roll, makes this point in his booklet *The Suppression of Knowledge*. He was referring here to those in high places within the system, but the principles apply to everyone and everything, be it religion, science, or economics:

"If a baby from birth is told by loving parents that 2 + 2 = 3; and later at Sunday school, kindergarten, preparatory school, public school, and university this young mind is again told by apparently clever and often highly respected teachers that 2 + 2 = 3; and if this same teaching comes through the mass media, backed by the weight of law, is it any wonder that many people, often in very responsible positions, seriously believe that 2 + 2 = 3?"

The System is geared to the setting and passing of examinations.

This immediately creates 'successes' (those with the ability to absorb and remember mostly irrelevant and inaccurate information) and 'failures' (those who do not have that ability or are too bored to use it). The 'successes' go on to university to absorb yet more irrelevant and inaccurate information and the 'failures' go off to look for jobs that are more likely to be given to the 'successes.' What a way to start your life, be you a success or failure.

I was a failure under that definition. I was bored stiff at school. I could not see how most of the tidal wave of information I was being forced to listen to day after day could have any relevance to my future life. I also had the underlying feeling that most of what I was being told was baloney anyway. I was talked at by the teachers and rarely consulted for my view or asked to express creativity. I never passed an exam and I left school at the first opportunity to become a professional soccer player. All my education in its true sense has happened since. I enjoyed school for the sport and my friends. I liked most of the teachers, too, because they were very nice people. But the lessons and examinations were something I had to endure in order to play soccer and be with my mates.

I can see why The System loves examinations. They are an excellent way of making children and young people absorb the system's view. There is little margin for personal opinion. If you are going to pass you must tell the status quo what it wants to hear. Who sets the questions in exams? The status quo. Who decides what the answers must be if you are going to pass? The status quo. Whatever is the conventional wisdom of the day provides the criteria under which you pass or fail. A few centuries ago you would have failed your exam if you had said the Earth was round!

Like all aspects of The System, education is in desperate trouble. Its role is to produce robots to fill the jobs the system requires them to do and to condition out of young people any idea of rebellion against the status quo. The System does not evolve to encompass the gifts and creativity of people; people have to be conditioned and prepared to fit the system. People blindly accepted that while take-make-and-throwaway could employ the robots, most accepted that you went to school to be prepared for work and then you worked in a trade until you retired or died. But now that is no longer happening in the same way. Millions of young people can see no prospect of a job at the end of the line. Even the 'successes', the university graduates, are struggling to find employment. A feeling of 'what's the point?' is growing. Truancy is mostly caused through boredom and a lack of self worth and involvement at school. Everyone, but *everyone*, has latent creativity and gifts they have come to offer the world. Human education is only seriously interested in the gifts that fit The System and that leaves out a terrific number of alienated people.

Within this perversion of the word education are a number of enlightened teachers and, to a lesser extent in my experience, university lecturers. They do the best they can to lessen the indoctrination. There are schools which try to tap the full potential of their students. But, like the doctors, nurses, politicians, journalists, economists and scientists who are opening their consciousness to greater understanding, teachers and lecturers are subject to severe limitations of action by the structure and control they have to endure. As the demise of take-make-and-throwaway quickens we are hearing government ministers talking of a 'return to basics' in all things. This is their way of finding some illusion of security in a mythical 1950s utopia in which everyone had their place and everyone knew what it was. This back to basics policy when applied to education, puts an emphasis on 'talking at' teaching, an expansion of tests and exams and, to quote one former Education Secretary, a return to teaching a fear of God. Give me strength.

I see a very different approach surfacing as consciousness expands its understanding of life. Like everything I have discussed in this book, the transition period for education will be one of opposites. The status quo and those who support it will try to hold back change by returning to 'basics' as they call them. They will wish to make education even more rigid and impose more dogma as a reaction to changes that will eventually sweep it away. Against that will be a growing demand from awakening people for education to replace indoctrination.

There are things we all need to learn in our early years, like how to count, write, and communicate. We also require a summary of the ideas that claim to explain what is happening around us. But, like history, these need to be presented as ideas, opinions and views, not facts, unless they can be shown to be so. You only have to read government papers which are released thirty years after events to see how the state re-writes history every day – look at the information in this book! Secret Illuminati documents which have come to light say that it has rewritten history to suit its own ends. To present all but the outlines of history as fact is to mislead. Children in the United States were brought up to believe the

Indians were backward savages. When those children grew up, many treated the Indians appallingly from that indoctrinated perspective. British children are taught by law in the schools that the Christian story is historical fact, not a story that Christians choose to believe. I was never told at school about Constantine's Council of Nicaea, the Jesus-style saviour figures of the pre-Christians, or the 'crusade' against the Cathars. Nor are my children. Every Christmas, pupils in primary schools perform nativity plays. That's fine if the story of the Nativity is portrayed as art, the acting-out of a Christian belief. But it isn't. It's mostly presented to the children as history.

I am looking forward to an education which teaches written and verbal communication, the mathematics we will need in our everyday lives, and the information that will help young people to have a wide understanding of the world. They need to be given access to all views and to be encouraged to have their own opinions. In the teaching of religion, for example, the course would include explanations of what all religions believe and why. There would be no imposition of one Christian, Muslim, or Jewish dogma. Explanations of karma, reincarnation, and Earth energies would be added to the curriculum along with the principles of astrology and alternative forms of healing to allow children and students the opportunity to have access to all views, not only those which the status quo wants us to believe.

Education of the future will encourage self-reliance. The basic skills people need to live without dependence on The System will be at the heart of this. How to grow food, cook, build a house, repair and maintain a home and its contents and the other skills necessary to be independent. This gives young people choices throughout their lives. The education system of today is teaching more and more about less and less. It is producing people who are dependent on earning money from one specialised skill to pay for all the other things they need. This is the opposite of independence. And look at the consequences when that skill is no longer required by take-make-and- throwaway. But making people dependent serves The System magnificently.

The main motivation of the new education will be to identify and encourage the gifts the student has brought into incarnation. The students themselves will decide this. Ask young people what they most enjoy and you will invariably be looking at their natural potential. We reveal our gifts in our enthusiasms and interests.

Many young people who are less than 'successful' at school will be doing some marvellous things in their spare time when they are in control of what they can and cannot do. I have known people who were regarded as failures at maths at school but who can work out the odds and pay-outs for a horse race at lightning speed. This is possible because the maths involved – in this case when applied to horse racing – has become part of their enthusiasm. You may not agree with horse racing or betting, but that's another subject. The point I am making is that, if you encourage people's enthusiasms and use those as a basis for teaching other skills, you are going to be very much more successful than if you only talk at them from the front of the class or tell them to read text books.

The new education will not concentrate on the skills demanded by throughput. There will be greater opportunities to develop gifts in the arts, crafts and sport. With everyone's gifts encouraged, there will be no 'failures'. Youngsters will not be leaving school thinking they have failed because the examination results say so. Once the basic diversity of knowledge has been taught, the opportunities will be there to specialise and develop to a level of excellence whatever the student has decided he or she wishes to do. But this will happen with the wide range of skills and understanding underpinning that specialisation and the choices they offer, always available.

Respect and love for the Earth and all life will be encouraged throughout the new education. From an early age, children will spend time, as part of their curriculum, working in the community with old people, the infirm and those in need for whatever reason. Loving and caring for each other will be the guiding principles of education. Professional teachers won't be the only vehicles for educating the young. In every community there are thousands of people with skills and knowledge which would benefit students. But, instead of using that wealth of knowledge, The System relies on teachers and lecturers alone to give insights into subjects for which they often have no practical experience. There needs to be a better balance between the teachers' classroom skills and the practical experience of others in the community.

It is time for the teaching profession to rebel and refuse to serve this system of indoctrination any longer. They are just being used by those in control to feed the children in their care the information The System wants them to hear and believe. Come on teachers and teachers' unions. Refuse to be used as system fodder programmed to turn out more fodder to replace you. Stop cooperating, Say No. The same applies to parents. Insist on real education. Stop cooperating with the programming of your children. The circle must be broken.

During the transition period, I expect more people to take their children out of the state system. They will either teach them at home or get together in groups to form their own schools. These will not be giant comprehensives. They will be much smaller and more personal. A typical one could be composed of just a few families getting together. Far less of a student's day will be spent sitting and being talked at; far more in doing and talking themselves. The move away from formal state education will increase through this decade and across the Millennium. Economic collapse will add further to the demise of the present education system. Further in the future, the whole concept of education will be unrecognisable when compared to what we have today or even to the new approach to learning which I have been promoting.

We need to appreciate that going through the state education indoctrination machine and coming out with examination passes and letters after your name does not, in itself, make you intelligent, wise or inspired. It can actually suppress all three. While I was writing this chapter I saw a 'highly-qualified' scientist giving a television lecture about the new frontiers of science. At the end he posed a number of questions which he said science will need to answer about the mysteries of life. People without his paper qualifications have been answering those questions since before he was born, but The System has not listened. In the next twenty years, it will be shown, even to the satisfaction of mainstream thinking, that the themes in this book and others about life and Creation are correct. The media could have printed these answers years ago, but they ignored them because I and people like me do not have letters after our name or have our explanations pored over in scientific journals. Nor are we supporters of the status quo. The education system of today doesn't just indoctrinate the population during their time at school and university. It decides throughout our lives who we should listen to and who we should not, especially when science is involved.

Yet, if you can access higher levels of consciousness, you can bring into this world understandings and knowledge that are light years ahead of human science, the bulk of which is only interested in the physical world. Coming into incarnation now through many of our babies are aspects of universal consciousness of considerable evolution. With the frequencies rising, they are able to tune consciously much earlier in their lives to frequency levels that were denied to us. We have had to work to stay with the rising frequencies while babies today can come in at the highest levels available to this planet. They will be manifesting their higher knowledge and understanding of who they are and what they are doing here much earlier than we could. This doesn't mean they are necessarily more evolved than many others on Earth today. It means they can connect earlier in their lives with the higher frequencies the planet is moving into. I have heard many people say that babies today are different. Well this is why.

This phenomenon alone will ensure that education will become a two-way process, as it should always have been anyway. We will tell the children what we know, or think we know, and they will tell us what they know. Encouraging them to connect with their highest potential will be the most important gift we can give to them and the world. The education of the future will be designed to bring out all the skills and knowledge that we possess and to help to lead us along the life path we have chosen before incarnation.

Today we indoctrinate for The System. Tomorrow we will educate for life.

19

Exploitation of the Spirit

THEY'RE after your mind. If they can control the way you think and feel they can control your behaviour and hijack your individuality. They can take you over.

'They' can take many forms: entities on other frequencies, religions, elements of the New Age and the technology of mind-control under the guidance of those groups outside of governmental and democratic control who seek to rule the world. In this chapter I am looking at some of the ways 'they' exploit the spirit and the minds of the human race, how we can stop it happening and how 'they' are likely to react to the challenge of the changing consciousness that threatens their ambitions so fundamentally. It is important to know what is going on because the mind controllers in all their forms will be trying even harder today to prevent the sort of changes I have outlined in the second half of the book.

Religions like Christianity, Islam, Judaism and so many others have only survived this long by fear, indoctrination and imposition. Without these, they would have been long gone. In their extreme forms they amount to nothing less than spiritual fascism. Their fear, guilt and prejudice have been indoctrinated through the generations over thousands of years and they have made a fundamental contribution to the division and pain on the Earth today. How ironic that those who proclaim the Jewish religion and condemn Islam could well have experienced Islamic lives in the past and vice-versa. It's the same with Protestants and Catholics, those two expressions of the Christian creed which have often been in conflict. Whenever I see Ian Paisley, the vehement Protestant spokesman in Northern Ireland, a voice in my mind says, 'He was a pope!'.

While the major religions speak of a world of spirit, they have been created by and motivated by the misunderstandings in the world of matter under the guidance of highly negative and imbalanced aspects of the Luciferic consciousness working on the minds of those involved – not all of them, but enough. The religions have sought material and political power and that has been their driving force. They have wished to control and deny free expression. The Inquisitions, the torture and the mass murder of non-believers are evidence of that. Any creed which has to indoctrinate, frighten and impose itself through violence and genocide has no respect for human life and freedom of thought and expression, nor for the very values it is supposed to proclaim. If they are so confident that what they say is true and credible, why do they feel the need to impose it and suppress alternative explanations? The answer to that is that, without imposition, it would not be here today.

We now have endless factions of Christianity, Mormons, Methodists, Baptists and more far right mind-controlling sects springing up to take advantage of humanity's spiritual emptiness and lack of meaning, particularly among the young. 'Give us your money, do as we say and we'll give you all the answers because we are the representatives of God. If you don't do what we say, you will be rejected by Jesus and go into the fires of hell.' That sums up the basic message of so many sick and misguided groups which prey on the minds of those seeking meaning in this crazy world. Exploitation of the spirit is a growth industry.

For nearly two thousand years Christianity had a free hand to force its creed upon the population of, particularly, the Western world. British people were forced to go to church by law and even today Christianity is given free air time quite outrageously day after day by the BBC and others to broadcast its propaganda. The Christian view is taught, again by law, in the schools. The Church of England is part of the institution of State. Prime Ministers are involved in the selection of bishops and the monarch is crowned as 'Defender of the Faith'. Most people have forgotten that the church became part of the state in the first place only because Henry VIII wanted a divorce and the Pope refused to allow it. As we have seen, Henry's decision to ignore the Pope and the determination of his daughter, Elizabeth I, to become supreme head of a Protestant Church of England led to Church and State becoming linked at all levels. To this day, bishops are given automatic places in the House of Lords and most of the clergy are often reluctant or frightened to speak out strongly against governments who abuse the values for which the Church claims to stand. There are exceptions to this, but the general rule remains. Christianity and other religions have instigated, supported or watched without challenge, some of the most horrendous atrocities against humanity and the Earth. Roman Catholicism, that most arrogant of dictatorships controlled by the Brotherhood, still tries to force people to behave in ways it deems acceptable.

Yet, despite all its imposition, privileges and advantages, the Christian Church is crumbling before our eyes. Attendances continue to fall and churches to close because the money is no longer there to pay the bills. The Church of England has been financed mostly from its land holdings and inherited wealth. The largest part of this land, and therefore the Church's wealth, came into its possession through force of various kinds, violent or psychological. In some cases, landowners who went off to fight for God (Christian power and influence) in the Crusades were persuaded by the Church to sign over all their land and property in the event of their death. Giving all that to the Church would ensure a place in Heaven. Purely by coincidence it would also ensure that the Church became richer. They could always come up with a biblical passage to support them:

"And everyone that hath forsaken houses, or brethren, or sisters, or father or mother, or wife or children, or lands for my name's sake, shall receive an hundredfold, and shall inherit everlasting life."

But falling attendances and ill-fated property speculation from the late 1980s have dramatically reduced the wealth of the Church of England, and others are also, or will soon be, in similar trouble. Around three-quarters of a billion pounds have been wiped off the Church of England's assets and that is only what they have publicly admitted to. Parish churches have been told they will now have to raise more of their money for themselves because the central fund cannot afford to continue with donations at the level they have been in the past. Even the ability of the Church to pay pensions to its clergy has been questioned.

Alongside this blow to its finances has come the public questioning of its dogma. I have said before that part of the plan for the transformation has been for some of the volunteers to incarnate with the task of becoming part of the bastions of mind-control, like the Church, the media, the monarchy, and science. They would not remember this yet but they are being activated at the right time to undermine these organisations from within. A wonderful example of this, I believe, is the former Bishop of Durham, David Jenkins. He has attracted fierce criticism from fanatics for questioning the Christian version of the Virgin Birth, much of the Christmas story, the Second Coming and the existence of a place called Hell to which sinners are supposed to be condemned for all eternity. Like most people who stand up and speak out with courage he was only articulating what others believe but are too frightened say. It speaks much for the feeble foundations of Christianity that those who attack the Bishop say he is questioning the whole basis on which the Christian religion stands or falls. If a creed depends on events that supposedly happened two thousand years ago, as reported in a book written by who knows who and who knows when, in who knows what circumstances, it doesn't say much for the creed, does it? But the Bishop has had the courage to keep on speaking out and, slowly, others within the Protestant and Catholic churches are beginning to do the same. The realisation is beginning to dawn that ancient texts have to be read symbolically, not literally, most of the time, and that you cannot use them as an infallible record of truth. Such people have a long way to move before they encompass the sort of themes included in this book but they are already questioning the dogmatic view of the Church. We will see more people breaking ranks and saying what they have long believed – that the dogma of the Christian creed is simply not credible. You only have to read some Christian literature to realise that:

"If you ignore him (Jesus) and reject him now, at the Day Of Judgment when we must all stand before him he will ignore and reject you. 'I do not know you, depart from me'." (This is the 'loving' Jesus and the Prince of Peace?)

"...after death there is no more opportunity to turn to Christ. It will be too late." (This is clearly bad news for the babies who die after a few minutes or the little children who have not had the opportunity to know what Jesus is demanding of them. And what about the children in parts of the world who do not even know of Jesus?)

"The good news of the Gospel is that Jesus, the perfect substitute, made the ultimate once and for all payment on our behalf. It cost Him His life. As a result God gives the free gift of salvation to those who believe in His Son."

(The publication from which this quote is taken included a chapter attacking alternative thought called 'The Fine Art Of Baloney Detection'!).

Throughout the Christian Church there are many thousands of people, like the Quakers, who have been attracted by the laudable values attributed to Jesus in the Gospels. They have suffered the dogma but lived the values. They have used the Church to work for the good of the community. Indeed, there are some magnificent human beings working within Christianity and other religions. These are people who would have found other ways to express their decency if the Church had never existed. They are prisoners of the dogma within the Church structure but not within their own consciousness. When that structure is no more, and that time is not far away, these Church people will be freed to live and promote the values of caring, sharing, love and tolerance without being forced to insist that everything in the Bible is true and the word of God. Such values have been devalued by the dogma which anyone with a mind they can genuinely call their own knows to be invention and not even inspired invention at that.

The rising frequencies will be affecting open minded, value-led, Church people in the same way that they are awakening others. As we have seen with the former Bishop of Durham, the awakening to their role in this life will be so powerful that they will not be able to stop themselves from speaking out, no matter what the short-term consequences for them might be. Tensions will grow between this awakening consciousness within the Church and the closed minds who will seek security in the face of these changes by the promotion of dogma in its most extreme forms. The demise of the economic system will bring the political right to the surface and the religious right will rise in the wake of the Church's collapse. Both will fail as the transition proceeds, but they could cause considerable pain and disruption in the short term. There are likely to be witch-hunts by the extremists against those within the religions who disagree with them.

I see in all the religions the rejection of dogma by sensible, open-minded Muslims, Jews, Christians and others in the light of the changing consciousness. They will start to think for themselves and demand freedom of thought and expression. Summon your courage, thinkers within the Church, and speak out. The religious robots also need to rebel. The extremes will react against this challenge, creating potential for conflict. Mind-controlled fanatics who will be befuddled even more by the rising vibrations could resort to violence and inquisition in an attempt to impose their will. There will be attempts to portray the upheavals of the transition, including the weather and geological events, as God's reprisals against a human race which does not behave as he says, (i.e. what the religious dogmatists say). This will succeed with a few people and there will be a temporary turning to these religions by those who fear what is happening but don't wish to take responsibility for their own thoughts and actions. I believe that the Brotherhood and the scientists of the underground bases, may use their Walt Disney technology to project illusions of great religious miracles to suggest that the Second Coming is upon us and that people must repent (for repent, read 'do as they say').

The Brotherhood will at the same time use the Church and destroy it when the moment arrives to introduce its own "Messiah" or "World king", whatever form that is supposed to take. Having manipulated the Vatican for its own ends, it will bring down the Roman Catholic Church. It is vital that people do not buy their ludicious, but sinister, alternative:

"We shall not overtly lay a finger on existing churches, but we shall fight against them by criticism calculated to produce schism... only years divide us from the moment of the complete wrecking of the Christian religion. As for the other religions, we will have still less difficulty in dealing with them." (Illuminati Protocol 17).

Religion is under challenge on two fronts, the Brotherhood and the changing consciousness, and the way we react to its demise is going to decide which one will hold sway in the collective human mind.

The greatest potential for trouble is from those countries where religious fascist regimes are already in control. To the people of such countries I would offer again these words: '100,000 Englishmen cannot control 300 million Indians if those Indians will not cooperate'. Sadly, after a lifetime, often many lifetimes, of severe indoctrination, many of those in countries controlled by the religious right have layers of conditioning to remove before they will challenge that control in large enough numbers. As always in looking ahead, exactly what will happen is impossible to say because that will depend on how many open up to the new frequencies and how humanity as a whole reacts to events.

Christianity is already well aware of the consequences for its influence and existence being posed by the new consciousness. Its reaction to this has been painfully predictable. It is turning to the weapons it always uses in times of trouble – fear and misrepresentation. Nothing encapsulates this approach and what we are likely to see from the dogma-supporters in the near future better than a book called *New Age versus the Gospel: Christianity's Greatest Challenge*. It was put through my letter box by a local Christian offering to 'save' me from my misguided ways. He did this with the best of intentions I am sure but all the book achieved was to confirm to me (a) the pathetic nature of dogmatic Christianity and (b) the way in which that dogma reacts to alternative thought. This is some of the blurb on the book cover:

"Suddenly it is chic to be 'spiritual'." (Implication: you can only be spiritual if you are a Christian).

"But the roots of today's 'spirituality' are in Paganism, and not Christianity." (A breathtaking statement when Christianity is recycled Paganism!)

"...(The New Age)...a heady mix of Hinduism, Buddhism, and the hard core occult represents the greatest threat to Christianity in the history of the faith." (The term 'hard core occult' is designed to frighten people. Occult is another word, like Paganism, that Christianity has assassinated. Originally it meant 'hidden'. To investigate occult mysteries is to say you are investigating hidden mysteries. The word occult has been changed to imply devil worship. No single body has promoted the cause of extreme negativity more than Christianity through the centuries, except the Brotherhood. And the greatest threat to Christianity is, and has always been, itself.)

"Christians need to know where New Age is coming from and how to counter its claims." (misrepresent them.)

"New Age Versus the Gospel analyses the menace, comes to grips with the Gospel and points to the Power for revival." (The rise of evangelical dogmatists to condemn awakening peoples as evil followers of the Devil and to condemn other members of their own creed who disagree with them as not real Christians).

I have already been rebuked 'in the name of the Lord' by Christian evangelists and been dubbed 'the anti-Christ' and it was no surprise that a whole chapter was devoted to me in that book. I had to read the account about me a couple of times to confirm I wasn't dreaming. It was hysterical. The writer said that I had claimed on a television programme to be a 'New Age priest'. I am more likely to call myself Nellie The Elephant than that. As you will see, I have great reservations about some areas of what is termed New Age, although not for the reasons expressed in that book. What is more, the whole idea of priests is abhorrent to me. Stand by for more of such insults to the intelligence as the Christian dogmatists cling on to their sinking ship and thrash out at all who are heading for the lifeboats.

The foreword to the book was written by a cleric from All Souls Church, Langham Place, London. This is opposite the headquarters of BBC Radio and it is from All Souls that much free Christian propaganda is broadcast to the nation by the 'independent' BBC. The author of the foreword has a real problem with the idea that all is One and all is God. Christianity is obsessed with portraying God as an outside force which is not part of us. Humans cannot find answers from within, the book informs us, we have to be 'rescued' and that can only happen if we 'find' Jesus. Only by accepting that Jesus had to suffer horribly on the cross, in order for his father to agree to forgive the sins of the rest of us, can we be 'saved', apparently.

He says that *"from beginning to end, the New Age Movement expresses a preoccupation, even an infatuation, with self. It puts self in the place of God and even declares that we ARE God."*

Dogmatic Christianity is based on division and lack of self-worth – a division between different parts of Creation and the belief that we are born sinners. Love of self is seen as arrogant, selfish and offensive to God. In fact, it is the lack of self love and, through that, love for others which is at the heart of humanity's malaise. We cannot love, forgive and respect others until we can love, forgive and respect ourselves. This link between love for self and love for others is highlighted in my book *Heal The World*. People who are aggressive in their behaviour towards others are people who hate themselves. Their hatred of self is projected outwards in an apparent hatred of the world. Yet, I was banned from speaking at the Central Hall in Westminster, London, because I am saying love yourself, love the world.

I had wanted to hire the hall for a talk. I rang them and learned that the date I wanted was available. All was going well. Then, after the details had been agreed, the lady asked for my name. When I told her, there was a silence. After a few seconds she recovered her voice but her attitude had changed. The hall was run by the Methodist Church, she told me. I would have to write in and outline what I would be saying before permission to hire the hall would be granted. So much for freedom of speech, I thought. I wrote to them but they asked for more details. I wrote again to inform them that, in part, I would be saying that we need to love, forgive and respect ourselves if we are do the same for others. I was not surprised that the Methodist trustees of the Central Hall replied that I would not be allowed to speak there. But I was rather taken aback by the reason they gave for this ban. Part of their letter said:

"….The doctrines of the evangelical faith which Methodism has held from the beginning and still holds, are based upon the Divine revelation recorded in the Holy Scriptures. The Methodist Church acknowledges this revelation as the supreme rule of faith and practice.."

In other words, I take it, they believe that the Bible, despite all its contradictions, incitements to violence, and (according to research in the 19th Century) 36,191 translation errors in the King James version alone, is one hundred per cent accurate and infallible. The letter continued:

"Central to the evangelical Christian doctrine is the belief that to love God is the first commandment, and that implicit trust in Him is the path to salvation. It is our feeling that the promotion of a world-view which is based on 'self-love' would be contrary to the Christian Gospel which Methodism seeks to expound."

What have we come to? Someone is barred from speaking because a view which involves loving, respecting and forgiving yourself and others is 'contrary to the Christian Gospel…'. Well, if that is the case, there is something seriously wrong with the Gospels or the interpretation of them. No wonder the Church is dying on its feet when people hear this proclaimed from the pulpits; nor is it surprising that Christianity has sought and fought to crush other views that threaten to expose its gigantic confidence trick on the minds of humanity. In the face of the new consciousness, this centuries-old prison of the mind has no chance of surviving, no matter how it presents the beliefs of those who are putting a different view. In his criticism of the New Age, the cleric from All Souls gives us an excellent insight into the misunderstandings and desperation of Christianity. He says in his introduction:

"To New Agers 'transformation' has nothing to do with people's morality or behaviour. It refers rather to the transformation of their consciousness, the discovery and development of their own potential."

He says that as a criticism? And what will a transformation of consciousness do if not change the way people think and behave?

Christianity lives in a dream world in which one generation indoctrinates the next. It speaks of Divine Will and revelation when, in reality, its dogma was decided by a Roman Emperor, sundry bishops and misguided popes who sought economic and political power above spiritual insight. Its beliefs and ceremonies have their origin in the Pagan beliefs they so despise. Nothing will be affected more by the transformation, all over the planet, than Christianity and its like. Open-minded true scientists are going to be inspired to confirm that all consciousness is eternal, that Creation is made up of frequencies and that everything is the same energy in different states of being. All is One. This and other discoveries and exposures will hasten the end of Christianity. We will see real science (not the system-serving variety) and spirituality (not religion) speaking the same language. In fact, they already are.

The new spirituality will have no rules and regulations. It will respect the right of all to believe what they think is correct. Its only challenge will be to those who wish to force others, through subtle and less subtle means, to believe what they want them to believe. My problem with Christianity and other dogmatic religions is not with their right to believe what they wish, but with the way they have tried to impose their beliefs through fear, violence and support from the State. Had that not been the case, this chapter would not have needed to be written, for the Christian religion would no longer be with us.

During the transformation, people will be guided together, naturally, as higher selves reconnect powerfully with our physical personalities. It will be a free spirituality in which we can link with the Source and the higher levels when we are alone at home, with a few friends, or in vast groups. The choice will be ours and one will be no more valid than the other. With so many churches built on energy points, I believe many could be used by spiritual groups as Christianity continues to fold and the churches close. They could be used for energy-channelling and healing, rather than for the obsession with events which took place two thousand years ago. They will be places of love and joy where the gift of life can be celebrated with others. They will not be places of fear and guilt which emphasise 'sin' at the expense of people loving themselves. With science and spirituality working as one, we will be visiting and interacting with other loving civilisations in the Universe and moving across frequencies. This will give a fantastic understanding of life and Creation compared with what we have now. Our spirituality will evolve rapidly as a result, if we are open to it.

There are dangers on this road, however, even for those who accept the themes of this book. You can believe in reincarnation without serving others. You can speak of peace and love without really meaning it at the core of your being. It is easy for love and peace to become the spiritual equivalent of 'have a nice day'. All that glitters is not gold and all that speaks of love and peace is not loving and peaceful. I have had several experiences, some very extreme, which have shown me this. So much of what is termed 'New Age' is merely the Old Age in disguise. It is, too often, the old thought patterns and reactions at work under a different cloak, that's all.

The New Age is a vast tapestry of people and beliefs and should not be seen as a movement or entity which thinks and believes the same. I refuse to call myself 'New Age' because, like tens of millions of others, I am an aspect of consciousness awakening to my true self and that does not require titles or all-encompassing 'movements'. It requires me to follow my own intuition at all times. Within the New Age field, there is substantial exploitation and there are many who complicate simple themes. The more complicated you can make it appear, the more people will be dependent on others to decide what is best and to sell them endless paraphernalia – rebirthing tanks, counselling, karma sessions and goodness knows what else. The idea is to free people from spiritual dependency and dependency of all kinds – not to create a new dependency on a guru, teacher, channeller or piece of equipment. That is not to say that some of these New Age services are not helpful when enlightened people are involved, they certainly are. But too much is irrelevant and emotionally-dangerous exploitation. It can hold back your awakening and, in areas like karmic counselling, can, possibly, make you feel really bad about yourself if the counsellor tells you of unpleasant things he or she claims you were responsible for in past lives. It is the same with many channellers. Much channelled information is claptrap and needs to be treated with great caution. There is a woman I met briefly with Yeva who now sends me a stream of strange letters claiming the most outrageous things. She is quite obviously in a state of considerable confusion and in need of some enlightened help yet, on her business cards, she describes herself as a past life and present life counsellor. Be careful.

The Brotherhood has infiltrated New Age and UFO groups and negative extra-terrestrials could have been using channellers for thousands of years. Remember, they know this consciousness shift is planned and they want to stop it because they know the consequences of it for them. What better way than to feed a load of trash through channellers and 'gurus' to those who are being affected by that shift? I read in one American New Age magazine some channelling, purporting to come from extra-terrestrials, that was calling for a world government. I have reservations, too, about some of the communications which allegedly come from 'Ascended Masters'. Whenever I hear that term, I feel really bad about it. I have had bad vibes about some of the groups who have promoted this idea of 'Masters', not least the 'I am' movement in the United States. The Masters, according to New Age belief, are part of something called the Great White Brotherhood who are said to be guiding humanity and the Earth through this time of change. But are they? Someone is, for sure, but is it the entities who are said to be Masters? I'm not yet convinced, you know. It could be that it is the hierarchal tone of Ascended Masters that makes me feel less than positive about it and maybe the blind worship of these entities is not something they wish to happen. But, even if the ideas of Masters is correct, is every channelled entity who claims to be from that consciousness stream really telling the truth? The answer to the latter is definitely "No", because negative ETs and the Luciferic consciousness use some channellers tuning to the lower frequencies as a means to manipulate. Claiming to be from what is so widely accepted to be a positive consciousness stream like the Masters in an excellent way of doing it. I have no doubt that consciousness of a very high evolution is trying to guide us, and so are streams of positive, loving ETs from other Universal civilizations, but we always have to be selective and wary about who is on the other end of the line. Being spiritual is vital to the transformation but being streetwise is equally so.

Once again, the key is to follow our intuition, to listen to channelling while being very selective. It is what *we* feel is right within our hearts that matters and that doesn't need the name of some Master of other to give it legitimacy. It has no name. It just is.

A danger I see is that parts of the New Age could become nothing more than another religion. The signs are already there. We have the gurus, the teachers, and the 'living gods on Earth'. We see 'disciples' giving over their responsibility to think and act to these people in the same way that Christians do to the Bible and Jesus, and Muslims do to the Koran and Mohammed. I have met people who have been diverted from the journey to enlightenment by becoming obsessed with Indian gurus. I have seen how they have turned their homes into shrines to them. I am not saying that we should not listen to the views of the guru figures, but no more so than anyone else. What I challenge is the unquestioning worship of them. This is another expression of humanity's collective desire to pass on their responsibility to others for the way they think and act. This is precisely what the Brotherhood wants. All over the New Age arena are cosy little niches where people can become trapped and cease to evolve their understanding. Some have a certain belief about karma and they stick with it, no matter what other information comes to light; some channel the same non-physical entities all their lives instead of expanding their conscious-ness to access higher and higher levels of information and know-ledge; others mix only with those who agree with them and avoid the sometimes-unpleasant and painful necessity of taking their knowledge to sceptical audiences who have as much right to hear it as everyone else.

I understand why some people find a nice little spot on the path and pitch their tent. There have been many times in the past when I have wished to step off the road and take a rest for a while from the frustration and aggravation of speaking to closed minds. But, if we are to speed the emergence of the new consciousness and free humanity from the prison of indoctrination as smoothly as pos-sible, we must continually work to expand our own understanding and to pass on what we believe for others to accept or reject. No-one said it would be easy and turning the New Age into another religion or giving our responsibility to guru figures will hold back the spiritual revolution. Respect and love are the foundations of the new thinking – the worship of others is not, I would suggest.

That's the old way recycled.

But the positive contribution of what is termed the New Age movement and which I term the Spiritual Renaissance far out-weighs the negative. I have met thousands of wonderful, loving, non-judgmental human beings who are doing a superb job in helping people to awaken. No-one wants to stop the exploitation of the new consciousness more than they do and, whenever I talk in these terms at meetings, the audience invariably shows its en-thusiastic support for this view. What I am saying is, be careful. Just because someone claims to be a channeller, astrologer, karmic counsellor or healer does not mean that they are proficient in those skills. Not even the well-known ones, necessarily. Look for those who are recommended and respected by others in their field or by previous clients. More than anything, our own intuition should be our guide.

I believe we could see three clearly identifiable groups during the transition. There will be those who reject the rising frequencies and who, as the years pass, will be easy to recognise. There will be those who move so far and stop when they find a comfortable niche. And there will be others, the few probably, who go on searching, seeking and challenging, no matter what the personal consequences in the short term. The further you walk along the road the lonelier it can become, as others stop through weariness, material gain or fear. With every step, you are tuning to a higher wavelength which evolves your understanding and behaviour. From the perspective of those who have chosen to stop back down the road you may appear extreme and strange. If you keep walking and seeking, you will be ridiculed and increasingly condemned by the first group of padlocked minds. But I feel the second group, many of which will be within what is termed the New Age Movement, will also be less than supportive of those on the front of the snowplough who will be questioning many of the themes on which some New Age niches depend. The road to enlightenment is never-ending. Just as we are leaving dogmatic religion behind, so we will eventually do the same with many elements of current New Age dogma.

The third example of the exploitation of the spirit and the mind is the Brotherhood with the behaviour-controlling technology I talked about in an earlier chapter. We are getting help with this from the higher levels who are taking steps to block it as the transformation proceeds. The more who ask for this to be done, the better. Mass forms of mind control can only affect us if we allow ourselves to de-link from the frequency of love to which our heart chakras are tuned. If we think love and live love we can resist it.

Another crucial way our minds are attacked is the programming by the messages which are projected at us through the media and our general lives every day. We should not underestimate their power to exploit our minds and spirits. An Illuminati document called "Silent Weapons for a Quiet War" was found in 1986 in an IBM copier bought at a second hand sale. It was dated 1979. It encapsulates all that I have been saying in this book, and has been the policy of the Bilderberg Group since the 1950s:

"Experience has proven that the simplest method of securing a silent weapon and gaining control of the public is to keep them undisciplined and ignorant of basic systems principles on the one hand, while keeping them confused, disorganised, and distracted with matters of no real importance on the other hand.

"This is achieved by:

1.   disengaging their minds; sabotaging their mental activities; providing a low-quality program of public education in mathematics, logic, systems design and economics, and discouraging technical creativity.

2.   engaging their emotions, increasing their self-indulgence and their indulgence in emotional and physical activities by:

(a)   unrelenting emotional affrontations and attacks (mental and emotional rape) by way of a constant barrage of sex, violence, and wars in the media – especially the TV and newspapers.

(b)   giving them what they desire – in excess – "junk food for thought" – and depriving them of what they really need.

(c)   Re-writing history and law and subjecting the public to the deviant creation, thus being able to shift their thinking from personal needs to highly fabricated outside priorities.

These preclude their interest in and discovery of the silent weapons of social automation technology. The general rule is that there is profit in confusion; the more confusion, the more profit. Therefore the best approach is to create problems and then offer solutions.

"In Summary:

Media: Keep the adult public attention diverted away from the real social issues, and captivated by matters of no real importance.

Schools: Keep the young public ignorant of real mathematics, real economics, real law, and real history.

Entertainment: Keep the public entertainment below a sixth grade level.

Work: Keep the public busy, busy, busy, with no time to think; back on the farm with the other animals."

Recognise all that? Of course you do. It is the world we live in and it is exactly what the Illuminati have sought to create. If we are going to repel this form of spiritual and mental exploitation we must start to think for ourselves; to get involved and to get informed about what is really going on; to make sure our children are informed and realise how they are being manipulated; to get off our knees and start to use our minds to their full potential; to reject the pressure to accept the drip, drip, drip of trivia designed to deaden our consciousness.

The best way to challenge the negative is with joy, laughter, peace – and knowledge. The negative does not understand love and peace. And never underestimate your own potential and the power of your own psyche. You own it. It belongs to no-one else, not a church, guru, ascended master, piece of technology or ET. You are connected through your higher self to all Creation. Tap into that and no-one, but no-one, can exploit your spirit.

20

The Earth Needs Rebels

"All that is necessary for evil to triumph is for good men to do nothing" –
Edmund Burke.

A journey of a thousand miles begins with one step and a
transformation of human understanding can begin with one
thought and one rebel.

Every improvement in the human condition has come from
someone pushing against the tide and speaking out, no matter
what the consequences. That person is within all of us. Rebellion
and the desire for positive change is at the heart of the human
spirit.

But what is rebellion?

The meaning of the word is often misunderstood. Many of
those who once came to heckle and laugh when I have spoken in
public have been under the impression that they were rebels. Yet
they are system servers doing exactly what they are programmed
to do – undermine anyone prepared to challenge its control. Beers
and jeers are not a rebellion. Others see rebels as those who wage
war against the State. I am sure those in Northern Ireland who
daily kill and maim think they are rebels. But, again, they are
merely puppets of the Luciferic consciousness and the Brotherhood working through both sides. The rebellion of which I speak
does not involve armed uprisings or violence of any kind. It is a
rebellion against indoctrination and mind control; a refusal to be
programmed a moment longer by the 'values' imposed upon us by
other generations and by the super robots in politics, economics,
science, religion and the Brotherhood networks.

Thinking for yourself and having the confidence and courage to
live what you believe – that's rebellion.

From this will come change in every aspect of life on Earth.
Such rebellion will show itself in this transition period in a refusal

to cooperate with the system and the Brotherhood elite. Awakening people will seek ways of disconnecting themselves as much as possible from dependency upon its destructive delusions. They will have the courage to speak loudly and confidently, for they will know that the Robots' Rebellion cannot be stopped. It is not for me to tell people what to do. I have no desire or stomach for that. But I support the campaign of non-cooperation and peaceful resistance which is gathering across the world. I believe it will continue to grow and that some of its manifestations could be:

 * A boycott of all banks which create money out of nothing and charge interest on it. I hope people will withdraw their money from these banks and even refuse to pay interest on their loans. The latter decision needs to be well coordinated so that millions do it at the same time.

 * Support for community banks and ethical banking which invest in projects designed to benefit people and the planet.

 * A refusal to cooperate with and in schools, universities and government departments in every country, until we have the free flow of information about what is *really* going on in secret and all the knowledge available.

 * Constant sit-ins, peaceful occupation and mass protests at government headquarters in every country, particularly the key players like the United States, Russia, Britain, Australia, Japan, the European Community and the United Nations.

 * The peaceful disruption of all occasions of state in every country until we are told the truth and the closing down, by mass sit-ins, of roads and entrances to parliamentary buildings.

 * Mass peaceful resistance to projects that harm the environment. If they face such protests everywhere, the authorities will soon have to re-think and listen.

 * The boycotting of all court proceedings that may arise from such actions and mass sit-ins at the court buildings to disrupt them, also.

 * The bombardment of phone-in programmes and audience participation programmes with questions and information about the secret government and what people can do to stop its manipulation.

 * Protests and sit-ins at the headquarters of media organisations until they refuse to be Brotherhood poodles and start to report the truth to people. Boycotts of system-serving newspapers.

 * The same at the headquarters and branches of the Freemasons

in each country and district and the immediate resignation by all members of the Freemasons and other secret organisations who no longer wish to be used as a front for the manipulation of the world.

    * A refusal to vote for or support any politician who refuses to disclose whether he or she is a member of a secret society or closely-connected to anyone who is. A refusal to support any politician who is a member of any Brotherhood front organisation, such as the Council on Foreign Relations, the Trilateral Commission or, in London, connected to the Royal Institute of International Affairs.

The three most important words here are *peaceful, determined* and *constant*. Those who serve either knowingly or, more often, unknowingly, the forces who control us do not deserve our hatred. They need our love and we can protest with laughter and joy. They know not what they do and they are in prison as well. I always find it sad that some who protest against the activities of far right groups, do so with aggression and hatred in their hearts – the very same emotions that motivate the far right. We need to protest with love because that is the energy we wish to spread across the world. But our love must not be blind, it must be streetwise. We must remember that in the world of the Brotherhood black is white and white is black. Remember this also: Silence is connivance. It is time to think, to take responsibility, and to speak and act against the silent, secret, tyranny. The Brotherhood acknowledge the threat to their ambitions of individuals thinking for themselves and responding with action:

"(We wish to) discourage any kind of personal initiative which might hinder our affair. There is nothing more dangerous than personal initiative; if it has genius behind it, such initiative can do more than can be done by millions of people among whom we have sown discord." (Protocol 5).

One individual *can* make a difference. We are not helpless, and the manipulation is not invincible, nor the ills of the world insurmountable. It depends on your state of mind. Problems can become solutions with a change of thought.

    If we are going to return freedom to the Earth, we have seriously to harass the system into realising that the robots are not cooperating any more. We will not be lied to and manipulated. There are billions of us and only a relative handful who operate the secret world government. They cannot impose their will on us unless we allow them to. Are you going to be a robot or a rebel? That is your choice for there will be no in-betweens.

Rebellion may appear on the surface to be the opposite of peace and love, but I don't believe that it is. Through this book I have strongly questioned the thought-patterns which control economics, politics, the media, science, religion and parts of the New Age. Some may see this as judgmental. But we are all responsible for what has happened since Atlantis and we have all done things we would rather not have done. It is pointless trying to be holier than thou and judging others from that lofty and misguided perspective. Speaking out against negative thought-patterns is not being judgmental or unloving. After all, what is love? Is it loving to ignore what these patterns are doing to people and the planet? Is it loving to say that all is well and that there is no need to change what we do? Is it loving to avoid upsetting some people when, by speaking out, you may be able to alert others to the dangers and the exploitation? I think not. There are times when love is calling a spade a shovel if that is what is needed for positive change. One of the most important channelled messages I have been given said:

"True love does not always give the receiver what it would like to receive, but it will always give that which is best for it."

Or, to add some humility to that, what we believe is best for it. I have met many people who think that protest and direct action, even of the peaceful kind I am advocating, is unloving. I would not agree with that and I feel that unless we begin a campaign of non-cooperation with The System, we will allow the Brotherhood elite to do some desperately unpleasant things in the wake of our inaction. There have been some negative themes running through this book, but they are not there to frighten, they are there to inform and alert. Have no fear. A new dawn awaits us and it will bring an end to such horrors.

We are on the threshold of incomprehensible change as Mother Earth moves back into alignment with the rest of the Universe and raises her consciousness to a higher dimension of love and harmony. When you think of all the wonderful things that happen in the world, even against the background I have described, think what life will be like when that disruption and disharmony is no more. That day is near. We will see the truth that humanity is not

evil or stupid, but loving, intelligent and overflowing with the
love and creativity which it is desperate to express. It may not
seem like that sometimes, but there are reasons for this, as we have
seen, and the period of Luciferic opportunity is almost over.

We shall love the Earth and love each other. We shall love those
who love us and love those who hate us. We shall not choose
between them, for all are we and we are all. We are each other and
the truth of that is re-emerging in our consciousness. Open your
heart, follow your heart, and your life and all life on this planet will
be transformed.

We are here to change the world. We chose to come and our
time has come. We cannot and we will not fail.

Bibliography

Allan , Derek & Delair, Bernard, *When the Earth Nearly Died – Compelling Evidence of World Catastrophe, 10,500BC:* Gateway Books, Bath, & Atrium Publishers Group, Lower Lake, CA, 1994.

Blumrich, Joseph F, *The Space Ships of Ezekiel:* Corgi, London 1974.

Bowen, Russell S, *The Immaculate Deception:* dist. by American West, Boulder, CO.

Bramley, William, *Gods of Eden:* Avon Books, New York.

Cooper, Bill, *Behold a Pale Horse:* Light Technology Publishing, PO Box 1495, Sedona, AZ 86336

Dauncey, Guy, *After the Crash – Emergence of the Rainbow Economy:* Green Print, London, 1988.

Findlay, Arthur, *The Curse of Ignorance (2 vols):* Arthur Findlay College, Stansted Hall, Stansted Mountfichet, Essex.

Good, Timothy, *Above Top Secret – Worldwide UFO Cover-up:* Grafton, London, 1989. *Alien Liason:* Sidgwick & Jackson, London 1991. *UFO Reports, 1990, 1991:* Sidgwick & Jackson, London.

Hassnain, Fida, *A Search for the Historical Jesus – From Apocryphal, Buddhist, Islamic & Sanskrit Sources:* Gateway Books, Bath; & Atrium Publishers Group, Lower Lake, CA, 1994.

Keith, Jim, *Casebook on Alternative Three:* PO Box 20593, Sun Valley, NV 1433

Koestler, Arthur, *The Thirteenth Tribe:* Hutchinson, London.

Nexus Magazine: Provides hard-to-get information on the transformative changes in society. Available by subscription from: (a) PO Box 30, Mapleton, Qld 4560, Australia. (b) PO Box 177, Kempton, IL 60946–0177, USA. (c) PO Box 66, Gorredjik 8400 AB, The Netherlands. (d) 55 Queens Rd, E. Grinstead, W. Sussex, RH19 1BG, UK.

Rosa, Peter Da, *The Vicars of Christ – The Dark Side of the Papacy:* Bantam Press, London, 1988

Schlemmer, Phyllis (ed), *The Only Planet of Choice – Essential Briefings from Deep Space:* Gateway Books, Bath; & Atrium Publishers Group, Lower Lake, CA, 1994.

Tarpley, Webster G & Chaitkin, Anton, *George Bush – the Unauthorised Biography:* Executive Intelligence Review, PO Box 17390, Washington DC.

USEFUL CONTACTS:

The American Academy of Dissident Sciences, 10970 Ashton Ave, #310, Los Angeles, CA 90024, USA.

Contact Network International, PO Box 66, Gorredjik 8400AB, The Netherlands.

Dennis Lee (free energy scientist), c/o Better World Technology, PO Box 653, McAfee, NJ 07428, USA.

David Icke, 35 Dover St, Ryde, Isle of Wight, PO33 2BW (for newsletter and information on lectures, worksmops, tapes & books – please send s.a.e.).

INDEX

Other books by David Icke published by Gateway:
"This is the man I've been waiting for, for ages" - Sir GEORGE TREVELYAN
(British pioneer of holistic education)

Heal the World: *A do-it-yourself guide to human & planetary trans-formation*

Healing the world starts with self-healing, love and self-respect. In this easy-to-read book, David brings together his proven environmental commitment with his vision for a transformed society and shows us how to work together to make the world better.

112pp   Paperback   £5.95 $9.95

Truth Vibrations: *From TV celebrity to world visionary*

The gripping story of David Icke's personal journey of discovery and of his vision of a decade of world transformation. An excellent starting book for readers new to his ideas.

144p   Paperback   £5.95 $9.95

Days of Decision (audio tape): *A speech by David Icke*

You've read his words - now hear his voice.
The Great Awakening is upon us. All over the world, people are freeing themselves from Church and State to find new motivation for living. We are in a period of transition, seeing the old order crumble and political turmoil making way for a new era of peace and harmony. This powerful and inspired speech will not leave you unmoved.

audio tape   running time 45 mins   £6.95 $10.95

Also from Gateway Books:

A Search for the Historical Jesus: *Apocryphal, Buddhist, Islamic and Sanskrit Sources* - by Professor Fida Hassnain

Millions of people have been brought up to believe that Jesus's life-mission ended with the crucifixion. Here, a respected Sufi historian finds evidence of information suppressed by the Church that Jesus survived the Cross and undertook an Essene-backed extended ministry in India and the East. Riveting reading.

272pp including colour photographs and maps paperback   £8.95 $14.95

When the Earth Nearly Died: *Compelling Evidence of World Catastrophe, 9,500 BC* - by D S Allan & J B Delair

Evidence from many disciplines, traditions and cultures of a cataclysm which nearly destroyed Earth 11,500 years ago. The authors draw on decades of research to describe how a golden age disappeared with appalling devastation and show how their findings could have relevance for present world changes.

386pp including photos, maps, charts   paperback   £12.95 $19.95

The Only Planet of Choice: *Essential Briefings from Deep Space* - by Phyllis Schlemmer & The Council of Nine. New edition.
Gateway's bestseller, compiled from nearly 20 years of communications with a circle of high-level universal beings, is widely-acknowledged as one of the most significant books for our time. For anyone who wants to know more about the place of Planet Earth in the Cosmos, the origin of humanity, ETs, God, the present traumas facing the world and how they can be resolved.
"Everything you ever wanted to know about the Universe, but didn't know who to ask." - Kindred Spirit magazine, UK.

352pp   paperback   £9.95 $15.95

Living Energies: *Viktor Schauberger's Brilliant Work with Natural Energy Explained* - by Callum Coats
Schauberger was the pioneer of new technologies using the subtle energies of Nature - for water purification, transportation, free energy heating and home power generation. Describes clearly how the creative processes of Nature actually work.

320pp   354 illustrations   £12.95 $19.95

The Vortex: *Key to Future Science* - by David Ash & Peter Hewitt.
About matter and energy and a deeper purpose of our existence. Merges physics and metaphysics in a study first researched by Lord Kelvin 130 years ago. Convincing light is cast on traditional beliefs about life after death, miracles, UFOs and clairvoyance.

192pp   photos   paperback   £6.95 $11.95

The Cosmic Connection: *Worldwide crop formations and ET contacts* - by Michael Hesemann.
The failure of rationalists to address these phenomena and the inaccuracies of the media has led to new observation of events and related phenomena, making the ET connection more obvious. Packed with information.

234pp   70 colour photos   paperback   £12.95 $19.95

Kombucha - Miracle Fungus: *The Essential Handbook* by Harald Tietze
This remarkable fermented drink you make at home at almost no cost has well-documented benefits: cleansing the blood, detoxifying the liver, enhancing the immune system. It produces a 'baby' every week and is now widely networked throughout the world.

112pp   illustrations   £6.95 $9.95

Gateway Books' experience in alternative publishing spans 25 years. Its policy is to challenge conventional or establishment thinking in all areas, and positively to promote spirituality and holistic awareness.
Write for our catalogue and join Gateway's growing band of supportive networkers.